THE
ROYAL &
ANCIENT
GOLFER'S
HANDBOOK
2002 EDITOR RENTON LAIDLAW

First published 1984 by Macmillan
This edition published 2001 by Macmillan
an imprint of Pan Macmillan Ltd
Pan Macmillan, 20 New Wharf Road, London N1 9RR
Basingstoke and Oxford
Associated companies throughout the world
www.panmacmillan.com

ISBN 0 333 90531 8 (Hardback)
ISBN 0 333 90532 6 (Paper laminate case)

Note
Whilst every care has been taken in compiling the information contained
in this book, the Publishers, Editor and Sponsors accept no responsibility
for any errors or omissions.

Correspondence
Letters on editorial matters should be addressed to:
The Editor, Royal & Ancient Golfer's Handbook, Pan Macmillan,
20 New Wharf Road, London N1 9RR

Advertising
Enquiries about advertising in this book should be addressed to:
Communications Management International, Chiltern House, 120
Eskdale Avenue, Chesham, Bucks HP5 3BD

Mailing lists
The information on golf courses and clubs contained in this
Handbook is available for purchase on disk as mailing labels.
For further information please call 020 7014 6034 or e-mail
s.bierwerth@macmillan.co.uk

9 8 7 6 5 4 3 2 1

A CIP catalogue record for this book is available from the British Library

Cover photographs of David Duval © Phil Sheldon

Typeset by Penrose Typography, Maidstone, Kent

Printed by Mackays of Chatham plc, Chatham, Kent

Contents

Part I The Major Championships

Part II Men's Professional Tournaments

Tee Off

with
Corus and Regal hotels

Corus and Regal hotels have always been known for their great character, friendly staff, comfortable surroundings and excellent value for money.

- 18 hole and 9 hole courses
- PGA qualified golf professionals
- Driving ranges
- Short game practice areas
- Changing rooms
- Private function rooms
- Extensive leisure facilities
- Quality overnight accommodation

Less well known is that we have three eighteen-hole and two nine-hole golf courses within our group. Located at Tewkesbury, Telford and Washington (Tyne and Wear) our eighteen-hole locations combine the best hotel facilities with a golf product that focuses on delivering an enjoyable experience to our customers. In addition, nine hole courses at Briggens House (Hertford) and Hall Garth (Darlington) offer opportunities to enjoy this relaxing game combined with the added attraction of AA Rosette restaurants. ■

For further details on our hotels and courses please see our listings in each of the regional sections.

For a copy of our FREE full colour brochure call

01905 730 370

or visit our website at www.corushotels.co.uk

Corus and Regal hotels

Part IX The Government of the Game

Part X Golf History

Part XI Guide to Golfing Services and Places to Stay in the British Isles and Ireland

Part XII Clubs and Courses in the British Isles and Europe

CENTENARY CLUBS
2002

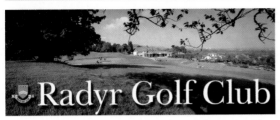

RADYR GOLF CLUB
Drysgol Road,
Radyr, Cardiff CF15 8BS
Tel: 029 2084 2408
Fax: 029 2084 3914

Following its foundation in 1902 the newly established course and clubhouse was officially opened by Lord Windsor in 1903. In 1904 the club staged the first ever Welsh Professional Championship and an exhibition match involving three of the world's greatest golfers - Harry Vardon, James Braid and J H Taylor.

Extensive refurbishment includes comfortable lounge bar commanding magnificent views, and the dining room which can convert into excellent conference facilities leading to our splendid new patio. Our fully equipped pro shop has everything to suit a golfer's needs at competitive prices.

E-mail: manager@radyrgolf.co.uk Website: www.radyrgolf.co.uk

NELSON GOLF CLUB
Kings Causeway, Brierfield,
Nelson, Lancashire BB9 0EU.

Tel: 01282 611834 Fax: 01282 606226

The club was founded in 1902 and is situated on a plateau overlooking Nelson and Burnley. The late Dr MacKenzie, who laid out the course, managed a design which does not include any wearisome climbing and created many interesting holes. Visitors will find a warm welcome and the friendliness extends to the recently refurbished clubhouse which caters to all needs and has wonderful panoramic views of the surrounding Pendle area.

TULLIALLAN GOLF CLUB
Kincardine on Forth,
Alloa, Fife FK10 4BB.

Tel: 01259 730798 Fax: 01259 733950

Tulliallan is a fine parkland course in Fife about a mile north of the Kincardine bridge and close to the Ocnil hills. The fairways are tree lined and the course presents a good test of golf at 5,965 yards and a par of 69. Excellent clubhouse and bar facilities are available to all visitors.

BULWELL FOREST GOLF CLUB
Hucknall Road,
Bulwell, Nottingham NG6 9LQ.

Tel: 0115-977 0526   (Pro Shop) 0115-976 3172

In the 1870s a seven hole course (later 18-holes) was laid out by John Doleman "The Father of Nottinghamshire Golf". The Nottinghamshire Golf Club spent their early years at Bulwell leaving in 1901. 1902 saw the present club formed. Council owned, few course changes have occurred. Constructed on sandstone gives excellent drainage and play throughout the year. The length is 5,611 yards par 68 SSS 67 and each undulating hole is different. Challenging par 3's are a feature. DON'T BE FOOLED - THIS COURSE IS NOT EASY!

ATHENRY GOLF CLUB
Palmerstown, Oranmore,
Co Galway, Ireland.

Office Telephone +353 91 794466
Fax: +353 91 794971
Pro Shop +353 91 790599
E-mail: athenrygc@eircom.net

Situated in the west coast of Ireland on the outskirts of Galway City (ten minutes' drive, East, off N6 on R348) Athenry golf club offers a challenge to all levels of golfing ability with its unique mixture of parkland and heathland set on a limestone base with excellent drainage allowing the course to remain playable all year long. Par 70 of 6,200 yards from Medal Tees. Other facilities available include bar, restaurant, pro shop, club hire, tuition and practice area.

ASHTON-IN-MAKERFIELD GOLF CLUB
Garswood Park,
Ashton-in-Makerfield,
Wigan WN4 0YT.

Telephone 01942 719330 (Secretary)
01942 724229 (Professional)

Ashton-in-Makerfield Golf Club is situated on the A58 adjacent to the M6. Parkland in nature, the course measures 6,205 yards with a par of 70. Visitors are invited to enjoy the excellent bar and catering facilities in the clubhouse, which was extended and modernised in 1996.

BEREHAVEN GOLF CLUB
Castletownbere, Co Cork, Ireland.
Tel/Fax: +353 27 70700
E-mail: bearagolf@eircom.net

Berehaven Golf Club is set on the rugged, picturesque coastline of the Beara Peninsula, on the south western tip of Ireland. The course was originally laid down by the British Admiralty in 1902 and known as the Channel Fleet Golf Club until the hand-over of the ports to the Irish government in 1938. Although only a 9-hole links course, water and wind are prominent hazards on many holes, and totally different teeboxes for the second nine increase the range of skilled shotmaking required to make a score. Full clubhouse and bar facilities are available as well as on-site crazy golf, tennis, camper park, camping and shore angling. Visitors are welcome all year round. Course 5,527 yards par 69 SSS 66 - Green fees 20 Euro's.

HESWALL GOLF CLUB
Cottage Lane,
Gayton,
Wirral CH60 8PB

Tel: 0151-342 1237
Fax: 0151-342 6140

Founded in 1902 and enjoying a splendid aspect on the Dee Estuary, Heswall Golf Club is one of the very best of golfing venues. The gently rolling parkland course in superb conditions affords the golfer all that is good in the game.

LA MOYE GOLF CLUB
La Moye, St Brelade, Jersey JE3 8GQ,
Channel Islands.

Telephone 01534 743401 (Secretary)
742701 (Clubhouse) Fax: 01534 747289

Not numbered as the sands on the shore or the stars in the sky but certainly over the past 100 years many thousands of men and women have enjoyed the pleasures of La Moye Golf Club. The stunning views on sunny days and the thrill of good shots on windy ones have always been there, but perhaps most of all the making of friendships which is so much part of our club life.
As we look forward to our next Centenary the welcome we give to new members and visitors alike will be of the highest standards that will not fall.

LINKS GOLF CLUB
**Cambridge Road,
Newmarket,
Suffolk CB8 0TG**

**Tel: 01638 663000
Fax: 01638 661476**

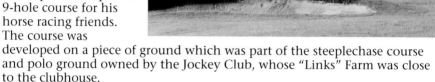

Golf came to
Newmarket when
Colonel Henry
McCalmont decided to
develop his own private
9-hole course for his
horse racing friends.
The course was
developed on a piece of ground which was part of the steeplechase course
and polo ground owned by the Jockey Club, whose "Links" Farm was close
to the clubhouse.

The attractive and mature 18-hole (par 72) course of some 6,582 yards was
re-designed by Colonel Hotchkin, whose golf courses include Woodhall Spa
and Ashridge. From the point of view of design, The Links at Newmarket
conforms to his very high standards

SUNNINGDALE LADIES GOLF CLUB
**Cross Road,
Sunningdale,
Berkshire SL5 9RX**

Tel: 01344 620507

The course was developed
on land originally
forming part of Windsor
forest and acquired by St
John's College
Cambridge in 1524
following the closure of the monasteries by Henry VIII. The club was
founded by Mr E E Villiers and is considered to be the second oldest ladies'
club in England.

The course is a very pleasant heathland course - 3,616 yards in length with
a standard scratch score of 60. We are privileged to have HM Queen
Elizabeth the Queen Mother as our patron having been captain in 1932.
Visitors are welcome to our friendly club.

Open competitions include September Foursomes knockout over three
consecutive days, Fleming Foursomes mixed knockout played during the
winter, open to amateurs and professionals and a Mixed Greensomes on the
first Sunday in each month except January.

FAVERSHAM GOLF CLUB

Belmont Park, Faversham,
Kent ME13 0HB.

Tel: 01795 890251 (Clubhouse)
01795 890561 (Secretary)
01795 890275 (Professional)
Fax: 01795 890760

Founded in 1902 by twelve fervent disciples, the club was originally on Nagden Marshes before moving to its present home. The land in Belmont Park was generously leased to the club by Lord Harris the then Kent and England cricket captain. A slightly unusual clause in the lease, which is still in force today, is that the pheasant shoots have priority!!! The club mascot and emblem is a cock pheasant and many of them can be seen wandering the fairways.

The great storm of 1987 had a devastating effect on this beautiful woodland course but it has now regained much of its former splendour. The addition of the impressive new clubhouse, which was opened formally in December 1997, complements the course and provides a friendly welcoming atmosphere.

WALMLEY GOLF CLUB

Brooks Road,
Wylde Green,
Sutton Coldfield,
West Midlands
B72 1HR.

Tel/Fax: 0121-377 7272

Walmley Golf Club began in 1902; nine holes over meadow land were extended to 18 in 1908.

The course, now well wooded, slopes from the clubhouse to a brook and to two pools that affect the play of three holes. Birmingham, its centre only six miles away, can easily be forgotten. The clubhouse, built in 1965, replaced another that had served for 55 years. It commands a delightful view in which the first and the 18th holes can be followed from tee to green.

British Golf Museum
St Andrews

HEROIC

SURPRISING

STRIKING

HISTORIC

you can't miss this

Bruce Embankment, St Andrews, Fife KY16 9AB Telephone 01334 478880. Fax 01334 473306.
Opening Times Summer Hours: Easter to Mid October • 9.30am - 5.30pm Open 7 days
Winter Hours: 11am - 3pm Closed Tuesday & Wednesday.

Foreword

Renton Laidlaw

Renton Laidlaw

Bringing forward publication from March to a date which allows *The Golfer's Handbook* to be in the shops before Christmas has proved commercially successful and popular too with our readers. Of course it means that we cannot get all the results of the current year in the book but we have ensured a continuity of results by printing in this year's edition all those results and end of season tables from around the world that were too late for publication in the last edition. Any late results this year will be included in the 2003 edition.

As always I have been fortunate to persuade a host of top-name golf writers from both sides of the Atlantic to provide the important editorial substance to the book. David Davies, the long-serving golf correspondent of *The Guardian* took on the task of encapsulating the four majors into one literary piece with his usual relish and there was a similarly enthusiastic response from Jerry Tarde, executive editor of *Golf Digest* to my request that he outline just how golf's greatest corporate 'high flier' Tiger Woods has changed the game for all of us. Göran Zachrisson, the polished Swedish golf-writing doyen, tells us in his own inimitable way why so many of his countrymen and women have been so successful at the game and that makes for interesting reading as does the *Daily Telegraph*'s Lewine Mair's review of the year in women's golf which, I am delighted to say, singles out the very special role Laura Davies has played on the European and, more importantly, the world scene. Mark Garrod, the hard-working correspondent of the Press Association, had no problem deciding what to lead with in his annual review of the amateur game. Was there a more dramatic golfing moment in 2001 than the first ever successful defence by a Great Britain and Ireland side of the Walker Cup on American soil? That was an award-winning performance all round. John Hopkins of *The Times* had hoped to report on an equally impressive European performance at The Belfry in the Ryder Cup. The match was cancelled but as he reports still made the headlines.

Ian Wooldridge, who has been writing for the *Daily Mail* for more than 40 years, enjoyed reminiscing, in his now annual essay, about the golf writers of the past – the gentlemen of the press who might be surprised at what now appears in some papers. Completing our line-up Keith Mackie, the St Andrews-based author, was asked to cast his experienced eye over Muirfield, venue of the 2002 Open, and highlight the Rules decisions which made the headlines including Ian Woosnam's famous 15th club at the Open.

No reference book could ever be produced without the help of a host of experts behind the scenes. I would be remiss were I not to mention the sterling work Jan Bennett puts in ensuring the clubs section is as up-to-date as possible and the efforts of Alan and Heather Elliott who spend hours collecting and collating addresses and results. Val Rice is learning much about golf as our cheerful proof reader and if there was concern at Jayne Jenkinson's decision to retire from her key production role we need not have been worried. Mick Card was her chosen replacement and he has fitted in to the team brilliantly. To all of them I owe a debt of gratitude and to our readers, whether regulars for many years or new to a publication with a history stretching back to the 19th century, have a great golfing year.

The Royal and Ancient Golf Club of St Andrews

New captain has worthy sporting links

© GSR Photographic

Graeme Maxwell Simmers, CBE, the new 2001–2002 captain of the Royal and Ancient Golf Club of St Andrews, comes from a well-known sporting family. His father Max was a Scottish Rugby Union international, his mother Gwen played Wightman Cup tennis; his grandmother Charlotte Sterry (née Cooper) was nine times Wimbledon champion and his daughter Corinne was a Scottish lacrosse player. He himself played 17 years for Glasgow Academicals, captaining the side for four seasons, or Glasgow XV and also for Scottish Districts against the Springboks. Currently playing off six he is a member of Loch Lomond, Buchanan Castle and Prestwick Golf Clubs as well as the R & A and is a member, too, of the All-England Lawn Tennis Club.

Formerly a partner in Kidson Simmers Chartered Accountants and a director of the Scottish Highland Hotels Group from 1962 until 1992, he received an OBE for his services to tourism. He served as Chairman of the Scottish Sports Council from 1992 to 1999 and is a former director of the Scottish Institute of Sport. He was awarded the CBE for his services in this field. He has held a non-executive directorship at the Stirling Royal Infirmary NHS Trust and is currently on the Forth Valley Acute Hospitals NHS Trust. For seven years from 1979 he was a member of the Scottish Tourist Board. He has been a governor of Loretto School in Musselburgh since 1968 serving as the chairman from 1992 to 1999. He is president of the Old Lorettonian Golfing Society and played for Loretto in the Halford Hewitt on 12 occasions. During his national service he was commissioned in the Royal Marine Corps and since 2000 has been Honorary Colonel Royal Marines Reserve Scotland.

The 66-year-old captain has been married to his wife Jennifer for 36 years and has two sons, Mark and Peter, and two daughters, Corinne and Kirsty. His golfing experience has been extensive. A member of the R & A since 1975 he served on the Rules of Golf Committee from 1978 to 1982 and was a member of the Championship committee from 1983 to 1991 serving as chairman for the 1989 Open won at Royal Troon by Mark Calcavecchia, the 1990 event won by Nick Faldo at St Andrews and the 1991 Championship which Ian Baker-Finch won at Royal Birkdale. He also acted as chairman of the committee running the Loch Lomond Invitational from 1996 to 1999.

He admits being nominated as captain is particularly satisfying and is looking forward immensely to his busy year which will involve overseas trips to, among other places, Japan (which in 2001 celebrated 100 years of golf in that country), Brazil and Switzerland which are also celebrating a century of involvement in the game. He is deeply conscious of the key role the Royal and Ancient Golf Club of St Andrews plays in world golf and is determined to uphold those traditions. 'Golf is the best governed of all games and the reputation we all have for fair play and sportsmanship is well worth protecting,' he says. Sir Michael Bonallack OBE and John Uzielli, his immediate predecessors as captain, did much to encourage clubs to improve conditions for juniors and to underline the importance of maintaining the etiquette that makes golf so special. During his term of office he will attend up to 60 dinners and in his speeches he will re-emphasise these points, encouraged by the behaviour of both teams and the manner in which the 2001 Walker Cup was played at Sea Island.

Review of the Year

Renton Laidlaw

The year began with so much expectation. Tiger Woods with his second Masters win became the first player to hold all four major titles simultaneously – an incredible performance but one that even his own father did not recognise as a Grand Slam nor as his son's greatest achievement in golf. That, he insisted, was his three US junior titles won in succession followed by three US Amateurs in a row. Tiger has rewritten the record book but still has something to aim at every year. He wants to win all four majors in the same season but despite his fast start it did not happen for him in 2001. Maybe 2002 will be the year he achieves that magical target.

Tiger won his second Masters with less flourish than he did in 1997 when his winning margin was 12 shots. This time it was much tenser among the bougainvilleas and tall pines as he battled with regular rivals David Duval and Phil Mickelson. He ended up winning by two. He had made just the start he wanted, but then he played what for him were only supporting roles in the US Open won by South African Retief Goosen, the Open at Lytham where Duval finally made his deserved major title debut and the US PGA Championship where David Toms ensured that Mickelson remains the most talented player on the American side of the Atlantic not to have won one of those titles that reflect greatness. Maybe 2002 will see the long-awaited major triumphs for the unlucky American left-hander and for Europe's Colin Montgomerie. Few would argue with this but if they do win that will scupper Tiger's Grand Slam hopes again.

Elsewhere David Davies recalls in more detail the major title challenges in 2001 but surely the saddest story of all was that involving a revitalised Ian Woosnam, whose charge for glory on the final day at Lytham was dramatically halted when he discovered he had an extra driver in his bag. It would never have happened at any other Open venue. Only Lytham starts with a par 3. Woosnam did not notice his error until the second hole but by then he had incurred his two shot penalty for having that second driver – one he had been trying out minutes earlier on the range. It was his fault as much as that of the caddie (who did not last much longer on the bag) but it underlined the necessity for an official to make a fail-safe cross-check with players on the first tee.

Woosnam rallied well enough to finish joint third and later in the season won the Cisco World Match Play Championship – an event which lost little from the fact that for the first time since its inception in 1964 no American was willing to travel to Britain in the aftermath of the September 11 terrorist attacks. Woosnam that week swept to victory beating US Open champion Goosen, surprisingly not seeded, Colin Montgomerie, defending champion Lee Westwood and Padraig Harrington. It was a bravura performance by a golfer who might well but for the extra club incident have made the European Ryder Cup team as a player rather than vice-captain.

For two years we had been looking forward to the Cup re-match. These days the transatlantic competition is a much closer affair and after the events that marred the otherwise superb last day performance of the Americans at Brookline there was a real chance to restore the Cup's reputation at The Belfry last September. The European captain Sam Torrance and Curtis Strange, who was leading the American side, had committed themselves to ensuring the match would be played in the highly competitive but friendly spirit that Samuel Ryder always wanted it to be.

Sadly it never happened. The terrible events of September 11 in New York, Washington and Philadelphia put paid to that. The match has been delayed for 12 months. Morally it was the only thing to do but ironically 2001 may well be remembered as much for the match that did not take place as for the match that did and produced a result that had all of us on this side of the Atlantic cheering to the echo.

Former British champion Peter McEvoy, who had a lengthy Walker Cup history as a player, has become the ultimate team captain. He led his men to a 15–9 victory at Nairn in 1999 and inspired them to come from behind in Georgia on the last day in 2001 to retain the trophy – a history-making performance. It was only the second win on American soil and the first time a Great Britain and Ireland side had successfully defended the trophy in the 79 years history of the encounter. To cross the Atlantic with the Cup and bring it back was stunning. Derek Lawrenson in the *Daily Mail* described the Walker Cup success as 'quite simply the greatest day in the history of British amateur golf.' With both players and spectators behaving as you might expect them to at a golf event Martin Johnson's article in the *Daily Telegraph* highlighted the difference between the last day scenes at the 1999 Ryder Cup at Boston and the 2001 Walker Cup. It was headed 'Gentleman's Guide to good pot hunting.' Bill Jones, the millionaire owner of Sea Island, where the Cup match was played, declared that the Walker Cup represented everything that is pure in golf. Nobody disagreed.

The victory will have a far reaching effect on the golf scene in Europe. So many of the McEvoy boys – Paul Casey, Luke Donald, Steven O'Hara, Nick Dougherty, to name just four, could become the backbone of the European professional scene in the years to come. Casey has already scored his first Tour victory at Gleneagles Hotel in the Scottish PGA Championship.

Golfing standards continue to improve. Sweden's Annika Sörenstam, who finished top money earner on the LPGA Tour for the fourth time in seven years, fired a first ever 59 in the Tour's 52 year history and in Canada Jason Bohn did even better with a 58. Nobody has yet broken 60 in Europe but the time cannot be long off when it will happen. Today players

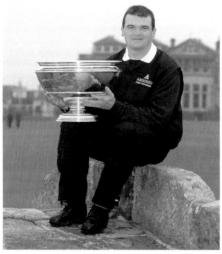

He had not won since taking the 1999 Open title but Paul Lawrie hit the jackpot in the Dunhill Links Championship

© Phil Sheldon

practice more, are aware, because of Tiger Woods, of the importance of keeping themselves fit and they take advantage of the advances in technology which have forced even Augusta National to make radical changes to the Masters layout.

At Augusta they have made changes at nine holes including seven par 4s and two par 5s. The overall yardage is now 7270 instead of 6985 all in an effort, as Hootie Johnson, the Augusta National Club chairman, explains, to 'keep the course current'. Cliff Roberts and Bobby Jones made changes in the past and what has been done to strengthen the course is in keeping with their philosophy.

Mark O'Meara who has already played the new courses with Tiger Woods predicts that winning scores now may not be much under par. Both agree that the integrity of the course has not been compromised in any way. Their summing up – 'It looks as if it has always been this way.'

These days the top professionals are driving close to 300 yards on average taking full advantage of the new technology. Following the death just over a year ago of Karsten Solheim, whose technical know-how revolutionised the game in the latter part of the 20th century with Ping, the game lost another giant in that field with the death at the age of 82 from pancreatic cancer of Ely Callaway, distantly related to Bobby Jones.

Callaway, who had spent 30 years in the textile industry, so loved golf that he bought a small golf company called Hickory Stick in 1984 for $400,000 and built it up in 16 years to a company worth $1.5 billion. Sales of Callaway clubs which earned a modest $5 million in 1988 had rocketed to $800 million annually by 1998. His 'Big Bertha', big headed drivers were hugely successful but he ran into problems with the authorities with his ERC titanium driver. It's spring-like effect on the hitting surface produces significant distance gains on the tee.

The Royal and Ancient Golf Club of St Andrews gave its approval for the new driver to be used but the United States Golf Association, who look after the game in the US and Mexico, banned it arguing that it was their responsibility to control unchecked technology. In this instance the Canadians, normally with the R & A, sided with the Americans. To date it is still possible for a player using a club that is illegal in America to win the Open with it in Britain where it is legal. It is essential that the two ruling bodies resolve this issue – the problem is how to do so without one side losing face. The importance of having one set of rules worldwide is evident enough.

Not everyone is in favour of golf being introduced into the Olympics but the World Amateur Golf Association has lodged a bid for golf to be

(From left): *Gary Player, Bob Charles and Sergio Garcia. Player and Charles, both former winners of the Open at Royal Lytham and St Annes, made their final appearance at the Championship there last year while Spain's Garcia continued to provide exciting golf wherever he played but mostly on t he other side of the Atlantic. He did play the required 11 events, however, to stay a full member of the European Tour.*

included officially in the 2008 Games scheduled for Beijing. Professionals could take part as well if the bid is accepted and that seems likely. The Chinese would relish seeing Tiger Woods attempt to become the first golfer since Canada's George Lyon in 1904 to win an official golfing gold. The game has not been part of the Olympics since 1936 and even then it was an unofficial sport. Inclusion does, however, bring benefits in the form of grants that could enable some countries to improve their facilities and training programmes.

Just how the events of September 11 will affect golf in general is still too early to say. The game is booming worldwide as a result of Tiger Woods and certainly there can be no worries in America or in Europe for the time being – most of the tournament contracts have several seasons to run. As George O'Grady, deputy executive director of the PGA European Tour states: 'Sponsors realise the value of the product they are backing. They know there are considerable global advantages in putting money in to golf.' These are difficult times for everyone but at any rate the bigger Tours seem safe.

Despite the traumatic happenings in September it was not a bad year. There were plenty of new winners and the older brigade Mark McNulty, Ian Woosnam, and the incredible Bernhard Langer on both sides of the Atlantic, reminded the younger fellows they are still competitively sharp. Sadly this did not stretch to Seve Ballesteros and Sandy Lyle who continue to struggle. Even Nick Faldo is finding it tough these days although he played well in the 2001 Volvo PGA Championship at Wentworth. It was a rare flash of the old brilliance but it would be unwise to write him off.

It was US Open champion Retief Goosen's year in Europe as he became the first non-European since Greg Norman in 1982 and the first South African since Dale Hayes in 1975 to win the Volvo Order of Merit ... and with two tournaments to spare. Darren Clarke looked like finishing second.

The sadness, for me, was the desperately bad luck suffered by long-time Tour sponsors Dunhill with their much-hyped pro-am celebration of links golf – on reflection a perhaps over-ambitious successor (in light of the time of year) to the Dunhill Cup at St Andrews in October.

The weather was as bad as it could be, the press coverage, on the sports pages at any rate, was less than complimentary and at times downright nasty. Yet celebrating links golf is a good idea and deserves to find a permanent place on the European calendar. Ironically the weather at either side of Dunhill week was glorious. The complicated television link up of three courses worked well and was watched by millions around the world and Paul Lawrie left the Old course with a cheque for £551,040.11p in his pocket.

Scotsman Lawrie had been worried that he had not won since taking the 1999 Open at Carnoustie from Justin Leonard and Jean Van de Velde, happily playing in Europe again in 2002. He felt some people were beginning to think of him as a flash in the pan although he never doubted his own ability to win again. When he rolled in a 60 foot winning birdie putt from the Valley of Sin he and his sponsor with whom, he played in the pro-am were all smiles. Come to think of it, is that putt from the Valley not as difficult as we thought? Costantino Rocca got himself into an Open play-off by holing from down there in the 1995 Open and Miguel Angel Martin did the same as he helped Spain to their successful defence of the sadly missed Dunhill Cup in 2000.

Impressive Tiger but not always invincible

David Davies reviews the 2001 majors

Tiger Woods won the US Masters, the first major championship of the 2001 season. Of course. Hadn't he won the last three of the season 2000? And five of the last six majors overall? It had become a custom; his habit.

Now though, he held all four major championships at the same time and the only problem confronting the golfing world was what to call it: the Simultaneous Slam perhaps, the Straight Slam, the Not-So-Grand Slam, the Tiger Slam?

Almost everyone was agreed it was not what was meant originally by the term Grand Slam, which would have had to be completed in a calendar year. Some of the players, Colin Montgomerie among them, thought that it was such a fantastic achievement that you could call it what you liked, including Grand Slam, but there were plenty of voices strongly against that appellation.

Surprisingly, perhaps, Tiger's father, Earl, was among the antis, as were Jack Nicklaus and Arnold Palmer and even Tiger was ambivalent. In the moment of his triumph – the greatest golfing feat of modern times – he never once uttered the words Grand Slam. At the press conference immediately after his Masters win, when he was asked directly if he thought he now held the Grand Slam he said only: 'I've got all four,' and he smiled a truly enigmatic smile.

Actions not words

That smile could have been taken to mean: 'You know, it really doesn't matter what you call it now, because I'll just win the next three and stifle the life out of the argument anyway.' Certainly no one in Augusta in April 2001 would have bet much against that, such was the aura of invincibility that Woods had draped around himself. Nothing, if he set his mind to it, seemed to be beyond his reach. He was the greatest and, unlike the conqueror of that corrupt sport, boxing, who had previously and repeatedly proclaimed himself The Greatest, Woods had allowed his skills and his clubs to do that type of talking. Woods did many wonderful things at Augusta, including holing five successive single putts from the seventh in the final round. They were of 8, 10, 7, 11 and 18 feet, each was huge-

ly important psychologically, keeping the chasers at arms length and making David Duval and Phil Mickelson, his principal challengers, wonder what they had to do to get through to the Tiger. But perhaps the biggest blow Woods inflicted was on his playing partner, Mickelson.

The perfect answer

The two men stood on the par five 13th tee knowing that this wonderful risk and reward hole could offer anything from an eagle to a triple bogey and could make or break either of them. Mickelson, a left-hander, had the honour and hit a magnificent controlled fade of a drive round the dog-leg, and as he stepped away, he smiled. He had produced his best when it was needed.

David Duval played superbly over the last two days to win his first major last July.

© Phil Sheldon

What he didn't know, however, was that Woods had the answer. He had been practising a shot since January which, he thought, could be used at this particular hole should he need extra length. He called it his 'slinger' and he duly slung it, low and, as if on rails, round the corner, where it finished 25 yards past Mickelson's best.

Misplaced expectations

Woods kept his face impassive. There was no glance at his opponent, no silent 'take that' and there was no need. Mickelson had been put in his place and Woods duly occupied his, which was top spot on the rostrum. The expectations for the remainder of the season then, were great, but as it turned out, misplaced. After the Masters there were too many times when you couldn't see Woods for the trees. His driving, so spectacular in the wide-open spaces of Augusta, was not so impressive when confined by the narrower fairways of Southern Hills for the US Open, of Royal Lytham and St Annes for the Open and of the Atlanta Athletic Club for the US PGA.

He began to miss fairways and that, in a major, is fatal. The rough, in these modern times, is so severe that to be in it is to drop a shot and with the quality of fields nowadays that cannot be afforded. Amazingly, Woods did not even contend for the three majors after the Masters and aside from the driving, several reasons were advanced for this relative decline.

Perhaps the most convincing came from one of the men closest to Woods, his friend and frequent

After missing from two feet to win the title South African Retief Goosen held his nerve to win the US Open play-off.

travelling companion David Duval. He said: 'If it had been me at the start of the season needing to win the Masters to have all four, that is what I would have put everything into. If I achieved it, well, that would have been that. I'm not saying that Tiger is not trying to win, just that he may have used everything up for a little while.'

Duval had won his Open Championship when he said that and so knew what goes into the winning of one major, never mind four in succession and five out of six. 'Believe me,' he said, 'it beats you up.'

The other theory of consequence was that Woods was not working quite so hard on the practice range. He swings so quickly, that it needs constant repetition in order to preserve the timing. Woods, who has always been one of the hardest workers in the game, became less so in the latter half of the year. In the period between the Open and the US PGA, for instance, he did not hit a competitive shot, preferring to go on two fishing trips, on one of which in Alaska his group were attacked by a bear. He wanted the salmon that Mark O'Meara had caught and it was only by running and wading to their boat in mid-stream that Woods, O'Meara and John Cook escaped.

The US Open, with Woods never in contention, plodded a fairly dreary way round Southern Hills, until it hit the 72nd hole. There the astonished spectators witnessed a finish to a major that may never be repeated, given that three men had the chance to win the title there and then, and none of them did. Mark Brooks, Stewart Cink and Retief Goosen were the contestants and they, in effect, played pass the parcel with the US Open Championship trophy.

Brooks, playing in front of the others, three-putted the last green, his first putt, from 35 feet being hit so badly that it was both seven feet long and seven feet left. That put him in the clubhouse at four-under and eventually Goosen and Cink arrived on the 18th tee five-under. Goosen then proceeded to hit two first-class shots to within 18 feet of the pin. Cink proceeded to hit two poor shots, the second of which nestled in deep rough on the left of the green.

His chip was 20 feet short, his first putt ran two feet past and then, instead of marking his ball, he tried to tap it in. He was anxious to get out of Goosen's way, because Cink and the whole golfing world anticipated that the South African would two-putt from where he was, and win. But Cink, in his hurry, missed, took 6 and went back to three-under.

A few moments later there was no more horrified man in world sport than Cink, for Goosen ran his first putt maybe two feet past and then, with the most tentative of jabs, missed the one to win the title. Goosen holed his third putt, to be in a play-off with Brooks – but not, of course, with Cink. It was a cruel way to lose a chance of your first major championship. The United States Golf Association clong doggedly to the 18-hole play-off the following day. It is almost always an anti-climax, and this ran true to form. Goosen birdied the 9th and 10th holes, Brooks bogied both and the US Open went to a third South African, Gary Player and Ernie Els having won it in earlier years.

Deserving Duval

Goosen deserves all credit for not allowing his 72nd hole miss destroy him completely. He did not have a history of winning before Southern Hills, with only four titles in his nine years on the European tour, and many a chance wasted. Brooks was the strong favourite for the play-off, having won the US PGA in 1996, but in fact he was outplayed throughout and lost by two.

The Open was played on a course, Royal Lytham and St Annes, that received, rightly, rave reviews. They achieved that most difficult of feats – one that, for instance, eluded Carnoustie completely – of making the course relatively fair. Not completely fair, of course, for no golf course can or should be that, but the players were given a chance to use their drivers, the first and second cuts of rough allowed the ball to be advanced significant distances and the greens, firm and fast, were not *too* firm or fast.

The course deserved a decent winner, and it got one of the best. David Duval has long been one of the great ball strikers in the game, generating enormous clubhead speed despite a slight physique. In the US PGA he *averaged* 320 yards off the tee. What of this man? He was briefly the world No.1, the last before Woods took over; he won the first three US tour events of 1999, including the best 59 recorded in the last round of the Bob Hope Chrysler Classic enabling him to win it but never before had he put together all aspects of his game in a major as he did in the final two rounds at Lytham. As he said: 'I played indifferently for the first two rounds, but holed everything, and then played really nicely for the last two rounds – and carried on holing everything.'

The last round was a confusing affair with as many would-be winners as a Florida election ballot paper has candidates. As many as eight men could have won it, although for long periods it seemed that the only way out would be a play-off. Among those in contention were Niclas Fasth, Darren Clarke, Ian Woosnam, Miguel Angel Jiménez, Bernhard Langer, Ernie Els and Billy Mayfair. There was so much going on that it was almost as if there was a great dust storm concealing proceedings, until suddenly it cleared and out of the wreckage stepped the winner, Duval.

David Toms was the third first-time major title winner of the year when he held off Phil Mickelson in the USPGA Championhip.

Two players in particular had their chance at the title and while Clarke contributed to his own misfortune, Woosnam's was effectively taken away from him by a bizarre set of circumstances.

Clarke got as far as the 17th before retreating. He went for a big drive at this exceedingly difficult hole and actually hit it too far, the ball rolling into a bunker. A double-bogey 6 dropped him back to joint third, but Woosnam will rue the day both he and his caddie, Miles Byrne, forgot one of the basic routines of professional golf: always count the clubs on the first tee.

The Welshman had been practising with two drivers and, after opening with a birdie at Lytham's short first hole – unusual in Championship golf – the man on the bag uttered the immortal words: "You're going to go ballistic," and he was right! The second driver was still in the bag, the bag now contained 15 clubs and under Rule 4-4 that was a two-stroke penalty.

Woosnam hurled the offending instrument into the undergrowth, hurled invective at all and sundry but particularly at the unfortunate Byrne, pointing out (in a cleaned up version) that it was 'the only thing I've asked you to do.' Without the two shots penalty Woosnam, who was jointly third, would have been clear second, would have won £218,333 more than he did and would have been, from that moment, in the Ryder Cup team. After it was over he did well to display a sense of humour. Asked if he had a routine for counting his clubs, he said: 'Well you usually start at one and stop when you get to fourteen ....' Of course without the penalty there's no saying where he would have finished – first or worse than third. We'll never know.

Meanwhile Duval was playing monumentally steady golf, typified by the par 4 15th, Lytham's hardest. His drive was long, but drifted just off the fairway. He had 215 yards to go and, anticipating a flier, took a six-iron and hit it flush. It finished 15-feet from the pin, a superb shot and after that the American knew he was going to win.

He made a lovely acceptance speech afterwards, telling a couple of tales about how he loved British golf and British crowds and saying how much he relished the thought of the name David Duval being on the trophy directly after that of Tiger Woods. It was only a year since he and Woods had gone out together for the final round at St Andrews, and Duval had been humiliated. He took 43 for the back nine, including four shots in the Road Hole Bunker, as he collapsed completely. Now he was the champion golfer of 2001: from chump to champ.

Experience no help

It has to be admitted that the season which slammed its way into our consciousness so dramatically at Augusta in April ended with a bit of a whimper. Before the start of the 83rd US PGA at the Atlanta Athletic Club, David Toms was not a man who was thought to be major championship material. A well-considered golfer, yes; a player capable of winning ordinary US Tour events but a man who had never really challenged at the top level, although he had impressed many when finishing joint fourth in the 2000 Open. That was to change, though, in the final round at Atlanta in which he was paired with Phil Mickelson who, with the relative decline of Colin Montgomerie for the moment at any rate, carries the tag of 'Best Player Never To Have Won A Major.'

Mickelson had a chance in the Masters, and in the US Open final round had three-putted the 13th from three feet to fade away there. Now, though, with Woods not in contention – Tiger had food poisoning and had lost nine pounds in eight days – Mickelson was only two behind the journeyman Toms with 18 to go. It was time for Mickelson's first major.

Earlier in the week he had spoken of his frustration at not being able to win at the top level because, he said, he was not aiming to win just one, but 'a whole bunch of them.' Here was his best chance so far and when, at the short 15th, Mickelson rolled in a huge birdie putt and Toms, having hit his tee shot into a bunker, took a bogey 4, it seemed Mickelson must win. They were level with three to play: surely Mickelson's major experience, his Ryder Cup experience, his

ranking of number two in the world, must help him prevail? He was level for as long as it took to play the 16th. Mickelson is one of the best putters in the world, but, as an American magazine was to remark, he is too often the best putter in the world *for three rounds*. Sure enough, he three-putted, hitting a 50-footer eight feet past, a mistake that was to be vital.

It meant that eventually Toms stood on the 18th tee with a one stroke lead, enabling him to play this 490-yards long par 4 the way he did. Toms' drive leaked away to the right; Mickelson was down the middle and long, easily able to carry the lake in front of the green. When Toms got to his ball, however, he found a dilemma. It was on a hump, above his feet, and his assessment of it was: 'A sidehill, downhill lie – that translates into a low hook with no spin on it.'

Knowing that Mickelson was almost certain of a par four and could quite possibly get a birdie, Toms had to decide whether to go for the green, or lay up and hope for a pitch-and-putt 4. The spectators had no doubt as to what they thought he should do. 'Go for it, go for it,' they yelled and then 'You wimp' when he showed signs of laying up. Back in the locker-room Hal Sutton, like Toms, from Shreveport, Louisiana was also yelling, but his advice was 'Lay up for chrissake.' On the fairway, Mickelson admitted later, he was hoping against hope that Toms would go for it.

Common sense

The situation was beautifully summed up in the *Atlanta Journal-Constitution* by Steve Hummer, as Toms weighed the merits of his options. Hummer wrote: 'David Toms stood there like forever, gripping the 5-wood, while testosterone squared off with common sense. In one ear a voice whispered: "Be a man, go for it. You're going to lay it up on a par 4? What next, hitting from the red tees? Lace doily head covers?" In the other cooed sweet reason: "It's 209 to the pin, water in the front, cabbage in the back. Lay up. Show 'em your sensitive side."'

Toms, of course, showed good sense. He took the pitching wedge to give himself an 88-yard third shot over the water. To have gone for the green would have been next to suicidal. 'I could have hit 100 balls', he said later, 'and I might have hit the green a few times but more likely I would have finished in the water, or the grandstand'. Toms then showed additional skill by hitting a lob wedge to 12 feet, and after Mickelson had missed his birdie attempt, holed for the Championship. It was another major disappointment for Mickelson, but Major Toms, as he was quickly and inevitably dubbed, will never forget the day that common sense squared off with testosterone, and won.

Cup postponement the correct decision

John Hopkins on Ryder Cup affairs

The 2001 Ryder Cup was the one that was on, then postponed and finally rearranged to take place almost exactly one year later. If this sounds complicated then it is – because of events in the US on September 11, events so unbelievably stunning they need no further elucidation.

The month had begun normally enough. On a Sunday evening in Munich at the beginning of September Sam Torrance, the European team captain, announced that Sergio García and Jesper Parnevik were his choices to round out his team to face the Americans at The Belfry four weeks later. Europe's leading golfers dispersed, some to play in Switzerland, some to rest, many to fly to St Louis to compete in the American Express tournament, one of the World Golf Championship events scheduled to begin on September 13. Then came the awful events of September 11 and, suddenly, golf seemed completely irrelevant compared with what had happened in New York, Washington and outside Pittsburgh. The American Express event in St Louis was first postponed and then cancelled, and while this was going on officials from the PGA of America and the PGA in Birmingham and the European Tour at Wentworth began a frantic series of transatlantic telephone calls, conference calls, faxes and e-mails as they tried to determine what to do about the biennial event that was now barely two weeks away.

Opinions differed on the best course of action. Out of respect for the thousands who had died in the terrorist attacks at the World Trade Center in New York, the Pentagon in Washington and in Philadelphia, it was surely only right and proper the Cup should be rescheduled. On the other hand by not playing would this be tantamount to giving in to the terrorists? By playing the event,

albeit with heavy hearts, would this give out a message of unity against those who had perpetrated such horrendous acts?

On Sunday September 16 it was announced the Ryder Cup was being postponed for a year. The PGA of America told officials in Europe that the scope of the tragedy of September 11 was so overwhelming it would be impossible for the US Ryder Cup team and officials to travel. This meant the European Ryder Cup Board had been placed in a position beyond its control and therefore the match, out of necessity, had been postponed. The compromise reached was that as much as possible of the 2001 event, including the two teams and the venue, would remain the same for 2002.

There was no surprise at the postponement. There had been indications of an American unwillingness to travel in the circumstances

Sam Torrance and Curtis Strange, the respective Ryder Cup captains, all smiles before the horror of the September 11 attacks.

© Phil Sheldon

when Tiger Woods had withdrawn from the Trophée Lancôme in Paris the week after the American Express, and the week before the Ryder Cup, Phil Mickelson and Mark Calcavecchia had also indicated, through their manager, that they would not travel to Europe at this time.

The postponement seemed a compromise between American expediency and British tact, but it raised hundreds of questions to do with the event. What about tickets? What about accommodation? What woud be done about this and about that? The loss adjusters had a field day.

Would it have been better to have cancelled the 2001 Ryder Cup and let everyone move on to the 2003 Ryder Cup? Financially, of course, that was not the answer. Was it a mistake to name the identical teams for the 2002 match as had been selected for 2001, when someone who had been in form in 2001 might be spectacularly out of form a year later? Maybe, but on the other hand there was some merit in saying 'these were the men who had won their places in the 2001 match and they should not be denied the opportunity to represent their continent, especially as, for some, it might be their only appearance.'

Wales successful

On 19 September it was announced that the 2001 match would take place at The Belfry from 27–29 September 2002, a week after the American Express Championship at Mount Juliet in Ireland. This was the date the PGA of America wanted. At the same time it was announced that the Ryder Cup would switch to even years so that the match at Oakland Hills, Michigan, which should have taken place in 2003 would now be held in 2004 and the one at the K-Club, south west of Dublin, would be in 2006 instead of 2005.

An extraordinarily eventful month ended with more animated discussion and controversy when Wales, for the first time in the match's history, was named as the venue for the 2010 event at Celtic Manor Resort and that Scotland would host the 2014 Cup match at Gleneagles

Hotel in Perthshire, where, back in the early 1920s, Walter Hagen had helped organise an unofficial Britain v America match – a forerunner of the Ryder Cup. This time the new Monarch's Course, renamed the PGA Millenium and designed by Jack Nicklaus, would be used. Wales, preferred choice of European Tour excutive director Ken Schofield months before the bidding ended, had won the day after an excellent campaign headed by former Test cricketer Tony Lewis. Now the wonderful Ryder Cup records of Dai Rees, Dave Thomas, Brian Huggett and Ian Woosnam were being recognised. The next four home Ryder Cups – 2018, 2022, 2026 and 2030 – would be held on the Continent. Arithmeticians quickly calculated that this meant there would not be a Ryder Cup in Britain or Ireland for 20 years from 2014.

The match may not have taken place in September 2001 for the most understandable of reasons but the Ryder Cup kept making the headlines for so many different reasons. What is certain is that the re-arranged match will be very different in character from the one at Brookline in 1999. The events of September 11 have reminded us all that golf – even when played at its most competitive – is just a game.

When the Cup match is played in September 2002 the teams chosen for the match in 2001 will line up. This is how they match up.

Eurupe: Darren Clarke, Padraig Harrington, Thomas Bjorn and Colin Montgomerie; Pierre Fulke, Lee Westwood, Paul McGinley and Niclas Fasth; Bernhard Langer and Phillip Price with wild cards Sergio García and Jesper Parnevik. Fasth, Fulke, McGinley and Price will be making their débuts. Langer will be making a tenth appearance having first played in 1981.

USA: Tiger Woods, Phil Mickelson, David Duval and Mark Calcavecchia; David Toms, Davis Love III, Scott Hoch and Jim Furyk; Hal Sutton, Stewart Cink and wild cards Scott Verplank and Paul Azinger. Toms, Cink ancl Verplank will be making their débuts.

The Ryder Cup no longer runs at a loss

The commercial value to the PGA European Tour and the PGA of the Ryder Cup now that the matches are much closer is apparent from the figures. In 1981 when the match was staged at Walton Heath and Europe lost to perhaps the strongest ever US side there was a loss of £50,000. Since then, however, each match played in Europe has shown an increasing profit.

In 1985 when Europe won for the first time since 1957 there was a £300,000 profit. This jumped to £l million profit in 1989 and £4 million in 1993 when the match was again played at The Belfry. The Valderrama Ryder Cup made £4.25 million of a surplus and the predicted profit for the 2001 match was £8.5 million. They are predicting a £10 million profit on the 2006 match at the K Club just outside Dublin and when the match is played in Wales for the first time in 2010 the profit could be £12 million. In future too, profits will be shared by the Tour, the PGA and the PGA of Europe

Americans stunned as McEvoy and his men make history

Mark Garrod salutes a brilliant Walker Cup side

Eight years ago anybody who wanted to denigrate the Walker Cup had an easy time doing so.

Thirty-four matches played and only three wins for Great Britain and Ireland. It made for such lop-sided reading that inevitably some people questioned whether the event should continue unaltered in the aftermath of a record 19–5 defeat in Minnesota, and with the Ryder Cup enjoying its revival following the introduction of continental Europe into the arrangements, the argument for change was strengthened.

If the amateur equivalent had continued in similar vein for perhaps even one more match it is hard to imagine the clamour for change being resisted, however difficult choosing a European team would have been and however strongly held the view that the true purpose of the series was as a medium of international friendship and understanding between the Royal and Ancient Golf Club of St Andrews and the United States Golf Association. Then came the victory at Royal Porthcawl in 1995 over an American side which contained Tiger Woods. Although the 1997 contest at Quaker Ridge did produce another crushing US win, the match two years later at Nairn saw Great Britain and Ireland stage a stunning second day comeback to register their biggest-ever winning margin.

Non-playing captain at Nairn Peter McEvoy felt that if he could harness the same spirit when the 'Class of 2001' travelled to Sea Island in Georgia then a first-ever successful defence for GB & I might be on the cards.

Hopes of that were dented when Paul Casey, unbeaten at Nairn and twice the English champion, decided to turn professional and not wait for a second cap. Yet against a United States side which the previous season had recaptured the Eisenhower Trophy world team title, the loss of Casey, the player who had been the second leading individual in that event, was overcome … and how!

In an extraordinary performance considering the extreme humidity, Great Britain and Ireland repeated their 15–9 win of two years earlier. It was the Americans who were left licking their wounds and wondering how to go about redressing the balance next time.

The match was a personal triumph for McEvoy. He had been in winning Eisenhower and Walker Cup teams as a player (as well as taking two Amateur Championship titles and winning more England caps than anyone in history) and had gone on to be the captain of sides who had done the same and become the first to take the trophy across the Atlantic and return with it.

Just as they did at Nairn, McEvoy's side came from behind on the second day. At one point in the Saturday singles the United States led in seven and were level in the other. That was as good as it got for them and 24 hours later it got very, very bad.

To be trailing only by a point at halfway maintained Great Britain and Ireland's belief that they had the winning of the match. In the end they did not just win it, they cruised home. Only one of the morning foursomes was lost and only one of the concluding eight singles.

Luke Donald confirmed himself as a star-in-the-making. Along with Casey, Donald had won four points out of four in 1999, and by making that seven out of eight the Beaconsfield player, out-standing on the American college circuit, was only one short of Sir Michael Bonallack's record number of wins for Great Britain and Ireland. To underline what an achievement that was, Sir Michael played in nine matches, Donald had done it in two.

The results page details the success of others as well, but special mention has to be made of one more member of the victorious side – and one American too. Forty-year-old Gary Wolstenholme now has the distinction of being on three winning Great Britain and Ireland teams, while 21-year-old Erik Compton, from Florida, became the first player to appear in the match after undergoing a heart transplant operation.

Danny Yates, retained as United States captain after the defeat at Nairn, was magnanimous again in the circumstances. 'You have figured out a way to play very good team golf and you do an excellent job of getting ready for the Walker Cup,' he told McEvoy.

Why have things changed so dramatically in so short a space of time? The increased number of British and Irish players in the American collegiate system has obviously made a big difference, and even those who do not look for golf scholarships are given more international experience at an early age. McEvoy pointed out, for instance, that 19-year-old Nick Dougherty, who like Donald turned professional straight after the match, had already won on four different continents.

Youngsters are generally better coached now as well and exposure to professional events has helped. There has been nothing for a while to match the astonishing fourth place achieved by 17-year-old Justin Rose in the 1998 Open, but Dougherty finished joint 12th at the Benson and Hedges International Open and Amateur champion Michael Hoey had a closing round of 64 to be joint 11th in the Scottish Open. Furthermore, David Dixon, a player who did not even make it into the Walker Cup side, came through regional and final qualifying to finish in a tie for 30th place in the Open at Royal Lytham and St Annes.

It was at Prestwick, home of the very first Open in 1860, that Northern Irishman Hoey won the Amateur, 31 years after his father Brian had been beaten by American Bill Hyndman in the semifinals. Hoey junior had to go to the seventh extra hole to defeat Scotland's Simon Mackenzie at the same stage, having been two down with three to play, then overcame Wales's Ian Campbell by one hole in the final.

The home nations filled four of the top five places in the European team championships in Sweden, with pride of place going to Scotland. Only fifth in the qualifying stages, they knocked out favourites England in the semi-finals and then Ireland 5–2 in the final. It was the Scots' fifth victory in an event where they have reached the final on 10 of the last 16 occasions.

England's revenge came at the home internationals at Woodhall Spa. Wooden spoonists the previous year – and that after seven successive victories – they recaptured the title from Scotland, with teenager Zane Scotland winning all his five games and Walker Cupper Jamie Elson five out of six.

What will be interesting to monitor now is how the four home countries fare in the Eisenhower Trophy in Malaysia next October. It will be the first time they have competed separately rather than as a combined Great Britain and Ireland side. As well as ratifying the individual membership applications, the World Amateur Golf Council has decided to reduce the size of all teams from four players to three so that more countries can participate.

A reminder of the emerging talent abroad, however, came at Chantilly in France, where Great Britain and Ireland's boys suffered a record 16–8 hiding at the hands of the Continent of Europe, who interestingly dropped only half a point from eight foursomes games.

The national championships went to Scott Godfrey (England), Gavin McNeill (Ireland), Barry Hume (Scotland) and Craig Williams (Wales), while former professional Richard Walker won the Brabazon Trophy, Richard McEvoy the Lytham, Greg Evans the Berkshire and Steven O'Hara the St Andrews Links Trophy, a success which enabled the 21-year-old to be named Scottish Golfer of the Year for the second season running. He will not be making it three, however. The Walker Cup was O'Hara's farewell to the amateur ranks and he can join Donald and Dougherty in saying: 'What a farewell.'

© Phil Sheldon

The victorious Walker Cup side with captain Peter McEvoy after their stunning success at Sea Island. They retained the Cup with a 15–9 victory.

Se Ri said she would never come back but did – and won

Lewine Mair reports on women's golf's newest major

European women's golf acquired an important new status symbol in 2001, as the Weetabix Women's British Open joined the Nabisco, the US Women's Open and the McDonald's LPGA championship as a major.

For Sir Richard George, the Weetabix chairman, the news that his tournament had been recognised must have rekindled many of the feelings he had when word came of his impending knighthood.

No less than the knighthood, the 'major' was well deserved, because no-one has poured more into the distaff side of the game than Sir Richard, a man who has always been engagingly conscious of the fact that women professionals have had few of the monetary advantages of their men.

Women golfers from around the world wanted to participate in the 2001 Weetabix. As is the case at the Open, the Americans started arriving four or even five days in advance in order to get the feel of Sunningdale. Yet there were two players, and important ones at that, who did not turn up till rather later ...

Annika Sörenstam and Karrie Webb, the No.1 and No.2 in the world, had been playing alongside Tiger Woods and David Duval in an exhibition match in California on the Monday and ended up flying into Heathrow on Tuesday night.

Webb was on the defensive when people asked if she was adequately prepared for the defence of her title and was given a hard time because of it. Sörenstam, though, was endearingly honest. She admitted that she had been unable to resist playing with Woods. 'I thought to myself that there were plenty more majors but that this might be my only chance to play with Tiger.'

No real impact

As you would expect, neither Sörenstam nor Webb made any real impact on the 2001 Weetabix but such is the strength in depth in the modern women's game that it was not the issue it might have been. There was good golf in progress on almost every fairway.

Se Ri Pak appeared like a genie on the last afternoon. Four behind Scotland's Catriona Matthew at the start of the day, she went from nowhere to somewhere with an opening eagle.

By the time she reached the 14th, she was topping the Leaderboard, with no one more surprised than she was when it became apparent that such early leaders as Lora Fairclough, Janice Moodie, Catriona Matthew and Laura Diaz had all taken a slide.

At the same time, she could not but think how very different this was to her first appearance in the Weetabix in 1998. Then, the combination of wind, rain and a share of 34th place had her vowing that she would never return to these shores.

It was Pak's caddie, Colin Cann, a young man who had previously worked with Annika, who persuaded her to think again. Cann, a member of the same West Byfleet club as Laura Davies, told the player that the more she tangled with the British game, the more she would grow to love it.

Se Ri Pak played the par 5s at Sunningdale in the Weetabix in an impressive 13-under en route to victory.

In particular, the Korean made telling use of Sunningdale's par 5s which, like most European par 5s, are generally more accessible than their American counterparts. She was 13 under for those holes, whereas Davies, who is still the longest and strongest of them all, was only four under.

Ultimately, Pak finished birdie, birdie for a closing 66 and an 11-under-par tally. There was then a long and tearfully anxious wait with her mother while the earlier leaders played the last few holes. Matthew gave the Pak family a fright when she made a birdie at the 14th to go 10 under, but the Scot retreated straightaway, catching sand at the 15th where she had made a hole-in-one on the Friday.

Hudston stays amateur

All of which left Pak winning what was her third major by two shots from her sister Korean, Mi Hyun Kim, who tackled Sunningdale with an assortment of woods from a No.11 to a driver.

As for the amateur medal, that went to the 22-year-old Rebecca Hudson who played with Pak on the last afternoon. To no-one's great surprise, Hudson demonstrated that she was not remotely out of place in that lofty company but, for the moment, she will stay put in the amateur game. She won the 2001 English Championship and the British Women's Stroke Play Championship and now has her heart set on playing in the 2002 Curtis Cup at Fox Chapel, Pittsburgh.

When the two of them got talking at Sunningdale, Laura Davies told Hudson that she was right not to rush into the professional game at a time when she was revelling in her amateur experiences. "You're lucky," she told her. "I couldn't afford to stay amateur for as long as I would have wanted." There had been no lottery funding for the top amateurs of her day.

The rake which contributed to Davies' undoing at Sunningdale was not some cad culled from the pages of a PG Wodehouse story. Instead, it was of the garden implement variety and had been carelessly tossed aside to the right of the bunker guarding the first green. It diverted Davies' perfectly struck second into the trap, leaving her with an impossible lie in which she had to hit her third with the ball some way above her feet. As if that were not enough, her recovery involved a double-hit, costing her a penalty shot and an eventual 6.

If the Weetabix was the tournament of 2001, there is no question that Annika Sörenstam's 59 was the round of the year. It happened on Friday 16th March, 2001, at the Standard Register Ping tournament at the Moon Valley Country Club in Phoenix.

Precisely nine years earlier, at that same event and that same venue, the then 21-year-old Swede had said something more than a little prophetic.

Annika Sörenstam fired a first-ever 59 on the LPGA tour.

© Phil Sheldon

At the time, she was in the second year of a golf scholarship at the University of Arizona. Already, she had made something of a name for herself in the college arena and, because the university was local, the Standard Register people had issued her with a special invitation.

Among the leaders

After having initially been turned away by the car park attendant, who protested that she could not possibly be old enough to play in a professional tournament, the elfin Annika went on to hand in an opening 68 which left her among the leaders. The golf writers already knew that she had won the previous year's NCAA championship but now they summoned her to the press room to hear about her golfing roots. Annika told them that she had started golf at 12 and that she had been playing for the Swedish women's team since she was 16.

The formal interview over, there was some informal chat in which a British journalist asked where her ambitions lay. Then, as now, Annika spoke quietly and, when she volunteered, "I want to shoot in the 50s," the journalist said she was sorry but she had not caught what she said. "I want to shoot in the 50s," repeated the player.

Although, at the time, the writer put it down to an extraordinarily talented young golfer getting a little carried away, Pia Nilsson, who captained the European team in the 1998 Solheim Cup at Muirfield Village, stepped in with an explanation. What Annika was saying, she said, had not been plucked from the world of dreams. Kjell Enhager, the Swedish psychologist who nowadays works with Nick Faldo, had been telling all aspiring Swedes that there was no reason why they should go along with the rest of the golfing globe in accepting that two putts per green were the norm. They should be aiming at one.

Sörenstam's win in the Standard Register was the second of four consecutive wins on an American tour which had known no such sequence since 1978 when Nancy Lopez, in her rookie season, won a record five tournaments in a row.

Pak interrupted Annika's run when she captured the Long Drugs Challenge in California but, as early as the middle of September, it was certain that no one was going to stop the Swede from winning the LPGA's Order of Merit for a fourth time. Webb and the aforementioned Pak were the players best placed to make a fight of it over the closing weeks.

If the Weetabix Women's British Open was the title which Davies would have wanted above the rest, she eventually matched her triumph in the 2001 LPGA Rochester International with a win in the WPGA International Match Play championship at Gleneagles.

The European women's Evian tour, like the men's Tour, is currently alive with up-and-coming players, with the women boasting such as Suzann Peterson, Raquel Corriedo and Paula Marti. Yet it has to be said that Davies remains the most popular of them all. She, more than any other, is the golfer who has been the making of the women's professional game on this side of the Atlantic, the process having started when she beat her American sisters in the 1987 US Open at Plainfield.

In an era when competitors everywhere are advised they would do better to keep their emotions in check, this great personality lets everyone share in the joys and frustrations of her every golfing day.

Sörenstam's Record 59

For her record 13-birdie score at the par 72 Moon Valley in Phoenix Arizona, Annika Sörenstam started her round at the 10th. This is how she compiled the lowest round on the LPGA Tour. She had 11 single putts and missed only one fairway – at the sixth (her 15th).

10th	534 yds	par 5	sand wedge to 9ft	1P 4	1st	349 yds	par 4	sand wedge to 9ft	1P 3
11th	157 yds	par 3	9 iron to 7ft	1P 2	2nd	169 yds	par 3	7 iron to 22ft	1P 2
12th	394 yds	par 4	8 iron to 30ft	1p 3	3rd	336 yds	par 4	sand wedge to 12ft	1P 3
13th	506 yds	par 5	7 wood to 18ft	2P 4	4th	511 yds	par 5	chip to 18in	1P 4
14th	355 yds	par 4	sand wedge to 4ft	1P 3	5th	136 yds	par 3	9 iron to 9ft	2P 3
15th	177 yds	par 3	7 iron to 11ft	1P 2	6th	393 yds	par 4	8 iron to 20ft	2P 4
16th	414 yds	par 4	7 iron to 10ft	1P 3	7th	401 yds	par 4	9 iron to 30ft	2P 4
17th	360 yds	par 4	sand wedge to 18ft	1P 3	8th	476 yds	par 5	7 wood to 25ft	2P 4
18th	408 yds	par 4	8 iron to 25ft	2P 4	9th	383 yds	par 4	sand wedge to 9ft	2P 4

Front nine 28

Back nine 31

Total 59

36

Tiger's global impact has changed golf forever

Jerry Tarde on an incredible achievement

When the disaster of September 11 struck New York City and Washington, D.C. and the anticipation of even worse nightmares hung in the air, Tiger Woods was waiting to play a golf tournament in the American Midwest. With airports closed and the tournament cancelled, Tiger's reaction was to get in a car – it will be left unsaid whether it was a Buick – and drive by himself the 987 miles home. It took him 18 hours, interrupted only by cell phone calls from his minder at Nike, who naturally worried for his safety.

A man who has made it this far, however, who has delivered on every outlandish prediction his father ever made could find his own way from St. Louis, Missouri, to the wrought-iron gates of Orlando, Florida, without any trouble. That trip was nothing compared to where he's taking the game of golf.

Interplanetary

Tiger's impact can be summed up in a single word: globalization. The sport had been played worldwide before he came along, but the stakes and the volume and the consequences are at the outer edges of even Earl Woods' imagination.

Never before, not in Bobby Jones' time, not in Arnold Palmer's, has the most famous athlete in the world been a golfer. When Jones played, only Britain and America cared. Palmer added the whole of Europe in resuscitating the Open Championship, but Tiger's oyster is almost interplanetary. He stands at the gates of Asia, the Third World, a China opening up and the Internet Galaxy.

Tiger will reach emerging markets like no other product spokesman. The wind beneath his swoosh is a global company that will promote his celebrity worldwide for decades to come.

One of the things Tiger has brought to golf, or returned to it, depending on your point of view, is the sense that money doesn't matter. His own personal wealth crossed the threshold of ever having to care about earning a living, for himself or even for his children's children. (This, of course, was the unspoken goal that always drove, still drives, Jack Nicklaus.)

Tournament winnings aside, Tiger's endorsement income now tops $70 million annually, and, even were I to be handling his investments, it's a foregone conclusion that he will be our first billion dollar athlete. Greg Norman may have had the Ferraris and yachts of a rock star, but

Not even Jack Nicklaus, Arnold Palmer or Seve Ballesteros enjoyed the universal popularity of Tiger Woods. He has transformed the game.

Tiger's got the complete package of riches and celebrity.

His rising tide floats all the boats of professional golf. Just as Frank Beard once said that every pro should get down on his hands and knees and thank Arnie for 25 cents out of each dollar earned, today's pros owe $250,000 out of every million to Tiger.

PGA Tour purses doubled in his first four years as a pro, and despite a poorer economy, they will probably double again in the next four years. The $5 million American purse has had an odd chain reaction: it's hurt the European Tour as more players choose to play in the U.S.; it's allowed pros at the end of their career, like Bernhard Langer, to win millions more; if anything, it's become more difficult for women's golf to survive; and it's driven golf equipment companies to the sidelines, replaced by multinational corporate sponsors.

Just at a time when team players were signing ever bigger contracts and becoming increasingly less fan friendly, and the perception of them was growing as overpaid and arrogant, golf stood out as shiningly different. Our players are accessible – too accessible in this age perhaps – and they only take home the money they earn. Golfers don't wear uniforms, making them easier to 'logo', and they don't get arrested.

Tiger super-heated this phenomenon, and his greatest impact may be as the game's unlimited partner in translating golf spectators into players. If he delivers even ten per cent of his potential, he will be credited with stimulating the first significant growth of the game since the early age of Palmer.

TV loves Tiger

The American television network CBS studied his effects on viewing habits in 2000 and the results were astounding, even by his standards. When Tiger was in contention (defined as being among the top five on Sunday), the TV ratings were 113% higher than average. Tiger simply being in the field increases the tournament audience by 30 to 40 per cent.

Of course, Tiger can also be credited with popularizing the power game. Ironically he uses clubs that do not push the leading edge of technology, but the distance he nevertheless achieves has ushered in an era of power-hitters.

To keep up with him, tour players have conditioned their bodies, maximized their equipment and honed their technique in an all-out effort to become 300-yard men. In the past, long-knockers were freak shows and carnival acts who entertained the crowds but disappeared on weekends. Now, for the first time in history, the best players in the world are the longest hitters.

'Tiger Distance' is a requirement for playing the game at the highest level, and the result has been a mad dash by course architects to roll back the tee boxes on golf's museum pieces. Augusta National, horrified by the 78-yard pitch he played into its 18th hole in winning the 2001 Masters, signalled this land rush by picking up and moving the tee 60 yards to the rear.

The distinguished writer for *Golf World* magazine, Ron Sirak, makes the point that unlike in previous generations, great athletes are turning to golf as a legitimate pursuit. Before Tiger, says Sirak, the pro game was populated by failed athletes from other sports. Golf was rarely the first choice. The tour was filled with people in Dow Finsterwald bodies.

Now, as a direct result of the exciting potentials offered up by Tiger, really good young athletes have taken up golf ahead of all other sports. And they are focusing on golf from an early age. Imagine the talent of a Greg Norman, introduced to the game at 17, if he knew he were going to be a professional golfer from age 5, as Tiger seemingly did.

Tiger legitimizes golf in the eyes of young people, who no longer see the game as something their oddly-dressed dad performs, but as a genuinely cool sport. My own daughters, now aged 6 and 7, have followed Tiger on television since infancy, and he remains the only golfer aside from me and my erratic friends they can identify. There is something about his countenance, the smile, the baby face, that leads children to think of Tiger as one of their own. The seeds he's planting now may take 15 or 20 years to mature, but the game will be indebted to him for a changed image among young people.

Lee Trevino used to say that nobody ever got a full set: 'The good Lord always held back at least one of the 14 clubs.' Even the great Jack Nicklaus, who seemed to have everything, didn't have a wedge.

Magical happenings

Tiger lays that thinking to rest. Tiger has the wedge through the driver, and the putter, too. He has the smile and the smarts, the personality and the raw ability to make magical things happen when they are needed most. He has the world's greatest name for a golfer – could you invent one better than 'Tiger Woods'? Not since Cassius Clay has an athlete had a better handle.

Tiger transcends his sport. He even has a father who is a war hero. As we've come to realize now, it's not Nicklaus that the son of the father is chasing. It's Gandhi.

GOLF IRELAND ™

IRELAND'S NATIONAL GOLF MAGAZINE

IRELAND'S LARGEST DISTRIBUTED SPORTS MAGAZINE. 100% IRISH.

Going direct to
over 250,000
Irish golfers

Reach over half a million high spending golfers in European's most lucrative market

Contact Gregory Francis for details

Phone: 00353-1-4734100   Fax: 00353-1-4731056
Email: sales@121golf.com

The Golden Age that ended with Herbert Warren Wind

Ian Wooldridge writes about golf writers

I have never been a golf correspondent. By trade I am a sort of gypsy sports columnist who briefly pitches his tent at Twickenham, the Olympics, Sydney Cricket Ground, Royal Ascot, at a Las Vegas ringside or America's Cup yachting. Occasionally I get an esoteric assignment like the Iditerod dog-sled race across 1000 miles of Alaska which is damned cold, I can tell you.

Generosity of spirit

Yet the warmest I ever feel is when writing off-beat pieces from some golf tournament: the Open Championship, the US Masters, the Walker Cup, wherever. It has nothing to do with the climate. It has everything to do with the generosity of spirit of specialist round-the-year golf writers to this occasional intruder – something that does not apply in

Henry Longhurst's secret – he did what he liked doing best and got someone else to pay.

all sports. I once had the wire of my telephone cut by a British colleague just before reporting a big fight from New York.

I first learned of the generosity of golf writers at the very first major event I attended. It was The Ryder Cup at Palm Desert, California, in 1959, when, nervous and wet behind the ears, I met the great Henry Longhurst for the first time. God, this was the supreme Longhurst for whose magical golf column in the *Sunday Times* I used to jump on my bicycle and get down to the newsagent's to read at crack of dawn.

Instantly he treated *me* as an equal in a deplorable trade. 'I am glad to see', he said, 'that already you have learned the secret of life. It is to find out what you like doing best and then get someone to pay for it.' It was probably that evening when I acquired my lifelong affinity with dry martinis!

Golf writing has changed dramatically since then. The ferocious circulation wars between the red-top tabloids some 20 years ago introduced another element: news reporters who see golf as a soft target for scandal, marital discord and strife which frequently hits the front pages and leads to headlines like 'Is Nick Faldo the Most Hated Man in Sport?' which I am ashamed to say appeared in my own newspaper. The writer had never met Nick Faldo in his life. Other pop-papers sent men and posses of photographers to discover the identity of Tiger Wood's latest girl friend. Sports editors with no affinity with the game wanted dirt.

Playing it straight

It is essential to make this distinction before writing about golf writers down the ages. By and large, golf writers play it pretty straight. They realise they have no chance of getting a 1000 word essay about the beautiful links at Portmarnock or Turnberry into their papers. News and controversy are what sell newspapers today and most of them can tread that line, particularly since the introduction of the ubiquitous press conference.

There is no denying the convenience of the press conference, particularly in these days of ever more demanding deadlines. Instantly everybody in the press is privy to the wisdom of men such as

Jack Nicklaus or the experience of Arnold Palmer. Most would acknowledge, however, that the press conference has had a detrimental affect on golf writing. It is far easier to dash off 'quotes' than construct an original sentence or description or comment. It is a field day for the popular press when a significant golfer can be lured into an indiscretion. *That*, you may rest assured, will make tomorrow's dominant headline even if two players have just shot 62s.

Another contributing factor is the propensity of golfers to put their names to autobiographies, mostly produced by ghost-writers. This can be a very lucrative sideline when aimed at newspaper serialisation but this is dodgy ground. Newspapers want revelation, hopefully sensation. The book is filleted down to two or three articles, sometimes completely rewritten from the original text, which are topped by eye-catching headlines. It was this that led to the very public in-fighting between ex-Ryder Cup captain Mark James and Nick Faldo in 2000. It was an unpleasant episode and, sadly, it will not be the last.

Imaginary England

But this is writing *about* golf. It is not golf-*writing*. Golden ages are often mirages but I think one ended when Mr Herbert Warren Wind, an American besotted by the English class system, wrote an article at least 6000 words long about The Sacred Nine, in other words the nine-hole Royal Worlington course just outside Cambridge.

I read it in the Algonquin Hotel in New York and the astonishing thing was that it covered page after page of the *New Yorker* magazine, a publication as unlikely to carry an article about golf, let alone some pint-sized course in England, as it would the sexual depravity of Bangkok. Mr Warren Wind – I would never call him Herbert since we have not been introduced – was an intense wordsmith. His feature article was beautifully written and very snobbish, introducing vulgar New Yorkers to an England that had not really existed, except in Warren Wind's imagination, since Evelyn Waugh's society novels of the mid 1930s. I wondered, and still do, whether we shall see its like again, even in specialist golf magazines which now tend to concentrate on features about how to add 30 yards to your drive.

Warren Wind was clearly a disciple of Bernard Darwin, the acknowledged father of great golf essayists, a vivid writer whose reports in *The Times* under the by-line 'Our Golf Correspondent' spanned the Open Championship at Prestwick in 1914 to Ben Hogan's only Open appearance at Carnoustie in 1953. With his fascination for English eccentricity, however, Warren Wind couldn't keep his eyes off three other writers,

Henry Longhurst, of the *Sunday Times*, Leonard Crawley of the *Daily Telegraph* and Pat Ward-Thomas, of *The Guardian*. He christened them The Crazy Gang.

Longhurst, squat and remarkably brilliant, had covered and been involved in everything from war to motor racing, from Parliament to the Cresta Run, and was the best writer of the three. His *Sunday Times* column exemplified a great principle of journalism: people not things are the best subjects.

'Dear boy,' he would say – his invariable introduction if he took a shine to you – 'a tip. Always take a pencil and a piece of paper with you to a party or dinner and when you hear a good story write down a trigger word so that you will recall it when you are sober in the morning.' It probably cost me half a dozen large gins to learn that trick.

Leonard Crawley, a brilliant all-round sportsman, impressed Warren Wind in a different way. Leonard would arrive in America for a golf tournament and send for a stenographer to take down his mighty words. He was belligerent but authoritative whereas Ward-Thomas was a meticulous sentence-constructor whose wartime experiences in the battlefield made his impatience with militant trades union copy-takers, in the days when every word had to be transmitted by telephone, spectacular and noisy. He never actually burst a blood vessel but there were many times we thought he would.

Salute true genius

This is the great divide between golf-writing then and now and there was only one man who bridged the gulf and he, too, is no longer with us. He was a tall, lugubrious, shambling man who only turned to golf-writing half-way through his journalistic career. His name was Peter Dobereiner, once features editor of my newspaper, the *Daily Mail*. Occasionally, when I had struggled with some article, he would saunter over to my desk and say 'Look, pal, wouldn't this paragraph read better if we did it like this?' He was a genius.

One day he said: 'I've had enough of all this. I've had enough of office life. I love that golf and I'm going to have a crack at writing about it'.

Walk now into the luxurious Valderrama Golf Club in southern Spain and they will direct you to the Peter Dobereiner Room, upon whose walls are framed examples of his always witty, perceptive and penetrating columns. Was Dobereiner the last of the great golf writers? I truly hope not but scanning the publishing horizon it may just be that my trade of journalism may have decreed otherwise.

Muirfield – always a fair and demanding Open challenge

Keith Mackie on this year's venue for the oldest major

When the clamour of the 2002 Open Championship has died away, television cameras have been swiftly moved to the next sporting extravaganza and stands have been dismantled, life at Muirfield, home of the Honourable Company of Edinburgh Golfers, will settle back into the style of a byegone age.

The Honourable Company has the distinction of being the world's oldest golf club with records that date back to 7 March , 1744, and members today keep a firm grip on the standards and traditions more closely in tune with the early days of the game.

This reactionary club has no professional's shop, no souvenir-crested sweaters, the small tee markers carry no yardages or stroke index. Foursomes is the preferred choice of play and lunch is served at one long table where each new entrant into the dining room takes the next available seat.

Sampling the delights of golf at Muirfield is not easy and the club has a fearsome reputation for repelling visitors, fuelled mainly by stories

© Phil Sheldon

Nick Faldo won two of his three Open titles at Muirfield. In 1987 he shot 18 straight pars in the final round to beat Paul Azinger and Rodger Davis. In 1992 he came from behind to edge out John Cook.

of former secretary, ex-Navy Captain Paddy Hanmer, whose bark was so ferocious that few were tempted to risk what proved to be a less intimidating bite. Jack Nicklaus, an Open winner at Muirfield, made a personal plea for a member of his golf course design team to play. There was no chance of a game said Hanmer, 'but send him along and we'll let him walk the course'.

A limited number of starting times is available to those who write in advance with a letter of introduction from their home club. The fortunate few find that, once through the doors, the rather frosty, aloof face that Muirfield presents to the world is totally contradicted by the warm and gracious atmosphere within.

The club's place in the annals of the game began on the day in 1744 when a request for the donation of a silver club, to be offered as the prize in an annual open competition, was agreed by the magistrates and council of Edinburgh City following the traditions already well established by companies of archers, who competed for silver arrow trophies.

In the city archives, in a flowing if faded hand, one of the most momentous incidents in the history of golf is faithfully recorded: 'It being represented in council that gentlemen of honour, skilful in the ancient and healthful exercise of the golf, had applied for a silver club to be annually played for on the Links of Leith at such times and upon such conditions as the Magistrates and Council should think proper.

'And it being reported that the Gentlemen Golfers had drawn up a scroll at the desire of the Magistrates of such articles and conditions as to them seemed most expedient, as proper regulations to be observed by the Gentlemen who should yearly offer to play for the said Silver Club, which were produced and read in council.'

Then follow the conditions laid down for the event which included five shilling entry fees from each competitor which were to be 'solely at the disposal of the victor'.

Not only did these regulations signal the birth of the world's oldest golf club (The Royal Burgess Golfing Society in Edinburgh claims it was founded in 1735 but has no records dating back to then), but they also set down for the first time a set of rules to govern play. The rather primitive condition of Leith's five-hole course can be judged by those original 13 rules. If a ball was stopped by any object or person, or by a horse or dog, it had to be played where it lay. Players were not able to remove stones, bones or broken clubs that interfered with play, except on the green, and then only if they were within one club's length of the ball. And there was a one-stroke penalty for lifting the ball from 'watter or any wattery filth'.

The first winner of the silver club was Edinburgh surgeon John Rattray. The following year he exercised his professional skills to treat the wounded at the Battle of Prestonpans and stayed with Bonnie Prince Charlie and his army as they drove deep into English territory, but was taken prisoner after the retreat and final defeat at Culloden. Scotland's senior judge and fellow golfer Duncan Forbes finally arranged his release and he again competed for the silver club in 1748.

The golfers of the Honourable Company continued to play at Leith until 1836 when they moved to the longer and less crowded nine-hole course a few miles to the east at Musselburgh. It was here, in 1874, that they first staged the Open Championship, having been invited by Prestwick, the originators of the event 14 years earlier, to join a three-way agreement with the Royal and Ancient Golf Club of St Andrews to promote the championship.

Six Opens were played at Musselburgh before the Honourable Company found an ideal site at Muirfield, 20 miles to the east of Edinburgh, on which to build their own 18-hole private course in 1891. Andrew Kirkaldy, who was to become the first honorary professional of the Royal and Ancient Golf Club of St Andrews but a man not renowned for his diplomatic turn of phrase, judged the new course to be nothing more than 'an old water meadow'. Yet it was the venue little more than a year later, of the first Open to be played over 72 holes and has since built a justified reputation as one of the great championship courses, an intrinsically fair and demanding challenge.

Amateur Harold Hilton, playing against his father's wishes and arriving by train only an hour or so before the Championship began, won that first four-round Open and was followed by Harry Vardon and James Braid, two of the great players who dominated the game in the decades that bracketed the turn of the century. Then came Ted Ray and Walter Hagen, Alf Perry and Henry Cotton, before Gary Player ushered in the modern era by overcoming an eight-stroke deficit to overhaul the leaders over the final 36-holes in 1959 to capture the first of his three Open titles.

The roll call of great Muirfield champions continued with a period of American supremacy led by Jack Nicklaus, Lee Trevino, who edged out Tony Jacklin dramatically in 1972, and Tom Watson (1980) – a stars and stripes invasion ended by Britain's own emerging champion Nick Faldo, who played every hole of the final round in par in foul weather conditions in 1987 to claim his first major title of six.

When the championship returned in 1992 to mark the centenary of Muirfield's association with the Open, it was again Faldo who took the honours, becoming only the second player since James Braid in 1901 and 1906, to score an Open double at the home of the Honourable Company.

Brad and Faldo double winners

Year	Winner	Club/Nationality	Scores — Total	First prize £
1892	Harold Hilton	Royal Liverpool (am)	78-81-72-74—305	—
1896	Harry Vardon	Ganton	83-78-78-77—316	30
	(after a play-off with JH Taylor (Winchester): Vardon 157, Taylor 161)			
1901	James Braid	Romford	79-76-74-80—309	30
1906	James Braid	Walton Heath	77-76-74-73—300	30
1912	Ted Ray	Oxhay	71-73-76-75—295	50
1929	Walter Hagen	USA	75-67-75-75—292	100
1935	Alf Perry	Leatherhead	69-75-67-72—283	100
1948	Henry Cotton	Royal Mid-Surrey	71-66-75-72—284	150
1959	Gary Player	South Africa	75-71-70-68—284	1,000
1966	Jack Nicklaus	USA	70-67-75-70—282	2,100
1972	Lee Trevino	USA	71-70-66-71—278	5,500
1980	Tom Watson	USA	68-70-64-69—271	25,000
1987	Nick Faldo	England	68-69-71-71—279	75,000
1992	Nick Faldo	England	66-64-69-73—272	95,000

James Braid and Nick Faldo each won two Opens at Muirfield

The Swedish life-style that breeds winners

Göran Zachrisson on a remarkable success story

Swedes have done quite well at golf lately, particularly the women. This has led many to believe that there is a system in Sweden: one that breeds good players. In a sense that is true, for we have a way of finding youngsters who show promise, not only at golf but at all sports.

Having found them, we care for their needs for a while, coach them, school them and, once they are in their late teens, we let them go.

Traditionally, sports in Sweden are run by volunteers, an extensive and intricate network of people who manage clubs, drive buses to events, provide for, coach and, above all, encourage. It is a unique set-up that has no social barriers, no matter in which sport you participate. I believe this will always be the country's great equaliser.

Sweden is twice the size of Great Britain and Ireland and has a population of 8.5 million, fewer people than live in London. As a fifth of the country lies within the Arctic Circle, there is not much opportunity for outdoor sports. The golfing season on average lasts no more than four months. Yet it is a great country for sports, especially in the winter. Almost everyone growing up in Sweden will know how to ski and skate. Being able to swim at least 200 metres is obligatory in schools. There is an indoor swimming pool in most villages, as well as an indoor ice rink and floodlit track for running or cross-country skiing.

The major sport is football and, with 500,000 registered players in 450 clubs, golf is placed fourth. What is interesting is that in spite of a governmental pledge to make all sports accessible to everyone, there is not one public course in Sweden and only a handful of pay-as-you-play layouts. If you want to play at any of the private clubs, you have to show membership at another club.

We have an enormous amount of land available for the game. In fact, the whole country looks like a golf course, with streams, rivers, lakes, hills, and natural characteristics. All you need to do is cut down a few trees, locate a good site for a green and off you go.

Formal organisation

Sweden's sports world is organised formally as a pyramid. The government gives an annual allowance to the General Sports Organisation which distributes the monies to the different National Federations. Last year the Golf Federation received 4 million SKr, equal to £300,000. In addition it received fees paid to it by the clubs – each individual club donation based on its membership.

The Swedish Federation has a division that deals with marketing and sponsorship: it runs a golf magazine distributed to every golfing household in Sweden, operates a website, has an organisation handling the annual Scandinavian Masters, the Compaq Open on the Evian Tour and the Swedish Golf Tour, two tournaments of which are on the European Challenge Tour. Altogether more than 60 people are employed by the Federation, which has become one of the richest Sports Federations in the country.

Before turning to specifics, let me point out that all Federations are basically run the same

© Phil Sheldon

Jesper Parnevik, the first Swede to win a European Tour event in Sweden

way, using very similar methods to seek out the talented athletes. As a country Sweden is not particularly diverse – there are not that many people, so everyone knows everyone and talent cannot be hidden. We seem to be good at organising things.

This is why the best woman golfer in the world is a Swede and why we have three Swedes in the Ryder Cup team. In the latest Solheim Cup half the European team were from Sweden. But it also explains why we annually export many footballers to different leagues around the world, at least 20 youngsters to the National Hockey League, and just as many handball players. At the moment some of the best swimmers come from Sweden, some of the best in speedway, car racing, table tennis, bandy – a type of outside hockey played with a red ball and crooked stick – skiing, skateboarding, sailing, orienteering and wrestling.

Developing talent

I am not trying to impress. I am only reporting facts and suggesting that the main reason why so many Swedish sports people have reached prominence is that they were given the chance and were supported and encouraged when they were young to develop their talents.

The junior golfers are treated like any other full member at the golf club. They can play whenever they like and if they show aptitude, they get coaching. Some clubs have practice facilities and experienced committee members looking after the juniors. Parents and others chauffeur the kids to Teen Tour Events, a national series of competitions run by the Federation. Later many are given the opportunity to go to special Golf College, where they can study at a pace that suits them and fits in with their other sporting, educational and social commitments. The aim is still to pass their Baccalaureate but not at the expense of their sporting abilities and desires.

Some, with help, end up in the USA on golf scholarships. Some stay on in Sweden to plan the foundation of a professional career. During their amateur years all the best players are observed by swing experts, psychologists, administrators and others. Often these tutors have visited the US and European Tours to learn from the Parneviks, Sörenstams, Forsbrands and Karlssons and each year there is a conference where the good young player get to meet and talk and play golf with the best tour players. All experiences are shared. The older players enjoy this too because they feel like the sailor coming back from a long voyage. They are giving something back.

There is also constant cross-referencing . The golfers will hear boxers speaking of timing; rifle shooters will discuss concentration and breathing; sailors will speak of endurance and eating; weightlifters of balance; ice hockey players of the technique of the slap shot.

This is the Swedish system, if that is the word for it. I am suspicious of the word, for systems aim to suit everyone and are therefore seldom good for anyone, and I also believe that what we are doing in Sweden might not work in any other country. Like great wines, systems sometimes do not travel well but the Swedish way may well be worth trying because it is proving so successful. Yet speaking of greatness, how do we explain such individuals as Björn Borg or Ingemar Stenmark? Are they products of the Swedish way of life and system, or would they have come through, no matter what, because of their very special qualities and ambitions?

Swedish Winners in Europe

Men		Women	
Anders Forsbrand	7	Helen Alfredsson	12
PU Johansson	5	Liselotte Neumann	12
Jesper Parnevik	4	Sophie Gustafson	8
Robert Karlsson	4	Annika Sörenstam	6
Jarmo Sandelin	4	Sofia Grönberg-Whitmore	3
Mathias Gronberg	3	Kirstin Ehrnlund	3
Ove Sellberg	3	Karin Koch	2
Mats Lanner	3	Catrin Nilsmark	2
Pierre Fulke	3	Maria Wennersten	1
Patrik Sjöland	2	Anna Oxenstierna	1
Joakim Haeggman	2	*50 events won since 1979*	
Michael Jonzon	2		
Niclas Fasth	1		
Henrik Stenson	1		
Peter Hedblom	1		
45 wins in 15 years			

Venues and Dates for the US Majors and the Ryder Cup

	The Masters	US Open	USPGA Championship
2002	**April 11–14** Augusta National, Augusta, Georgia	**June 13–16** Bethpage State Park, New York	**15–18 August** Hazeltine National, Massachusetts
2003	**April 10–13** Augusta National, Augusta, Georgia	**June 12–15** Olympia Fields, Illinois	**14–17 August** Oak Hill CC, New York
2004	**April 8–11** Augusta National, Augusta, Georgia	**June 17–20** Shinnecock Hills, Southampton, NY	**August** Whistling Straits, Kohler, Wisonsin
2005	**April 7–10** Augusta National, Augusta, Georgia	**June 16–19** Pinehurst No.2, Pinehurst, NC	**August** The Country Club, Brookline, MA
2006	**April** Augusta National, Augusta, Georgia	**June 15–18** Winged Foot GC, Mamaroneck, NY	**August** Medinah CC, Medinah, IL

The US Masters normally begins on the Thursday following the first Sunday in April.
The US Open Championship normally begins on the Thursday following the second
Sunday in June.
The USPGA Championship normally begins on the second Thursday in August.

Ryder Cup

The 2001 Ryder Cup was postponed to 2002 and the Cup will now be played in even
years.

2002 at The Belfry, Sutton Coldfield, West Midlands on September 27–29
2004 at Oakland Hills Country Club, Birmingham, Michigan on September 26–28
2006 at The K Club, County Kildare, Ireland
2008 at Valhalla Golf Club, Louisville, Kentucky
2010 at Celtic Manor Resort, Newport, Wales
2012 at Medinah Country Club, Illinois
2014 at Gleneagles Hotel, Perthshire, Scotland

Presidents Cup (USA *v* Rest of the World except Europe)
2003 at Fancourt Hotel and CC Estate (The Links Course), George, South Africa

R&A Venues and Dates for Championships 2002–2004

	2002	2003	2004
The Amateur Championship	**June 3–8** Royal Porthcawl/ Pyle & Kenfig	**June 2–7** Royal Troon/ Irvine (Bogside)	**May 31–June 5** St Andrews Old & Jubilee
The Open Championship Regional Qualifying	**July 8**	**July 7**	**July 5**
The Open Championship Final Qualifying	**July 8–15** Dunbar Gullane No.1 Luffness New North Berwick	**July 13–14** TBA	**July 11–12** TBA
The Junior Open Championship	**July 15–16** Royal Musselburgh	**Not Played**	**July 13–14**
The Open Championship	**July 18–21** Muirfield	**July 17–20** Royal St George's	**July 15–18** Royal Troon
The Senior British Open	**TBA** Muirfield	**TBA** Royal St George's	**TBA** Royal Troon
The Seniors' Open Amateur Championship	**August 7–9** Woodhall Spa, Hotchkin and Bracken Courses	**August 6–8** Blairgowrie, Rosemount and Lansdowne	**August 4–6** The Berkshire, Red and Blue Courses
The Boys' Home Internationals	**August 6–8** Blairgowrie	**August 5–7** Royal St David's	**August 3–5** Royal Dublin
The Boys' Amateur Championship	**August 12–17** Carnoustie	**August 11–16** Royal Liverpool	**August 9–14** Conwy (Caernarvonshire)
British Mid-Amateur Championship	**August 14–18** Formby	**August 13–17** Jubilee Course, St Andrews	**August 11–15** Royal Liverpool
The Jacques Léglise Trophy	**August 30–31** Lausanne, Switzerland	**August 29–30** Lahinch, Ireland	**August 27–28** Nairn, Scotland
The St Andrews Trophy	**August 30–31** Lausanne, Switzerland	**Not Played**	**August 27–28** Nairn, Scotland
The Walker Cup	**Not Played**	**September 6–7** Ganton	**Not Played**
The Eisenhower Trophy	**October 10–13** Kuala Lumpur, Malaysia	**Not Played**	**TBA** Puerto Rico

Schedules for the 2002 Season

USPGA Senior Tour

Jan 14–20	MasterCard Championship, Hualalai Golf Course, Kaupulehu-Kona, HI
Jan 21–27	†Senior Skins Game, Wailea Golf Resort, Maui, HI
Jan 28–Feb 3	Royal Caribbean Classic, Crandon Park Golf Club, Key Biscayne, FL
Feb 4–10	ACE Group Classic, Pelican Marsh Country Club, Naples FL
Feb 11–17	Verizon Classic, TPC of Tampa Bay, Lutz, FL
Feb 18–24	Audi Senior Classic, La Vista Country Club & Golf, AC, Puebla, MX
Feb 25–Mar 3	SBC Senior Classic, Valencia Country Club, Valencia, CA
Mar 4–10	Toshiba Senior Classic, Newport Beach Country Club, Newport Beach, CA
Mar 11–17	Siebel Classic in Silicon Valley, Coyote Creek Golf Club, San Jose, CA
Mar 25–31	Emerald Coast Classic, The Moors Golf Club, Milton, FL
Apr 1–7†	Liberty Mutual Legends of Golf, The King & The Bear at WGV, St Augustine, FL
Apr 15–21	World Seniors Invitational, TPC at Piper Glen, Charlotte, NC
Apr 22–28	The Countrywide Tradition, TBA
Apr 29–May 3	Bruno's Memorial Classic, Greystone Golf Club and CC, Birmingham, AL
May 6–12	TD Waterhouse Championship, Tiffany Greens Golf Club, Kansas City, MO
May 13–19	The Instinet Classic, TPC at Jasna Polana, Princeton, NJ
May 20–26	Farmers Charity Classic, Egypt Valley Country Club, Ada, MI
May 27–Jun 2	NFL Golf Classic, Upper Montclair Country Club, Clifton, NJ
Jun 3–9	Senior PGA Championship, Firestone Country Club, South Akron, OH
Jun 10–16	BellSouth Senior Classic at Opryland, Springhouse GC, Nashville, TN
Jun 17–23	Greater Baltimore Classic, Hayfields Country Club, Hunt Valley, MD
Jun 24–30	US Senior Open, Coves Valley Golf Club, Wings Mills, MD
Jul 1–7	AT&T Canadian Senior Open, Essex G and C Club, LaSalle, Ontario
Jul 8–14	Ford Senior Players Championship, TPC of Michigan, Dearborn, MI
Jul 15–21	SBC Senior Open, TBA, Chicago, IL
Jul 22–18	FleetBoston Classic, Nashawtuc Country Club, Concord, MA
Jul 29–Aug 4	Lightpath Long Island Classic, Meadow Brook Club, Jericho, NY
Aug 5–11	3M Championship, TPC of the Twin Cities, Minneapolis, MN
Aug 19–25	Novell Utah Showdown, Park Meadows Country Club, Park City, UT
Aug 26–Sep 1	Alianz Championship, Glen Oak Country Club, West Des Moines, Iowa
Sep 2–8	Kroger Senior Classic, TPC at River's Bend, Maineville, OH
Sep 9–15	RJR Championship, Tanglewood Park, Clemmons, Winston-Salem, NC
Sep 16–22	SAS Championship, Prestonwood Country Club, Cary, NC
Sep 23–29	Gold Rush Classic, Serrano Country Club, El Dorado Hills, Sacramento, CA
Sep 30–Oct 6	Turtle Bay Championship, The Palmer Couse at Turtle Bay, Kahuku, HI
Oct 7–13	The Napa Championships, Silverado Resort, Napa, CA
Oct 14–20	SBC Championship, TBA, San Antonio, TX
Oct 22–28	Senior Tour Championship at Gaillardia G and C Club, Oklahoma City, OK
Nov 4–10	†Our Lucaya Senior Slam, Lucaya Course, Grand Bahama Island, Bahamas
Nov 11–17	†Wendy's Three Tour Challenge, Lake Las Vegas Resort, Las Vegas, NV
Dec 9–15	†Office Depot Father-Son Challenge, The Ocean Club, Nassau, Bahamas
Dec 16–22	†Hyundai Team Matches, Monarch Beach Golf Links, Dana Point, CA

US Men's Amateur Championship

Aug 19–25	Oakland Hills CC, Broomfield Hills, MI

† Not PGA Tour

US PGA Tour

The first nine events constitute the St Paul West Coast swing (i.e. Mercedes Championship through Touchstone Energy Tucson Open and Accenture Match Play Championship). The last 12 events constitute the PriceWaterhouseCooper Fall Finish (i.e. Air Canada Championship to the Tour Championship and Southern Farm Bureau Classic)

Dec 31–Jan 6	Mercedes Championships, The Plantation Course at Kapalua, Kapalua, HI
Jan 7–13	Sony Open in Hawaii, Waialae Country Club, Honolulu, HI
Jan 14–20	†Bob Hope Chrysler Classic, PGA West-Arnold Palmer Private Course, Tamarisk
Jan 21–27	Phoenix Open, TPC of Scottsdale, Scottsdale, AZ
Jan 28–Feb 3	†AT&T Pebble Beach National Pro-Am, Pebble Beach, CA
Feb 4–10	Buick Invitational, Torrey Pines Golf Course, LaJolla, CA
Feb 11–17	Nissan Open, Riviera Country Club, Pacific Palisades, CA
Feb 18–24	**WGC: Accenture Match Play Championship**, La Costa, Carlsbad, CA
Feb 18–24	Touchstone Energy Tucson Open, Omni Tucson National Golf Resort, AZ
Feb 25–Mar 3	Genuity Championship, Doral Golf Resort and Spa, Miami, FL
Mar 4–10	Honda Classic, TPC at Heron Bay, Coral Springs, FL
Mar 11–17	Bay Hill Invitational Presented by Cooper Tires, Bay Hill, Orlando, FL
Mar 18–24	The Players Championship, TPC at Sawgrass, Ponte Vedra Beach, FL
Mar 25–31	Shell Houston Open, TPC at The Woodlands, TX
Apr 1–7	BellSouth Classic, TPC at Sugarloaf, Duluth, GA
Apr 8–14	**The Masters**, Augusta National Golf Club, Augusta, GA
Apr 15–21	WorldCom Classic, Harbour Town Golf Links, Hilton Head Island, SC
Apr 22–28	Greater Greensboro Chrysler Classic, Forest Oaks Country Club, Greensboro, NC
Apr 29–May 5	Compaq Classic of New Orleans, English Turn Golf and Country Club, LA
May 6–12	Verizon Byron Nelson Classic, TPC at Four Seasons-Las Colinas, Irving, TX
May 13–19	Mastercard Colonial, Colonial Ccountry Club, Fort Worth, TX
May 20–26	Memorial Tournament, Muirfield Village GC, Dublin, OH
May 27–Jun 2	Kemper Insurance Open, TPC at Avenel, Potomac, MD
Jun 3–9	Buick Classic, Westchester Country Club, Harrison, NY
Jun 10–16	**US Open Championship**, Bethpage State Park, Farmingdale, NY
Jun 17–23	Canon Greater Hartford Open, TPC at River Highlands, Cromwell, CT
Jun 24–30	FedEx St Jude Classic, TPC at Southwind, Memphis, TN
July 1–7	Advil Western Open, Cog Hill Golf and Country Club, Lemont, IL
Jul 9–15	Greater Milwaukee Open, Brown Deer Park Golf Course, Milwaukee, WI
Jul 15–21	**Open Championship**, Honourable Company of Edinburgh Golfers, Muirfield
Jul 15–21	BC Open, En-Joie GC, Endicott, NY
Jul 22–28	John Deere Classic, TPC at Deere Run, Silvis, IL
Jul 29–Aug 4	The International Presented by Owest, Castle Pines Golf Club, Castle Rock, CO
Aug 5–11	Buick Open, Warwick Hills Golf and Country Club, Grand Blanc, MI
Aug 12–18	**USPGA Championship**, Hazeltine National Golf Club, Chaska, MN
Aug 19–25	**WGC: NEC Invitational**, Sahalee Country Club, Sammanish, WA
Aug 19–25	Reno-Tahoe Open, Montreux Golf and Country Club, Reno, NV
Aug 26–Sep 1	Air Canada Championship, Northview Golf and Country Club, Surrey, BC, Canada
Sep 2–8	Bell Canadian Open, Angus Glen Golf Club, Markham, Ontario, Canada
Sep 9–15	SEI Pennsylvania Classic, Waynesborough Country Club, Paoli, PA
Sep 16–22	**WGC: American Express Championship**, Mount Juliet Estate, Thomastown, CO
Sep 16–22	Tampa Bay Classic presented by Buick, Westin Innisbrook Resort, Palm Harbor, FL
Sep 23–29	**Ryder Cup**, The De Vere Belfry, Sutton Coldfield, England
Sep 23–29	Texas Open at LaCantera, LaCantera Golf Club, San Antonio, TX
Sep 30–Oct 6	Michelob Championship at Kingsmill, Kingsmill Golf Club, Williamsburg, VA
Oct 7–13	†Invensys Classic at Las Vegas, TPC at Summerlin, Las Vegas, NV
Oct 14–20	†National Car Rental Golf Classic at Walt Disney World Resort, Lake Buena Vista, FL
Oct 21–27	Buick Challenge, Callaway Gardens Resort, Pine Mountain, GA
Oct 28–Nov 3	The Tour Championship presented by Dynegy, East Lake Golf Club, Atlanta, GA
Oct 28–Nov 3	Southern Farm Bureau Classic, Annandale Golf Club, Madison, MS

US Women's Amateur Championship

Aug 12–17	Sleepy Hollow CC, Scarborough, NY

Bold type indicates a major   † *Host Club*

PGA European Tour

Nov 22–25	BMW Asian Open, Westin Resort, Ta Shee, Taiwan
Nov 29–Dec 2	Omega Hong Kong Open, Hong Kong GC, Hong Kong
Jan 10–13	South African Open, The Country Club, Durban, South Africa
Jan 17–20	Alfred Dunhill Championship, Houghton GC, Johannesburg, South Africa
Jan 24–27	Johnnie Walker Classic, Lake Karrinyup GC, Victoria, Australia
Jan 31–Feb 3	Heineken Classic, Royal Melbourne GC, Victoria, Australia
Feb 7–10	The ANZ Championship, The Lakes Golf Club, Sydney, Australia
Feb 20–24	**WGC: Accenture Match Play**, La Costa Resort & Spa, Carlsbad, California, USA
Feb 21–24	Caltex Singapore Masters, Laguna G&CC, Singapore
Feb 28–Mar 3	Carlsberg Malaysian Open, Royal Selangor GC, Kuala Lumpur, Malaysia
Mar 7–10	Dubai Desert Classic, Emirates GC
Mar 14–17	Qatar Masters, Doha GC, Qatar
Mar 21–24	Madeira Island Open, Santo da Serra, Madeira
Mar 28–31	Open de Canarias, El Cortijo Club de Campo, Gran Canarias
Apr 4–7	Algarve Portuguese Open, TBC
Apr 11–14	**The Masters**, Augusta National, GA, USA
Apr 19–21	The Seve Trophy, Druids Glen, Wicklow, Ireland
Apr 25–28	Open d'España, TBC
May 2–5	Novotel Perrier Open de France, Le Golf National, Paris, France
May 9–12	Benson & Hedges International Open, The De Vere Belfry, Sutton Coldfield, England
May 16–19	Deutsche Bank – SAP Open TPC of Europe, St Leon-Rot, Heidelberg, Germany
May 23–26	**Volvo PGA Championship**, Wentworth Club, Surrey, England
May 30–Jun 2	Victor Chandler British Masters, Woburn, Milton Keynes, England
Jun 6–9	The Compass Group English Open, Marriott Forest of Arden, Warwickshire, England
Jun 13–16	**US Open**, Bethpage State Park, Farmingdale, New York, USA
Jun 20–23	The Great North Open, De Vere Slaley Hall, Northumberland, England
Jun 27–30	Murphy's Irish Open, Fota Island, Cork, Ireland
Jul 4–7	Smurfit European Open, The K Club, Dublin, Ireland
Jul 11–14	The Scottish Open at Loch Lomond, Loch Lomond, Glasgow, Scotland
Jul 18–21	**131st Open Golf Championship**, Muirfield, East Lothian, Scotland
Jul 25–28	The TNT Open, Hilversumche GC, Hilversum, Netherlands
Aug 1–4	Volvo Scandinavian Masters, Kungsängen, Stockholm, Sweden
Aug 8–11	The Celtic Manor Resort Wales Open, Newport, Wales
Aug 15–18	**US PGA Championship**, Hazeltine National GC, Chaska, Minnesota, USA
Aug 15–18	North West of Ireland Open, Ballyliffin GC, Co Donegal, Ireland
Aug 22–25	**WGC: NEC Invitational**, Sahalee CC, Redmond, Washington, USA
Aug 22–25	Gleneagles Scottish PGA Championship, The Gleneagles Hotel, Pethshire, Scotland
Aug 29–Sep 1	BMW International Open, Golfclub München Nord-Eichenried, Munich, Germany
Sep 5–8	Omega European Masters, Crans-sur-Sierre, Switzerland
Sep 12–15	Linde German Masters, Gut Lärchenhof, Cologne, Germany
Sep 19–22	**WGC: American Express Championship**, Mount Juliet, Co. Kilkenny, Ireland
Sep 27–29	**The 34th Ryder Cup**, The De Vere Belfry, Sutton Coldfield, England
Oct 10–13	Trophée Lancôme, Saint-Nom-la-Bretèche, Paris, France
Oct 17–20	†Cisco World Match Play Championship, Wentworth Club, Surrey, England
Oct 24–27	Telefonica Open de Madrid, Club de Campo, Madrid, Spain
Oct 31–Nov 3	Atlanet Italian Open, Is Molas, Sardinia Italy
Nov 7–10	**Volvo Masters Andalucia**, TBC
Dec 12–15	**WGC: EMC World Cup**

Bold type indicates a major   † *denotes approved special events*

European Amateur Championships

Championships in italics have not been confirmed yet

Feb 27–Mar 3	Spanish Ladies Amateur Championship, Montecastillo
	Spanish Amateur Championship, Costa Ballena
Mar 13–17	Portuguese Ladies Amateur Championship, Marvao
	Portuguese Amateur Championship, Marvao
Mar 28–Apr 1	French Lady Juniors Championship, Golf de Saint-Cloud
	French Boys Championship, Golf de Toulouse-Scilla\
Apr 26–28	German Ladies Amateur Championship, GC Am Alten Fliess, Cologne
	German Amateur Championship, GC Am Alten Fliess, Cologne
Apr 27–28	Scottish Ladies Open Stroke Play Championship, Portlad & Royal Troon
May 4–5	Lytham Tropy, Roya Lytham & St Annes
May 10–12	Irish Amateur Open Championship, Royal Dublin
May 17–19	English Open Stroke Play (Brabazon Trophy), Royal Cinque Ports
May 17–20	Austrian Ladies Amateur Championship, GC Fontana, Oberwaltersdorf
	Austrian Amateur Championship, GC Fontana, Oberwaltersdorf
May 22–26	Spanish Junior Championship, Léon Glub de Golf
Jun 1–2	Welsh Open Youths Championship, Cardiff
Jun 3–8	**The Amateur Championship**, Royal Porthcawl/Pyle & Kenfig
Jun 11–15	**Ladies' British Open Amateur Championship**, Ashburnham
Jun 13-15	**Polish Open Amateur Championship**, Gdansk G&CC
Jun 14–16	*Coupe Marat*, Chantilly
Jun 14–16	Scottish Open Amateur Stroke Play Championship, Southerness
Jun 17–20	Spanish Lady Juniors Championship, El Fresnillo
Jun 21–23	Welsh Open Stroke Play Championship, Pyle & Kenfig
Jun 22–23	Scottish Youths Open Amateur Stroke Play Championship, Murrayshall
Jun 26–30	Russian Ladies Amateur Championship, Moscow CC
	Russian Amateur Championship, Moscow CC
Jun 27–28	Irish Youths Amateur Open Championship, Seapoint
Jun 28–30	Welsh Ladies' Open Stroke Play Championship, Northop Country Park
Jul 3–7	Luxembourg Ladies Amateur Championship, GC Grand Ducal
	Luxembourg Amateur Championship, GC Grand Ducal
Jul 3–5	Dutch Junior International, Toxandria
Jul 16–18	*Slovak Amateur Championship*, TBA
Jul 23–25	English Boys (under 18) Amateur Stroke Play Championship (Carris Trophy), Beau Desert
Jul 27–28	Irish Ladies Open Stroke Play Championship, Dundalk GC
Jul 29–31	Danish Girls Championship, Smorum GC, Copenhagen
	Danish Boys Championship, Smorum GC, Copenhagen
Jul 30–31	Scottish Lady Junior Stroke Play Championship, Baberton GC
Aug 1–4	Finnish Ladies Amateur Championship, Helsinki GC
	Finnish Amateur Championship, Helsinki GC
Aug 2–4	Swiss Ladies Amateur Championship, Zürich-Zumikon
	Swiss Amateur Championship, Zürich-Zumikon
Aug 6–10	**Girls British Open Amateur Championship**, Sandiway
Aug 7–9	**British Senior Championship**, Woodhall Spa
Aug 12–17	**British Boys Championship**, Carnoustie
Aug 13–16	English Ladies' Open Intermediate Championship, Littlestone GC
Aug 14–17	Czech Ladies Amateur Championship, GC Marianske Lazne
	Czech Amateur Championship, GC Marianske Lazne
Aug 14–18	**British Mid-Amateur Championship**, Formby
Aug 27–31	Belgian Lady Junior Championship, Royal GC de Belgique, Ravenstein
	Belgian Junior Championship, Royal GC de Belgique, Ravenstein
Aug 29–31	Hungarian Open Ladies Amateur Championship, Old Lake GC
Sep 5–8	*Slovenian Ladies Amateur Championship*, TBA
	Slovenian Amateur Championship, TBA
Sep 11–13	Ladies British Open Amateur Stroke Play Championship, Hunstanton
Sep 18–22	Italian International Ladies Amateur Championship, Villa d'Este GC
	Italian International Amateur Championship, Villa d'Este GC
Sep 20–22	Polish Junior Open Championship, Binowo Park
Sep 24–26	*Senior Ladies British Open Amateur Championship*, Longniddry

European Amateur Championships *continued*

Sep 26–29	French Ladies Amateur Stroke Play Championship, Paris
	French Amateur Stroke Play Championship, Paris
	Hellenic Ladies Amateur Championship, Glyfada GC
	Hellenic Amateur Championship, Glyfada GC
Oct 14–17	Israel Ladies Amateur Open Championship, Caesarea GC
Oct 14–17	Israel Amateur Open Championship, Caesarea GC
Oct 26–29	Turkish Open Amateur Championship (Men), National GC-Belek-Antalya

European Team Championships

Jul 9–13	Lady Juniors, Moscow G&CC, Russia
	Youths, Gdansk G&CC, Poland
	Girls, Torino GC, Italy
	Boys, Reykjavik GC, Iceland

International European Championships

Jun 6–8	Mid-Amateur, Kärntner GC Dellach, Austria
Jun 13–15	Seniors, La Manga, Spain
Jun 28–30	EGA Challenge Trophy – Men, Bled GC, Slovenia
Jul 25–27	European Young Masters, GC Augsburg, Germany
Aug 21–24	Amateur, TBA
Aug 28–31	Ladies, Kristianstad GC, Sweden
Oct 3–5	European Club Cup Trophy – Ladies, Racing Club de France, La Boulie
Nov 6–9	European Club Cup Trophy – Albacom Trophy, parco de Medici GC, Italy

International Matches

May 8–10	Europe v Asia/Pacific, Hirono GC, Japan
Aug 30–31	St Andrews Trophy, Lausanne GC, Switzerland
	Jacques Léglise Trophy, Lausanne GC, Switzerland

Tournaments recommended by the European Golf Association

Apr 10–13	*Sherry Cup, European Nations Championship,* Sotogrande, Spain
Jul 15–16	Junior Open Championships, Royal Musselburgh, Scotland
Aug 28–31	*IFJG World Junior Golf Championship,* TBA

World Championships

Oct 16–19	Espirito Santo Trophy, Saujana G&CC, Malaysia
Oct 24–27	Eisenhower Trophy, Saujana G&CC, Malaysia

Dates courtesy of the European Golf Association

US LPGA Tour

Schedules can be found on p.226

Abbreviations

Alb	Albania	Ind	India	Pol	Poland
Arg	Argentina	Irl	Ireland	Por	Portugal
Aus	Australia	Isl	Iceland	Pur	Puerto Rico
Aut	Austria	Ita	Italy	Rus	Russia
Bel	Belgium	Jam	Jamaica	Sin	Singapore
Bra	Brazil	Jpn	Japan	RSA	South Africa
Can	Canada	Kor	Korea (South)	Sco	Scotland
Chi	China	Mex	Mexico	Swe	Sweden
Col	Colombia	Nam	Namibia	Sui	Switzerland
Den	Denmark	Ned	Netherlands	Tai	Taiwan
Eng	England	NI	Northern Ireland	Tha	Thailand
Esp	Spain	Nor	Norway	Tri	Trinidad and
Fij	Fiji	NZ	New Zealand		Tobago
Fin	Finland	Pan	Panama	USA	United States
Fra	France	Par	Paraquay	Ven	Venezuela
Ger	Germany	Per	Peru	Wal	Wales
Hun	Hungary	Phi	Philippines	Zim	Zimbabwe

(am)	Amateur	(M)	Match play	jr	Junior
		(S)	Stroke play	sr	Senior

Where available, total course yardage and the par for a course are displayed in square brackets, i.e. [6686–70]

* indicates winner after play-off

Late Results

Results and related items that were obtained too late for inclusion in their pertinent sections can be found on pages 202 and 203

PART I

The Major Championships

The Open Championship

130th Open Championship at Royal Lytham & St Anne's (7115 yds, Par 72)

Prize Money £3,229,748. Entries 2255. Regional qualifying courses: Alwoodley, Blackmoor, Burnham & Berrow, Carlisle, County Louth, Copt Heath, Coxmoor, Hadley Wood, Hindhead, Little Aston, Northamptonshire County, Orsett, Renfrew, Stockport, Wildernesse, Wilmslow. Final qualifying courses: Fairhaven, Hillside, St Anne's Old Links, Southport & Ainsdale. Final field comprised 156 players, of whom 70 (including one amateur) made the half-way cut on 144 or better.

1	David Duval (USA)	69-73-65-67—274	£600000	€984756
2	Niclas Fasth (Swe)	69-69-72-67—277	360000	590854
3	Bernhard Langer (Ger)	71-69-67-71—278	141667	232512
	Ian Woosnam (Wal)	72-68-67-71—278	141667	232512
	Miguel Angel Jiménez (Esp)	69-72-67-70—278	141667	232512
	Billy Mayfair (USA)	69-72-67-70—278	141667	232512
	Ernie Els (RSA)	71-71-67-69—278	141667	232512
	Darren Clarke (NI)	70-69-69-70—278	141667	232512
9	Sergio García (Esp)	70-72-67-70—279	63750	104630
	Jesper Parnevik (Swe)	69-68-71-71—279	63750	104630
	Mikko Ilonen (Fin)	68-75-70-66—279	63750	104630
	Kevin Sutherland (USA)	75-69-68-67—279	63750	104630
13	Des Smyth (Irl)	74-65-70-71—280	40063	65753
	Loren Roberts (USA)	70-70-70-70—280	40063	65753
	Raphaël Jacquelin (Fra)	71-68-69-72—280	40063	65753
	Colin Montgomerie (Sco)	65-70-73-72—280	40063	65753
	Billy Andrade (USA)	69-70-70-71—280	40063	65753
	Vijay Singh (Fij)	70-70-71-69—280	40063	65753
	Alex Cejka (Ger)	69-69-69-73—280	40063	65753
	Retief Goosen (RSA)	74-68-67-71—280	40063	65753
21	Nick Price (Zim)	73-67-68-73—281	32500	53341
	Davis Love III (USA)	73-67-74-67—281	32500	53341
23	Greg Owen (Eng)	69-68-72-73—282	30500	50058
	Michael Campbell (NZ)	71-72-71-69—282	30500	50058
25	Eduardo Romero (Arg)	70-68-72-73—283	27500	45135
	Tiger Woods (USA)	71-68-73-71—283	27500	45135
	Bob Estes (USA)	74-70-73-66—283	27500	45135
	Joe Ogilvie (USA)	69-68-71-75—283	27500	45135
29	Barry Lane (Eng)	70-72-72-70—284	25000	41032
30	Stewart Cink (USA)	71-72-72-70—285	21500	35287
	Justin Rose (Eng)	69-72-74-70—285	21500	35287
	Scott Verplank (USA)	71-72-70-72—185	21500	35287
	Phillip Price (Wal)	74-69-71-71—285	21500	35287
	Nicolas Vanhootegem (Bel)	72-68-70-75—285	21500	35287
	Phil Mickelson (USA)	70-72-72-71—285	21500	35287
	David Dixon (am) (Eng)	70-71-70-74—285		
37	Padraig Harrington (Irl)	75-66-74-71—286	16300	26753
	Dudley Hart (USA)	74-69-69-74—286	16300	26753
	Toru Taniguchi (Jpn)	72-69-72-73—286	16300	26753
	Andrew Coltart (Sco)	75-68-70-73—286	16300	26753
	Frank Lickliter (USA)	71-71-73-71—286	16300	26753
42	Mark O'Meara (USA)	70-69-72-76—287	13500	22157
	Steve Stricker (USA)	71-69-72-75—287	13500	22157
	Richard Green (Aus)	71-70-72-74—287	13500	22157
	JP Hayes (USA)	69-71-74-73—287	13500	22157

42T	Paul Lawrie (Sco)	72-70-69-76—287	13500	22157
47	Brad Faxon (USA)	68-71-74-75—288	10629	17444
	Peter Lonard (Aus)	72-70-74-72—288	10629	17444
	Robert Allenby (Aus)	73-71-71-73—288	10629	17444
	Lee Westwood (Eng)	73-70-71-74—288	10629	17444
	Chris DiMarco (USA)	68-74-72-74—288	10629	17444
	Adam Scott (Aus)	73-71-70-74—288	10629	17444
	Matt Gogel (USA)	73-70-71-74—288	10629	17444
54	José María Olazábal (Esp)	69-74-73-73—289	8943	14678
	Paul Curry (Eng)	72-71-71-75—289	8943	14678
	Mark Calcavecchia (USA)	72-70-N-75—289	8943	14678
	Carlos Daniel Franco (Par)	71-71-73-74—289	8943	14678
	Paul McGinley (Irl)	69-72-72-76—289	8943	14678
	Duffy Waldorf (USA)	70-73-69-77—289	8943	14678
	Rory Sabbatini (RSA)	70-69-76-74—289	8943	14678
61	Stuart Appleby (Aus)	69-75-72-74—290	8500	13951
62	Gordon Brand jr (Sco)	70-72-75-74—291	8400	13787
	Brandel Chamblee (USA)	72-69-74-76—291	8400	13787
	Pierre Fulke (Swe)	69-67-72-83—291	8400	13787
65	Neil Cheetham (Eng)	72-72-73-78—295	8300	13622
66	Alexandre Balicki (Fra)	69-75-75-77—296	8225	13499
	Thomas Levet (Fra)	72-72-77-75—296	8225	13499
68	David Smail (NZ)	71-72-76-79—298	8150	13376
69	Sandy Lyle (Sco)	72-71-77-81—301	8075	13253
	Scott Henderson (Sco)	75-69-81-76—301	8075	13253

The following players missed the half-way cut:

71	Steve Flesch (USA)	74-71—145
	Søren Kjeldsen (Den)	73-72—145
	Justin Leonard (USA)	74-71—145
	Stephen Leaney (Aus)	76-69—145
	Gary Birch (Eng)	75-70—145
	Jean Hugo (RSA)	73-72—145
	Joe Durant (USA)	75-70—145
	Peter O'Malley (Aus)	71-74—145
	Mathias Grönberg (Swe)	75-70—145
	Fredrik Jacobson (Swe)	74-71—145
	Markus Brier (Aut)	74-71—145
	John Bickerton (Eng)	74-71—145
83	Nick Faldo (Eng)	75-71—146
	Corey Pavin (USA)	71-75—146
	Bradford Vaughan (RSA)	72-74—146
	Shigeki Maruyama (Jpn)	75-71—146
	Taichi Teshima (Jpn)	74-72—146
	Søren Hansen (Den)	71-75—146
	Dinesh Chand (Fij)	75-71—146
	Robert Karlsson (Swe)	75-71—146
	Robert Coles (Eng)	73-73—146
	Mark Brooks (USA)	73-73—146
	Matthew Cort (Eng)	77-69—146
94	David Howell (Eng)	74-73—147
	Mark Wiebe (USA)	73-74—147
	Olle Karlsson (Swe)	72-75—147
	Scott Hoch (USA)	75-72—147
	Mark Pilkington (Wal)	77-70—147
	Tom Lehman (USA)	75-72—147
	David Toms (USA)	74-73—147
	Aaron Baddeley (Aus)	75-72—147
	Stuart Wilson (am) (Eng)	77-70—147
103	David Frost (RSA)	74-74—148
	Nobuhito Sato (Jpn)	76-72—148
	José Coceres (Arg)	71-77—148
	Gary Orr (Sco)	73-75—148

103T	Jeff Maggert (USA)	72-76—148
	John Daly (USA)	72-76—148
	Daren Lee (Eng)	76-72—148
	Dennis Paulson (USA)	78-70—148
	Brian Gay (USA)	72-76—148
112	Seve Ballesteros (Esp)	78-71—149
	Bob Charles (NZ)	75-74—149
	Tony Jacklin (Eng)	75-74—149
	Andrew Oldcorn (Sco)	73-76—149
	Steve Elkington (Aus)	77-72—149
	Mark McNulty (Zim)	70-79—149
	Fred Couples (USA)	71-78—149
	Michael Hoey (am) (NI)	73-76—149
	Bob May (USA)	77-72—149
	Jeff Quinney (am) (USA)	76-73—149
	Carl Paulson (USA)	72-77—149
123	Naomichi 'Joe' Ozaki (Jpn)	77-73—150
	Mike Weir (Can)	78-72—150
	Dean Wilson (USA)	72-78—150
	Simon Dyson (Eng)	77-73—150
	Shingo Katayama (Jpn)	75-75—150
	Matthew Griffiths (am) (Eng)	73-77—150
	Nathan Green (Aus)	75-75—150
130	Mark Roe (Eng)	73-78—151
	Jerry Kelly (USA)	74-77—151
	Geoff Ogilvy (Aus)	76-75—151
	Steve Jones (USA)	74-77—151
	John Huston (USA)	76-75—151
	Thomas Bjørn (Den)	76-75—151
	Brett Rumford (Aus)	73-78—151
137	Roger Chapman (Eng)	76-76—152
	Tom Watson (USA)	74-78—152
	Gregg Turner (NZ)	79-73—152
	Jim Furyk (USA)	77-75—152

130th Open Championship continued

137T	Henrik Stenson (Swe)	75-77—152		148T	Angel Cabrera (Arg)	80-75—155
	Jean Van de Velde (Fra)	77-75—152		150	Matthew McGuire (Eng)	71-85—156
	Mark Sanders (Eng)	79-73—152			Toshiaki Odate (Jpn)	76-80—156
144	Graham Rankin (Sco)	79-75—154		152	Gary Player (RSA)	77-82—159
	Juan Carlos Aguero (Esp)	77-77—154			Simon Vale (Eng)	85-74—159
	Hidemichi Tanaka (Jpn)	76-78—154		154	Stuart Callan (Eng)	78-82—160
	John Kemp (am) (Eng)	76-78—154		155	Chris Perry (USA)	78-W/D—78
148	Wayne Riley (Aus)	78-77—155			Rocco Mediate (USA)	74-W/D—74

2000 Open Championship at St Andrews (7115 yds, Par 72)

Prize Money £2,722,150. Entries 2372. Regional qualifying courses: Alwoodley, Beau Desert, Blackmoor, Burnham & Berrow, Camberley Heath, Carlisle, Copt Heath, County Louth, Coxmoor, Hadley Wood, Hindhead, Northamptonshire County, Ormskirk, Renfrew, Romford, Stockport, Wildernesse. Final qualifying courses: Ladybank, Leven, Lundin, Scotscraig. Final field comprised 156 players, of whom 74 (none amateur) made the half-way cut on 144 or better.

1	Tiger Woods (USA)	67-66-67-69—269	£500000	20T	Padraig Harrington		
2	Ernie Els (RSA)	66-72-70-69—277	245000		(Irl)	68-72-70-72—282	25500
	Thomas Bjørn (Den)	69-69-68-71—277	245000		Steve Pate (USA)	73-70-71-68—282	25500
4	Tom Lehman (USA)	68-70-70-70—278	130000		Bob Estes (USA)	72-69-70-71—282	25500
	David Toms (USA)	69-67-71-71—278	130000		Paul McGinley (Irl)	69-72-71-70—282	25500
6	Fred Couples (USA)	70-68-72-69—279	100000		Notah Begay III (USA)	69-73-69-71—282	25500
7	Loren Roberts (USA)	69-68-70-73—280	66250	26	Mark O'Meara (USA)	70-73-69-71—283	20000
	Paul Azinger (USA)	69-72-72-67—280	66250		Colin Montgomerie		
	Pierre Fulke (Swe)	69-72-70-69—280	66250		(Sco)	71-70-72-70—283	20000
	Darren Clarke (NI)	70-69-68-73—280	66250		Miguel Angel Jiménez		
11	Bernhard Langer (Ger)	74-70-66-71—281	37111		(Esp)	73-71-71-68—283	20000
	Mark McNulty (Zim)	69-72-70-70—281	37111		Mark Calcavecchia		
	David Duval (USA)	70-70-66-75—281	37111		(USA)	73-71-71-69—283	20000
	Stuart Appleby (Aus)	73-70-68-70—281	37111		Dean Robertson (Sco)	73-70-68-72—283	20000
	Davis Love III (USA)	74-66-74-67—281	37111	31	José Maria Olazábal		
	Vijay Singh (Fij)	70-70-73-68—281	37111		(Esp)	72-70-71-71—284	16750
	Phil Mickelson (USA)	72-66-71-72—281	37111		Jean Van de Velde		
	Bob May (USA)	72-72-66-71—281	37111		(Fra)	71-68-72-73—284	16750
	Dennis Paulson (USA)	68-71-69-73—281	37111		Steve Jones (USA)	70-70-72-72—284	16750
20	Steve Flesch (USA)	67-70-71-74—282	25500		Jarmo Sandelin (Swe)	70-70-75-69—284	16750

Other Totals: Eduardo Romero (Arg), Sergio García (Esp), Jesper Parnevik (Swe), Craig Parry (Aus), José Coceres (Arg), Robert Allenby (Aus) 286; Nick Faldo (Eng), Justin Leonard (USA), Stewart Cink (USA), Jim Furyk (USA), Nick O'Hern (Aus), Jarrod Moseley (Aus), Gary Orr (Sco), Jeff Maggert (USA), Retief Goosen (RSA), Lucas Parsons (Aus), Tsuyoshi Yoneyama (Jpn) 287; Mike Weir (Can), Ian Garbutt (Eng), Rocco Mediate (USA), 288; David Frost (RSA), Tom Watson (USA), Shigeki Maruyama (Jpn), Greg Owen (Eng), Andrew Coltart (Sco) 289; Christy O'Connor jr (Irl), Jeff Sluman (USA), Steve Elkington (Aus), Kirk Triplett (USA) 290; Desvonde Botes (RSA), Ian Poulter (Eng), Per-Ulrik Johansson (Swe), Lee Westwood (Eng) 291; Gordon Brand jr (Sco), Ian Woosnam (Wal), 292; Tom Kite (USA), Kazuhiko Hosokawa (Jpn) 294; Peter Senior (Aus), Lionel Alexandre (Fra) 295; Dudley Hart (USA) RETD

1999 Open Championship at Carnoustie (7361 yds, Par 71)

Prize Money £2,009,550. Entries 2222. Regional qualifying courses: Beau Desert, Blackmoor, Burnham & Berrow, Carlisle, Copt Heath, County Louth, Coxmoor, Glenbervie, Hankley Common, Moortown, Northamptonshire County, Ormskirk, Romford, South Herts, Stockport, Wildernesse. Final qualifying courses: Downfield, Monifieth Links, Montrose Links, Panmure. Final field comprised 156 players, of whom 73 (none amateurs) made the half-way cut on 154 or better.

1	P Lawrie* (Sco)	73-74-76-67—290	£350000	10	J Parnevik (Swe)	74-71-78-72—295	34800
2	J Leonard (USA)	73-74-71-72—290	185000		S Dunlap (USA)	72-77-76-70—295	34800
	J Van de Velde (Fra)	75-68-80-77—290	185000		R Goosen (RSA)	76-75-73-71—295	34800
*Lawrie won four-hole play-off					H Sutton (USA)	73-78-72-72—295	34800
4	C Parry (Aus)	76-75-67-73—291	100000		J Furyk (USA)	78-71-76-70—295	34800
	A Cabrera (Arg)	75-69-77-70—291	100000	15	T Yoneyama (Jpn)	74-74-73-72—296	26000
6	G Norman (Aus)	76-70-75-72—293	70000		C Montgomerie (Sco)	74-76-72-74—296	26000
7	D Frost (RSA)	80-69-71-74—294	50000		S Verplank (USA)	80-74-73-69—296	26000
	D Love III (USA)	74-74-77-69—294	50000	18	B Langer (Ger)	72-77-73-75—297	20500
	T Woods (USA)	74-72-74-74—294	50000		A Coltart (Sco)	74-74-72-77—297	20500

18T	F Nobilo (NZ)	76-76-70-75—297	20500		29	P Harrington (Irl)	77-74-74-74—299	13500
	P Sjöland (Swe)	74-72-77-74—297	20500		30	J Maggert (USA)	75-77-75-73—300	11557
	L Westwood (Eng)	76-75-74-72—297	20500			D Clarke (NI)	76-75-76-73—300	11557
	C Rocca (Ita)	81-69-74-73—297	20500			P Stewart (USA)	79-73-74-74—300	11557
24	P O'Malley (Aus)	76-75-74-73—298	15300			P Fulke (Swe)	75-75-77-73—300	11557
	E Els (RSA)	74-76-76-72—298	15300			T Bjørn (Den)	79-73-75-73—300	11557
	B Watts (USA)	74-73-77-74—298	15300			T Herron (USA)	81-70-74-75—300	11557
	I Woosnam (Wal)	76-74-74-74—298	15300			L Mattiace (USA)	73-74-75-78—300	11557
	MA Martin (Esp)	74-76-72-76—298	15300					

Other Totals: M McNulty (Zim), D Hart (USA), P Baker (Eng), N Price (Zim), M Weir (Can), P Affleck (Wal) 301; D Waldorf (USA), M James (Eng) 302; S Pate (USA), N Ozaki (Jpn), J Sluman (USA), D Howell (Eng) 303; N Price (Eng), T Levet (Fra), K Tomori (Jpn), Kyoung-Ju Choi (Kor), B Hughes (Aus), D Robertson (Sco), B Estes (USA), S Allan (Aus), P Lonard (Aus) 304; D Paulson (USA), J Robinson (Eng), S Luna (Esp), P Price (Wal) 305; J Ryström (Swe), D Duval (USA), M Brooks (USA) 306; J Sandelin (Swe) 307; S Strüver (Ger) 308; L Thompson (Eng) 309; B Davis (Eng), J Huston (USA) 310; L Janzen (USA) 311; K Shingo (Jpn) 312; M Thompson (Eng), D Cooper (Eng) 313.

1998 Open Championship *at Royal Birkdale* (7018 yds, Par 70)

Prize money: £1,750,000. Entries: 2336. Regional qualifying courses: Beau Desert, Blackmoor, Burnham & Berrow, Carlisle, Copt Heath, County Louth, Coxmoor, Glenbervie, Hankley Common, Moortown, Northamptonshire County, Ormskirk, Romford, South Herts, Stockport and Wildernesse. Final qualifying courses: Hesketh, Hillside, Southport & Ainsdale and West Lancashire. Final field comprised 151 players, of whom 78 (including 3 amateurs) made the half-way cut on 146 or better.

1	M O'Meara (USA)*	72-68-72-68—280	£300000		19	C Strange (USA)	73-73-74-70—290	17220
2	B Watts (USA)	68-69-73-70—280	188000			V Singh (Fij)	67-74-78-71—290	17220
	O'Meara won four-hole play-off					S Lyle (Sco)	71-72-75-72—290	17220
3	T Woods (USA)	65-73-77-66—281	135000			R Allenby (Aus)	67-76-78-69—290	17220
4	J Furyk (USA)	70-70-72-70—282	76666			M James (Eng)	71-74-74-71—290	17220
	J Parnevik (Swe)	68-72-72-70—282	76666		24	S Torrance (Sco)	69-77-75-70—291	12480
	R Russell (Sco)	68-73-75-66—282	76666			B Estes (USA)	72-70-76-73—291	12480
	J Rose (Eng) (am)	72-66-75-69—282				S Ames (Tri)	68-72-79-72—291	12480
8	D Love III (USA)	67-73-76-85—285	49500			P O'Malley (Aus)	71-71-78-71—291	12480
9	T Björn (Den)	68-71-76-71—286	40850			L Janzen (USA)	72-69-80-70—291	12480
	C Rocca (Ita)	72-74-70-70—286	40850		29	S Dunlap (USA)	72-69-80-71—292	10030
11	J Huston (USA)	65-77-73-72—287	33333			N Price (Zim)	66-72-82-72—292	10030
	B Faxon (USA)	67-74-74-72—287	33333			S Maruyama (Jpn)	70-73-75-74—292	10030
	D Duval (USA)	70-71-75-71—287	33333			L Roberts (USA)	66-76-76-74—292	10030
14	G Brand jr (Sco)	71-70-76-71—288	29000			E Els (RSA)	72-74-74-72—292	10030
15	P Baker (Eng)	69-72-77-71—289	23650			S Garcia (am) (Esp)	69-75-76-72—292	
	G Turner (NZ)	68-75-75-71—289	23650		35	M Calcavecchia (USA)	69-77-73-74—293	8900
	JM Olazábal (Esp)	73-72-75-69—289	23650			S Luna (Esp)	70-72-80-71—293	8900
	D Smyth (Irl)	74-69-75-71—289	23650			S Strüver (Ger)	75-70-80-68—293	8900

Other Totals: P Sjöland (Swe), J Haeggman (Swe), P Walton (Irl), N Ozaki (Jpn), T Kite (USA), S Tinning (Den) 294; K Tomori (Jpn), D Howell (Eng), D Frost (RSA), R Davis (Aus), D Carter (Eng), N Faldo (Eng), P Stewart (USA), A Coltart (Sco) 295; S Stricker (USA), B Mayfair (USA), B Jobe (USA), L Mize (USA), F Minoza (Phi) 296; T Dodds (Nam), E Romero (Arg), S Jones (USA), J Leonard (USA), I Garrido (Esp), I Woosnam (Wal), L Westwood (Eng), C Daniel Franco (Par) 298; S Cink (USA), M Brooks (USA), M Campbell (NZ), F Couples (USA), M Long (NZ); D De Vooght (am) (Bel) 299; A Clapp (Eng) 300; G Evans (Eng) 301; B May (USA) 303; A McLardy (RSA) 304; F Jacobson (Swe) 305; K Hosokawa (Jpn) 306; R Giles (Irl) 307; P Mickelson (USA) 308; A Oldcorn (Sco) 309; D Hart (USA) 310.

1997 Open Championship *at Royal Troon* (7079 yds, Par 71)

Prize money: £1,586,300. Entries: 2133. Regional qualifying courses: Beau Desert, Burnham & Berrow, Carlisle, Copt Heath, Coxmoor, Glenbervie, Hankley Common, Moortown, North Hants, Romford, South Herts, Sundridge Park, Wilmslow. Final qualifying courses: Irvine Bogside, Glasgow Gailes, Kilmarnock Barassie, Western Gailes. 156 players took part, 70 (including 1 amateur) qualified for final 36 holes.

1	J Leonard (USA)	69-66-72-65—272	£250000		7T	E Romero (Arg)	74-68-67-72—281	40666
2	D Clarke (NI)	67-66-71-71—275	150000			P O'Malley (Aus)	73-70-70-68—281	40666
	J Parnevik (Swe)	70-66-66-73—275	150000		10	R Goosen (RSA)	75-69-70-68—282	24300
4	J Furyk (USA)	67-72-70-70—279	90000			L Westwood (Eng)	73-70-67-72—282	24300
5	S Ames (Tri)	74-69-66-71—280	62500			T Watson (USA)	71-70-70-71—282	24300
	P Harrington (Irl)	75-69-69-67—280	62500			M Calcavecchia (USA)	74-67-72-69—282	24300
7	F Couples (USA)	69-68-70-74—281	40666			R Allenby (Aus)	76-68-66-72—282	24300

1999 Open Championship continued

10T	S Maruyama (Jpn)	74-69-70-69—282	24300	24T	D A Russell (Eng)	75-72-68-69—284	10362
	T Kite (USA)	72-67-74-69—282	24300		T Woods (USA)	72-74-64-74—284	10362
	D Love III (USA)	70-71-74-67—282	24300		T Lehman (USA)	74-72-72-66—284	10362
	E Els (RSA)	75-69-69-69—282	24300		J Haas (USA)	71-70-73-70—284	10362
	F Nobilo (NZ)	74-72-68-68—282	24300		P Mickelson (USA)	76-68-69-71—284	10362
20	JM Olazábal (Esp)	75-68-73-67—283	14500	32	M McNulty (Zim)	78-67-72-68—285	8750
	M James (Eng)	76-67-70-70—283	14500	33	J Lomas (Eng)	72-71-69-74—286	8283
	B Faxon (USA)	77-67-72-67—283	14500		D Duval (USA)	73-69-73-71—286	8283
	S Appleby (Aus)	72-72-68-71—283	14500		R Davis (Aus)	73-73-70-70—286	8283
24	P Lonard (Aus)	72-70-69-73—284	10362	36	A Magee (USA)	70-75-72-70—287	7950
	C Montgomerie (Sco)	76-69-69-70—284	10362		G Norman (Aus)	69-73-70-75—287	7950
	I Woosnam (Wal)	71-73-69-71—284	10362				

Other Totals: R Russell (Sco), M O'Meara (USA), J Kernohan (USA), M Bradley (USA), B Langer (Ger), V Singh (Fij) 288; J Coceres (Arg), D Tapping (Eng), C Strange (USA), J Kelly (USA) 289; S Jones (USA), J Payne (Eng), R Boxall (Eng) 290; A Cabrera (Arg), J Maggert (USA), W Riley (Aus), P Senior (Aus), C Pavin (USA), P Mitchell (Eng), N Faldo (Eng), G Turner (NZ) 291; P Stewart (USA) 292; J Nicklaus (USA), B Howard (am) (Sco) 293; T Purtzer (USA), J Spence (Eng), S Stricker (USA), P Teravainen (USA) 294; P McGinley (Irl), P-U Johansson (Swe), G Clark (Eng) 295; T Tolles (USA) 296; B Andrade (USA) 298.

1996 Open Championship at Royal Lytham & St Annes (6892 yds, Par 71)

Prize money: £1,400,000. Entries: 1918. Regional qualifying courses: Beau Desert, Burnham & Berrow, Carlisle, Copt Heath, Coxmoor, Glenbervie, Hankley Common, Moortown, North Hants, Romford, South Herts, Sundridge Park, Wilmslow. Final qualifying courses: Fairhaven, Formby, St Anne's Old Links, Southport & Ainsdale. Qualified for final 36 holes: 77 (including 1 amateur).

1	T Lehman (USA)	67-67-64-73—271	£200000	18T	R Mediate (USA)	69-70-69-72—280	15500
2	M McCumber (USA)	67-69-71-66—273	125000	22	M James (Eng)	70-68-75-68—281	11875
	E Els (RSA)	68-67-71-67—273	125000		J Haas (USA)	70-72-71-68—281	11875
4	N Faldo (Eng)	68-68-68-70—274	75000		T Woods (am) (USA)	75-66-70-70—281	
5	J Maggert (USA)	69-70-72-65—276	50000		C Mason (Eng)	68-70-70-73—281	11875
	M Brooks (USA)	67-70-68-71—276	50000		S Stricker (USA)	71-70-66-74—281	11875
7	P Hedblom (Swe)	70-65-75-67—277	35000	27	B Crenshaw (USA)	73-68-71-70—282	9525
	G Norman (Aus)	71-68-71-67—277	35000		T Kite (USA)	77-66-69-70—282	9525
	G Turner (NZ)	72-69-68-68—277	35000		P Broadhurst (Eng)	65-72-74-71—282	9525
	F Couples (USA)	67-70-69-71—277	35000		C Pavin (USA)	70-66-74-72—282	9525
11	A Cejka (Ger)	73-67-71-67—278	27000		P Mitchell (Eng)	71-68-71-72—282	9525
	D Clarke (NI)	70-68-69-71—278	27000		F Nobilo (NZ)	70-72-68-72—282	9525
	V Singh (Fij)	69-67-69-73—278	27000	33	E Romero (Arg)	70-71-75-67—283	7843
14	M McNulty (Zim)	69-71-70-69—279	20250		T Tolles (USA)	73-70-71-69—283	7843
	D Duval (USA)	76-67-66-70—279	20250		S Simpson (USA)	71-69-73-70—283	7843
	P McGinley (Irl)	69-65-74-71—279	20250		E Darcy (Irl)	73-69-71-70—283	7843
	S Maruyama (Jpn)	68-70-69-72—279	20250		D Gilford (Eng)	71-67-71-74—283	7843
18	M Welch (Eng)	71-68-73-68—280	15500		M O'Meara (USA)	67-69-72-75—283	7843
	P Harrington (Irl)	68-68-73-71—280	15500		H Tanaka (Jpn)	67-71-70-75—283	7843
	L Roberts (USA)	67-69-72-72—280	15500		B Faxon (USA)	67-73-68-75—283	7843

Other Totals: M Calcavecchia (USA), P Mickelson (USA), K Eriksson (Swe), D Frost (RSA) 284; C Stadler (USA), B Mayfair (USA), P Jacobsen (USA), T Hamilton (Can), B Hughes (Aus), P Stewart (USA), R Boxall (Eng), J Nicklaus (USA), N Price (Zim), J Furyk (USA), J Parnevik (Swe) 285; J Payne (Eng), S Lyle (Sco), R Allenby (Aus), S Ames (Tri) 286; M Jonzon (Swe), DA Weibring (USA), J Sluman (USA), B Barnes (Sco) 287; C Suneson (Eng), C Rocca (Ita), G Law (Sco) 288; DA Russell (Eng), B Ogle (Aus), J Daly (USA) 289; H Clark (Eng) 290; B Charles (NZ) 291; D Hospital (Esp), R Todd (Can), C Strange (USA), R Chapman (Eng) 292; R Goosen (RSA) 293; A Langenaeken (Bel) 298.

1995 Open Championship at St Andrews (6933 yds, Par 72)

Prize money: £1,250,000. Entries: 1836. Regional qualifying courses: Beau Desert, Blackwell, Glenbervie, Hankley Common, Lanark, Moortown, North Hants, Romford, Sherwood Forest, South Herts, Sundridge, Wilmslow. Final qualifying courses: Ladybank, Leven Links, Lundin, Scotscraig. Qualified for final 36 holes: 103 (including 4 amateurs).

1	J Daly (USA)*	67-71-73-71—282	£125000	3T	M Campbell (NZ)	71-71-65-76—283	65666
2	C Rocca (Ita)	69-70-70-73—282	100000	6	V Singh (Fij)	68-72-73-71—284	40500
	Daly won four-hole play-off				S Elkington (Aus)	72-69-69-74—284	40500
3	S Bottomley (Eng)	70-72-72-69—283	65666	8	M James (Eng)	72-75-68-70—285	33333
	M Brooks (USA)	70-69-73-71—283	65666		B Estes (USA)	72-70-71-72—285	33333
	M Brooks (USA)	70-69-73-71—283	65666		C Pavin (USA)	69-70-72-74—285	33333

11	P Stewart (USA)	72-68-75-71—286	26000	24T	B Langer (Ger)	72-71-73-73—289	10316
	B Ogle (Aus)	73-69-71-73—286	26000		J Parnevik (Swe)	75-71-70-73—289	10316
	S Torrance (Sco)	71-70-71-74—286	26000		M Calcavecchia (USA)	71-72-72-74—289	10316
	E Els (RSA)	71-68-72-75—286	26000		B Glasson (USA)	68-74-72-75—289	10316
15	G Norman (Aus)	71-74-72-70—287	18200		K Tomori (Jpn)	70-68-73-78—289	10316
	R Allenby (Aus)	71-74-71-71—287	18200	31	R Drummond (Sco)	74-68-77-71—290	8122
	B Crenshaw (USA)	67-72-76-72—287	18200		JM Olazábal (Esp)	72-72-74-72—290	8122
	P-U Johansson (Swe)	69-78-68-72—287	18200		D Frost (RSA)	72-72-74-72—290	8122
	B Faxon (USA)	71-67-75-74—287	18200		H Sasaki (Jpn)	74-71-72-73—290	8122
20	P Mitchell (Eng)	73-74-71-70—288	13500		J Huston (USA)	71-74-72-73—290	8122
	D Duval (USA)	71-75-70-72—288	13500		P Jacobsen (USA)	71-76-70-73—290	8122
	A Coltart (Sco)	70-74-71-73—288	13500		D Clarke (NI)	69-77-70-74—290	8122
	B Lane (Eng)	72-73-68-75—288	13500		D Feherty (NI)	68-75-71-76—290	8122
24	L Janzen (USA)	73-73-71-72—289	10316		T Watson (USA)	67-76-70-77—290	8122
	S Webster (am) (USA)	70-72-74-73—289					

Other Totals: S Ballesteros (Esp), W Bennett (am) (Eng), P Mickelson (USA), M McNulty (Zim), N Faldo (Eng), B Watts (USA), G Sherry (am) (Sco), J Cook (USA), N Price (Zim) 291; I Woosnam (Wal), A Forsbrand (Swe), M O'Meara (USA), T Nakajima (Jpn), B Claar (USA), K Green (USA) 292; J Gallagher (USA), P O'Malley (Aus), R Claydon (Eng) 293; P Senior (Aus), P Broadhurst (Eng), D Cooper (Eng), E Herrera (Col), T Kite (USA), P Lawrie (Sco), M Gates (Eng), R Floyd (USA), J Leonard (USA), D Gilford (Eng) 294; P Baker (Eng), J Maggert (USA), J Lomas (Eng), F Nobilo (NZ), G Player (RSA), O Karlsson (Swe), M Hallberg (Swe), S Hoch (USA), G Hallberg (USA), J Rivero (Esp), T Woods (am) (Sco) 295.

1994 Open Championship *at Turnberry* (6957 yds, Par 70)

Prize money: £1,100,000. Entries 1701. Regional qualifying courses: Blackwell, Glenbervie, Hankley Common, Lanark, Moortown, North Hants, Orsett, Sherwood Forest, South Herts, Sundridge Park, Wilmslow. Final qualifying courses: Glasgow Gailes, Irvine Bogside, Kilmarnock Barassie, Western Gailes. Qualified for final 36 holes: 81 (including 1 amateur). Non-qualifiers after 36 holes with scores of 143 or more: 75 (71 professionals, 4 amateurs)

1	N Price (Zim)	69-66-67-66—268	£110000	20	M Brooks (USA)	74-64-71-68—277	12500
2	J Parnevik (Swe)	68-66-68-67—269	88000		V Singh (Fij)	70-68-69-70—277	12500
3	F Zoeller (USA)	71-66-64-70—271	74000		G Turner (NZ)	65-71-70-71—277	12500
4	A Forsbrand (Swe)	72-71-66-64—273	50666		P Senior (Aus)	68-71-67-71—277	12500
	M James (Eng)	72-67-66-68—273	50666	24	B Estes (USA)	72-68-72-66—278	7972
	D Feherty (NI)	68-69-66-70—273	50666		T Price (Aus)	74-65-71-68—278	7972
7	B Faxon (USA)	69-65-67-73—274	36000		P Lawrie (Sco)	71-69-70-68—278	7972
8	N Faldo (Eng)	75-66-70-64—275	30000		J Maggert (USA)	69-74-67-68—278	7972
	T Kite (USA)	71-69-66-69—275	30000		T Lehman (USA)	70-69-70-69—278	7972
	C Montgomerie (Sco)	72-69-65-69—275	30000		E Els (RSA)	69-69-69-71—278	7972
11	R Claydon (Eng)	72-71-68-65—276	19333		M Springer (USA)	72-67-68-71—278	7972
	M McNulty (Zim)	71-70-68-67—276	19333		L Roberts (USA)	68-69-69-72—278	7972
	F Nobilo (NZ)	69-67-72-68—276	19333		P Jacobsen (USA)	69-70-67-72—278	7972
	J Lomas (Eng)	66-70-72-68—276	19333		C Stadler (USA)	71-69-66-72—278	7972
	M Calcavecchia (USA)	71-70-67-68—276	19333		A Coltart (Sco)	71-69-66-72—278	7972
	G Norman (Aus)	71-67-69-69—276	19333	35	M Davis (Eng)	75-68-69-67—279	6700
	L Mize (USA)	73-69-64-70—276	19333		L Janzen (USA)	74-69-69-67—279	6700
	T Watson (USA)	68-65-69-74—276	19333		G Evans (Eng)	69-69-73-68—279	6700
	R Rafferty (NI)	71-66-65-74—276	19333				

Other Totals: D Gilford (Eng), D Hospital (Esp), JM Olazábal (Esp), S Ballesteros (Esp), B Marchbank (Eng), D Clarke (NI) 280; J Van De Velde (Fra), D Love III (USA), M Ozaki (Jpn) 280; J Gallagher jr (USA), D Edwards (USA), G Kraft (USA), H Twitty (USA) 281; D Frost (RSA), M Lanner (Swe), K Tomori (Jpn), T Watanabe (Jpn) 282; P Baker (Eng), J Cook (USA), T Nakajima (Jpn), B Watts (USA), R McFarlane (Eng) 283; G Brand jr (Sco), H Meshiai (Jpn), B Langer (Ger), C O'Connor jr (Irl), P-U Johansson (Swe), R Allenby (Aus), W Grady (Aus) 284; S Elkington (Aus), M Roe (Eng), L Clements (USA), C Mason (Eng), R Alvarez (Arg) 285; W Bennett (am) (Eng), W Riley (Aus) 286; A Lyle (Sco) 287; C Ronald (Eng), C Gillies (Eng) 288; B Crenshaw (USA), C Parry (Aus), J Haeggman (Swe) 289; N Henning (RSA) 291; J Daly (USA) 292.

1993 Open Championship *at Royal St George's* (6860 yds, Par 70)

Prize money: £1,017,000. Entries 1827. Regional qualifying courses: Beau Desert, Blackwell, Coxmoor, Hankley Park, Lanark, Langley Park, North Hants, Orsett, Sherwood Forest, South Herts, Sundridge Park, Wilmslow. Final qualifying courses: Littlestone, North Foreland, Prince's and Royal Cinque Ports. Qualified for final 36 holes: 78 (77 professionals, 1 amateur). Non-qualifiers after 36 holes: 78 (73 professionals, 5 amateurs) with scores of 144 and above.

1	G Norman (Aus)	66-68-69-64—267	£100000	4T	P Senior (Aus)	66-69-70-67—272	50500
2	N Faldo (Eng)	69-63-70-67—269	80000	6	N Price (Zim)	68-70-67-69—274	33166
3	B Langer (Ger)	67-66-70-67—270	67000		E Els (RSA)	68-69-69-68—274	33166
4	C Pavin (USA)	68-66-68-70—272	50500		P Lawrie (Sco)	72-68-69-65—274	33166

1993 **Open Championship** *continued*

9	W Grady (Aus)	74-68-64-69—275	25500	24	R Davis (Aus)	68-71-71-70—280	8400
	F Couples (USA)	68-66-72-69—275	25500		D Frost (RSA)	69-73-70-68—280	8400
	S Simpson (USA)	68-70-71-66—275	25500		M Roe (Eng)	70-71-73-66—280	8400
12	P Stewart (USA)	71-72-70-63—276	21500	27	L Mize (USA)	67-69-74-71—281	7225
13	B Lane (Eng)	70-68-71-68—277	20500		S Ballesteros (Esp)	68-73-69-71—281	7225
14	J Daly (USA)	71-66-70-71—278	15214		M James (Eng)	70-70-70-71—281	7225
	F Zoeller (USA)	66-70-71-71—278	15214		D Smyth (Irl)	67-74-70-70—281	7225
	G Morgan (USA)	70-68-70-70—278	15214		Y Mizumaki (Jpn)	69-69-73-70—281	7225
	J Rivero (Esp)	68-73-67-70—278	15214		M Mackenzie (Eng)	72-71-71-67—281	7225
	M McNulty (Zim)	67-71-71-69—278	15214		I Pyman (am) (Eng)	68-72-70-71—281	
	M Calcavecchia (USA)	66-73-71-68—278	15214	34	H Twitty (USA)	71-71-67-73—282	6180
	T Kite (USA)	72-70-68-68—278	15214		R Floyd (USA)	70-72-67-73—282	6180
21	H Clark (Eng)	67-72-70-70—279	10000		W Westner (RSA)	67-73-72-70—282	6180
	J Parnevik (Swe)	68-74-68-69—279	10000		P Broadhurst (Eng)	71-69-74-68—282	6180
	P Baker (Eng)	70-67-74-68—279	10000		J Van de Velde (Fra)	75-67-73-67—282	6180

Other Totals: D Clarke (NI), C O'Connor jr (Irl), A Sorensen (Den), D Waldorf (USA), P Moloney (Aus), G Turner (NZ), C Mason (Eng), A Magee (USA), R Mediate (USA) 283; L Janzen (USA), S Elkington (Aus), J Huston (USA) 284; J Sewell (Eng), M Pinero (Esp), F Nobilo (NZ), S Torrance (Sco), MA Jiménez (Esp), I Woosnam (Wal), S Ames (Tri), I Garbutt (Eng) 285; C Parry (Aus), T Lehman (USA), V Singh (Fij), P Azinger (USA) 286; J Spence (Eng), O Karlsson (Swe), R Drummond (Eng) 287; T Pernice (USA), W Guy (Eng), J Cook (USA), M Sunesson (Swe) 288; I Baker-Finch (Aus), T Purtzer (USA), M Miller (Eng) 289; M Harwood (Aus), P Mitchell (Eng), P Fowler (Aus), D Forsman (USA) 290; M Krantz (Swe) 292; R Willison (Eng) 293.

1992 **Open Championship** *at Muirfield* (6970 yds, Par 71)

Prize money: £950,000. Entries 1666. Regional qualifying courses: Beau Desert, Blackwell, Coxmoor, Glenbervie, Lanark, North Hants, Orsett, Sherwood Forest, South Herts, Sundridge Park, Wilmslow. Final qualifying courses: Dunbar, Gullane, Luffness New, North Berwick. Qualified for final 36 holes: 75 (74 professionals, 1 amateur). Non-qualifiers after 36 holes: 81 (77 professionals, 4 amateurs) with scores of 143 and above.

1	N Faldo (Eng)	66-64-69-73—272	£95000	19T	I Baker-Finch (Aus)	71-71-72-68—282	11066
2	J Cook (USA)	66-67-70-70—273	75000		T Kite (USA)	70-69-71-72—282	11066
3	JM Olazábal (Esp)	70-67-69-68—274	64000	22	P Mitchell (Eng)	69-71-72-71—283	8950
4	S Pate (USA)	64-70-69-73—276	53000		P Lawrie (Sco)	70-72-68-73—283	8950
5	D Hammond (USA)	70-65-70-74—279	30071		T Purtzer (USA)	68-69-75-71—283	8950
	A Magee (USA)	67-72-70-70—279	30071	25	B Andrade (USA)	69-71-70-74—284	7700
	E Els (RSA)	66-69-70-74—279	30071		D Waldorf (USA)	69-70-73-72—284	7700
	I Woosnam (Wal)	65-73-70-71—279	30071		P Senior (Aus)	70-69-70-75—284	7700
	G Brand jr (Sco)	65-68-72-74—279	30071	28	M Calcavecchia (USA)	69-71-73-72—285	6658
	M Mackenzie (Chi)	71-67-70-71—279	30071		M McNulty (Zim)	71-70-70-74—285	6658
	R Karlsson (Swe)	70-68-70-71—279	30071		J Mudd (USA)	71-69-74-71—285	6658
12	J Spence (Eng)	71-68-70-71—280	17383		C Parry (Aus)	67-71-76-71—285	6658
	C Beck (USA)	71-68-67-74—280	17383		R Cochran (USA)	71-68-72-74—285	6658
	R Floyd (USA)	64-71-73-72—280	17383		M Lanner (Swe)	72-68-71-74—285	6658
	A Lyle (Sco)	68-70-70-72—280	17383	34	A Forsbrand (Swe)	70-72-70-74—286	5760
	M O'Meara (USA)	71-68-72-69—280	17383		C Pavin (USA)	69-74-73-70—286	5760
	L Rinker (USA)	69-68-70-73—280	17383		P Stewart (USA)	70-73-71-72—286	5760
18	G Norman (Aus)	71-72-70-68—281	13200		S Elkington (Aus)	68-70-75-73—286	5760
19	H Irwin (USA)	70-73-67-72—282	11066		T Johnstone (Zim)	72-71-74-69—286	5760

Other Totals: DW Basson (RSA), L Janzen (USA), L Trevino (USA), S Richardson (Eng), W Grady (Aus), R Rafferty (Irl) 287; M Harwood (Aus), L Wadkins (USA), J Coceres (Arg), R Mediate (USA), C Mann (Aus), B Marchbank (Eng) 288; R Mackay (Aus), V Singh (Fij), N Price (Zim), B Lane (Eng) 289; C Rocca (Ita), D Feherty (NI), M Brooks (USA), O Vincent III (USA) 290; P Azinger (USA), B Langer (Ger), W Riley (Aus), W Guy (Eng), M Clayton (Aus) 291; C Stadler (USA), R Chapman (Eng), D Mijovic (Can), H Buhrmann (RSA) 292; P-U Johansson (Swe), P O'Malley (Aus), A Sherborne (Eng), J Robson (Eng), D Lee (am) (Eng) 293; F Funk (USA) 294; P Mayo (Eng) (am) 295; J Daly (USA) 298.

OPEN CHAMPIONSHIP HISTORY

The Belt

Year	Winner	Score	Venue	Entrants
1860	W Park, Musselburgh	174	Prestwick	8
1861	T Morris sr, Prestwick	163	Prestwick	12
1862	T Morris sr, Prestwick	163	Prestwick	6
1863	W Park, Musselburgh	168	Prestwick	14
1864	T Morris Sr, Prestwick	167	Prestwick	6
1865	A Strath, St Andrews	162	Prestwick	10
1866	W Park, Musselburgh	169	Prestwick	12
1867	T Morris sr, St Andrews	170	Prestwick	10
1868	T Morris jr, St Andrews	154	Prestwick	12
1869	T Morris jr, St Andrews	157	Prestwick	14
1870	T Morris jr, St Andrews	149	Prestwick	17

Having won it three times in succession the Belt became the property of Young Tom Morris and the Championship was held in abeyance for a year. In 1872 the Claret Jug was, and still is, offered for annual competition.

The Claret Jug

Year	Winner	Score	Venue	Entrants
1872	T Morris jr, St Andrews	166	Prestwick	8
1873	T Kidd, St Andrews	179	St Andrews	26
1874	M Park, Musselburgh	159	Musselburgh	32
1875	W Park, Musselburgh	166	Prestwick	18
1876	B Martin, St Andrews	176	St Andrews	34
(D Strath tied but refused to play off)				
1877	J Anderson, St Andrews	160	Musselburgh	24
1878	J Anderson, St Andrews	157	Prestwick	26
1879	J Anderson, St Andrews	169	St Andrews	46
1880	B Ferguson, Musselburgh	162	Musselburgh	30
1881	B Ferguson, Musselburgh	170	Prestwick	22
1882	B Ferguson, Musselburgh	171	St Andrews	40
1883	W Fernie, Dumfries	159	Musselburgh	41
(After a tie with B Ferguson, Musselburgh)				
1884	J Simpson, Carnoustie	160	Prestwick	30
1885	B Martin, St Andrews	171	St Andrews	51
1886	D Brown, Musselburgh	157	Musselburgh	46
1887	W Park jr, Musselburgh	161	Prestwick	36
1888	J Burns, Warwick	171	St Andrews	53
1889	W Park Jr, Musselburgh	155	Musselburgh	42
(After a tie with A Kirkaldy)				
1890	J Ball, Royal Liverpool (am)	164	Prestwick	40
1891	H Kirkaldy, St Andrews	166	St Andrews	82

After 1891 the competition was extended to 72 holes and for the first time entry money was imposed

1892	H Hilton, Royal Liverpool (am)	305	Muirfield	66
1893	W Auchterlonie, St Andrews	322	Prestwick	72
1894	J Taylor, Winchester	326	Sandwich, R St George's	94
1895	J Taylor, Winchester	322	St Andrews	73
1896	H Vardon, Ganton	316	Muirfield	64
(Vardon won a 36 hole play-off after a tie with a score of 157 to Taylor's 161)				
1897	H Hilton, Royal Liverpool (am)	314	Hoylake, R Liverpool	86
1898	H Vardon, Ganton	307	Prestwick	78
1899	H Vardon, Ganton	310	Sandwich, R St George's	98
1900	J Taylor, Mid-Surrey	309	St Andrews	81
1901	J Braid, Romford	309	Muirfield	101
1902	A Herd, Huddersfield	307	Hoylake, R Liverpool	112
1903	H Vardon, Totteridge	300	Prestwick	127
1904	J White, Sunningdale	296	Sandwich, R St George's	144
1905	J Braid, Walton Heath	318	St Andrews	152
1906	J Braid, Walton Heath	300	Muirfield	183
1907	A Massy, La Boulie	312	Hoylake, R Liverpool	193

Open Championship Claret Jug winners history *continued*

Year	Winner	Score	Venue	Entrants
1908	J Braid, Walton Heath	291	Prestwick	180
1909	J Taylor, Mid-Surrey	295	Deal, R Cinque Ports	204
1910	J Braid, Walton Heath	299	St Andrews	210
1911	H Vardon, Totteridge	303	Sandwich, R St George's	226

(After a tie with A Massy. The tie was over 36 holes, but Massy picked up at the 35th hole before holing out. He had taken 148 for 34 holes, and when Vardon holed out at the 35th hole his score was 143.)

Year	Winner	Score	Venue	Entrants
1912	E Ray, Oxhey	295	Muirfield	215
1913	J Taylor, Mid-Surrey	304	Hoylake, R Liverpool	269
1914	H Vardon, Totteridge	306	Prestwick	194
1915–19	*No Championship owing to Great War*			

Year	Winner	Score	Venue	Qualifiers	Entrants
1920	G Duncan, Hanger Hill	303	Deal, R Cinque Ports	81	190
1921	J Hutchison, Glenview, Chicago	296	St Andrews	85	158

(After a tie with R Wethered (am). Play-off scores: Hutchison 150; Wethered 159)

Year	Winner	Score	Venue	Qualifiers	Entrants
1922	W Hagen, Detroit, USA	300	Sandwich, R St George's	80	225
1923	A Havers, Coombe Hill	295	Troon	88	222
1924	W Hagen, Detroit, USA	301	Hoylake, R Liverpool	86	277
1925	J Barnes, USA	300	Prestwick	83	200
1926	R Jones, USA (am)	291	R Lytham and St Annes	117	293
1927	R Jones, USA (am)	285	St Andrews	108	207
1928	W Hagen, USA	292	Sandwich, R St George's	113	271
1929	W Hagen, USA	292	Muirfield	109	242
1930	R Jones, USA (am)	291	Hoylake, R Liverpool	112	296
1931	T Armour, USA	296	Carnoustie	109	215
1932	G Sarazen, USA	283	Sandwich, Prince's	110	224
1933	D Shute, USA	292	St Andrews	117	287

(After a tie with C Wood, USA. Play-off scores: Shute 149; Wood 154)

Year	Winner	Score	Venue	Qualifiers	Entrants
1934	T Cotton, Waterloo, Belgium	283	Sandwich, R St George's	101	312
1935	A Perry, Leatherhead	283	Muirfield	109	264
1936	A Padgham, Sundridge Park	287	Hoylake, R Liverpool	107	286
1937	T Cotton, Ashridge	290	Carnoustie	141	258
1938	R Whitcombe, Parkstone	295	Sandwich, R St George's	120	268
1939	R Burton, Sale	290	St Andrews	129	254
1940–45	*No Championship owing to Second World War*				
1946	S Snead, USA	290	St Andrews	100	225
1947	F Daly, Balmoral	293	Hoylake, R Liverpool	100	263
1948	T Cotton, Royal Mid-Surrey	284	Muirfield	97	272
1949	A Locke, South Africa	283	Sandwich, R St George's	96	224

(After a tie with H Bradshaw, Kilcroney. Play-off scores: Locke 135; Bradshaw 147)

Year	Winner	Score	Venue	Qualifiers	Entrants
1950	A Locke, South Africa	279	Troon	93	262
1951	M Faulkner, England	285	R Portrush	98	180
1952	A Locke, South Africa	287	R Lytham and St Annes	96	275
1953	B Hogan, USA	282	Carnoustie	91	196
1954	P Thomson, Australia	283	Birkdale	97	349
1955	P Thomson, Australia	281	St Andrews	94	301
1956	P Thomson, Australia	286	Hoylake, R Liverpool	96	360
1957	A Locke, South Africa	279	St Andrews	96	282
1958	P Thomson, Australia	278	R Lytham and St Annes	96	362

(After a tie with D Thomas, Sudbury. Play-off scores: Thomson 139; Thomas 143)

Year	Winner	Score	Venue	Qualifiers	Entrants
1959	G Player, South Africa	284	Muirfield	90	285
1960	K Nagle, Australia	278	St Andrews	74	410
1961	A Palmer, USA	284	Birkdale	101	364
1962	A Palmer, USA	276	Troon	119	379
1963	R Charles, New Zealand	277	R Lytham and St Annes	119	261

(After a tie with P Rodgers, USA. Play-off scores: Charles 140; Rodgers 148)

Year	Winner	Score	Venue	Qualifiers	Entrants
1964	T Lema, USA	279	St Andrews	119	327
1965	P Thomson, Australia	285	R Birkdale	130	372
1966	J Nicklaus, USA	282	Muirfield	130	310
1967	R De Vicenzo, Argentina	278	Hoylake, R Liverpool	130	326
1968	G Player, South Africa	289	Carnoustie	130	309
1969	A Jacklin, England	280	R Lytham and St Annes	129	424
1970	J Nicklaus, USA	283	St Andrews	134	468

(After a tie with Doug Sanders, USA. Play-off scores: Nicklaus 72; Sanders 73)

Year	Winner	Score	Venue	Qualifiers	Entrants
1971	L Trevino, USA	278	R Birkdale	150	528
1972	L Trevino, USA	278	Muirfield	150	570
1973	T Weiskopf, USA	276	Troon	150	569

Year	Winner	Score	Venue	Qualifiers	Entrants
1974	G Player, South Africa	282	R Lytham and St Annes	150	679
1975	T Watson, USA	279	Carnoustie	150	629

(After a tie with J Newton, Australia. Play-off scores: Watson 71; Newton 72)

Year	Winner	Score	Venue	Qualifiers	Entrants
1976	J Miller, USA	279	R Birkdale	150	719
1977	T Watson, USA	268	Turnberry	150	730
1978	J Nicklaus, USA	281	St Andrews	150	788
1979	S Ballesteros, Spain	283	R Lytham and St Annes	150	885
1980	T Watson, USA	271	Muirfield	151	994
1981	B Rogers, USA	276	Sandwich, R St George's	153	971
1982	T Watson, USA	284	R Troon	150	1,121
1983	T Watson, USA	275	R Birkdale	151	1,107
1984	S Ballesteros, Spain	276	St Andrews		1,413
1985	A Lyle, Scotland	282	Sandwich, R St George's	149	1,361
1986	G Norman, Australia	280	Turnberry	152	1,347
1987	N Faldo, England	279	Muirfield	153	1,407
1988	S Ballesteros, Spain	273	R Lytham and St Annes	153	1,393
1989	M Calcavecchia, USA	275	R Troon	156	1,481

(Calcavecchia won a four-hole play-off after a tie with W Grady, Australia, and G Norman, Australia)

Year	Winner	Score	Venue	Qualifiers	Entrants
1990	N Faldo, England	270	St Andrews	152	1,707
1991	I Baker-Finch, Australia	272	R Birkdale	156	1,496
1992	N Faldo, England	272	Muirfield	156	1,666
1993	G Norman, Australia	267	Sandwich, R St George's	156	1,827
1994	N Price, Zimbabwe	268	Turnberry	156	1,701
1995	J Daly, USA	282	St Andrews	159	1,836

(Daly won a four-hole play-off after a tie with C Rocca, Italy)

Year	Winner	Score	Venue	Qualifiers	Entrants
1996	T Lehman, USA	271	R Lytham and St Annes	156	1,918
1997	J Leonard, USA	272	R Troon	156	2,133
1998	M O'Meara, USA	280	R Birkdale	152	2,336

(O'Meara won a four-hole play-off after a tie with B Watts, USA)

Year	Winner	Score	Venue	Qualifiers	Entrants
1999	P Lawrie, Scotland	290	Carnoustie	156	2,222

(Lawrie won a four-hole play-off after a tie with J Leonard, USA, and J Van de Velde, France)

Year	Winner	Score	Venue	Qualifiers	Entrants
2000	T Woods, USA	269	St Andrews	156	2,722
2001	David Duval, USA	274	R Lytham and St Annes	156	2,255

The Richest Golf Tournaments

Prize-money in golf is booming. Here is the 2001 list of the eleven richest events with the total prize-fund and first prize.

1	The Players Championship	$6m	$1.08m
2	Accenture Match Play Championship	$5m	$1m
	NEC Invitational	$5m	$1m
	American Express Championship	$5m	$1m
	EMC World Cup	$5m	$1m
	The Tour Championship	$5m	$1m
7	US PGA Championship	$5m	$900,000
8	Dunhill Links Championship	$5m	$800,000
9	The Open Championship	$4.62m	$840,000
10	US Open Championship	$4.5m	$800,000
11	The Masters	$3.88m	$1.008m

The US Open Championship

Players are of American nationality unless stated

101st US Open at *Southern Hills CC, Tulsa, Oklahoma* (6978 yds, Par 70)

Prize money: $5,000,000. Entries: 8300. Final field: 156, of whom 79 (including one amateur) made the half-way cut on 146 or better.

1	Retief Goosen (RSA)	66-70-69-71—276	$900000
2	Mark Brooks	72-64-70-70—276	530000
3	Stewart Cink	69-69-67-72—277	325310
4	Rocco Mediate	71-68-67-72—278	226777
5	Tom Kite	73-72-72-64—281	172912
	Paul Azinger	74-67-69-71—281	172912
7	Davis Love III	72-69-71-70—282	125172
	Vijay Singh (Fij)	74-70-74-64—282	125172
	Angel Cabrera (Arg)	70-71-72-69—282	125172
	Phil Mickelson	70-69-68-75—282	125172
	Kirk Triplett	72-69-71-70—282	125172
12	Tiger Woods	74-71-69-69—283	91734
	Sergio García (Esp)	70-68-68-77—283	91734
	Michael Allen	77-68-67-71—283	91734
	Matt Gogel	70-69-74-70—283	91734
16	David Duval	70-69-71-74—284	75337
	Scott Hoch	73-73-69-69—284	75337
	Chris DiMarco	69-73-70-72—284	75337
19	Corey Pavin	70-75-68-72—285	63426
	Chris Perry	72-71-73-69—285	63426
	Mike Weir (Can)	67-76-68-74—285	63426
22	Scott Verplank	71-71-73-71—286	54813
	Thomas Bjørn (Den)	72-69-73-72—286	54813
24	Steve Lowery	71-73-72-71—287	42523
	Joe Durant	71-74-70-72—287	42523
	Mark Calcavecchia	70-74-73-70—287	42523
	Hal Sutton	70-75-71-71—287	42523
	Tom Lehman	76-68-69-74—287	42523
	Olin Browne	71-74-71-71—287	42523
30	Padraig Harrington (Irl)	73-70-71-74—288	30055
	Jesper Parnevik (Swe)	73-73-74-68—288	30055
	Dean Wilson	71-74-72-71—288	30055
	Bob Estes	70-72-75-71—288	30055
	Steve Jones	73-73-72-70—288	30055
	Gabriel Hjertstedt (Swe)	72-74-70-72—288	30055
	Darren Clarke (NI)	74-71-71-72—288	30055
	Bob May	72-72-69-75—288	30055
	Bryce Molder (am)	75-71-68-74—288	
	JL Lewis	68-68-77-75—288	30055
40	Bernhard Langer (Ger)	71-73-71-74—289	23933
	Tim Herron	71-74-73-71—289	23933
	Briny Baird	71-72-70-76—289	23933
	Shaun Micheel	73-70-75-71—289	23933
44	Fred Funk	78-68-71-73—290	18780
	Toshimitsu Izawa (Jpn)	69-74-74-73—290	18780
	Brandel Chamblee	72-71-71-76—290	18780
	Jeff Maggert	69-73-72-76—290	18780
	Duffy Waldorf	75-68-69-78—290	18780
	Kevin Sutherland	73-72-73-72—290	18780
	Tom Byrum	74-72-72-72—290	18780
51	Eduardo Romero (Arg)	74-72-72-73—291	15035

52	Loren Roberts	69-76-69-78—292	13164
	Colin Montgomerie (Sco)	71-70-77-74—292	13164
	Mark Wiebe	73-72-74-73—292	13164
	Bob Tway	75-71-72-74—292	13164
	Hale Irwin	67-75-74-76—292	13164
	José Coceres (Arg)	70-73-75-74—292	13164
	Scott Dunlap	74-70-73-75—292	13164
	Brandt Jobe	77-68-71-76—292	13164
	Frank Lickliter	75-71-70-76—292	13164
	Jimmy Walker	79-66-74-73—292	13164
62	Jim Furyk	70-70-71-82—293	11443
	Dudley Hart	71-73-74-75—293	11443
	Richard Zokol (Can)	72-71-74-76—293	11443
	Tim Petrovic	74-71-75-73—293	11443
66	Ernie Els (RSA)	71-74-77-72—294	10368
	Peter Lonard (Aus)	76-69-70-79—294	10368
	Dan Forsman	75-71-77-71—294	10368
	David Toms	71-71-77-75—294	10368
	Harrison Frazar	73-73-76-72—294	10368
	David Peoples	73-73-72-76—294	10368
72	Nick Faldo (Eng)	76-70-74-75—295	9508
	Franklin Langham	75-71-75-74—295	9508
74	Anthony Kang (Kor)	74-72-77-73—296	8863
	Mathias Grönberg (Swe)	74-69-74-79—296	8863
	Gary Orr (Sco)	74-72-74-76—296	8863
	Thongchai Jaidee (Tha)	73-73-72-78—296	8863
78	Jim McGovern	71-73-77-76—297	8325
79	Stephen Gangluff	74-72-78-77—301	8105

The following players missed the half-way cut and received $1000 each:

80	Brad Faxon	73-74—147
	Gary Koch	75-72—147
	Robert Damron	73-74—147
	Mike Hulbert	75-72—147
	Lee Janzen	77-70—147
	Tom Pernice	74-73—147
	Chad Campbell	76-71—147
	Rich Beem	74-73—147
	Brett Quigley	71-76—147
	Pete Jordan	77-70—147
90	Mark O'Meara	74-74—148
	Nick Price (Zim)	74-74—148
	Steve Stricker	73-75—148
	Kyoung-Ju Choi (Kor)	78-70—148
	Skip Kendall	74-74—148
	Robert Gamez	74-74—148
	Dennis Paulson	75-73—148
97	José María Olazábal (Esp)	77-72—149
	Billy Andrade	75-74—149
	Toru Taniguchi (Jpn)	78-71—149
	Robert Allenby (Aus)	74-75—149
	Charles Howell III	75-74—149
	Carl Paulson	73-76—149
103	Steve Flesch	81-69—150
	Fred Couples	76-74—150
	Miguel Angel Jiménez (Esp)	77-73—150

103T	Paul Lawrie (Sco)	73-77—150
	Kyle Blackman	74-76—150
	Joey Maxon	74-76—150
	Ronnie Black	76-74—150
	Tripp Isenhour	73-77—150
	Chris Gonzalez	75-75—150
112	Justin Leonard	78-73—151
	Paul Goydos	76-75—151
	Donnie Hammond	76-75—151
	John Huston	75-76—151
	Esteban Toledo (Mex)	74-77—151
	Jay Don Blake	75-76—151
	Mike Sposa	78-73—151
	Lee Westwood (Eng)	75-76—151
	Todd Fischer	76-75—151
	Joel Kribel	74-77—151
	Jason Dufner	74-77—151
122	Gary Nicklaus	78-74—152
	Charles Raulerson	77-75—152
	Jeff Freeman	77-75—152
	Shingo Katayama (Jpn)	77-75—152
	Jess Daley	80-72—152
	Chris Smith	74-78—152
	Jason Dufner	74-77—151
	Bradley Klapprott	75-77—152
	John Douma	77-75—152
131	John Harris (am)	76-77—153
	Kevin Johnson	77-76—153

131T	Glen Day	77-76—153
	Brian Henninger	75-78—153
135	Michael Campbell (NZ)	77-77—154
136	Jeff Hart	80-75—155
	Stuart Appleby (Aus)	80-75—155
	Carlos Daniel Franco (Par)	76-79—155
	Dicky Pride	77-78—155
	Jeff Quinney (am)	82-73—155
	Scott Johnson	82-73—155
	Benjamin Bates	75-80—155
	John Maginnes	79-76—155
144	Notah Begay III	78-78—156
	Willie Wood	75-81—156
	Dennis Clark	79-77—156
	Wes Heffernan	77-79—156
	Christopher Anderson	77-79—156
149	Marty Schienne	78-79—157
150	Jeff Barlow	78-81—159
151	Chris Wall	81-79—160
152	George Frake II	84-77—161
153	Pierre Fulke (Swe)	76 Retd
	Jarmo Sandelin (Swe)	72 Wd
	Jay Williamson	Disq
	Phillip Price (Wal)	Retd

2000 US Open at *Pebble Beach, CA* (6874 yds, Par 71)

Prize money: $4,500,000. Entries: 8457 (record high)

1	Tiger Woods	65-69-71-67—272	$800000	22	Notah Begay III	74-75-72-73—294	53105
2	Miguel Angel Jiménez			23	Hal Sutton	69-73-83-70—295	45537
	(Esp)	66-74-76-71—287	391150		Bob May	72-76-75-72—295	45537
	Ernie Els (RSA)	74-73-68-72—287	391150		Tom Lehman	71-73-78-73—295	45537
4	John Huston	67-75-76-70—288	212779		Mike Brisky	71-73-79-72—295	45537
5	Padraig Harrington			27	Tom Watson	71-74-78-73—296	34066
	(Irl)	73-71-72-73—289	162526		Nick Price (Zim)	77-70-78-71—296	34066
	Lee Westwood (Eng)	71-71-76-71—289	162526		Steve Stricker	75-74-75-72—296	34066
7	Nick Faldo (Eng)	69-74-76-71—290	137203		Steve Jones	75-73-75-73—296	34066
8	Loren Roberts	68-78-73-72—291	112766		Hale Irwin	68-78-81-69—296	34066
	David Duval	75-71-74-71—291	112766	32	Tom Kite	72-77-77-71—297	28247
	Stewart Cink	77-72-72-70—291	112766		Chris Perry	75-72-78-72—297	28247
	Vijay Singh (Fij)	70-73-80-68—291	112766		Richard Zokol (Can)	74-74-80-69—297	28247
12	José María Olazábal				Rocco Mediate	69-76-75-77—297	28247
	(Esp)	70-71-76-75—292	86223		Lee Porter	74-70-83-70—297	28247
	Paul Azinger	71-73-79-69—292	86223	37	Woody Austin	77-70-78-73—298	22056
	Retief Goosen (RSA)	77-72-72-71—292	86223		Jerry Kelly	73-73-81-71—298	22056
	Michael Campbell				Larry Mize	73-72-76-77—298	22056
	(NZ)	71-77-71-73—292	86223		Craig Parry (Aus)	73-74-76-75—298	22056
16	Justin Leonard	73-73-75-72—293	65214		Bobby Clampett	68-77-76-77—298	22056
	Mike Weir (Can)	76-72-76-79—293	65214		Angel Cabrera (Arg)	69-76-79-74—298	22056
	Fred Couples	70-75-75-73—293	65214		Lee Janzen	71-73-79-75—298	22056
	Scott Hoch	73-76-75-69—293	65214		Ted Tryba	71-73-79-75—298	22056
	Phil Mickelson	71-73-73-76—293	65214		Charles Warren	75-74-75-74—298	22056
	David Toms	73-76-72-72—293	65214				

Other players who made the cut: Rick Hartmann, Sergio García (Esp), Colin Montgomerie (Sco), Scott Verplank, Thomas Bjørn (Den) 299; Warren Schutte (SA), Mark O'Meara 300; Darren Clarke (NI), Keith Clearwater, Jeff Coston 301; Kirk Triplett 302; Dave Eichelberger, Jimmy Green 303; Jeffrey Wilson (am) 304; Jim Furyk 305; Brandel Chamblee, Carlos Daniel Franco (Par) 306; Robert Damron 313

1999 US Open at *Pinehurst No. 2, North Carolina* (7175 yds, Par 70)

Prize money: $3,500,000. Entries: 7889 (record high)

1	P Stewart	68-69-72-70—279	$625000	17T	S Verplank	72-73-72-74—291	46756
2	P Mickelson	67-70-73-70—280	370000	23	MA Jiménez (Esp)	73-70-72-77—292	33505
3	V Singh (Fij)	69-70-73-69—281	196791		N Price (Zim)	71-74-74-73—292	33505
	T Woods	68-71-72-70—281	196791		T Scherrer	72-72-74-74—292	33505
5	S Stricker	70-73-69-73—285	130655		B Watts	69-73-77-73—292	33505
6	T Herron	69-72-70-75—286	116935		DA Weibring	69-74-74-75—292	33505
7	D Duval	67-70-75-75—287	96260	28	D Berganio jr	68-77-76-72—293	26185
	J Maggert	71-69-74-73—287	96260		T Lehman	73-74-73-73—293	26185
	H Sutton	69-70-76-72—287	96260	30	B Estes	70-71-77-76—294	23804
10	D Clarke (NI)	73-70-74-71—288	78862		G Sisk	71-72-76-75—294	23804
	B Mayfair	67-72-74-75—288	78862	32	S Cink	72-74-78-71—295	22448
12	P Azinger	72-72-75-70—289	67347		S Strüver (Ger)	70-76-75-74—295	22448
	P Goydos	67-74-74-74—289	67347	34	B Fabel	69-75-78-74—296	19083
	D Love III	70-73-74-72—289	67347		C Franco (Par)	69-77-73-77—296	19083
15	J Leonard	69-75-73-73—290	58214		G Hjertstedt (Swe)	75-72-79-70—296	19083
	C Montgomerie (Sco)	72-72-74-72—290	58214		R Mediate	69-72-76-79—296	19083
17	J Furyk	69-73-77-72—291	46756		C Parry (Aus)	69-73-79-75—296	19083
	J Haas	74-72-73-72—291	46756		S Pate	70-75-75-76—296	19083
	D Hart	73-73-76-69—291	46756		C Pavin	74-71-78-73—296	19083
	J Huston	71-69-75-76—291	46756		E Toledo (Mex)	70-75-72-78—296	19083
	J Parnevik (Swe)	71-71-76-73—291	46756				

Other players who made the cut: S Allan (Aus), G Hallberg, L Mattiace, C Perry 297; R Allenby (Aus), B Chamblee, L Janzen, D Lebeck, 298; S Elkington (Aus), C Tidland 299; G Kraft, S McRoy, P Price (Wal), J Tyska 300; J Kelly, T Watson, K Yokoo (Jpn) 301; J Cook, T Kite 302; C Smith, B Tway 303; L Mize 304; H Kuehne (am) 306; B Burns, T Tryba 308; J Daly 309

1998 US Open at The Olympic Club, San Francisco (6797 yds, Par 70)

Prize money: $3,000,000. Entries: 7117

1	L Janzen	73-66-73-68—280	$535000	18T	JM Olazábal (Esp)	68-77-71-74—290	41833
2	P Stewart	66-71-70-74—281	315000		T Woods	74-72-71-73—290	41833
3	B Tway	68-70-73-73—284	201730	23	C Martin	74-71-74-72—291	34043
4	N Price (Zim)	73-68-71-73—285	140597		G Day	73-72-71-75—291	34043
5	S Stricker	73-71-69-73—286	107392	25	DA Weibring	72-72-75-73—292	25640
	T Lehman	68-75-68-75—286	107392		P-U Johansson (Swe)	71-75-73-73—292	25640
7	D Duval	75-68-75-69—287	83794		E Romero (Arg)	72-70-76-74—292	25640
	L Westwood (Eng)	72-74-70-71—287	83794		C Perry	74-71-72-75—292	25640
	J Maggert	69-69-75-74—287	83794		V Singh (Fij)	73-72-73-74—292	25640
10	J Sluman	72-74-74-68—288	64490		T Björn (Den)	72-75-70-75—292	25640
	P Mickelson	71-73-74-70—288	64490		M Carnevale	67-73-74-78—292	25640
	S Appleby (Aus)	73-74-70-71—288	64490	32	M O'Meara	70-76-78-69—293	18372
	S Cink	73-68-73-74—288	64490		P Harrington (Irl)	73-72-76-72—293	18372
14	P Azinger	75-72-77-65—289	52214		B Zabriski	74-71-74-74—293	18372
	J Parnevik (Swe)	69-74-76-70—289	52214		S Pate	72-75-73-73—293	18372
	M Kuchar (am)	70-69-76-74—289			J Huston	73-72-72-76—293	18372
	J Furyk	74-73-68-74—289	52214		J Durant	68-73-76-76—293	18372
18	C Montgomerie (Sco)	70-74-77-69—290	41833		C DiMarco	71-71-74-77—293	18372
	L Roberts	71-76-71-72—290	41833		L Porter	72-67-76-78—293	18372
	F Lickliter II	73-71-72-74—290	41833				

Other players who made the cut: J Leonard, S McCarron, F Nobilo (NZ) 294; D Clarke (NI), J Sindelar, T Kite, J Acosta Jr, O Browne, J Nicklaus 295; E Els (RSA), M Reid, B Faxon, S Verplank 296; F Couples, T Herron, J Johnston, J Daly 297; M Brooks 298; S Simpson 300; R Walcher 303; T Sipula 305.

1997 US Open at Congressional CC, Bethesda, Maryland (7213 yds, Par 70)

Prize money: $2,600,000. Entries: 7013

1	E Els (SA)	71-67-69-69—276	$465000		P Stankowski	75-70-68-73—286	31915
2	C Montgomerie (Sco)	65-76-67-69—277	275000		H Sutton	66-73-73-74—286	31915
3	T Lehman	67-70-68-73—278	172828	24	L Mattiace	71-75-73-68—287	24173
4	J Maggert	73-66-68-74—281	120454		E Fryatt	72-73-73-69—287	24173
5	B Tway	71-71-70-70—282	79875		S Dunlap	75-66-75-71—287	24173
	O Browne	71-71-69-71—282	79875	24T	S Elkington (Aus)	75-68-72-72—287	24173
	J Furyk	74-68-69-71—282	79875	28	P Goydos	73-72-74-69—288	17443
	J Haas	73-69-68-72—282	79875		P Azinger	72-72-74-70—288	17443
	T Tolles	74-67-69-72—282	79875		P Stewart	71-73-73-71—288	17443
10	S McCarron	73-71-69-70—283	56949		M McNulty (Zim)	67-73-75-73—288	17443
	S Hoch	71-68-72-72—283	56949		H Kase	68-73-73-74—288	17443
	D Ogrin	70-69-71-73—283	56949		F Zoeller	72-73-69-74—288	17443
13	L Roberts	72-69-72-71—284	47348		K Gibson	72-69-72-75—288	17443
13T	S Cink	71-67-74-72—284	47348	28T	J Sluman	69-72-72-75—288	17443
	B Andrade	75-67-69-73—284	47348	36	J Leonard	69-72-78-70—289	13483
16	B Hughes (Aus)	75-70-71-69—285	40086		G Waite	72-74-72-71—289	13483
	JM Olazábal (Esp)	71-71-72-71—285	40086		S Stricker	66-76-75-72—289	13483
	D Love III	75-70-69-71—285	40086		M O'Meara	73-73-71-72—289	13483
19	N Price (Zim)	71-74-71-70—286	31915		S Appleby (Aus)	71-75-70-73—289	13483
	L Westwood (Eng)	71-71-73-71—286	31915		F Nobilo (NZ)	71-74-70-74—289	13483
	T Woods	74-67-73-72—286	31915		J Cook	72-71-71-75—289	13483

Other players who made the cut: D Clarke (NI), P Mickelson, F Funk, C Perry, C Parry (Aus) 290; J Parnevik (Swe), D Duval, N Faldo (Eng) 291; D White 292; L Janzen, J Nicklaus, H Irwin, F Couples, P Teravainen, P Broadhurst (Eng) 293; L Mize, C Rose 294; C Smith, D Waldorf, R Butcher, S Jones 295; T Watson 296; D Schreyer, B Crenshaw, B Faxon 297; T Kite, M Hulbert, G Kraft, J Morse, S Ames (T&T), T Björn (Den) 298; J Green 299; R Wylie, A Coltart (Sco) 300; D Mast, G Towne, V Singh (Fij), P Parker, D Hammond 301; J Ferenz 303; M Dawson 304; S Adams 306.

1996 US Open at Oakland Hills, Birmingham, Michigan (6990 yds, Par 70)

Prize money: $2,400,000. Entries: 5925

1	S Jones	74-66-69-69—278	$425000	16T	S Cink	69-73-70-73—285	33188
2	D Love III	71-69-70-69—279	204801		S Torrance (Sco)	71-69-71-74—285	33188
	T Lehman	71-72-65-71—279	204801	23	B Bryant	73-71-74-68—286	23806
4	J Morse	68-74-68-70—280	111235		P Jacobsen	71-74-70-71—286	23806
5	E Els (RSA)	72-67-72-70—281	84964		B Andrade	72-69-72-73—286	23806
	J Furyk	72-69-70-70—281	84964		W Austin	67-72-72-75—286	23806
7	S Hoch	73-71-71-67—282	66294	27	C Strange	74-73-71-69—287	17809
	V Singh (Fij)	71-72-70-69—282	66294		P Jordan	71-74-72-70—287	17809
	K Green	73-67-72-70—282	66294		J Nicklaus	72-74-69-72—287	17809
10	L Janzen	68-75-71-69—283	52591		P Stewart	67-71-76-73—287	17809
	G Norman (Aus)	73-66-74-70—283	52591		J Daly	72-69-73-73—287	17809
	C Montgomerie (Sco)	70-72-69-72—283	52591	32	M Swartz	72-72-74-70—288	14070
13	D Forsman	72-71-70-71—284	43725		T Purtzer	76-71-71-70—288	14070
	T Watson	70-71-71-72—284	43725		B Mayfair	72-71-74-71—288	14070
	F Nobilo (NZ)	69-71-70-74—284	43725		B Ogle (Aus)	70-75-72-71—288	14070
16	N Faldo (Eng)	72-71-72-70—285	33188		S Gotsche	72-70-74-72—288	14070
	D Begganio	69-72-72-72—285	33188		M Campbell (NZ)	70-73-73-72—288	14070
	M Brooks	76-68-69-72—285	33188		A Forsbrand (Swe)	74-71-71-72—288	14070
	M O'Meara	72-73-68-72—285	33188		S Murphy	71-75-68-74—288	14070
	J Cook	70-71-71-73—285	33188				

Other players who made the cut: L Parsons, JL Lucas, B Ford, S Simpson, W Riley (Aus), S Elkington (Aus), T Tolles, C Pavin, K Triplett, L Roberts 289; W Westner (RSA), B Gilder, K Perry, J Sluman, J Gullion, H Irwin, A Cejka (Ger), M Bradley, K Gibson, J Leonard 290; S Stricker, S Lowery, B Porter, W Murchison, R Leen (am), D Gilford (Eng), D Harrington 291; D Duval, A Morse, P Azinger, F Linkliter II, M Ozaki (Jpn), C Rocca (Ita), W Grady (Aus), D Ogrin, P O'Malley (Aus), C Byrum, J Gallagher jr, B Tway 292; T Kuehne (am), M Christie, I Woosnam (Wal) 293; T Woods (am), J Huston, K Jones, S Kendall, S McCarron, T Kite, B Faxon, N Lancaster 294; C Parry (Aus), J Sanchez, J O'Keefe, J Haas 295; A Rodriguez, T Pernice jr, P Mickelson 296; J Maggert, J Thorpe, B McCallister (Aus), P Walton (Irl) 297; O Uresti, O Browne 298; G Trevisonno 299; M Wiebe 300; S Scott (Am), R Yokota (Jpn) 301; M Burke jr 302; S Kelly 309.

1995 US Open at Shinnecock Hills, New York (6944 yds, Par 70)

Prize money: $2,000,000. Entries: 6,001

1	C Pavin	72-69-71-68—280	$350000	21T	B Ogle (Aus)	71-75-72-69—287	20085
2	G Norman (Aus)	68-67-74-73—282	207000		P Jordan	74-71-71-71—287	20085
3	T Lehman	70-72-67-74—283	131974		B Andrade	72-69-74-72—287	20085
4	N Lancaster	70-72-77-65—284	66633		S Verplank	72-69-71-75—287	20085
	J Maggert	69-72-77-66—284	66633		I Woosnam (Wal)	72-71-69-75—287	20085
	B Glasson	69-70-76-69—284	66633	28	C Montgomerie (Sco)	71-74-75-68—288	13912
	J Haas	70-73-72-69—284	66633		MA Jiménez (Esp)	72-72-75-69—288	13912
	D Love III	72-68-73-71—284	66633		M Hulbert	74-72-72-70—288	13912
	P Mickelson	68-70-72-74—284	66633		M Ozaki (Jpn)	69-68-80-71—288	13912
10	F Nobilo (NZ)	72-72-70-71—285	44184		S Simpson	67-75-74-72—288	13912
	V Singh (Fij)	70-71-72-72—285	44184		D Duval	70-73-73-72—288	13912
	B Tway	69-69-72-75—285	44184		JM Olazábal (Esp)	73-70-72-73—288	13912
13	M McCumber	70-71-77-68—286	30934		G Hallberg	70-76-69-73—288	13912
	D Waldorf	72-70-75-69—286	30934	36	B Porter	73-70-79-67—289	9812
	Brad Bryant	71-75-70-70—286	30934		R Floyd	74-72-76-67—289	9812
13T	J Sluman	72-69-74-71—286	30934		H Sutton	71-74-76-68—289	9812
	M Roe (Eng)	71-69-74-72—286	30934		C Strange	70-72-76-71—289	9812
	L Janzen	70-72-72-72—286	30934		G Boros	73-71-74-71—289	9812
	N Price (Zim)	66-73-73-74—286	30934		S Elkington (Aus)	72-73-73-71—289	9812
	S Stricker	71-70-71-74—286	30934		C Byrum	70-70-76-73—289	9812
21	F Zoeller	69-74-76-68—287	20085		B Langer (Ger)	74-67-74-74—289	9812
	P Stewart	74-71-73-69—287	20085				

Other players who made the cut: B Lane (Eng) 290; J McGovern, C Pena, O Uresti, J Daly, N Faldo (Eng), B Hughes 291; B Burns, E Romero (Arg), T Tryba, P Jacobsen, M Gogel 292; B Faxon, T Watson, C Perry, S Lowery, S Hoch, G Bruckner 293; J Gallagher, J Cook, B Jobe, D Edwards, P Goydos 294; T Kite, M Brisky, T Armour III 295; J Connelly 296; B Crenshaw, J Maginnes 297; J Gullion 301.

1994 US Open at Oakmont, Pennsylvania (6946 yds, Par 71)

Prize money: $1,700,000. Entries: 6010

1	E Els (RSA)*	69-71-66-73—279	$320000	18T	S Ballesteros (Esp)	72-72-70-73—287	22477
2	L Roberts	76-69-64-70—279	141828		H Irwin	69-69-71-78—287	22477
	C Montgomerie (Sco)	71-65-73-70—279	141828	21	S Torrance (Sco)	72-71-76-69—288	19464
*Els won at second sudden-death play-off hole against Roberts					S Pate	74-66-71-77—288	19464
after both shot 74 in 18-hole play-off. Montgomerie shot 78.				23	B Langer (Ger)	72-72-73-72—289	17223
4	C Strange	70-70-70-70—280	75728		K Triplett	70-71-71-77—289	17223
5	J Cook	73-65-73-71—282	61318	25	M Springer	74-72-73-71—290	14705
6	C Dennis	71-71-70-71—283	49485		C Parry (Aus)	78-68-71-73—290	14705
	G Norman (Aus)	71-71-69-72—283	49485		C Beck	73-73-70-74—290	14705
	T Watson	68-73-68-74—283	49485	28	D Love III	74-72-74-72—292	11514
9	D Waldorf	74-68-73-69—284	37179		J Furyk	74-69-74-75—292	11514
	J Maggert	71-68-75-70—284	37179		L Clements	73-71-73-75—292	11514
	J Sluman	72-69-72-71—284	37179		J Nicklaus	69-70-77-76—292	11514
	F Nobilo (NZ)	69-71-68-76—284	37179		M Ozaki (Jpn)	70-73-69-80—292	11514
13	J McGovern	73-69-74-69—285	29767	33	M Carnevale	75-72-76-70—293	9578
	S Hoch	72-72-70-71—285	29767		T Lehman	77-68-73-75—293	9578
	D Edwards	73-65-75-72—285	29767		F Allen	73-70-74-76—293	9578
16	F Couples	72-71-69-74—286	25899		T Kite	73-71-72-77—293	9578
	S Lowery	71-71-68-76—286	25899		B Crenshaw	71-74-70-78—293	9578
18	S Verplank	70-72-75-70—287	22477		B Faxon	73-69-71-80—293	9578

Other players who made the cut: B Hughes, P Baker (Eng), G Brand Jr (Sco), B Jobe 294; F Quinn jr 295;
P Goydos, F Funk, D Walsworth 296; T Dunlavey, O Browne, B Lane (Eng), M Emery, D Bergano, J Gallagher Jr,
W Levi, P Mickelson 297; T Armour III, H Royer III, S Simpson 298; S Richardson (Eng), F Zoeller 299;
D Rummells, D Martin 301; E Humenik, M Smith, M Aubrey 302.

1993 US Open at Baltusrol, Springfield, NJ (7155 yds, Par 70)

Prize money: $1,600,000. Entries: 5905

1	L Janzen	67-67-69-69—272	$290000	16T	F Couples	68-71-71-71—281	21576
2	P Stewart	70-66-68-70—274	145000		M Standly	70-69-70-72—281	21576
3	C Parry (Aus)	66-74-69-68—277	78556	19	B McCallister	68-73-73-68—282	18071
	P Azinger	71-68-69-69—277	78556		D Forsman	73-71-70-68—282	18071
5	S Hoch	66-72-72-68—278	48730		C Pavin	68-69-75-70—282	18071
	T Watson	70-66-73-69—278	48730		T Lehman	71-70-71-70—282	18071
7	E Els (RSA)	71-73-68-67—279	35481		S Pate	70-71-71-70—282	18071
	R Floyd	68-73-70-68—279	35481		I Baker-Finch (Aus)	70-70-70-72—282	18071
	N Henke	72-71-67-69—279	35481	25	C Strange	73-68-75-67—283	14531
	F Funk	70-72-67-70—279	35481		J Ozaki (Jpn)	70-70-74-69—283	14531
11	L Roberts	70-70-71-69—280	26249		R Mediate	68-72-73-70—283	14531
	J Sluman	71-71-69-69—280	26249		C Beck	72-68-72-71—283	14531
	J Adams	70-70-69-71—280	26249		K Perry	74-70-68-71—283	14531
	D Edwards	70-72-66-72—280	26249		M Calcavecchia	70-70-71-72—283	14531
	N Price (Zim)	71-66-70-73—280	26249		J Cook	75-66-70-72—283	14531
16	B Lane (Eng)	74-68-70-69—281	21576		W Levi	71-69-69-74—283	14531

Other players who made the cut: S Lowery, C Montgomerie (Sco), B Gilder, J Ozaki (Jpn), G Twiggs, B Andrade,
L Rinker, J Daly, C Stadler, R Allenby (Aus), D Love III, S Elkington (Aus), M Donald 284; S Simpson, M Brooks,
M McCumber, B Claar, R Fehr, L Nelson 285; K Triplett, I Woosnam (Wal), F Allem (RSA), V Heafner, E Kirby,
M Christie, K Clearwater, A Lyle (Sco), B Estes, J Maggert 286; M Hulbert, H Irwin, M Smith, A Knoll, J Edwards,
JD Blake 287; F Zoeller, S Gotsche, J Leonard (am), B Faxon 288; J Nicklaus, N Faldo (Eng), G Waite, P Jordan,
D Waldorf 289; M Wiebe, T Johnstone (Zim), J Haas, B Thompson 290; W Grady (Aus), T Schulz 291; S Stricker 292;
S Flesch 294; D Weaver, J Flannery 295; R Wrenn 297; R Gamez 298.

1992 US Open at Pebble Beach, Monterey, California (6809 yds, Par 72)

Prize money: $1,500,000. Entries: 6244

1	T Kite	71-72-70-72—285	$275000	17	T Tyner		74-72-78-70—294	18069
2	J Sluman	73-74-69-71—287	137500		W Grady (Aus)		74-66-81-73—294	18069
3	C Montgomerie (Sco)	70-71-77-70—288	84245		F Couples		72-70-78-74—294	18069
4	N Faldo (Eng)	70-76-68-77—291	54924		W Wood		70-75-75-74—294	18069
	N Price (Zim)	71-72-77-71—291	54924		A Magee		77-69-72-76—294	18069
6	I Woosnam (Wal)	72-72-69-79—292	32315		A Dillard		68-70-79-77—294	18069
	JD Blake	70-74-75-73—292	32315	23	B Bryant		71-76-75-73—295	13906
	B Gilder	73-70-75-74—292	32315		B Mayfair		74-73-75-73—295	13906
	B Andrade	72-74-72-74—292	32315		C Strange		67-78-76-74—295	13906
	M Hulbert	74-73-70-75—292	32315		J Haas		70-77-74-74—295	13906
	T Lehman	69-74-72-77—292	32315		J Kane		73-71-76-75—295	13906
	J Sindelar	74-72-68-78—292	32315		B Langer (Ger)		73-72-75-75—295	13906
13	M McCumber	70-76-73-74—293	22531		D Hammond		73-73-73-76—295	13906
	J Cook	72-72-74-75—293	22531		J Ozaki (Jpn)		77-70-72-76—295	13906
	I Baker-Finch (Aus)	74-71-72-76—293	22531		D Hart		76-71-71-77—295	13906
	G Morgan	66-69-77-81—293	22531		S Ballesteros (Esp)		71-76-69-79—295	13906

Other players who made the cut: F Funk, J Delsing, C Parry (Aus), R Cochran, A Forsbrand, T Purtzer, M Calcavecchia, R Zokol (Can), P Azinger, C Stadler, M McNulty (Zim) 296; D Pooley, D Pruitt, B Estes, R Floyd, R Mediate, G Hallberg, M Brooks 297; S Gump, A Lyle (Sco), H Irwin, B Wolcott, T Schulz, P Stewart 298; D Donovan, D Waldorf, J Gallagher Jr 299; D Love III, D Forsman 300; M Smith 301; P Jacobsen 302; G Twiggs, S Simpson 303; K Triplett 305.

US OPEN CHAMPIONSHIP HISTORY

Year	Winner	Runner-up	Venue	By
1894	W Dunn	W Campbell	St Andrews, NY	2 holes

After 1894 decided by stroke play

1895	HJ Rawlins	Newport	173
1896	J Foulis	Southampton	152
1897	J Lloyd	Wheaton, IL	162
1898	F Herd	Shinnecock Hills	328
72 holes played from 1898			
1899	W Smith	Baltimore	315
1900	H Vardon (Eng)	Wheaton, IL	313
1901	W Anderson	Myopia, MA	315
(After a tie with A Smith Play-off: Anderson 85, Smith 86)			
1902	L Auchterlonie	Garden City	305
1903	W Anderson	Baltusrol	307
(After a tie with D Brown Play-off: Anderson 82, Brown 84)			
1904	W Anderson	Glenview	304
1905	W Anderson	Myopia, MA	335
1906	A Smith	Onwentsia	291
1907	A Ross	Chestnut Hill, PA	302
1908	F McLeod	Myopia, MA	322
(After a tie with W Smith Play-off: McLeod 77, Smith 83)			
1909	G Sargent	Englewood, NJ	290
1910	A Smith	Philadelphia	289
(After a tie with J McDermott and M Smith)			
1911	J McDermott	Wheaton, IL	307
(After a tie with M Brady and G Simpson Play-off: McDermott 80, Brady 82, Simpson 85)			
1912	J McDermott	Buffalo, NY	294
1913	F Ouimet (am)	Brookline, MA	304
(After a tie with H Vardon and E Ray)			
1914	W Hagen	Midlothian	297
1915	J Travers (am)	Baltusrol	290
1916	C Evans (am)	Minneapolis	286
1917-18	*No Championship*		
1919	W Hagen	Braeburn	301
(After a tie with M Brady Play-off: Hagen 77, Brady 78)			

1920	E Ray (Eng)	Inverness	295
1921	J Barnes	Washington	289
1922	G Sarazen	Glencoe	288
1923	R Jones jr (am)	Inwood, LI	295
(After a tie with R Cruikshank. Play-off: Jones 76, Cruikshank 78)			
1924	C Walker	Oakland Hills	297
1925	W MacFarlane	Worcester	291
(After a tie with R Jones jr Play-off: MacFarlane 75-72, Jones 75-73)			
1926	R Jones jr (am)	Scioto	293
1927	T Armour	Oakmont	301
(After a tie with H Cooper. Play-off: Armour 76, Cooper 79)			
1928	J Farrell	Olympia Fields	294
(After a tie with R Jones Jr. Play-off: Farrell 143, Jones 144)			
1929	R Jones jr (Am)	Winged Foot, NY	294
(After a tie with A Espinosa. Play-off: Jones 141, Espinosa 164)			
1930	R Jones jr (am)	Interlachen	287
1931	B Burke	Inverness	292
(After a tie with G von Elm. Play-off: Burke 149-148, von Elm 149-149)			
1932	G Sarazen	Fresh Meadow	286
1933	J Goodman (am)	North Shore	287
1934	O Dutra	Merion	293
1935	S Parks	Oakmont	299
1936	T Manero	Springfield	282
1937	R Guldahl	Oakland Hills	281
1938	R Guldahl	Cherry Hills	284
1939	B Nelson	Philadelphia	284
(After a tie with C Wood and D Shute)			
1940	W Lawson Little	Canterbury, OH	287
(After a tie with G Sarazen. Play-off: Little 70, Sarazen 73)			
1941	C Wood	Fort Worth, TX	284

1942–45	*No Championship*		
1946	L Mangrum	Canterbury	284
(After a tie with B Nelson and V Ghezzie)			
1947	L Worsham	St Louis	282
(After a tie with S Snead. Play-off: Worsham 69, Snead 70)			
1948	B Hogan	Los Angeles	276
1949	Dr C Middlecoff	Medinah, IL	286
1950	B Hogan	Merion, PA	287
(After a tie with L Mangrum and G Fazio. Play-off: Hogan 69, Mangrum 73, Fazio 75)			
1951	B Hogan	Oakland Hills, MI	287
1952	J Boros	Dallas, TX	281
1953	B Hogan	Oakmont	283
1954	E Furgol	Baltusrol	284
1955	J Fleck	San Francisco	287
(After a tie with B Hogan. Play-off: Fleck 69, Hogan 72)			
1956	Dr C Middlecoff	Rochester, NY	281
1957	D Mayer	Inverness	282
(After a tie with Dr C Middlecoff. Play-off: Mayer 72, Middlecoff 79)			
1958	T Bolt	Tulsa, OK	283
1959	W Casper	Winged Foot, NY	282
1960	A Palmer	Denver, CO	280
1961	G Littler	Birmingham, MI	281
1962	J Nicklaus	Oakmont	283
(After a tie with A Palmer. Play-off: Nicklaus 71, Palmer 74)			
1963	J Boros	Brookline, MA	293
(After a tie. Play-off: J Boros 70, J Cupit 73, A Palmer 76)			
1964	K Venturi	Washington	278
1965	G Player (RSA)	St Louis, MO	282
(After a tie with K Nagle. Play-off: Player 71, Nagle 74)			
1966	W Casper	San Francisco	278
(After a tie with A Palmer. Play-off: Casper 69, Palmer 73)			
1967	J Nicklaus	Baltusrol	275
1968	L Trevino	Rochester, NY	275
1969	O Moody	Houston, TX	281
1970	A Jacklin (Eng)	Hazeltine, MN	281
1971	L Trevino	Merion, PA	280
(After a tie with J Nicklaus. Play-off: Trevino 68, Nicklaus 71)			

1972	J Nicklaus	Pebble Beach	290
1973	J Miller	Oakmont, PA	279
1974	H Irwin	Winged Foot, NY	287
1975	L Graham	Medinah, IL	287
(After a tie with Mahaffey. Play-off: Graham 71, Mahaffey 73)			
1976	J Pate	Atlanta, GA	277
1977	H Green	Southern Hills, Tulsa	278
1978	A North	Cherry Hills	285
1979	H Irwin	Inverness, OH	284
1980	J Nicklaus	Baltusrol	272
1981	D Graham (Aus)	Merion, PA	273
1982	T Watson	Pebble Beach	282
1983	L Nelson	Oakmont, PA	280
1984	F Zoeller	Winged Foot	276
(After a tie with G Norman. Play-off: Zoeller 67, Norman 75)			
1985	A North	Oakland Hills, MI	279
1986	R Floyd	Shinnecock Hills, NY	279
1987	S Simpson	Olympic, San Francisco	277
1988	C Strange	Brookline, MA	278
(After a tie with N Faldo. Play-off: Strange 71, Faldo 75)			
1989	C Strange	Rochester, NY	278
1990	H Irwin	Medinah	280
(After a tie with M Donald won at 1st extra hole after 18-hole play-off tie)			
1991	P Stewart	Hazeltine, MN	282
(After a tie with S Simpson Play-off: Stewart 75, Simpson 77)			
1992	T Kite	Pebble Beach, FL	285
1993	L Janzen	Baltusrol	272
1994	E Els (RSA)	Oakmont, PA	279
(After a tie with L Roberts and C Montgomerie Play-off: Els 74, Roberts 74, Montgomerie 78. Els then defeated Roberts at the second hole of a sudden death play-off)			
1995	C Pavin	Shinnecock Hills, NY	280
1996	S Jones	Oakland Hills, MI	278
1997	E Els (RSA)	Congressional, Bethesda	276
1998	L Janzen	Olympic, San Francisco	280
1999	P Stewart	Pinehurst No. 2, NC	279
2000	T Woods	Pebble Beac , CA	272
2001	R Goosen (RSA)	Southern Hills CC, OK	276

Lawrie's putt wins Shot of the Year

Paul Lawrie's putt from the Valley of Sin on the 18th hole at St Andrews, which secured for him the inaugural Dunhill Links Championship, has won The European Tour Shot of the Year for 2001. The putt earned him a £551,040 first prize.

Lawrie explained: 'I reckoned it was a double-breaker with a bit of left to right movement at the start and from right to left near the hole. It worked out perfectly and as soon as I hit it, I knew it wasn't going to be far away. It was to be the most important putt of my life'.

'When I won the 1999 Open Championship I had three putts from about three feet to win, but this was real pressure knowing what was riding on one stroke. It was a great tournament to play in, and it doesn't get much better than to win at the Home of Golf'.

The Masters

Players are of American nationality unless stated

65th Masters *at Augusta National GC, Georgia* (6985 yds, Par 72)

Prize money: $5,574,920. Final field comprised 93 players, of whom two withdrew and 47 (including no amateurs) made the half-way cut on 145 or better.

1	Tiger Woods	70-66-68-68—272	$1008000
2	David Duval	71-66-70-67—274	604800
3	Phil Mickelson	67-69-69-70—275	380800
4	Toshimitsu Izawa (Jpn)	71-66-74-67—278	246400
	Mark Calcavecchia	72-66-68-72—278	246400
6	Bernhard Langer (Ger)	73-69-68-69—279	181300
	Jim Furyk	69-71-70-69—279	181300
	Ernie Els (RSA)	71-68-68-72—279	181300
	Kirk Triplett	68-70-70-71—279	181300
10	Brad Faxon	73-68-68-71—280	128800
	Steve Stricker	66-71-72-71—280	128800
	Miguel Angel Jiménez (Esp)	68-72-71-69—280	128800
	Angel Cabrera (Arg)	66-71-70-73—280	128800
	Chris DiMarco	65-69-72-74—280	128800
15	José María Olazábal (Esp)	70-68-71-72—281	95200
	Paul Azinger	70-71-71-69—281	95200
	Rocco Mediate	72-70-66-73—281	95200
18	Vijay Singh (Fij)	69-71-73-69—282	81200
	Tom Lehman	75-68-71-68—282	81200
20	Mark O'Meara	69-74-72-68—283	65240
	Jesper Parnevik (Swe)	71-71-72-69—283	65240
	John Huston	67-75-72-69—283	65240
	Jeff Maggert	72-70-70-71—283	65240
24	Darren Clarke (NI)	72-67-72-73—284	53760
25	Tom Scherrer	71-71-70-73—285	49280
26	Fred Couples	74-71-73-68—286	44800
27	Padraig Harrington (Irl)	75-69-72-71—287	40600
	Justin Leonard	73-71-72-71—287	40600
	Mike Weir (Can)	74-69-72-72—287	40600
	Steve Jones	74-70-72-71—287	40600
31	Stuart Appleby (Aus)	72-70-70-76—288	33208
	Mark Brooks	70-71-77-70—288	33208
	Duffy Waldorf	72-70-71-75—288	33208
	Lee Janzen	67-70-72-79—288	33208
	David Toms	72-72-71-73—288	33208
36	Hal Sutton	74-69-71-75—289	28840
37	Loren Roberts	71-74-73-72—290	26320
	Chris Perry	68-74-74-74—290	26320
	Scott Hoch	74-70-72-74—290	26320
40	Steve Lowery	72-72-78-70—292	22960
	Shingo Katayama (Jpn)	75-70-73-74—292	22960
	Franklin Langham	72-73-75-72—292	22960
43	Dudley Hart	74-70-78-71—293	19600
	Bob May	71-74-73-75—293	19600
	Jonathan Kaye	74-71-74-74—293	19600
46	Carlos Franco (Par)	71-71-77-75—294	17360
47	Robert Allenby (Aus)	71-74-75-75—295	16240

The following players missed the half-way cut. Each professional player received $5000:

48	Sergio García (Esp)	70-76—146	59T	Nick Price (Zim)	73-75—148	79	Seve Ballesteros		
	Davis Love III	71-75—146		Larry Mize	74-74—148		(Esp)	76-76—152
	José Coceres (Arg)	77-69—146		Rory Sabbatini			Craig Stadler	79-73—152
	Thomas Bjørn			(RSA)	73-75—148		Charles Coody	80-72—152
	(Den)	70-76—146	67	Gary Player (RSA)	73-76—149		Pierre Fulke (Swe)	73-79—152
	Dennis Paulson	73-73—146		Fuzzy Zoeller	77-72—149	83	Greg Norman (Aus)	71-82—153
	Notah Begay III	73-73—146		Stewart Cink	75-74—149		Michael Campbell	
	James Driscoll			Colin Montgomerie			(NZ)	78-75—153
	(am)	68-78—146		(Sco)	73-76—149		DJ Trahan (am)	78-75—153
55	Sandy Lyle (Sco)	74-73—147		Paul Lawrie (Sco)	73-76—149	86	Jeff Quinney (am)	80-76—156
	Shigeki Maruyama			Retief Goosen			Greg Puga (am)	76-80—156
	(Jpn)	77-70—147		(RSA)	75-74—149	88	Arnold Palmer	82-76—158
	Scott Verplank	69-78—147	73	Steve Flesch	74-76—150	89	Ben Crenshaw	81-78—159
	Joe Durant	73-74—147		Grant Waite (NZ)	79-71—150	90	Tommy Aaron	81-82—163
59	Jack Nicklaus	73-75—148		Aaron Baddeley		91	Billy Casper	87-80—167
	Eduardo Romero			(Aus)	75-75—150	92	Gay Brewer	84 Retd 190
	(Arg)	75-73—148	76	Nick Faldo (Eng)	75-76—151	93	Doug Ford	W/D 190
	Tom Watson	78-70—148		Raymond Floyd	76-75—151			
	Ian Woosnam (Wal)	71-77—148		Mikko Ilonen (am)				
	Greg Chalmers			(Fin)	72-79—151			
	(Aus)	76-72—148						

2000 Masters *at Augusta National GC, Georgia* (6985 yds, Par 72)

Prize money: $4,617,000. Entries: 95, of whom 57 made the half-way cut.

1	Vijay Singh (Fij)	72-67-70-69—278	$828000	28T	Justin Leonard	72-71-77-73—293	28673
2	Ernie Els (RSA)	72-67-74-68—281	496800		Stewart Cink	75-72-72-74—293	28673
3	Loren Roberts	73-69-71-69—282	266800		Mike Weir (Can)	75-70-70-78—293	28673
	David Duval	73-65-74-70—282	266800		Dudley Hart	75-71-72-75—293	28673
5	Tiger Woods	75-72-68-69—284	184000		Paul Azinger	72-72-77-72—293	28673
6	Tom Lehman	69-72-75-69—285	165600		Masashi Ozaki (Jpn)	72-72-74-75—293	28673
7	Davis Love III	75-72-68-71—286	143367		Thomas Bjørn (Den)	71-77-73-72—293	28673
	Carlos Franco (Par)	79-68-70-69—286	143367	37	Fred Funk	75-68-78-73—294	21620
	Phil Mickelson	71-68-76-71—286	143367		Jay Haas	75-71-75-73—294	21620
10	Hal Sutton	72-75-71-69—287	124200		Notah Begay III	74-74-73-73—294	21620
11	Greg Norman (Aus)	80-68-70-70—288	105800	40	Ian Woosnam (Wal)	74-70-76-75—295	17480
	Nick Price (Zim)	74-69-73-72—288	105800		Sergio García (Esp)	70-72-75-78—295	17480
	Fred Couples	76-72-70-70—288	105800		Jesper Parnevik (Swe)	77-71-70-77—295	17480
14	Chris Perry	73-75-72-69—289	80500		Darren Clarke (NI)	72-71-78-74—295	17480
	Jim Furyk	73-74-71-71—289	80500		Mark Brooks	72-76-73-74—295	17480
	John Huston	77-69-72-71—289	80500		Retief Goosen (RSA)	73-69-79-74—295	17480
	Dennis Paulson	68-76-73-72—289	80500	46	Shigeki Maruyama (Jpn)	76-71-74-75—296	13800
18	Jeff Sluman	73-69-77-71—290	69000		Scott Gump	75-70-78-73—296	13800
19	Padraig Harrington (Irl)	76-69-75-71—291	53820	48	Brandt Jobe	73-74-76-74—297	12604
	Steve Stricker	70-73-75-73—291	53820	49	Miguel Angel Jiménez		
	Jean Van de Velde (Fra)	76-70-75-70—291	53820		(Esp)	76-71-79-72—298	11623
	Colin Montgomerie				Steve Pate	78-69-77-74—298	11623
	(Sco)	76-69-77-69—291	53820		David Toms	74-72-73-79—298	11623
	Bob Estes	72-71-77-71—291	53820	52	Steve Elkington (Aus)	74-74-78-73—299	10948
	Glen Day	79-67-74-71—291	53820		Rocco Mediate	71-74-75-79—299	10948
25	Larry Mize	78-67-73-74—292	37567	54	Jack Nicklaus	74-70-81-78—303	10672
	Craig Parry (Aus)	75-71-72-74—292	37567		David Gossett (am)	75-71-79-78—303	10672
	Steve Jones	71-70-76-75—292	37567	56	Skip Kendall	76-72-77-83—308	10580
28	Nick Faldo (Eng)	72-72-74-75—293	28673	57	Tommy Aaron	72-74-86-81—313	10488
	Bernhard Langer (Ger)	71-71-75-76—293	28673				

1999 Masters *at Augusta* (6985 yds, Par 72)

Prize money: $3,200,000. Entries: 96, of whom 56 made the half-way cut.

1	JM Olazábal (Esp)	70-66-73-71—280	$720000	27	TE Els (RSA)	71-72-69-80—292	29000
2	D Love III	69-72-70-71—282	432000		R Mediate	73-74-69-76—292	29000
3	G Norman (Aus)	71-68-71-73—283	272000	31	T Lehman	73-72-73-75—293	23720
4	B Estes	71-72-69-72—284	176000		S Maruyama (Jpn)	78-70-71-74—293	23720
	S Pate	71-75-65-73—284	176000		M O'Meara	70-76-69-78—293	23720
6	D Duval	71-74-70-70—285	125200		J Sluman	70-75-70-78—293	23720
	C Franco (Par)	72-72-68-73—285	125200		B Watts	73-73-70-77—293	23720
	P Mickelson	74-69-71-71—285	125200	36	J Huston	74-72-71-77—294	20100
	N Price (Zim)	69-72-72-72—285	125200		A Magee	70-77-72-75—294	20100
	L Westwood (Eng)	75-71-68-71—285	125200	38	B Andrade	76-72-72-75—295	18800
11	S Elkington (Aus)	72-70-71-74—287	92000		M Brooks	76-72-75-72—295	18800
	B Langer (Ger)	76-66-72-73—287	92000		R Floyd	74-73-72-76—295	18800
	C Montgomerie (Sco)	70-72-71-74—287	92000		C Stadler	72-76-70-77—295	18800
14	J Furyk	72-73-70-73—288	70000		S Stricker	75-72-69-79—295	18800
	L Janzen	70-69-73-76—288	70000		S García (Esp) (am)	72-75-75-73—295	
	B Jobe	72-71-74-71—288	70000	44	J Haas	74-69-79-75—297	14000
	I Woosnam (Wal)	71-74-71-72—288	70000		T Herron	75-69-74-79—297	14000
18	B Chamblee	69-73-75-72—289	52160		S Hoch	75-73-70-79—297	14000
	B Glasson	72-70-73-74—289	52160		T McKnight (am)	73-74-73-77—297	
	J Leonard	70-72-73-74—289	52160	48	S Lyle (Sco)	71-77-70-80—298	12000
	S McCarron	69-68-76-76—289	52160		C Parry (Aus)	75-73-73-77—298	12000
	T Woods	72-72-70-75—289	52160	50	C Perry	73-72-74-80—299	10960
23	L Mize	76-70-72-72—290	41600		M Kuchar (am)	77-71-73-78—299	
24	B Faxon	74-73-68-76—291	35200	52	O Browne	74-74-72-80—300	9980
	P-U Johansson (Swe)	75-72-71-73—291	35200		J Daly	72-76-71-81—300	9980
	V Singh (Fij)	72-76-71-72—291	35200		P Stewart	73-75-77-75—300	9980
27	S Cink	74-70-71-77—292	29000		B Tway	75-73-78-74—300	9980
	F Couples	74-71-76-71—292	29000	56	T Immelman (RSA) (am)	72-76-78-79—305	

1998 Masters *at Augusta* (6905 yds, Par 72)

Prize money: $3,200,000. Entries: 88, of whom 46 made the half-way cut.

1	M O'Meara	74-70-68-67—279	$576000	23T	J Huston	77-71-70-71—289	33280
2	D Duval	71-68-74-67—280	281600		J Maggert	72-73-72-72—289	33280
	F Couples	69-70-71-70—280	281600	26	D Frost (RSA)	72-73-74-71—290	26133
4	J Furyk	76-70-67-68—281	153600		S Jones	75-70-75-70—290	26133
5	P Azinger	71-72-69-70—282	128000		B Faxon	73-74-71-72—290	26133
6	J Nicklaus	73-72-70-68—283	111200	29	M Bradley	73-74-72-72—291	23680
	D Toms	75-72-72-64—283	111200	30	S Elkington (Aus)	75-75-71-71—292	22720
8	D Clarke (NI)	76-73-67-69—285	89600	31	A Magee	74-72-74-73—293	21280
	J Leonard	74-73-69-69—285	89600		J Parnevik (Swe)	75-73-73-72—293	21280
	C Montgomerie (Sco)	71-75-69-70—285	89600	33	L Janzen	76-74-72-72—294	18112
	T Woods	71-72-72-70—285	89600		F Zoeller	71-74-75-74—294	18112
12	J Haas	72-71-71-72—286	64800		P Blackmar	71-78-75-70—294	18112
	P-U Johansson (Swe)	74-75-67-70—286	64800		J Daly	77-71-71-75—294	18112
	P Mickelson	74-69-69-74—286	64800		D Love III	74-75-67-78—294	18112
	JM Olazábal (Esp)	70-73-71-72—286	64800	38	T Kite	73-74-74-74—295	15680
16	M Calcavecchia	74-74-69-70—287	48000	39	B Langer (Ger)	75-73-74-74—296	14720
	E Els (RSA)	75-70-70-72—287	48000		P Stankowski	70-80-72-74—296	14720
	S Hoch	70-71-73-73—287	48000	41	C Pavin	73-77-72-75—297	13440
	I Woosnam (Wal)	74-71-72-70—287	48000		C Stadler	79-68-73-77—297	13440
	S McCarron	73-71-72-71—287	48000	43	J Cook	75-73-74-76—298	12480
21	W Wood	74-74-70-70—288	38400	44	L Westwood (Eng)	74-76-72-78—300	11840
	M Kuchar (am)	72-76-68-72—288			J Kribel (am)	74-76-76-75—301	
23	S Cink	74-76-69-70—289	33280	46	G Player (RSA)	77-72-78-75—302	11200

1997 Masters *at Augusta* (6925 yds, Par 72)

Prize money: $2,500,000. Entries: 86, of whom 46 made the half-way cut.

1	T Woods	70-66-65-69—270	$486000	24	N Price (Zim)	71-71-75-74—291	24840
2	T Kite	77-69-66-70—282	291600		L Westwood (Eng)	77-71-73-70—291	24840
3	T Tolles	72-72-72-67—283	183600	26	L Janzen	72-73-74-73—292	21195
4	T Watson	75-68-69-72—284	129600		C Stadler	77-72-71-72—292	21195
5	C Rocca (Ita)	71-69-70-75—285	102600	28	P Azinger	69-73-77-74—293	19575
	P Stankowski	68-74-69-74—285	102600		J Furyk	74-75-72-72—293	19575
7	F Couples	72-69-73-72—286	78570	30	S McCarron	77-71-72-74—294	17145
	B Langer (Ger)	72-72-74-68—286	78570		L Mize	79-69-74-72—294	17145
	J Leonard	76-69-71-70—286	78570		C Montgomerie (Sco)	72-67-74-81—294	17145
	D Love III	72-71-72-71—286	78570		M O'Meara	75-74-70-75—294	17145
	J Sluman	74-67-72-73—286	78570	34	A Lyle (Sco)	73-73-74-75—295	14918
12	S Elkington (Aus)	76-72-72-67—287	52920		F Zoeller	75-73-69-78—295	14918
	P-U Johansson (Swe)	72-73-73-69—287	52920	36	D Waldorf	74-75-72-75—296	13905
	T Lehman	73-76-69-69—287	52920	37	D Frost (SA)	74-71-73-79—297	13230
	JM Olazábal (Esp)	71-70-74-72—287	52920	38	S Hoch	79-68-73-78—298	12690
	W Wood	72-76-71-68—287	52920	39	J Nicklaus	77-70-74-78—299	11610
17	M Calcavecchia	74-73-72-69—288	39150		S Torrance (Sco)	75-73-73-78—299	11610
	E Els (RSA)	73-70-71-74—288	39150		I Woosnam (Wal)	77-68-75-79—299	11610
	F Funk	73-74-69-72—288	39150	42	M Ozaki (Jpn)	74-74-74-78—300	10530
	V Singh (Fij)	75-74-69-70—288	39150	43	C Pavin	75-74-78-74—301	9720
21	S Appleby (Aus)	72-76-70-71—289	30240		C Rose	73-75-79-74—301	9720
	J Huston	67-77-75-70—289	30240	45	B Crenshaw	75-73-74-80—302	8910
	J Parnevik (Swe)	73-72-71-73—289	30240	46	F Nobilo (NZ)	76-72-74-81—303	8370

1996 Masters *at Augusta* (6925 yds, Par 72)

Prize money: $2,500,000. Entries: 92, of whom 44 made the half-way cut.

1	N Faldo (Eng)	69-67-73-67—276	$450000	23	L Mize	75-71-77-68—291	25000
2	G Norman (Aus)	63-69-71-78—281	270000		L Roberts	71-73-72-75—291	25000
3	P Mickelson	65-73-72-72—282	170000	25	R Floyd	70-74-77-71—292	21000
4	F Nobilo (NZ)	71-71-72-69—283	120000		B Faxon	69-77-72-74—292	21000
5	S Hoch	67-73-73-71—284	95000	27	B Estes	71-71-79-72—293	18900
	D Waldorf	72-71-69-72—284	95000		J Leonard	72-74-75-72—293	18900
7	D Love III	72-71-74-68—285	77933	29	J Furyk	75-70-78-71—294	15571
	J Maggert	71-73-72-69—285	77933		J Gallagher jr	70-76-77-71—294	15571
	C Pavin	75-66-73-71—285	77933		H Irwin	74-71-77-72—294	15571
10	S McCarron	70-70-72-74—286	65000		S Simpson	69-76-76-73—294	15571
	D Frost (RSA)	70-68-74-74—286	65000		C Stadler	73-72-71-78—294	15571
12	B Tway	67-72-76-72—287	52500		J Daly	71-74-71-78—294	15571
	L Janzen	68-71-75-73—287	52500		I Woosnam (Wal)	72-69-73-80—294	15571
	E Els (RSA)	71-71-72-73—287	52500	36	F Funk	71-72-76-76—295	12333
15	F Couples	78-68-71-71—288	43750		J Haas	70-73-75-77—295	12333
	M Calcavecchia	71-73-71-73—288	43750		B Langer (Ger)	75-70-72-78—295	12333
17	J Huston	71-71-71-76—289	40000	39	C Montgomerie (Sco)	72-74-75-75—296	11050
18	P Azinger	70-74-76-70—290	32600		V Singh (Fij)	69-71-74-82—296	11050
	M O'Meara	72-71-75-72—290	32600	41	S Lowery (Sco)	71-74-75-77—297	10050
	T Lehman	75-70-72-73—290	32600		J Nicklaus	70-73-76-78—297	10050
	N Price (Zim)	71-75-70-74—290	32600	43	S Ballesteros (Esp)	73-73-77-76—299	9300
	D Duval	73-72-69-76—290	32600	44	A Cejka (Ger)	73-71-78-80—302	8800

1995 Masters at Augusta (6905 yds, Par 72)

Prize money: $2,132,000. Entries: 86, of whom 47 made the half-way cut.

1	B Crenshaw	70-67-69-68—274	$396000	24T	D Edwards	69-73-73-71—286	18260
2	D Love III	69-69-71-66—275	237600		L Roberts	72-69-72-73—286	18260
3	J Haas	71-64-72-70—277	127600		N Faldo (Eng)	70-70-71-75—286	18260
	G Norman (Aus)	73-68-68-68—277	127600		D Waldorf	74-69-67-76—286	18260
5	S Elkington (Aus)	73-67-67-72—279	83600	29	B Estes	73-70-76-68—287	15300
	D Frost (RSA)	66-71-71-71—279	83600		M Ozaki (Jpn)	70-74-70-73—287	15300
7	S Hoch	69-67-71-73—280	70950	31	B Lietzke	72-71-71-74—288	13325
	P Mickelson	66-71-70-73—280	70950		P Jacobsen	72-73-69-74—288	13325
9	C Strange	72-71-65-73—281	63800		B Langer (Ger)	71-69-73-75—288	13325
10	F Couples	71-69-67-75—282	57200		M O'Meara	68-72-71-77—288	13325
	B Henninger	70-68-68-76—282	57200	35	D Forsman	71-74-74-71—290	10840
12	K Perry	73-70-71-69—283	48400		W Grady (Aus)	69-73-74-74—290	10840
	L Janzen	69-69-74-71—283	48400		J Nicklaus	67-78-70-75—290	10840
14	JM Olazábal (Esp)	66-74-72-72—284	39600		C Beck	68-76-69-77—290	10840
	T Watson	73-70-69-72—284	39600		M McCumber	73-69-69-79—290	10840
	H Irwin	69-72-71-72—284	39600	40	T Lehman	71-72-74-75—292	9500
17	C Montgomerie (Sco)	71-69-76-69—285	28786	41	M Calcavecchia	70-72-78-73—293	8567
	P Azinger	70-72-73-70—285	28786		T Woods (am)	72-72-77-72—293	
	B Faxon	76-69-69-71—285	28786		J Sluman	73-72-71-77—293	8567
	I Woosnam (Wal)	69-72-71-73—285	28786		P Stewart	71-72-72-78—293	8567
	R Floyd	71-70-70-74—285	28786	45	S Ballesteros (Esp)	75-68-78-75—296	7500
	C Pavin	67-71-72-75—285	28786		J Daly	75-69-71-81—296	7500
	J Huston	70-66-72-77—285	28786	47	R Fehr	76-69-69-83—297	6800
24	D Gilford (Eng)	67-73-75-71—286	18260				

1994 Masters at Augusta (6905 yds, Par 72)

Prize money: $1,960,000. Entries: 86, of whom 51 made the half-way cut.

1	JM Olazábal (Esp)	74-67-69-69—279	$360000	27	S Simpson	74-74-73-73—294	14800
2	T Lehman	70-70-69-72—281	216000		V Singh (Fij)	70-75-74-75—294	14800
3	L Mize	68-71-72-71—282	136000		C Strange	74-70-75-75—294	14800
4	T Kite	69-72-71-71—283	96000	30	L Janzen	75-71-76-73—295	13300
5	J Haas	72-72-72-69—285	73000		C Parry (Aus)	75-74-73-73—295	13300
	J McGovern	72-70-71-72—285	73000	32	N Faldo (Eng)	76-73-73-74—296	12400
	L Roberts	75-68-72-70—285	73000	33	R Cochran	71-74-74-79—297	11500
8	E Els (RSA)	74-67-74-71—286	60000		S Torrance (Sco)	76-73-74-74—297	11500
	C Pavin	71-72-73-70—286	60000	35	D Frost (RSA)	74-71-75-78—298	10300
10	I Baker-Finch (Aus)	71-71-71-74—287	50000		N Price (Zim)	74-73-74-77—298	10300
	R Floyd	70-74-71-72—287	50000		F Zoeller	74-72-74-78—298	10300
	J Huston	72-72-74-69—287	50000	38	F Allem (RSA)	69-77-76-77—299	9000
13	T Watson	70-71-73-74—289	42000		F Funk	79-70-75-75—299	9000
14	D Forsman	74-66-76-73—289	38000		A Lyle (Sco)	75-73-78-73—299	9000
15	C Beck	71-71-75-74—291	34000	41	W Grady (Aus)	74-73-73-80—300	7400
	B Faxon	71-73-73-74—291	34000		A Magee	74-74-76-76—300	7400
	M O'Meara	75-70-76-70—291	34000		H Meshiai (Jpn)	71-71-80-78—300	7400
18	S Ballesteros (Esp)	70-76-75-71—292	24343		C Rocca (Ita)	79-70-78-73—300	7400
	B Crenshaw	74-73-73-72—292	24343		M Standly	77-69-79-75—300	7400
	D Edwards	73-72-73-74—292	24343	46	J Cook	77-72-77-75—301	6000
	B Glasson	72-73-75-72—292	24343		I Woosnam (Wal)	76-73-77-75—301	6000
	H Irwin	73-68-79-72—292	24343	48	J Daly	76-73-77-78—304	5250
	G Norman (Aus)	70-70-75-77—292	24343		H Twitty	73-76-74-81—304	5250
	L Wadkins	73-74-73-72—292	24343	50	J Maggert	75-73-82-75—305	5000
25	B Langer (Ger)	74-74-72-73—293	16800		J Harris (am)	72-76-80-77—305	
	J Sluman	74-75-71-73—293	16800				

1993 Masters *at Augusta* (6905 yds, Par 72)

Prize money: $1,705,700. Entries: 90, of whom 61 made the half-way cut.

1	B Langer (Ger)	68-70-69-70—277	$306000
2	C Beck	72-67-72-70—281	183600
3	T Lehman	67-75-73-68—283	81600
	J Daly	70-71-73-69—283	81600
	S Elkington (Aus)	71-70-71-71—283	81600
	L Wadkins	69-72-71-71—283	81600
7	JM Olazábal (Esp)	70-72-74-68—284	54850
	D Forsman	69-69-73-73—284	54850
9	P Stewart	74-70-72-69—285	47600
	B Faxon	71-70-72-72—285	47600
11	A Forsbrand (Swe)	71-74-75-66—286	34850
	S Ballesteros (Esp)	74-70-71-71—286	34850
	C Pavin	67-75-73-71—286	34850
	S Simpson	72-71-71-72—286	34850
	R Floyd	68-71-74-73—286	34850
	F Zoeller	76-67-71-73—286	34850
17	I Woosnam (Wal)	71-74-73-69—287	24650
	M Calcavecchia	71-70-74-72—287	24650
	H Twitty	70-71-73-73—287	24650
	J Sluman	71-72-71-73—287	24650
21	M O'Meara	75-69-73-71—288	17000
	F Couples	72-70-74-72—288	17000
	L Mize	67-74-74-73—288	17000
	A Lyle (Sco)	73-71-71-73—288	17000
	J Maggert	70-67-75-76—288	17000
	R Cochran	70-69-73-76—288	17000
27	J Nicklaus	67-75-76-71—289	12350
	H Irwin	74-69-74-72—289	12350
	J Sindelar	72-69-76-72—289	12350
	N Henke	76-69-71-73—289	12350
31	B Lietzke	74-71-71-74—290	10533
31T	A Magee	75-69-70-76—290	10533
	G Norman (Aus)	74-68-71-77—290	10533
34	G Sauers	74-71-75-71—291	8975
	B Gilder	69-76-75-71—291	8975
	P Mickelson	72-71-75-73—291	8975
	C Stadler	73-74-69-75—291	8975
38	J Haas	70-73-75-74—292	8000
39	N Faldo (Eng)	71-76-79-67—293	6817
	T Schulz	69-76-76-72—293	6817
	D Waldorf	72-75-73-73—293	6817
	K Clearwater	74-70-75-74—293	6817
	J Cook	76-67-75-75—293	6817
	L Janzen	67-73-76-77—293	6817
45	M Ozaki (Jpn)	75-71-77-71—294	4940
	N Ozaki (Jpn)	74-70-78-72—294	4940
	T Watson	71-75-73-75—294	4940
	JD Blake	71-74-73-76—294	4940
	C Parry (Aus)	69-72-75-78—294	4940
50	G Morgan	72-74-72-77—295	4250
	B Ogle (Aus)	70-74-71-80—295	4250
52	D Peoples	71-73-78-74—296	4050
	C Montgomerie (Sco)	71-72-78-75—296	4050
54	I Baker-Finch (Aus)	73-72-73-80—298	3900
	D Edwards	73-73-76-76—298	3900
	D Love III	73-72-76-77—298	3900
57	C Coody	74-72-75-78—299	3800
	G Hallberg	72-74-78-75—299	3800
59	J Huston	68-74-84-75—301	3800
60	G Player (RSA)	71-76-75-80—302	3700
61	B Andrade	73-74-80-76—303	3700

1992 Masters *at Augusta* (6905 yds, Par 72)

Prize money: $1,500,000. Entries: 83, of whom 63 made the half-way cut.

1	F Couples	69-67-69-70—275	$270000
2	R Floyd	69-68-69-71—277	162000
3	C Pavin	72-71-68-67—278	102000
4	J Sluman	65-74-70-71—280	66000
	M O'Meara	74-67-69-70—280	66000
6	S Pate	73-71-70-67—281	43829
	N Henke	70-71-70-70—281	43829
	I Baker-Finch (Aus)	70-69-68-74—281	43829
	N Price (Zim)	70-71-67-73—281	43829
	G Norman (Aus)	70-70-73-68—281	43829
	L Mize	73-69-71-68—281	43829
	T Schulz	68-69-72-72—281	43829
13	D Pruitt	75-68-70-69—282	26500
	W Grady (Aus)	68-75-71-68—282	26500
	S Simpson	70-71-71-70—282	26500
	B Leitzke	69-72-68-73—282	26500
	N Faldo (Eng)	71-72-68-71—282	26500
	C Parry (Aus)	69-66-69-78—282	26500
19	BR Brown	70-74-70-69—283	17550
	A Magee	73-70-70-70—283	17550
19T	I Woosnam (Wal)	69-66-73-75—283	17550
	F Zoeller	71-70-73-69—283	17550
	J Daly	71-71-73-68—283	17550
25	B Fleisher	73-70-72-69—284	11467
	J Huston	69-73-73-69—284	11467
	C Stadler	70-71-70-73—284	11467
	J Gallagher jr	74-68-71-71—284	11467
	D Love III	68-72-72-72—284	11467
	D A Weibring	71-68-72-73—284	11467
31	B Langer (Ger)	69-73-69-74—285	8717
	B Faxon	71-71-69-74—285	8717
	S Richardson (Eng)	69-75-70-71—285	8717
	C Strange	73-72-71-69—285	8717
	P Azinger	70-73-70-72—285	8717
	M Calcavecchia	73-72-75-65—285	8717
37	C Montgomerie (Sco)	72-71-73-70—286	6800
	S Elkington	69-71-74-72—286	6800
	M McCumber	72-70-76-68—286	6800
	A Lyle (Sco)	72-69-70-75—286	6800
37T	R Mediate	70-73-70-73—286	6800
42	B Gilder	72-71-73-71—287	5450
	J Nicklaus	69-75-69-74—287	5450
	JM Olazábal (Esp)	76-69-72-70—287	5450
	B Mayfair	71-71-72-73—287	5450
46	B Crenshaw	72-71-71-74—288	4700
47	H Irwin	72-70-72-75—289	4400
48	B McCallister	71-71-76-72—290	3933
	L Wadkins	65-75-76-74—290	3933
	T Watson	73-70-76-71—290	3933
51	G Archer	74-69-76-72—291	3700
52	F Allem (RSA)	69-71-78-74—292	3550
52T	D Feherty (NI)	73-72-77-70—292	3550
54	B Andrade	73-71-73-76—293	3440
	J Cook	72-73-71-77—293	3440
	L Janzen	74-71-74-74—293	3440
	T Aaron	76-69-77-71—293	3440
	D Peoples	73-71-72-77—293	3440
59	M Zerman (am)	70-71-76-77—294	
	S Ballesteros (Esp)	75-68-70-81—294	3300
61	P Jacobsen	72-70-77-76—295	3300
	T Purtzer	76-69-75-75—295	3300
63	R Davis (Aus)	77-68-77-79—301	3200

THE MASTERS HISTORY

* Winner after play-off

1934	H Smith	284	1970	W Casper*	279
1935	G Sarazen*	282	1971	C Coody	279
1936	H Smith	285	1972	J Nicklaus	286
1937	B Nelson	283	1973	T Aaron	283
1938	H Picard	285	1974	G Player (RSA)	278
1939	R Guldahl	279	1975	J Nicklaus	276
1940	J Demaret	280	1976	R Floyd	271
1941	C Wood	280	1977	T Watson	276
1942	B Nelson*	280	1978	G Player (RSA)	277
1946	H Keiser	282	1979	F Zoeller*	280
1947	J Demaret	281	1980	S Ballesteros (Esp)	275
1948	C Harmon	279	1981	T Watson	280
1949	S Snead	283	1982	C Stadler*	284
1950	J Demaret	282	1983	S Ballesteros (Esp)	280
1951	B Hogan	280	1984	B Crenshaw	277
1952	S Snead	286	1985	B Langer (Ger)	282
1953	B Hogan	274	1986	J Nicklaus	279
1954	S Snead*	289	1987	L Mize*	285
1955	C Middlecoff	279	1988	A Lyle (Sco)	281
1956	J Burke	289	1989	N Faldo (Eng)*	283
1957	D Ford	283	1990	N Faldo (Eng)*	278
1958	A Palmer	284	1991	I Woosnam (Wal)	277
1959	A Wall	284	1992	F Couples	275
1960	A Palmer	282	1993	B Langer (Ger)	277
1961	G Player (RSA)	280	1994	JM Olazábal (Esp)	279
1962	A Palmer*	280	1995	B Crenshaw	274
1963	J Nicklaus	286	1996	N Faldo (Eng)	276
1964	A Palmer	276	1997	T Woods	270
1965	J Nicklaus	271	1998	M O'Meara	279
1966	J Nicklaus*	288	1999	JM Olazábal (Esp)	280
1967	G Brewer	280	2000	V Singh (Fij)	278
1968	R Goalby	277	2001	T Woods	272
1969	G Archer	281			

US PGA Championship

Players are of American nationality unless stated

83rd US PGA Championship *at Atlanta Athletic Club, Atlanta, Georgia*

(7213 yds, Par 70) Prize money: $5,205,049. Final field: 150, of whom 76 made the half-way cut on 141 or better.

1	David Toms	66-65-65-69—265	$936000
2	Phil Mickelson	66-66-66-68—266	562000
3	Steve Lowery	67-67-66-68—268	354000
4	Mark Calcavecchia	71-68-66-65—270	222500
	Shingo Katayama (Jpn)	67-64-69-70—270	222500
6	Billy Andrade	68-70-68-66—272	175000
7	Jim Furyk	70-64-71-69—274	152333
	Scott Verplank	69-68-70-67—274	152333
	Scott Hoch	68-70-69-67—274	152333
10	David Duval	66-68-67-74—275	122000
	Justin Leonard	70-69-67-69—275	122000
	Kirk Triplett	68-70-71-66—275	122000
13	Steve Flesch	73-67-70-66—276	94666
	Jesper Parnevik (Swe)	70-68-70-68—276	94666
	Ernie Els (RSA)	67-67-70-72—276	94666
16	Stuart Appleby (Aus)	66-70-68-73—277	70666
	Mike Weir (Can)	69-72-66-70—277	70666
	Dudley Hart	66-68-73-70—277	70666
	José Coceres (Arg)	69-68-73-67—277	70666
	Robert Allenby (Aus)	69-67-73-68—277	70666
	Chris DiMarco	68-67-71-71—277	70666
22	Mark O'Meara	72-63-70-73—278	44285
	Shigeki Maruyama (Jpn)	68-72-71-67—278	44285
	Paul Azinger	68-67-69-74—278	44285
	Paul McGinley (Irl)	68-72-71-67—278	44285
	Briny Baird	70-69-72-67—278	44285
	J Brian Gay	70-68-69-71—278	44285
	Charles Howell III	71-67-69-71—278	44285
29	Greg Norman (Aus)	70-68-71-70—279	29437
	Tiger Woods	73-67-69-70—279	29437
	Nick Price (Zim)	71-67-71-70—279	29437
	Kyoung-Ju Choi (Kor)	66-68-72-73—279	29437
	Bob Tway	69-69-71-70—279	29437
	Carlos Franco (Par)	67-72-71-69—279	29437
	Niclas Fasth (Swe)	66-69-72-72—279	29437
	Christopher Smith	69-71-68-71—279	29437
	José María Olazábal (Esp)	70-70-68-71—279	29437
37	Fred Couples	70-69-70-71—280	21000
	Davis Love III	71-67-65-77—280	21000
	Bob Estes	67-65-75-73—280	21000
	Angel Cabrera (Arg)	69-69-70-72—280	21000
	Andrew Coltart (Sco)	67-72-71-70—280	21000
	Retief Goosen (RSA)	69-70-66-75—280	21000
44	Andrew Oldcorn (Sco)	73-67-74-67—281	14250
	Greg Chalmers (Aus)	68-70-69-74—281	14250
	Jerry Kelly	69-67-72-73—281	14250
	Hal Sutton	67-71-73-70—281	14250
	Kenny Perry	68-70-71-72—281	14250
	Lee Westwood (Eng)	71-68-68-74—281	14250

93rd US PGA Championship *continued*

44T	Rick Schuller	68-70-72-71—281	14250
51	Nick Faldo (Eng)	67-74-71-70—282	11343
	Ian Woosnam (Wal)	71-70-73-68—282	11343
	Joe Durant	68-71-72-71—282	11343
	Vijay Singh (Fij)	73-68-70-71—282	11343
	Scott Dunlap	69-72-70-71—282	11343
	Tom Pernice	69-69-74-70—282	11343
	Chris Riley	68-71-73-70—282	11343
	Frank Lickliter	71-69-71-71—282	11343
59	Brad Faxon	66-70-74-73—283	10650
	Stewart Cink	68-72-71-72—283	10650
	Phillip Price (Wal)	68-69-76-70—283	10650
	Grant Waite (NZ)	64-74-73-72—283	10650
63	Skip Kendall	72-67-73-72—284	10300
	Thomas Bjørn (Den)	67-71-73-73—284	10300
	Jonathan Kaye	67-68-78-71—284	10300
	Rocco Mediate	70-65-73-76—284	10300
66	Tom Watson	69-70-76-70—285	9950
	Steve Stricker	75-65-75-70—285	9950
	Robert Damron	68-73-71-73—285	9950
70	Fred Funk	66-74-71-75—286	9725
	Scott McCarron	69-67-73-77—286	9725
72	John Huston	67-68-75-77—287	9650
73	Bob May	71-70-76-74—291	9600
74	Paul Stankowski	67-71-76-79—293	9550
75	Steve Pate	71-69-71-83—294	9500
76	Colin Montgomerie (Sco)	71-69-74 DQ	2000

The following players missed the half-way cut. Each received $2000:

77	Stephen Keppler		
	(Eng)	72-70—142	
	Bernhard Langer		
	(Ger)	69-73—142	
	Larry Nelson	68-74—142	
	Garrett Willis	70-72—142	
	Darren Clarke (NI)	73-69—142	
	Mark Brooks	71-71—142	
	Jeff Maggert	70-72—142	
	Olin Browne	70-72—142	
85	Tom Kite	72-71—143	
	Loren Roberts	74-69—143	
	Sergio García		
	(Esp)	68-75—143	
	Jerry Pate	73-70—143	
	Gary Orr (Sco)	73-70—143	
	Paul Lawrie (Sco)	69-74—143	
	Glen Day	74-69—143	
	Kevin Sutherland	73-70—143	
	Brett Quigley	71-72—143	
	Adam Scott (Aus)	71-72—143	
	David Gossett	72-71—143	
96	Tom Lehman	72-72—144	
	Lee Janzen	70-74—144	
98	Eduardo Romero		
	(Arg)	73-72—145	
	Bruce Zabriski	69-76—145	
	Nick O'Hern (Aus)	73-72—145	
	Billy Mayfair	73-72—145	
	Len Mattiace	74-71—145	

98T	Tim Thelen	74-71—145
	Carl Paulson	72-73—145
	Don Berry	73-72—145
106	Tim Herron	72-74—146
	Ian Poulter (Eng)	73-73—146
	Dennis Paulson	73-73—146
	Notah Begay III	78-68—146
	Steve Schneiter	72-74—146
	Harrison Frazar	73-73—146
	Franklin Langham	70-76—146
113	Robert Karlsson	
	(Swe)	74-73—147
	Duffy Waldorf	75-72—147
	John Mazza	70-77—147
	John Aber	74-73—147
	Tim Fleming	75-72—147
118	Jeff Sluman	72-76—148
	Chris Perry	74-74—148
	Miguela Angel	
	Jiménez (Esp)	74-74—148
	Mark Brown	75-73—148
	Michael Clark II	70-78—148
123	Padraig Harrington	
	(Irl)	75-74—149
	Mathias Grönberg	
	(Swe)	75-74—149
	Pierre Fulke (Swe)	71-78—149
	John Daly	72-77—149
	Craig Stevens	73-76—149
128	Darrell Kestner	73-77—150

128T	Toru Taniguchi	
	(Jpn)	72-78—150
	Wayne	
	Defrancesco	76-74—150
	Jim Woodward	77-73—150
	Bob Sowards	78-72—150
133	Curtis Strange	74-77—151
	Mark McNulty	
	(Zim)	71-80—151
	Naomichi 'Joe'	
	Ozaki (Jpn)	78-73—151
	Michael Campbell	
	(NZ)	72-79—151
	Ken Schall	74-77—151
	Jeffrey Lankford	77-74—151
139	Larry W Emery	74-78—152
140	Hidemichi Tanaka	
	(Jpn)	80-73—153
	Steve Brady	77-76—153
142	Rory Sabbatini	
	(RSA)	78-76—154
	James Blair III	80-74—154
144	Mark Mielke	80-77—157
	Mike Northern	78-79—157
	Dean Prowse	78-79—157
147	Bill Loeffler	78-81—159
148	Robert Wilkin	86-75—161
149	Lanny Wadkins	86-85—171
150	Steve Elkington	
	(Aus)	77 W/D

2000 US PGA Championship at Valhalla GC, Louisville, Kentucky
(7167 yds, Par 72) Prize money: $5,000,000. Entries: 150, of whom 80 made the half-way cut.

1	Tiger Woods	66-67-70-67—270	$900000	19T	JP Hayes	69-68-68-86—281	56200
2	Bob May	72-66-66-66—270	540000		Angel Cabrera (Arg)	72-71-71-67—281	56200
Woods won after play-off					Robert Allenby (Aus)	73-71-68-69—281	56200
3	Thomas Bjørn (Den)	72-68-67-68—275	340000		Lee Janzen	76-70-70-65—281	56200
4	Greg Chalmers (Aus)	71-69-66-70—276	198667	24	Paul Azinger	72-71-66-73—282	41000
	José María Olazábal				Steve Jones	72-71-70-69—282	41000
	(Esp)	76-68-63-69—276	198667		Jarmo Sandelin (Swe)	74-72-68-68—282	41000
	Stuart Appleby (Aus)	70-69-68-69—276	198667	27	Brad Faxon	71-74-70-68—283	34167
7	Franklin Langham	72-71-65-69—277	157000		Skip Kendall	72-72-69-70—283	34167
8	Notah Begay III	72-66-70-70—278	145000		Tom Pernice	74-69-70-70—283	34167
9	Tom Watson	76-70-65-68—279	112500	30	Mike Weir (Can)	76-69-68-71—284	28875
	Fred Funk	69-68-74-68—279	112500		Jean Van de Velde		
	Davis Love III	68-69-72-70—279	112500		(Fra)	70-74-69-71—284	28875
	Darren Clarke (NI)	68-72-72-67—279	112500		Stephen Ames (Tri)	69-71-71-73—284	28875
	Scott Dunlap	66-68-70-75—279	112500		Kenny Perry	78-68-70-68—284	28875
	Phil Mickelson	70-70-69-70—279	112500	34	Sergio García (Esp)	74-69-73-69—285	24000
15	Stewart Cink	72-71-70-67—280	77500		Chris Perry	72-74-70-69—285	24000
	Lee Westwood (Eng)	72-72-69-67—280	77500		Mark Calcavecchia	73-74-71-67—285	24000
	Chris Dimarco	73-70-69-68—280	77500		Ernie Els (RSA)	74-68-72-71—285	24000
	Michael Clark II	73-70-67-70—280	77500		Blaine McCallister	73-71-70-71—285	24000
19	Tom Kite	70-72-69-70—281	56200				

Other Totals: Toshimitsu Izawa (Jpn), Colin Montgomerie (Sco) 286; Jeff Sluman, Justin Leonard, Paul Stankowski, Steve Pate, David Toms 287; Bernhard Langer (Ger), Mark O'Meara, Shigeki Maruyama (Jpn), Duffy Waldorf, Brian Henninger 288; Nick Faldo (Eng), Jesper Parnevik (Swe), Steve Lowery, Brian Watts, Glen Day, Andrew Coltart (Sco), Jonathan Kaye 289; Padraig Harrington (Irl), Loren Roberts, Curtis Strange, Carlos Franco (Par), Dennis Paulson, Joe Ogilvie 290; Wayne Grady (Aus), Craig Stadler, Bill Glasson, Miguel Angel Jiménez (Esp), Jay Haas 291; Greg Kraft, Kirk Triplett 292; John Huston 293; Jim Furyk, Paul Lawrie (Sco) 294; Robert Damron, Billy Mayfair, Scott Hoch 297; Masashi Ozaki (Jpn), Rory Sabbatini 299; Hidemichi Tanaka (Jpn) 301; Frank Dobbs 313

1999 US PGA Championship at Medinah, Illinois
(7401 yds, Par 72) Prize money: $3,000,000. Entries: 149, of whom 74 made the half-way cut.

1	T Woods	70-67-68-72—277	$630000	21	D Frost (RSA)	75-68-74-71—288	33200
2	S García (Esp)	66-73-68-71—278	378000		S Hoch	71-71-75-71—288	33200
3	S Cink	69-70-68-73—280	203000		S Kendall	74-65-71-78—288	33200
	J Haas	68-67-75-70—280	203000		JL Lewis	73-70-74-71—288	33200
5	N Price (Zim)	70-71-69-71—281	129000		K Wentworth	72-70-72-74—288	33200
6	B Estes	71-70-72-69—282	112000	26	F Couples	73-69-75-72—289	24000
	C Montgomerie (Sco)	72-70-70-70—282	112000		C Franco (Par)	72-71-71-75—289	24000
8	J Furyk	71-70-69-74—284	96500		J Kelly	69-74-71-75—289	24000
	S Pate	72-70-73-69—284	96500		H Sutton	72-73-73-71—289	24000
10	D Duval	70-71-72-72—285	72166		J Van de Velde (Fra)	74-70-75-70—289	24000
	MA Jiménez (Esp)	70-70-75-70—285	72166	31	P Goydos	73-70-71-76—290	20000
	J Parnevik (Swe)	72-70-73-70—285	72166		M James (Eng)	70-74-79-67—290	20000
	C Pavin	69-74-71-71—285	72166		T Tryba	70-72-76-72—290	20000
	C Perry	70-73-71-71—285	72166	34	S Flesch	73-71-72-75—291	15428
	M Weir (Can)	68-68-69-80—285	72166		P Lawrie (Sco)	73-72-72-74—291	15428
16	M Brooks	70-73-70-74—287	48600		T Lehman	70-74-76-71—291	15428
	G Hjertstedt (Swe)	72-70-73-72—287	48600		B Mayfair	75-69-75-72—291	15428
	B Jobe	69-74-69-75—287	48600		K Perry	74-69-72-76—291	15428
	G Turner (NZ)	73-69-70-75—287	48600		S Verplank	73-72-73-73—291	15428
	L Westwood (Eng)	70-68-74-75—287	48600		L Wadkins	72-69-74-76—291	15428

Other Totals: P Azinger, Angel Cabrera (Arg), C DiMarco, N Faldo (Eng), H Irwin, R Karlsson (Swe), D Waldorf, B Watts 292; O Browne, D Love III, R Mediate, V Singh (Fij), K Triplett 293; JP Hayes, A Magee, J Sluman 294; P Mickelson, M O'Meara, P Stewart, B Tway 295; M Calcavecchia, B Faxon, G Kraft, B Langer (Ger) 296; A Cejka (Ger), A Coltart (Sco), M Reid 297; S Dunlap, B Zabriski 298; R Beem, T Bjørn (Den), N Ozaki (Jpn) 299; F Funk 300

1998 US PGA Championship *at Sahalee, Seattle*
(6906 yds, Par 70) Prize money: $3,000,000. Entries: 150, of whom 75 made the half-way cut.

1	V Singh (Fij)	70-66-67-68—271	$540000	21	E Els (RSA)	72-72-71-66—281	32000
2	S Stricker	69-68-66-70—273	324000		A Magee	70-68-72-71—281	32000
3	S Elkington (Aus)	69-69-69-67—274	204000	23	P-U Johansson (Swe)	69-74-71-68—282	26000
4	F Lickliter	68-71-69-68—276	118000		F Funk	70-71-71-70—282	26000
	M O'Meara	69-70-69-68—276	118000		S Gump	68-69-72-73—282	26000
	N Price (Zim)	70-73-68-65—276	118000		G Kraft	71-73-65-73—282	26000
7	B Mayfair	73-67-67-70—277	89500	27	J Sluman	71-73-70-69—283	20500
	D Love III	70-68-69-70—277	89500		H Sutton	72-68-72-71—283	20500
9	J Cook	71-68-70-69—278	80000	29	G Day	68-71-75-70—284	17100
10	K Perry	69-72-70-68—279	69000		T Lehman	71-71-70-72—284	17100
	T Woods	66-72-70-71—279	69000		I Woosnam (Wal)	70-75-67-72—284	17100
	S Kendall	72-68-68-71—279	69000		L Rinker	70-70-71-73—284	17100
13	B Faxon	70-68-74-68—280	46000		S Hoch	72-69-70-73—284	17100
	F Couples	74-71-67-68—280	46000	34	P Mickelson	70-70-78-67—285	14250
	B Tway	69-76-67-68—280	46000		B Estes	68-76-69-72—285	14250
	P Azinger	68-73-70-69—280	46000		P Goydos	70-70-72-73—285	14250
	B Glasson	68-74-69-69—280	46000		R Cochran	69-71-70-75—285	14250
	S Flesch	75-69-67-69—280	46000	38	C Stadler	69-74-71-72—286	12750
	J Huston	70-71-68-71—280	46000		D Waldorf	74-70-70-72—286	12750
	R Allenby (Aus)	72-68-69-71—280	46000				

Other Totals: J Sindelar, J Haas, J Durant, C Franco (Par) 287; J Ozaki (Jpn), J Maggert, S Lowery, D Ogrin, K Sutherland, C Montgomerie (Sco), PH Horgan III, M Calcavecchia, D Hart, B Andrade 288; N Faldo (Eng), S Verplank 289; T Tryba, M Brooks, B Watts, J Carter, D Frost (RSA), JD Blake 290; T Dodds (Nam), T Byrum, O Browne 291; R Karlsson (Swe), S Maruyama (Jpn), L Roberts 292; S Leaney (Aus) 293; A Coltart (Sco) 294; D Sutherland 295; B Geiberger, C Parry (Aus), B Fabel 296; C Perry 297; T Herron 298

1997 US PGA Championship *at Winged Foot CC, New York*
(6987 yds, Par 70) Prize money: $2,600,000. Entries: 150, of whom 77 made the half-way cut.

1	D Love III	66-71-66-66—269	470000	13T	B Tway	68-75-72-69—284	35100
2	J Leonard	68-70-65-71—274	280000		M O'Meara	69-73-75-67—284	35100
3	J Maggert	69-69-73-65—276	175000	23	M Calcavecchia	71-74-73-67—285	22500
4	L Janzen	69-67-74-69—279	125000		B Langer (Ger)	73-71-72-69—285	22500
5	T Kite	68-71-71-70—280	105000		D Martin	69-75-74-67—285	22500
6	P Blackmar	70-68-74-69—281	85000		S Maruyama (Jpn)	68-70-74-73—285	22500
	J Furyk	69-72-72-68—281	85000		K Perry	73-68-73-71—285	22500
	S Hoch	71-72-68-70—281	85000		J Cook	71-71-74-69—285	22500
9	T Byrum	69-73-70-70—282	70000	29	P Azinger	68-73-71-74—286	13625
10	T Lehman	69-72-72-70—283	60000		R Black	76-69-71-70—286	13625
	S McCarron	74-71-67-71—283	60000		F Couples	71-67-73-75—286	13625
	J Sindelar	72-71-71-69—283	60000		J Daly	66-73-77-70—286	13625
13	D Duval	70-70-71-73—284	35100		P Goydos	70-72-71-73—286	13625
	T Herron	72-73-68-71—284	35100		H Irwin	73-70-71-72—286	13625
	C Montgomerie (Sco)	74-71-67-72—284	35100		P Mickelson	69-69-73-75—286	13625
	G Norman (Aus)	68-71-74-71—284	35100		F Nobilo (NZ)	72-73-67-74—286	13625
	N Price (Zim)	72-70-72-70—284	35100		D Pooley	72-74-70-70—286	13625
	V Singh (Fij)	73-66-76-69—284	35100		P Stewart	70-70-72-74—286	13625
	T Tolles	75-70-73-66—284	35100		L Westwood (Eng)	74-68-71-73—286	13625
	K Triplett	73-70-71-70—284	35100		T Woods	70-70-71-75—286	13625

Other Totals: I Garrido (Esp), S Jones, D Ogrin, E Romero (Arg) 287; T Bjørn (Den), S Elkington (Aus), J Parnevik (Swe), S Torrance (Sco) 288; R Allenby (Aus), B Henninger, C Perry, L Roberts 289; O Browne, E Els (RSA), B Mayfair, T Smith, C Stadler 290; S Lowery, L Mize, L Wadkins 291; S Appleby (Aus), J Haas, R Cochran, F Funk, R Goosen (RSA), L Rinker 292; P Jacobsen, P-U Johansson (Swe), P Stankowski 293; C Franco (Par) 294; M Bradley, Y Kaneko (Jpn), L Nelson, C Rocca (Ita) 295; A Magee 296; P Jordan, K Sutherland 297.

1996 US PGA Championship at Valhalla, Louisville, Kentucky

(7144 yds, Par 72) Prize money: $2,400,000. Entries: 150, of whom 87 made the half-way cut.

1	M Brooks*	68-70-69-70—277	$430000	17T	D Edwards	69-71-72-70—282	27285
2	K Perry	66-72-71-68—277	260000		J Furyk	70-70-73-69—282	27285
*Brooks won play-off at extra hole					G Norman (Aus)	68-72-69-73—282	27285
3	S Elkington (Aus)	67-74-67-70—278	140000	24	E Aubrey	69-74-72-68—283	21500
	T Tolles	69-71-71-67—278	140000		MA Jiménez (Esp)	71-71-71-70—283	21500
5	J Leonard	71-66-72-70—279	86666	26	F Funk	73-69-73-69—284	18000
	J Parnevik (Swe)	73-67-69-70—279	86666		M O'Meara	71-70-74-69—284	18000
	V Singh (Fij)	69-69-69-72—279	86666		C Pavin	71-74-70-69—284	18000
8	L Janzen	68-71-71-70—280	57500		C Strange	73-70-68-73—284	18000
	P-U Johansson (Swe)	73-72-66-69—280	57500		S Stricker	73-72-72-67—284	18000
	P Mickelson	67-67-74-72—280	57500	31	P Azinger	70-75-71-69—285	13000
	L Mize	71-70-69-70—280	57500		M Bradley	73-72-70-70—285	13000
	F Nobilo (NZ)	69-72-71-68—280	57500		P Burke	71-72-69-73—285	13000
	N Price (Zim)	68-71-69-72—280	57500		J Haas	72-71-69-73—285	13000
14	M Brisky	71-69-69-72—281	39000		T Herron	71-73-68-73—285	13000
	T Lehman	71-71-69-70—281	39000	36	M Calcavecchia	70-74-70-72—286	9050
	J Sindelar	73-72-69-67—281	39000		R Mediate	71-72-67-76—286	9050
17	B Faxon	72-68-73-69—282	27285		D Ogrin	75-70-68-73—286	9050
	T Watson	69-71-73-69—282	27285		I Woosnam (Wal)	68-72-75-71—286	9050
	D A Weibring	71-73-71-67—282	27285		F Zoeller	76-67-72-71—286	9050
	R Cochran	68-72-65-77—282	27285				

Other Totals: G Day, D Duval, G Morgan, J Morse 287; J Sluman, F Couples 287; P Blackmar, J Cook, S McCarron, P Stankowski, B Watts 288; J Adams, B Boyd, A Cejka (Ger), J Gallagher Jr, L Rinker, C Rocca (Ita), N Lancaster, B Mayfair, T Nakajima (Jpn) 289; E Els (RSA), D Forsman, S Hoch, M Wiebe 290; N Faldo (Eng), W Grady (Aus), C Parry (Aus), W Wood 291; W Austin, B Crenshaw, N Henke, P Stewart 292; P Goydos, J Maggert 293; M Dawson 294; B Langer (Ger) 295; J Edwards 296; S Higashi (Jpn), S Ingraham 297; H Clark (Eng), J Reeves 298.

1995 US PGA Championship at Riviera, Los Angeles

(6956 yds, Par 71) Prize money: $2,000,000. Entries: 150, of whom 72 made the half-way cut.

1	S Elkington (Aus)*	68-67-68-64—267	$360000	20	G Norman (Aus)	66-69-70-72—277	21000
2	C Montgomerie (Sco)	68-67-67-65—267	216000		J Parnevik (Swe)	69-70-69-69—277	21000
*Elkington won at first play-off hole					D Waldorf	69-69-67-72—277	21000
3	E Els (RSA)	66-65-66-72—269	116000	23	W Austin	70-70-70-68—278	15500
	J Maggert	66-69-65-69—269	116000		N Henke	68-73-67-70—278	15500
5	B Faxon	70-67-71-63—271	80000		P Jacobsen	69-67-71-71—278	15500
6	B Estes	69-68-68-68—273	68500		L Janzen	66-70-72-70—278	15500
	M O'Meara	64-67-69-73—273	68500		B Lietzke	73-68-67-70—278	15500
8	J Haas	69-71-64-70—274	50000		B Mayfair	68-68-72-70—278	15500
	J Leonard	68-66-70-70—274	50000		S Stricker	75-64-69-70—278	15500
	S Lowery	69-68-68-69—274	50000		S Torrance (Sco)	69-69-69-71—278	15500
	J Sluman	69-67-68-70—274	50000	31	P Azinger	70-70-72-67—279	8906
	C Stadler	71-66-66-71—274	50000		M Brooks	67-74-69-69—279	8906
13	J Furyk	68-70-69-68—275	33750		F Couples	70-69-74-66—279	8906
	MA Jiménez (Esp)	69-69-67-70—275	33750		N Faldo (Eng)	69-73-70-67—279	8906
	P Stewart	69-70-69-67—275	33750		G Morgan	66-73-74-66—279	8906
	K Triplett	71-69-68-67—275	33750		JM Olazábal (Esp)	72-66-70-71—279	8906
17	M Campbell (NZ)	71-65-71-69—276	26000		Joe Ozaki (Jpn)	71-70-65-73—279	8906
	C Rocca (Ita)	70-69-68-69—276	26000		DA Weibring	74-68-69-68—279	8906
	C Strange	72-68-68-68—276	26000				

Other Totals: L Clements, F Funk, A Lyle (Sco) 280; N Price (Zim), P Walton (Eng) 280; C Beck, B Crenshaw, J Gallagher jr, G Sauers, P Senior (Aus) 281; J Adams, B Claar, R Freeman, Jumbo Ozaki (Jpn), K Perry 282; M Bradley, H Irwin, T Kite, S Simpson 283; E Dougherty, P-U Johansson (Swe), S Pate, L Roberts, T Watson 284; B Lane (Eng), M Sullivan, L Wadkins 285; D Pruitt 286; D Frost (RSA), J Nicklaus 287; F Zoeller 288; B Kamm 289; C Byrum, W Defrancesco 291.

1994 US PGA Championship *at Southern Hills, Tulsa, Oklahoma*
(6834 yds, Par 70) Prize money: $1,750,000. Entries: 151, of whom 76 made the half-way cut.

1	N Price (Zim)	67-65-70-67—269	$310000	19T	M McCumber	73-70-71-68—282	18666
2	C Pavin	70-67-69-69—275	160000		F Zoeller	69-71-72-70—282	18666
3	P Mickelson	68-71-67-70—276	110000		B Glasson	71-73-68-70—282	18666
4	N Faldo (Eng)	73-67-71-66—277	76666		C Strange	73-71-68-70—282	18666
	G Norman (Aus)	71-69-67-70—277	76666		C Parry (Aus)	70-69-70-73—282	18666
	J Cook	71-67-69-70—277	76666	25	B Lane (Eng)	70-73-68-72—283	13000
7	S Elkington (Aus)	73-70-66-69—278	57500		B Langer (Ger)	73-71-67-72—283	13000
	JM Olazábal (Esp)	72-66-70-70—278	57500		D Frost (RSA)	70-71-69-73—283	13000
9	I Woosnam (Wal)	68-72-73-66—279	41000		E Els (RSA)	68-71-69-75—283	13000
	T Kite	72-68-69-70—279	41000		J Sluman	70-72-66-75—283	13000
	T Watson	69-72-67-71—279	41000	30	B Faxon	72-73-73-66—284	8458
	L Roberts	69-72-67-71—279	41000		W Grady (Aus)	75-68-71-70—284	8458
	B Crenshaw	70-67-70-72—279	41000		B Boyd	72-71-70-71—284	8458
14	J Haas	71-66-68-75—280	32000		L Clements	74-70-69-71—284	8458
15	K Triplett	71-69-71-70—281	27000		S Torrance (Sco)	69-75-69-71—284	8458
	L Mize	72-72-67-70—281	27000		R Zokol (Can)	77-67-67-73—284	8458
	M McNulty (Zim)	72-68-70-71—281	27000	36	C Beck	72-70-72-71—285	7000
	G Day	70-69-70-72—281	27000		B McAllister	74-64-75-72—285	7000
19	C Stadler	70-70-74-68—282	18666		C Montgomerie (Sco)	67-76-70-72—285	7000

Other Totals: F Couples, B Mayfair, G Morgan, T Lehman, H Irwin 286; N Lancaster, D Edwards, D Gilford (Eng) 287; B Andrade, F Allem (RSA), B Estes, A Magee, F Nobilo (NZ), G Kraft, J Ozaki (Jpn), DA Weibring 288; D Hart, F Funk, H Sutton, T Dolby, K Perry, M Springer 289; R Floyd, T Nakajima (Jpn), R McDougal, L Wadkins, B Fleisher 290; L Janzen, JD Blake, P Stewart, J Inman, T Smith 291; D Hammond, P Senior (Aus) 292; A Lyle (Sco), D Pride 297; B Henninger, H Meshiai (Jpn) 298.

1993 US PGA Championship *at Inverness, Toledo, Ohio*
(6982 yds, Par 71) Prize money: $1,700,000. Entries: 151, of whom 74 made the half-way cut.

1	P Azinger*	69-66-69-68—272	300000	22	G Sauers	68-74-70-69—281	14500
2	G Norman (Aus)	68-68-67-69—272	155000		F Nobilo (NZ)	69-66-74-72—281	14500
*Azinger won at second play-off hole					L Janzen	70-68-71-72—281	14500
3	N Faldo (Eng)	68-68-69-68—273	105000		I Woosnam (Wal)	70-71-68-72—281	14500
4	V Singh (Fij)	68-63-73-70—274	90000		G Twiggs	70-69-70-72—281	14500
5	T Watson	69-65-70-72—276	75000		J McGovern	71-67-69-74—281	14500
6	S Hoch	74-68-68-67—277	47812	28	P Jacobsen	71-67-76-72—282	10166
	N Henke	72-70-67-68—277	47812		B Mayfair	68-73-70-71—282	10166
	P Mickelson	67-71-69-70—277	47812		L Roberts	67-67-77-68—282	10166
	J Cook	72-66-68-71—277	47812	31	M Calcavecchia	68-70-77-68—283	7057
	S Simpson	64-70-71-72—277	47812		M McCumber	67-72-75-69—283	7057
	D Hart	66-68-71-72—277	47812		D Love III	70-72-72-69—283	7057
	B Estes	69-66-69-73—277	47812		S Ingraham	74-69-71-69—283	7057
	H Irwin	68-69-67-73—277	47812		F Zoeller	72-70-71-70—283	7057
14	B Fleisher	69-74-67-68—278	25000		N Price (Zim)	74-66-72-71—283	7057
	R Zokol (Can)	66-71-71-70—278	25000		T Wargo	71-70-71-71—283	7057
	S Elkington (Aus)	67-66-74-71—278	25000		F Allem (RSA)	70-71-70-72—283	7057
	G Hallberg	70-69-68-71—278	25000		M Hulbert	67-72-72-72—283	7057
	B Faxon	70-70-65-73—278	25000		H Sutton	69-72-70-72—283	7057
	L Wadkins	65-68-71-74—278	25000		C Parry (Aus)	70-73-68-72—283	7057
20	E Romero (Arg)	67-67-74-71—279	18500		F Couples	70-68-71-74—283	7057
	J Haas	69-68-70-72—279	18500		W Levi	69-73-66-75—283	7057

Other Totals: F Funk, DA Weibring, R Cochran, J Huston, D Forsman, P Stewart, J Ozaki (Jpn) 284; A Magee, J Daly, J Maggert, H Green, P Senior (Aus) 285; L Nelson, J M Olazábal (Esp), T Kite, R Fehr, A Lyle (Sco) 286; M Allen, J Sluman, B Crenshaw, D Hammond, M Standly 287; I Baker-Finch (Aus) 288; M Wiebe 289; B Ford, R Mediate 290; S Pate 292; K Burton, B Lane (Eng) 294; B Borowicz 295; J Adams 296.

1992 US PGA Championship *at Bellerive, St Louis, Missouri*

(7148 yds, Par 71) Prize money: $1,400,000. Entries: 151, of whom 85 made the half-way cut.

1	N Price (Zim)	70-70-68-70—278	$280000	21	T Purtzer	72-72-74-70—288	14000
2	N Faldo (Eng)	68-70-76-67—281	101250		L Janzen	74-71-72-71—288	14000
	J Gallagher jr	72-66-72-71—281	101250		B Britton	70-77-70-71—288	14000
	J Cook	71-72-67-71—281	101250		F Couples	69-73-73-73—288	14000
	G Sauers	67-69-70-75—281	101250		T Kite	73-73-69-73—288	14000
6	J Maggert	71-72-65-74—282	60000		T Nakajima (Jpn)	71-75-69-73—288	14000
7	R Cochran	69-69-76-69—283	52500		G Morgan	71-69-73-75—288	14000
	D Forsman	70-73-70-70—283	52500	28	N Ozaki (Jpn)	76-72-74-67—289	9000
9	D Waldorf	74-73-68-69—284	40000		M Hulbert	74-74-70-71—289	9000
	A Forsbrand (Swe)	73-71-70-70—284	40000		T Wargo	72-72-73-72—289	9000
	B Claar	68-73-73-70—284	40000		P Jacobsen	73-71-72-73—289	9000
12	J Sluman	73-71-72-69—285	30166		L Nelson	72-68-75-74—289	9000
	C Pavin	71-73-70-71—285	30166	33	B Fabel	72-76-74-68—290	7000
	B Andrade	72-71-70-72—285	30166		D Love III	77-71-70-72—290	7000
15	B Faxon	72-69-75-70—286	24000		B Fleisher	70-72-75-73—290	7000
	G Norman (Aus)	71-74-71-70—286	24000		F Nobilo (NZ)	69-74-74-73—290	7000
	M Brooks	71-72-68-75—286	24000		C Montgomerie (Sco)	72-76-69-73—290	7000
18	J Huston	73-75-71-68—287	19000		D Pruitt	73-70-73-74—290	7000
	R Fehr	74-73-71-69—287	19000		P Azinger	72-73-68-77—290	7000
	S Elkington (Aus)	74-70-71-72—287	19000				

Other Totals: D Edwards, M James, BR Brown, L Mize, F Allem (RSA), B Langer (Ger), L Wadkins, R Mediate 291; P Senior (Aus), B Bryant, S Pate, M Calcavecchia, V Singh (Fij), C Stadler, S Richardson, R Floyd 292; J Sindelar, L Rinker, A Magee, K Clearwater, B Tway, G Hallberg 293; J Overton, B McCallister, J Haas, T Watson 294; J Kane, H Irwin, R Mackay 295; P Stewart, I Baker-Finch (Aus), D Peoples, T Schulz 296; B Lietzke, D Frost (RSA), B Crenshaw 298; D Blake, B Estes, S Veriato 300; T Smith, R Gamez, S Gump 303; J Daly 304; H Perry 305; N Lancaster, K McDonald 307.

US PGA CHAMPIONSHIP HISTORY

Year	Winner	Runner-up	Venue	By
1916	J Barnes	J Hutchison	Siwanoy	1 hole
1919	J Barnes	F McLeod	Engineers' Club	6 and 5
1920	J Hutchison	D Edgar	Flossmoor	1 hole
1921	W Hagen	J Barnes	Inwood Club	3 and 2
1922	G Sarazen	E French	Oakmont	4 and 3
1923	G Sarazen	W Hagen	Pelham	38th hole
1924	W Hagen	J Barnes	French Lick	2 holes
1925	W Hagen	W Mehlhorn	Olympic Fields	6 and 4
1926	W Hagen	L Diegel	Salisbury	4 and 3
1927	W Hagen	J Turnesa	Dallas, TX	1 hole
1928	L Diegel	A Espinosa	Five Farms	6 and 5
1929	L Diegel	J Farrell	Hill Crest	6 and 4
1930	T Armour	G Sarazen	Fresh Meadow	1 hole
1931	T Creavy	D Shute	Wannamoisett	2 and 1
1932	O Dutra	F Walsh	St Paul, MN	4 and 3
1933	G Sarazen	W Goggin	Milwaukee	5 and 4
1934	P Runyan	C Wood	Buffalo	38th hole
1935	J Revolta	T Armour	Oklahoma	5 and 4
1936	D Shute	J Thomson	Pinehurst	3 and 2
1937	D Shute	H McSpaden	Pittsburgh	37th hole
1938	P Runyan	S Snead	Shawnee	8 and 7
1939	H Picard	B Nelson	Pomonok	37th hole
1940	B Nelson	S Snead	Hershey, PA	1 hole
1941	V Ghezzie	B Nelson	Denver, CO	38th hole
1942	S Snead	J Turnesa	Atlantic City, NJ	2 and 1
1943	*No Championship*			
1944	B Hamilton	B Nelson	Spokane, WA	1 hole
1945	B Nelson	S Byrd	Dayton, OH	4 and 3
1946	B Hogan	E Oliver	Portland	6 and 4
1947	J Ferrier	C Harbert	Detroit	2 and 1
1948	B Hogan	M Turnesa	Norwood Hills	7 and 6
1949	S Snead	J Palmer	Richmond, VA	3 and 2

United States PGA Championship History *continued*

Year	Winner	Runner-up	Venue	By
1950	C Harper	H Williams	Scioto, OH	4 and 3
1951	S Snead	W Burkemo	Oakmont, PA	7 and 6
1953	W Burkemo	F Lorza	Birmingham, MI	2 and 1
1954	C Harbert	W Burkemo	St Paul, MN	4 and 3
1955	D Ford	C Middlecoff	Detroit	4 and 3
1956	J Burke	T Kroll	Boston	3 and 2
1957	L Hebert	D Finsterwald	Miami Valley, Dayton	3 and 1

Changed to stroke play

Year	Winner	Venue	Score		Year	Winner	Venue	Score
1958	D Finsterwald	Llanerch, PA	276		1981	L Nelson	Atlanta, GA	273
1959	B Rosburg	Minneapolis, MN	277		1982	R Floyd	Southern Hills, OK	272
1960	J Hebert	Firestone, Akron, OH	281		1983	H Sutton	Pacific Palisades, CA	274
1961	J Barber*	Olympia Fields, IL	277		1984	L Trevino	Shoal Creek, AL	273
1962	G Player (RSA)	Aronimink, PA	278		1985	H Green	Cherry Hills, Denver, CO	278
1963	J Nicklaus	Dallas, TX	279		1986	R Tway	Inverness, Toledo, OH	276
1964	B Nichols	Columbus, OH	271		1987	L Nelson*	PGA National, FL	287
1965	D Marr	Laurel Valley, PA	280		1988	J Sluman	Oaktree, OK	272
1966	A Geiberger	Firestone, Akron, OH	280		1989	P Stewart	Kemper Lakes, IL	276
1967	D January*	Columbine, CO	281		1990	W Grady (Aus)	Shoal Creek, AL	282
1968	J Boros	Pecan Valley, TX	281		1991	J Daly	Crooked Stick, IN	276
1969	R Floyd	Dayton, OH	276		1992	N Price (Zim)	Bellerive, MS	278
1970	D Stockton	Southern Hills, OK	279		1993	P Azinger*	Inverness, Toledo, OH	272
1971	J Nicklaus	PGA National, FL	281		1994	N Price (Zim)	Southern Hills, OK	269
1972	G Player (RSA)	Oakland Hills, MI	281		1995	S Elkington (Aus)*	Riviera, LA	267
1973	J Nicklaus	Canterbury, OH	277		1996	M Brooks*	Valhalla, Kentucky	277
1974	L Trevino	Tanglewood, NC	276		1997	D Love III	Winged Foot, NY	269
1975	J Nicklaus	Firestone, Akron, OH	276		1998	V Singh (Fij)	Sahalee, Seattle, WA	271
1976	D Stockton	Congressional, MD	281		1999	T Woods	Medinah, IL	277
1977	L Wadkins*	Pebble Beach, CA	287		2000	T Woods*	Valhalla, Louisville KY	270
1978	J Mahaffey*	Oakmont, PA	276		2001	D Toms	Atlanta Athletic Club, GA	265
1979	D Graham (Aus)*	Oakland Hills, MI	272					
1980	J Nicklaus	Oak Hill, NY	274					

The Golden Bear well out in front

Jack Nicklaus leads the table of major professional title winners with 18 victories in the Open Championship, The Masters and the US PGA Championship. Walter Hagen won 11 of those titles, Ben Hogan and Gary Player nine, Tom Watson eight and Bobby Jones, Arnold Palmer, Gene Sarazen, Sam Snead and Harry Vardon seven. Tiger Woods has joined Nick Faldo and Lee Trevino with six victories in modern Grand Slam events.

Men's Major Title Table

Jack Nicklaus

Bobby Jones

Walter Hagen

All photographs © Phil Sheldon

	Open	US Open	Masters	US PGA	Amateur	US Amateur	Total Titles
Jack Nicklaus	3	4	6	5	0	2	20
Bobby Jones	3	4	0	0	1	5	13
Walter Hagen	4	2	0	5	0	0	11
John Ball	1	0	0	0	8	0	9
Ben Hogan	1	4	2	2	0	0	9
Gary Player	3	1	3	2	0	0	9
Tiger Woods	1	1	2	2	0	3	9
Arnold Palmer	2	1	4	0	0	1	8
Tom Watson	5	1	2	0	0	0	8
Harold Hilton	2	0	0	0	4	1	7
Gene Sarazen	1	2	1	3	0	0	7
Sam Snead	1	0	3	3	0	0	7
Harry Vardon	6	1	0	0	0	0	7
Lee Trevino	2	2	0	2	0	0	6
Nick Faldo	3	0	3	0	0	0	6

Weetabix Women's British Open Championship

2001 Weetabix Women's British Open Championship

at Sunningdale, Berkshire (6255 yds, Par 72)   Prize money: £1,000,000
Final field comprised 134, of whom 70 (one amateur) made the half-way cut.

1	Se Ri Pak (Kor)	71-70-70-66—277	£155000	€253022
2	Mi Hyun Kim (Kor)	72-65-71-71—279	100000	163240
3	Laura Diaz (USA)	74-70-69-67—280	51813	84579
	Iben Tinning (Den)	71-69-72-68—280	51813	84579
	Janice Moodie (Sco)	67-70-71-72—280	51813	84579
	Catriona Matthew (Sco)	70-65-72-73—280	51813	84579
7	Kristal Parker (USA)	72-71-71-67—281	25600	41789
	Marina Arruti (Esp)	71-73-70-67—281	25600	41789
	Kathryn Marshall (Sco)	75-71-68-67—281	25600	41789
	Kelli Kuehne (USA)	71-70-71-69—281	25600	41789
	Kasumi Fujii (Jpn)	71-71-69-70—281	25600	41789
12	Raquel Carriedo (Esp)	73-70-70-69—282	17750	28975
	Tracy Hanson (USA)	72-69-70-71—282	17750	28975
	Rosie Jones (USA)	70-69-71-72—282	17750	28975
15	Brandie Burton (USA)	72-71-73-67—283	14400	23507
	Pearl Sinn (USA)	74-70-72-67—283	14400	23507
	Jill McGill (USA)	70-70-72-71—283	14400	23507
	Karrie Webb (Aus)	74-67-68-74—283	14400	23507
19	Becky Morgan (Wal)	73-68-71-72—284	12575	20527
	Trish Johnson (Eng)	70-67-72-75—284	12575	20527
21	Johanna Head (Eng)	68-70-75-72—285	11125	18160
	Marlene Hedblom (Swe)	70-74-69-72—285	11125	18160
	Emilee Klein (USA)	71-70-71-73—285	11125	18160
	Lora Fairclough (Eng)	71-70-67-77—285	11125	18160
25	Danielle Ammaccapane (USA)	75-68-74-69—286	9071	14808
	Dina Ammaccapane (USA)	72-71-74-69—286	9071	14808
	Silvia Cavalleri (Ita)	71-73-72-70—286	9071	14808
	Maria Hjörth (Swe)	72-73-71-70—286	9071	14808
	Gloria Park (Kor)	71-73-71-71—286	9071	14808
	Lee Ji Hee (Kor)	75-71-69-71—286	9071	14808
	Laura Davies (Eng)	68-73-69-76—286	9071	14808
32	Annika Sörenstam (Swe)	70-74-74-69—287	6767	11046
	Marisa Baena (Col)	72-74-72-69—287	6767	11046
	Suzann Pettersen (Nor)	78-64-74-71—287	6767	11046
	Wendy Doolan (Aus)	72-68-75-72—287	6767	11046
	Grace Park (USA)	70-71-74-72—287	6767	11046
	Kelly Robbins (USA)	69-72-73-73—287	6767	11046
	Mhairi McKay (Sco)	70-72-72-73—287	6767	11046
	Hee Won Han (Kor)	72-73-69-73—287	6767	11046
	Hiromi Kobayashi (Jpn)	72-70-71-74—287	6767	11046
	Rebecca Hudson (am) (Eng)	71-70-70-76—287		
42	Sophie Gustafson (Swe)	74-70-78-66—288	5125	8366
	Kellee Booth (USA)	72-73-73-70—288	5125	8366
	Joanne Morley (Eng)	74-71-72-71—288	5125	8366

42T	Vicki Goetze-Ackerman (USA)	75-68-72-73—288	5125	8366
46	Lorie Kane (Can)	70-75-75-69—289	4000	6530
	Suzanne Strudwick (Eng)	74-71-73-71—289	4000	6530
	Tina Barrett (USA)	77-69-71-72—289	4000	6530
	Cindy Schreyer (USA)	73-72-71-73—289	4000	6530
	Elisabeth Esterl (Ger)	69-71-75-74—289	4000	6530
	Riikka Hakkarainen (Fin)	73-72-69-75—289	4000	6530
52	Joanne Mills (Aus)	75-70-77-68—290	3300	5387
53	Becky Iverson (USA)	71-72-74-74—291	3000	4897
	Yu Ping Lin (Tai)	72-73-72-74—291	3000	4897
55	Liselotte Neumann (Swe)	73-71-75-73—292	2700	4407
56	Carin Koch (Swe)	73-72-76-72—293	2325	3795
	Jenny Lidback (Per)	72-73-76-72—293	2325	3795
	Marine Monnet (Fra)	70-72-76-75—293	2325	3795
	Diane Barnard (Eng)	73-73-71-76—293	2325	3795
60	Kaori Harada (Jpn)	74-70-76-74—294	1800	2938
	Laurette Maritz (RSA)	74-72-73-75—294	1800	2938
	Karin Icher (Fra)	71-74-73-76—294	1800	2938
	Lisa Hed (Swe)	71-75-72-76—294	1800	2938
64	Nicola Moult (Eng)	74-71-74-76—295	1550	2530
	Helen Alfredsson (Swe)	71-69-78-77—295	1550	2530
	Patricia Meunier-Lebouc (Fra)	72-70-73-80—295	1550	2530
67	Kirsty Taylor (Eng)	72-73-77-74—296	1000	1632
68	Judith Van Hagen (Ned)	75-70-81-71—297	1000	1632
	Claire Duffy (Eng)	73-71-76-77—297	1000	1632
70	Dorothy Delasin (USA)	71-69-83-75—298	1000	1632

The following players missed the cut. Each player received £300:

71	Karen Stupples (Eng)	76-71—147
	Heather Bowie (USA)	75-72—147
	Michelle Estill (USA)	75-72—147
	Karen Pearce (Aus)	76-71—147
	Laurel Kean (USA)	75-72—147
	Smriti Mehra (Ind)	75-72—147
	Rachel Teske (Aus)	76-71—147
	Meg Mallon (USA)	72-75—147
	Caroline McMillan (Eng)	75-72—147
80	Sophie Sandolo (Ita)	75-73—148
	Michele Redman (USA)	76-72—148
	Catrin Nilsmark (Swe)	75-73—148
	Juli Inkster (USA)	75-73—148
	Dottie Pepper (USA)	75-73—148
	Vibeke Stensrud (Nor)	77-71—148
	Sara Eklund (Swe)	76-72—148
	Jen Hanna (USA)	76-72—148
88	Beth Daniel (USA)	73-76—149
	Kris Tschetter (USA)	77-72—149
	Cherie Byrnes (Aus)	77-72—149
	Karen Weiss (USA)	78-71—149
	Denise Killeen (USA)	73-76—149
	Anna Berg (Swe)	75-74—149
	Paula Marti (Esp)	74-75—149
	Wendy Ward (USA)	78-71—149
	Corinne Dibnah (Aus)	75-74—149
	Maggie Will (USA)	76-73—149
98	Ana Belen Sanchez (Esp)	76-74—150
	Chirhiro Nakajima (Jpn)	75-75—150
	Jackie Gallagher-Smith (USA)	79-71—150
	Giulia Sergas (Ita)	76-74—150
	Tammie Durdin (Aus)	75-75—150

98T	Mardi Lunn (Aus)	77-73—150
	Sherri Steinhauer (USA)	75-75—150
	Akiko Fukushima (Jpn)	79-71—150
	Marta Prieto (am) (Esp)	74-76—150
	Cindy Figg-Currier (USA)	76-74—150
	Charlotta Sörenstam (Swe)	79-71—150
	Valerie Van Ryckeghem (Bel)	78-72—150
110	Samantha Head (Eng)	78-73—151
	Catherine Schmitt (Fra)	80-71—151
	Chieko Amanuma (Jpn)	76-75—151
113	Pat Hurst (USA)	81-71—152
	Alison Nicholas (Eng)	76-76—152
	Michelle McGann (USA)	80-72—152
	LaRee Pearl Sugg (USA)	78-74—152
	Jeong Jang (Kor)	72-80—152
	Jennifer Rosales (Phi)	80-72—152
119	Cecilie Lundgreen (Nor)	75-78—153
	Natascha Fink (Aut)	80-73—153
	Shani Waugh (Aus)	78-75—153
122	Christina Kuld (Den)	77-77—154
	Nancy Scranton (USA)	76-78—154
	Asa Gottmo (Swe)	79-75—154
125	Alison Munt (Aus)	79-76—155
	Leslie Spalding (USA)	77-78—155
	Karen Lunn (Aus)	81-74—155
	Lynnette Brooky (NZ)	75-80—155
129	Sara Sanders (USA)	77-79—156
	Cristie Kerr (USA)	79-77—156
	Gina Scott (NZ)	74-82—156
	Wendy Dicks (Eng)	78-78—156
	Nicole Stillig (Ger)	81-75—156
134	Dale Reid (Sco)	76-81—157

2000 Women's British Open Championship

at Royal Birkdale, Southport, England (6285 yds, Par 73)   Prize money: £730,000

1	Sophie Gustafson (Swe)	70-66-71-75—282	£120000	17T	Annika Sörenstam (Swe)	70-76-71-72—289	9850
2	Kirsty Taylor (Eng)	71-74-72-67—284	50713	20	Kelly Robbins (USA)	73-74-73-70—290	8475
	Becky Iverson (USA)	70-70-75-69—284	50713		Karen Weiss (USA)	73-70-75-72—290	8475
	Liselotte Neumann				Rachel Hetherington		
	(Swe)	71-73-71-69—284	50713		(Aus)	71-74-73-72—290	8475
	Meg Mallon (USA)	74-69-71-70—284	50713		Brandie Burton (USA)	72-74-71-73—290	8475
6	Laura Philo (USA)	72-73-72-68—285	27500	24	Michele Redman		
7	Karrie Webb (Aus)	68-75-72-71—286	23250		(USA)	74-73-73-71—291	7275
8	Janice Moody (Sco)	73-74-73-67—287	19500		Alicia Dibos (Per)	72-73-74-72—291	7275
	Vicki Goetze-Ackerman				Marine Monnet (Fra)	72-73-74-72—291	7275
	(USA)	77-69-73-68—287	19500		Raquel Carriedo (Esp)	76-71-72-72—291	7275
10	Maggie Will (USA)	74-72-76-66—288	13250	28	Riko Higashio (Jpn)	74-72-76-70—292	6313
	Michelle McGann				Susan Redman (USA)	70-78-71-73—292	6313
	(USA)	72-76-69-71—288	13250		Jill McGill (USA)	71-71-76-74—292	6313
	Juli Inkster (USA)	70-69-77-72—288	13250		Mhairi McKay (Sco)	74-71-71-76—292	6313
	Jenny Lidback (Per)	71-71-73-73—288	13250	32	Shani Waugh (Aus)	73-74-76-70—293	5400
	Trish Johnson (Eng)	71-72-72-73—288	13250		Michelle Estill (USA)	72-75-75-71—293	5400
	Kellee Booth (USA)	73-71-71-73—288	13250		Sofia Grönberg		
	Kathryn Marshall (Sco)	72-69-73-74—288	13250		Whitmore (Swe)	80-69-73-71—293	5400
17	Pat Bradley (USA)	74-71-74-70—289	9850		Gail Graham (Can)	79-71-71-72—293	5400
	Rosie Jones (USA)	72-72-73-72—289	9850		Betsey King (USA)	74-73-73-73—293	5400

Other players who made the cut: Giulia Sergas (Ita), Maria Hjörth (Swe), Tina Barrett (USA), Leigh Ann Mills (USA), Julie Forbes (Sco), Wendy Daden (Eng), Pernilla Sterner (Swe), Laura Davies (Eng) 294; Anna Berg (Swe), Yu Ping Lin (Tai), Aki Takamura (Jpn), Karen Pearce (Aus) 295; Silvia Cavalleri (Ita), Stephanie Arricau (Fra), Sara Eklund (Swe), Karen Stupples (Eng), Sandrine Mendiburu (Fra), Jenifer Feldott (USA), Helen Alfredsson (Swe), Anne-Marie Knight (Aus) 296; Federica Dassu (Ita) 297; Kristal Parker-Gregory (USA), Elizabeth Esterl (Ger) 298; Catrin Nilsmark (Swe), Smriti Mehra (Ind), Johanna Head (Eng) 299; Mardi Lunn (Aus), Mandy Adamson (RSA), Dale Reid (Sco) 300; Hiromi Kobayashi (Jpn), Lisa De Paulo (USA) 301; Hsui Feng Tseng (Chn), Nina Karlsson (Swe), Judith Van Hagen (Ned) 303; Emilee Klein (USA), Gina Marie Scott (NZ), Laurette Maritz (RSA) 304; Lora Fairclough (Eng) 306

1999 Women's British Open Championship

at Woburn G&CC (6463 yds, Par 73)   Prize money: £575,000

1	S Steinhauer (USA)	71-71-68-73—283	£100000	17T	C Figg-Currier (USA)	69-76-72-73—290	6614
2	A Sörenstam (Swe)	69-71-72-72—284	60000		V Van		
3	H Dobson (Eng)	71-72-72-70—285	31666		Ryckeghem (Bel)	72-75-70-73—290	6614
	C Flom (USA)	71-74-69-71—285	31666		K Taylor (Eng)	73-71-72-74—290	6614
	F Pike (Aus)	70-70-71-74—285	31666	24	G Sergas (am) (Ita)	71-73-74-73—291	
6	E Klein (USA)	72-70-73-71—286	16000		J Morley (Eng)	70-75-73-73—291	5300
	S Gustafson (Swe)	73-69-72-72—286	16000		A Nicholas (Eng)	73-71-73-74—291	5300
	M Lunn (Aus)	71-72-70-73—286	16000		M Hjörth (Swe)	71-68-77-75—291	5300
	I Tinning (Den)	68-69-75-74—286	16000		S Lowe (Eng)	72-74-70-75—291	5300
	C McCurdy (USA)	73-70-68-75—286	16000		P Meunier-		
11	S Mehra (Ind)	70-70-76-71—287	11000		Lebouc (Fra)	73-70-72-76—291	5300
12	C Koch (Swe)	74-72-72-70—288	9625		M Yoneyama (Jpn)	73-70-72-76—291	5300
	S Strudwick (Eng)	71-70-76-71—288	9625	31	C Nilsmark (Swe)	72-71-76-73—292	4150
14	R Jones (USA)	73-71-73-72—289	8033		M Hirase (Jpn)	73-72-74-73—292	4150
	L Philo (USA)	69-71-75-74—289	8033		D Barnard (Eng)	73-72-74-73—292	4150
	L Neumann (Swe)	72-70-72-75—289	8033		K Marshall (Sco)	72-75-72-73—292	4150
17	D Richard (USA)	72-73-73-72—290	6614		S Cavalleri (Ita)	73-72-73-74—292	4150
	L Navarro (Esp)	70-70-77-73—290	6614		Yu Chen Huang (Tai)	71-75-72-74—292	4150
	M McNamara (Aus)	72-70-75-73—290	6614		R Hudson (am) (Eng)	72-69-75-76—292	
	T Kimura (Jpn)	69-74-74-73—290	6614				

Other players who made the cut: L Davies (Eng), T Barrett (USA), M McKay (Sco), C Dibnah (Aus), K Webb (Aus) J Head (Eng), R Higashio (Jpn) 293; C Sörenstam (Swe), J Moodie (Sco), L Hackney (Eng), J Forbes (Sco), J McGill (USA), K Orum (Den), F Dassu (Ita), A Belen Sanchez (Esp) 294; N Scranton (USA), M Baena (Col), H Kobayashi (Jpn), L Lambert (Aus), T Johnson (Eng), A Takamura (Jpn), E Poburski (Ger), M Dunn (USA), B Pestana (RSA) 297; J Mills (Aus), M Sutton (Eng), B Morgan (Wal) (am), C Schmitt (Fra) 299; P Wright (Sco), S Croce (Ita) 300; N Nijenhuis (Ned) (am), C Matthew (Sco) 301; M Hageman (Ned) 302; Le Kreutz (Fra), V Stensrud (Nor) 303

1998 Women's British Open Championship

at Royal Lytham & St Annes (6355 yds, Par 72) Prize money: £575,000

1	S Steinhauer	81-72-70-69—292	£100000	20T	J Gallacher-Smith	76-74-74-79—303	6300
2	S Gustafson	78-71-74-70—293	50000		K Marshall	79-74-71-79—303	6300
	B Burton	71-74-77-71—293	50000	24	D Andrews	81-72-76-75—304	5600
4	J Moodie	75-72-72-75—294	30000		J Morley	79-74-74-77—304	5600
5	K Webb	76-76-71-73—296	25000		P Hurst	76-77-70-81—304	5600
6	L Spalding	76-70-75-76—297	17000	27	C Johnstone-Forbes	78-76-79-72—305	5100
	W Ward	76-71-74-76—297	17000		S Strudwick	75-72-75-83—305	5100
	S Mehra	73-77-71-76—297	17000	29	C Koch	79-74-76-77—306	4700
	B King	71-77-72-77—297	17000		K Saiki	80-76-73-77—306	4700
10	C Nilsmark	77-77-69-75—298	12000	31	C McCurdy	80-77-75-75—307	4216
11	T Johnson	72-77-77-73—299	9687		F Dassu	82-72-77-76—307	4216
	J Inkster	75-75-76-73—299	9687		A Nicholas	79-72-76-80—307	4216
	A Sörenstam	75-73-77-74—299	9687	34	L Fairclough	77-77-78-76—308	3300
	ML de Lorenzi	79-70-76-74—299	9687		SR Pak	78-74-79-77—308	3300
15	M McKay	75-74-75-76—300	8000		W Doolan	83-72-76-77—308	3300
16	M Murray	81-76-69-75—301	7300		L Baugh	77-80-74-77—308	3300
	D Reid	73-79-73-76—301	7300		C Dibnah	77-80-74-77—308	3300
	H Wadsworth	79-74-72-76—301	7300		H Dobson	80-71-79-78—308	3300
19	H Kobayashi	77-74-75-76—302	6800		C McMillan	76-78-76-78—308	3300
20	M Hjörth	82-73-76-72—303	6300		C Figg-Currier	78-78-74-78—308	3300
	K Tschetter	79-75-73-76—303	6300		V Odegard	82-73-74-79—308	3300

Other players who made the cut: E Klein, C Sörenstam, R Carriedo, S Lowe 309; S Dallongeville, L Philo 310; A Munt, C Hall, T Fischer 311; K Pearce, L Kane, B Whitehead, J Forbes, D Barnard 312; I Tinning, L Neumann 313; L Maritz, T Barrett, H Stacy 314; R Hakkerainen, A Berg 316; M Hirase 317; C Johnson 318; M Spencer-Devlin 319; E Knuth 321

1997 Women's British Open Championship

at Sunningdale (6255 yds, Par 72) Prize money: £525,000

1	K Webb	65-70-63-71—269	£82500	19T	C Dibnah	72-71-70-73—286	5837
2	R Jones	70-70-66-71—277	52000		A Dibos	71-72-70-73—286	5837
3	A Sörenstam	72-70-69-67—278	36750	23	L Davies	74-73-69-71—287	5300
4	B Burton	73-69-71-67—280	27000		R Hetherington	75-70-71-71—287	5300
5	L Hackney	74-69-67-71—281	20000		K Tschetter	73-70-72-72—287	5300
	C Matthew	70-70-70-71—281	20000	26	E Klein	69-74-74-75—288	5000
7	W Doolan	74-70-68-70—282	14000	27	S Farron	72-75-75-67—289	4475
	T Barrett	70-72-70-70—282	14000		B Whitehead	71-74-77-67—289	4475
9	C Johnson	71-71-73-68—283	11500		J Morley	75-69-76-69—289	4475
10	C Sörenstam	71-70-72-71—284	10100		L Brooky	72-73-72-72—289	4475
	B King	71-72-68-73—284	10100		H Alfredsson	69-76-72-72—289	4475
12	J Lidback	71-74-70-70—285	7414		J Moodie	74-71-71-73—289	4475
	M Hirase	76-65-74-70—285	7414	33	K Lunn	74-71-75-70—290	3875
	L Neumann	68-75-71-71—285	7414		P Hurst	76-72-70-72—290	3875
	J Inkster	69-71-73-72—285	7414		S Cavalleri (am)	70-73-73-74—290	
	B Mucha	72-67-73-73—285	7414	36	S Maynor	72-74-74-71—291	3650
	H Dobson	73-69-69-74—285	7414	37	S Strudwick	72-74-74-72—292	3350
	K Marshall	70-68-73-74—285	7414		D Richard	71-72-75-74—292	3350
19	C Koch	76-71-71-68—286	5837		G Graham	73-73-71-75—292	3350
	L Lambert	70-73-73-70—286	5837				

Other players who made the cut: M Estill, S Steinhauer, K Parker-Gregory 293; P Meunier Lebouc, A Gottmo, S Prosser, A Fruhwirth, S Waugh 294; M Spencer-Devlin, H Kobayashi, F Dassu 295; T Green, A Yamaoka, T Johnson, E Esterl (Am) 296; S Croce, C Pierce, J Lee, W Dicks 297; M Koch, K Taylor, H Wadsworth, L Fairclough, L Kane, M Murray 298; C Figg-Currier 299; N Moult, D Barnard, S Gustafson 301; S Dallongeville 302.

1996 Women's British Open Championship

at Woburn G&CC, Milton Keynes (6309 yds, Par 73) Prize money: £500,000

1	E Klein	68-66-71-72—277	£80000	19T	L Davies	72-75-71-70—288	5675
2	P Hammel	71-70-72-71—284	42500		D Reid	68-74-74-72—288	5675
	A Alcott	72-70-70-72—284	42500		K Yamazaki	71-70-74-73—288	5675
4	J Geddes	72-73-70-70—285	20416		H Alfredsson	69-76-69-74—288	5675
	L Hackney	71-69-73-72—285	20416		J Lidback	68-73-73-74—288	5675
	A Nicholas	68-71-74-72—285	20416	25	J Morley	72-71-74-72—289	4850
7	B Whitehead	76-70-71-69—286	9571		K Marshall	71-72-73-73—289	4850
	D Richard	71-73-71-71—286	9571		T Abitbol	70-75-70-74—289	4850
	ML de Lorenzi	74-72-68-72—286	9571		T Barrett	71-74-69-75—289	4850
	P Bradley	70-75-69-72—286	9571		M Hjörth	70-70-71-78—289	4850
	C Johnson	72-69-73-72—286	9571	30	S Grönberg-Whitmore	75-73-71-71—290	4100
	R Jones	69-71-73-73—286	9571		A Fukushima	74-74-69-73—290	4100
	T Kerdyk	70-70-72-74—286	9571		C Sörenstam	76-70-71-73—290	4100
14	B Mucha	73-71-74-69—287	6600		V Goetze	74-70-72-74—290	4100
	D Eggeling	69-77-71-70—287	6600		J Piers	68-73-72-77—290	4100
	C Nilsmark	72-76-68-71—287	6600	35	B Daniel	77-71-71-72—291	3300
	K Webb	69-70-74-74—287	6600		C Matthew	71-73-75-72—291	3300
	A Sörenstam	69-70-73-75—287	6600		S Maynor	73-73-71-74—291	3300
19	D Andrews	80-65-74-69—288	5675		T Fischer	72-71-74-74—291	3300

Other players who made the cut: H Kobayashi, T Hanson, M Hirase 292; E Knuth, K Parker-Gregory 293; M Mallon, S Strudwick, L Brooky, S Croce, E Orley, L Navarro 294; A-M Knight, P Sterner, S Redman, C Dibnah, P Rigby-Jinglov, M Figueras-Dotti, M Berteotti, C Figg-Currier 295; R Hetherington, J Crafter, B Hackett (Am) 296; R Carriedo, J Forbes, X Wunsch-Ruiz, M Estill 297; S Farwig, J Mcgill, C Hj Koch 298; N Harvey 300; K Weiss 302; M Sutton, K Harada 303.

1995 Women's British Open Championship

at Woburn G&CC, Milton Keynes (6257 yds, Par 73) Prize money: £360,000

1	K Webb	69-70-69-70—278	£60000	19T	A Gottmo	70-73-74-74—291	4032
2	J McGill	71-73-71-69—284	30000		B Burton	72-70-74-75—291	4032
	A Sörenstam	70-72-71-71—284	30000	23	R Hetherington	74-76-76-66—292	3710
4	M Berteotti	73-71-71-70—285	14333		J Morley	72-72-74-74—292	3710
	C Pierce	70-70-72-73—285	14333		E Orley	71-73-74-74—292	3710
	V Skinner	74-68-67-76—285	14333	26	V Michaud	76-73-75-69—293	3215
7	S Strudwick	73-68-71-74—286	9500		A Nicholas	73-72-76-72—293	3215
8	ML de Lorenzi	68-74-73-73—288	6937		S Dallongeville	76-72-72-73—293	3215
	W Doolan	73-71-70-74—288	6937		M McGuire	68-78-73-74—293	3215
	N Lopez	71-73-70-74—288	6937		T Fischer	76-66-77-74—293	3215
	L Neumann	67-74-71-76—288	6937		L Hackney	74-74-70-75—293	3215
12	K Tschetter	73-75-74-67—289	4957		L Fairclough	76-68-72-77—293	3215
	C Matthew	74-71-73-71—289	4957		M Lunn	73-67-73-80—293	3215
	V Goetze	73-72-71-73—289	4957	34	M McNamara	76-73-74-71—294	2585
	P Meunier	73-71-74-74—289	4957		T Johnson	75-74-74-71—294	2585
16	J Forbes	69-73-77-71—290	4430		Li Wen-Lin	74-71-75-74—294	2585
	S Prosser	70-74-74-72—290	4430		L West	73-75-71-75—294	2585
	H Kobayashi	72-70-74-74—290	4430		S Waugh	68-75-72-79—294	2585
19	L Brooky	69-74-76-72—291	4032		S Croce	71-71-73-79—294	2585
	K Pearce	74-71-72-74—291	4032				

Other players who made the cut: D Barnard, C Hall, T Hanson, C Hjalmarsson, P Hammel 296; L Davies, LA Mills, S Burnell, P Wright, W Dicks, E Klein, K Peterson-Parker 297; C Duffy, E Knuth 298; A Brighouse, K Orum, J Geddes 298; A Rogers, K Marshall, L Weima, C Eliasson-Wharton, S Gr-Whitmore 299; A Arruti, A Shapcott, T Barrett, K Davies 300; G Stewart, L Dermott (am) 301; S Moon, D Reid 302; J Soulsby, P Sterner 303; H Hopkins, C Evelyn Louw 304; K Stupples (am) 305; N Buxton 307.

1994 Women's British Open Championship

at Woburn G&CC, Milton Keynes (6224 yds, Par 73) Prize money: £335,000

1	L Neumann	71-67-70-72—280	£52500	17T	E Knuth	78-69-72-73—292	4100
2	D Mochrie	73-66-74-70—283	27250	21	P Wright	68-75-78-72—293	3740
	A Sörenstam	69-75-69-70—283	27250		K Pearce	70-74-75-74—293	3740
4	L Davies	74-66-73-71—284	14625		K Tschetter	68-76-75-74—293	3740
	C Dibnah	75-70-67-72—284	14625	24	K Cockerill	71-77-73-73—294	3425
6	C Figg-Currier	69-74-68-74—285	10750		A Alcott	74-74-75-71—294	3425
7	H Alfredsson	71-76-71-68—286	9250		B King	73-74-69-78—294	3425
8	T Hanson	74-73-66-74—287	8000		A Ritzman	69-76-75-74—294	3425
9	S Strudwick	71-71-71-75—288	6250	28	S Moon	72-78-74-71—295	2930
	V Skinner	77-71-66-74—288	6250		A Nicholas	72-73-70-80—295	2930
	C Pierce	70-75-71-72—288	6250		D Reid	76-72-75-72—295	2930
12	H Kobayashi	73-73-69-74—289	5100		M Lunn	73-75-75-72—295	2930
13	S Gautrey	69-74-72-75—290	4800		K Marshall	76-72-75-72—295	2930
14	T Abitbol	76-68-75-72—291	4526		L Fairclough	75-72-72-76—295	2930
	P Grice-Whittaker	77-72-72-70—291	4526		S Redman	74-71-76-74—295	2930
	M McGuire	71-73-78-69—291	4526	35	T Johnson	75-75-72-74—296	2480
17	S Grönberg-Whitmore	71-69-74-78—292	4100		E Orley	73-76-74-73—296	2480
	Li Wen-Lin	73-70-73-76—292	4100		K Albers	75-67-78-76—296	2480
	J Geddes	74-72-72-74—292	4100				

Other players who made the cut: LA Mills, H Person, C Hall, L Navarro, L West 297; T Barrett 298;
M Figueras-Dotti, K Orum, W Doolan, T Fischer (am), J Forbes 299; ML de Lorenzi, C Hjalmarsson, I Maconi 300;
X Wunsch-Ruiz, LR Sugg, K Noble 301; F Dassu, M De Boer, G Steward, F Descampe, C Nilsmark, S Prosser,
M Spencer-Devlin, S Waugh, H Wadsworth, S Mendiburu, S Robinson 302; N Scranton 303; D Barnard, L Hackney,
E Crosby 304; M Hageman 306; B New, M Burstrom, N Moult, M Lawrence Wengler 307; J Lawrence, S Gustafson
309.

1993 Women's British Open Championship

at Woburn G&CC, Milton Keynes (6224 yds, Par 73) Prize money: £300,000

1	K Lunn	71-69-68-67—275	£50000	21	J Soulsby	76-75-73-72—296	3685
2	B Burton	75-70-68-70—283	32000		C Figg-Currier	75-75-72-74—296	3685
3	K Marshall	73-71-69-73—286	21000	23	G Stewart	74-75-76-72—297	3505
4	Li Wen-Lin	70-71-74-72—287	14350		P Meunier (am)	73-76-77-71—297	
	J Geddes	76-75-72-64—287	14350		J Morley (am)	77-74-74-72—297	
6	P Sheehan	75-70-72-72—289	10500		V Michaud	79-73-70-75—297	3505
7	L Davies	69-76-75-70—290	7300	27	T Abitbol	77-74-74-73—298	3145
	ML de Lorenzi	73-77-72-68—290	7300		F Dassu	70-75-75-78—298	3145
	S Strudwick	72-71-73-74—290	7300		X Wunsch-Ruiz	73-79-71-75—298	3145
	C Nilsmark	76-71-74-69—290	7300		D Hanna	74-73-73-78—298	3145
11	A Nicholas	74-73-70-74—291	5400		K Cathrein	74-76-73-75—298	3145
12	T Johnson	72-75-77-69—293	4670		A Gottmo	77-70-74-77—298	3145
	D Reid	76-75-74-68—293	4670		N Buxton (am)	74-74-74-76—298	
	C Hjalmarsson	77-74-68-74—293	4670	34	L Neumann	74-72-80-73—299	2740
	H Alfredsson	77-71-74-71—293	4670		S Waugh	77-75-74-73—299	2740
16	S Grönberg-Whitmore	76-70-79-69—294	4180		C Hall	75-71-75-78—299	2740
	K Orum	75-72-73-74—294	4180	37	K Espinasse	77-74-74-75—300	2470
	S Gautrey	76-75-69-74—294	4180		F Descampe	75-77-74-74—300	2470
19	C Duffy	75-76-71-73—295	3880		A-C Jonasson (am)	72-74-78-76—300	
	R Hast	77-71-72-75—295	3880		L Cowan	74-77-75-74—300	2470

Other players who made the cut: C Dibnah, K Weiss, S Dallongeville (am) 301; S Moon, D Patterson, C Lambert
(am) 302; C Soules 303; L Brooky (am), V Palli 304; R Lautens, S Van Wyk, MG Estuesta, S Burnell (am), T Loveys,
S Bennett 305; M Sutton (am), H Wadsworth 306; K Leadbetter 307; D Barnard, C Sörenstam (am) 309; D Petrizzi
310; M Hageman 311.

1992 Women's British Open Championship

at Woburn G&CC, Milton Keynes (6224 yds, Par 73) Prize money: £300,000

1	P Sheehan	68-72-67—207	£50000	20	T Abitbol	72-71-78—221	3550	
2	C Dibnah	70-69-71—210	32000		F Dassu	73-77-71—221	3550	
3	ML de Lorenzi	71-71-70—212	21000		T Johnson	73-73-75—221	3550	
4	L Neumann	69-74-70—213	16000		Li Wen-Lin	74-70-77—221	3550	
5	P Rizzo	72-70-72—214	11600		C Hjalmarsson	74-75-72—221	3550	
	H Alfredsson	74-72-68—214	11600		C Figg-Currier	71-77-73—221	3550	
7	D Mochrie	74-68-73—215	9000		K Marshall	74-73-74—221	3550	
8	J Arnold	70-74-72—216	6120	27	C Soules	78-73-71—222	3100	
	S Strudwick	75-72-69—216	6120		D Petrizzi	76-72-74—222	3100	
	F Descampe	71-73-72—216	6120		S Croce	79-73-70—222	3100	
	M Burstrom	72-73-71—216	6120	30	A Shapcott	74-75-74—223	2830	
	E Orley	70-75-71—216	6120		L Sugg	76-71-76—223	2830	
13	K Davies	75-70-73—218	4560		S Robinson	75-76-72—223	2830	
	P Wright	73-76-69—218	4560	33	G Stewart	76-75-73—224	2425	
	K Parker	72-74-72—218	4560		K Cornelius	73-77-74—224	2425	
16	J Geddes	78-69-72—219	4300		K Lasken	76-74-74—224	2425	
17	D Reid	73-73-74—220	4060		LA Mills	74-76-74—224	2425	
	A Dibos	75-75-70—220	4060		J Sevil	74-75-75—224	2425	
	V Michaud	71-76-73—220	4060		L Hackney	74-74-76—224	2425	

Other players who made the cut: L Davies, L Maritz-Atkins, A Nicholas, A Fukushima (am), H Wadsworth 225;
K Douglas, P Smillie, M Lunn, N Hall, S Rule, C Savy, M Hageman 226; C Duffy, S Grönberg, C Nilsmark,
K Pearce 227; D Dowling, E Farquharson 228; R Comstock, L Fairclough 229; K Orum 230; S Mendiburu 231;
V Marvin 232; J Posener 235.

WOMEN'S BRITISH OPEN HISTORY

Year	Winner	Country	Venue	Score
1976	J Lee Smith	England	Fulford	299
1977	V Saunders	England	Lindrick	306
1978	J Melville	England	Foxhills	310
1979	A Sheard	South Africa	Southport and Ainsdale	301
1980	D Massey	USA	Wentworth (East)	294
1981	D Massey	USA	Northumberland	295
1982	M Figueras-Dotti	Spain	Royal Birkdale	296
1983	*Not played*			
1984	A Okamoto	Japan	Woburn	289
1985	B King	USA	Moor Park	300
1986	L Davies	England	Royal Birkdale	283
1987	A Nicholas	England	St Mellion	296
1988	C Dibnah*	Australia	Lindrick	296
* Won play-off after a tie with S Little				
1989	J Geddes	USA	Ferndown	274
1990	H Alfredsson*	Sweden	Woburn	288
* Won play-off at fourth extra hole after a tie with J Hill				
1991	P Grice-Whittaker	England	Woburn	284
1992	P Sheehan	USA	Woburn	207
Reduced to 54 holes by rain				
1993	K Lunn	Australia	Woburn	275
1994	L Neumann	Sweden	Woburn	280
1995	K Webb	Australia	Woburn	278
1996	E Klein	USA	Woburn	277
1997	K Webb	Australia	Sunningdale	269
1998	S Steinhauer	USA	Royal Lytham & St Annes	292
1999	S Steinhauer	USA	Woburn	283
2000	S Gustafson	Sweden	Royal Birkdale	282
2001	SR Pak	Korea	Sunningdale	277

US Women's Open Championship

Players are of American nationality unless stated

2001 US Women's Open Championship

at Pine Needles Lodge and Golf Cousrse, Southern Pines, NC (6256 yds, Par 70)

Prize Money $2,900,000. Final field comprised 150 players, of whom 60 (including three amateurs) made the half-way cut on 150 or better.

1	Karrie Webb (Aus)	70-65-69-69—273	$520000
2	Se Ri Pak (Kor)	69-70-70-72—281	310000
3	Dottie Pepper	74-69-70-69—282	202580
4	Cristie Kerr	69-73-71-70—283	118697
	Sherri Turner	72-70-71-70—283	118697
	Catriona Matthew (Sco)	72-68-70-73—283	118697
7	Lorie Kane (Can)	75-68-72-69—284	80726
	Kristi Albers	71-69-74-70—284	80726
	Kelli Kuehne	70-71-72-71—284	80726
	Wendy Doolan	71-70-70-73—284	80726
11	Sophie Gustafson (Swe)	74-66-74-71—285	66581
12	Kelly Robbins	72-68-76-70—286	57088
	AJ Eathorne (Can)	67-71-75-73—286	57088
	Juli Inkster	68-72-71-75—286	57088
	Yuri Fudoh (Jpn)	73-68-70-75—286	57088
16	Emilee Klein	72-69-75-71—287	46885
	Michele Redman	70-72-73-72—287	46885
	Annika Sörenstam (Swe)	70-72-73-72—287	46885
19	Maria Hjörth (Swe)	70-71-77-70—288	37327
	Marisa Baena (Col)	71-72-75-70—288	37327
	Jill McGill	68-76-72-72—288	37327
	Wendy Ward	70-71-74-73—288	37327
	Dorothy Delasin	75-70-70-73—288	37327
24	Beth Daniel	73-70-71-75—289	30091
	Audra Burks	70-72-72-75—289	30091
26	Brandie Burton	73-70-77-70—290	24649
	Helen Alfredsson (Swe)	71-73 74-72—290	24649
	Mi Hyun Kim (Kor)	68-76-72-74—290	24649
	Janice Moodie (Sco)	71-70-73-76—290	24649
30	Kris Tschetter	72-74-77-68—291	20472
	Michelle Ellis	75-69-75-72—291	20472
	Candy Hannemann (am)	73-73-72-73—291	
	Meg Mallon	72-70-76-73—291	20472
34	Pat Hurst	73-71-76-72—292	18408
	Natalie Gulbis (am)	73-71-75-73—292	
	Catrin Nilsmark (Swe)	70-76-72-74—292	18408
	Dina Ammaccapane	69-73-75-75—292	18408
	Karen Weiss	74-71-71-76—292	18408
39	Marcy Newton	74-72-74-73—293	16061
	Liselotte Neumann (Swe)	70-73-76-74—293	16064
	Rosie Jones	73-68-75-77—293	16061
	Grace Park (Kor)	76-70-69-78—293	16061
43	Leta Lindley	71-75-76-72—294	13145
	Paula Marti (Esp)	74-70-76-74—294	13145
	Amy Fruhwirth	75-71-73-75—294	13145

2001 US Women's Open Championship *continued*

43T	Aki Nakano	70-74-75-75—294	13145
	Cindy Figg-Currier	67-76-75-76—294	13145
	Alison Nicholas (Eng)	73-70-72-79—294	13145
49	Pearl Sinn (Kor)	70-74-77-74—295	11104
50	Stephanie Keever (am)	69-72-83-72—296	
	Christina Kim (am)	73-73-75-75—296	
	Sherri Steinhauer	70-73-76-77—296	10522
53	Smriti Mehra (Ind)	72-73-77-75—297	9467
	Jean Bartholamew	70-75-76-76—297	9467
	Raquel Carriedo (Esp)	74-71-73-79—297	9467
56	Terry-Jo Myers	70-75-81-72—298	8874
57	Yu Ping Lin (Twn)	73-70-82-74—299	8342
	Jamie Hullett	74-72-77-76—299	8342
	Lynnette Brooky	72-74-77-76—299	8342
	Lisa Strom	73-73-76-77—299	8342

The following players missed the cut:

61	Michelle McGann	74-73—147	90T	Tanya Maree Holl	76-74—150	123 T	Lynn Valentine	75-80—155
	Becky Iverson	72-75—147		Jenna Daniels	77-73—150		Marine Monnet	
	Jenny Lidback	74-73—147		Danielle			(Fra)	78-77—155
	Laurel Kean	76-71—147		Ammaccapane	74-76—150		Joan Pitcock	77-78—155
	Laura Myerscough			Marianne Morris	73-77—150		Leigh Anne	
	(am)	76-71—147		Jackie Gallagher-			Hardin (am)	78-77—155
	Angela Buzminski	74-73—147		Smith	73-77—150		Kathryn Marshall	
	Nancy Harvey	71-76—147		Allison Finney	74-76—150		(Sco)	77-78—155
	Ashli Bunch	74-73—147		Tina Barrett	75-75—150	130	Laura Coble (am)	79-77—156
69	Jennifer Rosales	77-71—148	100	Shani Waugh	74-77—151		Celeste Troche	
	Akiko Fukushima	76-72—148		Laurie Brower	78-73—151		(am)	80-76—156
	Laura Davies			Vicki Goetze-		132	Susan Redman	80-77—157
	(Eng)	75-73—148		Ackerman	76-75—151		Carrie	
	Karine Icher (Fra)	75-73—148		Angela Jerman			Summerhays	
	Johanna Head			(am)	79-72—151		(am)	79-78—157
	(Eng)	72-76—148	104	Amy Langhals	78-74—152	134	Linda Ishii	78-81—159
	Suzanne Strudwick			Betsy King	76-76—152		Diana Ramage	
	(Eng)	75-73—148		Charlotta			(am)	80-79—159
	Rachel Teske			Sörenstam			Shelly Stouffer	82-77—159
	(Aus)	76-72—148		(Swe)	76-76—152		Eve Lux	81-78—159
	Barb Mucha	74-74—148		Marnie McGuire	76-76—152		Laura Brown	77-82—159
77	Nicole Jeray	77-72—149		Mary Beth		139	Dominique	
	Joanne Morley			Zimmerman	78-74—152		Gagnon (am)	76-84—160
	(Eng)	73-76—149		Marilyn Lovander	75-77—152		Carol Semple	
	Jean Zedlitz	76-73—149		Nancy Scranton	78-74—152		Thompson	
	Kimberly Williams	74-75—149		Donna Andrews	77-75—152		(am)	80-80—160
	Penny Hammel	75-74—149		Kellee Booth	78-74—152	141	Stacy Orschell	79-82—161
	Laura Diaz	72-77—149		Heather Wilbur	78-74—152		Patricia Liscio	79-82—161
	Patricia Baxter-			Trish Johnson			Claudia	
	Johnson	74-75—149		(Eng)	75-77—152		Beauchesne	83-78—161
	Jennifer Brody	74-75—149	115	Tonya Gill	77-76—153	144	Amber Marsh	
	Michelle Murphy	75-74—149		Kim Bauer	77-76—153		(am)	82-80—162
	Marie-Josee			Jennifer Greggain	79-74—153	145	Brenda Corrie	
	Rouleau	77-72—149		Angela Stanford	77-76—153		Kuehn (am)	79-84—163
	Jane Geddes	74-75—149		Marcela Leon (am)	79-74—153	146	Deborah Harmon	80-84—164
	Leslie Spalding	74-75—149	120	Meredith Duncan		147	Nina Foust	77-90—167
	Stacy			(am)	76-78—154	148	Sofia Grönberg-	
	Prammanasudh			Morgan Pressel			Whitmore (Swe)	80-89—169
	(am)	71-78—149		(am)	77-77—154	149	Kathleen	
90	Lisa Depaulo	73-77—150		Carin Koch	78-76—154		Robinson	88-88—176
	Nicole Materne	72-78—150	123	Lindsay Steelman	76-79—155			
	Heather Daly-			Kris Derdenger	80-75—155			
	Donofrio	73-77—150						

2000 US Women's Open Championship

at Merit Club, Libertyville, IL (6540 yds, Par 72) Prize money: $2,700,000

1	Karrie Webb (Aus)	69-72-68-73—282	$500000	21T	Wendy Doolan (Aus)	77-69-74-75—295	34113
2	Cristie Kerr	72-71-74-70—287	240228	23	Donna Andrews	73-75-79-70—297	28404
	Meg Mallon	68-72-73-74—287	240228		Kristi Albers	71-77-73-76—297	28404
4	Rosie Jones	73-71-72-72—288	120119		Michele Redman	74-74-73-76—297	28404
	Mi Hyun Kim (Kor)	74-72-70-72—288	120119		Juli Inkster	70-74-73-80—297	28404
6	Grace Park (Kor)	74-72-73-70—289	90458	27	Charlotta Sörenstam		
	Kelli Kuehne	71-74-73-71—289	90458		(Swe)	75-74-76-73—298	21740
8	Beth Daniel	71-74-72-73—290	79345		AJ Eathorne (Can)	73-77-73-75—298	21740
9	Annika Sörenstam				Silvia Cavalleri (Ita)	72-73-75-78—298	21740
	(Swe)	73-75-73-70—291	67369		Joanne Morley (Eng)	73-72-74-79—298	21740
	Kelly Robbins	74-73-71-73—291	67369	31	Tina Barrett	72-78-75-74—299	17067
	Laura Davies (Eng)	73-71-72-75—291	67369		Danielle Ammaccapane	72-73-79-75—299	17067
12	Jennifer Rosales (Phi)	75-75-69-73—292	55355		Emilee Klein	77-72-75-75—299	17067
	Pat Hurst	73-72-72-75—292	55355		Fiona Pike (Aus)	72-74-77-76—299	17067
	Dorothy Delasin	76-68-72-76—292	55355		Kate Golden	75-72-76-76—299	17067
15	Se Ri Pak (Kor)	74-75-75-69—293	47846		Jenny Lidback (Per)	73-74-76-76—299	17067
	Kellee Booth	70-78-75-70—293	47846		Carin Koch (Swe)	75-73-73-78—299	17067
17	Janice Moodie (Sco)	73-77-75-69—294	40586		Sophie Gustafson		
	Kathryn Marshall (Sco)	72-72-77-73—294	40586		(Swe)	72-78-71-78—299	17067
	Shani Waugh (Aus)	69-75-73-77—294	40586		Hiromi Kobayashi		
	Lorie Kane (Can)	71-74-72-77—294	40586		(Jpn)	77-72-70-80—299	17067
21	Jackie Gallagher Smith	71-77-73-74—295	34113				

Other players who made the cut: Michelle Ellis (Aus), Valerie Skinner, Mary Beth Zimmerman, Naree Wongluekiet (am) 300; Catriona Matthew (Sco), Jill McGill (Sco); Leta Lindley, Nancy Scranton, Nancy Lopez, Jan Stephenson (Aus), Jae Jean Ro (am), Betsy King, Sara Sanders 302; Jean Zedlitz 304; Marisa Baena (Col), Anna Macosko 305; Hilary Homeyer (am) 306; Carri Wood 307; Barb Mucha 308; Pearl Sinn (Kor) 310; Michelle McGann 311

1999 US Women's Open Championship

at Old Waverley, West Point, MS (6421 yds, Par 72) Prize money: $1,750,000

1	J Inkster	65-69-67-71—272	$315000	20T	L Lindley	72-72-73-70—287	21832
2	S Turner	69-69-68-71—277	185000		S Gustafson (Swe)	72-72-70-73—287	21832
3	K Kuehne	64-71-70-74—279	118227		D Andrews	69-71-72-75—287	21832
4	L Kane	70-64-71-75—280	82399		H Fukushima (Jpn)	69-70-71-77—287	21832
5	C Koch (Swe)	72-69-68-72—281	62938	25	K Saiki	70-71-73-74—288	16006
	M Mallon	70-70-69-72—281	62938		S Croce (Ita)	71-71-71-75—288	16006
7	K Webb (Aus)	70-70-68-74—282	53132		R Jones	71-70-72-75—288	16006
8	H Dobson (Eng)	71-70-73-69—283	45244		L Kiggens	71-67-73-77—288	16006
	M Hjörth (Swe)	73-69-70-71—283	45244		S Steinhauer	68-69-73-78—288	16006
	C Matthew (Sco)	69-68-74-72—283	45244	30	M Lunn (Aus)	72-71-74-72—289	11652
	G Park (Kor) (am)	70-67-73-73—283			J Zedlitz	75-67-75-72—289	11652
12	H Alfredsson (Swe)	72-68-70-74—284	37666		M McKay (Sco)	73-68-76-72—289	11652
	B Iverson	72-64-73-75—284	37666		N Scranton	69-72-75-73—289	11652
14	M Redman	72-71-75-67—285	32389		D Coe Jones	73-71-71-74—289	11652
	Se Ri Pak (Kor)	68-70-74-73—285	32389		A Acker Macosko	73-71-71-74—289	11652
	D Pepper	68-69-72-76—285	32389		K Robbins	70-70-74-75—289	11652
17	L Neumann (Swe)	73-71-69-73—286	27422	37	H Kobayashi (Jpn)	74-70-76-70—290	10078
	AJ Eathorne (Can)	69-71-71-75—286	27422		D Dormann	74-70-73-73—290	10078
	C Nilsmark (Swe)	69-71-70-76—286	27422		K Booth (am)	71-73-70-76—290	
20	C McCurdy	72-72-74-69—287	21832				

Other players who made the cut: M Estill, M Berteotti, K Tschetter, W Ward, M Dunn 291; P Kerrigan, S Strudwick (Eng) 292; B King, B Daniel, B Mucha, A Munt, W Doolan, V Odegard 293; M Will, R Hetherington (Aus) 294; J Lidback, L Hackney, C Figg-Currier, A Nicholas (Eng) 295; P Rizzo 296; J Feldott, P Hammel 297; K Millies 298; T Green 299

1998 US Women's Open Championship

at *Blackwolf Run, Wisconsin, WI* (6412 yds, Par 71) Prize money: $1,500,000

1	Se Ri Pak* (Kor)	69-70-75-76—290	$267500	19T	J Lidback (Per)	71-73-79-75—298	18998
2	J Chuasiriporn (am)	72-71-75-72—290			A Fukushima (Jpn)	72-71-79-76—298	18998

*Se Ri Pak won at second extra hole after both were tied
after 18 extra holes*

				R Jones	74-74-74-76—298	18998
				W Ward	76-69-75-78—298	18998
3	L Neumann (Swe)	70-70-75-76—291	157500	D Andrews	70-75-75-78—298	18998
4	Dani Ammaccapane	76-71-74-71—292	77351	L Walters (Can)	76-70-74-78—298	18998
	P Hurst	69-75-75-73—292	77351	26	D Dormann	72-76-79-72—299	12972
	C Johnson	72-70-76-74—292	77351	N Scranton	76-72-78-73—299	12972
7	S Croce	74-71-76-72—293	46737	M Estill	75-74-76-74—299	12972
	T Green	73-71-76-73—293	46737	H Dobson (Eng)	71-75-77-76—299	12972
	M McKay (Sco)	72-70-73-78—293	46737	L Rinker Graham	75-71-77-76—299	12972
10	T Johnson (Eng)	73-71-77-73—294	39015	31	K Williams	68-81-79-72—300	10093
11	L Davies (Eng)	68-75-78-74—295	34929	P Hammel	71-79-77-73—300	10093
	D Pepper	71-71-78-75—295	34929	B Daniel	77-69-78-76—300	10093
13	C Koch (Swe)	72-74-77-73—296	30684	D Eggeling	71-72-79-78—300	10093
	H Alfredsson (Swe)	75-75-73-73—296	30684	K Webb (Aus)	76-73-73-78—300	10093
15	H Stacy	76-68-82-71—297	25871	36	D Coe Jones	71-74-83-73—301	8897
	A Acker Macosko	74-74-76-73—297	25871	I Blais (am)	74-73-78-76—301	
	Dina Ammaccapane	75-70-78-74—297	25871	K Tschetter	75-72-77-77—301	8897
	B Burton	74-72-77-74—297	25871	B Corrie Kuehn (am)	70-72-80-79—301	
19	L Kane (Can)	74-72-82-70—298	18998	L Spalding	69-74-78-80—301	8897

Other players who made the cut: H Wadsworth, E Klein, N Bowen, A Sörenstam, B Mucha 302; P Bradley, P Rizzo, P Sinn 304; K Albers, M Redman, M Lovander, K Booth (am), A De Luca 305; H Kobayashi 306; ML de Lorenz 307; S Lowe 308; J Stephenson, TJ Myers 309; JJ Robertson (am) 310; C Kerr 311; K Parker 314; K Baue 316

1997 US Women's Open Championship

at *Pumpkin Ridge GC, Cornelius, OR* (6365 yds, Par 71) Prize money: $1,300,000

1	A Nicholas	70-66-67-71—274	$232500	21	K Kuehne	72-73-74-67—286	13800
2	N Lopez	69-68-69-69—275	137500	K Weiss	74-72-72-68—286	13800
3	K Robbins	68-69-74-66—277	86708	Se Ri Pak	68-74-75-69—286	13800
4	K Webb	73-72-65-68—278	60432	P Hurst	72-74-70-70—286	13800
5	S Croce	72-69-71-67—279	46159	L Bemvenuti	73-71-72-70—286	13800
	L Hackney	71-70-67-71—279	46159	C Pierce	71-71-73-71—286	13800
7	T Green	74-70-71-65—280	37542	27	C Matthew	76-69-70-72—287	10961
	M Redman	74-67-70-69—280	37542	28	S Smyers	71-71-75-71—288	9188
9	P Sheehan	72-71-71-68—282	28769	P Bradley	72-71-73-72—288	9188
	C Johnson	72-68-73-69—282	28769	K Marshall	72-71-73-72—288	9188
	D Coe-Jones	72-67-73-70—282	28769	B King	74-72-69-73—288	9188
	D Andrews	74-71-66-71—282	28769	J Pitcock	71-69-75-73—288	9188
	A Fukushima	71-71-69-71—282	28769	33	D Eggeling	71-74-76-70—291	7392
14	B Burton	73-72-69-70—284	21287	E Makings	72-73-75-71—291	7392
	D Pepper	72-70-72-70—284	21287	V Fergon	72-75-71-73—291	7392
	J Inkster	72-66-76-70—284	21287	M Morris	75-69-74-73—291	7392
	L Neumann	67-70-76-71—284	21287	R Jones	70-74-73-74—291	7392
	D Richard	68-70-73-73—284	21287	P Sinn	70-73-74-74—291	7392
19	T Johnson	69-74-71-71—285	17407	M McGann	73-70-73-75—291	7392
	K Williams	71-71-67-76—285	17407	C Nilsmark	76-70-69-76—291	7392

Other players who made the cut: A Dibos, J McGill 292; N Bowen, M McGeorge, M Mallon, J Lidback, E Wicoff 293; J Stephenson, H Alfredsson, L Kane 294; B Iverson, B Mucha 295; E Klein, J Gallagher-Smith, M Spencer-Devlin 296; T Hanson, S Redman, J Chuasiriporn (am) 297; D Dormann, N Harvey 298; M Edge, R Walton 299; B Corrie Kuehn (am) 302; P Dunlap 303.

1996 US Women's Open Championship

at Pine Needles Lodge & GC, Southern Pines, NC (6207 yds, Par 70)
Prize money: $1,200,000

1	A Sörenstam	70-67-69-66—272	$212500	19T	B Daniel	69-78-68-72—287	14374
2	K Tschetter	70-74-68-66—278	125000		W Ward	76-68-71-72—287	14374
3	P Bradley	74-70-67-69—280	60372		M Hirase	74-69-69-75—287	14374
	J Geddes	71-69-70-70—280	60372	25	M Hattori	74-71-74-69—288	10482
	B Burton	70-70-69-71—280	60372		K Williams	69-78-69-72—288	10482
6	L Davies	74-68-70-69—281	40077		B Iverson	73-71-71-73—288	10482
7	C Nilsmark	72-73-68-69—282	35995		N Harvey	72-71-69-76—288	10482
8	C Rarick	73-70-72-68—283	29584	29	K Weiss	74-72-73-70—289	8134
	L Neumann	74-69-70-70—283	29584		S Redman	73-73-71-72—289	8134
	V Skinner	74-68-71-70—283	29584		R Jones	71-70-76-72—289	8134
	T Green	72-70-69-72—283	29584		T Kerdyk	73-72-69-75—289	8134
12	J Lidback	70-76-68-70—284	24654		E Klein	71-69-73-76—289	8134
13	A Nicholas	74-70-74-67—285	23243	34	C Pierce	72-75-73-70—290	7294
14	P Sheehan	74-71-72-69—286	19664		J Inkster	74-71-71-74—290	7294
	S Croce	72-70-74-70—286	19664	36	G Graham	72-70-76-73—291	6479
	C Schreyer	74-70-70-72—286	19664		H Kobayashi	77-71-66-77—291	6479
	M Will	71-72-70-73—286	19664		S Steinhauer	72-73-71-75—291	6479
	M Redman	70-73-69-74—286	19664		K Saiki	73-70-73-75—291	6479
19	C Johnston-Forbes	72-75-71-69—287	14374		B Mucha	74-71-70-76—291	6479
	M Mallon	77-68-72-70—287	14374		C Kerr (am)	73-73-76-69—291	
	K Webb	74-73-68-72—287	14374				

Other players who made the cut: K Albers, C Mockett, J Piers, M McGeorge, M McGann, I Shiotani, J Pitcock 292; J McGill, K Golden, T Johnson 293; Dani. Ammaccapane, C Matthew 294; S Farwig, J Stephenson, M Bell, M Baena (am) 295; K Robbins, S Turner, C Johnson 296; E Dahllof, N Foust 300.

1995 US Women's Open Championship

at The Broadmoor, Colorado Springs, CO (6398 yds, Par 70) Prize money: $1,000,000

1	A Sörenstam	67-71-72-68—278	$175000	21	L Neumann	70-71-75-71—287	11154
2	M Malon	70-69-66-74—279	103500		A Okamoto	70-73-71-73—287	11154
3	B King	72-69-72-67—280	56238		A Ritzman	75-69-69-74—287	11154
	P Bradley	67-71-72-70—280	56238	24	C Hill	74-73-70-71—288	9287
5	L Lindley	70-68-74-69—281	35285		J Pitcock	72-73-72-71—288	9287
	R Jones	69-70-70-72—281	35285		L Davies	72-73-69-74—288	9287
7	T Green	68-70-75-69—282	28009		MB Zimmerman	72-72-68-76—288	9287
	D Coe-Jones	68-70-74-70—282	28009	28	A Fruhwirth	75-72-72-70—289	6841
	J Larsen	68-71-68-75—282	28009		B Burton	72-74-73-70—289	6841
10	M Morris	73-73-70-67—283	22190		N Lopez	72-73-74-70—289	6841
	P Sheehan	70-73-71-69—283	22190		M Hirase	70-74-73-72—289	6841
	V Skinner	68-72-72-71—283	22190		C Walker	69-73-75-72—289	6841
13	D Mochrie	73-70-66-72—284	18007		P Wright	72-73-71-73—289	6841
	K Tschetter	68-74-69-73—284	18007		D Miho Koyama	74-68-73-74—289	6841
	K Robbins	74-68-68-74—284	18007		J Bartholomew	67-71-77-74—289	6841
16	C Johnson	71-70-74-70—285	14454		G Graham	71-72-71-75—289	6841
	J Briles-Hinton	66-72-74-73—285	14454	37	S Strudwick	75-70-73-72—290	5218
	T Abitbol	67-72-72-74—285	14454		J Inkster	72-73-72-73—290	5218
	D Eggeling	70-68-73-74—285	14454		H Stacy	69-72-75-74—290	5218
20	M Redman	70-75-71-70—286	12449				

Other players who made the cut: H Alfredsson, J Dickinson, M McGann, A Dibos, C Hjalmarsson, J Geddes 291; K Peterson-Parker 292; L Kean, M McGeorge, P Hurst, A Nicholas 293; S Turner, J Stephenson, S Lebrun Ingram (am) 294; K Marshall, E Hayashida, V Goetze 295; K Albers, L Rinker-Graham, M Nause, K Noble, W Ward (am), K Booth (am) 296; A Alcott, E Crosby, A Benz, M Will, L Rittenhouse, M Estill, G Park (am) 297; S Rule, S Maynor, C Keggi 298; B Mucha, A Acker-Macosko 299; M Platt 303; A Munt 306.

1994 US Women's Open Championship

at Indianwood G&CC, Lake Orion, MI (6244 yds, Par 71)   Prize money: $850,000

1	P Sheehan	66-71-69-71—277	$155000	22T	S Maynor	73-70-76-69—288	9011
2	T Green	66-72-69-71—278	85000		L Walters	72-73-72-71—288	9011
3	L Neumann	69-72-71-69—281	47752		S Steinhauer	68-72-74-74—288	9011
4	T Abitbol	72-68-73-70—283	31132	25	K Tschetter	71-73-72-73—289	8089
	A Dibos	69-68-73-73—283	31132		D Richard	68-74-72-75—289	8089
6	M Mallon	70-72-73-69—284	21486		P Bradley	72-69-70-78—289	8089
	A Alcott	71-67-77-69—284	21486		P Wright	74-65-71-79—289	8089
	B King	69-71-72-72—284	21486	29	K Lunn	72-72-77-69—290	7371
9	K Robbins	71-72-70-72—285	16445		V Goetze	71-73-73-73—290	7371
	D Andrews	67-72-70-76—285	16445	31	D Eggeling	67-73-79-72—291	6929
	H Alfredsson	63-69-76-77—285	16445		J Carner	69-74-75-73—291	6929
12	L Merten	74-68-75-69—286	12805		A Read	68-72-76-75—291	6929
	D Mochrie	72-72-71-71—286	12805		C Semple		
	L Grimes	72-73-69-72—286	12805		Thompson (am)	66-75-76-74—291	
	J Dickinson	66-73-73-74—286	12805	35	C Walker	73-73-75-71—292	6048
	M Estill	69-68-75-74—286	12805		H Vaughn	74-70-76-72—292	6048
	L Davies	68-68-75-75—286	12805		K Williams	72-74-72-74—292	6048
18	M McGann	71-70-77-69—287	10202		J Geddes	73-72-73-74—292	6048
	J Inkster	75-72-69-71—287	10202		D Coe-Jones	73-73-71-75—292	6048
	B Daniel	69-74-71-73—287	10202		N Lopez	73-71-73-75—292	6048
	J Pitcock	74-72-67-74—287	10202		M McGeorge	69-73-75-75—292	6048

Other players who made the cut: V Fergon, M Berteotti, E Crosby, M Hirase, B Burton, S Little 293; N Bowen, A Okamoto 294; S Turner, D Dormann, E Klein (am) 295; J Stephenson, H Kobayashi, N Ramsbottom 296; C Pierce, T Fleming, A Ritzman, M Edge, S LeBrun Ingram (am) 297; T Kimura, L Kiggens 298; P Sinn, P Dunlap 300; J Sams 303; S McGuire 304

1993 US Women's Open Championship

at Crooked Stick GC, Carmel, IN (6311 yds, Par 72)   Prize money: $800,000

1	L Merten	71-71-70-68—280	$144000	17T	K Tschetter	73-71-69-75—288	9978
2	D Andrews	71-69-69-71—281	62431	21	M Mallon	73-72-69-75—289	9061
	H Alfredsson	68-70-69-74—281	62431	22	Dani Ammaccapane	73-74-73-70—290	8334
4	P Bradley	72-70-68-73—283	29249		A Finney	74-72-73-71—290	8334
	H Kobayashi	71-67-71-74—283	29249		M Redman	75-71-72-72—290	8334
6	P Sheehan	73-71-69-71—284	22379		D Coe-Jones	69-72-76-73—290	8334
7	B King	74-70-72-69—285	17525	26	L West	73-73-73-72—291	6894
	M McGann	70-66-78-71—285	17525		A Miller	73-68-78-72—291	6894
	N Lopez	70-71-70-74—285	17525		L Brower	73-73-72-73—291	6894
	A Okamoto	68-72-71-74—285	17525		J Larsen	76-71-70-74—291	6894
11	L Davies	73-71-69-73—286	13993		A Alcott	70-74-73-74—291	6894
	J Carner	71-69-73-73—286	13993		C Mah-Lyford	73-73-70-75—291	6894
13	T Barrett	73-73-70-71—287	11999		S Hamlin	74-68-73-76—291	6894
	C Johnson	71-75-69-72—287	11999		K Robbins	71-70-74-76—291	6894
	S Steinhauer	73-67-75-72—287	11999		Dina Ammaccapane	71-70-70-80—291	6894
	N Foust	71-71-71-74—287	11999		D Miho Koyama (am)	70-74-72-75—291	
17	D Mochrie	72-71-74-71—288	9978	36	J Dickinson	74-73-72-73—292	5907
	G Graham	72-73-70-73—288	9978		M Estill	74-70-75-73—292	5907
	B Mucha	75-69-71-73—288	9978		M Berteotti	72-75-70-75—292	5907

Other players who made the cut: Melissa McNamara, C Rarick, E Crosby, D Richard, J Inkster, B Burton 293; M McGeorge, P Wright, F Descampe, N Ramsbottom, L Rittenhouse 294; L Walters, J Geddes, V Goetze 295; A Read, B Daniel 296; B Bunkowsky 297; K Cathrein, J Anschutz 298; K Guadagnino, A Benz, S Ingram (am) 299; A Munt 301; L Neumann 303; J Myers 305.

1992 US Women's Open Championship

at Oakmont CC, Oakmont, PA (6312 yds, Par 71) Prize money: $700,000

1	P Sheehan*	69-72-70-69—280	$130000	16T	B King	74-73-73-75—295	8674
2	J Inkster	72-68-71-69—280	65000	22	A Ritzman	74-69-77-76—296	7327
P Sheehan won play-off 72–74					L Walters	74-72-72-78—296	7327
3	D Andrews	69-73-72-70—284	38830		A Benz	73-71-73-79—296	7327
4	M Mallon	73-72-72-70—287	28336	25	K Monaghan	75-72-75-75—297	6578
5	D Coe	71-71-74-72—288	22295		V Fergon	74-73-75-75—297	6578
6	D Mochrie	70-74-72-73—289	17472		R Jones	73-75-73-76—297	6578
	M McGann	72-73-70-74—289	17472		J Dickinson	75-72-74-76—297	6578
	G Graham	72-71-71-75—289	17472	29	A Fukushima	77-72-78-71—298	5643
9	J Geddes	73-70-78-70—291	13372		P Bradley	74-74-78-72—298	5643
	T Green	73-75-70-73—291	13372		M Figueras-Dotti	74-77-74-73—298	5643
	P Wright	70-69-76-76—291	13372		B Mucha	78-71-75-74—298	5643
12	M Edge	73-74-72-73—292	11731		T Barrett	73-75-75-75—298	5643
13	A Alcott	76-74-73-70—293	10887		T Kerdyk	69-77-76-76—298	5643
	H Alfredsson	71-79-72-71—293	10887		N Ramsbottom	69-75-77-77—298	5643
15	L Neumann	76-72-72-74—294	10111	36	S Steinhauer	74-75-76-74—299	4788
16	N Lopez	75-76-71-73—295	8674		M Spencer-Devlin	69-80-76-74—299	4788
	S Strudwick	75-73-73-74—295	8674		J Stephenson	75-71-78-75—299	4788
	M Estill	74-74-73-74—295	8674		S Little	74-74-74-77—299	4788
	Ok-Hee Ku	73-74-74-74—295	8674		K Albers	72-76-74-77—299	4788
	N Foust	73-74-74-74—295	8674		K Tschetter	70-74-76-79—299	4788

Other players who made the cut: S Turner, K Davies, K Skalicky, C Keggi, J Carner, D Eggeling 300; K Peterson-Parker, V Goetze (am), N Bowen, D Richard, M Murphy, M McNamara, C Johnson 301; K Robbins, L Depaulo 303; J Anschutz, L Rinker-Graham, B Bunkowsky 304; P Sinn, K Saiki 306; C Schreyer 307; A Sörenstam (am), S Hamlin, C Mackey 308; M Berteotti 313.

US WOMEN'S OPEN HISTORY

Year	Winner	Venue	By
1946	P Berg beat B Jamieson	Spokane	5 and 4

Changed to strokeplay

Year	Winner	Venue	Score
1947	B Jamieson	Greensboro	300
1948	B Zaharias	Atlantic City	300
1949	L Suggs	Maryland	291
1950	B Zaharias	Wichita	291
1951	B Rawls	Atlanta	294
1952	L Suggs	Bala, PA	284
1953	B Rawls*	Rochester, NY	302

* Won play-off after a tie with J Pung 71–77

1954	B Zaharias	Peabody, MA	291
1955	F Crocker	Wichita	299
1956	K Cornelius*	Duluth	302

* Won play-off after a tie with B McIntire (am) 75–82

1957	B Rawls	Mamaroneck	299
1958	M Wright	Bloomfield Hills, MI	290
1959	M Wright	Pittsburgh, PA	287
1960	B Rawls	Worchester, MA	292
1961	M Wright	Springfield, NJ	293
1962	M Lindstrom	Myrtle Beach	301
1963	M Mills	Kenwood	289
1964	M Wright*	San Diego	290

* Won play-off after a tie with R Jessen, Seattle 70–72

1965	C Mann	Northfield, NJ	290

US Women's Open Championship History *continued*

Year	Winner	Venue	Score
1966	S Spuzich	Hazeltine National, MN	297
1967	C Lacoste (am) (Fra)	Hot Springs, VA	294
1968	S Berning	Moselem Springs, PA	289
1969	D Caponi	Scenic-Hills	294
1970	D Caponi	Muskogee, OK	287
1971	J Gunderson-Carner	Erie, PA	288
1972	S Berning	Mamaroneck, NY	299
1973	S Berning	Rochester, NY	290
1974	S Haynie	La Grange, IL	295
1975	S Palmer	Northfield, NJ	295
1976	J Carner*	Springfield, PA	292

* Won play-off after a tie with S Palmer 76-78

Year	Winner	Venue	Score
1977	H Stacy	Hazeltine, MN	292
1978	H Stacy	Indianapolis	299
1979	J Britz	Brooklawn, CN	284
1980	A Alcott	Richland, TN	280
1981	P Bradley	La Grange, IL	279
1982	J Alex	Del Paso, Sacramento, CA	283
1983	J Stephenson (Aus)	Broken Arrow, OK	290
1984	H Stacy	Salem, MA	290
1985	K Baker	Baltusrol, NJ	280
1986	J Geddes*	NCR	287

* Won play-off after a tie with S Little 71-73

1987	L Davies (Eng)*	Plainfield	285

* Won play-off after a tie with J Carner and A Okamoto – Davies 71, Okamoto 73, Carner 74

Year	Winner	Venue	Score
1988	L Neumann (Swe)	Baltimore	277
1989	B King	Indianwood, MI	278
1990	B King	Atlanta Athletic Club, GA	284
1991	M Mallon	Colonial, TX	283
1992	P Sheehan*	Oakmont, PA	280

* Won play-off after a tie with J Inkster 72-74

1993	L Merton	Crooked Stick	280
1994	P Sheehan	Indianwood, MI	277
1995	A Sörenstam (Swe)	The Broadmore, CO	278
1996	A Sörenstam (Swe)	Pine Needles Lodge, NC	272
1997	A Nicholas (Eng)	Pumpkin Ridge, OR	274
1998	SR Pak (Kor)*	Blackwolf Run, WI	290

* Won play-off after a tie with J Chausiriporn (am). Both shot 73 then Pak 5, 3 to 5, 4

1999	J Inkster	Old Waverley, West Point, MS	272
2000	K Webb (Aus)	Merit Club, Libertyville, IL	282
2001	K Webb (Aus)	Pine Needles Lodge & GC, NC	273

McDonald's LPGA Championship

Players are of American nationality unless stated

2001 McDonald's LPGA Championship *at Du Pont CC, Wilmington,*
Delaware (6408 yds, Par 71) Prize money: $1,500,000. Final field comprised 142, of whom 71 (all professionals) made the half-way cut on 145 or better.

1	Karrie Webb (Aus)	67-64-70-69—270	$225000
2	Laura Diaz	67-71-66-68—272	139639
3	Maria Hjörth (Swe)	71-67-66-70—274	90577
	Wendy Ward	65-69-71-69—274	90577
5	Annika Sörenstam (Swe)	68-69-71-67—275	64157
6	Laura Davies (Eng)	67-68-70-71—276	48684
	Becky Iverson	66-73-67-70—276	48684
8	Mi Hyun Kim (Kor)	70-70-68-69—277	39250
9	Helen Alfredsson (Swe)	68-66-74-70—278	35476
10	Michele Redman	69-66-73-71—279	30245
	Maggie Will	68-74-67-70—279	30245
12	Rosie Jones	71-69-71-69—280	25013
	Lorie Kane (Can)	69-71-71-69—280	25013
	Liselotte Neumann (Swe)	69-72-68-71—280	25013
15	Wendy Doolan (Aus)	70-71-72-68—281	21239
	Juli Inkster	71-71-69-70—281	21239
17	Pat Hurst	72-68-72-70—282	16819
	Carin Koch (Swe)	69-73-71-69—282	16819
	Leta Lindley	71-71-70-70—282	16819
	Meg Mallon	71-74-67-70—282	16819
	Mhairi McKay (Sco)	68-72-70-72—282	16819
	Terry-Jo Myers	70-71-69-72—282	16819
	Dottie Pepper	71-72-71-68—282	16819
	Kelly Robbins	69-74-71-68—282	16819
	Rachel Teske (Aus)	68-72-70-72—282	16819
26	Heather Daly-Donofrio	75-68-71-69—283	13162
	Beth Daniel	71-71-70-71—283	13162
	Akiko Fukushima (Jpn)	66-72-73-72—283	13162
	Nancy Scranton	73-68-70-72—283	13162
30	Dawn Coe-Jones	72-69-71-72—284	11603
	Catriona Matthew (Sco)	71-72-72-69—284	1 603
	Grace Park (Kor)	71 72-71-70—284	11633
33	Danielle Ammaccapane	69-71-71-74—285	10257
	Jane Crafter (Aus)	71-71-69-74—285	10257
	Patricia Meunier-Lebouc (Fra)	70-73-71-71—285	10257
	Sherri Turner	71-72-72-70—285	10257
37	Brandie Burton	69-74-68-75—286	9125
	Hee Won Han (Kor)	70-75-72-69—286	9125
39	Kathryn Marshall (Sco)	71-73-71-72—287	8011
	Se Ri Pak (Kor)	71-73-69-74—287	8011
	Deb Richard	72-71-73-71—287	8011
	Kris Tschetter	71-74-69-73—287	8011
43	Alicia Dibos	72-73-71-72—288	6747
	Vicki Goetze-Ackerman	73-68-70-77—288	6747
	Gloria Park (Kor)	72-69-76-71—288	6747
	Kristal Parker	69-72-73-74—288	6747
47	Suzy Green	75-69-71-74—289	5690

2001 McDonald's LPGA Championship *continued*

47T	Jenny Lidback (Per)	72-72-71-74—289	5690
	Marnie McGuire	74-69-76-70—289	5690
50	Mitzi Edge	69-71-77-73—290	4746
	Jackie Gallagher-Smith	71-74-71-74—290	4746
	Emilee Klein	71-69-75-75—290	4746
	Sara Sanders	73-71-72-74—290	4746
54	Amy Alcott	70-75-75-71—291	3511
	Donna Andrews	72-71-73-75—291	3511
	Marisa Baena (Col)	71-73-73-74—291	3511
	Susan Ginter	73-70-75-73—291	3511
	Betsy King	72-70-70-79—291	3511
	Charlotta Sörenstam (Swe)	72-72-74-73—291	3511
	Leslie Spalding	71-72-75-73—291	3511
61	Dorothy Delasin	73-72-74-73—292	2671
	Alison Nicholas (Eng)	72-71-75-74—292	2671
63	Jean Bartholomew	70-71-73-79—293	2369
	Gail Graham (Can)	72-73-75-73—293	2369
	Joanne Morley (Eng)	70-73-75-75—293	2369
66	Janice Moodie (Sco)	70-74-72-78—294	2142
	Barb Mucha	71-71-71-81—294	2142
	Joan Pitcock	70-73-73-78—294	2142
69	Annette DeLuca	70-74-76-76—296	1992
70	Michelle McGann	70-75-81-73—299	1917
71	Cathy Gerring	72-73-80-76—301	1840

The following players missed the cut:

72	Sherri Steinhauer	75-71—146
	Lauri Brower	75-71—146
	Jeong Jang	74-72—146
	Vickie Odegard	73-73—146
	AJ Eathorne (Can)	73-73—146
	Heather Bowie	73-73—146
	Jennifer Feldott	73-73—146
	Helen Dobson (Eng)	73-73—146
	Shani Waugh (Aus)	72-74—146
	Dina Ammaccapane	71-75—146
	Diann D'Alessio	69-77—146
83	Lisa Kiggens	79-68—147
	Dodie Mazzuca	76-71—147
	Amy Fruhwirth	75-72—147
	Pamela Kerrigan	75-72—147
	Fiona Pike	74-73—147
	Jane Geddes	74-73—147
	Jill McGill	73-74—147
	Tammie Green	73-74—147
	Dale Eggeling	73-74—147
	Tamie Durdin (Aus)	72-75—147
	Kristi Albers	72-75—147
	Tina Barrett	72-75—147
	Cristie Kerr	70-77—147
	Silvia Cavalleri (Ita)	70-77—147

97	Beth Bader	77-71—148
	Caroline McMillan	77-71—148
	Mardi Lunn (Aus)	76-72—148
	Tracy Hanson	75-73—148
	Penny Hammel	74-74—148
	Michelle Estill	73-75—148
	Audra Burks	73-75—148
	Cathy Johnston Forbes	72-76—148
	Cindy Flom	72-76—148
	Michelle Ellis (Aus)	71-77—148
	Kelli Kuehne	71-77—148
	Sophie Gustafson (Swe)	71-77—148
	Laurel Kean	71-77—148
110	Denise Killeen	76-73—149
	Susie Redman	74-75—149
	Hiromi Kobayashi (Jpn)	74-75—149
	Kim Saiki	72-77—149
	Angela Stanford	71-78—149
	Marcy Newton	70-79—149
116	Kristin Lindstrom	76-74—150
	Cindy Figg Currier	76-74—150
	Suzanne Strudwick (Eng)	76-74—150

116T	Karen Weiss	74-76—150
	Val Skinner	74-76—150
	Becky Morgan (Wal)	71-79—150
122	Yu Ping Lin (Twn)	78-73—151
	Moira Dunn	76-75—151
124	Kate Golden	75-77—152
	Pearl Sinn (Kor)	75-77—152
	Luciana Bemvenuti (Bra)	74-78—152
127	Nancy Lopez	79-74—153
128	Ashli Bunch	77-77—154
	Nam Kyong Ha (Kor)	77-77—154
130	C McCurdy	78-77—155
	Kellee Booth	76-79—155
	Kim Williams	76-79—155
133	Vicki Fergon	81-75—156
	Jan Stephenson (Aus)	77-79—156
135	Connie Baker	80-77—157
	Peggy Gustafson	78-79—157
137	Jennifer Rosales (Phi)	76-82—158
138	Heather Zakhar	83-76—159
	L Eller	81-78—159
140	Diane Daugherty	79-81—160
141	Sally Litte (RSA)	80-82—162
142	Jennie Hinkle	83-81—164

2000 McDonald's LPGA Championship

at Du Pont CC, Wilmington, Delaware (6376 yds, Par 71) Prize money: $1,400,000

1	Juli Inkster*	72-69-65-75—281	$210000	23T	Betsy King	68-78-67-74—287	13304
Winner after second play-off hole					Janice Moodie (Sco)	72-73-71-71—287	13304
2	Stefania Croce (Ita)	72-67-74-68—281	130330		Alison Nicholas (Eng)	72-72-71-72—287	13304
3	Se Ri Pak (Kor)	73-69-69-71—282	76319		Dottie Pepper	71-73-69-74—287	13304
	Nancy Scranton	72-70-67-73—282	76319	28	Rosie Jones	70-74-74-70—288	11191
	Wendy Ward	69-69-68-76—282	76319		Jenny Lidback (Per)	75-71-71-71—288	11191
6	Heather Bowie	74-70-70-69—283	42503		Gloria Park (Kor)	68-75-75-70—288	11191
	Jane Crafter (Aus)	72-69-69-73—283	42503		Karen Weiss	73-71-70-74—288	11191
	Laura Davies (Eng)	70-66-75-72—283	42503		Barb Whitehead	73-72-70-73—288	11191
9	Akiko Fukushima (Jpn)	71-72-71-70—284	29839	33	Beth Daniel	72-72-70-75—289	9698
	Jan Stephenson (Aus)	70-69-69-76—284	29839		Emilee Klein	74-71-71-73—289	9698
	Karrie Webb (Aus)	72-70-69-73—284	29839		Kim Saiki	77-69-71-72—289	9698
12	Amy Fruhwirth	74-71-70-70—285	21885	36	Jean Bartholomew	71-71-74-74—290	8464
	Mi Hyun Kim (Kor)	70-73-70-72—285	21885		Alicia Dibos (Per)	72-74-74-70—290	8464
	Leta Lindley	71-73-71-70—285	21885		Cindy McCurdy	73-74-71-72—290	8464
	Kelly Robbins	72-72-73-68—285	21885		Maggie Will	74-72-67-77—290	8464
	Annika Sörenstam (Swe)	70-73-70-72—285	21885	40	Sophie Gustafson		
17	Dawn Coe-Jones	71-73-72-70—286	16602		(Swe)	76-70-69-76—291	6820
	Wendy Doolan (Aus)	69-71-71-75—286	16602		Carin Koch (Swe)	74-70-73-74—291	6820
	Jane Geddes	66-74-73-73—286	16602		Barb Mucha	72-72-70-77—291	6820
	Pat Hurst	71-70-71-74—286	16602		Laura Philo	72-74-73-72—291	6820
	Meg Mallon	72-73-69-72—286	16602		Jennifer Rosales (Phi)	71-73-74-73—291	6820
	Michele Redman	70-70-70-76—286	16602		Sherri Steinhauer	70-75-68-78—291	6820
23	Pat Bradley	68-76-67-76—287	13304				

Other players who made the cut: Cindy Flom, Kathryn Marshall (Sco), Leigh Ann Mills, Patty Sheehan, Kris Tschetter, Mary Beth Zimmerman 292; Cindy Figg-Currier, Yu Ping Lin (Tre), 293; Jill McGill, Joanne Morley (Eng) 293; Marisa Baena (Col), AJ Eathorne (Can), Vicki Goetze-Ackerman, Kate Golden, Tracy Hanson, Catrin Nilsmark (Swe) 294; Ashli Bunch, Val Skinner, Leslie Spalding 295; Pamela Kerrigan, Nancy Lopez, Shani Waugh (Aus) 296; Danielle Ammaccapane, Debbi Koyama (Jpn) 298; Moira Dunn 299; Carmen Hajjar 300; Julie Piers 301; Dina Ammaccapane 305

1999 McDonald's LPGA Championship

at Du Pont CC, Wilmington, Delaware (6376 yds, Par 71) Prize money: $1,400,000

1	J Inkster	68-66-69-65—268	$210000	22	L Kiggens	68-74-69-68—279	14063
2	L Neumann (Swe)	67-67-70-68—272	130330		A Fukushima (Jpn)	70-70-69-70—279	14063
3	M Lunn (Aus)	68-74-65-66—273	84538		V Odegard	69-70-70-70—279	14063
	N Scranton	69-68-66-70—273	84538		A Finney	67-69-71-72—279	14063
5	R Jones	64-72-68-70—274	54596	26	P Sinn	71-71-70-68—280	11087
	C Kerr	70-64-69-71—274	54596		Mi Hyun Kim (Kor)	70-70-71-69—280	11087
7	E Klein	72-68-67-68—275	35224		V Fergon	67-73-70-70—280	11087
	J McGill	70-69-68-68—275	35224		J Crafter	70-69-71-70—280	11087
	L Davies (Eng)	65-71-71-68—275	35224		L Lindley	70-72-67-71—280	11087
	Se Ri Pak (Kor)	68-69-67-71—275	35224		B Mucha	70-70-69-71—280	11087
11	M Hirase	70-73-68-65—276	23487		K Kuehne	68-67-72-73—280	11087
	S Sanders	70-68-68-70—276	23487		A Nicholas (Eng)	67-73-66-74—280	11087
	T Green	68-70-68-70—276	23487		T Johnson (Eng)	67-69-70-74—280	11087
	J Lidback	67-67-72-70—276	23487		L Kane	70-66-70-74—280	11087
	M Mallon	70-71-63-72—276	23487	36	T Tombs	71-71-69-70—281	8164
16	A Sörenstam (Swe)	73-68-68-68—277	18415		H Stacy	73-68-70-70—281	8164
	S Redman	70-68-70-69—277	18415		C Koch	68-73-70-70—281	8164
	J Stephenson	69-69-69-70—277	18415		N Bowen	70-72-68-71—281	8164
19	D Pepper	71-72-68-67—278	16301		S Waugh	70-69-71-71—281	8164
	S Steinhauer	74-69-65-70—278	16301		C Figg-Currier	71-70-67-73—281	8164
	H Kobayashi (Jpn)	70-67-71-70—278	16301				

Other players who made the cut: Dana Dormann, W Doolan, J Moodie (Sco), R Hetherington (Aus), M Spencer-Devlin 282; C Flom, M Nause, B Iverson, M McGann, D Eggeling, S Croce (Ita), T Barrett 283; K Coats, K Tschetter, P Hammel, C Nilsmark (Swe), K Saiki, D Richard, S Little, C Johnson, S Gustafson (Swe) 284; M Hjörth (Swe), M Will 285; PBradley 286; K Robbins 287; D Barnard 288; M McGeorge 289; B King, D Killeen 290; K Lunn (Aus) 299

1998 McDonald's LPGA Championship

at Du Pont CC, Wilmington, Delaware (6386 yds, Par 71)   Prize money: $1,300,000

1	Se Ri Pak	65-68-72-68—273	$195000	21T	P Hurst	71-73-68-72—284	13558
2	D Andrews	71-67-69-69—276	104666		J Lidback	70-73-68-73—284	13558
	L Hackney	70-66-69-71—276	104666	25	D Dormann	71-74-74-66—285	11579
4	K Webb	71-73-67-66—277	62145		M McGann	68-74-73-70—285	11579
	W Ward	71-67-69-70—277	62145		N Scranton	73-73-67-72—285	11579
6	M Mallon	71-69-68-70—278	39467		S Redman	68-76-69-72—285	11579
	C Johnson	69-71-67-71—278	39467		D Eggeling	68-69-74-74—285	11579
	E Klein	72-67-68-71—278	39467	30	W Doolan	73-72-71-70—286	9365
9	C Nilsmark	69-73-70-67—279	29110		V Odegard	69-74-73-70—286	9365
	K Robbins	69-71-68-71—279	29110		A Sörenstam	73-71-71-71—286	9365
11	J Pitcock	69-75-70-66—280	23180		R Hetherington	71-71-72-72—286	9365
	A DeLuca	70-70-71-69—280	23180		L Kane	72-73-68-73—286	9365
	J Geddes	69-69-70-72—280	23180		K Tschetter	71-71-71-73—286	9365
14	T Green	72-68-70-71—281	19691		J Morley	73-69-69-75—286	9365
	L Walters	66-69-73-73—281	19691	37	S Steinhauer	73-73-71-70—287	7093
16	M Hjörth	71-70-73-68—282	17402		B King	71-73-72-71—287	7093
	J Inkster	70-71-69-72—282	17402		M Spencer-Devlin	74-71-70-72—287	7093
18	M Redman	70-71-74-68—283	15767		L Neumann	73-69-73-72—287	7093
	C Koch	71-73-69-70—283	15767		M Halpin	73-73-68-73—287	7093
	C Johnston-Forbes	71-70-70-72—283	15767		M Estill	72-70-72-73—287	7093
21	J Moodie	75-69-73-67—284	13558		C Matthew	74-70-68-75—287	7093
	H Dobson	76-70-70-68—284	13558				

Other players who made the cut: D Coe-Jones, S Little, N Lopez, L Davies, C McCurdy, M Figueras-Dotti, P Bradley 288; C Figg-Currier, K Saiki, B Mucha, D Barnard, H Alfredsson 289; E Dahllof, C Sörenstam 290; C McMillan, K Albers, K Monaghan, B Daniel, M Berteotti 291; H Stacy, M Dobek, P Hammel 292; G Graham, T Hanson 293; M McGeorge, B Burton 295; J Gallagher-Smith, M Morris 297; H Daly-Donofrio 298

1997 McDonald's LPGA Championship

at Du Pont CC, Wilmington, Delaware (6386 yds, Par 71)   Prize money: $1,200,000

1	C Johnson*	68-73-69-71—281	$180000	16T	K Saiki	68-75-69-77—289	15397
2	L Lindley	72-69-69-71—281	111711	20	A Fruhwirth	72-75-73-70—290	13586
*Johnson won play-off at second extra hole					J Wyatt	73-75-71-71—290	13586
3	A Sörenstam	70-73-72-67—282	81519	22	M Lunn	72-77-75-67—291	12176
4	L Davies	67-75-74-68—284	57365		M Mallon	72-76-73-70—291	12176
	S Steinhauer	68-71-73-72—284	57365		T Barrett	69-77-75-70—291	12176
6	G Graham	69-79-71-66—285	38947	25	D Reid	74-75-73-70—292	10446
	D Coe-Jones	70-75-71-69—285	38947		W Ward	72-78-71-71—292	10446
8	T Johnson	70-73-72-71—286	31400		C Matthew	71-75-75-71—292	10446
9	K Webb	71-79-70-67—287	26871		M McGeorge	73-74-73-72—292	10446
	B Mucha	68-73-72-74—287	26871		A Dibos	71-76-73-72—292	10446
11	K Robbins	73-74-74-67—288	20047		C Figg-Currier	71-76-72-73—292	10446
	P Bradley	70-75-76-67—288	20047	31	S Strudwick	72-74-77-70—293	8423
	B Burton	71-73-76-68—288	20047		M McGann	74-76-71-72—293	8423
	D Dormann	70-73-75-70—288	20047		H Dobson	78-72-69-74—293	8423
	J Dickinson	75-72-68-73—288	20047		K Weiss	73-75-71-74—293	8423
16	W Doolan	74-72-74-69—289	15397		C Walker	72-74-73-74—293	8423
	L Kane	73-74-71-71—289	15397		N Bowen	73-72-73-75—293	8423
	D Andrews	73-71-73-72—289	15397				

Other players who made the cut: N Lopez, K Monaghan, D Richard, N Ramsbottom, D Pepper, M Edge, M Estill, K Parker-Gregory, B Whitehead 294; A Miller, K Albers, A Finney, K Marshall, J Lidback, M Morris, J Pitcock 295; B King, H Stacy, C Hj Koch, M Berteotti, S Redman, J Inkster 296; MB Zimmerman 297; J McGill, V Goetze-Ackerman, H Kobayashi, J Crafter, R Hetherington, K Peterson-Parker, N Scranton 298; C Mockett, H Alfredsson, Danielle Ammaccapane, J Geddes, D Killeen, A Alcott, J Gallagher-Smith, E Klein 299; M Hirase, M Spencer-Devlin, C Johnston-Forbes, A-M Palli, P Hurst 300; L Walters, V Skinner 301; Vickie Odegard 302.

1996 McDonald's LPGA Championship

at Du Pont CC, Wilmington, Delaware (6386 yds, Par 71)   Prize money: $1,200,000

1	L Davies	72-71-70—213	$180000	18T	S Steinhauer	74-71-74—219	13080
2	J Piers	72-72-70—214	111711		D Richard	74-70-75—219	13080
3	P Hammel	73-72-70—215	72461		A Benz	73-71-75—219	13080
	J Crafter	75-68-72—215	72461		N Lopez	70-73-76—219	13080
5	J Dickinson	71-74-71—216	37800		K Robbins	69-71-79—219	13080
	J Inkster	70-73-73—216	37800	26	J McGill	76-70-74—220	9744
	S Furlong	70-73-73—216	37800		S Redman	74-72-74—220	9744
	V Skinner	73-69-74—216	37800		D Pepper	70-76-74—220	9744
	H Kobayashi	71-70-75—216	37800		T-J Myers	74-71-75—220	9744
10	M Dobek	72-75-70—217	22342		J Geddes	71-74-75—220	9744
	P Sheehan	72-74-71—217	22342		C Pierce	75-69-76—220	9744
10T	M Mallon	69-75-73—217	22342	26T	M McGeorge	74-70-76—220	9744
	K Albers	72-71-74—217	22342		B Daniel	72-72-76—220	9744
14	L Kiggens	75-70-73—218	17058	34	B Mucha	76-72-73—221	7366
	B King	72-72-74—218	17058		P Hurst	76-72-73—221	7366
	J Briles-Hinton	73-69-76—218	17058		T Johnson	75-73-73—221	7366
	A Sörenstam	69-73-76—218	17058		C Figg-Currier	73-74-74—221	7366
18	CH Koch	73-74-72—219	13080		L Grimes	74-70-77—221	7366
	K Tschetter	75-71-73—219	13080		E Dahllof	72-72-77—221	7366
	K Marshall	73-73-73—219	13080		R Hood	71-73-77—221	7366

Other players who made the cut: T Kerdyk, A Dibos, M Redman, K Monaghan, K Webb, M McGann, M Hirase, L Neumann, S Croce, T Hanson 222; D Dormann, P Bradley, G Graham, MB Zimmerman, B Whitehead, A Nicholas, M Nause 223; M Lunn, E Klein, S Maynor, S Strudwick, C Johnson 224; L West, D Andrews, B Iverson, B Burton, T Green, K Parker-Gregory 225; K Williams, R Jones, M Dunn 226; M Will, M Berteotti 227; M Morris, C Johnston-Forbes 228; A-M Palli, V Goetze 229; M Spencer-Devlin 231; M Estill 232.

1995 McDonald's LPGA Championship

at Du Pont CC, Wilmington, Delaware (6386 yds, Par 71)   Prize money: $1,200,000

1	K Robbins	66-68-72-68—274	$180000	18T	S Redman	73-71-71-71—286	13080
2	L Davies	68-68-69-70—275	111711		L Garbacz	71-71-72-72—286	13080
3	J Larsen	71-68-70-71—280	65416		K Tschetter	73-69-71-73—286	13080
	M Morris	67-71-70-72—280	65416		N Lopez	73-71-68-74—286	13080
	P Sheehan	67-68-72-73—280	65416		C Walker	70-70-72-74—286	13080
6	B Thomas	70-66-73-72—281	38947		A Finney	71-68-70-77—286	13080
	D Mochrie	67-70-71-73—281	38947	26	S Turner	73-74-70-70—287	10626
8	P Bradley	71-70-70-71—282	29890		K Guadagnino	72-73-68-74—287	10626
	T Green	69-72-70-71—282	29890		N Bowen	71-71-71-74—287	10626
10	A Sörenstam	71-71-72-69—283	25362	29	K Williams	72-71-75-70—288	9374
11	K Albers	71-71-72-70—284	20681		M Redman	75-68-72-73—288	9374
	D Eggeling	72-72-68-72—284	20681		J Geddes	71-71-71-75—288	9374
	J Pitcock	75-66-71-72—284	20681		M Estill	72-73-67-76—288	9374
	B King	69-71-72-72—284	20681	33	P Hurst	74-72-74-69—289	7970
15	L Kiggens	70-70-75-70—285	16504		K Peterson-Parker	74-73-71-71—289	7970
	M Mallon	70-72-71-72—285	16504		V Fergon	73-71-74-71—289	7970
	B Mucha	71-69-71-74—285	16504		E Gibson	73-69-74-73—289	7970
18	B Daniel	71-73-72-70—286	13080		R Jones	72-71-68-78—289	7970
	N Scranton	71-75-69-71—286	13080				

Other players who made the cut: J Carner, S Little, J Lidback, R Heiken, L Neumann, H Alfredsson, C Johnson, B Iverson, T Johnson 290; D Coe-Jones, A Nicholas, L Walters, T Kerdyk, J Inkster, M Edge, K Noble, V Skinner 291; A Ritzman, M Berteotti, J Dickinson, C Hill, J Crafter, M Figueras-Dotti 292; C Pierce, M McGeorge, C Johnston-Forbes, H Dobson, MB Zimmerman 293; D Massey, V Goetze, B Scherbak, C Mockett, A Benz 294; C Rarick 295; E Klein, T Hanson 296; J Briles-Hinton 297; E Dahllof 298; S Strudwick 299; L Tatum 300.

1994 McDonald's LPGA Championship

at Du Pont CC, Wilmington, Delaware (6386 yds, Par 71) Prize money: $1,100,000

1	L Davies	70-72-69-68—279	$165000	17T	D Andrews	73-76-69-71—289	12257
2	A Ritzman	68-73-71-70—282	102402		B King	74-73-71-71—289	12257
3	E Crosby	76-71-69-67—283	54660		M McGeorge	75-71-70-73—289	12257
	P Bradley	73-73-70-67—283	54660		K Monaghan	72-72-72-73—289	12257
	H Kobayashi	72-73-71-67—283	54660		M Lunn	70-75-70-74—289	12257
	L Neumann	74-73-67-69—283	54660		R Walton	70-70-75-74—289	12257
7	S Steinhauer	75-70-72-68—285	27676	26	J Carner	73-75-74-68—290	9907
	A Alcott	71-75-70-69—285	27676		M McGann	70-76-75-69—290	9907
	B Daniel	72-74-68-71—285	27676	28	J Lidback	73-73-74-71—291	8460
	P Sheehan	72-68-72-73—285	27676		M Berteotti	75-70-75-71—291	8460
11	D Mochrie	68-78-70-70—286	20203		G Graham	73-71-76-71—291	8460
	M Mallon	71-71-69-75—286	20203		B Burton	76-70-73-72—291	8460
13	V Skinner	74-69-72-72—287	18266		A Okamoto	74-72-73-72—291	8460
14	J Inkster	69-76-74-69—288	16051		J Wyatt	72-74-73-72—291	8460
	D Dormann	71-76-71-70—288	16051		T Barrett	73-77-68-73—291	8460
	C Johnson	70-74-73-71—288	16051	35	D Eggeling	76-74-71-71—292	6891
17	B Mucha	73-74-75-67—289	12257		P Dunlap	71-74-75-72—292	6891
	N Bowen	73-75-73-68—289	12257		A Arruti	75-73-71-73—292	6891
	T Green	71-76-74-68—289	12257		H Alfredsson	73-74-71-74—292	6891

Other players who made the cut: J Dickinson, C Schreyer, M Spencer-Devlin, L Kiggens, K Guadagnino, L West 293; H Stacy 294; B Bunkowsky, L Merten, MB Zimmerman 295; M Morris, N Daghe, N Scranton, N Foust, K Tschetter 296; A Finney, L Walters, C Figg-Currier 297; P Sinn, K Noble, P Allen, M Estill, M Figueras-Dotti, J Anschutz 298; J Stephenson, A Benz, C Rarick 299; J Larsen, N Ramsbottom, C Johnston-Forbes, K Saiki, A Miller, C Keggi, M Edge 300; S Hamlin, N Harvey, V Goetze, M Will 301; D Coe-Jones 303; K Marshall 304; L Rinker-Graham,

1993 McDonald's LPGA Championship

at Du Pont CC, Wilmington, Delaware (6398 yds, Par 71) Prize money: $900,000

1	L Davies	66-69-73-69—277	$135000	20T	J Inkster	69-74-72-70—285	9747
2	S Steinhauer	69-72-70-67—278	83783		B Burton	74-74-66-71—285	9747
3	H Alfredsson	74-68-70-67—279	54346		J Carner	70-73-69-73—285	9747
	L Merten	68-69-72-70—279	54346	24	P Wright	75-73-70-68—286	8106
5	H Kobayashi	72-71-69-68—280	38494		R Hood	69-71-76-70—286	8106
6	P Bradley	73-70-71-67—281	25814		D Mochrie	70-71-74-71—286	8106
	MB Zimmerman	72-74-65-70—281	25814		D Lofland-Dormann	70-70-72-74—286	8106
	P Sheehan	68-73-70-70—281	25814		R Walton	74-65-72-75—286	8106
	G Graham	66-69-74-72—281	25814		A Dibos	70-71-69-76—286	8106
10	C Johnson	71-74-71-66—282	16756	30	P Sinn	72-75-70-70—287	6781
	N Lopez	73-69-70-70—282	16756		B Thomas	72-73-71-71—287	6781
	V Skinner	70-72-72-70—282	16756		L Kean	73-69-73-72—287	6781
	H Stacy	73-67-70-72—282	16756		M Berteotti	72-67-76-72—287	6781
14	B King	71-67-78-67—283	12793	34	D Coe-Jones	80-68-71-69—288	6090
	A Nicholas	73-74-67-69—283	12793		C Pierce	71-72-73-72—288	6090
	D Eggeling	70-76-68-69—283	12793	36	K Peterson-Parker	74-73-74-68—289	5411
	A Fukushima	72-69-68-74—283	12793		K Robbins	74-71-72-72—289	5411
18	J Dickinson	75-71-71-67—284	11095		L Neumann	71-75-69-74—289	5411
	T Barrett	73-72-71-68—284	11095		L Garbacz	73-69-72-75—289	5411
20	L Walters	69-73-76-67—285	9747				

Other players who made the cut: M Will, B Daniel, N Scranton, M Mallon, D Wilkins 290; N Ramsbottom, M Spencer-Devlin, J Larsen, A Alcott, M Murphy, E Crosby, E Gibson, J Crafter 291; K Albers, D Baldwin, J Briles-Hinton, M McGeorge, T Kerdyk, D Massey 292; T Green, P Rizzo, Dina Ammaccapane, J Pitcock, T-J Myers, C Figg-Currier, K Tschetter, P Dunlap, L Rinker-Graham 293; S Hamlin, Dani Ammaccapane, K Williams, S Turner 294; M Redman, J Wyatt, T Johnson 295; D Andrews, B Mucha, C Semple Thompson (am)

1992 McDonald's LPGA Championship

at Du Pont CC, Wilmington, Delaware (6398 yds, Par 71) Prize money: $750,000
Rain reduced event to 54 holes

1	A Okamoto	67-69-69—205	$112500	17T	J Anschutz	72-72-69—213	7928
2	P Bradley	72-70-66—208	53465		D Andrews	72-72-69—213	7928
	D Richard	68-70-70—208	53465		E Gibson	73-70-70—213	7928
	B Burton	73-63-72—208	53465		S Turner	72-70-71—213	7928
5	J Dickinson	70-68-71—209	32079		D McHaffie	72-70-71—213	7928
6	J Geddes	77-65-68—210	24342		N White	71-71-71—213	7928
	D Mochrie	71-70-69—210	24342		F Descampe	75-66-72—213	7928
8	M McGann	74-69-68—211	16888		D Lasker	72-69-72—213	7928
	C Walker	72-70-69—211	16888		A Benz	69-71-73—213	7928
	N Scranton	70-72-69—211	16888	29	J Inkster	75-71-68—214	5371
	N Lopez	67-73-71—211	16888		Ok-Hee Ku	75-69-70—214	5371
12	H Alfredsson	72-71-69—212	11699		J Carner	73-71-70—214	5371
	K Shipman	71-72-69—212	11699		E Crosby	72-71-71—214	5371
	Dani. Ammaccapane	72-70-70—212	11699		T Green	71-72-71—214	5371
	J Crafter	72-69-71—212	11699		M Mackall	74-68-72—214	5371
	C Keggi	70-70-72—212	11699		S McGuire	72-69-73—214	5371
17	M Mallon	74-70-69—213	7928		B Daniel	72-69-73—214	5371
	S Steinhauer	73-71-69—213	7928		M Redman	71-69-74—214	5371
	P Sheehan	72-72-69—213	7928				

Other players who made the cut: M Nause, H Stacy, B King, T Barrett, L Neumann 215; T Kerdyk, N Ramsbottom, M Berteotti, L Davies, K Peterson-Parker 216; D Eggeling, K Robbins, B Pearson, P Sinn, J Briles-Hinton, G Hull, A Miller, L Rinker-Graham, V Fergon, S Hamlin, V Skinner 217; P Hammel, M Edge, B Mucha, P Wright, J Thobois, S Little, K Albers, J Lidback 218; S Palmer, R Hood, K Davies 219; K Postlewait, M Spencer-Devlin, G Graham 221; A Finney 222; A Alcott, A Ritzman, R Walton, M McGeorge 223; K Rogerson 225; L Baugh 230.

LPGA CHAMPIONSHIP HISTORY

The Championship was known simply as the LPGA Championship from its inauguration in 1955 until 1987. It was sponsored by Mazda from 1988 until 1993 when the sponsorship was taken over by McDonald's.

1955	B Hanson	Orchard Ridge	4 and 3
1956	M Hagg	Forest Lake	291
(After a tie with P Berg)			
1957	L Suggs	Churchill Valley	285
1958	M Wright	Churchill CC	288
1959	B Rawls	Churchill CC	288
1960	M Wright	French Lick	292
1961	M Wright	Stardust	287
1962	J Kimball	Stardust	282
1963	M Wright	Stardust	294
1964	M Mills	Stardust	278
1965	S Haynie	Stardust	279
1966	G Ehret	Stardust	282
1967	K Whitworth	Pleasant Valley	284
1968	S Post	Pleasant Valley	294
(After a tie with K Whitworth)			
1969	B Rawls	Concord	293
1970	S Englehorn	Pleasant Valley	285
(After a tie with K Whitworth)			
1971	K Whitworth	Pleasant Valley	288
1972	K Ahern	Pleasant Valley	293
1973	M Mills	Pleasant Valley	288

LPGA Championship History *continued*

1974	S Haynie	Pleasant Valley	288
1975	K Whitworth	Pine Ridge	288
1976	B Burfeindt	Pine Ridge	287
1977	C Higuchi (Jpn)	Bay Tree	279
1978	N Lopez	Kings Island	275
1979	D Caponi	Kings Island	279
1980	S Little (SA)	Kings Island	285
1981	D Caponi	Kings Island	280
1982	J Stephenson (Aus)	Kings Island	279
1983	P Sheehan	Kings Island	279
1984	P Sheehan	Kings Island	272
1985	N Lopez	Kings Island	273
1986	P Bradley	Kings Island	277
1987	J Geddes	Kings Island	275
1988	S Turner	Kings Island	281
1989	N Lopez	King's Island	274
1990	B Daniel	Bethesda	280
1991	M Mallon	Bethesda	274
1992	B King	Bethesda	267
1993	P Sheehan	Bethesda	275
1994	L Davies (Eng)	Wilmington, Delaware	275
1995	K Robbins	Wilmington, Delaware	274
1996	L Davies (Eng)	Wilmington, Delaware	213
(Reduced to 54 holes – bad weather)			
1997	C Johnson	Wilmington, Delaware	281
1998	Se Ri Pak (Kor)	Wilmington, Delaware	273
1999	J Inkster	Wilmington, Delaware	268
2000	J Inkster	Wilmington, Delaware	281
(After a tie with Stefania Croce (Ita))			
2001	Karrie Webb (Aus)	Wilmington, Delaware	270

Palm Springs home for famous Starter's Box

When the St Andrews links committee decided to put the Old Course Starter's Box up for on-line auction, bidders from America and Denmark competed fiercely until the final second that bidding was allowed. John Hagen, acting on behalf of the Country Club of the Desert, a new three-course complex in Palm Springs, was successful paying £59,000 for a piece of golfing memorabilia.

The money raised will go to further boost the development of junior golf at St Andrews. The decision to auction the box was taken as part of a redesigning of the first tee area at the Old Course.

Nabisco Dinah Shore

Players are of American nationality unless stated

2001 Nabisco Dinah Shore

at Mission Hills CC, Rancho Mirage, California (6520 yds, Par 72)

Prize Money $1,250,000. Final field comprised 103 players, of whom 74 (including three amateurs) made the half-way cut on 151 or better.

1	Annika Sörenstam (Swe)	72-70-70-69—281	$225000
2	Karrie Webb (Aus)	73-72-70-69—284	87557
	Janice Moodie (Sco)	72-72-70-70—284	87557
	Dottie Pepper	71-71-71-71—284	87557
	Akiko Fukushima (Jpn)	74-68-70-72—284	87557
	Rachel Teske (Aus)	72-73-66-73—284	87557
7	Sophie Gustafson (Swe)	72-74-70-69—285	41891
	Brandie Burton	74-69-72-70—285	41891
9	Laura Diaz	71-74-69-72—286	33589
	Pat Hurst	70-68-74-74—286	33589
11	Laura Davies (Eng)	71-73-75-68—287	25957
	Dorothy Delasin	73-70-74-70—287	25957
	Se Ri Pak (Kor)	73-69-73-72—287	25957
	Tina Barrett	71-73-70-73—287	25957
15	Mi Hyun Kim (Kor)	74-71-70-73—288	20736
	Carin Koch (Swe)	70-69-75-74—288	20736
	Juli Inkster	70-75-68-75—288	20736
18	Liselotte Neumann (Swe)	70-74-74-71—289	18220
	Jeong Jang (Kor)	74-71-71-73—289	18220
	Michele Redman	71-72-71-75—289	18220
21	Jill McGill	75-71-70-74—290	16711
	Loreno Ochoa (Mex) (am)	72 71-74-73—290	
23	Becky Iverson	75-70-72-74—291	15955
24	Maria Hjörth	73-72-75-72—292	14540
	Tammie Green	72-73-75-72—292	14540
	Kelly Robbins	75-72-72-73—292	14540
	Penny Hammel	70-75-72-75—292	14540
28	Meg Mallon	74-71-78-70—293	12063
	Grace Park (Kor)	75-75-72-71—293	12063
	Dina Ammaccapane	74-74-73-72—293	12063
	Rosie Jones	73-73-75-72—293	12063
	Alison Nicholas (Eng)	71-75-75-72—293	12063
	Stefania Croce (Ita)	74-72-73-74—293	12063
	Emilee Klein	72-74-72-75—293	12063
35	Kelli Kuehne	75-70-75-74—294	10446
36	Jan Crafter (Aus)	78-73-74-70—295	9124
	Heather Bowie	77-73-74-71—295	9124
	Charlotte Sörenstam (Swe)	78-71-75-71—295	9124
	Nancy Scranton	72-75-75-73—295	9124
	Moira Dunn	78-73-70-74—295	9124
	Wendy Ward	76-73-70-76—295	9124
42	Amy Fruhwirth	75 75-72-74—296	7350
	Joanne Morley (Eng)	72-74-76-74—296	7350
	Danielle Ammaccapane	74-74-73-75—296	7350
	Lorie Kane (Can)	74-71-74-77—296	7350
46	Helen Alfredsson (Swe)	73-73-74-77—297	6597
	Aree Wongluekiet (am)	76-73-74-74—297	

2001 Nabisco Dinah Shore *continued*

48	Jenny Lidback (Per)	78-72-77-71—298	5420
	Cindy Figg Currier	73-78-74-73—298	5420
	Nanci Bowen	73-75-76-74—298	5420
	Leta Lindley	74-77-71-76—298	5420
	Chris Johnson	74-72-75-77—298	5420
	Cathy Johnston Forbes	78-67-74-79—298	5420
	Donna Andrews	72-72-72-82—298	5420
55	Beth Daniel	76-73-79-71—299	4180
	Laurie Kean	76-73-75-75—299	4180
	Pearl Sinn (Kor)	75-75-73-76—299	4180
58	Jackie Gallagher Smith	76-74-76-74—300	3387
	Vickie Goetze Ackerman	74-75-77-74—300	3387
	Caroline McMillan	75-75-74-76—300	3387
	Vicki Fergon	74-75-74-77—300	3387
	Naree Wongluekiet (am)	74-73-76-77—300	
63	Wendy Doolan (Aus)	73-78-77-73—301	2746
	Nancy Lopez	74-74-77-76—301	2746
	Hiromi Kobayashi (Jpn)	75-73-74-79—301	2746
66	Cristie Kerr	78-73-79-72—302	2407
	Susie Redman	76-75-77-74—302	2407
68	Joan Pitcock	73-75-80-75—303	2218
	Catrin Nilsmark (Swe)	77-71-78-77—303	2218
	Kellee Booth	74-73-78-78—303	2218
71	Ok Hee Ku (Jpn)	72-76-76-81—305	2066
72	Dawn Coe-Jones	76-73-80-77—306	1954
	Marine Monnet (Fra)	76-75-78-77—306	1954
74	Betsy King	73-76-85-75—309	1840

The following players missed the cut:

Barb Mucha	75-77—152	Mardi Lunn (Aus)	76-78—154
Terry-Jo Myers	75-77—152	Patty Sheehan	73-81—154
Deb Richard	75-77—152	Gail Graham (Can)	77-78—155
Sherri Steinhauer	73-79—152	Shani Waugh (Aus)	75-80—155
Helen Dobson (Eng)	84-69—153	Aki Nakano	75-81—156
AJ Eathorne (Can)	80-73—153	Amy Alcott	83-76—159
Catriona Matthew (Sco)	78-75—153	Lisa Ferrero	79-80—159
Michelle McGann	78-75—153	Leigh Ann Hardin	76-83—159
Kim Saiki	77-76—153	Yuri Fodoh (Jpn)	83-77—160
Kristi Albers	77-77—154	JoAnne Carner	77 DQ
Dale Eggeling	76-78—154		

2000 Nabisco Dinah Shore
at Mission Hills CC, Rancho Mirage, CA (6460 yds, Par 72)   Prize money: $1,250,000

1	Karrie Webb (Aus)	67-70-67-70—274	$187500	17T	Kaori Higo (Jpn)	76-72-73-71—292	14321
2	Dottie Pepper	68-72-72-72—284	116366		Sherri Steinhauer	73-71-77-71—292	14321
3	Meg Mallon	75-70-73-67—285	84916		Charlotta Sörenstam		
4	Cathy Johnston-				(Swe)	75-75-70-72—292	14321
	Forbes	74-71-71-70—286	59755		Juli Inkster	76-71-73-72—292	14321
5	Michele Redman	73-73-69-71—286	59755		Nancy Bowen	75-72-73-72—292	14321
6	Helen Dobson (Eng)	73-74-72-68—287	40750		Carin Koch (Swe)	79-70-70-73—292	14321
	Chris Johnson	73-68-73-73—287	40750		Nancy Scranton	78-70-71-73—292	14321
8	Rosie Jones	74-71-74-69—288	31135		Barb Mucha	77-71-70-74—292	14321
	Kim Saiki	72-77-68-71—288	31135	27	Jane Geddes	74-72-78-69—293	10969
10	Jenny Lidback (Per)	75-72-74-68—289	24170		Leta Lindley	73-76-73-71—293	10969
	Wendy Doolan (Aus)	73-73-69-74—289	24170		Catriona Matthew		
	Pat Hurst	72-72-70-75—289	24170		(Sco)	72-77-73-71—293	10969
	Aree Song				Alison Nicholas (Eng)	71-74-74-74—293	10969
	Wongluekiet (am)	75-71-68-75—289		31	Susie Redman	73-75-74-72—294	9507
14	Kristi Albers	77-71-72-70—290	20845		Caroline McMillan		
	Se Ri Pak (Kor)	73-71-77-70—291	18957		(Eng)	73-74-74-73—294	9507
	Janice Moodie (Sco)	74-72-70-75—291	18957		Gail Graham (Can)	71-75-75-73—294	9507
17	Kelly Robbins	79-69-73-71—292	14321		Brandie Burton	74-75-71-74—294	9507
	Annika Sörenstam						
	(Swe)	76-72-73-71—292	14321				

Other players who made the cut: Akiko Fukushima (Jpn), Tina Barrett, Dawn Coe Jones, Laura Davies (Eng), Cristie Kerr, Fumiko Muraguchi (Jpn), Lorie Kane (Can), Beth Bauer (am) 295; Pearl Sinn (Kor), Nancy Lopez, Wendy Ward, Barb Whitehead 296; Cindy McCurdy, Becky Iverson, Mi Hyun Kim (Kor), Jill McGill, Patty Sheehan, Beth Daniel 297; Kris Tschetter, Donna Andrews, Mary Beth Zimmerman, Jan Stephenson (Aus) 298; Helen Alfredsson (Swe), Eva Dahlloff (Swe), Jackie Gallagher Smith, Catrin Nilsmark (Swe), Amy Fruhwirth 299; Mayumi Hirase (Jpn), Penny Hammel, Tammie Green, Sherri Turner, Rachel Hetherington (Aus) 300; Maggie Will, Ayako Okamoto (Jpn), Julie Piers, Kathryn Marshall (Sco) 301; Marnie McGuire (NZ) 302; Liselotte Neumann (Swe) 306; Dale Eggeling 309

1999 Nabisco Dinah Shore
at Mission Hills CC, Rancho Mirage, CA (6460 yds, Par 72)   Prize money: $1,000,000

1	D Pepper	70-66-67-66—269	$150000	13T	K Tschetter	68-70-73-75—286	13712
2	M Mallon	66-69-71-69—275	93093	21	M Spencer-Devlin	72-69-77-69—287	9692
3	K Webb (Aus)	73-71-70-66—280	67933		H Stacy	74-74-69-70—287	9692
4	K Robbins	69-73-67-72—281	52837		M Estill	70-76-71-70—287	9692
5	C Sörenstam (Swe)	72-68-76-66—282	42772		R Hetherington (Aus)	70-74-71-72—287	9692
6	J Inkster	72-66-71-74—283	35224		N Lopez	72-73-69-73—287	9692
7	C Matthew (Sco)	72-73-69-70—284	26502		D Eggeling	73-70-70-74—287	9692
	A Sörenstam (Swe)	70-73-71-70—284	26502		H Kobayashi (Jpn)	70-69-74-74—287	9692
	J Moodie (Sco)	69-68-75-72—284	26502		D Andrews	70-69-74-74—287	9692
10	S Steinhauer	70-72-72-71—285	19289	29	H Dobson (Eng)	74-72-74-68—288	7812
	M Hjörth (Swe)	77-68-68-72—285	19289		D Dormann	74-73-71-70—288	7812
	H Alfredsson (Swe)	69-71-73-72—285	19289		L Kane	73-74-71-70—288	7812
13	R Jones	73-70-73-70—286	13712		J Pitcock	77-68-73-70—288	7812
	M Will	72-71-73-70—286	13712	33	W Ward	74-73-72-70—289	6516
	M Redman	71-74-69-72—286	13712		A Alcott	74-71-71-73—289	6516
	P Bradley	73-69-72-72—286	13712		J Geddes	73-72-71-73—289	6516
	C McCurdy	70-74-69-73—286	13712		T Green	70-75-71-73—289	6516
	Se Ri Pak (Kor)	73-69-69-75—286	13712		B Mucha	73-75-67-74—289	6516
	M Hirase	70-72-69-75—286	13712		J Crafter	70-74-71-74—289	6516

Other players who made the cut: K Saiki, T Tombs, N Bowen, G Park (Am) 290; K Marshall (Sco), E Klein, M Nause, P Hurst, B Daniel 291; G Graham, T Johnson, C Figg-Currier 292; T Barrett, C Johnson, M McGeorge, D Coe-Jones, K Albers, S Turner, A Nicholas (Eng) 293; L Neumann (Swe), M McGann, T Hanson, M Hattori 294; C Johnston-Forbes, P Sinn, L Kiggens 295; V Fergon, Dina Ammaccapane 296; D Richard, J Piers, J Chuasiriporn (am) 297; E Crosby, C Flom, L Davies (Eng) 298; P Sheehan, TJ Myers, Dani Ammaccapane, K Harada 299; B King 300; B Iverson 301; V Skinner, S Gustafson 302

1998 Nabisco Dinah Shore
at Mission Hills CC, Rancho Mirage, CA (6460 yds, Par 72) Prize money: $1,000,000

1	P Hurst	68-72-70-71—281	$150000	18T	M Spencer-Devlin	72-70-76-73—291	12147
2	H Dobson	70-74-71-67—282	93093		L Hackney	71-71-73-76—291	12147
3	L Davies	75-70-70-68—283	60385	23	G Park (am)	77-73-71-71—292	
	H Alfredsson	70-73-70-70—283	60385	24	E Klein	76-74-73-70—293	9256
5	D Andrews	71-72-71-70—284	38998		J Inkster	74-75-74-70—293	9256
	L Neumann	69-71-71-73—284	38998		C Figg-Currier	74-72-77-70—293	9256
7	A Sörenstam	76-71-69-70—286	27928		B Iverson	74-72-77-70—293	9256
	K Webb	71-72-70-73—286	27928		B Mucha	72-75-74-72—293	9256
9	D Pepper	73-72-74-68—287	22393		T Green	72-72-76-73—293	9256
	S Steinhauer	69-76-71-71—287	22393		Dani Ammaccapane	75-73-71-74—293	9256
11	A Fruhwirth	73-71-73-71—288	18438		M McGann	74-71-72-76—293	9256
	D Coe-Jones	70-72-74-72—288	18438		M Hirase	73-69-73-78—293	9256
13	C Matthew	75-74-70-70—289	15670	33	H Kobayashi	77-71-77-69—294	6964
	P Hammel	73-72-71-73—289	15670		T Barrett	76-73-74-71—294	6964
	N Lopez	71-71-73-74—289	15670		M Halpin	72-77-74-71—294	6964
16	M Mallon	75-69-76-70—290	13658		G Graham	71-75-74-74—294	6964
	B Bauer (am)	76-70-72-72—290			A Nicholas	75-70-75-74—294	6964
18	L Kane	76-71-74-70—291	12147		J Geddes	73-75-71-75—294	6964
	R Jones	75-66-78-72—291	12147		D Dormann	73-74-72-75—294	6964
	J Carner	73-72-73-73—291	12147				

Other players who made the cut: A Alcott, J Stephenson 295; C McCurdy, K Saiki, J Crafter, P Sheehan, M Redman, J Pitcock, P Bradley, K Robbins 296; V Fergon, D Richard, D Eggeling, J Piers, B Burton 297; J Lidback, MB Zimmerman, K Marshall, L Walters 298; T Tombs, R Hetherington 299; C Rarick, B King, K Weiss 300; V Skinner 301; S Redman, P Rizzo, N Bowen 302; S Hamlin, T Johnson 303; M Morris 304; L Kiggens 305; B Daniel 306

1997 Nabisco Dinah Shore
at Mission Hills CC, CA (6460 yds, Par 72) Prize money: $900,000

1	B King	71-67-67-71—276	$135000	16T	L Davies	70-70-74-72—286	10898
2	K Tschetter	66-76-66-70—278	83783		K Marshall	66-73-73-74—286	10898
3	A Fruhwirth	69-70-68-72—279	54346	23	C Schreyer	72-74-73-68—287	8690
	K Robbins	70-67-68-74—279	54346		M Baena (am)	74-71-73-69—287	
5	N Bowen	70-74-70-68—282	35097		P Hammel	76-72-67-72—287	8690
	L Hackney	70-72-72-68—282	35097		T Johnson	70-72-73-72—287	8690
7	T Barrett	70-71-70-72—283	26720		N Lopez	70-74-69-74—287	8690
8	MB Zimmerman	75-74-72-63—284	21285	28	B Mucha	71-72-73-72—288	8000
	H Kobayashi	72-69-71-72—284	21285	29	K Webb	69-74-71-75—289	7728
	A Sörenstam	70-72-68-74—284	21285	30	M Hirase	70-77-72-71—290	6940
11	M Morris	71-75-72-67—285	15065		M Estill	72-73-73-72—290	6940
	D Andrews	73-71-72-69—285	15065		D Coe-Jones	73-72-72-73—290	6940
	J Geddes	68-75-72-70—285	15065		D Richard	68-75-74-73—290	6940
	J Crafter	70-71-72-72—285	15065		D Eggeling	68-72-75-75—290	6940
	D Pepper	69-70-71-75—285	15065	35	J Briles-Hinton	72-76-74-69—291	5668
16	T Green	72-73-71-70—286	10898		C Johnson	75-72-72-72—291	5668
	J Inkster	72-74-69-71—286	10898		E Klein	73-74-71-73—291	5668
	M McGann	74-70-71-71—286	10898		A-M Palli	73-74-70-74—291	5668
	L Neumann	74-71-69-72—286	10898		H Stacy	72-73-72-74—291	5668
	P Hurst	74-69-71-72—286	10898		P Bradley	69-72-73-77—291	5668

Other players who made the cut: A Nicholas, C Walker 292; V Skinner, J Lidback, C Rarick, B Iverson, L Walters 293; S Turner, B Burton, S Steinhauer, K Harada, J Pitcock, V Goetze-Ackerman 294; J Piers, R Hood, H Alfredsson 295; T Hanson, A Finney, A Alcott, K Monaghan 296; N Ramsbottom, R Walton 298; P Sheehan 299; A Okamoto 300; M Spencer-Devlin 301; A Ritzman, TJ Myers 302; B Bunkowsky-Scherbak, A Fukushima, L Kiggens 303; V Fergon, B Whitehead 304; T Kerdyk, A Benz 305.

1996 Nabisco Dinah Shore

at Mission Hills CC, CA (6460 yds, Par 72)   Prize money: $900,000

1	P Sheehan	71-72-67-71—281	$135000	19T	T Kerdyk	67-72-77-72—288	10189
2	K Robbins	71-72-71-68—282	64158		J Inkster	70-70-74-74—288	10189
	M Mallon	71-70-71-70—282	64158	23	P Bradley	73-76-71-69—289	8111
	A Sörenstam	67-72-73-70—282	64158		J Geddes	74-72-74-69—289	8111
5	A Fruhwirth	71-73-68-71—283	32305		D Andrews	74-70-76-69—289	8111
	K Webb	72-70-70-71—283	32305		A Fukushima	74-68-78-69—289	8111
	B Burton	75-67-68-73—283	32305		A Alcott	68-78-71-72—289	8111
8	H Stacy	69-71-74-70—284	23550		P Hammel	75-69-73-72—289	8111
9	K Tschetter	71-74-70-70—285	21285		D Pepper	71-71-75-72—289	8111
10	D Richard	73-71-73-69—286	16212		N Bowen	76-70-70-73—289	8111
	L Neumann	73-69-75-69—286	16212	31	B Iverson	76-71-73-70—290	6544
	V Skinner	74-71-71-70—286	16212		S Redman	73-75-71-71—290	6544
	R Jones	72-67-75-72—286	16212		A Nicholas	75-72-72-71—290	6544
	T Hanson	69-69-74-74—286	16212		H Kobayashi	72-74-72-72—290	6544
15	N Lopez	73-72-73-69—287	12114	35	C Pierce	72-71-75-73—291	5411
	M McGeorge	74-70-74-69—287	12114		T Johnson	74-72-71-74—291	5411
	J Pitcock	71-74-71-71—287	12114		D Coe-Jones	72-73-72-74—291	5411
	L Davies	72-70-70-75—287	12114		P Sinn	73-73-70-75—291	5411
19	M Morris	76-71-71-70—288	10189		C Schreyer	72-71-73-75—291	5411
	S Farwig	71-73-73-71—288	10189		S Little	69-73-71-78—291	5411

Other players who made the cut: C Johnston-Forbes, K Parker-Gregory, N Ramsbottom, R Walton, B Mucha, G Graham, M Nause 292; J Piers, H Alfredsson, A Okamoto, T Barrett, J Wyatt, S Furlong 293; I Shiotani, L Lindley, V Fergon, M Redman 294; C Walker, K Marshall, M Estill, K Albers 295; J Dickinson, M McGann, MB Zimmerman, Dani Ammaccapane, A Ritzman 296; K Shipman, L Rinker-Graham 297; J Crafter 298; A Dibos, A Finney, S Strudwick, P Wright 299; A Benz, K Guadagnino, 301; S Palmer, E Klein 302; J Stephenson 303; J Carner, C Mackey 305.

1995 Nabisco Dinah Shore

at Mission Hills CC, CA (6460 yds, Par 72)   Prize money: $850,000

1	N Bowen	69-75-71-70—285	$127500	16T	P Bradley	74-75-71-72—292	10056
2	S Redman	75-70-70-71—286	79129		J Inkster	76-70-73-73—292	10056
3	B Burton	76-71-71-69—287	42237		T-J Myers	77-68-73-74—292	10056
	S Turner	72-74-71-70—287	42237		M Estill	72-72-74-74—292	10056
	L Davies	75-69-70-73—287	42237		M Mallon	74-72-71-75—292	10056
	N Lopez	74-71-68-74—287	42237	24	A Sörenstam	76-74-74-69—293	8040
7	C Walker	74-73-69-72—288	23738		M Spencer-Devlin	69-79-74-71—293	8040
	T Green	71-70-70-77—288	23738		K Albers	76-72-72-73—293	8040
9	D Coe-Jones	71-75-71-72—289	20103	27	J Geddes	76-75-74-69—294	7014
10	C Pierce	77-71-73-69—290	17964		K Tschetter	75-74-73-72—294	7014
11	B King	77-75-71-68—291	14200		L West	74-75-71-74—294	7014
	D Mochrie	78-73-70-70—291	14200		K Robbins	76-67-76-75—294	7014
	B Mucha	74-74-72-71—291	14200		B Thomas	79-69-70-76—294	7014
	S Palmer	72-73-74-72—291	14200	32	D Eggeling	72-78-75-70—295	5859
	D Massey	71-75-72-73—291	14200		C Rarick	74-73-78-70—295	5859
16	A Dibos	77-74-75-66—292	10056		L Neumann	75-74-74-72—295	5859
	S Steinhauer	78-74-72-68—292	10056		J Larsen	74-76-72-73—295	5859
	A Nicholas	75-74-73-70—292	10056		K Noble	71-77-71-76—295	5859

Other players who made the cut: C Keggi, V Skinner, H Kobayashi, A Okamoto, N Ramsbottom, L Merten 296; P Sheehan, A Benz, L Walters, MB Zimmerman 297; Danielle Ammaccapane, C Schreyer, A Ritzman, B Daniel, P Jordan 298; R Jones, F Descampe, J Crafter, J Briles-Hinton, M McNamara 299; Jean Zedlitz, M McGann, I Shiotani, T Johnson, C Johnson, P Hammel 300; K Guadagnino, M Figueras-Dotti 301; L Kiggens, C Johnston-Forbes 302; P Sinn 303; A Finney, T Barrett, K Peterson-Parker, S Farwig, C Hill 304; J Stephenson, M Nause, D Andrews 305; M Berteotti 307; J Anschutz 311.

1994 Nabisco Dinah Shore

at Mission Hills CC, CA (6446 yds, Par 72)   Prize money: $700,000

1	D Andrews	70-69-67-70—276	$105000	19T	C Keggi	72-73-72-71—288	7204
2	L Davies	70-68-69-70—277	65165		C Johnson	74-73-69-72—288	7204
3	T Green	70-72-69-68—279	47553		P Sheehan	73-71-72-72—288	7204
4	J Stephenson	70-69-70-71—280	36985		D Mochrie	74-73-68-73—288	7204
5	M McGann	70-68-70-73—281	29940		A Okamoto	69-74-72-73—288	7204
6	G Graham	73-71-71-68—283	21251		M McGeorge	72-71-70-75—288	7204
	K Robbins	73-70-69-71—283	21251	28	T Tombs	73-74-72-70—289	5670
	B Burton	73-73-65-72—283	21251		S Turner	72-74-71-72—289	5670
9	H Stacy	72-72-70-70—284	15674		V Skinner	72-72-72-73—289	5670
	N Lopez	68-72-73-71—284	15674		M Berteotti	71-73-72-73—289	5670
11	M Mallon	72-75-69-69—285	12064	32	T-J Myers	76-73-71-70—290	4913
	L Neumann	76-71-68-70—285	12064		H Kobayashi	72-77-71-70—290	4913
	D Dormann	73-71-70-71—285	12064		K Tschetter	73-69-76-72—290	4913
	D Eggeling	71-71-71-72—285	12064		S Steinhauer	76-68-72-74—290	4913
15	K Monaghan	70-76-70-70—286	9862	36	J Larsen	76-70-75-70—291	3949
	V Fergon	69-74-72-71—286	9862		K Albers	77-73-70-71—291	3949
17	L Merten	74-74-71-68—287	8982		C Rarick	72-74-74-71—291	3949
	N Scranton	75-70-69-73—287	8982		D Coe-Jones	74-70-75-72—291	3949
19	B Daniel	76-72-70-70—288	7204		Toshimi Kimura	71-74-73-73—291	3949
	J Geddes	70-77-71-70—288	7204		M Nause	74-71-72-74—291	3949
	P Bradley	71-75-71-71—288	7204		A Miller	68-71-77-75—291	3949

Other players who made the cut: M Spencer-Devlin, E Crosby, Danielle Ammaccapane, D Richard, T Johnson 292; J Crafter, J Carner, K Noble, S Strudwick, H Alfredsson, C Schreyer, J Dickinson, L Kean, B King, L Walters 293; C Figg-Currier, A Alcott, S Redman, M McNamara, T Kerdyk, L Garbacz 295; A Ritzman, M Will, R Hood, A Benz 296; M Estill 297; B Mucha, S Little, K Guadagnino 298; S Palmer, C Walker, P Wright 299; E Klein (am) 300; C Mackey 305; S Farwig 306; A-M Palli 307.

1993 Nabisco Dinah Shore

at Mission Hills CC, CA (6437 yds, Par 72)   Prize money: $700,000

1	H Alfredsson	69-71-72-72—284	$105000	19T	N Scranton	73-72-71-75—291	8101
2	A Benz	72-73-71-70—286	49901	22	M McGann	78-70-75-69—292	7237
	T Barrett	70-73-72-71—286	49901		S Barrett	69-77-72-74—292	7237
	B King	71-74-67-74—286	49901	24	L Garbacz	75-75-72-71—293	6304
5	H Stacy	72-74-71-70—287	25126		C Keggi	74-74-73-72—293	6304
	M Berteotti	68-74-73-72—287	25126		Dani Ammaccapane	69-75-74-75—293	6304
	D Coe-Jones	72-68-72-75—287	25126		C Schreyer	75-70-72-76—293	6304
8	N Lopez	68-78-72-70—288	15762		A-M Palli	70-71-76-76—293	6304
	B Burton	73-73-68-74—288	15762		M Figueras-Dotti	68-72-75-78—293	6304
	T Johnson	74-68-72-74—288	15762	30	D Lofland-Dormann	76-75-75-68—294	4740
	J Crafter	71-72-70-75—288	15762		D Mochrie	77-73-74-70—294	4740
12	P Sheehan	73-70-76-70—289	10625		H Drew	79-70-74-71—294	4740
	D Massey	70-74-74-71—289	10625		V Skinner	73-75-74-72—294	4740
	T Green	72-73-72-72—289	10625		A Finney	70-73-79-72—294	4740
	L Davies	72-72-73-72—289	10625		C Rarick	76-75-70-73—294	4740
	P Wright	74-68-75-72—289	10625		S Turner	73-72-76-73—294	4740
	P Bradley	71-69-75-74—289	10625		T-J Myers	74-73-73-74—294	4740
18	K Monaghan	76-71-74-69—290	8806		J Pitcock	70-72-76-76—294	4740
19	D Andrews	73-74-72-72—291	8101		S Steinhauer	72-74-71-77—294	4740
	K Noble	74-72-70-75—291	8101				

Other players who made the cut: L Neumann, J Carner, P Rizzo, J Inkster, M Will, S Hamlin, K Postlewait, B Mucha, J Stephenson 295; F Descampe, J Dickinson, J Geddes, C Walker, M Mallon, S Little, L Walters 296; A Ritzman, A Alcott, C Figg-Currier, A Miller 297; K Tschetter, D Richard 298; R Jones, M Estill, V Fergon 299; S Redman, S Farwig, L Connelly, L Adams 300; E Crosby, B Daniel 301; N Foust, M Spencer-Devlin, P Jordan, L Merten 302; C Johnson, S Palmer, B Pearson 305; A Okamoto 307; S Furlong, V Goetze (am) 308.

1992 Nabisco Dinah Shore

at Mission Hills CC, CA (6437 yds, Par 72)   Prize money: $700,000

1	D Mochrie*	69-71-70-69—279	$105000	17T	J Geddes	75-68-73-72—288	8517
2	J Inkster	72-68-68-71—279	65165		P Bradley	73-71-69-75—288	8517
Winner after play-off				22	Dani Ammaccapane	74-73-70-72—289	7046
3	B Burton	70-72-71-68—281	42269		S Little	71-75-71-72—289	7046
	P Sheehan	71-69-69-72—281	42269		Ok-Hee Ku	71-73-73-72—289	7046
5	M Mallon	73-69-72-68—282	29940		V Fergon	72-72-71-74—289	7046
6	S Steinhauer	72-73-69-70—284	22719	26	C Marino	70-74-73-73—290	5946
	D Eggeling	67-78-69-70—284	22719		L Kean	70-71-76-73—290	5946
8	K Tschetter	73-71-73-68—285	15778		C Figg-Currier	73-74-69-74—290	5946
	P Wright	74-71-71-69—285	15778		B Mucha	73-72-71-74—290	5946
	B Daniel	70-68-76-71—285	15778		L Walters	72-72-71-75—290	5946
	M McGann	68-74-71-72—285	15778		L Neumann	68-76-71-75—290	5946
12	E Crosby	72-70-73-71—286	11335	32	C Keggi	71-77-72-71—291	4712
	A Okamoto	71-71-72-72—286	11335		L Rinker	73-72-75-71—291	4712
	M Spencer-Devlin	73-69-71-73—286	11335		C Rarick	70-76-73-72—291	4712
	J Stephenson	72-72-68-74—286	11335		D Coe	71-68-79-73—291	4712
16	T Green	70-70-74-73—287	9574		T Barrett	74-73-70-74—291	4712
17	K Postlewait	73-74-72-69—288	8517		R Jones	74-71-72-74—291	4712
	C Johnson	71-71-75-71—288	8517		A Alcott	74-73-69-75—291	4712
	J Carner	70-72-75-71—288	8517				

Other players who made the cut: A Benz, H Stacy, A Miller, MB Zimmerman 292; M Estill, J Coles, M Berteotti 293; A Ritzman, T Johnson, I Shiotani, M McNamara, M Will 294; M McGeorge, C Mackey, M Nause, M Figueras-Dotti, A Fruhwirth (am) 295; B King 296; T-J Myers, C Dibnah, N Scranton, A-M Palli, B Bunkowsky, D Lofland 297; C Walker 298; M Faulconer, C Hill 300; J Anschutz, H Drew, L Adams 301; V Goetze (am) 302; P Pulz 304; S LeBrun Ingram (am) 305; T Purtzer 306.

NABISCO DINAH SHORE HISTORY

This event was inaugurated in 1972 as the Colgate Dinah Shore and continued to be sponsored by Colgate until 1981. Nabisco took over the sponsorship in 1982; and the Nabisco Dinah Shore was designated a Major Championship in 1983. Mission Hills CC, Rancho Mirage, California, is the event's permanent venue.

1972	J Blalock	213		1988	A Alcott	274
1973	M Wright	284		1989	J Inkster	279
1974	J Prentice	289		1990	B King	283
1975	S Palmer	283		1991	A Alcott	273
1976	J Rankin	285		1992	D Mochrie*	279
1977	K Whitworth	289		*Won play-off after a tie with J Inkster*		
1978	S Post	283		1993	H Alfredsson (Swe)	284
1979	S Post	276		1994	D Andrews	276
1980	D Caponi	275		1995	N Bowen	285
1981	N Lopez	277		1996	P Sheehan	281
1982	S Little	278		1997	B King	276
1983	A Alcott	282		1998	P Hurst	281
1984	J Inkster*	280		1999	D Pepper	269
Won play-off after a tie with P Bradley				2000	K Webb (Aus)	274
1985	A Miller	278		2001	A Sörenstam (Swe)	281
1986	P Bradley	280				
1987	B King*	283				

* *Won play-off after a tie with P Sheehan*

du Maurier Classic History

The du Maurier Classic was inaugurated in 1973 and designated a Major Championship in 1979. It was discontinued after 2000 and was replaced as a major on the US LPGA schedule by the Weetabix Women's British Open.

Players are of American nationality unless stated

Year	Winner	Venue	Score
1973	J Bourassa*	Montreal GC, Montreal	214
* Won play-off after a tie with S Haynie, J Rankin			
1974	CJ Callison	Candiac GC, Montreal	208
1975	J Carner*	St George's CC, Toronto	214
* Won play-off after a tie with C Mann			
1976	D Caponi*	Cedar Brae G&CC, Toronto	212
* Won play-off after a tie with J Rankin			
1977	J Rankin	Lachute G&CC, Montreal	214
1978	J Carner	St George's CC, Toronto	278
1979	A Alcott	Richelieu Valley CC, Montreal	285
1980	P Bradley	St George's CC, Toronto	277
1981	J Stephenson (Aus)	Summerlea CC, Dorian, Quebec	278
1982	S Haynie	St George's CC, Toronto	280
1983	H Stacy	Beaconsfield CC, Montreal	277
1984	J Inkster	St George's CC, Toronto	279
1985	P Bradley	Beaconsfield CC, Montreal	278
1986	P Bradley*	Board of Trade CC, Toronto	276
* Won play-off after a tie with A Okamoto			
1987	J Rosenthal	Islesmere GC, Laval, Quebec	272
1988	S Little (RSA)	Vancouver GC, Coquitlam, BC	279
1989	T Green	Beaconsfield CC, Montreal	279
1990	C Johnston	Westmount G&CC, Kitchener, Ontario	276
1991	N Scranton	Vancouver GC, Coquitlam, BC	279
1992	S Steinhauer	St Charles CC, Winnipeg, Manitoba	277
1993	B Burton*	London H&CC, Ontario	277
* Won play-off after a tie with B King			
1994	M Nause	Ottawa Hunt Club, Ontario	279
1995	J Lidback	Beaconsfield CC, Montreal	280
1996	L Davies (Eng)	Edmonton CC, Edmonton, Alberta	277
1997	C Walker	Glen Abbey GC, Toronto	278
1998	B Burton	Essex G&CC, Ontario	270
1999	K Webb (Aus)	Priddis Greens G&CC, Calgary, Alberta	277
2000	M Mallon	Royal Ottawa GC, Aylmer, Quebec	282

Women's Major Title Table

Juli Inkster   *Mickey Wright*   *Karrie Webb*

All photographs © Phil Sheldon

	#British Open	US Open	LPGA	†Dinah Shore	*du Maurier	British Amateur	US Amateur	*Total titles*
Juli Inkster	0	1	2	2	1	0	3	9
Mickey Wright	0	4	4	0	0	0	0	8
Jo Anne Carner	0	2	0	0	0	0	5	7
Betsy King	1	2	1	3	0	0	0	7
Karrie Webb (Aus)	2	2	1	1	1	0	0	7
Pat Bradley	0	1	1	1	3	0	0	6
Betsy Rawls	0	4	2	0	0	0	0	6
Glenna Collett Vare	0	0	0	0	0	0	6	6
Louise Suggs	0	2	1	0	0	1	1	5
Babe Zaharias	0	3	0	0	0	1	1	5
Amy Alcott	0	1	0	3	1	0	0	5
Laura Davies (Eng)	1	1	2	0	1	0	0	5

 # Designated a major on the US LPGA circuit from 2001   † Designated a major in 1983
★ Designated a major in 1979, discontinued after 2000

PART II

Men's Professional Tournaments

Official World Rankings, Top 50 (at end 2001 US and European Seasons)

Ranking		Name	Country	Points Average	Total Points	No. of Events	1999/2000 Pts Lost	2001 Pts Gained
1	(1)	Tiger Woods	USA	18.06	794.84	44	−757.77	+568.11
2	(3)	Phil Mickelson	USA	10.01	480.48	48	−329.25	+411.85
3	(5)	David Duval	USA	8.55	350.39	41	−234.46	+308.89
4	(2)	Ernie Els	RSA	6.79	353.08	52	−338.19	+234.77
5	(8)	Davis Love III	USA	6.52	293.24	45	−232.07	+275.25
6	(15)	Sergio Garcia	Esp	6.30	327.44	52	−203.07	+306.66
7	(21)	David Toms	USA	6.26	356.66	57	−198.51	+320.60
8	(10)	Vijay Singh	Fij	6.09	365.27	60	−294.87	+349.35
9	(7)	Darren Clarke	NI	5.43	325.59	60	−218.36	+232.31
10	(20)	Padraig Harrington	Irl	5.36	268.00	50	−154.84	+221.19
11	(18)	Mike Weir	Can	5.30	270.26	51	−187.88	+221.94
12	(36)	Retief Goosen	RSA	5.17	315.28	61	−158.27	+299.33
13	(6)	Colin Montgomerie	Sco	4.90	254.67	52	−265.71	+184.11
14	(63)	Bernhard Langer	Ger	4.84	256.48	53	−107.97	+251.60
15	(17)	Jim Furyk	USA	4.67	238.22	51	−193.95	+219.35
16	(48)	Scott Verplank	USA	4.67	252.19	54	−108.07	+228.55
17	(43)	José Coceres	Arg	4.43	181.77	41	−85.40	+156.34
18	(73)	Bob Estes	USA	4.43	208.10	47	−80.89	+204.91
19	(54)	Scott Hoch	USA	4.32	237.62	55	−117.27	+224.92
20	(62)	Chris DiMarco	USA	4.24	262.96	62	−105.09	+232.94
21	(47)	Toshimitsu Izawa	Jpn	4.20	197.29	47	−99.81	+167.15
22	(16)	Thomas Björn	Den	4.16	232.72	56	−178.41	+161.86
23	(31)	Paul Azinger	USA	4.09	163.65	40	−105.88	+134.66
24	(11)	Tom Lehman	USA	4.03	181.46	45	−190.77	+152.83
25	(50)	Mark Calcavecchia	USA	4.00	199.83	50	−128.48	+192.17
26	(33)	Robert Allenby	Aus	3.92	243.30	62	−136.98	+188.54
27	(4)	Lee Westwood	Eng	3.71	200.60	54	−266.22	+48.41
28	(19)	Stewart Cink	USA	3.68	206.07	56	−170.10	+160.11
29	(38)	Rocco Mediate	USA	3.67	157.66	43	−123.86	+145.15
30	(12)	Michael Campbell	NZ	3.57	193.04	54	−166.43	+116.09
31	(9)	Hal Sutton	USA	3.57	182.18	51	−212.99	+139.02
32	(13)	Jesper Parnevik	Swe	3.57	178.40	50	−187.64	+142.33
33	(14)	Nick Price	Zim	3.56	167.43	47	−174.11	+117.22
34	(42)	Angel Cabrera	Arg	3.42	164.27	48	−107.91	+149.30
35	(66=)	Paul McGinley	Irl	3.36	174.68	52	−77.12	+156.29
36	(85)	Kenny Perry	USA	3.34	150.09	45	−63.46	+144.15
37	(40)	Shingo Katayama	Jpn	3.21	173.61	54	−84.07	+117.48
38	(185)	Joe Durant	USA	3.10	161.29	52	−67.40	+187.34
39	(22)	Justin Leonard	USA	3.05	180.01	59	−154.76	+125.86
40	(148)	Niclas Fasth	Swe	2.98	128.29	43	−36.53	+126.39
41	(35)	Kirk Triplett	USA	2.95	159.46	54	−119.35	+118.01
42	(64)	Steve Lowery	USA	2.90	165.53	57	−85.48	+140.42
43	(91)	Frank Lickliter	USA	2.60	153.32	59	−87.56	+153.97
44	(69)	Brad Faxon	USA	2.57	141.46	55	−97.13	+152.77
45	(324)	Charles Howell III	USA	2.52	100.85	40	−17.69	+102.63
46	(206)	Scott McCarron	USA	2.42	132.98	55	−50.48	+143.48
47	(41)	Steve Flesch	USA	2.40	153.44	64	−110.93	+99.50
48	(95)	Billy Andrade	USA	2.39	136.09	57	−63.50	+121.09
49	(507)	John Daly	USA	2.38	135.69	57	−17.54	+144.57
50	(30)	Pierre Fulke	Swe	2.32	92.91	40	−9.81	+850.46

Ranking in brackets indicates position at 31st Decemvber 2000

European Tour – 2001 and Past Results

2001 VOLVO ORDER OF MERIT (at end of season)

South African Retief Goosen topped the Volvo Order of Merit for the first time when he earned £1,770,180. Padraig Harrington came second and Darren Clarke third. Goosen won the US Open, Scottish Open and Telefonica Madrid Open during the year.

1	Retief Goosen (RSA)	£1,770,180.19	41	Barry Lane (Eng)	295,001.62
2	Padraig Harrington (Irl)	1,292,427.59	42	Nick O'Hern (Aus)	292,985.91
3	Darren Clarke (NI)	1,292,288.99	41	Gary Orr (Sco)	280,519.05
4	Ernie Els (RSA)	1,061,244.78	42	Henrik Stenson (Swe)	273,398.41
5	Colin Montgomerie (Sco)	976,154.49	43	Daren Lee (Eng)	264,898.23
6	Bernhard Langer (Ger)	975,198.29	44	John Bickerton (Eng)	264,066.55
7	Thomas Bjørn (Den)	911,925.47	47	Mark McNulty (Zim)	256,563.02
8	Paul McGinley (Irl)	905,514.13	48	Anthony Wall (Eng)	253,135.79
9	Paul Lowrie (Sco)	883,499.38	49	Richard Green (Aus)	251,608.40
10	Niclas Fasth (Swe)	757,208.35	50	Soren Kjeldsen (Den)	247,765.37
11	Angel Cabrera (Arg)	731,709.36	51	Alex Cejka (Ger)	246,931.76
12	Michael Campbell (NZ)	658,816.76	52	Lee Westwood (Eng)	241,530.59
13	Adam Scott (Aus)	555,653.94	53	Brian Davis (Eng)	239,180.15
14	David Howell (Eng)	547,937.48	54	Peter Lonard (Aus)	227,200.47
15	Robert Karlsson (Swe)	542,393.01	55	Greg Turner (NZ)	223,476.10
16	Mathias Grönberg (Swe)	528,243.20	56	Ian Garbutt (Eng)	223,445.03
17	Peter O'Malley (Aus)	524,070.15	57	Brett Rumford (Aus)	219,623.27
18	Ian Woosnam (Wal)	518,048.38	58	Roger Wessels (RSA)	219,482.41
19	Thomas Levet (Fra)	495,750.38	59	Gary Evans (Eng)	218,099.12
20	Miguel Angel Jiménez (Esp)	487,374.69	60	Gregory Havret (Fra)	212,201.04
21	Phillip Price (Wal)	472,324.93	61	Carl Petersson (Swe)	211,974.09
22	Paul Casey (Eng)	470,364.39	62	Mark Mouland (Wal)	209,061.32
23	Pierre Fulke (Swe)	464,479.16	63	Mikael Lundberg (Swe)	201,211.79
24	Ian Poulter (Eng)	455,380.83	64	Raymond Russell (Sco)	201,209.79
25	Ricardo Gonzalez (Arg)	446,348.89	65	Stephen Gallacher (Sco)	198,744.59
26	Andrew Oldcorn (Sco)	443,560.83	66	Nick Faldo (Eng)	195,306.93
27	Sergia Garcia (Esp)	442,289.12	67	Sven Strüver (Ger)	194,334.30
28	Raphael Jacquelin (Fra)	405,973.15	68	Olle Karlsson (Swe)	187,378.63
29	Warren Bennett (Eng)	404,066.42	69	Tony Johnstone (Zim)	180,513.56
30	Steve Webster (Eng)	400,724.63	70	Markus Brier (Aut)	175,261.35
31	Andrew Coltart (Sco)	400,068.28	71	Jarrod Moseley (Aus)	173,238.14
32	Greg Owen (Eng)	387,203.56	72	Bradley Dredge (Wal)	171,267.08
33	Justin Rose (Eng)	383,983.14	73	Eduardo Romero (Arg)	169,844.28
34	Jean Hugo (RSA)	367,308.39	74	Costantino Rocca (Ita)	160,499.28
35	José Maria Olazabal (Esp)	357,766.81	75	Roger Chapman (Eng)	159,401.54
36	Dean Robertson (Sco)	354,262.42	76	Jorge Berendt (Arg)	157,156.29
37	Soren Hansen (Den)	334,030.40	77	Jonathan Lomas (Eng)	155,904.89
38	Frederik Jacobson (Swe)	329,059.62	78	Gary Emerson (Eng)	155,384.76
39	Anders Hansen (Den)	309,505.28	79	Des Smyth (Irl)	154,306.50
40	David Lynn (Eng)	301,927.57	80	Joakim Haeggman (Swe)	153,662.02

CAREER MONEY LIST (at end of 2001 season)

1	Colin Montgomerie	(Sco)	€13,531,275	51	Miguel Angel Martin	(Esp)	2,547,202
2	Bernhard Langer	(Ger)	10,031,834	52	Howard Clark	(Eng)	2,507,193
3	Darren Clarke	(NI)	9,196,016	53	Des Smyth	(Irl)	2,436,450
4	Ian Woosnam	(Wal)	7,978,407	54	Greg Norman	(Aus)	2,386,352
5	Lee Westwood	(Eng)	7,684,940	55	Mark Roe	(Eng)	2,364,672
6	José Maria Olazabal	(Esp)	7,147,112	56	David Howell	(Eng)	2,301,715
7	Ernie Els	(RSA)	6,610,014	57	Eamonn Darcy	(Irl)	2,297,984
8	Retief Goosen	(RSA)	6,432,348	58	Frank Nobilo	(NZ)	2,282,061
9	Nick Faldo	(Eng)	6,297,316	59	Russell Claydon	(Eng)	2,259,276
10	Miguel Angel			60	Ignacio Garrido	(Esp)	2,250,930
	Jiménez	(Esp)	5,898,299	61	Patrik Sjöland	(Swe)	2,250,473
11	Padraig Harrington	(Irl)	5,531,076	62	Jarmo Sandelin	(Swe)	2,201,127
12	Thomas Bjørn	(Den)	5,390,892	63	Joakim Haeggman	(Swe)	2,200,324
13	Seve Ballesteros	(Esp)	5,315,148	64	Alex Cejka	(Ger)	2,175,506
14	Sam Torrance	(Sco)	5,118,214	65	Sven Strüver	(Ger)	2,138,092
15	Vijay Singh	(Fij)	4,691,858	66	Peter Senior	(Aus)	2,013,301
16	Mark McNulty	(Zim)	4,667,262	67	Philip Walton	(Irl)	1,996,625
17	Mark James	(Eng)	4,399,278	68	Andrew Oldcorn	(Sco)	1,994,538
18	Eduardo Romero	(Arg)	4,320,915	69	Santiago Luna	(Esp)	1,922,452
19	Costantino Rocca	(Ita)	4,175,779	70	Bob May	(USA)	1,921,213
20	Michael Campbell	(NZ)	4,120,473	71	Steven Richardson	(Eng)	1,876,238
21	Paul McGinley	(Irl)	4,097,474	72	Niclas Fasth	(Swe)	1,869,222
22	Paul Lawrie	(Sco)	3,870,318	73	Mark Mouland	(Wal)	1,839,612
23	Phillip Price	(Wal)	3,709,253	74	Wayne Riley	(Aus)	1,772,443
24	Gordon Brand jr	(Sco)	3,603,284	75	Mats Lanner	(Swe)	1,719,398
25	Barry Lane	(Eng)	3,533,115	76	Carl Mason	(Eng)	1,717,708
26	Andrew Coltart	(Sco)	3,471,023	77	David Carter	(Eng)	1,629,376
27	Robert Karlsson	(Swe)	3,345,149	78	Dean Robertson	(Sco)	1,577,072
28	Peter O'Malley	(Aus)	3,315,509	79	Malcolm Mackenzie	(Eng)	1,557,986
29	Angel Cabrera	(Arg)	3,307,964	80	Steve Webster	(Eng)	1,548,082
30	Per-Ulrik Johansson	(Swe)	3,206,224	81	Raymond Russell	(Sco)	1,546,368
31	Peter Baker	(Eng)	3,179,874	82	Gary Evans	(Eng)	1,508,671
32	Gary Orr	(Sco)	3,101,085	83	Stephen Leaney	(Aus)	1,495,831
33	Jesper Parnevik	(Swe)	3,089,457	84	Jonathan Lomas	(Eng)	1,573,773
34	Ronan Rafferty	(NI)	3,082,369	85	Mike Harwood	(Aus)	1,448,990
35	Pierre Fulke	(Swe)	2,932,527	86	Peter Fowler	(Aus)	1,431,689
36	David Gilford	(Eng)	2,922,470	87	Andrew Sherborne	(Eng)	1,429,834
37	Anders Forsbrand	(Swe)	2,918,617	88	Paul Eales	(Eng)	1,404,964
38	Sandy Lyle	(Sco)	2,899,418	89	Fredrik Jacobson	(Swe)	1,382,701
39	Jean Van De Velde	(Fra)	2,888,593	90	Richard Boxall	(Eng)	1,376,169
40	Greg Turner	(NZ)	2,827,946	91	Steen Tinning	(Den)	1,373,150
41	Peter Mitchell	(Eng)	2,743,692	92	Derrick Cooper	(Eng)	1,363,875
42	José Rivero	(Esp)	2,742,507	93	Christy O'Connor jr	(Irl)	1,354,539
43	José Coceres	(Arg)	2,717,249	94	Wayne Westner	(RSA)	1,331,916
44	Paul Broadhurst	(Eng)	2,691,533	95	Ricardo Gonzalez	(Arg)	1,297,047
45	Tony Johnstone	(Zim)	2,685,394	96	Brian Davis	(Eng)	1,293,473
46	Mathias Grönberg	(Swe)	2,684,213	97	Greg Owen	(Eng)	1,275,478
47	Sergio Garcia	(Esp)	2,632,222	98	Thomas Levet	(Fra)	1,265,727
48	Roger Chapman	(Eng)	2,631,444	99	Richard Green	(Aus)	1,249,459
49	Jamie Spence	(Eng)	2,589,838	100	Roger Wessels	(RSA)	1,245,385
50	Rodger Davis	(Aus)	2,552,905				

2001 TOUR STATISTICS (Reuters Performance Data)

Stroke averages

Pos	Name	Avg
1	Padraig Harrington (Irl)	69.23
2	Retief Goosen (RSA)	69.32
3	Sergio Garcia (Esp)	69.53
4	Colin Montgomerie (Sco)	69.75
5T	Paul McGinley (Irl)	69.82
	Bernhard Langer (Ger)	69.82
7	Ernie Els (RSA)	69.90
8	Angel Cabrera (Arg)	69.95
9	Ricardo Gonzalez (Arg)	70.00
10	Darren Clarke (NI)	70.02
11	Adam Scott (Aus)	70.12
12	Thomas Bjørn (Den)	70.19
13	Niclas Fasth (Swe)	70.27
14T	Peter O'Malley (Aus)	70.35
	Anthony Wall (Eng)	70.35
16	Warren Bennett (Eng)	70.37
17	Robert Karlsson (Swe)	70.39
18	Phillip Price (Wal)	70.42
19	Ian Woosnam (Wal)	70.45
20	Anders Hansen (Den)	70.47

Driving accuracy

Pos	Name	%
1	Peter O'Malley (Aus)	83.7
2	Richard Green (Aus)	81.9
3	John Bickerton (Eng)	77.1
4	Gary Orr (Sco)	76.0
5	Mark Pilkington (Wal)	75.1
6	Michele Reale (Ita)	75.0
7	Anders Hansen (Den)	73.7
8	Matthew Blackey (Eng)	73.4
9	Paul Eales (Eng)	72.7
10	Sergio Garcia (Esp)	72.6

Average putts per round

Pos	Name	Avg
1	Seve Ballesteros (Esp)	27.9
2	Pierre Fulke (Swe)	28.1
3T	Thomas Bjørn (Den)	28.2
	Joakim Haeggman (Swe)	28.2
5	Jeev Milkha Singh (Ind)	28.3
6T	Nick Faldo (Eng)	28.4
	Mathias Grönberg (Swe)	28.4
8	Gerry Norquist (USA)	28.5
	Olle Karlsson (Swe)	28.5
10T	Gary Emerson (Eng)	28.6
	Robert Karlsson (Swe)	28.6
	Andrew Marshall (Eng)	28.6
	Fredrik Jacobson (Swe)	28.6
	Henrik Bjornstad (Nor)	28.6
	Bradley Dredge (Wal)	28.6
	Phillip Price (Wal)	28.6

Driving distance

Pos	Name	Yds
1	Angel Cabrera (Arg)	303.5
2	Ricardo Gonzalez (Arg)	303.3
3	Emanuele Canonica (Ita)	298.8
4	Jean Hugo (RSA)	297.6
5	Adam Scott (Aus)	297.4
6	Mark Pilkington (Wal)	295.7
7T	Robert Karlsson (Swe)	295.3
	Elliot Boult (NZ)	295.3
9	Carl Suneson (Esp)	294.5
10	Scott Gardiner (Aus)	293.4

Sand saves

Pos	Name	%
1	Jean Van De Velde (Fr)	85.2
2	Tony Johnstone (Zim)	81.6
3	Bernhard Langer (Ger)	78.9
4	Miguel Angel Jiménez (Esp)	78.7
5	Brett Rumford (Aus)	78.3
6	Simon Hurd (Eng)	76.9
7	John Senden (Aus)	76.0
8	Seve Ballesteros (Esp)	72.5
9	José Maria Olazabal (Esp)	72.2
10	Padraig Harrington (Irl)	71.1

Greens in regulation

Pos	Name	%
1T	Greg Owen (Eng)	77.1
	Sergio Garcia (Esp)	77.1
	Padraig Harrington (Irl)	77.1
4T	Peter O'Malley (Aus)	76.5
	Retief Goosen (RSA)	76.5
6	Paul McGinley (Irl)	75.6
7	Steve Webster (Eng)	75.5
8	Richard Green (Aus)	75.4
9	Colin Montgomerie (Sco)	75.1
10	Adam Scott (Aus)	74.6

Putts per green in regulation

Pos	Name	Avg
1	Padraig Harrington (Irl)	1.723
2T	Michael Campbell (NZ)	1.731
	Thomas Bjørn (Den)	1.731
4T	Colin Montgomerie (Sco)	1.738
	Retief Goosen (RSA)	1.738
6	Pierre Fulke (Swe)	1.739
7	Darren Clarke (NI)	1.742
8	José Maria Olazabal (Esp)	1.744
9	Niclas Fasth (Swe)	1.745
10T	Phillip Price (Wal)	1.746
	Brian Davis (Eng)	1.746

TOUR RESULTS (in chronological order)

Johnnie Walker Classic

1992	I Palmer	Bangkok	268	1996	I Woosnam	Tanah Merah, Singapore	272
1993	N Faldo	Singapore Island	269	1997	E Els	Hope Island, Queensland	278
1994	G Norman	Blue Canyon, Phuket	277	1999	Not played		
1995	F Couples	Orchard GC, Manila	277	2000	M Campbell	Ta Shee, Taiwan	276

2001 at Alpine Club, Bangkok, Thailand   [6989-72]

1	Tiger Woods (USA)	68-65-65-65—263	£133330	€221134
2	Geoff Ogilvy (Aus)	68-67-67-64—266	88880	147411
3	Michael Campbell (NZ)	71-67-63-69—270	50080	83060

WGC Accenture Match Play

2000   Darren Clarke (NI) beat Tiger Woods (USA) 4 and 3 at Carlsbad, CA, USA

2001 at Metropolitan, Melbourne, Australia

Final: Steve Stricker (USA) ($1000000) beat Pierre Fulke (Swe) ($500000) 2 and 1

Consolation match: Toru Taniguchi (Jpn) ($400000) beat Ernie Els (RSA) ($300000) 4 and 3

Fuller details of this event are to be found on p.171

Alfred Dunhill Championship at Houghton, Johannesburg, RSA

(1995–99 combined with South African PGA Championship)

1995	E Els	Wanderers Club	271	1998	T Johnstone	Houghton GC	271
1996	S Strüver	Houghton GC	202 (54)	1999	E Els	Houghton GC	273
1997	N Price	Houghton GC	269	2000	A Wall	Houghton GC	204

2001   [7284-72]

1	Adam Scott (Aus)	67-66-65-69—267	£79000	€123072
2	Justin Rose (Eng)	66-67-66-69—268	57500	89578
3	Nick Faldo (Eng)	68-65-68-68—269	29625	46152
	Dean Robertson (Sco)	62-70-67-70—269	29625	46152

Mercedes Benz Vodacom South African Open

1992	E Els	1995	R Goosen	1998	E Els
1993	C Whitelaw	1996	E Els	1999	D Frost
1994	T Johnstone	1997	V Singh	2000	M Grönberg

2001 at East London, RSA   [6847-72]

1	Mark McNulty (Zim)	69-71-69-71—280	£107948	€169283
2	Justin Rose (Eng)	72-69-68-72—281	78322	122824
3	Thomas Bjørn (Den)	72-67-71-72—282	40251	63121
	Roger Wessels (RSA)	67-69-72-74—282	40251	63121

Heineken Classic

1996	I Woosnam (Wal)	277	1999	Jarrod Moseley (Aus)	274
1997	MA Martin (Esp)	273	2000	M Campbell (NZ)	268
1998	T Bjørn (Den)	280			

2001 at Vines Resort, Perth, Australia   [7101-72]

1	Michael Campbell (NZ)	69-70-67-64—270	£123450	€195499
2	David Smail (NZ)	71-72-66-66—275	69955	110783
3	Nick O'Hern (Aus)	66-69-69-72—276	46294	73312

Greg Norman Holden International

2000   L Parsons   Sydney, Australia   273

2001 *at Lakes Course, Sydney, Australia* [6904-73]

1	Aaron Baddeley (Aus)	67-68-68-68—271	£142402	€223594
2	Sergio García (Esp)	64-69-70-68—271	80694	126703
3	Ian Poulter (Eng)	70-69-65-68—272	53401	83848

Carlsberg Malaysian Open

1992	V Singh	1995	C Devers	1998	E Fryatt
1993	G Norquist	1996	S Fiesch	1999	G Norquist
1994	J Haegmann	1997	L Westwood	2000	Y Wei Tze

2001 *at Saujana, Malaysia* [6945-72]

1	Vijay Singh (Fij)	68-70-68-68—274	£104665	€163656
2	Padraig Harrington (Irl)	70-66-68-70—274	69779	109107
3	Ahmad Dan Bateman (USA)	72-69-68-67—276	35357	55285
	Charlie Wi (PRK)	70-70-67-69—276	35357	55285

Caltex Singapore Masters *at Singapore Island CC, Singapore* [6751-71]

1	Vijay Singh* (Fij)	64-63-68-68—263	£97663	€154617
2	Warren Bennett (Eng)	63-69-65-68—265	65109	103078
3	Maarten Lafeber (Ned)	64-67-70-65—266	32992	52232
	Colin Montgomerie (Sco)	66-67-70-65—266	32992	52232

Dubai Desert Classic *at Emirates GC, Dubai*

1989	M James*	277	1995	F Couples	268
1990	E Darcy	276	1996	C Montgomerie	270
1991	*Not played*		1997	R Green	272
1992	S Ballesteros*	272	1998	JM Olazábal	269
1993	W Westner	274	1999	D Howell	275
1994	E Els	268			

2001 [7127-72]

1	Thomas Bjørn (Den)	64-66-67-69—266	£166660	€265153
2	Padraig Harrington (Irl)	66-69-64-69—268	86855	138185
	Tiger Woods (USA)	64-64-68-72—268	86855	138185

Qatar Masters *at Doha, Qatar* [6500-72]

1998	A Coltart	270	1999	P Lawrie	268	2000	R Muntz	280

2001

1	Tony Johnstone (Zim)	68-70-66-70—274	£84890	€133833
2	Robert Karlsson (Swe)	63-70-70-73—276	56591	89218
3	Elliot Boult (NZ)	68-67-72-71—278	31885	50268

Madeira Island Open

1993	M James	Campo de Golf da Madeira	281	
1994	M Lanner	Campo de Golf da Madeira	206	(54)
1995	S Luna	Campo de Golf da Madeira	272	
1996	J Sandelin	Campo de Golf da Madeira	279	
1997	P Mitchell	Santo de Serra GC	204	(54)
1998	M Lanner	Santo de Serra GC	277	
1999	P Linhart	Santo da Serra GC	276	
2000	N Fasth	Santo de Serra GC	279	

Madeira Island Open *continued*

2001 *at Santo da Serra GC, Madeira*

1	Des Smyth (Irl)	66-70-68-66—270	£58181	€91660
2	John Bickerton (Eng)	67-67-69-69—272	38790	61110
3	Stephen Dodd (Wal)	71-67-66-70—274	16583	26125
	Niclas Fasth (Swe)	69-63-72-70—274	16583	26125
	Massimo Florioli (Ita)	68-68-65-73—274	16583	26125
	Massimo Scarpa (Ita)	69-68-70-67—274	16583	26125

Sao Paulo Brazil Open *at Sao Paulo*

1998   A Coltart   270

1	Darren Fichardt (RSA)	67-61-67—195	£78242	€125000
2	José Coceres (Arg)	68-64-68—200	35007	55927
	Richard S Johnson (Swe)	68-67-65—200	35007	55927
	Brett Rumford (Aus)	66-65-69—200	35007	55927

Open de Argentina *The Jockey Club, Buenos Aires, Argentina*   [6686-70]

1	Angel Cabrera (Arg)	67-65-69-67—268	£81626	€130697
2	Carl Pettersson (Swe)	65-69-67-69—270	54415	87128
3	Graeme Storm (Eng)	68-66-69-69—272	30661	49093

MASTERS *at Augusta National, Georgia, USA*   [6985-72]

1	Tiger Woods (USA)	70-66-68-68—272	£710359	€1146236
2	David Duval (USA)	71-66-70-67—274	426216	687742
3	Phil Mickelson (USA)	67-69-69-70—275	268358	433023

Fuller details of this event are included in Part I The Majors p.74

Moroccan Open *at Royal Golf, Dar Es Salam, Rabat, Morocco*   [7359-73]

1987	H Clark	Dar-es-Salam	284	1996	P Hedblom	Dar-es-Salam	281
1992	D Gilford*	Dar-es-Salam	287	1997	C Whitelaw	Golf Royal d'Agadir	277
1993	D Gilford	Golf Royal d'Agadir	279	1998	S Leaney	Golf Royal d'Agadir	271
1994	A Forsbrand	Golf Royal d'Agadir	276	1999	MA Martin*	Golf Royal d'Agadir	276
1995	M James	Golf Royal d'Agadir	275	2000	J Spence	Golf d'Amelkis	266

1	Ian Poulter (Eng)	71-67-69-70—277	£66660	€106507
2	David Lynn (Eng)	72-72-68-67—279	44440	71004
3	Peter Lonard (Aus)	71-75-66-68—280	25040	40008

Via Digital Open de España *El Saler, Valencia, Spain*   [6952-72]

1	Robert Karlsson (Swe)	68-68-71-70—277	£123840	€200000
2	Jean-François Remesy (Fra)	66-72-75-66—279	82558	133330
3	Søren Hansen (Den)	68-71-70-71—280	41833	67560
	Miguel Angel Jiménez (Esp)	71-69-70-70—280	41833	67560

Algarve Open de Portugal Quinta do Lago, Algarve, Portugal [7099-72]

1953	EC Brown	Estoril	260	1977	M Ramos	Penina	287
1954	A Miguel	Estoril	263	1978	H Clark	Penina	291
1955	F van Donck	Estoril	267	1979	B Barnes	Vilamoura	287
1956	A Miguel	Estoril	268	1982	S Torrance	Penina	207 (54)
1958	P Alliss	Estoril	264	1983	S Torrance	Troia	286
1959	S Miguel	Estoril	265	1984	A Johnstone	Quinta do Lago	274
1960	K Bousfield	Estoril	268	1985	W Humphreys	Quinta do Lago	279
1961	K Bousfield	Estoril	263	1986	M McNulty	Quinta do Lago	270
1962	A Angelini	Estoril	269	1987	R Lee	Estoril	195 (54)
1963	R Sota	Estoril	204 (54)	1988	M Harwood	Quinta do Lago	280
1964	A Miguel	Estoril	279	1989	C Montgomerie	Quinta do Lago	264
1966	A Angelini	Estoril	273	1990	M McLean	Quinta do Lago	274
1967	A Gallardo	Estoril	214 (54)	1991	S Richardson	Estela	283
1968	M Faulkner	Estoril	273	1992	R Rafferty	Vila Sol	273
1969	R Sota	Estoril	270	1993	D Gilford*	Vila Sol	275
1970	R Sota	Estoril	274	1994	P Price	Penha Longa	278
1971	L Platts	Estoril	277	1995	A Hunter*	Penha Longa	277
1972	G Garrido	Estoril	196 (54)	1996	W Riley	Aroeira	271
1973	J Benito*	Penina	294	1997	M Jonzon	Aroeira	269
1974	BGC Huggett	Estoril	272	1998	P Mitchell	Algarve	274
1975	H Underwood	Penina	292	1999	V Phillips*	Penina	276
1976	S Balbuena	Quinta do Lago	283	2000	G Orr	Penina	275

1	Phillip Price (Wal)	72-67-70-64—273	£104330	€166660
2	Padraig Harrington (Irl)	64-70-71-70—275	54372	86855
	Sven Strüver (Ger)	70-70-65-70—275	54372	86855

Novotel Perrier Open de France

1906	A Massy	La Boulie	292	1956	A Miguel	Deauville	277
1907	A Massy	La Boulie	294	1957	F van Donck	St Cloud	266
1908	JH Taylor	La Boulie	300	1958	F van Donck	St Germain	276
1909	JH Taylor	La Boulie	290	1959	DC Thomas	La Boulie	276
1910	J Braid	La Boulie	298	1960	R De Vicenzo	St Cloud	275
1911	A Massy	La Boulie	284	1961	KDG Nagle	La Boulie	271
1912	J Gassiat	La Boulie	284	1962	A Murray	St Germain	274
1913	G Duncan	Chantilly	304	1963	B Devlin	St Cloud	273
1914	JD Edgar	Le Touquet	284	1964	R de Vicenzo	Chantilly	272
1920	W Hagen	La Boulie	298	1965	R Sota	St Nom-la-Bretêche	268
1921	A Boomer	Le Touquet	284	1966	DJ Hutchinson	La Boulie	274
1922	A Boomer	La Boulie	284	1967	BJ Hunt	St Germain	271
1923	J Ockenden	Dieppe	284	1968	PJ Butler	St Cloud	272
1924	CJH Tolley (am)	La Boulie	290	1969	J Garaialde	St Nom-la-Bretêche	277
1925	A Massy	Chantilly	291	1970	D Graham	Chantaco	268
1926	A Boomer	St Cloud	280	1971	Lu Liang Huan	Biarritz	262
1927	G Duncan	St Germain	290	1972	B Jaeckel*	Biarritz & La Nivelle	265
1928	CJH Tolley (am)	La Boulie	283	1973	P Oosterhuis	La Boulie	280
1929	A Boomer	Fourqueux	283	1974	P Oosterhuis	Chantilly	284
1930	ER Whitcombe	Dieppe	282	1975	B Barnes	La Boulie	281
1931	A Boomer	Deauville	291	1976	V Tshabalaia	Le Touquet	272
1932	AJ Lacey	St Cloud	296	1977	S Ballesteros	Le Touquet	282
1933	B Gadd	Chantilly	283	1978	D Hayes	La Baule	269
1934	SF Brews	Dieppe	284	1979	B Gallacher	Lyons	284
1935	SF Brews	Le Touquet	292	1980	G Norman	St Cloud	268
1936	M Dallemagne	St Germain	277	1981	A Lyle	St Germain	270
1937	M Dallemagne	St Cloud	278	1982	S Ballesteros	St Nom-la-Bretêche	278
1938	M Dallemagne	Fourqueux	282	1983	N Faldo*	La Boulie	277
1939	M Pose	Le Touquet	285	1984	B Langer	St Cloud	270
1946	TH Cotton	St Cloud	269	1985	S Ballesteros	St Germain	263
1947	TH Cotton	Chantilly	285	1986	S Ballesteros	La Boulie	269
1948	F Cavalo	St Cloud	287	1987	J Rivero	St Cloud	269
1949	U Grappasonni	St Germain	275	1988	N Faldo	Chantilly	274
1950	R De Vicenzo	Chantilly	279	1989	N Faldo	Chantilly	273
1951	H Hassanein	St Cloud	278	1990	P Walton*	Chantilly	275
1952	AD Locke	St Germain	268	1991	E Romero	National GC	281
1953	AD Locke	La Boulie	276	1992	MA Martin	National GC	276
1954	F van Donck	St Cloud	275	1993	C Rocca*	National GC	273
1955	B Nelson	La Boulie	271	1994	M Roe	National GC	274

Novotel Perrier Open de France *continued*

1995	P Broadhurst	National GC	274	1998	S Torrance	National GC	276
1996	R Allenby*	National GC	272	1999	R Goosen*	Golf du Médoc	272
1997	R Goosen	National GC	271	2000	C Montgomerie	Le Golf National	272

2001 *at Lyon GC, Villette d'Anthon, France*   [7175-70]

1	José María Olazábal (Esp)	66-69-66-67—268	£134624	€216660
2	Paul Eales (Eng)	66-69-67-68—270	60235	96940
	Costantino Rocca (Ita)	68-69-64-69—270	60235	96940
	Greg Turner (NZ)	69-67-67-67—270	60235	96940

Benson and Hedges International Open

1971	A Jacklin*	Fulford	279	1986	M James*	Fulford	274
1972	J Newton	Fulford	281	1987	N Ratcliffe	Fulford	275
1973	V Baker	Fulford	276	1988	P Baker*	Fulford	271
1974	P Toussaint*	Fulford	276	1989	G Brand Jr	Fulford	272
1975	V Fernandez	Fulford	266	1990	JM Olazábal	St Mellion	279
1976	G Marsh	Fulford	272	1991	B Langer	St Mellion	286
1977	A Garrido	Fulford	280	1992	P Senior*	St Mellion	287
1978	L Trevino*	Fulford	274	1993	P Broadhurst	St Mellion	276
1979	M Bembridge	St Mellion	272	1994	S Ballesteros	St Mellion	281
1980	G Marsh	Fulford	272	1995	P O'Malley	St Mellion	280
1981	T Weiskopf	Fulford	272	1996	S Ames	The Oxfordshire	283
1982	G Norman	Fulford	283	1997	B Langer	The Oxfordshire	276
1983	J Bland	Fulford	273	1998	D Clarke	The Oxfordshire	273
1984	S Torrance	Fulford	270	1999	C Montgomerie	The Oxfordshire	273
1985	A Lyle	Fulford	274	2000	JM Olazábal	The Belfry	275

2001 *at The Belfry, Sutton Coldfield, England*   [7118-72]

1	Henrik Stenson (Swe)	66-68-71-70-275	£166660	€267918
2	Angel Cabrera (Arg)	70-70-69-69-278	86855	139626
	Paul McGinley (Irl)	66-72-70-70-278	86855	139626

Deutsche Bank – SAP Open TPC of Europe

1977	N Coles	Foxhills	288	1989	C Montgomerie	Quinta do Lago	264
1978	B Waites	Foxhills	286	1990	M McLean	Quinta do Lago	274
1979	M King	Moor Park	281	1991	*not played*		
1980	B Gallacher	Moortown	268	1992	*not played*		
1981	B Barnes*	Dalmahoy	276	1993	*not played*		
1982	N Faldo	Notts	270	1994	*not played*		
1983	B Langer	St Mellion	269	1995	B Langer	Gut Kaden	270
1984	J Gonzalez*	St Mellion	265	1996	F Nobilo	Gut Kaden	270
1985	*Not played*			1997	R McFarlane	Gut Kaden	282
1986	I Woosnam	The Belfry	277	1998	L Westwood	Gut Kaden	265
1987	*Not played*			1999	T Woods	St Leon Rot	273
1988	*Not played*			2000	L Westwood	Gut Kaden, Hamburg	273

2001 *at St Leon-Rot, Heidelberg, Germany*   [7207-72]

1	Tiger Woods (USA)	69-68-63-66—266	£278025	€450000
2	Michael Campbell (NZ)	62-65-73-70—270	185350	300000
3	Søren Kjeldsen (Den)	70-67-69-65—271	93914	152005
	Peter O'Malley (Aus)	71-68-63-69—271	93914	152005

Volvo PGA Championship

1955	K Bousfield	Pannal	277		1978	N Faldo	R Birkdale	278
1956	CH Ward	Maesdu	282		1979	V Fernandez	St Andrews	288
1957	P Alliss	Maesdu	286		1980	N Faldo	R St George's	283
1958	H Bradshaw	Llandudno	287		1981	N Faldo	Ganton	274
1959	DJ Rees	Ashburnham	283		1982	A Jacklin*	Hillside	284
1960	AF Stickley	Coventry	247 (63)		1983	S Ballesteros	R St George's	278
1961	BJ Bamford	R Mid-Surrey	266		1984	H Clark	Wentworth Club	204 (54)
1962	P Alliss	Little Aston	287		1985	P Way*	Wentworth Club	282
1963	PJ Butler	R Birkdale	306		1986	R Davis*	Wentworth Club	281
1964	AG Grubb	Western Gailes	287		1987	B Langer	Wentworth Club	270
1965	P Alliss	Prince's	286		1988	I Woosnam	Wentworth Club	274
1966	GB Wolstenholme	Saunton	278		1989	N Faldo	Wentworth Club	272
1967	BGC Huggett	Thorndon Park	271		1990	M Harwood	Wentworth Club	271
1967	ME Gregson	Hunstanton	275		1991	S Ballesteros*	Wentworth Club	271
1968	PM Townsend	R Mid-Surrey	275		1992	T Johnstone	Wentworth Club	272
1968	D Talbot	Dunbar	276		1993	B Langer	Wentworth Club	274
1969	B Gallacher	Ashburnham	293		1994	JM Olazábal	Wentworth Club	271
1972	A Jacklin	Wentworth Club	279		1995	B Langer	Wentworth Club	279
1973	P Oosterhuis	Wentworth Club	280		1996	C Rocca	Wentworth Club	274
1974	M Bembridge	Wentworth Club	278		1997	I Woosnam	Wentworth Club	275
1975	A Palmer	R St George's	285		1998	C Montgomerie	Wentworth Club	274
1976	NC Coles*	R St George's	280		1999	C Montgomerie	Wentworth Club	270
1977	M Piñero	R St George's	283		2000	C Montgomerie	Wentworth Club	271

2001 *at Wentworth Club, Virginia Water, Surrey* [7047-72]

1	Andrew Oldcorn (Sco)	66-66-69-71--272		£333330	€544521
2	Angel Cabrera (Arg)	63-71-72-68--274		222220	363014
3	Nick Faldo (Eng)	72-66-70-67--275		125200	204524
4	Phillip Price (Wal)	65-69-72-71--277		84933	138745
	Mathias Grönberg (Swe)	71-69-72-65--277		84933	138745
	Michael Campbell (NZ)	70-70-67-70--277		84933	138745
7	Vijay Singh (Fij)	73-65-70-70--278		60000	98015
8	Peter Baker (Eng)	67-72-75-65--279		44933	73402
	Darren Clarke (NI)	72-69-68-70--279		44933	73402
	Gary Orr (Sco)	74-67-69-69--279		44933	73402
11	José María Olazábal (Esp)	72-68-67-73--280		34467	56304
	Steve Webster (Eng)	67-68-72-73--280		34467	56304
	Dean Robertson (Sco)	68-68-75-69--280		34467	56304
14	John Senden (Aus)	71-67-72-71--281		29400	48027
	Niclas Fasth (Swe)	69-68-69-75--281		29400	48027
	Simon Dyson (Eng)	68-72-72-69--281		29400	48027
17	Richard Green (Aus)	73-68-70-71--282		25400	41493
	Anthony Wall (Eng)	70-70-72-70--282		25400	41493
	Colin Montgomerie (Sco)	73-69-69-71--282		25400	41493
	Paul Lawrie (Sco)	69-68-72-73--282		25400	41493
21	Ian Woosnam (Wal)	71-68-73-71--283		22000	35939
	Anders Hansen (Den)	71-70-72-70--283		22000	35939
	Stephen Leaney (Aus)	70-64-74-75--283		22000	35939
	Gary Emerson (Eng)	70-69-71-73--283		22000	35939
	Mikael Lundberg (Swe)	67-72-70-74--283		22000	35939
26	Raphaël Jacquelin (Fra)	69-68-74-73--284		18700	30548
	Thomas Levet (Fra)	72-71-72-69--284		18700	30548
	Peter O'Malley (Aus)	69-71-71-73--284		18700	30548
	Paul McGinley (Irl)	66-74-73-71--284		18700	30548
	Ian Garbutt (Eng)	71-71-70-72--284		18700	30548
	Diego Borrego (Esp)	72-70-69-73--284		18700	30548
32	Søren Kjeldsen (Den)	71-66-72-76--285		15086	24644
	Justin Rose (Eng)	72-69-73-71--285		15086	24644
	Joakim Haeggman (Swe)	68-73-74-70--285		15086	24644
	Greg Owen (Eng)	69-74-68-74--285		15086	24644
	Markus Brier (Aut)	72-71-71-71--285		15086	24644
	Andrew Coltart (Sco)	68-69-71-77--285		15086	24644

Volvo PGA Championship *continued*

37T	Adam Scott (Aus)	70-69-74-72--285	15086	24644
39	Henrik Stenson (Swe)	76-66-71-73--286	12400	20256
	Ernie Els (RSA)	70-72-68-76--286	12400	20256
	Rolf Muntz (Ned)	71-67-74-74--286	12400	20256
	Thomas Bjørn (Den)	68-69-72-77--286	12400	20256
	Henrik Nystrom (Swe)	69-72-72-73--286	12400	20256
	Christopher Hanell (Swe)	72-71-72-71--286	12400	20256
45	Eamonn Darcy (Irl)	72-71-71-73--287	9200	15029
	Des Smyth (Irl)	70-68-75-74--287	9200	15029
	Padraig Harrington (Irl)	67-75-69-76--287	9200	15029
	Carlos Rodiles (Esp)	69-70-78-70--287	9200	15029
	Steen Tinning (Den)	70-73-73-71--287	9200	15029
	Jonathan Lomas (Eng)	72-67-73-75--287	9200	15029
	Nicolas Vanhootegem (Bel)	69-71-72-75--287	9200	15029
	David Lynn (Eng)	72-71-75-69--287	9200	15029
	Patrik Sjöland (Swe)	70-73-74-70--287	9200	15029
	John Bickerton (Eng)	69-71-76-71--287	9200	15029
55	Paul Broadhurst (Eng)	69-74-73-72--288	6600	10782
	David Higgins (Irl)	72-71-74-71--288	6600	10782
	Alastair Forsyth (Sco)	67-73-75-73--288	6600	10782
58	Miguel Angel Martin (Esp)	69-70-75-75--289	5600	9148
	Damian McGrane (Irl)	68-72-70-79--289	5600	9148
	Nick O'Hern (Aus)	66-71-78-74--289	5600	9148
	Søren Hansen (Den)	71-70-73-75--289	5600	9148
	Raymond Russell (Sco)	72-69-76-72--289	5600	9148
63	Warren Bennett (Eng)	71-68-76-75--290	4700	7678
	Jean Hugo (RSA)	72-70-75-73--290	4700	7678
	Emanuele Canonica (Ita)	71-70-72-77--290	4700	7678
63T	Peter Lonard (Aus)	71-71-72-76--290	4700	7678
67	Robert Karlsson (Swe)	72-70-73-76--291	4000	6534
	Alex Cejka (Ger)	73-70-75-73--291	4000	6534
	Pierre Fulke (Swe)	71-70-79-71--291	4000	6534
70	Gary Evans (Eng)	71-71-77-74--293	3650	5963
71	Jarmo Sandelin (Swe)	71-72-73-78--294	3000	4901
72	Jeev Milkha Singh (Ind)	76-67-76-80--299	2998	4898

Victor Chandler British Masters

1946T	AD Locke	Stoneham	286	1969	C Legrange	Little Aston	281
	J Adams			1970	B Huggett	R Lytham & St Annes	293
1947	A Lees	Little Aston	283	1971	M Bembridge	St Pierre	273
1948	N Von Nida	Sunningdale	272	1972	R J Charles	Northumberland	277
1949	C Ward	St Andrews	290	1973	A Jacklin	St Pierre	272
1950	D Rees	Hoylake	281	1974	B Gallacher*	St Pierre	282
1951	M Faulkner	Wentworth Club	281	1975	B Gallacher	Ganton	289
1952	H Weetman	Mere	281	1976	B Dassu	St Pierre	271
1953	H Bradshaw	Sunningdale	272	1977	G Hunt*	Lindrick	291
1954	AD Locke	Prince's	291	1978	T Horton	St Pierre	279
1955	H Bradshaw	Little Aston	277	1979	G Marsh	Woburn	283
1956	C O'Connor	Prestwick	277	1980	B Langer	St Pierre	270
1957	E Brown	Hollinwell	275	1981	G Norman	Woburn	273
1958	H Weetman	Little Aston	276	1982	G Norman	St Pierre	267
1959	C O'Connor	Portmarnock	276	1983	L Woosnam	St Pierre	269
1960	J Hitchcock	Sunningdale	275	1985	L Trevino	Woburn	278
1961	P Thomson	Porthcawl	284	1986	S Ballesteros	Woburn	275
1962	D Rees	Wentworth Club	278	1987	M McNulty	Woburn	274
1963	B Hunt	Little Aston	282	1988	A Lyle	Woburn	273
1964	C Legrange	Royal Birkdale	288	1989	N Faldo	Woburn	267
1965	B Hunt	Portmarnock	283	1990	M James	Woburn	270
1966	N Coles	Lindrick	278	1991	S Ballesteros	Woburn	275
1967	A Jacklin	R St George's	274	1992	C O'Connor jr*	Woburn	270
1968	P Thomson	Sunningdale	274	1993	P Baker	Woburn	266

1994	I Woosnam	Woburn	271	1998	C Montgomerie	Forest of Arden	281
1995	S Torrance	Collingtree Park	270	1999	B May	Woburn	269
1996	R Allenby*	Collingtree Park	284	2000	G Orr	Woburn	267
1997	G Turner	Forest of Arden	275					

2001 *at Woburn, Milton Keynes, England*

1	Thomas Levet* (Fra)	69-69-67-69—274	£208330	€345080
2	Mathias Grönberg (Swe)	69-70-67-68—274	93210	154394
	David Howell (Eng)	68-65-68-73—274	93210	154394
	Robert Karlsson (Swe)	66-67-69-72—274	93210	154394

The Compass Group English Open

1979	S Ballesteros	The Belfry	286	1993	I Woosnam	Forest of Arden	269
1980	M Piñero	The Belfry	286	1994	C Montgomerie	Forest of Arden	274
1981	R Davis	The Belfry	283	1995	P Walton*	Forest of Arden	274
1982	G Norman	The Belfry	279	1996	R Allenby	Forest of Arden	278
1983	H Baiocchi*	The Belfry	279	1997	P-U Johansson	Hanbury Manor	269
1988	H Clark	Royal Birkdale	279	1998	L Westwood	Hanbury Manor	271
1990	M James*	The Belfry	284	1999	D Clarke	Hanbury Manor	268
1991	D Gilford	The Belfry	278	2000	D Clarke	Forest of Arden	275
1992	V Fernandez	The Belfry	283				

2001 *at Forest of Arden, Warwickshire* [7182-72]

1	Peter O'Malley (Aus)	70-69-70-66—275	£133330	€223373
2	Raphaël Jacquelin (Fra)	73-67-66-70—276	88880	148904
3	Adam Scott (Aus)	67-70-67-73—277	50080	83901

US OPEN

2001 *at Southern Hills, Tulsa, OK* [6973-70]

1	Retief Goosen* (RSA)	66-70-69-71—276	£651372	€1058199
2	Mark Brooks (USA)	72-64-70-70—276	383585	623161
3	Stewart Cink (USA)	69-69-67-72—277	235442	382492

Fuller details of this event are included in Part I The Majors p.66

The Great North Open *at Slaley Hall, Northumberland, England* [7088-72]

1996	R Goosen	277	1998	cancelled		2000	L Westwood	276
1997	C Montgomerie	270	1999	D park	274			

2001

1	Andrew Coltart (Sco)	68-68-69-72—277	£133330	€217209
2	Paul Casey (Eng)	71-66-72-69—278	69480	113191
	Stephen Gallacher (Sco)	76-67-67-68—278	69480	113191

Murphy's Irish Open

1927	G Duncan	Portmarnock	312	1948	D Rees	Portmarnock	295
1928	E Whitcombe	Newcastle	288	1949	H Bradshaw	Belvoir Park	286
1929	A Mitchell	Portmarnock	309	1950	H Pickworth	Royal Dublin	287
1930	C Whitcombe	Portrush	289	1953	E Brown	Belvoir Park	272
1931	E Kenyon	Royal Dublin	291	1975	C O'Connor Jr	Woodbrook	275
1932	A Padgham	Cork	283	1976	B Crenshaw	Portmarnock	284
1933	E Kenyon	Malone	286	1977	H Green	Portmarnock	283
1934	S Easterbrook	Portmarnock	284	1978	K Brown	Portmarnock	281
1935	E Whitcombe	Newcastle	292	1979	M James	Portmarnock	282
1936	R Whitcombe	Royal Dublin	281	1980	M James	Portmarnock	284
1937	B Gadd	Portrush	284	1981	S Torrance	Portmarnock	276
1938	A Locke	Portmarnock	292	1982	J O'Leary	Portmarnock	287
1939	A Lees	Newcastle	287	1983	S Ballesteros	Royal Dublin	271
1946	F Daly	Portmarnock	288	1984	B Langer	Royal Dublin	267
1947	H Bradshaw	Portrush	290	1985	S Ballesteros*	Royal Dublin	278

Murphy's Irish Open *continued*

1986	S Ballesteros	Portmarnock	285	1994	B Langer	Mount Juliet	275
1987	B Langer	Portmarnock	269	1995	S Torrance*	Mount Juliet	277
1988	I Woosnam	Portmarnock	278	1996	C Montgomerie	Druid's Glen	279
1989	I Woosnam*	Portmarnock	278	1997	C Montgomerie	Druid's Glen	269
1990	JM Olazábal	Portmarnock	282	1998	D Carter	Druid's Glen	278
1991	N Faldo	Killarney	283	1999	S García	Druid's Glen	268
1992	N Faldo*	Killarney	274	2000	P Sjöland	Ballybunion	270
1993	N Faldo*	Mount Juliet	276				

2001 *at Fota Island, Cork, Ireland*   [6927-71]

1	Colin Montgomerie (Sco)	63-69-68-66—266	£161618	€266660
2	Darren Clarke (NI)	70-72-65-64—271	72312	119310
	Niclas Fasth (Swe)	68-71-69-63—271	72312	119310
	Padraig Harrington (Irl)	67-72-68-64—271	72312	119310

Smurfit European Open

1978	B Wadkins*	Walton Heath	283	1990	P Senior	Sunningdale	267
1979	A Lyle	Turnberry	275	1991	M Harwood	Walton Heath	277
1980	T Kite	Walton Heath	284	1992	N Faldo	Sunningdale	262
1981	G Marsh	Royal Liverpool	275	1993	G Brand jr	E. Sussex National	275
1982	M Piñero	Sunningdale	266	1994	D Gilford	E. Sussex National	275
1983	L Aoki	Sunningdale	274	1995	B Langer*	The K Club	280
1984	G Brand jr	Sunningdale	270	1996	P-U Johansson	The K Club	277
1985	B Langer	Sunningdale	269	1997	P-U Johansson	The K Club	267
1986	G Norman*	Sunningdale	269	1998	M Grönberg	The K Club	275
1987	P Way	Walton Heath	279	1999	L Westwood	The K Club	271
1988	I Woosnam	Sunningdale	260	2000	L Westwood	The K Club	276
1989	A Murray	Walton Heath	277				

2001 *at The K Club, Dublin, Ireland*   [7227-72]

1	Darren Clarke (NI)	68-68-71-66-273	£333330	€553728
2	Thomas Bjørn (Den)	69-66-73-68-276	149140	247751
	Padraig Harrington (Irl)	70-67-69-70-276	149140	247751
	Ian Woosnam (Wal)	69-66-73-68-276	149140	247751

The Scottish Open

1986	D Feherty*	Haggs Castle	270	1994	C Mason	Gleneagles	265
1987	I Woosnam	Gleneagles	264	1995	W Riley	Carnoustie	276
1988	B Lane	Gleneagles	271	1996	I Woosnam	Carnoustie	289
1989	M Allen	Gleneagles	272		T Bjørn	Loch Lomond	277
1990	I Woosnam	Gleneagles	269	1997	T Lehman	Loch Lomond	265
1991	C Parry	Gleneagles	268	1998	L Westwood	Loch Lomond	276
1992	P O'Malley	Gleneagles	262	1999	C Montgomerie	Loch Lomond	268
1993	J Parnevik	Gleneagles	271	2000	E Els	Loch Lomond	273

2001 *at Loch Lomond, Glasgow, Scotland*   [7050-71]

1	Retief Goosen (RSA)	62-69-66-71-268	£366660	€610999
2	Thomas Bjørn (Den)	68-67-69-67-271	244440	407332
3	John Daly (USA)	68-68-66-70-272	104500	174138
	Barry Lane (Eng)	70-65-69-68-272	104500	174138
	Paul McGinley (Irl)	68-67-67-70-272	104500	174138
	Adam Scott (Aus)	65-68-67-72-272	104500	174138

It has been decided officially that results in the Standard Life Invitational at Loch Lomond
(1996–2000) will be counted as the Scottish Open results.

OPEN CHAMPIONSHIP

2001 *at Royal Lytham & St Annes*   [6905-71]

1	David Duval (USA)	69-73-65-67—274	£600000	€984756
2	Niclas Fasth (Swe)	69-69-72-67—277	360000	590854
3	Darren Clarke (NI)	70-69-69-70—278	141667	232512
	Ernie Els (RSA)	71-71-67-69—278	141667	232512
	Miguel Angel Jiménez (Esp)	69-72-67-70—278	141667	232512
	Bernhard Langer (Ger)	71-69-67-71—278	141667	232512
	Billy Mayfair (USA)	69-72-67-70—278	141667	232512
	Ian Woosnam (Wal)	72-68-67-71—278	141667	232512

Past results and fuller details in Part I The Majors p.56

TNT Dutch Open

1919	D Oosterveer	The Hague	158		1963	R Waltman	Wassenaar	279
1920	H Burrows	Kennemer	155		1964	S Sewgolum	Eindhoven	275
1921	H Burrows	Domburg	151		1965	A Miguel	Breda	278
1922	G Pannell	Noordwijk	160		1966	R Sota	Kennemer	276
1923	H Burrows	Hilversumsche	153		1967	P Townsend	The Hague	282
1924	A Boomer	The Hague	138		1968	J Cockin	Hilversumsche	292
1925	A Boomer	The Hague	144		1969	G Wolstenholme	Utrecht	277
1926	A Boomer	The Hague	151		1970	V Fernandez	Eindhoven	279
1927	P Boomer	The Hague	147		1971	R Sota	Kennemer	277
1928	ER Whitcombe	The Hague	141		1972	J Newton	The Hague	277
1929	JJ Taylor	Hilversumsche	153		1973	D McClelland	The Hague	279
1930	J Oosterveer	The Hague	152		1974	B Barnes	Hilversumsche	211 (54)
1931	F Dyer	Kennemer	145		1975	H Baiocchi	Hilversumsche	279
1932	A Boyer	The Hague	137		1976	S Ballesteros	Kennemer	275
1933	M Dallemagne	Kennemer	143		1977	R Byman	Kennemer	278
1934	SF Brews	Utrecht	286		1978	R Byman	Noordwijkse	21 (54)
1935	SF Brews	Kennemer	275		1979	G Marsh	Noordwijkse	285
1936	F van Donck	Hilversumsche	285		1980	S Ballesteros	Hilversumsche	280
1937	F van Donck	Utrecht	286		1981	H Henning	The Hague	280
1938	AH Padgham	The Hague	281		1982	P Way	Utrecht	276
1939	AD Locke	Kennemer	281		1983	K Brown	Kennemer	274
1946	F van Donck	Hilversumsche	290		1984	B Langer	Rosendaelsche	275
1947	G Ruhl	Eindhoven	290		1985	G Marsh	Noordwijkse	282
1948	C Denny	Hilversumsche	290		1986	S Ballesteros	Noordwijkse	271 (70)
1949	J Adams	The Hague	294		1987	G Brand jr	Hilversumsche	272
1950	R De Vicenzo	Breda	269		1988	M Mouland	Hilversumsche	274
1951	F van Donck	Kennemer	281		1989	JM Olazábal*	Kennemer	277
1952	C Denny	Hilversumsche	284		1990	S McAllister	Kennemer	274
1953	F van Donck	Eindhoven	286		1991	P Stewart	Noordwijkse	267
1954	U Grappasonni	The Hague	295		1992	B Langer*	Noordwijkse	277
1955	A Angelini	Kennemer	280		1993	C Montgomerie	Noordwijkse	281
1956	A Cerda	Eindhoven	277		1994	MA Jiménez	Hilversumsche	270
1957	J Jacobs	Hilversumsche	284		1995	S Hoch	Hilversumsche	269
1958	D Thomas	Kennemer	277		1996	M McNulty	Hilversumsche	266
1959	S Sewgolum	The Hague	283		1997	S Strüver	Hilversumsche	266
1960	S Sewgolum	Eindhoven	280		1998	S Leaney	Hilversumsche	266
1961	BBS Wilkes	Kennemer	279		1999	L Westwood	Hilversumsche	269
1962	BGC Huggett	Hilversumsche	274		2000	S Leaney	Nordwijkse	269

2001 *at Nordwijkse, The Netherlands*   [6741-71]

1	Bernhard Langer*(Ger)	69-67-67-66—269	£182918	€300000
2	Warren Bennett (Eng)	68-67-67-67—269	121945	200000
3	Miguel Angel Jiménez (Esp)	71-65-71-66—273	68704	112680

Volvo Scandinavian Masters

1991	C Montgomerie	Drottningholm	270	1996	L Westwood	Forsgårdens	281
1992	N Faldo	Barsebäck	277	1997	J Haeggman	Barsebäck	270
1993	P Baker*	Forsgårdens	278	1998	J Parnevik	Kungsängen	273
1994	V Singh	Drottningholm	268	1999	C Montgomerie	Barsebåck	268
1995	J Parnevik	Barsebäck	270	2000	L Westwood	Kungsängen	270

2001 *at Kungsängen, Stockholm, Sweden*   [7323-72]

1	Colin Montgomerie (Sco)	66-69-69-70—274	£184112	€300000
2	Ian Poulter (Eng)	70-65-68-72—275	95947	156340
	Lee Westwood (Eng)	67-67-69-72—275	95947	156340

The Wales Open *at Celtic Manor Resort, Newport, Wales*   [7324-72]

2000	S Tinning	Newport	223

2001

1	Paul McGinley*(Irl)	67-71—138	£125000	€201685
2	Paul Lawrie (Sco)	67-71—138	65140	105102
	Daren Lee (Eng)	69-69—138	65140	105102

Rain washed out further rounds. Winner won on 5th hole of play-off.

US PGA CHAMPIONSHIP

2001 *at Atlanta Athletic Club, GA, USA*   [7213-70]

1	David Toms (USA)	66-65-65-69—265	£655783	€1046978
2	Phil Mickelson (USA)	66-66-66-68—266	393750	628634
3	Steve Lowery (USA)	67-67-66-68—268	248021	395973

Past results and fuller details in Part I The Majors p.81

North West of Ireland Open

2001 *at Co. Cavan, Ireland*   [7061-72]

1	Tobias Dier (Ger)	66-68-66-71—271	£36535	€58330
2	Stephen Dodd (Wal)	67-68-68-69—272	24353	38880
3	Mark Pilkington (Wal)	68-69-69-68—274	13724	21910

WGC: NEC Invitational *at Firestone CC, Akron, Ohio, USA*   [7139-70]

1	Tiger Woods* (USA)	66-67-66-69—268	£691324	€1091096
2	Jim Furyk (USA)	65-66-66-71—268	345662	545548
3	Darren Clarke (NI)	66-68-68-69—271	259246	409161

Fuller details of this event are included in *World Championship Events*

Scottish PGA Championship

1999	W Bennett
2000	P Fulke

2001 *at King's Course, Gleneagles, Scotland*   [7060-72]

1	Paul Casey (Eng)	69-69-67-69—274	£166660	€263035
2	Alex Cejka (Ger)	71-67-66-71—275	111110	175362
3	David Howell (Eng)	70-71-66-70—277	62600	98800

BMW International Open

1989	D Feherty	Golfplatz, Munich	269	1996	M Farry	St Eurach L&GC	132
1990	P Azinger*	Golfplatz, Munich	277	*(36 holes only)*			
.1991	A Lyle	Golfplatz, Munich	268	1997	R Karlsson	GC München	264
1992	P Azinger*	Golfplatz, Munich	266	1998	R Claydon	GC München	270
1993	P Fowler	Golfplatz, Munich	267	1999	C Montgomerie	GC München	268
1994	M McNulty	St Eurach L&GC	274	2000	T Bjørn	GC München	368
1995	F Nobilo	St Eurach L&GC	272				

2001 *at Golfclub München Nord-Eichenried, Munich* [6914-72]

1	John Daly (USA)	63-64-68-66—261	£189352	€300000
2	Padraig Harrington (Irl)	69-63-62-68—262	126235	200000
3	Thomas Levet (Fra)	70-66-64-68—268	71121	112680

Omega European Masters *at Crans-sur-Sierre, Switzerland* (since 1939)

1923	A Ross	Engen	149	1968	R Bernardini		272
1924	P Boomer	Engen	150	1969	R Bernardini		277
1925	A Ross	Engen	148	1970	G Marsh		274
1926	A Ross	Lucerne	145	1971	PM Townsend		270
1929	A Wilson	Lucerne	142	1972	G Marsh		270
1930	A Boyer	Samedan	150	1973	H Baiocchi		278
1931	M Dallemagne	Lucerne	145	1974	RJ Charles		275
1934	A Boyer	Lausanne	133	1975	D Hayes		273
·1935	A Boyer	Lausanne	137	1976	M Piñero		274
1936	F Francis (am)	Lausanne	134	1977	S Ballesteros		273
1937	M Dallemagne	Samedan	138	1978	S Ballesteros		272
1938	J Saubaber	Zumikon	139	1979	H Baiocchi		275
1939	F Cavalo	Crans-sur-Sierre	273	1980	N Price		267
1948	U Grappasonni		285	1981	M Piñero*		277
1949	M Dallemagne		270	1982	I Woosnam*		272
1950	A Casera		276	1983	N Faldo*		268
1951	EC Brown		267	1984	J Anderson		261
1952	U Grappasonni		267	1985	C Stadler		267
1953	F van Donck		267	1986	JM Olazábal		262
1954	AD Locke		276	1987	A Forsbrand		263
1955	F van Donck		277	1988	C Moody		268
1956	DJ Rees		278	1989	S Ballesteros		266
1957	A Angelini		270	1990	R Rafferty		267
1958	K Bousfield		272	1991	J Hawkes		268
1959	DJ Rees		274	1992	J Spence*		271
1960	H Henning		270	1993	B Lane		270
1961	KDG Nagle		268	1994	E Romero		266
1962	RJ Charles*		272	1995	M Grönberg		270
1963	DJ Rees*		278	1996	C Montgomerie		260
1964	HR Henning		276	1997	C Rocca		266
1965	HR Henning		208 (54)	1998	S Strüver		263
1966	A Angelini		271	1999	L Westwood		270
1967	R Vines		272	2000	E Romero		261

2001

1	Ricardo Gonzalez (Arg)	65-67-68-68—268	£156616	€250000
2	Soren Hansen (Den)	70-65-68-68—271	104407	166660
3	Gary Orr (Sco)	67-66-71-69—273	52905	84450
	Craig Stadler (USA)	69-69-67-68—273	52905	84450

WGC: American Express Championship
This event was cancelled

Trophée Lancôme *at Saint-Nom-La-Bretèche, Paris*

1970	A Jacklin	206	(54)	1986T	S Ballesteros*	274
1971	A Palmer	202	(54)		B Langer*	
1972	T Aaron	279		1987	I Woosnam	264
1973	J Miller	277		1988	S Ballesteros	269
1974	W Casper	283		1989	E Romero	266
1975	G Player	278		1990	JM Olazábal	269
1976	S Ballesteros	283		1991	F Nobilo	267
1977	G Marsh*	273		1992	M Roe	267
1978	L Trevino	272		1993	I Woosnam	267
1979	J Miller	281		1994	V Singh	263
1980	L Trevino	280		1995	C Montgomerie	269
1981	D Graham	280		1996	J Parnevik	268
1982	D Graham	276		1997	M O'Meara	271
1983	S Ballesteros	269		1998	MA Jiménez	273
1984	A Lyle*	278		1999	P Fulke	270
1985	N Price*	275		2000	R Goosen	271

2001

1	Sergio García (Esp)	68-65-68-65—266	£150000	€239782
2	Retief Goosen (RSA)	64-71-65-67—267	100000	159855
3	Jean Hugo (RSA)	66-68-69-66—269	56340	90062

RYDER CUP *Postponed until 2002*

Linde German Masters

2001 *at Gut Lärchenhof, Cologne*   [7289–72]

1987	A Lyle*	Stuttgart	278	1994	S Ballesteros*	Motzener See	270
1988	JM Olazábal	Stuttgart	279	1995	A Forsbrand	Motzener See	264
1989	B Langer	Stuttgart	276	1996	D Clarke	Motzener See	264
1990	S Torrance	Stuttgart	272	1997	B Langer	Berliner G & CG	267
1991	B Langer*	Stuttgart	275	1998	C Montgomerie	Gut Lärchenhof	266
1992	B Lane	Stuttgart	272	1999	S García	Gut Lärchenhof	277
1993	S Richardson	Stuttgart	271	2000	M Campbell (NZ)	Gut Lärchenhof	197

1	Bernhard Langer (Ger)	67-64-68-67—266	€450000
2	John Daly (USA)	71-67-64-65—267	234510
	Fredrik Jacobson (Swe)	67-66-67-67—267	234510

Cannes Open *at Cannes Mougins, Cannes, France*   [6860–72]

1984	D Frost	1989	P Broadhurst	1994	I Woosnam	1999	*not played*
1985	R Lee	1990	M McNulty	1995	A Bossert	2000	*not played*
1986	J Bland	1991	D Feherty	1996	R Russell		
1987	S Ballesteros	1992	A Forsbrand	1997	S Cage		
1988	M McNulty	1993	R Davis	1998	T Levet		

1	Jorge Berendt (Arg)	67-66-67-68—268	€92500
2	Jean Van De Velde (Fra)	70-66-68-65—269	61660
3	Thomas Levet (Fra)	69-66-69-68—272	28675
	Santiago Luna (Esp)	70-66-68-68—272	28675
	Andrew Marshall (Eng)	65-68-69-70—272	28675

Cisco World Matchplay Championship

1964	A Palmer	N Coles	2 and 1		1983	G Norman	N Faldo	3 and 2
1965	G Player	P Thomson	3 and 2		1984	S Ballesteros	B Langer	2 and 1
1966	G Player	J Nicklaus	6 and 4		1985	S Ballesteros	B Langer	6 and 5
1967	A Palmer	P Thomson	1 hole		1986	G Norman	A Lyle	2 and 1
1968	G Player	R Charles	1 hole		1987	I Woosnam	A Lyle	1 hole
1969	R Charles	G Littler	37th hole		1988	A Lyle	N Faldo	2 and 1
1970	J Nicklaus	L Trevino	2 and 1		1989	N Faldo	I Woosnam	1 hole
1971	G Player	J Nicklaus	5 and 4		1990	I Woosnam	M McNulty	4 and 2
1972	T Weiskopf	L Trevino	4 and 3		1991	S Ballesteros	N Price	3 and 2
1973	G Player	G Marsh	40th hole		1992	N Faldo	J Sluman	8 and 7
1974	H Irwin	G Player	3 and 1		1993	C Pavin	N Faldo	1 hole
1975	H Irwin	A Geiberger	4 and 2		1994	E Els	C Montgomerie	4 and 2
1976	D Graham	H Irwin	38th hole		1995	E Els	S Elkington	2 and 1
1977	G Marsh	R Floyd	5 and 3		1996	E Els	V Singh	3 and 2
1978	I Aoki	S Owen	3 and 2		1997	V Singh	E Els	1 hole
1979	W Rogers	I Aoki	1 hole		1998	M O'Meara	T Woods	1 hole
1980	G Norman	A Lyle	1 hole		1999	C Montgomerie	M O'Meara	3 and 2
1981	S Ballesteros	B Crenshaw	1 hole		2000	L Westwood	C Montgomerie	38th hole
1982	S Ballesteros	A Lyle	37th hole					

2001 *at Wentworth, Surrey, England*

First Round
Thomas Bjørn (Den) beat Adam Scott (Aus) 4 and 3
Ian Woosnam (Wal) beat Retief Goosen (RSA) 4 and 3
Padraig Harrington (Irl) beat Nick Faldo (Eng) 9 and 8
Sam Torrance (Sco) beat Seve Ballesteros (Esp) 3 and 2

Quarter Finals
Lee Westwood (Eng) beat Bjørn 1 hole
Woosnam beat Colin Montgomerie (Sco) 4 and 3
Harrington beat Darren Clarke (NI) 5 and 4
Torrance beat Vijay Singh (Fij) 1 hole

Semi-Finals
Woosnam beat Westwood 10 and 9
Harrington beat Torrance 4 and 3

Final
Ian Woosnam beat Padraig
Harrington 2 and 1

Dunhill Links Championship

2001 *at St Andrews Old Course* [7115–72]; *Kingsbarn* [7126–72]; *Carnoustie* [7361–72]

1	Paul Lawrie (Sco)	71-68-63-68—270	£551040
2	Ernie Els (RSA)	65-70-68-68—271	367357
3	David Howell (Eng)	67-68-69-68—272	206970

Telefonica Madrid Open

formerly BBVA Open Turespaña Masters de la Communidad de Madrid [6957–71]

1968	G Garrido	1977	A Garrido	1986	H Clark	1995	A Cejka
1969	R Soto	1978	H Clark	1987	I Woosnam	1996	D Borrego
1970	M Cabrera	1979	S Hobday	1988	D Cooper	1997	JM Olazábal
1971	V Barrios	1980	S Ballesteros	1989	S Ballesteros	1998	MA Jiménez
1972	J Kinsetta	1981	M Pineto	1990	B Langer	1999	MA Jiménez
1973	G Garrido	1982	S Ballesteros	1991	A Sherborne	2000	P Harrington
1974	M Pineto	1983	A Lyle	1992	D Feherty		
1975	K Shearer	1984	H Clark	1993	D Smyth		
1976	F Abreu	1985	M Pineto	1994	C Mason		

2001 *at Club de Campo, Madrid, Spain*

1	Retief Goosen (RSA)	66-64-66-68—264	£145904	€233330
2	Steven Webster (Eng)	68-62-68-66—264	97267	155550
3	Brian Davis (Eng)	66-64-73-62—265	49287	78220
	Diego Borrego (Esp)	69-65-69-67—265	49287	78220

Italian Open

1925	F Pasquali	Stresa	154	1973	A Jacklin	Rome	284
1926	A Boyer	Stresa	147	1974	P Oosterhuis	Venice	249 (63)
1927	P Alliss	Stresa	145	1975	W Casper	Monticello	286
1928	A Boyer	Villa d'Este	145	1976	B Dassu	Is Molas	280
1929	R Golias	Villa d'Este	143	1977	A Gallardo*	Monticello	286
1930	A Boyer	Villa d'Este	140	1978	D Hayes	Pevero	293
1931	A Boyer	Villa d'Este	141	1979	B Barnes*	Monticello	281
1932	A Boomer	Villa d'Este	143	1980	M Mannelli	Rome	276
1934	N Nutley	San Remo	132	1981	J M Canizares*	Milan	280
1935	P Alliss	San Remo	262	1982	M James	Is Molas	280
1936	H Cotton	Sestriere	268	1983	B Langer*	Ugolino	271
1937	M Dallemagne	San Remo	276	1984	A Lyle	Milan	277
1938	F van Donck	Villa d'Este	276	1985	M Piñero	Molinetto	267
1947	F van Donck	San Remo	263	1986	D Feherty*	Albarella, Venice	270
1948	A Casera	San Remo	267	1987	S Torrance*	Monticello	271
1949	H Hassanein	Villa d'Este	263	1988	G Norman	Monticello	270
1950	U Grappasonni	Rome	281	1989	R Rafferty	Monticello	273
1951	J Adams	Milan	289	1990	R Boxall	Milan	267
1952	E Brown	Milan	273	1991	C Parry	Castelconturbia	279
1953	F van Donck	Villa d'Este	267	1992	A Lyle	Monticello	270
1954	U Grappasonni	Villa d'Este	272	1993	G Turner	Modena	267
1955	F van Donck	Venice	287	1994	E Romero	Marco Simone	272
1956	A Cerda	Milan	284	1995	S Torrance	Le Rovedine	269
1957	H Henning	Villa d'Este	273	1996	J Payne	Bergamo GC	275
1958	P Alliss	Varese	282	1997	B Langer	Gardagolf	273
1959	P Thomson	Villa d'Este	269	1998	JM Olazábal	Castelconturbia	195 (54)
1960	B Wilkes	Venice	285	1999	D Robertson	Circolo GC, Torino	271
1961	R Sota	Garlenda	282	2000	I Poulter	Is Molas	267
1972	N Wood	Villa d'Este	271				

2001 *at Is Molas, Cagliari, Sardinia*   [7013–72]

1	Gregory Havret (Fra)	65-66-68-69—268	€166660
2	Bradley Dredge (Wal)	69-66-65-69—269	111110
3	Mark Roe (Eng)	63-69-73-66—271	47500
	Shaun Webster (Eng)	63-69-73-66—271	47500
	Ian Poulter (Eng)	67-69-68-67—271	47500
	Diego Borrego (Esp)	70-66-65-70—271	47500

Volvo Masters Andalucia

1988	N Faldo	Valderrama	284	1995	A Cejka	Valderrama	282
1989	R Rafferty	Valderrama	282	1996	M McNulty	Valderrama	276
1990	M Harwood	Valderrama	286	1997	L Westwood	Montecastillo	200 (54)
1991	R Davis	Valderrama	280	1998	D Clarke	Montecastillo	271
1992	A Lyle	Valderrama	287	1999	MA Jiménez	Montecastillo	269
1993	C Montgomerie	Valderrama	274	2000	P Fulke	Montecastillo	272
1994	B Langer	Valderrama	276				

2001 *at Montecastillo GC, Jerez de la Frontera, Spain*   [7069–72]

1	Padraig Harrington (Irl)	61-71-66—204	€539074
2	Paul McGinley (Irl)	66-69-70—205	359383
3	Adam Scott (Aus)	67-74-65—296	202478

only three rounds played due to bad weather

WGC: EMC² World Cup

1	South Africa* (E Els and R Goosen)	64-71-63-66—264	
2	Denmark (T Bjørn and S Hansen)	65-69-65-65—264	
	New Zealand (M Campbell and D Smail)	63-66-65-70—264	
	USA (T Woods and D Duval)	66-68-63-67—264	

* South Africa won at second hole of sudden-death play-off

European Challenge Tour 2001

FINAL ORDER OF MERIT

Because Jamie Donaldson earned his card off the Main Tour, the top 16 earned cards off the Challenge Tour ranking

1	Mark Foster	(Eng)	€97,736		51	James Hepworth	(Eng)	24,578
2	Jamie Donaldson	(Wal)	92,740		52	Damien McGrane	(Irl)	22,732
3	Philip Golding	(Eng)	79,731		53	Jean-François Lucquin	(Fra)	22,405
4	Andrew Marshall	(Eng)	75,840		54	Paul Dwyer	(Eng)	21,828
5	Gary Clark	(Eng)	72,949		55	Fredrik Widmark	(Swe)	21,807
6	Sebastien Delagrange	(Fra)	71,236		56	Simon Khan	(Eng)	21,062
7	Kas Eriksson	(Swe)	66,933		57	Daniel Chopra	(Swe)	20,708
8	Robert Jan Derksen	(Ned)	61,595		58	Peter Lawrie	(Irl)	20,469
9	Chris Gane	(Eng)	60,778		59	Gary Murphy	(Irl)	19,709
10	Richard Bland	(Eng)	60,693		60	Andreas Ljunggren	(Swe)	19,326
11	Mads Vibe-Hastrup	(Den)	60,677		61	Sam Little	(Eng)	19,264
12	Peter Hanson	(Swe)	60,432		62	Thomas Havemann	(Den)	18,945
13	Grant Hamerton	(Eng)	59,580		63	Dennis Edlund	(Swe)	18,828
14	Stuart Little	(Eng)	58,649		64	Gianiuca Baruffaldi	(Ita)	18,425
15	Mårten Olander	(Swe)	58,306		65	Tony Edlund	(Swe)	18,264
16	Peter Hedblom	(Swe)	57,680		66	Nieis Kraaij	(Ned)	18,129
					67	Peter Malmgren	(Swe)	17,999
17	Greig Hutcheon	(Sco)	56,387		68	Kalie Vainola	(Fin)	17,777
18	Scott Drummond	(Sco)	54,058		69	Pasi Purhonen	(Fin)	17,705
19	Andrew Sherborne	(Eng)	53,173		70	Simon Hurd	(Eng)	17,265
20	André Bossert	(Sui)	51,080		71	Per Larsson	(Swe)	17,100
21	Michael Archer	(Eng)	50,401		72	Massimo Florioli	(Ita)	16,804
22	Benn Barham	(Eng)	49,664		73	Andrew Butterfield	(Eng)	16,334
23	Iain Pyman	(Eng)	47,749		74	Bjorn Pettersson	(Swe)	15,697
24	Mattias Eliasson	(Swe)	47,025		75	Tino Schuster	(Ger)	15,122
25	Alberto Binaghi	(Ita)	46,104		76	Adam Mednick	(Swe)	14,961
26	Ashley Roestoff	(RSA)	44,466		77	Knud Storgaard	(Den)	14,941
27	Dominique Nouailhac	(Fra)	43,639		78	Ulrik Gustafsson	(Swe)	14,780
28	Mattias Nilsson	(Swe)	39,392		79	Marcel Siem	(Ger)	14,286
29	Didier De Vooght	(Bel)	38,192		80	Francesco Guermani	(Ita)	13,524
30	Euan Little	(Sco)	36,965		81	Marceito Santi	(Ita)	13,522
31	Jesus Maria Arruti	(Esp)	36,047		82	Patrik Gottfridson	(Swe)	13,153
32	Simon Wakefield	(Eng)	33,882		83	Hampus Von Post	(Swe)	13,043
33	Sam Walker	(Eng)	33,031		84	Robert McGuirk	(Eng)	12,194
34	Kenneth Ferrie	(Eng)	32,915		85	David Drysdale	(Scot)	12,139
35	Joakim Rask	(Swe)	32,231		86	Martin Erlandsson	(Swe)	12,073
36	Magnus Persson	(Swe)	31,735		87	Ben Mason	(Eng)	11,885
37	Kariem Baraka	(Ger)	31,636		88	Carlos Larrain	(Ven)	11,680
38	Fan Hutchings	(RSA)	31,443		89	Raimo Sjöberg	(Swe)	11,656
39	Hennie Walters	(RSA)	31,122		90	Franck Aumonier	(Fra)	11,639
40	Marc Pendaries	(Fra)	30,867		91	Kalle Brink	(Swe)	11,500
41	Christophe Pottier	(Fra)	30,219		92	Lee Thompson	(Eng)	11,433
42	Miles Tunnicliff	(Eng)	30,214		93	Paul Nilbrink	(Swe)	11,412
43	Federico Bisazza	(Ita)	29,871		94	Frédéric Cupillard	(Fra)	11,319
44	Wolfgang Huget	(Ger)	29,090		95	Thomas Besancenez	(Fra)	11,242
45	Johan Skold	(Swe)	28,847		96	Benoit Teilleria	(Fra)	10,822
46	Pehr Magnebrant	(Swe)	26,536		97	Thomas Norret	(Den)	10,639
47	Simon D Hurley	(Eng)	26,214		98	Olivier David	(Fra)	10,569
48	Mikael Piltz	(Fin)	25,856		99	Richard Dinsdale	(Wal)	10,312
49	Lee S James	(Eng)	25,364		100	Jamie Little	(Eng)	9,740
50	Alvaro Salto	(Esp)	24,766					

TOUR RESULTS

Tusker Kenya Open	Muthaiga, Kenya	Ashley Roestoff (RSA)	271 (-13)
Stanbic Zambia Open	Lusaka, Zambia	Mark Foster (Eng)	278 (-14)
Challenge de España	Villamartin, Alicante, Spain	Euan Little (Sco)	277 (-11)
Challenge Open Golf Montecchia	Montecchia, Padova, Italy	Andrew Sherborne (Eng)	269 (-19)
Credit Suisse Private Banking Open	Patriziale Ascona, Switzerland	Greig Hutcheon (Sco)	266 (-18)
Austrian Open	Murhof, Graz, Austria	Chris Gane (Eng)	270 (-18)
5th Aa Open de Saint Omer	Aa Saint Omer, France	Sebastien Delagrange (Fra)	272 (-20)
NCC Open	Söderåsens, Sweden	Benn Barham (Eng)	273 (-11)
Nykredit Danish Open	Aalborg, Denmark	Sebastien Delagrange (Fra)	282 (-2)
Galeria Kaufhof Pokal Challenge	Rittergut Birkhof, Germany	Wolfgang Huget (Ger)	270 (-22)
DEXIA-BIL Luxembourg Open	Kikuoka CC, Canach, Luxembourg	Grant Hamerton (Eng)	271 (-17)
Open des Volcans	Golf des Volcans, France	Scott Drummond (Sco)	271 (-17)
Challenge Total Fina Elf	Joyenval, Chambourcy, France	Kenneth Ferrie (Eng)	268 (-20)
Volvo Finnish Open	Espoon Golfseura, Finland	Peter Hedblom (Swe)	274 (-14)
Günther Hamburg Classics	Treudelberg, Germany	Peter Hanson (Swe)	265 (-23)
Charles Church European Challenge Tour Championship	Bowood, Wiltshire, England	Mark Foster (Eng)	277 (-11)
BMW Russian Open	Moscow, Russia	Jamie Donaldson (Wal)	270 (-18)
Finnish Challenge	Talma, Finland	Klas Eriksson (Swe)	272 (-16)
North West of Ireland Open	Slieve Russell Hotel, Co Cavan, Ireland	Tobias Dier (Ger)	271 (-17)
Rolex Trophy	Genève, Switzerland	Stuart Little (Eng)	271 (-17)
Skandia PGA Open	Bokskogens, Sweden	Christophe Pottier (Fra)	272 (-16)
Formby Hall Challenge	Formby Hall, England	Sam Little (Eng)	276 (-12)
Muermans Real Estate Challenge Open	Herkenbosch, Roermond, Netherlands	Dominique Nouailhat (Fra)	261 (-19)
Telia Grand Prix	Bro Bålsta, Stockholm, Sweden	Jamie Donaldson (Wal)	270 (-22)
PGA Masters of Austria	Kitzbuhel, Austria	Iain Pyman (Eng)	268 (-16)
San Paolo Vita Open	Margara, Italy	Mads Vibe-Hastrup (Den)	267 (-21)
Hardelot Challenge de France	Hardelot, France	Mårten Olander (Swe)	268 (-16)
Terme Euganee International Open Padova	Padova, Valsansibio, Italy	Chris Gane (Eng)	265 (-23)
Challenge Tour Grand Final	Golf du Medoc, France	Richard Bland (Eng)	266 (-18)

European Senior Tour 2001

FINAL RANKING

1	Ian Stanley	(Aus)	€287025	51	Trevordowning	(Aus)	33886
2	Denis Durnian	(Eng)	276623	52	Roberto Bernardini	(Ita)	32063
3	Noel Ratcliffe	(Aus)	218685	53	Renato Campagnoli	(Ita)	29268
4	David Good	(Aus	214500	54	John Chillas	(Sco)	26602
5	Jerry Bruner	(USA)	214457	55	Antonio Garrido	(Esp)	24627
6	Simon Owen	(NZ)	199341	56	Ross Metherell	(Aus)	24587
7	David Oakley	(USA)	188061	57	John Fourie	(RSA)	24099
8	Seiji Ebihara	(Jpn)	187077	58	Liam Higgins	(Irl)	24064
9	Delroy Cambridge	(Jam)	177871	59	Lawrence Farmer	(Wal)	23681
10	John Morgan	(Eng)	171750	60	Randall Vines	(Aus)	22931
11	Bernard Gallacher	(Sco)	166623	61	Rodger Davis	(Aus)	21535
12	Denis O'Sullivan	(Irl)	165919	62	Kenny Stevenson	(NI)	21357
13	Maurice Bembridge	(Eng)	143651	63	Brian Waites	(Eng)	20346
14	Jay Horton	(USA)	134576	64	David Ojala	(USA)	20250
15	Priscillo Diniz	(Bra)	126670	65	Graham Burroughs	(Eng)	19863
16	Bob Shearer	(Aus)	121619	66	Manuel Sanchez	(Esp)	18665
17	Barry Vivian	(NZ)	117312	67	Geoff Parslow	(Aus)	18500
18	Keith MacDonald	(Eng)	114243	68	Joe McDermott	(Irl)	18174
19	Nick Job	(Eng)	111083	69	Gordon MacDonald	(Sco)	17736
20	Malcolm Gregson	(Eng)	107364	70	Lan Mosey	(Eng)	16199
21	Peter Dawson	(Eng)	107174	71	Manuel Ballesteros	(Esp)	13698
22	Bob Lendzion	(USA)	105483	72	Jan Björnsson	(Swe)	13289
23	Jim Rhodes	(Eng)	104274	73	Antero Baburin	(Swe)	12900
24	David Creamer	(Eng)	101523	74	Leonard Owens	(Irl)	12155
25	Craig Defoy	(Wal)	97787	75	Peter Ward	(Eng)	11743
26	Terry Gale	(Aus)	94912	76	JR Delich	(USA)	11112
27	John Grace	(USA)	93615	77	Glenn MacDonald	(Can)	11094
28	Mike Miller	(Sco)	89715	78	Raymond Kane	(Irl)	10189
29	Tommy Horton	(Eng)	85342	79	Pat Kaylor	(USA)	9762
30	David Huish	(Sco)	84052	80	John Tolhurst	(Aus)	8869
31	Eddie Polland	(NI)	83266	81	Barry Sandry	(Eng)	7886
32	Bill Hardwick	(Can)	82922	82	Norman Wood	(Sco)	7834
33	Jeffvan Wagenen	(USA)	78943	83	Tienie Britz	(RSA)	7282
34	Bobby Verwey	(RSA)	75749	84	Paul Van Biljon	(RSA)	6987
35	John McTear	(Sco)	75002	85	Arnold O'Connor	(Irl)	6573
36	Alan Tapie	(USA)	70491	86	Rick Uhlir	(USA)	6301
37	Russell Weir	(Scot)	69548	87	Michael Steadman	(Eng)	5729
38	Paul Leonard	(NI)	64440	88	William Milne	(Sco)	5168
39	Alberto Croce	(Ita)	56530	89	Robert Webster	(Sco)	4998
40	Neil Coles	(Eng)	55371	90	John Benda	(USA)	4790
41	John Irwin	(Can)	51835	91	Paul Herbert	(Eng)	4622
42	Hank Woodrome	(USA)	50536	92	Tomas Persson	(Swe)	4426
43	Peter Townsend	(Eng)	47274	93	Brad Franks	(USA)	4369
44	Ray Carrasco	(USA)	42281	94	Hugh Dolan	(Aus)	4309
45	Brian Huggett	(Wal)	40278	95	Ian Richardson	(Eng)	4213
46	Steve Wild	(Eng)	38185	96	John Garner	(Eng)	4025
47	Tommy Price	(USA)	36748	97	David Snell	(Eng)	3965
48	Silvano Locatelli	(Ita)	35520	98	Bill Lockie	(Sco)	3734
49	Jay Dolan III	(USA)	34697	99	Richard Beer	(Aus)	3703
50	David Vaughan	(Wal)	34441	100	TR Jones	(USA)	3225

CAREER MONEY LIST

1	Tommy Horton (Eng)	€1232903	51	Peter Butler (Eng)		155984
2	Noel Ratcliffe (Aus)	727546	52	Hugh Inggs (RSA)		153047
3	Neil Coles (Eng)	710790	53	Ray Carrasco (USA)		146828
4	Brian Huggett (Wal)	629926	54	John Garner (Eng)		142685
5	John Morgan (Eng)	588115	55	Chick Evans (USA)		141711
6	Malcolm Gregson (Eng)	559593	56	David Butler (Eng)		141202
7	David Oakley (USA)	495907	57	Peter Townsend (Eng)		137632
8	Antonio Garrido (Esp)	495663	58	John McTear (Sco)		130561
9	Maurice Bembridge (Eng)	492508	59	Joe McDermott (Irl)		128224
10	Jim Rhodes (Eng)	488609	60	Ian Richardson (Eng)		125870
11	Ian Stanley (Aus)	478586	61	Vincent Tshabalala (RSA)		122481
12	Brian Waites (Eng)	477332	62	Barry Vivian (NZ)		122209
13	David Huish (Sco)	467620	63	David Snell (Eng)		121707
14	Bobby Verwey (RSA)	457407	64	Jay Dolan III (USA)		118693
15	David Creamer (Eng)	440441	65	Deray Simon (USA)		118482
16	Eddie Polland (NI)	435125	66	Keith MacDonald (Eng)		114243
17	Bob Charles (NZ)	433246	67	JR Delich (USA)		113165
18	Denis O'Sullivan (Irl)	432470	68	Michael Murphy (Irl)		112561
19	Jerry Bruner (USA)	413465	69	Doug Dalziel (USA)		112220
20	Gary Player (RSA)	363507	70	Tony Grubb (Eng)		111240
21	Alberto Croce (Ita)	363345	71	Barry Sandry (Eng)		108183
22	Liam Higgins (Irl)	357038	72	Agim Bardha (Alb)		108153
23	Terry Gale (Aus)	355430	73	Geoff parslow (Aus)		105388
24	Bob Shearer (Aus)	346066	74	Randall Vines (Aus)		104772
25	John Fourie (RSA)	337750	75	Roger Fidler (Eng)		103403
26	David Jones (NI)	319369	76	Joe Carr (USA)		102745
27	Denis Durnian (Eng)	307714	77	Snell Lancaster (USA)		101667
28	Renato Campagnoli	297615	78	Steve Wild (Eng)		100011
29	Seiji Ebihara (Jpn)	288604	79	Tienie Britz (RSA)		94555
30	Bernard Gallacher (Sco)	287776	80	Trevor Downing (Aus)		91130
31	David Good (Aus)	284208	81	Mike Miller (Sco)		89715
32	John Grace (USA)	276569	82	Robert Bernardini (Ita)		88779
33	Bill Hardwick (Can)	273131	83	Tommy Price (USA)		86619
34	Craig Defoy (Eng)	259376	84	José Maria Roca (Esp)		85082
35	Priscillo Diniz (Bra)	259807	85	Harry Flatman (Eng)		83946
36	Paul Leonard (NI)	252605	86	Hugh Boyle (NI)		82616
37	Brian Barnes (Sco)	234957	87	Bernard Hunt (Eng)		82382
38	Christy O'Connor jr (Irl)	230134	88	TR Jones (USA)		81356
39	Alan Tafte (USA)	228744	89	Bryan Carter (Eng)		74392
40	Bob Lendzion (USA)	219344	90	Manuel Ballesteros (Esp)		72344
41	Nick Job (Eng)	109191	91	Hedley Muscroft (Eng)		72187
42	John Bland (RSA)	109107	92	Arnold O'Connor (Irl)		70961
43	Simon Owen (NZ)	199341	93	Bob Menne (USA)		70631
44	Peter Dawson (Eng)	190696	94	Christy O'Connor sr (Irl)		70082
45	Jeff Van Wagenen (USA)	185770	95	Russell Weir (Sco)		69548
46	Ross Metherell (Aus)	183206	96	Francisco Abreu (Esp)		69341
47	Jay Horton (USA)	181670	97	José Maria Canizares (Esp)		69321
48	Delroy Cambridge (Jam)	177871	98	John Irwin (Eng)		68962
49	Norman Wood (Sco)	171410	99	Arnold Palmer (USA)		68069
50	Bill Brask (USA)	162109	100	Gordon Parkhill (Eng)		65331

TOUR RESULTS

Tournament	Venue	Winner	Score
Royal Westmoreland Barbados Open	Royal Westmoreland	Priscillo Diniz (Bra)	200 (-16)
Beko Classic	Gloria Golf Resort, Turkey	Noel Ratcliffe (Aus)	209 (-7)
AIB Irish Seniors Open	Tulfarris, Ireland	Seiji Ebihara (Jpn)	207 (-9)
De Vere PGA Seniors Championship	Carden Park, England	Ian Stanley (Aus)	278 (-10)
Wales Seniors Open	Royal St David's, Wales	Denis Durnian (Eng)	208 (+1)
The Microlease Jersey Senior Open	La Moye, Jersey	Seiji Ebihara (Jpn)	213 (-3)
Palmerston Trophy Berlin	Palmerston, Berlin, Germany	Denis O'Sullivan (Irl)	212 (-4)
Lawrence Batley Seniors	Huddersfield, England	Nick Job (Eng)	204 (-9)
STC Scandinavian International	Kungsängen, Sweden	Denis O'Sullivan (Irl)	205 (-8)
SENIOR BRITISH OPEN	Royal Co Down, N Ireland	Ian Stanley (Aus)	278 (-6)
De Vere Hotels Senior Classic	Slaley Hall, England	Noel Ratcliffe (Aus)	205 (-11)
Bad Ragaz PGA Seniors Open	Bad Ragaz, Engadine, Switzerland	David Huish (Sco)	198 (-12)
Energis Senior Masters	Wentworth, Surrey, England	David Oakley (USA)	208 (-8)
Legends in Golf	Crayestein, Dordrecht, The Netherlands	David Good (Aus)	204 (-9)
Scottish Seniors Open	The Roxburghe, Scotland	David Oakley (USA)	210 (-6)
STC Bovis Lend Lease European Invitational	Woburn, England	Bob Shearer (Aus)	208 (-8)
Big 3 Records Monte Carlo Invitational	Monte Carlo, France	*Not played*	
TEMES Seniors Open	Glyfada, Greece	Russell Weir (Sco)	202 (-14)
Dan Technology Senior Tournament of Champions	Mere, England	Delroy Cambridge (Jam)	205 (-8)
Egyptian Seniors Open	Katameya Heights, Egypt	*Not played*	
Tunisian Seniors Open	Port El Kantaoui, Tunisia	Simon Owen (NZ)	208 (-8)
SSL International/Sodexho Match Play	Le Meridien Penina, Portugal	Jim Rhodes (Eng)	3 and 2
STC Seniors Tour Championship	PGA Golf de Catalunya, Spain	Jerry Bruner (USA)	210 (-6)

US PGA Tour 2001

Players are of US nationality unless stated

FINAL RANKING

Tiger Woods topped the US money table for a fourth successive year and the fifth time in six years. He has now made $26,191,227 from 109 tournaments since joining the Tour as a professional in late 1996. His nearest rivals on the career money list, David Duval and Phil Mickelson, have made just short of $18 million. In 2001 Woods played 19 US Tour events to earn $5,687,777 with Phil Mickelson next best earner with $4,403,883. The top 115 on the money list retained their cards.

1	Tiger Woods	$5,687,777	38	Kirk Triplett	1,388,202	78	Esteban Toledo	
2	Phil Mickelson	4,403,883	39	Tom Pernice jr	1,318,762		(Mex)	683,751
3	David Toms	3,791,595	40	Billy Andrade	1,313,047	79	Jonathan Kaye	683,210
4	Vijay Singh (Fij)	3,440,829	41	Brian Gay	1,299,361	80	Neal Lancaster	657,580
5	Davis Love III	3,169,463	42	Nick Price (Zim)	1,286,756	81	Joey Sindelar	654,864
6	Sergio Garcia		43	Fred Funk	1,237,004	82	JP Hayes	622,964
	(Esp)	2,898,635	44	Steve Flesch	1,207,552	83	Paul Gow (Aus)	608,382
7	Scott Hoch	2,875,319	45	Chris Riley	1,198,225	84	Len Mattiace	592,781
8	David Duval	2,801,760	46	Joel Edwards	1,193,528	85	Jerry Smith	592,030
9	Bob Estes	2,795,477	47	Retief Goosen		86	Loren Roberts	584,072
10	Scott Verplank	2,783,401		(RSA)	1,126,985	87	Brandel Chamblee	582,086
11	Mike Weir (Can)	2,777,936	48	Bob Tway	1,121,858	88	Mike Sposa	576,312
12	Chris DiMarco	2,595,201	49	JJ Henry	1,073,847	89	Stephen Ames	
13	Jim Furyk	2,540,734	50	Cameron			(Tri)	574,451
14	Joe Durant	2,381,684		Beckman	1,071,343	90	Edward Fryatt	572,820
15	Ernie Els (RSA)	2,336,456	51	Robert Damron	1,059,187	91	Chris Perry	568,391
16	Robert Allenby		52	Rory Sabbatini		92	Jay Haas	565,141
	(Aus)	2,309,029		(RSA)	1,038,590	93	Grant Waite (NZ)	539,227
17	Mark		53	Dudley Hart	1,035,710	94	Bob May	534,936
	Calcavecchia	1,991,576	54	John Cook	1,022,778	95	Geoff Ogilvy (Aus)	525,338
18	Brad Faxon	1,951,412	55	Stuart Appleby		96	Scott Simpson	512,530
19	Frank Lickliter II	1,941,911		(Aus)	1,004,528	97	Per-Ulrik	
20	Tom Lehman	1,907,660	56	Brett Quigley	956,934		Johansson (Swe)	510,488
21	Jeff Sluman	1,841,952	57	Tim Herron	945,441	98	J.L. Lewis	508,618
22	Bernhard Langer		58	Chris Smith	932,810	99	Carl Paulson	508,208
	(Ger)	1,810,363	59	Lee Janzen	905,628	100	John Huston	505,252
23	Scott McCarron	1,793,506	60	Mark Brooks	899,444	101	David Frost (RSA)	504,376
24	Kenny Perry	1,786,066	61	John Daly	828,914	102	Craig Parry	503,923
25	Justin Leonard	1,783,842	62	Olin Browne	815,636	103	Greg Kraft	503,605
26	Stewart Cink	1,743,028	63	Briny Baird	812,001	104	Carlos Franco (Per)	486,665
27	Steve Lowery	1,738,820	64	Dennis Paulson	811,105	105	Kaname Yokoo	
28	Hal Sutton	1,723,946	65	KJ Choi (Kor)	800,326		(Jpn)	477,989
29	Billy Mayfair	1,716,002	66	Harrison Frazar	792,456	106	Jay Williamson	476,031
30	Steve Stricker	1,676,229	67	Skip Kendall	753,701	107	Miguel A. Jimenez	
31	Jesper Parnevik		68	David Gossett	748,126		(Esp)	464,457
	(Swe)	1,574,208	69	Paul Stankowski	743,603	108	Frank Nobilo	
32	Kevin		70	Matt Gogel	729,783		(NZ)	462,650
	Sutherland	1,523,573	71	Glen Day	715,780	109	Rich Beem	460,565
33	Paul Azinger	1,509,130	72	Jeff Maggert	713,607	110	Jose Maria	
34	Jose Coceres		73	David Peoples	712,657		Olazabal (Esp)	458,678
	(Arg)	1,502,888	74	Brent Geiberger	711,194	111	Corey Pavin	458,401
35	Jerry Kelly	1,491,607	75	Greg Chalmers		112	Brian Watts	457,293
36	Rocco Mediate	1,474,435		(Aus)	692,170	113	Craig Perks	457,127
37	Shigeki		76	David Berganio jr	685,082	114	Dan Forsman	456,194
	Maruyama (Jpn)	1,441,455	77	Garrett Willis	684,038	115	Larry Mize	440,179

CAREER MONEY LIST (at end of 2001 season)

1	Tiger Woods	$26,191,227	51	Andrew Magee	6,837,432
2	Davis Love III	17,994,690	52	Billy Andrade	6,783,158
3	Phil Mickelson	17,837,998	53	Duffy Waldorf	6,580,748
4	David Duval	15,312,553	54	Steve Lowery	6,535,290
5	Scott Hoch	14,553,202	55	Bruce Lietzke	6,474,794
6	Vijay Singh (Fij)	14,524,452	56	Steve Stricker	6,451,844
7	Nick Price (Zim)	14,477,425	57	Lanny Wadkins	6,355,681
8	Hal Sutton	13,885,946	58	Scott Simpson	6,351,463
9	Mark Calcavecchia	13,409,349	59	Chip Beck	6,199,550
10	Greg Norman (Aus)	13,344,142	60	Bill Glasson	6,132,054
11	Fred Couples	12,681,268	61	Joey Sindelar	5,969,691
12	Tom Lehman	12,088,396	62	Hale Irwin	5,966,031
13	Mark O'Meara	12,025,198	63	Stuart Appleby (Aus)	5,892,274
14	Ernie Els (RSA)	12,016,635	64	Steve Jones	5,813,955
15	Payne Stewart	11,737,008	65	Fuzzy Zoeller	5,803,343
16	Paul Azinger	11,687,965	66	Peter Jacobsen	5,788,270
17	Jim Furyk	11,493,593	67	Jack Nicklaus	5,713,991
18	Justin Leonard	10,919,999	68	Chris DiMarco	5,680,474
19	Tom Kite	10,865,959	69	Dudley Hart	5,678,502
20	Jeff Sluman	10,634,572	70	Jim Gallagher jr	5,647,072
21	Loren Roberts	9,866,485	71	Ray Floyd	5,323,075
22	Brad Faxon	9,777,678	72	Mark McCumber	5,309,688
23	Tom Watson	9,593,631	73	Gil Morgan	5,259,164
24	Corey Pavin	9,536,170	74	Dan Forsman	5,240,555
25	David Toms	9,412,686	75	Bernhard Langer (Ger)	5,238,139
26	John Cook	9,381,679	76	Nick Faldo (Eng)	5,237,051
27	Jeff Maggert	9,272,821	77	Russ Cochran	5,064,876
28	John Huston	9,267,529	78	Robert Allenby (Aus)	4,961,348
29	Lee Janzen	9,002,576	79	Glen Day	4,831,450
30	Steve Elkington (Aus)	8,780,272	80	Tim Herron	4,830,607
31	Craig Stadler	8,502,884	81	Jay Don Blake	4,824,557
32	Bob Estes	8,481,255	82	Blaine McCallister	4,767,636
33	Jay Haas	8,433,856	83	D.A. Weibring	4,712,371
34	Bob Tway	8,388,384	84	Wayne Levi	4,688,679
35	Fred Funk	8,387,851	85	Mike Reid	4,686,774
36	Jesper Parnevik (Swe)	8,311,970	86	Frank Lickliter II	4,664,229
37	Billy Mayfair	8,273,562	87	Sergio Garcia (Esp)	4,583,889
38	Scott Verplank	7,757,523	88	Steve Flesch	4,562,864
39	Kenny Perry	7,628,415	89	Scott McCarron	4,508,564
40	Curtis Strange	7,583,744	90	Craig Parry (Aus)	4,449,875
41	David Frost (RSA)	7,491,392	91	David Edwards	4,352,039
42	Kirk Triplett	7,439,256	92	Mark Wiebe	4,289,025
43	Steve Pate	7,393,536	93	Tom Purtzer	4,134,028
44	Rocco Mediate	7,230,798	94	Mike Hulbert	4,118,760
45	Mark Brooks	7,155,021	95	Jose Maria Olazabal (Esp)	4,117,263
46	Ben Crenshaw	7,091,166	96	Joe Durant	4,078,422
47	Mike Weir (Can)	7,082,144	97	Rick Fehr	4,012,299
48	Stewart Cink	6,978,220	98	Skip Kendall	4,005,545
49	Chris Perry	6,866,671	99	Carlos Franco (Par)	3,997,869
50	Larry Mize	6,866,366	100	Kevin Sutherland	3,963,246

TOUR STATISTICS

Stroke averages

Pos	Name	Rds	Avg
1	Tiger Woods	76	68.81
2	Davis Love III	75	69.06
3	Sergio Garcia (Esp)	60	69.13
4T	Phil Mickelson	82	69.21
	Vijay Singh (Fij)	92	69.21
6	Nick Price (Zim)	74	69.66
7T	David Duval	74	69.73
	Bob Estes	88	69.73
9	Scott Hoch	84	69.85
10	Chris DiMarco	103	69.87

Driving accuracy
(Percentage of fairways in regulation)

Pos	Name	Rds	%
1	Joe Durant	80	81.10
2	Glen Hnatiuk	101	77.80
3	Fred Funk	117	77.20
4	John Cook	88	76.60
5	Billy Mayfair	100	76.50
6	Olin Browne	96	75.80
7	Jim Furyk	88	75.70
8T	Tom Byrum	85	75.60
	José Coceres (Arg)	57	75.60
	Brian Gay	112	75.60

Driving distance (Average yards per drive)

Pos	Name	Rds	Yds
1	John Daly	82	306.7
2	Brett Quigley	63	298.5
3T	Davis Love III	75	297.6
	Tiger Woods	76	297.6
5	David Duval	74	297.6
6T	Charles Howell III	85	293.9
	Phil Mickelson	82	293.9
8	Steve Allen	86	293.3
9	Chris Smith	98	293.2
10	Kenny Perry	89	292.3

Sand saves

Pos	Name	Rds	%
1	Frank Langham	60	68.9
2	Scott Verplank	97	66.20
3	Brad Faxon	87	64.90
4	Nick Price (Zim)	74	64.80
5	Jose Coceres (Arg)	57	63.70
6	Kevin Sutherland	98	63.00
7	Scott McCarron	94	62.10
8	Edward Fryatt (Eng)	89	61.80
9	Ronnie Black	51	61.30
10T	Ernie Els (RSA)	60	60.60
	Paul Gow (Aus)	75	60.60
	Billy Mayfair	100	60.60

Greens in regulation

Pos	Name	Rds	%
1	Tom Lehman	79	74.50
2	Charles Howell III	85	73.50
3	John Cook	88	72.90
4	David Toms	96	72.60
5	Joe Durant	80	72.10
6T	Bob Tway	106	71.90
	Tiger Woods	76	71.90
8	Kenny Perry	89	71.40
9	Hal Sutton	95	71.10
10T	Donnie Hammond	51	71.00
	Glen Hnatiuk	101	71.00
	Rocco Mediate	69	71.00

Putting averages

Pos	Name	Rds	Avg
1	David Frost (RSA)	87	1.708
2	Phil Mickelson	82	1.717
3	Brian Gay	112	1.722
4	Vijay Singh (Fij)	92	1.723
5	Jeff Sluman	104	1.725
6T	Bob Estes	88	1.726
	Craig Kanada	78	1.726
8	Bernhard Langer (Ger)	61	1.729
9	Skip Kendall	108	1.730
10	David Toms	96	1.732

TOUR RESULTS (in chronological order)

Players are of American nationality unless stated

WGC Accenture Match Play
Metropolitan, Melbourne, Australia
Final: Steve Stricker (USA) ($1000000) beat Pierre Fulke (Swe) ($500000) 2 and 1
Consolation match: Toru Taniguchi (Jpn) ($400000) beat Ernie Els (RSA) ($300000) 4 and 3

Fuller details of this event are to be found on p.171

Mercedes Championships
Plantation Course, Kapalua, Hawaii   [7263-73]

1	Jim Furyk	69-69-69-67—274	$630000
2	Rory Sabbatini (RSA)	69-69-65-72—275	380000
3	Ernie Els (RSA)	68-66-73-69—276	203000
	Vijay Singh (Fij)	71-67-67-71—276	203000

Touchstone Energy Tucson Open
Omni Tucson National, AZ   [7109-72]

1	Garrett Willis	71-69-64-69—273	$540000
2	Kevin Sutherland	67-72-67-68—274	324000
3	Geoff Ogilvy (Aus)	67-72-68-68—275	174000
	Bob Tway	73-69-67-66—275	174000

Sony Open
Waialae CC, Honolulu, Hawaii   [7060-70]

1	Brad Faxon	64-64-67-65—260	$720000
2	Tom Lehman	66-67-65-66—264	432000
3	Ernie Els (RSA)	68-65-65-69—267	272000

Phoenix Open
TPC Scottsdale, AZ   [7098-71]

1	Mark Calcavecchia	65-60-64-67—256	$720000
2	Rocco Mediate	68-63-64-69—264	432000
3	Steve Lowery	69-67-64-68—268	272000

AT&T Pebble Beach National Pro-Am
Pebble Beach, CA   [6816-72]

1	Davis Love III	71-69-69-63—272	$720000
2	Vijay Singh (Fij)	66-68-70-69—273	432000
3	Olin Browne	68-69-65-73—275	232000
	Phil Mickelson	70-66-66-73—275	232000

Buick Invitational
Torrey Pines, CA   [S 7033-72; N 6854-72]

1	Phil Mickelson*	68-64-71-66—269	$630000
2	Frank Lickliter II	68-67-68-66—269	308000
	Davis Love III	65-67-70-67—269	308000

Bob Hope Chrysler Classic
Bermuda Dunes [6829-71]; *Indian Wells* [6478-72];
La Quinta [7060-72]; *West Arnold Palmer* [6950-72]

1	Joe Durant	65-61-67-66-65—324	$630000
2	Paul Stankowski	67-64-65-69-63—328	378000
3	Mark Calcavecchia	64-66-69-65-66—330	238000

Nissan Open
Riviera CC, Pacific Palisades, CA   [6987-71]

1	Robert Allenby* (Aus)	73-64-69-70—276	$612000
2	Brandel Chamblee	68-68-73-67—276	204000
	Toshi Izawa (Jpn)	73-68-69-66—276	204000
	Dennis Paulson	70-68-68-70—276	204000
	Jeff Sluman	68-69-70-69—276	204000
	Bob Tway	67-71-70-68—276	204000

Genuity Championship
Doral (Blue), Miami, FL   [7125-72]

1	Joe Durant	68-70-67-65—270	$810000
2	Mike Weir (Can)	62-70-69-71—272	486000
3	Vijay Singh (Fij)	70-71-66-67—274	234000
	Jeff Sluman	69-66-69-70—274	234000
	Hal Sutton	66-66-70-72—274	234000

Honda Classic
Heron Bay, Coral Springs, FL   [7268-72]

1	Jesper Parnevik (Swe)	65-67-66-72—270	$576000
2	Mark Calcavecchia	67-68-66-70—271	238933
	Geoff Ogilvy (Aus)	65-72-65-69—271	238933
	Craig Perks	67-70-68-66—271	238933

Bay Hill Invitational
Orlando, FL   [7239-72]

1	Tiger Woods	71-67-66-69—273	$630000
2	Phil Mickelson	66-72-70-66—274	378000
3	Grant Waite (NZ)	66-71-72-69—278	238000

The Players Championship
Sawgrass, Ponte Vedra Beach, FL   [7093-72]

1	Tiger Woods	72-69-66-67—274	$1080000
2	Vijay Singh (Fij)	67-70-70-68—275	648000
3	Bernhard Langer (Ger)	73-68-68-67—276	408000

BellSouth Classic
TPC Sugarloaf, Duluth   [7259-72]

1	Scott McCarron	68-67-72-73—280	$594000
2	Mike Weir (Can)	76-67-73-67—283	356400
3	Phil Mickelson	70-66-73-75—284	171600
	Dennis Paulson	72-65-72-75—284	171600
	Chris Smith	73-70-72-69—284	171600

MASTERS
Augusta National, GA   [6985-72]

1	Tiger Woods	70-66-68-68—272	$1008000
2	David Duval	71-66-70-67—274	604800
3	Phil Mickelson	67-69-69-70—275	380800

Fuller details of this will be found in Part I The Majors p.74

Worldcom Classic – The Heritage of Golf
Harbour Town, Hilton Head Island, SC   [6976-71]

1	José Coceres* (Arg)	68-70-64-71—273	$630000
2	Billy Mayfair	65-68-69-71—273	378000
3	Bernhard Langer (Ger)	69-69-67-69—274	168000
	Carl Paulson	71-63-71-69—274	168000
	Vijay Singh (Fij)	65-68-67-74—274	168000
	Scott Verplank	68-67-69-70—274	168000

Shell Houston Open
TPC, The Woodlands, TX   [7018-72]

1	Hal Sutton	70-68-71-69—278	$612000
2	Joe Durant	67-69-71-74—281	299200
	Lee Janzen	67-68-73-73—281	299200

Greater Greensboro Chrysler Classic
Forest Oaks CC, NC   [7062-72]

1	Scott Hoch	68-68-67-69—272	$630000
2	Brett Quigley	68-71-67-67—273	308000
	Scott Simpson	66-69-70-68—273	308000

Compaq Classic of New Orleans
English Turn, New Orleans, LA   [7116-72]

1	David Toms	66-73-63-64—266	$720000
2	Phil Mickelson	66-66-64-72—268	432000
3	Ernie Els (RSA)	67-69-65-68—269	272000

Verizon Byron Nelson Classic
TPC Las Colinas, Irving, TX   [6846–70]

1	Robert Damron*	66-64-67-66—263	$4810000
2	Scott Verplank	62-67-68-66—263	486000
3	David Duval	64-65-70-67—266	234000
	Nick Price (Zim)	69-65-65-67—266	234000
	Tiger Woods	66-68-69-63—266	234000

MasterCard Colonial
Colonial CC, Fort Worth, TX   [7080-70]

1	Sergio García (Esp)	69-69-66-63—267	$720000
2	Brian Gay	66-69-69-65—269	352000
	Phil Mickelson	65-68-66-70—269	352000

Kemper Insurance Open
TPC Avenal, Potomac, MD   [7005-71]

1	Frank Lickliter II	69-65-66-68—268	$630000
2	JJ Henry	65-71-67-66—269	378000
3	Bradley Hughes (Aus)	70-63-72-67—272	182000
	Spike McRoy	71-66-67-68—272	182000
	Phil Mickelson	68-67-72-65—272	182000

Memorial Tournament
Muirfield Village, Dublin, OH   [7221-72]

1	Tiger Woods	68-69-68-66—271	$738000
2	Paul Azinger	68-67-69-74—278	360800
	Sergio García (Esp)	68-69-70-71—278	360800

FedEx St Jude Classic
TPC Southwind, Memphis, TN   [7030-71]

1	Bob Estes	61-66-69-71—267	$630000
2	Bernhard Langer (Ger)	69-65-68-66—268	378000
3	Tom Lehman	69-68-66-66—269	203000
	Scott McCarron	66-65-66-72—269	203000

US OPEN
Southern Hills CC, Tulsa, OK   [6973-70]

1	Retief Goosen* (RSA)	66-70-69-71—276	$900000
2	Mark Brooks	72-64-70-70—276	530000
3	Stewart Cink	69-69-67-72—277	325310

Fuller details of this event are included in Part I The Majors p.66

Buick Classic
Westchester CC, Rye, NY   [6722-71]

1	Sergio García (Esp)	68-67-66-67—268	$630000
2	Scott Hoch	67-68-68-68—271	378000
3	Billy Andrade	70-69-68-66—273	182000
	Stewart Cink	65-72-69-67—273	182000
	JP Hayes	68-69-67-69—273	182000

Canon Greater Hartford Open
TPC River Highlands, Cromwell, CT   [6820-70]

1	Phil Mickelson	67-68-61-68—264	$558000
2	Billy Andrade	68-65-66-66—265	334800
3	D Berganio	67-66-64-69—266	161200
	C DiMarco	65-67-66-68—266	161200
	D Hart	70-63-70-63—266	161200

Advil Western Open
Cog Hill, Lemont, IL   [7073-72]

1	Scott Hoch	69-68-66-64—267	$648000
2	Davis Love III	66-67-69-66—268	388800
3	Brandel Chamblee	69-67-70-69—275	208800
	Mike Weir (Can)	71-70-67-67—275	208800

Greater Milwaukee Open
Brown Deer Park, Milwaukee, WI   [6759-71]

1	Shigeki Maruyama* (Jpn)	68-65-67-66-266	$558000
2	Charles Howell III	66-69-67-64-266	334800
3	JP Hayes	69-66-71-63-269	179800
	Tim Herron	69-69-64-67-269	179800

OPEN CHAMPIONSHIP
Royal Lytham & St Annes   [6905-71]

1	David Duval	69-73-65-67-274	$858300
2	Niclas Fasth (Swe)	69-69-72-67-277	514980
3	Darren Clarke (NI)	70-69-69-70-278	202655
	Ernie Els (RSA)	71-71-67-69-278	202655
	Miguel Angel Jiménez (Esp)	69-72-67-70-278	202655
	Bernhard Langer (Ger)	71-69-67-71-278	202655
	Billy Mayfair	69-72-67-70-278	202655
	Ian Woosnam (Wal)	72-68-67-71-278	202655

Fuller details of this event are included in Part I The Majors

BC Open
En-Joie, Endicott, NY   [6974-72]

1	Jeff Sluman*	67-68-65-66-266	$360000
2	Paul Gow	69-65-66-66-266	216000
3	Jonathan Kaye	67-65-70-67-269	136000

John Deere Classic
TPC Deere Run, Silvas, IL   [7183-71]

1	David Gossett	67-64-68-66-265	$504000
2	Briny Baird	69-65-66-66-266	302400
3	Pete Jordan	69-68-65-65-267	190400

Buick Open
Warwick Hills, Grand Blanc, MI   [7127-72]

1	Kenny Perry	66-64-64-69—263	$558000
2	Chris DiMarco	68-67-65-65—265	272800
	Jim Furyk	64-69-66-66—265	272800

US PGA CHAMPIONSHIP
Atlanta Athletic Club, GA, USA   [7213-70]

1	David Toms	66-65-65-69—265	$936000
2	Phil Mickelson	66-66-66-68—266	562000
3	Steve Lowery	67-67-66-68—268	354000

Fuller details of this event are included in Part I The Majors p.81

WGC: NEC Invitational
Firestone CC, Akron, OH, USA   [7139-70]

1	Tiger Woods*	66-67-66-69—268	$1000000
2	Jim Furyk	65-66-66-71—268	500000
3	Darren Clarke (NI)	66-68-68-69—271	375000

Fuller details of this event are to be found on p.172

Reno-Tahoe Open
Montreux GCC, Reno, NV, USA   [7552–72]

1	John Cook	69-64-74-64—271	$540000
2	Jerry Kelly	66-68-67-71—272	324000
3	Bryce Molder	70-65-67-71—273	204000

Air Canada Championship
Northview, Surrey, British Columbia, Canada   [7072-71]

1	Joel Edwards	65-67-68-65—265	$612000
2	Steve Lowery	73-65-68-66—272	367200
3	Fred Funk	70-67-67-69—273	197200
	Matt Kuchar	68-66-72-67—273	197200

Bell Canadian Open
Royal Montreal, Canada   [6859-70]

1	Scott Verplank	70-63-66-67—266	$684000
2	Bob Estes	69-65-67-68—269	334400
	Joey Sindelar	66-69-69-65—269	334400

WGC Amex Championship
This was cancelled

Tampa Bay Classic
This was cancelled

Marconi Pennsylvania Classic
Laurel Valley, Ligonier, PA   [6939-71]

1	Robert Allenby (Aus)	70-65-66-68—269	$594000
2	Rocco Mediate	69-68-67-68—272	290400
	Larry Mize	73-67-67-65—272	290400

Texas Open
La Cantera, San Antonio, TX   [6905-71]

1	Justin Leonard	65-64-68-69—266	$540000
2	J J Henry	70-64-68-66—268	264000
	Matt Kuchar	67-68-64-69—268	264000

RYDER CUP
Postponed until 2002

Michelob Championship at Kingsmill
Kingsmill, Williamsburg, VA   [6853-71]

1	David Toms	64-70-67-68—269	$630000
2	Kirk Triplett	67-68-69-66—270	378000
3	Charles Howell III	70-65-71-67—273	203000
	Esteban Toleda (Mex)	68-67-68-70—273	203000

Invensys Classic at Las Vegas
TPC Summerlin [7243-72]; Southern Highlands [7103-72];
The Canyons [7381-71]

1	Bob Estes	65-66-67-68-63—329	$810000
2	Tom Lehman	63-62-72-67-66—330	396000
	Rory Sabatini	64-67-72-63-64—330	396000

National Car Rental Golf Classic
Walt Disney Magnolia GC, Palm Golf Course   [6967-72]

1	Jose Coceres (Arg)	68-65-64-68—265	$612000
2	Davis Love III	67-66-67-66—266	367000
3	David Peoples	69-65-68-66—268	197000
	Jeremy Smith	66-66-73-63—268	197000

Buick Challenge
Callaway Gardens Mountain View Course, Pine Mountain, GA
[7057-72]

1	Chris DiMarco*	67-64-71-65—267	$612000
2	David Duval	67-69-68-63—267	367000
3	Bob Estes	71-63-69-66—269	197200
	Neal Lancaster	65-67-68-69—269	197200

Southern Farm Bureau Classic
Annandale GC, Madison, MA   [7199–72]

1	Cameron Beckman	66-69-67-67—269	$432000
2	Chad Campbell	70-64-65-71—270	259000
3	Fred Funk	65-69-69-68—271	163200

The Tour Championship
Champions GC, Houston, TX   [7220–72]

1	Mike Weir* (Can)	68-66-68-68—270	$900000
2	Ernie Els (RSA)	69-68-65-68—270	375000
	Sergio Garcia (Esp)	69-67-66-68—270	375000
	David Toms	73-66-64-67—270	375000

WGC: EMC² World Cup
Gotemba, Tokyo

1	South Africa* (E Els and R Goosen)	64-71-63-66—264
2	Denmark (T Bjørn and S Hansen)	65-69-65-65—264
	New Zealand (M Campbell and D Smail)	63-66-65-70—264
	USA (T Woods and D Duval)	66-68-63-67—264

* South Africa won at second hole of sudden-death play-off

Ace expert Art Wall dies

The 1959 Masters champion Art Wall, who has died aged 77, is credited with having shot 40 holes-in-one during his professional career.

Wall, who played in three Ryder Cup sides, came from five behind with seven to play in the 1959 Masters to win. He made birdies at five of the last six holes to beat defending champion Arnold Palmer by two strokes and Cary Middlecoff by one.

That year Wall was top earner on the US Tour, led the stroke averages and was PGA Golfer of the Year.

US Senior Tour 2001

Players are of American nationality unless stated

FINAL RANKING

1	Allen Doyle	$2553582	26	John Bland	718632
2	Bruce Fleisher	2411543	27	John Schroeder	716197
3	Hale Irwin	2147422	28	Stewart Ginn (Aus)	699254
4	Larry Nelson	2109936	29	Terry Mauney	695474
5	Gil Morgan	1885871	30	Hugh Baiocchi (RSA)	693131
6	Jim Thorpe	1827223	31	Isao Aoki (Jpn)	676735
7	Doug Tewell	1721339	32	Graham Marsh (Aus)	629260
8	Bob Gilder	1684988	33	Bobby Wadkins	549657
9	Dana Quigley	1537931	34	Ray Floyd	546190
10	Tom Kite	1398802	35	Steven Veriato	527703
11	Walter Hall	1339059	36	Dave Stockton	522444
12	Mike McCullough	1335040	37	Jay Sigel	516027
13	Ed Dougherty	1330818	38	JC Snead	500854
14	José Maria Canizares (Esp)	1191094	39	Bobby Walzel	487452
15	Tom Jenkins	1156576	40	Bob Eastwood	482993
16	Bruce Lietzke	1119573	41	Dave Eichelberger	479724
17	Tom Watson	986547	42	Joe Inman	468056
18	Sammy Rachels	932031	43	John Mahaffey	467985
19	Jim Colbert	930096	44	Howard Twitty	431932
20	Bruce Summerhays	904617	45	Mike Smith	426313
21	Leonard Thompson	893881	46	Walter Morgan	421687
22	Vicente Fernandez (Arg)	852442	47	Ted Goin	394516
23	Gary McCord	851132	48	Andy North	391538
24	Jim Ahern	831480	49	Jim Holtgrieve	376498
25	John Jacobs (Eng)	743421	50	Mike Hill	355974

CAREER MONEY LIST

1	Hale Irwin	$19,887,905	18	Mike Hill	7,953,520
2	Gil Morgan	15,008,481	19	Chi Chi Rodriguez	
3	Ray Floyd	13,552,580		(Pur)	7,595,140
4	Tom Kite	13,464,418	20	Bruce Lietzke	7,594,368
5	Lee Trevino	12,904,970	21	Gary Player (RSA)	7,459,067
6	Jim Colbert	12,107,076	22	Dale Douglass	7,022,420
7	Tom Watson	11,934,778	23	Lanny Wadkins	6,933,562
8	Larry Nelson	11,913,798	24	Graham Marsh	
9	Dave Stockton	10,444,151		(Aus)	6,662,508
10	George Archer	9,882,770	25	Al Geiberger	6,521,268
11	Bob Charles (NZ)	9,111,445	26	Jay Sigel	6,422,862
12	Bruce Fleisher	8,999,990	27	John Mahaffey	6,413,274
13	Jack Nicklaus	8,755,116	28	Allen Doyle	6,392,152
14	Isao Aoki (Jpn)	8,518,519	29	Dana Quigley	6,291,605
15	JC Snead	8,489,691	30	Jim Thorpe	6,287,317
16	Jim Dent	8,396,851	31	Hubert Green	6,114,602
17	Bob Murphy	8,202,294	32	Bruce Crampton (Aus)	6,028,877

US Senior Tour *continued*

33	Bruce Summerhays	34	6,022,286	43	John Jacobs	36	5,110,565
34	Tom Wargo	23	5,956,708	44	John Bland (RSA)	30	5,045,078
35	Doug Tewell	28	5,905,207	45	Vicente Fernandez		
36	Dave Eichelberger	31	5,701,191		(Arg)	29	5,024,224
37	David Graham (Aus)	18	5,692,346	46	Kermit Zarley	7	4,988,802
38	Leonard Thompson	31	5,683,400	47	Ed Dougherty	36	4,971,712
39	Jim Albus	31	5,682,617	48	Mike McCullough	35	4,951,694
40	Miller Barber	25	5,595,317	49	Charles Coody	17	4,941,660
41	Mark McCumber	3	5,330,056	50	Bob Gilder	30	4,820,747
42	Gibby Gilbert	21	5,260,117				

TOUR STATISTICS

Stroke averages

Pos	Name	Avg
1	Gil Morgan	69.20
2	Hale Irwin	69.29
3	Allen Doyle	69.41
4	Bruce Fleisher	69.52
5	Tom Kite	69.80
6	Larry Nelson	69.91
7	Doug Tewell	69.94
8	Gary McCord	70.11
9	Jim Thorpe	70.15
10	Tom Watson	70.21

Driving accuracy

Pos	Name	%
1	John Bland (RSA)	82.30
	Doug Tewell	82.30
3	Allen Doyle	80.90
4	Bruce Fleisher	80.70
5	Bob Murphy	79.50
6T	John Mahaffey	79.00
	Walter Zembriski	79.00
8	Hale Irwin	77.20
9	Graham Marsh	77.00
10	Hubert Green	76.70

Driving distance

(Average yards per drive)

Pos	Name	Yds
1	Lon Hinkle	289.3
2	Jim Ahern	285.4
3	Terry Dill	284.3
4	Bobby Walzel	284.2
5	Bruce Summerhays	283.2
6	JohnSchroeder	282.8
7	Tom Kite	282.5
8	Jim Holtgrieve	281.4
9	Jim Thorpe	280.7
10T	Walter Hall	280.6
	Dana Quigley	280.6
	Sammy Rachels	280.6

Putting leaders

(Average putts per hole)

Pos	Name	Avg
1	Hale Irwin	1.728
2	Larry Nelson	1.730
3	Bruce Fleisher	1.736
4	Tom Watson	1.738
5T	Terry Mauney	1.742
	Bob Gilder	1.742
	Gil Morgan	1.742
8	Allen Doyle	1.743
9T	Ray Floyd	1.744
	Walter Hall	1.744

Sand saves

Pos	Name	%
1	Bob Eastwood	62.60
2	Jose Maria Canizares (Esp)	60.40
3T	Gary McCord	58.60
	Steven Veriato	58.60
5	Isao Aoki (Jpn)	57.90
6	Gary Player (RSA)	56.40
7	Hubert Green	55.80
8	Lee Trevino	55.70
9	Howard Twitty	55.60
10	Tom Kite	55.40

Greens in regulation

Pos	Name	%
1	Tom Kite	75,20
2	Bruce Fleisher	74.00
3	Doug Tewell	73.80
4T	Hale Irwin	73.10
	Gil Morgan	73.10
6	John Mahaffey	73.00
7	Allen Doyle	72.90
8T	Tom Jenkins	72.40
	Gary McCord	72.40
10	Jim Ahern	71.90

TOUR RESULTS

MasterCard Championship	Hualalai, Kaupulehu-Kona, HI	Larry Nelson	197 (-19)
Senior Skins Game	Wailea, Maui, HI	Hale Irwin	
Royal Caribbean Classic	Crandon Park, Key Biscayne, FL	Larry Nelson	29 pts
ACE Group Classic	Pelican Marsh, Naples, FL	Gil Morgan	204 (-12)
Verizon Classic	TPC Tampa Bay, Lutz, FL	Bob Gilder	205 (-8)
Mexico Senior Classic	La Vista, Cholula, Puebla, Mexico	Mike McCullough	204 (-12)
Toshiba Senior Classic	Newport Beach, CA	José Maria Canizares	202 (-11)
SBC Senior Classic	Los Angeles CA	Jim Colbert	204 (-12)
Siebel Classic in Silicon Valley	Coyote Creek, San Jose, CA	Hale Irwin	206 (-10)
Emerald Coast Classic	The Moors, Milton, Pensacola, FL	Mike McCullough	200 (-10)
Liberty Mutual Legends of Golf	St Augustine, FL	Jim Colbert/ Andy North	124 (-20)
The Tradition	Desert Mountain, Scottsdale, AZ	Doug Tewell	265 (-23)
Las Vegas Senior Classic	TPC Summerlin, Las Vegas, NV	Bruce Fleisher	208 (-8)
Bruno's Memorial Classic	Greystone, Birmingham, AL	Hale Irwin	195 (-21)
The Home Depot Invitational	TPC Piper Glen, Charlotte, NC	Bruce Fleisher	201 (-15)
Enterprise Rent-a-Car Match Play Championship	Boone Valley, Augusta, MO	Leonard Thompson	
TD Waterhouse Ch'p	Tiffany Greens, Kansas City, MO	Ed Dougherty	194 (-22)
Senior PGA Championship	Ridgewood, Paramus	Tom Watson	274 (-14)
BellSouth Senior Classic	Springhouse, Nashville, TN	Sammy Rachels	199 (-17)
NFL Golf Classic	Upper Montclair, Clifton, NJ	John Schroeder	207 (-9)
Instinet Classic	TPC Jasna Polana, Princeton, NJ	Gil Morgan	201 (-15)
FleetBoston Classic	Nashawtuc, Concord, MA	Larry Nelson	201 (-15)
US Senior Open	Salem CC, Peabody,	Bruce Fleisher	280 (even)
Farmers Charity Classic	Egypt Valley, Ada, MI	Larry Nelson	202 (-14)
Ford Senior Players Ch'p	TPC Michigan, Dearborn, MI	Allen Doyle	273 (-15)
SBC Senior Open	Kemper Lakes, Long Grove, IL	Dana Quigley	200 (-16)
State Farm Senior Classic	Hayfields, Hunt Valley, MD	Allen Doyle*	205 (-11)
Lightpath Long Island Classic	Meadow Brook, Jericho, NY	Bobby Wadkins	202 (-14)
3M Championship	TPC Twin Cities, Minneapolis	Bruce Lietzke	207 (-9)
Novell Utah Showdown	Park Meadows, Park City, UT	Steve Veriato	204 (-12)
AT&T Canada Senior Open	Mississauga, Ontario, Canada	Walter Hall	269 (-19)
Kroger Senior Classic	Kings Island, Mason, OH	Jim Thorpe	130 (-10)
Allianz Championship	Des Moines, IA	Jim Thorpe	199 (-14)
Vantage Championship	Tanglewood Park, Clemmons, NC	*Event cancelled*	
SAS Championship	Prestonwood, Cary, NC	Bruce Lietzke	201 (-15)
Gold Rush Classic	Serrano CC, El Dorado Hills, CA	Tom Kite	194 (-22)
Turtle Bay Championship	The Palmer course at Turtle Bay, Kahuku, HI	Hale Irwin	205 (-11)
The Transamerica	Silverado, Napa, CA	Sammy Rachels	202 (-14)
SBC Championship	Dominion CC, San Antonio, TX	Larry Nelson	199 (-17)
Senior Tour Championship	Oklahoma City, OK	Bob Gilder	277 (-11)
Senior Slam	The World Golf Village, St Augustin, FL	Allen Doyle	134 (-10)

US Buy.com Tour 2001

Players are of American nationality unless stated

FINAL RANKING   (Top 15 earned US Tour Card)

Pos	Name	Events	Prize $	Pos	Name	Events	Prize $
1	Chad Campbell	23	394552	51	Mike Heinen	15	90766
2	Pat Bates	24	352261	52	David Sutherland	3	89383
3	Heath Slocum)	18	339670	53	Don Reese	23	88733
4	Rod Pampling (Aus)	26	306573	54	Darron Stiles	26	83779
5	Deane Pappas (RSA)	24	271169	55	Joe Daley	24	83108
6	John Rollins	25	242841	56	Jay Hobby	26	77149
7	Tim Petrovic	23	239010	57	Mark Wurtz	20	76122
8	Jonathan Byrd	2o	222224	58	Brian Bateman	24	75343
9	Jeff Gove	25	198812	59	Tim O'Neal	23	75109
10	Brendan Pappas (RSA)	26	188152	60	Chad Wright	19	74744
11	Bo Van Pelt	24	175947	61	Mike Brisky	20	71759
12	Matt Peterson	21	169947	62	Jamie Rogers (Aus)	25	68715
13	Richard Zokol (Can)	21	167192	63	Bobby Gage	22	62972
14	Jason Hill	26	166899	64	Gary Hallberg	16	62819
15	Michael Long (NZ)	23	161665	65	Jeff Sanday	24	61654
16	Todd Barranger	27	159392	66	FranQuinn	23	61015
17	Paul Claxton	26	158920	67	David Kirkpatrick (Sco)	25	60983
18	Tjaart Van Der Walt (RSA)	23	155291	68	Shane Bertsch	24	60900
19	Steve Haskins	25	153739	69	Bob Heintz	25	60272
20	Ryuji Imada (Jpn)	25	151711	70	Rick Price	23	60237
21	Jason Dufner	13	151394	71	Michael Allen	21	59864
22	Tom Carter	25	149576	72	Phil Tataurangi (NZ)	10	59119
23	Ben Crane	26	147474	73	Todd Rose	20	54864
24	Kelly Gibson	24	145551	74	John Wilson	21	54303
25	Chris Couch	26	145536	75	Charley Hoffman	23	54052
26	Sonny Skinner	24	143951	76	Steve Runge	24	53428
27	Keoke Cotner (Mex)	26	143317	77	Brad Klapprott	20	53395
28	Brian Kamm	22	138714	78	Robert Gaus	26	50922
29	Jim Benepe	17	128987	79	Scott Hebert	23	50206
30	DA Points	20	126366	80	Lee Rinker	25	49772
31	Jay Delsing	18	125374	81	Rob McMillan (Can)	18	49648
32	Pat Perez	26	124818	82	Anthony Painter (Aus)	12	49222
33	Todd Fischer	12	118622	83	Chris Wollmann	25	48592
34	Jeff Freeman	24	118038	84	David McKenzie (Aus)	17	47136
35	Eric Meeks	24	117816	85	Andy Morse	21	46798
36	Charles Raulerson	25	116966	86	Scott Petersen	24	46756
37	David Gossett	12	116288	87	Bob Friend	24	46664
38	Jason Caron	26	116147	88	RW Eaks	26	45966
39	Jason Buha	25	115527	89	Jim McGovern	9	45308
40	Trevor Dodds (Nam))	21	114966	90	Stiles Mitchell	19	41502
41	John Elliott	26	112987	91	Stan Utley	18	40134
42	Omar Uresti	24	110969	92	Ryan Howison	23	40084
43	Guy Boros	23	109802	93	Patrick Sheehan	23	39395
44	Danny Briggs	23	109696	94	Joel Kribel	11	39075
45	John Maginnes	20	108268	95	Matt Kuchar	3	38739
46	Rob McKelvey	25	104852	96	Pete Morgan	21	37350
47	Brett Quigley	4	101776	97	John Patterson	19	36653
48	Billy Judah	25	98001	98	Willie Wood	7	36562
49	Tommy Biershenk	23	96304	99	Don Pooley	7	36295
50	Vic Wilk	26	94588	100	Craig Bowden	22	36190

TOUR RESULTS

Florida Classic	Gainesville, FL	Chris Couch	269 (-15)
Monterrey Open	Monterrey, Mexico	Deane Pappas (RSA)	271 (-17)
Louisiana Open	Le Triomphe, Broussard, LA	Paul Claxton	271 (-17)
Arkansas Classic	Hot Springs Village, AR	Brett Quigley	276 (-12)
Charity Pro-Am at the Cliffs	Cliffs Valley, Greenville, SC	Jonathan Byrd	269 (-18)
Carolina Classic	Raleigh, NC	John Maginnes	269 (-15)
Virginia Beach Open	TPC Virginia Beach, VA	Trevor Dodds (Nam)	277 (-11)
Richmond Open	Richmond, VA	Chad Campbell	263 (-21)
Steamtown Classic	Glenmaura National, Scranton, PA	Jason Hill	272 (-8)
Samsung Canadian PGA Championship	DiamondBack, Toronto, Ontario	Richard Zokol (Can)	271 (-17)
Greater Cleveland Open	Quail Hollow, Concord, OH	Heath Slocum	267 (-21)
Dayton Open	Yankee Trace, Centerville, OH	Todd Barranger	262 (-26)
Knoxville Open	Fox Den, Knoxville, TN	Heath Slocum	265 (-23)
Hershey Open	Hershey, PA	John Rollins	273 (-11)
Wichita Open	Crestview, Wichita, KS	Jason Dufner	266 (-22)
Siouxland Open	Dakota Dunes, SD	Pat Bates	273 (-15)
Ozarks Open	Highland Springs, Springfield, MO	Steve Haskins	131 (-13)
Omaha Classic	Omaha, NE	Heath Slocum	266 (-22)
Fort Smith Classic	Hardscrabble CC, Fort Smith, AR	Jay Delsing	263 (-17)
Permian Basin Open	Mission Dorado, Odessa, TX	Chad Campbell	264 (-24)
Utah Classic	Willow Creek, Salt Lake City, UT	David Sutherland	272 (-16)
Tri-Cities Open	Meadow Springs, Richland, WA	Guy Boros	274 (-14)
Oregon Classic	Shadow Hills, Eugene, OR	Event cancelled	
Boise Open	Hillcrest, Boise, ID	Michael Long (NZ)	270 (-14)
Inland Empire Open	Empire Lakes, Rancho Cucamonga, CA	DA Points	267 (-21)
Monterey Peninsula Classic	Bayonet Golf Cousrse, Seaside, CA	Chad Campbell	208 (-8)
Gila River Classic	Whirlwind GC, Chandler, AZ	Ben Crane	261 (-23)
Shreveport Open	Southern Trace, Shreveport, LA	Pat Bates	268 (-20)
Buy.com Tour Championship	Senator Course, Capitol Hill Golf Facility, Prattville, AL	Pat Bates	284 (-4)

Japan PGA Tour

Players are of Japanese nationality unless stated

Results 2000

Dunlop Phoenix	Phoenix CC, Miyazaki	Shingo Katayama	265 (-19)
Casio World Open	Ibusuki, Kagoshima	Toru Suzuki	267 (-21)
Golf Nippon Series JT Cup	Yomiuri, Tokyo	Shingo Katayama	271 (-9)
Fancl Okinawa Open	Daikyo, Okinawa	Shingo Katayama	277 (-11)

Final Ranking 2000

1	Shingo Katayama	¥177 116 489	6	Hirofumi Miyase	106 622 452
2	Toru Taniguchi	175 827 742	7	Masashi Ozaki	88 940 087
3	Nobuhito Sato	155 246 900	8	Keiichiro Fukabori	81 471 008
4	Toshimitsu Izawa	120 316 633	9	Toru Suzuki	77 513 374
5	Hidemichi Tanaka	108 807 851	10	Kaname Yokoo	76 634 601

Results 2001

Token Corporation Cup	Kedoin GC, Kagoshima	Shingo Katayama	205 (-8)
DyDo-Drinco Shizuoka Open	Hamaoka Course, Shizuoka	Eiji Mizoguchi	279 (-9)
Tsuruya Open	Sports Shinko CC, Hyogo	Hidemichi Tanaka	274 (-14)
Kirin Open	East Course, Ibaragi	Shingo Katayama	271 (-13)
The Crowns	Nagoya, Aichi	Darren Clarke (NI)	267 (-13)
Fujisankei Classic	Kawana, Shizuoka	Frankie Minoza (Phi)	267 (-8)
JPGA Championship	Caledonian GC, Chiba	Dean Wilson (USA)	281 (-3)
Munsingwear Open KSB Cup	Tojigaoka Marin Hills, Okayama	Dinesh Chand (Fij)	271 (-17)
Diamond Cup	Oarai, Ibaragi	Toshimitsu Izawa	277 (-11)
JCB Classic Sendai	Omotezao Kokusai, Miyagi	Toshiaki Odate	275 (-9)
Tamanoi Yomiuri Open	Yomiuri Hyogo	Yoshimitsu Fukuzawa	272 (-16)
Mizuno Open	Sentonaikai, Okayama	Hidemichi Tanaka	272 (-16)
Iiyama Cup JGT Championship	Tour Players Championship Hiroshima	Katsumasa Miyamoto	273 (-15)
Jyuken Sangyo Open		Keiichiro Fukabori	203 (-13)
Aiful Cup	Ajigasawa Kogen, Aomori	Keng Chi Lin (Twn)	270 (-18)
NST Niigata Open	Nakajyo, Niigata	Go Higaki	264 (-26)
Sunychlorella Classic	Sapporo Bay, Hokkaido	Hiroyuki Fujita	283 (-5)
Hisamitsu-KBC Augusta	Keya, Fukuoka	Takenori Hiraishi	273 (-15)
Japan Match Play Promis Cup	Nidom, Hokkaido	Dean Wilson (USA)	
Suntory Open	Sobu CC, Chiba	Shingo Katayama	268 (-16)
ANA Open	Sapporo, Hokkaido	Keng Chi Lin	273 (-15)
Sumitomo Visa Taiheyo Masters	Taiheiyo, Shizuoka	Toshimitsu Izawa	270 (-18)
Acom International	Ishioka, Ibaragi	Kazuhiko Hosokawa	267 (-17)
Tokai Classic	Miyoshi CC, Aichi	Toshimitsu Izawa	272 (-16)
Japan Open	Saitama, Tokyo	Taichi Teshima	277 (-7)
Bridgestone Open	Sodegaura, Chiba	Toshimitsu Izawa	274 (-14)
Ube Kosan Open	Ube 72 CC, Yamaguchi	Dean Wilson (USA)	267 (-21)
Dunlop Phoenix Tournament	Phoenix CC, Miyazaki	David Duval (USA)	269 (-19)
Philip Morris Championship	ABC GC, Hyogo	Toru Taniguchi	(D)
Casio World Open	Ibusuki GC, Kagoshima	Toru Suzuki	(D)
Golf Nippon Series Cup	Tokyo Yomiori, Tokyo	Shingo Katayama	(D)

Latest Ranking (after Dunlop Phoenix Open)

1	Toshimitzu Izawa	¥171 688 883	11	Toru Taniguchi	56 458 250
2	Dean Wilson (USA)	115 114 750	12	Scott Laycock (Aus)	55 948 275
3	Taichi Teshima	108 313 878	13	Hajime Meshiai	55 488 914
4	Shingo Katayama	98 118 950	14	Tsuneyuki Nakajima	55 270 345
5	Keng Chi Lin (Twn)	94 937 000	15	Frankie Minoza (Phi)	53 863 875
6	Hidemichi Tanaka	69 435 544	16	Katsuyoshi Tomori	45 362 752
7	Hiroyuki Fujita	62 977 788	17	Shinichi Yokota	42 045 302
8	Kenchiro Fukabori	60 274 731	18	Dinesh Chand (Fij)	41 223 400
9	Katsumasa Miyamoto	57 455 177	19	David Duval (USA)	40 000 000
10	Masashi Ozaki	57 325 945	20	Nobuhito Sato	39 856 780

Davidoff Asian PGA Tour

Results 2000

Johnnie Walker	Alpine CC, Bangkok, Thailand	Tiger Woods (USA)	263 (-25)
Thailand Open	Springfield Royal CC, Pataya	Des Terblanche (RSA)	269 (-19)
Singapore Open	Singapore Island CC, Island Course	Jyoti Randhawa (Ind)	268 (-20)
Omega Hong Kong Open	Hong Kong GC, Fanling	Simon Dyson (Eng)	263 (-21)

Final Ranking 2000

1	Simon Dyson (Eng)	$282371	6	Thongchai Jaidee (Tha)	155518
2	Jyoti Randhawa (Ind)	224898	7	Prayed Marksaeng (Tha)	141929
3	Yeh Wei Zze (Twn)	224357	8	Des Terblanche (RSA)	131749
4	Craig Kamps (RSA)	165325	9	James Kingston (RSA)	113790
5	Arjun Atwal (Ind)	163049	10	Kang Wook Soon (Kor)	111359

Results 2001

Thailand Masters	Windmill Park CC, Bangkokj	Kang Wock Soon (Kor)	264 (-24)
London Myanmar Open	Yangon GC	Anthony Kang (Kor)	282 (-6)
Carlsberg Malaysian Open	Saujana GC, Kuala Lumpur	Vijay Singh (Fij)	274 (-14)
Caltex Singapore masters	Bukit, Singapore Island	Vijay Singh (Fij)	263 (-21)
Wills Indian Open	Classic GR, New Delhi	Thongchai Jaidee (Tha)	271 (-17)
Maekyung LG Fashion			
Open	Nam Seoul CC, Seoul	Choi-Gwang Soo (Kor)	271 (-17)
Macau Open	Macau GCC	Zhang Lian Wei (Chn)	273 (-11)
SK Telecom Open	Il Dong Lake GC	Charlie Wi (Kor)	281 (-7)
Alcatel Singapore Open	Jurong CC	Thoworn Wirachant (Tha)	272 (-16)
Volvo Masters of Malaysia	Kota Permae GCC,		
	Kuala Lumpur	Thoworn Wirachant (Tha)	271 (-17)
Acer Taiwan Open	Sunrise GBC	Andrew Pitts (USA)	197 (-19)

Davidoff Tour *continued*

Mercuries Masters	Tamsui Course, Taiwan GCC	Daniel Chopra (Swe)	284 (-4)
Kolon Cup Korean Open	Seoul Hanyang GC	Kim Dre Sub (am) (Kor)	272 (-16)
Shin Hang Dong Hae Open	Kaya GCC	Charlie Wi (Kor)	276 (-12)
Volvo China Open	Shanghai Silport GC	Charlie Wi (Kor)	272 (-14)

Two events remain to be played on the Davidoff Tour, both joint ventures with the European Tour which includes them on their 2002 schedule:

BMW Asian Open	Western Resort Ta Shee	*New event*
Hong Kong Open	Hong Kong GC	Simon Dyson (D)

Latest Ranking (after Volvo China Open and with two events to play)

1	Charlie Wi (Kor)	US$289092	11	Yang Yong-eun (Kor)	77528
2	Thongchai Jaidee (Tha)	212428	12	Mardan Mamat (Sin)	76986
3	Andrew Pitts (USA)	135178	13	Anthony Kang (Kor)	73496
4	Thaworn Wirachant (Tha)	112842	14	Park Do-kyo (Kor)	70381
5	Arjun Atwal (Ind)	95212	15	Choi Gwang-soo	64312
6	Simon Yates (Sco)	91164	16	Clay Devers (USA)	61044
7	Kang Wook-soon (Kor)	87151	17	Thammanoon Sriroj (Tha)	60224
8	Vivek Bhandari (Ind)	85339	18	Zhang Lian-wei (Chi)	53898
9	James Kingston	84922	19	Ahmad Bateman (USA)	58398
10	Daniel Chopra (Swe)	83686	20	Arjun Singh (Ind)	49473

Eamonn Darcy hits the 600 mark

Ireland's Eamonn Darcy become only the second European Tour player to go through the 600 tournament barrier when he played in the 2001 Cannes Open. The only other player to have teed up more than 600 times is Sam Torrance the Ryder Cup captain.

Malcom Mackenzie, the 40-year-old professional from Barrow-upon-Soar, made it through 500 when he played in the Telefonica Open de Madrid. Four others have played 500 events – Des Smyth (whose 2001 Madeira Island Open win at age 48 years and 31 days earned him the oldest winner in our record from previous holder Neil Coles), Carl Mason, Mark James and Roger Chapman. Unlike the other four Mackenzie has never won on Tour although he did come second in the 1990 Murphy's Cup at Fulford to Tony Johnstone.

The full list at the end of the 2001 season reads:

660	Sam Torrance (Sco)	501	Malcolm Mackenzie (Eng)
602	Eamonn Darcy (Ire)	494*	Howard Clark (Eng)
571	Des Smyth (Ire)	492	Gordon Brand jr (Sco)
543*	Carl Mason (Eng)	488	Mark Mouland (Wal)
524	Mark James (Eng)	485*	Christy O'Connor jr (Ire)
518	Roger Chapman (Eng)		

*No longer plays on main Tour

Australasian Tour

Players are of Australian nationality unless stated

Results 2000–2001

Johnnie Walker Classic	Alpine CC, Bangkok, Thailand	Tiger Woods (USA)	263 (-25)
Holden Australian Open	Kingston Heath, Melbourne	Aaron Baddeley (Aus)	278 (-10)
Australian PGA	Royal Queensland, Brisbane	Robert Allenby (Aus)	275 (-13)
Ford Open	Kooyonga, Adelaide	Peter Lonard (Aus)	269 (-19)
WGC – Accenture Match Play Championship	Metropolitan, Melbourne	Steve Stricker (USA)	
Victorian Open	Cranbourne, Melbourne	Scott Laycock	270 (-18)
New Zealand Open	Grange, Auckland, NZ	David Smail	273 (-7)
Canon Challenge	Castle Hill, Sydney, NSW	David Smail	269 (-19)
Heineken Classic	The Vines, Perth, WA	Michael Campbell	270 (-18)
Greg Norman Holden International	The Lakes, Sydney, NSW	Aaron Baddeley	271 (-21)
Ericsson Masters	Huntingdale, Melbourne	Colin Montgomerie (Sco)	278 (-10)
ANZ Championship	Concord, Sydney, NSW	Peter Lonard	269 (-15)

Final Ranking 2000–2001

1	Aaron Baddeley	AUS$662125	11	Rod Pampling	200491
2	Peter Lonard	579387	12	Peter O'Malley	185534
3	Michael Campbell (NZ)	484732	13	Scott Laycock	179444
4	David Smail (NZ)	428889	14	Scott Gardiner	175876
5	Nick O'Hern	385730	15	Richard Green	162725
6	Robert Allenby	307500	16	Brett Rumford	158241
7	Nathan Green	301212	17	Anthony Painter	153252
8	Geoff Ogilvy	287836	18	Jim Benepe	143650
9	Jarrod Moseley	202945	19	Paul Gow	139614
10	Greg Norman	202483	20	Kenny Druce	136463

Fixtures 2001-2002 (season ends December 15)

Australian PGA Championship	Royal Queensland GC Robert Allenby 273 (-15)
Nov 22–25	Holden Australian Open Championship, The Grand GC, Queensland
Jan 10–13	Telstra Saturn Hyundai New Zealand Open Championship, Paraparaumu Beach GC
Jan 24–27	*Johnnie Walker Classic, Lake Karrinyup CC, Western Australia
Jan 31–Feb 3	†Heineken Classic, Royal Melbourne GC, Victoria
Feb 7–10	†ANZ Championship, The Lakes GC, Sydney
Mar 7–10	‡Jacobs Creek Open, Kooyonga GC
Mar 14–17	‡Clearwater Classic, Clearwater Resort
Nov 14–17	Perth International, Lake Karrinyup CC, Western Australia
Nov 21–24	Holden Australian Open, Victoria GC, Melbourne
Nov 28–Dec 2	Australian PGA Championship, Royal Queensland GC
Dec 5–8	Ericsson Masters, Huntingdale GC, Melbourne
Dec 12–15	Tour Championship, Concord GC, Sydney

* *co-sanctioned with European and Davidoff Tours*   † *co-sanctioned with European Tour*
‡ *co-sanctioned with US Buy.com Tour*

South African Sunshine Tour

Players are of South African nationality unless stated

Results 2000–2001

Platinum Classic	Moonooi	Desvonde Botes	202 (-14)
Riviera Resort Classic	Riviera CC	Ulrich Van den Berg	130 (-10)
Cabs Old Mutual Zimbabwe Open	Royal Harare GC	Mark McNulty (Zim)	269 (-19)
Vodacom Players Championship	Royal Cape GC, Cape Town	Trevor Immelman	279 (-9)
Nashua Nedtel Cellular Masters	Wild Coast Sun CC	Mark McNulty (Zim)	274 (-6)
Alfred Dunhill Championship	Houghton GC, Johannesburg	Adam Scott (Aus)	267 (-21)
Mercedes Benz SA Open	East London GC	Mark McNulty (Zim)	280 (-8)
Dimension Data Pro-Am	Gary Player CC and Lost City GC, Sun City	Darren Clarke (NI)	274 (-14)
South African PGA Championship	Woodhill CC, Pretoria	Dean Pappas	269 (-19)
Royal Swazi Sun Open	Royal Swazi Sun CC, Mbabane	Bradford Vaughan	263 (-25)
The Tour Championship	Leopard Creek, near Malalene	Darren Fichardt	270 (-14)

Final Ranking 2000–2001

1	Mark McNulty (Zim)	SAR1603481	*	Malcolm Mackenzie (Eng)	427927
2	Bradford Vaughan	686414	7	Titch Moore	418191
3	Roger Wessels	632383	*	Darren Clarke (NI)	407200
4	Hennie Otto	620210	8	Darren Fichardt	402270
5	Trevor Immelman	619765	9	Justin Hobday	353358
6	Retief Goosen	516852	10	Grant Muller	295703

* Denotes member who has won enough money to be in the top 25 but who has not played the minimum required number of events to be given an Order-of-Merit ranking

Results and Fixtures 2000–2001

Stanbic Zambia Open	Lusaka GC	Mark Foster (Eng)	278 (-14)
Cock o' the North	Ndola GC	Sean Farrell (Zim)	209 (-10)
FNB Botswana Open	Gaberone GC	Marc Cayeux (Zim)	197 (-16)
Royal Swazi Sun Classic	Royal Swazi Sun CC, Mbabane	Titch Moore	200 (-16)
Pietersburg Industrelek Classic	Pietersburg GC	Ryan Reid	204 (-12)
Goldfields Powerade Classic	Oppenheimer Park, Welkom	Callie Stewart	207 (-9)
Bloemfontein Classic	Shoeman Park, Bloemfontein	André Cruse	207 (-9)
Randfontein Classic	Randfontein GC	James Kingston	205 (-11)
Bearing Man Highfield Classic	Withbank GC	Justin Hobday	203 (-13)
Atlantic Beach Classic	Atlantic Beach, Cape Town	James Kingston	213 (-3)
Western Cape Classic	Rondebosch GC, Cape Town	Lindani Ndwandwe	207 (-9)
Vodacom Trophy	Zwartkop CC	Ulrich van den Berg	198 (-18)
Graceland Challenge	Graceland, Secunda	Warren Abery	205 (-11)

Nov 16–18	Platinum Classic, Mooinoi GC, Rustenburg
Nov 22–25	CABS/Old Mutual Zimbabwe Open, Chapman GC, Harare
Nov 29–Dec 2	*Nedbank Golf Challenge, Gary Player CC, Sun City

Dec 6–9	Vodacom Players Championship, Royal Cape GC, Cape Town
Jan 10–13	†South African Open, Durban CC, Durban
Jan 17–20	†Alfred Dunhill Championship, Houghton GC, Johannesburg
Jan 24–27	Telkom PGA Championship, Woodhill CC, Pretoria
Jan 31–Feb 3	Dimension Data Pro-am, Gary Player CC and Lost City GC, Sun City
Feb 7–10	Nashua Masters, Wild Coast CC, near Port Edward
Feb 14–17	The Tour Championship, Leopard Creek CC, near Malelane

non order of merit   † co-sanctioned with European Tour

Latest Ranking (after Graceland Challenge)

1	André Cruse	12	SAR113,996	11	Sean Farrell (Zim)	10	60,264
2	Marc Cayeux (Zim)	11	96,361	12	Keith Horne	11	58,411
3	Mark Foster (Eng)	1	87,361	13	Naithen Moore	11	55,720
4	Ulrich van den Berg	11	83,236	14	Wallie Coatsee	11	54,010
5	Ryan Reid	12	76,935	15	Stuart Little (Eng)	1	53,544
6	Justin Hobday	5	69,653	16	Jaco Van Zyl	9	53,212
7	Jaco Oliver	10	68,763	17	Sean Ludgater	11	49,270
8	Warren Abery	11	68,266	18	Graeme van der Nest	10	47,334
9	James Kingston	4	67,370	19	Hendrik Buhrmann	8	44,575
10	Titch Moore	9	60,736	20	Lindani Nowandwe		44,469

Canadian Tour 2001

Results

Panama Open	Coronado GC, Coronado Beach	Steve Runge (USA)	272 (-16)
Myrtle Beach Open	Barefoot Resort, Myrtle Beach SC	Eamonn Brady (Irl)	277 (-7)
Barefoot Classic	Barefoot Resort, Myrtle Beach SC	Aaron Barber (USA)	204 (-12)
South Carolina Challenge	Barefoot Resort, Myrtle Beach SC	Jace Bugg	274 (-14)
CanAm Days Championship	Barefoot Resort, Myrtle Beach SC	Scott Ford (USA)	206 (–10)
Shell Payless Open	Gorge Vale GC, Victoria, BC	Paul Devenport (NZ)	271 (-13)
Telus Vancouver Open	Point Grey GC, Vancouver BC	Steve Scott (USA)	276 (-12)

After play-off with Steve Alker, Roger Tambellini, Scott Hend, Mark Slawter and Jess Daley

Telus Edmonton Open	Edmonton GC, Edmonton AB	Aaron Barber (USA)	264 (-20)
Ontario Open Heritage Classic	Fort Williams GC, Thunder Bay, ON	Craig Matthew (Can)	272 (-16)

After play-off with Bob Conford

Grant Forest Products/ NRCS Classic	Timberwolf, Sudbury, ON	Derek Gilchrist (USA)	270 (-18)

After play-off with Ken Duke

MTS Classic	Pine Ridge, Winnipeg, Manitoba	Ken Staton (USA)	266 (-18)
Telus Open	Les Quatre Domaines, Mirabel, QC	Paul Devenport (NZ)	269 (-19)
Eagle Creek Classic	Eagle Creek GC, Ottawa, ON	Mark Slawter (USA)	266 (-22)
Aliant Cup	Clovelly, St John's, Newfoundland	Brian Payne (USA)	281 (-7)

Canadian Tour *continued*

Casino de Charlevoix Cup	Le Manoir, Richelieu, Pointe-au-Pic, QC	Drew Symons and Darren Griff (Can)	2 and 1
Bayer Championship	Huron Oaks GC, Sarnia, ON	Jason Bohn	260 (-24)
Niagara Classic	Whirlpool GC, Niagara Falls, ON	Ken Staton	134 (-10)

Final Ranking 2000

1	Aaron Barber (USA)	$75337	11	Rich Massey (USA)	52133
2	Paul Devenport (NZ)	72629	12	Brian Payne (USA)	46461
3	Jason Bohn (USA)	69957	13	Jess Daley (USA)	45225
4	Jace Bugg (USA)	64717	14	Scott Ford (USA)	41044
5	Mark Slawter (USA)	63005	15	Steven Alker (NZ)	40268
6	Ken Staton (USA)	62653	16	Patrick Moore (USA)	37915
7	Steve Scott (USA)	55400	17	Chris Greenwood (USA)	34151
8	Craig Matthew (Can)	53932	18	Ken Duke (USA)	30638
9	Dave Christensen (USA)	53093	19	Todd Fanning (Can)	29442
10	Derek Gilchrist (USA)	52285	20	Bob Conrad (USA)	26311

Tour de las Americas

Results 2000–2001

TPG Movilnet Classic	Lagunita CC	Angel Franco (Par)	267 (-13)
Abierto de Peru	Los Incas CC	Scott Dunlap (USA)	278 (-10)
Abierto del Litoral	Rosario	Jesus Amaya (Col)	134 (-10)
Abierto de la Rep Argentina	Jockey Club	Vicente Fernandez (Arg)	277 (-3)
Abierto Chevrolet de Brazil	Guarapiranga	Jesus Amaya (Col)	274 (-6)
Abierto de Paraguay	Yacht & GC Paraguayo	Carlos Franco (Par)	279 (-5)
Masters de Chile	Brisas de Chicureo	Alexandre Rodia (Bra)	265 (-15)
Masters de Mexico	Atlas CC	Raul Fretes (Par)	276 (-12)
Campeonato PGA de las Americas		Angel Romero (Col)	269 (-19)

Final Ranking 2000–2001

1	Angel Romero (Col)	US$49396	11	Pedro Martinez (Par)	13340
2	Jesus Amaya (Col)	48583	12	Mauricio Molina (Arg)	12654
3	Angel Franco (Par)	40248	13	David Schuster (USA)	11538
4	Adam Arnadost (USA)	34088	14	Kim Hegna (USA)	11441
5	Donald Donahue (USA)	28412	15	Rafael Gomez (Arg)	11095
6	Raul Fretes (Par)	27998	16	Alan McDonald (Sco)	10062
7	Dave Bishop (USA)	27388	17	Damian Hale (Tri)	9658
8	Shannon Sykora (USA)	25850	18	Gustavo Mendoza (Col)	9620
9	Alex Balicki (Fra)	15412	19	Daniel Nunez (Arg)	9600
10	Rigoberto Velazquez (Col)	13829	20	Eduardo Pesenti (Bra)	9165

World Championship Events

Accenture Match Play Championship
2001 *at Metropolitan GC, Melbourne Australia*

First Round
Ernie Els (RSA) beat Greg Kraft (USA) 4 and 2
Hidemachi Tanaka (Jpn) beat Bernhard Langer (Ger) 1 hole
Jean Van de Velde (Fra) beat Duffy Waldorf (USA) 1 hole
Retief Goosen (RSA) beat Steve Lowery (USA) 2 and 1
Craig Stadler (USA) beat John Huston (USA) 4 and 2
Craig Parry (Aus) beat Dennis Paulson (USA) 1 hole
David Toms (USA) beat Hirofumi Miyase (Jpn) 1 hole
Andrew Coltart (Sco) beat Phillip Price (Wal) 3 and 2

Tom Lehman (USA) beat Greg Chalmers (Aus) 2 and 1
Jeff Sluman (USA) beat Naomichi (Joe) Ozaki (Jpn) 3 and 2
Chris Perry (USA) beat Jonathan Kaye (USA) 2 holes
Brad Faxon (USA) beat José Coceres (Arg) 3 and 2
Michael Campbell (NZ) beat Mathias Grönberg (Swe) 4 and 3
Toshi Izawa (Jpn) beat Steve Pate (USA) 1 hole
Glen Day (USA) beat Kirk Triplett (USA) 3 and 1
Pierre Fulke (Swe) beat Fred Funk (USA) 5 and 4

Nick O'Hern (Aus) beat Hal Sutton (USA) 1 hole
Tim Herron (USA) beat Franklin Langham (USA) 3 and 1
Robert Allenby (Aus) beat Nobuhito Sato (Jpn) 2 and 1
Dudley Hart (USA) beat Skip Kendall (USA) 6 and 5
Justin Leonard (USA) beat Patrick Sjöland (Swe) 6 and 5
Gary Orr (Sco) beat Paul McGinley (Irl) 2 and 1
Steve Stricker (USA) beat Padraig Harrington (Irl) 2 and 1
Scott Verplank (USA) beat Brent Geiberger (USA) 1 hole

Vijay Singh (Fij) beat Kevin Sutherland (USA) 4 and 2
Toru Taniguchi (Jpn) beat Bob Estes (USA) 3 and 2
Stuart Appleby (Aus) beat Kenny Perry (USA) 2 holes
Per-Ulrik Johansson (Swe) beat Steve Flesch (USA) 5 and 4
Mark McNulty (Zim) beat Stewart Cink (USA) 1 hole
Paul Lawrie (Sco) beat Chris DiMarco (USA) 5 and 4
Bob May (USA) beat Tom Scherrer (USA) 2 and 1
Shigeki Maruyama (Jpn) beat Scott Dunlap (USA) 2 and 1

Second Round
Els beat Tanaka 1 hole
Van de Velde beat Goosen 4 and 3
Stadler beat Parry 7 and 6
Coltart beat Toms 4 and 2
Lehman beat Sluman 3 and 2
Faxon beat Perry 1 hole
Campbell beat Izawa 6 and 4
Fulke beat Day at 20th

O'Hern beat Herron 5 and 3
Allenby beat Hart 5 and 4
Leonard beat Orr at 20th
Stricker beat Verplank 3 and 2
Taniguchi beat Singh 1 hole
Appleby beat Johansson 4 and 3
McNulty beat Lawrie 5 and 4
Maruyama beat May at 22nd

Third Round
Els beat Van de Velde at 19th
Stadler beat Coltart at 19th
Faxon beat Lehman 1 hole
Fulke beat Campbell 1 hole
O'Hern beat Hart 5 and 4
Stricker beat Leonard 6 and 5
Taniguchi beat Appleby 2 and 1
Maruyama beat McNulty 4 and 3

Quarter-finals
Els beat Stadler 1 hole
Fulke beat Faxon at 19th
Stricker beat O'Hern at 20th
Taniguchi beat Maruyama 2 and 1

Semi-finals
Fulke beat Els 2 and 1
Stricker beat Taniguchi 2 and 1

Final (36 holes)
Steve Stricker beat Pierre Fulke 2 and 1

Consolation Match
Toru Taniguchi beat Ernie Els 4 and 3

Winner:	$1,000,000	€1,065,188
Runner-up:	500,000	532,592
3rd place:	400,000	426,075
4th place:	300,000	319,556

NEC World Series *at Firestone, Akron, Ohio* [7139-70]

2000 Tiger Woods (USA) 259

1	Tiger Woods* (USA)	66-67-66-69—268	$691324	€1091096
2	Jim Furyk (USA)	65-66-66-71—268	345662	545548
3	Darren Clarke (NI)	66-68-68-69—271	259246	409161
4	Colin Montgomerie (Sco)	66-71-66-70—273	207397	327329
5	Stuart Appleby (Aus)	70-64-70-70—274	139417	220038
	Paul Azinger (USA)	67-70-65-72—274	139417	220038
	Davis Love III (USA)	68-68-70-68—274	139417	220038
8	Ernie Els (RSA)	67-70-66-72—275	101970	160937
	Phil Mickelson (USA)	67-66-70-72—275	101970	160937
10	Retief Goosen (RSA)	72-69-64-71—276	90563	142934
11	Bernhard Langer (Ger)	69-67-68-73—277	81922	129295
	Hal Sutton (USA)	69-71-67-70—277	81922	129295
13	Stewart Cink (USA)	69-67-70-72—278	69478	109655
	Ian Poulter (Eng)	67-72-69-70—278	69478	109655
	Vijay Singh (Fij)	68-68-69-73—278	69478	109655
	David Toms (USA)	68-70-70-70—278	69478	109655
17	Pierre Fulke (Swe)	73-71-65-70—279	57380	90561
	Padraig Harrington (Irl)	68-66-73-72—279	57380	90561
	Scott Verplank (USA)	69-71-70-69—279	57380	90561
20	Carlos Franco (Par)	68-71-68-73—280	50467	79650
21	Niclas Fasth (Swe)	74-67-68-72—281	45627	72012
	Scott Hoch (USA)	71-70-69-71—281	45627	72012
23	Robert Allenby (Aus)	68-67-75-72—282	40097	63284
	Steve Elkington (Aus)	73-68-73-68—282	40097	63284
25	Mike Weir (Can)	69-70-71-73—283	36640	57828
26	Paul McGinley (Irl)	68-73-71-72—284	35258	55646
27	David Duval (USA)	69-69-72-75—285	33875	53464
28	Phillip Price (Wal)	70-71-74-71—286	32492	51282
29	Nick Price (Zim)	71-70-71-76—288	30418	48008
	Loren Roberts (USA)	72-70-67-79—288	30418	48008
31	Notah Begay III (USA)	77-71-72-69—289	26270	41462
	Thomas Bjørn (Den)	66-79-73-71—289	26270	41462
	Michael Campbell (NZ)	71-71-75-72—289	26270	41462
	Shigeki Maruyama (Jpn)	68-75-73-73—289	26270	41462
35	Greg Norman (Aus)	65-71-74-80—290	22814	36006
36	Mark Calcavecchia (USA)	72-69-72-79—292	21431	33824
	Miguel Angel Jimenéz (Esp)	70-72-74-76—292	21431	33824
DQ	Kirk Triplett (USA)	70-70-69	17974	28368
W/D	Lee Westwood (Eng)	70-78	17974	28368

American Express Challenge

This event was cancelled

World Cup of Golf (Known as the Canada Cup until 1966)

Year	Winner	Runners-up	Venue	Score
1953	Argentina	Canada	Montreal	287
	(A Cerda and R De Vincenzo)	(S Leonard and B Kerr)		
	(Individual: A Cerda, Argentina, 140)			
1954	Australia	Argentina	Laval-Sur-Lac	556
	(P Thomson and K Nagle)	(A Cerda and R De Vincenzo)		
	(Individual: S Leonard, Canada, 275)			
1955	United States	Australia	Washington	560
	(C Harbert and E Furgol)	(P Thomson and K Nagle)		
	(Individual: E Furgol, USA, after a play-off with P Thomson and F van Donck, 279)			
1956	United States	South Africa	Wentworth	567
	(B Hogan and S Snead)	(A Locke and G Player)		
	(Individual: B Hogan, USA, 277)			
1957	Japan	United States	Tokyo	557
	(T Nakamura and K Ono)	(S Snead and J Demaret)		
	(Individual: T Nakamura, Japan, 274)			
1958	Ireland	Spain	Mexico City	579
	(H Bradshaw and C O'Connor)	(A Miguel and S Miguel)		
	(Individual: A Miguel, Spain, after a play-off with H Bradshaw, 286)			
1959	Australia	United States	Melbourne	563
	(P Thomson and K Nagle)	(S Snead and C Middlecoff)		
	(Individual: S Leonard, Canada, 275, after a tie with P Thomson, Australia)			
1960	United States	England	Portmarnock	565
	(S Snead and A Palmer)	(H Weetman and B Hunt)		
	(Individual: F van Donck, Belgium, 279)			
1961	United States	Australia	Puerto Rico	560
	(S Snead and J Demaret)	(P Thomson and K Nagle)		
	(Individual: S Snead, USA, 272)			
1962	United States	Argentina	Buenos Aires	557
	(S Snead and A Palmer)	(F de Luca and R De Vicenzo)		
	(Individual: R De Vicenzo, Argentina, 276)			
1963	United States	Spain	St Nom-La-Breteche	482
	(A Palmer and J Nicklaus)	(S Miguel and R Sota)		
	(Individual: J Nicklaus, USA, 237 [63 holes])			
1964	United States	Argentina	Maui, Hawaii	554
	(A Palmer and J Nicklaus)	(R De Vicenzo and L Ruiz)		
	(Individual: J Nicklaus, USA, 276)			
1965	South Africa	Spain	Madrid	571
	(G Player and H Henning)	(A Miguel and R Sota)		
	(Individual: G Player, South Africa, 281)			
1966	United States	South Africa	Tokyo	548
	(J Nicklaus and A Palmer)	(G Player and H Henning)		
	(Individual: G Knudson, Canada, and H Sugimoto, Japan, each 272; Knudson won play-off)			
1967	United States	New Zealand	Mexico City	557
	(J Nicklaus and A Palmer)	(R Charles and W Godfrey)		
	(Individual: A Palmer, USA, 276)			
1968	Canada	United States	Olgiata, Rome	569
	(A Balding and G Knudson)	(J Boros and L Trevino)		
	(Individual: A Balding, Canada, 274)			
1969	United States	Japan	Singapore	552
	(O Moody and L Trevino)	(T Kono and H Yasuda)		
	(Individual: L Trevino, USA, 275)			
1970	Australia	Argentina	Buenos Aires	545
	(B Devlin and D Graham)	(R De Vicenzo and V Fernandez)		
	(Individual: R De Vicenzo, Argentina, 269)			
1971	United States	South Africa	Palm Beach, Florida	555
	(J Nicklaus and L Trevino)	(H Henning and G Player)		
	(Individual: J Nicklaus, USA, 271)			
1972	Taiwan	Japan	Melbourne	438
	(H Min-Nan and LL Huan)	(T Kono and T Murakami)		
	(Individual: H Min-Nan, Taiwan, 217 [3 rounds only])			
1973	United States	South Africa	Marbella, Spain	558
	(J Nicklaus and J Miller)	(G Player and H Baiocchi)		
	(Individual: J Miller, USA, 277)			
1974	South Africa	Japan	Caracas	554
	(R Cole and D Hayes)	(I Aoki and M Ozaki)		
	(Individual: R Cole, South Africa, 271)			
1975	United States	Taiwan	Bangkok	554
	(J Miller and L Graham)	(H Min-Nan and KC Hsiung)		
	(Individual: J Miller, USA, 275)			
1976	Spain	United States	Palm Springs	574
	(S Ballesteros and M Pinero)	(J Pate and D Stockton)		
	(Individual: EP Acosta, Mexico, 282)			

World Cup of Golf *continued*

Year	Winner	Runners-up	Venue	Score
1977	Spain (S Ballesteros and A Garrido) (Individual: G Player, South Africa, 289)	Philippines (R Lavares and B Arda)	Manilla, Philippines	591
1978	United States (J Mahaffey and A North) (Individual: J Mahaffey, USA, 281)	Australia (G Norman and W Grady)	Hawaii	564
1979	United States (J Mahaffey and H Irwin) (Individual: H Irwin, USA, 285)	Scotland (A Lyle and K Brown)	Glyfada, Greece	575
1980	Canada (D Halldorson and J Nelford) (Individual: A Lyle, Scotland, 282)	Scotland (A Lyle and S Martin)	Bogota	572
1981	*Not played*			
1982	Spain (M Pinero and JM Canizares) (Individual: M Pinero, Spain, 281)	United States (B Gilder and B Clampett)	Acapulco	563
1983	United States (R Caldwell and J Cook) (Individual: D Barr, Canada, 276)	Canada (D Barr and J Anderson)	Pondok Inah, Jakarta	565
1984	Spain (JM Canizares and J Rivero) (Individual: JM Canizares, Spain, 205. Played over 54 holes due to storm)	Scotland (S Torrance and G Brand Jr)	Olgiata, Rome	414
1985	Canada (D Halidorson and D Barr) (Individual: H Clark, England, 272)	England (H Clark and P Way)	La Quinta, Calif.	559
1986	*Not played*			
1987	Wales (won play-off) (I Woosnam and D Llewelyn) (Individual: I Woosnam, Wales, 274)	Scotland (S Torrance and A Lyle)	Kapalua, Hawaii	574
1988	United States (B Crenshaw and M McCumber) (Individual: B Crenshaw, USA, 275)	Japan (T Ozaki and M Ozaki)	Royal Melbourne, Australia	560
1989	Australia (P Fowler and W Grady) (Individual: P Fowler. Played over 36 holes due to storms.)	Spain (JM Olazábal and JM Canizares)	Las Brisas, Spain	
1990	Germany (B Langer and T Giedeon) (Individual: P Stewart, USA, 271)	T England (M James and R Boxall) Ireland (R Rafferty and D Feherty)	Grand Cypress Resort, Orlando, Florida	556
1991	Sweden (A Forsbrand and P-U Johansson) (Individual: I Woosnam, Wales, 273)	Wales (I Woosnam and P Price)	La Querce, Rome	563
1992	USA (F Couples and D Love III) (Individual: B Ogle, Australia, 270 after a tie with I Woosnam, Wales)	Sweden (A Forsbrand and P-U Johansson)	La Moraleja II, Madrid, Spain	548
1993	USA (F Couples and D Love III) (Individual: B Langer, Germany, 272)	Zimbabwe (N Price and M McNulty)	Lake Nona, Orlando, FL	556
1994	USA (F Couples and D Love III) (Individual: F Couples, USA, 265)	Zimbabwe (M McNulty and T Johnstone)	Dorado Beach, Puerto Rico	536
1995	USA (F Couples and D Love III) (Individual: D Love III, USA, 267)	Australia (B Ogle and R Allenby)	Mission Hills, Shenzhen, China	543
1996	South Africa (E Els and W Westner) (Individual: E Els, S. Africa, 272)	USA (T Lehman and S Jones)	Erinvale, Cape Town South Africa	547
1997	Ireland (P Harrington and P McGinley) (Individual: C Montgomerie, Scotland, 266)	Scotland (C Montgomerie and R Russell)	Kiawah Island, SC	545
1998	England (N Faldo and D Carter) (Individual: Scott Verplank, USA, 279)	Italy (C Rocca and M Florioli)	Gulf Harbour, Auckland New Zealand	568
1999	USA (T Woods and M O'Meara) (Individual: Tiger Woods, USA, 263)	Spain (S Luna and MA Martin)	The Mines Resort, KL Malaysia	545
2000	USA (T Woods & D Duval)	Argentina (A Cabrera & E Romero)	Buenos Aires GC Argentina	

The 47th EMC^2 World Cup of Golf was played at the Taiheiyo Club, Gotemba, Shizuoka, Japan with a prize fund of $3 million. Results can be found on page 158.

Other International Events

Hassan II Trophy

1971	O Moody (USA)	1980	E Sneed (USA)	1993	P Stewart (USA)
1972	R Cerrudo (USA)	1981	B Eastwood (USA)	1994	M Gates (Eng)
1973	W Casper (USA)	1982	F Connor (USA)	1995	N Price (Zim)
1974	L Ziegler (USA)	1983	R Streck (USA)	1996	I Garrido (Esp)
1975	W Casper (USA)	1984	R Maltbie (USA)	1997	C Montgomerie (Sco)
1976	S Balbuena (USA)	1985	K Green (USA)	1998	S Luna (Esp)
1977	L Trevino (USA)	1986–90	Not played	1999	D Toms* (USA)
1978	P Townsend (Eng)	1991	V Singh (Fij)	2000	R Chapman (Eng)
1979	M Brannan (USA)	1992	P Stewart (USA)		

2001 at *Royal Dar Es Salam Red course, Rabat, Morocco*

1	Joakim Haegmann (Swe)	67-70-75-72—284	$50000
2	Santiago Luna (Esp)	71-73-67-74—285	34000
	Mark Roe (Eng)	79-69-71-74—285	34000

Million Dollar Challenge

at *Sun City, Bophutatswana, South Africa* (7597 yds, Par 72)

1982 (Jan)	J Miller (USA)	277	1988	F Allem (RSA)	278	1995	C Pavin (USA)	276
1982 (Dec)	R Floyd (USA)	280	1989	D Frost (RSA)	276	1996	C Montgomerie	
1983	S Ballesteros (Esp)	274	1990	D Frost (RSA)	284		(Sco)	274
1984	S Ballesteros (Esp)	279	1991	B Langer (Ger)	272	1997	N Price (Zim)	275
1985	B Langer (Ger)	278	1992	D Frost (RSA)	276	1998	N Price* (Zim)	273
1986	M McNulty (Zim)	282	1993	N Price (Zim)	264	1999	E Els (RSA)	263
1987	I Woosnam (Wal)	274	1994	N Faldo (Eng)	272	2000	E Els (RSA)	268

2001 event being played in December

International Team Events

Ryder Cup

This event will next be played in 2002 and thereafter in even-numbered years

Home team names first

Great Britain v USA

1926 at Wentworth
Result: GB 13½, USA 1½

Singles
Abe Mitchell beat Jim Barnes   8 and 7
George Duncan beat Walter Hagen   6 and 5
Aubrey Boomer beat Tommy Armour   2 and 1
Archie Compston lost to Bill Mehlhorn   1 hole
George Gadd beat Joe Kirkwood   8 and 7
Ted Ray beat Al Watrous   6 and 5
Fred Robson beat Cyril Walker   5 and 4
Arthur Havers beat Fred McLeod   10 and 9
Ernest Whitcombe halved with Emmett French
Herbert Jolly beat Joe Stein   3 and 2

Foursomes
Mitchell & Duncan beat Barnes & Hagen   9 and 8
Boomer & Compston beat Armour & Kirkwood
   3 and 2
Gadd & Havers beat Mehlhorn & Watrous   3 and 2
Ray & Robson beat Walker & McLeod   3 and 2
Whitcombe & Jolly beat French & Stein   3 and 2

RYDER CUP – Inaugurated 1927

1927 at Worcester, MA
Result: USA 9½, GBI 2½
Captains: W Hagen (USA), E Ray (GBI)
Foursomes
Hagen & Golden beat Ray & Robson   2 and 1
Farrell & Turnesa beat Duncan & Compston   8 and 6
Sarazen & Watrous beat Havers & Jolly   3 and 2
Diegel & Mehlhorn lost to Boomer & Whitcombe
   7 and 5

Singles
Bill Mehlhorn beat Archie Compston   1 hole
Johnny Farrell beat Aubrey Boomer   5 and 4
Johnny Golden beat Herbert Jolly   8 and 7
Leo Diegel beat Ted Ray   7 and 5
Gene Sarazen halved with Charles Whitcombe
Walter Hagen beat Arthur Havers   2 and 1
Al Watrous beat Fred Robson   3 and 2
Joe Turnesa lost to George Duncan   1 hole

1929 at Moortown
Result: GBI 7, USA 5
*Captains: George Duncan (GBI),
   Walter Hagen (USA)*
Foursomes
C Whitcombe & Compston halved with Farrell &
   Turnesa

Boomer & Duncan lost to Diegel & Espinosa   7 and 5
Mitchell & Robson beat Sarazen & Dudley   2 and 1
E Whitcombe & Cotton lost to Golden & Hagen   2
holes

Singles
Charles Whitcombe beat Johnny Farrell   8 and 6
George Duncan beat Walter Hagen   10 and 8
Abe Mitchell lost to Leo Diegel   9 and 8
Archie Compston beat Gene Sarazen   6 and 4
Aubrey Boomer beat Joe Turnesa   4 and 3
Fred Robson lost to Horton Smith   4 and 2
Henry Cotton beat Al Watrous   4 and 3
Ernest Whitcombe halved with Al Espinosa

1931 at Scioto, Columbus, OH
Result: USA 9, GBI 3
*Captains: Walter Hagen (USA),
   Charles Whitcombe (GBI)*

Foursomes
Sarazen & Farrell beat Compston & Davies   8 and 7
Hagen & Shute beat Duncan & Havers   10 and 9
Diegel & Espinosa lost to Mitchell & Robson   3 and 1
Burke & Cox beat Easterbrook & E Whitcombe
   3 and 2

Singles
Billy Burke beat Archie Compston   7 and 6
Gene Sarazen beat Fred Robson   7 and 6
Johnny Farrell lost to William H Davies   4 and 3
Wilfred Cox beat Abe Mitchell   3 and 1
Walter Hagen beat Charles Whitcombe   4 and 3
Densmore Shute beat Bert Hodson   8 and 6
Al Espinosa beat Ernest Whitcombe   2 and 1
Craig Wood lost to Arthur Havers   4 and 3

1933 at Southport & Ainsdale
Result: GBI 6½, USA 5½
*Captains: JH Taylor (GBI),
   Walter Hagen (USA)*

Foursomes
Alliss & Whitcombe halved with Sarazen & Hagen
Mitchell & Havers beat Dutra & Shute   3 and 2
Davies & Easterbrook beat Wood & Runyan   1 hole
Padgham & Perry lost to Dudley & Burke   1 hole

Singles
Alf Padgham lost to Gene Sarazen   6 and 4
Abe Mitchell beat Olin Dutra   9 and 8
Arthur Lacey lost to Walter Hagen   2 and 1
William H Davies lost to Craig Wood   4 and 3
Percy Alliss beat Paul Runyan   2 and 1

1933 Singles continued
Arthur Havers beat Leo Diegel 4 and 3
Syd Easterbrook beat Densmore Shute 1 hole
Charles Whitcombe lost to Horton Smith 2 and 1

1935 at Ridgewood, NJ
Result: USA 9, GBI 3
Captains: Walter Hagen (USA),
Charles Whitcombe (GBI)

Foursomes
Sarazen & Hagen beat Perry & Busson 7 and 6
Picard & Revolta beat Padgham & Alliss 6 and 5
Runyan & Smith beat Cox & Jarman 9 and 8
Dutra & Laffoon lost to C Whitcombe &
  E Whitcombe 1 hole

Singles
Gene Sarazen beat Jack Busson 3 and 2
Paul Runyon beat Dick Burton 5 and 3
Johnny Revolta beat Charles Whitcombe 2 and 1
Olin Dutra beat Alf Padgham 4 and 2
Craig Wood lost to Percy Alliss 1 hole
Horton Smith halved with Bill Cox
Henry Picard beat Ernest Whitcombe 3 and 2
Sam Parks halved with Alf Perry

1937 at Southport & Ainsdale
Result: USA 8, GBI 4
Captains: Charles Whitcombe (GBI),
Walter Hagen (USA)
Foursomes
Padgham & Cotton lost to Dudley & Nelson 4 and 2
Lacey & Bill Cox lost to Guldahl & Manero 2 and 1
Whitcombe & Rees halved with Sarazen & Shute
Alliss & Burton beat Picard & Johnny Revolta 2 and 1
Singles
Alf Padgham lost to Ralph Guldahl 8 and 7
Sam King halved with Densmore Shute
Dai Rees beat Byron Nelson 3 and 1
Henry Cotton beat Tony Manero 5 and 3
Percy Alliss lost to Gene Sarazen 1 hole
Dick Burton lost to Sam Snead 5 and 4
Alf Perry lost to Ed Dudley 2 and 1
Arthur Lacey lost to Henry Picard 2 and 1

1947 at Portland, OR
Result: USA 11, GBI 1
Captains: Ben Hogan (USA),
Henry Cotton (GBI)
Foursomes
Oliver & Worsham beat Cotton & Lees 10 and 9
Snead & Mangrum beat Daly & Ward 6 and 5
Hogan & Demaret beat Adams & Faulkner 2 holes
Nelson & Herman Barron beat Rees & King 2 and 1
Singles
Dutch Harrison beat Fred Daly 5 and 4
Lew Worsham beat Jimmy Adams 3 and 2
Lloyd Mangrum beat Max Faulkner 6 and 5
Ed Oliver beat Charlie Ward 4 and 3
Byron Nelson beat Arthur Lees 2 and 1
Sam Snead beat Henry Cotton 5 and 4
Jimmy Demaret beat Dai Rees 3 and 2
Herman Keiser lost to Sam King 4 and 3

1949 at Ganton
Result: USA 7, GBI 5
Captains: Charles Whitcombe (GBI),
Ben Hogan (USA)
Foursomes
Faulkner & Adams beat Harrison & Palmer 2 and 1
Daly & Ken Bousfield beat Hamilton & Alexander
  4 and 2
Ward & King lost to Demaret & Heafner 4 and 3
Burton & Lees beat Snead & Mangrum 1 hole
Singles
Max Faulkner lost to Dutch Harrison 8 and 7
Jimmy Adams beat Johnny Palmer 2 and 1
Charlie Ward lost to Sam Snead 6 and 5
Dai Rees beat Bob Hamilton 6 and 4
Dick Burton lost to Clayton Heafner 3 and 2
Sam King lost to Chick Harbert 4 and 3
Arthur Lees lost to Jimmy Demaret 7 and 6
Fred Daly lost to Lloyd Mangrum 1 hole

1951 at Pinehurst, NC
Result: USA 9½, GBI 2½
Captains: Sam Snead (USA),
Arthur Lacey (GBI)
Foursomes
Heafner & Burke beat Faulkner & Rees 5 and 3
Oliver & Henry Ransom lost to Ward & Lees 2 and 1
Mangrum & Snead beat Adams & Panton 5 and 4
Hogan & Demaret beat Daly & Bousfield 5 and 4
Singles
Jack Burke beat Jimmy Adams 4 and 3
Jimmy Demaret beat Dai Rees 2 holes
Clayton Heafner halved with Fred Daly
Lloyd Mangrum beat Harry Weetman 6 and 5
Ed Oliver lost to Arthur Lees 2 and 1
Ben Hogan beat Charlie Ward 3 and 2
Skip Alexander beat John Panton 8 and 7
Sam Snead beat Max Faulkner 4 and 3

1953 at Wentworth
Result: USA 6½, GBI 5½
Captains: Henry Cotton (GBI),
Lloyd Mangrum (USA)
Foursomes
Weetman & Alliss lost to Douglas & Oliver 2 and 1
Brown & Panton lost to Mangrum & Snead 8 and 7
Adams & Hunt lost to Kroll & Burke 7 and 5
Daly & Bradshaw beat Burkemo & Middlecoff 1 hole
Singles
Dai Rees lost to Jack Burke 2 and 1
Fred Daly beat Ted Kroll 9 and 7
Eric Brown beat Lloyd Mangrum 2 holes
Harry Weetman beat Sam Snead 1 hole
Max Faulkner lost to Cary Middlecoff 3 and 1
Peter Alliss lost to Jim Turnesa 1 hole
Bernard Hunt halved with Dave Douglas
Harry Bradshaw beat Fred Haas jr 3 and 2

1955 at Palm Springs, CA
Result: USA 8, GBI 4
Captains: Chick Harbert (USA),
Dai Rees (GBI)
Foursomes
Harper & Barber lost to Fallon & Jacobs 1 hole
Ford & Kroll beat Brown & Scott 5 and 4
Burke & Bolt beat Lees & Weetman 1 hole
Snead & Middlecoff beat Rees & Bradshaw 3 and 2

1965 *continued*

Singles
Tommy Bolt beat Christy O'Connor 4 and 2
Chick Harbert beat Syd Scott 3 and 2
Cary Middlecoff lost to John Jacobs 1 hole
Sam Snead beat Dai Rees 3 and 1
Marty Furgol lost to Arthur Lees 3 and 1
Jerry Barber lost to Eric Brown 3 and 2
Jack Burke beat Harry Bradshaw 3 and 2
Doug Ford beat Harry Weetman 3 and 2

1957 *at Lindrick*
Result: GBI 7½, USA 4½
Captains: Dai Rees (GBI), Jack Burke (USA)

Foursomes
Alliss & Hunt lost to Ford & Finsterwald 2 and 1
Bousfield & Rees beat Art Wall jr & Hawkins 3 and 2
Faulkner & Weetman lost to Kroll & Burke 4 and 3
O'Connor & Brown lost to Mayer & Bolt 7 and 5

Singles
Eric Brown beat Tommy Bolt 4 and 3
Peter Mills beat Jack Burke 5 and 3
Peter Alliss lost to Fred Hawkins 2 and 1
Ken Bousfield beat Lionel Hebert 4 and 3
Dai Rees beat Ed Furgol 7 and 6
Bernard Hunt beat Doug Ford 6 and 5
Christy O'Connor beat Dow Finsterwald 7 and 6
Harry Bradshaw halved with Dick Mayer

1959 *at Palm Desert, CA*
Result: USA 8½, GBI 3½
Captains: Sam Snead (USA), Dai Rees (GBI)

Foursomes
Rosburg & Souchak beat Hunt & Brown 5 and 4
Ford & Wall lost to O'Connor & Alliss 3 and 2
Boros & Finsterwald beat Rees & Bousfield 2 holes
Snead & Middlecoff halved with Weetman & Thomas

Singles
Doug Ford halved with Norman Drew
Mike Souchak beat Ken Bousfield 3 and 2
Bob Rosburg beat Harry Weetman 6 and 5
Sam Snead beat Dave Thomas 6 and 5
Dow Finsterwald beat Dai Rees 1 hole
Jay Hebert halved with Peter Alliss
Art Wall jr beat Christy O'Connor 7 and 6
Cary Middlecoff lost to Eric Brown 4 and 3

1961 *at Royal Lytham & St Anne's*
Result: USA 14½, GBI 9½
Captains: Jerry Barber (USA), Dai Rees (GBI)

First Day: Foursomes – Morning
O'Connor & Alliss beat Littler & Ford 4 and 3
Panton & Hunt lost to Wall & Hebert 4 and 3
Rees & Bousfield lost to Casper & Palmer 2 and 1
Haliburton & Coles lost to Souchak & Collins 1 hole

Foursomes – Afternoon
O'Connor & Alliss lost to Wall & Hebert 1 hole
Panton & Hunt lost to Casper & Palmer 5 and 4
Rees & Bousfield beat Souchak & Collins 4 and 2
Haliburton& Coles lost to Barber & Finsterwald
    1 hole

Second Day: Singles – Morning
Harry Weetman lost to Doug Ford 1 hole
Ralph Moffitt lost to Mike Souchak 5 and 4
Peter Alliss halved with Arnold Palmer
Ken Bousfield lost to Billy Casper 5 and 3

Dai Rees beat Jay Hebert 2 and 1
Neil Coles halved with Gene Littler
Bernard Hunt beat Jerry Barber 5 and 4
Christy O'Connor lost to Dow Finsterwald 2 and 1

Singles – Afternoon
Weetman lost to Wall 1 hole
Alliss beat Bill Collins 3 and 2
Hunt lost to Souchak 2 and 1
Tom Haliburton lost to Palmer 2 and 1
Rees beat Ford 4 and 3
Bousfield beat Barber 1 hole
Coles beat Finsterwald 1 hole
O'Connor halved with Littler

1963 *at Atlanta, GA*
Result: USA 23, GBI
Captains: Arnold Palmer (USA),
    John Fallon (GBI)

First Day: Foursomes – Morning
Palmer & Pott lost to Huggett & Will 3 and 2
Casper & Ragan beat Alliss & O'Connor 1 hole
Boros & Lema halved with Coles & B Hunt
Littler & Finsterwald halved with Thomas & Weetman

Foursomes – Afternoon
Maxwell & Goalby beat Thomas & Weetman 4 and 3
Palmer & Casper beat Huggett & Will 5 and 4
Littler & Finsterwald beat Coles & G Hunt 2 and 1
Boros & Lema beat Haliburton & B Hunt 1 hole

Second Day: **Fourball – Morning**
Palmer & Finsterwald beat Huggett & Thomas
    5 and 4
Littler & Boros halved with Alliss & B Hunt
Casper & Maxwell beat Weetman & Will 3 and 2
Goalby & Ragan lost to Coles & O'Connor 1 hole

Fourball – Afternoon
Palmer & Finsterwald beat Coles & O'Connor
    3 and 2
Lema & Pott beat Alliss & B Hunt 1 hole
Casper & Maxwell beat Haliburton & G Hunt
    2 and 1
Goalby & Ragan halved with Huggett & Thomas

Third Day: **Singles – Morning**
Tony Lema beat Geoffrey Hunt 5 and 3
Johnny Pott lost to Brian Huggett 3 and 1
Arnold Palmer lost to Peter Alliss 1 hole
Billy Casper halved with Neil Coles
Bob Goalby beat Dave Thomas 3 and 2
Gene Littler lost to Tom Haliburton 6 and 5
Julius Boros lost to Harry Weetman 1 hole
Dow Finsterwald lost to Bernard Hunt 2 holes

Singles – Afternoon
Arnold Palmer beat George Will 3 and 2
Dave Ragan beat Neil Coles 2 and 1
Tony Lema halved with Peter Alliss
Gene Littler beat Tom Haliburton 6 and 5
Julius Boros beat Harry Weetman 2 and 1
Billy Maxwell beat Christy O'Connor 2 and 1
Dow Finsterwald beat Dave Thomas 4 and 3
Bob Goalby beat Bernard Hunt 2 and 1

1965 *at Royal Birkdale*
Result: GBI 12½, USA 19½
Captains: Harry Weetman (GBI),
    Byron Nelson (USA)

First Day: Foursomes – Morning
Thomas & Will beat Marr & Palmer 6 and 5
O'Connor & Alliss beat Venturi & January 5 and 4

Platts & Butler lost to Boros & Lema 1 hole
Hunt & Coles lost to Casper & Littler 2 and 1
Foursomes – Afternoon
Thomas & Will lost to Marr & Palmer 6 and 5
Martin & Hitchcock lost to Boros & Lema 5 and 4
O'Connor & Alliss beat Casper & Littler 2 and 1
Hunt & Coles beat Venturi & January 3 and 2
Second Day: **Fourball – Morning**
Thomas & Will lost to January & Jacobs 1 hole
Platts & Butler halved with Casper & Littler
Alliss & O'Connor lost to Marr & Palmer 5 and 4
Coles & Hunt beat Boros & Lema 1 hole
Fourball – Afternoon
Alliss & O'Connor beat Marr & Palmer 1 hole
Thomas & Will lost to January & Jacobs 1 hole
Platts & Butler halved with Casper & Littler
Coles & Hunt lost to Lema & Venturi 1 hole
Third Day: **Singles – Morning**
Jimmy Hitchcock lost to Arnold Palmer 3 and 2
Lionel Platts lost to Julius Boros 4 and 2
Peter Butler lost to Tony Lema 1 hole
Neil Coles lost to Dave Marr 2 holes
Bernard Hunt beat Gene Littler 2 holes
Peter Alliss beat Billy Casper 1 hole
Dave Thomas lost to Tommy Jacobs 2 and 1
George Will halved with Don January
Singles – Afternoon
Butler lost to Palmer 2 holes
Hitchcock lost to Boros 2 and 1
Christy O'Connor lost to Lema 6 and 4
Alliss beat Ken Venturi 3 and 1
Hunt lost to Marr 1 hole
Coles beat Casper 3 and 2
Will lost to Littler 2 and 1
Platts beat Jacobs 1 hole

1967 *at Houston, TX*
Result: USA 23½, GBI 8½
Captains: Ben Hogan (USA), Dai Rees (GBI)
First Day: **Foursomes – Morning**
Casper & Boros halved with Huggett & Will
Palmer & Dickinson beat Alliss & O'Connor 2 and 1
Sanders & Brewer lost to Jacklin & Thomas 4 and 3
Nichols & Pott beat Hunt & Coles 6 and 5
Foursomes – Afternoon
Boros & Casper beat Huggett & Will 1 hole
Dickinson & Palmer beat Gregson & Boyle 5 and 4
Littler & Geiberger lost to Jacklin & Thomas 3 and 2
Nichols & Pott beat Alliss & O'Connor 2 and 1
Second Day: **Fourball – Morning**
Casper & Brewer beat Alliss & O'Connor 3 and 2
Nichols & Pott beat Hunt & Coles 1 hole
Littler & Geiberger beat Jacklin & Thomas 1 hole
Dickinson & Sanders beat Huggett & Will 3 and 2
Fourball – Afternoon
Casper & Brewer beat Hunt & Coles 5 and 3
Dickinson & Sanders beat Alliss & Gregson 4 and 3
Palmer & Boros beat Will & Boyle 1 hole
Littler & Geiberger halved with Jacklin & Thomas
Third Day: **Singles – Morning**
Gay Brewer beat Hugh Boyle 4 and 3
Billy Casper beat Peter Alliss 2 and 1
Arnold Palmer beat Tony Jacklin 3 and 2
Julius Boros lost to Brian Huggett 1 hole
Doug Sanders lost to Neil Coles 2 and 1
Al Geiberger beat Malcolm Gregson 4 and 2
Gene Littler halved with Dave Thomas
Bobby Nichols halved with Bernard Hunt

Singles – Afternoon
Palmer beat Huggett 5 and 3
Brewer lost to Alliss 2 and 1
Gardner Dickinson beat Jacklin 3 and 2
Nichols beat Christy O'Connor 3 and 2
Johnny Pott beat George Will 3 and 1
Geiberger beat Gregson 2 and 1
Boros halved with Hunt
Sanders lost to Coles 2 and 1

1969 *at Royal Birkdale*
Result: USA 16, GBI 16
Captains: Eric Brown (GBI),
Sam Snead (USA)
First Day: **Foursomes – Morning**
Coles & Huggett beat Barber & Floyd 3 and 2
Gallacher & Bembridge beat Trevino & Still
2 and 1
Jacklin & Townsend beat Hill & Aaron 3 and 1
O'Connor & Alliss halved with Casper & Beard
Foursomes – Afternoon
Coles & Huggett lost to Hill & Aaron 1 hole
Gallacher & Bembridge lost to Trevino & Littler
2 holes
Jacklin & Townsend beat Casper & Beard 1 hole
Hunt & Butler lost to Nicklaus & Sikes
Second Day: **Fourball – Morning**
O'Connor & Townsend beat Hill & Douglass
1 hole
Huggett & Alex Caygill halved with Floyd & Barber
Barnes & Alliss lost to Trevino & Littler 1 hole
Jacklin & Coles beat Nicklaus & Sikes 1 hole
Fourball – Afternoon
Townsend & Butler lost to Casper & Beard 2 holes
Huggett & Gallacher lost to Hill & Still 2 and 1
Bembridge & Hunt halved with Aaron & Floyd
Jacklin & Coles halved with Trevino & Barber
Third Day: **Singles – Morning**
Peter Alliss lost to Lee Trevino 2 and 1
Peter Townsend lost to Dave Hill 5 and 4
Neil Coles beat Tommy Aaron 1 hole
Brian Barnes lost to Billy Casper 1 hole
Christy O'Connor beat Frank Beard 5 and 4
Maurice Bembridge beat Ken Still 1 hole
Peter Butler beat Ray Floyd 1 hole
Tony Jacklin beat Jack Nicklaus 4 and 3
Singles – Afternoon
Barnes lost to Hill 4 and 2
Bernard Gallacher beat Trevino 4 and 3
Bembridge lost to Miller Barber 7 and 6
Butler beat Dale Douglass 3 and 2
O'Connor lost to Gene Littler 2 and 1
Brian Huggett halved with Casper
Coles lost to Dan Sikes 4 and 3
Jacklin halved with Nicklaus

1971 *at St Louis, MO*
Result: USA 18½, GBI 13½
Captains: Jay Hebert (USA),
Eric Brown (GBI)
First Day: **Foursomes – Morning**
Casper & Barber lost to Coles & O'Connor
2 and 1
Palmer & Dickinson beat Townsend & Oosterhuis
2 holes
Nicklaus & Stockton lost to Huggett & Jacklin
3 and 2
Coody & Beard lost to Bembridge & Butler 1 hole

1971 *continued*

Foursomes – Afternoon
Casper & Barber lost to Bannerman & Gallacher
2 and 1
Palmer & Dickinson beat Townsend & Oosterhuis
1 hole
Trevino & Rudolph halved with
Nicklaus & Snead beat Bembridge & Butler 5 and 3
***Second Day:* Fourball – Morning**
Trevino & Rudolph beat O'Connor & Barnes
2 and 1
Beard & Snead beat Coles & John Garner 2 and 1
Palmer & Dickinson beat Oosterhuis & Gallacher
5 and 4
Nicklaus & Littler beat Townsend & Bannerman
2 and 1
Fourball – Afternoon
Trevino & Casper lost to Oosterhuis & Gallacher
1 hole
Littler & Snead beat Huggett & Jacklin 2 and 1
Palmer & Nicklaus beat Townsend & Bannerman
1 hole
Coody & Beard halved with Coles & O'Connor
***Third Day:* Singles – Morning**
Lee Trevino beat Tony Jacklin 1 hole
Dave Stockton halved with Bernard Gallacher
Mason Rudolph lost to Brian Barnes 1 hole
Gene Littler lost to Peter Oosterhuis 4 and 3
Jack Nicklaus beat Peter Townsend 3 and 2
Gardner Dickinson beat Christy O'Connor 5 and 4
Arnold Palmer halved with Harry Bannerman
Frank Beard halved with Neil Coles
Singles – Afternoon
Trevino beat Brian Huggett 7 and 6
JC Snead beat Jacklin 1 hole
Miller Barber lost to Barnes 2 and 1
Stockton beat Townsend 1 hole
Charles Coody lost to Gallacher 2 and 1
Nicklaus beat Coles 5 and 3
Palmer lost to Oosterhuis 3 and 2
Dickinson lost to Bannerman 2 and 1

1973 *at Muirfield*
Result: USA 19, GBI 13
Captains: Bernard Hunt (GBI),
Jack Burke (USA)
***First Day:* Foursomes – Morning**
Barnes & Gallacher beat Trevino & Casper 1 hole
O'Connor & Coles beat Weiskopf & Snead 3 and 2
Jacklin & Oosterhuis halved with Rodriguez &
Graham
Bembridge & Polland lost to Nicklaus & Palmer
6 and 5
Fourball – Afternoon
Barnes & Gallacher beat Aaron & Brewer 5 and 4
Bembridge & Huggett beat Nicklaus & Palmer
3 and 1
Jacklin & Oosterhuis beat Weiskopf & Casper
3 and 1
O'Connor & Coles lost to Trevino & Blancas
2 and 1
***Second Day:* Foursomes – Morning**
Barnes & Butler lost to Nicklaus & Weiskopf 1 hole
Jacklin & Oosterhuis beat Palmer & Hill 2 holes
Bembridge & Huggett beat Rodriguez & Graham
5 and 4
O'Connor & Coles lost to Trevino & Casper
2 and 1

Fourball – Afternoon
Barnes & Butler lost to Snead & Palmer 2 holes
Jacklin & Oosterhuis lost to Brewer & Casper
3 and 2
Clark & Polland lost to Nicklaus & Weiskopf 3 and 2
Bembridge & Huggett halved with Trevino &
Blancas
***Third Day:* Singles – Morning**
Brian Barnes lost to Billy Casper 2 and 1
Bernard Gallacher lost to Tom Weiskopf 3 and 1
Peter Butler lost to Homero Blancas 5 and 4
Tony Jacklin beat Tommy Aaron 3 and 1
Neil Coles halved with Gay Brewer
Christy O'Connor lost to JC Snead 1 hole
Maurice Bembridge halved with Jack Nicklaus
Peter Oosterhuis halved with Lee Trevino
Singles – Afternoon
Brian Huggett beat Blancas 4 and 2
Barnes lost to Snead 3 and 1
Gallacher lost to Brewer 6 and 5
Jacklin lost to Casper 2 and 1
Coles lost to Trevino 6 and 5
O'Connor halved with Weiskopf
Bembridge lost to Nicklaus 2 holes
Oosterhuis beat Arnold Palmer 4 and 2

1975 *at Laurel Valley, PA*
Result: USA 21, GBI 11
Captains: Arnold Palmer (USA),
Bernard Hunt (GBI)
***First Day:* Foursomes – Morning**
Nicklaus & Weiskopf beat Barnes & Gallacher
5 and 4
Littler & Irwin beat Wood & Bembridge 4 and 3
Geiberger & Miller beat Jacklin & Oosterhuis 3 and 1
Trevino & Snead beat Horton & O'Leary 2 and 1
Fourball – Afternoon
Casper & Floyd lost to Jacklin & Oosterhuis 2 and 1
Weiskopf & Graham beat Darcy &
Christy O'Connor jr 3 and 2
Nicklaus & Murphy halved with Barnes & Gallacher
Trevino & Irwin beat Horton & O'Leary 2 and 1
***Second Day:* Fourball – Morning**
Casper & Miller halved with Jacklin & Oosterhuis
Nicklaus & Snead beat Horton & Wood 4 and 2
Littler & Graham beat Barnes & Gallacher 5 and 3
Geiberger & Floyd halved with Darcy & Hunt
Foursomes – Afternoon
Trevino & Murphy lost to Jacklin & Barnes 3 and 2
Weiskopf & Miller beat O'Connor & O'Leary 5 and 3
Irwin & Casper beat Oosterhuis & Bembridge
3 and 2
Geiberger & Graham beat Darcy & Hunt 3 and 2
***Third Day:* Singles – Morning**
Bob Murphy beat Tony Jacklin 2 and 1
Johnny Miller lost to Peter Oosterhuis 2 holes
Lee Trevino halved with Bernard Gallacher
Hale Irwin halved with Tommy Horton
Gene Littler beat Brian Huggett 4 and 2
Billy Casper beat Eamonn Darcy 3 and 2
Tom Weiskopf beat Guy Hunt 5 and 3
Jack Nicklaus lost to Brian Barnes 4 and 2
Singles – Afternoon
Ray Floyd beat Jacklin 1 hole
JC Snead lost to Oosterhuis 3 and 2
Al Geiberger halved with Gallacher
Lou Graham lost to Horton 2 and 1

Irwin beat John O'Leary 2 and 1
Murphy beat Maurice Bembridge 2 and 1
Trevino lost to Norman Wood 2 and 1
Nicklaus lost to Barnes 2 and 1

1977 at Royal Lytham & St Anne's
Result: USA 12½, GBI 7½
*Captains: Brian Huggett (GBI),
    Dow Finsterwald (USA)*
First Day: Foursomes
Gallacher & Barnes lost to Wadkins & Irwin 3 and 1
Coles & Dawson lost to Stockton & McGee 1 hole
Faldo & Oosterhuis beat Floyd & Graham 2 and 1
Darcy & Jacklin halved with Sneed & January
Horton & James lost to Nicklaus & Watson 5 and 4
Second Day: Fourball
Barnes & Horton lost to Watson & Green 5 and 4
Coles & Dawson lost to Sneed & Wadkins 5 and 3
Faldo & Oosterhuis beat Nicklaus & Floyd 3 and 1
Darcy & Jacklin lost to Hill & Stockton 5 and 3
James & Brown lost to Irwin & Graham 1 hole
Third Day: Singles
Howard Clark lost to Lanny Wadkins 4 and 3
Neil Coles lost to Lou Graham 5 and 3
Peter Dawson beat Don January 5 and 4
Brian Barnes beat Hale Irwin 1 hole
Tommy Horton lost to Dave Hill 5 and 4
Bernard Gallacher beat Jack Nicklaus 1 hole
Eamonn Darcy lost to Hubert Green 1 hole
Mark James lost to Ray Floyd 2 and 1
Nick Faldo beat Tom Watson 1 hole
Peter Oosterhuis beat Jerry McGee 2 holes

From 1979 GBI became a European team

1979 at Greenbrier, WV
Result: USA 17, Europe 11
*Captains: Billy Casper (USA),
    John Jacobs (Eur)*
First Day: Fourball – Morning
Wadkins & Nelson beat Garrido & Ballesteros
    2 and 1
Trevino & Zoeller beat Brown & James 3 and 2
Bean & Elder beat Oosterhuis & Faldo 2 and 1
Irwin & Mahaffey lost to Gallacher & Barnes 2 and 1
Foursomes – Afternoon
Irwin & Kite beat Brown & Smyth 7 and 6
Zoeller & Green lost to Garrido & Ballesteros 3 and 2
Trevino & Morgan halved with Lyle & Jacklin
Wadkins & Nelson beat Gallacher & Barnes 4 and 3
Second Day: Foursomes – Morning
Elder & Mahaffey lost to Lyle & Jacklin 5 and 4
Bean & Kite lost to Oosterhuis & Faldo 6 and 5
Zoeller & Hayes halved with Gallacher & Barnes
Wadkins & Nelson beat Garrido & Ballesteros 3 and 2
Fourball – Afternoon
Wadkins & Nelson beat Garrido & Ballesteros
    5 and 4
Irwin & Kite beat Lyle & Jacklin 1 hole
Trevino & Zoeller lost to Gallacher & Barnes 3 and 2
Elder & Hayes lost to Oosterhuis & Faldo 1 hole
Third Day: Singles
Lanny Wadkins lost to Bernard Gallacher 3 and 2
Larry Nelson beat Seve Ballesteros 3 and 2
Tom Kite beat Tony Jacklin 1 hole
Mark Hayes beat Antonio Garrido 1 hole

Andy Bean beat Michael King 4 and 3
John Mahaffey beat Brian Barnes 1 hole
Lee Elder lost to Nick Faldo 3 and 2
Hale Irwin beat Des Smyth 5 and 3
Hubert Green beat Peter Oosterhuis 2 holes
Fuzzy Zoeller lost to Ken Brown 1 hole
Lee Trevino beat Sandy Lyle 2 and 1
Gil Morgan, Mark James: injury; match a half

1981 at Walton Heath
Result: USA 18½, Europe 9½
*Captains: John Jacobs (Eur),
    Dave Marr (USA)*
First Day: Foursomes – Morning
Langer & Pinero lost to Trevino & Nelson 1 hole
Lyle & James beat Rogers & Lietzke 2 and 1
Gallacher & Smyth beat Irwin & Floyd 3 and 2
Oosterhuis & Faldo lost to Watson & Nicklaus
    4 and 3
Fourball – Afternoon
Torrance & Clark halved with Kite & Miller
Lyle & James beat Crenshaw & Pate 3 and 2
Smyth & Canizares beat Rogers & Lietzke 6 and 5
Gallacher & Darcy lost to Irwin & Floyd 2 and 1
Second Day: Fourball – Morning
Faldo & Torrance lost to Trevino & Pate 7 and 5
Lyle & James lost to Nelson & Kite 1 hole
Langer & Pinero beat Irwin & Floyd 2 and 1
Smyth & Canizares lost to Watson & Nicklaus
    3 and 2
Foursomes – Afternoon
Oosterhuis & Torrance lost to Trevino & Pate
    2 and 1
Langer & Pinero lost to Watson & Nicklaus 3 and 2
Lyle & James lost to Rogers & Floyd 3 and 2
Gallacher & Smyth lost to Nelson & Kite 3 and 2
Third Day: Singles
Sam Torrance lost to Lee Trevino 5 and 3
Sandy Lyle lost to Tom Kite 3 and 2
Bernard Gallacher halved with Bill Rogers
Mark James lost to Larry Nelson 2 holes
Des Smyth lost to Ben Crenshaw 6 and 4
Bernhard Langer halved with Bruce Lietzke
Manuel Pinero beat Jerry Pate 4 and 2
José Maria Canizares lost to Hale Irwin 1 hole
Nick Faldo beat Johnny Miller 2 and 1
Howard Clark beat Tom Watson 4 and 3
Peter Oosterhuis lost to Ray Floyd 2 holes
Eamonn Darcy lost to Jack Nicklaus 5 and 3

1983 at PGA National, FL
Result: USA 14½, Europe 13½
*Captains: Jack Nicklaus (USA),
    Tony Jacklin (Eur)*
First Day: Foursomes – Morning
Watson & Crenshaw beat Gallacher & Lyle 5 and 4
Wadkins & Stadler lost to Faldo & Langer 4 and 2
Floyd & Gilder lost to Canizares & Torrance 4 and 3
Kite & Peete beat Ballesteros & Way 2 and 1
Fourball – Afternoon
Morgan & Zoeller lost to Waites & Brown 2 and 1
Watson & Haas beat Faldo & Langer 2 and 1
Floyd & Strange lost to Ballesteros & Way 1 hole
Crenshaw & Peete halved with Torrance &
    Woosnam

1983 *continued*

Second Day: Foursomes - Morning
Floyd & Kite lost to Faldo & Langer 3 and 2
Wadkins & Morgan beat Canizares & Torrance
7 and 5
Gilder & Watson lost to Ballesteros & Way 2 and 1
Haas & Strange beat Waites & Brown 3 and 2

Fourball - Afternoon
Wadkins & Stadler beat Waites & Brown 1 hole
Crenshaw & Peete lost to Faldo & Langer 2 and 1
Haas & Morgan halved with Ballesteros & Way
Gilder & Watson beat Torrance & Woosnam
5 and 4

Third Day: Singles
Fuzzy Zoeller halved with Seve Ballesteros
Jay Haas lost to Nick Faldo 2 and 1
Gil Morgan lost to Bernhard Langer 2 holes
Bob Gilder beat Gordon J Brand 2 holes
Ben Crenshaw beat Sandy Lyle 3 and 1
Calvin Peete beat Brian Waites 1 hole
Curtis Strange lost to Paul Way 2 and 1
Tom Kite halved with Sam Torrance
Craig Stadler beat Ian Woosnam 3 and 2
Lanny Wadkins halved with José Maria Canizares
Ray Floyd lost to Ken Brown 4 and 3
Tom Watson beat Bernard Gallacher 2 and 1

1985 *at The Belfry*
Result: Europe 16½, USA 11½
Captains: Tony Jacklin (Eur),
Lee Trevino (USA)

First Day: Foursomes - Morning
Ballesteros & Pinero beat Strange & O'Meara
2 and 1
Faldo & Langer lost to Kite & Peete 3 and 2
Brown & Lyle lost to Floyd & Wadkins 4 and 3
Clark & Torrance lost to Stadler & Sutton 3 and 2

Fourball - Afternoon
Way & Woosnam beat Green & Zoeller 1 hole
Ballesteros & Pinero beat Jacobsen & North 2 and 1
Canizares & Langer halved with Stadler & Sutton
Clark & Torrance lost to Floyd & Wadkins 1 hole

Second Day: Fourball - Morning
Clark & Torrance beat Kite & North 2 and 1
Way & Woosnam beat Green & Zoeller 4 and 3
Ballesteros & Pinero lost to O'Meara & Wadkins
3 and 2
Langer & Lyle halved with Stadler & Strange

Foursomes - Afternoon
Canizares & Rivero beat Kite & Peete 7 and 5
Ballesteros & Pinero beat Stadler & Sutton 5 and 4
Way & Woosnam lost to Jacobsen & Strange
4 and 3
Brown & Langer beat Floyd & Wadkins 3 and 2

Third Day: Singles
Manuel Pinero beat Lanny Wadkins 3 and 1
Ian Woosnam lost to Craig Stadler 2 and 1
Paul Way beat Ray Floyd 2 holes
Seve Ballesteros halved with Tom Kite
Sandy Lyle beat Peter Jacobsen 3 and 2
Bernhard Langer beat Hal Sutton 5 and 4
Sam Torrance beat Andy North 1 hole
Howard Clark beat Mark O'Meara 1 hole
Nick Faldo lost to Hubert Green 3 and 1
José Rivero lost to Calvin Peete 1 hole
José Maria Canizares beat Fuzzy Zoeller 2 holes
Ken Brown lost to Curtis Strange 4 and 2

1987 *at Muirfield Village, OH*
Result: Europe 15, USA 13
Captains: Jack Nicklaus (USA),
Tony Jacklin (Eur)

First Day: Foursomes - Morning
Kite & Strange beat Clark & Torrance 4 and 2
Pohl & Sutton beat Brown & Langer 2 and 1
Mize & Wadkins lost to Faldo & Woosnam 2 holes
Nelson & Stewart lost to Ballesteros & Olazábal
1 hole

Fourball - Afternoon
Crenshaw & Simpson lost to Brand & Rivero
3 and 2
Bean & Calcavecchia lost to Langer & Lyle 1 hole
Pohl & Sutton lost to Faldo & Woosnam 2 and 1
Kite & Strange lost to Ballesteros & Olazábal
2 and 1

Second Day: Foursomes - Morning
Kite & Strange beat Brand & Rivero 3 and 1
Mize & Sutton halved with Faldo & Woosnam
Nelson & Wadkins lost to Langer & Lyle 2 and 1
Crenshaw & Stewart lost to Ballesteros & Olazábal
1 hole

Fourball - Afternoon
Kite & Strange lost to Faldo & Woosnam 5 and 4
Bean & Stewart beat Brand & Darcy 3 and 2
Mize & Sutton beat Ballesteros & Olazábal 2 and 1
Nelson & Wadkins lost to Langer & Lyle 1 hole

Third Day: Singles
Andy Bean beat Ian Woosnam 1 hole
Dan Pohl lost to Howard Clark 1 hole
Larry Mize halved with Sam Torrance
Mark Calcavecchia beat Nick Faldo 1 hole
Payne Stewart beat José Maria Olazábal 2 holes
Scott Simpson beat José Rivero 2 and 1
Tom Kite beat Sandy Lyle 3 and 2
Ben Crenshaw lost to Eamonn Darcy 1 hole
Larry Nelson halved with Bernhard Langer
Curtis Strange lost to Seve Ballesteros 2 and 1
Lanny Wadkins beat Ken Brown 3 and 2
Hal Sutton halved with Gordon Brand jr

1989 *at The Belfry*
Result: Europe 14, USA 14
Captains: Tony Jacklin (Eur),
Ray Floyd (USA)

First Day: Foursomes - Morning
Faldo & Woosnam halved with Kite & Strange
Clark & James lost to Stewart & Wadkins 1 hole
Ballesteros & Olazábal halved with Beck & Watson
Langer & Rafferty lost to Calcavecchia & Green
2 and 1

Fourball - Afternoon
Brand & Torrance beat Azinger & Strange 1 hole
Clark & James beat Couples & Wadkins 3 and 2
Faldo & Woosnam beat Calcavecchia & McCumber
1 hole
Ballesteros & Olazábal beat O'Meara & Watson
6 and 5

Second Day: Foursomes - Morning
Faldo & Woosnam beat Stewart & Wadkins
3 and 2
Brand & Torrance lost to Azinger & Beck 4 and 3
O'Connor & Rafferty lost to Calcavecchia & Green
3 and 2
Ballesteros & Olazábal beat Kite & Strange 1 hole

Fourball – Afternoon
Faldo & Woosnam lost to Azinger & Beck 2 and 1
Canizares & Langer lost to Kite & McCumber
    2 and 1
Clark & James beat Stewart & Strange 1 hole
Ballesteros & Olazábal beat Calcavecchia & Green
    4 and 2
Third Day: Singles
Seve Ballesteros lost to Paul Azinger 1 hole
Bernhard Langer lost to Chip Beck 3 and 1
José Maria Olazábal beat Payne Stewart 1 hole
Ronan Rafferty beat Mark Calvecchia 1 hole
Howard Clark lost to Tom Kite 8 and 7
Mark James beat Mark O'Meara 3 and 2
Christy O'Connor jr beat Fred Couples 1 hole
José Maria Canizares beat Ken Green 1 hole
Gordon Brand jr lost to Mark McCumber 1 hole
Sam Torrance lost to Tom Watson 3 and 1
Nick Faldo lost to Lanny Wadkins 1 hole
Ian Woosnam lost to Curtis Strange 1 hole

1991 *at Kiawah Island, SC*
Result: USA 14½, Europe 13½
Captains: Dave Stockton (USA),
    Bernard Gallacher (Eur)
First Day: Morning – Foursomes
Ballesteros & Olazábal beat Azinger & Beck 2 and 1
Langer & James lost to Floyd & Couples 2 and 1
Gilford & Montgomerie lost to Wadkins & Irwin
    4 and 2
Faldo & Woosnam lost to Stewart & Calcavecchia
    1 hole
Afternoon – Fourball
Torrance & Feherty halved with Wadkins &
    O'Meara
Ballesteros & Olazábal beat Azinger & Beck 2 and 1
Richardson & James beat Pavin & Calcavecchia
    5 and 4
Faldo & Woosnam lost to Floyd & Couples 5 and 3
Second Day: Morning – Foursomes
Torrance & Feherty lost to Irwin & Wadkins 4 and 2
James & Richardson lost to Calcavecchia &
    Stewart 1 hole
Faldo & Gilford lost to Azinger & O'Meara 7 and 6
Ballesteros & Olazábal beat Couples & Floyd
    3 and 2
Afternoon – Fourball
Woosnam & Broadhurst beat Azinger & Irwin 2 and 1
Langer & Montgomerie beat Pate & Pavin 2 and 1
James & Richardson beat Wadkins & Levi 3 and 1
Ballesteros & Olazábal halved with Couples &
    Stewart
Third Day – Singles
Nick Faldo beat Ray Floyd 2 holes
David Feherty beat Payne Stewart 2 and 1
Colin Montgomerie halved with Mark Calcavecchia
José Maria Olazábal lost to Paul Azinger 2 holes
Steven Richardson lost to Corey Pavin 2 and 1
Seve Ballesteros beat Wayne Levi 3 and 2
Ian Woosnam lost to Chip Beck 3 and 1
Paul Broadhurst bat Mark O'Meara 3 and 1
Sam Torrance lost to Fred Couples 3 and 2
Mark James lost to Lanny Wadkins 3 and 2
Bernhard Langer halved with Hale Irwin
David Gilford (withdrawn) halved with Steve Pate
    (withdrawn – injured)

1993 *at The Belfry*
Result: Europe 13, USA 15
Captains: Bernard Gallacher (Eur)
    Tom Watson (USA)
First Day: Morning – Foursomes
Torrance & James lost to Wadkins & Pavin 4 and 3
Woosnam & Langer beat Azinger & Stewart 7 and 5
Ballesteros & Olazábal lost to Kite & Love 2 and 1
Faldo & Montgomerie beat Floyd & Couples
    4 and 3
Afternoon – Fourball
Woosnam & Baker beat Gallagher & Janzen 1 hole
Lane & Langer lost to Wadkins & Pavin 4 and 2
Faldo & Montgomerie halved with Azinger &
    Couples
Ballesteros & Olazábal beat Kite & Love 4 and 3
Second Day: Morning – Foursomes
Faldo & Montgomerie beat Wadkins & Pavin
    3 and 2
Langer & Woosnam beat Couples & Azinger 2 and 1
Baker & Lane lost to Floyd & Stewart 3 and 2
Ballesteros & Olazábal beat Kite & Love 2 and 1
Afternoon – Fourball
Faldo & Montgomerie lost to Beck & Cook 2 holes
James & Rocca lost to Pavin & Gallagher 5 and 4
Woosnam & Baker beat Couples & Azinger 6 and 5
Olazábal & Haeggman lost to Floyd & Stewart
    2 and 1
Third Day – Singles
Ian Woosnam halved with Fred Couples
Barry Lane lost to Chip Beck 1 hole
Colin Montgomerie beat Lee Janzen 1 hole
Peter Baker beat Corey Pavin 2 holes
Joakim Haeggman beat J Cook 1 hole
Sam Torrance (withdrawn at start of day) halved with
    Lanny Wadkins (withdrawn at start of day)
Mark James lost to Payne Stewart 3 and 2
Constantino Rocca lost to Davis Love III 1 hole
Seve Ballesteros lost to Jim Gallagher jr 3 and 2
José Maria Olazábal lost to Ray Floyd 2 holes
Bernhard Langer lost to Tom Kite 5 and 3
Nick Faldo halved with Paul Azinger

1995 *at Oak Hill, Rochester, NY*
Result: USA 13½, Europe 14½
Captains: Lanny Wadkins (USA),
    Bernard Gallacher (Eur)
First Day: Morning – Foursomes
Faldo & Montgomerie lost to Pavin & Lehman
    1 hole
Torrance & Rocca beat Haas & Couples 3 and 2
Clark & James lost to Love & Maggert 4 and 3
Langer & Johansson beat Crenshaw & Strange 1 hole
Afternoon – Fourball
Gilford & Ballesteros beat Faxon & Jacobsen 4 and 3
Torrance & Rocca lost to Maggert & Roberts 6 and 5
Faldo & Montgomerie lost to Couples & Love
    3 and 2
Langer & Johansson lost to Pavin & Mickelson
    6 and 4
Second Day: Morning – Foursomes
Faldo & Montgomerie beat Haas & Strange 4 and 2
Torrance & Rocca beat Love & Maggert 6 and 5
Woosnam & Walton lost to Roberts & Jacobsen
    1 hole
Langer & Gilford beat Pavin & Lehman 4 and 3

1995 *continued*

Afternoon – Fourball
Torrance & Montgomerie lost to Faxon & Couples
4 and 2
Woosnam & Rocca beat Love & Crenshaw
3 and 2
Ballesteros & Gilford lost to Haas & Mickelson
3 and 2
Faldo & Langer lost to Pavin & Roberts 1 hole

Third Day – Singles
Seve Ballesteros lost to Tom Lehman 4 and 3
Howard Clark beat Peter Jacobsen 1 hole
Mark James beat Jeff Maggert 4 and 3
Ian Woosnam halved with Fred Couples
Costantino Rocca lost to Davis Love III 3 and 2
David Gilford beat Brad Faxon 1 hole
Colin Montgomerie beat Ben Crenshaw 3 and 1
Nick Faldo beat Curtis Strange 1 hole
Sam Torrance beat Loren Roberts 2 and 1
Bernhard Langer beat Corey Pavin 3 and 2
Philip Walton beat Jay Haas 1 hole
Per-Ulrik Johansson lost to Phil Mickelson
2 and 1

1997 Ryder Cup *at Valderrama, Spain*

Result: Europe 14½, USA 13½,
Captains: Seve Ballesteros (Eur),
  Tom Kite (USA)
First Day: Morning – Fourball
Olazábal & Rocca beat Love & Mickelson 1 hole
Faldo & Westwood lost to Couples & Faxon 1 hole
Parnevik & Johansson beat Lehman & Furyk 1 hole
Montgomerie & Langer lost to Woods & O'Meara
3 and 2

Afternoon – Foursomes
Rocca & Olazábal lost to Hoch & Janzen 1 hole
Langer & Montgomerie beat O'Meara & Woods
5 and 3
Faldo & Westwood beat Leonard & Maggert 3 and 2
Parnevik & Garrido halved with Lehman & Mickelson

Second Day: Morning – Fourball
Montgomerie & Clarke beat Couples & Love 1 hole
Woosnam & Bjørn beat Leonard & Faxon 2 and 1
Faldo & Westwood beat Woods & O'Meara 2 and 1
Olazábal & Garrido halved with Mickelson &
Lehman

Afternoon – Foursomes
Montgomerie & Langer beat Janzen & Furyk 1 hole
Faldo & Westwood lost to Hoch & Maggert
2 and 1
Parnevik & Garrido halved with Leonard & Woods
Olazábal & Rocca beat Love & Couples 5 and 4

Third Day – Singles
Ian Woosnam lost to Fred Couples 8 and 7
Per-Ulrik Johansson beat Davis Love III 3 and 2
Costantino Rocca beat Tiger Woods 4 and 2
Thomas Bjørn halved with Justin Leonard
Darren Clarke lost to Phil Mickelson 2 and 1
Jesper Parnevik lost to Mark O'Meara 5 and 4
José Maria Olazábal lost to Lee Janzen 1 hole
Bernhard Langer beat Brad Faxon 2 and 1
Lee Westwood lost to Jeff Maggert 3 and 2
Colin Montgomerie halved with Scott Hoch
Nick Faldo lost to Jim Furyk 3 and 2
Ignacio Garrido lost to Tom Lehman 7 and 6

1999 Ryder Cup *at Brookline, MA*

Result: USA 14½, Europe 13½
Captains: Ben Crenshaw (USA),
  Mark James (Eur)
First Day: Morning – Foursomes
Montgomerie & Lawrie beat Duval & Mickelson
3 and 2
Parnevik & García beat Lehman & Woods 2 and 1
Jiménez & Harrington halved halved with Love &
Stewart
Clarke & Westwood lost to Sutton & Maggert 3 and 2

Afternoon – Fourball
Montgomerie & Lawrie halved with Love & Leonard
Parnevik & García beat Mickelson & Furyk 1 hole
Jiménez & Olazábal beat Sutton & Maggert 2 and 1
Clarke & Westwood beat Duval & Woods 1 hole

Second Day: Morning – Foursomes
Montgomerie & Lawrie lost to Sutton & Maggert
1 hole
Clarke & Westwood beat Furyk & O'Meara 3 and 2
Jiménez & Harrington lost to Pate & Woods 1 hole
Parnevik & García beat Stewart & Leonard 3 and 2

Afternoon – Fourball
Clarke & Westwood lost to Mickelson & Lehman
2 and 1
Parnevik & García halved with Love & Duval
Jiménez & Olazábal halved with Leonard & Sutton
Montgomerie & Lawrie beat Pate & Woods 2 and 1

Third Day – Singles
Lee Westwood lost to Tom Lehman 3 and 2
Darren Clarke lost to Hal Sutton 4 and 2
Jarmo Sandelin lost to Phil Mickelson 4 and 3
Jean Van de Velde lost to Davis Love III 6 and 5
Andrew Coltart lost to Tiger Woods 3 and 2
Jesper Parnevik lost to David Duval 5 and 4
Padraig Harrington beat Mark O'Meara 1 hole
Miguel Angel Jiménez lost to Steve Pate 2 and 1
José Maria Olazábal halved with Justin Leonard
Colin Montgomerie beat Payne Stewart 1 hole
Sergio García lost to Jim Furyk 4 and 3
Paul Lawrie beat Jeff Maggert 4 and 3

INDIVIDUAL RECORDS

Matches were contested as Great Britain v USA from 1927–71; as Great Britain & Ireland v USA from 1973–77; and as Europe v USA from 1979. Bold type indicates captain; non-playing in brackets.

† Selected to play in the postponed 2001 tournament; will now play in the 2002 event

Europe

Name	Year	Played	Won	Lost	Halved
Jimmy Adams	*1939-47-49-51-53	7	2	5	0
Percy Alliss	1929-33-35-37	6	3	2	1
Peter Alliss	1953-57-59-61-63-65-67-69	30	10	15	5
Laurie Ayton	1949	0	0	0	0
Peter Baker	1993	4	3	1	0
Severiano Ballesteros (Esp)	1979-83-85-87-89-91-93-95-(97)	37	20	12	5
Harry Bannerman	1971	5	2	2	1
Brian Barnes	1969-71-73-75-77-79	25	10	14	1
Maurice Bembridge	1969-71-73-75	16	5	8	3
Thomas Bjørn (Den)	1997-†2001	2	1	0	1
Aubrey Boomer	1927-29	4	2	2	0
Ken Bousfield	1949-51-55-57-59-61	10	5	5	0
Hugh Boyle	1967	3	0	3	0
Harry Bradshaw	1953-55-57	5	2	2	1
Gordon J Brand	1983	1	0	1	0
Gordon Brand jr	1987-89	7	2	4	1
Paul Broadhurst	1991	2	2	0	0
Eric Brown	1953-55-57-59-(69)-(71)	8	4	4	0
Ken Brown	1977-79-83-85-87	13	4	9	0
Stewart Burns	1929	0	0	0	0
Dick Burton	1935-37-*39-49	5	2	3	0
Jack Busson	1935	2	0	2	0
Peter Butler	1965-69-71-73	14	3	9	2
José Maria Canizares (Esp)	1981-83-85-89	11	5	4	2
Alex Caygill	1969	1	0	0	1
Clive Clark	1973	1	0	1	0
Howard Clark	1977-81-85-87-89-95	15	7	7	1
Darren Clarke	1997-99-†2001	7	3	4	0
Neil Coles	1961-63-65-67-69-71-73-77	40	12	21	7
Andrew Coltart	1999	1	0	1	0
Archie Compston	1927-29-31	6	1	4	1
Henry Cotton	1929-37-*39-47-(53)	6	2	4	0
Bill Cox	1935-37	3	0	2	1
Allan Dailey	1933	0	0	0	0
Fred Daly	1947-49-51-53	8	3	4	1
Eamonn Darcy	1975-77-81-87	11	1	8	2
William Davies	1931-33	4	2	2	0
Peter Dawson	1977	3	1	2	0
Norman Drew	1959	1	0	0	1
George Duncan	1927-**29**-31	5	2	3	0
Syd Easterbrook	1931-33	3	2	1	0
Nick Faldo	1977-79-81-83-85-87-89-91-93-95-97	46	23	19	4
John Fallon	1955-(63)	1	1	0	0
Niclas Fasth	†2001				
Max Faulkner	1947-49-51-53-57	8	1	7	0
David Feherty	1991	3	1	1	1
Pierre Fulke (Swe)	†2001				
George Gadd	1927	0	0	0	0
Bernard Gallacher	1969-71-73-75-77-79-81-83-(91)-(93)-(95)	31	13	13	5
Sergio García (Esp)	1999-†2001	5	3	1	1
John Garner	1971-73	1	0	1	0
Antonio Garrido (Esp)	1979	5	1	4	0
Ignacio Garrido (Esp)	1997	4	0	1	3
David Gilford	1991-95	6	3	3	0
Eric Green	1947	0	0	0	0
Malcolm Gregson	1967	4	0	4	0
Joakim Haeggman (Swe)	1993	2	1	1	0
Tom Haliburton	1961-63	6	0	6	0
Jack Hargreaves	1951	0	0	0	0
Padraig Harrington	1999-†2001	3	1	1	1
Arthur Havers	1927-31-33	6	3	3	0
Jimmy Hitchcock	1965	3	0	3	0
Bert Hodson	1931	1	0	1	0

★ *In 1939 a GB&I team was named but the match was not played because of the Second World War*

Ryder Cup European Individual Records *continued*

Name	Year	Played	Won	Lost	Halved
Reg Horne	1947	0	0	0	0
Tommy Horton	1975-77	8	1	6	1
Brian Huggett	1963-67-69-71-73-75-(77)	25	9	10	6
Bernard Hunt	1953-57-59-61-63-65-67-69-(73)-(75)	28	6	16	6
Geoffrey Hunt	1963	3	0	3	0
Guy Hunt	1975	3	0	2	1
Tony Jacklin	1967-69-71-73-75-77-79-(83)-(85)-(87)-(89)	35	13	14	8
John Jacobs	1955-(79)-(81)	2	2	0	0
Mark James	1977-79-81-89-91-93-95-(99)	24	8	15	1
Edward Jarman	1935	1	0	1	0
Miguel Angel Jiménez (Esp)	1999	5	1	2	2
Per-Ulrik Johansson (Swe)	1995-97	5	3	2	0
Herbert Jolly	1927	2	0	2	0
Michael King	1979	1	0	1	0
Sam King	1937-*39-47-49	5	1	3	1
Arthur Lacey	1933-37-(51)	3	0	3	0
Barry Lane	1993	3	0	3	0
Bernhard Langer (Ger)	1981-83-85-87-89-91-93-95-97-†2001	38	18	15	5
Paul Lawrie	1999	5	3	1	1
Arthur Lees	1947-49-51-55	8	4	4	0
Sandy Lyle	1979-81-83-85-87	18	7	9	2
Pau;l McGinley (Irl)	†2001				
Jimmy Martin	1965	1	0	1	0
Peter Mills	1957-59	1	1	0	0
Abe Mitchell	1929-31-33	6	4	2	0
Ralph Moffitt	1961	1	0	1	0
Colin Montgomerie	1991-93-95-97-99-†2001	23	12	7	4
Christy O'Connor jr	1975-89	4	1	3	0
Christy O'Connor sr	1955-57-59-61-63-65-67-69-71-73	36	11	21	4
José Maria Olazábal (Esp)	1987-89-91-93-97-99	28	15	8	5
John O'Leary	1975	4	0	4	0
Peter Oosterhuis	1971-73-75-77-79-81	28	14	11	3
Alf Padgham	1933-35-37-*39	6	0	6	0
John Panton	1951-53-61	5	0	5	0
Jesper Parnevik (Swe)	1997-99-†2001	9	4	2	3
Alf Perry	1933-35-37	4	0	3	1
Manuel Pinero (Esp)	1981-85	9	6	3	0
Lionel Platts	1965	5	1	2	2
Eddie Polland	1973	2	0	2	0
Phillip Price	†2001				
Ronan Rafferty	1989	3	1	2	0
Ted Ray	1927	2	0	2	0
Dai Rees	1937-*39-47-49-51-53-55-57-59-61-(67)	18	7	10	1
Steven Richardson	1991	4	2	2	0
José Rivero (Esp)	1985-87	5	2	3	0
Fred Robson	1927-29-31	6	2	4	0
Costantino Rocca (Ita)	1993-95-97	11	6	5	0
Jarmo Sandelin (Swe)	1999	1	0	1	0
Syd Scott	1955	2	0	2	0
Des Smyth	1979-81	7	2	5	0
Dave Thomas	1959-63-65-67	18	3	10	5
Sam Torrance	1981-83-85-87-89-91-93-95-†**2001**	27	7	15	5
Peter Townsend	1969-71	11	3	8	0
Jean Van de Velde (Fra)	1999	1	0	1	0
Brian Waites	1983	4	1	3	0
Philip Walton	1995	2	1	1	0
Charlie Ward	1947-49-51	6	1	5	0
Paul Way	1983-85	9	6	2	1
Harry Weetman	1951-53-55-57-59-61-63-(65)	15	2	11	2
Lee Westwood	1997-99-†2001	5	2	3	0
Charles Whitcombe	1927-29-31-33-35-37-*39-(49)	9	3	2	4
Ernest Whitcombe	1929-31-35	6	1	4	1
Reg Whitcombe	1935-*39	1	0	1	0
George Will	1963-65-67	15	2	11	2
Norman Wood	1975	3	1	2	0
Ian Woosnam	1983-85-87-89-91-93-95-97	31	14	12	5

* In 1939 a GB&I team was named but the match was not played because of the Second World War

United States of America

Name	Year	Played	Won	Lost	Halved
Tommy Aaron	1969-73	6	1	4	1
Skip Alexander	1949-51	2	1	1	0
Paul Azinger	1989-91-93-†2001	14	5	7	2
Jerry Barber	1955-61	5	1	4	0
Miller Barber	1969-71	7	1	4	2
Herman Barron	1947	1	1	0	0
Andy Bean	1979-87	6	4	2	0
Frank Beard	1969-71	8	2	3	3
Chip Beck	1989-91-93	9	6	2	1
Homero Blancas	1973	4	2	1	1
Tommy Bolt	1955-57	4	3	1	0
Julius Boros	1959-63-65-67	16	9	3	4
Gay Brewer	1967-73	9	5	3	1
Billy Burke	1931-33	3	3	0	0
Jack Burke	1951-53-55-57-59-(73)	8	7	1	0
Walter Burkemo	1953	1	0	1	0
Mark Calcavecchia	1987-89-91-†2001	11	5	5	1
Billy Casper	1961-63-65-67-69-71-73-75-(79)	37	20	10	7
Stewart Cink	†2001				
Bill Collins	1961	3	1	2	0
Charles Coody	1971	3	0	2	1
John Cook	1993	2	1	1	0
Fred Couples	1989-91-93-95-97	20	7	9	4
Wilfred Cox	1931	2	2	0	0
Ben Crenshaw	1981-83-87-95-(99)	12	3	8	1
Jimmy Demaret	*1941-47-49-51	6	6	0	0
Gardner Dickinson	1967-71	10	9	1	0
Leo Diegel	1927-29-31-33	6	3	3	0
Dale Douglass	1969	2	0	2	0
Dave Douglas	1953	2	1	0	1
Ed Dudley	1929-33-37	4	3	1	0
Olin Dutra	1933-35	4	1	3	0
David Duval	1999-†2001	4	1	2	1
Lee Elder	1979	4	1	3	0
Al Espinosa	1927-29-31	4	2	1	1
Johnny Farrell	1927-29-31	6	3	2	1
Brad Faxon	1995-97	6	2	4	0
Dow Finsterwald	1957-59-61-63-(77)	13	9	3	1
Ray Floyd	1969-75-77-81-83-85-(89)-91-93	31	12	16	3
Doug Ford	1955-57-59-61	9	4	4	1
Ed Furgol	1957	1	0	1	0
Marty Furgol	1955	1	0	1	0
Jim Furyk	1997-99-†2001	6	2	4	0
Jim Gallagher jr	1993	3	2	1	0
Al Geiberger	1967-75	9	5	1	3
Vic Ghezzi	*1939-*41	0	0	0	0
Bob Gilder	1983	4	2	2	0
Bob Goalby	1963	5	3	1	1
Johnny Golden	1927-29	3	3	0	0
Lou Graham	1973-75-77	9	5	3	1
Hubert Green	1977-79-85	7	4	3	0
Ken Green	1989	4	2	2	0
Ralph Guldahl	1937-*39	2	2	0	0
Fred Haas, Jr	1953	1	0	1	0
Jay Haas	1983-95	8	3	4	1
Walter Hagen	**1927-29-31-33-35-(37)**	9	7	1	1
Bob Hamilton	1949	2	0	2	0
Chick Harbert	1949-55	2	2	0	0
Chandler Harper	1955	1	0	1	0
EJ (Dutch) Harrison	1947-49-51	3	2	1	0
Fred Hawkins	1957	2	1	1	0
Mark Hayes	1979	3	1	2	0
Clayton Heafner	1949-51	4	3	0	1
Jay Hebert	1959-61-(71)	4	2	1	1
Lionel Hebert	1957	1	0	1	0
Dave Hill	1969-73-77	9	6	3	0
Jimmy Hines	*1939	0	0	0	0
Scott Hoch	1997-†2001	3	2	0	1
Ben Hogan	*1941-47-(49)-51-(67)	3	3	0	0
Hale Irwin	1975-77-79-81-91	20	13	5	2
Tommy Jacobs	1965	4	3	1	0

* US teams were selected in 1939 and 1941, but did not play because of the Second World War

Ryder Cup American Individual Records *continued*

Name	Year	Played	Won	Lost	Halved
Peter Jacobsen	1985-95	6	2	4	0
Don January	1965-77	7	2	3	2
Lee Janzen	1993-97	5	2	3	0
Herman Keiser	1947	1	0	1	0
Tom Kite	1979-81-83-85-87-89-93-(97)	28	15	9	4
Ted Kroll	1953-55-57	4	3	1	0
Ky Laffoon	1935	1	0	1	0
Tom Lehman	1995-97-99	10	5	3	2
Tony Lema	1963-65	11	8	1	2
Justin Leonard	1997-99	8	0	3	5
Wayne Levi	1991	2	0	2	0
Bruce Lietzke	1981	3	0	2	1
Gene Littler	1961-63-65-67-69-71-75	27	14	5	8
Davis Love III	1993-95-97-99-†2001	17	6	8	3
Jeff Maggert	1995-97-99	11	6	5	0
John Mahaffey	1979	3	1	2	0
Mark McCumber	1989	3	2	1	0
Jerry McGee	1977	2	1	1	0
Harold McSpaden	*1939-*41	0	0	0	0
Tony Manero	1937	2	1	1	0
Lloyd Mangrum	*1941-47-49-51-**53**	8	6	2	0
Dave Marr	1965-(**81**)	6	4	2	0
Billy Maxwell	1963	4	4	0	0
Dick Mayer	1957	2	1	0	1
Bill Mehlhorn	1927	2	1	1	0
Dick Metz	*1939	0	0	0	0
Phil Mickelson	1995-97-99-†2001	11	6	3	2
Cary Middlecoff	1953-55-59	6	2	3	1
Johnny Miller	1975-81	6	2	2	2
Larry Mize	1987	4	1	1	2
Gil Morgan	1979-83	6	1	2	3
Bob Murphy	1975	4	2	1	1
Byron Nelson	1937-*39-*41-47-(**65**)	4	3	1	0
Larry Nelson	1979-81-87	13	9	3	1
Bobby Nichols	1967	5	4	0	1
Jack Nicklaus	1969-71-73-75-77-81-(**83**)-(**87**)	28	17	8	3
Andy North	1985	3	0	3	0
Ed Oliver	1947-51-53	5	3	2	0
Mark O'Meara	1985-89-91-97-99	14	4	9	1
Arnold Palmer	1961-**63**-65-67-71-73-(**75**)	32	22	8	2
Johnny Palmer	1949	2	0	2	0
Sam Parks	1935	1	0	0	1
Jerry Pate	1981	4	2	2	0
Steve Pate	1991-99	4	2	2	0
Corey Pavin	1991-93-95	8	5	3	0
Calvin Peete	1983-85	7	4	2	1
Henry Picard	1935-37-*39	4	3	1	0
Dan Pohl	1987	3	1	2	0
Johnny Pott	1963-65-67	7	5	2	0
Dave Ragan	1963	4	2	1	1
Henry Ransom	1951	1	0	1	0
Johnny Revolta	1935-37	3	2	1	0
Loren Roberts	1995	4	3	1	0
Chi Chi Rodriguez	1973	2	0	1	1
Bill Rogers	1981	4	1	2	1
Bob Rosburg	1959	2	2	0	0
Mason Rudolph	1971	3	1	1	1
Paul Runyan	1933-35-*39	4	2	2	0
Doug Sanders	1967	5	2	3	0
Gene Sarazen	1927-29-31-33-35-37-*41	12	7	2	3
Densmore Shute	1931-33-37	6	2	2	2
Dan Sikes	1969	3	2	1	0
Scott Simpson	1987	2	1	1	0
Horton Smith	1929-31-33-35-37-*39-*41	4	3	0	1
JC Snead	1971-73-75	11	9	2	0
Sam Snead	1937-*39-*41-47-49-51-**53**-55-**59**-(**69**)	13	10	2	1
Ed Sneed	1977	2	1	0	1
Mike Souchak	1959-61	6	5	1	0
Craig Stadler	1983-85	8	4	2	2
Payne Stewart	1987-89-91-93-99	19	7	10	2
Ken Still	1969	3	1	2	0

* *US teams were selected in 1939 and 1941, but did not play because of the Second World War*

Name	Year	Played	Won	Lost	Halved
Dave Stockton	1971-77-(91)	5	3	1	1
Curtis Strange	1983-85-87-89-95-†2001	20	6	12	2
Hal Sutton	1985-87-99-†2001	14	6	4	4
David Toms	†2001				
Lee Trevino	1969-71-73-75-79-81-(85)	30	17	7	6
Jim Turnesa	1953	1	1	0	0
Joe Turnesa	1927-29	4	1	2	1
Ken Venturi	1965	4	1	3	0
Lanny Wadkins	1977-79-83-85-87-89-91-93-(95)	33	20	11	2
Art Wall, Jnr	1957-59-61	6	4	2	0
Al Watrous	1927-29	3	2	1	0
Tom Watson	1977-81-83-89-(93)	15	10	4	1
Tom Weiskopf	1973-75	10	7	2	1
Craig Wood	1931-33-35-*41	4	1	3	0
Tiger Woods	1997-99-†2001	10	3	6	1
Lew Worsham	1947	2	2	0	0
Fuzzy Zoeller	1979-83-85	10	1	8	1

PGA Cup (Instituted 1973)

Great Britain and Ireland Club Professionals v United States Club Professionals

1973	USA	Pinehurst, NC	13–3	1984	GB&I	Turnberry, Scotland	12½–8½
1974	USA	Pinehurst, NC	11½–4½				
1975	USA	Hillside, Southport, England	9½–6½	*Played alternate years from 1984*			
1976	USA	Moortown, Leeds, England	9½–6½	1986	USA	Knollwood, Lake Fore, IL	16–9
1977	Halved	Mission Hills, Palm Springs	8½–8½	1988	USA	The Belfry, England	15½–10½
1978	GB&I	St Mellion, Cornwall	10½–6½	1990	USA	Turtle Point, Kiawah Island, SC	19–7
1979	GB&I	Castletown, Isle of Man	12½–4½	1992	USA	K Club, Ireland	15–11
1980	USA	Oak Tree, Edmond, OK	15–6	1994	USA	Palm Beach, Florida	15–11
1981	Halved	Turnberry Isle, Miami, FL	10½–10½	1996	Halved	Gleneagles, Scotland	13–13
1982	USA	Holston Hills, Knoxville, TN	13–7	1998	USA	The Broadmoor, Colorado	
1983	GB&I	Muirfield, Scotland	14½–6½			Springs, CO	11½–4½

2000 *at Celtic Manor, Newport, Wales*

Non-playing captains: GB&I, David Llewellyn; USA, Ken Lindsay

GB&I		USA	

First Day – **Foursomes**

P Wesselingh and B Cameron	0	T Dunlavey and B Boyd (2 and 1)	1
S Hamill and R Weir (4 and 3)	1	K Burton and J Freeman	0
S Bebb and H Stott	0	T Thelen and M Brown (2 and 1)	1
C Halla nd D McGrane (2 and 1)	1	F Dobbs and M Gill	0
	2		2

Fourball

S Bebb and J Dwyer	0	B Gaffney and J Freeman (4 and 3)	1
S Hamill and E Weir (4 and 3)	1	S Kelly and T Dunlavey	0
P Wesselingh and T Nash (halved)	½	B Boyd and F Dobbs (halved)	½
C Hall and D McGrane	0	M Brown and M Gill (2 and 1)	1
	1½		2½

Match position: GB&I 3½, USA 4½

Second Day – **Foursomes**

B Cameron and T Nash	0	J Freeman and B Boyd (2 and 1)	1
S Bebb and P Wesselingh (2 and 1)	1	B Gaffney and S Kelly	0
C Hall and D McGrane	0	M Gill and T Dunlavey (2 and 1)	1
S Hamill and R Weir	0	F Dobbs and M Brown (2 and 1)	1
	1		3

---

* *US teams were selected in 1939 and 1941, but did not play because of the Second World War*

PGA Cup *continued*

Fourball

B Cameron and H Stott	0	J Freeman and T Thelen (4 and 3)	1
P Wesselingh and T Nash (1 hole)	1	T Dunlavey and F Dobbs	0
S Bebb and J Dwyer (3 and 2)	1	K Burton and M Brown	0
C Hall and S Hamill	0	M Gill and B Boyd (4 and 3)	1
	2		2

Match position: GB&I 6½, USA 9½

Third Day – Singles

Stephen Hamill (2 and 1)	1	Tim Thelen	0
Russell Weir	0	Tim Dunlavey (2 and 1)	1
Paul Wesselingh (2 and 1)	1	Mark Brown	0
Damien McGrane (3 and 2)	1	Kevin Burton	0
Hogan Stott	0	Brian Gaffney (2 and 1)	1
Sion Bebb (2 and 1)	1	Shawn Kelly	0
Bob Cameron	0	Bob Boyd (3 and 1)	1
John Dwyer	0	Jeff Freeman (2 and 1)	1
Tony Nash (1 hole)	1	Frank Dobbs	0
Chris Hall (6 and 5)	1	Mike Gill	0
	6		4

Result: GB&I 12½, USA 13½

Presidents Cup (Instituted 1994)

1994	USA	Lake Manassas, Virginia	20–12
1996	USA	Lake Manassas, Virginia	16½–15½
1998	International	Royal Melbourne, Australia	20½–11½

2000 *at Robert Trent Jones GC, Gainsville*

Non-playing captains: Ken Venturi, US; Peter Thomson, Internationals

USA		International Team	
First Day – Foursomes			
P Mickelson and T Lehman (5 and 4)	1	G Norman (Aus) and S Elkington (Aus)	0
H Sutton and J Furyk (1 hole)	1	R Allenby (Aus) and S Appleby (Aus)	0
S Cink and K Triplett (3 and 2)	1	M Weir (Can) and R Goosen (RSA)	0
T Woods and N Begay III (1 hole)	1	V Singh (Fij) and E Els (RSA)	0
D Duval and D Love III (1 hole)	1	N Price (Zim) and C Franco (Par)	0
	5		0

Match position: US 5, Internationals 0

Second Day – Fourball			
H Sutton and P Azinger	0	M Campbell (NZ) and R Goosen (4 and 3)	1
J Furyk and D Duval	0	N Price and G Norman (6 and 5)	1
T Lehman and L Roberts	0	M Weir and S Elkington (3 and 2)	1
T Woods and B Begay III	0	S Maruyama (Jpn) and C Franco (3 and 2)	1
P Mickelson and D Love III (2 and 1)	1	V Singh and E Els	0
	1		4

Foursomes

T Woods and N Begay III (6 and 5)	1	V Singh and E Els	0
P Azinger and L Roberts (5 and 4)	1	C Franco and S Maruyama	0
H Sutton and T Lehman (3 and 2)	1	M Campbell and R Goosen	0
S Cink and K Triplett (2 and 1)	1	R Allenby and S Appleby	0
P Mickelson and D Duval	0	N Price and M Weir (6 and 4)	1
	4		1

Match position: US 10, Internationals 5

Third Day – Fourball

H Sutton and J Furyk (6 and 5)	1	G Norman and M Campbell	0
D Duval and D Love III (3 and 2)	1	E Els and N Price	0
T Lehman and P Mickelson (2 and 1)	1	M Weir and S Elkington	0
T Woods and N Begay III	0	V Singh and R Goosen (2 and 1)	1
K Triplett and S Cink (1 hole)	1	R Allenby and C Franco	0
	4		1

Match position: US 14, Internationals 6

Fourth Day – Singles

Paul Azinger	0	Robert Allenby (2 and 1)	1
David Duval (2 and 1)	1	Nick Price	0
Phil Mickelson	0	Mike Weir (4 and 3)	1
Loren Roberts (3 and 2)	1	Stuart Appleby	0
Davis Love III (4 and 3)	1	Ernie Els	0
Tom Lehman	0	Steve Elkington (1 hole)	1
Tiger Woods (2 and 1)	1	Vijay Singh	0
Stewart Cink (2 and 1)	1	Greg Norman	0
Hal Sutton	0	Carlos Franco (6 and 5)	1
Jim Furyk (5 and 4)	1	S Maruyama	0
Kirk Triplett (halved)	½	Michael Campbell (halved)	½
N Begay III (1 hole)	1	R Goosen	0
	7½		4½

Result: US 21½, Internationals 10½

Praia d'el Rey Rover European Cup (European Seniors v Ladies'

European PGA, instituted 1997) *at Praia d'el Rey, Obidos, Portugal*

1997	European PGA Seniors beat ELPGA	13–7
1998	European PGA Seniors halved with ELPGA	10–10
1999	Ladies' European Tour beat European PGA Seniors	11–9
2000	*Not played*	
2001	*Not played*	

Alfred Dunhill Cup (Held at St Andrews from 1985 to 2000)

Year	Winner	Runner-up	Score
1985	Australia	USA	3–0
	(G Norman, G Marsh, D Graham)	(M O'Meara, R Floyd, C Strange)	
1986	Australia	Japan	3–0
	(R Davis, D Graham, G Norman)	(T Ozaki, N Ozaki, T Nakajima)	
1987	England	Scotland	2–1
	(N Faldo, G Brand, H Clark)	(S Lyle, S Torrance, G Brand Jr)	
1988	Ireland	Australia	2–1
	(D Smyth, R Rafferty, E Darcy)	(R Davis, D Graham, G Norman)	
1989	USA	Japan	3½–2½
	(M Calcavecchia, T Kite, C Strange)	(H Meshiai, N Ozaki, K Suzuki)	
1990	Ireland	England	3½–2½
	(P Walton, R Rafferty, D Feherty)	(M James, R Boxall, H Clark)	
1991	Sweden	South Africa	2–1
	(A Forsbrand, P-U Johansson, M Lanner)	(J Bland, D Frost, G Player)	
1992	England	Scotland	2–0
	(S Richardson, J Spence, D Gilford)	(G Brand Jr, C Montgomerie, S Lyle)	
1993	USA	England	2–1
	(P Stewart, F Couples, J Daly)	(M James, N Faldo, P Baker)	
1994	Canada	USA	2–1
	(D Barr, R Gibson, R Stewart)	(T Kite, C Strange, F Couples)	
1995	Scotland	Zimbabwe	2–1
	(A Coltart, C Montgomerie, S Torrance)	(T Johnstone, M McNulty, N Price)	
1996	USA	New Zealand	2–1
	(M O'Meara, P Mickelson, S Stricker)	(F Nobilo, G Turner, G Waite)	
1997	South Africa	Sweden	2–1
	(R Goosen, D Frost, E Els)	(J Parnevik, P-U Johansson, J Haeggman)	

Dunhill European Cup *continued*

Year	Winner	Runner-up	Score
1998	South Africa	Spain	2–1
	(R Goosen, D Frost, E Els)	(MA Jiménez, S Luna, JM Olazábal)	
1999	Spain	Australia	2–1
	(S García, JM Olazábal, MA Jiménez)	(C Parry, PO'Malley, S Leaney)	
2000	Spain	South Africa	2–1
	(MA Martin, MA Jiménez, JM Olazábal)	(D Frost, R Goosen, E Els)	

Tournament discontinued

Eurobet Seve Ballesteros Trophy   (Instituted 2000)

2000 *at Sunningdale, Berkshire, England*

Captains: Colin Montgomerie, GB&I; Seve Ballesteros, Continental Europe

GB&I		Continental Europe	
First Day – **Foursomes**			
C Montgomerie and I Woosnam (2 and 1)	1	JM Olazábal and JA Jiménez	0
D Clarke and L Westwood (4 and 3)	1	A Cejka and B Langer	0
P Harrington and P Price (1 hole)	1	T Bjørn and R Karlsson	0
P Lawrie and G Orr	0	S García and J Van de Velde	1
	3		1

Fourball			
L Westwood and D Howell (2 and 1)	1	JM Olazábal and S Ballesteros	0
D Clarke and J Bickerton	0	T Bjørn and MA Jiménez (1 hole)	1
I Woosnam and P Harrington	0	A Cejka and B Langer (2 and 1)	1
P Lawrie and C Montgomerie	0	J Sandelin and S García (3 and 2)	1
	1		3

Match position: GB&I, 4; Continental Europe, 4

Second Day – **Fourball**			
I Woosnam and C Montgomerie	0	MA Jiménez and J Olazábal (6 and 5)	1
P Lawrie and G Orr (1 hole)	1	J Sandelin and R Karlsson	0
J Bickerton and P Price	0	T Bjørn and S García (1 hole)	1
D Clarke and L Westwood (3 and 1)	1	A Cejka and J Van de Velde	0
	2		2

Greensomes			
P Lawrie and G Orr (halved)	½	MA Jiménez and JM Olazábal (halved)	½
C Montgomerie and D Howell (2 and 1)	1	S García and J Van de Velde	0
D Clarke and L Westwood	0	B Langer and T Bjørn (4 and 3)	1
P Harrington and P Price (halved)	½	A Cejka and R Karlsson (halved)	½
	2		2

Match position: GB&I, 8; Continental Europe 8

Singles

C Montgomerie	0	S Ballestetos (2 and 1)	1
D Clarke (halved)	½	S García (halved)	½
J Bickerton	0	J Sandelin (2 and 1)	1
L Westwood (1 hole)	1	T Bjørn	0
P Price (2 and 1)	1	A Cejka	0
I Woosnam	0	B Langer (4 and 3)	1
D Howell	0	R Karlsson (2 and 1)	1
G Orr	0	JM Olazábal (2 and 1)	1
P Lawrie (5 and 4)	1	J Van de Velde	0
P Harrington (1 hole)	1	MA Jiménez	0
	4½		5½

Result: GB&I, 12½; Continental Europe 13½

Davidoff Nations Cup

2000   Korea

2001 *at Royal Selangor GC, Malaysia*

1	China (Zhang Lian-Wei, Kiang Wen Chong)	62-70-66-67—265
2	Malaysia (Danny Chia, P Gunasegaran)	66-66-63-71—266
	Norway (Per Haugsrud, Henrik Bjornstad)	60-72-64-70—266
4	Mexico (Octavio Gonzalez, Alejandro Quiroz)	62-74-64-67—267
5	Philippines (Rodrigo Cuello, Danny Zarate)	64-70-66-69—269
	Holland (Maarten LaFeber, Robert Jan Derkson)	63-74-62-70—269

Top six qualified for EMC² World Cup, Taiheiyo Club, Gotemba, Japan

Other finishers: 7 Hong Kong; 8 Germany; 9 Taiwan, South Korea, Singapore; 12 Myanmar; 13 Chile, Brazil; 15 Pakistan; 16 Jamaica; 17 Thailand; 18 Colombia; 19 Switzerland; 20 Italy; 21 Slovenia; 22 India; 23 Nepal; 24 Finland; 25 Mauritius; 26 Poland

Warburg Cup

at Kiawah Island, South Carolina

USA 12½, World 11½

Full result on page 203

National and Regional Championships

NATIONAL CHAMPIONSHIPS

Maxfli PGA Assistants' Championship

1984	G Weir	Coombe Hill	286	1993	C Everett	Oaklands	280
1985	G Coles	Coombe Hill	284	1994	M Plummer	Burnham & Berrow	278
1986	J Brennand	Sand Moor	280	1995	I Sparkes	The Warwickshire	285
1987	J Hawksworth	Coombe Hill	282	1996	S Purves	Moor Allerton	281
1988	J Oates	Coventry	284	1997	P Sefton	De Vere, Blackpool	273
1989	C Brooks	Hillside	291	1998	A Raitt	Bearwood Lakes	280
1990	A Ashton	Hillside	213 (54)	1999	I Harrison	Bearwood Lakes	274
1991	S Wood	Wentworth	288	2000	T Anderson	St Anne's Old Links	273
1992	P Mayo	E Sussex National	285				

2001 *at St Anne's Old Links*

1	Craig Goodfellow (Eden)	65-67-65—207	
2	Philip Edwards (Springwater)	69-70-73—212	
3	Daniel Poulter (Chadwell Springs)	73-73-67—213	

The De Vere PGA Seniors' Championship

1970	M Faulkner	Longniddry	288	1986	N Coles	Mere, Cheshire	276
1971	K Nagle	Elie	269	1987	N Coles	Turnberry	279
1972	K Bousfield	Longniddry	291	1988	P Thomson	North Berwick	287
1973	K Nagle	Elie	270	1989	N Coles	West Hill	277
1974	E Lester	Lundin	282	1990	B Waites	Brough	269
1975	K Nagle	Longniddry	268	1991	B Waites	Wollaton Park	277
1976	C O'Connor	Cambridgeshire Hotel	284	1992	T Horton	R Dublin	290
1977	C O'Connor	Cambridgeshire Hotel	288	1993	B Huggett	Sunningdale	204 (54)
1978	P Skerritt	Cambridgeshire Hotel	288	1994	J Morgan	Sunningdale	203
1979	C O'Connor	Cambridgeshire Hotel	280	1995	J Morgan	Sunningdale	204
1980	P Skerritt	Gleneagles Hotel	286	1996	T Gale	The Belfry	284
1981	C O'Connor	North Berwick	287	1997	W Hall	The Belfry	277
1982	C O'Connor	Longniddry	285	1998	T Horton	The Belfry	277
1983	C O'Connor	Burnham and Berrow	277	1999	R Metherall	The Belfry	276
1984	E Jones	Stratford-upon-Avon	280	2000	J Grace*	The Belfry	282
1985	N Coles	Pannal, Harrogate	284				

2001 *at Carden Park, Chester*

1	Ian Stanley (Aus)	71-66-68-73—278	
2	Maurice Bembridge (Eng)	65-75-68-72—280	
3	Barry Vivian (NZ)	72-71-69-72—284	

Glenmuir Club Professionals' Championship

1973	DN Sewell	Calcot Park	276	1981	M Steadman	Woburn	289
1974	WB Murray	Calcot Park	275	1982	D Durnian	Hill Valley	285
1975	DN Sewell	Calcot Park	276	1983	J Farmer	Heaton Park	270
1976	WJ Ferguson	Moortown	283	1984	D Durnian	Bolton Old Links	278
1977	D Huish	Notts	284	1985	R Mann	The Belfry	291
1978	D Jones	Pannal	281	1986	D Huish	R Birkdale	278
1979	D Jones	Pannal	278	1987	R Weir	Sandiway	273
1980	D Jagger	Turnberry	286	1988	R Weir	Harlech	269

1989	B Barnes	Sandwich, Prince's	280	1995	P Carman	West Hill	269
1990	A Webster	Carnoustie	292	1996	B Longmuir	Co Louth	280
1991	W McGill	King's Lynn	285	1997	B Rimmer	Northop	268
1992	J Hoskison	St Pierre	275	1998	M Jones	Royal St David's	280
1993	C Hall	Coventry	274	1999	S Bebb*	Kings Lynn	283
1994	D Jones	North Berwick	278	2000	R Cameron*	St Andrews	295

2001 *at County Louth GC, Baltray*

1	Simon Edwards (Carden Park)	65-70-71-69—756
2	Bob Cameron (Sundridge Park)	69-67-76-66—278
3	Gordon Law (Uphall)	71-65-74-69—279
	Alun Evans (Newport Pembs)	71-68-71-69—279
	Sion Bebb (Mountain Lakes)	70-67-72-70—279
	Alan Reid (Brunstone Castle)	71-69-68-71—279

Smurfit Irish PGA Championship

1960	C O'Connor	Warrenpoint	271	1981	D Jones	Woodbrook	283
1961	C O'Connor	Lahinch	280	1982	D Feherty	Woodbrook	287
1962	C O'Connor	Bangor	264	1983	L Higgins	Woodbrook	275
1963	C O'Connor	Little Island	271	1984	M Sludds	Skerries	277
1964	E Jones	Knock	279	1985	D Smyth	Co Louth	204 (54)
1965	C O'Connor	Mullingar	283	1986	D Smyth	Waterville	282
1966	C O'Connor	Warrenpoint	269	1987	P Walton	Co Louth	144 (36)
1967	H Boyle	Tullamore	214 (54)	1988	E Darcy	Castle, Dublin	269
1968	C Greene	Knock	282	1989	P Walton	Castle, Dublin	266
1969	J Martin	Dundalk	268	1990	D Smyth	Woodbrook	271
1970	H Jackson	Massareene	283	1991	P Walton	Woodbrook	277
1971	C O'Connor	Galway	278	1992	E Darcy	K Club	285
1972	J Kinsella	Bundoran	289	1993	M Sludds	K Club	285
1973	J Kinsella	Limerick	284	1994	D Clarke	Galway Bay	285
1974	E Polland	Portstewart	277	1995	P Walton	Belvoir Park	273
1975	C O'Connor	Carlow	275	1996	D Smyth	Slieve Russell GC	281
1976	P McGuirk	Waterville	291	1997	P McGinley	Fota Island	285
1977	P Skerritt	Woodbrook	281	1998	P Harrington*	Powerscourt	216 (54)
1978	C O'Connor	Dollymount	286	1999	N Manchip	The Island	271
1979	D Smyth	Dollymount	215 (54)	2000	P McGinley	Co Louth	270
1980	D Feherty	Dollymount	283				

2001 *at Castle Rock GC, County Londonderry*

1	Des Smyth	73-66-66-68—273
2	Paul McGinley	73-64-70-69—276
3	Michael Allen	72-69-67-71—279

Irish Club Professionals' Championship

1993	D Mooney	Royal Tara	208	1997	N Manchip	Mount Wolseley	141
1994	K O'Donnell	Knockanally	216	1998	L Robinson	Nuremore	140
1995	D Jones	Fota Island	145	1999	N Manchip	Nuremore	139
1996	B McGovern	Headfort	140	2000	L Walker	Nuremore	134

2001 *at The Nuremore Golf Hotel, Co Monahan*

1	Michel Allan*	69–73—142
2	Raymond Burns	74-68—142
3	Neil Lane	73-70—143
	Robert Hutton	72-71—143
	Eamonn Logue	71-72—143
	Leslie Walker	69-74—143

Macallan Spey Bay Scottish Assistants' Championship

1980	F Mann	Dunbar	294	1991	G Hume	Kilmarnock Barassie	299
1981	M Brown	West Kilbride	290	1992	E McIntosh	Turnberry Hotel	266
1982	R Collinson	West Kilbride	294	1993	J Wither	Alloa	280
1983	A Webster	Stirling	285	1994	S Henderson	Newmacher	283
1984	C Elliott	Stirling	285	1995	A Tait	Newmacher	276
1985	C Elliott	Falkirk Tryst	284	1996	S Thompson	Newmacher	278
1986	P Helsby	Erskine	295	1997	M Hastie	Balbirnie Park	275
1987	C Innes	Hilton Park	284	1998	D Orr	Balbirnie Park	272
1988	G Collinson	Turnberry	289	1999	A Forsyth	Balbirnie Park	269
1989	C Brooks	Windyhill	282	2000	C Lee	Balbirnie Park	275
1990	P Lawrie	Cruden Bay	279				

2001 *at Spey Bay*

1	Chris Kelly (Clober)	69-67-68-71—275
2	Andrew Erskine (Ratho Park)	68-73-69-68—278
	Scott Garrett (Gleddoch House)	69-69-69-71—278

Scottish Match Play Championship

Sponsored by Aberdeen Asset Management at Meldrum House, Aberdeen

Semi-Finals

Mark King (Deer Park) beat Paul Lawrie (Meldrum House) 1 hole

Russell Weir (Cowal) beat Colin Gillies (Braid Hills) 3 and 2

Final

King beat Weir 5 and 4

Scottish Professionals' Championship

1965	EC Brown	Forfar	271	1983	B Gallacher	Dalmahoy	276
1966T	EC Brown	Cruden Bay	137 (36)	1984	I Young	Dalmahoy	276
	J Panton			1985	S Torrance	Dalmahoy	277
1967	H Bannerman	Montrose	279	1986	R Drummond	Glenbervie	270
1968	EC Brown	Monktonhall	286	1987	R Drummond	Glenbervie	268
1969	G Cunningham	Machrihanish	284	1988	S Stephen	Haggs Castle	283
1970	RDBM Shade	Montrose	276	1989	R Drummond	Monktonhall	274
1971	NJ Gallacher	Lundin Links	282	1990	R Drummond	Deer Park	278
1972	H Bannerman	Strathaven	268	1991	S Torrance	Erskine	274
1973	BJ Gallacher	Kings Links	276	1992	P Lawrie	Cardross	273
1974	BJ Gallacher	Drumpellier	276	1993	S Torrance	Dalmahoy	269
1975	D Huish	Duddingston	279	1994	A Coltart	Dalmahoy	281
1976	J Chillas	Haggs Castle	286	1995	C Gillies	Dalmahoy	278
1977	BJ Gallacher	Barnton	282	1996	B Marchbank	Dalmahoy	276
1978	S Torrance	Strathaven	269	1997	G Law	Downfield	284
1979	AWB Lyle	Glasgow Gailes	274	1998	C Gillies	Newmacher	273
1980	S Torrance	East Kilbride	273	1999	G Hutcheon	Gleneagles	288
1981	B Barnes	Dalmahoy	275	2000	A Forsyth	Gleneagles	255
1982	B Barnes	Dalmahoy	286				

2001 *at Gleneagles Hotel's PGA Centenary Course*

1	John Chillas (Glenbervie)	70-72-72-70—284
2	Murray Urquhart (Inverness)	69-74-72-69—284
3	Colin Gillies (Braid Hills)	73-73-73-69—288
	Ross Drummond (unattached)	73-72-73-70—288

Welsh Professionals Championship

1960	RH Kemp jr	Llandudno	288		1981	C DeFoy	Cardiff	139
1961	S Mouland	Southerndown	286		1982	C DeFoy	Cardiff	137
1962	S Mouland	Porthcawl	302		1983	S Cox	Cardiff	136
1963	H Gould	Wrexham	291		1984	K Jones	Cardiff	135
1964	B Bielby	Tenby	297		1985	D Llewellyn	Whitchurch	132
1965	S Mouland	Penarth	281		1986	P Parkin	Whitchurch	142
1966	S Mouland	Conway	281		1987	A Dodman	Cardiff	132
1967	S Mouland	Pyle and Kenfig	219 (54)		1988	I Woosnam	Cardiff	137
1968	RJ Davies	Southerndown	292		1989	K Jones	Royal Porthcawl	140
1969	S Mouland	Llandudno	277		1990	P Mayo	Fairwood Park	136
1970	W Evans	Tredegar Park	289		1991	P Mayo	Fairwood Park	138
1971	J Buckley	St Pierre	291		1992	C Evans	Asburnham	142
1972	J Buckley	Porthcawl	298		1993	P Price	Caerphilly	138
1973	A Griffiths	Newport	289		1994	M Plummer	Northop	133
1974	M Hughes	Cardiff	284		1995	S Dodd	Northop	139
1975	C DeFoy	Whitchurch	285		1996	M Stanford	Northop	137
1976	S Cox	Radyr	284		1997	M Ellis	Vale of Glamorgan	139
1977	C DeFoy	Glamorganshire	135		1998	L Bond	Vale of Glamorgan	69 (18)
1978	BCC Huggett	Whitchurch	145		1999	R Dinsdale	Vale of Glamorgan	134
1979	*Cancelled*				2000	M Plummer	Newport	136
1980	A Griffiths	Cardiff	139					

2001 *at Ashburnham*

1	Stephen Dodd	64–64–76—214
2	Sion Bebb	74–71–74—219
3	Richard Dinsdale	70–79–71—220
	David Wood	70–79–71—220

PGA of Europe Championship

1983	Cees Renders (Ned)		1989	Russell Weir (Sco)	1997	Claude Grenier (Aut)
1984	Donald Armour (Ned)		1990	John Woof (Ned)	1998	Simon Brown (Eng)
1985	John Woof (Ned)		1991	Paul Carman (Eng)	1999	Richard Dinsdale (Wal)
1986	Stuart Brown (Eng)		1992	Tim Giles (Eng)	2000	Sion Bebb (Wal)
1987	Jim Rhodes (Eng)		1993	Russell Weir (Sco)		
1988	Russell Weir (Sco)		1994/1996 – *not played*			

2001 *at Pevero, Sardinia* [6117m–72]

1	Andrew George (Eng)	68–75–71–70—284 (–4)
2	Fraser Man (Sco)	70–73–74–70—287 (–1)
	Bob Cameron (Eng)	67–75–70–75—287 (–1)

REGIONAL CHAMPIONSHIPS

Derbyshire Professionals

1992	J Proctor	1997	A Carnall
1993	K Cross	1998	J Mellor
1994	D Stafford	1999	D Russell
1995	A Carnall	2000	M Smith
1996	C Cross	2001	M Smith

Devon Open

1992	R Troake	1997	J Langmead
1993T	D Sheppard	1998	D Sheppard
	T McSherry	1999	J Langmead
1994	I Higgins	2000	B Austin
1995	B Austin	2001	B Austin
1996	J Langmead		

Dorset PGA

2000	Mark Wiggett

East Anglian Open

1992	L Fickling	1997	I Poulter
1993	A George	1998	P Curry
1994	R Mann	1999	P Curry
1995	N Brown	2000	J Bevan
1996	N Brown	2001	D Parker

East Region PGA

1995	L Fickling	1999	S Khan
1996	T Charnley	2000	I Ellis
1997	R Mann	2001	P Barham
1998	T Charnley		

Essex Open

1992	C Platts	1997	V Cox
1993	A Blackburn	1998	J Robson
1994	D Jones	1999	P Joiner
1995	J Robson	2000	S Khan
1996	S Khan	2001	R Coles

Essex Professionals

1992	P Barham	1997	M Stokes
1993	T Wheals	1998	G Carter
1994	V Cox	1999	P Curry
1995	M Stokes	2000	W McColl
1996	P Joiner	2001	J Fryatt

Hampshire PGA

1992	I Benson	1997	J Lovell
1993	R Edwards	1998	G Hughes
1994	G Hughes	1999	J Barnes
1995	I Benson	2000	K Saunder
1996	R Bland	2001	S Cowie

Hampshire Match Play

1992	J Hay	1997	D Harris
1993	K Saunders	1998	D Harris
1994	M Wheeler	1999	J Lovell
1995	M Wheeler	2000	M Robbins
1996	J Le Roux	2001	P Bryden

Hampshire, Isle of Wight and Channel Islands Open

1992	I Benson	1997	M Blackey
1993	R Bland	1998	R Bland
1994	R Bland	1999	R Bland
1995	R Bland	2000	R Bland
1996	G Hughes	2001	S Cowie

Herts Professionals

1992	P Cherry	1997	P Winston
1993	L Jones	1998T	R Mitchell
1994T	N Brown		I Parker
	D Tapping	1999	L Jones
1995	N Brown	2000	R Mitchell
1996	R Hurd	2001	A Bailey

Kent Open

1992	S Barr	1997	S Page
1993	N Haynes	1998	D Parris
1994	T Berry	1999	R Cameron
1995	T Milford	2000	M McLean
1996	S Green	2001	J Marshall

Kent Professionals

1992	M Lawrence	1997	P Lyons
1993	R Cameron	1998	T Milford
1994	M Lawrence	1999	R Cameron
1995	T Poole	2000	B Coomber
1996	A Butterfield	2001	S Wood

Lancashire Open

1992	S Townend	1997	G Furey
1993	L Edwards	1998	J Cheetham
1994	A Lancaster	1999	C Corrigan
1995	G Furey	2000	G Furey
1996	G Furey	2001	M Hollingsworth

Leicestershire and Rutland Open

1992	*Not played*	1997	N Bland
1993	P Frith	1998	J Caylis (am)
1994	J Herbert	1999	I Ball
1995	I Lyner	2000	M Cort
1996	D Gibson	2001	I Ball

Lincolnshire Open

1992	P Streeter (am)	1997	M King (am)
1993	S Bennett	1998	M King (am)
1994	S Brewer	1999	M King (am)
1995	S Cox	2000	M King (am)
1996	S Bennett	2001	S Emery

Middlesex Open

1992	GA Homewood	1997	L Fickling
1993	GA Homewood	1998	T Sheaff
1994	N Wichelow	1999	L Fickling
1995	N Wichelow	2000	L Fickling
1996	C Austin (am)	2001	—

Midland Professionals

1992	J Higgins (M and S)	1997	J Higgins (M and S)
1993	C Clark (M) P Baker (S)	1998	J Robinson (M) S Webster (S)
1994	N Turley (M) P Baker (S)	1999	I Ball (M) C Hall (S)
1995	D Eddiford (M) S Rose (S)	2000	R Rock (M) DJ Russell (S)
1996	S Bennett (M) DJ Russell (S)	2001	J Robinson (M) T Rouse (S)

Midland Seniors

1992	A Guest	1998	I Clark
1993	J Humphries	1999	S Wild
1994	G Pope	2000	T Squires
1995	T Squires	2001	*Not played*
1996	JC Thomas		
1997T	EW Hammond		
	C Moir		
	MA Smith		

Norfolk Open

1992	C Green	1998	R Wilson
1993	A Collison	1999	P Little
1994	J Hill	2000	M Jubb
1995	M Barrett	2001	D Henderson
1996	M Barrett		(am)
1997	N Lythgoe		

Norfolk Professionals

1992	A Collison	1997	T Varney
1993	A Collison	1998	R Wilson
1994	A Collison	1999	I Ellis
1995	P Briggs	2000	M Jubb
1996	P Bower	2001	A Collison

Northern Region PGA

1992	P Cowen	1997	G Furey
1993	C Smiley	1998	P Carman
1994	P Wesselingh	1999	R Wragg
1995	G Furey	2000	C Hislop
1996	S Townend	2001	B Sharrock

Northern Open

1992	P Smith	1997	D Thomson
1993	K Stables	1998	L James
1994	K Stables	1999	A Forsyth
1995	J Higgins	2000	J Payne
1996	S Henderson	2001	G Rankin

Nottinghamshire Open

1992	J King	1997	R Ellis
1993	J King	1998	P Wheatcroft
1994	J King	1999	O Wilson (am)
1995	J King	2000	TA Payne
1996	D McJannet	2001	M Scothern (am)

South West PGA

1994	G Emerson	1998	S Little
1995	G Howell	1999	G Ryall
1996	M Stanford	2000	K Spurgeon
1997	M Stanford	2001	M Wiggett

Southern Assistants

1992	G Orr	1997	A Lovelace
1993	R Edwards	1998	D Parris
1994	M Wheeler	1999	C Fromant
1995	P Lyons	2000	N Reilly
1996	D Parris	2001	C Roake

Southern Assistants Match Play

1992	G McQuitty	1997	B Hodkin
1993	N Gorman	1998	B Hodkin
1994	M Groombridge	1999	M Nichols
1995	M Groombridge	2000	S Wells
1996	A Butterfield	2001	S Crooks

Southern Professionals

1992	J Hoskison	1997	P Sherman
1993	G Smith	1998	P Simpson
1994	R Edwards	1999	S Wood
1995	P Sefton	2000	P Robshaw
1996	P Hughes	2001	K Saunders

Staffordshire Open

1992	J Rhodes	1997	A Roger
1993	M McGuire	1998	R Peace
1994	D Scott	1999	G Beddow
1995	I Proverbs	2000	J Cookson (am)
1996	B Rimmer	2001	R Maxfield (am)

Staffordshire and Shropshire Stroke Play

1992	S Russell	1997	R Fisher
1993	J Rhodes	1998	A Feriday
1994	J Rhodes	1999	P Wesselingh
1995	B Stevens	2000	P Wesselingh
1996	J Higgins	2001	S Russell

Suffolk Open

1992	R Mann	1997	P Wilby
1993	R Mann	1998	J Wright
1994	L Patterson	1999	S MacPherson
1995	R Mann	2000	J Keeley
1996	S MacPherson	2001	J Moul (am)

Suffolk Professionals

1992	R Mann	1998	K Golding (M)
1993	K Golding		S MacPherson (S)
1994	C Jenkins (M)	1999	R Mann (M)
	L Patterson (S)		S MacPherson (S)
1995	C Jenkins (M)	2000	R Hitchcock (M)
	R Mann (S)		J Bevan (S)
1996	K Vince (M)	2001	J Moul (am) (M)
	T Cooper (S)		A Cotton (S)
1997T	A Cotton (M)		
	A Lucas (S)		
	C Jenkins (S)		

Warwickshire Professionals

1992	C Harrison (M)	1997	L Bashford (M)
	A Allen (S)		C Phillips (S)
1993	A Bands (M)	1998	C Phillips (M)
	G Marston (S)		J Corns* (S)
1994	C Wicketts (M)	1999	D Clayton (M)
	S Webster (am)		A Bownes (S)
	(S)	2000	A Carey (M)
1995	J Cook		A Stokes (S)
	(M and S)	2001	A Stokes (M)
1996	C Phillips (M)		A Bownes (S)
	S Edwards (S)		

Sunderland of Scotland Masters

1992	K Walker	1997	L Vennet
1993	A Oldcorn	1998	M Miller*
1994	R Weir	1999	C Gillies
1995	M Jones	2000	S Martin
1996	C Ronald	2001	J Bevan

West Region PGA

1992	M Thomas	1997	M Thompson
1993	P Mayo	1998	J Taylor
1994	S Little	1999	S Little
1995	M Thompson	2000	M Higley
1996	M McEwan	2001	I Ferrie

Surrey Open

1992	C Defoy	1997	M Nichols
1993	R Dickman	1998	P Sefton
1994	M Nichols	1999	H Stott
1995	A Wall	2000	C Gane
1996	P Hughes	2001	N Reilly

Hills Wiltshire Pro Champ

1992	G Emerson	1997	M Smith
1993T	G Emerson	1998	R Blake
	D Ray	1999	S McDonald
1994	S Robertson	2000	A Beal
1995	G Laing	2001	S Robertson
1996	B Sandry		

Sussex Open

1992	P Harrison	1997	K Macdonald
1993	N Burke	1998	J Doherty (am)
1994	K Hinton	1999	P Lyons
1995	J Blamires	2000	P Lyons
1996	K Macdonald	2001	G Murray

Worcestershire Open

1992	A Robinson	1997	P Scarrett
1993	P Scarrett	1998	D Eddiford*
1994	S Edwards	1999	S Edwards
1995	C Clark	2000	N Turley
1996	D Clee	2001	N Turley

Ulster Professionals

1992	D Clarke	1997	D Mooney
1993	D Jones	1998	D Mooney
1994	P Russell	1999	D Mooney
1995	R Burns	2000	P Collins
1996	J Heggarty	2001	J Dwyer

Worcestershire Stroke Play

1992	R Cameron	1997	I Clark
1993	F Clark	1998	D Eddiford
1994	C Clark	1999	F Clark
1995	I Clark	2000	J Jones
1996	F Clark	2001	N Turley

Warwickshire Open

1992	P Chalkley	1997	D Barton
1993	A Bownes	1998	SJ Walker
1994	D White	1999	D Clayton
1995	C Dowling	2000	T Whitehouse (am)
1996	P Chalkley	2001	A Carey

Yorkshire Professionals

1992	L Turner	1997	S Robinson
1993	A Nicholson	1998	G Brown
1994	L Turner	1999	G Brown
1995	R Golding	2000	G Walker
1996	N Ludwell	2001	A Ambler

Overseas National Championships

(Excluding European Tour or Affiliated Events)

Australian Open

1904	Hon Michael Scott (am)
1905	Dan Soutar
1906	Carnegie Clark (am)
1907	Hon Michael Scott (am)
1908	Clyde Pearce (am)
1909	C Felstead (am)
1910	Carnegie Clark (am)
1911	Carnegie Clark (am)
1912	Ivo Whitton (am)
1913	Ivo Whitton (am)
1914-1919	*not played*
1920	Joe Kirkwood
1921	A Le Fevre
1922	C Campbell
1923	T Howard
1924	A Russell (am)
1925	Fred Popplewell
1926	Ivo Whitton (am)
1927	R Stewart
1928	Fred Popplewell
1929	Ivo Whitton (am)
1930	F Eyre
1931	Ivo Whitton (am)
1932	Mick Ryan (am)
1933	M Kelly
1934	Bill Bolger
1935	F McMahon
1936	Gene Sarazen
1937	George Naismith
1938	Jim Ferrier (am)
1939	Jim Ferrier (am)
1940-1945	*not played*
1946	Ossie Pickworth
1947	Ossie Pickworth
1948	Ossie Pickworth
1949	Eric Cremin
1950	Norman Von Nida
1951	Peter Thomson
1952	Norman Von Nida
1953	Norman Von Nida
1954	Ossie Pickworth
1955	Bobby Locke
1956	Bruce Crampton
1957	Frank Phillips
1958	Gary Player
1959	Kel Nagle
1960	Bruce Devlin (am)
1961	Frank Phillips
1962	Gary Player
1963	Gary Player
1964	Jack Nicklaus
1965	Gary Player
1966	Arnold Palmer
1967	Peter Thomson
1968	Jack Nicklaus
1969	Gary Player
1970	Gary Player
1971	Jack Nicklaus
1972	Peter Thomson
1973	J C Snead
1974	Gary Player
1975	Jack Nicklaus
1976	Jack Nicklaus
1977	David Graham
1978	Jack Nicklaus
1979	Jack Newton
1980	Greg Norman
1981	Bill Rogers
1982	Bob Shearer
1983	Peter Fowler
1984	Tom Watson
1985	Greg Norman
1986	Rodger Davis
1987	Greg Norman
1988	Mark Calcavecchia
1989	Peter Senior
1990	John Morse
1991	Wayne Riley
1992	Steve Elkington
1993	Brad Faxon
1994	Robert Allenby
1995	Greg Norman
1996	Greg Norman
1997	Lee Westwood
1998	Greg Chalmers
1999	Aaron Baddeley (am)
2000	Aaron Baddeley
2001	*To be played*

Canadian Open

Inaugurated 1904	
1904	J H Oke
1905	G Cumming
1906	C Murray
1907	P Barrett
1908	A Murray
1909	K Keffer
1910	D Kenny
1911	C Murray
1912	G Sargent
1913	A Murray
1914	K Kesser
1915-1918	*not played*
1919	J D Edgar
1920	J D Edgar
1921	W H Trovinger .
1922	A Watrous
1923	C W Hackney
1924	L Diegel
1925	L Diegel
1926	M Smith
1927	T Armour
1928	L Diegel
1929	L Diegel
1930	T Armour
1931	W Hagen
1932	H Cooper
1933	J Kirkwood
1934	T Armour
1935	G Kunes
1936	L Little
1937	H Cooper
1938	S Snead
1939	H McSpaden
1940	S Snead
1941	S Snead
1942	C Wood
1943-1944	*not played*
1945	B Nelson
1946	G Fazio
1947	AD Locke
1948	CW Congdon
1949	E J Harrison
1950	J Ferrier
1951	J Ferrier
1952	J Palmer
1953	D Douglas
1954	P Fletcher
1955	A Palmer
1956	D Sanders (am)
1957	G Bayer
1958	W Ellis jr
1959	D Ford
1960	A Wall jr
1961	J Cupit
1962	T Kroll
1963	D Ford
1964	KDG Nagle
1965	G Littler
1966	D Massengale
1967	W Casper
1968	RJ Charles
1969	T Aaron
1970	D Zarley
1971	L Trevino
1972	G Brewer jr
1973	T Weiskopf
1974	B Nichols
1975	T Weiskopf
1976	J Pate
1977	L Trevino
1978	B Lietzke
1979	L Trevino
1980	B Gilder
1981	P Oosterhuis
1982	B Lietzke
1983	J Cook
1984	G Norman
1985	C Strange
1986	B Murphy
1987	C Strange
1988	K Green
1989	S Jones
1990	W Levi
1991	N Price
1992	G Norman
1993	D Frost
1994	N Price
1995	M O'Meara
1996	D Hart
1997	S Jones
1998	B Andrade
1999	H Sutton
2000	T Woods
2001	S Verplank

Austrian Open

1992	P Mitchell	1997	E Simsek
1993	R Rafferty	1998	K Carissimi
1994	M Davis	1999	J Ciola
1995	A Cejka	2000	*Not played*
1996	P McGinley	2001	C Gane

Hong Kong Open

1992	T Watson	1997	F Nobilo
1993	B Watts	1998	WS Kang
1994	D Frost	1999	P Sjöland
1995	G Webb	2000	S Dyson
1996	G Webb	2001	*To be played*

Some of these events were to be played after we went to press

Indian Open

1992	S Ginn	1997	E Fryatt
1993	A Sher	1998	A Firoz
1994	E Aubrey	1999	A Atwal
1995	J Rutledge	2000	J Randhawa
1996	H Shirakata	2001	T Jaidee

New Zealand Open

1992	G Waite	1997	G Turner
1993	P Fowler	1998	G Turner
1994	C Jones	1999	M Lane
1995	L Parsons	2000	M Campbell
1996	M Long	2001	*To be played*

Japanese Open

1992	M Ozaki	1997	C Parry
1993	S Okuda	1998	H Tanaka
1994	M Ozaki	1999	N Ozaki
1995	T Izwa	2000	N Ozaki
1996	P Teravainen	2001	T Teshima

Singapore Open

1992	B Israelson	1997	Z Moe
1993	P Maloney	1998	S Micheel
1994	KH Han	1999	J Milkha Singh
.1995	S Conran	2000	J Randhawa
1996	J Kernohan	2001	T Warachant

Kenyan Open

1992	A Bossert	1997	J Berendt
1993	C Maltman	1998	R Gonzalez
1994	P Carman	1999	M Lafeber
1995	J Lee	2000	T Immelman
1996	M Miller	2001	A Roestoff

Thailand Open

1997	C Chernock	2000	D Terblanche
1998	J Kingston	2001	*Not played*
1999	F Quinn		

Zambian Open

1992	J Robinson	1997	*Not played*
1993	P Harrison	1998	M Cayeux
1994	*Not played*	1999	*Not played*
1995	*Not played*	2000	J Loughnane
1996	D Botes	2001	M Foster

Korean Open

1992	T Hamilton	1997	K Jong-Duck
1993	Y Kun Han	1998	DS Kim (am)
1994	M Cunning	1999	Choi Kyung Ju
1995	B Jobe	2000	T Jaidee
1996	Choi Kyung-Ju	2001	DS Kim (am)

Zimbabwe Open

1992	M McNulty	1997	M McNulty
1993	*Not played*	1998	H Alberts
1994	C Williams	1999	J Hugo
1995	N Price	2000	M McNulty
1996	N Price	2001	*To be played*

Mauritius Open

1994	M McLean	1998	R Davis
1995	M Santi	1999	J Lomas
1996	P Golding	2000	Mike McLean
1997	G Sherry	2001	*To be played*

Some of these events were to be played after we went to press

Late Results

US SENIOR TOUR: FINAL QUALIFERS

Top eight receive full 2002 cards

1	H Twitty	276	3T	R Davis (Aus)	280	7T	C Hughey	284	
2	L Ziegler	279	6	D Pooley	283		B Sheehan	284	
3	J Spradlin	280	7	D Mast (am)	284		RW Eakes	284	
	D O'Neill	280		F Gibson	284		B Brask	284	

Late Results

UBS Warburg Cup (Instituted 2001)

Rest of World *v* USA   *Captains:* Arnold Palmer (USA); Gary Player (Rest of World)
at Kiawah Island, South Carolina

First Day – **Foursomes**
Cook & Hoch lost to Langer & Nobilo 2 and 1
Roberts & Watson lost to Canizares & Ginn
1 hole
Nelson & Strange halved with Torrance &
Woosnam
Calcavecchia & Irwin lost to Aoki & Faldo
2 and 1
O'Meara & Palmer lost to Player & Smyth
3 and 2
Floyd & Quigley beat Durnian & Stanley 1 hole
First day result: USA 1½, Rest of World 4½

Second Day – **Fourball**
Calcavecchia & Floyd halved with Langer &
Nobilo
Cook & O'Meara halved with Torrance &
Woosnam
Strange & Watson halved with Aoki & Faldo
Palmer & Quigley lost to Player & Smyth
2 holes
Irwin & Nelson beat Canizares & Ginn 2 holes
Hoch & Roberts beat Durnian & Stanley
4 and 2

Second day result: USA 3½. World 2½

Overall result after two days: USA 5, World 7

Third Day – **Singles**
Arnold Palmer beat Gary Player (RSA)
2 and 1
Scott Hoch beat Isao Aoki (Jpn) 2 and 1
Loren Roberts lost to Des Smyth (Irl)
4 and 3
Hale Irwin halved with Bernhard Langer
(Ger)
Tom Watson lost to Nick Faldo (Eng)
3 and 2
Curtis Strange halved with Sam Torrance
(Sco)
Mark O'Meara beat Stewart Ginn (Aus)
5 and 4
John Cook beat José María Canizares (Esp)
2 and 1
Dana Quigley lost to Denis Durnian (Eng)
1 hole
Ray Floyd halved with Ian Stanley (Aus)
Mark Calcavecchia beat Ian Woosnam (Wal)
1 hole
Larry Nelson beat Frank Nobilo (NZ)
3 and 2
Third day result: USA 7½. World 4½

Overall result: USA 12½, World 11½

EUROPEAN TOUR: FINAL QUALIFERS

The top 36 players earned Main Tour cards for 2002

1 Johan Skold (Swe)	415	13 Russell Claydon		26 Erol Simsek (Ger)	425
2 Christophe Pottier		(Eng)	423	27 Fredrik Andersson
(Fra)	417	14 David Park (Wal)	423	(Swe)	426
3 Nick Dougherty		15 Arjun Atwal (Ind)	424	28 Peter Fowler (Aus)	426
(Eng)	418	16 Kenneth Ferrie		29 Benoit Teilleria
4 David Drysdale (Sco)	419	(Eng)	424	(Fra)	426
5 Didier de Vooght		17 Sam Walker (Eng)	424	30 Michele Reale (Fra)	426
(Bel)	419	18 Matthew Cort (Eng)	424	31 Adam Mednick
6 Nicolas Vanhootegen		19 Iain Pyman (Eng)	424	(Swe)	426
(Bel)	419	20 Magnus Persson		32 Dennis Edlund
7 Andrew Butterfield		(Swe)	424	(Swe)	426
(Eng)	420	21 Alvaro Salto (Esp)	424	33 Robert Coles (Eng)	427
8 Jeremy Robinson		22 Mattias Eliasson		34 Nicolas Kalouguine
(Eng)	421	(Swe)	424	(Fra)	427
9 Santiago Luna (Esp)	421	23 Graham Fox (Sco)	425	35 Mattias Nilsson
10 Ian Hutchings (RSA)	421	24 Simon Khan (Eng)	425	(Swe)	427
11 Carl Suneson (Esp)	422	25 Roger Winchester		36 Marcel Siem (Ger)	427
12 Gustavo Rojas (Arg)	423	(Eng)	425	

British Golf Museum
St Andrews

Willie and Laurie Auchterlonie in their workshop

Bruce Embankment, St. Andrews, Fife KY16 9AB
Phone 01334 460046 • Fax 01334 460064
Website www.britishgolfmuseum.co.uk

Opening Times:
Summer: Easter to Mid-October 9.30am–5.30pm • Open 7 days
Winter: 11am–3pm • Closed Tuesday and Wednesday

PART III

Women's Professional Tournaments

Golf Weekly *World Ranking* for *Women's Professional Golf*

Latest ranking after Mizuno Classic

1	Annika Sörenstam (Swe)	533.48	39	Chieko Amanuma (Jpn)	90.31
2	Karrie Webb (Aus)	476.94	40	Beth Daniel (USA)	88.18
3	Se Ri Pak (Kor)	418.58	41	Brandie Burton (USA)	84.87
4	Laura Diaz (USA)	297.22	42	Michie Ohba (Jpn)	81.89
5	Mi Hyun Kim (Kor)	284.57	43	Kelli Kuehne (USA)	80.96
6	Lorie Kane (Can)	288.73	44	Becky Iverson (USA)	80.25
7	Sophie Gustafson (Swe)	265.56	45	Wendy Doolan (USA)	79.18
8	Dottie Pepper (USA)	241.61	46	Akiko Fukushima (Jpn)	76.34
9	Laura Davies (Eng)	218.52	47	Iben Tinning (Den)	75.83
10	Catriona Matthew (Sco)	212.79	48	Junko Yasui (Jpn)	73.23
11	Maria Hjörth (Swe)	198.10	49	Moira Dunn (USA)	72.85
12	Rosie Jones (USA)	195.05	49	Mineko Nasu (Jpn)	72.77
13	Meg Mallon (USA)	182.98	51	Betsy King (USA)	71.63
14	Juli Inkster (USA)	180.70	52	Mhairi McKay (Sco)	71.05
15	Janice Moodie (Sco)	179.75	53	Miyuki Shimabukuro (Jpn)	68.25
16	Yuri Fudoh (Jpn)	175.38	54	Aki Nakano (Jpn)	67.83
17	Rachel Teske (Aus)	172.66	55	Paula Marti (Esp)	67.63
18	Raquel Carriedo (Esp)	164.86	56	Kaori Harada (Jpn)	67.40
19	Wendy Ward (USA)	160.97	57	Sherri Steinhauer (USA)	64.87
20	Michele Redman (USA)	145.79	58	Charlotta Sörenstam (Swe)	64.41
21	Pat Hurst (USA)	145.30	59	Trish Johnson (Eng)	64.23
22	Carin Koch (Swe)	124.01	60	Patricia Meunier Lebouc (Fra)	63.58
23	Dorothy Delasin (USA)	120.98	61	Midori Yoneyama (Jpn)	61.78
24	Nancy Scranton (USA)	119.98	62	Marina Arruti (Esp)	61.75
25	Aki Takamura (Jpn)	118.33	63	Yu Chen Huang (Chn)	58.74
26	Marine Monnet (Fra)	114.80	64	Helen Alfredsson (Swe)	56.96
27	Kasumi Fujii (Jpn)	112.43	65	Kirsty Taylor (Eng)	56.45
28	Karine Icher (Fra)	110.83	66	Marisa Baena (USA)	55.76
29	Grace Park (USA)	110.48	67	Kathryn Marshall (Sco)	55.53
30	Emilee Klein (USA)	110.16	68	Leta Lindley (USA)	53.09
31	Woo Soon Ko (Kor)	103.28	69	Dale Reid (Sco)	51.50
32	Elisabeth Esterl (Ger)	100.91	70	Liselotte Neumann (Swe)	51.26
33	Suzann Pettersen (Nor)	99.50	71	Kris Tschetter (USA)	50.93
34	Kelly Robbins (USA)	99.19	72	Corinne Dibnah (Aus)	50.55
35	Kaori Higo (Jpn)	97.41	73	Tina Fischer (Ger)	50.25
36	Cristie Kerr (USA)	97.08	74	Gina Scott (NZ)	49.25
37	Toshimi Kimura (Jpn)	96.39	75	Michelle McGann (USA)	48.96
38	Ok Hee Ku (Kor)	95.35			

Evian Ladies European Tour, 2001

FINAL ORDER OF MERIT

1	Raquel Carriedo (Esp)	10661	23	Johanna Head (Eng)	1964
2	Suzann Pettersen (Nor)	8014	24	Valerie Van Ryckeghem (Bel)	1855
3	Karine Icher (Fra)	6927	25	Kirsty Taylor (Eng)	1853
4	Marine Monnet (Fra)	6590	26	Ana Belen Sánchez (Esp)	1794
5	Sophie Gustafson (Swe)	5916	27	Lynnette Brooky (NZ)	1766
6	Paula Marti (Esp)	5459	28	Cecilie Lundgren (Nor)	1756
7	Elisabeth Esterl (Ger)	4836	29	Lora Fairclough (Eng)	1744
8	Iben Tinning (Den)	3887	30	Rachel Kirkwood (Eng)	1619
9	Marina Aruti (Esp)	3509	31	Laurette Maritz (RSA)	1615
10	Becky Morgan (Wal)	3194	32	Sophie Sandolo (Ita)	1534
11	Laura Davies (Eng)	3117	33	Giulia Sergas (Ita)	1507
12	Corinne Dibnah (Aus)	2816	34	Joanne Mills (Aus)	1484
13	Nicola Moult (Eng)	2461	35	Marlene Hedblom (Swe)	1450
14	Samantha Head (Eng)	2385	36	Joanne Morley (Eng)	1361
15	Asa Gottmo (Swe)	2295	37	Patricia Meunier Lebouc (Fra)	1350
16	Trish Johnson (Eng)	2151	38	Alison Nicholas (Eng)	1285
17	Alison Munt (Aus)	2090	39	Diane Barnard (Eng)	1231
18	Kathryn Marshall (Sco)	2057	40	Catrin Nilsmark (Swe)	1175
19	Dale Reid OBE (Sco)	2054	41	Karen Pearce (Aus)	1156
20	Gina Scott (NZ)	2000	42	Judith Van Hagen (Ned)	1140
21	Anna Berg (Swe)	1992	43	Riikka Hakkarainen (Fin)	1139
22	Lisa Hed (Swe)	1986	44	Sara Eklund (Swe)	1082

FINAL MONEY LIST

1	Raquel Carriedo (Esp)	£160441	26	Giulia Sergas (Ita)	25444
2	Suzann Petersen (Nor)	129546	27	Marlene Hedblom (Swe)	25176
3	Marine Monnet (Fra)	121193	28	Gina Scott (NZ)	24838
4	Karine Icher (Fra)	101016	29	Anna Berg (Swe)	23722
5	Sophie Gustafson (Swe)	98612	30	Laurette Maritz (RSA)	23564
6	Iben Tinning (Den)	78152	31	Alison Nicholas (Eng)	23276
7	Paula Marti (Esp)	73815	32	Kirsty Taylor (Eng)	23019
8	Elisabeth Esterl (Ger)	67193	33	Karen Pearce (Aus)	22918
9	Laura Davies (Eng)	57123	34	Catrin Nilsmark (Swe)	22263
10	Becky Morgan (Wal)	57077	35	Ana Belen Sánchez (Esp)	21662
11	Marina Aruti (Esp)	53402	36	Joanne Mills (Aus)	21234
12	Kathryn Marshall (Sco)	44634	37	Cecilie Lundgren (Nor)	21076
13	Asa Gottmo (Swe)	40894	38	Patricia Meunier Lebouc (Fra)	20957
14	Trish Johnson (Eng)	40457	39	Silvia Cavalleri (Ita)	19965
15	Corinne Dibnah (Aus)	40224	40	Sophie Sandolo (Ita)	18576
16	Johanna Head (Eng)	36214	41	Shani Waugh (Aus)	18106
17	Alison Munt (Aus)	34110	42	Riikka Hakkarainen (Fin)	18024
18	Lisa Hed (Swe)	31111	43	Sara Eklund (Swe)	17273
19	Nicola Moult (Eng)	28985	44	Rachel Kirkwood (Eng)	17012
20	Joanne Morley (Eng)	28977	45	Diane Barnard (Eng)	15973
21	Lora Fairclough (Eng)	28973	46	Judith Van Hagen (Ned)	14966
22	Dale Reid OBE (Sco)	28732	47	Loraine Lambert (Aus)	13655
23	Samantha Head (Eng)	28488	48	Esther Poburski (Ger)	12291
24	Valerie Van Ryckeghem (Bel)	26335	49	Pernilla Sterner (Swe)	12146
25	Lynnette Brooky (NZ)	25844	50	Ludivine Kreutz (Fra)	10283

TOUR RESULTS (in chronological order)

Australian Ladies Masters
Royal Pines, Gold Coast, Queensland   [6397-72]

1	Karrie Webb (Aus)	67-70-65-69—271	£30392	€49611
2	Rachel Teske (Aus)	71-68-71-69—279	20261	33074
3	Catriona Matthew (Sco)	70-70-72-68—280	12157	19845

AAMI Women's Australian Open
Yarra Yarra, East Bentleigh, Victoria, Australia   [5534-72]

1	Sophie Gustafson (Swe)	70-69-66-71—276	£24313	€39689
2	Karrie Webb (Aus)	70-70-69-68—277	16209	26459
3	Jane Crafter (Aus)	68-71-70-74—283	9725	15875

Taiwan Ladies Masters   *Ta Shee GCC,*
Taiwan   [7004-72]

1	Raquel Carriedo (Esp)	69-67-75—211	£15000	€24486
2	Anna Berg (Swe)	74-66-72—212	8575	13998
	Elisabeth Esterl (Ger)	72-70-70—212	8575	13998

Nedbank MasterCard SA Masters
Sun City, RSA   [6330-72]

1	Samantha Head (Eng)	70-72-68—210	£15000	€24486
2	Raquel Carriedo (Esp)	74-70-67—211	7516	12270
	Elisabeth Esterl (Ger)	70-69-72—211	7516	12270
	Cecilie Lundgreen (Nor)	71-72-68—211	7516	12270

Ladies Italian Open
Poggio Dei Medici, Tuscany, Italy   [6252-73]

1	Paula Marti *(Esp)	70-73-72-68—283	£18000	€29383
2	Raquel Carriedo (Esp)	72-69-73-69—283	12180	19883
3	Corinne Dibnah (Aus)	65-73-72-74—284	8400	13712

Ladies French Open
Arras, Anzin St Aubin, France   [5800-72]

1	Suzann Pettersen* (Nor)	71-70-70-69—280	£24450	€39912
2	Becky Morgan (Wal)	72-67-70-71—280	16545	27007
3	Karine Icher (Fra)	70-69-69-73—281	10106	16497
	Giulia Sergas (Ita)	69-72-68-72—281	10106	16497

Evian Masters

Evian Les Bains, France [5975-72]

1	Rachel Teske (Aus)	71-68-66-68—273	£222426	€363088
2	Maria Hjörth (Swe)	69-65-71-69—274	148372	242202
3	Beth Daniel (USA)	67-68-70-72—277	108994	177922

Kellogg's Ladies' British Masters

Mottram Hall, Cheshire [6322-73]

1	Paula Marti (Esp)	71-70-68—209	£15000	€24486
2	Raquel Carriedo (Esp)	70-70-70—210	10150	16569
3	Dale Reid (Sco)	70-69-72—211	7000	11427

WPGA Championship of Europe

Royal Porthcawl, Wales [6277-72]

1	Helen Alfredsson (Swe)	67-70-68-71—276	£60000	€97944
2	Suzann Pettersen (Nor)	70-68-68-74—280	40600	66275
3	Asa Gottmo (Swe)	71-73-71-68—283	28000	45707

WEETABIX WOMEN'S BRITISH OPEN

Sunningdale, Berkshire [6255-72]

1	Se Ri Pak (Kor)	71-70-70-66—277	£155000	€253022
2	Mi Hyun Kim (Kor)	72-65-71-71—279	100000	163240
3	Laura Diaz (USA)	74-70-69-67—280	51813	84579
	Catriona Matthew (Sco)	70-65-72-73—280	51813	84579
	Janice Moodie (Sco)	67-70-71-72—280	51813	84579
	Iben Tinning (Den)	71-69-72-68—280	51813	84579

Fuller details of this event are included in Part I The Majors p.90

Compaq Open

Österåkers, Stockholm, Sweden [6213-73]

1	Raquel Carriedo (Esp)	72-67-73-72—284	£48750	€79580
2	Karine Icher (Fra)	66-67-76-76—285	32988	53849
3	Sophie Gustafson (Swe)	69-77-66-74—286	22750	37137

Ladies German Open

Treudelberg, Hamburg, Germany [6213-72]

1	Karine Icher (Fra)	71-69-70—210	£22500	€36729
2	Suzann Pettersen (Nor)	72-67-72—211	15225	24853
3	Nicola Moult (Eng)	74-69-69—212	10500	17140

Ladies Irish Open
Faithlegg, Waterford, Ireland   [6001-72]

1	Raquel Carriedo (Esp)	68-66-66—200	£15000	€24486
2	Sophie Gustafson (Swe)	69-67-65—201	10150	16569
3	Laura Davies (Eng)	70-67-65—202	6200	10121
	Ana Belen Sanchez (Esp)	66-68-68—202	6200	10121

MEXX Sport Open
Kennemer G&CC, Zandvoort, Netherlands   [5993-72]

1	Karine Icher (Fra)	70-70-72—212	£15000	€24486
2	Suzann Pettersen (Nor)	69-70-73—212	10150	16569
3	Valerie Van Ryckeghem (Bel)	68-73-72—213	62000	10121
	Gina Scott (NZ)	68-73-72—213	62000	10121

International Match Play
PGA Centenary Course, Gleneagles, Scotland

Quarter Finals:
Sophie Gustafson (Swe) beat Suzann Pettersen (Nor) at 19th
Laura Davies (Eng) beat Laura Diaz (USA) at 19th
Janice Moodie (Sco) beat Maria Hjörth (Swe) 3 and 2
Carin Koch (Swe) beat Marie-Laure de Lorenzi (Fra) 1 hole

Semi-Finals:
Davies beat Gustafson at 19th
Moodie beat Koch 2 and 1

Final
L Davies (£110000) beat J Moodie (£70,000) 5 and 4

3rd Place:
S Gustafson (£50,000) beat C Koch (£38,000) 4 and 3

Biarritz Ladies Classic
Biarritz Le Phare, France   [5688-70]

1	Rachel Kirkwood (Eng)★	70-65-67—202	£15000	€24486
2	Marina Arruti (Esp)	68-66-68—202	10150	16569
3	Sophie Giquel (am) (Fra)	63-73-67—203		

Meriam Cup (unofficial event)
Dar Es Salam Golf Glub, Rabat, Morocco

1	Marine Monnet (Fra)	75-70-73—218	$11,000
2	Joanna Head (Eng)	73-73-73—223	
	Patricia Meunier-Lebouc (Fra)	72-75-74—223	
	Elisabeth Esterl (Ger)	71-72-80—223	

US LPGA Tour 2001

Players are of American nationality unless stated

FINAL RANKING

1	Annika Sörenstam (Swe)	$2,105,868	51	Helen Alfredsson (Swe)	223,745
2	Se Ri Pak (Kor)	1,623,009	52	Jackie Gallagher-Smith	216,940
3	Karrie Webb (Aus)	1,535,404	53	Michelle McGann	212,937
4	Lorie Kane (Can)	947,489	54	Tammie Green	203,734
5	Maria Hjorth (Swe)	848,105	55	Amy Fruhwirth	188,984
6	Rosie Jones	785,010	56	Karen Weiss	186,228
7	Dottie Pepper	776,482	57	Sherri Steinhauer	175,431
8	Mi Hyun Kim (Kor)	762,363	58	Dina Ammaccapane	173,306
9	Laura Diaz	751,466	59	Barb Mucha	172,526
10	Catriona Matthew (Sco)	747,970	60	Kathryn Marshall (Sco)	162,170
11	Rachel Teske (Aus)	713,129	61	Liselotte Neumann (Swe)	159,719
12	Wendy Ward	686,906	62	AJ Eathorne (Can)	157,833
13	Emilee Klein	649,380	63	Audra Burks	147,012
14	Dorothy Delasin	620,442	64	Marnie McGuire	145,237
15	Sophie Gustafson (Swe)	617,327	65	Leslie Spalding	144,918
16	Janice Moodie (Sco)	595,463	66	Alicia Dibos (Per)	139,251
17	Michele Redman	552,317	67	Penny Hammel	139,034
18	Laura Davies (Eng)	492,143	68	Jenny Lidback	136,115
19	Meg Mallon	488,125	69	Charlotta Sörenstam (Swe)	132,917
20	Kelly Robbins	483,671	70	Hee-Won Han (Kor)	131,669
21	Nancy Scranton	465,673	71	Michelle Estill	130,541
22	Juli Inkster	455,087	72	Dawn Coe-Jones	130,366
23	Grace Park (Kor)	446,670	73	Hiromi Kobayashi (Jpn)	129,810
24	Mhairi McKay (Sco)	439,024	74	Kristi Albers	128,912
25	Carin Koch (Swe)	421,329	75	Jean Bartholomew	126,209
26	Beth Daniel	410,540	76	Jane Crafter (Aus)	117,597
27	Wendy Doolan	405,135	77	Tina Barrett	116,241
28	Cristie Kerr	373,947	78	Silvia Cavalleri (Ita)	114,007
29	Pat Hurst	367,303	79	Cindy Figg-Currier	113,283
30	Betsy King	358,756	80	Kristal Parker	109,716
31	Jill McGill	340,991	81	Kellee Booth	108,110
32	Moira C Dunn	335,307	82	Patricia Meunier-Lebouc (Fra)	108,000
33	Marisa Baena (Col)	318,819	83	Becky Morgan (Wal)	101,955
34	Kelli Kuehne	300,729	84	Denise Killeen	100,746
35	Gloria Park (Kor)	289,468	85	Jeong Jang (Kor)	99,872
36	Kris Tschetter	288,839	86	Shani Waugh (Aus)	97,776
37	Brandie Burton	265,853	87	Jenny Rosales (Phi)	94,879
38	Donna Andrews	263,754	88	Alison Nicholas (Eng)	94,475
39	Vicki Goetze-Ackerman	261,446	89	Karen Stupples (Eng)	91,027
40	Akiko Fukushima (Jpn)	256,894	90	Cindy Schreyer	90,010
41	Yu Ping Lin (Twn)	253,771	91	Pearl Sinn (Kor)	87,119
42	Sherri Turner	253,724	92	Tamie Durdin	86,869
43	Danielle Ammaccapane	251,992	93	Maggie Will	82,623
44	Tracy Hanson	249,978	94	Sara Sanders	78,610
45	Tina Fischer (Ger)	245,662	95	Mitzi Edge	70,944
46	Leta Lindley	243,597	96	Vickie Odegard	70,773
47	Heather Daly-Donofrio	242,176	97	Deb Richard	69,310
48	Becky Iverson	233,602	98	Angela Stanford	66,956
49	Heather Bowie	226,291	99	Jamie Hullett	65,695
50	Kate Golden	223,879	100	Terry-Jo Myers	64,399

TOUR RESULTS (in chronological order)

YourLife Vitamins LPGA Classic

Grand Cypress, Orlando, FL   [6220-72]

1	Se Ri Pak (Kor)	71-68-64—203	$150000
2	Penny Hammel	67-72-68—207	80513
	Carin Koch (Swe)	69-68-70—207	80513

Subaru Memorial of Naples

The Club at the Strand, Naples, FL   [6328-72]

1	Sophie Gustafson (Swe)	68-64-70-70—272	$150000
2	Karrie Webb (Aus)	68-70-68-69—275	93093
3	Dottie Pepper	68-69-72-67—276	67933

The Office Depot

Doral Resort Blue/Red, Miami, FL [B 6388-72; R 5842-70]

1	Grace Park (Kor)	70-69-70-71—280	$123750
2	Karrie Webb (Aus)	69-72-69-71—281	76801
3	Jenny Rosales (Phi)	70-72-70-70—282	49817
	Karen Weiss	76-69-67-70—282	49817

LPGA Takefuji Classic

Kona CC, Kailua-Kona, HI   [6257-72]

1	Lorie Kane (Can)	70-69-66—205	$127500
2	Annika Sörenstam (Swe)	70-67-70—207	79129
3	Cristie Kerr	70-69-69—208	57743

Cup Noodles Hawaiian Ladies Open

Kapolei, Oahu, HI   [6100-72]

1	Catriona Matthew (Sco)	67-71-72—210	$112500
2	Annika Sörenstam		
	(Swe)	74-69-70—213	69819
3	Danielle Ammaccapane	75-70-69—214	40884
	Nancy Scranton	76-64-74—214	40884
	Wendy Ward	74-67-73—214	40884

Welch's/Circle K Championship

Randolph Park, Tucson, AZ [6222-72]

1	Annika Sörenstam (Swe)	65-68-67-65—265	$112500
2	Laura Diaz	68-69-68-66—271	48118
	Michelle McGann	70-66-71-64—271	48118
	Se Ri Pak (Kor)	68-67-67-69—271	48118
	Dottie Pepper	67-67-70-67—271	48118

Standard Register Ping

Moon Valley, Phoenix, AZ [6459-72]

1	Annika Sörenstam (Swe)	65-59-69-68—261	$150000
2	Se Ri Pak (Kor)	65-68-63-67—263	93093
3	Yu Ping Lin (Twn)	72-65-68-70—275	60384
	Dottie Pepper	68-67-73-67—275	60384

NABISCO CHAMPIONSHIP

Mission Hills, Rancho Mirage, CA [6520-72]

1	Annika Sörenstam (Swe)	72-70-70-69—281	$225000
2	Akiko Fukushima (Jpn)	74-68-70-72—284	87557
	Janice Moodie (Sco)	72-72-70-70—284	87557
	Dottie Pepper	71-71-71-71—284	87557
	Rachel Teske (Aus)	72-73-66-73—284	87557
	Karrie Webb (Aus)	73-72-70-69—284	87557

Fuller details of this event are included in Part I The Majors p.113

The Office Depot

Wilshire CC, Los Angeles, CA [6531-72]

1	Annika Sörenstam* (Swe)	71-73-66—210	$120000
2	Mi Hyun Kim (Kor)	70-75-65—210	74474
3	Pat Hurst	67-67-77—211	54346

Longs Drugs Challenge

Twelve Bridges GC, Lincoln, CA [6388-72]

1	Se Ri Pak (Kor)	66-71-71—208	$120000
2	Laura Diaz	70-72-68—210	74474
3	Michele Redman	68-70-73—211	54346

Kathy Ireland Championship

Onion Creek GC, Austin, TX [6067-70]

1	Rosie Jones*	66-67-68-67—268	$135000
2	Mi Hyun Kim (Kor)	70-68-64-66—268	83783
3	Marisa Baena (Col)	70-67-64-68—269	61139

Chick-fil-A Charity Championship

Eagles Landing, Stockbridge, GA   [6218-72]

1	Annika Sörenstam* (Swe)	70-66-67—203	$180000
2	Sophie Gustafson (Swe)	70-65-68—203	111711
3	Beth Daniel	67-68-69—204	72461
	Dottie Pepper	66-74-64—204	72461

Electrolux USA Championship

The Legends Club, Franklin, TN   [6425-72]

1	Juli Inkster	73-67-69-65—274	$120000
2	Catriona Matthew (Sco)	66-71-69-69—275	74474
3	Annika Sörenstam (Swe)	69-67-70-70—276	54346

The Champions Classic

CC of the North, Beavercreek, OH [6331-72] weather affected

1	Wendy Doolan* (Aus)	68-64—132	$112500
2	Wendy Ward	64-68—132	69819
3	Beth Daniel	68-65—133	45288
	Maria Hjörth (Swe)	68-65—133	45288

LPGA Corning Classic

Corning, NY   [6062-72]

1	Carin Koch (Swe)	68-67-69-66—270	$135000
2	Maria Hjörth (Swe)	71-69-63-69—272	72461
	Mhairi McKay (Sco)	69-65-68-70—272	72461

US WOMEN'S OPEN

Pine Needles Lodge GC, Southern Pines, NC   [6256-70]

1	Karrie Webb (Aus)	70-65-69-69—273	$520000
2	Se Ri Pak (Kor)	69-70-70-72—281	310000
3	Dottie Pepper	74-69-70-69—282	202580

Fuller details of this event are included in Part I The Majors p.97

Wegmans Rochester International

Locust Hill, Pittsford, NY   [6190-72]

1	Laura Davies (Eng)	68-68-69-74—279	$150000
2	Maria Hjörth (Swe)	70-71-69-72—282	80513
	Wendy Ward	72-71-72-67—282	80513

Evian Masters

Evian-les-Bains, France [6091-72]

1	Rachel Teske (Aus)	71-68-66-68—273	$315000
2	Maria Hjörth (Swe)	69-65-71-69—274	210125
3	Beth Daniel	67-68-70-72—277	154357

McDONALDS LPGA CHAMPIONSHIP

DuPont CC, Wilmington, DE [6408-71]

1	Karrie Webb (Aus)	67-64-70-69—270	$225000
2	Laura Diaz	67-71-66-68—272	139639
3	Maria Hjörth (Swe)	71-67-66-70—274	90577
	Wendy Ward	65-69-71-69—274	90577

Fuller details of this event are included in Part I The Majors p.105

ShopRite LPGA Classic

Seaview (Bay), Atlantic City, NJ [6051-71]

1	Betsy King	65-69-67—201	$180000
2	Lorie Kane (Can)	65-68-70—203	111711
3	Donna Andrews	68-74-65—207	50923
	Tamie Durdin (Aus)	68-72-67—207	50923
	Rosie Jones	70-66-71—207	50923
	Cristie Kerr	67-66-74—207	50923
	Catriona Matthew (Sco)	68-69-70—207	50923
	Leslie Spalding	71-72-64—207	50923

Jamie Farr Kroger Classic

Highland Meadows, Sylvania, OH [6365-71]

1	Se Ri Pak (Kor)	70-62-69-68—269	$150000
2	Maria Hjörth (Swe)	76-65-66-64—271	93093
3	Heather Bowie	68-66-71-68—273	60384
	Marnie McGuire (NZ)	70-69-69-65—273	60384

Michelob Light Classic

Fox Run, St Louis, MO [6452-72]

1	Emilee Klein	64-72-69—205	$120000
2	Jill McGill	71-76-63—210	64410
	Annika Sörenstam (Swe)	68-72-70—210	64410

Big Apple Classic

Wykagyl, New Rochelle, NY [6161-71]

1	Rosie Jones	70-66-66-70—272	$142500
2	Laura Diaz	68-71-68-66—273	88438
3	Kris Tschetter	68-70-70-66—274	64536

Giant Eagle LPGA Classic
Squaw Creek, Vienna, OH   [6565-72]

1	Dorothy Delasin	69-69-65—203	$150000
2	Tammie Green	69-67-68—204	93093
3	Se Ri Pak (Kor)	67-67-71—205	67933

WEETABIX WOMEN'S BRITISH OPEN
Sunningdale, Berkshire, England   [6255-72]

1	Se Ri Pak (Kor)	71-70-70-66—277	$221650
2	Mi Hyun Kim (Kor)	72-65-71-71—279	143000
3	Laura Diaz (USA)	74-70-69-67—280	74092
	Catriona Matthew (Sco)	70-65-72-73—280	74092
	Janice Moodie (Sco)	67-70-71-72—280	74092
	Iben Tinning (Den)	71-69-72-68—280	74092

Fuller details of this event are included in Part I The Majors p.90

Wendy's Championship for Children
New Albany, OH   [6279-72]

1	Wendy Ward	65-62-68—195	$150000
2	Moira Dunn	67-64-67—198	80513
3	Annika Sörenstam (Swe)	67-65-66—198	80513

Bank of Montreal Canadian Women's Open
Magna, Asurora, Ontario, Canada   [6411-72]

1	Annika Sörenstam (Swe)	71-68-64-69—272	$180000
2	Kelly Robbins	65-69-69-71—274	111711
3	Lorie Kane (Can)	69-69-68-70—276	72461
	Se Ri Pak (Kor)	65-72-71-68—276	72461

First Union Betsy King Classic
Berkleigh, Kutztown, PA   [6197-72]

1	Heather Daly-Donofrio	65-71-68-69—273	$120000
2	Moira Dunn	68-66-68-72—274	64410
	Mhairi McKay (Sco)	69-67-68-70—274	64410

State Farm Rail Classic
The Rail Course, Springfield, IL   [xxxx-72]

1	Kate Golden	69-65-70-63—267	$150000
2	Annika Sörenstam (Swe)	65-66-67-70—268	93093
3	Moira Dunn	69-68-67-67—271	67933

Williams Championship

Tulsa, OK   [xxxx-70]

1	Gloria Park (Kor)	68-69-64—201	$150000
2	Donna Andrews	70-62-70—202	93093
3	Rachel Teske (Aus)	69-67-71—207	67933

Safeway LPGA Championship

Columbia Edgewater, Portland, OR

This event was cancelled

Asalu Ryokuken International Championship

Mount Vintage Plantation, North Augusta, GA   [6321-72]

1	Gloria Park (Kor)	68-69-64—201	$150000
2	Donna Andrews	70-62-70—202	93093
3	Rachel Teske (Aus)	69-67-71—207	67933

AFLAC Champions

Magnolia Groves Mobile, AL   [6253-72]

1	Se Ri Pak (Kor)	70-67-64-71—272	$122000
2	Lorie Kane (Can)	72-69-67-69—277	75500
3	Grace Park (Kor)	69-69-71-70—279	54250

Samsung World Championship

Hiddenbrooke GC, Vallejo, CA

1	Dorothy Delasin (USA)	70-71-67-69—277	$157000
2	Karrie Webb (Aus)	72-67-70-72—281	81500
	Se Ri Pak (Kor)	70-72-67-72—281	81500

Sports Today CJ Nine Bridges Classic

CJ Nine Bridges Golf Resort, Jeju Island

This event was cancelled

Cisco World Ladies' Match Play Challenge

at Chiba, Japan

Quarter-finals

Annika Sörenstam (Swe) beat Mhairi McKay (Sco) 3 and 1
Lorie Kane (Can) beat Emilee Klein (USA) 4 and 3
Se Ri Pak (Kor) beat Rachel Teske (Aus) 3 and 2
Huang Yu-Chen (Jpn) beat A Takamura (Jpn) 1 hole

Cisco World Ladies' Match Play Challenge *continued*

Semi-finals
Annika Sörenstam (Swe) beat Lorie Kane (Can) 4 and 2
Se Ri Pak (Kor) beat Huang Yu-Chen (Jpn) 6 and 4.

Final
Sörenstam beat Se Ri Pak 1 hole

Mizuno Classic
Musashigaoka GC   [6344–72]

1	Annika Sörenstam (Swe)	66-67-70—203	$162000
2	Laura Davies (Eng)	66-71-71—208	100540
3	Marisa Baena (Col)	67-71-70—208	65215
	Woo-Soon-ko (Kor)	67-71-70—208	65215

Tyco/ADT Championship
Trump International, West Palm Beach, Florida

1	Karrie Webb (Aus)	67-71-73-68—279	$215000
2	Annika Sörenstam (Swe)	68-74-74-65—281	115000
3	Janice Moodie (Sco)	70-75-69-74—288	686000

Annika Sörenstam hits US$2 million

Sweden's Annika Sörenstam became the first player on the US PGA Tour to pass through the US$2 million earnings mark. She earned $2,105,868. In addition she set a new scoring average of 69.42 – .01 better than the previous best by Karrie Webb. To break both records Sörenstam had to shoot 65 in the last round of the last event of the year and did just that.

Japan LPGA Tour

Players are of Japanese nationality unless stated

Results 2000

Itoen Ladies	Great Island Club, Chiba	Ok Hee Ku (Kor)	208 (-8)
Daiohseishi Elleair Open	Elleair, Kagawa	Ok Hee Ku (Kor)	212 (-4)
JLPGA Tour Championship	Hibiscus, Miyazaki	Aki Nakano	282 (-6)

Final Ranking 2000

1	Yuri Fudoh	¥120 443 924	6	Kaori Higo	52 834 487
2	Aki Nakano	73 622 445	7	Midori Yoneyama	51 711 737
3	Ok Hee Ku (Kor)	69 281 930	8	Kasumi Fujii	50 398 766
4	Aki Takamura	65 081 375	9	Woo Soon Ko (Kor)	46 936 202
5	Junko Yasui	59 336 310	10	Yu-Chen Huang	37 879 721

Results 2001

Daikin Orchid Ladies	Ryukyu, Okinawa	Yuri Fudoh	213 (-3)
Saishunkan Ladies	Kumamoto Kuukou	Kaori Higo	216 (even)
Nasu Ogawa Ladies	Nasu Ogawa, Tochigi	Michie Ohba	209 (-7)
Katokichi Queens	Yashima	Chieko Amanuma	208 (-8)
Nichirei Cup World Ladies	Tokyo Yomiuri CC	Karrie Webb (Aus)	278 (-10)
Varnal Ladies	Fukuoka Century	Ikuyo Shiotani	216 (even)
Chukyo TV Bridgestone Open	Chukyo	Michie Ohba	207 (-9)
Kosaido Ladies Cup	Kosaido CC, Chiba	Aki Takamura	212 (-4)
Resort Trust Ladies	Grandee Naruto GC	Aki Takamura	209 (-7)
Suntory Ladies Open	Japan Memorial	Michiko Hattori	279 (-9)
Apita Circle K Sankus Ladies	Nakatsugawa, Gifu	Midori Yoneyama	205 (-11)
Friskie Osaka Ladies Open	Hanna, Osaka	Midori Yoneyama	211 (-5)
Toyo Suisan Ladies Hokkaido	Sapporo Kitahiroshima	Chieko Amanuma	211 (-5)
Taiheiyo Club Ladies	Sherwood Course, Oarai	Kaori Higo	204 (-12)
Golf 5 Ladies	Mizunami, Gifu	Hsiao-Thuan Ku	215 (-1)
Varnal Open	The Privilege GC	Yuri Fudoh	207 (-9)
NEC Karuizawa 72	Karuizawa 72, Nagano	Chieko Amanuma	207 (-9)
New Caterpillar Mitsubishi	Daihakone CC	Chieko Amanuma	212 (-4)
Yonex Ladies	Yonex, Teradomari	Yuri Fudoh	204 (-12)
Fuji Sankei Ladies Classic	Fujizakura, Yamanash	Miyuki Shimabukuro	214 (+1)
JLPGA Championship Konica Cup	Rope GC	Kumiko Hiyoshi	282 (-6)
Munsingwear Tokai Classic	Ryosen, Mie	Kumiko Hiyoshi	282 (-6)
Miyagi TV Cup Dunlop Open	Rainbow Hills, Tomiya	Toshimi Kimura	213 (-3)
Japan Women's Open	Muroran	Miyuki Shimabukuro	302 (+14)
Sankyo Ladies Open	Akagi GC	Hiroko Yamaguchi	207 (-9)
Fujitsu Ladies	Tokyo 700, Chiba	Yuri Fudoh	203 (-13)
Chako-Higuchi Kibun Ladies Classic	Caledonian GC	Chickp Amanua	210 (-6)

Japan LPGA Tour Results *continued*

Cisco World Ladies Match Play	Sousei CC, Chiba	Annika Sörenstam (Swe)	
Mizuno Classic	Musashigaoka GC, Saitama	Annika Sörenstam (Swe)	203 (-13)
Tyco-ADT Championship	West Palm Beach, FL	*To be played*	
Itoen Ladies	Great Island C, Chiba	Laura Davies	267 (-9)
Elleair Ladies Open	Ehime Prefecture	Ok Hee Ku	(D)
Japan LPGA Championship (Iicoh Cup)	Miazaki	Aki Nakano	(D)

Latest Ranking 2001 (after Ito-En Ladies)

1	Yuri Fudoh	¥83 248 793	11	Woo Soon Ko	45 292 061
2	Chieko Amanuma	89 543 902	12	Yu Chen Huan	38 580 218
3	Kaori Higo	55 926 360	13	Fuki Kido	37 721 802
4	Toshimi Kumura	55 142 288	14	Ikuyo Shiotani	37 487 447
5	Miyuki Shimbukuro	54 417 916	15	Mineko Nasu	26 646 440
6	Kasumi Fujii	53 861 626	16	Midori Yonayama	35 946 988
7	Aki Takamura	51 524 004	17	Michiko Hattori	31 470 443
8	Kaori Harada	51 368 852	18	Ok Hee Ku	29 832 970
9	Michie Obba	49 566 162	19	Hiroko Yamaguchi	29 247 918
10	Ji Hee Lee	48 308 650	20	Junko Yasui	29 188 623

Two events had still to be played on the 2001 Japan LPGA circuit

Rules from 13-to-34

The first written Rules of Golf were drawn up in 1744 by the Gentleman Golfers at Leith, later to be known as the Honourable Company of Edinburgh Golfers. Ten years later they were adopted, with one minor change, by the Society of St Andrews Golfers which in 1834 became the Royal and Ancient Golf Club of St Andrews who 50 years later appointed the first Rules of Golf committee to ensure a uniform code was used throughout the world.

Today the R & A is recognised as the governing authority except in the United States, Canada and Mexico. The Royal Canadian Golf Association, which is affiliated to the R & A, legislates for Canada while the United States Golf Association is the legislative body for the United States and Mexico.

Although there were only 13 rules, originally witten on one piece of paper, the modern rule book includes 34, plus appendices and definitions.

For the complete Rules of Golf, see page 431.

International Team Events

Solheim Cup *(Home team names first)*

1990 *at Lake Nona, FL*
Result: USA 11½, Europe 4½
Captains: Kathy Whitworth (USA),
Mickey Walker (Europe)
First Day **– Foursomes**
Bradley & Lopez lost to Davies & Nicholas 2 and 1
Gerring & Mochrie beat Wright & Neumann 6 and 5
Sheehan & Jones beat Reid & Alfredsson 6 and 5
Daniel & King beat Johnson & de Lorenzi 5 and 4
Second Day **– Fourball**
Sheehan & Jones beat Johnson & de Lorenzi 2 and 1
Bradley & Lopez beat Reid & Alfredsson 2 and 1
King & Daniel beat Davies & Nicholas 4 and 3
Gerring & Mochrie lost to Neumann & Wright 4 and 2
Third Day **– Singles**
Cathy Gerring beat Helen Alfredsson 4 and 3
Rosie Jones lost to Laura Davies 3 and 2
Nancy Lopez beat Alison Nicholas 6 and 4
Betsy King halved with Pam Wright
Beth Daniel beat Liselotte Neumann 7 and 6
Patty Sheehan lost to Dale Reid 2 and 1
Dottie Mochrie beat Marie Laure de Lorenzi
  4 and 2
Pat Bradley beat Trish Johnson 8 and 7

1992 *at Dalmahoy*
Result: Europe 11½, USA 6½
Captains: Mickey Walker (Europe),
Kathy Whitworth (USA)
First Day **– Foursomes**
Davies & Nicholas beat King & Daniel 1 hole
Neumann & Alfredsson beat Bradley & Mochrie
  2 and 1
Descampe & Johnson lost to Ammaccapane & Mallon
  1 hole
Reid & Wright halved with Sheehan & Inkster
Second Day **– Fourball**
Davies & Nicholas beat Sheehan & Inkster 1 hole
Johnson & Descampe halved with Burton & Richard
Wright & Reid lost to Mallon & King 1 hole
Alfredsson & Neumann halved with Bradley & Mochrie
Third Day **– Singles**
Laura Davies beat Brandie Burton 4 and 2
Helen Alfredsson beat Danielle Ammaccapane 4 and 3
Trish Johnson beat Patty Sheehan 2 and 1
Alison Nicholas lost to Juli Inkster 3 and 2
Florence Descampe lost to Beth Daniel 2 and 1
Pam Wright beat Pat Bradley 4 and 3
Catrin Nilsmark beat Meg Mallon 3 and 2
Kitrina Douglas lost to Deb Richard 7 and 6
Liselotte Neumann beat Betsy King 2 and 1
Dale Reid beat Dottie Pepper Mochrie 3 and 2

1994 *at the Greenbrier, WA*
Result: USA 13, Europe 7
Captains: JoAnne Carner (USA),
Mickey Walker (Europe)
First Day **– Foursomes**
Burton & Mochrie beat 3 and 2
Daniel & Mallon lost to Nilsmark & Sörenstam 1 hole
Green & Robbins lost to Fairclough & Reid 2 and 1
Andrews & King lost to Davies & Nicholas 2 holes
Sheehan & Steinhauer beat Johnson & Wright
  2 holes
Second Day **– Fourball**
Burton & Mochrie beat Davies & Nicholas 2 and 1
Daniel & Mallon beat Nilsmark & Sörenstam
  6 and 5
Green & Robbins lost to Fairclough & Reid 4 and 3
Andrews & King beat Johnson & Wright 3 and 2
Sheehan & Steinhauer lost to Alfredsson & Neumann
  1 hole
Third Day **– Singles**
Betsy King lost to Helen Alfredsson 2 and 1
Dottie Pepper Mochrie beat Catrin Nilsmark 6 and 5
Beth Daniel beat Trish Johnson 1 hole
Kelly Robbins beat Lora Fairclough 4 and 2
Meg Mallon beat Pam Wright 1 hole
Patty Sheehan lost to Alison Nicholas 3 and 2
Brandie Burton beat Laura Davies 1 hole
Tammie Green beat Annika Sörenstam 3 and 2
Sherri Steinhauer beat Dale Reid 2 holes
Donna Andrews beat Liselotte Neumann 3 and 2

1996 *at St Pierre, Chepstow*
Result: USA 17, Europe 11
Captains: (USA), Mickey Walker (Europe)
First Day **– Foursomes**
Sörenstam & Nilsmark halved with Robbins &
  McGann
Davies & Nicholas lost to Sheehan & Jones 1 hole
de Lorenzi & Reid lost to Daniell & Skinner 1 hole
Alfredsson & Neumann lost to Pepper & Burton
  2 and 1
Fourball
Davies & Johnson beat Robbins & Bradley 6 and 5
Sörenstam & Marshall beat Skinner & Geddes 1 hole
Neumann & Nilsmark lost to Pepper & King 1 hole
Alfredsson & Nicholas halved with Mallon & Daniel
Second Day **– Foursomes**
Davies & Johnson beat Daniel & Skinner 4 and 3
Sörenstam & Nilsmark beat Pepper & Burton 1 hole
Neumann & Marshall halved with Mallon & Geddes
de Lorenzi & Alfredsson beat Robbins & McGann
  4 and 3

Solheim Cup *continued*

Fourball
Davies & Hackney beat Daniel & Skinner 6 and 5
Sörenstam & Johnson halved with McGann & Mallon
de Lorenzi & Morley lost to Robbins & King 2 and 1
Nilsmark & Neumann beat Sheehan & Geddes
  2 and 1

Third Day – **Singles**
Annika Sörenstam beat Pat Bradley 2 and 1
Kathryn Marshall lost to Val Skinner 2 and 1
Laura Davies lost to Michelle McGann 3 and 2
Liselotte Neumann halved with Beth Daniel
Lisa Hackney lost to Brandie Burton 1 hole
Trish Johnson lost to Dottie Pepper 3 and 2
Alison Nicholas halved with Kelly Robbins
Marie Laure de Lorenzi lost to Betsy King 6 and 4
Joanne Morley lost to Rosie Jones 5 and 4
Dale Reid lost to Jane Geddes 2 holes
Catrin Nilsmark lost to Patty Sheehan 2 and 1
Helen Alfredsson lost to Meg Mallon 4 and 2

1998 *at Muirfield Village, Dublin, OH*
Result: USA 16, Europe 12
Captains: Judy Rankin (USA),
  Pia Nilsson (Europe)

First Day – **Foursomes**
Pepper & Inkster beat Davies & Johnson 3 and 1
Mallon & Burton beat Alfredsson & Nicholas 3 and 1
Robbins & Hurst beat Hackney & Neumann 1 hole
A Sörenstam & Matthew beat Andrews & Green
  3 and 2

Fourball
King & Johnson halved with Davies & C Sörenstam
Hurst & Jones beat Hackney & Gustafson 7 and 5
Robbins & Steinhauer lost to Alfredsson & de Lorenzi
  2 and 1
Pepper & Burton beat A Sörenstam & Nilsmark
  2 holes

Second Day – **Foursomes**
Andrews & Steinhauer beat A Sörenstam & Matthew
  3 and 2
Mallon & Burton lost to Davies & C Sörenstam
  3 and 2
Pepper & Inkster beat Alfredsson & de Lorenzi 1 hole
Robbins & Hurst beat Neumann & Nilsmark 1 hole

Fourball
King & Jones lost to A Sörenstam & Nilsmark 5 and 3
Johnson & Green lost to Davies & Hackney 2 holes
Andrews & Steinhauer beat Alfredsson & de Lorenzi
  4 and 3
Mallon & Inkster beat Neumann & C Sörenstam
  2 and 1

Third Day – **Singles**
Pat Hurst lost to Laura Davies 1 hole
Juli Inkster lost to Helen Alfredsson 2 and 1
Donna Andrews lost to Annika Sörenstam 2 and 1
Brandie Burton lost to Liselotte Neumann 1 hole
Dottie Pepper beat Trish Johnson 3 and 2
Kelly Robbins beat Charlotta Sörenstam 2 and 1
Chris Johnson lost to Marie Laure de Lorenzi 1 hole
Rosie Jones beat Catrin Nilsmark 6 and 4
Tammie Green beat Alison Nicholas 1 hole
Sherri Steinhauer beat Catriona Matthew 3 and 2
Betsy King lost to Lisa Hackney 6 and 5
Meg Mallon halved with Sophie Gustafson

2000 *at Loch Lomond*
Result: Europe 14½, USA 11½
Captains: Dale Reid (Europe),
Pat Bradley (USA)

First Day – **Foursomes**
Davies & Nicholas beat Pepper & Inkster 4 and 3
Johnson & Gustafson beat Robbins & Hurst 3 and 2
Nilsmark & Koch beat Burton & Iverson 2 and 1
Sörenstam & Moodie beat Mallon & Daniel 1 hole

Foursomes
Davies & Nicholas lost to Iverson & Jones 6 and 5
Johnson & Gustafson halved with Inkster & Steinhauer
Neumann & Alfredsson lost to Robbins & Hurst
  2 holes
Moodie & Sörenstam beat Mallon & Daniel 1 hole

Second Day – **Fourball**
Nilsmark & Koch beat Scranton & Redman 2 and 1
Neumann & Meunier Labouc halved with Pepper &
  Burton
Davies & Carriedo halved with Mallon & Daniel
Sörenstam & Moodie lost to Hurst & Robbins
  2 and 1
Johnson & Gustafson beat Jones & Iverson 3 and 2
Nicholas & Alfredsson beat Inkster & Steinhauer
  3 and 2

Third Day – **Singles**
Annika Sörenstam lost to Juli Inkster 5 and 4
Sophie Gustafson lost to Brandie Burton 4 and 3
Helen Alfredsson beat Beth Daniel 4 and 3
Trish Johnson lost to Dottie Pepper 2 and 1
Laura Davies lost to Kelly Robbins 3 and 2
Liselotte Neumann halved with Pat Hurst
Alison Nicholas halved with Sherri Steinhauer
Patricia Meunier Labouc lost to Meg Mallon 1 hole
Catrin Nilsmark beat Rosie Jones 1 hole
Raquel Carriedo lost to Becky Iverson 3 and 2
Carin Koch beat Michele Redman 2 and 1
Janice Moodie beat Nancy Scranton 1 hole

Solheim Cup – INDIVIDUAL RECORDS

Brackets indicate non-playing captain

Europe

Name		Year	Played	Won	Lost	Halved
Helen Alfredsson	Swe	1990-92-94-96-98-2000	21	9	10	2
Requel Carriedo	Esp	2000	2	0	1	1
Laura Davies	Eng	1990-92-94-96-98-2000	23	13	8	2
Florence Descampe	Bel	1992	3	0	2	1
Kitrina Douglas	Eng	1992	1	0	1	0
Lora Fairclough	Eng	1994	3	2	1	0
Sophie Gustafson	Swe	1998-2000	6	2	2	2
Lisa Hackney	Eng	1996-98	6	3	3	0
Trish Johnson	Eng	1990-92-94-96-98-2000	19	5	11	3
Carin Koch	Swe	2000	3	3	0	0
Marie Laure de Lorenzi	Fra	1990-96-98	11	3	8	0
Kathryn Marshall	Sco	1996	3	1	1	1
Catriona Matthew	Sco	1998	3	1	2	0
Patricia Meunier Lebouc	Fra	2000	2	0	1	1
Janice Moodie	Sco	2000	4	3	1	0
Joanne Morley	Eng	1996	2	0	2	0
Liselotte Neumann	Swe	1990-92-94-96-98-2000	21	6	10	5
Alison Nicholas	Eng	1990-92-94-96-98-2000	18	7	8	3
Catrin Nilsmark	Swe	1992-94-96-98-2000	16	8	7	1
Pia Nilsson	Swe	(1998)	0	0	0	0
Dale Reid	Sco	1990-92-94-96-(2000)	11	4	6	1
Annika Sörenstam	Swe	1994-96-98-2000	17	9	6	2
Charlotta Sörenstam	Swe	1998	4	1	2	1
Mickey Walker	Eng	(1990)-(92)-(94)-(96)	0	0	0	0
Pam Wright	Sco	1990-92-94	6	1	4	1

United States

Name	Year	Played	Won	Lost	Halved
Danielle Ammaccapane	1992	2	1	1	0
Donna Andrews	1994-98	7	4	3	0
Pat Bradley	1990-92-96-(2000)	8	2	5	1
Brandie Burton	1992-94-96-98-2000	14	8	4	2
Jo Anne Carner	(1994)	0	0	0	0
Beth Daniel	1990-92-94-96-2000	16	7	6	3
Jane Geddes	1996	4	1	2	1
Cathy Gerring	1990	3	2	1	0
Tammie Green	1994-98	6	2	4	0
Pat Hurst	1998-2000	8	5	2	1
Juli Inkster	1992-98-2000	11	5	4	2
Becky Iverson	2000	4	2	2	0
Chris Johnson	1998	3	0	2	1
Rosie Jones	1990-96-98-2000	12	7	5	0
Betsy King	1990-92-94-96-98	15	7	6	2
Nancy Lopez	1990	3	2	1	0
Michelle McGann	1996	4	1	1	2
Meg Mallon	1992-94-96-98-2000	18	8	5	5
Alice Miller	(1992)*	0	0	0	0
Dottie Pepper	1990-92-94-96-98-2000	20	13	5	2
Judy Rankin	(1996)-(98)	0	0	0	0
Michele Redman	2000	2	0	2	0
Deb Richard	1992	2	1	0	1
Kelly Robbins	1994-96-98-2000	16	8	6	2
Nancy Scranton	2000	2	0	2	0
Patty Sheehan	1990-92-94-96	13	5	7	1
Val Skinner	1996	4	2	2	0
Sherri Steinhauer	1994-98-2000	10	5	1	2
Kathy Whitworth	(1990)-(92)*	0	0	0	0

Professional Women's Overseas Championships

Australian Ladies Masters

1998	K Webb	2000	K Webb
1999	K Webb	2001	K Webb

AAMI Australian Women's Open

1995	L Neumann	1999	*Not played*
1996	C Matthew	2000	K Webb
1997	J Crafter	2001	S Gustafson
1998	M McGuire		

Austrian Ladies Open

1994	F Descampe	1998	L Brooky
1995	A Sorenstam	1999	M Arrutti
1996	M Koch	2000	P Meunier-Lebouc
1997	*Not played*	2001	*Not played*

French Ladies Open

1992	*Not played*	1997	K Lunn
1993	*Not played*	1998	*Not played*
1994	J Forbes	1999	T Johnson
1995	L Kreutz	2000	P Meunier-Lebouc
1996	L Rolner	2001	S Pettersen

German Ladies Open
(Became Hennessy Cup in 1993)

1992	*Not played*	1997	L Davies
1993	L Neumann	1998	L Fairclough
1994	L Neumann	1999	A-M Knight
1995	A Sorenstam	2000	J Morley
1996	H Alfredsson	2001	K Icher

Italian Ladies Open

1992	L Davies	1997	V Van Ryckegham
1993	A Arruti	1998	*Not played*
1994	C Dibnah	1999	S Head
1995	D Booker	2000	S Gustafson
1996	L Davies	2001	P Marti

Malaysian Ladies Open

1992	C Nishida	1997	P Rigby-Jinglov
1993	S Prosser	1998	S Mendiburu
1994	J-S Won	1999	J Head
1995	C Dibnah	2000	Kang Soo Yun
1996	C Dibnah	2001	*Not played*

Swedish Ladies Open

1992	C Hjalmarsson	1997	C Nilsmark
1993	M Hjörth	1998	H Koch
1994	L Neumann	1999	F Hansson (am)
1995	M Löjdahl	2000	M Burström
1996	A Berg	2001	*Not played*

South African Ladies Masters

2001   S Head

Taiwan Ladies

2001   R Carriedo

US LPGA Tour

Feb 28–Mar 2	LFGA Takefuji Classic, Waikoloa Beach Resort, Big Island, HI
Mar 14–17	PING Banner Health, Moon Valley Country Club, Phoenix, AZ
Mar 21–24	Welch's/Circle K Championship, Randolph North Golf Course, Tucson, AZ
Mar 28–31	**Kraft Nabisco Championship,** Mission Hills Country Club, Dinah Shore Tournament Course, Rancho Mirage, CA
Apr 5–7	The Office Depot Championship, El Caballero Country Club, Tarzana, CA
Apr 18–21	Longs Drugs Challenge, Twelve Bridges Golf Club, Lincoln, CA
Apr 25–28	TBD
May 3–5	Chick-fil-A Charity Championship, Eagle's Landing Country Club, Stockbridge, GA
May 9–12	Aerus Electrolux USA Championship, Legends Club of Tennessee, Franklin, TN
May 16–19	Asahi Ryokuken International Championship at Mount Vintage, Mount Vintage Plantation Golf Club, North Augusta, SC
May 23–26	LPGA Corning Classic, Corning Country Club, Corning, NY
May 31–Jun 2	Kellog Keebler Classic, Stonebridge Country Club, Aurora, IL
Jun 6–9	**McDonald's LPGA Championship,** Dupont Country Club, Wilmington, DE
Jun 12–15	Evian Masters, Evian Masters Golf Club, Evian-les-Bains, France
Jun 20–23	Wegmans Rochester LPGA, Locust Hill Country Club, Pinsford, NY
Jun 28–30	ShopRite LFGA Classic, Marriott Seaview Resort, Bay Course, Galloway, NJ
Jul 4–7	**U.S. Women's Open,** Prairie Dunes Country Club, Hutchinson, KS
Jul 11–14	Jamie Farr Kroger Classic, Highland Meadows Golf Club, Sylvania, OH
Jul 19–21	Giant Eagle LPGA Classic, Squaw Creek Country Club, Vienna, OH
Jul 25–28	Sybase Big Apple Classic, Wykegyl Country Club, New Rochelle, NY
Jul 29–Aug 4	Wendy's Championship for Children at Tartan Fields, Tartan Fields Golf Club, Dublin, OH
Aug 8–11	**Weetabix Women's British Open,** Turnberry Golf Club, Ayrshire, Scotland
Aug 15–18	Bank of Montreal Canadian Women's Open, Summerlea Golf and Country Club, Vaudreuil-Dorian, Quebec, Canada
Aug 22–25	First Union Betsy King Classic, Berkleigh Country Club, Kutztown, PA
Aug 29–Sep 1	State Farm Classic, The Rail Golf Course, Springfield, IL
Sep 6–8	Williams Championship, Tulsa Country Club, Tulsa, OK
Sep 13–15	Safeway Classic, Columbia Edgewater Country Club, Portland, OR
Sep 20–22	**The Solheim Cup,** Interlachen Country Club, Edina, MN
Sep 26–29	TBD
Oct 3–6	Samsung World Championship, Hiddenbrooke Golf Club, Vallejo, CA
Oct 10–13	TBD
Oct 25–27	Sports Today CJ Nine Bridges Classic, Nine Bridges Golf Club, Villa & Spa, Jeju Island, Korea
Oct 31–Nov 3	CISCO World Ladies Match Play Championship, TBD, Japan
Nov 8–10	Mizimo Classic, TBD, Japan
Nov 16–17	Hyundai Team Matches, Monarch Beach Golf Links, Dana Point, CA
Nov 21–24	Tyco/ADT Championship, Trump International Golf Club, West Palm Beach, FL
Dec 21–22	Wendy's Three-Tour Challenge, Lake Las Vegas Resort, Henderson, NV

Other Tournament Schedules can be found on pp.48–52

PART IV

Men's Amateur

PART IV

Men's Amateur Tournaments

National and International Championships

Amateur Championship

Year	Winner	Runner-up	Venue	By	Ent
1885	A MacFie	H Hutchinson	Hoylake, Royal Liverpool	7 and 6	44
1886	H Hutchinson	H Lamb	St Andrews	7 and 6	42
1887	H Hutchinson	J Ball	Hoylake, Royal Liverpool	1 hole	33
1888	J Ball	J Laidlay	Prestwick	5 and 4	38
1889	J Laidlay	L Melville	St Andrews	2 and 1	40
1890	J Ball	J Laidlay	Hoylake, Royal Liverpool	4 and 3	44
1891	J Laidlay	H Hilton	St Andrews	20th hole	50
1892	J Ball	H Hilton	Sandwich, Royal St George's	3 and 1	45
1893	P Anderson	J Laidlay	Prestwick	1 hole	44
1894	J Ball	S Fergusson	Hoylake, Royal Liverpool	1 hole	64
1895	L Melville	J Ball	St Andrews	19th hole	68
From 1896 36 holes played					
1896	F Tait	H Hilton	Sandwich, Royal St George's	8 and 7	64
1897	A Allan	J Robb	Muirfield	4 and 2	74
1898	F Tait	S Fergusson	Hoylake, Royal Liverpool	7 and 5	77
1899	J Ball	F Tait	Prestwick	37th hole	101
1900	H Hilton	J Robb	Sandwich, Royal St George's	8 and 7	68
1901	H Hilton	J Low	St Andrews	1 hole	116
1902	C Hutchings	S Fry	Hoylake, Royal Liverpool	1 hole	114
1903	R Maxwell	H Hutchinson	Muirfield	7 and 5	142
1904	W Travis (USA)	E Blackwell	Sandwich, Royal St George's	4 and 3	104
1905	A Barry	Hon O Scott	Prestwick	3 and 2	148
1906	J Robb	C Lingen	Hoylake, Royal Liverpool	4 and 3	166
1907	J Ball	C Palmer	St Andrews	6 and 4	200
1908	E Lassen	H Taylor	Sandwich, Royal St George's	7 and 6	197
1909	R Maxwell	Capt C Hutchison	Muirfield	1 hole	170
1910	J Ball	C Aylmer	Hoylake, Royal Liverpool	10 and 9	160
1911	H Hilton	E Lassen	Prestwick	4 and 3	146
1912	J Ball	A Mitchell	Westward Ho!, Royal North Devon	38th hole	134
1913	H Hilton	R Harris	St Andrews	6 and 5	198
1914	J Jenkins	C Hezlet	Sandwich, Royal St George's	3 and 2	232
1915–19 No Championship owing to the Great War					
1920	C Tolley	R Gardner (USA)	Muirfield	37th hole	165
1921	W Hunter	A Graham	Hoylake, Royal Liverpool	12 and 11	223
1922	E Holderness	J Caven	Prestwick	1 hole	252
1923	R Wethered	R Harris	Deal, Royal Cinque Ports	7 and 6	209
1924	E Holderness	E Storey	St Andrews	3 and 2	201
1925	R Harris	K Fradgley	Westward Ho!, Royal North Devon	13 and 12	151
1926	J Sweetser (USA)	A Simpson	Muirfield	6 and 5	216
1927	Dr W Tweddell	D Landale	Hoylake, Royal Liverpool	7 and 6	197
1928	T Perkins	R Wethered	Prestwick	6 and 4	220
1929	C Tolley	J Smith	Sandwich, Royal St George's	4 and 3	253
1930	R Jones (USA)	R Wethered	St Andrews	7 and 6	271
1931	E Smith	J De Forest	Westward Ho!, Royal North Devon	1 hole	171
1932	J De Forest	E Fiddian	Muirfield	3 and 1	235
1933	Hon M Scott	T Bourn	Hoylake, Royal Liverpool	4 and 3	269
1934	W Lawson Little (USA)	J Wallace	Prestwick	14 and 13	225
1935	W Lawson Little (USA)	Dr W Tweddell	R Lytham and St Annes	1 hole	232
1936	H Thomson	J Ferrier (Aus)	St Andrews	2 holes	283
1937	R Sweeney jr (USA)	L Munn	Sandwich, Royal St George's	3 and 2	223
1938	C Yates (USA)	R Ewing	Troon	3 and 2	241
1939	A Kyle	A Duncan	Hoylake, Royal Liverpool	2 and 1	167
1940–45 Suspended during Second World War					
1946	J Bruen	R Sweeny (USA)	Birkdale	4 and 3	263
1947	W Turnesa (USA)	R Chapman (USA)	Carnoustie	3 and 2	200

Year	Winner	Runner-up	Venue	By	Ent
1948	F Stranahan (USA)	C Stowe	Sandwich, Royal St George's	5 and 4	168
1949	S McCready	W Turnesa (USA)	Portmarnock	2 and 1	204
1950	F Stranahan (USA)	R Chapman (USA)	St Andrews	8 and 6	324
1951	R Chapman (USA)	C Coe (USA)	Royal Porthcawl	5 and 4	192
1952	E Ward (USA)	F Stranahan (USA)	Prestwick	6 and 5	286
1953	J Carr	E Harvie Ward (USA)	Hoylake, Royal Liverpool	2 holes	279
1954	D Bachli (Aus)	W Campbell (USA)	Muirfield	2 and 1	286
1955	J Conrad (USA)	A Slater	Royal Lytham and St Annes	3 and 2	240
1956	J Beharrell	L Taylor	Troon	5 and 4	200
1957	R Reid Jack	H Ridgley (USA)	Formby	2 and 1	200
In 1956 and 1957 the Quarter Finals, Semi-Finals and Final were played over 36 holes					
1958	J Carr	A Thirlwell	St Andrews	3 and 2	488
In 1958, Semi-Finals and Final only were played over 36 holes					
1959	D Beman (USA)	W Hyndman (USA)	Sandwich, Royal St George's	3 and 2	362
1960	J Carr	R Cochran (USA)	Royal Portrush	8 and 7	183
1961	MF Bonallack	J Walker	Turnberry	6 and 4	250
1962	R Davies (USA)	J Povall	Hoylake, Royal Liverpool	1 hole	256
1963	M Lunt	J Blackwell	St Andrews	2 and 1	256
1964	G Clark	M Lunt	Ganton	39th hole	220
1965	MF Bonallack	C Clark	Royal Porthcawl	2 and 1	176
1966	R Cole (RSA)	R Shade	Carnoustie (18 holes)	3 and 2	206
1967	R Dickson (USA)	R Cerrudo (USA)	Formby	2 and 1	
1968	MF Bonallack	J Carr	Royal Troon	7 and 6	249
1969	MF Bonallack	W Hyndman (USA)	Hoylake, Royal Liverpool	3 and 2	245
1970	MF Bonallack	W Hyndman (USA)	Newcastle, Royal Co Down	8 and 7	256
1971	S Melnyk (USA)	J Simons (USA)	Carnoustie	3 and 2	256
1972	T Homer	A Thirlwell	Sandwich, Royal St George's	4 and 3	253
1973	R Siderowf (USA)	P Moody	Royal Porthcawl	5 and 3	222
1974	T Homer	J Gabrielsen (USA)	Muirfield	2 holes	330
1975	M Giles (USA)	M James	Hoylake, Royal Liverpool	8 and 7	206
1976	R Siderowf (USA)	J Davies	St Andrews	37th hole	289
1977	P McEvoy	H Campbell	Ganton	5 and 4	235
1978	P McEvoy	P McKellar	Royal Troon	4 and 3	353
1979	J Sigel (USA)	S Hoch (USA)	Hillside	3 and 2	285
1980	D Evans	D Suddards (RSA)	Royal Porthcawl	4 and 3	265
1981	P Ploujoux (Fra)	J Hirsch (USA)	St Andrews	4 and 2	256
1982	M Thompson	A Stubbs	Deal, Royal Cinque Ports	4 and 3	245
Qualifying round introduced					
1983	P Parkin	J Holtgrieve (USA)	Turnberry	5 and 4	288
1984	JM Olazábal (Esp)	C Montgomerie	Formby	5 and 4	291
1985	G McGimpsey	G Homewood	Royal Dornoch	8 and 7	457
1986	D Curry	G Birtwell	Royal Lytham and St Annes	11 and 9	427
1987	P Mayo	P McEvoy	Prestwick	3 and 1	373
1988	C Hardin (Swe)	B Fouchee (RSA)	Royal Porthcawl	1 hole	391
1989	S Dodd	C Cassells	Royal Birkdale	5 and 3	378
1990	R Muntz (Ned)	A Macara	Muirfield	7 and 6	510
1991	G Wolstenholme	B May (USA)	Ganton	8 and 6	345
1992	S Dundas	B Dredge	Carnoustie	7 and 6	364
1993	I Pyman	P Page	Royal Portrush	37th hole	279
1994	L James	G Sherry	Nairn	2 and 1	288
1995	G Sherry	M Reynard	Hoylake, Royal Liverpool	7 and 6	288
1996	W Bladon	R Beames	Turnberry	1 hole	288
1997	C Watson	T Immelman (RSA)	Royal St Georges, Royal Cinque Ports	3 and 2	369
1998	S García (Esp)	C Williams	Muirfield	7 and 6	537
1999	G Storm	A Wainwright	Royal County Down, Kilkeel	7 and 6	433
2000	M Ilonen	C Reimbold	Royal Liverpool and Wallasey	2 and 1	376

106th Amateur Championship *at Prestwick & Kilmarnock (Barassie)*

288 entrants from 23 countries played in the 36-hole qualifying competition, 65 of whom qualified on 145 or better for the match play stage.
Leading Qualifier: 138 Nicholas Dougherty (Shaw Hill)

First Round
Andrew Webster (Aus) beat Craig Williams (Creigiau) 2 holes

Second Round
Stuart Davis (Kedleston Park) beat Nicholas Dougherty (Shaw Hill) at 20th
John Morgan (Clevedon) beat Craig Heap (East Kilbride) 4 and 3

Second Round *continued*
Barry Hume (Haggs Castle) beat Randy Haag (USA) 6 and 5
Graeme Clark (Doncaster) beat Geoffrey Harris (Reading) 1 hole
Zane Scotland (Woodcote Park) beat Stuart Wilson (Forfar) 5 and 4
Paul Bradshaw (Gainsborough) beat Graeme McDowell (Rathmore) 2 holes

Amateur Championship *continued*

Second Round *continued*
Nicky Bell (Carlisle) beat Scott Godfrey (St Enodoc) 1 hole
Martin Wiegele (Aut) beat Ryan Grant (USA) 3 and 2

Ian Campbell (Marlborough) beat Gareth Paddison (NZ) 2 and 1
Tim Rice (Limerick) beat Jonathan Evans (Guildford) 4 and 3
Gary Birch (Ger) beat Jack Doherty (Vale of Glamorgan) 1 hole
Lee Corfield (Burnham & Berrow) beat Clemens Conrad-Prader (Aut) 4 and 3
Gareth Maybin (Ballyclare) beat David Inglis (Glencorse) 2 holes
Scott Strange (Aus) beat Richard Walker (Walton Hall) 1 hole
Richard Sterne (RSA) beat Rafael Cabrera (Esp) 6 and 5
John Pitt (USA) beat Inder Van Weerelt (Ned) 1 hole

Mikko Korhonen (Fin) beat Michael Kanski (Hesketh) 2 and 1
David Skinns (Lincoln) beat Dean Lambert (RSA) 6 and 5
Daniel Wardrop (Didsbury) beat Nathan Kent (Aus) at 22nd
Michael Hoey (Shandon Park) beat Niklas Bruzelius (Swe) at 24th
Brian Adam (Ratho Park) beat Marcus Fraser (Aus) 2 and 1
Kyron Sullivan (Brynhill) beat Ari Savolainen (Fin) 5 and 4
Matthew Griffiths (Woodlake Park) beat François Delamontagne (Fra) 1 hole
Steven O'Hara (Colville Park) beat Erik Herberth (USA) 4 and 2

Gavin Lawrie (Prestwick St Nicholas) beat Joel Hendry (Elgin) 1 hole
Gary Wolstenholme (Kilworth Springs) beat Andrea Romano (Ita) 3 and 2
Jonathan King (Cardross) beat Jody Fanagan (Milltown) 3 and 2
Guido Van Der Valk (Ned) beat Richard Caldwell (Sunningdale) 1 hole
Simon Young (Seascale) beat Eric Ramsay (Carnoustie) 2 and 1

Second Round *continued*
Simon Mackenzie (West Linton) beat Craig Watson (East Renfrewshire) 3 and 1
David Dixon (Enmore Park) beat Marc Warren (East Kilbride) 2 and 1
Andrew Webster (Aus) beat Adam Frayne (St Mellion) 1 hole

Third Round
Davis beat Morgan 2 and 1
Clark beat Hume 2 holes
Bradshaw beat Scotland 2 and 1
Bell beat Wiegele at 19th
Campbell beat Rice 1 hole
Corfield beat Birch at 19th
Strange beat Maybin at 20th
Sterne beat Pitt 5 and 4
Skinns beat Korhonen 5 and 4
Hoey beat Wardrop 2 and 1
Sullivan beat Adam 2 and 1
O'Hara beat Griffiths 4 and 3
Wolstenholme beat Lawrie 3 and 2
King beat Van Der Valk 3 and 2
Mackenzie beat Young 1 hole
Dixon beat Webster 4 and 2

Fourth Round
Davis beat Clark 2 and 1
Bradshaw beat Bell at 20th
Campbell beat Corfield 1 hole
Strange beat Sterne 1 hole
Hoey beat Skinns 1 hole
O'Hara beat Sullivan 2 and 1
Wolstenholme beat King 4 and 3
Mackenzie beat Dixon 3 and 2

Quarter Finals
Davis beat Bradshaw 3 and 2
Campbell beat Strange 5 and 4
Hoey beat O'Hara 3 and 2
Mackenzie beat Wolstenholme 3 and 2

Semi-Finals
Campbell beat Davis at 20th
Hoey beat Mackenzie at 25th

Final
Michael Hoey (Shandon Park) beat Ian Campbell (Marlborough) 1 hole

British Seniors' Open Amateur Championship

1969	R Pattinson	Formby	154	1979	RJ White	Harlech, R St David's	226
1970	K Bamber	Prestwick	150	1980	JM Cannon	Prestwick St Nicholas	218
1971	GH Pickard	Royal Cinque Ports;		1981	T Branton	Hoylake, R Liverpool	227
		Royal St George's	150	1982	RL Glading	Blairgowrie	218
1972	TC Hartley	St Andrews	147	1983	AJ Swann (USA)	Walton Heath	222
1973	JT Jones	Longniddry	142	1984	JC Owens (USA)	Western Gailes	222
1974	MA Ivor-Jones	Moortown	149	1985	D Morey (USA)	Hesketh	223
1975	HJ Roberts	Turnberry	138	1986	AN Sturrock	Panmure	229
1976	WM Crichton	Berkshire	149	1987	B Soyars (USA)	Royal Cinque Ports	226
1977	Dr TE Donaldson	Panmure	228	1988	CW Green	Royal Burgess	221
1978	RJ White	Formby	225	1989	CW Green	Moortown, Alwoodley	226

1990	CW Green	The Berkshire	207
1991	CW Green	Prestwick	219
1992	C Hartland	Purdis Heath	221
1993	CW Green	Royal Aberdeen	150
1994	CW Green	Formby,	
		Southport & Ainsdale	223
1995	G Steel	Hankley Common	218

1996	J Hirsch	Blairgowrie	210
1997	G Bradley (USA)	Sherwood Forest	216
1998	D Lane	Western Gailes/	
		Glasgow Gailes	221
1999	W Shean (USA)	Frilford Heath	219
2000	J Hirsch (USA)	Gullane	218

2001 *at Royal Portrush*

1	Kemp Richardson (USA)	71-73-73—217
2	David Carroll (USA)	77-70-71—218
3	Joel Hirsch (USA)	75-68-76—219

British Mid-Amateur Championship

1995	GP Wolstenholme	S Vale	Sunningdale
1996	GP Wolstenholme	G Steel	Hillside, Lancs
1997	S Philipson	G Thomson	Prestwick
1998	GP Wolstenholme	S Twynholm	Ganton
1999	J Kemp	S East	Walton Heath
2000	A Farmer	J Kemp	Royal Troon

2001 *at Royal Troon*

Quarter Finals

Hugh Hamilton (Seaton Carew) beat Danny
Dantzler (USA) 7 and 5

Stephen East (Moortown) beat Sandy Twynholm
(Morpeth) 1 hole

James McGroarty (Dumbarton) beat Jay
Blumenfeld (USA) 3 and 2

Ian Mackenzie (Hallamshire) beat Steven
Barwick (East Berkshire) 2 holes

Semi-Finals

East beat Hamilton 6 and 4

McGroarty beat Mackenzie 1 hole

Final

Stephen East beat James McGroarty
6 and 5

English Amateur Championship

1925	TF Ellison	S Robinson	Royal Liverpool	1 hole
1926	TF Ellison	Sq Ldr CH Hayward	Walton Heath	6 and 4
1927	TP Perkins	JB Beddard	Little Aston	2 and 1
1928	JA Stout	TP Perkins	R Lytham and St Annes	3 and 2
1929	W Sutton	EB Tipping	Northumberland	3 and 2
1930	TA Bourn	CE Hardman	Burnham & Berrow	3 and 2
1931	LG Crawley	W Sutton	Hunstanton	1 hole
1932	EW Fiddian	AS Bradshaw	Royal St George's	1 hole
1933	J Woollam	TA Bourn	Ganton	4 and 3
1934	S Lunt	LG Crawley	Formby	37th hole
1935	J Woollam	EW Fiddian	Hollinwell	2 and 1
1936	HG Bentley	JDA Langley	Royal Cinque Ports	5 and 4
1937	JJ Pennink	LG Crawley	Saunton	6 and 5
1938	JJ Pennink	SE Banks	Moortown	2 and 1
1939	AL Bentley	W Sutton	Royal Birkdale	5 and 4
1946	IR Patey	K Thom	Mid-Surrey	5 and 4
1947	GH Micklem	C Stow	Ganton	1 hole
1948	AGB Helm	HJR Roberts	Little Aston	2 and 1
1949	RJ White	C Stowe	Formby	5 and 4
1950	JDA Langley	IR Patey	Royal Cinque Ports	1 hole
1951	GP Roberts	H Bennett	Hunstanton	39th hole
1952	E Millward	TJ Shorrock	Burnham and Berrow	2 holes
1953	GH Micklem	RJ White	Royal Birkdale	2 and 1
1954	A Thirlwell	HG Bentley	Royal St George's	2 and 1
1955	A Thirlwell	M Burgess	Ganton	7 and 6
1956	GB Wolstenholme	H Bennett	R Lytham and St Annes	1 hole
1957	A Walker	G Whitehead	Royal Liverpool	4 and 3
1958	DN Sewell	DA Procter	Walton Heath	8 and 7
1959	GB Wolstenholme	MF Bonallack	Formby	1 hole
1960	DN Sewell	MJ Christmas	Hunstanton	41st hole
1961	I Caldwell	GJ Clark	Wentworth	37th hole
1962	MF Bonallack	MSR Lunt	Moortown	2 and 1
1963	MF Bonallack	A Thirlwell	Burnham and Berrow	4 and 3
1964	Dr D Marsh	R Foster	Hollinwell	1 hole

English Amateur Championship *continued*

1965	MF Bonallack	CA Clark	The Berkshire	3 and 2
1966	MSR Lunt	DJ Millensted	R Lytham and St Annes	3 and 2
1967	MF Bonallack	GE Hyde	Woodhall Spa	4 and 2
1968	MF Bonallack	PD Kelley	Ganton	12 and 11
1969	JH Cook	P Dawson	Royal St George's	6 and 4
1970	Dr D Marsh	SG Birtwell	R Birkdale	6 and 4
1971	W Humphreys	JC Davies	Burnham and Berrow	9 and 8
1972	H Ashby	R Revell	Northumberland	5 and 4
1973	H Ashby	SC Mason	Formby	5 and 4
1974	M James	JA Watts	Woodhall Spa	6 and 5
1975	N Faldo	D Eccleston	Royal Lytham and St Annes	6 and 4
1976	P Deeble	JC Davies	Ganton	3 and 1
1977	TR Shingler	J Mayell	Walton Heath	4 and 3
1978	P Downes	P Hoad	Royal Birkdale	1 hole
1979	R Chapman	A Carman	Royal St George's	6 and 5
1980	P Deeble	P McEvoy	Moortown	4 and 3
1981	D Blakeman	A Stubbs	Burnham & Berrow	3 and 1
1982	A Oldcorn	I Bradshaw	Royal Liverpool	4 and 3
1983	G Laurence	A Brewer	Wentworth	7 and 6
1984	D Gilford	M Gerrard	Woodhall Spa	4 and 3
1985	R Winchester	P Robinson	Little Aston	1 hole
1986	J Langmead	B White	Hillside	2 and 1
1987	K Weeks	R Eggo	Frilford Heath	37th hole
1988	R Claydon	D Curry	R Birkdale	38th hole
1989	S Richardson	R Eggo	Royal St George's	2 and 1
1990	I Garbutt	G Evans	Woodhall Spa	8 and 7
1991	R Willison	M Pullan	Formby	10 and 8
1992	S Cage	R Hutt	Royal Cinque Ports	3 and 2
1993	D Fisher	R Bland	Saunton	3 and 1
1994	M Foster	A Johnson	Moortown	8 and 7
1995	M Foster	S Jarman	Hunstanton	6 and 5
1996	S Webster	D Lucas	Hollinwell	6 and 4
1997	A Wainwright	P Rowe	Royal Liverpool	2 and 1
1998	M Sanders	S Gorry	Woodhall Spa	6 and 5
1999	P Casey	S Dyson	St Mellion	2 and 1
2000	P Casey	G Wolstenholme	Royal Lytham and St Annes	4 and 2

2001 *at Saunton*

Quarter Finals

Simon Robinson (Seaton Carew) beat
Andrew Smith (Enville) 4 and 3

Ricky Blaxill (Wanstead) beat Martin Young
(Brokenhurst Manor) 5 and 4

Ashley Siddle (Rossendale) beat Geoff Harris
(Reading) 1 hole

Scott Godfrey (St Enodoc) beat Ben
Cummings (Basingstoke) 4 and 3

Semi-Finals

Robinson beat Blaxill 3 and 2
Godfrey beat Siddle 7 and 6

Final

Scott Godfrey beat Simon Robinson 4 and 3

English Open Amateur Stroke Play Championship
(Brabazon Trophy) (Inaugurated 1957)

1957	D Sewell	Moortown	287	1970	R Foster	Little Aston	287
1958	AH Perowne	Birkdale	289	1971	MF Bonallack	Hillside	294
1959	D Sewell	Hollinwell	300	1972	PH Moody	Hoylake, R Liverpool	296
1960	GB Wolstenholme	Ganton	286	1973	R Revell	Hunstanton	294
1961	RDBM Shade	Hoylake, R Liverpool	284	1974	N Sundelson	Moortown	291
1962	A Slater	Woodhall Spa	209	1975	A Lyle	Hollinwell	298
1963	RDBM Shade	R Birkdale	306	1976	P Hedges	Saunton	294
1964	MF Bonallack	Deal, R Cinque Ports	290	1977	A Lyle	Royal Liverpool	293
1965T	CA Clark	Formby	289	1978	G Brand Jr	Woodhall Spa	289
	DJ Millensted			1979	D Long	Little Aston	291
	MJ Burgess			1980T	R Rafferty		
1966	PM Townsend	Hunstanton	282		P McEvoy	Hunstanton	293
1967	RDBM Shade	Saunton	299	1981	P Way	Hillside	292
1968	MF Bonallack	Walton Heath	210	1982	P Downes	Woburn	299
1969T	R Foster			1983	C Banks	Hollinwell	294
	MF Bonallack	Moortown	290	1984	M Davis	Deal, R Cinque Ports	286

1985T	R Roper			1992	I Garrido	Notts	280
	P Baker	Seaton Carew	296	1993	D Fisher	Stoneham	277
1986	R Kaplan	Sunningdale	286	1994	G Harris	Little Aston	280
1987	JG Robinson	Ganton	287	1995T	M Foster		
1988	R Eggo	Saunton	289		CS Edwards	Hillside	283
1989T	C Rivett			1996	P Fenton	R St Georges	297
	RN Roderick	Hoylake, R Liverpool	293	1997	D Park	Saunton	271
1990T	O Edmond			1998	P Hansson	Formby	287
	G Evans	Burnham and Berrow	287	1999	M Side	Moortown	279
1991T	G Evans			2000	J Lupprien (Ger)	Woodhall Spa	284
	M Pullan	Hunstanton	284				

2001 Brabazon Trophy *at Royal Birkdale*

1	Richard Walker (Walton Hall)	72-68-73-67—280
2	Steven O'Hara (Colville Park)	68-67-72-74—281
3	David Porter (Stoneham)	73-71-66-73—283

English Seniors' Amateur Championship

1981	CR Spalding	Copt Heath	152	1992	B Cawthray	Fulford	223
1982	JL Whitworth	Lindrick	152	1993	G Edwards	John O'Gaunt	221
1983	B Cawthray	Ross-on-Wye	154	1994T	G Steel	Parkstone,	
1984	RL Glading	Thetford	150		F Jones	Broadstone	72 (18)
1985	JR Marriott	Bristol and Clifton	153	1995	H Hopkinson	Copt Heath	226
1986	R Hiatt	Northants County	153	1996T	G Edwards		
1987	I Caldwell	North Hants	72 (18)		B Berney	West Lancs	224
1988	G Edwards	Bromborough	222	1997	D Lane	West Hill	215
1989	G Clark	West Sussex	212	1998	J Marks	Saunton	217
1990	N Paul	Enville, Bridgnorth	217	1999	D Lane	Shifnal	73 (18)
1991	W Williams	Gerrards Cross	217	2000	R Smethurst	Moor Park	212

2001 *at Sherwood Forest & Coxmoor*

1	Roy Smethurst (Crewe)	71-74-75—220
2	Andrew Morrison (Appleby)	74-70-79—223
3	Robert Turner (Wearside)	74-76-75—225

English Open Mid-Amateur Championship (Logan Trophy)

1988	P McEvoy	Little Aston	284	1995	C Banks	Seacroft	222
1989	A Mew	Moortown	290	1996	C Banks	Pannal	222
1990	A Mew	Wentworth	214	1997	C Banks	Stockport	211
1991	I Richardson	West Lancashire	223	1998	S East	Broadstone	216
1992	A Mew	King's Lynn	222	1999	S East	Little Aston	217
1993	R Godley	Southport & Ainsdale	210	2000	B Downing	Ponteland	208
1994T	I Richardson						
	A McLure	Trentham	217				

2001 *at Lindrick*

1	Stephen East (Moortown)	73-66-67—206
2	David Gibson (Cosby)	69-67-74—210
3	Martin Haddock (Wheatley)	69-73-69—211

English County Champions' Tournament

(Formerly President's Bowl)

1962T	G Edwards, Cheshire	1969	A Holmes, Herts
	A Thirwell, Northumberland	1970	M King, Berks, Bucks and Oxon
1963T	M Burgess, Sussex/R Foster, Yorks	1971	M Lee, Yorks
1964	M Attenborough, Kent	1972	P Berry, Glos
1965	M Lees, Lincs	1973	A Chandler, Lancs
1966	R Stephenson, Middx	1974T	G Hyde, Sussex/A Lyle, Shrops & Hereford
1967	P Benka, Surrey	1975	N Faldo, Herts
1968	G Hyde, Sussex	1976	R Brown, Devon

English County Champions' Tournament *continued*

1977	M Walls, Cumbria		1989	R Willison, Middlesex
1978	I Simpson, Notts		1990T	P Streeter, Lincs/R Sloman, Kent
1979	N Burch, Essex		1991	T Allen, Warwickshire
1980	D Lane, Berks, Bucks and Oxon		1992	L Westwood, Notts
1981	M Kelly, Yorks		1993	R Walker, Durham
1982	P Deeble, Northumberland		1994	GP Wolstenholme, Glos
1983	N Chesses, Warwickshire		1995	S Webster, Warwickshire
1984T	N Briggs, Herts/P McEvoy, Warwickshire		1996T	J Herbert, Leics/G Wolstenholme, Glos
1985	P Robinson, Herts		1997	J Herbert, Leicestershire & Rutland
1986	A Gelsthorpe, Yorks		1998	GP Wolstenholme, Leics
1987T	F George, Berks, Bucks & Oxon		1999	D Griffiths, Herts
	D Fay, Surrey		2000	P Bradshaw, Lincolnshire
1988	R Claydon, Cambridge			

2001 *at Woodhall Spa*

1	Gary Wolstenholme (Leics & Rutland)	68-71—139
2	Chris McDonnell (Northumberland)	69-72—141
3	Ricky Blaxill (Essex)	72-70—142

Irish Amateur Open Championship (Inaugurated 1892)

1946	JB Carr	AT Kyle	Portrush
1947	J Burke	JB Carr	Dollymount
1948	C Ewing	JB Carr	Newcastle
1949	WM O'Sullivan	BJ Scannell	Killarney
1950	JB Carr	C Ewing	Rosses Point
1951	C Ewing	JB Carr	Portmarnock
1952	NV Drew	CH Beamish	Portrush
1953	NV Drew	WM O'Sullivan	Killarney
1954	JB Carr	C Ewing	Dollymount
1955	JF Fitzgibbon	JW Hulme	Newcastle
1956	JB Carr	JR Mahon	Portmarnock
1957	JL Bamford	W Meharg	Portrush
1958	T Craddock	JW Hulme/JB Carr	Dollymount
1959	J Duncan	AG Gordon	Newcastle
1960–94 *No Championship*			
1995	P Harrington	G McGimpsey	Fota Island
1996	K Nolan	P Lawrie	Fota Island
1997	K Nolan	R Coughlan	Fota Island
1998	M Hoey	G Cullen	Royal Dublin
1999	G Cullen	J Fanagan	Royal Dublin
2000	N Fox	K Kearney	Royal Dublin

2001 *at Royal Dublin*

1	Richard McEvoy*(Thorpe Hall)	69-67-68-73—277 at 3rd extra hole
2	Michael Hoey (Shandon Park)	70-69-71-67—277
3	Richard Sterne (RSA)	68-69-71-70—278

Irish Amateur Close Championship (Inaugurated 1893)

1960	M Edwards	N Fogarty	Portstewart	6 and 5
1961	D Sheahan	J Brown	Rosses Point	5 and 4
1962	M Edwards	J Harrington	Baltray	42nd hole
1963	JB Carr	EC O'Brien	Killarney	2 and 1
1964	JB Carr	A McDade	Co Down	6 and 5
1965	JB Carr	T Craddock	Rosses Point	3 and 2
1966	D Sheahan	J Faith	Dollymount	3 and 2
1967	JB Carr	PD Flaherty	Lahinch	1 hole
1968	M O'Brien	F McCarroll	Portrush	2 and 1
1969	V Nevin	J O'Leary	Co Sligo	1 hole
1970	D Sheahan	M Bloom	Grange	2 holes
1971	P Kane	M O'Brien	Ballybunion	3 and 2
1972	K Stevenson	B Hoey	Co Down	2 and 1
1973	RKM Pollin	RM Staunton	Rosses Point	1 hole
1974	R Kane	M Gannon	Portmarnock	5 and 4

1975	MD O'Brien	JA Bryan	Cork	5 and 4
1976	D Brannigan	D O'Sullivan	Portrush	2 holes
1977	M Gannon	A Hayes	Westport	19th hole
1978	M Morris	T Cleary	Carlow	1 hole
1979	J Harrington	MA Gannon	Ballybunion	2 and 1
1980	R Rafferty	MJ Bannon	Co Down	8 and 7
1981	D Brannigan	E McMenamin	Co Sligo	19th hole
1982	P Walton	B Smyth	Woodbrook	7 and 6
1983	T Corridan	E Power	Killarney	2 holes
1984	CB Hoey	L McNamara	Malone	20th hole
1985	D O'Sullivan	D Branigan	Westport	1 hole
1986	J McHenry	P Rayfus	Dublin	4 and 3
1987	E Power	JP Fitzgerald	Tranmore	2 holes
1988	G McGimpsey	D Mulholland	Portrush	2 and 1
1989	P McGinley	N Goulding	Rosses Point	3 and 2
1990	D Clarke	P Harrington	Baltray	3 and 2
1991	G McNeill	N Goulding	Ballybunion	3 and 1
1992	G Murphy	JP Fitzgerald	Portstewart	2 and 1
1993	E Power	D Higgins	Enniscrone	3 and 2
1994	D Higgins	P Harrington	Portmarnock	20th hole
1995	P Harrington	D Coughlan	Lahinch	3 and 2
1996	P Lawrie	G McGimpsey	Royal Co Down	3 and 2
1997	K Kearney	P Lawrie	Fota Island	5 and 4
1998	E Power	B Omelia	The Island	1 hole
1999	C McMonagle	M Sinclair	Killarney	2 and 1
2000	G McDowell	A McCormick	Royal Portrush	7 and 6

2001 *at Co Sligo*

Leading Qualifier: G Maybin (Ballyclare) 137
Match Play: 64 qualified on 150 or better (3 out of 5 on 150)

Quarter Finals

S Browne (Hermitage) beat E O'Sullivan
(The Island) 1 hole
D Crowe (Dunmurray) beat P Martin
(Balmoral) 2 and 1
D Sugrue (Killarney) beat D Mortimer
(Connemara) at 19th
G McNeill (Waterford) beat S McTernan
(Co Sligo) 4 and 3

Semi-Finals

Browne beat Crowe 3 and 2
McNeill beat Sugrue 4 and 3

Final

G McNeill beat S Browne at 20th

Irish Seniors' Open Amateur Championship

1980	GN Fogarty	Galway	144	1991	C Hartland	Mullingar	147
1981	GN Fogarty	Bundoran	149	1992	C Hartland	Athlone	145
1982	J Murray	Douglas	141	1993	P Breen	Bangor	147
1983	F Sharpe	Courtown	153	1994	B Buckley	Tramore	151
1984	J Boston	Connemara	147	1995	B Hoey	Dundalk	151
1985	J Boston	Newcastle	155	1996	E Condren	Oughterard	148
1986	J Coey	Waterford	141	1997	B Wilson	The Knock	152
1987	J Murray	Castleroy	150	1998	J Harrington	Thurles	149
1988	WB Buckley	Westport	154	1999	A Lee	Thurles	150
1989	B McCrea	Royal Belfast	150	2000	D Jackson	Westport	151
1990	C Hartland	Cork	149				

2001 *at Clandeboye*

1	D Jackson (Clandeboye)	77-76—153
2	D White (Moate)	77-77—154
3	P Cowley (Cork)	75-80—155
	H McKinney (European)	78-77—155

Scottish Amateur Championship

1922	J Wilson	E Blackwell	St Andrews	19th hole
1923	TM Burrell	Dr A McCallum	Troon	1 hole
1924	WW Mackenzie	W Tulloch	Aberdeen	3 and 2
1925	JT Dobson	W Mackenzie	Muirfield	3 and 2
1926	WJ Guild	SO Shepherd	Leven	2 and 1
1927	A Jamieson jr	Rev D Rutherford	Gailes	22nd hole
1928	WW Mackenzie	W Dodds	Muirfield	5 and 3
1929	JT Bookless	J Dawson	Aberdeen	5 and 4
1930	K Greig	T Wallace	Carnoustie	9 and 8
1931	J Wilson	A Jamieson Jr	Prestwick	2 and 1
1932	J McLean	K Greig	Dunbar	5 and 4
1933	J McLean	KC Forbes	Aberdeen	6 and 4
1934	J McLean	W Campbell	Western Gailes	3 and 1
1935	H Thomson	J McLean	St Andrews	2 and 1
1936	ED Hamilton	R Neill	Carnoustie	1 hole
1937	H McInally	K Patrick	Barassie	6 and 5
1938	ED Hamilton	R Rutherford	Muirfield	4 and 2
1939	H McInally	H Thomson	Prestwick	6 and 5
1946	EC Brown	R Rutherford	Carnoustie	3 and 2
1947	H McInally	J Pressley	Glasgow Gailes	10 and 8
1948	AS Flockhart	G Taylor	Royal Aberdeen	7 and 6
1949	R Wright	H McInally	Muirfield	1 hole
1950	WC Gibson	D Blair	Prestwick	2 and 1
1951	JM Dykes	J Wilson	St Andrews	4 and 2
1952	FG Dewar	J Wilson	Carnoustie	4 and 3
1953	DA Blair	J McKay	Western Gailes	3 and 1
1954	JW Draper	W Gray	Nairn	4 and 3
1955	RR Jack	AC Miller	Muirfield	2 and 1
1956	Dr FWG Deighton	A MacGregor	Troon	8 and 7
1957	JS Montgomerie	J Burnside	Balgownie	2 and 1
1958	WD Smith	I Harris	Prestwick	6 and 5
1959	Dr FWG Deighton	R Murray	St Andrews	6 and 5
1960	JR Young	S Saddler	Carnoustie	5 and 3
1961	J Walker	ST Murray	Western Gailes	4 and 3
1962	SWT Murray	R Shade	Muirfield	2 and 1
1963	RDBM Shade	N Henderson	Troon	4 and 3
1964	RDBM Shade	J McBeath	Nairn	8 and 7
1965	RDBM Shade	G Cosh	St Andrews	4 and 2
1966	RDBM Shade	C Strachan	Western Gailes	9 and 8
1967	RDBM Shade	A Murphy	Carnoustie	5 and 4
1968	GB Cosh	R Renfrew	Muirfield	4 and 3
1969	JM Cannon	A Hall	Troon	6 and 4
1970	CW Green	H Stuart	Royal Aberdeen	1 hole
1971	S Stephen	C Green	St Andrews	3 and 2
1972	HB Stuart	A Pirie	Prestwick	3 and 1
1973	IC Hutcheon	A Brodie	Carnoustie	3 and 2
1974	GH Murray	A Pirie	Western Gailes	2 and 1
1975	D Greig	G Murray	Montrose	7 and 6
1976	GH Murray	H Stuart	St Andrews	6 and 5
1977	A Brodie	P McKellar	Troon	1 hole
1978	IA Carslaw	J Cuddihy	Downfield	7 and 6
1979	K Macintosh	P McKellar	Prestwick	5 and 4
1980	D Jamieson	C Green	Royal Aberdeen	2 and 1 (18)
1981	C Dalgleish	A Thomson	Western Gailes	7 and 6
1982	CW Green	G Macgregor	Carnoustie	1 hole
1983	CW Green	J Huggan	Gullane	1 hole
1984	A Moir	K Buchan	Renfrew	3 and 3
1985	D Carrick	D James	Southerness	4 and 2
1986	C Brooks	A Thomson	Monifieth	3 and 2
1987	C Montgomerie	A Watt	Nairn	9 and 8
1988	J Milligan	A Coltart	Kilmarnock (Barassie)	1 hole
1989	A Thomson	A Tait	Moray	1 hole
1990	C Everett	M Thomson	Gullane	7 and 5
1991	G Lowson	L Salariya	Downfield	4 and 3
1992	S Gallacher	D Kirkpatrick	Glasgow Gailes	37th hole
1993	D Robertson	R Russell	Royal Dornoch	2 holes
1994	H McKibben	A Reid	Renfrew	39th hole
1995	S Mackenzie	H McKibben	Southerness	8 and 7
1996	M Brooks	A Turnbull	Dunbar	7 and 6
1997	C Hislop	S Cairns	Carnoustie	5 and 3
1998	G Rankin	M Donaldson	Prestwick	6 and 5
1999	C Heap	M Loftus	Cruden Bay	7 and 5
2000	S O'Hara	C Heap	Royal Dornoch	1 hole

2001 *at Downfield*

Quarter Finals
Craig Watson (East Renfrewshire) beat Jonathan King (Cardross) at 19th
Martin Laird (Hilton Park) beat Stuart Wilson (Forfar) 2 and 1
Barry Hume (Haggs Castle) beat Fraser McLaughlan (Wishaw) 4 and 3
Jamie McLeary (Glenrothes) beat George Crawford (Williamwood) 2 and 1

Semi-Finals
Watson beat Laird 5 and 4
Hume beat McLeary 6 and 4

Final
Barry Hume beat Craig Watson 4 and 3

Scottish Open Amateur Stroke Play Championship

1967	BJ Gallacher	Muirfield and Gullane	291
1968	RDBM Shade	Prestwick and Prestwick St Nicholas	282
1969	JS Macdonald	Carnoustie and Monifieth	288
1970	D Hayes	Glasgow Gailes and Barassie	275
1971	IC Hutcheon	Leven and Lundin	277
1972	BN Nicholas	Dalmahoy and Ratho Park	290
1973T	DM Robertson/GJ Clark	Dunbar and North Berwick	284
1974	IC Hutcheon	Blairgowrie and Alyth	283
1975	CW Green	Nairn and Nairn Dunbar	295
1976	S Martin	Monifieth and Carnoustie	299
1977	PJ McKellar	Muirfield and Gullane	299
1978	AR Taylor	Cawder	281
1979	IC Hutcheon	Blairgowrie	286
1980	G Brand jr	Musselburgh and R Musselburgh	207 (54 holes)
1981	F Walton	Erskine and Renfrew	287
1982	C Macgregor	Downfield and Camperdown	287
1983	C Murray	Irvine and Irvine Ravenspark	291
1984	CW Green	Blairgowrie	287
1985	C Montgomerie	Dunbar and North Berwick	274
1986	KH Walker	Carnoustie	289
1987	D Carrick	Lundin and Ladybank	282
1988	S Easingwood	Cathkin Braes and East Kilbride	277
1989	F Illouz	Blairgowrie	281
1990	G Hay	Royal Aberdeen and Murcar	133 (36 holes)
1991	A Coltart	Royal Troon and Troon Portland	291
1992	D Robertson	Mortonhall and Bruntsfield Links	281
1993	A Reid	St Andrews Jubilee and New	289
1994	D Downie	Letham Grange	288
1995	S Gallacher	Paisley and Renfrew	284
1996	A Forsyth	Cardross and Helensburgh	279
1997	DB Howard	Monifieth and Panmure	271
1998	L Kelly	Moray and Elgin	275
1999	G Rankin	St Andrews Old and Jubilee	286
2000	S McKenzie*	Letham Grange	278

2001 *at Nairn and Nairn Dunbar*

1	John Sutherland* (Aus)	74-64-70-71—279
2	Steven Carmichael (Cardross)	69-68-71-71—279
3	Marcus Fraser (Aus)	68-71-72-69—280
	Steven Horne (Tulliallan)	70-73-69-68—280
	Craig Watson (East Renfrewshire)	73-70-69-68—280
	Stuart Wilson (Forfar)	70-74-72-64—280

Scottish Senior Championship

1978T	JM Cannon	Glasgow	149	1983	WD Smith	Glasgow	145
	GR Carmichael			1984	A Sinclair	Royal Burgess	148
1979	A Sinclair	Glasgow	143	1985	AN Sturrock	Glasgow	143
1980	JM Cannon	Royal Burgess	149	1986	RL Glading	Royal Burgess	153
1981T	IR Harris	Glasgow	146	1987	I Hornsby	Glasgow	145
	Dr J Hastings			1988	J Hayes	Royal Burgess	143
	AN Sturrock			1989	AS Mayer	Glasgow	139
1982T	JM Cannon	Royal Burgess	143	1990	C Hartland	Royal Burgess	146
	J Niven			1991	CW Green	Glasgow	140

Scottish Senior Championship *continued*

1992	G Clark	Royal Burgess	148	1997	CW Green	Glasgow	137
1993	J Maclean	Glasgow	141	1998	CW Green	Ladybank	146
1994	DM Lawrie	Ladybank	149	1999	G Steel*	Glasgow	145
1995	CW Green	Glasgow	141	2000	N Grant	Falkirk Tryst	142
1996	CW Green	Western Gailes	146				

2001 *at Glasgow*

1	David Lane (Goring & Streatley)		72-68—140
2	Charlie Green (Cardross)		71-69—140
3	Borje Back (Swe)		72-70—142

Scottish Champion of Champions *at Leven*

1970	A Horne	1981	I Hutcheon	1992	D Robertson
1971	D Black	1982	G Macgregor	1993	R Russell
1972	R Strachan	1983	D Carrick	1994	G Sherry
1973	*Not held*	1984	S Stephen	1995	S Gallacher
1974	M Niven	1985	I Brotherston	1996	M Brooks
1975	A Brodie	1986	I Hutcheon	1997	G Rankin
1976	A Brodie	1987	G Shaw	1998	G Rankin
1977	V Reid	1988	I Hutcheon	1999	D Patrick
1978	D Greig	1989	J Milligan	2000	G Fox
1979	B Marchbank	1990	J Milligan		
1980	I Hutcheon	1991	G Hay		

2001

1 Mark Loftus (Cowglen)	65-68-68-75—276
2 Marc Warren (East Kilbride)	67-69-70-71—277
3 Steven O'Hara (Colville Park)	66-70-70-73—279
Stuart Wilson (Forfar)	67-68-71-73—279

Scottish Mid-Amateur Championship

1994	C Watson	1997	H McDonald	2000	J Cameron
1995	M Thomson	1998	G Campbell		
1996	B Smith	1999	G Crawford		

2001 *at Bruntsfield*

Semi-Finals
Mike Thomson (Torwoodlee) beat Kevin Cattanach (Bruntsfield) 2 and 1
James McGroarty (Dumbarton beat Brian Adam (Ratho Park) at 19th

Final
Mike Thomson beat James McGroarty 2 and 1

Welsh Amateur Championship

1934	SB Roberts	GS Noon	Prestatyn	4 and 3
1935	R Chapman	GS Noon	Tenby	1 hole
1936	RM de Lloyd	G Wallis	Aberdovey	1 hole
1937	DH Lewis	R Glossop	Porthcawl	2 holes
1938	AA Duncan	SB Roberts	Rhyl	2 and 1
1946	JV Moody	A Marshman	Porthcawl	9 and 8
1947	SB Roberts	G Breen Turner	Harlech	8 and 7
1948	AA Duncan	SB Roberts	Porthcawl	2 and 1
1949	AD Evans	MA Jones	Aberdovey	2 and 1
1950	JL Morgan	DJ Bonnell	Southerndown	9 and 7
1951	JL Morgan	WI Tucker	Harlech	3 and 2
1952	AA Duncan	JL Morgan	Ashburnham	4 and 3
1953	SB Roberts	D Pearson	Prestatyn	5 and 3
1954	AA Duncan	K Thomas	Tenby	6 and 5
1955	TJ Davies	P Dunn	Harlech	38th hole
1956	A Lockley	WI Tucker	Southerndown	2 and 1

1957	ES Mills	H Griffiths	Harlech	2 and 1
1958	HC Squirrell	AD Lake	Conway	4 and 3
1959	HC Squirrell	N Rees	Porthcawl	8 and 7
1960	HC Squirrell	P Richards	Aberdovey	2 and 1
1961	AD Evans	J Toye	Ashburnham	3 and 2
1962	J Povall	HC Squirrell	Harlech	3 and 2
1963	WI Tucker	J Povall	Southerndown	4 and 3
1964	HC Squirrell	WI Tucker	Harlech	1 hole
1965	HC Squirrell	G Clay	Porthcawl	6 and 4
1966	WI Tucker	EN Davies	Aberdovey	6 and 5
1967	JK Povall	WI Tucker	Asburnham	3 and 2
1968	J Buckley	J Povall	Conway	8 and 7
1969	JL Toye	EN Davies	Porthcawl	1 hole
1970	EN Davies	J Povall	Harlech	1 hole
1971	CT Brown	HC Squirrell	Southerndown	6 and 5
1972	EN Davies	JL Toye	Prestatyn	40th hole
1973	D McLean	T Holder	Ashburnham	6 and 4
1974	S Cox	EN Davies	Caernarvonshire	3 and 2
1975	JL Toye	WI Tucker	Porthcawl	5 and 4
1976	MPD Adams	WI Tucker	Harlech	6 and 5
1977	D Stevens	JKD Povall	Southerndown	3 and 2
1978	D McLean	A Ingram	Caernarvonshire	11 and 10
1979	TJ Melia	MS Roper	Ashburnham	5 and 4
1980	DL Stevens	G Clement	Prestatyn	10 and 9
1981	S Jones	C Davies	Porthcawl	5 and 3
1982	D Wood	C Davies	Harlech	8 and 7
1983	JR Jones	AP Parkin	Southerndown	2 holes
1984	JR Jones	A Llyr	Prestatyn	1 hole
1985	ED Jones	MA Macara	Ashburnham	2 and 1
1986	C Rees	B Knight	Conwy	1 hole
1987	PM Mayo	DK Wood	Porthcawl	2 holes
1988	K Jones	RN Roderick	Harlech	40th hole
1989	S Dodd	K Jones	Tenby	2 and 1
1990	A Barnett	A Jones	Prestatyn	1 hole
1991	S Pardoe	S Jones	Ashburnham	7 and 5
1992	H Roberts	R Johnson	Pyle & Kenfig	3 and 2
1993	B Dredge	M Ellis	Southerndown	3 and 1
1994	C Evans	M Smith	Royal Porthcawl	5 and 4
1995	G Houston	C Evans	R St David's	3 and 2
1996	Y Taylor	DH Park	Ashburnham	3 and 2
1997	JR Donaldson	M Pilkington	Pyle & Kenfig	5 and 4
1998	M Pilkington	K Sullivan	Prestatyn	2 and 1
1999	M Griffiths	R Brookman	Tenby	7 and 6
2000	JG Jermine	R Brookman	Royal St David's	1 hole

2001 *at Royal Porthcawl*

Quarter Finals

Nigel Edwards (Whitchurch) beat Adam
  Campbell (Marlborough) 4 and 3
Craig Williams (Creigiau) beat Matthew
  Griffiths (Woodlake Park) 2 and 1
Lee Harpin (North Wales) beat Eurig
  Williams (Royal St David's) at 19th
Ian Campbell (Marlborough) beat David
  Price (Vale of Glamorgan) 2 and 1

Semi-Finals

Williams beat Edwards 4 and 3
Harpin beat Campbell 3 and 2

Final

Craig Williams beat Lee Harpin 1 hole

Welsh Amateur Stroke Play Championship

1967	EN Davies	Harlech	295	1976	WI Tucker	Newport	282
1968	JA Buckley	Harlech	294	1977	JA Buckley	Prestatyn	302
1969	DL Stevens	Tenby	288	1978	HJ Evans	Pyle & Kenfig	300
1970	JK Povall	Newport	292	1979	D McLean	Holyhead	289
1971T	EN Davies	Harlech	296	1980	TJ Melia	Tenby	291
	JL Toye			1981	D Evans	Wrexham	270
1972	JR Jones	Pyle & Kenfig	299	1982	JR Jones	Cradoc	287
1973	JR Jones	Llandudno (Maesdu)	300	1983	G Davies	Aberdovey	287
1974	JL Toye	Tenby	307	1984	RN Roderick	Newport	292
1975	D McLean	Wrexham	288	1985	MA Macara	Harlech	291

Welsh Amateur Stroke Play Championship *continued*

1986	M Calvert	Pyle & Kenfig	299	1993	M Macara	Maesdu	280
1987	MA Macara	Llandudno (Maesdu)	290	1994	N Van Hootegem	St Pierre	290
1988	RN Roderick	Tenby	283	1995	M Peet	Prestatyn	282
1989	SC Dodd	Conwy	304	1996	M Blackey	Tenby	276
				1997	G Wolstenholme	Conwy	286
Open event since 1990				1998	DAJ Patrick	Southerndown	279
1990	G Houston	Pyle & Kenfig	288	1999	C Williams	Northop	288
1991	A Jones	R Porthcawl	290	2000	J Donaldson	Ashburnham	283
1992	AJ Barnett	R St David's	278				

2001 *at Maesdu*

1	Jonathan Lupton (Middlesborough)	69-67-62-68—266
2	Simon Robinson (Seaton Carew)	73-64-67-67—271
3	Craig Williams (Creigiau)	70-69-68-66—273

Welsh Seniors' Amateur Championship *at Aberdovey*

1975	A Marshman	77 (18)	1989	WI Tucker	160
1976	AD Evans	156	1990	I Hughes	159
1977	AE Lockley	154	1991	RO Ward	155
1978	AE Lockley	75 (18)	1992	I Hughes	150
1979	CR Morgan	158	1993	G Perks	149
1980	ES Mills	152	1994T	G Perks/I Hughes/	
1981	T Branton	153		A Prytherch	157
1982	WI Tucker	147	1995	I Hughes	147
1983	WS Gronow	153	1996	G Isaac	152
1984	WI Tucker	150	1997	I Hughes	148
1985	NA Lycett	149	1998	D Reidford	158
1986	E Mills	154	1999	G Isaac	150
1987	WS Gronow	146	2000	JR Jones*	145
1988	NA Lycett	150			

2001

1	William Stowe (Aberdovey)	72-76-74—222
2	John Dinsdale (Newport)	77-71-75—223
	Gareth Isaac (Newport)	70-75-78—223

Welsh Champion of Champions *at Cradoc*

1999	R Williams	143	2000	J Davidson	143

2001

1	Neil Oakley (St Mellons)	71-72—143
2	Richard Scott (Haverfordwest)	75-71—146
3	Leon Clark (Pontnewydd)	69-77—146

European Amateur Championship

1986	A Haglund (Swe)	Eindhoven, Netherlands	1995	S García (Esp)	El Prat, Spain
1988	D Ecob (Aus)	Falkenstein, Germany	1996	D Olsson (Swe)	Karlstad, Sweden
1990	K Erikson (Swe)	Aalborg, Denmark	1997	D de Vooght (Bel)	Domaine Imperial,
1991	J Payne (Eng)	Hillside, England			Switzerland
1992	M Scarpa (Ita)	Le Querce, Italy	1998	P Gribben (Irl)	Golf du Medoc, France
1993	M Backhausen (Den)	Dalmahoy, Scotland	1999	G Havret (Fra)	Ascona, Switzerland
1994	S Gallacher (Sco)	Aura, Finland	2000	C Pettersson (Swe)	Murhof, Austria

2001 *at Odense, Denmark*

1	Stephen Browne (Irl)	65-69-67-69—270
2	Stuart Wilson (Sco)	66-69-71-69—275
3	Graeme Clark (Eng)	73-69-71-63—276
	Panu Kylliainen (Fin)	66-71-70-69—276

European Seniors' Championship

1999   H-J Ecklebe (Ger)   Switzerland   216   2000   HH Giesen (Ger)   Spain   217

2001 *at Torremirona, Spain*
1   Graham Steel (Eng)   71-72-73—216
2   Luis Javier Trenor (Esp)   72-73-74—219
3   Peter Cowley (Irl)   73-75-76—224

European Mid-Amateur Championship

1999   H-G Reiter (Ger)   Luxembourg   215   2000   F Illouz (Fra)   England   221

2001 *at Gloria, Turkey*
1   Barry Downing (Hallamshire)   69-77-70—216
2   François Illouz (Fra)   74-70-73—217
3   Tomas Nilsson (Swe)   74-72-72—218

NATIONAL ORDERS OF MERIT

Ireland – Willie Gill Award 2001
1   Stephen Browne (Hermitage)   180
2   Michael Hoey (Shandon Park)   110
3   Michael McDermott (Stackstown)   110

Scotland – Johnnie Walker Order of Merit 2001
1   Steven O'Hara (Colville Park)   545
2   Jonathan King (Cardross)   510
3   Steven Carmichael (Cardross)   476

Wales – Konica Order of Merit 2001
1   Nigel Edwards (Whitchurch)   671
2   Craig Williams (Creigiau)   629
3   Ian Campbell (Marlborough)   474

Daily Telegraph/JJB Amateur Order of Merit
1   Gary Wolstenholme (Kilworth Springs)   2751.12
2   Steven O'Hara (Colville Park)   2483.58
3   Peter McEvoy (Thorpe Hall)   2071.96

TEAM EVENTS

Walker Cup *(Home team names first)*

2001 *at Ocean Forest, Sea Island, Georgia*

Captains: Danny Yates jr (USA), Peter McEvoy (GBI)

USA		Great Britain and Ireland	
First Day – Foursomes			
D Green & DJ Trahan	0	S O'Hara & GP Wolstenholme (5 and 3)	1
N Cassini & L Glover (4 and 3)	1	L Donald & N Dougherty	0
D Eger & B Molder	½	J Elson & R McEvoy	½
J Driscoll & J Quinney	0	G McDowell & M Hoey (3 and 1)	1
	1½		2½
Singles			
E Compton (3 and 2)	1	G Wolstenholme	0
DJ Trahan (2 and 1)	1	S O'Hara	0
J Driscoll	0	N Dougherty (2 and 1)	1
N Cassini (5 and 4)	1	N Edwards	0
J Harris	0	M Warren (5 and 4)	1
J Quinney	0	L Donald (3 and 2)	1
B Molder (2 and 1)	1	G McDowell	0
L Glover (1 hole)	1	M Hoey	0
	5		3
Second Day – Foursomes			
E Compton & J Harris	0	L Donald & N Dougherty (3 and 2)	1
N Cassini & L Glover	0	G McDowell & M Hoey (2 and 1)	1
D Eger & B Molder (7 and 6)	1	S O'Hara & M Warren	0
D Green & DJ Trahan	0	J Elson & R McEvoy (1 hole)	1
	1		3
Singles			
L Glover	0	L Donald (3 and 2)	1
J Harris	0	S O'Hara (4 and 3)	1
DJ Trahan	0	N Dougherty (1 hole)	1
J Driscoll	0	M Warren ((2 and 1)	1
B Molder (1 hole)	1	G McDowell	0
D Green	0	M Hoey (1 hole)	1
E Compton	½	J Elson	½
N Cassini	0	GP Wolstenholme (4 and 3)	1
	1½		6½

Result: Great Britain and Ireland 15, USA 9

---

21 May 1921 *at Hoylake*	**1922** *at National Golf Links, New York*
Unofficial match — GBI v USA	*Officially named the Walker Cup*
Result: USA 9, GBI 3	**Result: USA 8, GBI 4**
Foursomes	*Captains: WC Fownes (USA), R Harris (GBI)*
Simpson & Jenkins lost to Evans & Jones 5 and 3	**Foursomes**
Tolley & Holderness lost to Ouimet & Guilford 3 and 2	Guilford & Ouimet beat Tolley & Darwin 8 and 7
de Montmorency & Wethered lost to Hunter & Platt 1 hole	Evans & Gardner lost to Wethered & Aylmer 5 and 4
	Jones & Sweetser beat Torrance & Hooman 3 and 2
Aylmer & Armour lost to Wright & Fownes 4 and 2	Marston & Fownes beat Caven & Mackenzie 2 and 1
Singles	**Singles**
CJH Tolley beat C Evans jr 4 and 3	JP Guilford beat CJH Tolley 2 and 1
JLC Jenkins lost to FD Ouimet 6 and 5	RT Jones jr beat RH Wethered 3 and 2
RH de Montmorency lost to RT Jones jr 4 and 3	C Evans jr beat J Caven 5 and 4
JG Simpson lost to JP Guilford 2 and 1	FD Ouimet beat CC Aylmer 8 and 7
CC Aylmer beat P Hunter 2 and 1	RA Gardner beat WB Torrance 7 and 5
TD Armour beat JW Platt 2 and 1	MR Marston lost to WW Mackenzie 6 and 5
EWE Holderness lost to F Wright 2 holes	WC Fownes jr lost to B Darwin 3 and 1
RH Wethered lost to WC Fownes jr 3 and 1	JW Sweetser lost to CVL Hooman at 37th

1923 *at St Andrews*
Result: USA 6½, GBI 5½
Captains: R Harris (GBI), RA Gardner (USA)
Foursomes
Tolley & Wethered beat Ouimet & Sweetser 6 and 5
Harris & Hooman lost to Gardner & Marston 7 and 6
Holderness & Hope beat Rotan & Herron 1 hole
Wilson & Murray beat Johnston & Neville
4 and 3
Singles
RH Wethered halved with FD Ouimet
CJH Tolley beat JW Sweetser 4 and 3
R Harris lost to RA Gardner 1 hole
WW Mackenzie lost to GV Rotan 5 and 4
WL Hope lost to MR Marston 6 and 5
EWE Holderness lost to FJ Wright jr 1 hole
J Wilson beat SD Herron 1 hole
WA Murray lost to OF Willing 2 and 1

1924 *at Garden City, New York*
Result: USA 9, GBI 3
*Captains: RA Gardner (USA), CJH Tolley
(GBI)*
Foursomes
Marston & Gardner beat Storey & Murray 3 and 1
Guilford & Ouimet beat Tolley & Hezlet 2 and 1
Jones & Fownes jr lost to Scott & Scott jr 1 hole
Sweetser & Johnston beat Torrance & Bristowe 4 and 3
Singles
MR Marston lost to CJH Tolley 1 hole
RT Jones jr beat CO Hezlet 4 and 3
C Evans jr beat WA Murray 2 and 1
FD Ouimet beat EF Storey 1 hole
JW Sweetser lost to Hon M Scott 7 and 6
RA Gardner beat WL Hope 3 and 2
JP Guilford beat TA Torrance 2 and 1
OF Willing beat DH Kyle 3 and 2

1926 *at St Andrews*
Result: USA 6½, GBI 5½
Captains: R Harris (GBI), RA Gardner (USA)
Foursomes
Wethered & Holderness beat Ouimet &
Guilford 5 and 4
Tolley & Jamieson lost to Jones & Gunn 4 and 3
Harris & Hezlet lost to Von Elm & Sweetser 8 and 7
Storey & Brownlow lost to Gardner & MacKenzie
1 hole
Singles
CJH Tolley lost to RT Jones jr 12 and 11
EWE Holderness lost to JW Sweetser 4 and 3
RH Wethered beat FD Ouimet 5 and 4
CO Hezlet halved with G Von Elm
R Harris beat JP Guilford 2 and 1
Hon WGE Brownlow lost to W Gunn 9 and 8
EF Storey beat RR MacKenzie 2 and 1
A Jamieson jr beat RA Gardner 5 and 4

1928 *at Wheaton, Chicago, IL*
Result: USA 11, GBI 1
*Captains: RT Jones jr (USA), W Tweddell
(GBI)*
Foursomes
Sweetser & Von Elm beat Perkins & Tweddell 7 and 6
Jones & Evans beat Hezlet & Hope 5 and 3
Ouimet & Johnston beat Torrance & Storey 4 and 2
Gunn & MacKenzie beat Beck & Martin 7 and 5

Singles
RT Jones jr beat TP Perkins 13 and 12
G Von Elm beat W Tweddell 3 and 2
FD Ouimet beat CO Hezlet 8 and 7
JW Sweetser beat WL Hope 5 and 4
HR Johnston beat EF Storey 4 and 2
C Evans jr lost to TA Torrance 1 hole
W Gunn beat RH Hardman 11 and 10
RR MacKenzie beat GNC Martin 2 and 1

1930 *at St George's, Sandwich*
Result: USA 10, GBI 2
*Captains: RH Wethered (GBI),
RT Jones jr (USA)*
Foursomes
Tolley & Wethered beat Von Elm & Voigt 2 holes
Hartley & Torrance lost to Jones & Willing 8 and 7
Holderness & Stout lost to MacKenzie & Moe 2 and 1
Campbell & Smith lost to Johnston & Ouimet 2 and 1
Singles
CJH Tolley lost to HR Johnston 5 and 4
RH Wethered lost to RT Jones jr 9 and 8
RW Hartley lost to G Von Elm 3 and 2
EWE Holderness lost to GJ Voigt 10 and 8
JN Smith lost to OF Willing 2 and 1
TA Torrance beat FD Ouimet 7 and 6
JA Stout lost to DK Moe 1 hole
W Campbell lost to RR MacKenzie 6 and 5

1932 *at Brookline, MA*
Result: USA 9½, GBI 2½
Captains: FD Ouimet (USA), TA Torrance (GBI)
Foursomes
Sweetser & Voigt beat Hartley & Hartley 7 and 6
Seaver & Moreland beat Torrance & de Forest
6 and 5
Ouimet & Dunlap beat Stout & Burke 7 and 6
Moe & Howell beat Fiddian & McRuvie 5 and 4
Singles
FD Ouimet halved with TA Torrance
JW Sweetser halved with JA Stout
GT Moreland beat RW Hartley 2 and 1
J Westland halved with J Burke
GJ Voigt lost to LG Crawley 1 hole
MJ McCarthy jr beat WL Hartley 3 and 2
CH Seaver beat EW Fiddian 7 and 6
GT Dunlap jr beat EA McRuvie 10 and 9

1934 *at St Andrews*
Result: USA 9½, GBI 2½
*Captains: Hon M Scott (GBI),
FD Ouimet (USA)*
Foursomes
Wethered & Tolley lost to Goodman & Little
8 and 6
Bentley & Fiddian lost to Moreland & Westland
6 and 5
Scott & McKinlay lost to Egan & Marston 3 and 2
McRuvie & McLean beat Ouimet & Dunlap 4 and 2
Singles
Hon M Scott lost to JG Goodman 7 and 6
CJH Tolley lost to WL Little jr 6 and 5
LG Crawley lost to FD Ouimet 5 and 4
J McLean lost to GT Dunlap 4 and 3
EW Fiddian lost to JW Fischer 5 and 4
SL McKinlay lost to GT Moreland 3 and 1
EA McRuvie halved with J Westland
TA Torrance beat MR Marston 4 and 3

1936 at Pine Valley, NJ
Result: USA 10½, GBI 1½
Captains: FD Ouimet (USA),
  W Tweddell (GBI)
Foursomes
Goodman & Campbell beat Thomson & Bentley
  7 and 5
Smith & White beat McLean & Langley 8 and 7
Yates & Emery halved with Peters & Dykes
Givan & Voigt halved with Hill & Ewing
Singles
JG Goodman beat H Thomson 3 and 2
AE Campbell beat J McLean 5 and 4
JW Fischer beat RC Ewing 8 and 7
R Smith beat GA Hill 11 and 9
W Emery beat GB Peters 1 hole
CR Yates beat JM Dykes 8 and 7
GT Dunlap jr halved with HG Bentley
E White beat JDA Langley 6 and 5

1938 at St Andrews
Result: GBI 7½, USA 4½
Captains: JB Beck (GBI), FD Ouimet (USA)
Foursomes
Bentley & Bruen halved with Fischer & Kocsis
Peters & Thomson beat Goodman & Ward 4 and 2
Kyle & Stowe lost to Yates & Billows 3 and 2
Pennink & Crawley beat Smith & Haas 3 and 1
Singles
J Bruen jr lost to CR Yates 2 and 1
H Thomson beat JG Goodman 6 and 4
LG Crawley lost to JW Fischer 3 and 2
C Stowe beat CR Kocsis 2 and 1
JJF Pennink lost to MH Ward 12 and 11
RC Ewing beat RE Billows 1 hole
GB Peters beat R Smith 9 and 8
AT Kyle beat F Haas jr 5 and 4

1947 at St Andrews
Result: USA 8, GBI 4
Captains: JB Beck (GBI), FD Ouimet (USA)
Foursomes
Carr & Ewing lost to Bishop & Riegel 3 and 2
Crawley & Lucas beat Ward & Quick 5 and 4
Kyle & Wilson lost to Turnesa & Kammer 5 and 4
White & Stowe beat Stranahan & Chapman 4 and 3
Singles
LG Crawley lost to MH Ward 5 and 3
JB Carr beat SE Bishop 5 and 4
GH Micklem lost to RH Riegel 6 and 5
RC Ewing lost to WP Turnesa 6 and 5
C Stowe lost to FR Stranahan 2 and 1
RJ White beat AF Kammer jr 4 and 3
JC Wilson lost to SL Quick 8 and 6
PB Lucas lost to RD Chapman 4 and 3

1949 at Winged Foot, New York
Result: USA 10, GBI 2
Captains: FD Ouimet (USA), PB Lucas (GBI)
Foursomes
Billows & Turnesa lost to Carr & White 3 and 2
Kocsis & Stranahan beat Bruen & McCready 2 and 1
Bishop & Riegel beat Ewing & Micklem 9 and 7
Dawson & McCormick beat Thom & Perowne
  8 and 7

Singles
WP Turnesa lost to RJ White 4 and 3
FR Stranahan beat SM McCready 6 and 5
RH Riegel beat J Bruen jr 5 and 4
JW Dawson beat JB Carr 5 and 3
CR Coe beat RC Ewing 1 hole
RE Billows beat KG Thom 2 and 1
CR Kocsis beat AH Perowne 4 and 2
JB McHale jr beat GH Micklem 5 and 4

1951 at Birkdale
Result: USA 7½, GBI 4½
Captains: RH Oppenheimer (GBI),
  WP Turnesa (USA)
Foursomes
White & Carr halved with Stranahan & Campbell
Ewing & Langley halved with Coe & McHale
Kyle & Caldwell lost to Chapman & Knowles jr
  1 hole
Bruen jr & Morgan lost to Turnesa & Urzetta 5 and 4
Singles
SM McCready lost to S Urzetta 4 and 3
JB Carr beat FR Stranahan 2 and 1
RJ White beat CR Coe 2 and 1
JDA Langley lost to JB McHale jr 2 holes
RC Ewing lost to WC Campbell 5 and 4
AT Kyle beat WP Turnesa 2 holes
I Caldwell halved with HD Paddock jr
JL Morgan lost to RD Chapman 7 and 6

1953 at Kittansett, MA
Result: USA 9, GBI 3
Captains: CR Yates (USA), AA Duncan (GBI)
Foursomes
Urzetta & Venturi beat Carr & White 6 and 4
Ward & Westland beat Langley & AH Perowne 9 and 8
Jackson & Littler beat Wilson & MacGregor 3 and 2
Campbell & Coe lost to Micklem & Morgan
  4 and 3
Singles
EH Ward jr beat JB Carr 4 and 3
RD Chapman lost to RJ White 1 hole
GA Littler beat GH Micklem 5 and 3
J Westland beat RC MacGregor 7 and 5
DR Cherry beat NV Drew 9 and 7
K Venturi beat JC Wilson 9 and 8
CR Coe lost to JL Morgan 3 and 2
S Urzetta beat JDA Langley 3 and 2

1955 at St Andrews
Result: USA 10, GBI 2
Captains: GA Hill (GBI), WC Campbell (USA)
Foursomes
Carr & White lost to Ward & Cherry 1 hole
Micklem & Morgan lost to Patton & Yost 2 and 1
Caldwell & Millward lost to Conrad & Morey 3 and 2
Blair & Cater lost to Cudd & Jackson 5 and 4
Singles
RJ White lost to EH Ward jr 6 and 5
PF Scrutton lost to WJ Patton 2 and 1
I Caldwell beat D Morey 1 hole
JB Carr lost to DR Cherry 5 and 4
DA Blair beat JW Conrad 1 hole
EB Millward lost to BH Cudd 2 holes
RC Ewing lost to JG Jackson 6 and 4
JL Morgan lost to RL Yost 8 and 7

1957 at Minikahda, MN
Result: USA 8½, GBI 3½
Captains:CR Coe (USA), GH Micklem (GBI)
Foursomes
Baxter & Patton beat Carr & Deighton 2 and 1
Campbell & Taylor beat Bussell & Scrutton 4 and 3
Blum & Kocsis lost to Jack & Sewell 1 hole
Robbins & Rudolph halved with Shepperson & Wolstenholme
Singles
WJ Patton beat RR Jack 1 hole
WC Campbell beat JB Carr 3 and 2
R Baxter jr beat A Thirlwell 4 and 3
W Hyndman III beat FWG Deighton 7 and 6
JE Campbell lost to AF Bussell 2 and 1
FM Taylor jr beat D Sewell 1 hole
EM Rudolph beat PF Scrutton 3 and 2
H Robbins jr lost to GB Wolstenholme 2 and 1

1959 at Muirfield
Result: USA 9, GBI 3
Captains:GH Micklem (GBI), CR Coe (USA)
Foursomes
Jack & Sewell lost to Ward & Taylor 1 hole
Carr & Wolstenholme lost to Hyndman & Aaron 1 hole
Bonallack & Perowne lost to Patton & Coe 9 and 8
Lunt & Shepperson lost to Wettlander & Nicklaus 2 and 1
Singles
JB Carr beat CR Coe 3 and 1
GB Wolstenholme lost to EH Ward jr 9 and 8
RR Jack beat WJ Patton 5 and 3
DN Sewell lost to W Hyndman III 4 and 3
AE Shepperson beat TD Aaron 2 and 1
MF Bonallack lost to DR Beman 2 holes
MSR Lunt lost to HW Wettlander 6 and 5
WD Smith lost to JW Nicklaus 5 and 4

1961 at Seattle, WA
Result: USA 11, GBI 1
Captains: J Westland (USA), CD Lawrie (GBI)
Foursomes
Beman & Nicklaus beat Walker & Chapman 6 and 5
Coe & Cherry beat Blair & Christmas 1 hole
Hyndman & Gardner beat Carr & G Huddy 4 and 3
Cochran & Andrews beat Bonallack & Shade 4 and 3
Singles
DR Beman beat MF Bonallack 3 and 2
CR Coe beat MSR Lunt 5 and 4
FM Taylor jr beat J Walker 3 and 2
W Hyndman III beat DW Frame 7 and 6
JW Nicklaus beat JB Carr 6 and 4
CB Smith lost to MJ Christmas 3 and 2
RW Gardner beat RDBM Shade 1 hole
DR Cherry beat DA Blair 5 and 4

1963 at Turnberry
Result: USA 14.GBI 10
Captains: CD Lawrie (GBI), RS Tufts (USA)
First Day – Foursomes
Bonallack & Murray beat Patton & Sikes 4 and 3
Carr & Green lost to Gray & Harris 2 holes
Lunt & Sheahan lost to Beman & Coe 5 and 3
Madeley & Shade halved with Gardner & Updegraff

Singles
SWT Murray beat DR Beman 3 and 1
MJ Christmas lost to WJ Patton 3 and 2
JB Carr beat RH Sikes 7 and 5
DB Sheahan beat LE Harris 1 hole
MF Bonallack beat RD Davies 1 hole
AC Saddler halved with CR Coe
RDBM Shade beat AD Gray jr 4 and 3
MSR Lunt halved with CB Smith
Second Day – Foursomes
Bonallack & Murray lost to Patton & Sikes 1 hole
Lunt & Sheahan lost to Gray & Harris 3 and 2
Green & Saddler lost to Gardner & Updegraff 3 and 1
Madeley & Shade lost to Beman & Coe 3 and 2
Singles
Murray lost to Patton 3 and 2
Sheahan beat Davies 1 hole
Carr lost to Updegraff 4 and 3
Bonallack lost to Harris 3 and 2
Lunt lost to Gardner 3 and 2
Saddler halved with Beman
Shade beat Gray 2 and 1
Green lost to Coe 4 and 3

1965 at Five Farms, MD
Result: USA 12, GBI 12
Captains: JW Fischer (USA), JB Carr (GBI)
First Day – Foursomes
Campbell & Gray lost to Lunt & Cosh 1 hole
Beman & Allen halved with Bonallack & Clark
Patton & Tutwiler beat Foster & Clark 5 and 4
Hopkins & Eichelberger lost to Townsend & Shade 2 and 1
Singles
WC Campbell beat MF Bonallack 6 and 5
DR Beman beat R Foster 2 holes
AD Gray jr lost to RDBM Shade 3 and 1
JM Hopkins lost to CA Clark 5 and 3
WJ Patton lost to P Townsend 3 and 2
D Morey lost to AC Saddler 2 and 1
DC Allen lost to GB Cosh 2 holes
ER Updegraff lost to MSR Lunt 2 and 1
Second Day – Foursomes
Campbell & Gray beat Saddler & Foster 4 and 3
Beman & Eichelberger lost to Townsend & Shade 2 and 1
Tutwiler & Patton beat Cosh & Lunt 2 and 1
Allen & Morey lost to CA Clark & Bonallack 2 and 1
Singles
Campbell beat Foster 3 and 2
Beman beat Saddler 1 hole
Tutwiler beat Shade 5 and 3
Allen lost to Cosh 4 and 3
Gray beat Townsend 1 hole
Hopkins halved with CA Clark
Eichelberger beat Bonallack 5 and 3
Patton beat Lunt 4 and 2

1967 at St George's, Sandwich
Result: USA 15, GBI 9
Captains: JB Carr (GBI), JW Sweetser (USA)
First Day – Foursomes
Shade & Oosterhuis halved with Murphy & Cerrudo
Foster & Saddler lost to Campbell & Lewis 1 hole
Bonallack & Attenborough lost to Gray & Tutwiler 4 and 2
Carr & Craddock lost to Dickson & Grant 3 and 1

Singles
RDBM Shade lost to WC Campbell 2 and 1
R Foster lost to RJ Murphy jr 2 and 1
MF Bonallack halved with AD Gray jr
MF Attenborough lost to RJ Cerrudo 4 and 3
P Oosterhuis lost to RB Dickson 6 and 4
T Craddock lost to JW Lewis jr 2 and 1
AK Pirie halved with DC Allen
AC Saddler beat MA Fleckman 3 and 2

Second Day – Foursomes
Bonallack & Craddock beat Murphy & Cerrudo
   2 holes
Saddler & Pirie lost to Campbell & Lewis 1 hole
Shade & Oosterhuis beat Gray & Tutwiler 3 and 1
Foster & Millensted beat Allen & Fleckman
   2 and 1

Singles
Shade lost to Campbell 3 and 2
Bonallack beat Murphy 4 and 2
Saddler beat Gray 3 and 2
Foster halved with Cerrudo
Pirie lost to Dickson 4 and 3
Craddock beat Lewis 5 and 4
Oosterhuis lost to Grant 1 hole
Millensted lost to Tutwiler 3 and 1

1969 *at Milwaukee, WI*
Result: USA 13, GBI 11
Captains: WJ Patton (USA),
   MF Bonallack (GBI)

First Day – Foursomes
Giles & Melnyk beat Bonallack & Craddock
   3 and 2
Fleisher & Miller halved with Benka & Critchley
Wadkins & Siderowf lost to Green & A Brooks
W Hyndman III & Inman jr beat Foster & Marks
   2 and 1

Singles
B Fleisher halved with MF Bonallack
M Giles III beat CW Green 1 hole
AL Miller III beat B Critchley 1 hole
RL Siderowf beat LP Tupling 6 and 5
S Melnyk lost to PJ Benka 3 and 1
L Wadkins lost to GC Marks 1 hole
J Bohmann beat MG King 2 and 1
ER Updegraff beat R Foster 6 and 5

Second Day – Foursomes
Giles & Melnyk halved with Green & Brooks
Fleisher & Miller lost to Benka & Critchley 2 and 1
Siderowf & Wadkins beat Foster & King 6 and 5
Updegraff & Bohmann lost to Bonallack & Tupling
   4 and 3

Singles
Fleisher lost to Bonallack 5 and 4
Siderowf halved with Critchley
Miller beat King 1 hole
Giles halved with Craddock
Inman beat Benka 2 and 1
Bohmann lost to Brooks 4 and 3
Hyndman halved with Green
Updegraff lost to Marks 3 and 2

1971 *at St Andrews*
Result: GBI 13, USA 11
Captains: MF Bonallack (GBI),
   JM Winters jr (USA)

First Day – Foursomes
Bonallack & Humphreys beat Wadkins & Simons
   1 hole
Green & Carr beat Melnyk & Giles 1 hole
Marsh & Macgregor beat Miller & Farquhar
   2 and 1
Macdonald & Foster beat Campbell & Kite 2 and 1

Singles
CW Green lost to L Wadkins 1 hole
MF Bonallack lost to M Giles III 1 hole
GC Marks lost to AL Miller III 1 hole
JS Macdonald lost to S Melnyk 3 and 2
RJ Carr halved with W Hyndman III
W Humphreys lost to JR Gabrielsen 1 hole
HB Stuart beat J Farquhar 3 and 2
R Foster lost to T Kite 3 and 2

Second Day – Foursomes
Marks & Green lost to Melnyk & Giles 1 hole
Stuart & Carr beat Wadkins & Gabrielsen 1 hole
Marsh & Bonallack lost to Miller & Farquhar 5 and 4
Macdonald & Foster halved with Campbell & Kite

Singles
Bonallack lost to Wadkins 3 and 1
Stuart beat Giles 2 and 1
Humphreys beat Melnyk 2 and 1
Green beat Miller 1 hole
Carr beat Simons 2 holes
Macgregor beat Gabrielsen 1 hole
Marsh beat Hyndman 1 hole
Marks lost to Kite 3 and 2

1973 *at Brookline, MA*
Result: USA 14, GBI 10
Captains: JW Sweetser (USA), DM Marsh (GBI)

First Day – Foursomes
Giles & Koch halved with King & Hedges
Siderowf & Pfeil beat Stuart & Davies 5 and 4
Edwards & Ellis beat Green & Milne 2 and 1
West & Ballenger beat Foster & Homer 2 and 1

Singles
M Giles III beat HB Stuart 5 and 4
RL Siderowf beat MF Bonallack 4 and 2
G Koch lost to JC Davies 1 hole
M West lost to HK Clark 2 and 1
D Edwards beat R Foster 2 holes
M Killian lost to MG King 1 hole
W Rodgers lost to CW Green 1 hole
M Pfeil lost to WT Milne 4 and 3

Second Day – Foursomes
Giles & Koch & Homer & Foster 7 and 5
Siderowf & Pfeil halved with Clark & Davies
Edwards & Ellis beat Hedges & King 2 and 1
Rodgers & Killian beat Stuart & Milne 1 hole

Singles
Ellis lost to Stuart 5 and 4
Siderowf lost to Davies 3 and 2
Edwards beat Homer 2 and 1
Giles halved with Green
West beat King 1 hole
Killian lost to Milne 2 and 1
Koch halved with Hedges
Pfeil beat Clark 1 hole

1975 at St Andrews
Result: USA 15½, GBI 8½
*Captains: DM Marsh (GBI),
ER Updegraff (USA)*

First Day – Foursomes
James & Eyles beat Pate & Siderowf 1 hole
Davies & Poxon lost to Burns & Stadler
5 and 4
Green & Stuart lost to Haas & Strange 2 and 1
Macgregor & Hutcheon lost to Giles & Koch 5 and 4

Singles
M James beat J Pate 2 and 1
JC Davies halved with C Strange
P Mulcare beat RL Siderowf 1 hole
HB Stuart lost to G Koch 3 and 2
MA Poxon lost to J Grace 3 and 1
IC Hutcheon halved with WC Campbell
GRD Eyles lost to J Haas 2 and 1
G Macgregor lost to M Giles III 5 and 4

Second Day – Foursomes
Mulcare & Hutcheon beat Pate & Siderowf 1 hole
Green & Stuart lost to Burns & Stadler 1 hole
James & Eyles beat Campbell & Grace 5 and 3
Hedges & Davies lost to Haas & Strange 3 and 2

Singles
Hutcheon beat Pate 3 and 2
Mulcare lost to Strange 4 and 3
James lost to Koch 5 and 4
Davies beat Burns 2 and 1
Green lost to Grace 2 and 1
Macgregor lost to Stadler 3 and 2
Eyles lost to Campbell 2 and 1
Hedges halved with Giles

1977 at Shinnecock Hills, NY
Result: USA 16, GBI 8
*Captains: LW Oehmig(USA),
AC Saddler (GBI)*

First Day – Foursomes
Fought & Heafner beat Lyle & McEvoy 4 and 3
Simpson & Miller beat Davies & Kelley 5 and 4
Siderowf & Hallberg lost to Hutcheon & Deeble
1 hole
Sigel & Brannan beat Brodie & Martin 1 hole

Singles
L Miller beat P McEvoy 2 holes
J Fought beat IC Hutcheon 4 and 3
S Simpson beat GH Murray 7 and 6
V Heafner beat JC Davies 4 and 3
B Sander lost to A Brodie 4 and 3
G Hallberg lost to S Martin 3 and 2
F Ridley beat AWB Lyle 2 holes
J Sigel beat P McKellar 5 and 3

Second Day – Foursomes
Fought & Heafner beat Hutcheon & Deeble 4 and 3
Miller & Simpson beat McEvoy & Davies 2 holes
Siderowf & Sander lost to Brodie & Martin 6 and 4
Ridley & Brannan lost to Murray & Kelley 4 and 3

Singles
Miller beat Martin 1 hole
Fought beat Davies 2 and 1
Sander lost to Brodie 2 and 1
Hallberg beat McEvoy 4 and 3
Siderowf lost to Kelley 2 and 1
Brannan lost to Hutcheon 2 holes
Ridley beat Lyle 5 and 3
Sigel beat Deeble 1 hole

1979 at Muirfield
Result: USA 151/2, GBI 81/2
Captains: R Foster (GBI), RL Siderowf (USA)

First Day – Foursomes
McEvoy & Marchbank lost to Hoch & Sigel 1 hole
Godwin & Hutcheon beat West & Sutton
2 holes
Brand jr & Kelley lost to Fischesser & Holtgrieve
1 hole
Brodie & Carslaw beat Moody & Gove 2 and 1

Singles
P McEvoy halved with J Sigel
JC Davies lost to D Clarke 8 and 7
J Buckley lost to S Hoch 9 and 7
IC Hutcheon lost to J Holtgrieve 6 and 4
B Marchbank beat M Peck 1 hole
G Godwin beat G Moody 3 and 2
MJ Kelley beat D Fischesser 3 and 2
A Brodie lost to M Gove 3 and 2

Second Day – Foursomes
Godwin & Brand lost to Hoch & Sigel 4 and 3
McEvoy & Marchbank beat Fischesser & Holtgrieve
2 and 1
Kelley & Hutcheon halved with West & Sutton
Carslaw & Brodie halved with Clarke & Peck

Singles
McEvoy lost to Hoch 3 and 1
Brand lost to Clarke 2 and 1
Godwin lost to Gove 3 and 2
Hutcheon lost to Peck 2 and 1
Brodie beat West 3 and 2
Kelley lost to Moody 3 and 2
Marchbank lost to Sutton 3 and 1
Carslaw lost to Sigel 2 and 1

1981 at Cypress Point, CA
Result: USA 15, GBI 9
*Captains: J Gabrielsen (USA),
R Foster (GBI)*

First Day – Foursomes
Sutton & Sigel lost to Walton & Rafferty 4 and 2
Holtgrieve & Fuhrer beat Chapman & McEvoy
1 hole
Lewis & von Tacky beat Deeble & Hutcheon 2 and 1
Commans & Pavin beat Evans & Way 5 and 4

Singles
H Sutton beat R Rafferty 3 and 1
J Rassett beat CR Dalgleish 1 hole
R Commans lost to P Walton 1 hole
B Lewis lost to R Chapman 2 and 1
J Mudd beat G Godwin 1 hole
C Pavin beat IC Hutcheon 4 and 3
D von Tacky lost to P Way 3 and 1
J Sigel beat P McEvoy 4 and 2

Second Day – Foursomes
Sutton & Sigel lost to Chapman & Way 1 hole
Holtgrieve & Fuhrer lost to Walton & Rafferty 6 and 4
Lewis & von Tacky lost to Evans & Dalgleish 3 and 2
Rassett & Mudd beat Hutcheon & Godwin 5 and 4

Singles
Sutton lost to Chapman 1 hole
Holtgrieve beat Rafferty 2 and 1
Fuhrer beat Walton 4 and 3
Sigel beat Way 6 and 5
Mudd beat Dalgleish 7 and 5
Commans halved with Godwin
Rassett beat Deeble 4 and 3
Pavin halved with Evans

1983 *at Hoylake*
Result: USA 13½, GBI 10½
Captains: CW Green (GBI), J Sigel (USA)

First Day – Foursomes
Macgregor & Walton beat Sigel & Fehr 3 and 2
Keppler & Pierse lost to Wood & Faxon 3 and 1
Lewis & Thompson lost to Lewis & Holtgrieve
 7 and 6
Mann & Oldcorn beat Hoffer & Tentis 5 and 4

Singles
P Walton beat J Sigel 1 hole
SD Keppler lost to R Fehr 1 hole
G Macgregor halved with W Wood
DG Carrick lost to B Faxon 3 and 1
A Oldcorn beat B Tuten 4 and 3
P Parkin beat N Crosby 5 and 4
AD Pierse lost to B Lewis jr 3 and 1
LS Mann lost to J Holtgrieve 6 and 5

Second Day – Foursomes
Macgregor & Walton lost to Crosby & Hoffer 2 holes
Parkin & Thompson beat Faxon & Wood 1 hole
Mann & Oldcorn beat Lewis & Holtgrieve 1 hole
Keppler & Pierse halved with Sigel & Fehr

Singles
Walton beat Wood 2 and 1
Parkin lost to Faxon 3 and 2
Macgregor lost to Fehr 2 and 1
Thompson lost to Tuten 3 and 2
Mann halved with Tentis
Keppler lost to Lewis 6 and 5
Oldcorn beat Holtgrieve 3 and 2
Carrick lost to Sigel 3 and 2

1985 *at Pine Valley, NJ*
Result: USA 13, GBI 11
Captains: J Sigel (USA), CW Green (GBI)

First Day – Foursomes
Verplank & Sigel beat Montgomerie & Macgregor
 1 hole
Waldorf & Randolph lost to Hawksworth &
 McGimpsey 4 and 3
Sonnier & Haas lost to Baker & McEvoy 6 and 5
Podolak & Love halved with Bloice & Stephen

Singles
S Verplank beat G McGimpsey 2 and 1
S Randolph beat P Mayo 5 and 4
R Sonnier halved with J Hawksworth
J Sigel beat CS Montgomerie 5 and 4
B Lewis lost to P McEvoy 2 and 1
C Burroughs lost to G Macgregor 2 holes
D Waldorf beat D Gilford 4 and 2
J Haas lost to AR Stephen 2 and 1

Second Day – Foursomes
Verplank & Sigel halved with Mayo & Montgomerie
Randolph & Haas beat Hawksworth & McGimpsey
 3 and 2
Lewis & Burroughs beat Baker & McEvoy 2 and 1
Podolak & Love beat Bloice & Stephen 3 and 2

Singles
Randolph halved with McGimpsey
Verplank beat Montgomerie 1 hole
Sigel lost to Hawksworth 4 and 3
Love beat McEvoy 5 and 3
Sonnier lost to Baker 5 and 4 .
Burroughs lost to Macgregor 3 and 2
Lewis beat Bloice 4 and 3
Waldorf lost to Stephen 2 and 1

1987 *at Sunningdale*
Result: USA 16½, GBI 7½
Captains: GC Marks (GBI), F Ridley (USA)

First Day – Foursomes
Montgomerie & Shaw lost to Alexander & Mayfair
 5 and 4
Currey & Mayo lost to Kite & Mattice 2 and 1
Macgregor & Robinson lost to Lewis & Loeffler
 2 and 1
McHenry & Girvan lost to Sigel & Andrade 3 and 2

Singles
D Currey beat B Alexander 2 holes
J Robinson lost to B Andrade 7 and 5
CS Montgomerie beat J Sorenson 3 and 2
R Eggo lost to J Sigel 3 and 2
J McHenry lost to B Montgomery 1 hole
P Girvan lost to B Lewis 3 and 2
DG Carrick lost to B Mayfair 2 holes
G Shaw beat C Kite 1 hole

Second Day – Foursomes
Currey & Carrick lost to Lewis & Loeffler 4 and 3
Montgomerie & Shaw lost to Kite & Mattice 5 and 3
Mayo & Macgregor lost to Sorenson & Montgomery
 4 and 3
McHenry & Robinson beat Sigel & Andrade 4 and 2

Singles
Currey lost to Alexander 5 and 4
Montgomerie beat Andrade 4 and 2
McHenry beat Loeffler 3 and 2
Shaw halved with Sorenson
Robinson beat Mattice 1 hole
Carrick lost to Lewis 3 and 2
Eggo lost to Mayfair 1 hole
Girvan lost to Sigel 6 and 5

1989 *at Peachtree, GA*
Result: GBI 12½, USA 11½
Captains: F Ridley (USA), GC Marks (GBI)

First Day – Foursomes
Gamez & Martin beat Claydon & Prosser 3 and 2
Yates & Mickelson halved with Dodd & McGimpsey
Lesher & Sigel lost to McEvoy & O'Connell 6 and 5
Eger & Johnson lost to Milligan & Hare 2 and 1

Singles
R Gamez beat JW Milligan 7 and 6
D Martin lost to R Claydon 5 and 4
E Meeks halved with SC Dodd
R Howe lost to E O'Connell 5 and 4
D Yates lost to P McEvoy 2 and 1
P Mickelson beat G McGimpsey 4 and 2
G Lesher lost to C Cassells 1 hole
J Sigel halved with RN Roderick

Second Day – Foursomes
Gamez & Martin halved with McEvoy & O'Connell
Sigel & Lesher lost to Claydon & Cassells 3 and 2
Eger & Johnson lost to Milligan & Hare 2 and 1
Mickelson & Yates lost to McGimpsey & Dodd
 2 and 1

Singles
Gamez beat Dodd 1 hole
Martin halved with Hare
Lesher beat Claydon 3 and 2
Yates beat McEvoy 4 and 3
Mickelson halved with O'Connell
Eger beat Roderick 4 and 2
Johnson beat Cassells 4 and 2
Sigel halved with Milligan

1991 *at Portmarnock*

Result: USA 14, GBI 10

*Captains: G Macgregor (GBI),
   JR Gabrielsen (USA)*

First Day – Foursomes

Milligan & Hay lost to Mickelson & May 5 and 3
Payne & Evans lost to Duval & Sposa 1 hole
McGimpsey & Willison lost to Voges & Eger
   1 hole
McGinley & Harrington lost to Sigel & Doyle 2 and 1

Singles

A Coltart lost to P Mickelson 4 and 3
J Payne beat F Langham 2 and 1
G Evans beat D Duval 2 and 1
R Willison lost to B May 2 and 1
G McGimpsey beat M Sposa 1 hole
P McGinley lost to A Doyle 6 and 4
G Hay beat T Scherrer 1 hole
L White lost to J Sigel 4 and 3

Second Day – Foursomes

Milligan & McGimpsey beat Voges & Eger 2 and 1
Payne & Willison lost to Duval & Sposa 1 hole
Evans & Coltart beat Langham & Scherrer 4 and 3
White & McGinley beat Mickelson & May 1 hole

Singles

Milligan lost to Mickelson 1 hole
Payne beat Doyle 3 and 1
Evans lost to Langham 4 and 2
Coltart beat Sigel 1 hole
Willison beat Scherrer 3 and 2
Harrington lost to Eger 3 and 2
McGimpsey lost to May 4 and 3
Hay lost to Voges 3 and 1

1993 *at Interlachen, Edina, MN*

Result: USA 19, GBI 5

*Captains: M Giles III (USA),
   G Macgregor (GBI)*

First Day – Foursomes

Abandoned – rain & flooding

Singles

A Doyle beat I Pyman 1 hole
D Berganio lost to M Stanford 3 and 2
J Sigel lost to D Robertson 3 and 2
K Mitchum halved with S Cage
T Herron beat P Harrington 1 hole
D Yates beat P Page 2 and 1
T Demsey beat R Russell 2 and 1
J Leonard beat R Burns 4 and 3
B Gay lost to V Phillips 2 and 1
J Harris beat B Dredge 4 and 3

Second Day – Foursomes

Doyle & Leonard beat Pyman & Cage 4 and 3
Berganio & Demsey beat Stanford & Harrington
   3 and 2
Sigel & Mitchum beat Dredge & Phillips 3 and 2
Harris & Herron beat Russell & Robertson 1 hole

Singles

Doyle beat Robertson 4 and 3
Harris beat Pyman 3 and 2
Yates beat Cage 2 and 1
Gay halved with Harrington
Sigel beat Page 5 and 4
Herron beat Phillips 3 and 2
Mitchum beat Russell 4 and 2
Berganio lost to Burns 1 hole
Demsey beat Dredge 3 and 2
Leonard beat Stanford 5 and 4

1995 *at Royal Porthcawl*

Result: GBI 14, USA 10

*Captains: C Brown (GBI),
   AD Gray jr (USA)*

First Day – Foursomes

Sherry & Gallacher lost to Harris & Woods 4 and 3
Foster & Howell halved with Bratton & Riley
Rankin & Howard lost to Begay & Jackson 4 and 3
Harrington & Fanagan beat Cox & Kuehne
   5 and 3

Singles

G Sherry beat N Begay 3 and 2
L James lost to K Cox 1 hole
M Foster beat B Marucci 4 and 3
S Gallacher beat T Jackson 4 and 3
P Harrington beat J Courville jr 2 holes
B Howard halved with A Bratton
G Rankin lost to J Harris 1 hole
GP Wolstenholme beat T Woods 1 hole

Second Day – Foursomes

Sherry & Gallacher lost to Bratton & Riley 4 and 2
Howell & Foster beat Cox & Kuehne 3 and 2
Wolstenholme & James lost to Marucci & Courville
   6 and 5
Harrington & Fanagan beat Harris & Woods 2 and 1

Singles

Sherry beat Riley 2 holes
Howell beat Begay 2 and 1
Gallacher beat Kuehne 3 and 2
Fanagan beat Courville 3 and 2
Howard halved with Jackson
Foster halved with Marucci
Harrington lost to Harris 3 and 2
Wolstenholme lost to Woods 4 and 3

1997 *at Quaker Ridge, NY*

Result: USA 18, GBI 6

Captains: AD Gray jr (USA), C Brown(GBI)

First Day – Foursomes

Howard & Young lost to Elder & Kribel 4 and 3
Rose & Brooks lost to Courville & Marucci 5 and 4
Wolstenholme & Nolan lost to Gore & Harris
   6 and 4
Coughlan & Park lost to Leen & Wollman 1 hole

Singles

S Young beat D Delcher 5 and 4
C Watson beat S Scott 1 hole
B Howard lost to B Elder 5 and 4
J Rose beat J Kribel 1 hole
K Nolan lost to R Leen 3 and 2
G Rankin lost to J Gore 3 and 2
R Coughlan halved with C Wollman
GP Wolstenholme lost to J Harris 1 hole

Second Day – Foursomes

Young & Watson lost to Harris & Elder 3 and 2
Howard & Rankin lost to Courville & Marucci 5 and 4
Coughlan & Park lost to Delcher & Scott 1 hole
Wolstenholme & Rose beat Leen & Wollman 2 and 1

Singles

Young beat Kribel 2 and 1
Watson halved with Gore
Rose lost to Courville 3 and 2
Nolan lost to Elder 2 and 1
Brooks lost to Harris 6 and 5
Park lost to Marucci 4 and 3
Wolstenholme lost to Delcher 2 and 1
Coughlan lost to Scott 2 and 1

1999 *at Nairn*
Result: GBI 15, USA 9
Captains: P McEvoy (GBI), D Yates (USA)

First Day – Foursomes
Rankin & Storm lost to Haas & Miller 1 hole
Casey & Donald beat Byrd & Scott 5 and 3
Gribben & Kelly lost to Gossett & Jackson 3 and 1
Rowe & Wolstenholme beat Kuchar & Molder 1 hole

Singles
G Rankin lost to E Loar 4 and 3
L Donald beat T McKnight 4 and 3
G Storm lost to H Haas 5 and 3
P Casey beat S Scott 4 and 3
D Patrick lost to J Byrd 6 and 5
S Dyson halved with D Gossett
P Gribben halved with B Molder
L Kelly lost to T Jackson 3 and 1

Second Day – Foursomes
Rankin & Storm beat Loar & McKnight 4 and 3
Dyson & Gribben lost to Haas & Miller 1 hole
Casey & Donald beat Gossett & Jackson 1 hole
Rowe & Wolstenholme beat Kuchar & Molder 4 and 3

Singles
Rankin beat Scott 1 hole
Dyson lost to Loar 5 and 4
Casey beat Miller 3 and 2
Storm beat Byrd 1 hole
Donald beat Molder 3 and 2
Rowe beat Kuchar 1 hole
Gribben beat Haas 3 and 2
Wolstenholme beat Gossett 1 hole

Walker Cup – INDIVIDUAL RECORDS

Notes: Bold type indicates captain; in brackets, did not play
† indicates players who have also played in the Ryder Cup

Great Britain and Ireland

Name		Year	Played	Won	Lost	Halved
MF Attenborough	Eng	1967	2	0	2	0
CC Aylmer	Eng	1922	2	1	1	0
†P Baker	Eng	1985	3	2	1	0
JB Beck	Eng	1928-(38)-(47)	1	0	1	0
PJ Benka	Eng	1969	4	2	1	1
HG Bentley	Eng	1934-36-38	4	0	2	2
DA Blair	Sco	1955-61	4	1	3	0
C Bloice	Sco	1985	3	0	2	1
MF Bonallack	Eng	1957-59-61-63-65-67-**69-71-73**	25	8	14	3
†G Brand jr	Sco	1979	3	0	3	0
OC Bristowe	Eng	(1923)-24	1	0	1	0
A Brodie	Sco	1977-79	8	5	2	1
A Brooks	Sco	1969	3	2	0	1
M Brooks	Sco	1997	2	0	2	0
C Brown	Wal	**1995-(97)**	0	0	0	0
Hon WGE Brownlow	Eng	1926	2	0	2	0
J Bruen	Irl	1938-49-51	5	0	4	1
JA Buckley	Wal	1979	1	0	1	0
J Burke	Irl	1932	2	0	1	1
R Burns	Irl	1993	2	1	1	0
AF Bussell	Sco	1957	2	1	1	0
S Cage	Eng	1993	3	0	2	1
I Caldwell	Eng	1951-55	4	1	2	1
W Campbell	Sco	1930	2	0	2	0
JB Carr	Irl	1947-49-51-53-55-57-59-61-63-(65)-67	20	5	14	1
RJ Carr	Irl	1971	4	3	0	1
DG Carrick	Sco	1983-87	5	0	5	0
IA Carslaw	Sco	1979	3	1	1	1
P Casey	Eng	1999	4	4	0	0
C Cassells	Eng	1989	3	2	1	0
JR Cater	Sco	1955	1	0	1	0
J Caven	Sco	1922	2	0	2	0
BHG Chapman	Eng	1961	1	0	1	0
R Chapman	Eng	1981	4	3	1	0
MJ Christmas	Eng	1961-63	3	1	2	0
†CA Clark	Eng	1965	4	2	0	2
GJ Clark	Eng	1965	1	0	1	0
†HK Clark	Eng	1973	3	1	1	1
R Claydon	Eng	1989	4	2	2	0

Name		Year	Played	Won	Lost	Halved
†A Coltart	Sco	1991	3	2	1	0
GB Cosh	Sco	1965	4	3	1	0
R Coughlan	Irl	1997	4	0	3	1
T Craddock	Irl	1967-69	6	2	3	1
LG Crawley	Eng	1932-34-38-47	6	3	3	0
B Critchley	Eng	1969	4	1	1	2
D Curry	Eng	1987	4	1	3	0
CR Dalgleish	Sco	1981	3	1	2	0
B Darwin	Eng	1922	2	1	1	0
JC Davies	Eng	1973-75-77-79	13	3	8	2
P Deeble	Eng	1977-81	5	1	4	0
FWG Deighton	Sco	(1951)-57	2	0	2	0
SC Dodd	Wal	1989	4	1	1	2
L Donald	Eng	1999-01	8	7	1	0
N Dougherty	Eng	2001	4	3	1	0
B Dredge	Wal	1993	3	0	3	0
†NV Drew	Irl	1953	1	0	1	0
AA Duncan	Wal	**(1953)**	0	0	0	0
JM Dykes	Sco	1936	2	0	1	1
S Dyson	Eng	1999	3	0	2	1
N Edwards	Wal	2001	1	0	1	0
R Eggo	Eng	1987	2	0	2	0
J Elson	Eng	2001	3	1	0	2
D Evans	Wal	1981	3	1	1	1
G Evans	Eng	1991	4	2	2	0
RC Ewing	Irl	1936-38-47-49-51-55	10	1	7	2
GRD Eyles	Eng	1975	4	2	2	0
J Fanagan	Irl	1995	3	3	0	0
EW Fiddian	Eng	1932-34	4	0	4	0
J de Forest	Eng	1932	1	0	1	0
M Foster	Eng	1995	4	2	0	2
R Foster	Eng	1965-67-69-71-73-(**79**)-(**81**)	17	2	13	2
DW Frame	Eng	1961	1	0	1	0
S Gallacher	Sco	1995	4	2	2	0
†D Gilford	Eng	1985	1	0	1	0
P Girvan	Sco	1987	3	0	3	0
G Godwin	Eng	1979-81	7	2	4	1
CW Green	Sco	1963-69-71-73-75-(**83**)-(**85**)	17	4	10	3
P Gribben	Irl	1999	4	1	2	1
RH Hardman	Eng	1928	1	0	1	0
A Hare	Eng	1989	3	2	2	0
†P Harrington	Irl	1991-93-95	9	3	5	1
R Harris	Sco	(**1922**)-23-**26**	4	1	3	0
RW Hartley	Eng	1930-32	4	0	4	0
WL Hartley	Eng	1932	2	0	2	0
J Hawksworth	Eng	1985	4	2	1	1
G Hay	Sco	1991	3	1	2	0
P Hedges	Eng	1973-75	5	0	2	3
CO Hezlet	Irl	1924-26-28	6	0	5	1
GA Hill	Eng	1936-(**55**)	2	0	1	1
M Hoey	Irl	2001	4	3	1	0
Sir EWE Holderness	Eng	1923-26-30	6	2	4	0
TWB Homer	Eng	1973	3	0	3	0
‡CVL Hooman	Eng	1922-23	3	†1	2	†0
WL Hope	Sco	1923-24-28	5	1	4	0
DB Howard	Sco	1995-97	6	0	4	2
D Howell	Eng	1995	3	2	0	1
G Huddy	Eng	1961	1	0	1	0
W Humphreys	Eng	1971	3	2	1	0
IC Hutcheon	Sco	1975-77-79-81	15	5	8	2
RR Jack	Sco	1957-59	4	2	2	0
L James	Eng	1995	2	0	2	0
†M James	Eng	1975	4	3	1	0
A Jamieson jr	Sco	1926	2	1	1	0
MJ Kelley	Eng	1977-79	7	3	3	1
L Kelly	Sco	1999	2	0	2	0
SD Keppler	Eng	1983	4	0	3	1
†MG King	Eng	1969-73	7	1	5	1
AT Kyle	Sco	1938-47-51	5	2	3	0
DH Kyle	Sco	1924	1	0	1	0

‡*In 1922 Hooman beat Sweetser at the 37th – on all other occasions halved matches have counted as such.*

Walker Cup Individual Records *continued*

Name		Year	Played	Won	Lost	Halved
JA Lang	Sco	(1930)	0	0	0	0
JDA Langley	Eng	1936-51-53	6	0	5	1
CD Lawrie	Sco	(1961)-(63)	0	0	0	0
ME Lewis	Eng	1983	1	0	1	0
PB Lucas	Eng	(1936)-47-(49)	2	1	1	0
MSR Lunt	Eng	1959-61-63-65	11	2	8	1
†AWB Lyle	Sco	1977	3	0	3	0
AR McCallum	Sco	1928	1	0	1	0
SM McCready	Irl	1949-51	3	0	3	0
JS Macdonald	Sco	1971	3	1	1	1
G McDowell	Irl	2001	4	2	2	0
P McEvoy	Eng	1977-79-81-85-89-(99)-(01)	18	5	11	2
R McEvoy	Eng	2001	2	1	0	1
G McGimpsey	Irl	1985-89-91	11	4	5	2
P McGinley	Irl	1991	3	1	2	0
G Macgregor	Sco	1971-75-83-85-87-(91)-(93)	14	5	8	1
RC MacGregor	Sco	1953	2	0	2	0
J McHenry	Irl	1987	4	2	2	0
P McKellar	Sco	1977	1	0	1	0
WW Mackenzie	Sco	1922-23	3	1	2	0
SL McKinlay	Sco	1934	2	0	2	0
J McLean	Sco	1934-36	4	1	3	0
EA McRuvie	Sco	1932-34	4	1	2	1
JFD Madeley	Irl	1963	2	0	1	1
LS Mann	Sco	1983	4	2	1	1
B Marchbank	Sco	1979	4	2	2	0
GC Marks	Eng	1969-71-(87)-(89)	6	2	4	0
DM Marsh	Eng	71-(73)-(75)	3	2	1	0
GNC Martin	Irl	1928	1	0	1	0
S Martin	Sco	1977	4	2	2	0
P Mayo	Wal	1985-87	4	0	3	1
GH Micklem	Eng	1947-49-53-55-(57)-(59)	6	1	5	0
DJ Millensted	Eng	1967	2	1	1	0
JW Milligan	Sco	1989-91	7	3	3	1
EB Millward	Eng	(1949)-55	2	0	2	0
WTG Milne	Sco	1973	4	2	2	0
†CS Montgomerie	Sco	1985-87	8	2	5	1
JL Morgan	Wal	1951-53-55	6	2	4	0
P Mulcare	Irl	1975	3	2	1	0
GH Murray	Sco	1977	2	1	1	0
SWT Murray	Sco	1963	4	2	2	0
WA Murray	Sco	1923-24-(26)	4	1	3	0
K Nolan	Irl	1997	3	0	3	0
E O'Connell	Irl	1989	4	2	0	2
S O'Hara	Sco	2001	4	2	2	0
A Oldcorn	Eng	1983	4	4	0	0
†PA Oosterhuis	Eng	1967	4	1	2	1
R Oppenheimer	Eng	(1951)	0	0	0	0
P Page	Eng	1993	2	0	2	0
D Park	Wal	1997	3	0	3	0
P Parkin	Wal	1983	3	2	1	0
D Patrick	Sco	1999	1	0	1	0
J Payne	Eng	1991	4	2	2	0
JJF Pennink	Eng	1938	2	1	1	0
TP Perkins	Eng	1928	2	0	2	0
GB Peters	Sco	1936-38	4	2	1	1
V Phillips	Eng	1993	3	1	2	0
AD Pierse	Irl	1983	3	0	2	1
AH Perowne	Eng	1949-53-59	4	0	4	0
AK Pirie	Sco	1967	3	0	2	1
MA Poxon	Eng	1975	2	0	2	0
D Prosser	Eng	1989	1	0	1	2
I Pyman	Eng	1993	3	0	3	0
†R Rafferty	Irl	1981	4	2	2	0
G Rankin	Sco	1995-97-99	8	2	6	0
D Robertson	Sco	1993	3	1	2	0
J Robinson	Eng	1987	4	2	2	0
RN Roderick	Wal	1989	2	0	1	1

Name		Year	Played	Won	Lost	Halved
J Rose	Eng	1997	4	2	2	0
P Rowe	Eng	1999	3	3	0	0
R Russell	Sco	1993	3	0	3	0
AC Saddler	Sco	1963-65-67-(77)	10	3	5	2
Hon M Scott	Eng	1924-**34**	4	2	2	0
R Scott, jr	Sco	1924	1	1	0	0
PF Scrutton	Eng	1955-57	3	0	3	0
DN Sewell	Eng	1957-59	4	1	3	0
RDBM Shade	Sco	1961-63-65-67	14	6	6	2
G Shaw	Sco	1987	4	1	2	1
DB Sheahan	Irl	1963	4	2	2	0
AE Shepperson	Eng	1957-59	3	1	1	1
G Sherry	Sco	1995	4	2	2	0
AF Simpson	Sco	(1926)	0	0	0	0
JN Smith	Sco	1930	2	0	2	0
WD Smith	Sco	1959	1	0	1	0
M Stanford	Eng	1993	3	1	2	0
AR Stephen	Sco	1985	4	2	1	1
EF Storey	Eng	1924-26-28	6	1	5	0
G Storm	Eng	1999	4	2	2	0
JA Stout	Eng	1930-32	4	0	3	1
C Stowe	Eng	1938-47	4	2	2	0
HB Stuart	Sco	1971-73-75	10	4	6	0
A Thirlwell	Eng	1957	1	0	1	0
KG Thom	Eng	1949	2	0	2	0
MS Thompson	Eng	1983	3	1	2	0
H Thomson	Sco	1936-38	4	2	2	0
CJH Tolley	Eng	1922-23-**24**-26-30-34	12	4	8	0
TA Torrance	Sco	1924-28-30-**32**-34	9	3	5	1
WB Torrance	Sco	1922	2	0	2	0
†PM Townsend	Eng	1965	4	3	1	0
LP Tupling	Eng	1969	2	1	1	0
W Tweddell	Eng	**1928**-(36)	2	0	2	0
J Walker	Sco	1961	2	0	2	0
†P Walton	Irl	1981-83	8	6	2	0
M Warren	Sco	2001	3	2	1	0
C Watson	Sco	1997	3	1	1	1
†P Way	Eng	1981	4	2	2	0
RH Wethered	Eng	1922-23-26-**30**-34	9	5	3	1
L White	Eng	1991	2	1	1	0
RJ White	Eng	1947-49-51-53-55	10	6	3	1
R Willison	Eng	1991	4	1	3	0
J Wilson	Sco	1923	2	2	0	0
JC Wilson	Sco	1947-53	4	0	4	0
GB Wolstenholme	Eng	1957-59	4	1	2	1
GP Wolstenholme	Eng	1995-97-99-01	13	7	6	0
S Young	Sco	1997	4	2	2	0

United States of America

Name	Year	Played	Won	Lost	Halved
†TD Aaron	1959	2	1	1	0
B Alexander	1987	3	2	1	0
DC Allen	1965-67	6	0	4	2
B Andrade	1987	4	2	2	0
ES Andrews	1961	1	1	0	0
D Ballenger	1973	1	1	0	0
R Baxter, jr	1957	2	2	0	0
N Begay III	1995	3	1	2	0
DR Beman	1959-61-63-65	11	7	2	2
D Berganio	1993	3	1	2	0
RE Billows	1938-49	4	2	2	0
SE Bishop	1947-49	3	2	1	0
AS Blum	1957	1	0	1	0
J Bohmann	1969	3	1	2	0
M Brannan	1977	3	1	2	0
A Bratton	1995	3	1	0	2

Walker Cup Individual Records *continued*

Name	Year	Played	Won	Lost	Halved
GF Burns	1975	3	2	1	0
C Burroughs	1985	3	1	2	0
J Byrd	1999	3	1	2	0
AE Campbell	1936	2	2	0	0
JE Campbell	1957	1	0	1	0
WC Campbell	1951-53-(55)-57-65-67-71-75	18	11	4	3
N Cassini	2001	4	2	2	0
RJ Cerrudo	1967	4	1	1	2
RD Chapman	1947-51-53	5	3	2	0
D Cherry	1953-55-61	5	5	0	0
D Clarke	1979	3	2	0	1
RE Cochran	1961	1	1	0	0
CR Coe	1949-51-53-(57)-59-61-63	13	7	4	2
R Commans	1981	3	1	1	1
E Compton	2001	3	1	1	1
JW Conrad	1955	2	1	1	0
J Courville jr	1995-97	6	4	2	0
K Cox	1995	3	1	2	0
N Crosby	1983	2	1	1	0
BH Cudd	1955	2	2	0	0
RD Davies	1963	2	0	2	0
JW Dawson	1949	2	2	0	0
D Delcher	1997	3	2	1	0
T Demsey	1993	3	3	0	0
RB Dickson	1967	3	3	0	0
A Doyle	1991-93	6	5	1	0
J Driscoll	2001	3	0	3	0
GT Dunlap jr	1932-34-36	5	3	1	1
†D Duval	1991	3	2	1	0
D Edwards	1973	4	4	0	0
HC Egan	1934	1	1	0	0
D Eger	1991-01	5	3	1	1
HC Eger	1989	3	1	2	0
D Eichelberger	1965	3	1	2	0
B Elder	1997	4	4	0	0
J Ellis	1973	3	2	1	0
W Emery	1936	2	1	0	1
C Evans jr	1922-24-28	5	3	2	0
J Farquhar	1971	3	1	2	0
†B Faxon	1983	4	3	1	0
R Fehr	1983	4	2	1	1
JW Fischer	1934-36-38-(65)	4	3	0	1
D Fischesser	1979	3	1	2	0
MA Fleckman	1967	2	0	2	0
B Fleisher	1969	4	0	2	2
J Fought	1977	4	4	0	0
WC Fownes jr	**1922-24**	3	1	2	0
F Fuhrer	1981	3	2	1	0
JR Gabrielsen	1977-(81)-(91)	3	1	2	0
R Gamez	1989	4	3	0	1
RA Gardner	1922-**23**-24-**26**	8	6	2	0
RW Gardner	1961-63	5	4	0	1
B Gay	1993	2	0	1	1
M Giles	1969-71-73-75	15	8	2	5
HL Givan	1936	1	0	0	1
L Glover	2001	4	2	2	0
JG Goodman	1934-36-38	6	4	2	0
J Gore	1997	3	2	0	1
D Gossett	1999	4	1	2	1
M Gove	1979	3	2	1	0
J Grace	1975	3	2	1	0
JA Grant	1967	2	2	0	0
AD Gray jr	1963-65-67-**(95)**-**(97)**	12	5	6	1
D Green	2001	3	0	3	0
JP Guilford	1922-24-26	6	4	2	0
W Gunn	1926-28	4	4	0	0
†F Haas jr	1938	2	0	2	0
H Haas	1999	4	3	1	0

Name	Year	Played	Won	Lost	Halved
†J Haas	1975	3	3	0	0
J Haas	1985	3	1	2	0
G Hallberg	1977	3	1	2	0
GS Hamer jr	(1947)	0	0	0	0
J Harris	1993-95-97-01	14	10	4	0
LE Harris jr	1963	4	3	1	0
V Heafner	1977	3	3	0	0
SD Herron	1923	2	0	2	0
T Herron	1993	3	3	0	0
†S Hoch	1979	4	4	0	0
W Hoffer	1983	2	1	1	0
J Holtgrieve	1979-81-83	10	6	4	0
JM Hopkins	1965	3	0	2	1
R Howe	1989	1	0	1	0
W Howell	1932	1	1	0	0
W Hyndman	1957-59-61-69-71	9	6	1	2
J Inman	1969	2	2	0	0
JG Jackson	1953-55	3	3	0	0
T Jackson	1995-99	6	3	2	1
K Johnson	1989	3	1	2	0
HR Johnston	1923-24-28-30	6	5	1	0
RT Jones jr	1922-24-26-**28-30**	10	9	1	0
AF Kammer	1947	2	1	1	0
M Killian	1973	3	1	2	0
C Kite	1987	3	2	1	0
†TO Kite	1971	4	2	1	1
RE Knepper	(1922)	0	0	0	0
RW Knowles	1951	1	1	0	0
G Koch	1973-75	7	4	1	2
CR Kocsis	1938-49-57	5	2	2	1
J Kribel	1997	3	1	2	0
M Kuchar	1999	3	0	3	0
T Kuehne	1995	3	0	3	0
F Langham	1991	3	1	2	0
R Leen	1997	3	2	1	0
†J Leonard	1993	3	3	0	0
G Lesher	1989	4	1	3	0
B Lewis jr	1981-83-85-87	14	10	4	0
JW Lewis	1967	4	3	1	0
WL Little jr	1934	2	2	0	0
†GA Littler	1953	2	2	0	0
E Loar	1999	3	2	1	0
B Loeffler	1987	3	2	1	0
†D Love III	1985	3	2	0	1
RR Mackenzie	1926-28-30	6	5	1	0
MJ McCarthy jr	(1928)-32	1	1	0	0
BN McCormick	1949	1	1	0	0
T McKnight	1999	2	0	2	0
JB McHale	1949-51	3	2	0	1
MR Marston	1922-23-24-34	8	5	3	0
D Martin	1989	4	1	1	2
B Marucci	1995-97	6	4	1	1
L Mattiace	1987	3	2	1	0
R May	1991	4	3	1	0
B Mayfair	1987	3	3	0	0
E Meeks	1989	1	0	0	1
SN Melnyk	1969-71	7	3	3	1
†P Mickelson	1989-91	8	4	2	2
AL Miller	1969-71	8	4	3	1
J Miller	1999	3	2	1	0
L Miller	1977	4	4	0	0
K Mitchum	1993	3	2	0	1
DK Moe	1930-32	3	3	0	0
B Molder	1999-01	8	3	3	2
B Montgomery	1987	2	2	0	0
G Moody	1979	3	1	2	0
GT Moreland	1932-34	4	4	0	0
D Morey	1955-65	4	1	3	0
J Mudd	1981	3	3	0	0
†RJ Murphy	1967	4	1	2	1

Walker Cup Individual Records *continued*

Name	Year	Played	Won	Lost	Halved
JF Neville	1923	1	0	1	0
†JW Nicklaus	1959-61	4	4	0	0
LW Oehmig	(1977)	0	0	0	0
FD Ouimet	1922-23-24-26-30-**32-34**-(**36**)-(**38**)-(**47**)-(**49**)	16	9	5	2
HD Paddock jr	1951	1	0	0	1
†J Pate	1975	4	0	4	0
WJ Patton	1955-57-59-63-65-(**69**)	14	11	3	0
†C Pavin	1981	3	2	0	1
M Peck	1979	3	1	1	1
M Pfeil	1973	4	2	1	1
M Podolak	1985	2	1	0	1
SL Quick	1947	2	1	1	0
J Quinney	2001	2	0	2	0
S Randolph	1985	4	2	1	1
J Rassett	1981	3	3	0	0
F Ridley	1977-(**87**)-(**89**)	3	2	1	0
RH Riegel	1947-49	4	4	0	0
C Riley	1995	3	1	1	1
H Robbins jr	1957	2	0	1	1
†W Rogers	1973	2	1	1	0
GV Rotan	1923	2	1	1	0
†EM Rudolph	1957	2	1	0	1
B Sander	1977	3	0	3	0
T Scherrer	1991	3	0	3	0
S Scott	1997-99	6	2	4	0
CH Seaver	1932	2	2	0	0
RL Siderowf	1969-73-75-77-(**79**)	14	4	8	2
J Sigel	1977-79-81-**83**-85-87-89-91-93	33	18	10	5
RH Sikes	1963	3	1	2	0
JB Simons	1971	2	0	2	0
†S Simpson	1977	3	3	0	0
CB Smith	1961-63	2	0	1	1
R Smith	1936-38	4	2	2	0
R Sonnier	1985	3	0	2	1
J Sorensen	1987	3	1	1	1
M Sposa	1991	3	2	1	0
†C Stadler	1975	3	3	0	0
FR Stranahan	1947-49-51	6	3	2	1
†C Strange	1975	4	3	0	1
†H Sutton	1979-81	7	2	4	1
‡JW Sweetser	1922-23-24-26-28-32-(**67**)-(**73**)	12	7	†4	†1
FM Taylor	1957-59-61	4	4	0	0
D Tentis	1983	2	0	1	1
DJ Trahan	2001	4	1	3	0
RS Tufts	(**1963**)	0	0	0	0
WP Turnesa	1947-49-**51**	6	3	3	0
B Tuten	1983	2	1	1	0
EM Tutweiler	1965-67	6	5	1	0
ER Updegraff	1963-65-69-(**75**)	7	3	3	1
S Urzetta	1951-53	4	4	0	0
K Venturi	1953	2	2	0	0
S Verplank	1985	4	3	0	1
M Voges	1991	3	2	1	0
GJ Voigt	1930-32-36	5	2	2	1
G Von Elm	1926-28-30	6	4	1	1
D von Tacky	1981	3	1	2	0
†JL Wadkins	1969-71	7	3	4	0
D Waldorf	1985	3	1	2	0
EH Ward	1953-55-59	6	6	0	0
MH Ward	1938-47	4	2	2	0
M West	1973-79	6	2	3	1
J Westland	1932-34-53-(**61**)	5	3	0	2
HW Wettlaufer	1959	2	2	0	0
E White	1936	2	2	0	0
OF Willing	1923-24-30	4	4	0	0
JM Winters jr	(**1971**)	0	0	0	0
C Wollman	1997	3	1	1	1
W Wood	1983	4	1	2	1

‡ *In 1922 Hooman beat Sweetser at the 37th – on all other occasions halved matches have counted as such.*

Name	Year	Played	Won	Lost	Halved
†T Woods	1995	4	2	2	0
FJ Wright	1923	1	1	0	0
CR Yates	1936-38-(53)	4	3	0	1
D Yates jr	1989-93-(99)-01	6	3	2	1
RL Yost	1955	2	2	0	0

World Amateur Team Championship (Eisenhower Trophy)

Year	Winners	Runners-up	Venue	Score
1958	Australia	United States	St Andrews	918

(After a tie, Australia won the play-off by two strokes: Australia 222, United States 224)

Year	Winners	Runners-up	Venue	Score
1960	United States	Australia	Ardmore, USA	834
1962	United States	Canada	Kawana, Japan	854
1964	Great Britain & Ireland	Canada	Olgiata, Rome	895
1966	Australia	United States	Mexico City	877
1968	United States	Great Britain & Ireland	Melbourne	868
1970	United States	New Zealand	Madrid	857
1972	United States	Australia	Buenos Aires	865
1974	United States	Japan	Dominican Rep.	888
1976	Great Britain & Ireland	Japan	Penina, Portugal	892
1978	United States	Canada	Fiji	873
1980	United States	South Africa	Pinehurst, USA	848
1982	United States	Sweden	Lausanne	859
1984	Japan	United States	Hong Kong	870
1986	Canada	United States	Caracas, Venezuela	860
1988	Great Britain & Ireland	United States	Ullva, Sweden	882
1990	Sweden	New Zealand	Christchurch, New Zealand	879
1992	New Zealand	United States	Capilano, Canada	823
1994	United States	Great Britain & Ireland	Paris, France	838
1996	Australia	Sweden	Manila, Philippines	838
1998	Great Britain and Ireland	Australia	Los Leones/La Dehesa, Chile	852
2000	United States	Great Britain & Ireland	Sporting Club, Berlin	841

Europe v Asia-Pacific

2000 *at Puerta de Hierro, Spain*

Europe 20, Asia-Pacific 12

European Amateur Team Championship

Year	Winner	Second	Venue
1959	Sweden		
1961	Sweden	England	Brussels, Belgium
1963	England	Sweden	Falsterbo, Sweden
1965	Ireland	Scotland	St George's, England
1967	Ireland	France	Turin, Italy
1969	England	W Germany	Hamburg, W Germany
1971	England	Scotland	Lausanne, Switzerland
1973	England	Scotland	Penina, Portugal
1975	Scotland	Italy	Killarney, Ireland
1977	Scotland	Sweden	The Haagsche, Holland
1979	England	Wales	Esbjerg, Denmark
1981	England	Scotland	St Andrews, Scotland
1983	Ireland	Spain	Chantilly, France
1985	Scotland	Sweden	Halmstad, Sweden
1987	Ireland	England	Murhof, Austria
1989	England	Scotland	Royal Porthcawl
1991	England	Italy	Puerta de Hierro
1993	Wales	England	Marianske Lasne, Czech Republic
1995	Scotland	England	Royal Antwerp, Belgium
1997	Spain	Scotland	Portmarnock
1999	France	England	Monticello, Italy
2001	Scotland	Ireland	Ljunghusens, Sweden

European Club Cup

1975	Club de Campo, Spain	Club de Campo	1989	Ealing, England	Aloha
1976	Växjö Golfklub, Sweden	El Prat	1990	Ealing, England	Aloha
1977	Chantilly, France	RC Belgique	1991	Club de Golf Terramar, Spain	La Quinta
1978	Hamburger, Germany	Deauville	1992	Hillerod, Denmark	La Quinta
1979	Hamburger, Germany	Santa Ponsa	1993	Lahden, Finland	La Quinta
1980	Limerick, Ireland	Santa Ponsa	1994	Kilmarnock (Barassie),	
1981	El Prat, Spain	Aloha		Scotland	Vilamoura
1982	El Prat, Spain	Aloha	1995	Racing C de France, France	Vilamoura
1983	Rapallo, Italy	Aloha	1996	Racing C de France, France	Vilamoura
1984	Hamburger, Germany	Aloha	1997	Racing C de France, France	Parco de Medici
1985	El Prat, Spain	Aloha	1998	Aalborg, Denmark	Parco de Medici
1986	Hamburger, Germany	Aloha	1999	Aalborg, Denmark	Parco de Medici
1987	Puerto de Hierro, Spain	Aloha	2000	Shandon Park,	
1988	Brokenhurst Manor, England	Aloha		Northern Ireland	Parco de Medici

St Andrews Trophy (Great Britain & Ireland v Continent of Europe) Match instituted 1956, trophy presented 1962

1956	Great Britain & Ireland	Wentworth	12½–2½
1958	Great Britain & Ireland	St Cloud, France	10–5
1960	Great Britain & Ireland	Walton Heath	13–5
1962	Great Britain & Ireland	Halmstead, Sweden	18–12
1964	Great Britain & Ireland	Muirfield	23–7
1966	Great Britain & Ireland	Bilbao, Spain	19½–10½
1968	Great Britain & Ireland	Portmarnock	20–10
1970	Great Britain & Ireland	La Zoute, Belgium	17½–12½
1972	Great Britain & Ireland	Berkshire	19½–10½
1974	Continent of Europe	Punta Ala, Italy	16–14
1976	Great Britain & Ireland	St Andrews	18½–11½
1978	Great Britain & Ireland	Bremen, Germany	20½–9½
1980	Great Britain & Ireland	Sandwich, R St George's	19½–10½
1982	Continent of Europe	Rosendaelsche, Netherlands	14–10
1984	Great Britain & Ireland	Saunton, Devon	13–11
1986	Great Britain & Ireland	Halmstead, Sweden	14½–9½
1988	Great Britain & Ireland	St Andrews	15½–8½
1990	Great Britain & Ireland	El Saler, Spain	13–11
1992	Great Britain & Ireland	R Cinque Ports	14–10
1994	Great Britain & Ireland	Chantilly, France	14–10
1996	Great Britain & Ireland	Woodhall Spa	16–8
1998	Continent of Europe	Villa d'Este, Italy	14–10

2000 *at The Ailsa Course, Turnberry*

GB&I		Continent of Europe	
First Day – **Foursomes**			
Luke Donald and Paul Casey (halved)	½	Jochen Lupprian and Stefano Reale (halved)	½
Mark Loftus and Steven O'Hara	0	Tino Schuster and Michael Thannhauser (2/1)	1
Gary Wolstenholme and Nick Dougherty	0	Mikko Ilonen and Panu Kylliainen (7 and 6)	1
Max Harris and Noel Fox (4 and 3)	1	Thomas Besancenez and Jacques Thalamy	0
	1½		2½
Singles			
Luke Donald (6 and 5)	1	Rafel Vera	0
Paul Casey (1 hole)	1	Stefano Reale	0
Mark Loftus	0	Jochen Lupprian (1 hole)	1
Jamie Donladson (5 and 4)	1	Tino Schuster	0
Steven O'Hara (4 and 3)	1	Michael Thannhauser	0
Max Harris (halved)	½	Jacques Thalamy (halved)	½
Nick Dougherty (5 and 4)	1	Panu Kylliainen	0
Gary Wolstenholme	0	Mikko Ilonen (1 hole)	1
	5½		2½

Match position: GB&I 7, Continent of Europe 5

Second Day – **Foursomes**

Loftus and O'Hara	0	Schuster and Thannhauser (1 hole)	1
Harris and Fox	0	Reale and Lupprian (4 and 2)	1
Donald and Casey (3 and 2)	1	Thalamy and Vera	0
Donaldson and Dougherty	0	Ilonen and Kylliainen (1 hole)	1
	1		**3**

Singles

Wolstenholme	0	Thannhauser (2 and 1)	1
O'Hara (2 and 1)	1	Schuster	0
Harris (3 and 1)	1	Besancenez	0
Dougherty	0	Reale (2 and 1)	1
Casey (1 hole)	1	Thalamy	0
Donald (2 and 1)	1	Lupprian	0
Donaldson (3 and 2)	1	Kylliainen	0
Fox	0	Ilonen (4 and 2)	1
	5		**3**

Match Result: GB&I 13, Continent of Europe 11

Home Internationals

1932	Scotland	1958	England	1977	England
1933	Scotland	1959T	England/Ireland/Scotland	1978	England
1934	Scotland	1960	England	1979	No Internationals held
1935T	England/Ireland/Scotland	1961	Scotland	1980	England
1936	Scotland	1962T	England/Ireland/Scotland	1981	Scotland
1937	Scotland	1963T	England/Ireland/Scotland	1982	Scotland
1938	England	1964	England	1983	Ireland
1939–46	No Internationals held	1965	England	1984	England
1947	England	1966	England	1985	England
1948	England	1967	Scotland	1986	Scotland
1949	England	1968	England	1987	Ireland
1950	Ireland	1969	England	1988	England
1951T	Ireland and Scotland	1970	Scotland	1989	England
1952	Scotland	1971	Scotland	1990	Ireland
1953	Scotland	1972T	Scotland/England	1991	Ireland
1954	England	1973	England	1992T	England and Ireland
1955	Ireland	1974	England	1993	England
1956	Scotland	1975	Scotland		
1957	England	1976	Scotland		

1994 *at Ashburnham, Dyfed*

England beat Scotland	9½ matches to 5½
Ireland beat Wales	10½ matches to 4½
England beat Wales	10 matches to 5
Ireland beat Scotland	11 matches to 4
Scotland beat Wales	8 matches to 7
England beat Ireland	9 matches to 6

Winners: England

1995 *at Royal Portrush, Co Antrim*

Ireland beat Scotland	8½ matches to 6½
Wales beat England	8½ matches to 6½
Scotland beat Wales	11 matches to 4
England beat Ireland	9 matches to 6
Ireland beat Wales	10 matches to 5
England beat Scotland	9½ matches to 5½

Winners: England beat Ireland on countback
25 wins to 24½

1996 *at Moray, Scotland*

England beat Wales	9 matches to 6
Ireland beat Scotland	8½ matches to 6½
England halved with Scotland	7½ matches each
Ireland beat Wales	9½ matches to 5½
England beat Ireland	10 matches to 5
Scotland beat Wales	9 matches to 6

Winners: England

1997 *at Burnham & Berrow*

England beat Wales	10½ matches to 4½
Ireland beat Scotland	10½ matches to 4½
England beat Scotland	10½ matches to 4½
Ireland beat Wales	8½ matches to 6½
England halved with Ireland	7½ matches to 7½
Scotland beat Wales	9 matches to 6

Winners: England

Home Internationals *continued*

1998 *at Royal Porthcawl*

Ireland beat Scotland	11 matches to 4
England beat Wales	11 matches to 4
Ireland halved with Wales	7½ matches each
England beat Scotland	9 matches to 6
England beat Ireland	8 matches to 7
Wales beat Scotland	11½ matches to 3½

Winners: England

1999 *at Royal County Down*

England beat Scotland	10 matches to 5
Ireland beat Wales	8 matches to 7
England beat Wales	11½ matches to 3½
Ireland beat Scotland	10½ matches to 4½
Scotland beat Wales	10½ matches to 4½
England beat Ireland	8½ matches to 6½

Winners: England

2000 *at Carnoustie*

England halved with Wales	7½ matches to 7½
Ireland halved with Scotland	7½ matches to 7½
England halved with Scotland	7½ matches to 7½
Wales beat Ireland	8 matches to 7
Scotland beat Wales	8½ matches to 6½
Ireland beat England	9½ matches to 5½

Winners: Scotland

2001 *at Woodhall Spa*

England beat Scotland	9 matches to 6
Ireland beat Wales	10½ matches to 4½
England halved with Wales	7½ matches to 7½
Scotland beat Ireland	8½ matches to 6½
Scotland beat Wales	10½ matches to 4½
England beat Ireland	11½ matches to 3½

Winners: England

Senior Internationals

2001 *at Portmarnock*

1 England, 2 Ireland, 3 Sweden, 4 Wales

English County Championship

1928	Warwickshire	1957	Surrey	1980	Surrey
1929	Lancashire	1958	Surrey	1981	Surrey
1930	Lancashire	1959	Northumberland	1982	Yorkshire
1931	Yorkshire	1961	Lancashire	1983	Berks, Bucks, Oxon
1932	Surrey	1962	Northumberland	1984	Yorkshire
1933	Yorkshire	1963	Yorkshire	1985T	Devon/Hertfordshire
1934	Worcestershire	1964	Northumberland	1986	Hertfordshire
1935	Worcestershire	1965	Northumberland	1987	Yorkshire
1936	Surrey	1966	Surrey	1988	Warwickshire
1937	Lancashire	1967	Lancashire	1989	Middlesex
1938	Staffordshire	1968	Surrey	1990	Warwickshire
1939	Worcestershire	1969	Berks, Bucks, Oxon	1991	Middlesex
1947	Staffordshire	1970	Gloucestershire	1992	Dorset
1948	Staffordshire	1971	Staffordshire	1993	Yorkshire
1949	Lancashire	1972	Berks, Bucks, Oxon	1994	Middlesex
1950	*Not played*	1973	Yorkshire	1995	Lancashire
1951	Lancashire	1974	Lincolnshire	1996	Hampshire
1952	Yorkshire	1975	Staffordshire	1997	Yorkshire
1953	Yorkshire	1976	Warwickshire	1998	Yorkshire
1954	Cheshire	1977	Warwickshire	1999	Yorkshire
1955	Yorkshire	1978	Kent	2000	Surrey
1956	Staffordshire	1979	Gloucestershire		

2001 *at Burnham & Berrow*

Berks, Bucks & Oxford beat Gloucestershire 5–4
Yorkshire beat Lincolnshire 8½–½
Yorkshire beat Berks, Bucks & Oxford 6–3
Gloucestershire halved with Lincolnshire 4½–4½
Berks, Bucks & Oxford beat Lincolnshire 5–4
Yorkshire beat Gloucestershire 7–2

Result: 1 Yorkshire, 2 Berks, Bucks & Oxford, 3 Gloucestershire, 4 Lincolnshire

English Club Championship

1989	Ealing	Southport and Ainsdale		1995	Sandmoor	Ipswich
1990	Ealing	Goring and Streatley		1996	Hartlepool	Frilford Heath
1991	Trentham	Porters Park		1997	Royal Mid-Surrey	Sandiway
1992	Bristol & Clifton	South Staffs		1998	Moor Park	Northumberland
1993	Worksop	Rotherham		1999	Royal Mid-Surrey	Moor Park
1994	Sandmoor	Coxmoor		2000	Coxmoor	Berkhampstead

2001 *at Minchinhampton*

1	St Mellion (Cornwall)	274	[Adam Frayne, Ben Welch, Richard Ackland]
2	Hull (Yorkshire)	281	
3	Worthing (Sussex)	281	

All-Ireland Inter-County Championship

Year	Winner	Runner-up	Venue	Score
1995	Down	Waterford	Rosslare	3½–1½
1996	Down	Dublin	Co Sligo	4–1
1997	Cork	Wicklow	Doneghal	4–1
1998	Dublin	Kerry	Lahinch	4–1
1999	Louth	Londonderry	Carlow	3½–1½
1999	Louth	Londonderry	Carlow	3½–1½
2000	Cork	Roscommon	Athlone	3–2

2001 *at Ballyliffin*

Semi-Finals

Co Dublin beat Co. Antrim	3½–1½
Co Waterford beat Co. Sligo	4–1

Final

Co Dublin beat Co. Waterford	3½–1½

Scottish Club Championship

2001 *at North Berwick*

1	Blairgowrie*	281	[C Mitchell, G Campbell, S Graham]
2	Dumfries & Galloway	281	(countback)
3	Earlsferry Thistle	282	

Scottish Area Team Championship

1990	North East		1994	Lothians	1998	Lanarkshire
1991	Glasgow		1995	North	1999	Lothians
1992	North East		1996	Renfrewshire	2000	North
1993	Lothians		1997	Lothians		

2001 *at Panmure*

Semi-finals

Lothians 8, Stirlingshire 1
Perth and Kinross 5, Fife 4

Final

Perth and Kinross 5½, Lothians 3½

Scottish Foursomes Tournament –
Glasgow Evening Times Trophy

1990	Dunblane New	1994	Standard Life	1998	Haggs Castle
1991	Irvine Ravenspark	1995	Ratho Park	1999	Scottish Life
1992	Cochrane Castle	1996	Cardross	2000	Colville
1993	Baberton	1997	Cardross		

2001 *at Hamilton*

Final
Hamilton beat Drumpellier

Welsh Inter-Counties Championship

2001 *at Borth & Ynslas*

1	Caernarvonshire	737
2	Gwent	751
3	Glamorgan	762

Welsh Team Championship

2001 *at Porthmadog*

Final
Pontnewydd beat Newport 3–2

Two aces in one round

Steve Fear, a 44-year-old police detective, will not forget the round of golf he played last summer at the Dunstanburgh Castle Golf Club in Northumberland. He had not had an ace in almost 30 years of playing the game but then he made two in the same round! Mr Fear, who plays off 12, holed in one with a 9-iron at the 166 yards fourth and then did the same with a wedge at the 122 yards fifteenth.

Principal 72 hole Tournaments

Including the National District Championships

Aberconwy Trophy (Inaugurated 1976) at Conwy/Llandudno (Maesdu), Gwynedd

1976	JR Jones	1985	MA Macara	1994	G Marsden
1977	EN Davies	1986	JR Berry	1995	S Andrew
1978	MG Mouland	1987	M Sheppard	1996	R Williams
1979	JM Morrow	1988	MG Hughes	1997	I Campbell
1980	JM Morrow	1989	JN Lee	1998	J Donaldson
1981	D Evans	1990	S Wilkinson	1999	J Donaldson
1982	G Tuttle	1991	S Wilkinson	2000	J Donaldson
1983	GH Brown	1992	MJ Ellis		
1984	D McLean	1993	S Wilkinson		

2001

1	Lee Harpin* (North Wales)	70-75-74-75—294
2	Adam Campbell (Marlborough)	75-68-79-72—294
3	Stephen Dixon (Bromborough)	76-72-75-73—296

Berkshire Trophy (Inaugurated 1946) at The Berkshire

1946	R Sweeney	148	1964	R Foster	281	1983	S Hamer	288
1947	PB Lucas	298	1965	MF Bonallack	278	1984	JL Plaxton	276
1948	LG Crawley	301	1966	P Oosterhuis	287	1985	P McEvoy	279
1949	PB Lucas	300	1967	DJ Millensted	283	1986	R Muscroft	280
1950	PF Scrutton	296	1968	MF Bonallack	273	1987	J Robinson	275
1951	PF Scrutton	301	1969	JC Davies	278	1988	R Claydon	276
1952	PF Scrutton	286	1970	MF Bonallack	274	1989	J Metcalfe	272
1953	JL Morgan	289	1971T	MF Bonallack	277	1990	J O'Shea	271
1954T	Ft Lt K Hall	303		J Davies		1991	J Bickerton	280
	E Bromley-Davenport		1972	DP Davidson	280	1992	V Phillips	274
1955	GH Micklem	282	1973	PJ Hedges	278	1993	V Phillips	271
1956	GB Wolstenholme	285	1974	J Downie	280	1994T	J Knight	274
1957	MF Bonallack	291	1975	N Faldo	281		A Marshall	
1958T	GB Wolstenholme	284	1976	PJ Hedges	284	1995	G Harris	275
	AH Perowne		1977	A Lyle	279	1996	GP Wolstenholme	274
1959	JB Carr	279	1978	PJ Hedges	281	1997	GP Wolstenholme	275
1960	GB Wolstenholme	276	1979	D Williams	274	1998	M Hilton	284
1961	MF Bonallack	275	1980	P Downes	280	1999	D Henley	275
1962	SC Saddler	279	1981	D Blakeman	280	2000	C Edwards	281
1963	DW Frame	289	1982	SD Keppler	278			

2001

1	Greg Evans (Ealing)	72-67-73-71—283
2	Gary Wolstenholme (Kilworth Springs)	72-71-70-73—286
3	Carlos Aldecoa (Esp)	68-71-69-79—287
	Cennydd Mills (Vale of Glamorgan)	71-71-73-72—287

Cameron Corbett Vase (Inaugurated 1897) *at Haggs Castle, Glasgow*

1897	AF Duncan	1933	W Tulloch	1970T	J McTear
1898	AF Duncan	1934	JM Dykes		D Hayes
1899	W Laidlaw	1935	H Thomson	1971	G Macgregor
1900	GH Hutcheson	1936	J Gray	1972	HB Stuart
1901	G Fox jr	1937	Tl Craig jr	1973	MJ Miller
1902	AF Duncan	1938	JS Logan	1974	M Rae
1903	G Fox jr	1939	A Steel	1975	D Barclay Howard
1904	R Bone	1940–41	*No competition*	1976	GH Murray
1905	R Bone	1942	AC Taylor	1977	MJ Miller
1906	W Gemmill	1943–45	*No competition*	1978	GH Murray
1907	G Wilkie	1946	JS Montgomerie	1979	KW Macintosh
1908	AF Duncan	1947	W Maclaren	1980	IA Carslaw
1909	EB Tipping	1948	J Pressley	1981	GH Murray
1910	JH Irons	1949	GB Peters	1982	GH Murray
1911	G Morris	1950	J Gray	1983	AS Oldcorn
1912	R Scott jr	1951	GB Peters	1984	D Barclay Howard
1913	R Scott jr	1952	J Stewart Thomson	1985	J McDonald
1914	D Martin	1953	J Orr	1986	JW Milligan
1915–18	*Not played due to First*	1954	JR Cater	1987	J Semple
	World War	1955	RC Macgregor	1988	C Everett
1919	HR Orr	1956	RC Macgregor	1989	AG Tait
1920	DJ Murray Campbell	1957	I Rennie	1990	D Robertson 290
1921	HM Dickson	1958	DH Reid	1991	K Gallacher 281
1922	WS Macfarlane	1959	AS Kerr	1992	D Kirkpatrick 284
1923	JO Stevenson	1960	J Mackenzie	1993	R Russell 278
1924	JO Stevenson	1961	GB Cosh	1994	J Hodson 280
1925	A Jamieson jr	1962	JH Richmond	1995	D Barclay Howard 268
1926	G Chapple	1963	JA Davidson	1996	C Watson 282
1927	RS Rodger	1964	IA MacCaskill	1997	C Watson 268
1928	SL McKinlay	1965	H Frazer	1998	E Wilson 140 (36)
1929	D McBride	1966	D Black	1999	W Bryson 278
1930	HM Dickson	1967	JRW Walkinshaw	2000	P McKechnie 277
1931	HM Dickson	1968	CW Green		
1932	W Stringer	1969	A Brooks		

2001

1	Paul Gault (Westerwood)	69-73-72-77—291
2	Wilson Bryson (Drumpellier)	74-70-76-72—292
3	Neil MacRae (Cawder)	71-73-72-77—293

Carad Trophy *at Radyr/Cardiff*

1971	TA Rickard	292	1981	SR Davidson		1991	AV Jones	
1972	EN Davies	280	1982	LR Absolem	292	1992	MJ Ellis	287
1973	RJ Jones	279	1983	P Mayo	283	1993	H Roberts	285
1974	WI Tucker	283	1984	AP Parkin	277	1994	C Evans	267
1975	A Disley	284	1985	P Mayo	277	1995	A Harrhy	280
1976	WI Tucker	277	1986	P Mayo	274	1996	NB Edwards	275
1977	AB Morgan	287	1987	P Mayo	274	1997	NB Edwards	277
1978	N Davies	293	1988	CS Dodd (54 holes)	204	1998	NB Edwards	279
1979	R Broad	291	1989	JL Peters	275	1999	S Roberts	276
1980	AP Parkin	284	1990	R Johnson	278	2000	N Edwards	275

2001

1	David Price (Vale of Glamorgan)	67-72-68-70—277
2	Stuart Manley (Mountain Ash)	69-74-69-68—280
3	Alex Smith (Pyle & Kenfig)	74-71-69-67—281

Clwyd Open (Inaugurated 1991) *at Prestatyn/Wrexham*

1991	G Houston	1995	M Ellis	1999	L Harpin
1992	C O'Carrol	1996	M Ellis	2000	K Sullivan
1993	M Ellis	1997	D Park		
1994	G Houston	1998	R Donovan		

2001

1	Adam Campbell (Marlborough)	70-69-76-77—292
	Tim Dykes (Wrexham)	70-71-76-75—292
3	Steven Merrill (Wrexham)	69-70-79-77—295

Craigmillar Park Open (Inaugurated 1961) *at Craigmillar Park, Edinburgh*

1961	RDBM Shade	1975	IC Hutcheon	1989	RM Roper
1962	A Sinclair	1976	NA Faldo	1990	SJ Bannerman
1963	HM Campbell	1977	CW Green	1991	N Walton
1964	RDBM Shade	1978	DM McCart	1992	SJ Knowles
1965	GB Cosh	1979	IC Hutcheon	1993	R Russell
1966	RDBM Shade	1980	JB Dunlop	1994	BW Collier
1967	RDBM Shade	1981	GK MacDonald	1995	C Watson
1968	RDBM Shade	1982	AS Oldcorn	1996	GW Tough
1969	GB Cosh	1983	G Macgregor	1997	CD Hislop
1970	PJ Smith	1984	G Macgregor	1998	G Rankin
1971	CW Green	1985	C Bloice	1999	S Mackenzie
1972	CW Green	1986	SR Easingwood	2000	M Warren
1973	DF Campbell	1987	RM Roper		
1974	GH Murray	1988	B Shields		

2001

1	Steven O'Hara (Colville Park)	63-67-66-69—265
2	Ewan Forbes (Turriff)	70-66-69-65—270
3	Mark Loftus (Cowglen)	70-71-66-66—273

Duncan Putter (Inaugurated 1959) *at Southerndown, Bridgend, Glamorgan*

1959	G Huddy	301	1973	JKD Povall	299	1986	D Wood	300
1960	Wl Tucker	289	1974	S Cox	302	1987	P McEvoy	278
1961T	G Huddy	295	1975	JG Jermine	295	1988	S Dodd	290
	Wl Tucker		1976T	Wl Tucker	286	1989	RN Roderick	280
1962	EN Davies	297		H Stott		1990	R Willison	311
1963	Wl Tucker	296	1977	H Stott	295	1991	R Willison	267
1964	JL Toye	293	1978	P McEvoy	295	1992	R Dinsdale	213
1965	P Townsend	305	1979	HJ Evans	292	1993	M Thomson	289
1966	MF Attenborough	291	1980	P McEvoy	296	1994	GP Wolstenholme	226
1967	D Millensted	297	1981T	R Chapman	294	1995	B Dredge	293
1968	JL Morgan	299		PG Way		1996	GP Wolstenholme	291
1969	Wl Tucker	304	1982	D McLean	283	1997	M Pilkington	283
1970	JL Toye	305	1983	JG Jermine	297	1998	M King	291
1971	W Humphreys	295	1984	JP Price	284	1999	GP Wolstenholme	216 (54)
1972	P Berry (3 rounds)	230	1985	P McEvoy	299	2000	J Donaldson	285

2001

1	Nigel Edwards (Whitchurch)	71-69—140
2	Matthew Griffiths (Woodlake Park)	70-75—145
3	Lee Harpin (North Wales)	73-73—146

First day cancelled due to fog

Hampshire Salver (Inaugurated 1979) at North Hants/Blackmoor

1979	P McEvoy	280	1987	A Rogers	286	1995	M Treleaven	275
1980	J Morrow	282	1988	N E Holman	279	1996	J Knight	272
1981	A P Sherborne	211*	1989	P Dougan	286	1997	J P Rose	275
1982	I Gray	293	1990	J Metcalfe	272	1998	S J Dyson	275
1983	D G Lane	281	1991	G Evans	281	1999	B Mason	273
1984	D H Currie	283	1992	S R Cage	276	2000	M Young	207*
1985	A J Clapp	285	1993	D J Hamilton	281			
1986	D Gilford	287	1994	W Bennett	279			

2001

1	Gary Wolstenholme (Kilworth Springs)	69-69-64-69—271
2	Jonathan Lupton (Middlesbrough)	69-67-72-69—277
3	Richard Finch (Hull)	68-70-72-68—278

Lagonda Trophy (Inaugurated 1975) at Camberley Heath; from 1990 at Gog Magog

1975	WJ Reid	143	1984	MS Davis	289	1993	L James	279
1976	JC Davies	142	1985	J Robinson	283	1994	S Webster	276
1977	WS Gronow	145	1986	D Gilford	282	1995	P Nelson	274
1978	JC Davies	135	1987	DG Lane	290	1996	S Collingwood	283
1979	JG Bennett	142	1988	R Claydon	275	1997	L Donald	279
1980	P McEvoy	139	1989	T Spence	280	1998	K Ferrie	284
1981	N Mitchell	138	1990	L Parsons	273	1999	Z Scotland	284
1982	A Sherborne	290	1991	J Cook	277	2000	M Young	279
1983	I Sparkes	216 (54)	1992	L Westwood	279			

2001

1	David Skinns (Lincoln)	64-66-68-73—271
2	James Heath (Coombe Wood)	70-66-72-70—278
3	Mark Payne (Brickendon Grange)	73-69-66-72—280

Standard Life Leven Gold Medal

(Inaugurated 1870) at Leven Links, Fife

1870	J Elder	85	1901	R Simpson	76	1935	EG Stoddart	71
1871	R Wallace	91	1902	J Bell	76	1936	GA Buist	73
1872	P Anderson	91	1903	W Henderson	76	1937	JY Strachan	75
1873	R Armit	95	1904	W Henderson	77	1938	S Macdonald	71
1874	D Campbell	93	1905	G Wilkie	76	1939	D Jamieson	72
1875	AM Ross	90	1906	G Wilkie	78	1940–45	No competition	
1876	AM Ross	88	1907	M Goodwillie	73	1946	EA McRuvie	77
1877	J Wilkie	88	1908	W Henderson	77	1947	JE Young	74
1878	R Wallace	90	1909	W Henderson	77	1948	J Imrie	77
1879	C Anderson	89	1910	W Whyte	76	1949	WM Ogg	76
1880	C Anderson	89	1911	G Wilkie	73	1950	E McRuvie	77
1881	J Foggo	91	1912	G Wilkie	73	1951	J Imrie	72
1882	J Wilkie	89	1913	W Whyte	73	1952	HVS Thomson	69
1883	J Foggo	86	1914	GB Rattray	76	1953	O Rolland	70
1884	C Anderson	89	1915–18	No competition		1954	JW Draper	73
1885	R Adam	84	1919	G Wilkie	77	1955	JW Draper	72
1886	R Adam	87	1920	JJ Smith	76	1956	R Dishart	72
1887	J Foggo	81	1921	GV Donaldson	77	1957	I Pearson	72
1888	DA Leitch	86	1922	SO Shepperd	72	1958	W McIntyre	71
1889	R Adam	81	1923	GV Donaldson	73	1959	W Moyes	71
1890	W Marshall	80	1924	JN Smith	76	1960	T Taylor	69
1891	DM Jackson	80	1925	A Robertson	73	1963	W Moyes	68
1892	Col DW Mackinnon	85	1926	T Ainslie	75	1961	A Cunningham	69
1893	HS Colt	79	1927	EA McRuvie	72	1962	W Moyes	71
1894	J Bell jr	82	1928	EA McRuvie	70	1964	A Cunningham	68
1895	C Wllkie jr	80	1929	EA McRuvie	72	1965	PG Buchanan	71
1896	J Bell jr	78	1930	EA McRuvie	68		*Two rounds played from 1966*	
1897	J Bell jr	79	1931	A Dunsire	71			
1898	G Wilkie jr	82	1932	J Ballingall	72	1966	GM Rutherford	144
1899	G Wilkie jr	78	1933	CA Danks	73	1967	AO Maxwell	140
1900	W Henderson	78	1934	EA McRuvie	67	1968	A Cunningham	140

Four rounds played from 1966			1979	B Marchbank	274	1991	GA Lowson	284
			1980	J Huggan	279	1992	D Robertson	279
1969	P Smith	284	1981	IC Hutcheon	282	1993	L Westwood	276
1970	JC Farmer	277	1982	IC Hutcheon	272	1994	B Howard	265
1971	J Scott Macdonald	207	1983	J Huggan	274	1995	S Mackenzie	273
1972	J Rankine	282	1984	S Stephen	278	1996	M Eliasson	267
1973	S Stephen	288	1985	AD Turnbull	281	1997	S Carmichael	278
1974	P Smith	282	1986	P-U Johansson	275	1998	G Rankin	268
1975	HB Stuart	286	1987	G Macgregor	271	1999	J Mathers	291
1976	IC Hutcheon	266	1988	CE Everett	280	2000	G Gordon	269
1977	IC Hutcheon	289	1989	AJ Coltart	280			
1978	R Wallace	287	1990	CE Everett	280			

2001

1	Peter Whiteford* (Lundin)	66-72-68-65—271
2	George Crawford (Williamwood)	68-69-71-63—271
	Ewan Forbes (Turriff)	66-73-65-67—271
	Barry Hume (Haggs Castle)	69-72-65-65—271

Lytham Trophy (Inaugurated 1965) *at Royal Lytham & St Annes and Fairhaven*

1965T	MF Bonallack	295	1975	G Macgregor	299	1990	G Evans	291
	CA Clark		1976	MJ Kelley	292	1991	G Evans	284
1966	PM Townsend	290	1977	P Deeble	296	1992	S Cage	294
1967	R Foster	296	1978	B Marchbank	288	1993	T McLure	292
1968	R Foster	286	1979	P McEvoy	279	1994	W Bennett	285
1969T	T Craddock	290	1980	IC Hutcheon	293	1995	S Gallacher	281
	SG Birtwell		1981	R Chapman	221	1996	M Carver	284
1970T	JC Farmer	296	1982	MF Sludds	306	1997	G Rankin	279
	CW Green		1983	S McAllister	299	1998	L Kelly	288
	GC Marks		1984	J Hawksworth	289	1999	T Schuster	283
1971	W Humphreys	292	1985	MPD Walls	291	2000	D Dixon	285
1972	MF Bonallack	281	1986	S McKenna	297			
1973T	MG King	292	1987	D Wood	293			
1973T	SG Birtwell	292	1988	P Broadhurst	296			
1974	CW Green	291	1989	N Williamson	286			

2001

1	Richard McEvoy (Thorpe Hall)	71-67-72-66—276 [record total]
2	Paul Bradshaw (Gainsborough)	69-70-72-73—284
	Marc Warren (East Kilbride)	72-72-70-70--284

St Andrews Links Trophy (Inaugurated 1989) *at St Andrews (Old and New)*

1989	R Claydon	284	1993	G Hay	280	1997	J Rose	284
1990	S Bouvier (Aus)	280	1994	DB Howard	294	1998	C Watson	276
1991	R Willison	289	1995	G Rankin	276	1999	D Patrick	(36) 152
1992	C Watson	281	1996	DB Howard	282	2000	M King	140

2001

1	Steven O'Hara (Colville Park)	73-68-67-73—281
2	Paul Bradshaw (Gainsborough)	73-70-71-71—285
3	Craig Heap (East Kilbride)	73-70-67-76—286

St David's Gold Cross (Inaugurated 1930) *at Royal St David's, Gwynedd*

1930	GC Stokoe	1957	CD Lawrie	1979	MA Smith
1931	EW Fiddian	1958	GB Turner	1980	CP Hodgkinson
1932	Dr W Tweddell	1959	MSR Lunt	1981	G Broadbent
1933	IS Thomas	1960	LJ Ranells	1982	MW Calvert
1934	SB Roberts	1961	MSR Lunt	1983	RD James
1935	IS Thomas	1962	PD Kelley	1984	RJ Green
1936	RMW Pritchard	1963	JKD Povall	1985	KH Williams
1937	IS Thomas	1964	MSR Lunt	1986	RN Roderick
1938	SB Roberts	1965	MSR Lunt	1987	SR Andrew
1939	IS Thomas	1966	MSR Lunt	1988	MW Calvert
1940–45	*No competition*	1967	MSR Lunt	1989	AJ Barnett
1946	SB Roberts	1968	AW Holmes	1990	MA Macara
1947	G Mills	1969	AJ Thomson	1991	RJ Dinsdale
1948	CH Eaves	1970	AJ Thomson	1992	B Dredge
1949	SB Roberts	1971	A Smith	1993	B Dredge
1950	DMG Sutherland	1972	EN Davies	1994	C Evans
1951	JL Morgan	1973	RD James	1995	M Skinner
1952	SB Roberts	1974	GC Marks	1996	L Harpin
1953	S Lunt	1975	CP Hodgkinson	1997	M Pilkington
1954	GB Turner	1976	JR Jones	1998	L Harpin
1955	JL Morgan	1977	JA Fagan	1999	D Jones
1956	W Cdr CH Beamish	1978	S Wild	2000	D Price

2001

1	Craig Williams (Creigiau)	69-65-73-66—273
2	Stuart Manley (Mountain Ash)	71-65-69-74—279
	David Price (Vale of Glamorgan)	66-72-71-70—279

Sherry Cup

1990	Alvaro Prat	1994	Francisco Cea	1998	Sergio García
1991	Padraig Harrington	1995	José Maria Zamora	1999	Marcel Siem
1992	Frederic Cupillard	1996	Alvaro Salto	2000	G Wolstenholme
1993	Francisco Valera	1997	Sergio García		

2001 *at Sotogrande, Spain*

1	Gary Wolstenholme★ (Kilworth Springs)	69-69-71-71—280
2	David Griffiths (West Herts)	72-72-67-69—280
3	M Juan Tomas (Esp)	71-70-68-73—282

Sutherland Chalice (Inaugurated 2000)

2000	G Gordon	275

2001 *at Dumfries & Galloway*

1	Steven Carmichael (Cardross)	72-69-65-68—274
2	Jonathan King (Cardross)	70-68-67-71—276
3	Wilson Bryson (Drumpellier)	71-69-71-66—277

Tennant Cup (Inaugurated 1880) *at Glasgow GC*

1880	AW Smith	1893	W Doleman	1906	JG Macfarlane
1881	AW Smith	1894	W Doleman	1907	R Andrew
1882	AM Ross	1895	JA Shaw	1908	R Carson
1883	J Kirk	1896	J Thomson	1909	WS Colville
1884	W Doleman	1897	D Bone	1910	R Andrew
1885	TR Lamb	1898	R Bone	1911	WS Colville
1886	D Bone	1899	W Hunter	1912	R Scott jr
1887	JR Motion	1900	JG Macfarlane	1913	SO Shepherd
1888	D Bone	1901	R Bone	1914	John Caven
1889	W Milne	1902	CB Macfarlane	1915–19	*No competition*
1890	W Marshall	1903	CB Macfarlane	1920	G Lockhart
1891	D Bone	1904	WS Colville	1921	R Scott jr
1892	D Bone	1905	TW Robb	1922	WD Macleod

1923	FW Baldie	1953	AD Gray	1978	IA Carslaw
1924	J Barrie Cooper	1954	H McInally	1979	G Hay
1925	R Scott jr	1955	LG Taylor	1980	Allan Brodie
1926	W Tulloch	1956	JM Dykes	1981	G MacDonald
1927	W Tulloch	1957	LG Taylor	1982	LS Mann
1928	A Jamieson jr	1958	Dr FWG Deighton	1983	C Dalgleish
1929	R Scott jr	1959	JF Milligan	1984	E Wilson
1930	JE Dawson	1960	Dr FWG Deighton	1985	CJ Brooks
1931	GNS Tweedale	1961	R Reid Jack	1986	PG Girvan
1932	SL McInlay	1962	WS Jack	1987	J Rasmussen
1933	H Thomson	1963	SWT Murray	1988	C Dalgleish
1934	K Lindsay jr	1964	Dr FWG Deighton	1989	DG Carrick
1935	JM Dykes jr	1965	J Scott Cochran	1990	C Everett
1936	JNW Dall	1966	AH Hall	1991	C Everett
1937	WS McCleod	1967	BJ Gallacher	1992	D Robertson
1938	A Jamieson jr	1968	CW Green	1993	D Robertson
1939	GB Peters	1969	J Scott Cochran	1994	G Rankin
1940–45	*No competition*	1970	CW Green	1995	S Gallacher
1946	JB Stevenson	1971	Andrew Brodie	1996	G Rankin
1947	JC Wilson	1972	Allan Brodie	1997	C Hislop
1948	J Wallace	1973	PJ Smith	1998	G Rankin
1949	W Irvine	1974	D McCart	1999	G Fox
1950	JW Mill	1975	CW Green	2000	G Fox
1951	WS McCleod	1976	IC Hutcheon		
1952	GT Black	1977	S Martin		

2001

1	Craig Watson (East Renfrewshire)	69-66-66-69—270
2	Jonathan King (Cardross)	74-66-66-65—271
3	Graham Gordon (Newmachar)	68-68-69-71—276
	David Inglis (Glencorse)	69-70-73-64—276

Tillman Trophy (Inaugurated 1989)

1989	J Cook	1993	C Nowicki	1997	M Searle
1990	M Wiggett	1994	*Not played*	1998	R Blaxhill
1991	A Tillman	1995	P Stuart	1999	J Conteh
1992	D Probert	1996	S Wakefield	2000	B Welch

2001 *at Hunstanton*

1	Ross Fisher (Wentworth)	75-68-74-69—286
2	Steve Barwick (East Berkshire)	72-73-74-72—291
3	Nick Knighton (Longcliffe)	74-71-72-76—293

Trubshaw Cup (Inaugurated 1989) *at Ashburnham and Tenby*

1989	MA Macara	1993	B Dredge	1997	M Pilkington
1990	TSM Wilkinson	1996	M Ellis	1998	M Pilkington
1991	S Pardoe	1994	C Evans	1999	N Matthews
1992	B Dredge	1995	B Dredge	2000	N Edwards

2001

1	Nigel Edwards (Whitchurch)	73-77-69-69—288
2	Gareth Maybin (Ireland)	72-74-74-69—289
	Kyron Sullivan (Brynhill)	76-76-70-67—289

Tucker Trophy

1999	J Donaldson	2000	I Campbell

2001 *at Newport/Whitchurch*

1	Nigel Edwards (Whitchurch)	68-65-69-64—266
2	Kyron Sullivan (Brynhill)	70-68-68-69—275
3	Ian Campbell (Marlborough)	71-71-70-66—278

NATIONAL DISTRICT CHAMPIONSHIPS

Midland Open (Inaugurated 1976) at Little Aston & Sutton Coldfield

1976	P Downes	1983	CA Banks	1990	J Bickerton	1997	P Streeter
1977	P Downes	1984	K Valentine	1991	P Sefton	1998	L Donald
1978	P McEvoy	1985	MC Hassall	1992	M McGuire	1999	G Davies
1979	M Tomlinson	1986	G Wolstenholme	1993	N Williamson	2000	D Dixon
1980	P Downes	1987	C Suneson	1994	D Howell		
1981	P Baxter	1988	R Winchester	1995	G Harris		
1982	NJ Chesses	1989	J Cook	1996	M Carver		

2001

1	Matt Lock (Tall Pines)	69-70-69-71—279
2	Lee Nash (Walton Heath)	75-69-69-69—282
3	David Skinns (Lincoln)	67-71-69-76—283

West of England Open Match Play (Inaugurated 1912)

at Burnham & Berrow

1912	RA Riddell	1936	PH White		McCrea	1983	C Peacock
1913	Hon M Scott	1937	O Austreng	1963	KT Warren	1984	GB Hickman
1914–18	No competition	1938	HJ Roberts	1964	DC Allen	1985	AC Nash
1919	Hon M Scott	1939–45	No competition	1965	DE Jones	1986	J Bennett
1920	Hon D Scott	1946	JH Neal	1966	A Forrester	1987	D Rosier
1921	CVL Hooman	1947	WF Wise	1967	A Forrester	1988	N Holman
1922	Hon M Scott	1948	WF Wise	1968	SR Warrin	1989	N Holman
1923	D Grant	1949	J Payne	1969	SR Warrin	1990	I West
1924	D Grant	1950	EB Millward	1970	C Ball	1991	S Amor
1925	D Grant	1951	J Payne	1971	G Irlam	1992	K Baker
1926	K Whetstone	1952	EB Millward	1972	JA Bloxham	1993	D Haines
1927	GC Brooks	1953	F Griffin	1973	SC Mason	1994	A Emery
1928	JA Pierson	1954	EB Millward	1974	CS Mitchell	1995	A March
1929	DE Landale	1955	SJ Fox	1975	MR Lovett	1996	M Carver
1930	RH de	1956	SJ Fox	1976	No competition	1997	SJ Martin
	Montmorency	1957	D Gardner	1977	AR Dunlop	1998	D Dixon
1931	DR Howard	1958	AJN Young	1978	R Broad	1999	D Dixon
1932	R Straker	1959	DM Woolmer	1979	N Burch	2000	J Morgan
1933	DM Anderson	1960	AW Holmes	1980	JM Durbin		
1934	Hon M Scott	1961	JM Leach	1981	M Mouland		
1935	JJF Pennink	1962	Sq Ldr WE	1982	M Higgins		

2001

Semi-Finals

Martin Fell (Wrag Barn) beat Jon Sutherland (Cirencester) 3 and 2
Lee Corfield (Burnham & Berrow) beat Brian Lee (Newport) 2 holes

Final

L Corfield beat M Fell 2 and 1

West of England Open Stroke Play (Inaugurated 1968)

1968	PJ Yeo	Saunton	297	1980	PE McEvoy	R North Devon	288
1969	A Forrester	Saunton	304	1981	N Taee	Saunton	245 (54)
1970	PJ Yeo	R North Devon	312	1982	MP Higgins	R North Devon	286
1971	P Berry	Saunton	303	1983	PE McEvoy	Saunton	298
1972	P Berry	R North Devon	310	1984	A Sherborne	R North Devon	288
1973	SC Mason	Saunton	287	1985	PE McEvoy	Saunton	307
1974	R Abbott	R North Devon	301	1986	P Baker	R North Devon	282
1975	BG Steer	Saunton	290		*Won at second extra hole after play-off with P McEvoy*		
1976	R Abbott	R North Devon	304	1987	G Wolstenholme	Saunton	296
1977	PE McEvoy	Saunton	298	1988	MC Evans	R North Devon	291
1978	JG Bennett	R North Devon	291	1989	AD Hare	Saunton	289
	After play-off with PE McEvoy			1990	J Payne	Saunton	290
1979	R Kane	Saunton	296	1991	D Lee	Saunton	286

1992	M Stanford	R North Devon	291		1997	M Reynard	R North Devon	280
1993	PR Trew	Saunton	279		1998	C Edwards	R North Devon	287
1994	CP Nowicki	R North Devon	294		1999	D Griffiths	Saunton	286
1995	G Clark	Saunton	141 (36)		2000	S Grewal	R North Devon	279
1996	R Wiggins	Saunton	288					

2001 *at Saunton*

1	Richard Finch (Hull)	70-70-70-69—279
2	Jonathan Lupton (Middlesbrough)	73-71-69-68—281
	Gary Wolstenholme (Kilworth Springs)	67-70-72-72—281

East of Ireland Open

1989	D Clarke	1992	R Burns	1995	D Brannigan	1998	G McGimpsey
1990	D O'Sullivan	1993	R Burns	1996	N Fox	1999	K Kearney
1991	P Hogan	1994	G McGimpsey	1997	S Quinlivan	2000	N Fox*

2001 *at Co Louth*

1	Ken Kearney (Roscommon)	72-74-65-72—283
2	Michael McDermott (Stackstown)	74-68-72-73—287
	Pat Murray (Kinsale)	72-68-77-70—287

North of Ireland Open

1989	N Anderson	1992	G McGimpsey	1995	F Nolan	1998	P Gribben
1990	D Clarke	1993	G McGimpsey	1996	M McGinley	1999	P Gribben
1991	G McGimpsey	1994	N Ludwell	1997	M Sinclair	2000	M Hoey

2001 *at Royal Portrush*

Semi-Finals
Graeme McDowell (UCD/Rathmore) beat David Jones (City of Derry) 1 hole
Stuart Paul (Tandragee) beat Mark O'Sullivan (UCD/Galway) 3 and 1

Final: S Paul beat G McDowell 2 and 1   **Leading Qualifier:** Stuart Paul (Tandragee) 134

South of Ireland Open

1989	S Keenan	1992	L MacNamara	1995	J Fanagan	1998	J Foster
1990	D Clarke	1993	P Sheehan	1996	A Morrow	1999	M Campbell
1991	P McGinley	1994	D Higgins	1997	P Collier	2000	G McDowell

2001 *at Lahinch*

Semi-Finals
Stephen Browne (Hermitage) beat David Mortimer (Connemara) 6 and 5
J Kehoe (UCD/Birr) beat Michael McGinley (Grange) 2 and 1

Final: Justin Kehoe beat S Browne 6 and 4

West of Ireland Open

1989	P McInerney	1992	K Kearney	1995	E Brady	1998	N Fox
1990	N Goulding	1993	G McGimpsey	1996	G McGimpsey	1999	M Ilonen (Fin)
1991	N Goulding	1994	P Harrington	1997	J Fanagan	2000	E Brady

2001 *at Co Sligo (Rosses Point)*

Semi-Finals
Michael McDermott (Stackstown) beat S Browne (Hermitage) 2 holes
Michael Hoey (Shandon Park) beat Garth McGimpsey (Bangor) 3 and 2

Final: Michael McDermott beat Michael Hoey 2 and 1

Leading Qualifier: Michael McDermott (Stackstown)

East of Scotland Open Stroke Play

1989	K Hird	1992	ST Knowles	1995	G Davidson	1998	B Lamb (Aus)
1990	G Lawrie	1993	S Meiklejohn	1996	C Hislop	1999	R Beames
1991	R Clark	1994	A Reid	1997	S Meiklejohn	2000	C Watson

2001 *at Lundin GC*

1	Jonathan King (Cardross)	66-70-69-75—280
2	Steven Carmichael (Cardross)	72-71-71-68—282
	Steven Wallace (Prestwick St Cuthbert)	72-68-69-73—282

North of Scotland Open Stroke Play

1989	G Hickman	1992	K Buchan	1995	R Beames	1998	C Taylor
1990	S McIntosh	1993	D Downie	1996	C Dunan	1999	N Steven*
1991	S Henderson	1994	E Forbes	1997	G Crawford	2000	C Watson

2001 *at Moray*

1	Gary Thomson (Moray)	69-66-63-69—277
2	Andrew McKay (Cochrane Castle)	68-70-71-69—278
3	Steven Horne (Tulliallan)	70-73-66-70—279

North-East Scotland District Championship

1999	BA Innes	2000	E Forbes

2001 *at Duff House Royal*

1	Graham Gordon (Newmachar)	68-69-68-63—268
2	Wallace Booth (Crieff)	65-66-70-69—270
3	Colin Mitchell (Blairgowrie)	74-64-69-65—272

South-East Scotland District Championship

1999	S Carmichael	2000	J King

2001 *at Mortonhall*

1	Jack Doherty (Vale of Glamorgan)	66-68-72-73—279
2	Simon Mackenzie (West Linton)	70-66-70-76—282
3	Colin Swanston (Uphall)	72-72-70-70—284

West of Scotland Open

1989	A Elliot	1992	S Henderson	1995	G Rankin	1998	L Kelly
1990	S Knowles	1993	B Howard	1996	C Hislop	1999	L Kelly
1991	A Coltart	1994	J Hodgson	1997	C Hislop	2000	S O'Hara

2001 *at Bishopbriggs*

1	Brian Fitzsimmons (Clydebank & District)	67-69-67-73—276
2	Wilson Bryson (Drumpellier)	68-68-69-72—277
3	Steven O'Hara (Colville Park)	71-66-73-68—278

Other Men's Amateur Tournaments

Berkhamsted Trophy (Inaugurated 1960)

1960	HC Squirrell	150	1974	P Fisher	144	1988	J Cowgill	146
1961	DW Frame	147	1975	PG Deeble	147	1989	J Payne	142
1962	DG Neech	149	1976	JC Davies	144	1990	J Barnes	144
1963	HC Squirrell	149	1977	AWB Lyle	144	1991	G Homewood	141
1964	PD Flaherty	149	1978	JC Davies	146	1992	P Page	141
1965	LF Millar	153	1979	JC Davies	147	1993	S Burnell	143
1966	P Townsend	150	1980	R Knott	143	1994	M Treleaven	140
1967	DJ Millensted	150	1981	P Dennett	146	1995	J Crampton	142
1968	PD Flaherty	144	1982	DG Lane	148	1996	L Donald	139
1969	MM Niven	149	1983	J Hawksworth	146	1997	P Streeter	143
1970	R Hunter	145	1984	R Willison	139	1998	G Storm	69 (18)
1971	A Millar	144	1985	F George	144	1999	GP Wolstenholme*	140
1972	C Cieslewicz	148	1986	P McEvoy	144	2000	J Wormald*	141
1973	SC Mason	141	1987	F George	141			

2001

1	Scott Godfrey (St Enedoc)	68-72—140
2	Tom Whitehouse (Maxstoke Park)	72-69—141
3	David Skinns (Lincoln)	73-70—143

John Cross Bowl (Inaugurated 1957) *at Worplesdon, Surrey*

1957	DW Frame	1972	AR Kerr	1987	B White
1958	G Evans	1973	DW Frame	1988	B White
1959	G Evans	1974	RPF Brown	1989	KG Jones
1960	DW Frame	1975	BJ Winteridge	1990	D Lee
1961	DW Frame	1976	DW Frame	1991	P Sefton
1962	DW Frame	1977	DW Frame	1992	R Watts
1963	PO Green	1978	RPF Brown	1993	J Collier
1964	RL Glading	1979	JG Bennett	1994	P Benka
1965	P Townsend	1980	JG Bennett	1995	M Galway
1966	P Townsend	1981	ME Johnson	1996	B Barham
1967	MJ Burgess	1982	R Boxall	1997	C Banks
1968	PJ Benka	1983	DG Lane	1998	J Wormald
1969	DW Frame	1984	I Gray	1999	M Galway
1970	P Dawson	1985	M Devetta	2000	R Mann*
1971	PBQ Drayson	1986	C Rotheroe		

2001

1	Jonathan Bint (Chigwell)	69-68—137
2	David Childs (Purley Downs)	70-69—139
3	Lloyd Godwin (Charthills)	70-70—140

Frame Trophy (Inaugurated 1986 for players aged 50+) at *Worplesdon, Surrey*

1988	DW Frame	229	1993	DW Frame	216	1998	DG Lane	211
1989	JRW Walkinshaw	219	1994	DG Lane	222	1999	NH Barnes	220
1990	WJ Williams	224	1995	M Christmas	223	20001	DW Frame	213
1991	DB Sheahan	223	1996	DG Lane	217			
1992	DW Frame	223	1997	B Turner	226			

2001

1	DW Frame (Worplesdon)	71-71-75—217
2	DG Lane (Goring & Streatley)	76-70-72—218
3	NH Barnes (Brokenhurst Manor)	69-74-76—219

Golf Illustrated Gold Vase (Inaugurated 1909)

1909	CK Hutchison	1949	RJ White	1975	MF Bonallack
1910	Abe Mitchell	1950	AW Whyte	1976	A Brodie
1911	R Harris	1951	JB Carr	1977	J Davies
1912	R Harris	1952	JDA Langley	1978	P Thomas
1913	Abe Mitchell	1953	JDA Langley	1979	KJ Miller
1914	H Hilton	1954	H Ridgeley	1980	G Brand jr
1919	D Darwin	1955	Major DA Blair	1981	P Garner
1920	DS Crowther	1956	Major DA Blair	1982	I Carslaw
1921	M Seymour	1957	GB Wolstenholme	1983	S Keppler
1922	WA Murray	1958	M Lunt	1984	JV Marks
1923	CJH Tolley	1959	A Bussell	1985	M Davis
1924	CC Aylmer	1960	D Sewell	1986	R Eggo
1925	JB Beck	1961T	DJ Harrison/MF Bonallack	1987	D Lane
1926T	CJH Tolley/TA Torrance	1962	BHG Chapman	1988	M Turner
1927	RH Wethered	1963	RH Mummery	1989	GP Wolstenholme
1928	CJH Tolley	1964	D Moffat	1990	A Rogers
1929	D Grant	1965	C Clark	1991	R Scott
1930	RT Jones (US)	1966	PM Townsend	1992	P Page
1931	WA Murray	1967T	MF Bonallack/	1993T	C Challen/V Phillips
1932	RW Hartley		RA Durrant	1994	S Burnell
1933	RW Hartley	1968	MF Bonallack	1995	A Wall
1934	WL Hartley	1969T	MF Bonallack/J Hayes	1996	*Not played*
1935	J Thomas	1970	D Harrison	1997	M James
1936	J Ferrier	1971	MF Bonallack	1998	R Rea★
1937	R Sweeney	1972T	H Ashby/DP Davidson/	1999	M Side
1938	CJ Anderson		R Hunter	2000	J Kemp
1939	SB Robert	1973	J Davies		
1948	RD Chapman	1974	P Hedges		

2001 at *Walton Heath*

1	James Heath (Walton Heath)	69-72—141
2	Ben Smith (East Berkshire)	73-69—142
3	Steven Barwick (East Berkshire)	71-73—144
	Scott Nightingale (Worthing)	72-72—144
	Paul Stanford (Berkhamsted)	74-70—144

Hampshire Hog (Inaugurated 1957) at *Northants*

1957	MF Bonallack	1972	R Revell	1987	A Rogers
1958	PF Scrutton	1973	SC Mason	1988	S Richardson
1959	Col AA Duncan	1974	TJ Giles	1989	P McEvoy
1960	MF Attenborough	1975	HAN Stott	1990	J Metcalfe
1961	HC Squirrell	1976	MC Hughesdon	1991	M Welch
1962	FD Physick	1977	AWB Lyle	1992	S Graham
1963	Sqn Ldr WE McCrea	1978	GF Godwin	1993	D Hamilton
1964	DF Wilkie	1979	MF Bonallack	1994	B Ingleby
1965	T Koch de Gooreynd	1980	RA Durrant	1995	J Rose
1966	Major DA Blair	1981	G Brand jr	1996	R Tate
1967	Major DA Blair	1982	A Sherborne	1997	GP Wolstenholme
1968	MJ Burgess	1983	I Gray	1998	P Rowe
1969	B Critchley	1984	J Hawksworth	1999	C Rodgers
1970	Major DA Blair	1985	A Clapp	2000	M Booker
1971	DW Frame	1986	R Eggo		

2001

1	Jon Lupton (Middlesborough)	69-67—136
2	Gary Wolstenholme (Kilworth Springs)	69-69—138
3	Richard Finch (Hull)	68-70—138

King George V Coronation Cup *at Porters Park, Herts.*

1990	C Boal	141	1994	S Webster	146	1998	M King	65 (18)
1991	S Hoffman	142	1995	S Jarvis	140	1999	J Field*	141
1992	R Watts	141	1996	N Swaffield	134	2000	R Chattaway	142
1993	D Hamilton	134	1997	J Knight	136			

2001

1	Mark Payne* (Brickendon Grange)	68-75—143
2	Lee Boxall (West Surrey)	69-74—143
3	Steven Barwick ((East Berkshire)	72-72—144

Prince of Wales Challenge Cup (Inaugurated 1928) *at Royal Cinque Ports*

1928	D Grant	142	1958T	BAF Belmore	158	1980T	B Nicholson	149
1929	NR Reeves	153	1959	D Johnstone	149	1981	JM Baldwin	146
1930	R Harris	156	1960	CG Moore	162	1982	SG Homewood	145
1931	RW Hartley	149	1961	RH Bazell	151	1983	M Davis	141
1932	EN Layton	151	1962	Dr J Pittar	154	1984T	F Wood	146
1933	JB Nash	148	1963	Sq Ldr WE McCrea	155		DH Niven	
1934	R Sweeney	304	1964	NA Paul	153.	1985	RJ Tickner	141
1935	HG Bentley	301	1965T	NA Paul	150	1986	JM Baldwin	149
1936	LOM Munn	301		VE Barton		1987	S Finch	148
1937	DHR Martin	291	1966	P Townsend	150	1988	MP Palmer	144
1938	EA Head	291	1967	MF Bonallack	141	1989T	T Lloyd	146
1939–46	*No competition*		1968T	NA Paul	144		NA Farrell	
1947	PB Lucas	154		GC Marks		1990T	G Homewood	
1948	Capt DA Blair	151	1969	MF Attenborough	152			
1949	C Stowe	142	1970	J Butterworth	153	1991	S Pardoe	145
1950	I Caldwell	151	1971	VE Barton	147	1992	L Westwood	160
1951	I Caldwell	151	1972	PJ Hedges	162	1993	ML Welch	143
1952	I Caldwell	150	1973	PJ Hedges	138	1994	I Hardy	149
1953	JG Blackwell	159	1974	PJ Hedges	146	1995	L Ferris	152
1954	DLW Woon	143	1975	JC Davies	150	1996	J Maddock	142
1955T	C Taylor	153	1976	MJ Inglis	162	1997	J Carter	154
	GT Duncan		1977	PJ Hedges	154	1998	G Woodman	144
1956	PF Scrutton	151	1978	ER Dexter	145	1999	A Webster (Aus)	147
1957	*No competition*		1979	GF Godwin	148	2000	JM Bint	145
1958T	KR Mackenzie	158	1980T	GM Dunsire	149			

2001

1	A Webster (Metropolitan)	70-70—140
2	Yasin Ali (Ealing)	74-71—145
3	G Homewood (Ashford Manor)	75-73—148
	P Wheatcroft (Worksop)	72-76—148

Rosebery Challenge Cup (Inaugurated 1933) *at Ashridge*

1962	PR Johnston	1975	JA Watts	1988	N Leconte
1963	CA Murray	1976	G Stradling	1989	C Slattery
1964	A Millar	1977	J Ambridge	1990	C Tingey
1965	EJ Wiggs	1978	RJ Bevan	1991	M Thompson
1966	A Holmes	1979	JB Berney	1992	R Harris
1967	A Holmes	1980	JA Watts	1993	M Hooper
1968	A Holmes	1981	RY Mitchell	1994	P Wilkins
1969	A Holmes	1982	DG Lane	1995	P Wilkins
1970	PW Bent	1983	N Briggs	1996	J Kemp
1971	AW Holmes	1984	DG Lane	1997	L Watcham
1972	AW Holmes	1985	P Wharton	1998	S Vinnicombe
1973	AJ Mason	1986	JE Ambridge	1999	J Kemp
1974	G Stradling	1987	HA Wilkerson	2000	J Kemp

2001

1	James Ruebotham (Welwyn Garden City)	69-71—140
2	Bob Peacock (South Herts)	74-67—141
3	Steven Walsom (Muswell Hill)	72-71—143

St George's Grand Challenge Cup (Inaugurated 1888)

at Royal St George's, Sandwich, Kent

1888	J Ball	180	1927	WL Hartley	153	1968	MF Bonallack	142
1889	J Ball	169	1928	D Grant	146	1969	PJ Benka	150
1890	J Ball	175	1929	TA Torrance	148	1970	PJ Hedges	150
1891	J Ball	174	1930	RW Hartley	148	1971	EJS Garrett	143
1892	FA Fairlie	167	1931	WL Hartley	149	1972	JC Davies	149
1893	HH Hilton	165	1932	HG Bentley	151	1973	JC Davies	141
1894	HH Hilton	167	1933	JB Beck	151	1974	JC Davies	140
1895	E Blackwell	176	1934	AGS Penman	153	1975	JC Davies	147
1896	FG Tait	165	1935	Maj WHH Aitken	158	1976	JC Davies	158
1897	CE Hambro	162	1936	DHR Martin	150	1977	JC Davies	154
1898	FG Tait	163	1937	DHR Martin	144	1978	C Phillips	145
1899	FG Tait	155	1938	JJF Pennink	142	1979	CF Godwin	146
1900	R Maxwell	155	1939	AA McNair	153	1980	J Simmance	150
1901	SH Fry	165	1940–46	*No competition*		1981	MF Bonallack	151
1902	H Castle	162	1947	PB Lucas	147	1982	SJ Wood	145
1903	CK Hutchison	158	1948	M Gonzalez	144	1983	R Willison	155
1904	J Graham jr	154	1949	PF Scrutton	143	1984	SJ Wood	142
1905	R Harris	154	1950	E Bromley-Davenport	148	1985	SJ Wood	144
1906	S Mure Fergusson	155	1951	PF Scrutton	142	1986	RC Claydon	143
1907	CE Dick	161	1952	GH Micklem	148	1987	MR Coodwin	147
1908	AC Lincoln	157	1953	Major DA Blair	148	1988	T Ryan	143
1909	SH Fry	153	1954	H Berwick (Aus)	141	1989	S Green	149
1910	Capt CK Hutchison	157	1955	PF Scrutton	150	1990	P Sullivan	144
1911	E Martin Smith	148	1956	DAC Marr	148	1991	D Fisher	141
1912	Hon Michael Scott	146	1957	PF Scrutton	148	1992	L Westwood	146
1913	HD Gillies	153	1958	PF Scrutton	144	1993	P Sefton	137
1914	J Graham jr	146	1959	J Nicklaus (USA)	149	1994	M Welch	142
1915–19	*No competition*		1960	JG Blackwell	152	1995	J Harris	142
1920	R Harris	162	1961	Sq Ldr WE McCrea	143	1996	M Brooks	137
1921	WB Torrance	154	1962	Sq Ldr WE McCrea	145	1997	*Abandoned due to rain*	
1922	WI Hunter	156	1963	Sq Ldr WE McCrea	150	1998	C Gold*	145
1923	F Ouimet (USA)	153	1964	Major DA Blair	153	1999	M Williamson (Aus)	149
1924	RH Wethered	149	1965	MF Bonallack	144	2000	P Appleyard	151
1925	D Grant	149	1966	P Townsend	148			
1926	Maj CO Hezlet	158	1967	Major DA Blair	154			

2001

1	Adam Gee (Leatherhead)	73-67—140
2	John Sutherland (Aus)	69-74—143
3	Marcus Fraser (Aus)	78-71—149

* Winner after play-off

Selborne Salver (Inaugurated 1976) *at Blackmoor*

1976	A Miller	1985	SM Bottomley	1994	W Bennett
1977	CS Mitchell	1986	TE Clarke	1995	S Drummond
1978	GM Brand	1987	A Clapp	1996	J Knight
1979	P McEvoy	1988	NE Holman	1997	R Binney
1980	P McEvoy	1989	M Stamford	1998	M Side
1981	A Sherborne	1990	J Metcalfe	1999	B Mason
1982	IA Cray	1991	J Payne	2000	J Franks
1983	DG Lane	1992	M Treleaven		
1984	D Curry	1993	M Welch		

2001

1	Gary Wolstenholme (Kilworth Springs)	64-69—133
2	Darren Henley (Stoneham)	70-66—136
3	Stephen East (Moortown)	70-68—138

Ryder Cupper Charlie Ward dies

Charlie Ward, one of the PGA's longest serving members, has died a few weeks short of his 90th birthday. He had been a member since 1928 and was made an honorary member in 1978. In the five years after the end of World War II he won the Vardon Trophy twice and 14 other tournaments.

He finished third behind his close friend Max Faulkner in the 1951 Open Championship at Royal Portrush and played in the 1947, 1949 and 1951 Ryder Cups.

Foursomes Events

The Antlers (Inaugurated 1933) *at Royal Mid-Surrey*

1933	TFB Law and PWL Risdon	147		1970	JB Carr and R Carr	142
1934	GA Hill and HS Malik	153		1971	I Mosey and I Gradwell	144
1935	EF Storey and Sir WS Worthington Evans	152		1972	MJ Kelley and W Smith	144
1936	HG Bentley and F Francis	144		1973	DOJ Albutt and P Flaherty	148
1937	LG Crawley and C Stowe	145		1974	BF Critchley and MC Hughesdon	140
1938	RW Hartlev and PWL Risdon	149		1975	JC Davies and PJ Davies	140
1939	LG Crawley and H Thomson	148		1976	JK Tate and P Deeble	144
1940–47	*Not played due to Second World War*			1977	JC Davies and PJ Davies	141
1948	RC Quilter and E Bromley-Davenport	151		1978	R Chapman and R Fish	148
1949	LG Crawley and JC Wilson	143		1979	N Roche and D Williams	143
1950	L Gracey and I Caldwell	151		1980	G Coles and M Johnson	148
1951	LG Crawley and JC Wilson	147		1981	R Boxall and R Chapman	143
1952T	Major DA Blair and GH Micklem	145		1982	IA Carslaw and J Huggan	139
	LG Crawley and JC Wilson			1983	N Fox and G Lashford	147
1953	D Wilson and G Simmons	148		1984	M Palmer and M Belsham	147
1954	JR Thornhill and PF Scrutton	147		1985	S Blight and R Wilkins	143
1955	G Evans and D Sewell	147		1986	M Gerrard and B White	146
1956	GH Micklem and AF Bussell	141		1987	IA Carslaw and J Huggan	141
1957	Major DA Blair and CD Lawrie	138		1988	A Raitt and P Thornley	143
1958	D Sewell and G Evans	143		1989	A Howard and R Hunter	146
1959	HC Squirrell and P Dunn	146		1990	AC Livesey and RG Payne	143
1960	MSR Lunt and JC Behrrell	139		1991	WM Hopkinson and MR Cook	143
1961	HC Squirrell and P Dunn	145		1992	J C Davies and P J Davies	148
1962	AW Holmes and JM Leach	142		1993	M Benka and S Seman	138
1963	RC Pickering and MJ Cooper	146		1994	D Cowap and J Brant	142
1964	MF Bonallack and Dr DM Marsh	145		1995	R Neill and G Evans	141
1965	MSR Lunt and DE Rodway	146		1996	I Tottingham and R Harris	144
1966	PD Kelley and Dr DM Marsh	144		1997	S Kay and R Peacock	143
1967	Play abandoned			1998	G Willman and B Willman	142
1968	H Broadbent and G Birtwell	144		1999	D Lomas and K Staunton*	104
1969T	SR Warrin and JH Cook	146		2000	M Booker and R Rae	143
	J Povall and K Dabson					
1969T	JC Davies and W Humphreys	146				
	RD Watson-Jones and LOM Smith					

2001

1	Rupert Rea (Royal Mid-Surrey) & Mark Booker (Royal Mid-Surrey)	142
2	Simon Cooper (Roehampton) & Tom Williamson (Gog Magog)	146
3	Robert Mann (Thames Ditton & Esher) & Andrew Inglis (Sunningdale Artisans)	148

Burhill Family Foursomes (Inaugurated 1937) *at Burhill, Surrey*

1937	Captain JR Stroyan and Miss S Stroyan		1959	Jack and Anna van Zwanenberg
1938	W Price and Miss E Price		1960	Mrs M Kippax and JM Kippax
1939–1946	*No competition*		1961	Mrs R Sutherland Pilch and J Sutherland Pilch
1947	Mrs GH Brooks and PJ Brooks		1962	JC Hubbard and Miss Trudi Hubbard
1948	W Price and Miss E Price		1963	GA Rowan-Robinson and
1949	Mrs EC Pepper and W Pepper			Miss 'Pooh' Rowan Robinson
1950	A Forbes Ilsley and Miss J Ilsley		1964	Mrs P Todhunter and T Todhunter
1951	Major E Loxley Land and Miss J Land		1965	Mrs WT Warrin and SR Warrin
1952	CHV Elliot and Miss S Elliott		1966	Mrs WT Warrin and SR Warrin
1953	JC Hubbard and Miss A Hubbard		1967	Mrs WT Warrin and SR Warrin
1954	JC Hubbard and Miss A Hubbard		1968	Mrs CHP Trollope and Nigel Trollope
1955	Mrs HP Thornhill and JR Thornhill		1969	Mrs EPP D'A Walton and JF Walton
1956	Mrs HP Thornhill and JR Thornhill		1970	JF Young and Miss EJ Young
1957	CH Young and Mrs PBK Gracey		1971	PHA Brownrigg and Miss D Brownrigg
1958	Mrs HM Winckley and JB Winckley		1972	Mrs S Grant and NJ Grant

1973	MV Blake and Miss B Blake	1987	Mrs A Croft and M Croft
1974	Mrs NR Bailhache and WJ Bailhache	1988	Mrs V Hargreaves and R Hargreaves
1975	Mrs PR Williams and PM Williams	1989	Mrs J Lawson and P Lawson
1976	Mrs D Gotla and C Gotla	1990	Mrs M Maisey and S Maisey
1977	Mrs J Maudsley and C Maudsley	1991	Mrs M Pollitt and R Pollitt
1978	Mrs H Calderwood and WR Calderwood	1992	R Stocks and Miss Joanna Stocks
1979	Dr AG Wells and Miss E Wells	1993	Mrs M Bartlett and Jerome Bartlett
1980	JL Hall and Miss Cynthia Hall	1994	MJ Toole and Miss SJ Toole
1981	Mrs J Fox and N Fox	1995	Mrs G Warner and R Warner
1982	Mrs J Fox and N Fox	1996	Mrs AP Croft and MC Croft
1983	Mrs J Rowe and D Rowe	1997	Mrs J Clink and T Clink
1984	Mrs JS Gilbert and AS Gilbert	1998	MJ Toole and Miss SJ Toole
1985	Mrs MM Pollitt and R Pollitt	1999	MJ Toole and Miss SJ Toole
1986	Mrs J Maudesley and C Maudesley	2000	Mrs V Marchbanks and R Marchbanks

2001 Final: Mrs C Warren & R Warren (Clandon Regis) beat SR Stradling (Rye) & Miss A Stradling (Worplesdon)

Fathers and Sons Foursomes *at West Hill, Surrey*

1991	DM and WK Laing	1995	J and D Niven	1999	R and K Boxall
1992	JA and R Piggott	1996	MJ and J Hickey	2000	G and M Steele
1993	B and R Groce	1997	DR and M Baxter		
1994	RJ and P Hill	1998	SF and P Brown		

2001 Final: J & D Niven (Newbury & Cookham) beat I & J Sangster (Orsett)

Sunningdale Foursomes (Inaugurated 1934) *at Sunningdale*

1934	Miss D Fishwick and EN Layton	1971	A Bird and H Flatman
1935	Miss J Wethered and JSF Morrison	1972	JC Davies and MG King
1936	Miss J Wethered and JSF Morrison	1973	J Putt and Miss M Everard
1937	AS Anderson and Dai Rees	1974	PJ Butler and CA Clark
1938	Miss P Barton and Alf Padgham	1975	*Cancelled due to snow*
1939	C Rissik and EWH Kenyon	1976	CA Clark and M Hughesdon
1940–47	*Not played due to Second World War*	1977	GN Hunt and D Matthew
1948	Miss Wanda Morgan and Sam King	1978	GA Caygill and Miss J Greenhalgh
1949	RG French and SS Field	1979	G Will and R Chapman
1950	M Faulkner and J Knipe	1980	NC Coles and D McClelland
1951	Miss J Donald and TB Haliburton	1981	A Lyddon and G Brand jr
1952	PF Scrutton and Alan Waters	1982	Miss MA McKenna and Miss M Madill
1953	Miss J Donald and TB Haliburton	1983	J Davies and M Devetta
1954	PF Scrutton and Alan Waters	1984	Miss M McKenna and Miss M Madill
1955	W Sharp and SS Scott	1985	J O'Leary and S Torrance
1956	G Knipe and DC Smalldon	1986	R Rafferty and R Chapman
1957	BGC Huggett and R Whitehead	1987	I Mosey and W Humphreys
1958	Miss J Donald and Peter Alliss	1988	SC Mason and A Chandler
1959	MF Bonallack and D Sewell	1989	AD Hare and R Claydon
1960	Miss B McCorkindale and MJ Moir	1990	Miss D Reid and Miss C Dibnah
1961	Mrs J Anderson and Peter Alliss	1991	J Robinson and W Henry
1962	ER Whitehead and NC Coles	1992	R Boxall and D Cooper
1963	L Platts and D Snell	1993	A Beal and L James
1964	B Critchley and R Hunter	1994	S Webster and A Wall
1965	Mrs AD Spearman and T Fisher	1995	D Cooper and R Boxall
1966	RRW Davenport and A Walker	1996	L Donald and M O'Connor
1967	NC Coles and K Warren	1997	Mrs J Hall and Miss H Wadsworth
1968	JC Davies and W Humphreys	1998	D Fisher and W Bennett
1969	P Oosterhuis and PJ Benka	1999	L Walters and R McEvoy
1970	R Barrell and Miss A Willard	2000	S Head and J Head

2001 Quarter Finals

C Lipscombe (Cirencester) & S Little (Lilley Brook) beat S Nightingale (Worthing) & J Doherty (Worthing) 5 and 4

A Ambler (Walton Heath) & A Wainwright (Garforth) beat R Rea (Royal Mid-Surrey) & M Booker (Royal Mid-Surrey) 3 and 2

Sunningdale Foursomes *continued*

Semi-Finals *continued*
S Andrew (Clitheroe) & Kim Andrew (Clitheroe) beat J Carter (Kingshill) & D Lomas (Woodcote Park) 6 and 5
J Spence (PGAET) & Trish Johnson (Evian Tour) beat H Hodgkinson (Lindrick) & P Carr (Sunningdale) 1 hole

Semi-Finals
Lipscombe & Little beat Ambler & Wainwright at 20th
Spence & Johnson beat Andrew & Andrew 4 and 3

Final
C Lipscombe & S Little beat J Spence & T Johnson 2 and 1

Worplesdon Mixed Foursomes (Inaugurated 1921) *at Worplesdon, Surrey*

1921	Miss Helme and TA Torrance	1964	Mrs G Valentine and JE Behrend
1922	Miss Joyce Wethered and R Wethered	1965	Mrs G Valentine and JE Behrend
1923	Miss Joyce Wethered and CJ Tolley	1966	Mrs C Barclay and DJ Miller
1924	Miss SR Fowler and EN Layton	1967	JF Gancedo and Mlle C Lacoste
1925	Miss Cecil Leitch and E Esmond	1968	JD van Heel and Miss Dinah Oxley
1926	Mlle de la Chaume and R Wethered	1969	Mrs R Ferguson and Alistair Wilson
1927	Miss Joyce Wethered and CJH Tolley	1970	Miss R Roberts and RL Glading
1928	Miss Joyce Wethered and JSF Morrison	1971	Mrs D Frearson and A Smith
1929	Miss M Gourlay and Maj CO Hezlet	1972	Miss B Le Garreres and CA Strang
1930	Miss M Gourlay and Maj CO Hezlet	1973	Miss T Perkins and RJ Evans
1931	Miss J Wethered and Hon M Scott	1974	Mrs S Birley and RL Glading
1932	Miss J Wethered and RH Oppenheimer	1975	Mr and Mrs JR Thornhill
1933	Miss J Wethered and B Darwin beat	1976	Mrs B Lewis and J Caplan
1934	Miss M Gourlay and TA Torrance	1977	Mrs D Henson and J Caplan
1935,	Miss G and J Craddock-Hartopp	1978	Miss T Perkins and R Thomas
1936	Miss J Wethered and Hon T Coke	1979	Miss J Melville and A Melville
1937	Mrs Heppel and LG Crawley	1980	Mrs L Bayman and I Boyd
1938	Mrs MR Garon and EF Storey	1981	Mrs J Nicholsen and MN Stern
1939–45	*Not played due to First World War*	1982	Miss B New and K Dobson
1946	Miss J Gordon and AA Duncan	1983	Miss B New and K Dobson
1947	Miss J Gordon and AA Duncan	1984	Mrs L Bayman and MC Hughesdon
1948	Miss W Morgan and EF Storey	1985	Mrs H Kaye and D Longmuir
1949	Miss F Stephens and LG Crawley	1986	Miss P Johnson and RN Roderick
1950	Miss F Stephens and LG Crawley	1987	Miss J Nicholson and B White
1951	Mrs AC Barclay and G Evans	1988	Mme A Larrezac and JJ Caplan
1952	Mrs RT Peel and GW Mackie	1989	Miss J Kershaw and M Kershaw
1953	Miss J Gordon and G Knipe	1990	Miss S Keogh and A Rodgers
1954	Miss F Stephens and WA Slark	1991	J Rhodes and C Banks
1955	Miss P Garvey and PF Scrutton	1992	D Henson and B Turner
1956	Mrs L Abrahams and Maj WD Henderson	1993	A Macdonald and S Skeldon
1957	Mrs B Singleton and WD Smith	1994	Mr and Mrs K Quinn
1958	Mr and Mrs M Bonallack	1995	Mrs C Caldwell and P Carr
1959	Miss J Robertson and I Wright	1996	Miss L Walters and M Naylor
1960	Miss B Jackson and MJ Burgess	1997	Miss K Burton and G Wolstenholme
1961	Mrs R Smith and B Critchley	1998	Miss K Burton and J Smith
1962	Viscomtesse de Saint Sauveur and DW Frame	1999	Miss AM Boatman and RG Hodgkinson
1963	Mrs G Valentine and JE Behrend	2000	Mr and Mrs Galway

2001 Semi-Finals
Mr and Mrs M Galway beat Mrs L Webb and GP O'Connor 6 and 5
Miss K Fisher and J Harper beat Miss A Boatman and SP Benka 6 and 5

Final
Miss K Fisher and J Harper beat Mr and Mrs M Galway 2 and 1

University and School Events

Halford-Hewitt Cup (Inaugurated 1924) *at Deal*

1924	Eton	1954	Rugby	1978	Harrow
1925	Eton	1955	Eton	1979	Stowe
1926	Eton	1956	Eton	1980	Shrewsbury
1927	Harrow	1957	George Watson's	1981	George Watson's
1928	Eton	1958	Harrow	1982	Charterhouse
1929	Harrow	1959	Wellington	1983	Charterhouse
1930	Charterhouse	1960	Rossall	1984	Charterhouse
1931	Harrow	1961	Rossall	1985	Harrow
1932	Charterhouse	1962	Oundle	1986	Repton
1933	Rugby	1963	Repton	1987	Merchiston
1934	Charterhouse	1964	Fettes	1988	Stowe
1935	Charterhouse	1965	Rugby	1989	Eton
1936	Charterhouse	1966	Charterhouse	1990	Tonbridge
1937	Charterhouse	1967	Eton	1991	Shrewsbury
1938	Marlborough	1968	Eton	1992	Tonbridge
1939	Charterhouse	1969	Eton	1993	Shrewsbury
1940–46	*No competition*	1970	Merchiston	1994	Tonbridge
1947	Harrow	1971	Charterhouse	1995	Harrow
1948	Winchester	1972	Marlborough	1996	Radley
1949	Charterhouse	1973	Rossall	1997	Oundle
1950	Rugby	1974	Charterhouse	1998	Charterhouse
1951	Rugby	1975	Harrow	1999	George Watson's
1952	Harrow	1976	Merchiston	2000	Epsom
1953	Harrow	1977	George Watson's		

2001

Semi-Finals Bradfield beat Merchiston
Tonbridge beat Whitgift

Final Tonbridge beat Bradfield

Grafton Morrish Trophy (Inaugurated 1963) *at Hunstanton and Brancaster*

1963	Tonbridge	1976	Charterhouse	1989	Tonbridge
1964	Tonbridge	1977	Haileybury	1990	Clifton
1965	Charterhouse	1978	Charterhouse	1991	Repton
1966	Charterhouse	1979	Harrow	1992	Charterhouse
1967	Charterhouse	1980	Charterhouse	1993	Malvern
1968	Wellington	1981	Charterhouse	1994	George Heriot's
1969	Sedbergh	1982	Marlborough	1995	Repton
1970	Sedbergh	1983	Wellington	1996	Coventry
1971	Dulwich	1984	Sedbergh	1997	George Heriot's
1972	Sedbergh	1985	Warwick	1998	Solihull
1973	Pangbourne	1986	Tonbridge	1999	George Heriot's
1974	Millfield	1987	Harrow	2000	Lancing
1975	Oundle	1988	Robert Gordon's		

2001

Final
King's College School, Wimbledon beat Epsom 2½–1½

Oxford v Cambridge Varsity Match (Inaugurated 1878)

1878	Oxford	Wimbledon	1938	Cambridge	Westward Ho!
1879	Cambridge	Wimbledon	1939	Cambridge	Royal St George's
1880	Oxford	Wimbledon	1940–45	*No competitions due to Second World War*	
1881	*Not played*		1946	Cambridge	Royal Lytham & St Annes
1882	Cambridge	Wimbledon	1947	Oxford	Rye
1883	Oxford	Wimbledon	1948	Oxford	Royal St George's
1884	Oxford	Wimbledon	1949	Cambridge	Hoylake
1885	Oxford	Wimbledon	1950	Oxford	Royal Lytham & St Annes
1886	Oxford	Wimbledon	1951	Cambridge	Rye
1887	Cambridge	Wimbledon	1952	Cambridge	Rye
1888	Cambridge	Wimbledon	1953	Cambridge	Rye
1889	Oxford	Wimbledon	1954	Cambridge	Rye
1890	Cambridge	Wimbledon	1955	Cambridge	Rye
1891	Cambridge	Wimbledon	1956	Oxford	Formby
1892	Cambridge	Wrlmbledon	1957	Oxford	Royal St George's
1893	Cambridge	Wimbledon	1958	Cambridge	Rye
1894	Oxford	Sandwich	1959	Cambridge	Burnham & Berrow
1895	Cambridge	Sandwich	1960	Cambridge	Royal Lytham & St Annes
1896	Halved	Wimbledon	1961	Oxford	Royal St George's
1897	Cambridge	Sandwich	1962	Halved	Hunstanton
1898	Cambridge	Sandwich	1963	Cambridge	Royal Birkdale
1899	Oxford	Sandwich	1964	Oxford	Rye
1900	Oxford	Sandwich	1965	Cambridge	Royal St George's
1901	Oxford	Sandwich	1966	Cambridge	Hunstanton
1902	Oxford	Sandwich	1967	Cambridge	Rye
1903	Oxford	Sandwich	1968	Cambridge	Porthcawl
1904	Oxford	Woking	1969	Cambridge	Formby
1905	Cambridge	Sunningdale	1970	Halved	Royal St George's
1906	Cambridge	Hoylake	1971	Oxford	Rye
1907	Cambridge	Hoylake	1972	Cambridge	Formby
			1973	Oxford	Saunton

After 1907 the result was arrived at by matches won

			1974	Cambridge	Ganton
1908	Cambridge	Sunningdale	1975	Cambridge	Hoylake
1909	Oxford	Royal St George's	1976	Cambridge	Woodhall Spa
1910	Cambridge	Hoylake	1977	Cambridge	Porthcawl
1911	Oxford	Rye	1978	Oxford	Rye
1912	Halved	Prince's,	1979	Oxford	Harlech
1913	Halved	Hoylake	1980	Oxford	Hoylake
1914	Oxford	Rye	1981	Cambridge	Formby
1915–19	*No competitions due to First World War*		1982	Cambridge	Hunstanton
1920	Cambridge	Sunningdale	1983	Cambridge	Royal St George's
1921	Oxford	Hoylake	1984	Cambridge	Sunningdale
1922	Cambridge	Prince's, Sandwich	1985	Oxford	Rye
1923	Oxford	Rye	1986	Oxford	Ganton
1924	Cambridge	Hoylake	1987	Cambridge	Formby
1925	Oxford	Hunstanton	1988	Cambridge	Royal Porthcawl
1926	Cambridge	Burnham and Berrow	1989	Cambridge	Rye
1927	Cambridge	Hoylake	1990	Cambridge	Muirfield
1928	Cambridge	Prince's, Sandwich	1991	Cambridge	Royal St George's
1929	Cambridge	Rye	1992	Oxford	Royal Cinque Ports
1930	Oxford	Hoylake	1993	Oxford	Royal Liverpool
1931	Oxford	Prince's, Sandwich	1994	Oxford	Rye
1932	Oxford	Lytham St Annes	1995	Oxford	Royal Lytham & St Annes
1933	Cambridge	Prince's, Sandwich	1996	Oxford	Royal West Norfolk
1934	Oxford	Formby	1997	Oxford	Royal St Georges
1935	Cambridge	Burnham and Berrow	1998	Cambridge	Rye
1936	Cambridge	Hoylake	1999	Oxford	Royal Cinque Ports
1937	Cambridge	Prince's, Sandwich	2000	Cambridge	Porthcawl

2001 *at Formby*

Oxford beat Cambridge 8–7

Oxford and Cambridge Golfing Society
for the President's Putter (Inaugurated 1920) at Rye

1920	EWE Holderness	1951	LG Crawley	1977	AWJ Holmes
1921	EWE Holderness	1952	LG Crawley	1978	MJ Reece
1922	EWE Holderness	1953	GH Micklem	1979	*Cancelled due to snow*
1923	EWE Holderness	1954	G Huddy	1980	S Melville
1924	B Darwin	1955	G Huddy	1981	AWJ Holmes
1925	HD Gillies	1956	GT Duncan	1982	DMA Steel
1926T	EF Storey	1957	AE Shepperson	1983	ER Dexter
	RH Wethered	1958	Lt-Col AA Duncan	1984	A Edmond
1927	RH Wethered	1959	ID Wheater	1985	ER Dexter
1928	RH Wethered	1960	JME Anderson	1986	J Caplan
1929	Sir EWE Holderness	1961	ID Wheater	1987	CD Meacher
1930	TA Bourn	1962	MF Attenborough	1988	G Woollett
1931	AG Pearson	1963	JG Blackwell	1989	M Froggatt
1932	LG Crawley	1964	DMA Steel	1990	G Woollett
1933	AJ Peech	1965	WJ Uzielli	1991	B Ingleby
1934	DHR Martin	1966	MF Attenborough	1992	M Cox
1935	RH Wethered	1967	JR Midgley	1993	C Weight
1936	RH Wethered	1968	AWJ Holmes	1994	S Seman
1937	JB Beck	1969	P Moody	1995	A Woolnough
1938	CJH Tolley	1970	DMA Steel	1996	C Rotheroe
1939	JOH Greenly	1971	GT Duncan	1997	C Rotheroe
1940–46	*No competition*	1972	P Moody	1998	N Pabari
1947	LG Crawley	1973	AD Swanston	1999	C Dale
1948	Major AA Duncan	1974	R Biggs	2000	CJ Dale
1949	PB Lucas	1975	CJ Weight		
1950	DHR Martin	1976	MJ Reece		

2001

Quarter Finals
B Streather O beat AP Stracey C at 19th
JTA Martin-Jenkins O beat RD Marrett O 1 hole
ADC West O beat MM Williamson C 2 holes
RAN Perkins C beat IM Henderson O 4 & 3

Semi-Finals
B Streather beat JTA Martin Jenkins 6 & 5
RAN Perkins beat ADC West 3 & 2

Final
Bruce Streather beat Rob Perkins 2 holes

Palmer Cup (USA university students v Great Britain & Ireland students)

1997	USA	19–5	Bay Hill, Orlando, Florida
1998	USA	12–12	St Andrews, Scotland
1999	USA	17½–6½	Honors, Tennessee
2000	GB&I	12½–11½	Royal Liverpool

2001 at Springfield, NJ

First Day: Fourball – Morning
Engler & Glover beat Rowe & Sullivan 4 and 3
Lander & Cassini beat McDowell & Kehoe
  4 and 3
Quinney & Wisler halved with O Wilson & Elson
Molder & Compton beat S Wilson & Inglis
  1 hole

Foursomes – Afternoon
Cassini & Glover beat McDowell & Elson
  5 and 3
Quinney & Lander beat Rowe & Sullivan
  5 and 3
Engler & Wisler beat O Wilson & Kehoe
  2 and 1
Molder & Compton lost to S Wilson & Inglis
  4 and 3

Second Day: Singles – Morning
Bryce Molder halved with Graeme McDowell
Lucas Glover beat Jamie Elson 3 and 2
Nick Cassini beat David Inglis 1 hole
John Engler beat Stuart Wilson 2 holes
Erik Compton beat Justin Kehoe 6 and 4
Scott Lander beat Kyron Sullivan 1 hole
Jeff Quinney beat Philip Rowe 6 and 5
Chris Wisler beat Oliver Wilson 4 and 2

Singles – Afternoon
L Glover lost to G McDowell 1 hole
B Molder lost to D Inglis 2 holes
J Quinney beat J Elson 3 and 2
N Cassini halved withS Wilson
E Compton beat K Sullivan 5 and 4
J Engler halved with P Rowe
C Wisler beat J Kehoe 6 and 5
S Lander lost to O Wilson 3 and 2

Result: United States 14, Great Britain & Ireland 2

Boyd Quaich (University Championship) *at St Andrews*

1946	AS Mayer	Glasgow	161	1974	G Cairns	Edinburgh	297
1947T	H Brews	Johannesburg	148	1975	S Dunlop	Trinity, Dublin	291
	FWG Deighton	Glasgow	148	1976	R Watson	Dundee	297
1948	JL Lindsay	St Andrews	203	1977	R Watson	Dundee	297
1949	FD Tatum	Oxford	217	1978	R Watson	Dundee	298
1950	GP Roberts	Liverpool	294	1979	D McLeary	St Andrews	302
1951	H Dooley	Nottingham	299	1980	ME Lewis	Bath	290
1952	G Parker	Glasgow	297	1981	P Gallagher	Heriot-Watt	302
1953	JL Bamford	Trinity, Dublin	290	1982	ME Lewis	Bath	297
1954	I Caldwell	London	287	1983	R Risan	Lund, Sweden	296
1955	HC Squirrll	Birmingham	292	1984	J Huggan	Stirling	297
1956	JL Bamford	Trinity, Dublin	295	1985	S Elgie	W. Ontario, Canada	299
1957	DM Marsh	Liverpool	293	1986	A Roberts	Hull	291
1958	R Mummery	London	299	1987	M Pask	St Andrews	293
1959-61	*Not played*			1988	A Mathers	Stirling	289
1962	DB Sheahan	Univ. Coll., Dublin	217	1989	A Mathers	Stirling	300
1963	S MacDonald	Edinburgh	295	1990	A Mathers	Stirling	297
1964	AJ Low	St Andrews	299	1991	C Somner	Friberg, Switzerland	302
1965	S MacDonald	Edinburgh	295	1992	L Walker	Trinity, Dublin	286
1966	FE McCarroll	Queen's, Belfast	291	1993	G Sherry	Stirling	298
1967	B Nicholson	Aberdeen	294	1994	C Sanderson	Stellenbosch, SA	283
1968	JW Johnston	Aberdeen	291	1995	C Sanderson	Stellenbosch, SA	290
1969	PH Moody	Cambride	286	1996	B Templeton	Heriot-Watt	294
1970	JT Moffat	Strathclyde	297	1997	G Maly	St Andrews	289
1971	JW Johnston	Aberdeen	289	1998	D Simpson	Edinburgh	283
1972	D Greig	Aberdeen	288	1999	O Lindsay	St Andrews	290
1973	J Rube	Sweden	285	2000	G Greer	Glasgow	288

2001

1	Pieter Botha* (Pretoria)	69-73-76-74—292
2	Andy Smith (SE Louisiana)	69-76-72-75—292
3	Finlay Miller (St Andrews)	73-80-72-69—294

Queen Elizabeth Coronation Schools Trophy (Inaugurated 1953)

at Royal Burgess, Barnton

1953	Watsonians	1977	Glasgow High School FP
1954	Daniel Stewart's FP	1978	Old Lorettonians
1955	Watsonians	1979	Gordonians
1956	Watsonians	1980	George Heriot's FP
1957	Hillhead High School FP	1981	Ayr Academicals
1958	Watsonians	1982	George Heriot's FP
1959	Glasgow High School FP	1983	Perth Academy FP
1960	Glasgow High School FP	1984	Glasgow High School FP
1961	Watsonians	1985	Glasgow High School FP
1962	Glasgow High School FP	1986	Watsonians
1963	Glasgow High School FP	1987	Daniel Stewart's/Melville FP
1964	Dollar Academicals	1988	Watsonians
1965	Old Lorettonians	1989	Kelvinside Academicals
1966	Merchistonians	1990	Hutchesons' Grammar School FP
1967	Merchistonians	1991	Glasgow High School FP
1968	Hillhead High School FP	1992	Daniel Stewart's/Melville FP
1969	Kelvinside Academicals	1993	Merchistonians
1970	Dollar Academicals	1994	Perth Academy FP
1971	Merchistonians	1995	Glasgow High School FP
1972	Merchistonians	1996	Glasgow High School FP
1973	Merchistonians	1997	Old Uppinghamians
1974	Old Carthusians	1998	Watsonians
1975	Old Lorettonians	1999	Morrisonians
1976	Watsonians	2000	Breadalbane Academicals

2001

Old Carthusians beat Campbellians 2½–½
Glasgow High School FP beat Dollar Academicals 2–1

Final
Old Carthusians beat Glasgow High School FP 2–1

County and Other Regional Championships

Anglesey

1992	D McLean	1997	M Perdue
1993	M Perdue	1998	EO Jones
1994	J Campbell	1999	A Williams
1995	D McLean	2000	H Hughes
1996	A Williams	2001	H Hughes

Angus

1992	D Downie	1998	E Ramsay
1993	G Tough	1999	J Flynn
1994	E Wilson	2000	S Wilson
1995	J Rae	2001	M Lindsay (M)
1996	G Bell		A Johnston (S)
1997	P Cunningham		

Argyll and Bute

1992	G Bolton	1998	J Sharp
1993	G Tyre-Cole	1999	G Bolton
1994	G Bolton	2000	G McMillan
1995	G Tyre	2001	G Bolton (M)
1996	L Kelly		G Reynolds (S)
1997	S Campbell		

Ayrshire

1992	G Sherry (M)	1997	G Fox (M)
	G Lawrie (S)		B Aitken (S)
1993	H McKibben (M)	1998	I Robertson (M)
	G Sherry (S)		D Glass (S)
1994	J Cairney (M)	1999	G Holland
	G Lawrie (S)		(M and S)
1995	A Reid (M)	2000	L Bagnall (M)
	A Gourlay (S)		A Gourlay (S)
1996	J Cairney (M)	2001	A Gourlay (M)
	G Lawrie (S)		G Bryden (S)

Bedfordshire

1992	L Watcham	1997	K Kemp
1993	C Beard	1998	M Wharton
1994	J Kemp	1999	J Kemp
1995	I Tottingham	2000	S Vinnecombe
1996	M Wharton	2001	J Kemp

Berks, Bucks and Oxon

1992	VL Phillips	1997	L Donald
1993	R Walton	1998	L Donald
1994	.D Fisher	1999	L Rusher
1995	D Lane	2000	K Freeman
1996	J Carlsen	2001	C Bowler

Border Golfers' Association

1992	M Thomson	1997	W Simpson
1993	D Valentine	1998	D Ballantyne
1994	M Thomson	1999	J Paterson
1995	M Thomson	2000	M Thomson
1996	D Ballantyne	2001	M Thomson

Caernarfon and District

1992	D McLean	1997	*Not played*
1993	E Jones	1998	A Clishem
1994	D McLean	1999	R Williams
1995	S Pritchard	2000	H Hughes
1996	A Williams	2001	M Tottey

Caernarfonshire Cup

1992	MA Macara	1997	*Not played*
1993	L Harpin	1998	M Pilkington
1994	J Dabecki	1999	E Angel
1995	J Dabecki	2000	M Wyn Jones
1996	M Pilkington	2001	A Thomas

Cambridgeshire

1992	LG Yearn	1997	O Cousins
1993	LG Yearn	1998	L Yearn
1994	A Emery	1999	O Cousins
1995	S Jarvis	2000	LG Yearn
1996	P Rains	2001	LG Yearn

Channel Islands

1992	C Chevalier	1997	R Williamson
1993	B Eggo	1998	DA Rowlinson
1994	C Chevalier	1999	N Voudin
1995	C Chevalier	2000	R Eggo
1996	R Eggo	2001	P Le Chevalier

Cheshire

1992	A Hill	1997	N Pabari
1993	J Hodgson	1998	J Donaldson
1994	J Hodgson	1999	SS Grewal
1995	C Smethurst	2000	FA Bibby
1996	D Vaughan	2001	GJ Bradley

Clackmannanshire

1992	G Kennedy	1998	B Stewart
1993	S Horne	1999	M Crichton
1994	P McLeod	2000	AC Fairbrother
1995	I Ross	2001	I Macaulay
1996	R Stewart		(M and S)
1997	G Bowie		

Cornwall

1992	P Clayton	1997	P Darlington
1993	C Phillips	1998	I Atkinson
1994	R Binney	1999	I Veale
1995	M Lock	2000	S Chapman
1996	I Veale	2001	C Llewellyn

Cumbria

1992	A Greenbank	1997	G Watson
1993	R Secular	1998	P Jack
1994	B Story	1999	J Longcake
1995	N Mitchell	2000	J Carr
1996	R Secular	2001	S Young

Denbigh

2001	P Grimby

Derbyshire

1992	J Feeney	1997	AS Humpston
1993	G Shaw	1998	L Walley
1994	J Feeney	1999	JP Feeney
1995	G Shaw	2000	N Vowles
1996	J Feeney	2001	P Gration

Devon

1992	D Lewis	1997	G Ruth
1993	R Goodey	1998	S Pike
1994	M Crossfield	1999	G Ruth
1995	A Capping	2000	S Davey
1996	D Eva	2001	G Ruth

Dorset

1992	L James	1997	J Baldwin
1993	A Lawrence	1998	J Pounder
1994	M Davies	1999	C Jessup
1995	M Davies	2000	M Davies
1996	A Lawrence	2001	A Lawrence

Dunbartonshire

1992	D Shaw (M)	1997	S Carmichael (M)
	R Blair (S)		S McLeitch (S)
1993	F Jardine	1998	S Carmichael (M)
	(M and S)		G Murphy (S)
	F Jardine (S)	1999	G Greer (M)
1994	D Carrick (M)		J Hughes (S)
	F Hutchison (S)	2000	J Devonney (M)
1995	T McKeown (M)		SR McIntosh (S)
	F Jardine (S)	2001	F Bone (M)
1996	K MacNair (M)		P Gault (S)
	A Leitch (S)		

Durham

1992	A McLure	1997	J Dryden
1993	R Walker	1998	C Hamilton
1994	J Kennedy	1999	A McLure
1995	A McLure	2000	AJ McLure
1996	S Ord	2001	M Ridley

Dyfed

2001	P Davies

Essex

1992	D Lee	1997	B Taylor
1993	R Coles	1998	B Taylor
1994	R Coles	1999	R Blaxhill
1995	D Salisbury	2000	S Middleton
1996	G Clark	2001	R Blaxill

Fife

1992	N Urquhart	1998	J Bunch
1993	DA Paton	1999	J McLeary
1994	C MacDougall	2000	R Bremner
1995	D Paton	2001	J McLeary (M)
1996	B Erskine		S Meiklejohn (S)
1997	S Meiklejohn		

Flint

2001	MB Jones

Glamorgan

1992	CM Rees	1997	Y Taylor
1993	M Stimson	1998	C Williams
1994	N Edwards	1999	S Roberts
1995	S Roberts	2000	N Edwards
1996	N Edwards	2001	N Edwards

Gloucestershire

1992	G Wolstenholme	1997	M Unwin
1993	G Wolstenholme	1998	TP Smith
1994	G Wolstenholme	1999	D Young
1995	T Smith	2000	C Newman
1996	G Wolstenholme	2001	M Unwin

Gwent (Formerly Monmouthshire Amateur)

1992	CN Evans	1997	R Price
1993	A Harray	1998	N Povall
1994	B Dredge	1999	A Williams
1995	C Dinsdale	2000	CJ Dinsdale
1996	M Hayward	2001	S Westley

Hampshire, Isle of Wight and Channel Islands

1992	C Chevalier	1997	S Stanley
1993	M Blackey	1998	C Hudson
1994	R Bland	1999	D Henley
1995	M Le Mesurier	2000	C McLaughlin
1996	M Blackey	2001	D Henley

Hertfordshire

1992	S Burnell	1997	C Duke
1993	S Burnell	1998	R Conway-Lye
1994	G Maly	1999	D Griffiths
1995	H Steel	2000	I Farrant
1996	S Little	2001	M Payne

Isle of Man

1992	G Wilson	1997	P McMullan
1993	G Wilson	1998	P McMullan
1994	R Sayle	1999	G Wilson
1995	G Wilson	2000	S Ellis
1996	G Wilson	2001	G Wilson

Kent

1992	P Sherman	1997	D Ottoway
1993	G Brown	1998	D Ottaway
1994	B Barham	1999	J Carter
1995	T Milford	2000	D Curtis
1996	B Barham	2001	L Godwin

Lanarkshire

1992	W Bryson (M and S)	1998	R Hinshelwood (M)
1993	K Gallacher (M)		M Warren (S)
	D Brown (S)	1999	W Bryson
1994	M Moir (M)		(M and S)
	W Bryson (S)		W Bryson (S)
1995	W Bryson (M)	2000	I Duff (M)
	K Nisbet (S)		C Heap (S)
1996	J Ralston (M)	2001	C Gibson (M)
	K Ralston (S)		W Bryson (S)
1997	W Bryson (M)		
	E Moir (S)		

Lancashire

1992	R Hutt	1997	D Johnson
1993	G Helsby	1998	P Wiliams
1994	K Wallbank	1999	A Jackson
1995	G Boardman	2000	M Cox
1996	G Boardman	2001	R Bardsley

Leicestershire and Rutland

1992	D Gibson	1997	J Herbert
1993	P Frith	1998	G Wolstenholme
1994	I Lyner	1999	D Gibson
1995	P Frith	2000	N Knighton
1996	J Herbert	2001	G Wolstenholme

Lincolnshire

1992	P Streeter	1997	P Streeter
1993	J Crampton	1998	A White
1994	J Crampton	1999	D Skinns
1995	J Crampton	2000	P Bradshaw
1996	P Streeter	2001	LJ Toyne

Lothians

1992	C MacPhail	1998	K Nicholson
1993	S Smith	1999	C Swanston
1994	S Smith	2000	M Timmins
1995	S Smith	2001	K Nicholson (M)
1996	N Shillinglaw		D Thomson (S)
1997	K Nicholson		

Middlesex

1992	WJ Bennett	1997	C Austin
1993	GA Homewood	1998	R Vaney
1994	WJ Bennett	1999	G Evans
1995	G Clark	2000	S Samphire
1996	S Kay	2001	S Samphire

Norfolk

1992	A Marshall	1997	G Price
1993	DA Edwards	1998	CJ Lamb
1994	J Durrant	1999	CJ Lamb
1995	I Ellis	2000	NJ Williamson
1996	P Little	2001	D Henderson

North (Scotland)

2001	NG Pears

North-East (Scotland)

2001	N Pears (M)
	G Gordon (S)

Northamptonshire

1992	AJ Wilson	1997	P Langrish-Smith
1993	S McIlwain	1998	G Keates
1994	A Print	1999	N Soto
1995	A Lord	2000	A Print
1996	I Dallas	2001	N Soto

Northumberland

1992	S Philipson	1997	D Clark
1993	P Taylor	1998	J McCallum
1994	S Twynholm	1999	SE Philipson
1995	M Hall	2000	AR Paisley
1996	K Cademy-Taylor	2001	C McDonnell

Nottinghamshire

1992	L Westwood	1997	O Wilson
1993	L Westwood	1998	AJ Liddle
1994	D Lucas	1999	AJ Liddle
1995	H Hopkinson	2000	M Allen
1996	D McJannet	2001	D McJannet

Perth and Kinross

1992	B Grieve	1998	K Grant
1993	T McLevy	1999	N Macdonald
1994	E Lindsay	2000	G Campbell
1995	S Herd	2001	G Campbell
1996	M Rose		(M and S)
1997	N Macdonald		

Renfrewshire

1992	G Urquhart	1998	A McKay
1993	R Clark	1999	A McKay
1994	M Carmichael	2000	S Robertson
1995	R Adam	2001	A Craig (M)
1996	S Nicol		G Murphy (S)
1997	D Owens		

Shropshire and Herefordshire

1992	M Welch	1997	K Preece
1993	M Welch	1998	O Pughe
1994	M Welch	1999	K Baker
1995	D Park	2000	R Brown
1996	D Harris	2001	D McDonnell

Somerset

1992	C Edwards	1997	R Swords
1993	C Edwards	1998	J Morgan
1994	C Edwards	1999	G Legg
1995	B Whittock	2000	D Dixon
1996	D Dixon	2001	C Edwards

South of Scotland

1992	J Wright	1998	D Sutton
1993	D Wallis	1999	I Thomson
1994	I Reid	2000	BJ Scott
1995	B Scott	2001	I Brotherston (M)
1996	E Little		C Haddow (S)
1997	I Brotherston		

South-Western Counties Match Play

1992	S Edgley	1997	S McCarthy
1993	B Sandry	1998	S McCarthy
1994	A Lawrence	1999	M Davies
1995	S McCarthy	2000	S Godfrey
1996	D Marsh	2001	D Dixon

Staffordshire

1992	M McGuire	1997	SD Wakefield
1993	C Poxon	1998	KD Hale
1994	R Mayfield	1999	R Chattaway
1995	T Ryder	2000	C Russell
1996	R Parkes	2001	MA Payne

Stirlingshire

1992	H Anderson	1998	JR Johnson
1993	D Smith	1999	K McArthur
1994	K McArthur	2000	H Anderson
1995	K Brunton	2001	H Anderson (M)
1996	G McDonald		D Todd (S)
1997	A Ellison		

Suffolk

1992	P Buckle	1997	J Maddock
1993	J Maddock	1998	J Wright
1994	J Maddock	1999	P Barnard
1995	D Quinney	2000	L Dodd
1996	J Keely	2001	L Dodd

Surrey

1992	A Wall	1997	T Paterson
1993	A Raitt	1998	C Rodgers
1994	M Ellis	1999	N Pimm
1995	A Wall	2000	J Franks
1996	M Palmer	2001	Z Scotland

Wiltshire

1992	D Howell	1997	P Bicknell
1993	RE Searle	1998	P Bicknell
1994	R Searle	1999	P Bicknell
1995	N Mumford	2000	S Surry
1996	A Mutch	2001	I Campbell

Sussex

1992	M Galway	1997	M Harris
1993	M Galway	1998	M Harris
1994	P Clevely	1999	M Galway
1995	M Allen	2000	J Doherty
1996	M Harris	2001	S Nightingale

Worcestershire

1992	M Reynard	1997	S Braithwaite
1993	M Reynard	1998	D Glover
1994	R Sadler	1999	P Scarrett
1995	M Reynard	2000	R Wassell
1996	M Reynard	2001	M Reynard

Warwickshire

1992	G Lord	1997	T Whitehouse
1993	G Marston	1998	T Whitehouse
1994	N Connolly	1999	T Whitehouse
1995	S Webster	2000	T Whitehouse
1996	A Carey	2001	T Whitehouse

Wigtownshire

1992	R O'Keefe	1997	R Shaw
1993	K Hardie	1998	R Shaw
1994	K Hardie	1999	G Sharp
1995	R O'Keefe	2000	R Shaw
1996	E Little	2001	D Brodie

Yorkshire

1992	ID Pyman (M)	1998	S Tarplett (M)
	J Docker (S)		M Bugg (S)
1993	J Healey (M)		R Hodgkinson
	J Roberts (S)		(S)
1994	P Wood (M)	1999	GA Clark (M)
	N Ludwell (S)		SJ Dyson (S)
1995	J Ellis (M)	2000	JB Godbold (M)
	N Gibson (S)		GA Clark (S)
	J Hepworth (S)		RM Hollins (S)
1996	R Jones (M)	2001	R Finch (M)
	N Emmerson		R Finch (S)
	(S)		
1997	R Jones (M)		
	A Wright (S)		

Five albatrosses on 2001 European circuit

Five players made rare albatrosses or double-eagles on the 2001 European Tour, two of them being achieved in the Open Championship at Royal Lytham and St Annes. The double eagle men were:

1. Andrew Richter (RSA), Alfred Dunhill Championship, Houghton, 16th hole, Round One
2. Jeff Maggert (USA), Open Championship, Royal Lytham and St Annes, 6th hole, Round One
3. Greg Owen (Eng), Open Championship, Royal Lytham and St Annes, 11th hole, Round Three
4. José Maria Olazabal (Esp), BMW International, Nord Eichenreid, Munich, 11th Hole, Round Two
5. Johnathan Lomas (Eng), Scottish Cup PGA Championship, PGA Centenary Course, Gleneagles Hoel, 12th Hole, Round One

Overseas Amateur Championships

Australian Amateur	Steven Bowditch
Austrian Amateur	Achim Spannagel
Canadian Amateur	Dareth Paddison
Caribbean Amateur	Robert Chilman
Czech Amateur	Petr Nic
Danish Amateur Strokeplay	Allan Høgh Madsen
French Amateur	François Delamontagne
German Amateur	Markus Zoller
Hungarian Amateur	Richard Sárközi
Italian Amateur	Edoardo Molinari
Luxembourg Amateur	Alan Dowling
Netherlands	Wil Besseling
New Zealand Amateur	Ben Gallie
New Zealand Amateur Stroke Play	Sam Hunt
Portuguese Open	David Price (Wal)
Singapore Open	Tim Wilkinson (NZ)
South African Amateur	David Dixon (Eng)
South African Amateur Stroke Play	Richard Sterne
Spanish Open	Tom Whitehouse (Eng)
Swiss Amateur	Raphaël de Sousa

United States Amateur Championship

Year	Winner	Runner-up	Venue	By
1895	CB Macdonald	C Sands	Newport, RI	12 and 11
1896	HJ Whigham	JG Thorp	Shinnecock Hills, NY	8 and 7
1897	HJ Whigham	WR Betts	Wheaton, IL	8 and 6
1898	FS Douglas	WB Smith	Morris County, NJ	5 and 3
1899	HM Harriman	FS Douglas	Onwentsia, IL	3 and 2
1900	WJ Travis	FS Douglas	Garden City, NY	2 holes
1901	WJ Travis	WE Egan	Atlantic City, NJ	5 and 4
1902	LN James	EM Byers	Glenview, IL	4 and 3
1903	WJ Travis	EM Byers	Nassau, NY	5 and 4
1904	HC Egan	F Herreshof	Baltusrol, NJ	8 and 6
1905	HC Egan	DE Sawyer	Wheaton, IL	6 and 5
1906	EM Byers	GS Lyon	Englewood, NJ	2 holes
1907	JD Travers	A Graham	Cleveland, OH	6 and 5
1908	JD Travers	MH Behr	Garden City, NY	8 and 7
1909	RA Gardner	HC Egan	Wheaton, IL	4 and 3
1910	WC Fownes jr	WK Wood	Brookline, MA	4 and 3
1911	HH Hilton	F Herreshof	Apawamis, NY	37th
1912	JD Travers	C Evans jr	Wheaton, IL	7 and 6
1913	JD Travers	JG Anderson	Garden City, NY	5 and 4
1914	F Ouimet	JD Travers	Ekwanok, VT	6 and 5
1915	RA Gardner	JG Anderson	Detroit, MI	5 and 4
1916	C Evans jr	RA Gardner	Merion, PA	4 and 3
1917–18	*Not played due to First World War*			
1919	SD Herron	RT Jones jr	Oakmont, PA	5 and 4
1920	C Evans jr	F Ouimet	Roslyn, NY	7 and 6
1921	JP Guildford	RA Gardner	Clayton, MO	7 and 6
1922	JW Sweetser	C Evans jr	Brookline, MA	3 and 2
1923	MR Marston	JW Sweetser	Flossmoor, IL	38th
1924	RT Jones jr	G Von Elm	Merion, PA	9 and 8

Year	Winner	Runner-up	Venue	By
1925	RT Jones jr	W Gunn	Oakmont, PA	8 and 7
1926	G Von Elm	RT Jones jr	Baltusrol, NJ	2 and 1
1927	RT Jones jr	C Evans jr	Minikahda, MN	8 and 7
1928	RT Jones jr	TP Perkins	Brae Burn, MA	10 and 9
1929	HR Johnston	OF Willing	Pebble Beach, CA	4 and 3
1930	RT Jones jr	EV Homans	Merion, PA	8 and 7
1931	F Ouimet	J Westland	Beverley, IL	6 and 5
1932	CR Somerville	J Goodman	Baltimore, MD	2 and 1
1933	GT Dunlap jr	MR Marston	Kenwood, OH	6 and 5
1934	W Lawson Little jr	D Goldman	Brookline, MA	8 and 7
1935	W Lawson Little jr	W Emery	Cleveland, OH	4 and 2
1936	JW Fischer	J McLean	Garden City, NY	37th
1937	J Goodman	RE Billows	Portland, OR	2 holes
1938	WP Turnesa	BP Abbott	Oakmont, PA	8 and 7
1939	MH Ward	RE Billows	Glenview, IL	7 and 5
1940	RD Chapman	WB McCullough	Winged Foot, NY	11 and 9
1941	MH Ward	BP Abbott	Omaha, NE	4 and 3
1946	SE Bishop	S Quick	Baltusrol, NJ	37th
1947	RH Riegel	JW Dawson	Pebble Beach, CA	2 and 1
1948	WP Turnesa	RE Billows	Memphis, TN	2 and 1
1949	CR Coe	R King	Rochester, NY	11 and 10
1950	S Urzetta	FR Stranahan	Minneapolis, MN	39th
1951	WJ Maxwell	J Gagliardi	Saucon Valley, PA	4 and 3
1952	J Westland	A Mengert	Seattle, WA	3 and 2
1953	G Littler	D Morey	Oklahoma City, OK	1 hole
1954	A Palmer	R Sweeney	Detroit, MI	1 hole
1955	E Harvie Ward	W Hyndman	Richmond, VA	9 and 8
1956	E Harvie Ward	C Kocsis	Lake Forest, IL	5 and 4
1957	H Robbins	FM Taylor	Brookline, MA	5 and 4
1958	CR Coe	TD Aaron	San Francisco, CA	5 and 4
1959	JW Nicklaus	CR Coe	Broadmoor, CO	1 hole
1960	DR Beman	RW Gardner	St Louis, MO	6 and 4
1961	JW Nicklaus	HD Wysong	Pebble Beach, CA	8 and 6
1962	LE Harris jr	D Gray	Pinehurst, NC	1 hole
1963	DR Beman	RH Sikes	Des Moines, IA	2 and 1
1964	WC Campbell	EM Tutweiler	Canterbury, OH	1 hole

Changed to stroke play

Year	Winner	Venue	Score
1965	RJ Murphy	Tulsa, OK	291
1966	G Cowan	Merion, PA	285
1967	RB Dickson	Broadmoor, CO	285
1968	B Fleisher	Columbus, OH	284
1969	S Melnyk	Oakmont, PA	286
1970	L Wadkins	Portland, OR	280
1971	G Cowan	Wilmington, DE	280
1972	M Giles	Charlotte, NC	285

Reverted to match play

Year	Winner	Runner-up	Venue	By
1973	C Stadler	D Strawn	Inverness, OH	6 and 5
1974	J Pate	J Grace	Ridgewood, NJ	2 and 1
1975	F Ridley	K Fergus	Richmond, VA	2 holes
1976	B Sander	CP Moore	Bel-Air, CA	8 and 6
1977	J Fought	D Fischesser	Aronimink, PA	9 and 8
1978	J Cook	S Hoch	Plainfield, NJ	5 and 4
1979	M O'Meara	J Cook	Cleveland, OH	8 and 7
1980	H Sutton	B Lewis	Pinehurst, NC	9 and 8
1981	N Crosby	B Lindley	San Francisco, CA	37th
1982	J Sigel	D Tolley	Brookline, MA	8 and 7
1983	J Sigel	C Perry	Glenview, IL	8 and 7
1984	S Verplank	S Randolph	Oak Tree, OK	4 and 3
1985	S Randolph	P Persons	Montclair, NJ	1 hole
1986	S Alexander	C Kite	Shoal Creek, AL	5 and 3
1987	W Mayfair	E Rebmann	Jupiter Hills, FL	4 and 3
1988	E Meeks	D Yates	Hot Springs, VA	7 and 6
1989	C Patton	D Green	Merion, PA	3 and 1
1990	P Mickelson	M Zerman	Cherry Hills, CO	5 and 4
1991	M Voges	M Zerman	Chattanooga, TN	7 and 6

United States Amateur Championship *continued*

Year	Winner	Runner-up	Venue	By
1992	J Leonard	T Scherrer	Muirfield Village, OH	8 and 7
1993	J Harris	D Ellis	Houston, TX	5 and 3
1994	T Woods	T Kuehne	Sawgrass, FL	2 holes
1995	T Woods	G Marucci	Newport, RI	2 holes
1996	T Woods	S Scott	Pumpkin Ridge, OR	38th
1997	M Kuchar	J Kribel	Cog Hill, Lemont, IL	2 and 1
1998	H Kuehne	T McKnight	Oak Hill, Rochester, NY	2 and 1
1999	D Gossett	Sung Yoon Kim	Pebble Beach, CA	9 and 8
2000	J Quinney	J Driscoll	Springfield, NJ	39th hole

2001 *at East Lake, Atlanta, GA*

Quarter Finals
Robert Hamilton Beat Daniel Summerhayes 4 and 3
Manuel Merizalde (Col) beat Taichiro Kiyota (Jpn) 6 and 5
Brian Nosler beat Jeff Quinney 1 hole
Babba Dickerson beat Michael Sims (Ber) 1 hole

Semi-Finals
Hamilton beat Merizalde 2 and 1
Dickerson beat Nosler 1 hole

Final
Babba Dickerson beat Robert Hamilton 1 hole

PART V

Women's Amateur Tournaments

National and International Tournaments

Ladies British Amateur Championship

1893	M Scott	I Pearson	St Annes	7 and 5
1894	M Scott	I Pearson	Littlestone	3 and 2
1895	M Scott	E Lythgoe	Portrush	5 and 4
1896	Miss Pascoe	L Thomson	Hoylake, Royal Liverpool	3 and 2
1897	EC Orr	Miss Orr	Gullane	4 and 2
1898	L Thomson	EC Neville	Yarmouth	7 and 5
1899	M Hezlet	Magill	Newcastle Co Down	2 and 1
1900	Adair	Neville	Westward Ho!, R North Devon	6 and 5
1901	Graham	Adair	Aberdovey	3 and 1
1902	M Hezlet	E Neville	Deal	19th hole
1903	Adair	F Walker-Leigh	Portrush	4 and 3
1904	L Dod	M Hezlet	Troon	1 hole
1905	B Thompson	ME Stuart	Cromer	3 and 2
1906	Kennon	B Thompson	Burnham	4 and 3
1907	M Hezlet	F Hezlet	Newcastle Co Down	2 and 1
1908	M Titterton	D Campbell	St Andrews	19th hole
1909	D Campbell	F Hezlet	Birkdale	4 and 3
1910	Miss Grant Suttie	L Moore	Westward Ho!, R North Devon	6 and 4
1911	D Campbell	V Hezlet	Portrush	3 and 2
1912	G Ravenscroft	S Temple	Turnberry	3 and 2

(Final played over 36 holes after 1912)

1913	M Dodd	Chubb	St Annes	8 and 6
1914	C Leitch	G Ravenscroft	Hunstanton	2 and 1
1915–18	*No Championship owing to the Great War*			
1919	*Should have been played at Burnham in October, but abandoned owing to railway strike*			
1920	C Leitch	M Griffiths	Newcastle Co Down	7 and 6
1921	C Leitch	J Wethered	Turnberry	4 and 3
1922	J Wethered	C Leitch	Prince's, Sandwich, Royal St George's	9 and 7
1923	D Chambers	A Macbeth	Burnham, Somerset	2 holes
1924	J Wethered	Mrs Cautley	Portrush	7 and 6
1925	J Wethered	C Leitch	Troon	37th hole
1926	C Leitch	Mrs Garon	Harlech	8 and 7
1927	T de la Chaume (Fra)	Miss Pearson	Newcastle Co Down	5 and 4
1928	N Le Blan (Fra)	S Marshall	Hunstanton	3 and 2
1929	J Wethered	G Collett (USA)	St Andrews	3 and 1
1930	D Fishwick	G Collett (USA)	Formby	4 and 3
1931	E Wilson	W Morgan	Portmarnock	7 and 6
1932	E Wilson	CPR Montgomery	Saunton	7 and 6
1933	E Wilson	D Plumpton	Gleneagles	5 and 4
1934	AM Holm	P Barton	Porthcawl	6 and 5
1935	W Morgan	P Barton	Newcastle Co Down	3 and 2
1936	P Barton	B Newell	Southport and Ainsdale	5 and 3
1937	J Anderson	D Park	Turnberry	6 and 4
1938	AM Holm	E Corlett	Burnham	4 and 3
1939	P Barton	T Marks	Portrush	2 and 1
1940–45	*No Championship owing to Second World War*			
1946	GW Hetherington	P Garvey	Hunstanton	1 hole
1947	B Zaharias (USA)	J Gordon	Gullane	5 and 4
1948	L Suggs (USA)	J Donald	Lytham St Annes	1 hole
1949	F Stephens	V Reddan	Harlech	5 and 4
1950	Vicomtesse de St Sauveur (Fra)	J Valentine	Newcastle Co Down	3 and 2
1951	PJ MacCann	F Stephens	Broadstone	4 and 3
1952	M Paterson	F Stephens	Troon	39th hole
1953	M Stewart (Can)	P Garvey	Porthcawl	7 and 6
1954	F Stephens	E Price	Ganton	4 and 3
1955	J Valentine	B Romack (USA)	Portrush	7 and 6

1956	M Smith (USA)	M Janssen (USA)	Sunningdale	8 and 7
1957	P Garvey	J Valentine	Gleneagles	4 and 3
1958	J Valentine	E Price	Hunstanton	1 hole
1959	E Price	B McCorkindale	Ascot	37th hole
1960	B McIntyre (USA)	P Garvey	Harlech	4 and 2
1961	M Spearman	DJ Robb	Carnoustie	7 and 6
1962	M Spearman	A Bonallack	Royal Birkdale	1 hole
1963	B Varangot (Fra)	P Garvey	Newcastle Co Down	3 and 1
1964	C Sorenson (USA)	BAB Jackson	Sandwich, Prince's, Royal St George's	37th hole
1965	B Varangot (Fra)	IC Robertson	St Andrews	4 and 3
1966	E Chadwick	V Saunders	Ganton	3 and 2
1967	E Chadwick	M Everard	Harlech	1 hole
1968	B Varangot (Fra)	C Rubin (Fra)	Walton Heath	20th hole
1969	C Lacoste (Fra)	A Irvin	Portrush	1 hole
1970	D Oxley	IC Robertson	Gullane	1 hole
1971	M Walker	B Huke	Alwoodley	3 and 1
1972	M Walker	C Rubin (Fra)	Hunstanton	2 holes
1973	A Irvin	M Walker	Carnoustie	3 and 2
1974	C Semple (USA)	A Bonallack	Porthcawl	2 and 1
1975	N Syms (USA)	S Cadden	St Andrews	3 and 2
1976	C Panton	A Sheard	Silloth	1 hole
1977	A Uzielli	V Marvin	Hillside	6 and 5
1978	E Kennedy (Aus)	J Greenhalgh	Notts	1 hole
1979	M Madill	J Lock (Aus)	Nairn	2 and 1
1980	A Quast (USA)	L Wollin (Swe)	Woodhall Spa	3 and 1
1981	IC Robertson	W Aitken	Conway	20th hole
1982	K Douglas	G Stewart	Walton Heath	4 and 2
1983	J Thornhill	R Lautens (Sui)	Silloth	4 and 2
1984	J Rosenthal (USA)	J Brown	Royal Troon	4 and 3
1985	L Beman (Irl)	C Waite	Ganton	1 hole
1986	McGuire (NZ)	L Briars (Aus)	West Sussex	2 and 1
1987	J Collingham	S Shapcott	Harlech	19th hole
1988	J Furby	J Wade	Deal	4 and 3
1989	H Dobson	E Farquharson	Royal Liverpool	6 and 5
1990	J Hall	H Wadsworth	Dunbar	3 and 2
1991	V Michaud (Fra)	W Doolan (Aus)	Pannal	3 and 2
1992	P Pedersen (Den)	J Morley	Saunton	1 hole
1993	C Lambert	K Speak	Royal Lytham	3 and 2
1994	E Duggleby	C Mourgue d'Algue	Newport	3 and 1
1995	J Hall	K Mourgue d'Algue	Royal Portrush	3 and 2
1996	K Kuehne (USA)	B Morgan	Royal Liverpool	5 and 3
1997	A Rose	M McKay	Cruden Bay	4 and 3
1998	K Rostron	C Nocera	Little Aston	3 and 2
1999	M Monnet (Fra)	R Hudson	Royal Birkdale	1 hole
2000	R Hudson	E Duggleby	Royal Birkdale	5 and 4

2001 *at Ladybank, Fife*

First Round

Rebecca Hudson (Wheatley) beat Jo Pritchard (Tredegar Park) 8 and 7
Linzi Morton (Tulliallan) beat Jessica Issler (Ger) 2 holes
Kerry Knowles (Worplesdon) beat Maria Beautell (Esp) 4 and 3
Marta Prieto (Esp) beat Louise Kenney (Pitreavie) at 21st
Anna Gertsson (Swe) beat Anne Laing (Vale of Leven) 1 hole
Pia Odefey (Ger) beat Heather Stirling (Bridge of Allan) 2 and 1
Camilla Guriby Hilland (Nor) beat Elaine Dowdell (Wexford) 5 and 4
Michaela Parmlid (Swe) beat Renata Young (Can) 5 and 4
Becky Brewerton (Abergele) beat Rebecca Prout (Betchworth Park) 4 and 3
Kelly Hutcherson (Porters Park) beat Marie Allen (Moor Park) 2 and 1
Nuria Clau (Esp) beat Yvonne Cassidy (Dundalk) 3 and 2
Kerry Smith (Waterlooville) beat Alexandra Keighley (Lightcliffe) 1 hole
Carmen Alonso (Esp) beat Nicola Timmins (Sene Valley) 4 and 2
Ryley Webb (Can) beat Emma Weeks (Hockley) 4 and 3
Fiona Brown (Heswall) beat Lyndsey Devenish (Cruden Bay) 4 and 3
Christine Boucher (Can) beat Skye Matthews (Porters Park) 4 and 2

Ladies British Amateur Championship *continued*

First Round *continued*

Celestine de Vos (Bel) beat Kirsty Fisher (Royal Lytham & St Annes) 5 and 3
Maitena Alsuguren (Fra) beat Nina Reiss (Swe) 3 and 2
Fame More (Chesterfield) beat Annemieke de Goederen (Ned) at 20th
Kristina Engstrom (Swe) beat Vikki Laing (Musselburgh) 3 and 1
Nadina Taylor (Aus) beat Tullia Calzavara (Ita) 1 hole
Jessica Shepley (Can) beat Tracy Atkin (Leamington & County) 2 holes
Alison Coffey (Warrenpoint) beat Lisa Holm Sørensen (Den) 3 and 2
Federica Piovano (Ita) beat Deirdre Smith (Co. Louth) at 19th

Kate Phillips (Creigiau) beat Natalie Parkinson (Aus) 6 and 5
Laura Henderson (Can) beat Stephanie Coverley (Woodsome Hall) 2 and 1
Sara Garbutt (Knaresborough) beat Claire Grignolo (Ita) 5 and 3
Claire Hargan (Cardross) beat Anna Knuttson (Swe) 3 and 2
Kirsty Taylor (Sandford Springs) beat Alison Waller (Harpenden) 3 and 2
Sarah Jones (Pennard) beat Mahault Passerat de Silans (Fra) 1 hole
Fany Shaeffer (Fra) beat Kim Andrew (Clitheroe) 4 and 3
Emma Duggleby (Malton & Norton) beat Claire Coughlan (Cork) 4 and 3

Second Round

Morton beat Hudson 2 and 1
Prieto beat Knowles 6 and 5
Gertsson beat Odefey 2 and 1
Parmlid beat Hilland 6 and 4
Brewerton b Hutcherson 2 and 1
Smith beat Clau 3 and 2
Alonso beat Webb 5 and 3
Boucher beat Brown 1 hole

Alsuguren beat de Vos 5 and 4
More beat Engstrom at 21st
N Taylor beat Shepley 2 holes
Coffey beat Piovano 2 and 1
Phillips beat Henderson 4 and 3
Hargan beat Garbutt at 19th
K Taylor beat Jones 3 and 2
Duggleby beat Shaeffer 1 hole

Third Round

Prieto beat Morton 3 and 1
Parmlid beat Gertsson 1 hole

Third Round *continued*

Brewerton beat Smith 4 and 3
Alonso beat Boucher 2 and 1
More beat Alsuguren 1 hole
N Taylor beat Coffey 3 and 2
Hargan beat Phillips at 20th
Duggleby beat K Taylor 2 and 1

Quarter Finals

Prieto beat Parmlid 2 and 1
Alonso beat Brewerton 4 and 3
N Taylor beat More 3 and 2
Duggleby beat Hargan 2 holes

Semi-Finals

Prieto beat Alonso 3 and 1
Duggleby beat N Taylor at 21st

Final

Marta Prieto (Esp) beat Emma Duggleby (Eng)
   4 and 3

Ladies British Open Amateur Stroke Play Championship

1969	A Irvin	Gosforth Park	295	1985	IC Robertson	Formby	300
1970	M Everard	Birkdale	313	1986	C Hourihane	Blairgowrie	291
1971	IC Robertson	Ayr Belleisle	302	1987	L Bayman	Ipswich	297
1972	IC Robertson	Silloth	296	1988	K Mitchell	Porthcawl	317
1973	A Stant	Purdis Heath	298	1989	H Dobson	Southerness	298
1974	J Greenhalgh	Seaton Carew	302	1990	V Thomas	Strathaven	287
1975	J Greenhalgh	Gosforth Park	298	1991	J Morley	Long Ashton	297
1976	J Lee Smith	Fulford	299	1992	J Hockley	Frilford Heath	287
1977	M Everard	Lindrick	306	1993	J Hall	Gullane	290
1978	J Melville	Foxhills	310	1994	K Speak	Woodhall Spa	297
1979	M McKenna	Moseley	305	1995	MJ Pons (Esp)	Princes	289
1980	M Mahill	Brancepeth Castle	304	1996	C Kuld (Den)	Conwy (Caernarvonshire)	289
1981	J Soulsby	Norwich	300	1997	KM Juul (Den)	Silloth-on-Solway	293
1982	J Connachan	Downfield	294	1998	N Nijenhuis	Stirling	297
1983	A Nicholas	Moortown	292	1999	B Brewerton	Huddersfield	294
1984	C Waite	Caernarvonshire	295	2000	R Hudson	Newcastle, NI	294

2001 *at Kilmarnock (Barassie)*

1	Rebecca Hudson (Wheatley)	75-78-69-78—300
2	Alison Coffey (Warrenpoint)	75-77-75-75—302
3	Kerry Smith (Waterlooville)	76-81-78-71—306

Senior Ladies British Open Amateur Stroke Play Championship

1981	BM King	Formby	159	1991	A Uzielli	Ladybank	154
1982	P Riddiford	Ilkley	161	1992	A Uzielli	Stratford-upon-Avon	148
1983	M Birtwistle	Troon Portland	167	1993	J Thornhill	Ashburnham	151
1984	O Semelaigne	Woodbridge	152	1994	D Williams	Nottingham	154
1985	Dr G Costello	Prestatyn	158	1995	A Uzielli	Blairgowrie	152
1986	P Riddiford	Longniddry	154	1996	V Hassett	Pyle & Kenfig	236
1987	O Semelaigne	Copt Heath	152	1997	T Wiesner (USA)	Frilford Heath	231
1988	C Bailey	Littlestone	156	1998	A Uzielli	Powfoot	227
1989	C Bailey	Wrexham	149	1999	A Uzielli	Malone	229
1990	A Uzielli	Harrogate	153	2000	B Mogensen (Den)	West Kilbride	242

2001 *at Aberdovey*

1	Mary McKenna (Donabate)	74-76-80—230
2	Rosalind Page (Henbury)	76-76-79—231
3	Claudeen Lindberg (USA)	78-83-73—234

English Ladies Close Amateur Championship

1960	M Nichol	A Bonallack	Burnham	3 and 1
1961	R Porter	P Reece	Littlestone	2 holes
1962	J Roberts	A Bonallack	Woodhall Spa	3 and 1
1963	A Bonallack	E Chadwick	Liphook	7 and 6
1964	M Spearman	M Everard	R Lytham and St Annes	6 and 5
1965	R Porter	C Cheetham	Whittington Barracks	6 and 5
1966	J Greenhalgh	JC Holmes	Hayling Island	3 and 1
1967	A Irwin	A Pickard	Alwoodley	3 and 2
1968	S Barber	D Oxley	Hunstanton	5 and 4
1969	B Dixon	M Wenyon	Burnham and Berrow	6 and 4
1970	D Oxley	S Barber	Rye	3 and 2
1971	D Oxley	S Barber	Hoylake	5 and 4
1972	M Everard	A Bonallack	Woodhall Spa	2 and 1
1973	M Walker	C Le Feuvre	Broadstone	6 and 5
1974	A Irvin	J Thornhill	Sunningdale	1 hole
1975	B Huke	L Harrold	R Birkdale	2 and 1
1976	L Harrold	A Uzielli	Hollinwell	3 and 2
1977	V Marvin	M Everard	Burnham and Berrow	1 hole
1978	V Marvin	R Porter	West Sussex	2 and 1
1979	J Greenhalgh	S Hedges	Hoylake	2 and 1
1980	B New	J Walker	Aldeburgh	3 and 2
1981	D Christison	S Cohen	Cotswold Hills	2 holes
1982	J Walter	C Nelson	Brancepeth Castle	4 and 3
1983	L Bayman	C Mackintosh	Hayling Island	4 and 3
1984	C Waite	L Bayman	Hunstanton	3 and 2
1985	P Johnson	L Bayman	Ferndown	1 hole
1986	J Thornhill	S Shapcott	Sandwich, Princes	3 and 1
1987	J Furby	M King	Alwoodley	4 and 3
1988	J Wade	S Shapcott	Little Aston	19th hole
1989	H Dobson	S Morgan	Burnham and Berrow	4 and 3
1990	A Uzielli	L Fletcher	Rye	2 and 1
1991	N Buxton	K Stupples	Sheringham	2 holes
1992	C Hall	J Hockley	St Annes Old Links	1 hole
1993	N Buxton	S Burnell	St Enodoc	2 and 1
1994	J Hall	S Sharpe	The Berkshire	1 hole
1995	J Hall	E Ratcliffe	Ipswich	2 and 1
1996	J Hockley	L Educate	Silloth	4 and 3
1997	K Rostron	K Burton	Saunton	4 and 2
1998	E Ratcliffe	L Walters	Walton Heath	19th hole

English Ladies Close Amateur Championship continued

| 1999 | F Brown | K Smith | Ganton | 2 and 1 |
| 2000 | E Duggleby | R Hudson | Hunstanton | 4 and 3 |

2001 at West Sussex GC, Pulborough

Quarter Finals

Rebecca Hudson (Wheatley) beat K Evans (Moor Park) 2 and 1

Kerry Knowles (Worplesdon) beat Kirsty Taylor (Sandford Springs) 3 and 2

Sara Garbutt (Knaresborough) beat Nicola Timmins (Sene Valley) 2 holes

Emma Duggleby (Malton & Norton) beat Fame More (Chesterfield) 1 hole

Semi-Finals

Hudson beat Knowles 2 holes

Duggleby beat Garbutt 1 hole

Final

R Hudson beat E Duggleby at 20th

English Ladies Close Amateur Stroke Play Championship

1984	P Grice	Moor Park	300	1993	J Hall	King's Norton	298
1985	P Johnson	Northants County	301	1994	F Brown	Ferndown	289
1986	S Shapcott	Broadstone	301	1995	L Walton	Hallamshire	289
1987	J Wade	Northumberland	296	1996	S Gallagher	Little Aston	290
1988	S Prosser	Wentworth	297	1997	L Tupholme	Hankley Common	293
1989	S Robinson	Notts	302	1998	E Duggleby	Broadstone	306
1990	K Tebbet	Saunton	299	1999	C Lipscombe	Gog Magog	300
1991	J Morley	Ganton	301	2000	R Hudson	Silloth-on-Solway	290
1992	J Morley	Littlestone	289				

2001 at Stoneham

1	Caroline Marron* (Bromborough)	75-71-70-75—291
2	Clare Lipscombe (Cirencester)	67-73-76-75—291
	Christine Quinn (South Winchester)	74-76-70-71—291
	Emma Weeks (Hockley)	69-72-70-80—291

English Ladies Under-23 Championship

1978	S Bamford	Caldy	228	1990	K Tebbet	Saunton	299
1979	B Cooper	Coxmoor	223	1991	J Hockley	Saunton	303
1980	B Cooper	Porters Park	226	1992	N Buxton	Littlestone	292
1981	J Soulsby	Willesley Park	220	1993	R Millington	King's Norton	302
1982	M Gallagher	High Post	221	1994	F Brown	Ferndown	289
1983	P Grice	Hallamshire	219	1995	E Fields	Hallamshire	297
1984	P Johnson	Moor Park	300	1996	R Hudson	Little Aston	299
1985	P Johnson	Northants County	301	1997	R Bailey	Hankley Common	306
1986	S Shapcott	Broadstone	301	1998	L Meredith	Broadstone	307
1987	J Wade	Northumberland	296	1999	C Lipscombe	Gog Magog	300
1988	J Wade	Wentworth	299	2000	R Hudson	Silloth-on-Solway	290
1989	A Shapcott	Notts Ladies	302				

2001 at Stoneham

1	Emma Weeks (Hockley)	69-72-70-80—291
2	Deana Rushworth (Woodsome Hall)	69-77-73-73—292
3	Rebecca Prout (Betchworth Park)	71-71-73-78—293

English Senior Ladies Stroke Play Championship

1988	A Thompson	Wentworth	158	1995	V Morgan	Tandridge	151
1989	C Bailey	Notts Ladies	163	1996	A Uzielli	Royal North Devon	153
1990	A Thompson	Fairhaven	162	1997	A Thompson	Formby Ladies	152
1991	C Bailey	Burnham and Berrow	155	1998	E Boatman	Royal Liverpool	154
1992	A Thompson	Pleasington	154	1999	S Westall	Northants County	151
1993	A Uzielli	Hunstanton	150	2000	E McCombe	Formby	162
1994	S Bassindale	Littlestone	163				

2001 *at Woodhall Spa*

1	Mrs Ros Page (Henbury)	81-78—159
2	Mrs Geraldine Bray (Faversham)	82-78—160
3	Mrs Denise Parker (Woodhall Spa)	81-79—160

English Senior Ladies Match Play Championship

1994	E Annison	S Bassindale	Whitting Heath
1995	A Thompson	G Palmer	R Ashdown Forest
1996	R Farrow	V Morgan	Lindrick
1997	G Palmer	C Means	S Winchester
1998	E McCombe	J Thornhill	West Sussex
1999	E McCombe	V Morgan	Lindrick
2000	E McCombe	M Griffiths	Burnham & Berrow

2001 *at Beau Desert*

Quarter Finals

Alanna Vine (Bramhall) beat Carolyn Howell (Woburn) 2 holes

Carole Caldwell (Sunningdale) beat Jenny Tootell (Blackburn North Shore) 3 and 2

Kathy Wells (Falmouth) beat Sarah Millar (Langley Park) 4 and 3

Vibeke Morgan (Denham) beat Rosemary Farrow (St Neots) 5 and 4

Semi-Finals

Vine beat Caldwell at 20th

Morgan beat Wells 3 and 2

Final

A Vine beat V Morgan 3 and 1

English Ladies Intermediate Championship

1982	J Rhodes	Headingley	19th hole	1992	K Speak	South Staffs	3 and 1
1983	L Davies	Worksop	2 and 1	1993	K Speak	Seascale	2 and 1
1984	P Grice	Whittington Barracks	3 and 2	1994	J Oliver	Beaconsfield	2 up
1985	S Lowe	Caldy	2 and 1	1995	K Smith	Clitheroe	5 and 4
1986	S Moorcroft	Hexham	6 and 5	1996	R Bailey	Sandiway	3 and 2
1987	J Wade	Sheringham	2 and 1	1997	K Smith	Abbotsley	2 and 1
1988	S Morgan	Enville, Staffs	20th hole	1998	J Lamb	Hornsea	1 hole
1989	L Fairclough	Warrington	4 and 3	1999	K Fisher	Woodbury Park	1 hole
1990	L Fletcher	Whitley Bay	7 and 6	2000	K Keogh	Woodbury Park	1 hole
1991	J Morley	West Lancashire	6 and 5				

2001 *at Pleasington*

Quarter Finals

Alex Keighley (Lightcliffe) beat Sara Garbutt (Knaresborough) 3 and 2

Rebecca Prout (Betchworth Park) beat Natalee Evans (Pleasington) 7 and 5

Marie Allen (Moor Park) beat Emma Weeks (Hockley) 4 and 2

Kerry Smith (Waterlooville) beat Georgina Simpson (Cleckheaton & District) 4 and 3

Semi-Finals

Keighley beat Prout at 22nd

Allen beat Smith 1 hole

Final

A Keighley beat M Allen at 22nd

Irish Ladies Close Amateur Championship

1960	P Garvey	PG McGann	Cork	5 and 3
1961	K McCann	A Sweeney	Newcastle	5 and 3
1962	P Garvey	M Earner	Baltray	7 and 6
1963	P Garvey	E Barnett	Killarney	9 and 7
1964	Z Fallon	P O'Sullivan	Portrush	37th hole
1965	E Purcell	P O'Sullivan	Mullingar	3 and 2
1966	E Bradshaw	P O'Sullivan	Rosslare	3 and 2
1967	G Brandom	P O'Sullivan	Castlerock	3 and 2
1968	E Bradshaw	M McKenna	Lahinch	3 and 2

Irish Ladies Close Amateur Championship *continued*

1969	M McKenna	C Hickey	Ballybunion	3 and 2
1970	P Garvey	M Earner	Portrush	2 and 1
1971	E Bradshaw	M Mooney	Baltray	3 and 1
1972	M McKenna	I Butler	Killarney	5 and 4
1973	M Mooney	M McKenna	Bundoran	2 and 1
1974	M McKenna	V Singleton	Lahinch	3 and 2
1975	M Gorry	E Bradshaw	Tramore	1 hole
1976	C Nesbitt	M McKenna	Rosses Point	20th hole
1977	M McKenna	R Hegarty	Ballybunion	2 holes
1978	M Gorry	I Butler	Grange	4 and 3
1979	M McKenna	C Nesbitt	Donegal	6 and 5
1980	C Nesbitt	C Hourihane	Lahinch	1 hole
1981	M McKenna	M Kenny	Laytown & Bettystown	1 hole
1982	M McKenna	M Madill	Portrush	2 and 1
1983	C Hourihane	V Hassett	Cork	6 and 4
1984	C Hourihane	M Madill	Rosses Point	19th hole
1985	C Hourihane	M McKenna	Waterville	4 and 3
1986	T O'Reilly	E Higgins	Castlerock	4 and 3
1987	C Hourihane	C Hickey	Lahinch	5 and 4
1988	L Bolton	E Higgins	Tramore	2 and 1
1989	M McKenna	C Wickham	West Port	19th hole
1990	ER McDaid	L Callan	The Island	2 and 1
1991	C Hourihane	E McDaid	Ballybunion	1 hole
1992	ER Power	C Hourihane	Co. Louth	1 hole
1993	E Higgins	A Rogers	R Belfast	2 and 1
1994	L Webb	H Kavanagh	Rosses Point	20th hole
1995	ER Power	S O'Brien-Kenney	Cork	1 hole
1996	B Hackett	L Behan	Tullamore	3 and 2
1997	S Fanagan	ER Power	Enniscrone	4 and 3
1998	L Behan	O Purfield	Clandeboye	19th hole
1999	C Coughlan	ER Power	Carlow	4 and 3
2000	A Coffey	C Coughlan	Co Louth	3 and 2

2001 *at The European Club*

Quarter Finals

Alison Coffey (Warrenpoint) beat Jennifer
  Gannon (Co. Louth) 3 and 2
Mary Dowling (New Ross) beat Eileen Rose
  Power (Kilkenny) 1 hole
Joanne Black (Knock) beat Sue Phillips
  (Woodbrook) 5 and 4
Claire Coughlan (Cork) beat Elaine Dowdall
  (Wexford) 1 hole

Semi-Finals

Coffey beat Dowling 4 and 3
Coughlan beat Black 4 and 3

Final

A Coffey beat C Coughlan 4 and 3

Irish Ladies Open Amateur Stroke Play Championship

1993	T Eakin	Milltown	293
1994	H Kavanagh	Milltown	286
1995	N Quigg	Grange	300
1996	ER Power	Grange	218
1997	Y Cassidy	Waterford Castle	217
1998	S O'Brien	Waterford Castle	141
1999	H Kavanagh	Waterford Castle	217
2000	R Cookley	Birr	205

2001 *at Birr*

1	Anne Laing (Vale of Leven)	71-70-73—214
2	Vikki Laing (Musselburgh)	72-72-74—218
3	R Coakley (Carlow)	74-73-72—219

Irish Senior Ladies Amateur Championship

1991	C Hickey	77	1995	A Gaynor	81	1999	R Fanagan	80
1992	C Hickey	79	1996	M Stuart	81	2000	S Kearney	80
1993	G Costello	81	1997	M O'Donnell	85			
1994	G Costello	80	1998	M Moran	78			

2001 *at Co. Louth*

1	Mary McKenna* (Donabate)	84-78—162	[better last round]
2	Pam Williamson (Baberton)	82-80—162	
3	E MacMullen (Donegal)	85-78—163	

Scottish Ladies Close Amateur Championship

1960	JS Robertson	DT Sommerville	Turnberry	2 and 1
1961	JS Wright (*née* Robertson)	AM Lurie	St Andrews	1 hole
1962	JB Lawrence	C Draper	R Dornoch	5 and 4
1963	JB Lawrence	IC Robertson	Troon	2 and 1
1964	JB Lawrence	SM Reid	Gullane	5 and 3
1965	IC Robertson	JB Lawrence	Nairn	5 and 4
1966	IC Robertson	M Fowler	Machrihanish	2 and 1
1967	J Hastings	A Laing	North Berwick	5 and 3
1968	J Smith	J Rennie	Carnoustie	10 and 9
1969	JH Anderson	K Lackie	West Kilbride	5 and 4
1970	A Laing	IC Robertson	Dunbar	1 hole
1971	IC Robertson	A Ferguson	R Dornoch	3 and 2
1972	IC Robertson	CJ Lugton	Machrihanish	5 and 3
1973	I Wright	Dr AJ Wilson	St Andrews	2 holes
1974	Dr AJ Wilson	K Lackie	Nairn	22nd hole
1975	LA Hope	JW Smith	Elie	1 hole
1976	S Needham	T Walker	Machrihanish	3 and 2
1977	CJ Lugton	M Thomson	R Dornoch	1 hole
1978	IC Robertson	JW Smith	Prestwick	2 holes
1979	G Stewart	LA Hope	Gullane	2 and 1
1980	IC Robertson	F Anderson	Carnoustie	1 hole
1981	A Gemmill	W Aitken	Stranraer	2 and 1
1982	J Connachan	P Wright	R Troon	19th hole
1983	G Stewart	F Anderson	North Berwick	3 and 1
1984	G Stewart	A Gemmill	R Dornoch	3 and 2
1985	A Gemmill	D Thomson	Barassie	2 and 1
1986	IC Robertson	L Hope	St Andrews	3 and 2
1987	F Anderson	C Middleton	Nairn	4 and 3
1988	S Lawson	F Anderson	Southerness	3 and 1
1989	J Huggon	L Anderson	Lossiemouth	5 and 4
1990	E Farquharson	S Huggan	Machrihanish	3 and 2
1991	C Lambert	F Anderson	Carnoustie	3 and 2
1992	J Moody	E Farquharson	R Aberdeen	2 and 1
1993	C Lambert	M McKay	Prestwick St Nicholas	5 and 4
1994	C Matthew	V Melvin	Gullane	1 hole
1995	H Monaghan	S McMaster	Portpatrick	21st hole
1996	A Laing	A Rose	R Dornoch	1 hole
1997	A Rose	H Monaghan	W Kilbride	3 and 2
1998	E Moffat	C Agnew	North Berwick	4 and 3
1999	J Smith	A Laing	Nairn Dunbar	2 and 1
2000	L Kenny	H Stirling	Machrihanish	1 hole

2001 *at Carnoustie*

Quarter Finals

Anne Laing (Vale of Leven) beat Heather Stirling (Bridge of Allan) 3 and 2

Lesley Mackay (Stirling University) beat Claire Hargan (Cardross) 1 hole

Alison Davidson (Stirling) beat Fiona Lockhart (St Regulus) 3 and 2

Linzi Morton (Tulliallan) beat Katrina Milne (Dunfermline) 5 and 4

Semi-Finals

Mackay beat Laing 4 and 3

Morton beat Davidson 1 hole

Final

L Morton beat L Mackay 6 and 4

Scottish Ladies Open Strokeplay Championship (Helen Holm Trophy)

1988	E Farquharson	1993	J Hall	1998	K-M Juul Esbjerg
1989	S Robinson	1994	K Tebbet	1999	L Nicholson
1990	C Lambert	1995	M Hjörth	2000	R Hudson
1991	J Hall	1996	J Hockley		
1992	M McKay	1997	K Rostron		

2001 *at Royal Troon and Troon Portland*

1	Fiona Brown (Heswall)	67-74-74—215
2	Rebecca Hudson (Wheatley)	72-74-71—217
3	Eleanor Pilgrim (St Pierre)	73-71-76—220

Scottish Senior Ladies Amateur Championship

1997	A Wilson	1999	P Williamson
1998	I McIntosh	2000	P Hutton

2001 *at*

1	Frances Liddle (Dunblane New)	79-81—160
2	Jennifer Mack (Haggs Castle)	84-78—162
3	Anna Telfer (Milngavie)	78-84—162

Welsh Ladies Amateur Championship

1960	M Barron	E Brown	Tenby	8 and 6
1961	M Oliver	N Sneddon	Aberdovey	5 and 4
1962	M Oliver	P Roberts	Radyr	4 and 2
1963	P Roberts	N Sneddon	Harlech	7 and 5
1964	M Oliver	M Wright	Southerndown	1 hole
1965	M Wright	E Brown	Prestatyn	3 and 2
1966	A Hughes	P Roberts	Ashburnham	5 and 4
1967	M Wright	C Phipps	Harlech	21st hole
1968	S Hales	M Wright	Porthcawl	3 and 2
1969	P Roberts	A Hughes	Caernarvonshire	3 and 2
1970	A Briggs	J Morris	Newport	19th hole
1971	A Briggs	EN Davies	Harlech	2 and 1
1972	A Hughes	J Rogers	Tenby	3 and 2
1973	A Briggs	J John	Holyhead	3 and 2
1974	A Briggs	Dr H Lyall	Ashburnham	3 and 2
1975	A Johnson (née Hughes)	K Rawlings	Prestatyn	1 hole
1976	T Perkins	A Johnson	Porthcawl	4 and 2
1977	T Perkins	P Whitley	Aberdovey	5 and 4
1978	P Light	A Briggs	Newport	2 and 1
1979	V Rawlings	A Briggs	Caernarvonshire	2 holes
1980	M Rawlings	A Briggs	Tenby	2 and 1
1981	M Rawlings	A Briggs	Harlech	5 and 3
1982	V Thomas (née Rawlings)	M Rawlings	Ashburnham	7 and 6
1983	V Thomas	T Thomas (née Perkins)	Llandudno	1 hole
1984	S Roberts	K Davies	Newport	5 and 4
1985	V Thomas	S Jump	Prestatyn	1 hole
1986	V Thomas	L Isherwood	Porthcawl	7 and 6
1987	V Thomas	S Roberts	Aberdovey	3 and 1
1988	S Roberts	F Connor	Tenby	4 and 2
1989	H Lawson	V Thomas	Conwy	2 and 1
1990	S Roberts	H Wadsworth	Ashburnham	3 and 2
1991	V Thomas	H Lawson	R St David's	4 and 3
1992	J Foster	S Boyes	Newport	4 and 3
1993	A Donne	V Thomas	Abergele & Pensarn	19th hole
1994	V Thomas	L Dermott	Royal Porthcawl	19th hole
1995	L Dermott	K Stark	Aberdovey	19th hole
1996	L Dermott	V Thomas	Tenby	4 and 3
1997	E Pilgrim	L Davis	Northop	4 and 2
1998	L Davis	R Morgan	Ashburnham	1 hole
1999	R Brewerton	R Morgan	Conwy	19th hole
2000	K Evans	K Phillips	Pyle & Kenfig	19th hole

2001 *at Royal St David's*

Quarter Finals
Becky Brewerton beat Ann Lewis 7 and 6
Sara Mountford (Wrexham) beat Jo Nicolson
    3 and 2
Anna Highgate (Cottrell Park) beat El Pilgrim
    3 and 2
Sarah Jones (Pennard) beat Kathryn Evans
    2 and 1

Semi-Finals
Brewerton beat Mountford 5 and 4
Jones beat Highgate 5 and 3

Final
Becky Brewerton beat Sarah Jones 2 and 1

Welsh Ladies Open Amateur Strokeplay Championship

1981	V Thomas	Aberdovey	224	1991	M Sutton	R Porthcawl	224
1982	V Thomas	Aberdovey	225	1992	C Lambert	R Porthcawl	218
1983	J Thornhill	Aberdovey	239	1993	J Hall	Newport	221
1984	L Davies	Aberdovey	230	1994	A Rose	Newport	217
1985	C Swallow	Aberdovey	219	1995	F Brown	Newport	221
1986	H Wadsworth	Aberdovey	223	1996	E Duggleby	Whitchurch	223
1987	S Shapcott	Newport	225	1997	K Edwards	Whitchurch	216
1988	S Shapcott	Newport	218	1998	G Simpson	Rolls of Monmouth	154
1989	V Thomas	Newport	220	1999	A Walker	Celtic Manor	230
1990	L Hackney	Newport	218	2000	R Prout	Ashburnham	228

2001 *at Royal Porthcawl*

1	Vicki Laing (Musselburgh)	229
2	Stephanie Coverley (Woodsome Hall)	232
3	Anna Highgate (Cottrell Park)	232
	Fame More (Chesterfield)	232
	Alison Waller (Harpenden)	232

Welsh Senior Ladies Championship

1990	E Higgs	Vale of Llangollen	171	1996	C Thomas	Vale of Llangollen	157
1991	H Lyall	Pyle and Kenfig	160	1997	C Thomas	Fairwood Park	160
1992	P Morgan	Cardigan	83	1998	C Thomas	Padeswood	163
1993	P Morgan	Pwllheli	157	1999	V Mackenzie	St Mellons	153
1994	C Thomas	Llandudno	163	2000	F Shehan	Carmarthen	159
1995	C Thomas	Tredegar Park	157				

2001 *at Porthmadog*

1	Frances Shehan	159
2	Verona MacKenzie	171
3	Ruth James	172

Ladies European Open Amateur Championship

1986	M Koch (Ger)	Morfontaine, France	286
1988	F Descampe (Bel)	Pedrena, Spain	289
1990	M Koch (Ger)	Zumicon, Switzerland	295
1991	D Bourson (Fra)	Schönborn, Austria	294
1992	J Morley (Eng)	Estoril, Portugal	284
1993	V Steinsrud (Nor)	Torino, Italy	277
1994	M Fischer (Ger)	Bastad, Sweden	288
1995	M Hjörth (Swe)	Berlin, Germany	284
1996	S Cavalleri (Ita)	Furesoe, Denmark	288
1997	S Cavalleri (Ita)	Formby, England	297
1998	G Sergas (Ita)	Noordwijk, Netherlands	295
1999	S Sandolo (Ita)	Karlovy Vary, Czech Republic	284
2000	E Duggleby (Eng)	Amber Baltic GC, Poland	283

2001 *at Biella, Italy*

1	Martina Eberl (Ger)	71-72-74—217
2	Nuria Clau (Esp)	69-75-77—221
3	Pia Odefey (Ger)	72-74-76—222

European Senior Ladies Championship

2000	C Mourgue d'Algue (Fra)	La Manga	226

2001 *at Torremirona, Spain*

1	Cecilia Mourgue d'Algue (Fra)	71-75-73—219
2	Vicky Pertierra (Esp)	76-74-75—225
3	Eva Maeker (Ger)	77-73-77—227

NATIONAL ORDERS OF MERIT

ILGU Irish Order of Merit, 2001

1	Alison Coffey (Warrenpoint)	1640
2	Claire Coughlan (Cork)	965
3	Elaine Dowdell (Wexford)	665

Dunfermline Building Society Scottish Order of Merit, 2001

1 Anne Laing (Vale of Leven)
2 Heather Stirling (Bridge of Allan)
3 Linzi Morton (Tulliallan)

Welsh Order of Merit, 2001

1	Becky Brewerton	1395
2	El Pilgrim (St Pierre)	855
3	Anna Highgate (Cottrell Park)	805

ELGA Order of Merit, 2001

1	Rebecca Hudson (Wheatley)	1485
2	Kerry Smith (Waterlooville)	975
3	Emma Duggleby (Malton & Norton)	965

TEAM EVENTS

Great Britain & Ireland *v* USA for the Curtis Cup

Home team names first

1932 *at Wentworth*
Result: USA 5½, GBI 3½
Captains: J Wethered (GBI), M Hollins (USA)
Foursomes
Wethered & Morgan lost to Vare & Hill 1 hole
Wilson & JB Watson lost to Van Wie & Hicks 2 and 1
Gourlay & Doris Park lost to Orcutt & Cheney 1 hole
Singles
Joyce Wethered beat Glenna Collett Vare 6 and 4
Enid Wilson beat Helen Hicks 2 and 1
Wanda Morgan lost to Virginia Van Wie 2 and 1
Diana Fishwick beat Maureen Orcutt 4 and 3
Molly Gourlay halved with Opal Hill
Elsie Corlett lost to Leona Pressley Cheney 4 and 3

1934 *at Chevy Chase, MD*
Result: USA 6½, GBI 2½
Captains: Glenna Collett Vare (USA),
Doris Chambers (GBI)
Foursomes
Van Wie & Glutting halved with Gourlay & Barton
Orcutt & Cheney beat Fishwick & Morgan 2 holes
Hill & Lucille Robinson lost to Plumpton & Walker
2 and 1
Singles
Virginia Van Wie beat Diana Fishwick 2 and 1
Maureen Orcutt beat Molly Gourlay 4 and 2
Leona Pressley Cheney beat Pamela Barton 7 and 5
Charlotte Glutting beat Wanda Morgan
Opal Hill beat Diana Plumpton 3 and 2
Aniela Goldthwaite lost to Charlotte Walker
3 and 2

1936 *at Gleneagles*
Result: USA 4½, GBI 4½
Captains: Doris Chambers (GBI),
Glenna Collett Vare (USA)
Foursomes
Morgan & Garon halved with Vare & Berg
Barton & Walker lost to Orcutt & Cheney 2 and 1
Anderson & Holm beat Hill & Glutting 3 and 2
Singles
Wanda Morgan lost to Glenna Collett Vare 3 and 2
Helen Holm beat Patty Berg 4 and 3
Pamela Barton lost to Charlotte Glutting 1 hole
Charlotte Walker lost to Maureen Orcutt 1 hole
Jessie Anderson beat Leona Pressley Cheney 1 hole
Marjorie Garon beat Opal Hill 7 and 5

1938 *at Essex, MA*
Result: USA 5½, GBI 3½
Captains: Frances Stebbins (USA),
Mrs RH Wallace-Williamson(GBI)
Foursomes
Page & Orcutt lost to Holm & Tiernan 2 holes
Vare & Berg lost to Anderson & Corlett 1 hole
Miley & Kathryn Hemphill halved with Walker &
Phyllis Wade

Singles
Estelle Lawson Page beat Helen Holm 6 and 5
Patty Berg beat Jessie Anderson 1 hole
Marion Miley beat Elsie Corlett 2 and 1
Glenna Collett Vare beat Charlotte Walker 2 and 1
Maureen Orcutt lost to Clarrie Tiernan 2 and 1
Charlotte Glutting beat Nan Baird 1 hole

1948 *at Birkdale*
Result: USA 6½, GBI 2½
Captains: Doris Chambers (GBI),
Glenna Collett Vare (USA)
Foursomes
Donald & Gordon beat Suggs & Lenczyk 3 and 2
Garvey & Bolton lost to Kirby & Vare 4 and 3
Ruttle & Val Reddan lost to Page & Kielty 5 and 4
Singles
Philomena Garvey halved with Louise Suggs
Jean Donald beat Dorothy Kirby 2 holes
Jacqueline Gordon lost to Grace Lenczyk 5 and 3
Helen Holm lost to Estelle Lawson Page 3 and 2
Maureen Ruttle lost to Polly Riley 3 and 2
Zara Bolton lost to Dorothy Kielty 2 and 1

1950 *at Buffalo NY*
Result: USA 7½, GBI 1½
Captains: Glenna Collett Vare (USA),
Diana Fishwick Critchley (GBI)
Foursomes
Hanson & Porter beat Valentine & Donald
3 and 2
Helen Sigel & Kirk lost to Stephens & Price 1 hole
Dorothy Kirby & Kielty beat Garvey & Bisgood
6 and 5
Singles
Dorothy Porter halved with Frances Stephens
Polly Riley beat Jessie Anderson Valentine 7 and 6
Beverly Hanson beat Jean Donald 6 and 5
Dorothy Kielty beat Philomena Garvey 2 and 1
Peggy Kirk beat Jeanne Bisgood 1 hole
Grace Lenczyk beat Elizabeth Price 5 and 4

1952 *at Muirfield*
Result: GBI 5, USA 4
Captains: Lady Katherine Cairns (GBI),
Aniela Goldthwaite (USA)
Foursomes
Donald & Price beat Kirby & DeMoss 3 and 2
Stephens & JA Valentine lost to Doran & Lindsay
6 and 4
Paterson & Garvey beat Riley & Patricia O'Sullivan
2 and 1
Singles
Jean Donald lost to Dorothy Kirby 1 hole
Frances Stephens beat Marjorie Lindsay 2 and 1
Moira Paterson lost to Polly Riley 6 and 4
Jeanne Bisgood beat Mae Murray 6 and 5
Philomena Garvey lost to Claire Doran 3 and 2
Elizabeth Price beat Grace DeMoss 3 and 2

1954 at Merion, PA
Result: USA 6, GBI 3
Captains: Edith Flippin (USA),
Mrs JB Beck (GBI)
Foursomes
Faulk & Riley beat Stephens & Price 6 and 4
Doran & Patricia Lesser beat Garvey & Valentine
6 and 5
Kirby & Barbara Romack beat Marjorie Peel &
Robertson 6 and 5
Singles
Mary Lena Faulk lost to Frances Stephens 1 hole
Claire Doran beat Jeanne Bisgood 4 and 3
Polly Riley beat Elizabeth Price 9 and 8
Dorothy Kirby lost to Philomena Garvey 3 and 1
Grace DeMoss Smith beat Jessie Anderson Valentine
4 and 3
Joyce Ziske lost to Janette Robertson 3 and 1

1956 at Prince's, Sandwich
Result: GBI 5, USA 4
Captains: Zara Davis Bolton (GBI),
Edith Flippin (USA)
Foursomes
Valentine & Garvey lost to Lesser & Smith 2 and 1
Smith & Price beat Riley & Romack 5 and 3
Robertson & Veronica Anstey lost to Downey &
Carolyn Cudone 6 and 4
Singles
Jessie Anderson Valentine beat Patricia Lesser 6 and 4
Philomena Garvey lost to Margaret Smith 9 and 8
Frances Stephens Smith beat Polly Riley 1 hole
Janette Robertson lost to Barbara Romack 6 and 4
Angela Ward beat Mary Ann Downey 6 and 4
Elizabeth Price beat Jane Nelson 7 and 6

1958 at Brae Burn, MA
Result: GBI 4½, USA 4½
Captains: Virginia Dennehy (USA),
Daisy Ferguson (GBI)
Foursomes
Riley & Romack lost to Bonallack & Price 2 and 1
Gunderson & Quast lost to Robertson & Smith
3 and 2
Johnstone & McIntire beat Jackson & Valentine
6 and 5
Singles
JoAnne Gunderson beat Jessie Anderson Valentine
2 holes
Barbara McIntire halved with Angela Ward Bonallack
Anne Quast beat Elizabeth Price 4 and 2
Anna Johnstone lost to Janette Robertson 3 and 2
Barbara Romack beat Bridget Jackson 3 and 2
Polly Riley lost to Frances Stephens Smith 2 holes

1960 at Lindrick
Result: USA 6½, GBI 2½
Captains: Maureen Garrett (GBI),
Mildred Prunaret (USA)
Foursomes
Price & Bonallack beat Gunderson & McIntyre 1 hole
Robertson & McCorkindale lost to Eller & Quast
4 and 2
Frances Smith & Porter lost to Goodwin & Anna
Johnstone 3 and 2

Singles
Elizabeth Price halved with Barbara McIntyre
Angela Ward Bonallack lost to JoAnne Gunderson
2 and 1
Janette Robertson lost to Anne Quast 2 holes
Philomena Garvey lost to Judy Eller 4 and 3
Belle McCorkindale lost to Judy Bell 8 and 7
Ruth Porter beat Joanne Goodwin 1 hole

1962 at Broadmoor, Colorado Springs, CO
Result: USA 8, GBI 1
Captains: Polly Riley (USA), Frances Stephens
Smith (GBI)
Foursomes
Decker & McIntyre beat Spearman & Bonallack
7 and 5
Jean Ashley & Anna Johnstone beat Ruth Porter &
Frearson 8 and 7
Creed & Gunderson beat Vaughan & Ann Irvin
4 and 3
Singles
Judy Bell lost to Diane Frearson 8 and 7
JoAnne Gunderson beat Angela Ward Bonallack
2 and 1
Clifford Ann Creed beat Sally Bonallack 6 and 5
Anne Quast Decker beat Marley Spearman
7 and 5
Phyllis Preuss beat Jean Roberts 1 hole
Barbara McIntyre beat Sheila Vaughan 5 and 4

1964 at Porthcawl
Result: USA 10½, GBI 1½
Captains: Elsie Corlett (GBI),
Helen Hawes (USA)
First Day: Foursomes
Spearman & Bonallack beat McIntyre & Preuss
2 and 1
Sheila Vaughan & Porter beat Gunderson & Roth
3 and 2
Jackson & Susan Armitage lost to Sorenson & White
8 and 6
Singles
Angela Ward Bonallack lost to JoAnne Gunderson
6 and 5
Marley Spearman halved with Barbara McIntyre
Julia Greenhalgh lost to Barbara White 3 and 2
Bridget Jackson beat Carol Sorenson 4 and 3
Joan Lawrence lost to Peggy Conley 1 hole
Ruth Porter beat Nancy Roth 1 hole
Second Day: Foursomes
Spearman & Bonallack beat McIntyre & Preuss
6 and 5
Armitage & Jackson lost to Gunderson & Roth
2 holes
Porter & Vaughan halved with Sorenson & White
Singles
Spearman halved with Gunderson
Lawrence lost to McIntyre 4 and 2
Greenhalgh beat Phyllis Preuss 5 and 3
Bonallack lost to White 3 and 2
Porter lost to Sorenson 3 and 2
Jackson lost to Conley 1 hole

1966 at Hot Springs, VA
Result: USA 13, GBI 5
Captains: Dorothy Germain Porter (USA),
Zara Bolton (GBI)
First Day
Foursomes
Ashley & Preuss beat Armitage & Bonallack 1 hole
Barbara McIntire & Welts halved with Joan Hastings &
Robertson
Boddie & Flenniken beat Chadwick & Tredinnick
1 hole
Singles
Jean Ashley beat Belle McCorkindale Robertson
1 hole
Anne Quast Welts halved with Susan Armitage
Barbara White Boddie beat Angela Ward Bonallack
3 and 2
Nancy Roth Syms beat Elizabeth Chadwick 2 holes
Helen Wilson lost to Ita Burke 3 and 1
Carol Sorenson Flenniken beat Marjory Fowler
3 and 1
Second Day: Foursomes
Ashley & Preuss beat Armitage & Bonallack 2 and 1
McIntire & Welts lost to Burke & Chadwick 1 hole
Boddie & Flenniken beat Hastings & Robertson
2 and 1
Singles
Ashley lost to Bonallack 2 and 1
Welts halved with Robertson
Boddie beat Armitage 3 and 2
Syms halved with Pam Tredinnick
Phyllis Preuss beat Chadwick 3 and 2
Flenniken beat Burke 2 and 1

1968 at Newcastle, Co Down
Result: USA 10½, GBI 7½
Captains: Zara Bolton (GBI),
Evelyn Monsted (USA)
First Day: Foursomes
Irvin & Robertson beat Hamlin & Welts 6 and 5
Pickard & Saunders beat Conley & Dill 3 and 2
Howard & Pam Tredinnick lost to Ashley & Preuss
1 hole
Singles
Ann Irvin beat Anne Quast Welts 3 and 2
Vivien Saunders lost to Shelley Hamlin 1 hole
Belle McCorkindale Robertson lost to Roberta Albers
1 hole
Bridget Jackson halved with Peggy Conley
Dinah Oxley halved with Phyllis Preuss
Margaret Pickard beat Jean Ashley 2 holes
Second Day: Foursomes
Oxley & Tredinnick lost to Ashley & Preuss 5 and 4
Irvin & Robertson halved with Conley & Dill
Pickard & Saunders lost to Hamlin & Welts 2 and 1
Singles
Irvin beat Hamlin 3 and 2
Robertson halved with Welts
Saunders halved with Albers
Ann Howard lost to Mary Lou Dill 4 and 2
Pickard lost to Conley 1 hole
Jackson lost to Preuss 2 and 1

1970 at Brae Burn, MA
Result: USA 11½, GBI 6½
Captains: Carolyn Cudone (USA),
Jeanne Bisgood (GBI)
First Day: Foursomes
Bastanchury & Hamlin lost to McKenna & Oxley
4 and 3
Preuss & Wilkinson beat Irvin & Robertson 4 and 3
Jane Fassinger & Hill lost to Everard & Greenhalgh
5 and 3
Singles
Jane Bastanchury beat Dinah Oxley 5 and 3
Martha Wilkinson beat Ann Irvin 1 hole
Shelley Hamlin halved with Belle McCorkindale
Robertson
Phyllis Preuss lost to Mary McKenna 4 and 2
Nancy Hager beat Margaret Pickard 5 and 4
Alice Dye beat Julia Greenhalgh 1 hole
Second Day: Foursomes
Preuss & Wilkinson beat McKenna & Oxley 6 and 4
Dye & Hill halved with Everard & Greenhalgh
Bastanchury & Hamlin beat Irvin & Robertson
1 hole
Singles
Bastanchury beat Irvin 4 and 3
Hamlin halved with Oxley
Preuss beat Robertson 1 hole
Wilkinson lost to Greenhalgh 6 and 4
Hager lost to Mary Everard 4 and 3
Cindy Hill beat McKenna 2 and 1

1972 at Western Gailes
Result: USA 10, GBI 8
Captains: Frances Stephens Smith (GBI),
Jean Ashley Crawford (USA)
First Day: Foursomes
Everard & Beverly Huke lost to Baugh & Kirouac
2 and 1
Frearson & Robertson beat Booth & McIntyre
2 and 1
McKenna & Walker beat Barry & Hollis Stacy 1 hole
Singles
Mickey Walker halved with Laura Baugh
Belle McCorkindale Robertson lost to Jane
Bastanchury Booth 3 and 1
Mary Everard lost to Martha Wilkinson Kirouac
4 and 3
Dinah Oxley lost to Barbara McIntire 4 and 3
Kathryn Phillips beat Lancy Smith 2 holes
Mary McKenna lost to Beth Barry 2 and 1
Second Day: Foursomes
McKenna & Walker beat Baugh & Kirouac 3 and 2
Everard & Huke lost to Booth & McIntyre 5 and 4
Frearson & Robertson halved with Barry & Stacy
Singles
Robertson lost to Baugh 6 and 5
Everard beat McIntyre 6 and 5
Walker beat Booth 1 hole
McKenna beat Kirouac 3 and 1
Diane Frearson lost to Smith 3 and 1
Phillips lost to Barry 3 and 1

1974 at San Francisco, CA
Result: USA 13, GBI 5
Captains: Sis Choate (USA),
  Belle McCorkindale Robertson (GBI)
First Day: Foursomes
Hill & Semple halved with Greenhalgh & McKenna
Booth & Sander beat Lee-Smith & LeFeuvre 6 and 5
Budke & Lauer lost to Everard & Walker 5 and 4
Singles
Carol Semple lost to Mickey Walker 2 and 1
Jane Bastanchury Booth beat Mary McKenna 5 and 3
Debbie Massey beat Mary Everard 1 hole
Bonnie Lauer beat Jennie Lee-Smith 6 and 5
Beth Barry beat Julia Greenhalgh 1 hole
Cindy Hill halved with Tegwen Perkins
Second Day: Foursomes
Booth & Sander beat McKenna & Walker 5 and 4
Budke & Lauer beat Everard & LeFeuvre 5 and 3
Hill & Semple lost to Greenhalgh & Perkins 3 and 2
Singles
Anne Quast Sander beat Everard 4 and 3
Booth beat Greenhalgh 7 and 5
Massey beat Carol LeFeuvre 6 and 5
Semple beat Walker 2 and 1
Mary Budke beat Perkins 5 and 4
Lauer lost to McKenna 2 and 1

1976 at Royal Lytham & St Annes
Result: USA 11½, GBI 6½
Captains: Belle McCorkindale Robertson (GBI),
  Barbara McIntyre (USA)
First Day: Foursomes
Greenhalgh & McKenna lost to Daniel & Hill 3 and 2
Cadden & Henson lost to Horton & Massey 6 and 5
Irvin & Perkins beat Semple & Syms 3 and 2
Singles
Ann Irvin lost to Beth Daniel 4 and 3
Dinah Oxley Henson beat Cindy Hill 1 hole
Suzanne Cadden lost to Nancy Lopez 3 and 1
Mary McKenna lost to Nancy Roth Syms 1 hole
Tegwen Perkins lost to Debbie Massey 1 hole
Julia Greenhalgh halved with Barbara Barrow
Second Day: Foursomes
Cadden & Irvin lost to Daniel & Hill 4 and 3
Henson & Perkins beat Semple & Syms 2 and 1
McKenna & Anne Stant lost to Barrow & Lopez
  4 and 3
Singles
Henson lost to Daniel 3 and 2
Greenhalgh beat Syms 2 and 1
Cadden lost to Donna Horton 6 and 5
Jennie Lee-Smith lost to Massey 3 and 2
Perkins beat Hill 1 hole
McKenna beat Carol Semple 1 hole

1978 at Apawamis, NY
Result: USA 12, GBI 6
Captains: Helen Wilson (USA),
  Carol Comboy (GBI)
First Day: Foursomes
Daniel & Brenda Goldsmith lost to Greenhalgh &
  Marvin 3 and 2
Cindy Hill & Smith lost to Everard & Thomson
  2 and 1
Cornett & Carolyn Hill halved with McKenna &
  Perkins

Singles
Beth Daniel beat Vanessa Marvin 5 and 4
Noreen Uihlein lost to Mary Everard 7 and 6
Lancy Smith beat Angela Uzielli 4 and 3
Cindy Hill beat Julia Greenhalgh 2 and 1
Carolyn Hill halved with Carole Caldwell
Judy Oliver beat Tegwen Perkins 2 and 1
Second Day: Foursomes
Cindy Hill & Smith beat Everard & Thomson 1 hole
Daniel & Goldsmith beat McKenna & Perkins 1 hole
Oliver & Uihlein beat Greenhalgh & Marvin 4 and 3
Singles
Daniel beat Mary McKenna 2 and 1
Patricia Cornett beat Caldwell 3 and 2
Cindy Hill lost to Muriel Thomson 2 and 1
Lancy Smith beat Perkins 2 holes
Oliver halved with Greenhalgh
Uihlein halved with Everard

1980 at St Pierre, Chepstow
Result: USA 13, GBI 5
Captains: Carol Comboy (GBI), Nancy Roth
  Syms (USA)
First Day: Foursomes
McKenna & Nesbitt halved with Terri Moody &
  Smith
Stewart & Thomas lost to Castillo & Sheehan 5 and 3
Caldwell & Madill halved with Oliver & Semple
Singles
Mary McKenna lost to Patty Sheehan 3 and 2
Claire Nesbitt halved with Lancy Smith
Jane Connachan lost to Brenda Goldsmith 2 holes
Maureen Madill lost to Carol Semple 4 and 3
Linda Moore halved with Mary Hafeman
Carole Caldwell lost to Judy Oliver 1 hole
Second Day: Foursomes
Caldwell & Madill lost to Castillo & Sheehan 3 and 2
McKenna & Nesbitt lost to Moody & Smith 6 and 5
Moore & Thomas lost to Oliver & Semple 1 hole
Singles
Madill lost to Sheehan 5 and 4
McKenna beat Lori Castillo 5 and 4
Connachan lost to Hafeman 6 and 5
Gillian Stewart beat Smith 5 and 4
Moore beat Goldsmith 1 hole
Tegwen Perkins Thomas lost to Semple 4 and 3

1982 at Denver, CO
Result: USA 14½, GBI 3½
Captains: Betty Probasco (USA),
  Maire O'Donnell (GBI)
First Day: Foursomes
Inkster & Semple beat McKenna & Robertson 5 and 4
Baker & Smith halved with Douglas & Soulsby
Benz & Hanlon beat Connachan & Stewart 2 and 1
Singles
Amy Benz beat Mary McKenna 2 and 1
Cathy Hanlon beat Jane Connachan 5 and 4
Mari McDougall beat Wilma Aitken 2 holes
Kathy Baker beat Belle McCorkindale Robertson
  7 and 6
Judy Oliver lost to Janet Soulsby 2 holes
Juli Inkster beat Kitrina Douglas 7 and 6
Second Day: Foursomes
Inkster & Semple beat Aitken & Connachan 3 and 2
Baker & Smith beat Douglas & Soulsby 1 hole
Benz & Hanlon lost to McKenna & Robertson 1 hole

Singles
Inkster beat Douglas 7 and 6
Baker beat Gillian Stewart 4 and 3
Oliver beat Vicki Thomas 5 and 4
McDougall beat Soulsby 2 and 1
Carol Semple beat McKenna 1 hole
Lancy Smith lost to Robertson 5 and 4

1984 *at Muirfield*
Result: USA 9½, GBI 8½
Captains: Diane Robb Bailey (GBI),
  Phyllis Preuss (USA)
First Day: Foursomes
New & Waite beat Pacillo & Sander 2 holes
Grice & Thornhill halved with Rosenthal & Smith
Davies & McKenna lost to Farr & Widman 1 hole
Singles
Jill Thornhill halved with Joanne Pacillo
Claire Waite lost to Penny Hammel 4 and 2
Claire Hourihane lost to Jody Rosenthal 3 and 1
Vicki Thomas beat Dana Howe 2 and 1
Penny Grice beat Anne Quast Sander 2 holes
Beverley New lost to Mary Anne Widman 4 and 3
Second Day: Foursomes
New & Waite lost to Rosenthal & Smith 3 and 1
Grice & Thornhill beat Farr & Widman 2 and 1
Hourihane & Thomas halved with Hammel & Howe
Singles
Thornhill lost to Pacillo 3 and 2
Laura Davies beat Sander 1 hole
Waite beat Lancy Smith 5 and 4
Grice lost to Howe 2 holes
New lost to Heather Farr 6 and 5
Hourihane beat Hammel 2 and 1

1986 *at Prairie Dunes, KS*
Result: GBI 13, USA 5
Captains: Judy Bell (USA),
  Diane Robb Bailey (GBI)
First Day: Foursomes
Kessler & Schreyer lost to Behan & Thornhill 7 and 6
Ammaccapane & Mochrie lost to Davies & Johnson
  2 and 1
Gardner & Scrivner lost to McKenna & Robertson
  1 hole
Singles
Leslie Shannon lost to Patricia (Trish) Johnson 1 hole
Kim Williams lost to Jill Thornhill 4 and 3
Danielle Ammaccapane lost to Lillian Behan 4 and 3
Kandi Kessler beat Vicki Thomas 3 and 2
Dottie Pepper Mochrie halved with Karen Davies
Cindy Schreyer beat Claire Hourihane 2 and 1
Second Day: Foursomes
Ammaccapane & Mochrie lost to Davies & Johnson
  1 hole
Shannon & Williams lost to Behan & Thornhill
  5 and 3
Gardner & Scrivner halved with McKenna & Belle
  McCorkindale Robertson
Singles
Shannon halved with Thornhill
Kathleen McCarthy Scrivner lost to Trish Johnson
  5 and 3
Kim Gardner beat Behan 1 hole
Williams lost to Thomas 4 and 3
Kessler halved with Davies
Schreyer lost to Hourihane 5 and 4

1988 *at Royal St George's*
Result: GBI 11, USA 7
Captains: Diane Robb Bailey (GBI),
  Judy Bell (USA)
First Day: Foursomes
Bayman & Wade beat Kerdyk & Scrivner 2 and 1
Davies & Shapcott beat Scholefield & Thompson
  5 and 4
Thomas & Thornhill halved with Keggi & Shannon
Singles
Linda Bayman halved with Tracy Kerdyk
Julie Wade beat Cindy Scholefield 2 holes
Susan Shapcott lost to Carol Semple Thompson
  1 hole
Karen Davies lost to Pearl Sinn 4 and 3
Shirley Lawson beat Pat Cornett-Iker 1 hole
Jill Thornhill beat Leslie Shannon 3 and 2
Second Day: Foursomes
Bayman & Wade lost to Kerdyk & Scrivner 1 hole
Davies & Shapcott beat Keggi & Shannon 2 holes
Thomas & Thornhill beat Scholefield & Thompson
  6 and 5
Singles
Wade lost to Kerdyk 2 and 1
Shapcott beat Caroline Keggi 3 and 2
Lawson lost to Kathleen McCarthy Scrivner 4 and 3
Vicki Thomas beat Cornett-Iker 5 and 3
Bayman beat Sinn 1 hole
Thornhill lost to Thompson 3 and 2

1990 *at Somerset Hills, NJ*
Result: USA 14, GBI 4
Captains: Leslie Shannon (USA),
  Jill Thornhill (GBI)
First Day: Foursomes
Goetze & Anne Quast Sander beat Dobson & Lambert
  4 and 3
Noble & Margaret Platt lost to Wade & Imrie 2 and 1
Thompson & Weiss beat Farquharson & Helen
  Wadsworth 3 and 1
Singles
Vicki Goetze lost to Julie Wade 2 and 1
Katie Peterson beat Kathryn Imrie 3 and 2
Brandie Burton beat Linzi Fletcher 3 and 1
Robin Weiss beat Elaine Farquharson 4 and 3
Karen Noble beat Catriona Lambert 1 hole
Carol Semple Thompson lost to Vicki Thomas 1 hole
Second Day: Foursomes
Goetze & Sander beat Wade & Imrie 3 and 1
Noble & Platt lost to Dobson & Lambert 1 hole
Burton & Peterson beat Farquharson & Wadsworth
  5 and 4
Singles
Goetze beat Helen Dobson 4 and 3
Burton beat Lambert 4 and 3
Peterson beat Imrie 1 hole
Noble beat Wade 2 holes
Weiss beat Farquharson 2 and 1
Thompson beat Thomas 3 and 1

1992 at Hoylake
Result: GBI 10, USA 8
Captains: Elizabeth Boatman (GBI),
Judy Oliver (USA)
First Day: Foursomes
Hall & Wade halved with Fruhwirth & Goetze
Lambert & Thomas beat Ingram & Shannon 2 and 1
Hourihane & Morley beat Hanson & Thompson
2 and 1
Singles
Joanne Morley halved with Amy Fruhwirth
Julie Wade lost to Vicki Goetze 3 and 2
Elaine Farquharson beat Robin Weiss 2 and 1
Nicola Buxton lost to Martha Lang 2 holes
Catriona Lambert beat Carol Semple Thompson
3 and 2
Caroline Hall beat Leslie Shannon 6 and 5
Second Day: Foursomes
Hall & Wade halved with Fruhwirth & Goetze
Hourihane & Morley halved with Lang & Weiss
Lambert & Thomas lost to Hanson & Thompson
3 and 2
Singles
Morley beat Fruhwirth 2 and 1
Lambert beat Tracy Hanson 6 and 5
Farquharson lost to Sarah LeBrun Ingram 2 and 1
Vicki Thomas lost to Shannon 2 and 1
Claire Hourihane lost to Lang 2 and 1
Hall beat Goetze 1 hole

1994 at Chattanooga, TN
Result: GBI 9, USA 9
Captains: Lancy Smith (USA),
Elizabeth Boatman (GBI)
First Day: Foursomes
Sarah LeBrun Ingram & McGill halved with Matthew
& Moodie
Klein & Thompson beat McKay & Kirsty Speak
7 and 5
Kaupp & Port lost to Wade & Walton 6 and 5
Singles
Jill McGill halved with Julie Wade
Emilee Klein beat Janice Moodie 3 and 2
Wendy Ward lost to Lisa Walton 1 hole
Carol Semple Thompson beat Myra McKinlay
2 and 1
Ellen Port beat Mhairi McKay 2 and 1
Stephanie Sparks lost to Catriona Lambert Matthew
1 hole
Second Day: Foursomes
Ingram & McGill lost to Wade & Walton 2 and 1
Klein & Thompson beat McKinlay & Eileen Rose
Power 4 and 2
Sparks & Ward lost to Matthew & Moodie 3 and 2
Singles
McGill beat Wade 4 and 3
Klein lost to Matthew 2 and 1
Port beat McKay 7 and 5
Wendy Kaupp lost to McKinlay 3 and 2
Ward beat Walton 4 and 3
Thompson lost to Moodie 2 holes

1996 at Killarney
Result: GBI 11½, USA 6½
Captains: Ita Burke Butler (GBI),
Martha Lang (USA)
First Day: Foursomes
Lisa Walton Educate & Wade lost to K Kuehne & Port
2 and 1
Lisa Dermott & Rose beat B Corrie Kuehn & Jemsek
3 and 1
McKay & Moodie halved with Kerr & Thompson
Singles
Julie Wade lost to Sarah LeBrun Ingram 4 and 2
Karen Stupples beat Kellee Booth 3 and 2
Alison Rose beat Brenda Corrie Kuehn 5 and 4
Elaine Ratcliffe halved with Marla Jemsek
Mhairi McKay beat Cristie Kerr 1 hole
Janice Moodie beat Carol Semple Thompson 3 and 1
Second Day: Foursomes
McKay & Moodie beat Booth & Ingram 3 and 2
Dermott & Rose beat B Corrie Kuehn & Jemsek
2 and 1
Educate & Wade lost to K Kuehne & Port 1 hole
Singles
Wade lost to Kerr 1 hole
Ratcliffe beat Ingram 3 and 1
Stupples lost to Booth 3 and 2
Rose beat Ellen Port 6 and 5
McKay halved with Thompson
Moodie beat Kelli Kuehne 2 and 1

1998 at Minikahda, Minneapolis, MN
Result: USA 10, GBI 8
Captains: Barbara McIntire (USA),
Ita Burke Butler (GBI)
First Day: Foursomes
Bauer & Chuasiriporn lost to Ratcliffe & Rostron
1 hole
Booth & Corrie Kuehn beat Brown & Stupples
2 and 1
Burke & Derby Grimes beat Morgan & Rose 3 and 2
Singles
Kellee Booth beat Kim Rostron 2 and 1
Brenda Corrie Kuehn beat Alison Rose 3 and 2
Jenny Chuasiriporn halved with Rebecca Hudson
Beth Bauer beat Hilary Monaghan 5 and 3
Jo Jo Robertson lost to Becky Morgan 2 and 1
Carol Semple Thompson lost to Elaine Ratcliffe
3 and 2
Second Day: Foursomes
Booth & Corrie Kuehn beat Morgan & Rose 6 and 5
Bauer & Chuasiriporn lost to Brown & Hudson
2 holes
Burke & Derby Grimes beat Ratcliffe & Rostron
2 and 1
Singles
Booth beat Rostron 2 and 1
Corrie Kuehn beat Morgan 2 and 1
Thompson lost to Karen Stupples 1 hole
Robin Burke lost to Hudson 2 and 1
Robertson lost to Fiona Brown 1 hole
Virginia Derby Grimes halved with Ratcliffe

2000 *at Ganton*
Result: USA 10, GBI 8
Captains: Claire Hourihane Dowling (GBI),
Jane Bastanchury Booth (USA)
First Day: Foursomes
Andrew & Morgan lost to Bauer & Carol Semple
  Thompson 1 hole
Brewerton & Hudson lost to Keever & Stanford
  1 hole
Duggleby & O'Brien halved with Derby Grimes &
  Homeyer
Singles
Kim Rostron Andrew lost to Beth Bauer 3 and 2
Fiona Brown lost to Robin Weiss 1 hole
Rebecca Hudson lost to Stephanie Keever 4 and 2
Lesley Nicholson halved with Angela Stanford

Singles *continued*
Suzanne O'Brien beat Leland Beckel 3 and 1
Emma Duggleby lost to Hilary Homeyer 1 hole
Second Day: Foursomes
Brewerton & Hudson beat Bauer & Thompson
  2 and 1
Duggleby & O'Brien beat Keever & Stanford
  7 and 6
Andrew & Morgan lost to Derby Grimes & Homeyer
  3 and 1
Singles
Hudson lost to Bauer 1 hole
O'Brien beat Weiss 3 and 2
Duggleby beat Keever 4 and 2
Becky Brewerton lost to Homeyer 3 and 2
Becky Morgan beat Stanford 5 and 4
Andrew beat Virginia Derby Grimes 6 and 5

Curtis Cup INDIVIDUAL RECORDS

Bold print: captain; bold print in brackets: non-playing captain
Maiden name in parentheses, former surname in square brackets

Great Britain and Ireland

Name		Year	Played	Won	Lost	Halved
Jean Anderson (Donald)	Sco	1948	6	3	3	0
Kim Andrew (Rostron)	Eng	1999-2000	8	2	6	0
Diane Bailey [Frearson] (Robb)	Eng	1962-72-(84)-(86)-(88)	5	2	2	1
Sally Barber (Bonallack)	Eng	1962	1	0	1	0
Pam Barton	Eng	1934-36	4	0	3	1
Linda Bayman	Eng	1988	4	2	1	1
Baba Beck (Pym)	Irl	(1954)	0	0	0	0
Charlotte Beddows [Watson] (Stevenson)	Sco	1932	1	0	1	0
Lilian Behan	Irl	1986	4	3	1	0
Veronica Beharrell (Anstey)	Eng	1956	1	0	1	0
Pam Benka (Tredinnick)	Eng	1966-68	4	0	3	1
Jeanne Bisgood	Eng	1950-52-54-(70)	4	1	3	0
Elizabeth Boatman (Collis)	Eng	(1992)-(94)	0	0	0	0
Zara Bolton (Davis)	Eng	1948-(56)-(66)-(68)	2	0	2	0
Angela Bonallack (Ward)	Eng	1956-58-60-62-64-66	15	6	8	1
Becky Brewerton	Wal	2000	3	1	2	0
Fiona Brown	Eng	1998-2000	4	2	2	0
Ita Butler (Burke)	Irl	1966-(96)	3	2	1	0
Lady Katherine Cairns	Eng	(1952)	0	0	0	0
Carole Caldwell (Redford)	Eng	1978-80	5	0	3	2
Doris Chambers	Eng	(1934)-(36)-(48)	0	0	0	0
Carol Comboy (Grott)	Eng	(1978)-(80)	0	0	0	0
Jane Connachan	Sco	1980-82	5	0	5	0
Elsie Corlett	Eng	1932-38-(64)	3	1	2	0
Diana Critchley (Fishwick)	Eng	1932-34-(50)	3	1	2	0
Alison Davidson (Rose)	Sco	1996-98	7	4	3	0
Karen Davies	Wal	1986-88	7	4	1	2
Laura Davies	Eng	1984	2	1	1	0
Lisa Dermott	Wal	1996	2	2	0	0
Helen Dobson	Eng	1990	3	1	2	0
Kitrina Douglas	Eng	1982	4	0	3	1
Claire Dowling (Hourihane)	Irl	1984-86-88-90-92-(2000)	8	3	3	2
Marjorie Draper [Peel] (Thomas)	Sco	1954	1	0	1	0
Emma Duggleby	Eng	2000	4	2	1	1
Lisa Educate (Walton)	Eng	1994-96	6	3	3	0
Mary Everard	Eng	1970-72-74-78	15	6	7	2
Elaine Farquharson	Sco	1990-92	6	1	5	0
Daisy Ferguson	Irl	(1958)	0	0	0	0
Marjory Ferguson (Fowler)	Sco	1966	1	0	1	0
Elizabeth Price Fisher (Price)	Eng	1950-52-54-56-58-60	12	7	4	1
Linzi Fletcher	Eng	1990	1	0	1	0

Curtis Cup Individual Records *continued*

Name		Year	Played	Won	Lost	Halved
Maureen Garner (Madill)	Irl	1980	4	0	3	1
Marjorie Ross Garon	Eng	1936	2	1	0	1
Maureen Garrett (Ruttle)	Eng	1948-(60)	2	0	2	0
Philomena Garvey	Irl	1948-50-52-54-56-60	11	2	8	1
Carol Gibbs (Le Feuvre)	Eng	1974	3	0	3	0
Jacqueline Gordon	Eng	1948	2	1	1	0
Molly Gourlay	Eng	1932-34	4	0	2	2
Julia Greenhalgh	Eng	1964-70-74-76-78	17	6	7	4
Penny Grice-Whittaker (Grice)	Eng	1984	4	2	1	1
Caroline Hall	Eng	1992	4	2	0	2
Julie Hall (Wade)	Eng	1988-90-92-94-96	19	6	10	3
Marley Harris [Spearman] (Baker)	Eng	1960-62-64	6	2	2	2
Dorothea Hastings (Sommerville)	Sco	1958	0	0	0	0
Lady Heathcoat-Amory (Joyce Wethered)	Eng	**1932**	2	1	1	0
Dinah Henson (Oxley)	Eng	1968-70-72-76	11	3	6	2
Helen Holm (Gray)	Sco	1936-38-48	5	3	2	0
Ann Howard (Phillips)	Eng	1956-68	2	0	2	0
Rebecca Hudson	Eng	1998-2000	7	3	3	1
Beverley Huke	Eng	1972	2	0	2	0
Kathryn Imrie	Sco	1990	4	1	3	0
Ann Irvin	Eng	1962-68-70-76	12	4	7	1
Bridget Jackson	Eng	1958-64-68	8	1	6	1
Patricia Johnson	Eng	1986	4	4	0	0
Susan Langridge (Armitage)	Eng	1964-66	6	0	5	1
Joan Lawrence	Sco	1964	2	0	2	0
Shirley Lawson	Sco	1988	2	1	1	0
Wilma Leburn (Aitken)	Sco	1982	2	0	2	0
Jenny Lee Smith	Eng	1974-76	3	0	3	0
Kathryn Lumb (Phillips)	Eng	1970-72	2	1	1	0
Mhairi McKay	Sco	1994-96	7	2	3	2
Mary McKenna	Irl	1970-72-74-76-78-80-82-84-86	30	10	16	4
Myra McKinlay	Sco	1994	3	1	2	0
Suzanne McMahon (Cadden)	Sco	1976	4	0	4	0
Sheila Maher (Vaughan)	Eng	1962-64	4	1	2	1
Vanessa Marvin	Eng	1978	3	1	2	0
Catriona Matthew (Lambert)	Sco	1990-92-94	12	7	4	1
Tegwen Matthews [Thomas] (Perkins)	Wal	1974-76-78-80	14	4	8	2
Moira Milton (Paterson)	Sco	1952	2	1	1	0
Hilary Monaghan	Sco	1998	1	0	1	0
Janice Moodie	Sco	1994-96	8	5	1	2
Becky Morgan	Wal	1998-2000	7	2	5	0
Wanda Morgan	Eng	1932-34-36	6	0	5	1
Joanne Morley	Eng	1992	4	2	0	2
Nicola Murray (Buxton)	Eng	1992	1	0	1	0
Beverley New	Eng	1984	4	1	3	0
Lesley Nicholson	Sco	2000	1	0	0	1
Suzanne O'Brien	Irl	2000	4	3	0	1
Maire O'Donnell	Irl	(1982)	0	0	0	0
Margaret Pickard (Nichol)	Eng	1968-70	5	2	3	0
Diana Plumpton	Eng	1934	2	1	1	0
Elizabeth Pook (Chadwick)	Eng	1966	4	1	3	0
Doris Porter (Park)	Sco	1932	1	0	1	0
Eileen Rose Power (McDaid)	Irl	1994	1	0	1	0
Elaine Ratcliffe	Eng	1996-98	6	3	1	2
Clarrie Reddan (Tiernan)	Irl	1938-48	3	2	1	0
Joan Rennie (Hastings)	Sco	1966	2	0	1	1
Maureen Richmond (Walker)	Sco	1974	4	2	2	0
Jean Roberts	Eng	1962	1	0	1	0
Belle Robertson (McCorkindale)	Sco	1960-66-68-70-72-(74)-(76)-82-86	24	5	12	7
Claire Robinson (Nesbitt)	Irl	1980	3	0	1	2
Kim Rostron	Eng	1998	4	1	3	0
Vivien Saunders	Eng	1968	4	1	2	1
Susan Shapcott	Eng	1988	4	3	1	0
Linda Simpson (Moore)	Eng	1980	3	1	1	1
Ruth Slark (Porter)	Eng	1960-62-64	7	3	3	1
Anne Smith [Stant] (Willard)	Eng	1976	1	0	1	0

Name		Year	Played	Won	Lost	Halved
Frances Smith (Stephens)	Eng	1950-52-54-56-58-60-(62)-(72)	11	7	3	1
Janet Soulsby	Eng	1982	4	1	2	1
Kirsty Speak	Eng	1994	1	0	1	0
Gillian Stewart	Sco	1980-82	4	1	3	0
Karen Stupples	Eng	1996-98	4	2	2	0
Vicki Thomas (Rawlings)	Wal	1982-84-86-88-90-92	13	6	5	2
Muriel Thomson	Sco	1978	3	2	1	0
Jill Thornhill	Eng	1984-86-88	12	6	2	4
Angela Uzielli (Carrick)	Eng	1978	1	0	1	0
Jessie Valentine (Anderson)	Sco	1936-38-50-52-54-56-58	13	4	9	0
Helen Wadsworth	Wal	1990	2	0	2	0
Claire Waite	Eng	1984	4	2	2	0
Mickey Walker	Eng	1972-74	4	3	0	1
Pat Walker	Irl	1934-36-38	6	2	3	1
Verona Wallace-Williamson	Sco	(1938)	0	0	0	0
Nan Wardlaw (Baird)	Sco	1938	1	0	1	0
Enid Wilson	Eng	1932	2	1	1	0
Janette Wright (Robertson)	Sco	1954-56-58-60	8	3	5	0
Phyllis Wylie (Wade)	Eng	1938	1	0	0	1

United States of America

Name	Year	Played	Won	Lost	Halved
Roberta Albers	1968	2	1	0	1
Danielle Ammaccapane	1986	3	0	3	0
Kathy Baker	1982	4	3	0	1
Barbara Barrow	1976	2	1	0	1
Beth Barry	1972-74	5	3	1	1
Beth Bauer	1998-2000	7	4	3	0
Laura Baugh	1972	4	2	1	1
Leland Beckel	2000	1	0	1	0
Judy Bell	1960-62-(86)-(88)	2	1	1	0
Peggy Kirk Bell (Kirk)	1950	2	1	1	0
Amy Benz	1982	3	2	1	0
Patty Berg	1936-38	4	1	2	1
Barbara Fay Boddie (White)	1964-66	8	7	0	1
Jane Booth (Bastanchury)	1970-72-74-(2000)	12	9	3	0
Kellee Booth	1996-98	7	5	2	0
Mary Budke	1974	3	2	1	0
Robin Burke	1998	3	2	1	0
Brandie Burton	1990	3	3	0	0
Jo Anne Carner (Gunderson)	1958-60-62-64	10	6	3	1
Lori Castillo	1980	3	2	1	0
Leona Cheney (Pressler)	1932-34-36	6	5	1	0
Sis Choate	(1974)	0	0	0	0
Jenny Chuasiriporn	1998	3	0	2	1
Peggy Conley	1964-68	6	3	1	2
Mary Ann Cook (Downey)	1956	2	1	1	0
Patricia Cornett	1978-88	4	1	2	1
Brenda Corrie Kuehn	1996-98	7	4	3	0
Jean Crawford (Ashley)	1962-66-68-(72)	8	6	2	0
Clifford Ann Creed	1962	2	2	0	0
Grace Cronin (Lenczyk)	1948-50	3	2	1	0
Carolyn Cudone	1956-(70)	1	1	0	0
Beth Daniel	1976-78	8	7	1	0
Virginia Dennehy	(1958)	0	0	0	0
Virginia Derby Grimes	1998-2000	6	3	1	2
Mary Lou Dill	1968	3	1	1	1
Alice Dye	1970	2	1	0	1
Heather Farr	1984	3	2	1	0
Jane Fassinger	1970	1	0	1	0
Mary Lena Faulk	1954	2	1	1	0
Carol Sorensen Flenniken (Sorensen)	1964-66	8	6	1	1
Edith Flippin (Quier)	(1954)-(56)	0	0	0	0
Amy Fruhwirth	1992	4	0	1	3
Kim Gardner	1986	3	1	1	1
Charlotte Glutting	1934-36-38	5	3	1	1
Vicki Goetze	1990-92	8	4	2	2
Brenda Goldsmith	1978-80	4	2	2	0

Curtis Cup Individual Records *continued*

Name	Year	Played	Won	Lost	Halved
Aniela Goldthwaite	1934-(52)	1	0	1	0
Joanne Goodwin	1960	2	1	1	0
Mary Hafeman	1980	2	1	0	1
Shelley Hamkin	1968-70	8	3	3	2
Penny Hammel	1984	3	1	1	1
Nancy Hammer (Hager)	1970	2	1	1	0
Cathy Hanlon	1982	3	2	1	0
Beverley Hanson	1950	2	2	0	0
Tracy Hanson	1992	3	1	2	0
Patricia Harbottle (Lesser)	1954-56	3	2	1	0
Helen Hawes	(1964)	0	0	0	0
Kathryn Hemphill	1938	1	0	0	1
Helen Hicks	1932	2	1	1	0
Carolyn Hill	1978	2	0	0	2
Cindy Hill	1970-74-76-78	14	5	6	3
Opel Hill	1932-34-36	6	2	3	1
Marion Hollins	(1932)	0	0	0	0
Hilary Homeyer	2000	4	3	0	1
Dana Howe	1984	3	1	1	1
Juli Inkster	1982	4	4	0	0
Maria Jemsek	1996	3	0	2	1
Ann Casey Johnstone	1958-60-62	4	3	1	0
Mae Murray Jones (Murray)	1952	1	0	1	0
Wendy Kaupp	1994	2	0	2	0
Stephanie Keever	2000	4	2	2	0
Caroline Keggi	1988	3	0	2	1
Tracy Kerdyk	1988	4	2	1	1
Cristie Kerr	1996	3	1	1	1
Kandi Kessler	1986	3	1	1	1
Dorothy Kielty	1948-50	4	4	0	0
Dorothy Kirby	1948-50-52-54	7	4	3	0
Martha Kirouac (Wilkinson)	1970-72	8	5	3	0
Emilee Klein	1994	4	3	1	0
Nancy Knight (Lopez)	1976	2	2	0	0
Kelli Kuehne	1996	3	2	1	0
Martha Lang	1992-(96)	3	2	0	1
Bonnie Lauer	1974	4	2	2	0
Sarah Le Brun Ingram	1992-94-96	7	2	4	1
Marjorie Lindsay	1952	2	1	1	0
Patricia Lucey (O'Sullivan)	1952	1	0	1	0
Mari McDougall	1982	2	2	0	0
Jill McGill	1994	4	1	1	2
Barbara McIntire	1958-60-62-64-66-72-(76)	16	6	6	4
Lucile Mann (Robinson)	1934	1	0	1	0
Debbie Massey	1974-76	5	5	0	0
Marion Miley	1938	2	1	0	1
Dottie Mochrie (Pepper)	1986	3	0	2	1
Evelyn Monsted	(1968)	0	0	0	0
Terri Moody	1980	2	1	0	1
Karen Noble	1990	4	2	2	0
Judith Oliver	1978-80-82-(92)	8	5	1	2
Maureen Orcutt	1932-34-36-38	8	5	3	0
Joanne Pacillo	1984	3	1	1	1
Estelle Page (Lawson)	1938-48	4	3	1	0
Katie Peterson	1990	3	3	0	0
Margaret Platt	1990	2	0	2	0
Frances Pond (Stebbins)	(1938)	0	0	0	0
Ellen Port	1994-96	6	4	2	0
Dorothy Germain Porter	1950-(66)	2	1	0	1
Phyllis Preuss	1962-64-66-68-70-(84)	15	10	4	1
Betty Probasco	(1982)	0	0	0	0
Mildred Prunaret	(1960)	0	0	0	0
Polly Riley	1948-50-52-54-56-58-(62)	10	5	5	0
Jo Jo Robertson	1998	2	0	2	0
Barbara Romack	1954-56-58	5	3	2	0
Jody Rosenthal	1984	3	2	0	1
Anne Sander [Welts] [Decker] (Quast)	1958-60-62-66-68-74-84-90	22	11	7	4
Cindy Scholefield	1988	3	0	3	0

Name	Year	Played	Won	Lost	Halved
Cindy Schreyer	1986	3	1	2	0
Kathleen McCarthy Scrivner (McCarthy)	1986-88	6	2	3	1
Carol Semple Thompson	1974-76-80-82-90-92-94-96-**98**-2000	31	14	13	4
Leslie Shannon	1986-88-90-92	9	1	6	2
Patty Sheehan	1980	4	4	0	0
Pearl Sinn	1988	2	1	1	0
Grace De Moss Smith (De Moss)	1952-54	3	1	2	0
Lancy Smith	1972-78-80-82-84-(**94**)	16	7	5	4
Margaret Smith	1956	2	2	0	0
Stephanie Sparks	1994	2	0	2	0
Hollis Stacy	1972	2	0	1	1
Claire Stancik (Doran)	1952-54	4	4	0	0
Angela Stanford	2000	4	1	2	1
Judy Street (Eller)	1960	2	2	0	0
Louise Suggs	1948	2	0	1	1
Nancy Roth Syms (Roth)	1964-66-76-(**80**)	9	3	5	1
Noreen Uihlein	1978	3	1	1	1
Virginia Van Wie	1932-34	4	3	0	1
Glenna Collett Vare (Collett)	1932-(**34**)-**36**-38-48-(**50**)	7	4	2	1
Wendy Ward	1994	3	1	2	0
Jane Weiss (Nelson)	1956	1	0	1	0
Robin Weiss	1990-92-2000	7	4	2	1
Donna White (Horton)	1976	2	2	0	0
Mary Anne Widman	1984	3	2	1	0
Kimberley Williams	1986	3	0	3	0
Helen Sigel Wilson (Sigel)	1950-66-(**78**)	2	0	2	0
Joyce Ziske	1954	1	0	1	0

Women's World Amateur Team Championship for the Espirito Santo Trophy

Year	Winners	Runners-up	Venue	Score
1964	France	United States	St Germain	588
1966	United States	Canada	Mexico	580
1968	United States	Australia	Melbourne	616
1970	United States	France	Madrid	598
1972	United States	France	Buenos Aires	583
1974	United States	GB&I, South Africa	Dominican Republic	620
1976	United States	France	Vilamoura, Portugal	605
1978	Australia	Canada	Fiji	596
1980	United States	Australia	Pinehurst, USA	588
1982	United States	New Zealand	Geneva, Switzerland	579
1984	United States	France	Hong Kong	585
1986	Spain	France	Caracas, Venezuela	580
1988	United States	Sweden	Drottningholm, Sweden	587
1990	United States	New Zealand	Christchurch, New Zealand	585
1992	Spain	GB&I	Vancouver, Canada	588
1994	United States	Korea	Paris, France	569
1996	Korea	Italy	Manila, Philippines	438
1998	United States	Italy	Santiago, Chile	558
2000	France	Korea	Sporting Club, Berlin	580

Commonwealth Tournament (Instituted 1959, played every four years)

1959	Great Britain	St Andrews
1963	Great Britain	Royal Melbourne, Australia
1967	Great Britain	Ancaster, Ontario, Canada
1971	Great Britain	Hamilton, New Zealand
1975	Great Britain	Ganton, England
1979	Canada	Lake Karrinup, Perth, Australia
1983	Australia	Glendale, Edmonton, Canada
1987	Canada	Christchurch, New Zealand
1991	Great Britain	Northumberland, England
1995	Australia	Royal Sydney, Australia
1999	Australia	Marine Drive, Vancouver, Canada

Women's European Amateur Team Championship

Year	Winner	Second	Venue	Year	Winner	Second	Venue
1967	England	France	Penina, Portugal	1985	England	Italy	Stavanger, Norway
1969	France	England	Tylosand, Sweden	1987	Sweden	Wales	Turnberry, Scotland
1971	England	France	Ganton, England	1989	France	England	Pals, Spain
1973	England	France	Brussels, Belgium	1991	England	Sweden	Wentworth, England
1975	France	Spain	Paris, France	1993	England	Spain	Royal Haagshe
1977	England	Spain	Sotogrande, Spain	1995	Spain	Scotland	Milan, Italy
1979	Ireland	Germany	Hermitage, Ireland	1997	Sweden	Scotland	Nordcenter, Finland
1981	Sweden	France	Troia, Portugal	1999	France	England	St Germain, France
1983	Ireland	England	Waterloo, Belgium				

2001 *at Golf de Meis, Pontevedra, Spain*

1 Sweden, 2 Spain (semi-finals & final cancelled due to adverse weather conditions)

Vagliano Trophy – Great Britain & Ireland *v* Continent of Europe

1959	GB & I	12–3	Wentworth	1981	Europe	14–10	P de Hierro
1961	GB & I	8–7	Villa d'Este	1983	GB & I	14–10	Woodhall Spa
1963	GB & I	20–10	Muirfield	1985	GB & I	14–10	Hamburg
1965	Europe	17–13	Cologne	1987	GB & I	15–9	The Berkshire
1967	Europe	15½–14½	Lytham	1989	GB & I	14½–9½	Venice
1969	Europe	16–14	Chantilly	1991	GB & I	13½–10½	Nairn
1971	GB & I	17½–12½	Worplesdon	1993	GB & I	13½–10½	Morfontaine
1973	GB & I	20–10	Eindhoven	1995	Europe	14–10	Ganton
1975	GB & I	13½–10½	Muirfield	1997	Europe	14–10	Halmstad
1977	GB & I	15½–8½	Malmo	1999	Europe	13–11	North Berwick
1979	Halved	12–12	R Porthcawl				

2001 *at Venezia, Italy*
Result: Continent of Europe 7, GB & I 5
Captains: Macarena Campomanes (Eur), Claire Dowling (GB & I)

First Day: Foursomes
Eberl & Simon lost to Duggleby & More 1 hole
Elosegui & Prieto beat Andrew & Brown 2 and 1
Piovano & Grignolo lost to Coffey & Smith 1 hole
Dertsson & Engstrom lost to Fisher & Hudson 1 hole

Second Day: Foursomes
Piovano & Grignolo lost to Duggleby & More 4 and 2
Dertsson & Engstrom lost to Fisher & Hudson 2 and 1
Elosegui & Prieto beat Coffey & Smith 2 and 1
Eberl & Simon lost to 4 and 3

Singles
Prieto beat Duggleby 1 hole
Nocera lost to More 5 and 3
Simon beat Brown 2 and 1
Grignolo beat Brewerton 2 and 1
Dertsson beat Andrew 7 and 6
Engstrom beat Smith 2 holes
Elosegui lost to Coffey 2 and 1
Eberl beat Hudson 4 and 3

Singles
Simon lost to Hudson 1 hole
Prieto beat Duggleby 2 holes
Engstrom lost to More 3 and 2
Federica Piovano beat Alison Coffey 2 and 1
Grignolo lost to Brown 2 and 1
Dertsson beat Andrew 1 hole
Eberl beat Kirsty Fisher 2 and 1
Elosegui beat Smith 4 and 3

Women's Home Internationals

1948	England	R Lytham and St Annes		1972	England	R Lytham and St Annes
1949	Scotland	Harlech		1973	England	Harlech
1950	Scotland	Newcastle Co Down		1974T	England/Scotland/	
1951	Scotland	Broadstone			Ireland	Sandwich, Princes
1952	Scotland	Troon		1975	England	Newport
1953	England	Porthcawl		1976	England	Troon
1954T	England/Scotland	Ganton, Scotland		1977	England	Cork
1955	England	Western Gailes		1978	England	Moortown
1956	Scotland	Sunningdale		1979T	Scotland/Ireland	Harlech
1957	Scotland	Troon		1980	Ireland	Cruden Bay
1958	England	Hunstanton		1981	Scotland	Portmarnock
1959	England	Hoylake		1982	England	Burnham and Barrow
1960	England	Gullane		1983	*Matches abandoned due to weather*	
1961	Scotland	Portmarnock		1984	England	Gullane
1962	Scotland	Porthcawl		1985	England	Waterville
1963	England	Formby		1986	Ireland	Whittington Barracks
1964	England	Troon		1987	England	Ashburnham
1965	England	Portrush		1988	Scotland	Kilmarnock (Barassie)
1966	England	Woodhall Spa		1989	England	Westport
1967	England	Sunningdale		1990	Scotland	Hunstanton
1968	England	Porthcawl		1991	Scotland	Aberdovey
1969T	England/Scotland	Western Gailes		1992	England	Hamilton
1970	England	Killarney		1993	England	Dublin
1971	England	Longniddry				

1994 at Huddersfield, Yorkshire

England beat Ireland	6½ matches to 2½
Scotland beat Wales	8½ matches to ½
England beat Wales	8 matches to 1
Scotland halved with Ireland	4½ matches to 4½
England beat Scotland	6 matches to 3
Ireland beat Wales	5½ matches to 3½

Result: England 3; Scotland 1½; Ireland 1½; Wales 0

1995 at Wrexham, Clwyd

Ireland beat Scotland	6 matches to 3
Ireland halved with Wales	4½ matches to 4½
Ireland beat Scotland	5 matches to 4
Wales beat England	5 matches to 4
England beat Ireland	9 matches to 0
Scotland beat Wales	5 matches to 4

Result: England 2; Wales 1½; Ireland 1½; Scotland 1

1996 at Longniddry

Scotland beat Ireland	5½ matches to 3½
England beat Wales	6 matches to 3
Scotland beat Wales	5 matches to 4
England beat Ireland	6 matches to 3
England beat Scotland	5 matches to 4
Ireland beat Wales	5½ matches to 3½

Result: England 3; Scotland 2; Ireland 1; Wales 0

1997 at Lahinch, Ireland

Ireland beat Wales	6½ matches to 2½
England beat Scotland	6½ matches to 2½
England beat Ireland	6 matches to 3
Scotland beat Wales	5½ matches to 3½
England beat Wales	5 matches to 4
Ireland beat Scotland	7 matches to 2

Result: England 3; Ireland 2; Scotland 1; Wales 0

1998 at Burnham & Berrow

Ireland beat Wales	6 matches to 3
England beat Scotland	6 matches to 3
England beat Ireland	5 matches to 4
Ireland halved with Scotland	4½ matches to 4½
England beat Wales	6½ matches to 2½
Scotland halved with Wales	4½ matches to 4½

Result: England 3; Ireland 1½; Scotland 1; Wales ½

1999 at Royal Dornoch

Ireland beat Scotland	5 matches to 4
England halved with Wales	4½ matches to 4½
Wales beat Ireland	7½ matches to 1½
England beat Scotland	5 matches to 4
England beat Ireland	7 matches to 2
Wales beat Scotland	5½ matches to 3½

Result: Wales 2½; England 2½; Ireland 1; Scotland 0
(Wales won on individual games countback 17½–16½)

2000 at Royal St David's

Ireland halved with Wales	4½ matches to 4½
England beat Scotland	6 matches to 3
Wales beat Scotland	8 matches to 1
England beat Ireland	8 matches to 1
Ireland beat Scotland	5 matches to 4
England beat Wales	5 matches to 4

Result: England 3; Wales 1½; Ireland 1½; Scotland 0

2001 at Carlow

Ireland beat Wales 6 matches to 3
England beat Scotland 5½ matches to 3½
Wales halved with Scotland 4½ matches to 4½
England beat Ireland 5½ matches to 3½
England beat Wales 5 matches to 4
Ireland beat Scotland 5½ matches to 3½

Result: 1 England; 2 Ireland; 3 Scotland & Wales

England and Wales Ladies County Championship

1908	Lancashire	1949	Surrey	1976	Staffordshire
1909	Surrey	1950	Yorkshire	1977	Essex
1910	Cheshire	1951	Lancashire	1978	Glamorgan
1911	Cheshire	1952	Lancashire	1979	Essex
1912	Cheshire	1953	Surrey	1980	Lancashire
1913	Surrey	1954	Warwickshire	1981	Glamorgan
1920	Middlesex	1955	Surrey	1982	Surrey
1921	Surrey	1956	Kent	1983	Surrey
1922	Surrey	1957	Middlesex	1984	Surrey/Yorkshire
1923	Surrey	1958	Lancashire	1985	Surrey
1924	Surrey	1959	Middlesex	1986	Glamorgan
1925	Surrey	1960	Lancashire	1987	Lancashire
1926	Surrey	1961	Middlesex	1988	Surrey
1927	Yorkshire	1962	Staffordshire	1989	Cheshire
1928	Cheshire	1963	Warwickshire	1990	Cheshire
1929	Yorkshire	1964	Lancashire	1991	Glamorgan
1930	Surrey	1965	Staffordshire	1992	Hampshire
1931	Middlesex	1966	Lancashire	1993	Lancashire
1932	Cheshire	1967	Lancashire	1994	Staffordshire
1933	Yorkshire	1968	Surrey	1995	Hampshire
1934	Surrey	1969	Lancashire	1996	Cheshire
1935	Essex	1970	Yorkshire	1997	Surrey
1936	Surrey	1971	Kent	1998	Yorkshire
1937	Surrey	1972	Kent	1999	Yorkshire
1938	Lancashire	1973	Northumberland	2000	Yorkshire
1947	Surrey	1974	Surrey		
1948	Yorkshire	1975	Glamorgan		

2001 *at Moortown*

1 Yorkshire;   2 Hertfordshire;   3 Staffordshire;   4 Gloucestershire

Scottish Ladies County Championship

1992	Dunbartonshire & Argyll	1997	Dunbartonshire & Argyll
1993	East Lothian	1998	East Lothian
1994	East Lothian	1999	East Lothian
1995	Fife	2000	Northern Counties
1996	East Lothian		

2001 *at Prestwick St Nicholas*

1 Stirlingshire & Clackmannanshire;   2 Lanarkshire;   3 Northern Counties;   4 Borders

Scottish Ladies Foursomes

1992	Haggs Castle	1997	Stirling
1993	North Berwick	1998	Prestonfield
1994	Turnberry	1999	Dunblane New
1995	Gullane	2000	Windyhill
1996	Hilton Park		

2001 *at Haggs Castle*

Stirling [E Allison, A Davidson]

Welsh Ladies Team Championship

1992	Whitchurch	1997	St Pierre
1993	Pennard	1998	Wrexham
1994	St Pierre	1999	Pennard
1995	R. St Davids	2000	Pennard
1996	R. St Davids		

2001 *at Pennard GC, Swansea*

Whitchurch GC

(R Mackenzie, P Chugg, L Dingwall, K Hollyman and M Davies)

Other Women's Amateur Tournaments

Astor Salver (Inaugurated 1951)

1992	L Walton	1998	R Morgan
1993	S Lambert	1999	*Not played*
1994	S Lambert	2000T	C Court
1995	J Oliver		K Taylor
1996	S Gallagher	2001	E Pilgrim
1997	J Lamb		

Bridget Jackson Bowl *at Handsworth*

1992	F Brown	1997	K Macintosh
1993	S Morgan	1998	C Dowling
1994	K Speak	1999	S McKevitt
1995	K Stupples	2000	R Hudson
1996	R Hudson	2001	Laura Wright

Hampshire Rose (Inaugurated 1973) *at North Hants*

1992	A Uzielli	1997	S Sanderson
1993	C Hourihane	1998	C Court
1994T	K Shepherd/K Egford	1999	C Court
1995	J Oliver	2000	K Fisher
1996	K Stupples	2001	K Smith

Liphook Scratch Cup (Inaugurated 1992) *at Liphook*

1992	T Kernan, K Shepherd	1997	E Weeks
1993	K Egford	1998	K Knowles
1994	S Sharpe	1999	R Prout
1995	K Shepherd	2000	K Smith
1996	K Shepherd	2001	N Timmins

St Rule Trophy (Inaugurated 1984) *at St Andrews*

1984	P Hammel (US)	149	1993	C Lambert	215	
1985	K Imrie	151	1994	C Matthew	217	
1986	T Hammond	153	1995	M Hjörth	220	
1987	J Morley	153	1996	A Laing	227	
1988	C Middleton	152	1997	K Rostron	217	
1989	C Middleton	232	1998	N Clau[†]	154 (36)	
1990	A Sörenstam	228	1999	L Nicholson	227	
1991	A Rose	237	2000	V Laing*	153 (36)	
1992	M Wright	222				

2001

1	Alison Coffey (Warrenpoint)	74-72-75—221
2	Rebecca Hudson (Wheatley)	75-74-74—223
3	Vikki Laing (Musselburgh)	76-77-73—226

---

† *At 16 years, the youngest ever winner*

Sherry Cup *at Sotogrande, Cadiz, Spain*

1991	Caterina Quintarelli	1995	Maria Hjörth	1999	Martina Eberl
1992	Estafania Knuth	1996	Maria Hjörth	2000	Martina Eberl
1993	Ana F Johansson	1997	Marieke Zelsman		
1994	Ada O'Sullivan	1998	Nicole Stillia		

2001

1	Carmen Alonso Fuentes (Esp)	75-71-71-71—288
2	Diana Luna (Ita)	78-75-70-73—296
3	Rille Rasmussen (Den)	77-74-75-72—298

Final Ranking: 1 Spain, 2 Italy, 3 Denmark and Switzerland

Roehampton Gold Cup *inaugurated 1926*

2001

1   Miss T Loveys

WOMEN'S FOURSOMES EVENTS

London Ladies Foursomes

1992	Chelmsford	1997	The Berkshire
1993	Knebworth	1998	The Berkshire
1994	Knebworth	1999	The Berkshire
1995	The Berkshire	2000	Worplesdon
1996	The Berkshire	2001	Porter's Park

Mothers and Daughters Foursomes
at Royal Mid-Surrey

1992	Mrs P Carrick and Mrs A Uzielli		1997	Mrs S Lines and Miss K Lines
1993	Mrs P Carrick and Mrs A Uzielli		1998	Mrs H Joyce and Miss C Joyce
1994	Mrs P Carrick and Mrs A Uzielli		1999	Mrs E Boatman and Miss A Boatman
1995T	Mrs P Carrick and Mrs A Uzielli		2000	Lady Bonallack and Mrs G Beasley
	Mrs P Huntley and Miss J Huntley		2001	Mrs and Miss Gay
1996T	Mrs A Uzielli and Miss C Uzielli			
	Mrs E Boatman and Miss A Boatman			
	Mrs S Lines and Miss K Lines			

Women's Regional Amateur Championships

Aberdeenshire Ladies

1992	R MacLennan	1997	K Moggach
1993	G Penny	1998	L Urquhart
1994	C Hunter	1999	L Urquhart
1995	J Matthews	2000	S Wood
1996	S Wood	2001	S Wood

Angus Ladies

1992	M Summers	1997	S Raitt
1993	M Summers	1998	L Fenton
1994	M Summers	1999	L Fenton
1995	K Sutherland	2000	A Ramsay
1996	S Simpson	2001	K Sutherland

Ayrshire Ladies

1992	C Gibson	1997	A Gemmill
1993	M Wilson	1998	S Lambie
1994	A Gemmill	1999	S Lambie
1995	R Kennedy	2000	R Kennedy
1996	A Gemmill	2001	L Keohone

Bedfordshire Ladies

1992	S Cormack	1997	J Faris
1993	S Cormack	1998	S Cormack
1994	T Gale	1999	E Bruce
1995	A Bradley	2000	C Hoskin
1996	C Hoskin	2001	P Gale

Berkshire Ladies

1992	J Guntrip	1997	L Meredith
1993	A Uzielli	1998	S Sanderson
1994	J Guntrip	1999	L Webb
1995	A Uzielli	2000	L Webb
1996	S Sanderson	2001	E Cooper

Border Counties Ladies

1992	J Anderson	1997	J Anderson
1993	D Turnbull	1998	A Hunter
1994	W Wells	1999	J Anderson
1995	A Fleming	2000	M Pow
1996	K Inkpen	2001	M Pow

Buckinghamshire Ladies

1992	C Watson	1997	C Watson
1993	C Watson	1998	C Watson
1994	P Williamson	1999	C Watson
1995	C Dowling	2000	C Watson
1996	C Watson	2001	S Mace

Caernarfonshire and Anglesey Ladies

1992	S Turner	1997	F Vaughan-Thomas
1993	A Lewis	1998	F Vaughan-Thomas
1994	C Thomas	1999	K Evans
1995	L Davies	2000	L Davies
1996	L Davies	2001	L Davies

Cambridgeshire and Huntingdonshire Ladies

1992	T Eakin	1997	J Walter
1993	T Eakin	1998	J Walter
1994	T Eakin	1999	R Farrow
1995	P Parker	2000	J Walter
1996	J Walter	2000	P Parker

Cheshire Ladies

1992	J Morley	1997	E Ratcliffe
1993	J Morley	1998	E Ratcliffe
1994	F Brown	1999	R Adby
1995	E Ratcliffe	2000	O Briggs
1996	L Dermott	2001	R Adby

Cornwall Ladies

1992	G Fields	1997	L Simpson
1993	J Ryder	1998	G Dowling
1994	E Fields	1999	G Dowling
1995	L Simpson	2000	G Dowling
1996	L Simpson	2001	S Sanderson

Cumbria Ladies

1992	J Currie	1997	J Blaydes
1993	J Currie	1998	A Wood
1994	J Currie	1999	J Blaydes
1995	J Viles	2000	J Viles
1996	R Bruce	2001	J Blades

Denbighshire and Flintshire Ladies

1992	B Jones	1997	R Brewerton
1993	S Lovatt	1998	B Jones
1994	A Donne	1999	R Brewerton
1995	S Lovatt	2000	S Mountford
1996	B Jones	2001	J Nicholson

Derbyshire Ladies

1992	L Holmes	1997	L Walters
1993	L Holmes	1998	L Shaw
1994	L Walters	1999	L Walters
1995	L Holmes	2000	R Wood
1996	L Shaw	2001	L Shaw

Devon Ladies

1992	K Tebbet	1997	J Roberts
1993	K Tebbet	1998	C Copping
1994	K Tebbet	1999	K Clarke
1995	J Roberts	2000	K Clarke
1996	R Cirin	2001	K Clarke

Dorset Ladies

1992	S Lowe	1997	A Monk
1993	S Sanderson	1998	A Monk
1994	W Russell	1999	S Phillips
1995	A Monk	2000	J Topp
1996	C Brown	2001	C Jones

Dumfriesshire Ladies

1992	D Douglas	1997	L Wells
1993	G Adamson	1998	D MacDonald
1994	F Watson	1999	L Wells
1995	D Douglas	2000	L Wells
1996	C Adamson	2001	K Wells

Dunbartonshire and Argyll Ladies

1992	J Moodie	1997	K Burns
1993	M McKinlay	1998	A Laing
1994	V Melvin	1999	V Melvin
1995	A Laing	2000	V Melvin
1996	V Melvin	2001	A Laing

Durham Ladies

1992	L Still	1997	K Lee
1993	L Keers	1998	P Dobson
1994	P Dobson	1999	L Keers
1995	K Lee	2000	P Simpson
1996	A Dobson	2001	A Dobson

East Lothian Ladies

1992	C Lambert	1997	S McMaster
1993	S McMester	1998	S McEwan
1994	C Matthew	1999	L Nicholson
1995	H Monaghan	2000	L Nicholson
1996	H Monaghan	2001	J Smith

Eastern Division Ladies (Scotland)

1992	J Ford	1997	S Grant
1993	A Rose	1998	F Lockhart
1994	J Ford	1999	L Kenny
1995	L Nicholson	2000	H Stirling
1996	H Monaghan	2001	H Stirling

Essex Ladies

1992	F Edmond	1997	S Barber
1993	T Poulton	1998	M Williams
1994	T Wilson	1999	E Gibson
1995	G Scase	2000	S Smith
1996	G Scase	2001	J Dartford

Fife County Ladies

1992	A Watson	1997	J Hall
1993	K Milne	1998	K Milne
1994	L Bennett	1999	L Fury
1995	K Milne	2000	E Moffat
1996	E Moffat	2001	L Kenney

Galloway Ladies

1992	C Meldrum	1997	S McMurtrie
1993	H Nesbit	1998	S McMurtrie
1994	C Meldrum	1999	S Booth
1995	T Dodds	2000	S McMurtrie
1996	A Cairns	2001	S McMurtrie

Glamorgan County Ladies

1992	J Foster	1997	V Thomas
1993	V Thomas	1998	P Chugg
1994	V Thomas	1999	K Phillips
1995	J Thomas	2000	V Thomas
1996	V Thomas	2001	A Highgate

Gloucestershire Ladies

1992	C Hall	1997	C Lipscombe
1993	C Hamilton	1998	C Lipscombe
1994	K Hamilton	1999	N Lumb
1995	N Sutton	2000	L Occleshaw
1996	J Clingan	2001	C Lipscombe

Hampshire Ladies

1992	A MacDonald	1997	H Wheeler
1993	K Egford	1998	E Weekes
1994	K Egford	1999	K Taylor
1995	H Wheeler	2000	K Taylor
1996	C Stirling	2201	N Booth

Hertfordshire Ladies

1992	S Alison	1997	K Evans
1993	C Hawkes	1998	M Allen
1994	J Oliver	1999	H Skinner
1995	J Oliver	2000	K Evans
1996	K Evans	2001	S Matthews

Kent Ladies

1992	C Caldwell	1997	S Butchers
1993	M Sutton	1998	K Stupples
1994	M Sutton	1999	N Timmins
1995	C Caldwell	2000	D Masters
1996	K Stupples	2001	N Timmins

Lanarkshire Ladies County

1992	F McKay	1997	L Lloyd
1993	M Hughes	1998	F Prior
1994	J Gardner	1999	F Prior
1995	R Rankin	2000	A Bell
1996	A Prentice	2001	C Queen

Lancashire Ladies

1992	J Collingham	1997	G Nutter
1993	K Rostron	1998	A Murray
1994	G Nutter	1999	K Fisher
1995	G Nutter	2000	C Blackshaw
1996	A Murray	2001	K Fisher

Leicestershire and Rutland Ladies

1992	H Summ	1997	J Morris
1993	M Page	1998	C Gay
1994	M Page	1999	J Morris
1995	C Gay	2000	H Lowe
1996	H Lowe	2001	C Gay

Lincolnshire Ladies

1992	R Jones	1997	A Thompson
1993	R Broughton	1998	M Willerton
1994	S Brook	1999	S Hunter
1995	A Thompson	2000	S Walker
1996	M Willerton	2001	N Chantry

Middlesex Ladies

1992	J Sadler	1997	J Barnett
1993	L Housman	1998	J Sadler
1994	M Henderson	1999	P Costello
1995	J Sadler	2000	D McCormack
1996	P Ramchand	2001	C Irons

Midland Ladies

1992	R Bolas	1997	R Bailey
1993	R Bolas	1998	N Lawrenson
1994	J Morris	1999	S Pidgeon
1995	K Edwards	2000	S Walker
1996	S Gallagher	2001	K Hanwell

Midlothian Ladies

1992	K Marshall	1997	P Silver
1993	E Bruce	1998	V Laing
1994	E Bruce	1999	C Williamson
1995	P Silver	2000	B Murphy
1996	M Quigley	2001	F Hunter

Mid-Wales Ladies

1992	P Morgan	1997	K Humphries
1993	A Owen	1998	A Hubbard
1994	G Gibb	1999	S Hughes
1995	J James	2000	J Dyer
1996	L Davies	2001	J Dyer

Monmouthshire Ladies

1992	R Morgan	1997	S O'Sullivan
1993	S Musto	1998	S O'Sullivan
1994	E Pilgrim	1999	R Morgan
1995	E Pilgrim	2000	J Pritchard
1996	C Waite	2001	L Diggle

Norfolk Ladies

1992	T Williamson	1997	T Williamson
1993	T Williamson	1998	T Williamson
1994	J Wilkerson	1999	R Shubrook
1995	J Wilkerson	2000	J Wilkerson
1996	C Grady	2001	J Wilkerson

Northamptonshire Ladies

1992	G Gibbs	1997	S Carter
1993	S Sharpe	1998	C Gibbs
1994	S Sharpe	1999	S Turbayne
1995	S Sharpe	2000	C Gibbs
1996	S Carter	2001	S Carter

Northern Counties (Scotland) Ladies

1992	I Shannon	1997	E Vass
1993	S Alexander	1998	L Vass
1994	L Roxburgh	1999	L Mackay
1995	F McKay	2000	L Mackay
1996	F McLennan	2001	C Gruber

Northern Women's (ELGA)

1992	G Simpson	1997	G Nutter
1993	A Brighouse	1998	R Lomas
1994	G Nutter	1999	C Ritson
1995	K Rostron	2000	L Mackay
1996	K Rostron	2001	N Evans

Northern Women's Counties Championship

1993	Lancashire	1998	Yorkshire
1994	Lancashire	1999	Yorkshire
1995	Cheshire	2000	Yorkshire
1996	Lancashire	2001	Yorkshire
1997	Lancashire		

Northern Division Ladies (Scotland)

1992	S Alexander	1997	C Hunter
1993	S Alexander	1998	J Tough
1994	J Matthews	1999	L McLardy
1995	J Harrison	2000	J Yellowlees
1996	J Harrison	2001	S Wood

Northumberland Ladies

1992	C Hall	1997	C Hall
1993	H Wilson	1998	C Hall
1994	D Glenn	1999	J Ross
1995	H Wilson	2000	J Ross
1996	C Hall	2001	J Ross

Nottinghamshire Ladies

1992	S Bishop	1997	J Collingham
1993	L Rayner	1998	J Collingham
1994	G Palmer	1999	L Wright
1995	G Palmer	2000	L Wright
1996	L Wright	2001	*Event cancelled*

Oxfordshire Ladies

1992	L King	1997	L King
1993	N Sparks	1998	N Woolford
1994	L King	1999	K Humphris
1995	L King	2000	N Woolford
1996	L King	2001	N Woolford

Perth and Kinross Ladies

1992	I Shannon	1997	N Harding
1993	E Wilson	1998	J Yellowlees
1994	C Dunbar	1999	A Murray
1995	F Farquharson	2000	C Meir
1996	E Wilson	2001	J Yellowlees

Renfrewshire County Ladies

1992	D Jackson	1997	L Robertson
1993	K Fitzgerald	1998	K Fitzgerald
1994	C Agnew	1999	D Jackson
1995	D Jackson	2000	D Jackson
1996	D Jackson	2001	D Jackson

Shropshire Ladies

1992	A Johnson	1997	S Heath
1993	A Johnson	1998	L Archer
1994	A Johnson	1999	S Heath
1995	B Smith	2000	L Archer
1996	B Smith	2001	S Heath

Somerset Ladies

1992	C Whiting	1997	L Wixon
1993	R Murr	1998	G Pritchard
1994	S Burnell	1999	V McFarlane
1995	L Wixon	2000	A Pitt
1996	L Wixon	2001	B New

South-Eastern Ladies

1992	A MacDonald	1997	L Evans
1993	K Smith	1998	A Waller
1994	K Egford	1999	K Knowles
1995	K Smith	2000	A Waller
1996	J Oliver	2001	K Smith

Southern Division Ladies (Scotland)

1992	D Douglas	1997	J Anderson
1993	C Meldrum	1998	D MacDonald
1994	D Douglas	1999	J Anderson
1995	J Anderson	2000	M Pow
1996	D Douglas	2001	

South of Scotland Ladies

1992	M Wilson	1997	J Anderson
1993	D Douglas	1998	D Sutton
1994	F Rennie	1999	D MacDonald
1995	C Meldrum	2000	M Pow
1996	S McMurtrie	2001	M Pow

South-Western Women's

1992	C Hall	1997	E Pilgrim
1993	E Fields	1998	C Lipscombe
1994	R Morgan	1999	J Clingan
1995	E Fields	2000	E Pilgrim
1996	B Morgan	2001	C Lipsombe

Warwickshire Ladies

1992	N Moutt	1997	C Dowling
1993	S Morgan	1998	C Dowling
1994	S Westhall	1999	C Dowling
1995	S Westhall	2000	T Atkin
1996	C Dowling	2001	C Dowling

Staffordshire Ladies

1992	P Hale	1997	K Edwards
1993	R Bolas	1998	K Edwards
1994	S Gallagher	1999	C Champion
1995	K Edwards	2000	J Peacock
1996	S Gallagher	2001	R Bolas

Western Division Ladies (Scotland)

1992	M McKinlay	1997	C Malcolm
1993	J Moodie	1998	A Laing
1994	V Melvin	1999	A Laing
1995	A Hendry	2000	A Laing
1996	K Fitzgerald	2001	C Hargan

Stirling and Clackmannan County Ladies

1992	A Rose	1997	S Grant
1993	H Stirling	1998	L Kenny
1994	H Stirling	1999	H Stirling
1995	S Grant	2000	H Stirling
1996	H Hume	2001	L Kenny

Wiltshire Ladies

1992	S Sutton	1997	J Lamb
1993	V Hanks	1998	W Martin
1994	S Sutton	1999	J Wheaton
1995	J Lamb	2000	J Wheaton
1996	J Lamb	2001	G Loughrey

Suffolk Ladies

1992	J Hall	1997	L Wright
1993	J Hall	1998	J Hockley
1994	J Hockley	1999	A Boatman
1995	J Hall	2000	L Steadman
1996	J Hockley	2001	A Boatman

Worcestershire Ladies

1992	L Montgomery	1997	N Lawrenson
1993	L Jones	1998	N Lawrenson
1994	N Lawrenson	1999	S Haslam
1995	S Tufnall	2000	S Nicklin
1996	N Lawrenson	2001	K Greenfield

Surrey Ladies

1992	J Thornhill	1997	J Thornhill
1993	S Lambert	1998	K Burton
1994	S Lambert	1999	R Prout
1995	J Thornhill	2000	K Knowles
1996	L McGowan	2001	L McGowan

Yorkshire Ladies

1992	N Buxton	1997	R Hudson
1993	N Buxton	1998	R Hudson
1994	N Buxton	1999	R Hudson
1995	R Hudson	2000	E Duggleby
1996	J Aldersley	2001	A Keighley

Sussex Ladies

1992	J Head	1997	C Court
1993	C Titcomb	1998	J Galway
1994	J Head	1999	P Carver
1995	Z Steel	2000	C Court
1996	C Court	2001	C Court

Women's Amateur Championships Overseas

Argentine Ladies Amateur	Astrid Gulesserian
Australian Ladies Amateur	Helen Beatty
Austrian Ladies Amateur	Kristina Rothengatter
Canadian Ladies Amateur	Lisa Meldrum
Czechoslovak Ladies Amateur	Petra Kvidova
Danish Ladies Amateur	Mira Bendevis
French Ladies Amateur	Maïtena Alsuguren
German Ladies Amateur	K Schallenberg
Italian Ladies Amateur	Virginia Costa
Japan Ladies Amateur	Mihoko Iseri
Luxembourg Ladies Amateur	Stephanie Doering (Ger)
Netherlands Ladies Amateur	Charlotte Heeres
New Zealand Ladies Amateur	Wendy Hawkes
Portuguese Ladies Amateur	Kirsty Taylor (Eng)
Spanish Ladies Open Amateur	Neloufar Azam (Sui)
Swiss Ladies Open Amateur	Denise Simon (Ger)

United States Ladies Amateur Championship (Inaugurated 1895)

Year	Winner	Runner-up	Venue	By
1895	CS Brown	N Sargent	Meadowbrook, NY	132
Changed to match play				
1896	B Hoyt	A Tunure	Morristown, NJ	2 and 1
1897	B Hoyt	N Sargent	Essex County, MA	5 and 4
1898	B Hoyt	M Wetmore	Ardsley, NY	5 and 3
1899	R Underhill	M Fox	Philadelphia, PA	2 and 1
1900	FC Griscom	M Curtis	Shinnecock Hills, NY	6 and 5
1901	G Hecker	L Herron	Baltusrol, NJ	5 and 3
1902	G Hecker	LA Wells	Brookline, MA	4 and 3
1903	B Anthony	JA Carpenter	Wheaton, IL	7 and 6
1904	GM Bishop	EF Sanford	Merion, PA	5 and 3
1905	P Mackay	M Curtis	Morris County, NJ	1 hole
1906	HS Curtis	MB Adams	West Newton, MA	2 and 1
1907	M Curtis	HS Curtis	Blue Island, IL	7 and 6
1908	KC Harley	TH Polhemus	Chevy Chase, MD	6 and 5
1909	D Campbell	N Barlow	Merion, PA	3 and 2
1910	D Campbell	GM Martin	Homewood, IL	2 and 1
1911	M Curtis	LB Hyde	Baltusrol, NJ	5 and 4
1912	M Curtis	N Barlow	Essex County, MA	3 and 2
1913	G Ravenscroft	M Hollins	Wilmington, DE	2 holes
1914	KC Harley	EV Rosenthal	Nassau, NY	1 hole
1915	F Vanderbeck	M Gavin (Eng)	Onwentsia, IL	3 and 2
1916	A Stirling	M Caverly	Belmont Springs, MA	2 and 1
In abeyance due to Word War I				
1919	A Stirling	M Gavin (Eng)	Shawnee, PA	6 and 5
1920	A Stirling	D Campbell Hurd	Cleveland, OH	5 and 4
1921	M Hollins	A Stirling	Deal, NJ	5 and 4
1922	G Collett	M Gavin (Eng)	Greenbrier, WV	5 and 4
1923	E Cummings	A Stirling	Westchester, NY	3 and 2
1924	D Campbell Hurd	MK Browne	Nyatt, RI	7 and 6
1925	G Collett	A Stirling Fraser	Clayton, MO	9 and 8
1926	H Stetson	E Goss	Merion, PA	2 and 1

Year	Winner	Runner-up	Venue	By
1927	MB Horn	M Orcutt	Garden City, NY	5 and 4
1928	G Collett	V Van Wie	Hot Springs, VA	13 and 12
1929	G Collett	L Pressler	Oakland Hills, MI	4 and 3
1930	G Collett	V Van Wie	Beverly Hills, CA	6 and 5
1931	H Hicks	G Collett Vare	Williamsville, NY	2 and 1
1932	V Van Wie	G Collett Vare	Peabody, MA	10 and 8
1933	V Van Wie	H Hicks	Highland Park, IL	4 and 3
1934	V Van Wie	D Traung	Whitemarsh Valley, PA	2 and 1
1935	G Collett Vare	P Berg	Interlachen, MN	3 and 2
1936	P Barton (Eng)	M Orcutt	Canoe Brook, NJ	4 and 3
1937	EL Page	P Berg	Memphis, TN	7 and 6
1938	P Berg	EL Page	Westmoreland, IL	6 and 5
1939	B Jameson	D Kirby	Wee Burn, CT	3 and 2
1940	B Jameson	J Cochran	Pebble Beach, CA	6 and 5
1941	E Hicks Newell	H Sigel	Brookline, MA	5 and 3
In abeyance due to Word War II				
1946	B Zaharias	C Sherman	Tulsa, OK	11 and 9
1947	L Suggs	D Kirby	Franklin, MI	2 holes
1948	G Lenczyk	H Sigel	Pebble Beach, CA	4 and 3
1949	D Porter	D Kielty	Merion, PA	3 and 2
1950	B Hanson	M Murray	Atlanta, GA	6 and 4
1951	D Kirby	C Doran	St Paul, MN	2 and 1
1952	J Pung	S McFedters	Portland, OR	2 and 1
1953	ML Faulk	P Riley	West Barrington, RI	3 and 2
1954	B Romack	M Wright	Sewickley, PA	4 and 2
1955	P Lesser	J Nelson	Charlotte, NC	7 and 6
1956	M Stewart	J Gunderson	Indianapolis, IN	2 and 1
1957	J Gunderson	AC Johnstone	Del Paso, CA	8 and 6
1958	A Quast	B Romack	Wee Burn, CT	3 and 2
1959	B McIntyre	J Goodwin	Washington, DC	4 and 3
1960	J Gunderson	J Ashley	Tulsa, OK	6 and 5
1961	A Quast	P Preuss	Tacomac, WA	14 and 13
1962	J Gunderson	A Baker	Rochester, NY	9 and 8
1963	A Quast	P Conley	Williamstown, MA	2 and 1
1964	B McIntyre	J Gunderson	Prairie Dunes, KA	3 and 2
1965	J Ashley	A Quast	Denver, CO	5 and 4
1966	J Gunderson Carner	JD Stewart Streit	Sewickley, PA	41st hole
1967	ML Dill	J Ashley	Pasadena, CA	5 and 4
1968	J Gunderson Carner	A Quast	Birmingham, MI	5 and 4
1969	C Lacoste (Fra)	S Hamlin	Las Colinas, TX	3 and 2
1970	M Wilkinson	C Hill	Wee Burn, CT	3 and 2
1971	L Baugh	B Barry	Atlanta, GA	1 hole
1972	M Budke	C Hill	St Louis, MO	5 and 4
1973	C Semple	A Quast	Montclair, NJ	1 hole
1974	C Hill	C Semple	Seattle, WA	5 and 4
1975	B Daniel	D Horton	Brae Burn, MA	3 and 2
1976	D Horton	M Bretton	Del Paso, CA	2 and 1
1977	B Daniel	C Sherk	Cincinnati, OH	3 and 1
1978	C Sherk	J Oliver	Sunnybrook, PA	4 and 3
1979	C Hill	P Sheehan	Memphis, TN	7 and 6
1980	J Inkster	P Rizzo	Prairie Dunes, KA	2 holes
1981	J Inkster	L Goggin (Aus)	Portland, OR	1 hole
1982	J Inkster	C Hanlon	Colorado Springs, CO	4 and 3
1983	J Pacillo	S Quinlan	Canoe Brook, NJ	2 and 1
1984	D Richard	K Williams	Seattle, WA	37th hole
1985	M Hattori (Jpn)	C Stacy	Pittsburgh, PA	5 and 4
1986	K Cockerill	K McCarthy	Pasatiempo, CA	9 and 7
1987	K Cockerill	T Kerdyk	Barrington, RI	3 and 2
1988	P Sinn	K Noble	Minikahda, MN	6 and 5
1989	V Goetze	B Burton	Pinehurst, NC	4 and 3
1990	P Hurst	S Davis	Canoe Brook, NJ	37th hole
1991	A Fruhwirth	H Voorhees	Prairie Dunes, KA	5 and 4
1992	V Goetze	A Sörenstam (Swe)	Kemper Lakes, IL	1 hole
1993	J McGill	S Ingram	San Diego, CA	1 hole
1994	W Ward	J McGill	Hot Springs, VA	2 and 1
1995	K Kuehne	A-M Knight	Brookline, MA	4 and 2
1996	K Kuehne	M Baena	Lincoln, NE	2 and 1
1997	S Cavalleri (It)	R Burke	Brae Burn, MA	5 and 4
1998	G Park (Kor)	J Chuasiriporn	Blackwolf Run, WI	7 and 6
1999	D Delasin	J Kang	Biltmore Forest, NC	4 and 3
2000	N Newton	L Myerscough	Biltmore Forest, NC	8 and 7

United States Ladies' Amateur Championship *continued*

2001 *at Flint Hills, Andover, KS*

Quarter Finals
Joo-Mi Kim (Kor) beat Virada Nirapathpongporn (Tha) 4 and 3
Nicole Perrot (Chi) beat Malinda Johnson 5 and 3
Meredith Duncan beat Kelli Kamimura 3 and 2
Emily Bastel beat Hilary Homeyer 2 and 1

Semi-Finals
N Perrot beat J-M Kim 3 and 2
M Duncan beat E Bastel 3 and 1

Final
Meredith Duncan beat Nicole Perrot at 37th

PART VI

Junior Tournaments and Events

Boys and Youths Tournaments

Boys Amateur Championship

Year	Winner	Runner-up	Venue	By
1921	ADD Mathieson	GH Lintott	Ascot	37th hole
1922	HS Mitchell	W Greenfield	Ascot	4 and 2
1923	ADD Mathieson	HS Mitchell	Dunbar	3 and 2
1924	RW Peattie	P Manuevrier (Fra)	Coombe Hill	2 holes
1925	RW Peattie	A McNair	Barnton	4 and 3
1926	EA McRuvie	CW Timmis	Coombe Hill	1 hole
1927	EW Fiddian	K Forbes	Royal Burgess	4 and 2
1928	S Scheftel	A Dobbie	Formby	6 and 5
1929	J Lindsay	J Scott-Riddell	Royal Burgess	6 and 4
1930	J Lindsay	J Todd	Fulwell	9 and 8
1931	H Thomson	F McGloin	Glasgow (Killermont)	5 and 4
1932	IS MacDonald	LA Hardie	Royal Lytham and St Annes	2 and 1
1933	PB Lucas	W McLachlan	Carnoustie	3 and 2
1934	RS Burles	FB Allpass	Moortown	12 and 10
1935	JDA Langley	R Norris	Royal Aberdeen	6 and 5
1936	J Bruen	W Innes	Birkdale	11 and 9
1937	IM Roberts	J Stewart	Bruntsfield	8 and 7
1938	W Smeaton	T Snowball	Moor Park	3 and 2
1939	SB Williamson	KG Thom	Carnoustie	4 and 2
1940-45	*Suspended during War*			
1946	AFD MacGregor	DF Dunstan	Bruntsfield	7 and 5
1947	J Armour	I Caldwell	Hoylake	5 and 4
1948	JD Pritchett	DH Reid	Kilmarnock (Barasssie)	37th hole
1949	H MacAnespie	NV Drew	St Andrews	3 and 2
1950	J Glover	I Young	Royal Lytham and St Annes	2 and 1
1951	N Dunn	MSR Lunt	Prestwick	6 and 5
1952	M Bonallack	AE Shepperson	Formby	37th hole
1953	AE Shepperson	AT Booth	Dunbar	6 and 4
1954	AF Bussell	K Warren	Hoylake	38th hole
1955	SC Wilson	BJK Aitken	Kilmarnock (Barassie)	39th hole
1956	JF Ferguson	CW Cole	Sunningdale	2 and 1
1957	D Ball	J Wilson	Carnoustie	2 and 1
1958	R Braddon	IM Stungo	Moortown	4 and 3
1959	AR Murphy	EM Shamash	Pollok	3 and 1
1960	P Cros (Fra)	PO Green	Olton	5 and 3
1961	FS Morris	C Clark	Dalmahoy	3 and 2
1962	PM Townsend	DC Penman	Royal Mid-Surrey	1 hole
1963	AHC Soutar	DI Rigby	Prestwick	2 and 1
1964	PM Townsend	RD Gray	Formby	9 and 8
1965	GR Milne	DK Midgley	Gullane	4 and 2
1966	A Phillips	A Muller	Moortown	12 and 11
1967	LP Tupling	SC Evans	Western Gailes	4 and 2
1968	SC Evans	K Dabson	St Annes Old Links	3 and 2
1969	M Foster	M Gray	Dunbar	37th hole
1970	ID Gradwell	JE Murray	Hillside	1 hole
1971	H Clark	G Harvey	Kilmarnock (Barassie)	6 and 5
1972	G Harvey	R Newsome	Moortown	7 and 5
1973	DM Robertson	S Betti (Ita)	Blairgowrie	5 and 3
1974	TR Shannon	A Lyle	Hoylake	10 and 9
1975	B Marchbank	A Lyle	Bruntsfield	1 hole
1976	M Mouland	G Hargreaves	Sunningdale	6 and 5
1977	I Ford	CR Dalgleish	Downfield	1 hole
1978	S Keppler	M Stokes	Seaton Carew	3 and 2
1979	R Rafferty	D Ray	Kilmarnock (Barassie)	6 and 5
1980	D Muscroft	A Llyr	Formby	7 and 6

1981	J Lopez (Esp)	R Weedon	Gullane	4 and 3
1982	M Grieve	G Hickman	Burnham and Barrow	37th hole
1983	JM Olazábal (Esp)	M Pendaries	Glenbervie	6 and 5
1984	L Vannett	A Mednick (Swe)	Royal Porthcawl	2 and 1
1985	J Cook	W Henry	Royal Burgess	5 and 4
1986	L Walker	G King	Seaton Carew	5 and 4
1987	C O'Carrol	P Olsson (Swe)	Barassie	3 and 1
1988	S Pardoe	D Haines	Formby	3 and 2
1989	C Watts	C Fraser	Nairn	5 and 3
1990	M Welch	M Ellis	Hunstanton	3 and 1
1991	F Valera (Esp)	R Walton	Montrose	4 and 3
1992	L Westerberg (Swe)	F Jacobson (Swe)	Royal Mid-Surrey	3 and 2
1993	D Howell	V Gustavsson (Swe)	Glenbervie	3 and 1
1994	C Smith	C Rodgers	Little Aston	2 and 1
1995	S Young	S Walker	Dunbar	7 and 6
1996	K Ferrie	M Pilkington	Littlestone	2 and 1
1997	S García (Esp)	R Jones	Saunton	6 and 5
1998	S O'Hara	S Reale (Ita)	Ladybank	1 hole
1999	A Gutierrez (Esp)	M Skelton	Royal St David's	1 hole
2000	D Inglis	D Skinns	Hillside	1 hole

2001 *at Ganton*

Quarter Finals
Pablo Martin (Esp) beat Stephen Lewton (Woburn) 1 hole
James Heath (Coombe Wood) beat Michael Skelton
(Hunley Hall) 2 and 1
Chris Clarke (Wath) beat Damian Ulrich (Sui) 4 and 3
Rafael Cabrera (Esp) beat Jorge Campillo (Esp) 1 hole

Semi-Finals
Martin beat Heath 1 hole
Cabrera beat Clarke 3 and 1

Final
P Martin beat R Cabrera 3 and 2

British Youths Open Amateur Championship

This championship bridged the gap between the Boys and the Men's tournaments from 1954 until 1995, when it was discontinued because it was no longer needed. The date on the schedule was used to introduce the Mid-Amateur (over 25s).

Year	Winner	Club	Venue	Score
1954	JS More	Swanston	Erskine	287
1955	B Stockdale	Royal Lytham & St Annes	Pannal	287
1956	AF Bussell	Coxmoor	Royal Burgess	287
1957	G Will	St Andrews	Pannal	290
1958	RH Kemp	Glamorganshire	Dumfries & County	281
1959	RA Jowle	Moseley	Pannal	286
1960	GA Caygill	Sunningdale	Pannal	279
1961	JS Martin	Kilbirnie Place	Bruntsfield	284
1962	GA Caygill	Sunningdale	Pannal	287
1963	AJ Low	St Andrews U	Pollok	283
1964	BW Barnes	Burnham & Berrow	Pannal	290
1965	PM Townsend	Porters Park	Gosforth Park	281
1966	PA Easterhouse	Dulwich & Sydenham Hill	Dalmahoy	219 (54 holes)
1967	PJ Benka	Addington	Copt Heath	278
1968	PJ Benka	Addington	Ayr Belleisle	281
1969	JH Cook	Calcot Park	Lindrick	289
1970	B Dassu	Italy	Royal Burgess	276
1971	P Elson	Coventry	Northamptonshire County	277
1972	AH Chandler	Regent Park (Bolton)	Glasgow Gailes	281
1973	SC Mason	Goring & Streatley	Southport & Ainsdale	284
1974	DM Robertson	Dunbar	Downfield	284
1975	N Faldo	Welwyn Garden City	Pannal	278
1976	ME Lewis	Henbury	Gullane	277
1977	AWB Lyle	Hawkstone Park	Moor Park	285
1978	B Marchbank	Auchterarder	East Renfrewshire	278
1979	G Brand jr	Knowle	Woodhall Spa	291
1980	G Hay	Hilton Park	Royal Troon	303
1981	T Antevik	Sweden	West Lancashire	290
1982	AP Parkin	Newtown	St Andrews New	280
1983	P Mayo	Newport	Sunningdale	290

British Youths Open Amateur Championship *continued*

Year	Winner	Club	Venue	Score
1984	R Morris	Padeswick & Buckley	Blairgowrie	281
1985	JM Olazábal	Spain	Ganton	281
1986	D Gilford	Trentham Park	Carnoustie	283
1987	J Cook*	Leamington & County	Hollinwell	283
1988	C Cevaer*	France	Royal Aberdeen	275
1989	M Smith*	Brokenhurst Manor	Ashburnham	285
1990	M Gronberg	Sweden	Southerness	275
1991	J Payne	Sandilands	Woodhall Spa	287
1992	W Bennett	Ruislip	Northumberland	283
1993	L Westwood	Worksop	Glasgow Gailes	278
1994	F Jacobson	Sweden	Royal St Davids	277

English Boys Stroke Play Championship (formerly Carris Trophy)

1935	R Upex	75 (18)	1961	DJ Miller	143	1981	D Gilford	290
1936	JDA Langley	152	1962	FS Morris	145	1982	M Jarvis	298
1937	RJ White	149	1963	EJ Threlfall	147	1983	P Baker	288
1938	IP Garrow	147	1964	PM Townsend	148	1984	J Coe	283
1939	CW Warren	149	1965	G McKay	145	1985	P Baker	286
1946	AH Perowne	158	1966	A Black	151	1986	G Evans	292
1947	I Caldwell	159	1967	RF Brown	147	1987	D Bathgate	289
1948	I Caldwell	152	1968	P Dawson	149	1988	P Page	284
1949	PB Hine	148	1969	ID Gradwell	150	1989	I Garbutt	285
1950	J Glover	144	1970	MF Foster	146	1990	M Welch	276
1951	I Young	154	1971	RJ Evans	146	1991	I Pyman	284
1952	N Thygesen	150	1972	L Donovan	143	1992	M Foster	286
1953	N Johnson	148	1973	S Hadfield	148	1993	J Harris	285
1954	K Warren	149	1974	KJ Brown	304	1994	R Duck	280
1955	ID Wheater	151	1975	A Lyle	270	1995	J Rose	266
1956	G Maisey	141	1976	H Stott	285	1996	G Storm	281
1957	G Maisey	145	1977	R Mugglestone	293	1997	D Griffiths	283
1958	J Hamilton	149	1978	J Plaxton	144	1998	S Godfrey	286
1959	RT Walker	152	1979	P Hammond	288	1999	D Porter	275
1960	PM Baxter	150	1980	MP McLean	290	2000	G Lockerbie	279

2001 *at Formby*

1	Matthew Richardson* (Pinner Hill)	70-68—138
2	Raphael De Sousa (Sui)	68-70—138
3	Farren Keenan (Royal Mid-Surrey)	68-71—139
	Alejandro Cañizares (Esp)	67-72—139

English Boys Under-16 Championship (McGregor Trophy)

1994	G Storm	291	1997	R Paolillo	285	2000	M Skelton	289
1995	J Rose	287	1998	MY Ali	280			
1996	E Molinari	291	1999	J Heath	280			

2001 *at Radcliffe-on-Trent*

1	Paul Waring (Bromborough)	69-70-73—212
2	Paul Fiddes (Bedlingtonshire)	74-71-72—217
3	Matthew Baldwin (Hesketh)	72-75-71—218

Fourth round abandoned – thunderstorm

IMSL Irish Boys Championship

Year	Winner	Runner Up	Venue	Score
1990	R Burns		Kilkenny	213
1991	R Coughlan	R Burns	Thurles	207
1992	J O'Sullivan	D Dunne	Athlone	210
1993	H Armstrong	C McMonagle/P Byrne	Warrenpoint	222
1994	P Byrne	R Leonard/A Thomas	Nenagh	209
1995	L Dalton	M McGreedy	Mullingar	222
1996	M Campbell	L Dalton	Galway	213
1997	M Hoey	D Jones	Galway	217
1998	D Jones	D O'Connor	Youghal	214
1999	M McTernan	M O'Sullivan	Kilkenny	210
2000	D McNamara	C Doran	Strandhill	268

2001 *at Donaghadee*

1	Michael McHugh* (Ballinasloe)	74-72-68-66—280
2	Kenneth Fahey (Connemara)	66-76-67-71—280
3	D Gleeson (Old Conna)	74-71-65-72—282
	M Mulryan (Athenry)	69-75-72-66—282

Irish Youths Open Amateur Championship

Year	Winner	Venue	Score	Year	Winner	Venue	Score
1980	J McHenry	Clandeboye	296	1991	R Coughlan	Lahinch	288
1981	J McHenry	Westport	303	1992	K Nolan	Clandeboye	275
1982	K O'Donnell	Mullingar	286	1993	CD Hislop	Co Sligo	279
1983	P Murphy	Cork	287	1994	B O'Melia	Tullamore	272
1984	JC Morris	Bangor	292	1995	S Young	Ballybunion	286
1985	J McHenry	Co Sligo	287	1996	S Young	Royal Portrush	291
1986	JC Morris	Carlow	280	1997	N Howley	Galway	284
1987	C Everett	Killarney	300	1998	A Murray	Headfort	281
1988	P McGinley	Malone	283	1999	G McDowall	Cork	284
1989	A Mathers	Athlone	280	2000	G McDowall	Malone	276
1990	D Errity	Dundalk	293				

2001 *at Enniscrone*

1	Michael Ryan (Grange)	77-71-78-72—298
2	Mark O'Sullivan (UCD/Galway)	74-77-76-72—299
3	Darren Crowe (Dunmurry)	73-78-73-79—303

Scottish Boys Championship

Year	Winner	Runner-up	Venue	By
1960	L Carver	S Wilson	North Berwick	6 and 5
1961	K Thomson	G Wilson	North Berwick	10 and 8
1962	HF Urquhart	S MacDonald	North Berwick	3 and 2
1963	FS Morris	I Clark	North Berwick	9 and 8
1964	WR Lockie	MD Cleghorn	North Berwick	1 hole
1965	RL Penman	J Wood	North Berwick	9 and 8
1966	J McTear	DG Greig	North Berwick	4 and 3
1967	DG Greig	I Cannon	North Berwick	2 and 1
1968	RD Weir	M Grubb	North Berwick	6 and 4
1969	RP Fyfe	IP Doig	North Berwick	4 and 2
1970	S Stephen	M Henry	North Berwick	38th hole
1971	JE Murray	AA Mackay	North Berwick	4 and 3
1972	DM Robertson	G Cairns	North Berwick	9 and 8
1973	R Watson	H Alexander	North Berwick	8 and 7
1974	DM Robertson	J Cuddihy	North Berwick	6 and 5
1975	A Brown	J Cuddihy	North Berwick	6 and 4
1976	B Marchbank	J Cuddihy	Dunbar	2 and 1
1977	JS Taylor	GJ Webster	Dunbar	3 and 2
1978	J Huggan	KW Stables	Dunbar	2 and 1
1979	DR Weir	S Morrison	West Kilbride	5 and 3
1980	R Gregan	AJ Currie	Dunbar	2 and 1
1981	C Stewart	G Mellon	Dunbar	3 and 2
1982	A Smith	J White	Dunbar	39th hole

Scottish Boys Championship *continued*

Year	Winner	Runner-up	Venue	By
1983	C Gillies	C Innes	Dunbar	38th hole
1984	K Buchan	L Vannet	Dunbar	2 and 1
1985	AD McQueen	FJ McCulloch	Dunbar	1 hole
1986	AG Tait	EA McIntosh	Dunbar	6 and 5
1987	AJ Coltart	SJ Bannerman	Dunbar	37th hole
1988	CA Fraser	F Clark	Dunbar	9 and 8
1989	M King	D Brolls	Dunbar	8 and 7
1990	B Collier	D Keeney	West Kilbride	2 and 1
1991	C Hislop	R Thorton	West Kilbride	11 and 9
1992	A Reid	A Forsyth	West Kilbride	2 and 1
1993	S Young	A Campbell	West Kilbride	4 and 2
1994	S Young	E Little	Dunbar	2 and 1
1995	S Young	M Donaldson	Royal Aberdeen	7 and 6
1996	S Whiteford	I McLaughlin	West Kilbride	3 and 2
1997	M Donaldson	L Rhind	Dunbar	1 hole
1998	S O'Hara	D Sutton	Murcar	2 holes
1999	L Harper	M Syme	West Kilbride	6 and 5
2000	S Buckley	M Risbridger	Dunbar	7 and 6

2001 *at Royal Aberdeen*

Quarter Finals

Steven Brown (Carnoustie) beat David Brodie (Newton Stewart) 5 and 3

Robert Kelly (Haddington) beat Scott Mann (Carnoustie) 4 and 3

Richard Gill (Craigmillar Park) beat Ross Nicol (Milngavie) 4 and 3

Richie Ramsay (Royal Aberdeen) beat Steven Taylor (Wishaw) 3 and 2

Semi-Finals

Brown beat Kelly 5 and 4

Gill beat Nicol 1 hole

Final

Steven Brown beat Richard Gill 6 and 4

Scottish Boys Stroke Play Championship

Year	Winner	Venue	Score	Year	Winner	Venue	Score
1970	D Chillas	Carnoustie	298	1985	G Matthew	Baberton	297
1971	JE Murray	Lanark	274	1986	G Cassells	Edzell	294
1972	S Martin	Montrose	280	1987	C Ronald	Lanark	287
1973	S Martin	Royal Burgess	284	1988	M Urquhart	Dumfries and County	280
1974	PW Gallacher	Lundin Links	290	1989	C Fraser	Stirling	282
1975	A Webster	Kilmarnock (Barassie)	286	1990	N Archibald	Monifieth	292
1976	A Webster	Forfar	292	1991	S Gallacher	Crieff	280
1977T	J Huggan	Renfrew	303	1992	S Gallacher	Monifieth	288
	L Mann			1993	J Bunch	Powfoot	292
1978	R Fraser	Arbroath	283	1994	S Young	Drumpellier	288
1979	L Mann	Stirling	289	1995	C Lee	Arbroath	284
1980	ASK Glen	Forfar	288	1996	M Brown	Dullatur	286
1981	J Gullen	Bellshill	296	1997	L Rhind	Downfield	287
1982	D Purdie	Monifieth	296	1998	G Holland	Burntisland	281
1983	L Vannet	Kilmarnock (Barassie)	286	1999	B Hume	Nairn Dunbar	281
1984	K Walker	Carnoustie	280	2000	C Ries (RSA)	Cawder	275

2001 *at Lanark*

1	Scott Jamieson (Cathkin Braes)	67-65-68-75—275
2	James McGhee (Duddingston)	71-71-68-68—278
3	Wallace Booth (Crieff)	71-65-70-72—278+

Scottish Boys Under-16 Stroke Play Championship

1990	G Davidson	W Linton	148	1996	P Whiteford	Bothwell	143
1991	D Patrick	R Musselburgh	152	1997	D Inglis	Glenbervie	139
1992	*Not played*			1998	D Inglis	Braehead	139
1993	S Lamond	Old Ranfurly	150	1999	G Murray	Lundin	141
1994	S Fraser	Crieff	142	2000	W Booth	The Hirsel	138
1995	C Campbell	Shotts	73 (18)				

2001 *at Edzell*

1	Chris Johnston (Dunbar)	71-72—143
2	Frazer Bone (Cardross)	75-70—145
3	Marc Gentle (Edzell)	73-73—146

Scottish Youths Stroke Play Championship

1979	A Oldcorn	Dalmahoy	217	1990	S Bannerman	Portpatrick & Stranraer	213
1980	G Brand jr	Monifieth & Ashludie	281	1991	D Robertson	Hilton Park	273
1981	S Campbell	Cawder and Keir	279	1992	R Russell	Nairn	296
1982	LS Mann	Leven and Scoonie	270	1993	CD Hislop	West Kilbride	284
1983	A Moir	Mortonhall	284	1994	S Gallacher	Crieff	275
1984	B Shields	Eastwood, Renfrew	280	1995	E Little	Irvine, Ayr	280
1985	H Kemp	East Kilbride	282	1996	E Little	Stranraer & Portpatrick	280
1986	A Mednick	Cawder	282	1997	S Young	Cawder	269
1987	K Walker	Bogside	291	1998	T Rice*	Bruntsfield/R. Burgess	287
1988	P McGinley	Ladybank & Glenrothes	281	1999	J Hendry*	Crieff & Aucterarder	142
1989	J Mackenzie	Longniddry	281	2000	J Hendry	Newmachar	285

2001 *at Crail*

1	Jamie McLeary (Glenrothes)	77-66-72-72 –287
2	Lee Harper (Musselburgh)	74-73-71-70—288
3	Martin Laird (Hilton Park)	73-70-74-73—290
	Kevin McAlpine (Alyth)	72-69-72-77—290

Welsh Boys' Championship

Year	Winner	Runner–up	Venue	By
1960	C Gilford	JL Toye	Llandrindod Wells	5 and 4
1961	AR Porter	JL Toye	Llandrindod Wells	3 and 2
1962	RC Waddilove	W Wadrup	Harlech	20th hole
1963	G Matthews	R Witchell	Penarth	6 and 5
1964	D Lloyd	M Walters	Conway	2 and 1
1965	G Matthews	DG Lloyd	Wenvoe Castle	7 and 6
1966	J Buckley	DP Owen	Holyhead	4 and 2
1967	J Buckley	DL Stevens	Glamorganshire	2 and 1
1968	J Buckley	C Brown	Maesdu	1 hole
1969	K Dabson	P Light	Glamorganshire	5 and 3
1970	P Tadman	A Morgan	Conway	2 and 1
1971	R Jenkins	TJ Melia	Ashburnham	3 and 2
1972	MG Chugg	RM Jones	Wrexham	3 and 2
1973	R Tate	N Duncan	Penarth	2 and 1
1974	D Williams	S Lewis	Llandudno	5 and 4
1975	G Davies	PG Garrett	Glamorganshire	20th hole
1976	JM Morrow	MG Mouland	Caernarvonshire	1 hole
1977	JM Morrow	MG Mouland	Glamorganshire	2 and 1
1978	JM Morrow	A Laking	Harlech	2 and 1
1979	P Mayo	M Hayward	Penarth	24th hole
1980	A Llyr	DK Wood	Llandudno (Maesdu)	2 and 1
1981	M Evans	P Webborn	Pontypool	5 and 4
1982	CM Rees	KH Williams	Prestatyn	2 holes
1983	MA Macara	RN Roderick	Radyr	1 hole
1984	GA Macara	D Bagg	Llandudno	1 hole
1985	B Macfarlane	R Herbert	Cardiff	1 hole
1986	C O'Carroll	GA Macara	Rhuddlan	1 hole
1987	SJ Edwards	A Herbert	Abergavenny	19th hole
1988	C Platt	P Murphy	Holyhead	2 and 1

Welsh Boys Championship *continued*

Year	Winner	Runner–up	Venue	By
1989	R Johnson	RL Evans	Southerndown	2 holes
1990	M Ellis	C Sheppard	Llandudno (Maesdu)	3 and 2
1991	B Dredge	A Cooper	Tenby	2 and 1
1992	Y Taylor	J Pugh	Wrexham	1 hole
1993	R Davies	S Raybould	Pyle and Kenfig	3 and 2
1994	R Peet	K Sullivan	Abergele & Pensarn	7 and 6
1995	M Palmer	O Pughe	Newport	4 and 3
1996	A Smith	M Griffiths	Borth & Ynyslas	at 19th hole
1997	A Lee	I Campbell	Glamorganshire	4 and 3
1998	M Setterfield	D Price	Llandudno	3 and 2
1999	C Mills	D Price	Neath	3 and 2
2000	R Narduzzo	G Dobson-Jones	Pwllheli	1 hole

2001 *at St Mellons*

Quarter Finals

Ben Briscoe (Old Colwyn) beat James Evans (Mold) 1 hole

Llewellyn Matthews (Southerndown) beat Ian Grove (Pontardawe) 5 and 4

Chris Cole (Monmouthshire) beat Stuart Clark (Whitchurch) 2 and 1

James Morgan (Alice Springs) beat Greg Williams (Pontypridd) 5 and 4

Semi-Finals

Briscoe beat Matthews 1 hole

Morgan beat Cole 1 hole

Final

J Morgan beat B Briscoe 3 and 2

Welsh Boys Stroke Play Championship *at Borth & Ynyslas*

1	J Morgan (Alice Springs)	74-75—149
2	C Chamberlain (Borth & Ynyslas)	72-78—150
3	O Duckett (Tenby)	76-77—153

Welsh Boys Under-15 Championship *at Creigiau*

1998	BM Briscoe	Aberdare	152
1999	L James	Aberdare	140
2000	Matthew Jones	Pontypridd	159

2001

1	Phillip Smith (Dewstow)	74-74—148
2	Adam Partington (Wrexham)	70-79—149
3	Rhys Williams (Brynhill)	79-72—151

Welsh Open Youths Championship

1998	M Hearne	Carmarthen	294
1999	D Price	Carmarthen	281
2000	Ben Welch	Cottrell Park	276

2001 *at Wrexham*

1	Tim Dykes (Wrexham)	68-68-76-69—281
2	J Williams (Pontypridd)	68-74-69-71—282
3	C Mills (Vale of Glamorgan)	69-73-72-73—287

Peter McEvoy Trophy *at Copt Heath*

1988	P Sefton	1993	S Webster	1998	J Rose
1989	D Bathgate	1994	J Harris	1999	D Porter
1990	P Sherman	1995	C Duke	2000	Z Scotland
1991	L Westwood	1996	M Pilkington		
1992	B Davis	1997	P Rowe		

2001

1	Ben Harvey (Didsbury)	73-67-74-66—280
2	Stephen Lewton Woburn)	72-73-70-73—288
3	Scott Jackson (Bramall Park)	72-73-74-70—289

R&A Junior Open (Boys and Girls)

1994	Orn Aevar Hjartanson (Isl)
1996	Antti Hiltunen (Fin)
1998	David Inglis (Sco)
2000	Steven Jeppeson (Swe) (Gold)
	Luis Cargiulo (Pan) (Silver)

International Foundation for Junior Golf (Boys)

1990	M Welch (Eng)	276	1996	M Eibe-Hastrup	281
1991	D Chopra (Ind)	281	1997	A Scott (Aus)	281
1992	F Jacobsen (Swe)	276	1998	A Smith (Eng)	292
1993	G Morales (Ven)	272	1999	S Robinson (Eng)	289
1994	S Webster (Eng)	275	2000	E Stenman (Fin)	203
1995	D Gleeson (Aus)	302			

2001 *at Augsburg, Germany*

1	Rick Kulacz (Aus)	68-69-72-73—282
2	Steven Bowditch (Aus)	68-74-71-70—283
3	Charl Schwartzel (RSA)	73-70-71-74—288

Team result [Boys/Girls]:1 Australia, 2 Africa, 3 South America, 4 Europe, 5 North America

Nick Faldo Junior Series

1997	N Dougherty		
1998	G Hyde	Loch Lomond	138
1999	N Dougherty	The Belfry	109 (27 holes)
2000	N Dougherty	Royal Liverpool	140

2001 *at Saunton*

1	Grigory Bondarenko* (Rus)	78-74—152
2	Roberto Laino (Bedford & County)	77-75—152

Under 18 winner: Stewart Clare (Horsley Lodge)   78-75—153

Under 17 winner: Stewart Clare (Horsley Lodge)   78-75—153

Under 16 winner: James Cundy (King's Lynn)   75-78—153

Under 15 winner: Roberto Laino (Bedford & County)   77-75—152

---

* *Winner after play-off*

Nick Faldo Junior Series (International Trophy)

1999	Etienne Bond (Fra)	The Belfry	111 (27 holes)
2000	A Kruger (RSA)	Royal Liverpool	150

2001 *at Saunton*

1	Peter Erofejeff (Fin)	76-77—153
2	Jacob Furland	83-76—159
3	Nicol Van Wyk	92-70—162

Midland Boys Amateur Championship

1989	M Wilson	1994	R Duck	1998	E Vernon
1990	ML Welch	1995	C Richardson	1999	C Stevenson
1991	S Drummond	1996T	S Walker	2000	J Prince
1992	S Drummond		K Cliffe		
1993	S Webster	1997	K Hale		

2001 *at Olton*

Oliver West (Robin Hood)	70-67—137

TEAM EVENTS

World Junior Team Championship

1995	USA	643
1996	Japan	625
1997	USA	864
1998	England	874
1999	England	863
2000	USA	859

2001 *at Asahi Kokusai, Japan*

1	South Africa	856
2	New Zealand	857
3	United States	858

European Boys Team Championship

1980	Spain	El Prat, Barcelona	1991	Sweden	Oslo, Norway
1981	England	Olgiata, Rome	1992	Scotland	Conwy, Wales
1982	Italy	Frankfurt, Germany	1993	Sweden	Ascona, Switzerland
1983	Sweden	Helsinki, Finland	1994	England	Vilamoura, Portugal
1984	Scotland	Royal St George's, England	1995	England	Woodhall Spa
1985	England	Troia, Portugal	1996	Spain	Gut Murstatten, Austria
1986	England	Turin, Italy	1997	Spain	Bled, Slovenia
1987	Scotland	Chantilly, France	1998	Ireland	Gullane, Scotland
1988	France	Renfrew, Scotland	1999	England	Uppsala, Sweden
1989	England	Lyckoma, Sweden	2000	Scotland	Noord Nederlandse
1990	Spain	Reykjavik, Iceland			

2001 *at Amber Baltic, Poland*

Final: Sweden beat Switzerland 4½-2½

Final Ranking: 1 Sweden 2 Switzerland 3 England 4 Spain

European Youths Team Championship

1990	Italy	Sweden	Turin, Italy
1992	Sweden	England	Helsinki, Finland
1994	Ireland	Sweden	Esbjerg, Denmark
1996	Scotland	Spain	Madeira
1998	Wales	Sweden	Royal Waterloo, Belgium
2000	England	Scotland	Kilmarnock (Barassie), Scotland

Great Britain & Ireland v Continent of Europe (Jacques Léglise Trophy)

1958	GB&I	11½–½	Moortown	1984	GB&I	6½–5½	Royal Porthcawl
1959	GB&I	7–2	Pollok	1985	GB&I	7½–4½	Royal Burgess
1960	GB&I	8–7	Olton	1986	Europe	8½–3½	Seaton Carew
1961	GB&I	11–4	Dalmahoy	1987	GB&I	7½–4½	Kilmarnock (Barassie)
1962	GB&I	11–4	Royal Mid-Surrey	1988	GB&I	5½–2½	Formby
1963	GB&I	12–3	Prestwick	1989	GB&I	7½–4½	Nairn
1964	GB&I	12–1	Formby	1990	GB&I	10–2	Hunstanton
1965	GB&I	12–1	Gullane	1991	GB&I	6½–5½	Montrose
1966	GB&I	10–2	Moortown	1992	GB&I	8–7	Royal Mid-Surrey
1967–76		Not played		1993	GB&I	8–7	Glenbervie
1977	Europe	7–6	Downfield	1994	GB&I	12½–2½	Little Aston
1978	Europe	7–6	Seaton Carew	1995	GB&I	9–6	Dunbar
1979	GB&I	9½–2½	Kilmarnock (Barassie)	1996	Europe	13–11	Woodhall Spa
1980	GB&I	7–5	Formby	1997	Europe	12½–11½	Aberdeen
1981	GB&I	8–4	Gullane	1998	GB&I	14–10	Villa d'Este, Italy
1982	GB&I	11–1	Burnham & Berrow	1999	GB&I	15–9	Burnham & Berrow
1983	GB&I	6½–5½	Glenbervie	2000	GB&I	16–8	Turnberry

2001 *at Chantilly, France* (European names first):

Captains: Charlie Westrup (Nor), Scott Macdonald (GBI)

First Day – **Foursomes**
de Sousa & Perrot beat Jackson & Wardrop
3 and 2
Adell & Lemke halved with Bowe & Turner
Brizzolari & Joachim Fourquet (Fra) beat Heath
& Keenan 4 and 3
Cabrera & Cañizares beat Porter & Buckley
5 and 4

Singles
Raphael de Sousa (Sui) beat Daniel Wardrop
(Didsbury) 5 and 3
Peter Erofejeff (Fin) lost to Niall Turner
(Muskerry) 2 and 1
Bilbo Perrot (Sui) lost to Scott Jackson
(Bramall Park) 2 holes
Niklas Lemke (Swe) beat Clancy Bowe
(Tramore) 5 and 4
Alejandro Cañizares (Esp) beat Chris
Cousins (Aberdare) 1 hole
Simone Brizzolari (Ita) halved with Stephen
Buckley (Prestonfield)
Gustav Adell (Swe) lost to Farren Keenan
(Royal Mid-Surrey) 2 and 1
Rafael Cabrera (Esp) lost to David Porter
(Stoneham) 4 and 3

Second Day – **Foursomes**
de Sousa & Perrot beat Jackson & Wardrop
2 and 1
Adell & Lemke beat Bowe & Turner 4 and 3
Brizzolari & Fourquet beat Buckley & Keenan
3 and 1
Cabrera & Cañizares beat Heath & Porter
1 hole

Singles
de Sousa halved with Wardrop
Perrot halved with Jackson
Adell beat Buckley 4 and 3
Erofejeff lost to Turner 5 and 3
Brizzolari beat James Heath (Coombe Wood)
2 and 1
Cañizares beat Cousins 6 and 5
Cabrera beat Keenan 3 and 2
Lemke lost to Porter 2 holes

Result: Europe 16, GBI 8

Boys Home Internationals (R&A Trophy) (Instituted 1985)

1985T	England/Ireland	Royal Burgess	1993	England	Glenbervie
1986	Ireland	Seaton Carew	1994	England	Little Aston
1987	Scotland	Barassie	1995	Scotland	Dunbar
1988	England	Formby	1996	England	Littlestone
1989	England	Nairn	1997	Ireland	Royal North Devon
1990	Scotland	Hunstanton	1998	England	St Andrews
1991	England	Montrose	1999	England	Conwy
1992T	Wales/Scotland	Royal Mid-Surrey	2000	England	Portmanock

2001 *at Moortown*

England beat Wales	9–6
Scotland beat Ireland	11–4
England halved with Ireland	7½–7½
Scotland beat Wales	11–3
Ireland beat Wales	10–4
England beat Scotland	11–4

Result: 1 England; 2 Ireland; 3 Scotland; 4 Wales

English Boys County Finals

2000   Surrey

2001 *at Longcliffe*

1   Lancashire
2   Warwickshire
3   Hampshire, Isle of Wight & Channel Islands
4   Gloucestershire

Scottish Boys Team Championship

2000   Lothians   355

2001 *at Prestwick*

1   Dunbartonshire   347
2   Renfrewshire   356
3   North-East   358

Girls and Junior Ladies Tournaments

Girls British Open Championship

Year	Winner	Runner–up	Venue	By
1960	S Clarke	AL Irvin	Kilmarnock (Barassie)	2 and 1
1961	D Robb	J Roberts	Beaconsfield	3 and 2
1962	S McLaren-Smith	A Murphy	Foxton Hall	2 and 1
1963	D Oxley	B Whitehead	Gullane	2 and 1
1964	P Tredinnick	K Cumming	Camberley Heath	2 and 1
1965	A Willard	A Ward	Formby	3 and 2
1966	J Hutton	D Oxley	Troon Portland	20th hole
1967	P Burrows	J Hutton	Liphook	2 and 1
1968	C Wallace	C Reybroeck	Leven	4 and 3
1969	J de Witt Puyt	C Reybroeck	Ilkley	2 and 1
1970	C Le Feuvre	Michelle Walker	North Wales	2 and 1
1971	J Mark	Maureen Walker	North Berwick	4 and 3
1972	Maureen Walker	S Cadden	Norwich	2 and 1
1973	AM Palli	N Jeanson	Northamptonshire	2 and 1
1974	R Barry	T Perkins	Dunbar	1 hole
1975	S Cadden	L Isherwood	Henbury	4 and 3
1976	G Stewart	S Rowlands	Pyle and Kenfig	5 and 4
1977	W Aitken	S Bamford	Formby Ladies	2 and 1
1978	M L de Lorenzi	D Glenn	Largs	2 and 1
1979	S Lapaire	P Smilie	Edgbaston	19th hole
1980	J Connachan	L Bolton	Wrexham	2 holes
1981	J Connachan	P Grice	Woodbridge	20th hole
1982	C Waite	M Mackie	Edzell	6 and 5
1983	E Orley	A Walters	Leeds	7 and 6
1984	C Swallow	E Farquharson	Maesdu	1 hole
1985	S Shapcott	E Farquharson	Hesketh	3 and 1
1986	S Croce	S Bennett	West Kilbride	5 and 4
1987	H Dobson	S Croce	Barnham Broom	19th hole
1988	A Macdonald	J Posener	Pyle and Kenfig	3 and 2
1989	M McKinlay	S Eriksson	Carlisle	19th hole
1990	S Cavalleri	E Valera	Penrith	5 and 4
1991	M Hjorth	J Moodie	Whitchurch	3 and 2
1992	M McKay	L Navarro	Northamptonshire	2 holes
1993	M McKay	A Vincent	Helensburgh	4 and 3
1994	A Vincent	R Hudson	Gog Magog	1 up
1995	A Lemoine	J Krantz	Northop Park	3 and 2
1996	M Monnet	C Laurens	Formby	4 and 3
1997	C Laurens	M Nagl	West Kilbride	2 and 1
1998	M Beautell	M Nagl	Holyhead	4 and 3
1999	S Pettersen	M Nagl	High Post	3 and 1
2000	T Calzavara	R Bell	Blairgowrie	1 hole

2001 *at Brough*

Quarter Finals

Clare Queen (Drumpellier) beat Dewi Claire Schreefel (Ned) 4 and 3

Azahara Munoz (Esp) beat Immaculda de la Lama (Esp) 2 and 1

Carmen Alonso (Esp) beat Louise Stahle (Swe) 2 and 1

Cassandra Kirkland (Fra) beat Guisy Paolillo (Ita) 5 and 3

Semi-Finals

Queen beat Munoz at 21st

Alonso beat Kirkland 3 and 2

Final

Clare Queen beat Carmen Alonso 1 hole

English Girls Close Championship

Year	Winner	Runner–up	Venue	By
1964	S Ward	P Tredinnick	Wollaton Park	2 and 1
1965	D Oxley	A Payne	Edgbaston	2 holes
1966	B Whitehead	D Oxley	Woodbridge	1 hole
1967	A Willard	G Holloway	Burhill	1 hole
1968	K Phillips	C le Feuvre	Harrogate	6 and 5
1969	C le Feuvre	K Phillips	Hawkstone Park	2 and 1
1970	C le Feuvre	M Walker	High Post	2 and 1
1971	C Eckersley	J Stevens	Liphook	4 and 3
1972	C Barker	R Kelly	Trentham	4 and 3
1973	S Parker	S Thurston	Lincoln	19th hole
1974	C Langford	L Harrold	Knowle	2 and 1
1975	M Burton	R Barry	Formby	6 and 5
1976	H Latham	D Park	Moseley	3 and 2
1977	S Bamford	S Jolly	Chelmsford	21st hole
1978	P Smillie	J Smith	Willesley Park	3 and 2
1979	L Moore	P Barry	Cirencester	1 hole
1980	P Smillie	J Soulsby	Kedleston Park	3 and 2
1981	J Soulsby	C Waite	Worksop	7 and 5
1982	C Waite	P Grice	Wilmslow	3 and 2
1983	P Grice	K Mitchell	West Surrey	2 and 1
1984	C Swallow	S Duhig	Bath	3 and 1
1985	L Fairclough	K Mitchell	Coventry	6 and 5
1986	S Shapcott	N Way	Huddersfield	7 and 6
1987	S Shapcott	S Morgan	Sandy Lodge	1 hole
1988	H Dobson	S Shapcott	Long Ashton	1 hole
1989	H Dobson	A MacDonald	Edgbaston	3 and 1
1990	C Hall	J Hockley	Bolton Old Links	20th hole
1991	N Buxton	C Hall	Knole Park	2 and 1
1992	F Brown	L Nicholson	Finham Park	2 and 1
1993	G Simpson	L Wixon	Cotswold Hills	7 and 5
1994	K Hamilton	S Forster	Whitley Bay	3 and 2
1995	R Hudson	G Nutter	Porters Park	2 and 1
1996	R Hudson	D Rushworth	Bedford	8 and 6
1997	S McKevitt	C Ritson	Kingsdown	3 and 2
1998	L Walters	K Lawton	Harrogate	5 and 4
1999	S Heath	A Cook	Chigwell	6 and 4
2000	S Walker	R Wood	Sheringham	1 hole

2001 *at Long Ashton*

Quarter Finals
Alex Marshall (North Foreland) beat Danielle
Roseberry (Durham City) 2 and 1
Samantha Lovell (Stock Brook Manor) beat
Zandie Lennox (Shirehampton Park) 2 and 1
Sophie Walker (Kenwick Park) beat Hayley
Charlick (Sundridge Park) 4 and 3
Lydia Sampson (Wentworth) beat Danielle
Masters (Rochester & Cobham) at 20th

Semi-Finals
Marshall beat Lovell 7 and 5
Walker beat Sampson 4 and 3

Final
Alex Marshall beat Sophie Walker 3 and 2

Irish Girls Championship

Year	Winner	Runner–up	Venue	By
1961	M Coburn	C McAuley	Portrush	6 and 5
1962	P Boyd	P Atkinson	Elm Park	4 and 3
1963	P Atkinson	C Scarlett	Donaghadee	8 and 7
1964	C Scarlett	A Maher	Milltown	6 and 5
1965	V Singleton	P McKenzie	Ballycastle	7 and 6
1966	M McConnell	D Hulme	Dun Laoghaire	3 and 2
1967	M McConnell	C Wallace	Portrush	6 and 5
1968	C Wallace	A McCoy	Louth	3 and 1
1969	EA McGregor	M Sheenan	Knock	6 and 5
1970	EA McGregor	J Mark	Greystones	3 and 2
1971	J Mark	C Nesbitt	Belfast	3 and 2

Year	Winner	Runner-up	Venue	By
1972	P Smyth	M Governey	Elm Park	1 hole
1973	M Governey	R Hegarty	Mullingar	3 and 1
1974	R Hegarty	M Irvine	Castletroy	2 holes
1975	M Irvine	P Wickham	Carlow	2 and 1
1976	P Wickham	R Hegarty	Castle	5 and 3
1977	A Ferguson	R Walsh	Birr	3 and 2
1978	C Wickham	B Gleeson	Killarney	1 hole
1979	L Bolton	B Gleeson	Milltown	3 and 2
1980	B Gleeson	L Bolton	Kilkenny	5 and 3
1981	B Gleeson	E Lynn	Donegal	1 hole
1982	D Langan	S Lynn	Headfort	5 and 4
1983	E McDaid	S Lynn	Ennis	20th hole
1984	S Sheehan	L Tormey	Thurles	6 and 4
1985	S Sheehan	D Hanna	Laytown/Bettystown	5 and 4
1986	D Mahon	T Eakin	Mallow	4 and 3
1987	V Greevy	B Ryan	Galway	8 and 7
1988	L McCool	P Gorman	Courtown	3 and 2
1989	A Rogers	R MacGuigan	Athlone	2 and 1
1990	G Doran	L McCool	Royal Portrush	3 and 1
1991	A Rogers	D Powell	Mallow	2 and 1
1992	M McGreevy	N Gorman	Kilkenny	2 and 1
1993	M McGreevy	E Dowdall	Strandhill	2 and 1
1994	A O'Leary	D Doyle	Mullingar	23rd hole
1995	P Murphy	G Hegarty	Douglas	5 and 4
1996	P Murphy	C Smyth	Warren Point	2 holes
1997	J Gannon	C Coughlan	Lay/Bettystown	3 and 2
1998	P Murphy	C Coughlan	Galway	5 and 4
1999	P Murphy	M Gillen	Tullamore	20th hole
2000	M Gillen	N Mullooly	Limerick	6 and 5

2001 *at Belvoir Park*

Quarter Finals

Amy Duggan (Killarney) beat Susie Hayes
  (Hermitage) 2 and 1
Dawn Marie Conaty {Ashbourne) beat Norma
  Mullooly (Donegal) 5 and 4
Heather Nolan (Shannon) beat Catherine Tucker
  (Limerick) 5 and 4
Karen Delaney (Carlow) beat Maria Dunne (Skerries)
  at 20th

Semi-Finals

Conaty beat Duggan 2 and 1
Nolan beat Delaney 5 and 4

Final

Dawn Marie Conaty beat Heather Nolan

Scottish Ladies Junior Open Stroke Play Championship

1960	J Greenhalgh	Ranfurly Castle	1981	K Douglas	Downfield
1961	D Robb	Whitecraigs	1982	J Rhodes	Dumfries & Galloway
1962	S Armitage	Dalmahoy	1983	S Lawson	Largs
1963	A Irvin	Dumfries	1984	S Lawson	Dunbar
1964	M Nuttall	Dalmahoy	1985	K Imrie	Ballater
1965	I Wylie	Carnoustie	1986	K Imrie	Dumfries and County
1966	J Smith	Douglas Park	1987	K Imrie	Douglas Park
1967	J Bourassa	Dunbar	1988	C Lambert	Baberton
1968	K Phillips	Dumfries	1989	C Lambert	Dunblane New
1969	K Phillips	Prestonfield	1990	J Moodie	Royal Troon
1970	B Huke	Leven	1991	C Macdonald	Alyth
1971	B Huke	Dalmahoy	1992	L McCool	North Berwick
1972	L Hope	Troon, Portland	1993	J Moodie	Dumfries and County
1973	G Cadden	Edzell	1994	C Agnew	Dumfries and County
1974	S Lambie	Stranraer	1995	R Hakkarainen (Fin)	Lanark
1975	S Cadden	Lanark	1996	L Moffat	Auchterarder
1976	S Cadden	Prestonfield	1997	L Nicholson	Stranraer
1977	S Cadden	Edzell	1998	V Laing	Duff House Royal
1978	J Connachan	Peebles	1999	L Kenny	Alyth
1979	A Gemmill	Royal Troon, Portland	2000	L Morton	Cardross
1980	J Connachan	Kirkcaldy			

Scottish Ladies Junior Open Stroke Play Championship *continued*

2001 *at Southerness*

1	Lynn Kenny (Stirling University)	72-70-75—217
2	Louise Kenney (Pitreavie)	76-71-76—223
3	Clare Queen (Drumpellier)	76-73-75—224

Scottish Girls Close Championship

Year	Winner	Runner–up	Venue	By
1960	J Hastings	A Lurie	Kilmacolm	6 and 4
1961	I Wylie	W Clark	Murrayfield	3 and 1
1962	I Wylie	U Burnet	West Kilbride	3 and 1
1963	M Norval	S MacDonald	Carnoustie	6 and 4
1964	JW Smith	C Workman	West Kilbride	2 and 1
1965	JW Smith	I Walker	Leven	7 and 5
1966	J Hutton	F Jamieson	Arbroath	2 holes
1967	J Hutton	K Lackie	West Kilbride	4 and 2
1968	M Dewar	J Crawford	Dalmahoy	2 holes
1969	C Panton	A Coutts	Edzell	23rd hole
1970	M Walker	L Bennett	Largs	3 and 2
1971	M Walker	S Kennedy	Edzell	1 hole
1972	G Cadden	C Panton	Stirling	3 and 2
1973	M Walker	M Thomson	Cowal, Dunoon	1 hole
1974	S Cadden	D Reid	Arbroath	3 and 1
1975	W Aitken	S Cadden	Leven	1 hole
1976	S Cadden	D Mitchell	Dumfries and County	4 and 2
1977	W Aitken	G Wilson	West Kilbride	2 holes
1978	J Connachan	D Mitchell	Stirling	7 and 5
1979	J Connachan	G Wilson	Dunbar	3 and 1
1980	J Connachan	P Wright	Dumfries and County	21st hole
1981	D Thomson	P Wright	Kilmarnock (Barassie)	2 and 1
1982	S Lawson	D Thomson	Montrose	1 hole
1983	K Imrie	D Martin	Leven	2 and 1
1984	T Craik	D Jackson	Peebles	3 and 2
1985	E Farquharson	E Moffat	West Kilbride	2 holes
1986	C Lambert	F McKay	Nairn	4 and 3
1987	S Little	L Moretti	Stirling	3 and 2
1988	J Jenkins	F McKay	Dumfries and County	4 and 3
1989	J Moodie	V Melvin	Kilmacolm	19th hole
1990	M McKay	J Moodie	Duff House Royal	3 and 2
1991	J Moodie	M McKay	Leven Links	5 and 4
1992	M McKay	L Nicholson	Powfoot	2 and 1
1993	C Agnew	H Stirling	Baberton	19th hole
1994	C Nicholson	L Moffat	Deeside	3 and 1
1995	L Moffat	F Lockhart	Paisley	2 and 1
1996	V Laing	C Hunter	Peebles	5 and 4
1997	V Laing	A Walker	Dunfermline	5 and 4
1998	V Laing	L Moffat	Kilmarnock Barassie	at 21st hole
1999	V Laing	L Wells	Edzell	3 and 2
2000	L Kenney	F Gilbert	Dunblane New	3 and 2

2001 *at Glenbervie*

Quarter Finals

Louise Kenney (Pitreavie) beat Clare Queen (Drumpellier) at 19th

Jenna Wilson (Strathaven) beat Rowena Hay (Nairn Dunbar) 3 and 2

Heather MacRae (Dunblane) beat Sjavon Dee Wilson (Brechin) 1 hole

Kate O'Sullivan (Paisley Bushes) beat Fiona Gilbert (Carnoustie) 2 and 1

Semi-Finals

Kenney beat Wilson 3 and 2

MacRae beat O'Sullivan 7 and 5

Final

Heather MacRae beat Louise Kenney 1 hole

Welsh Girls Championship

Year	Winner	Runner–up	Venue	By
1960	A Hughes	D Wilson	Llandrindod Wells	6 and 4
1961	J Morris	S Kelly	North Wales	3 and 2
1962	J Morris	P Morgan	Southerndown	4 and 3
1963	A Hughes	A Brown	Conway	8 and 7
1964	A Hughes	M Leigh	Holyhead	5 and 3
1965	A Hughes	A Reardon-Hughes	Swansea Bay	19th hole
1966	S Hales	J Rogers	Prestatyn	1 hole
1967	E Wilkie	L Humphreys	Pyle and Kenfig	1 hole
1968	L Morris	J Rogers	Portmadoc	1 hole
1969	L Morris	L Humphreys	Wenvoe Castle	5 and 3
1970	T Perkins	P Light	Rhuddlan	2 and 1
1971	P Light	P Whitley	Glamorganshire	4 and 3
1972	P Whitley	P Light	Llandudno (Maesdu)	2 and 1
1973	V Rawlings	T Perkins	Whitchurch	19th hole
1974	L Isherwood	S Rowlands	Wrexham	4 and 3
1975	L Isherwood	S Rowlands	Swansea Bay	1 hole
1976	K Rawlings	C Parry	Rhuddlan	5 and 4
1977	S Rowlands	D Taylor	Clyne	7 and 5
1978	S Rowlands	G Rees	Abergele	3 and 2
1979	M Rawlings	J Richards	St Mellons	19th hole
1980	K Davies	M Rawlings	Vale of Llangollen	19th hole
1981	M Rawlings	F Connor	Radyr	4 and 3
1982	K Davies	K Beckett	Wrexham	6 and 5
1983	N Wesley	J Foster	Whitchurch	4 and 2
1984	J Foster	J Evans	Pwllheli	6 and 5
1985	J Foster	S Caley	Langland Bay	6 and 5
1986	J Foster	L Dermott	Holyhead	3 and 2
1987	J Lloyd	S Bibbs	Cardiff	2 and 1
1988	L Dermott	A Perriam	Builth Wells	2 holes
1989	L Dermott	N Stroud	Carmarthen	4 and 2
1990	L Dermott	N Stroud	Padeswood and Buckley	6 and 4
1991	S Boyes	R Morgan	Clyne	3 and 1
1992	B Jones	S Musto	Rhuddlan	2 and 1
1993	K Stark	S Tudor-Jones	Radyr	3 and 2
1994	K Stark	J Evans	Wrexham	4 and 3
1995	E Pilgrim	L Davis	Borth and Ynyslas	2 holes
1996	K Stark	S Bourne	Monmouth	4 and 3
1997	R Brewerton	K Stark	Perhos	19th hole
1998	B Brewerton	L Archer	Old Padeswood	3 and 1
1999	K Phillips	R Last	Pontardawe	6 and 5
2000	K Phillips	J Pritchard	Northop Country Park	1 hole

2001 *at Carmarthen*

Quarter Finals

Sarah Jones (Pennard) beat Kate Phillips (Creigiau) 3 and 2

Natasha Morgan (Alice Springs) beat Lucy Gould (Bargoed) 2 and 1

Rosie Vaughan-Jones (Cardigan) beat Melanie Peake (Rhuddlan) 3 and 2

Janet Dyer (Aberystwyth) beat Stephanie Evans (Vale of Llangollen) 1 hole

Semi-Finals

Jones beat Morgan 3 and 2

Dyer beat Vaughan-Jones at 21st

Final

Sarah Jones beat Janet Dyer 3 and 2

International Foundation for Junior Golf (Girls)

2000	L Holm-Sorensem (Den)	1 hole

2001 *at Augsburg, Germany*

1	Nicole Perrot (Chi)	72-73-73-75—293
2	Sarah-Jane Kenyon (Aus)	70-72-73-80—295
3	Leandre Pieterse (RSA)	76-71-79-80—306

Nick Faldo Junior Series

1998	K Philips	Loch Lomond	154
1999	A Highgate	The Belfry	114 (27 holes)
2000	A Highgate	Royal Liverpool	146

2001 *at Saunton*

1	Ouliana Rotmistrova (Rus)	76-79—155
2	Natalie Haywood (Rotherham)	83-80—163
3	Kate Phillips (Creigiau)	79-86—165

TEAM EVENTS

European Girls Team Championship

2001 *at Oporto, Portugal*

Final: Spain beat Sweden 3½–1½

Final Ranking: 1 Spain, 2 Sweden, 3 France, 4 Germany

European Lady Juniors Team Championship

Year	Winner	Second	Venue
1990	Sweden	England	Shannon, Ireland
1992	Spain	Sweden	St Nom–la–Breteche, France
1994	Sweden	France	Gutenhof, Vienna, Austria
1996	France	Spain	Nairn, Scotland
1998	Spain	Italy	Oslo, Norway
2000	Italy	England	Castelconturbia GC, Italy

Girls Home Internationals (Stroyan Cup)

1966	Scotland	Troon (Portland)	1984	Scotland	Llandudno (Maesdu)
1967	England	Liphook	1985	England	Hesketh GC
1968	England	Leven	1986	England	West Kilbride
1969	England	Ilkley	1987	England	Barnham Broom
1970	England	North Wales	1988	England	Pyle and Kenfig
1971	England	North Berwick	1989	England	Carlisle
1972	Scotland	Royal Norwich	1990	England	Penrith
1973	Scotland	Northamptonshire County	1991	England	Whitchurch
1974	England	Dunbar	1992	Scotland	Moseley
1975	England	Henbury	1993	Scotland	Helensburgh
1976	Scotland	Pyle and Kenfig	1994	Scotland	Gog Magog
1977	England	Formby Ladies	1995	England	Northop
1978	England	Largs	1996	England	Formby
1979	England	Edgbaston	1997	England	Forfar
1980	England	Wrexham	1998	England	Mullingar
1981	England	Woodbridge	1999	Wales	High Post
1982	England	Edzell	2000	England	Downfield
1983	England	Alwoodley			

2001 *at Brough*

England beat Ireland	6–3
Scotland beat Wales	5–4
Ireland beat Wales	6–3
England beat Scotland	5½–3½
England beat Wales	7½–1½
Scotland beat Ireland	6½–2½

Result: 1 England   2 Scotland   3 Ireland   4 Wales

Golf Foundation Events

WEETABIX AGE GROUP CHAMPIONSHIPS

at The Warwickshsire

Boys

Year	Under 16	Under 15	Under 14
1990	C Lane (Kingsthorpe)	G Harris (Broome Manor)	P Collier (Limerick)
1991	G Harris (Broome Manor)	C Richardson (Burghley Park)	J Bajcer (Church Stretton)
1992	C Leach (Gillingham)	S Walker (Walmley)	D Kirton (Worksop)
1993	K Godfrey (St Enodoc)	S Young (Seascale)	J Rose (North Hants)
1994	A Smith (Rhondda)	T Hilton (Lewes)	A Smith (Enville)
1995	G Legg (Enmore Park)	S Robinson (Seaton Carew)	D Inglis (Glencorse)
1996	S Fromant (Orsett)	D Skinns (Canwick Park)	C Smith (Cotgrave Place)
1997	M Stam (Royal Liverpool)	G Lockerbie (Keswick)	S Robinson (Thames Ditton)
1998	D Rix (Malton and Norton)	M Skelton (Hunley Hall)	L Shepherd (Cleckheaton & District)
1999	W Schucksmith (Sand Moor)	J Moul (Stoke by Nayland)	T Robinson (Middlesbrough)
2000	M Jones (Upton-by-Chester)	S Taylor (Blundells Hill)	S Hufton (Copt Heath)

Year	Under 13
1990	S Walker (Boldmere)
1991	N Rossin (John O'Gaunt)
1992	D Main (Moray)
1993	S Godfrey (St Enodoc)
1994	D Tarbotton (Hull)
1995	D Porter (Wellow)
1996	J Maxwell (Muckhart)
1997	J Turner (Newmarket Links)
1998	C Paisley (Stocksfield)
1999	J Haugh (Salisbury and S Wilts)
2000	J Stevenson (Torrington)

2001

Under 16

James Cundy (Kings Lynn)	75-70—145
James Milmore (Whickham)	73-75—148
Darren Gould (Thornton)	74-75—149
Daniel Reilly (Birchwood)	77-73—150
Sean Fleming (Waterford)	71-80—151
Philip Ashenden (Forrester Park)	78-74—152

Under 15

Matthew Baldwin (Hesketh)	73-74—147
Damien McCartan (Ashbourne)	75-73—148
Alex Stevenson (Whittington Heath)	72-76—148
Phil Smith (Dewstow)	80-71—151
Ben Evans (East Sussex)	77-76—153

Under 14

Tom Chambers (Coxmoor)	76-76—152
Tom Murtagh (Truro)	76-77—153
Ben Smith (Bowood Park)	80-76—156
Ian Winstanley (Warrington)	81-78—159

Weetabix Age Group Championships *continued*

Under 13

Zach Gould (Vale of Glamorgan)	74-71—145
Tony Mitchell (Redbourn)	78-72—150
Lewis Edmunds (West Cornwall)	81-71—152
Leigh Pritchard (Maxstoke Park)	80-75—155
Alex Kippen (Enmore Park)	76-81—157

Girls

Year	Under 17	Under 16	Under 15
1990		T Poulton (Boyce Hill)	V Hanks (Broome Manor)
1991		G Simpson (Cleckheaton & District)	D Doyle (Lahinch)
1992		H Stirling (Bridge of Allan)	G Nutter (Prestwich)
1993		K Wrigglesworth (Hornsea)	R Hudson (Wheatley)
1994		L Meredith (Wentworth)	L Moffat (W. Kilbride)
1995	R Hudson (Wheatley)	L Moffat (W. Kilbride)	V Laing (Musselburgh)
1996	K Fisher (Leyland)	F More (Lindrick)	L Archer (Lilleshall Hall)
1997	V Laing (Musselburgh)	R Bell (Northcliff)	L Kenney (Pitreavie)
1998	J Pritchard (Tredegar Park)	L Archer (Lilleshall Hall)	A Marshall (Burghley Park)
1999	P Willett (Enfield)	H MacRae (Callander)	A Marshall (Burghley Park)
2000	C Queen (Drumpelier)	L Eastwood (Yelverton)	N Haywood (Rotherham)

2001

Under 17

Laura Eastwood (Yelverton)	75-78—153
Stephanie Evans (Vale of Llangollen)	80-84—164
Rebecca Godfrey (Dewstow)	84-81—165
Laura Bee (Boldon)	87-79—166
Gillian Davidson (Saline)	88-80—168
Merelina Byford (Bury St Edmunds)	85-84—169

Under 16

Natalie Haywood (Rotherham)	74-71—145
Louise Fleming (The Hirsel)	80-85—165
Laura Weatherill (Gower)	81-85—166
Katie Gellatly (Hornsea)	85-85—170
Katie Thomson (Kintore)	87-85—172

Under 15

Felicity Johnson (Harborne)	82-74—156
Kyung Hae Lee (Castle)	83-76—159
Laura Harvey (Huddersfield)	82-80—162
Melissa Reid (Chevin)	81-81—162
Kerry-Anne Haskell (Knighton Heath)	89-74—163
Hannah Ralph (Goodwood)	87-77—164

Duke of York Trophy Winners (For best 36-hole aggregate)

Year	Boys	Girls
1991	Gary Harris (Broome Manor)	Georgina Simpson (Cleckheaton)
1992	Christopher Leach (Gillingham)	Heather Stirling (Bridge of Allan)
1993	Kristian Godfrey (St Enodoc)	Katy Wrigglesworth (Hornsea)
1994	Alex Smith (Rhondda)	Lisa Meredith (Wentworth)
1995	Gavin Legg (Enmore Park)	Rebecca Hudson (Wheatley)
1996	Stuart Fromant (Orsett)	Fame More (Lindrick)
1997	Marcus Stam (Royal Liverpool)	Louise Kenney (Pitreavie)
1998	Darren Rix (Malton & Norton)	Laura Archer (Lilleshall Hall)
1999	William Shucksmith (Sand Moor)	Alexandra Marshall (Burghley Park) and Polly Willett (Enfield)
2000	Sam Hufton (Copt Heath)	Natalie Haywood (Rotherham)
2001	James Cundy (King's Lynn)	Natalie Haywood (Rotherham)

Golf Foundation Schools Team Championship (for the R&A Trophy)

Year	Winner	Country	Venue
1990	Lycée Bellevue	France	St Andrews
1991	Lycée Bellevue	France	Sunningdale
1992	Lycée Bellevue	France	St Andrews
1993	Lycée Bellevue	France	Gleneagles
1994	Lycée Bellevue	France	St Andrews
1995	Kelvin Grove High School	Australia	Sunningdale
1996	Welkom Gymnasium	South Africa	Blairgowrie
1997	Lycée Bellevue	France	Loch Lomond
1998	Damelin College, Randburg	South Africa	Sunningdale
1999	Kooralbyn International School	Australia	St Andrews
2000	Rotorua Boys' High School	New Zealand	Royal County Down

2001 *at The Berkshire GC*

1 New Zealand
Rotorua Boys' High School, Rotorua

Bradley Iles	70-72—142	
Sam Hunt	72-68—140	
Mathew Holten	75-73—148	
		430

2 Australia
St Bede's College, Victoria

Richard Slade	72-72—144	
Andrew Tampion	75-69—144	
Fraser Tull	74-72—146	
		434

3 France
Lycée Bellevue, Toulouse

Yohann Alazard	76-73—149	
Benjamin Blanchard	83-72—155	
Loic Salgado	79-73—152	
		456

4 England
Millfield School, Somerset

Sam Clark	81-79—160	
Harry Diamond	77-73—150	
Ben Evans	80-74—154	
		464

5 South Africa
Pretoria Boys High School

Sean Gillmer	86-82—168	
Corne Maritz	80-73—153	
Chris Thiart	79-76—155	
		476

6 Sweden
Njudungs Gymnasie Skola, Vetlanda

Daniel Gustavsson	83-74—157	
Linda Svensson†	80-84—164	
Maria Svensson†	77-80—157	
		478

7 Germany
Gymnasium Auf Der Karthouse

Daniel Froreich	74-82—156	
Patrick Niederdrenk	80-73—153	
Gunar Petersen	88-84—172	
		481

8 Ireland
Garbally College, Co.Galway

James Barton	80-73—153	
Michael McHugh	88-72—160	
John Paul O'Gara	86-82—168	
		481

9 Scotland
Dunfermline High School

Callum Macaulay	73-70—143	
John Maxwell	81-79—160	
Barry Nelson	93-87—180	
		483

10 Wales
Hawthorn High School, Pontypridd

Nicholas Davies	86-88—174	
Huw Priestland	82-85—167	
Owen Rees	83-79—162	
		503

11 Netherlands
Thorbecke Lyceum

Stefan Kalmeyer	90-96—186	
Varin Schilperoord	80-76—156	
Viktor Tybout	93-79—172	
		514

† *Girls received two courtesy shots per round*

PGA European Tour Trophy (For best individual)

Sam Hunt, New Zealand   72-68—140

Golf Foundation Award Winners

Year	Winner	Club
1982	Lindsey Anderson	Tain
1983	Nigel Osborne Clarke	Shirehampton
1984	Wayne Henry	Redbourn
1985	David Grantham	Hull
1986	Matthew Stanford	Saltford
1987	Jane Marchant	Whittington Barracks
1988	*Boys:* Ian Garbutt	Wheatley
	Girls: Lisa Dermott	St Melyd
1989	*Boys:* Lee Westwood	Worksop
	Girls: Lynn McCool	Strabane
1990	*Boys:* Keith Law	Forfar
	Girls: Mhairi McKay	Turnberry
1991	*Boys:* Gary Harris	Broome Manor
	Girls: Nicola Buxton	Woodsome Hall
1992	*Boys:* Shaun Devenney	Strabane
	Girls: Mhairi McKay	Turnberry
1993	*Boys:* Craig Williams	Greigiau
	Girls: Georgina Simpson	Cleckheaton & Dist
1994	*Boys:* Denny Lucas	Worksop
	Girls: Rebecca Hudson	Wheatley
1995	*Boys:* Justin Rose	North Hants
	Girls: Rebecca Hudson	Wheatley
1996	*Boys:* Mark Pilkington	Nefyn & District GC and Pwllheli
	Girls: Fame More	Chesterfield GC and Lindrick GC
1997	*Boys:* Nicholas Dougherty	Shaw Hill, Lancs
	Girls: Rebecca Brewerton	Abergele & Pensarn
1998	*Boys:* Steven O'Hara	Colville Park
	Girls: Vikki Laing	Musselburgh
1999	*Boys:* Barry Hume	Haggs Castle
	Girls: Rebecca Brewerton	Abergele
2000	*Boys:* David Inglis (Glencorse)	
	Girls: Sophie Walker (Kenwick Park)	

2001 winners to be decided in early 2002

† *Girls received two courtesy shots per round*

New region added to Faldo Junior Series for 2002

Nick Faldo has reacted to record demand for his Faldo Junior Series by adding an extra region and three new venues to the itinerary for 2002. The revamped 2002 itinerary will feature six regions:

Region	Venue	Date
SE England	Walton Heath (Surrey)	March 28
	Royal St George's (Kent)	April 24
	Frilford Heath (Oxon)	May 8
SW England & S Wales	St Mellion (Cornwall)	May 2
	Saunton (Devon)	May 23
	Royal Porthcawl (Mid Glamorgan)	June 24
Midland & E Anglia	Royal West Norfolk (Norfolk)	March 22
	Woburn (Bucks)	April 5
	Marriott Forest of Arden (Warwicks)	August 28
NW England & N Wales	Portal (Cheshire)	April 23
	Royal St David's (Gwynedd)	July 18
	Royal Liverpool (Merseyside)	August 5
NE England	Lindrick (Notts)	May 16
	De Vere Slaley Hall (Northumberland)	May 31
	Ganton (North Yorkshire)	August 22
Scotland	Royal Dornoch (Highland)	April 9
	Loch Lomond (Dunbartonshire)	April 16
	Blairgowrie (Perthshire)	July 2
Final	Date and venue to be confirmed	

Schoolboys set junior record for fastest round

Eighteen junior golfers (all aged under 18) have established a junior record for the fastest round in golf. Last October at the Cranford School Golf Course, an English Golf Union affiliated course, they completed 18 holes in 13 minutes and two seconds.

They achieved their time at their third attempt having trimmed two minutes off their first time. They failed, however, to beat the existing adult record set by 91 golfers at the Paradise Golf Club in Arizona in 1992. The time: 11 minutes 24 seconds.

PART VII
Awards

Awards

Association of Golf Writers' Trophy (Awarded to the man or woman who, in the opinion of golf writers, has done most for European golf during the year)

1951 Max Faulkner	1975 Golf Foundation
1952 Miss Elizabeth Price	1976 GB&I Eisenhower Trophy Team
1953 Joe Carr	1977 Christy O'Connor
1954 Mrs Roy Smith (Miss Frances Stephens)	1978 Peter McEvoy
1955 Ladies' Golf Union's Touring Team	1979 Severiano Ballesteros
1956 John Beharrell	1980 Sandy Lyle
1957 Dai Rees	1981 Bernhard Langer
1958 Harry Bradshaw	1982 Gordon Brand Jr
1959 Eric Brown	1983 Nick Faldo
1960 Sir Stuart Goodwin (sponsor of international golf)	1984 Severiano Ballesteros
1961 Commdr Charles Roe (ex-hon secretary, PGA)	1985 European Ryder Cup Team
1962 Mrs Marley Spearman, British Ladies' Champion 1961–1962	1986 GB&I Curtis Cup Team
	1987 European Ryder Cup Team
1963 Michael Lunt, Amateur Champion, 1963	1988 Sandy Lyle
1964 GB&I Eisenhower Trophy Team	1989 Great Britain & Ireland Walker Cup Team
1965 Gerald Micklem, golf administrator, President, English Golf Union	1990 Nick Faldo
	1991 Severiano Ballesteros
1966 Ronnie Shade	1992 European Solheim Cup Team
1967 John Panton	1993 Bernhard Langer
1968 Michael Bonallack	1994 Laura Davies
1969 Tony Jacklin	1995 European Ryder Cup Team
1970 Tony Jacklin	1996 Colin Montgomerie
1971 Great Britain & Ireland Walker Cup Team	1997 Alison Nicholas
1972 Miss Michelle Walker	1998 Lee Westwood
1973 Peter Oosterhuis	1999 Sergio García
1974 Peter Oosterhuis	2000 Lee Westwood

Harry Vardon Trophy (Awarded to the PGA member heading the Order of Merit at the end of the season)

1937	Charles Whitcombe	1962	Christy O'Connor	1982	Greg Norman
1938	Henry Cotton	1963	Neil Coles	1983	Nick Faldo
1939	Roger Whitcombe	1964	Peter Alliss	1984	Bernhard Langer
1940–45	In abeyance	1965	Bernard Hunt	1985	Sandy Lyle
1946	Bobby Locke	1966	Peter Alliss	1986	Severiano Ballesteros
1947	Norman Von Nida	1967	Malcolm Gregson	1987	Ian Woosnam
1948	Charlie Ward	1968	Brian Huggett	1988	Severiano Ballesteros
1949	Charlie Ward	1969	Bernard Gallacher	1989	Ronan Rafferty
1950	Bobby Locke	1970	Neil Coles	1990	Ian Woosnam
1951	John Panton	1971	Peter Oosterhuis	1991	Severiano Ballesteros
1952	Harry Weetman	1972	Peter Oosterhuis	1992	Nick Faldo
1953	Flory van Donck	1973	Peter Oosterhuis	1993	Colin Montgomerie
1954	Bobby Locke	1974	Peter Oosterhuis	1994	Colin Montgomerie
1955	Dai Rees	1975	Dale Hayes	1995	Colin Montgomerie
1956	Harry Weetman	1976	Severiano Ballesteros	1996	Colin Montgomerie
1957	Eric Brown	1977	Severiano Ballesteros	1997	Colin Montgomerie
1958	Bernard Hunt	1978	Severiano Ballesteros	1998	Colin Montgomerie
1959	Dai Rees	1979	Sandy Lyle	1999	Colin Montgomerie
1960	Bernard Hunt	1980	Sandy Lyle	2000	Lee Westwood
1961	Christy O'Connor	1981	Bernhard Langer	2001	Retief Goosen

Sir Henry Cotton
European Rookie of the Year

1960 Tommy Goodwin	1982 Gordon Brand Jr
1961 Alex Caygill	1983 Grant Turner
1962 *No Award*	1984 Philip Parkin
1963 Tony Jacklin	1985 Paul Thomas
1964 *No Award*	1986 José Maria Olazàbal
1966 Robin Liddle	1987 Peter Baker
1967 *No Award*	1988 Colin Montgomerie
1968 Bernard Gallacher	1989 Paul Broadhurst
1969 Peter Oosterhuis	1990 Russell Claydon
1970 Stuart Brown	1991 Per-Ulrik Johansson
1971 David Llewellyn	1992 Jim Payne
1972 Sam Torrance	1993 Gary Orr
1973 Philip Elson	1994 Jonathan Lomas
1974 Carl Mason	1995 Jarmo Sandelin
1975 *No Award*	1996 Thomas Bjorn
1976 Mark James	1997 Scott Henderson
1977 Nick Faldo	1998 Olivier Edmond
1978 Sandy Lyle	1999 Sergio García
1979 Mike Miller	2000 Ian Poulter
1980 Paul Hoad	2001 Paul Casey
1981 Jeremy Bennett	

Daily Telegraph Woman Golfer of the Year

1982	Jane Connachan
1983	Jill Thornhill
1984	Gillian Stewart and Claire Waite
1985	Belle Robertson
1986	GB&I Curtis Cup Team
1987	Linda Bayman
1988	GB&I Curtis Cup Team
1989	Helen Dobson
1990	Angela Uzielli
1991	Joanne Morley
1992	GB&I Curtis Cup Team, Captain Liz Boatman
1993	Catriona Lambert and Julie Hall
1994	GB&I Curtis Cup Team, Captain Liz Boatman
1995	Julie Hall
1996	GB&I Curtis Cup Team
1997	Alison Rose
1998	Kim Andrew
1999	Welsh International Team
2000	Rebecca Hudson
2001	Rebecca Hudson

Arnold Palmer Award

Awarded to the US PGA Tour leading money-winner

1981 Tom Kite	1992 Fred Couples
1982 Craig Stadler	1993 Nick Price
1983 Hal Sutton	1994 Nick Price
1984 Tom Watson	1995 Greg Norman
1985 Curtis Strange	1996 Tom Lehman
1986 Greg Norman	1997 Tiger Woods
1987 Paul Azinger	1998 David Duval
1988 Curtis Strange	1999 Tiger Woods
1989 Tom Kite	2000 Tiger Woods
1990 Greg Norman	2001 Tiger Woods
1991 Corey Pavin	

Bobby Jones Award
Awarded by USGA for distinguished sportsmanship in golf

1955 Francis Ouimet	1979 Tom Kite
1956 Bill Campbell	1980 Charles Yates
1957 Babe Zaharias	1981 JoAnne Carner
1958 Margaret Curtis	1982 Billy Joe Patton
1959 Findlay Douglas	1983 Maureen Garrett
1960 Charles Evans Jr	1984 Jay Sigel
1961 Joe Carr	1985 Fuzzy Zoeller
1962 Horton-Smith	1986 Jess W Sweetser
1963 Patty Berg	1987 Tom Watson
1964 Charles Coe	1988 Isaac B Grainger
1965 Mrs Edwin Vare	1989 Chi-Chi Rodriquez
1966 Gary Player	1990 Peggy Kirk Bell
1967 Richard Tufts	1991 Ben Grenshaw
1968 Robert Dickson	1992 Gene Sarazen
1969 Gerald Micklem	1993 PJ Boatwright Jr
1970 Roberto De Vicenzo	1994 Lewis Oehmig
1971 Arnold Palmer	1995 Herbert Warren
1972 Michael Bonallack	Wind
1973 Gene Littler	1996 Betsy Rawls
1974 Byron Nelson	1997 Fred Brand
1975 Jack Nicklaus	1998 Nancy Lopez
1976 Ben Hogan	1999 Ed Updegraff
1977 Joseph C Dey	2000 Barbara McIntyre
1978 Bob Hope and	2001 Thomas Cousins
Bing Crosby	

The US Vardon Trophy

The award is made by the PGA of America to the member of the US Tour who completes 60 rounds or more, with the lowest scoring average over the calendar year.

1948 Ben Hogan	1975 Bruce Crampton
1949 Sam Snead	1976 Don January
1950 Sam Snead	1977 Tom Watson
1951 Lloyd Mangrum	1978 Tom Watson
1952 Jack Burke	1979 Tom Watson
1953 Lloyd Mangrum	1980 Lee Trevino
1954 Ed Harrison	1981 Tom Kite
1955 Sam Snead	1982 Tom Kite
1956 Cary Middlecoff	1983 Ray Floyd
1957 Dow Finsterwald	1984 Calvin Peete
1958 Bob Rosburg	1985 Don Pooley
1959 Art Wall	1986 Scott Hoch
1960 Billy Casper	1987 Dan Pohl
1961 Arnold Palmer	1988 Chip Beck
1962 Arnold Palmer	1989 Greg Norman
1963 Billy Casper	1990 Greg Norman
1964 Arnold Palmer	1991 Fred Couples
1965 Billy Casper	1992 Fred Couples
1966 Billy Casper	1993 Nick Price
1967 Arnold Palmer	1994 Greg Norman
1968 Billy Casper	1995 Steve Elkington
1969 Dave Hill	1996 Tom Lehman
1970 Lee Trevino	1997 Nick Price
1971 Lee Trevino	1998 David Duval
1972 Lee Trevino	1999 Tiger Woods
1973 Bruce Crampton	2000 Tiger Woods
1974 Lee Trevino	2001 Tiger Woods

Jack Nicklaus Award
Decided by US PGA Tour members ballot

1990	Wayne Levi	1996	Tom Lehman
1991	Fred Couples	1997	Tiger Woods
1992	Fred Couples	1998	Mark O'Meara
1993	Nick Price	1999	Tiger Woods
1994	Nick Price	2000	Tiger Woods
1995	Greg Norman	2001	*Not yet decided*

US PGA Player of the Year

1948	Ben Hogan	1975	Jack Nicklaus
1949	Sam Snead	1976	Jack Nicklaus
1950	Ben Hogan	1977	Tom Watson
1951	Ben Hogan	1978	Tom Watson
1952	Julius Boros	1979	Tom Watson
1953	Ben Hogan	1980	Tom Watson
1954	Ed Furgol	1981	Bill Rogers
1955	Doug Ford	1982	Tom Watson
1956	Jack Burke	1983	Hal Sutton
1957	Dick Mayer	1984	Tom Watson
1958	Dow Finsterwald	1985	Lanny Wadkins
1959	Art Wall	1986	Bob Tway
1960	Arnold Palmer	1987	Paul Azinger
1961	Jerry Barner	1988	Curtis Strange
1962	Arnold Palmer	1989	Tom Kite
1963	Julius Boros	1990	Nick Faldo
1964	Ken Venturi	1991	Corey Pavin
1965	Dave Marr	1992	Fred Couples
1966	Billy Casper	1993	Nick Price
1967	Jack Nicklaus	1994	Nick Price
1968	*not awarded*	1995	Greg Norman
1969	Orville Moody	1996	Tom Lehman
1970	Billy Casper	1997	Tiger Woods
1971	Lee Trevino	1998	Mark O'Meara
1972	Jack Nicklaus	1999	Tiger Woods
1973	Jack Nicklaus	2000	Tiger Woods
1974	Johnny Miller	2001	Tiger Woods

US PGA Rookie of the Year
Decided by PGA Tour members ballot

1990	Robert Gamez	1996	Tiger Woods
1991	John Daly	1997	Stewart Cink
1992	Mark Carnevale	1998	Steve Flesch
1993	Vijay Singh	1999	Carlos Franco
1994	Ernie Els	2000	Michael Clark II
1995	Woody Austin	2001	*Not yet decided*

US LPGA Rookie of the Year

1980	M Van Hoose	1991	B Burton
1981	P Sheehan	1992	H Alfredsson (Swe)
1982	P Rizzo	1993	S Strudwick (Eng)
1983	S Farwig	1994	A Sörenstam (Swe)
1984	J Inkster	1995	P Hurst
1985	P Hammel	1996	K Webb (Aus)
1986	J Rosenthal	1997	L Hackney (Eng)
1987	T Green	1998	Se Ri Pak (Kor)
1988	L Neumann (Swi)	1999	Mi Hyun Kim (Kor)
1989	P Wright (Sco)	2000	Dorothy Delason
1990	H Kobayashi (Jpn)	2001	Hee Won Han (Kor)

US LPGA Rolex Player of the Year

1980	Beth Daniel	1991	Pat Bradley
1981	Jo Anne Carner	1992	Dottie Mochrie
1982	Jo Anne Carner	1993	Betsy King
1983	Patty Sheehan	1994	Beth Daniel
1984	Betsy King	1995	Annika Sörenstam
1985	Nancy Lopez	1996	Laura Davies
1986	Pat Bradley	1997	Annika Sörenstam
1987	Ayako Okamoto	1998	Annika Sörenstam
1988	Nancy Lopez	1999	Karrie Webb
1989	Betsy King	2000	Karrie Webb
1990	Beth Daniel	2001	Annika Sörenstam

US LPGA Vare Trophy

		Scoring average
1980	Amy Alcott	71.51
1981	Jo Anne Carner	71.75
1982	Jo Anne Carner	71.49
1983	Jo Anne Carner	71.41
1984	Patty Sheehan	71.40
1985	Nancy Lopez	70.73
1986	Pat Bradley	71.10
1987	Betsy King	71.14
1988	Colleen Walker	71.26
1989	Beth Daniel	70.38
1990	Beth Daniel	70.54
1991	Pat Bradley	70.66
1992	Dottie Mochrie	70.80
1993	Nancy Lopez	70.83
1994	Beth Daniel	70.90
1995	Annika Sörenstam	71.00
1996	Annika Sörenstam	70.47
1997	Karrie Webb	70.01
1998	Annika Sörenstam	69.99
1999	Karrie Webb	69.43
2000	Karrie Webb	70.05
2001	*Not yet decided*	

Evian Tour Stroke Average Winners

		Scoring average
1991	Alison Nicholas	71.71
1992	Laura Davies	70.35
1993	Laura Davies	71.63
1994	Liselotte Neumann	69.56
1995	Annika Sörenstam	69.75
1996	Marie Laure de Lorenzi	71.39
1997	Marie Laure de Lorenzi	72.20
1998	Laura Davies	71.96
1999	Elaine Ratcliffe	73.76
2000	Laura Davies	70.50
2001	Catriona Mathew	70.08

Joyce Wethered Trophy

Awarded to the outstanding amateur under 25

1994	Janice Moodie	1998	Liza Walters
1995	Rebecca Hudson	1999	Becky Brewerton
1996	Mhairi McKay	2000	Sophie Walker
1997	Rebecca Hudson	2001	Clare Queen

Bill Johnson Trophy

Awarded to the Rookie of the Year on the Evian Tour

1984	Katrina Douglas (Eng)
1085	Laura Davies (Eng)
1986	Patricia Gonzales
1987	Trish Johnson (Eng)
1988	Laurette Maritz (USA)
1989	Helen Alfredsson (Swe)
1990	Pearl Sinn (Kor)
1991	Helen Wdsworth (Wal)
1992	Sandrine Mendiburu (Fra)
1993	Annika Sörenstam (Swe)
1994	Tracy Hansen (USA)
1995	Karrie Webb (Aus)
1996	Anne-Marie Knight (Aus)
1997	Anna Berg (Swe)
1998	Laura Philo (USA)
1999	Elaine Ratcliffe (Eng)
2000	Guila Sergas (Ita)
2001	Suzann Pettersen (Nor)

Bohn shoots historic 58

Jason Bohn, a 28-year-old American from Atlanta, Georgia, made golfing history when he fired a 58 on the way to winning the Bayer Championship on the Canadian Tour.

Bohn, who won $1 million for an ace in 1992 during his college days at the University of Alabama, had ten birdies and two eagles on his card which also included a dropped shot at the par three eighth hole. Despite that he covered the first nine holes in nine-under-par and the back nine in four-under, grazing the hole at the last for a 57!

'It was wild, it was crazy,' said Bohn, who was nine-under after just seven holes, 'and more satisfying than my $1m ace because this was no lucky shot. My caddie Bill Spencer kept me calm.'

Adding to his delight, Bohn's parents were in the gallery watching him play for the first time on his five years on the Canadian Tour.

'Having my parents here to see me do this meant so much to me', said Bohn who with his win moved from 14th to 3rd in the end-of-season McDonald's Order of Merit. It is believe that his score was the first 58 shot in top-line competition.

PART VIII

Who's Who
in Golf

Great Britain and Ireland Players

Alliss, Peter
Born Berlin, 28 February 1931
Turned professional 1946
Following a distinguished career as a tournament golfer in which he won 18 titles between 1954 and 1966 and played eight times in the Ryder Cup between 1953 and 1969, he turned to golf commentating. In Britain he works for the BBC and in America for the ABC network. Twice captain of the PGA in 1962 and 1987 he won the Spanish, Italian and Portuguese Opens in 1958. Author or co-author of several golf books and a novel with a golfing background, he has also designed several courses including the Brabazon course at The Belfry in association with Dave Thomas.

Andrew, Kim *(née* Rostron)
Born 12 February 1974
After taking the English and Scottish Ladies stroke play titles in 1997 she won the Ladies British Open Amateur a year later. She played in the 1998 and 2000 Curtis Cup matches.

Bailey MBE, Mrs Diane (Frearson *née* Robb)
Born Wolverhampton, 31 August 1943
After playing in the 1962 and 1972 Curtis Cup matches she captained the side in 1984, 1986 and 1988. In 1988 at Muirfield the Great Britain and Ireland side lost narrowly to the Americans but she led the side to a first ever victory on American soil at Prairie Dunes in Kansas two years later. The result was a convincing 13-5. She was in charge again when the GB and I side held on to the Cup two years later this time by 11-7 at Royal St George's.

Baker, Peter
Born Shifnal, Shropshire, 7 October 1967
Rookie of the year in 1987, Peter was hailed as the best young newcomer by Nick Faldo when he beat Faldo in a play-off for the Benson and Hedges International in 1988. Several times a winner since then he played in the 1993 Ryder Cup scoring three points out of four. In the singles he beat Corey Pavin.

Barnes, Brian
Born Addington, Surrey, 3 June 1945
Turned professional 1964
Extrovert Scottish professional whose father-in-law is former Open champion Max Faulkner. He was a ten times winner on the European Tour between 1972 and 1981 and was twice British Seniors champion successfully defending the title in 1996. He played in six Ryder Cup matches most notably at Laurel Valley

in 1975 when, having beaten Jack Nicklaus in the morning, he beat him again in the afternoon. Now troubled by injury he is expanding his career as a commentator on American television.

Beharrell, John Charles
Born Birmingham, 14 January 1935
Youngest winner of the Amateur Championship when he took the title at Troon (now Royal Troon) in 1956. Held the post of captain of the Royal and Ancient Golf Club of St Andrews in 1998/99. Married Veronica Anstey, former Curtis Cup player, Australian and New Zealand Ladies champion.

Benka, Peter
Born London, 18 September 1946
Former Walker Cup player who won the British Youths Championship in 1967 and 1968. Now chairman of the R&A Selection Committee.

Bennett, Warren
Born Ruislip, 20 August 1971
Turned professional 1994
Leading amateur in the 1994 Open Championship and winner of the Australian Centennial Amateur Championship the same year. Now a professional, he won the 1999 Scottish PGA Championship.

Bisgood CBE, Jeanne
Born Richmond, Surrey, 11 August 1923
Three times English Ladies champion in 1951, 1953 and 1957. Having played in three Curtis Cups she captained the side in 1970. Between 1952 and 1955 she won the Swedish, Italian, German, Portuguese and Norwegian Ladies titles.

Bonallack Kt OBE, Sir Michael Francis
Born Chigwell, Essex, 31 December 1934
One of only three golfing knights (the others are the late Sir Henry Cotton and Sir Bob Charles) he won the Amateur Championship five times between 1961 and 1970 and was five times English champion between 1962 and 1968. He also won the English stroke play title four times and was twice leading amateur in the Open in 1968 and 1971. In his hugely impressive career he played in nine Walker Cup matches captaining the side on two occasions. He participated in five Eisenhower Trophy matches and five Commonwealth team competitions. He scored his first national title win in the 1952 British Boys' Championship and took his Essex County title 11 times between 1954 and 1972. After serving as secretary of the R&A from 1983

to 1999 he was captain in 1999/2000. Twice winner of the Association of Golf Writers' award in 1968 and 1999, he also received the Bobby Jones award in 1972, the Donald Ross and Gerald Micklem awards in 1991, the Ambassador of Golf award in 1995. In 2000 he was inducted into the World Hall Golf of Fame. A former chairman of the R&A selection committee, he served as chairman of the PGA from 1976 to 1981 and is now a non-executive director of the PGA European Tour. He was chairman of the Golf Foundation in 1977 and president of the English Golf Union in 1982. His wife Lady Angela is the former English champion Angela Ward.

Bonallack, Lady Angela (née Ward)

Born Birchington, Kent, 7 April 1937

Wife of Sir Michael Bonallack OBE she played in six Curtis Cup matches. She was leading amateur in the 1975 and 1976 Colgate European Opens, won two English Ladies titles and had victories, too, in the Swedish, German, Scandinavian and Portuguese Championships.

Brown, Kenneth

Born Harpenden, Hertfordshire, 9 January 1957
Turned professional 1974

Renowned as a great short game exponent, especially with his hickory-shafted putter, he won four times in Europe between 1978 and 85, and took the Southern Open on the US tour in 1987. He played in two winning Ryder Cup sides in 1985 and 1987 having previously played in the 1977, 1979 and 1983 matches. Latterly he has carved out a new career for himself as a television commentator initially, for Sky TV, now with the BBC.

Butler, Ita (née Burke)

Born Nenagh, County Tipperary

Having played in the Curtis Cup in 1966, she captained the side that beat the Americans by 5 points at Killarney thirty years later.

Carr, Joseph B

Born Dublin, 18 February 1922

Winner of the Amateur Championship in 1953, 1958 and 1960, he is Ireland's most successful post-war amateur golfer. Between 1954 and 1967 he won six Irish championships, and was Irish Open Amateur champion four times between 1946 and 1956. He won the south of Ireland Open Amateur Championship three times, but took the East of Ireland title and West of Ireland title twelve times each. He played in ten Walker cups and captained the side twice. He was leading amateur in the Open in 1956 and 1958, was awarded the Association of Golf Writers' Trophy in 1953 and was presented with the Bobby Jones Award in 1961 and the Walter Hagen Award in 1967. He captained the R&A in 1991/92.

Casey, Paul

Born Cheltenham, 21 July 1977
Turned professional 2001

Winner of the English Amateur Championship in 1999 and 2000, he attended Arizona State University where he was a three time All American in NCAA Golf. In the 1999 Walker Cup match, which the Great Britain and

Ireland side won at Nairn, he won all of his four games. After turning professional he earned his European Tour card after just five events helped by a second-equal finish in the Great North Open 2001 and twelfth place finishes in the Compass English Open and Benson and Hedges International. He became a winner in his 11th event when taking the Gleneagles Scottish PGA title over the PGA Centenary course. His coach is Peter Kostis.

Chapman, Roger

Born Nakuru, Kenya, 1 May 1959
Turned professional 1981

After playing on the European Tour for eighteen years without success, he lost his card and had to return to the qualifying school in 1999. Regaining his playing privileges with a twelfth place finish in the six round competition, he made his break-through win by beating Padraig Harrington at the second hole of a play-off in the Brazil Rio de Janeiro Five Hundred Years Open. A former English Amateur Champion in 1981 he played in the Walker Cup the same year beating Hal Sutton twice in a day at Cypress Point.

Clark, Clive Anthony

Born Winchester, 27 June 1945
Turned professional 1965

In the 1965 Walker Cup at Five Farms East in Maryland, he holed a 35-foot putt to earn a half point against Mark Hopkins and ensure a drawn match against the Americans. After turning professional he played in the 1973 Ryder Cup and was a four time winner of titles between 1966 and 1974. Following a career as commentator with the BBC he continued his golf course architecture work in America, and has received awards for his innovative designs.

Clark, Howard

Born Leeds, 26 August 1954
Turned professional 1973

A scratch player by the age of 16 he turned professional after playing in the 1973 Walker Cup. An eleven-time winner on the European tour he played in six Ryder Cups and was in the winning team three times – in 1985 at The Belfry, 1987 at Muirfield Village, when the Europeans won for the first time on American soil, and in 1995 when he gained a vital point helped by a hole in one in the last day singles against Peter Jacobsen. In the 1985 World Cup played at La Quinta in Palm Springs he was the individual champion. He played 494 tournaments before giving up full-time competition to concentrate on his job as a golf analyst on the Sky TV commentary team.

Clarke, Darren

Born Dungannon, Northern Ireland, 14 August 1968
Turned professional 1990

He became the first European Tour player to shoot 60 twice when he returned that record low score at the European Open at the K Club in 1999. Seven years earlier he had shot a nine under par 60 at Mont Agel in the European Monte Carlo Open, but his 60 in Dublin was 12 under par. With his second 60 he also equalled two other records. With twelve birdies on the card he matched the best birdie total in a round and he also scored a record equalling eight birdies in a row. Tied second in the 1997 Open behind Justin Leonard, he was third equal in 2001 at Lytham, Clarke played particularly well in the 2000 Andersen Consulting Match Play Championship at La Costa in California beating Paul Azinger, Mark O'Meara, Thomas Bjørn, Hal Sutton and David Duval to reach the final against Tiger Woods. He became the first European to win a World Golf Championship event when he beat Woods 4 and 3 and picked up the million dollar first prize. He played in the 1997 and 1999 Ryder Cup and is in the 2001 team.

Coles MBE, Neil Chapman
Born 26 September 1934
Turned professional 1950
Remarkably he has won golf tournaments in six decades. In 1956 he won the Gor-Ray tournament and made golfing history when he took the Microlease Jersey Seniors Open at La Moye in 2000. From 1973 to 1979 he played in 68 events on the main European Tour without missing a half-way cut and became the then oldest winner when he won the Sanyo Open in Barcelona in 1982 at the age of 48 years and 14 days. (Des Smyth has since become an even older winner.) Coles remains, however, the oldest winner on the European Senior tour scoring his Jersey win when aged 65 years and 10 months. A member of eight Ryder Cup teams, he has represented his country nineteen times since turning professional at the age of sixteen with a handicap of 14. He has been chairman of the PGA European Tour's Board of Directors since its inception in 1971 and in 2000 was inducted into the World Golf Hall of Fame. Internationally respected he might well have won more in America but for an aversion to flying caused by a bad experience on an internal flight from Edinburgh to London.

Coltart, Andrew John
Born Dumfries, 12 May 1970
Turned professional 1991
Twice Australian PGA champion in 1994 and 1997 he was the Australasian circuit's top money earner for the 1997/98 season. He made his Ryder Cup debut at Brookline in 1999 as a captain's pick and on the final day found himself up against Tiger Woods. A former Walker Cup and Eisenhower Trophy player he was a member of the only Scottish team to win the Alfred Dunhill Cup at St Andrews in 1995. His European tour successes include the 1998 Qatar Masters and 2001 Great North Open. His sister Laurae is married to fellow professional Lee Westwood.

Darcy, Eamonn Christopher
Born Dalgeny, 7 August 1952
Turned professional 1969
One of Ireland's best known players who is closing in on 600 tournament appearances on the European Tour despite suffering for many years with back trouble. First played when he was 10 years old and is renowned for his very distinctive swing incorporating a flying right elbow. He played in four Ryder Cups including the memorable one at Muirfield Village in 1987 when Europe won for the first time in America. He scored a vital point in the last day singles holing a tricky left to right downhill seven footer for a valuable point against Ben Crenshaw.

Davidson, Alison (née Rose)
Born Stirling, Scotland, 18 June 1968
Twice a Curtis Cup player in 1996 and 1998. She won the Ladies British Open Amateur in 1997.

Davies CBE, Laura
Born 10 October 1963
Turned professional 1985
Record-breaking performer who has won over 60 events worldwide including the US and British Women's Opens. For six days in 1987 she held both titles having won the American event before joining the US Tour. Was a founder member of the Women's Tour in Europe where she has won a record 32 times. Still holds the record for the number of birdies in a round – 11 which she scored in the 1987 Open de France Feminin. Her 16-shot victory, by a margin of five shots, in the 1995 Guardian Irish Holidays Open at St Margaret's remains the biggest in European Tour history. Her 267 totals in the 1988 Biarritz Ladies Open and the 1995 Guardian Irish Holidays Open are the lowest on Tour. Other major victories include the LPGA Championship twice and the du Maurier Championship. A big-hitting 5ft 10 ins blonde she has won every year in America since 1988 except in 1990, 1992 and 1999 when her best finish was second. Between 1985 and 1999 she had won in Europe at least once a season. In 1999 became the first European Tour player to pass through the £1 million in prize-money earnings and finished European No 1 that year for a record fifth time. The 1996 Rolex Player of the Year in America she has won almost $5.5 million in US prize-money. Originally honoured with an MBE by Her Majesty the Queen in 1988, she became a CBE in 2000. Enjoys all sports including soccer (she supports Liverpool FC). Among other awards she has received during her career have been the Association of Golf Writers' Trophy for her contribution to European golf in 1994 and the American version in 1994 and 1996 for her performances on the US Tour. In 1994 she became the first golfer to score victories on five different Tours – European, American, Australasian, Japanese and Asian in one calendar year. As an amateur she played for Surrey and was a Curtis Cup player in 1984. She has competed in all six Solheim Cup matches. In 2000 was recognised by the LPGA in their top 50 players and teachers.

Donald, Luke
Born Hemel Hempstead, Hertfordshire, 7 December 1977
Member of the winning Great Britain and Ireland team against the Americans in the 1999 Walker Cup at Nairn and again in 2001 before turning professional. In 1999 won the NCAA Championship and was named NCAA Player of the Year.

Dowling, Clare (née Hourihane)
Born 18 February 1958
Won three Irish Ladies Championships in a row – 1983, 1984 and 1985 and won the title again in 1987 and 1991. She won the 1986 British Ladies Stroke play amateur title. Two years earlier she had made the first of five playing appearances in the Curtis Cup before acting as non-playing captain in 2000.

Drew, Norman Vico
Born Belfast, 25 May 1932
Turned professional 1958
Twice Irish Open Amateur champion in 1952 and 1953 he played in the 1953 Walker Cup and six years later represented Great Britain and Ireland in the Ryder Cup.

Duggelby, Emma
Born Fulford, York, 5 October 1971
Talented English golfer who won the British Ladies Open Amateur Championship in 1994 and the English Ladies in 2000 when she also made her Curtis Cup début.

Faldo MBE, Nicholas Alexander
Born Welwyn Garden City, 18 July 1957
Turned professional 1976
Decided to turn professional after watching the US Masters on television and being impressed by Jack Nicklaus's performance. Europe's most successful major title winner having won three Open Championships in 1987, 1990 at St Andrews and 1992 and three Masters titles in 1989, 1990 and 1996. Of current day players only Tom Watson with eight wins has won more majors. When he successfully defended the Masters in 1990 he became only the second man (after Nicklaus) to win in successive years. Staged a dramatic last day revival to win the 1996 Masters having started the last round six behind Greg Norman. When he realised his swing was not good enough to win majors he completely revamped it with the help of coach David Leadbetter. His 31 European Tour victories include a record three Irish Open victories in a row. In 1992 became the first player to win over £1 million in prize-money during a season. He played with distinction in 11 Ryder Cup matches including the winning teams in 1985, 1987, 1995 and 1997. He holds the record for most games played in the Cup – 46 – and most points won – 25. In 1995 at Oak Hill came from behind to score a vital last day point against Curtis Strange, the American who had beaten him in a play-off for the US Open title in 1988 at The Country Club in Boston. He became the first international player to be named USPGA Player of the Year in 1990 and led the official World Golf Rankings for 81 weeks in 1993-1994. After having teamed up with Swedish caddie Fanny Sunesson for ten years they split only to be reunited as one of golf's best-known partnerships in 2001.

Faulkner, Max
Born Bexhill, Sussex, 29 July 1916
Turned professional 1933
One of the game's most extrovert and colourful characters who played in five Ryder Cups but whose career highlight was winning the Open at Royal in 1951. Curiously and disappointingly the only British Open champion not to have been honoured by Her Majesty the Queen. Father-in-law of Brian Barnes.

Feherty, David
Born Bangor, Northern Ireland, 13 August 1958
Turned professional 1976
Quick-witted Ulsterman who gave up his competitive golfing career to become a hugely successful commentator for CBS in America where his one-liners are legendary. Had five European title wins and three

victories on the South African circuit before switching his golf clubs for a microphone.

Fiddian, Eric Westwood
Born Stourbridge, Worcestershire, 28 March 1910
Best remembered for having had two holes in one during the final of the 1933 Irish Open Amateur Championship but still lost by 3 and 2 to J McLean.

Foster, Rodney
Born Shipley, Yorkshire, 13 October 1941
Played in the Walker Cup five times between 1965 and 1973 and captained the side in 1979. He also captained the Eisenhower Trophy team in 1980.

Gallacher CBE, Bernard
Born Bathgate, Scotland, 9 February 1949
Turned professional 1967
For many years combined tournament golf with the club professional's post at Wentworth where he was honoured in 2000 by being appointed captain. He took up golf at the age of 11 and nine years later was European no.1 with over 30 victories worldwide. Gallacher was the youngest Ryder Cup player when he made his début in the 1969 match in which he beat Lee Trevino in the singles. He played in eight Cup matches and captained the side three times losing narrowly in 1991 at Kiawah Island and 1993 at The Belfry before leading the team to success at Oak Hill in 1995. He is a member of the European Tour's Board of Directors. Now plays on the European Senior Tour.

Garrett, Maureen (*née* Ruttle)
Born 22 August 1922
President of the Ladies' Golf Union from 1982 to 1985, she captained the Curtis Cup (1960) and Vagliano Trophy (1961) teams. In 1983 won the Bobby Jones award presented annually by the United States Golf Association to a person who emulates Jones' spirit, personal qualities and attitude to the game and its players.

Garvey, Philomena
Born Drogheda, Co Louth, 27 April 1927
Turned professional 1964 but later reinstated
Winner of the Irish Ladies title 15 times between 1946 and 1970 and six times a Curtis Cup player between 1948 and 1960 she remains one of Ireland's most successful players. In 1957 she won the British Ladies Open Amateur title.

Glover, John
Born Belfast, 3 March 1933
He was secretary of the R&A Rules of Golf committee from 1980 until his retirement in 1995. He played eight times for Ireland between 1951 and 1970.

Green OBE, Charles Wilson
Born Dumbarton, 2 August 1932
One of Scotland's most successful amateur golfers who was leading amateur in the 1962 Open Championship. A prolific winner he took the Scottish Amateur title three times in 1970, 1982 and 1983. He played in five and was non-playing captain in two more Walker Cups

and was awarded the Frank Moran Trophy for his services to Scottish sport in 1974.

Harrington, Padraig

Born Dublin, Ireland, 31 August 1971
Turned professional 1995

A qualified accountant, he was Irish Open and Close Amateur champion (1995) and played three times in the Walker Cup player before turning professional. Played in the 1999 Ryder Cup at Brookline and beat Mark O'Meara in the singles. He is in the 2001 European team for the postponed match. Best remembered in 2000 for being disqualified on the final day of the Benson and Hedges International at The Belfry after having moved into a five shot lead at the 54-hole stage. It was only then discovered that one of his playing partners had signed Harrington's card on the first day and not Harrington himself. The manner in which he accepted this disappointment greatly impressed observers.

Harris, Marley (*née* Spearman)

Born January 11 1982

Superb ambassadress for golf in the 1950s and 1960s whose exuberance and joie de vivre is legendary. Three times a Curtis Cup player she won the British Ladies in 1961 and again in 1962. She was English champion in 1964. In 1962 was awarded the Association of Golf Writers' Trophy for her services to golf.

Horton MBE, Thomas Alfred

Born St Helens, Lancashire, 16 June 1961
Turned professional 1957

A former Ryder Cup player who was no.1 earner on the European Seniors Tour in 1993 and for four successive seasons between 1996 and 1999. Awarded an MBE by Her Majesty the Queen for his services to golf, Tommy is a member of the European Tour Board and is chairman of the European Seniors Tour committee. A distinguished coach, broadcaster, author and golf course architect, Tommy retired as club professional at Royal Jersey in 1999 after 25 years in the post.

Howard, Barclay

Born Johnstone, Scotland, 27 January 1953

Leading amateur in the Open Championship at Royal Troon in 1997, he has successfully battled cancer which affected his golfing career after he had played in both the 1995 and 1997 Walker Cup matches. When Dean Robertson won the Italian Open at Turin in 1999 he dedicated his victory to him as a tribute to his courage in adversity.

Hudson, Rebecca

Born Doncaster, Yorkshire, 13 June 1979

A member of the 1998 and 2000 Curtis Cup teams Rebecca is one of the most gifted of younger players. In 2000 she won both the British Match Play and Stroke Play titles, the Scottish and English Stroke play Championships and the Spanish Women's Open. In addition she made the birdie that ensured Great Britain and Ireland won a medal in the World Team Championship for the Espirito Santo Trophy in Berlin in 2000.

Huggett MBE, Brian George Charles

Born Porthcawl, Wales, 18 November 1936
Turned professional 1951

Brian won the first of his 16 European Tour titles in Holland in 1962 and was still winning in 2000 when he landed the Beko Seniors Classic in Turkey after a play-off. A dogged competitor he played in six Ryder Cup matches before being given the honour of captaining the side in 1977 – the last year the Americans took on players from only Great Britain and Ireland. A respected golf course designer, Huggett was awarded the MBE for his services to golf and in particular Welsh golf.

Hunt MBE, Bernard John

Born Atherstone, Warwickshire, 2 February 1930
Turned professional 1946

One of Britain's most accomplished professionals he won 22 times between 1953 and 1973. He was third in the 1960 Open at the Old Course behind Kel Nagle and fourth in 1964 when Tony Lema took the title at St Andrews. Among his other victories were successes in Egypt and Brazil. Having made eight appearances in the Ryder Cup he captained the side in 1973 and again in 1975. He was PGA captain in 1966 and won the Harry Vardon Trophy as leading player in the Order of Merit on three occasions.

Irvin, Ann Lesley

Born 11 April 1943

Winner of the British Ladies' title in 1973, she played in four Curtis Cup matches between 1962 and 1976. She was Daks Woman Golfer of the Year in 1968 and 1969 and has been active in administration at junior and county level.

Jacklin CBE, Tony

Born Scunthorpe, 7 July 1944
Turned professional 1962

Played an important and often under-rated role in the growth of the PGA European Tour after it became a self-supporting organisation in 1971. Although playing most of his golf in America he was encouraged by John Jacobs, the then executive director of the European Tour, to return to Europe to help build up the circuit. In 1969 he won the Open Championship at Royal Lytham and St Annes – the first British winner of the title since Max Faulkner in 1951. A year later he led from start to finish to win the US Open at Hazeltine – the first British player to win that event since Ted Ray had been successful in 1920. He was the first player since Harry Vardon to hold the British and American Open titles simultaneously. He might well have won further Opens but a thunderstorm halted his bid for the title at St Andrews in 1970, he came third in 1971 and in 1972 Lee Trevino chipped in at the 17th at Muirfield and went on to win a title the British player had seemed set to win.

Jackson, Barbara Amy Bridget

Born Birmingham, 10 July 1936

A former President of the Ladies Golf Union she played in three Curtis Cup matches and captained the Vagliano Trophy side twice after having played four times. Although the best she managed in the British Championship was runner-up in 1964 she did win the English, German and Canadian titles.

Jacobs OBE, John Robert Maurice

Born Lindrick, Yorkshire, 14 March 1925
The first Executive Director of the independently run PGA European Tour, John Jacobs was awarded the OBE in 2000 for his services to golf as a player, administrator and coach. Known as 'Dr Golf' Jacobs has built up an awesome reputation as a teacher around the world and is held in high esteem by the golfing world. Tiger Woods' coach Butch Harmon summed up Jacobs' contribution in this field of golf when he said: 'There is not one teacher who does not owe something to John. He wrote the book on coaching.' With 75 per cent of the votes he was inducted into the World Golf Teachers Hall of Fame and was described at that ceremony as 'the English genius'. Last year he was also, quite correctly, welcomed into the World Golf Hall of Fame in America. Having played in the 1955 Ryder Cup match he captained the side in 1979 when Continental players were included for the first time and again in 1981. Ken Schofield who succeeded him as European Tour supremo believes that Jacobs changed the face of golf sponsorship allowing, as he points out, more than 10 players a season to earn a living.

James, Mark Hugh

Born Manchester, 28 October 1953
Turned professional 1976
Veteran of over 500 European tournaments who is now chairman of the European Tour's Tournament committee. A seven-time Ryder Cup player including the 1995 match at Oak Hill when he scored a vital early last day point against Jeff Maggert, he captained the side at Brookline in 1999. Four times a top five finisher in the Open Championship Mark has been involved in his fair share of controversy especially in the early days. He has won 18 European Tour events and four elsewhere but these days having successfully battled cancer, he is just as happy working in his Yorkshire garden. Caused some raised eyebrows with some of his comments in his book reviewing the 1999 Ryder Cup entitled 'Into the Bear Pit'. Affectionately known as Jesse to his friends.

Johnson, Trish

Born Bristol, 17 January 1966
Turned professional 1987
Another stalwart of the Women's Tour in Europe who learned the game at windy Westward Ho. Regular winner on Tour both in Europe and America, she scored two and a half points out of four in Europe's dramatic Solheim Cup win over the Americans at Loch Lomond in 2000. She has played in all six Solheim Cup matches. She was European no.1 earner in 1990. A loyal supporter of Arsenal FC she regularly attends games at Highbury.

King, Sam

Born Sevenoaks, Kent, 27 March 1911
Turned professional 1933
He played Ryder Cup golf immediately before and after World War II and came third in the 1939 Open Championship

Lane, Barry Douglas

Born Hayes, Middlesex, 21 June 1960
Turned professional 1976
After winning his way into the 1993 Ryder Cup he hit the headlines when he won the first prize of $1 million in the Andersen Consulting World Championship in beating David Frost in the final at Greyhawk in Arizona. He has played over 400 European events.

Lawrence, Joan

Born Kinghorn, Fife, 20 April 1930
After a competitive career in which she three times won the Scottish championship and played in the 1964 Curtis Cup, she has played her part in golf administration. She had two four-year spells as an LGU selector, is treasurer of the Scottish Ladies Golf Association and has also served on the LGU executive.

Lawrie MBE, Paul Stewart

Born Aberdeen, 1 January 1969
Turned professional 1986
Made golfing history when he came from 10 shots back on the final day to win the 1999 Open Championship at Carnoustie after a play-off against former winner Justin Leonard and Frenchman Jean Van de Velde. With his win he became the first home-based Scot since Willie Auchterlonie in 1893 to take the title. Still based in Aberdeen he hit the opening tee shot in the 1999 Ryder Cup and played well in partnership with Colin Montgomerie in foursomes and four balls and in the singles earned a point against Jeff Maggert. Originally an assistant at Banchory Golf Club on Royal Deeside Lawrie has had a hole named after him at the club. Coached by former Tour player Adam Hunter and Scottish Rugby Union psychologist Dr Richard Cox, Lawrie has been awarded an MBE for his achievements in golf.

Lee-Smith, Jennifer

Born Newcastle-upon-Tyne, 2 December 1948
Turned professional 1977
After winning the Ladies British Open as an amateur in 1976 was named Daks Woman Golfer of the Year. She played twice in the Curtis Cup before turning professional and winning nine times in a six year run from 1979. For a time she ran her own driving range in southern England but now lives in Florida.

Lunt, Michael Stanley Randle

Born Birmingham, 20 May 1935
Won the Amateur Championship in 1963 beating John Blackwell in the final then reached the final again the following year. He was English Amateur champion in 1966 and played four times in the Walker Cup.

Lyle MBE, Alexander Walter Barr

Born Shrewsbury, 9 February 1958
Turned professional in 1977
With his win in the 1985 Open Championship at Royal St. George's became the first British player to take the title since Tony Jacklin in 1969. He was also the first British player to win a Green Jacket in the Masters at Augusta in 1988 helped by a majestic 7-iron second shot out of sand at the last for a birdie 3. Although he represented England as an amateur at boys', youths'

and senior level he became Scottish when he turned professional, something he was entitled to do at the time because his father, the professional at Hawkstone Park, was a Scot. This is no longer allowed. He made his international début at age 14 and, two years later, qualified for and played 54 holes in the 1974 Open at Royal Lytham and St Annes. A tremendously talented natural golfer he fell a victim later in his career to becoming over-technical. Now lives in Perthshire in Scotland but still competes when possible on the US Tour.

McEvoy, Peter

Born London, 22 March 1953
The most capped player for England who has had further success as a captain of Great Britain and Ireland's Eisenhower Trophy and Walker Cup sides. The Eisenhower win came in 1998 and the Walker Cup ttriumphs at Nairn in 1999 and at Ocean Forest, Sea Island, Georgia in 2001. On both occasions his team won 15-9. A regular winner of amateur events McEvoy was amateur champion in 1977 and 1978 and won the English stroke play title in 1980. He reached the final of the English Amateur the same year. In 1978 he played all four rounds in the Masters at Augusta and that year received the Association of Golf Writers' Trophy for his contribution to European golf. He was leading amateur in two Open Championships – 1978 and 1979.

McGimpsey, Garth

Born 17 July 1955
A long hitter who was Irish long-driving champion in 1977 and UK long-driving title holder two years later. He was amateur champion in 1985 and Irish champion the same year and again in 1988. He played in three Walker Cup matches and competed in the home internationals for Ireland in 1978 and from 1980 to 1998.

McGinley, Paul

Born Dublin, 16 December 1966
Turned Professional 1991
Popular Irish golfer who turned to the game after breaking his left kneecap playing Gaelic football. With Padraig Harrington won the 1977 World Cup at Kiawah and will make his Ryder Cup début when the postponed 2001 match is played this year.

Macgregor, George

Born Edinburgh, 19 August 1944
After playing in five Walker Cup matches he captained the side in 1991 and later served as chairman of the R&A Selection committee. He won the Scottish Stroke Play title in 1982 after having been runner up three times.

McKenna, Mary A

Born Dublin, 29 April 1949
Winner of the British Ladies Amateur Stroke play title in 1979 and eight times Irish champion between 1969 and 1989. One of Ireland's most successful golfers she played in nine Curtis Cup matches and nine Vagliano Trophy matches between 1969 and 1987. She captained the Vagliano team in 1995. Three times a member of the Great Britain and Ireland Espirito

Santo Trophy side she went on to captain the team in 1986. She was Daks Woman Golfer of the Year in 1979.

Marks, Geoffrey C

Born Hanley, Stoke-on-Trent November 1938
President of the English Golf Union in 1995 he captained the Walker Cup side in 1987 after having played on two previous occasions. He made eight appearances for England in the home internationals before captaining the team in a non-playing capacity at the start of the 1980s. He is a former England selector and was chairman of the R&A selection committee for four years from 1989.

Marsh, Dr David Max

Born Southport, Lancashire, 29 April 1934
Twice winner of the English Amateur Championship in 1964 and 1970, he was captain of the R&A in 1990/1991. He played in the 1971 Walker Cup match at St Andrews and helped the home side win by scoring a vital one hole victory in the Singles against Bill Hyndman. He captained the team in 1973 and 1975 and had a distinguished career as a player and then captain for England between 1956 and 1972. He was chairman of the R&A selection committee from 1979 to 1983 and in 1987 was president of the English Golf Union.

Milligan, James

Born Irvine, Ayrshire, 15 June 1963
The 1988 Scottish Amateur champion had his moment of international glory in the 1989 Walker Cup which was won by the Great Britain and Ireland side for only the third time in the history of the event and for the first time on American soil. With the visitors leading by a point at Peachtree in Atlanta only Milligan and his experienced opponent Jay Sigel were left on the course. The American looked favourite to gain the final point and force a draw. The American was two up with three to play but Milligan hit his approach from 100 yards to a few inches to win the 16th with a birdie then chipped in after both had fluffed chips to square at the 17th. The last was halved leaving the Great Britain and Ireland side historic winners by a point.

Montgomerie MBE, Colin Stuart

Born Glasgow, 23 June 1963
Turned professional 1987
Europe's most consistent golfer who topped the Volvo Order of Merit an unprecedented seven years in a row between 1993 and 1999. Although he has yet to win a major he has come close losing a play-off for the US Open to Ernie Els in 1994 and again being pipped by Els in the 1997 Championship. He was third behind Tom Kite in the 1992 US Open. In 1995 he was beaten in a play-off for the US PGA Championship by Australian Steve Elkington. He has had 31 victories around the world and has played with distinction in five Ryder Cups and is in the 2001 team. At Brookline in 1999 he was a pillar of strength for the team in difficult on-course conditions. He has twice won the Association of Golf Writers' Golfer of the Year award and has been three times Johnnie Walker Golfer of the Year in Europe. His low round in Europe is 61 achieved at Crans-sur-Sierre in the Canon European Masters in

1996. He has been honoured by Her Majesty the Queen for his record-breaking golfing exploits.

Moodie, Janice
Born Glasgow, 31 May 1973
Turned professional 1997
The 1992 Scottish Women's Stroke play champion played in two winning Curtis Cup teams and earned All American honours at San Jose State University where she graduated with a degree in psychology. She plays both the European and American Tours and in 2000 finished 17th in America and ninth in Europe. Started playing at age 11 and has been helped considerably by Cawder professional Ken Stevely. In the 2000 Solheim Cup she won three out of four points.

Nicholas MBE, Alison
Born Gibraltar, 6 February 1978
In Solheim Cup golf had a successful partnership with Laura Daviesn. In addition they have both won the British and US Open Championship. Alison's first win on the European Tour came in the 1987 Weetabix British Open and she added the US Open ten years later after battling with Nancy Lopez who was trying to win her national title for the first time. Alison is a former winner of the Association of Golf Writers' Golfer of the Year award and has been honoured with an MBE.

O'Connor Sr, Christy
Born Galway, 21 December 1924
Turned professional 1946
Never managed to win the Open but came close on three occasions finishing runner-up to Peter Thomson in 1965 and being third on two other occasions. Played in ten Ryder Cup matches between 1955 and 1973 and scored 24 wins in tournament play between 1955 and 1972. Known affectionately as 'Himself' by Irish golfing fans who have long admired his talent with his clubs.

O'Connor Jr, Christy
Born Galway, 19 August 1948
Turned professional 1965
Nephew of Christy Sen. he finished third in the 1985 Open Championship. A winner on the European and Safari circuits he won the 1999 and 2000 Senior British Open – only the second man to successfully defend. Played in two Ryder Cup matches hitting a career best 2-iron to the last green at The Belfry in 1989 to beat Fred Couples and ensure a drawn match enabling Europe to keep the trophy.

O'Leary, John E
Born Dublin, 19 August 1949
Turned professional 1979
After a successful career as a player including victory in the Carrolls Irish Open in 1982 he retired because of injury and now is director of golf at the Buckinghamshire Club. He is a member of the PGA European Tour Board of Directors.

Oosterhuis, Peter
Born London, 3 May 1948
Turned professional 1968
Twice runner up in the Open Championship in 1974 and 1982, he was also the leading British player in 1975 and 1978. He finished third in the US Masters in 1973, had multiple wins on the European tour and in Africa and won the Canadian Open on the US tour in 1981. He played in six Ryder Cups partnering Nick Faldo at Royal Lytham and St Annes in 1977 when Faldo made his début. He was top earner in Europe four years in a row from 1971. Following his retirement from top-line golf he moved to America and is now a respected member of the CBS commentary team.

Panton-Lewis, Catherine Rita
Born Bridge of Allan, Stirlingshire, 14 June 1955
Turned professional 1978
A former Ladies British Open Amateur Champion in 1976 when she was named Scottish Sportswoman of the year. She notched up thirteen victories as a professional on the European tour between 1979 and 1988. Daughter of John Panton, MBE.

Panton MBE, John
Born Pitlochry, Perthshire, 9 October 1916
Turned professional 1935
Honorary professional since 1988 to the Royal & Ancient Golf Club of St Andrews, he is one of Scotland's best known and admired professionals. He was leading British player in the 1956 Open and as a senior golfer beat Sam Snead for the World Senior's title in 1967. He played in three Ryder Cup matches and was twelve times a contestant in the World Cup with the late Eric Brown as his regular partner. He won the Association of Golf Writer's Trophy for his contribution to the game in 1967 and has been honoured with an MBE.

Price Fisher, Elizabeth
Born London, 17 January 1923
Turned professional 1968 but reinstated as an amateur three years later
Between 1950 and 1960 she played in six Curtis Cup matches and, in addition to her 1959 victory in the British Ladies Championship, also won national titles in Denmark and Portugal.

Price, Phillip
Born Pontypridd, 21 October 1966
Turned professional 1989
Winner of the 1994 Portuguese Open he plans to play the US Tour in 2002. Will make his Ryder Cup début this year having made the 2001 side for the postponed match.

Rafferty, Ronan
Born Newry, Northern Ireland, 13 January 1964
Turned professional 1981
Won the Irish Amateur Championship as a 16 year old in 1980 when he also won the English Amateur Open Stroke Play title, competed in the Eisenhower Trophy and played against Europe in the home internationals. Winner of the British Boys, Irish Youths' and Ulster Youths' titles in 1979, he also played in the senior Irish side against Wales that year. A regular winner on the European tour between 1988 and 1993 he was also victorious in tournaments played in South America, Australia and New Zealand. A wrist injury has curtailed his career but he is active on the corporate golf front and often commentates for Sky TV.

Reid MBE, Dale

Born Ladybank, Fife, 20 March 1959
Turned professional 1979

Scored twenty-one wins in her professional career between 1980 and 1991 and was so successful in leading Europe's Solheim Cup side to victory against the Americans at Loch Lomond in 2000 that she will again captain the side in 2002. Following the team's success in the Solheim Cup she received an MBE.

Robertson MBE, Isabella (Belle)

Born Southend, Argyll, 11 April 1936

One of Scotland's most talented amateur golfers who was Scottish Sportswoman of the Year in 1968, 1971, 1978 and 1981. She was Woman Golfer of the Year in 1971, 1981 and 1985. A former Ladies British Open Amateur Champion and six times Scottish Ladies Champion, she competed in nine Curtis Cups acting as non-playing captain in 1974 and 1976.

Rose, Justin Peter

Born Johannesburg, South Africa, 30 July 1980
Turned professional 1998

Walker Cup player who shot to attention in the 1998 Open Championship when he finished top amateur and third behind winner Mark O'Meara after holing his third shot at the last on the final day for a closing birdie. Immediately after that Open he turned professional and missed his first 21 half-way cuts before finding his feet.

Saunders, Vivien Inez

Born Sutton, Surrey, 24 November 1946
Turned professional 1969

Founder of the Women's Professional Golfers' Association (European Tour) in 1978 and chairman for the first two years. In 1969 she was the first European golfer to qualify for the LPGA Tour in America.

Sinclair OBE, Alexander (Sandy)

Born West Kilbride, Ayrshire, 6 July 1920

Captain of the Royal and Ancient Golf Club of St Andrews in 1988/1989 he was chairman of the R&A Selection committee from 1969 to 1975 and chairman of the R&A Amateur Status committee from 1979 to 1981. One of Scotland's top golfing administrators he was President of the Scottish Golf Union from 1976 to 1978.

Smyth, Des

Born Drogheda, Ireland, 12 February 12
Turned professional 1973

Became the oldest winner on the PGA European Tour when he won the Madeira Island Open in 2001. Smyth was several months older than Neil Coles had been when he won the Sanyo Open in Barcelona. One of the Tour's most consistent performers he has teed up in over 550 events since 1974. Five times Irish National Champion he was a member of the winning Irish side in the 1988 Alfred Dunhill Cup.

Thomas, David

Born Newcastle-upon-Tyne, 16 August 1934

Twice runner-up in the Open Championship Welshman Thomas lost a play-off to Peter Thomson in 1958. He played 11 times in the World Cup for Wales and four times in the Ryder Cup. In all he won 10 tournaments between 1961 and 1969 before retiring to concentrate on golf course design. Along with Peter Alliss designed the Ryder Cup course at The Belfry. Was appointed captain of the Professional Golfers' Association for 2001 – their Centenary year – and for 2002.

Thomas, Vicki (*née* Rawlings)

Born Northampton, 27 October 1954

One of Wales' most accomplished players who took part in six Curtis Cup matches between 1982 and 1992. She won the Welsh Championship eight times between 1979 and 1994 as well as the British Ladies Stroke Play in 1990.

Torrance MBE, Sam

Born Largs, Ayrshire, 24 August 1953
Turned professional 1970

Between 1976 and 1998 he won 21 times on the European Tour in which he has played over 650 events. Captain of the 2001 European Ryder Cup side having previously played in eight matches notably holing the winning putt in 1985 to end a 28-year run of American domination. His father Bob, who has been his only coach, looks after the swings these days of several others on the European Tour. He was awarded the MBE in 1996. European Tour officials worked out that in his first 28 years Torrance walked an estimated 14,000 miles and played 15,000 shots earning at the rate of £22 per stroke.

Valentine MBE, Jessie (*née* Anderson)

Born Perth, Scotland, 18 March 1915
Turned professional 1960

A winner of titles before and after World War II, she was an impressive competitor and was one of the first ladies to make a career out of professional golf. She won the British Ladies as an amateur in 1937 and again in 1955 and 1958 and was Scottish champion in 1938 and 1939 and four times between 1951 and 1956. But for the war years it is certain she would have had more titles and victories. She played in seven Curtis Cups between 1936 and 1958 and represented Scotland in the Home Internationals on 17 occasions between 1934 and 1958.

Wade, Julie

Born Ipswich, Suffolk, 10 March 1967

Secretary of the Ladies Golf Union from 1996 to 2000 she was one of the most successful competitors in both individual and team golf. Among the many titles she won were the English Stroke Play in 1987 and 1993, the British Ladies Stroke Play in 1993 and the Scottish Stroke Play in 1991 and 1993. She shared Britain's Golfer of the Year award in 1993 and won it again in 1995 on her own. She played in five Curtis Cups matches including the victories at Royal Liverpool in 1992 and Killarney in 1996 and the drawn match in 1994 at Chattanooga. Now works with the R&A.

Walker OBE, Carole Michelle (Mickey)

Born Alwoodley, Yorkshire 17 December 1952
Turned professional 1973

Always a popular and modest competitor she followed up an excellent amateur career by doing well as a professional. Twice a Curtis Cup player she won the Ladies British Open Amateur in 1971 and 1972, the English Ladies in 1973 and had victories, too, in Portugal, Spain and America where she won the 1972 Trans-Mississippi title. She won six times as a professional but is perhaps best known for her stirring captaincy of the first four European Solheim Cup sides leading them to a five point success at Dalmahoy. In 1992 she galvanised her side by playing them tapes of the men's Ryder Cup triumphs. Now a club professional she also works regularly as a television commentator.

Walton, Philip
Born Dublin, 28 March 1962
Turned professional 1983
Twice a Walker Cup player he is best remembered for two-putting the last to beat Jay Haas by one hole and clinch victory in the 1995 Ryder Cup at Oak Hill. He played in five Alfred Dunhill Cup competitions at St Andrews and was in the winning side in 1990.

Westwood, Lee
Born Worksop, Nottinghamshire, 24 April 1973
Turned professional 1993
A former British Youths champion who missed out on Walker Cup honours, he quickly made the grade in the professional ranks. In 2000 he ended the seven-year reign of Colin Montgomerie by taking the top spot in the Volvo Order of Merit. He was six-time winner that year in Europe taking five order of merit titles and beating Montgomerie at the second extra hole of the Cisco World match play final at Wentworth. Among his overseas victories are three successful Taiheiyo Masters titles in Japan, the Australian Open in 1997 when he beat Greg Norman in a play-off and the Freeport McDermott Classic at New Orleans on the US Tour. He has already won titles on every major circuit. He is married to Laurae Coltart, sister of fellow professional Andrew Coltart. He has been a member of the last three Ryder Cup teams.

White, Ronald James
Born Wallasey, Cheshire, 9 April 1921
A five times Walker Cup team member between 1947 and 1953 he was one of the most impressive players in post-war amateur golf. He won six and halved one of the 10 Walker Cup matches he played and won the English Amateur in 1949 and the English Open stroke play title the following two years.

Wolstenholme, Gary Peter
Born Egham, Surrey, 21 August 1960
The 1991 Amateur champion he has been one of the most regular title winners in the past 11 years. Son of

former professional the late Guy Wolstenholme he won the 1995 and 1996 British Mid- Amateur Championship, the Chinese Amateur title in 1993, the Emirates Amateur in 1995 and the Finnish Amateur in 1996. He was England County champion of champions in 1994 and 1996 and he highlighted his appearances in Walker Cup golf by beating Tiger Woods by one hole in the first day singles of the 1995 match at Royal Porthcawl. Great Britain and Ireland won that year but Woods gained his revenge on Wolstenholme by beating him on the second day.

Woosnam MBE, Ian Harold
Born Oswestry, Shropshire, 2 March 1958
Turned professional 1976
Highlight of his career was winning the Green Jacket at the Masters in 1991 after a last day battle with Spaniard José Maria Olazábal who went on to win in 1994 and again in 1999. Teamed up very successfully with Nick Faldo in Ryder Cup golf and was in four winning teams in 1985, 1987, 1995 and 1997. Was vice-captain in 2001 to Sam Torrance. He has scored 28 European Tour victories and twice won the World Match Play Championship in 1987 when he beat Sandy Lyle with whom he used to play boys' golf in Shropshire and 1990 when his opponent was Zimbabwean Mark McNulty. In 1989 he lost a low-scoring final to Nick Faldo on the last green. His lowest round was a 60 he returned in the 1990 Monte Carlo Open at Mont Agel. Partnered by David Llewellyn he won the World Cup of Golf in 1987 beating Scotland's Sam Torrance and Sandy Lyle in a play-off. Honoured with an MBE from Her Majesty the Queen he now lives with his family in Jersey. Finished joint third in the 2001 Open at Lytham after having been penalised two shots for discovering on the second tee he had 15 clubs (one over the limit) in his bag.

Wright, Janette *(née Robertson)*
Born Glasgow, 7 January 1935
Another of Scotland's most accomplished amateur players she competed four times in the Curtis Cup and was four times Scottish champion between 1959 and 1973. Married to golf professional Innes Wright her daughter Pamela plays professionally on the LPGA Tour in America.

Wright, Pamela
Born Aboyne, Scotland, 26 June 1964
Turned professional 1988
Daughter of former Scottish champion and Curtis Cup golfer Janette Wright and Aboyne professional Innes Wright. She played in the first three Solheim Cup matches being a member of the winning team at Dalmahoy in 1992. She was an All-American in 1987 and again in 1988 when she also won Collegiate Golfer of the Year honours.

Overseas Players

Aaron, Tommy (USA)
Born Gainesville, Georgia, 22 February 1937
Turned professional 1961
After finishing runner-up in the 1972 US PGA Championship he won the 1973 Masters. He was a member of the 1969 and 1973 Ryder Cup teams. Inadvertently marked down a 4 on Roberto de Vicenzo's card for the 17th hole in the 1968 Masters when the Argentinian took 3. De Vicenzo signed for the 4 and lost out by one shot on a play-off for the Green Jacket.

Alfredsson, Helen (Swe)
Born Gothenburg, 9 April 1965
Turned professional 1989
After earning Rookie of the Year on the 1989 European Tour she won the 1992 Ladies' British Open. Two years later she was Gatorade Rookie of the Year on the American LPGA Tour. She has competed in the six Solheim Cup matches played to date and has won titles in Europe, America. Japan and Australia.

Allenby, Robert (Aus)
Born Melbourne, 12 July 1971
Turned professional 1992
Pipped by a shot from winning the Australian Open as an amateur in 1991 by Wayne Riley's birdie, birdie, birdie finish at Royal Melbourne he won the title three years later as a professional. After competing on the European Tour and winning four times, he now plays on the US Tour. He has played in two Presidents Cup matches in 1996 and 2000.

Isao, Aoki (Jpn)
Born Abiko, Chiba, 31 August 1942
Turned professional 1964
Successful international performer whose only victory on the main US Tour came dramatically in Hawaii in 1983 when he holed a 128 yards pitch for an eagle 3 at the last at Waialae to beat Jack Renner. Only Japanese golfer to win on the main European Tour taking the European Open in 1983. He also won the World Match Play in 1978 beating Simon Owen and was runner up the following year. He holed in one at Wentworth in that event to win a condominium at Gleneagles. He was top earner five times in his own country and is the Japanese golfer who has come closest to winning a major title finishing runner-up two shots behind Jack Nicklaus in the 1980 US Open at Baltusrol.

Azinger, Paul William (USA)
Born Holyoke, Massachusetts, 6 January 1960
Turned professional 1981
Helped by a second hole play-off victory against Greg Norman in the 1993 US PGA Championship at Inverness he made almost $1.5 million to finish second on the US money list to Nick Price. The following year he played only four events after having been diagnosed with lymphoma in his right shoulder blade. Happily he made a good recovery and scored his 12th US Tour victory in 2000 and his first since his 1993 US PGA win when he opened with a 63 and led from start to finish in the Sony Open in Hawaii. He played in three Ryder Cup matches in 1989, 1991 and 1993 and is on the 2001 team. In 1987 he was joint runner-up with Rodger Davis in the Open at Muirfield won by Nick Faldo.

Baddeley, Aaron (Aus)
Born New Hampshire, USA, 17 March 1981
Turned professional 2000
Became the first amateur to win the Australian Open since Bruce Devlin in 1969 and the youngest when he took the title at Royal Sydney in 2000. Then, having turned professional he successfully defended it at Kingston Heath. He had shown considerable promise when at age 15, he qualified for the Victorian Open. Represented Australia in the Eisenhower Trophy and holds both Australian and American passports.

Baiocchi, Hugh John (RSA)
Born Johannesburg, 17 August 1946
Turned professional 1971
A scratch golfer when he was 15, Hugh Baiocchi joined the Senior PGA Tour after playing with distinction for 23 years on the European Tour. He has played in 31 different countries around the world winning in many of them. He gained an extra special delight at winning the 1978 South African Open emulating his long-time golfing hero Gary Player who is a multiple winner of that title.

Baker-Finch, Ian (Aus)
Born Namour, Queensland, 24 October 1960
Turned professional 1979
Impressive winner of the Open Championship in 1991 he emerged as a tremendous ambassador for golf. Sadly in attempting to hit the ball further off the tee he lost his game completely when teeing up in Tour events and was forced, after an agonising spell, to retire prematurely. After having been given the chance to commentate in Australia, he took up the opportunity to do a similar job for the American ABC network.

Ballesteros, Severiano (Esp)
Born Pedrena, 9 April 1957
Turned professional 1974
Charismatic and stubbornly proud Spaniard who won 52 titles between 1976 and 1999 including three Opens

(1979, 1984 at St Andrews and 1988) and The Masters at Augusta in 1980 and again in 1983. One of four brothers all of whom play golf. He was introduced to the game by big brother Manuel and first hit the headlines when in 1976 he and Jack Nicklaus finished second to Johnny Miller at Royal Birkdale. He played in eight Ryder Cups and captained the side to victory at Valderrama in 2000. Never one of golf's straightest hitters his powers of recovery from seemingly impossible positions have been legendary throughout his career. He was the driving force in getting a match started between the British and Irish golfers and the Continentals in 2000. Sadly has lost his game but not his hope that one day it will return.

Berg, Patty (USA)

Born Minneapolis, 13 February 1918
Turned professional 1940
A founder member of the LPGA Tour in America, she won 57 times in her career including the 1946 US Women's Open. She was leading US money winner in 1954, 1955 and 1957. The first president of the LPGA she was honoured several times winning, among others, the Bobby Jones award in 1963 and the Ben Hogan award and Hall of Fame in 1976.

Bjørn, Thomas (Den)

Born Silkeborg, 18 February 1971
Turned professional 1993
A former Danish Amateur champion in 1990 and 1991, he became the first Dane to play in the Ryder Cup when he made the team in 1997. Four down after four holes against Justin Leonard in the last day singles at Valderrama he fought back to halve the match and gain a valuable half-point in the European victory. He missed out on the 1999 match but is in the 2001 side. Won four times in the Challenge Tour before gaining his full European card. He came joint second to Tiger Woods in the 2000 Open at St Andrews just a few weeks after finishing third behind Woods in the US Open at Pebble Beach. In Japan in 1999 he beat Sergio Garcia at the fourth hole of a play-off for the Dunlop Phoenix title.

Bradley, Pat (USA)

Born Westford, Massachusetts, 24 March 1951
Turned professional 1974
Winner of four US LPGA majors – the Nabisco Championship, the US Women's Open, the LPGA Championship and the du Maurier Classic, she won 31 times on the American circuit. An outstanding skier and ski instructor as well she started playing golf when she was 11. Every time she won her mother would ring a bell on the porch of the family home whatever the time of day. The bell is now in the World Golf Hall of Fame. She played in four Solheim Cup sides and captained the team in 2000 at Loch Lomond. Inducted into the LPGA Hall of Fame in 1991 she was Rolex Player of the Year in 1986 and 1991.

Brooks, Mark (USA)

Born Fort Worth, Texas, 25 March 1961
Turned professional 1983
A seven-time winner on the US Tour between 1988 and 1996 he took the US PGA Championship title in 1996 after a play-off with Kenny Perry at Valhalla. On

that occasion he birdied the 72nd hole and the first extra hole to win but he was beaten by South African Retief Goosen in the 18-hole play-off for the 2000 US Open at Southern Hills in Tulsa. Goosen shot 70, Brooks 72.

Calcavecchia, Mark (USA)

Born Laurel, Nebraska, 12 June 1960
Turned professional 1981
Winner of the 1989 Open Championship at Royal Troon after the first ever four-hole play-off against Australians Greg Norman and Wayne Grady. He was runner-up in the 1987 Masters at Augusta to Sandy Lyle and came second to Jodie Mudd in the 1990 Players' Championship. He played in the 1987, 1989 and 1991 Ryder Cup sides and is in the 2001 team.

Campbell, William Cammack (USA)

Born West Virginia, 5 May 1923
One of America's most distinguished players and administrators. He won the US Amateur Championship in 1964 ten years after finishing runner-up in the Amateur Championship in Britain to Australian Doug Bachli at Muirfield. One of a select group who have been both President of the United States Golf Association (in 1983) and captain of the Royal and Ancient Golf Club of St Andrews (in 1987/1988). He played in eight Ryder Cup matches between 1951 and 1975 captaining the side in 1955.

Canizares, José Maria (Esp)

Born Madrid, 18 February 1947
Turned professional 1967
A seven-time winner on the European Tour between 1972 and 1992 the popular Spaniard now plays full time on the US Senior Tour where his consistency has enabled him to earn $3.47 million from his first 104 events. A former caddie, he played in four Ryder Cup matches in the 80s winning five and halving two of his 11 games.

Caponi, Donna (USA)

Born Detroit, Michigan, 29 January 1945
Turned professional 1965
Twice winner of the US Women's Open in 1969 and 1970 she collected 24 titles between 1969 and 1981 on the LPGA Tour. Winner of the 1975 Colgate European Open at Sunningdale, she is now a respected commentator/analyst for The Golf Channel.

Carner, Jo Anne (née Gunderson) (USA)

Born Kirkland, Washington, 4 April 1939
Turned professional 1970
Had five victories in the US Ladies' Amateur Championship (1957, 1960, 1962, 1966 and 1968) before turning professional and winning the 1971 and 1976 US Women's Open. She remains the last amateur to win on the LPGA Tour after having taken the 1969 Burdine's Invitational. Between 1970 and 1985 scored 42 victories on the LPGA Tour and was Rolex Player of the Year in 1974, 1981 and 1982. She was inducted into the LPGA Hall of Fame in 1982 and the World Golf Hall of Fame in 1985. She won the Bobby Jones award in 1981 and the Mickey Wright award in 1974 and 1982.

Casper, Billy (USA)

Born San Diego, California, 24 June 1931
Turned professional 1954
A three-time major title winner he took the US Open in 1959 and 1966 and the US Masters in 1970. In 1966 he came back from seven strokes behind Arnold Palmer with nine to play to force a play-off which he then won. Between 1956 and 1975 he picked up 51 first prize cheques on the US Tour. His European victories were the 1974 Trophée Lancôme and Lancia D'Oro and the 1975 Italian Open. As a senior golf he won nine times between 1982 and 1989 including the US Senior Open in 1983. Played in eight Ryder Cups and captained the American side in 1979 at Greenbrier. He and wife Shirley have 11 children several of them adopted. He was named Father of the Year in 1966. Started playing golf aged 5 and rates Ben Hogan, Byron Nelson and Sam Snead as his heroes. Five times Vardon Trophy winner (for low season stroke-average) and twice top money earner he was US PGA Player of the Year in 1966 and 1970. He was inducted into the World Golf Hall of Fame in 1978 and the US PGA Hall of Fame in 1982.

Cavalleri, Silvia (Ita)

Born Milan, 10 October 1972
Turned professional 1997
Became the first Italian to win the US Amateur when she beat R Burke 5 and 4 at Brae Burn in the final. She was five times Italian National Junior champion and won the British Girls title in 1990 with a 5 and 4 success over E Valera at Penrith. As a professional her best finish to date is tied second in the 2000 Ladies' Italian Open.

Charles, Sir Robert James (Bob) (NZ)

Born Auckland, 14 March 1936
Turned professional 1960
Three years after turning professional he became the first and still the only New Zealander and left-hander to win the Open Championship. He defeated Phil Rodgers in the last 36-hole play-off for the title at Royal Lytham and St Annes then was runner-up in 1968 to Gary Player at Carnoustie and in 1969 to Tony Jacklin again at Lytham. Earlier in 1954 he had won the first of his four New Zealand Opens as an amateur. Between 1954 and 1960 worked in a bank before embarking on a golf career which has seen him win extensively around the world on golf's main Tours and the US Senior Tour. He won seven times on the US Tour, nine times in Europe, 24 times in New Zealand and has also won in Canada Japan and South Africa. He does everything right-handed except games requiring two hands. In 1972 received the OBE from Her Majesty the Queen, the CBE in 1992 and was knighted in 1999 for his services to golf.

Cink, Stewart Ernest (USA)

Born Huntsville, Alabama, 21 May 1973
Turned professional 1995
The Rookie of the Year on the US Tour in 1997 when he won the Canon Greater Hartford Classic. The year before he had been top rookie on the Buy.Com tour. Although he made the 2001 Ryder Cup side he missed a two foot putt on the last and a play-off for the US Open with Mark Brooks and winner Retief Goosen.

Coe, Charles (USA)

Born Oklahoma City, 26 October 1923
Another fine American amateur golfer who finished runner-up with Arnold Palmer to Gary Player in the 1961 Masters at Augusta. Twice US Amateur champion in 1949 and 1958, he played in six Walker Cup matches and was non-playing captain in 1959. He won seven and halved two of the 13 games he played. Winner of the Bobby Jones award in 1964.

Cole, Bobby (RSA)

Born Springs, 11 May 1948
Turned professional 1966
Winner of the Amateur Championship in 1966 when he beat RDBM Shade in the final which because of haar (fog) was reduced to 18 holes. Among his victories when he turned professional were two South African Opens in 1974 and 1980.

Cook, John (USA)

Born Toledo, Ohio, 2 October 1957
Turned professional 1979
A regular winner on the US Tour he gave Nick Faldo a fright in the 1992 Open at Muirfield. Three strokes behind with eight to play Cook had moved out in front after 16 holes on the final day but finished 5,5 to Faldo's 4,4. He was also tied second that year in the US PGA Championship. Given much help in his early years by Jack Nicklaus and Tom Weiskopf.

Couples, Frederick Steven (Fred) (USA)

Born Seattle, Washington, 3 October 1959
Turned professional 1980
Troubled continually with a back problem he has managed to win only one major – the 1992 US Masters but is one of the most popular of all American players. Although he has been known to say he enjoys watching television lying on the sofa, he is no stay-at-home in a golfing sense. He has always been willing to travel and his overseas victories include two Johnnie Walker World Championships, the Johnnie Walker Classic, the Dubai Desert Classic and the Tournoi Perrier de Paris. On the US Tour he won 14 times between 1983 and 1998. He played five Ryder Cup matches and three times teed up for the US in the Presidents Cup.

Crenshaw, Ben (USA)

Born Austin, Texas, 11 January 1952
One of golf's great putters who followed up his victory in the 1984 US Masters with an emotional repeat success in 1995 just a short time after the death of his long-time coach and mentor Harvey Pennick. He played in four Ryder Cup matches between 1981 and 1995 before captaining the side at Brookline in 1999 when the Americans came from four points back to win the trophy with a scintillating last day performance. Winner of the Byron Nelson award in 1976 he was also named Bobby Jones award winner in 1991. Now combines playing with an equally successful career as a golf course designer and is an acknowledged authority on every aspect of the history of the game.

Daly, John Patrick (USA)
Born Sacramento, California, 28 April 1966
Turned professional 1987
Winner of two majors – the 1991 US PGA Championship and the 1995 Open Championship at St Andrews after a play-off with Costantino Rocca, his career has not been without its ups and downs. He admits he has battled alcoholism and, on occasions, has been his own worst enemy when having run-ins with officialdom but he remains one of the most popular and likeable if sometimes unorthodox players on Tour because of his long hitting. His average drive is over 300 yards. When he won the US PGA Championship at Crooked Stick he got in as ninth alternate, drove through the night to tee it up without a practice round and shot 69, 67, 69, 71 to beat Bruce Lietzke by three. Given invaluable help at times by Fuzzy Zoeller he writes his own songs and is a mean performer on the guitar. In 2001 took the BMW International Open title at Munich.

Daniel, Beth (USA)
Born Charleston, South Carolina, 14 October 1956
Turned professional 1978
A member of the LPGA Hall of Fame she won 32 times between 1979 and 1995 including the 1990 US LPGA Championship. She was Rolex Player of the Year in 1980, 1990 and 1994. Before turning professional she won the US Women's Amateur title in 1975 and 1977 and played in the 1976 and 1978 Curtis Cup teams. She has played in five Solheim Cup competitions since it began in 1990, missing only the 1998 match.

Davis, Rodger (Aus)
Born Sydney, 18 May 1951
Turned professional 1974
Experienced Australian competitor who came joint second in the 1987 Open Championship behind Nick Faldo at Muirfield. A regular on the European Tour he hopes to extend his playing career on the US Senior circuit. Winner of 27 titles, 19 of them on the Australasian circuit where, in 1988, he picked up an Aus$1 million first prize in the Bicentennial event at Royal Melbourne. Gave up golf for a while but lost all his money in a hotel venture that went wrong and took up tournament play again. For many years played in trade mark 'plus twos' and is wearing them again on the European Tour.

Dibnah, Corinne (Aus)
Born Brisbane, 29 July 1962
Turned professional 1984
A former Australian and New Zealand amateur champion, she joined the European Tour after turning professional and won 13 times between 1986 and 1994. A pupil of Greg Norman's first coach Charlie Earp, she was Europe's top earner in 1991.

Dickson, Robert B (USA)
Born McAlester, Oklahoma, 25 January 1944
Turned professional 1968
Best remembered for being one of only four players to complete a Transatlantic amateur double. In 1967 he won the US Amateur Championship at Broadmoor with a total of 285 (the Championship was played over 72 holes from 1965 to 1972) and the British Amateur title with a 2 and 1 win over fellow American Ron Cerrudo at Formby. After turning professional scored two wins on the US Tour.

Duval, David Robert (USA)
Born Jacksonville, Florida, 19 November 1971
Turned professional 1993
A regular winner on the US Tour who wears dark glasses because of an eye stigmatism which is sensitive to light, he won his first major at Royal Lytham and St Annes last year when he became only the second American professional to win the Open over that course. He was the first player in US Tour history to win titles by play-off in consecutive weeks. Played 86 events and had seven second-place finishes and four thirds before making his break-through win in the Michelob Championship then won the following week as well. His father Bob plays the US Senior Tour. He is a winner of the US Tour Championship in 1997 and the Players' Championship in 1999. In the 1998 and 2001 Masters he came second and was third in that event in 2000. He played in 1991 Walker Cup and was a member of the winning Ryder Cup side on his début in 1999. He is also a member of the 2001 Cup side.

Elkington, Stephen John (Steve) (Aus)
Born Inverell, 8 December 1962
Turned professional 1985
A former Australian (1990 and 1991) and New Zealand (1990) champion he is a regular winner these days on the US Tour despite an allergy to grass. At Riviera CC in Los Angeles in 1995 he beat Colin Montgomerie in a play-off for the US PGA Championship, the only major he has won to date. Winner of the 1992 Australian Open he has one of the finest swings in golf. He is also an accomplished artist in his spare time. He has played four times since 1994 in the Presidents Cup.

Els, Theodore Ernest (Ernie) (RSA)
Born Johannesburg, 17 October 1969
Turned professional 1989
Teenage winner of the South African Amateur Championship in 1996 he is renowned as one of the game's big hitters. His short game can be deadly too and when on song he is one of the most impressive international performers. He has won two US Opens – in 1994 at Oakmont after a play-off against Loren Roberts and Colin Montgomerie and at Congressional where he beat Montgomerie into second place. Although proficient at Rugby Union and cricket he decided to concentrate on golf when he played off scratch at age 14. He has matched Gary Player's record of winning three successive South African Opens and has collected the South African PGA and Masters titles as well. In 1994 equalled the European Tour record of 12 birdies in the 61 he fired en route to victory in the Dubai Desert Classic. He was made an honorary member of the PGA European Tour in recognition of his two US Open wins and his three successive World Match Play title successes round the famous West Course. Going for a fourth successive win in 1997 he lost on the last green to Vijay Singh.

Fasth, Niclas (Swe)
Born Gothenburg, Sweden, 29 April 1972
Turned professional 1989
One of the three Swedes who made the 2001 European Ryder Cup side helped by his second place finish to David Duval in the 2001 Open at Royal Lytham and St Annes where he shot 69, 69, 72 and 67. That earned him over 590,000 Cup points. Played in the US Tour in 1998 but found the travelling too demanding..

Faxon, Brad (USA)
Born Oceanport, New Jersey, 1 August 1961
Turned professional 1983
A former Walker Cup player who competed in the 1983 match he has played twice in the Ryder Cup (1995 and 1997). A seven-time winner on the US Tour he also putted superbly to win the Australian Open at Metropolitan in 1993.

Fernandez, Vicente (Arg)
Born Corrientes, 5 May 1946
Turned professional 1964
After playing on the European Tour where he won five times between 1975 and 1992 he joined the US Senior Tour competing with considerable success. In this respect he was following in the footsteps of fellow Argentinian Roberto de Vicenzo. Born with one leg shorter than the other which is why he limps, he is remembered in Europe for the 87 foot putt he holed up three tiers on the final green at The Belfry in 1992 to win the Murphy's English Open. His nickname is 'Chino'.

Finsterwald, Dow (USA)
Born Athens, Ohio, 6 September 1929
Turned professional 1951
Winner of the 1958 US PGA Championship he won 11 other competitions between 1955 and 1963. He played in four Ryder Cup matches in a row from 1957 and captained the side in 1977. He was US PGA Player of the Year in 1958.

Floyd, Raymond Loran (USA)
Born Fort Bragg, North Carolina, 4 September 1942
Turned professional 1961
A four time major winner whose failure to win an Open Championship title prevented his completing a Slam of Majors. He won the US Open in 1986, the Masters in 1976 when he matched the then 72-hole record set by Jack Nicklaus to win by eight strokes and took the US PGA title in 1969 and 1982. In addition to coming second and third in the Open he was also runner-up three times in the Masters and in the US PGA once. After scoring 22 victories on the main US Tour he has continued to win as a senior. Inducted into the World Golf Hall of Fame in 1989 he is an avid Chicago Cubs baseball fan. Played in eight Ryder Cup matches between 1969 and 1993 making history with his last appearance by being the oldest player to take part in the match. He was 49. He was non-playing captain in 1989 when the match was drawn at The Belfry.

Ford, Doug (USA)
Born West Haven, Connecticut, 6 August 1922
Turned professional 1949
His 25 wins on the US Tour between 1955 and 1963 included the 1975 US Masters. US PGA Player of the Year in 1955, he competed in four Ryder Cup matches in succession from 1955.

Franco, Carlos (Par)
Born Asunción, 24 May 1965
Turned professional 1986
Emerged on to the international stage from humble beginnings. He was one of a family of nine who shared a one-room home at the course where his father was greens superintendent and caddie. All five of his brothers play golf and he was appointed Paraguayan Minister of Sport in 1999. Won twice in his rookie year on the US Tour and became the first player to make more than $1 million in his first two seasons. Has scored three wins on the US circuit, five times in Japan where he had 11 top 10 finishes in 1997, once in the Philippines and 19 times in South America. First made headlines at St Andrews when he beat Sam Torrance in the Alfred Dunhill Cup.

Frost, David Laurence (RSA)
Born Cape Town, 11 September 1959
Turned professional 1981
Although now based permanently in the United States has won as many titles overseas as on the US Tour. The 1993 season was his best in America when he made over $1 million in prize money and finished fifth on the money list. He has established a vineyard in South Africa growing 100 acres of vines on the 300-acre estate. He has very quickly earned a reputation for producing quality wines.

Falke, Pierre (Swe)
Born Nyköping, Sweden, 21 February 1971
Turned professional 1993
Victory in the 2000 Volvo Masters at Montecastillo and a runner-up cheque when losing the final of the Accenture Championship Cup in the WGC Circuit to Steve Stricker catapulted him into the Ryder Cup side in 2001 long before the points counting period was over. Son of a former Swedish swimming champion Falke was out of the game for nine months after winning the 1999 Lancôme Trophy because of a wrist injury.

Furyk, Jim (USA)
Born West Chester, Pennsylvania, 12 May 1970
Turned professional 1992
Clearly enjoys playing in Las Vegas where he has won three Invitational events in 1995, 1999 and 1998. Has teed it up in two Presidents Cups and two Ryder Cups beating Nick Faldo in the singles at Valderrama in 1997. He is also in the 2001 side for the postponed match being played this year. Has one of the most easily recognisable if idiosyncratic swings in top line golf. His father Mike has been his only coach.

Garcia, Sergio Fernandez (Esp)
Born Castellon, 9 January 1980
Turned professional 1999
The extrovert Spaniard having won the French and Amateur Championships in 1997 took the British title in 1998 and in both years was European Amateur Masters champion. Son of a greenkeeper his future was always going to be in professional golf but he waited until after the 1999 Masters in which he was leading

amateur before joining the paid ranks at the Spanish Open. Although only just starting to collect Ryder Cup points he easily made the 1999 team and formed an invaluable partnership with Jesper Parnevik at Brookline scoring three and a half points out of four on the first two days. Victories in the Murphy's Irish Open and Linde German Masters helped him to the 1999 Rookie of the Year title in Europe but arguably an even better performance was finishing runner-up to Tiger Woods in the US PGA Championship at Medinah outside Chicago. Although he did not win in 2000 he won the Mastercard Colonial and Buick Classic on the US Tour in 2001. He is a member of the 2001 Ryder Cup side.

Garrido, Ignacio Villacieros (Esp)
Born Madrid, 27 March 1972
Turned professional 1993
Eldest son of Antonio Garrido who played in the 1979 Ryder Cup, Ignacio emulated his father when he made the team at the 1997 match at Valderrama having earlier that year won the Volvo German Open. Before turning professional with a handicap of 4 he won the English Amateur Stroke Play title (the Brabazon Trophy) in 1992. In the 80s used to caddie for his father who has since caddied for him on occasion.

Geddes, Jane (USA)
Born Huntingdon, New York, 5 February 1960
Turned professional 1983
In 1986 she was the 13th player on the LPGA Tour to score her first victory at the US Women's Open. A year later she won the US LPGA title and took the British Women's title in 1989. She won 11 times on the US Tour between 1986 and 1994.

Goldschmid Isa (*née* Bevione) (Ita)
Born Italy, 15 October 1925
One of Italy's greatest amateurs she won her national title 21 times between 1947 and 1974 and was ten times Italian Open champion between 1952 and 1969. Among her other triumphs were victories in the 1952 Spanish Ladies and the 1973 French Ladies.

Goosen, Retief (RSA)
Born Pietersburg, 3 February 1969
Turned professional 1990
Introduced to golf at the age of 11 he scored his first major success when leading from start to finish at the 2001 US Open at Tulsa and then beating Mark Brooks in the 18-hole play-off by two shots. Although he suffered health problems after being hit by lightning as a teenager he has enjoyed a friendly rivalry with South Africa's other talented young player Ernie Els. Winner of the 1990 South African Amateur title, he scored his first professional victory in the Iscor Newcastle Classic a year later. In Europe where he has been helped by Belgian psychologist Jos Vanstiphout, golf's quiet achiever enjoys playing in France where he has won two French Championships (1997 and 1999) and the Trophée Lancôme in 2000. Just weeks after his US Open win in 2001 he led again from start to finish to win the Scottish Open at Loch Lomond.

Grady, Wayne (Aus)
Born Brisbane, 26 July 1957
Turned professional 1973 and again in 1978
One of Australia's most popular players he won the US PGA Championship at Shoal Creek by three shots over

Fred Couples. A year earlier he had tied with Greg Norman and eventual winner Mark Calcavecchia for the Open Championship losing out in the first ever four-hole play-off for the title. Took over in 2001 as chairman of the Australasian Tour from Jack Newton.

Graham, David (Aus)
Born Windsor, Tasmania, 23 May 1946
Turned professional 1962
Played superbly for a closing 67 round Merion to win the 1981 US Open Championship from George Burns and Bill Rogers. That day he hit every green in regulation. Two years earlier he had beaten Ben Crenshaw at the third extra hole at Oakland Hills to win the US PGA Championship. When he took up the game at age 14 he played with left-handed clubs before making the switch to a right-handed set. Awarded the Order of Australia for his services to golf he is a member of the Cup and Tee committee that sets up Augusta each year for the Masters. A regular winner around the world in the 70s and 80s he won eight times on the US Tour between 1972 and 1983. Now plays on the US Senior Tour but also has gained a considerable reputation as a course designer.

Graham, Lou (USA)
Born Nashville, Tennessee, 7 January 1938
Turned professional 1962
Won the US Open at Medinah in 1975 after a play-off against John Mahaffey.

Green, Hubert (USA)
Born Birmingham, Alabama, 18 December 1946
Turned professional 1970
Beat Lou Graham for the 1977 US Open at Southern Hills despite being told with four holes to play that he had received a death threat. Three times a Ryder Cup player he also won the 1985 US PGA Championship. His only European Tour victory was the 1977 Irish Open. Best known for his unorthodox swing and distinctive crouching putting style.

Gustafson, Sophie (Swe)
Born Saro, 27 December 1973
Turned professional 1992
Winner of the 2000 Weetabix Women's British Open she had studied marketing, economics and law before turning to professional golf. Credits Seve Ballesteros and Laura Davies as the two players most influencing her career. Her first European victory was the 1996 Swiss Open and her first on the US LPGA Tour was the Chick-fil-A Charity Cup in 2000.

Haeggman, Joakim (Swe)
Born Kalmar, 28 August 1969
Turned professional 1989
Became the first Swedish player to play in the Ryder Cup when he made the side which lost to the Americans at The Belfry in 1993. He received one of team captain Bernard Gallacher's 'wild cards' and beat John Cook in his last day singles. Gave up ice hockey after dislocating his shoulder and breaking ribs in 1994. Realised then that ice hockey and golf do not mix but has become an enthusiastic angler when not on the links. Equalled the world record of 27 for the first nine holes in the Alfred Dunhill Cup over the Old

course at St Andrews in 1997. Occasionally acts as commentator for Swedish TV and was a member of Sam Torrance's Ryder Cup back-room team at The Belfry in 2001.

Harper, Chandler (USA)
Born Portsmouth, Virginia, 10 March 1914
Turned professional 1934
Winner of the 1950 US PGA Championship he won over ten tournaments and was elected to the US PGA Hall of Fame in 1969. Once shot 58 (29-29) round a 6100 yards course in Portsmouth.

Hayes, Dale (RSA)
Born Pretoria, 1 July 1952
Turned professional 1970
Former South African amateur stroke play champion who was a regular winner in South Africa and Europe after turning professional. He was Europe's top money earner in 1975 but retired from competitive golf to move into business. He is now a successful television commentator in South Africa with a weekly programme of his own.

Haynie, Sandra (USA)
Born Fort Worth, Texas, 4 June 1943
Turned professional 1961
Twice a winner of the US Open (1965 and 1974) she won 42 times between 1962 and 1982 on the US LPGA Tour. She was elected to the LPGA Hall of Fame in 1977.

Henning, Harold (RSA)
Born Johannesburg, 3 October 1934
Turned professional 1953
One of three brothers from a well-known South African golf family he was a regular winner of golf events in his home country and Europe and had two wins on the US Tour. Played ten times for South Africa in the World Cup winning the event with Gary Player in Madrid in 1965.

Hjörth, Maria (Swe)
Born Falun, 10 October 1973
Turned professional 1996
After an excellent amateur career when she won titles in Finland, Norway and Spain) she attended the prestigious Sherry Cup) she attended Stirling University in Scotland on a golf bursary and graduated with a BA honours degree in English before turning professional.

Hoch, Scott (USA)
Born Raleigh, North Carolina, 24 November 1955
Turned professional 1979
Ryder Cup, Presidents Cup, Walker Cup and Eisenhower Trophy player who is a regular winner on the US Tour. Has scored 10 wins on the US Tour between 1980 and 2001 and has had six more victories worldwide. In 1989 he donated $100,000 of his Las Vegas Invitational winnings to the Arnold Palmer Children's Hospital in Orlando where his son Cameron had been successfully treated for a rare bone infection in his right knee.

Ilonen, Mikko (Fin)
Born Lahti, 18 December 1979
Turned professional 2001
Became the first Finnish golfer to win the Amateur Championship when he beat Christian Reimbold from Germany 2 and 1 in the final at Royal Liverpool. He has won both the Finnish match play and stroke play titles.

Inkster, Juli (USA)
Born Santa Cruz, California, 24 June 1960
Turned professional 1983
Winner of two majors in 1984 (the Nabisco Championship and the du Maurier) she also had a double Major year in 1999 when she won the US Women's Open and the LPGA Championship which she won for a second time in 2000. In her amateur career she became the first player since 1934 to win the US Women's amateur title three years in a row (1980, 81, 82). Only four other women and one man (Tiger Woods) have successfully defended the national titles twice in a row. Coached for a time by London-based Leslie King at Harrods Store.

Irwin, Hale (USA)
Born Joplin, Montana, 3 June 1945
Turned professional 1968
A three time winner of the US Open (1974, 1979 and 1990) he has been a prolific winner on the main US Tour and, since turning 50, on the US Senior Tour. He had 20 wins on the main Tour including the 1990 US Open triumph where he holed a 45-foot putt on the final green at Medinah to force a play-off with Mike Donald then after both were still tied following a further 18 holes became the oldest winner of the Championship at 45 when he sank a 10-foot birdie putt at the first extra hole of sudden death. Joint runner-up to Tom Watson in the 1983 Open at Royal Birkdale where he stubbed the ground and missed a tap-in putt on the final day – a slip that cost him the chance of a play-off. Three times top earner on the Senior Tour where, prior to the start of the 2001 season, he had averaged $90,573 per start in 130 events coming in the top three in 63 of those events and finishing over par in only nine of them.

January, Don (USA)
Born Plainview, Texas, 20 November 1929
Turned professional 1955
Winner of the US Open in 1967 he followed up his successful main Tour career in which he had 11 wins between 1956 and 1976 with double that success as a Senior winning 22 times. Much admired for his easy rhythmical style.

Janzen, Lee (USA)
Born Austin, Minnesota, 28 August 1964
Turned professional 1986
Twice a winner of the US Open in 1993 and again in 1998 when he staged the best final round comeback since Johnny Miller rallied from six back to win the title 25 years earlier. Five strokes behind the late Payne Stewart after 54 holes at Baltusrol he closed with a 67 to beat Stewart with whom he had also battled for the title in 1993.

Jimenez, Miguel Angel (Esp)
Born Malaga, 4 January 1954
Turned professional 1982
Talented Spaniard who was runner-up to Tiger Woods in the 2000 US Open. This was a year after making his successful début in the Ryder Cup. One of seven brothers he did not take up golf until his mid-teens. He loves cars, drives a Ferrari and has been nicknamed 'The Mechanic' by his friends. His best-remembered shot was the 3-wood he hit into the hole for an albatross 2 at the infamous 17th hole at Valderrama in the Volvo Masters but he was credited with having played the Canon Shot of the Year when he chipped in at the last to win 1998 Trophée Lancôme. In 2000 lost in a play-off at Valderrama in a World Championship to Tiger Woods.

Johansson, Per-Ulrik (Swe)
Born Uppsala, 6 December 1966
Turned professional 1990
A former amateur international at both junior and senior level he became the first Swede to play in two Ryder Cups when he made the 1995 and 1997 teams. In 1997 he played Phil Mickelson with whom he had studied at Arizona State University in the singles. In 1991 he was winner of the Sir Henry Cotton Rookie of the Year award in Europe.

Jones, Steve (USA)
Born Artesia, New Mexico, 27 December 1958
Turned professional 1981
First player since Jerry Pate in 1976 to win the US Open after having had to qualify in 1996. That victory was the result of inspiration he received from reading a Ben Hogan book given to him the week before the Championship at Oakland Hills. Uses a reverse overlapping grip as a result of injury. Indeed his career was put on hold for three years after injury to his left index finger following a dirt-bike accident. He dominated the 1997 Phoenix Open shooting 62, 64, 65 and 67 for an 11 shot victory over Jesper Parnevik That week his 258 winning total was just one outside the low US Tour record set by Mike Souchak in 1955.

King, Betsy (USA)
Born Reading, Pennsylvania, 13 August 1955
Turned professional 1977
Another stalwart of the LPGA Tour in America she has won 34 times between 1984 and 2001. Winner of the British Open in 1985 she has also won the US Open in 1989 and 1990, the Nabisco Championship three times in 1987, 1990 and 1997 and the LPGA Championship in 1990. She never managed to win the du Maurier event although finishing in the top six on nine occasions. Three times Rolex Player of the Year in 1984, 1989 and 1993 she was elected to the LPGA Hall of Fame in 1995.

Kite, Tom (USA)
Born Austin, Texas, 9 December 1949
Turned professional 1972
He won the US Open at Pebble Beach in 1992 in difficult conditions when aged 42 to lose the 'best player around never to have won a Major' tag. With 19 wins on the main Tour he was the first to top $6million, $7 million, $8 million and $9 million dollars in prize money. Has been playing since he was 11 and

after a lifetime wearing glasses had laser surgery to correct acute near-sightedness. The Ryder Cup captain in 1997 he now plays the US Senior Tour.

Klein, Emilee (USA)
Born Santa Monica, California, 11 June 1974
Turned professional 1994
A former Curtis Cup player who played in the 1994 match she scored her biggest triumph as a professional when winning the Weetabix British Women's Open at Woburn in 1996.

Kuchar, Matt (USA)
Born Lake Mary, Florida, 21 June 1978
Winner of the US Amateur in 1997 he was leading amateur in the 1998 Masters and US Open Championship.

Kuehne, Kelli (USA)
Born Dallas, Texas, 11 May 1977
Turned professional 1998
Having won the US Women's Amateur Championship in 1995 she successfully defended the title the following year when she also won the British Women's title – the first player to win both in the same year. She was also the first player to follow up her win in the US Junior Girls Championship in 1994 with victory in the US Women's event the following year. Her brother Hank is also a professional.

Langer, Bernhard (Ger)
Born Anhausen, 27 August 1957
Turned professional 1972
One of the game's most respected figures and consistent performers he is best known for having conquered the putting yips on more than one occasion. Twice winner of the US Masters in 1985 and 1993 he has never managed to win the Open despite coming second twice and third on three occasions. Deeply religious he was for many years Germany's only top player. He has been an inspiration to many taking his own National title on 12 occasions and winning 37 titles in Europe between 1980 and 2000. In 1979 he won the Cacherel Under 25s Championship by 17 shots. He played nine times in the Ryder Cup between 1981 and 1997 proving a mainstay in foursomes and fourballs with 11 different partners. He regained his place for the 2001 match being played later this year after having been overlooked for a captain's pick in 1999. Now plays both the US and European Tours. Has won ten times in Germany including five German Opens.

Lehman, Tom (USA)
Born Austin, Minnesota, 7 March 1959
Turned professional 1982
Winner of the Open Championship at Royal Lytham and St Annes in 1996 he was runner-up in the US Open in 1996 and third in 1997. He was runner-up in the 1994 US Masters having come third the previous year. Has played in four Ryder Cup matches.

Leonard, Justin (USA)
Born Dallas, Texas, 15 June 1972
Turned professional 1994
Winner of the 1997 Open at Royal Troon when he beat Jesper Parnevik and Darren Clarke into second place

with a closing 65 and nearly won the title again in 1999 when he lost a four-hole play-off with Jean Van de Velde and Paul Lawrie to the Scotsman at Carnoustie. In 1998 came from five back to beat Lee Janzen in the Players Championship and is remembered for his fight back against José Maria Olazábal on the final day of the 1999 Ryder Cup at Brookline. Four down after 11 holes he managed to share a half-point with the Spaniard to help America win the Cup.

Littler, Gene (USA)
Born San Diego, California, 21 July 1930
Turned professional 1954
Winner of the 1953 US Amateur Championship he had a distinguished professional career scoring 26 victories on the US Tour between 1955 and 1977. He scored his only major triumph at Pebble Beach in 1971 when he beat Bob Goalby and Doug Sanders at Oakland Hills. He had been runner-up in the US Open in 1954 and was runner-up in the 1977 US PGA Championship and the 1970 US Masters. A seven-time Ryder Cup player between 1961 and 1977 he is a former winner of the Ben Hogan, Bobby Jones and Byron Nelson awards. He won the Hogan award after successfully beating cancer.

Lopez, Nancy (née Knight) (USA)
Born Torrance, California, 6 January 1957
Turned professional 1977
One of the game's bubbliest personalities and impressive performers who took her first title – the New Mexico Women's Amateur title at age 12. Between 1978 and 1995 she won 48 times on the LPGA Tour and was Rolex Player of the Year on four occasions (1978, 79, 85 and 88). In 1978, her rookie year, she won nine titles including a record five in a row. That year she also lost two play-offs and remains the only player to have won the Rookie of the Year, Player of the Year and Vare Trophy (scoring average) in the same season. A year later she won eight tournaments. Three times a winner of the LPGA Championship in 1978, 1985 and 1989 she has never managed to win the US Open although she was runner-up in 1975 as an amateur, in 1977, 1989 and most recently 1997 when she lost out to Britain's Alison Nicholas.

De Lorenzi, Marie-Laure (Fra)
Born Biarritz, 21 January 1961
Turned professional 1986
The stylish French golfer won 20 titles in Europe between 1987 and 1997 setting a record in 1988 when she won eight times but for family reasons never spent time on the US Tour. Jointly holds the record for 54 holes on the European Tour with her 201 total in the 1995 Dutch Open.

Love III, Davis (USA)
Born Charlotte, North Carolina, 13 April 1964
Turned professional 1985
Son of one of America's most highly rated teachers who died in a plane crash in 1988, Love has won only one major – the 1997 US PGA Championship at Winged Foot where he beat Justin Leonard by five shots. He has been runner-up in the US Open (1996) and the US Masters (1999). In the World Cup of Golf won the title in partnership with Fred Couples four years in a row

(1992-1995). He has played in four Ryder Cups and is in the 2001 team to meet Europe in the postponed match this year.

Lunn, Karen (Aus)
Born Sydney, 21 March 1966
Turned professional 1985
A former top amateur she won the British Women's Open in 1993 at Woburn following the success in the European Ladies Open earlier in the year by her younger sister Mardi.

McIntire, Barbara (USA)
Born Toledo, Ohio, 1935
One of America's best amateurs who finished runner-up in the 1956 US Women's Open to Kathy Cornelius at Northland Duluth. Winner of the US Women's Amateur title in 1959 and 1964 she also won the British Amateur title in 1960. She played in six Curtis Cups between 1958 and 1962.

McNulty, Mark (Zim)
Born Zimbabwe, 25 October 1953
Turned professional 1977
Recognised as one of the best putters in golf he was runner-up to Nick Faldo in the 1990 Open at St Andrews. Although hampered throughout his career by a series of injuries and illness he has scored 16 wins on the European Tour and 33 around the world including 23 on the South African Sunshine circuit. He won the South African Open in 1987 and again in 2001 holing an 18-foot putt on the last at East London to beat Justin Rose.

Maggert, Jeff (USA)
Born Columbia, Missouri, 20 February 1964
Turned professional 1986
A three times Ryder Cup player who competed in the 1995, 1997 and 1999 matches he won the World Golf Championship Match Play event in 1999 to land a million. A quiet achiever he has come third in the US PGA twice in 1995 and 1997.

Mallon, Meg (USA)
Born Natwick, Maryland, 14 April 1963
Turned professional 1986
Winner of the 1991 US Women's Open and nine other events on the LPGA Tour between 1991 and 2000.

Mann, Carole (USA)
Born Buffalo, New York, 3 February 1940
Turned professional 1960
Winner of 38 events on the LPGA Tour in her 22 years on Tour. A former president of the LPGA she was a key figure in the founding of the Tour and received the prestigious Babe Zaharias award. In 1964 she won the Western Open, then a Major, and in 1965 the US Women's Open but in 1968 she had a then record 23 rounds in the 60s, won 11 times and won the scoring averages prize with a score of 72.04.

Marsh, Graham (Aus)
Born Kalgoorlie, Western Australia, 14 January 1944
Turned professional 1968
A notable Australian who followed up his international playing career by gaining a reputation for designing fine

courses. Although he played in Europe, America and Australasia he spent most of his time on the Japanese circuit where he had 17 wins between 1971 and 1982 but won 11 times in Europe and scored victories also in the United States, India, Thailand and Malaysia.

Massey, Debbie (USA)
Born Grosse Pointe, Michigan, 5 November 1950
Turned professional 1977
Best known for winning the British Women's Open in 1980 and 1981.

Melnyk, Steve (USA)
Born Brunswick, Georgia, 26 February 1947
Turned professional 1971
US Amateur champion in 1969 and British champion in 1971. His professional career was cut short because of an ankle injury. Today he commentates for CBS, one of the US networks.

Mickelson, Phil (USA)
Born San Diego, California, 16 June 1970
Turned professional 1992
Plays all sports right-handed except golf and claims to have started hitting golf balls at 18 months. Although he won the 2000 Tour Championship is still without a major victory. His best finishes in Majors are second in the 2001 US PGA Championship and the 1999 US Open and third in the 1994 US PGA Championship. His 19 victories on the US Tour include a win as an amateur in the 1995 Tucson Open. His 65 at the Masters in 1996 is lowest score by a left-hander at that event. One of only three players to win the NCAA Championship and US Amateur in the same year. The others – Jack Nicklaus and Tiger Woods. He has played in two Walker Cups, four times in Presidents Cup and in five Ryder Cup matches including the still to be played 2001 match.

Miller, Johnny Lawrence (USA)
Born San Francisco, California, 29 April 1947
Turned professional 1969
Dreamed of winning the Open after Tony Lema, another member of the Olympic Club in San Francisco, did so in 1964. Realised his dream when he beat Jack Nicklaus and Seve Ballesteros into second place in the 1976 Open at Royal Birkdale. His US Open win in 1973 came with the help of a brilliant last round 63 which set the record since equalled for the lowest round in the Championship. Was involved with Tom Weiskopf and Jack Nicklaus in one of the greatest finishes to a US Masters in 1975 which Nicklaus won. He scored 24 wins between 1971 and 1984 and in 1975 shot 49 under par when winning the Phoenix and Tucson Opens in successive weeks. Now commentates for NBC.

Mize, Larry Hogan (USA)
Born Augusta, Georgia, 23 September 1958
Turned professional 1980
Only local player ever to win the Masters and he did it in dramatic style holing a 140-foot pitch and run at the second extra hole to edge out Greg Norman and Seve Ballesteros. He had made the play-off by holing a 10-foot birdie on the final green. In 1993 he beat an international field to take the Johnnie Walker World Championship title at Tryall in Jamaica.

Nagle, Kel (Aus)
Born North Sydney, 21 December 1920
Turned professional 1946
In the dramatic Centenary Open at St Andrews in 1960 he edged out Arnold Palmer, winner already that year of the Masters and US Open, to become champion. It was the finest moment in the illustrious career of a golfer who has been a wonderful ambassador for his country. Along with Peter Thomson he competed nine times in the World Cup winning the event in 1954. He is an honorary member of the Royal and Ancient Golf Club of St Andrews.

Nelson, Byron (USA)
Born Fort Worth, Texas, 4 February 1912
Turned professional 1932
In the 1945 US season he won 18 times including 11 events in a row between March and August – a record unlikely ever to be broken. Between 1935 and 1946 he won 54 times but although he won the US Open in 1939, the US PGA Championship in 1940 and 1945 and the US Masters in 1937 and 1942 he never managed to complete the set of four majors. His only win in Europe was the 1955 French Open. He remains a father figure in US golf and until he retired in 2001 was one of the Masters honorary starters along with Sam Snead and the late Gene Sarazen.

Nelson, Larry Gene (USA)
Born Fort Payne, Alabama, 10 September 1947
Turned professional 1971
Often underrated he learned to play by reading Ben Hogan's *The Five Fundamentals of Golf* and broke 100 first time out and 70 after just nine months. Active as well these days on course design he has won the Jack Nicklaus award. He has been successful in the US Open (1983 at Oakmont) and two US PGA Championships (in 1981 at the Atlanta Athletic Club and in 1987 after a play-off with Lanny Wadkins at PGA National). Three times a Ryder Cup player he has competed equally successfully as a Senior having won 15 titles (at end of July 2001). He did not play as a youngster but visited a driving range after completing his military service and was hooked. He was named Senior PGA Tour Player of the Year for finishing top earner and winning six times in 2000. At the end of his third full season on the Senior Tour and after 87 events he had won just short of $10 million.

Neumann, Liselotte (Swe)
Born Finspang, 20 May 1966
Turned professional 1985
Having won the US Women's Open in 1988 she won the Weetabix British Women's title in 1990 to become one of six players to complete the Transatlantic double. The others are Laura Davies, Alison Nicholas, Jane Geddes, Betsy King and Patty Sheehan. The 1988 Rookie of the Year on the LPGA Tour she has played in all six Solheim Cup matches.

Newton, Jack (Aus)
Born Sydney, 30 January 1950
Turned professional 1969
Runner-up to Tom Watson after a play-off in the 1975 Open at Carnoustie and runner-up to Seve Ballesteros in the 1980 Masters at Augusta, he was a popular

personality on both sides of the Atlantic and in his native Australia only to have his playing career ended prematurely when he walked into the whirling propeller of a plane at Sydney airport. He lost an eye, an arm and had considerable internal injuries but the quick action of a surgeon who happened to be around probably saved his life. Learned to play one-handed and still competes in pro-ams successfully. Until his retirement in 2000 he was chairman of the Australasian Tour and remains Australia's most successful golf commentator working exclusively for Channel Seven.

Nicklaus, Jack William (USA)

Born Columbus, Ohio, 21 January 1940
Turned professional 1961
The greatest golfer of the 20th century and possibly of all time depending on what Tiger Woods manages to achieve. After winning two US Amateurs he went on to win 18 professional major titles. His record is phenomenal. He won the Open in 1966, 1970 and 1978, the last two at St Andrews and was runner-up seven times and third on two further occasions. He won the US Open in 1962, 1967, 1972 and 1980 and came second four times. He won five US PGA titles in 1963, 1971, 1973, 1975 and 1980 and was runner-up four times and third on two further occasions and he won six Masters in 1963, 1965, 1966, 1972, 1975 and 1986 when at the age of 46 he became the oldest winner of a Green Jacket. In addition he was runner-up four times and third twice. In 1966 he became the first player to successfully defend the Masters (a feat later matched by Nick Faldo in 1990). He won six Australian Opens (1964, 1968, 1971, 1975, 1976 and 1978) and played in six Ryder Cups, captaining two more in 1983 at Palm Beach Gardens when America won and in 1987 at Muirfield Village where his side were losers for the first time on home soil. Credited with saving the Cup match after suggesting that Continental golfers should be included in the side from 1979. Ten years earlier he conceded the 18-inch putt that Jacklin had for a half at the last when the result of the match depended on the result of that game. The match was drawn. After winning 71 times between 1962 and 1984 on the main Tour he won a further ten times on the Senior US Tour. He has won almost every honour you can win in golf including the Byron Nelson, Ben Hogan and Walter Hagen awards. He was the US top money earner in seasons 1964, 1965, 1967, 1971, 1972, 1973, 1975 and 1976 and is a honorary member of the Royal and Ancient Golf Club of St Andrews. Bobby Jones once said of Nicklaus that 'he played a game with which I am not familiar'. With the constant support of his wife Barbara, Nicklaus has been the personification of all that is good about the game.

Nobilo, Frank (NZ)

Born Auckland, 14 May 1960
Turned professional 1979
Injury has affected his career in recent years but he remains one of his country's most popular players with an excellent swing. After winning regularly in Europe he moved to America where in 1997 he won the Greater Greensboro Classic. He has represented New Zealand in nine World Cup matches between 1982 and 1999, played in 11 Alfred Dunhill Cups and three Presidents Cup sides.

Norman, Greg (Aus)

Born Mount Isa, Queensland, 10 February 1955
Turned professional 1976
Australia's most prolific winner in recent years credited with 77 victories worldwide (as of July 2001) but has slowed down because of injury and trimmed his schedule in recent times. He won the Open in tough conditions at Turnberry in 1986 and again in glorious weather at Royal St George's in 1993 when he fired the lowest winning aggregate of 267 (66, 68, 69, 64). Decided to take up golf after caddying for his mother and abandoned plans to join the Australian Air Force. One of the few golfers to have topped the official money lists on both sides of the Atlantic he received his first winner's cheque in the Westlake Classic on the Australian Tour in 1976. Has the unhappy reputation of having lost Majors in three different types of play-off – the 1987 Masters to Larry Mize and the 1993 US PGA to Paul Azinger in sudden death, the Open to Mark Calcavecchia at Royal Troon n a four-hole play-off in 1989 and the US Open over 18 holes to Fuzzy Zoeller at Winged Foot in 1984. In 1986 he led going into the final round of all four Majors that year and won only the Open. During his career he has set all kinds of money records on the US Tour but is jinxed at the US Masters where he has finished second three times. He has also been runner-up on five other occasions in Majors. Today spends as much time in the boardroom looking after his business interests as he does playing.

North, Andy (USA)

Born Thorp, Wisconsin, 9 March 1950
Turned professional 1972
Although this tall American found it difficult to win Tour events he did pick up two US Open titles. His first Championship success came at Cherry Hills in Denver in 1986 when he edged out Dave Stockton and JC Snead and the second at Oakland Hills in 1985 when he finished just a shot ahead of Dave Barr, TC Chen and Denis Watson who had been penalised a shot during the Championship for waiting longer than the regulation 10 seconds at one hole to see if his ball would drop into the cup. North is now a very successful golf commentator whose analytical comments are much admired.

Okamoto, Ayako (Jpn)

Born Hiroshima, 12 April 1951
Turned professional 1976
Although she won the British Women's Open in 1984 she managed only a runner-up spot in the US Women's Open and US LPGA Championships despite finishing in the top 20 28 times and missing the cut only four times. In the LPGA Championships she finished second or third five times in six years from 1986. She scored 17 victories in the USA between 1982 and 1992, won the 1990 German Open and was Japanese Women's champion in 1993 and 1997.

Olazábal, José Maria (Esp)

Born Fuenterrabia, 5 February 1966
Turned professional 1985
Twice a winner of the Masters, his second triumph was particularly emotional. He had won in 1994 but had to withdraw from the 1995 Ryder Cup with a foot problem eventually diagnosed as rheumatoid

polyarthritis in three joints of the right foot and two of the left. He was out of golf for eighteen months but treatment from Munich doctor Hans-Wilhelm Muller-Wohlfahrt helped him back to full fitness after a period when he was house bound and unable to walk. At that point it seemed as if his career was over, but he came back in 1999 to beat Davis Love III by two shots at Augusta. With over twenty victories in Europe and a further seven abroad, the son of a Real Sebastian greenkeeper who took up the game at the age of four has been one of the most popular players in the game. He competed in six Ryder Cups frequently partnering Severiano Ballesteros. He is a former British Boys Youths and Amateur champion. His best performance in the Open was third in 1992 when Nick Faldo won at Muirfield.

O'Meara, Mark (USA)

Born Goldsboro, North Carolina, 13 January 1957
Turned professional 1980

A former US Amateur Champion in 1979 Mark was 41 when he won his first Major – the US Masters at Augusta. That week in 1998 he did not three putt once on Augusta's glassy greens. Three months later he won the Open at Royal Birkdale battling with, among others, Tiger Woods with whom he has had a particular friendship. They both live at Isleworth in Florida. He is the oldest player to win two Majors in the same year and was chosen as PGA Player of the Year that season. When he closed birdie, birdie to win the Masters he joined Arnold Palmer and Art Wall as the only players to do that and became only the fifth player in Masters history to win without leading in the first three rounds. He won his Open championship title in a four hole play-off against Brian Watts. O'Meara has played in five Ryder Cups between 1985 and 1999.

Ozaki, Masashi (Jumbo) (Jpn)

Born Kaiman Town, Tokushima, 24 January 1947
Turned professional 1980

Along with Isao Aoki is Japan's best known player, but unlike Aoki has maintained his base in Japan where he has scored over 80 victories. His only overseas win was the New Zealand Open early in his career. He is a golfing icon in his native country. His two brothers Joe (Naomichi) and Jet also play professionally.

Pak, Se Ri (Kor)

Born Daejeon, 28 September 1977
Turned professional 1996

In 1998 she was awarded the Order of Merit by the South Korean government – the highest honour given to an athlete – for having won two Majors in her rookie year on the US Tour. She won the McDonald LPGA Championship matching Liselotte Neumann in making a major her first tour success. When she won the US Women's Open later that year after an 18-hole play-off followed by two extra holes of sudden death against amateur Jenny Chuasiriporn, she became the youngest golfer to take that title. By the middle of 2001 she had won 12 events on the US tour including the Weetabix Women's British Open at Sunningdale – an event included on the US Tour as well as the European Circuit for the first time. As an amateur in Korea she won 30 titles.

Palmer, Arnold (USA)

Born Latrobe, Pennsylvania, 10 September 1929
Turned professional 1954

Winner of 61 titles on the US Tour between 1956 and 1980, he is one of the most charismatic players in golf who has been credited with starting the golfing boom in the latter part of the 20th century. A former US Amateur champion in 1954, his performances were always exciting to watch and for years he was followed around by his own ever-loyal army of fans... indeed still is when he tees up on the US Senior Tour. He won eight Major titles – the 1960 US Open and the 1961 and 1962 Opens at Royal Birkdale in very stormy weather and at Royal Troon where he beat Kel Nagle by six shots and the rest of the field by 13. He won the US Masters in 1958, 1960, 1962 and 1964 but never managed to win the US PGA although he finished second three times. The first player to pass the $1 million mark in earnings he helped Keith Mackenzie the then secretary of the Royal and Ancient Golf Club of St Andrews revive the Open and is now a distinguished honorary member of the club. In 1960 having won the US Masters and US Open he came to St Andrews for the Centenary Open hoping to match three majors in a season – a record held at the time by Ben Hogan but he was beaten by Australian Kel Nagle. Son of the greenkeeper at Ligonier in the Pennsylvanian mountains – he later bought the club – he has remained a respected golfing idol noted for his remarkable strength and his attacking golf. With Jack Nicklaus and Gary Player he became a member of the modern Big Three – a concept developed by his manager Mark McCormack whose first client he was.

Parnevik, Jesper (Swe)

Born Danderyd, Stockholm, 7 March 1965
Turned professional 1986

Son of a well-known Swedish entertainer he is one of the most extrovert of golfers best known for his habit of wearing a baseball cap with the brim turned up and brightly coloured drain-pipe style trousers. Winner of events on both sides of the Atlantic he plays most of his golf these days in America where he has won five times since 1998 and made history in 1995 when he became the first Swede to win in Sweden when he took the Scandinavian Masters at Barseback in Malmo. Has twice finished runner-up in the Open at Turnberry in 1994 when he was two ahead but made a bogey at the last and was passed by Nick Price who finished with an eagle and a birdie in the last three holes. He led by two with a round to go in 1998 but shot 73 and finished tied second with Darren Clarke behind Justin Leonard. Played in the 1997 and 1999 Ryder Cup teaming up successfully with Sergio Garcia to win three and a half points in 1999. Is also in the 2001 team. Has had health problems suffering injuries and illness and has resorted at times to unusual remedies including eating volcanic dust to cleanse the system.

Pate, Jerry (USA)

Born Macon, Georgia, 16 September 1953
Turned professional 1975

Winner of the 1976 US Open when he hit a 5-iron across water to three feet at the 72nd hole at the Atlanta Athletic Club. He was a member of what is regarded as the strongest ever Ryder Cup side that beat the Europeans at Walton Heath in 1981. Has now retired from golf and commentates for one of the American networks

Pavin, Corey (USA)

Born Oxnard, California, 26 May 1961
Turned professional 1983
Although not one of golf's longer hitters he battled with powerful Greg Norman to take the 1995 US Open title at Shinnecock Hills. A runner-up in the 1994 US PGA Championship and third in the 1992 US Masters he won 13 times between 1984 and 1996. His only victory in Europe came when he took the German Open title in 1983 while on honeymoon.

Pepper (Mochrie, Scarinzi), Dottie (USA)

Born Saratoga Springs, Florida, 17 August 1965
Turned professional 1987
Winner of 17 events (through to July 2001) on the US LPGA Tour including two majors. A fierce competitor she took the Nabisco Dinah Shore title in 1992 and again in 1999. She has played in all Solheim Cup matches to date and along with Laura Davies has earned a record 14 points.

Player, Gary (RSA)

Born Johannesburg, 1 November 1935
Turned professional 1953
One of the modern Big Three with Arnold Palmer and Jack Nicklaus, he has won 167 titles worldwide including nine Majors between 1959 and 1978 and nine senior Majors between 1986 and 1997. His Major wins include three Open Championships in 1959 at Muirfield, 1968 at Carnoustie and 1974 at Royal Lytham and St Annes, three US Masters in 1961, 1974 and 1978, the US Open in 1965 when he completed a Grand Slam of major titles and the US PGA Championship in 1962 and 1972. A life-long fitness fanatic who has won titles in five decades he is one of only five players to have won all four Major titles. Gene Sarazen, Ben Hogan, Jack Nicklaus and Tiger Woods are the others. He considers the greatest thrill of his life was becoming the third man in history to do so. Having never based himself full-time in the US he has travelled more miles than any other golfer during his career – an estimated 12 million by the end of 2000. He entered his first Open in 1955 and failed to qualify but finished fourth in 1956 and played for the last time at Royal Lytham and St Annes in 2001 when 66. One of his most dramatic major performances came when he went into the last round seven shots behind Hubert Green at the 1974 US Masters, came home in 30 and equalled the then record 64 to win. He scored a record seven wins in the Australian Open, took the South African Open a record 13 times and won the World Match Play title a record-equalling five times coming from seven down after 19 holes in one tie in 1965 to beat Tony Lema at the 37th. Credited as being one of the game's greatest bunker players he remains as enthusiastic about competing today as he did when he first took up the game.

Prado, Catherine (*née* Lacoste) (Fra)

Born Paris 27 June 1945
The only amateur golfer ever to win the US Women's Open she won the title at Hot Springs, Virginia in 1967. She was also the first non-American to take the title and the youngest. Two years later she won both the US and British Amateur titles. She was a four times winner of her own French Championship in 1967, 1969, 1970 and 1972 and won the Spanish title in 1969, 1972 and 1976. She comes from a well-known French sporting family.

Price, Nick (Zim)

Born Durban, South Africa, 28 January 1957
Turned professional 1977
One of the game's most popular players his greatest season was 1990 when he took six titles including the Open at Turnberry when he beat Jesper Parnevik and the US PGA at Southern Hills when Corey Pavin was second. He had scored his first Major triumph two years earlier when he edged out John Cook, Nick Faldo, Jim Gallagher Jr and Gene Sauers at the US PGA at Bellerive, St Louis. Along with Tiger Woods his record of 15 wins in the 90s was the most by any player. One of only seven players to win consecutive Majors, the others being Ben Hogan, Jack Nicklaus, Arnold Palmer, Lee Trevino, Tom Watson and Tiger Woods. Four times a Presidents Cup player he jointly holds the Augusta National record of 63 with Greg Norman. One of only two players in the 90s to win two Majors in a year, the others being Nick Faldo in 1990 and Mark O'Meara in 1998. Born of English parents but brought up in Zimbabwe he played his early golf with Mark McNulty and Tony Johnstone. Winner of 39 titles by end of July 2001.

Rawls, Betsy (USA)

Born Spartanburg, South Carolina, 4 May 1928
Turned professional 1951
Winner of the 1951, 1953, 1957 and 1960 US Women's Open and the US LPGA Championship in 1959 and 1969 as well as two Western Opens when the Western Open was a Major, she scored 55 victories on the LPGA Tour between 1951 and 1972. One of the best shot makers in women's golf who was noted for her game around and on the greens.

Rivero, José (Esp)

Born Madrid, 20 September 1955
Turned professional 1973
One of only eight Spaniards who have played in the Ryder Cup he competed in the winning 1985 and 1987 sides. Worked as a caddie but received a grant from the Spanish Federation to pursue his golf career. With José Maria Canizares won the World Cup in 1984 at Olgiata in Italy.

Rocca, Costantino (Ita)

Born Bergamo, 4 December 1956
Turned professional 1981
The first and to date only Italian to play in the Ryder Cup. In the 1999 match at Valderrama he beat Tiger Woods 4 and 2 in a vital singles. Left his job in a polystyrene box making factory to become a club professional and graduated to the tournament scene through Europe's Challenge Tour. In 1995 he fluffed a chip at the final hole in the Open at St Andrews only to hole from 60 feet out of the Valley of Sin to force a play-off against John Daly which he then lost.

Rogers, William (Bill) (USA)
Born Waco, Texas, 10 September 1951
Turned professional 1974
US PGA Player of the Year in 1981 when he won the Open at Royal St George's and was runner-up in the US Open. That year he also won the Australian Open but retired from top line competitive golf not long after because he did not enjoy all the travelling. A former Walker Cup player in 1973 he only entered the Open in 1981 at the insistence of Ben Crenshaw. Now a successful club professional and sometime television commentator.

Romero, Eduardo (Arg)
Born Cordoba, Argentina, 12 July 1954
Turned professional 1982
Son of the Cordoba club professional he learned much from former Open champion Roberto de Vicenzo and has inherited his grace and elegance as a competitor. A wonderful ambassador for Argentina he briefly held a US Tour card in 1994 but prefers to play his golf these days on the European Tour where he has won seven times including impressively at the 1999 Canon European Masters where he improved his concentration after studying Indian yoga techniques. Used his own money to sponsor Angel Cabrera with whom he finished second in the 2000 World Cup in Buenos Aries behind Tiger Woods and David Duval.

Sandelin, Jarmo (Swe)
Born Imatra, Finland, 10 May 1967
Turned professional 1987
Extrovert Swede who made his début in the Ryder Cup at Brookline in 1999 although he did not play until the singles. Has always been a snazzy dresser on course where he is one of the game's longest hitters often in the early days with a 54-inch shafted driver. Four time winner on Tour (at end of July 2001) he met his partner Linda when she asked to caddie for him at a Stockholm pro-am.

Sander, Anne (Welts, Decker, *née* Quast) (USA)
Born ?Marysville, 1938
A three time winner of the US Ladies title in 1958, 1961 and 1963, she also won the British Ladies title in 1980. She made eight appearances in the Curtis Cup stretching from 1958 to 1990. Only Carole Semple Thompson has played more often having played ten times.

Scott, Adam (Aus)
Born Adelaide, 16 July 1980
Turned professional 2000
Highly regarded young Australian who was ranked World No 2 amateur when he turned professional in 2000. Coached in the early days by his father Phil, himself a golf professional Scott now uses Butch Harmon whom he met while attending the University of Las Vegas. Swings very much like another Harmon client Tiger Woods. He made headlines as an amateur when he fired a 10-under-par 63 at the Lakes in the Greg Norman Holden International in 2000 but has shot 62 in the US Junior Championship at Los Coyotes CC. Made his European Tour card in just eight starts and secured his first Tour win when beating Justin Rose in the 2001 Alfred Dunhill Championship at Houghton in Johannesburg.

Segard, Mme Patrick (de St Saveur, *née* Lally Vagliano) (Fra)
Former chairperson of the Women's Committee of the World Amateur Golf Council holding the post from 1964 to 1972. A four times French champion (1948, 50, 51 and 52) she also won the British (1950), Swiss (1949 and 1965), Luxembourg (1949), Italian (1949 and 1951) and Spanish (1951) amateur titles. She represented France from 1937 to 1939, from 1947 to 1965 and again in 1970.

Semple Thompson, Carol (USA)
Born 1950
Winner of the US Ladies Amateur title in 1973 and the British Ladies in 1974 she has played in ten Curtis Cup matches between 1974 and 2000 playing in 31 games.

Senior, Peter (Aus)
Born Singapore, 31 July 1959
Turned professional 1978
One of Australia's most likeable and underrated performers who has been a regular winner over the years on the Australian, Japanese and European circuits. Converted to the broomstick putter by Sam Torrance – a move that saved his playing career. A former winner of the Australian Open, Australian PGA and Australian Masters titles he had considerable success off the course when he bought a share in a pawn-broking business.

Sheehan, Patty (USA)
Born Middlebury, Vermont, 27 October 1956
Turned professional 1980
Scored 35 victories between 1981 and 1996 including six Majors – the LPGA Championship in 1983, 1984 and 1994, the US Women's Open in 1993 and 1994 and the Nabisco Championship in 1996. As an amateur she won all her four games in the 1980 Curtis Cup. She is a member of the LPGA Hall of Fame.

Siderowf, Dick (USA)
Twice a winner of the British Amateur title in 1973 when he beat Peter Moody at Royal Porthcawl and again in 1976 when he had to go to the 37th hole to beat John Davies. He was leading amateur in the 1968 US Open and played in four Walker Cups (1969, 1973, 1975 and 1977) before captaining the winning side in 1979.

Sigel, Jay ((USA)
Born Narbeth, Pennsylvania, 13 November 1943
Turned professional 1993
Winner of the Amateur Championship in 1979 when he beat Scott Hoch 3 and 2 at Hillside, he also won the US Amateur in successive years 1982 and 1983. He was leading amateur in the US Open in 1984 and leading amateur in the US Masters in 1981, 1982 and 1988. He played in nine Walker Cup matches between 1977 and 1993 and has a record 18 points to his credit. Turned professional in order to join the US Senior Tour where he has had several successes.

Simpson, Scott (USA)

Born San Diego, California, 17 September 1955
Turned professional 1977

Winner of the US Open in 1987 at San Francisco's Olympic Club, he was beaten in a play-off for the title four years later at Hazeltine when the late Payne Stewart won the 18-hole play-off.

Singh, Vijay (Fij)

Born Lautoka, 22 February 1963
Turned professional 1982

An international player who began his career in Australasia he became the first Fijian to win a major when he won the 1998 US PGA Championship at Sahalee but may well be remembered more for his victory in the 2000 US Masters which effectively prevented Tiger Woods winning all four Majors in a year. Tiger went on to win the US Open, Open and US PGA Championship that year and won the Masters the following year to hold all four Major titles at the one time. Introduced to golf by his father, an aeroplane technician, Vijay modelled his swing on that of Tom Weiskopf. Before making the grade on the European Tour where he won the 1992 Volvo German Open by 11 shots he was a club professional in Borneo. He has won tournaments in South Africa, Malaysia, the Ivory Coast, Nigeria, France, Zimbabwe, Morocco, Spain, England, Germany, Sweden, Taiwan and the United States. He ended Ernie Els' run of victories in the World Match Play Championship when he beat him in the final by one hole in 1997 when the South African was going for a fourth successive title. One of the game's most dedicated practisers.

Snead, Samuel Jackson (Sam) (USA)

Born Hot Springs, Virginia, 27 May 1912
Turned professional 1934

Did not want to come to the 1946 Open at St Andrews but came after all and won the title. This golfing legend still acts as an honorary starter at Augusta. He won three US PGA Championships in 1942, 1949 and 1951 and three US Masters in 1949, 1952 and 1954 but never managed to complete a Grand Slam. His national title evaded him despite the fact that he came second four times. He played in seven Ryder Cups between 1939 and 1959 and captained the team that drew with Britain and Ireland in 1969 at Royal Birkdale. Not all the statistics are available but he claims to have won 165 titles during his illustrious career. In 1965 when 52 he became the oldest professional to win on the US Tour when he took the Greater Greensboro Open for the eighth time – a US Tour record. In the 1979 Quad Cities Open became the first player to beat and equal his age when shooting 67 and 66 at age 67. A winner in six decades from the 1936 West Virginian Closed to the Legends of Golf with Don January in 1982, he was a founder member of the US Senior Tour in 1980 and won 11 senior major titles.

Sörenstam, Annika (Swe)

Born Stockholm, 9 October 1970
Turned professional 1992

Winner of the US Open in 1995 and 1996 she and Karrie Webb of Australia have battled for the headlines on the US LPGA Tour over the past few years. A prolific winner of titles in America (24 wins to the end July 2001) she won four in a row in early summer 2000 as she and Webb battled again for the No 1 spot in 2001. Sörenstam was the No 1 earner in 1995, 1997 and 1998, Webb in 1996, 1999 and 2000. At the Standard Register Ping event she became the first golfer to shoot 59 on the LPGA Tour. Her second round score 59 included 13 birdies, 11 of them in her first 12 holes. Her 36-hole total of 124 beat the previous record set by Webb the previous season by three. Her 54-hole score of 193 matched the record set by Karrie Webb and her 72-hole total of 261 which gave her victory by three shots from Se Ri Pak matched the low total on Tour set by Se Ri Pak in 1998. Sörenstam's 27-under-par winning score was a new record for the Tour beating the 26-under-par score Webb returned in the Australian Ladies' Masters in 1999. Her sister Charlotta also plays on the LPGA and Evian Tours. Before turning professional she finished runner-up in the 1992 US Women's Championship.

Stadler, Craig (USA)

Born San Diego, California, 2 June 1953
Turned professional 1975

Nicknamed 'The Walrus' because of his moustache and stocky build, he was the winner of the 1982 Masters at Augusta. Winner of 12 titles on the US Tour between 1980 and 1996 he played in two Ryder Cups (1983 and 1985). As an amateur he played in the 1975 Walker Cup two years after winning the US Amateur.

Steinhauer, Sherri (USA)

Born Madison, Wisconsin, 27 December 1962
Turned professional 1985

Winner of the Women's British Open in 1998 at Royal Lytham and St Annes and the following year at Woburn. She has played in the last three Solheim Cup matches.

Stephenson, Jan (Aus)

Born Sydney, 22 December 1951
Turned professional 1973

She won three majors on the LPGA Tour – the 1981 du Maurier Classic, the 1982 UPGA Championship and the 1983 US Women's Open. She was twice Australian Ladies champion in 1973 and 1977.

Stockton, Dave (USA)

Born San Bernardino, California, 2 November 1941
Turned professional 1964

Winner of two US PGA Championships in 1970 and 1976, he has won more Senior Tour titles (14 as of end July 2001) than he did on the main Tour (11). Captained the American Ryder Cup team at Kiawah Island in 1991.

Stranahan, Frank R (USA)

Born Toledo, Ohio, 5 August 1922
Turned professional 1954

One of America's most successful amateurs he won the Amateur championship at Royal St George's in 1948 and 1950. He also won the US Amateur in 1950, the Mexican Amateur in 1946, 1948 and 1951 and the Canadian title in 1947 and 1948. He was also leading amateur in the Open in 1947, 1949, 1950, 1951 and 1953 behind Ben Hogan. He played in three Walker Cups in 1947, 1949 and 1951.

Strange, Curtis (USA)
Born Norfolk, Virginia, 20 January 1955
Turned professional 1976
Winner of successive US Opens in 1988 and again in 1989 when he beat Nick Faldo in an 18-hole play-off at The Country Club Brookline after getting up and down from a bunker at the last to tie on 278. Winner of 17 US Tour titles he won at least one event for seven successive years from 1983. Having played in five Ryder Cup matches he will captain the US side when the 2001 match is played at The Belfry in 2002 after being postponed in 2001. Now commentates for the ABC Network.

Streit, Marlene Stewart (Can)
Born Cereal, Alberta, 9 March 1934
One of Canada's most successful amateurs she won her national title ten times between 1951 and 1973. She won the 1953 British Amateur, the US Amateur in 1956 and the Australian Ladies in 1963. She was Canadian Woman Athlete of the Year in 1951, 1953, 1956, 1960 and 1963.

Stricker, Steve (USA)
Born Egerton, Wisconsin, 23 February 1967
Turned professional 1990
Started 2001 by winning the $1 million first prize in the Accenture Match Play Championship, one of the World Golf Championship series. In the final he beat Pierre Fulke. Was a member of the winning American Alfred Dunhill Cup side in 1996.

Suggs, Louise (USA)
Born Atlanta, Georgia, 7 September 1923
Turned professional 1948
Winner of 58 titles on the LPGA Tour after a brilliant amateur career which included victories in the 1947 US Amateur and the 1948 British Amateur Championships. She won 11 Majors including the US Open in 1949 and 1952 and the LPGA Championship in 1957. A founder member of the US Tour she was an inaugural honoree when the LPGA Hall of Fame was instituted in 1967.

Sutton, Hal (USA)
Born Shreveport, Louisiana, 28 April 1958
Turned professional 1981
Winner of the 1983 US PGA Championship at the Riviera CC in Los Angeles beating Jack Nicklaus into second place. Played in the 1985 and 1987 Ryder Cup matches and returned to the side in 1999 at Brookline when he beat Darren Clarke 4 and 2 in the singles. Is a member of the 2001 Cup side.

Thomson CBE, Peter W (Aus)
Born Melbourne, 23 August 1929
Turned professional 1949
He is one of only four players who have won five Open Championships. At the start of the 20th century JH Taylor and James Braid won five, and Tom Watson won five in eight years from 1975 while Thomson completed his five victories between 1954 and 1965. In one seven-year spell from 1952 Thomson never finished worse than second in the Championship. His run of finishes from 1952 was 2, 2, 1, 1, 1, 2, 1. His fifth victory, arguably his most impressive, came at Royal Birkdale in 1965 when more Americans were in the field. He played only three times in the US Open finishing fourth in 1956. He played in five US Masters with his best finish in 1957. He won three Australian Opens and in Europe had 24 victories between 1954 and 1972. With one of the most fluent and reliable swings he made golf look easy. Instrumental in developing the game throughout Asia, Africa and the Middle East he was ready to retire from golf and pursue a career in Australian politics but he was not elected and turned instead to the US Senior Tour with great success. In 1985 he won nine Senior Tour titles. Has captained three Rest of the World Presidents Cup sides, was elected to the World Golf Hall of Fame in 1988 and is an honorary member of the Royal and Ancient Golf Club of St Andrews. After his retirement from top-line golf he concentrated on his hugely successful golf course designing business based in Melbourne completing projects in many countries around the world.

Toms, David (USA)
Born Monroe, LA, 4 January 1967
Turned professional 1989
Most important of his six wins on the US Tour was his first Major success by beating Phil Nickelson into second place in the 2001 USPGA Championship. Toms shot 66, 65, 65 and 69 for a 265 record winning aggregate at the Atlanta Athletic Club. This is the lowest aggregate in any Major. The previous year he had come joint fourth to Tiger Woods in the Open. Made his Ryder Cup début in 2001.

Trevino, Lee (USA)
Born Dallas, Texas, 1 December 1939
Turned professional 1961
Twenty times a winner on the US Tour between 1968 and 1981 'Supermex', as he was nicknamed by his peers, hit the headlines in 1971 when he won the US Open beating Jack Nicklaus in a play-off at Merion, the Canadian Open at Montreal and the Open at Royal Birkdale in succession. One of the most extrovert of golfers who followed up his 27 victories on the main Tour with 29 on the US Senior Tour was entirely self-taught. He won six Majors – the Open in 1971 and 1972 when he chipped in at the 71st hole to end Tony Jacklin's hopes of winning, the US Open in 1968 and 1971 and the US PGA Championship in 1974 and 1984 but he never finished better than tenth twice in the Masters at Augusta – a course with so many right to left dog-legs that he felt it did not suit his game. In 1975 he was hit by lightning while playing in the Western Open in Chicago and had to undergo back surgery in order to keep competing. He was involved in one of the low scoring matches in the World Match Play Championship with Tony Jacklin in 1972 when he again came out on top.

Van de Velde, Jean (Fra)
Born Mont de Marsan, 29 May 1966
Turned professional 1987
Who ever remembers who came second? Everybody will remember Jean Van de Velde, however, for

finishing runner-up after a play-off with eventual winner Paul Lawrie and American Justin Leonard when the Open returned to a somewhat tricked-up Carnoustie in 1999. Playing the last hole he led by three but refused to play safe and paid a severe penalty. He ran up a triple bogey 7 after seeing his approach ricochet off a stand into the rough and his next into the Barry Burn. He appeared to contemplate playing the half-submerged ball when taking off his shoes and socks and wading in but that was never a possibility. Took up the game as a youngster when holidaying with his parents in Biarritz. Has scored only one win in Europe (the Roma Masters in 1993) and now plays full time on the US Tour. Made his Ryder Cup début at Brookline in 1999.

Varangot, Brigitte (Fra)
Born Biarritz May 1 1940
Winner of the French Amateur title five times in six years from 1961 and again in 1973. Her run in the French Championship was impressive from 1960 when her finishes were 2, 1, 1, 2, 1, 1, 1, 2. She was also a triple winner of the British Championship in 1963, 1965 and 1968. One of France's most successful players she also won the Italian title in 1970.

Verplank, Scott Rachal (USA)
Born Dallas, Texas, 9 July 1964
When he won the Western Open as an amateur in 1985 he was the first to do so since Doug Sanders took the 1956 Canadian Open. Missed most of the 1991 and 1992 seasons because of an elbow injury and the injury also affected his 1996 season. He has diabetes and wears an insulin pump while playing to regulate his medication. Curtis Strange chose him as one of his two 'picks' for the 2001 US Ryder Cup side.

De Vicenzo, Roberto (Arg)
Born Buenos Aires, 14 April 1923
Turned professional 1938
Although he won the Open in 1967 at Royal Liverpool this impressive South American is perhaps best known for the Major title he might have won. In 1968 he finished tied with Bob Goalby at Augusta or he thought he had. He had finished birdie, bogey to do so but sadly signed for the par 4 that had been inadvertently and carelessly put down for the 17th by Tommy Aaron who was marking his card Although everyone watching on television and at the course saw the Argentinian make 3 the fact that he signed for 4 was indisputable and he had to accept that there would be no play-off. It remains one of the saddest incidents in golf with the emotion heightened by the fact that that Sunday was de Vicenzo's 45th birthday. The gracious manner in which he accepted the disappointments was remarkable. What a contrast to the scenes at Hoylake nine months earlier when, after years of trying, he finally won the Open beating Jack Nicklaus and Clive Clark in the process thanks to a pressure-packed brilliant last round 70. In fact he was runner-up in the event in 1950 and came third six times. The father of South American golf he was a magnificent driver and is credited with having won over 200 titles in his extraordinary career including nine Argentinian Opens between 1944 and 1974 plus the 1957 Jamaican, 1950 Belgian, 1950 Dutch, 1950, 1960 and 1964 French, 1964 German Open and 1966 Spanish Open titles. He

played 15 times for Argentina in the World Cup and four times for Mexico. Inducted into the World Golf Hall of Fame in 1989 he is an honorary member of the Royal and Ancient Golf Club of St Andrews.

Wadkins, Lanny (USA)
Born Richmond, Virginia, 5 December 1949
Turned professional 1971
His 21 victories on the US Tour between 1972 and 1992 include the 1977 US PGA Championship, only Major. He won that after a play-off with Gene Littler at Pebble Beach but lost a play-off for the same title in 1987 to Larry Nelson at Palm Beach Gardens. He was second on two other occasions to Ray Floyd in 1982 and to Lee Trevino in 1984. In other Majors his best finish was third three times in the US Masters (1990, 1991 and 1993), tied second in the US Open (1986) and tied fourth in the 1984 Open at St Andrews. One of the fiercest of competitors he played eight Ryder Cups between 1977 and 1993 winning 20 of his 33 games, but was a losing captain at Oak Hill in 1995.

Ward, Harvie (USA)
Born Tarboro, North Carolina 1926
Turned professional 1973
Winner of the Amateur Championship in 1952 when he beat Frank Stranahan 6 and 5 at Prestwick, he went on to win the US title in 1955 and 1956 and the Canadian Amateur in 1964. He played in the 1953, 1955 and 1959 Walker Cup matches and won all of his six games.

Watson, Tom (USA)
Born Kansas City, Missouri, 4 September 1949
Turned professional 1971
Winner of 34 career titles, he won at least three a year on the main US Tour in a six-year spell between 1977 and 1982. He is best known for having won five Open championships in eight years between 1975 and 1983 to match the feat of JH Taylor, James Braid and Peter Thomson. When he had a chance to win a sixth Open and tie Harry Vardon's record at St Andrews in 1984 he hit his second close to the wall through the green at the 17th and lost out to Seve Ballesteros. Watson's wins came at Carnoustie in 1975 after a play-off with Jack Newton; a memorable 1977 triumph in which he edged out Jack Nicklaus at Turnberry shooting 65, 65 over the weekend to Nicklaus' 65, 66; 1980 at Muirfield where he beat Lee Trevino; 1982 at Royal Troon where Peter Oosterhuis and Nick Price came second and 1983 when Andy Bean and Hale Irwin were runners-up. Watson also won the 1982 US Open chipping in from the rough at the 17th on the final day to go on and beat Nicklaus and two US Masters in 1977 and 1981 but he never did better than tied second in the 1977 US PGA Championship to miss out joining Gene Sarazen, Ben Hogan, Gary Player, Jack Nicklaus and Tiger Woods as a winner of all four Majors. Became the oldest winner on the US Tour when he won the Mastercard Colonial in 1998 nearly 24 years after scoring his first win in the Western Open. He was 48, two years older than the previous oldest Ben Hogan, when he won the same event for the fifth time in 1959. Six times Player of the Year he played in four Ryder Cups and captained the side to

victory in 1993 at The Belfry. Now plays on the US Senior Tour Inducted into the World Golf Hall of Fame in 1988, he is an honorary member of the Royal and Ancient Golf Club of St Andrews.

Webb, Karrie (Aus)

Born Ayr, Queensland, 21 December 1974
Turned professional 1994
Blonde Australian who is rewriting the record books with her performances on the LPGA Tour. Peter Thomson, the five times Open champion considers she is the best golfer male or female there is and Greg Norman, who was her inspiration as a teenager, believes she can play at times better than Tiger Woods although Webb herself hates comparisons. She scored her first Major win in 1995 when she took the Weetabix Women's British Open – a title she won again in 1997. When she joined the LPGA Tour she won the 1999 du Maurier Classic, the 2000 Nabisco Championship and the 2000 and 2001 US Women's Open – five Majors out of eight (by the end of July 2001) – the most impressive run since Mickey Wright won five out of six in the early 1960s. Enjoys a close rivalry with Annika Sörenstam.

Weir, Mike (Can)

Born Sarnia, Ontario, 12 May 1970
Turned professional 1992
A left-hander, he was the first Canadian to play in the Presidents Cup when he made the side in 2000 and the first from his country to win a World Golf Championship event when he took the American Express Championship at Valderrama in 2000. Wrote to Jack Nicklaus as a 13-year-old to enquire whether or not he should switch from playing golf left-handed to right-handed and was told not to switch. In 1997 he led the scoring averages on the Canadian Tour with a score of 69.29.

Weiskopf, Tom (USA)

Born Massillon, Ohio, 9 November 1942
Turned professional 1946
Winner of only one Major – the 1973 Open Championship at Royal Troon, he lived in the shadow of Jack Nicklaus throughout his competitive career. He was runner-up in the 1976 US Open to Jerry Pate and was twice third in 1973 and 1977. His best finish in the US PGA Championship was third in 1975 – the year he had to be content for the fourth time with second place at the US Masters. He had been runner-up for a Green Jacket in 1969, 1972 and 1974 previously but played perhaps his best golf ever in 1975 only to be pipped at the post by Nicklaus. With 22 wins to his name he now plays the US Senior Tour with a curtailed schedule because of his course design work for which he and his original partner Jay Morrish have received much praise. One of their designs is Loch Lomond, venue of the revived Scottish Open. Played in just two Ryder Cup matches giving up a place in the team one year in order to go Bighorn sheep hunting in Alaska.

Whitworth, Kathy (USA)

Born Monahans, Texas, 27 September 1939
Turned professional 1958
Won 88 titles on the LPGA Tour between 1959 and 1991 – more than any one else male or female. Her golden period was in the 1960s when she won eight events in 1965, nine in 1966, eight in 1967 and 10 in 1968. When she finished third in the 1981 US Women's Open she became the first player to top $1 million in prize money on the LPGA Tour. She was the seventh member of the LPGA Tour Hall of Fame when inducted in 1975. Began playing golf at the age of 15 and made golfing history when she teamed up with Mickey Wright to play in the previously all male Legends of Golf event. Winner of six Majors – including three LPGA Championship wins in 1967, 1971 and 1975. In addition she won two Titleholders Championships (1966 and 1967) and the 1967 Western Open when they were Majors. Enjoyed a winning streak of 17 successive years on the LPGA Tour.

Woods, Eldrick 'Tiger' (USA)

Born Cypress, California, 30 December 1975
Turned professional 1996
First golfer in history to hold all four Majors simultaneously. He won the 2000 US Open, the Open at St Andrews and the US PGA Championship after a play-off with Bob May then scored his second victory at Augusta when he won the 2001 US Masters. He is rewriting the record books. As an amateur he successfully made two defences of the US Championship to win the event a record three years in a row but the meteoric start to his professional career gives rise to the view that he might beat Jack Nicklaus' 18 major title wins record. In 2000 he was 53-under-par for the four Majors with Ernie Els next best at 17-under. His nine Tour victories in a season was the most by anyone since Ben Hogan won 11 in 1950. When he won the AT and T at Pebble Beach in 2000 he became the first player since Ben Hogan in 1948 to win on six successive starts on the US Tour. At Pebble Beach in the US Open he shot 65, 69, 71, 67 to tie the US Open record of 272 but his 12-under-par score was a new sub-par record. Having won the US Masters for the first time with a record 270 total which gave him a 12 shot victory in 1997 and taken the US PGA title in 1999 he needed only to win the Open in Britain to become the youngest and only the fifth player in history (the others were Gene Sarazen, Ben Hogan, Gary Player and Jack Nicklaus) to have won all four Majors. At the Old Course at St Andrews he romped home by eight shots with a new British Open and major Championship record total of 269 – 19-under-par. He needed extra holes to beat Bob May at Valhalla to successfully defend the US PGA title a few weeks later. With that victory he joined Ben Hogan (1953) as a winner of three Majors in a season but beat that record when he took the US Masters Green Jacket for a second time in 2001. His current Majors tally is six. His chance of winning all four Majors in one season was lost when he did not successfully defend his US Open title later in the year. During the 2000 season he set or tied 27 records and his average score on the US Tour of 68.1 beat Sam Snead's record of 69.23 set in 1945. Named Tiger after a Vietnamese soldier who was a friend of his father's he was born to play golf, hitting shots on the Bob Hope Show when aged two and shooting 48 for nine holes at age three. He is the youngest player to have won 20 events on the US Tour. He is so far ahead in the World rankings that he is unlikely to be deposed for some considerable time. He played in the 1997 and 1999 Ryder Cup matches and is a member of the 2001 side.

388 Who's Who in Golf

Wright, Mary Kathryn (Mickey) (USA)

Born San Diego, California 14 February 1935
Turned professional 1954
Her 82 victories on the LPGA Tour between 1956 and 1973 was bettered only by Kathy Whitworth who has 88 official victories. One of the greatest golfers in the history of the Tour she had a winning streak of 14 successive seasons. Winner of 13 Major titles she is the only player to date to have won three in one season. In 1961 she took the US Women's Open, the LPGA Championship and the Titleholders Championship. That year she became only the second player to win both the US Women's Open and LPGA Championship in the same year having done so previously in 1958. Scored 79 of her victories between 1956 and 1969 when averaging almost eight wins a season. During this time she enjoyed a tremendous rivalry with Miss Whitworth. Truly a golfing legend.

Yates, Charles Richard (Charlie) (USA)

Born Atlanta, Georgia 9 September 1913
Great friend of the late Bobby Jones he was top amateur in the US Masters in 1934, 1939 and 1940. In 1938 came to Royal Troon and won the British Amateur title beating R Ewing 3 and 2. For many years acted as chairman of the press committee at the US Masters and annually stages an overseas golf writers party in the Augusta Clubhouse.

Zoeller, Frank Urban (Fuzzy) (USA)

Born New Albany, Indiana 11 November 1951
Turned professional 1973
Winner of the US Masters in 1979 after a play-off with Ed Sneed (who had dropped shots at the last three holes in regulation play) and Tom Watson and the US Open in 1984 at Winged Foot after an 18-hole play-off with Greg Norman. A regular winner on the US Tour between 1979 and 1986, he played in three Ryder Cups (1979, 1983 and 1985).

British Isles International Players, Professional Men

Captaincy is indicated by the year printed in bold type
* indicates winning team   [2001] or [01] = selected for Ryder Cup, postponed to 2002

Adams, J
(GBI): Ryder Cup 1947-49-51-53.
(Scotland): v England 1932-33-34-
35-36-37-38; v Wales 1937-38;
v Ireland 1937-38

Affleck, P
(Wales): Dunhill Cup 1995-96

Ainslie, T
(Scotland): v Ireland 1936

Alliss, Percy
(GBI): v France 1929; Ryder Cup
1929-31-33-35-37. (England):
v Scotland 1932-33-34-35-36-37;
v Ireland 1932-38; v Wales 1938

Alliss, Peter
(GBI): Ryder Cup 1953-57-59-61-
63-65-67-69. (England): Canada
Cup 1954-55-57-58-59-61-62-64-
66; World Cup 1967

Anderson, Joe
(Scotland): v Ireland 1932

Anderson, W
(Scotland): v Ireland 1936;
v England 1937; v Wales 1937

Ayton, LB
(Scotland): v England 1910-12-13-
33-34

Ayton, JB, Jr
(GBI): Ryder Cup 1949.
(Scotland): v England 1937

Baker, P
(Eur): Ryder Cup 1993. (England):
Dunhill Cup 1993 (r/u)-98; World
Cup 1999

Ballantine, J
(Scotland): v England 1932-36

Ballingall, J
(Scotland): v England 1938; Ireland
1938; v Wales 1938

Bamford, BJ
(England): Canada Cup 1961

Bannerman, H
(Eur): Ryder Cup 1993. (Scotland):
World Cup 1967-72

Barber, T
(England): v Ireland 1932-33

Barnes, BW
(GBI): Ryder Cup 1969-71-73-75-
77-79; v Europe 1974-76-78-80;
v South Africa 1976. (Scotland):
World Cup 1974-75-76-77

Batley, JB
(England): v Scotland 1912

Beck, AG
(England): v Wales 1938; v Ireland
1938

Bembridge, M
(GBI): Ryder Cup 1969-71-73-75;
v South Africa 1976. (Sen) European
Cup 1997. (England): World Cup
1974-75

Bickerton, J
(GBI): v Europe 2000

Boomer, A
(GBI): v America 1926; Ryder Cup
1927-29

Bousfield, K
(GBI): Ryder Cup 1949-51-55-57-
59-61. (England): Canada Cup
1956-57

Boxall, R
(England): Dunhill Cup 1990;
World Cup 1990

Boyle, HF
(GBI): Ryder Cup 1967. (Ireland):
World Cup 1967

Bradshaw, H
(GBI): Ryder Cup 1953-55-57.
(Ireland): Canada Cup 1954-55-56-
57-58-59; v Scotland 1937-38;
v Wales 1937; v England 1938

Braid, J
(GBI): v America 1921.
(Scotland): v England 1903-04-
05-06-07-09-10-12.

Branch, WJ
(England): v Scotland 1936

Brand, G, Jr
(GBI): Ryder Cup 1987-89;
v Australia 1988. (Eur): Nissan
Cup 1985; Kirin Cup 1988; Four
Tours World Chp 1989.
(Scotland): World Cup 1984-85-
88-89-90-92-94; Dunhill Cup

1985-86-87-88-89-91-92-93-94-
97

Brand, GJ
(GBI): Ryder Cup 1983; (Eur)
Nissan Cup 1986. (England): World
Cup 1983; Dunhill Cup 1986-87*

Broadhurst, P
(England): Dunhill Cup 1991;
World Cup 1997. (Eur) Ryder Cup
1991; Four Tours World Chp 1991-
95

Brown, EC
(GBI): Ryder Cup 1953-55-57-59.
(Scotland): Canada Cup 1954-55-56-
57-58-59-60-61-62-65-66; World
Cup 1987-68

Brown, K
(GBI): Ryder Cup 1977-79-83-85-
87; v Europe 1978; (Eur) Kirin
Cup 1987. (Scotland): World Cup
1977-78-79-83.

Burns, S
(GBI): Ryder Cup 1929.
(Scotland): v England 1932

Burton, J
(England): v Ireland 1933

Burton, R
(GBI): Ryder Cup 1935-37-49.
(England): v Scotland 1935-36-
37-38; v Ireland 1938; v Wales 1938

Busson, JH
(England): v Scotland 1938

Busson, JJ
(GBI): Ryder Cup 1935. (England):
v Scotland 1934-35-36-37

Butler, PJ
(GBI): Ryder Cup 1965-69-71-73;
v Europe 1976. (England): World
Cup 1969-70-73

Callum, WS
(Scotland): v Ireland 1935

Campbell, J
(Scotland): v Ireland 1936

Carrol, LJ
(Ireland): v Scotland 1937-38;
v Wales 1937; v England 1938

Carter, D
(England): Dunhill Cup 1998;
World Cup 1998*

Cassidy, D
(Ireland): v Scotland 1936-37;
v Wales 1937

Cassidy, J
(Ireland): v England 1933;
v Scotland 1934-35

Cawsey, GH
(England): v Scotland 1906-07

Caygill, GA
(GBI): Ryder Cup 1969

Chapman, R
(England): Dunhill Cup 2000

Clark, C
(GBI): Ryder Cup 1973

Clark, HK
(GBI): Ryder Cup 1977-81-85-87-89-95; v Australia 1988; v Europe 1978-84. (Eur): Nissan Cup 1985. (England): World Cup 1978-84-85-87; Dunhill Cup 1985-86-87*-89-90(r/u)-94-95

Clarke, D
(GBI): v Europe 2000. (Eur): Ryder Cup 1997-99-[01]. (Ireland): Dunhill Cup 1994-95-96-97-98-99; World Cup 1994-95-96

Claydon, R
(England): Dunhill Cup 1997

Coles, NC
(GBI): Ryder Cup 1961-63-65-67-69-71-73-77; v Europe 1974-76-78-80. (Sen) European Cup 1998-99. (England): Canada Cup 1963; World Cup 1968

Collinge, T
(England): v Scotland 1937

Collins, JF
(England): v Scotland 1903-04

Coltart, A
(Eur): Ryder Cup 1999. (Scotland): Dunhill Cup 1994-95* -96-98-2000; World Cup 1994-95-96-98

Coltart, F
(Scotland): v England 1909

Compston, A
(GBI): v America 1926, Ryder Cup 1927-29-31; v France 1929. (England): v Scotland 1932-35; v Ireland 1932

Cotton, TH
(GBI): Ryder Cup 1929-37-47; v France 1929

Cox, S
(Wales): World Cup 1975

Cox, WJ
(GBI): Ryder Cup 1935-37. (England): v Scotland 1935-36-37

Curtis, D
(England): v Scotland 1934-38;
v Ireland 1938; v Wales 1938

Dabson, K
(Wales): World Cup 1972

Dailey, A
(GBI): Ryder Cup 1933.
(Scotland): v England 1932-33-34-35-36-38; v Ireland 1938; v Wales 1938

Daly, F
(GBI): Ryder Cup 1947-49-51-53.
(Ireland): v Scotland 1936-37-38;
v England 1938; v Wales 1937;
Canada Cup 1954-55

Darcy, E
(GBI): Ryder Cup 1975-77-81-87;
v Europe 1976-84; v South Africa 1976. (Ireland): World Cup 1976-77-83-84-85-87; Dunhill Cup 1987-88*-91

Davis, B
(England): Dunhill Cup 2000

Davies, R
(Wales): World Cup 1968

Davies, WH
(GBI): Ryder Cup 1931-33.
(England): v Scotland 1932-33;
v Ireland 1932-33

Davis, W
(Scotland): v Ireland 1933-34-35-36-37-38; v England 1937-38;
v Wales 1937-38

Dawson, P
(GBI): Ryder Cup 1977. (England): World Cup 1977

De Foy, CB
(Wales): World Cup 1971-73-74-75-76-77-78

Denny, CS
(England): v Scotland 1936

Dobson, T
(Scotland): v England 1932-33-34-35-36-37; v Ireland 1932-33-34-35-36-37-38; v Wales 1937-38

Don, W
(Scotland): v Ireland 1935-36

Donaldson, J
(Scotland): v England 1932-35-38;
v Ireland 1937; v Wales 1937

Dornan, R
(Scotland): v Ireland 1932

Drew, NV
(GBI): Ryder Cup 1959. (Ireland):
Canada Cup 1960-61

Duncan, G
(GBI): v America 1921-26, Ryder Cup 1927-29-31. (Scotland):
v England 1906-07-09-10-12-13-32-34-35-36-37

Durnian, D
(England): World Cup 1989;
Dunhill Cup 1989

Durward, JG
(Scotland): v Ireland 1934;
v England 1937

Easterbrook, S
(GBI): Ryder Cup 1931-33.
(England): v Scotland 1932-33-34-35-38; v Ireland 1933

Edgar, J
(Ireland): v Scotland 1938

Fairweather, S
(Ireland): v England 1932;
v Scotland 1933. (Scotland):
v England 1933-35-36; v Ireland 1938; v Wales 1938

Faldo, NA
(GBI): Ryder Cup 1977-79-81-83-85-87-89-91-93-95-97; v Europe 1978-80-82-84; v Rest of World 1982. (Eur): Nissan Cup 1986. Kirin Cup 1987; Four Tours World Chp 1990. (England): World Cup 1977-91-98*; Dunhill Cup 1985-86-87* -88-91-93 (r/u)

Fallon, J
(GBI): Ryder Cup 1955.
(Scotland): v England 1936-37-38;
v Ireland 1937-38; v Wales 1937-38

Faulkner, M
(GBI): Ryder Cup 1947-49-51-53-57

Feherty, D
(Eur): Ryder Cup 1991; Four Tours World Chp 1990-91.
(Ireland): World Cup 1990;
Dunhill Cup 1985-86-90*-91-93

Fenton, WB
(Scotland): v England 1932;
v Ireland 1932-33

Fernie, TR
(Scotland): v England 1910-12-13-33

Foster, M
(GBI): v Europe 1976. (England):
World Cup 1976

Gadd, B
(England): v Scotland 1933-35-38;
v Ireland 1933-38; v Wales 1938

Gadd, G
(GBI): v America 1926, Ryder Cup 1927

Gallacher, BJ
(GBI): Ryder Cup 1969-71-73-75-77-79-81-83-91-93-95; v Europe 1974-78-82-84; v South Africa 1976; v Rest of World 1982.
(Scotland): World Cup 1969-71-74-82-83

Garner, JR
(GBI): Ryder Cup 1971-73

Gaudin, PJ
(England): v Scotland 1905-06-07-09-12-13

Gilford, D
(Eur): Ryder Cup 1991-95. (England): World Cup 1992-93; Dunhill Cup 1992*

Good, G
(Scotland): v England 1934-36

Gould, H
(Wales): Canada Cup 1954-55

Gow, A
(Scotland): v England 1912

Grabham, C
(Wales): v England 1938; v Scotland 1938

Grant, T
(Scotland): v England 1913

Gray, E
(England): v Scotland 1904-05-07

Green, E
(GBI): Ryder Cup 1947

Green, T
(England): v Scotland 1935. (Wales): v Scotland 1937-38; v Ireland 1937; v England 1938

Greene, C
(Ireland): Canada Cup 1965

Gregson, M
(GBI): Ryder Cup 1967.(England): World Cup 1967. (Sen) European Cup 1997

Haliburton, TB
(GBI): Ryder Cup 1961-63. (Scotland): v Ireland 1935-36-38; v England 1938; v Wales 1938; Canada Cup 1954

Hamill, J
(Ireland): v Scotland 1933-34-35; v England 1932-33

Hargreaves, J
(GBI): Ryder Cup 1951

Harrington, P
(GBI): v Europe 2000. (Eur): Ryder Cup 1999-[01]. (Ireland): Dunhill Cup 1996-97-98-99; World Cup 1996-97*-98-99-2000

Hastings, W
(Scotland): England 1937-38; v Wales 1937-38; v Ireland 1937-38

Havers, AG
(GBI): v America 1921-26, Ryder Cup 1927-31-33; v France 1929. (England): v Scotland 1932-33-34; v Ireland 1932-33

Healing, SF
(Wales): v Scotland 1938

Hepburn, J
(Scotland): v England 1903-05-06-07-09-10-12-13

Herd, A
(Scotland): v England 1903-04-05-06-09-10-12-13-32

Hill, EF
(Wales): v Scotland 1937-38; v Ireland 1937; v England 1938

Hitchcock, J
(GBI): Ryder Cup 1965

Hodson, B
(GBI): Ryder Cup 1931. (England): v Ireland 1933. (Wales): v Scotland 1937-38; v Ireland 1937; v England 1938

Holley, W
(Ireland): v Scotland 1933-34-35-36-38; v England 1932-33-38

Horne, R
(GBI): Ryder Cup 1947

Horton, T
(GBI): v Europe 1974-76; Ryder Cup 1975-77. (Sen) European Cup 1997-98-99. (England): World Cup 1976

Houston, D
(Scotland): v Ireland 1934

Howell, D
(GBI): v Europe 2000. (England): Dunhill Cup 1999

Huggett, BGC
(GBI): Ryder Cup 1963-67-69-71-73-75; v Europe 1974-78. (Wales): Canada Cup 1963-64-65; World Cup 1968-69-70-71-76-79. (Sen) European Cup 1998

Huish, D
(Scotland): World Cup 1973

Hunt, BJ
(GBI): Ryder Cup 1953-57-59-61-63-65-67-69. (England): Canada Cup 1958-59-60-62-63-64; World Cup 1968

Hunt, GL
(GBI): v Europe 1974; Ryder Cup 1975. (England): World Cup 1972-75

Hunt, Geoffrey M
(GBI): Ryder Cup 1963

Hunter, W
(Scotland): v England 1906-07-09-10

Hutton, GC
(Scotland): v Ireland 1936-37; v England 1937-38; v Wales 1937

Ingram, D
(Scotland): World Cup 1973

Jacklin, A
(GBI): Ryder Cup 1967-69-71-73-75-77-79-**83**-85-87-89; v Europe

1976-82; v Rest of World 1982. (England): Canada Cup 1966; World Cup 1970-71-72

Jackson, H
(Ireland): World Cup 1970-71

Jacobs, JRM
(GBI): Ryder Cup 1955

Jagger, D
(GBI): v Europe 1976

James, G
(Wales): v Scotland 1937; v Ireland 1937

James, MH
(GBI): Ryder Cup 1977-79-81-89-91-93-95-**99**; v Europe 1978-80-82; v Rest of World 1982; v Australia 1988; (Eur): Kirin Cup 1988; Four Tours World Chp 1989-90. (England): World Cup 1978-79-82-84-87-88-93-97-99; Dunhill Cup 1988-89-90(r/u)-93(r/u)-95-97-99

Jarman, EW
(GBI): Ryder Cup 1935. (England): v Scotland 1935

Job, N
(GBI): v Europe 1980

Jolly, HC
(GBI): v America 1926, Ryder Cup 1927; v France 1929

Jones, D
(Sen) European Cup 1998-99

Jones, DC
(Wales): v Scotland 1937-38; v Ireland 1937; v England 1938

Jones, E
(Ireland): Canada Cup 1965

Jones, R
(England): v Scotland 1903-04-05-06-07-09-10-12-13

Jones, T
(Wales): v Scotland 1936; v Ireland 1937; v England 1938

Kenyon, EWH
(England): v Scotland 1932; v Ireland 1932

King, M
(GBI): Ryder Cup 1979. (England): World Cup 1979

King, SL
(GBI): Ryder Cup 1937-47-49. (England): v Scotland 1934-36-37-38; v Wales 1938; v Ireland 1938

Kinsella, J
(Ireland): World Cup 1968-69-72-73

Kinsella, W
(Ireland): v Scotland 1937-38; v England 1938

Knight, G
(Scotland): v England 1937

Lacey, AJ
(GBI): Ryder Cup 1933-37.
(England): v Scotland 1932-33-34-
36-37-38; v Ireland 1932-33-38;
v Wales 1938

Laidlaw, W
(Scotland): v England 1935-36-38;
v Ireland 1937; v Wales 1937

Lane, B
(Eur): Ryder Cup 1993. (England):
World Cup 1988-94; Dunhill Cup
1988-94-95-96

Lawrie, P
(GBI): v Europe 2000. (Eur): Ryder
Cup 1999. (Scotland): World Cup
1996; Dunhill Cup 1999

Lees, A
(GBI): Ryder Cup 1947-49-51-55.
(England): v Scotland 1938;
v Wales 1938; v Ireland 1938

Llewellyn, D
(GBI): v Europe 1984. (Wales):
World Cup 1974-85-87*-88;
Dunhill Cup 1985-88

Lloyd, F
(Wales): v Scotland 1937-38;
v Ireland 1937; v England 1938

Lockhart, G
(Scotland): v Ireland 1934-35

Lomas, J
(England): Dunhill Cup 1996

Lyle, AWB
(GBI): Ryder Cup 1979-81-83-85-
87; v Europe 1980-82-84;
v Rest of World 1982; v Australia
1988. (Eur): Nissan Cup 1985-86;
Kirin Cup 1987. (Scotland): World
Cup 1979-80-87; Dunhill Cup
1985-86-87-88-89-90-92

McCartney, J
(Ireland): v Scotland 1932-33-34-
35-36-37-38; v England 1932-33-
38; v Wales 1937

McCulloch, D
(Scotland): v England 1932-33-34-
35-36-37; v Ireland 1932-33-34-35

McDermott, M
(Ireland): v England 1932;
v Scotland 1932

McDowall, J
(Scotland): v England 1932-33-34-
35-36; v Ireland 1933-34-35-36

McEwan, P
(Scotland): v England 1907

McGinley, P
(Eur) Ryder Cup [2001]; (Ireland):
Dunhill Cup 1993-94-96-97-98-99;
World Cup 1993-94-97*-98-99-
2000

McIntosh, G
(Scotland): v England 1938;
v Ireland 1938; v Wales 1938

McKenna, J
(Ireland): v Scotland 1936-37-38;
v Wales 1937-38; v England 1938

McKenna, R
(Ireland): v Scotland 1933-35;
v England 1933

McMillan, J
(Scotland): v England 1933-34-35;
v Ireland 1933-34

McMinn, W
(Scotland): v England 1932-33-34

McNeill, H
(Ireland): v England 1932

Mahon, PJ
(Ireland): v Scotland 1932-33-34-
35-36-37-38; v Wales 1937-38;
v England 1932-33-38

Martin, J
(GBI): Ryder Cup 1965. (Ireland):
Canada Cup 1962-63-64-66; World
Cup 1970

Martin, S
(Scotland): World Cup 1980

Mason, SC
(GBI): v Europe 1980. (England):
World Cup 1980

Mayo, CH
(England): v Scotland 1907-09-10-
12-13

Mayo, P
(Wales): Dunhill Cup 1993

Mills, RP
(GBI): Ryder Cup 1957

Mitchell, A
(GBI): v America 1921-26, Ryder
Cup 1929-31-33. (England):
v Scotland 1932-33-34

Mitchell, P
(England): World Cup 1996

Moffitt, R
(GBI): Ryder Cup 1961

Montgomerie, C
(GBI) v Europe 2000. (Eur): Ryder
Cup 1991-93-95-97-99-[01]; Four
Tours World Chp 1991. (Scotland):
World Cup 1988-91-92-93-97
(individual winner)-98-99; Dunhill
Cup 1988-91-92-93-94-95*-96-97-
98-2000

Morgan, J
(Sen) European Cup 1997-99

Mouland, M
(Eur): Kirin Cup 1988. (Wales):
World Cup 1988-89-90-92-93-95-
96; Dunhill Cup 1986-87-88-89-93-
95-96

Mouland, S
(Wales): Canada Cup 1965-66;
World Cup 1967

O'Brien, W
(Ireland): v Scotland 1934-36-37;
v Wales 1937

Ockenden, J
(GBI): v America 1921

O'Connor, C
(GBI): Ryder Cup 1955-57-59-61-
63-65-67-69-71-73. (Ireland):
Canada Cup 1956-57-58-59-60-61-
62-63-64-66; World Cup 1967-68-
69-71-73

O'Connor, C, Jr
(GBI): Ryder Cup 1975-89;
v Europe 1974-84; v South Africa
1976. (Sen) European Cup 1998.
(Ireland): World Cup 1974-75-78-
85-89-92; Dunhill Cup 1985-89-92

O'Connor, CJ
(Sen) European Cup 1998

O'Connor, P
(Ireland): v Scotland 1932-33-34-
35-36; v England 1932-33

Oke, WG
(England): v Scotland 1932

O'Leary, JE
(GBI): Ryder Cup 1975; v Europe
1976-78-82; v Rest of World 1982.
(Ireland): World Cup 1972-80-82

O'Neill, J
(Ireland): v England 1933

O'Neill, M
(Ireland): v Scotland 1933-34;
v England 1933

Oosterhuis, PA
(GBI): Ryder Cup 1971-73-75-77-
79-81; v Europe 1974. (England):
World Cup 1971

Orr, G
(GBI): v Europe 2000. (Scotland):
Dunhill Cup 1998-99-2000

O'Sullivan, DF
(Sen) European Cup 1998

Padgham, AH
(GBI): Ryder Cup 1933-35-37.
(England): v Scotland 1932-33-34-
35-36-37-38; v Ireland 1932-33-38;
v Wales 1938

Panton, J
(GBI): Ryder Cup 1951-53-61.
(Scotland): Canada Cup 1955-56-
57-58-59-60-61-62-63-64-65-66;
World Cup 1968

Park, D
(Wales): Dunhill Cup 2000

Park, J
(Scotland): v England 1909

Parkin, P
(GBI): v Europe 1984. (Wales):
World Cup 1984-89; Dunhill Cup
1985-86-87-89-90-91

Patterson, E
(Ireland): v Scotland 1933-34-35-36; v England 1933; v Wales 1937

Payne, J
(England): World Cup 1996

Perry, A
(GBI): Ryder Cup 1933-35-37.
(England); v Ireland 1932;
v Scotland 1933-36-38

Pickett, C
(Wales): v Scotland 1937-38;
v Ireland 1937; v England 1938

Platts, L
(GBI): Ryder Cup 1965

Polland, E
(GBI): Ryder Cup 1973; v Europe 1974-76-78-80; v South Ryder Cup 1976. (Sen) European Cup 1998-99. (Ireland): World Cup 1973-74-76-77-78-79

Pope, CW
(Ireland): v England 1932;
v Scotland 1932

Price, P
(Eur) Ryder Cup [2001]; (GBI): v Europe 2000. (Wales): Dunhill Cup 1991-96; World Cup 1994-95-97-98-2000

Rafferty, R
(Ireland): World Cup 1983-84-87-88-90-91-92-93; Dunhill Cup 1986-87-88*-89-90*-91-92-93-95.
(GBI): v Europe 1984;
v Australia 1988. (Eur): Ryder Cup 1989; Kirin Cup 1988; Four Tours World Chp 1989-90-91

Rainford, P
(England): v Scotland 1903-07

Ray, E
(GBI): v America 1921-26, Ryder Cup 1927. (England): v Scotland 1903-04-05-06-07-09-10-12-13

Rees, DJ
(GBI): Ryder Cup 1937-47-49-51-53-55-57-59-61. (Wales): v Scotland 1937-38; v Ireland 1937; England 1938; Canada Cup 1954-56-57-58-59-60-61-62-64

Reid, W
(England): v Scotland 1906-07

Renouf, TG
(England): v Scotland 1903-04-05-10-13

Rhodes, J
(England): (Sen) European Cup 1998

Richardson, S
(Eur): Ryder Cup 1991; Four Tours World Chp 1991. (England): Dunhill Cup 1991-92*; World Cup 1992

Ritchie, WL
(Scotland): v England 1913

Robertson, F
(Scotland): v Ireland 1933;
v England 1938

Robertson, P
(Scotland): v England 1932;
v Ireland 1932-34

Robson, F
(GBI): v America 1926, Ryder Cup 1927-29-31. (England): v Scotland 1909-10

Roe, M
(England): World Cup 1989-94-95; Dunhill Cup 1994

Rowe, AJ
(England): v Scotland 1903-06-07

Russell, R
(Scotland): Dunhill Cup 1996-97; World Cup 1997

Sayers, B, Jr
(Scotland): v England 1906-07-09

Scott, SS
(GBI): Ryder Cup 1955

Seymour, M
(England): v Scotland 1932-33;
v Ireland 1932-33. (Scotland):
v Ireland 1932

Shade, RDBM
(Scotland): World Cup 1970-71-72

Sherlock, JG
(GBI): v America 1921. (England):
v Scotland 1903-04-05-06-07-09-10-12-13

Simpson, A
(Scotland): v England 1904

Smalldon, D
(Wales): Canada Cup 1955-56

Smith, CR
(Scotland): v England 1903-04-07-09-13

Smith, GE
(Scotland): v Ireland 1932

Smyth, D
(GBI): Ryder Cup 1979-81;
v Europe 1980-82-84; v Rest of World 1982. (Ireland): World Cup 1979-80-82-83-88-89; Dunhill Cup 1985-86-87-88*-2000

Snell, D
(England): Canada Cup 1965

Spark, W
(Scotland): v Ireland 1933-35-37;
v England 1935; v Wales 1937

Spence, J
(England): Dunhill Cup 1992*-2000

Stevenson, P
(Ireland): v Scotland 1933-34-35-36-38; v England 1933-38

Sutton, M
(England): Canada Cup 1955

Taylor, JH
(GBI): v America 1921. (England):
v Scotland 1903-04-05-06-07-09-10-12-13

Taylor, JJ
(England): v Scotland 1937

Taylor, Josh
(England): v Scotland 1913.
(GBI): v America 1921

Thomas, DC
(GBI): Ryder Cup 1959-63-65-67.
(Wales): Canada Cup 1957-58-59-60-61-62-63-66; World Cup 1967-69-70

Thompson, R
(Scotland): v England 1903-04-05-06-07-09-10-12

Tingey, A
(England): v Scotland 1903-05

Torrance, S
(GBI): v Europe 1976-78-80-82-84; Ryder Cup 1981-83-85-87-89-91-93-95-[01]; v Rest of World 1982. (Eur): Nissan Cup 1985; Four Tours World Chp 1991.
(Scotland): World Cup 1976-78-82-84-85-87-89-90-93-95; Dunhill Cup 1985-86-87-89-90-91-93-95*

Townsend, P
(GBI): Ryder Cup 1969-71;
v Europe 1974) (England): World Cup 1969-74

Twine, WT
(England): v Ireland 1932

Vardon, H
(England): v America 1921

Vaughan, DI
(Wales): World Cup 1972-73-77-78-79-80

Waites, BJ
(GBI): v Europe 1980-82-84;
v Rest of World 1982; Ryder Cup 1983. (England): World Cup 1980-82-83. (Sen) European Cup 1997-98

Walker, RT
(Scotland): Canada Cup 1964

Wallace, L
(Ireland): v England 1932;
v Scotland 1932

Walton P
(Eur): Ryder Cup 1995. (Ireland): Dunhill Cup 1989-90*-92-94-95; World Cup 1995

Ward, CH
(GBI): Ryder Cup 1947-49-51.
(England): v Ireland 1932

Watt, T
(Scotland): *v* England 1907

Watt, W
(Scotland): *v* England 1912-13

Way, P
(Eur): Ryder Cup 1983-85-99.
(England): Dunhill Cup 1985-99;
World Cup 1985

Weetman, H
(GBI): Ryder Cup 1951-53-55-57-
59-61-63. (England): Canada Cup
1954-56-60

Westwood, L
(GBI): *v* Europe 2000. (Eur):
Ryder Cup 1997-99-[01].
(England): Dunhill Cup 1996-97-
98-99

Whitcombe, CA
(GBI): Ryder Cup 1927-29-31-33-
35-37; *v* France 1929. (England):
v Scotland 1932-33-34-35-36-37-
38; *v* Ireland 1933

Whitcombe, EE
(England): *v* Scotland 1938;
v Wales 1938; *v* Ireland 1938

Whitcombe, ER
(GBI): *v* America 1926, Ryder Cup
1929-31-35; *v* France 1929.
(England): *v* Scotland 1932;
v Ireland 1933

Whitcombe, RA
(GBI): Ryder Cup 1935. (England):
v Scotland 1933-34-35-36-37-38

White, J
(Scotland): *v* England 1903-04-05-
06-07-09-12-13

Wilcock, P
(England): World Cup 1973

Will, G
(GBI): Ryder Cup 1963-65-67.
(Scotland): Canada Cup 1963;
World Cup 1969-70

Williams, K
(Wales): *v* Scotland 1937-38;
v Ireland 1937; *v* England 1938

Williamson, T
(England): *v* Scotland 1904-05-06-
07-09-10-12-13

Wilson, RG
(England): *v* Scotland 1913

Wilson, T
(Scotland): *v* England 1933-34;
v Ireland 1932-33-34

Wolstenholme, GB
(England): Canada Cup 1965

Wood, N
(GBI): Ryder Cup 1975.
(Scotland): World Cup 1975

Woosnam, I
(GBI): *v* Europe 1982-84-2000;
v Rest of World 1982; Ryder Cup
1983-85-87-89-91-93-95-97;
v Australia 1988. (Eur): Nissan
Cup 1985-86. Kirin Cup 1987;
Four Tours World Chp 1989-90.
(Wales): World Cup 1980-82-83-
84-85-87*-90-91-92-93-94-96-97-
98; Dunhill Cup 1985-86-87-88-
89-90-91-93-95-2000

British Isles International Players, Amateur Men

Adams, MPD
(Wales): Home Int 1969-70-71-72-75-76-77; Eur T Ch 1971

Aitken, AR
(Scotland): v England 1906-07-08

Alexander, DW
(Scotland): Home Int 1958; v Scandinavia 1958

Allison, A
(Ireland): v England 1928; v Scotland 1929

Anderson, N
(GBI): v Europe 1988. (Ireland): Home Int 1985 to 90-93. Eur T Ch 1989

Anderson, RB
(Scotland): v Scandinavia 1960-62; Home Int 1962-63

Andrew, R
(Scotland): v England 1905 to 1910

Armour, A
(Scotland): v England 1922

Armour, TD
(GBI): v America 1921

Ashby, H
(GBI): Dominican Int 1973; v Europe 1974. (England): Home Int 1972-73-74

Atkinson, HN
(Wales): v Ireland 1913

Attenborough, M
(GBI): Walker Cup 1967; v Europe 1966-68. (England): Home Int 1964-66-67-68; Eur T Ch 1967

Aylmer, CC
(GBI): v America 1921, Walker Cup 1922. (England): v Scotland 1911-22-23-24

Babington, A
(Ireland): v Wales 1913

Baker, P
(GBI): Walker Cup 1985; v Europe 1986. (England): Home Int 1985

Baker, RN
(Ireland): Home Int 1975

Ball, J
(England): v Scotland 1902-03-04-05-06-07-08-09-10-11-12

Bamford, JL
(Ireland): Home Int 1954-56

Banks, C
(England): Home Int 1983

Banks, SE
(England): Home Int 1934-38

Bannerman, SJ
(Scotland): Home Int 1988; v Sweden 1990

Bardsley, R
(England): Home Int 1987; v France 1988

Barker, HH
(England): v Scotland 1907

Barnett, A
(Wales): Home Int 1989-90-91; Eur T Chp 1991

Barrie, GC
(Scotland): Home Int 1981-83; v Sweden 1983

Barry, AG
(England): v Scotland 1906-07

Bathgate, D
(England): Home Int 1990

Bayliss, RP
(England): v Ireland 1929; Home Int 1933-34

Bayne, PWGA
(Wales): Home Int 1949

Beames, R
(GBI) v Europe 1996. (Scotland): Home Int 1995-96-99; v Spain 1996; v France, Sweden 1997

Beamish, CH
(Ireland): Home Int 1950-51-53-56

Beck, JB
(GBI): Walker Cup 1928-**38**-**47**. (England): v Scotland 1926-30; Home Int 1933.

Beddard, JB
(England): v Wales/Ireland 1925; v Ireland 1929; v Scotland 1927-28-29

Beharrell, JC
(England): Home Int 1956

Bell, HE
(Ireland): v Wales 1930; Home Int 1932

Bell, RK
(England): Home Int 1947

Benka, PJ
(GBI): Walker Cup 1969; v Europe 1970. (England): Home Int 1967-68-69-70; Eur T Ch 1969

Bennett, H
(England): Home Int 1948-49-51

Bennett, S
(England): v Scotland 1979

Bennett, W
(GBI) v Europe 1994; Eisenhower Trophy 1994. (England): Home Int 1992-93-94; v France 1994

Bentley, AL
(England): Home Int 1936-37; v France 1937-39

Bentley, HG
(GBI): Walker Cup 1934-36-38. (England): v Ireland 1931;

v Scotland 1931. Home Int 1932-33-34-35-36-37-38-47; *v* France 1934-35-36-37-39-54

Berry, P
(GBI): *v* Europe 1972. (England): Home Int 1972

Bevan, RJ
(Wales): Home Int 1964-65-66-67-73-74

Beveridge, HW
(Scotland): *v* England 1908

Birnie, J
(Scotland): *v* Ireland 1927

Birtwell, SG
(England): Home Int 1968-70-73

Black, D
(Scotland): Home Int 1966-67

Black, FC
(GBI): *v* Europe 1966. (Scotland): Home Int 1962-64-65-66-68; *v* Scandinavia 1962; Eur T Ch 1965-67

Black, GT
(Scotland): Home Int 1952-53; *v* South Africa 1954

Black, JL
(Wales): Home Int 1932-33-34-35-36

Black, WC
(Scotland): Home Int 1964-65

Blackey, M
(England): *v* France 1994-96; *v* Spain 1995; Home Int 1995-96-97; Eur T Ch 1997

Blackwell, EBH
(Scotland): *v* England 1902-04-05-06-07-09-10-12-23-24-25

Bladon, W
(GBI) *v* Europe 1996. (England): Home Int 1996

Blair, DA
(GBI): Walker Cup 1955-61; CW 1954. (Scotland): Home Int 1948-49-51-52-53-55-56-57; *v* Scandinavia 1956-58-62

Blakeman, D
(England): Home Int 1981; *v* France 1982

Bland, R
(England): Home Int 1994-95; *v* Spain 1995

Bloice, C
(GBI): Walker Cup 1985. (Scotland): Home Int 1985-86; *v* France 1985; Eur T Ch 1985; *v* Italy 1986; *v* Sweden 1986

Bloxham, JA
(England): Home Int 1966

Blyth, AD
(Scotland): *v* England 1904

Bonallack, MF
(GBI): Walker Cup 1957 to 73;

v Europe 1958 and 1962 to 72; CW 1959-63-67-71; Eisenhower Trophy 1960 to 72. (England): Home Int 1957 to 74; Eur T Ch 1969-71

Bonnell, DJ
(Wales): Home Int 1949-50-51

Bookless, JT
(Scotland): *v* England 1930-31; *v* Ireland 1930; *v* Wales 1931

Bottomley, S
(England): Home Int 1986

Bourn, TA
(GBI): *v* Australia 1934. (England): Home Int 1933-34; *v* Ireland 1928; *v* Scotland 1930; *v* France 1934

Bowen, J
(Ireland): Home Int 1961

Bowman, TH
(England): Home Int 1932

Boxall, R
(England): Home Int 1980-81-82; *v* France 1982

Boyd, HA
(Ireland): *v* Wales 1913-23

Bradshaw, AS
(England): Home Int 1932

Bradshaw, EI
(England): *v* Scotland 1979; Eur T Ch 1979

Brady, E
(Ireland): Home Int 1995-98; Eur T Ch 1999

Braid, HM
(Scotland): *v* England 1922-23

Bramston, JAT
(England): *v* Scotland 1902

Brand, GJ
(England): Home Int 1976. (GBI) *v* Europe 1976

Brand Jr, G
(GBI): Walker Cup 1979; *v* Europe 1978-80; Eisenhower Trophy 1978-80. (Scotland): Home Int 1978-80; *v* England 1979; Eur T Ch 1979; *v* Italy 1979; *v* Belgium 1980; *v* France 1980-81

Branigan, D
(Ireland): Home Int 1975-76-77-80-81-82-86; Eur T Ch 1977-81; *v* West Germany, France, Sweden 1976

Bretherton, CF
(England): *v* Scotland 1922-23-24-25; *v* Wales/Ireland 1925

Briscoe, A
(Ireland): *v* England 1928-29-30-31; *v* Scotland 1929-30-31; *v* Wales 1929-30-31; Home Int 1932-33-38

Bristowe, OC
(GBI): Walker Cup 1923-24

Broad, RD
(Wales): *v* Ireland 1979; Home Int 1980-81-82-84; Eur T Ch 1981

Broadhurst, P
(GBI) *v* Europe 1988. (England): Home Int 1986-87; *v* France 1988

Brock, J
(Scotland) *v* Ireland 1929; Home Int 1932

Brodie, Allan
(GBI): Walker Cup 1977-79; *v* Europe 1974-76-78-80; Eisenhower Trophy 1978. (Scotland): Home Int 1970-72 to 78-80; Eur T Ch 1973-77-79; *v* England 1979; *v* Italy 1979; *v* Belgium 1977; *v* Spain 1977; *v* France 1978

Brodie, Andrew
(Scotland): Home Int 1968-69; *v* Spain 1974

Bromley-Davenport, E
(England): Home Int 1938-51

Brooks, A
(GBI): Walker Cup 1969. (Scotland): Home Int 1968-69; Eur T Ch 1969

Brooks, CJ
(GBI): *v* Europe 1986. (Scotland): Home Int 1984-85; *v* Sweden 1984-86; *v* Italy 1986

Brooks, M
(GBI) Walker Cup 1997; *v* Europe 1996; Eisenhower Trophy 1996. (Scotland): *v* Austria 1994; Home Int 1995-96; *v* Spain 1996; *v* France, Sweden 1997; Eur T Ch 1997

Brookman, R
(Wales): Home Int 1999-2000

Brotherston, IR
(Scotland): Home Int 1984-85; *v* France 1985; Eur T Ch 1985

Brough, S
(GBI): *v* Europe 1960. (England): Home Int 1952-55-59-60; *v* France 1952-60

Brown, CT
(GBI) *v* Walker Cup 1995; *v* Europe 1996. (Wales): Home Int 1970 to 75-77-78-80-88; Eur T Ch 1973; *v* Denmark 1977-80; *v* Ireland 1979; *v* Switzerland, Spain 1980

Brown, D
(Wales): *v* Ireland 1923-30-31; *v* England 1925; *v* Scotland 1931

Brown, JC
(Ireland): Home Int 1933-34-35-36-37-38-48-52-53

Browne, S
(Ireland): Home Int 2001; Eur T Ch 2001

Brownlow, Hon WGE
(GBI): Walker Cup 1926

Bruen, J
(GBI): Walker Cup 1938-49-51. (Ireland): Home Int 1937-38-49-50

Bryson, WS
(Scotland): Home Int 1991-92-93;

v Sweden 1992; v Italy 1992; v France 1993; v Spain 1994

Bucher, AMM
(Scotland): Home Int 1954-55-56; v Scandinavia 1956

Buckley, JA
(GBI): Walker Cup 1979. (Wales): Home Int 1967-68-69-76-77-78; Eur T Ch 1967-69; v Denmark 1976-77

Burch, N
(England): Home Int 1974

Burgess, MJ
(England): Home Int 1963-64-67; Eur T Ch 1967

Burke, J
(GBI): Walker Cup 1932. (Ireland): v England 1929-30-31; v Wales 1929-30-31; v Scotland 1930-31; Home Int 1932 to 38-47-48-49

Burns, M
(Ireland): Home Int 1973-75-83

Burns, R
(GBI): Walker Cup 1993; v Europe 1992; Eisenhower Trophy 1992. (Ireland): Home Int 1991-92

Burnside, J
(Scotland): Home Int 1956-57

Burrell, TM
(Scotland): v England 1924

Bussell, AF
(GBI): Walker Cup 1957; v Europe 1956-62. (Scotland): Home Int 1956-57-58-61; v Scandinavia 1956-60

Butterworth, JR
(England): v France 1954

Cage, S
(GBI): Walker Cup 1993. (England): Home Int 1992

Cairnes, HM
(Ireland): v Wales 1913-25; v England 1904; v Scotland 1904-27

Cairns, S
(Scotland): Home Int 1997

Caldwell, I
(GBI): Walker Cup 1951-55. (England): Home Int 1950-51-52-53-54-55-56-57-58-59-61; v France 1950

Calvert, M
(Wales): Home Int 1983-84-86-87-89-91

Cameron, D
(Scotland): Home Int 1938-51

Campbell, A
(Wales): Home Int 1996-97-2000-01

Campbell, C
(Scotland): Home Int 1999

Campbell, Bart, Sir Guy C
(Scotland): v England 1909-10-11

Campbell, HM
(GBI): v Europe 1964. (Scotland): Home Int 1962-64-68; v Scandinavia 1962; v Australia 1964; Eur T Ch 1965-79

Campbell, I
(Wales): Home Int 1998-99-2001; Eur T Ch 1999-2001

Campbell, JGS
(Scotland): Home Int 1947-48

Campbell, MK
(Ireland): Home Int 1999

Campbell, W
(GBI): Walker Cup 1930. (Scotland): v Ireland 1927-28-29-30-31; v England 1928-29-30-31; v Wales 1931; Home Int 1933-34-35-36

Cannon, JHS
(England): v Ireland/Wales 1925

Cannon, JM
(Scotland): Home Int 1969; v Spain 1974

Carman, A
(England): v Scotland 1979; Home Int 1980

Carmichael, S
(Scotland): Home Int 1998-99-2001; v Sweden 1999

Carr, FC
(England): v Scotland 1911

Carr, JB
(GBI): Walker Cup 1947 to 67; v Europe 1954-56-64-66-68; Eisenhower Trophy 1958-60. (Ireland): Home Int 1947 to 1969; Eur T Ch 1965-67-69

Carr, JJ
(Ireland): Home Int 1981-82-83

Carr, JP
(Wales): v Ireland 1913

Carr, JR
(Ireland): v Wales 1930-31; v England 1931; Home Int 1933

Carr, R
(GBI): Walker Cup 1971. (Ireland): Home Int 1970-71; Eur T Ch 1971

Carrigill, PM
(England): Home Int 1978

Carrick, DG
(GBI): Walker Cup 1983-87; v Europe 1986. (Scotland): Home Int 1981 to 1989; v West Germany 1987; v Italy 1984-86-88; v France 1987-89; v Sweden 1983-84-86; Eur T Ch 1987-89-91

Carroll, CA
(Ireland): v Wales 1924

Carroll, JP
(Ireland): Home Int 1948-49-50-51-62

Carroll, W
(Ireland): v Wales 1913-23-24-25; v England 1925; v Scotland 1929; Home Int 1932

Carslaw, IA
(GBI): Walker Cup 1979; v Europe 1978. (Scotland): Home Int 1976-77-78-80-81; Eur T Ch 1977-79; v England 1979; v Italy 1979; v Spain 1977; v Belgium 1978; v France 1978-83

Carver, M
(England): Home Int 1996; Eur T Ch 1997

Carvill, J
(GBI): v Europe 1990. (Ireland): Home Int 1989; Eur T Ch 1989

Casey, P
(GBI): Walker Cup 1999; Eisenhower Trophy 2000; v Europe 2000. (England): Home Int 1999

Cashell, BG
(Ireland): Home Int 1978; v France, West Germany, Sweden 1978

Cassells, C
(England): Home Int 1989

Castle, H
(England): v Scotland 1903-04

Cater, JR
(GBI): Walker Cup 1955. (Scotland): Home Int 1952-53-54-55-56; v South Africa 1954; v Scandinavia 1956

Caul, P
(Ireland): Home Int 1968-69-71-72-73-74-75

Caven, J
(Scotland): v England 1926. (GBI): Walker Cup 1922

Chapman, BHG
(GBI): Walker Cup 1961; v Europe 1962. (England): Home Int 1961-62

Chapman, JA
(Wales): v Ireland 1923-29-30-31; v Scotland 1931; v England 1925

Chapman, R
(Wales): v Ireland 1929; Home Int 1932-34-35-36

Chapman, R
(GBI): Walker Cup 1981; v Europe 1980. (England): v Scotland 1979; Home Int 1980-81; Eur T Ch 1981

Charles, WB
(Wales): v Ireland 1924

Chillas, D
(Scotland): Home Int 1971

Christmas, MJ
(GBI): Walker Cup 1961-63; v Europe 1962-64; Eisenhower Trophy 1962. (England): Home Int 1960-61-62-63-64

Clark, CA
(GBI): Walker Cup 1965; v Europe 1964. (England): Home Int 1964

Clark, G
(England): Home Int 1995-2001;
Eur T Ch 2001; v Spain 2001

Clark, GJ
(GBI): Walker Cup 1965; v Europe
1964-66. (England): Home Int
1961-64-66-67-68-71

Clark, HK
(GBI): Walker Cup 1973.
(England): Home Int 1973

Clark, MD
(Wales): v Ireland 1947

Clarke, D
(GBI): v Europe 1990. (Ireland):
Home Int 1987-89

Clay, G
(Wales): Home Int 1962

Claydon, R
(GBI): Walker Cup 1989.
(England): Home Int 1988; Eur T
Ch 1989

Cleary, T
(Ireland): Home Int 1976-77-78-
82-83-84-85-86; v Wales 1979;
v France, West Germany, Sweden
1976

Clement, G
(Wales): v Ireland 1979

Cochran, JS
(Scotland): Home Int 1966

Collier, B
(Scotland): Home Int 1994;
v Austria 1994

Colt, HS
(England): v Scotland 1908

Coltart, A
(GBI): Walker Cup 1991; v Europe
1990; Eisenhower Trophy 1990.
(Scotland): Home Int 1988-89-90;
Eur T Ch 1989-91; v Sweden 1990;
v Italy 1990; Nixdorf Nations Cup
1990; v France 1991

Cook, J
(England): Home Int 1989-90

Cook, JH
(England): Home Int 1969

Corcoran, DK
(Ireland): Home Int 1972-73; Eur
T Ch 1973

Corridan, T
(Ireland): Home Int 1983-84-91-92

Cosh, GB
(GBI): Walker Cup 1965; v Europe
1966-68; CW 1967; Eisenhower
Trophy 1966-68. (Scotland): Home
Int 1964-65-66-67-68-69; Eur T Ch
1965-**69**

Coughlan, R
(GBI): Walker Cup 1997. (Ireland):
Home Int 1991-94; Eur T Ch 1997

Coulter, JG
(Wales): Home Int 1951-52

Coutts, FJ
(Scotland): Home Int 1980-81-82;
Eur T Ch 1981-83; v France 1981-
82-83

Cox, S
(Wales): Home Int 1970-71-72-73-
74; Eur T Ch 1971-73

Crabbe, JL
(Ireland): v Wales 1925; v Scotland
1927-28

Craddock, T
(GBI): Walker Cup 1967-69.
(Ireland): Home Int 1955-56-57-
58-59-60-67-68-69-70; Eur T Ch
1971

Craigan, RM
(Ireland): Home Int 1963-64

Crawford, DR
(Scotland): Home Int 1990-91; Eur
T Ch 1991; v France 1991

Crawley, LG
(GBI): Walker Cup 1932-34-38-47.
(England): v Ireland 1931;
v Scotland 1931; Home Int 1932-
33-34-36-37-38-47-48-49-54-55;
v France 1936-37-38-49

Critchley, B
(GBI): Walker Cup 1969; v Europe
1970. (England): Home Int 1962-
69-70; Eur T Ch 1969

Crosbie, GF
(Ireland): Home Int 1953-55-56-
57-**88**

Crowley, M
(Ireland): v England 1928-29-30-31;
v Wales 1929-31; v Scotland 1929-
30-31; Home Int 1932

Cuddihy, J
(Scotland): Home Int 1977-78

Cullen, G
(Ireland): Home Int 1999; Eur T
Ch 1999. (Eur): v Asia Pacific 2000

Curry, DH
(GBI): Walker Cup 1987; v Europe
1986-88; Eisenhower Trophy 1986.
(England): Home Int 1984-86-87;
v France 1988

Dalgleish, CR
(GBI): Walker Cup 1981; v Europe
1982. (Scotland): Home Int 1981-
82-83-89-**95**; v France 1982; Eur T
Ch 1981-83-**93**-95; Nixdorf
Nations Cup 1989

Darwin, B
(GBI): Walker Cup 1922.
(England): v Scotland 1902-04-05-
08-09-10-23-24

Davies, EN
(Wales): Home Int 1959-60-61-62-
63-64-65-66-67-68-69-70-71-72-
73-74; Eur T Ch 1969-71-73

Davies, FE
(Ireland): v Wales 1923

Davies, G
(Wales): v Denmark 1977; Home
Int 1981-82-83

Davies, HE
(Wales): Home Int 1933-34-36

Davies, JC
(GBI): Walker Cup 1973-75-77-79;
v Europe 1972-74-76-78; Eisenhower
Trophy 1974-76*. (England) Home
Int 1969-71-72-73-74-78; Eur T Ch
1973-75-77

Davies, M
(England): Home Int 1984-85

Davies, TJ
(Wales): Home Int 1954-55-56-57-
58-58-60

Davison, C
(England): Home Int 1989

Dawson, JE
(Scotland): v Ireland 1927-29-30-
31; v England 1930-31; v Wales
1931; Home Int 1932-33-34-37

Dawson, M
(Scotland): Home Int 1963-65-66

Dawson, P
(England): Home Int 1969

De Bendern, Count J (John
de Forest)
(GBI): Walker Cup 1932.
(England): v Scotland, Ireland 1931

Deboys, A
(Scotland): Home Int 1956-59-60;
v Scandinavia 1960

Deeble, P
(GBI): Walker Cup 1977-81;
v Europe 1978; Colombian Int 1978.
(England): Home Int 1975-76-77-
78-80-81-83-84; v France 1982;
v Scotland 1979; Eur T Ch 1979-81

Deighton, FWG
(GBI): Walker Cup 1951-57; CW
1954-59. (Scotland): Home Int
1950-52-53-56-58-59-60; v South
Africa 1954; v New Zealand 1954;
v Scandinavia 1956

Denholm, RB
(Scotland): v Ireland 1927-29-31;
v Wales 1931; v England 1931;
Home Int 1932-33-34

Dewar, FG
(Scotland): Home Int 1952-53-55;
v South Africa 1954; Eur T Ch
1971-73

Dick, CE
(Scotland): v England 1902-03-04-
05-09-12

Dickson, HM
(Scotland): v Ireland 1929-31

Dickson, JR
(Ireland): Eur T Ch 1977; Home
Int 1980

Dinsdale, R
(Wales): Home Int 1991-92-93

Disley, A
(Wales): Home Int 1976-77-78-(99);
v Denmark 1977; v Ireland 1979

Dixon, D
(England): Home Int 2000; v Spain
2001; v South Africa 2001

Dodd, SC
(GBI): Walker Cup 1989. (Wales):
Home Int 1985-87-88-89

Doherty, J
(Scotland): Home Int 2001; v
Sweden 2001

Donald, L
(GBI): Walker Cup 1999-2001;
Eisenhower Trophy 1998*-2000; v
Europe 2000. (England): Home Int
1996-97-98; v France 1996; Eur T
Ch 1999-2001

Donaldson, J
(GBI): Eisenhower Trophy 2000; v
Europe 2000. (Wales): Home Int
1996-97-98-99-2000; Eur T Ch
1997-99

Donellan, B
(Ireland): Home Int 1952

Dougherty, N
(GBI): Walker Cup 2001; Eur T
Ch 2001; v Spain 2001, v South
Africa 2001; v Europe 2000.
(England): v France 2000; Home
Int 2000

Dowie, A
(Scotland): Home Int 1949

Downes, P
(GBI): v Europe 1980. (England):
Home Int 1976-77-78-80-81-82;
Eur T Ch 1977-79-81

Downie, D
(Scotland): Home Int 1993-94;
v Italy 1994; v Spain 1994;
v Sweden 1995; v France 1995

Downie, JJ
(England): Home Int 1974

Draper, JW
(Scotland): Home Int 1954

Dredge, B
(GBI): Walker Cup 1993;
Eisenhower Trophy 1992; v Europe
1994. (Wales): Home Int 1992-93-
94-95; Eur T Ch 1995

Drew, NV
(GBI): Walker Cup 1953. (Ireland):
Home Int 1952-53

Drummond, S
(England): Home Int 1995

Duck, R
(England): Home Int 1997

Duffy, I
(Wales): Home Int 1975

Duncan, AA
(GBI): Walker Cup 1953. (Wales):
Home Int 1933-34-36-38-47-48-
49-50-51-52-53-54-55-56-57-58-59

Duncan, GT
(Wales): Home Int 1952-53-54-55-
56-57-58

Duncan, J, Jr
(Wales): v Ireland 1913

Duncan, J
(Ireland): Home Int 1959-60-61

Dundas, S
(Scotland): Home Int 1992-93

Dunn, NW
(England): v Ireland 1928

Dunn, P
(Wales): Home Int 1957-58-59-60-
61-62-63-65-66

Dunne, D
(Ireland): Home Int 1997

Dunne, E
(Ireland): Home Int 1973-74-76-
77-(2001); v Wales 1979; Eur T Ch
1975

Durrant, RA
(England): Home Int 1967; Eur T
Ch 1967

Dykes, JM
(GBI): Walker Cup 1936.
(Scotland): Home Int 1934-35-36-
48-49-51

Dykes, T
(Wales): Home Int 2001

Dyson, S
(GBI) Walker Cup 1999.
(England): Home Int 1998-99; Eur
T Ch 1999; v Spain 1999

Easingwood, SR
(Scotland): Home Int 1986-87-88-
90; v Italy 1988-90; v France 1987-
89; Eur T Ch 1989

Eaves, CH
(Wales): Home Int 1935-36-38-47-
48-49

Edwards, B
(Ireland): Home Int 1961-62-64-
65-66-67-68-69-73

Edwards, CS
(England): Home Int 1991-92-93-
94-95-97-98; v France 1992-94-96-
2000; v Spain 1993-95-99-2001;
Eur T Ch 1995-99

Edwards, M
(Ireland): Home Int 1956-57-58-
60-61-62

Edwards, N
(GBi): Walker Cup 2001; (Wales):
Home Int 1995-96-97-98-99-2000-
01; Eur T Ch 1997-99-2001

Edwards, S
(Wales): Home Int 1992

Edwards, TH
(Wales): Home Int 1947

Egan, TW
(Ireland): Home Int 1952-53-59-
60-62-67-68; Eur T Ch 1967-69

Eggo, R
(GBI): Walker Cup 1987; v Europe
1988. (England): Home Int 1986-
87-88-89-90; v France 1988

Elliot, A
(Scotland): Home Int 1989;
v France 1989; Eur T Ch 1989

Elliot, C
(Scotland): Home Int 1982;
v France 1983

Elliot, IA
(Ireland): Home Int 1975-77-78;
Eur T Ch 1975, v France, West
Germany, Sweden 1978

Ellis, HC
(England): v Scotland 1902-12

Ellis, M
(GBI): v Europe 1996. (Wales):
Home Int 1992-93-94-95-96

Ellison, TF
(England): v Scotland 1922-25-26-
27

Elson, J
(GBI): Walker Cup 2001; (England):
v France 2000, v Spain 2001; Home
Int 2000-01

Emerson, T
(Wales): Home Int 1932

Emery, G
(Wales): v Ireland 1925; Home Int
1933-36-38

Errity, D
(Ireland): Home Int 1990

Evans, AD
(Wales): v Scotland 1931-35;
v Ireland 1931; Home Int 1932 to
35-38-47 to 56-61

Evans, C
(Wales): Home Int 1990-91-92-93-
94-95; Eur T Ch 1995

Evans, Duncan
(GBI): Walker Cup 1981; v Europe
1980. (Wales): Home Int 1978-80-
81; v Ireland 1979; Eur T Ch 1981

Evans, G
(England): Home Int 1961

Evans, G
(GBI): Walker Cup 1991;
Eisenhower Trophy 1990.
(England): Home Int 1990; Eur T
Ch 1991

Evans, HJ
(Wales): Home Int 1976-77-78-80-
81-84-85-87-88; v France 1976;
v Denmark 1977-80; v Ireland
1979; Eur T Ch 1979-81;
v Switzerland, Spain 1980

Evans, M Gear
(Wales): v Ireland 1930-31;
v Scotland 1931

Everett, C
(Scotland): Home Int 1988-89-90;

v Italy 1988-90; *v* France 1988-89-91; Eur T Ch 1989-91; Nixdorf Nations Cup 1989-90; *v* Sweden 1990

Ewing, RC
(GBI): Walker Cup 1936-38-47-49-51-55. (Ireland): Home Int 1934 to 38-47 to 51-53 to 58

Eyles, GR
(GBI): Walker Cup 1975; *v* Europe 1974; Eisenhower Trophy 1974. (England): Home Int 1974-75; Eur T Ch 1975

Fairbairn, KA
(England): Home Int 1988

Fairchild, CEL
(Wales): *v* Ireland 1923; *v* England 1925

Fairchild, LJ
(Wales): *v* Ireland 1924

Fairlie, WE
(Scotland): *v* England 1912

Faldo, N
(England): Home Int 1975. (GBI): CW 1975

Fanagan, J
(GBI): Walker Cup 1995; *v* Europe 1992-96. (Ireland): Home Int 1989 to 1997; Eur T Ch 1995-97

Farmer, A
(Scotland): Home Int 1997; *v* Sweden 1999

Farmer, JC
(Scotland): Home Int 1970

Fenton, P
(England): Home Int 1996

Ferguson, M
(Ireland): Home Int 1952

Ferguson, WJ
(Ireland): Home Int 1952-54-55-58-59-61

Fergusson, S Mure
(Scotland): *v* England 1902-03-04

Ferrie, K
(England): Home Int 1998

French, WF
(Ireland): *v* Scotland 1929; Home Int 1932

Fiddian, EW
(GBI): Walker Cup 1932-34. (England): *v* Scotland 1929-30-31; *v* Ireland 1929-30-31; Home Int 1932-33-34-35; *v* France 1934

Finch, R
(England): *v* France 2000; Home Int 2000

Fisher, D
(GBI): *v* Europe 1994. (England): Home Int 1993-94; *v* France 1994

Fitzgibbon, JF
(Ireland): Home Int 1955-56-57

Fitzsimmons, J
(Ireland): Home Int 1938-47-48

Flaherty, JA
(Ireland): Home Int 1934-35-36-37

Flaherty, PD
(Ireland): Home Int 1967; Eur T Ch 1967-69

Fleming, J
(Scotland): Home Int 1987

Fleury, RA
(Ireland): Home Int 1974

Flockhart, AS
(Scotland): Home Int 1948-49

Fogarty, GN
(Ireland): Home Int 1956-58-63-64-67

Fogg, HN
(England): Home Int 1933

Forbes, E
(Scotland): Home Int 1996-98-2000-01; *v* Italy 1996-2000; *v* France 1997, *v* Sweden 1997-99

Forsyth, A
(Scotland): Home Int 1996; *v* Italy 1996; *v* France, Sweden 1997; Eur T Ch 1997

Foster, J
(Ireland): Home Int 1998-2000-01

Foster, M
(GBI): Walker Cup 1995. (England): Home Int 1994-95; *v* Spain 1995; Eur T Ch 1995

Foster, MF
(England): Home Int 1973

Foster, R
(GBI): Walker Cup 1965-67-69-71-73-**79**-81; *v* Europe 1964-66-68-70; CW 1967-71; Eisenhower Trophy 1964-70-(**80**). (England): Home Int 1963-64-66-67-68-69-70-71-72; Eur T Ch 1967-69-71-73

Fowler, WH
(England): *v* Scotland 1903-04-05

Fox, G
(Scotland): Home Int 1997-98-99; Eur T Ch 1999; *v* Sweden 1999

Fox, N
(GBI): *v* Europe 2000. (Ireland): Home Int 1996-97-98-99-2001; Eur T Ch 1997-2001

Fox, SJ
(England): Home Int 1956-57-58

Frame, DW
(GBI): Walker Cup 1961. (England): Home Int 1958-59-60-61-62-63

Francis, F
(England): Home Int 1936; *v* France 1935-36

Frazier, K
(England): Home Int 1938

Froggatt, P
(Ireland): Home Int 1957

Fry, SH
(England): *v* Scotland 1902 to 1909

Gairdner, JR
(Scotland): *v* England 1902

Gallacher, BJ
(Scotland): Home Int 1967

Gallacher, S
(GBI): Walker Cup 1995; Eisenhower Trophy 1994. (Scotland): Home Int 1992-93-94-95; *v* Italy 1994; *v* Spain 1994; *v* Sweden 1995; *v* France 1995; Eur T Ch 1993-95

Galloway, RF
(Scotland): Home Int 1957-58-59; *v* Scandinavia 1958

Gannon, MA
(GBI): *v* Europe 1974-78. (Ireland): Home Int 1973-74-77-78-80-81-83-84-87-88-89-90; *v* France, West Germany, Sweden 1978-80; Eur T Ch 1979-81-89

Garbutt, I
(GBI): *v* Europe 1992. (England): Home Int 1990-91-92; Eur T Ch 1991; *v* France 1992

Garner, PF
(England): Home Int 1977-78-80; *v* Scotland 1979

Garnet, LG
(GBI): *v* Australia 1934. (England): *v* France 1934

Garson, R
(Scotland): *v* Ireland 1927-28-29

Gent, J
(England): *v* Ireland 1930; Home Int 1938

Gibb, C
(Scotland): *v* England 1927; *v* Ireland 1928

Gibson, WC
(Scotland): Home Int 1950-51

Gilford, CF
(Wales): Home Int 1963 to 1967

Gilford, D
(GBI): Walker Cup 1985; *v* Europe 1986; Eisenhower Trophy 1984. (England): Home Int 1983-84-85

Gill, WJ
(Ireland): *v* Wales 1931; Home Int 1932 to 1937

Gillies, HD
(England): *v* Scotland 1908-25-26-27

Girvan, P
(GBI): Walker Cup 1987. (Scotland): Home Int 1986; West Germany 1987; Eur T Ch 1987

Glossop, R
(Wales): Home Int 1935-37-38-47

Glover, J
(Ireland): Home Int 1951-52-53-55-59-60-70

Godfrey, S
(England): Home Int 2001

Godwin, G
(GBI): Walker Cup 1979-81.
(England): Home Int 1976-77-78-80-81; v Scotland 1979; v France 1982; Eur T Ch 1979-81

Gordon, G
(Scotland): Home Int 2000

Goulding, N
(Ireland): Home Int 1988-89-90-91-92; Eur T Ch 1991

Graham, AJ
(Scotland): v England 1925

Graham, J
(Scotland): v England 1902-03-04-05-06-07-08-09-10-11

Graham, JSS
(Ireland): Home Int 1938-50-51

Gray, CD
(England): Home Int 1932

Green, CW
(GBI): Walker Cup 1963-69-71-73-75-**83-85**; v Europe 1962-66-68-70-72-74-76; CW 1971; Eisenhower Trophy 1970-72-**84-86**.
(Scotland): Home Int 1961 to 1978; Eur T Ch 1965-67-69-71-73-75-77-79-81-83; v Scandinavia 1962; v Australia 1964; v Belgium 1973-75-77-78; v Spain 1977; v Italy 1979; v England 1979

Green, HB
(England): v Scotland 1979

Green, PO
(GBI): CW 1963. (England): Home Int 1961-62-63

Greene, R
(Ireland): Home Int 1933

Greig, DG
(GBI): CW 1975. (Scotland): Home Int 1972-73-75

Greig, K
(Scotland): Home Int 1933

Gribben, P
(GBI) Eisenhower Trophy 1998*; Walker Cup 1999. (Ireland): Home Int 1997-98-99

Griffiths, D
(England): Home Int 1999-2000-01; v France 2000; v Spain 2001; v South Africa 2001

Griffiths, HGB
(Wales): v Ireland 1923-24-25

Griffiths, HS
(Wales): v England 1958

Griffiths, JA
(Wales): Home Int 1933

Griffiths, M
(Wales): Home Int 1999-2000-01; Eur T Ch 2001

Guerin, M
(Ireland): Home Int 1961-62-63

Guild, WJ
(Scotland): v England 1925-27-28; v Ireland 1927-28

Hales, JP
(Wales): v Scotland 1963

Hall, A
(Wales): Home Int 1994

Hall, AH
(Scotland): Home Int 1962-66-69

Hall, D
(Wales): Home Int 1932-37

Hall, K
(Wales): Home Int 1955-59

Hambro, AV
(England): v Scotland 1905-08-09-10-22

Hamilton, CJ
(Wales): v Ireland 1913

Hamilton, ED
(Scotland): Home Int 1936-37-38

Hamer, S
(England): Home Int 1983-84

Hanway, M
(Ireland): Home Int 1971-74

Hardman, RH
(GBI): Walker Cup 1928.
(England): v Scotland 1927-28

Hare, A
(GBI) Walker Cup 1989. (England): Home Int 1988; Eur T Ch 1989

Hare, WCD
(Scotland): Home Int 1953; v New Zealand 1954

Harpin, L
(Wales): Home Int 1996-98-99-2000-01; Eur T Ch 1999-2001

Harrhy, A
(Wales): Home Int 1988-89-95

Harrington, J
(Ireland): Home Int 1960-61-74-75-76; Eur T Ch 1975; v Wales 1979

Harrington, P
(GBI): Walker Cup 1991-93-95; v Europe 1992-94. (Ireland): Home Int 1990-91-92-93-94-95; Eur T Ch 1991-95

Harris, D
(Wales): Home Int 1997

Harris, G
(England): Home Int 1994; v Spain 1995; Eur T Ch 1995

Harris, IR
(Scotland): Home Int 1955-56-58-59

Harris, M
(GBI): v Europe 2000. (England): Home Int 1998-99

Harris, R
(GBI): Walker Cup **1922-23-26**.
(Scotland): v England 1905-08-10-11-12-22-23-24-25-26-27-28

Harrison, JW
(Wales): Home Int 1937-50

Hartley, RW
(GBI): Walker Cup 1930-32.
(England): v Scotland 1926-27-28-29-30-31; v Ireland 1928-29-30-31; Home Int 1933-34-35

Hartley, WL
(GBI): Walker Cup 1932.
(England): v Ireland/Wales 1925; v Scotland 1927-31; v Ireland 1928-31; Home Int 1932-33; v France 1935

Hassall, JE
(England): v Scotland 1923; v Ireland/Wales 1925

Hastings, JL
(Scotland): Home Int 1957-58; v Scandinavia 1958

Hawksworth, J
(GBI): Walker Cup 1985.
(England): Home Int 1984-85

Hay, G
(GBI): v Europe 1980; Walker Cup 1991. (Scotland): v England 1979; Home Int 1980-88-90-91-92; v Belgium 1980; v France 1980-82-89-91-93; v Italy 1988-92-94; v Sweden 1992; v Spain 1994; Eur T Ch 1991-93

Hay, J
(Scotland): Home Int 1972

Hayes, JA
(Ireland): Home Int 1977

Hayward, CH
(England): v Scotland 1925; v Ireland 1928

Healy, TM
(Ireland): v Scotland 1931; v England 1931

Heap, C
(Scotland): Home Int 1999-2001; Eur T Ch 2001

Heather, D
(Ireland): Home Int 1976; v France, West Germany, Sweden 1976

Hedges, PJ
(GBI): Walker Cup 1973-75; v Europe 1974-76; Eisenhower Trophy 1996. (England): Home Int 1970-73-74-75-76-77-78-82-83; Eur T Ch 1973-75-77

Hegarty, J
(Ireland): Home Int 1975

Hegarty, TD
(Ireland): Home Int 1957

Helm, AGB
(England): Home Int 1948

Henderson, J
(Ireland): v Wales 1923

Henderson, N
(Scotland): Home Int 1963-64

Henriques, GLQ
(England): v Ireland 1930

Henry, W
(England): Home Int 1987;
v France 1988

Herlihy, B
(Ireland): Home Int 1950

Herne, KTC
(Wales): v Ireland 1913

Heverin, AJ
(Ireland): Home Int 1978; v France,
West Germany, Sweden 1978

Hezlet, CO
(GBI): Walker Cup 1924-26-28;
v South Africa 1927. (Ireland):
v Wales 1923-25-27-29-31;
v Scotland 1927-28-29-30-31;
v England 1929-30-31

Higgins, D
(Ireland): Home Int 1993-94

Higgins, L
(Ireland): Home Int 1968-70-71

Hill, GA
(GBI): Walker Cup 1936-55.
(England): Home Int 1936-37

Hilton, HH
(England): v Scotland 1902-03-04-
05-06-07-09-10-11-12

Hilton, M
(England): v Spain 1999

Hird, K
(Scotland): Home Int 1987-88-89;
Nixdorf Nations Cup 1989; v Italy
1990

Hislop, C
(Scotland): Home Int 1994-96;
v Austria 1994; v Italy 1996

Hoad, PGJ
(England): Home Int 1978;
v Scotland 1979

Hodgson, C
(England): v Scotland 1924

Hodgson, J
(England): Home Int 1994

Hoey, M
(GBI): Walker Cup 2001; (Ireland):
Home Int 1999-2000-01; Eur T Ch
1999-2001

Hoey, TBC
(Ireland): Home Int 1970-71-72-
73-77-84; Eur T Ch 1971-77

Hogan, P
(Ireland): Home Int 1985-86-87-
88; Eur T Ch 1991

Holderness, Sir EWE
(GBI): v America 1921, Walker
Cup 1923-26-30. (England):
v Scotland 1922-23-24-25-26-28

Holmes, AW
(England): Home Int 1962

Homer, TWB
(GBI): Walker Cup 1973; v Europe
1972; Eisenhower Trophy 1972.
(England): Home Int 1972-73; Eur
T Ch 1973

Homewood, G
(England): Home Int 1985-91; Eur
T Ch 1991

Hooman, CVL
(GBI): Walker Cup 1922-23.
(England): v Scotland 1910-22

Hope, WL
(GBI): Walker Cup 1923-24-28.
(Scotland): v England 1923-25-26-
27-28-29

Horne, A
(Scotland): Home Int 1971

Horne, S
(Scotland): Home Int 1997-98

Hosie, JR
(Scotland): Home Int 1936

Houston, G
(Wales): Home Int 1990-91-92-93-
94-95; Eur T Ch 1991-95

Howard, DB
(GBI): Walker Cup 1995-97;
v Europe 1980-94-96; Eisenhower
Trophy 1996. (Scotland):
v England 1979; Home Int 1980-
81-82-83-93-94-95-96; v Belgium
1980; v France 1980-81-83-95-97;
v Italy 1984-94; v Spain 1994-96;
v Sweden 1995-97. Eur T Ch
1981-95-97

Howell, D
(GBI) Walker Cup 1995.
(England): Home Int 1994-95;
v Spain 1995; Eur T Ch 1995

Howell, HR
(Wales): v Ireland 1923-24-25-29-
30-31; v England 1925; v Scotland
1931; Home Int 1932-34-35-36-37-
38-47

Howell, H Logan
(Wales): v Ireland 1925

Huddy, G
(GBI): Walker Cup 1961.
(England): Home Int 1960-61-62

Huggan, J
(Scotland): Home Int 1981-82-83-
84; v France 1982-83; v Sweden
1983; v Italy 1984; Eur T Ch 1981

Hughes, I
(Wales): Home Int 1954-55-56

Hulme, WJ
(Ireland): Home Int 1955-56-57

Hume, B
(Scotland): Home Int 1999-2000-
01; Eur T Ch 2001; v Italy 2000;
Sweden 2001

Humphrey, JG
(Wales): v Ireland 1925

Humphreys, AR
(Ireland): v England 1957

Humphreys, DI
(Wales): Home Int 1972

Humphreys, W
(GBI): Walker Cup 1971; v Europe
1970. (England): Home Int 1970-
71; Eur T Ch 1971

Hunter, NM
(Scotland): v England 1903-12

Hunter, R
(Scotland): Home Int 1966

Hunter, WI
(Scotland): v England 1922

Hutcheon, I
(GBI): Walker Cup 1975-77-79-81;
v Europe 1974-76; Eisenhower
Trophy 1974-76*-80; CW 1975;
Dominican Int 1973; Colombian
Int 1975. (Scotland): Home Int
1971-72-73-74-75-76-77-78-80;
v Belgium 1973-75-77-78-80;
v Spain 1977; v France 1978-80-
81; v Italy 1979; v Sweden 1983;
Eur T Ch 1973-75-77-79-81

Hutchings, C
(England): v Scotland 1902

Hutchinson, HG
(England): v Scotland 1902-03-04-
06-07-09

Hutchison, CK
(Scotland): v England 1904-05-06-
07-08-09-10-11-12

Hutt, R
(England): Home Int 1991-92-93

Hutton, R
(Ireland): Home Int 1991

Hyde, GE
(England): Home Int 1967-68

Illingworth, G
(England): v Scotland 1929;
v France 1937

Inglis, D
(Scotland): Home Int 2001

Inglis, MJ
(England): Home Int 1977

Isitt, GH
(Wales): v Ireland 1923

Jack, RR
(GBI): Walker Cup 1957-59;
v Europe 1956; Eisenhower Trophy
1958; CW 1959. (Scotland): Home
Int 1950-51-54-55-56-57-58-59-61;
v New Zealand 1954; v Scandinavia
1956-58

Jack, WS
(Scotland): Home Int 1955

Jacob, NE
(Wales): Home Int 1932 to 1936

James, D
(Scotland): Home Int 1985

James, L
(GBI): Walker Cup 1995; v Europe
1994; Eisenhower Trophy 1994.
(England): Home Int 1993-94-95;
v France 1994; v Spain 1995; Eur
T Ch 1995

James, M
(GBI): Walker Cup 1975. (England):
Home Int 1974-75; Eur T Ch 1975

James, RD
(England): Home Int 1974-75

Jameson, JF
(Ireland): v Wales 1913-24

Jamieson, A, jr
(GBI): Walker Cup 1926.
(Scotland): v England 1927-28-31;
v Ireland 1928-31; v Wales 1931;
Home Int 1932-33-36-37

Jamieson, D
(Scotland): Home Int 1980

Jenkins, JLC
(GBI): v America 1921. (Scotland):
v England 1908-12-22-24-26-28;
v Ireland 1928

Jermine, JG
(Wales): Home Int 1972-73-74-75-
76-82-2000; Eur T Ch 1975-77;
v France 1975

Jobson, RH
(England): v Ireland 1928

Johnson, R
(GBI) v Europe 1994. (Wales):
Home Int 1990-92-93-94; Eur T
Ch 1991

Johnson, TWG
(Ireland): v England 1929

Johnston, JW
(Scotland): Home Int 1970-71

Jones, A
(Wales): Home Int 1989-90; Eur T
Ch 1991

Jones, D
(Ireland): Home Int 1998

Jones, DK
(Wales): Home Int 1973

Jones, EO
(Wales): Home Int 1983-85-86

Jones, JG Parry
(Wales): Home Int 1959-60

Jones, JL
(Wales): Home Int 1933-34-36

Jones, JR
(Wales): Home Int 1970-72-73-77-
78-80-81-82-83-84-85; Eur T Ch
1973-79-81; v Denmark 1976-80;
v Ireland 1979; v Switzerland,
Spain 1980; v Ireland 1979

Jones, JW
(England): Home Int 1948-49-50-
51-52-54-55

Jones, KG
(Wales): Home Int 1988

Jones, MA
(Wales): Home Int 1947-48-49-50-
51-53-54-57

Jones, Malcolm F
(Wales): Home Int 1933

Jones, SP
(Wales): Home Int 1981-82-83-84-
85-86-88-89-91-93

Kane, RM
(GBI): v Europe 1974. (Ireland):
Home Int 1967-68-71-72-74-78;
Eur T Ch 1971-79; v Wales 1979

Kearney, K
(Ireland): Home Int 1988-89-90-
92-94-95-97-98; Eur T Ch 1999

Keenan, S
(Ireland): Home Int 1989

Kehoe, J
(Ireland): Home Int 2000-01

Kelleher, WA
(Ireland): Home Int 1962

Kelley, MJ
(GBI): Walker Cup 1977-79;
v Europe 1976-78; Eisenhower
Trophy 1976*; Colombian Int 1978.
(England): Home Int 1974-75-76-77-
78-80-81-82-**88**; v France 1982; Eur
T Ch 1977-79

Kelley, PD
(England): Home Int 1965-66-68

Kelly, L
(GBI): Eisenhower Trophy 1998*;
Walker Cup 1999. (Scotland):
Home Int 1997-98; Eur T Ch
1999; v Sweden 1999

Kelly, NS
(Ireland): Home Int 1966

Keppler, SD
(GBI): Walker Cup 1983. (England):
Home Int 1982-83; v France 1982

Kilduff, AJ
(Ireland): v Scotland 1928

Killey, GC
(Scotland): v Ireland 1928

King, J
(Scotland): Home Int 2001; v
Sweden 2001

King, M
(GBI): Walker Cup 1969-73;
v Europe 1970-72; CW 1971.
(England): Home Int 1969-70-71-
72-73; Eur T Ch 1971-73

Kirkpatrick, D
(Scotland): Home Int 1992;
v France 1993; Eur T Ch 1993

Kissock, B
(Ireland): Home Int 1961-62-74-76;
v France, Germany, Sweden 1978

Kitchin, JE
(England): v France 1949

Knight, B
(Wales): Home Int 1986

Knight, J
(England): v France 1996

Knipe, RG
(Wales): Home Int 1953- to 1956

Knowles, ST
(Scotland): Home Int 1990-91-92;
v France 1991

Knowles, WR
(Wales): v England 1948

Kyle, AT
(GBI): Walker Cup 1938-47-51;
v South Africa 1952. (Scotland):
Home Int 1938-47-49-50-51-52-53

Kyle, DH
(GBI): Walker Cup 1924.
(Scotland): v England 1924-30

Kyle, EP
(Scotland): v England 1925

Laidlay, JE
(Scotland): v England 1902 to 1911

Lake, AD
(Wales): Home Int 1958

Lang, JA
(GBI): Walker Cup 1930.
(Scotland): v England 1929-31;
v Ireland 1929-30-31; v Wales 1931

Langley, JDA
(GBI): Walker Cup 1936-51-53.
(England): Home Int 1950 to 1953;
v France 1950

Langmead, J
(England): Home Int 1986

Lassen, EA
(England): v Scotland 1909 to 1912

Last, CN
(Wales): Home Int 1975

Laurence, C
(England): Home Int 1983-84-85

Lawrie, CD
(GBI): Walker Cup **1961-63**; v South
Africa 1952; v Europe **1960-62**;
Eisenhower Trophy **1960-62**.
(Scotland): Home Int 1949-50-55-
56-57-58; v Sweden 1950;
v Scandinavia 1956-58

Lawrie, GA
(Scotland): Home Int 1990-91; Eur
T Ch 1991

Lawrie P
(Ireland): Home Int 1996; Eur T
Ch 1997

Layton, EN
(England): v Scotland 1922-23-26;
v Ireland/Wales 1925

Lee, IGF
(Scotland): Home Int 1958-59-60-
61-62; v Scandinavia 1960

Lee, JN
(Wales): Home Int 1988-89; Eur T
Ch 1991

Lee, M
(England): Home Int 1950

Lee, MG
(England): Home Int 1965

Lehane, N
(Ireland): Home Int 1976; v France,
West Germany, Sweden 1976

Lewis, DH
(Wales): Home Int 1935-36-37-38

Lewis, DR
(Wales): v Ireland 1925-29-30-31;
v Scotland 1931; Home Int 1932-34

Lewis, ME
(GBI): Walker Cup 1983.
(England): Home Int 1980-81-82-
(99)-(2001); v France 1982

Lewis, R Cofe
(Wales): v Ireland 1925

Leyden, PJ
(Ireland): Home Int 1953-55-56-
57-59

Lincoln, AC
(England): v Scotland 1907

Lindsay, J
(Scotland): Home Int 1933 to 1936

Little, E
(Scotland): v Italy 1996

Lloyd, HM
(Wales): v Ireland 1913

Lloyd, RM de
(Wales): v Scotland 1931; v Ireland
1931; Home Int 1932 to 1938-47-48

Llyr, A
(Wales): Home Int 1984-85

Lockhart, G
(Scotland): v England 1911-12

Lockley, AE
(Wales): Home Int 1956-57-58-62

Loftus, M
(GBI): v Europe 2000. (Scotland):
Home Int 1999-2000; v Italy 2000

Logan, GW
(England): Home Int 1973

Long, D
(Ireland): Home Int 1973-74-80-
81-82-83-84; v Wales 1979; Eur T
Ch 1979

Low, AJ
(Scotland): Home Int 1964-65; Eur
T Ch 1965; v Australia 1964

Low, JL
(Scotland): v England 1904

Lowdon, CJ
(Scotland): v Ireland 1927

Lowe, A
(Ireland): v Wales 1924; v England
1925-28; v Scotland 1927-28

Lowson, AG
(Scotland): Home Int 1989-90-91-
97; v Sweden 1990-92; v Italy 1992

Lucas, D
(England): Home Int 1996

Lucas, PB
(GBI): Walker Cup 1936-47-49.
(England): Home Int 1936-48-49;
v France 1936

Ludwell, N
(England): Home Int 1991;
v France 1992

Lunt, MSR
(GBI): Walker Cup 1959-61-63-65;
v Europe 1964; CW 1963;
Eisenhower Trophy 1964.
(England): Home Int 1956-57-58-
59-60-62-63-64-66

Lunt, S
(England): Home Int 1932-33-34-
35; v France 1934-35-39

Lupton, J
(England): Home Int 2001

Lygate, M
(Scotland): Home Int 1970-75-88;
Eur T Ch 1971-85-87

Lyle, AWB
(GBI): Walker Cup 1977; CW 1975;
v Europe 1976. (England): Home
Int 1975-76-77; Eur T Ch 1977

Lynn, D
(England): Home Int 1995

Lyon, JS
(England): Home Int 1937-38

Lyons, P
(Ireland): Home Int 1986

McAllister, SD
(Scotland): Home Int 1983;
v Sweden 1983; Eur T Ch 1983

Macara, MA
(Wales): Home Int 1983-84-85-87-
89-90-91-92-93

McArthur, W
(Scotland): Home Int 1952-54;
v South Africa 1954

McBeath, J
(Scotland): Home Int 1964

McBride, D
(Scotland): Home Int 1932

McCallum, AR
(GBI): Walker Cup 1928.
(Scotland): v England 1929

McCarroll, F
(Ireland): Home Int 1968-69

McCart, DM
(Scotland): Home Int 1977-78;
v Belgium 1978; v France 1978

McCarthy, L
(Ireland): Home Int 1953-54-55-56

McCarthy, S
(England): Home Int 1998

McConnell, FP
(Ireland): v Wales 1929-30-31;
v England 1929-30-31;v Scotland
1930-31; Home Int 1934

McConnell, RM
(Ireland): v Wales 1924-25-29-30-
31; v England 1925-28-29-30-31;
v Scotland 1927-28-29-31; Home
Int 1934-35-36-37

McConnell, WG
(Ireland): v England 1925

McCormack, JD
(Ireland): v Wales 1913-24;
v England 1928, Home Int 1932-
33-34-35-36-37

McCormick, A
(Ireland): Home Int 1997-98-99-
2000-01

McCrea, WE
(Ireland): Home Int 1965-66-67;
Eur T Ch 1965

McCready, SM
(GBI): Walker Cup 1949-51.
(Ireland): Home Int 1947-49-50-
52-54

McDaid, B
(Ireland): v Wales 1979

McDermott, M
(Ireland): Home Int 2000-01; Eur
T Ch 2001

MacDonald, GK
(Scotland): Home Int 1978-81-82;
v England 1979; v France 1981-82-
83

McDonald, H
(Scotland): Home Int 1970

Macdonald, JS
(GBI): Walker Cup 1971; v Europe
1970. (Scotland): Home Int 1969-
70-71-72; v Belgium 1973; Eur T
Ch 1971

McDowell, G
(GBI): Walker Cup 2001; Eur T
Ch 2001; (Ireland): Home Int 2000

McEvoy, P
(GBI): Walker Cup 1977-79-81-85-
89-(99)-(2001); v Europe 1978-80-
86-88; Eisenhower Trophy 1978-
80-84-86-88*. (England): Home
Int 1976-77-78-80-81-83-84-85-
86-87-88-89-91, 94 to 97;
v Scotland 1979; v France 1982-
88-92; Eur T Ch 1977-79-81-89

McEvoy, R
(GBI): Walker Cup 2001;
(England): v France 2000; Home
Int 2000-01; Eur T Ch 2001; v
Spain 2001

Macfarlane, CB
(Scotland): v England 1912

McGimpsey, G
(GBI): Walker Cup 1985-89-91;
v Europe 1986-88-90-92;
Eisenhower Trophy 1984-86-88*.
(Ireland): Home Int 1978 and 1980
to 1999; v Wales 1979; Eur T Ch
1981-89-91-95-97-99

McGinley, M
(Ireland): Home Int 1996

McGinley, P
(GBI): Walker Cup 1991. (Ireland):
Home Int 1989-90; Eur T Ch 1991

Macgregor, A
(Scotland): v Scandinavia 1956

Macgregor, G
(GBI): Walker Cup 1971-75-83-85-

87-91-93; *v* Europe 1970-74-84; CW 1971-75; Eisenhower Trophy 1982. (Scotland): Home Int 1969 to 1976, 1980 to 1987-(**99**); *v* Belgium 1973-75-80; *v* England 1979; *v* Sweden 1983-84-86; *v* Italy 1984-86; *v* France 1981-82-85-87; Eur T Ch 1971-73-75-81-83-85-87

MacGregor, RC
(GBI): Walker Cup 1953.
(Scotland): Home Int 1951-52-53-54; *v* New Zealand 1954

McGuire, M
(England): Home Int 1992

McHenry, J
(GBI): Walker Cup 1987. (Ireland): Home Int 1985-86

McInally, H
(Scotland): Home Int 1937-47-48

McInally, RH
(Ireland): Home Int 1949-51

McIntosh, EA
(Scotland): Home Int 1989

Macintosh, KW
(GBI): *v* Europe 1980. (Scotland): *v* England 1979; Home Int 1980; *v* France 1980; *v* Belgium 1980

McKay, G
(Scotland): Home Int 1969

McKay, JR
(Scotland): Home Int 1950-51-52-54; *v* New Zealand 1954

McKechnie, P
(Scotland): Home Int 1998

McKellar, PJ
(GBI): Walker Cup 1977; *v* Europe 1978. (Scotland): Home Int 1976-77-78; *v* Belgium 1978; *v* France 1978; *v* England 1979

Mackenzie, F
(Scotland): *v* England 1902-03

Mackenzie, S
(Scotland): Home Int 1990-93-94-95-96-97-98-99-2000-01; *v* Italy 1994-2000; *v* Spain 1994-96; *v* France 1997, *v* Sweden 1997-99; Eur T Ch 1999-2001

Mackenzie, WW
(GBI): Walker Cup 1922-23.
(Scotland): *v* England 1923-26-27-29; *v* Ireland 1930

Mackeown, HN
(Ireland): Home Int 1973; Eur T Ch 1973

McKibbin, H
(Scotland): Home Int 1994-95; *v* Sweden 1995; *v* France 1995; Eur T Ch 1995; *v* Spain 1996

Mackie, GW
(Scotland): Home Int 1948-50

McKinlay, SL
(GBI): Walker Cup 1934.
(Scotland): *v* England 1929-30-31;

v Ireland 1930; *v* Wales 1931; Home Int 1932-33-35-37-47

McKinna, RA
(Scotland): Home Int 1938

McKinnon, A
(Scotland): Home Int 1947-52

McLean, D
(Wales): Home Int 1968-69-70-71-72-73-74-75-76-77-78-80-81-82-83-85-86-88-90; Eur T Ch 1975-77-79-81; *v* France 1975-76; *v* Denmark 1976-80; *v* Ireland 1979; *v* Switzerland, Spain 1980

McLean, J
(GBI): Walker Cup 1934-36;
v Australia 1934. (Scotland): Home Int 1932-33-34-35-36

McLeod, AE
(Scotland): Home Int 1937-38

McLeod, WS
(Scotland): Home Int 1935-37-38-47-48-49-50-51; *v* Sweden 1950

McMenamin, E
(Ireland): Home Int 1981

McMonagle, C
(Ireland): Home Int 1999-2000; Eur T Ch 1999

McMullan, C
(Ireland): Home Int 1933-34-35

McNair, AA
(Scotland): *v* Ireland 1929

MacNamara, L
(Ireland): Home Int 1977-83-84-85-86-87-88-89-90-91-92; Eur T Ch 1977-91

McNeill, G
(Ireland): Home Int 1991-93-2001

McRuvie, EA
(GBI): Walker Cup 1932-34.
(Scotland): *v* England 1929-30-31; *v* Ireland 1930-31; *v* Wales 1931; Home Int 1932-33-34-35-36

McTear, J
(Scotland): Home Int 1971

Madeley, JFD
(GBI): Walker Cup 1963; *v* Europe 1962. (Ireland): Home Int 1959-60-61-62-63-64

Mahon, RJ
(Ireland): Home Int 1938-52-54-55

Maliphant, FR
(Wales): Home Int 1932

Malone, B
(Ireland): Home Int 1959-64-69-71-75; Eur T Ch 1971-75

Manford, GC
(Scotland): *v* England 1922-23

Manley, N
(Ireland): *v* Wales 1924; *v* England 1928; *v* Scotland 1927-28

Manley, S
(Wales) Home Int 2001

Mann, LS
(GBI): Walker Cup 1983.
(Scotland): Home Int 1982-83; *v* Sweden 1983; Eur T Ch 1983

Marchbank, B
(GBI): Walker Cup 1979; *v* Europe 1976-78; Eisenhower Trophy 1978. (Scotland): Home Int 1978; *v* Italy 1979; Eur T Ch 1979

Marks, GC
(GBI): Walker Cup 1969-71-**87-89**; *v* Europe 1968-70; Eisenhower Trophy 1970; CW 1975; Colombian Int 1975. (England): Home Int 1963-67-68-69-70-71-74-75-82; Eur T Ch 1967-69-71-75; *v* France **1982**

Marren, JM
(Ireland): *v* Wales 1925

Marsden, G
(Wales): Home Int 1994

Marsh, DM
(GBI): Walker Cup 1959-71-**73-75**; *v* Europe 1958. (England): Home Int 1956-57-58-59-60-64-66-68-69-70-71-72; Eur T Ch 1971

Marshman, A
(Wales): Home Int 1952

Marston, CC
(Wales): *v* Ireland 1929-30-31; *v* Scotland 1931

Martin, DHR
(England): Home Int 1938; *v* France 1934-49

Martin, GNC
(GBI): Walker Cup 1928. (Ireland): *v* Wales 1923-29; *v* Scotland 1928-29-30; *v* England 1929-30

Martin, S
(GBI): Walker Cup 1977; *v* Europe 1976; Eisenhower Trophy 1976*. (Scotland): Home Int 1975-76-77; Eur T Ch 1977; *v* Belgium 1977; *v* Spain 1977

Mason, B
(England): Home Int 1998-99; *v* Spain 1999

Mason, SC
(England): Home Int 1973

Mathias-Thomas, FEL
(Wales): *v* Ireland 1924-25

Matthews, N
(Wales): Home Int 1999; Eur T Ch 1999

Matthews, RL
(Wales): Home Int 1935-37

Maxwell, R
(Scotland): *v* England 1902-03-04-05-06-07-09-10

Mayo, PM
(GBI): Walker Cup 1985-87.
(Wales): Home Int 1982-8

Meharg, W
(Ireland): Home Int 1957

Melia, TJ
(Wales): Home Int 1976-77-78-80-81-82; *v* Ireland 1979; Eur T Ch 1977-79; *v* Denmark 1976-80; *v* Switzerland, Spain 1980

Mellin, GL
(England): *v* Scotland 1922

Melville, LM Balfour
(Scotland): *v* England 1902-03

Melville, TE
(Scotland): Home Int 1974

Menzies, A
(Scotland): *v* England 1925

Metcalfe, J
(GBI) *v* Europe 1990. (England): Home Int 1989

Micklem, GH
(GBI): Walker Cup 1947-49-53-55-57-59; Eisenhower Trophy 1958. (England): Home Int 1947-48-49-50-51-52-53-54-55

Mill, JW
(Scotland): Home Int 1953-54

Millensted, DJ
(GBI): Walker Cup 1967; CW 1967. (England): Home Int 1966; Eur T Ch 1967

Miller, AC
(Scotland): Home Int 1954-55

Miller, MJ
(Scotland): Home Int 1974-75-77-78; *v* Belgium 1978; *v* France 1978

Milligan, JW
(GBI): Walker Cup 1989-91; Eisenhower Trophy 1988*-90; *v* Europe 1988-92. (Scotland): Home Int 1986-87-88-89-90-91-92; *v* West Germany 1987; *v* Italy 1988-90-92; *v* France 1987-89-91; Eur T Ch 1987-89-91; Nixdorf Nations Cup 1989; *v* Sweden 1986-90-92

Mills, ES
(Wales): Home Int 1957

Millward, EB
(GBI): Walker Cup 1949-55. (England): Home Int 1950-52-53-54-55

Milne, WTG
(GBI): Walker Cup 1973. (Scotland): Home Int 1972-73; Eur T Ch 1973; *v* Belgium 1973

Mitchell, A
(England): *v* Scotland 1910-11-12

Mitchell, CS
(England): Home Int 1975-76-78

Mitchell, FH
(England): *v* Scotland 1906-07-08

Mitchell, JWH
(Wales): Home Int 1964-65-66

Moffat, DM
(England): Home Int 1961-63-67; *v* France 1959-60

Moir, A
(GBI): *v* Europe 1984. (Scotland): Home Int 1983-84; *v* Sweden 1984; *v* Italy 1984; *v* France 1985; Eur T Ch 1985

Montgomerie, CS
(GBI): Walker Cup 1985-87; *v* Europe 1986; Eisenhower Trophy 1984-86. (Scotland): Home Int 1984-85-86; *v* West Germany 1987; *v* Sweden 1984-86; *v* Italy 1984; *v* France 1985; Eur T Ch 1985-87

Montgomerie, JS
(Scotland): Home Int 1957; *v* Scandinavia 1958; Eur T Ch 1965

Montmorency, RH de
(GBI): *v* America 1921. (England): *v* Scotland 1908; *v* Wales/Ireland 1925; *v* South Africa 1927

Moody, JV
(Wales): Home Int 1947-48-49-51-56-58-59-60-61

Moody, PH
(GBI): *v* Europe 1972. (England): Home Int 1971-72

Moore, GJ
(Ireland): *v* England 1928; *v* Wales 1929

Morgan, J
(England): *v* France 2000

Morgan, JL
(GBI): Walker Cup 1951-53-55. (Wales): 1948-49-50-51-52-53-54-55-56-57-58-59-60-61-62-64-68

Moriarty, C
(Ireland): Home Int 2001

Morris, FS
(Scotland): Home Int 1963

Morris, JC
(Ireland): Home Int 1993-94-95-96-97-98; Eur T Ch 1995

Morris, MF
(Ireland): Home Int 1978-80-82-83-84; *v* Wales 1979; Eur T Ch 1979; *v* France, W. Germany, Sweden 1980

Morris, R
(Wales): Home Int 1983-86-87

Morris, TS
(Wales): *v* Ireland 1924-29-30

Morrison, JH
(Scotland): *v* Scandinavia 1960

Morrison, JSF
(England): *v* Ireland 1930

Morrow, AJC
(Ireland): Home Int 1975-83-92-93-96-97-99-2000

Morrow, JM
(Wales): *v* Ireland 1979; Home Int 1980-81; Eur T Ch 1979-81; *v* Denmark 1980, *v* Switzerland 1980, *v* Spain 1980

Mosey, IJ
(England): Home Int 1971

Moss, AV
(Wales): Home Int 1965-66-68

Mouland, MG
(Wales): Home Int 1978-81; *v* Ireland 1979; Eur T Ch 1979

Moxon, GA
(Wales): *v* Ireland 1929-30

Mulcare, P
(GBI): Walker Cup 1975; *v* Europe 1972. (Ireland): Home Int 1968-69-70-71-72-74-78-80; *v* France, West Germany, Sweden 1978-80; Eur T Ch 1975-79

Mulholland, D
(Ireland): Home Int 1988

Munn, E
(Ireland): *v* Wales 1913-23-24; *v* Scotland 1927

Munn, L
(Ireland): *v* Wales 1913-23-24; Home Int 1936-37

Munro, RAG
(Scotland): Home Int 1960

Murdoch, D
(Scotland): Home Int 1964

Murphy, AR
(Scotland): Home Int 1961-67

Murphy, G
(Ireland): Home Int 1992-93-94-95; Eur T Ch 1995

Murphy, M
(Ireland): Home Int 2000

Murphy, P
(Ireland): Home Int 1985-86

Murray, GH
(GBI): Walker Cup 1977; *v* Europe 1978. (Scotland): Home Int 1973-74-75-76-77-78-83; *v* Spain 1974-77; *v* Belgium 1975-77; Eur T Ch 1975-77

Murray, P
(Ireland): Home Int 1995-96

Murray, SWT
(GBI): Walker Cup 1963; *v* Europe 1958-62. (Scotland): Home Int 1959-60-61-62-63; *v* Scandinavia 1960

Murray, WA
(GBI): Walker Cup 1923-24. (Scotland): *v* England 1923-24-25-26-27

Murray, WB
(Scotland): Home Int 1967-68-69; Eur T Ch 1969

Muscroft, R
(England): Home Int 1986

Nash A
(England): Home Int 1988-89

Neech, DG
(England): Home Int 1961

Neill, JH
(Ireland): Home Int 1938-47-48-49

Neill, R
(Scotland): Home Int 1936

Nelson, P
(England): v France 1996

Nestor, JM
(Ireland): Home Int 1962-63-64

Nevin, V
(Ireland): Home Int 1960-63-65-67-69-72; Eur T Ch 1967-69-73

Newey, AS
(England): Home Int 1932

Newman, JE
(Wales): Home Int 1932

Newton, H
(Wales): v Ireland 1929

Nicholson, J
(Ireland): Home Int 1932

Nolan, K
(GBI): Walker Cup 1997; v Europe 1996; Eisenhower Trophy 1996. (Ireland): Home Int 1992-93-94-95-96; Eur T Ch 1995-97

Noon, GS
(Wales): Home Int 1935-36-37

Noon, J
(Scotland): Home Int 1987

O'Boyle, P
(Ireland): Eur T Ch 1977

O'Brien, MD
(Ireland): Home Int 1968-69-70-71-72-75-76-77; Eur T Ch 1971; v France, West Germany, Sweden 1976

O'Carroll, C
(Wales): Home Int 1989-90-91-92-93; Eur T Ch 1991

O'Connell, A
(Ireland): Home Int 1967-70-71

O'Connell, E
(GBI): Walker Cup 1989; v Europe 1988; Eisenhower Trophy 1988*. (Ireland): Home Int 1985; Eur T Ch 1989

O'Hara, S
(GBI): Walker Cup 2001; Eur T Ch 2001; v Sweden 2001; Eisenhower Trophy 2000; v Europe 2000. (Scotland): Home Int 1999-2000; v Italy 2000

O'Leary, JE
(Ireland): Home Int 1969-70; Eur T Ch 1969

O'Neill, JJ
(Ireland): Home Int 1968

O'Rourke, P
(Ireland): Home Int 1980-81-82-84-85

O'Sullivan, DF
(Ireland): Home Int 1976-85-86-87-91; Eur T Ch 1977

O'Sullivan, WM
(Ireland): Home Int 1934-35-36-37-38-47-48-49-50-51-53-54

Oldcorn, A
(GBI): Walker Cup 1983; Eisenhower Trophy 1982. (England): Home Int 1982-83

Omelia, B
(Ireland): Home Int 1994-95-96-97

Oosterhuis, PA
(GBI): Walker Cup 1967; v Europe 1968; Eisenhower Trophy 1968. (England): Home Int 1966-67-68

Oppenheimer, RH
(GBI): Walker Cup 1957. (England): v Ireland 1928-29-30; v Scotland 1930

Osgood, TH
(Scotland): v England 1925

Owen, JB
(Wales): Home Int 1971

Owens, GF
(Wales): Home Int 1960-61

Ownes, GH
(Ireland): Home Int 1935-37-38-47

Page, P
(GBI): Walker Cup 1993. (England): Home Int 1993

Palferman, H
(Wales): Home Int 1950-53

Palmer, DJ
(England): Home Int 1962-63

Palmer, M
(Wales): Home Int 1998

Pardoe, S
(Wales): Home Int 1991

Parfitt, RWM
(Wales): v Ireland 1924

Park, D
(GBI): Walker Cup 1997. (Wales): Home Int 1994-95-96-97; Eur T Ch 1995-97

Parkin, AP
(GBI): Walker Cup 1983. (Wales): Home Int 1980-81-82

Parry, JR
(Wales): Home Int 1966-75-76-77; v France 1976

Patey, IR
(England): Home Int 1952; v France 1948-49-50

Paton, DA
(Scotland): Home Int 1991

Patrick, D
(GBI): Walker Cup 1999-2000. (Scotland): Home Int 1997-98-99; Eur T Ch 1999; v Sweden 1999. (Eur): v Asia Pacific 2000

Patrick, KG
(Scotland): Home Int 1937

Patterson, AH
(Ireland): v Wales 1913

Pattinson, R
(England): Home Int 1949

Paul, S
(Ireland): Home Int 2001

Payne, J
(England): Home Int 1950-51

Payne, J
(GBI): Walker Cup 1991; v Europe 1990. (England): Home Int 1989-90; Eur T Ch 1991

Pearson, AG
(GBI): v South Africa 1927

Pearson, MJ
(England): Home Int 1951-52

Pease, JWB (later Lord Wardington)
(England): v Scotland 1903-04-05-06

Peet, M
(Wales): Home Int 1995-96

Pennink, JJF
(GBI): Walker Cup 1938. (England): Home Int 1937-38-47; v France 1937-38-39

Perkins, TP
(GBI): Walker Cup 1928. (England): v Scotland 1927-28-29

Perowne, AH
(GBI): Walker Cup 1949-53-59; Eisenhower Trophy 1958. (England): Home Int 1947-48-49-50-51-53-54-55-57

Peters, GB
(GBI): Walker Cup 1936-38. (Scotland): Home Int 1934-35-36-37-38

Peters, JL
(Wales): Home Int 1987-88-89

Philipson, S
(England): Home Int 1997

Phillips, LA
(Wales): v Ireland 1913

Phillips, V
(GBI): Walker Cup 1993

Pierse, AD
(GBI): Walker Cup 1983; v Europe 1980; Eisenhower Trophy 1982. (Ireland): Home Int 1976-77-78-80-81-82-83-84-85-87-88; v Wales 1979; v France, West Germany, Sweden 1980; Eur T Ch 1981

Pilkington, M
(Wales): Home Int 1997-98; Eur T Ch 1997

Pinch, AG
(Wales): Home Int 1969

Pirie, AK
(GBI): Walker Cup 1967; v Europe 1970. (Scotland): Home Int 1966 to 1975; Eur T Ch 1967-69; v Belgium 1973-75; v Spain 1974

Plaxton, J
(England): Home Int 1983-84

Pollin, RKM
(Ireland): Home Int 1971; Eur T
Ch 1973

Pollock, VA
(England): v Scotland 1908

Povall, J
(GBI): v Europe 1962. (Wales):
Home Int 1960 to 63, 65 to 1977;
Eur T Ch 1967-69-71-73-75-77;
v France 1975-76; v Denmark 1976

Powell, WA
(England): v Scotland 1923-24;
v Wales/Ireland 1925

Power, E
(Ireland): Home Int 1987-88-93-
94-95-97-98-99

Power, M
(Ireland): Home Int 1947-48-49-
50-51-52-54

Poxon, MA
(GBI): Walker Cup 1975.
(England): Home Int 1975-76; Eur
T Ch 1975

Pressdee, RNG
(Wales): Home Int 1958-59-60-61-62

Pressley, J
(Scotland): Home Int 1947-48-49

Price, D
(Wales): Home Int 1999-2000-01

Price, JP
(Wales): Home Int 1986-87-88

Price, R
(Wales): Home Int 1994-96-97

Prosser, D
(England): Eur T Ch 1989

Pughe, O
(Wales): Home Int 1997-98

Pugh, RS
(Wales): v Ireland 1923-24-29

Pullan, M
(England): Home Int 1991-92

Purcell, J
(Ireland): Home Int 1973

Pyman, I
(GBI): Walker Cup 1993.
(England): Home Int 1993

Raeside, A
(Scotland): v Ireland 1929

Rafferty, R
(GBI): Walker Cup 1981; v Europe
1980; Eisenhower Trophy 1980.
(Ireland): v Wales 1979; Home Int
1980-81; v France, West Germany,
Sweden 1980; Eur T Ch 1981

Rainey, WHE
(Ireland): Home Int 1962

Rankin, G
(GBI): Walker Cup 1995-97-99.
(Scotland): Home Int 1994-95-97-
98; v Sweden 1995-97-99; v France

1995-97; Eur T Ch 1995-97-99;
v Spain 1996

Rawlinson, D
(England): Home Int 1949-50-52-
53

Ray, D
(England): Home Int 1982;
v France 1982

Rayfus, P
(Ireland): Home Int 1986-87-88

Reade, HE
(Ireland): v Wales 1913

Reddan, B
(Ireland): Home Int 1987

Rees, CN
(Wales): Home Int 1986-88-89-91-
92-94-95-96-97

Rees, DA
(Wales): Home Int 1961 to 1964

Reid, A
(Scotland): Home Int 1993-94-95;
Eur T Ch 1993-95; v Spain 1994;
v Italy 1994; v France 1995

Renfrew, RL
(Scotland): Home Int 1964

Renwick, G, Jr
(Wales): v Ireland 1923

Revell, RP
(England): Home Int 1972-73; Eur
T Ch 1973

Reynard, M
(England): Home Int 1996-97;
v France 1996

Ricardo, W
(Wales); v Ireland 1930-31;
v Scotland 1931

Rice, JH
(Ireland): Home Int 1947-52

Rice, T
(Ireland): Home Int 2000-01; Eur
T Ch 2001

Rice-Jones, L
(Wales): v Ireland 1924

Richards, PM
(Wales): Home Int 1960-61-62-63-
71

Richardson, S
(England): Home Int 1986-87-88

Risdon, PWL
(England): Home Int 1935-36

Robb, J, Jr
(Scotland): v England 1902-03-05-
06-07

Robb, WM
(Scotland): Home Int 1935

Roberts, AT
(Scotland): v Ireland 1931

Roberts, GP
(England): Home Int 1951-53;
v France 1949

Roberts, GW
(Scotland): Home Int 1937-38

Roberts, H
(Wales): Home Int 1992-93

Roberts, HJ
(England): Home Int 1947-48-53

Roberts, J
(Wales): Home Int 1937

Roberts, S
(Wales): Home Int 1998-99

Roberts, SB
(Wales): Home Int 1932 to 35-37-
38-47 to 54

Roberts, WJ
(Wales): Home Int 1948 to 54

Robertson, A
(England): Home Int 1986-87;
v France 1988

Robertson, CW
(Ireland): v Wales 1930; v Scotland
1930

Robertson, D
(GBI): Walker Cup 1993; v Europe
1992; Eisenhower Trophy 1992.
(Scotland): Home Int 1991-92-93;
v Sweden 1992; v Italy 1992;
v France 1993; Eur T Ch 1993

Robertson, DM
(Scotland): Home Int 1973-74;
v Spain 1974

Robertson-Durham, JA
(Scotland): v England 1911

Robinson, J
(England): v Ireland 1928

Robinson, J
(GBI): Walker Cup 1987.
(England): Home Int 1986

Robinson, S
(England): v Scotland 1925;
v Ireland 1928-29-30

Roderick, RN
(GBI): v Europe 1988; Walker Cup
1989. (Wales): Home Int 1983 to
1988

Rodgers, C
(England): Home Int 1999; v Spain
1999

Rogers, A
(England): Home Int 1991;
v France 1992

Rolfe, B
(Wales): Home Int 1963-65

Roobottom, EL
(Wales): Home Int 1967

Roper, HS
(Ireland): v Wales 1931;
v Scotland 1931

Roper, MS
(Wales): v Ireland 1979

Roper, R
(England): Home Int 1984 to 1987

Rose, J
(GBI) Walker Cup 1997.
(England): Home Int 1997; Eur T
Ch 1997

Rothwell, J
(England): Home Int 1947-48

Rowe, P
(GBI): Walker Cup 1999. (Eur):
v Asia Pacific 2000. (England):
Home Int 1997-98-2000; Eur T Ch
1999; v Spain 1999

Russell, R
(GBI): Walker Cup 1993.
(Scotland): Home Int 1992-93;
v France 1993; Eur T Ch 1993

Rutherford, DS
(Scotland): v Ireland 1929

Rutherford, R
(Scotland): Home Int 1938-47

Ryles, D
(England): Home Int 2000

Saddler, AC
(GBI): Walker Cup 1963-65-67-77;
v Europe 1960-62-64-66; CW
1959-63-67; Eisenhower Trophy
1962-76*. (Scotland): Home Int
1959-60-61-62-63-64-66;
v Scandinavia 1962; Eur T Ch
1965-67-(75)-(77)

Sanders, M
(England): Home Int 1998-99;
v Spain 1999

Sandywell, A
(England): Home Int 1990; Eur T
Ch 1991

Scannel, BJ
(Ireland): Home Int 1947-48-49-
50-51-53-54

Scotland, Z
(England): v France 2000; Home
Int 2000-01

Scott, KB
(England): Home Int 1937-38;
v France 1938

Scott, Hon M
(GBI): Walker Cup 1924-**34**;
v Australia 1934. (England):
v Scotland 1911-12-23-24-25-26

Scott, Hon O
(England): v Scotland 1902-05-06

Scott, R, Jr
(GBI): Walker Cup 1924.
(Scotland): v England 1924-28

Scott, WGF
(Scotland): v Ireland 1927

Scratton, EWHB
(England): v Scotland 1912

Scroggie: FH
(Scotland): v England 1910

Scrutton, PF
(GBI): Walker Cup 1955-57.
(England): Home Int 1950-55

Sewell, D
(GBI): Walker Cup 1957-59; CW
1959; Eisenhower Trophy 1960.
(England): Home Int 1956-57-58-
59-60

Shade, RDBM
(GBI): Walker Cup 1961-63-65-67;
v Europe 1962-64-66-68;
Eisenhower Trophy 1962-64-66-68;
CW 1963-67; v Australia 1964.
(Scotland): Home Int 1957, 1960
to 1968; v Scandinavia 1960-62;
Eur T Ch 1965-67

Shaw, G
(GBI): Walker Cup 1987.
(Scotland): Home Int 1984-86-87-
88-90; v West Germany 1987;
v Sweden 1984; v France 1987; Eur
T Ch 1987

Sheals, HS
(Ireland): v Wales 1929; v England
1929-30-31; v Scotland 1930;
Home Int 1932-33

Sheahan, D
(GBI): Walker Cup 1963; v Europe
1962-64-67. (Ireland): Home Int
1961-62-63-64-65-66-67-70

Sheppard, M
(Wales): Home Int 1990

Shepperson, AE
(GBI): Walker Cup 1957-59.
(England): Home Int 1956-57-58-59-
60-62

Sherborne, A
(England): Home Int 1982-83-84

Sherry, G
(GBI): Walker Cup 1995; v Europe
1994; Eisenhower Trophy 1994.
(Scotland): Home Int 1993-94-95;
v France 1993-95; v Spain 1994;
v Sweden 1995; Eur T Ch 1995

Shields, B
(Scotland):Home Int 1986

Shingler, TR
(England): Home Int 1977

Shorrock, TJ
(England): v France 1952

Side, M
(England): Home Int 1999

Simcox, R
(Ireland): v Wales 1930-31;
v Scotland 1930-31; v England
1931; Home Int 1932-33-34-35-36-
38

Simpson, AF
(Scotland): v Ireland 1928;
v England 1927

Simpson, JG
(GBI): v America 1921. (Scotland):
v England 1906-07-08-09-11-12-
22-24-26

Sinclair, A
(Scotland): Home Int 1950; Eur T
Ch 1967 (Captain)

Sinclair, M
(Ireland): Home Int 1999

Skinns, D
(England): Home Int 2001

Slark, WA
(England): Home Int 1957

Slater, A
(England): Home Int 1955-62

Slattery, B
(Ireland): Home Int 1947-48

Sludds, MF
(Ireland): Home Int 1982

Smith, A
(Wales): Home Int 1998-2000

Smith, Eric M
(England): v Ireland 1931;
v Scotland 1931

Smith, Everard
(England): v Scotland 1908-09-10-12

Smith, GF
(England): v Scotland 1902-03

Smith, JN
(GBI): Walker Cup 1930.
(Scotland): v Ireland 1928-30-31;
v England 1929-30-31; v Wales
1931; Home Int 1932-33-34

Smith, JR
(England): Home Int 1932

Smith, LOM
(England): Home Int 1963

Smith, M
(Wales): Home Int 1993-94-95-96-
97; Eur T Ch 1995-97

Smith, S
(Scotland): v Austria 1994

Smith, VH
(Wales): v Ireland 1924-25

Smith, W
(England): Home Int 1972.
(GBI): v Europe 1972

Smith, WD
(GBI): Walker Cup 1959; v Europe
1958. (Scotland): Home Int 1957-
58-59-60-63; v Scandinavia 1958-60

Smyth, D
(Ireland): Home Int 1972-73; Eur
T Ch 1973

Smyth, DW
(Ireland): v Wales 1923-30;
v England 1930; v Scotland 1931;
Home Int 1933

Smyth, HB
(GBI): v Europe 1976. (Ireland):
Home Int 1974-75-76-78; Eur T
Ch 1975-79; v France, West
Germany, Sweden 1976

Smyth, V
(Ireland): Home Int 1981-82

Snowdon, J
(England): Home Int 1934

Soulby, DEB
(Ireland): v Wales 1929-30;
v England 1929-30; v Scotland
1929-30

Spiller, EF
(Ireland): *v* Wales 1924; *v* England 1928; *v* Scotland 1928-29

Spring, G
(Ireland): Home Int 1996

Squirrell, HC
(Wales): Home Int 1955 to 1971, 1973 to 1975; Eur T Ch 1967-69-71-75; *v* France 1975

Stanford, M
(GBI): Walker Cup 1993; *v* Europe 1992; Eisenhower Trophy 1992. (England): Home Int 1991-92-93; *v* France 1992

Staunton, R
(Ireland): Home Int 1964-65-72; Eur T Ch 1973

Steel, DMA
(England): Home Int 1970

Stephen, AR
(GBI): Walker Cup 1985; *v* Europe 1972. (Scotland): Home Int 1971-72-73-74-75-76-77-84-85; Eur T Ch 1975-85; *v* France 1985; *v* Spain 1974; *v* Belgium 1975-77-78

Stevens, DI
(Wales): Home Int 1968-69-70-74-75-76-77-78-80-82; Eur T Ch 1969-77; *v* France 1976; *v* Denmark 1977

Stevens, LB
(England): *v* Scotland 1912

Stevenson, A
(Scotland): Home Int 1949

Stevenson, JB
(Scotland): *v* Ireland 1931; Home Int 1932-38-47-49-50-51

Stevenson, JF
(Ireland): *v* Wales 1923-24; *v* England 1925

Stevenson, K
(Ireland): Home Int 1972

Stockdale, B
(England): Home Int 1964-65

Stoker, K
(Wales): *v* Ireland 1923-24

Stokoe, GC
(Wales): *v* England 1925; *v* Ireland 1929-30

Storey, EF
(GBI): Walker Cup 1924-26-28. (England): *v* Scotland 1924-25-26-27-28-30; Home Int 1936; *v* France 1936

Storm, G
(GBI): Walker Cup 1999. (England): Home Int 1999; Eur T Ch 1999

Stott, HAN
(England): Home Int 1976-77

Stout, JA
(GBI): Walker Cup 1930-32.

(England): *v* Scotland 1928-29-30-31; *v* Ireland 1929-31

Stowe, C
(GBI): Walker Cup 1938-47. (England): Home Int 1935-36-37-38-47-49-54; *v* France 1938-39-49

Strachan, CJL
(Scotland): Home Int 1965-66-67; Eur T Ch 1967

Straker, R
(England): Home Int 1932

Streeter, P
(England): Home Int 1992; *v* France 1994-96

Stuart, HB
(GBI): Walker Cup 1971-73-75; *v* Europe 1968-72-74; CW 1971; Eisenhower Trophy 1972. (Scotland): Home Int 1967-68-69-70-71-72-73-74-76; Eur T Ch 1969-71-73-75; *v* Belgium 1973-75

Stuart, JE
(Scotland): Home Int 1959

Stubbs, AK
(England): Home Int 1982

Sullivan, K
(Wales): Home Int 1998-99-2000-01; Eur T Ch 2001

Suneson, C
(England): Home Int 1988; Eur T Ch 1989

Sutherland, DMG
(England): Home Int 1947

Sutton, W
(England): *v* Scotland 1929-31; *v* Ireland 1929-30-31

Symonds, A
(Wales): *v* Ireland 1925

Taggart, J
(Ireland): Home Int 1953

Tait, AG
(Scotland): Home Int 1987-88-89; Nixdorf Nations Cup 1989

Tate, JK
(England): Home Int 1954-55-56

Taylor, GN
(Scotland): Home Int 1948

Taylor, HE
(England): *v* Scotland 1911

Taylor, JS
(Scotland): *v* England 1979; Home Int 1980; *v* Belgium 1980; *v* France 1980

Taylor, LG
(Scotland): Home Int 1955-56

Taylor, TPD
(Wales): Home Int 1963

Taylor, Y
(Wales): Home Int 1995-96-97; Eur T Ch 1995-97

Thirlwell, A
(GBI): Walker Cup 1957; *v* Europe

1956-58-64; CW 1953-64. (England): Home Int 1951-52-54-55-56-57-58-63-64

Thirsk, TJ
(England): *v* Ireland 1929; Home Int 1933-34-35-36-37-38; *v* France 1935-36-37-38-39

Thom, KG
(GBI): Walker Cup 1949. (England): Home Int 1947-48-49-53

Thomas, I
(England): Home Int 1933

Thomas, KR
(Wales): Home Int 1951-52

Thompson, ASG
(England): Home Int 1935-37

Thompson, MS
(GBI): Walker Cup 1983. (England): Home Int 1982

Thomson, AP
(Scotland): Home Int 1970; Eur T Ch 1971

Thomson, G
(Scotland): Home Int 1996

Thomson, H
(GBI): Walker Cup 1936-38. (Scotland): Home Int 1934 to 1938

Thomson, JA
(Scotland): Home Int 1981 to 89-91-92; Eur T Ch 1983; *v* West Germany 1987; *v* Italy 1984-86-88-90; *v* Sweden 1990

Thomson, M
(Scotland): Home Int 1998

Thorburn, K
(Scotland): *v* England 1928; *v* Ireland 1927

Timbey, JC
(Ireland): *v* Scotland 1928-31; *v* Wales 1931

Timmis, CW
(England): *v* Ireland 1930; Home Int 1936-37

Tipping, EB
(England): *v* Ireland 1930

Tipple, ER
(England): *v* Ireland 1928-29; Home Int 1932

Tolley, CJH
(GBI): *v* America 1921, Walker Cup 1922-23-24-26-30-34; *v* South Africa 1927. (England): *v* Scotland 1922 to 30; Home Int 1936-37-38; *v* Ireland/Wales 1925; *v* France 1938

Tooth, EA
(Wales): *v* Ireland 1913

Torrance, TA
(GBI): Walker Cup 1924-28-30-32-34. (Scotland): *v* England 1922-23-25-26-28-29-30; Home Int 1933

Torrance, WB
(GBI): Walker Cup 1922.

(Scotland): v England 1922-23-24-26-27-28-30; v Ireland 1928-29-30

Townsend, PM
(GBI): Walker Cup 1965; v Europe 1966; Eisenhower Trophy 1966.
(England): Home Int 1965-66

Toye, JL
(Wales): Home Int 1963-64-65-66-67-69-70-71-72-73-74-76-78; Eur T Ch 1971-73-75-77; v France 1975

Tredinnick, SV
(England): Home Int 1950

Tucker, WI
(Wales): Home Int 1949 to 1972, 1974-75; Eur T Ch 1967-69-75; v France 1975

Tulloch, W
(Scotland): v England 1927-29-30-31; v Ireland 1930-31; v Wales 1931; Home Int 1932

Tupling, LP
(GBI): Walker Cup 1969.
(England): Home Int 1969; Eur T Ch 1969

Turnbull, A
(Scotland): Home Int 1995-96-97; v France 1995; v Spain 1996

Turnbull, CH
(Wales): v Ireland 1913-25

Turner, A
(England): Home Int 1952

Turner, GB
(Wales): Home Int 1947-48-49-50-51-52-55-56

Tweddell, W
(GBI): Walker Cup **1928-36**.
(England): v Scotland 1928-29-30; Home Int 1935

Twynholm, S
(Scotland): Home Int 1990.
Nixdorf Nations Cup 1990

Urquhart, M
(Scotland): Home Int 1993; v Italy 1996

Vannet, L
(Scotland): Home Int 1984

Waddell, G
(Ireland): v Wales 1925

Wainwright, A
(England): Home Int 1997-99

Walker, J
(GBI): Walker Cup 1961; v Europe 1958-60. (Scotland): Home Int 1954-55-57-58-60-61-62-63; v Scandinavia 1958-62

Walker, KH
(Scotland): Home Int 1985-86

Walker, MS
(England): v Ireland/Wales 1925

Walker, RS
(Scotland): Home Int 1935-36

Walker, R
(England): Home Int 2001

Wallbank, K
(England): Home Int 1996-97; v France 1996

Wallis, G
(Wales): Home Int 1934-36-37-38

Walls, MPD
(England): Home Int 1980-81-85

Walters, EM
(Wales): Home Int 1967-68-69; Eur T Ch 1969

Walton, AR
(England): Home Int 1934-35

Walton, P
(GBI): Walker Cup 1981-83; Eisenhower Trophy 1982.
(Ireland): v Wales 1979: Home Int 1980-81; v France, Germany, Sweden 1980; Eur T Ch 1981

Warren, KT
(England): Home Int 1962

Warren, M
(GBI): Walker Cup 2001;
(Scotland): Home Int 2000-01; v Italy 2000; Eur T Ch 2001; v Sweden 2001

Watson, CR
(GBI) Walker Cup 1997.
(Scotland): Home Int 1991-92 and 94 to 2000-**2001**; v Sweden 1992-97; v Italy 1992; v Austria 1994; v Spain 1996; v France 1997; Eur T Ch 1997-99-2001; v Sweden 2001

Watt, AW
(Scotland): Home Int 1987

Watts, C
(England): Home Int 1991-92; v France 1992

Way, P
(GBI): Walker Cup 1981.
(England): Home Int 1981; Eur T Ch 1981

Webster, AJ
(Scotland): Home Int 1978

Webster, F
(Ireland): Home Int 1949

Webster, S
(England): Home Int 1995-96; Eur T Ch 1997

Weeks, K
(England): Home Int 1987-88; v France 1988

Welch, L
(Ireland): Home Int 1936

Welch, M
(England): Home Int 1993-94; v France 1994

Wells, J
(England): Home Int 1999

Wemyss, DS
(Scotland): Home Int 1937

Werner, LE
(Ireland): v Wales 1925

West, CH
(Ireland): v England 1928; Home Int 1932

Westwood, L
(England): Home Int 1993

Wethered, RH
(GBI): v America 1921, Walker Cup 1922-23-26-**30**-34. (England): v Scotland 1922-23-24-25-26-27-28-29-30

White, L
(GBI): Walker Cup 1991.
(England): Home Int 1990; Eur T Ch 1991

White, RJ
(GBI): Walker Cup 1947-49-51-53-55. (England): Home Int 1947-48-49-53-54

Whitehouse, T
(England): Home Int 2000

Whyte, AW
(Scotland): Home Int 1934

Wiggett, M
(England): Home Int 1990

Wiggins, R
(GBI): v Europe 1996. (England): Home Int 1996; Eur T Ch 1997

Wight, R
(Scotland): v Sweden 1950

Wilkie, DF
(Scotland): Home Int 1962-63-65-67-68

Wilkie, G
(Scotland): v England 1911

Wilkie, GT
(Wales): Home Int 1938

Wilkinson, S
(Wales): Home Int 1990-91

Willcox, FS
(Wales): v Scotland 1931; v Ireland 1931

Williams, C
(Eur): v Asia Pacific 2000. (Wales): Home Int 1998-99-2000-01; Eur T Ch 1999-2001

Williams, DF
(England): v Scotland 1979

Williams, J
(Wales): Home Int 2001

Williams KH
(Wales): Home Int 1983 to 1987

Williams, PG
(Wales): *v* Ireland 1925

Williamson, SB
(Scotland): Home Int 1947-48-49-
51-52

Willison, R
(GBI): Walker Cup 1991; *v* Europe
1990; Eisenhower Trophy 1990.
(England): Home Int 1988-89-90;
Eur T Ch 1989-91

Wills, M
(Wales): Home Int 1990

Wilson, E
(Scotland): Home Int 1985

Wilson, J
(GBI): Walker Cup 1923.
(Scotland): *v* England 1922-23-24-
26; *v* Ireland 1932

Wilson, JC
(GBI): Walker Cup 1947-53;
v South Africa 1954; CW 1954.
(Scotland): Home Int 1947-48-49-
51-52-53; *v* Sweden 1950; *v* New
Zealand 1954

Wilson, P
(Scotland): Home Int 1976;
Belgium 1977

Wilson, S
(Scotland): Home Int 2000

Winchester, R
(England): Home Int 1985-87-89

Winfield, HB
(Wales): *v* Ireland 1913

Winter, G
(England): Home Int 1991

Wise, WS
(England): Home Int 1947

Wolstenholme, GB
(GBI): Walker Cup 1957-59;
Eisenhower Trophy 1958-60; CW
1959. (England): Home Int 1953-
55-56-57-58-59-60

Wolstenholme, GP
(GBI): Walker Cup 1995-97-99-
2001; *v* Europe 1992-94;
Eisenhower Trophy 1996-98*.
(Eur): *v* Asia Pacific 2000;
(England): Home Int 1988 to 2001;
v France 1988-92-94-2000; *v* Spain
1989-91-95-99; Eur T Ch 1995-97-
99-2001; *v* Spain 2001; *v* South
Africa 2001

Wood, DK
(Wales): Home Int 1982 to 1987

Woollam, J
(England): Home Int 1933-34-35;
v France 1935

Woolley, FA
(England): *v* Scotland 1910-11-12

Woosnam, I
(Wales): *v* France 1976

Worthington, JS
(England): *v* Scotland 1905

Wright, I
(Scotland): Home Int 1958-59-60-
61; *v* Scandinavia 1960-62

Yeo, J
(England): Home 1971

Young, D
(Ireland): Home Int 1969-70-77

Young, ID
(GBI): *v* Europe 1982. (Scotland):
Home Int 1981-82; *v* France 1982

Young, JR
(GBI): *v* Europe 1960. (Scotland):
Home Int 1960-61-65; *v* Scandinavia
1960

Young, S
(GBI) Walker Cup 1997.
(Scotland): Home Int 1996; *v* Italy
1996; Eur T Ch 1997

Zacharias, JP
(England): Home Int 1935

Zoete, HW de
(England): *v* Scotland 1903-04-06-
07

British Isles International Players, Amateur Women

Abbreviations

CW   Commonwealth Team

Eur T Ch   played in European Team Championship for home country

Home Int   played in Home International matches

*   indicates winning team

Captaincy is indicated by the year printed in bold type; non-playing captaincy in brackets

[1998] indicates Espirito Santo Team selection which was subsequently advised not to travel to Chile

Maiden names are shown in brackets; other surnames in square brackets

Agnew, C
(Scotland): Home Int 1995

Aitken, E (Young)
(Scotland): Home Int 1954

Alexander, M
(Ireland): Home Int 1920-21-22-30

Allen, F
(England): Home Int 1952

Allington Hughes, Miss
(Wales): Home Int 1908-09-10-12-14-22-25

Anderson, E
(Scotland): Home Int 1910-11-12-21-25

Anderson, F
(GBI): Vagliano Trophy 1987.
(Scotland): Home Int 1977-79-80-81-83-84-86-87-88-89-90-91-92;
Eur(L) T Ch 1979-83-87-91

Anderson, H
(GBI): Vagliano Trophy 1969.
(Scotland): Home Int 1964-65-68-69-70-71; Eur(L) T Ch 1969

Anderson, J (Donald)
(GBI): Curtis Cup 1948-50-52.
(Scotland): Home Int 1947 to 1952

Anderson, L
(Scotland): Home Int 1986-87-88-89; Eur(L) T Ch 1987-89

Anderson, VH
(Scotland): Home Int 1907

Andrew, K (Rostron)
(GBI): Curtis Cup 1998-2000;
Vagliano Trophy 1997-99-2001;
Espirito Santo [1998]; CW 1999.
(England): Home Int 1996-97-99-2001; Eur(L) T Ch 1997-2001

Arbuthnot, M
(Ireland): Home Int 1921

Archer, A (Rampton)
(England): Home Int **1968**

Archer, L
(Wales): Home Int 1999

Armstrong, M
(Ireland): Home Int 1906

Ashcombe, Lady
(Wales): Home Int 1950 to 1954

Aubertin, Mrs
(Wales): Home Int 1908-09-10

Bailey, D [Frearson] (Robb)
(GBI): Curtis Cup 1962-72-**84-86-88**; Vagliano Trophy 1961-**83-85**;
CW 1983. (England): Home Int
1961-62-71; Eur(L) T Ch 1968-**93**

Baker, J
(Wales): Home Int 1990

Bald, J
(Scotland): Home Int 1968-69-71;
Eur(L) T Ch 1969

Barber, S (Bonallack)
(GBI): Curtis Cup 1962; Vagliano
Trophy 1961-63-69; CW **1995**;
Espirito Santo **1996**. (England):
Home Int 1960-61-62-68-70-72-77-**78**; Eur(L) T Ch 1969-71

Barclay, C (Brisbane)
(Scotland): Home Int 1953-61-68

Bargh Etherington, B
(Whitehead)
(England): Home Int 1974

Barlow, Mrs
(Ireland): Home Int 1921

Barron, M
(Wales): Home Int 1929 to 31, 34-to 39, 47 to 58, 60 to 63

Barry, L
(England): Home Int 1911-12-13-14

Barry, P
(England): Home Int 1982

Barton, P
(GBI): Curtis Cup 1934-36.
(England): Home Int 1935-36-37-38-39

Bastin, G
(England): Home Int 1920-21-22-23-24-25

Bayliss, Mrs
(Wales): Home Int 1921

Bayman, L (Denison Pender)
(GBI): Curtis Cup 1988; Vagliano
Trophy 1971-85-87; Espirito Santo
1988. (England): Home Int 1971-72-73-83-84-85-87-88-**95-96**;
Eur(L) T Ch 1985-87-89-**97**-(**2001**)

Baynes, Mrs CE
(Scotland): Home Int 1921-22

Beck, B (Pim)
(Ireland): Home Int 1930-31-32-33-34-36-37-47-48-49-50-51-52-53-54-55-56-58-59-61

Beckett, J
(Ireland): Home Int 1962-66-67-68: Eur(L) T Ch 1967

Beddows, C [Watson]
(Stevenson)
(GBI): Curtis Cup 1932.
(Scotland): Home Int 1913-14-21-22-23-27-29-30-31-32-33-34-35-36-37-39-47-48-49-50-51.

Behan, L
(GBI): Curtis Cup 1986; Vagliano
Trophy 1985. (Ireland): Home Int
1984-85-86-96-98

Beharrell, V (Anstey)
(GBI): Curtis Cup 1956.
(England): Home Int 1955-56-57-**61**

Benka, P (Tredinnick)
(GBI): Curtis Cup 1966-68;
Vagliano Trophy 1967. (England):
Home Int 1967

Bennett, L
(Scotland): Home Int 1977-80-81

Benton, MH
(Scotland): Home Int 1914

Biggs, A (Whittaker)
(GBI): Vagliano Trophy 1959

Birmingham, M
(Ireland): Home Int **1967**

Bisgood, J
(GBI): Curtis Cup 1950-52-54-**70**.
(England): Home Int 1949-50-51-
52-53-54-56-58

Blair, N (Menzies)
(Scotland): Home Int 1955

Blake, Miss
(Ireland): Home Int 1931 to 1936

Blaymire, J
(England): Home Int 1971-88-**89**

Bloodworth, D (Lewis)
(Wales): Home Int 1954-55-56-57-
60

Boatman, EA (Collis)
(GBI): Curtis Cup 1992-**94**; CW
1987-**91**. (England): Home Int
1974-80-**84-85-90-91**; Eur(L) T Ch
1985-87

Bolas, R
(England): Home Int 1992

Bolton, Z (Bonner Davis)
(GBI): Curtis Cup 1948-**56-66-68-
94**; CW 1967. (England): Home Int
1939-48-49-50-51-**55**-56

Bonallack, A (Ward)
(GBI): Curtis Cup 1956-58-60-62-
64-66; Vagliano Trophy 1959-61-
63. (England): Home Int 1956 to
1966 and 72.

Bostock, M
(England): Home Int **1954**

Bourn, Mrs
(England): Home Int 1909-12

Bowhill, M (Robertson-
Durham)
(Scotland): Home Int 1936-37-38

Boyd, J
(Ireland): Home Int 1912-13-14

Boyes, S
(Wales): Home Int 1992

Bradley, K (Rawlings)
(Wales): Home Int 1975-76-77-78-
79-82-83

Bradshaw, E
(GBI): Vagliano Trophy 1969-71.
(Ireland): Home Int 1964-66-67-
68-69-70-71-74-75-**80-81**; Eur(L)
T Ch 1969-71-75

Brandom, G
(GBI): Vagliano Trophy 1967.
(Ireland): Home Int 1965-66-67-
68; Eur(L) T Ch 1967

Brearley, M
(Wales): Home Int 1937-38

Brennan, R (Hegarty)
(Ireland): Home Int 1974-75-76-
77-78-79-81

Brewerton, R
(GBI): Curtis Cup 2000.
(Wales): Vagliano Trophy 2001;
Home Int 1997-98-99-2000-01;
Eur(L) T Ch 1999-2001

Brice, Mrs
(Ireland): Home Int 1948

Bridges, Mrs
(Wales): Home Int 1933-38-39

Briggs, A (Brown)
(GBI): Vagliano Trophy 1971-75.
(Wales): Home Int 1969-70-71-72-
73-74-75-76-77-78-79-80-**81-82-83**
-84-**93**; Eur(L) T Ch 1971-75

Brinton, Mrs
(Ireland): Home Int 1922

Bromley-Davenport, I
(Rieben)
(Wales): Home Int 1932-33-34-35-
36-48-50-51-52-53-54-55-56

Brook, D
(Wales): Home Int 1913

Brooks, E
(Ireland): Home Int 1953-54-56

Broun, JG
(Scotland): Home Int 1905-06-07-21

Brown, B
(Ireland): Home Int 1960

Brown, E (Jones)
(Wales): Home Int 1947-48-49-50-
52-53-57-58-59-60-61-62-63-64-
65-66-68-69-70

Brown, F
(GBI): Curtis Cup 1998-2000;
Vagliano Trophy 1999-2001; CW
1999. (England): Home Int 1994-
96-97-98-99-2000-01; Eur(L) T
Ch 1997-99-2001

Brown, Mrs FW (Gilroy)
(Scotland): Home Int 1905-06-07-
08-09-10-11-13-21

Brown, J
(Wales): Home Int 1960-61-62-64-
65; Eur(L) T Ch 1965-69

Brown, J
(England): Home Int 1984

Brown, TWL
(Scotland): Home Int 1924-25

Brown, Mrs
(Wales): Home Int 1924-25-27

Brownlow, Miss
(Ireland): Home Int 1923

Bryan-Smith, S
(Wales): Home Int 1947-48-49-50-
51-52-56

Burnell, S
(England): Home Int 1993; Eur(L)
T Ch 1993

Burns, K
(Scotland): Home Int 1999

Burrell, Mrs
(Wales): Home Int 1939

Burton, H (Mitchell)
(GBI): Vagliano Trophy 1961.
(Scotland): Home Int 1931-55-56-
59

Burton, M
(England): Eur(L) T Ch 1997

Burton, M
(England): Home Int 1975-76

Butler, I (Burke)
(GBI): Curtis Cup 1966-**96**;
Vagliano Trophy 1965; Espirito
Santo 1964-66. (Ireland): Home Int
1962-63-64-65-66-68-70-71-72-73-
76-77-78-79-**86-87**; Eur(L) T Ch
1967

Byrne, A (Sweeney)
(Ireland): Home Int 1959-60-61-
62-63-**90-91**

Cadden, G
(GBI): Vagliano Trophy **1997**.
(Scotland): Home Int 1974-75-**95-
96**; Eur(L) T Ch **1997**

Cairns, Lady Katherine
(GBI): Curtis Cup **1952**. (England):
Home Int 1947-48-50-51-52-53-54

Caldwell, C (Redford)
(GBI): Curtis Cup 1978-80;
Vagliano Trophy 1973. (England):
Home Int 1973-78-79-80

Callen, L
(Ireland): Home Int 1990

Campbell, J (Burnett)
(Scotland): Home Int 1960

Cann, M (Nuttall)
(England): Home Int 1966

Carrick, P (Bullard)
(England): Home Int 1939-47

Caryl, M
(Wales): Home Int 1929

Casement, M (Harrison)
(Ireland): Home Int 1909-10-11-
12-13-14

Cassidy, Y
(Ireland): Home Int 1994-95-2000-
01

Cautley, B (Hawtrey)
(England): Home Int 1912-13-14-
22-23-24-25-27

Chambers, D
(GBI): Curtis Cup 1934-36-38.

(England): Home Int 1906-07-09-10-11-12-20-24-25

Christison, D
(England): Home Int 1981

Chugg, P (Light)
(Wales): Home Int 1973-74-75-76-77-78-86-87-88-96; Eur(L) T Ch 1975-87-(**2001**)

Clark, G (Atkinson)
(England): Home Int 1955

Clarke, Mrs ML
(England): Home Int 1933-35

Clarke, P
(England): Home Int 1981

Clarke, Mrs
(Ireland): Home Int 1922

Clarkson, H (Reynolds)
(Wales): Home Int 1935-38-39

Clay, E
(Wales): Home Int 1912

Clement, V
(England): Home Int 1932-34-35

Close, M (Wenyon)
(GBI): Vagliano Trophy 1969.
(England): Home Int 1968-69;
Eur(L) T Ch 1969

Coats, Mrs G
(Scotland): Home Int 1931 to 1934

Cochrane, K
(Scotland): Home Int 1924-25-28-29-30

Coffey, A
(GBI): Espirito Santo 2000;
Vagliano Trophy 1999-2001.
(Ireland): Home Int 1995-96-97-98-99-2000-01; Eur(L) T Ch 1997-99-2001

Cole, C
(Wales): Home Int 1998

Collett, P
(England): Home Int 1910

Collingham, J (Melville)
(GBI): Vagliano Trophy 1979-87;
CW 1987. (England): Home Int 1978-79-81-84-86-87-92; Eur(L) T Ch 1989

Colquhoun, H
(Ireland): Home Int 1959-60-61-63

Comboy, C (Grott)
(GBI): Curtis Cup 1978-**80**;
Vagliano Trophy 1977-**79**; Espirito Santo 1978; CW 1979. (England):
Home Int **1975-76**

Connachan, J
(GBI): Curtis Cup 1980-82; Vagliano Trophy 1981-83; Espirito Santo 1980-82; CW 1983. (Scotland):
Home Int 1979-80-81-82-83

Coote, Miss
(Ireland): Home Int 1925-28-29

Copley, K (Lackie)
(Scotland): Home Int 1974-75

Corlett, E
(GBI): Curtis Cup 1932-38-**64**.
(England): Home Int 1927-29-30-31-32-33-35-36-37-38-39

Costello, G
(Ireland): Home Int 1973-**84-85**

Cotton, S (German)
(GBI): Vagliano Trophy 1967.
(England): Home Int 1967-68;
Eur(L) T Ch 1967

Coughlan, C
(Ireland): Home Int 1999-2000-01;
Eur(L) T Ch 1999-2001

Couper, M
(Scotland): Home Int 1929-34-35-36-37-39-56

Court, C
(England): Home Int 2000

Cowley, Lady
(Wales): Home Int 1907-09

Cox, Margaret
(Wales): Home Int 1924-25

Cox, Nell
(Wales): Home Int 1954

Craik, T
(Scotland): Home Int 1988

Cramsie, F (Hezlet)
(Ireland): Home Int 1905-06-07-08-09-10-13-20-24

Crawford, I (Wylie)
(Scotland): Home Int 1970-71-72

Cresswell, K (Stuart)
(Scotland): Home Int 1909-10-11-12-14

Critchley, D (Fishwick)
(GBI): Curtis Cup 1932-34-**50**.
(England): Home Int 1930-31-32-33-35-36-47

Croft, A
(England): Home Int 1927

Cross, M
(Wales): Home Int 1922

Cruickshank, DM (Jenkins)
(Scotland): Home Int 1910-11-12

Crummack, Miss
(England): Home Int 1909

Cuming, Mrs
(Ireland): Home Int 1910

Cunninghame, S
(Wales): Home Int 1922-25-29-31

Cuthell, R (Adair)
(Ireland): Home Int 1908

Dampney, S
(Wales): Home Int 1924-25-27-28-29-30

David, Mrs
(Wales): Home Int 1908

Davidson, A (Rose)
(GBI): Curtis Cup 1996-98; Vagliano Trophy 1995-97; CW 1995.
(Scotland): Home Int 1990 to 1998, 2000; Eur(L) T Ch 1991-93-95-97-99

Davidson, B (Inglis)
(Scotland): Home Int 1928

Davies, K
(GBI): Curtis Cup 1986-88;
Vagliano Trophy 1987; CW 1987.
(Wales): Home Int 1981-82-83;
Eur(L) T Ch 1987

Davies, L
(GBI): Curtis Cup 1984; CW 1987.
(England): Home Int 1983-84

Davies, P (Griffiths)
(Wales): Home Int 1965-66-67-68-70-71-73; Eur(L) T Ch 1971

Davis, L
(Wales): Home Int 1997-98-2000-01; Eur(L) T Ch 1997-99

Deacon, Mrs
(Wales): Home Int 1912-14

Denny, A (Barrett)
(England): Home Int 1951

Dering, Mrs
(Ireland): Home Int 1923

Dermott, L
(GBI): Curtis Cup 1996. (Wales):
Home Int 1987-88-89-91-92-93-94-95-96; Eur(L) T Ch 1991-93

Dickson, E
(Ireland): Home Int 1999-2000;
Eur(L) T Ch 1999

Dickson, M
(Ireland): Home Int 1909

Dobson, H
(GBI): Curtis Cup 1990; Vagliano Trophy 1989. (England): Home Int 1987-88-89; Eur(L) T Ch 1989

Dod, L
(England): Home Int 1905

Donne, A
(Wales): Home Int 1993-94;
Eur(L) T Ch 1993

Douglas, K
(GBI): Curtis Cup 1982; Vagliano Trophy 1983. (England): Home Int 1981-82-83

Dowdall, E
(Ireland): Home Int 1997-98-99-2000-01

Dowling, C (Hourihane)
(GBI): Curtis Cup 1984-86-88-90-92-**2000**; Vagliano Trophy 1981-83-85-87-89-91-(**99**); Espirito Santo 1986-90-[**98**]. (Ireland):
Home Int 1979 to 1992; Eur(L) T Ch 1981-83-85-87-89-**97**

Dowling, D
(England): Home Int 1979

Draper, M [Peel] (Thomas)
(GBI): Curtis Cup 1954; Vagliano
Trophy 1963. (Scotland): Home Int
1929-34-38-49-50-51-52-53-**54**-55-
56-57-58-**61**-62

Duggleby, E
(GBI): Curtis Cup 2000; Vagliano
Trophy 1995-2001. (England):
Home Int 1994-95-96-99-2000-01;
Eur(L) T Ch 1995-99-2001

Duncan, B
(Wales): Home Int 1907-08-09-10-12

Duncan, M
(Wales): Home Int 1922-23-28-34

Duncan, MJ (Wood)
(Scotland): Home Int 1925-27-28-
39

Durlacher, Mrs
(Ireland): Home Int 1905-06-07-
08-09-10-14

Durrant, B [Green] (Lowe)
(England): Home Int 1954

Dwyer, Mrs
(Ireland): 1928

Eakin, P (James)
(Ireland): Home Int 1967

Eakin, T
(Ireland): Home Int 1990-91-92-
93-94; Eur(L) T Ch 1993

Earner, M
(Ireland): Home Int 1960-61-62-
63-70

Edmond, F (Macdonald)
(GBI): Vagliano Trophy 1991.
(England): Home Int 1991; Eur(L)
T Ch 1991

Educate, L (Walton)
(GBI): Curtis Cup 1994-96;
Vagliano Trophy 1993-95; CW
1995. (England): Home Int 1991-
94-95; Eur(L) T Ch 1993-95

Edwards, E
(Wales): Home Int 1949-50

Edwards, J
(Wales): Home Int 1932-33-34-36-37

Edwards, J (Morris)
(Wales): Home Int 1962-63-66-67-
68-69-70-77-**78**-79; Eur(L) T Ch
1967-69-**93**

Egford, K
(England): Home Int 1992-94

Ellis, E
(Ireland): Home Int 1932-35-37-38

Ellis Griffiths (Mrs)

(Wales): Home Int 1907-08-09-12-
13

Emery, MJ
(Wales): Home Int 1928-29-30-31-
32-33-34-35-36-37-38-47

Evans, H
(England): Home Int 1908

Evans, K
(Wales): Home Int 1999-2000-01

Evans, N
(Wales): Home Int 1908-09-10-13

Evans, N
(Wales): Home Int 1996-97-98-99;
Eur(L) T Ch 1997-99

Everard, M
(GBI): Curtis Cup 1970-72-74-78;
Vagliano Trophy 1967-69-71-73;
Espirito Santo 1968-72-78; CW
1971. (England): Home Int 1964-
67-69-70-72-73-77-78; Eur(L) T
Ch 1967-71-77

Fairclough, L
(GBI): Vagliano Trophy 1989.
(England): Home Int 1988-89-90;
Eur(L) T Ch 1989

Falconer, V (Lamb)
(Scotland): Home Int 1932-36-37-
47-48-49-50-51-52-53-54-55-56

Farie-Anderson, J
(Scotland): Home Int 1924

Farquharson-Black, E
(GBI): Curtis Cup 1990-92;
Vagliano Trophy 1989-91; CW
1991. (Scotland): Home Int 1987-
88-89-90-91-97-98; Eur(L) T Ch
1989-91

Ferguson, A
(Ireland): Home Int 1989

Ferguson, D
(GBI): Curtis Cup 1958. (Ireland):
Home Int 1927-28-29-30-31-32-
34-35-36-37-38-**61**

Ferguson, M (Fowler)
(GBI): Curtis Cup 1966; Vagliano
Trophy 1965. (Scotland): Home Int
1959-62-63-64-65-66-67-69-70-85;
Eur(L) T Ch 1965-67-71

Ferguson R (Ogden)
(England): Home Int 1957

Fields, E
(England): Home Int 1995-96

Fisher, K
(England): Vagliano Trophy 2001;
Home Int 1998-99-2000-01;
Eur(L) T Ch 1999-2001

Fitzgibbon, M
(Ireland): Home Int 1920-21-29-
30-31-32-33

FitzPatrick, O (Heskin)
(Ireland): Home Int 1967

Fletcher, L
(GBI): Curtis Cup 1990; CW 1991.
(England): Home Int 1989-90;
Eur(L)T Ch 1991

Fletcher, P (Sherlock)
(Ireland): Home Int 1932-34-35-
36-38-39-54-55-**66**

Forbes, J
(Scotland): Home Int 1985-86-87-
88-89; Eur(L) T Ch 1987-89

Ford, J
(Scotland): Home Int 1993-94-95

Foster, C
(England): Home Int 1905-06-09

Fowler, J
(England): Home Int 1928

Franklin Thomas, E
(Wales): Home Int 1909

Freeguard, C
(Wales): Home Int 1927

Furby, J
(England): Home Int 1987-88;
Eur(L) T Ch 1987

Fyshe, M
(England): Home Int 1938

Gallagher, S
(Scotland): Home Int 1983-84

Gardiner, A
(Ireland): Home Int 1927-29

Garfield Evans, PR
(Whittaker)
(Wales): Home Int 1948-49-50-51-
52-53-54-**55**-**56**-57-**58**

Garon, MR
(GBI): Curtis Cup 1936.
(England): Home Int 1927-28-32-
33-34-36-37-38

Garrett, M (Ruttle)
(GBI): Curtis Cup 1948-**60**;
Vagliano Trophy 1959. (England):
Home Int 1947-48-50-53-**59**-**60**-**63**

Garvey, P
(GBI): Curtis Cup 1948-50-52-54-
56-60; Vagliano Trophy 1959-63.
(Ireland): Home Int 1947-48-49-
50-51-52-53-**54**-56-57-**58**-**59**-**60**-61-
62-63-68-69

Gaynor, Z (Fallon)
(GBI): Espirito Santo 1964.
(Ireland): Home Int 1952-53-54-
55-56-57-58-59-60-61-62-63-64-
65-68-69-70-**72**

Gear Evans, A
(Wales): Home Int 1932-33-34

Gee, Hon. J (Hives)
(England): Home Int 1950-51-52

Gemmill, A
(Scotland): Home Int 1981-82-84-
85-86-87-88-89-91-**97**

Gethin Griffith, S
(Wales): Home Int 1914-22-23-24-
28-29-30-31-35

Gibb, M (Titterton)
(England): Home Int 1906-07-08-
10-12

Gibbs, C (Le Feuvre)
(GBI): Curtis Cup 1974; Vagliano
Trophy 1973. (England): Home Int
1971-72-73-74

Gibbs, S
(Wales): Home Int 1933-34-39

Gildea, Miss
(Ireland): Home Int 1936-37-38-39

Gillen, M
(Ireland): Home Int 1999-2001;
Eur(L) T Ch 2001

Glendinning, D
(Ireland): Home Int 1937-54

Glennie, H
(Scotland): Home Int 1959

Glover, A
(Scotland): Home Int 1905-06-08-
09-12

Gold, N
(England): Home Int 1929-31-32

Gordon, J
(GBI): Curtis Cup 1948.
(England): Home Int 1947-48-49-
52-53

Gorman, S
(Ireland): Home Int 1976-79-80-
81-82-**92-93**; Eur(L) T Ch **1993**

Gorry, Mary
(GBI): Vagliano Trophy 1977.
(Ireland): Home Int 1971-72-73-
74-75-76-77-78-79-80-88-**89**;
Eur(L) T Ch 1971-75

Gotto, Mrs C
(Ireland): Home Int 1923

Gotto, Mrs L
(Ireland): Home Int 1920

Gourlay, M
(GBI): Curtis Cup 1932-34.
(England): Home Int 1923-24-27-
28-29-30-32-33-34-38-**57**

Gow, J
(Scotland): Home Int 1923-24-27-
28

Graham, MA
(Scotland): Home Int 1905-06

Graham, N
(Ireland): Home Int 1908-09-10-12

Granger Harrison, Mrs
(Scotland): Home Int 1922

Grant-Suttie, E
(Scotland): Home Int 1908-10-11-
14-22-23

Grant-Suttie, R
(Scotland): Home Int 1914

Green, B (Pockett)
(England): Home Int 1939

Grice-Whittaker, P (Grice)
(GBI): Curtis Cup 1984; Espirito
Santo 1984. (England): Home Int
1983-84

Griffith, W
(Wales): Home Int 1981

Griffiths, M
(England): Home Int 1920-21

Greenlees, E
(Scotland): Home Int 1924

Greenlees, Y
(Scotland): Home Int 1928-30-31-
33-34-35-38

Guadella, E (Leitch)
(England): Home Int 1908-10-20-
21-22-27-28-29-30-33

Gubbins, Miss
(Ireland): Home Int 1905

Hackett, B
(Ireland): Home Int 1993-94-96

Hackney, L
(England): Home Int 1990

Haig, J (Mathias Thomas)
(Wales): Home Int 1938-39

Hall, C
(GBI): Curtis Cup 1992; Vagliano
Trophy 1991. (England): Home Int
1991-92; Eur LT Ch 1991

Hall, CM
(England): Home Int 1985

Hall, J (Wade)
(GBI): Curtis Cup 1988-90-92-94-
96; Espirito Santo 1988-90-94;
Vagliano Trophy 1989-91-93-95;
CW 1991-95. (England): Home Int
1987 to 1995; Eur(L) T Ch 1987-
89-91-93-95

Hall, Mrs
(Ireland): Home Int 1927-30

Hamilton, S (McKinven)
(Scotland): Home Int 1965

Hambro, W (Martin Smith)
(England): Home Int 1914

Hamilton, J
(England): Home Int 1937-38-39

Hammond, T
(England): Home Int 1985

Hampson, M
(England): Home Int 1954

Hanna, D
(Ireland): Home Int 1987-88

Hargan, C
(Scotland): Home Int 1999-2000-
=01; Eur(L) T Ch 2001

Harrington, D
(Ireland): Home Int 1923

Harris, M [Spearman]
(GBI): Curtis Cup 1960-62-64;
Vagliano Trophy 1959-61-65;
Espirito Santo 1964. (England):
Home Int 1955-56-57-58-59-60-
61-62-63-64-65; Eur(L) T Ch
1965-71

Harrold, L
(England): Home Int 1974-75-76

Hartill, D
(England): Home Int 1923

Hartley, E
(England): Home Int 1964

Hartley, R
(Wales): Home Int 1958-59-62

Hastings, D (Sommerville)
(GBI): Curtis Cup 1958; Vagliano
Trophy 1963. (Scotland): Home Int
1955-56-57-58-59-60-61-62-63

Hay, J (Pelham Burn)
(Scotland): Home Int 1959

Hayter, J (Yuille)
(England): Home Int 1956

Hazlett, VP
(Ireland): Home Int 1956

Healy, B
(Ireland): Home Int 1980-82

Heath S (Gleeson)
(England): Home Int 2001; Eur(L)
T Ch 2001

Heathcoat-Amory, Lady
(Joyce Wethered)
(GBI): Curtis Cup 1932. (England):
Home Int 1921-22-23-24-25-29

Hedges, S (Whitlock)
(GBI): Vagliano Trophy 1979; CW
1979. (England): Home Int 1979

Hedley Hill, Miss
(Wales): Home Int 1922

Hegarty, G
(Ireland): Home Int 1955-56-**64**

Helme, E
(England): Home Int 1911-12-13-20

Heming Johnson, G
(England): Home Int 1909-11-13

Henson, D (Oxley)
(GBI): Curtis Cup 1968-70-72-76;
Vagliano Trophy 1967-69-71;
Espirito Santo 1970; CW 1967-71.
(England): Home Int 1967-68-69-70-
75-76-77-78; Eur(L) T Ch 1971-77

Heskin, A
(Ireland): Home Int 1968-69-70-
72-75-77-**82-83**

Hetherington, Mrs (Gittens)
(England): Home Int 1909

Hewett, G
(Ireland): Home Int 1923-24

Hezlet, Mrs
(Ireland): Home Int 1910

Hickey, C
(Ireland): Home Int 1969-**75-76**

Higgins, E
(Ireland): Home Int 1981 to 1988,
1991 to 1996; Eur(L) T Ch 1987-
93-(**2001**)

Highgate, A
(Wales): Home Int 1999-2001;
Eur(L) T Ch 2001

Hill, J
(England): Home Int 1986

Hill, Mrs
(Wales): Home Int 1924

Hockley, J
(GBI): Espirito Santo 1992;
Vagliano Trophy 1993. (England):
Home Int 1991-92-93-96

Hodge, S (Shapcott)
(GBI): Curtis Cup 1988; Vagliano
Trophy 1987; CW 1987; Espirito
Santo 1988. (England): Home Int
1986-88; Eur(L) T Ch 1987

Hodgson, M
(England): Home Int 1939

Holland, I (Hurst)
(Ireland): Home Int 1958

Holm, H (Gray)
(GBI): Curtis Cup 1936-38-48.
(Scotland): Home Int 1932-33-34-
35-36-37-38-47-48-50-51-55-57

Holmes, A
(England): Home Int 1931

Holmes, J [Hetherington]
    (McClure)
(England): Home Int 1957-66-**67**

Hooman, EM [Gavin]
(England): Home Int 1910-11

Hope, LA
(Scotland): Home Int 1975-76-80-
84-85-86-87-**88-89-90**

Hort, K
(Wales): Home Int 1929

Howard, A (Phillips)
(GBI): Curtis Cup 1956-58.
(England): Home Int 1953-54-55-
56-57-58-**79-80**.

Hudson, R
(GBI): Curtis Cup 1998-2000;
Vagliano Trophy 1997-2001;
Espirito Santo [1998]-2000; CW
1999. (England): Home Int 1996-
97-98-99-2000-01; Eur(L) T Ch
1997-99-2001

Huggan, S (Lawson)
(GBI): Curtis Cup 1988, Vagliano
Trophy 1989. (Scotland): Home Int
1985-86-87-88-89; Eur(L) T Ch
1985-87-89

Hughes, J
(Wales): Home Int 1967-71-88-**89**;
Eur(L) T Ch 1971

Hughes, Miss
(Wales): Home Int 1907

Huke, B
(GBI): Curtis Cup 1972; Vagliano
Trophy 1975. (England): Home Int
1971-72-75-76-77

Hulton, V (Hezlet)
(Ireland): Home Int 1905-07-09-
10-11-12-20-21

Humphreys, A (Coulman)
(Wales): Home Int 1969-70-71

Humphreys, D (Forster)
(Ireland): Home Int 1951-52-53-
55-57

Hunter, D (Tucker)
(England): Home Int 1905

Hurd, D [Howe] (Campbell)
(Scotland): Home Int 1905-06-08-
09-11-28-30

Hurst, Mrs
(Wales): Home Int 1921-22-23-25-
27-28

Hyland, B
(Ireland): Home Int 1964-65-66

Inghram, E (Lever)
(Wales): Home Int 1947-48-49-50-
51-52-53-54-55-56-57-58-64-65

Irvin, A
(GBI): Curtis Cup 1962-68-70-76;
Vagliano Trophy 1961-63-65-67-
69-71-73-75; Espirito Santo **1982**;
CW 1967-75. (England): Home Int
1962-63-65-67-68-69-70-71-72-73-
75; Eur(L) T Ch 1965-67-69-71

Irvine, Miss
(Wales): Home Int 1930

Isaac, Mrs
(Wales): Home Int 1924

Isherwood, L
(Wales): Home Int 1972-76-77-78-
80-86-88-89-90-91

Jack, E (Philip)
(Scotland): Home Int 1962-63-64-
81-82

Jackson, B
(Ireland): Home Int 1937-38-39-50

Jackson, B
(GBI): Curtis Cup 1958-64-68;
Vagliano Trophy 1959-63-65-67-**73**-
75; Espirito Santo 1964; CW 1959-
67. (England): Home Int 1955-56-
57-58-59-63-64-65-66-**73-74**

Jackson, D
(Scotland): Home Int 1990

Jackson, Mrs H
(Ireland): Home Int 1921

Jackson, J
(Ireland): Home Int 1912-13-14-
20-21-22-23-24-25-27-28-29-30

Jackson, Mrs L
(Ireland): Home Int 1910-12-14-
20-22-25

Jameson, S (Tobin)
(Ireland): Home Int 1913-14-20-
24-25-27

Jenkin, B
(Wales): Home Int 1959

Jenkins, J (Owen)
(Wales): Home Int 1953-56

John, J
(Wales): Home Int 1974

Johns, A
(England): Home Int 1987-88-89

Johnson, A (Hughes)
(Wales): Home Int 1964, 1966 to
1976, 1978-79-85-**95**; Eur(L) T Ch
1965-67-69-71

Johnson, J (Roberts)
(Wales): Home Int 1955

Johnson, M
(England): Home Int 1934-35

Johnson, PM
(GBI): Curtis Cup 1986; Vagliano
Trophy 1985; Espirito Santo 1986.
(England): Home Int 1984-85-86;
Eur(L) T Ch 1985

Johnson, R
(Wales): Home Int 1955

Jones, A (Gwyther)
(Wales): Home Int 1959

Jones, B
(Wales): Home Int 1994-95-96-98;
Eur(L) T Ch 1993

Jones, K
(Wales): Home Int **1959-60-61**

Jones, M (De Lloyd)
(Wales): Home Int 1951

Jones, S
(Wales): Home Int 2000-01;
Eur(L) T Ch 2001

Jones, Mrs
(Wales): Home Int 1932-35

Justice, M
(Wales): Home Int 1931-32

Kavanagh, H
(GBI): Vagliano Trophy 1995.
(Ireland): Home Int 1993-94-95-
97-98-2001; Eur(L) T Ch 1997-
2001

Kaye, H (Williamson)
(England): Home Int **1986-87**

Keane, S
(Ireland): Home Int 2000; Eur(L)
T Ch 2001

Keenan, D
(Ireland): Home Int 1989

Keiller, G [Style]
(England): Home Int 1948-49-52

Kelway Bamber, Mrs
(Scotland): Home Int 1923-27-33

Kennedy, D (Fowler)
(England): Home Int 1923-24-25-
27-28-29

Kennion, Mrs (Kenyon Stow)
(England): Home Int 1910

Kenny, L
(Scotland): Home Int 2000-01

Kerr, J
(Scotland): Home Int 1947-48-49-54

Kidd, Mrs
(Ireland): Home Int 1934-37

King Mrs
(Ireland): Home Int 1923-25-27-29

Kinloch, Miss
(Scotland): Home Int 1913-14

Kirkwood, Mrs
(Ireland): Home Int 1955

Knight, Mrs
(Scotland): Home Int 1922

Kyle, B [Rhodes] (Norris)
(England): Home Int 1937-38-39-48-49

Kyle, E
(Scotland): Home Int 1909-10

Laing, A
(GBI): Vagliano Trophy 1967.
(Scotland): Home Int 1966-67-70-71-73-74-2001; Eur(L) T Ch 1967-2001

Laing, A
(GBI): Vagliano Trophy 1999; CW
1999. (Scotland): Home Int 1995-96-97-98-99; Eur(L) T Ch 1997-99

Laing, V
(Scotland): Home Int 1997-98;
Eur(L) T Ch 2001

Lamb, J
(England): Home Int 1998-99

Lambert, S (Cohen)
(GBI): Vagliano Trophy 1979-95.
(England): Home Int 1979-80-93-94-95; Eur(L) T Ch 1995

Lambie, S
(Scotland): Home Int 1976

Laming Evans, Mrs
(Wales): Home Int 1922-23

Langford, Mrs
(Wales): Home Int 1937

Langridge, S (Armitage)
(GBI): Curtis Cup 1964-66;
Vagliano Trophy 1963-65.
(England): Home Int 1963-64-65-66; Eur(L) T Ch 1965

Large, P (Davies)
(England): Home Int 1951-52-**81-82**

Larkin, C (McAuley)
(Ireland): Home Int 1966-67-68-69-70-71-72; Eur(L) T Ch 1971

Latchford, B
(Ireland): Home Int 1931-33

Latham Hall, E (Chubb)
(England): Home Int 1928

Lauder, G
(Ireland): Home Int 1911

Lauder, R
(Ireland): Home Int 1911

Lawrence, JB
(GBI): Curtis Cup 1964; Vagliano
Trophy 1963-65; Espirito Santo
1964; CW 1971. (Scotland): Home
Int 1959-60-61-62-63-64-65-66-

67-68-69-70-77; Eur(L) T Ch
1965-67-69-71

Lawson, H
(Wales): Home Int 1989-90-91-92-97-98; Eur(L) T Ch 1991-93-97

Lebrun, W (Aitken)
(GBI): Curtis Cup 1982; Vagliano
Trophy 1981-83. (Scotland): Home
Int 1978-79-80-81-82-83-85

Leaver, B
(Wales): Home Int 1912-14-21

Lee Smith, J
(GBI): Curtis Cup 1974-76; Espirito
Santo 1976; CW 1975. (England):
Home Int 1973-74-75-76

Leete, Mrs IG
(Scotland): Home Int 1933

Leitch, C
(England): Home Int 1910-11-12-13-14-20-21-22-24-25-27-28

Leitch, M
(England): Home Int 1912-14

Lipscombe, C
(England): Home Int 1999

Little, S
(Scotland): Home Int 1993

Llewellyn, Miss
(Wales): Home Int 1912-13-14-21-22-23

Lloyd, J
(Wales): Home Int 1988

Lloyd, P
(Wales): Home Int 1935-36

Lloyd Davies, VH
(Wales): Home Int 1913

Lloyd Roberts, V
(Wales): Home Int 1907-08-10

Lloyd Williams, Miss
(Wales): Home Int 1909-10-12-14

Lobbett, P
(England): Home Int 1922-24-27-29-30

Lovatt, S
(Wales): Home Int 1994-95

Lowry, Mrs
(Ireland): Home Int 1947

Luckin, B (Cooper)
(England): Home Int 1980

Lugton, C
(Scotland): Home Int 1968-72-73-75-**76**-77-78-80

Lumb, K (Phillips)
(GBI): Curtis Cup 1972; Vagliano
Trophy 1969-71. (England): Home
Int 1968-69-70-71; Eur(L) T Ch
1969

Lyons, T (Ross Steen)
(GBI): Vagliano Trophy 1959.
(England): Home Int 1959

MacAndrew, F
(Scotland): Home Int 1913-14

Macbeth, M (Dodd)
(England): Home Int 1913-14-20-21-22-23-24-25

MacCann, K
(Ireland): Home Int 1984-85-86

MacCann, K (Smye)
(Ireland): Home Int 1947-48-49-50-51-52-53-54-56-57-58-60-61-62-64-**65**

McCarthy, A
(Ireland): Home Int 1951-52

McCarthy, D
(Ireland): Home Int 1988-90-91-95; Eur(L) T Ch 1993

McCool, L
(Ireland): Home Int 1993

McCulloch, J
(Scotland): Home Int 1921-22-23-24-27-29-30-31-32-33-35-(**60**)

McDaid, E (O'Grady)
(Ireland): Home Int 1959

Macdonald, F
(England): Home Int 1990

Macdonald, K
(Scotland): Home Int 1928-29

MacGeach, C
(Ireland): Home Int 1938-39-48-49-50

McGreevy, M
(Ireland): Home Int 1996-97-98;
Eur(L) T Ch 1997

McGreevy, V
(Ireland): Home Int 1987-90-92

McIntosh, B (Dixon)
(GBI): Vagliano Trophy 1969.
(England): Home Int 1969-70;
Eur(L) T Ch 1969

MacIntosh, I
(Scotland): Home Int **1991-92-93**;
Eur(L) T Ch **1993**

McIntyre, J
(England): Home Int 1949-54

McKay, F
(Scotland): Home Int 1992-93-94;
Eur(L) T Ch 1993

Mackay, L
(Scotland): Home Int 1999-2000-01; Eur(L) T Ch 2001

MacKay, M
(GBI): Curtis Cup 1994-96;
Vagliano Trophy 1993-95-97; CW
1995; Espirito Santo 1996.
(Scotland): Home Int 1991-93-94-96; Eur(L) T Ch 1993-95

MacKean, Mrs
(Wales): Home Int 1938-39-47

McKenna, M
(GBI): Curtis Cup 1970-72-74-76-78-80-82-84-86; Vagliano Trophy
1969-71-73-75-77-79-81-85-87-**95**;
Espirito Santo 1970-74-76-**86-90**.
(Ireland): Home Int 1968 to 1991-93; Eur(L) T Ch 1969-71-75-87

Mackenzie, A
(Scotland): Home Int 1921

McKinlay, M
(GBI): Curtis Cup 1994.
(Scotland): Home Int 1990-92-93;
Eur(L) T Ch 1993

McLarty, E
(Scotland): Home Int **1966-67-68**

McMahon, S (Cadden)
(Scotland): Home Int 1974-75-76-77-79. (GBI): Curtis Cup 1976;
Vagliano Trophy 1975

McMaster, S
(Scotland): Home Int 1994-95-96-97; Eur(L) T Ch 1995-97

McNair, W
(England): Home Int 1921

McNeil, K
(Scotland): Home Int **1969-70**

McNeile, CL
(Ireland): Home Int 1906

McQuillan, Y
(Ireland): Home Int 1985-86

MacTier, Mrs
(Wales): Home Int 1927

Madeley, M (Coburn)
(Ireland): Home Int 1964-69;
Eur(L) T Ch 1969

Madill, M
(GBI): Curtis Cup 1980; Vagliano
Trophy 1979-81-85; Espirito Santo
1980; CW 1979. (Ireland): Home
Int 1978-79-80-81-82-83-84-85

Madill, Mrs
(Ireland): Home Int 1920-24-25-27-28-29-33

Magee, A-M
(Wales): Home Int 1991-92-93-94

Magill, J
(Ireland): Home Int 1907-11-13

Maher, S (Vaughan)
(GBI): Curtis Cup 1962-64;
Vagliano Trophy 1961; CW 1963.
(England): Home Int 1960-61-62-63-64

Mahon, D
(Ireland): Home Int 1989-90

Main, M (Farquhar)
(Scotland): Home Int 1950-51

Maitland, M
(Scotland): Home Int 1905-06-08-12-13

Mallam, Mrs S
(Ireland): Home Int 1922-23

Margan, T
(Ireland): Home Int 1998-2000

Marks, Mrs T
(Ireland): Home Int 1950

Marks, Mrs
(Ireland): Home Int 1930-31-33-35

Marley, MV
(Wales): Home Int 1921-22-23-30-37

Marr, H (Cameron)
(Scotland): Home Int 1927-28-29-30-31

Marshall, K (Imrie)
(GBI): Curtis Cup 1990; Vagliano
Trophy 1989. (Scotland): Home Int
1984-85-89. Eur(L) T Ch 1987-89

Martin, P [Whitworth Jones]
(Low)
(Wales): Home Int 1948-50-56-59-60-61

Marvin, V
(England): Home Int 1977-78;
Eur(L) T Ch 1977. (GBI): Curtis
Cup 1978; Vagliano Trophy 1977

Mason, Mrs
(Wales): Home Int 1923

Mather, H
(Scotland): Home Int 1905-09-12-13-14

Matthew, C (Lambert)
(GBI): Curtis Cup 1990-92-94;
Vagliano Trophy 1989-91-93;
Espirito Santo 1992; CW 1991.
(Scotland): Home Int 1989-90-91-92-93; Eur(L) T Ch 1989-91-93

Matthews, T [Thomas]
(Perkins)
(GBI): Curtis Cup 1974-76-78-80;
Vagliano Trophy 1973-75-77-79;
Espirito Santo 1974; CW 1975-79.
(Wales): Home Int 1972-73-74-75-76-77-78-79-80-81-82-83-84;
Eur(L) T Ch 1975

Mellis, Mrs
(Scotland): Home Int 1924-27

Melvin, V
(Scotland): Home Int 1994-96

Menton, D
(Ireland): Home Int 1949

Menzies, M
(Scotland): Home Int **1962**

Merrill, J (Greenhalgh)
(GBI): Curtis Cup 1964-70-74-76-78; Vagliano Trophy 1961-65-75-77; Espirito Santo 1970-74-78; CW
1963. (England): Home Int 1960-61-63-66-69-70-71-75-76-77-78;
Eur(L) T Ch 1971-77

Millar, D
(Ireland): Home Int 1928

Milligan, J (Mark)
(Ireland): Home Int 1971-72-73

Mills, I
(Wales): Home Int 1935-36-37-39-47-48

Milton, M (Paterson)
(GBI): Curtis Cup 1952.
(Scotland): Home Int 1948-49-50-51-52

Mitchell, J
(Ireland): Home Int 1930

Moffat, L
(GBI): Vagliano Trophy 1999.
(Scotland): Home Int 1996-98-2001; Eur(L) T Ch 1999-2001

Monaghan, H
(GBI): Curtis Cup 1998; Vagliano
Trophy 1999. (Scotland): Home Int
1995-96-97-98-2000; Eur(L) T Ch
1997-99

Moodie, J
(GBI): Curtis Cup 1994-96;
Vagliano Trophy 1993-95-97;
Espirito Santo 1996; CW 1995.
(Scotland): Home Int 1990-91-92;
Eur(L) T Ch 1991-93-95-97

Mooney, M
(GBI): Vagliano Trophy 1973.
(Ireland): Home Int 1972-73;
Eur(L) T Ch 1971

Moorcroft, S
(England): Home Int 1985-86;
Eur(L) T Ch 1985-87

Moore, S
(Ireland): Home Int 1937-38-39-47-48-49-**68**

Moran, V (Singleton)
(Ireland): Home Int 1970-71-73-74-75; Eur(L) T Ch 1971-75

Morant, E
(England): Home Int 1906-10

More, F
(England): Vagliano Trophy 2001;
Home Int 2000-01; Eur(L) T Ch
2001

Morgan, R
(GBI): Curtis Cup 1998-2000;
Vagliano Trophy 1997-99; Espirito
Santo [1998]; CW 1999. (Wales):
Home Int 1996-97-98-99; Eur(L)
T Ch 1997-99

Morgan, S
(England): Home Int 1989; Eur(L)
T Ch 1989

Morgan, W
(GBI): Curtis Cup 32-34-36.
(England): Home Int 1931-32-33-34-35-36-37

Morgan, Miss
(Wales): Home Int 1912-13-14

Moriarty, M (Irvine)
(Ireland): Home Int 1979

Morley, J
(GBI): Curtis Cup 1992; Vagliano
Trophy 1991-93; Espirito Santo
1992. (England): Home Int 1990-91-92-93; Eur(L) T Ch 1991-93

Morris, L (Moore)
(England): Home Int 1912-13

Morris, Mrs de B
(Ireland): Home Int 1933

Morrison, G (Cheetham)
(GBI): Vagliano Trophy 1965.
(England): Home Int 1965-**69**

Morrison, G (Cradock-Hartopp)
(England): Home Int 1936

Morton, L
(Scotland): Home Int 2000-01;
Eur(L) T Ch 2001

Mountford, S
(Wales): Home Int 1989-90-91-92;
Eur(L) T Ch 1991-2001

Murray, N (Buxton)
(GBI): Curtis Cup 1992; Vagliano
Trophy 1991-93. (England): Home
Int 1991-92-93; Eur LT Ch 1991-93

Murray, Rachel
(Ireland): Home Int 1952

Murray, S (Jolly)
(England): Home Int 1976

Musgrove, Mrs
(Wales): Home Int 1923-24

Myles, M
(Scotland): Home Int 1955-57-59-60-67

Neill-Fraser, M
(Scotland): Home Int 1905-06-07-08-09-10-11-12-13-14

Nes, K (Garnham)
(England): Home Int 1931-32-33-36-37-38-39

Nevile, E
(England): Home Int 1905-06-08-10

New, B
(GBI): Curtis Cup 1984; Vagliano
Trophy 1983. (England): Home Int
1980-81-82-83

Newell, B
(England): Home Int 1936

Newman, L
(Wales): Home Int 1927-31

Newton, B (Brown)
(England): Home Int 1930-33-34-35-36-37

Nicholls, M
(Wales): Home Int **1962**

Nicholson, J (Hutton)
(GBI): CW 1971. (Scotland):
Home Int 1969-70; Eur(L) T Ch
1971

Nicholson, L
(GBI): Curtis Cup 2000; Vagliano
Trophy 1999. (Scotland): Home Int
1994-95-96-97-98-99; Eur(L) T
Ch 1995-97-99

Nicholson, Mrs WH
(Scotland): Home Int 1910-13

Nimmo, H
(Scotland): Home Int 1936-38-39

Norris, J (Smith)
(GBI): Vagliano Trophy 1977.

(Scotland): Home Int 1966-67-68-69-70-71-72-75-76-77-78-79-**83**-84; Eur(L) T Ch 1971

Norwell, I (Watt)
(Scotland): Home Int 1954

Nutting, P (Jameson)
(Ireland): Home Int 1927-28

O'Brien, A
(Ireland): Home Int 1969

O'Brien, S (Fanagan)
(GBI): Curtis Cup 2000; Espirito
Santo 2000; Vagliano Trophy 1999.
(Ireland): Home Int 1995-96-97-98-99-2000; Eur L T Ch 1997-99

O'Brien Kenney, S
(Ireland): Home Int 1977-78-83-84-85-86

O'Donnell, M
(GBI): Curtis Cup 1982; Vagliano
Trophy **1981**. (Ireland): Home Int
1974-77 -78-79 Eur(L) T Ch **1980**

O'Donohoe, A
(Ireland): Home Int 1948-49-50-51-53-**73**-74

O'Hare, S
(Ireland): Home Int 1921-22

O'Reilly, T (Moran)
(Ireland): Home Int 1977-78-86-88-**95**; Eur(L) T Ch 1987

O'Sullivan, A
(Ireland): Home Int 1982-83-84-92-94-95-96; Eur(L) T Ch 1993-97

O'Sullivan, P
(Ireland): Home Int 1950-51-52-53-54-55-56-57-58-59-60-63-64-65-66-67-**69-70-71**; Eur(L) T Ch **1971**

Oliver, J
(England): Home Int 1995

Oliver, M (Jones)
(GBI): Espirito Santo 1964.
(Wales): Home Int 1955-60-61-62-63-64-65-66

Ormsby, Miss
(Ireland): Home Int 1909-10-11

Orr, P (Boyd)
(Ireland): Home Int 1971

Orr, Mrs
(Wales): Home Int 1924

Owen, E
(Wales): Home Int 1947

Panton-Lewis, C (Panton)
(GBI): Vagliano Trophy 1977;
Espirito Santo 1976. (Scotland):
Home Int 1972-73-76-77-78

Park, Mrs
(Scotland): Home Int 1952

Parker, S
(England): Home Int 1973

Patey, Mrs
(Scotland): Home Int 1922-23

Pearson, D
(England): Home Int 1928-29-30-31-32-34

Percy, G (Mitchell)
(Scotland): Home Int 1927-28-30-31

Perriam, A
(Wales): Home Int 1988-90-91-92;
Eur(L) T Ch 1991

Phelips, M
(Wales): Home Int 1913-14-21

Phillips, K
(Wales): Home Int 1999-2000-01;
Eur(L) T Ch 2001

Phillips, ME
(England): Home Int 1905

Phillips, Mrs
(Wales): Home Int 1921

Pickard, M (Nichol)
(GBI): Curtis Cup 1968-70;
Vagliano Trophy 1959-61-67.
(England): Home Int 1958-59-60-61-67-69-**83**

Pilgrim, E
(Wales): Home Int 1995-97-2000-01; Eur(L) T Ch 1997-99-2001

Pim, Mrs
(Ireland): Home Int 1908

Pook, E (Chadwick)
(GBI): Curtis Cup 1966; Vagliano
Trophy 1963-67; CW 1967.
(England): Home Int 1963-65-66-67; Eur(L) T Ch 1967

Porter, D (Park)
(GBI): Curtis Cup 1932.
(Scotland): Home Int 1922-25-27-29-30-31-32-33-34-35-37-38-47-48

Porter, M (Lazenby)
(England): Home Int 1931-32

Powell, M
(Wales): Home Int 1908-09-10-12

Power, ER (McDaid)
(GBI): Curtis Cup 1994; Vagliano
Trophy 1995-97. (Ireland): Home
Int 1987 to 1997-2001; Eur(L) T
Ch 1987-93-97-99

Price, M (Greaves)
(England): Home Int 1956

Price Fisher, E (Price)
(GBI): Curtis Cup 1950-52-54-56-58-60; Vagliano Trophy 1959; CW
1959. (England): Home Int 1948-51-52-53-54-55-56-57-58-59-60

Proctor, Mrs
(Wales): Home Int 1907

Prout, R
(England): Home Int 2000

Provis, I (Kyle)
(Scotland): Home Int 1910-11

Purcell, E
(Ireland): Home Int 1965-66-67-72-73

Purfield, O
(Ireland): Home Int 1998-99

Purvis-Russell-
Montgomery, C
(Scotland): Home Int 1921-22-23-
25-28-29-30-31-32-33-34-35-36-
37-38-39-47-48-49-50-52

Pyman, B
(Wales): Home Int 1925-28-29-30-
32-33-34-35-36-37-38

Rabbidge, R
(England): Home Int 1931

Ratcliffe, E
(GBI): Curtis Cup 1998; Espirito
Santo 1996; Vagliano Trophy 1997.
(England): Home Int 1995-96-97;
Eur(L) T Ch 1995-97

Rawlings, M
(GBI): Vagliano Trophy 1981.
(Wales): Home Int 1979-80-81-83-
84-85-86-87

Rawlinson, T (Walker)
(GBI): Vagliano Trophy 1973.
(Scotland): Home Int 1970-71-73-76

Read, P
(England): Home Int 1922

Reddan, C (Tiernan)
(GBI): Curtis Cup 1938-48.
(Ireland): Home Int 1935-36-38-
39-47-48-49

Reddan, MV
(Ireland): Home Int 1955

Reece, P (Millington)
(England): Home Int 1966

Rees, G
(Wales): Home Int 1981

Rees, MB
(Wales): Home Int 1927-31

Reid, A (Lurie)
(GBI): Vagliano Trophy 1961.
(Scotland): Home Int 1960-61-62-
63-64-66

Reid, A (Kyle)
(Scotland): Home Int 1923-24-25

Reid, D
(Scotland): Home Int 1978-79

Remer, H
(England): Home Int 1909

Rennie, J (Hastings)
(GBI): Curtis Cup 1966; Vagliano
Trophy 1961-67. (Scotland): Home
Int 1961-65-66-67-71-72; Eur(L) T
Ch 1967

Rhys, J
(Wales): Home Int 1979

Rice, J
(Ireland): Home Int 1924-27-29

Richards, D
(Wales): Home Int 1994-95-96

Richards, J
(Wales): Home Int 1980-82-83-85

Richards, S
(Wales): Home Int 1967

Richardson, Mrs
(England): Home Int 1907-09

Richmond, M (Walker)
(GBI): Curtis Cup 1974; Vagliano
Trophy 1975. (Scotland): Home Int
1972-73-74-75-77-78

Rieben, Mrs
(Wales): Home Int 1927-28-29-30-
31-32-33

Rigby, F (Macbeth)
(Scotland): Home Int 1912-13

Ritchie, C (Park)
(Scotland): Home Int 1939-47-48-
51-52-53-**64**

Roberts, B
(Wales): Home Int **1984-85-86**

Roberts, E (Pentony)
(Ireland): Home Int 1932-33-34-
35-36-39

Roberts, E (Barnett)
(Ireland): Home Int 1961-62-63-
64-65; Eur(L) T Ch 1964

Roberts, G
(Wales): Home Int 1949-52-53-54

Roberts, M (Brown)
(GBI): Espirito Santo 1964.
(Scotland): Home Int **1965**

Roberts, P
(GBI): Espirito Santo 1964.
(Wales): Home Int 1950-51-53-55-
56-57-58-59-60-61-62-63-**64-65-**
66-67-68-69-70; Eur(L) T Ch
1965-67-69

Roberts, S
(Wales): Home Int 1983-84-85-86-
87-88-89-90; Eur(L) T Ch 1983-87

Robertson, B (McCorkindale)
(GBI): Curtis Cup 1960-66-68-70-
72-**74-76**-82-86; Vagliano Trophy
1959-63-69-71-81-85; CW 1971-
75; Espirito Santo 1964-66-**68**-72-
80-82. (Scotland): Home Int 1958-
59-60-61-62-63-64-65-66-69-72-
73-78-80-81-82-84 -85-86; Eur(L)
T Ch 1965-**67**-69-**71**

Robertson, D
(Scotland): Home Int 1907

Robertson, E
(Scotland): Home Int 1924

Robertson, G
(Scotland): Home Int 1907-08-09

Robinson, C (Nesbitt)
(GBI): Curtis Cup 1980; Vagliano
Trophy 1979. (Ireland): Home Int
1974-75-76-77-78-79-80-81

Robinson, R (Bayly)
(Ireland): Home Int 1947-56-57

Robinson, S
(England): Home Int 1989

Roche, Mrs
(Ireland): Home Int 1922

Rogers, A
(Ireland): Home Int 1992-93;
Eur(L) T Ch 1993

Rogers, J
(Wales): Home Int 1972

Roskrow, M
(England): Home Int 1948-50

Ross, M (Hezlet)
(Ireland): Home Int 1905-06-07-
08-11-12

Roxburgh, L
(Scotland): Home Int 1993-94-95

Roy, S (Needham)
(GBI): Vagliano Trophy 1973-75.
(Scotland): Home Int 1969-71-72-
73-74-75-76-83

Rudgard, G
(England): Home Int 1931-32-50-
51-52

Rusack, J
(Scotland): Home Int 1908

Sabine, D (Plumpton)
(GBI): Curtis Cup 1934.
(England): Home Int 1934-35

Saunders, V
(GBI): Curtis Cup 1968; Vagliano
Trophy 1967; CW 1967.
(England): Home Int 1967-68;
Eur(L) T Ch 1967

Scott Chard, Mrs
(Wales): Home Int 1928-30

Seddon, N
(Wales): Home Int 1962-63-**74** -**75**-
76

Selkirk, H
(Wales): Home Int 1925-28

Shapcott, A
(England): Home Int 1989

Shaw, P
(Wales): Home Int 1913

Sheldon, A
(Wales): Home Int 1981

Sheppard, E (Pears)
(England): Home Int 1947

Simpson, L (Moore)
(England): Home Int 1979-80

Singleton, B (Henderson)
(Scotland): Home Int 1939-52-53-
54-55-56-57-58-60-61-62-63-64-65

Slade, Lady
(Ireland): Home Int 1906

Slark, R (Porter)
(GBI): Curtis Cup 1960-62-64;
Vagliano Trophy 1959-61-65;
Espirito Santo 1966; CW 1963.
(England): Home Int 1959-60-61-
62-64-65-66-68-78; Eur(L) T Ch
1965; Espirito Santo 1964

Slocombe, E (Davies)
(Wales): Home Int 1974-75

Smalley, Mrs A
(Wales): Home Int 1924-25-31-32-33-34

Smillie, P
(England): Home Int 1985-86

Smith, A [Stant] (Willard)
(GBI): Curtis Cup 1976; Vagliano Trophy 1975; CW 1959-63. (England): Home Int 1974-75-76

Smith, D
(Ireland): Home Int 1999; Eur(L) T Ch 2001

Smith, E
(England): Home Int 1991

Smith, F (Stephens)
(GBI): Curtis Cup 1950-52-54-56-58-60-(**62**)-(**72**); Vagliano Trophy 1959-71; CW 1959-63. (England): Home Int 1947-48-49-50-51-52-53-54-55-59-**62**-**71**-**72**

Smith, J
(Scotland): Home Int 1999; Eur(L) T Ch 1999

Smith, K
(England): Vagliano Trophy 2001; Home Int 1997-98-99-2000-01; Eur(L) T Ch 1999

Smith, Mrs L
(Ireland): Home Int 1913-14-21-22-23-25

Smythe, M
(Ireland): Home Int 1947-48-49-50-51-52-53-54-55-56-58-59-**62**

Sowter, Mrs
(Wales): Home Int 1923

Speak, K
(GBI): Curtis Cup 1994; Vagliano Trophy 1993; Espirito Santo 1994. (England): Home Int 1993-94; Eur(L) T Ch 1993

Speir, M
(Scotland): Home Int 1957-64-68-**71**-**72**

Stark, K
(Wales): Home Int 1995-96

Starrett, L (Malone)
(Ireland): Home Int 1975-76-77-78-80

Stavert, M
(Scotland): Home Int 1979

Steel, Mrs DC
(Scotland): Home Int 1925

Steel, E
(England): Home Int 1905-06-07-08-11

Stewart, G
(GBI): Curtis Cup 1980-82; Vagliano Trophy 1979-81-83; CW 1979-83. (Scotland): Home Int 1979-80-81-82-83-84; Eur(L) T Ch 1982-84

Stewart, L (Scraggie)
(Scotland): Home Int 1921-22-23

Stirling, H
(Scotland): Home Int 1999-2000-01

Stocker, J
(England): Home Int 1922-23

Stockton, Mrs
(Wales): Home Int 1949

Storry, Mrs
(Wales): Home Int 1910-14

Stroud, N
(Wales): Home Int 1989

Stuart, M
(Ireland): Home Int 1905-07-08

Stuart-French, Miss
(Ireland): Home Int 1922

Stupples, K
(GBI): Curtis Cup 1996-98; Vagliano Trophy 1997. (England): Home Int 1995-96-97-98; Eur(L) T Ch 1995-97

Sugden, J (Machin)
(England): Home Int 1953-54-55

Summers, M (Mackie)
(Scotland): Home Int 1986

Sumpter, Mrs
(England): Home Int 1907-08-12-14-24

Sutherland Pilch, R (Barton)
(England): Home Int 1947-49-50-58

Swallow, C
(England): Home Int 1985; Eur(L) T Ch 1985

Sweeney, L
(Ireland): Home Int 1991

Tamworth, Mrs
(England): Home Int 1908

Taylor, I
(Ireland): Home Int 1930

Teacher, F
(Scotland): Home Int 1908-09-11-12-13

Tebbet, K
(England): Home Int 1990-94

Temple, S
(England): Home Int 1913-14

Temple Dobell, G (Ravenscroft)
(England): Home Int 1911-12-13-14-20-21-25-30

Thomas, C (Phipps)
(Wales): Home Int 1959-63-64-65-66-67-68-69-70-71-72-73-76-77-80

Thomas, I
(Wales): Home Int 1910

Thomas, J (Foster)
(Wales): Home Int 1984-85-86-87-92-93-95; Eur(L) T Ch 1987-89-91-93

Thomas, O
(Wales): Home Int 1921

Thomas, S (Rowlands)
(Wales): Home Int 1977-82-84-85

Thomas, V (Rawlings)
(GBI): Curtis Cup 1982-84-86-88-90; Vagliano Trophy 1979-83-85-87-89-91; CW 1979-83-87-91; Espirito Santo 1990. (Wales): Home Int 1971 to 1998; Eur(L) T Ch 1973-75-77-79-81-83-87-91-97-99

Thompson, M
(Wales): Home Int 1937-38-39

Thompson, M (Wallis)
(England): Home Int 1948-49

Thompson, M
(Scotland): Home Int 1949

Thomson, D
(Scotland): Home Int 1982-83-85-87

Thomson, M
(Scotland): Home Int 1907

Thomson, M
(GBI): Curtis Cup 1978; Vagliano Trophy 1977. (Scotland): Home Int 1974-75-76-77-78; Eur(L) T Ch 1978

Thornhill, J (Woodside)
(GBI): Curtis Cup 1984-86-88; Vagliano Trophy 1965-83-85-87-89; CW 1983-87. (England): Home Int 1965-74-82-83-84-85-86-87-88; Eur(L) T Ch 1965-85-87

Thornhill, Miss
(Ireland): Home Int 1924-25

Thornton, Mrs
(Ireland): Home Int 1924

Todd, Mrs
(Ireland): Home Int 1931 to 1936

Thomlinson, J [Evans] (Roberts)
(GBI): Curtis Cup 1962; Vagliano Trophy 1963. (England): Home Int 1962-64

Treharne, A [Mills]
(Wales): Home Int 1952-61

Turner, B
(England): Home Int 1908

Turner, S (Jump)
(Wales): Home Int 1982-84-85-86-91-93

Tynte, V
(Ireland): Home Int 1905-06-08-09-11-12-13-14

Uzielli, A (Carrick)
(GBI): Curtis Cup 1978; Vagliano Trophy 1977. (England): Home Int 1976-77-78-90-**92**-**93**; Eur(L) T Ch 1977

Valentine, J (Anderson)
(GBI): Curtis Cup 1938-48-50-52

54-56-58; CW 1959. (Scotland):
Home Int 1934-35-36-37-38-39-
47-49-50-51-52-53-54-55-**56**-57-58

Valentine, P (Whitley)
(Wales): Home Int 1973-74-75-77-
78-79-80-**90**

Veitch, F
(Scotland): Home Int 1912

Wadsworth, H
(GBI): Curtis Cup 1990. (Wales):
Home Int 1987-88-89-90; Eur(L)
T Ch 1987-90

Waite, C
(GBI): Curtis Cup 1984; Vagliano
Trophy 1983; Espirito Santo 1984;
CW 1983. (England): Home Int
1981-82-83-84, Eur(L) T Ch 1985

Wakelin, H
(Wales): Home Int 1955

Walker, B (Thompson)
(England): Home Int 1905-06-07-
08-09-11

Walker, M
(GBI): Curtis Cup 1972; Vagliano
Trophy 1971; CW 1971. (Eng-
land): Home Int 1970-72; Eur(L) T
Ch 1971

Walker, P
(Ireland): Home Int 1928-29-30-
31-32-33-34-35-36-37-38-39-48.
(GBI): Curtis Cup 1934-36-38

Walker-Leigh, F
(Ireland): Home Int 1907-08-09-
11-12-13-14

Wallace-Williamson, V
(GBI): Curtis Cup **1938**. (Scotland): Home Int 1932

Walsh, R
(Ireland): Home Int 1987

Walter, J
(England): Home Int 1974-79-80-
82-86

Walters, L
(England): Home Int 1998

Wardlaw, N (Baird)
(GBI): Curtis Cup 1938. (Scotland): Home Int 1932-35-36-37-
38-39-47-48

Watson, C (Nelson)
(England): Home Int 1982

Webb, L (Bolton)
(Ireland): Home Int 1981-82-88-
89-91-92-94

Webster, S (Hales)
(Wales): Home Int 1968-69-72-**91**

Wesley, N
(Wales): Home Int 1986

Westall, S (Maudsley)
(England): Home Int 1973

Weston, R
(Wales): Home Int 1927

Whieldon, Miss
(Wales): Home Int 1908

Wickham, C
(Ireland): Home Int 1983-89

Wickham, P
(Ireland): Home Int 1976-83-87;
Eur(L) T Ch 1987

Williams, M
(Wales): Home Int 1936

Williamson, C (Barker)
(England): Home Int 1979-80-81

Willock-Pollen, G
(England): Home Int 1907

Wilson, A
(Scotland): Home Int 1973-74-**85**

Wilson, E
(GBI): Curtis Cup 1932. (England): Home Int 1928-29-30

Wilson, Mrs
(Ireland): Home Int 1931

Wilson Jones, D
(Wales): Home Int 1952

Winn, J
(England): Home Int 1920-21-23-25

Wood, S
(Scotland): Home Int 1999-2000

Wooldridge, W (Shaw)
(Scotland): Home Int 1982

Wragg, M
(England): Home Int 1929

Wright, J (Robertson)
(GBI): Curtis Cup 1954-56-58-60;
Vagliano Trophy 1959-61-63; CW
1959. (Scotland): Home Int 1952-
53-54-55-56-57-58-59-60-61-63-
65-67-73-**78-79-80-86**; Eur(L) T
Ch 1965

Wright, M
(Scotland): Home Int 1990-91-92;
Eur(L) T Ch 1991

Wright, N (Cook)
(GBI): Espirito Santo 1964.
(Wales): Home Int 1938-47-48-49-
51-52-53-54-57-58-59-60-62-63-
64-66-67-68-**71-72-73**; Eur(L) T
Ch 1965-**71**

Wright, P
(GBI): Vagliano Trophy 1981.
(Scotland): Home Int 1981-82-83-
84; Eur(L) T Ch 1987

Wylie, P (Wade)
(GBI): Curtis Cup 1938. (England):
Home Int 1934-35-36-37-38-47

PART IX

Government of the Game

The Royal and Ancient and the modern game

The Royal and Ancient Golf Club of St Andrews holds a unique position within the game. Formed in 1754 as a private members' club, it has evolved through two and a half centuries as golf's senior authority. There are now three distinct areas of responsibility within the framework of administration undertaken by the R&A.

At international level, excluding the USA, the club has been the governing authority for the Rules of Golf since 1897, with more than 120 countries, unions and associations affiliated to it.

The running of the Open and Amateur Championships has also been part of the R&A remit since 1920, a national commitment now enlarged with the running of the Boys, Mid-Amateur and Seniors Championships and the Junior Open. The R&A selects teams to represent Great Britain & Ireland in events such as the Walker Cup, St Andrews Trophy and World Amateur Team Championships, and organises these events when they are played in Britain and Ireland.

As a private club the R&A has 2,500 members throughout the world, many of whom are leading administrators within their own country's golf authority. This wealth of expertise makes a wide range of experience available to all R&A committees.

In addition to these responsibilities the R&A, from time to time, appoints specialist subcommittees to examine particular areas of the game. One of these, the Golf Course Advisory Panel, brings together experts in golf course design, construction and maintenance to carry out in-depth studies on greenkeeping, conservation and the environment for the benefit of those responsible for the upkeep of courses and ultimately all those who play them.

Another major aspect of the R&A's leadership is the allocation of funds from Open Championship revenues to help finance projects large and small which promote and expand the game world-wide. Over £40 million has been ploughed back into grass roots golf in this way.

The Royal and Ancient staged the first international golf conference in 1980 at which 33 affiliated countries were represented. At the sixth conference in 2001, more than 150 delegates from 69 organisations around the world were involved in discussing topics vital to the growth and development of the game.

Judgements made by the R&A on all aspects of the game are made against a background of history and tradition established over six centuries, but always with an understanding of modern demands.

Refining the laws of the ancient game

During a 10-year period towards the end of the 19th century, when the number of golf clubs in Britain rose from fewer than 200 to almost 1,000, the need for a governing body to bring conformity to the rules became a matter of serious debate. Until that time each club could set and administer its own regulations for playing the game.

The R&A was already recognised as something of a father figure and eventually agreed to pressure from the leading clubs to take responsibility for the laws of the game. On September 28, 1897, the Rules of Golf Committee was formed and the R&A moved from its position as a highly regarded adviser to a firmly established governing authority with well defined powers.

With the exception of the United States, whose allegiance lies with the United States Golf Association, and Canada, which is self-governing but affiliated to the R&A, every country where the game is played has affiliated to the Royal and Ancient and accepts the club's authority over the laws of the game and the regulation on amateur status. Following a four-day meeting in the House of Lords between the R&A and the USGA, a uniform code of rules has been applied world-wide since 1952. Yet, even today, the R&A does not impose the Rules of Golf, but rather governs by consent.

The main thrust of the work of the Rules of Golf Committee is in the area of interpretation and constant review, revision and simplification of the laws. To this end the R&A and USGA meet twice a year to discuss possible changes which will then be examined at great length in consultation with amateur and professional golfing bodies world-wide. Any agreed changes to the rules are made every four years.

The Rules Committee is composed of 12 members of the R&A with up to a further 12 representatives from golfing bodies at home and abroad. In addition to the USGA there are advisory members from Britain's Council of National

Golf Unions and the Ladies Golf Union, plus delegates from Europe, Australia, New Zealand, Canada, South Africa, South America, Asia and the Pacific, and Japan.

Since the creation of the first Rules Committee in 1897, the R&A has spawned two further offspring to meet the ever-increasing pressures of administration. The Implements and Ball Committee investigates and rules on the admissibility or otherwise of newly developed clubs and golf balls, and the Amateur Status Committee defines the laws which govern acceptable levels of prizes, tournament rules, grants and scholarships and applications for reinstatement to the amateur ranks.

The Open Championship

The R&A first became involved with the Open Championship after Young Tom Morris won the original championship belt outright in 1870 and Prestwick Golf Club, which had inaugurated the event 10 years earlier, asked the Royal and Ancient and the Honourable Company of Edinburgh Golfers to join them in providing a new trophy and staging the championship.

By 1919 a total of 26 golf clubs had become involved in the organisation of the Open and Amateur Championships. It was a cumbersome and at times chaotic situation which was resolved when the clubs invited the R&A to take full responsibility for both events from 1920.

Significant changes had taken place over the first 60 years since the first championship in 18860. Entries had increased from eight to more than 250, qualifying rounds were introduced and play changed from three rounds of Prestwick's 12-hole course in one day to four rounds of 18 holes over two days.

Those changes pale into insignificance when set beside the modern championship. Well over 2,000 entries are received each year. Prize money has reached more than £3 million and spectators number more than 200,000. The tented village is virtually a small township, with more than 7,000 people involved as volunteers or paid employees.

But it is not just the Open which occupies the talents of Championship Committee members. They are also responsible for the Amateur, Boys, Mid-Amateur and Seniors Championships and the Junior Open. International events also come under their umbrella. These include organisation of the Walker Cup, World Amateur Team Championships, St Andrews and Jacques Léglise Trophies when they are played in Great Britain and Ireland.

The Selection Committee, which reports directly to the General Committee, has the responsibility for teams representing Great Britain & Ireland and involves members from each of the four home countries.

Profits from the Open Championship are channelled back into the game through the External Funds Supervisory Committee which recommends grants and loans for projects throughout the world, particularly those concerned with the training and development of junior golf and with the creation of new facilities.

The R&A as a private club

Although the world-wide membership of the R&A is 2,500, those resident in St Andrews barely number three figures. Many who wear the R&A tie are also members of leading clubs in golfing nations around the globe and bring with them a wealth of experience to committee discussions. The R&A has never been a narrowly parochial institution run by and for local golfers.

Yet despite its pre-eminent position, the club has no golf course. For many years the upkeep of the Old Course was paid for by the R&A and the New course was built and maintained at the members' expense. That arrangement came to an end in 1946 when an Act of Parliament allowed St Andrews Town Council to charge local golfers for the right to play on the links. Until then golf had been free to St Andreans.

How the Open benefits golf

Keith Mackie

The success of the Open Championship has enabled the Royal and Ancient Golf Club of St Andrews to pump well in excess of £40 million into the grass roots of the game.

Profits from the Championship have been distributed around the world, principally to fund the development of junior golf and to expand and improve facilities for the ever-growing number of amateur golfers.

More than £20 million has been given to good golfing causes as outright grants, with a further substantial amount distributed as interest-free loans. When the Open Championship first began to make a profit, the R&A made two fundamental decisions. None of the money was to be used to support the R&A as a private members club and all proceeds were to be spread as widely as possible 'for the benefit of golf'. An External Funds Supervisory Committee was set up to determine where the money would achieve the best results.

As the Open continues to generate greater funding reserves and the demand for grants and loans increases, the R&A has created the new executive position of Golf Development Secretary to search out the areas where help is most needed and strengthen the management of policies and funding.

The task has been entrusted to Duncan Weir, who moved from his position as Assistant Secretary (Championships). He joined the R&A in 1985 after graduating with a BA in Economics from the College of William and Mary in Williamsburg, Virginia, where he had gained a golf scholarship. He was Scottish Boys and Schools champion in 1979 and a member of the Great Britain and Ireland team which played against the Continent of Europe that same year. He reached the semi-finals of the Scottish Amateur in 1989.

A major part of the funding under his control will continue to go towards coaching and the encouragement of junior golf. The Golf Foundation receives extensive grants for its wide-ranging schemes for juniors which include coaching at 2,500 schools in Britain and the opening of Starter Centres throughout the country. The annual Golf Foundation Team Championship for Schools attracts a world-wide entry of more than 2,000 schools competing for places in the finals.

Grants

Help with golf instruction stretches around the world and more than 40 countries have been given grants to improve the coaching of amateur golfers.

In countries like Russia, where it has often been difficult to transfer money or where there was no opportunity to buy golf equipment, grants initially took the form of equipment rather than cash. The Czech Republic originally requested a consignment of clubs, balls and golf shoes. Hungary asked simply for a mower to keep the country's only nine-hole course in trim.

Closer to home, efforts are being made to stem the tide of young golfers accepting golf scholarships in America and a series of golf bursaries was started at Stirling University in 1987. There are now over 150 places available at more than 20 universities in Britain.

Yet it is not only the amateur game that benefits from the Open. The Professional Golfers' Association receives regular grants for its training programmes and the PGA European Tour has had support from the R&A since the inception of its Challenge Tour, the training ground for the next generation of tournament stars.

The Women's Professional Golfers Association European Tour was saved from going into liquidation in its formative years by a substantial donation from the R&A.

At grass roots level hundreds of clubs have been helped to extend and improve their playing facilities. The underlying principle is to create an environment where greater numbers of members and visitors can enjoy the game. Initially the R&A will want to know what action clubs have taken to help themselves and will usually provide cash to top up amounts already raised rather than funding entire projects.

Clubs have been helped with the construction costs of additional holes and practice facilities, installation of irrigation systems and the building of defences against coastal erosion.

R&A Contacts

The history of the Royal and Ancient Golf Club of St Andrews and up-to-date news of its activities worldwide can be found at the website **www.randa.org**

Full details of the Open Championship can be found at **www.opengolf.com**

R&A officials can be contacted on: Tel 01334 460000   Fax 01334 460001

Secretary: Peter Dawson
Championship Secretary: Angus Farquhar
Financial Secretary: Mark Dobell
Golf Development Secretary: Duncan Weir
Golf Heritage Secretary: Peter Lewis
Members' Secretary: Aubyn Stewart-Wilson
Projects Secretary: Lachlan McIntosh
Rules Secretary: David Rickman

Training, research and development

In addition to this direct input to individual clubs, the R&A also makes funds available for training, research and development in greenkeeping and increasingly in ecological and conservation matters.

The formation of the British and International Golf Greenkeepers' Association was funded by a grant and the work of their training committee is supported annually. The Sports Turf Research Institute also gets regular funding and a contribution is made to the Research and Test Centre operated by the United States Golf Association.

The R&A has also established its own think tank – the Golf Course Advisory Committee – which calls on experts in many fields. The four home golfing unions are represented, together with agronomists, greenkeepers, golf course architects, constructors and environmentalists.

The Committee has a wide remit, looking at issues such as the future demand for golf, new and improved greenkeeping techniques, the restriction on use of chemicals in the upkeep of courses, the importance of correct enviromnental management and the conservation of natural terrain and animal habitats. The production of booklets and video-tapes on these issues has also been funded by the R&A.

British Golf Musuem

As well as projects designed to safeguard the future of golf, R&A funding also created the British Golf Museum to preserve the game's history, allowing the creation of a wonderful collection of clubs, balls, pictures, paintings and memorabilia which together with interactive touch-screen techniques bring the story of golf to life.

The Open Championship not only continues to be the oldest and greatest challenge in the ancient game, the profits it generates go back into golf at all levels to pave the way for new and expanding generations to enjoy its enduring qualities.

The history of the club and up-to-date news of its world-wide activities is included on the website www.randa.org. Full details of the Open Championship are at www.opengolf.com.

Woosnam beaten with extra club

Keith Mackie relates the history of the 14 club limit

The two-shot penalty suffered by Ian Woosnam in the final round of the 2001 Open Championship at Royal Lytham and St Annes was imposed under a rule first introduced in Britain in 1939. At that time the punishment for the crime of carrying more than the permitted 14 clubs was draconian – instant disqualification. It was only in 1956 that the sentence was reduced to two strokes per hole up to a maximum of four shots.

The idea of limiting the number of clubs was introduced by Robert Harris, a member of the R&A Rules of Golf Committee, who had won the 1925 Amateur Championship at Royal North Devon by a margin of 13 and 12 over K Fragley.

He felt that the rigidity of the new steel shafts could not be made to work as well as the more flexible hickory and the consequent loss of finesse led to a wider variety of lofts being introduced. Instead of manufacturing shots with a few clubs golfers were carrying a plethora of clubs to do the job for them. The matter was getting out of hand however when Lawson Little was reported to have as many as 31 clubs in his bag when he won the Amateur title, ironically, at Lytham, in 1935 by beating Dr W Tweddle by one hole.

Harris discussed his ideas with United States Golf Association president John Jackson and both the R&A and the USGA issued statements on January 1, 1937, to warn of the new limit of 14 clubs which would be applied a year later. The USGA gave the reasoning behind the change: "The limitation of clubs will tend to restore the making of individual shots and increase the skill of the player. The multiplicity of clubs tends towards mechanisation of the game. In earlier days players used to change their swings in order to execute the various types of shots. In recent years the tendency has been merely to take a different club."

While the new rule came into force in America as planned in 1938, there was dissent within the R&A and the motion failed to gain the necessary two-thirds majority when members were asked to vote for its ratification. After much behind the scenes lobbying, it was a year later, on January 1, 1939, that the 14-club limit was first imposed on the rest of the golfing world.

In his autobiography, Harris wrote colourfully of his campaign to stop golfers buying a specific club for each shot rather than developing the skill of playing half-shots. "Lack of imagination brought ruin, and the scramble of the buying of the shot forced the set up to 20 and even 25 clubs being carried by some players in a quest for results which before were obtainable from five or six shafts of hickory. Golf became a caricature of a game. Knickerbockered, hobnailed, clothcapped British sportsmen were inflicting unnecessary hardship and stunting the growth of the small boys and girls of France and Belgium by the weight of their golf bags."

And why 14 clubs? There is no evidence of how this number was arrived at. Harris merely records that the decision was made "without the why and wherefore of only 14 clubs being questioned or debated."

Many years after his idea became universal golf law he was convinced that he had been too generous in his limitation. "It is apparent that 14 is too many," he said. "These debates with caddies regarding digits, when the player is afraid of the shot, are slowing up the game."

How to avoid a putting penalty

During the Women's Professional Golf Association International Match Play Championship at Gleneagles, one competitor called a penalty on herself when her ball was moved on a sloping green by the strong wind.

Rule 18-2b says: "If a player's ball in play moves after he has addressed it (other than as a result of a stroke), the player shall be deemed to have moved the ball and shall incur a penalty stroke. The player shall replace the ball unless the movement of the ball occurs after he has begun his swing and he does not discontinue his swing."

In windy conditions players can avoid this penalty by taking their putting stance without letting the head of the putter touch the ground. A player has addressed the ball "when he has taken his stance and has also grounded his club." By keeping the head of the club off the ground the address position is incomplete and no penalty is imposed if the ball moves. The ball must be replaced before putting out.

In a hazard, where grounding the club is prohibited, the player is considered to have addressed the ball when he has completed his stance. The definition is: "taking the stance consists in a player placing his feet in position for and preparatory to making a stroke."

Rules Booklet

The Rules of Golf are available in booklet form free from the Royal and Ancient Golf Club of St Andrews, which also has for sale a book detailing decisions taken regarding the rules.

RULES
OF GOLF

As Approved by
The Royal and Ancient Golf Club
of St. Andrews, Scotland
and the
United States Golf Association

29th EDITION
EFFECTIVE 1st JANUARY 2000

HOW TO USE THE RULE BOOK

Understand the words

The Rules book is written in a very precise and deliberate fashion. You should be aware of and understand the following differences in word use.

may	=	optional
should	=	recommendation
shall/must	=	instruction (and penalty if not carried out)
a ball	=	you may substitute another ball (e.g. Rules 26, 27 or 28)
the ball	=	you may not substitute another ball (e.g. Rules 24-2 or 25-1)

Know the definitions

There are over forty defined terms and these form the foundation around which the Rules of play are written. A good knowledge of the defined terms (which are italicised throughout the book) is very important to the correct application of the Rules.

Which rule applies?

The Contents pages may help you find the relevant Rule, alternatively there is an Index at the back of the book.

What is the ruling

To answer any question on the Rules you must first establish the facts of the case. To do so, you should identify:

1. The form of play (e.g. match play or stroke play, single, foursome or four-ball?)
2. Who is involved (e.g. the player, his partner or caddie, an outside agency?)
3. Where the incident occurred (e.g. on the teeing ground, in a bunker or water hazard, on the putting green or elsewhere on the course).

In some cases it might also be necessary to establish:

4. The player's intentions (e.g. what was he doing and what does he want to do?)
5. Any subsequent events (e.g. the player has returned his score card or the competition has closed).

Refer to the book

It is recommended that you carry a Rule book in your golf bag and use it whenever a question arises. If in doubt, play the course as you find it and play the ball as it lies. Once back in the Clubhouse, reference to Decisions on the Rules of Golf should help resolve any outstanding queries.

CONTENTS

SECTION I — ETIQUETTE

COURTESY ON THE COURSE

Safety
Prior to playing a stroke or making a practice swing, the player should ensure that no one is standing close by or in a position to be hit by the club, the ball or any stones, pebbles, twigs or the like which may be moved by the stroke or swing.

Consideration for Other Players
The player who has the honour should be allowed to play before his opponent or fellow-competitor tees his ball.

No one should move, talk or stand close to or directly behind the ball or the hole when a player is addressing the ball or making a stroke.

No player should play until the players in front are out of range.

Pace of Play
In the interest of all, players should play without delay.

If a player believes his ball may be lost outside a water hazard or out of bounds, to save time, he should play a provisional ball.

Players searching for a ball should signal the players behind them to pass as soon as it becomes apparent that the ball will not easily be found. They should not search for five minutes before doing so. They should not continue play until the players following them have passed and are out of range.

When the play of a hole has been completed, players should immediately leave the putting green.

If a match fails to keep its place on the course and loses more than one clear hole on the players in front, it should invite the match following to pass.

PRIORITY ON THE COURSE

In the absence of special rules, two-ball matches should have precedence over and be entitled to pass any three- or four-ball match, which should invite them through.

A single player has no standing and should give way to a match of any kind.

Any match playing a whole round is entitled to pass a match playing a shorter round.

CARE OF THE COURSE

Holes in Bunkers
Before leaving a bunker, a player should carefully fill up and smooth over all holes and footprints made by him.

Repair Divots, Ball-Marks and Damage by Spikes
A player should ensure that any divot hole made by him and any damage to the putting green made by a ball is carefully repaired. On completion of the hole by all players in the group, damage to the putting green caused by golf shoe spikes should be repaired.

Damage to Greens — Flagsticks, Bags, etc.
Players should ensure that, when putting down bags or the flagstick, no damage is done to the putting green and that neither they nor their caddies damage the hole by standing close to it, in handling the flagstick or in removing the ball from the hole. The flagstick should be properly replaced in the hole before the players leave the putting green. Players should not damage the putting green by leaning on their putters, particularly when removing the ball from the hole.

Golf Carts
Local notices regulating the movement of golf carts should be strictly observed.

Damage Through Practice Swings
In taking practice swings, players should avoid causing damage to the course, particularly the tees, by removing divots.

SECTION II — DEFINITIONS

The Definitions are placed in alphabetical order and some are also repeated at the beginning of their relevant Rule.

In the Rules themselves, defined terms which may be important to the application of a Rule are italicised the first time they appear.

Abnormal Ground Conditions

An 'abnormal ground condition' is any casual water, ground under repair or hole, cast or runway on the course made by a burrowing animal, a reptile or a bird.

Addressing the Ball

A player has 'addressed the ball' when he has taken his stance and has also grounded his club, except that in a hazard a player has addressed the ball when he has taken his stance.

Advice

'Advice' is any counsel or suggestion which could influence a player in determining his play, the choice of a club or the method of making a stroke.

Information on the Rules or on matters of public information, such as the position of hazards or the flagstick on the putting green, is not advice.

Ball Deemed to Move

See 'Move or Moved'.

Ball Holed

See 'Holed'.

Ball Lost

See 'Lost Ball'.

Ball in Play

A ball is 'in play' as soon as the player has made a stroke on the teeing ground. It remains in play until holed out, except when it is lost, out of bounds or lifted, or another ball has been substituted whether or not such substitution is permitted; a ball so substituted becomes the ball in play.

Bunker

A 'bunker' is a hazard consisting of a prepared area of ground, often a hollow, from which turf or soil has been removed and replaced with sand or the like. Grass-covered ground bordering or within a bunker is not part of the bunker. The margin of a bunker extends vertically downwards, but not upwards. A ball is in a bunker when it lies in or any part of it touches the bunker.

Burrowing Animal

A 'burrowing animal' is an animal that makes a hole for habitation or shelter, such as a rabbit, mole, ground hog, gopher or salamander.

Note: A hole made by a non-burrowing animal, such as a dog, is not an abnormal ground condition unless marked or declared as ground under repair.

Caddie

A 'caddie' is one who carries or handles a player's clubs during play and otherwise assists him in accordance with the Rules.

When one caddie is employed by more than one player, he is always deemed to be the caddie of the player whose ball is involved, and equipment carried by him is deemed to be that player's equipment, except when the caddie acts upon specific directions of another player, in which case he is considered to be that other player's caddie.

Casual Water

'Casual water' is any temporary accumulation of water on the course which is visible before or after the player takes his stance and is not in a water hazard. Snow and natural ice, other than frost, are either casual water or loose impediments, at the option of the player. Manufactured ice is an obstruction. Dew and frost are not casual water. A ball is in casual water when it lies in or any part of it touches the casual water.

Committee

The 'Committee' is the committee in charge of the competition or, if the matter does not arise in a competition, the committee in charge of the course.

Competitor

A 'competitor' is a player in a stroke competition. A 'fellow-competitor' is any person with whom the competitor plays. Neither is partner of the other.

In stroke play foursome and four-ball competitions, where the context so admits, the word 'competitor' or 'fellow-competitor' includes his partner.

Course

The 'course' is the whole area within which play is permitted (see Rule 33-2).

Equipment

'Equipment' is anything used, worn or carried by or for the player except any ball he has played at the hole being played and any small object, such as a coin or a tee, when used to mark the position of a ball or the extent of an area in which a ball is to be dropped. Equipment includes a golf cart, whether or not motorised. If such a cart is shared by two or more players, the cart and everything in it are deemed to be the equipment of the player whose ball is involved except that, when the cart is being moved by one of the players sharing it, the cart and everything in it are deemed to be that player's equipment.

Note: A ball played at the hole being played is equipment when it has been lifted and not put back into play.

Fellow-Competitor
See 'Competitor".

Flagstick
The 'flagstick' is a movable straight indicator, with or without bunting or other material attached, centred in the hole to show its position. It shall be circular in cross-section.

Forecaddie
A 'forecaddie' is one who is employed by the Committee to indicate to players the position of balls during play. He is an outside agency.

Ground Under Repair
'Ground under repair' is any part of the course so marked by order of the Committee or so declared by its authorised representative. It includes material piled for removal and a hole made by a greenkeeper, even if not so marked.

All ground and any grass, bush, tree or other growing thing within the ground under repair is part of the ground under repair. The margin of ground under repair extends vertically downwards, but not upwards. Stakes and lines defining ground under repair are in such ground. Such stakes are obstructions. A ball is in ground under repair when it lies in or any part of it touches the ground under repair.

Note 1: Grass cuttings and other material left on the course which have been abandoned and are not intended to be removed are not ground under repair unless so marked.

Note 2: The Committee may make a Local Rule prohibiting play from ground under repair or an environmentally sensitive area which has been defined as ground under repair.

Hazards
A 'hazard' is any bunker or water hazard.

Hole
The 'hole' shall be 4¼ inches (108 mm) in diameter and at least 4 inches (100 mm) deep. If a lining is used, it shall be sunk at least 1 inch (25 mm) below the putting green surface unless the nature of the soil makes it impracticable to do so; its outer diameter shall not exceed 4¼ inches (108 mm).

Holed
A ball is 'holed' when it is at rest within the circumference of the hole and all of it is below the level of the lip of the hole.

Honour
The player who is to play first from the teeing ground is said to have the 'honour".

Lateral Water Hazard
A 'lateral water hazard' is a water hazard or that part of a water hazard so situated that it is not possible or is deemed by the Committee to be impracticable to drop a ball behind the water hazard in accordance with Rule 26-1b.

That part of a water hazard to be played as a lateral water hazard should be distinctively marked. A ball is in a lateral water hazard when it lies in or any part of it touches the lateral water hazard.

Note 1: Lateral water hazards should be defined by red stakes or lines.

Note 2: The Committee may make a Local Rule prohibiting play from an environmentally-sensitive area which has been defined as a lateral water hazard.

Note 3: The Committee may define a lateral water hazard as a water hazard.

Line of Play
The 'line of play' is the direction which the player wishes his ball to take after a stroke, plus a reasonable distance on either side of the intended direction. The line of play extends vertically upwards from the ground, but does not extend beyond the hole.

Line of Putt
The 'line of putt' is the line which the player wishes his ball to take after a stroke on the putting green. Except with respect to Rule 16-1e, the line of putt includes a reasonable distance on either side of the intended line. The line of putt does not extend beyond the hole.

Loose Impediments
'Loose impediments' are natural objects such as stones, leaves, twigs, branches and the like, dung, worms and insects and casts or heaps made by them, provided they are not fixed or growing, are not solidly embedded and do not adhere to the ball.

Sand and loose soil are loose impediments on the putting green, but not elsewhere.

Snow and natural ice, other than frost, are either casual water or loose impediments, at the option of the player. Manufactured ice is an obstruction.

Dew and frost are not loose impediments.

Lost Ball
A ball is 'lost' if:

a. It is not found or identified as his by the player within five minutes after the player's side or his or their caddies have begun to search for it; or

b. The player has put another ball into play under the Rules, even though he may not have searched for the original ball; or

c. The player has played any stroke with a provisional ball from the place where the original ball is likely to be or from a point nearer the hole than that place, whereupon the provisional ball becomes the ball in play.

Time spent in playing a wrong ball is not counted in the five-minute period allowed for search.

Marker

A 'marker' is one who is appointed by the Committee to record a competitor's score in stroke play. He may be a fellow-competitor. He is not a referee.

Matches

See 'Sides and Matches'.

Move or Moved

A ball is deemed to have 'moved' if it leaves its position and comes to rest in any other place.

Nearest Point of Relief

The 'nearest point of relief' is the reference point for taking relief without penalty from interference by an immovable obstruction (Rule 24-2), an abnormal ground condition (Rule 25-1) or a wrong putting green (Rule 25-3).

It is the point on the course, nearest to where the ball lies, which is not nearer the hole and at which, if the ball were so positioned, no interference (as defined) would exist.

Note: The player should determine his nearest point of relief by using the club with which he expects to play his next stroke to simulate the address position and swing for such stroke.

Observer

An 'observer' is one who is appointed by the Committee to assist a referee to decide questions of fact and to report to him any breach of a Rule. An observer should not attend the flagstick, stand at or mark the position of the hole, or lift the ball or mark its position.

Obstructions

An 'obstruction' is anything artificial, including the artificial surfaces and sides of roads and paths and manufactured ice, except:

a. Objects defining out of bounds, such as walls, fences, stakes and railings;

b. Any part of an immovable artificial object which is out of bounds; and

c. Any construction declared by the Committee to be an integral part of the course.

An obstruction is a movable obstruction if it may be moved without unreasonable effort, without unduly delaying play and without causing damage. Otherwise, it is an immovable obstruction.

Note: The Committee may make a Local Rule declaring a movable obstruction to be an immovable obstruction.

Out of Bounds

'Out of bounds' is beyond the boundaries of the course or any part of the course so marked by the Committee.

When out of bounds is defined by reference to stakes or a fence, or as being beyond stakes or a fence, the out of bounds line is determined by the nearest inside points of the stakes or fence posts at ground level excluding angled supports. Objects defining out of bounds such as walls, fences, stakes and railings, are not obstructions and are deemed to be fixed.

When out of bounds is defined by a line on the ground, the line itself is out of bounds.

The out of bounds line extends vertically upwards and downwards.

A ball is out of bounds when all of it lies out of bounds.

A player may stand out of bounds to play a ball lying within bounds.

Outside Agency

An 'outside agency' is any agency not part of the match or, in stroke play, not part of the competitor's side, and includes a referee, a marker, an observer and a forecaddie. Neither wind nor water is an outside agency.

Partner

A 'partner' is a player associated with another player on the same side.

In a threesome, foursome, best-ball or four-ball match, where the context so admits, the word 'player' includes his partner or partners.

Penalty Stroke

A 'penalty stroke' is one added to the score of a player or side under certain Rules. In a three-some or foursome, penalty strokes do not affect the order of play.

Provisional Ball

A 'provisional ball' is a ball played under Rule 27-2 for a ball which may be lost outside a water hazard or may be out of bounds.

Putting Green

The 'putting green' is all ground of the hole being played which is specially prepared for putting or otherwise defined as such by the Committee. A ball is on the putting green when any part of it touches the putting green.

Referee

A 'referee' is one who is appointed by the Committee to accompany players to decide questions of fact and apply the Rules. He shall act on any breach of a Rule which he observes or is reported to him.

A referee should not attend the flagstick, stand at or mark the position of the hole, or lift the ball or mark its position.

Rub of the Green
A 'rub of the green' occurs when a ball in motion is accidentally deflected or stopped by any outside agency (see Rule 19-1).

Rule or Rules
The term 'Rule' includes:

a. The Rules of Golf;
b. Any Local Rules made by the Committee under Rule 33-8a and Appendix I; and
c. The specifications on clubs and the ball in Appendices II and III.

Sides and Matches
Side: A player, or two or more players who are partners.

Single: A match in which one plays against another.

Threesome: A match in which one plays against two, and each side plays one ball.

Foursome: A match in which two play against two, and each side plays one ball.

Three-ball: A match play competition in which three play against one another, each playing his own ball. Each player is playing two distinct matches.

Best-ball: A match in which one plays against the better ball of two or the best ball of three players.

Four-ball: A match in which two play their better ball against the better ball of the two other players.

Stance
Taking the 'stance' consists in a player placing his feet in position for and preparatory to making a stroke.

Stipulated Round
The 'stipulated round' consists of playing the holes of the course in their correct sequence unless otherwise authorised by the Committee. The number of holes in a stipulated round is 18 unless a smaller number is authorised by the Committee. As to extension of stipulated round in match play, see Rule 2-3.

Stroke
A 'stroke' is the forward movement of the club made with the intention of fairly striking at and moving the ball, but if a player checks his down-swing voluntarily before the clubhead reaches the ball he is deemed not to have made a stroke.

Teeing Ground
The 'teeing ground' is the starting place for the hole to be played. It is a rectangular area two club-lengths in depth, the front and the sides of which are defined by the outside limits of two tee-markers. A ball is outside the teeing ground when all of it lies outside the teeing ground.

Through the Green
'Through the green' is the whole area of the course except:

a. The teeing ground and putting green of the hole being played; and
b. All hazards on the course.

Water Hazard
A 'water hazard' is any sea, lake, pond, river, ditch, surface drainage ditch or other open water course (whether or not containing water) and anything of a similar nature.

All ground or water within the margin of a water hazard is part of the water hazard. The margin of a water hazard extends vertically upwards and downwards. Stakes and lines defining the margins of water hazards are in the hazards. Such stakes are obstructions. A ball is in a water hazard when it lies in or any part of it touches the water hazard.

Note 1: Water hazards (other than lateral water hazards) should be defined by yellow stakes or lines.

Note 2: The Committee may make a Local Rule prohibiting play from an environmentally-sensitive area which has been defined as a water hazard.

Wrong Ball
A 'wrong ball' is any ball other than the player's:

a. Ball in play,
b. Provisional ball, or
c. Second ball played under Rule 3-3 or Rule 20-7b in stroke play.

Note: Ball in play includes a ball substituted for the ball in play whether or not such substitution is permitted.

Wrong Putting Green
A 'wrong putting green' is any putting green other than that of the hole being played. Unless otherwise prescribed by the Committee, this term includes a practice putting green or pitching green on the course.

SECTION III — THE RULES OF PLAY

THE GAME

Rule 1. The Game

1-1. General
The Game of Golf consists in playing a ball from the *teeing ground* into the *hole* by a *stroke* or successive strokes in accordance with the *Rules*.

1-2. Exerting Influence on Ball
No player or caddie shall take any action to influence the position or the movement of a ball except in accordance with the *Rules*.

(Removal of movable obstructions – see Rule 24-1.)

PENALTY FOR BREACH OF RULE 1-2:
Match play – Loss of hole;
Stroke play – Two strokes.

Note: In the case of a serious breach of Rule 1-2, the *Committee* may impose a penalty of disqualification.

1-3. Agreement to Waive Rules
Players shall not agree to exclude the operation of any *Rule* or to waive any penalty incurred.

PENALTY FOR BREACH OF RULE 1-3:
Match play – Disqualification of both sides;
Stroke play – Disqualification of competitors concerned.

(Agreeing to play out of turn in stroke play – see Rule 10-2c.)

1-4. Points Not Covered by Rules
If any point in dispute is not covered by the *Rules*, the decision shall be made in accordance with equity.

Rule 2. Match play

2-1. Winner of Hole; Reckoning of Holes
In match play the game is played by holes.

Except as otherwise provided in the *Rules*, a hole is won by the side which holes its ball in the fewer strokes. In a handicap match the lower net score wins the hole.

The reckoning of holes is kept by the terms: so many 'holes up' or 'all square', and so many 'to play'.

A side is 'dormie' when it is as many holes up as there are holes remaining to be played.

2-2. Halved Hole
A hole is halved if each side holes out in the same number of strokes.

When a player has holed out and his opponent has been left with a stroke for the half, if the player thereafter incurs a penalty, the hole is halved.

2-3. Winner of Match
A match (which consists of a *stipulated round*, unless otherwise decreed by the *Committee*) is won by the side which is leading by a number of holes greater than the number of holes remaining to be played.

The Committee may, for the purpose of settling a tie, extend the stipulated round to as many holes as are required for a match to be won.

2-4. Concession of Next Stroke, Hole or Match
When the opponent's ball is at rest or is deemed to be at rest under Rule 16-2, the player may concede the opponent to have holed out with his next *stroke* and the ball may be removed by either side with a club or otherwise.

A player may concede a hole or a match at any time prior to the conclusion of the hole or the match.

Concession of a stroke, hole or match may not be declined or withdrawn.

2-5. Claims
In match play, if a doubt or dispute arises between the players and no duly authorised representative of the *Committee* is available within a reasonable time, the players shall continue the match without delay. Any claim, if it is to be considered by the Committee, must be made before any player in the match plays from the next *teeing ground* or, in the case of the last hole of the match, before all players in the match leave the *putting green*.

No later claim shall be considered unless it is based on facts previously unknown to the player making the claim and the player making the claim had been given wrong information (Rules 6-2a and 9) by an opponent. In any case, no later claim shall be considered after the result of the match has been officially announced, unless the Committee is satisfied that the opponent knew he was giving wrong information.

2-6. General Penalty
The penalty for a breach of a *Rule* in match play is loss of hole except when otherwise provided.

Rule 3. Stroke Play

3-1. Winner
The competitor who plays the *stipulated round* or rounds in the fewest strokes is the winner.

3-2. Failure to Hole Out
If a competitor fails to hole out at any hole and does not correct his mistake before he plays a *stroke* from the next *teeing ground* or, in the case of the last hole of the round, before he leaves the *putting green*, he shall be disqualified.

3-3. Doubt as to Procedure
a. Procedure
In stroke play only, when during play of a hole a competitor is doubtful of his rights or procedure, he may, without penalty, play a second ball. After the situation which caused the doubt has arisen, the competitor should, before taking further action, announce to his *marker* or a *fellow-competitor* his decision to invoke this Rule and the ball with which he will score if the *Rules* permit.

The competitor shall report the facts to the *Committee* before returning his score card unless he scores the same with both balls; if he fails to do so, he shall be disqualified.

b. Determination of Score for Hole
If the *Rules* allow the procedure selected in advance by the competitor, the score with the ball selected shall be his score for the hole.

If the competitor fails to announce in advance his decision to invoke this Rule or his selection, the score with the original ball or, if the original ball is not one of the balls being played, the first ball put into play shall count if the Rules allow the procedure adopted for such ball.

Note 1: If a competitor plays a second ball, *penalty strokes* incurred solely by playing the ball ruled not to count and *strokes* subsequently taken with that ball shall be disregarded.

Note 2: A second ball played under Rule 3-3 is not a *provisional ball* under Rule 27-2.

3-4. Refusal to Comply with a Rule
If a competitor refuses to comply with a *Rule* affecting the rights of another competitor, he shall be disqualified.

3-5. General Penalty
The penalty for a breach of a *Rule* in stroke play is two strokes except when otherwise provided.

Rule 4. Clubs

A player in doubt as to the conformity of a club should consult the Royal and Ancient Golf Club of St. Andrews.

A manufacturer should submit to the Royal and Ancient Golf Club of St. Andrews a sample of a club which is to be manufactured for a ruling as to whether the club conforms with the *Rules*. If a manufacturer fails to submit a sample before manufacturing and/or marketing the club, the manufacturer assumes the risk of a ruling that the club does not conform to the Rules. Any sample submitted to the Royal and Ancient Golf Club of St. Andrews will become its property for reference purposes.

4-1. Form and Make of Clubs
a. General
The player's clubs shall conform with this Rule and the provisions, specifications and interpretations set forth in Appendix II.

b. Wear and Alteration
A club which conforms with the *Rules* when new is deemed to conform after wear through normal use. Any part of a club which has been purposely altered is regarded as new and must, in its altered state, conform with the Rules.

4-2. Playing Characteristics Changed and Foreign Material
a. Playing Characteristics Changed
During a *stipulated round*, the playing characteristics of a club shall not be purposely changed by adjustment or by any other means.

b. Foreign Material
Foreign material must not be applied to the club face for the purpose of influencing the movement of the ball.

PENALTY FOR BREACH
OF RULE 4-1 or -2: Disqualification.

4-3. Damaged Clubs:
Repair and Replacement
a. Damage in Normal Course of Play
If, during a *stipulated round*, a player's club is damaged in the normal course of play, he may:
(i) use the club in its damaged state for the remainder of the *stipulated round*; or
(ii) without unduly delaying play, repair it or have it repaired; or
(iii) as an additional option available only if the club is unfit for play, replace the damaged club with any club. The replacement of a club must not unduly delay play and must not be made by borrowing any club selected for play by any other person playing on the *course*.

PENALTY FOR BREACH OF RULE 4-3a:
See Penalty Statement for Rule 4-4a or b.

CLUBS AND THE BALL
The Royal and Ancient Golf Club of St. Andrews reserves the right to change the *Rules* and make and change the interpretations relating to clubs, balls and other implements at any time.

Note: A club is unfit for play if it is substantially damaged, e.g. the shaft breaks into pieces or the clubhead becomes loose, detached or significantly deformed. A club is not unfit for play solely because the shaft is bent, the club's lie or loft has been altered or the clubhead is scratched.

b. Damage Other Than in Normal Course of Play

If, during a *stipulated round*, a player's club is damaged other than in the normal course of play rendering it non-conforming or changing its playing characteristics, the club shall not subsequently be used or replaced during the round.

c. Damage Prior to Round

A player may use a club damaged prior to a round provided the club, in its damaged state, conforms with the *Rules*.

Damage to a club which occurred prior to a round may be repaired during the round, provided the playing characteristics are not changed and play is not unduly delayed.

PENALTY FOR BREACH OF
RULE 4-3b or c: Disqualification.
(Undue delay – see Rule 6-7.)

4-4. Maximum of Fourteen Clubs
a. Selection and Addition of Clubs

The player shall start a *stipulated round* with not more than fourteen clubs. He is limited to the clubs thus selected for that round except that, if he started with fewer than fourteen clubs, he may add any number provided his total number does not exceed fourteen.

The addition of a club or clubs must not unduly delay play (Rule 6-7) and must not be made by borrowing any club selected for play by any other person playing on the course.

b. Partners May Share Clubs

Partners may share clubs, provided that the total number of clubs carried by the partners so sharing does not exceed fourteen.

PENALTY FOR BREACH OF
RULE 4-4a or b, *regardless of number of excess clubs carried*: Match play – At the conclusion of the hole at which the breach is discovered, the state of the match shall be adjusted by deducting one hole for each hole at which a breach occurred. Maximum deduction per round: two holes.

Stroke play – Two strokes for each hole at which any breach occurred; maximum penalty per round: four strokes.

Bogey and par competitions – Penalties as in match play.

Stableford competitions – see Note 1 to Rule 32-1b.

c. Excess Club Declared Out of Play

Any club carried or used in breach of this Rule shall be declared out of play by the player immedi-ately upon discovery that a breach has occurred and thereafter shall not be used by the player during the round.

PENALTY FOR BREACH OF RULE 4-4c:
Disqualification.

Rule 5. The Ball

5-1. General

The ball the player uses shall conform to requirements specified in Appendix III.

Note: The *Committee* may require, in the conditions of a competition (Rule 33-1), that the ball the player uses must be named on the current List of Conforming Golf Balls issued by the Royal and Ancient Golf Club of St. Andrews.

5-2. Foreign Material

Foreign material must not be applied to a ball for the purpose of changing its playing characteristics.

PENALTY FOR BREACH OF
RULE 5-1 or 5-2: Disqualification.

5-3. Ball Unfit for Play

A ball is unfit for play if it is visibly cut, cracked or out of shape. A ball is not unfit for play solely because mud or other materials adhere to it, its surface is scratched or scraped or its paint is damaged or discoloured.

If a player has reason to believe his ball has become unfit for play during the play of the hole being played, he may during the play of such hole lift his ball without penalty to determine whether it is unfit.

Before lifting the ball, the player must announce his intention to his opponent in match play or his *marker* or a *fellow-competitor* in stroke play and mark the position of the ball. He may then lift and examine the ball without cleaning it and must give his opponent, marker or fellow-competitor an opportunity to examine the ball.

If he fails to comply with this procedure, he shall incur a penalty of one stroke.

If it is determined that the ball has become unfit for play during play of the hole being played, the player may substitute another ball, placing it on the spot where the original ball lay. Otherwise, the original ball shall be replaced.

If a ball breaks into pieces as a result of a *stroke*, the stroke shall be cancelled and the player shall play a ball without penalty as nearly as possible at the spot from which the original ball was played (see Rule 20-5).

*PENALTY FOR BREACH OF RULE 5-3:
Match play – Loss of hole;
Stroke play – Two strokes.
*If a player incurs the general penalty for breach of Rule 5-3, no additional penalty under the Rule shall be applied.

Note: If the opponent, marker or fellow-competitor wishes to dispute a claim of unfitness, he must do so before the player plays another ball. (Cleaning ball lifted from putting green or under any other Rule – see Rule 21.)

PLAYER'S RESPONSIBILITIES

Rule 6. The Player

Definition
A **marker** is one who is appointed by the *Committee* to record a *competitor's* score in stroke play. He may be a *fellow-competitor*. He is not a *referee*.

6-1. Rules; Conditions of Competition
The player is responsible for knowing the *Rules* and the conditions under which the competition is to be played (Rule 33-1).

6-2. Handicap
a. Match Play
Before starting a match in a handicap competition, the players should determine from one another their respective handicaps. If a player begins the match having declared a higher handicap which would affect the number of strokes given or received, he shall be disqualified; otherwise, the player shall play off the declared handicap.

b. Stroke Play
In any round of a handicap competition, the competitor shall ensure that his handicap is recorded on his score card before it is returned to the *Committee*. If no handicap is recorded on his score card before it is returned, or if the recorded handicap is higher than that to which he is entitled and this affects the number of strokes received, he shall be disqualified from the handicap competition; otherwise, the score shall stand.
Note: It is the player's responsibility to know the holes at which handicap strokes are to be given or received.

6-3. Time of Starting and Groups
a. Time of Starting
The player shall start at the time laid down by the *Committee*.

b. Groups
In stroke play, the competitor shall remain throughout the round in the group arranged by the *Committee* unless the Committee authorises or ratifies a change.

PENALTY FOR BREACH OF RULE 6-3:
Disqualification.
(Best-ball and four-ball play – see Rules 30-3a and 31-2.)

Note: The *Committee* may provide in the conditions of a competition (Rule 33-1) that, if the

player arrives at his starting point, ready to play, within five minutes after his starting time, in the absence of circumstances which warrant waiving the penalty of disqualification as provided in Rule 33-7, the penalty for failure to start on time is loss of the first hole in match play or two strokes at the first hole in stroke play instead of disqualification.

6-4. Caddie
The player may have only one *caddie* at any one time, under penalty of disqualification.
For any breach of a *Rule* by his caddie, the player incurs the applicable penalty.

6-5. Ball
The responsibility for playing the proper ball rests with the player. Each player should put an identification mark on his ball.

6-6. Scoring in Stroke Play
a. Recording Scores
After each hole the *marker* should check the score with the competitor and record it. On completion of the round the marker shall sign the card and hand it to the competitor. If more than one marker records the scores, each shall sign for the part for which he is responsible.

b. Signing and Returning Card
After completion of the round, the competitor should check his score for each hole and settle any doubtful points with the *Committee*. He shall ensure that the *marker* has signed the card, countersign the card himself and return it to the Committee as soon as possible.

PENALTY FOR BREACH OF RULE 6-6b:
Disqualification.

c. Alteration of Card
No alteration may be made on a card after the competitor has returned it to the *Committee*.

d. Wrong Score for Hole
The competitor is responsible for the correctness of the score recorded for each hole on his card. If he returns a score for any hole lower than actually taken, he shall be disqualified. If he returns a score for any hole higher than actually taken, the score as returned shall stand.
Note 1: The *Committee* is responsible for the addition of scores and application of the handicap recorded on the card – see Rule 33-5.
Note 2: In four-ball stroke play, see also Rule 31-4 and -7a.

6-7. Undue Delay; Slow Play
The player shall play without undue delay and in accordance with any pace of play guidelines which may be laid down by the *Committee*. Between completion of a hole and playing from

the next *teeing ground*, the player shall not unduly delay play.

PENALTY FOR BREACH OF RULE 6-7:
Match play – Loss of hole;
Stroke play – Two strokes.
Bogey and par competitions – See Note 2
to Rule 32-1a.
Stableford competitions – See Note 2
to Rule 32-1b.
For subsequent offence – Disqualification.

Note 1: If the player unduly delays play between holes, he is delaying the play of the next hole and, except for bogey, par and Stableford competitions (see Rule 32), the penalty applies to that hole.

Note 2: For the purpose of preventing slow play, the *Committee* may, in the conditions of a competition (Rule 33-1), lay down pace of play guidelines including maximum periods of time allowed to complete a stipulated round, a hole or a stroke.

In stroke play only, the Committee may, in such a condition, modify the penalty for a breach of this Rule as follows:
First offence – One stroke;
Second offence – Two strokes.
For subsequent offence – Disqualification.

6-8. Discontinuance of Play; Resumption of Play
a. When Permitted
The player shall not discontinue play unless:

(i) the *Committee* has suspended play;
(ii) he believes there is danger from lightning;
(iii) he is seeking a decision from the *Committee* on a doubtful or disputed point (see Rules 2-5 and 34-3); or
(iv) there is some other good reason such as sudden illness.

Bad weather is not of itself a good reason for discontinuing play.

If the player discontinues play without specific permission from the *Committee*, he shall report to the Committee as soon as practicable. If he does so and the Committee considers his reason satisfactory, the player incurs no penalty. Otherwise, the player shall be disqualified.

Exception in match play: Players discontinuing match play by agreement are not subject to disqualification unless by so doing the competition is delayed.

Note: Leaving the course does not of itself constitute discontinuance of play.

b. Procedure When Play Suspended by Committee
When play is suspended by the *Committee*, if the players in a match or group are between the play of two holes, they shall not resume play until the Committee has ordered a resumption of play. If they are in the process of playing a hole, they may

continue provided they do so without delay. If they choose to continue, they shall discontinue either before or immediately after completing the hole.

The players shall resume play when the Committee has ordered a resumption of play.

PENALTY FOR BREACH OF RULE 6-8b:
Disqualification.

Note: The *Committee* may provide in the conditions of a competition (Rule 33-1) that, in potentially dangerous situations, play shall be discontinued immediately following a suspension of play by the Committee. If a player fails to discontinue play immediately, he shall be disqualified unless circumstances warrant waiving such penalty as provided in Rule 33-7.

c. Lifting Ball When Play Discontinued
When a player discontinues play of a hole under Rule 6-8a, he may lift his ball without penalty only if the *Committee* has suspended play or there is a good reason to lift it. Before lifting the ball the player must mark its position. If the player discontinues play and lifts his ball without specific permission from the Committee, when reporting to the Committee (Rule 6-8a), he shall, at that time, report the lifting of the ball.

If the player lifts the ball without a good reason to do so, fails to mark the position of the ball before lifting it or fails to report the lifting of the ball, he shall incur a penalty of one stroke.

d. Procedure When Play Resumed
Play shall be resumed from where it was discontinued, even if resumption occurs on a subsequent day. The player shall, either before or when play is resumed, proceed as follows:

(i) if the player has lifted the ball, he shall, provided he was entitled to lift it under Rule 6-8c, place a ball on the spot from which the original ball was lifted. Otherwise, the original ball must be replaced;
(ii) if the player entitled to lift his ball under Rule 6-8c has not done so, he may lift, clean and replace the ball, or substitute a ball on the spot from which the original ball was lifted. Before lifting the ball he must mark its position; or
(iii) if the player's ball or ball-marker is moved (including by wind or water) while play is discontinued, a ball or ball-marker shall be placed on the spot from which the original ball or ball-marker was moved.

(Spot not determinable – see Rule 20-3c.)

*PENALTY FOR BREACH OF RULE 6-8d:
Match play – Loss of hole;
Stroke play – Two strokes.
*If a player incurs the general penalty for a breach of Rule 6-8d, no additional penalty under Rule 6-8c shall be applied.

Rule 7. Practice

Definition
The **course** is the whole area within which play is permitted (see Rule 33-2).

7-1. Before or Between Rounds
a. Match Play
On any day of a match play competition, a player may practise on the competition *course* before a round.

b. Stroke Play
On any day of a stroke competition or play-off, a competitor shall not practise on the competition *course* or test the surface of any *putting green* on the course before a round or play-off. When two or more rounds of a stroke competition are to be played over consecutive days, a competitor shall not practise between those rounds on any competition course remaining to be played, or test the surface of any putting green on such course.
Exception: Practice putting or chipping on or near the first *teeing ground* before starting a round or play-off is permitted.

PENALTY FOR BREACH OF RULE 7-1b:
    Disqualification.

Note: The *Committee* may in the conditions of a competition (Rule 33-1) prohibit practice on the competition course on any day of a match play competition or permit practice on the competition course or part of the course (Rule 33-2c) on any day of or between rounds of a stroke competition.

7-2. During Round
A player shall not play a practice *stroke* either during the play of a hole or between the play of two holes except that, between the play of two holes, the player may practise putting or chipping on or near the *putting green* of the hole last played, any practice putting green or the *teeing ground* of the next hole to be played in the round, provided such practice stroke is not played from a hazard and does not unduly delay play (Rule 6-7).
Strokes played in continuing the play of a hole, the result of which has been decided, are not practice strokes.
Exception: When play has been suspended by the *Committee*, a player may, prior to resumption of play, practise (a) as provided in this Rule, (b) anywhere other than on the competition *course* and (c) as otherwise permitted by the Committee.

PENALTY FOR BREACH OF RULE 7-2:
    Match play – Loss of hole;
    Stroke play – Two strokes.
In the event of a breach between the play of two holes, the penalty applies to the next hole.

Note 1: A practice swing is not a practice *stroke* and may be taken at any place, provided the player does not breach the *Rules*.
Note 2: The *Committee* may prohibit practice on or near the *putting green* of the hole last played.

Rule 8. Advice; Indicating Line of Play

Definitions
Advice is any counsel or suggestion which could influence a player in determining his play, the choice of a club or the method of making a *stroke*.
Information on the *Rules* or on matters of public information, such as the position of *hazards* or the *flagstick* on the *putting green*, is not advice.
The **line of play** is the direction which the player wishes his ball to take after a *stroke*, plus a reasonable distance on either side of the intended direction. The line of play extends vertically upwards from the ground, but does not extend beyond the *hole*.

8-1. Advice
During a *stipulated round*, a player shall not give *advice* to anyone in the competition except his partner and may ask for advice only from his partner or either of their caddies.

8-2. Indicating Line of Play
a. Other Than on Putting Green
Except on the *putting green*, a player may have the *line of play* indicated to him by anyone, but no one shall be positioned by the player on or close to the line or an extension of the line beyond the hole while the *stroke* is being played. Any mark placed during the play of a hole by the player or with his knowledge to indicate the line shall be removed before the stroke is played.
Exception: Flagstick attended or held up – see Rule 17-1.

b. On the Putting Green
When the player's ball is on the *putting green*, the player, his partner or either of their caddies may, before but not during the *stroke*, point out a line for putting, but in so doing the putting green shall not be touched. No mark shall be placed anywhere to indicate a line for putting.

PENALTY FOR BREACH OF RULE:
    Match play – Loss of hole;
    Stroke play – Two strokes.

Note: The *Committee* may, in the conditions of a team competition (Rule 33-1), permit each team to appoint one person who may give *advice* (including pointing out a line for putting) to members of that team. The Committee may lay down conditions relating to the appointment and permitted conduct of such person, who must be identified to the Committee before giving advice.

Rule 9. Information as to Strokes Taken

9-1. General
The number of *strokes* a player has taken shall include any penalty strokes incurred.

9-2. Match Play
A player who has incurred a penalty shall inform his opponent as soon as practicable, unless he is obviously proceeding under a *Rule* involving a penalty and this has been observed by his opponent. If he fails so to inform his opponent, he shall be deemed to have given wrong information, even if he was not aware that he had incurred a penalty.

An opponent is entitled to ascertain from the player, during the play of a hole, the number of strokes he has taken and, after play of a hole, the number of strokes taken on the hole just completed.

If during the play of a hole the player gives or is deemed to give wrong information as to the number of strokes taken, he shall incur no penalty if he corrects the mistake before his opponent has played his next stroke. If the player fails so to correct the wrong information, he shall lose the hole.

If after play of a hole the player gives or is deemed to give wrong information as to the number of strokes taken on the hole just completed and this affects the opponent's understanding of the result of the hole, he shall incur no penalty if he corrects his mistake before any player plays from the next *teeing ground* or, in the case of the last hole of the match, before all players leave the *putting green*. If the player fails so to correct the wrong information, he shall lose the hole.

9-3. Stroke Play
A competitor who has incurred a penalty should inform his *marker* as soon as practicable.

ORDER OF PLAY

Rule 10. Order of Play

Definition
The player who is to play first from the *teeing ground* is said to have the **honour**.

10-1. Match Play
a. Teeing Ground
The side which shall have the *honour* at the first *teeing ground* shall be determined by the order of the draw. In the absence of a draw, the honour should be decided by lot.

The side which wins a hole shall take the honour at the next teeing ground. If a hole has been halved, the side which had the honour at the previous teeing ground shall retain it.

b. Other Than on Teeing Ground
When the balls are *in play*, the ball farther from the hole shall be played first. If the balls are equidistant from the hole, the ball to be played first should be decided by lot.

Exception: Rule 30-3c (best-ball and four-ball match play).

c. Playing Out of Turn
If a player plays when his opponent should have played, the opponent may immediately require the player to cancel the stroke so played and, in correct order, play a ball without penalty as nearly as possible at the spot from which the original ball was last played (see Rule 20-5).

10-2. Stroke Play
a. Teeing Ground
The competitor who shall have the *honour* at the first *teeing ground* shall be determined by the order of the draw. In the absence of a draw, the honour should be decided by lot.

The competitor with the lowest score at a hole shall take the honour at the next teeing ground. The competitor with the second lowest score shall play next and so on. If two or more competitors have the same score at a hole, they shall play from the next teeing ground in the same order as at the previous teeing ground.

b. Other Than on Teeing Ground
When the balls are *in play*, the ball farthest from the hole shall be played first. If two or more balls are equidistant from the hole, the ball to be played first should be decided by lot.

Exceptions: Rules 22 (ball interfering with or assisting play) and 31-5 (four-ball stroke play).

c. Playing Out of Turn
If a competitor plays out of turn, no penalty is incurred and the ball shall be played as it lies. If, however, the *Committee* determines that competitors have agreed to play in an order other than that set forth in Clauses 2a, 2b and 3 of this Rule to give one of them an advantage, they shall be disqualified.

(Playing stroke while another ball in motion after stroke from putting green - see Rule 16-1f.)

(Incorrect order of play in threesomes and foursomes stroke play – see Rule 29-3.)

10-3. Provisional Ball or Second Ball from Teeing Ground
If a player plays a *provisional ball* or a second ball from a *teeing ground*, he shall do so after his opponent or *fellow-competitor* has played his first

stroke. If a player plays a provisional ball or a second ball out of turn, Clauses 1c and 2c of this Rule shall apply.

10-4. Ball Moved in Measuring
If a ball is moved in measuring to determine which ball is farther from the hole, no penalty is incurred and the ball shall be replaced.

TEEING GROUND
Rule 11. Teeing Ground

Definition
The **teeing ground** is the starting place for the hole to be played. It is a rectangular area two club-lengths in depth, the front and the sides of which are defined by the outside limits of two tee-markers. A ball is outside the teeing ground when all of it lies outside the teeing ground.

11-1. Teeing
In teeing, the ball may be placed on the ground, on an irregularity of surface created by the player on the ground or on a tee, sand or other substance in order to raise it off the ground.

A player may stand outside the *teeing ground* to play a ball within it.

11-2. Tee-Markers
Before a player plays his first *stroke* with any ball from the *teeing ground* of the hole being played, the tee-markers are deemed to be fixed. In such circumstances, if the player moves or allows to be moved a tee-marker for the purpose of avoiding interference with his stance, the area of his intended swing or his line of play, he shall incur the penalty for a breach of Rule 13-2.

11-3. Ball Falling Off Tee
If a ball, when not *in play*, falls off a tee or is knocked off a tee by the player in addressing it, it may be re-teed without penalty, but if a *stroke* is made at the ball in these circumstances, whether the ball is moving or not, the stroke counts but no penalty is incurred.

11-4. Playing from Outside Teeing Ground
a. Match Play
If a player, when starting a hole, plays a ball from outside the *teeing ground*, the opponent may immediately require the player to cancel the *stroke* so played and play a ball from within the teeing ground, without penalty.

b. Stroke Play
If a competitor, when starting a hole, plays a ball from outside the *teeing ground*, he shall incur a penalty of two strokes and shall then play a ball from within the teeing ground.

If the competitor plays a stroke from the next teeing ground without first correcting his mistake or, in the case of the last hole of the round, leaves the *putting green* without first declaring his intention to correct his mistake, he shall be disqualified.

The stroke from outside the teeing ground and any subsequent strokes by the competitor on the hole prior to his correction of the mistake do not count in his score.

11-5. Playing from Wrong Teeing Ground
The provisions of Rule 11-4 apply.

PLAYING THE BALL

Rule 12. Searching for and Identifying the Ball

Definitions
A **hazard** is any bunker or water hazard.

A **bunker** is a *hazard* consisting of a prepared area of ground, often a hollow, from which turf or soil has been removed and replaced with sand or the like. Grass-covered ground bordering or within a bunker is not part of the bunker. The margin of a bunker extends vertically downwards, but not upwards. A ball is in a bunker when it lies in or any part of it touches the bunker.

A **water hazard** is any sea, lake, pond, river, ditch, surface drainage ditch or other open water course (whether or not containing water) and anything of a similar nature.

All ground or water within the margin of a water hazard is part of the water hazard. The margin of a water hazard extends vertically upwards and downwards. Stakes and lines defining the margins of water hazards are in the hazards. Such stakes are *obstructions*. A ball is in a water hazard when it lies in or any part of it touches the water hazard.

Note 1: Water hazards (other than *lateral water hazards*) should be defined by yellow stakes or lines.

Note 2: The *Committee* may make a Local Rule prohibiting play from an environmentally-sensitive area which has been defined as a water hazard.

12-1. Searching for Ball; Seeing Ball
In searching for his ball anywhere on the *course*, the player may touch or bend long grass, rushes, bushes, whins, heather or the like, but only to the extent necessary to find and identify it, provided that this does not improve the lie of the ball, the area of his intended swing or his *line of play*.

A player is not necessarily entitled to see his ball when playing a *stroke*.

In a *hazard*, if a ball is believed to be covered by *loose impediments* or sand, the player may remove by probing, raking or other means as much thereof as will enable him to see a part of a ball. If an excess is removed, no penalty is incurred and the ball shall be re-covered so that only a part of the ball is visible. If the ball is moved in such removal, no penalty is incurred; the ball shall be replaced and, if necessary, re-covered. As to removal of loose impediments outside a hazard, see Rule 23.

If a ball lying in an *abnormal ground condition* is accidentally moved during search, no penalty is incurred; the ball shall be replaced, unless the player elects to proceed under Rule 25-1b. If the player replaces the ball, he may still proceed under Rule 25-1b if applicable.

If a ball is believed to be lying in water in a *water hazard*, the player may probe for it with a club or otherwise. If the ball is moved in so doing, no penalty is incurred; the ball shall be replaced, unless the player elects to proceed under Rule 26-1.

PENALTY FOR BREACH OF RULE 12-1:
Match play – Loss of hole;
Stroke play – Two strokes.

12-2. Identifying Ball
The responsibility for playing the proper ball rests with the player. Each player should put an identification mark on his ball.

Except in a *hazard*, the player may, without penalty, lift a ball he believes to be his own for the purpose of identification and clean it to the extent necessary for identification. If the ball is the player's ball, he shall replace it. Before lifting the ball, the player must announce his intention to his opponent in match play or his *marker* or a *fellow-competitor* in stroke play and mark the position of the ball. He must then give his opponent, marker or fellow-competitor an opportunity to observe the lifting and replacement. If he lifts his ball without announcing his intention in advance, marking the position of the ball or giving his opponent, marker or fellow-competitor an opportunity to observe, or if he lifts his ball for identification in a hazard, or cleans it more than necessary for identification, he shall incur a penalty of one stroke and the ball shall be replaced.

If a player who is required to replace a ball fails to do so, he shall incur the penalty for a breach of Rule 20-3a, but no additional penalty under Rule 12-2 shall be applied.

Rule 13. Ball Played as It Lies

Definitions
A **hazard** is any *bunker* or *water hazard*.
A **bunker** is a *hazard* consisting of a prepared area of ground, often a hollow, from which turf or soil has been removed and replaced with sand or the like. Grass-covered ground bordering or within a bunker is not part of the bunker. The margin of a bunker extends vertically downwards, but not

upwards. A ball is in a bunker when it lies in or any part of it touches the bunker.

A **water hazard** is any sea, lake, pond, river, ditch, surface drainage ditch or other open water course (whether or not containing water) and anything of a similar nature.

All ground or water within the margin of a water hazard is part of the water hazard. The margin of a water hazard extends vertically upwards and downwards. Stakes and lines defining the margins of water hazards are in the hazards. Such stakes are *obstructions*. A ball is in a water hazard when it lies in or any part of it touches the water hazard.

Note 1: Water hazards (other than *lateral water hazards*) should be defined by yellow stakes or lines.

Note 2: The *Committee* may make a Local Rule prohibiting play from an environmentally-sensitive area which has been defined as a water hazard.

The **line of play** is the direction which the player wishes his ball to take after a *stroke*, plus a reasonable distance on either side of the intended direction. The line of play extends vertically upwards from the ground, but does not extend beyond the *hole*.

Taking the **stance** consists in a player placing his feet in position for and preparatory to making a *stroke*.

13-1. General
The ball shall be played as it lies, except as otherwise provided in the Rules. (Ball at rest moved – see Rule 18.)

13-2. Improving Lie, Area of Intended Stance or Swing, or Line of Play
Except as provided in the *Rules*, a player shall not improve or allow to be improved:
the position or lie of his ball,
the area of his intended stance or swing,
his *line of play* or a reasonable extension of that line beyond the *hole*, or
the area in which he is to drop or place a ball

by any of the following actions:
moving, bending or breaking anything growing or fixed (including immovable *obstructions* and objects defining *out of bounds*),
creating or eliminating irregularities of surface,
removing or pressing down sand, loose soil, replaced divots or other cut turf placed in position, or
removing dew, frost or water

except as follows:
as may occur in fairly taking his *stance*,
in making a *stroke* or the backward movement of his club for a stroke,

on the *teeing ground* in creating or eliminating irregularities of surface, or on the *putting green* in removing sand and loose soil as provided in Rule 16-1a or in repairing damage as provided in Rule 16-1c.

The club may be grounded only lightly and shall not be pressed on the ground.

Exception: Ball in hazard – see Rule 13-4.

13-3. Building Stance
A player is entitled to place his feet firmly in taking his *stance*, but he shall not build a stance.

13-4. Ball in Hazard
Except as provided in the *Rules*, before making a *stroke* at a ball which is in a *hazard* (whether a *bunker* or a *water hazard*) or which, having been lifted from a hazard, may be dropped or placed in the hazard, the player shall not:

a. Test the condition of the hazard or any similar hazard,
b. Touch the ground in the hazard or water in the water hazard with a club or otherwise, or
c. Touch or move a *loose impediment* lying in or touching the hazard.

Exceptions:
1. Provided nothing is done which constitutes testing the condition of the hazard or improves the lie of the ball, there is no penalty if the player (a) touches the ground in any hazard or water in a water hazard as a result of or to prevent falling, in removing an *obstruction*, in measuring or in retrieving, lifting, placing or replacing a ball under any Rule or (b) places his clubs in a hazard.
2. The player after playing the *stroke*, or his *caddie* at any time without the authority of the player, may smooth sand or soil in the hazard, provided that, if the ball is still in the hazard, nothing is done which improves the lie of the ball or assists the player in his subsequent play of the hole.

Note: At any time, including at address or in the backward movement for the *stroke*, the player may touch with a club or otherwise any *obstruction*, any construction declared by the *Committee* to be an integral part of the course or any grass, bush, tree or other growing thing.

PENALTY FOR BREACH OF RULE:
Match play – Loss of hole;
Stroke play – Two strokes.
(Searching for ball – see Rule 12-1.)

Rule 14. Striking the Ball

Definition
A **stroke** is the forward movement of the club made with the intention of fairly striking at and moving the ball, but if a player checks his downswing voluntarily before the clubhead reaches the ball he is deemed not to have made a stroke.

14-1. Ball to be Fairly Struck At
The ball shall be fairly struck at with the head of the club and must not be pushed, scraped or spooned.

14-2. Assistance
In making a *stroke*, a player shall not:

a. accept physical assistance or protection from the elements, or
b. allow his *caddie*, his partner or his partner's caddie to position himself on or close to an extension of the *line of play* or the *line of putt* behind the ball.

PENALTY FOR BREACH OF
RULE 14-1 or -2: Match play – Loss of hole;
Stroke play – Two strokes.

14-3. Artificial Devices and Unusual Equipment
A player in doubt as to whether use of an item would constitute a breach of Rule 14-3 should consult the Royal and Ancient Golf Club of St. Andrews.

A manufacturer may submit to the Royal and Ancient Golf Club of St. Andrews a sample of an item which is to be manufactured for a ruling as to whether its use during a *stipulated round* would cause a player to be in breach of Rule 14-3. Such sample will become the property of the Royal and Ancient Golf Club of St. Andrews for reference purposes. If a manufacturer fails to submit a sample before manufacturing and/or marketing the item, he assumes the risk of a ruling that use of the item would be contrary to the *Rules*.

Except as provided in the Rules, during a stipulated round the player shall not use any artificial device or unusual equipment:

a. Which might assist him in making a *stroke* or in his play; or
b. For the purpose of gauging or measuring distance or conditions which might affect his play; or
c. Which might assist him in gripping the club, except that:
   (i) plain gloves may be worn;
   (ii) resin, powder and drying or moisturising agents may be used; and
   (iii) a towel or handkerchief may be wrapped around the grip.

PENALTY FOR BREACH OF RULE 14-3:
Disqualification.

14-4. Striking the Ball More Than Once
If a player's club strikes the ball more than once in the course of a *stroke*, the player shall count the stroke and add a penalty stroke, making two strokes in all.

14-5. Playing Moving Ball

A player shall not play while his ball is moving.

Exceptions:
Ball falling off tee – Rule 11-3.
Striking the ball more than once – Rule 14-4.
Ball moving in water – Rule 14-6.

When the ball begins to move only after the player has begun the *stroke* or the backward movement of his club for the stroke, he shall incur no penalty under this Rule for playing a moving ball, but he is not exempt from any penalty incurred under the following Rules:

Ball at rest moved by player – Rule 18-2a.
Ball at rest moving after address – Rule 18-2b.
Ball at rest moving after loose impediment touched – Rule 18-2c.

(Ball purposely deflected or stopped by player, partner or caddie – see Rule 1-2.)

14-6. Ball Moving in Water

When a ball is moving in water in a *water hazard*, the player may, without penalty, make a *stroke*, but he must not delay making his stroke in order to allow the wind or current to improve the position of the ball. A ball moving in water in a water hazard may be lifted if the player elects to invoke Rule 26.

PENALTY FOR BREACH OF
RULE 14-5 or -6: Match play – Loss of hole;
Stroke play – Two strokes.

Rule 15. Wrong Ball; Substituted Ball

Definition
A **wrong ball** is any ball other than the player's:

a. *Ball in play,*
b. *Provisional ball,* or
c. Second ball played under Rule 3-3 or Rule 20-7b in stroke play.

Note: Ball in play includes a ball substituted for the ball in play whether or not such substitution is permitted.

15-1. General

A player must hole out with the ball played from the *teeing ground* unless a *Rule* permits him to substitute another ball. If a player substitutes another ball when not so permitted, that ball is not a *wrong ball*; it becomes the *ball in play* and, if the error is not corrected as provided in Rule 20-6, the player shall incur a penalty of loss of hole in match play or two strokes in stroke play. (Playing from wrong place – see Rule 20-7.)

15-2. Match Play

If a player plays a *stroke* with a *wrong ball* except in a *hazard*, he shall lose the hole.

If a player plays any strokes in a hazard with a wrong ball, there is no penalty. Strokes played in a hazard with a wrong ball do not count in the player's score. If the wrong ball belongs to another player, its owner shall place a ball on the spot from which the wrong ball was first played.

If the player and opponent exchange balls during the play of a hole, the first to play the wrong ball other than from a hazard shall lose the hole; when this cannot be determined, the hole shall be played out with the balls exchanged.

15-3. Stroke Play

If a competitor plays a *stroke* or strokes with a *wrong ball*, he shall incur a penalty of two strokes, unless the only stroke or strokes played with such ball were played when it was in a *hazard*, in which case no penalty is incurred.

The competitor must correct his mistake by playing the correct ball. If he fails to correct his mistake before he plays a stroke from the next *teeing ground* or, in the case of the last hole of the round, fails to declare his intention to correct his mistake before leaving the *putting green*, he shall be disqualified.

Strokes played by a competitor with a wrong ball do not count in his score.

If the wrong ball belongs to another competitor, its owner shall place a ball on the spot from which the wrong ball was first played.
(Lie of ball to be placed or replaced altered – see Rule 20-3b.)

THE PUTTING GREEN

Rule 16. The Putting Green

Definitions
The **putting green** is all ground of the hole being played which is specially prepared for putting or otherwise defined as such by the *Committee*. A ball is on the putting green when any part of it touches the putting green.

The **line of putt** is the line which the player wishes his ball to take after a *stroke* on the *putting green*. Except with respect to Rule 16-1e, the line of putt includes a reasonable distance on either side of the intended line. The line of putt does not extend beyond the *hole*.

A ball is **holed** when it is at rest within the circumference of the *hole* and all of it is below the level of the lip of the hole.

16-1. General
a. Touching Line of Putt

The *line of putt* must not be touched except:

(i) the player may move sand and loose soil on the *putting green* and other *loose impediments* by picking them up or by brushing them aside with his hand or a club without pressing anything down;

(ii) in *addressing the ball*, the player may place the club in front of the ball without pressing anything down;

(iii) in measuring – Rule 10-4;

(iv) in lifting the ball –Rule 16-1b;

(v) in pressing down a ball-marker;

(vi) in repairing old hole plugs or ball marks on the putting green – Rule 16-1c; and

(vii) in removing movable *obstructions* – Rule 24-1.

(Indicating line for putting on putting green – see Rule 8–2b.)

b. Lifting Ball
A ball on the *putting green* may be lifted and, if desired, cleaned. A ball so lifted shall be replaced on the spot from which it was lifted.

c. Repair of Hole Plugs, Ball Marks and Other Damage
The player may repair an old hole plug or damage to the *putting green* caused by the impact of a ball, whether or not the player's ball lies on the putting green. If a ball or ball-marker is accidentally moved in the process of such repair, the ball or ball-marker shall be replaced, without penalty. Any other damage to the putting green shall not be repaired if it might assist the player in his subsequent play of the hole.

d. Testing Surface
During the play of a hole, a player shall not test the surface of the *putting green* by rolling a ball or roughening or scraping the surface.

e. Standing Astride or on Line of Putt
The player shall not make a *stroke* on the *putting green* from a *stance* astride, or with either foot touching, the *line of putt* or an extension of that line behind the ball.

f. Playing Stroke While Another Ball in Motion
The player shall not play a *stroke* while another ball is in motion after a stroke from the *putting green*, except that, if a player does so, he incurs no penalty if it was his turn to play.

(Lifting ball interfering with or assisting play while another ball in motion – see Rule 22.)

PENALTY FOR BREACH OF RULE 16-1:
Match play – Loss of hole;
Stroke play – Two strokes.
(Position of caddie or partner - see Rule 14-2.)
(Wrong putting green - see Rule 25-3.)

16-2. Ball Overhanging Hole
When any part of the ball overhangs the lip of the *hole*, the player is allowed enough time to reach the hole without unreasonable delay and an additional ten seconds to determine whether the ball is at rest. If by then the ball has not fallen into the hole, it is deemed to be at rest. If the ball subsequently falls into the hole, the player is deemed to have holed out with his last stroke, and he shall add a penalty stroke to his score for the hole; otherwise there is no penalty under this Rule.

(Undue delay – see Rule 6-7.)

Rule 17. The Flagstick

Definition
The **flagstick** is a movable straight indicator, with or without bunting or other material attached, centred in the hole to show its position. It shall be circular in cross-section.

17-1. Flagstick Attended, Removed or Held Up
Before and during the *stroke*, the player may have the *flagstick* attended, removed or held up to indicate the position of the *hole*. This may be done only on the authority of the player before he plays his stroke.

If, prior to the stroke, the flagstick is attended, removed or held up by anyone with the player's knowledge and no objection is made, the player shall be deemed to have authorised it. If anyone attends or holds up the flagstick or stands near the hole while a stroke is being played, he shall be deemed to be attending the flagstick until the ball comes to rest.

17-2. Unauthorised Attendance
a. Match Play
In match play, an opponent or his *caddie* shall not, without the authority or prior knowledge of the player, attend, remove or hold up the *flagstick* while the player is making a *stroke* or his ball is in motion.

b. Stroke Play
In stroke play, if a *fellow-competitor* or his *caddie* attends, removes or holds up the *flagstick* without the competitor's authority or prior knowledge while the competitor is making a *stroke* or his ball is in motion, the fellow-competitor shall incur the penalty for breach of this Rule. In such circumstances, if the competitor's ball strikes the flagstick, the person attending it or anything carried by him, the competitor incurs no penalty and the ball shall be played as it lies, except that, if the stroke was played from the *putting green*, the stroke shall be cancelled, the ball replaced and the stroke replayed.

PENALTY FOR BREACH OF
RULE 17-1 or -2: Match play – Loss of hole;
Stroke play – Two strokes.

17-3. Ball Striking Flagstick or Attendant

The player's ball shall not strike:

a. The *flagstick* when attended, removed or held up by the player, his *partner* or either of their *caddies*, or by another person with the player's authority or prior knowledge; or

b. The player's *caddie*, his partner or his partner's caddie when attending the *flagstick*, or another person attending the flagstick with the player's authority or prior knowledge or anything carried by any such person; or

c. The *flagstick* in the hole, unattended, when the ball has been played from the *putting green*.

PENALTY FOR BREACH OF RULE 17-3:
Match play – Loss of hole;
Stroke play – Two strokes,
and the ball shall be played as it lies.

17-4. Ball Resting Against Flagstick

If the ball rests against the *flagstick* when it is in the *hole*, the player or another person authorised by him may move or remove the flagstick and if the ball falls into the hole, the player shall be deemed to have holed out with his last stroke; otherwise the ball, if *moved*, shall be placed on the lip of the hole, without penalty.

BALL MOVED, DEFLECTED OR STOPPED

Rule 18. Ball at Rest Moved

Definitions

A ball is deemed to have **moved** if it leaves its position and comes to rest in any other place.

An **outside agency** is any agency not part of the match or, in stroke play, not part of the competitor's *side*, and includes a *referee*, a *marker*, an *observer* and a *forecaddie*. Neither wind nor water is an outside agency.

Equipment is anything used, worn or carried by or for the player except any ball he has played at the hole being played and any small object, such as a coin or a tee, when used to mark the position of a ball or the extent of an area in which a ball is to be dropped. Equipment includes a golf cart, whether or not motorised. If such a cart is shared by two or more players, the cart and everything in it are deemed to be the equipment of the player whose ball is involved except that, when the cart is being moved by one of the players sharing it, the cart and everything in it are deemed to be that player's equipment.

Note: A ball played at the hole being played is equipment when it has been lifted and not put back into play.

A player has **addressed the ball** when he has taken his *stance* and has also grounded his club, except that in a *hazard* a player has addressed the ball when he has taken his stance.

Taking the **stance** consists in a player placing his feet in position for and preparatory to making a *stroke*.

18-1. By Outside Agency

If a ball at rest is moved by an *outside agency*, the player shall incur no penalty and the ball shall be replaced before the player plays another *stroke*.

(Player's ball at rest moved by another ball – see Rule 18–5.)

18-2. By Player, Partner, Caddie or Equipment

a. General

When a player's ball is *in play*, if:

(i) the player, his *partner* or either of their *caddies* lifts or *moves* it, touches it purposely (except with a club in the act of addressing it) or causes it to *move* except as permitted by a *Rule*, or

(ii) *equipment* of the player or his *partner* causes the ball to *move*,

the player shall incur a penalty stroke. The ball shall be replaced unless the movement of the ball occurs after the player has begun his swing and he does not discontinue his swing.

Under the *Rules* no penalty is incurred if a player accidentally causes his ball to move in the following circumstances:

In measuring to determine which ball farther from hole – Rule 10-4

In searching for covered ball in *hazard* or for ball in an *abnormal ground condition* – Rule 12-1

In the process of repairing hole plug or ball mark – Rule 16-1c

In the process of removing *loose impediment* on *putting green* – Rule 18-2c

In the process of lifting ball under a Rule – Rule 20-1

In the process of placing or replacing ball under a Rule – Rule 20-3a

In removal of movable *obstruction* – Rule 24-1.

b. Ball Moving After Address

If a player's *ball in play moves* after he has *addressed* it (other than as a result of a *stroke*), the player shall be deemed to have moved the ball and shall incur a penalty stroke. The player shall replace the ball unless the movement of the ball occurs after he has begun his swing and he does not discontinue his swing.

c. Ball Moving After Loose Impediment Touched

Through the green, if the ball *moves* after any *loose impediment*, lying within a club-length of it has been touched by the player, his *partner* or either of their *caddies* and before the player has *addressed* it, the player shall be deemed to have moved the ball and shall incur a penalty stroke. The player shall replace the ball unless the movement of the ball occurs after he has begun his swing and he does not discontinue his swing.

On the *putting green*, if the ball or the ball-marker moves in the process of removing any loose impediment, the ball or the ball-marker shall be replaced. There is no penalty provided the movement of the ball or the ball-marker is directly attributable to the removal of the loose impediment. Otherwise, the player shall incur a penalty stroke under Rule 18-2a or 20-1.

18-3. By Opponent, Caddie or Equipment in Match Play
a. During Search

If, during search for a player's ball, the ball is *moved* by an opponent, his *caddie* or his *equipment*, no penalty is incurred and the player shall replace the ball.

b. Other Than During Search

If, other than during search for a ball, the ball is touched or *moved* by an opponent, his *caddie* or his *equipment*, except as otherwise provided in the *Rules*, the opponent shall incur a penalty stroke. The player shall replace the ball.

(Ball moved in measuring to determine which ball farther from the hole – see Rule 10-4.)

(Playing a wrong ball – see Rule 15-2.)

18-4. By Fellow-Competitor, Caddie or Equipment in Stroke Play

If a competitor's ball is *moved* by a *fellow-competitor*, his *caddie* or his *equipment*, no penalty is incurred. The competitor shall replace his ball.

(Playing a wrong ball – see Rule 15-3.)

18-5. By Another Ball

If a *ball in play* and at rest is *moved* by another ball in motion after a *stroke*, the moved ball shall be replaced.

*PENALTY FOR BREACH OF RULE:
  Match play – Loss of hole;
  Stroke play – Two strokes.

*If a player who is required to replace a ball fails to do so, he shall incur the general penalty for breach of Rule 18 but no additional penalty under Rule 18 shall be applied.

Note 1: If a ball to be replaced under this Rule is not immediately recoverable, another ball may be substituted.

Note 2: If it is impossible to determine the spot on which a ball is to be placed, see Rule 20-3c.

Rule 19. Ball in Motion Deflected or Stopped

Definitions

An **outside agency** is any agency not part of the match or, in stroke play, not part of the com-

petitor's side, and includes a *referee*, a *marker*, an *observer* and a *forecaddie*. Neither wind nor water is an outside agency.

Equipment is anything used, worn or carried by or for the player except any ball he has played at the hole being played and any small object, such as a coin or a tee, when used to mark the position of a ball or the extent of an area in which a ball is to be dropped. Equipment includes a golf cart, whether or not motorised. If such a cart is shared by two or more players, the cart and everything in it are deemed to be the equipment of the player whose ball is involved except that, when the cart is being moved by one of the players sharing it, the cart and everything in it are deemed to be that player's equipment.

Note: A ball played at the hole being played is equipment when it has been lifted and not put back into play.

19-1. By Outside Agency

If a ball in motion is accidentally deflected or stopped by any *outside agency*, it is a *rub of the green*, no penalty is incurred and the ball shall be played as it lies except:

a. If a ball in motion after a *stroke* other than on the *putting green* comes to rest in or on any moving or animate *outside agency*, the player shall, *through the green* or in a *hazard*, drop the ball, or on the putting green place the ball, as near as possible to the spot where the outside agency was when the ball came to rest in or on it, and

b. If a ball in motion after a *stroke* on the *putting green* is deflected or stopped by, or comes to rest in or on, any moving or animate *outside agency* except a worm or an insect, the stroke shall be cancelled, the ball replaced and the stroke replayed.

If the ball is not immediately recoverable, another ball may be substituted.

(Player's ball deflected or stopped by another ball – see Rule 19-5.)

Note: If the *referee* or the *Committee* determines that a player's ball has been purposely deflected or stopped by an *outside agency*, Rule 1-4 applies to the player. If the outside agency is a *fellow-competitor* or his *caddie*, Rule 1-2 applies to the fellow-competitor.

19-2. By Player, Partner, Caddie or Equipment
a. Match Play

If a player's ball is accidentally deflected or stopped by himself, his *partner* or either of their *caddies* or *equipment*, he shall lose the hole.

b. Stroke Play

If a competitor's ball is accidentally deflected or stopped by himself, his *partner* or either of their *caddies* or *equipment*, the competitor shall incur a penalty of two strokes. The ball shall be played as it lies, except when it comes to rest in or on the competitor's, his partner's or either of their caddies' clothes or equipment, in which case the competitor shall *through the green* or in a *hazard* drop the ball, or on the *putting green* place the ball, as near as possible to where the article was when the ball came to rest in or on it.

Exception: Dropped ball – see Rule 20-2a.

(Ball purposely deflected or stopped by player, partner or caddie – see Rule 1-2.)

19-3. By Opponent, Caddie or Equipment in Match Play

If a player's ball is accidentally deflected or stopped by an opponent, his *caddie* or his *equipment*, no penalty is incurred. The player may play the ball as it lies or, before another *stroke* is played by either side, cancel the stroke and play a ball without penalty as nearly as possible at the spot from which the original ball was last played (see Rule 20-5).

If the ball has come to rest in or on the opponent's or his caddie's clothes or equipment, the player may *through the green* or in a *hazard* drop the ball, or on the *putting green* place the ball, as near as possible to where the article was when the ball came to rest in or on it.

Exception: Ball striking person attending flagstick – see Rule 17-3b.

(Ball purposely deflected or stopped by opponent or caddie – see Rule 1-2.)

19-4. By Fellow-Competitor, Caddie or Equipment in Stroke Play

See Rule 19-1 regarding ball deflected by *outside agency*.

19-5. By Another Ball
a. At Rest

If a player's ball in motion after a *stroke* is deflected or stopped by a *ball in play* and at rest, the player shall play his ball as it lies.

In match play, no penalty is incurred. In stroke play, there is no penalty unless both balls lay on the *putting green* prior to the stroke, in which case the player incurs a penalty of two strokes.

b. In Motion

If a player's ball in motion after a *stroke* is deflected or stopped by another ball in motion after a stroke, the player shall play his ball as it lies. There is no penalty unless the player was in breach of Rule 16-1f, in which case he shall incur the penalty for breach of that Rule.

Exception: If the player's ball is in motion after a *stroke* on the *putting green* and the other ball in motion is an *outside agency* – see Rule 19-1b.

PENALTY FOR BREACH OF RULE:
Match play – Loss of hole;
Stroke play – Two strokes.

RELIEF SITUATIONS AND PROCEDURE

Rule 20. Lifting, Dropping and Placing; Playing from Wrong Place

20-1. Lifting and Marking

A ball to be lifted under the *Rules* may be lifted by the player, his partner or another person authorised by the player. In any such case, the player shall be responsible for any breach of the Rules.

The position of the ball shall be marked before it is lifted under a Rule which requires it to be replaced. If it is not marked, the player shall incur a penalty of one stroke and the ball shall be replaced. If it is not replaced, the player shall incur the general penalty for breach of this Rule but no additional penalty under Rule 20-1 shall be applied.

If a ball or ball-marker is accidentally moved in the process of lifting the ball under a Rule or marking its position, the ball or the ball-marker shall be replaced. There is no penalty provided the movement of the ball or the ball-marker is directly attributable to the specific act of marking the position of or lifting the ball. Otherwise, the player shall incur a penalty stroke under this Rule or Rule 18-2a.

Exception: If a player incurs a penalty for failing to act in accordance with Rule 5-3 or 12-2, no additional penalty under Rule 20-1 shall be applied.

Note: The position of a ball to be lifted should be marked by placing a ball-marker, a small coin or other similar object immediately behind the ball. If the ball-marker interferes with the play, *stance* or *stroke* of another player, it should be placed one or more clubhead-lengths to one side.

20-2. Dropping and Re-Dropping
a. By Whom and How

A ball to be dropped under the *Rules* shall be dropped by the player himself. He shall stand erect, hold the ball at shoulder height and arm's length and drop it. If a ball is dropped by any other person or in any other manner and the error is not corrected as provided in Rule 20-6, the player shall incur a penalty stroke.

If the ball touches the player, his partner, either of their *caddies* or their *equipment* before or after it strikes a part of the *course*, the ball shall be re-dropped, without penalty. There is no limit to the number of times a ball shall be re-dropped in such circumstances.

(Taking action to influence position or movement of ball – see Rule 1-2.)

b. Where to Drop

When a ball is to be dropped as near as possible to a specific spot, it shall be dropped not nearer the hole than the specific spot which, if it is not precisely known to the player, shall be estimated.

A ball when dropped must first strike a part of the *course* where the applicable *Rule* requires it to be dropped. If it is not so dropped, Rules 20-6 and -7 apply.

c. When to Re-Drop
A dropped ball shall be re-dropped without penalty if it:

(i) rolls into and comes to rest in a *hazard*;
(ii) rolls out of and comes to rest outside a *hazard*;
(iii) rolls onto and comes to rest on a *putting green*;
(iv) rolls and comes to rest *out of bounds*;
(v) rolls to and comes to rest in a position where there is interference by the condition from which relief was taken under Rule 24-2b (immovable obstruction), Rule 25-1 (abnormal ground conditions), Rule 25-3 (wrong putting green) or a Local Rule (Rule 33-8a) or rolls back into the pitch-mark from which it was lifted under Rule 25-2 (embedded ball);
(vi) rolls and comes to rest more than two club-lengths from where it first struck a part of the course; or
(vii) rolls and comes to rest nearer the hole than:
  (a) its original position or estimated position (see Rule 20-2b) unless otherwise permitted by the *Rules*; or
  (b) the nearest point of relief or maximum available relief (Rule 24-2, 25-1 or 25-3); or
  (c) the point where the original ball last crossed the margin of the *water hazard* or *lateral water hazard* (Rule 26-1).

If the ball when re-dropped rolls into any position listed above, it shall be placed as near as possible to the spot where it first struck a part of the course when re-dropped.

If a ball to be re-dropped or placed under this Rule is not immediately recoverable, another ball may be substituted.

Note: If a ball when dropped or re-dropped comes to rest and subsequently *moves*, the ball shall be played as it lies, unless the provisions of any other *Rule* apply.

20-3. Placing and Replacing
a. By Whom and Where
A ball to be placed under the *Rules* shall be placed by the player or his partner. If a ball is to be replaced, the player, his partner or the person who lifted or moved it shall place it on the spot from which it was lifted or moved. In any such case, the player shall be responsible for any breach of the Rules.

If a ball or ball-marker is accidentally *moved* in the process of placing or replacing the ball, the ball or the ball-marker shall be replaced. There is no penalty provided the movement of the ball or the ball-marker is directly attributable to the specific act of placing or replacing the ball or removing the ball-marker. Otherwise, the player shall incur a penalty stroke under Rule 18-2a or 20-1.

b. Lie of Ball to be Placed or Replaced Altered
If the original lie of a ball to be placed or replaced has been altered:

(i) except in a *hazard*, the ball shall be placed in the nearest lie most similar to the original lie which is not more than one club-length from the original lie, not nearer the hole and not in a *hazard*;
(ii) in a *water hazard*, the ball shall be placed in accordance with Clause (i) above, except that the ball must be placed in the water hazard;
(iii) in a *bunker*, the original lie shall be recreated as nearly as possible and the ball shall be placed in that lie.

c. Spot Not Determinable
If it is impossible to determine the spot where the ball is to be placed or replaced:

(i) *through the green*, the ball shall be dropped as near as possible to the place where it lay but not in a *hazard* or on a *putting green*;
(ii) in a *hazard*, the ball shall be dropped in the hazard as near as possible to the place where it lay;
(iii) on the *putting green*, the ball shall be placed as near as possible to the place where it lay but not in a *hazard*.

d. Ball Fails to Come to Rest on Spot
If a ball when placed fails to come to rest on the spot on which it was placed, it shall be replaced without penalty. If it still fails to come to rest on that spot:

(i) except in a *hazard*, it shall be placed at the nearest spot where it can be placed at rest which is not nearer the hole and not in a hazard;
(ii) in a hazard, it shall be placed in the hazard at the nearest spot where it can be placed at rest which is not nearer the hole.

If a ball when placed comes to rest on the spot on which it is placed, and it subsequently *moves*, there is no penalty and the ball shall be played as it lies, unless the provisions of any other *Rule* apply.

PENALTY FOR BREACH OF RULE 20-1,
-2 or -3: Match play – Loss of hole;
Stroke play – Two strokes.

20-4. When Ball Dropped or Placed Is in Play
If the player's *ball in play* has been lifted, it is again in play when dropped or placed.

A substituted ball becomes the ball in play when it has been dropped or placed.
(Ball incorrectly substituted – see Rule 15-1.)
(Lifting ball incorrectly substituted, dropped or placed – see Rule 20-6.)

20-5. Playing Next Stroke from Where Previous Stroke Played

When, under the *Rules*, a player elects or is required to play his next *stroke* from where a previous stroke was played, he shall proceed as follows: if the stroke is to be played from the *teeing ground*, the ball to be played shall be played from anywhere within the teeing ground and may be teed; if the stroke is to be played from *through the green* or a *hazard*, it shall be dropped; if the stroke is to be played on the *putting green*, it shall be placed.

PENALTY FOR BREACH OF RULE 20-5:
Match play – Loss of hole;
Stroke play – Two strokes.

20-6. Lifting Ball Incorrectly Substituted, Dropped or Placed

A ball incorrectly substituted, dropped or placed in a wrong place or otherwise not in accordance with the *Rules* but not played may be lifted, without penalty, and the player shall then proceed correctly.

20-7. Playing from Wrong Place

For a ball played from outside the *teeing ground* or from a wrong teeing ground – see Rule 11-4 and -5.

a. Match Play

If a player plays a *stroke* with a ball which has been dropped or placed in a wrong place, he shall lose the hole.

b. Stroke Play

If a competitor plays a *stroke* with his *ball in play* (i) which has been dropped or placed in a wrong place or (ii) which has been *moved* and not replaced in a case where the *Rules* require replacement, he shall, provided a serious breach has not occurred, incur the penalty prescribed by the applicable Rule and play out the hole with the ball.

If, after playing from a wrong place, a competitor becomes aware of that fact and believes that a serious breach may be involved, he may, provided he has not played a stroke from the next *teeing ground* or, in the case of the last hole of the round, left the *putting green*, declare that he will play out the hole with a second ball dropped or placed in accordance with the Rules. The competitor shall report the facts to the *Committee* before returning his score card; if he fails to do so, he shall be disqualified. The Committee shall determine whether a serious breach of the Rule occurred. If so, the score with the second ball shall count and the competitor shall add two penalty strokes to his score with that ball.

If a serious breach has occurred and the competitor has failed to correct it as prescribed above, he shall be disqualified.

Note: If a competitor plays a second ball, *penalty strokes* incurred solely by playing the ball ruled not to count and *strokes* subsequently taken with that ball shall be disregarded.

Rule 21. Cleaning Ball

A ball on the *putting green* may be cleaned when lifted under Rule 16-1b. Elsewhere, a ball may be cleaned when lifted except when it has been lifted:

a. To determine if it is unfit for play (Rule 5-3);

b. For identification (Rule 12-2), in which case it may be cleaned only to the extent necessary for identification; or

c. Because it is interfering with or assisting play (Rule 22).

If a player cleans his ball during play of a hole except as provided in this Rule, he shall incur a penalty of one stroke and the ball, if lifted, shall be replaced.

If a player who is required to replace a ball fails to do so, he shall incur the penalty for breach of Rule 20-3a, but no additional penalty under Rule 21 shall be applied.

Exception: If a player incurs a penalty for failing to act in accordance with Rule 5-3, 12-2 or 22, no additional penalty under Rule 21 shall be applied.

Rule 22. Ball Interfering With or Assisting Play

Any player may:

a. Lift his ball if he considers that the ball might assist any other player or

b. Have any other ball lifted if he considers that the ball might interfere with his play or assist the play of any other player,

but this may not be done while another ball is in motion. In stroke play, a player required to lift his ball may play first rather than lift. A ball lifted under this Rule shall be replaced.

PENALTY FOR BREACH OF RULE:
Match play – Loss of hole;
Stroke play – Two strokes.

Note: Except on the *putting green*, the ball may not be cleaned when lifted under this Rule – see Rule 21.

Rule 23. Loose Impediments

Definition

Loose impediments are natural objects such as stones, leaves, twigs, branches and the like, dung, worms and insects and casts or heaps made by them, provided they are not fixed or growing, are not solidly embedded and do not adhere to the ball.

Sand and loose soil are loose impediments on the *putting green* but not elsewhere.

Snow and natural ice, other than frost, are either *casual water* or loose impediments, at the option of the player. Manufactured ice is an *obstruction*.

Dew and frost are not loose impediments.

23-1. Relief

Except when both the *loose impediment* and the ball lie in or touch the same *hazard,* any loose impediment may be removed without penalty. If the ball *moves*, see Rule 18-2c.

When a ball is in motion, a loose impediment which might influence the movement of the ball shall not be removed.

PENALTY FOR BREACH OF RULE:
Match play – Loss of hole;
Stroke play – Two strokes.

(Searching for ball in hazard – see Rule 12-1.)
(Touching line of putt – see Rule 16-1a.)

Rule 24. Obstructions

Definitions

The **nearest point of relief** is the reference point for taking relief without penalty from interference by an immovable *obstruction* (Rule 24-2), an *abnormal ground condition* (Rule 25-1) or a *wrong putting green* (Rule 25-3).

It is the point on the *course,* nearest to where the ball lies, which is not nearer the hole and at which, if the ball were so positioned, no interference (as defined) would exist.

Note: The player should determine his nearest point of relief by using the club with which he expects to play his next stroke to simulate the address position and swing for such stroke.

An **obstruction** is anything artificial, including the artificial surfaces and sides of roads and paths and manufactured ice, except:

a. Objects defining *out of bounds,* such as walls, fences, stakes and railings;

b. Any part of an immovable artificial object which is *out of bounds*; and

c. Any construction declared by the *Committee* to be an integral part of the course.

An obstruction is a movable obstruction if it may be moved without unreasonable effort, without unduly delaying play and without causing damage. Otherwise, it is an immovable obstruction.

Note: The *Committee* may make a Local Rule declaring a movable obstruction to be an immovable obstruction.

24-1. Movable Obstruction

A player may obtain relief from a movable *obstruction* as follows:

a. If the ball does not lie in or on the *obstruction*, the obstruction may be removed. If the ball *moves*, it shall be replaced, and there is no penalty provided that the movement of the ball is directly attributable to the removal of the obstruction. Otherwise, Rule 18-2a applies.

b. If the ball lies in or on the *obstruction*, the ball may be lifted, without penalty, and the obstruction removed. The ball shall *through the green* or in a *hazard* be dropped, or on the *putting green* be placed, as near as possible to the spot directly under the place where the ball lay in or on the obstruction, but not nearer the hole.

The ball may be cleaned when lifted under Rule 24-1.

When a ball is in motion, an obstruction which might influence the movement of the ball, other than an attended *flagstick* or *equipment* of the players, shall not be removed.

(Exerting influence on the ball – see Rule 1-2.)

Note: If a ball to be dropped or placed under this Rule is not immediately recoverable, another ball may be substituted.

24-2. Immovable Obstruction
a. Interference

Interference by an immovable *obstruction* occurs when a ball lies in or on the obstruction, or so close to the obstruction that the obstruction interferes with the player's *stance* or the area of his intended swing. If the player's ball lies on the *putting green*, interference also occurs if an immovable obstruction on the putting green intervenes on his *line of putt*. Otherwise, intervention on the *line of play* is not, of itself, interference under this Rule.

b. Relief

Except when the ball is in a *water hazard* or a *lateral water hazard*, a player may obtain relief from interference by an immovable *obstruction*, without penalty, as follows:

(i) Through the Green: If the ball lies *through the green*, the *nearest point of relief* shall be determined which is not in a *hazard* or on a *putting green*. The player shall lift the ball and drop it within one club-length of and not nearer the hole than the nearest point of relief, on a part of the *course* which avoids interference (as defined) by the immovable *obstruction* and is not in a hazard or on a putting green.

(ii) In a Bunker: If the ball is in a *bunker,* the player shall lift and drop the ball in accordance with Clause (i) above, except that the *nearest point of relief* must be in the bunker and the ball must be dropped in the bunker.

(iii) On the Putting Green: If the ball lies on the *putting green*, the player shall lift the ball and place it at the nearest *point of relief* which is not in a *hazard*. The nearest point of relief may be off the putting green.

The ball may be cleaned when lifted under Rule 24-2b.

(Ball rolling to a position where there is interference by the condition from which relief was taken – see Rule 20-2c(v).)

Exception: A player may not obtain relief under Rule 24–2b if (a) it is clearly unreasonable for him to play a stroke because of interference by anything other than an immovable *obstruction* or (b) interference by an immovable obstruction would occur only through use of an unnecessarily abnormal *stance*, swing or direction of play.

Note 1: If a ball is in a *water hazard* (including a *lateral water hazard*), the player is not entitled to relief without penalty from interference by an immovable *obstruction*. The player shall play the ball as it lies or proceed under Rule 26-1.

Note 2: If a ball to be dropped or placed under this Rule is not immediately recoverable, another ball may be substituted.

Note 3: The *Committee* may make a Local Rule stating that the player must determine the *nearest point of relief* without crossing over, through or under the *obstruction*.

c. Ball Lost
It is a question of fact whether a ball lost after having been struck toward an immovable *obstruction* is lost in the obstruction. In order to treat the ball as lost in the obstruction, there must be reasonable evidence to that effect. In the absence of such evidence, the ball must be treated as a *lost ball* and Rule 27 applies.

If a ball is lost in an immovable obstruction, the spot where the ball last entered the obstruction shall be determined and, for the purpose of applying this Rule, the ball shall be deemed to lie at this spot.

(i) Through the Green: If the ball last entered the immovable *obstruction* at a spot *through the green*, the player may substitute another ball without penalty and take relief as prescribed in Rule 24-2b(i).

(ii) In a Bunker: If the ball last entered the immovable *obstruction* at a spot in a *bunker*, the player may substitute another ball without penalty and take relief as prescribed in Rule 24-2b(ii).

(iii) In a Water Hazard (including a Lateral Water Hazard): If the ball last entered the immovable *obstruction* at a spot in a *water hazard*, the player is not entitled to relief without penalty. The player shall proceed under Rule 26-1.

(iv) On the Putting Green: If the ball last entered the immovable *obstruction* at a spot on the *putting green*, the player may substitute another ball without penalty and take relief as prescribed in Rule 24-2b(iii).

PENALTY FOR BREACH OF RULE:
Match play – Loss of hole;
Stroke play – Two strokes.

Rule 25. Abnormal Ground Conditions, Embedded Ball and Wrong Putting Green

Definitions
An **abnormal ground condition** is any *casual water*, *ground under repair* or hole, cast or runway on the *course* made by a *burrowing animal*, a reptile or a bird.

A **burrowing animal** is an animal that makes a hole for habitation or shelter, such as a rabbit, mole, ground hog, gopher or salamander.

Note: A hole made by a non-burrowing animal, such as a dog, is not an *abnormal ground condition* unless marked or declared as *ground under repair*.

Casual water is any temporary accumulation of water on the *course* which is visible before or after the player takes his *stance* and is not in a *water hazard*. Snow and natural ice, other than frost, are either casual water or *loose impediments*, at the option of the player. Manufactured ice is an *obstruction*. Dew and frost are not casual water. A ball is in casual water when it lies in or any part of it touches the casual water.

Ground under repair is any part of the *course* so marked by order of the *Committee* or so declared by its authorised representative. It includes material piled for removal and a hole made by a greenkeeper, even if not so marked.

All ground and any grass, bush, tree or other growing thing within the ground under repair is part of the ground under repair. The margin of ground under repair extends vertically downwards, but not upwards. Stakes and lines defining ground under repair are in such ground. Such stakes are *obstructions*. A ball is in ground under repair when it lies in or any part of it touches ground under repair.

Note 1: Grass cuttings and other material left on the *course* which have been abandoned and are not intended to be removed are not ground under repair unless so marked.

Note 2: The *Committee* may make a Local Rule prohibiting play from ground under repair or an environmentally-sensitive area which has been defined as ground under repair.

The **nearest point of relief** is the reference point for taking relief without penalty from interference by an immovable *obstruction* (Rule 24-2), an *abnormal ground condition* (Rule 25-1) or a *wrong putting green* (Rule 25-3).

It is the point on the *course*, nearest to where the ball lies, which is not nearer the hole and at which, if the ball were so positioned, no interference (as defined) would exist.

Note: The player should determine his nearest point of relief by using the club with which he expects to play his next stroke to simulate the address position and swing for such stroke.

A **wrong putting green** is any *putting green* other than that of the hole being played. Unless otherwise prescribed by the *Committee*, this term includes a practice putting green or pitching green on the *course*.

25-1. Abnormal Ground Conditions
a. Interference
Interference by an *abnormal ground condition* occurs when a ball lies in or touches the condition or when such a condition interferes with the player's *stance* or the area of his intended swing. If the player's ball lies on the *putting green*, interference also occurs if such condition on the putting green intervenes on his *line of putt*. Otherwise, intervention on the *line of play* is not, of itself, interference under this Rule.

Note: The *Committee* may make a Local Rule denying the player relief from interference with his *stance* by an *abnormal ground condition*.

b. Relief
Except when the ball is in a *water hazard* or a *lateral water hazard*, a player may obtain relief from interference by an *abnormal ground condition* as follows:

(i) **Through the Green:** If the ball lies *through the green*, the *nearest point of relief* shall be determined which is not in a *hazard* or on a *putting green*. The player shall lift the ball and drop it without penalty within one club-length of and not nearer the hole than the nearest point of relief, on a part of the *course* which avoids interference (as defined) by the condition and is not in a *hazard* or on a putting green.

(ii) **In a Bunker:** If the ball is in a *bunker*, the player shall lift and drop the ball either:

  (a) Without penalty, in accordance with Clause (i) above, except that the *nearest point of relief* must be in the bunker and the ball must be dropped in the bunker, or if complete relief is impossible, in the bunker as near as possible to the spot where the ball lay, but not nearer the hole, on a part of the *course* which affords maximum available relief from the condition; or

  (b) Under penalty of one stroke, outside the bunker keeping the point where the ball lay directly between the hole and the spot on which the ball is dropped, with no limit to how far behind the bunker the ball may be dropped.

(iii) **On the Putting Green:** If the ball lies on the *putting green*, the player shall lift the ball and place it without penalty at the *nearest point of relief* which is not in a *hazard*, or if complete relief is impossible, at the nearest position to where it lay which affords maximum available relief from the condition, but not nearer the hole nor in a *hazard*. The nearest point of relief or maximum available relief may be off the putting green.

The ball may be cleaned when lifted under Rule 25-1b.

(Ball rolling to a position where there is interference by the condition from which relief was taken – see Rule 20-2c(v).)

Exception: A player may not obtain relief under Rule 25-1b if (a) it is clearly unreasonable for him to play a stroke because of interference by anything other than an *abnormal ground condition* or (b) interference by such a condition would occur only through use of an unnecessarily abnormal *stance*, swing or direction of play.

Note 1: If a ball is in a *water hazard* (including a *lateral water hazard*), the player is not entitled to relief without penalty from interference by an *abnormal ground condition*. The player shall play the ball as it lies (unless prohibited by Local Rule) or proceed under Rule 26-1.

Note 2: If a ball to be dropped or placed under this Rule is not immediately recoverable, another ball may be substituted.

c. Ball Lost
It is a question of fact whether a ball lost after having been struck toward an *abnormal ground condition* is lost in such condition. In order to treat the ball as lost in the abnormal ground condition, there must be reasonable evidence to that effect. In the absence of such evidence, the ball must be treated as a *lost ball* and Rule 27 applies.

If a ball is lost in an abnormal ground condition, the spot where the ball last entered the condition shall be determined and, for the purposes of applying this Rule, the ball shall be deemed to lie at this spot.

(i) **Through the Green:** If the ball last entered the *abnormal ground condition* at a spot *through the green*, the player may substitute another ball without penalty and take relief as prescribed in Rule 25-1b(i).

(ii) **In a Bunker:** If the ball last entered the *abnormal ground condition* at a spot in a *bunker*, the player may substitute another ball without penalty and take relief as prescribed in Rule 25-1b(ii).

(iii) **In a Water Hazard (including a Lateral Water Hazard):** If the ball last entered the *abnormal ground condition* at a spot in a *water hazard*, the player is not entitled to relief without penalty. The player shall proceed under Rule 26-1.

(iv) On the Putting Green: If the ball last entered the *abnormal ground condition* at a spot on the *putting green*, the player may substitute another ball without penalty and take relief as prescribed in Rule 25-1b(iii).

25-2. Embedded Ball
A ball embedded in its own pitch-mark in the ground in any closely-mown area *through the green* may be lifted, cleaned and dropped, without penalty, as near as possible to the spot where it lay but not nearer the hole. The ball when dropped must first strike a part of the *course* through the green. 'Closely-mown area' means any area of the course, including paths through the rough, cut to fairway height or less.

25-3. Wrong Putting Green
a. Interference
Interference by a *wrong putting green* occurs when a ball is on the wrong putting green.

Interference to a player's *stance* or the area of his intended swing is not, of itself, interference under this Rule.

b. Relief
If a player has interference by a *wrong putting green*, the player must take relief, without penalty, as follows:

The *nearest point of relief* shall be determined which is not in a *hazard* or on a *putting green*. The player shall lift the ball and drop it within one club-length of and not nearer the hole than the nearest point of relief, on a part of the *course* which avoids interference (as defined) by the wrong putting green and is not in a hazard or on a putting green. The ball may be cleaned when so lifted.

PENALTY FOR BREACH OF RULE:
  Match play – Loss of hole;
  Stroke play – Two strokes.

Rule 26. Water Hazards (including Lateral Water Hazards)

Definitions
A **water hazard** is any sea, lake, pond, river, ditch, surface drainage ditch or other open water course (whether or not containing water) and anything of a similar nature.

All ground or water within the margin of a water hazard is part of the water hazard. The margin of a water hazard extends vertically upwards and downwards. Stakes and lines defining the margins of water hazards are in the hazards. Such stakes are *obstructions*. A ball is in a water hazard when it lies in or any part of it touches the water hazard.

Note 1: Water hazards (other than *lateral water hazards*) should be defined by yellow stakes or lines.

Note 2: The *Committee* may make a Local Rule prohibiting play from an environmentally-sensitive area which has been defined as a water hazard.

A **lateral water hazard** is a *water hazard* or that part of a water hazard so situated that it is not possible or is deemed by the *Committee* to be impracticable to drop a ball behind the water hazard in accordance with Rule 26-1b.

That part of a water hazard to be played as a lateral water hazard should be distinctively marked. A ball is in a lateral water hazard when it lies in or any part of it touches the lateral water hazard.

Note 1: Lateral water hazards should be defined by red stakes or lines.

Note 2: The *Committee* may make a Local Rule prohibiting play from an environmentally-sensitive area which has been defined as a lateral water hazard.

Note 3: The Committee may define a lateral water hazard as a water hazard.

26-1. Ball in Water Hazard
It is a question of fact whether a ball lost after having been struck toward a *water hazard* is lost inside or outside the hazard. In order to treat the ball as lost in the hazard, there must be reasonable evidence that the ball lodged in it. In the absence of such evidence, the ball must be treated as a *lost ball* and Rule 27 applies.

If a ball is in or is lost in a water hazard (whether the ball lies in water or not), the player may under penalty of one stroke:

a. Play a ball as nearly as possible at the spot from which the original ball was last played (see Rule 20-5); or

b. Drop a ball behind the water hazard, keeping the point at which the original ball last crossed the margin of the water hazard directly between the hole and the spot on which the ball is dropped, with no limit to how far behind the water hazard the ball may be dropped; or

c. As additional options available only if the ball last crossed the margin of a lateral water hazard, drop a ball outside the water hazard within two club-lengths of and not nearer the hole than (i) the point where the original ball last crossed the margin of the water hazard or (ii) a point on the opposite margin of the water hazard equidistant from the hole.

The ball may be cleaned when lifted under this Rule.

(Ball moving in water in a water hazard – see Rule 14-6.)

26-2. Ball Played Within Water Hazard
a. Ball Comes to Rest in the Hazard
If a ball played from within a *water hazard* comes to rest in the same hazard after the *stroke*, the player may:

(i) proceed under Rule 26-1; or

(ii) under penalty of one stroke, play a ball as nearly as possible at the spot from which the last stroke from outside the hazard was played (see Rule 20-5).

If the player proceeds under Rule 26-1a, he may elect not to play the dropped ball. If he so elects, he may:

(a) proceed under Rule 26-1b, adding the additional penalty of one stroke prescribed by that Rule; or

(b) proceed under Rule 26-1c, if applicable, adding the additional penalty of one stroke prescribed by that Rule; or

(c) add an additional penalty of one stroke and play a ball as nearly as possible at the spot from which the last stroke from outside the hazard was played (see Rule 20-5).

b. Ball Lost or Unplayable Outside Hazard or Out of Bounds

If a ball played from within a *water hazard* is *lost* or declared unplayable outside the hazard or is *out of bounds*, the player, after taking a penalty of one stroke under Rule 27-1 or 28a, may:

(i) play a ball as nearly as possible at the spot in the hazard from which the original ball was last played (see Rule 20-5); or

(ii) proceed under Rule 26-1b, or if applicable Rule 26-1c, adding the additional penalty of one stroke prescribed by the Rule and using as the reference point the point where the original ball last crossed the margin of the hazard before it came to rest in the hazard; or

(iii) add an additional penalty of one stroke and play a ball as nearly as possible at the spot from which the last stroke from outside the hazard was played (see Rule 20-5).

Note 1: When proceeding under Rule 26-2b, the player is not required to drop a ball under Rule 27-1 or 28a. If he does drop a ball, he is not required to play it. He may alternatively proceed under Clause (ii) or (iii).

Note 2: If a ball played from within a water hazard is declared unplayable outside the hazard, nothing in Rule 26-2b precludes the player from proceeding under Rule 28b or c.

PENALTY FOR BREACH OF RULE:
Match play – Loss of hole;
Stroke play – Two strokes.

Rule 27. Ball Lost or Out of Bounds; Provisional Ball

Definitions

A ball is **lost** if:

a. It is not found or identified as his by the player within five minutes after the player's

side or his or their *caddies* have begun to search for it; or

b. The player has put another ball into play under the *Rules*, even though he may not have searched for the original ball; or

c. The player has played any stroke with a *provisional ball* from the place where the original ball is likely to be or from a point nearer the hole than that place, whereupon the provisional ball becomes the *ball in play*.

Time spent in playing a *wrong ball* is not counted in the five-minute period allowed for search.

Out of bounds is beyond the boundaries of the *course* or any part of the course so marked by the *Committee*.

When out of bounds is defined by reference to stakes or a fence, or as being beyond stakes or a fence, the out of bounds line is determined by the nearest inside points of the stakes or fence posts at ground level excluding angled supports.

Objects defining out of bounds such as walls, fences, stakes and railings, are not *obstructions* and are deemed to be fixed.

When out of bounds is defined by a line on the ground, the line itself is out of bounds.

The out of bounds line extends vertically upwards and downwards.

A ball is out of bounds when all of it lies out of bounds.

A player may stand out of bounds to play a ball lying within bounds.

A **provisional ball** is a ball played under Rule 27-2 for a ball which may be *lost* outside a *water hazard* or may be *out of bounds*.

27-1. Ball Lost or Out of Bounds

If a ball is *lost* or is *out of bounds*, the player shall play a ball, under penalty of one stroke, as nearly as possible at the spot from which the original ball was last played (see Rule 20-5).

Exceptions:

1. If there is reasonable evidence that the original ball is lost in a *water hazard*, the player shall proceed in accordance with Rule 26-1.

2. If there is reasonable evidence that the original ball is lost in an immovable *obstruction* (Rule 24-2c) or an *abnormal ground condition* (Rule 25-1c) the player may proceed under the applicable Rule.

PENALTY FOR BREACH OF RULE 27-1:
Match play – Loss of hole;
Stroke play – Two strokes.

27-2. Provisional Ball
a. Procedure

If a ball may be *lost* outside a *water hazard* or may be *out of bounds*, to save time the player may play another ball provisionally in accordance with Rule 27-1. The player shall inform his opponent in match play or his *marker* or a *fellow-competitor* in stroke play that he intends to play a *provisional ball*, and he shall play it before he or his partner goes forward to search for the original ball.

If he fails to do so and plays another ball, such ball is not a provisional ball and becomes the *ball in play* under penalty of stroke and distance (Rule 27-1); the original ball is deemed to be lost.

(Order of play from teeing ground - see Rule 10-3.)

b. When Provisional Ball Becomes Ball in Play

The player may play a *provisional ball* until he reaches the place where the original ball is likely to be. If he plays a *stroke* with the provisional ball from the place where the original ball is likely to be or from a point nearer the hole than that place, the original ball is deemed to be *lost* and the provisional ball becomes the *ball in play* under penalty of stroke and distance (Rule 27-1).

If the original ball is lost outside a *water hazard* or is *out of bounds*, the provisional ball becomes the ball in play, under penalty of stroke and distance (Rule 27-1).

If there is reasonable evidence that the original ball is lost in a water hazard, the player shall proceed in accordance with Rule 26-1.

Exception: If there is reasonable evidence that the original ball is lost in an immovable *obstruction* (Rule 24-2c) or an *abnormal ground condition* (Rule 25-1c), the player may proceed under the applicable Rule.

c. When Provisional Ball to be Abandoned

If the original ball is neither *lost* nor *out of bounds*, the player shall abandon the *provisional ball* and continue play with the original ball. If he fails to do so, any further *strokes* played with the provisional ball shall constitute playing a *wrong ball* and the provisions of Rule 15 shall apply.

Note: Strokes taken and *penalty strokes* incurred solely in playing a *provisional ball* subsequently abandoned under Rule 27-2c shall be disregarded.

Rule 28. Ball Unplayable

The player may declare his ball unplayable at any place on the *course* except when the ball is in a *water hazard*. The player is the sole judge as to whether his ball is unplayable.

If the player deems his ball to be unplayable, he shall, under penalty of one stroke:

a. Play a ball as nearly as possible at the spot from which the original ball was last played (see Rule 20-5); or

b. Drop a ball within two club-lengths of the spot where the ball lay, but not nearer the hole; or

c. Drop a ball behind the point where the ball lay, keeping that point directly between the hole and the spot on which the ball is dropped, with no limit to how far behind that point the ball may be dropped.

If the unplayable ball is in a *bunker*, the player may proceed under Clause a, b or c. If he elects to proceed under Clause b or c, a ball must be dropped in the bunker.

The ball may be cleaned when lifted under this Rule.

PENALTY FOR BREACH OF RULE:
Match play – Loss of hole;
Stroke play – Two strokes.

OTHER FORMS OF PLAY

Rule 29. Threesomes and Foursomes

Definitions
Threesome: A match in which one plays against two, and each side plays one ball.
Foursome: A match in which two play against two, and each side plays one ball.

29-1. General
In a *threesome* or a *foursome*, during any *stipulated round* the *partners* shall play alternately from the *teeing grounds* and alternately during the play of each hole. *Penalty strokes* do not affect the order of play.

29-2. Match Play
If a player plays when his *partner* should have played, his side shall lose the hole.

29-3. Stroke Play
If the *partners* play a *stroke* or *strokes* in incorrect order, such stroke or strokes shall be cancelled and the side shall incur a penalty of two strokes. The side shall correct the error by playing a ball in correct order as nearly as possible at the spot from which it first played in incorrect order (see Rule 20-5). If the side plays a stroke from the next *teeing ground* without first correcting the error or, in the case of the last hole of the round, leaves the *putting green* without declaring its intention to correct the error, the side shall be disqualified.

Rule 30. Three-Ball, Best-Ball and Four-Ball Match Play

Definitions
Three-Ball: A match play competition in which three play against one another, each playing his own ball. Each player is playing two distinct matches.

Best-Ball: A match in which one plays against the better ball of two or the best ball of three players.

Four-Ball: A match in which two play their better ball against the better ball of two other players.

30-1. Rules of Golf Apply
The Rules of Golf, so far as they are not at variance with the following special Rules, shall apply to three-ball, best-ball and four-ball matches.

30-2. Three-Ball Match Play
a. Ball at Rest Moved by an Opponent
Except as otherwise provided in the *Rules*, if the player's ball is touched or *moved* by an opponent, his *caddie* or *equipment* other than during search, Rule 18-3b applies. That opponent shall incur a penalty stroke in his match with the player, but not in his match with the other opponent.

b. Ball Deflected or Stopped by an Opponent Accidentally
If a player's ball is accidentally deflected or stopped by an opponent, his *caddie* or *equipment,* no penalty shall be incurred. In his match with that opponent the player may play the ball as it lies or, before another stroke is played by either side, he may cancel the stroke and play a ball without penalty as nearly as possible at the spot from which the original ball was last played (see Rule 20-5). In his match with the other opponent, the ball shall be played as it lies.

   Exception: Ball striking person attending flagstick – see Rule 17-3b.

   (Ball purposely deflected or stopped by opponent – see Rule 1-2.)

30-3. Best-Ball and Four-Ball Match Play
a. Representation of Side
A side may be represented by one *partner* for all or any part of a match; all partners need not be present. An absent partner may join a match between holes, but not during play of a hole.

b. Maximum of Fourteen Clubs
The side shall be penalised for a breach of Rule 4-4 by any partner.

c. Order of Play
Balls belonging to the same side may be played in the order the side considers best.

d. Wrong Ball
If a player plays a *stroke* with a *wrong ball* except in a *hazard,* he shall be disqualified for that hole, but his *partner* incurs no penalty even if the wrong ball belongs to him. If the wrong ball belongs to another player, its owner shall place a ball on the spot from which the wrong ball was first played.

e. Disqualification of Side
(i) A side shall be disqualified for a breach of any of the following by any *partner:*
   Rule 1-3 – Agreement to Waive Rules.
   Rule 4-1 or -2 – Clubs.
   Rule 5-1 or -2 – The Ball.
   Rule 6-2a – Handicap (playing off higher handicap).
   Rule 6-4 – Caddie.
   Rule 6-7 – Undue Delay; Slow Play (repeated offence).
   Rule 14-3 – Artificial Devices and Unusual Equipment.

(ii) A side shall be disqualified for a breach of any of the following by all *partners:*
   Rule 6-3 – Time of Starting and Groups.
   Rule 6-8 – Discontinuance of Play.

f. Effect of Other Penalties
If a player's breach of a *Rule* assists his *partner's* play or adversely affects an opponent's play, the partner incurs the applicable penalty in addition to any penalty incurred by the player.

In all other cases where a player incurs a penalty for breach of a Rule, the penalty shall not apply to his partner. Where the penalty is stated to be loss of hole, the effect shall be to disqualify the player for that hole.

g. Another Form of Match Played Concurrently
In a best-ball or four-ball match when another form of match is played concurrently, the above special Rules shall apply.

Rule 31. Four-Ball Stroke Play

In four-ball stroke play two competitors play as *partners*, each playing his own ball. The lower score of the partners is the score for the hole. If one partner fails to complete the play of a hole, there is no penalty.

31-1. Rules of Golf Apply
The Rules of Golf, so far as they are not at variance with the following special Rules, shall apply to four-ball stroke play.

31-2. Representation of Side
A *side* may be represented by either *partner* for all or any part of a *stipulated round*; both partners need not be present. An absent competitor may join his partner between holes, but not during play of a hole.

31-3. Maximum of Fourteen Clubs
The *side* shall be penalised for a breach of Rule 4-4 by either *partner*.

31-4. Scoring

The *marker* is required to record for each hole only the gross score of whichever *partner's* score is to count. The gross scores to count must be individually identifiable; otherwise the *side* shall be disqualified. Only one of the partners need be responsible for complying with Rule 6-6b.

(Wrong score – see Rule 31-7a.)

31-5. Order of Play

Balls belonging to the same *side* may be played in the order the side considers best.

31-6. Wrong Ball

If a competitor plays a *stroke* or strokes with a *wrong ball* except in a *hazard*, he shall add two penalty strokes to his score for the hole and shall then play the correct ball. His *partner* incurs no penalty even if the wrong ball belongs to him.

If the wrong ball belongs to another competitor, its owner shall place a ball on the spot from which the wrong ball was first played.

31-7. Disqualification Penalties
a. Breach by One Partner

A *side* shall be disqualified from the competition for a breach of any of the following by either *partner*:

Rule 1-3 –	Agreement to Waive Rules.
Rule 3-4 –	Refusal to Comply with Rule.
Rule 4-1 or -2 –	Clubs.
Rule 5-1 or -2 –	The Ball.
Rule 6-2b –	Handicap (playing off higher handicap; failure to record handicap).
Rule 6-4 –	Caddie.
Rule 6-6b –	Signing and Returning Card.
Rule 6-6d –	Wrong Score for Hole, i.e. when the recorded score of the partner whose score is to count is lower than actually taken. If the recorded score of the partner whose score is to count is higher than actually taken, it must stand as returned.
Rule 6-7 –	Undue Delay; Slow Play (repeated offence).
Rule 7-1 –	Practice Before or Between Rounds.
Rule 14-3 –	Artificial Devices and Unusual Equipment.
Rule 31-4 –	Gross Scores to Count Not Individually Identifiable.

b. Breach by Both Partners

A *side* shall be disqualified:

(i) for a breach by both *partners* of Rule 6-3 (Time of Starting and Groups) or Rule 6-8 (Discontinuance of Play), or

(ii) if, at the same hole, each *partner* is in breach of a *Rule* the penalty for which is disqualification from the competition or for a hole.

c. For the Hole Only

In all other cases where a breach of a *Rule* would entail disqualification, the competitor shall be disqualified only for the hole at which the breach occurred.

31-8. Effect of Other Penalties

If a competitor's breach of a *Rule* assists his *partner's* play, the partner incurs the applicable penalty in addition to any penalty incurred by the competitor.

In all other cases where a competitor incurs a penalty for breach of a Rule, the penalty shall not apply to his partner.

Rule 32. Bogey, Par and Stableford Competitions

32-1. Conditions

Bogey, par and Stableford competitions are forms of stroke competition in which play is against a fixed score at each hole. The Rules for stroke play, so far as they are not at variance with the following special Rules, apply.

a. Bogey and Par Competitions

The reckoning for bogey and par competitions is made as in match play. Any hole for which a competitor makes no return shall be regarded as a loss. The winner is the competitor who is most successful in the aggregate of holes.

The *marker* is responsible for marking only the gross number of strokes for each hole where the competitor makes a net score equal to or less than the fixed score.

Note 1: Maximum of 14 Clubs – Penalties as in match play – see Rule 4-4.

Note 2: Undue Delay; Slow Play (Rule 6-7) – The competitor's score shall be adjusted by deducting one hole from the overall result.

b. Stableford Competitions

The reckoning in Stableford competitions is made by points awarded in relation to a fixed score at each hole as follows:

Hole Played in	*Points*
More than one over fixed score or no score returned	0
One over fixed score	1
Fixed score	2
One under fixed score	3
Two under fixed score	4
Three under fixed score	5
Four under fixed score	6

The winner is the competitor who scores the highest number of points.

The *marker* shall be responsible for marking only the gross number of strokes at each hole where the competitor's net score earns one or more points.

Note 1: Maximum of 14 Clubs (Rule 4-4) – Penalties applied as follows: From total points scored for the round, deduction of two points for each hole at which any breach occurred; maximum deduction per round: four points.

Note 2: Undue Delay; Slow Play (Rule 6-7) – The competitor's score shall be adjusted by deducting two points from the points total scored for the round.

32-2. Disqualification Penalties
a. From the Competition
A competitor shall be disqualified from the competition for a breach of any of the following:

Rule 1-3 –	Agreement to Waive Rules.
Rule 3-4 –	Refusal to Comply with Rule.
Rule 4-1 or -2 –	Clubs.
Rule 5-1 or -2 –	The Ball.
Rule 6-2b –	Handicap (playing off higher handicap; failure to record handicap).
Rule 6-3 –	Time of Starting and Groups.
Rule 6-4 –	Caddie.
Rule 6-6b –	Signing and Returning Card.
Rule 6-6d –	Wrong Score for Hole, except that no penalty shall be incurred when a breach of this Rule does not affect the result of the hole.
Rule 6-7 –	Undue Delay; Slow Play (repeated offence).
Rule 6-8 –	Discontinuance of Play.
Rule 7-1 –	Practice Before or Between Rounds.
Rule 14-3 –	Artificial Devices and Unusual Equipment.

b. For a Hole
In all other cases where a breach of a *Rule* would entail disqualification, the competitor shall be disqualified only for the hole at which the breach occurred.

ADMINISTRATION

Rule 33. The Committee

33-1.   Conditions; Waiving Rule
The *Committee* shall lay down the conditions under which a competition is to be played.

The Committee has no power to waive a Rule of Golf.

Certain special rules governing stroke play are so substantially different from those governing match play that combining the two forms of play is not practicable and is not permitted. The results of matches played and the scores returned in these circumstances shall not be accepted.

In stroke play the Committee may limit a *referee's* duties.

33-2. The Course
a. Defining Bounds and Margins
The *Committee* shall define accurately:
(i)   the *course* and *out of bounds*,
(ii) the margins of *water hazards* and *lateral water hazards*,
(iii) *ground under repair*, and
(iv) *obstructions* and integral parts of the course.

b. New Holes
New *holes* should be made on the day on which a stroke competition begins and at such other times as the *Committee* considers necessary, provided all competitors in a single round play with each hole cut in the same position.

Exception: When it is impossible for a damaged *hole* to be repaired so that it conforms with the Definition, the *Committee* may make a new hole in a nearby similar position.

Note: Where a single round is to be played on more than one day, the *Committee* may provide in the conditions of a competition that the *holes* and *teeing grounds* may be differently situated on each day of the competition, provided that, on any one day, all competitors play with each hole and each teeing ground in the same position.

c. Practice Ground
Where there is no practice ground available outside the area of a competition *course*, the *Committee* should lay down the area on which players may practise on any day of a competition, if it is practicable to do so. On any day of a stroke competition, the Committee should not normally permit practice on or to a *putting green* or from a *hazard* of the competition course.

d. Course Unplayable
If the *Committee* or its authorised representative considers that for any reason the *course* is not in a playable condition or that there are circumstances which render the proper playing of the game impossible, it may, in match play or stroke play, order a temporary suspension of play or, in stroke play, declare play null and void and cancel all scores for the round in question. When a round is cancelled, all penalties incurred in that round are cancelled.

(Procedure in discontinuing and resuming play – see Rule 6-8.)

33-3. Times of Starting and Groups
The *Committee* shall lay down the times of starting and, in stroke play, arrange the groups in which competitors shall play.

When a match play competition is played over an extended period, the Committee shall lay down the limit of time within which each round shall be completed. When players are allowed to arrange the date of their match within these limits, the Committee should announce that the match must be played at a stated time on the last day of the period unless the players agree to a prior date.

33-4. Handicap Stroke Table
The *Committee* shall publish a table indicating the order of holes at which handicap strokes are to be given or received.

33-5. Score Card
In stroke play, the Committee shall issue for each competitor a score card containing the date and the competitor's name or, in foursome or four-ball stroke play, the competitors' names.

In stroke play, the Committee is responsible for the addition of scores and application of the handicap recorded on the card.

In four-ball stroke play, the Committee is responsible for recording the better-ball score for each hole and in the process applying the handicaps recorded on the card, and adding the better-ball scores.

In bogey, par and Stableford competitions, the Committee is responsible for applying the handicap recorded on the card and determining the result of each hole and the overall result or points total.

33-6. Decision of Ties
The *Committee* shall announce the manner, day and time for the decision of a halved match or of a tie, whether played on level terms or under handicap.

A halved match shall not be decided by stroke play. A tie in stroke play shall not be decided by a match.

33-7. Disqualification Penalty; Committee Discretion
A penalty of disqualification may in exceptional individual cases be waived, modified or imposed if the *Committee* considers such action warranted.

Any penalty less than disqualification shall not be waived or modified.

33-8. Local Rules
a. Policy
The *Committee* may make and publish Local Rules for local abnormal conditions if they are consistent with the policy set forth in Appendix I.

b. Waiving or Modifying a Rule
A Rule of Golf shall not be waived by a Local Rule. However, if a *Committee* considers that local abnormal conditions interfere with the proper playing of the game to the extent that it is necessary to make a Local Rule which modifies the

Rules, the Local Rule must be authorised by the Royal and Ancient Golf Club of St. Andrews.

Rule 34. Disputes and Decisions

34-1. Claims and Penalties
a. Match Play
In match play if a claim is lodged with the *Committee* under Rule 2-5, a decision should be given as soon as possible so that the state of the match may, if necessary, be adjusted.

If a claim is not made within the time limit provided by Rule 2-5, it shall not be considered unless it is based on facts previously unknown to the player making the claim and the player making the claim had been given wrong information (Rules 6-2a and 9) by an opponent. In any case, no later claim shall be considered after the result of the match has been officially announced, unless the Committee is satisfied that the opponent knew he was giving wrong information.

There is no time limit on applying the disqualification penalty for a breach of Rule 1-3.

b. Stroke Play
Except as provided below, in stroke play, no penalty shall be rescinded, modified or imposed after the competition has closed. A competition is deemed to have closed when the result has been officially announced or, in stroke play qualifying followed by match play, when the player has teed off in his first match.

Exceptions: A penalty of disqualification shall be imposed after the competition has closed if a competitor:

(i) was in breach of Rule 1-3 (Agreement to Waive Rules); or

(ii) returned a score card on which he had recorded a handicap which, before the competition closed, he knew was higher than that to which he was entitled, and this affected the number of strokes received (Rule 6-2b); or

(iii) returned a score for any hole lower than actually taken (Rule 6-6d) for any reason other than failure to include a penalty which, before the competition closed, he did not know he had incurred; or

(iv) knew, before the competition closed, that he had been in breach of any other *Rule* for which the prescribed penalty is disqualification.

34-2. Referee's Decision
If a *referee* has been appointed by the *Committee*, his decision shall be final.

34-3. Committee's Decision
In the absence of a *referee*, any dispute or doubtful point on the *Rules* shall be referred to the *Committee*, whose decision shall be final.

If the Committee cannot come to a decision, it shall refer the dispute or doubtful point to the Rules of Golf Committee of the Royal and Ancient Golf Club of St. Andrews, whose decision shall be final.

If the dispute or doubtful point has not been referred to the Rules of Golf Committee, the player or players have the right to refer an agreed statement through the Secretary of the Club to the Rules of Golf Committee for an opinion as to the correctness of the decision given. The reply will be sent to the Secretary of the Club or Clubs concerned.

If play is conducted other than in accordance with the Rules of Golf, the Rules of Golf Committee will not give a decision on any question.

APPENDIX I
LOCAL RULES; CONDITIONS OF THE COMPETITION
Part A: Local Rules

As provided in Rule 33-8a, the Committee may make and publish Local Rules for local abnormal conditions if they are consistent with the policy set forth in this Appendix.

In addition, detailed information regarding acceptable and prohibited Local Rules is provided in 'Decisions on the Rules of Golf' under Rule 33-8.

If local abnormal conditions interfere with the proper playing of the game and the Committee considers it necessary to modify a Rule of Golf, authorisation from the Royal and Ancient Golf Club of St. Andrews must be obtained.

1. Defining Bounds and Margins
Specifying means used to define out of bounds, water hazards, lateral water hazards, ground under repair, obstructions and integral parts of the course (Rule 33-2a).

2. Water Hazards
a. Lateral Water Hazards
Clarifying the status of water hazards which may be lateral water hazards (Rule 26).

b. Provisional Ball
Permitting play of a provisional ball for a ball which may be in a water hazard of such character that if the original ball is not found, there is reasonable evidence that it is lost in the water hazard and it would be impracticable to determine whether the ball is in the hazard or to do so would unduly delay play. The ball shall be played provisionally under any of the available options under Rule 26-1 or any applicable Local Rule. In such a case, if a provisional ball is played and the original ball is in a water hazard, the player may play the original ball as it lies or continue with the provisional ball in play, but he may not proceed under Rule 26-1 with regard to the original ball.

3. Areas of the Course Requiring Preservation; Environmentally-Sensitive Areas
Assisting preservation of the course by defining areas, including turf nurseries, young plantations and other parts of the course under cultivation, as 'ground under repair' from which play is prohibited.

When the Committee is required to prohibit play from environmentally-sensitive areas which are on or adjoin the course, it should make a Local Rule clarifying the relief procedure.

4. Temporary Conditions - Mud, Extreme Wetness, Poor Conditions and Protection of Course
a. Lifting an Embedded Ball, Cleaning
Temporary conditions which might interfere with the proper playing of the game, including mud and extreme wetness, warranting relief for an embedded ball anywhere through the green or permitting lifting, cleaning and replacing a ball anywhere through the green or on a closely-mown area through the green.

b. 'Preferred Lies' and 'Winter Rules'
Adverse conditions, including the poor condition of the course or the existence of mud, are sometimes so general, particularly during winter months, that the Committee may decide to grant relief by temporary Local Rule either to protect the course or to promote fair and pleasant play. Such Local Rule shall be withdrawn as soon as the conditions warrant.

5. Obstructions
a. General
Clarifying the status of objects which may be obstructions (Rule 24).

Declaring any construction to be an integral part of the course and, accordingly, not an obstruction, e.g. built-up sides of teeing grounds, putting greens and bunkers (Rules 24 and 33-2a).

b. Stones in Bunkers
Allowing the removal of stones in bunkers by declaring them to be 'movable obstructions' (Rule 24-1).

c. Roads and Paths
(i) Declaring artificial surfaces and sides of roads and paths to be integral parts of the course, or
(ii) Providing relief of the type afforded under Rule 24-2b from roads and paths not having artificial surfaces and sides if they could unfairly affect play.

d. Fixed Sprinkler Heads
Providing relief from intervention by fixed sprinkler heads on or within two club-lengths of the

putting green when the ball lies within two club-lengths of the sprinkler head.

e. Protection of Young Trees
Providing relief for the protection of young trees.

f. Temporary Obstructions
Providing relief from interference by temporary obstructions (e.g. grandstands, television cables and equipment, etc.).

6. Dropping Zones (Ball Drops)
Establishing special areas on which balls may or shall be dropped when it is not feasible or practicable to proceed exactly in conformity with Rule 24-2b or 24-2c (Immovable Obstruction), Rule 25-1b or 25-1c (Abnormal Ground Conditions), Rule 25-3 (Wrong Putting Green), Rule 26-1 (Water Hazards and Lateral Water Hazards) or Rule 28 (Ball Unplayable).

Part B: Specimen Local Rules

Within the policy set out in Part A of this Appendix, the Committee may adopt a Specimen Local Rule by referring, on a score card or notice board, to the examples given below. However, Specimen Local Rules 3a, 3b, 3c, 6a and 6b should not be printed or referred to on a score card as they are all of limited duration.

1. Areas of the Course Requiring Preservation; Environmentally-Sensitive Areas
a. Ground Under Repair; Play Prohibited
If the Committee wishes to protect any area of the course, it should declare it to be ground under repair and prohibit play from within that area. The following Local Rule is recommended:

'The _____ (defined by ____) is ground under repair from which play is prohibited. If a player's ball lies in the area, or if it interferes with the player's stance or the area of his intended swing, the player must take relief under Rule 25-1.

PENALTY FOR BREACH OF LOCAL RULE: Match play - Loss of hole; Stroke play - Two strokes.'

b. Environmentally-Sensitive Areas
If an appropriate authority (i.e. a Government Agency or the like) prohibits entry into and/or play from an area on or adjoining the course for environmental reasons, the Committee should make a Local Rule clarifying the relief procedure.

The Committee has some discretion in terms of whether the area is defined as ground under repair, a water hazard or out of bounds. However, it may not simply define such an area to be a water hazard if it does not meet the Definition of a 'Water Hazard' and it should attempt to preserve the character of the hole.

The following Local Rule is recommended:

'#### 1. Definition
An environmentally-sensitive area is an area so declared by an appropriate authority, entry into and/or play from which is prohibited for environmental reasons. Such an area may be defined as ground under repair, a water hazard, a lateral water hazard or out of bounds at the discretion of the Committee provided that, in the case of an environmentally-sensitive area which has been defined as a water hazard or a lateral water hazard, the area is, by Definition, a water hazard.

Note: The Committee may not declare an area to be environmentally-sensitive.

2. Ball in Environmentally-Sensitive Area
a. Ground Under Repair
If a ball is in an environmentally-sensitive area which is defined as ground under repair, a ball must be dropped in accordance with Rule 25-1b.

If there is reasonable evidence that a ball is lost within an environmentally-sensitive area which is defined as ground under repair, the player may take relief without penalty as prescribed in Rule 25-1c.

b. Water Hazards and Lateral Water Hazards
If a ball is in or there is reasonable evidence that it is lost in an environmentally-sensitive area which is defined as a water hazard or lateral water hazard, the player must, under penalty of one stroke, proceed under Rule 26-1.

Note: If a ball dropped in accordance with Rule 26 rolls into a position where the environmentally-sensitive area interferes with the player's stance or the area of his intended swing, the player must take relief as provided in Clause 3 of this Local Rule.

c. Out of Bounds
If a ball is in an environmentally-sensitive area which is defined as out of bounds, the player shall play a ball, under penalty of one stroke, as nearly as possible at the spot from which the original ball was last played (see Rule 20-5).

3. Interference with Stance or Area of Intended Swing
Interference by an environmentally-sensitive area occurs when such a condition

interferes with the player's stance or the area of his intended swing. If interference exists, the player must take relief as follows:

(i) **Through the Green:** If the ball lies through the green, the point on the course nearest to where the ball lies shall be determined which (a) is not nearer the hole, (b) avoids interference by the condition and (c) is not in a hazard or on a putting green. The player shall lift the ball and drop it without penalty within one club-length of the point thus determined on a part of the course that fulfils (a), (b) and (c) above.

(ii) **In a Hazard:** If the ball is in a hazard, the player shall lift the ball and drop it either:

(a) Without penalty, in the hazard, as near as possible to the spot where the ball lay, but not nearer the hole, on a part of the course which provides complete relief from the condition; or

(b) Under penalty of one stroke, outside the hazard, keeping the point where the ball lay directly between the hole and the spot on which the ball is dropped, with no limit to how far behind the hazard the ball may be dropped.

Additionally, the player may proceed under Rule 26 or 28 if applicable.

(iii) **On the Putting Green:** If the ball lies on the putting green, the player shall lift the ball and place it without penalty in the nearest position to where it lay which affords complete relief from the condition, but not nearer the hole or in a hazard.

The ball may be cleaned when so lifted under Clause 3 of this Local Rule.

Exception: A player may not obtain relief under Clause 3 of this Local Rule if (a) it is clearly unreasonable for him to play a stroke because of interference by anything other than a condition covered by this Local Rule or (b) interference by such a condition would occur only through use of an unnecessarily abnormal stance, swing or direction of play.

PENALTY FOR BREACH OF LOCAL
RULE: Match play – Loss of hole;
Stroke play – Two strokes.

Note: In case of a serious breach of this Local Rule, the Committee may impose a penalty of disqualification.'

2. Protection of Young Trees

When it is desired to prevent damage to young trees, the following Local Rule is recommended:

'Protection of young trees identified by _____ . If such a tree interferes with a player's stance or the area of his intended swing, the ball must be lifted, without penalty, and dropped in accordance with the procedure prescribed in Rule 24-2b (Immovable Obstruction). If the ball lies in a water hazard, the player shall lift and drop the ball in accordance with Rule 24-2b(i) except that the nearest point of relief must be in the water hazard and the ball must be dropped in the water hazard or the player may proceed under Rule 26. The ball may be cleaned when so lifted.

Exception: A player may not obtain relief under this Local Rule if (a) it is clearly unreasonable for him to play a stroke because of interference by anything other than such tree or (b) interference by such tree would occur only through use of an unnecessarily abnormal stance, swing or direction of play.

PENALTY FOR BREACH OF LOCAL
RULE: Match play – Loss of hole;
Stroke play – Two strokes.'

3. Temporary Conditions - Mud, Extreme Wetness, Poor Conditions and Protection of the Course

a. Relief for Embedded Ball; Cleaning Ball

Rule 25-2 provides relief without penalty for a ball embedded in its own pitch-mark in any closely-mown area through the green. On the putting green, a ball may be lifted and damage caused by the impact of a ball may be repaired (Rules 16-1b and c). When permission to take relief for an embedded ball anywhere through the green would be warranted, the following Local Rule is recommended:

'Through the green, a ball which is embedded in its own pitch-mark in the ground, other than sand, may be lifted without penalty, cleaned and dropped as near as possible to where it lay but not nearer the hole. The ball when dropped must first strike a part of the course through the green.

Exception: A player may not obtain relief under this Local Rule if it is clearly unreasonable for him to play a stroke because of interference by anything other than the condition covered by this Local Rule.

PENALTY FOR BREACH OF LOCAL
RULE: Match play – Loss of hole;
Stroke play – Two strokes.'

Alternatively, conditions may be such that permission to lift, clean and replace the ball will suffice. In such circumstances, the following Local Rule is recommended:

'(Specify area) a ball may be lifted, cleaned and replaced without penalty.

Note: The position of the ball shall be marked before it is lifted under this Local Rule - see Rule 20-1.

PENALTY FOR BREACH OF LOCAL RULE: Match play – Loss of hole; Stroke play – Two strokes.'

b. 'Preferred Lies' and 'Winter Rules'

The R&A does not endorse 'preferred lies' or 'winter rules' and recommends that the Rules of Golf be observed uniformly. Ground under repair is provided for in Rule 25 and occasional local abnormal conditions which might interfere with fair play and are not widespread should be defined as ground under repair.

However, adverse conditions are sometimes so general throughout a course that the Committee believes 'preferred lies' or 'winter rules' would promote fair play or help protect the course. Heavy snows, spring thaws, prolonged rains or extreme heat can make fairways unsatisfactory and sometimes prevent use of heavy mowing equipment.

When a Committee adopts a Local Rule for 'preferred lies' or 'winter rules' it should be set out in detail and should be interpreted by the Committee, as there is no established code for 'winter rules'. Without a detailed Local Rule, it is meaningless for a Committee to post a notice merely saying 'Winter Rules today.'

The following Local Rule would seem appropriate for the conditions in question, but the R&A will not interpret it:

'A ball lying on a closely-mown area through the green may, without penalty, be moved or may be lifted, cleaned and placed within (specify area, e.g., six inches, one club-length, etc.) of where it originally lay, but not nearer the hole and not in a hazard or on a putting green. A player may move or place his ball once and after the ball has been so moved or placed, it is in play.

PENALTY FOR BREACH OF LOCAL RULE: Match play – Loss of hole; Stroke play – Two strokes.'

Before a Committee adopts a Local Rule permitting 'preferred lies' or 'winter rules', the following facts should be considered:
1. Such a Local Rule conflicts with the Rules of Golf and the fundamental principle of playing the ball as it lies.
2. 'Winter rules' are sometimes adopted under the guise of protecting the course when, in fact, the practical effect is just the opposite - they permit moving the ball to the best turf, from which divots are then taken to injure the course further.
3. 'Preferred lies' or 'winter rules' tend generally to lower scores and handicaps, thus penalising the players in competition with players whose scores for handicaps are made under the Rules of Golf.
4. Extended use or indiscriminate use of 'preferred lies' or 'winter rules' will place players at a disadvantage when competing at a course where the ball must be played as it lies.

c. Aeration Holes

When a course has been aerated, a Local Rule permitting relief, without penalty, from an aeration hole may be warranted. The following Local Rule is recommended:

'Through the green, a ball which comes to rest in or on an aeration hole may be lifted without penalty, cleaned and dropped, as near as possible to the spot where it lay but not nearer the hole. The ball when dropped must first strike a part of the course through the green.

On the putting green, the player shall place the ball at the nearest spot not nearer the hole which avoids such situation.

PENALTY FOR BREACH OF LOCAL RULE: Match play – Loss of hole; Stroke play – Two strokes.'

4. Stones in bunkers

Stones are, by definition, loose impediments and, when a player's ball is in a hazard, a stone lying in or touching the hazard may not be touched or moved (Rule 13-4). However, stones in bunkers may represent a danger to players (a player could be injured by a stone struck by the player's club in an attempt to play the ball) and they may interfere with the proper playing of the game.

When permission to lift a stone in a bunker would be warranted, the following Local Rule is recommended:

'Stones in bunkers are movable obstructions (Rule 24-1 applies).'

5. Fixed Sprinkler Heads

Rule 24-2 provides relief without penalty from interference by an immovable obstruction, but it also provides that, except on the putting green, intervention on the line of play is not, of itself, interference under this Rule.

However, on some courses, the aprons of the putting greens are so closely mown that players may wish to putt from just off the green. In such conditions, fixed sprinkler heads on the apron may interfere with the proper playing of the game and the introduction of the following Local Rule providing additional relief without penalty from intervention by a fixed sprinkler head would be warranted:

'All fixed sprinkler heads are immovable obstructions and relief from interference by them may be obtained under Rule 24-2. In addition, if a ball lies off the putting green but not in a hazard and such an obstruction on or within two club-lengths of the putting green and within two club-lengths of the ball intervenes on the line of play between the ball and the hole, the player may take relief as follows:

The ball shall be lifted and dropped at the nearest point to where the ball lay which (a) is not nearer the hole, (b) avoids such intervention and (c) is not in a hazard or on a putting green. The ball may be cleaned when so lifted.

PENALTY FOR BREACH OF LOCAL RULE:Match play – Loss of hole; Stroke play – Two strokes.'

6. Temporary Obstructions

When temporary obstructions are installed on or adjoining the course, the Committee should define the status of such obstructions as movable, immovable or temporary immovable obstructions.

a. Temporary Immovable Obstructions

If the Committee defines such obstructions as temporary immovable obstructions, the following Local Rule is recommended:

'1. Definition

A temporary immovable obstruction is a non-permanent artificial object which is often erected in conjunction with a competition and which is fixed or not readily movable.

Examples of temporary immovable obstructions include, but are not limited to, tents, scoreboards, grandstands, television towers and lavatories.

Supporting guy wires are part of the temporary immovable obstruction unless the Committee declares that they are to be treated as elevated power lines or cables.

2. Interference

Interference by a temporary immovable obstruction occurs when (a) the ball lies in front of and so close to the obstruction that the obstruction interferes with the player's stance or the area of his intended swing, or (b) the ball lies in, on, under or behind the obstruction so that any part of the obstruction intervenes directly between the player's ball and the hole; interference also exists if the ball lies within one club-length of a spot where such intervention would exist.

Note: A ball is under a temporary immovable obstruction when it is below the outer most edges of the obstruction, even if these edges do not extend downwards to the ground.

3. Relief

A player may obtain relief from interference by a temporary immovable obstruction, including a temporary immovable obstruction which is out of bounds, as follows:

a. Through the Green - If the ball lies through the green, the point on the course nearest to where the ball lies shall be determined which (a) is not nearer the hole, (b) avoids interference as defined in Clause 2 and (c) is not in a hazard or on a putting green. The player shall lift the ball and drop it without penalty within one club-length of the point thus determined on a part of the course which fulfils (a), (b) and (c) above.

b. In a Hazard: If the ball is in a hazard, the player shall lift and drop the ball either:

(i) Without penalty, in the hazard, on the nearest part of the course affording complete relief within the limits specified in Clause 3a above or, if complete relief is impossible, on a part of the course within the hazard which affords maximum available relief; or

(ii) Under penalty of one stroke, outside the hazard as follows: the point on the course nearest to where the ball lies shall be determined which (a) is not nearer the hole, (b) avoids interference as defined in Clause 2 and (c) is not in a hazard. The player shall drop the ball within one club-length of the point thus determined on a part of the course which fulfils (a), (b) and (c) above.

The ball may be cleaned when lifted under Clause 3.

Note 1: If the ball lies in a hazard, nothing in this Local Rule precludes the player from proceeding under Rule 26 or Rule 28, if applicable.

Note 2: If the ball to be dropped under this Local Rule is not immediately recoverable, another ball may be substituted.

Note 3: A Committee may make a Local Rule (a) permitting or requiring a player to use a dropping zone or ball drop when taking relief from a temporary immovable obstruction or (b) permitting a player, as an additional relief option, to drop the ball on the opposite side of the obstruction from the point established under Clause 3, but otherwise in accordance with Clause 3.

Exceptions:

If a player's ball lies in front of or behind the temporary immovable obstruction (not in, on or under the obstruction) he may not obtain relief under Clause 3 if:

1. It is clearly unreasonable for him to play a stroke or, in the case of intervention, to play a stroke such that the ball could finish

on a direct line to the hole, because of interference by anything other than the temporary immovable obstruction;

2. Interference by the temporary immovable obstruction would occur only through use of an unnecessarily abnormal stance, swing or direction of play; or

3. In the case of intervention, it would be clearly unreasonable to expect the player to be able to strike the ball far enough towards the hole to reach the temporary immovable obstruction.

Note: A player not entitled to relief due to these exceptions may proceed under Rule 24-2, if applicable.

4. Ball Lost
If there is reasonable evidence that the ball is lost in, on or under a temporary immovable obstruction, a ball may be dropped under the provisions of Clause 3 or Clause 5, if applicable. For the purpose of applying Clauses 3 and 5, the ball shall be deemed to lie at the spot where it last entered the obstruction (Rule 24-2c).

5. Dropping Zones (Ball Drops)
If the player has interference from a temporary immovable obstruction, the Committee may permit or require the use of a dropping zone or ball drop. If the player uses a dropping zone in taking relief, he must drop the ball in the dropping zone nearest to where his ball originally lay or is deemed to lie under Clause 4 (even though the nearest dropping zone may be nearer the hole).

Note 1: A Committee may make a Local Rule prohibiting the use of a dropping zone or ball drop which is nearer the hole.

Note 2: If the ball is dropped in a dropping zone, the ball shall not be re-dropped if it comes to rest within two club-lengths of the spot where it first struck a part of the course even though it may come to rest nearer the hole or outside the boundaries of the dropping zone.

PENALTY FOR BREACH OF LOCAL RULE: Match play – Loss of hole; Stroke play – Two strokes.'

b. Temporary Power Lines and Cables
When temporary power lines, cables, or telephone lines are installed on the course, the following Local Rule is recommended:

'Temporary power lines, cables, telephone lines and mats covering or stanchions supporting them are obstructions:
1. If they are readily movable, Rule 24-1 applies.
2. If they are fixed or not readily movable, the player may, if the ball lies through the green

or in a bunker, obtain relief as provided in Rule 24-2b. If the ball lies in a water hazard, the player may obtain relief under Rule 24-2b(i) except that the nearest point of relief must be in the water hazard and the ball must be dropped in the water hazard or the player may proceed under Rule 26.

3. If a ball strikes an elevated power line or cable, the stroke shall be cancelled and replayed, without penalty (see Rule 20-5). If the ball is not immediately recoverable another ball may be substituted.

Note: Guy wires supporting a temporary immovable obstruction are part of the temporary immovable obstruction unless the Committee, by Local Rule, declares that they are to be treated as elevated power lines or cables.

Exception: Ball striking elevated junction section of cable rising from the ground shall not be replayed.

4. Grass-covered cable trenches are ground under repair even if not so marked and Rule 25-1b applies.'

Part C: Conditions of the Competition

Rule 33-1 provides, 'The Committee shall lay down the conditions under which a competition is to be played.' Such conditions should include many matters such as method of entry, eligibility, number of rounds to be played, etc. which it is not appropriate to deal with in the Rules of Golf or this Appendix. Detailed information regarding such conditions is provided in 'Decisions on the Rules of Golf' under Rule 33-1.

However, there are seven matters which might be covered in the Conditions of the Competition to which the Committee's attention is specifically drawn by way of a Note to the appropriate Rule. These are:

1. Specification of the Ball (Note to Rule 5-1)
The following two conditions are recommended only for competitions involving expert players:

a. List of Conforming Golf Balls
The R&A periodically issues a List of Conforming Golf Balls which lists balls that have been tested and found to conform. If the Committee wishes to require use of a brand of golf ball on the List, the List should be posted and the following condition of competition used:

'The ball the player uses shall be named on the current List of Conforming Golf Balls issued by the Royal and Ancient Golf Club of St Andrews.

PENALTY FOR BREACH OF CONDITION: Disqualification.'

b. One Ball Condition
If it is desired to prohibit changing brands and types of golf balls during a stipulated round, the following condition is recommended:

> 'Limitation on Balls Used During Round:
> (Note to Rule 5-1)
>
> (i) 'One Ball' Condition
> During a stipulated round, the balls a player uses must be of the same brand and type as detailed by a single entry on the current List of Conforming Golf Balls.
>
>   PENALTY FOR BREACH OF CONDITION: Match play – At the conclusion of the hole at which the breach is discovered, the state of the match shall be adjusted by deducting one hole for each hole at which a breach occurred; maximum deduction per round: Two holes.
> Stroke play – Two strokes for each hole at which any breach occurred; maximum penalty per round: Four strokes.
>
> (ii) Procedure When Breach Discovered
> When a player discovers that he has used a ball in breach of this condition, he shall abandon that ball before playing from the next teeing ground and complete the round using a proper ball; otherwise, the player shall be disqualified. If discovery is made during play of a hole and the player elects to substitute a proper ball before completing that hole, the player shall place a proper ball on the spot where the ball used in breach of the condition lay.'

2. Time of Starting (Note to Rule 6-3a)
If the Committee wishes to act in accordance with the Note, the following wording is recommended:

> 'If the player arrives at his starting point, ready to play, within five minutes after his starting time in the absence of circumstances which warrant waiving the penalty of disqualification as provided in Rule 33-7, the penalty for failure to start on time is loss of the first hole to be played in match play or two strokes in stroke play. Penalty for lateness beyond five minutes is disqualification.'

3. Pace of Play
The Committee may lay down pace of play guidelines to help prevent slow play, in accordance with Note 2 to Rule 6-7.

4. Suspension of Play Due to a Dangerous Situation (Note to Rule 6-8b)
As there have been many deaths and injuries from lightning on golf courses, all clubs and sponsors of golf competitions are urged to take precautions for the protection of persons against lightning. Attention is called to Rules 6-8 and 33-2d. If the Committee desires to adopt the condition in the Note under Rule 6-8b, the following wording is recommended:

> 'When play is suspended by the Committee for a dangerous situation, if the players in a match or group are between the play of two holes, they shall not resume play until the Committee has ordered a resumption of play. If they are in the process of playing a hole, they shall discontinue play immediately and shall not thereafter resume play until the Committee has ordered a resumption of play. If a player fails to discontinue play immediately, he shall be disqualified unless circumstances warrant waiving such penalty as provided in Rule 33-7.
>
>   The signal for suspending play due to a dangerous situation will be a prolonged note of the siren.'

The following signals are generally used and it is recommended that all Committees do similarly:
Discontinue Play Immediately: One prolonged note of siren.
Discontinue Play: Three consecutive notes of siren, repeated.
Resume Play: Two short notes of siren, repeated.

5. Practice
a. General
The Committee may make regulations governing practice in accordance with the Note to Rule 7-1, Exception (c) to Rule 7-2, and Rule 33-2c.

b. Practice Between Holes (Note 2 to Rule 7)
It is recommended that a condition of competition prohibiting practice putting or chipping on or near the putting green of the hole last played is only introduced in stroke play competitions. The following wording is recommended:

> 'A player shall not play any practice stroke on or near the putting green of the hole last played. If a practice stroke is played on or near the putting green of the hole last played, the player shall incur a penalty of two strokes at the next hole, except that in the case of the last hole of the round, he incurs the penalty at that hole.'

6. Advice in Team Competitions
If the Committee wishes to act in accordance with the Note under Rule 8, the following wording is recommended:

> 'In accordance with the Note to Rule 8 of the Rules of Golf, each team may appoint one person (in addition to the persons from whom advice may be asked under the Rule) who may give advice to members of that team. Such person (if it is desired to insert

any restriction on who may be nominated insert such restriction here) shall be identified to the Committee before giving advice.'

7. New Holes

The Committee may provide, in accordance with the Note to Rule 33-2b, that the holes and teeing grounds for a single round competition, being held on more than one day, may be differently situated on each day.

Other conditions of the competition might include:

Transportation

If it is desired to require players to walk in a competition, the following condition is recommended:

'Players shall walk at all times during a stipulated round.

PENALTY FOR BREACH OF CONDITION:

Match play – At the conclusion of the hole at which the breach is discovered, the state of the match shall be adjusted by deducting one hole for each hole at which a breach occurred. Maximum deduction per round: Two holes.

Stroke play – Two strokes for each hole at which any breach occurred; maximum penalty per round: Four strokes. In the event of a breach between the play of two holes, the penalty applies to the next hole.

Match or stroke play – Use of any unauthorised form of transportation shall be discontinued immediately upon discovery that a breach has occurred. Otherwise, the player shall be disqualified.'

How to Decide Ties

Rule 33-6 empowers the Committee to determine how and when a halved match or a stroke play tie shall be decided. The decision should be published in advance.

The R&A recommends:

Match Play

A match which ends all square should be played off hole by hole until one side wins a hole. The play-off should start on the hole where the match began. In a handicap match, handicap stokes should be allowed as in the prescribed round.

Stroke Play

(a) In the event of a tie in a scratch stroke play competition, a play-off is recommended. Such a play-off may be over 18 holes or a smaller number of holes as specified by the Committee. If that is not feasible or there is still a tie, a hole-by-hole play-off is recommended.

(b) In the event of a tie in a handicap stroke play competition, a play-off with handicaps is recommended. Such a play-off may be over 18 holes or a smaller number of holes as specified by the Committee. If the play-off is less than 18 holes, the percentage of 18 holes to be played should be applied to the players' handicaps to determine their play-off handicaps. Handicap stroke fractions of one-half stroke or more should count as a full stroke and any lesser fraction should be disregarded.

(c) In either a scratch or handicap stroke play competition, if a play-off of any type is not feasible, matching score cards is recommended. The method of matching cards should be announced in advance. An acceptable method of matching cards is to determine the winner on the basis of the best score for the last nine holes. If the tying players have the same score for the last nine, determine the winner on the basis of the last six holes, last three holes and finally the 18th hole. If such a method is used in a handicap stroke play competition, one-half, one-third, one-sixth, etc. of the handicaps should be deducted. Fractions should not be disregarded. If such a method is used in a competition with a multiple tee start, it is recommended that the 'last nine holes, last six holes, etc.' is considered to be holes 10-18, 13-18, etc.

(d) If the conditions of the competition provide that ties shall be decided over the last nine, last six, last three and last hole, they should also provide what will happen if this procedure does not produce a winner.

Draw for Match Play

Although the draw for match play may be completely blind or certain players may be distributed through different quarters or eighths, the General Numerical Draw is recommended if matches are determined by a qualifying round.

General Numerical Draw

For purposes of determining places in the draw, ties in qualifying rounds other than those for the last qualifying place shall be decided by the order in which scores are returned, with the first score to be returned receiving the lowest available number, etc. If it is impossible to determine the order in which scores are returned, ties shall be determined by a blind draw.

Upper half	Lower Half	Upper Half	Lower Half
64 Qualifiers		32 Qualifiers	
1 vs 64	2 vs 63	1 vs 32	2 vs 31
32 vs 33	31 vs 34	16 vs 17	15 vs 18
16 vs 49	15 vs 50	8 vs 25	7 vs 26
17 vs 48	18 vs 47	9 vs 24	10 vs 23
8 vs 57	7 vs 58	4 vs 29	3 vs 30
25 vs 40	26 vs 39	13 vs 20	14 vs 19
9 vs 56	10 vs 55	5 vs 28	6 vs 27
24 vs 41	23 vs 42	12 vs 21	11 vs 22
4 vs 61	3 vs 62	16 Qualifiers	
29 vs 36	30 vs 35	1 vs 16	2 vs 15
13 vs 52	14 vs 51	8 vs 9	7 vs 10
20 vs 45	19 vs 46	4 vs 13	3 vs 14
5 vs 60	6 vs 59	5 vs 12	6 vs 11
28 vs 37	27 vs 38	8 Qualifiers	
12 vs 53	11 vs 54	1 vs 8	2 vs 7
21 vs 44	22 vs 43	4 vs 5	3 vs 6

APPENDICES II AND III

Any design in a club or ball which is not covered by Rules 4 and 5 and Appendices II and III, or which might significantly change the nature of the game, will be ruled on by the Royal and Ancient Golf Club of St. Andrews.

The dimensions contained in Appendices II and III are referenced in imperial measurements. A metric conversion is also referenced for information, calculated using a conversion rate of 1 inch = 25.4 mm. In the event of any dispute over the conformity of a club or ball, the imperial measurement shall take precedence.

APPENDIX II
Design of Clubs

A player in doubt as to the conformity of a club should consult the Royal and Ancient Golf Club of St. Andrews.

A manufacturer should submit to the Royal and Ancient Golf Club of St. Andrews a sample of a club which is to be manufactured for a ruling as to whether the club conforms with the *Rules*. If a manufacturer fails to submit a sample before manufacturing and/or marketing the club, the manufacturer assumes the risk of a ruling that the club does not conform with the Rules. Any sample submitted to the Royal and Ancient Golf Club of St. Andrews will become its property for reference purposes.

The following paragraphs prescribe general regulations for the design of clubs, together with specifications and interpretations.

Where a club, or part of a club, is required to have some specific property, this means that it must be designed and manufactured with the intention of having that property. The finished club or part must have that property within manufacturing tolerances appropriate to the material used.

1. Clubs
a. General

A club is an implement designed to be used for striking the ball and generally comes in three forms: woods, irons and putters distinguished by shape and intended use. A putter is a club with a loft not exceeding ten degrees designed primarily for use on the putting green.

The club shall not be substantially different from the traditional and customary form and make. The club shall be composed of a shaft and a head. All parts of the club shall be fixed so that the club is one unit, and it shall have no external attachments except as otherwise permitted by the *Rules*.

b. Adjustability

Woods and irons shall not be designed to be adjustable except for weight. Putters may be designed to be adjustable for weight and some other forms of adjustability are also permitted. All methods of adjustment permitted by the *Rules* require that:

(i) the adjustment cannot be readily made;
(ii) all adjustable parts are firmly fixed and there is no reasonable likelihood of them working loose during a round; and
(iii) all configurations of adjustment conform with the Rules.

The disqualification penalty for purposely changing the playing characteristics of a club during a *stipulated round* (Rule 4-2a) applies to all clubs including a putter.

c. Length

The overall length of the club shall be at least 18 inches (457.2 mm) measured from the top of the grip along the axis of the shaft or a straight line extension of it to the sole of the club.

d. Alignment

When the club is in its normal address position the shaft shall be so aligned that:

(i) the projection of the straight part of the shaft on to the vertical plane through the toe and heel shall diverge from the vertical by at least 10 degrees (see Fig. I).
(ii) the projection of the straight part of the shaft on to the vertical plane along the intended line of play shall not diverge from the vertical by more than 20 degrees (see Fig. II).

Except for putters, all of the heel portion of the club shall lie within 0.625 inches (15.88 mm) of the plane containing the axis of the straight part of the shaft and the intended (horizontal) line of play (see Fig. III).

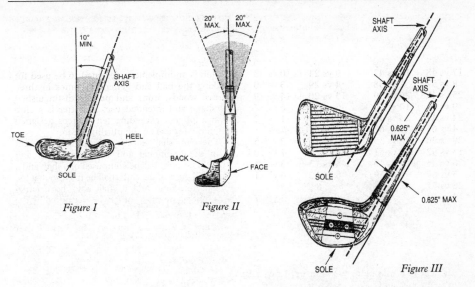

Figure I   Figure II   Figure III

2. Shaft
a. Straightness
The shaft shall be straight from the top of the grip to a point not more than 5 inches (127mm) above the sole, measured from the point where the shaft ceases to be straight along the axis of the bent part of the shaft and the neck and/or socket (see Fig. IV).

b. Bending and Twisting Properties
At any point along its length, the shaft shall:

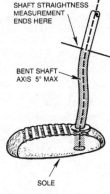

Figure IV

(i) bend in such a way that the deflection is the same regardless of how the shaft is rotated about its longitudinal axis; and

(ii) twist the same amount in both directions.

c. Attachment to Clubhead
The shaft shall be attached to the clubhead at the heel either directly or through a single plain neck and/or socket. The length from the top of the neck and/or socket to the sole of the club shall not exceed 5 inches (127mm), measured along the axis of, and following any bend in, the neck and/or socket (see Fig. V).

Exception for Putters: The shaft or neck or socket of a putter may be fixed at any point in the head.

3. Grip (See Fig. VI)
The grip consists of material added to the shaft to enable the player to obtain a firm hold. The grip shall be straight and plain in form, shall extend to the end of the shaft and shall not be moulded for any part of the hands. If no material is added, that portion of the shaft designed to be held by the player shall be considered the grip.

(i) For clubs other than putters the grip must be circular in cross-section, except that a continuous, straight, slightly raised rib may be incorporated along the full length of the grip, and a slightly indented spiral is permitted on a wrapped grip or a replica of one.

(ii) A putter grip may have a non-circular cross-section, provided the cross-section has no concavity, is symmetrical and remains generally similar throughout the length of the grip. (See Clause (v) below.)

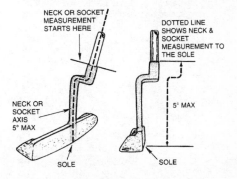

Figure V

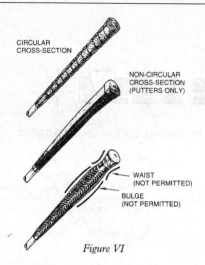

CIRCULAR
CROSS-SECTION

NON-CIRCULAR
CROSS-SECTION
(PUTTERS ONLY)

WAIST
(NOT PERMITTED)

BULGE
(NOT PERMITTED)

Figure VI

(iii) The grip may be tapered but must not have any bulge or waist. Its cross-sectional dimensions measured in any direction must not exceed 1.75 inches (44.45 mm).

(iv) For clubs other than putters the axis of the grip must coincide with the axis of the shaft.

(v) A putter may have two grips provided each is circular in cross-section, the axis of each coincides with the axis of the shaft, and they are separated by at least 1.5 inches (38.1 mm).

4. Clubhead
a. Plain in Shape

The clubhead shall be generally plain in shape. All parts shall be rigid, structural in nature and functional. It is not practicable to define plain in shape precisely and comprehensively but features which are deemed to be in breach of this requirement and are therefore not permitted include:

(i) holes through the head,

(ii) transparent material added for other than decorative or structural purposes,

(iii) appendages to the main body of the head such as knobs, plates, rods or fins,

for the purpose of meeting dimensional specifications, for aiming or for any other purpose. Exceptions may be made for putters.

Any furrows in or runners on the sole shall not extend into the face.

b. Dimensions

The distance from the heel to the toe of the clubhead shall be greater than the distance from the face to the back. These dimensions are measured, with the clubhead in its normal address position, on horizontal lines between vertical projections of the outermost points of (i) the heel and the toe and (ii) the face and the back (see Fig. VII, dimension A). If the outermost point of the heel is not clearly defined, it is deemed to be 0.625 inches (15.88 mm) above the horizontal plane on which the club is resting in its normal address position (see Fig. VII, dimension B).

c. Striking Faces

The clubhead shall only have one striking face, except that a putter may have two such faces if their characteristics are the same, and they are opposite each other.

5. Club Face
a. General

The material and construction of, or any treatment to, the face or clubhead shall not have the effect at impact of a spring (test on file), or impart significantly more spin to the ball than a standard steel face, or have any other effect which would unduly influence the movement of the ball.

The face of the club shall be hard and rigid (some exceptions may be made for putters) and, except for such markings listed below, shall be smooth and shall not have any degree of concavity.

b. Impact Area Roughness and Material

Except for markings specified in the following paragraphs, the surface roughness within the area where impact is intended (the 'impact area') must not exceed that of decorative sandblasting, or of fine milling (see Fig. VIII).

The whole of the impact area must be of the same material. Exceptions may be made for wooden clubs.

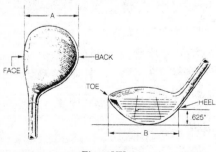

FACE

BACK

TOE

HEEL

A

B

625°

Figure VII

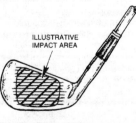

ILLUSTRATIVE
IMPACT AREA

Figure VIII

c. Impact Area Markings
Markings in the impact area must not have sharp edges or raised lips as determined by a finger test. Grooves or punch marks in the impact area must meet the following specifications:

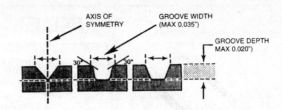

EXAMPLES OF PERMISSIBLE GROOVE CROSS-SECTIONS

Figure IX

(i) Grooves. A series of straight grooves with diverging sides and a symmetrical cross-section may be used (see Fig. IX). The width and cross-section must be consistent across the face of the club and along the length of the grooves. Any rounding of groove edges shall be in the form of a radius which does not exceed 0.020 inches (0.508 mm). The width of the grooves shall not exceed 0.035 inches (0.9mm), using the 30 degree method of measurement on file with the Royal and Ancient Golf Club of St. Andrews. The distance between edges of adjacent grooves must not be less than three times the width of a groove, and not less than 0.075 inches (1.905 mm). The depth of a groove must not exceed 0.020 inches (0.508 mm).

(ii) Punch Marks. Punch marks may be used. The area of any such mark must not exceed 0.0044 square inches (2.84 sq.mm). A mark must not be closer to an adjacent mark than 0.168 inches (4.27 mm) measured from centre to centre. The depth of a punch mark must not exceed 0.040 inches (1.02 mm). If punch marks are used in combination with grooves, a punch mark must not be closer to a groove than 0.168 inches (4.27 mm), measured from centre to centre.

d. Decorative Markings
The centre of the impact area may be indicated by a design within the boundary of a square whose sides are 0.375 inches (9.53 mm) in length. Such a design must not unduly influence the movement of the ball. Decorative markings are permitted outside the impact area.

e. Non-metallic Club Face Markings
The above specifications apply to clubs on which the impact area of the face is of metal or a material of similar hardness. They do not apply to clubs with faces made of other materials and whose loft angle is 24 degrees or less, but markings which could unduly influence the movement of the ball are prohibited. Clubs with this type of face and a loft angle exceeding 24 degrees may have grooves of maximum width 0.040 inches (1.02 mm) and maximum depth 1½ times the groove width, but must otherwise conform to the markings specifications above.

f. Putter Face
The specifications above with regard to roughness, material and markings in the impact area do not apply to putters.

APPENDIX III
The Ball

1. Weight
The weight of the ball shall not be greater than 1.620 ounces avoirdupois (45.93 gm).

2. Size
The diameter of the ball shall be not less than 1.680 inches (42.67mm). This specification will be satisfied if, under its own weight, a ball falls through a 1.680 inches diameter ring gauge in fewer than 25 out of 100 randomly selected positions, the test being carried out at a temperature of $23 \pm 1°C$.

3. Spherical Symmetry
The ball must not be designed, manufactured or intentionally modified to have properties which differ from those of a spherically symmetrical ball.

4. Initial Velocity
The initial velocity of the ball shall not exceed the limit specified (test on file) when measured on apparatus approved by the Royal and Ancient Golf Club of St. Andrews.

5. Overall Distance Standard
The combined carry and roll of the ball, when tested on apparatus approved by the Royal and Ancient Golf Club of St. Andrews, shall not exceed the distance specified under the conditions set forth in the Overall Distance Standard for golf balls on file with the Royal and Ancient Golf Club of St. Andrews.

INDEX

The Rules of Golf are here indexed according to the
pertinant rule number, definition or appendix that has gone before.

HANDICAPS

The Rules of Golf do not legislate for the allocation and adjustment of handicaps. Such matters are within the jurisdiction of the National Union concerned and queries should be directed accordingly.

RULES OF AMATEUR STATUS

As approved by the Royal and Ancient Golf Club of St Andrews
Effective from 1st January 2000

Preamble
The Royal and Ancient Golf Club of St. Andrews reserves the right to change the Rules and to make and change the interpretations relating to Amateur Status at any time.

Definitions

The Definitions are placed in alphabetical order and some are also repeated at the beginning of their relevant Rule.

In the Rules themselves, defined terms are italicised.

Amateur Golfer
An 'Amateur Golfer' is one who plays the game as a non-remunerative and non-profit-making sport and who does not receive remuneration for teaching golf or for other activities because of *golf skill or reputation*, except as provided in the *Rules*.

Committee
The 'Committee' is the appropriate Committee of the *Governing Body*.

Golf Skill or Reputation
Generally, an *Amateur golfer* is only considered to have golf skill if he has gained representative honours at county or national level. Golf reputation can only be gained through golf skill and does not include prominence for service to the game of golf as an administrator. It is a matter for a *Governing Body* to decide whether a particular *Amateur golfer* has 'golf skill or reputation'.

Governing Body
The 'Governing Body' for the Rules of Amateur Status in any country is the national union of that country.

Note: In Great Britain and Ireland, the Royal and Ancient Golf Club of St. Andrews is the *Governing Body*.

Instruction
'Instruction' covers teaching the physical aspects of playing golf i.e. the actual mechanics of swinging a golf club and hitting a golf ball.

Junior Golfer
A 'junior golfer' is an *Amateur golfer* who has not reached his 18th birthday in the year prior to the event, unless a different age is decided by the *Governing Body*.

Prize Voucher
A 'prize voucher' is a voucher issued by the Committee in charge of a competition for the purchase of goods from a Professional's shop or other retail source.

Retail Value
The 'retail value' of a prize is the normal recommended selling price at which merchandise is available to anyone at a retail source.

Rule or Rules
The term 'Rule' or 'Rules' refers to the Rules of Amateur Status as determined by the *Governing Body*.

Symbolic Prize
A 'symbolic prize' is a trophy made of gold, silver, ceramic, glass or the like which is permanently and distinctively engraved.

Testimonial Award
A 'testimonial award' relates to notable performances or contributions to golf as distinguished from competition prizes. A testimonial award may not be a monetary award.

Rule 1. Amateurism

Definitions
An **Amateur golfer** is one who plays the game as a non-remunerative and non-profit-making sport and who does not receive remuneration for teaching golf or for other activities because of *golf skill or reputation*, except as provided in the *Rules*.

The term **Rule** or **Rules** refers to the Rules of Amateur Status as determined by the *Governing Body*.

1-1. General
An *Amateur golfer* must play the game and conduct himself in accordance with the *Rules*.

1-2. Amateur Status
Amateur Status is a universal condition of eligibility for playing in golf competitions as an *Amateur golfer*. A person who acts contrary to the *Rules* may forfeit his status as an *Amateur golfer* and as a result will be ineligible to play in Amateur competitions.

1-3. Purpose and Spirit of the Rules
The purpose and spirit of the *Rules* is to maintain the distinction between Amateur golf and Professional golf and keep the Amateur game as free as possible from the abuses which may follow from uncontrolled sponsorship and financial incentive. It is considered necessary to safeguard Amateur golf, which is largely self-regulating with regard to the Rules of play and handicapping, so that it may be fully enjoyed by all *Amateur golfers*.

1-4. Doubt as to Rules
Any person who wishes to be an *Amateur golfer* and who is in doubt as to whether taking a proposed course of action is permitted under the *Rules* should consult the *Governing Body*.

Any organiser or sponsor of an Amateur golf competition or a competition involving *Amateur golfers*, who is in doubt as to whether a proposal is in accordance with the *Rules* should consult the *Governing Body*.

Rule 2. Professionalism

2-1. General
An *Amateur golfer* must not take any action for the purpose of becoming a Professional golfer, including entering into an agreement, written or oral, with a sponsor or Professional agent.

Exception: Applying unsuccessfully for the position of an Assistant Professional.

Note: An *Amateur golfer* may enquire as to his likely prospects as a Professional and he may work in a Professional's shop and receive a salary, provided he does not infringe the *Rules* in any other way.

2-2. Professional Golfers' Associations
An *Amateur golfer* must not hold or retain membership of any Professional Golfers' Association.

2-3. Professional Tournament Players
An *Amateur golfer* must not file an application to a final or sole qualifying competition for a Professional Tour.

Note: If an *Amateur golfer* must pre-qualify for a final qualifying competition, he may enter such a pre-qualifying competition without forfeiting his Amateur Status.

Rule 3. Prizes

Definitions
The **Governing Body** for the Rules of Amateur Status in any country is the national union of that country.

Note: In Great Britain and Ireland, the Royal and Ancient Golf Club of St. Andrews is the *Governing Body*.

A **prize voucher** is a voucher issued by the Committee in charge of a competition for the purchase of goods from a Professional's shop or other retail source.

The **retail value** of a prize is the normal recommended selling price at which merchandise is available to anyone at a retail source.

A **symbolic prize** is a trophy made of gold, silver, ceramic, glass or the like which is permanently and distinctively engraved.

A **testimonial award** relates to notable performances or contributions to golf as distinguished from competition prizes. A testimonial award may not be a monetary award.

3-1. Playing for Prize Money
An *Amateur golfer* must not play golf for prize money.

3-2. Prize Limits
a. General
An *Amateur golfer* must not accept a prize (other than a *symbolic prize*) or *prize voucher* of *retail value* in excess of the prescribed limits. These limits apply to the total prizes or *prize vouchers* received by an *Amateur golfer* in any one competition or series of competitions, excluding any hole-in-one prize.

In Europe	£300	or the equivalent
Elsewhere	$US500	or the equivalent

or such lesser figure as may be decided by the *Governing Body*.

b. Hole-in-One Prizes
The limits prescribed in Rule 3-2a apply to a prize for a hole-in-one. However, such a prize may be accepted in addition to any other prize won in the same competition.

c. Exchanging Prizes

An *Amateur golfer* must not exchange a prize or *prize voucher* for cash.

Exception: An *Amateur golfer* may submit a *prize voucher* to a national or county union and thereafter be reimbursed from the value of that voucher for expenses incurred in participating in a golf competition, provided the reimbursement of such expenses is permitted under Rule 4-2.

Note 1: The onus of proving the *retail value* of a particular prize rests with the Committee in charge of the competition.

Note 2: It is recommended that the total value of scratch prizes, or each division of handicap prizes, should not exceed twice the prescribed limit in an 18-hole competition, three times in a 36-hole competition, four times in a 54-hole competition and five times in a 72-hole competition.

3-3. Testimonial Awards
a. General

An *Amateur golfer* must not accept a *testimonial award* of *retail value* in excess of the limits prescribed in Rule 3-2a.

b. Multiple Awards

An *Amateur golfer* may accept more than one *testimonial award* from different donors, even though their total *retail value* exceeds the prescribed limit, provided they are not presented so as to evade the limit for a single award.

Rule 4. Expenses

Definitions

The **Governing Body** for the Rules of Amateur Status in any country is the national union of that country.

Note: In Great Britain and Ireland, The Royal and Ancient Golf Club of St. Andrews is the *Governing Body*.

A **junior golfer** is an *Amateur golfer* who has not reached his 18th birthday in the year prior to the event, unless a different age is decided by the *Governing Body*.

4-1. General

Except as provided in the *Rules*, an *Amateur golfer* must not accept expenses, in money or otherwise, from any source to play in a golf competition or exhibition.

4-2. Receipt of Expenses

An *Amateur golfer* may receive expenses, not exceeding the actual expenses incurred, to play in a golf competition or exhibition as follows:-

a. Family support

An *Amateur golfer* may receive expenses from a member of his family or a legal guardian.

b. Junior Golfers

A *junior golfer* may receive expenses when competing in a competition limited exclusively to *junior golfers*.

c. Team Events

(i) An *Amateur golfer*, who is representing his country, county or club (or similar body) in a team competition or at a training camp may receive expenses; and

(ii) An *Amateur golfer*, who is representing his country by taking part in a national championship abroad immediately before or after an international team competition may receive expenses.

The expenses must be paid by the body he represents or the body controlling golf in the country he is visiting.

d. Individual Events

An *Amateur golfer* may receive expenses when competing in individual events provided he complies with the following provisions:

(i) The player must be nominated to play in the competition by either his club, county or national union.

(ii) Where the competition is to take place in the player's own country and the nomination has been made by a club or county union, the approval of the national union, or the county union in the area in which the competition is to be staged, must first be obtained.

(iii) Where the competition is to take place in another country, the approval of the national union of the country in which the competition is to be staged and, if the nominating body is not the national union of the country from which the nomination is made, the approval of the national union must first be obtained by the nominating body.

(iv) The expenses must be paid only by the national union or county union responsible in the area from which the nomination is made or, subject to the approval of the nominating body, by the body controlling golf in the territory he is visiting.

(v) The expenses must be limited to a specific number of competitive days in any one calendar year as may be determined by the *Governing Body* in the country from which the nomination is made. The expenses are deemed to include reasonable travelling time and practice days in connection with the competitive days.

e. Celebrities, Business Associates, etc.

An *Amateur golfer* who is invited to take part in a competition for reasons unrelated to *golf skill* may receive expenses.

f. Exhibitions

An *Amateur golfer* who is participating in an exhibition in aid of a recognised charity may receive expenses, provided that the exhibition is not run in connection with another golfing event.

g. Sponsored Handicap Competitions

An *Amateur golfer* may receive expenses when competing in a sponsored handicap competition, provided the competition has been approved as follows:

(i) Where the competition is to take place in the player's own country, the annual approval of the *Governing Body* must first be obtained in advance by the sponsor; and

(ii) Where the competition is to take place in more than one country or involves golfers from another country, the approval of the two or more *Governing Bodies* must first be obtained in advance by the sponsor. The application for this approval should be sent to the *Governing Body* in the country where the competition commences.

Rule 5. Instruction

Definitions

Instruction covers teaching the physical aspects of playing golf, i.e. the actual mechanics of swinging a golf club and hitting a golf ball.

A **junior golfer** is an *Amateur golfer* who has not reached his 18th birthday in the year prior to the event, unless a different age is decided by the *Governing Body*.

5-1. General

Except as provided in the *Rules*, an *Amateur golfer* must not receive payment or compensation for giving *instruction* in playing golf.

5-2. Where Payment Permitted
a. Schools, Colleges, etc.

An *Amateur golfer*, who is an employee of an educational institution or system, may receive payment or compensation for golf *instruction* to students of the institution or system, provided that during a year the total time devoted to golf *instruction* comprises less than 50 percent of the time spent in the performance of all duties as such an employee.

b. Junior Golfers

An *Amateur golfer* may receive expenses, not exceeding the actual expenses incurred, for giving golf *instruction* to *junior golfers* as part of a programme which has been approved in advance by the *Governing Body*.

5-3. Instruction in Writing

An *Amateur golfer* may receive payment or compensation for *instruction* in writing, provided his ability or reputation as a golfer was not a major factor in his employment or in the commission or sale of his work.

Note: *Instruction* does not cover the many psychological aspects of the game or the Rules or Etiquette of Golf.

Rule 6. Use of Golf Skill or Reputation

Definitions

Generally, an *Amateur golfer* is only considered to have golf skill if he has gained honours at county or national level. Golf reputation can only be gained through golf skill and does not include prominence for service to the game of golf as an administrator. It is a matter for a *Governing Body* to decide whether a particular *Amateur golfer* has **golf skill or reputation**.

The **Governing Body** for the Rules of Amateur Status in any country is the national union of that country.

Note: In Great Britain and Ireland, the Royal and Ancient Golf Club of St. Andrews is the *Governing Body*.

Instruction covers teaching the physical aspects of playing golf, i.e. the actual mechanics of swinging a golf club and hitting a golf ball.

6-1. General

Except as provided in the *Rules*, an *Amateur golfer* of *golf skill or reputation* must not use that skill or reputation to promote, advertise or sell anything or for any financial gain.

6-2. Lending Name or Likeness

An *Amateur golfer* of *golf skill or reputation* must not use that skill or reputation to obtain payment, compensation, personal benefit or any financial gain for allowing his name or likeness to be used for the advertisement or sale of anything.

Note: An *Amateur golfer* may accept equipment from anyone dealing in such equipment provided no advertising is involved.

6-3. Personal Appearance

An *Amateur golfer* of *golf skill or reputation* must not use that skill or reputation to obtain payment, compensation, personal benefit or any financial gain for a personal appearance.

Exception: An *Amateur golfer* may receive actual expenses in connection with a personal appearance provided no golf competition or exhibition is involved.

6-4. Broadcasting and Writing

An *Amateur golfer* of *golf skill or reputation* must not use that skill or reputation to obtain payment, compensation, personal benefit or any financial gain for broadcasting concerning golf or writing golf articles or books.

Exception: An *Amateur golfer* may receive payment, compensation, personal benefit or any financial gain from broadcasting or writing provided:

(a) the player is actually the author of the commentary, article or books; and

(b) *instruction* in playing golf is not included.

6-5. Grants, Scholarships and Bursaries
An *Amateur golfer* of *golf skill or reputation* must not accept the benefits of a grant, scholarship or bursary, except one whose terms and conditions have been approved by the *Governing Body*.

6-6. Membership
An *Amateur golfer* of *golf skill or reputation* must not accept an offer of membership in a Golf Club without full payment for the class of membership if such an offer is made as an inducement to play for that Club.

Rule 7. Other Conduct Incompatible with Amateurism

Definitions
An **Amateur golfer** is one who plays the game as a non-remunerative and non-profit-making sport and who does not receive remuneration for teaching golf or for other activities because of *golf skill or reputation*, except as provided in the *Rules*.

The term **Rule** or **Rules** refers to the Rules of Amateur Status as determined by the *Governing Body*.

7-1. Conduct Detrimental to Golf
An *Amateur golfer* must not act in a manner which is considered detrimental to the best interests of the game.

7-2. Conduct Contrary to the Purpose and Spirit of the Rules
An *Amateur golfer* must not take any action, including actions relating to golf gambling, which is contrary to the purpose and spirit of the *Rules*.

Rule 8. Procedure for Enforcement of the Rules

Definitions
The **Committee** is the appropriate Committee of the *Governing Body*.

The **Governing Body** for the Rules of Amateur Status in any country is the national union of that country.

Note: In Great Britain and Ireland, the Royal and Ancient Golf Club of St. Andrews is the *Governing Body*.

8-1. Decision on a Breach
If a possible breach of the *Rules* by a person claiming to be an *Amateur golfer* comes to the attention of the *Committee*, it is a matter for the *Committee* to decide whether a breach has occurred. Each case will be investigated to the extent deemed appropriate by the *Committee* and considered on its merits. The decision of the *Committee* shall be final, subject to an Appeal as provided in these *Rules*.

8-2. Enforcement
Upon a decision that a person has breached the *Rules*, the *Committee* may declare the Amateur Status of the person forfeited or require the person to refrain or desist from specified actions as a condition of retaining his Amateur Status.

The *Committee* must use its best endeavours to ensure that the person is notified and may notify any interested golf union of any action taken under Rule 8-2.

8-3. Appeals Procedure
A person affected by a decision made by the Amateur Status Committee of the Royal and Ancient Golf Club of St. Andrews in respect of the enforcement of these *Rules*, may raise an appeal of that decision with the Amateur Status Appeals Committee.

Note: Each *Governing Body* should put in place a procedure whereby any decision in respect of forfeiture of Amateur Status may be appealed by the person affected by such decision.

Rule 9. Reinstatement of Amateur Status

Definitions
The **Committee** is the appropriate Committee of the *Governing Body*.

The **Governing Body** for the Rules of Amateur Status in any country is the national union of that country.

Note: In Great Britain and Ireland, the Royal and Ancient Golf Club of St. Andrews is the *Governing Body*.

9-1. General
The *Committee* has sole power to reinstate a person to Amateur Status or to deny reinstatement, subject to an Appeal as provided in these *Rules*. Each application for reinstatement shall be considered on its merits.

9-2. Applications for Reinstatement
In considering an application for reinstatement, the *Committee* shall normally be guided by the following principles:

a. Awaiting Reinstatement
The Professional is considered to hold an advantage over the *Amateur golfer* by reason of having devoted himself to the game as his profession; other persons infringing the *Rules* also obtain advantages not available to the *Amateur golfer*. They do not necessarily lose such advantages merely by deciding to cease infringing the *Rules*. Therefore, an applicant for reinstatement to Amateur Status must undergo a period awaiting reinstatement as prescribed by the *Committee*.

The period awaiting reinstatement starts from the date of the person's last breach of the *Rules* unless the *Committee* decides that it starts from the date when the person's last breach became known to the *Committee*.

b. Period Awaiting Reinstatement
(i) Professionalism
The period awaiting reinstatement is normally related to the period the person was in breach. However, no applicant is normally eligible for reinstatement until he has conducted himself in accordance with the *Rules* for a period of at least one year.

It is recommended that the following guidelines on periods awaiting reinstatement are applied by the *Committee:*

Period of Breach:	Period Awaiting Reinstatement:
under 2 years	1 year
2-10 years	2 years
over 10 years	3 years

The *Committee* reserves the right to extend or to shorten such a period. Players of national prominence who have been in breach for more than five years are not normally eligible for reinstatement.

(ii) Other Breaches of the Rules
The period awaiting reinstatement is normally related to the seriousness of the breach, i.e. the value of the excessive prize, the amount of unauthorised expenses received, etc. However, no applicant is normally eligible for reinstatement until he has conducted himself in accordance with the *Rules* for a period of at least two years.

The *Committee* reserves the right to extend or shorten such a period.

(iii) Second Reinstatement
The period awaiting reinstatement is normally three years irrespective of the period of breach.

The *Committee* reserves the right to extend or shorten such a period.

c. Number of Reinstatements
A person is not normally reinstated more than twice.

d. Status While Awaiting Reinstatement
During the period awaiting reinstatement an applicant for reinstatement must comply with these *Rules* as they apply to an *Amateur golfer*.

He is not eligible to enter competitions as an *Amateur golfer*. However, he may enter competitions and win a prize solely among members of a Club of which he is a member, subject to the approval of the Club; but he may not represent such Club against other Clubs.

9-3. Procedure for Applications
Each application for reinstatement must be submitted to the *Committee*, in accordance with such procedures as may be laid down and it must include such information as the *Committee* may require.

9-4. Appeals Procedure
A person affected by a decision made by the Amateur Status Committee of the Royal and Ancient Golf Club of St. Andrews in respect of reinstatement of Amateur Status, may raise an appeal of that decision with the Amateur Status Appeals Committee.

Note: Each *Governing Body* should put in place a procedure whereby any decision in respect of reinstatement of Amateur Status may be appealed by the person affected by such a decision.

Rule 10. Committee Decision

Definition
The **Committee** is the appropriate Committee of the *Governing Body*.

10-1. Committee's Decision
The *Committee's* decision is final, subject to an Appeal as provided in Rules 8-3 and 9-4.

10-2. Doubt as to Rules
If the *Committee* considers the case to be doubtful or not covered by the *Rules*, it may, prior to making its decision, consult with the Amateur Status Committee of the Royal and Ancient Golf Club of St. Andrews.

Other Governing Bodies

Home Unions

The English Golf Union

The English Golf Union was founded in 1924 and embraces 34 County Unions with 1895 affiliated clubs, 24 clubs overseas, and 500 Golfing Societies and Associations. Its objects are:

(1) To further the interests of Amateur Golf in England.
(2) To assist in maintaining a uniform system of handicapping.
(3) To arrange an English Championship; an English Strokeplay Championship; an English County Championship, International and other Matches and Competitions.
(4) To cooperate with the Royal & Ancient Golf Club of St Andrews and the Council of National Golf Unions.
(5) To cooperate with other National Golf Unions and Associations in such manner as may be decided.

The Scottish Golf Union

The Scottish Golf Union was founded in 1920 and embraces 695 clubs. Subject to the stipulation and declaration that the Union recognises the Royal & Ancient Golf Club of St Andrews as the Ruling Authority in the game of golf, the objects of the Union are:

(a) To foster and maintain a high standard of amateur golf in Scotland and to administer and organise and generally act as the governing body of amateur golf in Scotland.
(b) To institute and thereafter carry through annually a Scottish Amateur Championship, a Scottish Open Amateur Strokeplay Championship and other such competitions and matches as they consider appropriate.
(c) To administer and apply the rules of the Standard Scratch Score and Handicapping Scheme as approved by the Council of National Golf Unions from time to time.
(d) To deal with other matters of general or local interest to amateur golfers in Scotland.

The Union's organisation consists of Area Committees covering the whole of Scotland. There are 16 Areas, each having its own Association or Committee elected by the Clubs in that particular area and each Area Association or Committee elects one delegate to serve on the Executive of the Union.

Golfing Union of Ireland

The Golfing Union of Ireland, founded in 1891, embraces 398 Clubs. Its objects are:

(1) Securing the federation of the various Clubs.
(2) Arranging Amateur Championships, Inter-Provincial and Inter-Club Competitions, and International Matches.
(3) Securing a uniform standard of handicapping.
(4) Providing for advice and assistance, other than financial, to affiliated Clubs in all matters appertaining to Golf, and generally to promote the game in every way, in which this can be better done by the Union than by individual Clubs.

Its functions include the holding of the Close Championship for Amateur Golfers and Tournaments for Team Matches.

Its organisation consists of Provincial Councils in each of the four Provinces elected by the Clubs in the Province – each province electing a limited number of delegates to the Central Council which meets annually.

Welsh Golfing Union

The Welsh Golfing Union was founded in 1895 and is the second oldest of the four National Unions. Unlike the other Unions it is an association of Golf Clubs and Golfing Organisations. The present membership is 159. For the purpose of electing the Executive Council, Wales is divided into ten districts which between them return 22 members. The objects of the Union are:

(a) To take any steps which may be deemed necessary to further the interests of the amateur game in Wales.
(b) To hold a Championship Meeting or Meetings each year.
(c) To encourage, financially and/or otherwise, Inter-Club, Inter-County, and International Matches, and such other events as may be authorised by the Council.

(d) To assist in setting up and maintaining a uniform system of Handicapping.

(e) To assist in the establishment and maintenance of high standards of greenkeeping.

Note: The union recognises the Royal & Ancient Golf Club of St Andrews as the ruling authority.

The Council of National Golf Unions

At a meeting of Representatives of Golf Unions and Associations in Great Britain and Ireland, called at the special request of the Scottish Golf Union, and held in York, on 14th February, 1924, resolutions were adopted from which the Council of National Golf Unions was constituted.

The Council holds an Annual Meeting in March, and such other meetings as may be necessary. Two representatives are elected from each national Home Union – England, Scotland, Ireland and Wales and one from the Royal and Ancient Golf Club of St Andrews – and hold office until the next Annual meeting when they are eligible for re-election.

The principal function of the Council, as laid down by the York Conference, was to formulate a system of Standard Scratch Scores and Handicapping, and to co-operate with the Royal & Ancient Championship Committee in matters coming under their jurisdiction. The responsibilities undertaken by the Council at the instance of the Royal & Ancient Golf Club or the National Unions are as follows:

1   The Standard Scratch Score and Handicapping Scheme, formulated in March, 1926, approved by the Royal & Ancient, and last revised in 2001.

2   The nomination of one member on the Board of Management of The Sports Turf Research Institute, with an experimental station at St Ives, Bingley, Yorkshire.

3   The management of the Annual Amateur International Matches between the four countries – England, Scotland, Ireland and Wales.

United States Golf Association

The USGA is the national governing body of golf in the United States, dedicated to promoting and conserving the best interests and true spirit of the game.

Founded on 22 December 1894 by representatives of five American golf clubs, the USGA was originally charged with conducting national championships, implementing a uniform code of rules, and maintaining a national system of handicapping.

Today, the principal functions of the association remain lagely unchanged. Each year, the USGA conducts thirteen national championships for amateur and professional golfers; biennial competitions include State Team Championships for men and women, the Walker Cup, Curtis Cup, and World Amateur Team Championships. In cooperation with the Royal & Ancient Golf Club of St. Andrews, Scotland, the USGA continues to write and interpret the Rules of Golf, and oversees the standards regulating the equipment used to play the game. The association also maintains a national handicapping system, providing handicap computation services to state and regional golf associations through the Golf Handicap and Information Network.

Additional responsibilities assumed by the association encompass turfgrass and environmental research conducted by the USGA Green Section; preservation and promotion of the game's rich history in the Museum and Archives; oversight of the Rules of Amateur Status; publication of *Golf Journal*, the USGA's official magazine; and direction of the USGA Members Program, with over 900,000 members globally. Since 1965, the USGA Foundation has functioned as the association's broad-based philanthropic arm, dedicated to maintaining and improving the opportunities for all individuals to participate fully in the game.

Tel: +1 908 234 2300   Fax: +1 908 234 9687

The Professional Golfers' Association

The Professional Golfers' Association was founded in 1901 to promote interest in the game of golf; to protect and advance the mutual and trade interests of its members; to arrange and hold meetings and tournaments periodically for the members; to institute and operate funds for the benefit of the members; to assist the members to obtain employment; and effect any other objects of a like nature as may be determined from time to time by the Association.

Classes of Membership

There shall be nine classes of membership:

(i)   **Class A** Members engaged as the nominated professional on a full-time basis at a PGA Club, PGA Course or PGA Driving Range in one of the seven Regions; and members engaged as the nominated professional on a full-time basis, at an establishment in one of the seven Regions at which the public can play and/or practise which, in the opinion of the Executive Committee does not qualify as a PGA Club, Course or Driving Range but does warrant Class A status.

Note: Class A(T) – Class A members currently engaged at an establishment which has been inspected and approved as a PGA Training Establishment and currently holds that status will be identified where appropriate by the suffix (T) after their classification.

(ii) **Class B** Members engaged by a Class A or D member to assist the nominated professional at any PGA Establishment in one of the seven Regions on a full-time basis.

(iii) **Class C** Tournament playing members (men and women).

(iv) **Class D** Members engaged as the nominated professional on a full-time basis at a PGA Establishment within the seven Regions which does not qualify as a 'Class A' establishment, or engaged on a full-time basis within the seven Regions by any other Company or any other individual designated by the Executive Committee for this purpose. (Former Class G.)

(v) **Class E** Honorary Associate Members (HAM). Those who in the opinion of the Executive Committee through their past or continuing membership justify retaining the full privileges of membership as Honorary Associate Members (HAM).

(vi) **Class F** Associate Members (AM).

(a) Those who have ceased to be eligible for other categories of membership who in the opinion of the Executive Committee through their past membership justify retaining limited privileges of membership as Associate Members; and (b) Members of the PGA European Tour or WPGET who do not qualify for Class C membership but who in the opinion of the Executive Committee justify limited privileges of membership as Associate Members.

(vii) **Class G** Honorary Life Members (HLM). Those recommended by the Board to a Special General Meeting of the Association for election as Honorary Life Members. No form of application is needed nor need reference be made to the Regional Committee concerned.

(viii) **Class H** Members who are qualified members of the Association, and ineligible for any other class of membership, engaged on a full-time basis at an establishment acceptable to the Association outside the jurisdiction of the seven Regions. (Overseas)

(ix) **Class O** Members who have not qualified at the official training centre of the Association, who are ineligible for any other class of membership, and who are current members of another PGA approved by the Association and have held such membership for not less than two years.

The Management of the Association is under the overall direction and control of a Board. The Association is divided into seven Regions each of which employs a full-time secretary and runs tournaments for the benefit of members within its Region.

The Association is responsible for arranging and obtaining sponsorship of the Ryder Cup, Club Professionals' Championship, PGA Cup matches, Seniors' Championship, PGA Assistants' Championship, Assistants' Matchplay Championship and other National Championships.

Anyone who intends to become a club professional must serve a minimum of three years in registration and qualify at the PGA Training School before election as a full Member.

The Professional Golfers' Associations of Europe

The PGA of Europe was created in 1989 as an Association of national European PGAs to ensure uniformity of professional standards and objectives.

In its first ten years the PGAE grew to a body comprising 33 member PGAs, five of them Associate Members from outside the continent of Europe. These 33 PGAs are made up of a total of 12,000 professionals comprising Directors of Golf, Club Professionals, Teaching Professionals, all of whom provide a comprehensive service to the entire golfing community.

The purpose of the PGA or Europe is to:

(1) Unify and improve standards of education and qualification;

(2) Advise and assist golf professionals to achieve properly rewarded employment;

(3) Provide relevant playing opportunities;

(4) Be the central point of advice, information and support;

(5) Be a respected link with other golfing bodies throughout Europe and the rest of the world – all for the benefit of its members and the enhancement of the sport.

PGA European Tour

To be eligible to become a member of the PGA European Tour a player must possess certain minimum standards which shall be determined by the Tournament Committee. In 1976 a Qualifying School for potential new members was introduced to be held annually. The leading players are awarded cards allowing them to compete in PGA European Tour tournaments.

In 1985 the PGA European Tour became ALL EXEMPT with no more Monday pre-qualifying. Full details can be obtained from the Wentworth Headquarters.

The Evian Tour (Ladies' European Tour)

The Evian Tour was founded in 1988 to further the development of women's professional golf throughout Europe and its membership is open to all nationalities. A qualifying school is held annually and an amateur wishing to participate must be 18 years of age and have a handicap of 1 or less. Full details can be obtained from the Tour Headquarters at Tytherington.

Government of the Amateur and Open Golf Championship

In December 1919, on the invitation of the clubs who had hitherto controlled the Amateur and Open Golf Championships, the Royal & Ancient took over the government of those events. These two championships are now controlled by a committee appointed by the Royal & Ancient Golf Club of St Andrews. The Committee is called the Royal and Ancient Golf Club Championship Committee and consists of eight members of the Club elected by the Club.

Ladies' Golf Union (LGU)

The Ladies' Golf Union was founded in 1893 with the following objectives:

(1) To promote the interests of the game of Golf.
(2) To obtain a uniformity of the rules of the game by establishing a representative legislative authority.
(3) To establish a uniform system of handicapping.
(4) To act as a tribunal and court of reference on points of uncertainty.
(5) To arrange the Annual Championship Competition and obtain the funds necessary for that purpose.

After 100 years, only the language has changed, the present Constitution defines the objectives as:

(1) To uphold the rules of the game, to advance and safeguard the interests of women's golf and to decide all doubtful and disputed points in connection therewith.
(2) To maintain, regulate and enforce the LGU Handicapping System.

(3) To employ the funds of The Union in such a manner as shall be deemed best for the interests of women's golf, with power to borrow or raise money to use for the same purpose.
(4) To maintain and regulate International events, Championships and Competitions held under the LGU regulations and to promote the interests of Great Britain and Ireland in Ladies International Golf.
(5) To make, maintain and publish such regulations as may be considered necessary for the above purposes.

The constituents of the LGU are:

Home Countries. The English Ladies' Golf Association (founded 1952), the Irish Ladies' Golf Union (founded 1893), the Scottish Ladies' Golfing Association (founded 1904), the Welsh Ladies' Golf Union (founded 1904), plus ladies' societies, girls' schools and ladies' clubs affiliated to these organisations.

Overseas. Affiliated ladies' golf unions and golf clubs in the Commonwealth and any other overseas ladies' golfing organisation affiliated to the LGU.

Individual lady members of clubs within the above categories are regarded as members of the LGU.

The Rules of the Game and of Amateur Status, which the LGU is bound to uphold, are those published by the Royal & Ancient Golf Club of St Andrews.

In endeavouring to fulfil its responsibilities towards advancing and safeguarding women's golf, the LGU maintains contact with other golfing organisations – the Royal & Ancient Golf Club of St Andrews, the Council of National Golf Unions, the Golf Foundation, the Central Council of Physical Recreation, the Sports Council, the Women Professional Golfers' European Tour and the Women's Committee of the United States Golf Association. This contact ensures that the LGU is informed of developments and projected developments and has an opportunity to comment upon and to influence the future of the game for women.

Either directly or through its constituent national organisations the LGU advises and is the ultimate authority on doubts or disputes which may arise in connection with the handicapping system and regulations governing competitions played under LGU conditions.

The handicapping system, together with the system for assessment of Scratch Scores, is formulated and published by the LGU. Handicap Certificates are provided by the LGU and distributed through the National Organisations and appointed club officials to every member of every affiliated club which has fulfilled the requisite conditions for obtaining an LGU handicap.

The funds of the LGU are administered by the Hon. Treasurer on the authority of the Executive

Council, and the accounts are submitted annually for adoption in General Meeting.

The Women's British Open Championship, Ladies' British Open Amateur Championship, Ladies' British Open Amateur Stroke Play Championship, Girls' British Open Amateur Championship, Senior Ladies' British Open Amateur Championship, Ladies British Open Mid-Amateur Championship and the Home International matches are organised annually by the LGU. International events involving a British or a combined British and Irish team are organised and controlled by the LGU when held in this country and the LGU acts as the coordinating body for the Commonwealth Tournament in whichever of the five participating countries it is held, four-yearly, by rotation. The LGU selects and trains the teams, provides the uniforms and pays all the expenses of participation, whether held in this country or overseas. The LGU also maintains and regulates certain competitions played under handicap, such as Medal Competitions, Coronation Foursomes, Challenge Bowls, Australian Spoons and the LGU Pendant Competition.

The day-to-day administration of certain of the LGU responsibilities in the home countries is undertaken by the National Organisations, such as that concerned with handicapping regulations, Scratch Scores, and the organisation of Challenge Bowls and Australian Spoons Competitions.

Membership subscriptions to the LGU are assessed on a per capita basis of the club membership. To save unnecessary expense and duplication of administrative work in the home countries LGU subscriptions are collected by the National Organisations along with their own, and transmitted in bulk to the LGU.

Policy is determined and control over all the LGU's activities is exercised by an Executive Council of eight members – two each elected by the English, Irish, Scottish and Welsh national organisations. The Chairman is elected annually by the Councillors. During her chairmanship her place on the Council is taken by her Deputy and she has no vote other than a casting vote. The President and the Hon. Treasurer of the Union also attend and take part in Council meetings but with no vote. The Council meets five times a year.

The Annual General Meeting is held in January. The formal business includes presentation of the Report of the Executive Council for the previous year and of the Accounts for the last completed financial year, the election or re-election of President, Vice-Presidents, Hon. Treasurer and Auditors, and a report of the election of Councillors and their Deputies for the ensuing year and of the European Championship Committee representative. Voting is on the following basis: Executive Council, one each (8); members in the four home countries, one per national organisation (4) and in addition one per 100 affiliated clubs or part thereof; one per overseas Commonwealth Union with a membership of 50 or more clubs, and one per 100 individually affiliated clubs.

The Lady Golfer's Handbook is published annually by the LGU and is distributed free to all affiliated clubs and organisations and to appointed Handicap Advisers. It is also available for sale to anyone interested. It contains the regulations for British Championships and international matches (with results for the past twenty years) and for LGU competitions, and sets out the Rules of the Union. It also lists every affiliated organisation, with names and addresses of officials, and every affiliated club, with Scratch Score, county of affiliation, number of members, and other useful information.

Championship and International Match Conditions

CHAMPIONSHIP CONDITIONS

Men

The Amateur Championship

The Championship, until 1982, was decided entirely by match play over 18 holes except for the final which was over 36 holes. Since 1983 the Championship has comprised two stroke play rounds of 18 holes each from which the leading 64 players and ties over the 36 holes qualify for the match play stages. Matches are over 18 holes except for the final which is over 36 holes. Full particulars can be obtained from the Championship Entries Department, Royal and Ancient Golf Club, St Andrews, Fife KY16 9JD. Tel: 01334 460000   Fax: 01334 460001

The Seniors Open Amateur Championship

The Championship consists of 18 holes on each of two days, the leading 50 players and ties over the 36 holes then playing a further 18 holes the following day. Entrants must have attained the age of 55 years prior to the first day of the Championship. Full particulars can be obtained from the Championship Entries Department, Royal and Ancient Golf Club, St Andrews, Fife KY16 9JD. Tel: 01334 460000 Fax: 01334 460001

National Championships

The English, Scottish, Irish and Welsh Amateur Championships are played by holes, each match consisting of one round of 18 holes except the final which is contested over 36 holes. Full particulars of conditions of entry and method of play can be obtained from the secretaries of the respective national Unions.

English Open Amateur Stroke Play Championship

The Championship consists of one round of 18 holes on each of two days after which the leading 40 and those tying for 40th place play a further two rounds. The remainder are eliminated.

Conditions for entry include: entrants must have a handicap not exceeding three; where the entries exceed 130, an 18-hole qualifying round is held the day before the Championship. Certain players are exempt from qualifying.

Full particulars of conditions of entry and method of play can be obtained from the Secretary, English Golf Union, National Golf Centre, The Broadway, Woodhall Spa, Lincs LN10 6PU. Tel: 01526 354500   Fax: 01526 354020

Scottish Open Amateur Stroke Play Championship

The Championship consists of one round of 18 holes on each of two days after which the leading 40 and those tying for 40th place play a further two rounds. The remainder are eliminated. Full particulars of conditions of entry and method of play can be obtained from the Scottish Golf Union, Scottish National Golf Centre, Drumoig, Leuchars, St Andrews, Fife KY 16 0DW. Tel: 01382 549500 Fax: 01382 549510

British Mid-Amateur Championship

The Championship comprises two stroke play rounds of 18 holes from which the leading 64 players over the 36 holes qualify for the match play stages. All matches including the final are over 18 holes. Entrants must have attained the age of 25 years prior to the first day of the Championship. Full particulars can be obtained from the Championship Entries Department, Royal and Ancient Golf Club, St Andrews, Fife KY16 9JD. Tel: 01334 460000   Fax: 01334 460001

Boys

Boys Amateur Championship

The Championship is played by match play, each match including the final consisting of one round of 18 holes. Entrants must be under 18 years of age at 00.00 hours on 1st January in the year of the Championship. Full particulars can be obtained from the Championship Entries Department, Royal and Ancient Golf Club, St Andrews, Fife KY16 9JD. Tel: 01334 460000   Fax: 01334 460001

Ladies

Ladies' British Open Amateur Championship

The Championship consists of one 18-hole qualifying round on each of two days. The players returning the 64 lowest scores over 36 holes shall qualify for match play. Ties for 64th place shall be decided by hole-by-hole play-off.

Ladies' British Open Amateur Stroke Play Championship

The Championship consists of 72 holes stroke play; 18 holes are played on each of two days after which the first 40 and all ties for 40th place qualify for a further 36 holes on the third day. Handicap limit is 6.4.

Ladies' British Open Championship

The Championship consists of 72 holes stroke play. 18 holes are played on each of four days, the field being reduced after the first 36 holes.

Entries accepted from lady amateurs with a handicap not exceeding scratch and from lady professionals. Full particulars for all three Championships can be obtained from the LGU, The Scores, St Andrews, Fife KY16 9AT. Tel: 01334 475811   Fax: 01334 472818

National Championships

Conditions of entry and method of play for the English, Scottish, Welsh and Irish Ladies' Close Championships can be obtained from the Secretaries of the respective associations.

Other championships organised by the respective national associations, from whom full particulars can be obtained, include English Ladies', Intermediate, English Ladies' Stroke Play, Scottish Girls' Open Amateur Stroke Play (under 21) and Welsh Ladies' Open Amateur Stroke Play.

Girls

Girls' British Open Amateur Championship

The Championship consists of two 18-hole qualifying rounds, followed by match play in two flights, the first of 32 and the second of 16 players.

Conditions of entry include:
Entrants must be under 18 years of age on the 1st January in the year of the Championship.
Competitors are required to hold a certified LGU international handicap not exceeding 12.4.
Full particulars can be obtained from the Administrator, LGU, The Scores, St Andrews, Fife KY16 9AT. Tel: 01334 475811   Fax: 01334 472818

National Championships

The English, Scottish, Irish and Welsh Girls' Close Championships are open to all girls of relevant nationality and appropriate age which may vary from country to country. A handicap limit may be set by some countries. Full particulars can be obtained via the secretaries of the respective associations.

International European Amateur Championships

Founded in 1986 by the European Golf Association, the International Amateur and Ladies Amateur Championships are held on an annual basis since 1990. These Championships consist of one round of 18 holes on each of three days after which the leading 70 and those tying for 70th place play one further round.

Full particulars of conditions of entry and method of play can be obtained from the European Golf Association.

Since 1991, the European Golf Association also holds an International Mid-Amateur Championship on an annual basis. The Championship consist of one round of 18 holes on each of two days after which the leading 90 and those tying for 90th place play one further round.

Full particulars of conditions of entry and method of play can be obtained from the European Golf Association.

Since 1996, the European Golf Association holds an International Seniors Championship for ladies and men on an annual basis.

The Championship consists of one round of 18 holes on each of two days after which there is a cut in both ladies and men categories. The competitors who pass the cut play one further round.

Additionally, a nation's cup is played within the tournament on the first two days. Teams are composed of three players. The two best gross scores out of three will count each day. The total aggregate of the four scores over two days will constitute the team's score.

Full particulars of conditions of entry and method of play can be obtained from the European Golf Association, Place de la Croix-Blanche 19, PO Box CH-1066 Epilanges, Switzerland. Tel: +41 21 784 32 32   Fax: +412 1 784 35 91

INTERNATIONAL MATCH CONDITIONS

Men's Amateur Matches

Walker Cup – Great Britain and Ireland v United States of America

Mr GH Walker of the United States presented a Cup for international competition to be known as *The United States Golf Association International Challenge Trophy*, popularly described as *The Walker Cup*.

The Cup shall be played for by teams of amateur golfers selected from Clubs under the jurisdiction of the United States Golf Association on the one side and from England, Ireland, Scotland and Wales on the other.

The Walker Cup shall be held every two years in the United States of America and Great Britain and Ireland alternately.

The teams shall consist of not more than ten players and a captain.

The contest consists of four foursomes and eight singles matches over 18 holes on each of two days.

St Andrews Trophy – Great Britain and Ireland v Continent of Europe

First staged in 1956, the St Andrews Trophy is a biennial international match played between two selected teams of amateur golfers representing Great Britain and Ireland and the Continent of Europe. Each team consists of nine players and the match is played over two consecutive days with four morning foursomes followed each afternoon by eight singles. Selection of the Great Britain and Ireland team is carried out by the Selection Committee of The Royal and Ancient Golf Club. The European Golf Association select the Continent of Europe team.

Eisenhower Trophy – Men's World Team Championship

Founded in recognition of the need for an official world amateur team championship, the first event was played at St Andrews in 1958 and the Trophy has been played for every second year in different countries around the world.

Each country enters a team of four players who play strokeplay over 72 holes, the total of the three best individual scores to be counted for each round.

European Team Championship

Founded in 1959 by the European Golf Association for competition among member countries of the Association. The Championship is held biennially and played in rotation round the countries, which are grouped in four geographical zones.

Each team consists of six players who play two qualifying rounds of 18 holes, the five best scores of each round constituting the team aggregate. Flights for match play are then arranged according to qualifying rankings. The match play consists of two foursomes and five singles on each of three days.

A similar championship is held in alternate years for Youths teams, under 21 years of age and every year for Boys teams, under 18 years of age.

Raymond Trophy – Home Internationals

The first official International Match recorded was in 1902 at Hoylake between England and Scotland who won 32 to 25 on a holes up basis.

In 1932 International Week was inaugurated under the auspices of the British Golf Unions' Joint Advisory Council with the full approval of the four National Golf Unions. The Council of National Golf Unions is now responsible for running the matches. Teams of 11 players from England, Scotland, Ireland and Wales engage in matches consisting of five foursomes and ten singles over 18 holes, the foursomes being in the morning and the singles in the afternoon. Each team plays every other team.

The eligibility of players to play for their country shall be their eligibility to play in the Amateur Championship of their country.

Sir Michael Bonallack Trophy – Europe v Asia /Pacific

First staged in 1998, the Sir Michael Bonallack Trophy is a biennial international match played between two selected teams of amateur golfers representing Europe and Asia/Pacific. Each team consists of 12 players and the match is played over three days with five four balls in the morning and five foursomes in the afternoon of the first two days, followed by 12 singles on the last day. Selection of the European team is carried out by the European Golf Association. The Asia/Pacific Golf Confederation selects the Asia/Pacific team.

Men's Professional Matches

Ryder Cup – Europe v United States of America

This Cup was presented by Mr Samuel Ryder, St Albans, England (who died 2nd January, 1936), for competition between a team of British professionals and a team of American professionals. The trophy was first competed for in 1927. In 1929 the original conditions were varied to confine the British team to British-born professionals resident in Great

Britain, and the American team to American-born professionals resident in the United States, in the year of the match. In 1979 the British team was extended to include European players. The matches are played biennially, in alternate continents, in accordance with the conditions as agreed between the respective PGAs.

World Cup *(formerly Canada Cup)*

Founded in America by John Jay Hopkins in 1955 as a team event for professional golfers with the object of spreading international goodwill. Each country is represented by two players with the best team score over 72 holes producing the winners of the World Cup and the best individual score the winner of the International Trophy. Played for annually (but not in 1986) the event was run until 1999 by the International Gold Association but it is now organised as part of the new World Championship series of events by representatives of the leading professional golf tours.

Seve Ballesteros Trophy – Great Britain and Ireland *v* Continent of Europe

A match instituted in 2000 at Sunningdale and played along Ryder Cup lines in alternate years.

Llandudno Trophy (PGA Cup) – Great Britain and Ireland *v* United States of America

The Llandudno International Trophy was first awarded to England in 1939 after winning the first Home Tournament Series against Ireland, Scotland and Wales. With the outbreak of war the series was abolished and the Trophy formed part of Percy Alliss's personal collection. After Percy's death his son Peter donated the Llandudno Trophy to be awarded to the winner of the then annual PGA Cup Match. Now it is a biennial match played since 1973 in Ryder Cup format between Great Britain and Ireland and the United States of America involving top club professionals. No prize money is awarded to the competitors who compete solely for their country. Selection of the Great Britain and Ireland team is determined following completion of the Glenmuir PGA Club Professionals Championship.

Ladies Amateur Matches

Curtis Cup – Great Britain and Ireland *v* United States

For a trophy presented by the late Misses Margaret and Harriot Curtis of Boston, USA, for biennial competition between amateur teams from the United States of America and Great Britain and Ireland. The match is sponsored jointly by the United States Golf Association and the Ladies' Golf Union who may select teams of not more than eight players.

The match consists of three foursomes and six singles of 18 holes on each of two days, the foursomes being played each morning.

Vagliano Trophy – Great Britain and Ireland *v* Continent of Europe

For a trophy presented to the Comité des Dames de la Fédération Française de Golf and the Ladies' Golf Union by Monsieur AA Vagliano, originally for annual competition between teams of women amateur golfers from France and Great Britain and Ireland but, since 1959, by mutual agreement, for competition between teams from the Continent of Europe and Great Britain and Ireland.

The match is played biennially, alternately in Great Britain and Ireland and on the Continent of Europe, with teams of not more than nine players plus a non-playing captain. The match consists of four foursomes and eight singles, of 18 holes on each of two days. The foursomes are played each morning.

Espirito Santo Trophy – Women's World Team Championship

Presented by Mrs Ricardo Santo of Portugal for biennial competition between teams of not more than three women amateur golfers who represent a national association affiliated to the World Amateur Golf Council. First competed for in 1964. The Championship consists of 72 holes strokeplay, 18 holes on each of four days, the two best scores in each round constituting the team aggregate.

Lady Astor Trophy – Commonwealth Tournament

For a trophy presented by the late Viscountess Astor CH, and the Ladies' Golf Union for competition once in every four years between teams of women amateur golfers from Commonwealth countries.

The inaugural Commonwealth Tournament was played at St Andrews in 1959 between teams from Australia, Canada, New Zealand, South Africa and Great Britain and was won by the British team. The tournament is played in rotation in the competing countries, for the present Great Britain, Australia, Canada, and New Zealand, each country being entitled to nominate six players including a playing or non-playing captain.

Each team plays every other team and each team match consists of two foursomes and four singles over 18 holes. The foursomes are played in the morning and the singles in the afternoon.

European Team Championships

Founded in 19S9 by the European Golf Association for competition among member countries of the Association. The Championship is held biennially and played in rotation round the countries, which are grouped in four geographical zones.

Each team consists of six players who play two qualifying rounds of 18 holes, the five best scores of each round constituting the team aggregate. Flights for matchplay are then arranged according to qualifying rankings. The matchplay consists of two foursomes and five singles on each of three days.

A similar championship is held in alternate years for Lady Juniors teams, under 21 years of age and every year for Girls teams, under 18 years of age.

Home Internationals

Teams from England, Scotland, Ireland and Wales compete annually for a trophy presented to the LGU by the late Mr TH Miller. The qualifications for a player being eligible to play for her country are the same as those laid down by each country for its Close Championship.

Each team plays each other team. The matches consist of six singles and three foursomes, each of 18 holes. Each country may nominate teams of not more than eight players.

Ladies Professional Matches

Solheim Cup – Europe v United States

The Solheim Cup, named after Karsten Solheim who founded the sponsoring Ping company, is the women's equivalent of the Ryder Cup. In 1990 the inaugural competition between the top women professional golfers from Europe and America took place in Florida.

The matches are played biennially in alternate continents. The format is foursomes and fourball matches on the first two days, followed by singles on the third in accordance with the conditions as agreed between the Evian Tour and the United States LPGA Tour.

World Cup

Started in 2000 by the LPGA and the International management Group, the event is held along similar lines to the men's World Cup with each country represented by two players. There is also an individual competiton incorporated in the regulations. It had been planned as an annual fixture but the 2001 Championship scheduled for Adelaide was cancelled.

Boys Matches

R & A Trophy – Home Internationals

Teams comprising 11 players from England, Scotland, Ireland and Wales compete against one another over three days in a single round robin format. Each fixture comprises five morning foursomes followed by ten afternoon singles.

To be eligible for selection, players must be under the age of 18 at 00.00 hours on 1st January in the year of the matches and have eligibility to play in their national championships

Jacques Léglise Trophy – Great Britain and Ireland v Continent of Europe

The Jacques Léglise Trophy is an annual international match played between two selected teams of amateur boy golfers representing Great Britain and Ireland and the Continent of Europe. Each team consists of nine players and the match is played over two consecutive days with four morning foursomes followed each afternoon by eight singles. Selection of the Great Britain and Ireland team is carried out by the Selection Committee of The Royal and Ancient Golf Club. The European Golf Association selects the Continent of Europe team

To be eligible for selection, players must be under the age of 18 at 00.00 hours on 1st January in the year of the matches.

Junior Ryder Cup

First staged in 1995, the Junior Ryder Cup is a biennial international match played between two selected teams of amateur golfers representing Europe and the USA, prior to the Ryder Cup. Each team consists of four girls and four boys under 16 as well as two girls and two boys under 18. The match is played over two consecutive days with six four balls on the first day and six mixed four balls on the second day.

Selection of the European team is carried out by the European Golf Association. Players and captains are then invited to watch the Ryder Cup.

Girls

Home Internationals

Teams from England, Scotland, Ireland and Wales compete annually for the Stroyan Cup. The qualifications for a player for the Girls' International Matches shall be the same as those laid down by each country for its Girls' Close Championship except that a player shall be under 18 years on the 1st January in the year of the Championship.

Each team, consisting of not more than eight players, plays each other team, a draw taking place to decide the order of play between the teams. The matches consist of three foursomes and six singles, each of 18 holes.

Golf Associations

The National Association of Public Golf Courses (Affiliated to English Golf Union)

The Association was founded in 1927 by golf course architect FG Hawtree and five-times Open Champion JH Taylor who saw the need for cohesion of private golf, public golf and the local councils. Until 1939 the Association was sustained by a small amount of financial support from the *News of the World*, which enabled the the Public Courses Championship of England, the so-called Unofficial Championship to be staged. After the War the Association was revitalised and the Championship was recognised by the National Union. Some 3500 public course golfers now try to qualify for the Unofficial Championship.

The success and importance of this prompted the inauguration of the Ladies' Championship and, subsequently, the Junior Championship. Various club team events came soon after, and these have now progressed to national level with a vast following from club members. Thus the Association now organises some 14 national events annually.

Many of the local councils' course management authorities (CMAs) are now full subscribing members, and many others permit the courtesy of the course for all the Association's national and zonal tournaments. Advice is offered to CMAs, when requested, on such matters as course construction, club formation and integration, establishment of Standard Scratch Score and par values, and many other topics concerned with the management of the game of golf. Overseas organisations and councils can seek advice and help in forming their own courses, clubs and associations.

The constitutional aims have not changed over the years, and the Association is proud to have maintained them. The aims are:

1. To unite the clubs formed on public courses in England and Wales, and their course managements in the furtherance of the interests of amateur golf.
2. To promote annual public course championships and such other matches, competitions and tournaments as shall be authorised by the executive of the Association.
3. To afford direct representation of public course interests in the National Union.

The organisation of the Association is wholly voluntary and honorary. Contact details p.503.

Association of Golf Club Secretaries

Membership is over 2,300, consisting of secretaries/managers and retired secretaries of clubs and golfing associations situated in the UK and Europe.

The Association offers advice on all aspects of managing a golf club, including the use of an extensive information library, mainly available direct to members through its website. A national conference is held every three years. Potential and newly appointed secretaries can attend a residential training course while regular seminars are available to all members. The Association's journal, *Golf Club Management*, is published monthly and circulated to all members. The regular business of the Association is conducted from the 17 regions of the UK, along with a number of golf meetings. After five years members can apply for membership of the Institute of Golf Club Management, which is part of the Association. Contact details p.502.

The Association of Golf Writers

A group of 30 newspapermen attending the Walker Cup Match at St Andrews on 2 June 1938 decided there was a need for an organisation to 'protect the interests of golf writers'. Their main objective was to establish close liaison with the governing bodies and promoters of golf. Thus was born The Association of Golf Writers, now solidly established and rightly respected as the official negotiating body of the golfing press. The Association owes much to a membership which has included many internationally recognised names who have contributed to elevating the Association to a unique level among British sports writers' associations. Contact details p.503.

The Sports Turf Research Institute (STRI)
(Bingley, West Yorkshire)

The STRI is officially recognised as the national centre for sports and amenity turf and is the official agronomist to the Championship Committee of the R&A. It is a non-profit distributing company limited by guarantee, its affairs managed by a small Executive Committee drawn from its Members Body comprising most sports controlling bodies. Golf is represented by the nominees of the R&A, the four home Golf Unions and the Council of National Golf Unions. The British Institute of Golf Course Architects, the British & International Greenkeepers Association and the PGA European Tour are also represented on its Members Body and Golf Committee.

STRI's mission is to carry out research and promote innovation; to provide advisory and consultancy services; and to provide education and publications for subscribing clubs, sports controlling bodies and the turfgrass industry at large. Contact details on p.503.

The European Institute of Golf Course Architects (EIGCA)

The European Institute of Golf Course Architects reprsents the vast majority of qualified and experienced golf course architects throughout Europe. EIGCA's goals include enhancing the professional status of the profession, developing the role of eduation and increasing the opportunities for its members to practise in countries throughout the world. EIGCA also provides educational courses to train future golf course architects and is the authoritative voice on all related matters, being recognised by the Royal and Ancient Golf Club of St Andrews. Contact details p.503.

The British Association of Golf Course Constructors

The BAGCC has always maintained its small though highly prestigious membership by 'invitation only', those selected proven by example to have performed work to the highest standard in every aspect of golf course construction: from initial consultation, survey, through design and construction to regular course maintenance. New members are admitted only if they satisfy the criteria of experience, professionalism and quality of workmanship set by the association. Membership remains an identity of considerable pride, worn in the same way, as, say, that of a qualified architect or surveyor. In simple terms it indicates that "This organisationis skilled at its job, it is highly professional and is recognised by its peers". Contact details p.503.

British and International Golf Greenkeepers' Association (BIGGA)

Formed in 1987 from an amalgamation of the British, English and Scottish Associations. Objectives are to promote and advance all aspects of greenkeeping; to assist and encourage the proficiency of members; to arrange an international annual conference, educational seminars, functions and competitions; to collaborate with any body or organisation which may benefit the Association or its members or with which there may be a common interest; to carry out and perform any other duties which shall be in the general interests of the Association or its members. The Association has an official magazine, *Greenkeeping International*, which is issued free to all members. The Association also organised the annual BIGGA Turf Management Exhibition (BTME) which is Europe's largest indoor turf show. Currently the Association has over 7,300 members in the United Kingdom and world wide. Contact details p.503.

National Golf Clubs' Advisory Association

Founded in 1922, the Association's objectives are to protect the interests of golf clubs in general and to give legal advice and direction, under the opinion of Counsel, on the administrative and legal responsibilities of golf clubs. Financial assistance may sometimes be given in cases taken to the courts for decisions on points which, in the opinion of the Executive Committee, involve principles affecting the general interests of affiliated clubs. Contact details p.503.

European Golf Association
Association Européenne de Golf

Formed at a meeting held 20 November 1937 in Luxembourg, membership is restricted to European national amateur golf associations or unions. The Association concerns itself solely with matters of an international character. The association is presently composed of 30 member countries and is governed by the following committees:

- Executive Committee
- Championship Committee
- Professional Technical Committee
- EGA Handicapping & Course Rating Committee

Prime objectives are:

(a) To encourage international development of golf, to strengthen bonds of friendship existing between it members.

(b) To encourage the formation of new golf organisations representing the golf activities of European countries.

(c) To co-ordinate the dates of the Open and Amateur championships of its members and to arrange, in conjuction with host Federations, European championships and specific matches of international character.

(d) To ratify and publish the calendar dates of the major Amateur and Professional championships and international matches in Europe.

(e) To create and maintain international relationships in the field of golf and undertake any action useful to the cause of golf on an international level.

The headquarters are situated in Epalinges, Switzerland. Contact details p.511.

Golf Club Stewards' Association

The Golf Club Stewards' Association was founded as early as 1912. Its members are Stewards in golf clubs throughout the UK and Ireland. It has a National Committee and Regional Branches in the South, North-West, Midlands, East Anglia, Yorkshire, Wales and the West, North-East Scotland and Ireland. The objectives of the Association are to promote the interests of members; to administer a Benevolent Fund for members in need; and to arrange golf competitions and matches. It also serves as an agency for the employment of Stewards in golf clubs. Contact details p.503.

Directory of Golfing Organisations Worldwide

NATIONAL ASSOCIATIONS

Great Britain and Ireland

Royal and Ancient Golf Club
Sec, Peter Dawson, St Andrews, Fife
KY16 9JD
Tel (01334) 460000   *Fax* (01334) 460001
E-mail thesecretary@randagc.org
Website www.randa.org

Council of National Golf Unions
Hon Sec, A Thirlwell, 19 Birch Green, Formby,
Liverpool L37 1NG
Tel/Fax (01704) 831800

The Evian Tour (Ladies European Tour)
Ch Execs, I Randall and R Gibson, The
Tytherington Club, The Old Hall,
Macclesfield, SK10 2JP
Tel (01625) 611444   *Fax* (01625) 610406
E-mail mail@elpga.com
Website www.eviantour.com

Ladies' Golf Union
Sec, The Scores, St Andrews, Fife KY16 9AT
Tel (01334) 475811   *Fax* (01334) 472818
E-mail info@lgu.org
Website www.lgu.org

The Professional Golfers' Association
Ch Exec, Sandy Jones, Centenary House,
The De Vere Belfry, Sutton Coldfield,
B76 9PT
Tel (01675) 470333   *Fax* (01675) 477888
Website www.pga.org.uk
East Region: *Sec*, John Smith, John O'Gaunt
GC, Sutton Park, Sandy, Beds SG19 2LY
Tel (01767) 261888   *Fax* (01767) 261381
Midland Region: *Sec*, Jon Sewell, King's
Norton GC, Brockhill Lane, Weatheroak,
Nr Alvechurch, Worcs B48 7ED
Tel (01564) 824909   *Fax* (01564) 822805
North Region: *Sec*, J Croxton, No 2 Cottage,
Bolton GC, Lostock Park, Chorley New Road,
Bolton, Lancs BL6 4AJ
Tel (01204) 496137   *Fax* (01204) 847959
South Region: *Sec*, P Ward, Clandon Regis
GC, Epsom Road, West Clandon, Guildford,
Surrey GU4 7TT

Tel (01483) 224200
Fax (01483) 223224
West Region: *Sec*, R Ellis, Exeter G&CC,
Topsham Road, Countess Wear, Exeter
EX2 7AE
Tel (01392) 877657
Fax (01392) 876382
Irish Region: *Sec*, M McCumiskey, Dundalk
GC, Blackrock, Dundalk, Co Louth, Eire
Tel (00 353) 42 932 1193
Fax (00 353) 42 932 1899
Scottish Region: *Sec*, Peter Lloyd, King's
Lodge, Gleneagles, Auchterarder PH3 1NE
Tel 01764 661840   *Fax* 01764 661841

PGA European Tour
Exec Dir, KD Schofield CBE, PGA European
Tour, Wentworth Drive, Virginia Water, Surrey
GU25 4LX
Tel (01344) 840400
Fax (01344) 840500
E-mail kschofield@europeantour.com
Website www.europeantour.com

PGA of Europe
Sec, LE Thornton, Centenary House, The De
Vere Belfry, Sutton Coldfield, B76 9PT
Tel (01675) 477899   *Fax* (01675) 477890
E-mail pgae@netcomuk.co.uk
Website www.pgae.com

Artisan Golfers' Association
Hon Sec, K Stevens, 85 The Avenue,
Highwater, Surrey GU18 5RG
Tel 01276 475103

Association of Golf Club Secretaries
Sec, R Burniston, 7a Beaconsfield Road,
Weston-super-Mare BS23 1YE
Tel (01934) 641166   *Fax* (01934) 644254
E-mail hq@agcs.org.uk
Website www.agcs.org.uk

Association of Golf Writers
Sec, M Garrod, 106 Byng Drive, Potters Bar, EN6 1UJ
Tel/Fax (01707) 654112
E-mail pasport@markgarrod.fsbusiness.co.uk

British Association of Golf Course Constructors
Sec, D White, Fore! The Dormy House, Cooden Beach GC, Bexhill-on-Sea, TN39 4TR
Tel (01424) 842380   *Fax* (01424) 843375
E-mail mightyspyder@aol.com
Website www.bagcc.org.uk

British Golf Collectors' Society
Sec, CH Ibbetson, PO Box 13704, North Berwick, EH39 4ZB
Tel/Fax (01620) 895561
E-mail bgcs@globalnet.co.uk
Website www.britgolfcollectors.wyenet.co.uk

The British Golf Museum
Dir, PN Lewis; *Curator*, Kathryn Baker, Bruce Embankment, St Andrews, Fife KY16 9AB
Tel (01334) 460046   *Fax* (01334) 460064
E-mail kathrynbaker@randagc.org
Website www.britishgolfmuseum.co.uk

British & International Golf Greenkeepers' Association
Exec Dir, N Thomas, Bigga House, Aldwark, Alne, York Y061 1UF
Tel (01347) 833800   *Fax* (01347) 833801
E-mail reception@bigga.co.uk
Website www.bigga.org.uk

British Turf & Landscape Irrigation Association
PO Box 709, Garstang PR3 1GT
Tel/Fax (07041) 363 130
Website www.btlia.org.uk

The European Institute of Golf Course Architects (EIGCA)
Pres, D Williams, Merrist Wood House, Worplesdon, Surrey GU3 3PE
Tel (01483) 884036   *Fax* (01483) 884037
E-mail info@eigca.org
Website www.eigca.org

Golf Club Stewards' Association
Sec, Peter Payne, 3 St George's Drive, Ickenham, Middx UB10 4HW
Tel (01895) 674325

Golf Foundation
Foundation House, The Spinney, Hoddesdon Rd, Stanstead Abbots, SG12 8GF
Tel (01920) 876200   *Fax* (01920) 876211
E-mail info@golf-foundation.org
Website www.golf-foundation.org

Golf Society of Great Britain
Sec, Mrs J Hesketh, Inglewood Farm, Minshull

Vernon, Middlewich, Cheshire CW10 0LS
Tel/Fax (01270) 522533
E-mail jackie@hesketh2000.freeserve.co.uk

Hole in One Golf Society
Sec, B Dickinson, PO Box 109, New Line, Greengates, Bradford, BD10 9UY
Tel (01274) 598878   *Fax* (01274) 590878

National Association of Public Golf Courses
Hon Sec, E Mitchell, 12 Newton Close, Redditch B98 7YR
Tel (01527) 542106   *Fax* (01527) 455320

National Golf Clubs' Advisory Association
Sec, Michael Shaw LLM, Suite 2 Angel House, Portland Square, Bakewell, Derbyshire DE45 1HB
Tel (01629) 813844   *Fax* (01629) 812614
Website www.ngcaa.org.uk

Public Schools Old Boys Golf Association
Hon Sec: P de Pinna, Bruins, Wythwood, Haywards Heath, West Sussex RH16 4RD
Tel (01444) 454883   *Fax* (01444) 415117

Public Schools' Golfing Society
Hon Sec, JNS Lowe, Basement, Magdalen House, 148 Tooley St, London SE1 2TU
Tel (020) 7234 0007   *Fax* (020) 7234 0008
E-mail jlowe@solo-di.demon.co.uk

The Sports Turf Research Institute (STRI)
Ch Exec, Dr IG McKillop; *Head Ext Affairs*, Anne Wilson, St Ives Estate, Bingley, West Yorks BD16 1AU.
Tel (01274) 565131   *Fax* (01274) 561891
E-mail info@stri.co.uk
Website www.stri.co.uk

REGIONAL ASSOCIATIONS

England

English Golf Union
Sec, PM Baxter, National Golf Centre, The Broadway, Woodhall Spa, Lincs LN10 6PU
Tel (01526) 354500   *Fax* (01526) 354020
E-mail info@englishgolfunion.org
Website www.englishgolfunion.org

Midland Group: *Sec*, RJW Baldwin, Chantry Cottage, Friar Street, Droitwich, Worcs WR9 8EQ
Tel (01905) 778560   *Fax* (01905) 795848
Website www.midland.golfunion.com

Northern Group: *Sec*, IG Black, 683 Chorley New Road, Lostock, Bolton BL6 4AG
Tel/Fax (01204) 492651

South Eastern Group: *Sec*, JW Gilding, 10 Mansion Lane, Iver, Bucks SL0 9RH
Tel (01753) 819686   *Fax* (01753) 771809

South Western Group: *Sec*, DR King, 41 West Town Lane, Brislington, Bristol BS4 5DD
Tel (01179) 773330

English Men's County Unions

Bedfordshire County Golf Union
Hon Sec, C Allen, 102 Tyne Crescent, Bedford MK41 7UW
Tel/Fax (01234) 216835
E-mail bedsgusec@aol.com
Website www.bedsgolfunion.org

Berks, Bucks & Oxon Union of Golf Clubs
Sec, PMJ York, Unit 1d Saxeway Business Park, Chartridge Lane, Chartridge, Chesham HP5 2SH
Tel (01494) 778804   *Fax* (01494) 782030
E-mail bbogolf@aol.com
Website www.bbogolf.com

Cambridgeshire Area Golf Union
Sec, RAC Blows, 73 Pheasant Rise, Bar Hill, Cambridge CB3 8SB
Tel (01954) 780887

Cheshire Union of Golf Clubs
Hon Sec, BH Nattrass, 'Whitecliff', 6 Bryn Seiriol, Llandudno LL30 1PD
Tel/Fax (01492) 580518
E-mail secretary@cheshiregolf.org.uk
Website www.cheshiregolf.org.uk

Cornwall Golf Union
Hon Sec, JG Rowe, 11 St Winnall's Park, Looe PL13 1QG
Tel/Fax (01503) 465814

Cumbria Union of Golf Clubs
Hon Sec, W Ward, Moss View, Low Asby, Lamplugh, Workington CA14 4RT
Tel/Fax (01946) 861600

Derbyshire Union of Golf Clubs
Hon Sec, CRJ Ibbotson, 4 The Spinney, Luke Lane, Brailsford, nr Ashbourne DE6 3BS
Tel (01335) 361266
E-mail 'anyone'@dugc.co.uk
Website www.dugc.co.uk

Devon County Golf Union
Sec, RJ Hirst, c/o Yelverton GC, Golf Links Rd, Yelverton PL20 6BN
Tel/Fax (01822) 855850
E-mail info@devongolfunion.fg.co.uk
Website www.devon.golfunion.com

Dorset County Golf Union
Hon Sec, Lt Col MD Hutchins, 38 Carlton Road, Bournemouth BH1 3TG
Tel (01202) 290821   *Fax* (01202) 311288
Website www.dorset.golfunion.com

Durham County Golf Union
Hon Sec, GP Hope, 7 Merrion Close, Moorside, Sunderland SR3 2QP
Tel/Fax (0191) 522 8605

Essex County Amateur Golf Union
Sec, TJ Case, 2d Maldon Road, Witham, Essex CM8 2AB
Tel (01376) 500 998   *Fax* (01376) 500 842
E-mail info@essexgolfunion.org
Website www.essexgolfunion.org

Gloucestershire Golf Union
Sec, I Watkins, The Vyse, Olde Lane, Toddington, Glos GL54 5DQ
Tel/Fax (01242)612 476
E-mail secretary@gloucestershire.golfunion.com
Website www.gloucestershire.golfunion.com

Hampshire, Isle of Wight & Channel Islands Golf Union
Sec, K Maplesden, c/o Liphook GC, Wheatsheaf Enclosure, Liphook, Hants GU30 7EH
Tel/Fax (01428) 725580

Hertfordshire Golf Union
Hon Sec, JC Harkett, 5 Willow Way, Harpenden AL5 5JF
Tel (01582) 760841   *Fax* (01582) 462608
E-mail hertsgolfunionsec@lineone.net

Isle of Man Golf Union
Hon Sec, Joe Boyd, Cheu-Ny-Hawiney, Phildraw Rd, Ballasilla, Isle of Man IM9 3EG
Tel/Fax (01624) 823098

Kent County Golf Union
Sec, SS Fullager, St Andrew's Road, Littlestone, New Romney, Kent TN28 8RB
Tel (01797) 367725   *Fax* (01797) 367726
E-mail kcgu@kentgolf.co.uk
Website www.kentgolf.co.uk

Lancashire Union of Golf Clubs
Sec, AV Moss, 5 Dicconson Terrace, Lytham St Annes FY8 5JY
Tel (01253) 733323   *Fax* (01253) 795721

Leicestershire & Rutland Golf Union
Hon Sec, C Chamberlain, 10 Shipton Close, The Meadows, Wigston Magna, Leicester LE18 3WL
Tel/Fax (0116) 288 9862
E-mail colin@LR.golfunion.com
Website
    www.leicestershireandrutland.golfunion.com

Lincolnshire Union of Golf Clubs
Hon Sec, GH Moore OBE, Authorpe House, 36 Horncastle Road, Woodhall Spa LN10 6UZ
Tel/Fax (01526) 352792

Middlesex County Golf Union
Sec, JAL Williams, *Tele*vision House, 269 Field End Rd, Eastcote, Ruislip, HA4 9LS
Tel (0208) 429 9206   *Fax* (0208) 429 9156
E-mail mcgu@deal.pipex.com

Norfolk County Golf Union
Hon Sec, RJ Trower, 12a Stanley Avenue, Thorpe, Norwich, Norfolk NR7 0BE
Tel/Fax (01603) 431026

Northamptonshire Golf Union
Hon Sec, G Brooks, 17 Water Lane, Chelveston, Wellingborough NN9 6AP
Tel/Fax (01933) 625032
E-mail secretary@ngu.org.uk

Northumberland Union of Golf Clubs
Hon Sec, WE Procter, 5 Oakhurst Drive, Kenton Park, Gosforth, Newcastle-upon-Tyne NE3 4JS
Tel/Fax (0191) 285 4981
E-mail Elliott.Procter@online.co.uk

Nottinghamshire Union of Golf Clubs
Hon Sec, E Peters, 48 Weaverthorpe Road, Woodthorpe NG5 4NB
Tel/Fax (0115) 926 6560

Shropshire & Herefordshire Union of Golf Clubs
Hon Sec, JR Davies, 23 Poplar Crescent, Bayston Hill, Shrewsbury SY3 0QB
Tel (01743) 872655
E-mail bdavies@cableinet.co.uk

Somerset Golf Union
Hon Sec, GA Yates, Little Manor, Greinton, Nr Bridgwater TA7 9BW
Tel/Fax (01458) 210179
E-mail GrahamYates@Greinton.Freeserve.co.uk
Website www.somerset.golfunion.com

Staffordshire Union of Golf Clubs
Hon Sec, BA Cox, 34 Lordswood Square, Harborne, Birmingham B17 9BS
Tel (0121) 427 4962   *Fax* {0121) 426 6366
E-mail Staffs.Golf@virgin.net

Suffolk County Golf Union
Hon Sec, RA Kent, 77 Bennett Avenue, Bury St Edmunds IP33 3JJ
Tel/Fax (01284) 705765
E-mail golfsgu@aol.com

Surrey County Golf Union
Hon Sec, MW Ashton, Sutton Green GC, New Lane, Sutton Green GU4 7QF
Tel (01483) 755788   *Fax* (01483) 751771
E-mail cgu@surreygolf.org
Website www.surreygolf.org

Sussex County Golf Union
Sec, DJ Harmer, Suite 1, 216 South Coast Road, Peacehaven, East Sussex BN10 8JR
Tel (01273) 589791   *Fax* (01273) 585705
E-mail sussexgolf@tinyworld.co.uk
Website www.sussexgolf.org

Warwickshire Union of Golf Clubs
Sec, J Stubbings, Quaker Cottage, Wiggins Hill Road, Wishaw, Sutton Coldfield B76 9QE
Tel/Fax (01675) 470809
E-mail stubbings@wugc.fsnet.co.uk
Website www.warksgolf.co.uk

Wiltshire County Golf Union
Sec, BE Daniel, The Rowans, Church Rd, Derry Hill, Calne SN11 9NR
Tel (01249) 814368
E-mail brian@danielb.freeserve.co.uk

Worcestershire Union of Golf Clubs
Hon Sec, A Boyd, The Bears Den, Upper Street, Defford, Worcester WR8 9BG
Tel (01386) 750657
Fax (01386) 750472
E-mail yorkshiregolf@lineone.net

Yorkshire Union of Golf Clubs
Hon Sec, KH Dowswell, 33 George Street, Wakefield WF1 1LX.
Tel (01924) 383869
Fax (01924) 383634

English Ladies' Golf Association
Sec, Mrs S Dennis, Edgbaston GC, Church Road, Birmingham B15 3TB
Tel (0121) 456 2088
Fax (0121) 454 5542
E-mail office@englishladiesgolf.org
Website www.englishladiesgolf.org

Northern Division: *Hon Sec*, Mrs R Horsfall, Rock Bottom, Daisy Lea Lane, Edgerton, Huddersfield HD3 3LL
Tel (01484)533444
E-mail horsfall@rockbottom.fsnet.co.uk

Midlands Division: *Hon Sec*, Mrs J Latch, 3 The Barns, Soulbury Rd, Burcott, Leighton Buzzard LU7 0JU
Tel (01296) 681214
E-mail jill.latch@talk21.com

South-Eastern Division: *Hon Sec*, Mrs R Wallis, The Bungalow, The Green, Pirbright, Woking GU24 0JE
Tel (01483) 476528
E-mail rhwallis@ukgateway.net

South-Western Division: *Hon Sec*, Mrs A Bates, 25 Brinsea Rd, Congresbury, nr Bristol BS49 5JF
Tel (01934) 833470
E-mail audrey@batesinvestigations.fsnet.co.uk

English Ladies' County Associations

Bedfordshire Ladies' County Golf Association
Hon Sec, Mrs N Cole, 6 Church Lane, Eaton Bray, Beds LU6 2DJ
Tel (01525) 220479

Berkshire Ladies' County Golf Association
Hon Sec, Mrs M Shepherd, 40 Florence Road, College Town, Sandhurst GU47 0QD
Tel/Fax (01276) 35937

Buckinghamshire Ladies' County Golf Association
Hon Sec, Mrs C Hawkesworth, 22 Copthall Lane, Chalfont St Peter SL9 0DB
Tel (01753) 883088

Cambs & Hunts Ladies' County Golf Association
Hon Sec, Mrs S Ramsay, 25 Leighton, Orton Malbourne, Peterborough PE2 5QB
Tel (01733) 236502

Cheshire County Ladies' Golf Association
Hon Sec, Mrs B Walker, 12 Higher Downs, Knutsford, Cheshire WA16 8AW
Tel (01565) 634124

Cornwall Ladies' County Golf Association
Hon Sec, Mrs C Penhale, 2 Scolars Close, St Ive, Liskeard PL14 3UX
Tel (01579) 384595

Cumbria Ladies' County Golf Association
Hon Sec, Mrs L Mayne, Jasmine Cottage, Stainton, Nr Penrith CA11 0ES
Tel/Fax (01768) 865495

Derbyshire Ladies' County Golf Association
Hon Sec, Mrs J Morgan, Upper Burrows Farm, Brailsford, Derby DE6 3BW
Tel (01335) 360250

Devon County Ladies' Golf Association
Hon Sec, Mrs T Philp, 2 Coastguard Road, Budleigh Salterton EX9 6HB
Tel (01395) 443700

Dorset Ladies' County Golf Association
Hon Sec, Miss J Pomeroy, 10 Mill Close, East Coker, Yeovil, Somerset BA22 9LF
Tel (01935) 862574

Durham County Ladies' Golf Association
Sec, Mrs E Whittle, 23 Kitswell Road, Lanchester, Co Durham DH7 0JJ
Tel (01207) 520581

Essex Ladies' County Golf Association
Hon Sec, Mrs M Low, 15 Rushdene Road, Brentwood CM15 9ES
Tel (01277) 230849

Gloucestershire Ladies' County Golf Association
Hon Sec, Mrs G Merry, Myles House, Ashmead, Dursley GL11 3EN
Tel (01453) 542569

Hampshire Ladies' County Golf Association
Sec, Mrs A Grosvenor, 16A Salterns Lane, Hayling Island PO11 9PJ
Tel (023) 9246 5710

Hertfordshire County Ladies' Golf Association
Hon Sec, Mrs M Broadbent, 6 Earlsmead, Letchworth SG6 3UE
Tel (01452) 682767

Kent County Ladies' Golf Association
Hon Sec, Mrs S Daniel, 6 Wyvern Close, Dartford DA1 2NA
Tel (01322) 271583

Lancashire Ladies' County Golf Association
Hon Sec, Mrs J Rogers, 19 Lonsdale Rd, Formby, Liverpool L37 3HD
Tel (01704) 831009

Leicestershire & Rutland Ladies' County Golf Association
Hon Sec, Mrs AL Adams, 23 Fisher Close, Cossington, Leicester LE7 4US
Tel (01509) 812869

Lincolnshire Ladies' County Association
Hon Sec, Mrs K Craigs, 11 Sylvan Avenue, Woodhall Spa LN10 6SL
Tel (01526) 352293

Middlesex Ladies' County Golf Association
Hon Sec, Mrs E Thomas, 62 Highview Avenue, Edgware HA8 9UA
Tel (020)8905 3631

Norfolk Ladies' County Association
Hon Sec, Mrs J Foad, 28 St Leonard's Close, Wymondham NR18 0JF
Tel (01953) 602692

Northamptonshire Ladies' County Golf Association
Hon Sec, Mrs SE Clark, The Leys, 32 West St, Earls Barton, Northampton NN6 0EW
Tel (01604) 810257

Northumberland Ladies' County Golf Association
Hon Sec, Mrs PA Smith, Clonreher, Armstrong Cottages, Bamburgh, Northumberland NE69 7BA
Tel (01668) 214216

Nottinghamshire County Ladies' Golf Association
Hon Sec, Mrs BA Patrick, 18 Delville Avenue, Keyworth NG12 5JA
Tel (0115) 937 3237

Oxfordshire Ladies' County Golf Association
Hon Sec, Mrs EA Sadler, 84 Mably Grove, Wantage, Oxon OX12 9XN
Tel (01235) 760997

Shropshire Ladies' County Golf Association
Hon Sec, Mrs HF Davies, Brooklands, Old Woods, Bomere Heath, Shrewsbury SY4 3AX
Tel (01939) 290427

Somerset Ladies' County Golf Association
Hon Sec, Mrs D Bowerman, Ridgedown, Blagdon Hill, Taunton TA3 7SL
Tel (01823) 421256

Staffordshire Ladies' County Golf Association
Hon Sec, Mrs PM Barrow, Heron's Pool, Roman Rd, Little Aston, Sutton Coldfield B74 3AA
Tel/Fax (0121) 353 5753

Suffolk Ladies' County Golf Association
Hon Sec, Mrs W Wootton, Mill Cottage, Mill Lane, Great Blakenham, Ipswich IP19 8JZ
Tel (01986) 875554

Surrey Ladies' County Golf Association
Hon Sec, Mrs V Bell, Woodlands Common Lane, Claygate, Surrey KT10 0HY
Tel (01372) 462003   *Fax* (01372) 470516

Sussex County Ladies' Golf Association
Hon Sec, Mrs JM Scott, Preferred Lie, Rufwood, Crawley Down, West Sussex RH10 4HD
Tel (01342) 712213

Warwickshire Ladies' County Golf Association
Hon Sec, Mrs J Colley, Freshfield, Penn Lane, Tanworth-in-Arden, Solihull B94 5HH
Tel (01564) 742543

Wiltshire Ladies' County Golf Association
Sec, Mrs F Pinder, Pippins, Mill Orchard, Fovant, Salisbury SP3 5JS
Tel (01722) 714767

Worcestershire County Ladies' Golf Association
Hon Sec, Mrs S James, 408 Bromsgrove Road, Hunnington, West Midlands B62 0JN
Tel (0121) 550 2060

Yorkshire Ladies' County Golf Association
Hon Sec, Mrs S Dennis, 2 Hesp Hills, Beckfoot Lane, Bingley BD16 1AR
Tel (01274) 567500

English County PGAs

Bedfordshire & Cambridgeshire PGA
Sec, B Wake, 6 Gazelle Close, Eaton Socon, St Neots PE19 3QF
Tel (01480) 219760

Berks, Bucks & Oxon PGA
Hon Sec, Mrs M Green, Wayside, Aylesbury Road, Monks Risborough, Aylesbury HP27 0JS
Tel (01844) 343012

Cheshire and North Wales PGA
Sec, J Croxton, No 2 Cottage, Bolton GC, Lostock Park, Chorley New Road, Bolton BL6 4AJ
Tel (01204) 496137
Fax (01204) 847959

Cornwall PGA
Sec, B Gripe, 3 Redannick Crescent, Truro TR1 2DG
Tel (01872) 276989

Derbyshire PGA
Sec, F McCabe, Hillside, Lower Hall Close, Holbrook, Derby DE56 0TN
Tel (01332) 880411

Devon PGA
Sec, I Marshall, Staddon Heights GC, Plymstock, Plymouth PL9 9SP
Tel (01752) 492630

Dorset PGA
Sec/Treas, JM Nicholls, 230 St Michaels Avenue, Yeovil, Somerset BA21 4LZ
Tel (01935) 472839
E-mail nicholls.john@lineone.net

Essex PGA
Sec, J Stott, 1 The Paddocks, Great Totham, Maldon CM9 8PF
Tel (01621) 890113
E-mail jstott@essexpga.co.uk
Website www.essexpga.co.uk

Gloucestershire & Somerset PGA
Sec, E Goodwin, Cotswold Hills GC, Ullenwood, Cheltenham GL53 9QT
Tel (01242) 515263

Hampshire PGA
Sec, DL Wheeler, South Winchester GC, Pitt, Winchester SO22 5QW
Tel/Fax (01962) 860928
E-mail hampshirepga@yahoo.co.uk
Website www.hampshirepga.com

Hertfordshire PGA
Hon Sec, RA Gurney, 1 Field Lane, Letchworth, Herts SG6 3LF
Tel (01462) 627899

Kent PGA
Sec, Miss K Page, Kent PGA Office, West Malling GC, London Road, Addington, Maidstone ME19 5AR
Tel/Fax (01732) 843420
E-mail karen@kpga.fsnet.co.uk

Lancashire PGA
Sec, J Croxton, No 2 Cottage, Bolton GC,
Lostock Park, Chorley New Road, Bolton
BL6 4AJ
Tel (01204) 496137
Fax (01204) 847959

Leicestershire PGA
Sec, J Ashton, 2 Rose Tree Avenue, Birstall,
Leicester LE4 4CR
Tel (0116) 267 1316

Lincolnshire PGA
Sec, D Drake, Gainsborough GC, Thonock,
Gainsborough DN21 1PZ
Tel (01522) 703331

Middlesex PGA
Sec, B Eady, 8 Woodbank Drive, Chalfont
St Giles HP8 4RP
Tel (01494) 874487
E-mail brianeady@ukonline.co.uk

Norfolk PGA
Hon Sec, DM Bray, 11a Seaview Road,
Mundesley-on-Sea NR11 8DH
Tel (01263) 721224
E-mail norgolfe@aol.com

North East & North West PGA
Sec, R Sentance, 7 Larch Lea, Ponteland,
Newcastle-upon-Tyne NE20 9LG
Tel/Fax (01661) 821336

Northamptonshire PGA
Sec, Kash Naidu, Langholm, Kettering Rd,
Walgrave NN6 9PH
Tel (01604) 781353
Fax (01604) 781313
E-mail kashnaidu@hotmail.com

Nottinghamshire PGA
Sec, Mrs D Ashley, 31 Orchid Drive, Newark
NG24 3TX
Tel (01636) 686391
E-mail dianeashley@supanet.com

Shropshire & Hereford PGA
Sec, P Hinton, 1 Stanley Lane Cottages,
Bridgnorth, Shropshire
Tel (01746) 762045

Staffordshire PGA
Sec, DJ Lewis, 59 Chester Crescent, The
Westlands, Newcastle-under-Lyme ST5 3RR
Tel/Fax (01782) 613415

Suffolk PGA
Sec, A Sleath, 21 Hasketon Road, Woodbridge
IP12 4LD
Tel (01394) 380011

Surrey PGA
Sec, K Parry, Clandon Regis GC, Epsom Road,
West Clandon, Guildford GU4 7TT
Tel (01483) 223031

Fax (01483) 223224
E-mail celia.shipp@pga.org.uk

Sussex PGU
Sec, C Pluck, 96 Cranston Avenue, Bexhill,
East Sussex TN39 3NL
Tel/Fax (01424) 221298
E-mail cliff@spgu.freeserve.co.uk
Website www.spgu.freeserve.co.uk

Warwickshire PGA
Sec, J Tunnicliff, 80 Wychwood Ave, Knowle,
Solihull B93 9DQ
Tel (01564) 773168

Wiltshire PGA
Sec, R Blake, Upavon GC, Douglas Avenue,
Upavon, Pewsey SN9 6BQ
Tel (01980) 630281
Fax (01980) 635103
E-mail richard@upavongc.fsnet.co.uk

Worcestershire PGA
Sec, K Ball, 136 Alvechurch Road, West Heath,
Birmingham B31 3PW
Tel (0121) 475 7400

Yorkshire PGA
Sec, J Pape, 1 Summerhill Gardens, Leeds,
Yorks LS8 2EL
Tel (0113) 266 4746

English Blind Golf Association
Sec, R Tomlinson, 93 St Barnabas Road,
Woodford Green, Essex IG8 7BT
Tel/Fax (020) 8505 2085
E-mail ron@blindgolf.demon.co.uk
Website www.englishblindgolf,com

English Schools' Golf Association
Hon Sec, R Snell, 20 Dykenook Close,
Whickham, Newcastle-upon-Tyne NE16 5TD
Tel (0191) 488 3538   *Fax* (0191) 441 1146

Ireland

Golfing Union of Ireland
Gen Sec, S Smith, Glencar House, 81 Eglinton
Road, Donnybrook, Dublin 4
Tel +353 1 269 4111   *Fax* +353 1 269 5368
E-mail gui@iol.ie
Website www.gui.ie

Connacht Branch: *Gen Sec,* E Lonergan,
2 Springfield Terrace, Castlebar, Mayo
Tel +353 94 28141   *Fax* +353 94 28143
E-mail guieb@eircom.net

Leinster Branch: *Exec. Off,* P Smyth,
1 Clonskeagh Square, Clonskeagh Road,
Dublin 14
Tel +353 1 269 6977   *Fax* +353 1 269 3602
E-mail guilb@indigo.ie

Munster Branch: *Hon Sec*, S MacMahon,
6 Town View, Mallow, Co Cork
Tel +353 22 21026   *Fax* +353 22 42373
E-mail guimb@iol.ie
Ulster Branch: *Sec*, BG Edwards, MBE,
58a High Street, Holywood, Co Down
BT18 9AE
Tel (028) 9042 3708   *Fax* (028) 9042 6766
E-mail ulster.gui@virgin.net

Irish Ladies' Golf Union
Sec, Mrs T Thompson, 1 Clonskeagh Square,
Clonskeagh Road, Dublin 14
Tel +353 1 269 6244   *Fax* +353 1 283 8670
E-mail ilgu@ilgu.ie
Website www.ilgu.ie
Eastern District: *Hon Sec*, Miss E Foley,
10 Vale View Avenue, The Park, Cabinteely,
Dublin 18
Tel +353 1 285 6853
Midland District: *Hon Sec*, Mrs B McTague,
Athlone Rd, Ferbane, Co Offaly
Tel +353 902 54961
Northern District: *Hon Sec*, Ms A Dickson,
12 The Meadows, Strongford, Downpatrick,
Co Down BT20 6LN
Tel (028) 446 12286
Southern District: *Hon Sec*, Mrs M Power,
36 Tracton Avenue, Montenotte, Cork
Tel +353 21 551977
Western District: *Hon Sec*, Mrs K Reilly, Old
Church Street, Athenny, Co Galway
Tel +353 91 845417

Scotland

Scottish Golf Union
Sec, H Grey, Scottish National Golf Centre,
Drumoig, Leuchars, St Andrews KY16 0DW
Tel (01382) 549500   *Fax* (01382) 549510
E-mail sgu@scottishgolf.com
Website www.scottishgolf.com

Scottish Men's Area Associations

Angus: *Sec*, D Speed, 7 Eastgate, Friockheim,
Arbroath DD11 4TG
Tel (01241) 828544   *Fax* (01241) 828455
E-mail david@speedd.fsnet.co.uk
Argyll & Bute: *Sec*, G Duncanson, 4 Shore
Rd, Port Bannatyne, Bute PA20 0LQ
Tel (01700) 502468
Ayrshire: *Sec*, RL Crawford, 81 Connel
Crescent, Mauchline, Ayrshire KA5 5AU
Tel (01290) 551434   *Fax* (01290) 551078
E-mail secretaryaga@btinternet.com
Borders: *Sec*, RG Scott, 3 Whytbank Row,
Clovenfords, Galashiels TD1 3NE
Tel/Fax (01896) 850570

Clackmannanshire: *Sec*, T Johnson,
75 Dewar Avenue, Kincardine-on-Forth
FK10 4RR
Tel/Fax (01259) 731168
E-mail ronscott@bordergolf.freeserve.co.uk
Dunbartonshire: *Sec*, AW Jones, 107
Larkfield Road, Lenzie, Glasgow G66 3AS
Tel (0141) 776 7430
Fife: *Sec*, J Scott, Lauriston, East Links, Leven
KY8 4JL
Tel (01333) 423798
Fax (01333) 439910
E-mail jscott@care4free.net
Glasgow: *Sec*, RJG Jamieson, 32 Eglinton
Street, Beith KA15 1AH
Tel/Fax (01505) 503000
Lanarkshire: *Sec*, T Logan, 41 Woodlands
Drive, Coatbridge, ML5 1LB.
Tel (01236) 428799
Fax (01236) 429358
E-mail tlogan@btinternet.com
Lothians: *Sec*, J Wood, 28 Stoneyhill Avenue,
Musselburgh EH21 6SB
Tel/Fax 0131-665 4813
E-mail ilnwood@aol.com
North: *Sec*, J Macpherson, Pinetops,
11 Granary Park, Rafford, Forres IV36 2JZ
Tel (01309) 671576
E-mail js.macpherson@virgin.net
North-East: *Sec*, G McIntosh, 35 School
Road, Peterculter AB14 0TB
Tel (01224) 733836
Fax (01651) 863055
E-mail kayashish@msn.com
Perth & Kinross: *Sec*, DY Rae, 18 Carlownie
Place, Auchterarder PH3 1BT
Tel (01764) 662837
Fax (01764) 662886
Renfrewshire: *Sec*, JI McCosh, 'Muirfield', 20
Williamson Place, Johnstone, PA5 9DW
Tel (01505) 344613
South: *Sec*, James Burns, Glanavan, 14
Millfield Avenue, Stranraer DG9 0EG
Tel/Fax (01776) 704778
Stirlingshire: *Sec*, I Hutton, 18 Turret Drive,
Polmont FK2 0QW
Tel (01324) 712 585
Fax (01324) 717 087
E-mail iain@hutton-falkirk.demon.co.uk

Scottish Blind Golf Society
Co.Sec. Jim Gales, 38 Crawley Crescent,
Springfield, Cupar KY15 5SF
Tel/Fax (01334) 653 767
Scottish Golfers' Alliance
Sec/treas, Mrs MA Caldwell, 5 Deveron
Avenue, Giffnock, Glasgow G46 6NH
Tel (0141) 638 2066

Scottish Ladies' Golfing Association
Sec, Scottish National Golf Centre, Drumoig,
Leuchars, Fife KY16 0DW
Tel (01382) 549 502 *Fax* (01382) 549 512
E-mail slga@scottishgolf.com
Website www.scottishgolf.com

Aberdeen Ladies' County Golf Association
Hon Sec, Mrs M Robinson, 7 Carnegie
Gardens, Aberdeen AB15 4AW
Tel (01224) 313 582

Angus Ladies' County Golf Association
Hon Sec, Mrs D Gordon, 11 Golf Avenue,
Monifieth, DD5 4AS
Tel (01382) 532 799

Ayrshire Ladies' County Golf Association
Hon Sec, Miss AD Cree, 19 Woodfield Road,
Ayr KA8 8LZ
Tel (01292) 260 702

Border Counties' Ladies' Golf Association
Treas, Mrs E Crawford, Dunkeld, Fordel
Gardens, Melrose TD6 9SG
Tel (01896) 822 363

**Dumfriesshire Ladies' County Golf
Association**
Hon Sec, Miss MJ Greig, 10 Nelson Street,
Dumfries DG2 9AY
Tel (01387) 254 429

**Dunbartonshire & Argyll Ladies' County
Golf Association**
Hon Sec, Mrs M Johnston, Ardleish, 43 Hillside
Road, Cardross, Dumbarton G82 5LU
Tel (01389) 841 528

**East Lothian Ladies' County Golf
Association**
Hon Sec, Mrs C Bowe, Birkhill, Newbyth, East
Linton EH40 3DU
Tel (01620) 860 321

Fife County Ladies' Golf Association
Hon Sec, Mrs A Robertson, 24 Abbey Court,
St Andrews KY16 9TL
Tel (01334) 473 863

Galloway Ladies' County Golf Association
Hon Sec, Mrs P Magill, Church St, Kirkcolm,
Stranraer DG9 0NN
Tel (01776) 853 254

**Lanarkshire Ladies' County Golf
Association**
Hon Sec, Mrs M Heggie, 80 Weirwood Avenue,
Garrowhill, Glasgow G69 6LN
Tel (0141) 771 3802

**Midlothian County Ladies' Golf
Association**
Hon Sec, Mrs M Gammie, 4 Curriehall Castle
Drive, Balerno EH14 5TA
Tel (0131) 449 6652

**Northern Counties' Ladies' Golf
Association**
Hon Sec, Mrs J Corbett, Sandle Wood, 18
Edward Avenue, Banff
Tel (01261) 812 848

**Perth & Kinross Ladies' County Golf
Association**
Hon Sec, Mrs P Drysdale, Annandale, Park Hill
Road, Rattray, Blairgowrie PH10 7DS
Tel (01250) 873 641

**Renfrewshire Ladies' County Golf
Association**
Hon Sec, Mrs C Finlayson, Hazel Lodge,
Hazeldon Rd, Mearnskirk, Glasgow G77 6RR
Tel (0141) 639 5418

**Stirling & Clackmannan Ladies' Golf
Association**
Hon Sec, Mrs A Hunter, 22 Muirhead Road,
Stenhousemuir FK5 4JA
Tel (01324) 554 515

Wales

Welsh Golfing Union
Sec, R Dixon, Catsash, Newport, Gwent
NP18 1JQ
Tel (01633) 430 830
Fax (01633) 430 843
E-mail wgu@welshgolf.org
Website www.welshgolf.org

Welsh Men's Area Associations

Anglesey Golf Union
Hon Sec, GP Jones, 20 Gwelfor Estate, Cemaes
Bay, Anglesey LL67 0NL
Tel (01407) 710 755

Brecon & Radnor Golf Union
Hon Sec, DJ Davies, Garden House, Howey,
Llandrindod Wells, Powys LD1 5PU
Tel (01597) 824 316

Caernarfonshire & District Golfing Union
Hon Sec, RE Jones, 23 Bryn Rhos, Rhosbodrual,
Caernarfon, Gwynedd LL55 2BT
Tel (01286) 673 486

Denbighshire Golfing Union
Hon Sec, EG Howells, 10 Lon Howell,
Myddleton Park, Dinbych, LL16 4AN North
Wales
Tel/Fax (01745) 813 849

Dyfed Golfing Union
Hon Sec, AE Scott, 40 Clover Park,
Haverfordwest, Dyfed SA61 1UE
Tel (01437) 767 578
E-mail ascott4347@aol.com

Union of Flintshire Golf Clubs
Hon Sec, JF Snead, 1 Cornist Cottages, Cornist
Park, Flint, Clwyd CH6 5RH, North Wales
Tel (01352) 733 461

Glamorgan County Golf Union
Hon Sec, DC Thomas, 168 North Road,
Ferndale, Rhondda CF43 4RA
Tel (01443) 730 722

Gwent Golf Union
Sec, CM Buckley,
20 St Peters Drive, Libanus Fields, Blackwood,
NP12 2ER, Gwent
Tel (01495) 223 520

North Wales PGA *see* **Cheshire & North Wales PGA**

South Wales PGA
Sec, RC Thomas, 17 South Place, Porthcawl,
Mid Glamorgan CF36 3DB
Tel (01656) 783 377

Welsh Ladies' Golf Union
Sec, Mrs S Webster, Catsash, Newport
NP18 1JQ
Tel/Fax (01633) 422 911

Caernarvonshire & Anglesey Ladies' County Golf Association
Hon Sec, Mrs M Bromley, Ty'r Ysgol,
Borth-y-Gest, Porthmadog LL49 9UF
Tel (01766) 512 573

Denbighshire & Flintshire Ladies' County Golf Association
Sec, Mrs P Williams, 4 Green Meadows,
Hawarden, Flintshire CH5 3SL
Tel (01244) 534 549

Glamorgan Ladies' County Golf Association
Sec, Mrs S Williams, 19 Trem-y-Don, Barry,
South Glamorgan CF62 6QJ
Tel (01446) 734 865

Mid Wales Ladies' County Golf Association
Sec, Miss A James, Flat 4, Penbryn Court,
Lampeter, Dyfed SA48 7EU
Tel (01570) 422 463

Monmouthshire Ladies' County Golf Association
Hon Sec, Mrs E Davidson, Jon-Len, Goldcliff,
Newport NP18 2AU
Tel (01633) 274 477

Overseas Associations

Europe

European Golf Association
Gen Sec, JC Storjohann, Place de la Croix
Blanche 19, Case Postale CH-1066 Epalinges,
Switzerland
Tel +41 21 784 35 32
Fax +41 21 784 35 91

E-mail info@ega-golf.ch
Website www.ega-golf.ch

Austrian Golf Association
Sec, Mrs Waltraud Neuwirth, Haus des Sports,
Prinz-Eugen-Strasse 12, A-1040 Wien
Tel +43 1 505 3245
Fax +43 1 505 4962
E-mail oegv@golf.at
Website www.golf.at

Royal Belgian Golf Federation
Gen Sec, E Steghers, Chausée de la Hulpe 110,
B-1000 Brussels
Tel +32 2 672 2389
Fax +32 2 672 0897
E-mail info@golfbelgium.be
Website www.golfbelgium.be

Bulgarian National Golf Association
Chair, N Nedialkov, PO Box 844, Sofia 1000
Tel +359 2 931 1862
Fax +359 2 32 1845
E-mail: bnga@dir.bg

Croatian Golf Association
Sec, D Klisovic, Miramarska 15B, 10 000
Zagreb
Tel +385 1 538 169   *Fax* +385 1 457 7907

Czech Golf Federation
Gen Sec, M Dorníková, Erpet Golf Centre,
Strakonická 2860, CZ-150 00 Prague 5-
Smichov
Tel +420 2 5731 7865   *Fax* +420 2 5731 8618
E-mail cgf@cgf.cz
Website www.cgf.cz

Danish Golf Union
Sec, C Molholm, Idraettens Hus, Brøndby
Stadion 20, DK-2605 Brøndby
Tel +45 43 26 2700   *Fax* +45 43 26 2701
E-mail info@dgu-golf.dk
Website www.dgu-golf.dk

Estonian Golf Association
Pres, T Laak, 14 Tartu Rd, EE-10117
Tallinn
Tel +372 6 108 700   *Fax* +372 6 108 701
E-mail laak@online.ee

Finnish Golf Union
Gen Sec, K Hagfors, Radiokatu 20,
FIN-00093 Slu
Tel +358 9 3481 2520   *Fax* +358 9 147 145
E-mail office@golf.slu.fi
Website www.golf.fi

French Golf Federation
Dir Gen, H Chesneau, 68 Rue Anatole France,
F-92309 Levallois-Perret Cedex
Tel +33 1 41 49 7700   *Fax* +33 1 41 49 77 01
E-mail ffg@ffgolf.org
Website www.ffgolf.org

German Golf Association
Gen Sec, Ullrich Libor, Postfach 2106,
D-65011 Wiesbaden
Tel +49 611 990 2011
Fax +49 611 990 2015
E-mail info@dgv.golf.de
Website www.golf.de

Hellenic Golf Federation
Hon Sec, P Papalavrentis, PO Box 70003,
GR-166 10 Glyfada Athens
Tel +30 1 894 1933   *Fax* +30 1 894 5162
E-mail hgfederation@attglobal.net

Hungarian Golf Federation
Gen Sec, T Szlávy, Dózsa György út 1-3,
H-1143 Budapest
Tel/Fax +36 1 221 5923
E-mail hun.golf.fed@axelero.hu

Iceland Golf Union
Sec, H Thorsteinsson, Sport Center, Laugardal,
IS-104 Reykjavik
Tel +354 5 144 050   *Fax* +354 5 144 051
E-mail gsi@isisport.is
Website www.golf.is

Italian Golf Federation
Sec Gen, S Manca, Viale Tiziano 74, I-00196
Roma
Tel +39 06 323 1825   *Fax* +39 06 322 0250
E-mail fig@ntt.it
Website www.federgolf.it

Latvia Golf Federation
Gen Sec, N Mazjanis, Elizabetes Str.49
LV-1050 Riga
Tel +371 925 6220   *Fax* +371 782 8078
E-mail noris@navigators.lv

Luxembourg Golf Union
Sec, Jules Heisborg, 1 Route de Trèves,
L-2633 Senningerberg
Tel +352 34 0090   *Fax* +352 34 8394
E-mail gcgd@pt.lu

Malta Golf Federation
Hon Sec, Alexander Mangion, c/o Royal Malta
GC, Marsa LQA 06, Malta
Tel +356 23 9302   *Fax* +356 22 7020
E-mail info@maltagolf.org
Website www.maltagolf.org

Netherlands Golf Federation
Sec, HL Heyster, PO Box 221, NL-3454 ZL
De Meern.
Tel +31 30 242 6370   *Fax* +31 30 242 6380
E-mail golf@ngf.nl
Website www.golfsite.nl

Norwegian Golf Federation
Gen Sec, G.Ove Berg, PO Box 163, Lilleaker,
N-0216 Oslo
Tel +47 22 73 6620   *Fax* +47 22 73 6621
E-mail ngf@golf.no

Polish Golf Union
Sec, Andrzej Kalinski, ul.Kolektorska 30,
PL-01-692 Warszawa
Tel +48 22 832 15 91   *Fax* +48 22 832 15 92
Website www.golf.pl

Portuguese Golf Federation
Sec, J A Moreira, Av das Tulipas, Edifico
Miraflores 17°, Miraflores, P-1495-161 Algés
Tel +351 214 123 780
Fax +351 214 107 972
E-mail fpgolfe@mail.telepac.pt
Website www.fpg.pt

Russian Golf Association
Gen Sec, A Stepanov, Office 331, Luzhnetskaya
nab 8, RU-119871 Moskow
Tel +7 095 725 4719   *Fax* +7 095 147 6252
E-mail alstepanov@hotmail.com

San Marino Golf Federation
Gen Sec, F Sandro, Via XXV, Marzo 11, 47031
Domagnano
Tel +39 549 907 159   *Fax* +39 549 992 746

Slovak Golf Union
Gen Sec, Mliekarenska 10, SK-824 92
Bratislava
Tel +421 2 5557 1010
Fax +421 2 5557 7105
E-mail sgu@golfs.sk
Website www.sgu.sk

Slovenian Golf Association
Sec, M Azman, Dunajska 51, SLO-1000
Ljubljana
Tel +386 1 236 2492   *Fax* +386 1 436 9676
E-mail golfzveza@golfzveza-slovenije.si
Website www.golfzveza-slovenije.si

Royal Spanish Golf Federation
Sec, L Alvarez, Capitán Haya 9, E-28020
Madrid
Tel +34 91 555 2757   *Fax* +34 91 556 3290
E-mail webrfeg@ibm.net
Website www.golfspainfederacion.com

Swedish Golf Federation
Gen Sec, Bo Wickberg, PO Box 84, S-182 11
Danderyd
Tel +46 8 622 1500   *Fax* +46 8 755 8439
E-mail info@sgf.golf.se
Website www.golf.se

Swiss Golf Association
Sec, JC Storjohann, Place de la Croix Blanche
19, Case Postale, CH-1066 Epalinges
Tel +41 21 784 3531   *Fax* +41 21 784 3536
E-mail info@asg.ch
Website www.asg.ch

Turkish Golf Federation
Co-ord I Aktekin, GSGM Ulus Is Hani, A Blok
2, Kat205, Ulus 06050, Ankara
Tel/Fax +90 312 309 3945

European Professional Associations

Austria PGA
Sec, R Hagan, A-8724 Spielberg,
Frauenbachstrasse 51
Tel +43 664 304 5078   *Fax* +43 351 282 171
E-mail pga@pga-austria.at

Belgian PGA
Sec, B De Bruyckere, Grimstedestraat 53 B17,
B-2300 Turnhout
Tel +32 2672 2389   *Fax* +32 1472 0546
E-mail info@pga.be
Website www.pga.be

Denmark PGA
Sec, J Sunds, Centervej 1, Gatten 9640, Farso
Tel +45 98 100 041   *Fax* +45 98 100 037
E-mail pga@golfonline.dk
Website www.golfonline.dk.pga

Finland PGA
Sec, M Rantanen, Mynttilantie 1, FIN-02780
Espoo
Tel +358 9 8194 1420   *Fax* +358 9 8194 1425
E-mail pgafinland@pga.fi
Website www.pga.fi

French PGA
Dir, Alain Serra, National Golf Club, 2 Avenue
du Golf, 78 280 Guyancourt, France
Tel +33 1 34 52 0846   *Fax* +33 1 34 52 0548
E-mail pgafra@club-internet.fr
Website www.pgafrance.com

PGA of Germany
Sec, Rainer Goldrian, Werner Haas Str 6,
D-86153 Augsburg
Tel +49 821 568 710   *Fax* +49 821 568 7129
E-mail info@pga.de
Website www.pga.de

Italy PGA
Sec, L Rendina, Palazzo Galileo, Via
S Quintino 28, I-10121 Torino
Tel +39 011 561 2018   *Fax* +39 011 545 561
E-mail pgaitaly@tin.it
Website www.pga.it

Netherlands PGA
Sec, Mrs R Vonk Mundt, Burg van der
Borchlaan 1, 3722 GZ Bilthoven
Tel+31 30 228 7018   *Fax* +31 30 225 0261
E-mail npga@wxs.nl
Website www.PGAholland.com

Portugal PGA
Sec, R Pinto, Av das Tulipas, Edifico Miraflores
17°, Miraflores, P-1495-161 Algés
Tel +351 21 412 3788
Fax +351 21 410 7972
E-mail pga.portugal@neto.pt
Website www.fpg.pt

Spain PGA
Sec, M Santamaría, c/Capitán Haya 22-5C,
E-28020 Madrid
Tel +34 91 555 1393   *Fax* +34 91 597 0170
E-mail apge@wanadoo.es
Website www.golfexcel.com/apg

Swedish PGA
Sec, M Sorling, Tylösand, S-302 73
Halmstad
Tel +46 35 320 30   *Fax* +46 35 320 25
E-mail pga@golf.se
Website www.pga.golf.se

Swiss PGA
Gen Sec, C Blattmann, Hauserstrasse 14, PO
Box CH-8030 Zürich
Tel +41 1 267 3401   *Fax* +41 1 267 3411
E-mail info@swisspga.ch
Website www.swisspga.ch

North America: Canada and USA

Royal Canadian Golf Association
Exec Dir, SD Ross, Golf House, Glen Abbey,
1333 Dorval Drive, Oakville, Ontario L6J 4Z3
Tel +1 905 849 9700   *Fax* +1 905 845 7040
E-mail golfhouse@rcga.org
Website www.rcga.org

Canadian Ladies' Golf Association
Pres, Golf House, Glen Abbey, 1333 Dorval
Drive, Oakville, Ontario L6J 4Z3
Tel +1 905 849 2542   *Fax* +1 905 849 0188
E-mail clga@clga.org
Website www.clga.org

Canadian PGA
Pres, Ch Exec, David J Colling, 13450 Dublin
Line RR#1, Acton, Ontario L7J 2W7
Tel +1 519 853 5450   *Fax* +1 519 853 5449
E-mail cpga@canadianpga.org
Website www.cpga.com

Ladies' Professional Golf Association
Pres, 100 International Golf Drive, Daytona
Beach, Florida 32124-1092
Tel +1 386 274 6200   *Fax* +1 386 274 1099
Website www.lpga.com

National Golf Foundation
Pres, 1150 South US Highway One, Jupiter,
Florida 33477
Tel +1 561 744 6006
Website www.ngf.org

PGA of America
Pres, Box 109601, 100 Avenue of the
Champions, Palm Beach Gardens, Florida
33418.
Tel +1 407 624 8400   *Fax* +1 407 624 8448
Website www.pgaonline.com

PGA Tour
Pres, The Commissioner, PGA Tour, 112 PGA Tour Boulevard, Ponte Vedra Beach, Florida 32082
Tel +1 904 285 3700   *Fax* +1 904 285 7913
Website www.pgatour.com

United States Golf Association
Pres, Golf House, PO Box 708, Far Hills, NJ 07931-0708
Tel +1 908 234 2300   *Fax* +1 908 234 9687
E-mail usga@usga.org
Website www.usga.org

The Caribbean and Central America

Caribbean Golf Association
Sec, David G Bird, PO Box 31329 SMB, Grand Cayman, Cayman Islands
Tel +345 947 1903   *Fax* +345 947 3439
E-mail bird@candw.ky

Bahamas Golf Federation
Pres, Ambrose Gouthro, PO Box F-41790, Freeport, Grand Bahama
Tel +242 373 7295   *Fax* +242 373 7926
E-mail agouthro@blvdnet.com
Website www.bgfnet.com

Barbados Golf Association
Sec, PD Lashley, PO Box 585, Bridgetown, Barbados
Tel +246 428 8022   *Fax* +246 418 0342
E-mail mervholder@cyberseniors.bb
Website www.bajangolf.4mg.com

Bermuda Golf Association
Sec, Tom Smith, PO Box HM 433, Hamilton, Bermuda HM-BX
Tel +1 441 238 1367   *Fax* +1 441 238 0983
E-mail bdagolf@ibl.bm

Cayman Islands Golf Association
Sec, David G Bird, PO Box 31329 SMB, Grand Cayman
Tel +345 947 1903   *Fax* +345 947 3439
E-mail bird@candw.ky

National Golf Association of Costa Rica
Pres, F Solano, PO Box 10969, 1000 San Jose
Tel +506 221 8129   *Fax* +506 257 0439
E-mail fsolano@sol.racsa.co.cr
Website www.edenia.com/amagolf

Fedogolf (Dominican Republic)
Exec Dir, Rudys Soler, Campo Nacional de Golf, Las Lagunas S.A., Autopito Duarte Km 20, Santo Domingo
Tel +809 231 4719   *Fax* +809 372 7406
E-mail fedogolf@hotmail.com
Website www.fedogolf.org

El Salvador Golf Federation
Sec, G Aceto Marini, Apartado Postal 631, San Salvador C.A.
Tel +503 264 1584
E-mail gaceto@yahoo.com

Guatemalan Golf Federation
Exec Sec, Adolfo Rios, Diagonal 6 10-76, Zona 10, Guatemala
Tel +502 360 9435   *Fax* +502 360 9475

Hondurena Golf Association
Sec, LF Gutiérrez, Apartado Postal 3175, Tegucigalpa, Honduras
Tel +504 37 2084   *Fax* +504 38 0456

Jamaica Golf Association
Hon Sec, G Hutchinson, Constant Spring GC, PO Box 743, Kingston 8
Tel +1 876 925 2325   *Fax* +1 876 924 6330
E-mail jamaicagolf@cwjamaica.com
Website www.jamaicagolfassociation.com

Mexican Golf Federation
Sec, IA Herroz, Av.Lomas de Sotelo No.1112 int.2,Col.Lomas de Sotelo C.P.11200 Mexico
Tel +525 580 6121   *Fax* +525 580 2263
E-mail fedmexgolf@compuserve.com.mx
Website www.mexgolf.org

Nicaraguan Golf Association
Pres, Alfonso Llanes, Nicabox 538, PO Box 25640, Miami, FL 33102
Tel +350 441 7596   *Fax* +350 385 1464

OECS Golf Association
Sec, Joan Paul, PO Box 189, Castries, St Lucia
Tel +758 452 3079   *Fax* +758 452 3885
E-mail joanpaul@candw.lc

Panama Golf Association
Pres, Antonio DeRoux, PO Box 872115, Zona Panamá
Tel +507 266 7436   *Fax* +507 220 3994
E-mail master@pty.com

Puerto Rico Golf Association
Pres, Sidney Wolf, 58 Caribe St, San Juan, Puerto Rico 00907-1909
Tel +787 721 7742   *Fax* +787 723 5760
E-mail golfpuertorico@prga.org
Website www.prga.org

Trinidad & Tobago Golf Association
Pres, Clarence Wilcox, St Andrews GC, Moka, Maraval, Trinidad
Tel +868 625 2115   *Fax* +868 625 4764
E-mail wilent@wow.net

Turks & Caicos Golf Association
Pres, John Phillips, PO Box 64, Suite C12, Providenciales, Turks & Caicos Islands
Tel +649 946 4109   *Fax* +649 946 4939
E-mail claymore@tciway.tc

Virgin Islands Golfers' Federation
Pres, Cosmo Williams, PO Box 3457,
Christiansted, St Croix, US Virgin Islands
00822
Tel +340 773 3119   *Fax* +340 773 4032
E-mail cosanco@att.net

South America

South American Golf Federation
Exec Sec, Juan Pablo Gutiérrez, Carrera 49A
No 99-30, Bogotá, Colombia
Tel +57 1 226 3489   *Fax* +57 1 226 7788
E-mail fedesud@latino.net.co

Argentine Golf Association
Exec Dir, Jorge V Garasino, Corrientes 538-
Pisos 11y12, 1043 Buenos Aires
Tel +54 11 4325 1113   *Fax* +54 11 4325 8660
E-mail golf@aag.com.ar
Website www.aag.com.ar

Bolivian Golf Federation
Sec, Juan E Maclean, Edif.Camara de Comer-
cio Piso 6-Oficina 604, C.P. 10217, La Paz
Tel/Fax +591 2 315853
E-mail fbgolf@ceibo.entelnet.bo
Website www.bolivia-golf.com

Brazilian Golf Confederation
Sec, MA Aguiar Giusti, Rua Paes de
Araujo, 29cjs.42 e 43, CEP 04531-090-São
Paulo-SP.
Tel/Fax +55 11 3846
E-mail golfe@cbg.com.br
Website www.cbg.com.br

Chilean Golf Federation
Sec, Carlos Amenabar, Av el Golf 266,
Las Condes, Santiago
Tel +56 2 362 0777   *Fax* +56 2 362 0929
E-mail secretaria@chilegolf.cl
Website www.chilegolf.cl

Colombian Golf Union
Sec, Dr V Rodríguez Posada, Carrera 7A,
No 72-64 Int 26, Apartado aéreo 88768,
Bogotá
Tel +57 1 310 7664   *Fax* +57 1 235 5091
E-mail fedegolf@cable.net.co
Website www.federacioncolombianadegolf.com

Ecuador Golf Federation
Sec, Patricia Pazmiño, C.P. 17012411, Quito
Tel + 593 22 491 512   *Fax* + 593 22 491 254
E-mail fedecuat@feg.org.ec
Website www.feg.org.ec

Paraguay Golf Association
Pres, Victor M Ricciardi, Casilla de Correo No
76, Asunción
Tel +595 21 447 923   *Fax* +595 21 495 796
E-mail apg@mmail.com.py
Website www.apg.com.py

Peru Golf Federation
Sec, Juan Neira, Estadio Nacional Puerta 4 Piso
3, Lima 1
Tel +51 1 433 6515   *Fax* +51 1 433 8018
E-mail mail@fpg.org.pe
Website www.fpg.org.pe

Uruguay Golf Association
Sec, P Pereira Micoud, Casilla de Correo 1484,
Montevideo
Tel +598 2 701 721
E-mail augolf@adinet.com.uy

Venezuela Golf Federation
Exec Dir, Julio L Tories, Av. Juan B Arismendi,
Unidad Comercial La Florida, Mezzanina,
local 8.Urb.La Florida, Caracas 1050
Tel +582 731 7662   *Fax* +582 730 2731
E-mail direjec@fvg.org
Website www.fvg.org

Africa

Algerian Golf Federation
Sec, Benmiloud Noureddine, rue Ahmed
Quaked, Dely-Ibrahim
Tel +213 236 3059   *Fax* +213 261 4133

Botswana Golf Union
Sec, SE Palframan, PO Box 1033, Gaborone

Botswanu Ladies Golf Union
Hon Sec, Mrs M Baker, PO Box 1362,
Gaborone

The Egyptian Golf Federation
Chair, Khaled Abou Taleb, 29 Abdel Moneim
Hafaz Street, Heliopolis. Cairo
Tel +202 291 9101   *Fax* +202 291 9102
E-mail attar@internetalex.com

Ghana Golf Association
Hon Sec, Col JA Kabore, PO Box 8, Achimota,
Accra
Tel/Fax 233-21-400221
E-mail vaghq@ghana.com

Ghana Ladies Golf Union
Hon Sec, Miss E Adzakpo, PO Box 8,
Achimota, Accra

Côte d'Ivoire Golf Federation
Sec, I Keita, O8 BP 1297, Abidjan 08
Tel +225 213 874   *Fax* +225 227 112

Kenya Golf Union
Chair, Vishy Talwas, PO Box 49609, Nairobi
Tel +254 2 763 898   *Fax* +254 2 765 118
E-mail kgu@connect.co.ke
Website www.kgu.org.ke

KwaZulu–Natal Golf Union
Sec, RT Runge, PO Box 1939, Durban 4000
Tel +27 (0)31 202 7636
Fax +27 (0)31 202 1022
E-mail kzngu@kzngolf.co.za

Libyan Golf Federation
Pres, Mohamed El-Kheituni, PO Box 3674, Tripoli

Malawi Golf Union
Sec, J Hinde, PO Box 1198, Blantyre
Tel +265 643988   *Fax* +265 640135
E-mail jhinde@illovo.co.za

Malawi Ladies' Golf Union
Hon Sec, Mrs J Mullock, PO Box 5319, Limbe

Mauritius Golf Federation
Pres, Raj Ramlackhan, 42 Sir William Newton Street, Port Louis
Tel +230 208 2440   *Fax* +230 208 2438
E-mail ramn@intnet.mu

The Royal Moroccan Golf Federation
Sec, Sad Benkirane, Royal Golf Rabat Dar-es-Salam, Route des Zaers, Rabat
Tel +212 775 5636   *Fax* +212 775 1026

Namibian Golf Union
Treas, Hugh Mortimer, PO Box 2122, Windhoek, Namibia
E-mail wcc@iafrica.com.na

Nigeria Golf Union
Sec, IBB International G&CC, PO Box 6935, Wuse, Abuja
Tel +234 9 523 2015   *Fax* +234 9 523 2014
E-mail scovir@skannet.com

Nigerian Ladies Golf Union
Sec, Mrs P Ojebuoboh, c/o Ikoyi GC, PO Box 239, Ikoyi, Lagos

Sierra Leone Golf Federation
Pres, Freetown GC, PO Box 237, Lumley Beach, Freetown

South African Golf Association
Exec Dir, BA Younge, PO Box 391994, Bramley, South Africa 2018
Tel +27 11 442 3723   *Fax* +27 11 442 3753
E-mail sagolf@global.co.sa

South African Ladies' Golf Union
Pres, Hon Sec, Mrs V Horak, PO Box 209, Randfontein 1760, RSA
Tel/Fax +27 11 416 1263
E-mail salgu@golfing-sa.co.sa
Website www.safgu.co.za

South African PGA
Pres, PO Box 79432, Senderwood 2145
Tel +27 11 485 2327   *Fax* +27 11 485 1799

South African Women's PGA
Sec, Mrs V Harrington, PO Box 781547, Sandton 2146
Tel/Fax +27 11 477 8606

Swaziland Golf Union
Sec, J Resting, PO Box 1739, Mbabane
Tel/Fax +268 404 2227
E-mail johnrest@realnet.co.sz

Tanzania Golf Union
Sec, Rafik Meghji, PO Box 6018, Dar-es-Salaam
Tel +255 22 215 1706
Fax +255 22 215 0626
E-mail tgu@tzgolfun.com
Website www.tzgolfun.com

Tanzania Ladies' Golf Union
Hon Sec, Mrs T Kabani, PO Box 286, Dar-es-Salaam

Tunisian Golf Federation
Pres, Anror Atallah, Choutrana II, 2036 Soukra
Tel +216 1 865 745   *Fax* +216 1 865 700

Uganda Golf Union
Pres, GW Eggadu, Kitante Road, PO Box 2574, Kampala

Uganda Ladies Golf Union
Hon Sec, Mrs K Vnylsteke, PO Box 624, Kampala

Zambia Golf Union
Hon Sec, M Doogan, PO Box 71784, Ndola.
Tel +260 2 650697/621438
Fax +260 2 621834
E-mail collalum@coppernet.com

Zambia Ladies' Golf Union
Hon Sec, Mrs P Dyson, PO Box 90554, Luanshya

Zimbabwe Golf Association
Sec, JL Nixon, PO Box 3327, Harare
Tel +263 4 746 141   *Fax* +263 4 746 228

Zimbabwe Ladies' Golf Union
Hon Sec, Mrs F Benzon, 15 Brompton Rd, Highlands, Harare
E-mail benzon@africaonline.com.zw

Middle East

Bahrain Golf Committee
Gen Sec, Muneer Ahmed, PO Box 38938, Riffa
Tel +973 777 179   *Fax* +973 778 595
E-mail bgcom@batelco.com.bh

The Golf Federation of the Islamic Republic of Iran
Sec Gen, Mohammad Reza Naddaf Poor, PO Box 15815-1881, Tehran
Tel +98 21 829 671   *Fax* +98 21 834 333

Israel Golf Federation
Sec, Alon Ben David, PO Box 1010, Caesarea 38900
Tel +972 6636 1174   *Fax* +972 6636 1173

Lebanese Golf Federation
Pres, Faysal Alamldine, c/o GC of Lebanon, PO Box 11-3099, Beirut
Tel +961 1 822 470   *Fax* +961 1 822 474

Qatar Golf Association
Pres, Sheikh Ab, PO Box 6177, Doha
Tel +974 454 284   *Fax* +974 430 132

Saudi Golf Committee
Sec, PO Box 102201, Riyadh 11675, Saudi
Arabia

United Arab Emirates Golf Association
Sec Gen, Khalid Al Halyan, PO Box 31410,
Dubai, UAE
Tel +971 4 295 6440   *Fax* +971 4 295 6026
E-mail uaegolf@emirates.net.ae
Website www.uaegolf.com

Asia

Asia-Pacific Golf Confederation
Sec, Bertie To Jr, c/o HKR International Ltd,
Room 203, Discovery Bay Office Centre, No.2
Plaza Lane, Discovery Bay, Lantau Island,
Hong Kong
Tel +852 2238 3330   *Fax* +852 2987 6432
E-mail bertieto@dbgc.com.hk

Asian PGA
Sec, Ramlan Dato'harun, 415-417 Block A
Kelana Business Centre, 97 Jalan SS 7/2
Kelana Jaya, Selangor, Malaysia
Tel +603 7492 0099   *Fax* +603 7492 0098
Website www.asianpgatour.com

Asia PGA Tour
Chief Exec Off, Justin Strachan, 15/F,
One Harbourfront, 18 Tak Fung Street,
Hunghom, Kowloon, Hong Kong
Tel +852 2330 8227   *Fax* +852 2801 5743
E-mail apgatour@asiaonline.net
Website www.asianpgatour.com

China Golf Associaton
Sec, Mr Cui, 9 Tiya Guan Road, Beijing, China
100763

**Golf Association of the Republic of
China**
Sec Gen, Lung-Kuo Chien, 12 F-1, 125
Nan-King East Road, Section 2, Taipei,
Taiwan 104 R.O.C.
Tel +886 2 516 5611   *Fax* +886 2 516 3208

PGA Republic of China
2nd Floor 196 Cheng-Teh Road, Taipei,
Taiwan
Tel +886 2 8220318   *Fax* +886 2 8229684

Hong Kong Golf Association
Sec, WR Marshall QC, Room 2003, Sports
House, 1 Stadium Path, So Kon Po, Causeway
Bay, Hong Kong.
Tel +852 2522 8804   *Fax* +852 2845 1553
E-mail hkga@netvigator.com
Website www.hkga.com

Hong Kong PGA
Sec, Mr M Lai Wai Sing, Room 702 Landmark
North, Sheung Shui, NT Hong Kong
Tel +852 523 3171

Indian Golf Union
Sec, Mr PK Bhattacharyya, 'Sukh Sagar' 2nd
Floor, 2/5 Sarat Bose Road, Calcutta 700 020
Tel +91 33 4745 795   *Fax* +91 33 4748 914
E-mail ingolf.union@gems.vsnl.net.in

Indonesian Golf Association
Sec Gen Kusman Ismukanto, Rawamangun
Muka Raya, Jakarta 13220
Tel/Fax +62 21 470 1019
E-mail pgi@pgionline.org
Website www.pgionline.org

Japan Golf Association
Sec, Naomi Yokoyama, 606-6th Floor, Palace
Building, Marunouchi, Chiyoda-ku, Tokyo
100-0005
Tel +81 3 3215 0003   *Fax* +81 3 3214 2831

Japan Ladies PGA
7-16-3 Ginza, Nitetsu Kobiki Bldg 8F,
Chuo-ku, Tokyo 104-0061
Tel +81 3 3546 7801   *Fax* +81 3 3546 7805

Japan PGA
Int Com, Seien Kobayakawa, Top
Hamamatsucho Bldg, 1-5-12 Shiba.Minato-
Ku, 8FL, Tokyo 105-0014
Tel +81 3 5419 2614
Fax +81 3 5419 2622
E-mail bp@pga.or.jp

Korean Golf Association
Sec Gen, Dong Wook Kim, 1318 Rm
Manhattan Bldg, 36-2 Yeo Eui Du-Dong,
Yeong Deung Po Ku, Seoul
Tel +82 2 783 4748   *Fax* +82 2 783 4747
E-mail kogolf@chollian.net

Malaysian Golf Association
Sec, Tay Chong-Min, 12A Persiaran Ampang,
55000 Kuala Lumpur
Tel +60 3 4577931   *Fax* +60 3 4565596
E-mail mga@tm.net.my

PGA of Malaysia
Sec, Brig-Gen Mahendran, 1B Jalan Mamanda
7, Ampang Point, 6800 Selangor Darul Ehsan,
Malaysia

Myanmar Golf Federation
Sec, U Aung Kyi, c/o Aung San Stadium,
Rangoon
Tel +95 01 663 930   *Fax* +95 01 289 563

Pakistan Golf Federation
Hon Sec, W/Cdr Iftikhar Ahmed Khan,
Hamayun Rashid, Jhelum Road, PO Box
No 1295, Rawalpindi
Tel +92 51 256 995   *Fax* +92 51 584 566

Philippines Golf Association
Sec Gen, Alfredo M Masigan,
209 Administration Building, Rizal
Memorial Sports Complex, Vito Cruz,
Manila-1000
Tel +63 2 588845   *Fax* +63 2 521 1587

Singapore Golf Association
Hon Sec, Yik Nam Yeong, Tanglin Road Post
Office, PO Box 457, Singapore 912416
Tel +65 256 1318   *Fax* +65 256 1917
E-mail sga@pacific.net.sg

Sri Lanka Golf Union
Hon Sec, Shiran de Soysa, PO Box 309, 223
Model Farm Road, Colombo 8, Sri Lanka

Thailand Golf Association
Sec Gen, Pongnat Vatanasak, Room 212/213
Rajmangala National Stadium, 2088
Ramkamhaeng Rd, Hua Mark, Bangkapi,
Bangkok 10240
Tel +66 2 369 3777   *Fax* +66 2 369 3776
E-mail pongnat_v@yahoo.com
Website www.tga.or.th

Australasia and the Pacific

Australian Golf Union
Sec, Colin Phillips, Golf Australia House,
153-155 Cecil Street, South Melbourne,
Victoria 3205
Tel +61 3 9699 7944   *Fax* +61 3 9690 8510
E-mail agu@agn.org.au
Website www.agu.org.au

Womens' Golf Australia
Exec Dir, Maisie Mooney, 355 Moray Street,
South Melbourne, Victoria 3205
Tel +61 3 9690 9344   *Fax* +61 3 9696 2060
E-mail info@womensgolfaus.org.au
Website www.womensgolfaus.org.au

Australian PGA
Chief Exec, Max Garske, PO Box 1314, Crows
Nest, New South Wales

Tel +61 2 9439 8111   *Fax* +61 2 9439 7888
E-mail maxgpga@oze-mail.com.au
Website www.pga.org.au

Cook Islands Golf Association
Pres, Hugh M N Henry, Rarotonga GC,
PO Box 151, Rarotonga, Cook Islands
Tel +682 27 360   *Fax* +682 25 420

National Golf Association of Fiji
Hon Sec, CM Lenz, GPO Box 13843, Suva, Fiji
Tel +679 301 897   *Fax* +679 301 647
E-mail fasanoc@is.com.fj

New Zealand Golf Association
Chief Exec, P Aickin, PO Box 11842 Wellington
Tel +64 4 385 4330   *Fax* +64 4 385 4331
E-mail nzga@nzga.co.nz
Website www.nzga.co.nz

Womens' Golf New Zealand
Exec Dir, Mrs J Mackay, PO Box 11187,
65 Victoria Street, Wellington
Tel +64 4 4726 733   *Fax* +64 4 4726 732
E-mail golf@womensgolf.org.nz

New Zealand PGA
Exec Dir, PG Wyllie, PO Box 11-934,
Wellington
Tel +64 4 4722 687   *Fax* +64 4 4712 152
E-mail postmaster@pga.org.nz
Website www.pga.org.nz

Papua New Guinea Golf Association
Hon Sec, YoLae G.C., PO Box 164, Lae MP,
Papua New Guinea
Tel +675 323 1120   *Fax* +675 323 1300

**Papua New Guinea Ladies Golf
Association**
Hon Sec, Mrs L Illidge, PO Box 348, Lae
MP 411

Vanuatu Golf Association
Chairman, Bernie Cain, PO Box 358, Port Vila,
Vanuatu, Pacific Ocean
Tel +678 22178   *Fax* +678 25037
E-mail vilaref@vanuatu.com.vu

WEBSITES

Royal and Ancient Golf Club	www.randa.org
Ladies Golf Union	www.lgu.org
United States Golf Association	www.usga.org
European Golf Association	www.ega-golf.ch
English Golf Union	www.englishgolfunion.org
English Ladies (ELGA)	www.englishladiesgolf.org
Golf Union of Ireland	www.gui.ie
Irish Ladies (ILGU)	www.ilgu.ie
Scottish Golf Union & Scottish Ladies (SLGA)	www.scottishgolf.com
Welsh Golfing Union	www.welshgolf.org
Professional Golfers Association	www.pganet.net
PGA of Europe	www.pgae.com
European Tour	www.europeantour.com
Evian Tour	www.eviantour.com
PGA Tour	www.pgatour.com
LPGA Tour	www.lpga.com
Davidoff Tour	www.asianpgatour.com
ANZ Tour	www.pgatour.au
Sunshine Tour	**www.pgatour.co.za**
Other tours via Golf Web	www.golfweb.com
BBC Online – Golf	www.bbc.co.uk/sport
The Golf Channel	www.thegolfchannel.com
Golf Illustrated	www.golfillustrated.com
Nick Faldo (Junior Series)	www.nickfaldo.org
Jack Nicklaus	www.nicklaus.com
Tiger Woods	www.tigerwoods.com

PART X

Golf History

The Championships of Great Britain

The Open Championship

The Open Championship was initiated by Prestwick Golf Club in 1860 and was played there each year until 1870. Players competed for the Championship Belt, the winner holding it for the year unless it was won three years in succession in which case it would become the absolute property of that player. In those days the competition consisted of three rounds of the 12 hole course Prestwick then had, all played in one day (the Open did not become a four-round contest until 1892). There were few entrants in the early years and nearly all were professionals, who were sometimes also greenkeepers and clubmakers, though there were a few amateurs.

In 1870 Young Tom Morris won the Belt outright, and the following year there was no contest.

In 1872 three clubs, Prestwick, the Royal & Ancient Golf Club of St Andrews and the Honourable Company of Golfers (who at that time played at Musselburgh), together subscribed to provide the present trophy, which was not to be won outright. Had this condition not been changed, there have been only three winners who would have earned it: Jamie Anderson and Bob Ferguson both won three times in succession in the ten years after the trophy was instituted, and Peter Thomson in 1954–56.

Also from 1872 the Championship was to be held in turn on the courses of the three subscribing clubs. So it was that Young Tom Morris was the first to win the new cup at St Andrews, though this was to be his last time for he was to die tragically at the age of 24.

In 1890, at Prestwick, John Ball became the first amateur to win the cup. Only two other amateurs have followed him: Harold Hilton in 1892 and 1897, and Bobby Jones in 1926, 1927 and 1930. Roger Wethered tied with Jock Hutchison at St Andrews in 1921, but lost the play-off – had he not incurred a penalty stroke through treading on his ball in the third round, he may well have won.

The three courses continued to be used until 1892 when it was first played at Muirfield, to where the Honourable Company had moved. That year was also the first in which the Championship became a 72 hole contest over two days.

The Triumvirate

The year 1894 saw the first occasion the Open was played in England at Sandwich when J H Taylor became the first English professional to win. He won again the next year and for the fifth time in 1913. Harry Vardon and James Braid were the two others of the *great triumvirate* who together won sixteen Opens between 1894 and 1914. Taylor's five wins were spread over 20 years and Vardon's six over 19. Braid's wins were concentrated into ten years from 1901 to 1910, all of them in Scotland. Vardon won three times at Prestwick but never at St Andrews, where Taylor and Braid both won twice. Only Taylor managed a win at Hoylake. No other player won more than once during their supremacy. The winning scores at the time were very high by today's standards, for although the courses were marginally shorter, the equipment and clothing were primitive compared with those in use now. At Sandwich Taylor's score was 326, or 38 over an average of 4s. His 304 at Hoylake in 1913 was played in appalling weather, wearing a tweed jacket, cap and boots, and using wooden shafts and leather grips. He had no protective clothing or umbrella and won by eight strokes from Ted Ray. The last winning total over 300 was Hagen's 301 at Hoylake in 1924.

Better Standards

That improved equipment has helped combat the greater length and heavier rough of today's Championship courses is suggested by comparing the average winning scores for decades of this century.

Decade	Average winning score	Decade	Average winning score
1905–14	302	1956–65	280
1920–29	295	1966–75	280
1930–39	289	1976–85	277
1946–55	284	1986–95	273

Of the 130 Opens held so far, 23 Americans have won, 21 Scots, 16 English, four Australians, two South Africans and one each from France, Ireland,

New Zealand, Argentina, Spain and Zimbabwe. The Scots have won 40 times but only three times since Braid in 1910 (Duncan in 1920, Lyle in 1985 and Lawrie in 1999), the USA 34 times, England 29, Australia nine times, South Africa seven times, Spain three times and each of the others once. Since the triumvirate's day ended, the only Englishmen to win more than once have been Sir Henry Cotton and Nick Faldo, both with three victories. The Americans have won 35 out of the last 73 Opens played.

It will be seen that certain nationalities tend to dominate for a decade or so; the Scots until 1893, then the English until 1914, the USA in the 1920s and until 1933 when the English had a short resuscitation. The Commonwealth were to the fore from 1949 to 1965 (Locke, Thomson, Nagle and Charles) with the Americans coming back again to win in 13 out of 18 years between 1966 and 1983. Equally dominating in their periods were Hagen and Jones in the twenties, Cotton in the thirties, Locke and Thomson the fifties, and thereafter Palmer, Nicklaus, Player, Trevino, Watson, Faldo and Ballesteros.

Open Courses

Only 14 courses have accommodated the Open. St Andrews leads with 26, followed by Prestwick, which was discarded in 1925 as unsuitable for large crowds, with 24. The second group comprises Muirfield with 14, Royal St George's, Sandwich 12 and both Hoylake and Royal Lytham and St Annes with ten. Hoylake's last Open was in 1967 but agreement has now been reached for the Championship to return there. Deal appeared in 1909 and 1920, and was due again in 1949 but the sea broke across the course, and Sandwich came in for the last time until 1981. Troon and Royal Lytham and St Annes each held an Open between the wars, Carnoustie two and Princes, Sandwich, when Sarazen won in 1932, one; this course, which was used as a tank training ground during the Second World War, has not been asked again. In 1951, Portrush, the only Irish course to stage an Open, also provided the only English winner between Cotton and Jacklin in Max Faulkner. Birkdale and Turnberry are firmly established in the rota which for many years settled at four Scottish courses – St Andrews, Muirfield, Royal Troon and Turnberry – and three in England – Royal Lytham and St Annes, Royal Birkdale and Royal St George's, Sandwich. In 1999, however, Carnoustie returned to the championship rota for the first time since 1975. St Andrews hosted the event in 2000 – the 26th time it had done so since 1873.

Traditionally the Open is only played on links courses. While there may yet be new venues by the sea capable of being stretched and groomed to be worthy of holding an Open, the many other considerations to be weighed, such as an adequate road system to carry vast crowds and nearly as many acres as the course covers to accommodate the tented village and services, it is not easy to see where the Championship Committee will turn.

Qualifying

How does one qualify to play in an Open? Since qualifying was first introduced in 1914, there have been numerous changes. Regional qualifying was tried for a year in 1926. At one of the courses used, Sunningdale, Bobby Jones (and even he had to qualify!) played what many consider the classic round of golf: a 66, all 4s and 3s, never over par, 8 birdies, 33 putts and 33 other shots.

Until 1963 all competitors, even the holder, had to play two qualifying rounds on the Open course on the Monday and Tuesday of the Open week. The qualifiers then had one round on Wednesday, one on Thursday and the leading group of between 40 and 60 players finished with two rounds on Friday. In 1963 certain exemptions from qualifying were introduced. The two rounds on the Friday were dropped in 1966 in favour of one round each on Friday and Saturday; not until 1980 was the first round played on Thursday and the last on Sunday. As the entry continued to increase, in 1970 nearby courses were used for qualifying and in 1977 regional qualifying was reintroduced in the previous week with final qualifying on nearby courses later.

There have been surprisingly few ties involving a play-off, only 15 in 128 Championships. The first should have been in 1876 between David Strath and Bob Martin. However Strath took umbrage over a complaint against him and refused to play off. Until 1963 ties were decided over 36 holes; the next two, between Nicklaus and Sanders at St Andrews in 1970 and Watson and Newton at Carnoustie in 1975, were played over 18. Later it was decided that in the event of a tie, the winner would be found immediately by a play-off over specified holes, followed by 'sudden death' if necessary. This happened in 1989 when Mark Calcavecchia beat Greg Norman and Wayne Grady over four holes after finishing level on 275; in 1995 when John Daly beat Costantino Rocca at St Andrews; and in 1998 when Mark O'Meara defeated fellow American Brian Watts at Royal Birkdale to add the Open to the Masters title he had won three months previously. Then in 1999 Paul Lawrie, Jean Van de Velde and Justin Leonard played off over four holes at Carnoustie and Lawrie took the title with a birdie, birdie finish.

Prize Money

In 1863 the total prize money was £10, its distribution among the 14 entrants, six of whom were amateurs, is unknown. A year later it had risen by over 50% to £16; the winner taking £6. By 1993 the total prize fund reached £1,000,000 of which the winner received £100,000. In 2000 this had risen to £500,000 and in 2001 to £600,000. Until about 1955, the winner's and leaders' rewards were very modest; even in 1939 the cheque for the first man was £100 out of a total of £500. With some justification the prestige of winning the Open then was adjudged to be of much more value than any monetary award. The growth since the 1950s has been astonishing and is evidence that, while it is still a tremendous asset for any man to have won the Open, the authorities have recognised that it will not maintain its leading place without substantial reward.

The Amateur Championship

Early History

Golf has always been a competitive game and club medals have been keenly contested since the nineteenth century. Many of the leading amateurs were members of several clubs and, aided by an excellent railway system, they competed against each other at such venues as St Andrews, Prestwick, Hoylake and Musselburgh.

An embryonic open amateur competition was held in the late 1850s (the first being won by Robert Chambers, the publisher, in 1858), but there seems to have been little enthusiasm for such an event and it died around the time of the first Open Championship (1860). The best amateurs began to enter the Open from 1861.

By the 1870s, there was renewed interest in organising a tournament for amateurs only but nothing happened, probably because no one club took a strong enough lead. A proposal in 1877 to the membership of the R&A that it sponsor a sort of Amateur Championship (involving club members and others nominated by members) was defeated.

It fell to the Hoylake golfers to set in motion the championship we now know as The Amateur. In 1884 the Secretary of Royal Liverpool, Thomas Potter, proposed that an event – open to all amateurs – should be organised. This original intention was not carried out until 1886 and so the winner of 1885 (AF Macfie) triumphed over a strong, but limited, field drawn from certain clubs. The clubs that were responsible for the running of the championship until the R&A took over in 1920 – and who made contributions for the purchase of the trophy – were:

Royal & Ancient
Royal Burgess Golfing Society of Edinburgh
Royal Liverpool
Royal St George's
Royal Albert, Montrose
Royal North Devon
Royal Aberdeen
Royal Blackheath
Royal Wimbledon
Royal Dublin
Alnmouth
North Berwick, New Club
Panmure, Dundee
Prestwick
Bruntsfield Links Golfing Society, Edinburgh
Dalhousie
Gullane
Formby
Honourable Company of Edinburgh Golfers
Innerleven
King James VI, Perth
Kilspindie
Luffness
Tantallon
Troon
West Lancashire

The first championship was not without its teething troubles. The format which was adopted allowed both golfers to proceed to the next round if their match was halved, so the first championship had three semi-finalists – and Macfie got a bye into the final. From 1886, the usual format was adopted.

More serious than the problem of an idiosyncratic draw, however, was the question of amateur status, raised for the first time in 1886. The committee had to decide if it should accept the entries of John Ball III and Douglas Rolland. As a 15-year-old, Ball had finished fourth in the 1878 Open at Prestwick and on the advice of Jack Morris he accepted the prize money of 10s (50p). Rolland, a stonemason, had accepted second prize in the 1884 Open. Rolland's entry to the Amateur was refused while Ball's was accepted. Ball went on to win the championship a record eight times and the Open Championship of 1890.

The Format

After such a difficult start, the format of 18-hole matches with a 36-hole final remained until 1956. This arrangement made for many closely fought matches, as shown in 1930, the year of RT Jones' Grand Slam triumph. Jones' only victory in the event came in the right year and it is worth pointing out that, in making his way to the final, he won in the fourth round at the 19th (by laying a stymie) against Cyril Tolley, the holder, and his victories in the sixth round and in the semi-final were by the narrowest of margins.

In addition, the fact that the draw was not seeded sometimes meant early meetings between top golfers; for example, in 1926 the visiting American Walker Cup Team members, von Elm and Ouimet,

met in the second round and von Elm went on to meet Jesse Sweetser in the third.

As a result of such events, there was some pressure for the introduction of seeding the draw but it was not until 1958 that the practice was officially adopted. In the 50s and 60s there were other changes in format in an attempt to satisfy large numbers of golfers who wished to play and to ensure a worthy winner.

The popularity of the championship has posed difficulties for the R&A. The mathematically ideal number of entrants to be fitted into a convenient format is 256. In 1950, 324 entered the championship causing golf to be played on the Old Course for 14 hours a day.

In order to restrict the numbers turning up to the championship proper, an experiment in regional qualifying was held in 1958 (again a St Andrews year) and 488 players with handicaps of 5 and under played 36 holes of strokeplay on 14 courses.

Handicap Limits

This system was quickly replaced and, in 1961, the handicap limit was lowered to three and a balloting-out of higher handicaps was introduced so that 256 were left to play for the trophy. This method was followed until 1983 with the introduction of 36 holes of strokeplay to find 64 players for matchplay, from which to find the eventual winner. The handicap limit in 1997 was one.

There was also pressure for the introduction of 36-hole matches. As early as 1922 the R&A's championship committee canvassed the opinion of the 252 men who played that year. Nineteen of these voted in favour of 36-hole matches, seven for district qualification, two voted for a stroke play qualification followed by 18-hole matches and the others who replied wanted no change to the system. In 1956 and 1957 the last three rounds were played over 36 holes, in 1958 and 1959 the semi-final and final were over 36 holes and then the old format returned.

There is constant pressure on the organisers to find a format to satisfy the needs of large numbers of home and foreign players, to take into account differences in national handicapping systems, to preserve the atmosphere of the championship, to maintain matchplay as a central feature of top-level amateur golf and even to take into account the vagaries of the weather. The task is almost impossible.

The Winners

Any man who wins the Amateur is a considerable golfer but there are certain outstanding champions. John Ball of Royal Liverpool won the title eight times between 1888 and 1912. It is interesting to note that he never successfully defended his title. Michael Bonallack triumphed five times between 1961 and 1970, including an incredible hat-trick of victories in which he successively beat Joe Carr and Bill Hyndman twice.

Several golfers have successfully defended their title: Horace Hutchinson, Harold Hilton, Lawson Little and Peter McEvoy, while others have won twice or more – Johnny Laidlay, Freddie Tait, Bob Maxwell, Cyril Tolley, Edward Holderness, Frank Stranahan, Joe Carr and Trevor Homer.

The oldest man to win was the Hon Michael Scott, at the age of 54 in 1933. The youngest winners – John Beharrell and Bobby Cole – were both 18 years and 1 month old. Cole's victory over Ronnie Shade was achieved over 18 holes – play being affected by poor visibility. The first overseas winner was Walter Travis who won in 1904 – one consequence of his victory was the banning of the use of centre-shafted putters. The first Continental winner was the Frenchman Philippe Ploujoux, who won in 1981. A visiting Walker Cup team always made for an exciting championship, and from 17 visits to Great Britain the title crossed the Atlantic 12 times.

No doubt there have been hundreds of thrilling matches played in the Championship, but few can have been as pulsating as the 1899 final at Prestwick where Johnny Ball beat Freddie Tait at the 37th hole. The victory must have been a sweet one for Ball, since Tait, the hero of Scotland, had won the previous year over Ball's home links of Hoylake. Sadly, Tait was killed in the Boer War in 1900. 'The great battle', as Jones described his fourth round tie against Tolley in 1930, rivalled the Ball-Tait final for tense excitement, but for sheer brilliance of scoring, Michael Bonallack's first round in the 1968 final must take pride of place. He covered the first 18 holes in 61 with only one putt of less than two feet conceded. He went on to beat David Kelley by 12 and 11.

The Amateur Championship has been played for over a century and in essence it has changed remarkably little. The increasing popularity of the game at home and abroad, the lure of the professional ranks with its dependence on stroke play and the increasing commercialism of all sport notwithstanding, the Championship continues to stand for all that is great in golf.

Famous Players of the Past

In making the difficult choice of the names to be included, effort has been made to acknowledge the outstanding players and personalities of each successive era from the early pioneers to the stars of recent times.

Alliss, Percy   (1897–1975)

Finished in the top six in the Open Championship seven times, including joint third at Carnoustie in 1931, two strokes behind Tommy Armour. Twice winner of the Match Play Championship, five times German Open champion and twice winner of the Italian Open. Ryder Cup player in 1933-35-37, an international honour also gained by his son Peter. Spent much of his career as professional at the Wansee Club in Berlin.

Anderson, Jamie   (1842–1912)

Winner of three consecutive Open Championships – 1877-78-79. A native St Andrean, he once claimed to have played 90 consecutive holes on the Old Course without a bad or unintended shot. He was noted for his straight hitting and accurate putting.

Anderson, Willie   (1878–1910)

Took his typically Scottish flat swing to America where he won the US Open four times in a five year period from 1901. Only Bobby Jones, Ben Hogan and Jack Nicklaus have also won the US Open four times.

Armour, Thomas D   (1896–1968)

Born in Edinburgh, he played for Britain against America as an amateur and, after emigrating, for America against Britain as a professional in the forerunners of the Walker and Ryder Cup matches. Won the US Open in 1927, the USPGA in 1930 and the 1931 Open at Carnoustie. Became an outstanding coach and wrote several bestselling instruction books.

Auchterlonie, William   (1872–1963)

Won the Open at Prestwick in 1893 at the age of

21 with a set of seven clubs he had made himself Founded the famous family clubmaking business in St Andrews. He believed that golfers should master half, three-quarter and full shots with each club. Appointed Honorary Professional to the R&A in 1935.

Ball, John   (1861–1940)

Finished fourth in the Open of 1878 at the age of 16 and became the first amateur to win the title in 1890. He won the Amateur Championship eight times and shares with Bobby Jones the distinction of being the winner of the Open and Amateur in the same year. He grew up on the edge of the links area which became the Royal Liverpool Golf Club and the birthplace of the Amateur. He was a master at keeping the ball low in the wind, but with the same straight-faced club could cut the ball up for accurate approach shots. His run of success could have been greater but for military service in the South African campaign and the First World War.

Barton, Pamela   (1917–1943)

At the age of 19 she held both the British and American Ladies Championships in 1936. She was French champion at 17, runner-up in the British in both 1934 and '35 and won the title again in 1939. A Curtis Cup team member in 1934 and '36 she was a Flight Officer in the WAAF when she was killed in a plane crash at an RAF airfield in Kent.

Boros, Julius   (1920–1994)

Became the oldest winner of a major championship when he won the USPGA in 1968 at the age of 48. He twice won the US Open, in 1952 and again 11 years later at Brookline when he was 43. In a play-off he beat Jackie Cupit by three shots and Arnold Palmer by six. He played in four

Pam Barton   Popperfoto

Ryder Cup matches between 1959-67, winning nine of his 16 matches and losing only three.

Bousfield, Kenneth (1919–2000)

Although a short hitter even by the standards of his era, he won five out of 10 matches in six Ryder Cup appearances from 1949–61. He captured the PGA Match Play Championship in 1955, one of eight tournament victories in Britain, and also won six European Opens. He represented England in the World Cup at Wentworth in 1956 and Tokyo in 1957

Braid, James (1870–1950)

Together with Harry Vardon and JH Taylor he formed the Great Triumvirate and dominated the game for 20 years before the 1914-18 war. In a 10-year period from 1901 he became the first player in the history of the event to win the Open five times – and also finished second on three occasions. In that same period he won the Match Play Championship four times and the French Open. He was a tall, powerful player who hit the ball hard but always retained an appearance of outward calm. He was one of the founder members of the Professional Golfers' Association and did much to elevate the status of the professional golfer. He was responsible for the design of many golf courses and served as professional at Walton Heath for 45 years. He was an honorary member of that club for 25 years and became one of its directors. He was also an honorary member of the R&A.

Bruen, Jimmy (1920–1972)

Won the Irish Amateur at the age of 17 and defended his title the following year. At 18 he became the youngest ever Walker Cup player and in practice for the match at St Andrews in 1938 equalled the amateur course record of 68 set by Bobby Jones.

Campbell, Dorothy Iona (1883–1946)

One of only two golfers to win the British, American and Canadian Ladies titles. In total she won these three major championships seven times.

Compston, Archie (1893–1962)

Beat Walter Hagen 18 and 17 in a 72-hole challenge match at Moor Park in 1928 and tied for second place in the 1925 Open. Played in the Ryder Cup in 1927-29-31.

Cotton, Sir Henry (1907–1987)

The first player to be knighted for services to golf, he died a few days before the announcement of the award was made. He won the Open Championship three times, which included a round of 65 at Royal St George's in 1934 after which the famous Dunlop golf ball was named. His final 71 at Carnoustie to win the 1937 championship in torrential rain gave him great satisfaction and he set another record with a 66 at Muirfield on the way to his third triumph in 1948. He won the Match Play Championship three times and was runner-up on three occasion. He also won 11 Open titles in Europe, played three times in the Ryder Cup and was non-playing captain in 1953. Sir Henry worked hard to promote the status of professional golf and also championed the cause of young golfers, becoming a founder member of the Golf Foundation. He was a highly successful teacher, author and architect, spending much time at Penina, a course he created in southern Portugal. He was an honorary member of the R&A.

Crawley, Leonard (1903–1981)

Played four times in the Walker Cup in 1932-34-38-47 and won the English Amateur in 1931. He also played first-class cricket for Worcestershire and Essex and toured the West Indies with the MCC in 1936. After the Second World War he was golf correspondent for the *Daily Telegraph* for 30 years.

The Curtis sisters, Harriet (1878–1944) Margaret (1880-1965)

Donors of the Curtis Cup still contested biennially between the USA and GB&I. Harriet won the US Women's Amateur in 1906 and lost in the following year's final to her sister Margaret, who went on to win the championship three times.

Daly, Fred (1911–1990)

Daly won the Open at Royal Liverpool in 1947 and in four of the next five years was never out of the top four in the Championship. At Portrush, where he was born, he finished fourth to Max Faulkner in 1951, the only time the Open has been played in Northern Ireland. He was Ulster champion 11 times and three times captured the prestigious PGA Match Play Championship. He was a member of the Ryder Cup team four times, finishing on a high note at Wentworth in 1953 when he won his foursomes match in partnership with Harry Bradshaw and then beat Ted Kroll 9 and 7 in the singles.

Darwin, Bernard (1876–1961)

One of the most gifted and authoritative writers on golf, he was also an accomplished England international player for more than 20 years. While in America to report the 1922 Walker Cup match for The Times, he was called in to play and captain the side when Robert Harris became ill. A grandson of Charles Darwin, he was captain of the R&A in 1934-35. In 1937 he was awarded the CBE for services to literature.

Demaret, Jimmy (1910–1983)

Three times Masters champion, coming from five strokes behind over the final six holes to beat Jim Ferrier by two in 1950, he also won six consecutive tournaments in 1940 while still performing as a night club singer. He won all six Ryder Cup matches he played in the encounters of 1947-49-51.

Duncan, George (1884–1964)

Won the Open in 1920 by making up 13 shots on the leader over the last two rounds and came close to catching Walter Hagen for the title two years later. Renowned as one of the fastest players, his book was entitled Golf at the Gallop.

Ferguson, Bob (1848–1915)

The Open Championship winner three times in succession between 1880-82. He then lost a 36-hole play-off for the title by one stroke to Willie Fernie in 1883. At 18 he had won the Leith Tournament against the game's leading professionals.

Fernie, Willie (1851–1924)

In 1882 he was second to Bob Ferguson in the Open over his home course at St Andrews. The following year he beat the same player in a 36-hole play-off for the championship over Ferguson's home links at Musselburgh.

Hagen, Walter (1892–1969)

A flamboyant character who used a hired Rolls Royce as a changing room because professionals were not allowed in many clubhouses, he once gave his £50 cheque for winning the Open to his caddie. He won four consecutive USPGA Championships from 1924 when it was still decided by matchplay. He was four times a winner of the Open, in 1922-24-28-29 and captured the US Open title in 1914 and 1919. He captained and played in five Ryder Cup encounters between 1927-35, winning seven of his nine matches and losing only once. He was non-playing captain in 1937.

Herd, Alexander 'Sandy' (1868–1944)

When he first played in the Open at the age of 17 he possessed only four clubs. His only championship success came in the 1902 Open at Hoylake, the first player to capture the title using the new rubber-cored ball. He won the Match Play Championship at the age of 58 and took part in his last Open at St Andrews in 1939 at the age of 71.

Hilton, Harold (1869–1942)

Winner of the Amateur Championship four times between 1900 and 1913, he also became the first player and the only Briton to hold both the British and US Amateur titles in the same year 1911. He won the Open in 1892 at Muirfield, the first time the championships was extended to 72 holes. A small but powerful player he was the first editor of Golf Monthly.

Hogan, Ben (1912–1997)

One of only five players to have won all four major championships, his record of capturing three in the same season has been matched by Tiger Woods. He dominated the golfing scene in America after the Second World War and in 1953 won the Masters, US Open and the Open Championship. A clash of dates between the Open and USPGA prevented an attempt on the Grand Slam, but his poor state of health after a near fatal car crash four years earlier would have made the matchplay format of 10 rounds in six days in the USPGA an impossibility. After his car collided with a Greyhound bus in fog, it was feared that Hogan might never walk again. He had won three majors before the accident and he returned to capture six more. His only appearance in the Open was in his tremendous season of 1953 and he recorded rounds of 73-71-70-68 to win by four strokes at Camoustie. His dramatic life story was made into a Hollywood film entitled Follow the Sun.

Hutchinson, Horace (1859–1932)

Runner-up in the first Amateur Championship in 1885, he won the title in the next two years and reached the final again in 1903. Represented England from 1902–07. He was a prolific writer on golf and country life and became the first English captain of the R&A in 1908.

Jones, Bobby (1902–1971)

Always remembered for his incredible and unrepeatable achievement in 1930 of winning the Open and Amateur Championships of Britain and America in one outstanding season – the original and unchallenged Grand Slam. At the end of that year he retired from competitive golf at the age of 28. His victories included four US Opens, five US Amateur titles, three Opens in Britain and one Amateur Championship. Although his swing was stylish and fluent, he suffered badly from nerves and was often sick and unable to eat during championships.

He was also an accomplished scholar, gaining first-class honours degrees in law, English literature and mechanical engineering at three different universities. He subsequently opened a law practice in Atlanta and developed the idea of creating the Augusta National course and staging an annual invitation event which was to become known as the Masters.

He was made an honorary member of the Royal and Ancient Golf Club in 1956 and two years later was given the freedom of the Burgh of St Andrews at an emotional ceremony. He died after many years of suffering from a crippling spinal disease and a hole on the Old Course bears his name.

Bobby Jones   Popperfoto

Kirkaldy, Andrew (1860–1934)

First honorary professional appointed by the R&A, he lost a play-off for the Open Championship of 1889 to Willie Park at Musselburgh. He was second in the championship three times, a further three times finished third and twice fourth. A powerful player, he was renowned for speaking his mind.

Laidlay, John Ernest (1860–1940)

The man who first employed the overlapping grip which was later credited to Harry Vardon and universally known as the Vardon grip, Laidlay was a finalist in the Amateur Championship six times in seven years from 1888, winning the title twice at a time when John Ball, Horace Hutchinson and Harold Hilton were at their peak. He was runner-up in the Open to Willie Auchterlonie at Prestwick in 1893. Among the 130 medals he won, were the Gold Medal and Silver Cross in R&A competitions.

Leitch, 'Cecil' (1891–1977)

Christened Charlotte Cecilia, but universally known as Cecil, her list of international victories would undoubtedly have been greater but for the blank golfing years of the first world war. She first won the British Ladies Championship in 1908 at the age of 17. In 1914 she took the English, French and British titles and successfully defended all three when competition was resumed after the war. In all she won the French Championship five times, the British four times, the English twice, the Canadian once. Her total of four victories in the British has never been beaten and has been equalled only by her great rival Joyce Wethered. The victory in Canada was by a margin of 17 and 15 in the 36-hole final.

Lema, Tony (1934–1966)

His first visit to Britain, leaving time for only 27 holes of practice around the Old Course at St Andrews, culminated in Open Championship victory in 1964 by five shots over Jack Nicklaus. He had won three tournaments in four starts in America before arriving in Scotland and gave great credit for his Open success to local caddie Tip Anderson. He played in the Ryder Cup in 1963 and 1965 with an outstanding record. He lost only once in 11 matches, halved twice and won eight. Lema and his wife were killed when a private plane in which they were travelling to a tournament crashed in Illinois.

Little, Lawson   (1910–1968)

Won the Amateur Championships of Britain and America in 1934 and successfully defended both titles the following year. He then turned his amateur form into a successful professional career, starting in 1936 with victory in the Canadian Open. He won the US Open in 1940 after a play-off against Gene Sarazen.

Locke, Bobby   (1917–1987)

The son of Northern Irish emigrants to South Africa, Arthur D'Arcy Locke was playing off plus four by the age of 18 and won the South African Boys, Amateur and Open Championships. On his first visit to Britain in 1936 he was leading amateur in the Open Championship. Realising that his normal fade was leaving him well short of the leading players, he deliberately developed the hook shot to get more

Bobby Locke   Popperfoto

run on the ball. It was to become his trade-mark throughout a long career.

He was encouraged to try the American tour in 1947 and won five tournaments, one by the record margin of 16 shots. More successes followed and the USPGA framed a rule which banned him from playing in their events, an action described by Gene Sarazen as 'the most disgraceful action by any golf organisation'.

Disillusioned by the American attitude, Locke then played most of his golf in Europe, winning the Open four times. He shared a period of domination with Peter Thomson between 1949–1958 when they won the championship four times each, only Max Faulkner and Ben Hogan breaking the sequence. In his final Open victory at St Andrews in 1957 he failed to replace his ball in the correct spot on the 18th green after moving it from fellow competitor Bruce Crampton's line. The mistake, which could have led to disqualification, was only spotted on television replays. The R&A Championship Committee rightly decided that Locke, who had won by three strokes, had gained no advantage, and allowed the result to stand.

Following a career in which he won over 80 events around the world he was made an honorary member of the R&A in 1976.

Longhurst, Henry   (1909–1978)

Captain of Cambridge University golf team, runner-up in the French and Swiss Amateur Championships and winner of the German title in 1936, he became the most perceptive and readable golf correspondent of his time and a tele-vision commentator who never wasted a single word. His relaxed, chatty style was based on the premise that he was explaining the scene to a friend in his favourite golf club bar. For 25 years his Sunday Times column ran without a break and became compulsory reading for golfers and non-golfers alike. He had a brief spell as a member of parliament and was awarded the CBE for services to golf.

Mackenzie, Alister   (1870–1934)

A family doctor and surgeon, he became involved with Harry S. Colt in the design of the Alwoodley course in Leeds, where he was a founder member and honorary secretary and eventually abandoned his medical career and worked full time at golf course architecture. There are many outstanding examples of his work in Britain, Australia, New Zealand and America. His most famous creation, in partnership with Bobby Jones, is the Augusta National course in Georgia, home of the US Masters.

Massy, Arnaud   (1877–1958)

The first non-British player to win the Open Championship. Born in Biarritz, France, he defeated J.H. Taylor by two strokes at Hoylake in 1907. Four years later he tied for the title with Harry Vardon at Royal St George's, but conceded at the 35th hole when he was five strokes behind. He won the French Open four times, the Spanish on three occasions and the Belgian title once.

Micklem, Gerald   (1911–1988)

A pre-war Oxford Blue, he won the English Amateur Championship in 1947 and 1953 and played in the Walker Cup team four times between 1947 and 1955. He was non-playing captain in 1957 and 1959. In 1976 he set a record of 36 consecutive appearances in the President's Putter, an event that he won in 1953. In addition to his playing success he was a tireless administrator, serving as chairman of the R&A Rules, Selection and Championship Committees. He was president of the English Golf Union and the European Golf Association and captain of the R&A. In 1969 he received the Bobby Jones award for services to golf.

Middlecoff, Cary   (1921–1998)

Dentist turned golf professional, he became one of the most prolific winners on the US tour, with 37 victories that included two US Opens and a Masters victory. In the US Open of 1949 he beat Sam Snead and Clayton Heafner at Medinah, and seven years later recaptured the title by one shot ahead of Ben Hogan and Julius Boros at Oak Hill. His Masters success came in 1955 when he established a record seven-shot winning margin over Hogan.

Mitchell, Abe   (1897–1947)

Said by JH Taylor to be the finest player never to win an Open, he finished in the top six five times. He was more successful in the Match Play Championship, with victories in 1919, 1920 and 1929. He taught the game to St Albans seed merchant Samuel Ryder and is the figure depicted on top of the famous trophy.

Morgan, Wanda   (1910–1995)

Three-time English Amateur champion, in 1931–36–37, she also captured the British title in 1935 and played three times in the Curtis Cup from 1932-36.

Morris, Old Tom   (1821–1908)

Apprenticed as a feathery ball maker to Allan Robertson in St Andrews at the age of 18 he was one of the finest golfers of his day when he took up the position of Keeper of the Green at Prestwick, where he laid out the original 12-hole course. He was 39 when he finished second in the first Open in 1860, but subsequently won the title four times, and played in every Open until 1896 when he was 75. His success rate might have been much greater if he had been a better putter. His son once said: 'He would be a much better player if the hole was a yard closer.'

A man of fierce conviction, he returned to St Andrews to take up the duties of looking after the Old Course at a salary of £50 per year, paid by the R&A. He came to regard tjhe course as his own property and was once publicly reprimanded for closing it without authority because he considered it needed a rest. A testimonial in 1896 raised £1,240 pounds towards his old age from golfers around the world and when he retired in 1903 the R&A continued to pay his salary. He died after a fall on the stairs of the New Club in 1908, having outlived his wife, his daughter and his three sons.

Morris, Young Tom   (1851–1975)

Born in St Andrews, but brought up in Prestwick, where his father had moved to become Keeper of the Green, he won a tournament against leading professionals at the age of 13. He was only 17 when he succeeded his father as Open champion in 1868 and then defended the title successfully in the following two years to claim the winner's belt outright. There was no championship in 1871, but when the present silver trophy became the prize in 1872, Young Tom's was the first name engraved on its base.

His prodigious talent was best demonstrated in his third successive Open victory in 1870 when he played 36 holes at Prestwick in 149 strokes, 12 shots ahead of his nearest rival, superb scoring given the equipment and the condition of the courses at that time.

He married in November 1874 and was playing with his father in a money match at North Berwick the following year when a telegram from St Andrews sent them hurrying back across the Firth of Forth in a private yacht. Young Tom's wife and baby had both died in childbirth. He played golf only twice after that, in matches that had been arranged long in advance, and fell into moods of deep depression. He died on Christmas morning of that same year from a burst artery in the lung. He was 24 years old. A public subscription paid for a memorial which still stands above his grave in the cathedral cemetery.

Ouimet, Francis   (1893–1967)

He is often described as the player who started the golf boom in the US when, as a young amateur, he tied with Harry Vardon and Ted Ray for the 1913 US Open and went on to win the play-off. In an illustrious career he won the US Amateur twice and was a member of every Walker Cup team from 1922 to 1934 and was non-playing Captain from then until 1949. Ouimet was the first non-British national to be elected Captain of the R&A Golf Club in 1951. He was prominent in golf legislation and administration in America and a committee member of the USGA for many years.

The Parks

Brothers Willie and Mungo Park of Musselburgh are famous in the annals of golf for the numerous money matches they played.

Willie had the distinction of winning the very first Open Championship in 1860 and repeated his victory in 1863, 1866 and 1875. For twenty years Willie had a standing challenge in *Bell's Life*, London, to play any man in the world for £100-a-side. Willie took part in numerous matches against Tom Morris for very large stakes and in the last of these at Musselburgh in 1882, the match came to an abrupt end when Park was two up with six to play. The referee stopped play because spectators were interfering with the balls. Morris and the referee retired to Foreman's public house. Park sent a message saying if Morris did not come out and finish the match he would play the remaining holes alone and claim the stakes. This he did.

Mungo followed in his brother's footsteps by winning the Open Championship in 1874. He was for many years greenkeeper and professional at Alnmouth.

Willie's son, Willie Junior, kept up the golfing tradition of the family by winning the Open in 1887 and 1889. He designed many golf courses in Europe and America, sometimes in conjunction with property development, as at Sunningdale, and was the pioneer of the modern ideas of golf course construction. Like his forebears he took part in many private challenge matches, the one against Harry Vardon at North Berwick in 1899 being watched by the greatest crowd ever for that time and for many years afterwards. Willie Junior died in 1925 aged 61.

The third generation of this golfing family sustained a prominent golf association through Miss Doris Park (Mrs Aylmer Porter), daughter of Willie Junior, who established a distinguished record in ladies' international and championship golf.

Philp, Hugh

The master craftsman among the half-dozen club-makers located in St Andrews in the early days of the nineteenth century. He was especially skilled in making a wooden putter with a long head of pear-shaped design. He is believed to have made not many more than one hundred putters. The wooden putter was for centuries a favoured club at St Andrews for long approach putting. The creations of Hugh Philp are highly prized by golf club collectors. After his death in 1856 his business was carried on by Robert Forgan.

Picard, Henry (1907–1997)

The disappointment of finishing only fourth in the 1935 Masters after opening with rounds of 67 and 68 for a four-stroke lead was forgotten only three years later when, back in Augusta, scores of 71-72-72-70 proved good enough for a two-shot victory. The following year he added the United States PGA championship. One down with one to play against Byron Nelson, Picard made a four-foot birdie putt to force extra holes and at the 37th he holed from seven feet for another birdie while Nelson missed from five. Winner of 27 tournaments in total, ill-health affected his career thereafter, although he continued to play in the Masters until 1969. He can also be given some of the credit for Sam Snead's success, giving him a driver in 1937 which instantly solved Snead's hooking problems and turned him into the longest straight driver in the game.

Ray, Ted (1877–1943)

Born Jersey, his early days coincided with the famous Triumvirate and it was not until 1912 that he won the Open and was runner-up the following year to Taylor. He was again runner-up in 1925 at the age of 48. In 1913 he tied for the US Open with Ouimet and Vardon, but lost the play-off. After the war he returned to America and won the US Open title in 1920 and was the last British player to hold the title until Tony Jacklin, in 1970. He and Vardon were the only British players to win both the US Open and the Open until they were joined by Jacklin. Noted for his long driving and powers of recovery, he was invariably to be seen playing with a pipe clenched between his teeth.

Rees, Dai (1913–1983)

One of Britain's outstanding golfers from the 1930s to the 1960s. He played in nine Ryder Cup matches between 1937 and 1961, and was also non-playing captain in 1967. In 1957, he captained the only British team to win the Ryder Cup since 1933. He was three times a runner-up in the Open Championship and once third, and won the PGA Match Play Championship four times, and the Dunlop Masters twice, in addition to numerous other tournament successes in Britain, on the Continent of Europe and in Australasia. At the age of 60, he finished second in the Martini tournament. He was made an honorary member of the Royal & Ancient Golf Club in 1976.

Robertson, Allan   (1815–1958)

According to tradition, he was never beaten in an individual stake match on level terms. A short, thick-set man, he had a beautiful, well-timed swing, and several golfers who could recall Robertson, and who saw Harry Vardon at his best, were of the opinion that there was considerable similarity in the elegance and grace of the two players. Tom Morris, senior, worked in Allan Robertson's shop, where the principal trade was making feather balls. A disagreement occurred between Robertson and Morris on the advent of the gutta ball, because Old Tom decided to play with the invention, and Allan considered the gutta might damage his trade in featheries. Allan, through agents, endeavoured to buy up all gutta balls in order to protect his industry of feather balls. Allan Robertson and Tom Morris never seem to have come together in any single match for large stakes, but it is recorded that they never lost a foursome in which they were partners.

Ryder, Samuel   (1858–1936)

Sam Ryder was a prosperous seed merchant and the Mayor of St Albans. He did not take up golf until the age of 52 but became one of the most famous names in golf as donor of the Ryder Cup, played for in biennial competition between teams of professionals from Great Britain and Ireland (now Europe) and the United States. Ryder attended an unofficial international match between British and American professionals at Wentworth in 1926 and was greatly impressed by the chivalry and camaraderie of the two sides. He declared afterwards, 'We must do this again'. The first Ryder Cup match was played the following year at Worcester, Massachusetts, and the first in Britain in 1929 at Moortown, Yorkshire.

Sarazen, Gene   (1902–1999)

Born Eugene Saraceni in New York, 1902, he left school early to help his carpenter father, but for health reasons was advised to find an outdoor job. First a caddie, then an assistant professional, at the age of 20 he became the first player to win the US Open and USPGA titles in the same year. Five more Majors were to follow and, by adding the Open Championship at Prince's in 1932 and The Masters in 1935, he was the first of only five players to date who have have lifted all four 'Grand Slam' trophies during a career. On his way to winning at Augusta he produced one of the most famous shots of all time, a four-wood

Dai Rees   Popperfoto

into the 15th hole for an albatross two in the final round. It became known as 'the shot heard around the world' and enabled him to tie with Craig Wood and then win the play-off.

Credited with the invention of the sand wedge, Sarazen never lost his love of the game and at 71 entered the 1973 Open at Troon and holed-in-one at the 'Postage Stamp' eighth. The following day he holed from a bunker for a two there. Known as 'The Squire', he continued to act as an honorary starter for The Masters, hitting his final shot a month before his death.

Sayers, Ben   (1857–1924)

Of very small stature, one of the smallest Scottish professionals, and light of build, Bena Sayers nevertheless took a leading position in the game for over 40 years with his outstanding skill and rigid physical training. He engaged in numerous stake matches and played for Scotland against England in every match from 1903 to 1910 and in 1912 and 1913. He competed in every Open Championship from 1880 to 1923. Of a bright and sunny disposition, he contributed much to the merriment of championship and professional gatherings. He taught princes and nobles to play the game, was presented to King Edward, and received a presentation from King George, when Duke of York.

Smith, Mrs Frances (*née* Bunty Stephens) (1925–78)

Dominated post-war women's golf by winning the British Ladies' Championship in 1949 and 1954 (runner-up 1951-52), the English Ladies' in 1948-54-55 (runner-up 1959) and the French Ladies' in 1949. She represented Great Britain in the Curtis Cup on six consecutive occasions from 1950 to 1960. A pronounced pause at the top of her swing made her style most distinctive. She was awarded the OBE for her services to golf and was president of the English Ladies' Golf Association at the time of her death.

Smith, Horton (1908–1963)

Came to notice first from Joplin, Missouri, when 20 years old, and brilliantly embarked on the professional circuit in the winter of 1929 when he won all but one of the open tournaments in which he played. He was promoted to that year's Ryder Cup team and also played in 1933 and 1935. He won the first US Masters Tournament in 1934 and again in 1936 as well as more than thirty other major events. On his 21st birthday he won the French Open. He was President of the American PGA, 1952-54, and received two national distinctions: the Ben Hogan Award for overcoming illness or injury, and the Bobby Jones Award for distinguished sportsmanship in golf. The day after the Ryder Cup match which he attended in Atlanta in 1963 he collapsed and died in a Detroit hospital.

Smith, Macdonald (1890–1949)

Born at Carnoustie, he was one of the great golfers who never won the Open Championship, in which he consistently finished in a high place, coming second in 1930 and 1932, third in 1923 and 1924, fourth in 1925 and 1934 and fifth in 1931. He went to America before he was 20. In the Open Championship at Prestwick in 1925 he entered the last round with a lead of five strokes over the field, but a wildly enthusiastic Scottish crowd of 20,000 engulfed and overwhelmed him. The sequel to these unruly scenes was the introduction of gate money the following year and Prestwick was dropped from the rota for the Open. He died in Los Angeles.

Stewart, Payne (1957–1999)

Four months into his second reign as US Open Champion, Payne Stewart died in a tragic air accident, robbing the sport of one of its most colourful characters. He and five others boarded a private jet near his home in Florida, but soon after take-off air traffic controllers lost contact. Military aircraft flew alongside and reported that the windows had frosted over, indicating a loss of cabin pressure and the death of all those inside. The jet flew on auto-pilot for four hours and over 1800 miles before crashing in South Dakota.

Only a month earlier, Stewart had been on the winning United States Ryder Cup team, his fifth appearance in the match. Known for his plus-two trousers and flat caps, often in the brightest of colours, he won the 1989 US PGA Championship, then the 1991 US Open after a play-off with Scott Simpson. After losing a four-stroke lead in the 1998 US Open – Lee Janzen pushed him into second place, as he had in 1993 – Stewart returned the following year and made wonderful amends, holing an 18-foot putt on the final green to beat Phil Mickelson. He was also twice a runner-up in the Open Championship.

Tait, Freddie (1870–1900)

Born at 17 Drummond Place, in Edinburgh (his father PG Tait was a Professor at Edinburgh University). He joined the R&A in 1890, and that year beat all previous St Andrews' amateur records by holing the course in 77, and in 1894 he reduced the record to 72. He was first amateur in the Open Championship in 1894, 1896 and 1899 and third in 1896 and 1897. He won the Amateur Championship in 1896 at Sandwich, beating in successive rounds GC Broadwood, Charles Hutchings, JE Laidlay, John Ball, Horace Hutchinson and HH Hilton, the strongest amateurs of the day. He repeated his victory in 1898 at Hoylake, and in 1899 he fought and lost at the 37th the historic final with John Ball at Prestwick. There is a Freddie Tait Cup given annually to the best amateur in the South African Open Championship. This cup was purchased from the surplus of the fund collected during the visit of British amateur golfers to South Africa in 1928. He was killed in the South African War at Koodoosberg Drift, aged 30.

Taylor, John Henry (1871–1963)

Last survivor of the famous Triumvirate – Taylor, Braid and Vardon – died at his Devonshire home in February, 1963, within a month of his 92nd birthday. Born at Northam, Devon, he had been professional at Burnham, Winchester and Royal Mid-Surrey. JH won the Open Championship five times – 1894-95-1900-09-13 – and also tied with Harry Vardon in 1896, but lost the replay. He was runner-up in 1904-05-06-07-14. His brilliant career included the French and German Open Championships and he was second in the US Open in 1900. Among the many honours he received were honorary membership of the R&A Golf Club in 1949. He was regarded as the pioneer of British professionalism and helped to start the Professional Golfers' Association. He did much to raise the whole status of the professional and, in the words of Bernard Darwin, *turned a feckless company into a self-respecting and respected body of men.* On his retirement in 1957 the Royal North Devon Golf Club paid him their greatest compliment by electing him President.

Tolley, Cyril   (1896–1978)

A dominant figure in amateur golf in the interwar period. He won the first of two Amateur Championships in 1920 while still a student at Oxford and continued to win championships and represent England and Britain until 1938. Among other titles he won the Welsh Open (1921 and 1923) and remains the only amateur to have won the French Open (1924 and 1928). A powerful hitter with a delicate touch, Tolley was a crowd pleaser. He is remembered as much for a match he lost as for some of his victories. Having won the Amateur Championship in 1929, Tolley was a favourite to win at St Andrews in 1930. The draw was unseeded and he met Bobby Jones in the fourth round. A huge crowd turned out to watch a very exciting match which Jones won on the 19th with a stymie. Tolley was elected Captain of the R&A in 1948.

Travis, Walter   (1862–1925)

Born in Australia, Travis was the first overseas golfer to win the British Amateur, at Sandwich in 1904. He won the title using a centre-shafted putter, which was subsequently banned for many years. He won the US Amateur Championship in 1900, having taken up the game four years previously at the age of 35. He repeated his victory in 1901 and 1903 and was a semi-finalist five times between 1898 and 1914, winning also the stroke competition six times between 1900 and 1908. The *Old Man* as he was known is reckoned to have been one of the finest judges of distance who ever played golf. He died in New York.

Vardon, Harry   (1870–1937)

Born Grouville, Jersey, Vardon created a record by winning the Open Championship six times, his wins being in 1896, 1898, 1899, 1903, 1911 and 1914. He also won the American Open in 1900 and tied in 1913, subsequently losing the play-off. He had a serious illness in 1903 and it was said that he never quite regained his former dominance, particularly on the putting green.

That he was the foremost golfer of his time cannot be disputed and he innovated the modern upright swing and popularised the overlapping grip invented by JE Laidlay.

Had it not been for ill-health and the intervention of the First World War, his outstanding records both in the UK and America would almost certainly have been added to in later years. But in any event his profound influence on the game lives on. More than 100 years after his birth his achievements are still the standard of comparison with the latter-day giants of the game.

Vare, Glenna (*née* Collett)   (1903–1989)

A natural all-rounder at games, her six American Amateur championships set new standards. It was only achieved however by intense study of the mechanics of the swing and concentrated practice. She attacked the ball, with both irons and woods, with uncommon verve. Sadly, perhaps, a British Amateur title eluded her, despite being in successive finals in 1929 and 1930. In the first against Joyce Wethered at St Andrews she was three under 4s for the first 11 holes and 5-up but became victim of an outstanding counter-attack by the finest woman golfer of her time. A year later she lost again, this time unexpectedly to a little-known 19-year-old, Diana (Fishwick) Critchley, at Formby. She played in five Curtis Cup matches and was also captain, proving as popular with foe as with friend.

Walker, George   (1874–1953)

President of the United States Golf Association in 1920 and one of the instigators of the biennial Walker Cup matches between the leading amateurs of Great Britain and Ireland and the United States. He donated the trophy for the first match, played at Long Island, New York, on 29th August 1922, and won by the host country. Educated partly in England, at Stoneyhurst, Walker was an all-round sportsman and a good golfer, though not of international standard. His grandson, George Bush, became President of the United States.

Ward, Charles Harold   (1911–2001)

He played in three Ryder Cups in 1947, 1949 and 1951 and was twice tied in the Open Championship behind Henry Cotton at Muirfield in 1948 and Max Faulkner at Royal Portrush in 1951.

Wethered, Joyce (Lady Heathcoat-Amory)   (1899–1997)

Bobby Jones once stated that Joyce Wethered was, taking into account 'the unavoidable handicap of a woman's lesser physical strength', the finest golfer he had ever seen. Her brother Roger persuaded her into competitive golf after the First World War. She was just 18 when she entered her first English Ladies' Championship in 1920, but she won it at Sheringham by beating the holder Cecil Leitch in the final and was to remain unbeaten for the next four years, winning 33 successive matches. She also won four British Championships, equalling Leitch's record.

With her irons, her hands seldom went higher than shoulder level on either backswing or follow through and she made the game seem effortless. Jones's comment came after they played together at St Andrews. She scored 75 and he wrote: 'I had never played golf with anyone, man or woman, amateur or professional, who made me feel so utterly outclassed.' After playing in the inaugural Curtis Cup match in 1932, she forfeited her amateur status and toured America in 1935. She was reinstated as an amateur after the Second World War.

Wethered, Roger   (1899–1983)

One of the outstanding amateurs of the period between the two World Wars, Roger Wethered won the Amateur Championship in 1923 and was runner-up in 1928 and 1930. He won the President's Putter of the Oxford and Cambridge GS five times (once a tie) between 1926 and 1936, played in the Walker Cup against the United States six times between 1921 and 1934, and for England against Scotland every year from 1922 to 1930. He was captain of the Royal & Ancient in 1946. But he will probably be best remembered for the fact that he tied with Jock Hutchison, a Scot who had settled in the United States, in the 1921 Open Championship at St Andrews, despite having incurred a penalty stroke by inadvertently treading on his ball. Wethered was reluctant to stay on for the 36-hole play-off the following day because of a cricket engagement in England, but was persuaded to do so, only to be beaten by nine strokes, 150 to 159. No British amateur has come so close to winning the Open Championship since.

The Whitcombe Brothers:
Ernest (1890–1971)
Charles (1895–1978)
Reginald (1898–1957)

The story of the Whitcombes is told in a limited edition publication, *The Whitcombe Brothers – A Golfing Legend*, and what a remarkable story it is. They were born in Burnham, Somerset, and won many titles between them. All three played in the 1935 Ryder Cup contest at Ridgewood, New Jersey, but only Reg, the youngest, won the Open Championship (at Sandwich in 1938). Ernest finished second to Walter Hagen in 1924 at Hoylake after leading by three strokes at one time and Charles took 76 in the final round at Muirfield in 1935 to lose by five strokes and finish third.

Wilson, Enid   (1910–1996)

Between the wars of 1914–18 and then 1939–45 Enid Wilson was second only to Joyce Wethered among British women golfers. She had an outstanding record which was the result of her relish for the big occasion. Her finest years were between 1931–33 when she completed a hat-trick of victories in the British Women's Championship, all of them by wide margins. In 1931 she beat Wanda Morgan by seven and six in the final at Portmarnock. The following year at Saunton she similarly despatched Clementine Montgomery, and then in 1933 she defeated Diana Plumpton by 5 and 4 at Gleneagles. She had already won the English Championship twice, in 1928 and 1930, and, before that, the British Girls' title in 1925. Twice, in 1931 and 1933, she was a semi-finalist in the American Championship, and played for Britain in the inaugural Curtis Cup match against the United States at Wentworth in 1932, beating Helen Hicks.

Enid Wilson had a sound, rather graceful, swing, and, though a hard worker on the practice ground, she never allowed golf to rule her life – indeed she retired from the game at a comparatively early age. Instead she turned to journalism, and for many years was the women's golf correspondent of the *Daily Telegraph*, her pungent views frequently ruffling the feathers of the Ladies' Golf Union. Her book, *A Gallery of Women Golfers*, was widely acclaimed. She was a familiar figure in a long tweed skirt, which she wore in all weathers, and she compiled such a valuable collection of stamps that many of them had to be kept in the vaults of a bank. She saw out the last years of her life at her treasured Oast House at Crowborough in East Sussex.

Wood, Craig   (1901–1968)

Born at Lake Placid, New York, Wood was a player of 'near misses'. Like Greg Norman many years later, Wood lost play-offs for what are known now as all the major championships even if they were not then. They were the 1933 Open Championship to Densmore Shute at St Andrews, the 1934 PGA Championship to Paul Runyan at Buffalo, the 1935 Masters to Gene Sarazen at Augusta and the 1939 US Open to Byron Nelson at Philadelphia. However, success did finally come for Wood in 1941 when he won both the Masters and US Open. He was also a member of three American Ryder Cup teams.

Zaharias, Mrs George (Mildred Babe Didrikson)   (1915–1956)

In the 1932 Olympic Games she established three world records for women: 80 metres hurdles, javelin, and high jump. On giving up athletics she took up golf and won the Texas Women's Open in 1940-45-46; the Western Open, 1940-44-45-50; and the US National Women's Amateur, 1946. In 1947 she won the Ladies' Championship, the first American to do so. In August 1947 she turned professional and went on to win the US National Women's Open, 1948-50 and 1954. In winning the Tampa Open, 1951, she set up a women's world record aggregate, for the time, of 288 for 72 holes.

She was voted Woman Athlete of the year five times in 1932-45-46-47-50, and in 1949 was voted Greatest Female Athlete of the Half-Century. The first woman to hold the post of head professional to a golf club, the *Babe* was a courageous and fighting character who left her mark in the world of sport.

Eight birdies in a row for Marksaeng

Thailand's Prayed Marksaeng set a new Asian PGA record of eight birdies in a row when he equalled Simon Dyson's record 63 in the 2001 Volvo Masters of Malaysia. His birdie run began at the fifth and included no putt longer than 12 feet.

Several players have shot eight birdies in a row in European golf – Ian Woosnam at Fulford in 1985, Seve Ballesteros at Molinetto the same year, Tony Johnstone at Fulford in 1990 and John Bickerton at Penha Longa in 1996.

American Mark O'Meara fired eight straight birdies at St Andrews in 1996, Raymond Russell achieved the feat at Forest of Arden in 1997 and Darren Clarke and Marcello Santi both did it at The K Club and the Malaga Parador del Golf respectively in 1999.

In America, Fuzzy Zoeller had eight in a row at the 1976 Quad Cities Tournament, Dewey Arnette did it at the Buick Open in 1987 and Ed Fryatt made headlines when he strung together eight birdies in the 2000 Doral Ryder Open.

Interesting Facts and Unusual Incidents

Royal Golf Clubs

● The right to the designation *Royal* is bestowed by the favour of the Sovereign or a member of the Royal House. In most cases the title is granted along with the bestowal of royal patronage on the club. The Perth Golfing Society was the first to receive the designation *Royal*. That was accorded in June 1833. King William IV bestowed the honour on the Royal & Ancient Club in 1834. The most recent Club to be so designated is the Royal Troon in 1978.

Royal and Presidential Golfers

● In the long history of the Royal and Ancient game no reigning British monarch has played in an open competition. In 1922 the Duke of Windsor, when Prince of Wales, competed in the Royal & Ancient Autumn Medal at St Andrews. He also took part in competitions at Mid-Surrey, Sunningdale, Royal St George's and in the Parliamentary Handicap. He occasionally competed in American events, sometimes partnered by a professional. On a private visit to London in 1952, he competed in the Autumn competition of Royal St George's at Sandwich, scoring 97. As Prince of Wales he played on courses all over the world and, after his abdication, as Duke of Windsor he continued to enjoy the game for many years.

● King George VI, when still Duke of York, in 1930, and the Duke of Kent, in 1937, also competed in the Autumn Meeting of the Royal & Ancient, when they had formally played themselves into the Captaincy of the Club and each returned his card in the medal round.

● King Leopold of Belgium played in the Belgian Amateur Championship at Le Zoute, the only reigning monarch ever to have played in a national championship. The Belgian King played in many competitions subsequent to his abdication. In 1949 he reached the quarter-finals of the French Amateur Championship at St Cloud, playing as Count de Rethy.

● King Baudouin of Belgium in 1958 played in the triangular match Belgium-France-Holland and won his match against a Dutch player. He also took part in the Gleneagles Hotel tournament (playing as Mr B de Rethy), partnered by Dai Rees in 1959.

● United States President George Bush accepted an invitation in 1990 to become an Honorary Member of the Royal & Ancient Golf Club of St Andrews. The honour recognised his long connection and that of his family with golf and the R&A. Both President Bush's father, Prescott Bush Sr, and his grandfather, George Herbert Walker – who donated the Walker Cup – were presidents of the United States Golf Association. Other Honorary Members of the R&A include Kel Nagle, Jack Nicklaus, Arnold Palmer, Gene Sarazen, Peter Thomson, Roberto de Vicenzo, Gary Player and five-times Open Championship winner Tom Watson, who was made an honorary member in 1999 on his 50th birthday.

● In September 1992, the Royal & Ancient Golf Club of St Andrews announced that His Royal Highness The Duke of York had accepted the Club's invitation of Honorary Membership. The Duke of York is the third member of the Royal Family to accept membership along with Their Royal Highnesses The Duke of Edinburgh and The Duke of Kent. He has since become a single handicapper, and has appeared in a number of pro-ams, partnering Open and Masters champion Mark O'Meara to victory in the Alfred Dunhill Cup pro-am at St Andrews in 1998. His Royal Highness has been named captain-elect for 2004–5, when the club will celebrate its 250th anniversary.

First Lady Golfer

● Mary Queen of Scots, who was beheaded on 8th February, 1587, was probably the first lady golfer so mentioned by name. As evidence of her indifference to the fate of Darnley, her husband who was murdered at Kirk o' Field, Edinburgh, she was charged at her trial with having played at golf in the fields beside Seton a few days after his death.

Record Championship Victories

● In the Amateur Championship at Muirfield, 1920, Captain Carter, an Irish golfer, defeated an American entrant by 10 and 8. This is the only known instance where a player has won every hole in an Amateur Championship tie.

● In the final of the Canadian Ladies' Championship at Rivermead, Ottawa, in 1921, Cecil Leitch defeated Mollie McBride by 17 and 15. Miss Leitch lost only 1 hole in the match, the ninth. She was 14 up at the end of the first round, making only 3 holes necessary in the second. She won 18 holes out of 21 played, lost 1, and halved 2.

● In the final of the French Ladies' Open Championship at Le Touquet in 1927, Mlle de la Chaume (St Cloud) defeated Mrs Alex Johnston (Moor Park) by 15 and 14, the largest victory in a European golf championship.

● At Prestwick in 1934, W Lawson Little of Presidio, San Francisco, defeated James Wallace, Troon Portland, by 14 and 13 in the final of the Amateur Championship, the record victory in the Championship. Wallace failed to win a single hole.

Players who have won Two or More Majors in the Same Year

(The first Masters Tournament was played in 1934.)

    1922 Gene Sarazen – USPGA, US Open
    1924 Walter Hagen – USPGA, Open
    1926 Bobby Jones – US Open, Open
    1930 Bobby Jones – US Open, Open (Bobby
          Jones also won the US Amateur and
          British Amateur in this year.)
    1932 Gene Sarazen – US Open, Open
    1941 Craig Wood – Masters, US Open
    1948 Ben Hogan – USPGA, US Open
    1949 Sam Snead – USPGA, Masters
    1951 Ben Hogan – Masters, US Open
    1953 Ben Hogan – Masters, US Open, Open
    1956 Jack Burke – USPGA, Masters
    1960 Arnold Palmer – Masters, US Open
    1962 Arnold Palmer – Masters, Open
    1963 Jack Nicklaus – USPGA, Masters
    1966 Jack Nicklaus – Masters, Open
    1971 Lee Trevino – US Open, Open
    1972 Jack Nicklaus – Masters, Open
    1974 Gary Player – Masters, Open
    1975 Jack Nicklaus – USPGA, Masters
    1977 Tom Watson – Masters, Open
    1980 Jack Nicklaus – USPGA, US Open
    1982 Tom Watson – US Open, Open
    1990 Nick Faldo – Masters, Open
    1994 Nick Price – Open, US PGA
    1998 Mark O'Meara – Masters, Open
    2000 *Tiger Woods – US Open, Open, USPGA

*Woods also won the 2001 Masters to become the first player to hold all four Majors at the same time. He was 65-under-par for the four events.

Outstanding Records in Championships, International Matches and on the Professional Circuit

● The record number of victories in the Open Championship is six, held by Harry Vardon who won in 1896-98-99-1903-11-14.

● Five-time winners of the Championship are JH Taylor in 1894-95-1900-09-13; James Braid in 1901-05-06-08-10; Peter Thomson in 1954-55-56-58-65 and Tom Watson in 1975-77-80-82-83.

Thomson's 1965 win was achieved when the Championship had become a truly international event. In 1957 he finished second behind Bobby Locke. By winning again in 1958 Thomson was prevented only by Bobby Locke from winning five consecutive Open Championships.

● Four successive victories in the Open by *Young* Tom Morris is a record so far never equalled. He won in 1868-69-70-72. (The Championship was not played in 1871.) Other four-time winners are Bobby Locke in 1949-50-52-57, Walter Hagen 1922-24-28-29, Willie Park 1860-63-66-75, and *Old* Tom Morris 1861-62-64-67.

● Since the Championship began in 1860, players who have won three times in succession are Jamie Anderson, Bob Ferguson, and Peter Thomson.

● Robert Tyre Jones won the Open three times in 1926-27-30; the Amateur in 1930; the American Open in 1923-26-29-30; and the American Amateur in 1924-25-27-28-30. In winning the four major golf titles of the world in one year (1930) he achieved a feat unlikely ever to be equalled. Jones retired from competitive golf after winning the 1930 American Open, the last of these Championships, at the age of 28.

● Jack Nicklaus has had the most wins (six) in the US Masters Tournament, followed by Arnold Palmer with four.

● In modern times there are four championships generally regarded as standing above all others – the Open, US Open, US Masters, and USPGA. Five players have held all these titles, Gene Sarazen, Ben Hogan, Gary Player, Jack Nicklaus and Tiger Woods. In 1978 Nicklaus became the first player to have held each of them at least three times. His record in these events is: Open 1966-70-78; US Open 1962-67-72-80; US Masters 1963-65-66-72-75-86; USPGA 1963-71-73-75-80. His total of major championships is now 18. In 1998 at the age of 58, Nicklaus finished joint sixth in the Masters. By not playing in the Open Championship that year, he ended a run of 154 successive major championships for which he was eligible (stretching back to 1957).

In 1953 Ben Hogan won the Masters, US Open and Open, but did not compete in the USPGA because the date clashed with the Open.

In 2000 Tiger Woods won the US Open by 15 strokes (a major championship record), the Open by eight strokes, and the USPGA in the play-off. In 2001 he then added the Masters winning by two shots to become the first player to hold all four major titles at the same time. He was 65-under-par for the four events.

● In the 1996 English Amateur Championship at Hollinwell, Ian Richardson (50) and his son, Carl, of Burghley Park, Lincolnshire, both reached the semi-finals. Both lost.

● The record number of victories in the US Open is four, held by W Anderson, Bobby Jones, Ben Hogan and Jack Nicklaus.

● Bobby Jones (amateur), Gene Sarazen, Ben Hogan, Lee Trevino, Tom Watson and Tiger Woods are the only players to have won the Open and US Open Championships in the same year. Tony Jacklin won the Open in 1969 and the US Open in 1970 and for a few weeks was the holder of both.

● In winning the Amateur Championship in 1970 Michael Bonallack became the first player to win in three consecutive years.

● The English Amateur record number of victories is held by Michael Bonallack, who won the title five times.

● John Ball holds the record number of victories in the Amateur Championship, which he won eight times. Next comes Michael Bonallack (who was internationally known as *The Duke*) with five wins.

● Cecil Leitch and Joyce Wethered each won the British Ladies' title four times.

● The Scottish Amateur record was held by Ronnie Shade, who won five titles in successive years, 1963 to 1967. His long reign as Champion ended when he was beaten in the fourth round of the 1968 Championship after winning 44 consecutive matches.

● Joyce Wethered established an unbeaten record by winning the English Ladies' in five successive years from 1920 to 1924 inclusive.

● In winning the Amateur Championships of Britain and America in 1934 and 1935 Lawson Little won 31 consecutive matches. Other dual winners of these championships in the same year are RT Jones (1930) and Bob Dickson (1967).

● Peter Thomson's victory in the 1971 New Zealand Open Championship was his ninth in that championship.

● In a four-week spell in 1971, Lee Trevino won in succession the US Open, the Canadian Open and the Open Championships.

● Michael Bonallack and Bill Hyndman were the Amateur Championship finalists in both 1969 and 1970. This was the first time the same two players reached the final in successive years.

● On the US professional circuit the greatest number of consecutive victories is 11, achieved by Byron Nelson in 1945. Nelson also holds the record for most victories in one calendar year, again in 1945 when he won a total of 18 tournaments.

● Raymond Floyd, by winning the Doral Classic in March 1992, joined Sam Snead as the only winners of US Tour events in four different decades.

● Sam Snead won tournaments in six decades. His first win was the 1936 West Virginia PGA. In 1980 he won the *Golf Digest* Commemorative and in 1982 the Legends of Golf with Don January.

● Neil Coles became the second golfer to win a professional event in six different decades when he won the Microlease Jersey Seniors Open at La Moye in June 2000. He was 65 at the time and had won his maiden title in 1958.

● Jack Nicklaus and the late Walter Hagen have had five wins each in the USPGA Championship. All Hagen's wins were at match play; all Nicklaus's at stroke play.

● In 1953 Flori van Donck of Belgium had seven major victories in Europe, including the Open Championships of Switzerland, Italy, Holland, Germany and Belgium.

● Mrs Anne Sander won four major amateur titles each under a different name. She won the US Ladies' in 1958 as Miss Quast, in 1961 as Mrs Decker, in 1963 as Mrs Welts and the British Ladies' in 1980 as Mrs Sander.

● The highest number of appearances in the Ryder Cup matches is held by Nick Faldo who made his eleventh appearance in 1997.

● The greatest number of appearances in the Walker Cup matches is held by Irishman Joe Carr who made his tenth appearance in 1967.

● In the Curtis Cup Mary McKenna made her ninth consecutive appearance in 1986.

● Players who have represented their country in both Walker and Ryder Cup matches are: for the United States, Fred Haas, Ken Venturi, Gene Littler, Jack Nicklaus, Tommy Aaron, Mason Rudolph, Bob Murphy, Lanny Wadkins, Scott Simpson, Tom Kite, Jerry Pate, Craig Stadler, Jay Haas, Bill Rodgers, Hal Sutton, Curtis Strange, Davis Love III, Brad Faxon, Scott Hoch, Phil Mickelson, Corey Pavin, Justin Leonard, Tiger Woods and David Duval; and for Great Britain & Ireland, Norman Drew, Peter Townsend, Clive Clark, Peter Oosterhuis, Howard Clark, Mark James, Michael King, Gordon Brand Jr, Paul Way, Ronan Rafferty, Sandy Lyle, Philip Walton, David Gilford, Colin Montgomerie, Peter Baker, Padraig Harrington and Andrew Coltart.

Remarkable Recoveries in Matchplay

● There have been two remarkable recoveries in the Walker Cup Matches. In 1930 at Sandwich, JA Stout, Great Britain, round in 68, was 4 up at the end of the first round against Donald Moe. Stout started in the second round, 3, 3, 3, and was 7 up. He was still 7 up with 13 to play. Moe, who went round in 67, won back the 7 holes to draw level at the 17th green. At the 18th or 36th of the match, Moe, after a long drive placed his iron shot within three feet of the hole and won the match by 1 hole.

● In 1936 at Pine Valley, George Voigt and Harry Girvan for America were 7 up with 11 to play against Alec Hill and Cecil Ewing. The British pair drew level at the 17th hole, or the 35th of the match, and the last hole was halved.

● In the 1965 Piccadilly Match Play Championship Gary Player beat Tony Lema after being 7 down with 17 to play.

● Bobby Cruickshank, the old Edinburgh player, had an extraordinary recovery in a 36-hole match in a USPGA Championship for he defeated Al Watrous after being 11 down with 12 to play.

● In a match at the Army GC, Aldershot, on 5th July, 1974, for the Gradoville Bowl, MC Smart was 8 down with 8 to play against Mike Cook. Smart succeeded in winning all the remaining holes and the 19th for victory.

● In the 1982 Suntory World Match Play Championship Sandy Lyle beat Nick Faldo after being 6 down with 18 to play.

Oldest Champions

Open Championship: Belt Tom Morris in 1867 – 46 years 99 days. *Cup* Roberto de Vicenzo, 44 years 93 days, in 1967; Harry Vardon, 44 years 42 days, in 1914; JH Taylor, 42 years 97 days, in 1913.

Amateur Championship Hon. Michael Scot, 54, at Hoylake in 1933.

British Ladies Amateur Mrs Jessie Valentine, 43, at Hunstanton in 1958.

Scottish Amateur JM Cannon, 53, at Troon in 1969.

English Amateur Terry Shingler, 41 years 11 months at Walton Heath 1977; Gerald Micklem, 41 years 8 months, at Royal Birkdale 1947.

Welsh Amateur John Jermine, 56, at St David's, in 2000

US Open Hale Irwin, 45, at Medinah, Illinois, in 1990.

US Amateur Jack Westland, 47, at Seattle in 1952 (He had been defeated in the 1931 final, 21 years previously, by Francis Ouimet).

US Masters Jack Nicklaus, 46, in 1986.

European Tour Neil Coles, 48, in 1982

European Senior Tour Neil Coles, 65, in 2000

USPGA Julius Boros, 48, in 1968. Lee Trevino, 44, in 1984.

USPGA Tour Sam Snead, 52, at Greensborough Open in 1965. Sam Snead, 61, equal second in Glen Campbell Open 1974.

Youngest Champions

Open Championship: Belt Tom Morris, Jr, 17 years 5 months, in 1868. *Cup* Willie Auchterlonie, 21 years 24 days, in 1893; Tom Morris, Jr, 21 years 5 months, in 1872; Severiano Ballesteros, 22 years 103 days, in 1979.

Amateur Championship JC Beharrell, 18 years 1 month, at Troon in 1956; R Cole (SA) 18 years 1 month, at Carnoustie in 1966.

British Ladies Amateur May Hezlett, 17, at Newcastle, Co Down, in 1899; Michelle Walker, 18, at Alwoodley in 1971.

English Amateur Nick Faldo, 18, at Lytham St Annes in 1975; Paul Downes, 18, at Birkdale in 1978; David Gilford, 18, at Woodhall Spa in 1984; Ian Garbutt, 18, at Woodhall Spa in 1990; Mark Foster, 18, at Moortown in 1994.

English Amateur Strokeplay Ronan Rafferty, 16, at Hunstanton in 1980.

British Ladies Open Strokeplay Helen Dobson, 18, at Southerness in 1989.

Disqualifications

Disqualifications are now numerous, usually for some irregularity over signing a scorecard or for late arrival at the first tee. We therefore show here only incidents in major events involving famous players or players who were in a winning position or incidents which were in themselves unusual.

● JJ McDermott, the American Open Champion 1911-12, arrived for the Open Championship at Prestwick in 1914 to discover that he had made a mistake of a week in the date the championship began. The American could not play, as the qualifying rounds were completed on the day he arrived.

● In the Amateur Championship at Sandwich in 1937, Brigadier-General Critchley, arriving at Southampton from New York on the *Queen Mary*, which had been delayed by fog, flew by specially chartered aeroplane to Sandwich. He circled over the clubhouse, so the officials knew he was nearly there, but he arrived six minutes late, and his name had been struck out. At the same championship a player, entered from Burma, who had travelled across the Pacific and the American Continent, and was also on the *Queen Mary*, travelled from Southampton by motor car and arrived four hours after his starting time to find after journeying more than halfway round the world he was *struck out*.

● An unprecedented disqualification was that of A Murray in the New Zealand Open Championship, 1937. Murray, who was New Zealand Champion in 1935, was playing with JP Hornabrook, New Zealand Amateur Champion, and at the 8th hole in the last round, while waiting for his partner to putt, Murray dropped a ball on the edge of the green and made a practice putt along the edge. Murray returned the lowest score in the championship, but he was disqualified for taking the practice putt.

● At the Open Championship at St Andrews in 1946, John Panton, Glenbervie, in the evening practised putting on a green on the New Course, which was one of the qualifying courses. He himself reported his inadvertence to the Royal & Ancient and he was disqualified.

● At the Open Championship, Sandwich, 1949, C Rotar, an American, qualified by four strokes to compete in the championship but he was disqualified because he had used a putter which did not conform to the accepted form and make of a golf club, the socket being bent over the centre of the club head. This is the only case where a player has been disqualified in the Open Championship for using an illegal club.

● In the 1957 American Women's Open Championship, Mrs Jackie Pung had the lowest score,

298 over four rounds, but lost the championship. The card she signed for the final round read *five* at the 4th hole instead of the correct *six*. Her total of 72 was correct but the error, under rigid rules, resulted in her disqualification. Betty Jameson, who partnered Mrs Pung and also returned a wrong score, was also disqualified.

Longest Match

● WR Chamberlain, a retired farmer, and George New, a postmaster at Chilton Foliat, on 1st August, 1922, met at Littlecote, the 9-hole course of Sir Ernest Wills, and agreed to play every Thursday afternoon over the course. This continued until New's sudden death on 13th January, 1938. An accurate record of the match was kept, giving details of each round including wind direction and playing conditions. In the elaborate system nearly two million facts were recorded. They played 814 rounds, and aggregated 86,397 strokes, of which Chamberlain took 44,008 and New 42,371. New, therefore, was 1,637 strokes up. The last round of all was halved, a suitable end to such an unusual contest.

Longest Ties

● The longest known ties in 18-hole match play rounds in major events were in an early round of the News of the World Match Play Championship at Turnberry in 1960, when WS Collins beat WJ Branch at the 31st hole and in the third round of the same tournament at Walton Heath in 1961 when Harold Henning beat Peter Alliss also at the 31st hole.

● In the 1970 Scottish Amateur Championship at Balgownie, Aberdeen, E Hammond beat J McIvor at the 29th hole in their second round tie.

● CA Palmer beat Lionel Munn at the 28th hole at Sandwich in 1908. This is the record tie of the British Amateur Championship. Munn has also been engaged in two other extended ties in the Amateur Championship. At Muirfield, in 1932, in the semi-final, he was defeated by John de Forest, the ultimate winner, at the 26th hole, and at St Andrews, in 1936, in the second round he was defeated by JL Mitchell, again at the 26th hole.

The following examples of long ties are in a different category for they occurred in competitions, either stroke play or match play, where the conditions stipulated that in the event of a tie, a further stated number of holes had to be played – in some cases 36 holes, but mostly 18. With this method a vast number of extra holes was sometimes necessary to settle ties.

● The longest known was between two American women in a tournament at Peterson (New Jersey) when 88 extra holes were required before Mrs Edwin Labaugh emerged as winner.

● In a match on the Queensland course, Australia, in October, 1933, HB Bonney and Col

HCH Robertson versus BJ Canniffe and Dr Wallis Hoare required to play a further four 18-hole matches after being level at the end of the original 18 holes. In the fourth replay Hoare and Caniffe won by 3 and 2 which meant that 70 extra holes had been necessary to decide the tie.

● After finishing all square in the final of the Dudley GC's foursomes competition in 1950, FW Mannell and AG Walker played a further three 18-hole replays against T Poole and E Jones, each time finishing all square. A further 9 holes were arranged and Mannell and Walker won by 3 and 2 making a total of 61 extra holes to decide the tie.

● RA Whitcombe and Mark Seymour tied for first prize in the Penfold £750 Tournament at St Annes-on-Sea, in 1934. They had to play off over 36 holes and tied again. They were then required to play another 9 holes when Whitcombe won with 34 against 36. The tournament was over 72 holes. The first tie added 36 holes and the extra 9 holes made an aggregate of 117 holes to decide the winner. This is a record in first-class British golf but in no way compares with other long ties as it involved only two replays – one of 36 holes and one of 9.

● In the American Open Championship at Toledo, Ohio, in 1931, G Von Elm and Billy Burke tied for the title. Each returned aggregates of 292. On the first replay both finished in 149 for 36 holes but on the second replay Burke won with a score of 148 against 149. This is a record tie in a national open championship.

● Cary Middlecoff and Lloyd Mangrum were declared co-winners of the 1949 Motor City Open on the USPGA Tour after halving 11 sudden death holes.

● Australian David Graham beat American Dave Stockton at the tenth extra hole in the 1998 Royal Caribbean Classic, a record on the US Senior Tour.

● Paul Downes was beaten by Robin Davenport at the 9th extra hole in the 4th round of the 1981 English Amateur Championship, a record marathon match for the Championship.

● Severiano Ballesteros was beaten by Johnny Miller at the 9th extra hole of a sudden-death play-off at the 1982 Million Dollar Sun City Challenge.

● José Maria Olazabal beat Ronan Rafferty at the 9th extra hole to win the 1989 Dutch Open on the Kennemer Golf and Country Club course.

Long Drives

It is impossible to state with any certainty what is the longest ever drive. Many long drives have never been measured and many others have most likely never been brought to our attention. Then there are several outside factors which can produce freakishly long drives, such as a strong following wind, downhill terrain or bonehard ground. Where all three of these favourable conditions prevail outstandingly long drives can be achieved. Another consideration is that a long drive made during a tournament is a different proposition from one made for length alone, either on the practice ground, a long driving competition or in a game of no consequence. All this should be borne in mind when considering the long drives shown here.

● When professional Carl Hooper hit a wayward drive on the 3rd hole (456 yards) at the Oak Hills Country Club, San Antonio, during the 1992 Texas Open, he wrote himself into the record books but out of the tournament. The ball kept bouncing and rolling on a tarmac cart path until it was stopped by a fence – 787 yards away. It took Hooper two recovery shots with a 4-iron and then an 8-iron to return to the fairway. He eventually holed out for a double bogey six and failed to survive the half-way qualifying cut.
● Tommie Campbell of Portmarnock hit a drive of 392 yards at Dun Laoghaire GC in July 1964.
● Playing in Australia, American George Bayer is reported to have driven to within chipping distance of a 589 yards hole. *It was certainly a drive of over 500 yards,* said Bayer acknowledging the strong following wind, sharp downslope where his ball landed and the bone-hard ground.
● In September, 1934, over the East Devon course, THV Haydon, Wimbledon, drove to the edge of the 9th green which was a hole of 465 yards, giving a drive of not less than 450 yards.
● EC Bliss drove 445 yards at Herne Bay in August, 1913. The drive was measured by a government surveyor who also measured the drop in height from tee to resting place of the ball at 57 feet.

Long Carries

● At Sitwell Park, Rotherham, in 1935 the home professional, W Smithson, drove a ball which carried a dyke at 380 yards from the 2nd tee.
● George Bell, of Penrith GC, New South Wales, Australia, using a number 2 wood drove across the Nepean River, a certified carry of 309 yards in a driving contest in 1964.
● After the 1986 Irish Professional Championship at Waterville, Co. Kerry, four long-hitting professionals tried for the longest-carry record over water, across a lake in the Waterville Hotel grounds. Liam Higgins, the local professional, carried 310 yards and Paul Leonard 311, beating the previous record by 2 yards.
● In the 1972 Algarve Open at Penina, Henry Cotton vouched for a carry of 305 yards over a ditch at the 18th hole by long-hitting Spanish professional Francisco Abreu. There was virtually no wind assistance.
● At the Home International matches at Portmarnock in 1949 a driving competition was held in which all the players in all four teams competed. The actual carry was measured and the longest was 280 yards by Jimmy Bruen.
● On 6th April, 1976, Tony Jacklin hit a number of balls into Vancouver harbour, Canada, from

the 495-foot high roof of a new building complex. The longest carry was measured at 389 yards.

Long Hitting

There have been numerous long hits, not on golf courses, where an outside agency has assisted the length of the shot. Such an example was a 'drive' by Liam Higgins in 1986, on the Airport runway at Baldonal, near Dublin, of 632 yards.

Longest Albatrosses

● The longest-known albatrosses (three under par) recorded at par 5 holes are:
● 647 yards-2nd hole at Guam Navy Club by Chief Petty Officer Kevin Murray of Chicago on 3rd January, 1982.
● 609 yards-15th hole at Mahaka Inn West Course, Hawaii, by John Eakin of California on 12th November, 1972.
● 602 yards-16th hole at Whiting Field Golf Course, Milton, Florida, by 27-year-old Bill Graham with a drive and a 3-wood, aided by a 25 mph tail wind.
● The longest-known albatrosses in open championships are: 580 yards 14th hole at Crans-sur-Sierre, by American Billy Casper in the 1971 Swiss Open; 558 yards 5th hole at Muirfield by American Johnny Miller in the 1972 Open Championship.
● In the 1994 German Amateur Championship at Wittelsbacher GC, Rohrenfeld, Graham Rankin, a member of the visiting Scottish national team, had a two at the 592 yard 18th.

Eagles (Multiple and Consecutive)

● Wilf Jones scored three consecutive eagles at the first three holes at Moor Hall GC when playing in a competition there on August Bank Holiday Monday 1968. He scored 3, 1, 2 at holes measuring 529 yards, 176 yards and 302 yards.
● In a round of the 1980 Jubilee Cup, a mixed foursomes match play event of Colchester GC, Mrs Nora Booth and her son Brendan scored three consecutive gross eagles of 1, 3, 2 at the eighth, ninth and tenth holes.
● Three players in a four-ball match at Kington GC, Herefordshire, on 22nd July, 1948, all had eagle 2s at the 18th hole (272 yards). They were RN Bird, R Morgan and V Timson.
● Four Americans from Wisconsin on holiday at Gleneagles in 1977 scored three eagles and a birdie at the 300-yard par-4 14th hole on the King's course. The birdie was by Dr Kim Lulloff and the eagles by Dr Gordon Meiklejohn, Richard Johnson and Jack Kubitz.
● In an open competition at Glen Innes GC, Australia on 13th November, 1977, three players

in a four-ball scored eagle 3s at the 9th hole (442 metres). They were Terry Marshall, Roy McHarg and Jack Rohleder.

● David McCarthy, a member of Moortown Golf Club, Leeds, had three consecutive eagles (3,3,2) on the 4th, 5th and 6th holes during a Pro-Am competition at Lucerne, Switzerland, on 7th August, 1992.

Speed of Golf Ball and Club Head and Effect of Wind and Temperature

● In *The Search for the Perfect Swing*, a scientific study of the golf swing, a first class golfer is said to have the club head travelling at 100 mph at impact. This will cause the ball to leave the club at 135 mph. An outstandingly long hitter might manage to have the club head travelling at 130 mph which would produce a ball send-off speed of 175 mph. The resultant shot would carry 280 yards.

● According to Thomas Hardman, Wilson's director of research and development, wind will reduce or increase the flight of a golf ball by approximately 1½ yards for every mile per hour of wind. Every two degrees of temperature will make a yard difference in a ball's flight.

Most Northerly Course

● The most northerly course is the Akureyri Golf Club in Iceland which is situated 65°40' North of the equator. Not far south is the Luleò course in Sweden, at 65°35' North.

Most Southerly Course

● Golf's most southerly course is Scott Base Country Club, 13° north of the South Pole. The course is run by the New Zealand Antarctic Programme and players must be kitted in full survival gear. The most difficult aspect is finding the orange golf balls which tend to get buried in the snow. Other obstacles include penguins, seals and skuas. If the ball is stolen by a skua then a penalty of one shot is incurred; but if the ball hits a skua it counts as a birdie.

Highest Golf Courses

● The highest golf course in the world is thought to be the Tuctu GC in Peru which is 14,335 feet above sea-level. High courses are also found in Bolivia with the La Paz GC being about 13,500 feet. In the Himalayas, near the border with Tibet, a 9-hole course at 12,800 feet has been laid out by keen golfers in the Indian Army.

● The highest course in Europe is at Sestriere in the Italian Alps, 6,500 feet above sea-level.

● The highest courses in Great Britain are West Monmouthshire in Wales at 1,513 feet, Leadhills in Scotland at 1,500 feet and Church Stratton in England at 1,250 feet.

Longest Courses

● The longest course in the world is Dub's Dread GC, Piper, Kansas, USA measuring 8,101 yards (par 78).

● The longest course for the Open Championship was 7,252 yards at Carnoustie in 1968.

Longest Holes

● The longest hole in the world, as far as is known, is the 6th hole measuring 782 metres (860 yards) at Koolan Island GC, Western Australia. The par of the hole is 7. There are several holes over 700 yards throughout the world.

● The longest hole for the Open Championship is the 577 yards 6th hole at Royal Troon.

Longest Tournaments

● The longest tournament held was over 144 holes in the World Open at Pinehurst, N Carolina, USA, first held in 1973. Play was over two weeks with a cut imposed at the halfway mark.

● An annual tournament, played in Germany on the longest day of the year, comprises 100 holes' medal play. Best return, in 1995, was 399 strokes.

Largest Entries

● The Open – 2460, St Andrews, 2000.

● The Amateur – 537, Muirfield, 1998.

● US Open – 8457, Pebble Beach, 2000.

● The largest entry for a PGA European Tour event was 398 for the 1978 Colgate PGA Championship. Since 1985, when the all-exempt ruling was introduced, all PGA tournaments have had 144 competitors, slightly more or less.

● In 1952, Bobby Locke, the Open Champion, played a round at Wentworth against any golfer in Britain. Cards costing 2s. 6d. each (12½p), were taken out by 24,000 golfers. The challenge was to beat the local par by more than Locke could beat the par at Wentworth. 1,641 competitors, including women, succeeded in *beating* the Champion and each received a certificate signed by him. As a result of this challenge the British Golf Foundation benefited to the extent of £3,026, the proceeds from the sale of cards. A similar tournament was held in the US and Canada when 87,094 golfers participated; 14,667 players bettered Ben Hogan's score under handicap. The fund benefited by $80,024.

Largest Prize Money

● The Machrie Tournament of 1901 was the first tournament with a first prize of £100. It was won by JH Taylor, then Open Champion, who beat James Braid in the final.

● The richest event in the world is currently the Players' Championship in Florida. It has a total purse of $6 million and a first prize of $1.08 million.

Holing-in-One – Odds Against

● At the Wanderers Club, Johannesburg in January, 1951, forty-nine amateurs and professionals each played three balls at a hole 146 yards long. Of the 147 balls hit, the nearest was by Koos de Beer, professional at Reading Country Club, which finished 10½ inches from the hole. Harry Bradshaw, the Irish professional who was touring with the British team in South Africa, touched the pin with his second shot, but the ball rolled on and stopped 3 feet 2 inches from the cup.

● A competition on similar lines was held in 1951 in New York when 1,409 players who had done a hole-in-one held a competition over several days at short holes on three New York courses. Each player was allowed a total of five shots, giving an aggregate of 7,045 shots. No player holed-in-one, and the nearest ball finished 3½ inches from the hole.

● A further illustration of the element of luck in holing-in-one is derived from an effort by Harry Gonder, an American professional, who in 1940 stood for 16 hours 25 minutes and hit 1,817 balls trying to do a 160 yard hole-in-one. He had two official witnesses and caddies to tee and retrieve the balls and count the strokes. His 1,756th shot struck the hole but stopped an inch from the hole. This was his nearest effort.

● From this and other similar information an estimate of the odds against holing-in-one at any particular hole within the range of one shot was made at somewhere between 1,500 and 2,000 to 1 by a proficient player. Subsequently, however, statistical analysis in America has come up with the following odds: a male professional or top amateur 3,708 to 1; a female professional or top amateur 4,648 to 1; an average golfer 42,952 to 1.

Hole-in-One First Recorded

● Earliest recorded hole-in-one was in 1868 at the Open Championship when Tom Morris (Young Tom) did the 145-yard 8th hole Prestwick in one stroke. This was the first of four Open Championships won successively by Young Tom.

● The first hole-in-one recorded with the 1.66 in ball was in 1972 by John G Salvesen, a member of the R&A Championship Committee. At the time this size of ball was only experimental. Salvesen used a 7-iron for his historical feat at the 11th hole on the Old Course, St Andrews.

Holing-in-One in Important Events

Since the day of the first known hole-in-one by Tom Morris Jr, at the 8th hole (145 yards) at Prestwick in the 1868 Open Championship, holes-in-one, even in championships, have become too numerous for each to be recorded. Only where other unusual or interesting circumstances prevailed are the instances shown here.

● All hole-in-one achievements are remarkable. Many are extraordinary. Among the more amazing was that of 2-handicap Leicestershire golfer Bob Taylor, a member of the Scraptoft Club. During the final practice day for the 1974 Eastern Counties Foursomes Championship on the Hunstanton Links, he holed his tee shot with a one-iron at the 188-yard 16th. The next day, in the first round of the competition, he repeated the feat, the only difference being that because of a change of wind he used a six-iron. When he stepped on to the 16th tee the following day his partner jokingly offered him odds of 1,000,000 to one against holing-in-one for a third successive time. Taylor again used his six-iron – and holed in one!

● 1878–Jamie Anderson, competing in the Open Championship at Prestwick, holed the 17th hole in one. Anderson was playing the next to last hole, and though it seemed then that he was winning easily, it turned out afterwards that if he had not taken this hole in one stroke he would very likely have lost. Anderson was just about to make his tee shot when Andy Stuart (winner of the first Irish Open Championship in 1892), who was acting as marker to Anderson, remarked he was standing outside the teeing ground, and that if he played the stroke from there he would be disqualified. Anderson picked up his ball and teed it in a proper place. Then he holed-in-one. He won the Championship by one stroke.

● On a Friday the 13th in 1990, Richard Allen holed-in-one at the 13th at the Barwon Heads Golf Club, Victoria, Australia, and then lost the hole. He was giving a handicap stroke to his opponent, brother-in-law Jason Ennels, who also holed-in-one.

● 1906–R Johnston, North Berwick, competing in the Open Championship, did the 14th hole at Muirfield in one. Johnston played with only one club throughout – an adjustable head club.

● 1959–The first hole-in-one in the US Women's Open Championship was recorded. It was by Patty Berg on the 7th hole (170 yards) at Churchill Valley CC, Pittsburgh.

● 1962–On 6th April, playing in the second round of the Schweppes Close Championship at Little Aston, H Middleton of Shandon Park, Belfast, holed his tee shot at the 159-yard 5th hole, winning a prize of £1,000. Ten minutes later, playing two matches ahead of Middleton, RA Jowle, son of the professional, Frank Jowle, holed his tee shot at the 179-yard 9th hole. As an amateur he was rewarded by the sponsors with a £30 voucher.

● 1963–By holing out in one stroke at the 18th hole (156 yards) at Moor Park on the first day of the Esso Golden round-robin tournament, HR Henning, South Africa, won the £10,000 prize offered for this feat.

● 1967–Tony Jacklin in winning the Masters tournament at St George's, Sandwich, did the 16th hole in one. His ace has an exceptional place in the records for it was seen by millions on TV, the ball in view in its flight till it went into the hole in his final round of 64.

● 1971–John Hudson, 25-year-old professional at Hendon, achieved a near miracle when he holed two consecutive holes-in-one in the Martini Tournament at Norwich. They were at the 11th and 12th holes (195 yards and 311 yards respectively) in the second round.

● 1971–In the Open Championship at Birkdale, Lionel Platts holed-in-one at the 212-yard 4th hole in the second round. This was the first instance of an Open Championship hole-in-one being recorded by television. It was incidentally Platts' seventh ace of his career.

● There have been four holes-in-one in the Ryder Cup: by Peter Butler at Muirfield in 1973, Nick Faldo at the Belfry in 1993, and by Costantino Rocca and Howard Clark at Oak Hill in 1995.

● 1973–In the 1973 Open Championship at Troon, two holes-in-one were recorded, both at the 8th hole, known as the Postage Stamp, in the first round. They were achieved by Gene Sarazen and amateur David Russell, who were by coincidence respectively the oldest and youngest competitors.

● Mrs Argea Tissies, whose husband Hermann took 15 at Royal Troon's Postage Stamp 8th hole in the 1950 Open, scored a hole-in-one at the 2nd hole at Punta Ala in the second round of the Italian Ladies' Senior Open of 1978. Exactly five years later on the same date, at the same time of day, in the same round of the same tournament at the same hole, she did it again with the same club.

● In less than two hours play in the second round of the 1989 US Open at Oak Hill Country Club, Rochester, New York, four competitors – Doug Weaver, Mark Wiebe, Jerry Pate and Nick Price – each holed the 167-yard 6th hole in one. The odds against four professionals achieving such a record in a field of 156 are reckoned at 332,000 to 1.

● On 20th May, 1998, British golf journalist Derek Lawrenson, an eight-handicapper, won a Lamborghini Diablo car, valued at over £180,000, by holing his three-iron tee shot to the 175-yard 15th hole at Mill Ride, Berkshire. He was taking part in a charity day and was partnering England football stars Paul Ince and Steve McManaman.

● David Toms took the lead in the 2001 USPGA Championship at Atlanta Athletic Club with a hole-in-one at the 15th hole in the third round and went on to win. Nick Faldo (4th hole) and Scott Hoch (17th hole) also had holes-in-one during the event.

Holing-in-One – Longest Holes

● Bob Mitera, as a 21-year-old American student, standing 5 feet 6 inches and weighing under 12

stones, claimed the world record for the longest hole-in-one. Playing over the appropriately named Miracle Hill course at Omaha, on 7th October, 1965, Bob holed his drive at the 10th hole, 447 yards long. The ground sloped sharply downhill.

● Two longer holes-in-one have been achieved, but because they were at dog-leg holes they are not generally accepted as being the longest holes-in-one. They were 496 yards (17th hole, Teign Valley) by Shaun Lynch in July 1995 and 480 yards (5th hole, Hope CC, Arkansas) by L Bruce on 15th November, 1962.

● In March, 1961, Lou Kretlow holed his tee shot at the 427-yard 16th hole at Lake Hefner course, Oklahoma City, USA.

● The longest known hole-in-one in Great Britain was the 393-yard 7th hole at West Lancashire GC, where in 1972 the assistant professional Peter Parkinson holed his tee shot.

● Other long holes-in-one recorded in Great Britain have been 380 yards (5th hole at Tankersley Park) by David Hulley in 1961; 380 yards (12th hole at White Webbs) by Danny Dunne on 30th July, 1976; 370 yards (17th hole at Chilwell Manor, distance from the forward tee) by Ray Newton in 1977; 365 yards (10th hole at Harewood Downs) by K Saunders in 1965; 365 yards (7th hole at Catterick Garrison GC) by Leslie Bruckner on 18th July, 1980.

● The longest-recorded hole-in-one by a woman was that accomplished in September, 1949 by Marie Robie – the 393-yard hole at Furnace Brook course, Wollaston, Mass, USA.

Holing-in-One – Greatest Number by One Person

59–Amateur Norman Manley of Long Beach, California.

50–Mancil Davis, professional at the Trophy Club, Forth Worth, Texas.

31–British professional CT le Chevalier who died in 1973.

22–British amateur, Jim Hay of Kirkintilloch GC.

At One Hole

13–Joe Lucius at 15th hole of Mohawk, Ohio.

5–Left-hander, the late Fred Francis at 7th (now 16th) hole of Cardigan GC.

Holing-in-One – Greatest Frequency

● The greatest number of holes-in-one in a calendar year is 11, by JO Boydstone of California in 1962.

● John Putt of Frilford Heath GC had six holes-in-one in 1970, followed by three in 1971.

● Douglas Porteous, of Ruchill GC, Glasgow, achieved seven holes-in-one in the space of eight months. Four of them were scored in a five-day period from 26th to 30th September, 1974, in three consecutive rounds of golf. The first two were achieved at Ruchill GC in one round, the third there two days later, and the fourth at Clydebank and District GC after another two days. The following May, Porteous had three holes-in-one, the first at Linn Park GC incredibly followed by two more in the one round at Clober GC.

● Mrs Kathleen Hetherington of West Essex has holed-in-one five times, four being at the 15th hole at West Essex. Four of her five aces were within seven months in 1966.

● Mrs Dorothy Hill of Dumfries and Galloway GC holed-in-one three times in 11 days in 1977.

● James C Reid of Brodick, aged 59 and 8 handicap in 1987, achieved 14 holes-in-one, all but one on Isle of Arran courses. His success was in spite of severe physical handicaps of a stiff left knee, a damaged right ankle, two discs removed from his back and a hip replacement.

● Jean Nield, a member at Chorlton-cum-Hardy and Bramall Park, has had ten holes-in-one and her husband Nrian, who plays at Bramall Park, has had four – a husband and wife total of 14.

Holing Successive Holes-in-One

● Successive holes-in-one are rare; successive par 4 holes-in-one may be classed as near miracles. NL Manley performed the most incredible feat in September, 1964, at Del Valle Country Club, Saugus, California, USA. The par 4 7th (330 yards) and 8th (290 yards) are both slightly downhill, dog-leg holes. Manley had aces at both, en route to a course record of 61 (par 71).

● The first recorded example in Britain of a player holing-in-one stroke at each of two successive holes was achieved on 6th February, 1964, at the Walmer and Kingsdown course, Kent. The young assistant professional at that club, Roger Game (aged 17) holed out with a 4-wood at the 244-yard 7th hole, and repeated the feat at the 256-yard 8th hole, using a 5-iron.

● The first occasion of holing-in-one at consecutive holes in a major professional event occurred when John Hudson, 25-year-old professional at Hendon, holed-in-one at the 11th and 12th holes at Norwich during the second round of the 1971 Martini tournament. Hudson used a 4-iron at the 195-yard 11th and a driver at the 311-yard downhill 12th hole.

● Assistant professional Tom Doty (23 years), playing in a friendly match on a course near Chicago in October, 1971, had a remarkable four-hole score which included two consecutive holes-in-one, sandwiched either side by an albatross and an eagle: 4th hole (500 yards)-2; 5th hole (360 yards dog-leg)-1; 6th hole (175 yards)-1; 7th hole (375 yards)-2. Thus he was 10 under par for four consecutive holes.

● At the Standard Life Loch Lomond tournament on the European Tour in July 2000 Jarmo Sandelin holed-in-one at the 17th with the final

shot there in the third round and fellow Swede Mathias Gronberg holed-in-one with the first shot there in the last round. A prize of $100,000 was only on offer in the last round.

Holing-in-One Twice (or More) in the Same Round by the Same Person

What might be thought to be a very rare feat indeed – that of holing-in-one twice in the same round – has in fact happened on many occasions as the following instances show. It is, nevertheless, compared to the number of golfers in the world, still something of an outstanding achievement. The first known occasion was in 1907 when J Ireland playing in a three-ball match at Worlington holed the 5th and 18th holes in one stroke and two years later in 1909 HC Josecelyne holed the 3rd (175 yards) and the 14th (115 yards) at Acton on 24th November.

● The first mention of two holes-in-one in a round by a woman was followed later by a similar feat by another lady at the same club. On 19th May, 1942, Mrs W Driver, of Balgowlah Golf Club, New South Wales, holed out in one at the 3rd and 8th holes in the same round, while on 29th July, 1948, Mrs F Burke at the same club holed out in one at the second and eighth holes.

● The Rev Harold Snider, aged 75, scored his first hole-in-one on 9th June, 1976 at the 8th hole of the Ironwood course, near Phoenix. By the end of his round he had scored three holes-in-one, the other two being at the 13th (110 yards) and 14th (135 yards). Ironwood is a par-3 course, giving more opportunity of scoring holes-in-one, but, nevertheless, three holes-in-one in one round on any type of course is an outstanding achievement.

● When the Hawarden course in North Wales comprised only nine holes, Frank Mills in 1994 had two holes-in-one at the same hole in the same round. Each time, he hit a seven iron to the 134-yard 3rd and 12th.

● The youngest player to achieve two holes-in-one in the same round is thought to be Christopher Anthony Jones on 14 September, 1994. At the age of 14 years and 11 months he holed-in-one at the Sand Moor, Leeds, 137-yard 10th hole and then an at the 156-yard 17th.

● The youngest woman to have performed the feat was a 17-year-old, Marjorie Merchant, playing at the Lomas Athletic GC, Argentina, at the 4th (170 yards) and 8th (130 yards) holes.

● Tony Hannam, left-handed, handicap 16 and age 71, followed a hole-in-one at the 142 yards 4th of the Bude and North Cornwall Golf Club course with another at the 143-yard 10th on Friday, 18th September, 1992.

● Brothers Eric and John Wilkinson were playing together at the Ravensworth Golf Club on Tyneside in 2001 and both holed-in-one at the 148 yards eighth. Eric (46) played first and then John

to the hidden green but there is no doubting this unusual double ace. The club's vice-captain Dave Johnstone saw both balls go in! Postman Eric plays off 9. John, a county planner, has a handicap of 20. Next time they played the hole both missed the green.

Holes-in-One on the Same Day

● In July 1987, at the Skerries Club, Co Dublin, Rank Xerox sponsored two tournaments, a men's 18-hole four-ball with 134 pairs competing and a 9-hole mixed foursomes with 33 pairs. During the day each of the four par-3 holes on the course were holed-in-one: the 2nd by Noel Bollard, the 5th by Bart Reynolds, the 12th by Jackie Carr and the 15th by Gerry Ellis.
● Wendy Russell holed-in-one at the consecutive par threes in the first round of the British Senior Ladies' at Wrexham in 1989.
● Clifford Briggs, aged 65, holed-in-one at the 14th at Parkstone GC on the same day as his wife Gwen, 60, aced the 16th.
● In the final round of the 2000 Victor Chandler British Masters at Woburn Alastair Forsyth holed-in-one at the second. Playing partner Roger Chapman then holed-in-one at the eighth.

Two Holes-in-One at the Same Hole in the Same Game

● *First in World:* George Stewart and Fred Spellmeyer at the 18th hole, Forest Hills, New Jersey, USA in October 1919.
● *First in Great Britain:* Miss G Clutterbuck and Mrs HM Robinson at the 15th hole (120 yards), St Augustine GC, Ramsgate, on 8th May, 1925.
● *First in Denmark:* In a Club match in August 1987 at Himmerland, Steffan Jacobsen of Aalborg and Peter Forsberg of Himmerland halved the 15th hole in one shot, the first known occasion in Denmark.
● *First in Australia:* Dr & Mrs B Rankine, playing in a mixed 'Canadian foursome' event at the Osmond Club near Adelaide, South Australia in April 1987, holed-in-one in consecutive shots at the 2nd hole (162 metres); he from the men's tee with a 3-iron and his wife from the ladies' tee with a 1½ wood.
● Jack Ashton, aged 76, holed-in-one at the 8th hole of the West Kent Golf Club at Downe but only got a half. Opponent Ted Eagle, in receipt of shot, made a 2, net 1.

Holing-in-One – Youngest and Oldest players

● In January 1985 Otto Bucher of Switzerland holed-in-one at the age of 99 on La Manga's 130-yard 12th hole.

● Bob Hope had a hole-in-one at Palm Springs, California, at the age of 90.
● The youngest player ever to achieve a hole in one is now believed to be Matthew Draper, who was only five when he aced the 122-yard fourth hole at Cherwell Edge, Oxfordshire, in June 1997. He used a wood.
● Six-year-old Tommy Moore aced the 145-yard fourth hole at Woodbrier, West Virginia, in 1968. He had another at the same hole before his seventh birthday.
● Alex Evans, aged eight, holed-in-one with a 4-wood at the 136-yard 4th hole at Bromborough, Merseyside, in 1994.

Holing-in-One – Miscellaneous Incidents

● Chemistry student Jason Bohn, aged 19, of State College, Pennsylvania, supported a charity golf event at Tuscaloosa, Alabama, in 1992 when twelve competitors were invited to try to hole-in-one at the 135-yard second hole for a special prize covered by insurance. One attempt only was allowed. Bohn succeeded and was offered US$1m (paid at the rate of $5,000 a month for the next 20 years) at the cost of losing his amateur status. He took the money.
● The late Harry Vardon, who scored the greatest number of victories in the Open Championship, only once did a hole-in-one. That was in 1903 at Mundesley, Norfolk, where Vardon was convalescing from a long illness.
● In a guest day at Rochford Hundred, Essex, in 1994, there were holes-in-one at all the par threes. First Paul Cairns, of Langdon Hills, holed a 4-iron at the 205-yard 15th, next Paul Francis, a member of the home club, sank a 7-iron at the 156-yard seventh and finally Jim Crabb, of Three Rivers, holed a 9-iron at the 136-yard 11th.
● In April 1988, Mary Anderson, a biochemistry student at Trinity College, Dublin, holed-in-one at the 290-yard 6th hole at Island GC, Co Dublin.
● In April 1984 Joseph McCaffrey and his son, Gordon, each holed-in-one in the Spring Medal at the 164-yard 12th hole at Vale of Leven Club, Dunbartonshire.
● In 1977, 14-year-old Gillian Field after a series of lessons holed-in-one at the 10th hole at Moor Place GC in her first round of golf.
● When he holed-in-one at the second hole in a match against D Graham in the 1979 Suntory World Match Play at Wentworth, Japanese professional Isao Aoki won himself a Bovis home at Gleneagles worth, inclusive of furnishings, £55,000.
● On the morning after being elected captain for 1973 of the Norwich GC, JS Murray hit his first shot as captain straight into the hole at the 169-yard 1st hole.

● At Nuneaton GC in 1999 the men's captain and the ladies' captain both holed-in-one during their captaincies.

● Using the same club and ball, 11-handicap left-hander Christopher Smyth holed-in-one at the 2nd hole (170 yards) in two consecutive medal competitions at Headfort GC, Co Meath, in January, 1976.

● Playing over Rickmansworth course at Easter, 1960, Mrs AE (Paddy) Martin achieved a remarkable sequence of *aces*. On Good Friday she sank her tee shot at the 3rd hole (125 yards). The next day, using the same ball and the same 8-iron, at the same hole, she scored another *one*. And on the Monday (same ball, same club, same hole) she again holed out from the tee.

● At Barton-on-Sea in February 1989 Mrs Dorothy Huntley-Flindt, aged 91, holed-in-one at the par-3 13th. The following day Mr John Chape, a fellow member in his 80s, holed the par-3 5th in one.

● In 1995 Roy Marsland of Ratho Park, Edinburgh, had three holes in one in nine days: at Prestonfield's 5th, at Ratho Park's 3rd and at Sandilands' 2nd.

● Michael Monk, age 82, a member of Tandridge Golf Club, Surrey, waited until 1992 to record his first hole-in-one. It continued a run of rare successes for his family. In the previous 12 months, Mr Monk's daughter, Elizabeth, 52, daughter-in-law, Celia, 48, and grandson, Jeremy, 16, had all holed in one on the same course.

● Lou Holloway, a left-hander, recorded his second hole-in-one at the Mount Derby course in New Zealand 13 years after acing the same hole while playing right-handed.

● Ryan Procop, an American schoolboy, holed-in-one at a 168-yard par 3 at Glen Eagles GC, Ohio, with a putter. He confessed that he was so disgusted with himself after a 12 on the previous hole that he just grabbed his putter and hit from the tee.

● Ernie and Shirley Marsden, of Warwick Golf Club, are believed in 1993 to have equalled the record for holes-in-one by a married couple. Each has had three, as have another English couple, Mr and Mrs BE Simmonds.

● Russell Pugh, a 12-handicapper from Nottinghamshire, holed-in-one twice in three days at the 274-yard par-4 18th hole at Sidmouth in Devon in 1998. The hole has a blind tee shot.

Challenge Matches

One of the first recorded professional challenge matches was in 1843 when Allan Robertson beat Willie Dunn in a 20-round match at St Andrews over 360 holes by 2 rounds and 1 to play. Thereafter until about 1905 many matches are recorded, some for up to £200 a side – a considerable

sum for the time. The Morrises, the Dunns and the Parks were the main protagonists until Vardon, Braid and Taylor took over in the 1890s. Often matches were on a home-and-away basis over 72 holes or more, with many spectators; Vardon and Willie Park Jr attracted over 10,000 at North Berwick in 1899.

Between the wars Walter Hagen, Archie Compston, Henry Cotton and Bobby Locke all played several such matches. Compston surprisingly beat Hagen by 18 up and 17 to play at Moor Park in 1928; yet typically Hagen went on to win the Open the following week at Sandwich. Cotton played classic golf at Walton Heath in 1937 when he beat Densmore Shute for £500-a-side at Walton Heath by 6 and 5 over 72 holes.

Curious and Large Wagers
(See also bets recorded under **Cross-Country Matches** *and in* **Challenge Matches***)*

● In the Royal and Ancient Club minutes an entry on 3rd November, 1870 was made in the following terms:

> *Sir David Moncrieffe, Bart, of Moncrieffe, backs his life against the life of John Whyte-Melville, Esq, of Strathkinnes, for a new silver club as a present to the St Andrews Golf Club, the price of the club to be paid by the survivor and the arms of the parties to be engraved on the club, and the present bet inscribed on it. No balls to be attached to it. In testimony of which this bet is subscribed by the parties thereto.*

Thirteen years later, Mr Whyte-Melville, in a feeling and appropriate speech, expressed his deep regret at the lamented death of Sir Robert Moncrieffe, one of the most distinguished and zealous supporters of the club. Whyte-Melville, while lamenting the cause that led to it, had pleasure in fulfilling the duty imposed upon him by the bet, and accordingly delivered to the captain the silver putter. Whyte-Melville in 1883 was elected captain of the club a second time; he died in his eighty-sixth year in July, 1883, before he could take office and the captaincy remained vacant for a year. His portrait hangs in the Royal & Ancient clubhouse and is one of the finest and most distinguished pictures in the smoking room.

● In 1914 Francis Ouimet, who in the previous autumn had won the American Open Championship after a triangular tie with Harry Vardon and Ted Ray, came to Great Britain with Jerome D Travers, the holder of the American amateur title, to compete in the British Amateur Championship at Sandwich. An American syndicate took a bet of £30,000 to £10,000 that one or other of the two United States champions would be the winner. It only took two rounds to decide the bet against the Americans. Ouimet was beaten by a then quite unknown player, HS Tubbs, while Travers was defeated by Charles Palmer, who was 56 years of age at the time.

● 1907 John Ball for a wager undertook to go round Hoylake during a dense fog in under 90, in not more than two and a quarter hours and without losing a ball. Ball played with a black ball, went round in 81, and also beat the time.

● The late Ben Sayers, for a wager, played the 18 holes of the Burgess Society course scoring a four at every hole. Sayers was about to start against an American, when his opponent asked him what he could do the course in. *Fours* replied Sayers, meaning 72, or an average of 4s for the round. A bet was made, then the American added, *Remember a three or a five is not a four.* There were eight bogey 5s and two 3s on the Burgess course at the time Old Ben achieved his feat.

Feats of Endurance

Although golf is not a game where endurance, in the ordinary sense in which the term is employed in sport, is required, there are several instances of feats on the links which demanded great physical exertion.

● Four British golfers, Simon Gard, Nick Harley, Patrick Maxwell and his brother Alastair Maxwell, completed 14 rounds in one day at Iceland's Akureyri Golf Club, the most northern 18-hole course in the world, during June 1991 when there was 24-hour daylight. It was claimed a record and £10,000 was raised for charity.

● In 1971 during a 24-hour period from 6 pm on 27th November until 5.15 pm on 28th November, Ian Colston completed 401 holes over the 6,061 yards Bendigo course, Victoria, Australia. Colston was a top marathon athlete but was not a golfer. However prior to his golfing marathon he took some lessons and became adept with a 6-iron, the only club he used throughout the 401 holes. The only assistance Colston had was a team of harriers to carry his 6-iron and look for his ball, and a band of motor-cyclists who provided light during the night. This is, as far as is known, the greatest number of holes played in 24 hours on foot on a full-size course.

● In 1934 Col Bill Farnham played 376 holes in 24 hours 10 minutes at the Guildford Lake Course, Guildford, Connecticut, using only a mashie and a putter.

● To raise funds for extending the Skipton GC course from 12 to 18 holes, the club professional, 24-year-old Graham Webster, played 277 holes in the hours of daylight on Monday 20th June, 1977. Playing with nothing longer than a 5-iron he averaged 81 per 18-hole round. Included in his marathon was a hole-in-one.

● Michael Moore, a 7 handicap 26-year-old member of Okehampton GC, completed on foot 15 rounds 6 holes (276 holes) there on Sunday, 25th June, 1972, in the hours of daylight. He started at 4.15 am and stopped at 9.15 pm. The distance covered was estimated at 56 miles.

● On 21st June, 1976, 5-handicapper Sandy Small played 15 rounds (270 holes) over his home course Cosby GC, length 6,128 yards, to raise money for the Society of Physically Handicapped Children. Using only a 5-iron, 9-iron and putter, Small started at 4.10 am and completed his 270th hole at 10.39 pm with the aid of car headlights. His fastest round was his first (40 minutes) and slowest his last (82 minutes). His best round of 76 was achieved in the second round.

● During the weekend of 20th-21st June, 1970, Peter Chambers of Yorkshire completed over 14 rounds of golf over the Scarborough South Cliff course. In a non-stop marathon lasting just under 24 hours, Chambers played 257 holes in 1,168 strokes, an average of 84.4 strokes per round.

● Bruce Sutherland, on the Craiglockhart Links, Edinburgh, started at 8.15 pm on 21st June, 1927, and played almost continuously until 7.30 pm on 22nd June, 1927. During the night four caddies with acetylene lamps lit the way, and lost balls were reduced to a minimum. He completed fourteen rounds. Mr Sutherland, who was a physical culture teacher, never recovered from the physical strain and died a few years later.

● Sidney Gleave, motorcycle racer, and Ernest Smith, golf professional at Davyhulme Club, Manchester, on 12th June, 1939, played five rounds of golf in five different countries – Scotland, Ireland, Isle of Man, England and Wales. Smith had to play the five rounds under 80 in one day to win the £100 wager. They travelled by plane, and the following was their programme:

Start 3.40 a.m. at Prestwick St Nicholas (Scotland), finished 1 hour 35 minutes later on 70.

2nd Course – Bangor, Ireland. Started at 7.15 a.m. and took 1 hour 30 minutes to finish on 76.

3rd Course – Castletown, Isle of Man. Started 10.15 am, scored 76 in 1 hour 40 minutes.

4th Course – Blackpool, Stanley Park, England. Started at 1.30 pm and scored 72 in 1 hour 55 minutes.

5th Course – Hawarden, Wales, started at 6 pm and finished 2 hours 15 minutes later with a score of 72.

● On 19th June, 1995, Ian Botham, the former England cricketer, played four rounds of golf in Ireland, Wales, Scotland and England. His playing companions were Gary Price, the professional at Branston, and Tony Wright, owner of Craythorne, Burton-on-Trent, where the last 18 holes were completed. The other courses were St Margaret's, Anglesey and Dumfries & Galloway. The first round began at 4.30 am and the last was completed at 8.30 pm.

● On Wednesday, 3rd July, 1974, ES Wilson, Whitehead, Co Antrim and Dr GW Donaldson, Newry, Co Down, played a nine-hole match in each of seven countries in the one day. The first 9 holes was at La Moye (Channel Islands) followed by Hawarden (Wales), Chester (England), Turnberry (Scotland), Castletown (Isle of Man), Dundalk (Eire) and Warrenpoint (N Ireland). They started their first round at 4.25 am and their last round at 9.25 pm. Wilson piloted his own plane throughout.

● In June 1986 to raise money for the upkeep of his medieval church, the Rector of Mark with Allerton, Somerset, the Rev Michael Pavey, played a sponsored 18 holes on 18 different courses in the Bath & Wells Diocese. With his partner, the well-known broadcaster on music, Antony Hopkins, they played the 1st at Minehead at 5.55 am and finished playing the 18th at Burnham and Berrow at 6.05 pm. They covered 240 miles in the 'round' including the distances to reach the correct tee for the 'next' hole on each course. Par for the 'round' was 70. Together the pair raised £10,500 for the church.

● To raise funds for the Marlborough Club's centenary year (1988), Laurence Ross, the Club professional, in June 1987, played eight rounds in 12 hours. Against a par of 72, he completed the 576 holes in 3 under par, playing from back tees and walking all the way.

● As part of the 1992 Centenary Celebrations of the Royal Cinque Ports Golf Club at Deal, Kent, and to support charity, a six-handicap member, John Brazell, played all 37 royal courses in Britain and Ireland in 17 days. He won 22 matches, halved three, lost 12; hit 2,834 shots for an average score of 76.6; lost 11 balls and made 62 birdies. The aim was to raise £30,000 for Leukaemia Research and the Spastics Society.

● To raise more than £500 for the Guide Dogs for the Blind charity in the summer of 1992, Mrs Cheryle Power, a member of the Langley Park Golf Club, Beckenham, Kent, played 100 holes in a day – starting at 5 am and finishing at 8.45 pm.

● David Steele, a former European Tour player, completed 17½ rounds, 315 holes, between 6 am and 9.45 pm in 1993 at the San Roque club near Gibraltar in a total of 1,291 shots. Steele was assisted by a caddie cart and raised £15,000 for charity.

Fastest Rounds

● Dick Kimbrough, 41, completed a round on foot on 8th August, 1972, at North Platte CC, Nebraska (6,068 yards) in 30 minutes 10 seconds. He carried only a 3-iron.

● At Mowbray Course, Cape Town, November 1931, Len Richardson, who had represented South Africa in the Olympic Games, played a round which measured 6,248 yards in 31 minutes 22 seconds.

● The women's all-time record for the fastest round played on a course of at least 5,600 yards is held by Sue Ledger, 20, who completed the East Berks course in 38 minutes 8 seconds, beating the previous record by 17 minutes.

● In April, 1934, after attending a wedding in Bournemouth, Hants, Captain Gerald Moxom hurried to his club, West Hill in Surrey, to play in the captain's prize competition. With daylight fading and still dressed in his morning suit, he went round in 65 minutes and won the competition with a net 71 into the bargain.

● On 14th June, 1922, Jock Hutchison and Joe Kirkwood (Australia) played round the Old Course at St Andrews in 1 hour 20 minutes. Hutchison, out in 37, led by three holes at the ninth and won by 4 and 3.

● Fastest rounds can also take another form – the time taken for a ball to be propelled round 18 holes. The fastest known round of this type is 8 minutes 53.8 seconds on 25th August, 1979 by 42 members at Ridgemount CC Rochester, New York, a course measuring 6,161 yards. The Rules of Golf were observed but a ball was available on each tee; to be driven off the instant the ball had been holed at the preceding hole.

● The fastest round with the same ball took place in January 1992 at the Paradise Golf Club, Arizona. It took only 11 minutes 24 seconds; 91 golfers being positioned around the course ready to hit the ball as soon as it came to rest and then throwing the ball from green to tee.

● In 1992 John Daly and Mark Calcavecchia were both fined by the USPGA Tour for playing the final round of the Players' Championship in Florida in 123 minutes. Daly scored 80, Calcavecchia 81.

Curious Scoring

● CW Allen of Leek Golf Club chipped-in four times in a round in which he was partnered by K Brint against G Davies and R Hollins. The shortest chip was a yard, the longest 20 yards.

● Tony Blackwell, playing off a handicap of four, broke the course record at Bull Bay, Anglesey, by four strokes when he had a gross 60 (net 56) in winning the club's town trophy in 1996. The course measured 6,217 yards.

● In the third round of the 1994 Volvo PGA Championship at Wentworth, Des Smyth, of Ireland, made birdie twos at each of the four short holes, the 2nd, 5th, 10th and 14th. He also had a two at the second hole in the fourth round.

● Also at Wentworth, in the 1994 World Match Play Championship, Seve Ballesteros had seven successive twos at the short holes – and still lost his quarter-final against Ernie Els.

● RH Corbett, playing in the semi-final of the Tangye Cup at Mullion in 1916, did a score of 27. The remarkable part of Corbett's score was that it was made up of nine successive 3s, bogey being 5, 3, 4, 4, 5, 3, 4, 4, 3.

● At Little Chalfont in June 1985 Adrian Donkersley played six successive holes in 6, 5, 4,

3, 2, 1 from the 9th to the 14th holes against a par of 4, 4, 3, 4, 3, 3.

● On 2nd September, 1920, playing over Torphin, near Edinburgh, William Ingle did the first five holes in 1, 2, 3, 4, 5.

● In the summer of 1970, Keith McMillan, on holiday at Cullen, had a remarkable series of 1, 2, 3, 4, 5 at the 11th to 15th holes.

● Marc Osborne was only 14 years of age when he equalled the Betchworth Park amateur course record with a 66 in July, 1993. He was playing in the Mortimer Cup, a 36-hole medal competition, and had at the time a handicap of 6.8.

● Playing at Addington Palace, July, 1934, Ronald Jones, a member of Hendon Club, holed five consecutive holes in 5, 4, 3, 2, 1.

● Harry Dunderdale of Lincoln GC scored 5, 4, 3, 2, 1 in five consecutive holes during the first round of his club championship in 1978. The hole-in-one was the 7th, measuring 294 yards.

● At the Open Amateur Tournament of the Royal Ashdown Forest in 1936 Bobby Locke in his morning round had a score of 72, accomplishing every hole in 4.

● George Stewart of Cupar had a four at every hole over the Queen's course at Gleneagles despite forgetting to change into his golf shoes and therefore still wearing his street shoes.

● Henry Cotton told of one of the most extraordinary scoring feats ever. With some other professionals he was at Sestrieres in the 30s for the Italian Open Championship and Joe Ezar, a colourful character in those days on both sides of the Atlantic, accepted a wager from a club official – 1,000 lira for a 66 to break the course record; 2,000 for a 65; and 4,000 for a 64. *I'll do 64*, said Ezar, and proceeded to jot down the hole-by-hole score figures he would do next day for that total. With the exception of the ninth and tenth holes where his predicted score was 3, 4 and the actual score was 4, 3, he accomplished this amazing feat exactly as nominated.

● Nick Faldo scored par figures at all 18 holes in the final round of the 1987 Open Championship at Muirfield to win the title.

● During the Colts Championship at Knowle Golf Club, Bristol, Chris Newman (Cotswold Hills) scored eight consecutive 3s with birdies at four of the holes.

● At the Toft Hotel Golf Club captain's day event L Heffernan had an ace, D Patrick a 2, R Barnett a 3 and D Heffernan a 4 at the 240 yard par-4 ninth.

● In the European Club Championship played at the Parco de Medici Club in Rome in 1998, Belgian Dimitri van Hauwaert from Royal Antwerp had an albatross 2, Norwegian Marius Bjornstad from Oslo an eagle 3 and Scotsman Andrew Hogg from Turriff a birdie 4 at the 486 metre par-5 eighth hole.

High Scores

● In the qualifying competition at Formby for the 1976 Open Championship, Maurice Flitcroft, a 46-year-old crane driver from Barrow-in-Furness, took 121 strokes for the first round and then withdrew saying, *I have no chance of qualifying*. Flitcroft entered as a professional but had never before played 18 holes. He had taken the game up 18 months previously but, as he was not a member of a club, had been limited to practising on a local beach. His round was made up thus: 7, 5, 6, 6, 6, 6, 12, 6, 7-61; 11, 5, 6, 8, 4, 9, 5, 7, 5-60, total 121. After his round Flitcroft said, 'I've made a lot of progress in the last few months and I'm sorry I did not do better. I was trying too hard at the beginning but began to put things together at the end of the round.' R & A officials, who were not amused by the bogus professional's efforts, refunded the £30 entry money to Flitcroft's two fellow-competitors. Flitcroft has since tried to qualify for the Open under assumed names: Gerard Hoppy from Switzerland and Beau Jolley (as in the wine)!

● Playing in the qualifying rounds of the 1965 Open Championship at Southport, an American self-styled professional entrant from Milwaukee, Walter Danecki, achieved the inglorious feat of scoring a total of 221 strokes for 36 holes, 81 over par. His first round over the Hillside course was 108, followed by a second round of 113. Walter, who afterwards admitted he felt *a little discouraged and sad*, declared that he entered because he was *after the money*.

● The highest individual scoring ever known in the rounds connected with the Open Championship occurred at Muirfield, 1935, when a Scottish professional started 7, 10, 5, 10, and took 65 to reach the 9th hole. Another 10 came at the 11th and the player decided to retire at the 12th hole. There he was in a bunker, and after playing four shots he had not regained the fairway.

● In 1883 in the Open Championship at Musselburgh, Willie Fernie, the winner, had a 10, the only time double figures appeared on the card of the Open Champion of the year. Fernie won after a tie with Bob Ferguson, and his score for the last hole in the tie was 2. He holed from just off the green to win by one stroke.

● In the first Open Championship at Prestwick in 1860 a competitor took 21, the highest score for one hole ever recorded in this event. The record is preserved in the archives of the Prestwick Golf Club, where the championship was founded.

● In the first round of the 1980 US Masters, Tom Weiskopf hit his ball into the water hazard in front of the par-3 12th hole five times and scored 13 for the hole.

● In the French Open at St Cloud, in 1968, Brian Barnes took 15 for the short 8th hole in the second round. After missing putts at which he hurriedly snatched while the ball was moving he penalised himself further by standing astride the line of a putt. The amazing result was that he actually took 12 strokes from about three feet from the hole. The highest scores on the European Tour were also recorded in the French Open. Philippe Porquier had a 20 at La Baule in 1978 and Ian Woosnam a 16 at La Boulie in 1986.

● US professional Dave Hill 6-putted the fifth green at Oakmont in the 1962 US Open Championship.

● Many high scores have been made at the Road Hole at St Andrews. Davie Ayton, on one occasion, was coming in a certain winner of the Open Championship when he got on the road and took 11. In 1921, at the Open Championship, one professional took 13. In 1923, competing for the Autumn Medal of the Royal & Ancient, JB Anderson required a five and a four to win the second award, but he took 13 at the Road Hole. Anderson was close to the green in two, was twice in the bunkers in the face of the green, and once on the road. In 1935, RH Oppenheimer tied for the Royal Medal (the first award) in the Autumn Meeting of the Royal & Ancient. On the play-off he was one stroke behind Captain Aitken when they stood on the 17th tee. Oppenheimer drove three balls out of bounds and eventually took 11 to the Road Hole.

● British professional Mark James scored 111 in the second round of the 1978 Italian Open. He played the closing holes with only his right hand due to an injury to his left hand.

● In the 1927 Shawnee Open, Tommy Armour took 23 strokes to the 17th hole. Armour had won the American Open Championship a week earlier. In an effort to play the hole in a particular way, Armour hooked ball after ball out of bounds and finished with a 21 on the card. There was some doubt about the accuracy of this figure and on reaching the clubhouse Armour stated that it should be 23. This is the highest score by a professional in a tournament.

Freak Matches

● In 1912, the late Harry Dearth, an eminent vocalist, attired in a complete suit of heavy armour, played a match at Bushey Hall. He was beaten 2 and 1.

● In 1914, at the start of the First World War, JN Farrar, a native of Hoylake, was stationed at Royston, Herts. A bet was made of 10-1 that he would not go round Royston under 100 strokes, equipped in full infantry marching order, water bottle, full field kit and haversack. Farrar went round in 94. At the camp were several golfers, including professionals, who tried the same feat but failed.

● Captain Pennington took part in a match *from the air* against AJ Young, the professional at Sonning. Captain Pennington, with 80 golf balls in the locker of his machine, had to find the Sonning greens by dropping the balls as he circled over the course. The balls were covered in white cloth to ensure that they did not bounce once they struck the ground. The airman completed the course in 40 minutes, taking 29 *strokes*, while Young occupied two hours for his round of 68. Captain Pennington was eventually killed in an air crash in 1933.

● In April 1924, at Littlehampton, Harry Rowntree, an amateur golfer, played the better ball of Edward Ray and George Duncan, receiving an allowance of 150 yards to use as he required during the round. Rowntree won by 6 and 5 and had used only 50 yards 2 feet of his handicap. At one hole Duncan had a two – Rowntree, who was 25 yards from the hole, took this distance from his handicap and won the hole in one. Ray (died 1945) afterwards declared that, conceded a handicap of one yard per round, he could win every championship in the world. And he might, when reckoning is taken of the number of times a putt just stops an inch or two or how much difference to a shot three inches will make for the lie of the ball, either in a bunker or on the fairway. Many single matches on the same system have been played. An 18 handicap player opposed to a scratch player should make a close match with an allowance of 50 yards.

● The first known instance of a golf match by telephone occurred in 1957, when the Cotswold Hills Golf Club, Cheltenham, England, won a golf tournament against the Cheltenham Golf Club, Melbourne, Australia, by six strokes. A large crowd assembled at the English club to wait for the 12,000 miles telephone call from Australia. The match had been played at the suggestion of a former member of the Cotswold Hills Club, Harry Davies, and was open to every member of the two clubs. The result of the match was decided on the aggregate of the eight best scores on each side and the English club won by 564 strokes to 570.

Golf Matches Against Other Sports

● HH Hilton and Percy Ashworth, many times racket champion, contested a driving match, the former driving a golf ball with a driver, and the latter a racket ball with a racket. Best distances: Against breeze – Golfer 182 yards; Racket player 125 yards. Down wind – Golfer 230 yards; Racket player 140 yards. Afterwards Ashworth hit a golf ball with the racket ball, but was still a long way behind the ball driven by Hilton.

● In 1913, at Wellington, Shropshire, a match between a golfer and a fisherman casting a 2½ oz weight was played. The golfer, Rupert May, took 87; the fisherman JJD Mackinlay, in difficulty because of his short casts, 102. His longest cast, 105 yards, was within 12 yards of the world record at the time, held by French angler, Decautelle. When within a rod's length of a hole he ran the weight to the rod end and dropped into the hole. Five times he broke his line, and was allowed another shot without penalty.

● In December, 1913, FMA Webster, of the London Athletic Club, and Dora Roberts, with javelins, played a match with the late Harry Vardon and Mrs Gordon Robertson, who used the regulation clubs and golf balls. The golfers conceded two-thirds in the matter of distance, and they won by 5 up and 4 to play in a contest of 18 holes. The javelin throwers had a mark of two feet square in which to *hole out* while the golfers had to get their ball into the ordinary golf hole. Mr Webster's best throw was one of 160 feet.

● Several matches have taken place between a golfer on the one side and an archer on the other. The wielder of the bow and arrow has nearly always proved the victor. In 1953 at Kirkhill Golf Course, Lanarkshire, five archers beat six golfers by two games to one. There were two special rules for the match; when an archer's arrow landed six feet from the hole or the golfer's ball three feet from the hole, they were counted as holed. When the arrows landed in bunkers or in the rough, archers lifted their arrow and added a stroke. The sixth archer in this match called off and one archer shot two arrows from each of the 18 tees.

● In 1954, at the Southbroom Club, South Africa, a match over 9 holes was played between an archer and a fisherman against two golfers. The participants were all champions of their own sphere and consisted of Vernon Adams (archer), Dennis Burd (fisherman), Jeanette Wahl (champion of Southbroom and Port Shepstone), and Ron Burd (professional at Southbroom). The conditions were that the archer had holed out when his arrows struck a small leather bag placed on the green beside the hole and in the event of his placing his approach shot within a bow's length of the pin he was deemed to have 1-putted. The fisherman, to achieve a 1-putt, had to land his sinker within a rod's length of the pin. The two golfers were ahead for brief spells, but it was the opposition who led at the deciding 9th hole where *Robin Hood* played a perfect approach for a birdie.

● An *Across England* combined match was begun on 11th October, 1965, by four golfers and two archers from Crowborough Beacon Golf Club, Sussex, accompanied by *Penny*, a white Alsatian dog, whose duty it was to find lost balls. They teed off from Carlisle Castle via Hadrian's Wall, the Pennine Way, finally holing out in the 18th hole at Newcastle United GC in 612 teed shots. Casualties included 110 lost golf balls and 19 lost or broken arrows. The match took 5½ days, and the distance travelled was about 60 miles. The golfers were Miss P Ward, K Meaney, K Ashdown and CA Macey; the archers were WH Hulme and T Scott. The first arrow was fired from the battlements of Carlisle Castle, a distance of nearly 300 yards, by Cumberland Champion R Willis, who also fired the second arrow right across the River Eden. R Clough, president of Newcastle United GC, holed the last two putts. The match was in aid of *Guide Dogs for the Blind* and *Friends of Crowborough Hospital*.

Cross-country Matches

● Taking 1 year, 114 days, Floyd Rood golfed his way from coast to coast across the United States. He took 114,737 shots including 3,511 penalty shots for the 3,397 mile course.

● Two Californian teenagers, Bob Aube (17) and Phil Marrone (18) went on a golfing safari in 1974 from San Francisco to Los Angeles, a trip of over 500 miles lasting 16 days. The first six days they played alongside motorways. Over 1,000 balls were used.

● In 1830, the Gold Medal winner of the Royal & Ancient backed himself for 10 sovereigns to drive from the 1st hole at St Andrews to the toll bar at Cupar, distance nine miles, in 200 teed shots. He won easily.

● In 1848, two Edinburgh golfers played a match from Bruntsfield Links to the top of Arthur's Seat – an eminence overlooking the Scottish capital, 822 feet above sea level.

● On a winter's day in 1898, Freddie Tait backed himself to play a gutta ball in 40 teed shots from Royal St George's Clubhouse, Sandwich, to the Cinque Ports Club, Deal. He was to hole out by hitting any part of the Deal Clubhouse. The distance as the crow flies was three miles. The redoubtable Tait holed out with his 32nd shot, so effectively that the ball went through a window.

● In 1900 three members of the Hackensack (NJ) Club played a game of four-and-a-half hours over an extemporised course six miles long, which stretched from Hackensack to Paterson. Despite rain, cornfields, and wide streams, the three golfers – JW Hauleebeek, Dr ER Pfaare, and Eugene Crassons – completed the round, the first and the last named taking 305 strokes each, and Dr Pfaare 327 strokes. The players used only two clubs, the mashie and the cleek.

● On 3rd December, 1920, P Rupert Phillips and W Raymond Thomas teed up on the first tee of the Radyr Golf Club and played to the last hole at Southerndown. The distance as the crow flies was 15½ miles, but circumventing swamps, woods, and plough, they covered, approximately, 20 miles. The wager was that they would not do the hole in 1,000 strokes, but they holed out at their 608th stroke two days later. They carried large ordnance maps.

● On 12th March, 1921, A Stanley Turner, Macclesfield, played from his house to the Cat and Fiddle Inn, five miles distance, in 64 strokes. The route was broken and hilly with a rise of nearly 1,000 feet. Turner was allowed to tee up within two club lengths after each shot and the wagering was 6-4 against his doing the distance in 170 strokes.

● In 1919, a golfer drove a ball from Piccadilly Circus and, proceeding via the Strand, Fleet Street and Ludgate Hill, *holed out* at the Royal Exchange, London. The player drove off at 8 am on a Sunday, a time when the usually thronged thoroughfares were deserted.

● On 23rd April, 1939, Richard Sutton, a London stockbroker, played from Tower Bridge, London, to White's Club, St James's Street, in 142 strokes. The bet was he would not do *the course* in under 200 shots. Sutton used a putter, crossed the Thames at Southwark Bridge, and hit the ball short distances to keep out of trouble.

● Golfers produced the most original event in Ireland's three-week national festival of An Tostal, in 1953 – a cross-country competition with an advertised £1,000,000 for the man who could hole out in one. The 150 golfers drove off from the first tee at Kildare Club to hole out eventually on the 18th green, five miles away, on the nearby Curragh course, a distance of 8,800 yards. The unusual hazards to be negotiated included the main Dublin-Cork railway line and highway, the Curragh Racecourse, hoofprints left by Irish thoroughbred racehorses out exercising on the plains from nearby stables, army tank tracks and about 150 telephone lines. The Golden Ball Trophy, which is played for annually – a standard size golf ball in gold, mounted on a black marble pillar beside the silver figure of a golfer on a green marble base, designed by Captain Maurice Cogan, Army GHQ, Dublin – was for the best gross. And it went to one of the longest hitters in international golf – Amateur Champion, Irish internationalist and British Walker Cup player Joe Carr, with the remarkable score of 52.

● In 1961, as a University Charities Week stunt, four Aberdeen University students set out to golf their way up Ben Nevis (4,406 feet). About half-way up, after losing 63 balls and expending 659 strokes, the quartet conceded victory to Britain's highest mountain.

● Among several cross-country golfing exploits, one of the most arduous was faced by Iain Williamson and Tony Kent, who teed off from Cained Point on the summit of Fairfield in the Lake District. With the hole cut in the lawn of the Bishop of Carlisle's home at Rydal Park, it measured 7,200 yards and passed through the summits of Great Rigg Mann, Heron Pike and Nab Scar, descending altogether 1,900 feet. Eight balls were lost and the two golfers holed out in a combined total of 303 strokes.

Long-lived Golfers

● James Priddy, aged 80, played in the Seniors' Open at his home club, Weston-super-Mare, Avon, on 27th June, 1990, and scored a gross 70 to beat his age by ten shots.

● The oldest golfer who ever lived is believed to have been Arthur Thompson of British Columbia, Canada. He equalled his age when 103 at Uplands GC, a course of over 6,000 yards. He died two years later.

● Nathaniel Vickers celebrated his 103rd birthday on Sunday, 9th October, 1949, and died the following day. He was the oldest member of the United States Senior Golf Association and until 1942 he competed regularly in their events and won many trophies in the various age divisions. When 100 years old, he apologised for being able to play only nine holes a day. Vickers predicted he would live until 103 and he died a few hours after he had celebrated his birthday.

● American George Miller, who died in 1979 aged 102, played regularly when 100 years old.

● In 1999 94-year-old Mr W Seneviratne, a retired schoolmaster who lived and worked in Malaysia, was still practising every day and regularly competing in medal competitions at the Royal Colombo Golf Club which was founded in 1879.

● Phyllis Tidmarsh, aged 90, won a Stableford competition at Saltford Golf Club, near Bath, when she returned 42 points. Her handicap was cut from 28 to 27.

● George Swanwick, a member of Wallasey, celebrated his 90th birthday with a lunch at the club on 1st April, 1971. He played golf several times a week, carrying his own clubs, and had holed-in-one at the ages of 75 and 85. His ambition was to complete the sequence aged 95 . . . but he died in 1973 aged 92.

● The 10th Earl of Wemyss played a round on his 92nd birthday, in 1910, at Craigielaw. At the age of 87 the Earl was partnered by Harry Vardon in a match at Kilspindie, the golf course on his East Lothian estate at Gosford. After playing his ball the venerable earl mounted a pony and rode to the next shot. He died on 30th June, 1914.

● FL Callender, aged 78, in September 1932, played nine consecutive rounds in the Jubilee Vase, St Andrews. He was defeated in the ninth, the final round, by 4 and 2. Callender's handicap was 12. This is the best known achievement of a septuagenarian in golf.

● George Evans shot a remarkable one over par 71 at Brockenhurst Manor – remarkable because Mr Evans was 87 at the time. Playing with him that day was Hampshire, Isle of Wight and Channel Islands President John Nettell and former Ferndown pro Doug Sewell. 'It's good to shoot a score under your age, but when its 16 shots better that must be a record,' said Mr Nettell. Mr Evans qualified for four opens while professional at West Hill, Surrey.

● Bernard Matthews, aged 82, of Banstead Downs Club, handicap 6, holed the course in 72 gross in August 1988. A week later he holed it in 70, twelve shots below his age. He came back in

31, finishing 4, 3, 3, 2, 3, against a par of 5, 4, 3, 3, 4. Mr Matthews's eclectic score at his Club is 37, or one over 2's.

Playing in the Dark

On numerous occasions it has been necessary to hold lamps, lighted candles, or torches at holes in order that players might finish a competition. Large entries, slow play, early darkness and an eclipse of the sun have all been causes of playing in darkness.

● Since 1972, the Whitburn Golf Club at South Shields, Tyne and Wear, has held an annual Summer Solstice Competition. All competitors, who draw lots for starting tees, must begin before 4.24 and 13 seconds am, the time the sun rises over the first hole on the longest day of the year.

● At the Open Championship in Musselburgh in November 1889 many players finished when the light had so far gone that the adjacent street lamps were lit. The cards were checked by candlelight. Several players who had no chance of the championship were paid small sums to withdraw in order to permit others who had a chance to finish in daylight. This was the last championship at Musselburgh.

● At the Southern Section of the PGA tournament on 25th September, 1907, at Burnham Beeches, several players concluded the round by the aid of torch lights placed near the holes.

● In the Irish Open Championship at Portmarnock in September, 1907, a tie in the third round between WC Pickeman and A Jeffcott was postponed owing to darkness, at the 22nd hole. The next morning Pickeman won at the 24th.

● The qualifying round of the American Amateur Championship in 1910 could not be finished in one day, and several competitors had to stop their round on account of darkness, and complete it early in the morning of the following day.

● On 10th January, 1926, in the final of the President's Putter, at Rye, EF Storey and RH Wethered were all square at the 24th hole. It was 5 pm and so dark that, although a fair crowd was present, the balls could not be followed. The tie was abandoned and the Putter held jointly for the year. Each winner of the Putter affixes the ball he played; for 1926 there are two balls, respectively with the names of the finalists.

● In the 1932 Walker Cup contest at Brooklyn, a total eclipse of the sun occurred.

● At Perth, on 14th September, 1932, a competition was in progress under good clear evening light, and a full bright moon. The moon rose at 7.10 and an hour later came under eclipse to the earth's surface. The light then became so bad that on the last three greens competitors holed out by the aid of the light from matches.

● At Carnoustie, 1932, in the competition for the *Craw's Nest* the large entry necessitated competitors being sent off in 3-ball matches. The late players had to be assisted by electric torches flashed on the greens.

● In February, 1950, Max Faulkner and his partner, R Dolman, in a Guildford Alliance event finished their round in complete darkness. A photographer's flash bulbs were used at the last hole to direct Faulkner's approach. Several of the other competitors also finished in darkness. At the last hole they had only the light from the clubhouse to aim at and one played his approach so boldly that he put his ball through the hall doorway and almost into the dressing room.

● On the second day of the 1969 Ryder Cup contest, the last 4-ball match ended in near total darkness on the 18th green at Royal Birkdale. With the help of the clubhouse lights the two American players, Lee Trevino and Miller Barber, along with Tony Jacklin for Britain each faced putts of around five feet to win their match. All missed and their game was halved.

The occasions mentioned above all occurred in competitions where it was not intended to play in the dark. There are, however, numerous instances where players set out to play in the dark either for bets or for novelty.

● On 29th November, 1878, RW Brown backed himself to go round the Hoylake links in 150 strokes, starting at 11 pm. The conditions of the match were that Mr Brown was only to be penalised *loss of distance* for a lost ball, and that no one was to help him to find it. He went round in 147 strokes, and won his bet by the narrow margin of three strokes.

● In 1876 David Strath backed himself to go round St Andrews under 100, in moonlight. He took 95, and did not lose a ball.

● In September 1928, at St Andrews, the first and last holes were illuminated by lanterns, and at 11 pm four members of the Royal and Ancient set out to play a foursome over the 2 holes. Electric lights, lanterns, and rockets were used to brighten the fairway, and the headlights of motor cars parked on Links Place formed a helpful battery. The 1st hole was won in four, and each side got a five at the 18th. About 1,000 spectators followed the freak match, which was played to celebrate the appointment of Angus Hambro to the captaincy of the club.

● In 1931, Rufus Stewart, professional, Kooyonga Club, South Australia, and former Australian Open Champion, played 18 holes of exhibition golf at night without losing a single ball over the Kooyonga course, and completed the round in 77.

● At Ashley Wood Golf Club, Blandford, Dorset, a night-time golf tournament was arranged annually with up to 180 golfers taking part over four nights. Over £6000 has been raised in four years for the Muscular Dystrophy Charity.

● At Pannal, 3rd July, 1937, RH Locke, playing in bright moonlight, holed his tee shot at the 15th hole, distance 220 yards, the only known case of holing-in-one under such conditions.

Fatal and Other Accidents on the Links

The history of golf is, unfortunately, marred by a great number of fatal accidents on or near the course. In the vast majority of such cases they have been caused either by careless swinging of the club or by an uncontrolled shot when the ball has struck a spectator or bystander. In addition to the fatal accidents there is an even larger number on record which have resulted in serious injury or blindness. We do not propose to list these accidents except where they have some unusual feature. We would remind all golfers of the tragic consequences which have so often been caused by momentary carelessness. The fatal accidents which follow have an unusual cause and other accidents given may have their humorous aspect.

● English tournament professional Richard Boxall was three shots off the lead in the third round of the 1991 Open Championship when he fractured his left leg driving from the 9th tee at Royal Birkdale. He was taken from the course to hospital by ambulance and was listed in the official results as 'retired' which entitled him to a consolation prize of £3000.

A month later, Russell Weir of Scotland, was competing in the European Teaching Professionals' Championship near Rotterdam when he also fractured his left leg driving from the 7th tee in the first round.

● In July, 1971, Rudolph Roy, aged 43, was killed at a Montreal course; in playing out of woods, the shaft of his club snapped, rebounded off a tree and the jagged edge plunged into his body.

● Harold Wallace, aged 75, playing at Lundin Links with two friends in 1950, was crossing the railway line which separates the fifth green and sixth tee, when a light engine knocked him down and he was killed instantly.

● In the summer of 1963, Harold Kalles, of Toronto, Canada, died six days after his throat had been cut by a golf club shaft, which broke against a tree as he was trying to play out of a bunker.

● At Jacksonville, Florida, on 18th March, 1952, two women golfers were instantly killed when hit simultaneously by the whirling propeller of a navy fighter plane. They were playing together when the plane with a dead engine coming in out of control, hit them from behind.

● In May, 1993, at Ponoka Community GC, Alberta, Canada, Richard McCulough hit a poor tee shot on the 13th hole and promptly smashed his driver angrily against a golf cart. The head of the driver and six inches of shaft flew through the air, piercing McCulough's throat and severing his carotid artery. He died in hospital.

● Britain's first national open event for competitors aged over 80, at Moortown, Leeds in September, 1992, was marred when 81-year-old Frank Hart collapsed on the fourth tee and died. Play continued and Charles Mitchell, aged 80, won the Stableford competition with a gross score of 81 for 39 points.

● Playing in the 1993 Carlesburg-Tetley Cornish Festival at Tehidy Park, Ian Cornwell was struck on the leg by a wayward shot from a player two groups behind. Later, as he was leaving the 16th green, he was hit again, this time below the ear, by the same player, knocking him unconscious. This may be the first time that a player has been hit twice in the same round by the same player.

Lightning on the Links

There have been a considerable number of fatal and serious accidents through players and caddies having been struck by lightning on the course. The Royal & Ancient and the USGA have, since 1952, provided for discontinuance of play during lightning storms under the Rules of Golf (Rule 37, 6) and the United States Golf Association has given the following guide for personal safety during thunderstorms:

(a) Do not go out of doors or remain out during thunderstorms unless it is necessary. Stay inside of a building where it is dry, preferably away from fireplaces, stoves, and other metal objects.

(b) If there is any choice of shelter, choose in the following order:
   1. Large metal or metal-frame buildings.
   2. Dwellings or other buildings which are protected against lightning.
   3. Large unprotected buildings.
   4. Small unprotected buildings.

(c) If remaining out of doors is unavoidable, keep away from:
   1. Small sheds and shelters if in an exposed location.
   2. Isolated trees.
   3. Wire fences.
   4. Hilltops and wide open spaces.

(d) Seek shelter in:
   1. A cave.
   2. A depression in the ground.
   3. A deep valley or canyon.
   4. The foot of a steep or overhanging cliff.
   5. Dense woods.
   6. A grove of trees.

Note – Raising golf clubs or umbrellas above the head is dangerous.

● A serious incident with lightning involving well-known golfers was at the 1975 Western Open in Chicago when Lee Trevino, Jerry Heard and Bobby Nichols were all struck and had to be taken to hospital. At the same time Tony Jacklin had a club thrown 15 feet out of his hands.

● Two well-known competitors were struck by lightning in European events in 1977. They were Mark James of Britain in the Swiss Open and Severiano Ballesteros of Spain in the Scandinavian Open. Fortunately neither appeared to be badly injured.

● Two spectators were killed by lightning in 1991: one at the US Open and the other at US PGA Championship.

Spectators Interfering with Balls

● Deliberate interference by spectators with balls in play during important money matches was not unknown in the old days when there was intense rivalry between the *schools* of Musselburgh, St Andrews, and North Berwick, and disputes arose in stake matches caused by the action of spectators in kicking the ball into either a favourable or an unfavourable position.

● Tom Morris, in his last match with Willie Park at Musselburgh, refused to go on because of interference by the spectators, and in the match on the same course about 40 years later, in 1895, between Willie Park Jr and JH Taylor, the barracking of the crowd and interference with play was so bad that when the Park-Vardon match came to be arranged in 1899, Vardon refused to accept Musselburgh as a venue.

● Even in modern times spectators have been known to interfere deliberately with players' balls, though it is usually by children. In the 1972 Penfold Tournament at Queen's Park, Bournemouth, Christy O'Connor Jr had his ball stolen by a young boy, but not being told of this at the time had to take the penalty for a lost ball. O'Connor finished in a tie for first place, but lost the play-off.

● In 1912 in the last round of the final of the Amateur Championship at Westward Ho! between Abe Mitchell and John Ball, the drive of the former to the short 14th hit an open umbrella held by a lady protecting herself from the heavy rain, and instead of landing on the green the ball was diverted into a bunker. Mitchell, who was leading at the time by 2 holes, lost the hole and Ball won the Championship at the 38th hole.

● In the match between the professionals of Great Britain and America at Southport in 1937 a dense crowd collected round the 15th green waiting for the Sarazen-Alliss match. The American's ball landed in the lap of a woman, who picked it up and threw it so close to the hole that Sarazen got a two against Alliss' three.

● In a memorable tie between Bobby Jones and Cyril Tolley in the 1930 Amateur Championship at St Andrews, Jones' approach to the 17th green struck spectators massed at the left end of the green and led to controversy as to whether it would otherwise have gone on to the famous road. Jones himself had deliberately played for that part of the green and had requested stewards to get the crowd back. Had the ball gone on to the road, the historic Jones Quadrilateral of the year – the Open and Amateur Championships of Britain and the United States – might not have gone into the records.

● In the 1983 Suntory World Match Play Championship at Wentworth Nick Faldo hit his second shot over the green at the 16th hole into a group of spectators. To everyone's astonishment and discomfiture the ball reappeared on the green about 30ft from the hole, propelled there by a thoroughly misguided and anonymous spectator. The referee ruled that Faldo should play the ball where it lay on the green. Faldo's opponent, Graham Marsh, understandably upset by the incident, took three putts against Faldo's two, thus losing a hole he might well otherwise have won. Faldo won the match 2 and 1, but lost in the final to Marsh's fellow Australian Greg Norman by 3 and 2.

Golf Balls Killing Animals and Fish, and Incidents with Animals

● An astounding fatality to an animal through being hit by a golf ball occurred at St Margaret's-at-Cliffe Golf Club, Kent on 13th June, 1934, when WJ Robinson, the professional, killed a cow with his tee shot to the 18th hole. The cow was standing in the fairway about 100 yards from the tee, and the ball struck her on the back of the head. She fell like a log, but staggered to her feet and walked about 50 yards before dropping again. When the players reached her she was dead.

● JW Perret, of Ystrad Mynach, playing with Chas R Halliday, of Ralston, in the qualifying rounds of the Society of One Armed Golfers' Championship over the Darley course, Troon, on 27th August, 1935, killed two gulls at successive holes with his second shots. The *deadly* shots were at the 1st and 2nd holes.

● On the first day of grouse shooting of the 1975 season (12th August), 11-year-old schoolboy Willie Fraser, of Kingussie, beat all the guns when he killed a grouse with his tee shot on the local course.

● On 10th June, 1904, while playing in the Edinburgh High Constables' Competition at Kilspindie, Captain Ferguson sent a long ball into the rough at the Target hole, and on searching for it found that it had struck and killed a young hare.

● Playing in a mixed open tournament at the Waimairi Beach Golf Club in Christchurch, New Zealand, in the summer of 1961, Mrs RT Challis found her ball in fairly long spongy grass where a placing rule applied. She picked up, placed the ball and played her stroke. A young hare leaped into the air and fell dead at her feet. She had placed the ball on the leveret without seeing it and without disturbing it.

● In 1906 in the Border Championship at Hawick, a gull and a weasel were killed by balls during the afternoon's play.

● A golfer at Newark, in May, 1907, drove his ball into the river. The ball struck a trout 2lb in weight and killed it.

● On 24th April, 1975, at Scunthorpe GC, Jim Tollan's drive at the 14th hole, called *The Mallard*, struck and killed a female mallard duck in flight. The duck was stuffed and is displayed in the Scunthorpe Clubhouse.

● A Samuel, Melbourne Club, at Sandringham, was driving with an iron club from the 17th tee, when a kitten, which had been playing in the long grass, sprang suddenly at the ball. Kitten and club arrived at the objective simultaneously, with the result that the kitten took an unexpected flight through the air, landing some 20 yards away.

● As Susan Rowlands was lining up a vital putt in the closing stages of the final of the 1978 Welsh Girls' Championship at Abergele, a tiny mouse scampered up her trouser leg. After holing the putt, the mouse ran down again. Susan, who won the final, admitted that she fortunately had not known it was there.

Interference by Birds and Animals

● Crows, ravens, hawks and seagulls frequently carry off golf balls, sometimes dropping the ball actually on the green, and it is a common incident for a cow to swallow a golf ball. A plague of crows on the Liverpool course at Hoylake are addicted to golf balls – they stole 26 in one day – selecting only new balls. It was suggested that members should carry shotguns as a 15th club!

● A match was approaching a hole in a rather low-lying course, when one of the players made a crisp chip from about 30 yards from the hole. The ball trickled slowly across the green and eventually disappeared into the hole. After a momentary pause, the ball was suddenly ejected on to the green, and out jumped a large frog.

● A large black crow named Jasper which frequented the Lithgow GC in New South Wales, Australia, stole 30 golf balls in the club's 1972 Easter Tournament.

● As Mrs Molly Whitaker was playing from a bunker at Beachwood course, Natal, South Africa, a large monkey leaped from a bush and clutched her round the neck. A caddie drove it off by clipping it with an iron club.

● In Massachusetts a goose, having been hit rather hard by a golf ball which then came to rest by the side of a water hazard, took revenge by waddling over to the ball and kicking it into the water.

● In the summer of 1963, SC King had a good drive to the 10th hole at the Guernsey Club. His partner, RW Clark, was in the rough, and King helped him to search. Returning to his ball, he found a cow eating it. Next day, at the same hole, the positions were reversed, and King was in the rough. Clark placed his woollen hat over his ball, remarking, *I'll make sure the cow doesn't eat mine.* On his return he found the cow thoroughly enjoying his hat; nothing was left but the pompom.

● On 5 August 2000 in the first round of the Royal Westmoreland Club Championship in Barbados, Kevin Edwards, a five-handicapper, hit a tee shot at the short 15th to a few feet of the hole. A monkey then ran onto the green, picked up the ball, threw it into the air a few times, then placed it in the hole before running off. Mr Edwards had to replace his ball, but was obliged afterwards to buy everyone a drink at the bar by virtue of a newly written rule.

Armless, One-armed, Legless and Ambidextrous Players

● In September, 1933, at Burgess Golfing Society of Edinburgh, the first championship for one-armed golfers was held. There were 43 entries and 37 of the competitors had lost an arm in the 1914-18 war. Play was over two rounds and the championship was won by WE Thomson, Eastwood, Glasgow, with a score of 169 (82 and 87) for two rounds. The Burgess course was 6,300 yards long. Thomson drove the last green, 260 yards. The championship and an international match are played annually.

● In the Boys' Amateur Championship 1923, at Dunbar and 1949 at St Andrews, there were competitors each with one arm. The competitor in 1949, RP Reid, Cupar, Fife, who lost his arm working a machine in a butcher's shop, got through to the third round.

● There have been cases of persons with no arms playing golf. One, Thomas McAuliffe, who held the club between his right shoulder and cheek, once went round Buffalo CC, USA, in 108.

● Group Captain Bader, who lost both legs in a flying accident prior to the World War 1939-45, took part in golf competitions and reached a single-figure handicap in spite of his disability.

● In 1909, Scott of Silloth, and John Haskins of Hoylake, both one-armed golfers, played a home and away match for £20-a-side. Scott finished five up at Silloth. He was seven up and 14 to play at Hoylake but Haskins played so well that Scott eventually only won by 3 and 1. This was the first match between one-armed golfers. Haskins in 1919 was challenged by Mr Mycock, of Buxton, another one-armed player. The match was 36 holes, home and away. The first half was played over the Buxton and High Peak Links, and the latter half over the Liverpool Links, and resulted in a win for Haskins by 11 and 10. Later in the same year Haskins received another challenge to play against Alexander Smart of Aberdeen. The match was 18 holes over the Balgownie Course, and ended in favour of Haskins.

● In a match, November, 1926, between the Geduld and Sub Nigel Clubs – two golf clubs connected with the South African gold mines of the same names – each club had two players minus an arm. The natural consequence was that the quartet were matched. The players were – AWP Charteris and E Mitchell, Sub Nigel; and EP Coles and J Kirby, Geduld. This is the first record of four one-armed players in a foursome.

● At Joliet Country Club, USA, a one-armed golfer named DR Anderson drove a ball 300 yards.

● Left-handedness, but playing golf right-handed, is prevalent and for a man to throw with his left hand and play golf right-handed is considered an advantage, for Bobby Jones, Jesse Sweetser, Walter Hagen, Jim Barnes, Joe Kirkwood and more recently Johnny Miller were eminent golfers who were left-handed and ambidextrous.

● In a practice round for the Open Championship in July, 1927, at St Andrews, Len Nettlefold and Joe Kirkwood changed sets of clubs at the 9th hole. Nettlefold was a left-handed golfer and Kirkwood right-handed. They played the last nine, Kirkwood with the left-handed clubs and Nettlefold with the right-handed clubs.

● The late Harry Vardon, when he was at Ganton, got tired of giving impossible odds to his members and beating them, so he collected a set of left-handed clubs, and rating himself at scratch, conceded the handicap odds to them. He won with the same monotonous regularity.

● Ernest Jones, who was professional at the Chislehurst Club, was badly wounded in the war in France in 1916 and his right leg had to be amputated below the knee. He persevered with the game, and before the end of the year he went round the Clacton course balanced on his one leg in 72. Jones later settled in the United States where he built fame and fortune as a golf teacher.

● Major Alexander McDonald Fraser of Edinburgh had the distinction of holding two handicaps simultaneously in the same club – one when he played left-handed and the other for his right-handed play. In medal competitions he had to state before teeing up which method he would use.

● Former England test cricketer Brian Close once held a handicap of 2 playing right-handed, but after retiring from cricket in 1977 decided to apply himself as a left-handed player. His left-handed handicap at the time of his retirement was 7. Close had the distinction of once beating Ted Dexter, another distinguished test cricketer and noted golfer twice in the one day, playing right-handed in the morning and left-handed in the afternoon.

Blind and Blindfolded Golf

● Major Towse, VC, whose eyes were shot out during the South African War, 1899, was probably the first blind man to play golf. His only stipulations when playing the game were that he should be allowed to touch the ball with his hands to ascertain its position, and that his caddie could ring a small bell to indicate the position of the hole. Major Towse, who played with considerable skill, was also an expert oarsman and bridge player. He died in 1945, aged 81.

● The United States Blind Golfers' Association in 1946 promoted an Invitational Golf Tournament for the blind at Inglewood, California, to be held annually. In 1953 there were 24 competitors, of which 11 completed the two rounds of 36 holes. The winner was Charley Boswell who lost his eyesight leading a tank unit in Germany in 1944.

● In July, 1954, at Lambton Golf and Country Club, Toronto, the first international championship for the blind was held. It resulted in a win for Joe Lazaro, of Waltham, Mass, with a score of 220 for the two rounds. He drove the 215-yard 16th hole and just missed an ace, his ball stopping 18 inches from the hole. Charley Boswell, who won the United States Blind Golfers' Association Tournament in 1953, was second. The same Charles Boswell, of Birmingham, Alabama holed the 141-yard 14th hole at the Vestavia CC in one in October, 1970.

● Another blind person to have holed-in-one was American Ben Thomas while on holiday in South Carolina in 1978.

● Rick Sorenson undertook a bet in which, playing 18 holes blindfolded at Meadowbrook Course, Minneapolis, on 25th May, 1973, he was to pay $10 for every hole over par and receive $100 for every hole in par or better. He went round in 86 losing $70 on the deal.

● Alfred Toogood played blindfolded in a match against Tindal Atkinson at Sunningdale in 1912. Toogood was beaten 8 and 7. Previously, in 1908, I Millar, Newcastle-upon-Tyne, played a match blindfolded against AT Broughton, Birkdale, at Newcastle, County Down.

● Wing-Commander *Laddie* Lucas, DSO, DFC, MP, played over Sandy Lodge golf course in Hertfordshire on 7th August, 1954, completely blindfolded and had a score of 87.

Trick Shots

● Joe Kirkwood, Australia, specialised in public exhibitions of trick and fancy shots. He played all kinds of strokes after nominating them, and among his ordinary strokes nothing was more impressive than those hit for low flight. He played a full drive from the face of a wrist watch, and the toe of a spectator's shoe, full strokes at a suspended ball, and played for slice and pull at will, and exhibited his ambidexterity by playing left-handed strokes with right-handed clubs. Holing six balls, stymieing, a full shot at a ball catching it as it descended, and hitting 12 full shots in rapid succession, with his face turned away from the ball, were shots among his repertoire. In playing the last named Kirkwood placed the balls in a row, about six inches apart, and moved quickly along the line. Kirkwood, who was born in Australia lived for many years in America. He died in November, 1970 aged 73.

● On 2nd April, 1894, a 3-ball match was played over Musselburgh course between Messrs Grant, Bowden, and Waggot, the clubmaker, the latter teeing on the face of a watch at each tee. He finished the round in 41 the watch being undamaged in any way.

● In a match at Esher on 23rd November, 1931, George Ashdown, the professional, played his tee shot for each of the 18 holes from a rubber tee strapped to the forehead of Miss Ena Shaw.

● EA Forrest, a South African professional in a music hall turn of trick golf shots, played blindfolded shots, one being from the ball teed on the chin of his recumbent partner.

● The late Paul Hahn, an American trick specialist could hit four balls with two clubs Holding a club in each hand he hit two balls, hooking one and slicing the other with the same swing. Hahn had a repertoire of 30 trick shots. In 1955 he flew round the world, exhibiting in 14 countries and on all five continents.

Balls Colliding and Touching

● Competing in the 1980 Corfu International Championship, Sharon Peachey drove from one tee and her ball collided in mid-air with one from a competitor playing another hole. Her ball ended in a pond.

● Playing in the Cornish team championship in 1973 at West Cornwall GC Tom Scott-Brown, of West Cornwall GC, and Paddy Bradley, of Tehidy GC, saw their drives from the fourth and eighth tees collide in mid-air.

● During a fourball match at Guernsey Club in June, 1966, near the 13th green from the tee. Two of players, DG Hare and S Machin, chipped up simultaneously; the balls collided in mid-air and Machin's ball hit the green, then the flagstick, and dropped into the hole for a birdie 2.

● In May, 1926, during the meeting of the Army Golfing Society at St Andrews, Colonel Howard and Lieutenant-Colonel Buchanan Dunlop, while playing in the foursomes against J Rodger and J Mackie, hit full iron shots for the seconds to the 16th green. Each thought he had to play his ball first, and hidden by a bunker the players struck their balls simultaneously. The balls, going towards the hole about 20 yards from the pin and five feet in the air, met with great force and dropped either side of the hole five yards apart.

● In 1972, before a luncheon celebrating the centenary year of the Ladies' Section of Royal Wimbledon GC, a 12-hole competition was held during which two competitors, Mrs L Champion and Mrs A McKendrick, driving from the eighth and ninth tees respectively, saw their balls collide in mid-air.

● In 1928, at Wentworth Falls, Australia, Dr Alcorn and EA Avery, of Leura Club, were playing with professional E Barnes. The tee shots of Avery and Barnes at the 9th hole finished on opposite sides of the fairway. Both players unknowingly hit their seconds (chip shots) at the same time. Dr Alcorn, standing at the pin, suddenly saw two balls approaching the hole from different angles. They met in the air and dropped into the hole.

● At Rugby, 1931, playing in a 4-ball match, H Fraser pulled his drive from the 10th tee in the direction of the ninth tee. Simultaneously a club member, driving from the ninth tee, pulled his drive. The tees were about 350 yards apart. The two balls collided in mid-air.

● Two golf balls, being played in opposite directions, collided in flight over Longniddry Golf Course on 27th June, 1953. Immediately after Stewart Elder, of Longniddry, had driven from the third tee, another ball, which had been pulled off line from the second fairway, which runs alongside the third, struck his ball about 20 feet above the ground. SJ Fleming, of Tranent, who was playing with Elder, heard a loud crack and thought Elder's ball had exploded. The balls were found undamaged about 70 yards apart.

Three and Two Balls Dislodged by One Shot

● In 1934 on the short 3rd hole (now the 13th) of Olton Course, Warwickshire, JR Horden, a scratch golfer of the club, sent his tee shot into long wet grass a few feet over the back of the green. When he played an *explosion* shot three balls dropped on to the putting green, his own and two others.

● AM Chevalier, playing at Hale, Cheshire, March, 1935, drove his ball into a grass bunker, and when he reached it there was only part of it showing. He played the shot with a niblick and to his amazement not one but three balls shot into the air. They all dropped back into the bunker and came to rest within a foot of each other. Then came another surprise. One of the *finds* was of the same manufacture and bore the same number as the ball he was playing with.

● Playing to the 9th hole, at Osborne House Club, Isle of Wight, George A Sherman lost his ball which had sunk out of sight on the sodden fairway. A few weeks later, playing from the same tee, his ball again was plugged, only the top showing. Under a local rule he lifted his ball to place it, and exactly under it lay the ball he had lost previously.

Balls in Strange Places

● Playing at the John O' Gaunt Club, Sutton, near Biggleswade (Beds), a member drove a ball which did not touch the ground until it reached London – over 40 miles away. The ball landed in a vegetable lorry which was passing the golf course and later fell out of a package of cabbages when they were unloaded at Covent Garden, London.

● In the English Open Amateur Stroke Play at Moortown in 1974, Nigel Denham, a Yorkshire County player, in the first round saw his overhit second shot to the 18th green bounce up some steps into the clubhouse. His ball went through an open door, ricocheted off a wall and came to rest in the men's bar, 20 feet from the windows. As the clubhouse was not out of bounds Denham decided to play the shot back to the green and opened a window 4 feet by 2 feet through which he pitched his ball to 12 feet from the flag. (Several weeks later the R&A declared that Denham should have been penalised two shots for opening the window. The clubhouse was an immovable obstruction and no part of it should have been moved.)

● In the Open Championship at Sandwich, 1949, Harry Bradshaw, Kilcroney, Dublin, at the 5th hole in his second round, drove into the rough and found his ball inside a beer bottle with the neck and shoulder broken off and four sharp points sticking up. Bradshaw, if he had treated the ball as in an unplayable lie might have been involved in a disqualification, so he decided to play it where it lay. With his blaster he smashed the bottle and sent the ball about 30 yards. The hole, a par 4, cost him 6.

● Kevin Sharman of Woodbridge GC hit a low, very straight drive at the club's 8th hole in 1979. After some minutes' searching, his ball was found embedded in a plastic sphere on top of the direction post.

● On the Dublin Course, 16th July, 1936, in the Irish Open Championship, AD Locke, the South African, played his tee shot at the 100-yard 12th hole, but the ball could not be found on arrival on the green. The marker removed the pin and it was discovered that the ball had been entangled in the flag. It dropped near the edge of the hole and Locke holed the short putt for a birdie two.

● While playing a round on the Geelong Golf Club Course, Australia, Easter, 1923, Captain Charteris topped his tee shot to the short 2nd hole, which lies over a creek with deep and steep clay banks. His ball came to rest on the near slope of the creek bank. He elected to play the ball as it lay, and took his niblick. After the shot, the ball was nowhere to be seen. It was found later embedded in a mass of gluey clay stuck fast to the face of the niblick. It could not be shaken off. Charteris did what was afterwards approved by

the R&A, cleaned the ball and dropped it behind without penalty.

● In October, 1929, at Blackmoor Golf Club, Bordon, Hants, a player driving from the first tee holed out his ball in the chimney of a house some 120 yards distant and some 40 yards out of bounds on the right. The owner and his wife were sitting in front of the fire when they heard a rattle in the chimney and were astonished to see a golf ball drop into the fire.

● A similar incident occurred in an inter-club match between Musselburgh and Lothianburn at Prestongrange in 1938 when a member of the former team hooked his ball at the 2nd hole and gave it up for lost. To his amazement a woman emerged from one of the houses adjacent to this part of the course and handed back the ball which she said had come down the chimney and landed on a pot which was on the fire.

● In July, 1955, J Lowrie, starter at the Eden Course, St Andrews, witnessed a freak shot. A visitor drove from the first tee just as a north-bound train was passing. He sliced the shot and the ball disappeared through an open window of a passenger compartment. Almost immediately the ball emerged again, having been thrown back on to the fairway by a man in the compartment, who waved a greeting which presumably indicated that no one was hurt.

● At Coombe Wood Golf Club a player hit a ball towards the 16th green where it landed in the vertical exhaust of a tractor which was mowing fairway. The greenkeeper was somewhat surprised to find a temporary loss of power in the tractor. When sufficient compression had built up in the exhaust system, the ball was forced out with tremendous velocity, hit the roof of a house nearby, bounced off and landed some three feet from the pin on the green.

● When carrying out an inspection of the air conditioning system at St John's Hospital, Chelmsford, in 1993, a golf ball was found in the ventilator immediately above the operating theatre. It was probably the result of a hooked drive from the first tee at Chelmsford Golf Club, which is close by, but the ball can only have entered the duct on a re-bound through a three-inch gap under a ventilator hood and then descended through a series of sharp bends to its final resting place.

● There have been many occasions when misdirected shots have finished in strange places after an unusual line of flight and bounce. At Ashford, Middlesex, John Miller, aged 69, hit his tee shot out of bounds at the 12th hole (237 yards). It struck a parked car, passed through a copse, hit more cars, jumped a canopy, flew through the clubhouse kitchen window, finishing in a cooking stock-pot, without once touching the ground. Mr Miller had previously done the hole in one on four occasions.

Balls Hit To and From Great Heights

● In 1798 two Edinburgh golfers undertook to drive a ball over the spire of St Giles' Cathedral, Edinburgh, for a wager. Mr Sceales, of Leith, and Mr Smellie, a printer, were each allowed six shots and succeeded in sending the balls well over the weather-cock, a height of more than 160 feet from the ground.

● Some years later Donald McLean, an Edinburgh lawyer, won a substantial bet by driving a ball over the Melville Monument in St Andrew Square, Edinburgh – height, 154 feet.

● Tom Morris in 1860, at the famous bridge of Ballochmyle, stood in the quarry beneath and, from a stick elevated horizontally, attempted to send golf balls over the bridge. He could raise them only to the pathway, 400 feet high, which was in itself a great feat with the gutta ball.

● Captain Ernest Carter, on 28th September, 1922, drove a ball from the roadway at the 1st tee on Harlech Links against the wall of Harlech Castle. The embattlements are 200 feet over the level of the roadway, and the point where the ball struck the embattlements was 180 yards from the point where the ball was teed. Captain Carter, who was laid odds of £100 to £1, used a baffy.

● In 1896 Freddie Tait, then a subaltern in the Black Watch, drove a ball from the Rookery, the highest building on Edinburgh Castle, in a match against a brother officer to hole out in the fountain in Princes Street Gardens 350 feet below and about 300 yards distant.

● Prior to the 1977 Lancôme Tournament in Paris, Arnold Palmer hit three balls from the second stage of the Eiffel Tower, over 300 feet above ground. The longest was measured at 403 yards. One ball was hooked and hit a bus but no serious damage was done as all traffic had been stopped for safety reasons.

● Long drives have been made from mountain peaks, across the gorge at Victoria Falls, from the Pyramids, high buildings in New York, and from many other similar places. As an illustration of such freakish *drives* a member of the New York Rangers' Hockey Team from the top of Mount Edith Cavell, 11,033 feet high, drove a ball which struck the Ghost Glacier 5,000 feet below and bounced off the rocky ledge another 1,000 feet – a total drop of 2,000 yards. Later, in June, 1968, from Pikes Peak, Colorado (14,110 feet), Arthur Lynskey hit a ball which travelled 200 yards horizontally but 2 miles vertically.

Remarkable Shots

● Remarkable shots are as numerous as the grains of sand; around every 19th hole, legends are recalled of astounding shots. One shot is commemorated by a memorial tablet at the 17th hole at the Lytham and St Annes Club. It was made by Bobby Jones in the final round of the Open Championship in 1926. He was partnered by Al Watrous, another American player. They had been running neck and neck and at the end of the third round, Watrous was just leading Jones with 215 against 217. At the 16th Jones drew level then on the 17th he drove into a sandy lie in broken ground. Watrous reached the green with his second. Jones took a mashie-iron (the equivalent to a 4-iron today) and hit a magnificent shot to the green to get his 4. This remarkable recovery unnerved Watrous, who 3-putted, and Jones, getting another 4 at the last hole against 5, won his first Open Championship with 291 against Watrous' 293. The tablet is near the spot where Jones played his second shot.

● Arnold Palmer (USA), playing in the second round of the Australian Wills Masters tournament at Melbourne, in October, 1964, hooked his second shot at the 9th hole high into the fork of a gum tree. Climbing 20 feet up the tree, Palmer, with the head of his 1-iron reversed, played a hammer stroke and knocked the ball some 30 yards forward, followed by a brilliant chip to the green and a putt.

● In the foursome during the Ryder Cup at Moortown in 1929, Joe Turnesa hooked the American side's second shot at the last hole behind the marquee adjoining the clubhouse, Johnny Farrel then pitched the ball over the marquee on to the green only feet away from the pin and Turnesa holed out for a 4.

Miscellaneous Incidents and Strange Golfing Facts

● Gary Player of South Africa was honoured by his country by having his portrait on new postage stamps which were issued on 12th December, 1976. It was the first time a specific golfer had ever been depicted on any country's postage stamps. In 1981 the US Postal Service introduced stamps featuring Bobby Jones and Babe Zaharias. They are the first golfers to be thus honoured by the United States.

● Gary Harris, aged 18, became the first player to make five consecutive appearances for England in the European Boys Team Championship at Vilamoura, Portugal, in 1994.

● In February, 1971, the first ever golf shots on the moon's surface were played by Captain Alan Shepard, commander of the Apollo 14 spacecraft. Captain Shepard hit two balls with an iron head attached to a makeshift shaft. With a one-handed swing he claimed he hit the first ball 200 yards aided by the reduced force of gravity on the moon. Subsequent findings put this distance in doubt. The second was a shank. Acknowledging the occasion the R&A sent Captain Shepard the following telegram: *Warmest congratulations to all of you on your great achievement and safe return. Please refer to Rules of Golf section on etiquette, para-*

graph 6, quote – before leaving a bunker a player should carefully fill up all holes made by him therein, unquote. Shepard presented the club to the USGA Museum in 1974.

● Charles (Chick) Evans competed in every US Amateur Championship held between 1907 and 1962 by which time he was 72 years old. This amounted to 50 consecutive occasions discounting the six years of the two World Wars when the championship was not held.

● In winning the 1977 US Open at Southern Hills CC, Tulsa, Oklahoma, Hubert Green had to contend with a death threat. Coming off the 14th green in the final round, he was advised by USGA officials that a phone call had been received saying that he would be killed. Green decided that play should continue and happily he went on to win, unharmed.

● It was discovered at the 1977 USPGA Championship that the clubs with which Tom Watson had won the Open Championship and the US Masters earlier in the year were illegal, having grooves which exceeded the permitted specifications. The set he used in winning the 1975 Open Championship were then flown out to him and they too were found to be illegal. No retrospective action was taken.

● Mrs Fred Daly, wife of the former Open champion, saved the clubhouse of Balmoral GC, Belfast, from destruction when three men entered the professional's shop on 5th August, 1976, and left a bag containing a bomb outside the shop beside the clubhouse when refused money. Mrs Daly carried the bag over to a hedge some distance away where the bomb exploded 15 minutes later. The only damage was broken windows. On the same day several hours afterwards, Dungannon GC in Co Tyrone suffered extensive damage to the clubhouse from terrorist bombs. Co Down GC, proposed venue of the 1979 home international matches suffered bomb damage in May that year and through fear for the safety of team members the 1979 matches were cancelled.

● The Army Golfing Society and St Andrews on 21st April, 1934, played a match 200-a-side, the largest golf match ever played. Play was by foursomes. The Army won 58, St Andrews 31 and 11 were halved.

● Jamie Ortiz-Patino, owner of the Valderrama Golf Club at Sotogrande, Spain, paid a record £84,000 (increased to £92,400 with ten per cent buyers premium) for a late seventeenth- or early eighteenth-century rake iron offered at auction in Musselburgh in July, 1992. The iron, which had been kept in a garden shed, was bought to be exhibited in a museum being created in Valderrama.

● A Christie's golf auction during the week of the 1991 Open Championship created two world records. An American dealer bought a blacksmith-made iron club head dating from the seven-teenth century for £44,000. It had been found 10 years before in a hedge near the North Berwick Golf Club in Scotland. Also, £165,000 was paid by a Japanese collector for an oil painting by Sir Francis Grant (1810–1878) of the 1823 Royal & Ancient captain, John Whyte-Melville, standing beside the Swilcan Burn at St Andrews. The same Japanese buyer successfully bid £35,200 for a rare gutty golf ball marking device from the workshops of Old Tom Morris in St Andrews, while an unused feathery golf ball by Allan Robertson fetched £11,000.

● In 1986 Alistair Risk and three colleagues on the 17th green at Brora, Sutherland, watched a cow giving birth to twin calves between the markers on the 18th tee, causing them to play their next tee shots from in front of the tee. Their application for a ruling from the R&A brought a Rules Committee reply that while technically a rule had been broken, their action was considered within the spirit of the game and there should be no penalty. The Secretary added that the Rules Committee hoped that mother and twins were doing well.

● In view of the increasing number of people crossing the road (known as Granny Clark's Wynd) which runs across the first and 18th fairways of the Old Course, St Andrews, as a right of way, the St Andrews Links committee decided in 1969 to control the flow by erecting traffic lights, with appropriate green for go, yellow for caution and red for stop. The lights are controlled from the starter's box on the first tee. Golfers on the first tee must wait until the lights turn to green before driving off and a notice has been erected at the Wynd warning pedestrians not to cross at yellow or stop.

● A traffic light for golfers was also installed in 1971 on one of Japan's most congested courses. After putting on the uphill 9th hole of the Fukuoka course in Southern Japan, players have to switch on a go-ahead signal for following golfers waiting to play their shots to the green.

● A 22-year-old professional at Brett Essex GC, Brentwood, David Moore, who was playing in the Mufulira Open in Zambia in 1976, was shot dead it is alleged by the man with whom he was staying for the duration of the tournament. It appeared his host then shot himself.

● Peggy Carrick and her daughter, Angela Uzielli, won the Mothers and Daughters Tournament at Royal Mid-Surrey in 1994 for the 21st time.

● Patricia Shepherd has won the ladies' club championship at Turriff GC Aberdeenshire 30 consecutive times from 1959 to 1988.

● Mrs Jackie Mercer won the South African Ladies' Championship in 1979, 31 years after her first victory in the event as Miss Jacqueline Smith.

● During the Royal & Ancient Golf Club of St Andrews' medal meeting on 25th September, 1907, a member of the Royal & Ancient drove a ball which struck the sharp point of a hatpin in the hat of a lady who was crossing the course. The ball was so firmly impaled that it remained in position. The lady was not hurt.

● John Cook, former English Amateur Champion, narrowly escaped death during an attempted coup against King Hassan of Morocco in July 1971. Cook had been playing in a tournament arranged by King Hassan, a keen golfer, and was at the King's birthday party in Rabat when rebels broke into the party demanding that the King give up his throne. Cook and many others present were taken hostage.

● When playing from the 9th tee at Lossiemouth golf course in June, 1971, Martin Robertson struck a Royal Navy jet aircraft which was coming in to land at the nearby airfield. The plane was not damaged.

● At a court in Inglewood, California, in 1978, Jim Brown was convicted of beating and choking an opponent during a dispute over where a ball should have been placed on the green.

● During the Northern Ireland troubles a home-made hand grenade was found in a bunker at Dungannon GC, Co Tyrone, on Sunday, 12th September, 1976.

● Tiger Woods, 18, became both the youngest and the first black golfer to win the United States Amateur Championship at Sawgrass in 1994. He went on to win the title three years in a row and then won the first major championship he played as a professional, the 1997 Masters, by a record 12 strokes and with a record low aggregate of 270, 18 under par.

● To mark the centenary of the Jersey Golf Club in 1978, the Jersey Post Office issued a set of four special stamps featuring Jersey's most famous golfer, Harry Vardon. The background of the 13p stamp was a brief biography of Vardon's career reproduced from the *Golfer's Handbook*.

● Forty-one-year-old John Mosley went for a round of golf at Delaware Park GC, Buffalo, New York, in July, 1972. He stepped on to the first tee and was challenged over a green fee by an official guard. A scuffle developed, a shot was fired and Mosley, a bullet in his chest, died on the way to hospital. His wife was awarded $131,250 in an action against the City of Buffalo and the guard. The guard was sentenced to 7½ years for second-degree manslaughter.

● When three competitors in a 1968 Pennsylvania pro-am event were about to drive from the 16th tee, two bandits (one with pistol) suddenly emerged from the bushes, struck one of the players and robbed them of wristwatches and $300.

● In the 1932 Walker Cup match at Brooklyn, Leonard Crawley succeeded in denting the cup. An errant iron shot to the 18th green hit the cup, which was on display outside the clubhouse.

● In Johannesburg, South Africa, three golf officials appeared in court accused of violating a 75-year-old Sunday Observance Law by staging the final round of the South African PGA championship on Sunday, 28th February, 1971. The Championship should have been completed on the Saturday but heavy rain prevented any play.

● In the Open Championship of 1876, at St Andrews, Bob Martin and David Strath tied at 176. A protest was lodged against Strath alleging he played his approach to the 17th green and struck a spectator. The Royal & Ancient ordered the replay, but Strath refused to play off the tie until a decision had been given on the protest. No decision was given and Bob Martin was declared the Champion.

● At Rose Bay, New South Wales, on 11th July, 1931, DJ Bayly MacArthur, on stepping into a bunker, began to sink. MacArthur, who weighed 14 stone, shouted for help. He was rescued when up to the armpits. He had stepped on a patch of quicksand, aggravated by excess of moisture.

● The late Bobby Cruickshank was the victim of his own jubilation in the 1934 US Open at Merion. In the 4th round while in with a chance of winning he half-topped his second shot at the 11th hole. The ball was heading for a pond in front of the green but instead of ending up in the water it hit a rock and bounced on to the green. In his delight Cruickshank threw his club into the air only to receive a resounding blow on the head as it returned to earth.

● A dog with an infallible nose for finding lost golf balls was, in 1971, given honorary membership of the Waihi GC, Hamilton, New Zealand. The dog, called Chico, was trained to search for lost balls, to be sold back to the members, the money being put into the club funds.

● By 1980 Waddy, an 11-year-old beagle belonging to Bob Inglis, the secretary of Brokenhurst Manor GC, had found over 35,000 golf balls.

● Herbert M Hepworth, Headingley, Leeds, Lord Mayor of Leeds in 1906, scored one thousand holes in 2, a feat which took him 30 years to accomplish. It was celebrated by a dinner in 1931 at the Leeds club. The first 2 of all was scored on 12th June, 1901, at Cobble Hall Course, Leeds, and the 1,000th in 1931 at Alwoodley, Leeds. Hepworth died in November, 1942.

● Fiona MacDonald was the first female to play in the Oxford and Cambridge University match at Ganton in 1986.

● Mrs Sara Gibbon won the Farnham (Surrey) Club's Grandmother's competition 48 hours after her first grand-child was born.

● At Carnoustie in the first qualifying round for the 1952 Scottish Amateur Championship a competitor drove three balls in succession out of bounds at the 1st hole and thereupon withdrew.

● In 1993, the Clark family from Hagley GC, Worcs, set a record for the county's three major professional events. The Worcestershire Stroke Play Championship was won by Finlay Clark, the eldest son, who beat his father Iain and younger brother Cameron, who tied second. In the Match Play Iain beat his son Finlay by 2 and 1 in the final; Cameron won the play-off for third place. Then in the Worcestershire Annual Pro-Am it was Cameron's turn to win, with his brother Finlay coming second and father Iain third. To add to the achievements of the family, Cameron also won the Midland Professional Match Play Championship.

● During a Captain–Pro foursomes challenge match at Chelmsford in 1993, Club Professional Dennis Bailey, put the ball into a hole only once in all 18 holes – when he holed-in-one at the fourth.

Strange Local Rules

● The Duke of Windsor, who played on an extraordinary variety of the world's courses, once took advantage of a local rule at Jinja in Uganda and lifted his ball from a hippo's footprint without penalty.

● At the Glen Canyon course in Arizona a local rule provides that *If your ball lands within a club length of a rattlesnake you are allowed to move the ball.*

● Another local rule in Uganda read: *If a ball comes to rest in dangerous proximity to a crocodile, another ball may be dropped.*

● The 6th hole at Koolan Island GC, Western Australia, also serves as a local air strip and a local rule reads: *Aircraft and vehicular traffic have right of way at all times.*

● A local rule at the RAF Waddington GC reads: *When teeing off from the 2nd, right of way must be given to taxiing aircraft.*

Record Scoring

In the Major Championships nobody has shot lower than 63. There have been seven 63s in the Open, three 63s in the US Open, two 63s in The Masters and eight 63s in the USPGA Championship. The lowest first 36 holes is 130 by Nick Faldo in the 1992 Open at Muirfield and the lowest 72 hole total is 265 by David Toms in the 2001 USPGA Championship at the Atlanta Athletic Club.

The Open Championship

Most times champions

6   Harry Vardon, 1896-98-99-1903-11-14
5   James Braid, 1901-05-06-08-10; JH Taylor, 1894-95-1900-09-13; Peter Thomson, 1954-55-56-58-65; Tom Watson, 1975-77-80-82-83

Most times runner-up

7   Jack Nicklaus, 1964-67-68-72-76-77-79
6   JH Taylor, 1896-1904-05-06-07-14

Oldest winner

Old Tom Morris, 46 years 99 days, 1867
Roberto De Vicenzo, 44 years 93 days, 1967

Youngest winner

Young Tom Morris, 17 years 5 months 8 days, 1868
Willie Auchterlonie, 21 years 24 days, 1893
Severiano Ballesteros, 22 years 3 months 12 days, 1979

Youngest and oldest competitor

John Ball, 15 years 6 months, 1878
Gene Sarazen, 71 years 4 months 13 days, 1973

Widest margin of victory

13 strokes   Old Tom Morris, 1862
12 strokes   Young Tom Morris, 1870
8 strokes   JH Taylor, 1900 and 1913; James Braid, 1908; Tiger Woods, 2000
6 strokes   Harry Vardon, 1903; JH Taylor, 1909; Bobby Jones, 1927; Walter Hagen, 1929; Arnold Palmer, 1962; Johnny Miller, 1976

Lowest winning aggregates

267   Greg Norman, 66-68-69-64, Sandwich, 1993
268   Tom Watson, 68-70-65-65, Turnberry, 1977; Nick Price, 69-66-67-66, Turnberry, 1994
269   Tiger Woods, 67-66-67-69, St Andrews, 2000
270   Nick Faldo, 67-65-67-71, St Andrews, 1990

Lowest in relation to par

19 under   Tiger Woods, St Andrews, 2000
18 under   Nick Faldo, St Andrews, 1990

Lowest aggregate by runner-up

269   (68-70-65-66), Jack Nicklaus, Turnberry, 1977; (69-63-70-67) Nick Faldo, Sandwich, 1993; (68-66-68-67) Jesper Parnevik, Turnberry, 1994

Lowest aggregate by an amateur

281   (68-72-70-71), Iain Pyman, Sandwich, 1993; (75-66-70-70), Tiger Woods, R. Lytham, 1996

Lowest round

63   Mark Hayes, second round, Turnberry, 1977; Isao Aoki, third round, Muirfield, 1980; Greg Norman, second round, Turnberry, 1986; Paul Broadhurst, third round, St Andrews, 1990; Jodie Mudd, fourth round, Royal Birkdale, 1991; Nick Faldo, second round, Payne Stewart, fourth round, Sandwich, 1993

Lowest round by an amateur

66   Frank Stranahan, fourth round, Troon, 1950; Tiger Woods, second round, R. Lytham, 1996; Justin Rose, second round, R Birkdale, 1998

Lowest first round

64   Craig Stadler, Royal Birkdale, 1983; Christy O'Connor Jr, Royal St George's, 1985; Rodger Davis, Muirfield, 1987; Steve Pate, Ray Floyd, Muirfield, 1992

Lowest second round

63   Mark Hayes, Turnberry, 1977; Greg Norman, Turnberry, 1986; Nick Faldo, Sandwich, 1993

Lowest third round

63   Isao Aoki, Muirfield, 1980; Paul Broadhurst, St Andrews, 1990

Lowest fourth round

63   Jodie Mudd, Royal Birkdale, 1991; Payne Stewart, Sandwich, 1993

Lowest first 36 holes

130 (66-64), Nick Faldo, Muirfield, 1992
132 (67-65), Henry Cotton, Sandwich, 1934;
Nick Faldo (67-65) and Greg Norman (66-66),
St Andrews, 1990; Nick Faldo (69-63),
Sandwich, 1993

Lowest second 36 holes

130 (65-65), Tom Watson, Turnberry, 1977
(64-66) Ian Baker-Finch, R. Birkdale, 1991;
(66-64) Anders Forsbrand, Turnberry,
1994

Lowest first 54 holes

198 (67-67-64) Tom Lehman, Royal Lytham,
1996
199 (67-65-67), Nick Faldo, St Andrews, 1990;
(66-64-69) Nick Faldo, Muirfield, 1992

Lowest final 54 holes

199 (66-67-66) Nick Price, Turnberry, 1994
200 (70-65-65), Tom Watson, Turnberry,
1977 (63-70-67), Nick Faldo, Sandwich,
1993 (66-64-70), Fuzzy Zoeller, Turnberry,
1994 (66-70-64), Nick Faldo, Turnberry
1994

Lowest 9 holes

28 Denis Durnian, first 9, Royal Birkdale, 1983

Champions in three decades

Harry Vardon, 1986, 1903, 1911
JH Taylor, 1894, 1900, 1913
Gary Player, 1959, 1968, 1974

Biggest span between first and last victories

19 years, JH Taylor, 1894-1913
18 years, Harry Vardon, 1896-1914
15 years, Willie Park, 1860–75
15 years, Gary Player, 1959-74
14 years, Henry Cotton, 1934-48

Successive victories

4 Young Tom Morris, 1868-72 (no
championship in 1871)
3 Jamie Anderson, 1877-79; Bob Ferguson,
1880-82, Peter Thomson, 1954-56
2 Old Tom Morris, 1861-62; JH Taylor, 1894-
95; Harry Vardon, 1898-99; James Braid,
1905-06; Bobby Jones, 1926-27; Walter
Hagen, 1928-29; Bobby Locke, 1949-50;
Arnold Palmer, 1961-62; Lee Trevino, 1971-
72; Tom Watson, 1982-83

Victories by amateurs

3 Bobby Jones, 1926-27-30
2 Harold Hilton, 1892-97
1 John Ball, 1890
Roger Wethered lost a play-off in 1921

Highest number of top five finishes

16 JH Taylor and Jack Nicklaus
15 Harry Vardon and James Braid

Players with four rounds under 70

Greg Norman (66-68-69-64), Sandwich, 1993;
Ernie Els (68-69-69-68), Sandwich, 1993;
Nick Price (69-66-67-66), Turnberry, 1994;
Jesper Parnevik (68-66-68-67), Turnberry, 1994
Tiger Woods (67-66-67-69), St Andrews, 2000

Highest number of rounds under 70

33 Jack Nicklaus and Nick Faldo
27 Tom Watson
23 Greg Norman
21 Lee Trevino
20 Severiano Ballesteros and Nick Price

Outright leader after every round

Willie Auchterlonie, 1893; JH Taylor, 1894 (tied
with Harry Vardon 1900); James Braid, 1908; Ted
Ray, 1912; Bobby Jones, 1927; Gene Sarazen,
1932; Henry Cotton, 1934; Tom Weiskopf, 1973

Record leads (since 1892)

After 18 holes: 4 strokes, Bobby Jones, 1927;
Henry Cotton, 1934; Christy O'Connor Jr,
1985
After 36 holes: 9 strokes, Henry Cotton, 1934
After 54 holes: 10 strokes, Henry Cotton, 1934;
7 strokes, Tony Lema, 1964; 6 strokes,
James Braid, 1908; Tom Lehman, 1996;
Tiger Woods, 2000

Champions with each round lower than previous one

Jack White, 1904, Sandwich, 80-75-72-69
James Braid, 1906, Muirfield, 77-76-74-73
Ben Hogan, 1953, Carnoustie, 73-71-70-68
Gary Player, 1959, Muirfield, 75-71-70-68

Champion with four rounds the same

Densmore Shute, 1933, St Andrews, 73-73-73-73
(excluding the play-off)

Biggest variation between rounds of a champion

14 strokes, Henry Cotton, 1934, second round 65,
fourth round 79
11 strokes, Jack White, 1904, first round 80,
fourth round 69; Greg Norman, 1986, first
round 74, second round 63, third round 74

Biggest variation between two rounds

18 strokes: A Tingey Jr, 1923, first round 94,
second 76
17 strokes, Jack Nicklaus, 1981, first round 83,
second round 66; Ian Baker-Finch, 1986, first
round 86, second round 69

Best comeback by champions

After 18 holes: Harry Vardon, 1896, 11 strokes
behind the leader
After 36 holes: George Duncan, 1920, 13 strokes
behind leader
After 54 holes: Paul Lawrie, 1999, 10 strokes
behind the leader (won four-hole play-off)

Best comeback by non-champions

Of non-champions, Greg Norman, 1989, seven
strokes behind the leader and lost in a play-off

Best finishing round by a champion

64 Greg Norman, Sandwich, 1993
65 Tom Watson, Turnberry, 1977; Severiano
Ballesteros, Royal Lytham, 1988; Justin
Leonard, Royal Troon, 1997

Worst finishing round by a champion since 1920

79 Henry Cotton, Sandwich, 1934
78 Reg Whitcombe, Sandwich, 1938
77 Walter Hagen, Hoylake, 1924

Best opening round by a champion

66 Peter Thomson, Royal Lytham, 1958;
Nick Faldo, Muirfield, 1992; Greg Norman,
Sandwich, 1993
67 Henry Cotton, Sandwich, 1934; Tom Watson,
R. Birkdale, 1983; Severiano Ballesteros,
R. Lytham, 1988; Nick Faldo, St Andrews,
1990; John Daly, St Andrews, 1995, Tom
Lehman, R. Lytham, 1996, Tiger Woods, St
Andrews, 2000

Worst opening round by a champion since 1919

80 George Duncan, Deal, 1920 (he also had a
second round of 80)
77 Walter Hagen, Hoylake, 1924

Biggest recovery in 18 holes by a champion

George Duncan, Deal, 1920, was 13 strokes
behind the leader, Abe Mitchell, after 36 holes
and level after 54

Most consecutive appearances

47 Gary Player, 1955–2001

Championship since 1946 with the fewest rounds under 70

St Andrews, 1946; Hoylake, 1947; Portrush,
1951; Hoylake, 1956; Carnoustie, 1968. All had
only two rounds under 70

Longest course

Carnoustie, 1999, 7361 yds

Largest entries

2,460 in 2000, St Andrews

Courses most often used

St Andrews, 26; Prestwick, 24 (but not since
1925); Muirfield, 14; Sandwich, 12; Hoylake, 10;
Royal Lytham and St Annes, 10; Royal Birkdale,
8; Royal Troon 7; Musselburgh, 6; Carnoustie, 6;
Turnberry, 3; Deal, 2; Royal Portrush and
Prince's, 1

Albatrosses (Double-Eagles)

Both Jeff Maggert (6th hole, 2nd round) and Greg
Owen (11th hole, 3rd round) made albatrosses
during the 2001 Open Championship at Royal
Lytham and St Annes. No complete record of
albatrosses in the history of the event is available
but since 1980 there had been only three others –
by Johnny Miller (Muirfield 5th hole) in 1980, Bill
Rogers (Royal Birkdale 17th hole) 1983 and
Manny Zerman (St Andrews) 2000.

Prize Money

Year	Total	First Prize £	Year	Total	First Prize £	Year	Total	First Prize £
1860	nil	nil	1959	5,000	1,000	1985	530,000	65,000
1863	10	nil	1960	7,000	1,250	1986	600,000	70,000
1864	16	6	1961	8,500	1,400	1987	650,000	75,000
1876	20	20	1963	8,500	1,500	1988	700,000	80,000
1889	22	8	1965	10,000	1,750	1989	750,000	80,000
1891	28.50	10	1966	15,000	2,100	1990	815,000	85,000
1892	110	(Am)	1968	20,000	3,000	1991	900,000	90,000
1893	100	30	1969	30,000	4,250	1992	950,000	95,000
1910	125	50	1970	40,000	5,250	1993	1,000,000	100,000
1920	225	75	1971	45,000	5,500	1994	1,100,000	110,000
1927	275	100	1972	50,000	5,500	1995	1,250,000	125,000
1930	400	100	1975	75,000	7,500	1996	1,400,000	200,000
1931	500	100	1977	100,000	10,000	1997	1,586,300	250,000
1946	1,000	150	1978	125,000	12,500	1998	1,774,150	300,000
1949	1,700	300	1979	155,000	15,500	1999	2,029,950	350,000
1953	2,450	500	1980	200,000	25,000	2000	2,722,150	500,000
1954	3,500	750	1982	250,000	32,000	2001	3,229,748	600,000
1955	3,750	1,000	1983	300,000	40,000			
1958	4,850	1,000	1984	451,000	55,000			

Attendances

Year	Attendance	Year	Attendance	Year	Attendance	Year	Attendance
1962	37,098	1972	84,746	1982	133,299	1992	150,100
1963	24,585	1973	78,810	1983	142,892	1993	140,100
1964	35,954	1974	92,796	1984	193,126	1994	128,000
1965	32,927	1975	85,258	1985	141,619	1995	180,000
1966	40,182	1976	92,021	1986	134,261	1996	170,000
1967	29,880	1977	87,615	1987	139,189	1997	176,797
1968	51,819	1978	125,271	1988	191,334	1998	180,000
1969	46,001	1979	134,501	1989	160,639	1999	158,000
1970	82,593	1980	131,610	1990	207,000	2000	230,000
1971	70,076	1981	111,987	1991	192,154	2001	178,000

US Open

Most times champion
4   Willie Anderson, 1901-03-04-05; Bobby Jones, 1923-26-29-30; Ben Hogan, 1948-50-51-53; Jack Nicklaus, 1962-67-72-80

Most times runner-up
4   Bobby Jones, 1922-24-25-28; Sam Snead, 1937-47-49-53; Arnold Palmer, 1962-63-66-67; Jack Nicklaus, 1960 (am)-68-71-82

Oldest winner
Hale Irwin, 45 years, Medinah, 1990

Youngest winner
Johnny McDermott, 19 years, Chicago, 1911

Biggest winning margin
15 strokes Tiger Woods, Pebble Beach, 2000

Lowest winning aggregate
272 Jack Nicklaus, Baltusrol, 1980; Lee Janzen, Baltusrol, 1993; Tiger Woods, Pebble Beach, 2000

Lowest in relation to par
12 under Tiger Woods, Pebble Beach, 2000

Lowest round
63 Johnny Miller, fourth round, Oakmont, 1973; Jack Nicklaus, first round, Baltusrol, 1980; Tom Weiskopf, first round, Baltusrol, 1980

Lowest 9 holes
29 Neal Lancaster, Shinnecock Hills, 1995, and Oakland Hills, 1996

Lowest first 36 holes
134 Jack Nicklaus, Baltusrol, 1980; Tze-chung Chen, Oakland Hills, 1985; Tiger Woods, Pebble Beach, 2000

Lowest final 36 holes
132 Larry Nelson, Oakmont, 1983

Most consecutive appearances
44 Jack Nicklaus 1957 to 2000

Successive victories
3 Willie Anderson, 1903-04-05

Players with four rounds under 70
Lee Trevino, 69-68-69-69, Oak Hill, 1968; Lee Janzen, 67-67-69-69, Baltusrol, 1993

Wire to wire winners
Walter Hagen, Midlothian, 1914; Jim Barnes, Columbia, 1921; Ben Hogan, Oakmont, 1953; Tony Jacklin, Hazeltine, 1970; Tiger Woods, Pebble Beach, 2000

Best opening round by a champion
63 Jack Nicklaus, Baltusrol, 1980

Worst opening round by a champion
91 Horace Rawlins, Newport, RI, 1895
Since World War II: 76 Ben Hogan, Oakland Hills, 1951; Jack Fleck, Olympic, 1955

US Masters

Most times champion
6   Jack Nicklaus, 1963-65-66-72-75-86
4   Arnold Palmer, 1958-60-62-64

Most times runner-up
4   Ben Hogan, 1942-46-54-55; Jack Nicklaus, 1964-71-77-81

Oldest winner
Jack Nicklaus, 46 years, 1986

Youngest winner
Tiger Woods, 21 years, 3 months, 1997

Biggest winning margin
12 strokes Tiger Woods, 1997

Lowest winning aggregate
270 Tiger Woods, 1997

Lowest in relation to par
18 under Tiger Woods, Augusta, 1997

Lowest aggregate by an amateur
281 Charles Coe, 1961 (joint second)

Lowest round
63 Nick Price, 1986; Greg Norman, 1996

Lowest 9 holes
29 Mark Calcavecchia, 1992

Lowest first 36 holes
131 Raymond Floyd, 1976

Lowest final 36 holes
131 Johnny Miller, 1975

Most appearances
49 Doug Ford 1952 to 2001

Successive victories
2 Jack Nicklaus, 1965-66; Nick Faldo, 1989-90

Players with four rounds under 70
None

Wire to wire winners
Craig Wood, 1941; Arnold Palmer, 1960; Jack Nicklaus, 1972; Raymond Floyd, 1976

Best opening round by a champion
65 Raymond Floyd, 1976

Worst opening round by a champion
75 Craig Stadler, 1982

Albatrosses
There have been three albatross twos in the Masters at Augusta National: by Gene Sarazen at the 15th, 1935; by Bruce Devlin at the eighth, 1967; and by Jeff Maggert at the 13th, 1994.

USPGA Championship

Most times champion
5 Walter Hagen, 1921-24-25-26-27; Jack Nicklaus 1963-71-73-75-80

Most times runner-up
4 Jack Nicklaus, 1964-65-74-83

Oldest winner
Julius Boros, 48 years 4 months 18 days, Pecan Valley, 1968

Youngest winner
Gene Sarazen, 20 years 5 months 22 days, Oakmont, 1922

Biggest winning margin
7 strokes Jack Nicklaus, Oak Hill, 1980

Lowest winning aggregate
265 (-15) David Toms, Atlanta Athletic Club, 2001
267 Steve Elkington and Colin Montgomerie, Riviera, 1995 – Montgomerie lost sudden death play-off

Lowest aggregate by runner-up
266 (-14) Phil Michelson, Atlanta Athletic Club, 2001

Lowest in relation to par
18 under Tiger Woods and Bob May, Valhalla, 2000 (May lost three-hole play-off)

Lowest round
63 Bruce Crampton, Firestone, 1975; Raymond Floyd, Southern Hills, 1982; Gary Player, Shoal Creek, 1984; Vijay Singh, Inverness, 1993; Michael Bradley and Brad Faxon, Riviera, 1995; José Maria Olazábal, Valhalla, 2000; Mark O'Meara, Atlanta Athletic Club, 2001

Most successive victories
4 Walter Hagen, 1924-25-26-27

Lowest 9 holes
28 Brad Faxon, Riviera, 1995

Lowest first 36 holes
131 Hal Sutton, Riviera, 1983; Vijay Singh, Inverness, 1993; Ernie Els and Mark O'Meara, Riviera, 1995; Shingo Katayama and David Toms, Atlanta Athletic Club, 2001

Lowest final 36 holes
131 Mark Calcavecchia, Atlanta Athletic Club, 2001
132 Miller Barber, Dayton, 1969; Steve Elkington and Colin Montgomerie, Riviera, 1995

Most appearances
37 Arnold Palmer; Jack Nicklaus

Wire-to-wire winners
Bobby Nichols, Columbus, 1964; Raymond Floyd, Dayton, 1969; Jack Nicklaus, PGA National, 1971; Raymond Floyd, Southern Hills, 1982; Hal Sutton, Riviera, 1983

Best opening round by a champion
63 Raymond Floyd, Southern Hills, 1982

Worst opening round by a champion
75 John Mahaffey, Oakmont, 1978

European PGA Tour

Lowest 72-hole aggregate
258 (14 under par) David Llewellyn (Wal), AGF Biarritz Open, 1988; (18 under) Ian Woosnam (Wal), Monte Carlo Open, 1990.
259 (25 under par) Mark McNulty (Zim), German Open at Frankfurt, 1987; (21 under par) Tiger Woods (USA), NEC Invitational, 2000
Note: In relation to par, the 27-under 261 of Jerry Anderson (Can) to win the 1984 Ebel European Masters–Swiss Open at Crans-sur-Sierre is the record. John Daly equalled this at the 2001 BMW International Open at Munchen Nord-Richenreid, but preferred lies were in operation in the third round.

Lowest 9 holes
27 (9 under par) José María Canizares (Esp), Swiss Open at Crans-sur-Sierre, 1978; (7 under) Robert Lee (Eng), Johnnie Walker Monte Carlo Open at Mont Agel, 1985; (6 under) Robert Lee, Portuguese Open at Estoril, 1987; (9 under) Joakim Haeggman (Swe), Alfred Dunhill Cup at St Andrews, 1997

Lowest 18 holes
60 (-11) Baldovino Dassu (Ita), Swiss Open at Crans-sur-Sierre, 1971; David Llewellyn (Wal), AGF Biarritz Open, 1988; (-9) Ian Woosnam (Wal), Torras Monte Carlo Open at Mont Agel, 1990; (-12) Jamie Spence, Canon European Masters at Crans-sur-Sierre, 1992; (-10) Paul Curry, Bell's Scottish Open at Gleneagles, 1992; (-9) both Darren Clarke and Johan Rystrom, Monte Carlo Open at Mont Agel, 1992; (-12) Bernhard Langer (Ger), Linde German Masters at Motzener See, 1997; (-12) Darren Clarke, Smurfit European Open at K Club, 1999

Lowest 36 holes
124 (18 under par) Colin Montgomerie (Sco), Canon European Masters at Crans-sur-Sierre, 1996 (3rd and 4th rounds)

Lowest first 36 holes
125 Tiger Woods, NEC Invitational World Championship, Firestone, Akron, Ohio, 2000

Lowest 54 holes
192 (24 under par) Anders Forbrand (Swe), Ebel European Masters Swiss Open at Crans-sur-Sierre, 1987; (18 under) Tiger Woods, NEC Invitational, Firestone, Akron, Ohio, 2000

Largest winning margin
17 strokes Bernhard Langer, Cacharel Under-25s' Championship in Nîmes, 1979.

Highest winning score
306 Peter Butler (Eng), Schweppes PGA Close Championship at Royal Birkdale, 1963.

Youngest winner
Dale Hayes, 18 years 290 days, Spanish Open, 1971

Oldest winner
Des Smyth (Ire), 48 years 34 days, Madeira Island Open, 2001

Most wins in one season
7 Norman von Nida (Aus), 1947

US Tour

Lowest 72-hole aggregate
256 (28 under par) Mark Calcavecchia (USA), 65-60-64-67, Phoenix Open, TPC of Scottsdale, 2001

Note: John Huston's 260 at the 1998 Hawaiian Open was also 28 under

Lowest 18 holes
59 Sam Snead, 3rd round, Greenbrier Open (Sam Snead Festival), White Sulphur Springs, West Virginia, 1959; Al Geiberger, 2nd round, Danny Thomas Memphis Classic, Colonial CC, 1977 (when preferred lies were in operation); (-13) Chip Beck on the 6,914-yards Sunrise GC course, Las Vegas, 3rd round, Las Vegas Invitational, 1991 (finished third but won a bonus prize of $500,000 and another $500,000 for charities; (-13) David Duval on 6,940-yd PGA West Arnold Palmer course, CA, final round, Bob Hope Chrysler Classic, 1999 (won trn with last hole eagle)

Lowest 9 holes
27 Mike Souchak, Texas Open, 1955; Andy North, BC Open, 1975

Lowest 36 holes
124 (18 under) Mark Calcavecchia (USA), Phoenix Open, 2001 (2nd and 3rd rounds)

Lowest first 36 holes
125 (17 under) Mark Calcavecchia (USA), Phoenix Open, 2001; (15 under) Tiger Woods (USA), NEC Invitational World Championship, Firestone, Akron, Ohio, 2000

Lowest 54 holes
189 Chandler Harper, Texas Open (last three rounds), 1954; Mark Calcavecchia (USA), Phoenix Open (first three rounds), 2001

Largest winning margin
16 strokes J Douglas Edgar, Canadian Open Championship, 1919; Bobby Locke, Chicago Victory National Championship, 1948

Youngest winner
Johnny McDermott, 19 years 10 months, US Open, 1911

Oldest winner
Sam Snead, 52 years 10 months, Greater Greensboro Open, 1965

Most wins in one season
18 Byron Nelson, 1945

National opens – excluding Europe and USA

Lowest 72-hole aggregate
255 Peter Tupling, Nigerian Open, Lagos, 1981.

Lowest 36-hole aggregate
124 (18 under par) Sandy Lyle, Nigerian Open, Ikoyi GC, Lagos, 1978 (his first year as a professional)

Lowest 18 holes
59 Gary Player, second round, Brazilian Open, Gavea GC (6,185 yards), Rio de Janeiro, 1974.

Professional events– excluding Europe and USA

Lowest 72-hole aggregate
260 Bob Charles, Spalding Masters at Tauranga, New Zealand, 1969; Jason Bohn (USA), Bayer Classic, Huron Oaks, Canada, 2001.

Lowest 18-hole aggregate
58 (13 under) Jason Bohn (USA), Bayer Classic, Huron Oaks, Canada, 2001.

Lowest 9-hole aggregate
27 Bill Brask (USa) at Tauranga in the New Zealand PGA in 1976.

Miscellaneous British

72-hole aggregate
Andrew Brooks recorded a 72-hole aggregate of 259 in winning the Skol (Scotland) tournament at Williamwood in 1974.

Lowest rounds
Playing on the ladies' course (4,020 yards) at Sunningdale on 26th September, 1961, Arthur Lees, the professional there, went round in 52, 10 under par. He went out in 26 (2, 3, 3, 4, 3, 3, 3, 3, 2) and came back in 26 (2, 3, 3, 3, 2, 3, 4, 3, 3).

On 1st January, 1936, AE Smith, Woolacombe Bay professional, recorded a score of 55 in a game there with a club member. The course measured 4,248 yards. Smith went out in 29 and came back in 26 finishing with a hole-in-one at the 18th.

Other low scores recorded in Britain are by CC Aylmer, an English International who went round Ranelagh in 56; George Duncan, Axenfels in 56; Harry Bannerman, Banchory in 56 in 1971; Ian Connelly, Welwyn Garden City in 56 in 1972; James Braid, Hedderwick near Dunbar in 57; H Hardman, Wirral in 58; Norman Quigley, Windermere in 58 in 1937; Robert Webster, Eaglescliffe in 58, in 1970. Harry Weetman scored 58 in a round at the 6,171 yards Croham Hurst on 30th January, 1956.

D Sewell had a round of 60 in an Alliance Meeting at Ferndown, Bournemouth, a full-size course. He scored 30 for each half and had a total of 26 putts. In September 1986, Jeffrey Burn, handicap 1, of Shrewsbury GC, scored 60 in a club competition, made up of 8 birdies, an eagle and 9 pars. He was 30 out and 30 home and no 5

on his card. Andrew Sherborne, as a 20-year-old amateur, went round Cirencester in 60 strokes. Dennis Gray completed a round at Broome Manor, Swindon (6,906 yards, SSS 73) in the summer of 1976 in 60 (28 out, 32 in).

Playing over Aberdour on 13th June, 1936, Hector Thomson, British Amateur champion, 1936, and Jack McLean, former Scottish Amateur champion, each did 61 in the second round of an exhibition. McLean in his first round had a 63, which gave him an aggregate 124 for 36 holes.

Steve Tredinnick in a friendly match against business tycoon Joe Hyman scored a 61 over West Sussex (6,211 yards) in 1970. It included a hole-in-one at the 12th (198 yards) and a 2 at the 17th (445 yards).

Another round of 61 on a full-size course was achieved by 18-year-old Michael Jones on his home course, Worthing GC (6,274 yards), in the first round of the President's Cup in May, 1974.

In the Second City Pro-Am tournament in 1970, at Handsworth, Simon Fogarty did the second 9 holes in 27 against the par of 36.

Miscellaneous USA

Lowest rounds
The lowest known scores recorded for 18 holes in America are by 55 by EF Staugaard in 1935 over the 6,419 yards Montebello Park, California, and 55 by Homero Blancas in 1962 over the 5,002 yards Premier course in Longview, Texas. Staugaard in his round had 2 eagles, 13 birdies and 3 pars.

Equally outstanding is a round of 58 (13 under par) achieved by a 13-year-old boy, Douglas Beecher, on 6th July, 1976, at Pitman CC, New Jersey. The course measured 6,180 yards from the back tees, and the middle tees, off which Douglas played, were estimated by the club professional to reduce the yardage by under 180 yards.

In 1941 at a 6,100 yards course in Portsmouth, Virginia, Chandler Harper scored 58.

Jack Nicklaus in an exhibition match at Breakers Club, Palm Beach, California, in 1973 scored 59 over the 6,200-yard course.

The lowest 9-hole score in America is 25, held jointly by Bill Burke over the second half of the 6,384 yards Normandie CC, St Louis in May, 1970 at the age of 29; by Daniel Cavin, who had seven 3s and two 2s on the par 36 Bill Brewer Course, Texas, in September, 1959; and by Douglas Beecher over the second half of Pitman CC, New Jersey, on 6th July, 1976, at the amazingly young age of 13. The back 9 holes of the Pitman course measured 3,150 yards (par 35) from the back tees, but even though Douglas played off the middle tees, the yardage was still over 3,000 yards for the 9 holes. He scored 8 birdies and 1 eagle.

Horton Smith scored 119 for two consecutive rounds in winning the Catalina Open in California in December, 1928. The course, however, measured only 4,700 yards.

Miscellaneous – excluding GB and USA

Tony Jacklin won the 1973 Los Lagartos Open with an aggregate of 261, 27 under par.

Henry Cotton in 1950 had a round of 56 at Monte Carlo (29 out, 27 in).

In a Pro-Am tournament prior to the 1973 Nigerian Open, British professional David Jagger went round in 59.

Max Banbury recorded a 9-hole score of 26 at Woodstock, Ontario, playing in a competition in 1952.

Women

The lowest score recorded on a full-size course by a woman is 59 by Sweden's Annika Sörenstam on the 6,459 yards, par 72 Moon Valley course in Phoenix, Arizona. It broke by two the previous record of 61 by South Korean Se Ri Pak. Sörenstam had begun the tournament with a 65 and by adding rounds of 69 and 68 she equalled the LPGA record of 261 set by Pak (71-61-63-66) at Highland Meadows in Ohio in 1998. Sörenstam's score represents 27 under par, Pak's 23 under.

The lowest 9-hole score on the US Ladies' PGA circuit is 28, first achieved by Mary Beth Zimmerman in the 1984 Rail Charity Classic and since equalled by Pat Bradley, Muffin Spencer-Devlin, Peggy Kirsch and Renee Heiken.

The lowest round on the European LPGA is 62 (11 under par) by Trish Johnson in the 1996 French Open. A 62 was also achieved by New Zealand's Janice Arnold at Coventry in 1990 during a Women's Professional Golfers' Association tournament.

The lowest 9-hole score on the European LPGA circuit is 29 by Kitrina Douglas, Regine Lautens, Laura Davies, Anne Jones and Trish Johnson.

In the Women's World Team Championship in Mexico in 1966, Mrs Belle Robertson, playing for the British team, was the only player to break 70. She scored 69 in the third round.

At Westgate-on-Sea GC (measuring 5,002 yards), Wanda Morgan scored 60 in an open tournament in 1929.

Since scores cannot properly be taken in matchplay no stroke records can be made in matchplay events. Nevertheless we record here two outstanding examples of low scoring in the finals of national championships. Mrs Catherine Lacoste de Prado is credited with a score of 62 in the first round of the 36-hole final of the 1972 French

Ladies' Open Championship at Morfontaine. She went out in 29 and came back in 33 on a course measuring 5,933 yards. In the final of the English Ladies' Championship at Woodhall Spa in 1954, Frances Stephens (later Mrs Smith) did the first nine holes against Elizabeth Price (later Mrs Fisher) in 30. It included a hole-in-one at the 5th. The nine holes measured 3,280 yards.

Amateurs

National championships

The following examples of low scoring cannot be regarded as genuine stroke play records since they took place in match play. Nevertheless they are recorded here as being worthy of note.

Michael Bonallack in beating David Kelley in the final of the English championship in 1968 at Ganton did the first 18 holes in 61 with only one putt under two feet conceded. He was out in 32 and home in 29. The par of the course was 71.

Charles McFarlane, playing in the fourth round of the Amateur Championship at Sandwich in 1914 against Charles Evans did the first nine holes in 31, winning by 6 and 5.

This score of 31 at Sandwich was equalled on several occasions in later years there. Then, in 1948, Richard Chapman of America went out in 29 in the fourth round eventually beating Hamilton McInally, Scottish Champion in 1937, 1939 and 1947, by 9 and 7.

In the fourth round of the Amateur Championship at Hoylake in 1953, Harvie Ward, the holder, did the first nine holes against Frank Stranahan in 32. The total yardage for the holes was 3,474 yards and included one hole of 527 yards and five holes over 400 yards. Ward won by one hole.

Francis Ouimet in the first round of the American Amateur Championship in 1932 against George Voigt did the first nine holes in 30. Ouimet won by 6 and 5.

Open competitions

The 1970 South African Dunlop Masters Tournament was won by an amateur, John Fourie, with a score of 266, 14 under par. He led from start to finish with rounds of 65, 68, 65, 68, finally winning by six shots from Gary Player.

Jim Ferrier, Manly, won the New South Wales championship at Sydney in 1935 with 266. His rounds were: 67, 65, 70, 64, giving an aggregate 16 strokes better than that of the runner-up. At the time he did this amazing score Ferrier was 20 years old and an amateur.

Aaron Baddeley became the first amateur to win the Australian Open since Bruce Devlin in 1960 when he took the title at Royal Sydney in 1999. After turning pro he successfully defended the title the following year at Kingston Heath.

Holes below par

Most holes below par

EF Staugaard in a round of 55 over the 6,419 yards Montbello Park, California, in 1935, had two eagles, 13 birdies and three pars.

American Jim Clouette scored 14 birdies in a round at Longhills GC, Arkansas, in 1974. The course measured 6,257 yards.

Jimmy Martin in his round of 63 in the Swallow-Penfold at Stoneham in 1961 had one eagle and 11 birdies.

In the Ricarton Rose Bowl at Hamilton, Scotland, in August, 1981, Wilma Aitken, a women's amateur internationalist, had 11 birdies in a round of 64, including nine consecutive birdies from the 3rd to the 11th.

Mrs Donna Young scored nine birdies and one eagle in one round in the 1975 Colgate European Women's Open.

Jason Bohn had two eagles and 10 birdies in his closing 58 at the 2001 Bayer Classic on the Canadian Tour at the par 71 Huron Oaks.

Consecutive holes below par

Lionel Platts had ten consecutive birdies from the 8th to 17th holes at Blairgowrie GC during a practice round for the 1973 Sumrie Better-Ball tournament.

Roberto De Vicenzo in the Argentine Centre of the Republic Championship in April, 1974 at the Cordoba GC, Villa Allende, broke par at each of the first nine holes. (By starting his round at the 10th hole they were in fact the second nine holes played by Vicenzo.) He had one eagle (at the 7th hole) and eight birdies. The par for the 3,602 yards half was 37, completed by Vicenzo in 27.

Nine consecutive holes under par have been recorded by Claude Harmon in a friendly match over Winged Foot GC, Mamaroneck, NY, in 1931; by Les Hardie at Eastern GC, Melbourne, in April, 1934; by Jimmy Smith at McCabe GC, Nashville, Tenn, in 1969; by 13-year-old Douglas Beecher, in 1976, at Pitman CC, New Jersey; by Rick Sigda at Greenfield CC, Mass, in 1979; and by Ian Jelley at Brookman Park in 1994.

TW Egan in winning the East of Ireland Championship in 1962 at Baltray had eight consecutive birdies (2nd to 9th) in the third round.

On the United States PGA tour, eight consecutive holes below par have been achieved by three players – Bob Goalby in the 1961 St Petersburg Open, Fuzzy Zoeller in the 1976 Quad Cities Open and Dewey Arnette in the 1987 Buick Open.

Fred Couples set a PGA European Tour record with 12 birdies in a round of 61 during the 1991 Scandinavian Masters on the 72-par Drottningholm course. This has since been equalled by Ernie Els (1994 Dubai Desert Classic) and by Russell Claydon and Fredrik Lindgren (1995 German Masters). Ian Woosnam, Tony Johnstone, Severiano Ballesteros, John Bickerton, Mark O'Meara and Raymond Russell share another record with eight successive birdies.

The United States Ladies' PGA record is seven consecutive holes below par achieved by Carol Mann in the Borden Classic at Columbus, Ohio in 1975.

Miss Wilma Aitken recorded nine successive birdies (from the 3rd to the 11th) in the 1981 Ricarton Rose Bowl.

This has since been equalled by Ernie Els (1994 Dubai Desert Classic), Russell Claydon and Fredrik Lindgren (1995 Mercedes German Masters) and Darreb Clarke (1999 Smurfit European Open). Ian Woosnam, Tony Johnstone, Severiano Ballesteros, John Bickerton, Mark O'Meara, Raymond Russell, Darren Clarke and Marcello Santo share another record with eight successive birdies.

Low scoring rarities

At Standerton GC, South Africa, in May 1937, FF Bennett, playing for Standerton against Witwatersrand University, did the 2nd hole, 110 yards, in three 2s and a 1. Standerton ·is a 9-hole course, and in the match Bennett had to play four rounds.

In 1957 a fourball comprising HJ Marr, E Stevenson, C Bennett and WS May completed the 2nd hole (160 yards) in the grand total of six strokes. Marr and Stevenson both holed in one while Bennett and May both made 2.

The old Meadow Brook Club of Long Island, USA, had five par 3 holes and George Low in a round there in the 1950s scored two at each of them.

In a friendly match on a course near Chicago in 1971, assistant professional Tom Doty (23 years) had a remarkable low run over four consecutive holes: 4th (500 yards) 2; 5th (360 yards, dogleg) 1; 6th (175 yards) 1; 7th (375 yards) 2.

RW Bishop, playing in the Oxley Park, July medal competition in 1966, scored three consecutive 2s. They occurred at the 12th, 13th and 14th holes which measured 151, 500 and 136 yards respectively.

In the 1959 PGA Close Championship at Ashburnham, Bob Boobyer scored five 2s in one of the rounds.

American Art Wall scored three consecutive 2s in the first round of the US Masters in 1974. They were at the 4th, 5th and 6th holes, the par of which was 3, 4 and 3.

Nine consecutive 3s have been recorded by RH Corbett in 1916 in the semi-final of the Tangye Cup; by Dr James Stothers of Ralston GC over the 2,056 yards 9-hole course at Carradale, Argyll, during the summer of 1971; by Irish internationalist Brian Kissock in the Homebright Open at Carnalea GC, Bangor, in June, 1975; and by American club professional Ben Toski.

The most consecutive 3s in a British PGA event is seven by Eric Brown in the Dunlop at Gleneagles (Queen's Course) in 1960.

Hubert Green scored eight consecutive 3s in a round in the 1980 US Open.

The greatest number of 3s in one round in a British PGA event is 11 by Brian Barnes in the 1977 Skol Lager tournament at Gleneagles.

Fewest putts

The lowest known number of putts in one round is 14, achieved by Colin Collen-Smith in a round at Betchworth Park, Dorking, in June, 1947. He single-putted 14 greens and chipped into the hole on four occasions.

Professional Richard Stanwood in a round at Riverside GC, Pocatello, Idaho on 17th May, 1976 took 15 putts, chipping into the hole on five occasions.

Several instances of 16 putts in one round have been recorded in friendly games.

For 9 holes, the fewest putts is five by Ron Stutesman for the first 9 holes at Orchard Hills G&CC, Washington, USA in 1978.

Walter Hagen in nine consecutive holes on one occasion took only seven putts. He holed long putts on seven greens and chips at the other two holes.

In competitive stroke rounds in Britain and Ireland, the lowest known number of putts in one round is 18, in a medal round at Portpatrick Dunskey GC, Wilmslow GC professional Fred Taggart is reported to have taken 20 putts in one round of the 1934 Open Championship. Padraigh Hogan (Elm Park), when competing in the Junior Scratch Cup at Carlow in 1976, took only 20 putts in a round of 67.

The fewest putts in a British PGA event is believed to be 22 by Bill Large in a qualifying round over Moor Park High Course for the 1972 Benson and Hedges Match Play.

Overseas, outside the United States of America, the fewest putts is 19 achieved by Robert Wynn (GB) in a round in the 1973 Nigerian Open and by Mary Bohen (US) in the final round of the 1977 South Australian Open at Adelaide.

The USPGA record for fewest putts in one round is 18, achieved by Andy North (1990); Kenny Knox (1989); Mike McGee (1987) and Sam Trehan (1979). For 9 holes the record is eight putts by Kenny Knox (1989), Jim Colbert (1987) and Sam Trehan (1979).

The fewest putts recorded for a 72-hole US PGA Tour event is 93 by Kenny Knox in the 1989 Heritage Classic at Harbour Town Golf Links.

The fewest putts recorded by a woman is 17, by Joan Joyce in the Lady Michelob tournament, Georgia, in May, 1982.

PART XI

Guide to Golfing Services and Places to Stay in the British Isles and Ireland

Buyer's Guide to Good Golfing and Golf Course Maintenance

This compact but informative guide to manufacturers and organisations offering services to golf clubs and individual golfers includes a wide number of categories, from services to personal accessories and golfing equipment to golf course maintenance.

ACADEMIC QUALIFICATIONS
AGRONOMY
ANTIQUES
ARCHITECTS & CONSULTANTS
ASSOCIATIONS
AWARDS, PRIZES & TROPHIES
BAG/MEMBERSHIP TAGS
BAGS/GOLF ACCESSORIES
BALL COLLECTORS
BOOKSELLERS & PUBLISHERS
CARTS, TROLLEYS & BUGGIES
CLOTHING/GOLFWEAR
COMPUTER SOFTWARE/SYSTEMS
CORPORATE GIFTS & EVENTS
COURSE CONSTRUCTION & UPGRADING
COURSE MEASUREMENT
DISCOUNTED COURSE BOOKING SERVICE
DISTRIBUTORS & WHOLESALERS
DRIVING RANGE & PRACTICE EQUIPMENT
EDUCATION
ELECTRIC GOLF CARS
FITNESS CONSULTANTS
FIXTURE BOOKS
FLAGS, BANNERS & FLAGPOLES
FLOODLIGHTING & FENCING
FOOTWEAR/SHOE ACCESSORIES
GIFTS & NOVELTIES
GOLF & RESORT CONSULTANTS
GOLF & SPORTS PHOTOGRAPHY
GOLF BALL MANUFACTURES/SUPPLIERS
GOLF CLUB MANUFACTURERS/SUPPLIERS
GOLF CLUB PHOTOGRAPHS & SPORTS
    PHOTOGRAPHY
GOLF COURSE DESIGN CONSULTANTS
GOLF COURSE DISTANCE GUIDES
GOLF COURSE MAINTENANCE & UPGRADING
GOLF DEVELOPMENT/MANAGEMENT
GOLF HOLIDAYS

GOLF RANGE DESIGN
GOLFING AIDS/PRACTICE EQUIPMENT
GREEN KEEPING AND DRIVING RANGE VEHICLES
GRIPS & SHAFTS
INSURANCE
INTERNET TEE-TIME BOOKING
IRRIGATION EQUIPMENT/DESIGN & INSTALLATION
JEWELLERY
MAIL ORDER
PATHWAYS
PERSONAL EQUIPMENT & ACCESSORIES
PERSONALISED PRODUCTS
PICTURES & PRINTS
PLAY & STAY
PORTUGAL
PRACTICE NETTING/CAGES
PRINTING
PROPERTY CONSULTANTS
PUTTER/CHIPPER MANUFACTURERS & SUPPLIERS
RANGE BALL MANUFACTURERS/SUPPLIERS
RECRUITMENT CONSULTANTS
REMOTE CONTROLLED TROLLEYS
RIDE-ON BUGGIES
SCORECARDS & PLANNERS
SEEDS & FERTILISERS
SIMULATORS/ANALYSERS
SYNTHETIC SURFACES
TEE SIGNS
THERMAL WEAR
TRAINING & TEACHING AIDS
TROPHIES
TUITION
UMBRELLAS
WATER STORAGE/TANKS
WEATHERWEAR
WILD FLORA
WINTER ALL-WEATHER TEE MATS

ACADEMIC QUALIFICATIONS

Bournemouth University
School of Service Industries,
Fern Barrow,
Poole,
Dorset BH12 5BB.
Tel (01202) 595146 Fax (01202) 515707
E-mail: mcustard@bournemouth.ac.uk
Website: www.bournemouth.ac.uk/
service_industries

The university has developed a unique degree
for those interested in a career in golf and/or
sports management. With the support of local
golf clubs, the BSc(Hons) in Sports
Management (golf) is a 4-year sandwich degree
which provides graduates with the technical
expertise as well as the managerial skills
necessary to succeed in this dynamic industry.
Contact: Programme Administrator, School of
Service Industries

AGRONOMY

British Rootzone & Topdressing Manufacturers Association
Federation House,
NAC,
Stoneleigh Park,
Warwickshire CV8 2RF.
Tel (02476) 414999 Fax (02476) 414990

The Association is a collaboration of
experience and expertise in the manufacture of
rootzone materials to offer architects,
constructors and agronomists a recognised
focal point for the industry.

Grass Science
Victoria House,
Garside Street,
Bolton,
Lancashire BL1 4AE.
Tel (01204) 377757 Fax (01204) 377755
E-mail: j.pardon@grass-science.com
Website: www.grass-science.co.uk

UK based independent agronomy consultancy,
offers a complete service for the design,
construction and maintenance of your golf
course. We provide a most professional and
comprehensive service, utilising the latest
technology, techniques and concepts currently
available.

PSD Agronomy Ltd
42 Garstang Road,
Preston,
Lancashire PR1 1NA.
Tel (01772) 884450 Fax (01772) 884445
E-mail: psdgb@aol.com
Website: www.psdagronomy.com

A specialist team of golf course agronomists
working throughout the UK and Europe.
Whether building a new course, extending an
existing one or just making the best of what
you have - we have the technical expertise to
help.

STRI - The Sports Turf Research Institute
St Ives Estate,
Bingley,
West Yorkshire BD16 1AU.
Tel (01274) 565131 Fax (01274) 561891
E-mail: info@stri.co.uk
Website: www.stri.co.uk

Independent specialists offering you help and
advice for the design, construction,
management and maintenance, irrigation or
renovation of your golf course. Comprehensive
in-house support services for ecology, testing,
turf pathology and research.

ANTIQUES

Schotten Trophies - Manfred Schotten Antiques
109 High Street,
Burford,
Oxfordshire OX18 4RG.
Tel (01993) 822302 Fax (01993) 822055
Website: www.schotten.com

Exquisite hand crafted trophies in traditional
style, created and hand finished in our own
workshop by crafstmen using solid woods,
brass and bronze. Also available are golf
antiques, clubs, novelty items, desk sets etc,
and golf club furnishings. *(See advertisement
page 35 for further details.)*

ARCHITECTS & CONSULTANTS

David Griffith

20 Clwyd Avenue, Dyserth,
Denbighshire LL18 6HN.
Tel (01745) 570659 Fax (01745) 571382
E-mail: david@griffithgolf.co.uk
Mobile: 07778 494123

Golf course architect. Years of experience in a variety of golf projects ensures that no stone is left unturned in fulfilling the potential of a site. A satisfaction guarantee is given to all projects.

David Williams Golf Design

187 Llanelian Road,
Old Colwyn,
Colwyn Bay, North Wales LL29 8UW.
Tel (01492) 512070 Fax (01492) 512077
E-mail: williams@marketsite.co.uk

Golf course architects and project managers. Fully integrated service *from conception through construction to completion*. Over 20 new courses built in Britain within last ten years. Alterations, improvements and upgrades undertaken through the country. Member of the European Institute of Golf Course Architects (EIGCA).

J D Edgar - Golf Course Architect

Wheathampstead Pay & Play Golf Course,
Harpenden Road,
St Albans,
Hertfordshire AL4 8EZ.
Tel/Fax (01582) 833941

Doug Edgar the golf professional and golf course architect is a member of the PGA and PGAA. He designs and builds courses and can offer you a complete design consultancy service.

European Institute of Golf Course Architects - EIGCA

Merrist Wood House, Worplesdon,
Guildford, Surrey GU3 3PE.
Tel +44 (0) 1483 884036
Fax +44 (0) 1483 884037
E-mail: info@eigca.org
Website: www.eigca.org

The EIGCA represents the vast majority of qualified and experienced golf course architects throughout Europe. Our goals include enhancing the professional status of the profession, developing the role of education and increasing the opportunities for its members to practice in countries throughout the world. EIGCA also provides educational courses to train future golf course architects and is the authoritative voice on all related matters, being recognised by the R&A Golf Club of St Andrews. Contact: Julia Green, Executive Officer.

Gaunt & Marnoch - Golf Course Architects

Head Office: Hilltop,
Lakeside,
Bakewell, Derbyshire DE45 1GN.
Tel+44 (0) 1629 815453
Fax+44 (0) 1629 815170
E-mail: info@gauntandmarnoch.com
Website: www.gauntandmarnoch.com

Gaunt & Marnoch provides a comprehensive, cost-conscious and environmentally sympathetic golf course design service. An international and award-winning company who are flexible and offer a top quality service from feasibility through planning to construction supervision and opening the course for play. We are committed to better golf through good design. Ring for brochure. *(See advertisement page 26 for further details.)*

Grassform Ltd

3 Cricketers Row,
Herongate,
Brentwood, Essex CM13 3QA.
Tel (01277) 812973 Fax (01277) 812972

Grassform Limited undertakes all types of golf course projects. From new build to re-construction of tees, greens and bunkers. We also install land drainage systems, sand banding, lakes, water features, footpaths, buggy paths and driving ranges. For further information please contact Mark Dunning.

Hawtree Ltd - Golf Course Architects & Consultants

5 Oxford Street,
Woodstock,
Oxon OX20 1TQ.
Tel (01993) 811976 Fax (01993) 812448
E-mail: mail@hawtree.co.uk
Website: www.hawtree.co.uk

Founded in 1912, Hawtree Limited is the longest continuous golf course practice, having designed and renovated over 800 golf courses worldwide. Just some of these include the renowned Birkdale, Portmarnock, Lahinch and Vilamoura golf courses.

John Greasley Ltd
Ashfield House,
154 Melton Road,
Syston, Leicester LE7 2HB.
Tel 0116-269 6766 Fax 0116-269 6866

John Greasley established his company in 1984 and has specialised in the construction of new courses, along with alterations, improvements and refurbishment on existing ones. Works have been completed on some of the countries oldest and most prestigious courses.

Philip Sparks
Professional Golf Designs
Peak House,
Hawksdown,
Walmer, Deal, Kent CT12 5BE.
Tel (01304) 374119 Fax (01843) 853090

'Creating future links with the Past'. Specialising in golf course remodelling and renovation. Toro student architect of the year 2000. First golf professional in the world to gain an EIGCA diploma in golf course architecture.

Robin Hiseman
Golf Course Design
Berrymeadow Cottage,
4 West Cairnbeg Cottages,
Laurencekirk,
Aberdeenshire AB30 1SR.
Tel/Fax (01561) 320827
E-mail:
robin@hisemangolf.freeserve.co.uk

Scotland's EIGCA qualified golf architect provides a personal, professional and superior design service for existing clubs and new developers. A specialist in the alteration and extension of existing courses. Major projects completed for Royal Dornoch, Boat of Garten and Deeside.

STRI - The Sports Turf
Research Institute
St Ives Estate,
Bingley,
West Yorkshire BD16 1AU.
Tel (01274) 565131 Fax (01274) 561891
E-mail: info@stri.co.uk
Website: www.stri.co.uk

Independent specialists offering you help and advice for the design, construction, management and maintenance, irrigation or renovation of your golf course. Comprehensive in-house support services for ecology, testing, turf pathology and research.

Simon Gidman International
Golf Course Architects
Wychwood House,
43 Shipton Road,
Ascott Under Wychwood,
Oxon OX7 6AG.
Tel (01993) 830441 Fax (01993) 831860
E-mail:
simongidman@golfarch.freeserve.co.uk
Mobile: 0468 600102

A full member of the European Institute of Golf Course Architects (EIGCA), Simon Gidman has been involved with some 50 projects in Europe and throughout the world. The company also specialises in preparing reports and studies for the restoration and upgrading of existing golf courses.

Swan Golf Designs Ltd
Telfords Barn,
Willingale,
Ongar, Essex CM5 0QF.
Tel (01277) 896229 Fax (01277) 896300
E-mail: swangolfdesigns@btinternet.com
Website: www.swangolfdesigns.com

Professional golf course architects with traditional values, offering initial appraisals, conceptual designs, detailed design work and construction management. Specialising in improvements of existing golf courses, extensions, re-design of greens and tees etc, including restorations of classic old courses.

York & Martin
39 Salisbury Street,
Fordingbridge,
Hampshire SP6 1AB.
Tel (01425) 652087 Fax (01425) 652476
E-mail:
mike.martin@yorkandmartin.co.uk
Website: www.yorkandmartin.co.uk

Independent irrigation consultants providing objective advice on all irrigation related matters including water sourcing, existing system evaluation, system designs and specifications, project supervision etc. Operating throughout the UK and mainland Europe.

ASSOCIATIONS

Association of Golf Club Secretaries

7A Beaconsfield Road,
Weston-Super-Mare, Somerset BS23 1YE.
Tel (01934) 641166 Fax (01934) 644254
E-mail: hq@agcs.org.uk
Website: www.agcs.org.uk

Membership is available to golf secretaries and managers, course owners and others involved in golf club administration. The following services are available: monthly journal, information library, training courses. seminars, conferences, regional meetings and employment support.

British Association of Golf Course Constructors - BAGCC

The Dormy House, Cooden Beach Golf Club, Bexhill-on-Sea TN39 4TR.
Tel:(01424) 842380 Fax: (01424) 843375
Website: www.bagcc.org.uk

Secretary: David White. Constructors who appear on the BAGCC membership roster qualify only by passing a critical vetting process undertaken by their peers, who look for excellence in construction and a clear demonstration of skills pertinent only to the golf course industry. Utilising the services of a BAGCC member therefore ensures absolute professionalism.

British Rootzone & Topdressing Manufacturers Association

Federation House, NAC,
Stoneleigh Park, Warwickshire CV8 2RF.
Tel (02476) 414999 Fax (02476) 414990

The Association is a collaboration of experience and expertise in the manufacture of rootzone materials to offer architects, constructors and agronomists a recognised focal point for the industry.

English Golf Union - EGU

The National Golf Centre,
The Broadway, Woodhall Spa,
Lincolnshire LN10 6PU.
Tel (01526) 354500 Fax (01526) 354020
E-mail: info@englishgolfunion.org
Website: www.englishgolfunion.org

As the governing body for men's amateur golf in England the EGU organises championships and coaching for players and representative teams at all levels and offers an advisory service on all aspects of golf administration and management.

European Golf Industry Association

Federation House,
Stoneleigh Park, Warwickshire CV8 2RF.
Tel 024 7641 7141 Fax 024 7641 4990
E-mail: egia@sportslife.org.uk

Trade association for manufacturers and distributors of golf equipment.

EUROPEAN GOLF TEACHERS FEDERATION LTD

European Golf Teachers Federation - EGTF

5 Hastings Road, Bromley, Kent BR2 8NZ.
Tel 020 8462 4120 Fax 020 8462 3983
E-mail: egtf@dial.pipex.com
Website: www.egtf.co.uk

We offer intensive teaching courses for professionals and amateurs who would like to know how to teach the game simply. The EGTF is the leader in the field of golf instruction.

European Institute of Golf Course Architects - EIGCA

Merrist Wood House,
Worplesdon, Guildford, Surrey GU3 3PE.
Tel +44 (0) 1483 884036
Fax +44 (0) 1483 884037
E-mail: info@eigca.org
Website: www.eigca.org

The EIGCA represents the vast majority of qualified and experienced golf course architects throughout Europe. Our goals include enhancing the professional status of the profession, developing the role of education and increasing the opportunities for its members to practice in countries throughout the world. EIGCA also provides educational courses to train future golf course architects and is the authoritative voice on all related matters, being recognised by the R&A Golf Club of St Andrews. Contact: Julia Green, Executive Officer.

Golf Consultants Association - GCA

Federation House,
Stoneleigh Park, Warwickshire CV8 2RF.
Tel (02476) 414999 Fax (02476) 414990
E-mail: gca@sportstye.org.uk

The GCA provides a point of reference for those requiring independent, professional, golf consultancy services throughout the world.

Developing Junior Golf

The Golf Foundation - Developing Junior Golf

Foundation House, The Spinney,
Hoddesdon Road, Stanstead Abbotts,
Hertfordshire SG12 8GF.
Tel (01920) 876200 Fax (01920) 876211
Website: www.golf-foundation.org

An organisation dedicated to the promotion and development of grass roots junior golf

across the British Isles. (The Golf Foundation is a registered charity.)

National Association of Public Golf Courses - NAPGC

12 Newton Close, Redditch B98 7YR.
Tel (01527) 542106 Fax (01527) 455320
E-mail: eddiemitchell@blueyonder.co.uk
Website: www.napgc.org.uk

The Association provides competition golf for gentlemen and lady players of all handicaps and ages. It also offers help and advice to its member clubs - those playing over courses that they do not own.

STRI - The Sports Turf Research Institute

St Ives Estate, Bingley,
West Yorkshire BD16 1AU.
Tel (01274) 565131 Fax (01274) 561891
E-mail: info@stri.co.uk
Website: www.stri.co.uk

Independent specialists offering you help and advice for the design, construction, management and maintenance, irrigation or renovation of your golf course. Comprehensive in-house support services for ecology, testing, turf pathology and research.

AWARDS, PRIZES & TROPHIES

Birkdale Promotions

97 Old Watford Road, Bricket Wood,
Nr St Albans, Hertfordshire AL2 3UN.
Tel (01923) 671225 Fax (01923) 662522
E-mail: paulbirtro@tinyworld.co.uk
Website: www.birkdale-trophies.co.uk

An exclusive range of bronze figuerines, silverplated golf trophies, shields, antique replica plaques all suitable for clubs, societies and corporate events. Our in-house engraving enables each to be personalised to your specification and delivery can be made to any address worldwide. Please call for our free colour brochure and price list. *(See advertisement page 26 for further details.)*

Bryants of Leeds
Speedwell Street,
Meanwood Road,
Leeds LS6 2TD.
Tel 0113-242 8330 Fax 0113-242 6330
Website: www.dimplygolf.com

The leading supplier of personalised golf merchandise. Golf club membership tags and labels, green fee stationery. Captain's Day, Society events and Corporate Golf Day merchandise. Call for a free colour brochure or visit us on our website.

Derek Burridge (Wholesale) Ltd
Awards House,
Unit 15,
The Metro Centre,
Springfield Road, Hayes,
Middlesex UB4 0LE.
Tel 020 8569 0123 Fax 020 8569 0111

The country's leading suppliers of golf prizes, celebrating their 42nd year, offer a vast range of silverplate, crystal, china, clocks, leather goods and sporting trophies, all at trade prices. Glass and silverplate in-house engraving service. Next day delivery throughout the UK. Call for our brochure. *(See advertisement page 31 for further details.)*

Galloway Crystal & Glass Ltd
Beeswing, by Dumfries DG2 8ED.
Tel (01387) 760643 Fax (01387) 760537
E-mail: mccallum@gallowayglass.com
Websites: www.gallowayglass.com
www.crystalforgolfers.com

Specialist plain and cut crystal suppliers and engravers. Many innovative golfing gift ideas through our special collections. Personalisation our speciality. Ask for our catalogue along with club and reseller price lists.

Grandison Golf Gallery
'Gowanbank',
5 Sorley's Brae,
Dollar FK14 7AS.
Tel 01259 740318
E-mail: info@grandisongolfgallery.com
Website: www.grandisongolfgallery.com

Finest quality limited edition prints of the world's premier golfing venues by one of the world's leading golf artists, William Grandison. Each print is individually signed and numbered. Gifts and prizes of distinction for the discerning golfer. Private commissions. Free catalogue available.

Richard Chorley Golf Art
159 Lonsdale Road,
Stevenage, Hertfordshire SG1 5DG.
Tel/Fax (01438) 727901

Richard Chorley, England's premier golf artist. Private commissions, original oil paintings, drawings and limited edition prints. Prints signed by the artist, numbered and embossed. Collection of classic courses and golfing greats. Ideal corporate and captain's prizes gifts.

Schotten Trophies
- Manfred Schotten Antiques
109 High Street,
Burford,
Oxfordshire OX18 4RG.
Tel (01993) 822302 Fax (01993) 822055
Website: www.schotten.com

Exquisite hand crafted trophies in traditional style, created and hand finished in our own workshop by crafstmen using solid woods, brass and bronze. Also available are golf antiques, clubs, novelty items, desk sets etc, and golf club furnishings. *(See advertisement page 35 for further details.)*

Solent Souvenirs Ltd
Hamble Bank,
40 Newtown Road,
Warsash,
Southampton, Hampshire SO31 9FZ.
Tel (01489) 577985 Fax (01489) 577886
E-mail: solentsouvenirs@aol.com

Britain's premier supplier of specialised golf jewellery and quality gifts. Many items designed and manufactured exclusively for us and unobtainable elsewhere. Replace that traditional trophy with an elegant prize which will be both useful and cherished. Most items delivered overnight.

Sport Photo Gallery Ltd
P O Box 31327,
London SW11 5GJ.
Tel 020 7585 1820 Fax 020 7585 1830
E-mail: info@sportphotogallery.com
Website: www.sportphotogallery.com

Comprehensive range of great golf photographs making ideal gifts or golf day prizes. Framing, photo only or interior design options available and golf course photography service. New images added continuously including best shots from the top golf events as they happen. *(See advertisement page 26 for further details.)*

BAG/MEMBERSHIP TAGS

H M T Plastics Ltd
Fairway House,
31A Framfield Road,
Uckfield,
East Sussex TN22 5AH.
Tel (01825) 769393 Fax (01825) 769494
E-mail: hmt@aol.com
Website: www.hmt-plastics.com

Bag tags supplied in nine colours either round, pear shaped, shield maxi or sunrise to accommodate club logo, from a choice of print colours. Adhesive Year Stickers available in choice of nine colours and sold separately. *(See advertisement page 31 for further details.)*

BAGS/GOLF ACCESSORIES

Izzo (UK) Ltd
32 Queen Victoria Road,
Sheffield S17 4HT.
Tel/Fax 0114-236 4410

CARRY THE BEST. CARRY IZZO. Creators of the Dual Strap technology. The strap that lightens the load and is easy on easy off. Suppliers of top quality golf bags and golf club carrying systems.

Prosimmon Golf (UK) Ltd
21 Monkspath Business Park,
Highlands Road,
Shirley,
Solihull,
West Midlands B90 4NZ.
Tel 0121-744 9551 Fax 0121-744 9541

Manufacturers of premium golf clubs, bags and accessories. Designers of unique *Matchplay* computerised custom club fitting system. UK distributors for the STX putter range boasting *'the softest legal face in golf'*.

Teltale
6 Skye Road, Shawfarm Industrial Estate,
Prestwick KA9 2TA.
Tel/Fax (01292) 475125
E-mail: sales@teltale.uk.com
Website: www.teltale.uk.com

Waterproof nylon raincovers made from durable nylon with pocket for scorecard. Fits all bag sizes and packs into a neat zipped wallet. Available in six colours. Cost £11.50. *(See advertisement page 36 for further details.)*

BALL COLLECTORS

European Golf Machinery
Street Garage,
Bucklesham,
Ipswich, Suffolk IP10 0DN.
Tel (01473) 659815 Fax (01473) 659045
E-mail: sales@europeangolf.prestel.co.uk
Website: www.web-marketing.co.uk/
europeangolfmachinery

Manufacturers of driving range equipment including golf ball collectors, dispensers, ball washers and elevators. Kawasaki ATV and Mule distributors. *(See advertisement page 36 for further details.)*

BOOKSELLERS & PUBLISHERS

STRI - The Sports Turf Research Institute
St Ives Estate,
Bingley, West Yorkshire BD16 1AU.
Tel (01274) 565131 Fax (01274) 561891
E-mail: info@stri.co.uk
Website: www.stri.co.uk

A specialist provider and supplier of books and training courses. Over 200 titles available from our on-line bookshop (www.stri.co.uk). Catalogue and training course details on request.

Steve Schofield Golf Books
29 Nichols Way,
Wetherby,
West Yorkshire LS22 6AD.
Tel/Fax (01937) 581276
E-mail: golfbooks@steveschofield.com

Classic golf books for sale, new, old and antiquarian. Books on golf history, architecture, biography, club and ball collecting and instruction. Free catalogue on request.

CARTS, TROLLEYS & BUGGIES

A La Carts
Beechwood, Bakeham Lane,
Englefield Green TW20 9TU.
Tel/Fax (01784) 472982
Website: www.alacarts.tsx.org

Manufacturers and distributors of single and two-seater golf buggies. Also powered trolleys.

Callisto Golf Cars

**Cuparmuir, Cupar,
St Andrews, Fife KY15 5RL.
Tel +44 (0) 1334 657515
Fax +44 (0) 1334 652222**

*Official supplier of Scottish Golf Union and
Scottish National Golf Centre - St Andrews.*
Private Scottish organisation specialising in
supply of new and used golf cars for domestic
and export markets. We sell to clubs,
professionals and private individuals. Hiring/
Customised finance packages. Large selection
of cars in stock. Quick, personal service.

Middlemore Ltd

**Sharrocks Street,
Wolverhampton, West Midlands WV1 3RP.
Tel (01902) 870077 Fax (01902) 455200
E-mail: electra-caddie@thama.co.uk
Website: www.thama.co.uk**

Manufacturers of ELECTRA CADDIE
'Premier' and *'Compact'* one-piece foldaway
powered trolleys and the 4-wheel single seater
RYDEON '2000' buggy - simply load it into
the boot of your car! Break par, not your back!
Free colour brochure on request. *(See
advertisement page 31 for further details.)*

Patterson Products

**Unit 6, Fordwater Trading Estate,
Ford Road, Chertsey, Surrey KT16 8HG.
Tel (01932) 570016 Fax (01932) 570084
E-mail: info@patterson.co.uk
Website: www.patterson.co.uk**

Manufacturers and retailers of the Trio single-
seat, transportable golf cart. Major suppliers
and consultants to Handigolf, a charity for the
severely disabled golfer. The Trio is now in its
15th year with over 4,000 happy users.

Teltale

**6 Skye Road, Shawfarm Industrial Estate,
Prestwick KA9 2TA.
Tel/Fax (01292) 475125
E-mail: sales@teltale.uk.com
Website: www.teltale.uk.com**

The *TopCart* is sturdy, light (8kg) and
powerful. Folded size an incredible 33"x 14.7"
x 10" and available in three colours. Our new
Teltale ride-on buggy, being introduced in May
2002, is an innovative and user-friendly design,
quickly folded down in seconds to fit small
hatchback cars. High power motors and extra
wide tyres. Ideally suitable for hire. *(See
advertisement page 36 for further details.)*

Yamaha Motor (UK) Ltd

**Sopwith Drive, Brooklands,
Weybridge, Surrey KT13 0UZ.
Tel (01932) 358096 Fax (01932) 358090**

Suppliers of petrol and electric golf cars for
clubs and individuals. Fleet contracts with
optional purchase and lease schemes, full
maintenance and service support. On and off-
course utility vehicles, multi-passenger cars and
beverage units.

CLOTHING/GOLFWEAR

Sunderland of Scotland Ltd

**PO Box 14, Glasgow G2 1ER.
Tel 0141-572 5220 Fax 0141-572 5221
Website: www.sunderlandgolf.com**

Sunderland of Scotland manufacture high
quality golf rainwear in Scotland. All rainsuits
are tour-tested and guaranteed waterproof and
breathable, a variety of fabrics including
Goretex being used. Sunderlands also
manufacture the famous Sunderland Original
Weatherbeater, Classic windproof Pullovers
and Fleece. Official supplier to PGA, PGAE,
LPGA, LET and St Andrews Links Trust.

COMPUTER SOFTWARE/SYSTEMS

Links Software

**6 Ascot Avenue,
Westerlands Park, Glasgow G12 0AX.
Tel/Fax 0141-357 0199
E-mail: ac.provan@ntlworld.com
Website: www.linksgolf.co.uk**

The complete software solution for golf clubs.
Membership and subscriptions. Ladies and
gents handicaps. Booking system (with internet
link to Golfagent), point of sale, stock control
and accounts. Compatible with most swipe
cards (including GUI/SGU). Fully
networkable. Modular components start from
just £395. *(See advertisement page 36 for further
details.)*

CORPORATE GIFTS & EVENTS

Bryants of Leeds

**Speedwell Street,
Meanwood Road, Leeds LS6 2TD.
Tel 0113-242 8330 Fax 0113-242 6330
Website: www.dimplygolf.com**

The leading supplier of personalised golf
merchandise. Golf club membership tags and

labels, green fee stationery. Captain's Day, Society events and Corporate Golf Day merchandise. Call for a free colour brochure or visit us on our website.

Derek Burridge (Wholesale) Ltd
Awards House,
Unit 15,
The Metro Centre,
Springfield Road, Hayes,
Middlesex UB4 0LE.
Tel 020 8569 0123 Fax 020 8569 0111

The country's leading suppliers of golf prizes, celebrating their 42nd year, offer a vast range of silverplate, crystal, china, clocks, leather goods and sporting trophies, all at trade prices. Glass and silverplate in-house engraving service. Next day delivery throughout the UK. Call for our brochure. *(See advertisement page 31 for further details.)*

Newton Newton Flag & Banner Makers
The Bishop Tozers Chapel,
Middlemarsh Road,
Burgh-le-Marsh,
Lincolnshire PE24 5AD.
Tel (01754) 768401
Fax (01754) 610612
E-mail: newtonnewton@btinternet.com
Website: www.newtonnewtonflags.com

Manufacturers of superior golf club, captain, tournament, sponsor and pin flags. Appliqued and hand embroidered trophy presentation table covers, drapes, wall banners and badges of unsurpassed grace and beauty. PVC promotional banners and glassfibre flagpoles. *(See advertisement page 35 for further details.)*

COURSE CONSTRUCTION & UPGRADING

M J Abbott Ltd
Bratch Lane,
Dinton,
Salisbury, Wiltshire SP3 5EB.
Tel (01722) 716361 Fax (01722) 716828

M J Abbott Limited offer a range of specialist services to the golf and leisure industry. Recognised as one of Britain's leading companies offering Rain Bird irrigation systems. Land drainage, golf course construction and maintenance are all undertaken by experienced employees utilising the company's own specially adapted machinery.

Brian D Pierson
32 New Road, Ringwood,
Hampshire BH24 3AU.
Tel (01202) 822372 Fax (01202) 826447

The Golf Course Builder - 35 years' experience on over 200 golf courses. New construction - alterations - project management. Contracts completed in USA, Canada, mainland Europe and British Isles. Work completed on seven Open Championship courses.

British Association of Golf Course Constructors - BAGCC
The Dormy House,
Cooden Beach Golf Club,
Bexhill-on-Sea TN39 4TR.
Tel (01424) 842380 Fax (01424) 843375
Website: www.bagcc.org.uk

Secretary: David White: Constructors who appear on the BAGCC membership roster qualify only by passing a critical vetting process undertaken by their peers, who look for excellence in construction and a clear demonstration of skills pertinent only to the golf course industry. Utilising the services of a BAGCC member therefore ensures absolute professionalism.

David Williams Golf Design
187 Llanelian Road, Old Colwyn,
Colwyn Bay, North Wales LL29 8UW.
Tel (01492) 512070 Fax (01492) 512077
E-mail: williams@marketsite.co.uk

Golf course architects and project managers. Fully integrated service *from conception through construction to completion.* Over 20 new courses built in Britain within last ten years. Alterations, improvements and upgrades undertaken through the country. Member of the European Institute of Golf Course Architects (EIGCA).

Grass Science
Victoria House, Garside Street,
Bolton, Lancashire BL1 4AE.
Tel (01204) 377757 Fax (01204) 377755
E-mail: j.pardon@grass-science.com
Website: www.grass-science.co.uk

UK based independent agronomy consultancy, offers a complete service for the design, construction and maintenance of your golf course. We provide a most professional and comprehensive service, utilising the latest technology, techniques and concepts currently available.

Grassform Ltd

3 Cricketers Row,
Herongate,
Brentwood,
Essex CM13 3QA.
Tel (01277) 812973 Fax (01277) 812972

Grassform Limited undertakes all types of golf course projects. From new build to re-construction of tees, greens and bunkers. We also install land drainage systems, sand banding, lakes, water features, footpaths, buggy paths and driving ranges. For further information please contact Mark Dunning.

John Greasley Ltd

Ashfield House,
1154 Melton Road,
Syston,
Leicester LE7 2HB.
Tel 0116-269 6766 Fax 0116-269 6866

John Greasley established his company in 1984 and has specialised in the construction of new courses, along with alterations, improvements and refurbishment on existing ones. Works have been completed on some of the countries oldest and most prestigious courses.

Land Unit Construction Ltd

Hanslope,
Milton Keynes,
Buckinghamshire MK19 7BX.
Tel (01908) 510414 Fax (01908) 511056
E-mail: sales@landunitconstruction.co.uk
Website: www.landunitconstruction.co.uk

We have the knowledge and experience gained over 25 years in golf course construction and constantly work with many of the country's leading golf course architects to provide clients with unparalleled quality of service.

PSD Agronomy Ltd

42 Garstang Road,
Preston,
Lancashire PR1 1NA.
Tel (01772) 884450 Fax (01772) 884445
E-mail: psdgb@aol.com
Website: www.psdagronomy.com

A specialist team of golf course agronomists working throughout the UK and Europe. Whether building a new course, extending an existing one or just making the best of what you have - we have the technical expertise to help.

Robin Hiseman Golf Course Design

Berrymeadow Cottage,
4 West Cairnbeg Cottages, Laurencekirk,
Aberdeenshire AB30 1SR.
Tel/Fax (01561) 320827
E-mail:
robin@hisemangolf.freeserve.co.uk

Scotland's EIGCA qualified golf architect provides a personal, professional and superior design service for existing clubs and new developers. A specialist in the alteration and extension of existing courses. Major projects completed for Royal Dornoch, Boat of Garten and Deeside.

STRI - The Sports Turf Research Institute

St Ives Estate, Bingley,
West Yorkshire BD16 1AU.
Tel (01274) 565131 Fax (01274) 561891
E-mail: info@stri.co.uk
Website: www.stri.co.uk

Independent specialists offering you help and advice for the design, construction, management and maintenance, irrigation or renovation of your golf course. Comprehensive in-house support services for ecology, testing, turf pathology and research.

Simon Gidman International Golf Course Architects

Wychwood House, 43 Shipton Road,
Ascott Under Wychwood, Oxon OX7 6AG.
Tel (01993) 830441 Fax (01993) 831860
E-mail:
simongidman@golfarch.freeserve.co.uk
Mobile: 0468 600102

A full member of the European Institute of Golf Course Architects (EIGCA), Simon Gidman has been involved with some 50 projects in Europe and throughout the world. The company also specialises in preparing reports and studies for the restoration and upgrading of existing golf courses.

Swan Golf Designs Ltd

Telfords Barn, Willingale,
Ongar, Essex CM5 0QF.
Tel (01277) 896229 Fax (01277) 896300
E-mail: swangolfdesigns@btinternet.com
Website: www.swangolfdesigns.com

Professional golf course architects with traditional values, offering initial appraisals, conceptual designs, detailed design work and construction management. Specialising in improvements of existing golf courses, extensions, re-design of greens and tees etc, including restorations of classic old courses.

COURSE MEASUREMENT

Eagle Promotions Ltd
Eagle House,
1 Clearway Court,
139-141 Croydon Road,
Caterham,
Surrey CR3 6PF.
Tel (01883) 344244 Fax (01883) 341777
E-mail: info@eaglepromotions.co.uk
Website: www.eaglepromotions.co.uk

Eagle Promotions offer a comprehensive range of products from certified course measurement and tee signs through to scorecards, yardage books, green fee tickets, members' tags, event and leader boards, honours boards, clubhouse and general course signage. For further information please contact Philip McInley on 01883 344244.

Strokesport
Abbey Mill Business Centre,
Paisley PA1 1TJ.
Tel 0141-848 1199 Fax 0141-887 1642

Measurement and survey to professional standard. Certification accepted by National Golf unions. Leading specialists in course measurement. We are also publishers of *Strokesaver Distance Guides* which are recognised as the most accurate and useful golf course management aids worldwide. *Strokesaver* provides professionals and clubs with a constant profit centre. *(See advertisement page 31 for further details.)*

Vickers Sports Optics
Unit 9,
35 Revenge Road,
Lordswood,
Kent ME5 8DW.
Tel (01634) 201284 Fax (01634) 201286

Bushnell's Yardage Pros' instantaneously measures distances with incredible accuracy (± 1 yard). Know whether - you can reach the green in one - clear the water or bunker - it's safe to hit or how far you have driven/hit the ball.

DISCOUNTED COURSE BOOKING SERVICE

Portugal Fairways Go-Golf-Pay-Less
Estrada de Pera, Sesmarias,
8200 Albufeira, Portugal.
Tel +44 (0) 1908 311768
E-mail: info@go-golf-pay-less.com
Website: www.go-golf-pay-less.com

Algarve, Estoril and Costa Azul golfing breaks - let Go-Golf-Pay-Less book your courses, preferred dates and tee times at discounted prices at no charge to you! Accommodation in a choice of hotels, villas, motels and apartments. Car rental and airport transfers.

DISTRIBUTORS & WHOLESALERS

Aldila UK
12 Heather Road, Binley Woods,
Coventry CV3 2DE.
Tel/Fax 024 7654 5651

Aldila Golf equipment distributors: Diamond Golf Ltd, 4/5 Rudford Industrial Estate, Ford Road, Arundel BN18 0BS Tel (01903) 726999 Fax (01903) 726998; Golfsmith (Europe) Ltd, Ormond House, Nuffield Road, St Ives, Cambridgeshire PE27 3LX Tel (01480) 308800 Fax (01480) 308801; Oxygen Sports & Leisure Ltd, OSL House, Bow Beck, Bradford, West Yorkshire BD4 8SL. Tel (01274) 208080 Fax (01274) 208081.

Eaton Ltd - Golf Pride Grips
Units 1 & 2 The Stirling Centre,
Northfields Industrial Estate,
Market Deeping,
Nr Peterborough PE6 8EQ.
Tel (01778) 341555 Fax (01778) 344025

Manufacturers of golf grips for over 50 years, they have been the leader in golf grip technology and the leader in rubber and cord grip sales for both professional and amateur players alike.

European Golf Industry Association
Federation House,
Stoneleigh Park, Warwickshire CV8 2RF.
Tel 024 7641 7141 Fax 024 7641 4990
E-mail: egia@sportslife.org.uk

Trade association for manufacturers and distributors of golf equipment.

Yonex UK Ltd
Yonex House, 74 Wood Lane,
White City, London W12 7RH.
Tel 020 8742 9777 Fax 020 8742 9612
E-mail: cservice@yonex.uk.com

Manufacturer and distributor of Yonex
premium golf equipment. All models are
designed and manufactured using the latest in
high technology materials and world class
quality standards.

DRIVING RANGE
& PRACTICE EQUIPMENT

European Golf Machinery
Street Garage, Bucklesham,
Ipswich, Suffolk IP10 0DN.
Tel (01473) 659815 Fax (01473) 659045

Manufacturers of driving range equipment
including golf ball collectors, dispensers, ball
washers and elevators. Kawasaki ATV and
Mule distributors. *(See advertisement page 36 for
further details.)*

Tildenet Ltd
Hartcliffe Way,
Bristol BS3 5RJ.
Tel 0117-966 9684 Fax 0117-923 1251
Website: www.tildenet.co.uk

Tildenet supply and install a comprehensive
range of quality products to the Golfing World.
These include perimeter ball stop netting,
practice nets and mats for the professional
enthusiast. Anti-ball plug nets, target nets,
target greens and anti-dazzle netting for clubs,
and grass germination and bunker membranes
for the greenkeeper.

EDUCATION

Bournemouth University
School of Service Industries,
Fern Barrow, Poole, Dorset BH12 5BB.
Tel (01202) 595146 Fax (01202) 515707
E-mail: mcustard@bournemouth.ac.uk
*Website: www.bournemouth.ac.uk/
service_industries*

The university has developed a unique degree
for those interested in a career in golf and/or
sports management. With the support of local
golf clubs, the BSc(Hons) in Sports
Management (golf) is a 4-year sandwich degree
which provides graduates with the technical

expertise as well as the managerial skills
necessary to succeed in this dynamic industry.
Contact: Programme Administrator, School of
Service Industries.

ELECTRIC GOLF CARS

Middlemore Ltd
Sharrocks Street,
Wolverhampton,
West Midlands WV1 3RP.
Tel (01902) 870077 Fax (01902) 455200
E-mail: electra-caddie@thama.co.uk
Website: www.thama.co.uk

Manufacturers of ELECTRA CADDIE
'Premier' and 'Compact' one-piece foldaway
powered trolleys and the 4-wheel single seater
RYDEON '2000' buggy - simply load it into
the boot of your car! Break par, not your back!
Free colour brochure on request. *(See
advertisement page 31 for further details.)*

Yamaha Motor (UK) Ltd
Sopwith Drive,
Brooklands,
Weybridge,
Surrey KT13 0UZ.
Tel (01932) 358096 Fax (01932) 358090

Suppliers of petrol and electric golf cars for
clubs and individuals. Fleet contracts with
optional purchase and lease schemes, full
maintenance and service support. On and off-
course utility vehicles, multi-passenger cars and
beverage units.

FITNESS CONSULTANTS

Chartex Products
International Ltd
20 Grasmere,
Liden,
Swindon,
Wiltshire SN3 6LE.
Tel (01793) 530880 Fax (01793) 491035

Golf Fitness Programmes - *'Keeping Fit For
Golf'* is a new, unique programme of exercises
designed to help improve stamina, suppleness
and strength for enhanced control and greater
distance. The 36-page book, plus the warm-up
stretching booklet is supplemented with two
thera-band rubber tubes for progressive
strength training. Endorsed by the PGA of
Europe.

FIXTURE BOOKS

Iain Crosbie Printers
Beechfield Road,
Willowyard Industrial Estate,
Beith,
Ayrshire KA15 1LN.
Tel (01505) 504848 Fax (01505) 504674
E-mail: crosbieprinters@dial.pipex.com

At Crosbie Printers we have over 20 years' experience in printing associated with golf and commerce. We manufacture scorecards (standard and bespoke), fixture books/diaries, green fee tickets, marketing brochures/leaflets and all associated printed stationery. *(See advertisement page 35 for further details.)*

FLAGS, BANNERS & FLAGPOLES

Newton Newton Flag & Banner Makers
The Bishop Tozer's Chapel,
Middlemarsh Road,
Burgh-le-Marsh,
Lincolnshire PE24 5AD.
Tel (01754) 768401
Fax (01754) 610612
E-mail: mail@newtonnewtonflags.com
Website: www.newtonnewtonflags.com

Manufacturers of superior golf club, captain, tournament, sponsor and pin flags. Appliqued and hand embroidered trophy presentation table covers, drapes, wall banners and badges of unsurpassed grace and beauty. PVC promotional banners and glassfibre flagpoles. *(See advertisement page 35 for further details.)*

FLOODLIGHTING & FENCING

Mike Copson Associates Golf Driving Range Design & Construction Specialists
197 Comberton Road,
Kidderminster,
Worcestershire DY10 1UE.
Tel/Fax (01562) 863937
Mobile: 0836 371180

Mike Copson has been designing and building driving ranges since 1988. During this time he has completed 26 major golfing projects. Clients include: British Coal, Whitbread's, Bovis (La Manga) abroad and many private

golf clubs and local authorities. Our experience also extends to the design of high perimeter fencing and floodlighting designs. We can offer a full turnkey package or individually designed packages to suit each client or act as a consultant.

FOOTWEAR/SHOE ACCESSORIES

1000 Mile Sportswear Ltd
12 Shakespeare Industrial Estate,
Shakespeare Street,
Watford, Hertfordshire WD24 5RN.
Tel (01923) 242233 Fax (01923) 240066
E-mail: sales@1000mile.co.uk

The famous 1000 Mile blister-free guaranteed socks. Ray Cook putters - famous for over 35 years with over 200 tour wins. The award-winning GustBuster umbrella which will withstand winds up to 60 mph.

GIFTS & NOVELTIES

Birkdale Promotions
97 Old Watford Road,
Bricket Wood,
Nr St Albans, Hertfordshire AL2 3UN.
Tel (01923) 671225 Fax (01923) 662522
E-mail: paulbirtro@tinyworld.co.uk
Website: www.birkdale-trophies.co.uk

An exclusive range of bronze figuerines, silverplated golf trophies, shields, antique replica plaques all suitable for clubs, societies and corporate events. Our in-house engraving enables each to be personalised to your specification and delivery can be made to any address worldwide. Please call for our free colour brochure and price list. *(See advertisement page 26 for further details.)*

Derek Burridge (Wholesale) Ltd
Awards House,
Unit 15, The Metro Centre,
Springfield Road,
Hayes, Middlesex UB4 0LE.
Tel 020 8569 0123 Fax 020 8569 0111

The country's leading suppliers of golf prizes, celebrating their 42nd year, offer a vast range of silverplate, crystal, china, clocks, leather goods and sporting trophies, all at trade prices. Glass and silverplate in-house engraving service. Next day delivery throughout the UK. Call for our brochure. *(See advertisement page 31 for further details.)*

Schotten Trophies
- Manfred Schotten Antiques

109 High Street, Burford,
Oxfordshire OX18 4RG.
Tel (01993) 822302 Fax (01993) 822055
Website: www.schotten.com

Exquisite hand crafted trophies in traditional
style, created and hand finished in our own
workshop by craftsmen using solid woods,
brass and bronze. Also available are golf
antiques, clubs, novelty items, desks sets etc,
and golf club furnishings. *(See advertisement
page 35 for further details.)*

Solent Souvenirs Ltd

Hamble Bank, 40 Newtown Road,
Warsash, Southampton,
Hampshire SO31 9FZ.
Tel (01489) 577985 Fax (01489) 577886
E-mail: solentsouvenirs@aol.com

Britain's premier supplier of specialised golf
jewellery and quality gifts. Many items
designed and manufactured exclusively for us
and unobtainable elsewhere. Replace that
traditional trophy with an elegant prize which
will be both useful and cherished. Most items
delivered overnight.

Sport Photo Gallery Ltd

P O Box 31327, London SW11 5GJ.
Tel 020 7585 1820 Fax 020 7585 1830
E-mail: info@sportphotogallery.com
Website: www.sportphotogallery.com

Comprehensive range of great golf photographs
making ideal gifts or golf day prizes. Framing,
photo only or interior design options available
and golf course photography service. New
images added continuously including best shots
from the top golf events as they happen. *(See
advertisement page 26 for further details.)*

GOLF & RESORT CONSULTANTS

Portfolio International

5 Breams Buildings, London EC4A 1DY.
Tel +44 (0) 207 520 5000
Fax +44 (0) 207 520 5007
Website: www.portfoliointernational.com

Portfolio International can provide an exclusive
individual consultancy service, advising not
only on recruitment but also feasibility studies,
sales and marketing, strategy and interim
management, membership offerings and
trouble-shooting. For further information
please call Giles Greenwood.

GOLF & SPORTS PHOTOGRAPHY

Sport Photo Gallery Ltd

P O Box 31327,
London SW11 5GJ.
Tel 020 7585 1820 Fax 020 7585 1830
E-mail: info@sportphotogallery.com
Website: www.sportphotogallery.com

Comprehensive range of great golf photographs
making ideal gifts or golf day prizes. Framing,
photo only or interior design options available
and golf course photography service. New
images added continuously including best shots
from the top golf events as they happen. *(See
advertisement page 26 for further details.)*

GOLF BALL MANUFACTURES/SUPPLIERS

Wilson Sporting Goods Co Ltd

Ayr Road,
Irvine,
Ayrshire KA12 8HG.
Tel (01294) 316270 Fax (01294) 316300
Website: www.wilsonsports.com

Manufactures and supplies a full range of game
improvement products specifically designed to
enhance performance for golfers of all
standards. Superstar products for 2002 include
the new Deep Red family of drivers, fairway
woods, irons and putters. Also new for 2002 is
the Staff Pro Distance family of premium balls
available in five models, to cater for all
performance requirements. Call us or visit our
website for details of your nearest stockist.

GOLF CLUB PHOTOGRAPHS & SPORTS
PHOTOGRAPHY

Sport Photo Gallery Ltd

P O Box 31327,
London SW11 5GJ.
Tel 020 7585 1820 Fax 020 7585 1830
E-mail: info@sportphotogallery.com
Website: www.sportphotogallery.com

Comprehensive range of great golf photographs
making ideal gifts or golf day prizes. Framing,
photo only or interior design options available
and golf course photography service. New
images added continuously including best shots
from the top golf events as they happen. *(See
advertisement page 26 for further details.)*

34 GOLF CLUB MANUFACTURERS/ SUPPLIERS

Adams Golf UK Ltd
Unit 6 Corium House, Douglas Drive,
Catteshall Lane, Godalming,
Surrey GU7 1JX.
Tel (01483) 239333 Fax (01483) 239334
E-mail: sales@adamsgolf.co.uk
Website: www.adamsgolf.co.uk

Adams Golf supply the complete range of the
Tight Lie products with Multi Material
technology. Played by Tom Watson, these
consist of the ST (steel tip) range of drivers
and fairway woods and the GT (graphite tip)
range of irons and Watson wedges.

Aldila UK
12 Heather Road,
Binley Woods, Coventry CV3 2DE.
Tel/Fax 024 7654 5651

World's leading manufacturer of graphite golf
shafts, including Tour Grade series, Clubmaker
series, Value series, Speciality series, Classic
series and G Loomis shafts.

Bronty Golf
3 Musgrave Mount, Eccleshill,
Bradford, West Yorkshire BD2 3LA.
Tel/Fax +44 (0) 1274 773585
Mobile:+44 (0) 7950 397603
E-mail: brontygolf1@activemail.co.uk
Website: www.brontygolf.co.uk

Manufacturers of high quality British made
custom golf clubs, putters and specialist clubs.
Authentic replicas and hickory shafted putters
etc.

Callaway Golf Europe Ltd
Unit 27 Barwell Business Park,
Leatherhead Road,
Chessington, Surrey KT9 2NY.
Tel +44 (0) 20 8391 0111

Manufacturer of golf clubs and accessories.
Callaway Golf is now the distributor for
Odyssey Golf.

Prosimmon Golf (UK) Ltd
21 Monkspath Business Park,
Highlands Road, Shirley, Solihull,
West Midlands B90 4NZ.
Tel 0121-744 9551 Fax 0121-744 9541

Manufacturers of premium golf clubs, bags and
accessories. Designers of unique *Matchplay*
computerised custom club fitting system. UK

distributors for the STX putter range boasting
'the softest legal face in golf'.

True Temper UK/Europe
c/o Tucker Fasteners
Walsall Road,
Birmingham B42 1BP.
Tel 0121-331 2276 Fax 0121-331 2286

Golf shaft manufacturer both steel and
graphite. In 2000 achieved over 120
Tournament wins on PGA Tours. Dynamic
Gold used by leading players. Sensicore
continues to grow in usage by both
Tournament players and amateurs.

Wilson Sporting Goods Co Ltd
Ayr Road, Irvine,
Ayrshire KA12 8HG.
Tel (01294) 316270 Fax (01294) 316300
Website: www.wilsonsports.com

Manufactures and supplies a full range of game
improvement products specifically designed to
enhance performance for golfers of all
standards. Superstar products for 2002 include
the new Deep Red family of drivers, fairway
woods, irons and putters. Also new for 2002 is
the Staff Pro Distance family of premium balls
available in five models, to cater for all
performance requirements. Call us or visit our
website for details of your nearest stockist.

Yonex UK Ltd
Yonex House,
74 Wood Lane,
White City, London W12 7RH.
Tel 020 8742 9777 Fax 020 8742 9612
E-mail: cservice@yonex.uk.com

Manufacturer and distributor of Yonex
premium golf equipment. All models are
designed and manufactured using the latest in
high technology materials and world class
quality standards.

GOLF COURSE DESIGN CONSULTANTS

David Griffith
20 Clwyd Avenue, Dyserth,
Denbighshire LL18 6HN.
Tel (01745) 570659 Fax (01745) 571382
E-mail: david@griffithgolf.co.uk
Mobile: 07778 494123

Golf course architect. Years of experience in a
variety of golf projects ensures that no stone is
left unturned in fulfilling the potential of a site.
A satisfaction guarantee is given to all projects.

David Williams Golf Design
187 Llanelian Road,
Old Colwyn, Colwyn Bay,
North Wales LL29 8UW.
Tel (01492) 512070 Fax (01492) 512077
E-mail: williams@marketsite.co.uk

Golf Course architects and project managers.
Fully integrated service *from conception through
construction to completion.* Over 20 new courses
built in Britain within last ten years.
Alterations, improvements and upgrades
undertaken through the country. Member of
the European Institute of Golf Course
Architects (EIGCA).

European Institute of Golf Course Architects - EIGCA
Merrist Wood House, Worplesdon,
Guildford, Surrey GU3 3PE.
Tel +44 (0) 1483 884036
Fax +44 (0) 1483 884037
E-mail: info@eigca.org
Website: www.eigca.org

The EIGCA represents the vast majority of
qualified and experienced golf course architects
throughout Europe. EIGCA's goals include
enhancing the professional status of the
profession, developing the role of education
and increasing the opportunities for its
members to practice in countries throughout
the world. EIGCA also provids educational
courses to train future golf course architects is
the authoritative voice on all related matters,
being recognised by the R&A Golf Club of St
Andrews. Contact: Julia Green, Executive
Officer.

Gaunt & Marnoch - Golf Course Architects
Head Office: Hilltop, Lakeside,
Bakewell, Derbyshire DE45 1GN.
Tel+44 (0) 1629 815453
Fax+44 (0) 1629 815170
E-mail: info@gauntandmarnoch.com
Website: www.gauntandmarnoch.com

Gaunt & Marnoch provides a comprehensive,
cost-conscious and environmentally
sympathetic golf course design service. An
international and award-winning company who
are flexible and offer a top quality service from
feasibility through planning to construction
supervision and opening the course for play.
We are committed to better golf through good
design. Ring for brochure. *(See advertisement
page 26 for further details.)*

Grassform Ltd
3 Cricketers Row, Herongate,
Brentwood, Essex CM13 3QA.
Tel (01277) 812973 Fax (01277) 812972

Grassform Limited undertakes all types of golf
course projects. From new build to re-
construction of tees, greens and bunkers. We
also install land drainage systems, sand
banding, lakes, water features, footpaths, buggy
paths and driving ranges. For further
information please contact Mark Dunning.

Hawtree Ltd - Golf Course Architects & Consultants
5 Oxford Street,
Woodstock, Oxon OX20 1TQ.
Tel (01993) 811976 Fax (01993) 812448
E-mail: mail@hawtree.co.uk
Website: www.hawtree.co.uk

Founded in 1912, Hawtree Limited is the
longest continuous golf course practice, having
designed and renovated over 800 golf courses
worldwide. Just some of these include the
renowned Birkdale, Portmarnock, Lahinch and
Vilamoura golf courses.

Peter Alliss - Golf Ltd
25 St Johns Road, Farnham,
Surrey GU9 8NV.
Tel (01252) 717711 Fax (01252) 717722
E-mail: roy@allissgolf.demon.co.uk

Designers of golf courses and re-design of
existing courses. Contact Peter Alliss or Roy
Cooper.

Philip Sparks Professional Golf Designs
Peak House, Hawksdown,
Walmer, Deal, Kent CT12 5BE.
Tel (01304) 374119 Fax (01843) 853090

'Creating future links with the Past'. Specialising
in golf course remodelling and renovation.
Toro student architect of the year 2000. First
golf professional in the world to gain an
EIGCA diploma in golf course architecture.

GOLF COURSE DISTANCE GUIDES

Strokesport
Abbey Mill Business Centre,
Paisley PA1 1TJ.
Tel 0141-848 1199 Fax 0141-887 1642

We are publishers of *Strokesaver Distance Guides*
which are recognised as the most accurate and

useful golf course management aids worldwide. *Strokesaver* provides professionals and clubs with a constant profit centre. Course Measurement - Measurement and survey to professional standard. Certification accepted by National Golf unions. Leading specialists in course measurement. *(See advertisement page 31 for further details.)*

Vickers Sports Optics
Unit 9, 35 Revenge Road,
Lordswood, Kent ME5 8DW.
Tel (01634) 201284 Fax (01634) 201286

Bushnell's Yardage Pros' instantaneously measures distances with incredible accuracy (± 1 yard). Know whether - you can reach the green in one - clear the water or bunker - it's safe to hit or how far you have driven/hit the ball.

GOLF COURSE MAINTENANCE & UPGRADING

Brian D Pierson
32 New Road, Ringwood,
Hampshire BH24 3AU.
Tel (01202) 822372 Fax (01202) 826447

The Golf Course Builder - 35 years' experience on over 200 golf courses. New construction - alterations - project management. Contracts completed in USA, Canada, mainland Europe and British Isles. Work completed on seven Open Championship courses.

Grassform Ltd
3 Cricketers Row, Herongate,
Brentwood, Essex CM13 3QA.
Tel (01277) 812973 Fax (01277) 812972

Grassform Limited undertakes all types of golf course projects. From new build to re-construction of tees, greens and bunkers. We also install land drainage systems, sand banding, lakes, water features, footpaths, buggy paths and driving ranges. For further information please contact Mark Dunning.

Land Unit Construction Ltd
Hanslope, Milton Keynes,
Buckinghamshire MK19 7BX.
Tel (01908) 510414 Fax (01908) 511056
E-mail: sales@landunitconstruction.co.uk
Website: www.landunitconstruction.co.uk

We have the knowledge and experience gained over 25 years in golf course construction and constantly work with many of the country's leading golf course architects to provide clients with unparalleled quality of service.

Peter Alliss - Golf Ltd
25 St Johns Road, Farnham,
Surrey GU9 8NV.
Tel (01252) 717711 Fax (01252) 717722
E-mail: roy@allissgolf.demon.co.uk

Designers of golf courses and re-design of existing courses. Contact Peter Alliss or Roy Cooper.

Toro Commercial Products - Lely (UK) Ltd
Station Road, St Neots,
Huntingdon, Cambridgeshire PE19 1QH.
Tel (01480) 4226800 Fax (01480) 226801
E-mail: toro.info@lely.co.uk
Website: www.toro.com

Toro offer an extensive range of professional turf maintenance equipment which includes: greens mowers, fairway mowers, triplex mowers, rotary mowers, aeration and utility vehicles. *Toro* manufacture to an exceptionally high quality and give unrivalled quality of cut.

GOLF DEVELOPMENT/MANAGEMENT

Association of Golf Club Secretaries
7A Beaconsfield Road,
Weston-Super-Mare, Somerset BS23 1YE.
Tel (01934) 641166 Fax (01934) 644254
E-mail: hq@agcs.org.uk
Website: www.agcs.org.uk

Membership is available to golf secretaries and managers, course owners and others involved in golf club administration. The following services are available: monthly journal, information library, training courses. seminars, conferences, regional meetings and employment support.

Barrelfield Golf Ltd
302 Ewell Road,
Surbiton, Surrey KT6 7AQ.
Tel 020 8390 6566 Fax 020 8390 8830
Website: www.barrelfieldgolf.co.uk

Barrelfield Golf Limited has an unrivalled track record in the development, marketing, management and maintenance of profitable golf clubs in Britain. Other services include feasibility studies and arranging finance. For further information contact Melvin Thomas 020 8390 6566.

Bournemouth University

School of Service Industries,
Fern Barrow,
Poole, Dorset BH12 5BB.
Tel (01202) 595146 Fax (01202) 515707
E-mail: mcustard@bournemouth.ac.uk
Website: www.bournemouth.ac.uk/
service_industries

The university has developed a unique degree
for those interested in a career in golf and/or
sports management. With the support of local
golf clubs, the BSc(Hons) in Sports
Management (golf) is a 4-year sandwich degree
which provides graduates with the technical
expertise as well as the managerial skills
necessary to succeed in this dynamic industry.
Contact: Programme Administrator, School of
Service Industries.

English Golf Union - EGU

The National Golf Centre,
The Broadway,
Woodhall Spa, Lincolnshire LN10 6PU.
Tel (01526) 354500 Fax (01526) 354020
E-mail: info@englishgolfunion.org
Website: www.englishgolfunion.org

As the governing body for men's amateur golf
in England the EGU organises championships
and coaching for players and representative
teams at all levels and offers an advisory service
on all aspects of golf administration and
management.

Golf Consultants Association - GCA

Federation House,
Stoneleigh Park,
Warwickshire CV8 2RF.
Tel (02476) 414999 Fax (02476) 414990
E-mail: gca@sportstye.org.uk

The GCA provides a point of reference for
those requiring independent, professional, golf
consultancy services throughout the world.

The Golf Foundation - Developing Junior Golf

Foundation House, The Spinney,
Hoddesdon Road, Stanstead Abbotts,
Hertfordshire SG12 8GF.
Tel (01920) 876200 Fax (01920) 876211
Website: www.golf-foundation.org

An organisation dedicated to the promotion
and development of grass roots junior golf
across the British Isles. (The Golf Foundation
is a registered charity.)

Golf Search - The Golfing Recruitment Specialists

Kildare House, 102-104 Sheen Road,
Richmond-on-Thames, Surrey TW9 1UF.
Tel 020 8334 1125 Fax 020 8334 1112

Golf Search has years of recruitment
experience and the largest database of golf
management personnel in Europe. We carry
out comprehensive interviews, psychometric
tests and reference checks on all short-listed
candidates. The professional service provided
offers exceptional value for money. Please
phone for further information.

Portfolio International

5 Breams Buildings, London EC4A 1DY.
Tel +44 (0) 207 520 5000
Fax +44 (0) 207 520 5007
Website: www.portfoliointernational.com

Portfolio International can provide an exclusive
individual consultancy service, advising not
only on recruitment but also feasibility studies,
sales and marketing, strategy and interim
management, membership offerings and
trouble-shooting. For further information
please call Giles Greenwood.

GOLF HOLIDAYS

Irish Golf Tours Ltd

34 Sweetbriar Lawn, Tramore,
Co Waterford, Ireland.
Tel +353 51 381728 Fax +353 51 381961
E-mail: info@irishgolftours.com
Website: www.irishgolftours.com

The leading Irish golf travel company. For your
complete enjoyment let us design your personal
golf holiday in Ireland, to include your travel,
accommodation and guaranteed tee times. Visit
our website www.irishgolftours.com or contact
us on UK free phone 0800 169 5374. *(See
advertisement page 36 for further details.)*

Portugal Fairways Go-Golf-Pay-Less

Estrada de Pera,
Sesmarias, 8200 Albufeira, Portugal.
Tel +44 (0) 1908 311768
E-mail: info@go-golf-pay-less.com
Website: www.go-golf-pay-less.com

Algarve, Estoril and Costa Azul golfing breaks -
let Go-Golf-Pay-Less book your courses,
preferred dates and tee times at discounted

prices at no charge to you! Accommodation in a choice of hotels, villas, motels and apartments. Car rental and airport transfers.

GOLF RANGE DESIGN

Mike Copson Associates Golf Driving Range Design & Construction Specialists
197 Comberton Road,
Kidderminster, Worcestershire DY10 1UE.
Tel/Fax (01562) 863937
Mobile: 0836 371180

Mike Copson has been designing and building driving ranges since 1988. During this time he has completed 26 major golfing projects. Clients include: British Coal, Whitbread's, Bovis (La Manga) abroad and many private golf clubs and local authorities. Our experience also extends to the design of high perimeter fencing and floodlighting designs. We can offer a full turnkey package or individually designed packages to suit each client or act as a consultant.

GOLFING AIDS/PRACTICE EQUIPMENT

Pan European (Golf) 1973 (PEP)
Old Mill Works, High Street,
Maldon, Essex CM9 5EH.
Tel (01621) 851700 Fax (01621) 850417
E-mail: info@golfpep.co.uk
Website: www.golfpep.co.uk

Products include a wide range of practice nets and mats for beginners through to professionals. We also make a commercial range of nets and mats for clubs, stores and leisure centres. Worldwide export sales our speciality.

Sports Coach Systems Ltd
Curtis Road, Dorking, Surrey RH4 1XD.
Tel +44 (0) 1306 741888
Fax +44 (0) 1306 877333
E-mail: sportscoachsys@aol.com
Websites: www.sports-coach.com
www.euromats.com

Manufacturers of the world's finest range of golf electronics and software. Projected simulators from under £9,000, ball analysis, club analysis, driving range and swing analysis. As well as digital video with the world-famous Sports Coach 2001. Europe's largest manufacturer of golf mats, Portarange nets and cage nets.

GREEN KEEPING AND DRIVING RANGE VEHICLES

European Golf Machinery
Street Garage,
Bucklesham,
Ipswich, Suffolk IP10 0DN.
Tel (01473) 659815 Fax (01473) 659045

Manufacturers of driving range equipment including golf ball collectors, dispensers, ball washers and elevators. Kawasaki ATV and Mule distributors. *(See advertisement page 36 for further details.)*

Toro Commercial Products - Lely (UK) Ltd
Station Road,
St Neots,
Huntingdon, Cambridgeshire PE19 1QH.
Tel (01480) 4226800 Fax (01480) 226801
E-mail: toro.info@lely.co.uk
Website: www.toro.com

Toro offer an extensive range of professional turf maintenance equipment which includes: greens mowers, fairway mowers, triplex mowers, rotary mowers, aeration and utility vehicles. *Toro* manufacture to an exceptionally high quality and give unrivalled quality of cut.

GRIPS & SHAFTS

Eaton Ltd - Golf Pride Grips
Units 1 & 2 The Stirling Centre,
Northfields Industrial Estate,
Market Deeping,
Nr Peterborough PE6 8EQ.
Tel (01778) 341555 Fax (01778) 344025

Manufacturers of golf grips for over 50 years, they have been the leader in golf grip technology and the leader in rubber and cord grip sales for both professional and amateur players alike.

True Temper UK/Europe
c/o Tucker Fasteners
Walsall Road, Birmingham B42 1BP.
Tel 0121-331 2276 Fax 0121-331 2286

Golf shaft manufacturer both steel and graphite. In 2000 achieved over 120 Tournament wins on PGA Tours. Dynamic Gold used by leading players. Sensicore continues to grow in usage by both Tournament players and amateurs.

INSURANCE

Golfplan

International Golf & Travel Insurance
Redcliffe House,
Whitehouse Street, Bristol BS3 4AY.
Tel 0117-963 6198 Fax 0117-923 1058
E-mail: info@golfplan.co.uk
Website: www.golfplan.co.uk

Golfplan, endorsed by the PGA, is Europe's largest specialist golf insurance provider. A Golfplan policy covers individual golfers against personal liability; accidental damage to third party property; golf equipment; personal effects; equipment hire charges; tournament entry fees; membership fees; personal accident; Hole-in-One. Contact your professional or call Golfplan quoting Ref: GHB6.

INTERNET TEE-TIME BOOKING

Links Software

6 Ascot Avenue,
Westerlands Park, Glasgow G12 0AX.
Tel/Fax 0141-357 0199
E-mail: ac.provan@ntlworld.com
Website: www.linksgolf.co.uk

The complete software solution for golf clubs. Membership and subscriptions. Ladies and gents handicaps. Booking system (with internet link to Golfagent), point of sale, stock control and accounts. Compatible with most swipe cards (including GUI/SGU). Fully networkable. Modular components start from just £395. *(See advertisement page 36 for further details.)*

IRRIGATION EQUIPMENT/DESIGN & INSTALLATION

M J Abbott Ltd

Bratch Lane, Dinton, Salisbury,
Wiltshire SP3 5EB.
Tel (01722) 716361 Fax (01722) 716828

M J Abbott Limited offer a range of specialist services to the golf and leisure industry. Recognised as one of Britain's leading companies offering Rain Bird irrigation systems. Land drainage, golf course construction and maintenance are all undertaken by experienced employees utilising the company's own specially adapted machinery.

ISS Aquaturf Systems Ltd

Unit 18, Downton Industrial Estate,
Batten Road, Downton, Salisbury,
Wiltshire SP5 3HU.
Tel (01725) 513880 Fax (01725) 513003

ISS Aquaturf Systems Limited are master dealers for *Toro & Hunter* operating throughout southern England in the design, supply and installation of automatic pop-up irrigation systems for golf courses. The company has been in business for 20 years and specialises in providing quality systems at competitive prices.

Ocmis Irrigation (UK) Ltd

Head Office: Higher Burrow, Kingsbury,
Martock, Somerset TA12 6BU.
Tel (01460) 241939 Fax (01460) 242198

Scotland: Broadmeadow, Harburn,
West Calder, West Lothian EH55 8RT.
Tel 0131-220 2102 Fax 0131-220 6122

Ireland: 1 Glenageary Avenue,
Dun Laoghaire, Co Dublin.
Tel +353 1 235 4020

Ocmis Irrigation offer the complete irrigation service including the design, supply and installation of Rain Bird, Buckner and Hunter irrigation systems. Complete after-sales service, full maintenance and service contracts for all types and makes of irrigation systems.

STRI - The Sports Turf Research Institute

St Ives Estate, Bingley,
West Yorkshire BD16 1AU.
Tel (01274) 565131 Fax (01274) 561891
E-mail: info@stri.co.uk
Website: www.stri.co.uk

Independent specialists offering you help and advice for the design, construction, management and maintenance, irrigation or renovation of your golf course. Comprehensive in-house support services for ecology, testing, turf pathology and research.

York & Martin

39 Salisbury Street,
Fordingbridge, Hampshire SP6 1AB.
Tel (01425) 652087 Fax (01425) 652476
E-mail:
mike.martin@yorkandmartin.co.uk
Website: www.yorkandmartin.co.uk

Independent irrigation consultants providing objective advice on all irrigation related matters including water sourcing, existing system evaluation, system designs and specifications, project supervision etc. Operating throughout the UK and mainland Europe.

JEWELLERY

Solent Souvenirs Ltd
Hamble Bank, 40 Newtown Road,
Warsash, Southampton,
Hampshire SO31 9FZ.
Tel (01489) 577985 Fax (01489) 577886
E-mail: solentsouvenirs@aol.com

Britain's premier supplier of specialised golf jewellery and quality gifts. Many items designed and manufactured exclusively for us and unobtainable elsewhere. Replace that traditional trophy with an elegant prize which will be both useful and cherished. Most items delivered overnight.

MAIL ORDER

Steve Schofield Golf Books
29 Nichols Way, Wetherby,
West Yorkshire LS22 6AD.
Tel/Fax (01937) 581276
E-mail: golfbooks@steveschofield.com

Classic golf books for sale, new, old and antiquarian. Books on golf history, architecture, biography, club and ball collecting and instruction. Free catalogue on request.

PATHWAYS

Dura-Sport Ltd - Synthetic Surfaces for Golf
Road Barn Farm, Croft Road,
Cosby, Leicestershire LE9 1SG.
Tel 0116-286 3800 Fax 0116-286 3888
E-mail: sales@dura-sport.co.uk

The leading supplier of proven synthetic surface solutions for pathways, waiting areas, winter tees and putting/pitching areas

PERSONAL EQUIPMENT & ACCESSORIES

Izzo (UK) Ltd
32 Queen Victoria Road,
Sheffield S17 4HT.
Tel/Fax 0114-236 4410

CARRY THE BEST. CARRY IZZO. Creators of the Dual Strap technology. The strap that lightens the load and is easy on easy off. Suppliers of top quality golf bags and golf club carrying systems.

Mycoal Warm Packs Ltd
Unit 1, Imperial Park,
Empress Road,
Southampton, Hampshire SO14 0JW.
Tel 023 8021 1068 Fax 023 8023 1398
Website: www.mycoal.co.uk

Suppliers and manufacturers of the ever popular handwarmers and thermo-mittens. All enquiries welcome - small or large.

PERSONALISED PRODUCTS

Brollies Limited
45 Allerton Road,
Woolton Village,
Liverpool L25 7AL.
Tel 0151-421 0250 Fax 0151-421 0091
E-mail: jmyers105@hotmail.com
Website: www.brollies.ltd.uk

Brollies Limited carry a comprehensive range in best quality British made Hoyland and Fox Frame umbrellas. Also available seat sticks, twinbrellas, garden parasols, imported double ribbed golf umbrellas and golf ball retrievers. All printed or unprinted.

Bryants of Leeds
Speedwell Street,
Meanwood Road,
Leeds LS6 2TD.
Tel 0113-242 8330 Fax 0113-242 6330
Website: www.dimplygolf.com

The leading supplier of personalised golf merchandise. Golf club membership tags and labels, green fee stationery. Captain's Day, Society events and Corporate Golf Day merchandise. Call for a free colour brochure or visit us on our website.

Derek Burridge (Wholesale) Ltd
Awards House,
Unit 15,
The Metro Centre,
Springfield Road, Hayes,
Middlesex UB4 0LE.
Tel 020 8569 0123 Fax 020 8569 0111

The country's leading suppliers of golf prizes, celebrating their 42nd year. We offer a vast range of silverplate, crystal, china, clocks, leather goods and sporting trophies, all at trade prices. Glass and silverplate in-house engraving service. Next day delivery throughout the UK. Call for brochure. *(See advertisement page 31 for further details.)*

Galloway Crystal & Glass Ltd
Beeswing, by Dumfries DG2 8ED.
Tel (01387) 760643 Fax (01387) 760537
E-mail: mccallum@gallowayglass.com
Websites: www.gallowayglass.com
www.crystalforgolfer.com

Specialist plain and cut crystal suppliers and engravers. Many innovative golfing gift ideas through our special collections. Personalisation our speciality. Ask for our catalogue along with club and reseller price lists.

H M T Plastics Ltd
Fairway House, 31A Framfield Road,
Uckfield, East Sussex TN22 5AH.
Tel (01825) 769393 Fax (01825) 769494
E-mail: hmt@aol.com
Website: www.hmt-plastics.com

Bag tags supplied in nine colours either round, pear shaped, shield maxi or sunrise to accommodate club logo, from a choice of print colours. Adhesive Year Stickers available in choice of nine colours and sold separately. *(See advertisement page 31 for further details.)*

Newton Newton Flag & Banner Makers
The Bishop Tozers Chapel,
Middlemarsh Road,
Burgh-le-Marsh, Lincolnshire PE24 5AD.
Tel (01754) 768401 Fax (01754) 610612
E-mail: newtonnewton@btinternet.com
Website: www.newtonnewtonflags.com

Manufacturers of superior golf club, captain, tournament, sponsor and pin flags. Appliqued and hand embroidered trophy presentation table covers, drapes, wall banners and badges of unsurpassed grace and beauty. PVC promotional banners and glassfibre flagpoles. *(See advertisement page 35 for further details.)*

PICTURES & PRINTS

Grandison Golf Gallery
'Gowanbank',
5 Sorley's Brae, Dollar FK14 7AS.
Tel 01259 740318
E-mail: info@grandisongolfgallery.com
Website: www.grandisongolfgallery.com

Finest quality limited edition prints of the world's premier golfing venues by one of the world's leading golf artists, William Grandison. Each print is individually signed and numbered. Gifts and prizes of distinction for the discerning golfer. Private commissions. Free catalogue available.

Richard Chorley Golf Art
159 Lonsdale Road, Stevenage,
Hertfordshire SG1 5DG.
Tel/Fax (01438) 727901

Richard Chorley, England's premier golf artist. Private commissions, original oil paintings, drawings and limited edition prints. Prints signed by the artist, numbered and embossed. Collection of classic courses and golfing greats. Ideal corporate and captain's prizes gifts.

PLAY & STAY

Irish Golf Tours Ltd
34 Sweetbriar Lawn,
Tramore, Co Waterford, Ireland.
Tel +353 51 381728 Fax +353 51 381961
E-mail: info@irishgolftours.com
Website: www.irishgolftours.com

The leading Irish golf travel company. For your complete enjoyment let us design your personal golf holiday in Ireland, to include your travel, accommodation and guaranteed tee times. Visit our website *www.irishgolftours.com* or contact us on UK free phone 0800 169 5374. *(See advertisement page 36 for further details.)*

Portugal Fairways Go-Golf-Pay-Less
Estrada de Pera,
Sesmarias, 8200 Albufeira, Portugal.
Tel +44 (0) 1908 311768
E-mail: info@go-golf-pay-less.com
Website: www.go-golf-pay-less.com

Algarve, Estoril and Costa Azul golfing breaks - let Go-Golf-Pay-Less book your courses, preferred dates and tee times at discounted prices at no charge to you! Accommodation in a choice of hotels, villas, motels and apartments. Car rental and airport transfers.

PORTUGAL

Portugal Fairways Go-Golf-Pay-Less
Estrada de Pera,
Sesmarias, 8200 Albufeira, Portugal.
Tel +44 (0) 1908 311768
E-mail: info@go-golf-pay-less.com
Website: www.go-golf-pay-less.com

Algarve, Estoril and Costa Azul golfing breaks -

let Go-Golf-Pay-Less book your courses, preferred dates and tee times at discounted prices at no charge to you! Accommodation in a choice of hotels, villas, motels and apartments. Car rental and airport transfers.

PRACTICE NETTING/CAGES

Pan European (Golf) 1973 (PEP)
Old Mill Works,
High Street,
Maldon,
Essex CM9 5EH.
Tel (01621) 851700 Fax (01621) 850417
E-mail: info@golfpep.co.uk
Website: www.golfpep.co.uk

Products include a wide range of practice nets and mats for beginners through to professionals. We also make a commercial range of nets and mats for clubs, stores and leisure centres. Worldwide export sales our speciality.

Tildenet Ltd
Hartcliffe Way,
Bristol BS3 5RJ.
Tel 0117-966 9684 Fax 0117-923 1251
Website: www.tildenet.co.uk

Tildenet supply and install a comprehensive range of quality products to the Golfing World. These include perimeter ball stop netting, practice nets and mats for the professional enthusiast. Anti-ball plug nets, target nets, target greens and anti-dazzle netting for clubs, and grass germination and bunker membranes for the greenkeeper.

PRINTING

Iain Crosbie Printers
Beechfield Road,
Willowyard Industrial Estate,
Beith,
Ayrshire KA15 1LN.
Tel (01505) 504848 Fax: (01505) 504674
E-mail: crosbieprinters@dial.pipex.com

At Crosbie Printers we have over 20 years' experience in printing associated with golf and commerce. We manufacture scorecards (standard and bespoke), fixture books/diaries, green fee tickets, marketing brochures/leaflets and all associated printed stationery. *(See advertisement page 35 for further details.)*

PROPERTY CONSULTANTS

Edward Symmons Hotel & Leisure
11-14 Grafton Street,
London W1X 3LA.
Tel 020 7344 4500 Fax 020 7344 4555

Consultant surveyors providing specialist property advice to the golf and leisure industry. Established track record in sales, valuations, acquisitions, development appraisals, rating and feasibility studies throughout the UK and Europe.

PUTTER & CHIPPER MANUFACTURERS & SUPPLIERS

1000 Mile Sportswear Ltd
12 Shakespeare Industrial Estate,
Shakespeare Street,
Watford,
Hertfordshire WD24 5RN.
Tel (01923) 242233 Fax (01923) 240066
E-mail: sales@1000mile.co.uk

The famous 1000 Mile blister-free guaranteed socks. Ray Cook putters - famous for over 35 years with over 200 tour wins. The award-winning GustBuster umbrella which will withstand winds up to 60 mph.

Bronty Golf
3 Musgrave Mount,
Eccleshill,
Bradford,
West Yorkshire BD2 3LA.
Tel/Fax +44 (0) 1274 773585
Mobile: +44 (0) 7950 397603
E-mail: brontygolf1@activemail.co.uk
Website: www.brontygolf.co.uk

Manufacturers of high quality British made custom golf clubs, putters and specialist clubs. Authentic replicas and hickory shafted putters etc.

Callaway Golf Europe Ltd
Unit 27 Barwell Business Park,
Leatherhead Road,
Chessington,
Surrey KT9 2NY.
Tel +44 (0) 20 8391 0111

Manufacturer of golf clubs and accessories. Callaway Golf is now the distributor for Odyssey Golf.

RANGE BALL MANUFACTURERS/ SUPPLIERS

European Golf Machinery

Street Garage, Bucklesham,
Ipswich, Suffolk IP10 0DN.
Tel (01473) 659815 Fax (01473) 659045

Manufacturers of driving range equipment including golf ball collectors, dispensers, ball washers and elevators. Kawasaki ATV and Mule distributors. *(See advertisement page 36 for further details.)*

RECRUITMENT CONSULTANTS

Golf Search - The Golfing Recruitment Specialists

Kildare House, 1012-104 Sheen Road,
Richmond-on-Thames, Surrey TW9 1UF.
Tel 020 8334 1125 Fax 020 8334 1112

Golf Search has years of recruitment experience and the largest database of golf management personnel in Europe. We carry out comprehensive interviews, psychometric tests and reference checks on all short-listed candidates. The professional service provided offers exceptional value for money. Please phone for further information.

Portfolio International

5 Breams Buildings, London EC4A 1DY.
Tel +44 (0) 207 520 5000
Fax +44 (0) 207 520 5007
Website: www.portfoliointernational.com

Fifteen years' experience providing specialist recruitment services to the hospitality industry. Executive search, database search (over 36,000 contacts) or advertised search. Our golf division can save you valuable time and expense providing key management to golf clubs and resorts. Please phone for further information.

REMOTE CONTROLLED TROLLEYS

Middlemore Ltd

Sharrocks Street,
Wolverhampton, West Midlands WV1 3RP.
Tel (01902) 870077 Fax (01902) 455200
E-mail: electra-caddie@thama.co.uk
Website: www.thama.co.uk

European distributors of the world's foremost remote controlled powered golf trolley - the *LECTRONIC KADDY 'Dyna Steer 2000'* Your

hand held transmitter helps you to turn this amazing machine left to right and right to left with great ease. The Original all-alluminium lightweight machine that helps you break par, not your back. Free colour brochure on request. *(See advertisement page 36 for further details.)*

RIDE-ON BUGGIES

A La Carts

Beechwood, Bakeham Lane,
Englefield Green TW20 9TU.
Tel/Fax (01784) 472982
Website: www.alacarts.tsx.org

Manufacturers and distributors of single and two-seater golf buggies. Also powered trolleys.

Callisto Golf Cars

Cuparmuir, Cupar,
St Andrews, Fife KY15 5RL.
Tel +44 (0) 1334 657515
Fax +44 (0) 1334 652222

Official supplier Scottish Golf Union & Scottish National Golf Centre - St Andrews. Private Scottish organisation specialising in supply of new and used golf cars for domestic and export markets. We sell to clubs, professionals and private individuals. Hiring/customised finance packages. Large selection of cars in stock. Quick, personal service.

Patterson Products

Unit 6, Fordwater Trading Estate,
Ford Road, Chertsey, Surrey KT16 8HG.
Tel (01932) 570016 Fax (01932) 570084
E-mail: info@patterson.co.uk
Website: www.patterson.co.uk

Manufacturers and retailers of the Trio single-seat, transportable golf cart. Major suppliers and consultants to Handigolf, a charity for the severely disabled golfer. The Trio is now in its 15th year with over 4,000 happy users.

Teltale

6 Skye Road, Shawfarm Industrial Estate,
Prestwick KA9 2TA.
Tel/Fax (01292) 475125
E-mail: sales@teltale.uk.com
Website: www.teltale.uk.com

Teltale ride-on buggy available from May 2002. New design and innovative user-friendly buggy. Can be quickly folded down in a few seconds to fit into small hatchback car. High power motors and extra wide tyres. Ideally suitable for hire. *(See advertisement page 36 for further details.)*

SCORECARDS & PLANNERS

Eagle Promotions Ltd
Eagle House,
1 Clearway Court,
139-141 Croydon Road,
Caterham,
Surrey CR3 6PF.
Tel (01883) 344244 Fax (01883) 341777
E-mail: info@eaglepromotions.co.uk
Website: www.eaglepromotions.co.uk

Eagle Promotions offer a comprehensive range of products from certified course measurement and tee signs through to scorecards, yardage books, green fee tickets, members' tags, event and leader boards, honours boards, clubhouse and general course signage. For further information please contact Philip McInley on 01883 344244.

Iain Crosbie Printers
Beechfield Road,
Willowyard Industrial Estate,
Beith,
Ayrshire KA15 1LN.
Tel (01505) 504848 Fax: (01505) 504674
E-mail: crosbieprinters@dial.pipex.com

At Crosbie Printers we have over 20 years' experience in printing associated with golf and commerce. We manufacture scorecards (standard and bespoke), fixture books/diaries, green fee tickets, marketing brochures/leaflets and all associated printed stationery. *(See advertisement page 35 for further details.)*

SEEDS & FERTILISERS

British Seed Houses
Camp Road,
Witham St Hughs,
Swinderby,
Lincoln LN6 9QJ.
Tel (01522) 868714 Fax (01522) 868382
Website: www.britishseedhouses.com

British Seed Houses markets a comprehensive range of Grade A golf course seed mixtures and granular fertilisers. Avalon velvet bent and Providence creeping bent are also available.

SIMULATORS/ANALYSERS

Sports Coach Systems Ltd
Curtis Road,
Dorking,
Surrey RH4 1XD.
Tel +44 (0) 1306 741888
Fax +44 (0) 1306 877333
E-mail: sportscoachsys@aol.com
Websites: www.sports-coach.com
www.euromats.com

Manufacturers of the world's finest range of golf electronics and software. Projected simulators from under £9,000, ball analysis, club analysis, driving range and swing analysis. As well as digital video with the world-famous Sports Coach 2001. Europe's largest manufacturer of golf mats, Portarange nets and cage nets.

SYNTHETIC SURFACES

Dura-Sport Ltd - Synthetic Surfaces for Golf
Road Barn Farm,
Croft Road,
Cosby, Leicestershire LE9 1SG.
Tel 0116-286 3800 Fax 0116-286 3888
E-mail: sales@dura-sport.co.uk

The leading supplier of proven synthetic surface solutions for pathways, waiting areas, winter tees and putting/pitching areas

TEE SIGNS

Eagle Promotions Ltd
Eagle House,
1 Clearway Court,
139-141 Croydon Road,
Caterham,
Surrey CR3 6PF.
Tel (01883) 344244 Fax (01883) 341777
E-mail: info@eaglepromotions.co.uk
Website: www.eaglepromotions.co.uk

Eagle Promotions offer a comprehensive range of products from certified course measurement and tee signs through to scorecards, yardage books, green fee tickets, members' tags, event and leader boards, honours boards, clubhouse and general course signage. For further information please contact Philip McInley on 01883 344244.

THERMAL WEAR

Mycoal Warm Packs Ltd
Unit 1, Imperial Park, Empress Road,
Southampton, Hampshire SO14 0JW.
Tel 023 8021 1068 Fax 023 8023 1398
Website: www.mycoal.co.uk

Suppliers and manufacturers of the ever
popular handwarmers and thermo-mittens. All
enquiries welcome - small or large.

TRAINING & TEACHING AIDS

Chartex Products International Ltd
20 Grasmere, Liden,
Swindon, Wiltshire SN3 6LE.
Tel (01793) 530880 Fax (01793) 491035

Golf Fitness Programmes - *'Keeping Fit
Programme'* is a new, unique programme of
exercises designed to help improve stamina,
suppleness and strength for enhanced control
and greater distance. The 36-page book, plus
the warm-up stretching booklet is
supplemented with two thera-band rubber
tubes for progressive strenth training. Endorsed
by the PGA of Europe.

STRI - The Sports Turf Research Institute
St Ives Estate, Bingley,
West Yorkshire BD16 1AU.
Tel (01274) 565131 Fax (01274) 561891
E-mail: info@stri.co.uk
Website: www.stri.co.uk

A specialist provider and supplier of books and
training courses. Over 200 titles available from
our on-line bookshop (www.stri.co.uk).
Catalogue and training course details on
request.

Sports Coach Systems Ltd
Curtis Road, Dorking, Surrey RH4 1XD.
Tel +44 (0) 1306 741888
Fax +44 (0) 1306 877333
E-mail: sportscoachsys@aol.com
Websites: www.sports-coach.com
www.euromats.com

Manufacturers of the world's finest range of
golf electronics and software. Projected
simulators from under £9,000, ball analysis,
club analysis, driving range and swing analysis.
As well as digital video with the world-famous
Sports Coach 2001. Europe's largest

manufacturer of golf mats, Portarange nets and
cage nets.

TROPHIES

Birkdale Promotions
97 Old Watford Road, Bricket Wood,
Nr St Albans, Hertfordshire AL2 3UN.
Tel (01923) 671225 Fax (01923) 662522
E-mail: paulbirtro@tinyworld.co.uk
Website: www.birkdale-trophies.co.uk

An exclusive range of bronze figuerines,
silverplated golf trophies, shields, antique
replica plaques all suitable for clubs, societies
and corporate events. Our in-house engraving
enables each to be personalised to your
specification and delivery can be made to any
address worldwide. Please call for our free
colour brochure and price list. *(See
advertisement page 26 for further details.)*

Derek Burridge (Wholesale) Ltd
Awards House, Unit 15,
The Metro Centre, Springfield Road,
Hayes, Middlesex UB4 0LE.
Tel 020 8569 0123 Fax 020 8569 0111

The country's leading suppliers of golf prizes,
celebrating their 42nd year, offer a vast range of
silverplate, crystal, china, clocks, leather goods
and sporting trophies, all at trade prices. Glass
and silverplate in-house engraving service.
Next day delivery throughout the UK. Call for
our brochure. *(See advertisement page 31 for
further details.)*

Galloway Crystal & Glass Ltd
Beeswing, by Dumfries DG2 8ED.
Tel (01387) 760643 Fax (01387) 760537
E-mail: mccallum@gallowayglass.com
Websites:www.gallowayglass.com
www.crystalforgolfers.com

Specialist plain and cut crystal suppliers and
engravers. Many innovative golfing gift ideas
through our special collections. Personalisation
our speciality. Ask for our catalogue along with
club and reseller price lists.

Schotten Trophies - Manfred Schotten Antiques
109 High Street, Burford,
Oxfordshire OX18 4RG.
Tel (01993) 822302 Fax (01993) 822055
Website: www.schotten.com

Exquisite hand crafted trophies in traditional
style, created and hand finished in our own

workshop by crafstmen using solid woods, brass and bronze. Also available are golf antiques, clubs, novelty items, desk sets etc, and golf club furnishings. *(See advertisement page 35 for further details.)*

TUITION

Beaufort Golf Course
Churchtown,
Beaufort,
Killarney,
Co Kerry, Ireland.
Tel +353 64 44440 Fax +353 64 44752

A traditional Kerry welcome awaits you at *the Friendliest Course in Kerry*. Challenging 18-hole par 71 championship course, buggies and caddies for hire, excellent golf shop, bar food and snacks. Tuition can be arranged with our golf professional. Societies and groups welcome. *(See advertisement page 16 for further details.)*

Borth & Ynyslas Golf Club
Borth,
Ceredigion SY24 5JS.
Tel (01970) 871202
E-mail: secretary@borthgolf.co.uk

18-holes links course adjoining Borth beach. Humps and hollows provide great variation, although the topography and springy turf make for easy walking. Professional's shop, practice area, modern clubhouse with bar and catering. Tuition available.

Cannington Golf Course
Cannington College,
Cannington,
Bridgwater,
Somerset TA5 2LS.
Tel/Fax (01278) 655050

Designed by Martin Hawtree of Oxford and built to highest international specifications in 1992 by Brian Pierson Limited under the consultancy of top agronomists Jim Arthur and Gordon Child. Together they have produced arguably the best 9-hole golf course with its 18 tees in the west of England. With its 'Links-Like' appearance in high summer the subtle contours make for a testing round of golf for the scratch golfer, yet it is receptive to the beginner with its wide open spaces at 2,929 yards par 34. Beating par will take skill and courage.

European Golf Teachers Federation - EGTF
5 Hastings Road, Bromley, Kent BR2 8NZ.
Tel 020 8462 4120 Fax 020 8462 3983
E-mail: egtf@dial.pipex.com
Website: www.egtf.co.uk

We offer intensive teaching courses for professionals and amateurs who would like to know how to teach the game simply. The EGTF is the leader in the field of golf instruction.

Peter Ballingall Golf School
Barnham Broom Hotel,
Golf & Country Club
Norwich, Norfolk NR9 4DD.
Tel (01603) 759393 Fax (01603) 758224
Website: www.pbgolfschool.com

Based at Barnham Broom, the Peter Ballingall Golf School provides choice of tuition by experienced PGA professionals. Targeted at golfers of all levels of experience this golf school was voted best in UK in a *Golf Monthly* survey. Small groups and individual tuition ensures that progress is made. UK and overseas golf schools, overnight tuition breaks, golfing and leisure breaks available. Call for a brochure or visit our school website. *(See advertisement page 611 for further details.)*

Rodway Hill Golf Course
Newent Road, Highnam,
Gloucestershire GL2 8DN.
Tel (01452) 384222

An 18-hole, par 70 course, open to the public, two miles south west of Gloucester, with panoramic views of the Cotswolds. It has a well stocked shop, practice and teaching facilities. Hire kit available. Societies welcome.

UMBRELLAS

1000 Mile Sportswear Ltd
12 Shakespeare Industrial Estate,
Shakespeare Street,
Watford, Hertfordshire WD24 5RN.
Tel (01923) 242233 Fax (01923) 240066
E-mail: sales@1000mile.co.uk

The famous 1000 Mile blister-free guaranteed socks. Ray Cook putters - famous for over 35 years with over 200 tour wins. The award-winning GustBuster umbrella which will withstand winds up to 60 mph.

Brollies Limited
45 Allerton Road,
Woolton Village,
Liverpool L25 7AL.
Tel 0151-421 0250 Fax 0151-421 0091
E-mail: jmyers105@hotmail.com
Website: www.brollies.ltd.uk

Brollies Limited carry a comprehensive range
in best quality British made Hoyland and Fox
Frame umbrellas. Also available seat sticks,
twinbrellas, garden parasols, imported double
ribbed golf umbrellas and golf ball retrievers.
All printed or unprinted.

WATER STORAGE/TANKS

ISS Aquaturf Systems Ltd
Unit 18, Downton Industrial Estate,
Batten Road,
Downton,
Salisbury,
Wiltshire SP5 3HU.
Tel (01725) 513880 Fax (01725) 513003

ISS Aquaturf Systems Limited are master
dealers for *Toro & Hunter* operating throughout
southern England in the design, supply and
installation of automatic pop-up irrigation
systems for golf courses. The company has
been in business for 20 years and specialises in
providing quality systems at competitive prices.

Ocmis Irrigation (UK) Ltd
Head Office: Higher Burrow,
Kingsbury,
Martock,
Somerset TA12 6BU.
Tel (01460) 241939 Fax (01460) 242198

Scotland: Broadmeadow, Harburn,
West Calder, West Lothian EH55 8RT.
Tel 0131-220 2102 Fax 0131-220 6122

Ireland: 1 Glenageary Avenue,
Dun Laoghaire, Co Dublin.
Tel +353 1 235 4020

Ocmis Irrigation offer the complete irrigation
service including the design, supply and
installation of Rain Bird, Buckner and Hunter
irrigation systems. Complete after-sales service,
full maintenance and service contracts for all
types and makes of irrigation systems.

WEATHERWEAR

Mycoal Warm Packs Ltd
Unit 1, Imperial Park, Empress Road,
Southampton, Hampshire SO14 0JW.
Tel 023 8021 1068 Fax 023 8023 1398
Website: www.mycoal.co.uk

Suppliers and manufacturers of the ever
popular handwarmers and thermo-mittens. All
enquiries welcome - small or large.

Sunderland of Scotland Ltd
PO Box 14, Glasgow G2 1ER.
Tel 0141-572 5220 Fax 0141-572 5221
Website: www.sunderlandgolf.com

Sunderland of Scotland manufacture high
quality golf rainwear in Scotland. All rainsuits
are tour-tested and guaranteed waterproof and
breathable, a variety of fabrics including
Goretex being used. Sunderlands also
manufacture the famous Sunderland Original
Weatherbeater, Classic windproof Pullovers
and Fleece. Official supplier to PGA, PGAE,
LPGA, LET and St Andrews Links Trust.

WILD FLORA

British Seed Houses
Camp Road, Witham St Hughs,
Swinderby, Lincoln LN6 9QJ.
Tel (01522) 868714 Fax (01522) 868382
Website: www.britishseedhouses.com

All wild flora seed mixtures from British Seed
Houses use only UK native seed. All the
mixtures have been grown to meet specific
quality standards and they complement UK
wild flora habitats.

WINTER ALL-WEATHER TEE MATS

Dura-Sport Ltd - Synthetic Surfaces for Golf
Road Barn Farm, Croft Road,
Cosby, Leicestershire LE9 1SG.
Tel 0116-286 3800 Fax 0116-286 3888
E-mail: sales@dura-sport.co.uk

The leading supplier of proven synthetic
surface solutions for pathways, waiting areas,
winter tees and putting/pitching areas

Choose from among
the best Hotels in
the British Isles & Ireland

SOUTH LODGE HOTEL, West Sussex

Golfing Hotel Compendium

The Golfing Hotel Compendium is a comprehensive source of information for golfers wishing to find the most comfortable place to stay at or close to some of the finest courses in the country. This section has been compiled from the premier hotels, guest houses and self-catering facilities in the British Isles which include golf among their many attractions.

If readers wish especially to recommend an establishment which is not listed in this section of the Royal & Ancient Golfer's Handbook the editors will be happy to be advised.

ENGLAND

South West

Burnham & Berrow Golf Club
The Dormy,
St Christopher's Way,
Burnham-on-Sea,
Somerset TA8 2PE.
Tel (01278) 785760
*E-mail: secretary@burnhamandberrowgc.
2-golf.com*
*Website: www.burnhamandberrowgc.
2-golf.com*
18-hole championship links golf course and 9-hole course. Dormy accommodation available. *(See advertisement page 25 and 609 for further details.)*

China Fleet Country Club
Saltash,
Cornwall PL12 6LJ.
Tel (01752) 848668 Fax (01752) 848456
E-mail: sales@china-fleet.co.uk
Website: www.china-fleet.co.uk
Situated in 180 acres of Cornish countryside, 40 self-catering 4- and 6-berth apartments, 18-hole par 72 golf, 28-bay driving range, pool,

health suite, gymnasium, racket sports, bars, restaurant and coffee shop. *(See advertisement page 25 for further details.)*

East Dorset Golf Club
Bere Regis,
Dorset BH20 7NT.
Tel (01929) 472244 Fax (01929) 471294
E-mail: edgc@golf.co.uk
Website: www.golf.co.uk/edgc
3-Crown Commended golf lodge. 18-hole lakeland and 9-hole woodland courses. Floodlit covered driving range. Reputation for personal service. Excellent English cuisine. 12-twin and 4-double rooms, en suite facilities. Own lounge and games room. Two hours from London. In Hardy country overlooking the Purbeck Hills.

Fircroft Hotel
Owls Road,
Bournemouth,
Dorset BH5 1AE.
Tel (01202) 309771 Fax (01202) 395644
The hotel is situated close to sea and shops with many superb golf courses in the area. Fine restaurant with choice of menus. Large car park. Late bar. Free use of leisure club 9am to 6pm, with indoor pool, jacuzzi, sauna steam room and gym.

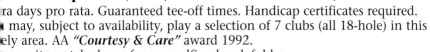

Golf View Hotel
Headland Road,
Newquay,
Cornwall TR7 1HN.
Tel/Fax (01637) 875082

An outstanding family run hotel overlooking
Newquay Golf Course and Newquay's world
famous Fistral beach (150 yards from the
hotel). Most rooms en suite. Own car park.
Reduced green fees on most local courses.
Special party rates.

Pines Hotel
Burlington Road,
Swanage,
Dorset BH19 1LT.
Tel (01929) 425211 Fax (01929) 422075
E-mail: reservations@pineshotel.co.uk
Website: www.pineshotel.co.uk

50-bedroom family run 3-Star hotel. All
bedrooms have private bathroom, telephone
and colour TV. One and a half miles from Isle
of Purbeck Golf Club. Within easy reach of all
Dorset courses. Award-winning restaurant.

Tewkesbury Park Hotel, Golf & Country Club - Regal
Lincoln Green Lane,
Tewkesbury, Gloucestershire GL20 7DN.
Tel (01684) 295405 Fax (01684) 292386
Website: www.corushotels.co.uk

An elegant extended 18th-century manor house
with stunning views across to the Malvern
Hills. The hotel has extensive leisure facilities
including an 18-hole par 3 parkland golf course
including wooded areas and water hazards.
(See advertisement page 4 for further details.)

Trevose Golf & Country Club
Constantine Bay, Padstow,
North Cornwall PL28 8JB.
Tel (01841) 520208 Fax (01841) 521057
E-mail: reception@trevose-gc.co.uk
Website: www.trevose-gc.co.uk/

Trevose offers not only great golf
(championship 18-hole course, a 9-hole full
length (3,100 yards) par 35 plus a 9-hole short
course) but also a first class clubhouse and
restaurant, three hard all-weather tennis courts,
a heated outdoor swimming pool in the
summer, a games room for the kids and a
boutique. Accommodation is available in
bungalows, chalets, trehuel flats, dormy flats
and cabins. Send for our detailed colour
brochure. Open all year. Societies welcome.

Woodbury Park Golf & Country Club
Woodbury Castle, Woodbury,
Exeter,
Devon EX5 1JJ.
Tel (01395) 233382 Fax (01395) 233384

Luxury 55-bedroom hotel with five superb
lodges. The Nigel Mansell owned resort
encompasses 27 holes, including the Oaks
championship course, in addition to extensive
leisure facilities. The ideal venue for your
golfing break.

South East

The Bell Hotel
The Quay, Sandwich, Kent CT13 9EF.
Tel (01304) 613388 Fax (01304) 615308
E-mail: hotel@princes-leisure.co.uk
Website: www.princes-leisure.co.uk

The perfect base when playing Royal St
Georges, Prince's and Royal Cinque Ports - all
within ten minutes' drive. Relax in traditional
comfort in historic surroundings. Individually
designed rooms with en suite throughout.
Special inclusive golf breaks with the *Prince's
Golf Club. (See advertisement page 611 for further
details.)*

Botley Park Hotel Golf & Country Club
Winchester Road, Boorley Green,
Botley, Southampton SO32 2UA.
Tel (01489) 780888 Fax (01489) 789242
E-mail:
info@botleypark.macdonald-hotels.co.uk
Website: www.macdonaldhotels.co.uk

Set in 176 acres of rolling Hampshire
countryside, this 4-Star hotel has 100 en suite
bedrooms, superb restaurant, extensive leisure
facilities and its own picturesque and
challenging 18-hole par 70 golf course and
driving range. *(See advertisement page 609 for
further details.)*

Briggens House Hotel - Regal
Briggens Park, Stanstead Road (A414),
Stanstead Abbotts, Nr. Harlow,
Hertfordshire SG12 8LD.
Tel (01279) 829955 Fax (01279) 793685
Website: www.corushotels.co.uk

A 17th-century house set in 80 acres of
parkland with a 9-hole professional golf course,
outdoor swimming pool and tennis courts. An

ideal base to visit Cambridge, London and the Bluewater Shopping Centre, all within a 45 minutes' drive. *(See advertisement page 4 for further details.)*

Corus and Regal Hotels
Blakelands House,
Yeomans Drive,
Blakelands, Milton Keynes MK14 5HG.
Reservations 0845 3000 2000
Website: www.corushotels.co.uk

Corus and Regal hotels have over 90 hotels throughout the country, ideally located for touring the best of Britain's golf courses. *(See advertisement page 4 for further details.)*

Coulsdon Manor
- Coulsdon Golf Centre
Coulsdon Court Road,
Coulsdon,
Surrey CR5 2LL.
Tel 020 8660 6083 Fax 020 8668 3118
E-mail:
coulsdonmanor@marstonhotels.com
Website: www.marstonhotels.com

A relaxing yet challenging par 70 golf course set in 140 acres of Surrey parkland. Golf societies made very welcome. Excellent restaurant and bar facilities at the Manor.

The Flackley Ash Hotel
Peasmarsh,
Rye, East Sussex TN31 6YH.
Tel (01797) 230651 Fax (01797) 230510

3-Star Georgian country house hotel set in beautiful grounds with putting green. Indoor swimming pool, whirlpool spa, saunas, steam room, gym, massage and beauty treatments. Extensive wine list, good food and a friendly welcome.

Gatton Manor Hotel
Golf & Country Club Ltd
Ockley,
Nr Dorking,
Surrey RH5 5PQ.
Tel (01306) 627555

Set amidst its own 18-hole golf course in 200 acres of parklands and lakes, situated between London and the south coast, in the heart of the Surrey countryside. Superb all en suite accommodation overlooking the golf course and grounds. À la carte restaurants, large lounge bar, conference suites, gym and health club.

Lansdowne Hotel
King Edward's Parade,
Eastbourne,
East Sussex BN21 4EE.
Tel (01323) 725174 Fax (01323) 739721

RAC/AA 3-Star. Play 36 holes a day on choice of seven courses; we book your tee-off time. Two nights with green fees, light lunch at club and use of our drying room. 18 January to 28 February £143; 1 to 31 March £153; 1 April to 31 May £161; 1 June to 30 September £171; 1 October to 31 December, £155. Extra days pro rata. *(See advertisement page 609 for further details.)*

Parasampia Golf & Country Club
Grove Road,
Donnington,
Newbury,
Berkshire RG14 2LA.
Tel (01635) 581000 Fax (01635) 552259
Website: www.parasampia.com

18-hole parkland/moorland championship course designed by Dave Thomas. The clubhouse and hotel are located within a beautifully renovated 18th-century gothic mansion. This will provide an ideal setting for your society, company golf day or conference stay.

Seaford - The Dormy House
Seaford Golf Club,
East Blatchington,
Seaford,
East Sussex BN25 2JD.
Tel (01323) 892442

The Dormy House provides comfortable accommodation for 20 guests in 10 twin-bedded en suit bedrooms on the first floor of the clubhouse, and 2 single rooms in our bungalow annexe. For latest brochure ring 01323 892442.

Wokefield Park Golf Club
Mortimer,
Reading,
Berkshire RG7 3AE.
Tel 0118-933 4013 Fax 0118-933 4162

Set amid the Berkshire countryside this challenging 7,000 yards golf course has mature trees, winding streams, nine lakes and large bunkers. Wokefield also features 320 bedrooms, teaching academy and leisure facilities. Call the golf sales team on 0118-933 4018 and 4017.

East Anglia

Abbotsley Golf Hotel & Country Club

Eynesbury Hardwicke,
St Neots,
Cambridgeshire PE19 4XN.
Tel (01480) 474000 Fax (01480) 471018

Set in 250 acres of idyllic countryside, offering two 18-hole courses, a par 3, driving range, squash courts, fitness centre and a 42-bedroom hotel. Golf breaks and residential packages available. Operated by American Golf (UK) Limited.

Barnham Broom Hotel, Golf & Country Club

Norwich,
Norfolk NR9 4DD.
Tel (01603) 759393 Fax (01603) 758224
Website: www.barnham-broom.co.uk

Set in 250 acres of peaceful Norfolk countryside just 15 minutes from the historical City of Norwich, Barnham Broom has 52 en suite bedrooms and suites, two superb 18-hole golf courses, a leisure club with indoor pool, SportsBar and Cafe with Sky TV, Flints restaurant and four versatile conference and banqueting suites. Golf and Leisure Breaks available throughout the year. Professional tuition by the Peter Ballingall Golf School. Corporate Golf and Society days. *(See advertisement page 611 for further details.)*

Beaumaris Hotel

15 South Street,
Sheringham,
Norfolk NR26 8LL.
Tel (01263) 822370 Fax (01263) 821421
E-mail: beauhotel@aol.com
Website: www.ecn.co.uk/beaumaris/

Established and run by the same family for 50 years with a reputation for personal service and excellent English cuisine. 21 en suite bedrooms. AA 2-Star Ashley Courtenay Recommended; ETC 2-Star. Three minutes' walk Sheringham's exhilarating cliff top golf course.

Brome Grange Hotel

Brome, Near Eye,
Suffolk IP23 8AP
Tel (01379) 870456 Fax (01379) 870921

Founded in the 16th century Brome Grange offers the traveller every modern comfort. English and international cuisine to the highest standard is served in our restaurant complemented by a bar with a range of cask conditioned ales. Surrounded by beautiful East Anglian countryside and the perfect base for golfers.

Cambridgeshire Moat House Hotel

Bar Hill,
Cambridge CB3 8EU.
Tel (01954) 249988 (Hotel) 780098 (Club)
Fax (01954) 780010

18-hole championship golf course set in 134 acres of parkland. Golf professional Paul Simpson. Newly built clubhouse and golf shop. 134 en suite bedrooms. Extensive leisure facilities. Five miles north of Cambridge on A14. Visitors welcome.

Thorpeness Hotel Golf Club

Thorpeness,
Nr Aldeburgh, Suffolk IP16 4NH.
Tel (01728) 452176 Fax (01728) 453868
E-mail: info@thorpeness.co.uk
Website: www.thorpeness.co.uk

One of East Anglia's finest and most challenging 18-hole courses. Handicap certificate required, advisable to book in advance. Accommodation, bars, restaurant, golf shop, tennis courts and course set adjacent to picturesque coastal village on Suffolk Heritage coast.

Virginia Court Hotel

Cliff Avenue,
Cromer, Norfolk NR27 0AN.
Tel (01263) 512398 Fax (01263) 515529
E-mail: virginiacourt.hotel@virgin.net
Website: www.virginiacourt.co.uk

Originally built as 'Cromer Clubhouse' in 1899 and converted to a hotel late in the 1920s. Now offering en suite bedrooms, the Billett Bar, Raffles Coffee Lounge, plus pleasant restaurant offering superb menus. Royal Cromer and other good courses nearby.

Wentworth Hotel

Wentworth Road,
Aldeburgh, Suffolk IP15 5BD.
Tel (01728) 452312 Fax (01728) 454343

Country house hotel with sea views. 38 bedrooms all with colour TV, radio and tea-maker. Two comfortable lounges, cosy bar, log fires and antique furniture. Our restaurant specialises in local, fresh produce and seafood.

Northamptonshire

Farthingstone Hotel & Golf Course

Farthingstone, Towcester,
Northamptonshire NN12 8HA.
Tel (01327) 361291 Fax (01327) 361645

Set in glorious wooded countryside, just 90 minutes outside London. Farthingstone Hotel offers 16 superb en suite rooms, a challenging 18-hole golf course, squash court, full size snooker tables, and a carvery restaurant. Highly competitive tariffs.

Hellidon Lakes Hotel Golf & Country Club

Hellidon, Daventry,
Northamptonshire NN11 6GG.
Tel (01327) 262550 Fax (01327) 262559
E-mail: hellidon@marstonhotels.com
Website: www.marstonhotels.com

27 holes of golf through woodland and over lakes. Buggies for hire. Corporate, Society and residential packages available. 71 well appointed bedrooms and suites, country club with extensive health and fitness facilities including pool, gym and treatment rooms. Indoor golf simulator and 10-pin bowling. Only 20 minutes from junction 11 of the M40 and junction 16 of the M1, one and a half hours from M25. *(See advertisement page 611 for further details.)*

East Midlands

Dower House Hotel

Manor Estate,
Woodhall Spa, Lincolnshire LN10 6PY.
Tel/Fax (01526) 352588

Situated within the Manor Estate the Dower House overlooks the new Woodhall 18-hole golf course. The hotel is renowned for food and wine. 3 Diamond. Golfing parties' tariff available.

The Grange & Links Hotel

Sea Lane, Sandilands,
Sutton-on-Sea, Lincolnshire LN12 2RA.
Tel (01507) 441334 Fax (01507) 443033
E-mail: grangelinks@ic24.net
Website: www.grangeandlinkshotel.com

3-Star 30-bedroom hotel with own 18-hole links course. Two tennis courts, snooker and ballroom. Award-winning hotel renowned for superb cuisine, friendliness, comfort and service.

North Shore Hotel Golf Club & Course

North Shore Road, Skegness PE25 1DN.
Tel (01754) 763298 Fax (01754) 761902
E-mail: golf@north-shore.co.uk
Website: www.north-shore.co.uk

A mature and challenging 18-hole part parkland and part links course with sea views on the edge of Skegness. Good all year round climate. Rarely closed in winter with no winter greens. Rarely closed bars, superb bar food and à la carte restaurant. 36 bedrooms available.

Petwood Hotel

Woodhall Spa, Lincolnshire LN10 6QF.
Tel (01526) 352411 Fax (01526) 353473
Website: www.petwood.co.uk

Built at the turn of the century, this luxurious hotel is set in a 30-acre estate, close to Woodhall Spa's championship golf course. 50 en suite bedrooms and a popular restaurant specialising in local produce. Special golf packages available - ask for our golf brochure for further details.

West Midlands

Nailcote Hall Hotel

Nailcote Lane, Berkswell,
Warwickshire CV7 7DE.
Tel 024 7646 6174 Fax 024 7647 0720
Website: www.nailcotehall.co.uk

Home of the British Professional Short Course. Delightful and challenging championship 9-hole par 3 course designed to test any golfers short game. Set in the grounds of this 17th-century black and white country house hotel, used by Cromwell in the English Civil War.

Telford Golf & Country Club - Regal

Great Hay Drive, Sutton Heights,
Telford, Shropshire TF7 4DT.
Tel (01952) 429977 Fax (01952) 586602
Website: www.corushotels.co.uk

The perfect place for a weekend away, this lovely hotel has its own 18-hole championship golf course together with well equipped leisure facilities. Visit the Ironbridge Gorge Museums and the nearby Tudor market town of Shrewsbury.

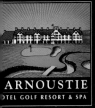

Welcombe Hotel & Golf Course

Warwick Road,
Stratford-upon-Avon,
Warwickshire CV37 0NR.
Tel (01789) 295252 Fax (01789) 414666
Corporate Golf Office:
Tel/Fax (01789) 413815

4-Star Jacobean-style mansion house hotel with
private 18-hole championship golf course set in
157 acres of wooded parkland with picturesque
lakes. Corporate golf and green fees most
welcome. *(See advertisement page 613 for further
details.)*

Whitefields Hotel Golf & Country Club

Coventry Road,
Thurlaston,
Nr Rugby,
Warwickshire CV23 9JR.
Tel (01788) 521800 Fax (01788) 521695
Website: www.whitefields/hotel.co.uk

18-hole course 6,223 yards. Driving range,
putting green 18. Four conference rooms. 50
en suite rooms. Bars and à la carte restaurant.
Societies welcome seven days. Call the
secretary on 01788 815555. Reservations
01788 521800.

Yorkshire & Humberside

Aldwark Manor Hotel Golf & Country Club

Aldwark,
Alne, York,
North Yorkshire YO61 1UF.
Tel (01347) 838146 (Hotel)
Fax (01347) 838867
Tel (01347) 838353 (Golf)
Fax(01347) 830007
E-mail: reception@aldwarkmanor.co.uk
Website: www.aldwarkmanor.co.uk

Victorian 28-bedroomed manor house set
within beautiful parkland with the river Ure
meandering through the 18-hole golf course.
Within easy reach of York, Harrogate and
Knaresborough. Ideal for visiting the Yorkshire
Dales and moors. Health spa with highly
trained therapists, swimming pool and sauna.
Aawrd-winning creative menus available in
both restaurant and brassiere with friendly,
efficient service. *(See advertisement page 613 for
further details.)*

Beiderbecke's Hotel

1-3 The Crescent,
Scarborough,
North Yorkshire YO11 2PW.
Tel (01723) 365766 Fax (01723) 367433
E-mail: info@beiderbeckes.com
Website: www.beiderbeckes.com

Refurbished 3-Star Georgian hotel in town
centre with own car park. 27 luxury bedrooms.
Incorporating Marmalade's 2-Rosette
restaurant (the BEST in Scarborough and 15
miles surrounding), Bix's Bar and Red Square.

Cave Castle Hotel & Country Club

South Cave,
East Yorkshire HU15 2EU.
Tel (01430) 422245 Fax (01430) 421118

Superb country manor house with 53 en suite
bedrooms in tranquil 160-acre parkland setting
with easy access to M62 motorway. Excellent,
traditional cuisine is served in our character
restaurant. Choice of two 18-hole golf courses
(Cave Castle and Boothferry Park), plus use of
leisure facilities, including 19m indoor pool,
gym, sauna, steam and spa. This is a Unique
Leisure Experience not to be missed! Golf and
leisure breaks, visiting parties and non-golfers
welcome.

Hotel Majestic - Scarborough

57 Northstead Manor Drive,
Scarborough,
North Yorkshire YO12 6AG.
Tel/Fax (01723) 363806

ETB 2-Star. Privately owned hotel overlooking
Peasholm Park. Minutes from Northcliffe Golf
Course. All 19 bedrooms have en suite, double
glazed, fully centrally heated. Cocktail bar.
Draught beers. Golf parties welcomed. Flexible
evening dinner times can be arranged.

The Royal Hotel - Scarborough

St Nicholas Street,
Scarborough,
North Yorkshire YO11 2HE.
Tel (01723) 364333 Fax (01723) 500618
E-mail: royalhotel@englishrosehotels.com
Website: www.englishrosehotels.com

The historic and famous Royal Hotel is a
quality 3-Star hotel in the central position
overlooking Scarborough's South Bay and close
to both North and South Cliff golf clubs. The
championship course at Ganton is a short
distance away. The hotel has been selected by

the US, Great Britain and Ireland teams together with the R&A officials as their base for the 2003 Walker Cup competition. *(See advertisement page 615 for further details.)*

Rudding Park Hotel & Golf
Follifoot,
Harrogate,
North Yorkshire HG3 1JH.
Tel (01423) 871350 Fax (01243) 872286
E-mail: sales@ruddingpark.com
Website: www.ruddingpark.com

The Rudding Park Estate, just two miles south of Harrogate, is an ideal venue for the discerning golfer. The contemporary award-winning 4-Star AA hotel and AA 2-Rosette Clocktower Restaurant, coupled with the magnificent 18-hole, par 72, parkland golf course, ensures a relaxing break. Golfing packages and special seasonal offers are available.

North West

The Allerdale Court Hotel
Market Place,
Cockermouth,
Cumbria CA13 9NQ.
Tel (01900) 823654 Fax (01900) 823033
Website: www.allerdalecourthotel.co.uk

2-Star Commended. Excellent restaurant, 24 en suite rooms, well stocked 19th hole. Two miles from Cockermouth Golf Club and near to Keswick and Silloth courses. Good value package deals for groups, societies and individuals.

Balmoral Lodge Hotel
41 Queens Road,
Southport,
Merseyside PR9 9EX.
Tel (01704) 544298 Fax (01704) 501224
Website: www.balmorallodge.co.uk

AA/RAC 2-Star; ETB 4-Crown Commended. All rooms superbly furnished with private bathroom, direct dial telephone, hospitality tray, hairdryer, trouser press, satellite TV and radio. Candlelit restaurant offering tantalising food and wines. Free sauna and club drying room. Golfing proprietor can arrange tee-times and caddies. Send for our golf package details.

The Dormy House
Royal Lytham & St Anne's Golf Club
Links Gate,
Lytham St Anne's,
Lancashire FY8 3LQ.
Tel (01253) 724206 Fax (01253) 780946

Ideal for small parties wishing to play the championship course. Accommodation for men only. Apply to the assistant secretary. *(See advertisement page 20 and 613 for further details.)*

The Fishermans Arms Hotel
The Coast Road,
Baycliff,
Ulverston,
Cumbria LA12 9RJ.
Tel (01229) 869387

Family run hotel built and styled in 1930's decor. Overlooking Morecombe Bay the ever changing real ales and good food add to the warm and welcoming atmosphere of the establishment. Nearest hotel to the Ulverston course.

Lancaster Golf Club
Ashton Hall,
Ashton with Stodday,
Lancaster LA2 0AJ.
Tel (01524) 751247 Fax (01524) 752742
E-mail: sec@lancastergc.freeserve.co.uk
Website: www.lancastergc.co.uk

Facilities to accommodate 18 guests, all en suite bedrooms mainly twin rooms with a limited number of singles. First class catering, well stocked bar with a wide selection of fine wines and malt whiskies. Resident club professional. *(See advertisement page 20 for further details.)*

Metropole Hotel
3 Portland Street,
Southport,
Merseyside PR8 1LL.
Tel (01704) 536836 Fax (01704) 549041
E-mail:
metropole.southport@btinternet.com
Website:
www.btinternet.com/metropole.southport

RAC/AA 2-Star hotel. Centrally situated and close to Royal Birkdale and other championship courses. Fully licensed - late bar facilities for residents. Full size snooker table. Reduced rates for golfers. Golfing proprietors will assist with tee reservations.

Northcote Manor
Northcote Road,
Langho,
Blackburn, Lancashire BB6 8BE.
Tel (01254) 240555 Fax (01254) 246568
E-mail: sales@northcotemanor.com
Website: www.northcotemanor.com

Premier country house hotel famous for its award-winning restaurant. Fabulous range of wines from our cellar. Fourteen excellent individual bedrooms. Within easy reach of five championship golf courses. Fully inclusive Golf Gourmet packages available - transport to all courses available. Fabulous venue for special occasions, weddings and corporate events. *(See advertisement page 615 for further details.)*

The Prince of Wales Hotel
Lord Street,
Southport,
Merseyside PR8 1JS.
Tel (01704) 536688 Fax (01704) 543932

Since 1876 the Prince of Wales Hotel has been the premier hotel in Southport - the Golfer's Paradise. Used as the base for the Ryder Cup and British Open over the years, the hotel provides quality 4-Star accommodation. 103 rooms, two restaurants and bars. We are able to arrange tee-times at any of the twelve courses in the area including Royal Birkdale. The hotel, located centrally in Southport, offers free car parking.

Shaw Hill Golf & Country Club
Preston Road,
Whittle-Le-Woods,
Chorley, Lancashire PR6 7PP.
Tel (01257) 269221 Fax (01257) 261223

Shaw Hill comprises a 72 par 18-hole golf course, a fully equipped leisure centre and an AA award-winning restaurant and we can offer wedding and conference facilities. *(See advertisement page 615 for further details.)*

Isle of Man

Castletown Golf Links Hotel
Derbyhaven, Castletown,
Isle of Man IM9 1UA.
Tel (01624) 822201 Fax (01624) 824633

Situated on our own peninsula, our championship golf course of 6,700 yards, with all holes having sea views, is a real test of links golf. The hotel facilities are of a luxurious 3-Star standard.

North East

George Washington Golf & Country Club - Regal
Stone Cellar Road,
High Usworth,
District 12, Washington,
Tyne & Wear NE37 1PH.
Tel 0191-402 9988 Fax 0191-415 1166
Website: www.corushotels.co.uk

A hotel with something for everyone with its own 18-hole championship golf course and leisure centre including an indoor pool and beauty treatments. Ideal for shopping or touring Northumbria's historical sites and beautiful coastlines. *(See advertisement page 4 for further details.)*

Hall Garth Golf & Country Club Hotel - Corus
Coatham Mundeville,
Darlington, Co Durham DL1 3LU.
Tel (01325) 300400 Fax (01325) 310083
Website: www.corushotels.co.uk

A 16th-century country house adjoining 67 acres of parkland with its own 9 par 72-hole golf course and extensive leisure club facilities. *(See advertisement page 4 for further details.)*

Linden Hall
Longhorsley, Morpeth,
Northumberland NE65 8XF.
Tel (01670) 500011 Fax (01670) 500001

Linden Hall golf course is located within the grounds of Linden Hall Hotel, a 4-Star luxury country house hotel. The 18-hole, 6,846 yard SSS 73 golf course, recently voted one of the ten best new golf courses built in the British Isles since 1996 by *Golf World*, is set within mature woodland, rolling parkland with established burns and lakes amidst a stunning backdrop of the Cheviot hills and Northumbrian coastline.

Ramside Hall Hotel & Golf Club
Carrville, Durham DH1 1TD.
Tel 0191-386 5282 Fax 0191-386 0399

Set in 220 acres on the outsksirts of the cathedral city of Durham and surrounded by a stimulating 27-hole golf course. 3-Star; 4-Crown Highly Commended. 80 luxury bedrooms, restaurant, grill room and carvery. Conference and banqueting facilities. Superb floodlit driving range and practice areas. *(See advertisement page 615 for further details.)*

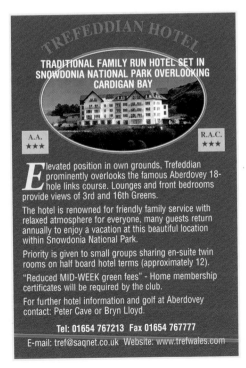

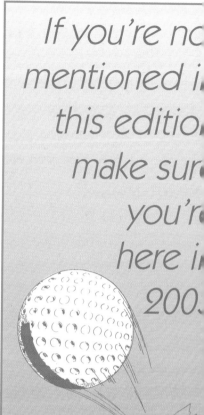

White Swan Hotel

Bondgate Within, Alnwick,
Northumberland NE66 1TD.
Tel (01665) 602109 Fax (01665) 510400

AA 3-Star 17th-century coaching inn. Over ten courses within 25 miles. Packages arranged, tee-times booked. Spectacular coastline. Also racing breaks. Visit our magnificent Olympic suite from the Titanic's sister ship.

SCOTLAND

Scottish Borders

Barniken House Hotel

18 Murray Street, Duns,
Berwickshire TD11 3DE.
Tel (01361) 882466 Fax (01361) 882594

Comfortable family run Georgian hotel. 105 malt whiskies in our cosy bar. Within 30 minutes of 20 golf courses in the Borders. Beautiful countryside, quiet roads. Comfortable beds and good food. £27.00 B&B - £36.00 DBB for 3 nights.

The Roxburghe Hotel & Golf Course

Heiton, By Kelso, Roxburghshire TD5 8JZ.
Tel (01573) 450331 Fax (01573) 450611
E-mail: golf@roxburghe.net
Website: www.roxburghe.net

22-bedroom hotel owned by the Duke and Duchess of Roxburghe. Luxury accommodation, superb cuisine. The 18-hole championship Roxburghe golf course, designed by Dave Thomas, is home to the Scottish Seniors Open.

Tweeddale Arms Hotel

High Street, Gifford,
East Lothian EH41 4QU.
Tel (01620) 810240 Fax (01620) 810488
E-mail: info@tweeddalearmshotel.co.uk
Website: www.tweeddalearmshotel.co.uk

Situated in the conservation village of Gifford eighteen miles from Edinburgh. We have eighteen of the finest golf courses to cater for everyone, from novice to champion, all within 20 minutes of the hotel. In addition to the excellent amenities and outstanding personal service the hotel offers warmth and hospitality in the true Scottish tradition. *(See advertisement page 617 for further details.)*

Central & East

Ballathie House Hotel

Kinclaven, Stanley, Perthshire PH1 4QN.
Tel (01250) 883268 Fax (01250) 883396
E-mail: email@ballathiehousehotel.com
Website: www.ballathiehousehotel.com

STB 4-Star, AA 2-Rosettes, Taste of Scotland and Thistle Award winner. Standing in its own grounds overlooking the river Tay near Perth, Ballathie House offers Scottish hospitality in a house of character and distinction. Fifteen minutes from Rosemount Golf Club and many other courses.

Carnoustie Hotel Golf Resort & Spa

The Links, Carnoustie, Angus DD7 7JE.
Tel (01241) 411999 Fax (01241) 411998
E-mail: enquiries@carnoustie-hotel.com
Website: www.carnoustie-hotel.com

Deluxe 4-Star hotel situated on the world class links, home to 128th Open Championship. Residents can take advantage of the first class facilities and reserve guaranteed starting times on the par 72 Championship Course, or the Burnside and Buddon 18-hole courses. *(See advertisement page 617 for further details.)*

Crusoe Hotel

2 Main Street, Lower Largo, Fife KY8 6BT.
Tel (01333) 320759 Fax (01333) 320865

Family run hotel on seafront of historic Lower Largo. Good food in bars and restaurant. Great golfing centre, St Andrews only fifteen minutes. Groups welcome - late bar.

Dalmunzie House Hotel

Spittal O'Glenshee, Blairgowrie,
Perthshire PH10 7QG.
Tel (01250) 885224 Fax (01250) 885225

Set in the Highlands with our own 9-hole course. This friendly country house offers an ideal base for a golfing holiday with excellent local courses at Blairgowrie, Pitlochry, Alyth and many more. *(See advertisement page 619 for further details.)*

Dean Park Hotel

Chapel Level, Kirkcaldy, Fife KY2 6QW.
Tel (01592) 261635 Fax (01592) 261371
Website: www.deanparkhotel.co.uk

Dean Park is centrally located within Fife and with its excellent cuisine, comprehensive facilities and friendly service, combined with its competitive rates, is a popular venue for the golfing fraternity. With over 100 courses within an hour's drive we provide a perfect location for your golfing break. *(See advertisement page 619 for further details.)*

Drumoig Hotel Golf Resort

Drumoig, Leuchars,
St Andrews,
Fife KY16 0BE.
Tel (01382) 541800 Fax (01382) 542211
E-mail: drumoig@sol.co.uk
Website: www.drumoigleisure.com

Picturesque AA 3-Star Drumoig Hotel Golf Resort has its own 18-hole championship golf course. The accommodation consists of 29 bedrooms including five suites with a comfortable bar and two restaurants. *(See advertisement page 617 for further details.)*

Goldenstones Hotel

Queens Road, Dunbar,
East Lothian EH42 1LG.
Tel (01368) 862356 Fax (01368) 865644
E-mail: goldenstones@cs.com
Website: www.goldenstones.co.uk

STB 3-Crown. We can arrange tee-times for you at some of the finest Scottish golf courses, including Muirfield, Dunbar and North Berwick. There are nineteen superb courses all within half an hour of the hotel. £30.00 B&B.

Golf Hotel

34 Dirleton Avenue,
North Berwick, East Lothian EH39 4BH.
Tel (01620) 892202 Fax (01620) 892290
Website: www.thegolfhotel.net

Family run hotel ideal for golfers wishing to play any of East Lothian's eighteen courses. Starting times arranged. Lounge bar, TV lounge, all rooms with private bathroom and colour TV.

Kinloch House Hotel

by Blairgowrie, Perthshire PH10 6SG.
Tel (01250) 884237 Fax: (01250) 884333

Kinloch House offers an almost unique proposition for golfers. 35 courses within an hour's drive, planning of rounds and booking of tee-times, sportsman's room with every facility and the best of Scottish hospitality. In-house health and fitness centre. AA 3-Red Star; 3-Rosette; STB 5-Star. *(See advertisement page 621 for further details.)*

Letham Grange

Colliston,
by Arbroath DD11 4RL.
Tel (01241) 890373 Fax (01241) 890725
E-mail: lethamgrange@sol.co.uk
Website: www.lethamgrange.co.uk/

The Leading Hotel in Carnoustie Country. 42-bedrooms, Victorian mansion, with 36-holes of superb golf. First class facilities set in the heartland of golf. Company/Society golf outings/breaks welcome. *(See advertisement page 619 for further details.)*

Loch Monzievaird Chalets

Ochtertyre,
Crieff, Perthshire PH7 4JR.
Tel (01764) 652586 Fax (01764) 652555

The beautiful grounds at Loch Monzievaird, are hidden away one mile from Crieff. Our Norwegian and Danish chalets are laid out amongst ancient oak, beech and scots pine. 20 golf courses within half an hour's drive!

The Marine Hotel

Cromwell Road,
North Berwick,
East Lothian EH39 4LZ.
Tel 0870 400 8129 Fax (01620) 894480

Superb 83-bedroom sporting hotel overlooking the North Berwick West Links with fabulous sea and golfing views. Home-from-home for many of the world's top golfers and famed for friendly service and traditional value for money holidays. For non-golfers there is swimming, tennis and snooker. Families, individuals and golfing parties enjoy the relaxed atmosphere of this all-year-round holiday hotel. Special seasonal leisure breaks and holiday rates. *(See advertisement page 617 for further details.)*

Old Course Hotel
- St Andrews Golf Resort & Spa

St Andrews,
Fife KY16 9SP.
Tel (01334) 474371 Fax (01334) 477668

This luxury 146-bedroom hotel overlooks the 17th Road Hole of the Old Course and is a five minute walk to the beach and town. Facilities include health spa with swimming pool, whirlpool, fitness room and full range of massage and beauty treatments. The hotel has its own championship golf course, the Duke's Course. Open to non-residents, with residents enjoying guaranteed tee-times and reduced green fees.

The Sandford
Country House Hotel
Newton Hill,
Wormit, (Nr St Andrews)
Fife DD6 8RG.
Tel (01382) 541802 Fax (01382) 542136

Cuisine at the Sandford is exceptional. The award-winning kitchen uses only the finest local produce to create varied and imaginative seasonal menus. Neighbouring Newton Hill Sports offer clay pigeon, fly fishing and off-roading.

The Scores Hotel
St Andrews,
Fife, KY16 9BB.
Tel (01334) 472451 Fax (01334) 473947

Overlooking the R&A clubhouse and first tee of the Old course, this famous golfers 3-Star hotel enjoys a commanding position with panoramic views over one of Scotland's most beautiful bays. The Scorecard bar offers a fascinating collection of golf memorabilia, including a comprehensive collection of the actual players' scorecards from *The Open* and *Dunhill Cups*. A stay at the Scores Hotel is part of the St Andrews Experience.

St Andrews Golf Hotel
St Andrews,
Fife KY16 9AS.
Tel (01334) 472611 Fax (01334) 472188
E-mail: reception@standrews-golf.co.uk
Website: www.standrews-golf.co.uk

AA 3-Star and 2-Rosettes; STB 4-Star. Most comfortable, traditional Scottish hotel (all bedrooms en suite). Fine restaurant. Extensive cellar. On the seafront 220 yards from the 'Old Course'. Let us arrange your golf in Scotland.

St Andrews Hazelbank Hotel
28 The Scores,
St Andrews,
Fife KY16 9AS.
Tel/Fax (01334) 472466
Website: www.hazelbank.com

Situated 200 yards from the R&A Clubhouse overlooking St Andrews Bay, this family run hotel offers quality accommodation (STB 3-Star) at affordable prices. All rooms en suite. Rates for 2002 £35 - £55 per person B&B. double/twin. Single supplement applies.

Highlands & Islands

Aurora Hotel
- Italian Restaurant
2 Academy Street,
Nairn, Inverness-shire IV12 4RJ.
Tel (01667) 453551 Fax (01667) 456577

A family run 10-bedroomed hotel with traditional Italian restaurant offers a warm welcome and comfortable accommodation. Close to both of Nairn's championship courses, many more within 30 miles. Beautiful beaches, whisky and castle trails.

Culloden House
Milton of Culloden,
Inverness IV2 7BZ.
Tel (01463) 790461 Fax (01463) 792181
Website: www.cullodenhouse.co.uk

Easy to access and a short drive to Royal Dornoch, Nairn and 28 other golf courses. This STB/AA 4-Star historical Georgian country house sits in 40 acres of tranquil parkland only minutes from Dalcross airport and Inverness. On-site or on-course PGA instruction/tour. *(See advertisement page 621 for further details.)*

Dornoch Castle
Castle Street,
Dornoch,
Sutherland IV25 3SD.
Tel (01862) 810216 Fax (01862) 810981
E-mail:
enquiries@dornochcastlehotel.com
Website: www.dornochcastlehotel.com

15th-century Dornoch Castle is situated across from Dornoch Cathedral and only five minutes' walk from the Royal Dornoch in this quaint village. Beautiful walled garden, comfortable rooms and excellent food, wines and malts are standard - along with a wonderful, warm Highland welcome.

Inverness Marriott Hotel
Culcabock Road,
Inverness IV2 3LP.
Tel (01463) 237166 Fax (01463) 225208
Website: www.marriotthotels.com/invkm

Overlooking Inverness Golf Club and centrally located for Royal Dornoch and the Nairn golf clubs, this 4-Star luxurious hotel offers purpose-built GOLF VILLAS and extensive leisure facilities with a 3-hole pitch and putt course.

Machrie Hotel & Golf Links

Port Ellen, Isle of Islay, Argyll PA42 7AN.
Tel (01496) 302310 Fax (01496) 302404
E-mail: machrie@machrie.com
Website: www.machrie.com

Play a hidden gem of a course. Traditional 18-hole championship links course situated on the doorstep of the Machrie Hotel. Excellent accommodation, fine food and friendly service. Self-catering and golf packages also available.

West

Dunduff House

Dunduff Farm, Dunure, Ayr KA7 4LH.
Tel (01292) 500225 Fax (01292) 500222

Situated on the edge of Dunure overlooking Arran and Firth of Clyde. Golf courses include Royal Troon, Turnberry and many more interesting courses. All rooms have TV, radio, tea-making facilities, wash hand basin. Two double rooms have en suite facilities. STB 4-Star; AA/RAC 5-Diamonds. Self-catering cottage available - sleeps four.

Fairfield House Hotel

12 Fairfield Road, Ayr KA7 2AR.
Tel (01292) 267461 Fax (01292) 261456
Website: www.fairfieldhotel.co.uk

The 4-Star Fairfield House is simply the most luxurious hotel of its type in the area, with a well deserved reputation for comfort and fine dining. Local courses include Turnberry and Royal Troon.

Langley Bank Guest House

39 Carrick Road, Ayr KA7 2RD.
Tel (01292) 264246 Fax (01292) 282628
Website: www.accommodation-ayr.co.uk

Langley Bank is an elegantly refurbished Victorian house offering quality accommodation at affordable prices. Centrally situated and in close proximity to all local golf courses. En suite facilities, direct dial telephone. Private car park.

Parkstone Hotel

Central Esplanade,
Prestwick, Ayrshire KA9 1QN.
Tel (01292) 477286 Fax (01292) 477671
E-mail: info@parkstonehotel.co.uk
Website: www.parkstonehotel.co.uk

Seafront location adjacent to Prestwick Golf Club and close to town centre. 22 bedrooms all en suite. AA 3-Star grading. Special breaks available and all golfing arrangements can be made.

Southern Gailes Ltd

29 Bothwell Road,
Hamilton ML3 0AS.
Freephone: 08000 285220
Tel (01698) 207080
Fax (01698) 891435
E-mail:
alancdaly@dalypartners.freeserve.co.uk
Website: www.southerngailes.com

A new and exciting development is now underway 'Southern Gailes'! The development will consist of an 18-hole championship golf course, a 9-hole course, leisure centre, hotel, driving range and luxury business managed residences. The golf course will be on a pay and play basis with corporate membership available. Full details can be seen on our website. *(See advertisement page 25 for further details.)*

The Westin Turnberry Resort, Scotland

Turnberry,
Ayrshire KA26 9LT.
Tel +44 (0) 1655 331000
Fax +44 (0) 1655 331707
E-mail: turnberry@westin.com
Website: www.turnberry.co.uk

World renowned hotel located in spectacular coastal surroundings with unrivalled facilities. Savour the finest international cuisine, stay in luxuriously appointed hotel and lodge bedrooms, relax in our award-winning spa or enjoy a range of exciting outdoor pursuits.

WALES

Welsh Borders

Belmont Lodge & Golf Course

Belmont,
Hereford HR2 9SA.
Tel (01432) 352666 Fax (01432) 358090

18-hole golf course running along the beautiful Wye Valley with a 30-bedroomed hotel on-site. Other facilities include bar, restaurant, fishing, bowling, tennis and snooker. Only a mile and a half from Hereford City centre.

Cadmore Lodge Hotel
St Michaels,
Tenbury Wells,
Worcestershire WR15 8TQ.
Tel/Fax (01584) 810044

A warm welcome awaits at Cadmore Lodge Hotel. Excellent cuisine from chefs with imagination and flair. Our own 9-hole golf course par 68 SSS 65 (18 holes). Two fishing lakes for trout and course fishing. Indoor swimming pool, with spa, steam room and cardio-vascular equipment. *(See advertisement page 621 for further details.)*

Hawkstone Park Hotel
Weston-under-Redcastle,
Shrewsbury,
Shropshire SY4 5UY.
Tel (01939) 200611 Fax (01939) 200311
E-mail: info@hawkstone.co.uk
Website: www.hawkstone.co.uk

Hawkstone Park Hotel with its 65 en suite bedrooms, has been accommodating golfing visitors since 1920. This tradition is enhanced by a purpose built golf centre, two 18-hole courses, 6-hole Academy course and friendly staff.

North

De Vere St David's Park Hotel
St David's Park,
Ewloe,
Nr Chester,
Flintshire CH5 3YB.
Tel (01244) 520800 Fax (01244) 520930
E-mail:reservations.stdavidspark@devere-hotels.com
Website: www.devereonline.co.uk

AA 4-Star hotel with extensive leisure facilities, including gym and swimming pool. 145 bedrooms and suites, excellent restaurant. Northop Country Park Golf Club only five minutes away. Special golf packages available. *(See advertisement page 621 for further details.)*

Deucoch Hotel
Sarn Bach,
Abersoch,
Pwllheli, Gwynedd LL53 7LD.
Tel (01758) 712680 Fax (01758) 712670

A 10-bedroom en suite country house hotel situated on the beautiful Llyn Peninsula, commanding extraordinary views over Cardigan Bay to Snowdonia. Associated with Abersoch, Caernarfon, Nefyn, Pwllheli, Porthmadog and Royal St Davids Harlech golf clubs. *(See advertisement page 623 for further details.)*

Imperial Hotel - Llandudno
The Promenade,
Llandudno, Gwynedd LL30 1AP.
Tel (01492) 877466 Fax (01492) 878043
Website: www.theimperial.co.uk

100-bedroomed hotel with extensive leisure facilities including 45' indoor swimming pool. Ideally situated for all North Wales' golf courses. Award-winning restaurant and private dining room for up to 30 available.

Soughton Hall
Northop,
Near Chester,
Flintshire CH7 6AB.
Tel (01352) 840811 Fax (01352) 840382

Stay in luxury - play championship golf course - we offer great value packages. Grand house amidst historic parkland. Setting for privately owned championship golf. Original stables adapted to bar restaurant, casual informal atmosphere. Real ales - wine shop inclusive. *(See advertisement page 623 for further details.)*

Trefeddian Hotel
Aberdovey,
Gwynedd LL35 0SB.
Tel (01654) 767213 Fax (01654) 767777

Elevated position in own grounds, Trefeddian prominently overlooks the famous Aberdovey links course. Lounges and front bedrooms provide views of 3rd and 16th Greens. Facilities include indoor swimming pool, tennis, 9-hole pitch and putt, snooker. Colour brochure by return. *(See advertisement page 623 for further details.)*

Central

Penrhos Golf & Country Club
Llanrhystud,
Ceredigion SY23 5AY.
Tel (01974) 202999 Fax (01974) 202100
Website: www.penrhosgolf.co.uk

Fifteen American-style suites. 18-hole championship length course, driving range, indoor swimming pool, sauna, steam room, gymnasium, tennis courts, spa, solarium and bowling green.

South & South West

The Best Western Lamphey Court Hotel
Lamphey,
Pembroke,
Pembrokeshire SA71 5NT.
Tel (01646) 672273 Fax (01646) 672480

One of Wales' leading country hotels. Deluxe bedrooms, superb leisure centre, swimming pool, jacuzzi, gym, sauna and floodlit tennis. Special arrangements with Tenby, South Pembrokeshire, Trefloyne and Haverfordwest golf clubs. Excellent food and wine - local produce. A Best Western Hotel.

The Dormy
Royal Porthcawl Golf Club,
Rest Bay, Porthcawl,
Mid Glamorgan CF36 3UW.
Tel (01656) 782251 Fax (01656) 771687
E-mail: royalporthcawl@cs.com
Website: www.royalporthcawl.com

Luxury dormy accommodation for parties of up to twelve persons. Apply to the secretary.
(See advertisement page 14 for further details.)

St Mary's Hotel Golf & Country Club
St Mary's Hill,
Pencoed,
Vale of Glamorgan CF35 5EA.
Tel (01656) 861100 Fax (01656) 863400

24-bedroom hotel, 18-hole membership and pay course. 9-hole pay as you play, 15-bay floodlit driving range, clubhouse and restaurant conservatory and three bars. Fully stocked golf shop. Floodlit chipping and putting area and resident golf professional Mr John Peters.

CHANNEL ISLANDS

La Grande Mare Hotel Golf Club
La Grande Mare,
Vazon,
Castel, Guernsey.
Tel (01481) 256576 & 253544
Fax (01481) 255194
Website: www.lgm.guernsey.net

Beautifully appointed luxury hotel with 18-hole golf course. Professional shop and tuition on-site. First class, well priced restaurant. 2-AA Rosettes. Beachside location. Golfing breaks catered for.

The Moorings Hotel & Restaurant
Gorey Pier,
Gorey, Jersey JE3 6EW.
Tel (01534) 853633 Fax (01534) 857618

3-Star intimate and luxurious 17-bedroom hotel overlooking the quaint Gorey harbour and the sandy bay of Grouville. Half a mile from the Royal Jersey Golf Club. Renowned for its superb food, seafood a speciality. Open all year. Special rates for golfers at any time.

St Pierre Park Hotel
Rohais,
St Peter Port,
Guernsey GYI 1FD.
Tel (01481) 728282 Fax (01481) 712041

This 4-Star hotel offers extensive leisure facilities including a 9-hole par 3 golf course, designed by Tony Jacklin. Three tennis courts and a health suite with heated indoor swimming pool, spa bath, saunas, steam rooms, solaria and exercise room.

NORTHERN IRELAND

Brown Trout Golf & Country Inn
209 Agivey Road,
Aghadowey,
Coleraine, Co Derry BT51 4AD.
Tel 028 7086 8209 Fax 028 7086 8878

3-Star country inn set on its own challenging 9-hole golf course. Only ten miles from the premier links of Royal Portrush, Portstewart and Castlerock. Good food and great craic guaranteed.

Bushmills Inn Hotel & Restaurant
9 Dunluce Road,
Bushmills,
Co Antrim BT57 8QG.
Tel 028 207 32339 Fax 028 207 32048
E-mail: rna@bushmillsinn.com
Website: www.bushmillsinn.com

'A living museum of Ulster Hospitality' With its turf fires, pitched pine and gas lights this faithfully restored coaching inn, and adjoining mill on the banks of the River Bush, is just four scenic miles from Royal Portrush. British Airways Tourism Awards 2000 'Best Hotel' and member of Ireland's Blue Book and Best-Loved Hotels of the World.

REPUBLIC OF IRELAND

Arnolds Hotel

Dunfanaghy,
Co Donegal,
Ireland.
Tel +353 74 36208 Fax +353 74 36352

Family hotel established since 1922 situated at the entrance to the village overlooking Horn Head and Sheephaven Bay. Ideal base to play the many scenic links of north west Donegal.

Bloomfield House Hotel & Leisure Club

Belvedere,
Mullingar,
Co Westmeath,
Ireland.
Tel +353 44 40894 Fax +353 44 43767
E-mail: sales@bloomfieldhouse.com
Website: www.bloomfieldhouse.com

This beautifully appointed hotel boasts 65 superb bedrooms, full leisure centre facilities, massage and reflexology all on-site. It is adjacent to Mullingar's Championship Golf Course. Glasson, Esker Hills and Tullamore golf courses are all nearby.

Caragh Lodge

Caragh Lake,
Near Killorglin,
Co Kerry,
Ireland.
Tel +353 66 9769115 Fax +353 66 9769316
E-mail: caragh@iol.ie
Website: www.caraghlodge.com

A country house situated on the shore of Caragh lake, the perfect location for Ballybunion, Waterville, Tralee, Killarney, Beaufort and Dooks. Member of Ireland's Blue Book, RAC Gold Ribbon, Johansen's Country House Award.

Casey's of Baltimore Hotel

Baltimore,
Co Cork, Ireland.
Tel +353 28 20197 Fax +353 28 20509
E-mail: caseys@eircom.net
Website: www.caseysofbaltimore.com

3-Star family run 14 en suite bedroom hotel. Seafood restaurant and traditional pub. Golf available at Skibbereen 18-hole golf course. Special rates for residents.

Castle Arms Hotel

Enniscrone, Co Sligo, Ireland.
Tel/Fax +353 96 36156

Castle Arms Hotel is a family run hotel renowned for its excellent home cooking. We are an ideal base for golfing in Enniscrone, Rosses Point, Strandhill and Carne. Let us help you organise your perfect golf holiday.

Castletroy Park Hotel

Dublin Road, Limerick, Ireland.
Tel +353 61 335566 Fax +353 61 331117
E-mail: sales@castletroy-park.ie
Website: www.castletroy-park.ie

The Castletroy Park Hotel lies at the heart of the south west of Ireland. The region boasts over 23 golf courses, including the renowned Ballybunion course, all within an hour's drive of the hotel.

Charleville Lodge

268-272 North Circular Road,
Phibsborough, Dublin 7, Ireland.
Tel +353 838 6633 Fax +353 838 5854
E-mail: charleville@indigo.ie
Website: www.charlevillelodge.ie

You are located in the heart of Dublin, surrounded by championship courses and beside all entertainment and restaurants. A warm welcome awaits you. Let us make your golf arrangements for you.

Citywest Hotel Conference, Leisure & Golf Resort

Saggart, Co Dublin, Ireland.
Tel +353 1 4010500 Fax +353 1 4588756

4-Star hotel with two golf courses and golf academy on-site. 5-Star leisure centre with 20 metre pool, hair and beauty salons. Conference facilities for up to 6,500 pax. Convention centre. 330 deluxe bedrooms and suites.

Clarion Hotel IFSC

International Financial Services Centre,
Dublin 1, Ireland.
Tel +353 1 4338800 Fax +353 1 4338801
E-mail: info@clarionhotelifsc.com
Website: www.clarionhotelifsc.com

In Dublin 1, overlooking the River Liffey, the Clarion is a contemporary 4-Star hotel. 147 air conditioned bedrooms, all with modern technology and comforts. Sinergie Restaurant, Kudos Bar and Sanovitae Health and Leisure Club complete with 18 metre pool. Ideal base for golf.

Coffey's Loch Lein House Hotel
Golf Course Road,
Fossa, Killarney,
Co Kerry, Ireland.
Tel +353 64 31260 Fax +353 64 36151
E-mail: ecoffey@indigo.ie
Website: www.lochlein.com

On the shores of Killarney's lower lake with magnificent views a warm welcome awaits at this family run hotel. Recently extended the relaxed atmosphere and service remains unchanged. Four excellent 18-hole championship golf courses nearby.

Dooly's Hotel
Emmet Square, Birr, Co Offaly, Ireland.
Tel +353 509 20032 Fax +353 509 21332

Modernised, historic 250 year old coaching inn with 18 en suite bedrooms. Table d'hôte and à la carte menu served in our award-winning Emmet Restaurant. An ideal base for golfing at Birr, Roscrea, Tullamore and surrounding courses.

Dromoland Castle
Newmarket-on-Fergus, Co Clare, Ireland.
Tel +353 61 368444 Fax +353 61 368498
Website: www.dromoland.ie

Dromoland Castle is a magnificent renaissance castle on 375 acres of parkland. It offers the highest accommodation standards, and award-winning restaurant. Activities include golf, clay pigeon shooting, horse riding and fishing, we also have a fully equipped health centre and swimming pool. The castle is located eight miles from Shannon International airport in County Clare.

Gormanstown Manor
- Farm Guest House
Gormanstown,
Nr Wicklow Town and Brittas Bay,
Co Wicklow, Ireland.
Tel +353 404 69432 Fax +353 404 61832
E-mail: gormanstownmanor@tinet.ie
Website: www.homepage.eircom.net/-gormanstownmanor

We have a spectactular par 3 golf course 18-hole pitch and putt and a golf driving range with a qualified golf professional in attendance daily. Gormanstown Manor is ideally located for the golfer who wishes to play golf on the top 25 golf courses in the area. We are just outside Dublin City off the N11. *(See advertisement page 624 for further details.)*

The Greenbrier Inn Guesthouse
Lahinch,
Co Clare, Ireland.
Tel +353 65 7081242 Fax +353 65 7081247
E-mail: gbrier@indigo.ie
Website: www.greenbrierinn.com

Luxurious 3-Star 14-bedroomed guesthouse overlooking Lahinch golf links and the Atlantic Ocean. An excellent base from which to play the famous Lahinch golf links or the spectacular Greg Norman designed Doonbeg golf links eighteen miles away. *'Come and enjoy our home while you are away from your own'.*

Hunter's Hotel
Rathnew,
Co Wicklow, Ireland.
Tel +353 404 40106 Fax +353 404 40338

270 year old coaching inn run by the same family for the past 170 years. Ideal centre for golf holidays. Twenty 18-hole courses within half an hour, nearest three minutes' drive away.

Inishowen Gateway Hotel
& Gateway Health & Fitness Club
Railway Road,
Buncrana, Inishowen,
Co Donegal, Ireland.
Tel +353 77 61144 Fax +353 77 62278
E-mail: inigatho@iol.ie
Website: www.inishowengateway.com

Stylish hotel, 63 en suite bedrooms, with adjoining luxurious health and fitness club. Enjoying a delightful location on the white sandy shores of Lough Swilly. Ideal for golf at the 'Faldo famous' Ballyliffin courses and North West Golf Club.

Island View Hotel
Coast Road, Malahide,
Co Dublin, Ireland.
Tel +353 1 84 50099 Fax +353 1 84 51498

There are many golf courses in the area of Malahide and Portmarnock. Other activities in this area would include swimming (we are beside the beach), horse riding and tennis.

Jurys Hotel Waterford
Ferrybank, Waterford, Ireland.
Tel +353 51 832111 Fax +353 51 832863

Situated on 38 acres of parkland and overlooking Waterford City, this hotel has 98 bedrooms. Facilities include an extensive leisure centre, bar and restaurant. There are six 18-hole courses within a ten mile radius.

The Killarney Park Hotel
Kenmare Place,
Killarney,
Co Kerry, Ireland.
Tel +353 64 35555 Fax +353 64 35266
E-mail: info@killarneyparkhotel.ie
Website: www.killarneyparkhotel.ie

Voted Irish Golf Hotel of the Year for 2001 by
the IGTOA. Superbly located in Killarney
town, this 5-Star hotel is the perfect location
for the finest golf courses in south west Ireland.
Spacious deluxe, air conditioned rooms or
magnificent suites. Relax and unwind in the
friendly Garden Bar, billiards room and library.
Leisure facilities, 20 metre pool, outdoor hot
tub and sauna. Drying room available for golf
club storage.

King Sitric Fish Restaurant & Accommodation
East Pier,
Howth, Co Dublin,
Ireland.
Tel +353 1 8325235 Fax +353 1 8392442

Beautifully located in picturesque Howth
harbour, with panoramic sea views. Famous
seafood restaurant, established 1971, now with
quality accommodation. Many golf courses of
Dublin and Fingal within half an hour. Dart
into Dublin 25 minutes; Dublin airport only 20
minutes.

Lake of Shadows Hotel
Grianan Park,
Buncrana,
Inishowen,
Co Donegal, Ireland.
Tel +353 77 61005 Fax +353 77 62131
Website: www.lakeofshadows.com

Family run hotel with 23 en suite bedrooms,
cosy, warm and just oozing with charm. Close
to beautiful sandy beaches and is an ideal
location for golfing at world famous Ballyliffin
(two courses) and North West Golf Club.

Mal Dua House
Clifden, Connemara,
Co Galway, Ireland.
Tel +353 95 21171 Fax +353 95 21739
E-mail: info@maldua.com
Website: www.maldua.com

AA/RAC-5-Star; Bord Failte 4-Star. In the
heart of Connemara, award-winning
guesthouse, close to Connemara Golf Club,
Mal Dua House offers luxury in a relaxed

atmosphere. Courtesy mini-bus. Bicycles for
hire. Visit our website.

Mount Juliet
Thomastown,
Co Kilkenny, Ireland.
Tel +353 56 73000 Fax +353 56 73019
E-mail: info@mountjuliet.ie
Website: www.mountjuliet.ie

Deluxe accommodation in the elegant Mount
Juliet House or the informal club rooms.
Ireland's premier sporting estate offers guests
on-site fishing, horse riding, tennis, leisure
centre and fully dedicated spa. Golf Academy
with PGA professionals. 18-hole putting
course. Irish Open venue 1993-95. Host to
WGC American Express Championship in
September 2002.

Renvyle House Hotel
Connemara,
Go Galway, Ireland.
Tel +353 95 43511 Fax +353 95 43515
E-mail: renvyle@iol.ie
Website: www.renvyle.com

Set in the wild splendour of Connemara in
truly magical surroundings. Originally the
home of Oliver St John Gogarty, Renvyle
House has played host to many famous people
- Augustus John, Yeats and Churchill to name
but a few. Warmth, comfort and award-
winning fare awaits. Excellent golf and golf
clinics are available on-site. *(See advertisement
page 623 for further details.)*

Rosapenna Hotel & Golf Links
Rosapenna, Downings, Donegal, Ireland.
Tel +353 74 55301 Fax +353 74 55128

Rosapenna Hotel is set in the middle of its own
27-hole golf links course. Half a mile from the
fishing village of Downings.

The Slieve Russell Hotel Golf & Country Club
Ballyconnell, Co Cavan, Ireland.
Tel +353 49 9526444 Fax +353 49 9526474
Website: www.quinnhotels.com

Located only two hours' drive from both
Dublin and Belfast, the Slieve Russell is a
complete resort with its 5-Star leisure facilities,
championship 18-hole golf course, 159
superbly appointed bedrooms and a selection
of restaurants and bars, conference and
banqueting suites - The Perfect location for
business or pleasure.

The Smugglers Inn
Cliff Road, Waterville,
Co Kerry, Ireland.
Tel +353 66 9474330 Fax +353 66 9474422
E-mail: thesmugglersinn@eircom.net
Website:
www.welcome.to/thesmugglersinn

Situated in a quiet location, 2km sandy beach, adjacent to Waterville golf links. Gourmet restaurant, chef proprietors Harry and Henry Hunt. 17 rooms all en suite. Wonderful views to the Atlantic and golf course.

St Helen's Bay
Golf & Country Club
St Helens, Kilrane,
Rosslare Harbour,
Co Wexford, Ireland.
Tel +353 53 33234 Fax +353 53 33803
E-mail: sthelens@iol.ie
Website: sthelensbay.com

Luxury on-site accommodation together with tennis courts. Full bar/catering facilities available in the clubhouse. Superbly located championship 18-hole golf course, which has blended the best of parkland characteristics with a finish that is true links and plenty of difficulty. Situated only five minutes from Rosslare ferryport. Green fee and society friendly, playable all year round.

Tinakilly Country House & Restaurant
Rathnew,
Wicklow,
Co Wicklow, Ireland.
Tel +353 404 69274 Fax +353 404 67806
E-mail: reservations@tinakilly.ie
Website: www.tinakilly.ie

4-Star ITB; RAC Gold Ribbon; AA Red Star and a Small Luxury Hotel of the World. Renowned for splendid fresh food in elegant Victorian surroundings, Tinakilly is situated in seven acres of gardens and has 51 bedrooms, mostly Junior Suites with sea views. 29 miles from Dublin, eight miles from Druid's Glen, home of the 1996-1999 Irish Open, and local to the European Club, Blainroe, Woodenbridge, Wicklow and Delgany. Don't miss Powerscourt Gardens, Glendalough, Wicklow mountains and BallyKissangel! Special golf brochure available.

Golf Club Facilities

This section lists clubs which can offer hotel accommodation, and hotels which have their own golf facilties. They are able to provide for society or corporate days, and in some instances offer an extensive range of other sports and leisure activities.

Abbotsley Golf Hotel & Country Club
Eynesbury Hardwicke, St Neots, Cambridgeshire PE19 4XN.
Tel (01480) 474000 Fax (01480) 471018

Set in 250 acres of idyllic countryside, offering two 18-hole courses, a par 3, driving range, squash courts, fitness centre and a 42-bedroom hotel. Golf breaks and residential packages available. Operated by American Golf (UK) Limited.

Aldwark Manor Hotel Golf & Country Club
Aldwark, Alne, York, North Yorkshire YO61 1UF.
Tel (01347) 838146 (Hotel)
Fax (01347) 838867
Tel (01347) 838353 (Golf)
Fax (01347) 830007
E-mail: reception@aldwarkmanor.co.uk
Website: www.aldwarkmanor.co.uk

Aldwark Manor extends a warm welcome to everyone. Situated in the Vale of York is a 6,154 yards par 71 golf course, laid out in easy walking parkland with the river Ure meandering beside a number of fairways. The ideal venue for your Society or company golf day. *(See advertisement page 613 for further details.)*

Barnham Broom Hotel, Golf & Country Club
Norwich, Norfolk NR9 4DD.
Tel (01603) 759393 Fax (01603) 758224
Website: www.barnham-broom.co.uk

Set in 250 acres of peaceful Norfolk countryside just 15 minutes from the historical City of Norwich, Barnham Broom has 52 en suite bedrooms and suites, two superb 18-hole golf courses, a leisure club with indoor pool, SportsBar and Cafe with Sky TV, Flints restaurant and four versatile conference and banqueting suites. Golf and Leisure Breaks available throughout the year. Professional tuition by the Peter Ballingall Golf School. Corporate Golf and Society days. *(See advertisement page 611 for further details.)*

Beaufort Golf Course
Churchtown, Beaufort, Killarney, Co Kerry, Ireland.
Tel +353 64 44440 Fax +353 64 44752

A traditional Kerry welcome awaits you at the *Friendliest Course in Kerry*. Challenging 18-hole par 71 championship course, buggies and caddies for hire, excellent golf shop, bar food and snacks. Tuition can be arranged with our golf professional. Societies and groups welcome. *(See advertisement page 16 for further details.)*

Belmont Lodge & Golf Course
Belmont, Hereford HR2 9SA.
Tel (01432) 352666 Fax (01432) 358090

18-hole golf course running along the beautiful Wye Valley with a 30-bedroomed hotel on-site. Other facilities include bar, restaurant, fishing, bowling, tennis and snooker. Only a mile and a half from Hereford City centre.

Borth & Ynyslas Golf Club

Borth,
Ceredigion SY24 5JS.
Tel (01970) 871202
E-mail: secretary@borthgolf.co.uk

18 holes links course adjoining Borth beach.
Humps and hollows provide great variation,
although the topography and springy turf make
for easy walking. Professional's shop, practice
area, modern clubhouse with bar and catering.
Tuition available.

Botley Park Hotel Golf & Country Club

Winchester Road,
Boorley Green,
Botley,
Southampton SO32 2UA.
Tel (01489) 780888 Fax (01489) 789242
E-mail:
info@botleypark.macdonald-hotels.co.uk
Website: www.macdonaldhotels.co.uk

Set in 176 acres of rolling Hampshire
countryside, this 4-Star hotel has 100 en suite
bedrooms, superb restaurant, extensive leisure
facilities and its own picturesque and
challenging 18-hole par 70 golf course and
driving range. *(See advertisement page 609 for
further details.)*

Brown Trout Golf & Country Inn

209 Agivey Road,
Aghadowey,
Coleraine,
Co Derry BT51 4AD.
Tel 028 7086 8209 Fax 028 7086 8878

3-Star country inn set on its own challenging
9-hole golf course. Only ten miles from the
premier links of Royal Portrush, Portstewart
and Castlerock. Good food and great craic
guaranteed.

Burnham & Berrow Golf Club

St Christopher's Way,
Burnham-on-Sea,
Somerset TA8 2PE.
Tel (01278) 785760
*E-mail: secretary@burnhamandberrowgc
.2-golf.com*
*Website: www.burnhamandberrowgc
.2-golf.com*

18-hole championship links golf course and 9-
hole course. Dormy accommodation available.
(See advertisement page 25 for further details.)

Bushey Hall Golf Club

Bushey Hall Drive,
Bushey,
Hertfordshire WD23 2EP.
Tel (01923) 222253
(01923) 225802 (Pro Shop)
Fax (01923) 229759
Website: www.golfclubuk.co.uk

Established in 1890 Bushey Hall Golf Club has
one of the oldest and best established courses
in Hertfordshire. Facilities include a fully
equipped pro shop, practice net, clubhouse
restaurant and bar. Open for membership. Pay
as you play operated. *(See advertisement page 20
for further details.)*

Cadmore Lodge Hotel

St Michaels,
Tenbury Wells,
Worcestershire WR15 8TQ.
Tel/Fax (01584) 810044

A warm welcome awaits at Cadmore Lodge
Hotel. Excellent cuisine from chefs with
imagination and flair. Our own 9-hole golf
course par 68 SSS 65 (18 holes). Two fishing
lakes for trout and course fishing. Indoor
swimming pool, with spa, steam room and
cardio-vascular equipment. *(See advertisement
page 621 for further details.)*

Cambridgeshire Moat House Hotel

Bar Hill, Cambridge CB3 8EU.
Tel (01954) 249988 (Hotel) 780098 (Club)
Fax (01954) 780010

18-hole championship golf course set in 134
acres of parkland. Golf professional Paul
Simpson. Newly built clubhouse and golf shop.
134 en suite bedrooms. Extensive leisure
facilities. Five miles north of Cambridge on
A14. Visitors welcome.

Cannington Golf Course

Cannington College, Cannington,
Bridgwater, Somerset TA5 2LS.
Tel/Fax (01278) 655050

Designed by Martin Hawtree of Oxford and
built to highest international specifications in
1992 by Brian Pierson Limited under the
consultancy of top agronomists Jim Arthur and
Gordon Child. Together they have produced
arguably the best 9-hole golf course with its 18
tees in the west of England. With its 'Links-
Like' appearance in high summer the subtle
contours make for a testing round of golf for

the scratch golfer yet it is receptive to the beginner with its wide spaces at 2,929 yards par 34. Beating par will take skill and courage.

Carnoustie Hotel Golf Resort & Spa

The Links, Carnoustie, Angus DD7 7JE.
Tel (01241) 411999 Fax (01241) 411998
E-mail: enquiries@carnoustie-hotel.com
Website: www.carnoustie-hotel.com

Deluxe 4-Star hotel situated on the world class links, home to 128th Open Championship. Residents can take advantage of the first class facilities and reserve guaranteed starting times on the par 72 Championship Course, or the Burnside and Buddon 18-hole courses. *(See advertisement page 617 for further details.)*

Castletown Golf Links Hotel

Derbyhaven,
Castletown,
Isle of Man IM9 1UA.
Tel (01624) 822201 Fax (01624) 824633

Situated on our own peninsula, our championship golf course of 6,700 yards, with all holes having sea views, is a real test of links golf. The hotel facilities are of a luxurious 3-Star standard.

Cave Castle Hotel & Country Club

South Cave, East Yorkshire HU15 2EU.
Tel (01430) 422245 Fax (01430) 421118

Superb country manor house with 53 en suite bedrooms in tranquil 160-acre parkland setting with easy access to M62 motorway. Excellent, traditional cuisine is served in our character restaurant. Choice of two 18-hole golf courses (Cave Castle and Boothferry Park), plus use of leisure facilities, including 19m indoor pool, gym, sauna, steam and spa. This is a Unique Leisure Experience not to be missed! Golf and leisure breaks, visiting parties and non-members welcome.

Charleville Golf Club

Charleville, Co Cork, Ireland.
Tel +353 63 81257 Fax +353 63 81274
E-mail: charlevillegolf@eircom.net

Located in the foothills of Ballyhoura mountains enjoy uncrowded golf at our 27-hole championship parkland course renowned for its lush fairways and excellent greens. Driving range, full bar and catering facilities in our friendly clubhouse. Open from 7.30am to sunset.

China Fleet Country Club

Saltash,
Cornwall PL12 6LJ.
Tel (01752) 848668 Fax (01752) 848456
E-mail: sales@china-fleet.co.uk
Website: www.china-fleet.co.uk

Situated in 180 acres of Cornish countryside, 40 self-catering 4- and 6-berth apartments, 18-hole par 72 golf, 28-bay driving range, pool, health suite, gymnasium, racket sports, bars, restaurant and coffee shop. *(See advertisement page 25 for further details.)*

Citywest Hotel Conference, Leisure & Golf Resort

Saggart,
Co Dublin,
Ireland.
Tel +353 1 4010500 Fax +353 1 4588756

4-Star hotel with two golf courses and golf academy on-site. 5-Star leisure centre with 20 metre pool, hair and beauty salons. Conference facilities for up to 6,500 pax. Convention centre. 330 deluxe bedrooms and suites.

Coulsdon Manor - Coulsdon Golf Centre

Coulsdon Court Road,
Coulsdon,
Surrey CR5 2LL.
Tel 020 8660 6083 Fax 020 8668 3118
E-mail:
coulsdonmanor@marstonhotels.com
Website: www.marstonhotels.com

A relaxing yet challenging par 70 golf course set in 140 acres of Surrey parkland. Golf societies made very welcome. Excellent restaurant and bar facilities at the Manor.

Courtown Golf Club

Kiltennel,
Gorey,
Co Wexford,
Ireland.
Tel +353 55 25166 Fax +353 55 25553
E-mail: courtown@iol.ie
Website: www.courtowngolfclub.com

This 18-hole heavily wooded parkland course features four challenging par 3's and three long par 5's. The variety (no two holes are alike) and excellence of this course is matched by its luxurious clubhouse and bar and catering facilities.

Dalmunzie House Hotel
Spittal O'Glenshee,
Blairgowrie,
Perthshire PH10 7QG.
Tel (01250) 885224 Fax (01250) 885225

Set in the Highlands with our own 9-hole course. This friendly country house offers an ideal base for a golfing holiday with excellent local courses at Blairgowrie, Pitlochry, Alyth and many more. *(See advertisement page 619 for further details.)*

De Vere Northop
Country Park Golf Club
Northop,
Flintshire CH7 6WA.
Tel (01352) 840440 Fax (01352) 840445
Website: www.devereonline.co.uk

John Jacob's designed par 72, 18-hole championship course in 247 acres of mature parkland. Driving range, pratice greens and pro shop plus two all-weather tennis courts, gym and sauna. Award-winning restaurant. Overnight accommodation available at nearby De Vere St David's Park Hotel five minutes away. *(See advertisement page 621 for further details.)*

Dromoland Castle
Newmarket-on-Fergus, Co Clare, Ireland.
Tel +353 61 368444 Fax +353 61 368498
Website: www.dromoland.ie

Dromoland Castle is a magnificent renaissance castle on 375 acres of parkland. It offers the highest accommodation standards, and award-winning restaurant. Activities include golf, clay pigeon shooting, horse riding and fishing, we also have a fully equipped health centre and swimming pool. The castle is located eight miles from Shannon International airport in County Clare.

Druids Glen Golf Club
Newtownmountkennedy,
Co Wicklow, Ireland.
Tel +353 1 287 3600 Fax +353 1 287 3699
E-mail: druids@indigo.ie
Website: www.druidsglen.ie

Venue for the 2001 Seve Trophy. European Golf Course of the Year 2000. Home of Murphy's Irish Open 1996 to 1999. Facilities include an 18-hole championship golf course, 3-hole teaching academy, practice ground and sumptuously converted 18th-century clubhouse with full bar and dining facilities. Visitors always welcome.

Drumoig Hotel Golf Resort
Drumoig, Leuchars,
St Andrews, Fife KY16 0BE.
Tel (01382) 541800 Fax (01382) 542211
E-mail: drumoig@sol.co.uk
Website: www.drumoigleisure.com

Picturesque AA 3-Star Drumoig Hotel Golf Resort has its own 18-hole championship golf course. The golf course with water and quarry features will prove challenging to golfers of all abilities. *(See advertisement page 617 for further details.)*

East Dorset Golf Club
Bere Regis, Dorset BH20 7NT.
Tel (01929) 472244 Fax (01929) 471294
E-mail: edgc@golf.co.uk
Website: www.golf.co.uk/edgc

Hawtree design. 7,027 yards SSS 74 with the record of 65. Other tees available! The lakeland course features all-the-year-round greens protected by large bunkers with water coming into play on several holes. A flat terrain in Hardy country overlooking Purbeck Hills. Attractive and challenging 9-hole Woodland course, surrounded by rhododendrons. Provides all-round golfing opportunities. Packages include accommodation, meals and all golf.

Edmondstown Golf Club
Rathfarnham, Dublin 16, Ireland.
Tel +353 1 493 1082 Fax +353 1 493 3152
E-mail: info@edmondstowngolfclub.ie
Website: www.edmondstowngolfclub.ie

Edmondstown Golf Club is situated amongst the most delightful surroundings on the foothills of the Dublin mountains, and only seven miles from Dublin City centre. A testing parkland course - it lends itself to the golfer who desires a socially enjoyable round of golf - on a well maintained and manicured golf course. *(See advertisement page 14 for further details.)*

Farthingstone Hotel
& Golf Course
Farthingstone, Towcester,
Northamptonshire NN12 8HA.
Tel (01327) 361291 Fax (01327) 361645

Set in glorious wooded countryside, just 90 minutes outside London. Farthingstone Hotel offers 16 superb en suite rooms, a challenging 18-hole golf course, squash court, full size snooker tables, and a carvery restaurant. Highly competitive tariffs.

Gainsborough Golf Club

Thonock, Gainsborough,
Lincolnshire DN21 1PZ.
Tel (01427) 613088 Fax (01427) 810172

The Karsten Lakes championship course, designed by Neil Coles, MBE, is part of a 36-hole complex set amongst undulating Lincolnshire parkland. The two courses are complemented with a 4-Star clubhouse offering restaurant and conference facilities. Visitors, Society and Corporate golf parties welcome.

Gatton Manor Hotel Golf & Country Club Ltd

Ockley, Nr Dorking, Surrey RH5 5PQ.
Tel (01306) 627555

Set amidst its own 18-hole golf course in 200 acres of parklands and lakes, situated between London and the south coast, in the heart of the Surrey countryside. Superb all en suite accommodation overlooking the golf course and grounds. À la carte restaurants, large lounge bar, conference suites, gym and health club.

Gormanstown Manor - Farm Guest House

Gormanstown,
Near Wicklow Town and Brittas Bay,
Co Wicklow, Ireland.
Tel +353 404 69432 Fax +353 404 61832
E-mail: gormanstownmanor@tinet.ie
Website: www.homepage.eircom.net/-gormanstownmanor

We have a spectactular par 3 golf course 18-hole pitch and putt and a golf driving range with a qualified golf professional in attendance daily. Gormanstown Manor is ideally located for the golfer who wishes to play golf on the top 25 golf courses in the area. We are just outside Dublin City off the N11. *(See advertisement page 624 for further details.)*

The Grange & Links Hotel

Sea Lane, Sandilands, Sutton-on-Sea,
Lincolnshire LN12 2RA.
Tel (01507) 441334 Fax (01507) 443033
E-mail: grangelinks@ic24.net
Website: www.grangeandlinkshotel.com

3-Star 30-bedroom hotel with own 18-hole links course. Two tennis courts, snooker and ballroom. Award-winning hotel renowned for superb cuisine, friendliness, comfort and service.

Harrogate Golf Club

Forest Lane Head, Harrogate,
North Yorkshire HG2 7TF.
Tel (01423) 862999

A long established 18-hole golf course set amongst mature trees formerly part of the Forest of Knaresborough. Visitors are assured of a warm reception in the extensively refurbished clubhouse and restaurant. *(See advertisement page 14 for further details.)*

Hawkstone Park Golf Centre

Weston-under-Redcastle,
Shrewsbury, Shropshire SY4 5UY.
Tel (01939) 200611 Fax (01939) 200311
E-mail: info@hawkstone.co.uk
Website: www.hawkstone.co.uk

Two championship golf courses, namely the Hawkstone and Windmill, a 6-hole Academy course, practice range and purpose built golf centre make Hawkstone Park a delight for any golfer. The famed historic park and follies and 65-bedroom hotel completes this enchanting venue.

Hellidon Lakes Hotel Golf & Country Club

Hellidon, Daventry,
Northamptonshire NN11 6GG.
Tel (01327) 262550 Fax (01327) 262559
E-mail: hellidon@marstonhotels.com
Website: www.marstonhotels.com

27 holes of golf through woodland and over lakes. Buggies for hire. Corporate, Society and residential packages available. 71 well appointed bedrooms and suites, country club with extensive health and fitness facilities including pool, gym and treatment rooms. Indoor golf simulator and 10-pin bowling. Only 20 minutes from junction 11 of the M40 and junction 16 of the M1, one and a half hours from M25. *(See advertisement page 611 for further details.)*

Hollywood Lakes Golf Club

Ballyboughal,
Co Dublin, Ireland.
Tel +353 1 843 3406/7
Fax +353 1 843 3002

Parkland course featuring water hazards and lakes at 5 holes and also the longest par 5 in Ireland at 639 yards (14th hole). Green fees weekday £20.00; weekend £25.00. *(See advertisement page 16 for further details.)*

Howth Golf Club
St Fintan's,
Carrickbrack Road,
Sutton, Dublin 13, Ireland.
Tel +353 1 832 3055 Fax +353 1 832 1793
E-mail: howthgc@gofree.indigo.ie
Website: www.howthgolfclub.ie

Howth Golf Club is a long established heathland course located within ten miles of Dublin City centre and Dublin airport. The club boasts a fine clubhouse and enjoys panoramic views of land and sea scapes.

The Island Golf Club
Corballis, Donabate,
Co Dublin, Ireland.
Tel +353 1 843 6462 Fax +353 1 843 6860
E-mail: islandgc@iol.ie
Website: www.theislandgolfclub.com

Continuing a tradition of links golf since its inception in 1890. The magnificent splendour and solitude associated with the Island, is highlighted by undulating fairways rolling through majestic sand dunes.

La Grande Mare Hotel Golf Club
La Grande Mare,
Vazon,
Castel, Guernsey.
Tel (01481) 256576 & 253544
E-mail: Fax (01481) 255194
Website: www.lgm.guernsey.net

Beautifully appointed luxury hotel with 18-hole golf course. Professional shop and tuition on-site. First class, well priced restaurant. 2-AA Rosettes. Beachside location. Golfing breaks catered for.

Lancaster Golf Club
Ashton Hall,
Ashton with Stodday,
Lancaster LA2 0AJ.
Tel (01524) 751247 Fax (01524) 752742
E-mail: sec@lancastergc.freeserve.co.uk
Website: www.lancastergc.co.uk

The parkland course laid out by James Braid is 6,500 yards par 71. Accommodation at the Dormy House at Ashton Hall is available. Inclusive packages (minimum two night stay) at very competitive rates. First class catering well stocked bar with a wide selection of fine wines and malt whiskies. Resident club professional. *(See advertisement page 20 for further details.)*

Letham Grange
Colliston,
by Arbroath DD11 4RL.
Tel (01241) 890373 Fax (01241) 890725
E-mail: lethamgrange@sol.co.uk
Website: www.lethamgrange.co.uk/

The Leading Hotel in Carnoustie Country. 42-bedrooms, Victorian mansion, with 36-holes of superb golf. First class facilities set in the heartland of golf. Company/Society golf outings/breaks welcome. *(See advertisement page 619 for further details.)*

Linden Hall
Longhorsley,
Morpeth,
Northumberland NE65 8XF.
Tel (01670) 500011 Fax (01670) 500001

Linden Hall golf course is located within the grounds of Linden Hall Hotel, a 4-Star luxury country house hotel. The 18-hole, 6,846 yard SSS 73 golf course, recently voted one of the ten best new golf courses built in the British Isles since 1996 by *Golf World*, is set within mature woodland, rolling parkland with established burns and lakes amidst a stunning backdrop of the Cheviot hills and Northumbrian coastline.

Machrie Hotel & Golf Links
Port Ellen,
Isle of Islay,
Argyll PA42 7AN.
Tel (01496) 302310 Fax (01496) 302404
E-mail: machrie@machrie.com
Website: www.machrie.com

Play a hidden gem of a course. Traditional 18-hole championship links course situated on the doorstep of the Machrie Hotel. Excellent accommodation, fine food and friendly service. Self-catering and golf packages also available.

Malone Golf Club
240 Upper Malone Road,
Dunmurry,
Belfast BT17 9LB.
Tel 028 9061 2758 Fax 028 9043 1394
E-mail: manager@malonegolfclub.co.uk
Website: www.malonegolfclub.co.uk

Superb 27-hole championship course set in 330 acres of rolling parkland. Five miles from Belfast City centre. Societies, groups and visitors welcome by arrangement. Full bar and catering facilities. *(See advertisement page 20 for further details.)*

Mersey Valley Golf Club (1995)
Warrington Road,
Bold Heath,
Widnes,
Cheshire WA8 3XL.
Tel 0151-424 6060 Fax 0151-257 9097

Conference facilities, corporate golf days and memberships, societies and visitors welcome. Buggy hire. We specialise in corporate golf days - easy walking course. 20 minutes from Liverpool and Manchester, two miles junction 7 on the M62. Superb bar and catering facilities.

Mount Juliet
Thomastown,
Co Kilkenny, Ireland.
Tel +353 56 73000 Fax +353 56 73019
E-mail: info@mountjuliet.ie
Website: www.mountjuliet.ie

Deluxe accommodation in the elegant Mount Juliet House or the informal club rooms. Ireland's premier sporting estate offers guests on-site fishing, horse riding, tennis, leisure centre and fully dedicated spa. Golf Academy with PGA professionals. 18-hole putting course. Irish Open venue 1993-95. Host to WGC American Express Championship in September 2002.

Nailcote Hall Hotel
Nailcote Lane,
Berkswell,
Warwickshire CV7 7DE.
Tel 024 7646 6174 Fax 024 7647 0720
Website: www.nailcotehall.co.uk

Home of the British Professional Short Course. Delightful and challenging championship 9-hole par 3 course designed to test any golfers short game. Set in the grounds of this 17th-century black and white country house hotel, used by Cromwell in the English Civil War.

National Association of Public Golf Courses - NAPGC
12 Newton Close,
Redditch B98 7YR.
Tel (01527) 542106 Fax (01257) 455320
E-mail: eddiemitchell@blueyonder.co.uk
Website: www.napgc.org.uk

The Association provides competition golf for men and lady players of all handicaps and ages. It also offers help and advice to its member clubs - those playing over courses that they do not own.

North Shore Hotel Golf Club & Course
North Shore Road,
Skegness PE25 1DN.
Tel (01754) 763298 Fax (01754) 761902
E-mail: golf@north-shore.co.uk
Website: www.north-shore.co.uk

A mature and challenging 18-hole part parkland and part links course with sea views on the edge of Skegness. Good all year round climate. Rarely closed in winter with no winter greens. Rarely closed bars, superb bar food and à la carte restaurant. 36 bedrooms available.

Old Course Hotel - St Andrews Golf Resort & Spa
St Andrews,
Fife KY16 9SP.
Tel (01334) 474371 Fax (01334) 477668

This luxury 146-bedroom hotel overlooks the 17th Road Hole of the Old Course and is a five minute walk to the beach and town. Facilities include health spa with swimming pool, whirlpool, fitness room and full range of massage and beauty treatments. The hotel has its own championship golf course, the Duke's Course. Open to non-residents, with residents enjoying guaranteed tee-times and reduced green fees.

Parasampia Golf & Country Club
Grove Road,
Donnington,
Newbury,
Berkshire RG14 2LA.
Tel (01635) 581000 Fax (01635) 552259
Website: www.parasampia.com

18-hole parkland/moorland championship course designed by Dave Thomas. The clubhouse and hotel are located within a beautifully renovated 18th-century gothic mansion. This will provide an ideal setting for your society, company golf day or conference stay.

Penrhos Golf & Country Club
Llanrhystud,
Ceredigion SY23 5AY.
Tel (01974) 202999 Fax (01974) 202100
Website: www.penrhosgolf.co.uk

Fifteen American-style suites. 18-hole championship length course, driving range, indoor swimming pool, sauna, steam room, gymnasium, tennis courts, spa, solarium and bowling green.

Penrith Golf Club
Salkeld Road,
Penrith,
Cumbria CA11 8SG.
Tel (01768) 891919

The club, which is 112 years old, is easily accessible from junction 41 on the M6 motorway and lies half a mile east of Penrith, enjoying panoramic views to the Lakeland hills. Visitors are very welcome to play this excellent course.

Powerscourt Golf Club
Enniskerry,
Co Wicklow, Ireland.
Tel +353 1 204 6033 Fax +353 1 276 1303
E-mail: golfclub@powerscourt.ie
Website: www.powerscourt.ie

An Inspiring Course in a Spectacular Location.
Powerscourt is a free draining course with links characteristics. Built to championship standard, with top quality tees and exceptional tiered greens, it is set in some of Ireland's most beautiful parkland. *(See advertisement page 16 for further details.)*

Prince's Golf Club
Sandwich Bay,
Sandwich,
Kent CT13 9QB.
Tel (01304) 611118 Fax (01304) 612000
E-mail: hotel@princes-leisure.co.uk
Website: www.princes-leisure.co.uk

This previous Open Championship venue offers a challenging 27-hole course 6,690 yards par 71-72 and excellent driving range with friendly clubhouse making visitors welcome. For overnight accommodation the Bell Hotel in Sandwich is within a ten minutes' drive where you can relax after a days golfing and enjoy imaginative cuisine and friendly service. *(See advertisement page 611 for further details.)*

Ramside Hall Hotel & Golf Club
Carrville,
Durham DH1 1TD.
Tel 0191-386 5282 Fax 0191-386 0399

Set in 220 acres on the outsksirts of the cathedral city of Durham and surrounded by a stimulating 27-hole golf course. 3-Star; 4-Crown Highly Commended. 80 luxury bedrooms, restaurant, grill room and carvery. Conference and banqueting facilities. Superb floodlit driving range and practice areas. *(See advertisement page 615 for further details.)*

Renvyle House Hotel
Connemara, Go Galway, Ireland.
Tel +353 95 43511 Fax +353 95 43515
E-mail: renvyle@iol.ie
Website: www.renvyle.com

Set in the wild splendour of Connemara in truly magical surroundings. Originally the home of Oliver St John Gogarty, Renvyle House has played host to many famous people - Augustus John, Yeats and Churchill to name but a few. Warmth, comfort and award-winning fare awaits. Excellent golf and golf clinics are available on-site. *(See advertisement page 623 for further details.)*

Rodway Hill Golf Course
Newent Road, Highnam,
Gloucestershire GL2 8DN.
Tel (01452) 384222

An 18-hole, par 70 course, open to the public, two miles south west of Gloucester, with panoramic views of the Cotswolds. It has a well stocked shop, practice and teaching facilities. Hire kit available. Societies welcome.

Rosapenna Hotel & Golf Links
Rosapenna, Downings, Donegal, Ireland.
Tel +353 74 55301 Fax +353 74 55128

Rosapenna Hotel is set in the middle of its own 27-hole golf links course. Half a mile from the fishing village of Downings.

The Roxburghe Hotel & Golf Course
Heiton, By Kelso, Roxburghshire TD5 8JZ.
Tel (01573) 450331 Fax (01573) 450611
E-mail: golf@roxburghe.net
Website: www.roxburghe.net

22-bedroom hotel owned by the Duke and Duchess of Roxburghe. Luxury accommodation, superb cuisine. The 18-hole championship Roxburghe golf course, designed by Dave Thomas, is home to the Scottish Seniors Open.

The Royal Dublin Golf Club
North Bull Island,
Dollymount, Dublin 3, Ireland.
Tel +353 1 833 6346 Fax +353 1 833 6504

The Royal Dublin Golf Club is Ireland's second oldest golf club and one of the country's premier sporting theatres. Royal Dublin provides visiting players with a combination of a superb championship links and a degree of hospitality that mirrors its historic development. *(See advertisement page 14 for further details.)*

Royal Lytham & St Anne's Golf Club

Links Gate,
Lytham St Anne's,
Lancashire FY8 3LQ.
Tel (01253) 724206 Fax (01253) 780946

Ideal for small parties wishing to play the championship course. Accommodation for men only. Apply to the assistant secretary. *(See advertisement page 20 and 613 for further details.)*

Royal Porthcawl Golf Club

Rest Bay,
Porthcawl,
Mid Glamorgan CF36 3UW.
Tel (01656) 782251 Fax (01656) 771687
E-mail: royalporthcawl@cs.com
Website: www.royalporthcawl.com

Luxury dormy accommodation for parties of up to twelve persons. Apply to the secretary. *(See advertisement page 14 for further details.)*

Rudding Park

Follifoot,
Harrogate,
North Yorkshire HG3 1DJ.
Tel (01423) 872100 Fax (01423) 873011
E-mail: sales@ruddingpark.com
Website: www.ruddingpark.com

Rudding Park, just two miles south of Harrogate provides the complete golfing experience. The 18-hole, par 72 Martin Hawtree designed parkland golf course together with the award-winning hotel, make for an enjoyable visit. The golf academy not only boasts an 18-bay floodlit covered driving range but also three PGA professionals. Corporate and Society events welcome.

Seaford Golf Club

East Blatchington,
Seaford,
East Sussex BN25 2JD.
Tel (01323) 892442

The Dormy House provides comfortable accommodation for 20 guests in 10 twin-bedded en suite bedrooms on the first floor of the clubhouse, and 2 single rooms in our bungalow annexe. For latest brochure ring 01323 892442.

Shaw Hill Golf & Country Club

Preston Road,
Whittle-Le-Woods,
Chorley, Lancashire PR6 7PP.
Tel (01257) 269221 Fax (01257) 261223

Shaw Hill comprises a 72 par 18-hole golf course, a fully equipped leisure centre and an AA award-winning restaurant and we can offer wedding and conference facilities. *(See advertisement page 615 for further details.)*

The Slieve Russell Hotel Golf & Country Club

Ballyconnell,
Co Cavan, Ireland.
Tel +353 49 9526444 Fax +353 49 9526474
Website: www.quinnhotels.com

Located only two hours' drive from both Dublin and Belfast, the Slieve Russell is a complete resort with its 5-Star leisure facilities, championship 18-hole golf course, 159 superbly appointed bedrooms and a selection of restaurants and bars, conference and banqueting suites - The *Perfect* location for business or pleasure.

Soughton Hall

Northop,
Nr Chester, Flintshire CH7 6AB.
Tel (01352) 840811 Fax (01352) 840382

Stay in luxury - play championship golf course - we offer great value packages. Grand house amidst historic parkland. Setting for privately owned championship golf. Original stables adapted to bar restaurant, casual informal atmosphere. Real ales - wine shop inclusive. *(See advertisement page 623 for further details.)*

Southern Gailes Ltd

29 Bothwell Road, Hamilton ML3 0AS.
Freephone: 08000 285220
Tel (01698) 207080 Fax (01698) 891435
E-mail:
alancdaly@dalypartners.freeserve.co.uk
Website: www.southerngailes.com

A new and exciting development is now underway 'Southern Gailes'! The development will consist of an 18-hole championship golf course, a 9-hole course, leisure centre, hotel, driving range and luxury business managed residences. The golf course will be on a pay and play basis with corporate membership available. Full details can be seen on our website. *(See advertisement page 25 for further details.)*

Sparkwell Golf Course
Blacklands,
Sparkwell,
Plymouth,
Devon PL7 5DF.
Tel/Fax (01752) 837219

A testing 9-hole, pay as you play course and a par 3 course, set in 60 acres of parkland. Facilities include a well equipped golf shop, excellent restaurant and friendly bar. Open to the public. Golf societies welcome.

St Helen's Bay
Golf & Country Club
St Helens,
Kilrane,
Rosslare Harbour,
Co Wexford, Ireland.
Tel +353 53 33234 Fax +353 53 33803
E-mail: sthelens@iol.ie
Website: www.sthelensbay.com

Superbly located championship 18-hole golf course, which has blended the best of parkland characteristics with a finish that is true links and plenty of difficulty. Luxury on-site accommodation together with tennis courts. Full bar and catering facilities available in the clubhouse. Situated only five minutes from Rosslare ferryport. Green fee and society-friendly, playable all year.

St Mary's Hotel
Golf & Country Club
St Mary's Hill,
Pencoed,
Vale of Glamorgan CF35 5EA.
Tel (01656) 861100 Fax (01656) 863400

24-bedroom hotel, 18-hole membership and pay course. 9-hole pay as you play, 15-bay floodlit driving range, clubhouse and restaurant conservatory and three bars. Fully stocked golf shop. Floodlit chipping and putting area and resident golf professional Mr John Peters.

St Pierre Park Hotel
Rohais,
St Peter Port,
Guernsey GYI 1FD.
Tel (01481) 728282 Fax (01481) 712041

This 4-Star hotel offers extensive leisure facilities including a 9-hole par 3 golf course, designed by Tony Jacklin. Three tennis courts and a health suite with heated indoor swimming pool, spa bath, saunas, steam rooms, solaria and exercise room.

Telford Golf & Country Club
Great Hay,
Sutton Heights,
Telford,
Shropshire TF7 4DT.
Tel (01952) 429977
Fax (01952) 586602
E-mail: golfsales.telford@corushotels.com
Website: www.corushotels.com/
telfordgolfandcountry

Overlooking the Ironbridge Gorge, the 96-bedroom hotel offers its own 18-hole championship course. Floodlit driving range and practice areas. The extensive leisure facilities include squash courts, snooker, swimming pool, gymnasium, whirlpool, sauna and steam rooms. Resident masseur. Corporate, Society and residential packages.

Thorpeness Hotel Golf Club
Thorpeness,
Nr Aldeburgh,
Suffolk IP16 4NH.
Tel (01728) 452176
Fax (01728) 453868
E-mail: info@thorpeness.co.uk
Website: www.thorpeness.co.uk

One of East Anglia's finest and most challenging 18-hole courses. Handicap certificate required, advisable to book in advance. Accommodation, bars, restaurant, golf shop, tennis courts and course set adjacent to picturesque coastal village on Suffolk Heritage coast.

Trevose Golf & Country Club
Constantine Bay,
Padstow,
North Cornwall PL28 8JB.
Tel (01841) 520208
Fax (01841) 521057
E-mail: reception@trevose-gc.co.uk
Website: www.trevose-gc.co.uk/

Trevose offers not only great golf (championship 18-hole course, a 9-hole full length (3,100 yards) par 35 plus a 9-hole short course) but also a first class clubhouse and restaurant, three hard all-weather tennis courts, a heated outdoor swimming pool in the summer, a games room for the kids and a boutique. Accommodation is available in bungalows, chalets, trehuel flats, dormy flats and cabins. Send for our detailed colour brochure. Open all year. Societies welcome.

Welcombe Hotel & Golf Course

Warwick Road,
Stratford-upon-Avon,
Warwickshire CV37 0NR.
Tel (01789) 295252
Fax (01789) 414666
Corporate Golf Office:
Tel/Fax(01789) 413815

4-Star Jacobean-style mansion house hotel with private 18-hole championship golf course set in 157 acres of wooded parkland with picturesque lakes. Corporate golf and green fees most welcome. *(See advertisement page 613 for further details.)*

The Westin Turnberry Resort, Scotland

Turnberry,
Ayrshire KA26 9LT.
Tel +44 (0) 1655 331000
Fax +44 (0) 1655 331707
E-mail: turnberry@westin.com
Website: www.turnberry.co.uk

One of the finest golfing destinations in the world. Turnberry has two championship links courses, the legendary Ailsa (host to three Open's) and the highly acclaimed new Kintyre. Whilst Colin Montgomerie Links Golf Academy offers world class teaching and practice facilities.

Wheathampstead Pay & Play Golf Course

Harpenden Road, St Albans,
Hertfordshire AL4 8EZ.
Tel/Fax (01582) 833941

A 9-hole par 33 golf course and large practice area. Everyone is welcome. Doug Edgar, who built and designed the course, will help you with all your golfing needs. Telephone 01582 833941.

Whitefields Hotel Golf & Country Club

Coventry Road,
Thurlaston,
Nr Rugby, Warwickshire CV23 9JR.
Tel (01788) 521800 Fax (01788) 521695
Website: www.whitefields/hotel.co.uk

18-hole course 6,223 yards. Driving range, putting green 18. Four conference rooms. 50 en suite rooms. Bars and a la carte restaurant. Societies welcome seven days. Call the secretary on 01788 815555. Reservations 01788 521800.

Wicklow Golf Club

Dunbur Road,
Wicklow, Ireland.
Tel +353 404 67361/67379
Fax +353 404 66122

A challenging and spectacular test of golf is promised here at Wicklow Golf Club. Par 71 SSS 70 5,720 metres featuring the natural contours of the terrain. Open from sunrise to sunset. Enjoy uncrowded golf and excellent clubhouse facilities. Visitors made very welcome.

Wokefield Park Golf Club

Mortimer,
Reading,
Berkshire RG7 3AE.
Tel 0118-933 4013 Fax 0118-933 4162

Set amid the Berkshire countryside this challenging 7,000 yards golf course has mature trees, winding streams, nine lakes and large bunkers. Wokefield also features 320 bedrooms, teaching academy and leisure facilities. Call the golf sales team on 0118-933 4018 and 4017.

Woodbury Park Golf & Country Club

Woodbury Castle,
Woodbury,
Exeter,
Devon EX5 1JJ.
Tel (01395) 233382 Fax (01395) 233384

Luxury 55-bedroom hotel with five superb lodges. The Nigel Mansell owned resort encompasses 27 holes, including the Oaks championship course, in addition to extensive leisure facilities. The ideal venue for your golfing break.

Index of Advertisers

PART XII

Clubs and Courses in the British Isles and Europe

Compiled by Jan Bennett

Club Centenaries

1902

Ashton-in-Makerfield
Athenry
Beaconsfield
Boston
Braemar
Brecon
Bulwell Forest
Chorlton-cum-Hardy
Cotswold Hills
East Devon
Faversham
Heswall
Kirkistown Castle
La Moye
Links (Newmarket)
Nelson
New Cumnock
New Galloway
New Golf Club
Portadown
Radyr
Rotherham
Rowlands Castle
Scarborough South Cliff
Sunningdale Ladies
Walmley

1903

Appleby
Arbroath
Ashford
Bangor
Barnehurst
Bishopshire
Bromborough
Caldwell
Castle Fields
Deeside
Diss
East Berkshire
Hale
Hendon
Kenmare
Killiney
Laleham
Leatherhead
Magdalene Fields
Newport
North Foreland
Oswestry

1903 *continued*

Pontypool
Portpatrick
Powfoot
Ralston
Rossendale
Ross-on-Wye
Shooter's Hill
Silecroft
St David's City
St Fillans
St Michaels
Walton Heath
Warrington

1904

Alness
Auchterderran
Bamburgh Castle
Banchory
Blackpool North Shore
Blankney
Bonar Bridge
Coombe Wood
Dundalk
Fereneze
Flackwell Heath
Fulwell
Haverfordwest
Highgate
Hindhead
Holywood
Isles of Scilly
Keighley
Kirkcaldy
Langland Bay
Lutterworth
Machynlleth
Morecambe
North Hants
Osborne
Piltdown
Roehampton
Roscommon
Saddleworth
Saltford
Spey Bay
Staddon Heights
Stand
Tuam
Wath

1904 *continued*

Whitehead
Wicklow
Wolstanton
Wrexham
Yelverton

1905

Bellshill
Blyth
Bramhall
Bridlington
Broomieknowe
Burley
Burnley
Caerphilly
Castle Douglas
Castlerea
Chapel-en-le-Frith
Clydebank & District
Colvend
Criccieth
Dunmurry
The Dunnerholme
Ellesborough
Erewash Valley
Hermitage
Hindley Hall
Huyton & Prescot
Knowle
Lee-on-the-Solent
Letchworth
Llandrindod Wells
Llanishen
Maryport
Mount Ellen
Nuneaton
Old Ranfurly
Pontypridd
Porthmadog
Prenton
Prestatyn
Queens Park
Rosslare
Sandyhills
Skerries
Sleaford
Southerndown
Stockport
Stranraer
Tenterden

1905 *continued*

Verulam
Whitecraigs
Worthing

1906

Alston Moor
Athy
Berehaven
Bradford Moor
Brandhall
Carholme
Chilwell Manor
Chipstead
Clayton
Cowglen
Deane
Dinsdale Spa
Dunfanaghy
Dunstable Downs
The Dyke
Elgin
Enmore Park
Fulford
The Glen
Gorleston
Gosforth
Halesowen
Halifax West End
Hartlepool
Harwich & Dovercourt
Holywell
Knighton
Kyles of Bute
Matlock
Morpeth
Otley
Pannal
Prince's
Serlby Park
Silverdale
South Bradford
Southport & Ainsdale
St Deiniol
Stafford Castle
Stanton-on-the-Wolds
Walmersley
West Byfleet
Whitsand Bay Hotel
Whittaker
Williamwood
Wrotham Heath

Golf Clubs and Courses in the British Isles and Europe

How to use this section

Clubs in England, Ireland and Wales are listed in alphabetical order by country and county. Note that some clubs and courses are affiliated to a county different to that in which they are physically located. Clubs in Scotland are grouped under recognised administrative regions. The Great Britain and Ireland county index can be found on page 650.

European clubs are listed alphabetically by country and grouped under regional headings. The index for this can be found on page 850. In most countries, only 18 hole courses are included.

All clubs and courses are listed in the the general index at back of the book.

Club details

The date after the name of the club indicates the year it was founded. Courses are private unless otherwise stated. Many public courses play host to members' clubs. Information on these can be obtained from the course concerned.

The address is the postal address.

Tel: club telephone number for general use.

Mem: total number of playing members. The number of lady members (L) and juniors (J) is sometimes shown separately.

Sec:/Pro: telephone numbers for secretaries and professionals are shown if different from the club telephone number.

Holes: the length of the course refers in most cases to the yardage from the medal tees.

V'tors: indicates the playing opportunities and restrictions for unaccompanied visitors.

Fees: green fees, the most up-to-date supplied, are quoted for visitors playing without a member. The basic cost per round or per day (D) is shown first, with the weekend and/or bank holiday rate in brackets. The cost of a weekly (W) ticket is sometimes shown.

Loc: general location.

Mis: other golf facilities and useful information.

Arch: course architect/designer.

Abbreviations

WD	Weekdays.
WE	Weekends.
BH	Bank Holidays.
H	Handicap certificate required.
M	With a member, i.e. casual visitors are not allowed: only visitors playing with a member are permitted on the days stated.
NA	No visitors allowed.
SOC	Recognised Golfing Societies welcome if previous arrangements made with secretary.
U	Unrestricted.
CR	Course Rating (Europe)
SR	Slope Rating (Europe)

We are indebted to club secretaries throughout Europe for the information.

GREAT BRITAIN AND IRELAND COUNTY INDEX

England

Bedfordshire

Aspley Guise & Woburn Sands (1914)
West Hill, Aspley Guise, Milton Keynes, MK17 8DX
Tel (01908) 583596
Fax (01908) 583596
Mem 560
Sec (01908) 583596
Pro C Clingan (01908) 582974
Holes 18 L 6079 yds Par 71 SSS 70
V'tors WD–H WE/BH–MH SOC–Wed & Fri
Fees £26 D–£35
Loc 2 miles W of M1 Junction 13
Arch Herd/Sandow

Aylesbury Vale (1991)
Wing, Leighton Buzzard, LU7 0UJ
Tel (01525) 240196
Fax (01525) 240848
Mem 500
Sec C Wright (Sec/Mgr)
Pro G Goble (01525) 240197
Holes 18 L 6612 yds Par 72 SSS 72
V'tors WD–U WE–U–phone first SOC–WD
Fees £13
Loc 3 miles W of Leighton Buzzard on Wing-Stewkley road
Mis Driving range
Arch Sq Ldr Don Wright

Beadlow Manor Hotel G&CC (1973)
Beadlow, Shefford, SG17 5PH
Tel (01525) 860800
Fax (01525) 861345
Mem 700
Sec R Tommey (01525) 843398
Pro P Hetherington (01525) 861292
Holes 18 L 6238 yds SSS 71
18 L 6042 yds SSS 70
V'tors U H SOC
Fees On application
Loc 2 miles W of Shefford on A507
Mis Driving range

Bedford (1999)
Carnoustie Drive, Great Denham, Biddenham, MK40 4BF
Tel (01234) 320022
Fax (01234) 320023
Sec M Rizzi (01234) 330559
Pro J Bodicoat
Holes 18 L 6560 yds Par 72
V'tors WD–U WE–M SOC–WD
Fees £25 (£40)
Loc 2 miles W of Bedford (A428)
Mis Driving range
Arch David Pottage

Bedford & County (1912)
Green Lane, Clapham, Bedford, MK41 6ET
Tel (01234) 352617
Fax (01234) 357195
Web www.bedfordandcountygolfclub.co.uk
Mem 600
Sec RP Walker (Mgr), O Ebsworth (Asst Mgr)
Pro R Tattersall (01234) 359189
Holes 18 L 6399 yds SSS 70
V'tors WD–U H WE–M SOC
Fees D–£30
Loc 2 miles NW of Bedford on A6

Bedfordshire (1891)
Spring Lane, Stagsden, Bedford, MK43 8SR
Tel (01234) 822555
Fax (01234) 825052
Mem 600
Sec DE Romans (Gen Mgr)
Pro P Saunders (01234) 826100
Holes 18 L 6565 yds SSS 72
V'tors WD–U (phone first) WE–M before noon SOC–WD
Fees On application
Loc 3 miles W of Bedford (A422)

Chalgrave Manor
Dunstable Road, Chalgrave, Toddington, LU5 6JN
Tel (01525) 876556
Fax (01525) 876556
Mem 450
Sec S Rumball
Pro T Bunyan
Holes 18 L 6382 yds Par 72 SSS 70
V'tors U SOC–WD
Fees £15 (£20)
Loc 2 miles W of M1 Junction 12 on A5120
Mis Practice range
Arch Mike Palmer

Colmworth (1992)
Proprietary
New Road, Colmworth, MK44 2NV
Tel (01234) 378181
Fax (01234) 376235
Web www.colmworthgolfclub.co.uk
Mem 200
Sec A Willis (01234) 402674
Pro M Fields
Holes 18 L 6435 yds Par 72 SSS 71
9 hole Par 3 course
V'tors U SOC
Fees £12 (£18)
Loc 6 miles N of Bedford, off B660. 4 miles W of A1
Mis Driving range
Arch John Glasgow

Colworth (1985)
Unilever Research, Sharnbrook, Bedford, MK44 1LQ
Tel (01933) 353269 (Sec)

Mem 405
Sec E Thompson
Holes 9 L 2626 yds Par 68 SSS 66
V'tors M
Fees D–£8
Loc Sharnbrook, 10 miles N of Bedford, off A6

Dunstable Downs (1906)
Whipsnade Road, Dunstable, LU6 2NB
Tel (01582) 604472
Fax (01582) 478700
Mem 640
Sec GB Woodcock
Pro M Weldon (01582) 662806
Holes 18 L 5903 yds SSS 69
V'tors WD–H WE–M SOC–WD exc Wed
Fees £25 D–£40
Loc 2 miles SW of Dunstable on B4541. M1 Junction 11
Arch James Braid

Griffin (1985)
Chaul End Road, Caddington, LU1 4AX
Tel (01582) 415573
Fax (01582) 415314
Mem 500
Sec M Smith
Pro D Marsden
Holes 18 L 6240 yds Par 71 SSS 70
V'tors WD–U WE/BH–phone first SOC
Fees £13 Fri–£15.50 (£18)
Loc 3 miles W of Luton on A505 between Dunstable and Caddington. M1 Junction 10/11

John O'Gaunt (1948)
Sutton Park, Sandy, Biggleswade, SG19 2LY
Tel (01767) 260360
Fax (01767) 262834
Mem 1450
Sec J Keight
Pro P Round (01767) 260094
Holes John O'Gaunt 18 L 6513 yds SSS 71;
Carthagena 18 L 5869 yds SSS 69
V'tors H–phone first SOC–WD
Fees £45 (£50)
Loc 3 miles NE of Biggleswade on B1040
Arch Hawtree

Leighton Buzzard (1925)
Plantation Road, Leighton Buzzard, LU7 7JF
Tel (01525) 373811/373812
Mem 650
Sec J Burchell (01525) 373811
Pro L Scarbrow (01525) 372143
Holes 18 L 6101 yds SSS 70

V'tors WD exc Tues–U H
WE/BH–MH
Fees £20 D–£27
Loc Heath and Reach, 1 mile N of
Leighton Buzzard. M1
Junction 12

Lyshott Heath (1980)
Ampthill, MK45 2JB
Tel (01525) 840252
Fax (01525) 406249
Web www.lyshott-heath.com
Mem 328
Sec DC Cooke
Pro D Armor (01525) 402269
Holes 18 L 7021 yds SSS 73
V'tors WD–U exc Thurs WE–NA
before 2pm SOC
Fees £20 (£35)
Loc 4 miles from M1 Junctions 12
or 13 on A507
Mis Practice range
Arch W Sutherland

Mount Pleasant (1992)
Proprietary
*Station Road, Lower Stondon, Henlow,
SG16 6JL*
Tel (01462) 850999
Fax (01462) 850257
Web www.mountpleasantgolfclub
.co.uk
Mem 300
Sec D Simkins (Prop)
(01462) 850999
Pro M Roberts
Holes 9 L 6003 yds Par 70 SSS 69
V'tors U SOC–WD
Fees 9 holes–£7.50 (£10)
18 holes–£13 (£17)
Loc 4 miles N of Hitchin, off A600
Arch Derek Young

Mowsbury (1975)
Public
Kimbolton Road, Bedford, MK41 8DQ
Tel (01234) 216374/771041
Mem 611
Sec LW Allan
Pro M Summers
Holes 18 L 6514 yds SSS 71
V'tors U
Fees £7.50 (£9.50)
Loc 2 miles N of Bedford on B660
Mis Driving range
Arch Hawtree

Pavenham Park (1994)
Pavenham, Bedford, MK43 7PE
Tel (01234) 822202
Fax (01234) 826602
Mem 700
Sec M Rizzi
Pro ZL Thompson
Holes 18 L 6353 yds SSS 71
V'tors WD–U WE–M SOC–WD
Fees £19
Loc 4 miles NW of Bedford on A6
Arch Zac Thompson

RAF Henlow (1985)
*RAF Henlow Camp, Henlow,
SG16 6DN*
Tel (01462) 851515 Ext 7083
Fax (01462) 816780
Mem 250
Sec W/O T Thomas
(01462) 851515 (Ext 8240)
Holes 9 L 5618 yds SSS 67
V'tors M
Fees D–£10
Loc 3 miles SE of Shefford on
A600
Mis Driving range

South Beds (1892)
Warden Hill Road, Luton, LU2 7AE
Tel (01582) 575201
Fax (01582) 495381
Mem 850
Sec RJ Wright (01582) 591500
Pro E Cogle (01582) 591209
Holes Galley 18 L 6397 yds SSS 71
Warden 9 L 4914 yds SSS 64
V'tors Galley WD–H (Ladies
Day–Tues) WE/BH–H exc
comp days–NA SOC
Warden–U
Fees Galley £22 D–£32 (£34
D–£43) Warden £10 (£13)
Loc 3 miles N of Luton, E of A6

Stockwood Park (1973)
Public
*Stockwood Park, London Rd, Luton,
LU1 4LX*
Tel (01582) 413704
Fax (01582) 481001
Mem 900
Sec Mrs B McMillan
Pro G McCarthy
Holes 18 L 6049 yds SSS 69
V'tors U
Fees £8.70 (£11.70)
Loc 1 mile S of Luton on A6. M1
Junction 10
Mis Driving range

Tilsworth (1972)
Pay and play
*Dunstable Rd, Tilsworth, Dunstable,
LU7 9PU*
Tel (01525) 210721/210722
Fax (01525) 210465
Web www.tilsworthgolf.co.uk
Mem 370
Sec G Brandon-White
Pro N Webb (Mgr)
Holes 18 L 5303 yds Par 69 SSS 67
V'tors U SOC
Fees £12 (£14)
Loc 2 miles N of Dunstable (A5)
Mis Driving range

Wyboston Lakes (1978)
Public
*Wyboston Lakes, Wyboston,
MK44 3AL*
Tel (01480) 223004
Fax (01480) 407330
Web www.wybostonlakes.co.uk
Mem 300
Sec DJ Little (Mgr)
Pro P Ashwell (01480) 223004
Holes 18 L 5995 yds Par 70 SSS
69
V'tors WD–U WE–booking SOC
Fees £13 (£17)
Loc S of St Neots, off A1 and St
Neots by-pass
Mis Driving range
Arch Neil Ockden

Berkshire

Bearwood (1986)
*Mole Road, Sindlesham, Wokingham,
RG41 5DB*
Tel (0118) 976 0060
Fax (0118) 977 2687
Mem 500
Sec BFC Tustin (Mgr)
(0118) 976 0060
Pro BJ Tustin (0118) 976 0156
Holes 9 L 5614 yds SSS 68
V'tors WD–H before 4pm –M after
4pm
Fees 18 holes–£18 (£22)
9 holes–£10 (£12)
Loc 1 mile SW of Winnersh, on
B3030. M4 Junction 10
Mis Driving range

Bearwood Lakes (1996)
*Bearwood Road, Sindlesham,
RG41 4SJ*
Tel (0118) 979 7900
Fax (0118) 979 2911
Web www.bearwoodlakes.co.uk
Mem 800
Sec S Evans (Gen Mgr)
Pro E Inglis (0118) 978 3030
Holes 18 L 6800 yds Par 72 SSS
72
V'tors M H
Loc 1 mile S of M4 Junction 10,
between Wokingham and
Sindlesham
Arch Martin Hawtree

The Berkshire (1928)
Swinley Road, Ascot, SL5 8AY
Tel (01344) 621495
Fax (01344) 623328
Mem 935
Sec Lt Col JCF Hunt
(01344) 621496
Pro P Anderson (01344) 622351
Holes Red 18 L 6379 yds SSS 71
Blue 18 L 6260 yds SSS 71
V'tors WD–I WE/BH–M
Fees On application
Loc 3 miles from Ascot on A332.
M3 Junction 3
Arch Herbert Fowler

For list of abbreviations see page 649

Billingbear Park

Pay and play
The Straight Mile, Wokingham,
RG40 5SJ

Tel	**(01344) 869259**
Fax	(01344) 869259
Mem	50
Sec	Mrs JR Blainey
Pro	MW Blainey
Holes	9 L 5700 yds Par 68
	9 hole Par 3 course
V'tors	U
Fees	£8 (£10)
Loc	2 miles E of Wokingham via
	B3034. M4 Junction 10

Bird Hills (1985)

Public
Drift Road, Hawthorn Hill,
Maidenhead, SL6 3ST

Tel	**(01628) 771030**
Fax	(01628) 631023
Mem	400
Sec	R Knott Gen Mgr)
Pro	N Slimming
Holes	18 L 6212 yds SSS 69
V'tors	U SOC–WD
Fees	On application
Loc	4 miles S of Maidenhead on
	A330
Mis	Floodlit driving range

Blue Mountain Golf Centre (1993)

Pay and play
Wood Lane, Binfield, RG42 4EX

Tel	**(01344) 300220**
Fax	(01344) 360960
Mem	500
Pro	I Looms (01344) 488858
Holes	18 L 6097 yds SSS 70
V'tors	U SOC
Fees	£18 Fri–£20 (£24)
Loc	1 mile W of Bracknell on
	B3408. M4 Junction 10
Mis	Driving range. Golf Academy

Calcot Park (1930)

Bath Road, Calcot, Reading,
RG31 7RN

Tel	**(0118) 942 7124**
Fax	(0118) 945 3373
Mem	750
Sec	JR Cox
Pro	IJ Campbell (0118) 942 7797
Holes	18 L 6216 yds SSS 70
V'tors	WD–H WE/BH–M SOC–WD
Fees	£36 After 4pm–£22
Loc	3 miles W of Reading on A4.
	1½ miles E of M4 Junction 12
Arch	HS Colt

Castle Royle (1994)

Knowl Hill, Reading, RG10 9XA

Tel	**(01628) 825442**
Sec	M Harris (Gen Mgr)
Pro	R Watts
Holes	18 L 6828 yds Par 72 SSS 73
V'tors	N/A
Fees	N/A

Loc	2 miles W of Maidenhead
	(A4). M4 Junction 8/9
Arch	Neil Coles

Datchet (1890)

Buccleuch Road, Datchet, SL3 9BP

Tel	**(01753) 543887 (Clubhouse)**
Fax	(01753) 541872
Mem	210 50(L) 25(J)
Sec	Mrs S Thompson
	(01753) 541872
Pro	I Godleman (01753) 545222
Holes	9 L 5978 yds SSS 69
V'tors	WD–U M after 3pm WE–M
	SOC
Fees	£18 D–£25
Loc	Slough, Windsor 2 miles
Arch	JH Taylor

Deanwood Park (1995)

Pay and play
Stockcross, Newbury, RG20 8JS

Tel	**(01635) 48772**
Fax	(01635) 48772
Mem	212
Sec	J Bowness
Pro	J Purton
Holes	9 L 4230 yds Par 64 SSS 61
V'tors	U
Fees	£12 (£15)
Loc	2 miles W of Newbury
	(B4000). M4 Junction 13,
	3 miles
Mis	Driving range

Donnington Valley (1985)

Snelsmore House, Snelsmore Common,
Newbury, RG14 3BG

Tel	**(01635) 568140**
Fax	(01635) 568141
Web	www.donningtonvalley.co.uk
Mem	500
Sec	LC Storey
Pro	E Lainchbury
Holes	18 L 6335 yds SSS 71
V'tors	U
Fees	£18 (£25)
Loc	N of Newbury, off Old Oxford
	Road

Downshire (1973)

Public
Easthampstead Park, Wokingham,
RG11 3DH

Tel	**(01344) 302030**
Fax	(01344) 301020
Sec	P Stanwick (Golf Mgr)
Pro	W Owers
Holes	18 L 6416 yds SSS 69
V'tors	U SOC
Fees	£13.50 (£17)
Loc	Off Nine Mile Ride
Mis	Driving range. Pitch & putt

East Berkshire (1903)

Ravenswood Ave, Crowthorne, RG45
6BD

Tel	**(01344) 772041**
Fax	(01344) 777378

Mem	700
Sec	DP Kelly
Pro	J Brant (01344) 774112
Holes	18 L 6345 yds SSS 70
V'tors	WD–H WE/BH–M SOC
Fees	£40
Loc	Nr Crowthorne Station
Arch	P Paxton

Goring & Streatley (1895)

Rectory Road, Streatley-on-Thames,
RG8 9QA

Tel	**(01491) 873229**
Fax	(01491) 875224
Web	www.goringgc.org
Mem	740 115(L) 50(J)
Sec	I McColl (Sec/Mgr)
Pro	J Hadland (01491) 873715
Holes	18 L 6355 yds SSS 70
V'tors	WD–U WE/BH–M SOC–WD
Fees	£28 D–£35 (£35)
Loc	10 miles NW of Reading on
	A417
Arch	Tom Dunne

Hennerton (1992)

Crazies Hill Road, Wargrave,
RG10 8LT

Tel	**(0118) 940 1000/4778**
Fax	(0118) 940 1042
Web	www.hennertongolfclub.co.uk
Mem	500
Sec	PJ Hearn
Pro	W Farrow (0118) 940 4778
Holes	9 L 2730 yds SSS 34
V'tors	WD–U WE–pm only SOC
Fees	18 holes–£15 (£18) 9
	holes–£10 (£14)
Loc	Between Maidenhead and
	Reading (A4/A321)
Mis	Driving range
Arch	Dion Beard

Hurst (1979)

Public
Sandford Lane, Hurst, Wokingham,
RG10 0SQ

Tel	**(01734) 344355**
Sec	AG Poncia (Hon)
Pro	P Watson
Holes	9 L 3015 yds SSS 70
Fees	On application
Loc	Reading 5 miles. Wokingham
	3 miles

Maidenhead (1896)

Shoppenhangers Road, Maidenhead,
SL6 2PZ

Tel	**(01628) 624693**
Mem	600
Sec	TP Jackson
Pro	S Geary (01628) 624067
Holes	18 L 6360 yds SSS 70
V'tors	WD–H Fri–M after noon
	WE–M
Fees	D–£35
Loc	Off A308, nr Maidenhead
	Station

For list of abbreviations see page 649

Mapledurham (1992)

Mapledurham, Reading, RG4 7UD
Tel   (0118) 946 3353
Fax (0118) 946 3363
Mem 400
Sec D Burton
Pro S O'Keefe
Holes 18 L 5625 yds SSS 69
V'tors U
Fees £14 (£17)
Loc 4 miles NW of Reading, off
      A4074
Arch MRM Sandow

Mill Ride (1990)

Mill Ride, Ascot, SL5 8LT
Tel   (01344) 886777
Fax (01344) 886820
Web www.mill-ride.com
Mem 300
Sec G Irvine (Gen Mgr)
Pro M Palmer
Holes 18 L 6752 yds SSS 72
V'tors H SOC
Fees On application
Loc 2 miles W of Ascot
Arch Donald Steel

Newbury & Crookham (1873)

*Bury's Bank Road, Greenham
Common, Newbury, RG19 8BZ*
Tel   (01635) 40035
Fax (01635) 40045
Mem 626
Sec Mrs JR Hearsey
Pro DW Harris (01635) 31201
Holes 18 L 5940 yds SSS 68
V'tors WD–U H WE–M (recognised
      club members)
Fees £20
Loc 2 miles SE of Newbury

Newbury Racecourse (1994)

The Racecourse, Newbury, RG14 7NZ
Tel   (01635) 551464
Fax (01635) 528354
Web www.nrgc.co.uk
Mem 300
Sec R Osgood (01635) 400015
Pro N Mitchell (01635) 551464
Holes 18 L 6311 yds Par 70 SSS 70
V'tors U SOC
Fees £13 (£17)
Loc 4 miles S of M4 Junction 13
      on A34/A39
Mis Driving range

Parasampia G&CC

*Donnington Grove, Grove Road,
Donnington, RG14 2LA*
Tel   (01635) 581000
Fax (01635) 552259
Web www.parasampia.com
Mem 350
Sec S Greenacre (Mgr)
Pro G Williams
Holes 18 L 7108 yds Par 72 SSS 74

V'tors U SOC–WD/BH
Fees £30 D–£40 (£35 D–£50)
Loc NW of Newbury, off old
      Oxford road (B4494). M4
      Junction 13, 3½ miles
Arch Dave Thomas

Reading (1910)

*17 Kidmore End Road, Emmer Green,
Reading, RG4 8SG*
Tel   (0118) 947 2909
Fax (0118) 946 4468
Mem 585
Sec R Brown (0118) 947 2909
Pro S Fotheringham (0118) 947
      6115
Holes 18 L 6212 yds SSS 70
V'tors Mon–Thurs–UH
      Fri/WE/BH–M
      SOC–Tues–Thurs
Fees £25 D–£40
Loc 2 miles N of Reading, off
      Peppard Road (B481)
Arch James Braid

Royal Ascot (1887)

Winkfield Road, Ascot, SL5 7LJ
Tel   (01344) 625175
Fax (01344) 872330
Mem 600
Sec T Berry
Pro A White (01344) 624656
Holes 18 L 5716 yds SSS 68
V'tors M SOC
Fees On application
Loc On Ascot Heath, inside Ascot
      racecourse. Windsor 4 miles
Arch JH Taylor

The Royal Household (1901)

*Invergelder Cottage, 53 Red Rose,
Binfield, RG42 5LJ*
Tel   (020) 7930 4832
Fax (020) 7839 5950
Mem 200
Sec B Crosbie
Holes 9 L 4560 yds SSS 62
V'tors Strictly by invitation
Loc Home Park, Windsor Castle
Arch Muir Ferguson

Sand Martins (1993)

*Finchampstead Road, Wokingham,
RG40 3RQ*
Tel   (0118) 979 2711
Fax (0118) 977 0282
Web www.sandmartins.com
Mem 750
Sec Ms E Roginski
Pro AJ Hall (0118) 977 0265
Holes 18 L 6204 yds Par 70 SSS 70
V'tors WD–U WE–NA SOC
Fees £30
Loc 1 mile S of Wokingham. M4
      Junction 10
Mis Driving range
Arch ET Fox

Sonning (1911)

*Duffield Road, Sonning, Reading,
RG4 6GJ*
Tel   (0118) 969 3332
Fax (0118) 944 8409
Mem 750
Sec AJ Tanner
Pro RT McDougall
      (0118) 969 2910
Holes 18 L 6366 yds SSS 70
V'tors WD–H WE–M
Fees On application
Loc 1½ miles E of A329(M). S of
      A4, nr Sonning

Sulham Valley (1992)

*Pincents Lane, Calcot, Reading,
RG3 5UQ*
Tel   (01734) 305959
Fax (01734) 305002
Mem 700
Sec To be appointed
Pro Tina Tetley
Holes 18 L 6121 yds Par 71
V'tors U SOC
Fees £20 (£25)
Loc M4 Junction 12, 1 mile

Swinley Forest (1909)

Coronation Road, Ascot, SL9 5LE
Tel   (01344) 620197
Fax (01344) 874733
Mem 350
Sec IL Pearce (01344) 874979
Pro RC Parker (01344) 874811
Holes 18 L 6045 yds Par 69 SSS 70
V'tors M
Fees £70
Loc S of Ascot
Arch HS Colt

Temple (1909)

*Henley Road, Hurley, Maidenhead,
SL6 5LH*
Tel   (01628) 824795
Fax (01628) 828119
Mem 534
Sec KGM Adderley
      (01628) 824795
Pro J Whiteley (01628) 824254
Holes 18 L 6248 yds SSS 70
V'tors H SOC
Fees £36 (£44)
Loc Between Maidenhead and
      Henley on A4130. M4
      Junction 8/9. M40 Junction 4
Arch Willie Park Jr

Theale

*North Street, Theale, Reading
RG6 5EX*
Tel   (01189) 305331
Fax (01189) 305331
Sec M Lowe
Pro L Newman
Holes 18 L 6392 yds Par 72 SSS 71
V'tors U SOC
Fees £16 (£20)
Loc 1 mile from M4 Junction 12
Arch M Lowe
Mis Driving range

West Berkshire (1975)

Chaddleworth, Newbury,
RG20 7DU

Tel	**(01488) 638574**
Mem	700
Sec	Mrs CM Clayton
Pro	P Simpson (01488) 638851
Holes	18 L 7001 yds SSS 74
V'tors	WD–U WE–M SOC–WD
Fees	£25 D–£35 (£35)
Loc	Off A338 to Wantage. M4 Junction 14

Winter Hill (1976)

Grange Lane, Cookham, SL6 9RP

Tel	**(01628) 527613**
Mem	800
Sec	JE Hoskings
Pro	R Frost (01628) 527610
Holes	18 L 6408 yds SSS 71
V'tors	WD–U WE–M SOC
Fees	D–£29 After 2pm–£21
Loc	Maidenhead 3 miles
Arch	Charles Lawrie

Wokefield Park

Mortimer, Reading, RG7 4AE

Tel	**(0118) 933 4013/4018/4017**
Fax	(0118) 933 4162
Sec	J Morgan (Hon)
Pro	G Smith (0118) 933 4078
Holes	18 L 6961 yds Par 72 SSS 73
V'tors	WD–U WE–NA before 9.30am SOC
Fees	£29 (£36)
Loc	8 miles SW of Reading, off A33. M4 Junction 11
Mis	Driving range
Arch	Jonathan Gaunt

Buckinghamshire

Abbey Hill (1975)

Monks Way, Two Mile Ash, Milton Keynes, MK8 8AA

Tel	**(01908) 563845**
Mem	300
Sec	J Falconer
Pro	G Woodham
Holes	18 L 6193 yds SSS 69 Par 3 course
V'tors	U
Fees	On application
Loc	2 miles S of Stony Stratford
Mis	Driving range

Aylesbury Golf Centre (1992)

Public

Hulcott Lane, Bierton, HP22 5GA

Tel	**(01296) 393644**
Sec	K Partington (Mgr)
Pro	A Saary
Holes	18 L 5965 yds SSS 69
V'tors	U
Fees	£10 (£15)
Loc	1 mile N of Aylesbury on A418
Mis	Driving range
Arch	TS Benwell

Aylesbury Park (1996)

Oxford Road, Aylesbury, HP17 8QQ

Tel	**(01296) 399166/395381**
Fax	(01296) 336830
Mem	340
Sec	Carole Barnes (01296) 399196
Pro	D Boot (01296) 399196
Holes	18 L 6150 yds SSS 69
V'tors	U
Fees	£12.50 (£18)
Loc	SW of Aylesbury (A418). M40 Junction 8, 12 miles
Mis	Driving range
Arch	Martin Hawtree

Beaconsfield (1902)

Seer Green, Beaconsfield, HP9 2UR

Tel	**(01494) 676545**
Fax	(01494) 681148
Mem	850
Sec	KR Wilcox
Pro	M Brothers (01494) 676616
Holes	18 L 6493 yds Par 72 SSS 71
V'tors	WD–H WE–M SOC
Fees	£35 D–£48
Loc	2 miles E of Beaconsfield. M40 Junction 2
Mis	Driving range
Arch	HS Colt

Buckingham (1914)

Tingewick Road, Buckingham, MK18 4AE

Tel	**(01280) 813282 (Clubhouse)**
Fax	(01280) 821812
Mem	680
Sec	T Gates (Gen Mgr) (01280) 815566
Pro	T Gates (01280) 815210
Holes	18 L 6082 yds SSS 69
V'tors	WD–U WE–M SOC–Tues & Thurs
Fees	£28
Loc	2 miles SW of Buckingham on A421

The Buckinghamshire (1992)

Denham Court, Denham Court Drive, Denham, UB9 5BG

Tel	**(01895) 835777**
Fax	(01895) 835210
Mem	650
Sec	M Murapa
Pro	J O'Leary
Holes	18 L 6880 yds SSS 72
V'tors	I or M SOC–WD exc Fri
Fees	£70 (£80)
Loc	Off A40(M). M25 Junction 16b/M40 Junction 1
Mis	Driving range (Members)
Arch	John Jacobs

Burnham Beeches (1891)

Green Lane, Burnham, Slough, SL1 8EG

Tel	**(01628) 661150**
Fax	(01628) 668968
Web	www.bbgc.co.uk
Mem	670
Sec	AJ Buckner (Mgr) (01628) 661448
Pro	R Bolton (01628) 661661
Holes	18 L 6449 yds SSS 71
V'tors	WD–I WE/BH–M H
Fees	£33 D–£50
Loc	4 miles W of Slough

Chartridge Park (1989)

Chartridge, Chesham, HP5 2TF

Tel	**(01494) 791772**
Web	www.cpgc.co.uk
Mem	700
Sec	Mr & Mrs P Gibbins
Pro	P Gibbins
Holes	18 L 5580 yds SSS 66
V'tors	U SOC
Fees	£25 (£30)
Loc	2 miles NW of Chesham. 9 miles W of M25 Junction 18
Arch	John Jacobs

Chesham & Ley Hill (1900)

Ley Hill, Chesham, HP5 1UZ

Tel	**(01494) 784541**
Fax	(01494) 785506
Mem	322
Sec	B Durand
Holes	9 L 5240 yds SSS 66
V'tors	WD–U exc Tues–NA before 3pm WE/BH–M SOC–Thurs & Fri
Fees	£13
Loc	Chesham 2 miles
Mis	Course closed Sun after 2pm from 1st Apr–30th Sept

Chiltern Forest

Aston Hill, Halton, Aylesbury, HP22 5NQ

Tel	**(01296) 631267**
Fax	(01296) 631267
Web	www.chilternforest.co.uk
Mem	650
Sec	S Thornton (01296) 631267
Pro	A Lavers (01296) 631817
Holes	18 L 5765 yds SSS 70
V'tors	WD–U WE–M SOC
Fees	£20 D–£25
Loc	5 miles SE of Aylesbury, off A4011

Denham (1910)

Tilehouse Lane, Denham, UB9 5DE

Tel	**(01895) 832022**
Fax	(01895) 835340
Mem	775
Sec	MJ Miller
Pro	S Campbell (01895) 832801
Holes	18 L 6462 yds SSS 71
V'tors	Mon–Thurs–I H Fri–Sun/BH–M

For list of abbreviations see page 649

Fees   £45 D–£63
Loc   2 miles NW of Uxbridge
Arch   HS Colt

Ellesborough (1905)

Butlers Cross, Aylesbury, HP17 0TZ
Tel   **(01296) 622114**
Fax   (01296) 622114
Web   www.ellesboroughgolf.com
Mem   700
Sec   B Weeds (Gen Mgr)
Pro   M Squire (01296) 623126
Holes   18 L 6283 yds SSS 71
V'tors   WE/BH–M WD–I or H
    SOC–Wed & Thurs only
Fees   On application
Loc   1 mile W of Wendover

Farnham Park (1974)

Public
*Park Road, Stoke Poges, Slough,
SL2 4PJ*
Tel   **(01753) 643332**
Mem   450
Sec   Mrs M Brooker
    (01753) 647065
Pro   P Warner
Holes   18 L 6172 yds SSS 71
V'tors   U
Fees   £14.50
Loc   2 miles N of Slough
Arch   Hawtree

Flackwell Heath (1904)

*Treadaway Road, Flackwell Heath,
High Wycombe, HP10 9PE*
Tel   **(01628) 520929**
Fax   (01628) 530040
Mem   700
Sec   SJ Chandler
Pro   P Watson (01628) 523017
Holes   18 L 6211 yds SSS 70
V'tors   WD–H WE–M SOC–Wed &
    Thurs
Fees   £24
Loc   Between High Wycombe and
    Beaconsfield, off A40. M40
    Junction 3/4
Arch   J Turner

Gerrards Cross (1921)

*Chalfont Park, Gerrards Cross,
SL9 0QA*
Tel   **(01753) 883263**
Fax   (01753) 883593
Mem   725
Sec   Inger Perkins
Pro   M Barr (01753) 885300
Holes   18 L 6212 yds SSS 70
V'tors   WD–H WE/BH–M SOC
Fees   £35 D–£48
Loc   1 mile from Station, off A413
Arch   B Pedlar

Harewood Downs (1907)

*Cokes Lane, Chalfont St Giles,
HP8 4TA*
Tel   **(01494) 762308**
Fax   (01494) 766869

Mem   700
Sec   SJ Thornton (01494) 762184
Pro   GC Morris (01494) 764102
Holes   18 L 5958 yds SSS 69
V'tors   H
Fees   £30 (£35)
Loc   2 miles E of Amersham, off
    A413

Harleyford (1996)

*Harleyford Estate, Henley Road,
Marlow, SL7 2SP*
Tel   **(01628) 402300**
Fax   (01628) 478434
Mem   850
Sec   NJ Brunner
Pro   A Barr (01628) 402149
Holes   18 L 6604 yds Par 72 SSS 72
V'tors   U H SOC–WD after 10am
    SOC–WE after 1pm
Fees   £40 (£60)
Loc   1 mile W of Marlow on A4155
Mis   Driving range
Arch   Donald Steel

Hazlemere (1982)

*Penn Road, Hazlemere, High Wycombe,
HP15 7LR*
Tel   **(01494) 719300**
Fax   (01494) 713914
Mem   500
Sec   BF Cable
Pro   P Harrison (01494) 719306
Holes   18 L 5807 yds SSS 69
V'tors   WD–U WE–booking req
    SOC–WD
Fees   £20 (£30)
Loc   3 miles NE of High Wycombe
    on B474
Arch   Terry Murray

Iver (1983)

Hollow Hill Lane, Iver, SL0 0JJ
Tel   **(01753) 655615**
Fax   (01753) 654225
Mem   500
Sec   G Noble
Pro   K Teschner
Holes   9 L 6300 yds SSS 72
V'tors   U SOC
Fees   18 holes–£11 (£14.50)
    9 holes–£6 (£7.50)
Loc   ½ mile from Langley station,
    off Langley Park Road. M4
    Junction 5, 2 miles

Ivinghoe (1967)

*Wellcroft, Ivinghoe, Leighton Buzzard,
LU7 9EF*
Tel   **(01296) 668696**
Fax   (01296) 662755
Mem   250
Sec   Mrs SE Garrad
    (01296) 662478
Pro   PW Garrad (01296) 668696
Holes   9 L 4508 yds SSS 62
V'tors   WD–U WE–U after 8am SOC
Fees   18 holes–£9. 9 holes–£6
Loc   3 miles N of Tring. M1
    Junction 11, 5 miles
Arch   R Garrad

The Lambourne Club (1992)

Dropmore Road, Burnham, SL1 8NF
Tel   **(01628) 666755**
Fax   (01628) 663301
Web   www.gch.co.uk
Mem   750
Sec   W Sheffield (Gen Mgr)
Pro   D Hart (Golf
    Dir) (01628) 662936
Holes   18 L 6771 yds SSS 73
V'tors   H
Fees   £38 (£48)
Loc   1 mile N of Burnham. M40
    Junction 2. M4 Junction 7
Mis   Driving range
Arch   Donald Steel

Little Chalfont (1981)

*Lodge Lane, Little Chalfont, Amersham,
HP8 4AJ*
Tel   **(01494) 764877**
Fax   (01494) 762860
Mem   400
Sec   JM Dunne
Pro   B Woodhouse
    (01494) 762942
Holes   9 L 5852 yds SSS 68
V'tors   U SOC
Fees   On application
Loc   Chalfont & Latimer Station ½
    mile
Arch   JM Dunne

Magnolia Park

Arncott Road, Boarstall, HP18 9XX
Tel   **(01844) 239700**
Fax   (01844) 238991
Mem   300
Sec   A Rutter (Gen Mgr)
Pro   A Taylor (Golf Dir)
Holes   18 holes Par 73 SSS 73
    9 hole course
V'tors   U SOC–WD
Fees   D–£40
Loc   10 miles NW of Thame
    (B4011)
Mis   Golf Academy
Arch   Jonathan Gaunt

Mentmore G&CC (1992)

*Mentmore, Leighton Buzzard,
LU7 0UA*
Tel   **(01296) 662020**
Fax   (01296) 662592
Mem   1100
Sec   K Whitehouse (Gen Mgr)
Pro   R Davies
Holes   Rothschild 18 L 6777 yds
    SSS 72;
    Rosebery 18 L 6850 yds
    SSS 73
V'tors   WD–H WE/BH–H by
    appointment SOC
Fees   £40 D–£50
Loc   4 miles S of Leighton Buzzard
Mis   Driving range
Arch   Bob Sandow

For list of abbreviations see page 649

Oakland Park (1994)

Three Households, Chalfont St Giles, HP8 4LW

Tel	**(01494) 871277**
Fax	(01494) 874692
Mem	790
Sec	SF Balmforth (Sec/Dir)
	A King (Gen Mgr)
Pro	A Thatcher
Holes	18 L 5246 yds Par 67 SSS 66
V'tors	U SOC–WD
Fees	£25
Loc	3 miles N of M40 Junction 2
Mis	Driving range
Arch	Jonathan Gaunt

Princes Risborough (1990)

Lee Road, Saunderton Lee, Princes Risborough, HP27 9NX

Tel	**(01844) 346989 (Clubhouse)**
Fax	(01844) 274938
Mem	400
Sec	JF Tubb (Man Dir)
Pro	A Mitchell 274567
Holes	9 L 5440 yds Par 68 SSS 66
V'tors	U SOC
Fees	£14 (£18)
Loc	7 miles NW of High Wycombe on A4010
Arch	Guy Hunt

Richings Park G&CC

(1996)

North Park, Iver, SL0 9DL

Tel	**(01753) 655352**
Fax	(01753) 655409
Web	www.richingspark.co.uk
Mem	650
Sec	A Garland (01753) 655370
Pro	S Kelly (01753) 655352
Holes	18 L 6094 yds Par 70 SSS 69
	Par 3 Academy course
V'tors	WD–U WE–M
Fees	£17
Loc	Nr M4 Junction 5
Mis	Driving range
Arch	Alan Higgins

Silverstone (1992)

Pay and play

Silverstone Road, Stowe, Buckingham, MK18 5LH

Tel	**(01280) 850005**
Fax	(01280) 850156
Mem	570
Sec	DG Allen
Pro	R Holt
Holes	18 L 6213 yds SSS 71
V'tors	U–booking advisable SOC
Fees	£14 (£18)
Loc	Opposite Silverstone Race Circuit, N of Buckingham
Mis	Driving range
Arch	David Snell

Stoke Poges (1908)

Park Road, Stoke Poges, SL2 4PG

Tel	**(01753) 717171**
Fax	(01753) 717181
Mem	850

Pro	S Collier
Holes	18 L 6721 yds SSS 72
	9 L 3074 yds
V'tors	U
Fees	£110 (£180)
Loc	5 miles N of Windsor
Arch	HS Colt

Stowe (1974)

Stowe, Buckingham, MK18 5EH

Mem	300
Sec	Mrs CM Shaw
	(01280) 818282
Holes	9 L 4472 yds SSS 62
V'tors	WD/WE 8am–1pm & after 7pm–M; School holidays–M
Fees	On application
Loc	M1 Junction 16. 4 miles NW of Buckingham

Thorney Park (1992)

Thorney Mill Lane, Iver, SL0 9AL

Tel	**(01895) 422095**
Fax	(01895) 431307
Mem	200
Sec	A Killing
Pro	A Killing
Holes	9 L 3000 yds SSS 34
V'tors	U SOC
Fees	9 holes–£8 (£9.50)
	18 holes–£13 (£16)
Loc	3 miles N of M4 Junction 5 (B470)

Three Locks (1992)

Great Brickhill, Milton Keynes, MK17 9BH

Tel	**(01525) 270470**
Fax	(01525) 270470
Mem	300
Sec	P Critchley
Holes	18 L 6025 yds Par 70 SSS 68
V'tors	U SOC exc Sun
Fees	£15 (£18)
Loc	N of Leighton Buzzard on A4146. M1 Junction 14
Arch	MRM Sandow

Wavendon Golf Centre

(1990)

Lower End Road, Wavendon, Milton Keynes, MK17 8DA

Tel	**(01908) 281811**
Fax	(01908) 281257
Mem	250
Sec	J Drake
Pro	G Iron
Holes	18 L 5460 yds Par 67 SSS 66
	9 hole Par 3 course
V'tors	U SOC
Fees	£12 (£17.50)
Loc	2 miles W of M1 Junction 13
Mis	Floodlit driving range

Weston Turville (1973)

New Road, Weston Turville, Aylesbury, HP22 5QT

Tel	**(01296) 424084**

Fax	(01296) 395376
Mem	600
Sec	D Allen
Pro	G George (01296) 425949
Holes	18 L 6008 yds SSS 69
V'tors	U
Fees	£20 (£25)
Loc	1½ miles SE of Aylesbury

Wexham Park (1979)

Pay and play

Wexham Street, Wexham, Slough, SL3 6ND

Tel	**(01753) 663271**
Fax	(01753) 663318
Web	www.wexhamparkgolfcourse .co.uk
Mem	850
Sec	J Dunne
Pro	J Kennedy
	(01753) 663425
Holes	18 L 5251 yds SSS 66
	Green 9 L 2219 yds SSS 32
	Red 9 L 2727 yds SSS 34
V'tors	U SOC–WD/Sat & Sun pm
Fees	18 hole:£12.50 (£16)
	9 hole:£7 (£9)
Loc	2 miles N of Slough. M4 Junction 4
Mis	Driving range
Arch	David Morgan

Whiteleaf (1904)

Whiteleaf, Princes Risborough, HP27 0LY

Tel	**(01844) 343097/274058**
Fax	(01844) 275551
Mem	300
Sec	D Hill
Pro	KS Ward (01844) 345472
Holes	9 L 5391 yds SSS 66
V'tors	WD–U WE–M SOC
Fees	£18
Loc	Princes Risborough 2 miles

Windmill Hill (1972)

Pay and play

Tattenhoe Lane, Bletchley, MK3 7RB

Tel	**(01908) 631113 (Bookings)**
Fax	(01908) 630034
Mem	134
Sec	B Smith
Pro	C Clingan (01908) 378623
Holes	18 L 6720 yds Par 73 SSS 72
V'tors	U SOC
Fees	£11 (£15)
Loc	W of Milton Keynes on A421. M1 Junctions 13 & 14
Mis	Driving range
Arch	Sir Henry Cotton

Woburn (1976)

Little Brickhill, Milton Keynes, MK17 9LJ

Tel	**(01908) 370756**
Fax	(01908) 378436
Mem	1200
Sec	E Bullock (Man Dir)
	Glenna Beasley (Sec)
Pro	L Blacklock (01908) 626600

Holes	Duke's 18 L 6979 yds SSS 74
	Duchess 18 L 6651 yds
	SSS 72
	Marquess 18 L 7180 yds
	SSS 74
V'tors	WD–H (by arrangement)
	WE–M
Fees	By arrangement
Loc	¹/₂ mile E of A5. 4 miles W of
	M1 Junction 13
Arch	Charles Lawrie (Duke's)

Wycombe Heights (1991)
Public
Rayners Avenue, Loudwater, High Wycombe, HP10 9SW

Tel	(01494) 816686
Fax	(01494) 816728
Mem	1200
Sec	P Talbot (01494) 813185
Pro	A Bishop (01494) 812862
Holes	18 L 6300 yds Par 70 SSS 72
	18 hole Par 3 course
V'tors	U SOC
Fees	£11 (£14.95)
Loc	¹/₂ mile from M40 Junction 3,
	on A40 to Wycombe
Mis	Driving range
Arch	John Jacobs

Cambridgeshire

Abbotsley (1986)
Proprietary
Eynesbury Hardwicke, St Neots, PE19 4XN

Tel	(01480) 474000
Fax	(01480) 403280
Mem	440
Sec	J Tubb (01480) 474000
Pro	S Connolly
Holes	18 L 6311 yds SSS 72
V'tors	WD/BH/U WE–M before
	1pm –U after 1pm SOC
Fees	£19 (£30)
Loc	2 miles SE of St Neots on
	B1046. M11 Junction 13
	(A428)
Arch	Vivien Saunders

Bourn (1991)
Toft Road, Bourn, Cambridge, CB3 7TT

Tel	(01954) 718057
Fax	(01954) 718908
Mem	600
Pro	C Watson (01954) 718958
Holes	18 L 6417 yds SSS 71
V'tors	U SOC–WD
Fees	On application
Loc	8 miles W of Cambridge, off
	B1046. M11 Junction 12

Brampton Park (1991)
Buckden Road, Brampton, Huntingdon, PE28 4NF

Tel	(01480) 434700
Fax	(01480) 411145

Web	www.bramptonparkgc.co.uk
Mem	650
Sec	RK Oakes (Gen Mgr)
Pro	A Currie (01480) 434705
Holes	18 L 6300 yds SSS 72
V'tors	U SOC
Fees	£25 (D–£35)
Loc	3 miles W of Huntingdon, off
	A1/A604
Arch	Simon Gidman

Cambridge
Station Road, Longstanton, Cambridge, CB4 5DR

Tel	(01954) 789388
Mem	300
Sec	K Green
Pro	G Huggett, A Engleman
Holes	18 L 6736 yds Par 72 SSS 74
V'tors	U SOC
Fees	£10 (£13)
Loc	5 miles NW of Cambridge, off
	A14 (B1050)
Mis	Floodlit driving range

Cambridge Meridian
Proprietary
Comberton Road, Toft, Cambridge, CB3 7RY

Tel	(01223) 264700
Fax	(01223) 264701
Web	www.golfsocieties.com
Mem	610
Sec	Ingrid van Rooyen
Pro	M Clemons (01223) 264702
Holes	18 L 6707 yds Par 73 SSS 72
V'tors	U SOC
Fees	£20 (£25)
Loc	3 miles SW of Cambridge on
	B1046. M11 Junction 12
Arch	Alliss/Clark

Cambridgeshire Moat House (1974)
Bar Hill, Cambridge, CB3 8EU

Tel	(01954) 249988 (Hotel)
Fax	(01954) 780010
Web	www.cambridgeshiregolf.co.uk
Mem	650
Sec	C Cooper
Pro	P Simpson (01954) 780098
Holes	18 L 6734 yds Par 72 SSS 73
V'tors	U SOC–WD
Fees	£20 (£30)
Loc	5 miles NW of Cambridge on
	A14

Cromwell
Proprietary
Eynesbury Hardwicke, St Neots, PE19 6XN

Tel	(01480) 215153
Fax	(01480) 406463
Mem	200
Sec	J Tubb (01480) 474000
Pro	S Connolly
Holes	18 L 6087 yds SSS 69
	9 hole Par 3 course
V'tors	U SOC
Fees	£10 (£17)

Loc	2 miles SE of St Neots on
	B1046. M11 Junction 13
	(A428)
Mis	Floodlit driving range
Arch	Vivien Saunders

Elton Furze (1993)
Bullock Road, Haddon, Peterborough, PE7 3TT

Tel	(01832) 280189
Fax	(01832) 280299
Web	www.eltonfurzegolfclub.co.uk
Mem	540
Sec	Barbara Knights
Pro	F Kiddie (01832) 280614
Holes	18 L 6289 yds SSS 70
V'tors	WD–phone in advance SOC
Fees	£22 (£32)
Loc	4 miles W of Peterborough on
	old A605
Mis	Driving range
Arch	Roger Fitton

Ely City (1961)
107 Cambridge Road, Ely, CB7 4HX

Tel	(01353) 662751
Fax	(01353) 668636
Web	www.elygolf.co.uk
Mem	840
Sec	MS Hoare (Mgr)
	(01353) 662751
Pro	A George (01353) 663317
Holes	18 L 6627 yds SSS 72
V'tors	WD–H WE–H
	SOC–Tues–Fri
Fees	£30 (£36)
Loc	12 miles N of Cambridge
Arch	Henry Cotton

Girton (1936)
Dodford Lane, Girton, CB3 0QE

Tel	(01223) 276169
Fax	(01223) 277150
Web	www.girtongolfclub.sagenet
	.co.uk
Mem	800
Sec	Miss VM Webb
Pro	S Thomson (01223) 276991
Holes	18 L 6012 yds SSS 69
V'tors	WD–U WE/BH–M SOC–WD
Fees	£20
Loc	3 miles N of Cambridge (A14)

The Gog Magog (1901)
Shelford Bottom, Cambridge, CB2 4AB

Tel	(01223) 247626
Fax	(01223) 414990
Mem	1300
Sec	D Knight
Pro	I Bamborough
	(01223) 246058
Holes	Old 18 L 6398 yds SSS 70
	Wandlebury 18 L 6735 yds
	SSS 72
V'tors	WD–I or H WE/BH–M
	SOC–Tues & Thurs
Fees	£35 D–£42
Loc	2 miles S of Cambridge on
	A1307 (A604)
Arch	Hawtree

Hemingford Abbots (1991)

Proprietary
New Farm Lodge, Cambridge Road, Hemingford Abbots, PE28 9HQ
Tel (01480) 495000
Fax (01480) 496000
Web www.astroman.co.uk
Mem 220
Sec RD Paton
Holes 9 L 5468 yds SSS 68
V'tors U
Fees On application
Loc 2 miles S of Huntingdon on A14
Mis Floodlit driving range

Heydon Grange G&CC (1994)

Heydon, Royston, SG8 7NS
Tel (01763) 208988
Fax (01763) 208926
Web www.heydongrange.co.uk
Mem 200
Sec C Barrett
Pro J Saxon-Mills
Holes 18 L 6512 yds SSS 72
9 L 3249 yds SSS 36
V'tors U SOC
Fees £12.50 (£17.50)
Loc 4 miles E of Royston on A505. M11 Junction 10
Mis Driving range
Arch Cameron Sinclair

Lakeside Lodge (1992)

Fen Road, Pidley, Huntingdon, PE17 3DD
Tel (01487) 740540
Fax (01487) 740852
Mem 550
Sec Mrs J Hopkins
Pro S Waterman (01487) 741541
Holes 18 L 6865 yds SSS 73
9 L 2601 yds SSS 33
V'tors U SOC
Fees £10 (£16)
Loc 4 miles N of St Ives on B1040
Mis Driving range
Arch A Headley

Malton (1993)

Pay and play
Malton Lane, Meldreth, Royston, SG8 6PE
Tel (01763) 262200
Fax (01763) 262209
Web www.maltongolf.co.uk
Mem 450
Sec A Boyce (01638) 751222
Pro None
Holes 18 L 6708 yds Par 72 SSS 72
V'tors U SOC–exc WE–NA before 11am
Fees £10 (£15)
Loc 8 miles SW of Cambridge, off A10. 5 miles SW of M11 Junction 11
Mis Driving range
Arch Bruce Critchley

March (1922)

Frogs Abbey, Grange Rd, March, PE15 0YH
Tel (01354) 652364
Mem 400
Sec Lt Cdr LE Taylor RN
Pro J Hadland
Holes 9 L 6210 yds SSS 70
V'tors H SOC–WD
Fees £17
Loc 18 miles E of Peterborough on A141

Old Nene G&CC (1992)

Muchwood Lane, Bodsey, Ramsey, PE26 2XQ
Tel (01487) 813519
Mem 200
Sec PB Cade
Pro I Galloway (01487) 710122
Holes 9 L 5605 yds SSS 68
V'tors U SOC
Fees 18 holes–£11 (£16)
9 holes–£7 (£9)
Loc 1 mile N of Ramsey, towards Ramsey Mereside
Mis Floodlit driving range
Arch Richard Edrich

Orton Meadows (1987)

Public
Ham Lane, Peterborough, PE2 5UU
Tel (01733) 237478
Web www.ortonmeadowsgolfcourse.co.uk
Mem 600
Sec Mrs S Ramsay (01733) 234769
Pro J Mitchell
Holes 18 L 5664 yds SSS 68
V'tors U–phone Pro
Fees £11.50 (£14.75)
Loc 2 miles SW of Peterborough on old A605
Mis 12 hole pitch & putt
Arch D & R Fitton

Peterborough Milton (1937)

Milton Ferry, Peterborough, PE6 7AG
Tel (01733) 380204
Fax (01733) 380489
Mem 850
Sec (01733) 380489
Pro M Gallagher (01733) 380793
Holes 18 L 6462 yds SSS 72
V'tors WD–U WE–M SOC H
Fees £25 (£35)
Loc 4 miles W of Peterborough on A47
Arch James Braid

Ramsey (1964)

4 Abbey Terrace, Ramsey, Huntingdon, PE26 1DD
Tel (01487) 812600
Fax (01487) 815746
Mem 750
Sec B Gazzard
Pro S Scott (01487) 813022
Holes 18 L 6163 yds Par 71 SSS 70

V'tors WD–H WE/BH–M SOC
Fees £25
Loc 12 miles SE of Peterborough
Arch J Hamilton Stutt

St Ives (1923)

St Ives, Huntingdon, PE27 6DH
Tel (01480) 64459
Fax (01480) 468392
Mem 385
Sec BE Dunn (01480) 468392
Pro D Glasby (01480) 466067
Holes 9 L 6180 yds SSS 70
V'tors WD–U H WE–M
Fees D–£20
Loc 5 miles E of Huntingdon

St Neots (1890)

Crosshall Road, St Neots, PE19 7GE
Tel (01480) 472363
Fax (01480) 472363
Mem 600
Sec PT Round (Mgr) (01480) 472363
Pro PT Round (01480) 476513
Holes 18 L 6074 yds SSS 69
V'tors WD–H WE–M
Fees On application
Loc By A1/B1048 Junction

Stilton Oaks

Proprietary
High Street, Stilton, Peterborough PE7 3RA
Tel (01733) 245233
Mem 200
Sec Mrs M Smith
Pro None
Holes 18 hole course
V'tors U
Fees £10 (£12)
Loc 5 miles S of Peterborough. A1(M) Junction 16

Thorney Golf Centre (1991)

Public
English Drove, Thorney, Peterborough, PE6 0TJ
Tel (01733) 270570
Fax (01733) 270842
Mem 400
Sec Jane Hind
Pro M Templeman
Holes Fen 18 L 6104 yds SSS 69
Lakes 18 L 6402 yds SSS 71
9 hole Par 3 course
V'tors Lakes WD–U SOC WE–M
Fees Fen £7 (£9) Lakes £11.50 (£18.50)
Loc 8 miles E of Peterborough, off A47
Mis Floodlit driving range
Arch A Dow

Thorpe Wood (1975)

Pay and play
Nene Parkway, Peterborough, PE3 6SE
Tel (01733) 267701
Fax (01733) 332774
Web www.thorpewoodgolfcourse.co.uk

Sec	R Palmer
Pro	R Fitton
Holes	18 L 7086 yds SSS 74
V'tors	U–booking required SOC–WD
Fees	£11.20 (£14.75)
Loc	3 miles W of Peterborough on A47 (Junction 15)
Arch	Alliss/Thomas

Waterbeach (1968)

Waterbeach Barracks, Waterbeach, Cambridge, CB5 9PA

Tel	(01223) 575260 (Sec)
Fax	(01223) 511525
Sec	ES Rowlands (Hon)
Holes	9 L 6236 yds Par 70 SSS 70
V'tors	M SOC–WD
Fees	£10
Loc	6 miles NE of Cambridge, off A10

Channel Islands

Alderney

Route des Carrieres, Alderney, GY9 3YD

Tel	(01481) 822835
Fax	(01481) 823609
Mem	420
Sec	Barbara Dale (01481) 823563
Holes	9 L 5006 yds Par 64 SSS 65
V'tors	U SOC H
Fees	D–£20 (D–£25)
Loc	1 mile E of St Anne

La Grande Mare (1994)

Vazon Bay, Castel, Guernsey, GY5 7LL

Tel	(01481) 255313
Fax	(01481) 255194
Web	www.LGM.Guernsey.net
Mem	650
Sec	J Vermeulen (01481) 253544
Pro	M Groves (01481) 253432
Holes	18 L 5112 yds SSS 66
V'tors	U–booking necessary SOC
Fees	D–£27 (£29)
Loc	Vazon Bay, W coast of Guernsey
Arch	Hawtree

Les Mielles G&CC (1994)

St Ouens Bay, Jersey, JE3 7FQ

Tel	(01534) 482787
Fax	(01534) 485414
Web	www.lesmielles.com
Mem	1500
Sec	J Le Brun (Golf Dir) (01534) 482787 Ext 4
Pro	L Elstone (01534) 483699 W Osmand (01534) 483252
Holes	18 L 5770 yds Par 70 SSS 69
V'tors	H or Green Card SOC
Fees	£22 (£25)
Loc	Five Mile Road, St Ouens Bay
Mis	Driving range
Arch	Le Brun/Whitehead

La Moye (1902)

La Moye, St Brelade, Jersey, JE3 8GQ

Tel	(01534) 743401, (01534) 747166 (Bookings)
Fax	(01534) 747289
Mem	1350
Sec	CHM Greetham
Pro	M Deeley (01534) 743130
Holes	18 L 6664 yds SSS 73
V'tors	I H SOC–9.30–11am and 2.30–4pm WE–after 2.30pm
Fees	£45 D–£75 (£50)
Loc	2 miles from Jersey Airport
Mis	Driving range
Arch	James Braid

Les Ormes (1996)

Pay and play

Mont à la Brune, St Brelade, Jersey, JE3 8FL

Tel	(01534) 497000
Fax	(01534) 499122
Mem	1200
Sec	M Graham (01534) 497002
Pro	A Chamberlain (01534) 497000
Holes	9 L 5018 yds Par 66 SSS 65
V'tors	U SOC
Fees	9 holes–£13 (£16) 18 holes–£19.50 (£24)
Loc	Mont à la Brune, nr Airport
Mis	Driving range

Royal Guernsey (1890)

L'Ancresse, Guernsey, GY3 5BY

Tel	(01481) 47022
Fax	(01481) 43960
Mem	1520
Sec	M de Laune (Club Mgr) R Eggo (Golf Mgr)
Pro	N Wood (01481) 45070
Holes	18 L 6215 yds SSS 70
V'tors	WD–H WE–M
Fees	£34
Loc	3 miles N of St Peter Port
Mis	Driving range

Royal Jersey (1878)

Grouville, Jersey, JE3 9BD

Tel	(01534) 854416
Fax	(01534) 854684
Mem	1300
Sec	DJ Attwood
Pro	D Morgan (01534) 852234
Holes	18 L 6100 yds SSS 70
V'tors	WD–H after 10am WE/BH–H after 2.30pm
Fees	£45 (£45)
Loc	4 miles E of St Helier

St Clements (1925)

Public

St Clements, Jersey, JE2 6QN

Tel	(01534) 821938
Pro	R Marks
Holes	9 L 3972 yds SSS 61
V'tors	U exc Sun am–NA
Fees	On application
Loc	1 mile E of St Helier

St Pierre Park

Rohais, St Peter Port, Guernsey, GY1 1FD

Tel	(01481) 727039
Mem	290
Pro	R Corbet (Mgr)
Holes	9 hole Par 3 course
V'tors	U SOC
Fees	18 holes–£15 (£17)
Loc	1 mile W of St Peter Port
Mis	Driving range
Arch	Tony Jacklin

Cheshire

Alder Root (1993)

Alder Root Lane, Winwick, Warrington, WA2 8RZ

Tel	(01925) 291919
Fax	(01925) 291961
Mem	450
Sec	E Lander
Pro	C McKevitt (01925) 291932
Holes	10 L 5820 yds Par 69 SSS 68
V'tors	WD–U SOC
Fees	£16 (£18)
Loc	4 miles N of Warrington (A49). M6 Junction 22. M62 Junction 9
Arch	Millington/Lander

Alderley Edge (1907)

Brook Lane, Alderley Edge, SK9 7RU

Tel	(01625) 585583
Web	www.aegc.co.uk
Mem	212 90(L) 40(J) 40(5)
Sec	JBD Page
Pro	P Bowring (01625) 584493
Holes	9 L 5823 yds SSS 68
V'tors	M or H SOC
Fees	£20 (£25)
Loc	12 miles S of Manchester

Aldersey Green

Aldersey, Chester, CH3 9EH

Tel	(01829) 782157
Sec	S Bradbury
Pro	S Bradbury (01829) 782157
Holes	18 L 6150 yds Par 70
V'tors	U SOC
Fees	£12 (£15)
Loc	8 miles S of Chester, off A41

Altrincham Municipal (1893)

Public

Stockport Road, Timperley, Altrincham, WA15 7LP

Tel	(0161) 928 0761
Mem	276
Sec	B Simpson
Pro	S Partington
Holes	18 L 6385 yds Par 71 SSS 70
V'tors	U SOC
Fees	£8.30 (£11.50)
Loc	1 mile W of Altrincham (A560)
Mis	Driving range

Alvaston Hall (1992)

Proprietary
Middlewich Road, Nantwich,
CW5 6PD

Tel	**(01270) 628473**
Fax	(01270) 623395
Mem	340
Sec	N Perkins (01270) 760206
Pro	K Valentine
Holes	9 L 3708 yds Par 64 SSS 59
V'tors	U
Fees	£10 (£10)
Loc	11 miles W of M6 Junction 16 on A530
Mis	Driving range
Arch	K Valentine

Antrobus

Foggs Lane, Antrobus, Northwich,
CW9 6JQ

Tel	**(01925) 730890**
Fax	(01925) 730100
Web	www.antrobusgolfclub.co.uk
Mem	550
Sec	Miss C Axford
Pro	P Farrance (01925) 730900
Holes	18 L 6220 yds Par 72 SSS 72
V'tors	H SOC
Fees	£20 (£24)
Loc	Nr M56 Junction 10, on A559 to Northwich
Mis	Driving range
Arch	Michael Slater

Ashton-on-Mersey (1897)

Church Lane, Sale, M33 5QQ

Tel	**(0161) 973 3220 (Clubhouse)**
Fax	(0161) 976 4390
Mem	180 70(L) 40(J)
Sec	R Tomlinson (0161) 976 4390
Pro	MJ Williams (0161) 962 3727
Holes	9 L 3073 yds SSS 69
V'tors	WD–U H exc Tues–NA before 3pm WE–M
Fees	£20.50
Loc	5 miles W of Manchester. M60 Junction 7, 1½ miles

Astbury (1922)

Peel Lane, Astbury, Congleton,
CW12 4RE

Tel	**(01260) 272772 (Clubhouse)**
Web	www.astburygolfclub.com
Mem	700
Sec	FM Reed (01260) 279139
Pro	A Salt (01260) 298663
Holes	18 L 6296 yds SSS 70
V'tors	WD–H or M WE–M SOC–Thurs only
Fees	£30 SOC–£25
Loc	1 mile S of Congleton, off A34

Birchwood (1979)

Kelvin Close, Birchwood, Warrington,
WA3 7PB

Tel	**(01925) 818819**
Fax	(01925) 822403
Mem	745
Sec	F Craig

Pro	P McEwan (01925) 816574
Holes	18 L 6727 yds Par 71 SSS 73
V'tors	U SOC–Mon/Wed/Thurs
Fees	£18 D–£26 (£34)
Loc	M62 Junction 11, 2 miles. Signs to 'Science Park North'
Arch	TJA Macauley

Bramall Park (1894)

20 Manor Road, Bramhall, Stockport,
SK7 3LY

Tel	**(0161) 485 3119 (Clubhouse)**
Fax	(0161) 485 7101
Mem	715
Sec	IR McNeill (0161) 485 7101
Pro	M Proffit (0161) 485 2205
Holes	18 L 6214 yds SSS 70
V'tors	I
Fees	£30 (£40)
Loc	8 miles S of Manchester (A5102)

Bramhall (1905)

Ladythorn Road, Bramhall, Stockport,
SK7 2EY

Tel	**(0161) 439 4057**
Fax	(0161) 439 0264
Web	www.bramhallgolfclub.com
Mem	325 155(L) 85(J)
Sec	B Hill (Hon) (0161) 439 6092
Pro	R Green (0161) 439 1171
Holes	18 L 6300 yds SSS 70
V'tors	U H exc Thurs SOC–Wed
Fees	£30 D–£35 (£37 D–£46)
Loc	S of Stockport, off A5102

Carden Park

Chester, CH3 9DQ

Tel	**(01829) 731600**
Fax	(01829) 731629
Mem	234
Sec	D Llewellyn
Pro	S Edwards (01829) 731500
Holes	Cheshire 18 L 6824 yds SSS 72; Nicklaus 18 L 7045 yds Par 72 9 hole Par 3 course
V'tors	H SOC
Fees	Cheshire–£40 Nicklaus–£60
Loc	10 miles S of Chester on A534
Mis	Golf Academy. Driving range

Cheadle (1885)

Shiers Drive, Cheadle Road, Cheadle,
SK8 1HW

Tel	**(0161) 491 4452**
Mem	350
Sec	BR Woodhouse
Pro	S Booth (0161) 428 9878
Holes	9 L 5006 yds SSS 65
V'tors	H or I exc Tues & Sat–NA SOC
Fees	£20 (£25)
Loc	1 mile S of Cheadle. M63 Junction 11, 2 miles

Chester (1901)

Curzon Park, Chester, CH4 8AR

Tel	**(01244) 675130**

Fax	(01244) 676667
Mem	840
Sec	VFC Wood (01244) 677760
Pro	G Parton (01244) 671185
Holes	18 L 6461 yds SSS 71
V'tors	U H SOC
Fees	£25 (£30)
Loc	Chester 1 mile

Congleton (1898)

Biddulph Road, Congleton
CW12 3LZ

Tel	**(01260) 273540**
Mem	440
Sec	R Brindley
Pro	JA Colclough
Holes	12 L 5103 yds Par 68 SSS 65
V'tors	U H SOC
Fees	£21 (£31)
Loc	1½ miles E of Congleton on A527

Crewe (1911)

Fields Road, Haslington, Crewe,
CW1 5TB

Tel	**(01270) 584227 (Steward)**
Fax	(01270) 584099
Web	www.crewegolfclub.co.uk
Mem	628
Sec	Mrs PM Rosenberg (01270) 584099
Pro	M Booker (01270) 585032
Holes	18 L 6424 yds SSS 71
V'tors	WD–U WE/BH–M SOC
Fees	£27 After 1pm–£22
Loc	2 miles NE of Crewe Station, off A534. 5 miles W of M6 Junction 17

Davenport (1913)

Worth Hall, Middlewood Road,
Poynton, SK12 1TS

Tel	**(01625) 876951**
Fax	(01625) 877489
Mem	650
Sec	TE Bonfield
Pro	G Norcott (01625) 877319
Holes	18 L 6027 yds SSS 69
V'tors	U exc Wed & Sat–NA SOC–Tues & Thurs
Fees	£30 (£40)
Loc	5 miles S of Stockport. 7 miles N of Macclesfield

Delamere Forest (1910)

Station Road, Delamere, Northwich,
CW8 2JE

Tel	**(01606) 883264**
Fax	(01606) 889444
Mem	400
Sec	TG Owen (01606) 883800
Pro	EB Jones (01606) 883307
Holes	18 L 6328 yds SSS 71
V'tors	WD–U WE–2 ball only SOC
Fees	£30 D–£45 (£45)
Loc	10 miles E of Chester, off B5152
Arch	Herbert Fowler

Disley (1889)

Stanley Hall Lane, Disley, Stockport, SK12 2JX

Tel	(01663) 762071
Fax	(01663) 762678
Mem	500
Sec	Dianne Bradley
Pro	AG Esplin (01663) 762884
Holes	18 L 5942 yds Par 70
V'tors	WD–U exc Thurs WE/BH–M
Fees	£25 (£30)
Loc	6 miles S of Stockport on A6

Dukinfield (1913)

Yew Tree Lane, Dukinfield, SK16 5DB

Tel	(0161) 338 2340
Mem	300 80(L) 65(J)
Sec	L Holmes (0161) 366 0542
Pro	J Lowe
Holes	18 L 5203 yds SSS 66
V'tors	WD–U exc Wed pm WE–M SOC
Fees	£16.50
Loc	6 miles E of Manchester

Dunham Forest G&CC (1961)

Oldfield Lane, Altrincham, WA14 4TY

Tel	(0161) 928 2605
Fax	(0161) 929 8975
Mem	600
Sec	Mrs S Klaus
Pro	I Wrigley (0161) 928 2727
Holes	18 L 6636 yds SSS 72
V'tors	WD–U WE/BH–M SOC exc 12–1pm
Fees	£40 (£45)
Loc	1 mile SW of Altrincham. M56 Junction 7

Eaton (1965)

Guy Lane, Waverton, Chester, CH3 7PH

Tel	(01244) 335885
Fax	(01244) 335782
Mem	550
Sec	K Brown
Pro	W Tye (01244) 335826
Holes	18 L 6562 yds SSS 71
V'tors	H SOC
Fees	On application
Loc	3 miles SE of Chester, off A41
Arch	Donald Steel

Ellesmere Port (1971)

Public

Chester Road, Childer Thornton, South Wirral, CH66 1QF

Tel	(0151) 339 7689
Mem	350
Sec	C Craggs
Pro	T Roberts
Holes	18 L 6432 yds SSS 71
V'tors	WD–U WE–arrange with Pro SOC–WD
Fees	£6.70 (£7.40)
Loc	9 miles N of Chester on A41. M53 Junction 5

Frodsham (1990)

Simons Lane, Frodsham, WA6 6HE

Tel	(01928) 732159
Fax	(01928) 734070
Web	www.frodshamgolfclub.co.uk
Mem	600
Sec	EI Roylance
Pro	G Tonge (01928) 739442
Holes	18 L 6298 yds SSS 70
V'tors	WD–U WE/BH–M SOC–WD
Fees	£30
Loc	9 miles NE of Chester (A56). M56 Junction 12, 3 miles
Arch	John Day

Gatley (1911)

Waterfall Farm, Styal Road, Heald Green, Cheadle SK8 3TW

Tel	(0161) 437 2091
Mem	450
Sec	CB Hamnett
Pro	J Hopley (0161) 436 2830
Holes	9 L 5934 yds SSS 68
V'tors	WD exc Tues–arrange with Pro WE/Tues–NA
Fees	£21
Loc	7 miles S of Manchester. Manchester Airport 2 miles

Hale (1903)

Rappax Road, Hale, WA15 0NU

Tel	(0161) 980 4225
Mem	350
Sec	JT Goodman
Pro	A Bickerdike (0161) 904 0835
Holes	9 L 5780 yds SSS 68
V'tors	WD–U exc Thurs–NA before 5pm WE/BH–M SOC
Fees	D–£25
Loc	2 miles SE of Altrincham

Hazel Grove (1913)

Buxton Road, Hazel Grove, Stockport, SK7 6LU

Tel	(0161) 483 3217 (Clubhouse)
Mem	550
Sec	FA Williams (0161) 483 3978
Pro	ME Hill (0161) 483 7272
Holes	18 L 6263 yds SSS 74
V'tors	U SOC–Thurs & Fri
Fees	£30 (£35)
Loc	3 miles S of Stockport (A6)

Heaton Moor (1892)

Mauldeth Road, Heaton Mersey, Stockport, SK4 3NX

Tel	(0161) 432 2134
Fax	(0161) 432 2134
Mem	550
Sec	JR Smith
Pro	SJ Marsh (0161) 432 0846
Holes	18 L 5968 yds SSS 69
V'tors	U SOC
Fees	£23 (£31)
Loc	2 miles from M63 Junction 12, off A5145

Helsby (1901)

Tower's Lane, Helsby, Frodsham, WA6 0JB

Tel	(01928) 722021
Fax	(01928) 725384
Mem	600
Sec	LJ Norbury
Pro	M Jones (01928) 725457
Holes	18 L 6229 yds SSS 70
V'tors	H WE–NA SOC–Tues & Thurs
Fees	£25
Loc	1 mile SE of M56 Junction 14, off Primrose Lane
Mis	Driving range
Arch	James Braid

Heyrose (1989)

Budworth Road, Tabley, Knutsford, WA16 0HZ

Tel	(01565) 733664
Fax	(01565) 734578
Mem	600
Sec	Mrs H March (01565) 733664
Pro	C Iddon (01565) 734267
Holes	18 L 6513 yds SSS 71
V'tors	U SOC
Fees	£20 (£25)
Loc	3 miles W of Knutsford, off Pickmere Lane. M6 Junction 19, 1 mile
Arch	CN Bridge

Houldsworth (1910)

Houldsworth Park, Houldsworth Street, Reddish, Stockport SK5 6BN

Tel	(0161) 442 9611
Fax	(0161) 442 1712
Mem	625
Sec	SW Zielinski (0161) 442 1712
Pro	D Naylor (0161) 442 1714
Holes	18 L 6209 yds Par 71 SSS 70
V'tors	U SOC
Fees	£20 (£25)
Loc	4 miles S of Manchester

Knights Grange (1983)

Public

Grange Lane, Winsford, CW7 2PT

Tel	(01606) 552780
Mem	144
Sec	Mrs P Littler (Mgr), J Burgess (Hon)
Pro	G Moore (01606) 853564
Holes	18 L 6253 yds SSS 70
V'tors	U SOC
Fees	£5 (£7)
Loc	Knights Grange Sports Complex. M6 Junctions 18 & 19

Knutsford (1891)

Mereheath Lane, Knutsford, WA16 6HS

Tel	(01565) 633355
Mem	250
Sec	DM Burgess
Pro	G Ogden
Holes	9 L 6288 yds SSS 70
V'tors	H exc Wed–NA SOC

For list of abbreviations see page 649

Fees £25 (£30)
Loc Knutsford ¹/₂ mile

Leigh (1906)

Kenyon Hall, Culcheth, Warrington, WA3 4BG

Tel **(01925) 763130**
Fax (01925) 765097
Mem 700
Sec PF Saunders (01925) 762943
Pro A Baguley (01925) 762013
Holes 18 L 5892 yds SSS 68
V'tors U H SOC
Fees £26 (£33)
Loc 5 miles NE of Warrington
Arch James Braid

Lymm (1907)

Whitbarrow Road, Lymm, WA13 9AN

Tel **(01925) 755020**
Fax (01925) 755020
Web www.lymm-golf-club.co.uk
Mem 400 100(L) 75(J) 50(5)
Sec S Nash
Pro S McCarthy (01925) 755054
Holes 18 L 6304 yds SSS 70
V'tors WD–H WE–M SOC–Wed
Fees £22 (£30)
Loc 5 miles SE of Warrington. M6
Junction 20

Macclesfield (1889)

The Hollins, Macclesfield, SK11 7EA

Tel **(01625) 423227**
Fax (01625) 260061
Web www.maccgolfclub.co.uk
Mem 600
Sec DJ English (01625) 615845
Pro T Taylor (01625) 616952
Holes 18 L 5752 yds SSS 68
V'tors WD/BH–H WE–M SOC–WD
Fees £25 (£30)
Loc SE edge of Macclesfield, off
A523
Arch Hawtree

Malkins Bank (1980)

Public
Malkins Bank, Sandbach, CW11 4XN

Tel **(01270) 765931**
Fax (01270) 764730
Pro D Wheeler
Holes 18 L 6071 yds SSS 69
V'tors U SOC
Fees £8.30 (£9.50)
Loc 2 miles S of Sandbach via
A534/A533. M6 Junction 17

Marple (1892)

Barnsfold Road, Hawk Green, Marple, Stockport SK6 7EL

Tel **(0161) 427 2311**
Fax (0161) 427 1125
Mem 435 100(L) 60(J)
Sec MR Baguley (0161) 427 1125
Pro D Myers (0161) 427 1195
Holes 18 L 5552 yds SSS 67
V'tors WD–U exc Thurs–NA
WE/BH–M SOC

Fees £20 (£30)
Loc 2 miles from High Lane
North, off A6

Mellor & Townscliffe (1894)

Tarden, Gibb Lane, Mellor, Stockport SK6 5NA

Tel **(0161) 427 9700 (Clubhouse)**
Fax (0161) 427 0103
Web www.mandtgc.demon.co.uk
Mem 700
Sec G Lee (0161) 427 2208
Pro G Broadley (0161) 427 5759
Holes 18 L 5925 yds SSS 69
V'tors WD–U WE–M SOC
Fees £22 (£31)
Loc 7 miles SE of Stockport, off
A626

Mere G&CC (1934)

Chester Road, Mere, Knutsford, WA16 6LJ

Tel **(01565) 830155**
Fax (01565) 830713
Mem 375 200(L) 40(J)
Pro P Eyre (01565) 830219
Holes 18 L 6817 yds SSS 73
V'tors WE/BH–M Wed & Fri–M
Mon/Tues/Thurs–H SOC
Fees D–£70
Loc 1 mile E of M6 Junction 19.
2 miles W of M56 Junction 7
Mis Driving range–members and
green fees only
Arch James Braid

Mersey Valley (1995)

Warrington Road, Bold Heath, Widnes, WA8 3XL

Tel **(0151) 424 6060**
Fax (0151) 257 9097
Mem 550
Sec A Stevenson
Pro A Stevenson
Holes 18 L 6300 yds SSS 70
V'tors U
Fees £18 (£20)
Loc M62 Junction 7, 2 miles
Arch RMR Bush

Mobberley

Burleyhurst Lane, Mobberley, Knutsford, WA16 7JZ

Tel **(01505) 880188**
Fax (01505) 880178
Sec N Donaghy
Pro S Dewhurst
Holes 9 L 5542 yds Par 67
V'tors U SOC
Fees £13.50 (£17)
Loc Mobberley. M56 Junction 6

Mollington Grange (1999)

Townfield Lane, Mollington, Chester, CH1 6NJ

Tel **(01244) 851185**
Fax (01244) 851349
Web www.mollingtongolfclub.co.uk

Mem 500
Sec MJ Olney-Smith
Pro L Corcoran
Holes 18 L 6696 yds Par 72 SSS 72
V'tors WD–U WE–NA before noon
SOC–WD
Fees £25 (£30)
Loc 2 miles N of Chester on A540.
End of M56, 2 miles
Mis Driving range

Mottram Hall Hotel (1991)

Wilmslow Road, Mottram St Andrew, Prestbury, SK10 4QT

Tel **(01625) 828135**
Fax (01625) 829284
Mem 500
Sec M Turnock
Pro T Rastall
Holes 18 L 7006 yds SSS 74
V'tors U H
Fees £45 (£50)
Loc 4 miles SE of Wilmslow
Mis Driving range
Arch Dave Thomas

Peover

Plumley Moor Road, Lower Peover, WA16 9SE

Tel **(01565) 723337**
Fax (01565) 723311
Mem 350
Sec PA Naylor
Holes 18 L 6702 yds Par 72
V'tors U SOC–WD
Fees £18 (£23)
Loc 3 miles SW of Knutsford, off
A556. M6 Junction 19
Arch Peter Naylor

Portal G&CC (1992)

Cobblers Cross Lane, Tarporley, CW6 0DJ

Tel **(01829) 733933**
Fax (01829) 733928
Web www.portalgolf.co.uk
Mem 250
Sec D Wills (Golf Dir)
Pro A Hill
Holes 18 L 7037 yds SSS 73
V'tors U H SOC
Fees £40
Loc 11 miles SE of Chester on
A51. M6 Junctions 16 or 19
Mis Driving range
Arch Donald Steel

Portal Premier (1990)

Forest Road, Tarporley, CW6 0JA

Tel **(01829) 733884**
Fax (01829) 733666
Mem 550
Sec D Wills (Golf Dir)
Pro Miss J Statham
(01829) 733703
Holes 18 L 6508 yds SSS 71
V'tors U SOC–WD
Fees £30 (£35)
Loc 1 mile N of Tarporley on A49
Warrington road

Mis Driving range
Arch Tim Rouse

Poulton Park (1980)
Dig Lane, Cinnamon Brow, WA2 0SH
Tel (01925) 812034/822802
Fax (01925) 822802
Mem 360
Sec E Caise
Pro A Matthews (01925) 825220
Holes 9 L 4978 metres SSS 66
V'tors WD–NA 5–6pm WE–NA
Fees £15 (£17)
Loc Off Crab Lane, Fearnhead

Prestbury (1920)
Macclesfield Road, Prestbury,
Macclesfield, SK10 4BJ
Tel (01625) 828241
Fax (01625) 828241
Mem 700
Sec N Wright
Pro N Summerfield
    (01625) 828242
Holes 18 L 6359 yds SSS 71
V'tors WD–I WE–M SOC–Thurs
Fees £42
Loc 2 miles NW of Macclesfield
Arch HS Colt

Pryors Hayes (1993)
Willington Road, Oscroft, Tarvin,
CH3 8NL
Tel (01829) 741250
Fax (01829) 749077
Web www.pryors-hayes.co.uk
Mem 600
Sec JM Quinn
Pro S O'Connor (01829) 740140
Holes 18 L 6054 yds Par 69 SSS 69
V'tors U SOC
Fees £20 (£25)
Loc Tarvin, 5 miles E of Chester
Arch John Day

Queens Park (1985)
Public
Queens Park Drive, Crewe, CW2 7SB
Tel (01270) 662378
Mem 250
Sec KF Lear (01270) 628352
Pro D Royle
Holes 9 L 4920 yds SSS 64
V'tors WD–U WE–U after 12 noon
    SOC
Fees £6.50 (£8.50)
Loc 2 miles from Crewe, off
    Victoria Avenue

Reaseheath (1987)
Reaseheath College, Reaseheath,
Nantwich, CW5 6DF
Tel (01270) 625131
Fax (01270) 625665
Mem 500
Sec GM Oakes (Hon)
Holes 9 L 3726 yds SSS 58
V'tors M SOC–WD
Fees £7

Loc 2 miles NW of Nantwich on
    College campus
Arch D Mortram

Reddish Vale (1912)
Southcliffe Road, Reddish, Stockport,
SK5 7EE
Tel (0161) 480 2359
Fax (0161) 477 8242
Web www.reddishvale.co.uk
Mem 600
Sec BJD Rendell JP
Pro RE Freeman (0161) 480 3824
Holes 18 L 6086 yds SSS 69
V'tors WD–U exc 12.30–1.30pm–M
    WE–M SOC–WD
Fees £25
Loc 1 mile NNE of Stockport
Arch Dr A MacKenzie

Ringway (1909)
Hale Mount, Hale Barns, Altrincham,
WA15 8SW
Tel (0161) 904 9609
Mem 345 165(L) 41(J)
Sec A Scully (0161) 980 2630
Pro N Ryan (0161) 980 8432
Holes 18 L 6494 yds SSS 71
V'tors Tues–NA before 3pm Fri–M
    Sun–NA before 11am
    SOC–Thurs
Fees £35 (£45)
Loc 8 miles S of Manchester, off
    M56 Junction 6 (A538)

Romiley (1897)
Goosehouse Green, Romiley, Stockport,
SK6 4LJ
Tel (0161) 430 2392
Fax (0161) 430 7258
Mem 625
Sec B Lindley
Pro RN Giles (0161) 430 7122
Holes 18 L 6412 yds Par 70 SSS 71
V'tors U SOC
Fees £30 (£40)
Loc Station 3/4 mile (B6104)

Runcorn (1909)
Clifton Road, Runcorn, WA7 4SU
Tel (01928) 572093 (Members)
Fax (01928) 574214
Mem 375 80(L) 80(J)
Sec WB Reading (01928) 574214
Pro A Franklin (01928) 564791
Holes 18 L 6035 yds SSS 69
V'tors WD–U H exc comp days
    WE–M SOC
Fees £22
Loc Runcorn (A557). M56
    Junction 12

St Michaels Jubilee (1977)
Public
Dundalk Road, Widnes, WA8 8BS
Tel (0151) 424 6230
Mem 200
Sec KB Stevenson
Pro R Bilton (01295) 65241

Holes 18 L 5612 yds SSS 67
V'tors U
Fees On application
Loc Widnes

Sale (1913)
Sale Lodge, Golf Road, Sale, M33 2XU
Tel (0161) 973 3404
Fax (0161) 962 4217
Mem 750
Sec KG Fraser (Hon)
    (0161) 973 1638
Pro M Stewart (0161) 973 1730
Holes 18 L 6126 yds SSS 70
V'tors U SOC–WD
Fees £28 (£33)
Loc N boundary of Sale. M60
    Junction 6

Sandbach (1895)
Middlewich Road, Sandbach,
CW11 1FH
Tel (01270) 762117
Mem 240 115(L) 50(J)
Sec GF Wood
Holes 9 L 5598 yds SSS 67
V'tors WD–U WE/BH–M
Fees D–£20
Loc 1 mile W of Sandbach (A533).
    M6 Junction 17

Sandiway (1921)
Chester Road, Sandiway, CW8 2DJ
Tel (01606) 883247
Fax (01606) 888548
Web www.sandiwaygolf.co.uk
Mem 730
Sec RH Owens
Pro W Laird (01606) 883180
Holes 18 L 6435 yds SSS 72
V'tors H SOC
Fees £35 (£40)
Loc 15 miles E of Chester on
    A556
Arch Ted Ray

Shrigley Hall Hotel & CC (1989)
Shrigley Park, Pott Shrigley,
Macclesfield, SK10 5SB
Tel (01625) 575757
Fax (01625) 575437
Mem 500
Sec Louisa Lawton
Pro T Stevens (01625) 575626
Holes 18 L 6281 yds SSS 71
V'tors U SOC
Fees £36 (£41)
Loc 15 miles from centre of
    Manchester. Airport 10 miles
Arch Donald Steel

Stamford (1901)
Oakfield House, Huddersfield Road,
Stalybridge, SK15 3PY
Tel (01457) 832126
Mem 700
Sec BD Matthews
Pro B Badger (01457) 834829

For list of abbreviations see page 649

Holes 18 L 5701 yds SSS 68
V'tors WD–U WE comp days–after 2.30pm SOC–WD
Fees £20 (£25)
Loc NE boundary of Stalybridge on B6175

Stockport (1905)

Offerton Road, Offerton, Stockport, SK2 5HL
Tel (0161) 427 2001 (Members)
Fax (0161) 449 8293
Mem 510
Sec JE Flanagan (0161) 427 8369
Pro M Peel (0161) 427 2421
Holes 18 L 6326 yds SSS 71
V'tors SOC–WD
Fees £40 (£50)
Loc 4 miles SE of Stockport on A627
Arch Herd/Hawtree

Styal (1994)

Station Road, Styal, SK9 4JN
Tel (01625) 531359 (Bookings)
Fax (01625) 530063
Web www.styalgolf.co.uk
Mem 850
Sec W Higham (01625) 530063
Pro S Forrest (01625) 528910
Holes 18 L 6301 yds Par 71 SSS 70
9 hole Par 3 course
V'tors U SOC
Fees £18 (£22)
Loc 2 miles from M56 Junction 5. Manchester Airport 5 mins
Mis Floodlit driving range
Arch T Holmes

Sutton Hall

Aston Lane, Sutton Weaver, Runcorn, WA7 3ED
Tel (01928) 790747
Fax (01928) 759174
Mem 600 30(J)
Sec M Faulkner
Pro I Smith (01928) 714872
Holes 18 L 6608 yds Par 72
V'tors U SOC–WD
Fees £20 (£24)
Loc 3 miles S of M56 Junction 12

The Tytherington Club (1986)

Macclesfield, SK10 2JP
Tel (01625) 506000
Fax (01625) 506040
Mem 800
Sec D Sheralte (Gen Mgr)
Pro N Coulson
Holes 18 L 6737 yds SSS 73
V'tors U H SOC–WD
Fees £28 D–£35 (£34 D–£45)
Loc N of Macclesfield (A523)
Mis Driving range
Arch Thomas/Dawson

Upton-by-Chester (1934)

Upton Lane, Chester, CH2 1EE
Tel (01244) 381183
Fax (01244) 376955
Mem 750
Sec F Hopley (01244) 381183
Pro PA Gardner (01244) 381183
Holes 18 L 5850 yds SSS 68
V'tors U SOC–WD
Fees £20 D–£30 (£20 D–£30)
Loc Off Liverpool road, near 'Frog' PH

Vale Royal Abbey (1998)

Whitegate, Northwich, CW8 2BA
Tel (01606) 301291
Fax (01606) 301414
Web www.crownsportsplc.com
Mem 650
Sec WG Squires
Pro R Stockdale (01606) 301702
Holes 18 holes Par 71 SSS 71
V'tors U SOC
Fees £35
Loc 2 miles W of Hartford, off A556
Arch Simon Gidman

Vicars Cross (1939)

Tarvin Road, Great Barrow, Chester, CH3 7HN
Tel (01244) 335174
Fax (01244) 335686
Mem 800
Sec Mrs K Hunt
Pro JA Forsythe (01244) 335595
Holes 18 L 6428 yds SSS 71
V'tors U SOC–Tues & Thurs
Fees £25 (£25)
Loc 3 miles E of Chester on A51
Mis Driving range
Arch E Parr

Walton Hall (1972)

Public
Warrington Road, Higher Walton, Warrington, WA4 5LU
Tel (01925) 266775
Mem 350
Sec I England
Pro J Jackson (01925) 263061
Holes 18 L 6843 yds Par 72 SSS 73
V'tors U SOC
Fees £9 (£11)
Loc 2 miles S of Warrington. M56 Junctions 10/11
Arch Thomas/Alliss

Warrington (1903)

Hill Warren, Appleton, WA4 5HR
Tel (01925) 261620
Fax (01925) 265933
Web www.warrington-golf-club.co.uk
Mem 875
Sec NF Morrall (01925) 261775
Pro R Mackay (01925) 265431
Holes 18 L 6210 yds SSS 70
V'tors U SOC–Wed
Fees On application
Loc 3 miles S of Warrington on A49. M56 Junction 10

Werneth Low (1912)

Werneth Low Road, Gee Cross, Hyde, SK14 3AF
Tel (0161) 368 2503
Fax (0161) 320 0053
Mem 315 60(L) 40(J)
Sec M Gregg (0161) 336 9496
Pro T Bacchus (0161) 367 9376
Holes 11 L 6113 yds Par 70 SSS 69
V'tors U exc Sun–NA Sat/BH–M SOC
Fees £18
Loc 2 miles SE of Hyde, nr Gee Cross. M67 Junction 4
Arch Peter Campbell

Widnes (1924)

Highfield Road, Widnes, WA8 7DT
Tel (0151) 424 2440
Fax (0151) 495 2849
Mem 600
Sec VA Rudder (0151) 424 2995
Pro J O'Brien (0151) 420 7467
Holes 18 L 5729 yds SSS 68
V'tors WD–U WE–H NA on comp days SOC–Wed & Thurs
Fees £18 (£24)
Loc Station ½ mile. M62 Junction 7

Wilmslow (1889)

Great Warford, Mobberley, Knutsford, WA16 7AY
Tel (01565) 872148
Fax (01565) 872172
Web www.wilmslowgolfclub.ukf.net
Mem 790
Sec Mrs MI Padfield
Pro J Nowicki (01565) 873620
Holes 18 L 6607 yds SSS 72
V'tors U H exc Wed–NA before 3pm
Fees £40 (£50)
Loc 3 miles W of Alderley Edge

Cornwall

Bowood Park (1992)

Valley Truckle, Lanteglos, Camelford, PL32 9RT
Tel (01840) 213017
Fax (01840) 212622
Mem 300
Pro R Jenkins
Holes 18 L 6692 yds SSS 72
V'tors H (phone first) SOC
Fees £23 (£25)
Loc 2 miles SW of Camelford, off A39, on to B3266
Mis Driving range

Bude & North Cornwall (1891)

Burn View, Bude, EX23 8DA
Tel (01288) 352006
Fax (01288) 356855
Web www.budegolf.co.uk
Mem 695 117(L) 42(J)

Sec Mrs PM Ralph
Pro J Yeo (01288) 353635
Holes 18 L 6057 yds Par 71 SSS 70
V'tors WD–U 9.30–12.30pm, 2–5pm
and after 6.30pm
WE–restricted
Fees D–£25 (£30)
Loc Bude town centre

Budock Vean Hotel
(1922)

Mawnan Smith, Falmouth,
TR11 5LG
Tel (01326) 252102
Fax (01326) 250892
Mem 150
Sec RM Whitwam
Pro A Ramsden (Golf Mgr)
Holes 9 L 5153 yds SSS 65
V'tors H
Fees D–£18 (D–£20)
Loc Falmouth 5 miles
Arch James Braid

Cape Cornwall G&CC
(1990)

St Just, Penzance, TR19 7NL
Tel (01736) 788611
Fax (01736) 788611
Mem 450
Sec M Waters
Pro M Atherton (01736) 788867
Holes 18 L 5650 yds SSS 68
V'tors WD/Sat–U Sun–NA before
noon SOC
Fees £20 (£20)
Loc 1 mile W of St Just. 8 miles W
of Penzance, off A3071
Arch R Hamilton

Carlyon Bay (1926)

Carlyon Bay, St Austell, PL25 3RD
Tel (01726) 814250
Fax (01726) 814250
Mem 500
Sec Y Lister, P Clemo
Pro M Rowe (01726) 814228
Holes 18 L 6560 yds SSS 71
V'tors U–book with Pro
Fees £35
Loc 2 miles E of St Austell
Arch J Hamilton Stutt

China Fleet CC (1991)

Saltash, PL12 6LJ
Tel (01752) 848668
Fax (01752) 848456
Mem 600
Sec DW O'Sullivan
Pro N Cook
Holes 18 L 6551 yds SSS 72
V'tors H–by arrangement SOC
Fees On application
Loc 1 mile from Tamar Bridge, off
A38
Mis Floodlit driving range
Arch Martin Hawtree

Culdrose

Royal Naval Air Station, Culdrose
Tel (01326) 574121 Ext 2413
Mem 173
Sec VC Williams (01326) 572540
Holes 18 L 6432 yds Par 72 SSS 71
V'tors M–play restricted to WE and
evenings
Fees D–£5 (D–£5)
Loc Culdrose, 1 mile S of Helston
on A3083

Falmouth (1894)

Swanpool Road, Falmouth,
TR11 5BQ
Tel (01326) 311262/314296
Fax (01326) 317783
Web www.falmouthgolfclub.co.uk
Mem 500
Sec R Wooldridge
(01326) 314296
Pro B Patterson (Golf Dir)
Holes 18 L 5937 yds Par 71 SSS 70
V'tors U H SOC
Fees £25 D–£35
Loc ¼ mile W of Swanpool Beach
Mis Driving range

Isles of Scilly (1904)

St Mary's, Isles of Scilly, TR21 0NF
Tel (01720) 422692
Fax (01720) 422049
Mem 130
Sec S Watt
Holes 9 L 6001 yds SSS 69
V'tors U
Fees £19
Loc Hughtown 1½ miles
Arch Horace Hutchinson

Killiow Park (1987)

Killiow, Kea, Truro, TR3 6AG
Tel (01872) 270246
Fax (01872) 240915
Mem 550
Sec J Crowson (01872) 240915
Holes 18 L 5274 yds Par 69 SSS 68
V'tors U
Fees £15
Loc 2½ miles S of Truro, off A39
Mis Driving range

Lanhydrock (1991)

Lostwithiel Road, Bodmin, PL30 5AQ
Tel (01208) 73600
Fax (01208) 77325
Web www.lanhydrock-golf.co.uk
Mem 400
Sec G Bond (Gen Mgr)
Pro J Broadway
Holes 18 L 6100 yds Par 70 SSS 70
V'tors U SOC
Fees On application
Loc 1 mile S of Bodmin, off
B3268
Mis Driving range
Arch J Hamilton Stutt

Launceston (1927)

St Stephen, Launceston, PL15 8HF
Tel (01566) 773442
Fax (01566) 777506
Web www.launcestongolfclub.com
Mem 900
Sec C Hicks
Pro J Tozer
Holes 18 L 6415 yds SSS 71
V'tors WD–U H WE–NA
Fees D–£20
Loc 1 mile N of Launceston, off
Bude road
Arch J Hamilton Stutt

Looe (1933)

Bin Down, Looe, PL13 1PX
Tel (01503) 240239
Fax (01503) 240864
Mem 600
Sec Mrs PJ Taroni
Pro A MacDonald
Holes 18 L 5940 yds SSS 68
V'tors U SOC
Fees On application
Loc 3 miles E of Looe
Arch Harry Vardon

Lostwithiel G&CC (1990)

Lower Polscoe, Lostwithiel, PL22 0HQ
Tel (01208) 873550
Fax (01208) 873479
Web www.golf-hotel.co.uk
Mem 350
Sec D Higman
Pro T Nash (01208) 873822
Holes 18 L 5984 yds Par 72
V'tors U SOC
Fees £25 (£29)
Loc ½ mile E of Lostwithiel, off
A390
Mis Driving range
Arch Stuart Wood

Merlin (1991)

Proprietary
Mawgan Porth, Newquay, TR8 4DN
Tel (01841) 540222
Fax (01841) 541031
Sec Mrs M Oliver
Holes 18 L 6210 yds Par 71 SSS 71
V'tors U SOC
Fees 18 holes–£14 9 holes–£10
Loc 4 miles N of Newquay
Mis Driving range
Arch Ross Oliver

Mullion (1895)

Cury, Helston, TR12 7BP
Tel (01326) 240685
Fax (01326) 240685
Mem 700
Sec G Fitter
Pro P Blundell (01326) 241176
Holes 18 L 6037 yds SSS 70
V'tors H (restricted comp days and
open days) SOC–WD
Fees D–£23 (£28)
Loc 6 miles S of Helston
Mis Golf academy
Arch W Sich

Newquay   (1890)

Tower Road, Newquay, TR7 1LT

Tel	**(01637) 872091**
Fax	(01637) 874066
Web	www.newquaygolfclub.com
Mem	600
Sec	G Binney (01637) 874354
Pro	M Bevan (01637) 874830
Holes	18 L 6151 yds SSS 69
V'tors	WD/Sat–H Sun–H SOC
Fees	£30 (£30) W–£90
Loc	Newquay town centre
Arch	HS Colt

Perranporth   (1927)

Budnic Hill, Perranporth, TR6 0AB

Tel	**(01872) 572454**
Fax	(01872) 573701
Mem	600
Sec	DC Mugford (01872) 573701
Pro	DC Michell (01872) 572317
Holes	18 L 6286 yds SSS 72
V'tors	WD–U WE–H SOC
Fees	£25 (£30)
Loc	½ mile NW of Perranporth
Arch	James Braid

Praa Sands   (1971)

Praa Sands, Penzance, TR20 9TQ

Tel	**(01736) 763445**
Fax	(01736) 763399
Mem	225
Sec	D & K Phillips (Props)
Holes	9 L 4122 yds Par 62 SSS 60
V'tors	U exc Sun am
Fees	£15 D–£20
Loc	7 miles E of Penzance on A394 Penzance-Helston road
Arch	RA Hamilton

St Austell   (1911)

Tregongeeves, St Austell, PL26 7DS

Tel	**(01726) 74756**
Mem	780
Sec	K Trahair
Pro	T Pitts (01726) 68621
Holes	18 L 5981 yds SSS 69
V'tors	SOC exc comp days
Fees	On application
Loc	1½ miles W of St Austell

St Enodoc   (1890)

Rock, Wadebridge, PL27 6LD

Tel	**(01208) 863216**
Fax	(01208) 862976
Mem	1360
Sec	Col I Waters MBE
Pro	NJ Williams (01208) 862402
Holes	Church 18 L 6243 yds SSS 70 Holywell 18 L 4103 yds SSS 61
V'tors	Church H–max 24 SOC Holywell–U
Fees	Church £35 (£40) Holywell £15 (£15)
Loc	6 miles NW of Wadebridge
Arch	James Braid

St Kew   (1993)

Pay and play

St Kew Highway, Wadebridge, Bodmin, PL30 3EF

Tel	**(01208) 841500**
Fax	(01208) 841500
Mem	250
Sec	J Brown
Pro	N Rogers
Holes	9 L 4543 yds SSS 62
V'tors	U SOC
Fees	9 holes–£9 18 holes–£14
Loc	2½ miles N of Wadebridge on A39
Mis	Covered driving range
Arch	David Derry

St Mellion Hotel G&CC   (1976)

St Mellion, Saltash, PL12 6SD

Tel	**(01579) 351351**
Fax	(01579) 350537
Web	www.stmellion.co.uk
Mem	850
Pro	D Moon
Holes	Old 18 L 5782 yds SSS 68 Nicklaus 18 L 6651 yds SSS 72
V'tors	U SOC
Fees	From £15
Loc	Tamar Bridge, 5 miles NW of Saltash
Mis	Driving range
Arch	Hamilton Stutt/Nicklaus

Tehidy Park   (1922)

Camborne, TR14 0HH

Tel	**(01209) 842208**
Fax	(01209) 843680
Mem	1000
Sec	R Parker
Pro	J Dumbreck (01209) 842914
Holes	18 L 6241 yds SSS 71
V'tors	H
Fees	£22 (£27)
Loc	3 miles N of Camborne

Tregenna Castle Hotel   (1982)

St Ives, TR26 2DE

Tel	**(01736) 795254 Ext 121**
Mem	297
Sec	J Goodman
Holes	18 L 3549 yds SSS 57
V'tors	U SOC
Fees	On application
Loc	St Ives 1 mile, off A3074

Treloy   (1991)

Treloy, Newquay, TR7 4JN

Tel	**(01637) 878554**
Mem	145
Sec	J Reid
Holes	9 L 2143 yds SSS 31
V'tors	U SOC
Fees	18 holes–£12.50 9 holes–£8
Loc	2 miles E of Newquay on A3059
Arch	MRM Sandow

Trethorne

Kennards House, Launceston, PL15 8QE

Tel	**(01566) 86903**
Fax	(01566) 86981
Mem	450
Sec	C Willis
Pro	M Boundy
Holes	18 L 6188 yds Par 71 SSS 71
V'tors	U
Fees	£24
Loc	2 miles SW of Launceston (A30)
Mis	Driving range
Arch	Frank Frayne

Trevose   (1924)

Constantine Bay, Padstow, PL28 8JB

Tel	**(01841) 520208**
Fax	(01841) 521057
Web	www.trevose-gc.co.uk
Mem	1500
Sec	P Gammon (Prop) PW O'Shea (Sec/Mgr)
Pro	G Alliss (01841) 520261
Holes	18 L 6608 yds SSS 72 9 L 3031 yds SSS 35 9 L 1360 yds SSS 29
V'tors	H SOC
Fees	On application
Loc	4 miles W of Padstow
Mis	3 & 4 ball times restricted (phone first)
Arch	HS Colt

Truro   (1937)

Treliske, Truro, TR1 3LG

Tel	**(01872) 272640**
Fax	(01872) 278684
Web	www.trurogolf.com
Mem	900
Sec	HWD Leicester (Sec/Mgr) (01872) 278684
Pro	NK Bicknell (01872) 276595
Holes	18 L 5347 yds SSS 66
V'tors	U H SOC
Fees	£20 (£25)
Loc	1 mile W of Truro on A390
Arch	Colt/Alison/Morrison

West Cornwall   (1889)

Lelant, St Ives, TR26 3DZ

Tel	**(01736) 753401**
Fax	(01736) 753401
Web	www.westcornwallgolfclub.co.uk
Mem	825
Sec	MC Lack
Pro	P Atherton (01736) 753177
Holes	18 L 5884 yds SSS 69
V'tors	H SOC
Fees	£25 (£30)
Loc	2 miles E of St Ives

Whitsand Bay Hotel   (1906)

Portwrinkle, Torpoint, PL11 3BU

Tel	**(01503) 230470 (Clubhouse)**
Fax	(01503) 230329
Mem	400

Sec   GG Dyer (01503) 230164
Pro   S Poole (01503) 230778
Holes 18 L 5953 yds SSS 69
V'tors U SOC
Fees   £20 (£22.50)
Loc   6 miles W of Plymouth
Arch   Willie Fernie

Cumbria

Alston Moor (1906)

The Hermitage, Alston, CA9 3DB
Tel   (01434) 381675
Fax   (01434) 381675
Mem   180
Sec   H Robinson (01434) 381354
Holes 10 L 5380 yds SSS 66
V'tors U SOC
Fees   D–£9 (D–£11)
Loc   2 miles S of Alston on B6277

Appleby (1903)

Brackenber Moor, Appleby, CA16 6LP
Tel   (017683) 51432
Mem   834
Sec   JMF Doig (Hon)
Pro   G Key (017683) 52922
Holes 18 L 5901 yds SSS 68
V'tors U H
Fees   £18 (£22)
Loc   2 miles SE of Appleby. ½ mile
       N of A66
Arch   Willie Fernie

Barrow (1921)

*Rakesmoor Lane, Hawcoat, Barrow-in-
Furness, LA14 4QB*
Tel   (01229) 825444
Mem   535 99(L) 61(J)
Sec   J Slater (Hon)
Pro   (01229) 832121
Holes 18 L 6184 yds Par 71 SSS 70
V'tors U H Ladies Day–Fri SOC
Fees   £20 W–£85
Loc   2 miles E of Barrow, off A590

Brampton (Talkin Tarn)
(1907)

Brampton, CA8 1HN
Tel   (016977) 2255
Fax   (016977) 41487
Mem   775
Sec   IJ Meldrum (01900) 827985
Pro   S Wilkinson (016977) 2000
Holes 18 L 6407 yds Par 72 SSS 71
V'tors U
Fees   D–£22 (D–£30)
Loc   B6413, 1 mile SE of
       Brampton
Mis   Driving range
Arch   James Braid

Brayton Park (1986)

Pay and play
*Lakeside Inn, Brayton Park, Aspatria,
CA5 3TD*
Tel   (016973) 20840

Mem   60
Sec   D Warwick
Holes 9 L 2521 yds SSS 65
V'tors U
Fees   9 holes–£5 (£6) 18 holes–£7
       (£8)
Loc   1 mile N of Aspatria. 10 miles
       N of Cockermouth

Carlisle (1908)

Aglionby, Carlisle, CA4 8AG
Tel   (01228) 513029
Fax   (01228) 513303
Mem   735
Sec   Mrs HM Rowell
Pro   M Heggie (01228) 513241
Holes 18 L 6278 yds SSS 70
V'tors WD–U exc Tues–NA Sat–M
       Sun–restricted
       SOC–Mon/Wed/Fri
Fees   £25 D–£40 (£30 D–£40)
Loc   ½ mile E of M6 Junction 43,
       on A69
Arch   Mackenzie Ross

Carus Green (1996)

Pay and play
Burneside Road, Kendal, LA9 6EB
Tel   (01539) 721097/737277
Fax   (01539) 721097
Mem   400
Sec   G Corrie
Pro   None
Holes 18 L 5642 yds Par 70 SSS 68
V'tors U SOC
Fees   £10 (£12)
Loc   1 mile N of Kendal on
       Burneside Road

Casterton

*Sedbergh Road, Casterton, Carnforth,
LA6 2LA*
Tel   (015242) 71592
Fax   (015242) 74387
Mem   300
Sec   J & E Makinson (Props)
Pro   R Williamson
Holes 9 L 3015 yds Par 35
V'tors U SOC
Fees   £10 (£14)
Loc   1 mile NE of Kirkby Lonsdale
       on A683. M6 Junction 36, 6
       miles
Arch   Will Adamson

Cockermouth (1896)

Embleton, Cockermouth, CA13 9SG
Tel   (017687) 76223/76941
Fax   (017687) 76941
Mem   539
Sec   RD Pollard (01900) 822650
Pro   None
Holes 18 L 5496 yds SSS 67
V'tors WD–U before 3.30pm exc
       Wed WE–restricted SOC
Fees   £15 (£20)
Loc   4 miles E of Cockermouth
Arch   James Braid

Dalston Hall (1990)

*Dalston Hall, Dalston, Carlisle,
CA5 7JX*
Tel   (01228) 710165
Mem   270
Sec   Jane Simpson
Holes 9 L 2700 yds SSS 67
V'tors U
Fees   9 holes–£6.50 (£7.50)
       18 holes–£10 (£13)
Loc   5 miles SW of Carlisle on
       B5299. 6 miles W of M6
       Junction 42

The Dunnerholme (1905)

*Duddon Road, Askam-in-Furness,
LA16 7AW*
Tel   (01229) 462675
Mem   400
Sec   Mrs ME Tyson
       (01229) 889326
Holes 10 L 6075 yds SSS 70
V'tors U
Fees   £10 (£12)
Loc   6 miles N of Barrow on A595

Eden (1992)

Crosby-on-Eden, Carlisle, CA6 4RA
Tel   (01228) 573003
Fax   (01228) 818435
Mem   700
Pro   S Harrison (01228) 573003
Holes 18 L 6368 yds SSS 72
V'tors U SOC
Fees   £22 (£27)
Loc   5 miles NE of Carlisle, off
       A689. M6 Junction 44
Mis   Driving range

Furness (1872)

*Walney Island, Barrow-in-Furness,
LA14 3LN*
Tel   (01229) 471232
Mem   625
Sec   WT French
Pro   None
Holes 18 L 6363 yds SSS 71
V'tors H SOC
Fees   £17 (£17)
Loc   Walney Island. M6 Junction
       36

Grange Fell (1952)

*Fell Road, Grange-over-Sands,
LA11 6HB*
Tel   (015395) 32536
Mem   300
Sec   M Higginson (015395) 34098
Holes 9 L 4826 metres SSS 66
V'tors U
Fees   £15 (£20)
Loc   W of Grange-over-Sands,
       towards Cartmel

Grange-over-Sands
(1919)

*Meathop Road, Grange-over-Sands,
LA11 6QX*
Tel   (015395) 33180

Fax (015395) 33754
Mem 430 170(L) 40(J)
Sec SD Wright (015395) 33754
Pro A Pickering (015395) 35937
Holes 18 L 5938 yds SSS 69
V'tors H SOC
Fees £20 D–£25 (£25 D–£30)
Loc E of Grange, off B5277
Arch A Mackenzie

Haltwhistle (1967)

*Wallend Farm, Greenhead, Carlisle,
CA6 7HN*
Tel (01697) 747367
Fax (01434) 344311
Mem 300
Sec JD Gilbertson (Hon)
Pro None
Holes 18 L 5522 yds Par 69 SSS 69
V'tors U SOC
Fees D–£12 (£15)
Loc 3 miles W of Haltwhistle on
A69
Arch Andrew Mair

Kendal (1891)

The Heights, Kendal, LA9 4PQ
Tel (01539) 724079 (Clubhouse),
(01539) 723499 (Bookings)
Fax (01539) 733708
Mem 731
Sec R Perry (01539) 733708
Pro P Scott (01539) 723499
Holes 18 L 5769 yds Par 70 SSS 68
V'tors U H SOC
Fees £22 (£27)
Loc 1 mile NW of Kendal

Keswick (1978)

Threlkeld Hall, Keswick, CA12 4SX
Tel (017687) 79010 (Bookings)
Fax (017687) 79861
Mem 900
Sec RC Jackson (017687) 79324
Pro P Rawlinson (017687) 79010
Holes 18 L 6225 yds SSS 72
V'tors U H–book with Pro SOC
Fees D–£20 (£25)
Loc 4 miles E of Keswick (A66)
Arch E Brown

Kirkby Lonsdale

*Scaleber Lane, Barbon, Carnforth,
LA6 2LJ*
Tel (015242) 76365
Fax (015242) 76503
Web www.klgolf.dial.pipex.com
Mem 600 75(J)
Sec G Hall (015242) 76365
Pro C Barrett (015242) 76366
Holes 18 L 6481 yds SSS 71
V'tors U SOC
Fees £24 (£28)
Loc 3 miles N of Kirkby Lonsdale,
off A683
Arch W Squires

Maryport (1905)

Bankend, Maryport, CA15 6PA
Tel (01900) 812605
Fax (01900) 815626

Mem 430
Sec JM Potter
Holes 18 L 6088 yds SSS 70
V'tors U SOC
Fees D–£17 (£22)
Loc 1 mile N of Maryport, off
B5300

Penrith (1890)

Salkeld Road, Penrith, CA11 8SG
Tel (01768) 891919/865429
Mem 750
Sec D Noble (01768) 891919
Pro G Key (01768) 891919
Holes 18 L 6026 yds SSS 69
V'tors WD–H WE/BH–H
10.06–11.30am & after 3pm
Fees £20 D–£25 (£25 D–£30)
Loc ½ mile E of Penrith

St Bees (1929)

*Peckmill, Beach Road, St Bees,
CA27 0EJ*
Tel (01946) 822515,
(01946) 824300 (Clubhouse)
Mem 400
Sec BG Ritson
Holes 9 L 5122 yds SSS 65
V'tors WD–U exc Wed–NA after
4pm WE–NA before 3.30pm
Fees £12 (£12)
Loc 4 miles S of Whitehaven

Seascale (1893)

Seascale, CA20 1QL
Tel (019467) 28202/28800
Fax (019467) 28202
Mem 650
Sec Mrs D Mansey
(019467) 28202
Pro S Rudd (019467) 21779
Holes 18 L 6416 yds Par 71 SSS 71
V'tors U SOC
Fees £21 D–£26 (£26 D–£31)
Loc 15 miles S of Whitehaven
Arch Campbell/Lowe

Sedbergh (1896)

Dent Road, Sedbergh, LA10 5SS
Tel (015396) 21551
Fax (015396) 20993
Mem 350
Sec AD Lord (015396) 20993
Pro J Garner
Holes 9 L 5588 yds Par 70 SSS 68
V'tors U–phone in advance SOC H
Fees £16 D–£22 (£18 D–£25)
Loc 1 mile S of Sedbergh on Dent
road. M6 Junction 37, 5 miles
Arch WG Squires

Silecroft (1903)

Silecroft, Millom, Cumbria
Tel (01229) 774250
Mem 300
Sec DLA MacLardie
(01229) 774342
Pro None
Holes 9 L 5877 yds Par 68 SSS 68

V'tors WD–U WE/BH–restricted
Fees D–£20 (£20)
Loc 3 miles W of Millom

Silloth-on-Solway (1892)

Silloth, Wigton, CA7 4BL
Tel (016973) 31304
Fax (016973) 31782
Mem 800
Pro (016973) 32404
Holes 18 L 6614 yds SSS 73
V'tors U H–booking advisable SOC
Fees D–£28 (£37)
Loc 22 miles W of Carlisle
(B5302). M6 Junction 43
Arch David Grant

Silverdale (1906)

*Red Bridge Lane, Silverdale, Carnforth,
LA5 0SP*
Tel (01524) 701300
Fax (01524) 702074
Mem 500
Sec KD Smith (01524) 702074
Holes 12 L 5559 yds Par 69 SSS 67
V'tors U exc Sun (Summer)–M
Fees £15 (£18)
Loc 3 miles NW of Carnforth, by
Silverdale Station
Mis Extension to 18 holes in 2002

Stony Holme (1974)

Public
St Aidan's Road, Carlisle, CA7 1LS
Tel (01228) 625511
Mem 375
Sec WJ Hodgson (01228) 527112
Pro S Ling
Holes 18 L 5775 yds Par 69 SSS 68
V'tors U SOC
Fees £7.80 (£9.75)
Loc 1 mile E of Carlisle, off A69.
M6 Junction 43
Arch Frank Pennink

Ulverston (1895)

Bardsea Park, Ulverston, LA12 9QJ
Tel (01229) 582824
Mem 745
Sec K Oliver
Pro MR Smith (01229) 582806
Holes 18 L 6201 yds SSS 70
V'tors H or I SOC
Fees £25 D–£30 (£30 D–£35)
Summer £14 D–£18 (£18
D–£22) Winter
Loc 1½ miles SW of Ulverston on
A5087
Arch Herd/Colt

Windermere (1891)

Cleabarrow, Windermere, LA23 3NB
Tel (015394) 43123
Fax (015394) 43123
Mem 700
Sec KR Moffat
Pro WSM Rooke (015394) 43550
Holes 18 L 5132 yds SSS 65
V'tors H SOC

Fees £24 (£28)
Loc 1½ miles E of Bowness
Arch George Lowe

Workington (1893)
Branthwaite Road, Workington, CA14 4SS
Tel (01900) 603460/67818
Fax (01900) 607122
Mem 600 110(L) 85(J)
Sec TF Stout
Pro A Drabble
Holes 18 L 6252 yds SSS 70
V'tors H SOC
Fees £20 (£25)
Loc 2 miles SE of Workington
Arch James Braid

Derbyshire

Alfreton (1892)
Oakerthorpe, Alfreton, DE55 7LH
Tel (01773) 832070
Mem 300
Sec E Brown
Pro J Mellor (01773) 831901
Holes 11 L 5393 yds SSS 66
V'tors WD–U H before 4.30pm –M
 after 4.30pm WE–M SOC H
Fees £16
Loc W of Alfreton (A38). M1
 Junction 28

Allestree Park (1949)
Public
Allestree Hall, Allestree, Derby, DE22 2EU
Tel (01332) 550616
Mem 200
Sec A Maguire
Pro L Woodward
Holes 18 L 5714 yds SSS 68
V'tors WD–U WE–booking req
 SOC
Fees £11
Loc 2 miles N of Derby on A6

Ashbourne (1886)
Wyaston Road, Ashbourne, DE6 1NB
Tel (01335) 342078
Fax (01335) 347937
Web www.ashbournegolfclub.co.uk
Mem 600
Sec P Cook
Pro A Smith (01335) 347960
Holes 18 L 6365 yds SSS 71
V'tors WD–U SOC
Fees £20 (£30)
Loc 1½ miles SW of Ashbourne,
 off A52
Arch David Hemstock

Bakewell (1899)
Station Road, Bakewell, DE4 1GB
Tel (01629) 812307
Mem 305 67(L) 25(J)
Sec F Parker
Pro None

Holes 9 L 5240 yds SSS 66
V'tors WD–U WE/BH–by
 arrangement SOC
Fees £15 (£20)
Loc ½ mile NE of Bakewell and
 A6

Birch Hall
Sheffield Road, Unstone, S18 5DH
Tel (01246) 291979
Mem 300
Sec G Jackson
Pro None
Holes 18 L 6509 yds Par 73 SSS 71
V'tors U
Fees On application
Loc 2 miles N of Chesterfield
 (B60557)
Arch David Tucker

Blue Circle (1985)
Cement Works, Hope, S33 2RP
Tel (01433) 622315
Mem 154
Sec DS Smith
Holes 9 L 5350 yds SSS 66
V'tors M
Loc Hope Valley

Bondhay (1991)
Bondhay Lane, Whitwell, Worksop, S80 3EH
Tel (01909) 723608
Fax (01909) 720226
Mem 470
Sec H Hardisty
Pro M Ramsden
Holes 18 L 6785 yds Par 72
 9 hole course
V'tors U SOC
Fees £17 (£22)
Loc 2 miles E of M1 Junction 30,
 off A619
Mis Driving range
Arch Donald Steel

Brailsford (1994)
Proprietary
Pools Head Lane, Brailsford, Ashbourne, DE6 3BU
Tel (01335) 360096
Mem 106
Sec K Wilson
Pro D McCarthy
Holes 9 L 3148 yds Par 36 SSS 35
V'tors U SOC
Fees 9 holes–£9 (£11.50)
 18 holes–£13.50 (£16.50)
Loc On A52 between Derby and
 Ashbourne
Mis Driving range

Breadsall Priory Hotel G&CC (1976)
Moor Road, Morley, Derby, DE7 6DL
Tel (01332) 832235
Fax (01332) 833509
Mem 900
Sec P Le Roi (Gen Mgr)

Pro D Steels (01332) 834425
Holes 18 L 6201 yds SSS 70
 18 L 6028 yds SSS 69
V'tors WD–U SOC–WD only
Fees £25–£38
Loc Morley, 5 miles N of Derby
 (A61)

Broughton Heath
Bent Lane, Church Broughton, DE65 5BA
Tel (01283) 521235
Fax (01283) 521235
Mem 435
Sec J Bentley
Pro S Stiff
Holes 18 L 3087 yds Par 54 SSS 53
V'tors WD–U WE–booking
 necessary SOC
Fees £8 (£9)
Loc Church Broughton, 1 mile N
 of A516 at Hatton
Arch K Tunnicliffe

Burton-on-Trent (1894)
43 Ashby Road East, Burton-on-Trent, DE15 0PS
Tel (01283) 568708 (Clubhouse)
Fax (01283) 544551
Mem 600
Sec D Hartley (01283) 544551
Pro G Stafford (01283) 562240
Holes 18 L 6579 yds SSS 71
V'tors I H WD–NA before 9am or
 1–2pm SOC
Fees £28 (£32)
Loc 3 miles E of Burton on A511
Arch HS Colt

Buxton & High Peak (1887)
Townend, Buxton, SK17 7EN
Tel (01298) 26263
Fax (01298) 26333
Mem 450
Sec D Roberts
Pro G Brown (01298) 23112
Holes 18 L 5954 yds SSS 69
V'tors U
Fees £23 (£29)
Loc NE boundary of Buxton (A6)

Carsington Water (1994)
Pay and play
Carsington, Wirksworth
Tel (01629) 85650
Mem 300
Sec GWR Coleman
 (Mgr) (01403) 784864
Pro To be appointed
Holes 9 L 6000yds SSS
V'tors U SOC
Fees On application
Loc 8 miles NE of Ashbourne, off
 B5035
Arch John Ludlow

Cavendish (1925)

Gadley Lane, Buxton, SK17 6XD

Tel (01298) 23494
Fax (01298) 79708
Mem 600
Sec JD Rushton (01298) 79708
Pro P Hunstone (01298) 25052
Holes 18 L 5833 yds SSS 68
V'tors U H SOC–by prior
   arrangement with Pro
Fees £26 (£35)
Loc ¾ mile W of Buxton Station.
   St John's Road (A53)
Mis Driving range
Arch Dr A Mackenzie

Chapel-en-le-Frith (1905)

*The Cockyard, Manchester Road,
Chapel-en-le-Frith, SK23 9UH*

Tel (01298) 812118
Fax (01298) 814990
Web www.chapelgolf.co.uk
Mem 640
Sec J Hilton (01298) 813943
Pro DJ Cullen (01298) 812118
Holes 18 L 6054 yds SSS 69
V'tors U
Fees £22 (£30)
Loc 13 miles SE of Stockport, off
   A6 (B5470)

Chesterfield (1897)

Walton, Chesterfield, S42 7LA

Tel (01246) 279256
Fax (01246) 276622
Mem 600
Sec BG Broughton
Pro M McLean (01246) 276297
Holes 18 L 6247 yds Par 71 SSS 70
V'tors WD–U H WE–M SOC–WD
Fees £26–£35
Loc 2 miles SW of Chesterfield on
   A623

Chesterfield Municipal

(1934)

Public

*Murray House, Crow Lane,
Chesterfield, S41 0EQ*

Tel (01246) 273887,
   (01246) 239500 (Bookings)
Fax (01246) 558024
Mem 350
Sec J Hearnshaw
Pro A Carnall (01246) 239500
Holes 18 L 6013 yds SSS 69
   9 hole course
V'tors U
Fees On application
Loc ¼ mile past Chesterfield
   station
Mis Pitch & putt

Chevin (1894)

Duffield, Derby, DE56 4EE

Tel (01332) 841864
Fax (01332) 841864
Mem 500 100(L) 80(J) 70(5D)
Sec JA Milner

Pro W Bird (01332) 841112
Holes 18 L 6057 yds SSS 69
V'tors WD–U WE–M SOC–WD
Fees £27
Loc 5 miles N of Derby on A6

Derby Sinfin (1923)

Public

*Wilmore Road, Sinfin, Derby,
DE24 9HD*

Tel (01332) 766323
Sec P Davidson
Pro J Siddons (01332) 766462
Holes 18 L 6163 yds SSS 69
V'tors U SOC
Fees On application
Loc 1 mile S of Derby, off A52

Erewash Valley (1905)

Stanton-by-Dale, DE7 4QR

Tel (0115) 932 3258
Fax (0115) 932 2984
Mem 675
Sec JA Beckett (0115) 932 2984
Pro MJ Ronan (0115) 932 4667
Holes 18 L 6547 yds SSS 71
V'tors WE/BH–NA before noon
   SOC–WD
Fees £24 D–£29 (D–£29)
Loc 10 miles E of Derby, off A52.
   M1 Junction 25, 3 miles

Glossop & District (1894)

Sheffield Road, Glossop, SK13 7PU

Tel (01457) 865247 (Clubhouse)
Mem 300
Sec DS Booth
Pro D Marsh (01457) 853117
Holes 11 L 5800 yds SSS 68
V'tors U SOC
Fees £20 (£25)
Loc 1 mile E of Glossop, off A57

Grassmoor Golf Centre

Pay and play

*North Wingfield Road, Grassmoor,
Chesterfield, S42 5EA*

Tel (01246) 856044
Fax (01246) 853486
Mem 390
Sec H Hagues
Pro G Hagues
Holes 18 L 5721 yds Par 69
V'tors U–advance booking required
   SOC
Fees £10 (£12)
Loc 2 miles S of Chesterfield on
   B6038. M1 Junction 29, 3
   miles
Mis Floodlit driving range
Arch Hawtree

Horsley Lodge (1992)

Smalley Mill Road, Horsley, DE21 5BL

Tel (01332) 780838
Fax (01332) 781118
Mem 600
Sec G Johnson
Pro G Lyall (01332) 780838

Holes 18 L 6336 yds SSS 70
V'tors WD–U H
Fees On application
Loc 4 miles NE of Derby. M1
   Junction 28
Mis Driving range
Arch GM White

Ilkeston (1929)

Public

*Peewit West End Drive, Ilkeston,
DE7 5GH*

Tel (0115) 930 4550
Mem 100
Sec M Ogden (0115) 944 2304
Pro None
Holes 9 L 4116 yds Par 62 SSS 60
V'tors U SOC–WD
Fees On application
Loc ½ mile E of Ilkeston

Kedleston Park (1947)

*Kedleston, Quarndon, Derby,
DE22 5JD*

Tel (01332) 840035
Fax (01332) 840035
Mem 784
Sec GR Duckmanton
Pro DJ Russell (01332) 841685
Holes 18 L 6675 yds SSS 72
V'tors WD–H–soft spikes only
Fees £30 (£40)
Loc 4 miles N of Derby. National
   Trust signs to Kedleston Hall
Arch James Braid

Matlock (1906)

*Chesterfield Road, Matlock Moor,
Matlock, DE4 5LZ*

Tel (01629) 582191
Mem 496 78(L) 55(J)
Sec J Odell (01629) 582191
Pro M Whithorn (01629) 584934
Holes 18 L 5804 yds SSS 68
V'tors WD–U exc
   12.30–1.30pm–NA
   WE/BH–M SOC–WD
Fees D–£25
Loc 1½ miles NE of Matlock
   (A632)

Maywood (1990)

Rushy Lane, Risley, Derby, DE7 3ST

Tel (0115) 939 2306
Mem 500
Sec T Barrell
Pro S Sherratt (0115) 949 0043
Holes 18 L 6424 yds Par 72 SSS 71
V'tors WD–U before 4pm
   WE–restricted SOC
Fees £15 (£20)
Loc Between Nottingham and
   Derby. M1 Junction 25
Arch P Moon

Mickleover (1923)

Uttoxeter Road, Mickleover, DE3 5AD

Tel (01332) 513339 (Clubhouse)
Fax (01332) 512092

Mem 800
Sec D Rodgers (01332) 512092
Pro T Coxon (01332) 518662
Holes 18 L 5708 yds SSS 68
V'tors U SOC–Tues & Thurs
Fees £22 (£25)
Loc 3 miles W of Derby on A516/B5020

New Mills (1907)
Shaw Marsh, New Mills, High Peak, SK22 4QE
Tel (01663) 743485
Mem 350
Sec P Jenkinson (01663) 744305
Pro S James (01663) 746161
Holes 9 L 5633 yds SSS 67
V'tors WD–U WE–M SOC
Fees £12
Loc 8 miles SE of Stockport
Mis Extension to 18 holes in 2002
Arch David Williams

Ormonde Fields (1906)
Nottingham Road, Codnor, Ripley, DE5 9RG
Tel (01773) 742987
Fax (01773) 744848
Mem 660
Sec K Constable
Holes 18 L 6504 yds SSS 72
V'tors U SOC
Fees On application
Loc A610 Ripley to Nottingham road. M1 Junction 26, 5 miles
Arch John Fearn

Pastures (1969)
Pastures Hospital, Mickleover, DE3 5DQ
Tel (01332) 521074
Mem 320
Sec S McWilliams
Holes 9 L 5095 yds SSS 65
V'tors M SOC–WD
Loc 4 miles W of Derby
Arch JF Pennink

Shirland (1977)
Lower Delves, Shirland, DE55 6AU
Tel (01773) 834935
Mem 450
Sec G Brassington (01246) 852816
Pro NB Hallam (01773) 834935
Holes 18 L 6072 yds SSS 70
V'tors WD–U WE–U after 3pm SOC
Fees £20 (£25)
Loc 1 mile N of Alfreton, off A61 by Shirland Church

Sickleholme (1898)
Bamford, Sheffield, S33 0BH
Tel (01433) 651306
Mem 250 100(L) 72(J)
Sec PH Taylor (Mgr)
Pro PH Taylor
Holes 18 L 6064 yds SSS 69
V'tors U exc Wed am
Fees £26 (£32)
Loc W of Sheffield, between Hathersage and Hope (A625)

Stanedge (1934)
Walton Hay Farm, Chesterfield, S45 0LW
Tel (01246) 566156
Mem 325
Sec W Tyzack (01246) 276568
Holes 9 L 5786 yds SSS 68
V'tors WD–U before 2pm –M after 2pm WE–M SOC
Fees £15
Loc 5 miles SW of Chesterfield, off B5057

Devon

Ashbury (1991)
Fowley Cross, Okehampton, EX20 4NL
Tel (01837) 55453
Fax (01837) 55468
Web www.ashburyhotel.co.uk
Mem 100
Sec N Agnew
Pro R Cade
Holes 18 L 5244 yds SSS 66
18 L 5881 yds SSS 68
18 hole Par 3 course
V'tors WD–U after 12 noon
Fees £15 (£20)
Loc 4 miles W of Okehampton, off A3079
Arch DJ Fensom

Axe Cliff (1894)
Squires Lane, Axmouth, Seaton, EX12 4AB
Tel (01297) 24371
Mem 400
Sec Mrs H Kenworthy
Pro M Dack (01297) 21754
Holes 18 L 5969 yds SSS 70
V'tors U H SOC
Fees £20 (£22)
Loc Nr Yacht Club at Axmouth Bridge

Bigbury (1923)
Bigbury-on-Sea, TQ7 4BB
Tel (01548) 810055 (Clubhouse)
Fax (01548) 810207
Mem 800
Sec MJ Lowry (01548) 810557
Pro S Lloyd (01548) 810412
Holes 18 L 6061 yds Par 70 SSS 69
V'tors H SOC
Fees £27 (£30)
Loc 15 miles SE of Plymouth on B3392
Arch JH Taylor

Chulmleigh (1976)
Pay and play
Leigh Road, Chulmleigh, EX18 7BL
Tel (01769) 580519
Fax (01769) 580519
Web www.chulmleighgolf.co.uk
Mem 100
Sec HM Meadows

Holes Summer 18 L 1450 yds SSS 54
Winter 9 L 2309 yds SSS 54
V'tors U
Fees £6.50 D–£12
Loc 1 mile N of A377 at Chulmleigh
Arch John Goodban

Churston (1890)
Churston, Brixham, TQ5 0LA
Tel (01803) 842751
Fax (01803) 845738
Web www.churstongolfclubunited .co.uk
Mem 983
Sec SR Bawden (01803) 842751
Pro N Holman (01803) 843442
Holes 18 L 6208 yds SSS 70
V'tors H exc Tues am–NA SOC–Mon/Thurs/Fri
Fees £30 (£35)
Loc 5 miles S of Torquay
Arch HS Colt

Dainton Park (1993)
Totnes Road, Ipplepen, Newton Abbot, TQ12 5TN
Tel (01803) 815000
Fax (01803) 815009
Mem 600
Sec M Penlington
Pro M Tyson
Holes 18 L 6210 yds SSS 70
V'tors U SOC
Fees £18 (£20)
Loc 2 miles S of Newton Abbot on A381
Mis Driving range
Arch Adrian Stiff

Dartmouth G&CC (1992)
Blackawton, Totnes, TQ9 7DE
Tel (01803) 712686
Fax (01803) 712628
Mem 800
Sec J Waugh
Pro S Dougan (01803) 712650
Holes Ch'ship 18 L 7191 yds SSS 74;
Dartmouth 18 L 4791 yds SSS 64
V'tors WD–U phone first WE–H SOC
Fees Ch'ship £27 (£35) Dartmouth £15 (£16)
Loc 4 miles NE of Dartmouth on A3122
Mis Driving range
Arch Jeremy Pern

Dinnaton (1989)
Ivybridge, PL21 9HU
Tel (01752) 892512/892452
Fax (01752) 698334
Mem 300
Sec B Rimes
Pro D Ridyard (01752) 691288
Holes 9 L 4100 yds SSS 59
9 hole course Par 64
V'tors U SOC

Fees D–£10 (D–£12.50)
Loc 12 miles SE of Plymouth, off A38/B3213
Arch Pink/Cotton

Downes Crediton (1976)

Hookway, Crediton, EX17 3PT
Tel (01363) 773991
Fax (01363) 775060
Mem 700
Sec PT Lee (01363) 773025
Pro H Finch (01363) 774464
Holes 18 L 5954 yds Par 70 SSS 69
V'tors H SOC
Fees £22 (£25)
Loc 2 miles S of Crediton, off A377

East Devon (1902)

North View Road, Budleigh Salterton, EX9 6DQ
Tel (01395) 442018
Fax (01395) 445547
Mem 850
Sec R Burley (01395) 443370
Pro T Underwood (01395) 445195
Holes 18 L 6231 yds SSS 70
V'tors WD–H NA before 10am SOC–Thurs only
Fees £28 (£36)
Loc 12 miles SE of Exeter

Elfordleigh Hotel G&CC (1932)

Colebrook, Plympton, Plymouth, PL7 5EB
Tel (01752) 336428
Fax (01752) 344581
Mem 660
Sec IC Roberts (01752) 348446
Pro S McAskeil (01752) 348425
Holes 18 L 5527 yds SSS 67
V'tors H–phone first
Fees £25 (£30)
Loc 4 miles E of Plymouth
Arch JH Taylor

Exeter G&CC (1895)

Countess Wear, Exeter, EX2 7AE
Tel (01392) 874139
Fax (01392) 874139
Mem 850
Sec KJ Ham (Golf Mgr) (01392) 874639
Pro M Rowett (01392) 875028
Holes 18 L 6008 yds SSS 69
V'tors WD–U WE–I SOC–Thurs
Fees On application
Loc 4 miles SE of Exeter
Arch James Braid

Fingle Glen (1992)

Tedburn St Mary, Exeter, EX6 6AF
Tel (01647) 61817
Fax (01647) 61135
Mem 450
Sec P Miliffe
Pro S Gould

Holes 9 L 2466 yds SSS 63
V'tors U SOC
Fees 18 holes–£11.50 (£15) 9 holes–£8 (£9)
Loc 5 miles W of Exeter on A30
Mis Driving range

Hartland Forest (1980)

Hartland Forest Golf Parc, Clovelly, EX39 5RA
Tel (01237) 431442
Fax (01237) 431734
Mem 90
Holes 18 L 6015 yds Par 71 SSS 69
V'tors U SOC
Fees £20
Loc 6 miles S of Clovelly, off A39
Arch Alan Cartwright

Hele Park Golf Centre

Pay and play
Ashburton Road, Newton Abbot, TQ12 6JN
Tel (01626) 336060
Fax (01626) 332661
Mem 300
Sec AJ Taylor (01626) 336060
Pro J Langmead
Holes 9 L 2584 yds SSS 65
V'tors U SOC
Fees £14 (£16)
Loc W of Newton Abbot on A383
Mis Driving range
Arch M Craig

Holsworthy (1937)

Kilatree, Holsworthy, EX22 6LP
Tel (01409) 253177
Fax (01409) 253177
Mem 650
Sec B Megson
Pro G Webb (01409) 254771
Holes 18 L 6100 yds SSS 69
V'tors WD–U Sun–U after 2.30pm
Fees £18
Loc 1 mile W of Holsworthy. 7 miles E of Bude (A3072)

Honiton (1896)

Middlehills, Honiton, EX14 9TR
Tel (01404) 44422
Fax (01404) 46383
Mem 800
Sec BM Young
Pro A Cave (01404) 42943
Holes 18 L 5902 yds Par 69 SSS 68
V'tors U (recognised club member) SOC
Fees £23 (£28)
Loc 2 miles S of Honiton

Hurdwick (1990)

Tavistock Hamlets, Tavistock, PL19 8PZ
Tel (01822) 612746
Mem 175
Sec Maj RW Cullen (Mgr)
Holes 18 L 5217 yds Par 68
V'tors U SOC
Fees £14 (£14)

Loc 1 mile N of Tavistock, on Brentor Church road
Arch Hawtree/Bartlett

Ilfracombe (1892)

Hele Bay, Ilfracombe, EX34 9RT
Tel (01271) 862176
Fax (01271) 867731
Mem 500
Sec B Wright
Pro M Davies (01271) 863328
Holes 18 L 5795 yds Par 69 SSS 68
V'tors WD–H SOC WE/BH–U after 10am –NA 12–1pm
Fees £20 (£24)
Loc 2 miles E of Ilfracombe, towards Combe Martin
Arch TK Weir

Libbaton (1990)

High Bickington, Umberleigh, EX37 9BS
Tel (01769) 560269
Mem 475
Sec JH Brough
Pro JN Phillips (01769) 560167
Holes 18 L 6494 yds SSS 72
V'tors U SOC
Fees £15 (£18)
Loc 1 mile S of High Bickington on B3217. M5 Junction 27
Mis Floodlit driving range

Manor House Hotel (1929)

Moretonhampstead, TQ13 8RE
Tel (01647) 440998
Fax (01647) 440961
Mem 250
Sec R Lewis
Pro R Lewis
Holes 18 L 6016 yds SSS 69 Par 3 course
V'tors U H SOC
Fees £30 (£35)
Loc 15 miles SW of Exeter on B3212. M5 Junction 31
Arch JF Abercromby

Mortehoe & Woolacombe (1992)

Easewell, Mortehoe, Ilfracombe, EX34 7EH
Tel (01271) 870225
Mem 225
Sec M Wilkinson (01271) 870745
Holes 9 L 4852 yds SSS 63
V'tors U
Fees 9 holes–£7 18 holes–£12
Loc E of Mortehoe village
Arch David Hoare

Newton Abbot (Stover) (1930)

Newton Abbot, TQ12 6QQ
Tel (01626) 352460
Fax (01626) 330210
Web www.stovergolfclub.com
Mem 750

For list of abbreviations see page 649

Sec GW Rees
Pro M Craig (01626) 362078
Holes 18 L 5764 yds SSS 68
V'tors U H SOC
Fees D–£30 (£28)
Loc 3 miles N of Newton Abbot on A382. A38 Drumbridges Junction
Arch James Braid

Okehampton (1913)

Okehampton, EX20 1EF
Tel (01837) 52113
Fax (01837) 52734
Web www.okehamptongc.co.uk
Mem 500
Sec C Yeo (Admin)
Pro S Jefferies (01837) 53541
Holes 18 L 5243 yds SSS 67
V'tors H SOC
Fees On application
Loc S boundary of Okehampton
Arch JH Taylor

Padbrook Park (1992)

Pay and play
Cullompton, EX15 1RU
Tel (01884) 38286
Mem 450
Sec R Chard (Mgr)
Pro S Adwick (01884) 820805
Holes L 6108 yds SSS 70
V'tors U SOC–WD
Fees 18 holes–£13 (£17) 9 holes–£9 (£12)
Loc 10 miles E of Exeter. M5 Junction 28, 1 mile
Arch Bob Sandow

Portmore Golf Park (1993)

Pay and play
Landkey Road, Barnstaple, EX32 9LB
Tel (01271) 378378
Fax (01271) 378378
Mem 400
Sec C Webber
Pro S Gould, D Everett
Holes 9 L 3048 yds Par 70 9 hole Par 3 course
V'tors U
Fees 9 holes–£10. 18 holes–£12 Par 3 course–£7–£10
Loc 1 mile E of Barnstaple, off A361
Mis Floodlit driving range
Arch Hawtree/Cox

Royal North Devon

(1864)
Golf Links Road, Westward Ho!, EX39 1HD
Tel (01237) 473824 (Clubhouse)
Fax (01237) 423456
Web www.royalnorthdevongolfclub .co.uk
Mem 1100
Sec R Fowler (01237) 473817
Pro R Herring (01237) 477598
Holes 18 L 6665 yds SSS 72
V'tors U H

Fees £32 D–£38 (£38 D–£42)
Loc 2 miles N of Bideford (A39)
Mis Golf Museum
Arch Old Tom Morris

Saunton (1897)

Saunton, Braunton, EX33 1LG
Tel (01271) 812436
Fax (01271) 814241
Web www.sauntongolf.co.uk
Mem 1350
Sec TC Reynolds
Pro AT Mackenzie (01271) 812013
Holes East 18 L 6729 yds SSS 72 West 18 L 6403 yds SSS 71
V'tors U H SOC
Fees £45 D–£65 inc lunch
Loc 6 miles W of Barnstaple
Arch Fowler/Pennink

Sidmouth (1889)

Cotmaton Road, Sidmouth, EX10 8SX
Tel (01395) 513023
Fax (01395) 514661
Mem 850
Sec IM Smith (01395) 513451
Pro G Tapper (01395) 516407
Holes 18 L 5068 yds SSS 65
V'tors U SOC
Fees £20 (£20)
Loc 1/2 mile W of Sidmouth. 12 miles SE of M5 Junction 30
Arch JH Taylor

Sparkwell (1993)

Pay and play
Sparkwell, Plymouth, PL7 5DF
Tel (01752) 837219
Fax (01752) 837219
Mem 108
Sec G Adamson
Pro None
Holes 9 L 5772 yds SSS 68
V'tors U SOC
Fees 18 holes–£10 (£12) 9 holes–£6 (£7)
Loc 8 miles NE of Plymouth. A38 Plympton Junction
Mis 9 hole pitch & putt
Arch J Gabb

Staddon Heights (1904)

Plymstock, Plymouth, PL9 9SP
Tel (01752) 402475
Fax (01752) 401998
Mem 740
Sec RW Brown
Pro I Marshall (01752) 492630
Holes 18 L 5845 yds SSS 70
V'tors WE–H SOC–WD
Fees D–£18 (D–£22)
Loc SE Plymouth, via Plymstock

Tavistock (1890)

Down Road, Tavistock, PL19 9AQ
Tel (01822) 612344
Fax (01822) 612344
Mem 700

Sec MJ O'Dowd
Pro D Rehaag (01822) 612316
Holes 18 L 6250 yds SSS 70
V'tors U SOC–WD
Fees £24 (£30)
Loc Whitchurch Down

Teign Valley (1995)

Christow, Exeter, EX6 7PA
Tel (01647) 253026
Fax (01647) 253026
Mem 300
Sec M Daniels
Pro S Amiet (01647) 253127
Holes 18 L 5913 yds Par 70 SSS 68
V'tors U SOC
Fees £17 (£20)
Loc SW of Exeter, via A38 (B3193)
Arch Peter Nicholson

Teignmouth (1924)

Exeter Road, Teignmouth, TQ14 9NY
Tel (01626) 773614
Fax (01626) 777070
Mem 900
Sec S Wright (01626) 777070
Pro P Ward (01626) 772894
Holes 18 L 6227 yds SSS 70
V'tors WD–H (recognised club member) WE–by appointment SOC–WD
Fees £25 (£27.50)
Loc 2 miles N of Teignmouth on B3192
Arch Dr A Mackenzie

Thurlestone (1897)

Thurlestone, Kingsbridge, TQ7 3NZ
Tel (01548) 560405
Fax (01548) 562149
Web www.thurlestonegc.co.uk
Mem 770
Sec JR Scott
Pro P Laugher (01548) 560715
Holes 18 L 6340 yds Par 71 SSS 70
V'tors I or H
Fees £30 W–£110
Loc 5 miles W of Kingsbridge, off A379
Arch HS Colt

Tiverton (1932)

Post Hill, Tiverton, EX16 4NE
Tel (01884) 252114 (Clubhouse)
Fax (01884) 251607
Mem 600 130(L) 45(J)
Sec C Lansdell (Sec/Mgr) (01884) 252187
Pro M Hawton (01884) 254836
Holes 18 L 6236 yds SSS 70
V'tors H
Fees On application
Loc 5 miles W of M5 Junction 27. 1 1/2 miles E of Tiverton on B3391
Arch Braid/Cotton

For list of abbreviations see page 649

Torquay (1909)

Petitor Road, St Marychurch, Torquay,
TQ1 4QF

Tel	**(01803) 327471**
Fax	(01803) 316116
Mem	800
Sec	BG Long (01803) 314591
Pro	M Ruth (01803) 329113
Holes	18 L 6198 yds Par 69 SSS 70
V'tors	H SOC
Fees	£24 (£28)
Loc	2 miles N of Torquay

Torrington (1895)

Weare Trees, Torrington, EX38 7EZ

Tel	**(01805) 622229**
Fax	(01805) 623878
Mem	400
Sec	Mrs JM Cudmore
Pro	None
Holes	9 L 4423 yds Par 64 SSS 63
V'tors	U exc Sun am–NA
	SOC–Tues/Wed am
Fees	D–£12
Loc	1 mile W of Torrington on
	Weare Giffard road

Warren (1892)

Dawlish Warren, EX7 0NF

Tel	**(01626) 862255**
Fax	(01626) 888005
Mem	600
Sec	T Aggett
Pro	D Prowse (01626) 864002
Holes	18 L 5965 yds Par 69 SSS 69
V'tors	H SOC–Mon/Wed/Fri
Fees	£21.50 (£24.50)
Loc	1½ miles E of Dawlish. M5
	Junction 30

Waterbridge (1992)

Pay and play
Down St Mary, Crediton, EX17 5LG

Tel	**(01363) 85111**
Web	www.waterbridge.business
	.co.uk
Sec	G & A Wren (Props)
Pro	D Ridyard (01837) 83406
Holes	9 L 1955 yds Par 32
V'tors	U
Fees	18 holes–£10 (£12)
	9 holes–£6 (£7)
Loc	1 mile N of Copplestone on
	A377
Arch	David Taylor

Woodbury Park (1992)

Woodbury Castle, Woodbury, EX5 1JJ

Tel	**(01395) 233382**
Fax	(01395) 234701
Mem	720
Sec	PJ Flavin
Pro	A Richards
Holes	18 L 6707 yds SSS 72
	9 L 4582 yds SSS 62
V'tors	U
Fees	18 hole:£35 9 hole:£9
Loc	10 miles E of Exeter on
	A3052. M5 Junction 30,
	6 miles

Mis / Arch

Mis	Driving range
Arch	J Hamilton Stutt

Wrangaton (1895)

Golf Links Road, Wrangaton, South
Brent, TQ10 9HJ

Tel	**(01364) 73229**
Fax	(01364) 73229
Mem	600
Sec	G Williams
Pro	A Whitehead (01364) 72161
Holes	18 L 6083 yds SSS 69
V'tors	H SOC
Fees	£18 (£24)
Loc	Dartmoor, 3 miles E of
	Ivybridge
Arch	Donald Steel

Yelverton (1904)

Golf Links Road, Yelverton,
PL20 6BN

Tel	**(01822) 852824**
Fax	(01822) 854869
Mem	600
Sec	SM Barnes (01822) 852824
Pro	T McSherry (01822) 853593
Holes	18 L 6351 yds Par 71 SSS 71
V'tors	H SOC
Fees	D–£30 (£40)
Loc	6 miles N of Plymouth on
	A386
Arch	Herbert Fowler

Dorset

The Ashley Wood (1896)

Wimborne Road, Blandford Forum,
DT11 9HN

Tel	**(01258) 452253**
Fax	(01258) 450590
Mem	670
Sec	NR Stone
Pro	J Shimmonds
Holes	18 L 6276 yds Par 70 SSS 70
V'tors	WD–U WE–H after 1pm
Fees	Phone in advance
Loc	1½ miles SE of Blandford on
	B3082
Arch	Patrick Tallack

Bournemouth & Meyrick Park (1890)

Pay and play
Central Drive, Meyrick Park,
Bournemouth, BH2 6LH

Tel	**(01202) 290307**
	(01202) 290862 (Bookings)
Mem	400
Pro	L Thompson
Holes	18 L 5637 yds Par 69
V'tors	U
Fees	£11 (£12)
Loc	½ mile behind Town Hall,
	Bournemouth
Arch	Dunn (1894)/Colt (1925)

Bridport & West Dorset (1891)

East Cliff, West Bay, Bridport,
DT6 4EP

Tel	**(01308) 421095/422597**
Fax	(01308) 421095
Mem	500
Sec	PJ Ridler (01308) 421095
Pro	D Parsons (01308) 421491
Holes	18 L 6028 yds Par 73 SSS 69
V'tors	WD/Sat–U after 9.30am
	Sun–U after 1pm SOC
Fees	£22 After noon–£16
Loc	2 miles S of Bridport at West
	Bay
Mis	9 hole pitch & putt course
	(Summer)
Arch	F Hawtree

Broadstone (1898)

Wentworth Drive, Broadstone,
BH18 8DQ

Tel	**(01202) 692595**
Fax	(01202) 692595
Web	www.broadstonegolfclub.com
Mem	650
Sec	C Robinson
Pro	N Tokely (01202) 692835
Holes	18 L 6315 yds SSS 70
V'tors	WD–H from 9.30–11.30am
	and 2–4pm WE/BH–restricted
	SOC–WD
Fees	£35 (£45)
Loc	4 miles N of Poole, off A349
Arch	Dunn(1898)/Colt(1920)

The Bulbury Club (1989)

Bulbury Lane, Lytchett Matravers,
Poole, BH16 6EP

Tel	**(01929) 459574**
Fax	(01929) 459000
Mem	400
Sec	IG Brooks
Pro	N Gravelle
Holes	18 L 6313 yds Par 72 SSS 70
V'tors	U SOC–WD
Fees	£20
Loc	3 miles NW of Poole, off A35

Came Down (1896)

Came Down, Dorchester, DT2 8NR

Tel	**(01305) 813494**
Fax	(01305) 813494
Mem	700
Sec	R Kelly (Mgr)
	(01305) 813494
Pro	N Rodgers (01305) 812670
Holes	18 L 6244 yds SSS 71
V'tors	H Sun am–NA SOC
Fees	£24 (£28)
Loc	2 miles S of Dorchester on
	A354
Arch	Taylor/Colt

Canford Magna

Knighton Lane, Wimborne, BH21 3AS

Tel	**(01202) 592552**
Fax	(01202) 592550
Web	www.canfordmagnagc.co.uk
Mem	1000

Sec T Smith (Mgr)
(01202) 592505
Pro R Tuddenham
(01202) 591212
Holes Parkland 18 L 6495 yds Par
71 SSS 71;
Riverside 18 L 6214 yds Par
70 SSS 70
9 L 1377 yds Par 27
V'tors U
Fees £10–£25
Loc 2 miles E of Wimborne on
A341
Mis Driving range. Golf Academy.
6 holes pitch & putt course
Arch Swan/Smith

Canford School

Canford School, Wimborne, BH21 3AD
Tel **(01202) 841254**
Fax (01202) 881009
Mem 360
Sec M Burley (Mgr)
Holes 9 L 5918 yds SSS 68
V'tors M SOC
Fees £12
Loc 1 mile SE of Wimborne, off
A341
Arch P Boult

Charminster

Proprietary
Wolfedale Golf Course, Charminster,
Dorchester DT2 7SG
Tel **(01305) 260186**
Fax (01305) 261376
Mem 140
Sec D Cox (Prop/Mgr)
(01305) 260186
Pro T Lovegrove (01305) 260186
Holes 9 L 5467 yds Par 69 SSS 67
V'tors U
Fees £11 (£11)
Loc 2 miles N of Dorchester

Chedington Court (1991)

South Perrott, Beaminster, DT8 3HU
Tel **(01935) 891413**
Fax (01935) 891217
Mem 450
Sec D Astill (Man Dir)
Pro S Cronin
Holes 18 L 5950 yds SSS 70
V'tors U SOC
Fees £16 (£20)
Loc 4 miles SE of Crewkerne on
A356
Arch Chapman/Hemstock/Astill

Christchurch (1977)

Pay and play
Riverside Avenue, Bournemouth,
BH7 7ES
Tel **(01202) 436436 (Bookings)**
Mem 320
Sec ME Harvey (01202) 436412
Pro L Moxon
Holes 18 L 6277 yds
9 hole short course
V'tors U SOC

Fees 18 hole: £14.50 (£17.50)
9 hole: £10 (£12)
Loc Bournemouth/Christchurch
boundary
Mis Driving range

Crane Valley (1992)

The Clubhouse, Verwood, BH31 7LE
Tel **(01202) 814088**
Fax (01202) 813407
Mem 600
Sec A Blackwell (Gen Mgr)
Pro D Ranson
Holes 18 L 6421 yds Par 72 SSS 71
9 L 2030 yds Par 33 SSS 60
V'tors H SOC 9 hole–U
Fees 18 hole:£25 (£35)
9 hole:£5.50 (£6.50)
Loc Nr Ringwood, on B3081
Verwood-Cranborne road
Mis Floodlit driving range
Arch Donald Steel

Dudsbury (1992)

64 Christchurch Road, Ferndown,
BH22 8ST
Tel **(01202) 593499**
Fax (01202) 594555
Sec GH Legg
Pro M Thomas (01202) 594488
Holes 18 L 6903 yds Par 71 SSS 73
V'tors U
Fees £32 (£37)
Loc 3 miles N of Bournemouth
(B3073)
Mis Driving range. Academy
course
Arch Donald Steel

East Dorset (1978)

Bere Regis, Wareham, BH20 7NT
Tel **(01929) 472244**
Fax (01929) 471294
Web www.golf.co.uk/edgc
Mem 620
Sec BR Lee (Gen Mgr)
Pro D Honan
Holes Lakeland 18 L 7027 yds
SSS 72;
Woodland 18 L 4887 yds
SSS 64
V'tors U SOC
Fees Lakeland–£30 (£35)
Woodland–£20 (£22)
Loc 5 miles S of Bere Regis, off
Wool road
Mis Driving range
Arch Martin Hawtree

Ferndown (1923)

119 Golf Links Road, Ferndown,
BH22 8BU
Tel **(01202) 874602**
Fax (01202) 873926
Mem 700
Sec T Pond (Mgr)
(01202) 874602
Pro IAB Parker (01202) 873825
Holes 18 L 6452 yds SSS 71
9 L 5604 yds SSS 68

V'tors WD–I H after 9.30am
SOC–Tues & Fri
Fees Old £45 (£60)
President's £18 (£20)
Loc 6 miles N of Bournemouth
Arch Harold Hilton

Ferndown Forest (1993)

Forest Links Road, Ferndown,
BH22 9QE
Tel **(01202) 876096**
Fax (01202) 894095
Web www.ferndown_forest_leisure
.co.uk
Mem 400
Sec M Dodd
Pro M Dodd (01202) 894990
Holes 18 L 5200 yds Par 68 SSS 65
V'tors U SOC
Fees £11 (£13)
Loc 5 miles N of Bournemouth.
N of Ferndown Bypass
Mis Floodlit driving range
Arch Hunt/Grafham

Halstock (1988)

Pay and play
Common Lane, Halstock, BA22 9SF
Tel **(01935) 891689**
Fax (01935) 891839
Mem 200
Sec LR Church (Mgr)
Holes 18 L 4481 yds Par 66
SSS 63
V'tors U SOC
Fees £11 (£13)
Loc 6 miles S of Yeovil, off A37
Mis Driving range

Highcliffe Castle (1913)

107 Lymington Road, Highcliffe-on-
Sea, Christchurch, BH23 4LA
Tel **(01425) 272210/272953**
Fax (01425) 272210
Mem 350 100(L) 50(J)
Sec BE Savery (01425) 272210
Holes 18 L 4776 yds Par 64
SSS 63
V'tors H SOC
Fees £25.50 (£35.50)
Loc 8 miles E of Bournemouth

Isle of Purbeck (1892)

Studland, BH19 3AB
Tel **(01929) 450361**
Fax (01929) 450501
Web www.purbeckgolf.co.uk
Mem 400
Sec Mrs J Robinson (Man Dir)
Pro I Brake (01929) 450354
Holes 18 L 6295 yds SSS 70
9 L 2007 yds SSS 30
V'tors U SOC
Fees £35 D–£45 (£40 D–£47.50)
Loc 3 miles N of Swanage on
B3351. Ferry from Sandbanks
to Studland
Arch HS Colt

Knighton Heath (1976)

Francis Avenue, West Howe,
Bournemouth, BH11 8NX
Tel (01202) 572633
Fax (01202) 590774
Mem 700
Sec R Bestwick
Holes 18 L 6094 yds SSS 69
V'tors WD–H after 9.30am WE–M
Fees On application
Loc 3 miles N of Poole, at junction
of A348/A3049

Lyme Regis (1893)

Timber Hill, Lyme Regis, DT7 3HQ
Tel (01297) 442043
(Clubhouse)
Mem 750
Sec B Wheeler (01297) 442963
Pro A Black (01297) 443822
Holes 18 L 6283 yds SSS 70
V'tors H WD–U after 9.30am
(2.30pm Thurs) Sun–U after
noon SOC
Fees £23 After 2pm–£20
Loc Between Lyme Regis and
Charmouth, off A3502/A35

Lyons Gate (1991)

Proprietary
Lyons Gate Farm, Lyons Gate,
Dorchester, DT2 7AZ
Tel (01300) 345239
Web www.lyonsgategolfclub.co.uk
Mem 80
Sec NW Pires (01300) 345239
Holes 9 L 3834 yds Par 60 SSS 60
V'tors U SOC
Fees 18 holes–£10 (£11)
9 holes–£6 (£7)
Loc Middle Marsh, 12 miles N of
Dorchester (A352)
Arch Ken Abel

Moors Valley (1988)

Public
Horton Road, Ringwood, BH24 2ET
Tel (01425) 480448
Fax (01425) 480799
Mem 310
Sec M Dean
Pro M Torrens (01425) 479776
Holes 18 L 6270 yds SSS 70
4-hole short course
V'tors U
Fees On application
Loc 4 miles SW of Ringwood, off
A31
Arch Martin Hawtree

Parkstone (1910)

Links Road, Parkstone, Poole,
BH14 9QS
Tel (01202) 707138
Fax (01202) 706027
Mem 500 160(L) 75(J)
Sec JM Harper
Pro M Thompson
(01202) 708092
Holes 18 L 6250 yds SSS 70

V'tors H WD–NA before 9.30am
and 12.30–2.10pm WE–NA
before 9.45am and
12.30–2.30pm
Fees £35 D–£50 (£45 D–£60)
Loc 3 miles W of Bournemouth,
off A35
Mis Practice range
Arch W Park Jr/Braid

Queens Park
(Bournemouth) (1905)

Public
Queens Park West Drive, Queens Park,
Bournemouth, BH8 9BY
Tel (01202) 302611,
(01202) 396198 (Bookings)
Fax (01202) 302611
Mem 370
Sec Mrs DJ Gibb (01202) 302611
Pro R Hill (01202) 396817
Holes 18 L 6305 yds SSS 70
V'tors U SOC
Fees £15.50 (£16.50)
Loc 2 miles NE of Bournemouth

Riversmeet Par Three

Stony Lane South, Christchurch,
BH23 1HW
Tel (01202) 477987
Fax (01202) 470853
Mem 250
Sec N Williams
Holes 18 L 1650 yds Par 54
V'tors U
Fees On application
Loc 2 miles W of Bournemouth

Sherborne (1894)

Higher Clatcombe, Sherborne,
DT9 4RN
Tel (01935) 812274
Fax (01935) 814218
Mem 700
Sec P Gamble
(01935) 814431
Pro A Tresidder
(01935) 812274
Holes 18 L 5882 yds Par 70
SSS 68
V'tors H
Fees £22 (£36)
Loc 1 mile N of Sherborne, off
B3145
Arch James Braid

Solent Meads Par
Three

Public
Rolls Drive, Hengistbury
Head, Bournemouth
Tel (01202) 420795
Holes 18 L 2325 yds Par 54
V'tors U
Fees On application
Loc Hengistbury Head, S of
Christchurch
Mis Driving range

Sturminster Marshall
(1992)

Moor Lane, Sturminster Marshall,
BH21 4AH
Tel (01258) 858444
Fax (01258) 858262
Mem 490
Sec DR Holdsworth
Pro G Howell
Holes 9 L 5026 yds SSS 65
V'tors U SOC
Fees 18 holes–£11. 9 holes–£8
Loc 8 miles N of Poole on A350
Arch John Sharkey

Wareham (1908)

Sandford Road, Wareham, BH20 4DH
Tel (01929) 554147/557995
Fax (01929) 557993
Web www.warehamgolfclub.com
Mem 550
Sec G Prince
Holes 18 L 5753 yds SSS 68
V'tors WD–H after 9.30am WE–H
after 1pm SOC–WD
Fees £22 D–£28 (£25)
Loc N of Wareham on A351
Arch C Whitcombe

Weymouth (1909)

Links Road, Weymouth, DT4 0PF
Tel (01305) 773981
Fax (01305) 788029
Web www.weymouthgc.co.uk
Mem 750
Sec BR Chatham
Pro D Lochrie (01305) 773997
Holes 18 L 5981 yds Par 70 SSS 69
V'tors H SOC–WD
Fees £24 (£30)
Loc 1 mile from town centre
(A354), off Manor
roundabout
Arch Braid/Hamilton Stutt

Durham

Barnard Castle (1898)

Harmire Road, Barnard Castle,
DL12 8QN
Tel (01833) 638355
Fax (01833) 695551
Web www.barnardcastlegolfclub
.org.uk
Mem 700
Sec WC Raine
Pro D Pearce (01833) 631980
Holes 18 L 6406 yds SSS 71
V'tors U SOC
Fees £20 D–£26 (£27 D–£32)
Loc N boundary of Barnard Castle
on B6278

Beamish Park (1950)

Beamish, Stanley, DH9 0RH
Tel (0191) 370 1382
Fax (0191) 370 2937

Mem 560
Sec G Cushlow (0191) 370 1382
Pro C Cole (0191) 370 1984
Holes 18 L 6205 yds SSS 70
V'tors WD/Sat–U before 4pm
Sun–NA SOC
Fees £16 (£24)
Loc Beamish, nr Stanley
Arch Henry Cotton

Billingham (1967)

Sandy Lane, Billingham, TS22 5NA
Tel (01642) 554494/533816
Fax (01642) 533816
Mem 850
Sec EI Douglas (01642) 533816
Pro M Ure (01642) 557060
Holes 18 L 6391 yds SSS 70
V'tors WD–H after 9am WE/BH–H
after 10am SOC
Fees D–£25 (£40)
Loc W boundary of Billingham by
A19, E of bypass
Arch Frank Pennink

Bishop Auckland (1894)

*High Plains, Durham Road, Bishop
Auckland, DL14 8DL*
Tel (01388) 602198
Fax (01388) 607005
Web www.bagc.co.uk
Mem 860
Sec A Milne (01388) 663648
Pro D Skiffington (01388) 661618
Holes 18 L 6420 yds SSS 70
V'tors H (closed Good Friday and
Christmas Day)
Fees £22 D–£26 (£28)
Loc ¹/₂ mile NE of Bishop
Auckland
Arch James Kay

Blackwell Grange (1930)

*Briar Close, Blackwell, Darlington,
DL3 8QX*
Tel (01325) 464464
Fax (01325) 464458
Mem 700
Sec PB Burkill (Hon)
(01325) 464458
Pro J Furby (01325) 462088
Holes 18 L 5621 yds Par 68 SSS 67
V'tors U exc Wed
11am–2.30pm–NA
Sat–booking req
Sun–restricted SOC
Fees £20 D–£25 (£30)
Loc 1 mile S of Darlington on A66
Arch Frank Pennink

Brancepeth Castle (1924)

Brancepeth Village, Durham, DH7 8EA
Tel (0191) 378 0075
Fax (0191) 378 3835
Web www.brancepeth-castle-
golf.co.uk
Mem 700 45(L) 100(J)
Sec B Cullen
Pro D Howdon (0191) 378 0183
Holes 18 L 6400 yds SSS 70
V'tors SOC–WD WE–NA

Fees £30 (£35)
Loc 4 miles W of Durham on
A690
Arch HS Colt

Castle Eden & Peterlee (1927)

Castle Eden, Hartlepool, TS27 4SS
Tel (01429) 836220
Web www.ceden-golf.co.uk
Mem 650
Sec D Livingston (01429) 836510
Pro P Jackson (01429) 836689
Holes 18 L 6262 yds SSS 70
V'tors U
Fees £24 (£34)
Loc 2 miles S of Peterlee
Arch Henry Cotton

Chester-Le-Street (1908)

*Lumley Park, Chester-Le-Street,
DH3 4NS*
Tel (0191) 388 3218
Fax (0191) 388 1220
Mem 435 130(L) 90(J)
Sec B Forster
Pro D Fletcher (0191) 389 0157
Holes 18 L 6437 yds SSS 71
V'tors WD–H after 9.30am –NA
12–1pm WE–NA before
10.30am or 12–2pm
Fees £20 (£25)
Loc E of Chester-Le-Street
Arch JH Taylor

Consett & District (1911)

Elmfield Road, Consett, DH8 5NN
Tel (01207) 502186
Fax (01207) 505060
Mem 650
Sec IB Murray (01207) 529324
Pro J Ord (01207) 580210
Holes 18 L 6020 yds SSS 69
V'tors WD–U SOC–exc Sat
Fees £18 (£26)
Loc 14 miles N of Durham on
A691
Arch Harry Vardon

Crook (1919)

Low Job's Hill, Crook, DL15 9AA
Tel (01388) 762429/767926
Mem 450
Sec R Hoggarth
Pro None
Holes 18 L 6102 yds SSS 69
V'tors U SOC
Fees £18 (£25)
Loc ¹/₂ mile E of Crook (A689)

Darlington (1908)

*Haughton Grange, Darlington,
DL1 3JD*
Tel (01325) 355324
Fax (01325) 488126
Mem 825
Sec GW Storey
Pro C Dilley (01325) 484198

Holes 18 L 6181 yds Par 70 SSS 69
V'tors WD–U from 10am–12 &
2–4pm WE–M
Fees £22 D–£31
Loc Off Salters Lane, NE of
Darlington
Arch Dr Alistair Mackenzie

Dinsdale Spa (1906)

*Middleton St George, Darlington,
DL2 1DW*
Tel (01325) 332222
Fax (01325) 332222
Mem 875
Sec EP Davison (01325) 332297
Pro N Metcalfe (01325) 332515
Holes 18 L 6090 yds Par 71 SSS 69
V'tors WD–U exc Tues–NA WE–M
Fees D–£25
Loc 5 miles SE of Darlington

Durham City (1887)

*Littleburn, Langley Moor, Durham,
DH7 8HL*
Tel (0191) 378 0069
Fax (0191) 378 4265
Mem 750
Sec LTI Wilson
(0191) 386 0200
Pro S Corbally (0191) 378 0029
Holes 18 L 6326 yds SSS 70
V'tors WD–U SOC
Fees £22 (£30)
Loc 1¹/₂ miles W of Durham, off
A690
Arch CC Stanton

Eaglescliffe (1914)

*Yarm Road, Eaglescliffe, Stockton-on-
Tees, TS16 0DQ*
Tel (01642) 780098
Web www.eaglescliffegolfclub.co.uk
Mem 835
Sec MR Sample (01642) 780238
Pro P Bradley (01642) 790122
Holes 18 L 6275 yds SSS 70
V'tors U SOC
Fees £26 D–£35 (£36 D–£50)
Loc 3 miles S of Stockton-on-Tees
on A135
Arch Braid (1926)/Cotton (1968)

Hartlepool (1906)

Hart Warren, Hartlepool, TS24 9QF
Tel (01429) 274398
Fax (01429) 274129
Web www.hartlepoolgolfclub.co.uk
Mem 700
Sec LG Gordon (01429) 261723
Pro G Laidlaw (01429) 267473
Holes 18 L 6255 yds SSS 70
V'tors WD–U SOC
Fees £25 (£36)
Loc N boundary of Hartlepool

High Throston (1997)

Hart Lane, Hartlepool, TS26 0UG
Tel (01429) 275325
Mem 240

Sec Mrs J Sturrock
      (01429) 268071
Pro None
Holes 18 L 6247 yds Par 71 SSS 70
V'tors U SOC
Fees £16 (£19)
Loc 2 miles NW of Hartlepool
      (A179)
Arch Jonathan Gaunt

Hobson Municipal

(1978)

Public
Hobson, Burnopfield, Newcastle-upon-Tyne, NE16 6BZ
Tel (01207) 271605
Sec RJ Handrick
Pro J Ord
Holes 18 L 6403 yds SSS 71
V'tors U SOC
Fees £15 (£18)
Loc Between Gateshead and
      Consett on A692

Knotty Hill Golf Centre

(1992)

Pay and play
*Sedgefield, Stockton-on-Tees,
TS21 2BB*
Tel (01740) 620320
Fax (01740) 622227
Sec D Craggs (Mgr)
Holes Princes 18 L 6577 yds Par 72
      SSS 71;
      Bishops 18 L 5886 yds
      Par 70
V'tors U SOC
Fees £13 (£13)
Loc 1 mile N of Sedgefield on
      A177. A1(M) Junction 60,
      2 miles
Mis Floodlit driving range
Arch Chris Stanton

Mount Oswald (1924)

South Road, Durham City, DH1 3TQ
Tel (0191) 386 7527
Fax (0191) 386 0975
Web www.mountoswald.co.uk
Mem 120
Sec N Galvin
Holes 18 L 5984 yds SSS 69
V'tors U SOC
Fees Mon–Thurs £12.50 D–£21
      Fri/WE–£15 D–£25
Loc SW of Durham on A177

Norton (1989)

Pay and play
Junction Road, Norton, Stockton-on-Tees, TS20 1SU
Tel (01642) 676385
Fax (01642) 608467
Holes 18 L 5870 yds SSS 71
V'tors U SOC
Fees £10 (£12)
Loc 1 mile E of A177 on B1274
Arch Tim Harper

Oakleaf Golf Complex

(1993)

Pay and play
*School Aycliffe Lane, Newton Aycliffe,
DL5 6QZ*
Tel (01325) 310820
Fax (01325) 300873
Sec A Bailey (Mgr)
      (01325) 300700
Pro A Waites
Holes 18 L 5821 yds SSS 68
V'tors WD–U WE–booking
      necessary
Fees £7.80 (£8.85)
Loc 1 mile W of Aycliffe on
      A6072, from A68
Mis Floodlit driving range

Ramside (1995)

*Ramside Hall Hotel, Carrville, Durham,
DH1 1TD*
Tel (0191) 386 9514
Fax (0191) 386 9519
Mem 300
Sec TI Flowers
Pro R Lister (0191) 386 9514
Holes 27 holes:
      6217-6851 yds SSS 70-73
V'tors U SOC Soft spikes only
Fees £28 (£35)
Loc 2 miles NE of Durham on
      A690. A1(M) Junction 62
Mis Driving range. Golf
      Academy
Arch J Gaunt

Roseberry Grange

(1986)

Public
*Grange Villa, Chester-Le-Street,
DH2 3NF*
Tel (0191) 370 0670
Fax (0191) 370 2047
Mem 500
Sec R McDermott (Hon)
Pro A Hartley (0191) 370 0660
Holes 18 L 5892 yds SSS 68
V'tors U SOC
Fees £12 (£15)
Loc 3 miles W of Chester-Le-
      Street on A693
Mis Driving range

Ryhope (1992)

Public
*Leechmere Way, Hollycarrside, Ryhope,
Sunderland SR2 0DH*
Tel (0191) 523 7333
Fax (0191) 521 3811
Mem 300
Sec A Brown
Pro None
Holes 18 L 4601 yds SSS 65
V'tors U
Fees £6 (£6)
Loc 2 miles SW of Sunderland, off
      A1018
Arch Jonathan Gaunt

Seaham (1908)

*Shrewsbury Street, Dawdon, Seaham,
SR7 7RD*
Tel (0191) 581 2354
Mem 550
Sec V Smith (0191) 581 1268
Pro G Jones (0191) 513 0837
Holes 18 L 5972 yds SSS 69
V'tors U SOC
Fees On application
Loc Dawdon, 2 miles NE of A19

Seaton Carew (1874)

Tees Road, Hartlepool, TS25 1DE
Tel (01429) 266249/261040
Mem 650
Sec PR Wilson (01429) 261473
Pro W Hector
Holes Old 18 L 6613 yds SSS 72
      Brabazon 18 L 6855 yds
      SSS 73
V'tors U SOC
Fees £27 (£38)
Loc Hartlepool 2 miles
Arch Dr A Mackenzie

South Moor (1923)

*The Middles, Craghead, Stanley,
DH9 6AG*
Tel (01207) 232848/283525
Fax (01207) 284616
Web www.south-
      moorgolfclub.co.uk
Mem 650
Sec B Davison (0191) 388 4523
Pro S Cowell (01207) 283525
Holes 18 L 6271 yds Par 72 SSS 70
V'tors WD–H WE/BH–M
      SOC–WD/Sat
Fees £15 (£26)
Loc 6 miles W of Chester-le-Street
Arch Dr A Mackenzie

Stressholme (1976)

Public
Snipe Lane, Darlington, DL2 2SA
Tel (01325) 461002
Fax (01325) 351826
Sec R Givens
Pro R Givens
Holes 18 L 6511 yds SSS 71
V'tors U
Fees On application
Loc 2 miles S of Darlington on
      A66
Mis Floodlit driving range

Woodham G&CC (1983)

Proprietary
*Burnhill Way, Newton Aycliffe,
DL5 4PN*
Tel (01325) 320574
Fax (01325) 315254
Mem 558
Sec JD Jenkinson
Pro E Wilson (01325) 315257
Holes 18 L 6688 yds Par 73 SSS 72
V'tors WD–U WE/BH–booking
      SOC
Fees £16.50 D–£22 (£26.50)

For list of abbreviations see page 649

Loc 1 mile N of Newton Aycliffe.
6 miles from A1 (A689)
Arch J Hamilton Stutt

The Wynyard Club
*Wellington Drive, Wynyard Park,
Billingham, TS22 5QJ*
Tel (01740) 644399
Fax (01740) 644592
Sec D Whelan (Golf Dir)
Pro A Oliphant
Holes 18 holes Par 72 SSS 73
V'tors M SOC–H
Fees On application
Loc 5 miles E of Sedgefield,
between A1 and A19
Mis Floodlit driving range. Golf
Academy
Arch Hawtree

Essex

Abridge G&CC (1964)
*Epping Lane, Stapleford Tawney,
RM4 1ST*
Tel (01708) 688396
Fax (01708) 688550
Mem 650
Sec Miss L Payne (01708) 688396
Pro S Layton (01708) 688333
Holes 18 L 6703 yds SSS 72
V'tors WD–H WE/BH–NA
Fees £30
Loc Theydon Bois/Epping Stations
3 miles
Arch Henry Cotton

Ballards Gore G&CC
(1980)
*Gore Road, Canewdon, Rochford,
SS4 2DA*
Tel (01702) 258917
Fax (01702) 258571
Mem 600
Sec J Watson
Pro R Emery
Holes 18 L 6874 yds SSS 73
V'tors WD–U WE–M after 12.30pm
(summer) 11.30am (winter)
SOC
Fees £20 D–£25
Loc 1½ miles NE of Rochford

Basildon (1967)
Public
*Clayhill Lane, Sparrow's Hearne,
Basildon, SS16 5JP*
Tel (01268) 533297
Fax (01268) 533849
Web www.basgolfclub.fsnet.co.uk
Mem 300
Sec AM Burch
Pro M Oliver (01268) 533532
Holes 18 L 6236 yds Par 72 SSS 70
V'tors U SOC
Fees £9.50 (£16)
Loc 1 mile S of Basildon, off A176
at Kingswood roundabout

Belfairs (1926)
Public
*Eastwood Road North, Leigh-on-Sea,
SS9 4LR*
Tel (01702) 525345 (Starter)
Holes 18 L 5802 yds SSS 68
V'tors WD–U exc Thurs am.
Booking necessary
Fees £11 (£16)
Loc Between A127 and A13

Belhus Park (1972)
Pay and play
*Belhus Park, South Ockendon,
RM15 4QR*
Tel (01708) 854260
Mem 280
Sec J Cleary
Pro G Lunn
Holes 18 L 5188 yds SSS 68
V'tors U
Fees £9.50 (£14)
Loc 1 mile N of A13/M25
Dartford Tunnel
Mis Floodlit driving range

Bentley G&CC (1972)
Ongar Road, Brentwood, CM15 9SS
Tel (01277) 373179
Fax (01277) 375097
Mem 550
Sec JA Vivers
Pro N Garrett (01277) 372933
Holes 18 L 6709 yds SSS 72
V'tors WD–UH WE–M after noon
BH–after 11am SOC–WD
Fees £22 D–£30
Loc 18 miles E of London. M25
Junction 28, 3 miles

Benton Hall (1993)
Wickham Hill, Witham, CM8 3LH
Tel (01376) 502454
Fax (01376) 521050
Sec M Orwin
Pro C Fairweather
Holes 18 L 6570 yds SSS 72
9 hole Par 3 course
V'tors U SOC–WD
Fees £25–£30
Loc Witham, 8 miles NE of
Chelmsford, off A12
Mis Driving range
Arch Walker/Cox

Birch Grove (1970)
Layer Road, Colchester, CO2 0HS
Tel (01206) 734276
Fax (01206) 734276
Mem 280
Sec Mrs M Marston
Holes 9 L 4532 yds SSS 63
V'tors U exc Sun–U after 1pm
SOC
Fees D–£12
Loc 3 miles S of Colchester on
B1026

Boyce Hill (1921)
Vicarage Hill, Benfleet, SS7 1PD
Tel (01268) 793625
Fax (01268) 750497
Mem 700
Sec PD Keeble
Pro G Burroughs (01268) 752565
Holes 18 L 6003 yds SSS 69
V'tors WD–UH WE/BH–MH
SOC–Thurs only
Fees D–£25
Loc 4 miles W of Southend
Arch James Braid

Braintree (1891)
*Kings Lane, Stisted, Braintree,
CM7 8DA*
Tel (01376) 346079
Fax (01376) 348677
Mem 700
Sec N Wells
Pro T Parcell (01376) 343465
Holes 18 L 6174 yds SSS 69
V'tors WD–U exc Fri–H Sat/BH–H
Sun–NA SOC
Fees £21 (£42)
Loc 1 mile E of Braintree, off
A120 towards Stisted
Arch Hawtree

Braxted Park (1953)
Braxted Park, Witham, CM8 3EN
Tel (01376) 572372
Fax (01621) 892840
Mem 100
Sec Mrs V Keeble
Pro J Hudson
Holes 9 L 5704 yds Par 70 SSS 68
V'tors WD–U SOC–WD
Fees 18 holes–£12.50
9 holes–£9.50
Loc 1½ miles off A12, nr
Kelvedon
Arch Sir Allen Clark

Bunsay Downs (1982)
Public
*Little Baddow Road, Woodham Walter,
Maldon, CM9 6RW*
Tel (01245) 412648/412369
Sec MFL Durham
Pro H Roblin (01245) 222648
Holes 9 L 2913 yds SSS 68
9 hole Par 3 course
V'tors WD–U WE/BH–book in
advance SOC–WD
Fees On application
Loc 7 miles E of Chelmsford, off
A414
Mis Indoor driving range

Burnham-on-Crouch
(1923)
*Ferry Road, Creeksea, Burnham-on-
Crouch, CM0 8PQ*
Tel (01621) 782282/785508
Fax (01621) 784489
Mem 600
Sec Mrs D Evers
Pro S Cardy (01621) 782282

Holes 18 L 6056 yds SSS 69
V'tors WD–H WE/BH–M
Fees £26
Loc 1¹/₂ miles W of Burnham
Arch D Swan

The Burstead (1995)

*Tye Common Road, Little Burstead,
Billericay, CM12 9SS*
Tel (01277) 631171
Fax (01277) 632766
Mem 800
Sec L Mence
Pro K Bridges
Holes 18 L 6275 yds SSS 70
V'tors WD–U H WE–NA pm SOC
Fees £20
Loc 2 miles S of Billericay, off
A176
Arch Patrick Tallack

Canons Brook (1962)

Elizabeth Way, Harlow, CM19 5BE
Tel (01279) 421482
Fax (01279) 626393
Web www.canonsbrook.com
Mem 700
Sec Mrs SJ Langton
Pro A McGinn (01279) 418357
Holes 18 L 6763 yds SSS 73
V'tors WD–U WE/BH–M
Fees £24 D–30
Loc 25 miles N of London
Arch Henry Cotton

Castle Point (1988)

Public
*Waterside Farm, Somnes Avenue,
Canvey Island, SS8 9FG*
Tel (01268) 510830
Mem 240
Sec Mrs D Archer
(01268) 696298
Pro M Utteridge (01268) 510830
Holes 18 L 6153 yds SSS 69
V'tors U SOC
Fees £9 (£13)
Loc On A130 to Canvey Island, off
A13 Eastbound
Mis Driving range
Arch Golf Landscapes

Channels (1974)

*Belsteads Farm Lane, Little Waltham,
Chelmsford, CM3 3PT*
Tel (01245) 440005
Fax (01245) 442032
Mem 650
Sec AM Squire
Pro IB Sinclair (01245) 441056
Holes 18 L 6402 yds Par 71 SSS 71
18 L 4779 yds Par 67 SSS 63
V'tors WD–U WE–M SOC
Fees £28 D–£40
Loc 3 miles NE of Chelmsford on
A130
Mis Pitch & putt course. Driving
range

Chelmsford (1893)

Widford, Chelmsford, CM2 9AP
Tel (01245) 256483
Fax (01245) 256483
Web www.chelmsfordgc.sagehost
.co.uk
Mem 650
Sec G Winckless (01245) 256483
Pro M Welch (01245) 257079
Holes 18 L 5981 yds SSS 69
V'tors WD–H WE/BH–M SOC
Fees £36 D–£46
Loc Off A1016 at Widford
roundabout
Arch HS Colt

Chigwell (1925)

High Road, Chigwell, IG7 5BH
Tel (020) 8500 2059
Fax (020) 8501 3410
Mem 700
Sec RH Danzey
Pro R Beard (020) 8500 2384
Holes 18 L 6279 yds SSS 70
V'tors WD–H WE/BH–M
Fees £35 D–£45
Loc 13 miles NE of London (A113)
Arch Hawtree/Taylor

Clacton-on-Sea (1892)

West Road, Clacton-on-Sea, CO15 1AJ
Tel (01255) 421919
Fax (01255) 424602
Mem 650
Sec JH Wiggam (01255) 421919
Pro SJ Levermore (01255) 426304
Holes 18 L 6532 yds SSS 71
V'tors H WE/BH–H after 11am SOC
Fees £20 (£30)
Loc On sea front

Colchester (1907)

Braiswick, Colchester, CO4 5AU
Tel (01206) 853396
Fax (01206) 852698
Mem 745
Sec T Peck
Pro M Angel (01206) 853920
Holes 18 L 6347 yds SSS 70
V'tors WD/WE–H BH–NA SOC
Fees £27.50 D–£37.50 (£40)
Loc ³/₄ mile NW of Colchester
North Station, towards West
Bergholt on B1508
Arch James Braid

Colne Valley (1991)

Station Road, Earls Colne, CO6 2LT
Tel (01787) 224343
Fax (01787) 224126
Mem 500
Sec T Smith (01787) 224343
Pro R Taylor (01787) 224233
Holes 18 L 6301 yds SSS 70
V'tors WD–U WE/BH–after 11am
SOC
Fees £25 (£30)
Loc 12 miles W of Colchester
(A1124)
Arch Howard Swann

Crondon Park (1994)

Proprietary
Stock Road, Stock, CM4 9DP
Tel (01277) 841115
Fax (01277) 841356
Web www.crondon.com
Mem 875
Sec P Cranwell
Pro P Barham
(01277) 841887
Holes 18 L 6585 yds SSS 71
9 hole course
V'tors WD–U WE–M SOC–WD
Fees £20 (£30)
Loc 5 miles S of Chelmsford on
B1007. M25 Junction 28
Mis Driving range
Arch Martin Gillett

Elsenham Golf Centre (1997)

*Hall Road, Elsenham, Bishop's
Stortford, CM22 6DH*
Tel (01279) 812865
Fax (01279) 816970
Sec O McKenna (Prop)
Pro O McKenna
Holes 9 L 5854 yds Par 70
V'tors U
Fees 9 holes–£10 (£12)
18 holes–£14 (£16)
Loc Off M11, by Stansted
Airport
Mis Driving range

Epping Forest G&CC (1994)

*Woolston Manor, Abridge Road,
Chigwell, IG7 6BX*
Tel (020) 8500 2549
Fax (020) 8501 5452
Mem 650
Sec M Williamson (Golf Dir)
(0181) 501 7614
Pro C Stephenson
(0181) 559 8272
Holes 18 L 6408 yds SSS 71
V'tors H SOC–WD
Fees £28 (£38)
Loc 1 mile from M11 Junction 5
Mis Floodlit driving range
Arch Neil Coles

Essex G&CC (1990)

Earls Colne, Colchester, CO6 2NS
Tel (01787) 224466
Fax (01787) 224410
Web www.the-essex.co.uk
Mem 600
Sec DJ Clark
Pro M Spooner
Holes 18 L 6982 yds Par 73
9 L 2771 yds Par 34
V'tors U SOC–WD
Fees £20 (£25)
Loc 2 miles N of A120 at
Coggeshall on B1024
Mis Floodlit driving range.
Arch Reg Plumbridge

The Essex Golf Complex
(1993)
Pay and play
Garon Park, Eastern Avenue, Southend-on-Sea, SS9 4PT
Tel   (01702) 601701
Fax   (01702) 601033
Mem   700
Sec   Mrs J Jacom
Pro   G Jacom
Holes 18 L 6237 yds SSS 70
           9 hole Par 3 course
V'tors U SOC
Fees   £16 (£21)
Loc   E side of Southend-on-Sea.
           M25 Junction 29
Mis   Floodlit driving range
Arch   Walker/Cox

Fairlop Waters (1987)
Public
Forest Road, Barkingside, Ilford, IG6 3JA
Tel   (020) 8500 9911
Mem   135
Sec   L Quinn
Pro   B Preston (0181) 501 1881
Holes 18 L 6288 yds SSS 72
           9 hole Par 3 course
V'tors U
Fees   £7.50 (£11)
Loc   2 miles from S end of M11, by
           Fairlop underground station
Mis   Driving range

Five Lakes Hotel G&CC
(1974)
Colchester Road, Tolleshunt Knights, Maldon, CM9 8HX
Tel   (01621) 868888
Fax   (01621) 869696
Mem   600
Sec   M Tucker (01621) 862307
Pro   G Carter (01621) 862326
Holes Links 18 L 6250 yds SSS 70
           Lakes 18 L 6765 yds SSS 72
V'tors U BH–U after 1pm SOC
Fees   Links £18 (£25) Lakes £25
           (£33)
Loc   8 miles S of Colchester, off
           B1026
Mis   Driving range
Arch   Neil Coles

Forrester Park (1975)
Beckingham Road, Great Totham, Maldon, CM9 8EA
Tel   (01621) 891406
Fax   (01621) 891406
Mem   900
Sec   T Forrester-Muir
Pro   G Pike (01621) 893456
Holes 18 L 6073 yds SSS 69
V'tors WD–U WE–NA before noon
           SOC–WD
Fees   £18 (£20)
Loc   3 miles NE of Maldon on
           B1022
Arch   Everett/Forrester-Muir

Frinton (1895)
1 The Esplanade, Frinton-on-Sea, CO13 9EP
Tel   (01255) 674618
Fax   (01255) 674618
Mem   850
Sec   Lt Col RW Attrill
Pro   P Taggart (01255) 671618
Holes 18 L 6259 yds SSS 70
           9 L 2508 yds SSS 33
V'tors 18 hole: H WE/BH–NA before
           11.30am SOC
Fees   18 hole: D–£26. 9 hole: £10
Loc   18 miles E of Colchester
Arch   W Park Jr/HS Colt

Gosfield Lake (1986)
The Manor House, Gosfield, Halstead, CO9 1SE
Tel   (01787) 474747
Fax   (01787) 476044
Web   www.gosfield-lake-golf-
           club.co.uk
Mem   800
Sec   JA O'Shea (Sec/Mgr)
Pro   R Wheeler (01787) 474488
Holes Lakes 18 L 6756 yds SSS 72
           Meadows 9 L 4180 yds Par 66
V'tors Lakes WD–H WE(pm)–H by
           arrangement SOC.
           Meadows–U
Fees   Lakes £25 D–£30
           Meadows £12 D–£15
Loc   7 miles N of Braintree
           (A1017)
Arch   Sir H Cotton/Swann

Hainault Forest (1912)
Public
Romford Road, Chigwell Row, IG7 4QW
Tel   (020) 8500 2131
           (Caddy Master),
           (020) 8500 2097 (Clubhouse)
Mem   630
Sec   Mrs V Krinks
           (0181) 500 0385
Pro   CS Hope (0181) 500 2131
Holes No 1 18 L 5754 yds SSS 67
           No 2 18 L 6600 yds SSS 71
V'tors U
Fees   On application
Loc   Hog Hill, Redbridge

Hanover G&CC (1991)
Owned privately
Hullbridge Road, Rayleigh, SS6 9QS
Tel   (01702) 232377
Fax   (01702) 231811
Mem   700
Sec   T Harrold
Pro   A Blackburn
Holes Georgian 18 L 6669 yds
           SSS 72;
           Regency 18 L 3700 yds
           SSS 58
V'tors Georgian:WD–H WE–M SOC
           Regency:U SOC
Fees   Georgian £25 D–£35 Regency
           £11.75 (£14.10)
Loc   3 miles NW of Southend
Arch   Reg Plumbridge

Hartswood (1967)
Public
King George's Playing Fields, Brentwood, CM14 5AE
Tel   (01277) 214830 (Bookings)
Mem   400
Sec   M Freeman (01227) 218850
Pro   S Cole (01277) 218714
Holes 18 L 6192 yds SSS 70
V'tors WD–U after 1pm SOC
Fees   On application
Loc   E of Brentwood on A128

Harwich & Dovercourt
(1906)
Station Road, Parkeston, Harwich, CO12 4NZ
Tel   (01255) 503616
Fax   (01255) 503323
Mem   400
Sec   JA Eldridge
Pro   None
Holes 9 L 2950 yds SSS 69
V'tors WD–H WE–M SOC
Fees   £18
Loc   A120 to roundabout to
           Harwich Port, course entrance
           20 yds on LHS

Ilford (1907)
Wanstead Park Road, Ilford, IG1 3TR
Tel   (020) 8554 2930
Fax   (020) 8554 0822
Mem   400
Sec   FLK Clapp
Pro   S Dowsett (020) 8554 0094
Holes 18 L 5299 yds SSS 66
V'tors WD–U WE–phone Pro SOC
Fees   £16 (£20)
Loc   S end of M11, off A406

Langdon Hills (1991)
Lower Dunton Road, Bulphan, RM14 3TY
Tel   (01268) 548444/544300
Fax   (01268) 490084
Mem   500
Sec   B Hardie
Pro   T Moncur (01268) 544300
Holes 27 holes:
           Langdon 9 L 3132 yds Par 35
           Bulphan 9 L 3372 yds Par 37
           Horndon 9 L 3054 yds Par 36
V'tors U SOC
Fees   £14.85 (£19.75)
Loc   SW of Basildon between A127
           and A13. M25 Junction 29, 8
           miles
Mis   Floodlit driving range
Arch   MRM Sandow

Lexden Wood (1993)
Pay and play
Bakers Lane, Colchester, CO3 4AU
Tel   (01206) 843333
Fax   (01206) 854775
Mem   850
Sec   J Rittzato
Pro   P Grice
Holes 18 L 5608 yds Par 67 SSS 64

V'tors U SOC
Fees £18 (£20)
Loc NW of Colchester, off A12
Mis Driving range. Pitch & putt course
Arch Jon Johnson

Loughton (1981)

Public
Clays Lane, Debden Green, Loughton, IG10 2RZ
Tel (020) 8502 2923
Mem 100
Sec A Day
Pro R Layton
Holes 9 L 4735 yds SSS 63
V'tors U–booking required SOC
Fees 18 holes–£11 (£13)
9 holes–£6.50 (£7.50)
Loc M25 Junction 26

Maldon (1891)

Beeleigh Langford, Maldon, CM9 6LL
Tel (01621) 853212
Fax (01621) 855232
Mem 400
Sec GR Bezant
Holes 9 L 6253 yds Par 71 SSS 70
V'tors WD–U H WE–M SOC
Fees £15 D–£20
Loc 3 miles NW of Maldon on B1019

Maylands (1936)

Harold Park, Romford, RM3 0AZ
Tel (017083) 42055
Fax (017083) 73080
Mem 600
Sec (017083) 73080
Pro JS Hopkin (017083) 46466
Holes 18 L 6351 yds SSS 70
V'tors WD–H WE/BH–M SOC H
Fees £20 (£30)
Loc 2 miles E of Romford on A12.
M25 Junction 28, 1 mile
Arch HS Colt

Nazeing (1992)

Middle Street, Nazeing, EN9 2LW
Tel (01992) 893798/893915
Fax (01992) 893882
Mem 350
Sec J Speller (01992) 893915
Pro R Green (01992) 893798
Holes 18 L 6598 yds SSS 71
V'tors WD–H WE/BH–H after 11am SOC
Fees £20 (£28)
Loc 3 miles SW of Harlow. M11 Junction 7
Mis Open air driving range
Arch Martin Gillett

North Weald (1996)

Rayley Lane, North Weald, Epping, CM16 6AR
Tel (01992) 522118
Fax (01992) 522881
Mem 500
Sec PH Newson

Pro D Rawlings (01992) 524725
Holes 18 L 6311 yds Par 71 SSS 70
V'tors H SOC–WD
Fees £20 (£27.50)
Loc 1½ miles E of M11 Junction 7 on A414
Mis Driving range
Arch David Williams

The Notleys (1995)

The Green, Black Notley, Witham, CM8 1RG
Tel (01376) 329328
Mem 300
Sec R Mortier
Pro D Bugg
Holes 18 L 6022 yds Par 71
9 hole Par 3 course
V'tors U SOC
Fees £11 (£15)
Loc Black Notley, S of Braintree, off A120
Mis Practice range
Arch John Day

Orsett (1899)

Brentwood Road, Orsett, RM16 3DS
Tel (01375) 891352
Fax (01375) 892471
Mem 700
Sec SL Sheppard (01375) 893409
Pro P Joiner (01375) 891797
Holes 18 L 6614 yds SSS 72
V'tors WD–H WE–M SOC–WD exc Thurs & Fri
Fees £25–£35
Loc 4 miles NE of Grays on A128.
M25 Junction 30/31
Arch James Braid

The Priors (1992)

Horseman's Side, Tysea Hill, Stapleford Abbotts, RM4 1JU
Tel (01708) 381108,
(01708) 373344 (Bookings)
Fax (01708) 386345
Sec D Eagle (Gen Mgr)
Pro J Stanion
Holes 18 L 5720 yds SSS 68
V'tors U SOC
Fees £11–£15
Loc 3 miles N of Romford. M25 Junction 28
Arch Howard Swann

Regiment Way Golf Centre (1995)

Pay and play
Back Lane, Little Waltham, Chelmsford, CM3 3PR
Tel (01245) 361100
Sec R Pamphilon
Pro D Marsh
Holes 9 L 4887 yds Par 65 SSS 64
V'tors U
Fees 9 holes–£8 (£9) 18 holes–£11 (£12)
Loc 3 miles NE of Chelmsford (A130)
Mis Floodlit driving range

Risebridge (1972)

Pay and play
Risebridge Chase, Lower Bedfords Road, Romford, RM1 4DG
Tel (01708) 741429
Mem 175
Sec L Bushell
Pro P Jennings
Holes 18 L 6394 yds SSS 71
9 hole Par 3 course
V'tors U
Fees £12 (£14)
Loc 2 miles from M25 Junction 28, off A12
Mis Driving range
Arch F Hawtree

Rochford Hundred (1893)

Rochford Hall, Hall Road, Rochford, SS4 1NW
Tel (01702) 544302
Fax (01702) 541343
Mem 375 90(L) 60(J)
Sec AH Bondfield
Pro GS Hill
Holes 18 L 6256 yds SSS 70
V'tors WD–U H WE–M
Fees On application
Loc 4 miles N of Southend-on-Sea
Arch James Braid

Romford (1894)

Heath Drive, Gidea Park, Romford, RM2 5QB
Tel (01708) 740007
(Members)
Fax (01708) 752157
Mem 680
Sec Mrs H Robinson
(01708) 740986
Pro H Flatman
(01708) 749393
Holes 18 L 6395 yds SSS 70
V'tors WD–I WE–NA SOC
Fees £25 D–£35
Loc 1 mile E of Romford. 3 miles W of M25 Junction 29
Arch HS Colt

Royal Epping Forest (1888)

Public
Forest Approach, Station Road, Chingford, London E4 7AZ
Tel (020) 8529 6407
Fax (020) 8559 4664
Mem 300 50(L) 25(J)
Sec Mrs P Runciman
(0181) 529 2195
Pro A Traynor
(0181) 529 5708
Holes 18 L 6220 yds SSS 70
V'tors U–booking necessary SOC
Fees £10.70 (£14.80)
Loc Nr Chingford station
Mis Red coats or trousers compulsory

For list of abbreviations see page 649

Saffron Walden (1919)

Windmill Hill, Saffron Walden,
CB10 1BX

Tel	**(01799) 522689**
Fax	(01799) 522786
Mem	950
Sec	DH Smith (Mgr)
	(01799) 522786
Pro	P Davis (01799) 527728
Holes	18 L 6606 yds SSS 72
V'tors	WD–U H WE/BH–M SOC
Fees	£35
Loc	Saffron Walden, on B184

St Cleres

St Cleres Hall, Stanford-le-Hope,
SS17 0LX

Tel	**(01375) 361565**
Mem	500
Sec	D Wood (01375) 361565
Pro	D Wood (01375) 361565
Holes	18 holes Par 72 SSS 71
V'tors	U H SOC
Fees	£15 (£20)
Loc	5 miles E of M25 Junction 30/31 (A13)
Mis	Driving range
Arch	Adrian Stiff

South Essex G&CC

Herongate, Brentwood, CM13 3LW

Tel	**(01277) 811289**
Fax	(01277) 811304
Web	www.americangolf.com
Mem	600
Sec	R Brewer (Gen Mgr)
Pro	G Stewart
Holes	18 L 6851 yds Par 72 SSS 73
	9 L 3102 yds Par 35
V'tors	U SOC
Fees	£16 (£21)
Loc	4 miles E of M25 Junction 29 (A127/A128)
Mis	Driving range. Golf Academy
Arch	Reg Plumbridge

Stapleford Abbotts (1989)

Horseman's Side, Tysea Hill, Stapleford
Abbotts, RM4 1JU

Tel	**(01708) 381108**
Fax	(01708) 386345
Mem	750
Sec	D Eagle (Gen Mgr)
Pro	J Stanion (01708) 381108
Holes	18 L 6501 yds SSS 71
	9 hole Par 3 course
V'tors	WD–U WE–H SOC
Fees	£25–£45
Loc	3 miles N of Romford. M25 Junction 28
Arch	Howard Swann

Stock Brook Manor (1992)

Queen's Park Avenue, Stock, Billericay,
CM12 0SP

Tel	**(01277) 653616**
Fax	(01277) 633063

Mem	750
Sec	K Roe (Dir)
Pro	K Merry
Holes	18 L 6905 yds SSS 73
	9 L 2952 yds SSS 69
V'tors	H–booking necessary
Fees	£25 (£30)
Loc	5 miles S of Chelmsford on B1007
Mis	Driving range. Par 3 course
Arch	Martin Gillett

Theydon Bois (1897)

Theydon Bois, Epping, CM16 4EH

Tel	**(01992) 813054**
Fax	(01992) 813054
Mem	600
Sec	RS Blower
Pro	RJ Hall (01992) 812460
Holes	18 L 5480 yds SSS 68
V'tors	U exc Thurs am–restricted SOC
Fees	£26 After 2pm–£22
Loc	1 mile S of Epping. M25 Junction 26
Arch	James Braid

Thorndon Park (1920)

Ingrave, Brentwood, CM13 3RH

Tel	**(01277) 810345**
Fax	(01277) 810645
Mem	450 140(L) 60(J)
Sec	Lt Col RM Estcourt
Pro	BV White (01277) 810736
Holes	18 L 6492 yds SSS 71
V'tors	WD–I WE/BH–M
Fees	£40 D–£55
Loc	2 miles SE of Brentwood on A128
Arch	HS Colt

Thorpe Hall (1907)

Thorpe Hall Avenue, Thorpe Bay,
SS1 3AT

Tel	**(01702) 582205**
Fax	(01702) 584498
Mem	750
Sec	RM O'Hara
Pro	WJ McColl
	(01702) 588195
Holes	18 L 6319 yds SSS 71
V'tors	WD–H SOC–Fri only
Fees	On application
Loc	E of Southend-on-Sea

Three Rivers (1973)

Stow Road, Purleigh, Chelmsford,
CM3 6RR

Tel	**(01621) 828631**
Fax	(01621) 828060
Web	www.clubhaus.com
Mem	800
Sec	J Martin (Gen Mgr)
Pro	S Clark
Holes	Kings 18 L 6449 yds Par 72 SSS 71
	Jubilee 18 L 4501 yds Par 64 SSS 62
V'tors	WD–U exc Mon & Wed–NA before 11.30am WE–U after 1.30pm SOC

Fees	Kings £20 (£25) Jubilee £10 (£12.50)
Loc	Cold Norton, 5 miles S of Maldon
Arch	Hawtree

Toot Hill (1991)

School Road, Toot Hill, Ongar,
CM5 9PU

Tel	**(01277) 365747**
Fax	(01277) 364509
Mem	400
Sec	Mrs Cameron
Pro	M Bishop
Holes	18 L 6053 yds Par 70 SSS 69
V'tors	H WE–NA before 1pm SOC–WD
Fees	£25 (£30)
Loc	2 miles W of Ongar
Mis	Practice range
Arch	Martin Gillett

Top Meadow (1986)

Fen Lane, North Ockendon,
RM14 3PR

Tel	**(01708) 852239 (Clubhouse)**
Sec	D Stock
Pro	K Smith (01708) 859545
Holes	18 L 6227 yds Par 72
V'tors	WD–U WE–M SOC
Fees	£12
Loc	N Ockendon, off B186
Mis	Driving range

Towerlands (1985)

Panfield Road, Braintree, CM7 5BJ

Tel	**(01376) 326802**
Fax	(01376) 552487
Mem	300
Sec	R Crane
Pro	(01376) 347951
Holes	9 L 5559 yds Par 68
V'tors	WD–U exc Wed & Fri–NA after 4.30pm WE–NA before 1pm SOC
Fees	18 holes–£10 (£12) 9 holes–£8
Loc	1 mile NW of Braintree (B1053)
Mis	Practice range

Upminster (1928)

114 Hall Lane, Upminster, RM14 1AU

Tel	**(01708) 222788**
Fax	(01708) 222484
Mem	1040
Sec	J Collantine
Pro	S Cipa (01708) 220000
Holes	18 L 6006 yds SSS 69
V'tors	WD–U H exc Tues am Ladies Day WE/BH–NA SOC
Fees	£25 D–£30
Loc	Station 3/4 mile

Wanstead (1893)

Wanstead, London, E11 2LW

Tel	**(020) 8989 0604**
Fax	(020) 8532 9138
Web	www.wanstead.golf.org.uk
Mem	650

For list of abbreviations see page 649

Sec K Jones (020) 8989 3938
Pro D Hawkins (020) 8989 9876
Holes 18 L 6262 yds SSS 69
V'tors WD–H WE/BH–M
Fees D–£28
Loc Off A12, nr Wanstead station
Arch James Braid

Warley Park (1975)
Magpie Lane, Little Warley, Brentwood, CM13 3DX
Tel (01277) 224891
Fax (01277) 200679
Mem 800
Sec K Regan
Pro J Groat (01277) 200441
Holes 27 hole course
V'tors WD–H
Fees £30
Loc 2 miles S of Brentwood. M25 Junction 29
Arch Reg Plumbridge

Warren (1932)
Woodham Walter, Maldon, CM9 6RW
Tel (01245) 223258/223198
Fax (01245) 223989
Web www.warrengolfclub.co.uk
Mem 800
Sec MFL Durham (01245) 223258
Pro D Brooks (01245) 224662
Holes 18 L 6211 yds SSS 69
V'tors WD–H WE–M SOC
Fees £30 D–£35
Loc 7 miles E of Chelmsford, off A414
Mis Golf Academy (01245) 223198

Weald Park (1994)
Coxtie Green Road, South Weald, Brentwood, CM14 5RJ
Tel (01277) 375101
Fax (01277) 374888
Web www.americangolf.com
Mem 600
Sec M Orwin (Gen Mgr)
Pro K Clark
Holes 18 L 6612 yds SSS 72
V'tors U–booking necessary WE–U after 11am SOC
Fees £18 (£24)
Loc 3 miles from M25 Junction 28 (A1023)
Mis Driving range
Arch Reg Plumbridge

West Essex (1900)
Bury Road, Sewardstonebury, Chingford, London E4 7QL
Tel (020) 8529 7558
Fax (020) 8524 7870
Mem 680
Sec D Wilson
Pro R Joyce (020) 8529 4367
Holes 18 L 6289 yds SSS 70
V'tors WD–U H WE/BH–M H SOC–Mon/Wed/Fri
Fees £28 D–£35

Loc 2 miles N of Chingford BR station. M25 Junction 26
Mis Driving range
Arch James Braid

Woodford (1890)
2 Sunset Avenue, Woodford Green, IG8 0ST
Tel (020) 8504 0553 (Clubhouse)
Fax (020) 8559 0504
Mem 430
Sec RS Crofts (020) 8504 3330
Pro R Layton (020) 8504 4254
Holes 9 L 5867 yds SSS 68
V'tors WD–U exc Tues am–NA Sat–M Sun–NA before noon SOC
Fees £10–£15
Loc 11 miles NE of London
Mis Major item of red clothing to be worn on course
Arch Tom Dunn

Gloucestershire

Brickhampton Court
Cheltenham Road, Churchdown, GL2 9QF
Tel (01452) 859444
Fax (01452) 859333
Web www.brickhampton.co.uk
Sec R East
Pro B Wilson
Holes Spa 18 L 6449 yds Par 71 SSS 71
Glevum 9 L 1859 yds Par 31
V'tors U SOC–WD
Fees £19 D–£30 (£25 D–£35)
Loc Between Cheltenham and Gloucester on B4063. M5 Junction 11, 3 miles
Mis Floodlit driving range
Arch Simon Gidman

Bristol & Clifton (1891)
Beggar Bush Lane, Failand, Clifton, Bristol BS8 3TH
Tel (01275) 393474/393117
Fax (01275) 394611
Web www.bristolgolf.co.uk
Mem 650
Sec CR Vane Percy (01275) 393474
Pro P Mawson (01275) 393031
Holes 18 L 6316 yds SSS 70
V'tors WD–UH WE/BH–MH SOC
Fees On request
Loc 2 miles W of suspension bridge. 4 miles S of M5 Junction 19
Mis Driving range

Broadway (1895)
Willersey Hill, Broadway, Worcs, WR12 7LG
Tel (01386) 858997
Fax (01386) 858643
Mem 515 165(L) 75(J)

Sec B Carnie (Sec/Mgr) (01386) 853683
Pro M Freeman (01386) 853275
Holes 18 L 6228 yds Par 72 SSS 70
V'tors H exc Sat–M SOC
Fees £30 (£37)
Loc 1½ miles E of Broadway (A44)
Arch James Braid

Canons Court (1982)
Bradley Green, Wotton-under-Edge, GL12 7PN
Tel (01453) 843128
Mem 200
Pro I Watts
Holes 9 L 5724 yds SSS 65
V'tors U
Fees £10
Loc 3 miles E of M5 Junction 14, off B4058

Chipping Sodbury
Chipping Sodbury, Bristol, BS37 6PU
Tel (01454) 312024 (Members)
Fax (01454) 320052
Web www.chippingsodurygolfclub.co.uk
Mem 750
Sec R Wilmott (01454) 319042
Pro M Watts (01454) 314087
Holes 18 L 6786 yds SSS 73
V'tors WD–U WE–pm only Sat/Sun am–XL SOC
Fees £22 (£27)
Loc 12 miles NE of Bristol. M4 Junction 18, 5 miles. M5 Junction 14, 9 miles.
Arch Fred Hawtree

Cirencester (1893)
Cheltenham Road, Bagendon, Cirencester, GL7 7BH
Tel (01285) 653939
Fax (01285) 650665
Web www.cirencestergolfclub.co.uk
Mem 800
Sec IA Gray (01285) 652465
Pro P Garratt (01285) 656124
Holes 18 L 6055 yds Par 70 SSS 69
V'tors H SOC–WD
Fees £25 (£30)
Loc 1½ miles N of Cirencester on A435
Arch James Braid

Cleeve Hill (1976)
Pay and play
Cleeve Hill, Cheltenham, GL52 3PW
Tel (01242) 672025
Sec S Gilman (Mgr)
Pro (01242) 672592
Holes 18 L 6444 yds SSS 71
V'tors U exc Sat 11–3pm/Sun am–NA SOC
Fees £8 (£10)
Loc 3 miles N of Cheltenham on A46 to Winchcombe
Mis Tee booking 7 days in advance

Cotswold Edge (1980)

Upper Rushmire, Wotton-under-Edge, GL12 7PT

Tel	(01453) 844167
Fax	(01453) 845120
Mem	800
Sec	NJ Newman
Pro	DJ Gosling (01453) 844398
Holes	18 L 5816 yds SSS 69
V'tors	WD–U WE–M SOC
Fees	£15
Loc	2 miles NE of Wotton-under-Edge on B4058 Tetbury road. M5 Junction 14

Cotswold Hills (1902)

Ullenwood, Cheltenham, GL53 9QT

Tel	(01242) 515264
Fax	(01242) 515317
Mem	750
Sec	P Burroughes (Gen Mgr)
Pro	N Allen (01242) 515263
Holes	18 L 6801 yds SSS 72
V'tors	U–recognised club members SOC
Fees	£27 D–£34 (£34 D–£40)
Loc	3 miles S of Cheltenham. M5 Junction 11A
Arch	MD Little

Dymock Grange (1995)

The Old Grange, Leominster Road, Dymock, GL18 2AN

Tel	(01531) 890840
Fax	(01531) 890852
Mem	180
Sec	BA Crossman (Gen Mgr)
Pro	None
Holes	9 L 2696 yds Par 36
	9 L 1695 yds Par 30
V'tors	U
Fees	£12 (£15)
Loc	14 miles NW of Gloucester (B4215)

Filton (1909)

Golf Course Lane, Bristol, BS34 7QS

Tel	(0117) 969 2021
Fax	(0117) 931 4359
Mem	700
Sec	Mrs E Mannering (0117) 969 4169
Pro	D Robinson (0117) 969 6968
Holes	18 L 6318 yds SSS 70
V'tors	WD–U WE/BH–M SOC–WD
Fees	£22 D–£27
Loc	4 miles N of Bristol
Arch	Hawtree

Forest Hills (1992)

Proprietary
Mile End Road, Coleford, GL16 7BY

Tel	(01594) 810620
Fax	(01594) 810823
Web	www.fweb.org.uk/forestgolf
Mem	550
Sec	N Antice (01594) 810620
Pro	R Ballard (01594) 810620
Holes	18 L 6300 yds SSS 72
V'tors	U SOC

Fees	£17 (£22)
Loc	1 mile E of Coleford (B4028)
Mis	Driving range
Arch	Adrian Stiff

Forest of Dean (1973)

Lords Hill, Coleford, GL16 8BE

Tel	(01594) 832583
Fax	(01594) 832584
Mem	500
Sec	R Sanzen-Baker
Pro	A Gray (01594) 833689
Holes	18 L 5682 yds SSS 69
V'tors	U SOC
Fees	£18 (£25)
Loc	½ mile SE of Coleford on Parkend road. M50, 10 miles
Arch	John Day

Gloucester Hotel (1976)

Matson Lane, Gloucester, GL4 9EA

Tel	(01452) 525653
Mem	750
Sec	P Darnell
Pro	P Darnell (01452) 411311
Holes	18 L 6127 yds SSS 69
	9 L 1980 yds SSS 27
V'tors	U
Fees	£19 (£25)
Loc	2 miles S of Gloucester, off Painswick road. M5 Junction 11
Mis	Driving range

Henbury (1891)

Westbury-on-Trym, Bristol, BS10 7QB

Tel	(0117) 950 0660
Fax	(0117) 959 1928
Web	www.henburygolfclub.co.uk
Mem	760
Sec	(0117) 950 0044
Pro	N Riley (0117) 950 2121
Holes	18 L 6007 yds SSS 70
V'tors	WD–H WE–M SOC–Tues & Fri
Fees	£25
Loc	3 miles N of Bristol, off A4018. M5 Junction 17

Hilton Puckrup Hall Hotel (1992)

Puckrup, Tewkesbury, GL20 6EL

Tel	(01684) 296200/271591
Fax	(01684) 850788
Mem	500
Sec	G Spring
Pro	K Pickett
Holes	18 L 6189 yds SSS 70
V'tors	WD–H SOC WE–residents
Fees	£25 (£30)
Loc	2 miles N of Tewkesbury on A38. M50 Junction 1. M5 Junction 8
Arch	Simon Gidman

Kendleshire

Henfield Road, Coalpit Heath, Bristol, BS36 2TG

Tel	(0117) 956 7007

Fax	(0117) 957 3433
Mem	750
Sec	P Murphy
Pro	M Bessell (0117) 956 7000
Holes	18 L 6500 yds Par 71 SSS 71
V'tors	U SOC
Fees	£25 (£40)
Loc	1 mile NE of Bristol. M32 Junction 1
Mis	Driving range. Golf Academy
Arch	Adrian Stiff

Knowle (1905)

Fairway, West Town Lane, Brislington, Bristol BS4 5DF

Tel	(0117) 977 6341
Fax	(0117) 972 0615
Mem	700
Sec	MJ Harrington (0117) 977 0660
Pro	R Hayward (0117) 977 9193
Holes	18 L 6016 yds SSS 69
V'tors	WD exc Thurs–H WE/BH–H SOC–Thurs
Fees	£22 D–£27 (£27 D–£32)
Loc	Brislington Hill, 3 miles S of Bristol, off A4
Arch	JH Taylor

Lilley Brook (1922)

Cirencester Road, Charlton Kings, Cheltenham, GL53 8EG

Tel	(01242) 526785
Fax	(01242) 256880
Mem	900
Sec	MF Jordan (Gen Mgr)
Pro	F Hadden (01242) 525201
Holes	18 L 6226 yds SSS 70
V'tors	WD–H or I (recognised club members) WE–M SOC–WD
Fees	£25 D–£30 (£30 D–£35)
Loc	3 miles SE of Cheltenham on A435. M5 Junction 11 or 11A

Long Ashton (1893)

Clarken Coombe, Long Ashton, Bristol, BS41 9DW

Tel	(01275) 392229
Fax	(01275) 394395
Web	www.longashtongolfclub.co.uk
Mem	750
Sec	R Williams (01275) 392229
Pro	M Hart (01275) 392229
Holes	18 L 6077 yds SSS 70
V'tors	WD–U H WE/BH–I H SOC–Wed & Fri
Fees	£30 (£35)
Loc	3 miles S of Bristol on B3128
Arch	JH Taylor

Lydney (1909)

Lakeside Avenue, Lydney, GL15 5QA

Tel	(01594) 842614
Mem	300
Sec	DA Barnard (01594) 843940
Holes	9 L 5382 yds SSS 66
V'tors	WD–U WE/BH–M SOC
Fees	£10

Loc 20 miles SW of Gloucester, off A48

Mangotsfield (1975)

Carsons Road, Mangotsfield, Bristol, BS17 3LW
Tel **(0117) 956 5501**
Mem 600
Sec C Main
Pro C Trewin
Holes 18 L 5337 yds SSS 66
V'tors U
Fees On application
Loc 6 miles NE of Bristol

Minchinhampton (1889)

Minchinhampton, Stroud, GL6 9BE
Tel **(01453) 832642 (Old), (01453) 833840 (New)**
Fax (01453) 837360
Mem 1860
Sec DT Calvert (01453) 833866
Pro C Steele (01453) 837351
Holes Old 18 L 6019 yds SSS 69; Avening 18 L 6263 yds SSS 70; Cherington 18 L 6387 yds SSS 70
V'tors H SOC
Fees Old–£10 (£13) New–£26 (£30)
Loc Old–3 miles E of Stroud. New–5 miles E of Stroud
Arch Old: R Wilson. Avening: F Hawtree. Cherington: M Hawtree

Naunton Downs (1993)

Naunton, Cheltenham, GL54 3AE
Tel **(01451) 850090**
Fax (01451) 850091
Web www.nauntondowns.fsnet.co.uk
Mem 750
Sec Charlotte Thomas
Pro N Ellis (01451) 850092
Holes 18 L 6135 yds Par 71 SSS 69
V'tors WD–U–by arrangement WE–NA before 11am
Fees £19 (£27.50)
Loc 5 miles SW of Stow-on-the-Wold, on B4068
Arch Jacob Pott

Newent (1994)

Pay and play
Coldharbour Lane, Newent, GL18 1DJ
Tel **(01531) 820478**
Fax (01531) 820478
Mem 50
Sec A Uppington
Pro T Brown
Holes 9 L 2100 yds Par 33 SSS 59
V'tors U SOC
Fees 9 holes–£6 (£7) 18 holes–£10 (£12)
Loc 10 miles NW of Gloucester on B4215. M50 Junct. 3, 4 miles

Painswick (1891)

Painswick, Stroud, GL6 6TL
Tel **(01452) 812180**
Fax (01452) 814423
Mem 430
Sec AB Layton-Smith (01452) 612622
Pro None
Holes 18 L 4780 yds SSS 63
V'tors WD/Sat–U Sun–M SOC
Fees £17.50 Sat–£22.50
Loc ½ mile N of Painswick on A46
Arch David Brown

Rodway Hill (1991)

Pay and play
Newent Road, Highnam, GL2 8DN
Tel **(01452) 384222**
Fax (01989) 766450
Mem 350
Sec R Howe
Pro T Grubb
Holes 18 L 6040 yds Par 70 SSS 69
V'tors U SOC
Fees 18 holes–£11 (£13.50) 9 holes–£7 (£8)
Loc 2 miles W of Gloucester (B4215)
Arch J Gabb

Sherdons Golf Centre (1993)

Pay and play
Tredington, Tewkesbury, GL20 7BP
Tel **(01684) 274782**
Fax (01684) 275358
Mem 300
Sec R Chatham
Pro P Clark, J Parker
Holes 9 L 2654 yds Par 34 SSS 66
V'tors U
Fees 18 holes–£11 (£14) 9 holes–£6.50 (£7.50)
Loc 2 miles S of Tewkesbury, off A38
Mis Driving range

Shirehampton Park (1907)

Park Hill, Shirehampton, Bristol, BS11 0UL
Tel **(0117) 982 3059**
Fax (0117) 982 5280
Mem 600
Sec W Hendry (0117) 982 2083
Pro B Ellis (0117) 982 2488
Holes 18 L 5430 yds Par 67 SSS 66
V'tors WD–H WE–M SOC
Fees £20 (£17)
Loc 2 miles E of M5 Junction 18, on B4054

Stinchcombe Hill (1889)

Stinchcombe Hill, Dursley, GL11 6AQ
Tel **(01453) 542015**
Fax (01453) 549545
Mem 550

Sec PH Jones
Pro P Bushell (01453) 543878
Holes 18 L 5734 yds SSS 68
V'tors U–phone Pro SOC
Fees £20 (£25)
Loc 1 mile W of Dursley. M5 Junction 14
Arch A Hoare

Tewkesbury Park Hotel (1976)

Lincoln Green Lane, Tewkesbury, GL20 7DN
Tel **(01684) 295405 (Hotel)**
Fax (01684) 292386
Web www.corushotels.com/tewkesburypark
Mem 600
Sec RS Nichol (01684) 272322
Pro C Boast (01684) 272320
Holes 18 L 6533 yds Par 73 SSS 71 6 hole Par 3 course
V'tors WD–U H WE–restricted SOC–WD
Fees £25 (£30)
Loc ½ mile S of Tewkesbury on A38. M5 Junction 9, 2 miles
Mis Driving range

Thornbury Golf Centre (1992)

Bristol Road, Thornbury
Tel **(01454) 281144**
Fax (01454) 281177
Mem 400
Sec I Gibson
Pro S Hubbard
Holes 18 L 6154 yds SSS 69 Par 71 18 L 2195 yds Par 54
V'tors U SOC–WD
Fees £14 (£16)
Loc 10 miles N of Bristol, off A38
Mis Driving range
Arch Hawtree

Tracy Park (1976)

Tracy Park, Bath Road, Wick, Bristol BS30 5RN
Tel **(0117) 937 2251, (0117) 303 9123 (Bookings)**
Fax (0117) 937 4288
Web www.tracypark.com
Mem 700
Sec D Knipe (Dir)
Pro T Thompson Green
Holes Crown 18 L 6443 yds SSS 71 Cromwell 18 L 6011 yds SSS 69
V'tors U–phone first SOC
Fees £30 (£38)
Loc 3 miles NW of Bath, off A420. M4 Junction 18
Mis Driving range

Westonbirt (1971)

Westonbirt, Tetbury, GL8 8QG
Tel **(01666) 880242**
Mem 200
Sec Bursar, Westonbirt School
Holes 9 L 4504 yds SSS 61

For list of abbreviations see page 649

V'tors U SOC–WD
Fees On application
Loc 3 miles S of Tetbury, off A433

Woodlands G&CC (1989)

Pay and play
Woodlands Lane, Almondsbury, Bristol,
BS32 4JZ
Tel (01454) 619319
Fax (01454) 619397
Web www.woodlands-golf.com
Sec I Knipe
Pro N Warburton
Holes 18 L 6100 yds SSS 70
V'tors U SOC
Fees £12 (£14)
Loc Nr M5 Junction 16

Woodspring G&CC
(1994)

Yanley Lane, Long Ashton, Bristol,
BS41 9LR
Tel (01275) 394378
Fax (01275) 394473
Sec M Pierce (Gen Mgr)
Pro N Beer
Holes 27 holes:
      6209-6587 yds Par 71
      SSS 70-71
V'tors W–H SOC
Fees £25 (£28.50)
Loc 2 miles S of Bristol on A38.
Mis Floodlit driving range
Arch Allis/Clark

Hampshire

Alresford (1890)

Cheriton Road, Alresford, SO24 0PN
Tel (01962) 733746
Fax (01962) 736040
Web www.alresfordgolf.com
Mem 720
Sec T Adams
Pro M Scott (01962) 733998
Holes 18 L 5905 yds Par 69 SSS 68
V'tors U H SOC–WD
Fees £23 D–£35 (£40)
Loc 1 mile S of Alresford on
      B3046
Arch Scott Webb Young

Alton (1908)

Old Odiham Road, Alton,
GU34 4BU
Tel (01420) 82042
Mem 370
Sec P Brown
Pro P Brown (01420) 86518
Holes 18 L 5744 yds SSS 68
V'tors WD–U WE–H or M
      SOC–WD
Fees 18 holes–£15 D–£20
      9 holes–£10
Loc 2 miles N of Alton. 6 miles S
      of Odiham, off B3349
Arch James Braid

Ampfield Par Three
(1963)

Winchester Road, Ampfield, Romsey,
SO51 9BQ
Tel (01794) 368480
Mem 500
Sec Ms L Hilman
Pro R Benfield (01794) 368750
Holes 18 L 2478 yds SSS 53
V'tors WD–U WE/BH–H (phone
      first) SOC
Fees £9 (£15.50)
Loc 5 miles E of Romsey on A31
Arch Henry Cotton

Andover (1907)

51 Winchester Road, Andover,
SP10 2EF
Tel (01264) 323980
Fax (01264) 358040
Mem 460 30(L) 45(J)
Sec D Dunn (01264) 358040
Pro D Lawrence (01264) 324151
Holes 9 L 6096 yds SSS 69
V'tors U H SOC–Mon–Wed
Fees £15 (£20)
Loc ½ mile S of Andover on
      A3057
Arch JH Taylor

Army (1883)

Laffan's Road, Aldershot, GU11 2HF
Tel (01252) 336776
Fax (01252) 337562
Web www.whichgolfclub.com/army
Mem 750
Sec Maj (Retd) JWG Douglass
      (01252) 337272
Pro G Cowley (01252) 336722
Holes 18 L 6579 yds SSS 71
V'tors WD–H–contact Sec/Mgr SOC
Fees Special rates for Forces
Loc Between Aldershot and
      Farnborough

Barton-on-Sea (1897)

Milford Road, New Milton, BH25 5PP
Tel (01425) 615308
Fax (01425) 621457
Web www.barton-on-sea-golf.co.uk
Mem 1000
Sec N Hallam-Jones
Pro P Rodgers (01425) 611210
Holes 27 holes:
      L 6289-6505 yds Par 72
V'tors H NA before 9am SOC–WD
      exc Tues
Fees D–£30 (D–£35)
Loc 1 mile from New Milton, off
      B3058. M27 Junction 1
Arch J Hamilton Stutt

Basingstoke (1928)

Kempshott Park, Basingstoke,
RG23 7LL
Tel (01256) 465990
Fax (01256) 331793
Mem 700
Sec WA Jefford
Pro G Shoesmith (01256) 351332

Holes 18 L 6350 yds SSS 70
V'tors WD–H WE–M SOC–Wed &
      Thurs
Fees £28 D–£38
Loc 3 miles W of Basingstoke on
      A30. M3 Junction 7
Arch James Braid

Bishopswood (1978)

Proprietary
Bishopswood Lane, Tadley, Basingstoke,
RG26 4AT
Tel (0118) 981 2200/5213
Fax (0118) 940 8606
Web www.bishopswoodgolfcourse
      .co.uk
Mem 400
Sec M Collins (0118) 982 0312
Pro S Ward
Holes 9 L 6474 yds Par 72 SSS 71
V'tors WD–U WE–M SOC
Fees 9 holes–£11. 18 holes–£16.50
Loc 6 miles N of Basingstoke, off
      A340
Mis Floodlit driving range
Arch Blake/Phillips

Blackmoor (1913)

Whitehill, Bordon, GU35 9EH
Tel (01420) 472775/475461
Fax (01420) 487666
Mem 680 100(L) 70(J)
Sec Mrs C Tupper
Pro S Clay (01420) 472345
Holes 18 L 6213 yds SSS 70
V'tors WD–H
Fees £34 D–£46
Loc ½ mile W of Whitehill on
      A325
Arch HS Colt

Blacknest (1993)

Frith End, Binsted, GU34 4QL
Tel (01420) 22888
Fax (01420) 22001
Mem 600
Sec GD Lawson
Pro I Benson
Holes 18 L 5858 yds SSS 69
      9 hole Par 3 course
V'tors U SOC
Fees £14 (£16) (1997)
Loc 7 miles SW of Farnham, off
      A325
Mis Driving range

Blackwater Valley

Chandlers Lane, Yateley, Surrey,
GU46 7SZ
Tel (01252) 874725
Fax (01252) 874725
Mem 50
Pro J Rodger
Holes 9 L 2365 yds Par 66
V'tors U SOC
Fees £7 (£9)
Loc 5 miles W of Camberley
      (B3272)
Mis Floodlit driving range
Arch HJ Allenby

Botley Park Hotel G&CC (1989)

Winchester Road, Boorley Green, Botley, SO3 2UA

Tel	**(01489) 780888 Ext 451**
Fax	(01489) 789242
Mem	700
Sec	Miss M Johnstone
Pro	T Barter (01489) 789771
Holes	18 L 6341 yds SSS 70
V'tors	H SOC
Fees	£30
Loc	6 miles E of Southampton on B3354. M27 Junction 7. 8 miles SE of M3 Junction 11
Mis	Driving range
Arch	Potterton/Murray

Bramshaw (1880)

Brook, Lyndhurst, SO43 7HE

Tel	**(023) 8081 3433**
Fax	(023) 8081 3460
Web	www.bramshaw.co.uk
Mem	1200
Sec	RD Tingey
Pro	C Bonner (023) 8081 3434
Holes	Forest 18 L 5774 yds SSS 68 Manor 18 L 6517 yds SSS 71
V'tors	U H
Fees	Forest–£25 Manor–£30
Loc	10 miles SW of Southampton. M27 Junction 1, 1 mile

Brokenhurst Manor (1919)

Sway Road, Brockenhurst, SO42 7SG

Tel	**(01590) 623332**
Fax	(01590) 624140
Mem	800
Sec	PE Clifford
Pro	B Parker (01590) 623092
Holes	18 L 6222 yds SSS 70
V'tors	WD–H after 9.30am NA–Tues–Ladies' Day SOC–Thurs
Fees	£36 D–£46 (£60)
Loc	1 mile SW of Brockenhurst on B3055
Arch	HS Colt

Burley (1905)

Cott Lane, Burley, Ringwood, BH24 4BB

Tel	**(01425) 403737 (Clubhouse)**
Fax	(01425) 402431
Mem	520
Sec	GJ Stride (01425) 402431
Holes	9 L 6149 yds Par 71 SSS 69
V'tors	U H–preferred
Fees	£16 (£20) W–£75
Loc	4 miles SE of Ringwood

Cams Hall Estate

Cams Hall Estate, Fareham, PO16 8UP

Tel	**(01329) 827222**
Fax	(01329) 827111
Mem	950
Sec	T Clagett (Sec/Mgr)
Pro	J Neve (01329) 837732

Holes	27 L 6244-6477 yds SSS 70-71
V'tors	U SOC
Fees	£20 (£27.50)
Loc	8 miles W of Portsmouth. M27 Junction 11
Arch	Alliss/Clarke

Chilworth (1989)

Main Road, Chilworth, Southampton, SO16 7JP

Tel	**(023) 8074 0544**
Fax	(023) 8073 3166
Mem	650
Sec	Mrs E Garner
Holes	18 L 5740 yds SSS 69
V'tors	U
Fees	£12 (£15)
Loc	Between Romsey and Southampton on A27
Mis	Floodlit driving range

Corhampton (1891)

Corhampton, Southampton, SO32 3LP

Tel	**(01489) 877279**
Fax	(01489) 877680
Web	www.corhamptongc.co.uk
Mem	800
Sec	Mrs L Collins
Pro	I Roper (01489) 877638
Holes	18 L 6444 yds SSS 71
V'tors	WD–U H WE/BH–M SOC–Mons & Thurs
Fees	£24 D–£34
Loc	9 miles S of Winchester

Dibden Golf Centre (1974)

Public

Main Road, Dibden, Southampton, SO45 5TB

Tel	**(023) 8020 7508 (Bookings)**
Web	www.nfdc.gov.uk/golf
Mem	700
Pro	P Smith (023) 8084 5596
Holes	18 L 5986 yds SSS 69 9 hole course
V'tors	U
Fees	£11.80 (£13.80)
Loc	10 miles W of Southampton, off A326 at Dibden roundabout
Mis	Floodlit driving range

Dummer (1993)

Dummer, Basingstoke, RG25 2AR

Tel	**(01256) 397888**
Fax	(01256) 397889
Web	www.dummergc.co.uk
Mem	750
Sec	R Corkhill
Pro	A Fannon
Holes	18 L 6377 yds SSS 70
V'tors	U SOC
Fees	£30 (£40)
Loc	4 miles SW of Basingstoke, by M3 Junction 7
Mis	Driving range
Arch	Alliss/Clark

Dunwood Manor (1969)

Danes Road, Awbridge, Romsey, SO51 0GF

Tel	**(01794) 340549**
Fax	(01794) 341215
Web	www.dunwood-golf.co.uk
Mem	700
Sec	JR Basford
Pro	H Teschner (01794) 340663
Holes	18 L 5767 yds SSS 69
V'tors	WE/BH–restricted SOC–WD
Fees	£24 (£35)
Loc	Romsey 4 miles, off A27

Fareham Woods (1997)

Skylark Meadows, Whiteley, Fareham, PO15 6RS

Tel	**(01329) 844441**
Fax	(01329) 844442
Mem	600
Sec	M Woodman
Pro	S Edwards
Holes	18 L 5622 yds Par 70 SSS 67
V'tors	WD–U WE–M SOC–WD
Fees	£15
Loc	6 miles W of Fareham. M27 Junction 9

Fleetlands (1961)

Fareham Road, Gosport, PO13 0AW

Tel	**(023) 9254 4492**
Mem	120
Sec	MR Sheehan (023) 9254 5195
Holes	9 L 4852 yds SSS 64
V'tors	M at all times
Loc	2 miles S of Fareham on A32 Gosport road. M27 Junction 12

Fleming Park (1973)

Public

Fleming Park, Magpie Lane, Eastleigh, SO50 9LH

Tel	**(023) 8061 2797**
Sec	A Wheavil
Pro	C Strickett
Holes	18 L 4436 yds SSS 62
V'tors	U SOC–WD
Fees	On application
Loc	6 miles N of Southampton

Four Marks (1994)

Headmore Lane, Four Marks, Alton, GU34 3ES

Tel	**(01420) 587214**
Fax	(01420) 587313
Mem	238
Sec	W Falloon
Pro	P Chapman (01420) 587214
Holes	9 L 2077 yds Par 62 SSS 61
V'tors	U SOC
Fees	9 holes–£7 (£8) 18 holes–£10.10 (£11.90)
Loc	6 miles SW of Alton (A31)
Arch	Don Wright

Furzeley (1993)

Pay and play

Furzeley Road, Denmead, PO7 6TX

Tel	**(023) 9223 1180**

Fax   (023) 9223 0921
Sec   T Brown
Pro   D Brown
Holes 18 L 4363 yds Par 62 SSS 61
V'tors U SOC
Fees £11 (£12.50)
Loc   2 miles NW of Waterlooville

Gosport & Stokes Bay
(1885)
Fort Road, Haslar, Gosport, PO12 2AT
Tel   (023) 9258 1625
Fax   (023) 9252 7941
Mem   450
Sec   P Lucas (023) 9252 7941
Holes 9 L 5995 yds SSS 69
V'tors U exc Sun–NA
      SOC–Mon/Wed/Fri
Fees £15 (£20)
Loc   S boundary of Gosport

The Hampshire
*Winchester Road, Goodworth Clatford,
Andover, SP11 7TB*
Tel   (01264) 357555
Fax   (01264) 356606
Mem   735
Sec   T Fiducia
Pro   S Cronin
Holes 18 L 6376 yds Par
      9 hole Par 3 course
V'tors U SOC
Fees £15 (£25)
Loc   1 mile SW of Andover
      (A3057)
Mis   Covered driving range
Arch T Fiducia

Hartley Wintney   (1891)
*London Road, Hartley Wintney,
Basingstoke, RG27 8PT*
Tel   (01252) 842214
Fax   (01252) 842214
Mem   750
Sec   RW Lamb (01252) 844211
Pro   M Smith (01252) 843779
Holes 18 L 6240 yds SSS 71
V'tors Wed–Ladies Day
      WE/BH–restricted SOC–Tues
      & Thurs
Fees £25 (£35)
Loc   A30 between Camberley and
      Basingstoke

Hayling   (1883)
Links Lane, Hayling Island, PO11 0BX
Tel   (023) 9246 3712/463777
Fax   (023) 9246 4446
Mem   900
Sec   CJ Cavill (023) 9246 4446
Pro   R Gadd (023) 9246 4491
Holes 18 L 6531 yds SSS 71
V'tors H WE/BH–after 10am
      SOC–Tues & Wed
Fees £36 (£44)
Loc   5 miles S of Havant on A3023
Arch Taylor(1905)/Simpson(1933)

Hockley   (1915)
Twyford, Winchester, SO21 1PL
Tel   (01962) 713165
Fax   (01962) 713612
Web   www.hockleygolfclub.org.uk
Mem   750
Sec   Mrs L Dyer
Pro   T Lane (01962) 713678
Holes 18 L 6336 yds SSS 70
V'tors U H SOC
Fees On application
Loc   2 miles S of Winchester on
      B3335
Arch James Braid

Leckford   (1929)
Leckford, Stockbridge, SO20 6JS
Tel   (01264) 810320
Fax   (01264) 810439
Mem   400
Sec   J Wood
Pro   T Ashton (01264) 338175
Holes Old 9 L 3251 yds SSS 71
      New 9 L 2281 yds SSS 62
V'tors M
Fees £10 (£14)
Loc   5 miles W of Andover

Lee-on-the-Solent   (1905)
*Brune Lane, Lee-on-the-Solent,
PO13 9PB*
Tel   (023) 9255 0207
Fax   (023) 9255 4233
Web   www.mod60.com/leegolf
Mem   715
Sec   P Clash (Mgr)
      (023) 92551170
Pro   J Richardson (01705) 551181
Holes 18 L 5959 yds SSS 69
V'tors WD–U H WE–M H
      SOC–Thurs
Fees D–£30 (£35)
Loc   3 miles S of Fareham. M27
      Junction 11

Liphook   (1922)
Liphook, GU30 7EH
Tel   (01428) 723271/723785
Fax   (01428) 724853
Mem   700
Sec   Maj JB Morgan MBE
      (01428) 723785/723271
Pro   G Lee
Holes 18 L 6167 yds SSS 70
V'tors I H (max 24) Sun–NA before
      1pm SOC
Fees £35 D–£45 (D–£53)
Loc   1 mile S of Liphook on B2070
      (old A3)
Arch ACG Groome

Marriott Meon Valley Hotel   (1977)
*Sandy Lane, Shedfield, Southampton,
SO32 2HQ*
Tel   (01329) 833455
Fax   (01329) 834411
Mem   730
Sec   GF McMenemy (Golf Dir)
Pro   R Cameron

Holes 18 L 6520 yds SSS 71
      9 L 2885 yds SSS 68
V'tors H SOC
Fees 18 hole: £36 (£45)
      9 hole: £12
Loc   2 miles NW of Wickham. N
      off A334
Mis   Driving range
Arch J Hamilton Stutt

New Forest   (1888)
*Southampton Road, Lyndhurst,
SO43 7BU*
Tel   (023) 8028 2752
Mem   750
Sec   Mrs B Shaw, R Macdonald
      (Prop) (023) 8028 2484
Pro   D Harris
Holes 18 L 5742 yds SSS 68
V'tors U exc Sun am SOC–WD
Fees £12 (£14)
Loc   8 miles W of Southampton on
      A35

North Hants   (1904)
Minley Road, Fleet, GU51 1RF
Tel   (01252) 616443
Fax   (01252) 811627
Mem   550
Sec   G Hogg
Pro   S Porter (01252) 616655
Holes 18 L 6519 yds Par 71
      SSS 72
V'tors WD–H by prior arrangement
      WE/BH–MH SOC–Tues &
      Wed
Fees On application
Loc   3 miles W of Farnborough on
      B3013. M3 Junction 4A
Arch James Braid

Old Thorns   (1982)
Pay and play
*Longmoor Road, Griggs Green,
Liphook, GU30 7PE*
Tel   (01428) 724555
Fax   (01428) 725036
Sec   GM Jones (Gen Mgr)
Pro   K Stevenson
Holes 18 L 6533 yds SSS 71
V'tors U SOC
Fees £35 (£45)
Loc   Griggs Green exit off A3
Mis   Driving range
Arch Cdr John Harris

Otterbourne Golf Centre   (1995)
*Poles Lane, Otterbourne, Winchester,
SO21 2EL*
Tel   (01962) 775225
Sec   JM Garner (Mgr)
Holes 9 L 1939 yds Par
V'tors U
Fees £4 (£5)
Loc   On A31 between Otterbourne
      and Hursley
Mis   Driving range

Park (1995)
Pay and play
Avington, Winchester, SO21 1DA
Tel	**(01962) 779945 (Clubhouse)**
Fax	(01962) 779530
Mem	350
Sec	R Stent (Prop)
	(01962) 779955
Pro	None
Holes	9 L 1907 yds Par 61 SSS 58
V'tors	U SOC
Fees	9 holes–£7 (£10) 18
	holes–£10.50 (£15)
Loc	4 miles E of Winchester. M3
	Junction 9

Paultons Golf Centre
Pay and play
Old Salisbury Road, Ower, Romsey,
SO51 6AN
Tel	**(023) 8081 3992**
Fax	(023) 8081 3993
Sec	R Pilbury
Pro	(023) 8081 4626
Holes	18 L 6238 yds SSS 71
	9 hole Academy course
V'tors	U SOC
Fees	18 holes–£16 (£20)
	9 holes–£6 (£6)
Loc	Nr M27 Junction 2, at Ower
Mis	Driving range

Petersfield (1892)
Tankerdale Lane, Liss, GU33 7QY
Tel	**(01730) 895165**
Fax	(01730) 894713
Mem	730
Sec	RR Hine
Pro	G Hughes (01730) 895216
Holes	18 L 6400 yds Par 72 SSS 71
V'tors	WD–U WE/BH–NA before
	noon SOC–Mon/Wed/Fri
Fees	£25 (£30)
Loc	Off A3, at Liss exit (B3006)
Arch	Hawtree

Petersfield Sussex Road
Pay and play
Sussex Road, Petersfield
Tel	**(01730) 267732**
Sec	RR Hine
Pro	G Hughes
Holes	9 L 3005 yds
V'tors	U
Fees	9 holes–£6 (£7) 18 holes–£10
	(£12)
Loc	Petersfield

Portsmouth (1926)
Public
Crookhorn Lane, Widley, Waterlooville,
PO7 5QL
Tel	**(023) 9237 2210**
Fax	(023) 9220 0766
Web	www.portsmouthgc.com
Mem	650
Sec	D Houlihan (023) 9220 1827
Pro	J Banting (023) 9237 2210
Holes	18 L 6139 yds SSS 70
V'tors	U SOC–arrange with Pro

Fees	£6.50–£13.50
Loc	1 mile N of Portsmouth, on
	B2177

Romsey (1900)
Nursling, Southampton, SO16 0XW
Tel	**(023) 8073 2218**
Fax	(023) 8074 1036
Mem	825
Sec	MTF Rees (023) 8073 4637
Pro	M Desmond (023) 8073 6673
Holes	18 L 5856 yds SSS 68
V'tors	WD–H WE/BH–M H
Fees	£23 D–£29
Loc	2 miles SE of Romsey on
	A3057. M27/M271 Junction 3

Rowlands Castle (1902)
Links Lane, Rowlands Castle,
PO9 6AE
Tel	**(023) 9241 2216**
Fax	(023) 9241 3649
Mem	800 150(L) 50(J)
Sec	KD Fisher (023) 9241 2784
Pro	P Klepacz (023) 9241 2785
Holes	18 L 6618 yds Par 72 SSS 72
V'tors	WD–U H exc Wed
	am–restricted WE–phone first
	Sat–M SOC–Tues & Thurs
Fees	£30 (£35)
Loc	9 miles S of Petersfield, off
	A3(M). 3 miles N of Havant
Arch	HS Colt

Royal Winchester (1888)
Sarum Road, Winchester, SO22 5QE
Tel	**(01962) 852462**
Fax	(01962) 865048
Mem	750
Sec	D Thomson (Mgr)
Pro	S Hunter (01962) 862473
Holes	18 L 6204 yds SSS 70
V'tors	WD–U H WE/BH–M
	SOC–Mon/Tues/Wed
Fees	On application
Loc	W of Winchester. M3 Junction
	11
Arch	JH Taylor

Sandford Springs (1988)
Wolverton, Tadley, RG26 5RT
Tel	**(01635) 296800**
Fax	(01635) 296801
Mem	700
Sec	K Brake (Man Dir)
Pro	G Edmunds (01635) 296808
Holes	27 L 6100 yds SSS 70
V'tors	WD–prior booking WE–M
	SOC–WD
Fees	£23 D–£29
Loc	8 miles N of Basingstoke on
	A339
Arch	Hawtree

Somerley Park (1995)
Somerley, Ringwood, BH24 3PL
Tel	**(01425) 461496**
Mem	169
Sec	J Staley, R Curtis (Props)

Pro	J Waring (01202) 821703
Holes	9 L 2155 yds Par 33 SSS 62
V'tors	M SOC
Fees	£10
Loc	5 miles W of Ringwood
Arch	John Jacobs OBE

South Winchester
Romsey Road, Winchester, SO22 5QW
Tel	**(01962) 877800**
Fax	(01962) 877900
Web	www.southwinchester.com
Mem	750
Sec	S Wright (Gen Mgr)
Pro	R Adams (01962) 840469
Holes	18 L 7086 yds SSS 74
V'tors	H SOC
Fees	£25 (£35)
Loc	S side of Winchester
Mis	Driving range
Arch	Thomas/Alliss

Southampton Municipal
(1935)
Public
Golf Course Road, Bassett,
Southampton, SO16 7AY
Tel	**(023) 8076 8407**
Pro	J Cave
Holes	18 L 6218 yds SSS 70
	9 L 2391 yds SSS 33
V'tors	U
Fees	On application
Loc	2 miles N of Southampton

Southsea (1914)
Public
The Clubhouse, Burrfields Road,
Portsmouth, PO3 5JJ
Tel	**(023) 9266 4549**
Fax	(023) 9265 0525
Mem	400
Sec	K Parker (023) 9266 8667
Pro	T Healy
Holes	18 L 5970 yds SSS 68
V'tors	U SOC
Fees	£10.30 (£12.30)
Loc	1 mile off M27 on A2030
Mis	Driving range

Southwick Park (1977)
Pinsley Drive, Southwick, PO17 6EL
Tel	**(023) 9238 0131**
Fax	(023) 9221 0289
Mem	650 80(L)
Sec	NW Price
Pro	J Green (023) 9238 0442
Holes	18 L 5884 yds SSS 69
V'tors	WD–U booking necessary
	WE–NA before 2pm SOC
Fees	On application. Service
	Personnel reduced rate
Loc	5 miles N of Portsmouth, off
	B2177

Southwood (1977)
Public
Ively Road, Farnborough, GU14 0LJ
Tel	**(01252) 548700**

Sec MJ Pettifor
Holes 18 L 5738 yds SSS 68
V'tors U
Fees £15 (£17.50)
Loc 1 mile W of Farnborough, off A325
Arch M Hawtree

Stoneham (1908)

Monks Wood Close, Bassett,
Southampton, SO16 3TT
Tel (023) 8076 8151
Fax (023) 8076 6320
Mem 800
Sec AL Bray (Mgr)
  (023) 8076 9272
Pro I Young (023) 8076 8397
Holes 18 L 6310 yds SSS 70
V'tors U SOC–Mon/Thurs/Fri
Fees £32 D–£36 (£44 D–£55)
Loc 2 miles N of Southampton on A27
Arch Willie Park

Test Valley (1992)

Micheldever Road, Overton,
Basingstoke, RG25 3DS
Tel (08707) 459020
Fax (08707) 459023
Mem 550
Sec A Briggs (Mgr)
  (08707) 459021
Pro A Briggs
Holes 18 L 6897 yds SSS 73
V'tors U SOC
Fees £18 (£24)
Loc 2 miles S of Overton on Micheldever road. M3 Junction 8 (A303)
Arch Wright/Darcy

Tournerbury Golf Centre (1993)

Pay and play
Tournerbury Road, Hayling Island,
PO11 9DL
Tel (023) 9246 2266
Pro R Brown
Holes 9 L 2956 yds SSS 35
V'tors U SOC
Fees 9 holes–£7 (£8.30)
Loc E coast of Hayling Island. 3 miles S of Havant
Mis Driving range

Tylney Park (1973)

Rotherwick, Basingstoke, RG27 9AY
Tel (01256) 762079
Fax (01256) 763079
Mem 700
Sec MR Alcock
Pro C de Bruin (Mgr)
Holes 18 L 6108 yds SSS 69
V'tors WD–U WE–M or H SOC
Fees On application
Loc 2 miles NW of Hook. M3 Junction 5

Waterlooville (1907)

Cherry Tree Ave, Cowplain,
Waterlooville, PO8 8AP
Tel (023) 9226 3388
Fax (023) 9234 7513
Web www.waterloovillegolfclub
  .co.uk
Mem 800
Sec D Nairne
Pro J Hay (023) 9225 6911
Holes 18 L 6602 yds SSS 72
V'tors WD/WE–M H (Sun am–XL) SOC
Fees £30 D–£35
Loc 10 miles N of Portsmouth on A3
Arch Henry Cotton

Wellow (1991)

Ryedown Lane, East Wellow, Romsey,
SO51 6BD
Tel (01794) 322872
Fax (01794) 323832
Mem 600
Sec Mrs C Gurd
Pro N Bratley (01794) 323833
Holes 27 L 6000 yds SSS 69
V'tors U SOC–WD
Fees £16 (£20)
Loc 2 miles W of Romsey. M27 Junction 2, via A36
Arch W Wiltshire

Weybrook Park (1971)

Rooksdown Lane, Basingstoke,
RG24 9NT
Tel (01256) 320347
Fax (01256) 812973
Mem 600
Sec GE Carpenter
Pro A Dillon (01256) 333232
Holes 18 L 6468 yds SSS 71
V'tors WD–U WE–contact Mgr SOC
Fees £19.50 (£24.50)
Loc 1½ miles N of Basingstoke

Wickham Park

Titchfield Lane, Wickham, Fareham,
PO17 5PJ
Tel (01329) 833342
Fax (01329) 834798
Web www.wickhampark.co.uk
Sec I Yates (Mgr)
Pro S Edwards
Holes 18 L 5898 yds Par 70 SSS 68
V'tors U SOC
Fees £12 (£15)
Loc 2 miles N of Fareham. M27 Junction 10
Arch Jon Payn

Worldham Park (1993)

Pay and play
Cakers Lane, Worldham, Alton,
GU34 3AG
Tel (01420) 543151/544606
Mem 500
Sec NV Harvey (01420) 544606

Pro J Le Roux (01420) 543151
Holes 18 L 6500 yds SSS 71
V'tors WD–U WE–U after 11am SOC–WD
Fees £11 (£14)
Loc ½ mile E of Alton on B3004 to Bordon
Mis Driving range
Arch Troth/Whidborne

Herefordshire

Belmont Lodge (1983)

Belmont, Hereford, HR2 9SA
Tel (01432) 352666
Fax (01432) 358090
Web www.belmontlodge.co.uk
Mem 500
Sec A Carver (Mgr)
Pro M Welsh (01432) 352717
Holes 18 L 6511 yds SSS 71
V'tors U SOC
Fees On application
Loc 1½ miles S of Hereford on A465
Arch B Sandow

Burghill Valley (1991)

Tillington Road, Burghill, Hereford,
HR4 7RW
Tel (01432) 760456
Fax (01432) 761654
Web www.bvgc.co.uk
Sec K Smith (Mgr)
Pro N Clarke (01432) 760808
Holes 18 L 6239 yds SSS 70
V'tors U SOC
Fees £20 (£25)
Loc 3 miles N of Hereford, off A4110

Cadmore Lodge (1990)

Pay and play
Berrington Green, Tenbury Wells,
Worcester, WR15 8TQ
Tel (01584) 810044
Fax (01584) 810044
Web www.cadmorelodge.demon
  .co.uk
Mem 150
Sec RV Farr
Pro None
Holes 9 L 5129 yds Par 68 SSS 65
V'tors U
Fees D–£10 (D–£14)
Loc 2 miles S of Tenbury Wells on A4112

Hereford Municipal (1983)

Public
Holmer Road, Hereford, HR4 9UD
Tel (01432) 344376
Fax (01432) 266281
Mem 200
Sec G Evans
Pro G Morgan (01432) 344376

Holes 9 L 3060 yds Par 70 SSS 69
V'tors U SOC
Fees 18 holes–£6.90 (£8.50) 9 holes–£4.60 (£5.60)
Loc Hereford Leisure Centre, A49 Leominster road

Herefordshire (1896)
Raven's Causeway, Wormsley, Hereford, HR4 8LY
Tel (01432) 830219
Fax (01432) 830095
Mem 770 150(L) 55(J)
Sec TG Horobin (Hon)
Pro D Hemming (01432) 830465
Holes 18 L 6069 yds SSS 69
V'tors U–phone first SOC
Fees £20 D–£25 (£25 D–£32)
Loc 6 miles NW of Hereford

Kington (1926)
Bradnor Hill, Kington, HR5 3RE
Tel (01544) 230340
Fax (01544) 340270
Mem 500
Sec GR Wictome (01544) 340270
Pro A Gealy (01544) 231320
Holes 18 L 5840 yds SSS 68
V'tors WE–NA before 10.15am –restricted 1.30–2.45pm SOC
Fees £16 D–£21 (£22 D–£27)
Loc 1 mile N of Kington
Arch CK Hutchinson

Leominster (1967)
Ford Bridge, Leominster, HR6 0LE
Tel (01568) 612863 (Clubhouse)
Fax (01568) 610055
Mem 550
Sec L Green (01568) 610055
Pro A Ferriday (01568) 611402
Holes 18 L 6026 yds SSS 69
V'tors U SOC
Fees £15.50 D–£19 (£22 D–£25)
Loc 3 miles S of Leominster on A49 (Leominster By-pass)
Arch R Sandow

Ross-on-Wye (1903)
Two Park, Gorsley, Ross-on-Wye, HR9 7UT
Tel (01989) 720267
Fax (01989) 720212
Web www.rossonwyegolfclub.co.uk
Mem 760
Sec PH Plumb
Pro N Catchpole (01989) 720439
Holes 18 L 6500 yds Par 72 SSS 71
V'tors U SOC–Wed–Fri (min 16 players)
Fees £36–£46 SOC–£28–£40
Loc 5 miles N of Ross-on-Wye, by M50 Junction 3
Mis Parkland driving range
Arch CK Cotton

Sapey (1991)
Upper Sapey, Worcester, WR6 6XT
Tel (01886) 853288
Fax (01886) 853485
Web www.sapeygolf.co.uk

Mem 500
Sec Miss L Stevenson
Pro C Knowles
Holes 18 L 5935 yds SSS 68 9 hole Par 3 course
V'tors WD–U WE–NA before 10am SOC
Fees £18 D–£25 (£23 D–£30) Par 3–£4 (£5)
Loc 6 miles N of Bromyard on B4203. M5 Junction 5

South Herefordshire (1992)
Twin Lakes, Upton Bishop, Ross-on-Wye, HR9 7UA
Tel (01989) 780535
Fax (01989) 740611
Mem 300
Sec RLA Lee (Mgr)
Pro E Litchfield
Holes 18 L 6672 yds Par 71 SSS 72 9 hole Par 3 course
V'tors U SOC
Fees £15 (£20)
Loc 3 miles NE of Ross-on-Wye. M50 Junction 4
Mis Floodlit driving range
Arch John Day

Hertfordshire

Aldenham G&CC (1975)
Church Lane, Aldenham, Watford, WD25 8NN
Tel (01923) 853929
Fax (01923) 858472
Mem 500
Sec Mrs J Phillips
Pro T Dunstan (01923) 857889
Holes 18 L 6500 yds SSS 71 9 L 2350 yds
V'tors U
Fees £25 (£35)
Loc 3 miles E of Watford, off B462. M1 Junction 5

Aldwickbury Park (1995)
Piggottshill Lane, Wheathampstead Road, Harpenden, AL5 1AB
Tel (01582) 765112
Fax (01582) 760113
Web www.wwsl.co.uk/aldwickbury
Mem 700
Sec A Knott
Pro S Plumb (01582) 760112
Holes 18 L 6032 yds Par 71 SSS 69 9 hole Par 3 course
V'tors WD–U booking necessary WE–U after 1pm SOC–WD
Fees £22 (£35)
Loc E of Harpenden on Wheathampstead road. M1 Junction 9. A1(M) Junction 4
Arch Gillett/Brown

Arkley (1909)
Rowley Green Road, Barnet, EN5 3HL
Tel (020) 8449 0394
Fax (020) 8440 5214
Mem 350
Sec D Reed
Pro M Porter (020) 8440 8473
Holes 9 L 6106 yds SSS 69
V'tors WD–U WE–M SOC–Wed–Fri
Fees £22
Loc NW of Barnet, off A1(M)
Arch James Braid

Ashridge (1932)
Little Gaddesden, Berkhamsted, HP4 1LY
Tel (01442) 842244
Fax (01442) 843770
Web www.ashridgegolfclub.ltd.uk
Mem 700
Sec MS Silver
Pro A Ainsworth (01442) 842307
Holes 18 L 6547 yds SSS 71
V'tors WD only–phone Sec
Fees On application
Loc 5 miles N of Berkhamsted on B4506
Arch Campbell/Hutchison/Hotchkin

Barkway Park (1992)
Nuthampstead Road, Barkway, Royston, SG8 8EN
Tel (01763) 849070
Mem 285
Sec GS Cannon
Pro J Bates (01763) 848215
Holes 18 L 6997 yds SSS 74
V'tors U
Fees £10 (£15)
Loc 5 miles SE of Royston, on B1368
Arch Vivien Saunders

Batchwood Hall (1935)
Pay and play
Batchwood Drive, St Albans, AL3 5XA
Tel (01727) 833349
Fax (01582) 833530
Mem 425
Sec B Hudson
Holes 18 L 6487 yds SSS 71
V'tors WD–U WE–NA before 10am
Fees £10.80 (£13.90)
Loc NW of St Albans on A5081. 5 miles S of M1 Junction 9
Arch JH Taylor

Batchworth Park (1996)
London Road, Rickmansworth, WD3 1JS
Tel (01923) 711400
Fax (01923) 710200
Mem 750
Sec D Cudmore (Gen Mgr)
Pro S Proudfoot (01923) 714922
Holes 18 L 6723 yds Par 72 SSS 72
V'tors M
Fees N/A

Loc   1 mile SE of Rickmansworth
       on A404. M25 Junction 18
Mis   Indoor Academy. Practice
       range
Arch   Dave Thomas

Berkhamsted (1890)

The Common, Berkhamsted, HP4 2QB
Tel   (01442) 865832
Fax   (01442) 863730
Mem   450 120(L) 50(J)
Sec   BJ Hill
Pro   BJ Proudfoot (01442) 865851
Holes 18 L 6605 yds Par 71 SSS 72
V'tors U H WE–M before 11.30am
       SOC–Wed & Fri
Fees   £30 (£40)
Loc   1 mile N of Berkhamsted.
       M25 Junction 21 (A41). M1
       Junction 8
Arch   HS Colt/James Braid

Bishop's Stortford (1910)

*Dunmow Road, Bishop's Stortford,
CM23 5HP*
Tel   (01279) 654715
Fax   (01279) 655215
Web   www.bsgc.co.uk
Mem   900
Sec   B Collins
Pro   SM Bryan (01279) 651324
Holes 18 L 6404 yds SSS 71
V'tors WD–U H WE–M SOC–WD
       exc Tues
Fees   £27 D–£35
Loc   E of Bishop's Stortford on
       A1250. M11 Junction
       8,¹/₂mile
Arch   James Braid

Boxmoor (1890)

*18 Box Lane, Hemel Hempstead,
HP3 0DJ*
Tel   (01442) 242434 (Clubhouse)
Web   www.boxmoorgolfclub.co.uk
Mem   290
Sec   CJ Horsted (07976) 747567
Pro   None
Holes 9 L 4854 yds SSS 64
V'tors U exc Sun–NA
Fees   £12 Sat–£14
Loc   1 mile W of Hemel
       Hempstead on B4505 to
       Chesham

Brickendon Grange (1964)

*Pembridge Lane, Brickendon, Hertford,
SG13 8PD*
Tel   (01992) 511258
Fax   (01992) 511411
Web   www.brickendongrangegc
       .co.uk
Mem   700
Sec   C Day
Pro   G Tippett (01992) 511218
Holes 18 L 6325 yds SSS 70
V'tors WD–U H WE/BH–M SOC
Fees   £28 D–£38
Loc   Bayford, 3 miles S of Hertford
Arch   CK Cotton

Bridgedown (1994)

St Albans Road, Barnet, EN5 4RE
Tel   (020) 8440 4120
Fax   (020) 8441 7649
Mem   400
Sec   Mrs A Menai-Davis
       (020) 8441 7649
Pro   L Jones
Holes 18 L 6626 yds Par 72 SSS 72
V'tors U
Fees   £15 (£17)
Loc   1 mile S of South Mimms on
       A1081. M25 Junction 23
Mis   Practice range
Arch   Howard Swann

Briggens House Hotel (1988)

*Briggens Park, Stanstead Road,
Stanstead Abbotts, SG12 8LD*
Tel   (01279) 793742
Fax   (01279) 793685
Mem   280
Sec   A Battle (Mgr)
Holes 9 L 5825 yds SSS 69
V'tors U SOC
Fees   9 holes–£10 (£14)
Loc   4 miles E of Hertford, off
       A414

Brocket Hall (1992)

Welwyn, AL8 7XG
Tel   (01707) 335241
Mem   790
Sec   P Densham (01707) 335241
Pro   K Wood (01707) 390063
Holes Melbourne 18 L 6616 yds
       SSS 72;
       Palmerston 18 L 6925 yds
       SSS 73
V'tors M H
Loc   On B653 to Wheathampstead.
       A1(M) Junction 4
Mis   Driving range. Golf Academy
Arch   Melbourne-Alliss/Clark.
       Palmerston-Steel

Brookmans Park (1930)

Brookmans Park, Hatfield, AL9 7AT
Tel   (01707) 652487
Fax   (01707) 661851
Mem   775
Sec   PA Gill
Pro   I Jelley (01707) 652468
Holes 18 L 6473 yds SSS 71
V'tors WD–UH WE/BH–M SOC
Fees   £30
Loc   3 miles S of Hatfield, off
       A1000
Arch   Hawtree/Taylor

Bushey G&CC (1980)

High Street, Bushey, WD2 1BJ
Tel   (020) 8950 2283
Fax   (020) 8386 1181
Mem   600
Sec   B Worthington
Pro   G Atkinson
       (020) 8950 2215
Holes 9 L 3000 yds SSS 69

V'tors WD–U before 6pm
       WE/BH–U after 3.30pm
       Wed–closed SOC–WD exc
       Wed
Fees   18 holes–£12 (17) 9 holes–£9
       (£11)
Loc   2 miles S of Watford on
       A4008
Mis   Driving range

Bushey Hall (1890)

Bushey Hall Drive, Bushey, WD2 2EP
Tel   (01923) 222253
Fax   (01923) 229759
Web   www.golfclubuk.co.uk
Mem   460
Sec   R Penman
Pro   K Wickham (01923) 225802
Holes 18 L 6099 yds SSS 69
V'tors U SOC–WD
Fees   £18 (£25)
Loc   1 mile SE of Watford. M1
       Junction 5

Chadwell Springs (1974)

Hertford Road, Ware, SG12 9LE
Tel   (01920) 463647
Mem   350
Sec   M Scott (01920) 461447
Pro   M Wall (01920) 462075
Holes 9 L 3021 yds SSS 69
V'tors WD–U WE–M
Fees   £20
Loc   Between Ware and Hertford
       on A119

Chesfield Downs (1991)

Pay and play
*Jack's Hill, Graveley, Stevenage,
SG4 7EQ*
Tel   (01462) 482929
Fax   (01462) 482930
Web   www.clubhaus.com
Mem   550
Sec   J Wright
Pro   Jane Fernley
Holes 18 L 6646 yds SSS 71
       9 holes Par 3 course
V'tors U SOC
Fees   18 hole:£16 (£24) 9 hole:£4
       (£5)
Loc   B197, N of Stevenage. A1(M)
       Junctions 8 or 9
Mis   Driving range
Arch   Jonathan Gaunt

Cheshunt (1976)

Public
Park Lane, Cheshunt, EN7 6QD
Tel   (01992) 29777
Mem   280
Sec   B Furne
Pro   D Banks (01992) 24009
Holes 18 L 6608 yds SSS 71
V'tors U–booking required
Fees   £12 (£16.50)
Loc   Off A10 at Church Lane,
       Cheshunt. M25 Junction 25, 3
       miles
Arch   Hawtree

Chorleywood   (1890)

Common Road, Chorleywood,
WD3 5LN

Tel	**(01923) 282009**
Fax	(01923) 286739
Mem	280
Sec	R Botham
Pro	None
Holes	9 L 2838 yds SSS 67
V'tors	WD–U exc Tues am WE–U after 11.30am SOC
Fees	£20 (£25)
Loc	3 miles N of Rickmansworth, off A404. M25 Junction 18

Danesbury Park   (1992)

Codicote Road, Welwyn, AL6 9SD

Tel	**(01438) 840100**
Fax	(01727) 846109
Mem	300
Sec	D Snowdon
Pro	G Harvey
Holes	9 L 4150 yds SSS 60
V'tors	U SOC–WD
Loc	¾ mile from A1(M) Junction 6 on B656 Hitchin road
Arch	Derek Snowdon

Dyrham Park CC   (1963)

Galley Lane, Barnet, EN5 4RA

Tel	**(020) 8440 3361**
Fax	(020) 8441 9836
Mem	600
Sec	K Sutton
Pro	W Large (020) 8440 3904
Holes	18 L 6422 yds SSS 71
V'tors	M SOC–Wed
Loc	10 miles N of London. M25 Junction 23
Arch	CK Cotton

East Herts   (1899)

Hamels Park, Buntingford, SG9 9NA

Tel	**(01920) 821923**
Fax	(01920) 823700
Mem	700
Sec	C Wilkinson (01920) 821978
Pro	G Culmer (01920) 821922
Holes	18 L 6456 yds SSS 71
V'tors	WD–H exc Wed–NA before 1pm WE–M
Fees	On application
Loc	¼ mile N of Puckeridge on A10

Elstree   (1984)

Watling Street, Elstree, WD6 3AA

Tel	**(020) 8953 6115**
Fax	(020) 8207 6390
Mem	500
Sec	K Roberts (020) 8238 6942
Pro	M Warwick
Holes	18 L 6556 yds Par 73 SSS 72
V'tors	U SOC
Fees	On application
Loc	A5183, 1 mile N of Elstree. M1 Junction 4
Mis	Floodlit driving range
Arch	Donald Steel

Forest Hills   (1994)

Newgate Street, SG13 8EW

Tel	**(01707) 876825**
Fax	(01707) 876825
Mem	170
Sec	G Spearpoint
Pro	C Easton
Holes	9 L 3220 yds Par 72 SSS 71
V'tors	WD–U WE/BH–by arrangement
Fees	£15 (£20)
Loc	3 miles W of Cheshunt. M25 Junction 25
Arch	Mel Flannagan

Great Hadham   (1993)

Great Hadham Road, Bishop's Stortford, SG10 6JE

Tel	**(01279) 843558**
Fax	(01279) 842122
Mem	700
Sec	T Streeter
Pro	K Lunt (01279) 843888
Holes	18 L 6854 yds Par 72 SSS 73
V'tors	WD–U WE/BH–NA before 12 noon SOC
Fees	£18 (£25)
Loc	3 miles SW of Bishops Stortford (B1004). M11 Junction 8
Mis	Driving range

Hadley Wood   (1922)

Beech Hill, Hadley Wood, Barnet, EN4 0JJ

Tel	**(020) 8449 4328**
Fax	(020) 8364 8633
Web	www.hadleywoodgc.com
Mem	635
Sec	CS Silcox (Gen Mgr)
Pro	P Jones (020) 8449 3285
Holes	18 L 6457 yds SSS 71
V'tors	WD–H WE/BH–M SOC
Fees	On application
Loc	10 miles N of London, off A111 between Potters Bar and Cockfosters. 2 miles S of M25 Junction 24
Mis	Practice range
Arch	Dr A Mackenzie

Hanbury Manor G&CC   (1990)

Ware, SG12 0SD

Tel	**(01920) 487722**
Fax	(01920) 487692
Mem	500
Sec	S Emms
Pro	P Blaze
Holes	18 L 7016 yds SSS 74
V'tors	M H + Hotel guests
Fees	£75
Loc	8 miles N of M25 Junction 25 on A10 at Thundridge
Arch	Jack Nicklaus II

Harpenden   (1894)

Hammonds End, Harpenden, AL5 2AX

Tel	**(01582) 712580**
Fax	(01582) 712725

Mem	800
Sec	FLK Clapp
Pro	P Cherry (01582) 767124
Holes	18 L 6381 yds SSS 70
V'tors	WD–U exc Thurs WE/BH–M SOC–WD exc Thurs
Fees	£26 D–£36
Loc	6 miles N of St Albans on B487
Arch	Hawtree/Taylor

Harpenden Common   (1931)

East Common, Harpenden, AL5 1BL

Tel	**(01582) 712856**
Fax	(01582) 715959
Mem	740
Sec	GD Eastwood (01582) 715959
Pro	D Fitzsimmons (01582) 460655
Holes	18 L 6214 yds SSS 70
V'tors	WD–U H WE–M SOC
Fees	£25 (£30)
Loc	4 miles N of St Albans, on A1081
Arch	K Brown (1995)

Hartsbourne G&CC   (1946)

Hartsbourne Avenue, Bushey Heath, WD2 1JW

Tel	**(020) 8950 1133**
Fax	(020) 8950 5357
Mem	750
Sec	S Whyte
Pro	A Cardwell (020) 8950 2836
Holes	18 L 6385 yds SSS 70 9 L 5773 yds SSS 68
V'tors	NA SOC
Loc	5 miles SE of Watford, off A4008
Arch	Hawtree/Taylor

Hatfield London CC   (1976)

Pay and play
Bedwell Park, Essendon, Hatfield, AL9 6JA

Tel	**(01707) 642624**
Fax	(01707) 646187
Mem	260
Sec	H Yoshikawa
Pro	N Greer (01707) 650431
Holes	18 L 6808 yds SSS 72
V'tors	U SOC
Fees	£17 (£27)
Loc	4 miles E of Hatfield on B158. M25 Junction 24. A1(M) Junction 4
Mis	9 hole pitch & putt course
Arch	Fred Hawtree

The Hertfordshire   (1995)

Pay and play
Broxbournebury Mansion, White Stubbs Lane, Broxbourne, EN10 7PY

Tel	**(01992) 466666**
Fax	(01992) 470326

Mem 690
Sec J Anderson (Dir)
Pro A Shearn
Holes 18 L 6400 yds Par 70 SSS 70
V'tors U H SOC
Fees £21 (£25)
Loc 8 miles N of M25 Junction 25,
off A10
Mis Floodlit driving range
Arch Jack Nicklaus II

Kingsway Golf Centre
(1991)
Cambridge Road, Melbourn, Royston,
SG8 6EY
Tel (01763) 262727
Fax (01763) 263298
Mem 200
Sec Teresa Russell
Pro M Sturgess, D Hastings
Holes 9 L 2500 yds Par 33
9 hole Par 3 course
V'tors U SOC
Fees 9 holes–£5. 18 holes–£8
Loc N of Royston on A10
Mis Driving range

Knebworth (1908)
Deards End Lane, Knebworth,
SG3 6NL
Tel (01438) 812752 (Clubhouse)
Fax (01438) 815216
Mem 1000
Sec M Parsons MBE
(01438) 812752
Pro G Parker (01438) 812757
Holes 18 L 6492 yds SSS 71
V'tors WD–U H WE–M
SOC–Mon/Tues/Thurs
Fees £30
Loc 1 mile S of Stevenage on B197
Arch Willie Park

Lamerwood (1996)
Codicote Road, Wheathampstead,
AL4 8GB
Tel (01582) 833013
Fax (01582) 832604
Sec S Takabatake (Golf Dir)
Pro J Coe
Holes 18 L 6953 yds Par 72
Par 3 course
V'tors U
Fees £24 (£35)
Loc 5 miles W of A1(M) Junction
4 on B653
Mis Driving range
Arch Cameron Sinclair

Letchworth (1905)
Letchworth Lane, Letchworth,
SG6 3NQ
Tel (01462) 683203
Fax (01462) 484567
Mem 900
Sec AR Bailey
Pro (01462) 682713
Holes 18 L 6181 yds SSS 69
V'tors WD–H WE–M
SOC–Wed–Fri

Fees £27
Loc S of Letchworth, off A505.
A1(M) Junction 9
Mis Driving range
Arch Harry Vardon

Little Hay Golf Complex
(1977)
Pay and play
Box Lane, Bovingdon, Hemel
Hempstead, HP3 0DQ
Tel (01442) 833798
Fax (01442) 831399
Sec C Gordon (Golf Mgr)
Pro N Allen
Holes 18 L 6592 yds SSS 71
V'tors U SOC
Fees £12 (£16.50)
Loc 2 miles W of Hemel
Hempstead, on B4505 to
Chesham
Mis Driving range. Pitch & putt
Arch Hawtree

Manor of Groves G&CC
(1991)
High Wych, Sawbridgeworth,
CM21 0LA
Tel (01279) 721486
Fax (01279) 726972
Mem 450
Pro C Laurence
Holes 18 L 6280 yds SSS 70
V'tors WD–U WE–NA before noon
SOC
Fees On application
Loc 1 mile N of Harlow
Arch S Sharer

Mid Herts (1892)
Gustard Wood, Wheathampstead,
AL4 8RS
Tel (01582) 832242
Fax (01582) 834834
Web www.mid-hertsgolfclub.co.uk
Mem 500(M) 125(L)
Sec RJH Jourdan
Pro B Puttick (01582) 832788
Holes 18 L 6060 yds SSS 70
V'tors WD–UH exc Tues & Wed pm
WE/BH–M SOC
Fees On application
Loc 6 miles N of St Albans on
B651

Mill Green (1994)
Gypsy Lane, Mill Green, Welwyn
Garden City, AL7 4TY
Tel (01707) 276900
Fax (01707) 276898
Sec RJ Jackson (Gen Mgr)
Pro I Parker (01707) 270542
Holes 18 L 6615 yds Par 72 SSS 72
Par 3 course
V'tors U SOC–WD
Fees £15–£21 (£25)
Loc S of Welwyn Garden City, off
A414. A1 Junction 4
Arch Clark/Alliss

Moor Park (1923)
Rickmansworth, WD3 1QN
Tel (01923) 773146
Fax (01923) 777109
Web www.moorparkgc.co.uk
Mem 1700
Sec JM Moore (01923) 773146
Pro L Farmer (01923) 774113
Holes High 18 L 6713 yds SSS 72
West 18 L 5823 yds SSS 68
V'tors WD–H WE/BH–M SOC
Fees High £60. West £35
Loc 1 mile SE of Rickmansworth,
off Batchworth roundabout
(A4145). M25 Junction 18, 2
miles
Arch HS Colt

Old Fold Manor (1910)
Old Fold Lane, Hadley Green, Barnet,
EN5 4QN
Tel (020) 8440 9185
Fax (020) 8441 4863
Web www.oldfoldmanor.co.uk
Mem 526
Sec AW Dickens (Mgr)
Pro P McEvoy (020) 8440 7488
Holes 18 L 6466 yds SSS 71
V'tors WD–H WE–M SOC–Thurs &
Fri
Fees £25 D–£35
Loc 1 mile N of Barnet on A1000

Oxhey Park
Prestwick Road, South Oxhey, Watford,
WD19 7EX
Tel (01923) 248213
Fax (01923) 248213
Mem 110
Sec AT Duggan (Prop)
Pro J Wright
Holes 9 L 1637 yds Par 58
V'tors U
Fees 9 holes–£5 (£7) 18 holes–£7
(£9)
Loc 2 miles SW of Watford. M1
Junction 5
Mis Driving range

Panshanger Golf
Complex (1976)
Old Herns Lane, Welwyn Garden City,
AL7 2ED
Tel (01707) 333312/333350
(Bookings)
Holes 18 L 6167 yds SSS 70
9 hole Par 3 course
V'tors U
Fees On application
Loc 2 miles off A1, via B1000 to
Hertford

Porters Park (1899)
Shenley Hill, Radlett, WD7 7AZ
Tel (01923) 854127
Fax (01923) 855475
Mem 850
Sec P Marshall
Pro D Gleeson (01923) 854366
Holes 18 L 6313 yds SSS 70

V'tors WD–H (phone first)
WE/BH–M SOC–Wed &
Thurs
Fees £30–£45
Loc E of Radlett on Shenley road.
M25 Junction 22

Potters Bar (1923)

Darkes Lane, Potters Bar, EN6 1DE
Tel (01707) 652020
Fax (01707) 655051
Web www.pottersbargolfclub.com
Mem 600
Sec PK Watson (Mgr)
Pro G A'ris, J Harding
(01707) 652987
Holes 18 L 6279 yds SSS 70
V'tors WD–H WE/BH–M SOC–WD
exc Wed
Fees £25 D–£35
Loc 1 mile N of M25 Junction 24,
off A1000
Arch James Braid

Redbourn (1970)

*Kinsbourne Green Lane, Redbourn, St
Albans, AL3 7QA*
Tel (01582) 793493
Fax (01582) 794362
Sec R Fay
Pro S Hunter
Holes 18 L 6506 yds SSS 71
9 hole Par 3 course
V'tors WD–U booking necessary
WE/BH–H SOC–WD
Fees 18 hole:£24 (£30)
9 hole:£7 (£10)
Loc 4 miles N of St Albans, off A5.
1 mile S of M1 Junction 9
Mis Target golf range

Rickmansworth (1937)

Public
Moor Lane, Rickmansworth, WD3 1QL
Tel (01923) 775278
Fax (01923) 775278
Mem 250
Pro A Dobbins (01923) 775278
Holes 18 L 4493 yds SSS 62
9 hole Par 3 course
V'tors U
Fees £11 (£15.50)
Loc 1/2 mile SE of Rickmansworth,
off Batchworth roundabout
(A4145). M25 Junction 18,
2 miles
Arch HS Colt

Royston (1892)

Baldock Road, Royston, SG8 5BG
Tel (01763) 242696
Fax (01763) 242696
Mem 750
Sec J Beech (01763) 242696
Pro S Clark (01763) 243476
Holes 18 L 6086 yds SSS 70
V'tors WD–H WE–M SOC–WD
Fees £25 D–£30
Loc SW of Royston on A505
Arch H Vardon

Sandy Lodge (1910)

*Sandy Lodge Lane, Northwood, Middx,
HA6 2JD*
Tel (01923) 825429
Fax (01923) 824319
Mem 700
Sec HE Inman
Pro J Pinsent (01923) 825321
Holes 18 L 6328 yds SSS 71
V'tors H or M SOC
Fees On application
Loc Adjacent Moor Park Station
Arch Harry Vardon

Shendish Manor (1988)

Pay and play
*Shendish House, Apsley, Hemel
Hempstead, HP3 0AA*
Tel (01442) 251806
Fax (01442) 230683
Sec M Thornberry
Holes 18 L 5660 yds Par 70 SSS 68
V'tors U SOC
Fees £15 (£20)
Loc S of Hemel Hempstead, off
A41. M25 Junction 20
Arch Cotton/Steel

South Herts (1899)

*Links Drive, Totteridge, London,
N20 8QU*
Tel (020) 8445 0117
Fax (020) 8445 7569
Mem 850
Sec KA Bravant (020) 8445 2035
Pro RY Mitchell (020) 8445 4633
Holes 18 L 6470 yds SSS 71
9 L 1581 yds
V'tors WD–IH WE/BH–M
Fees On application
Loc Totteridge Lane
Arch Harry Vardon

Stevenage (1980)

Public
Aston Lane, Stevenage, SG2 7EL
Tel (01438) 880424
Mem 450
Sec Mrs S Elwin (01438) 880322
Pro S Barker (01438) 880424
Holes 18 L 6451 yds SSS 71
9 hole Par 3 course
V'tors U
Fees £12 (£16)
Loc Off A602 to Hertford. A1(M)
Junction 7
Mis Driving range
Arch John Jacobs

Stocks Hotel G&CC (1994)

*Stocks Road, Aldbury, Tring,
HP23 5RX*
Tel (01442) 851341
Fax (01442) 851253
Mem 440
Sec R Darling (Golf Mgr)
Pro PR Lane (Ext 311)
Holes 18 L 7016 yds SSS 74
V'tors H SOC

Fees £30 (£40)
Loc Aldbury, 2 miles E of Tring.
A41(T), 2 miles
Mis Practice range
Arch M Billcliffe

Verulam (1905)

London Road, St Albans, AL1 1JG
Tel (01727) 853327
Fax (01727) 812201
Web www.verulamgolf.co.uk
Mem 712
Sec JR Maguire (Gen Mgr)
Pro N Burch (01727) 861401
Holes 18 L 6448 yds Par 72 SSS 71
V'tors WD–H exc Mon–U
WE/BH–M SOC–Tues &
Thurs
Fees £25 Mon–£20
Loc 1 mile SE of St Albans on
A1081. M25 Junction 21A or
22. M1 Junction 6
Mis Practice range
Arch Braid/Steel

Welwyn Garden City (1922)

*Mannicotts, High Oaks Road, Welwyn
Garden City, AL8 7BP*
Tel (01707) 325243
Fax (01707) 393213
Mem 900
Sec R Haslehurst (Gen Mgr)
(01707) 325243
Pro R May (01707) 325525
Holes 18 L 6100 yds SSS 69
V'tors WD–H WE/BH–NA
Fees On application
Loc 1 mile N of Hatfield. A1(M)
Junction 4 - B197 to Valley
Road
Arch Hawtree

West Herts (1890)

Cassiobury Park, Watford, WD3 3GG
Tel (01923) 236484
Fax (01923) 222300
Mem 700
Sec CC Dodman
Pro CS Gough (01923) 220352
Holes 18 L 6488 yds SSS 71
V'tors WD–U WE/BH–M
SOC–Wed & Fri
Fees £28 (£35)
Loc Off A412, between Watford
and Rickmansworth
Arch Morris/Mackenzie

Whipsnade Park (1974)

Studham Lane, Dagnall, HP4 1RH
Tel (01442) 842330
Fax (01442) 842090
Web www.whipsnadeparkgc.com
Mem 600
Sec Jane Mitchell
Pro M Green
Holes 18 L 6812 yds SSS 72
V'tors WD–U WE–M SOC–WD
Fees £26 D–£36
Loc 8 miles N of Hemel
Hempstead, off A4147

Whitehill (1990)
Dane End, Ware, SG12 0JS
Tel   (01920) 438495
Fax   (01920) 438891
Mem   650
Sec   Mr & Mrs A Smith (Props)
Pro   D Ling
Holes 18 L 6636 yds SSS 72
V'tors H–booking necessary
Fees   £19.50 (£22.50)
Loc   4 miles N of Ware (A10)
Mis   Floodlit driving range

Isle of Man

Castletown Hotel   (1892)
Fort Island, Derbyhaven, IM9 1UA
Tel   (01624) 822201
Fax   (01624) 824633
Mem   500
Sec   B Watts (Hon)
Pro   M Crowe (01624) 822211
Holes 18 L 6716 yds SSS 72
V'tors U SOC
Fees   £28 (£33)
Loc   1 mile E of Castletown
Arch   Mackenzie Ross

Douglas Municipal   (1927)
Public
Pulrose Park, Douglas, IM2 1AE
Tel   (01624) 675952 (Clubhouse)
Mem   300
Sec   M Murray
Pro   K Parry (01624) 661558
Holes 18 L 5922 yds Par 69 SSS 69
V'tors U
Fees   £8.50 (£10.50)
Loc   Douglas Pier 2 miles
Arch   Dr A Mackenzie

King Edward Bay   (1893)
Groudle Road, Onchan, IM3 2JR
Tel   (01624) 620430/673821
Fax   (01624) 676794
Mem   400
Sec   B Holt (01624) 670977
Pro   D Jones (01624) 672709
Holes 18 L 5457 yds SSS 65
V'tors U SOC
Fees   £10 (£12)
Loc   1 mile N of Douglas
Arch   Tom Morris (1893 course)

Mount Murray G&CC
(1994)
Santon, IM4 2HT
Tel   (01624) 661111
Fax   (01624) 611116
Mem   360
Sec   AD Dyson (Ext 3023)
Pro   AD Dyson (Ext 3023)
Holes 18 L 6664 yds SSS 72
V'tors U H SOC
Fees   £18 (£24)
Loc   3 miles SW of Douglas
Mis   Driving range

Peel   (1895)
Rheast Lane, Peel, IM5 1BG
Tel   (01624) 842227
Fax   (01624) 843456
Web   www.geocities.com/peelgc
Mem   600
Sec   GR Thompson
          (01624) 843456
Pro   M Crowe
Holes 18 L 5874 yds SSS 69
V'tors WD–U WE/BH–NA before
          10.30am SOC
Fees   £18 (£25)
Loc   10 miles W of Douglas via A1
Arch   James Braid

Port St Mary (1936)
Public
Kallow Road, Port St Mary, IM9 5EJ
Tel   (01624) 834932
Sec   T Boyle (Hon)
Pro   M Crowe (01624) 822221
Holes 9 L 2711 yds SSS 66
V'tors WD–U WE–NA before
          10.30am SOC
Fees   On application
Loc   6 miles S of Castletown via A5
Arch   George Duncan

Ramsey (1891)
Brookfield, Ramsey, IM8 2AH
Tel   (01624) 813365/812244
Fax   (01624) 815833
Mem   700
Sec   Mrs J Hignett (01624) 812244
Pro   C Wilson (01624) 814736
Holes 18 L 6019 yds SSS 69
V'tors WD–U after 10am WE–M
          SOC
Fees   £22 (£25)
Loc   N of Douglas via A18.
          W boundary of Ramsey
Arch   James Braid

Rowany (1895)
Rowany Drive, Port Erin, IM9 6LN
Tel   (01624) 834108
Fax   (01624) 834072
Mem   500
Sec   DG Street (Mgr)
          (01624) 834072
Holes 18 L 5774 yds SSS 69
V'tors U SOC
Fees   £14 (£18)
Loc   6 miles W of Castletown via
          A5

Isle of Wight

Cowes (1909)
Crossfield Avenue, Cowes, PO31 8HN
Tel   (01983) 280135 (Clubhouse)
Mem   300
Sec   D Weaver (01983) 292303
Holes 9 L 5878 yds SSS 68
V'tors H Thurs–NA before 3pm
          (Ladies Day) Fri–NA after
          5pm Sun am–NA

Fees   £15 (£18)
Loc   Nr Cowes High School
Arch   J Hamilton Stutt

Freshwater Bay   (1894)
Afton Down, Freshwater, PO40 9TZ
Tel   (01983) 752955
Fax   (01983) 756704
Web   www.isle-of-wight.uk.com/golf
Mem   500
Sec   T Riddett (01983) 752955
Holes 18 L 5725 yds SSS 68
V'tors H–NA before 9.30am SOC
Fees   £20 (£24)
Loc   400 yds off Military Road
          (A3055)

Newport   (1896)
St George's Down, Shide, Newport,
PO30 3BA
Tel   (01983) 525076
Mem   350
Sec   R Buchanan
Holes 9 L 5674 yds SSS 68
V'tors WD–U exc Wed–NA
          12–2.30pm Sat–NA before
          3.30pm Sun–NA before noon
          SOC
Fees   £15 (£17.50)
Loc   1 mile SE of Newport
Arch   Guy Hunt

Osborne (1904)
Osborne House Estate, East Cowes,
PO32 6JX
Tel   (01983) 295421
Mem   260 90(L)
Sec   RS Jones
Holes 9 L 6372 yds SSS 70
V'tors WD–U exc Ladies Day (Tues)
          9am–1pm–NA WE–NA
          before noon SOC
Fees   £20 (£22) 5D–£65
Loc   S of East Cowes in grounds of
          Osborne House

Ryde (1895)
Binstead Road, Ryde, PO33 3NF
Tel   (01983) 614809
Fax   (01983) 567418
Mem   450
Sec   ARJ Goodall
Pro   None
Holes 9 L 5287 yds SSS 66
V'tors WD–U exc Wed pm Sun–NA
          before noon
Fees   £15 (£20)
Loc   On main Ryde/Newport road
Arch   J Hamilton Stutt

Shanklin & Sandown
(1900)
The Fairway, Lake, Sandown,
PO36 9PR
Tel   (01983) 403217
Fax   (01983) 403217
Mem   700
Sec   AJ Messing
Pro   P Hammond (01983) 404424

Holes 18 L 6063 yds SSS 69
V'tors WD–U WE–NA before 12 noon
Fees £25 (£30) 3WD–£60
Loc 1 mile off A3055 in Lake
Arch James Braid

Ventnor (1892)
Steephill Down Road, Ventnor, PO38 1BP
Tel (01983) 853326
Mem 250
Sec S Blackmore
Holes 12 L 5767 yds Par 70 SSS 68
V'tors WD–U exc Mon Sun–NA before 1pm SOC
Fees On application
Loc NW boundary of Ventnor

Kent

Aquarius (1913)
Marmora Rd, Honor Oak, London, SE22 0RY
Tel (020) 8693 1626
Mem 400
Sec S Ridgeway
Pro F Private
Holes 9 L 5246 yds SSS 66
V'tors M

Ashford (1903)
Sandhurst Lane, Ashford, TN25 4NT
Tel (01233) 620180
Fax (01233) 622655
Mem 650
Sec AH Story (01233) 622655
Pro H Sherman (01233) 629644
Holes 18 L 6284 yds SSS 70
V'tors WD–H WE/BH–H SOC
Fees £28 D–£38 (£35)
Loc Ashford 1½ miles (A20)
Arch Cotton

Austin Lodge (1991)
Eynsford, Swanley, DA4 0HU
Tel (01322) 863000
Fax (01322) 862406
Mem 600
Sec S Bevan
Pro P Edwards
Holes 18 L 6600 yds Par 73 SSS 71
V'tors WD–U WE–NA before noon SOC
Fees £16 (£25)
Loc Off A225, nr Eynsford Station. M25 Junction 3, 3 miles
Mis Driving range for members and guests
Arch Peter Bevan

Barnehurst (1903)
Public
Mayplace Road East, Bexley Heath, DA7 6JU
Tel (01322) 523746

Fax (01322) 554612
Mem 300
Sec B Davies (01322) 552952
Pro P Tallack (01322) 552952
Holes 9 L 5448 yds SSS 69
V'tors U SOC
Fees £5.70 (£9.20)
Loc Between Crayford and Bexleyheath
Arch James Braid

Bearsted (1895)
Ware Street, Bearsted, Maidstone, ME14 4PQ
Tel (01622) 738389
Fax (01622) 738198
Mem 780
Sec Mrs LM Siems (01622) 738198
Pro T Simpson (01622) 738024
Holes 18 L 6253 yds SSS 70
V'tors WD–I H WE–H M (recognised GC members) SOC
Fees £27 D–£36
Loc 2½ miles E of Maidstone

Beckenham Place Park (1907)
Public
Beckenham Hill Road, Beckenham, BR3 2BP
Tel (020) 8650 2292
Fax (020) 8663 1201
Pro H Davies-Thomas
Holes 18 L 5722 yds SSS 68
V'tors U
Fees £7.60 (£12.40) WE–booking fee
Loc Off A21 on A222

Bexleyheath (1907)
Mount Road, Bexleyheath, BR8 7RJ
Tel (020) 8303 6951
Mem 350
Sec SE Squires
Holes 9 L 5239 yds SSS 66
V'tors WD–H before 4pm
Fees £20
Loc Station 1 mile

Birchwood Park (1990)
Birchwood Road, Wilmington, Dartford, DA2 7HJ
Tel (01322) 660554
Fax (01322) 667283
Web www.birchwoodgolf.co.uk
Mem 450
Sec Julie Smith (Mgr) (01322) 662038
Pro S Cranfield (01322) 615209
Holes 18 L 6364 yds Par 71 SSS 70 9 hole course
V'tors U SOC
Fees £16 (£21)
Loc 2 miles S of A2/A2018 Junction
Mis Driving range
Arch Howard Swann

Boughton (1993)
Pay and play
Brickfield Lane, Boughton, Faversham, ME13 9AJ
Tel (01227) 752277
Fax (01227) 752361
Mem 300
Sec S Hall
Pro T Poole
Holes 18 L 6452 yds SSS 71
V'tors U SOC–WD
Fees £16 (£22)
Loc NE of Boughton, nr M2/A2 interchange. 6 miles W of Canterbury
Mis Driving range
Arch Philip Sparks

Broke Hill (1993)
Sevenoaks Road, Halstead, TN14 7HR
Tel (01959) 533225
Fax (01959) 532680
Web www.brokehillgolf.co.uk
Sec C Winning (Gen Mgr)
Pro C West (01959) 533810
Holes 18 L 6374 yds Par 72 SSS 71
V'tors WD–U before 5pm WE–NA SOC–WD
Fees £35
Loc 4 miles S of Bromley on A21. M25 Junction 4
Arch David Williams

Bromley (1948)
Public
Magpie Hall Lane, Bromley, BR2 8JF
Tel (020) 8462 7014
Fax (020) 8462 6916
Mem 100
Pro A Hodgson
Holes 9 L 5538 yds SSS 66
V'tors U
Fees £5.30 (£6.95)
Loc Off Bromley Common (A21)

Broome Park (1981)
Broome Park Estate, Barham, Canterbury, CT4 6QX
Tel (01227) 830728
Fax (01227) 832591
Web www.broomepark.co.uk
Mem 600
Sec G Robins
Pro T Britz (01227) 831126
Holes 18 L 6610 yds SSS 72
V'tors H WE–NA before noon SOC–WD
Fees £30 (£35)
Loc M2/A2-A260 Folkestone road, 1½ miles on RH side
Mis Driving range
Arch Donald Steel

Canterbury (1927)
Scotland Hills, Littlebourne Road, Canterbury, CT1 1TW
Tel (01227) 453532
Fax (01227) 784277
Web www.canterburygolfclub .org.uk

Mem 680
Pro P Everard (01227) 462865
Holes 18 L 6249 yds SSS 70
V'tors WD–U H WE–NA before
11.30am
SOC–Tues/Thurs/Fri
Fees £27 D–£36 (£36)
Loc 1 mile E of Canterbury on
A257
Arch HS Colt

Chart Hills (1993)
*Weeks Lane, Biddenden, Ashford,
TN27 8JX*
Tel (01580) 292222
Fax (01580) 292233
Mem 495
Sec R Hyder (Gen Mgr)
Pro D French (01580) 292148
Holes 18 L 7135 yds SSS 74
V'tors U exc Mon/Wed/Sat–NA
SOC
Fees On application
Loc 12 miles W of Ashford (A262)
Mis Golf Academy
Arch Nick Faldo

Chelsfield Lakes Golf
Centre (1992)
Pay and play
Court Road, Orpington, BR6 9BX
Tel (01689) 896266
Fax (01689) 824577
Web www.clubhaus.com
Mem 650
Sec P Smith (Mgr)
Pro N Lee, B Hodkin
Holes 18 L 6077 yds Par 71 SSS 69
9 hole Par 3 course
V'tors U–booking required
Loc 1 mile from M25 Junction 4
(A224)
Mis Target golf range
Arch MRM Sandow

Cherry Lodge (1969)
*Jail Lane, Biggin Hill, Westerham,
TN16 3AX*
Tel (01959) 572250
Fax (01959) 540672
Mem 650
Sec AA Kemsley
Pro N Child (01959) 572989
Holes 18 L 6652 yds SSS 73
V'tors WD–U WE–M SOC–WD
before 3pm
Fees £30 D–£40
Loc 3 miles N of Westerham, off
A233
Mis Driving range
Arch John Day

Chestfield (1925)
*103 Chestfield Road, Whitstable,
CT5 3LU*
Tel (01227) 794411
Fax (01227) 794454
Web www.chestfield-golfclub.co.uk
Mem 550
Sec C Maxted

Pro J Brotherton (01227) 793563
Holes 18 L 6208 yds SSS 70
V'tors WD–U WE–NA before noon
SOC
Fees £22 (£25)
Loc ½ mile S of A2990 and
Chestfield Station
Arch Donald Steel

Chislehurst (1894)
*Camden Place, Camden Park Road,
Chislehurst, BR7 5HJ*
Tel (020) 8467 3055
Fax (020) 8295 0874
Mem 740
Sec D Bowles (020) 8467 2782
Pro J Bird (020) 8467 6798
Holes 18 L 5128 yds SSS 65
V'tors WD–H WE–M SOC
Fees D–£25
Loc M25 Junction 3/A20/A222

Cobtree Manor Park
(1984)
Public
*Chatham Road, Boxley, Maidstone,
ME14 3AZ*
Tel (01622) 753276
Sec A Ferras
Holes 18 L 5716 yds SSS 68
V'tors WD–U WE/BH–(book 1 wk
in advance) SOC–WD
Fees £10 (£18)
Loc 3 miles N of Maidstone on
A229
Arch F Hawtree

Cray Valley (1972)
Pay and play
*Sandy Lane, St Paul's Cray,
Orpington, BR5 3HY*
Tel (01689) 837909
Fax (01689) 891428
Mem 600
Sec J Scappatura (01689) 839677
Pro G Sheriff (01689) 837909
Holes 18 L 5624 yds SSS 67
9 L 2100 yds SSS 60
V'tors U
Fees £13 (£19)
Loc Off A20 Ruxley roundabout at
Sidcup

Darenth Valley (1973)
Pay and play
*Station Road, Shoreham, Sevenoaks,
TN14 7SA*
Tel (01959) 522944 (Clubhouse),
(01959) 522922 (Bookings)
Fax (01959) 525089
Sec JR Cooper (Mgr)
Pro D Copsey (01959) 522922
Holes 18 L 6302 yds Par 72 SSS 71
V'tors U–booking required SOC
Fees £16 (£21.50)
Loc 3 miles N of Sevenoaks, off
A225. M25 Junctions 1/3/5

Dartford (1897)
Heath Lane, Dartford, DA1 2TN
Tel (01322) 223616
Mem 600
Sec KJ Rawlins (01322) 226455
Pro J Gregory (01322) 226409
Holes 18 L 5914 yds Par 69 SSS 69
V'tors WD–I WE–M H
Fees £21
Loc Dartford 2 miles. Dartford
Heath turn off A2
Arch James Braid

Deangate Ridge (1972)
Public
*Duxcourt Road, Hoo, Rochester,
ME3 8RZ*
Tel (01634) 251950
Mem 560
Sec GW Harwood
(01634) 271754
Pro R Fox (01634) 251180
Holes 18 L 6300 yds SSS 70
V'tors U SOC
Fees On application
Loc 7 miles NE of Rochester on
A228. M2, 5 miles
Mis Driving range. Pitch & putt

Edenbridge G&CC (1973)
*Crouch House Road, Edenbridge,
TN8 5LQ*
Tel (01732) 867381
Fax (01732) 867029
Mem 800
Sec Mrs C Lloyd (Gen Mgr)
Pro K Burkin (01732) 865202
Holes 18 L 6577 yds SSS 72
18 L 5605 yds SSS 67
9 hole course
V'tors WD/WE–booking necessary
Fees £20 (£27.50)
Loc 2 miles W of Edenbridge.
M25 Junction 6
Mis Floodlit driving range
Arch David Williams

Eltham Warren (1890)
*Bexley Road, Eltham, London,
SE9 2PE*
Tel (020) 8850 1166
Web www.elthamwarrengolfclub
.co.uk
Mem 430
Sec DJ Clare (020) 8850 4477
Pro G Brett (020) 8859 7909
Holes 9 L 5840 yds SSS 68
V'tors WD–I WE/BH–M
SOC–Thurs only
Fees D–£25 (£10)
Loc ½ mile from Eltham station
on A210
Arch James Braid

Etchinghill (1995)
Pay and play
*Canterbury Road, Etchinghill,
Folkestone, CT18 8FA*
Tel (01303) 863863
Fax (01303) 863210
Mem 550
Sec S Garside (Mgr)

Pro C Hodgson (01303) 863966
Holes 27 L 6013-6116 yds Par 70
SSS 69
9 hole Par 3 course
V'tors WD–U WE–NA 7am–11am
Fees £18 (£24)
Loc 1 mile N of M20 Junction 12
on B2065
Mis Driving range
Arch John Sturdy

Faversham (1902)

Belmont Park, Faversham, ME13 0HB
Tel (01795) 890561
Fax (01795) 890760
Mem 850
Sec J Edgington
Pro S Rokes (01795) 890275
Holes 18 L 6030 yds Par 70 SSS 69
V'tors WD–I or H WE–M
Fees £30
Loc Faversham and M2, 2 miles

Fawkham Valley (1987)

Gay Dawn Farm, Fawkham, Dartford, DA3 8LZ
Tel (01474) 707144
Fax (01474) 707911
Web www.fawkhamvalley.co.uk
Mem 350
Sec A Dart
Pro C McKillop
Holes 9 L 6547 yds Par 72 SSS 72
V'tors WD–U H WE/BH–NA before
1pm SOC
Fees £20 (£27.50)
Loc 4 miles S of Dartford Tunnel.
E of Brands Hatch along
Fawkham Valley road

Gillingham (1908)

Woodlands Road, Gillingham, ME7 2AP
Tel (01634) 850999
Fax (01634) 574749
Mem 450 100(L) 50(J)
Sec Mrs M Scott (01634) 853017
Pro M Day (01634) 855862
Holes 18 L 5509 yds SSS 67
V'tors WD–I H WE/BH–M
Fees £18 D–£25
Loc A2/M2, 2 miles
Arch Braid/Steel

Hawkhurst (1968)

High Street, Hawkhurst, TN18 4JS
Tel (01580) 754074
Fax (01580) 754074
Mem 450
Sec B Morrison (Gen Mgr)
Pro T Collins (01580) 753600
Holes 9 L 5751 yds Par 70 SSS 68
V'tors WD–U WE–M SOC
Fees 18 holes–£18 (£20)
9 holes–£12
Loc 14 miles S of Tunbridge Wells
on A268

Hemsted Forest (1969)

Golford Road, Cranbrook, TN17 4AL
Tel (01580) 712833

Fax (01580) 714274
Sec K Stevenson
Holes 18 L 6305 yds SSS 70
V'tors WD–U WE/BH–restricted
SOC–H
Fees £27 (£35)
Loc 15 miles S of Maidstone. M25
Junction 5-A21/A262
Arch Cdr J Harris

Herne Bay (1895)

Eddington, Herne Bay, CT6 7PG
Tel (01227) 374097
Mem 500
Sec B Warren (01227) 373964
Pro S Dordoy (01227) 374727
Holes 18 L 5567 yds SSS 68
V'tors WD–U WE/BH–H after noon
SOC–WD
Fees £18 D–£25 (£25)
Loc A2299 Thanet road

Hever (1993)

Hever Road, Hever, TN8 7NP
Tel (01732) 700771
Fax (01732) 700775
Web www.hever.com
Mem 700
Pro R Tinworth
Holes 18 L 7002 yds SSS 75
9 L 2784 yds
V'tors H SOC
Fees £35 (£55)
Loc 2 miles E of Edenbridge
Mis Driving range
Arch Peter Nicholson

High Elms (1969)

Public
High Elms Road, Downe, Orpington, BR6 7SZ
Tel (01689) 858175
Fax (01689) 856326
Sec Mrs P O'Keeffe (Hon)
Pro P Remy
Holes 18 L 6221 yds Par 71
SSS 70
V'tors U
Fees On application
Loc Off A21 via Shire Lane

Hythe Imperial (1950)

Prince's Parade, Hythe, CT21 6AE
Tel (01303) 233745
Fax (01303) 267554
Mem 445
Sec B Duncan (01303) 267554
Pro G Ritchie (01303) 233745
Holes 9 L 5560 yds SSS 67
V'tors H SOC
Fees £20
Loc On coast, 4 miles W of
Folkestone

Kings Hill (1996)

Kings Hill, West Malling, ME19 4AF
Tel (01732) 875040/842121
(Bookings)
Fax (01732) 875019
Mem 530

Sec Margaret Gilbert (Mgr)
Pro D Hudspith (01732) 842121
Holes 18 L 6622 yds Par 72 SSS 72
V'tors WD–U SOC–WD
Fees £30
Loc 3 miles from M20 Junction 4,
off A228
Arch David Williams

Knole Park (1924)

Seal Hollow Road, Sevenoaks, TN15 0HJ
Tel (01732) 452709
Fax (01732) 463159
Web www.kentgolf.co.uk/knolepark
Mem 700
Sec PF Lamb (01732) 452150
Pro P Sykes (01732) 451740
Holes 18 L 6266 yds SSS 70
V'tors WD–restricted WE/BH–M H
SOC
Fees £35 D–£46
Loc 1/2 mile from Sevenoaks centre
Arch JF Abercromby

Lamberhurst (1890)

Church Road, Lamberhurst, TN3 8DT
Tel (01892) 890241
Fax (01892) 891140
Web www.lamberhurstgolfclub.com
Mem 700
Sec RJ Walden (01892) 890591
Pro BM Impett (01892) 890552
Holes 18 L 6364 yds SSS 70
V'tors WD–U H WE–NA before
noon
Fees £25 D–£35 (£40)
Loc 5 miles SE of Tunbridge
Wells, off A21

Langley Park (1910)

Barnfield Wood Road, Beckenham, BR3 6SZ
Tel (020) 8650 2090
Fax (020) 8658 6310
Mem 750
Sec C Staff (020) 8658 6849
Pro C Staff (020) 8650 1663
Holes 18 L 6488 yds SSS 71
V'tors WD–H WE–M SOC–WD
Fees £25 D–£35
Loc Bromley South Station 1
mile
Arch JH Taylor

Leeds Castle (1928)

Pay and play
Leeds Castle, Hollingbourne, Maidstone, ME17 1PL
Tel (01622) 880467/767828
Fax (01622) 735616
Sec Mrs A Knowlden
Pro S Purves
Holes 9 L 2451 yds Par 33
V'tors U SOC–WD
Fees 9 holes–£11 (£13)
Loc 4 miles E of Maidstone (A20).
M20 Junction 8, 1 mile
Mis 6-day advance booking
Arch Neil Coles

Littlestone (1888)

St Andrews Road, Littlestone, New Romney, TN28 8RB

Tel   (01797) 362310
Fax   (01797) 362740
Web   www.littlestonegolfclub.org
Mem   550
Sec   Col C Moorhouse
        (01797) 363355
Pro   A Jones (01797) 362231
Holes   18 L 6676 yds Par 71 SSS 73
V'tors WD–H WE–by arrangement
        SOC
Fees   £36 (£50)
Loc   2 miles E of New Romney.
        15 miles SE of Ashford
Arch   W Laidlaw Purves/Dr A
        Mackenzie

The London Golf Club (1993)

South Ash Manor Estate, Stansted Lane, Ash, TN15 7EN

Tel   (01474) 879899
Fax   (01474) 879912
Web   www.londongolf.co.uk
Mem   550
Sec   D Loh
Pro   B Longmuir
Holes   Heritage 18 L 7208 yds Par
        72 SSS 74;
        International 18 L 7005 yds
        Par 72 SSS 74
V'tors M I SOC–WD
Fees   On application
Loc   Off A20, nr Brands Hatch
Mis   Driving range. Academy
Arch   Nicklaus/Kirby

Lullingstone Park (1967)

Public

Parkgate Road, Chelsfield, Orpington, BR6 7PX

Tel   (01959) 533793
Sec   BMS Vallance
Pro   M Watt
Holes   18 L 6779 yds SSS 72
        9 L 2445 yds Par 33
V'tors U
Fees   On application
Loc   Off Orpington by-pass (A224)
        towards Well Hill. M25
        Junction 4
Mis   Driving range. 9 hole pitch &
        putt course

Lydd

Pay and play

Romney Road, Lydd, Romney Marsh, TN29 9LS

Tel   (01797) 320808
Fax   (01797) 321482
Web   www.lyddgolfclub.co.uk
Mem   475
Sec   BM Evans, S Balcomb
        (Gen Mgr)
Pro   AJ Jones (01797) 321201
Holes   18 L 6517 yds Par 71 SSS 71
        Driving range
V'tors U SOC
Fees   £17 (£23)

Loc   15 miles SE of Ashford, by
        Lydd Airport (B2075). M20
        Junction 10
Arch   M Smith

Mid Kent (1908)

Singlewell Road, Gravesend, DA11 7RB

Tel   (01474) 568035
Fax   (01474) 564218
Mem   1050
Pro   M Foreman (01474) 332810
Holes   18 L 6218 yds SSS 70
V'tors WD–H WE–M
Fees   On application
Loc   SE of Gravesend, nr A2
Arch   Frank Pennink

Moatlands (1993)

Watermans Lane, Brenchley, Tonbridge, TN12 6ND

Tel   (01892) 724400
Fax   (01892) 723300
Web   www.moatlands.com
Mem   600
Sec   K Wiley
Pro   S Wood (01892) 724252
Holes   18 L 7060 yds Par 72 SSS 74
V'tors WD–U H WE–H NA before
        noon SOC–WD exc Wed
Fees   £29 (£39)
Loc   Between Matfield and
        Paddock Wood, off B2160
Mis   Driving range
Arch   T Saito

Nizels (1992)

Nizels Lane, Hildenborough, Tonbridge, TN11 8NX

Tel   (01732) 833833
Fax   (01732) 833764
Web   www.clubhaus.com
Mem   700
Sec   J Martin (Gen Mgr)
Pro   A Mellor (01732) 838926
Holes   18 L 6297 yds SSS 71
V'tors WD–U SOC
Fees   £45 (£50)
Loc   4 miles from M25 on B245.
        A21 Tonbridge North
        Junction
Arch   Lennan/Purnell

North Foreland (1903)

Convent Road, Broadstairs, Thanet, CT10 3PU

Tel   (01843) 862140
Fax   (01843) 862663
Mem   1100
Sec   BJ Preston
Pro   D Parris (01843) 604471
Holes   18 L 6430 yds SSS 71
        18 hole Par 3 course
V'tors WD–H WE–NA am –H pm
Fees   £30 (£40)
Loc   B2052, 1½ miles N of
        Broadstairs
Arch   Fowler/Simpson

Oastpark (1992)

Malling Road, Snodland, ME6 5LG

Tel   (01634) 242661
Fax   (01634) 240744
Mem   300
Sec   Lesley Murrock
        (01634) 242818
Pro   D Porthouse (01634) 242661
Holes   9 L 2850 yds Par 34 SSS 34
V'tors U SOC
Fees   9 holes–£7 (£8) 18 holes–£12
        (£14)
Loc   1 mile E of M20 Junction 4
Mis   Driving range

Poult Wood (1974)

Public

Higham Lane, Tonbridge, TN11 9QR

Tel   (01732) 364039 (Bookings),
        (01732) 366180 (Clubhouse)
Mem   520
Sec   S Taylor
Pro   C Miller
Holes   18 L 5569 yds SSS 67
        9 hole course
V'tors U–booking required
        SOC–WD
Fees   £8.60 (£13.20)
Loc   1 mile N of Tonbridge, off
        A227
Arch   Hawtree

Prince's (1906)

Sandwich Bay, Sandwich, CT13 9QB

Tel   (01304) 611118
Fax   (01304) 612000
Mem   250
Sec   WM Howie (Dir)
Pro   D Barbour (01304) 613797
Holes   27 hole course (3 x 9 holes):
        Dunes/Himalayas/Shore
        Length 6813-7063 yds
        Par 71-72 SSS 72-73
V'tors U SOC
Fees   On application
Loc   Sandwich Bay (A256)
Mis   Driving range
Arch   Morrison/Campbell

Redlibbets

West Yoke, Ash, Nr Sevenoaks, TN15 7HT

Tel   (01474) 879190
Fax   (01474) 879290
Mem   600
Sec   J Potter
Pro   R Taylor (01474) 872278
Holes   18 L 6651 yds Par 72
V'tors U SOC
Fees   £28.50
Loc   Off A20 between Fawkham
        and Ash. M20 Junction 2.
        M25 Junction 3
Arch   Jonathan Gaunt

The Ridge (1993)

Chartway Street, East Sutton, Maidstone, ME17 3JB

Tel   (01622) 844382
Fax   (01622) 844168

Sec Miss V Jones
Pro J Cornish (01622) 844243
Holes 18 L 6254 yds SSS 72
V'tors WD–U WE–M before 12
noon SOC
Fees £20 (£25)
Loc 3 miles E of Maidstone, off
A274. M20 Junction 8
Mis Driving range
Arch Patrick Dawson

Riverside Golf Centre
(1991)
Pay and play
Fairway Drive, Summerton Way,
Thamesmead, London SE28 8PP
Tel (020) 8310 7975
Fax (020) 8312 3441
Web www.riversidegolf.co.uk
Sec BD Jarrett
Pro Sarah Jarrett
Holes 9 L 5462 yds Par 70 SSS 66
V'tors U SOC
Fees 18 holes–£10.50 (£12)
9 holes–£6.50 (£8.50)
Mis Floodlit driving range

Rochester & Cobham Park (1891)
Park Pale, by Rochester, ME2 3UL
Tel (01474) 823411
Fax (01474) 824446
Web www.rochesterandcobhamgc
.co.uk
Mem 720
Sec Maj JW Irvine (Mgr)
Pro I Higgins (01474) 823658
Holes 18 L 6596 yds SSS 71
V'tors WD–U H WE–M before 5pm
SOC–Tues & Thurs. Soft
spikes only
Fees £30
Loc 3 miles E of Gravesend exit
(A2)
Mis Driving range
Arch D Steel

Romney Warren (1993)
Pay and play
St Andrews Road, Littlestone, New
Romney, TN28 8RB
Tel (01797) 362231
Fax (01797) 362740
Web www.romneywarrengolfclub
.co.uk
Mem 250
Sec E Purkiss (Hon)
Pro S Watkins
Holes 18 L 5126 yds SSS 65
V'tors U SOC
Fees £13 (£18)
Loc 2 miles E of New Romney.
15 miles SE of Ashford
Arch Evans/Lewis

Royal Blackheath (1608)
Court Road, Eltham, London, SE9 5AF
Tel (020) 8850 1795
Fax (020) 8859 0150
Web www.rbgc.com

Mem 700
Sec AG Dunlop
Pro I McGregor (020) 8850 1763
Holes 18 L 6219 yds SSS 70
V'tors WD–I or H WE/BH–M SOC
Fees £35 D–£50
Loc 5 miles W of M25 Junction 3
Mis Golf Museum
Arch James Braid

Royal Cinque Ports (1892)
Golf Road, Deal, CT14 6RF
Tel (01304) 374007 (Office),
(01304) 374328 (Clubhouse)
Fax (01304) 379530
Web www.royalcinqueports.com
Mem 1000+
Sec CC Hammond
(01304) 367856
Pro A Reynolds (01304) 374170
Holes 18 L 6467 yds SSS 71
V'tors WD–H after 9.30am SOC
Fees On application
Loc A258, N of Deal
Mis Driving range

Royal St George's (1887)
Sandwich, CT13 9PB
Tel (01304) 613090
Fax (01304) 611245
Mem 675
Sec HCG Gabbey
Pro A Brooks (01304) 615236
Holes 18 L 6607 yds Par 70 SSS 72
V'tors WD–I H WE–M SOC–WD
Fees £70 D–£100
Loc 1 mile E of Sandwich
Arch Dr Laidlaw Purves

Ruxley Park (1975)
Pay and play
Sandy Lane, St Paul's Cray,
Orpington, BR5 3HY
Tel (01689) 871490
Fax (01689) 891428
Mem 500
Sec J Scappatura
Pro A Langoon
Holes 18 L 6027 yds SSS 69
9 hole Par 3 course
V'tors U
Fees £11 (£18)
Loc Off A20 Ruxley roundabout at
Sidcup
Mis Floodlit driving range

St Augustines (1907)
Cottington Road, Cliffsend, Ramsgate,
CT12 5JN
Tel (01843) 590333
Fax (01843) 590444
Mem 650 55(J)
Sec LP Dyke
Pro DB Scott (01843) 590222
Holes 18 L 5197 yds SS 65
V'tors H SOC–WD
Fees £21.50 (£23.50)
Loc 2 miles SW of Ramsgate from
A253 or A256. Signs to St
Augustines Cross
Arch Tom Vardon

Sene Valley (1888)
Sene, Folkestone, CT18 8BL
Tel (01303) 268513
Fax (01303) 237513
Mem 650
Sec G Sykes (Mgr)
Pro N Watson (01303) 268514
Holes 18 L 6215 yds SSS 70
V'tors H SOC
Fees £20 (£30)
Loc 2 miles N of Hythe on B2065
Arch Henry Cotton

Sheerness (1906)
Power Station Road, Sheerness,
ME12 3AE
Tel (01795) 662585
Fax (01795) 668100
Mem 700
Sec AF Jones
Pro L Stanford (01795) 583060
Holes 18 L 6460 yds SSS 71
V'tors WD–U SOC
Fees £18
Loc 9 miles N of Sittingbourne.
M20, M2 or A2 to A249

Shooter's Hill (1903)
Lowood, Eaglesfield Road, London,
SE18 3DA
Tel (020) 8854 1216
Fax (020) 8854 0469
Mem 596 69(L) 46(J)
Sec Sandy Watt (020) 8854 6368
Pro D Brotherton
(020) 8854 0073
Holes 18 L 5721 yds SSS 68
V'tors WD–I WE/BH–M SOC–Tues
& Thurs only
Fees £22 D–£27
Loc Off A207 nr Blackheath
Arch Willie Park

Shortlands (1894)
Meadow Road, Shortlands, Bromley,
BR2 0DX
Tel (020) 8460 2471
Fax (020) 8460 8828
Mem 525
Sec PS May (020) 8460 8828
Pro M Taylor (020) 8464 6182
Holes 9 L 5261 yds SSS 66
V'tors M
Fees £10
Loc Ravensbourne Ave,
Shortlands

Sidcup (1891)
7 Hurst Road, Sidcup, DA15 9AE
Tel (020) 8300 2864
Fax (020) 8300 2150
Mem 400
Sec J Auchterlony (020) 8300
2150
Pro N Willis (020) 8309 0679
Holes 9 L 5571 yds Par 68 SSS 68
V'tors WD–H WE/BH–M SOC–WD
Fees £18
Loc On A222. A2/A20, 2 miles

For list of abbreviations see page 649

Sittingbourne & Milton Regis (1929)

Wormdale, Newington, Sittingbourne, ME9 7PX

Tel	(01795) 842261
Fax	(01795) 844117
Mem	575 100(L) 50(J)
Sec	HDG Wylie
Pro	JR Hearn (01795) 842775
Holes	18 L 6291 yds SSS 70
V'tors	WD–H Sat–NA Sun–M SOC–Tues & Thurs
Fees	£25
Loc	N of M2 Junction 5, towards Danaway

Southern Valley (1999)

Pay and play

Thong Lane, Shorne, Gravesend, DA12 4LF

Tel	(01474) 740026, (01474) 568568 (Bookings)
Fax	(01474) 360366
Mem	380
Sec	Anne Green
Pro	L Batchelor
Holes	18 L 6100 yds Par 69 SSS 69
V'tors	U SOC
Fees	9 holes–£9.50 (£12) 18 holes–£15.50 (£18.50)
Loc	S of Gravesend, off A2
Arch	Weller/Richardson

Staplehurst Golf Centre

Cradducks Lane, Staplehurst, TN12 0DR

Tel	(01580) 893362
Sec	C Jenkins
Pro	C Jenkins
Holes	9 L 6114 yds Par 72 SSS 70
V'tors	U
Fees	£12 (£13)
Loc	8 miles S of Maidstone on A229
Mis	Driving range

Sundridge Park (1901)

Garden Road, Bromley, BR1 3NE

Tel	(020) 8460 1822
Fax	(020) 8289 3050
Mem	1200
Sec	R Burden (020) 8460 0278
Pro	B Cameron (020) 8460 5540
Holes	East 18 L 6538 yds SSS 71 West 18 L 6019 yds SSS 69
V'tors	H SOC–WD
Fees	£45
Loc	1 mile N of Bromley, by Sundridge Park Station. M25 Junctions 3/4

Sweetwoods Park (1994)

Cowden, Edenbridge, TN8 7JN

Tel	(01342) 850729
Fax	(01342) 850866
Web	www.sweetwoodspark.com
Mem	750
Sec	D Howe (01342) 850942
Pro	P Lyons (01342) 850729
Holes	18 L 6556 yds Par 72

V'tors	U SOC
Fees	£22 (£32)
Loc	5 miles E of E Grinstead on A264
Mis	Driving range
Arch	P Strand

Tenterden (1905)

Woodchurch Road, Tenterden, TN30 7DR

Tel	(01580) 763987
Fax	(01580) 763987
Web	www.tenterdengolfclub.co.uk
Mem	650
Sec	JM Wilson
Pro	K Kelsall (01580) 762409
Holes	18 L 6050 yds Par 70 SSS 69
V'tors	WD–U WE/BH–M Sun–NA before noon SOC–WD
Fees	On application
Loc	1 mile E of Tenterden on B2067

Tudor Park Hotel (1988)

Ashford Road, Bearsted, Maidstone, ME14 4NQ

Tel	(01622) 734334
Fax	(01622) 735360
Mem	750
Sec	J Ladbrook
Pro	N McNally (01622) 739412
Holes	18 L 6041 yds SSS 69
V'tors	H SOC
Fees	£25 (£30)
Loc	3 miles E of Maidstone on A20. M20 Junction 8
Mis	Driving range
Arch	Donald Steel

Tunbridge Wells (1889)

Langton Road, Tunbridge Wells, TN4 8XH

Tel	(01892) 523034
Fax	(01892) 536918
Mem	251 53(L) 58(J)
Sec	RF Mealing (01892) 536918
Pro	M Barton (01892) 541386
Holes	9 L 4725 yds SSS 62
V'tors	U H SOC
Fees	£15.75 (£26.25)
Loc	Tunbridge Wells, next to Spa Hotel

Upchurch River Valley (1991)

Pay and play

Oak Lane, Upchurch, Sittingbourne, ME9 7AY

Tel	(01634) 360626
Fax	(01634) 387784
Mem	640
Sec	D Candy (01634) 260594
Pro	R Cornwell (01634) 379592
Holes	18 L 6237 yds SSS 70 9 hole course
V'tors	U SOC–WD
Fees	18 hole:£11.45 (£14.45) 9 hole:£6.75 (£7.75)
Loc	3 miles NE of Rainham, off A2. M2 Junction 4

Mis	Floodlit driving range
Arch	David Smart

Walmer & Kingsdown (1909)

The Leas, Kingsdown, Deal, CT14 8EP

Tel	(01304) 373256
Fax	(01304) 382336
Mem	627
Sec	J Morgan
Pro	M Paget (01304) 363017
Holes	18 L 6444 yds Par 72 SSS 71
V'tors	WD–H WE–after noon SOC
Fees	D–£25 (£30)
Loc	2½ miles S of Deal on clifftop
Arch	James Braid

Weald of Kent (1992)

Pay and play

Maidstone Road, Headcorn, TN27 9PT

Tel	(01622) 890866
Fax	(01622) 891793
Mem	1000
Sec	D Etheridge (Mgr)
Holes	18 L 6169 yds SSS 69
V'tors	U–booking 3 days in advance SOC
Fees	£14.50 (£18.50)
Loc	5 miles S of Maidstone on A274. M20 Junction 8
Arch	John Millen

West Kent (1916)

West Hill, Downe, Orpington, BR6 7JJ

Tel	(01689) 851323
Fax	(01689) 858693
Web	www.wkgc.co.uk
Mem	750
Sec	AP Barclay
Pro	RS Fidler (01689) 856863
Holes	18 L 6399 yds SSS 70
V'tors	WD–H or I–phone to arrange WE/BH–M
Fees	On application
Loc	5 miles S of Orpington

West Malling (1974)

Addington, Maidstone, ME19 5AR

Tel	(01732) 844785
Fax	(01732) 844795
Web	www.westmallinggolf.com
Mem	900
Sec	MR Ellis
Pro	D Lambert
Holes	Spitfire 18 L 6142 yds Par 70 Hurricane 18 L 6240 yds Par 70
V'tors	WD–U WE–U H after noon
Fees	£25 (£35)
Loc	12 miles W of Maidstone (A20)
Mis	Driving range
Arch	Max Faulkner

Westerham

Valence Park, Brasted Road, Westerham, TN16 1LJ

Tel	(01959) 567100
Fax	(01959) 567101

Mem 700
Sec S Hodsdon (Gen Mgr)
Pro R Sturgeon
Holes 18 L 6272 yds Par 72
V'tors WD–U WE–after 12.30pm
Fees £25 (£35)
Loc E of Westerham (A25), off
M25 Junction 5
Mis Driving range
Arch David Williams

Westgate & Birchington (1893)

176 Canterbury Road, Westgate-on-Sea, CT8 8LT

Tel (01843) 831115/833905
Mem 325
Sec JM Wood
Pro R Game
Holes 18 L 4889 yds SSS 64
V'tors H or I WD–NA before 10am
WE–NA before 11am SOC
Fees £15 (£17)
Loc 1 mile W of Westgate (A28)

Whitstable & Seasalter (1911)

Collingwood Road, Whitstable, CT5 1EB

Tel (01227) 272020
Fax (01227) 280822
Mem 350
Sec C Chapman
Holes 9 L 5357 yds Par 63 SSS 63
V'tors U
Fees 18 holes–£15
Loc 1 mile W of Whitstable

Wildernesse (1890)

Seal, Sevenoaks, TN15 0JE

Tel (01732) 761526
Mem 700
Sec RA Foster (01732) 761199
Pro CA Walker (01732) 761527
Holes 18 L 6440 yds Par 72 SSS 71
V'tors WD–I H
SOC–Mon/Thurs/Fri
Fees £35 D–£50
Loc 2 miles E of Sevenoaks (A25).
M25 Junction 5

Woodlands Manor (1928)

Woodlands, Tinkerpot Lane, Sevenoaks, TN15 6AB

Tel (01959) 523806
Fax (01959) 524398
Mem 650
Sec CG Robins (01959) 523806
Pro P Womack (01959) 524161
Holes 18 L 6000 yds SSS 69
V'tors WD–U WE–H NA before
noon SOC–WD
Fees On application
Loc 4 miles S of M25 Junction 3.
Off A20 between West
Kingsdown and Otford
Mis Driving range
Arch Coles/Lyons

Wrotham Heath (1906)

Seven Mile Lane Comp, Sevenoaks, TN15 8QZ

Tel (01732) 884800
Mem 424 75(L) 50(J)
Sec LJ Byrne
Pro H Dearden (01732) 883854
Holes 18 L 5954 yds SSS 69
V'tors WD–H WE/BH–M
SOC–Thurs & Fri
Fees £25 D–£35
Loc 8 miles W of Maidstone on
B2016. M26/A20 Junction, 1
mile
Arch Donald Steel

Lancashire

Accrington & District (1893)

West End, Oswaldtwistle, Accrington, BB5 4LS

Tel (01254) 381614
Fax (01254) 233273
Web www.accrington-golf-
club.fsnet.co.uk
Mem 350
Sec GA Dixon (01254) 265620
Pro W Harling (01254) 231091
Holes 18 L 6044 yds SSS 69
V'tors WD/WE–U H SOC–H
Fees On application
Loc 3 miles SW of Accrington.
M65 Junctions 6/7

Ashton & Lea (1913)

Tudor Ave, Off Blackpool Rd, Lea, Preston PR4 0XA

Tel (01772) 726480
Fax (01772) 735762
Mem 750
Sec T Ashton (01772) 735282
Pro M Greenough
(01772) 720374
Holes 18 L 6334 yds SSS 70
V'tors U SOC
Fees £23 (£25)
Loc 3 miles W of Preston, off
A5085. Nr M6, M55 and
M65
Arch J Steer

Ashton-in-Makerfield (1902)

Garswood Park, Liverpool Road, Ashton-in-Makerfield, WN4 0YT

Tel (01942) 727267
Mem 500
Sec JR Hay (01942) 719330
Pro P Allan (01942) 724229
Holes 18 L 6212 yds SSS 70
V'tors WD–U exc Wed WE/BH–M
SOC
Fees £28
Loc 1 mile W of Ashton-in-
Makerfield on A58. M6
Junction 23/24

Ashton-under-Lyne (1912)

Gorsey Way, Hurst, Ashton-under-Lyne, OL6 9HT

Tel (0161) 330 1537
Fax (0161) 330 6673
Mem 600
Sec A Jackson (0161) 330 1537
Pro C Boyle (0161) 308 2095
Holes 18 L 6209 yds SSS 70
V'tors WD–U WE/BH–M SOC
Fees On application
Loc 8 miles E of Manchester. M60
Junction 23

Bacup (1910)

Maden Road, Bankside Lane, Bacup, OL13 8HN

Tel (01706) 873170
Fax (01706) 867726
Mem 396
Sec T Leyland (01706) 879644
Holes 9 L 6008 yds SSS 69
V'tors U
Fees On application
Loc Bankside Lane

Baxenden & District (1913)

Top o' th' Meadow, Baxenden, Accrington, BB5 2EA

Tel (01254) 234555
Web www.baxendengolf.co.uk
Mem 400
Sec N Turner (01706) 225423
Holes 9 L 5702 yds SSS 68
V'tors WD–U WE/BH–M
Fees £15
Loc 2 miles SE of Accrington

Beacon Park (1982)

Public

Beacon Lane, Dalton, Up Holland, WN8 7RU

Tel (01695) 627500
Mem 250
Sec T Harris
Pro R Peters (01695) 622700
Holes 18 L 5927 yds SSS 69
V'tors U–book 6 days in advance
SOC
Fees On application
Loc Nr Ashurst Beacon and
M58/M6 Junction 26
Mis Driving range

Blackburn (1894)

Beardwood Brow, Blackburn, BB2 7AX

Tel (01254) 51122
Fax (01254) 665578
Mem 476 65(L) 104(J)
Sec K Taylor (01254) 51122
Pro A Rodwell (01254) 55942
Holes 18 L 6144 yds SSS 70
V'tors U SOC–WD
WE/BH–restricted
Fees £24 (£28)
Loc 1 mile NW of Blackburn
(A677). M6 Junction 31

For list of abbreviations see page 649

Blackpool North Shore
(1904)
Devonshire Road, Blackpool, FY2 0RD
Tel   (01253) 351017
Fax   (01253) 591240
Mem   750
Sec   JM Ogden (01253) 352054
Pro   B Ward (01253) 354640
Holes   18 L 6443 yds SSS 71
V'tors   WD–U WE–restricted SOC
Fees   £30 (£35)
Loc   ½ mile E of Queens
Promenade (B5124)
Arch   HS Colt

Blackpool Park (1925)
Public
North Park Drive, Blackpool, FY3 8LS
Tel   (01253) 397910
Fax   (01253) 397910
Mem   700
Sec   D Stones (01253) 397916
Pro   B Purdie (01253) 391004
Holes   18 L 6192 yds SSS 69
V'tors   U–no telephone booking
Fees   £10.50 (£12.50)
Loc   2 miles E of Blackpool,
signposted off M55
Arch   Dr A Mackenzie

Bolton (1891)
Lostock Park, Bolton, BL6 4AJ
Tel   (01204) 843278
Fax   (01204) 843067
Web   www.golfagent.com/clubsites/
bolton_golf_club
Mem   600
Sec   Mrs HM Stuart
(01204) 843067
Pro   R Longworth (01204) 843073
Holes   18 L 6237 yds Par 70 SSS 70
V'tors   U SOC
Fees   £30 D–£36 (£33 D–£40)
Loc   3 miles W of Bolton. M61
Junction 6, 2 miles

Bolton Old Links (1891)
*Chorley Old Road, Montserrat, Bolton,
BL1 5SU*
Tel   (01204) 840050
Fax   (01204) 842307
Mem   600
Sec   Mrs J Boardman
(01204) 842307
Pro   P Horridge (01204) 843089
Holes   18 L 6469 yds SSS 71
V'tors   U H exc comp Sats SOC
Fees   £30 (£40)
Loc   3 miles NW of Bolton on
B6226
Arch   Dr A Mackenzie

Bolton Open Golf Course
Pay and play
*Longsight Park, Longsight Lane,
Harwood, BL2 4JX*
Tel   (01204) 597659/309778
Mem   250

Sec   D Fletcher (Sec/Mgr)
(01204) 597659
Pro   A Duncan (Golf Dir)
(01204) 309778
Holes   18 holes Par 70 SSS 68
V'tors   WD–U WE–booking
necessary SOC
Fees   £8 (£12)
Loc   2 miles NE of Bolton (A666)
Mis   Driving range

Brackley Municipal
(1977)
Public
*Bullows Road, Little Hulton, Worsley,
M38 9TR*
Tel   (0161) 790 6076
Pro   S Lomax (Mgr)
Holes   9 L 3003 yds SSS 69
V'tors   U
Fees   On application
Loc   2 miles NW of Walkden, off
A6

Breightmet (1911)
*Red Bridge, Ainsworth, Bolton,
BL2 5PA*
Tel   (01204) 527381
Mem   240
Sec   SP Griffiths
Holes   9 L 6416 yds SSS 71
V'tors   WD–H WE–NA SOC–WD
Fees   £15 (£18)
Loc   3 miles E of Bolton

Brookdale (1896)
*Medlock Road, Woodhouses, Failsworth,
M35 9WQ*
Tel   (0161) 681 4534
Fax   (0161) 688 6872
Web   www.brookdalegolfclub.co.uk
Mem   725
Sec   MJ Chadwick
Pro   T Cuppello (0161) 681 2655
Holes   18 L 5841 yds SSS 68
V'tors   WD–U SOC–WD
Fees   £22
Loc   5 miles NE of Manchester

Burnley (1905)
Glen View, Burnley, BB11 3RW
Tel   (01282) 421045
Fax   (01282) 451281
Web   www.burnleygolfclub@on the
green.co.uk
Mem   520
Sec   RDM Wills (01282) 451281
Pro   P McEvoy (01282) 455266
Holes   18 L 5939 yds SSS 69
V'tors   H SOC
Fees   £20 (£25)
Loc   Via Manchester Road to Glen
View Road

Bury (1890)
*Unsworth Hall, Blackford Bridge, Bury,
BL9 9TJ*
Tel   (0161) 766 4897
Fax   (0161) 796 3480

Mem   750
Sec   R Adams
Pro   D Procter (0161) 766 2213
Holes   18 L 5927 yds SSS 69
V'tors   H SOC
Fees   £26 (£30)
Loc   A56, 5 miles N of
Manchester. 3 miles N of
M62 Junction 17

Castle Hawk (1975)
*Chadwick Lane, Castleton, Rochdale,
OL11 3BY*
Tel   (01706) 640841
Fax   (01706) 860587
Mem   200
Sec   J Accleton
Pro   F Accleton
Holes   18 L 5398 yds SSS 68
9 L 3158 yds SSS 55
V'tors   U SOC
Fees   WD/Sat D–£8 Sun D–£10
Loc   Castleton Station 1 mile. M62
Junction 20
Mis   Driving range

Chorley (1897)
*Hall o' th' Hill, Heath Charnock,
Chorley, PR6 9HX*
Tel   (01257) 480263
Fax   (01257) 480722
Web   www.chorleygolfclub.co.uk
Mem   550
Sec   Mrs A Allen (01257) 480263
Pro   M Bradley (01257) 481245
Holes   18 L 6240 yds SSS 70
V'tors   WD–I or H WE–NA SOC
Fees   On application
Loc   1 mile S of Chorley at junction
A6/A673
Arch   JA Steer

Clitheroe (1891)
Whalley Road, Clitheroe, BB7 1PP
Tel   (01200) 422618 (Clubhouse)
Fax   (01200) 422292
Web   www.clitheroegolfclub.com
Mem   700
Sec   (01200) 422292
Pro   J Twissell (01200) 424242
Holes   18 L 6326 yds SSS 71
V'tors   WD–U H SOC
Fees   £33 (£39)
Loc   2 miles S of Clitheroe
Mis   Range
Arch   James Braid

Colne (1901)
*Law Farm, Skipton Old Road, Colne,
BB8 7EB*
Tel   (01282) 863391
Mem   354
Sec   JT Duerden (Hon)
Pro   None
Holes   9 L 5961 yds SSS 69
V'tors   U exc comp days SOC–WD
Fees   £16 (£20)
Loc   1½ miles N of Colne. From
end of M65, signs to Keighley
and then Lothersdale

Crompton & Royton (1913)

High Barn, Royton, Oldham, OL2 6RW

Tel	(0161) 624 2154
Fax	(0161) 652 4711
Mem	620
Sec	JB Lord (0161) 624 0086
Pro	DA Melling (0161) 624 2154
Holes	18 L 6214 yds SSS 70
V'tors	U SOC–WD
Fees	£20 (£30)
Loc	3 miles NW of Oldham

Darwen (1893)

Winter Hill, Duddon Avenue, Darwen, BB3 0LB

Tel	(01254) 701287
Fax	(01254) 773833
Mem	375 70(L) 60(J)
Sec	JR Lawson (01254) 704367
Pro	W Lennon (01254) 776370
Holes	18 L 5863 yds Par 69 SSS 68
V'tors	U exc Tues & Sat–NA
Fees	£25 (£30)
Loc	Darwen 1½ miles. M65 Junction 4

Dean Wood (1922)

Lafford Lane, Up Holland, Skelmersdale, WN8 0QZ

Tel	(01695) 622219
Fax	(01695) 622245
Mem	750
Sec	A McGregor
Pro	S Danchin
Holes	18 L 6148 yds SSS 70
V'tors	WD–U WE/BH–M SOC
Fees	£30 (£33)
Loc	4 miles W of Wigan (A577)
Arch	James Braid

Deane (1906)

Off Junction Road, Deane, Bolton, BL3 4NS

Tel	(01204) 61944
Mem	490
Sec	RY Hough (01204) 651808
Pro	D Martindale
Holes	18 L 5652 yds SSS 67
V'tors	WD–U WE–restricted SOC–Tues/Thurs/Fri
Fees	£20 (£25)
Loc	2 miles W of Bolton. M61 Junction 5, 1 mile

Dunscar (1908)

Longworth Lane, Bromley Cross, Bolton, BL7 9QY

Tel	(01204) 598228
Mem	600
Sec	JW Jennings (01204) 303321
Pro	G Treadgold (01204) 592992
Holes	18 L 6085 yds Par 71 SSS 69
V'tors	WD–U WE–restricted SOC
Fees	£20 (£30)
Loc	3 miles N of Bolton, off A666

Duxbury Park (1975)

Public

Duxbury Hall Road, Duxbury Park, Chorley, PR7 4AS

Tel	(01257) 265380
Fax	(01257) 241378
Sec	PA Smith
Pro	D Clarke
Holes	18 L 6270 yds SSS 70
V'tors	U
Fees	£8 (£10.50)
Loc	1½ miles S of Chorley, off Wigan Lane

Fairhaven (1895)

Lytham Hall Park, Ansdell, Lytham St Annes, FY8 4JU

Tel	(01253) 736741
Fax	(01253) 731461
Mem	900
Sec	H Fielding
Pro	(01253) 736976
Holes	18 L 6883 yds SSS 73
V'tors	WD–U WE–NA before 9am SOC–WD
Fees	£33 (£40)
Loc	Lytham 2 miles. St Annes 2 miles. M55 Junction 4

Fishwick Hall (1912)

Glenluce Drive, Farringdon Park, Preston, PR1 5TD

Tel	(01772) 798300
Fax	(01772) 704600
Mem	750
Sec	JP Davis
Pro	M Watson (01772) 795870
Holes	18 L 5857 yds SSS 69
V'tors	Apply to Sec SOC
Fees	£26 (£31)
Loc	1 mile E of Preston, nr junction of A59 and M6 Junction 31

Fleetwood (1932)

Golf House, Princes Way, Fleetwood, FY7 8AF

Tel	(01253) 873114 (Clubhouse)
Fax	(01253) 773573
Web	www.fleetwoodgolfclub.org.uk
Mem	548
Sec	N Robinson (01253) 773573
Pro	S McLaughlin (01253) 873661
Holes	L 18 L 6308 yds SSS 70
V'tors	U H exc Tues SOC
Fees	£30 (£40)
Loc	1 mile W of Fleetwood centre
Arch	A Steer

Gathurst (1913)

Miles Lane, Shevington, Wigan, WN6 8EW

Tel	(01257) 252861 (Clubhouse)
Fax	(01257) 255235
Mem	675
Sec	Mrs I Fyffe (01257) 255235
Pro	R Eastwood (01257) 255882
Holes	18 L 6089 yds Par 70 SSS 69

V'tors

V'tors	WD–U before 5pm WE/BH/Wed–M SOC–WD
Fees	£25
Loc	4 miles W of Wigan. 1 mile S of M6 Junction 27
Arch	N Pearson-ADAS

Ghyll (1907)

Ghyll Brow, Barnoldswick, Colne, BB18 6JH

Tel	(01282) 842466
Mem	310
Sec	JL Gill (01524) 412958
Holes	9 L 5708 yds SSS 68
V'tors	U exc Sun–NA
Fees	£15 (£18)
Loc	7 miles N of Colne, off A56

Great Harwood (1896)

Harwood Bar, Great Harwood, BB6 7TE

Tel	(01254) 884391
Fax	(01254) 879495
Mem	195 65(L) 45(J)
Sec	J Spibey (01254) 879494
Holes	9 L 6456 yds SSS 71
V'tors	U SOC
Fees	£16 (£22)
Loc	5 miles NE of Blackburn. M65 Junction 7

Green Haworth (1914)

Green Haworth, Accrington, BB5 3SL

Tel	(01254) 237580
Fax	(01254) 396176
Mem	250
Sec	W Halstead
Holes	9 L 5556 yds SSS 67
V'tors	WD–U exc Wed–Ladies only after 5pm WE/BH–M SOC
Fees	On application
Loc	Willows Lane

Greenmount (1920)

Greenmount, Bury, BL8 4LH

Tel	(01204) 883712
Mem	220
Sec	MD Barron (Hon)
Pro	J Seed
Holes	9 L 6208 yds SSS 70
V'tors	WD–U exc Tues WE–M
Fees	£15
Loc	3 miles N of Bury

Haigh Hall (1972)

Public

Haigh Hall Country Park, Haigh, Wigan, WN2 1PE

Tel	(01942) 833337 (Clubhouse)
Fax	(01942) 831417 (Pro)
Mem	300
Sec	W Fleetwood
Pro	I Lee (01942) 831107
Holes	9 L 1146 yds 18 L 6530 yds (open June 02)
V'tors	U
Fees	£3.60 (£4.60)
Loc	2 miles NW of Wigan. M6 Junction 27. M61 Junction 6
Arch	Gaunt/Marnoch

Harwood (1926)

Springfield, Roading Brook Road, Bolton, BL2 4JD

Tel	(01204) 522878
Fax	(01204) 524233
Mem	568
Sec	D Bamber (01204) 524233
Pro	(01204) 362834
Holes	18 L 5786 yds SSS 68
V'tors	WD–H WE–M SOC
Fees	£20
Loc	4 miles NE of Bolton (B6391)
Arch	J Shuttleworth

Heysham (1910)

Trumacar Park, Middleton Road, Heysham, Morecambe LA3 3JH

Tel	(01524) 851011
Fax	(01524) 853030
Mem	685
Sec	FA Bland (Sec/Mgr)
Pro	R Dône (01524) 852000
Holes	18 L 6258 yds SSS 70
V'tors	U H SOC
Fees	£23 D–£28 (£35)
Loc	2 miles S of Morecambe. M6 Junction 34, 5 miles
Arch	A Herd

Hindley Hall (1905)

Hall Lane, Hindley, Wigan, WN2 2SQ

Tel	(01942) 525020/523116
Fax	(01942) 253871
Mem	430
Sec	Louise Marrow (01942) 255131
Pro	N Brazell (01942) 255991
Holes	18 L 5913 yds SSS 68
V'tors	U SOC
Fees	£20 (£27)
Loc	2 miles S of Wigan. M61 Junction 6

Horwich (1895)

Victoria Road, Horwich, BL6 5PH

Tel	(01204) 696980
Fax	(01942) 205316
Mem	200
Sec	C Sherborne
Pro	B Sharrock
Holes	9 L 5404 yds SSS 67
V'tors	M SOC–WD
Fees	£16
Loc	5 miles W of Bolton
Arch	George Lowe

Hurlston Hall (1994)

Hurlston Lane, Southport Road, Scarisbrick, L40 8HB

Tel	(01704) 840400
Fax	(01704) 841404
Web	www.hurlstonhall.co.uk
Mem	650
Sec	M Atherton
Pro	J Esclapez (01704) 841120
Holes	18 L 6746 yds SSS 72
V'tors	H SOC
Fees	£28 (£34)
Loc	2 miles NW of Ormskirk (A570). M58 Junction 3

Mis	Floodlit driving range
Arch	Donald Steel

Ingol (1981)

Tanterton Hall Road, Ingol, Preston, PR2 7BY

Tel	(01772) 734556
Mem	700
Sec	H Parker
Pro	S Laycock
Holes	18 L 5868 yds SSS 68
V'tors	U SOC–WD
Fees	£15 (£25)
Loc	1½ miles NW of Preston (A6). M6 Junction 32

Knott End (1910)

Wyreside, Poulton-le-Fylde, FY6 0AA

Tel	(01253) 810254 (Clubhouse)
Fax	(01253) 813446
Mem	660
Sec	A Crossley (01253) 810576
Pro	P Walker (01253) 811365
Holes	18 L 5849 yds SSS 68
V'tors	WD–U WE/BH–by arrangement SOC–WD
Fees	D–£28 (£30)
Loc	Over Wyre, 12 miles NE of Blackpool (A588)
Arch	James Braid

Lancaster (1932)

Ashton Hall, Ashton-with-Stodday, Lancaster, LA2 0AJ

Tel	(01524) 752090 (Clubhouse)
Fax	(01524) 752742
Mem	530 170(L) 62(J)
Sec	KE Butcher (01524) 751247
Pro	DE Sutcliffe (01524) 751802
Holes	18 L 6500 yds SSS 71
V'tors	WD–H SOC–WD
Fees	£32
Loc	2 miles S of Lancaster (A588)
Mis	Dormy House
Arch	James Braid

Lansil (1947)

Caton Road, Lancaster, LA4 3PE

Tel	(01524) 39269
Mem	450
Sec	J Ollerton (01995) 601451
Holes	9 L 5608 yds Par 70 SSS 67
V'tors	WD–U Sun–U after 1pm
Fees	£12 (£12)
Loc	A683, 2 miles E of Lancaster

Leyland (1923)

Wigan Road, Leyland, PR25 2UD

Tel	(01772) 436457
Fax	(01772) 436457
Web	www.leylandgolfclub.com
Mem	750
Sec	J Ross
Pro	C Burgess (01772) 423425
Holes	18 L 6123 yds SSS 69
V'tors	WD–U WE–M SOC–WD
Fees	£25
Loc	M6 Junction 28, ½mile

Lobden (1888)

Whitworth, Rochdale, OL12 8XJ

Tel	(01706) 343228
Fax	(01706) 343228
Mem	220
Sec	N Danby (01706) 643241
Holes	9 L 5697 yds Par 70 SSS 68
V'tors	U
Fees	£12 (£15)
Loc	4 miles N of Rochdale

Longridge (1877)

Fell Barn, Jeffrey Hill, Longridge, Preston PR3 2TU

Tel	(01772) 783291
Fax	(01772) 783022
Mem	700
Sec	DC Wensley
Pro	S Taylor (01772) 783291
Holes	18 L 5969 yds SSS 69
V'tors	U
Fees	£15 (£20)
Loc	8 miles NE of Preston, off B6243

Lowes Park (1915)

Hilltop, Lowes Road, Bury, BL9 6SU

Tel	(0161) 764 1231
Fax	(0161) 763 9503
Mem	400
Sec	J Entwistle
Holes	9 L 6006 yds Par 70 SSS 69
V'tors	WD–U exc Wed–NA WE/BH–by arrangement
Fees	£15 (£25)
Loc	1 mile NE of Bury, off A56

Lytham Green Drive (1922)

Ballam Road, Lytham, FY8 4LE

Tel	(01253) 734782
Fax	(01253) 731350
Mem	700
Sec	S Higham (01253) 737390
Pro	A Lancaster (01253) 737379
Holes	18 L 6163 yds SSS 69
V'tors	WD–U H WE–NA SOC–WD
Fees	£27 (£37)
Loc	Lytham St Annes. M55 Junction 4
Arch	JA Steer

Marland (1928)

Public

Springfield Park, Bolton Road, Rochdale, OL11 4RE

Tel	(01706) 649801
Fax	(01706) 523082
Mem	300
Sec	J Wallis
Pro	D Wills
Holes	18 L 5237 yds SSS 66
V'tors	WD–U WE–booking necessary
Fees	£7.50 (£9.50)
Loc	W of Rochdale (A58). M62 Junctions 19/20, 2 miles

Marsden Park (1969)

Public
Townhouse Road, Nelson, BB9 8DG

Tel	**(01282) 661912**
Sec	BD Goodwin
	(01282) 450398
Pro	M Ross (01282) 661912
Holes	18 L 5813 yds Par 70 SSS 68
V'tors	U SOC
Fees	On application
Loc	M65 Junction 13, signposted Walton Lane

Morecambe (1904)

Bare, Morecambe, LA4 6AJ

Tel	**(01524) 418050**
Fax	(01524) 400088
Mem	850
Sec	Mrs J Atkinson
	(01524) 412841
Pro	S Fletcher (01524) 415596
Holes	18 L 5750 yds SSS 69
V'tors	U H SOC
Fees	On application
Loc	On coast road towards Carnforth (A5105)

Mossock Hall (1996)

Liverpool Road, Bickerstaffe, L39 0EE

Tel	**(01695) 421717**
Fax	(01695) 424961
Mem	600
Sec	K Brain
Pro	P Atkis (01695) 424969
Holes	18 L 6375 yds Par 71 SSS 71
V'tors	U exc comp days SOC
Fees	£25 (£30)
Loc	4 miles S of Ormskirk
Arch	Steve Marnoch

Mytton Fold Hotel (1994)

Whalley Road, Langho, BB6 8AB

Tel	**(01254) 240662 (Hotel)**
Fax	(01254) 248119
Web	www.smoothhound.co.uk/ hotels/mytton
Mem	300
Sec	DB Woodburn
Pro	G Coope (01254) 245392
Holes	18 L 6082 yds SSS 70
V'tors	U SOC
Fees	£14 (£16)
Loc	6 miles N of Blackburn, off A59. M6 Junction 31
Arch	F Hargreaves

Nelson (1902)

Kings Causeway, Brierfield, Nelson, BB9 0EU

Tel	**(01282) 614583**
Fax	(01282) 606226
Mem	550
Sec	BR Thomason
	(01282) 611834
Pro	N Sumner (01282) 617000
Holes	18 L 6007 yds SSS 69
V'tors	WD–U H exc Thurs–NA WE–U exc Sat before 4pm SOC

Fees	£25 (£30)
Loc	2 miles N of Burnley. M65 Junction 12
Arch	Dr A MacKenzie

Oldham (1892)

Lees New Road, Oldham, OL4 5PN

Tel	**(0161) 624 4986**
Mem	300 45(L) 35(J)
Sec	J Brooks
Pro	J Peel (0161) 626 8346
Holes	18 L 5045 yds SSS 65
V'tors	U SOC
Fees	On application
Loc	Off Oldham-Stalybridge road

Ormskirk (1899)

Cranes Lane, Lathom, Ormskirk, L40 5UJ

Tel	**(01695) 572112**
Mem	300
Sec	RDJ Lawrence
	(01695) 572227
Pro	J Hammond (01695) 572074
Holes	18 L 6358 yds SSS 70
V'tors	I exc Sat–NA SOC
Fees	£35 Wed–£40 Sun–£40 D–£50
Loc	2 miles E of Ormskirk

Pennington

Pennington Country Park, Leigh, WN7 3PA

Tel	**(01942) 682852**
Mem	122
Sec	A Wilson
Pro	T Kershaw (01942) 682852
Holes	9 L 5516 yds Par 70 SSS 68
V'tors	U SOC
Fees	£3.35 (£4.50)
Loc	¹/₂ mile off A580, on Leigh By-Pass

Penwortham (1908)

Blundell Lane, Penwortham, Preston, PR1 0AX

Tel	**(01772) 744630**
Fax	(01772) 740172
Mem	800
Sec	N Annandale
Pro	S Holden (01772) 742345
Holes	18 L 6056 yds SSS 69
V'tors	WD–U WE–no parties
Fees	£25 (£33)
Loc	1¹/₂ miles W of Preston (A59)

Pleasington (1891)

Pleasington, Blackburn, BB2 5JF

Tel	**(01254) 202177**
Fax	(01254) 201028
Mem	545
Sec	M Trickett
Pro	GJ Furey (01254) 201630
Holes	18 L 6445 yds SSS 71
V'tors	H
Fees	£38 (£42)
Loc	3 miles SW of Blackburn

Poulton-le-Fylde (1982)

Public
Myrtle Farm, Breck Road, Poulton-le-Fylde, FY6 7HJ

Tel	**(01253) 892444**
Mem	250
Sec	K Hoyle
Pro	L Ware
Holes	9 L 2979 yds SSS 69
V'tors	U
Fees	On application
Loc	3 miles NE of Blackpool
Mis	Indoor driving range

Preston (1892)

Fulwood Hall Lane, Fulwood, Preston, PR2 8DD

Tel	**(01772) 700011**
Fax	(01772) 794234
Mem	800
Sec	DJ Sanders
Pro	A Greenbank (01772) 700022
Holes	18 L 6312 yds SSS 71
V'tors	WD–U H WE–M SOC–WD
Fees	£27 D–£32
Loc	1¹/₂ miles W of M6 Junction 32
Mis	Driving range. Golf academy
Arch	James Braid

Regent Park (Bolton) (1931)

Public
Links Road, Chorley New Road, Bolton, BL6 4AF

Tel	**(01204) 844170**
Mem	260
Sec	J Rogers
Pro	B Longworth (01204) 842336
Holes	18 L 6221yds Par 70 SSS 69
V'tors	U SOC–WD
Fees	£8 (£10)
Loc	A673, 3 miles W of Bolton. M61 Junction 6

Rishton (1927)

Eachill Links, Hawthorn Drive, Rishton, BB1 4HG

Tel	**(01254) 884442**
Fax	(01254) 51946
Mem	302
Sec	T Charnock
Holes	9 L 6097 yds SSS 69
V'tors	WD–U WE–M
Fees	£12
Loc	3 miles E of Blackburn
Arch	Thomas/Alliss

Rochdale (1888)

Edenfield Road, Bagslate, Rochdale, OL11 5YR

Tel	**(01706) 646024 (Clubhouse)**
Fax	(01706) 861113
Mem	750
Sec	RV Platt (01706) 643818
Pro	A Laverty (01706) 522104
Holes	18 L 6031 yds SSS 69
V'tors	U
Fees	£30 (£35)

Loc 3 miles from M62 Junction 20 on A680
Arch George Lowe

Rossendale (1903)

Ewood Lane Head, Haslingden, Rossendale, BB4 6LH
Tel (01706) 831339
Fax (01706) 228669
Mem 713
Sec NC Readett
Pro SJ Nicholls (01706) 213616
Holes 18 L 6293 yds SSS 71
V'tors WD/Sun–U Sat–M
Fees £25 (£30) (1999)
Loc 7 miles N of Bury, nr end M66

Royal Lytham & St Annes (1886)

Links Gate, Lytham St Annes, FY8 3LQ
Tel (01253) 724206
Fax (01253) 780946
Mem 600
Sec LB Goodwin FCA
Pro E Birchenough (01253) 720094
Holes 18 L 6685 yds SSS 74
V'tors WD–I H
Fees £100 (incl lunch)
Loc St Annes 1 mile (A584)
Mis Dormy House

Saddleworth (1904)

Mountain Ash, Uppermill, Oldham, OL3 6LT
Tel (01457) 873653
Fax (01457) 820647
Mem 700
Sec AE Gleave
Pro RJ Johnson
Holes 18 L 5976 yds SSS 69
V'tors U
Fees £23 (£30)
Loc Uppermill, 5 miles E of Oldham
Arch Mackenzie/Leaver

St Annes Old Links (1901)

Highbury Road East, Lytham St Annes, FY8 2LD
Tel (01253) 723597
Fax (01253) 781506
Web www.saolgc.uk.com
Mem 945
Pro D Webster (01253) 722432
Holes 18 L 6684 yds SSS 72
V'tors WD–NA before 9.30am and 12–1.30pm WE/BH–arrange with Sec SOC
Fees £38 (£50)
Loc Between St Annes and Blackpool, off A584
Arch Herd

Shaw Hill Hotel G&CC (1925)

Preston Road, Whittle-le-Woods, Chorley, PR6 7PP
Tel (01257) 269221

Fax (01257) 261223
Mem 500
Sec DFW Dimsdale
Pro D Clarke (01257) 279222
Holes 18 L 6318 yds Par 72 SSS 70
V'tors WD–U H SOC
Fees £30 (£40)
Loc A6, 1½ miles N of Chorley. M61 Junction 8. M6 Junction 28

Standish Court (1995)

Rectory Lane, Standish, Wigan, WN6 0XD
Tel (01257) 425777
Fax (01257) 425888
Web www.standishgolf.co.uk
Mem 300
Sec ST Dawson
Pro T Kershaw
Holes 18 L 5650 yds Par 68 SSS 66
V'tors U SOC
Fees £12 (£16)
Loc M6 Junction 27, 2 miles
Arch Patrick Dawson

Stonyhurst Park (1980)

Stonyhurst, Hurst Green, Clitheroe, BB6 9QB
Tel (01254) 826478
Mem 380
Sec JM Aitken (01254) 823666
Holes 9 L 5572 yds SSS 67
V'tors WD–U WE–NA
Fees £15
Loc 5 miles SW of Clitheroe (B6243)
Mis Green fees payable at Bayley Arms, Hurst Green

Towneley (1932)

Public
Towneley Park, Todmorden Road, Burnley, BB11 3ED
Tel (01282) 451636
Mem 280
Sec N Clark (01282) 414555
Pro (01282) 438473
Holes 18 L 5811 yds Par 70 SSS 68
9 hole course
V'tors U
Fees £9.55 (£10.60)
Loc 1½ miles E of Burnley

Tunshill (1901)

Kiln Lane, Milnrow, Rochdale, OL16 3TS
Tel (01706) 342095
Mem 300
Sec G Hurst (01706) 650566
Holes 9 L 5745 yds SSS 68
V'tors WD–U WE–M SOC
Fees £16
Loc 2 miles E of Rochdale. M62 Junction 21

Turton (1908)

Wood End Farm, Chapeltown Road, Bromley Cross, Bolton BL7 9QH
Tel (01204) 852235
Mem 300 56(L) 51(J)
Sec D Fairclough (01204) 592024
Pro None
Holes 18 L 6159 yds Par 70 SSS 70
V'tors WD–U exc Wed–NA 11.30–3.30pm WE/BH–M SOC
Fees £20 (£25)
Loc 3½ miles N of Bolton, nr Last Drop Village

De Vere Herons Reach (1993)

Pay and play
East Park Drive, Blackpool, FY3 8LL
Tel (01253) 838866/766156
Fax (01253) 798800
Mem 550
Sec JA Honeysett
Pro D Naughton (01253) 766156
Holes 18 L 6461 yds SSS 71
V'tors U H SOC
Fees £40 (£45)
Loc M55 Junction 4. Follow signs to Blackpool Zoo
Mis Floodlit driving range
Arch Alliss/Clark

Walmersley (1906)

Garrett's Close, Walmersley, Bury, BL9 6TE
Tel (0161) 764 1429
Fax (0161) 764 7770
Mem 450
Sec RO Goldstein (0161) 764 7770
Pro P Thorpe (0161) 763 9050
Holes 18 L 5341 yds SSS 67
V'tors WD–U exc Tues–NA Sat–NA Sun–M SOC–Wed–Fri
Fees D–£20
Loc 2 miles N of Bury (A56). S of M66 Junction 1
Arch SG Marnoch

Werneth (1908)

Green Lane, Garden Suburb, Oldham, OL8 3AZ
Tel (0161) 624 1190
Mem 400
Sec JH Barlow
Pro R Penny
Holes 18 L 5363 yds SSS 66
V'tors WD–U WE–M SOC
Fees D–£18.50
Loc 2 miles S of Oldham
Arch Sandy Herd

Westhoughton (1929)

Long Island, Westhoughton, Bolton, BL5 2BR
Tel (01942) 811085/608958
Mem 230
Sec F Donohue
Pro J Seed
Holes 9 L 5834 yds SSS 68

V'tors WD–U WE/BH–M
Fees D–£16
Loc 4 miles SW of Bolton on A58

Whalley (1912)

Long Leese Barn, Clerkhill Road,
Whalley, BB7 9DR
Tel (01254) 822236
Mem 422
Sec P Lord (01282) 779167
Pro J Hunt (01254) 824766
Holes 9 L 6258 yds Par 72 SSS 71
V'tors U exc Sat (Apr–Oct)
SOC–WD
Fees £16 (£20)
Loc 7 miles NE of Blackburn

Whittaker (1906)

Littleborough, OL5 0LH
Tel (01706) 378310
Mem 200
Sec GA Smith (01484) 428546
Holes 9 L 5576 yds SSS 67
V'tors WD/Sat–U Sun–NA
Fees £12 (£16)
Loc 1½ miles N of Littleborough,
off A58
Arch NP Stott

Wigan (1898)

Arley Hall, Haigh, Wigan, WN1 2UH
Tel (01257) 421360
Mem 300
Sec E Walmsley
Holes 18 L 6008 yds SSS 70
V'tors U exc Tues & Sat
Fees £25 (£30)
Loc 4 miles N of Wigan, off
A5106/B5239. M6 Junction
27
Arch Gaunt/Marnoch

Wilpshire (1890)

72 Whalley Road, Wilpshire,
Blackburn, BB1 9LF
Tel (01254) 248260
Fax (01254) 248260
Mem 650
Sec HE Aspden
Pro W Slaven (01254) 249558
Holes 18 L 5911 yds SSS 69
V'tors WD–U WE/BH–on request
Fees £25 (£30)
Loc 3 miles NE of Blackburn, off
A666

Leicestershire

Beedles Lake (1993)

Pay and play
170 Broome Lane, East Goscote,
LE7 3WQ
Tel (0116) 260 6759
Mem 336
Sec L Emery (Gen Mgr)
Pro S Byrne
Holes 18 L 6732 yds Par 72 SSS 71

V'tors U SOC
Fees £10 (£13)
Loc 4 miles N of Leicester on
B5328, off A46. M1, 8 miles
Mis Driving range
Arch D Tucker

Birstall (1900)

Station Road, Birstall, Leicester,
LE4 3BB
Tel (0116) 267 4450
Fax (0116) 267 4322
Mem 420 100(L) 50(J)
Sec Mrs SE Chilton
(0116) 267 4322
Pro D Clark (0116) 267 5245
Holes 18 L 6222 yds SSS 70
V'tors Mon/Wed/Fri–I Other
days–M SOC
Fees £25 D–£30
Loc 3 miles N of Leicester (A6)

Blaby (1991)

Pay and play
Lutterworth Road, Blaby, LE8 3DB
Tel (0116) 278 4804
Pro B Morris
Holes 9 L 2600 yds SSS 68
V'tors U
Fees 18 holes–£6 (£8)
Loc S of Blaby village
Mis Driving range

Breedon Priory (1990)

Green Lane, Wilson, Derby, DE73 1LG
Tel (01332) 863081
Fax (01332) 865319
Mem 500
Sec M Mayfield
Pro J Broughton
Holes 18 L 5777 yds Par 69 SSS 68
V'tors WD–U WE–NA before 2pm
(phone first) SOC–WD
Fees £20 (£25)
Loc 3½ miles W of M1 Junction
23A on A453
Arch Snell/Ashton

Charnwood Forest
(1890)

Breakback Road, Woodhouse Eaves,
Loughborough, LE12 8TA
Tel (01509) 890259
Fax (01509) 890925
Mem 330
Sec Mrs J Bowler
Holes 9 L 5960 yds SSS 69
V'tors WD–H WE/BH–NA
SOC–Wed–Fri
Fees £20 (£25)
Loc M1 Junction 22/23, 3 miles

Cosby (1895)

Chapel Lane, Broughton Road, Cosby,
Leicester LE9 1RG
Tel (0116) 286 4759
Fax (0116) 286 4484
Web www.cosby-golf-club.co.uk
Mem 690

Sec GT Kirkpatrick
(0116) 286 4759
Pro M Wing (0116) 284 8275
Holes 18 L 6410 yds Par 71 SSS 71
V'tors WD–U H before 4pm
WE/BH–M H SOC–WD–H
Fees £18 D–£26
Loc ½ mile S of Cosby. 7 miles S
of Leicester

Enderby (1986)

Public
Mill Lane, Enderby, Leicester,
LE9 5NW
Tel (0116) 284 9388
Sec LJ Speake (0116) 284 1133
Pro C D'Araujo
Holes 9 L 5552 yds SSS 71
V'tors U
Fees 18 holes–£6.50 (£8.75)
Loc Enderby 2 miles. M1 Junction
21

Glen Gorse (1933)

Glen Road, Oadby, Leicester,
LE2 4RF
Tel (0116) 271 4159
Fax (0116) 271 4159
Mem 440 115(L) 60(J)
Sec M Goodson (0116) 271 4159
Pro D Fitzpatrick (0116) 271
3748
Holes 18 L 6648 yds SSS 72
V'tors WD–U WE/BH–M SOC–WD
Fees £25 D–£30
Loc 3 miles S of Leicester on A6

Hinckley (1894)

Leicester Road, Hinckley, LE10 3DR
Tel (01455) 615124
Fax (01455) 890841
Web www.hinckleygolfclub.com
Mem 650
Sec R Coley, L Jackson
(Admin)
Pro R Jones (01455) 615014
Holes 18 L 6527 yds SSS 71
V'tors WD–U exc Tues Sat–NA
before 4pm Sun–M after
11am SOC
Fees £25 D–£35
Loc NE of Hinckley on B4668, nr
M69

Humberstone Heights
(1978)

Public
Gipsy Lane, Leicester, LE5 0TB
Tel (0116) 299 5570/1
Fax (0116) 299 5569
Mem 350
Sec Mrs H Cotter
Pro P Highfield (0116) 299 5570
Holes 18 L 6343 yds SSS 70
V'tors U SOC
Fees On application
Loc 3 miles E of Leicester, off A47
Mis Driving range. Pitch & putt
course
Arch Hawtree

For list of abbreviations see page 649

Kibworth (1904)

Weir Road, Kibworth Beauchamp,
Leicester, LE8 0LP

Tel	(0116) 279 2301
Fax	(0116) 279 6434
Mem	700
Sec	J Noble (Mgr)
Pro	R Larratt (0116) 279 2283
Holes	18 L 6312 yds SSS 70
V'tors	WD–U WE–M SOC–WD
Fees	£23
Loc	9 miles SE of Leicester, off A6
Mis	Driving range

Kilworth Springs (1993)

South Kilworth Road, North Kilworth,
Lutterworth, LE17 6HJ

Tel	(01858) 575082
Fax	(01858) 575078
Mem	514
Sec	Ann Vicary
Pro	A Markert
Holes	18 L 6718 yds SSS 72
V'tors	U SOC
Fees	£18 (£21)
Loc	4 miles E of M1 Junction 20
Mis	Driving range

Kirby Muxloe (1893)

Station Road, Kirby Muxloe, Leicester,
LE9 2EP

Tel	(0116) 239 3457
Fax	(0116) 239 3457
Mem	425
Sec	R Wildsmith (0116) 239 3457
Pro	B Whipham (0116) 239 2813
Holes	18 L 6279 yds Par 71 SSS 70
V'tors	WD–U before 3.45pm exc Tues–NA WE–Captain's permission only SOC–H
Fees	£25 D–£30
Loc	3 miles W of Leicester
Mis	Driving range for members and green fees only

Langton Park G&CC
(1994)

Langton Hall, Leicester, LE16 7TY

Tel	(01858) 545374
Fax	(01858) 545358
Mem	200
Sec	J Window
Holes	18 L 6724 yds SSS 72
V'tors	H or I SOC
Fees	On application
Loc	12 miles SE of Leicester, off A6. 2 miles N of Market Harborough
Arch	Hawtree

Leicestershire (1890)

Evington Lane, Leicester, LE5 6DJ

Tel	(0116) 273 8825
Fax	(0116) 273 1900
Mem	750
Sec	CR Chapman
Pro	DT Jones (0116) 273 6730
Holes	18 L 6329 yds SSS 71
V'tors	U H SOC–arrange with Sec or Pro

Fees	£24 (£29)
Loc	2 miles E of Leicester

Leicestershire Forest (1991)

Markfield Lane, Botcheston,
LE9 9FJ

Tel	(01455) 824800
Mem	460
Sec	M Fixter
Pro	M Wing
Holes	18 L 6111 yds SSS 69
V'tors	U–phone first
Fees	On application
Loc	6 miles W of Leicester. M1 Junction 22, 4 miles
Mis	Driving range
Arch	York/Fixter

Lingdale (1967)

Joe Moore's Lane, Woodhouse Eaves,
Loughborough, LE12 8TF

Tel	(01509) 890703
Fax	(01509) 890703
Mem	685
Sec	M Green
Pro	P Sellears (01509) 890684
Holes	18 L 6545 yds SSS 71
V'tors	U SOC
Fees	D–£23 (£26)
Loc	6 miles S of Loughborough. M1 Junction 23, 4 miles

Longcliffe (1906)

Snells Nook Lane, Nanpantan,
Loughborough, LE11 3YA

Tel	(01509) 216321
Mem	650
Sec	P Keeling (01509) 239129
Pro	DC Mee (01509) 231450
Holes	18 L 6625 yds SSS 72
V'tors	WD–H WE–M
Fees	£29
Loc	3 miles SW of Loughborough. M1 Junction 23

Lutterworth (1904)

Rugby Road, Lutterworth, LE17 4HN

Tel	(01455) 552532
Fax	(01455) 553586
Mem	780
Sec	J Faulks
Pro	R Tisdall (01455) 557199
Holes	18 L 6226 yds SSS 70
V'tors	WD–U WE–M SOC–WD
Fees	£21 D–£30
Loc	By M1 Junction 20 and M6 Junction 1

Market Harborough
(1898)

Great Oxendon Road, Market
Harborough, LE16 8NF

Tel	(01858) 463684
Fax	(01858) 432906
Mem	650
Sec	AP Price-Jones
Pro	FJ Baxter (01858) 463684
Holes	18 L 6022 yds Par 70 SSS 69

V'tors	WD–U WE–M SOC–WD
Fees	£25 D–£30
Loc	1 mile S of Mkt Harborough on A508
Arch	Howard Swan

Melton Mowbray (1925)

Waltham Rd, Thorpe Arnold, Melton
Mowbray, LE14 4SD

Tel	(01664) 562118
Fax	(01664) 562118
Mem	575
Sec	Mrs EA Sallis
Pro	J Hetherington (01664) 569629
Holes	18 L 6222 yds SSS 70
V'tors	U H before 3pm –M after 3pm SOC
Fees	£20 (£23)
Loc	2 miles NE of Melton Mowbray on A607

Oadby (1974)

Public

Leicester Road, Oadby, Leicester,
LE2 4AJ

Tel	(0116) 270 9052/270 0215
Mem	450
Sec	P Goodall (0116) 270 3828
Pro	A Kershaw (0116) 270 9052
Holes	18 L 6311 yds Par 72 SSS 70
V'tors	WD–U WE/BH–book with Pro SOC–WD
Fees	£7 (£10)
Loc	Leicester Racecourse, 2 miles SE of Leicester (A6)

Park Hill (1994)

Park Hill, Seagrave, LE12 7NG

Tel	(01509) 815454
Fax	(01509) 816062
Web	www.parkhillgolf.co.uk
Mem	500
Sec	JP Hutson
Pro	M Ulyett (01509) 815775
Holes	18 L 7219 yds Par 73 SSS 74
V'tors	U SOC
Fees	£22 D–£30 (£26 D–£38)
Loc	6 miles N of Leicester on A46. M1 Junction 21A
Mis	Driving range

Rothley Park (1911)

Westfield Lane, Rothley, Leicester,
LE7 7LH

Tel	(0116) 230 2019
Fax	(0116) 230 2809
Web	www.rothleypark.com
Sec	SG Winterton (0116) 230 2809
Pro	A Collins (0116) 230 3023
Holes	18 L 6487 yds SSS 71
V'tors	WD–H exc Tues–NA WE/BH–NA SOC
Fees	£25 D–£30
Loc	6 miles N of Leicester, W of A6

Scraptoft (1928)

Beeby Road, Scraptoft, Leicester,
LE7 9SJ

Tel	(0116) 241 9000
Fax	(0116) 241 8863
Mem	563
Sec	H Taylor (0116) 241 8863
Pro	S Wood (0116) 241 9138
Holes	18 L 6235 yds Par 70 SSS 70
V'tors	WD–U WE–M SOC–WD
Fees	£20 D–£25
Loc	3 miles E of Leicester

Six Hills

Pay and play
Six Hills, Melton Mowbray, LE14 3PR

Tel	(01509) 881225
Fax	(01509) 889090
Mem	100
Sec	Mrs J Showler
Pro	T Westwood
Holes	18 L 5758 yds Par 71 SSS 69
V'tors	U
Fees	£10 (£13)
Loc	10 miles N of leicester, off A46

Ullesthorpe Court Hotel (1976)

Frolesworth Road, Ullesthorpe,
Lutterworth, LE17 5BZ

Tel	(01455) 209023
Fax	(01455) 202537
Web	www.ullesthorpecourt.co.uk
Mem	600
Sec	PE Woolley
Pro	D Bowring (01455) 209150
Holes	18 L 6650 yds SSS 72
V'tors	U SOC–WD
Fees	£20 D–£35
Loc	3 miles NW of Lutterworth, off B577. M1 Junction 20, 5 miles

Western Park (1920)

Public
Scudamore Road, Leicester, LE3 1UQ

Tel	(0116) 287 2339/287 6158
Mem	300
Sec	IA Nicholson
Pro	BN Whipham (0116) 287 2339
Holes	18 L 6532 yds SSS 71
V'tors	U
Fees	On application
Loc	4 miles W of Leicester. M1 Junction 21, 3 miles

Whetstone (1965)

Cambridge Road, Cosby, Leicester,
LE9 5SH

Tel	(0116) 286 1424
Fax	(0116) 286 1424
Mem	550
Sec	J Dalby
Pro	N Leatherland, D Raitt
Holes	18 L 5795 yds Par 68 SSS 68
V'tors	U SOC
Fees	£15
Loc	S boundary of Leicester

Mis	Driving range
Arch	E Callaway

Willesley Park (1921)

Measham Road, Ashby-de-la-Zouch,
LE65 2PF

Tel	(01530) 411532
Fax	(01530) 414596
Mem	600 99(L) 38(J)
Sec	RE Brown (01530) 414596
Pro	BJ Hill (01530) 414820
Holes	18 L 6304 yds SSS 70
V'tors	WD–H WE/BH–H after 9.30am SOC
Fees	£30 (£35)
Loc	2 miles S of Ashby on B5006. M1 Junctions 22/23/24. A42(M) Junction 12
Arch	James Braid

Lincolnshire

Ashby Decoy (1936)

Ashby Decoy, Burringham Road,
Scunthorpe, DN17 2AB

Tel	(01724) 842913
Fax	(01724) 271708
Mem	520 130(L) 65(J)
Sec	Mrs J Harrison (01724) 866561
Pro	A Miller (01724) 868972
Holes	18 L 6281 yds SSS 71
V'tors	WD–H Sat–M SOC–WD exc Tues
Fees	£18 (£23)
Loc	2 miles SW of Scunthorpe

Belton Park (1890)

Belton Lane, Londonthorpe Road,
Grantham, NG31 9SH

Tel	(01476) 567399
Fax	(01476) 592078
Web	www.greatgolfatbeltonpark .co.uk
Mem	900
Sec	T Ireland
Pro	B McKee (01476) 563911
Holes	27 holes:
	Brownlow L 6452 yds SSS 71
	Ancaster L 6305 yds SSS 70
	Belmont L 6075 yds SSS 69
V'tors	U H SOC–WD exc Tues
Fees	£27 (£33)
Loc	2 miles N of Grantham
Arch	T Williamson

Belton Woods Hotel (1991)

Belton, Grantham, NG32 2LN

Tel	(01476) 593200
Fax	(01476) 574547
Mem	350
Sec	A Ozolins (01636) 672305
Pro	S Sayers
Holes	Lakes 18 L 6831 yds SSS 73
	Woodside 18 L 6623 yds SSS 72
	9 hole Par 3 course
V'tors	U SOC

Fees	£27 D–£45 (£30 D–£50)
Loc	2 miles N of Grantham on A607 towards Lincoln
Mis	Driving range
Arch	Cayford

Blankney (1904)

Blankney, Lincoln, LN4 3AZ

Tel	(01526) 320263
Fax	(01526) 322521
Mem	664 138(L) 50(J)
Sec	DA Priest
Pro	G Bradley (01526) 320202
Holes	18 L 6638 yds SSS 73
V'tors	U H SOC
Fees	£22 (£30)
Loc	10 miles SE of Lincoln on B1188
Arch	Cameron Sinclair

Boston (1900)

Cowbridge, Horncastle Road, Boston,
PE22 7EL

Tel	(01205) 362306
Fax	(01205) 350589
Mem	650 115L) 60(J)
Sec	SP Shaw (01205) 350589
Pro	TR Squires (01205) 362306
Holes	18 L 6483 yds Par 72 SSS 71
V'tors	WD–U WE/BH–U H
Fees	£19 (£25)
Loc	2 miles N of Boston on B1183

Boston West (1995)

Hubbert's Bridge, Boston, PE20 3QX

Tel	(01205) 290670
Fax	(01205) 290725
Web	www.bostonwestgolfclub .co.uk
Mem	650
Sec	MJ Couture (01205) 290670
Pro	A Hare
Holes	18 L 6333 yds Par 72 SSS 70
	6 hole Par 3 course
V'tors	U
Fees	£13 (£15)
Loc	2 miles W of Boston on B1192
Mis	Floodlit driving range
Arch	Michael Zara

Burghley Park (1890)

St Martin's, Stamford, PE9 3JX

Tel	(01780) 753789
Fax	(01780) 753789
Mem	560 140(L) 100(J)
Sec	PH Mulligan (01780) 753789
Pro	G Davies (01780) 762100
Holes	18 L 6236 yds SSS 70
V'tors	WD–I or H WE/BH–M SOC–WD
Fees	£25
Loc	1 mile S of Stamford, off A1 to B1081
Arch	Rev JD Day

Canwick Park (1893)

Canwick Park, Washingborough Road,
Lincoln, LN4 1EF

Tel	(01522) 542912/522166

Fax   (01522) 526997
Web   www.canwickpark.co.uk
Mem   650
Sec   P Roberts (01522) 542912
Pro   S Williamson
       (01522) 536870
Holes 18 L 6150 yds SSS 69
V'tors WD–U WE–M before 2.30pm
       SOC–WD
Fees   £17 (£21)
Loc   1 mile SE of Lincoln
Arch   Hawtree

Carholme (1906)

Carholme Road, Lincoln, LN1 1SE
Tel   (01522) 523725
Fax   (01522) 533733
Web   www.carholme-golf-club.co.uk
Mem   600
Sec   J Lammin
Pro   R Hunter (01522) 536811
Holes 18 L 6215 yds Par 71 SSS 70
V'tors WD–U WE–U after 2pm
       BH–SOC
Fees   On application
Loc   Lincoln 1 mile (A57)

Cleethorpes (1894)

Kings Road, Cleethorpes, DN35 0PN
Tel   (01472) 814060 (Pro)
Mem   750
Sec   JG Ashton (01472) 816110
Pro   P Davies (01472) 814060
Holes 18 L 6349 yds SSS 70
V'tors WD–U exc Wed pm
Fees   D–£20 (D–£25)
Loc   1 mile S of Cleethorpes

Elsham (1900)

Barton Road, Elsham, Brigg,
DN20 0LS
Tel   (01652) 680291
Fax   (01652) 680308
Mem   650
Sec   T Hartley (Mgr)
       (01652) 680291
Pro   S Brewer (01652) 680432
Holes 18 L 6402 yds SSS 71
V'tors H SOC–WD
Fees   £21 D–£30
Loc   3 miles N of Brigg. M180
       Junction 5

Forest Pines (1996)

Ermine Street, Brigg, DN20 0AQ
Tel   (01652) 650756
Fax   (01652) 650495
Web   www.forestpines.co.uk
Mem   350
Sec   D Edwards (Golf Dir)
Pro   D Edwards
Holes 27 holes:6393-6859 yds
       Par 71-73 SSS 70-73
V'tors U SOC
Fees   £30 D–£40
Loc   M180 Junction 4, on A15 to
       Scunthorpe
Arch   John Morgan

Gainsborough (1894)

Thonock, Gainsborough, DN21 1PZ
Tel   (01427) 613088
Fax   (01427) 810172
Mem   600
Sec   D Bowers
Pro   S Cooper
Holes 18 L 6266 yds Par 70 SSS 70
       18 L 6724 yds Par 72 SSS 72
V'tors U
Fees   £25 D–£35
Loc   N of Gainsborough
Mis   Floodlit driving range
Arch   Neil Coles

Gedney Hill (1991)

Public
West Drove, Gedney End Hill,
PE12 0NT
Tel   (01406) 330922
Mem   400
Sec   M Page
Pro   D Hutton
Holes 18 L 5450 yds SSS 66
V'tors U SOC–WD
Fees   £6.50 (£11)
Loc   4 miles from A47 on B1166
Mis   Driving range
Arch   C Britton

Grange Park (1992)

Pay and play
Butterwick Road, Messingham,
Scunthorpe, DN17 3PP
Tel   (01724) 762945
Fax   (01724) 762851
Sec   I Cannon (Mgr)
Holes 13 L 4122 yds SSS 48
       9 hole Par 3 course
V'tors U
Fees   £6.50 (£8.50)
Loc   5 miles from Scunthorpe.
       M180 Junction 3
Mis   Floodlit driving range
Arch   RW Price

Grimsby (1922)

Littlecoates Road, Grimsby, DN34 4LU
Tel   (01472) 342823 (Clubhouse)
Fax   (01472) 342630
Mem   720 150(L) 70(J)
Sec   V McAfee (01472) 342630
Pro   R Smith (01472) 356981
Holes 18 L 6057 yds Par 70 SSS 69
V'tors WD–U Sat pm/Sun am–XL
       SOC–WD
Fees   £22 D–£28
Loc   1 mile W of Grimsby, off A46.
       1 mile from A180
Arch   HS Colt

Hirst Priory Park

Crowle, Scunthorpe, DN17 4BU
Tel   (07715) 420519
Mem   400
Sec   M Thompson
Pro   (01724) 711619
Holes 18 L 6199 yds Par 71 SSS 69
V'tors U SOC
Fees   £13.75 (£17.50)

Loc   ¾ mile N of M180 Junction 2,
       on A161 to Crowle
Arch   David Baxter

Holme Hall (1908)

Holme Lane, Bottesford, Scunthorpe,
DN16 3RF
Tel   (01724) 862078
Fax   (01724) 862078
Mem   470 90(L) 50(J)
Sec   Miss TL Curtis
Pro   R McKiernan (01724) 851816
Holes 18 L 6404 yds SSS 71
V'tors WD–U WE–M H SOC–WD
Fees   £20 D–£27
Loc   4 miles SE of Scunthorpe.
       M180 Junction 4

Horncastle (1990)

West Ashby, Horncastle, LN9 5PP
Tel   (01507) 526800
Mem   300
Sec   RC Chantry
Pro   EC Wright
Holes 18 L 5717 yds SSS 70
V'tors U SOC
Fees   £15 D–£20
Loc   1 mile N of Horncastle, off
       A158
Mis   Floodlit driving range
Arch   EC Wright

Humberston Park

Humberston Avenue, Humberston,
DN36 4SJ
Tel   (01472) 210404
Mem   230
Sec   R Bean (01472) 690361
Holes 9 L 3670 yds Par 60 SSS 57
V'tors U exc Wed pm/Thurs am/Sun
       am SOC
Fees   £8 (£10)
Loc   Humberston, 3 miles S of
       Grimsby (A1031)
Arch   T Barraclough

Immingham (1975)

St Andrews Lane, Off Church Lane,
Immingham, DN40 2EU
Tel   (01469) 575298
Fax   (01469) 577636
Web   www.immgc.com
Mem   650
Pro   N Harding (01469) 575493
Holes 18 L 6215 yds SSS 70
V'tors WD–U Sun–NA before noon
       SOC–WD
Fees   £16 D–£23
Loc   N of St Andrew's Church,
       Immingham
Arch   Hawtree/Pennink

Kenwick Park (1992)

Kenwick Hall, Louth, LN11 8NY
Tel   (01507) 605134
Fax   (01507) 606556
Sec   PG Shillington
Pro   E Sharp (01507) 607161
Holes 18 L 6815 yds Par 72 SSS 73
V'tors U SOC

Fees D–£25 (£35)
Loc 1 mile SE of Louth
Mis Teaching Academy. Driving range
Arch Patrick Tallack

Kingsway (1971)
Public
Kingsway, Scunthorpe, DN15 7ER
Tel (01724) 840945
Sec C Mann
Pro C Mann
Holes 9 L 1915 yds SSS 59
V'tors U
Fees On application
Loc ¾ mile W of Scunthorpe, off A18

Kirton Holme (1992)
Pay and play
Holme Road, Kirton Holme, Boston, PE20 1SY
Tel (01205) 290669
Mem 350
Sec Mrs T Welberry (01205) 290560
Pro Alison Johns (01205) 369948
Holes 9 L 2884 yds SSS 68
V'tors U SOC–WD
Fees D–£8.50 (£9.50)
Loc 3 miles W of Boston, off A52
Arch DW Welberry

Lincoln (1891)
Torksey, Lincoln, LN1 2EG
Tel (01427) 718721
Fax (01427) 718721
Mem 700
Sec DB Linton
Pro A Carter (01427) 718273
Holes 18 L 6438 yds SSS 71
V'tors WD–H SOC
Fees £26 D–£32
Loc 12 miles NW of Lincoln, off A156

Louth (1965)
Crowtree Lane, Louth, LN11 9LJ
Tel (01507) 602554
Fax (01507) 608501
Web www.louthgolfclub.com
Mem 700
Sec M Covey (Mgr) (01507) 603681
Pro AJ Blundell (01507) 604648
Holes 18 L 6430 yds SSS 71
V'tors U SOC–WD
Fees £18 D–£25 (£25 D–£30)
Loc W side of Louth

Manor (Laceby) (1992)
Laceby Manor, Laceby, Grimsby, DN37 7EA
Tel (01472) 873468
Fax (01472) 276706
Mem 550
Sec Mrs J Mackay, G Mackay (Mgr)
Holes 18 L 6354 yds SSS 70
V'tors U SOC

Fees D–£18 (£22)
Loc 5 miles W of Grimsby at Barton Street (A18)
Arch Nicholson/Rushton

Market Rasen & District (1912)
Legsby Road, Market Rasen, LN8 3DZ
Tel (01673) 842319
Mem 600
Sec JA Brown
Pro AM Chester (01673) 842416
Holes 18 L 6209 yds SSS 70
V'tors WD–I WE/BH–M SOC
Fees £20 D–£29
Loc 1 mile E of Market Rasen

Market Rasen Racecourse
Legsby Road, Market Rasen, LN8 3EA
Tel (01673) 843434
Fax (01673) 844532
Holes 9 L 2350 yds Par
V'tors U
Fees On application
Loc Market Rasen Racecourse

Martin Moor
Martin Road, Blankney, LN4 3BE
Tel (01526) 378243
Fax (01526) 378243
Mem 170
Sec B Wallis
Holes 9 L 6325 yds Par 72 SSS 70
V'tors U
Fees £7.50 (£9)
Loc 3 miles E of Metheringham (B1189)
Arch S Harrison

Millfield (1985)
Laughterton, Lincoln, LN1 2LB
Tel (01427) 718473
Fax (01427) 718473
Mem 500
Sec P Grey-Guthrie
Holes 18 L 6004 yds SSS 69
18 L 4585 yds
9 hole Par 3 course
V'tors U
Fees £5–£8
Loc 9 miles W of Lincoln, nr Torksey (B1133)
Mis Driving range
Arch C Watson

Normanby Hall (1978)
Public
Normanby Park, Scunthorpe, DN15 9HU
Tel (01724) 280444 Ext 852 (Bookings)
Mem 850
Sec P McNicholas (01724) 853212
Pro C Mann (01724) 720226
Holes 18 L 6548 yds SSS 71
V'tors U SOC–WD
Fees £11.50 D–£16 (£13.50)

Loc 5 miles N of Scunthorpe
Arch Hawtree

North Shore (1910)
North Shore Road, Skegness, PE25 1DN
Tel (01754) 763298
Fax (01754) 761902
Web www.north-shore.co.uk
Mem 450
Sec B Howard (01754) 763298
Pro J Cornelius (01754) 764822
Holes 18 L 6254 yds SSS 71
V'tors H–soft spikes only Apr–Oct SOC–WD
Fees £22 D–£33 (£31 D–£45)
Loc 1 mile N of Skegness
Arch James Braid

Pottergate
Moor Lane, Branston, Lincoln
Tel (01522) 794867
Mem 300
Sec G McFee
Pro L Tasker
Holes 9 L 5164 yds Par 68 SSS 65
V'tors U
Fees £8 (£8.50)
Loc 3 miles SE of Lincoln (B1188)
Arch WT Bailey

RAF Coningsby (1972)
RAF Coningsby, Lincoln, LN4 4SY
Tel (01526) 342581 Ext 6828
Mem 200
Sec S Ellis (01526) 347640
Holes 9 L 5354 yds Par 68 SSS 66
V'tors WD–U SOC–WD
Fees £6
Loc Between Woodhall Spa and Coningsby on B1192

RAF Waddington
Waddington, Lincoln, LN5 9NB
Tel (01522) 720271 Ext 7958
Mem 90
Sec D Bennett
Holes 9 L 5519 yds SSS 69
V'tors By prior arrangement
Fees On application
Loc 4 miles S of Lincoln (A607)

Sandilands (1900)
Sandilands, Sutton-on-Sea, LN12 2RJ
Tel (01507) 441432
Mem 400
Sec D Mumby (01507) 441617
Holes 18 L 5995 yds SSS 69
V'tors U SOC
Fees £15 (£20)
Loc 1 mile S of Sutton-on-Sea, off A52

Seacroft (1895)
Drummond Road, Seacroft, Skegness, PE25 3AU
Tel (01754) 763020
Fax (01754) 763020
Web www.seacroft-golfclub.co.uk

For list of abbreviations see page 649

Mem 310 120(L) 50(J)
Sec R England (Sec/Mgr)
Pro R Lawie (01754) 769624
Holes 18 L 6479 yds SSS 71
V'tors U H SOC
Fees £30 (£35)
Loc S boundary of Skegness, nr
Nature Reserve
Arch Willie Fernie

Sleaford (1905)

Willoughby Road, South Rauceby,
Sleaford, NG34 8PL
Tel (01529) 488326
Fax (01529) 488325
Mem 630
Sec TE Gibbons
Pro J Wilson (01529) 488644
Holes 18 L 6503 yds SSS 71
V'tors U H exc Sun–NA (Winter)
SOC–WD
Fees £22 (£36)
Loc 1 mile W of Sleaford on
A153
Arch Tom Williamson

South Kyme (1990)

Skinners Lane, South Kyme, Lincoln,
LN4 4AT
Tel (01526) 861113
Fax (01526) 861080
Sec P Chamberlain (Golf Dir)
Pro P Chamberlain
Holes 18 L 6597 yds SSS 71
V'tors U SOC
Fees £15 (£18)
Loc 2 miles from A17 on
B1395
Mis 6 hole practice course
Arch Graham Bradley

Spalding (1907)

Surfleet, Spalding, PE11 4EA
Tel (01775) 680386
Fax (01775) 680988
Mem 750
Sec BW Walker (01775) 680386
Pro J Spencer (01775) 680474
Holes 18 L 6478 yds SSS 71
V'tors U H SOC–Tues after 2pm &
Thurs
Fees £20 (£30)
Loc 4 miles N of Spalding, off A16
Arch Spencer/Ward/Price

Stoke Rochford (1924)

Great North Rd, Grantham,
NG33 5EW
Tel (01476) 530275
Mem 570
Sec J Martindale (01572) 756305
Pro A Dow (01476) 530218
Holes 18 L 6252 yds SSS 70
V'tors WD–U WE/BH–U after
10.30am
Fees On application
Loc 6 miles S of Grantham (A1)
Arch Maj Hotchkin (1935)

Sudbrook Moor (1991)

Public
Charity Street, Carlton Scroop,
Grantham, NG32 3AT
Tel (01400) 250796
Web www.sudbrookmoor.co.uk
Sec Judith Hutton
Pro T Hutton (01400) 250796
Holes 9 L 4827 yds Par 66 SSS 64
V'tors U
Fees D–£6 (D–£9)
Loc Carlton Scroop, 6 miles NE of
Grantham (A607)
Arch Tim Hutton

Sutton Bridge (1914)

New Road, Sutton Bridge, Spalding,
PE12 9RQ
Tel (01406) 350323 (Clubhouse)
Mem 320
Sec NE Davis (01945) 582447
Pro Alison Johns (01406) 351422
Holes 9 L 5820 yds SSS 68
V'tors WD–H WE–M SOC
Fees £18 (£10)
Loc 8 miles N of Wisbech (A17)

Tetney

Station Road, Tetney, Grimsby,
DN36 5HY
Tel (01472) 211644
Fax (01472) 211644
Mem 425
Sec J Abrams
Pro J Abrams
Holes 18 L 6100 yds Par 71 SSS 69
V'tors U SOC
Fees £10 (£11)
Loc 5 miles S of Grimsby, off A16
Mis Driving range

Toft Hotel (1988)

Toft, Bourne, PE10 0JT
Tel (01778) 590616
Fax (01778) 590264
Mem 500
Sec ND Frame
Pro M Jackson
Holes 18 L 6486 yds Par 72 SSS 71
V'tors U
Fees £20 (£25)
Loc 8 miles from Stamford on
A6121
Mis Driving range
Arch D & R Fitton

Waltham Windmill (1997)

Proprietary
Cheapside, Waltham, Grimsby,
DN37 0HT
Tel (01472) 824109
Fax (01472) 828391
Mem 600
Sec GW Fielding
Pro N Burkitt (01472) 823963
Holes 18 L 6400 yds Par 71 SSS 71
V'tors WD–U SOC
Fees £18 (£25)
Loc 2 miles S of Grimsby, off A16
Arch Fox/Payne

Woodhall Spa (1891)

Woodhall Spa, LN10 6PU
Tel (01526) 351835,
(01526) 352511 (Bookings)
Fax (01526) 352778
Mem 525
Sec BM Fawcett
Pro CC Elliot (01526) 351831
Holes Hotchkin 18 L 7047 yds
SSS 75;
Bracken 18 L 6735 yds
SSS 74
V'tors Booking essential SOC
Fees Hotchkin–£60 D–£100
Bracken–£40 D–£65
Loc 19 miles SE of Lincoln
(B1191)
Mis Driving range. Teaching
Academy
Arch Hotchkin/Steel

Woodthorpe Hall (1986)

Woodthorpe, Alford, LN13 0DD
Tel (01507) 450000
Fax (01507) 450000
Web www.woodthorpehall.co.uk
Mem 300
Sec EG Burton (01507) 450000
Holes 18 L 5140 yds Par 67 SSS 65
V'tors U SOC
Fees D–£10
Loc 3 miles N of Alford, off
B1373. 8 miles SE of Louth

London Clubs

Aquarius *Kent*
Beckenham Place Park *Kent*
Central London Golf Centre
Surrey
Dulwich & Sydenham Hill *Surrey*
Eltham Warren *Kent*
Finchley *Middlesex*
Hampstead *Middlesex*
Hendon *Middlesex*
Highgate *Middlesex*
Lee Valley *Middlesex*
London Scottish *Surrey*
Mill Hill *Middlesex*
Muswell Hill *Middlesex*
North Middlesex *Middlesex*
Richmond Park *Surrey*
Roehampton *Surrey*
Royal Blackheath *Kent*
Royal Epping Forest *Essex*
Royal Wimbledon *Surrey*
Shooter's Hill *Kent*
South Herts *Hertfordshire*
Trent Park *Middlesex*
Wanstead *Essex*
West Essex *Essex*
Wimbledon Common *Surrey*
Wimbledon Park *Surrey*

Manchester

Blackley (1907)

Victoria Avenue East, Manchester,
M9 7HW

Tel	**(0161) 643 2980**
Mem	800
Sec	CB Leggott (0161) 654 7770
Pro	C Gould (0161) 643 3912
Holes	18 L 6235 yds SSS 70
V'tors	WD–U WE–M SOC–WD exc Thurs
Fees	£24
Loc	North Manchester

Boysnope Park

Liverpool Road, Barton Moss, Eccles
M30 7RF

Tel	**(0161) 707 6125**
Fax	(0161) 707 3622
Web	www.boysnopegolfclub .co.uk
Sec	Jean Stringer (0161) 707 6125
Pro	S Currie (0161) 787 8687
Holes	18 L 3506 yds Par 72 SSS 71
V'tors	U SOC
Fees	£11 (£12)
Loc	SW of Manchester on A57. M60 Junction 11, 1 mile
Misc	Driving range

Chorlton-cum-Hardy

(1902)

Barlow Hall, Barlow Hall Road,
Manchester, M21 7JJ

Tel	**(0161) 881 3139**
Fax	(0161) 881 4532
Web	www.chorltoncumhardygolf club.sagenet.co.uk
Mem	800
Sec	Mrs K Poole (0161) 881 5830
Pro	DR Valentine (0161) 881 9911
Holes	18 L 5980 yds SSS 69
V'tors	U H SOC–Thurs & Fri
Fees	£25 (£30)
Loc	4 miles S of Manchester (A5103/A5145)

Davyhulme Park (1911)

Gleneagles Road, Davyhulme,
Manchester, M41 8SA

Tel	**(0161) 748 2260**
Fax	(0161) 747 4067
Mem	600
Sec	LB Wright
Pro	D Butler (0161) 748 3931
Holes	18 L 6237 yds SSS 70
V'tors	WD–H exc Wed & Fri–NA Sat–NA Sun–M SOC–Mon/Tues/Thurs
Fees	£24. 27 holes–£30
Loc	7 miles SW of Manchester

Denton (1909)

Manchester Road, Denton, Manchester,
M34 2GG

Tel	**(0161) 336 3218**
Fax	(0161) 336 4751

Mem	686
Sec	EW Tewson
Pro	M Hollingworth (0161) 336 2070
Holes	18 L 6496 yds SSS 71
V'tors	WD–U WE/BH–NA before 3pm SOC
Fees	£25 (£30)
Loc	M60 Junction 24, A57 to Manchester

Didsbury (1891)

Ford Lane, Northenden, Manchester,
M22 4NQ

Tel	**(0161) 998 9278**
Fax	(0161) 998 9278
Mem	760
Sec	AL Watson (Mgr)
Pro	P Barber (0161) 998 2811
Holes	18 L 6273 yds SSS 70
V'tors	WD–U H exc 9–10am & 12–1.30pm–NA WE–U H 10.30–11.30am & after 4pm
Fees	£26 (£30)
Loc	6 miles S of Manchester. M63 Junction 9

Ellesmere (1913)

Old Clough Lane, Worsley, Manchester,
M28 7HZ

Tel	**(0161) 790 2122**
Web	www.ellesmeregolf.co.uk
Mem	380 80(L) 75(J)
Sec	A Chapman (0161) 799 0554
Pro	T Morley (0161) 790 8591
Holes	18 L 6248 yds SSS 70
V'tors	U exc comp days (check with Pro) SOC–WD
Fees	£22 (£28)
Loc	6 miles W of Manchester, nr junction of M60/A580

Fairfield Golf & Sailing Club (1892)

Booth Road, Audenshaw, Manchester,
M34 5GA

Tel	**(0161) 370 1641**
Mem	550
Sec	H Jagger (0161) 370 1279
Pro	SA Pownell (0161) 370 2292
Holes	18 L 5664 yds SSS 68
V'tors	WD–U WE–NA before noon SOC–WD
Fees	£18 (£24)
Loc	5 miles E of Manchester on A635

Flixton (1893)

Church Road, Flixton, Urmston,
Manchester M41 6EP

Tel	**(0161) 748 2116**
Fax	(0161) 748 2116
Mem	400
Sec	F Baker (0161) 748 3456
Pro	D Wade (0161) 746 7160
Holes	9 L 6410 yds SSS 71
V'tors	WD–U exc Wed SOC

Fees	£16
Loc	6 miles SW of Manchester on B5213. M60 Junction 10

Great Lever & Farnworth (1901)

Plodder Lane, Farnworth, Bolton,
BL4 0LQ

Tel	**(01204) 656493**
Fax	(01204) 656137
Mem	730
Sec	MJ Ivill (01204) 656137
Pro	T Howarth (01204) 656650
Holes	18 L 6064 yds SSS 69
V'tors	H SOC–WD
Fees	£20 (£27)
Loc	2 miles S of Bolton. M61 Junction 4

Heaton Park Golf Centre (1912)

Public
Heaton Park, Prestwich, Manchester,
M25 2SW

Tel	**(0161) 654 9899**
Sec	JK Mort (Mgr)
Holes	18 L 5755 yds SSS 68
V'tors	U SOC
Fees	On application
Loc	North Manchester, via M60 to Middleton Road
Mis	Driving range
Arch	JH Taylor

Manchester (1882)

Hopwood Cottage, Rochdale Road,
Middleton, Manchester M24 6QP

Tel	**(0161) 643 2718,** **(0161) 643 0023 (Bookings)**
Fax	(0161) 643 9174
Web	www.manchestergc.co.uk
Mem	700
Sec	KG Flett (0161) 643 3202
Pro	B Connor (0161) 643 2638
Holes	18 L 6450 yds SSS 72
V'tors	WD–H WE–NA SOC
Fees	D–£30 (£45)
Loc	7 miles N of Manchester. M62 Junction 20
Mis	Driving range-members and green fees only
Arch	HS Colt

New North Manchester (1894)

Rhodes House, Manchester Old Road,
Middleton, Manchester M24 4PE

Tel	**(0161) 643 9033**
Fax	(0161) 643 7775
Web	www.nmgc.co.uk
Mem	700
Sec	D Parkinson
Pro	J Peel (0161) 643 7094
Holes	18 L 6598 yds SSS 72
V'tors	H
Fees	£25 (£28)
Loc	5 miles N of Manchester. M60 Junction 19
Arch	A Compston

Northenden (1913)

Palatine Road, Manchester, M22 4FR
Tel   **(0161) 998 4738**
Fax   (0161) 945 5592
Mem   700
Sec   RN Kemp (Sec/Mgr)
Pro   J Curtis
Holes 18 L 6503 yds SSS 71
V'tors U SOC
Fees   £28 (£32)
Loc   5 miles S of Manchester. M60 Junction 5

Old Manchester   (1818)

Club
Tel   **(0161) 766 4157**
Sec   PT Goodall, 9 Ashbourne Grove, Whitefield M45 7NJ
Holes Club without a course

Pike Fold (1909)

Hills Lane, Pole Lane, Unsworth, Bury BL9 8QP
Tel   **(0161) 766 3561**
Fax   (0161) 796 3569
Mem   250
Sec   J O'Donnell
Pro   A Cory
Holes 9 L 6312 yds Par 72 SSS 71
V'tors WD–U WE/BH–M
Fees   On application
Loc   8 miles N of Manchester, by M66

Prestwich (1908)

Hilton Lane, Prestwich, M25 9XB
Tel   **(0161) 773 2544**
Fax   (0161) 772 0700
Mem   500
Sec   S Wakefield (0161) 773 1404
Pro   S Wakefield (0161) 773 1404
Holes 18 L 4806 yds SSS 64
V'tors WD–H WE–NA before 3pm SOC
Fees   £20 (£20)
Loc   2½ miles N of Manchester, off A56. M63 Junction 17
Mis   Extension to 5103 yds by June 2002

Stand (1904)

The Dales, Ashbourne Grove, Whitefield, Manchester M45 7NL
Tel   **(0161) 766 2388**
Fax   (0161) 796 3234
Mem   700
Sec   TE Thacker (0161) 766 3197
Pro   M Dance (0161) 766 2214
Holes 18 L 6411 yds SSS 71
V'tors U SOC–WD
Fees   £25 (£30)
Loc   5 miles N of Manchester. M60 Junction 17
Arch   Alex Herd

Swinton Park (1926)

East Lancashire Road, Swinton, Manchester, M27 5LX
Tel   **(0161) 794 1785**

Fax   (0161) 281 0698
Mem   450 120(L) 50(J)
Sec   TH Glover (0161) 794 0861
Pro   J Wilson (0161) 793 8077
Holes 18 L 6726 yds SSS 72
V'tors WD–U WE–M SOC–Tues
Fees   On application
Loc   On A580, 5 miles NW of Manchester

Whitefield (1932)

Higher Lane, Whitefield, Manchester, M45 7EZ
Tel   **(0161) 351 2700**
Fax   (0161) 351 2712
Mem   538
Sec   Mrs A Schofield
Pro   P Reeves (0161) 351 2709
Holes 18 L 6045 yds SSS 69
               18 L 5755 yds SSS 68
V'tors U SOC–WD
Fees   £25 (£35)
Loc   4 miles N of Manchester. M60 Junction 17

William Wroe (1973)

Public
Pennybridge Lane, Flixton, Manchester, M31 3DL
Tel   **(0161) 748 8680**
Pro   B Parkinson
Holes 18 L 4395 yds SSS 61
V'tors U–booking necessary
Fees   On application
Loc   6 miles SW of Manchester, by M63 Junction 4

Withington   (1892)

243 Palatine Road, West Didsbury, Manchester, M20 2UE
Tel   **(0161) 445 3912**
Fax   (0161) 445 5210
Mem   340 97(L) 38(J)
Sec   B Grundy (0161) 445 9544
Pro   RJ Ling (0161) 445 4861
Holes 18 L 6410 yds SSS 70
V'tors WD–H exc Thurs SOC
Fees   On application
Loc   6 miles S of Manchester on B5166

Worsley (1894)

Stableford Avenue, Monton Green, Eccles, Manchester M30 8AP
Tel   **(0161) 789 4202**
Fax   (0161) 789 3200
Mem   625
Sec   R Pizzey MBE
Pro   C Cousins
Holes 18 L 6217 yds SSS 70
V'tors H SOC
Fees   £30 (£35)
Loc   5 miles W of Manchester

Merseyside

Allerton Municipal (1934)

Public
Allerton Road, Liverpool, L18 3JT
Tel   **(0151) 428 1046**
Pro   B Large
Holes 18 L 5494 yds SSS 65
               9 hole course
V'tors U SOC
Fees   On application
Loc   5 miles S of Liverpool

Arrowe Park (1931)

Public
Arrowe Park, Woodchurch, Birkenhead, CH49 5LW
Tel   **(0151) 677 1527**
Sec   C Jones
Pro   C Disbury
Holes 18 L 6396 yds SSS 70
V'tors U
Fees   £7.70 (£7.70)
Loc   3 miles S of Birkenhead on A552. M53 Junction 3, 1 mile

Bidston (1913)

Bidston Link Road, Wallasey, L44 2HR
Tel   **(0151) 638 3412**
Mem   500
Sec   F Taylor (Hon)
Pro   N McFarlane (0151) 630 6650
Holes 18 L 6207 yds SSS 70
V'tors WD–U WE–M SOC
Fees   On application
Loc   Off Bidston Link Road

Blundells Hill

Blundells Lane, Rainhill, L35 6NA
Tel   **(0151) 430 0100**
Fax   (0151) 426 5256
Web   www.blundellshill.co.uk
Mem   600
Sec   A Roberts
Pro   R Burbidge
Holes 18 L 6347 yds Par 71
V'tors U SOC
Fees   £25 (£30)
Loc   2 miles SW of St Helens. M62 Junction 7
Mis   Driving range
Arch   Steve Marnoch

Bootle (1934)

Dunnings Bridge Road, Litherland, L30 2PP
Tel   **(0151) 928 6196**
Mem   400
Sec   J Morgan
Pro   A Bradshaw (0151) 928 1371
Holes 18 L 6362 yds SSS 70
V'tors U–book by phone SOC
Fees   £7.20 (£9.20)
Loc   5 miles N of Liverpool (A565)
Arch   Fred Stevens

Bowring (1913)

Public

Bowring Park, Roby Road, Huyton, L36 4HD

Tel	(0151) 489 1901
Pro	D Weston
Holes	9 L 5592 yds SSS 66
V'tors	U
Fees	On application
Loc	6 miles N of Liverpool. M62 Junction 5

Brackenwood (1933)

Public

Brackenwood Lane, Bebington, Wirral, L63 2LY

Tel	(0151) 608 3093
Pro	C Disbury
Holes	18 L 6131 yds SSS 69
V'tors	U SOC
Fees	On application
Loc	Nr M53 Junction 4

Bromborough (1903)

Raby Hall Road, Bromborough, CH63 0NW

Tel	(0151) 334 2155
Fax	(0151) 334 7300
Web	www.bromborough-golf-club.freeserve.co.uk
Mem	800
Sec	JT Barraclough (0151) 334 2155
Pro	G Berry (0151) 334 4499
Holes	18 L 6547 yds SSS 72
V'tors	U–contact Pro in advance
Fees	£35 (£35)
Loc	Mid Wirral, M53 Junction 4

Caldy (1907)

Links Hey Road, Caldy, Wirral, CH48 1NB

Tel	(0151) 625 5660
Fax	(0151) 625 7394
Mem	875
Sec	Gail Copple
Pro	K Jones (0151) 625 1818
Holes	18 L 6675 yds SSS 73
V'tors	WD–U exc before 9.30am and from 1–2pm (booking necessary) SOC
Fees	On application
Loc	1½ miles S of West Kirby

Childwall (1913)

Naylor's Road, Gateacre, Liverpool, L27 2YB

Tel	(0151) 487 0654
Fax	(0151) 487 0882
Mem	650
Sec	J Tully (Mgr)
Pro	N Parr (0151) 487 9871
Holes	18 L 6425 yds SSS 71
V'tors	WE/BH/Tues–restricted
Fees	£26 (£35)
Loc	7 miles E of Liverpool. M62 Junction 6, 2 miles
Arch	James Braid

Eastham Lodge (1973)

117 Ferry Road, Eastham, Wirral, CH62 0AP

Tel	(0151) 327 1483 (Clubhouse)
Fax	(0151) 327 3003
Mem	686
Sec	CS Camden (0151) 327 3003
Pro	N Sargent (0151) 327 3008
Holes	18 L 5706 yds SSS 68
V'tors	WD–U WE/BH–M SOC–Tues
Fees	£22
Loc	6 miles S of Birkenhead, off A41. M53 Junction 5. Signs to Eastham Country Park
Arch	Hawtree/Hemstock

Formby (1884)

Golf Road, Formby, Liverpool, L37 1LQ

Tel	(01704) 872164
Fax	(01704) 833028
Web	www.formbygolfclub.co.uk
Mem	600
Sec	CCH Barker (01704) 872164
Pro	GH Butler (01704) 873090
Holes	18 L 6993 yds SSS 74
V'tors	WD–I H SOC
Fees	£65 (£65)
Loc	By Freshfield Station
Arch	Willie Park

Formby Hall

Southport Old Road, Formby, L37 0AB

Tel	(01704) 875699
Pro	D Lloyd
Holes	18 L 6875 yds Par 73
V'tors	WD–U SOC
Fees	On application
Loc	Off Formby by-pass
Mis	Floodlit driving range

Formby Ladies' (1896)

Golf Road, Formby, Liverpool, L37 1YH

Tel	(01704) 874127
Fax	(01704) 873493
Sec	Mrs J Houghton (01704) 873493
Pro	G Butler (01704) 873090
Holes	18 L 5426 yds SSS 71
V'tors	U–phone first SOC
Fees	£35 (£40)
Loc	Formby, off A565

Grange Park (1891)

Prescot Road, St Helens, WA10 3AD

Tel	(01744) 22980 (Members)
Fax	(01744) 26318
Web	www.ukgolfer.org
Mem	730
Sec	CV Hadley (01744) 26318
Pro	P Roberts (01744) 28785
Holes	18 L 6446 yds SSS 71
V'tors	I SOC–WD exc Tues
Fees	£26 (£33)
Loc	1½ miles W of St Helens on A58

Haydock Park (1877)

Golborne Park, Newton Lane, Newton-le-Willows, WA12 0HX

Tel	(01925) 224389
Fax	(01925) 228525
Mem	400 120(L)
Sec	JV Smith (01925) 228525
Pro	PE Kenwright (01925) 226944
Holes	18 L 6058 yds SSS 69
V'tors	H or I SOC–WD exc Tues
Fees	£27
Loc	1 mile E of M6 Junction 23

Hesketh (1885)

Cockle Dick's Lane, Cambridge Road, Southport, PR9 9QQ

Tel	(01704) 530226
Fax	(01704) 539250
Web	www.ukgolfer.org
Mem	650
Sec	MG Senior (01704) 536897
Pro	J Donoghue (01704) 530050
Holes	18 L 6587 yds SSS 72
V'tors	WD–U WE/BH–restricted SOC
Fees	£40 D–£50 (£50)
Loc	1 mile N of Southport (A565)
Arch	JOF Morris

Heswall (1902)

Cottage Lane, Gayton, Heswall, CH60 8PB

Tel	(0151) 342 1237
Fax	(0151) 342 6140
Mem	902
Sec	A Brooker
Pro	AE Thompson (0151) 342 7431
Holes	18 L 6492 yds SSS 72
V'tors	U H BH–NA SOC–Wed & Fri
Fees	£35 (£40)
Loc	8 miles NW of Chester off A540. M53 Junction 4

Hillside (1911)

Hastings Road, Hillside, Southport, PR8 2LU

Tel	(01704) 569902
Fax	(01704) 563192
Mem	800
Sec	JG Graham (01704) 567169
Pro	B Seddon (01704) 568360
Holes	18 L 6850 yds SSS 74
V'tors	By arrangement with Sec
Fees	D–£45 (£60)
Loc	Southport
Arch	Hawtree

Houghwood (1996)

Billinge Hill, Crank Road, Crank, St Helens WA11 8RL

Tel	(01744) 894754
Fax	(01744) 894754
Mem	630
Sec	AJ Martin
Pro	P Dickenson (01744) 894444
Holes	18 L 6202 yds SSS 69
V'tors	WD–U SOC–WD

Fees £17.50 (£25)
Loc 3 miles N of St Helens, off A580 (B5201). M6 Junctions 23 or 26
Arch N Pearson

Hoylake Municipal (1933)
Public
Carr Lane, Hoylake, Wirral, L47 4BQ
Tel (0151) 632 2956/4883 (Bookings)
Sec ME Down (0151) 632 6823
Pro S Hooton
Holes 18 L 6330 yds SSS 70
V'tors WD–U WE–phone booking 1 week in advance SOC
Fees £7.25
Loc 4 miles W of Birkenhead
Arch James Braid

Huyton & Prescot (1905)
Hurst Park, Huyton Lane, Huyton, L36 1UA
Tel (0151) 489 1138
Fax (0151) 489 0797
Mem 700
Sec D Ponsonby (0151) 489 3948
Pro J Fisher (0151) 489 2022
Holes 18 L 5839 yds SSS 68
V'tors WD–U WE–H SOC–WD
Fees On application
Loc 7 miles E of Liverpool. 1 mile S of Prescot on B5199. M57 Junction 2

Leasowe (1891)
Leasowe Road, Moreton, Wirral, CH46 3RD
Tel (0151) 677 5852
Fax (0151) 677 5852
Mem 610
Pro AJ Ayre (0151) 678 5460
Holes 18 L 6263 yds SSS 70
V'tors U SOC–H
Fees D–£23.50 (D–£30.50)
Loc 1 mile N of Queensway Tunnel. M53 Junction 1
Arch John Ball Jr

Lee Park (1954)
Childwall Valley Road, Gateacre, Liverpool, L27 3YA
Tel (0151) 487 9861 (Clubhouse)
Mem 550
Sec D Wise (0151) 487 3882
Holes 18 L 6024 yds SSS 69
V'tors SOC
Fees On application
Loc 7 miles SE of Liverpool (B5171)

Liverpool Municipal (1967)
Public
Ingoe Lane, Kirkby, Liverpool, L32 4SS
Tel (0151) 546 5435
Pro D Weston
Holes 18 L 6571 yds SSS 71

V'tors U WE–booking required SOC
Fees On application
Loc M57 Junction 6 to B5192

Prenton (1905)
Golf Links Road, Prenton, Birkenhead, CH42 8LW
Tel (0151) 608 1461
Fax (0151) 608 4659
Web www.prentongolfclub.co.uk
Mem 470 100(L) 80(J)
Sec N Brown (0151) 608 1053
Pro R Thompson (0151) 608 1636
Holes 18 L 6429 yds SSS 71
V'tors U SOC–Mon/Wed/Fri
Fees £30 (£35)
Loc Outskirts of Birkenhead. M53 Junction 3

RLGC Village Play (1895)
Club
Hoylake, Wirral, L47 4AL
Mem 35
Sec PD Williams (0151) 632 5156
Holes Play over Royal Liverpool

Royal Birkdale (1889)
Waterloo Road, Birkdale, Southport, PR8 2LX
Tel (01704) 567920
Fax (01704) 562327
Web www.royalbirkdale.com
Sec MC Gilyeat
Pro B Hodgkinson (01704) 568857
Holes 18 L 6703 yds SSS 73
V'tors I H SOC
Fees £108 D–£135 (£125)
Loc 1½ miles S of Southport (A565)
Arch George Lowe

Royal Liverpool (1869)
Meols Drive, Hoylake, L47 4AL
Tel (0151) 632 3101/3102
Fax (0151) 632 6737
Web www.royal-liverpool-golf.com
Mem 810
Sec Gp Capt CT Moore CBE
Pro J Heggarty (0151) 632 5868
Holes 18 L 7165 yds SSS 75
V'tors H SOC
Fees On application
Loc On A553 from M53 Junction 2

Sherdley Park Municipal
Public
Sherdley Park, St Helens
Tel (01744) 813149
Fax (01744) 817967
Sec B Collins (Mgr)
Holes 18 L 5974 yds SSS 69
V'tors U SOC
Fees £7.20 (£8.50)
Loc 2 miles E of St Helens (A570). M62 Junction 7, 2 miles
Mis Driving range

Southport & Ainsdale (1906)
Bradshaws Lane, Ainsdale, Southport, PR8 3LG
Tel (01704) 578000
Fax (01704) 570896
Web www.sandagolfclub.co.uk
Mem 462 101(L) 50(J)
Sec R Penley-Martin
Pro J Payne (01704) 577316
Holes 18 L 6687 yds SSS 73
V'tors WD–H WE–NA before noon
Fees £45 D–£60 (£60)
Loc 3 miles S of Southport on A565
Arch James Braid

Southport Municipal (1914)
Public
Park Road West, Southport, PR9 0JS
Tel (01704) 535286
Pro W Fletcher
Holes 18 L 6253 yds SSS 69
V'tors U SOC
Fees On application
Loc N end of Southport promenade

Southport Old Links (1926)
Moss Lane, Southport, PR9 7QS
Tel (01704) 228207
Fax (01704) 505353
Mem 450
Sec BE Kenyon
Holes 9 L 6349 yds SSS 71
V'tors U exc WE comp days/BH–NA SOC–WD
Fees £22 (£30)
Loc Churchtown, 3 miles NE of Southport

Wallasey (1891)
Bayswater Road, Wallasey, CH45 8LA
Tel (0151) 691 1024
Fax (0151) 638 8988
Web www.wallaseygolf.com
Mem 450 90(L) 50(J)
Sec CF Smith (0151) 691 1024
Pro M Adams (0151) 638 3888
Holes 18 L 6503 yds SSS 72
V'tors H SOC
Fees £45 (£60)
Loc M53–signs to New Brighton
Arch Tom Morris

Warren (1911)
Public
Grove Road, Wallasey, Wirral, CH45 0JA
Tel (0151) 639 8323 (Clubhouse)
Web www.warrengc.freeserve.co.uk
Sec DA Farrington
Pro S Konrad (0151) 639 5730
Holes 9 L 5914 yds SSS 68
V'tors U
Fees On application
Loc Wallasey

West Derby   (1896)

Yew Tree Lane, Liverpool, L12 9HQ
Tel   (0151) 228 1540
Fax   (0151) 259 0505
Mem   550
Sec   AP Milne (0151) 254 1034
Pro   A Witherup (0151) 220 5478
Holes   18 L 6277 yds SSS 70
V'tors   SOC–WD after 9.30am
Fees   £27 (£36)
Loc   2 miles E of Liverpool, off
A580-West Derby Junction

West Lancashire   (1873)

*Hall Road West, Blundellsands,
Liverpool, L23 8SZ*
Tel   (0151) 924 4115
Fax   (0151) 931 4448
Web   www.westlancashiregolf.co.uk
Mem   700
Sec   S King (0151) 924 1076
Pro   G Edge (0151) 924 5662
Holes   18 L 6767 yds SSS 73
V'tors   H SOC–WD exc Tues
Fees   £50 D–£65 (£70)
Loc   Between Liverpool and
Southport, off A565
Arch   CK Cotton

Wirral Ladies   (1894)

*93 Bidston Road, Birkenhead, Wirral,
CH43 6TS*
Tel   (0151) 652 1255
Fax   (0151) 653 4323
Mem   450
Sec   Mrs SA Headford
Pro   A Law (0151) 652 2468
Holes   18 L 4948 yds SSS 69
(Ladies)
18 L 5185 yds SSS 65 (Men)
V'tors   U H SOC–WD
Fees   £25 (£25)
Loc   Birkenhead ½ mile. M53,
2 miles

Woolton   (1900)

*Doe Park, Speke Road, Woolton,
Liverpool L25 7TZ*
Tel   (0151) 486 1601
Fax   (0151) 486 1664
Mem   750
Sec   K Hamilton (0151) 486 2298
Pro   D Thompson
(0151) 486 1298
Holes   18 L 5706 yds SSS 68
V'tors   U exc comp days
Fees   £24 (£35)
Loc   SE Liverpool. End of
M62/M57

Middlesex

Airlinks   (1984)

Public
Southall Lane, Hounslow, TW5 9PE
Tel   (020) 8561 1418
Fax   (020) 8813 6284
Sec   S Brewster

Pro   T Martin
Holes   18 L 6001 yds SSS 69
V'tors   U
Fees   £10 (£16)
Loc   Just off M4 Junction 3
Mis   Floodlit driving range
Arch   Alliss/Taylor

Ashford Manor   (1898)

Fordbridge Road, Ashford, TW15 3RT
Tel   (01784) 424644
Fax   (01784) 424649
Mem   800
Sec   DG Seward (01784) 424644
Pro   (01784) 255940
Holes   18 L 6352 yds SSS 70
V'tors   WD–H
Fees   £30 D–£35 WD only
Loc   Ashford, off A308

Brent Valley   (1938)

Public
*Church Road, Hanwell, London,
W7 3BE*
Tel   (020) 8567 4230 (Clubhouse),
(020) 8567 1287 (Bookings)
Mem   195
Sec   Ms M Griffin
Pro   P Bryant (020) 8567 1287
Holes   18 L 5426 yds SSS 66
V'tors   U SOC
Fees   On application

Bush Hill Park   (1895)

*Bush Hill, Winchmore Hill, London,
N21 2BU*
Tel   (020) 8360 5738
Fax   (020) 8360 5583
Web   www.bushhillparkgolfclub
.co.uk
Mem   630
Sec   Miss R Meade
Pro   A Andrews (020) 8360 4103
Holes   18 L 5825 yds SSS 68
V'tors   WD–H WE–NA SOC
Fees   £27
Loc   S of Enfield

C & L Country Club
(1991)

West End Road, Northolt UB5 6RD
Tel   (020) 8845 5662
Holes   9 L 4440 yds SSS 62
V'tors   U SOC
Fees   £10
Loc   A40, opp Northolt Airport
Arch   Patrick Tallack

Crews Hill   (1920)

*Cattlegate Road, Crews Hill, Enfield,
EN2 8AZ*
Tel   (020) 8363 0787
Fax   (020) 8364 5641
Mem   600
Sec   E Hollingsworth
(020) 8363 6674
Pro   N Wichelow
(020) 8366 7422
Holes   18 L 6208 yds SSS 70

V'tors   WD–I H WE/BH–M SOC
Fees   On application
Loc   2½ miles N of Enfield. M25
Junction 24
Arch   HS Colt

Ealing   (1898)

Perivale Lane, Greenford, UB6 8SS
Tel   (020) 8997 0937
Fax   (020) 8998 0756
Mem   600
Sec   June Mackison (Gen Mgr)
Pro   I Parsons (020) 8997 3959
Holes   18 L 6216 yds SSS 70
V'tors   WD–U H WE/BH–M
Fees   On application
Loc   Marble Arch 6 miles on A40-
Perivale junction
Arch   HS Colt

Enfield   (1893)

*Old Park Road South, Enfield,
EN2 7DA*
Tel   (020) 8363 3970
Fax   (020) 8342 0381
Web   www.enfieldgolfclub.co.uk
Mem   625
Sec   NA Challis
Pro   L Fickling (020) 8366 4492
Holes   18 L 6154 yds SSS 70
V'tors   WD–H WE/BH–M SOC–WD
Fees   £25 D–£30
Loc   1 mile NE of Enfield. M25
Junction 24-A1005
Arch   James Braid

Finchley   (1929)

*Nether Court, Frith Lane, London,
NW7 1PU*
Tel   (020) 8346 2436
Fax   (020) 8343 4205
Web   www.finchleygolfclub.co.uk
Mem   550
Sec   WD Keene
Pro   DM Brown (020) 8346 5086
Holes   18 L 6356 yds SSS 71
V'tors   WD–U WE–pm only SOC
Fees   On application
Loc   M1 Junction 2
Arch   James Braid

Fulwell   (1904)

*Wellington Road, Hampton Hill,
TW12 1JY*
Tel   (020) 8977 2733
Fax   (020) 8977 7732
Mem   750
Sec   PF Butcher
Pro   N Turner (020) 8977 3844
Holes   18 L 6544 yds SSS 71
V'tors   WD–I WE–M SOC
Fees   £30 (£35)
Loc   Opposite Fulwell Station

Grim's Dyke   (1910)

*Oxhey Lane, Hatch End, Pinner,
HA5 4AL*
Tel   (020) 8428 4093
Fax   (020) 8421 5494

Mem 600
Sec KA Connelly
(020) 8428 4539
Pro N Stephens (020) 8428 7484
Holes 18 L 5600 yds SSS 67
V'tors WD–U H WE–M SOC exc
BH–NA
Fees £26 D–£31
Loc 2 miles NW of Harrow
(A4008). M1 Junctions 4/5
Arch James Braid

Hampstead (1893)

Winnington Road, London, N2 0TU
Tel **(020) 8455 0203**
Fax (020) 8731 6194
Mem 435
Sec ACM Harris
Pro PJ Brown (020) 8455 7089
Holes 9 L 5812 yds SSS 68
V'tors H–phone Pro first
Fees £30 (£35)
Loc 1 mile from Hampstead, nr
Spaniards Inn
Arch Tom Dunn

Harrow School (1978)

*High Street, Harrow-on-the-Hill,
HA1 3HW*
Mem 440 100(L) 10(J)
Sec CV Davies (020) 8872 8232
Holes 9 L 3690 yds SSS 57
V'tors M H
Loc Harrow School, NW London
Arch Donald Steel

Haste Hill (1933)

Public
The Drive, Northwood, HA6 1HN
Tel **(01923) 825224**
Fax (01923) 826485
Mem 250
Sec M Groves
Pro C Smillie
Holes 18 L 5736 yds SSS 68
V'tors U SOC
Fees £12.50 (£17.50)
Loc Northwood-Hillingdon

Heath Park (1975)

Stockley Road, West Drayton
Tel **(01895) 444232**
Fax (01895) 444232
Web www.hpgc.co.uk
Mem 180
Sec B Sharma (Prop)
Holes 9 L 3236 yds SSS 56
V'tors WD–U Sun–NA before 11am
SOC
Fees £8 (£9)
Loc Crowne Plaza Hotel,
Heathrow
Arch Neil Coles

Hendon (1903)

*Ashley Walk, Devonshire Road,
London, NW7 1DG*
Tel **(020) 8346 6023**
Fax (020) 8343 1974
Mem 560

Sec DE Cooper
Pro M Deal (020) 8346 8990
Holes 18 L 6289 yds Par 70
SSS 70
V'tors WD–U WE/BH–bookings
SOC
Fees £30 D–£35 (£35)
Loc M1 Junction 2, on to Holders
Hill Road
Arch HS Colt

Highgate (1904)

*Denewood Road, Highgate, London,
N6 4AH*
Tel **(020) 8340 1906 (Clubhouse)**
Fax (020) 8348 9152
Web www.highgategolfclub
.freeserve.co.uk
Mem 700
Sec JG Wilson (020) 8340 3745
Pro R Turner (020) 8340 5467
Holes 18 L 5964 yds SSS 69
V'tors WD–U exc Wed–NA before
noon WE/BH–M SOC
Fees £30
Loc Off Sheldon
Avenue/Hampstead Lane
Arch Cuthbert Butchart

Hillingdon (1892)

*18 Dorset Way, Hillingdon, Uxbridge,
UB10 0JR*
Tel **(01895) 239810**
Fax (01895) 233956
Mem 375
Sec KJ Newton (01895) 233956
Pro PCR Smith (01895) 460035
Holes 9 L 5459 yds SSS 67
V'tors WD–U exc Thurs 12–4pm
WE pm–M H SOC–WD
Fees £15 D–£27
Loc Off Uxbridge Road, opposite
St John's Church

Horsenden Hill (1935)

Public
Woodland Rise, Greenford, UB6 0RD
Tel **(020) 8902 4555**
Mem 112
Sec AK Witte
Pro S Hoffman
Holes 9 L 3264 yds SSS 56
V'tors U
Fees On application
Loc Greenford

Hounslow Heath (1979)

Public
Staines Road, Hounslow, TW4 5DS
Tel **(020) 8570 5271**
Mem 140
Sec R Mulford
Holes 18 L 5901 yds Par 69 SSS 68
V'tors WD–U WE–booking essential
Fees £8.80 (£12.70)
Loc Opposite Green Lane, Staines
Road (A315)
Arch Fraser

Lee Valley (1973)

Pay and play
*Lee Valley Leisure, Picketts Lock Lane,
Edmonton, London N9 0AS*
Tel **(020) 8803 3611**
Pro RG Gerken
Holes 18 L 4974 yds SSS 64
V'tors WD–U WE–booking
advisable
Fees £12 (£15)
Loc 1 mile N of north Circular
Road, Edmonton on Meridian
Way
Mis Floodlit driving range

London Golf Centre (1984)

Public
Ruislip Road, Northolt, UB5 6QZ
Tel **(020) 8841 6162/845 2332**
Fax (020) 8842 2097
Sec JP Clifford (Gen Mgr)
Pro G Newall (020) 8845 3180
Holes 9 L 5838 yds SSS 69
V'tors U SOC
Fees 9 holes–£5. 18 holes–£9
Loc Off A40, nr Polish war
memorial
Mis Driving range

Mill Hill (1925)

*100 Barnet Way, Mill Hill, London,
NW7 3AL*
Tel **(020) 8959 2282**
Fax (020) 8906 0731
Mem 570
Sec DR Cromie (020) 8959 2339
Pro D Beal (020) 8959 7261
Holes 18 L 6309 yds SSS 70
V'tors WD–U H WE/BH–U H after
11.30am SOC–WD
Fees £25 (£30)
Loc ½ mile N of Apex Corner, nr
A1/A41 junction
Arch Abercromby/Colt

Muswell Hill (1893)

*Rhodes Avenue, Wood Green, London,
N22 7UT*
Tel **(020) 8888 2044**
Fax (020) 8889 9380
Mem 600
Sec J Underhill (020) 8888 1764
Pro D Wilton (020) 8888 8046
Holes 18 L 6474 yds SSS 71
V'tors WD–U WE–book with Pro
SOC
Fees £26 D–£36 (£35)
Loc 1 mile from Bounds Green
Station. Central London 7
miles
Arch Braid/Wilson

North Middlesex (1928)

*The Manor House, Friern Barnet Lane,
Whetstone, London N20 0NL*
Tel **(020) 8445 1732**
Fax (020) 8445 5023
Mem 500
Sec Ms A McDonald (Mgr)
(020) 8445 1604

Pro (020) 8445 3060
Holes 18 L 5594 yds SSS 67
V'tors WE/BH–restricted SOC–WD
Fees £23 (£29)
Loc 5 miles S of M25 Junction 23, between Barnet and Finchley
Arch Willie Park Jr

Northolt (1991)

Pay and play
Huxley Close, Northolt, UB5 5UL
Tel (020) 8841 5550
Mem 250
Sec L Gribben
Pro I Godleman
Holes 9 hole course Par 56 SSS 55
V'tors U SOC
Fees £5
Loc Nr M40 Target roundabout
Mis Driving range

Northwood (1891)

Rickmansworth Road, Northwood, HA6 2QW
Tel (01923) 825329
Fax (01923) 840150
Mem 560
Sec Maj (Retd) KP Loosemore (01923) 821384
Pro CJ Holdsworth (01923) 820112
Holes 18 L 6553 yds SSS 71
V'tors WD–H WE/BH–NA SOC
Fees £28 (£38)
Loc 3 miles SE of Rickmansworth (A404)
Arch James Braid

Perivale Park (1932)

Public
Stockdove Way, Argyle Road, Greenford, UB6 8EN
Tel (020) 8575 7116
Mem 140
Sec P Smith
Pro P Bryant (020) 8575 7116
Holes 9 L 5296 yds SSS 67
V'tors U
Fees 9 holes–£4.40 (£6.50) 18 holes–£11.50
Loc 1 mile E of Greenford, off A40

Pinner Hill (1927)

Southview Road, Pinner Hill, HA5 3YA
Tel (020) 8866 0963
Fax (020) 8868 4817
Web www.pinnerhillgc.co.uk
Mem 770
Sec IN Prentice (020) 8866 0963
Pro M Grieve (020) 8866 2109
Holes 18 L 6330 yds SSS 70
V'tors WD–H exc Wed & Thurs–U Sun/BH–M SOC
Fees £30 (£35) exc Wed & Thurs–£15
Loc 1 mile W from Pinner Green
Arch JH Taylor

Ruislip (1936)

Public
Ickenham Road, Ruislip, HA4 7DQ
Tel (01895) 638835
Fax (01895) 622172
Mem 325
Sec G Bannister (01895) 637659
Pro P Glozier
Holes 18 L 5571 yds Par 69 SSS 67
V'tors U SOC
Fees £12.50 (£17.50)
Loc W Ruislip BR/LTE Station
Mis Driving range
Arch A Herd

Stanmore (1893)

29 Gordon Avenue, Stanmore, HA7 2RL
Tel (020) 8954 2599
Fax (020) 8954 6418
Mem 590
Sec AW Schooling
Pro VR Law (020) 8954 2646
Holes 18 L 5860 yds SSS 68
V'tors WD–H WE/BH–M SOC–Wed & Thurs
Fees £29.50
Loc Between Stanmore and Belmont, off Old Church Lane

Stockley Park (1993)

Pay and play
The Clubhouse, Stockley Park, Uxbridge, UB11 1AQ
Tel (020) 8813 5700/561 6339 (Bookings)
Fax (020) 8813 5655
Sec N Munro
Pro A Knox
Holes 18 L 6548 yds SSS 71
V'tors U SOC
Fees £24 (£34)
Loc Heathrow Airport, 2 miles. M4 Junction 4, 1 mile
Arch Robert Trent Jones Sr

Strawberry Hill (1900)

Wellesley Road, Strawberry Hill, Twickenham, TW2 5SD
Tel (020) 8894 1246
Mem 350
Sec Mrs M King (020) 8894 0165
Pro P Buchan (020) 8898 2082
Holes 9 L 2381 yds Par 64 SSS 62
V'tors WD–U WE–M XL
Fees £20
Loc Strawberry Hill Station
Arch JH Taylor

Sudbury (1920)

Bridgewater Road, Wembley, HA0 1AL
Tel (020) 8902 3713
Fax (020) 8903 2966
Web www.sudburygolfclubltd.co.uk
Mem 640
Sec AJ Poole (Gen Mgr)
Pro N Jordan (020) 8902 7910
Holes 18 L 6282 yds SSS 70
V'tors WD–H WE–M SOC–Tues–Fri

Fees On application
Loc Junction of A4005/A4090

Sunbury (1993)

Pay and play
Charlton Lane, Shepperton, TW17 8QA
Tel (01932) 771414
Fax (01932) 789300
Mem 350
Sec S Hayes (Gen Mgr) (01932) 771414 ML Wadsworth (Hon)
Pro A Hardaway (01932) 772898
Holes 18 L 5540 yds Par 66 SSS 67 9 L 2607 yds Par 33
V'tors U–phone Pro SOC
Fees £14 (£18)
Loc SE of Queen Mary Reservoir, nr Chalton. M3 Junction 1, 2 miles
Mis Floodlit driving range

Trent Park (1973)

Public
Bramley Road, Southgate, London, N14 4UT
Tel (020) 8366 7432
Fax (020) 8368 3823
Pro T Sheaff
Holes 18 L 6008 yds SSS 69
V'tors WD–U SOC WE–NA before 11am
Fees £10.60 (£13.50)
Loc Nr Oakwood Tube station
Mis Driving range

Twickenham (1977)

Pay and play
Staines Road, Twickenham, TW2 5JD
Tel (020) 8783 1698
Fax (020) 8941 9134
Pro Suzy Watt (020) 8783 1698
Holes 9 L 6014 yds SSS 69
V'tors U
Fees £6.50 (£7)
Loc 2 miles NW of Hampton Court, nr end of M3
Mis Floodlit driving range

Uxbridge (1947)

Public
The Drive, Harefield Place, Uxbridge, UB10 8PA
Tel (01895) 231169
Fax (01895) 810262
Sec T Atkins (01895) 272457
Pro R Mullane (01895) 237287
Holes 18 L 5711 yds SSS 68
V'tors U SOC
Fees £12.50 (£17.50)
Loc 2 miles N of Uxbridge. B467 off A40 towards Ruislip. M25 Junction 16, 3 miles

West Middlesex (1891)

Greenford Road, Southall, UB1 3EE
Tel (020) 8574 3450
Fax (020) 8574 2383
Mem 650

Sec	E Marper
Pro	IP Harris (020) 8574 1800
Holes	18 L 6119 yds SSS 69
V'tors	WD–U WE–NA before 3pm (phone Pro) SOC–Tues/Thurs/Fri
Fees	Mon–£10 Tues/Thurs/Fri–£20 Wed–£12 (£25)
Loc	Junction of Uxbridge Road and Greenford Road
Arch	James Braid

Whitewebbs (1932)

Public
Beggars Hollow, Clay Hill, Enfield, EN2 9JN

Tel	(020) 8363 2951
Mem	200
Sec	IF Forsyth
Pro	P Garlick (020) 8363 4454
Holes	18 L 5863 yds SSS 68
V'tors	U
Fees	£10 (£12)
Loc	1 mile N of Enfield

Wyke Green (1928)

Syon Lane, Isleworth, Osterley, TW7 5PT

Tel	(020) 8560 8777
Fax	(020) 8569 8390
Mem	700
Sec	D Pearson
Pro	N Smith (020) 8847 0685
Holes	18 L 6211 yds SSS 70
V'tors	WD–U exc Fri–NA WE/BH–H after 4pm SOC
Fees	£25 D–£35 After 5pm–£20
Loc	1/2 mile from Gillette Corner (A4)
Mis	Practice range
Arch	Hawtree/Taylor

Norfolk

Barnham Broom Hotel (1977)

Honingham Road, Barnham Broom, Norwich, NR9 4DD

Tel	(01603) 759393 (Hotel), (01603) 759552 (Golf Shop)
Fax	(01603) 758224
Web	www.barnham-broom.co.uk
Mem	500
Sec	P Ballingall (Golf Dir) (01603) 759393 Ext 278
Pro	S Dicksee
Holes	Valley 18 L 6483 yds Par 72 SSS 71 Hill 18 L 6495 yds Par 71 SSS 71
V'tors	U SOC
Fees	£30 (£40)
Loc	10 miles SW of Norwich, off A47. 5 miles NW of Wymondham, off A11
Mis	3 Academy holes
Arch	Pennink/Steel

Bawburgh (1978)

Glen Lodge, Marlingford Road, Bawburgh, Norwich NR9 3LU

Tel	(01603) 740404
Fax	(01603) 740403
Mem	650
Sec	I Ladbrooke (Golf Dir), J Barnard
Pro	C Potter (01603) 742323
Holes	18 L 6224 yds SSS 70
V'tors	U–phone first SOC
Fees	£20 (£25)
Loc	2 miles W of Norwich, off A47 Norwich Southern Bypass
Mis	Floodlit driving range. Golf Academy
Arch	Shaun Manser

Caldecott Hall

Caldecott Hall, Beccles Road, Fritton, NR31 9EY

Tel	(01493) 488488
Fax	(01493) 488561
Mem	600
Sec	R Beales
Pro	S Shulver
Holes	18 L 6572 yds Par 72 SSS 71 9 hole Par 3 course
V'tors	H SOC
Fees	£20 (£25)
Loc	5 miles SW of Gt Yarmouth on A413
Mis	Floodlit driving range. 9 holes pitch & putt course

Costessey Park (1983)

Costessey Park, Costessey, Norwich, NR8 5AL

Tel	(01603) 746333
Fax	(01603) 746185
Mem	600
Sec	GC Stangoe
Pro	A Young (01603) 747085
Holes	18 L 5900 yds Par 71 SSS 69
V'tors	U SOC–WD
Fees	On application
Loc	3 miles W of Norwich, off A47 at Round Well PH

Dereham (1934)

Quebec Road, Dereham, NR19 2DS

Tel	(01362) 695900
Fax	(01362) 695904
Mem	400
Sec	W Sargeant
Pro	R Curtis (01362) 695631
Holes	9 L 6225 yds SSS 70
V'tors	H
Fees	£15 D–£20
Loc	Dereham 1/2 mile

Dunham (1979)

Proprietary
Little Dunham, Swaffham, PE32 2DF

Tel	(01328) 701718
Fax	(01328) 701906
Mem	200
Sec	G & S Potter (Props) (01328) 701906
Pro	G Potter (01328) 701906

Holes	9 L 2560 yds Par 66 SSS 64
V'tors	U SOC
Fees	£12 (£15)
Loc	4 miles NE of Swaffham, off A47. Signs from Necton
Arch	Cecil Denny

Eagles (1990)

39 School Road, Tilney All Saints, Kings Lynn, PE34 4RS

Tel	(01553) 827147
Fax	(01553) 829777
Web	www.eagles-golf-tennis.co.uk
Mem	200
Sec	D Horn (Prop)
Pro	N Pickerell
Holes	9 L 2142 yds SSS 61 9 hole Par 3 course
V'tors	U
Fees	9 holes–£7.50 (£8.50)
Loc	5 miles W of Kings Lynn on A47
Mis	Driving range
Arch	David Horn

Eaton (1910)

Newmarket Road, Norwich, NR4 6SF

Tel	(01603) 451686
Fax	(01603) 451686
Web	www.eatongc.co.uk
Mem	640 135(L) 70(J)
Sec	Mrs LA Bovill
Pro	M Allen (01603) 452478
Holes	18 L 6114 yds SSS 70
V'tors	H WE–NA before noon SOC–WD
Fees	£30 (£40)
Loc	S Norwich, off A11

Fakenham (1973)

The Race Course, Fakenham, NR21 7NY

Tel	(01328) 862867
Mem	510
Sec	G Cocker (01328) 855665
Pro	C Williams (01328) 863534
Holes	9 L 6174 yds SSS 69
V'tors	WD–U WE–NA before 12 noon SOC
Fees	£14 (£18)
Loc	Fakenham racecourse

Feltwell (1976)

Thor Ave, Wilton Road, Feltwell, IP26 4AY

Tel	(01842) 827644
Mem	400
Sec	SJ Waller
Pro	N Mitchell (01842) 827666
Holes	9 L 6488 yds SSS 71
V'tors	U SOC–WD pm
Fees	£15 (£24)
Loc	1 mile S of Feltwell on B1112
Mis	Former Feltwell aerodrome

Gorleston (1906)

Warren Road, Gorleston, Gt Yarmouth, NR31 6JT

Tel	(01493) 661911

Fax	(01493) 661911
Mem	900
Sec	NP Longbottom
	(01493) 661911
Pro	N Brown (01493) 662103
Holes	18 L 6400 yds SSS 71
V'tors	U H SOC
Fees	£25 (£30) W–£85
Loc	S of Gorleston, off A12
Arch	JH Taylor

Great Yarmouth & Caister (1882)

Beach House, Caister-on-Sea, Gt Yarmouth, NR30 5TD

Tel	**(01493) 728699**
Fax	(01493) 728831
Web	www.caistergolf.com
Mem	700
Sec	HJ Harvey
Pro	J Hill (01493) 720421
Holes	18 L 6330 yds SSS 70
V'tors	WE–NA before noon SOC
Fees	£30 (£35)
Loc	Caister-on-Sea

Hunstanton (1891)

Golf Course Road, Old Hunstanton, PE36 6JQ

Tel	**(01485) 532811**
Fax	(01485) 532319
Mem	650 250(L) 60(J)
Sec	MT Whybrow
Pro	J Dodds (01485) 532751
Holes	18 L 6759 yds SSS 73
V'tors	WD–H after 9.30am WE–H after 10.30am SOC
Fees	D–£55 (£65)
Loc	1½ miles NE of Hunstanton
Mis	2-ball play only
Arch	George Fernie

King's Lynn (1923)

Castle Rising, King's Lynn, PE31 6BD

Tel	**(01553) 631654**
Fax	(01553) 631036
Mem	910
Sec	MP Sackrée (01553) 631654
Pro	J Reynolds (01553) 631655
Holes	18 L 6609 yds SSS 73
V'tors	U H SOC
Fees	£40 (£50)
Loc	4 miles NE of King's Lynn, off A149
Arch	Alliss/Thomas

Links Country Park Hotel

West Runton, Cromer, NR27 9QH

Tel	**(01263) 838383**
Fax	(01263) 838264
Web	www.links-hotel.co.uk
Mem	300
Sec	CB Abbott
Pro	A Collison (01263) 838215
Holes	9 L 4814 yds Par 66 SSS 64
V'tors	U
Fees	£25 (£30)

Loc	3 miles W of Cromer (A149)
Arch	JH Taylor

Marriott Sprowston Manor Hotel (1980)

Wroxham Road, Sprowston, Norwich, NR7 8RP

Tel	**(01603) 410657**
Fax	(01603) 788884
Mem	500
Sec	J O'Malley (Golf Dir) (01603) 254294
Pro	G Ireson (01603) 417264
Holes	18 L 5982 yds SSS 70
V'tors	U SOC
Fees	£19 (£25)
Loc	2 miles NE of Norwich on A1151
Mis	Floodlit driving range

Mattishall (1990)

South Green, Mattishall, Dereham

Tel	**(01362) 850464**
Mem	180
Sec	B Hall
Holes	9 L 6170 yds Par 70 SSS 69
V'tors	WD–U WE–U before noon SOC
Fees	£8 (£10)
Loc	6 miles E of Dereham (B1063)
Mis	9 hole pitch & putt
Arch	BC Todd

Middleton Hall (1989)

Proprietary
Middleton, King's Lynn, PE32 1RH

Tel	**(01553) 841800**
Fax	(01553) 841800
Web	www.middletonhall.co.uk
Mem	600
Sec	J Holland
Pro	S White (01553) 841801
Holes	18 L 6004 yds Par 71 SSS 69
V'tors	U SOC
Fees	£25 (£30)
Loc	2 miles SE of King's Lynn on A47
Mis	Driving range
Arch	D Scott

Mundesley (1901)

Links Road, Mundesley, NR11 8ES

Tel	**(01263) 720279**
Fax	(01263) 720279
Mem	500
Sec	J Woodhouse (Sec/Mgr) (01263) 720095
Pro	TG Symmons (01831) 455461
Holes	9 L 5377 yds SSS 66
V'tors	WD–U H exc Wed 11.30–3.30pm WE–NA before 11.30am
Fees	£18 (£25)
Loc	5 miles SE of Cromer

The Norfolk G&CC (1993)

Hingham Road, Reymerston, Norwich, NR9 4QQ

Tel	**(01362) 850297**

Fax	(01362) 850614
Mem	530
Sec	T Varney (Gen Mgr)
Pro	A Rudge (01362) 850297
Holes	18 L 6609 yds SSS 72
V'tors	WD–U before 4pm –M after 4pm WE/BH–NA before noon SOC
Fees	£22 (£27)
Loc	14 miles W of Norwich, off B1135 Dereham to Wymondham road
Mis	**Driving range.** 9 hole pitch & putt course

RAF Marham (1974)

RAF Marham, Kings Lynn, PE33 9NP

Mem	290
Sec	WR Benton (01760) 337261 (Ext 6507)
Holes	9 L 5244 yds SSS 66
V'tors	By prior arrangement–U exc Sun am
Loc	11 miles SE of King's Lynn, nr Narborough
Mis	Course situated on MOD land, and may be closed without prior notice

Richmond Park (1990)

Saham Road, Watton, IP25 6EA

Tel	**(01953) 881803**
Fax	(01953) 881817
Mem	600
Sec	A Hemsley
Pro	A Hemsley
Holes	18 L 6300 yds SSS 70
V'tors	WD–U WE–H before noon SOC
Fees	£18 (£24)
Loc	½ mile NW of Watton
Mis	Driving range
Arch	Scott/Jessup

Royal Cromer (1888)

Overstrand Road, Cromer, NR27 0JH

Tel	**(01263) 512884**
Fax	(01263) 512430
Web	www.royal-cromer.com
Mem	700
Sec	R Fields
Pro	(01263) 512267
Holes	18 L 6508 yds SSS 72
V'tors	H SOC–WD
Fees	D–£35 (D–£40)
Loc	1 mile E of Cromer on B1159
Arch	Morris/Taylor/Braid/Pennink

Royal Norwich (1893)

Drayton High Road, Hellesdon, Norwich, NR6 5AH

Tel	**(01603) 425712**
Fax	(01603) 417945
Web	www.royalnorwichgolf.co.uk
Mem	700
Sec	J Meggy (Mgr) (01603) 429928
Pro	D Futter (01603) 408459
Holes	18 L 6506 yds SSS 72
V'tors	WE/BH–restricted SOC
Fees	D–£36 (£45)

Loc ¹/₂ mile W of Norwich ring
road, on Fakenham road
Arch James Braid

Royal West Norfolk (1892)

Brancaster, King's Lynn, PE31 8AX
Tel (01485) 210223
Fax (01485) 210087
Mem 760
Sec Maj NA Carrington Smith
(01485) 210087
Pro S Rayner (01485) 210616
Holes 18 L 6427 yds SSS 71
V'tors M No four balls allowed Mid
July–mid Sept WE–NA before
10am SOC
Fees £60 (£70)
Loc 7 miles E of Hunstanton on
A419
Arch Holcombe Ingleby

Ryston Park (1932)

*Ely Road, Denver, Downham Market,
PE38 0HH*
Tel (01366) 382133
Fax (01366) 383834
Mem 320
Sec WJ Flogdell
Pro None
Holes 9 L 6310 yds SSS 70
V'tors WD–H WE/BH–M SOC
Fees £15 D–£20
Loc 1 mile S of Downham Market
on A10
Arch James Braid

Sheringham (1891)

Sheringham, NR26 8HG
Tel (01263) 822038 (Clubhouse)
Fax (01263) 825189
Web www.sheringhamgolfclub
.co.uk
Mem 700
Sec MC Davies (01263) 823488
Pro MW Jubb (01263) 822980
Holes 18 L 6495 yds SSS 71
V'tors WD–U H after 9.30am SOC
Fees £45 (£50)
Loc ¹/₂ mile W of Sheringham
(A149)
Arch Tom Dunn

Swaffham (1922)

Cley Road, Swaffham, PE37 8AE
Tel (01760) 721621
Fax (01760) 721621
Mem 420
Sec RD Parry
Pro P Field
Holes 9 L 6252 yds SSS 70
V'tors WD–U WE–M exc Sun
am–NA
Fees £20
Loc 1¹/₂ miles SW of Swaffham
Mis Extension to 18 holes Sept
2001

Thetford (1912)

Brandon Road, Thetford, IP24 3NE
Tel (01842) 752258 (Clubhouse)

Fax (01842) 766212
Mem 700
Sec Mrs SA Redpath
(01842) 752169
Pro G Kitley (01842) 752662
Holes 18 L 6879 yds SSS 73
V'tors H SOC–Wed–Fri
Fees £34
Loc 2 miles W of Thetford
(B1107), off A11 By-pass
Arch CH Mayo

De Vere Dunston Hall (1994)

Pay and play
*Ipswich Road, Dunston, Norwich,
NR14 8PQ*
Tel (01508) 470178
Fax (01508) 471499
Mem 400
Sec P Briggs
Pro P Briggs
Holes 18 L 6200 yds Par 71 SSS 70
V'tors U
Fees £25 (£30)
Loc 5 miles S of Norwich on A140
Mis Floodlit driving range
Arch John Glasgow

Wensum Valley (1990)

*Beech Avenue, Taverham, Norwich,
NR8 6HP*
Tel (01603) 261012
Fax (01603) 261664
Web www.wensumvalleyhotel.co.uk
Mem 850
Sec Mrs B Hall
Pro P Whittle
Holes 18 L 6223 yds SSS 70
9 L 2906 yds SSS 68
V'tors U SOC
Fees £20
Loc 4 miles NW of Norwich on
A1067
Mis Floodlit driving range
Arch BC Todd

Weston Park (1993)

Weston Longville, Norwich, NR9 5JW
Tel (01603) 872363
Fax (01603) 873040
Web www.weston-park.co.uk
Mem 450
Sec RR Wright
Pro MR Few (01603) 872998
Holes 18 L 6603 yds SSS 72
V'tors WD–U H
Fees £28.50 (£33)
Loc 7 miles NW of Norwich, off
A1067
Arch John Glasgow

Northamptonshire

Brampton Heath

*Sandy Lane, Church Brampton,
NN6 8AX*
Tel (01604) 843939

Fax (01604) 843885
Web www.bhgc.co.uk
Mem 500
Sec S Lawrence (01604) 843939
Pro R Hudson (01604) 843939
Holes 18 L 6366 yds Par 71 SSS 70
9 hole short course
V'tors U SOC
Fees £14 (£18)
Loc 4 miles N of Northampton
between A50 and A428
Mis Driving range

Cold Ashby (1974)

*Stanford Road, Cold Ashby,
Northampton, NN6 6EP*
Tel (01604) 740548
Fax (01604) 740548
Web www.coldashbygolfclub.com
Mem 600 40(L) 40(J)
Sec DA Croxton (Prop)
Pro S Rose (01604) 740099
Holes 27 L 6308 yds Par 72 SSS 70
V'tors WD–U WE–U after 12 noon
(if booked) SOC
Fees £15 (£18)
Loc 11 miles N of Northampton,
nr A5199/A14 Junction 1.
7 miles E of M1 Junction 18
Arch David Croxton

Collingtree Park (1990)

*Windingbrook Lane, Northampton,
NN4 0XN*
Tel (01604) 700000
Fax (01604) 702600
Mem 900
Sec JH Laidler (Gen Mgr)
Pro G Pook
Holes 18 L 6776 yds SSS 72
V'tors H SOC
Fees £15 (£20)
Loc ¹/₂ mile E of M1 Junction 15
Mis Floodlit driving range
Arch Johnny Miller

Daventry & District (1911)

Norton Road, Daventry, NN11 5LS
Tel (01327) 702829
Mem 350
Sec E Smith
Pro None
Holes 9 L 5812 yds Par 69 SSS 68
V'tors WD–U Sun–NA before 11am
SOC–phone Sec
Fees £10 (£15)
Loc ¹/₂ mile E of Daventry

Delapre (1976)

Public
*Eagle Drive, Nene Valley Way,
Northampton, NN4 7DU*
Tel (01604) 764036/763957
Fax (01604) 706378
Web www.delapregolf.co.uk
Mem 1000
Sec JS Corby (01604) 763957
Pro J Corby, J Cuddihy
(01604) 764036

Holes Oaks 18 L 6293 yds SSS 70
Hardingstone 9 L 2146 yds
SSS 32
2 x 9 holes Par 3 courses
V'tors U SOC
Fees £12 (£16)
Loc 3 miles from M1 Junction 15,
on A508/A45
Mis Pitch & putt. Driving range
Arch Jacobs/Corby

Embankment (1975)

*The Embankment, Wellingborough,
NN8 1LD*

Tel **(01933) 228465**
Mem 175
Sec JB Andrew, E Walden (Mgr)
Holes 9 L 3400 yds SSS 56
V'tors WD–M
Fees £4
Loc 1 mile SE of Wellingborough
Arch TH Neal

Farthingstone Hotel
(1974)

Farthingstone, Towcester, NN12 8HA

Tel **(01327) 361291**
Fax (01327) 361645
Web www.farthingstone.co.uk
Mem 400
Sec DC Donaldson (Prop/Mgr)
Pro G Lunn (01327) 361533
Holes 18 L 6299 yds SSS 70
V'tors U SOC
Fees £17 D–£22 (£25 D–£30)
SOC–£19
Loc 4 miles W of A5 on
Farthingstone-Everdon road.
M1 Junction 16, 6 miles

Hellidon Lakes Hotel
G&CC (1991)

Hellidon, Daventry, NN11 6GG

Tel **(01327) 262550**
Fax (01327) 262559
Web www.hellidon.co.uk
Mem 500
Sec MA Thomas
Pro G Wills (01327) 262551
Holes 18 L 6700 yds SSS 72
9 L 5582 yds SSS 67
V'tors U H SOC
Fees £20 (£30)
Loc 7 miles SW of Daventry, via
A361. M40 Junction 11 and
M1 Junction 16,
Arch David Snell

Kettering (1891)

Headlands, Kettering, NN15 6XA

Tel **(01536) 511104**
Fax (01536) 511104
Web www.kettering-golf.co.uk
Mem 700 100(L) 50(J)
Sec DG Buckby
Pro K Theobald (01536) 81014
Holes 18 L 6087 yds SSS 69
V'tors WD–U WE/BH–M SOC
Fees D–£30
Loc S boundary of Kettering
Arch Tom Morris

Kingfisher Hotel

Proprietary
*Buckingham Road, Deanshanger,
Milton Keynes, MK19 6JY*

Tel **(01908) 560354/562332**
Fax (01908) 260857
Web www.kingfisher-
hotelandgolf.co.uk
Mem 98
Sec G de Carteret (Gen Mgr)
Pro B Mudge
Holes 9 L 5690 yds Par 70 SSS 67
V'tors U exc Sun–restricted SOC
Fees 9 holes–£7.50 (£10)
18 holes–£11 (£14)
Loc NW of Milton Keynes on
A422 to Buckingham. M1
Junction 15
Mis Driving range
Arch Donald Steel

Kingsthorpe (1908)

*Kingsley Road, Northampton,
NN2 7BU*

Tel **(01604) 711173**
Fax (01604) 710610
Mem 600
Sec JE Harris (01604) 710610
Pro P Armstrong (01604) 719602
Holes 18 L 5918 yds SSS 69
V'tors WD–U WE/BH–M H
SOC–WD
Fees D–£25
Loc 2 miles N of Northampton
centre, off A508

Northampton (1893)

Harlestone, Northampton, NN7 4EF

Tel **(01604) 845102**
Fax (01604) 820262
Mem 595 137(L) 75(J)
Sec S Malherbe (01604) 845155
Pro K Dickens (01604) 845167
Holes 18 L 6615 yds Par 72 SSS 72
V'tors WD–U H WE–M SOC
Fees £32
Loc 4 miles NW of Northampton,
on A428 beyond Harlestone
Arch Donald Steel

Northamptonshire
County (1909)

*Church Brampton, Northampton,
NN6 8AZ*

Tel **(01604) 842170**
Fax (01604) 843463
Mem 650
Sec ME Wadley (01604) 843025
Pro T Rouse (01604) 842226
Holes 18 L 6505 yds SSS 72
V'tors H SOC
Fees Summer–£45 (£45)
Winter–£30 (£30)
Loc 5 miles NW of Northampton,
between A428 and A50
Arch HS Colt

Oundle (1893)

Benefield Road, Oundle, PE8 4EZ

Tel **(01832) 273267**
Fax (01832) 273267

Mem 650
Sec D Foley
Pro R Keys (01832) 272273
Holes 18 L 6265 yds Par 72 SSS
70
V'tors WD–U H WE–M before
10.30am UH after 10.30am
SOC
Fees £25.50 (£35.50)
Loc 1½ miles W of Oundle on
A427

Overstone Park (1994)

*Watermark Leisure, Billing Lane,
Northampton, NN6 0AP*

Tel **(01604) 647666**
Fax (01604) 642635
Mem 450
Sec B Willoughby
Pro B Mudge (01604) 643555
Holes 18 L 6602 yds SSS 72
V'tors WD–U SOC
Fees £25 (£32)
Loc 4 miles E of Northampton, off
A45. M1 Junction 15
Mis Driving range
Arch Donald Steel

Priors Hall (1965)

Public
*Stamford Road, Weldon, Corby,
NN17 3JH*

Tel **(01536) 260756**
Fax (01536) 260756
Mem 400
Sec T Arnold
Pro G Bradbrook
Holes 18 L 6631 yds SSS 72
V'tors U SOC–WD
Fees On application
Loc 4 miles E of Corby (A43)
Arch Hawtree

Rushden (1919)

*Kimbolton Road, Chelveston,
Wellingborough, NN9 6AN*

Tel **(01933) 418511**
Mem 350
Sec SP Trayhorn
Holes 10 L 6335 yds Par 71
SSS 70
V'tors WD–U exc Wed pm
WE/BH–M SOC
Fees £18
Loc On B645, 2 miles E of
Higham Ferrers

Staverton Park (1977)

*Staverton Park, Staverton, Daventry,
NN11 6JT*

Tel **(01327) 302000/302118**
Fax (01327) 311428
Sec D Entwhistle (Gen Mgr),
Mrs A Radford (Sec)
Pro R Mudge (01327) 705506
Holes 18 L 6602 yds SSS 72
V'tors U SOC
Fees On application
Loc 1 mile SW of Daventry, off
A425. M1 Junctions 16/18.
M40 Junction 11
Mis Driving range

Stoke Albany (1997)

Ashley Road, Stoke Albany, Market Harborough, LE16 8PL

Tel	**(01858) 535208**
Fax	(01858) 535505
Mem	450
Sec	R Want
Pro	A Clifford
Holes	18 L 6132 yds Par 71 SSS 69
V'tors	U SOC
Fees	£13 (£18)
Loc	Between Market Harborough and Corby (A427)
Arch	Hawtree

Wellingborough (1893)

Harrowden Hall, Great Harrowden, Wellingborough, NN9 5AD

Tel	**(01933) 677234/673022**
Fax	(01933) 679379
Mem	850
Sec	R Tomlin (01933) 677234
Pro	D Clifford (01933) 678752
Holes	18 L 6620 yds SSS 72
V'tors	WD–U H exc Tues WE–M SOC–WD exc Tues
Fees	D–£40
Loc	2 miles N of Wellingborough on A509
Arch	Hawtree

Whittlebury Park G&CC (1992)

Whittlebury, Towcester, NN12 8XW

Tel	**(01327) 858092**
Fax	(01327) 858009
Mem	400
Sec	PJ Tomlin
Holes	36 holes: 5000-7000 yds SSS 66-72
V'tors	U H SOC
Fees	£18 D–£30 (£25 D–£35)
Loc	4 miles S of Towcester on A413
Mis	Driving range
Arch	Cameron Sinclair

Northumberland

Allendale (1906)

High Studdon, Allenheads Road, Allendale, Hexham NE47 9DH

Tel	**(01434) 683926**
Fax	(01434) 683926
Web	www.allendale-golf.org
Mem	145 26(L) 35(J)
Sec	PRF Mason (Hon)
Holes	18 L 4501 yds Par 66 SSS 64
V'tors	U Sun/BH–NA before 2pm SOC
Fees	D–£12 (D–£12) After 5pm–£7
Loc	1½ miles S of Allendale on B6295

Alnmouth (1869)

Foxton Hall, Alnmouth, NE66 3BE

Tel	**(01665) 830231**
Fax	(01665) 830922
Mem	750
Sec	M Tate
Pro	Shop (01665) 830043
Holes	18 L 6484 yds SSS 71
V'tors	Mon/Tues/Thurs–H (restricted) SOC
Fees	£25 D–£30
Loc	5 miles SE of Alnwick
Mis	Dormy House
Arch	HS Colt

Alnmouth Village (1869)

Marine Road, Alnmouth, NE66 2RZ

Tel	**(01665) 830370**
Fax	(01665) 602096
Mem	340
Sec	W Maclean (01665) 602096
Holes	9 L 6020 yds SSS 70
V'tors	H
Fees	£15 (£20)
Loc	Alnmouth

Alnwick (1907)

Swansfield Park, Alnwick, NE66 1AB

Tel	**(01665) 602632**
Mem	450
Sec	LE Stewart (01665) 602499
Holes	18 L 6250 yds SSS 70
V'tors	U
Fees	D–£20 (D–£25)
Loc	Alnwick, off A1
Arch	Rochester/Rae

Arcot Hall (1909)

Dudley, Cramlington, NE23 7QP

Tel	**(0191) 236 2794**
Fax	(0191) 217 0370
Mem	700
Sec	F Elliott (0191) 236 2794
Pro	J Metcalfe (0191) 236 2794
Holes	18 L 6389 yds SSS 70
V'tors	WD–H WE/BH–M SOC
Fees	D–£26 (£30) After 3pm–£21
Loc	7 miles N of Newcastle, off A1
Arch	James Braid

Bamburgh Castle (1904)

The Club House, 40 The Wynding, Bamburgh, NE69 7DE

Tel	**(01668) 214378**
Fax	(01668) 214607
Mem	730
Sec	RA Patterson (01668) 214321
Holes	18 L 5621 yds Par 68 SSS 67
V'tors	WD–U H WE/BH–M SOC
Fees	D–£30 (£30 D–£35)
Loc	5 miles E of A1, via B1341 or B1342
Arch	George Rochester

Bedlingtonshire (1972)

Acorn Bank, Hartford Road, Bedlington, NE22 6AA

Tel	**(01670) 822457**

Mem	750
Sec	FM Hanson
Pro	M Webb (01670) 822087
Holes	18 L 6224 metres SSS 73
V'tors	U
Fees	£16 (£28)
Loc	12 miles N of Newcastle (A1068)
Arch	Frank Pennink

Belford (1993)

South Road, Belford, NE70 7HY

Tel	**(01668) 213433**
Fax	(01668) 213919
Mem	300
Sec	AM Gilhome
Pro	None
Holes	9 L 6304 yds SSS 70
V'tors	U SOC
Fees	On application
Loc	15 miles N of Alnwick, off A1
Mis	Driving range
Arch	Nigel Williams

Bellingham (1893)

Boggle Hole, Bellingham, NE48 2DT

Tel	**(01434) 220530/220152**
Fax	(01434) 220160
Mem	630
Sec	P Cordiner (01434) 220182
Holes	18 L 6093 yds Par 70 SSS 70
V'tors	U SOC
Fees	£20 (£25)
Loc	15 miles N of Hexham, off B6320
Mis	Driving range
Arch	I Wilson

Berwick-upon-Tweed (1890)

Goswick, Berwick-upon-Tweed, TD15 2RW

Tel	**(01289) 387256**
Fax	(01289) 387334
Web	www.goswicklinksgc.co.uk
Mem	550
Sec	D Wilkinson
Pro	P Terras (01289) 387380
Holes	18 L 6449 yds SSS 71
V'tors	WD–U 9.30–11.30am & after 2pm WE–U 10–11.30am & after 2.30pm SOC
Fees	£25 (£30)
Loc	5 miles S of Berwick, off A1
Arch	James Braid

Blyth (1905)

New Delaval, Blyth, NE24 4DB

Tel	**(01670) 540110**
Fax	(01670) 540134
Mem	800
Pro	A Brown (01670) 356514
Holes	18 L 6456 yds SSS 71
V'tors	WD–U WE/BH–M SOC–WD before 3pm
Fees	£19 D–£25
Loc	W end of Plessey Road, Blyth

Burgham Park (1994)

Felton, Morpeth, NE65 8QP

Tel	(01670) 787898
Fax	(01670) 787164
Mem	630
Sec	J Carr
Pro	S McNally (01670) 787978
Holes	18 L 6751 yds SSS 72
V'tors	U SOC
Fees	£18 (£22)
Loc	7 miles N of Morpeth on A1
Mis	Pitch & putt course
Arch	Andrew Mair

Close House (1968)

*Close House, Heddon-on-the-Wall,
Newcastle-upon-Tyne, NE15 0HT*

Tel	(01661) 852953
Mem	900
Sec	ME Pearse
Holes	18 L 5606 yds SSS 67
V'tors	M SOC–WD
Fees	SOC D–£18
Loc	9 miles W of Newcastle on A69
Arch	Hawtree

Dunstanburgh Castle (1900)

Embleton, NE66 3XQ

Tel	(01665) 576562
Mem	396
Sec	PFC Gilbert (Mgr)
Holes	18 L 6298 yds SSS 70
V'tors	U
Fees	£16 (£20)
Loc	7 miles NE of Alnwick on B1339
Arch	James Braid

Hexham (1892)

Spital Park, Hexham, NE46 3RZ

Tel	(01434) 603072
Fax	(01434) 601865
Web	www.hexhamgolfclub.ntb.org.uk
Mem	750
Sec	Dawn Wylie (01434) 603072
Pro	MW Forster (01434) 604904
Holes	18 L 6272 yds SSS 70
V'tors	U
Fees	£30 (£40)
Loc	21 miles W of Newcastle (A69)
Arch	Vardon/Caird

Linden Hall (1997)

Longhorsley, Morpeth, NE65 8XF

Tel	(01670) 500011
Fax	(01670) 500001
Mem	250
Sec	D Curry (Sec/Mgr)
Pro	D Curry (01670) 500011
Holes	18 L 6846 yds Par 72 SSS 73
V'tors	U H SOC
Fees	£25 (£28)
Loc	8 miles NW of Morpeth, off A697
Mis	Driving range
Arch	Jonathan Gaunt

Longhirst Hall (1997)

Longhirst Hall, Longhirst, NE61 3LL

Tel	(01670) 791505 (Clubhouse), (01670) 858519 (Admin)
Fax	(01670) 791768
Web	www.longhirstgolf.co.uk
Mem	2250
Sec	J Boulton (01670) 812442
Pro	G Cant
Holes	18 L 6570 yds Par 72
V'tors	U SOC
Fees	£18 (£18)
Loc	4 miles NE of Morpeth, via A197/B1337
Mis	Driving range. Further 18 holes open 2003
Arch	B Poole

Magdalene Fields (1903)

Pay and play

*Magdalene Fields, Berwick-upon-Tweed,
TD15 1NE*

Tel	(01289) 306384
Web	www.magdalene-fields.co.uk
Mem	330
Sec	MJ Lynch
Holes	18 L 6407 yds SSS 71
V'tors	U SOC
Fees	£17 (£19)
Loc	Berwick-upon-Tweed 1 mile
Arch	Park/Jefferson/Thompson

Matfen Hall Hotel (1994)

Matfen, Hexham, NE20 0RH

Tel	(01661) 886500 (Hotel), (01661) 886400 (Bookings)
Fax	(01661) 886055
Web	www.matfenhall.com
Mem	500
Sec	D Burton
Pro	J Harrison
Holes	18 L 6516 yds Par 72 9 hole Par 3 course
V'tors	WD–U WE–U after 10am
Fees	£30
Loc	12 miles W of Newcastle, off B6318
Mis	Driving range
Arch	Mair/James/Gaunt

Morpeth (1906)

The Clubhouse, Morpeth, NE61 2BT

Tel	(01670) 504942
Fax	(01670) 504918
Mem	700
Sec	KD Cazaly (01670) 504942
Pro	MR Jackson (01670) 515675
Holes	18 L 5671 metres SSS 69
V'tors	H SOC
Fees	£22 (£27)
Loc	1 mile S of Morpeth on A197

Newbiggin (1884)

Newbiggin-by-the-Sea, NE64 6DW

Tel	(01670) 817344 (Clubhouse)
Fax	(01670) 520236
Mem	500
Sec	GW Beattie (01670) 852959
Pro	M Webb (01670) 817833
Holes	18 L 6452 yds SSS 71
V'tors	U after 10am exc comp days–NA SOC
Fees	D–£15 (D–£22)
Loc	Newbiggin, nr Church Point
Arch	Willie Park

Ponteland (1927)

53 Bell Villas, Ponteland, Newcastle-upon-Tyne, NE20 9BD

Tel	(01661) 822689
Fax	(01661) 860077
Mem	480 170(L) 115(J)
Sec	JN Dobson
Pro	A Robson-Crosby
Holes	18 L 6524 yds SSS 71
V'tors	WD–U SOC–Tues & Thurs
Fees	£25
Loc	6 miles NW of Newcastle on A696, nr Airport

Prudhoe (1930)

*Eastwood Park, Prudhoe-on-Tyne,
NE42 5DX*

Tel	(01661) 832466
Mem	450
Sec	GB Garratt
Pro	J Crawford (01661) 836188
Holes	18 L 5839 yds SSS 69
V'tors	WD–U
Fees	£20 (£25)
Loc	15 miles W of Newcastle (A695)

Rothbury (1891)

*Old Race Course, Rothbury, Morpeth,
NE65 7TR*

Tel	(01669) 621271
Mem	312
Sec	WT Bathgate (01669) 620718
Pro	None
Holes	9 L 5681 yds Par 68 SSS 67
V'tors	WD–U exc Tues after 4pm & Wed am WE–by arrangement
Fees	D–£11 (D–£16)
Loc	15 miles N of Morpeth on A697. W side of Rothbury
Arch	JB Radcliffe

Seahouses (1913)

Beadnell Road, Seahouses, NE68 7XT

Tel	(01665) 720794
Fax	(01665) 721994
Mem	600
Sec	JA Stevens
Holes	18 L 5516 yds SSS 67
V'tors	U SOC
Fees	£18 (£25)
Loc	14 miles N of Alnwick. 9 miles E of A1 on B1340

Stocksfield (1913)

New Ridley, Stocksfield, NE43 7RE

Tel	(01661) 843041
Fax	(01661) 843046
Web	www.sgcgolf.co.uk
Mem	426 100(L) 75(J)
Sec	B Slade
Pro	D Mather
Holes	18 L 5998 yds SSS 70
V'tors	U SOC–exc Wed & Sat
Fees	£25 (£30)

Loc 2 miles S of Stocksfield. 3
miles E of A68
Arch F Pennink

Swarland Hall (1993)
*Coast View, Swarland, Morpeth,
NE65 9JG*
Tel   **(01670) 787940
(Clubhouse)**
Sec K Rutter (01670) 787010
Pro Shop (01670) 787010
Holes 18 L 6628 yds SSS 72
V'tors U
Fees £15 (£20)
Loc 8 miles S of Alnwick, 1 mile
W of A1

Tynedale (1908)
Public
Tyne Green, Hexham, NE46 3HQ
Tel   **(01434) 608154**
Sec J McDiarmid
Pro Mrs C Brown
Holes 9 L 5706 yds SSS 68
V'tors U exc Sun–booking necessary
Fees £10 (£12) (1993)
Loc S side of Hexham

De Vere Slaley Hall
(1988)
Slaley, Hexham, NE47 0BY
Tel   **(01434) 673350**
Fax (01434) 673152
Web www.deverehotels.com
Mem 350
Sec M Stancer (Golf Mgr)
Pro M Stancer (01434) 673154
Holes Hunting 18 L 7073 yds Par 72
SSS 71-74;
Priestman 18 L 7010 Par 72
SSS 71-74
V'tors U SOC
Fees Hunting–£60.
Priestman–£40
Loc 20 miles W of Newcastle.
7 miles S of Corbridge, off
A68
Mis Driving range. Golf Academy
Arch Hunting-Dave Thomas.
Priestman-Neil Coles

Warkworth (1891)
*The Links, Warkworth, Morpeth,
NE65 0SW*
Tel   **(01665) 711596**
Mem 400
Sec JA Gray
Holes 9 L 5986 yds SSS 69
V'tors U exc Tues & Sat SOC
Fees D–£12 (D–£20)
Loc 9 miles SE of Alnwick
(A1068)
Arch Old Tom Morris

Wooler (1975)
*Dod Law, Doddington, Wooler,
NE71 6EA*
Tel   **(01668) 282135**
Mem 250
Sec S Lowrey (01668) 281631

Pro None
Holes 9 L 6372 yds SSS 70
V'tors U SOC
Fees D–£10 (D–£15)
Loc 3 miles N of Wooler on
B6525

Nottinghamshire

Beeston Fields (1923)
Beeston, Nottingham, NG9 3DD
Tel   **(0115) 925 7062**
Fax (0115) 925 4280
Web www.beestonfields.co.uk
Mem 510 148(L) 58(J)
Sec J Lewis
Pro A Wardle (0115) 922 0872
Holes 18 L 6404 yds SSS 71
V'tors U H SOC
Fees £26 (£31)
Loc 4 miles W of Nottingham. M1
Junction 25
Arch Tom Williamson

Brierley Forest (1993)
*Main Street, Huthwaite, Sutton-in-
Ashfield, NG17 2LG*
Tel   **(01623) 550761**
Fax (01623) 550761
Mem 130
Sec D Crafts
Pro None
Holes 18 L 6008 yds Par 72 SSS 69
V'tors WD–U bookings only
WE–NA before noon
Fees £11.50
Loc W of Sutton-in-Ashfield. M1
Junction 28, 2 miles

Bulwell Forest (1902)
Public
*Hucknall Road, Bulwell, Nottingham,
NG6 9LQ*
Tel   **(0115) 977 0576**
Fax (0115) 976 3172 (Pro)
Mem 400
Sec D Waddilove (Hon)
(0115) 960 8435
Pro L Rawlings
(0115) 976 3172
Holes 18 L 5746 yds SSS 68
V'tors U
Fees £11 (£11) 4ball–£32
Loc 4 miles N of Nottingham. M1
Junction 26, 3 miles

Chilwell Manor (1906)
*Meadow Lane, Chilwell, Nottingham,
NG9 5AE*
Tel   **(0115) 925 8958**
Fax (0115) 922 0575
Mem 700
Sec RA Westcott
Pro P Wilson (0115) 925 8993
Holes 18 L 6255 yds Par 70 SSS 71
V'tors U SOC
Fees £20 (£20)

Loc 4 miles W of Nottingham on
A6005
Arch Tom Williamson

College Pines (1994)
*Worksop College Drive, Sparken Hill,
Worksop, S80 3AP*
Tel   **(01909) 501431**
Fax (01909) 481227
Mem 550
Sec C Snell (Golf Dir)
Pro C Snell (01909) 501431
Holes 18 L 6716 yds SSS 72
V'tors U–phone first SOC
Fees £12 (£18)
Loc 1 mile SE of Worksop on
B6034, off Worksop Bypass
Mis Driving range
Arch David Snell

Cotgrave Place G&CC
(1991)
Owned privately
Stragglethorpe, NG12 3HB
Tel   **(0115) 933 3344/933 4567**
Mem 400
Sec DJ Mansfield
Pro R Smith
Holes Open 18 L 6303 yds SSS 70
Masters 18 L 5887 yds
SSS 68
V'tors U
Fees £14 (£17)
Loc 4 miles SE of Nottingham, off
A52
Mis Driving range
Arch Small/Glasgow/Alliss

Coxmoor (1913)
*Coxmoor Road, Sutton-in-Ashfield,
NG17 5LF*
Tel   **(01623) 557359**
Fax (01623) 557359
Mem 650
Sec JB Noble
Pro D Ridley (01623) 559906
Holes 18 L 6501 yds SSS 72
V'tors H exc Ladies Day–Tues
WE–NA SOC
Fees £35 D–£45
Loc 1½ miles S of Mansfield. 4
miles NE of M1 Junction 27
on A611

Edwalton (1982)
Public
Edwalton, Nottingham, NG12 4AS
Tel   **(0115) 923 4775**
Mem 700
Sec Mrs DJ Parkes (Hon)
Pro J Staples
Holes 9 L 3336 yds SSS 36
9 hole Par 3 course
V'tors U
Fees On application
Loc 2 miles S of Nottingham
(A606)

Kilton Forest (1978)

Public
Blyth Road, Worksop, S81 0TL
Tel (01909) 486563
Mem 364
Sec A Mansbridge (Hon)
(01909) 486269
Pro S Betteridge (01909) 486563
Holes 18 L 6424 yds Par 72 SSS 71
V'tors WD–U WE–booking necessary SOC
Fees £9.50 (£12)
Loc 1 mile NE of Worksop on B6045

Leen Valley Golf Centre (1994)

Pay and play
Wigwam Lane, Hucknall, NG15 7TA
Tel (0115) 964 2037
Fax (0115) 964 2724
Mem 670
Sec BR Goodman (Gen Mgr)
Pro J Lines (01623) 422764
Holes 18 L 6233 yds Par 72 SSS 70
V'tors U SOC–WD
Fees £10 (£14.50)
Loc ¹/₂ mile from Hucknall town centre
Mis 9 hole Par 3 course open 2001
Arch Tom Hodgetts

Mansfield Woodhouse (1973)

Public
Mansfield Woodhouse, NG19 9EU
Tel (01623) 23521
Sec M Stuart
Pro L Highfield Jr
Holes 9 L 2411 yds SSS 65
V'tors U
Fees £3
Loc 2 miles N of Mansfield (A60)

Mapperley (1907)

Central Avenue, Plains Road, Mapperley, Nottingham NG3 5RH
Tel (0115) 955 6672
Fax (0115) 955 6670
Mem 650
Sec A Newton
Pro J Barker (0115) 955 6673
Holes 18 L 6307 yds SSS 70
V'tors U SOC
Fees £17 D–£20
Loc 3 miles NE of Nottingham, off B684
Arch J Mason

Newark (1901)

Coddington, Newark, NG24 2QX
Tel (01636) 626241
Fax (01636) 626497
Mem 600
Sec P Snow (01636) 626282
Pro PA Lockley (01636) 626492
Holes 18 L 6458 yds SSS 71
V'tors H SOC

Fees £23 (£28)
Loc 4 miles E of Newark on A17

Norwood Park (1999)

Norwood Park, Southwell, NG25 0PF
Tel (01636) 816626
Fax (01636) 815702
Web www.norwoodpark.org.uk
Mem 350
Sec R Beckett
Pro P Thornton (01636) 816626
Holes 9 L 6666 yds Par 72 SSS 71
V'tors U SOC
Fees 9 holes–£7.50 (£10)
18 holes–£14 (£17.50)
Loc ¹/₂ mile W of Southwell, off Kirklington road
Mis Driving range
Arch Clyde Johnston

Nottingham City (1910)

Public
Lawton Drive, Bulwell, Nottingham, NG6 8BL
Tel (0115) 927 8021
Fax (0115) 927 6916
Mem 460
Sec (0115) 927 6916
Pro CR Jepson (0115) 927 2767
Holes 18 L 6218 yds SSS 70
V'tors WD–U WE–NA before noon SOC
Fees £11 (£11)
Loc 5 miles N of Nottingham. M1 Junction 26

Notts (1887)

Hollinwell, Kirkby-in-Ashfield, NG17 7QR
Tel (01623) 753225
Fax (01623) 753655
Mem 500
Sec NI Symington
Pro A Thomas (01623) 753087
Holes 18 L 7098 yds Par 72 SSS 75
V'tors WD–H WE/BH–M
Fees On application
Loc 4 miles S of Mansfield on A611. M1 Junction 27
Mis Driving range–green fees only
Arch Willie Park Jr

Oakmere Park (1974)

Oaks Lane, Oxton, NG25 0RH
Tel (0115) 965 3545
Fax (0115) 965 5628
Web www.ukgolf.net/oakmerepark
Mem 450
Sec D St-John Jones
Pro D St-John Jones (0115) 965 3545
Holes 18 L 6617 yds SSS 72
9 L 3495 yds SSS 37
V'tors WD–U WE/BH–arrange times with Mgr SOC
Fees 18 hole:£18 (£25) 9 hole:£6 (£8)
Loc 8 miles NE of Nottingham on A614
Mis Floodlit driving range
Arch F Pennink

Radcliffe-on-Trent (1909)

Dewberry Lane, Cropwell Road, Radcliffe-on-Trent, NG12 2JH
Tel (0115) 933 3000
Fax (0115) 911 6991
Web www.radcliffeontrentgc.com
Mem 670
Sec L Wake
Pro R Ellis (0115) 933 2396
Holes 18 L 6381 yds Par 70 SSS 71
V'tors H SOC–Wed only
Fees £23 (£28)
Loc 6 miles E of Nottingham, off A52
Arch Tom Williamson

Ramsdale Park Golf Centre (1992)

Pay and play
Oxton Road, Calverton, NG14 6NU
Tel (0115) 965 5600
Fax (0115) 965 4105
Web www.burhillgolf.net
Sec B Jenkinson (Mgr)
Pro R Macey
Holes 18 L 6546 yds SSS 71
18 hole Par 3 course
V'tors U SOC–WD
Fees £15 (£17.50)
Loc 5 miles NE of Nottingham on B6386
Mis Floodlit driving range
Arch Hawtree

Retford (1921)

Brecks Road, Ordsall, Retford, DN22 7UA
Tel (01777) 703733
Fax (01777) 710412
Mem 700
Sec Linda Colclough (01777) 860682
Pro C Morris
Holes 18 L 6370 yds SSS 70
V'tors WD–U WE–after 2pm SOC–WD
Fees £15 D–£20 (£18)
Loc 2 miles SW of Retford, off A638 or A620. M1 Junction 30

Ruddington Grange (1988)

Wilford Road, Ruddington, Nottingham, NG11 6NB
Tel (0115) 984 6141
Fax (0115) 940 5165
Mem 600
Sec AR Dessaur
Pro R Simpson (0115) 921 1951
Holes 18 L 6490 yds SSS 72
V'tors U H BH–U exc comp days SOC
Fees D–£15 (£22.50)
Loc 3 miles S of Nottingham

Rufford Park Golf Centre

Rufford Lane, Rufford, Newark,
NG22 9DG

Tel	(01623) 825253
Fax	(01623) 825254
Mem	450
Sec	Mrs K Whitehead
Pro	J Vaughan, J Thompson
Holes	18 L 6286 yds Par 70 SSS 70
V'tors	U–booking necessary
	SOC–WD/WEpm
Fees	£15 D–£20 (£20)
Loc	Nr Rufford Abbey on A614.
	8 miles S of A1/A614 junction
Mis	Floodlit driving range

Rushcliffe (1909)

Stocking Lane, East Leake,
Loughborough, LE12 5RL

Tel	(01509) 852959
Fax	(01509) 852688
Mem	704
Sec	KW Hodkinson
Pro	C Hall (01509) 852701
Holes	18 L 6090 yds SSS 69
V'tors	SOC–WD
Fees	£25 (£29)
Loc	9 miles S of Nottingham. M1
	Junction 24

Serlby Park (1906)

Serlby, Doncaster, DN10 6BA

Tel	(01777) 818268
Mem	250
Sec	KJ Crook (01302) 742280
Holes	9 L 5370 yds SSS 66
V'tors	M SOC–restricted
Loc	12 miles S of Doncaster,
	between A614 and A638

Sherwood Forest (1895)

Eakring Road, Mansfield, NG18 3EW

Tel	(01623) 626689
Fax	(01623) 420412
Mem	648
Sec	Mrs P Davies
Pro	K Hall (01623) 627403
Holes	18 L 6843 yds SSS 74
V'tors	H SOC–WD
Fees	On application to Sec
Loc	2 miles E of Mansfield (A617)
Arch	HS Colt/James Braid

Southwell (1993)

Southwell Racecourse, Rolleston,
Newark, NG25 0TS

Tel	(01636) 816501
Fax	(01636) 812271
Mem	400
Pro	S Meade (01636) 813706
Holes	18 L 5770 yds Par 70 SSS 68
V'tors	U SOC
Fees	£15
Loc	6 miles W of Newark on
	A617. Course adjacent to
	racetrack
Arch	RA Muddle

Springwater (1991)

Pay and play
Moor Lane, Calverton, Nottingham,
NG14 6FZ

Tel	(0115) 965 2129
Mem	400
Sec	W Turner (0115) 965 2565
Pro	P Drew (0115) 965 2129
Holes	18 L 6244 yds Par 71
V'tors	U SOC
Fees	£15 (£20)
Loc	Off A6097 between Lowdham
	and Oxton
Arch	ADAS/McEvoy

Stanton-on-the-Wolds

(1906)

Golf Road, Stanton-on-the-Wolds,
Nottingham, NG12 5BH

Tel	(0115) 937 2044
Fax	(0115) 937 4885
Mem	500 167(L) 100(J)
Sec	AR Evans (0115) 937 4885
Pro	N Hernon ((0115) 937 2390
Holes	18 L 6421 yds SSS 71
V'tors	WD–U exc comp days WE–M
	SOC
Fees	£23 D–£31 SOC–£25–£30
Loc	9 miles S of Nottingham

Trent Lock Golf Centre (1991)

Lock Lane, Sawley, Long Eaton,
NG10 3DD

Tel	(0115) 946 4398
Fax	(0115) 946 1183
Mem	550
Sec	R Gregory
Pro	M Taylor
Holes	18 L 5730 yds Par 69 SSS 68
	9 L 2908 yds Par 36
V'tors	U SOC
Fees	£12.50 (£15) 9 hole:£5
Loc	S of Long Eaton. M1 Junction
	25
Mis	Driving range
Arch	E McCausland

Wollaton Park (1927)

Wollaton Park, Nottingham, NG8 1BT

Tel	(0115) 978 7574
Fax	(0115) 970 0736
Mem	700
Sec	MT Harvey
Pro	J Lower (0115) 978 4834
Holes	18 L 6445 yds SSS 71
V'tors	U SOC
Fees	On application
Loc	2 miles SW of Nottingham
Arch	T Williamson

Worksop (1911)

Windmill Lane, Worksop, S80 2SQ

Tel	(01909) 472696
Fax	(01909) 477731
Mem	500
Sec	DA Dufall (01909) 477731
Pro	C Weatherhead
	(01909) 477732

Holes	18 L 6660 yds Par 72 SSS 73
V'tors	WD–H (phone first)
	WE/BH–M SOC
Fees	On application
Loc	1 mile SE of Worksop, off
	A6034 via by-pass (A57). M1
	Junction 30, 9 miles

Oxfordshire

Aspect Park (1988)

Remenham Hill, Henley-on-Thames,
RG9 3EH

Tel	(01491) 578306
Fax	(01491) 578306
Mem	600
Sec	T Winsland
Pro	T Notley (01491) 577562
Holes	18 L 6559 yds Par 72
	SSS 71
V'tors	WD–U WE–restricted before
	noon SOC
Fees	£20 (£25)
Loc	1 mile E of Henley. M40
	Junction 4, 8 miles
Mis	Driving range. Pitch & putt
Arch	T Winsland

Badgemore Park (1972)

Proprietary
Henley-on-Thames, RG9 4NR

Tel	(01491) 573667 (Clubhouse)
Fax	(01491) 576899
Web	www.badgemorepark.com
Mem	600
Sec	J Connell (Mgr)
	(01491) 572206
Pro	J Dunn (01491) 574175
Holes	18 L 6129 yds SSS 69
V'tors	WD–U exc Tues am–NA
	WE–U after 11am SOC–WD
Fees	£22 (£33)
Loc	1 mile NW of Henley on
	Rotherfield Greys road
Arch	B Sandow

Banbury Golf Centre (1993)

Aynho Road, Adderbury, Banbury,
OX17 3NT

Tel	(01295) 810419
Fax	(01295) 810056
Web	www.banburygolfcentre.co.uk
Mem	300
Sec	MA Reed (Prop)
Pro	S Kier (01295) 812880
Holes	27 holes :
	L 5766–6706 yds Par 72
	SSS 72
V'tors	U SOC
Fees	£14 (£20)
Loc	6 miles S of Banbury on
	B4100. M40 Junction 10/11
Arch	Reed/Payn

Bicester G&CC (1973)

Chesterton, Bicester, OX26 1TE

Tel	(01869) 241204

Mem	550
Sec	P Fox
Pro	J Goodman (01869) 242023
Holes	18 L 6224 yds SSS 70
V'tors	U SOC–WD
Fees	£16 (£20)
Loc	2 miles SW of Bicester. M40 Junction 9

Brailes (1992)

Sutton Lane, Lower Brailes, Banbury, OX15 5BB

Tel	(01608) 685336
Fax	(01608) 685205
Web	www.brailes-golf-club.co.uk
Mem	520
Sec	RAS Malir
Pro	A Brown (01608) 685633
Holes	18 L 6310 yds Par 71 SSS 70
V'tors	U SOC–WD
Fees	£18 (£28)
Loc	3 miles E of Shipston-on-Stour on B4035. M40 Junction 11, 10 miles
Arch	BA Hull

Burford (1936)

Burford, OX18 4JG

Tel	(01993) 822583
Fax	(01993) 822801
Mem	710
Sec	JP Quiney
Pro	M Ridge (01993) 822344
Holes	18 L 6432 yds SSS 71
V'tors	WD–H SOC
Fees	On application
Loc	19 miles W of Oxford on A40

Carswell CC (1993)

Carswell, Faringdon, SN7 8PU

Tel	(01367) 870422
Fax	(01367) 870592
Mem	300
Sec	G Lisi (Prop)
Pro	G Robbins
Holes	18 L 6133 yds Par 72
V'tors	U SOC–WD
Fees	£16 (£25)
Loc	12 miles W of Oxford on A420
Mis	Floodlit driving range

Cherwell Edge (1980)

Chacombe, Banbury, OX17 2EN

Tel	(01295) 711591
Fax	(01295) 712404
Mem	462
Sec	RA Beare
Pro	J Kingston
Holes	18 L 5947 yds SSS 68
V'tors	U SOC–WD
Fees	£12 (£16)
Loc	3 miles E of Banbury on B4525
Mis	Driving range

Chipping Norton (1890)

Southcombe, Chipping Norton, OX7 5QH

Tel	(01608) 642383

Fax	(01608) 645422
Mem	900
Sec	S Chislett
Pro	N Rowlands (01608) 643356
Holes	18 L 6280 yds SSS 70
V'tors	WD–U WE–M
Fees	£27
Loc	1 mile E of Chipping Norton on A44

Drayton Park (1992)

Pay and play
Steventon Road, Drayton, Abingdon, OX14 2RR

Tel	(01235) 550607/528989
Fax	(01235) 525731
Mem	600
Sec	(01235) 528989
Pro	P Morbey (01235) 550607
Holes	18 L 5535 yds SSS 67 9 hole Par 3 course
V'tors	U SOC
Fees	£12 (£15)
Loc	5 miles S of Oxford on A34. M4 Junction 13
Mis	Floodlit driving range
Arch	Hawtree

Frilford Heath (1908)

Frilford Heath, Abingdon, OX13 5NW

Tel	(01865) 390864
Fax	(01865) 390823
Mem	1200 210(L)
Sec	S Styles
Pro	DC Craik (01865) 390887
Holes	Red 18 L 6884 yds SSS 73 Green 18 L 6006 yds SSS 69 Blue 18 L 6728 yds SSS 72
V'tors	H SOC
Fees	£50 (£75)
Loc	3 miles W of Abingdon on A338
Arch	Blue–Simon Gidman

Hadden Hill (1990)

Wallingford Road, Didcot, OX11 9BJ

Tel	(01235) 510410
Fax	(01235) 510410
Web	www.haddenhillgolf.co.uk
Mem	420 62(L)
Sec	MV Morley
Pro	A Waters
Holes	18 L 6563 yds SSS 71
V'tors	WD–U SOC–WD
Fees	£15 (£20)
Loc	E of Didcot on A4130
Mis	Floodlit driving range
Arch	MV Morley

Henley (1907)

Harpsden, Henley-on-Thames, RG9 4HG

Tel	(01491) 575781
Fax	(01491) 412179
Mem	750
Sec	AM Chaundy (01491) 575742
Pro	M Howell (01491) 575710
Holes	18 L 6329 yds SSS 70
V'tors	WD–H WE–M SOC
Fees	D–£30
Loc	1 mile S of Henley (A4155)
Arch	James Braid

Hinksey Heights (1995)

Pay and play
South Hinksey, Oxford, OX1 5AB

Tel	(01865) 327775
Fax	(01865) 736930
Web	www.oxford-golf.co.uk
Mem	250
Sec	J Lidstone (Gen Mgr)
Pro	D Bolton (01865) 327775
Holes	18 L 7023 yds Par 74 SSS 74 9 hole Par 3 course
V'tors	U SOC
Fees	£15 (£20)
Loc	W of Oxford, off A34 between Oxford and Abingdon
Mis	Practice range
Arch	D Heads

Huntercombe (1901)

Nuffield, Henley-on-Thames, RG9 5SL

Tel	(01491) 641207
Fax	(01491) 642060
Mem	800
Sec	Lt Col TJ Hutchison
Pro	D Reffin (01491) 641241
Holes	18 L 6173 yds SSS 70
V'tors	H–by appointment only SOC–WD
Fees	D–£40
Loc	6 miles W of Henley on A4130
Mis	Foursomes and singles only
Arch	Willie Park Jr

Kirtlington (1995)

Kirtlington, OX5 3JY

Tel	(01869) 351133
Fax	(01869) 331143
Mem	350
Sec	P Smith (Sec/Mgr)
Holes	18 holes Par 70 SSS 69
V'tors	U SOC
Fees	£17 (£22)
Loc	1 mile from Kirtlington on A4095. M40 Junction 9
Mis	Driving range
Arch	G Webster

Lyneham (1992)

Proprietary
Lyneham, Chipping Norton, OX7 6QQ

Tel	(01993) 831841
Fax	(01993) 831775
Web	www.golf@lynehamgc .freeserve.co.uk
Mem	780
Sec	CJT Howkins
Pro	J Fincher
Holes	18 L 6669 yds SSS 72
V'tors	U SOC
Fees	£20 (£24)
Loc	4 miles W of Chipping Norton, off A361
Mis	Driving range
Arch	D Carpenter

North Oxford (1907)

Banbury Road, Oxford, OX2 8EZ

Tel	(01865) 554415
Fax	(01865) 515921

Web	www.nogc.co.uk
Mem	701
Sec	GW Pullin (01865) 554924
Pro	R Harris (01865) 553977
Holes	18 L 5805 yds SSS 67
V'tors	WD–U SOC–WD exc Thurs
Fees	£18 D–£25 After 5pm–£14
Loc	4 miles N of Oxford, off A4260 to Kidlington

The Oxfordshire (1993)

Rycote Lane, Milton Common, Thame, OX9 2PU

Tel	(01844) 278300
Fax	(01844) 278003
Mem	600
Sec	M Obata
Pro	N Pike
Holes	18 L 7187 yds SSS 76
V'tors	I H WE/BH–M
Fees	On application
Loc	1½ miles W of Thame on A329. M40 Junction 7, 1½ miles. M40 Junction 8, 4 miles
Mis	Driving range
Arch	Rees Jones

RAF Benson (1975)

Royal Air Force, Benson, Wallingford, OX10 6AA

Tel	(01491) 837766 Ext 7322
Mem	200
Sec	B Sowerby (01235) 848472
Holes	9 L 4395 yds Par 63 SSS 61
V'tors	M
Fees	£7
Loc	3½ miles NE of Wallingford

Rye Hill

Milcombe, Banbury, OX15 4RU

Tel	(01295) 721818
Fax	(01295) 720089
Pro	T Pennock
Holes	18 L 6919 yds Par 72
V'tors	U–booking necessary
Fees	£15 (£20)
Loc	5 miles SW of Banbury, off A361. M40 Junction 11
Mis	Academy holes

Southfield (1875)

Hill Top Road, Oxford, OX4 1PF

Tel	(01865) 242158
Fax	(01865) 242158
Mem	700
Sec	Sherrol Mathews (Asst)
Pro	A Rees (01865) 244258
Holes	18 L 6230 yds SSS 70
V'tors	WD–U WE/BH–M H SOC
Fees	£25
Loc	2 miles E of Oxford
Arch	HS Colt

The Springs Hotel (1998)

Wallingford Road, North Stoke, Wallingford, OX10 6BE

Tel	(01491) 827310
Fax	(01491) 827312
Web	www.thespringshotel.co.uk
Mem	550

Sec	D Allen (01491) 827300
Pro	L Atkins (01491) 827310
Holes	18 L 6470 yds Par 72 SSS 71
V'tors	By arrangement SOC
Fees	£26 (£33)
Loc	2 miles SW of Wallingford on B4009. M40 Junction 6
Arch	Brian Huggett

Studley Wood (1996)

The Straight Mile, Horton-cum-Studley, Oxford, OX33 1BF

Tel	(01865) 351144
Fax	(01865) 351166
Web	www.studleywoodgolf.co.uk
Mem	770
Sec	B Yates (01865) 351144
Pro	T Williams (01865) 351122
Holes	18 L 6722 yds Par 73 SSS 73
V'tors	U SOC
Fees	£30 (£50)
Loc	4 miles NE of Oxford. M40 Junction 8
Mis	Driving range. Golf academy
Arch	Simon Gidman

Tadmarton Heath (1922)

Wigginton, Banbury, OX15 5HL

Tel	(01608) 737278
Fax	(01608) 730548
Mem	650
Sec	IM Kirkwood
Pro	T Jones (01608) 730047
Holes	18 L 5917 yds SSS 69
V'tors	WD–H by appointment WE–M SOC–WD
Fees	£35 After 2.30pm–£25
Loc	5 miles SW of Banbury, off B4035
Arch	Maj CJ Hutchison

Waterstock (1994)

Pay and play

Thame Road, Waterstock, Oxford, OX33 1HT

Tel	(01844) 338093
Fax	(01844) 338036
Mem	500
Sec	AJ Wyatt
Pro	P Bryant
Holes	18 L 6535 yds Par 73
V'tors	U SOC
Fees	£15.50 (£18.50)
Loc	E of Oxford on A418. M40 Junction 8
Mis	Floodlit driving range
Arch	Donald Steel

Witney Lakes (1994)

Downs Road, Witney, OX8 5SY

Tel	(01993) 893010
Fax	(01993) 778866
Web	www.witney-lakes.co.uk
Mem	450
Sec	M Percival
Pro	A South, A Campbell
Holes	18 L 6460 yds SSS 71
V'tors	U
Fees	£16 (£22)
Loc	2 miles W of Witney on B4047

Mis	Floodlit driving range
Arch	Simon Gidman

Rutland

Greetham Valley (1992)

Greetham, Oakham, LE15 7NP

Tel	(01780) 460004
Fax	(01780) 460623
Mem	1000
Sec	FE Hinch
Pro	J Pengelly (01780) 460666
Holes	18 holes SSS 71
	18 holes SSS 68
	9 hole Par 3 course
V'tors	U SOC–WD
Fees	£28 (£32)
Loc	5 miles NE of Oakham (B668), nr A1
Mis	Floodlit driving range

Luffenham Heath (1911)

Ketton, Stamford, PE9 3UU

Tel	(01780) 720205
Fax	(01780) 722416
Mem	555
Sec	JR Ingleby
Pro	I Burnett (01780) 720298
Holes	18 L 6315 yds SSS 70
V'tors	U H SOC–WD
Fees	£35 D–£45 (£35 D–£45)
Loc	5 miles W of Stamford on A6121
Arch	James Braid

RAF Cottesmore (1982)

Oakham, Leicester, LE15 7BL

Tel	(01572) 812241 Ext 6706
Mem	150
Sec	GA Lawrence
Holes	9 L 5767 yds SSS 67
V'tors	By arrangement
Fees	£8 (£6)
Loc	RAF Cottesmore

RAF North Luffenham (1975)

RAF North Luffenham, Oakham, LE15 8RL

Tel	(01780) 720041 Ext 7523
Mem	350 62(L) 25(J)
Sec	S Nicholson
Holes	9 L 6048 yds Par 70 SSS 69
V'tors	U SOC
Fees	D–£8
Loc	½ mile from S shore of Rutland Water

Rutland County (1991)

Great Casterton, Stamford, PE9 4AQ

Tel	(01780) 460239/460330
Fax	(01780) 460437
Sec	S Lowe (Golf Dir)
Pro	J Darroch
Holes	18 L 6401 yds SSS 71
	9 hole Par 3 course
V'tors	U H SOC

Fees	£25 (£30)
Loc	3 miles N of Stamford on A1
Mis	Driving range
Arch	Cameron Sinclair

Shropshire

Aqualate
Pay and play
Stafford Road, Newport, TF10 9JT

Tel	**(01952) 811699**
Fax	(01952) 825343
Web	www.aqualategolf.f2s.com
Mem	160
Sec	HB Dawes (Mgr)
Pro	K Short (01952) 402991
Holes	18 L 5659 yds Par 69 SSS 67
V'tors	U
Fees	£10 (£15)
Loc	1 mile E of Newport (A518)
Mis	Floodlit driving range

Arscott (1992)
Arscott, Pontesbury, Shrewsbury, SY5 0XP

Tel	**(01743) 860114**
Fax	(01743) 860114
Mem	550
Sec	T Petersen
Pro	I Doran (01743) 860881
Holes	18 L 6112 yds SSS 69
V'tors	WD–U WE/BH–M before 2pm SOC
Fees	£16 (£20)
Loc	5 miles SW of Shrewsbury, off A488
Arch	Martin Hamer

Bridgnorth (1889)
Stanley Lane, Bridgnorth, WV16 4SF

Tel	**(01746) 763315**
Fax	(01746) 761381
Mem	690
Sec	KD Cole
Pro	P Hinton (01746) 762045
Holes	18 L 6638 yds SSS 72
V'tors	H SOC
Fees	£26 (£32)
Loc	1 mile N of Bridgnorth

Chesterton Valley
Chesterton, Worfield, Bridgnorth, WV15 5NX

Tel	**(01746) 783682**
Mem	350
Sec	P Hinton
Pro	P Hinton
Holes	18 L 5860 yds Par 69 SSS 67
V'tors	U–phone first SOC
Fees	£13.60 (£13.60)
Loc	10 miles W of Wolverhampton on B4176

Church Stretton (1898)
Trevor Hill, Church Stretton, SY6 6JH

Tel	**(01694) 722281**

Fax	(01694) 722633
Mem	530
Sec	R Broughton (01694) 722633
Pro	J Townsend (01694) 722281
Holes	18 L 5020 yds SSS 65
V'tors	H WE–NA before 10.30am SOC
Fees	£14 (£20)
Loc	½ mile W of Church Stretton, off A49
Arch	James Braid

Cleobury Mortimer
(1993)
Wyre Common, Cleobury Mortimer, DY14 8HQ

Tel	**(01299) 271112 (Clubhouse)**
Fax	(01299) 271468
Web	www.cleoburygolfclub.com
Mem	704
Sec	G Pain (Gen Mgr)
Pro	J Jones, M Payne
Holes	27 holes: L 6147–6438 yds SSS 69–71
V'tors	WD–U H WE–M H SOC
Fees	£20 (£30)
Loc	10 miles SW of Kidderminster on A4117

Hawkstone Park (1920)
Weston-under-Redcastle, Shrewsbury, SY4 5UY

Tel	**(01939) 200611**
Fax	(01939) 200311
Mem	700
Sec	KL Brazier
Pro	P Wesselingh
Holes	Hawkstone 18 L 6491 yds SSS 72; Windmill 18 L 6764 yds SSS 72 Academy 6 holes Par 3 course
V'tors	U
Fees	£28 D–£42 (£36 D–£50)
Loc	10 miles S of Whitchurch. 14 miles N of Shrewsbury on A49
Mis	Driving range
Arch	Braid/Huggett

Hill Valley G&CC (1975)
Terrick Road, Whitchurch, SY13 4JZ

Tel	**(01948) 663584**
Fax	(01948) 665927
Mem	600
Sec	JS Pickering
Pro	AR Minshall, CT Burgess
Holes	Emerald 18 L 6628 yds Par 73 Sapphire 18 L 4801 yds Par 66
V'tors	U
Fees	Emerald £20 (£25) Sapphire £11 (£15)
Loc	1 mile N of Whitchurch, off A41/A49 Bypass
Mis	6-bay practice range
Arch	Alliss/Thomas

Horsehay Village
Pay and Play
Wellington Road, Horsehay, Telford TF4 3BT

Tel	**(01952) 632070**
Fax	(01952) 632079
Mem	350
Sec	M Morgan
Pro	D Thorp (01952) 632070
Holes	9 L 5906 yds Par 69 SSS 69
V'tors	U
Fees	£11.50 (£13.50)
Loc	Nr M54 Junction 6
Mis	Driving range. Pitch & putt course
Arch	Howard Swan

Lilleshall Hall (1937)
Abbey Road, Lilleshall, Newport, TF10 9AS

Tel	**(01952) 603840/604776**
Fax	(01952) 604776
Mem	600
Sec	BC Stephens (01952) 604776
Pro	S McKane (01952) 604104
Holes	18 L 5813 yds SSS 68
V'tors	WD–U WE–M SOC
Fees	£22
Loc	3 miles S of Newport between Lilleshall and Sheriffhales. M54 Junction 4
Arch	HS Colt

Llanymynech (1933)
Pant, Oswestry, SY10 8LB

Tel	**(01691) 830542**
Mem	760
Sec	DR Thomas (01691) 830983
Pro	A Griffiths (01691) 830879
Holes	18 L 6114 yds Par 70 SSS 69
V'tors	U before 4.30pm –M after 4.30pm SOC–WD
Fees	£20 (£25)
Loc	5 miles S of Oswestry on A483

Ludlow (1889)
Bromfield, Ludlow, SY8 2BT

Tel	**(01584) 856285**
Fax	(01584) 856366
Mem	550
Sec	RJ Heath
Pro	R Price (01584) 856366
Holes	18 L 6277 yds SSS 70
V'tors	H SOC–WD
Fees	D–£18 (D–£24)
Loc	2 miles N of Ludlow (A49)

Market Drayton (1926)
Sutton, Market Drayton, TF9 1LX

Tel	**(01630) 652266**
Mem	550
Sec	DB Palmer
Pro	R Clewes (01630) 656237
Holes	18 L 6290 yds SSS 71
V'tors	WD–U WE–NA
Fees	£24
Loc	1 mile S of Market Drayton

Meole Brace (1976)
Public
Meole Brace, Shrewsbury SY2 6QQ
Tel   (01743) 364050
Fax   (01743) 364050
Pro   N Bramall
Holes 9 L 2915 yds SSS 68
V'tors WD–U WE–book in advance
Fees   On application
Loc   1 mile S of Shrewsbury, off
       A49

Mile End (1992)
Proprietary
Mile End, Oswestry, SY11 4JE
Tel   (01691) 671246
Fax   (01691) 670580
Web   www.mileendgolfclub.co.uk
Sec   R Thompson
Pro   S Carpenter (01691) 671246
Holes 18 L 6194 yds SSS 69
V'tors U SOC
Fees   £15 D–£22 (£20 D–£28)
Loc   1 mile SE of Oswestry, off A5
Mis   Driving range
Arch   Price/Gough

Oswestry (1903)
Aston Park, Oswestry, SY11 4JJ
Tel   (01691) 610221
Fax   (01691) 610535
Mem   880
Sec   A Jennings (01691) 610535
Pro   D Skelton (01691) 610448
Holes 18 L 6038 yds SSS 69
V'tors M or H SOC–WD
Fees   £23 (£31)
Loc   3 miles SE of Oswestry on A5
Arch   James Braid

Patshull Park Hotel G&CC (1980)
Pattingham, WV6 7HR, WV6 7HR
Tel   (01902) 700100
Fax   (01902) 700874
Web   www.patshull-park.co.uk
Mem   395
Sec   M Ellam
Pro   R Bissell (01902) 700342
Holes 18 L 6412 yds SSS 71
V'tors U H SOC
Fees   £30 (£40)
Loc   7 miles W of Wolverhampton,
       off A41. M54 Junction 3,
       5 miles
Arch   John Jacobs

Severn Meadows (1990)
Pay and play
Highley, Bridgnorth, WV16 6HZ
Tel   (01746) 862212
Mem   190
Sec   C Harrison
Pro   None
Holes 18 L 6357 yds Par 72 SSS 70
V'tors U WE–booking required
Fees   £12 (£14)
Loc   8 miles S of Bridgnorth on
       B4555

Shifnal (1929)
Decker Hill, Shifnal, TF11 8QL
Tel   (01952) 460467/460330
Fax   (01952) 461127
Web   www.shifnalgolfclub.co.uk
Mem   500
Sec   M Vanner (01952) 460330
Pro   J Flanaghan (01952) 460457
Holes 18 L 6422 yds SSS 71
V'tors WD–phone first WE/BH–M
Fees   On application
Loc   1 mile NE of Shifnal. M54
       Junction 4, 2 miles
Arch   Pennink

Shrewsbury (1891)
Condover, Shrewsbury, SY5 7BL
Tel   (01743) 872976
Fax   (01743) 874647
Web   www.shrewsbury-golf-
       club.co.uk
Mem   525 184(L) 70(J)
Sec   Mrs SM Kenny
       (01743) 872977
Pro   P Seal (01743) 874581
Holes 18 L 6178 yds Par 70 SSS 69
V'tors H SOC
Fees   £19 (£24)
Loc   4 miles S of Shrewsbury

The Shropshire (1992)
Pay and play
Muxton, Telford, TF2 8PQ
Tel   (01952) 677866
Fax   (01952) 677622
Web   www.theshropshire.co.uk
Mem   500
Sec   Gill White
Pro   S Marr
Holes 27 holes:
       L 6589-6637 yds SSS 70-72
V'tors U SOC
Fees   £17 (£24)
Loc   4 miles NW of Telford
       (B5060). M54 Junction 4
Mis   Floodlit driving range. Pitch &
       putt course
Arch   Martin Hawtree

Telford (1976)
*Great Hay, Sutton Heights, Telford,
TF7 4DT*
Tel   (01952) 429977
Fax   (01952) 586602
Web   www.telford-golfclub.co.uk
Mem   400
Sec   I Lucas (01952) 422960
Pro   D Bateman (01952) 586052
Holes 18 L 6761 yds SSS 72
V'tors H SOC
Fees   On application
Loc   4 miles SE of Telford, off
       A442
Mis   Driving range
Arch   John Harris

Worfield (1991)
Worfield, Bridgnorth, WV15 5HE
Tel   (01746) 716541
Fax   (01746) 716302

Mem   500
Sec   W Weaver (Gen Mgr)
       (01746) 716372
Pro   S Russell (01746) 716541
Holes 18 L 6660 yds SSS 72
V'tors U SOC
Fees   £20 (£25)
Loc   7 miles W of Wolverhampton
       on A454
Arch   Gough/Williams

Wrekin (1905)
Wellington, Telford, TF6 5BX
Tel   (01952) 244032
Fax   (01952) 252906
Mem   400 100(L) 90(J)
Sec   D Briscoe
Pro   K Housden (01952) 223101
Holes 18 L 5657 yds SSS 67
V'tors WD–U before 5pm –M after
       5pm SOC
Fees   £22 (£31)
Loc   Wellington, off B5061

Somerset

Bath (1880)
*Sham Castle, North Road, Bath,
BA2 6JG*
Tel   (01225) 425182
Fax   (01225) 331027
Web   www.bathgolfclub.org.uk
Mem   730
Sec   PE Ware (01225) 463834
Pro   P Hancox (01225) 466953
Holes 18 L 6442 yds SSS 71
V'tors H SOC
Fees   £27 (£32)
Loc   1½ miles SE of Bath, off
       A36
Arch   HS Colt

Brean (1973)
*Coast Road, Brean, Burnham-on-Sea,
TA8 2QY*
Tel   (01278) 752111
Fax   (01278) 752111
Mem   400
Sec   I Ross (Hon)
Pro   D Haines (01278) 752111
Holes 18 L 5565 yds SSS 67
V'tors WD–U WE–pm only
       SOC–WD
Fees   £15 (£20)
Loc   4 miles N of Burnham-on-Sea.
       M5 Junction 22, 6 miles

Burnham & Berrow (1890)
*St Christopher's Way, Burnham-on-
Sea, TA8 2PE*
Tel   (01278) 783137
Fax   (01278) 795440
Mem   800
Sec   Mrs EL Sloman
       (01278) 785760
Pro   M Crowther-Smith
       (01278) 784545

Holes 18 L 6606 yds SSS 73
9 L 6332 yds SSS 72
V'tors I SOC
Fees 18 hole:£40 (£60) 9 hole:£12
Loc 1 mile N of Burnham-on-Sea on B3140
Mis Dormy House

Cannington (1993)

Pay and play
Cannington College, Bridgwater, TA5 2LS
Tel (01278) 655050
Fax (01278) 652479
Mem 200
Sec R Macrow (Mgr)
Pro R Macrow
Holes 9 L 6072 yds Par 68 SSS 70
V'tors U exc Wed eve–restricted
Fees 18 holes–£13 (£16.50)
9 holes–£9 (£11)
Loc 4 miles NW of Bridgwater on A39. M5 Junction 24
Mis Driving range
Arch Hawtree

Clevedon

Castle Road, Clevedon, BS21 7AA
Tel (01275) 874057
Fax (01275) 341228
Mem 800
Sec J Cunning (01275) 874057
Pro R Scanlan (01275) 874704
Holes 18 L 6557 yds Par 72 SSS 72
V'tors WD–U H exc Wed am
WE/BH–U H (phone first)
SOC–WD
Fees £25 (£40)
Loc Off Holly Lane, Walton, Clevedon. M5 Junction 20
Arch JH Taylor

Enmore Park (1906)

Enmore, Bridgwater, TA5 2AN
Tel (01278) 671244 (Members)
Fax (01278) 671740
Web www.golfdirector.com/enmore
Mem 780
Sec D Weston (01278) 671481
Pro N Wixon (01278) 671519
Holes 18 L 6411 yds SSS 71
V'tors U SOC–WD
Fees £20 (£30)
Loc 3 miles W of Bridgwater, off Durleigh road. M5 Junction 23/24
Arch Hawtree

Entry Hill (1985)

Public
Entry Hill, Bath, BA2 5NA
Tel (01225) 834248
Sec J Sercombe
Pro T Tapley
Holes 9 L 4206 yds SSS 61
V'tors WD/WE–booking only
Fees 18 holes–£7.85 (£8.95)
9 holes–£4.95 (£5.60)
Loc 1 mile S of Bath, off A367

Farrington (1992)

Marsh Lane, Farrington Gurney, Bristol, BS39 6TS
Tel (01761) 453440 (Clubhouse)
Fax (01761) 241274
Mem 750
Sec Mrs PM Thompson
Pro P Thompson
(01761) 241787
Holes 18 L 6693 yds Par 72 SSS 72
9 L 3022 yds Par 54 SSS 53
V'tors U SOC–WD
Fees 18 hole: £20 (£30) 9 hole: £7
(£9)
Loc 12 miles S of Bristol (A37)
10 miles S of Bath (A39)
Mis Floodlit driving range
Arch Peter Thompson

Fosseway CC (1970)

Charlton Lane, Midsomer Norton, Radstock, BA3 4BD
Tel (01761) 412214
Fax (01761) 418357
Mem 270
Sec PJ Jordan (Mgr)
Holes 9 L 4565 yds SSS 63
V'tors WD–U exc Wed–M after 5pm
WE–NA before 1.30pm
Fees £15
Loc 10 miles SW of Bath on A367

Frome (1994)

Pay and play
Critchill Manor, Frome, BA11 4LJ
Tel (01373) 453410
Fax (01373) 453410
Web www.fromegolfclub.fsnet
.co.uk
Mem 330
Sec Mrs S Austin
Pro M McEwan
Holes 18 hole course Par 69 SSS 67
V'tors U
Fees £13 D–£18 (£15 D–£19)
Loc 12 miles S of Bath
Mis Driving range

Isle of Wedmore (1992)

Lineage, Lascots Hill, Wedmore, BS28 4QT
Tel (01934) 712452
Fax (01934) 713696
Mem 600
Sec AC Edwards
(01934) 713649
Pro G Coombe
(01934) 712452
Holes 18 L 6006 yds Par 70 SSS 69
V'tors U SOC–WD
Fees £18 (£22)
Loc ¾ mile N of Wedmore. M5 Junction 22
Arch Terry Murray

Kingweston (1983)

(Sec) Mead Run, Compton Street, Compton Dundon, Somerton TA11 6PP
Tel (01458) 43921
Mem 200

Sec JG Willetts
Holes 9 L 4516 yds SSS 62
V'tors M exc Wed & Sat 2–5pm–NA
Fees NA
Loc 1 mile SE of Butleigh. 2 miles SE of Glastonbury

Lansdown (1894)

Lansdown, Bath, BA1 9BT
Tel (01225) 422138
Fax (01225) 339252
Mem 750
Sec Mrs E Bacon
Pro T Mercer (01225) 420242
Holes 18 L 6316 yds SSS 70
V'tors H SOC
Fees £22
Loc 2 miles NW of Bath, by racecourse. M4 Junction 18, 6 miles
Arch HS Colt

Long Sutton (1991)

Pay and play
Long Load, Langport, TA10 9JU
Tel (01458) 241017
Fax (01458) 241022
Mem 600
Sec GC Bennett
Pro A Hayes
Holes 18 L 6367 yds SSS 71
V'tors WD–U WE–booking required
SOC
Fees £16 (£20)
Loc 3 miles E of Langport
Mis Floodlit driving range
Arch Patrick Dawson

The Mendip (1908)

Gurney Slade, Bath, BA3 4UT
Tel (01749) 840570
Fax (01749) 841439
Web www.mendipgolfclub.co.uk
Mem 800
Sec J Scott
Pro A Marsh (01749) 840793
Holes 18 L 6383 yds SSS 71
V'tors WD–U WE–H SOC–WD
Fees £21 (£31)
Loc 3 miles N of Shepton Mallet (A37)
Arch CK Cotton

Mendip Spring (1992)

Honeyhall Lane, Congresbury, BS49 5JT
Tel (01934) 853337/852322
Fax (01934) 853021
Mem 400
Sec I Harrison (Mgr)
Pro J Blackburn, R Moss
Holes 18 L 6334 yds SSS 70
9 L 4784 yds SSS 66
V'tors U
Fees 18 hole:£23 (£30) 9 hole:£8 (£8.50)
Loc Congresbury. M5 Junction 21.
Mis Driving range
Arch Langholt

Minehead & West Somerset (1882)

The Warren, Minehead, TA24 5SJ
Tel (01643) 702057
Fax (01643) 705095
Mem 604
Sec RAJ Rayner
Pro I Read (01643) 704378
Holes 18 L 6228 yds SSS 70
V'tors U after 9.30am SOC
Fees £24.50 (£27.50) W–£88
Loc E end of sea front

Oake Manor (1993)

Oake, Taunton, TA4 1BA
Tel (01823) 461993
Fax (01823) 461995
Web www.oakemanor.com
Mem 600
Sec R Gardner (Golf Mgr)
Pro R Gardner
Holes 18 L 6109 yds Par 70 SSS 69
V'tors U–phone first SOC
Fees £19 (£25)
Loc 4 miles W of Taunton, off B3227. M5 Junctions 25/26 onto A38
Mis Driving range. Academy course
Arch Adrian Stiff

Orchardleigh (1996)

Frome, BA11 2PH
Tel (01373) 454200/454206 (Bookings)
Fax (01373) 454202
Mem 500
Sec T Atkinson (Mgr)
Pro I Ridsdale
Holes 18 L 6810 yds Par 72 SSS 73
V'tors WD/BH–U WE–U after 11am SOC
Fees £22 D–£35 (£30)
Loc 2 miles NW of Frome on A362. 12 miles S of Bath
Mis Practice range
Arch Brian Huggett

Puxton Park (1992)

Pay and play
Puxton, Weston-super-Mare, BS24 6TA
Tel (01934) 876942
Pro C Ancsell
Holes 18 L 6600 yds Par 72
V'tors U SOC
Fees £8 (£10)
Loc A370, 2 miles E of M5 Junction 21

Saltford (1904)

Golf Club Lane, Saltford, Bristol, BS18 3AA
Tel (01225) 873220
Fax (01225) 873525
Mem 650
Sec V Radnedge (01225) 873513
Pro D Millensted (01225) 872043
Holes 18 L 6225 yds SSS 70
V'tors WD–U SOC–Mon & Thurs
Fees £24
Loc 7 miles SE of Bristol

Stockwood Vale (1991)

Public
Stockwood Lane, Keynsham, Bristol, BS31 2ER
Tel (0117) 986 6505
Fax (0117) 986 8974
Web www.stockwoodvale.com
Mem 500
Sec M Edenborough
Pro J Richards
Holes 18 L 6031 yds SSS 71
V'tors U SOC–WD
Fees £15 (£17)
Loc 1 mile SE of Bristol, off A4174
Mis Driving range
Arch Ramsay

Tall Pines (1991)

Cooks Bridle Path, Downside, Backwell, Bristol BS48 3DJ
Tel (01275) 472076
Fax (01275) 474869
Mem 500
Sec T Murray
Pro A Murray
Holes 18 L 6100yds Par 70 SSS 69
V'tors U SOC
Fees £18 (£18)
Loc 8 miles SW of Bristol (A470/A38)
Arch Terry Murray

Taunton & Pickeridge (1892)

Corfe, Taunton, TA3 7BY
Tel (01823) 421240
Fax (01823) 421742
Mem 660
Sec MPD Walls (01823) 421537
Pro G Milne (01823) 421790
Holes 18 L 5927 yds SSS 68
V'tors H SOC
Fees £22 (£30)
Loc 5 miles S of Taunton on B3170
Arch Hawtree

Taunton Vale (1991)

Creech Heathfield, Taunton, TA3 5EY
Tel (01823) 412220
Fax (01823) 413583
Mem 700
Pro M Keitch (01823) 412880
Holes 18 L 6167 yds Par 70 SSS 69
9 L 2004 yds Par 64 SSS 60
V'tors U SOC
Fees 18 hole: £19 (£23)
9 hole: £9 (£11)
Loc 3 miles N of Taunton, off A361. M5 Junctions 24/25
Mis Floodlit driving range
Arch John Pyne

Tickenham (1991)

Clevedon Road, Tickenham, Bristol, BS21 6RY
Tel (01275) 856626
Web www.tickenhamgolf.co.uk
Mem 1250

Pro A Sutcliffe
Holes 9 L 2000 yds
V'tors U–phone first SOC
Fees 18 holes–£10 (£12)
Loc 2 miles E of M5 Junction 20 on B3130, nr Nailsea
Mis Floodlit driving range
Arch Andrew Sutcliffe

Vivary (1928)

Public
Vivary Park, Taunton, TA1 3JW
Tel (01823) 289274 (Clubhouse)
Mem 500
Sec A Stone
Pro M Steadman (01823) 333875
Holes 18 L 4620 yds SSS 63
V'tors U SOC–WD
Fees £8.40
Loc Centre of Taunton
Arch Herbert Fowler

Wells (1893)

East Horrington Road, Wells, BA5 3DS
Tel (01749) 675005
Fax (01749) 675005
Mem 750
Pro A Bishop (01749) 679059
Holes 18 L 6015 yds SSS 69
V'tors WD–U WE–H SOC–WD
Fees £20 (£25)
Loc 1½ miles E of Wells, off Bath road (B3139)
Mis Floodlit driving range

Weston-super-Mare (1892)

Uphill Road North, Weston-super-Mare, BS23 4NQ
Tel (01934) 626968
Fax (01934) 621360
Mem 752
Sec Mrs K Drake (01934) 626968
Pro M La Band (01934) 633360
Holes 18 L 6251 yds SSS 70
V'tors H SOC
Fees £24 (£35) W–£75
Loc Weston-super-Mare
Arch T Dunn

Wheathill (1993)

Wheathill, Somerton, TA11 7HG
Tel (01963) 240667
Fax (01963) 240230
Mem 400
Sec A Lyddon (Sec/Mgr)
Pro A England
Holes 18 L 5362 yds SSS 66
4 holes Par 3 course
V'tors U SOC
Fees £15 (£20)
Loc 3 miles W of Castle Cary on B3153

Windwhistle (1932)

Cricket St Thomas, Chard TA20 4DG
Tel (01460) 30231
Fax (01460) 30055
Web www.windwhistlegolf.co.uk

Mem 550
Sec IN Dodd
Pro D Driver
Holes 18 L 6470 yds SSS 71
V'tors U–phone first SOC
Fees On application
Loc Windwhistle, 3 miles E of Chard on A30. M5 Junction 25, 12 miles
Mis Driving range
Arch JH Taylor/L Fisher

Worlebury (1908)

Monks Hill, Worlebury, Weston-super-Mare, BS22 9SX
Tel (01934) 625789
Fax (01934) 621935
Mem 640
Sec MW Wake
Pro G Marks (01934) 418473
Holes 18 L 5963 yds SSS 69
V'tors H SOC–WD
Fees £20 (£30)
Loc 2 miles NE of Weston, off A370
Arch H Vardon

Yeovil (1919)

Sherborne Road, Yeovil, BA21 5BW
Tel (01935) 475949 (Clubhouse)
Fax (01935) 411283
Mem 721 131(L) 81(J)
Sec GR Dodd (01935) 422965
Pro G Kite (01935) 473763
Holes 18 L 6144 yds SSS 70
9 L 4876 yds SSS 65
V'tors WD–U H WE/BH–H (WD/WE–phone Pro) SOC
Fees 18 hole:£25 (£30) 9 hole:£15 (£18)
Loc 1 mile from Yeovil on A30 to Sherborne
Arch Fowler/Alison

Staffordshire

Alsager G&CC (1992)

Audley Road, Alsager, Stoke-on-Trent, ST7 2UR
Tel (01270) 875700
Fax (01270) 882207
Web www.alsagergolfclub.com
Mem 660
Sec M Davenport
Pro R Brown
Holes 18 L 6225 yds SSS 70
V'tors WD–U before 5pm –M after 5pm SOC
Fees £25
Loc 5 miles W of Crewe. M6 Junction 16

Aston Wood (1994)

Blake Street, Sutton Coldfield, B74 4EU
Tel (0121) 580 7803
Fax (0121) 353 0354
Web www.astonwoodgolfclub.co.uk

Mem 850
Sec K Heathcote (0121) 580 7807
Pro S Smith (0121) 580 7801
Holes 18 holes Par 71 SSS 71
V'tors WD–M before 5pm WE–M SOC
Fees £22 (£33)
Loc 3 miles NE of Sutton Coldfield on A4026. M6 Junction 7. M42 Junction 9
Mis Driving range
Arch Alliss/Clarke

Barlaston (1987)

Meaford Road, Stone, ST15 8UX
Tel (01782) 372867
Fax (01782) 372867
Mem 650
Pro I Rogers (01782) 372795
Holes 18 L 5800 yds SSS 68
V'tors WD–U WE–NA before 10am
Fees On application
Loc ½ mile S of Barlaston. M6 Junction 14/15

Beau Desert (1921)

Hazel Slade, Cannock, WS12 5PJ
Tel (01543) 422626/422773
Fax (01543) 451137
Mem 500
Sec JN Bradbury (01543) 422626
Pro B Stevens (01543) 422492
Holes 18 L 6310 yds SSS 71
V'tors WD–U WE–phone in advance BH–NA SOC
Fees £38 (£48)
Loc 4 miles NE of Cannock, off A460
Mis Driving range
Arch WH Fowler

Bloxwich (1924)

Stafford Road, Bloxwich, WS3 3PQ
Tel (01922) 405724
Fax (01922) 493449
Mem 700
Sec DA Frost (01922) 476593
Pro RJ Dance (01922) 476889
Holes 18 L 6273 yds SSS 71
V'tors WD–U WE–M SOC
Fees £25 (£30)
Loc N of Walsall on A34

Branston G&CC (1975)

Burton Road, Branston, Burton-on-Trent, DE14 3DP
Tel (01283) 512211
Fax (01283) 566984
Mem 800
Sec G Pyle (Golf Mgr)
Pro J Sture
Holes 18 L 6697 yds Par 72 SSS 72
V'tors WD–U WE–M before noon SOC
Fees £28 (£38)
Loc ½ mile S of Burton (A38)
Mis Driving range
Arch G Hamshall

Brocton Hall (1894)

Brocton, Stafford, ST17 0TH
Tel (01785) 662627
Fax (01785) 661591
Mem 500
Sec G Ashley (01785) 661901
Pro R Johnson (01785) 661485
Holes 18 L 6095 yds SSS 69
V'tors I H SOC
Fees £33 (£40)
Loc 4 miles SE of Stafford, off A34
Arch Harry Vardon

Burslem (1907)

Wood Farm, High Lane, Stoke-on-Trent, ST6 7JT
Tel (01782) 837006
Mem 300
Sec Mrs J Mountford (01782) 258028
Holes 9 L 5274 yds SSS 66
V'tors WD–U WE–NA
Fees £16
Loc Burslem 2 miles

Calderfields (1983)

Aldridge Road, Walsall, WS4 2JS
Tel (01922) 646888 (Clubhouse)
(01922) 632243 (Bookings)
Fax (01922) 638787
Web www.calderfieldsgolf.com
Mem 550
Sec Mrs K Williams
Pro I Roberts (01922) 613725
Holes 18 L 6636 yds SSS 72
V'tors U SOC
Fees £18
Loc 1 mile N of Walsall (A454). M6 Junction 10
Mis Floodlit driving range

Cannock Park (1993)

Public
Stafford Road, Cannock, WS11 2AL
Tel (01543) 578850
Fax (01543) 578850
Mem 230
Sec CB Milne (01543) 571091
Pro D Dunk
Holes 18 L 5149 yds SSS 65
V'tors U SOC–WD
Fees £9 (£10.50)
Loc ½ mile N of Cannock on A34. M6 Junction 11, 2 miles
Arch John Mainland

The Chase (1999)

Pottall Pool Road, Penkridge, ST19 5RN
Tel (01785) 712191
Fax (01785) 712692
Mem 550
Sec M Clarke (01785) 712888
Pro A Preston (01785) 712191
Holes 18 L 6354 yds Par 72 SSS 72
V'tors U H
Fees £14 (£19.50)
Loc 10 miles S of Stafford, off A449. M6 Junctions 12 & 13
Mis Driving range

For list of abbreviations see page 649

The Craythorne (1972)

Craythorne Road, Stretton, Burton-on-Trent, DE13 0AZ

Tel	(01283) 564329
Fax	(01283) 511908
Web	www.craythorne.co.uk
Mem	450
Sec	AA Wright (Man Dir)
Pro	S Hadfield (01283) 533745
Holes	18 L 5650 yds Par 68 SSS 67 Pitch & putt course
V'tors	WD–U SOC
Fees	£22 (£28)
Loc	Stretton, 1½ miles N of Burton. A38/A5121 Junction
Mis	Floodlit driving range

Dartmouth (1910)

Vale Street, West Bromwich, B71 4DW

Tel	(0121) 588 2131
Mem	350
Sec	Mrs M Allen
Pro	G Dean
Holes	9 L 6036 yds SSS 71
V'tors	WD–U WE–M SOC–Tues & Thurs
Fees	D–£20
Loc	1 mile from W Bromwich, behind Churchfields High School. Junction M5/M6

Denstone College

Denstone, Uttoxeter, ST14 5HN

Tel	(01889) 590484
Sec	S Dean (Sec), M Raisbeck (Mgr)
Pro	None
Holes	9 L 4404 yds Par 64 SSS 62
V'tors	M SOC
Fees	£5
Loc	Grounds of Denstone College. 6 miles N of Uttoxeter
Arch	MP Raisbeck

Drayton Park (1897)

Drayton Park, Tamworth, B78 3TN

Tel	(01827) 251139
Fax	(01827) 284035
Mem	650
Sec	DO Winter
Pro	MW Passmore (01827) 251478
Holes	18 L 6401 yds SSS 71
V'tors	WD–H WE/BH–NA SOC–Tues & Thurs
Fees	R/D–£33
Loc	2 miles S of Tamworth (A4091)
Arch	James Braid

Druids Heath (1974)

Stonnall Road, Aldridge, WS9 8JZ

Tel	(01922) 55595
Mem	577 75(L) 45(J)
Sec	PJ Bradford
Pro	S Elliott (01922) 59523
Holes	18 L 6659 yds Par 72 SSS 73
V'tors	WD–U WE–M
Fees	£25 (£32)
Loc	6 miles NW of Sutton Coldfield, off A452

Enville (1935)

Highgate Common, Enville, Stourbridge, DY7 5BN

Tel	(01384) 872074
Fax	(01384) 873396
Mem	900
Sec	RJ Bannister (Sec/Mgr) (01384) 872074
Pro	S Power (01384) 872585
Holes	Highgate 18 L 6531 yds SSS 72; Lodge 18 L 6290 yds SSS 70
V'tors	WD–U WE/BH–M H SOC
Fees	£30–£40
Loc	6 miles W of Stourbridge

Goldenhill (1983)

Public

Mobberley Road, Goldenhill, Stoke-on-Trent, ST6 5SS

Tel	(01782) 784715
Fax	(01782) 775940
Mem	600
Sec	P Jones
Pro	A Clingan
Holes	18 L 5957 yds SSS 68
V'tors	U SOC–book with Pro
Fees	£6 (£7)
Loc	Between Tunstall and Kidsgrove, off A50

Great Barr (1961)

Chapel Lane, Birmingham, B43 7BA

Tel	(0121) 357 1232
Mem	600
Sec	Mrs HK Devey (0121) 358 4376
Pro	R Spragg (0121) 357 5270
Holes	18 L 6459 yds SSS 72
V'tors	WD–U WE–I (h'cap max 18) SOC
Fees	£30
Loc	6 miles NW of Birmingham. M6 Junction 7

Greenway Hall (1908)

Stockton Brook, Stoke-on-Trent, ST9 9LJ

Tel	(01782) 503158
Mem	550
Sec	A Pedley
Holes	18 L 5676 yds SSS 67
V'tors	WD–U SOC
Fees	£14
Loc	5 miles N of Stoke, off A53

Handsworth (1895)

11 Sunningdale Close, Handsworth Wood, Birmingham, B20 1NP

Tel	(0121) 554 3387
Fax	(0121) 554 6144
Mem	850
Sec	T Degge (Hon)
Pro	L Bashford (0121) 523 3594
Holes	18 L 6267 yds SSS 70
V'tors	WD–U WE/BH–M SOC
Fees	£35
Loc	3 miles NW of Birmingham. M5 Junction 1. M6 Junction 7

Himley Hall (1980)

Public

Himley Hall Park, Dudley, DY3 4DF

Tel	(01902) 895207
Mem	300
Sec	M Harris
Pro	J Nicholls
Holes	9 L 3145 yds SSS 36 9 hole short course
V'tors	WD–U WE/BH–restricted
Fees	18 holes–£9.50. 9 holes–£6.50
Loc	Grounds of Himley Hall Park. B4176, off A449
Arch	A & K Baker

Ingestre Park (1977)

Ingestre, Stafford, ST18 0RE

Tel	(01889) 270061
Fax	(01889) 270845
Mem	740
Sec	CJ Radmore (Mgr) (01889) 270845
Pro	D Scullion (01889) 270304
Holes	18 L 6268 yds SSS 70
V'tors	WD–H before 3.30pm WE/BH–M SOC–WD exc Wed
Fees	£25 D–£30
Loc	6 miles E of Stafford, off Tixall Road. M6 Junctions 13/14
Arch	Hawtree

Izaak Walton

Cold Norton, Stone, ST15 0NS

Tel	(01785) 760900
Mem	425
Sec	TT Tyler
Pro	J Brown
Holes	18 L 6281 yds SSS 72
V'tors	U SOC
Fees	£15 (£20)
Loc	7 miles NW of Stafford on B2056. M6 Junction 14
Mis	Driving range

Keele Golf Centre (1973)

Public

Keele Road, Newcastle-under-Lyme, ST5 5AB

Tel	(01782) 717417
Fax	(01782) 712972
Sec	GA Bytheway
Pro	C Smith
Holes	18 L 5822 metres SSS 70
V'tors	U
Fees	£6.50 (£8.40)
Loc	2 miles W of Newcastle on A525, opposite University. M6 Junction 15
Mis	Floodlit driving range
Arch	Hawtree

Lakeside (1969)

Rugeley Power Station, Rugeley, WS15 1PR

Tel	(01889) 575667
Mem	550

Sec   TA Yates
Holes 18 L 5765 yds Par 71 SSS 69
V'tors M
Loc   2 miles SE of Rugeley on
       A513

Leek (1892)
Big Birchall, Leek, ST13 5RE
Tel   (01538) 385889
Fax   (01538) 384535
Mem   500 130(L) 60(J)
Sec   JB Cooper (01538) 384779
Pro   I Benson (01538) 384767
Holes 18 L 6218 yds SSS 70
V'tors U H before 3pm –M after
       3pm SOC–Wed only
Fees   £24 (£30)
Loc   ½ mile S of Leek on A520

Little Aston (1908)
Streetly, Sutton Coldfield, B74 3AN
Tel   (0121) 353 2066
Fax   (0121) 580 8387
Web   www.littleastongolf.co.uk
Mem   250
Sec   AE Dibble (Mgr)
       (0121) 353 2942
Pro   J Anderson (0121) 353 0330
Holes 18 L 6670 yds SSS 73
V'tors H WE–by prior arrangement
       SOC–WD
Fees   £50 D–£60
Loc   4 miles NW of Sutton
       Coldfield, off A454
Arch   Harry Vardon

Manor (Kingstone) (1991)
*Leese Hill, Kingstone, Uttoxeter,
ST14 8QT*
Tel   (01889) 563234
Fax   (01889) 563234
Mem   300
Sec   A Campbell
Holes 18 hole course
V'tors U
Fees   £12 (£20)
Loc   4 miles W of Uttoxeter on
       A518
Arch   E Anderson

Newcastle-under-Lyme
(1908)
*Whitmore Road, Newcastle-under-
Lyme, ST5 2QB*
Tel   (01782) 616583
Fax   (01782) 617531
Mem   575
Sec   KP Geddes (Sec/Mgr)
       (01782) 617006
Pro   P Symonds (01782) 618526
Holes 18 L 6317 yds SSS 71
V'tors WD–U H WE/BH–M SOC
Fees   On application
Loc   2 miles SW of Newcastle-
       under-Lyme on A53

Onneley (1968)
Onneley, Crewe, Cheshire, CW3 5QF
Tel   (01782) 750577

Mem   410
Sec   P Ball (01782) 846759
Pro   None
Holes 13 L 5781 yds SSS 68
V'tors WD–U Sat/BH–M Sun–NA
       SOC–Thurs
Fees   D–£20
Loc   8 miles W of Newcastle, off
       A525
Arch   A Benson

Oxley Park (1913)
*Stafford Road, Bushbury,
Wolverhampton, WV10 6DE*
Tel   (01902) 420506
Fax   (01902) 712241
Mem   550
Sec   Mrs K Mann (01902) 425892
Pro   LA Burlison (01902) 425445
Holes 18 L 6226 yds SSS 70
V'tors U SOC
Fees   £25 (£25)
Loc   1 mile N of Wolverhampton,
       off A449
Arch   HS Colt

Parkhall (1989)
Public
*Hulme Road, Weston Coyney, Stoke-on-
Trent, ST3 5BH*
Tel   (01782) 599584
Sec   N Worrall (Mgr)
       (01831) 456409
Pro   A Clingan
Holes 18 L 2335 yds Par 54
V'tors WE–booking necessary SOC
Fees   On application
Loc   3 miles E of Stoke. Longton
       1 mile

Penn (1908)
*Penn Common, Wolverhampton,
WV4 5JN*
Tel   (01902) 341142
Fax   (01902) 620504
Mem   650
Sec   MH Jones
Pro   B Burlison (01902) 330472
Holes 18 L 6487 yds SSS 72
V'tors WD–U WE–M SOC
Fees   £20 (Nov–Feb £15)
Loc   2 miles SW of
       Wolverhampton, off A449

Perton Park (1990)
*Wrottesley Park Road, Perton,
Wolverhampton, WV6 7HL*
Tel   (01902) 380103/380073
Fax   (01902) 326219
Mem   300
Sec   E Greenway (Mgr)
Pro   J Harrold (01902) 380073
Holes 18 L 6520 yds SSS 72
V'tors U SOC
Fees   £12 (£18)
Loc   6 miles W of Wolverhampton,
       off A454
Mis   Driving range

Sandwell Park (1895)
*Birmingham Road, West Bromwich,
B71 4JJ*
Tel   (0121) 553 4637
Fax   (0121) 525 1651
Web   www.sandwellparkgolfclub
       .co.uk
Mem   600
Sec   DA Paterson
Pro   N Wylie (0121) 553 4384
Holes 18 L 6468 yds SSS 73
V'tors WD–U WE–MH SOC–WD
Fees   £30–£40
Loc   West Bromwich/Birmingham
       boundary. By M5 Junction 1
Arch   HS Colt

Sedgley (1992)
Pay and play
*Sandyfields Road, Sedgley, Dudley,
DY3 3DL*
Tel   (01902) 880503
Mem   150
Sec   JA Cox
Pro   G Mercer
Holes 9 L 3150 yds SSS 71
V'tors U
Fees   9 holes–£6. 18 holes–£8
Loc   ½ mile from Sedgley, off
       A463 between Dudley and
       Wolverhampton
Mis   Driving range
Arch   WG Cox

Seedy Mill (1991)
Pay and play
Elmhurst, Lichfield, WS13 8HE
Tel   (01543) 417333
Fax   (01543) 418098
Web   www.clubhaus.com
Mem   1200
Sec   S Dixon (Gen Mgr)
Pro   M Ashworth
Holes 18 L 6305 yds SSS 70
       9 hole Par 3 course
V'tors WD–U WE–U after 12 noon
       SOC
Fees   £21 (£26)
Loc   2 miles N of Lichfield on
       A515
Mis   Floodlit driving range
Arch   Hawtree

St Thomas's Priory (1995)
*Armitage Lane, Armitage, Rugeley,
WS15 1ED*
Tel   (01543) 491116
Fax   (01543) 492244
Web   www.st-thomass-golfclub.com
Mem   500
Sec   J Bissell
Pro   RMR O'Hanlon
       (01543) 492096
Holes 18 L 5969 yds SSS 70
V'tors H SOC–WD
Fees   £20 (£25)
Loc   1 mile SE of Rugeley on
       A513, opp Ash Tree Inn
Arch   Paul Mulholland

South Staffordshire
(1892)
Danescourt Road, Tettenhall,
Wolverhampton, WV6 9BQ
Tel (01902) 751065
Fax (01902) 741753
Mem 600
Sec JA Macklin
Pro M Sparrow (01902) 754816
Holes 18 L 6500 yds SSS 71
V'tors WD–U WE/BH–M or by
arrangement SOC
Fees £34 D–£40 (£47)
Loc 3 miles W of Wolverhampton,
off A41
Arch Harry Vardon

Stafford Castle (1906)
Newport Road, Stafford, ST16 1BP
Tel (01785) 223821
Mem 440
Sec PJ Ash (Admin)
Holes 9 L 6382 yds Par 71 SSS 70
V'tors WD–U WE–after 1pm
Fees £16 (£20)
Loc 1/2 mile W of Stafford

Stone (1896)
The Fillybrooks, Stone, ST15 0NB
Tel (01785) 813103
Mem 314
Sec PR Farley (01785) 284875
Holes 9 L 6299 yds Par 71 SSS 70
V'tors WD–U WE/BH–M SOC–WD
Fees £15
Loc 1/2 mile W of Stone on A34

Swindon (1976)
Bridgnorth Road, Swindon, Dudley,
DY3 4PU
Tel (01902) 897031
Fax (01902) 326219
Mem 500
Sec E Greenway (Mgr)
Pro P Lester (01902) 896191
Holes 18 L 6088 yds SSS 69
9 hole Par 3 course
V'tors U SOC–WD
Fees £18 (£27)
Loc 5 miles SW of
Wolverhampton on B4176
Mis Driving range

Tamworth (1976)
Public
Eagle Drive, Amington, Tamworth,
B77 4EG
Tel (01827) 709303
Fax (01827) 709304
Mem 500
Pro W Allcock
Holes 18 L 6695 yds SSS 72
V'tors U SOC–WD
Fees £13
Loc 21/2 miles E of Tamworth on
B5000. M42, 3 miles
Mis Driving range

Trentham (1894)
14 Barlaston Old Road, Trentham,
Stoke-on-Trent, ST4 8HB
Tel (01782) 642347
Fax (01782) 644024
Web www.trenthamgolf.org
Mem 420
Sec RN Portas (01782) 658109
Pro S Wilson (01782) 657309
Holes 18 L 6644 yds SSS 72
V'tors WD–U H WE/BH–M (or
enquire Sec) SOC–WD
Fees £40 (£50)
Loc 3 miles S of Newcastle-under-
Lyme on A5305, off A34. M6
Junction 15

Trentham Park (1936)
Trentham Park, Stoke-on-Trent,
ST4 8AE
Tel (01782) 642245
Fax (01782) 658800
Mem 500 100(L) 50(J)
Sec T Berrisford (01782) 658800
Pro B Rimmer (01782) 642125
Holes 18 L 6425 yds SSS 71
V'tors H SOC–Wed & Fri
Fees £22.50 (£30)
Loc 4 miles S of Newcastle on
A34. M6 Junction 15, 1 mile

Uttoxeter (1970)
Wood Lane, Uttoxeter, ST14 8JR
Tel (01889) 566552
Fax (01889) 567501
Mem 700
Sec R Orme
Pro AD McCandless
(01889) 564884
Holes 18 L 5801 yds Par 70 SSS 69
V'tors WD–U WE–by arrangement
SOC
Fees D–£20 (£30)
Loc Close to A50, by Uttoxeter
racecourse

Walsall (1907)
Broadway, Walsall, WS1 3EY
Tel (01922) 613512
Fax (01922) 616460
Mem 600
Sec JK Harding (01922) 613512
Pro R Lambert (01922) 626766
Holes 18 L 6259 yds SSS 71
V'tors WD–U WE–M SOC
Fees £33
Loc 1 mile S of Walsall, off A34.
M6 Junction 7
Arch McKenzie

Wergs (1990)
Pay and play
Keepers Lane, Tettenhall, WV6 8UA
Tel (01902) 742225
Fax (01902) 744748
Mem 150
Sec Mrs G Parsons
Holes 18 L 6949 yds Par 72 SSS 73
V'tors U
Fees D–£15 (£20)

Loc 3 miles W of Wolverhampton
on A41
Arch CW Moseley

Westwood (1923)
Newcastle Road, Wallbridge, Leek,
ST13 7AA
Tel (01538) 398385
Fax (01538) 382485
Mem 800
Sec C Plant
Pro N Hyde
Holes 18 L 6207 yds SSS 70
V'tors U SOC–WD
Fees WD–£18
Loc W boundary of Leek on A53

Whiston Hall (1971)
Whiston, Cheadle, ST10 2HZ
Tel (01538) 266260
Mem 500
Sec LC & RM Cliff (Mgr)
Holes 18 L 5742 yds SSS 69
V'tors U SOC
Fees £10
Loc 8 miles NE of Stoke-on-Trent
on A52, nr Alton Towers

Whittington Heath (1886)
Tamworth Road, Lichfield, WS14 9PW
Tel (01543) 432317 (Admin),
(01543) 432212 (Steward)
Fax (01543) 433962
Mem 670
Sec Mrs JA Burton
Pro AR Sadler (01543) 432261
Holes 18 L 6490 yds SSS 71
V'tors WD–H or I WE/BH–M
SOC–Wed & Thurs
Fees £35 D–£50
Loc 21/2 miles E of Lichfield on
Tamworth road (A51)

Wolstanton (1904)
Dimsdale Old Hall, Hassam Parade,
Wolstanton, Newcastle ST5 9DR
Tel (01782) 616995
Mem 625
Sec Mrs VJ Keenan
(01782) 622413
Pro S Arnold (01782) 622718
Holes 18 L 5807 yds SSS 68
V'tors WD–H WE–M SOC–WD
Fees £25
Loc 11/2 miles NW of Newcastle
(A34)

Suffolk

Aldeburgh (1884)
Aldeburgh, IP15 5PE
Tel (01728) 452890
Fax (01728) 452937
Web www.aldeburghgolfclub.co.uk
Mem 879
Sec GM Gadney
Pro K Preston (01728) 453309

Holes 18 L 6323 yds Par 68 SSS 71
9 L 2114 yds SSS 64
V'tors H–2 ball play only SOC
Fees On application
Loc 6 miles E of A12 (A1094)
Arch W Fernie/J Thompson

Beccles (1899)

The Common, Beccles, NR34 9BX
Tel (01502) 712244
Mem 150
Sec DW Trunks (01502) 714616
Holes 9 L 2696 yds SSS 67
V'tors WD–U Sun–M SOC
Fees £5 (£8)
Loc 10 miles W of Lowestoft
(A146)

Brett Vale (1992)

Noakes Road, Raydon, Ipswich,
IP7 5LR
Tel (01473) 310718
Fax (01473) 312270
Web www.brettvale.com
Mem 620
Sec JS Reid
Pro P Bate
Holes 18 L 5797 yds Par 70 SSS 67
V'tors U–booking advisable. Soft
spikes only. SOC–WD
Fees £22 (£28)
Loc 5 miles N of Colchester, off
A12 (B1070), towards
Hadleigh
Mis Driving range
Arch Howard Swan

Bungay & Waveney Valley (1889)

Outney Common, Bungay, NR35 1DS
Tel (01986) 892337
Fax (01986) 892222
Mem 673
Sec RW Stacey
Pro N Whyte
Holes 18 L 6044 yds Par 69 SSS 69
V'tors WD–U WE–M SOC–WD
Fees £24 D–£30
Loc ¹/₂ mile W of Bungay, on N
side of A143
Arch James Braid

Bury St Edmunds (1922)

Tut Hill, Bury St Edmunds, IP28 6LG
Tel (01284) 755979
Fax (01284) 763288
Web www.club-noticeboard.co.uk/
burystedmunds
Mem 750 180(L)
Sec JC Sayer
Pro M Jillings (01284) 755978
Holes 18 L 6669 yds Par 72 SSS 72
9 L 2217 yds Par 31 SSS 31
V'tors WD/BH–U WE–M SOC–WD
Fees 18 hole:£25 9 hole:£12 (£15)
Loc 2 miles W of Bury St
Edmunds on B1106, off A14
Arch Ted Ray

Cretingham (1984)

Grove Farm, Cretingham, Woodbridge,
IP13 7BA
Tel (01728) 685275
Fax (01728) 685037
Mem 300
Sec Mrs K Jackson
Pro N Jackson
Holes 9 L 2260 yds Par 33
V'tors U SOC
Fees 18 holes–£11 (£13)
Loc 2 miles SE of Earl Soham.
11 miles N of Ipswich
Mis Practice range. Pitch & putt
course
Arch J Austin

Diss (1903)

Stuston Common, Diss, IP22 4AA
Tel (01379) 641025
Fax (01379) 644586
Mem 750
Sec C Wellstead
Pro N Taylor (01379) 644399
Holes 18 L 6238 yds SSS 70
V'tors WD only
Fees £25
Loc 1 mile SE of Diss, off A140

Felixstowe Ferry (1880)

Ferry Road, Felixstowe, IP4 9RY
Tel (01394) 283060
Fax (01394) 273679
Web www.felixstowegolf.co.uk
Mem 1000
Sec R Tibbs (01394) 286834
Pro I Macpherson
(01394) 283975
Holes 18 L 6308 yds SSS 70
9 L 2986 yds Par 35
V'tors M H WD before 10.30am
SOC. 9 hole course–U
Fees £26
Loc 2 miles NE of Felixstowe,
towards Felixstowe Ferry
Arch Henry Cotton (1947)

Flempton (1895)

Bury St Edmunds, IP28 6HQ
Tel (01284) 728291
Mem 250
Sec JF Taylor
Pro M Jillings
Holes 9 L 6240 yds SSS 70
V'tors WD–H WE/BH–M
Fees £22 D–£28
Loc 4 miles NW of Bury St
Edmunds on A1101
Arch JH Taylor

Fynn Valley (1991)

Witnesham, Ipswich, IP6 9JA
Tel (01473) 785267
Fax (01473) 785632
Mem 650
Sec AR Tyrrell
Pro K Vince (01473) 785463
Holes 18 L 6310 yds Par 70 SSS 71
9 hole Par 3 course
V'tors U exc Sun am SOC

Fees £22 (£25)
Loc 2 miles N of Ipswich on
B1077
Mis Driving range
Arch AR Tyrrell

Halesworth (1990)

Bramfield Road, Halesworth, IP19 9XA
Tel (01986) 875567
Fax (01986) 874565
Mem 400
Pro R Whyte
Holes 18 L 6383 yds SSS 72
9 hole course SSS 33
V'tors H SOC
Fees 18 hole:£15 D–£19 (£21)
9 hole:£7.50
Loc 1 mile S of Halesworth, off
A144
Mis Floodlit driving range
Arch JW Johnson

Haverhill (1974)

Coupals Road, Haverhill, CB9 7UW
Tel (01440) 761951
Fax (01440) 761951
Mem 700
Sec Mrs J Edwards
D Renyard (Mgr)
Pro N Duc (01440) 712628
Holes 18 L 5898 yds SSS 70
V'tors U–phone Pro SOC–Tues &
Thurs
Fees £22 (£28)
Loc 1 mile E of Haverhill, off
A1107. Signs to Calford
Green
Arch Lawrie/Pilgrem

Hintlesham Hall (1991)

Hintlesham, Ipswich, IP8 3NS
Tel (01473) 652761
Fax (01473) 652750
Mem 475
Sec I Procter (Mgr)
Pro A Spink
Holes 18 L 6638 yds SSS 72
V'tors WD–U after 10.30am
WE–NA SOC
Fees £30–£38
Loc 4 miles W of Ipswich on
A1071
Arch Hawtree

Ipswich (Purdis Heath) (1895)

Purdis Heath, Bucklesham Road,
Ipswich, IP3 8UQ
Tel (01473) 727474 (Steward)
Fax (01473) 715236
Web www.ipswichgolfclub.com
Mem 740
Sec NM Ellice (01473) 728941
Pro SJ Whymark (01473) 724017
Holes 18 L 6435 yds Par 71 SSS 71
9 L 1930 yds Par 31
V'tors 18 hole: H SOC 9 hole: U
Fees 18 hole: £40 (£43)
9 hole: £12.50
Loc 3 miles E of Ipswich
Arch James Braid

Links (Newmarket)
(1902)

Cambridge Road, Newmarket,
CB8 0TG

Tel	**(01638) 663000**
Fax	(01638) 661476
Mem	750
Sec	Lt Col MI Botting
Pro	J Sharkey (01638) 662395
Holes	18 L 6424 yds SSS 72
V'tors	H exc Sun–M before 11.30am SOC
Fees	£30 (£34)
Loc	1 mile SW of Newmarket

Newton Green (1907)

Newton Green, Sudbury, CO10 0QN

Tel	**(01787) 77501**
Mem	650
Sec	K Mazdon (01787) 377217
Pro	T Cooper (01787) 313215
Holes	18 L 5893 yds SSS 69
V'tors	WD–U WE–M SOC
Fees	£15.50
Loc	4 miles S of Sudbury on A134

Rookery Park (1891)

Carlton Colville, Lowestoft, NR33 8HJ

Tel	**(01502) 560380**
Fax	(01502) 560380
Mem	1000
Sec	DP Kelly
Pro	M Elsworthy (01502) 515103
Holes	18 L 6714 yds SSS 72
	9 hole Par 3 course
V'tors	WD–U Sat/BH–after 11am Sun–NA SOC
Fees	£25 (£30)
Loc	3 miles W of Lowestoft (A146)

Royal Worlington & Newmarket (1893)

Golf Links Road, Worlington, Bury St Edmunds, IP28 8SD

Tel	**(01638) 712216 (Clubhouse)**
Fax	(01638) 717787
Mem	325
Sec	KJ Weston (01638) 717787
Pro	M Hawkins (01638) 715224
Holes	9 L 6210 yds SSS 70
V'tors	I or H–phone first (2 ball or foursomes only) WE–NA
Fees	D–£48 After 2pm–£35
Loc	6 miles NE of Newmarket, off A11
Arch	Tom Dunn

Rushmere (1927)

Rushmere Heath, Ipswich, IP4 5QQ

Tel	**(01473) 725648**
Fax	(01473) 273852
Mem	770
Sec	AN Harris (01473) 725648
Pro	NTJ McNeill (01473) 728076
Holes	18 L 6262 yds SSS 70
V'tors	WD–H WE/BH–H after 2.30pm

Fees	£25
Loc	3 miles E of Ipswich, off Woodbridge road (A1214)
Arch	David Williams (1999)

Seckford (1991)

Seckford Hall Road, Great Bealings, Woodbridge, IP13 6NT

Tel	**(01394) 388000**
Fax	(01394) 382818
Web	www.seckfordgolf.co.uk
Mem	400
Sec	BD Kinsey
	N Gruntvig (Mgr)
Pro	S Jay
Holes	18 L 5392 yds Par 68 SSS 66
V'tors	U–booking necessary SOC
Fees	£17 (£25)
Loc	SW of Woodbridge, off A12
Arch	J Johnson

Southwold (1884)

The Common, Southwold, IP18 6TB

Tel	**(01502) 723234**
Mem	450
Sec	PJ Obern (01502) 723248
Pro	B Allen (01502) 723790
Holes	9 L 6050 yds SSS 69
V'tors	U (subject to fixtures)
Fees	£20 (£22)
Loc	35 miles NE of Ipswich

Stoke-by-Nayland (1972)

Keepers Lane, Leavenheath, Colchester, CO6 4PZ

Tel	**(01206) 262836**
Fax	(01206) 263356
Web	www.stokebynaylandclub .co.uk
Mem	1400
Sec	D Howe (Gen Mgr)
Pro	K Lovelock (01206) 262769
Holes	Gainsborough 18 L 6498 yds SSS 71;
	Constable 18 L 6544 yds SSS 71
V'tors	WD–U WE/BH–H after 10am SOC
Fees	£25 (£35)
Loc	Off A134 Colchester-Sudbury road on B1068
Mis	Driving range

Stowmarket (1962)

Lower Road, Onehouse, Stowmarket, IP14 3DA

Tel	**(01449) 736392**
Fax	(01449) 736826
Web	www.club-noticeboard.co.uk/stowmarket
Mem	600
Sec	GR West (01449) 736473
Pro	D Burl
Holes	18 L 6119 yds SSS 69
V'tors	H SOC–Thurs & Fri
Fees	£25 (£31)
Loc	2½ miles SW of Stowmarket
Mis	Driving range

The Suffolk G&CC (1974)

St John's Hill Plantation, The Street, Fornham St Genevieve, IP28 6JQ

Tel	**(01284) 706777**
Fax	(01284) 706721
Mem	600
Sec	KJ Weston RAF (Rtd)
Pro	S Hall
Holes	18 L 6321 yds SSS 71
V'tors	U SOC
Fees	£25 (£30)
Loc	2 miles NW of Bury St Edmunds, off B1106

Thorpeness Hotel (1923)

Thorpeness, Leiston, IP16 4NH

Tel	**(01728) 452176**
Fax	(01728) 453868
Web	www.thorpeness.co.uk
Mem	300
Sec	J Montague
Pro	(01728) 454926
Holes	18 L 6281 yds SSS 71
V'tors	U
Fees	£32 (£37)
Loc	2 miles N of Aldeburgh
Arch	James Braid

Ufford Park Hotel (1992)

Yarmouth Road, Ufford, Woodbridge, IP12 1QW

Tel	**(01394) 382836**
Fax	(01394) 383582
Web	www.uffordpark.co.uk
Mem	350
Sec	B Tidy
Pro	S Robertson
Holes	18 L 6485 yds SSS 71
V'tors	U H SOC
Fees	£25 (£30)
Loc	2 miles N of Woodbridge, off A12
Mis	Golf Academy
Arch	P Pilgrim

Waldringfield Heath (1983)

Newbourne Road, Waldringfield, Woodbridge, IP12 4PT

Tel	**(01473) 736768**
Fax	(01473) 736436
Mem	640
Sec	LJ McWade
Pro	R Mann, A Lucas (01473) 736417
Holes	18 L 6141 yds SSS 69
V'tors	WD–U WE/BH–M before noon SOC–WD
Fees	On application
Loc	3 miles E of Ipswich, off A12
Arch	P Pilgrem

Woodbridge (1893)

Bromeswell Heath, Woodbridge, IP12 2PF

Tel	**(01394) 382038**
Fax	(01394) 382392
Mem	950
Sec	A Theunissen

For list of abbreviations see page 649

Pro   A Hubert (01394) 383213
Holes 18 L 6299 yds SSS 70
      9 L 6382 yds SSS 70
V'tors WD–H WE/BH–M SOC
Fees 18 hole:£33. 9 hole:£16
Loc   2 miles E of Woodbridge on
      A1152 towards Orford
Arch F Hawtree

Surrey

The Addington (1913)
205 Shirley Church Road, Croydon,
CR0 5AB
Tel   **(020) 8777 1055**
Fax   (020) 8777 1701
Sec   RAR Hill
Holes 18 L 6242 yds SSS 71
V'tors H SOC–WD
Fees On application
Loc   E Croydon 2½ miles
Arch JF Abercromby

Addington Court (1931)
Pay and play
Featherbed Lane, Addington, Croydon,
CR0 9AA
Tel   **(020) 8657 0281**
      (Bookings)
Fax   (020) 8651 0282
Mem   600
Sec   A Langdon (020) 8651 5270
Pro   T Healy (020) 8657 0281
Holes Championship 18 L 5577 yds
      SSS 67;
      Falconwood 18 L 5472 yds
      SSS 67
      9 L 1804 yds SSS 62
      18 hole pitch & putt course
V'tors U SOC
Fees Championship £15.35
      (£18.60)
      Falconwood £13.35 (£16.60)
      9 hole:£8 (£9)
Loc   3 miles SE of Croydon
Mis   Driving range
Arch F Hawtree Sr

Addington Palace (1923)
Addington Park, Gravel Hill,
Addington, CR0 5BB
Tel   **(020) 8654 3061**
Fax   (020) 8655 3632
Mem   700
Sec   Mrs P Argent
Pro   R Williams (020) 8654 1786
Holes 18 L 6410 yds SSS 71
V'tors WD–H WE/BH–M
Fees £35
Loc   2 miles E of Croydon Station

Banstead Downs (1890)
Burdon Lane, Belmont, Sutton,
SM2 7DD
Tel   **(020) 8642 2284**
Fax   (020) 8642 5252
Mem   650
Sec   RHA Steele
Pro   R Dickman (020) 8642 6884

Holes 18 L 6194 yds SSS 69
V'tors WD–H WE/BH–M
      SOC–Thurs
Fees £35 After 12 noon–£25
Loc   1 mile S of Sutton

Barrow Hills (1970)
Longcross, Chertsey, KT16 0DS
Tel   **(01344) 635770**
Mem   230
Sec   R Hammond (01483) 234807
Holes 18 L 3090 yds SSS 53
V'tors M
Fees On application
Loc   4 miles W of Chertsey

Betchworth Park (1911)
Reigate Road, Dorking, RH4 1NZ
Tel   **(01306) 882052**
Fax   (01306) 877462
Mem   725
Sec   J Holton (Mgr)
Pro   A Tocher (01306) 884334
Holes 18 L 6266 yds SSS 70
V'tors WD–by arrangement exc Tues
      & Wed am WE–NA exc Sun
      pm
Fees £34 (£45)
Loc   1 mile E of Dorking on A25
Arch HS Colt

Bletchingley (1993)
Church Lane, Bletchingley, RH1 4LP
Tel   **(01883) 744666**
Fax   (01883) 744284
Web   www.bletchingleygolfclub
      .co.uk
Mem   550
Sec   Mrs N Robinson (Mgr)
Pro   A Dyer (01883) 744848
Holes 18 L 6504 yds Par 72 SSS 71
V'tors WD–U WE–M before 2.15pm
      SOC
Fees £25 (£30)
Loc   1 mile S of M25 Junction 6 on
      A25
Arch Paul Wright

Bowenhurst Golf Centre
Mill Lane, Crondall, Farnham,
GU10 5RP
Tel   **(01252) 851695**
Fax   (01252) 852039
Mem   202
Sec   GL Corbey (01252) 851695
Pro   A Carter (01252) 851344
Holes 9 L 2007 yds Par 62 SSS 60
V'tors U SOC
Fees 18 holes–£11 (£14) 9
      holes–£7 (£8.50)
Loc   2 miles SW of Farnham on
      A287. M3 Junction 5
Mis   Driving range
Arch G Finn, N Finn

Bramley (1913)
Bramley, Guildford, GU5 0AL
Tel   **(01483) 892696**
Fax   (01483) 894673
Mem   800

Sec   Ms M Lambert
      (01483) 892696
Pro   G Peddie (01483) 893685
Holes 18 L 5990 yds SSS 69
V'tors WD–U WE–M SOC–WD
Fees £28 D–£34
Loc   3 miles S of Guildford on
      A281
Mis   Driving range–members and
      green fees only
Arch Mayo/Braid

Broadwater Park
Guildford Road, Farncombe,
Godalming, GU7 3BU
Tel   **(01483) 429955**
Mem   126
Sec   RJ Ashby
Pro   KD Milton
Holes 9 L 1301 yds Par 27
V'tors U
Fees £4.95 (£5.75)
Loc   1 mile SE of Godalming
      (A3100)
Arch KD Milton

Burhill (1907)
Burwood Road, Walton-on-Thames,
KT12 4BL
Tel   **(01932) 227345**
Fax   (01932) 267159
Mem   1100
Sec   D Cook (Gen Mgr)
Pro   L Johnson (01932) 221729
Holes 18 L 6479 yds SSS 71
      18 L 6597 yds SSS 71
V'tors WD–H WE/BH–M
Fees On application
Loc   Between Walton-on-Thames
      and Cobham, off Burwood
      Road
Mis   Game Improvement Centre
Arch Willie Park

Camberley Heath (1912)
Golf Drive, Camberley, GU15 1JG
Tel   **(01276) 23258**
Fax   (01276) 692505
Mem   725
Sec   J Greenwood
Pro   G Ralph (01276) 27905
Holes 18 L 6326 yds SSS 71
V'tors WD–H WE–M SOC H
Fees On application
Loc   1½ miles S of Camberley on
      A325
Arch HS Colt

Central London Golf Centre (1992)
Public
Burntwood Lane, Wandsworth, London,
SW17 0AT
Tel   **(020) 8871 2468**
Fax   (020) 8874 7447
Web   www.clgc.co.uk
Mem   200
Sec   J Robson
Pro   J Robson
Holes 9 L 4658 yds SSS 62
V'tors U SOC

Fees £8.50 (£10.50)
Loc Off Burntwood Lane SW17
Mis Driving range
Arch Patrick Tallack

Chessington Golf Centre (1983)

Pay and play
Garrison Lane, Chessington KT9 2LW
Tel (020) 8391 0948
Fax (020) 8397 2068
Mem 70
Sec M Bedford
Pro M Janes
Holes 9 L 1785 yds Par 62 SSS 57
V'tors U
Fees £7.50 (£9)
Loc Off A243, opp Chessington South Station. M25 Junction 9
Mis Driving range

Chiddingfold (1994)

Petworth Road, Chiddingfold, GU8 4SL
Tel (01428) 685888
Fax (01428) 685939
Mem 400
Sec Miss C Mentz (Gen Mgr)
Pro G Wallis
Holes 18 L 5482 yds Par 70 SSS 67
V'tors U SOC
Fees £16 (£22)
Loc On A283 between Petworth and Guildford
Arch Jonathan Gaunt

Chipstead (1906)

How Lane, Chipstead, Coulsdon, CR5 3LN
Tel (01737) 555781
Fax (01737) 555404
Web www.chipsteadgolf.co.uk
Mem 600
Sec Mrs SA Wallace (Admin) (01737) 555781
Pro G Torbett (Golf Dir) (01737) 554939
Holes 18 L 5450 yds SSS 67
V'tors WD-U WE/BH-M
Fees £30 After 2pm-£20
Loc M25 Junction 8 (A217)

Chobham (1994)

Chobham Road, Knaphill, Woking, GU21 2TZ
Tel (01276) 855584
Fax (01276) 855663
Web www.chobhamgolfclub.co.uk
Mem 750
Sec C Kennedy
Pro T Coombes (01276) 855748
Holes 18 L 5959 yds Par 69 SSS 69
V'tors M H-restricted SOC
Fees £36
Loc 3 miles E of M3 Junction 3 between Chobham and Knaphill (A3046)
Arch Alliss/Clark

Clandon Regis (1994)

Epsom Road, West Clandon, GU4 7TT
Tel (01483) 224888
Fax (01483) 211781
Mem 650
Sec Mrs WR Savage
Pro S Lloyd (01483) 223922
Holes 18 L 6419 yds Par 72 SSS 71
V'tors WD-U WE-NA before noon SOC-WD
Fees £25 (£35)
Loc 3 miles E of Guildford on A246
Arch David Williams

Coombe Hill (1911)

Golf Club Drive, Coombe Lane West, Kingston, KT2 7DF
Tel (020) 8336 7600
Fax (020) 8336 7601
Web www.coombehillgolf.com
Mem 553
Sec Mrs C De Foy
Pro C De Foy (020) 8949 3713
Holes 18 L 6293 yds SSS 71
V'tors WD-I or H WE-NA SOC
Fees £60 D-£80
Loc 1 mile W of New Malden on A238
Arch JF Abercromby

Coombe Wood (1904)

George Road, Kingston Hill, Kingston-upon-Thames, KT2 7NS
Tel (020) 8942 3828 (Clubhouse)
Fax (020) 8942 0388
Mem 640
Sec PM Urwin (020) 8942 0388
Pro D Butler (020) 8942 6764
Holes 18 L 5299 yds SSS 66
V'tors WD-U H WE/BH-M SOC-WD
Fees £25 (£35)
Loc 1 mile E of Kingston-upon-Thames, off A3 at Robin Hood roundabout or Coombe junction
Arch Williamson

Coulsdon Manor (1937)

Pay and play
Coulsdon Court Road, Old Coulsdon, Croydon, CR5 2LL
Tel (020) 8660 6083
Fax (020) 8668 3118
Pro D Copsey (020) 8660 6083
Holes 18 L 6037 yds SSS 70
V'tors U
Fees £13.50 (£16.75)
Loc 5 miles S of Croydon on B2030. M25 Junction 7
Arch HS Colt

The Cranleigh (1985)

Barhatch Lane, Cranleigh, GU6 7NG
Tel (01483) 268855
Fax (01483) 267251
Mem 650
Sec M Hale
Pro T Longmuir (01483) 277188

Holes 18 L 5648 yds SSS 67
V'tors WD-U WE/BH-pm only SOC-WD
Fees £24 (£26)
Loc 1 mile from Cranleigh, off A281
Mis Driving range

Croham Hurst (1911)

Croham Road, South Croydon, CR2 7HJ
Tel (020) 8657 5581
Fax (020) 8657 3229
Web www.crohamhurstgolfclub.co.uk
Mem 515 110(L) 50(J)
Sec HS Fleming
Pro E Stillwell (020) 8657 7705
Holes 18 L 6286 yds SSS 70
V'tors WD-I WE/BH-M
Fees £37 (£46)
Loc 1 mile from S Croydon. M25 Junction 6-A22-B270-B269
Arch Braid/Hawtree

Cuddington (1929)

Banstead Road, Banstead, SM7 1RD
Tel (020) 8393 0951
Fax (020) 8786 7025
Mem 760
Sec DM Scott (020) 8393 0952
Pro M Warner (020) 8393 5850
Holes 18 L 6595 yds SSS 71
V'tors WD-I WE-M
Fees £35 (£45)
Loc Nr Banstead Station
Arch HS Colt

Dorking (1897)

Deepdene Avenue, Chart Park, Dorking, RH5 4BX
Tel (01306) 886917
Fax (01306) 886917
Mem 360
Sec P Napier (Mgr)
Pro P Napier
Holes 9 L 5163 yds SSS 65
V'tors WD-U WE/BH-M SOC-WD
Fees £14
Loc 1 mile S of Dorking on A24
Arch James Braid

Drift (1976)

The Drift, East Horsley, KT24 5HD
Tel (01483) 284641
Fax (01483) 284642
Mem 700
Sec G Backett (Sec/Mgr)
Pro L Greasley (01483) 284772
Holes 18 L 6425 yds SSS 72
V'tors WD-U WE-U after 3pm SOC
Fees £30 (£45)
Loc 2 miles off A3 (B2039). M25 Junction 10
Mis Driving range
Arch Robert Sandow

Duke's Dene (1996)

Halliloo Valley Road, Woldingham, CR3 7HA

Tel	**(01883) 653501**
Fax	(01883) 653502
Mem	650
Sec	GJ Lewis
Pro	P Harrison (01883) 653541
Holes	18 L 6322 yds Par 71 SSS 70
V'tors	WD–U WE–NA before noon SOC
Fees	£25 (£40)
Loc	2¹/2 miles N of M25 Junction 6, off A22
Mis	Practice range
Arch	Bradford Benz

Dulwich & Sydenham Hill (1894)

Grange Lane, College Road, London, SE21 7LH

Tel	**(020) 8693 3961**
Fax	(020) 8693 2481
Mem	850
Sec	Mrs S Alexander
Pro	D Baillie (020) 8693 8491
Holes	18 L 6051 yds SSS 69
V'tors	WD–H WE/BH–M SOC
Fees	£25

Dunsfold Aerodrome (1965)

Dunsfold Aerodrome, Godalming, GU8 4BS

Tel	**(01483) 265403**
Fax	(01483) 265670
Mem	270
Sec	F Tuck
Pro	None
Holes	9 L 6236 yds Par 72 SSS 70
V'tors	M
Fees	£6 (£6)
Loc	10 miles S of Guildford, off A281
Arch	Sharkey/Hayward

Effingham (1927)

Guildford Road, Effingham, KT24 5PZ

Tel	**(01372) 452203**
Fax	(01372) 459959
Mem	980
Sec	JA Davies
Pro	S Hoatson (01372) 452606
Holes	18 L 6524 yds SSS 71
V'tors	WD–H WE/BH–M
Fees	£30
Loc	8 miles E of Guildford on A246. M25 Junction 10
Arch	HS Colt

Epsom (1889)

Longdown Lane South, Epsom Downs, Epsom, KT17 4JR

Tel	**(01372) 721666**
Fax	(01372) 817183
Mem	800
Sec	LR Anderson
Pro	R Goudie (01372) 741867
Holes	18 L 5701 yds SSS 68

V'tors	WD–U exc Tues am WE/BH–NA before noon SOC
Fees	£26
Loc	³/4 mile NE of Epsom Racecourse

Farleigh Court

Proprietary

Old Farleigh Road, Farleigh CR6 9PX

Tel	**(01883) 627733 (Bookings)**
Fax	(01883) 627722
Sec	C Dryden (Mgr) (01883) 627711
Pro	S Graham (01883) 627733
Holes	18 hole course Par 72 SSS 71 9 hole course Par 36
V'tors	WD–U after 10am WE–U after 12 noon
Fees	18 hole: £30 (£40) 9 hole: £14 (£17)
Loc	5 miles SE of Croydon. M25 Junction 6
Mis	Driving range
Arch	John Jacobs

Farnham (1896)

The Sands, Farnham, GU10 1PX

Tel	**(01252) 783163**
Fax	(01252) 781185
Mem	750
Sec	Judy Elliott (01252) 782109
Pro	G Cowlishaw (01252) 782198
Holes	18 L 6313 yds SSS 71
V'tors	WD–H WE–M SOC–Wed & Thurs
Fees	£35 D–£40
Loc	1 mile E of Farnham, off A31

Farnham Park Par Three (1966)

Pay and play

Farnham Park, Farnham, GU9 0AU

Tel	**(01252) 715216**
Fax	(01252) 718246
Mem	75
Sec	A Curtis
Pro	A Curtis
Holes	9 L 1163 yds Par 54
V'tors	U
Fees	£4.50 (£5)
Loc	By Farnham Castle
Arch	Henry Cotton

Foxhills (1975)

Stonehill Road, Ottershaw, KT16 0EL

Tel	**(01932) 872050**
Fax	(01932) 874762
Web	www.foxhills.co.uk
Mem	975
Sec	A Laking (Mgr)
Pro	A Good (01932) 873961
Holes	18 L 6680 yds SSS 73 18 L 6547 yds SSS 72 9 hole course
V'tors	WD–U WE–NA before noon SOC–WD am
Fees	£60 D–£80 (£70)
Loc	2 miles SW of Chertsey on B386

Mis	Driving range
Arch	FW Hawtree

Gatton Manor Hotel G&CC (1969)

Standon Lane, Ockley, Dorking, RH5 5PQ

Tel	**(01306) 627555**
Fax	(01306) 627713
Web	www.gattonmanor.co.uk
Mem	250
Sec	LC Heath
Pro	R Sargent (01306) 627557
Holes	18 L 6653 yds SSS 72
V'tors	U exc Sun before 1 pm–NA SOC–WD
Fees	£23 (£30)
Loc	1¹/2 miles SW of Ockley, off A29. M25 Junction 9, S on A24
Mis	Driving range
Arch	Henry Cotton

Goal Farm Par Three

Proprietary

Gole Road, Pirbright, GU24 0P2

Tel	**(01483) 473183/473205**
Sec	R & J Church (Props)
Holes	9 hole Par 3 course
V'tors	Sat/Thurs am–restricted SOC–WD
Fees	£4.50 (£4.75)
Loc	7 miles NW of Guildford

Guildford (1886)

High Path Road, Merrow, Guildford, GU1 2HL

Tel	**(01483) 563941**
Fax	(01483) 453228
Mem	600
Sec	BJ Green
Pro	PG Hollington (01483) 566765
Holes	18 L 6090 yds SSS 70
V'tors	WD–U WE–M SOC–WD
Fees	£30
Loc	2 miles E of Guildford on A246
Arch	Taylor/Hawtree

Hankley Common (1896)

Tilford, Farnham, GU10 2DD

Tel	**(01252) 792493**
Fax	(01252) 795699
Mem	700
Sec	JSW Scott
Pro	P Stow (01252) 793761
Holes	18 L 6438 yds SSS 71
V'tors	WD–U WE–H at discretion of Sec SOC
Fees	£50 (£65)
Loc	3 miles SE of Farnham on Tilford road

Happy Valley (1999)

Rook Lane, Chaldon, Caterham, CR3 5AA

Tel	**(01883) 344555**
Fax	(01883) 344422

Web www.happyvalley.co.uk
Mem 550
Sec S Hodsdon (Gen Mgr)
Pro D Kent
Holes 18 L 6858 yds Par 72 SSS 73
V'tors WD–U WE–NA before 11.30am SOC
Fees £20 (£25)
Loc 5 miles S of Croydon. M25 Junction 7
Mis Driving range
Arch David Williams

Hazelwood Golf Centre

Pay and play
Croysdale Avenue, Green Street, Sunbury-on-Thames, TW16 6QU
Tel (01932) 770932
Fax (01932) 770933
Mem 292
Sec J Reed
Pro F Sheridan (01932) 770932
Holes 9 L 5660 yds Par 35 SSS 67
V'tors U SOC
Fees £7 (£8.50)
Loc M3 Junction 1, 1 mile
Mis Driving range. Golf academy
Arch Jonathan Gaunt

Hersham Village

Assher Road, Hersham, Walton-on-Thames, KT12 4RA
Tel (01932) 267666
Fax (01932) 267146
Sec R Hutton (Golf Dir)
Pro J Noble
Holes 9 L 3097 yds Par 36
V'tors U
Fees 18 holes–£18.50
Loc 5 miles N of M25 Junction 10 (B365)
Mis Floodlit driving range

Hindhead (1904)

Churt Road, Hindhead, GU26 6HX
Tel (01428) 604614
Fax (01428) 608508
Mem 500 76(L) 90(J)
Sec PA Owen
Pro N Ogilvy (01428) 604458
Holes 18 L 6356 yds SSS 70
V'tors WD–U WE–by arrangement H SOC–Wed & Thurs
Fees £36 (£46)
Loc 1½ miles N of Hindhead on A287. M25 Junction 10, 25 miles

Hoebridge Golf Centre (1982)

Public
Old Woking Road, Old Woking, GU22 8JH
Tel (01483) 722611
Fax (01483) 740369
Web www.hoebridge.co.uk
Mem 480
Sec P Dawson (Mgr)
Pro TD Powell

Holes 18 L 6587 yds SSS 71
Inter 9 L 2294 yds Par 33
18 hole Par 3 course
V'tors U SOC–WD
Fees 18 hole: £17.50 (£21)
Inter: £9. Par 3: £7.20
Loc Between Old Woking and West Byfleet on B382
Mis Floodlit driving range
Arch Jacobs/Hawtree

Home Park (1895)

Hampton Wick, Kingston-upon-Thames, KT1 4AD
Tel (020) 8977 6645
Fax (020) 8977 4414
Mem 500
Sec BW O'Farrell
(020) 8977 2423
Pro L Roberts (020) 8977 2658
Holes 18 L 6584 yds SSS 71
V'tors U
Fees £22 (£25)
Loc 1 mile W of Kingston

Horton Park G&CC (1987)

Pay and play
Hook Road, Epsom, KT19 8QG
Tel (020) 8393 8400 (Enquiries),
(020) 8394 2626 (Bookings)
Fax (020) 8394 1369
Mem 450
Pro M Hirst (020) 8394 2626
Holes 18 L 6300 yds SSS 71
9 L 3274 yds Par 60
V'tors U SOC
Fees £16 (£18)
Loc 1 mile from A3, W of Epsom. M25 Junction 9
Mis Driving range
Arch P Nicholson

Hurtmore (1992)

Pay and play
Hurtmore Road, Hurtmore, Godalming, GU7 2RN
Tel (01483) 426492
Fax (01483) 426121
Mem 200
Sec Maxine Burton
Pro Maxine Burton
Holes 18 L 5530 yds SSS 67
V'tors U SOC
Fees £12 (£16)
Loc 6 miles S of Guildford on A3. M25 Junction 10
Arch Alliss/Clark

Kingswood (1928)

Sandy Lane, Kingswood, Tadworth, KT20 6NE
Tel (01737) 833316
Fax (01737) 833920
Mem 770
Sec L Andrews (Admin) (01737) 832188
Pro T Sims (01737) 832334
Holes 18 L 6904 yds SSS 73
V'tors U SOC
Fees £36 (£50)

Loc 5 miles S of Sutton on A217. M25 Junction 8, 2 miles
Mis Driving range
Arch James Braid

Laleham (1903)

Laleham Reach, Chertsey KT16 8RP
Tel (01932) 564211
Fax (01932) 564448
Web www.laleham-golf.co.uk
Mem 600
Sec Mrs PA Kennett
Pro H Stott (01932) 562877
Holes 18 L 6203 yds SSS 70
V'tors WD–U 9.30–4.30pm WE–M SOC–Mon–Wed
Fees £22–£30
Loc 2 miles S of Staines, opp Thorpe Park

Leatherhead (1903)

Proprietary
Kingston Road, Leatherhead, KT22 0EE
Tel (01372) 843966
Fax (01372) 842241
Web www.lgc-golf.co.uk
Mem 600
Sec A Norman (01372) 843966
Pro S Norman (01372) 843956
Holes 18 L 6203 yds Par 71 SSS 70
V'tors WD–U WE–NA before 2pm SOC
Fees £37.50 (£47.50)
Loc On A243 to Chessington. M25 Junction 9

Limpsfield Chart (1889)

Westerham Road, Limpsfield, RH8 0SL
Tel (01883) 723405/722106
Mem 300
Sec MA Baker
Pro None
Holes 9 L 5718 yds SSS 68
V'tors WD–U exc Thurs (Ladies Day) WE–M or by appointment SOC
Fees £18 (£20)
Loc 1 mile E of Oxted on A25

Lingfield Park (1987)

Racecourse Road, Lingfield, RH7 6PQ
Tel (01342) 834602
Fax (01342) 836077
Mem 700
Sec C Morley
Pro C Morley (01342) 832659
Holes 18 L 6500 yds SSS 72
V'tors WD–U WE/BH–M SOC–WD
Fees £36 (£50)
Loc Next to Lingfield racecourse. M25 Junction 6
Mis Driving range

London Scottish (1865)

Windmill Enclosure, Wimbledon Common, London, SW19 5NQ
Tel (020) 8788 0135
Fax (020) 8789 7517

Mem 250
Sec S Barr (020) 8789 7517
Pro S Barr (020) 8789 1207
Holes 18 L 5458 yds Par 68 SSS
66
V'tors WD–U WE/BH–NA SOC
Fees £15 Mon–£10
Loc Wimbledon Common
Mis Red upper garment must be
worn
Arch Willie Dunn/Tom Dunn

Malden (1893)

Traps Lane, New Malden, KT3 4RS
Tel (020) 8942 0654
Fax (020) 8336 2219
Mem 800
Sec Mrs A Besant (Mgr)
Pro R Hunter (Golf Mgr)
(020) 8942 6009
Holes 18 L 6295 yds SSS 70
V'tors WD–U WE–restricted
SOC–Wed–Fri
Fees On application
Loc Off A3, between Wimbledon
and Kingston

Merrist Wood (1997)

*Coombe Lane, Worplesdon, Guildford,
GU3 3PE*
Web www.merristwood-
golfclub.co.uk
Mem 700
Sec P Flavin
Pro A Kirk
Holes 18 L 6575 yds Par 72 SSS 71
V'tors H–soft spikes only SOC–WD
Fees £20 D–£35
Loc 2 miles W of Guildford, off
A323
Mis Driving range
Arch David Williams

Milford

Station Lane, Milford, GU8 5HS
Tel (01483) 419200
Fax (01483) 419199
Mem 750
Sec C Edwards (Mgr)
Pro N English (01483) 416291
Holes 18 L 5960 yds Par 69 SSS 68
V'tors WD–U WE–restricted SOC
Fees £22 (£27.50)
Loc 3 miles SW of Guildford, off
A3
Arch Alliss/Clark

Mitcham (1924)

*Carshalton Road, Mitcham Junction,
CR4 4HN*
Tel (020) 8648 1508,
(020) 8640 4280 (Bookings)
Fax (020) 8648 4197
Mem 500
Sec WJ Dutch (020) 8648 4197
Pro JA Godfrey (020) 8640 4280
Holes 18 L 5931 yds SSS 68
V'tors WD–U WE–NA before
1.30pm SOC
Fees £16 (£16)
Loc Mitcham Junction Station

Moore Place (1926)

Public
*Portsmouth Road, Esher,
KT10 9LN*
Tel (01372) 463533
Fax (01372) 460274
Mem 80
Sec P Hirsch
Pro D Allen
Holes 9 L 4216 yds SSS 58
V'tors U
Fees £5.80 (£7.70)
Loc Centre of Esher
Arch D Allen

New Zealand (1895)

*Woodham Lane, Addlestone,
KT15 3QD*
Tel (01932) 345049
Fax (01932) 342891
Mem 300
Sec RA Marrett (01932) 342891
Pro VR Elvidge
(01932) 349619
Holes 18 L 6075 yds SSS 69
V'tors By request
Fees On application
Loc Woking 3 miles. West Byfleet
1 mile. Weybridge 5 miles
Arch Simpson/Fergusson

North Downs (1899)

*Northdown Road, Woldingham,
Caterham, CR3 7AA*
Tel (01883) 652057
Fax (01883) 652832
Web www.northdownsgolfclub
.co.uk
Mem 550
Sec DM Sinden (Mgr)
(01883) 652057
Pro MJ Homewood
(01883) 653004
Holes 18 L 5843 yds Par 69 SSS 68
V'tors WD–U WE–M
SOC–Tues/Wed/Fri
Fees £20
Loc 3 miles E of Caterham. M25
Junction 6
Arch JF Pennink

Oak Park (1984)

*Heath Lane, Crondall, Farnham,
GU10 5PB*
Tel (01252) 850850
Fax (01252) 850851
Mem 600
Sec N Dainton
Pro G Murton (01252) 850066
Holes Woodland 18 L 6352 yds Par
70 SSS 70;
Village 9 L 3279 yds Par 36
V'tors U SOC
Fees Woodland £20 (£30) Village
£10 (£12)
Loc Off A287 Farnham-Odiham
road. M3 Junction 5, 4 miles
Mis Driving range
Arch Patrick Dawson

Oaks Sports Centre

(1973)
Public
*Woodmansterne Road, Carshalton,
SM5 4AN*
Tel (020) 8643 8363
Fax (020) 8770 7303
Mem 1000
Pro G Horley
Holes 18 L 6033 yds SSS 69
9 hole course
V'tors U
Fees 18 hole: £14.75 (£18)
9 hole: £7 (£8.50)
Loc 2 miles from Sutton on B278
Mis Floodlit driving range

Pachesham Park Golf
Centre (1990)

Pay and play
*Oaklawn Road, Leatherhead,
KT22 0BT*
Tel (01372) 843453
Fax (01372) 844076
Mem 250
Sec P Taylor
Pro P Taylor
Holes 9 L 2804 yds Par 35
V'tors U SOC
Fees 9 holes–£9 (£10.50)
Loc NW of Leatherhead, off A244.
M25 Junction 9
Mis Driving range
Arch P Taylor

Pine Ridge (1992)

Pay and play
*Old Bisley Road, Frimley, Camberley,
GU16 5NX*
Tel (01276) 20770
Fax (01276) 678837
Pro P Sefton
Holes 18 L 6458 yds SSS 71
V'tors U
Fees £20 (£25)
Loc Off Maultway, between
Lightwater and Frimley. M3
Junction 3, 2 miles
Mis Floodlit driving range
Arch Clive D Smith

Purley Downs (1894)

*106 Purley Downs Road, South
Croydon, CR2 0RB*
Tel (020) 8657 8347
Fax (020) 8651 5044
Web www.purleydowns.co.uk
Mem 660
Sec PC Gallienne
Pro G Wilson (020) 8651 0819
Holes 18 L 6275 yds SSS 70
V'tors WD–I WE–M SOC–WD exc
Tues am
Fees On application
Loc 3 miles S of Croydon (A235)

Puttenham (1894)

Puttenham, Guildford, GU3 1AL
Tel (01483) 810498

Fax (01483) 810988
Mem 500
Sec G Simmons
Pro D Lintott (01483) 810277
Holes 18 L 6212 yds SSS 71
V'tors WD–by prior appointment
WE/BH–M SOC–Wed &
Thurs
Fees On application
Loc Between Guildford and
Farnham, on Hog's Back

Pyrford (1993)

Warren Lane, Pyrford, GU22 8XR
Tel (01483) 723555
Fax (01483) 729777
Mem 650
Sec G Jones (Gen Mgr)
Pro N Sharratt (01483) 751070
Holes 18 L 6201 yds SSS 70
V'tors WD–U WE–M before noon
SOC
Fees £38 (£52)
Loc 2 miles from A3 at Ripley
Arch Alliss/Clark

Redhill (1993)

Pay and play
Canada Avenue, Redhill, RH1 5BF
Tel (01737) 770204
Fax (01737) 760046
Mem 90
Sec S Furlonger
Pro J Edgar
Holes 9 L 1903 yds Par 31 SSS 59
V'tors U SOC
Fees 9 holes–£4.95 (£5.95)
Loc 1½ miles S of Redhill on A23,
off Three Arch Road
Mis Floodlit driving range

Redhill & Reigate (1887)

*Clarence Lodge, Pendleton Road,
Redhill, RH1 6LB*
Tel (01737) 244626/244433
Fax (01737) 242117
Mem 500
Sec W Pike (01737) 240777
Pro W Pike (01737) 244433
Holes 18 L 5272 yds SSS 66
V'tors WD–U WE–phone first SOC
Fees £15 (£25)
Loc 1 mile S of Redhill on A23

Reigate Heath (1895)

*The Club House, Reigate Heath,
RH2 8QR*
Tel (01737) 242610
Fax (01737) 249226
Mem 330 80(L) 60(J)
Sec RJ Perkins (01737) 226793
Pro B Davies
Holes 9 L 5658 yds SSS 67
V'tors WD–U Sun/BH–M
SOC–Wed & Thurs
Fees On application
Loc W boundary of Reigate
Heath

Reigate Hill

Gatton Bottom, Reigate, RH2 0TU
Tel (01737) 645577
Fax (01737) 642650
Mem 550
Sec I Donnelly
Pro C Forsyth (01737) 646070
Holes 18 L 6175 yds Par 72 SSS 70
V'tors WD–U WE–M SOC
Fees £25
Loc 1 mile from M25 Junction 8,
off A217
Arch David Williams

Richmond (1891)

Sudbrook Park, Richmond, TW10 7AS
Tel (020) 8940 1463
Fax (020) 8332 7914
Mem 700
Sec RL Wilkins (020) 8940 4351
Pro N Job (020) 8940 7792
Holes 18 L 6007 yds SSS 69
V'tors WD–H
Fees £35
Loc Between Richmond and
Kingston-upon-Thames

Richmond Park (1923)

Public
*Roehampton Gate, Richmond Park,
London, SW15 5JR*
Tel (020) 8876 3205/1795
Fax (020) 8878 1354
Sec AJ Gourvish
Pro D Bown
Holes Dukes 18 L 6036 yds SSS 68
Princes 18 L 5868 yds SSS 67
V'tors WD–U WE–booking
necessary SOC–WD
Fees On application
Loc In Richmond Park
Mis Driving range
Arch Hawtree

Roehampton Club (1901)

Roehampton Lane, London, SW15 5LR
Tel (020) 8480 4200
Fax (020) 8480 4265
Mem 1500
Sec M Yates (Chief Exec)
(020) 8480 4205
JW Tucker (Games Mgr)
(020) 8480 4200
Pro AL Scott (020) 8876 3858
Holes 18 L 6065 yds Par 71
V'tors WD/WE–Introduced by
member
Fees On application
Loc 1 mile W of Putney, off South
Circular

Roker Park (1993)

Pay and play
*Holly Lane, Aldershot Road, Guildford,
GU3 3PB*
Tel (01483) 236677
Mem 200
Sec C Tegg
Pro K Warn (01483) 236677

Holes 9 L 3037 yds SSS 72
V'tors U SOC
Fees £8.50 (£10)
Loc 2 miles W of Guildford on
A323
Mis Driving range
Arch Alan Helling

Royal Automobile Club (1913)

Woodcote Park, Epsom, KT18 7EW
Tel (01372) 276311
Fax (01372) 276117
Sec D Adams
Pro I Howieson (01372) 279514
Holes Old 18 L 6709 yds SSS 72
Coronation 18 L 6223 yds
SSS 70
V'tors M SOC
Loc Epsom Station 2 miles
Arch Fowler/Myddleton

Royal Mid-Surrey (1892)

Old Deer Park, Richmond, TW9 2SB
Tel (020) 8940 1894
Fax (020) 8332 2957
Web www.rmsgc.co.uk
Mem 1420
Sec AT Marsden
Pro P Talbot (020) 8940 0459
Holes Outer 18 L 6385 yds SSS 70
Inner 18 L 5446 yds SSS 67
V'tors WD–H or M WE/BH–M SOC
Fees D–£68
Loc Nr Richmond roundabout, off
A316
Arch JH Taylor

Royal Wimbledon (1865)

*29 Camp Road, Wimbledon Common,
London, SW19 4UW*
Tel (020) 8946 2125
Fax (020) 8944 8652
Web www.rwgc.co.uk
Mem 800
Sec NI Smith
Pro H Boyle (020) 8946 4606
Holes 18 L 6348 yds SSS 70
V'tors WD–H by arrangement
Loc Wimbledon Common, 2 miles
S of A23 Tibbets Corner
Arch HS Colt

Rusper (1992)

Rusper Road, Newdigate, RH5 5BX
Tel (01293) 871456,
(01293) 871871 (Bookings)
Fax (01293) 871456
Mem 235
Sec Mrs J Thornhill
Pro Janice Arnold (01293) 871871
Holes 18 L 6597 yds SSS 69
V'tors U SOC
Fees 18 holes–£11.50 (£15.50)
9 holes–£8 (£10)
Loc 5 miles S of Dorking, off A24
Mis Driving range
Arch AW Blunden

St George's Hill (1912)

Golf Club Road, St George's Hill,
Weybridge, KT13 0NL

Tel	(01932) 847758
Fax	(01932) 821564
Web	www.stgeorgeshillgolfclub
	.co.uk
Mem	600
Sec	J Robinson
Pro	AC Rattue (01932) 843523
Holes	27 L 6097-6496 yds SSS 69-71
V'tors	WD–I H WE/BH–M SOC–Wed–Fri
Fees	£65 D–£90
Loc	2 miles N of M25/A3 Junction, on B374
Arch	HS Colt

Sandown Park Golf Centre (1970)

Public
More Lane, Esher, KT10 8AN

Tel	(01372) 461234
Fax	(01372) 461203
Web	www.sandown.co.uk
Mem	500
Sec	D Parr (Mgr)
Pro	J Skinner (01372) 461282
Holes	9 L 5658 yds SSS 67
	9 hole Par 3 course
V'tors	U–closed on race days
Fees	£6.75 (£8.50)
Loc	Sandown Park Racecourse
Mis	Floodlit driving range
Arch	John Jacobs

Selsdon Park Hotel (1929)

Addington Road, Sanderstead, South
Croydon, CR2 8YA

Tel	(020) 8657 8811
Fax	(020) 8657 3401
Sec	Mrs C Screene
Pro	M Churchill
	(020) 8657 4129
Holes	18 L 6473 yds SSS 71
V'tors	U SOC (min 12 golfers)
Fees	£20 (£30)
Loc	3 miles S of Croydon on A2022 Purley-Addington road
Mis	Driving range
Arch	JH Taylor

Shirley Park (1914)

194 Addiscombe Road, Croydon,
CR0 7LB

Tel	(020) 8654 1143
Fax	(020) 8654 6733
Web	www.shirleyparkgolfclub .co.uk
Mem	600
Sec	D Roy
Pro	W Grant (020) 8654 8767
Holes	18 L 6210 yds SSS 70
V'tors	WD–U WE/BH–M SOC
Fees	£35
Loc	On A232, 1 mile E of East Croydon Station

Silvermere (1976)

Pay and play
Redhill Road, Cobham, KT11 1EF

Tel	(01932) 867275
Fax	(01932) 868259
Web	www.crowngolf.co.uk
Mem	750
Sec	Mrs P Devereux
Pro	D McClelland
Holes	18 L 6027 yds SSS 71
V'tors	WD–U WE–NA before 11am SOC
Fees	£20 (£30)
Loc	¹/₂ mile from M25 Junction 10 on B366 to Byfleet
Mis	Floodlit driving range

Sunningdale (1900)

Ridgemount Road, Sunningdale, Berks,
SL5 9RR

Tel	(01344) 621681
Fax	(01344) 624154
Mem	900
Sec	S Zuill
Pro	K Maxwell (01344) 620128
Holes	Old 18 L 6581 yds SSS 72
	New 18 L 6617 yds SSS 73
V'tors	Mon–Thurs–I Fri/WE–M
Fees	Old–£120 New–£85
Loc	Sunningdale Station ¹/₄ mile, off A30
Arch	Willie Park/HS Colt

Sunningdale Ladies (1902)

Cross Road, Sunningdale, SL5 9RX

Tel	(01344) 620507
Mem	400
Sec	JF Darroch
Holes	18 L 3622 yds SSS 60
V'tors	WD/WE–by appointment. No 3 or 4 balls before 10.30 am
Fees	£22 (£25)
Loc	Sunningdale Station ¹/₄ mile
Arch	HS Colt

Surbiton (1895)

Woodstock Lane, Chessington,
KT9 1UG

Tel	(020) 8398 3101
Fax	(020) 8339 0992
Mem	800
Sec	DR Crockford
Pro	P Milton (020) 8398 6619
Holes	18 L 6055 yds SSS 69
V'tors	WD–H WE/BH–M
Fees	£30 D–£45
Loc	2 miles E of Esher

Sutton Green (1994)

New Lane, Sutton Green, Guildford,
GU4 7QF

Tel	(01483) 747898
Fax	(01483) 750289
Mem	600
Sec	J Buchanan
Pro	P Tedder (01483) 766849
Holes	18 L 6300 yds Par 71 SSS 70
V'tors	WD–U WE–U after 2pm

Fees	£40 (£50)
Loc	2 miles S of Woking
Arch	Walker/Davies

Tandridge (1925)

Oxted, RH8 9NQ

Tel	(01883) 712273 (Clubhouse)
Fax	(01883) 730537
Web	www.tandridgegolfclub.com
Mem	750
Sec	Lt Cdr SE Kennard RN (01883) 712274
Pro	C Evans (01883) 713701
Holes	18 L 6250 yds SSS 70
V'tors	Mon/Wed/Thurs only–H SOC–Mon/Wed/Thurs
Fees	On application
Loc	5 miles E of Redhill, off A25. M25 Junction 6
Arch	HS Colt

Thames Ditton & Esher (1892)

Portsmouth Road, Esher, KT10 9AL

Tel	(020) 8398 1551
Mem	150
Sec	A Barry
Pro	R Jones
Holes	9 L 5419 yds SSS 65
V'tors	WD–U WE–by arrangement
Fees	£10 (£12)
Loc	Esher

Tyrrells Wood (1924)

Tyrrells Wood, Leatherhead, KT22 8QP

Tel	(01372) 376025 (2 lines)
Fax	(01372) 360836
Web	www.tyrrellswood-golfclub.co.uk
Mem	744
Sec	CGR Kydd
Pro	S DeFoy (01372) 375200
Holes	18 L 6282 yds SSS 70
V'tors	WD–I BH/Sat–NA Sun–NA before noon SOC
Fees	£34 (£44)
Loc	2 miles SE of Leatherhead, off A24 nr Headley. M25 Junction 9, 1 mile

Walton Heath (1903)

Deans Lane, Walton-on-the-Hill,
Tadworth, KT20 7TP

Tel	(01737) 812060
Fax	(01737) 814225
Web	www.whgc.co.uk
Mem	900
Sec	M Bawden (01737) 812380
Pro	K Macpherson (01737) 812152
Holes	Old 18 L 6801 yds SSS 73
	New 18 L 6609 yds SSS 72
V'tors	WD–I H WE/BH–M SOC
Fees	On application
Loc	18 miles S of London on A217/B2032. 2 miles N of M25 Junction 8
Arch	WH Fowler

For list of abbreviations see page 649

Wentworth Club (1924)

*Wentworth Drive, Virginia Water,
GU25 4LS*

Tel	(01344) 842201
Fax	(01344) 842804
Web	www.wentworthclub.com
Mem	3622
Sec	S Christie (Admin)
Pro	D Rennie (01344) 846306
Holes	West 18 L 7047 yds SSS 74
	East 18 L 6201 yds SSS 70
	Edinburgh 18 L 7004 yds SSS 74
	Executive 9 L 1902 yds Par 27
V'tors	WD–H by prior arrangement WE–M SOC–WD
Fees	On application
Loc	21 miles SW of London at A30/A329 junction. M25 Junction 13, 3 miles
Mis	Driving range
Arch	HS Colt (East/West) Jacobs/Player (Edinburgh)

West Byfleet (1906)

*Sheerwater Road, West Byfleet,
KT14 6AA*

Tel	(01932) 345230
Fax	(01932) 340667
Mem	550
Sec	DG Lee (Gen Mgr) (01932) 343433
Pro	D Regan (01932) 346584
Holes	18 L 6211 yds SSS 70
V'tors	WD–U WE/BH–NA SOC
Fees	£32 D–£42
Loc	West Byfleet ½ mile on A245. M25 Junction 10 or 11
Arch	CS Butchart

West Hill (1907)

Bagshot Road, Brookwood, GU24 0BH

Tel	(01483) 474365/472110
Fax	(01483) 474252
Web	www.westhill-golfclub.co.uk
Mem	550
Sec	MC Swatton
Pro	JA Clements (01483) 473172
Holes	18 L 6368 yds Par 69 SSS 70
V'tors	WD–H WE–M SOC
Fees	£45 D–£60
Loc	5 miles W of Woking on A322
Arch	CS Butchart

West Surrey (1910)

Enton Green, Godalming, GU8 5AF

Tel	(01483) 421275
Fax	(01483) 415419
Mem	750
Sec	RT Crabb
Pro	A Tawse (01483) 417278
Holes	18 L 6300 yds SSS 70
V'tors	H SOC–Wed/Thurs/Fri
Fees	£27 (£48)
Loc	½ mile SE of Milford Station
Arch	Herbert Fowler

Wildwood (1992)

Horsham Road, Alfold GU6 8JE

Tel	(01403) 753255

Fax	(01403) 752005
Web	www.wildwoodgolf.co.uk
Mem	640
Sec	Sue Zacchetti (Gen Mgr)
Pro	N Parfrement
Holes	18 L 6655 yds SSS 73
V'tors	WE–NA before noon SOC
Fees	£30 (£45)
Loc	10 miles S of Guildford on A281
Mis	Driving range
Arch	Hawtree

Wimbledon Common (1908)

*19 Camp Road, Wimbledon Common,
London, SW19 4UW*

Tel	(020) 8946 0294
Fax	(020) 8947 8697
Mem	275
Sec	RJW Pierce (020) 8946 7571
Pro	JS Jukes
Holes	18 L 5438 yds SSS 66
V'tors	WD–U WE–M SOC
Fees	WD–£15 exc Mon–£10
Loc	Wimbledon Common
Mis	Pillarbox red outer garment must be worn. London Scottish play here
Arch	Willie Dunn/Tom Dunn

Wimbledon Park (1898)

Home Park Road, London, SW19 7HR

Tel	(020) 8946 1002
Fax	(020) 8944 8688
Web	www.wpgc.co.uk
Mem	650
Sec	Mrs E Inwood (020) 8946 1250
Pro	D Wingrove (020) 8946 4053
Holes	18 L 5492 yds SSS 66
V'tors	WD–H I WE/BH–after 3pm SOC
Fees	D–£40 (£40)
Loc	2 miles from A3 at Tibbets Corner

Windlemere (1978)

Pay and play
*Windlesham Road, West End, Woking,
GU24 9QL*

Tel	(01276) 858727
Fax	(01276) 678837
Sec	CD Smith
Pro	D Thomas
Holes	9 L 5346 yds SSS 66
V'tors	U
Fees	9 holes–£9 (£10.50)
Loc	A319 at Lightwater/West End
Mis	Floodlit driving range
Arch	Clive D Smith

Windlesham (1994)

Grove End, Bagshot, GU19 5HY

Tel	(01276) 452220
Fax	(01276) 452290
Web	www.windleshamgolf.com
Mem	800
Sec	CJ Lumley
Pro	L Mucklow (01276) 472323

Holes	18 L 6650 yds SSS 72
V'tors	H–phone first WE–pm only SOC–WD
Fees	£25 (£35)
Loc	½ mile N of M3 Junction 3, off A30/A322
Mis	Driving range
Arch	Tommy Horton

The Wisley (1991)

Ripley, Woking, GU23 6QU

Tel	(01483) 211022
Fax	(01483) 211662
Mem	700
Sec	AD Lawrence (Gen Mgr)
Pro	D Pugh (01483) 211213
Holes	27 holes SSS 73:
	Church 9 L 3356 yds;
	Garden 9 L 3385 yds;
	Mill 9 L 3473 yds
V'tors	M
Loc	1 mile S of M25 Junction 10
Arch	Robert Trent Jones Jr

Woking (1893)

*Pond Road, Hook Heath, Woking,
GU22 0JZ*

Tel	(01483) 760053
Fax	(01483) 772441
Mem	500
Sec	G Ritchie
Pro	C Bianco (01483) 769582
Holes	18 L 6340 yds SSS 70
V'tors	WD–H WE/BH–M SOC–WD
Fees	£55
Loc	W of Woking in St John's / Hook Heath area
Arch	Tom Dunn

Woodcote Park (1912)

*Meadow Hill, Bridle Way, Coulsdon,
CR5 2QQ*

Tel	(020) 8668 2788
Fax	(020) 8660 0918
Mem	630
Sec	KR Brabbins
Pro	I Golding (020) 8668 1843
Holes	18 L 6669 yds Par 71 SSS 72
V'tors	WD–U WE–M
Fees	£35 D–£45
Loc	Purley 2 miles. M25 Junction 7
Arch	HS Colt

Worplesdon (1908)

*Heath House Road, Woking,
GU22 0RA*

Tel	(01483) 472277
Fax	(01483) 473303
Mem	600
Sec	JT Christine
Pro	JT Christine (01483) 473287
Holes	18 L 6440 yds SSS 71
V'tors	WD–H WE–M
Fees	On application
Loc	E of Woking, off A322. 6 miles N of Guildford (A3). 6 miles S of M3 Junction 3

Sussex (East)

Brighton & Hove (1887)

Devils Dyke Road, Brighton, BN1 8YJ

Tel   (01273) 556482
Fax   (01273) 554247
Mem 320
Sec   P Bonsall (Golf Dir)
Pro   P Bonsall (01273) 540560
Holes 9 L 5704 yds SSS 68
V'tors U SOC Sun–NA before noon
Fees   £17 (£25)
Loc   4 miles N of Brighton
Arch James Braid

Cooden Beach (1912)

Cooden Beach, Bexhill-on-Sea, TN39 4TR

Tel   (01424) 842040
Fax   (01424) 842040
Mem 700
Sec   PJT Svehlik
Pro   J Sim (01424) 843938
Holes 18 L 6500 yds SSS 71
V'tors H SOC
Fees   £32 (£35)
Loc   W boundary of Bexhill
Arch Herbert Fowler

Crowborough Beacon (1895)

Beacon Road, Crowborough, TN6 1UJ

Tel   (01892) 661511
Fax   (01892) 611988
Web   www.crowboroughbeacongolf
      club.co.uk
Mem 700
Sec   Mrs V Harwood
      (01892) 661511
Pro   D Newnham (01892) 653877
Holes 18 L 6273 yds SSS 70
V'tors I H WE/BH–M
Fees   £27.50–£40
Loc   9 miles S of Tunbridge Wells
      on A26

Dale Hill Hotel (1973)

Ticehurst, Wadhurst, TN5 7DQ

Tel   (01580) 200112
Fax   (01580) 201249
Web   www.dalehill.co.uk
Mem 1000
Sec   Ms M Harris (Golf Dir)
Pro   A Good (01580) 201090
Holes 18 L 5856 yds SSS 69
      Woosnam 18 L 6512 yds
      SSS 71
V'tors U SOC
Fees   £20 (£30) Woosnam–£45
      (£55)
Loc   B2087, off A21 at Flimwell
Mis   Driving range

Dewlands Manor (1992)

Cottage Hill, Rotherfield, TN6 3JN

Tel   (01892) 852266
Fax   (01892) 853015
Sec   T Robins
Pro   N Godin
Holes 9 L 3186 yds Par 36
V'tors U–phone first
Fees   9 holes–£14 (£16)
      18 holes–£25 (£30)
Loc   1/2 mile S of Rotherfield, off
      A267/B2101. 10 miles S of
      Tunbridge Wells. M25
      Junction 5
Arch Reg Godin

The Dyke (1906)

Devil's Dyke, Devil's Dyke Road, Brighton, BN1 8YJ

Tel   (01273) 857296
Fax   (01273) 857078
Mem 750
Sec   MD Harrity (Sec/Mgr)
Pro   R Arnold (01273) 857260
Holes 18 L 6611 yds SSS 72
V'tors WD–U H WE–U H after
      noon SOC–WD
Fees   £28 D–£38 (£35)
Loc   4 miles N of Brighton
Arch Fred Hawtree

East Brighton (1893)

Roedean Road, Brighton, BN2 5RA

Tel   (01273) 604838
Fax   (01273) 680277
Mem 650
Sec   DM Jackson
Pro   M Stuart-William
      (01273) 603989
Holes 18 L 6346 yds SSS 70
V'tors WD–U H after 9am WE–NA
      before 11am SOC
Fees   £25 D–£35 (£30)
Loc   1 1/2 miles E of Town Centre,
      overlooking Marina
Arch James Braid

East Sussex National (1989)

Little Horsted, Uckfield, TN22 5ES

Tel   (01825) 880088
Fax   (01825) 880066
Web   www.eastsussexnational.co.uk
Mem 770
Sec   R Archer, B Street
Pro   S MacLennan
      (01825) 841111
Holes East 18 L 7138 yds SSS 74
      West 18 L 7154 yds SSS 74
V'tors U on one course
Fees   Summer–£50 (£55)
      Winter–£40 (£45)
Loc   2 miles S of Uckfield, on A22
Mis   Driving range. Golf academy
Arch Bob Cupp

Eastbourne Downs (1908)

East Dean Road, Eastbourne, BN20 8ES

Tel   (01323) 720827
Fax   (01323) 412506
Mem 550
Sec   AJ Reeves
Pro   T Marshall (01323) 732264
Holes 18 L 6601 yds SSS 72
V'tors WD–U WE–NA before 11am
Fees   D–£23
Loc   1/2 mile W of Eastbourne on
      A259
Arch JH Taylor

Eastbourne Golfing Park (1992)

Pay and play
Lottbridge Drove, Eastbourne, BN23 6QJ

Tel   (01323) 520400
Fax   (01323) 520400
Mem 250
Sec   R Parsons
Pro   B Finch
Holes 9 L 5046 yds SSS 65
V'tors U
Fees   £9 (£14)
Loc   1/2 mile S of Hampden Park
Mis   Floodlit driving range
Arch David Ashton

Hastings G&CC (1973)

Beauport Park, Battle Road, St Leonards-on-Sea, TN37 7BP

Tel   (01424) 854243
Fax   (01424) 854244
Web   www.hastingsgolfclub.com
Mem 300
Sec   M Strevett
Pro   C Giddins (01424) 852981
Holes 18 L 6180 yds SSS 71
V'tors U–booking necessary SOC
Fees   £14 (£17.50)
Loc   3 miles N of Hastings, off
      A2100 Battle road
Mis   Driving range

Highwoods (1925)

Ellerslie Lane, Bexhill-on-Sea, TN39 4LJ

Tel   (01424) 212625
Fax   (01424) 216866
Mem 800
Sec   LM Dennis-Smither
Pro   MJ Andrews (01424) 212770
Holes 18 L 6218 yds SSS 70
V'tors WD/Sat–H Sun am–M Sun
      pm–H
Fees   £28 (£33)
Loc   2 miles N of Bexhill
Arch JH Taylor

Hollingbury Park (1908)

Public
Ditchling Road, Brighton, BN1 7HS

Tel   (01273) 552010
Fax   (01273) 552010
Web   www.hollingburygolfclub
      .co.uk
Mem 300
Sec   Mrs M Bailey
Pro   G Crompton (01273) 500086
Holes 18 L 6415 yds SSS 71
V'tors U SOC
Fees   £12 (£17)
Loc   1 mile NE of Brighton

Holtye (1893)

Holtye, Cowden, Edenbridge, TN8 7ED
Tel   (01342) 850635
Fax   (01342) 850576
Mem   430
Sec   JP Holmes (01342) 850576
Pro   K Hinton (01342) 850957
Holes 9 L 5325 yds SSS 66
V'tors WD–U exc Wed/Thurs
         am–NA WE–NA before noon
         SOC–Tues & Fri
Fees   D–£16 (£18)
Loc   4 miles E of E Grinstead on
         A264

Horam Park (1985)

Pay and play
Chiddingly Road, Horam, TN21 0JJ
Tel   (01435) 813477
Fax   (01435) 813677
Web   www.horamparkgolf.co.uk
Mem   400
Sec   Mrs A Briggs
Pro   G Velvick
Holes 9 L 6128 yds SSS 70
V'tors U SOC
Fees   18 holes–£15.50 (£17)
         9 holes–£10.50 (£11)
Loc   ½ mile S of Horam towards
         Chiddingley. 12 miles N of
         Eastbourne on A267
Mis   Floodlit driving range. Pitch &
         putt course
Arch Glen Johnson

Lewes (1896)

Chapel Hill, Lewes, BN7 2BB
Tel   (01273) 473245
Fax   (01273) 483474
Mem   650
Sec   Miss J Raffety
         (01273) 483474
Pro   P Dobson (01273) 483823
Holes 18 L 6220 yds Par 71 SSS 70
V'tors WD–U WE–NA before 2pm
         SOC
Fees   £21 (£31)
Loc   ½ mile from Lewes at E end
         of Cliffe High Street

Mid Sussex (1995)

Spatham Lane, Ditchling, BN6 8XJ
Tel   (01273) 846567
Fax   (01273) 845767
Mem   600
Sec   J Tippett-Iles (Mgr)
Pro   C Connell
Holes 18 L 6450 yds Par 71 SSS 71
V'tors WD–U WE–pm only
         SOC–WD
Fees   £20
Loc   1 mile E of Ditchling
Mis   Driving range
Arch David Williams

Nevill (1912)

*Benhall Mill Road, Tunbridge Wells,
TN2 5JW*
Tel   (01892) 525818
Fax   (01892) 517861
Mem   550 142(L) 78(J)

Sec   TJ Fensom
Pro   P Huggett (01892) 532941
Holes 18 L 6349 yds SSS 70
V'tors WD–H WE/BH–M
Fees   £33
Loc   Tunbridge Wells 1 mile

Peacehaven (1895)

Brighton Road, Newhaven, BN9 9UH
Tel   (01273) 514049
Fax   (01273) 512571
Mem   290
Sec   Mrs D Corke (01273) 512571
Pro   I Pearson (01273) 512602
Holes 9 L 5488 yds SSS 69
V'tors WD–U WE/BH–after 11am
         SOC
Fees   £12 (£18)
Loc   8 miles E of Brighton on A259
Arch James Braid

Piltdown (1904)

Piltdown, Uckfield, TN22 3XB
Tel   (01825) 722033
Fax   (01825) 724192
Mem   400
Sec   CM Lewis (Hon)
Pro   J Partridge (01825) 722389
Holes 18 L 6070 yds SSS 69
V'tors I or H exc BH/Tues am/Thurs
         am/Sun am SOC
Fees   £30 D–£40
Loc   1 mile W of Maresfield, off
         A272 towards Isfield

Royal Ashdown Forest
(1888)

*Chapel Lane, Forest Row, East
Grinstead, RH18 5LR*
Tel   (01342) 822018/823014 (Old),
         (01342) 824866 (West)
Fax   (01342) 825211/824869
Web   www.royalashdown.co.uk
Mem   450
Sec   DED Neave
Pro   MA Landsborough
         (01342) 822247
Holes Old 18 L 6477 yds SSS 71
         West 18 L 5606 yds SSS 67
V'tors On application–phone first
Fees   Old–£45 D–£55 (£60 R/D)
         West £18 (£23)
Loc   4 miles S of E Grinstead on
         B2110 Hartfield road. M25
         Junction 6

Royal Eastbourne (1887)

Paradise Drive, Eastbourne, BN20 8BP
Tel   (01323) 729738
Fax   (01323) 729738
Mem   850
Sec   PG White
Pro   R Wooller (01323) 736986
Holes 18 L 6131 yds SSS 69
         9 L 2147 yds SSS 61
V'tors U H SOC
Fees   18 hole:£25 (£35) 9 hole:£15
Loc   ½ mile from Town Hall

Rye (1894)

Camber, Rye, TN31 7QS
Tel   (01797) 225241/225460
Fax   (01797) 225460
Mem   1000 125(L) 100(J)
Sec   JAL Smith
Pro   MP Lee (01797) 225218
Holes 18 L 6308 yds SSS 71
         9 L 6141 yds SSS 70
V'tors M
Loc   3 miles E of Rye on B2075
Arch HS Colt

Seaford (1887)

East Blatchington, Seaford, BN25 2JD
Tel   (01323) 892442
Fax   (01323) 894113
Web   www.seafordgolfclub.co.uk
Mem   420 110(L) 37(J)
Sec   PAA Court (Gen Mgr)
Pro   (01323) 894160
Holes 18 L 6233 yds SSS 70
V'tors WD–U after 10am exc Tues
         WE–M SOC
Fees   £25 D–£35
Loc   1 mile N of Seaford (A259)
Mis   Driving range
Arch JH Taylor

Seaford Head (1907)

Public
Southdown Road, Seaford, BN25 4JS
Tel   (01323) 890139
Sec   I Perkins (01323) 894843
Pro   AJ Lowles (01323) 890139
Holes 18 L 5812 yds SSS 68
V'tors U
Fees   £15 (£18)
Loc   8 miles W of Eastbourne. ¾
         mile S of A259

Sedlescombe (1990)

Owned privately
Kent Street, Sedlescombe, TN33 0SD
Tel   (01424) 870898
Fax   (01424) 870855
Mem   380
Sec   Mrs A Briggs
Pro   J Andrews
Holes 18 L 6218 yds Par 72
V'tors WD–H WE–M
Fees   On application
Loc   5 miles N of Hastings
Mis   Floodlit driving range
Arch Glen Johnson

Waterhall (1923)

Public
Waterhall Road, Brighton, BN1 8YR
Tel   (01273) 508658
Mem   300
Sec   LB Allen
Pro   P Charman
Holes 18 L 5775 yds SSS 68
V'tors WD–U WE–U after 8am
Fees   £11.50 (£11.50)
Loc   3 miles NW of Brighton between
         A23 and A27. 1 mile N of
         A2308

For list of abbreviations see page 649

Wellhurst G&CC (1992)

North Street, Hellingly, BN27 4EE

Tel   (01435) 813636
Fax   (01435) 812444
Mem   400
Sec   M Adams (Man Dir)
Pro   M Jarvis (01435) 813456
Holes   18 L 5771 yds SSS 68
V'tors   U SOC
Fees   £18 (£22)
Loc   2 miles N of Hailsham on A267
Mis   Driving range

West Hove (1910)

Church Farm, Hangleton, Hove, BN3 8AN

Tel   (01273) 413411 (Clubhouse)
Fax   (01273) 439988
Web   www.westhovegolfclub.co.uk
Mem   600
Sec   K Haste (Mgr) (01273) 419738
Pro   D Cook (01273) 413494
Holes   18 L 6201 yds SSS 70 Par 70
V'tors   U–phone first SOC
Fees   On application
Loc   N of Brighton By-pass. 2nd junction W from A23 flyover
Mis   Practice driving range
Arch   Hawtree

Willingdon (1898)

Southdown Road, Eastbourne, BN20 9AA

Tel   (01323) 410981
Fax   (01323) 411510
Mem   550
Sec   Mrs J Packham (01323) 410981
Pro   T Moore (01323) 410984
Holes   18 L 6049 yds SSS 69
V'tors   WD–U H WE–MH exc Sun am–NA SOC–H
Fees   D–£25 (£28)
Loc   ½ mile N of Eastbourne, off A22
Arch   JH Taylor/Dr A Mackenzie

Sussex (West)

Avisford Park (1990)

Pay and play
Yapton Lane, Walberton, Arundel, BN18 0LS

Tel   (01243) 554611
Mem   200
Sec   N Upjohn
Pro   R Beach
Holes   18 L 5390 yds Par 67 SSS 66
V'tors   U SOC
Fees   £12 (£15)
Loc   4 miles W of Arundel on A27

Bognor Regis (1892)

Downview Road, Felpham, Bognor Regis, PO22 8JD

Tel   (01243) 865867
Fax   (01243) 860719
Web   www.bognorgolfclub.co.uk
Mem   750
Sec   PD Badger (01243) 821929
Pro   S Bassil (01243) 865209
Holes   18 L 6238 yds Par 70 SSS 70
V'tors   WD–I or H after 9.30am WE/BH–M (Apr–Sept) –I H (Oct–Mar) SOC–WD
Fees   £25 (£30)
Loc   2 miles E of Bognor Regis, off A259
Arch   James Braid

Brinsbury College (1991)

North Heath, Pulborough, RH20 1DZ

Tel   (01798) 872218
Fax   (01798) 875222
Mem   200
Sec   S Hall (01798) 877421
Pro   S Hall (01798) 877421
Holes   9 holes Par 62 SSS 57
V'tors   WD–U WE–U exc Sun am–NA SOC–WD
Fees   £8 (£12)
Loc   2 miles N of Pulborough on A29
Mis   Driving range

Burgess Hill Golf Centre

Pay and play
Cuckfield Road, Burgess Hill

Tel   (01444) 258585
Fax   (01444) 247318
Web   www.golfsussex.co.uk
Sec   CJ Collins (Mgr)
Pro   M Green
Holes   9 hole Par 3 course
V'tors   U
Fees   On application
Loc   N of Burgess Hill
Mis   Floodlit driving range
Arch   Steel/Collins

Chartham Park (1993)

Proprietary
Felcourt, East Grinstead, RH19 2JT

Tel   (01342) 870340
Fax   (01342) 870719
Sec   PJ Smith (Gen Mgr)
Pro   D Hobbs (01342) 870008
Holes   18 L 6688 yds Par 72 SSS 72
V'tors   WD–U WE–U after 12 noon
Fees   £30 (£35)
Loc   2 miles N of East Grinstead, off A22. M25 Junction 6
Mis   Driving range
Arch   Neil Coles

Chichester (1990)

Hunston Village, Chichester, PO20 6AX

Tel   (01243) 533833
Fax   (01243) 539922
Web   www.chichestergolf.com
Mem   575
Pro   J Slinger
Holes   18 L 6442 yds SSS 71
        18 L 6109 yds SSS 69
        9 hole Par 3 course
V'tors   U SOC
Fees   £16–£21 (£21–£29)
Loc   2 miles S of A27 on B2145 to Selsey
Mis   Driving range
Arch   Phillip Sanders

Copthorne (1892)

Borers Arm Road, Copthorne, RH10 3LL

Tel   (01342) 712508
Fax   (01342) 717682
Web   www.copthornegolfclub.co.uk
Mem   565
Sec   JP Pyne (01342) 712033
Pro   J Burrell (01342) 712405
Holes   18 L 6505 yds SSS 71
V'tors   WD–U WE/BH–after 1pm SOC
Fees   £32 (£40)
Loc   1 mile E of M23 Junction 10, on A264
Arch   James Braid

Cottesmore (1975)

Buchan Hill, Pease Pottage, Crawley, RH11 9AT

Tel   (01293) 528256
Fax   (01293) 522819
Mem   900
Sec   B Pearmaine
Pro   C Callan (01293) 535399
Holes   Griffin 18 L 6248 yds Par 71 SSS 70;
        Phoenix 18 L 5514 yds Par 69 SSS 67
V'tors   U SOC
Fees   Griffin–£18 (£24) Phoenix–£15 (£20)
Loc   4 miles S of Crawley, off M23 Junction 11
Arch   MD Rogerson

Cowdray Park (1920)

Petworth Road, Midhurst, GU29 0BB

Tel   (01730) 813599
Fax   (01730) 815900
Mem   700
Sec   D Rodbard (Gen Mgr)
Pro   R Gough (01730) 812091
Holes   18 L 6212 yds SSS 70
V'tors   WD–H WE/BH–H NA before 11.30am SOC
Fees   £26 (£36)
Loc   1 mile E of Midhurst on A272
Arch   T Simpson

Effingham Park (1980)

West Park Road, Copthorne, RH10 3EU

Tel   (01342) 716528
Fax   (01342) 716039
Mem   300
Sec   IWB McRobbie (Hon)
Pro   M Root
Holes   9 L 1815 yds Par 30 SSS 57
V'tors   WD–U exc Wed & Thurs before 12 noon WE–U after 11.30am
Fees   £9 D–£14 (£11 D–£16)
Loc   B2028/B2039. M23 Junction 10

Mis Golf academy
Arch Francisco Escario

Foxbridge (1993)

Foxbridge Lane, Plaistow, RH14 0LB
Tel (01403) 753303
　　　(Bookings)
Fax (01403) 753433
Mem 300
Sec PA Clark
Pro S Hall
Holes 9 L 3118 yds SSS 70
V'tors U SOC
Fees £18 (£25)
Loc 15 miles S of Guildford, off B2133
Arch Paul Clark

Goodwood (1892)

Kennel Hill, Goodwood, Chichester, PO18 0PN
Tel (01243) 774968
Fax (01243) 781741
Mem 900
Sec Carole Davison
　　　(01243) 774968
Pro K MacDonald
　　　(01243) 774994
Holes 18 L 6401 yds SSS 71
V'tors WD–H after 9am WE–H after 10am SOC–Wed & Thurs
Fees £32 (£42)
Loc 3 miles NE of Chichester, on road to racecourse
Arch James Braid

Goodwood Park G&CC (1989)

Goodwood, Chichester, PO18 0QB
Tel (01243) 520117
Mem 700
Sec M Pierce
Pro A Wratting
Holes 18 L 6530 yds SSS 72
V'tors WD–H WE/BH–NA before noon H SOC
Fees £28 (£35)
Loc 4 miles N of Chichester
Mis Driving range
Arch Donald Steel

Ham Manor (1936)

West Drive, Angmering, Littlehampton, BN16 4JE
Tel (01903) 783288
Fax (01903) 850886
Web www.hammanor.co.uk
Mem 860
Sec VJ Chaszczewski
Pro S Buckley
　　　(01903) 783732
Holes 18 L 6216 yds SSS 70
V'tors WD/WE–H
Fees On application
Loc Between Worthing and Littlehampton
Arch HS Colt

Hassocks (1995)

Pay and play
London Road, Hassocks, BN6 9NA
Tel (01273) 846990
Fax (01273) 846070
Web www.hassocksgolfclub.co.uk
Mem 350
Sec Mrs J Brown (Gen Mgr)
　　　(01273) 846630
Pro C Ledger (01273) 846990
Holes 18 L 5754 yds Par 70 SSS 68
V'tors U
Fees £14.25 (£17.50)
Loc 1 mile S of Burgess Hill on A273. 7 miles N of Brighton
Arch Paul Wright

Haywards Heath (1922)

High Beech Lane, Haywards Heath, RH16 1SL
Tel (01444) 414457
Fax (01444) 458319
Mem 771
Sec GB Kullner
Pro M Henning (01444) 414866
Holes 18 L 6248 yds SSS 70
V'tors WD/WE–H–restricted SOC–Wed & Thurs
Fees £26 (£36)
Loc 2 miles N of Haywards Heath, off B2112

Hill Barn (1935)

Public
Hill Barn Lane, Worthing, BN14 9QE
Tel (01903) 237301
Pro AP Higgins
Holes 18 L 6224 yds SSS 70
V'tors U
Fees £12.50 (£13.50)
Loc NE of A27 at Warren Road roundabout
Arch Hawtree

Horsham (1993)

Pay and play
Worthing Road, Horsham, RH13 7AX
Tel (01403) 271525
Fax (01403) 274528
Mem 300
Sec E Purton (01403) 271525
Pro A Fitt
Holes 9 L 2061 yds Par 33 SSS 30
V'tors U SOC
Fees 9 holes–£6 (£7)
Loc 1 mile S of Horsham, off A24

Ifield (1927)

Rusper Road, Ifield, Crawley, RH11 0LN
Tel (01293) 520222
Fax (01293) 612973
Mem 875
Sec DJ Knight
Pro J Earl (01293) 523088
Holes 18 L 6330 yds SSS 70
V'tors WD–H WE–M SOC
Fees £26 D–£36
Loc W of Crawley. M23 Junction 11
Arch Hawtree/Taylor

Littlehampton (1889)

170 Rope Walk, Littlehampton, BN17 5DL
Tel (01903) 717170
Fax (01903) 726629
Mem 650
Sec A Sapsed
Pro G McQuitty
　　　(01903) 716369
Holes 18 L 6244 yds SSS 70
V'tors WD–U after 9.30am WE/BH–NA before noon SOC
Fees £28 (£35)
Loc W bank of River Arun, Littlehampton
Arch Hawtree

Mannings Heath (1905)

Fullers, Hammerpond Road, Mannings Heath, Horsham RH13 6PG
Tel (01403) 210228
Fax (01403) 270974
Web www.exclusivehotels.co.uk
Mem 730
Sec S Kershaw
Pro C Tucker (01403) 210228
Holes Waterfall 18 L 6378 yds SSS 70;
　　　Kingfisher 18 L 6217 yds SSS 70
V'tors U H SOC
Fees £34 (£42)
Loc 3 miles SE of Horsham (A281). M23 Junction 11
Mis Driving range
Arch Kingfisher-David Williams

Paxhill Park (1990)

East Mascalls Lane, Lindfield, RH16 2QN
Tel (01444) 484467
Fax (01444) 482709
Mem 540
Sec JD Bowen
Pro M Green
Holes 18 L 6196 yds SSS 68
V'tors WD–U WE–pm only
Fees £15 (£20)
Loc 1 mile N of Lindfield, off B2028. 4 miles NE of Haywards Heath
Mis Driving range
Arch Patrick Tallack

Pease Pottage (1986)

Horsham Road, Pease Pottage, Crawley, RH11 9AP
Tel (01293) 521706
Mem 56
Sec A Venn
Pro D Blair
Holes 9 L 3511 yds SSS 57
V'tors U
Fees £8.50 (£11)
Loc S of Crawley, off A23. M23 Junction 11
Mis Driving range

Petworth (1989)

Pay and play
London Road, Petworth, GU28 9LX
Tel   **(01798) 344097**
Fax   (01798) 342528
Mem 105
Sec   A Long (Mgr)
     (01798) 344097
Pro   J Little (01428) 605093
Holes 18 L 6191 yds Par 71 SSS 69
V'tors U SOC
Fees £10 D–£13.50
Loc   2¹/₂ miles N of Petworth on
     A283
Mis   Driving range
Arch C & T Duncton

Pyecombe (1894)

*Clayton Hill, Pyecombe, Brighton,
BN45 7FF*
Tel   **(01273) 845372**
Fax   (01273) 843338
Mem 650
Sec   IR Bradbery
Pro   CR White (01273) 845398
Holes 18 L 6278 yds SSS 70
V'tors WD–U exc Tues after 9.15am
     WE–U after 2pm
     SOC–Mon/Wed/Thurs
Fees £20 (£30)
Loc   6 miles N of Brighton on
     A273

Rustington (1992)

Public
Golfers Lane, Angmering, BN16 4NB
Tel   **(01903) 850790**
Fax   (01903) 850982
Web   www.rgcgolf.com
Sec   SP Langmead
Pro   (01903) 850790
Holes 18 L 5735 yds Par 70 SSS 68
     9 hole Par 3 course
V'tors U SOC
Fees On application
Loc   On A259 between Worthing
     and Littlehampton
Mis   Floodlit driving range
Arch David Williams

Selsey (1908)

Golf Links Lane, Selsey, PO20 9DR
Tel   **(01243) 605176 (Members)**
Fax   (01243) 602203
Mem 400
Sec   P Carter (01243) 602203
Pro   P Grindley
Holes 9 L 5834 yds SSS 68
V'tors U
Fees £12 (£17)
Loc   7 miles S of Chichester

Shillinglee Park (1980)

Pay and play
Chiddingfold, Godalming, GU8 4TA
Tel   **(01428) 653237**
Fax   (01428) 644391
Mem 400
Sec   G Baxter (Prop)
Pro   M Dowdell

Holes 9 L 2516 yds Par 32
V'tors U SOC exc Sat am
Fees 18 holes–£13 (£15)
     9 holes–£8.50 (£9.50)
Loc   2¹/₂ miles SE of Chiddingfold
Mis   Pitch & putt course
Arch Roger Mace

Singing Hills (1992)

Pay and play
Albourne, Brighton, BN6 9EB
Tel   **(01273) 835353**
Fax   (01273) 835444
Mem 400
Sec   B Hazelgrove
Pro   W Street
Holes 27 holes SSS 69-72:
     River 9 L 2826 yds
     Valley 9 L 3348 yds
     Lakes 9 L 3253 yds
V'tors U SOC
Fees £22 (£30)
Loc   6 miles N of Brighton, off
     B2117
Mis   Driving range
Arch MRM Sandow

Slinfold Park (1993)

*Stane Street, Slinfold, Horsham,
RH13 7RE*
Tel   **(01403) 791154 (Clubhouse)**
Fax   (01403) 791465
Web   www.slinfoldpark.co.uk
Mem 600
Sec   S Blake (Gen Mgr)
Pro   T Clingan (01403) 791555
Holes 18 L 6450 yds SSS 71
     9 hole course
V'tors U SOC
Fees £25 (£30)
Loc   3 miles W of Horsham (A29)
Mis   Driving range. Academy
     course
Arch John Fortune

Tilgate Forest (1982)

Public
*Titmus Drive, Tilgate, Crawley,
RH10 5EU*
Tel   **(01293) 530103**
Fax   (01293) 523478
Mem 320
Sec   T Reagan
Pro   S Trussell, D McClelland
Holes 18 L 6359 yds SSS 70
     9 hole Par 3 course
V'tors U SOC–Mon–Thurs
Fees 18 hole:£12 (£16) 9 hole:£4
     (£5.30)
Loc   1¹/₂ miles SE of Crawley. M23
     Junction 11
Mis   Driving range

West Chiltington (1988)

Pay and play
*Broadford Bridge Road, West
Chiltington, RH20 2YA*
Tel   **(01798) 813574**
Fax   (01798) 812631
Mem 500
Sec   GA Cotton

Pro   GA Cotton (01798) 812115
Holes 18 L 5969 yds Par 70 SSS 69
     9 hole Par 3 course
V'tors U SOC
Fees £15 (£17.50)
Loc   2 miles E of Pulborough
Mis   Driving range
Arch Faulkner/Barnes

West Sussex (1930)

*Golf Club Lane, Wiggonholt,
Pulborough, RH20 2EN*
Tel   **(01798) 872563**
Fax   (01798) 872033
Web   www.westsussexgolf.co.uk
Mem 800
Sec   CP Simpson
Pro   T Packham (01798) 872426
Holes 18 L 6223 yds SSS 70
V'tors WD–I H after 9.30am exc
     Fri–M SOC–Wed & Thurs
Fees On application
Loc   1¹/₂ miles E of Pulborough on
     A283
Mis   Driving range
Arch Campbell/Hutcheson

Worthing (1905)

Links Road, Worthing, BN14 9QZ
Tel   **(01903) 260801**
Fax   (01903) 694664
Web   www.worthinggolf.co.uk
Mem 1000
Sec   IJ Evans (01903) 260801
Pro   S Rolley (01903) 260718
Holes Lower 18 L 6530 yds Par 71
     SSS 72
     Upper 18 L 5243 yds Par 66
     SSS 66
V'tors WD–U H WE–confirm in
     advance with Pro
Fees On application
Loc   Central Station 1¹/₂ miles
     (A27), nr A24 Junction
Arch HS Colt

Tyne & Wear

Backworth (1937)

*The Hall, Backworth, Shiremoor,
Newcastle-upon-Tyne NE27 0AH*
Tel   **(0191) 268 1048**
Mem 400
Sec   D Carruthers
Pro   None
Holes 9 L 5930 yds SSS 69
V'tors Mon & Fri–U Tues–Thurs–M
     after 5pm WE–after 12.30pm
     exc comp Sats–after 6pm
Fees On application
Loc   Off Tyne Tunnel link road,
     Holystone roundabout

Birtley (1922)

Birtley Lane, Birtley, DH3 2LR
Tel   **(0191) 410 2207**
Mem 230
Sec   DM Dummett

Holes 9 L 5660 yds SSS 67
V'tors WD–U exc Fri pm–M
WE/BH–M SOC
Fees £12
Loc 3 miles from Birtley service
area on A1(M)

Boldon (1912)

Dipe Lane, East Boldon, NE36 0PQ

Tel **(0191) 536 4182**
(Clubhouse)
Fax (0191) 537 2270
Web www.boldongolfclub.co.uk
Mem 700
Sec RW Benton (0191) 536 5360
Pro Phipps Golf (0191) 536 5835
Holes 18 L 6348 yds SSS 70
V'tors WD–U WE/BH–NA before
3.30pm
Fees £20 (£24)
Loc 8 miles SE of Newcastle
Mis Driving range
Arch H Vardon

City of Newcastle (1891)

Three Mile Bridge, Gosforth, Newcastle-upon-Tyne, NE3 2DR

Tel **(0191) 285 1775**
Fax (0191) 284 0700
Mem 400 110(L) 60(J)
Sec AJ Matthew (Mgr)
Pro S McKenna (0191) 285 5481
Holes 18 L 6528 yds SSS 71
V'tors U SOC
Fees £24 (£28)
Loc B1318, 3 miles N of
Newcastle
Arch Harry Vardon

Garesfield (1922)

Chopwell, NE17 7AP

Tel **(01207) 561309**
Fax (01207) 561309
Mem 700
Sec WG Dunn
Pro D Race (01207) 563082
Holes 18 L 6458 yds SSS 71
V'tors WD–U WE/BH–NA before
4.30pm SOC
Fees On application
Loc 7 miles SW of Newcastle,
between High Spen and
Chopwell

Gosforth (1906)

Broadway East, Gosforth, Newcastle-upon-Tyne, NE3 5ER

Tel **(0191) 285 6710**
Fax (0191) 284 6274
Mem 380 100(L) 60(J)
Sec B Pluse (0191) 285 3495
Pro G Garland (0191) 285 0553
Holes 18 L 6024 yds SSS 69
V'tors WD–U WE–M before 4pm
–U after 4pm SOC
Fees £24
Loc 3 miles N of Newcastle, off
A6125

Hetton-le-Hole

Pay and play
*Elemore Golf Course, Elemore Lane,
DH5 0QB*

Tel **(0191) 517 3057**
Fax (0191) 517 3054
Sec E Booth
Holes 18 L 5950 yds Par 69
V'tors U SOC
Fees £9 (£12)
Loc 4 miles E of A1(M)/A690
junction

Heworth (1912)

*Gingling Gate, Heworth, Gateshead,
NE10 8XY*

Tel **(0191) 469 4424**
Mem 800
Sec G Holbrow
Pro A Marshall
Holes 18 L 6404 yds SSS 71
V'tors WD–U WE–NA before noon
Fees £15 (£15)
Loc SE boundary of Gateshead

Houghton-le-Spring (1908)

*Copt Hill, Houghton-le-Spring,
DH5 8LU*

Tel **(0191) 584 1198**
Mem 600
Sec N Wales (0191) 584 0048
Pro (0191) 584 7421
Holes 18 L 6416 yds Par 72 SSS 71
V'tors U SOC
Fees £20 (£27)
Loc 3 miles SW of Sunderland

Newcastle United (1892)

Ponteland Road, Cowgate, Newcastle-upon-Tyne, NE5 3JW

Tel **(0191) 286 4693 (Clubhouse)**
Mem 700
Sec J Simpson (Hon)
Pro (0191) 286 9998
Holes 18 L 6617 yds SSS 72
V'tors WD–U WE/BH–M
Fees On application
Loc Nuns Moor, 2 miles W of city
centre

Northumberland (1898)

High Gosforth Park, Newcastle-upon-Tyne, NE3 5HT

Tel **(0191) 236 2498**
Fax (0191) 236 2498
Mem 500
Sec JM Forteath QGM
Holes 18 L 6629 yds SSS 72
V'tors WD–I BH–M
Fees £35–£45
Loc 5 miles N of Newcastle
Arch HS Colt/James Braid

Parklands (1971)

High Gosforth Park, Newcastle-upon-Tyne, NE3 5HQ

Tel **(0191) 236 4480/4867**
Mem 600

Sec B Woof
Pro B Rumney
Holes 18 L 6060 yds Par 71 SSS 69
V'tors U
Fees £15 (£18)
Loc 5 miles N of Newcastle
Mis 9 hole pitch & putt course.
Driving range

Ravensworth (1906)

*Moss Heaps, Wrekenton, Gateshead,
NE9 7UU*

Tel **(0191) 487 6014/2843**
Mem 550
Sec RW Hill (0191) 442 1042
Pro S Cowell (0191) 491 3475
Holes 18 L 5872 yds SSS 68
V'tors U H SOC
Fees £19 (£28)
Loc 3 miles S of Newcastle on
B1296

Ryton (1891)

*Doctor Stanners, Clara Vale, Ryton,
NE40 3TD*

Tel **(0191) 413 3253**
Fax (0191) 413 1642
Mem 600
Sec S Dix
Holes 18 L 5499 metres SSS 69
V'tors WD–U WE–M SOC
Fees £16 (£21)
Loc 7 miles W of Newcastle, off
A695

South Shields (1893)

*Cleadon Hills, South Shields,
NE34 8EG*

Tel **(0191) 456 0475**
Mem 700
Sec R Stanness (0191) 456 8942
Pro G Parsons (0191) 456 0110
Holes 18 L 6264 yds SSS 70
V'tors U SOC
Fees On application
Loc Cleadon Hills

Tynemouth (1913)

*Spital Dene, Tynemouth, North Shields,
NE30 2ER*

Tel **(0191) 257 4578**
Fax (0191) 259 5193
Mem 855
Sec W Storey (0191) 257 3381
Pro J McKenna (0191) 258 0728
Holes 18 L 6359 yds SSS 71
V'tors WD–U 9.30am–5pm –NA
before 9.30am and after 5pm
WE/BH–M
Fees £20 D–£25
Loc 8 miles E of Newcastle
Arch Willie Park

Tyneside (1879)

Westfield Lane, Ryton, NE40 3QE

Tel **(0191) 413 2177**
Fax (0191) 413 2742
Mem 660
Sec E Stephenson
(0191) 413 2742

Pro M Gunn (0191) 413 1600
Holes 18 L 6042 yds SSS 69
V'tors WD–U exc 11.30–1.30pm
Sat–NA Sun–NA before 3pm
SOC
Fees £20 (£20)
Loc 7 miles W of Newcastle. S of
river, off A695
Arch HS Colt

Wallsend (1973)
Public
*Rheydt Avenue, Bigges Main, Wallsend,
NE28 8SU*
Tel (0191) 262 1973
Sec D Souter
Pro K Phillips (0191) 262 4231
Holes 18 L 6608 yds SSS 72
V'tors U
Fees £14.50 (£16.50)
Loc Between Newcastle and
Wallsend on coast road
Mis Driving range
Arch G Showball

Washington (1979)
*Stone Cellar Road, High Usworth,
District 12, Washington NE37 1PH*
Tel (0191) 402 9988
Fax (0191) 415 1166
Web www.corushotels.com/hotels/
wasgeo
Mem 600
Sec M Godfrey
Holes 18 L 6604 yds SSS 72
9 hole Par 3 course
V'tors U SOC
Fees £20
Loc Off A1(M), on A195
Mis Driving range

Wearside (1892)
Coxgreen, Sunderland, SR4 9JT
Tel (0191) 534 2518
Fax (0191) 534 6186
Mem 800
Sec M Gowland
Pro D Brolls (0191) 534 4269
Holes 18 L 6315 yds SSS 70
Par 3 course
V'tors H SOC
Fees £26 (£33)
Loc 2 miles W of Sunderland, off
A183, by A19

Westerhope (1941)
*Whorlton Grange, Westerhope,
Newcastle-upon-Tyne, NE5 1PP*
Tel (0191) 286 9125
Mem 778
Sec R Pears (0191) 286 7636
Pro N Brown (0191) 286 0594
Holes 18 L 6407 yds SSS 71
V'tors WD–U
Fees £16
Loc 5 miles W of Newcastle

Whickham (1911)
*Hollinside Park, Fellside Road,
Whickham, Newcastle-upon-Tyne
NE16 5BA*
Tel (0191) 488 7309 (Clubhouse)

Fax (0191) 488 1576
Mem 650
Sec BO Johnson (0191) 488 1576
Pro G Lisle (0191) 488 8591
Holes 18 L 5878 yds Par 68 SSS 68
V'tors U SOC–WD
Fees £20 (£25)
Loc 5 miles SW of Newcastle

Whitburn (1931)
Lizard Lane, South Shields, NE34 7AF
Tel (0191) 529 2144
Fax (0191) 529 4944
Mem 580 73(L) 85(J)
Sec Mrs V Atkinson
(0191) 529 4944
Pro D Stephenson
(0191) 529 4210
Holes 18 L 5899 yds Par 70 SSS 68
V'tors U SOC–WD exc Tues
Fees £20 (£26)
Loc 2 miles N of Sunderland on
coast
Arch Colt/Alison/Morrison

Whitley Bay (1890)
*Claremont Road, Whitley Bay,
NE26 3UF*
Tel (0191) 252 0180
Fax (0191) 297 0030
Web www.wbgolf.free-online.co.uk
Mem 700
Sec H Hanover
Pro G Shipley (0191) 252 5688
Holes 18 L 6529 yds SSS 71
V'tors WD–U WE–M
Fees £22 D–£30
Loc 10 miles E of Newcastle

Warwickshire

Ansty (1992)
*Brinklow Road, Ansty, Coventry,
CV7 9JH*
Tel (024) 7662 1341/7660 2568
Fax (024) 7660 2568
Mem 375
Sec S Firkins
Pro S Firkins
Holes 18 L 6079 yds Par 71 SSS 69
Par 3 course
V'tors U SOC
Fees £10 (£14)
Loc Between Ansty and Brinklow
(B4029). M6 Junction 2,
1 mile.
Mis Driving range
Arch D Morgan

Atherstone (1894)
*The Outwoods, Coleshill Road,
Atherstone, CV9 2RL*
Tel (01827) 713110
Fax (01827) 715686
Mem 400 40(L) 40(J)
Sec VA Walton (01827) 892568
Holes 18 L 6012 yds Par 72 SSS
70
V'tors WD–U BH/Sat–M Sun–M
after 5pm SOC–WD

Fees D–£20 Mon–£13
Loc 1/4 mile from Atherstone on
Coleshill road

The Belfry (1977)
Public
Lichfield Road, Wishaw, B76 9PR
Tel (01675) 470301
Fax (01675) 470174
Sec R Maxfield
Pro P McGovern
Holes Brabazon 18 L 7118 yds
SSS 74;
Derby 18 L 6009 yds SSS 69
PGA National 18 L 6737 yds
SSS 72
V'tors H SOC
Fees Brabazon £70–£130 PGA
National £40–£65 Derby
£20–£35
Loc 2 miles N of M42 Junction 9,
off A446
Mis Driving range
Arch Brabazon & Derby-
Alliss/Thomas; PGA National-
Thomas

Bidford Grange (1992)
*Stratford Road, Bidford-on-Avon,
B50 4LY*
Tel (01789) 490319
Fax (01789) 778184
Mem 310
Sec M Smith (Mgr)
Pro D Webber
Holes 18 L 7233 yds Par 72 SSS 74
V'tors U SOC
Fees £12 (£15)
Loc 5 miles W of Stratford-on-
Avon on B439
Arch Swann/Tillman/Granger

Boldmere (1936)
Public
*Monmouth Drive, Sutton Coldfield,
Birmingham, BJ3 6JR*
Tel (0121) 354 3379
Mem 300
Sec R Leeson
Pro T Short
Holes 18 L 4463 yds SSS 62
V'tors U
Fees £9 (£11)
Loc By Sutton Park, 1 mile W of
Sutton Coldfield

Bramcote Waters
Pay and play
*Bazzard Road, Bramcote, Nuneaton,
CV11 6QJ*
Tel (01455) 220807
Fax (01203) 388775
Pro N Gilks
Holes 9 L 4995 yds Par 66 SSS 64
V'tors U
Fees £12 (£13)
Loc 4 miles SE of Nuneaton, off
B4114
Arch David Snell

City of Coventry (Brandon Wood) (1977)

Public
Brandon Lane, Coventry, CV8 3GQ

Tel	(024) 7654 3141
Fax	(024) 7654 5108
Mem	500
Sec	C Gledhill
Pro	C Gledhill
Holes	18 L 6521 yds SSS 71
V'tors	U SOC
Fees	On application
Loc	6 miles SE of Coventry, off A45(S)
Mis	Floodlit driving range

Copt Heath (1907)

1220 Warwick Road, Knowle, Solihull, B93 9LN

Tel	(01564) 772650
Fax	(01564) 771022
Mem	700
Sec	CJ Hadley
Pro	BJ Barton (01564) 776155
Holes	18 L 6508 yds SSS 71
V'tors	WD–H WE/BH–M SOC
Fees	£40–£45
Loc	2 miles S of Solihull on A4141

Coventry (1887)

St Martins Road, Finham Park, Coventry, CV3 6RJ

Tel	(024) 7641 1123
Fax	(024) 7669 0131
Web	www.coventrygolfcourse.co.uk
Mem	750
Sec	B Fox (024) 7641 4152
Pro	P Weaver (024) 7641 1298
Holes	18 L 6601 yds SSS 73
V'tors	WD–H
Fees	£35
Loc	2 miles S of Coventry on A444/B4113
Arch	Vardon/Hawtree

Coventry Hearsall (1894)

Beechwood Avenue, Coventry, CV5 6DF

Tel	(024) 7671 3470
Fax	(024) 7669 1534
Mem	600
Sec	Mrs ME Hudson
Pro	M Tarn (024) 7671 3156
Holes	18 L 6005 yds SSS 69
V'tors	WD–U WE–M
Fees	D–£30
Loc	1¹/₂ miles S of Coventry, off A45

Edgbaston (1896)

Church Road, Edgbaston, Birmingham, B15 3TB

Tel	(0121) 454 1736
Fax	(0121) 454 2395
Web	www.edgbastongc.co.uk
Mem	980
Sec	P Heath
Pro	J Cundy (0121) 454 3226
Holes	18 L 6106 yds SSS 69
V'tors	H SOC

Fees	£40 (£50)
Loc	1¹/₂ miles S of Birmingham, off A38
Arch	HS Colt

Harborne (1893)

40 Tennal Road, Harborne, Birmingham, B32 2JE

Tel	(0121) 427 1728
Fax	(0121) 427 4039
Mem	650
Sec	GA Tozer (0121) 427 3058
Pro	A Quarterman (0121) 427 3512
Holes	18 L 6210 yds SSS 70
V'tors	WD–U WE/BH–M SOC
Fees	£30 D–£35
Loc	3 miles SW of Birmingham. M5 Junction 3
Arch	HS Colt

Harborne Church Farm (1926)

Public
Vicarage Road, Harborne, Birmingham, B17 0SN

Tel	(0121) 427 1204
Fax	(0121) 428 3126
Web	www.learnaboutgolf.co.uk
Mem	180
Sec	B Flanagan
Pro	P Johnson
Holes	9 L 4882 yds Par 66 SSS 64
V'tors	U
Fees	18 holes–£8.50 (£10) 9 holes–£6 (£7)
Loc	3 miles SW of Birmingham

Hatchford Brook (1969)

Public
Coventry Road, Sheldon, Birmingham, B26 3PY

Tel	(0121) 743 9821
Fax	(0121) 743 3420
Mem	500
Sec	ID Thomson (0121) 742 6643
Pro	M Hampton
Holes	18 L 6137 yds Par 70 SSS 69
V'tors	U SOC
Fees	£9 (£10)
Loc	City boundary close to airport. A45/M42 Junction

Henley G&CC (1994)

Birmingham Road, Henley-in-Arden, B95 5QA

Tel	(01564) 793715
Fax	(01564) 795754
Mem	600
Sec	G Wright (Chief Exec)
Pro	S Edwin
Holes	18 L 6933 yds SSS 73 9 hole Par 3 course
V'tors	U–booking required SOC–H
Fees	£20 D–£25 (£25 D–£30)
Loc	N of Stratford-on-Avon on A3400. M40 Junction 16, 3 miles
Mis	Driving range
Arch	N Selwyn-Smith

Hilltop (1979)

Public
Park Lane, Handsworth, Birmingham, B21 8LJ

Tel	(0121) 554 4463
Pro	K Highfield
Holes	18 L 6114 yds SSS 69
V'tors	U
Fees	On application
Loc	Sandwell Valley. M5 Junction 1

Ingon Manor (1993)

Ingon Lane, Snitterfield, Stratford-on-Avon, CV37 0QE

Tel	(01789) 731857
Mem	350
Pro	P Taylor
Holes	18 L 6575 yds Par 73 SSS 71
V'tors	U H SOC
Fees	£20 (£25)
Loc	3 miles N of Stratford-on-Avon, off A461. M40 Junction 15
Mis	Driving range
Arch	David Hemstock

Kenilworth (1889)

Crewe Lane, Kenilworth, CV8 2EA

Tel	(01926) 854296
Fax	(01926) 864453
Web	www.kenilworthgolfclub.org.uk
Mem	750
Sec	J McTavish (01926) 858517
Pro	S Yates (01926) 512732
Holes	18 L 6400 yds SSS 71
V'tors	U H BH–M SOC–WD
Fees	£30 (£38)
Loc	1¹/₂ miles E of Kenilworth. 5 miles S of Coventry
Arch	Hawtree

Ladbrook Park (1908)

Poolhead Lane, Tanworth-in-Arden, Solihull, B94 5ED

Tel	(01564) 742264
Fax	(01564) 742909
Mem	700
Sec	Mrs SE Burrows (Admin)
Pro	R Mountford (01564) 742581
Holes	18 L 6427 yds SSS 71
V'tors	WD–U H WE/BH–M H
Fees	On application
Loc	12 miles S of Birmingham. M42 Junction 3
Arch	HS Colt

Leamington & County (1908)

Golf Lane, Whitnash, Leamington Spa, CV31 2QA

Tel	(01926) 425961
Fax	(01926) 425961
Mem	650
Sec	SM Cooknell
Pro	J Mellor (01926) 428014
Holes	18 L 6439 yds SSS 71
V'tors	U SOC
Fees	£27 (£40)
Loc	1¹/₂ miles S of Leamington Spa
Arch	HS Colt

Marconi (Grange GC)

Copsewood, Coventry, CV3 1HS
Tel (024) 7656 3339
Mem 350
Sec REC Jones (Hon)
Holes 9 L 6048 yds SSS 71
V'tors WD–U before 2.30pm Sat–NA Sun–NA before noon
Fees £12 Sun–£15
Loc 2½ miles E of Coventry on A428
Arch TJ McAuley

Marriott Forest of Arden Hotel (1970)

Maxstoke Lane, Meriden, Coventry, CV7 7HR
Tel (01676) 522335
Fax (01676) 523711
Mem 650
Sec M Newey (Golf Dir)
Pro D Tudor
Holes Arden 18 L 6718 yds Par 72 SSS 73;
Aylesford 18 L 6525 yds Par 72 SSS 71
V'tors WD–U SOC–WD
Fees Arden–£50 (£60)
Aylesford–£35 (£40)
Loc 9 miles W of Coventry, off A45. M6 Junction 4
Mis Driving range
Arch Donald Steel

Maxstoke Park (1898)

Castle Lane, Coleshill, Birmingham, B46 2RD
Tel (01675) 466743
Fax (01675) 466743
Mem 630
Sec GE Crawford
Pro N McEwan
(01675) 464915
Holes 18 L 6442 yds SSS 71
V'tors WD–U H WE–M
Fees £27.50
Loc 3 miles SE of Coleshill

Moor Hall (1932)

Moor Hall Drive, Four Oaks, Sutton Coldfield, B75 6LN
Tel (0121) 308 6130
Fax (0121) 308 6130
Mem 668
Sec DJ Etheridge
Pro A Partridge (0121) 308 5106
Holes 18 L 6249 yds SSS 70
V'tors WD–U H exc Thurs–U after 1pm WE/BH–M
Fees £30 D–£40
Loc 1 mile E of Sutton Coldfield

Newbold Comyn (1973)

Public
Newbold Terrace East, Leamington Spa, CV32 4EW
Tel (01926) 421157
Mem 191
Sec CV Baker (01926) 887220
Pro R Carvell

Holes 18 L 6315 yds SSS 70
V'tors WD–U WE–booking 1 week in advance SOC
Fees £8 (£11.75)
Loc Off Willes Road (B4099)

North Warwickshire

(1894)
Hampton Lane, Meriden, Coventry, CV7 7LL
Tel (01676) 522464 (Clubhouse)
Fax (01676) 522915
Mem 450
Sec EG Barnes (Hon)
(01676) 522915
Pro A Bownes (01676) 522259
Holes 9 L 6374 yds SSS 71
V'tors WD–U WE/BH–M SOC
Fees £20
Loc 6 miles W of Coventry, off A45

Nuneaton (1905)

Golf Drive, Whitestone, Nuneaton, CV11 6QF
Tel (024) 7634 7810
Fax (024) 7632 7563
Mem 650
Sec P Smith
Pro J Salter (024) 7634 0201
Holes 18 L 6412 yds SSS 71
V'tors WD–U H WE–M SOC
Fees £25 D–£30
Loc 2 miles S of Nuneaton

Oakridge

Arley Lane, Ansley Village, Nuneaton, CV10 9PH
Tel (01676) 541389
Fax (01676) 542709
Mem 600
Sec Mrs S Lovric (Admin)
Pro I Sadler
Holes 18 L 6242 yds Par 71 SSS 70
V'tors U SOC–WD
Fees £15
Loc B4112 from Nuneaton. M6 Junction 3
Arch Algie Jayes

Olton (1893)

Mirfield Road, Solihull, B91 1JH
Tel (0121) 705 1083
Fax (0121) 711 2010
Mem 600
Sec BG Smith (0121) 704 1936
Pro C Haynes (0121) 705 7296
Holes 18 L 6232 yds SSS 74
V'tors WD–U exc Wed am WE–M
Fees £25–£35
Loc 7 miles SE of Birmingham (A41)

Purley Chase (1980)

Pipers Lane, Ridge Lane, Nuneaton, CV10 0RB
Tel (024) 7639 3118
Mem 600
Sec Linda Jackson

Holes 18 L 6772 yds SSS 72
V'tors WD/BH–U WE–U after 2.30pm SOC
Fees On application
Loc 4 miles WNW of Nuneaton on B4114 (A47) A5 Mancetter Island
Mis Driving range

Pype Hayes (1932)

Public
Eachelhurst Road, Walmley, Sutton Coldfield, B76 8EP
Tel (0121) 351 1014
Fax (0121) 313 0206
Mem 320
Sec L Brogan
Pro JF Bayliss
Holes 18 L 5996 yds SSS 69
V'tors U
Fees On application
Loc 5 miles NE of Birmingham

Robin Hood (1893)

St Bernards Road, Solihull, B92 7DJ
Tel (0121) 706 0061
Fax (0121) 706 0061
Mem 650
Pro A Harvey (0121) 706 0806
Holes 18 L 6635 yds SSS 72
V'tors WD–U WE/BH–M SOC–WD H
Fees £30 D–£35
Loc 7 miles S of Birmingham
Arch HS Colt

Rugby (1891)

Clifton Road, Rugby, CV21 3RD
Tel (01788) 544637
Fax (01788) 542306
Mem 750
Sec N Towler (01788) 542306
Pro N Summers (01788) 575134
Holes 18 L 5614 yds SSS 67
V'tors WD–U WE/BH–M SOC
Fees On application
Loc 1 mile N of Rugby on B5414

Shirley (1956)

Stratford Road, Monkspath, Shirley, Solihull B90 4EW
Tel (0121) 744 6001
Fax (0121) 745 8220
Mem 650
Sec Mrs VA Duggan
Pro S Bottrill (0121) 745 4979
Holes 18 L 6510 yds SSS 71
V'tors WD–U WE–M SOC
Fees £25 D–£35
Loc 8 miles S of Birmingham, nr M42 Junction 4
Arch John Morrison

Sphinx (1948)

Sphinx Drive, Coventry, CV3 1WA
Tel (024) 7645 1361
Mem 300
Sec GE Brownbridge
(024) 7659 7731
Holes 9 L 4262 yds SSS 60

V'tors Fri/WE–M after 4.30pm SOC
Fees £8 (£10)
Loc Nr Binley Road, Coventry

Stonebridge Golf Centre

Somers Road, Meriden, CV7 7PL
Tel (01676) 522442
Fax (01676) 522447
Mem 400
Sec R Grier
Pro R Grier
Holes 18 L 6250 yds Par 70
V'tors U
Fees £15.50 (£18.50)
Loc 2 miles E of M42 Junction 6
Mis Driving range

Stoneleigh Deer Park

(1992)
The Old Deer Park, Coventry Road, Stoneleigh, CV8 3DR
Tel (024) 7663 9991
Fax (024) 7651 1533
Mem 800
Sec A Wild
Pro M McGuire
Holes 18 L 6023 yds SSS 71
9 hole Par 3 course
V'tors WD–U WE–NA before 2pm
SOC–WD
Fees On application
Loc ½ mile E of Stoneleigh

Stratford Oaks (1991)

Bearley Road, Snitterfield, Stratford-on-Avon, CV37 0EZ
Tel (01789) 731982
Fax (01789) 731981
Mem 600
Sec ND Powell (Golf Dir)
Pro A Dunbar
Holes 18 L 6100 yds SSS 71
V'tors WD–U WE–U booking
necessary
Fees £15 (£20)
Loc 4 miles NE of Stratford-on-Avon
Mis Driving range
Arch Howard Swann

Stratford-on-Avon

(1894)
Tiddington Road, Stratford-on-Avon, CV37 7BA
Tel (01789) 205749
Fax (01789) 414909
Web www.stratfordgolf.co.uk
Mem 770
Sec NS Dodd (01789) 205749
Pro D Sutherland (01789) 205677
Holes 18 L 6374 yds SSS 70
V'tors U H SOC
Fees £35 (£40)
Loc ½ mile E of Stratford-on-Avon on B4086
Arch JH Taylor

Sutton Coldfield (1889)

110 Thornhill Road, Sutton Coldfield, B74 3ER
Tel (0121) 580 7878
Fax (0121) 353 5503
Mem 600
Sec RG MItchell, KM Tempest (0121) 353 9633
Pro JK Hayes (0121) 580 7878
Holes 18 L 6541 yds SSS 71
V'tors U H SOC
Fees £30 D–£35 (£40)
Loc 9 miles N of Birmingham, off B4138

Tidbury Green (1994)

Pay and play
Tilehouse Lane, Shirley, Solihull, B90 1HP
Tel (01564) 824460
Mem 300
Sec Lucy Broadhurst
Pro R Thompson
Holes 9 L 2473 yds Par 34
V'tors U SOC
Fees 18 holes–£9 (£9) 9 holes–£6 (£6)
Loc 2 miles from M42 Junction 4, nr Earlswood Lakes
Mis Driving range
Arch Derek Stevenson

Walmley (1902)

Brooks Road, Wylde Green, Sutton Coldfield, B72 1HR
Tel (0121) 377 7272
Fax (0121) 377 7272
Mem 700
Sec MJ Roberts
Pro CJ Wicketts (0121) 373 7103
Holes 18 L 6585 yds SSS 72
V'tors WD–U WE–M SOC
Fees £30 D–£35
Loc N boundary of Birmingham

Warwick (1971)

Public
Warwick Racecourse, Warwick, CV34 6HW
Tel (01926) 494316
Sec Mrs R Dunkley
Pro P Sharp (01926) 491284
Holes 9 L 2682 yds SSS 66
V'tors U exc while racing in progress
& Sun am
Fees £5 (£5.50)
Loc Centre of Warwick Racecourse
Mis Driving range
Arch DG Dunkley

The Warwickshire (1993)

Leek Wootton, Warwick, CV35 7QT
Tel (01926) 409409
Fax (01926) 408409
Mem 850
Sec B Fotheringham
Pro D Peck
Holes 18 L 7178 yds SSS 74
18 L 7154 yds SSS 74
9 hole Par 3 course

V'tors H SOC
Fees £45 (£45)
Loc 1 mile N of Warwick, off A46.
M40 Junction 15
Mis Driving range
Arch Karl Litton

Welcombe Hotel

Warwick Road, Stratford-on-Avon, CV37 0NR
Tel (01789) 413800
Fax (01789) 414666
Mem 200
Sec N Price (01789) 295252
Pro K Hayler (01789) 413800
Holes 18 L 6294 yds SSS 70
V'tors U H
Fees D–£40 (D–£50)
Loc 1½ miles NE of Stratford-on-Avon on A439 towards Warwick. M40 Junction 15
Mis Driving range
Arch T McAuley

Whitefields Hotel (1992)

Coventry Road, Thurlaston, Rugby, CV23 9JR
Tel (01788) 815555
Fax (01788) 521695
Web www.whitefields-hotel.co.uk
Mem 400
Sec B Coleman
Pro D Price
Holes 18 L 6223 yds Par 71 SSS 70
V'tors U SOC
Fees £16 (£22)
Loc 3 miles SW of Rugby at A45/M45 Junction
Mis Driving range

Widney Manor (1993)

Pay and play
Saintbury Drive, Widney Manor, Solihull, B91 3SZ
Tel (0121) 704 0704
Fax (0121) 704 7999
Mem 503
Sec M Harrhy (Sec/Mgr)
Pro T Atkinson
Holes 18 L 5284 yds Par 69
V'tors U–booking 5 days in advance SOC
Fees £9.95 (£14.95)
Loc 3 miles from M42 Junction 4, off A34
Mis Driving range

Windmill Village (1990)

Birmingham Road, Allesley, Coventry, CV5 9AL
Tel (024) 7640 4041
Fax (024) 7640 7016
Mem 700
Sec M Harrhy (Mgr)
Pro R Hunter (024) 7640 4041
Holes 18 L 5213 yds Par 70
V'tors U SOC
Fees £9.95 (£14.95)
Loc 3 miles W of Coventry on A45
Arch Hunter/Harrhy

Wishaw (1995)

Bulls Lane, Wishaw, Sutton Coldfield, B76 9AA

Tel	**(0121) 313 2110**
Mem	250
Sec	PM Lewington
Holes	18 L 5397 yds Par 71 SSS 66
V'tors	U SOC
Fees	£12 (£18)
Loc	3 miles NW of M42 Junction 9

Wiltshire

Bowood G&CC (1992)

Derry Hill, Calne, SN11 9PQ

Tel	**(01249) 822228**
Fax	(01249) 822218
Web	www.bowood.org
Mem	450
Sec	G Elliott
Pro	M Taylor
Holes	18 L 7317 yds Par 72 SSS 73
V'tors	U–booking required WE–M before noon SOC
Fees	£36 (£39)
Loc	3 miles SE of Chippenham on A342. M4 Junction 14 (A4)
Mis	Driving range. 3 Academy holes
Arch	David Thomas

Bradford-on-Avon (1991)

Trowbridge Road, Bradford-on-Avon

Tel	**(01225) 868268**
Pro	G Sawyer
Holes	9 L 2100 metres SSS 61
V'tors	WD–U WE–pm only
Fees	9 holes–£6.50. 18 holes–£10
Loc	SE of Bradford, nr River Avon

Brinkworth (1984)

Longmans Farm, Brinkworth, Chippenham, SN15 5DG

Tel	**(01666) 510277**
Mem	250
Sec	J Sheppard
Holes	18 L 5900 yds SSS 69
V'tors	U SOC
Fees	On application
Loc	2 miles from Brinkworth (B4042). 12 miles NE of Chippenham

Broome Manor (1976)

Public

Pipers Way, Swindon, SN3 1RG

Tel	**(01793) 532403**
Fax	(01793) 433255
Mem	800
Sec	JE Poolman (01793) 823462
Pro	B Sandry (01793) 532403
Holes	18 L 6283 yds SSS 70 9 L 2690 yds SSS 67
V'tors	U
Fees	18 hole: £12 9 hole: £7.20
Loc	Swindon 2 miles. M4 Junction 15
Mis	Floodlit driving range
Arch	F Hawtree

Chippenham (1896)

Malmesbury Road, Chippenham, SN15 5LT

Tel	**(01249) 652040**
Fax	(01249) 446681
Mem	650
Sec	D Maddison
Pro	W Creamer (01249) 655519
Holes	18 L 5540 yds SSS 67
V'tors	U WE–M SOC
Fees	£20 (£25)
Loc	1 mile N of Chippenham, off A350. M4 Junction 17

Cricklade Hotel (1992)

Common Hill, Cricklade SN6 6HA

Tel	**(01793) 750751**
Fax	(01793) 751767
Mem	70
Sec	C Withers
Pro	I Bolt
Holes	9 L 1830 yds Par 62 SSS 58
V'tors	WD–U SOC–WD
Fees	£16 D–£25
Loc	½ mile W of Cricklade on B4040. M4 Junctions 15/16
Arch	Bolt/Smith

Cumberwell Park (1994)

Bradford-on-Avon, BA15 2PQ

Tel	**(01225) 863322**
Fax	(01225) 868160
Web	www.cumberwellpark.co.uk
Mem	1050
Pro	J Jacobs (Golf Dir)
Holes	27 hole course
V'tors	U SOC
Fees	£22.50 (£28)
Loc	Between Bradford-on-Avon and Bath on A363. M4 Junction 18
Mis	Driving range
Arch	Adrian Stiff

Erlestoke Sands (1992)

Erlestoke, Devizes, SN10 5UB

Tel	**(01380) 831069**
Fax	(01380) 831284
Mem	740
Sec	M Pugsley
Pro	M Walters (01380) 831027
Holes	18 L 6406 yds Par 73 SSS 71
V'tors	U–book with Pro SOC
Fees	£20 (£27)
Loc	6 miles E of Westbury on B3098
Mis	Driving area. 3 Academy holes
Arch	Adrian Stiff

Hamptworth G&CC (1994)

Elmtree Farmhouse, Hamptworth Road, Landford, SP5 2DU

Tel	**(01794) 390155**
Fax	(01794) 390022
Web	www.hamptworthgolf.co.uk
Sec	P Stevens
Pro	M White
Holes	18 L 6516 yds SSS 71
V'tors	H

Fees	£25 D–£30
Loc	10 miles SE of Salisbury, off A36/B3079. M27 Junction 2, 6 miles
Mis	Driving range

High Post (1922)

Great Durnford, Salisbury, SP4 6AT

Tel	**(01722) 782356**
Fax	(01722) 782674
Mem	600
Sec	P Grimes (01722) 782356
Pro	I Welding (01722) 782219
Holes	18 L 6305 yds Par 70 SSS 70
V'tors	WD–U WE/BH–H SOC
Fees	£28 D–£37 (£35 D–£45) SOC–£30
Loc	4 miles N of Salisbury on A345
Arch	Hawtree

Highworth (1990)

Swindon Road, Highworth, SN6 7SJ

Tel	**(01793) 766014**
Sec	KW Loveday
Holes	9 L 3220 yds SSS 70
V'tors	U
Fees	£7.90
Loc	5 miles N of Swindon (A361). M4 Junction 15
Mis	9 hole pitch & putt course

Kingsdown (1880)

Kingsdown, Corsham, SN13 8BS

Tel	**(01225) 742530**
Mem	620 105(L) 45(J)
Sec	JE Elliott (01225) 743472
Pro	A Butler (01225) 742634
Holes	18 L 6445 yds SSS 71
V'tors	WD–H WE–M
Fees	£26
Loc	5 miles E of Bath

Manor House (1992)

Proprietary

Castle Combe, SN14 7JW

Tel	**(01249) 782982**
Fax	(01249) 782992
Web	www.exclusivehotels.co.uk
Mem	400
Sec	Susan Auld (Gen Mgr)
Pro	P Green
Holes	18 L 6286 yds SSS 71
V'tors	U H–booking necessary SOC
Fees	Mon–Thurs–£40. Fri–Sun–£50
Loc	N of Castle Combe, off B4039. M4 Junction 17, 4 miles
Mis	Driving range
Arch	Alliss/Clarke

Marlborough (1888)

The Common, Marlborough, SN8 1DU

Tel	**(01672) 512147**
Fax	(01672) 513164
Mem	750
Sec	JAD Sullivan
Pro	S Amor (01672) 512493

Holes 18 L 6491 yds SSS 71
V'tors WD/WE–H SOC
Fees £25 D–£33 (£30 D–£40)
Loc ½ mile N of Marlborough (A346). 7 miles S of M4 Junction 15

Monkton Park Par Three (1965)

Pay and play
Chippenham, SN15 3PP
Tel **(01249) 653928**
Fax (01249) 653928
Web www.pitchandputtgolf.com
Mem 100
Sec MR & BJ Dawson (Props)
Holes 9 hole Par 3 course
V'tors U
Fees 18 holes–£6 9 holes–£4
Loc Centre of Chippenham. M4 Junction 17
Arch M Dawson

North Wilts (1890)

Bishops' Cannings, Devizes, SN10 2LP
Tel **(01380) 860257**
Fax (01380) 860877
Web www.northwiltsgolf.com
Mem 625 105(L) 90(J)
Sec Mrs P Stephenson (01380) 860627
Pro GJ Laing (Golf Mgr) (01380) 860330
Holes 18 L 6414 yds SSS 71
V'tors U exc Xmas Day–Jan 31–M SOC
Fees £21 (£24)
Loc 1 mile from A4, E of Calne

Oaksey Park (1991)

Pay and play
Oaksey, Malmesbury, SN16 9SB
Tel **(01666) 577995**
Fax (01666) 577174
Holes 9 L 2900 yds SSS 68
V'tors U SOC
Fees £10 (£15)
Loc 8 miles NE of Malmesbury, off A429
Mis Driving range
Arch Chapman/Warren

Ogbourne Downs (1907)

Ogbourne St George, Marlborough, SN8 1TB
Tel **(01672) 841327**
Fax (01672) 841327
Mem 700
Sec Miss M Green (01672) 841327
Pro C Harraway (01672) 841287
Holes 18 L 6363 yds Par 71 SSS 70
V'tors WD–H WE–M SOC–WD
Fees £25 (£35)
Loc 5 miles S of M4 Junction 15, on A346
Arch JH Taylor

RMCS Shrivenham (1953)

RMCS Shrivenham, Swindon, SN6 8LA
Tel **(01793) 785725**
Mem 500
Sec R Humphrey (Mgr)
Holes 18 L 5684 yds SSS 69
V'tors M SOC
Fees £10 (£10)
Loc Grounds of Royal Military College of Science. Entry must be arranged with Mgr

Rushmore Park

Tollard Royal, Salisbury, SP5 5QB
Tel **(01725) 516326**
Fax (01725) 516466
Mem 370
Sec S McDonagh
Pro S McDonagh
Holes 18 hole course
V'tors U SOC
Fees £14 (£17)
Loc 8 miles SE of Shaftesbury (B3081)
Mis Driving range
Arch T Crouch

Salisbury & South Wilts (1888)

Netherhampton, Salisbury, SP2 8PR
Tel **(01722) 742645**
Fax (01722) 742645
Web www.salisburygolf.co.uk
Mem 1100
Sec GL Pearce (Gen Mgr)
Pro J Cave (01722) 742929
Holes 18 L 6485 yds SSS 71 9 hole course Par 34
V'tors WD–U SOC–WD
Fees £25 (£40)
Loc Wilton, 3 miles SW of Salisbury on A3094
Arch Taylor/Gidman

Shrivenham Park (1967)

Pay and play
Penny Hooks, Shrivenham, Swindon, SN6 8EX
Tel **(01793) 783853**
Fax (01793) 782999
Mem 400
Sec MJ Jefferies
Holes 18 L 5713 yds SSS 69
V'tors U SOC
Fees £15 (£17)
Loc 4 miles E of Swindon, off A420. M4 Junction 15

Thoulstone Park (1992)

Chapmanslade, Westbury, BA13 4AQ
Tel **(01373) 832825**
Fax (01373) 832821
Sec Mrs J Pearce
Pro T Isaacs (01373) 832808
Holes 18 L 6300 yds Par 71 SSS 70
V'tors U SOC–WD
Fees £18 (£24)

Loc 12 miles S of Bath, off A36
Mis Driving range
Arch MRM Sandow

Tidworth Garrison (1908)

Bulford Road, Tidworth, SP9 7AF
Tel **(01980) 842321 (Clubhouse)**
Fax (01980) 842301
Mem 800
Sec T Harris (01980) 842301
Pro T Gosden (01980) 842393
Holes 18 L 6320 yds Par 70 SSS 70
V'tors WD–U H SOC–Tues & Thurs
Fees £27.50
Loc 1 mile SW of Tidworth on Bulford road (A338)
Arch Donald Steel

Upavon (1913)

Douglas Avenue, Upavon, SN9 6BQ
Tel **(01980) 630787**
Fax (01980) 630787
Mem 550
Sec L Mitchell
Pro R Blake (01980) 630281
Holes 18 L 6415 yds SSS 71
V'tors WD–U WE–M before noon –U after noon SOC–WD
Fees £18 D–£24 (£20)
Loc 2 miles SE of Upavon on A342
Arch R Blake

West Wilts (1891)

Elm Hill, Warminster, BA12 0AU
Tel **(01985) 213133**
Fax (01985) 219809
Mem 570 70(L) 40(J)
Sec Mrs V Haydon-Foster
Pro S Swales (01985) 212110
Holes 18 L 5709 yds SSS 68
V'tors WD–U H WE–U H after noon –NA before noon
Fees £26 D–£30 (£30)
Loc Off A350, on Westbury road
Arch JH Taylor

Whitley (1993)

Pay and play
Corsham Road, Whitley, Melksham, SN12 7QE
Tel **(01225) 790099**
Mem 250
Sec C Tomkins (01225) 790099
Pro None
Holes 9 L 2200 yds Par 33 SSS 61
V'tors U
Fees 18 holes–£9. 9 holes–£7
Loc 1 mile N of Melksham on B3553
Mis Driving range
Arch Laurence Ross

The Wiltshire

Vastern, Wootton Bassett, Swindon, SN4 7PB
Tel **(01793) 849999**

Fax   (01793) 849988
Mem   600
Sec   RG Lipscombe (Gen Mgr)
Pro   A Gray
Holes   18 L 6666 yds SSS 72
V'tors   U SOC
Fees   £30 (£30)
Loc   1 mile S of Wootton Bassett
on A3102. M4 Junction 16
Arch   Alliss/Clark

Wrag Barn G&CC (1990)

Shrivenham Road, Highworth,
Swindon, SN6 7QQ
Tel   (01793) 861327
Fax   (01793) 861325
Web   www.wragbarn.com
Mem   600
Sec   M Betteridge
Pro   B Loughrey (01793) 766027
Holes   18 L 6600 yds SSS 71
V'tors   WD–U WE–NA before noon
SOC–WD
Fees   £25 (£30)
Loc   6 miles NE of Swindon on
B4000. M4 Junction 15, 8
miles
Mis   Driving range. 6-hole
Academy course
Arch   Hawtree

Worcestershire

Abbey Hotel G&CC
(1985)

Dagnell End Road, Redditch, B98 7BD
Tel   (01527) 63918
Fax   (01527) 584112
Mem   500
Pro   SD Edwards (01527) 68006
Holes   18 L 6499 yds SSS 72
V'tors   WD–U SOC
Fees   £15 (£21)
Loc   B4101, off A441 Birmingham
road. M42 Junction 2
Mis   Driving range
Arch   Donald Steel

Bank House Hotel
G&CC (1992)

Bransford, Worcester, WR6 5JD
Tel   (01886) 833551
Fax   (01886) 832461
Web   www.bankhousehotel.com
Mem   350
Sec   PAD Holmes
Pro   C George
Holes   18 L 6204 yds SSS 71
V'tors   U SOC
Fees   £18 (£25)
Loc   3 miles SW of Worcester on
A4103 Hereford road. M5
Junction 7
Mis   Driving range
Arch   Bob Sandow

Blackwell (1893)

Blackwell, Bromsgrove, Worcestershire,
B60 1PY
Tel   (0121) 445 1994
Fax   (0121) 445 4911
Mem   304 67(L) 6(J)
Sec   JT Mead
Pro   N Blake (0121) 445 3113
Holes   18 L 6230 yds SSS 71
V'tors   WD–U H WE/BH–M
Fees   £50 D–£60
Loc   3 miles E of Bromsgrove. M42
Junction 1 (South)

Brandhall (1906)

Public
Heron Road, Oldbury, Warley,
B68 8AQ
Tel   (0121) 552 7475
Mem   287
Pro   C Yates (0121) 552 2195
Holes   18 L 5813 yds SSS 68
V'tors   U exc first 1½ hrs Sat/Sun
Fees   £11
Loc   6 miles NW of Birmingham.
M5 Junction 2, 1½ miles

Bromsgrove Golf
Centre (1992)

Proprietary
Stratford Road, Bromsgrove,
B60 1LD
Tel   (01527) 575886
Fax   (01527) 570964
Web   www.bromsgrovegolfcentre
.co.uk
Mem   900
Sec   D Went
Pro   G Long (01527) 575886
Holes   18 L 5969 yds SSS 68
V'tors   U SOC
Fees   £14.50 (£19)
Loc   Junction of A38/A448. M42
Junction 1. M5 Junction 4/5
Mis   Driving range
Arch   Hawtree

Churchill & Blakedown
(1926)

Churchill Lane, Blakedown,
Kidderminster, DY10 3NB
Tel   (01562) 700018
Mem   300
Sec   MJ Taylor
Holes   9 L 6472 yds Par 72 SSS 71
V'tors   WD–U WE–M
Fees   £20
Loc   3 miles N of Kidderminster on
A456

Cocks Moor Woods (1926)

Public
Alcester Road, South King's Heath,
Birmingham, BK1 6ER
Tel   (0121) 444 3584
Pro   S Ellis
Holes   18 L 5742 yds SSS 67
V'tors   U
Fees   On application

Loc   6 miles S of Birmingham
(A435)

Droitwich G&CC (1897)

Ford Lane, Droitwich, WR9 0BQ
Tel   (01905) 774344
Fax   (01905) 797290
Mem   782
Sec   M Ashton (01905) 774344
Pro   CS Thompson
(01905) 770207
Holes   18 L 6058 yds SSS 69
V'tors   WD–U WE/BH–M
SOC–Wed & Fri
Fees   £26
Loc   1 mile N of Droitwich, off
A38. M5 Junction 5

Dudley (1893)

Turners Hill, Rowley Regis, B65 9DP
Tel   (01384) 253719
Fax   (01384) 233177
Mem   320
Sec   RP Fortune (01384) 233877
Pro   G Dean (01384) 254020
Holes   18 L 5654 yds SSS 69
V'tors   WD–U WE–M
Fees   On application
Loc   2 miles S of Dudley

Evesham (1894)

Craycombe Links, Fladbury, Pershore,
WR10 2QS
Tel   (01386) 860395
Fax   (01386) 861356
Mem   360
Sec   Mrs L Tattersall
(01386) 860395
Pro   D Cummins (01386) 861144
Holes   9 L 6415 yds SSS 71
V'tors   WD–H WE–M NA on
comp/match days SOC
Fees   D–£20
Loc   Fladbury, 4 miles W of
Evesham (A4538)

Fulford Heath (1933)

Tanners Green Lane, Wythall,
Birmingham, B47 6BH
Tel   (01564) 822806 (Clubhouse)
Fax   (01564) 822629
Mem   750
Sec   Mrs MA Tuckett
(01564) 824758
Pro   M Herbert (01564) 822930
Holes   18 L 6179 yds SSS 70
V'tors   WD–H WE/BH–M
SOC–Tues & Thurs
Fees   On application
Loc   8 miles S of Birmingham.
M42 Junction 3
Arch   Braid/Hawtree

Gay Hill (1913)

Hollywood Lane, Birmingham,
B47 5PP
Tel   (0121) 430 6523/7077
Fax   (0121) 436 7796
Mem   700
Sec   Mrs M Adderley
(0121) 430 8544

Pro   A Potter (0121) 474 6001
Holes 18 L 6532 yds SSS 72
V'tors WD–U H WE–M SOC
Fees   £28.50
Loc   7 miles S of Birmingham on
       A435. M42 Junction 3,
       3 miles

Habberley (1924)

*Low Habberley, Kidderminster,
DY11 5RG*

Tel   (01562) 745756
Fax   (01562) 745756
Mem   250
Sec   B Blakeway
Holes 9 L 5440 yds SSS 67
V'tors WD–U WE–M SOC
Fees   £12 (£15)
Loc   3 miles NW of
       Kidderminster

Hagley (1980)

Proprietary
*Wassell Grove, Hagley, Stourbridge,
DY9 9JW*

Tel   (01562) 883701
Fax   (01562) 887518
Web   www.hagleygolfandcountry
       club.co.uk
Mem   700
Sec   GF Yardley
       (01562) 883701
Pro   I Clark (01562) 883852
Holes 18 L 6353 yds SSS 72
V'tors WD–U WE–M after 10am
       SOC–WD
Fees   £20 D–£27
Loc   5 miles SW of Birmingham on
       A456. M5 Junction 3

Halesowen (1906)

The Leasowes, Halesowen, B62 8QF

Tel   (0121) 501 3606
Fax   (0121) 501 3606
Mem   680
Sec   P Crumpton
Pro   J Nicholas (0121) 503 0593
Holes 18 L 5754 yds SSS 69
V'tors WD–U WE–M SOC–WD exc
       Wed
Fees   £25 D–£30
Loc   M5 Junction 3, 2 miles

Kidderminster (1909)

*Russell Road, Kidderminster,
DY10 3HT*

Tel   (01562) 822303
Fax   (01562) 827866
Mem   900
Sec   M Burnand
Pro   NP Underwood
       (01562) 740090
Holes 18 L 6405 yds SSS 71
V'tors WD–H WE–M SOC–Thurs
Fees   £30 D–£40
Loc   Signposted off A449
       Wolverhampton-Worcester
       road

Kings Norton (1892)

*Brockhill Lane, Weatheroak,
Alvechurch, Birmingham B48 7ED*

Tel   (01564) 826789
Fax   (01564) 826955
Web   www.kingsnortongolfclub
       .co.uk
Mem   1050
Sec   T Webb (Mgr)
Pro   K Hayward (01564) 822822
Holes 9 L 3382 yds SSS 36
       9 L 3372 yds SSS 36
       9 L 3290 yds SSS 36
V'tors WD–U WE–NA SOC
Fees   £32 D–£40
Loc   7 miles S of Birmingham.
       1 mile N of M42 Junction 3
Mis   12 hole short course
Arch   Fred Hawtree

Lickey Hills (1927)

Public
*Lickey Hills, Rednal, Birmingham,
B45 8RR*

Tel   (0121) 453 3159
Sec   AG Cushing
Pro   J Kelly
Holes 18 L 6010 yds SSS 69
V'tors U
Fees   On application
Loc   10 miles SW of Birmingham.
       M5 Junction 4

Little Lakes (1975)

*Lye Head, Bewdley, Worcester,
DY12 2UZ*

Tel   (01299) 266385
Fax   (01299) 266398
Mem   400 50(L)
Sec   J Dean (01562) 741704
Pro   M Laing
Holes 18 L 5644 yds SSS 68
V'tors U SOC
Fees   £15 (£20)
Loc   3 miles W of Bewdley, off
       A456

Moseley (1892)

*Springfield Road, Kings Heath,
Birmingham, B14 7DX*

Tel   (0121) 444 2115
Fax   (0121) 441 4662
Mem   600
Sec   RA Jowle (0121) 444 4957
Pro   M Griffin (0121) 444 2063
Holes 18 L 6315 yds SSS 71
V'tors WD–H or M
Fees   £37
Loc   South Birmingham

North Worcestershire
(1907)

*Frankley Beeches Road, Northfield,
Birmingham, B31 5LP*

Tel   (0121) 475 1047
Fax   (0121) 476 8681
Mem   550
Sec   D Wilson
Pro   IF Clark (0121) 475 5721
Holes 18 L 5907 yds SSS 69

V'tors WD–U WE/BH–M
Fees   £25 D–£35
Loc   7 miles SW of Birmingham,
       off A38
Arch   James Braid

Ombersley (1991)

*Bishopswood Road, Ombersley,
Droitwich, WR9 0LE*

Tel   (01905) 620747
Fax   (01905) 620047
Mem   750
Sec   G Glenister (Gen Mgr)
Pro   G Glenister
Holes 18 L 6139 yds SSS 69
V'tors U
Fees   £11.50 (£15.50)
Loc   6 miles N of Worcester, off
       A449
Mis   Driving range
Arch   David Morgan

Perdiswell Park

Pay and play
Bilford Road, Worcester, WR3 8DX

Tel   (01905) 754668
Fax   (01905) 756608
Mem   286
Sec   R Gardner
Pro   M Woodward
       (01905) 754668
Holes 18 L 5297 yds SSS 68
V'tors U
Fees   9 holes–£5.50 (£7.15)
       18 holes–£8.70 (£11.20)
Loc   Worcester. M5 Junction 6

Pitcheroak (1973)

Public
Plymouth Road, Redditch, B97 4PB

Tel   (01527) 541054
Pro   D Stewart
Holes 9 L 4584 yds SSS 62
V'tors U
Fees   £5.75 (£6.75)
Loc   Redditch

Ravenmeadow

*Hindlip Lane, Clanes, Worcester,
WR3 8SA*

Tel   (01905) 757525
Fax   (01905) 759184
Mem   250
Sec   T Senter (Mgr)
       (01905) 458876
Pro   D Davis (01905) 757525
Holes 9 L 5440 yds Par 67
V'tors U
Fees   £10.75 (£14.75)
Loc   3 miles N of Worcester, off
       A38
Mis   Driving range
Arch   R Baldwyn

Redditch (1913)

*Lower Grinsty, Green Lane, Callow
Hill, Redditch B97 5PJ*

Tel   (01527) 543079
Fax   (01527) 547413

Mem 883
Sec SF Hickin
Pro D Down (01527) 546372
Holes 18 L 6494 yds SSS 72
V'tors WD–U SOC
Fees £28
Loc 3 miles SW of Redditch, off A441
Arch F Pennink

Stourbridge (1892)

Worcester Lane, Pedmore, Stourbridge, DY8 2RB
Tel (01384) 393062
Fax (01384) 444660
Web www.stourbridge-golf-club.co.uk
Mem 850
Sec Mrs MA Betts (01384) 395566
Pro M Male (01384) 393129
Holes 18 L 6231 yds SSS 70
V'tors WD–U exc Wed before 4pm–M WE/BH–M
Fees £30
Loc 1 mile S of Stourbridge on Worcester road. M5 Junction 3/4

Tolladine (1898)

The Fairway, Tolladine Road, Worcester, WR4 9BA
Tel (01905) 21074 (Clubhouse)
Mem 270
Sec D Turner
Pro M Slater
Holes 9 L 5174 yds SSS 67
V'tors WD–U before 4pm –M after 4pm WE/BH–M SOC
Fees On application
Loc M5 Junction 6, 1 mile

The Vale (1991)

Bishampton, Pershore, WR10 2LZ
Tel (01386) 462781
Fax (01386) 462597
Web www.crownsportsplc.com
Mem 800
Sec D Gutteridge (Gen Mgr)
Pro Caroline Griffiths (01386) 462520
Holes 18 L 6644 yds SSS 72
9 L 2628 yds SSS 65
V'tors WD–U WE–U after 1pm SOC–WD
Fees On application
Loc 6 miles NW of Evesham, off A4538. M5 Junction 6, 12 miles
Mis Driving range
Arch M Sandow

Warley (1921)

Public
Lightwoods Hill, Warley, B67 5EQ
Tel (0121) 429 2440
Sec A Woolridge
Pro D Owen
Holes 9 L 2606 yds SSS 64

V'tors U SOC
Fees On application
Loc 5 miles W of Birmingham, off A456

Wharton Park (1992)

Longbank, Bewdley, DY12 2QW
Tel (01299) 405222
Fax (01299) 405121
Mem 550
Pro A Hoare (01299) 405163
Holes 18 L 6435 yds Par 72 SSS 71
V'tors U SOC
Fees £20 (£25)
Loc Bewdley By-pass on A456
Arch Howard Swann

Worcester G&CC (1898)

Boughton Park, Worcester, WR2 4EZ
Tel (01905) 421132 (Clubhouse)
Fax (01905) 749090
Mem 1005
Sec DG Bettsworth (01905) 422555
Pro C Colenso (01905) 422044
Holes 18 L 6251 yds SSS 70
V'tors WD–H WE–M SOC
Fees £30
Loc 1 mile W of Worcester on A4103
Arch Dr A Mackenzie (1926)/ C Colenso (1991)

Worcestershire (1879)

Wood Farm, Malvern Wells, WR14 4PP
Tel (01684) 575992
Fax (01684) 575992
Mem 770
Sec Mrs JP Howe (Sec/Mgr) (01684) 575992
Pro RAF Lewis (01684) 564428
Holes 18 L 6449 yds SSS 71
V'tors WD–H WE–H after 10am
Fees £25 (£34) W–£100
Loc 2 miles S of Gt Malvern, off A449/B4209

Wyre Forest Golf Centre

Pay and play
Zortech Avenue, Kidderminster, DY11 7EX
Tel (01299) 822682
Fax (01299) 879433
Mem 363
Sec S Price (Mgr)
Pro S Price
Holes 18 L 5790 yds Par 70 SSS 68
V'tors U SOC
Fees £10 (£14.50)
Loc 18 miles S of Birmingham on A451, between Kidderminster and Stourport
Mis Floodlit driving range

Yorkshire (East)

Allerthorpe Park

Allerthorpe, York, YO42 4RL
Tel (01759) 306686
Fax (01759) 304308
Mem 475
Sec JD Atkinson (Sec/Mgr)
Pro None
Holes 18 L 5506 yds Par 67 SSS 66
V'tors U SOC
Fees £18 (£18)
Loc 2 miles W of Pocklington, off A1079
Arch JG Hatcliffe

Beverley & East Riding (1889)

The Westwood, Beverley, HU17 8RG
Tel (01482) 867190
Fax (01482) 868757
Mem 530
Sec M Drew (01482) 868757
Pro A Ashby (01482) 869519
Holes 18 L 5972 yds SSS 69
V'tors U SOC–WD
Fees £13 (£17)
Loc Beverley-Walkington road (B1230)

Boothferry Park (1982)

Spaldington Lane, Spaldington, Goole, DN14 7NG
Tel (01430) 430364
Fax (01430) 430567
Sec Christine Welton (Golf Admin) (01430) 430364
Pro N Bundy (01430) 430364
Holes 18 L 6593 yds SSS 72
V'tors U SOC
Fees £10 (£15)
Loc 3 miles N of Howden on B1288. M62 Junction 37, 2 miles
Arch Donald Steel

Bridlington (1905)

Belvedere Road, Bridlington, YO15 3NA
Tel (01262) 672092/606367
Fax (01262) 606367
Mem 623
Sec C Greenwood (01262) 606367
Pro ARA Howarth (01262) 674721
Holes 18 L 6638 yds Par 72 SSS 72
V'tors U exc Sun–NA
Fees £18 (£28)
Loc 1½ miles S of Bridlington, off A165
Arch James Braid

The Bridlington Links (1993)

Pay and play
Flamborough Road, Marton, Bridlington, YO15 1DW
Tel (01262) 401584

Fax   (01262) 401702
Mem   300
Sec   PM Hancock (Gen Mgr)
Pro   S Raybould
Holes 18 L 6720 yds SSS 72
           9 hole course
V'tors U
Fees   £12 (£15)
Loc   2 miles N of Bridlington on
           B1255
Mis   Floodlit driving range.
           3 Academy holes
Arch   Howard Swann

Brough (1893)

Cave Road, Brough, HU15 1HB
Tel   (01482) 667374
Fax   (01482) 669873
Web   www.brough-golfclub.co.uk
Mem   800
Sec   GW Townhill (Golf Dir)
           (01482) 667291
Pro   GW Townhill
           (01482) 667483
Holes 18 L 6183 yds SSS 69
V'tors WD–U exc Wed–NA
Fees   £30
Loc   10 miles W of Hull on A63

Cave Castle (1989)

South Cave, Nr Brough, HU15 2EU
Tel   (01430) 421286
Fax   (01430) 421118
Sec   C Welton (Admin)
Pro   S MacKinder (01430) 421286
Holes 18 L 6409 yds SSS 71
V'tors U SOC
Fees   £12.50 (£18)
Loc   10 miles W of Hull. Junction
           of A63/M62

Cherry Burton (1993)

Pay and play
*Leconfield Road, Cherry Burton,
Beverley, HU17 7RB*
Tel   (01964) 550924
Mem   220
Sec   A Ashby (Mgr)
Pro   A Ashby
Holes 9 L 2278 yds Par 33 SSS 62
V'tors U SOC
Fees   £7 (£10)
Loc   2 miles N of Beverley, off
           Malton road
Mis   Driving range

Cottingham

*Woodhill Way, Cottingham, Hull,
HU16 5RZ*
Tel   (01482) 842394
Fax   (01482) 845932
Web   www.golf-in-
           england.co.uk/cottingham
Mem   600
Sec   J Wiles (01482) 846030
Pro   CW Gray (01482) 842394
Holes 18 L 6459 yds Par 72 SSS 71
V'tors WD–U WE/BH–M before
           11am SOC
Fees   £16 D–£22 (£25 D–£35)

Loc   3 miles N of Hull, off A164
Mis   Driving range
Arch   Wiles/Litten

Driffield (1923)

Sunderlandwick, Driffield, YO25 9AD
Tel   (01377) 240448 (Clubhouse),
           (01377) 253116 (Office)
Fax   (01377) 240599
Mem   670
Sec   PJ Mounfield
Pro   K Wright (01377) 241224
Holes 18 L 6212 yds SSS 70
V'tors H I SOC
Fees   £20 D–£25 (£30 D–£40)
Loc   S of Driffield on A164

Flamborough Head
(1932)

*Lighthouse Road, Flamborough,
Bridlington, YO15 1AR*
Tel   (01262) 850333/850417
Fax   (01262) 850279
Web   www.fhgc.cwc.net
Mem   400
Sec   GS Thornton (01262) 850683
Holes 18 L 6189 yds Par 71 SSS 69
V'tors U
Fees   £18 (£20) 5D–£68
Loc   5 miles NE of Bridlington

Ganstead Park (1976)

*Longdales Lane, Coniston, Hull,
HU11 4LB*
Tel   (01482) 811280 (Steward)
Fax   (01482) 817754
Web   www.gansteadpark.co.uk
Mem   700
Sec   G Drewery (01482) 817754
Pro   M Smee (01482) 811121
Holes 18 L 6801 yds SSS 73
V'tors U H WE–NA before noon
           SOC
Fees   On application
Loc   5 miles E of Hull on A165
Arch   Peter Green

Hainsworth Park (1983)

Brandesburton, Driffield, YO25 8RT
Tel   (01964) 542362
Fax   (01964) 542362
Mem   550
Sec   GF Redshaw
           BW Atkin (Prop)
Pro   PR Binnington
           (01964) 542362
Holes 18 L 6362 yds SSS 71
V'tors U SOC
Fees   £16 (£20)
Loc   6 miles NW of Beverley, off
           A165 at Brandesburton
           roundabout

Hessle (1898)

*Westfield Road, Raywell, Cottingham,
HU16 5YL*
Tel   (01482) 650171
Fax   (01482) 652679
Mem   680
Sec   D Pettit

Pro   G Fieldsend
           (01482) 650190
Holes 18 L 6604 yds SSS 72
V'tors WD–U exc Tues 9am–1pm
           WE–NA before 11.30am
Fees   £23 (£30)
Loc   3 miles SW of Cottingham
Arch   Thomas/Alliss

Hornsea (1898)

Rolston Road, Hornsea, HU18 1XG
Tel   (01964) 532020
Fax   (01964) 532020
Mem   600
Sec   Angela Howard
           (01964) 532020
Pro   S Wright (01964) 534989
Holes 18 L 6685 yds SSS 72
V'tors WD–U WE–restricted SOC
Fees   £22 D–£30
Loc   300 yds past Hornsea Free
           Port
Arch   Mackenzie/Braid

Hull (1921)

*The Hall, 27 Packman Lane, Kirk Ella,
Hull HU10 7TJ*
Tel   (01482) 653026
Fax   (01482) 658919
Mem   821
Sec   R Toothill (Gen Mgr)
           (01482) 658919
Pro   D Jagger (01482) 653074
Holes 18 L 6246 yds SSS 70
V'tors WD–U WE–NA
Fees   £26.50 D–£32
Loc   5 miles W of Hull
Arch   James Braid

Kilnwick Percy (1995)

Pocklington, York, YO42 1UF
Tel   (01759) 303090
Mem   350
Sec   Mrs A Clayton (Sec/Mgr)
Pro   J Townhill
Holes 18 L 6214 yds Par 70 SSS 70
V'tors U SOC
Fees   £15 (£18)
Loc   1 mile E of Pocklington, off
           B1246
Arch   John Day

Springhead Park (1930)

Public
Willerby Road, Hull, HU5 5JE
Tel   (01482) 656309
Sec   Mrs J Garforth
           (01482) 656958
Holes 18 L 6402 yds SSS 71
V'tors U SOC–WD
Fees   £7.50 (£9)
Loc   4 miles W of Hull

Sutton Park (1935)

Public
Salthouse Road, Hull, HU8 9HF
Tel   (01482) 374242
Fax   (01482) 701428
Mem   300

Sec CR Alsop
Pro (01482) 711450
Holes 18 L 6251 yds SSS 70
V'tors U SOC–exc Sun
Fees £7.50 (£9.50)
Loc 3 miles E of Hull on A165

Withernsea (1909)

Chestnut Avenue, Withernsea,
HU19 2PG
Tel (01964) 612258 (Clubhouse)
Mem 329 30(L) 36(J)
Sec K Purdue (Admin)
 (01694) 612078
Holes 9 L 6207 yds Par 72 SSS 70
V'tors WD–U WE/BH–M before
 1pm SOC
Fees £10
Loc 17 miles E of Hull on A1033.
 S side of Withernsea

Yorkshire (North)

Aldwark Manor (1978)

Aldwark, Alne, York, YO61 1UF
Tel (01347) 838353
Fax (01347) 830007
Mem 420
Sec GF Platt (Mgr)
Pro P Harrison
Holes 18 L 6154 yds Par 71 SSS 70
V'tors U SOC
Fees £26 D–£35 (£32 D–£40)
Loc 5 miles SE of Boroughbridge,
 off A1. 13 miles NW of York,
 off A19

Ampleforth College

(1972)
Castle Drive, Gilling East, York,
YO62 4HP
Tel (01439) 788212
Web www.ampleforthgolf.co.uk
Mem 200
Sec Dr M Wilson (01904) 768861
Holes 9 L 5567 yds Par 69 SSS 69
V'tors U exc 2–4pm during term
 time
Fees £12 (£12)
Loc Gilling East, 18 miles N of
 York (B1363)
Mis Green fees payable at Fairfax
 Arms, Gilling East
Arch Rev Jerome Lambert OSB

Bedale (1894)

Leyburn Road, Bedale, DL8 1EZ
Tel (01677) 422568
Mem 600 60(J)
Sec G Brown (01677) 422451
Pro AD Johnson (01677) 422443
Holes 18 L 6610 yds SSS 72
V'tors U SOC
Fees £20 (£30)
Loc N boundary of Bedale

Bentham (1922)

Robin Lane, Bentham, Lancaster,
LA2 7AG
Tel (015242) 61018
Fax (015242) 62455
Web www.benthamgolfclub.co.uk
Mem 450
Sec T Tudor (015242) 62455
Holes 9 L 5820 yds SSS 69
V'tors U SOC
Fees £15 (£15)
Loc NE of Lancaster on B6480
 towards Settle. 13 miles E of
 M6 Junction 34

Catterick (1930)

Leyburn Road, Catterick Garrison,
DL9 3QE
Tel (01748) 833268
Fax (01748) 833268
Web www.catterickgolfclub.co.uk
Mem 700
Sec Mrs D Hopkins (Sec/Mgr)
Pro A Marshall (01748) 833671
Holes 18 L 6329 yds SSS 71
V'tors H WE–NA before 10am SOC
Fees £25 (£30)
Loc 6 miles SW of Scotch Corner,
 via A1
Arch Arthur Day

Cleveland (1887)

Queen Street, Redcar, TS10 1BT
Tel (01642) 471798
Fax (01642) 471798
Web www.clevelandgolfclub.co.uk
Mem 800
Sec P Fletcher (01642) 471798
Pro (01642) 483462
Holes 18 L 6746 yds SSS 72
V'tors WD–U WE/BH–by
 arrangement SOC
Fees £20 (£22)
Loc S bank of River Tees

Cocksford (1992)

Stutton, Tadcaster, LS24 9NG
Tel (01937) 834253
Fax (01937) 834253
Web www.cocksfordgolfclub
 .freeserve.co.uk
Sec F Judson
Pro G Thompson
Holes 18 L 5570 yds Par 71 SSS 69
V'tors WD–U WE–by arrangement
 SOC
Fees £18 D–£22 (£24 D–26)
Loc 1½ miles S of Tadcaster

Crimple Valley (1976)

Pay and play
Hookstone Wood Road, Harrogate,
HG2 8PN
Tel (01423) 883485
Fax (01423) 881018
Mem 200
Sec P Lumb
Pro P Lumb
Holes 9 L 2500 yds SSS 33
V'tors U

Fees 9 holes–£5 (£6) 18 holes–£8
 D–£11
Loc 1 mile S of Harrogate, off
 A61, by Yorkshire
 Showground
Arch R Lumb

Drax (1989)

Drax, Selby, YO8 8PQ
Mem 440
Sec K Onions (01405) 860872
Holes 9 L 5644 yds Par 68 SSS 67
V'tors M
Fees £6 (£8)
Loc 5 miles S of Selby, off A1041
Arch JM Scott

Easingwold (1930)

Stillington Road, Easingwold, York,
YO61 3ET
Tel (01347) 821486
Fax (01347) 822474
Web www.easingwold-golf-
 club.co.uk
Mem 690
Sec DB Stockley (01347) 822474
Pro J Hughes (01347) 821964
Holes 18 L 6627 yds Par 72 SSS 72
V'tors U
Fees D–£25 D–£30 (£30)
Loc 12 miles N of York on A19.
 S end of Easingwold
Mis Target golf
Arch Hawtree/OCM

Filey (1897)

West Ave, Filey, YO14 9BQ
Tel (01723) 513293
Fax (01723) 514952
Mem 768
Sec JR Nicholson
Pro GM Hutchinson
 (01723) 513134
Holes 18 L 6112 yds SSS 69
V'tors U H SOC
Fees £22 (£28) Summer £17
 (£22) Winter
Loc 1 mile S of Filey centre
Arch James Braid

Forest of Galtres (1993)

Moorlands Road, Skelton, York,
YO32 2RF
Tel (01904) 766198
Fax (01904) 769400
Mem 450
Sec Mrs SJ Procter
Pro P Bradley
Holes 18 L 6412 yds Par 72 SSS 70
V'tors U SOC–WD/Sun
Fees £18 (£25)
Loc Skelton, 4 miles N of York.
 1½ miles off A19
Mis Driving range
Arch Simon Gidman

Forest Park (1991)

Stockton-on Forest, York, YO32 9UW
Tel (01904) 400425
Mem 650

Sec N Crossley (01904) 400688
Pro None
Holes 18 L 6660 yds Par 71 SSS 72
9 L 3186 yds Par 70 SSS 70
V'tors U SOC
Fees £18 D–£24 (£23 D–£32)
9 hole:£8 (£10)
Loc 1½ miles from E end of A64
York By-pass
Mis Driving range

Fulford (1906)

Heslington Lane, York, YO10 5DY
Tel (01904) 413579
Fax (01904) 416918
Mem 750
Sec R Bramley MBE (Gen Mgr)
Pro M Brown (01904) 412882
Holes 18 L 6775 yds SSS 72
V'tors By arrangement with Mgr
Fees £37 D–£48 (£48)
Loc 2 miles S of York (A64)
Arch Major C McKenzie

Ganton (1891)

Station Road, Ganton, Scarborough,
YO12 4PA
Tel (01944) 710329
Fax (01944) 710922
Mem 550
Sec Maj RG Woolsey
Pro G Brown (01944) 710260
Holes 18 L 6734 yds SSS 73
V'tors By prior arrangement
Fees On application
Loc 11 miles SW of Scarborough
on A64
Arch Dunn/Vardon/Braid/Colt

Harrogate (1892)

Forest Lane Head, Harrogate,
HG2 7TF
Tel (01423) 863158 (Clubhouse)
Fax (01423) 860073
Web www.harrogate-gc.co.uk
Mem 700
Sec (01423) 862999
Pro P Johnson (01423) 862547
Holes 18 L 6241 yds SSS 70
V'tors WD–U WE/BH–enquire first
SOC–WD exc Tues
Fees £30 D–£35 (£40)
Loc 2 miles E of Harrogate on
Knaresborough road (A59)
Arch Sandy Herd

Heworth (1911)

Muncaster House, Muncastergate, York,
YO31 9JY
Tel (01904) 424618
Fax (01904) 426156
Mem 345 80(L) 50(J)
Sec RJ Hunt (01904) 426156
Pro S Burdett (01904) 422389
Holes 12 L 6141 yds Par 70 SSS 69
V'tors U
Fees £18 (£20)
Loc NE boundary of York
(A1036)

Hunley Hall (1993)

Brotton, Saltburn, TS12 2QQ
Tel (01287) 676216
Fax (01287) 678250
Web www.hunleyhall.co.uk
Mem 500
Sec E Lillie (01287) 676216
Pro A Brook (01287) 677444
Holes 27 holes:
5948-6918 yds Par/SSS 68-73
V'tors U SOC–exc Sun
Fees £20 (£30)
Loc 15 miles SE of Middlesbrough
on A174
Mis Floodlit driving range
Arch John Morgan

Kirkbymoorside (1951)

Manor Vale, Kirkbymoorside, York,
YO62 6EG
Tel (01751) 431525
Fax (01751) 433190
Web www.kirkbymoorsidegolf
.co.uk
Mem 630
Sec SH Morley
Pro C Tyson (01751) 430402
Holes 18 L 6112 yds SSS 69
V'tors U after 9 am
Fees £20 (£27)
Loc A170 between Helmsley and
Pickering

Knaresborough (1920)

Boroughbridge Road, Knaresborough,
HG5 0QQ
Tel (01423) 863219
Fax (01423) 869345
Mem 795
Sec JL Hall (Mgr)
(01423) 862690
Pro GJ Vickers (01423) 864865
Holes 18 L 6413 yds Par 70 SSS 71
V'tors U SOC
Fees £28.50 (£35.50)
Loc 1½ miles N of Knaresborough
on A6055
Arch Hawtree

Malton & Norton (1910)

Welham Park, Welham Road, Norton,
Malton YO17 9QE
Tel (01653) 692959
Fax (01653) 697912
Mem 820
Sec E Harrison (01653) 697912
Pro SI Robinson (01653) 693882
Holes 27 holes:
Welham L 6456 yds SSS 71
Park L 6242 yds SSS 70
Derwent L 6286 yds SSS 70
V'tors WD–U WE–restricted on
match days H SOC
Fees £25 (£30)
Loc 18 miles NE of York (A64)

Masham (1895)

Burnholme, Swinton Road, Masham,
Ripon HG4 4HT
Tel (01765) 689379
Fax (01765) 688054

Mem 327
Sec Mrs J McGee (01765) 688054
Holes 9 L 6120 yds SSS 69
V'tors WD–U before 5pm WE–M
BH–NA
Fees £20
Loc 10 miles N of Ripon, off
A6108

Middlesbrough (1908)

Brass Castle Lane, Marton,
Middlesbrough, TS8 9EE
Tel (01642) 311515
Fax (01642) 319607
Web www.middlesbroughgolfclub
.co.uk
Mem 975
Sec PM Jackson
Pro DJ Jones (01642) 311766
Holes 18 L 6278 yds SSS 70
V'tors WD–U H exc Tues–NA
before 1.30pm Sat–NA SOC
Fees D–£32 (£37)
Loc 3 miles S of Middlesbrough
Arch James Braid

Middlesbrough Municipal (1977)

Public
Ladgate Lane, Middlesbrough,
TS5 7YZ
Tel (01642) 315533
Fax (01642) 300726
Mem 625
Sec JC Taylor (Hon)
Pro A Hope (01642) 300720
Holes 18 L 6333 yds SSS 70
V'tors U
Fees £9.80 (£12.25)
Loc 2 miles S of Middlesbrough
on A174
Mis Floodlit driving range

Oakdale (1914)

Oakdale, Harrogate, HG1 2LN
Tel (01423) 567162
Fax (01423) 536030
Mem 775
Sec D Rodgers
Pro C Dell (01423) 560510
Holes 18 L 6456 yds SSS 71
V'tors WD–U 9.30–12.30 and after
2pm SOC–WD
Fees £30 D–£45
Loc ½ mile NE of Royal Hall,
Harrogate
Arch Dr A Mackenzie

The Oaks (1996)

Aughton Common, Aughton, York,
YO42 4PW
Tel (01757) 288001 (Clubhouse),
(01757) 288007 (Bookings)
Fax (01757) 289029
Web www.theoaksgolfclub.co.uk
Mem 675
Sec Mrs S Nutt (01757) 288577
Pro J Townhill
Holes 18 L 6743 yds Par 72 SSS 72
V'tors WD–U WE–M SOC–WD

Fees £22 D–£35
Loc 1 mile N of Bubwith on
B1228. 14 miles SE of York.
M62 Junction 37
Mis Driving range
Arch Julian Covey

Pannal (1906)

Follifoot Road, Pannal, Harrogate,
HG3 1ES
Tel (01423) 871641
Fax (01423) 870043
Mem 780
Sec R Braddon (01423) 872628
Pro D Padgett (01423) 872620
Holes 18 L 6622 yds SSS 72
V'tors WD–H 9.30–12 and after
1.30pm WE–H 11–12 and
after 2.30pm SOC
Fees £40 D–£50 (£50)
Loc 2½ miles S of Harrogate, on
A61
Arch Herd/Mackenzie

Pike Hills (1920)

Tadcaster Road, Askham Bryan, York,
YO23 3UW
Tel (01904) 700797
Fax (01904) 700797
Mem 750
Sec L Hargrave
Pro I Gradwell (01904) 708756
Holes 18 L 6146 yds SSS 70
V'tors WD–U H before 4.30pm –M
after 4.30pm SOC–WD
Fees £20 D–£26
Loc 3 miles SW of York on A64

Richmond (1892)

Bend Hagg, Richmond, DL10 5EX
Tel (01748) 825319
Mem 600
Sec BD Aston (01748) 823231
Pro P Jackson (01748) 822457
Holes 18 L 5886 yds SSS 68
V'tors U
Fees £20 D–£22 (£25 D–£30)
Loc 3 miles SW of Scotch Corner
Arch Frank Pennink

Ripon City (1907)

Palace Road, Ripon, HG4 3HH
Tel (01765) 603640
Fax (01765) 692880
Web www.ripongolf.com
Mem 650 100(L) 45(J)
Sec CJ Webb
Pro T Davis (01765) 600411
Holes 18 L 6084 yds SSS 69
V'tors U SOC
Fees £20 (£30)
Loc 1 mile N of Ripon on A6108
Mis Driving range
Arch ADAS

Romanby (1993)

Pay and play
Yafforth Road, Northallerton, DL7 0PE
Tel (01609) 779988
Fax (01609) 779084
Mem 550

Sec G McDonnell
(01609) 778855
Pro T Jenkins
Holes 18 L 6663 yds SSS 72
V'tors U SOC
Fees £18 (£25)
Loc 1 mile W of Northallerton on
B6271
Mis Floodlit driving range
Arch Will Adamson

Rudding Park (1995)

Pay and play
Rudding Park, Harrogate, HG3 1DJ
Tel (01423) 872100
Fax (01423) 873011
Web www.ruddingpark.com
Mem 430
Sec J Watson
Pro M Moore (01423) 873400
Holes 18 L 6871 yds SSS 72
V'tors U H SOC
Fees £19.50 (£22.50)
Loc 2 miles S of Harrogate (A658)
Mis Driving range. Golf Academy
Arch Hawtree

Saltburn (1894)

Hob Hill, Saltburn-by-the-Sea,
TS12 1NJ
Tel (01287) 622812
Fax (01287) 625988
Mem 900
Sec J Walton
Pro M Nutter (01287) 624653
Holes 18 L 5846 yds SSS 68
V'tors H SOC
Fees £22 (£28)
Loc 1 mile S of Saltburn

Scarborough North Cliff (1909)

North Cliff Avenue, Burniston Road,
Scarborough, YO12 6PP
Tel (01723) 360786
Fax (01723) 362134
Web www.ncgc.co.uk
Mem 860
Sec JR Freeman
Pro SN Deller (01723) 365920
Holes 18 L 6425 yds SSS 71
V'tors U H exc Sun before 10am and
comp days SOC–WD
Fees £21 D–£28 (£25 D–£30)
Loc 2 miles N of Scarborough on
coast road
Arch James Braid

Scarborough South Cliff (1902)

Deepdale Avenue, Scarborough,
YO11 2UE
Tel (01723) 374737
Fax (01723) 374737
Mem 565
Sec C Weir
Pro T Skingle (01723) 365150
Holes 18 L 6039 yds SSS 69
V'tors U H
Fees £22 (£27)

Loc 1 mile S of Scarborough, off
A165
Arch Dr A Mackenzie

Scarthingwell (1993)

Scarthingwell, Tadcaster, LS24 9DG
Tel (01937) 557878
Fax (01937) 557909
Mem 400
Pro S Footman (01937) 557864
Holes 18 L 6642 yds Par 71 SSS 72
V'tors U SOC
Fees £16 (£20)
Loc 4 miles S of Tadcaster on
A162

Selby (1907)

Mill Lane, Brayton, Selby, YO8 9LD
Tel (01757) 228622
Fax (01757) 228785
Web www.selbygolfclub.co.uk
Mem 749
Sec JN Proctor
Pro A Smith (01757) 228785
Holes 18 L 6374 yds SSS 71
V'tors WD–H WE–NA SOC–WD
Fees £30 D–£35
Loc 3 miles SW of Selby, off A19
at Brayton. 5 miles N of M62
Junction 34
Arch JH Taylor/Hawtree

Settle (1895)

Giggleswick, Settle, BD24 0DH
Tel (01729) 825288
Mem 250
Sec J Ketchell (01729) 823727
Holes 9 L 5414 yds SSS 66
V'tors U exc Sun–restricted SOC
Fees D–£15
Loc 1 mile N of Settle on A65
Arch Tom Vardon

Skipton (1893)

Off NW Bypass, Skipton, BD23 3LF
Tel (01756) 793922
Fax (01756) 796665
Mem 720
Sec EJ Paterson (01756) 795657
Pro R Robinson (01756) 793257
Holes 18 L 6087 yds SSS 70
V'tors U SOC
Fees £24 (£26)
Loc 1 mile N of Skipton on A59

Teesside (1901)

Acklam Road, Thornaby, TS17 7JS
Tel (01642) 676249
Fax (01642) 676252
Mem 690
Sec PB Hodgson (01642) 616516
Pro K Hall (01642) 673822
Holes 18 L 6535 yds Par 72 SSS 71
V'tors WD–U before 4.30pm WE–U
after 11am BH–M before
11am SOC
Fees D–£26 (£30)
Loc 2 miles S of Stockton on
A1130. ½ mile from A19 on
A1130
Arch Makepeace/Summerville

Thirsk & Northallerton (1914)

Thornton-le-Street, Thirsk, YO7 4AB

Tel	(01845) 522170
Fax	(01845) 525115
Mem	500
Sec	GS Batterbee (01845) 525115
Pro	R Garner (01845) 526216
Holes	18 L 6495 yds SSS 71
V'tors	WD/Sat–U H Sun–M SOC
Fees	£20 D–£25 Sat/BH–£25
Loc	2 miles N of Thirsk, nr A19 and A168 roundabout
Arch	ADAS

Whitby (1892)

Sandsend Road, Low Straggleton, Whitby, YO21 3SR

Tel	(01947) 602768
Fax	(01947) 600660
Mem	900
Sec	T Graham (01947) 600660
Pro	T Mason (01947) 602719
Holes	18 L 6134 yds SSS 69
V'tors	U H SOC
Fees	£22 (£28)
Loc	2 miles N of Whitby on A174

Wilton (1952)

Wilton, Redcar, Cleveland, TS10 4QY

Tel	(01642) 465265/465886
Fax	(01642) 465463
Mem	863
Sec	JCP Elder (01642) 465265
Pro	Pat Smillie (01642) 452730
Holes	18 L 6145 yds Par 70 SSS 69
V'tors	WD–U after 10am Sat–NA Sun/BH–U after 10am SOC–WD exc Tues & Thurs
Fees	D–£22 (D–£26)
Loc	3 miles W of Redcar on A174-signs to Wilton Castle

York (1890)

Lords Moor Lane, Strensall, York, YO32 5XF

Tel	(01904) 491840
Fax	(01904) 491852
Mem	400 129(L) 78(J)
Sec	SG Watson
Pro	AP Hoyles (01904) 490304
Holes	18 L 6301 yds SSS 70
V'tors	U–phone Sec SOC
Fees	£30–£40 (£40–£45)
Loc	4 miles N of York ring road (A1237)
Arch	JH Taylor

Yorkshire (South)

Abbeydale (1895)

Twentywell Lane, Dore, Sheffield, S17 4QA

Tel	(0114) 236 0763
Fax	(0114) 236 0762

Web	www.abbeydalegolf.co.uk
Mem	650
Sec	GL Lord
Pro	N Perry (0114) 236 5633
Holes	18 L 6407 yds SSS 71
V'tors	U SOC–H by arrangement
Fees	£30 (£45)
Loc	5 miles S of Sheffield, off A621
Arch	Herbert Fowler

Austerfield Park (1974)

Cross Lane, Austerfield, Doncaster, DN10 6RF

Tel	(01302) 710841/710850
Fax	(01302) 710841
Mem	350 52(L) 35(J)
Sec	R Whalley (01709) 719920
Pro	D Roberts
Holes	18 L 6900 yds Par 73 SSS 73 9 hole Par 3 course
V'tors	U SOC
Fees	£14 (£18)
Loc	2 miles NE of Bawtry, on A614
Mis	Driving range
Arch	E & M Baker

Barnsley (1925)

Public

Wakefield Road, Staincross, Barnsley, S75 6JZ

Tel	(01226) 382856
Mem	500
Sec	M Gillott
Pro	S Wyke (01226) 380358
Holes	18 L 5951 yds Par 69 SSS 69
V'tors	U
Fees	£10 (£12)
Loc	4 miles N of Barnsley on A61

Birley Wood (1974)

Public

Birley Lane, Sheffield, S12 3BP

Tel	(0114) 264 7262
Web	www.birleywood.free-online.co.uk
Mem	218
Sec	P Renshaw (0114) 265 3784
Pro	P Ball
Holes	18 L 5647 yds Par 68 SSS 67
V'tors	U
Fees	£10
Loc	4 miles S of Sheffield on A616. M1 Junction 30

Concord Park (1952)

Pay and play

Shiregreen Lane, Sheffield, S5 6AE

Tel	(0114) 257 7378
Sec	GR Gunnee
Pro	W Allcroft
Holes	18 L 4872 yds Par 67 SSS 64
V'tors	U
Fees	£8 (£10)
Loc	M1 Junction 34, 1 mile
Mis	Driving range

Crookhill Park (1974)

Public

Conisborough, Doncaster, DN12 2AH

Tel	(01709) 862979
Mem	500
Sec	TA Cusack
Pro	R Swaine
Holes	18 L 5839 yds SSS 68
V'tors	U
Fees	£8.75 (£9.95)
Loc	3 miles W of Doncaster (A630)

Doncaster (1894)

Bawtry Road, Bessacarr, Doncaster, DN4 7PD

Tel	(01302) 865632
Fax	(01302) 865994
Mem	375
Sec	DR Barton
Pro	G Bailey (01302) 868404
Holes	18 L 6220 yds SSS 70
V'tors	WD–U H WE/BH–NA before 11.30am SOC–WD
Fees	£27.50 D–£33 (£33)
Loc	4½ miles S of Doncaster on A638
Arch	Mackenzie/Hawtree

Doncaster Town Moor (1895)

Bawtry Road, Belle Vue, Doncaster, DN4 5HU

Tel	(01302) 533778
Mem	540
Sec	J Stoddart
Pro	S Shaw (01302) 535286
Holes	18 L 6001 yds SSS 69
V'tors	U exc Sun–NA before 3.30pm SOC
Fees	£16 (£17)
Loc	Inside racecourse. Clubhouse on A638

Dore & Totley (1913)

Bradway Road, Bradway, Sheffield, S17 4QR

Tel	(0114) 236 0492
Fax	(0114) 235 3436
Mem	580
Sec	JR Johnson (0114) 236 9872
Pro	G Roberts (0114) 236 6844
Holes	18 L 6265 yds Par 70 SSS 70
V'tors	WD–restricted Sat–NA Sun–restricted before 1pm SOC–Tues & Thurs
Fees	£26 (£30)
Loc	5 miles SW of Sheffield, off A61

Grange Park (1972)

Pay and play

Upper Wortley Road, Kimberworth, Rotherham, S61 2SJ

Tel	(01709) 558884
Mem	175
Sec	R Charity (01709) 558884
Pro	E Clark (01709) 559497
Holes	18 L 6461 yds SSS 71
V'tors	U SOC–phone Pro

Fees £11.75 (£12.75)
Loc 2 miles W of Rotherham on A629
Mis Driving range

Hallamshire (1897)

Sandygate, Sheffield, S10 4LA
Tel (0114) 230 1007
Fax (0114) 230 2153
Mem 600
Sec Mrs KE Renshaw (0114) 230 2153
Pro G Tickell (0114) 230 5222
Holes 18 L 6333 yds SSS 71
V'tors H SOC–WD
Fees £39 (£43)
Loc W boundary of Sheffield

Hallowes (1892)

Dronfield, Sheffield, S18 1UR
Tel (01246) 413734
Fax (01246) 411196
Mem 550
Sec T Marshall
Pro P Dunn (01246) 411196
Holes 18 L 6342 yds SSS 71
V'tors WD–U WE–M
Fees £30 D–£35
Loc 6 miles S of Sheffield on B6057

Hickleton (1909)

Hickleton, Doncaster, DN5 7BE
Tel (01709) 896081
Fax (01709) 896083
Mem 525
Sec JA Mills
Pro PJ Audsley (01709) 888436
Holes 18 L 6208 yds SSS 71
V'tors WD–U WE–NA before noon SOC
Fees £20 (£27)
Loc 6 miles W of Doncaster on A635
Arch Huggett/Coles

Hillsborough (1920)

Worrall Road, Sheffield, S6 4BE
Tel (0114) 234 3608
Fax (0114) 234 9151
Mem 519
Sec TC Pigott (0114) 234 9151
Pro L Horsman (0114) 233 2666
Holes 18 L 6035 yds SSS 70
V'tors H SOC
Fees £28 (£35)
Loc Wadsley, Sheffield
Mis Driving range

Lees Hall (1907)

Hemsworth Road, Norton, Sheffield, S8 8LL
Tel (0114) 255 4402
Fax (0114) 255 2900
Mem 550
Sec JW Poulson (0114) 255 2900
Pro S Berry
Holes 18 L 6171 yds SSS 70
V'tors U SOC

Fees £20 (£30)
Loc 3 miles S of Sheffield. E of A61

Lindrick (1891)

Lindrick Common, Worksop, Notts, S81 8BH
Tel (01909) 485802
Fax (01909) 488685
Web www.lindrickgolf.com
Mem 500
Sec Lt Cdr RJM Jack RN (01909) 475282
Pro JR King (01909) 475820
Holes 18 L 6486 yds Par 71 SSS 71
V'tors U H–by prior arrangement exc Tues SOC–WD
Fees £48 (£48)
Loc 4 miles W of Worksop on A57. M1 Junction 31

Owston Park (1988)

Public
Owston Hall, Owston, Doncaster, DN6 9JF
Tel (01302) 330821
Holes 9 L 6148 yds SSS 71
V'tors U
Fees On application
Loc 5 miles N of Doncaster on A19
Arch Michael Parker

Phoenix (1932)

Pavilion Lane, Brinsworth, Rotherham, S60 5PA
Tel (01709) 363788
Fax (01709) 363788
Mem 700
Sec J Burrows (01709) 370759
Pro M Roberts (01709) 382624
Holes 18 L 6145 yds SSS 70
V'tors U
Fees D–£21
Loc 2 miles S of Rotherham. M1 Junction 34
Mis Driving range
Arch H Cotton

Renishaw Park (1911)

Golf House, Mill Lane, Renishaw, Sheffield S21 3UZ
Tel (01246) 432044
Mem 450
Sec TJ Childs
Pro J Oates (01246) 435484
Holes 18 L 6262 yds SSS 70
V'tors H SOC
Fees £24.50 D–£34 (£38.50)
Loc 7 miles SE of Sheffield. 2 miles W of M1 Junction 30

Robin Hood (1996)

Owston Hall, Owston, Doncaster, DN6 9JF
Tel (01302) 722800
Fax (01302) 728885
Mem 200
Sec C Tanswell

Pro J Laszkowicz (01302) 722231
Holes 18 L 6937 yds Par 72 SSS 73
V'tors U SOC
Fees £12 (£15)
Loc 5 miles N of Doncaster on A19 (B1220)
Arch Will Adamson

Rother Valley Golf Centre (1997)

Mansfield Road, Wales Bar, Sheffield, S31 8PE
Tel (0114) 247 3000
Fax (0114) 247 6000
Mem 300
Sec Mrs M Goodman
Pro JK Ripley
Holes 18 L 6602 yds Par 72 SSS 72 9 hole Par 3 course
V'tors U SOC
Fees £12 (£16) Mon–£8
Loc Rother Valley Country Park, 2 miles S of M1 Junction 31
Mis Floodlit driving range
Arch Shattock/Roe

Rotherham (1903)

Thrybergh Park, Rotherham, S65 4NU
Tel (01709) 850466
Fax (01709) 859517
Mem 400
Sec G Smalley (01709) 850466
Pro S Thornhill (01709) 850480
Holes 18 L 6324 yds SSS 70
V'tors WD–U SOC
Fees £30 (£35)
Loc 4 miles E of Rotherham on A630

Roundwood (1976)

Green Lane, Rawmarsh, Rotherham, S62 6LA
Tel (01709) 523471
Mem 700
Sec M Pantry (01709) 527583
Holes 18 L 5620 yds Par 67 SSS 67
V'tors WE–NA before 5pm on comp days SOC–WD
Fees £15 (£18)
Loc 2 miles N of Rotherham on A633

Sandhill (1993)

Pay and play
Little Houghton, Barnsley, S72 0HW
Tel (01226) 753444
Fax (01226) 753444
Mem 275
Sec F Andrews
Holes 18 L 6250 yds SSS 70
V'tors U SOC
Fees £8.50 (£11)
Loc 6 miles E of Barnsley, off A635
Mis Driving range
Arch John Royston

For list of abbreviations see page 649

Sheffield Transport
(1923)
Meadow Head, Sheffield, S8 7RE
Tel   (0114) 237 3216
Mem   125
Sec   AE Mason
Holes   18 L 3966 yds SSS 62
V'tors M
Loc   S of Sheffield on A61

Silkstone (1893)
*Field Head, Elmhirst Lane, Silkstone,
Barnsley S75 4LD*
Tel   (01226) 790328
Fax   (01226) 792653
Mem   600
Sec   J Goulding
Pro   K Guy (01226) 790128
Holes   18 L 6069 yds SSS 70
V'tors WD–U SOC–WD
Fees   £22 D–£28 SOC(12+)–£40
Loc   1 mile W of M1 Junction 37
      on A628

Sitwell Park (1913)
*Shrogs Wood Road, Rotherham,
S60 4BY*
Tel   (01709) 541046
Fax   (01709) 703637
Mem   500
Sec   G Simmonite
Pro   N Taylor (01709) 540961
Holes   18 L 6250 yds SSS 70
V'tors WD–U Sat–M Sun–NA
      before 11.30am SOC
Fees   £24 D–£28 (£28)
Loc   2½ miles E of Rotherham on
      A631. M18 Junction 1
Arch   Dr A Mackenzie

Stocksbridge & District (1924)
*Royd Lane, Deepcar, Sheffield,
S36 2RZ*
Tel   (0114) 288 7479
Fax   (0114) 288 2003
Mem   300
Sec   J Willers (0114) 288 2003
Pro   T Brookes (0114) 288 2779
Holes   18 L 5200 yds Par 65 SSS 65
V'tors U SOC
Fees   £20 (£30)
Loc   9 miles W of Sheffield (A616)

Tankersley Park (1907)
*Park Lane, High Green, Sheffield,
S35 4LG*
Tel   (0114) 246 8247
Fax   (0114) 245 7818
Mem   574
Sec   A Brownhill
Pro   I Kirk (0114) 245 5583
Holes   18 L 6212 yds Par 69 SSS 70
V'tors WD–U WE–M SOC–WD
Fees   £26 D–£34 (£34)
Loc   Chapeltown, 7 miles N of
      Sheffield. M1 Junctions
      35A/36
Arch   Hawtree

Thorne (1980)
Pay and play
*Kirton Lane, Thorne, Doncaster,
DN8 5RJ*
Tel   (01405) 812084
Fax   (01405) 741899
Mem   120
Sec   R Highfield
Pro   ED Highfield (01405) 812084
Holes   18 L 5294 yds SSS 66
V'tors U
Fees   £9 (£10)
Loc   10 miles NE of Doncaster.
      M18 Junction 5/6
Arch   RD Highfield

Tinsley Park (1920)
Public
*High Hazels Park, Darnall, Sheffield,
S9 4PE*
Tel   (0114) 203 7435
Mem   500
Sec   ML Shillito
Pro   AP Highfield (0114) 203 7435
Holes   18 L 6084 yds SSS 69
V'tors WD–U WE–NA before 10am
      SOC
Fees   £10
Loc   M1 Junction 33, 3 miles
      (A6102)

Wath (1904)
Abdy Rawmarsh, Rotherham, S62 7SJ
Tel   (01709) 872149/878609
Fax   (01709) 878609
Mem   680
Sec   M Godfrey (01709) 583174
Pro   C Bassett (01709) 878677
Holes   18 L 6123 yds SSS 69
V'tors WD–U WE/BH–M SOC
Fees   £18 D–£23
Loc   Abdy Farm, 1½ miles S of
      Wath-upon-Dearne

Wheatley (1913)
Armthorpe Road, Doncaster, DN2 5QB
Tel   (01302) 831655
Fax   (01302) 812736
Mem   385 100(L) 50(J)
Sec   A Jones
Pro   S Fox (01302) 834085
Holes   18 L 6405 yds SSS 71
V'tors U SOC
Fees   £27 (£33)
Loc   3 miles NE of Doncaster

Wombwell Hillies (1989)
Public
*Wentworth View, Wombwell, Barnsley,
S73 0LA*
Tel   (01226) 754433
Fax   (01226) 758635
Sec   J Hayes (01226) 756761
Holes   9 L 2095 yds SSS 60
V'tors U
Fees   On application
Loc   4 miles SE of Barnsley

Wortley (1894)
*Hermit Hill Lane, Wortley, Sheffield,
S35 7DF*
Tel   (0114) 288 8469
Fax   (0114) 288 8469
Mem   400
Sec   WHM Hoyland
Pro   I Kirk (0114) 288 6490
Holes   18 L 6035 yds SSS 69
V'tors WD–U WE–NA before 10am
      SOC
Fees   £28 (£35)
Loc   2 miles W of M1 Junction 36,
      off A629

Yorkshire (West)

Alwoodley (1907)
*Wigton Lane, Alwoodley, Leeds,
LS17 8SA*
Tel   (0113) 268 1680
Fax   (0113) 293 9458
Web   www.alwoodley.co.uk
Mem   450
Sec   CD Wilcher
Pro   JR Green (0113) 268 9603
Holes   18 L 6785 yds SSS 73
V'tors U SOC–WD
Fees   £55 (£75)
Loc   5 miles N of Leeds on A61
Arch   Dr A Mackenzie

Bagden Hall Hotel (1993)
Wakefield Road, Scissett, HD8 9LE
Tel   (01484) 864835
Fax   (01484) 861001
Mem   175
Sec   J Gill
Pro   I Darren
Holes   9 L 3022 yds Par 56 SSS 55
V'tors U
Fees   £10 (£13)
Loc   On A636 between Derby Dale
      and Scissett. M1 Junction 39
Arch   F O'Donnell

Baildon (1896)
Moorgate, Baildon, Shipley, BD17 5PP
Tel   (01274) 584266
Fax   (01274) 530551
Mem   750
Sec   JA Cooley
Pro   R Masters (01274) 595162
Holes   18 L 6231 yds SSS 70
V'tors WD–U before 5pm (restricted
      Tues) WE/BH–restricted
Fees   £16 (£20)
Loc   5 miles N of Bradford, off
      A6038
Arch   Tom Morris/James Braid

Ben Rhydding (1947)
*High Wood, Ben Rhydding, Ilkley,
LS9 8SB*
Tel   (01943) 608759
Mem   195 60(L) 36(J)
Sec   A Leverton
Holes   9 L 4611 yds SSS 63

V'tors WD–U exc Wed pm & Thurs
am WE–M
Fees £12 (£17)
Loc 2 miles SE of Ilkley

Bingley St Ives (1931)
St Ives Estate, Bingley, BD16 1AT
Tel (01274) 562436
Fax (01274) 511788
Sec Mrs M Welch
Pro R Firth (01274) 562506
Holes 18 L 6480 yds SSS 71
V'tors WD–U before 4pm
Fees £25 D–£30
Loc 6 miles NW of Bradford, off
A650

Bracken Ghyll (1993)
*Skipton Road, Addingham, Ilkley,
LS29 0SL*
Tel (01943) 831207
Mem 400
Sec A Thompson
(01943) 831207
Pro None
Holes 18 L 5310 yds Par 69 SSS 66
V'tors WD/BH–U WE–NA before
noon on comp days SOC
Fees £18 (£20)
Loc 3 miles W of Ilkley on old A65
to Addingham
Mis Indoor practice area

Bradford (1891)
*Hawksworth Lane, Guiseley, Leeds,
LS20 8NP*
Tel (01943) 875570
Fax (01943) 875570
Mem 650
Sec T Eagle
Pro S Weldon (01943) 873719
Holes 18 L 6259 yds SSS 71
V'tors WD–U WE–NA before noon
SOC–WD
Fees On application
Loc 8 miles N of Bradford, off
A6038. 10 miles N of Leeds
on A650

Bradford Moor (1906)
*Scarr Hall, Pollard Lane, Bradford,
BD2 4RW*
Tel (01274) 771716
Mem 350
Sec CP Bedford (01274) 771693
Holes 9 L 5854 yds SSS 68
V'tors WD–U
Fees £8–£12
Loc 2 miles N of Bradford

Bradley Park (1978)
Public
Bradley Road, Huddersfield, HD2 1PZ
Tel (01484) 223772
Fax (01484) 451613
Mem 300
Sec K Blackwell
Pro PE Reilly
Holes 18 L 6202 yds SSS 70

9 hole Par 3 course
V'tors U SOC
Fees £12 (£14.50)
Loc 2 miles N of Huddersfield, off
A6107, M62 Junction 25
Mis Floodlit driving range

Branshaw (1912)
*Branshaw Moor, Oakworth, Keighley,
BD22 7ES*
Tel (01535) 643235
Fax (01535) 648011
Mem 525
Sec T O'Hara
Pro M Tyler (01535) 647441
Holes 18 L 5858 yds SSS 68
V'tors WD–U SOC–WD
Fees D–£20 (D–£30)
Loc 2 miles SW of Keighley on
B6143
Arch James Braid/Dr A Mackenzie

Calverley (1984)
Woodhall Lane, Pudsey, LS28 5QY
Tel (0113) 256 9244
Fax (0113) 256 4362
Mem 700
Sec D Johnson (Mgr)
Pro D Johnson
Holes 18 L 5527 yds SSS 67
9 L 2137 yds Par 33
V'tors WD–U WE–pm only
Fees £15 (£20)
Loc 4 miles NE of Bradford
Mis Driving range

Castlefields (1903)
*Rastrick Common, Brighouse,
HD6 3HL*
Tel (01484) 713276
Mem 180
Sec FC Tolley
Holes 6 L 2406 yds SSS 50
V'tors M
Fees £6 (£8)
Loc 1 mile S of Brighouse

City of Wakefield (1936)
Public
*Lupset Park, Horbury Road, Wakefield,
WF2 8QS*
Tel (01924) 367442
Sec Mrs P Ambler
Pro R Holland (01924) 360282
Holes 18 L 6319 yds SSS 70
V'tors U SOC–WD
Fees On application
Loc A642, 2 miles W of Wakefield.
2 miles E of M1 Junction
39/40
Arch JSF Morrison

Clayton (1906)
*Thornton View Road, Clayton,
Bradford, BD14 6JX*
Tel (01274) 880047
Mem 170 26(L) 54(J)
Sec DA Smith (01274) 572311
Holes 9 L 5515 yds SSS 67

V'tors WD–U Sat–U Sun–after 4pm
Fees £10 D–£12 (£12)
Loc 3 miles W of Bradford, off
A647

Cleckheaton & District (1900)
*483 Bradford Road, Cleckheaton,
BD19 6BU*
Tel (01274) 874118 (Clubhouse)
Fax (01274) 871382
Web www.cleckheatongolfclub
.fsnet.co.uk
Mem 572
Sec Mrs R Newsholme (Asst Sec)
(01274) 851266
Pro M Ingham (01274) 851267
Holes 18 L 5860 yds SSS 69
V'tors U SOC
Fees £25 D–£30 (£30)
Loc Nr M62 Junction 26–A638

Cookridge Hall G&CC
Cookridge Lane, Leeds, LS16 7NL
Tel (0113) 203 0002
Fax (0113) 285 7115
Mem 650
Sec P Hickling (Gen Mgr)
(0113) 203 0007
Pro M Pearson
Holes 18 L 6788 yds Par 72 SSS 72
V'tors WD–U WE–U after 2pm SOC
Fees £20 (£25)
Loc 5 miles NW of Leeds, via
A660
Mis Driving range. Golf Academy
Arch Karl Litten

Crosland Heath (1914)
*Felk Stile Road, Crosland Heath,
Huddersfield, HD4 7AF*
Tel (01484) 653216
Mem 600
Sec D Walker (Sec/Mgr)
(01484) 653216
Pro J Coverley (01484) 653877
Holes 18 L 6004 yds SSS 70
V'tors U SOC
Fees On application
Loc 3 miles W of Huddersfield, off
A62

Crow Nest Park (1994)
*Coach Road, Hove Edge, Brighouse,
HD6 2LN*
Tel (01484) 401121
Fax (01422) 203672
Mem 300
Sec A Naylor
Pro P Everitt (01484) 401121
Holes 9 L 6020 yds Par 70 SSS 69
V'tors WD–U WE–U before noon
Fees 18 holes–£20. 9 holes–£10
Loc 5 miles E of Halifax. M62
Junction 25
Mis Driving range
Arch Will Adamson

Dewsbury District (1891)

The Pinnacle, Sands Lane, Mirfield,
WF14 8HJ

Tel　(01924) 492399
Mem　650
Sec　CB Rhodes
Pro　N Hirst (01924) 496030
Holes　18 L 6360 yds SSS 71
V'tors　WD–U WE–M –U after 4pm
　　SOC
Fees　£18 (£18)
Loc　2 miles W of Dewsbury, off
　　A644
Arch　Tom Morris/Alliss/Thomas

East Bierley (1928)

South View Road, Bierley, Bradford,
BD4 6PP

Tel　(01274) 681023
Mem　156 47(L) 30(J)
Sec　RJ Welch (01274) 683666
Holes　9 L 4692 yds SSS 63
V'tors　U exc Mon–NA after 4pm
　　Sun–NA
Fees　£14 (£16)
Loc　4 miles SE of Bradford

Elland (1910)

Hammerstones Leach Lane, Hullen
Edge, Elland, HX5 0TA

Tel　(01422) 372505
Mem　280
Sec　AD Blackburn
　　(01422) 372014
Pro　N Krzywicki (01422) 374886
Holes　9 L 5498 yds Par 66 SSS 67
V'tors　U
Fees　£15 (£25)
Loc　Elland 1 mile. M62 Junction
　　24, signpost Blackley

Fardew (1993)

Pay and play
Nursery Farm, Carr Lane, East
Morton, Keighley BD20 5RY

Tel　(01274) 561229
Fax　(01274) 561229
Mem　100
Sec　GA Richardson
Pro　I Bottomley
Holes　9 L 3104 yds Par 72 SSS 70
V'tors　U SOC
Fees　9 holes–£7 (£8) 18 holes–£12
　　(£14)
Loc　2 miles W of Bingley on A650
Arch　Will Adamson

Ferrybridge 'C' (1976)

PO Box 39, Stranglands Lane,
Knottingley, WF11 8SQ

Tel　(01977) 884165
Mem　305
Sec　TD Ellis
Holes　9 L 5137 yds SSS 65
V'tors　M
Fees　D–£6 (D–£7)
Loc　¹/2 mile off A1, on B6136
Arch　NE Pugh

Fulneck (1892)

Fulneck, Pudsey, LS28 8NT

Tel　(0113) 256 5191
Mem　290
Sec　Mrs P Warburton
　　(0113) 256 2606
Holes　9 L 5456 yds SSS 67
V'tors　WD–U WE/BH–M SOC
Fees　£14
Loc　5 miles W of Leeds

Garforth (1913)

Long Lane, Garforth, Leeds, LS25 2DS

Tel　(0113) 286 2021
Fax　(0113) 286 3308
Web　www.garforthgolfclub.co.uk
Mem　550
Sec　NG Douglas (0113) 286 3308
Pro　K Findlater (0113) 286 2063
Holes　18 L 6304 yds SSS 70
V'tors　WD–U H WE/BH–M SOC
Fees　£28 D–£32
Loc　9 miles E of Leeds, between
　　Garforth and Barwick-in-
　　Elmet
Mis　Driving range

Gotts Park (1933)

Public
Armley Ridge Road, Armley, Leeds,
LS12 2QX

Tel　(0113) 234 2019
Mem　300
Sec　BJ Bond (0113) 263 5557
Pro　JK Simpson
Holes　18 L 4960 yds SSS 64
V'tors　U
Fees　On application
Loc　2 miles W of Leeds

Halifax (1895)

Union Lane, Ogden, Halifax,
HX2 8XR

Tel　(01422) 244171
Fax　(01422) 241459
Mem　450
Pro　M Allison (01422) 240047
Holes　18 L 6037 yds SSS 69
V'tors　U WD–parties welcome SOC
Fees　£20 (£25)
Loc　4 miles N of Halifax on A629
Arch　Alex Herd/James Braid

Halifax Bradley Hall (1907)

Holywell Green, Halifax, HX4 9AN

Tel　(01422) 374108
Mem　608
Sec　JR Burton (01484) 715797
Pro　P Wood (01422) 370231
Holes　18 L 6138 yds SSS 70
V'tors　U SOC
Fees　£18 (£28)
Loc　S of Halifax on A6112

Halifax West End (1904)

Paddock Lane, Highroad Well, Halifax,
HX2 0NT

Tel　(01422) 341878

Fax　(01442) 341878

Mem　340 100(L) 60(J)
Sec　G Gower (01422) 341878
Pro　D Rishworth (01422) 363293
Holes　18 L 5951 yds SSS 69
V'tors　U SOC
Fees　£21 (£26)
Loc　2 miles NW of Halifax

Hanging Heaton (1922)

Whitecross Road, Bennett Lane,
Dewsbury, WF12 7DT

Tel　(01924) 461606
Fax　(01924) 430100
Mem　400
Sec　K Wood (01924) 430100
Pro　(01924) 467077
Holes　9 L 2923 yds SSS 68
V'tors　WD–U WE–M
Fees　£16
Loc　Dewsbury ³/4 mile (A653)

Headingley (1892)

Back Church Lane, Adel, Leeds,
LS16 8DW

Tel　(0113) 267 3052 (Clubhouse)
Fax　(0113) 281 7334
Mem　675
Sec　JR Burns JP (Mgr)
　　(0113) 267 9573
Pro　SA Foster (0113) 267 5100
Holes　18 L 6298 yds SSS 70
V'tors　WD–U before 3.30pm SOC
Fees　£30 D–£35 (£40)
Loc　5 miles NW of Leeds, off
　　A660
Arch　Dr A MacKenzie

Headley (1907)

Headley Lane, Thornton, Bradford,
BD13 3LX

Tel　(01274) 833481
Fax　(01274) 833481
Mem　270 35(L) 35(J)
Sec　A Goodman
Holes　9 L 4914 yds SSS 64
V'tors　WD–U WE–M SOC
Fees　On application
Loc　5 miles W of Bradford
　　(B6145)

Hebden Bridge (1930)

Great Mount, Wadsworth, Hebden
Bridge, HX7 8PH

Tel　(01422) 842896
Mem　300
Sec　R Priestley (01422) 842896
Holes　9 L 5242 yds Par 68 SSS 67
V'tors　WD–U
Fees　£10–£12 (£15)
Loc　1 mile N of Hebden Bridge

Horsforth (1907)

Layton Rise, Layton Road, Horsforth,
Leeds LS18 5EX

Tel　(0113) 258 6819
Mem　365 90(L) 85(J)
Sec　Mrs J Kenny
Pro　(0113) 258 5200

Holes 18 L 6293 yds SSS 70
V'tors U SOC
Fees D–£25 (£35)
Loc 6 miles NW of Leeds

Howley Hall (1900)

Scotchman Lane, Morley, Leeds,
LS27 0NX
Tel **(01924) 350100**
Fax (01924) 350104
Mem 492
Sec D Jones (01924) 350100
Pro G Watkinson (01924) 350102
Holes 18 L 6058 yds Par 71 SSS 69
V'tors U SOC–WD/Sun before 5pm
Fees £27.50 D–£33 (£38)
Loc 4 miles SW of Leeds on
B6123

Huddersfield (1891)

Fixby Hall, Lightridge Road,
Huddersfield, HD2 2EP
Tel **(01484) 420110**
Fax (01484) 424623
Web www.huddersfield-golf.co.uk
Mem 682
Sec JM Seatter (Gen Mgr)
Mrs D Lockett
(01484) 426203
Pro P Carman (01484) 426463
Holes 18 L 6432 yds SSS 71
V'tors U SOC–WD
Fees £37 D–£47 (£47 D–£57)
Loc 2 miles N of Huddersfield, off
A6107. M62 Junction 24
Mis Driving range

Ilkley (1890)

Myddleton, Ilkley, LS29 0BE
Tel **(01943) 607277**
Fax (01943) 816130
Mem 530
Sec AK Hatfield (01943) 600214
Pro JL Hammond
(01943) 607463
Holes 18 L 6260 yds SSS 70
V'tors U
Fees £37 (£42)
Loc NW of Ilkley, off A65

Keighley (1904)

Howden Park, Utley, Keighley,
BD20 6DH
Tel **(01535) 604778**
Fax (01535) 610572
Mem 600
Sec G Cameron Dawson
Pro M Bradley (01535) 665370
Holes 18 L 6141 yds SSS 70
V'tors WD–U ex Tues Sat–NA
Sun/BH–NA before 2pm
Fees £27 D–£31 (£31 D–£37)
Loc 1 mile W of Keighley on A629

Leeds (1896)

Elmete Road, Roundhay, Leeds,
LS8 2LJ
Tel **(0113) 265 8775**
Fax (0113) 232 3369
Web www.leedsgolfclub.com

Mem 545
Sec SJ Clarkson (0113) 265 9203
Pro S Longster (0113) 265 8786
Holes 18 L 6092 yds SSS 69
V'tors WD–U WE–M SOC
Fees £25 D–£32
Loc 4 miles NE of Leeds, off A58

Leeds Golf Centre (1994)

Pay and play
Wike Ridge Lane, Shadwell, Leeds,
LS17 9JW
Tel **(0113) 288 6000**
Fax (0113) 288 6185
Web www.leedsgolfcentre.co.uk
Mem 500
Sec D Dourambeis
Pro N Harvey
Holes 18 L 6800 yds SSS 72
12 hole Par 3 course
V'tors U SOC
Fees £14.50 (£16.50)
Loc NE of Leeds, between A58
and A61
Mis Driving range. Golf Academy
Arch Donald Steel

Lightcliffe (1907)

Knowle Top Road, Lightcliffe,
HX3 8SW
Tel **(01422) 202459**
Mem 180 95(L) 84(J)
Sec CCD Balaam (01422) 201650
Pro R Kershaw
Holes 9 L 5368 metres SSS 68
V'tors U H–exc comp days Sun
am–M SOC
Fees £15 (£20)
Loc 3 miles E of Halifax (A58)

Lofthouse Hill

Leeds Road, Lofthouse Hill, Wakefield,
WF3 3LR
Tel **(01924) 823703**
Fax (01924) 823703
Sec N Todd
Pro B Janes (01924) 820048
Holes 9 L 3167 yds Par 35
V'tors M SOC
Fees 18 holes–£17.50 9 holes–£10
Loc Between Leeds and Wakefield
Mis Driving range

Longley Park (1910)

Maple Street, Huddersfield, HD5 9AX
Tel **(01484) 426932**
Mem 400
Pro N Leeming (01484) 422304
Holes 9 L 5212 yds Par 66 SSS 66
V'tors WD–U exc Thurs
WE–restricted
Fees £13.50 (£16)
Loc Huddersfield ½ mile

Low Laithes (1925)

Park Mill Lane, Flushdyke, Ossett,
WF5 9AP
Tel **(01924) 273275**
Fax (01924) 266067

Mem 575
Sec TJ White (01924) 266067
Pro P Browning (01924) 274667
Holes 18 L 6468 yds SSS 71
V'tors U WE–no parties SOC–WD
Fees £19 D–£23 (£32)
Loc 2 miles W of Wakefield. M1
Junction 40
Arch Dr A Mackenzie

The Manor

Bradford Road, Drighlington, Bradford,
BD11 1AB
Tel **(0113) 285 2644**
Mem 300
Sec J Crompton (Sec/Mgr)
Pro J Crompton
Holes 18 L 6508 yds Par 72 SSS 71
V'tors U SOC–exc Sat
Fees £15 (£15)
Loc 1 mile from M62 Junction 27,
off A650
Mis Floodlit driving range. 6 holes
pitch & putt course
Arch David Hemstock

Marriott Hollins Hall Hotel (1999)

Hollins Hill, Baildon, Shipley,
BD17 7QW
Tel **(01274) 534212**
Fax (01274) 534220
Mem 300
Sec Janice Dornom
(01274) 534250
Holes 18 L 6700 yds Par 71 SSS 72
V'tors H
Fees £40
Loc 6 miles N of Bradford on
A6038
Arch Ross McMurray

Marsden (1921)

Hemplow, Marsden, Huddersfield,
HD7 6NN
Tel **(01484) 844253**
Mem 200 50(L) 50(J)
Sec GM Sykes
Pro N Krzywicki
Holes 9 L 5702 yds SSS 68
V'tors WD–U Sat–NA before 4pm
Sun–M SOC
Fees £10
Loc 8 miles W of Huddersfield, off
A62
Arch Dr A Mackenzie

Meltham (1908)

Thick Hollins Hall, Meltham,
Huddersfield, HD9 4DA
Tel **(01484) 850227**
Fax (01484) 859051
Web www.meltham-golf.co.uk
Mem 650
Sec CJ Naylor (Hon)
Pro PF Davies (01484) 851521
Holes 18 L 6396 yds SSS 70
V'tors H
Fees £22 (£27)
Loc 5 miles SW of Huddersfield
(B6107)

Mid Yorkshire (1993)

Havercroft Lane, Darrington,
Pontefract, WF8 3BP

Tel	**(01977) 704522**
Fax	(01977) 600823
Mem	600
Sec	Linda Darwood
Pro	A Corbett (01977) 600844
Holes	18 L 6340 yds SSS 71
V'tors	U H SOC
Fees	£15 (£25)
Loc	Nr A1/M62 junction
Mis	Floodlit driving range
Arch	Steve Marnoch

Middleton Park (1933)

Public
Ring Road, Beeston Park, Middleton,
LS10 3TN

Tel	**(0113) 270 9506**
Mem	310
Sec	TC Foster (0113) 252 2215
Pro	S Shaw
Holes	18 L 5233 yds SSS 66
V'tors	U
Fees	On application
Loc	3 miles S of Leeds

Moor Allerton (1923)

Coal Road, Wike, Leeds, LS17 9NH

Tel	**(0113) 266 1154**
Fax	(0113) 237 1124
Mem	1000
Sec	N Lomas
Pro	R Lane (0113) 266 5209
Holes	27 holes:
	6470-6843 yds SSS 73-74
V'tors	WD/Sat–U Sun–NA SOC
Fees	£45 D–£50 (£72 D–£83)
Loc	5½ miles N of Leeds, off
	A61
Mis	Driving range
Arch	Robert Trent Jones Sr

Moortown (1909)

Harrogate Road, Leeds, LS17 7DB

Tel	**(0113) 268 6521**
Fax	(0113) 268 0986
Mem	600
Sec	KC Bradley
Pro	B Hutchinson
	(0113) 268 3636
Holes	18 L 6995 yds SSS 74
V'tors	H
Fees	£45 D–£55 (£50 D–£60)
Loc	5½ miles N of Leeds on A61
Arch	Dr A Mackenzie

Normanton (1903)

Hatfeild Hall, Aberford Road, Stanley,
Wakefield WF3 4JP

Tel	**(01924) 200900**
Fax	(01924) 200777
Mem	600
Sec	RJ Metcalfe
Pro	F Houlgate
Holes	18 L 6191 yds Par 72 SSS 69
V'tors	By arrangement
Fees	On application
Loc	3 miles N of Wakefield
	(A642). M62 Junction 30

Northcliffe (1921)

High Bank Lane, Shipley, Bradford,
BD18 4LJ

Tel	**(01274) 584085**
Fax	(01274) 596731
Web	www.northcliffegolfclub shipley.co.uk
Mem	867
Sec	I Collins (01274) 596731
Pro	M Hillas (01274) 587193
Holes	18 L 6113 yds SSS 70
V'tors	U SOC
Fees	£20 (£25)
Loc	3 miles NW of Bradford, off A650 Keighley road
Arch	James Braid

Otley (1906)

West Busk Lane, Otley, LS21 3NG

Tel	**(01943) 465329**
Fax	(01943) 850387
Web	www.otley-golfclub.co.uk
Mem	700
Sec	PJ Clarke Ext 202
Pro	S Tomkinson Ext 203
Holes	18 L 6225 yds SSS 70
V'tors	U exc Sat–NA SOC
Fees	£28 (£35)
Loc	1 mile W of Otley, off A6038

Oulton Park (1990)

Public
Oulton, Rothwell, Leeds, LS26 8EX

Tel	**(0113) 282 3152**
Fax	(0113) 282 6290
Mem	390
Sec	A Cooper (Mgr)
Pro	S Gromett
Holes	18 L 6479 yds SSS 71
	9 L 3287 yds SSS 35
V'tors	U SOC–WD
Fees	18 hole: £10.15 (£13.15)
	9 hole: £5.95 (£6.95)
Loc	5 miles SE of Leeds, off A642. N of M62 Junction 30
Mis	Driving range
Arch	Alliss/Thomas

Outlane (1906)

Slack Lane, Outlane, Huddersfield,
HD3 3YL

Tel	**(01422) 374762**
Fax	(01422) 311789
Mem	500
Sec	P Brennan
Pro	D Chapman
Holes	18 L 6010 yds SSS 70
V'tors	U SOC
Fees	£18 (£28)
Loc	4 miles W of Huddersfield, off A640. M62 Junction 23

Painthorpe House (1961)

Painthorpe Lane, Crigglestone,
Wakefield, WF4 3HE

Tel	**(01924) 255083**
Fax	(01924) 252022
Mem	180
Sec	H Kershaw (01924) 274527
Holes	9 L 4520 yds SSS 62
V'tors	U

Fees	£5 (£6)
Loc	1 mile SE of M1 Junction 39

Phoenix Park (1922)

Dick Lane, Thornbury, Bradford,
BD3 7AT

Tel	**(01274) 667573**
Mem	180
Sec	C Lally (01274) 668218
Pro	None
Holes	9 L 4982 yds SSS 64
V'tors	WD/BH–U WE–NA
Fees	On application
Loc	Thornbury Roundabout (A647)

Pontefract & District (1904)

Park Lane, Pontefract, WF8 4QS

Tel	**(01977) 792241**
Fax	(01977) 792241
Web	www.pdgc.cwc.net
Mem	841
Sec	RE Guiver (Mgr)
Pro	NJ Newman (01977) 706806
Holes	18 L 6227 yds SSS 70
V'tors	I SOC–WD exc Wed
Fees	£25 (£32)
Loc	Pontefract 1 mile on B6134. M62 Junction 32

Pontefract Park (1973)

Public
Park Road, Pontefract, WF8

Tel	**(01977) 702799**
Holes	18 L 4068 yds SSS 62
V'tors	U
Fees	On application
Loc	Between Pontefract and M62 roundabout, nr racecourse

Queensbury (1923)

Brighouse Road, Queensbury, Bradford,
BD13 1QF

Tel	**(01274) 882155**
Mem	421 52(L) 35(J)
Sec	B Cox
Pro	D Delaney (01274) 816864
Holes	9 L 5102 yds SSS 65
V'tors	U
Fees	£15 (£30)
Loc	4 miles SW of Bradford (A647)

Rawdon (1896)

Buckstone Drive, Micklefield Lane,
Rawdon, LS19 6BD

Tel	**(0113) 250 6040**
Mem	220 55(L) 50(J)
Sec	RA Adams (0113) 250 6064
Pro	(0113) 250 5017
Holes	9 L 5982 yds SSS 69
V'tors	WD–H WE/BH–M SOC
Fees	£16
Loc	6 miles NW of Leeds nr A65/A658 junction

Riddlesden (1927)

Howden Rough, Riddlesden, Keighley, BD20 5QN

Tel	(01535) 602148
Mem	400
Sec	Mrs KM Brooksbank
	(01535) 607646
Holes	18 L 4295 yds Par 63 SSS 61
V'tors	U exc Sun–NA before 2pm
Fees	£15 (£20)
Loc	1 mile from Riddlesden, off Scott Lane West. 3 miles N of Keighley, off A650

Roundhay (1923)

Public

Park Lane, Leeds, LS8 2EJ

Tel	(0113) 266 2695
Mem	290
Sec	RH McLauchlan
Pro	JA Pape (0113) 266 1686
Holes	9 L 5322 yds SSS 65
V'tors	U
Fees	On application
Loc	N of Leeds, off Moortown Ring Road

Ryburn (1910)

Norland, Sowerby Bridge, Halifax, HX6 3QP

Tel	(01422) 831355
Mem	200
Sec	J Hoyle (01422) 843070
Holes	9 L 4907 yds SSS 64
V'tors	U
Fees	£15 (£20)
Loc	3 miles S of Halifax

Sand Moor (1926)

Alwoodley Lane, Leeds, LS17 7DJ

Tel	(0113) 268 1685
Fax	(0113) 268 5180
Mem	540
Sec	K Spencer
Pro	P Tupling
	(0113) 268 3925
Holes	18 L 6429 yds SSS 71
V'tors	WD–H by arrangement WE–NA
Fees	£36 (£45)
Loc	5 miles N of Leeds, off A61
Arch	Dr A Mackenzie

Scarcroft (1937)

Syke Lane, Leeds, LS14 3BQ

Tel	(0113) 289 2311
Fax	(0113) 289 3835
Web	www.sgccwc.net
Mem	580
Sec	D Tear (Gen Mgr)
	(0113) 289 2311
Pro	D Tear (0113) 289 2780
Holes	18 L 6426 yds SSS 71
V'tors	WD–U WE/BH–M or by arrangement SOC–WD
Fees	£30 D–£38 (£40)
Loc	7 miles N of Leeds, off A58

Shipley (1896)

Beckfoot Lane, Cottingley Bridge, Bingley, BD16 1LX

Tel	(01274) 563212
Fax	(01274) 567739
Web	www.shipleygc.co.uk
Mem	600
Sec	Mrs MJ Bryan
	(01274) 568652
Pro	JR Parry (01274) 563674
Holes	18 L 6235 yds SSS 70
V'tors	WD–U exc Tues–NA before 2pm Sat–NA before 4pm
Fees	£25 D–£32 (£28 D–£35) Mon–£22 exc BH
Loc	6 miles N of Bradford on A650
Arch	Colt/Alison/Mackenzie/Braid

Silsden (1913)

Brunthwaite Lane, Brunthwaite, Silsden, BD20 0ND

Tel	(01535) 652998
Fax	(01535) 654273
Mem	300
Sec	J Bellerby
Holes	18 L 5259 yds Par 67 SSS 66
V'tors	Sat–restricted Sun–U after 1pm
Fees	£15 (£20)
Loc	5 miles N of Keighley, off A6034

South Bradford (1906)

Pearson Road, Odsal, Bradford, BD6 1BH

Tel	(01274) 679195
Mem	200
Sec	AI Moody
Pro	P Cooke (01274) 673346
Holes	9 L 6076 yds SSS 69
V'tors	WD–U WE–M
Fees	On application
Loc	Bradford 2 miles, nr Odsal Stadium

South Leeds (1914)

Gipsy Lane, Ring Road, Beeston, Leeds LS11 5TU

Tel	(0113) 270 0479
Mem	450
Sec	J Neal (0113) 277 1676
Pro	M Lewis (0113) 270 2598
Holes	18 L 5865 yds SSS 68
V'tors	WD–U WE–M SOC
Fees	£18 (£25)
Loc	4 miles S of Leeds. 2 miles from M62 and M1

Temple Newsam (1923)

Public

Temple Newsam Road, Halton, Leeds, LS15 0LN

Tel	(0113) 264 5624
Mem	500
Sec	G Hollins
Pro	J Pape (0113) 264 7362
Holes	Lord Irwin 18 L 6448 yds SSS 71; Lady Dorothy Wood 18 L 6229 yds SSS 70

Shipley / V'tors (continued)

V'tors	U SOC
Fees	£7.50 (£9) Summer £7 (£8.50) Winter
Loc	5 miles E of Leeds, off A63

Todmorden (1894)

Rive Rocks, Cross Stone, Todmorden, 0L14 8RD

Tel	(01706) 812986
Mem	179 44(L) 26(J)
Sec	G Holt (01706) 813653
Holes	9 L 5902 yds SSS 68
V'tors	WD/BH–U WE–M SOC–WD
Fees	£15 (£20)
Loc	1 mile N of Todmorden, off A646

Wakefield (1891)

28 Woodthorpe Lane, Sandal, Wakefield, WF2 6JH

Tel	(01924) 255104
Fax	(01924) 242752
Mem	500
Sec	AJ McVicar (01924) 258778
Pro	IM Wright (01924) 255380
Holes	18 L 6653 yds SSS 72
V'tors	U H SOC–Wed–Fri
Fees	On application
Loc	3 miles S of Wakefield on A61. M1 Junction 39
Arch	Alex Herd

Waterton Park (1995)

The Balk, Walton, Wakefield, WF2 6QL

Tel	(01924) 259525
Fax	(01924) 256969
Mem	650
Sec	L Lammas
Pro	N Wood (01924) 255557
Holes	18 L 6843 yds Par 72 SSS 73
V'tors	WD–H SOC
Fees	D–£30
Loc	4 miles SE of Wakefield centre
Mis	Driving range
Arch	Simon Gidman

West Bowling (1898)

Newall Hall, Rooley Lane, Bradford, BD5 8LB

Tel	(01274) 724449
Fax	(01274) 393207
Mem	500
Sec	IW Brogden (01274) 393207
Pro	IA Marshall (01274) 728036
Holes	18 L 5769 yds SSS 68
V'tors	WD–U H SOC
Fees	£24 (£30)
Loc	Junction of M606 and Bradford Ring Road East

West Bradford (1900)

Chellow Grange, Haworth Road, Bradford, BD9 6NP

Tel	(01274) 542767
Fax	(01274) 482079
Mem	450
Sec	IP Milnes (Hon)
Pro	NM Barber (01274) 542102
Holes	18 L 5738 yds SSS 68

V'tors U
Fees £21 (£21)
Loc 3 miles W of Bradford
(B6144)

Wetherby (1910)

Linton Lane, Linton, Wetherby,
LS22 4JF
Tel (01937) 580089
Fax (01937) 581915
Mem 630
Sec L McGrae (Mgr)
(01937) 580089
Pro M Daubney (01937) 583375
Holes 18 L 6235 yds SSS 70
V'tors WE–U after 10am SOC–WD
Fees £28 (£40)
Loc ³/4 mile W of Wetherby. A1
Wetherby roundabout
Mis Driving range

Whitwood (1987)

Public
Altofts Lane, Whitwood, Castleford,
WF10 5PZ
Tel (01977) 512835
Sec S Hicks (Hon)
Pro R Holland
Holes 9 L 6176 yds SSS 69
V'tors WD–U WE–booking
necessary
Fees On application
Loc 2 miles SW of Castleford
(A655). M62 Junction 31

Willow Valley (1993)

Pay and play
Clifton, Brighouse, HD6 4JB
Tel (01274) 878624
Fax (01274) 852805
Mem 280
Sec I Buckley
Pro J Haworth
Holes 18 & 9 hole courses
Academy course
V'tors U
Fees 18 hole:£22 (£26)
9 hole:£6.50 (£7.50)
Loc SW of Leeds, M62 Junction
25
Mis Driving range
Arch Jonathan Gaunt

Woodhall Hills (1905)

Woodhall Road, Calverley, Pudsey,
LS28 5UN
Tel (0113) 256 4771 (Clubhouse)
Fax (0113) 295 4594
Mem 550
Sec J Armitage (0113) 255 4594
Pro W Lockett (0113) 256 2857
Holes 18 L 6184 yds SSS 70
V'tors WD–U Sat–U after 4.30pm
Sun–U after 9.30am
Fees £20.50 (£25.50)
Loc 4 miles E of Bradford, off
A647, past Calverley GC

Woodsome Hall (1922)

Woodsome Hall, Fenay Bridge,
Huddersfield, HD8 0LQ
Tel (01484) 602971
Fax (01484) 608260
Web www.woodsomehall.co.uk
Mem 279 130(L) 85(J)
Sec TJ Mee (Mgr)
(01484) 602739
RB Shaw (Hon)
Pro M Higginbottom
(01484) 602034
Holes 18 L 6080 yds SSS 69
V'tors U H exc Tues–NA before
4pm SOC
Fees £30 D–£40 (£50 D–£60)
Loc 6 miles SE of Huddersfield on
A629 Penistone road

Woolley Park (1995)

Woolley, Wakefield, WF4 2JS
Tel (01226) 380144 (Bookings)
Fax (01226) 390295
Web www.woolleypark.co.uk
Mem 500
Sec D Rowbottom (Prop)
(01226) 382209
Pro J Baldwin
Holes 18 L 6606 yds Par 71 SSS 72
V'tors WD–U WE–restricted SOC
Fees £14 (£20)
Loc 5 miles S of Wakefield on
A61. M1 Junction 38, 2 miles
Arch M Shattock

Ireland

Co Antrim

Antrim (1997)

Allen Park Golf Centre, 45 Castle
Road, Antrim
Tel (028) 9442 9001
Fax (028) 9442 9001
Mem 500
Sec Marie Agnew (Mgr)
Pro S Hamill
Holes 18 L 6110 m Par 72 SSS 72
V'tors U
Fees £14 (£16)
Loc Antrim
Mis Driving range

Ballycastle (1890)

Cushendall Road, Ballycastle,
BT64 6QP
Tel (028) 2076 2536
Fax (028) 2076 9909
Mem 920
Sec BJ Dillon (Hon)
Pro I McLaughlin
(028) 2076 2506
Holes 18 L 5927 yds SSS 70
V'tors U H SOC

Fees £20 (£30)
Loc Between Portrush and
Cushendall (A2)

Ballyclare (1923)

25 Springvale Road, Ballyclare,
BT39 9JW
Tel (028) 9334 2352 (Clubhouse)
Fax (028) 9332 2696
Mem 440
Sec H McConnell
(028) 9332 2696
Holes 18 L 5840 yds SSS 71
V'tors WD–U WE–NA before 4pm
Fees £18 (£24)
Loc 1¹/2 miles N of Ballyclare. 14
miles N of Belfast
Arch T McAuley

Ballymena (1902)

128 Raceview Road, Ballymena,
BT42 4HY
Tel (028) 2586 1207/1487
Fax (028) 2586 1487
Mem 824
Sec C McAuley (Hon)
Pro K Revie

Holes 18 L 5299 m Par 68 SSS 67
V'tors WD/Sun–U SOC
Fees £17 (£22)
Loc 2 miles E of Ballymena on
A42

Bentra

Public
Slaughterford Road, Whitehead,
BT38 9TG
Tel (028) 9337 8996
Sec N Houston (028) 9335 1711
Holes 9 L 3155 yds Par 36 SSS 34
V'tors U
Fees £8 (£11)
Loc 4 miles N of Carrickfergus on
A2 Larne road
Arch James Braid

Bushfoot (1890)

50 Bushfoot Road, Portballintrae,
BT57 8RR
Tel (028) 2073 1317
Fax (028) 2073 1852
Mem 860
Sec J Knox Thompson
(Sec/Mgr)

Holes 9 L 6001 yds SSS 68
V'tors U Sat–NA after noon SOC
Fees £14 (£18)
Loc 1 mile N of Bushmills. 4 miles E of Portrush

Cairndhu (1928)

192 Coast Road, Ballygally, Larne, BT40 2QC

Tel (028) 2858 3324
Fax (028) 2858 3324
Mem 875
Sec N Moore (028) 2858 3324
Pro R Walker (028) 2858 3417
Holes 18 L 6112 yds SSS 69
V'tors U exc Sat–NA
Fees £20 (£25)
Loc 4 miles N of Larne
Arch JSF Morrison

Carrickfergus (1926)

35 North Road, Carrickfergus, BT38 8LP

Tel (028) 9336 3713
Fax (028) 9336 3023
Mem 385
Sec JW Thomson (Sec/Mgr)
Pro M Johnston
(028) 9335 1803
Holes 18 L 5752 yds SSS 68
V'tors U SOC
Fees £18 (£25)
Loc 7 miles E of Belfast, off M5

Cushendall (1937)

21 Shore Road, Cushendall, BT44 0NG
Tel (028) 2177 1318
Mem 834
Sec S McLaughlin
(028) 2175 8366
Holes 9 L 4834 m SSS 63
V'tors WE–restricted SOC
Fees £13 (£18)
Loc Cushendall, 25 miles N of Larne

Down Royal (1990)

Dungarton Road, Maze, Lisburn, BT27
Tel (028) 9262 1339
Fax (028) 9262 1339
Mem 52
Sec J Tinnion (Mgr)
Pro C Calder
Holes 18 L 6058 m Par 72 SSS 69
V'tors U
Fees £12 D–£17 (£24)
Loc Lisburn, W of Belfast City (M1)
Arch Stewart Assoc

Galgorm Castle (1997)

200 Galgorm Road, Ballymena, BT42 1HL
Tel (028) 2565 0210
Fax (028) 2565 1151
Web www.galgormcastle.co.uk
Mem 500
Sec B McGrown (Mgr)
Pro P Collins

Holes 18 L 6724 yds Par 72 SSS 72
V'tors U SOC
Fees £20 (£25)
Loc Ballymena
Mis Driving range

Gracehill (1995)

141 Ballinlea Road, Stranocum, Ballymoney, BT53 8PX
Tel (028) 2075 1209
Fax (028) 2075 1074
Web www.gracehillgolfclub.co.uk
Mem 360
Sec M McClure (Mgr)
Holes 18 L 6600 yds Par 72
V'tors U
Fees £15–£20 (£25)
Loc 6 miles N of Ballymoney (B66)
Arch Frank Ainsworth

Greenacres (1996)

153 Ballyrobert Road, Ballyclare, BT39 9RT
Tel (028) 9335 4111
Fax (028) 9335 4166
Web www.greenacresgolfclub .co.uk
Mem 340
Sec P Watson
Holes 18 L 5893 yds Par 70 SSS 68
V'tors U
Fees £12 (£18)
Loc 3 miles from Corrs Corner on B56
Mis Floodlit driving range

Greenisland (1894)

156 Upper Road, Greenisland, Carrickfergus, BT38 8RW
Tel (028) 9086 2236
Mem 740
Sec H Riddell (Hon) (028) 9086 6977
Holes 9 L 5536 m Par 71 SSS 69
V'tors WD–U WE–NA before 5pm SOC–exc Sat
Fees £12 (£18)
Loc 9 miles NE of Belfast
Arch H Middleton

Hilton Templepatrick

Castle Upton Estate, Paradise Walk, Templepatrick, BT39 0DD
Tel (028) 9443 5542
Fax (028) 9443 5511
Mem 350
Sec W Donald (Mgr)
Pro E Logue
Holes 18 L 7300 yds Par 71 SSS 71
V'tors U H
Fees £35 (£40)
Loc 12 miles N of Belfast. M2 Junction 5. Belfast Airport 6 miles
Mis Driving range
Arch Jones/Feherty

Lambeg (1986)

Bells Lane, Lambeg, Lisburn, BT27 4QH
Tel (028) 9266 2738
Fax (028) 9260 3432
Mem 200
Sec B Jackson (Hon)
Pro I Murdock
Holes 18 L 4139 m Par 66 SSS 62
V'tors U SOC
Fees £7.40 (£9.40)
Loc SW of Belfast, off Lisburn road

Larne (1894)

54 Ferris Bay Road, Islandmagee, Larne, BT40 3RJ
Tel (028) 9338 2228
Mem 420
Sec RI Johnston
Holes 9 L 6288 yds SSS 70
V'tors WD–U WE–M after 5pm SOC–WD/Sun
Fees £10 (£18)
Loc 6 miles N of Whitehead on Browns Bay road
Arch George Baillie

Lisburn (1891)

68 Eglantine Road, Lisburn, BT27 5RQ
Tel (028) 9267 7216
Fax (028) 9260 3608
Mem 1421
Sec GE McVeigh (Sec/Mgr)
Pro BR Campbell (028) 9267 7217
Holes 18 L 6647 yds Par 72 SSS 72
V'tors WD–U WE–M SOC–Mon & Thurs
Fees £25 (£30)
Loc 3 miles S of Lisburn on A1
Arch Hawtree

Mallusk (1992)

Mallusk, Newtownabbey, BT36 2RF
Tel (028) 9084 3799
Mem 75
Sec J Smith (Mgr)
Holes 9 L 4444 m SSS 62
V'tors U
Fees £6.50 (£8.75)
Loc 4 miles NW of Newtownabbey (B95)

Massereene (1895)

51 Lough Road, Antrim, BT41 4DQ
Tel (028) 9442 9293
Fax (028) 9448 7661
Mem 850
Sec Mrs S Greene (028) 9442 8096
Pro J Smyth (028) 9446 4074
Holes 18 L 6602 yds SSS 72
V'tors U SOC
Fees £25 (£30)
Loc 1 mile S of Antrim

Royal Portrush (1888)
Dunluce Road, Portrush, BT56 8JQ
Tel   **(028) 7082 2311**
Fax   (028) 7082 3139
Web www.royalportrushgolfclub
      .com
Mem 997 297(L)
Sec   Miss W Erskine
Pro   G McNeill (028) 7082 3335
Holes Dunluce 18 L 6772 yds
      SSS 73;
      Valley 18 L 6273 yds SSS 70;
      Skerries-9 hole course
V'tors WD–I H exc Wed & Fri
      pm–NA Sat–NA before 3pm
      Sun–NA before 10.30am
      SOC
Fees Dunluce £85 (£95) Valley
      £30 (£37.50)
Loc   Portrush Coastal Rd ½ mile
Arch HS Colt

Whitehead (1904)
McCrae's Brae, Whitehead,
Carrickfergus, BT38 9NZ
Tel   **(028) 9337 0820**
Fax   (028) 9337 0825
Mem 1076
Sec   J Niblock (Sec/Mgr)
Pro   C Farr (028) 9337 0821
Holes 18 L 6050 yds SSS 69
V'tors WD–U WE–M SOC–exc Sat
Fees £15 (£20)
Loc   ½ mile from Whitehead, off
      road to Island Magee
Arch AB Armstrong

Co Armagh

Ashfield (1990)
Freeduff, Cullyhanna, Newry,
BT35 0JJ
Tel   **(028) 3086 8180**
Mem 100
Sec   J Quinn (Sec/Mgr)
Pro   E Maney
Holes 18 L 5110 m Par 69 SSS 67
V'tors U
Fees £10 (£12)
Loc   6 miles S of
      Newtownhamilton (B135)
Mis   Driving range
Arch Frank Ainsworth

County Armagh (1893)
Newry Road, Armagh, BT60 1EN
Tel   **(028) 3752 2501**
Fax   (028) 3752 5861
Mem 1200
Sec   M Grant (028) 3752 5861
Pro   A Rankin (028) 3752 5864
Holes 18 L 6184 yds SSS 69
V'tors SOC
Fees £15 (£20)
Loc   40 miles SW of Belfast by M1

Edenmore (1992)
Drumnabreeze Road, Magheralin,
Craigavon, BT67 0RH
Tel   **(028) 9261 1310**
Fax   (028) 9261 3310
Mem 332
Sec   K Logan (Sec/Mgr)
Holes 18 L 6244 yds Par 71 SSS 70
V'tors U SOC
Fees £13 (£16)
Loc   4 miles E of Lurgan (A3)
Arch F Ainsworth

Lurgan (1893)
The Demesne, Lurgan, BT67 9BN
Tel   **(028) 3832 2087**
      (Clubhouse)
Fax   (028) 3832 5306
Mem 918
Sec   Mrs G Turkington
Pro   D Paul (028) 3832 1068
Holes 18 L 6257 yds SSS 70
V'tors U SOC–Mon/Thurs/Fri
      am/Sun am
Fees £15 (£20)
Loc   Nr Brownlow Castle, Lurgan
Arch Frank Pennink

Portadown (1902)
192 Gilford Road, Portadown,
BT63 5LF
Tel   **(028) 3835 5356**
Fax   (028) 3839 1394
Mem 959
Sec   Mrs ME Holloway
Pro   P Stevenson (028) 3833 4655
Holes 18 L 5691 m SSS 70
V'tors WD–U exc Tues
Fees £17 (£22)
Loc   3 miles S of Portadown,
      towards Gilford

Silverwood (1983)
Public
Turmoyra Lane, Silverwood, Lurgan,
BT66 6NG
Tel   **(028) 3832 6606**
Fax   (028) 3834 7272
Mem 280
Sec   G Coupland (Sec/Mgr)
Pro   D Paul (028) 3832 6606
Holes 18 L 6459 yds Par 72 SSS 71
V'tors U
Fees £12 (£15)
Loc   Lurgan 1 mile. M1 Junction
      10
Mis   Floodlit driving range

Tandragee (1922)
Markethill Road, Tandragee,
BT62 2ER
Tel   **(028) 3884 0727 (Clubhouse)**
Fax   (028) 3884 0664
Web www.tandragee.co.uk
Mem 976
Sec   D Clayton (028) 3884 1272
Pro   P Stevenson (028) 3884 1761
Holes 18 L 5754 m Par 71 SSS 70
V'tors U SOC
Fees £15 (£20)

Loc   8 miles S of Portadown on
      A27
Arch F Hawtree

Belfast

Ballyearl Golf Centre
Public
585 Doagh Road, Newtownabbey,
BT36 5RZ
Tel   **(028) 9084 8287**
Fax   (028) 9084 4896
Pro   J Robinson (028) 9084 0899
Holes 9 L 2362 yds Par 3 course
V'tors U
Fees £4.90 (£5.70)
Loc   N of Mossley on B59, via A8
Mis   Floodlit driving range

Balmoral (1914)
518 Lisburn Road, Belfast, BT9 6GX
Tel   **(028) 9038 1514**
Fax   (028) 9066 6759
Mem 925
Sec   RC McConkey (Mgr)
Pro   G Bleakley (028) 9066 7747
Holes 18 L 5909 m SSS 70
V'tors U exc Sat SOC–Mon & Thurs
Fees £20 (£30)
Loc   2 miles S of Belfast by Kings
      Hall

Belvoir Park (1927)
73 Church Road, Newtownbreda,
Belfast, BT8 4AN
Tel   **(028) 9049 1693**
Fax   (028) 9064 6113
Mem 1100
Sec   Ann Vaughan
      (028) 9049 1693
Pro   GM Kelly
Holes 18 L 6501 yds SSS 71
V'tors U–booking necessary
Fees £33 (£38)
Loc   3 miles S of Belfast centre, off
      Newcastle road
Arch HS Colt

Cliftonville (1911)
Westland Road, Belfast, BT14 6NH
Tel   **(028) 9074 4158**
Mem 429
Sec   JM Henderson
      (Hon) (028) 9074 6595
Holes 9 L 6242 yds SSS 70
V'tors U exc Sat
Fees £13 (£16)
Loc   Belfast

Dunmurry (1905)
91 Dunmurry Lane, Dunmurry, Belfast,
BT17 9JS
Tel   **(028) 9061 0834**
Fax   (028) 9060 2540
Mem 493 127(L) 117(J)
Sec   T Cassidy (Golf Mgr)
Pro   J Dolan (028) 9062 1314

Holes 18 L 6080 yds SSS 69
V'tors Tues & Thurs–NA after 5pm
Sat–NA before 5pm SOC
Fees £23 (£33) SOC–£20
Loc Belfast 5 miles
Arch T McAuley

Fortwilliam (1891)

Downview Avenue, Belfast, B15 4EZ
Tel (028) 9037 0770
Fax (028) 9078 1891
Mem 1100
Sec M Purdy
Pro P Hanna (028) 9077 0980
Holes 18 L 5973 yds SSS 69
V'tors U SOC
Fees £22 (£29)
Loc 2 miles N of Belfast on M2

Gilnahirk (1983)

Public
*Manns Corner, Upper Braniel Road,
Belfast, BT5 7TX*
Tel (028) 9044 8477
Mem 200
Sec H Moore
Pro K Gray
Holes 9 L 2699 m SSS 68
V'tors U
Fees On application
Loc 3 miles SE of Belfast, off A23

The Knock Club (1895)

*Summerfield, Dundonald, Belfast,
BT16 2QX*
Tel (028) 9048 2249
Fax (028) 9048 3251
Mem 900
Sec Anne Armstrong
(028) 9048 3251
Pro G Fairweather
(028) 9048 3825
Holes 18 L 6407 yds SSS 71
V'tors U SOC–Mon & Thurs
Fees D–£20 (£25)
Loc 4 miles E of Belfast on the
Upper Newtownards Road
Arch Colt/Mackenzie/Alison

Malone (1895)

*240 Upper Malone Road, Dunmurry,
Belfast, BT17 9LB*
Tel (028) 9061 2695
Fax (028) 9043 1394
Web www.malonegolfclub.co.uk
Mem 759 379(L) 211(J)
Sec JNS Agate
(028) 9061 2758
Pro M McGee
(028) 9061 4917
Holes 18 L 6599 yds SSS 71
9 L 3160 yds SSS 36
V'tors Tues/Wed pm–NA Sat–NA
before 3.30pm SOC–Mon &
Thurs
Fees £35 (£40)
Loc 6 miles S of Belfast
Arch J Harris/CK Cotton

Ormeau (1893)

50 Park Road, Belfast, BT7 2FX
Tel (028) 9064 1069 (Members)
Fax (028) 9064 6250
Mem 280 70(L) 45(J)
Sec R Barnes (028) 9064 0700
Pro (028) 9064 0999
Holes 9 L 5308 yds SSS 65
V'tors U SOC
Fees £12 (£15)
Loc 2 miles S of Belfast

Shandon Park (1926)

73 Shandon Park, Belfast, BT5 6NY
Tel (028) 9079 3730
Fax (028) 9040 2773
Mem 1100
Sec DG Jenkins (Mgr)
(028) 9040 1856
Pro B Wilson (028) 9079 7859
Holes 18 L 6261 yds SSS 70
V'tors WD–U Sat–NA before 5pm
SOC
Fees £22 (£27)
Loc 3 miles E of Belfast on the
Knock road

Co Carlow

Borris (1907)

Deerpark, Borris
Tel (0503) 73310
Fax (0503) 73750
Mem 475
Sec N Lucas (0503) 73310
Holes 9 L 5680 m Par 70 SSS 69
V'tors WD–U Sun–M SOC–WD/Sat
Fees £15
Loc Borris

Carlow (1899)

Deer Park, Dublin Road, Carlow
Tel (0503) 31695
Fax (0503) 40065
Web www.carlowgolfclub.com
Mem 1300
Sec Mrs M Meaney
Pro A Gilbert (0503) 41745
Holes 18 L 5844 m Par 70 SSS 71
V'tors U SOC–WD
Fees £35 (£45)
Loc 2 miles N of Carlow (N9) 50
miles S of Dublin (N7)
Arch Tom Simpson

Mount Wolseley (1996)

Tullow
Tel (0503) 51674
Fax (0503) 52123
Mem 250
Sec D Morrissey (Mgr)
Pro J Bolger
Holes 18 L 6497 m Par 72 SSS 74
V'tors U
Fees £20 (£25)
Loc 15 miles E of Carlow (R275)

Co Cavan

Belturbet (1950)

Erne Hill, Belturbet
Tel (049) 22287
Mem 110
Sec PF Coffey (049) 22498
Pro None
Holes 9 L 5347 yds Par 68 SSS 65
V'tors U SOC
Fees £10
Loc 1 mile E of Belturbet

Blacklion (1962)

Toam, Blacklion, via Sligo
Tel (072) 53024
Mem 250
Sec P Maguire (Hon)
Holes 9 L 5716 m SSS 69
V'tors U SOC
Fees D–£8 (D–£10)
Loc 12 miles SW of Enniskillen on
A4 to N16
Arch Eddie Hackett

Cabra Castle (1978)

Kingscourt
Mem 130
Holes 9 L 5308 m Par 70 SSS 68
V'tors U exc Sun–NA SOC
Fees On application
Loc 2 miles E of Kingscourt

County Cavan (1894)

Arnmore House, Drumelis, Cavan
Tel (049) 31541
Fax (049) 31541
Mem 800
Sec J Fraher
Pro C Carroll
Holes 18 L 5519 m SSS 69
V'tors U
Fees On application
Loc 2 miles W of Cavan on
Killeshandra road
Mis Driving range
Arch Eddie Hackett

Slieve Russell (1994)

Ballyconnell
Tel (049) 26444
Fax (049) 26474
Mem 350
Sec PJ Creamer (049) 26458
Pro L McCool (049) 26458
Holes 18 L 7053 yds Par 72 SSS 74
9 hole Par 3 course
V'tors U SOC
Fees £28 Sat–£36
Loc 15 miles N of Cavan Town
Mis Driving range
Arch Paddy Merrigan

Virginia (1945)

Park Hotel, Virginia
Tel (049) 854 8066
Mem 570
Sec S MacGabhann

Holes 9 L 4139 m Par 64 SSS 62
V'tors U
Fees £10
Loc 35 miles SE of Cavan, nr
Lough Ramor (N3)

Co Clare

Clonlara (1993)
Clonlara
Tel (061) 354141
Mem 85
Sec M O'Connell
Holes 12 L 5289 m Par 70 SSS 69
V'tors U
Fees £7 (£10)
Loc 8 miles NE of Limerick

Dromoland Castle
(1964)
Newmarket-on-Fergus
Tel (061) 368444
Fax (061) 368498
Web www.dromoland.ie
Mem 400
Sec J O'Halloran
Pro P Murphy
Holes 18 L 6098 yds SSS 71
V'tors U SOC
Fees D–£30 (£35)
Loc 18 miles NW of Limerick.
Shannon Airport 4 miles

East Clare (1992)
Bodyke
Tel (061) 921322
Mem 450
Sec P Nesbitt (Hon)
Holes 9 L 5639 m Par 71 SSS 69
V'tors U
Fees £15
Loc 20 miles E of Ennis (R352)

Ennis (1907)
Drumbiggle, Ennis
Tel (065) 682 4074
Fax (065) 684 1848
Web www.golfclub.ennis.ie
Mem 907
Sec N O'Donnell (Sec/Mgr)
Pro M Ward (065) 682 0690
Holes 18 L 5592 m Par 71 SSS 69
V'tors U SOC
Fees £20
Loc ½ mile NW of Ennis, off N18

Kilkee (1896)
East End, Kilkee
Tel (065) 905 6048
Fax (065) 905 6977
Mem 704
Sec J O'Regan
Holes 18 L 5928 m Par 71 SSS 71
V'tors U SOC

Fees £20
Loc End of Kilkee Promenade.
10 miles NW of Kilrush
Arch Eddie Hackett

Kilrush (1934)
Parknamoney, Kilrush
Tel (065) 905 1138
Fax (065) 905 2633
Web www.kilrushgolfclub.com
Mem 338
Sec DF Nagle (Sec/Mgr)
M Cody (Hon)
Pro J McDermott
Holes 18 L 5986 yds Par 70 SSS 69
V'tors U SOC
Fees £18 (£20)
Loc 25 miles SW of Ennis on
Lahinch-Ballybunion road
Arch Arthur Spring

Lahinch (1892)
Lahinch
Tel (065) 708 1003
Fax (065) 708 1592
Mem 1250
Sec A Reardon (Sec/Mgr)
Pro R McCavery (065) 708 1408
Holes Old 18 L 6699 yds SSS 73
Castle 18 L 5620 yds SSS 69
V'tors WD–U WE–NA 9–10.30am
and 1–2pm SOC
Fees Old–£50 Castle–£25
Loc 20 miles NW of Ennis on T69
Arch Morris/Gibson/Mackenzie/
Harris

Shannon (1966)
Shannon Airport
Tel (061) 471020
Fax (061) 471507
Mem 1050
Sec M Corry (061) 471849
Pro A Pike (061) 471551
Holes 18 L 6515 yds Par 72
SSS 72
V'tors WD–U SOC
Fees £22 (£27)
Loc Shannon Airport

Spanish Point (1915)
Spanish Point, Miltown Malbay
Tel (065) 84198
Mem 200
Sec D Fitzgerald
Holes 9 L 4624 m Par 64 SSS 63
V'tors U
Fees £15
Loc 2 mile S of Miltown Malbay
(N67). 20 miles W of Ennis

Woodstock (1993)
Shanaway Road, Ennis
Tel (065) 682 9463
Fax (065) 682 0304
Mem 350
Sec A Griffith (Sec/Mgr)
Holes 18 L 5879 m SSS 71
V'tors U
Fees £25 (£30)

Loc Ennis, 18 miles from Shannon
Airport
Arch Arthur Spring

Co Cork

Bandon (1909)
Castlebernard, Bandon
Tel (023) 41111
Fax (023) 44690
Mem 800
Sec N O'Sullivan (Hon)
Pro P O'Boyle (023) 42224
Holes 18 L 5663 m Par 70 SSS 69
V'tors U
Fees On application
Loc Bandon 1½ miles. 18 miles
SW of Cork

Bantry Bay (1975)
Donemark, Bantry, West Cork
Tel (027) 50579
Fax (027) 50579
Web www.bantrygolf.com
Mem 580
Sec Liz O'Shea (Mgr)
Holes 18 L 5914 m Par 71 SSS 72
V'tors WD–U before 4.30 pm
WE/BH–booking necessary
SOC
Fees £25–£30 (£25–£30)
Loc 1 mile N of Bantry on
Glengarriff road (N71)
Arch E Hackett/C O'Connor, Jnr

Berehaven (1902)
Millcove, Castletownbere
Tel (027) 70700
Fax (027) 70700
Mem 134
Sec P Lyne (Sec/Mgr)
(027) 70299
Holes 9 L 2605 yds SSS 66
V'tors U SOC
Fees £12
Loc 2 miles E of Castletownbere
on Glengarriff road
Arch James Healy

Charleville (1909)
Charleville
Tel (063) 81257/81515
Fax (063) 81274
Mem 650
Sec P Nagle (Sec/Mgr)
Pro D Keating
Holes 18 L 6430 yds SSS 69
9 L 6750 yds SSS 72
V'tors WD–U WE–book in advance
SOC
Fees £20 (£25) SOC–£17 (£20)
Loc 35 miles N of Cork on
Limerick road
Mis Driving range

Cobh (1987)

Ballywilliam, Cobh

Tel	**(021) 812399**
Fax	(021) 812615
Mem	120
Sec	H Cunningham
Holes	9 L 4576 m SSS 64
V'tors	WD–U WE–NA
Fees	£8 (£9)
Loc	1 mile N of Cobh. 16 miles SE of Cork
Arch	Eddie Hackett

Coosheen (1989)

Coosheen, Schull

Tel	**(028) 28182**
Mem	200
Sec	L Morgan
Holes	9 L 4001 m Par 60 SSS 61
V'tors	U
Fees	£12 (£12)
Loc	15 miles S of Bantry

Cork (1888)

Little Island, Cork

Tel	**(021) 435 3451/3037**
Fax	(021) 435 3410
Mem	366 176 (L)
Sec	M Sands (021) 435 3451
Pro	P Hickey (021) 435 3421
Holes	18 L 6065 m SSS 72
V'tors	WD–U H exc 12–2pm –M after 4pm Thurs–(Ladies Day)–phone in advance WE–NA before 2.30pm H
Fees	£50 (£55)
Loc	5 miles E of Cork, off N25
Arch	Dr A Mackenzie

Doneraile (1927)

Doneraile

Tel	**(022) 24137**
Mem	652
Sec	P Mannix (Hon) (022) 24509
Holes	9 L 5528 yds SSS 67
V'tors	WD–U
Fees	£15
Loc	8 miles NW of Mallow

Douglas (1909)

Douglas, Cork

Tel	**(021) 489 1086**
Fax	(021) 489 5297
Web	www.douglasgolfclub.ie
Mem	839
Sec	B Barrett (Mgr) (021) 489 5297
Pro	GS Nicholson (021) 436 2055
Holes	18 L 5972 m SSS 71
V'tors	WD–U WE–NA before 2pm SOC–WD
Fees	IR£35 (IR£42)
Loc	Cork 3 miles
Arch	P McEvoy

Dunmore (1967)

Clonakilty

Tel	**(023) 34644**
Mem	400
Sec	L Donovan (Hon)
Holes	9 L 4464 yds SSS 61
V'tors	WD–U exc Wed WE–M SOC–Sat
Fees	£15
Loc	3 miles S of Clonakilty
Arch	Eddie Hackett

East Cork (1971)

Gortacrue, Midleton

Tel	**(021) 631687**
Fax	(021) 613695
Mem	600
Sec	M Moloney (Sec/Mgr)
Pro	D MacFarlane
Holes	18 L 5207 m SSS 67
V'tors	WD–U WE–NA before noon BH–U
Fees	£15
Loc	2 miles N of Midleton on L35
Arch	Eddie Hackett

Fermoy (1892)

Corrin, Fermoy

Tel	**(025) 32694**
Fax	(025) 33072
Mem	1000
Sec	K Murphy
Pro	B Moriarty (025) 31472
Holes	18 L 5847 m SSS 70
V'tors	U SOC
Fees	£20 (£25)
Loc	2 miles S of Fermoy, off N8
Arch	Cdr John Harris

Fernhill (1994)

Carrigaline

Tel	**(021) 437 2226**
Fax	(021) 437 1011
Web	www.fernhillgolfhotel.com
Mem	120
Sec	J O'Reilly (Mgr)
Pro	W Callaghan
Holes	18 L 5766 m Par 70 SSS 67
V'tors	U
Fees	£14 (£16)
Loc	7 miles SE of Cork (R609)
Arch	ML Bowes

Fota Island (1993)

Carrigtwohill, Cork

Tel	**(021) 488 3710**
Fax	(021) 488 3713
Mem	400
Sec	K Mulcahy (Gen Mgr)
Pro	K Morris
Holes	18 L 6927 yds Par 71 SSS 73
V'tors	U
Fees	£60 (£70)
Loc	8 miles E of Cork on N25
Mis	Driving range
Arch	O'Connor Jr/McEvoy/Howes

Frankfield (1984)

Frankfield, Douglas

Tel	**(021) 363124**
Mem	320
Sec	A MacFarlane
Pro	D Whyte, M Ryan
Holes	9 L 4621 m SSS 65
V'tors	U SOC
Fees	£5
Loc	S of Cork
Mis	Driving range

Glengarriff (1935)

Glengarriff

Tel	**(027) 63150**
Fax	(027) 63575
Mem	250
Sec	N Deasy (Hon)
Holes	9 L 4094 m SSS 66
V'tors	U
Fees	D–£12 (£15)
Loc	1 mile E of Glengarriff (N71)

Harbour Point (1991)

Clash, Little Island

Tel	**(021) 353094**
Fax	(021) 354408
Mem	300
Sec	Mrs N Dwyer (Sec/Mgr)
Pro	M O'Donovan (021) 353719
Holes	18 L 6063 yds SSS 72
V'tors	U SOC
Fees	£17–£27
Loc	5 miles E of Cork
Mis	Floodlit driving range
Arch	Paddy Merrigan

Kanturk (1971)

Fairy Hill, Kanturk

Tel	**(029) 50534**
Mem	410
Sec	J Pigott (029) 50588
Pro	None
Holes	18 L 6262 yds Par 72 SSS 70
V'tors	U
Fees	£12 (£15)
Loc	2 miles SW of Kanturk (R579)
Arch	R Barry

Kinsale Farrangalway (1993)

Farrangalway, Kinsale

Tel	**(021) 477 4722**
Fax	(021) 477 3114
Mem	740
Sec	P Murray (Mgr)
Pro	G Broderick (021) 477 3258
Holes	18 L 6609 yds SSS 72
V'tors	WD–U WE–NA SOC
Fees	£22 (£30)
Loc	3 miles NW of Kinsale. 18 miles S of Cork
Arch	Jack Kenneally

Kinsale Ringenane (1912)

Ringenane, Belgooly, Kinsale

Tel	**(021) 477 2197**
Mem	740
Sec	P Murray (Mgr)
Pro	None
Holes	9 L 5332 yds SSS 68
V'tors	U SOC
Fees	£12

Loc   2 miles E of Kinsale (R600).
         16 miles S of Cork

Lee Valley G&CC (1993)

Clashanure, Ovens, Cork
Tel   **(021) 733 1721**
Fax   (021) 733 1695
Mem   450
Sec   J O'Reilly
Pro   J Savage (021) 733 1758
Holes   18 L 6800 yds SSS 72
V'tors   U SOC
Fees   £25 (£29)
Loc   8 miles W of Cork (N22)
Mis   Floodlit driving range
Arch   C O'Connor Jr

Macroom (1924)

Lackaduve, Macroom
Tel   **(026) 41072**
Fax   (026) 41391
Mem   650
Sec   C O'Sullivan (Mgr)
Pro   None
Holes   18 L 5574 m Par 72 SSS 70
V'tors   U SOC
Fees   D–IR£20 (IR£25)
Loc   Macroom Town, through
         Castle Arch. 25 miles W of
         Cork
Arch   Jack Kenneally

Mahon (1980)

Cloverhill, Blackrock, Cork
Tel   **(021) 294280**
Mem   450
Sec   B Ramsell (Hon)
Pro   T O'Connor
Holes   18 L 4818 m SSS 66
V'tors   U
Fees   £10 (£11)
Loc   SE of Cork City

Mallow (1948)

Ballyellis, Mallow
Tel   **(022) 21145**
Fax   (022) 42501
Mem   1500
Sec   D Curtin (Sec/Mgr)
Pro   S Conway
Holes   18 L 6559 yds SSS 72
V'tors   WD–U before 5pm SOC
Fees   £20 (£25)
Loc   1 mile SE of Mallow Bridge
         on Killavullen road
Arch   J Harris

Mitchelstown (1908)

Mitchelstown
Tel   **(025) 24072**
Mem   500
Sec   N Brennan
Holes   15 L 5057 m SSS 67
V'tors   U SOC
Fees   £12 (£15)
Loc   30 miles NE of Cork
Arch   David Jones

Monkstown (1908)

Parkgarriffe, Monkstown
Tel   **(021) 841376**
Fax   (021) 841376
Mem   900
Sec   J Long (Hon)
Pro   B Murphy (021) 841686
Holes   18 L 5669 m SSS 69
V'tors   U H SOC
Fees   £25 (£30)
Loc   7 miles SE of Cork

Muskerry (1907)

Carrigrohane
Tel   **(021) 438 5297**
Fax   (021) 438 5297
Mem   791
Sec   H Gallagher (Mgr)
Pro   WM Lehane (021) 438 1445
Holes   18 L 5786 m SSS 71
V'tors   Restricted at certain
         times–phone first SOC
Fees   £25 (£28)
Loc   7 miles NW of Cork. 2 miles
         W of Blarney

Old Head (1997)

Kinsale
Tel   **(021) 477 8444**
Fax   (021) 477 8022
Web   www.oldheadgolflinks.com
Sec   J O'Brien (Gen Mgr)
Pro   D Murray
Holes   18 L 7300 yds SSS 72
V'tors   U H
Fees   €250
Loc   7 miles S of Kinsale
Mis   Driving range
Arch   Kirby/Carr/
         Merrigan/Hackett/Higgins

Raffeen Creek (1989)

Ringaskiddy
Tel   **(021) 378430**
Mem   530
Holes   9 L 5098 m Par 70 SSS 67
V'tors   WD–U WE–U after noon
Fees   IR£10
Loc   1 mile from Ringaskiddy
         Ferryport
Arch   Eddie Hackett

Skibbereen (1931)

Licknavar, Skibbereen
Tel   **(028) 21227**
Fax   (028) 22994
Web   www.westcorkweb.ie/
         skibbereen/skibgolf
Mem   580
Sec   S Brett (Mgr)
Pro   None
Holes   18 L 5474 m Par 71 SSS 69
V'tors   U SOC–Sat
Fees   £18
Loc   1 mile W of Skibbereen. 52
         miles SW of Cork
Mis   Driving range
Arch   Eddie Hackett

Youghal (1898)

Knockaverry, Youghal
Tel   **(024) 92787/92861**
Fax   (024) 92641
Mem   827
Sec   Margaret O'Sullivan
Pro   L Burns (024) 92590
Holes   18 L 5646 m SSS 69
V'tors   U
Fees   D–IR£22 (IR£25)
Loc   30 miles E of Cork on N25
         from Rosslare
Arch   Cdr Harris

Co Donegal

Ballybofey & Stranorlar (1957)

The Glebe, Stranorlar
Tel   **(074) 31093**
Fax   (074) 31058
Mem   525
Sec   A Harkin (074) 31228
Holes   18 L 5922 yds Par 68 SSS 68
V'tors   U SOC
Fees   £15 (£18)
Loc   Stranorlar ¼ mile
Arch   PC Carr

Ballyliffin (1947)

Inishowen, Ballyliffin
Tel   **(077) 76119**
Fax   (077) 76672
Mem   828
Sec   KJ O'Doherty (Sec/Mgr)
Pro   None
Holes   Old 18 L 6611 yds SSS 72
         Glashedy 18 L 6837 yds
         Par 72
V'tors   U SOC–WD
Fees   Old IR£21 (IR£24) Glashedy
         IR£30 (IR£35)
Loc   8 miles N of Buncrana.
         15 miles N of Londonderry
Arch   Glashedy-Craddock/Ruddy

Buncrana (1951)

Buncrana
Tel   **(077) 62279**
Mem   175
Sec   F McGrory (Hon)
         (077) 20749
Pro   (Shop) J Doherty
Holes   9 L 4250 m SSS 62
V'tors   U
Fees   £6–£10
Loc   S of Buncrana

Bundoran (1894)

Bundoran
Tel   **(072) 41302**
Fax   (072) 42014
Mem   620
Sec   J McGagh (Sec/Mgr)
Pro   D Robinson
Holes   18 L 5688 m Par 70 SSS 70

V'tors WD–U WE–restricted SOC
Fees £20 (£25)
Loc E boundary of Bundoran. 20 miles S of Donegal
Arch H Vardon

Cruit Island (1985)
Kincasslagh, Dunglow
Tel (075) 43296
Fax (075) 48028
Web www.homepage.eircom.net/ ~cruitisland
Mem 350
Sec T Gallagher
Pro None
Holes 9 L 5297 yds Par 68 SSS 64
V'tors U SOC
Fees £10 (£15)
Loc 5 miles N of Dunglow, off R259

Donegal (1960)
Murvagh, Laghey
Tel (073) 34054
Fax (073) 34377
Web www.donegalgolfclub.ie
Mem 650
Sec J Nixon (073) 22166
J McBride (Admin)
Holes 18 L 7271 yds SSS 73
V'tors H SOC–exc Sun
Fees €40 (€55)
Loc 7 miles S of Donegal, off N15
Arch Eddie Hackett

Dunfanaghy (1906)
Kill, Dunfanaghy, Letterkenny
Tel (074) 36335
Fax (074) 36335
Web www.golfdunfanaghy.com
Mem 390
Sec J Moffitt
Holes 18 L 5066 m Par 68 SSS 66
V'tors U SOC
Fees IR£15 (IR£18)
Loc 25 miles NW of Letterkenny on N56
Mis Driving range
Arch Harry Vardon

Greencastle (1892)
Greencastle
Tel (077) 81013
Fax (077) 81015
Mem 750
Sec B McCaul
Pro None
Holes 18 L 5211 m SSS 67
V'tors WD–U WE–restricted SOC
Fees IR£15 (IR£20)
Loc 21 miles NE of Londonderry, nr Moville
Arch Eddie Hackett

Gweedore (1926)
Magheragallon, Derrybeg, Letterkenny
Tel (075) 31140
Mem 200

Sec O Ferry
Holes 9 L 6201 yds SSS 69
V'tors U
Fees £8 (£10)
Loc 3 miles N of Gweedore, off R257

Letterkenny (1913)
Barnhill, Letterkenny
Tel (074) 21150
Fax (074) 21175
Mem 790
Sec S Gildea (074) 22453
Holes 18 L 6239 yds SSS 71
V'tors U–booking necessary SOC
Fees £17 (£22)
Loc 1 mile E of Letterkenny
Arch Eddie Hackett

Narin & Portnoo (1931)
Narin, Portnoo
Tel (075) 45107
Fax (074) 45107
Mem 600
Sec E Bonner (Hon)
Pro None
Holes 18 L 5950 yds Par 69 SSS 68
V'tors WD/Sat–U H Sun–NA before 2pm SOC
Fees £17 (£20) SOC–£16
Loc 6 miles N of Ardara. West Donegal

North West (1891)
Lisfannon, Fahan
Tel (077) 61027
Fax (077) 63284
Mem 520
Sec D Coyle (Hon)
Pro S McBriarty (077) 61715
Holes 18 L 6239 yds SSS 70
V'tors U
Fees IR£17 (IR£22)
Loc 2 miles S of Buncrana. 12 miles N of Londonderry

Otway (1893)
Saltpans, Rathmullan, Letterkenny
Tel (074) 58319
Mem 97
Sec G McGivern (Hon)
Holes 9 L 4234 yds SSS 60
V'tors U
Fees £10
Loc 15 miles NE of Letterkenny, by Lough Swilly

Portsalon (1891)
Portsalon, Fanad
Tel (074) 59459
Fax (074) 59919
Mem 500
Sec P Doherty
Holes 18 L 5878 yds Par 68 SSS 66
V'tors U–phone in advance
Fees £18 (£22)
Loc 20 miles N of Letterkenny (R246)

Redcastle (1983)
Redcastle, Moville
Tel (077) 82073
Mem 120
Holes 9 L 6046 yds SSS 70
V'tors U
Fees £10 (£12)
Loc 15 miles NE of Londonderry, by Lough Foyle (R238)

Rosapenna (1894)
Downings, Rosapenna
Tel (074) 55301
Fax (074) 55128
Mem 300
Sec K Mooney, F Casey (Mgr)
Pro D Patterson
Holes 18 L 6254 yds Par 70 SSS 71
V'tors U
Fees €40 (€45)
Loc 20 miles N of Letterkenny
Mis Golf academy
Arch Morris/Vardon/Braid/Ruddy

Co Down

Ardglass (1896)
Castle Place, Ardglass, BT30 7PP
Tel (028) 4484 1219
Fax (028) 4484 1841
Mem 901
Sec Miss D Polly
Pro P Farrell (028) 4484 1022
Holes 18 L 5776 yds Par 70 SSS 69
V'tors U SOC
Fees £20 (£26)
Loc 7 miles SE of Downpatrick on B1

Ardminnan (1995)
15 Ardminnan Road, Portaferry, BT22 1QJ
Tel (028) 9177 1321
Fax (028) 9177 1321
Mem 170
Sec S McCrea (Mgr)
Pro J Peden
Holes 9 L 2766 m Par 70 SSS 69
V'tors U
Fees £10 (£15)
Loc 10 miles E of Downpatrick via ferry. 18 miles SE of Newtownards (A20)
Arch Frank Ainsworth

Banbridge (1913)
Huntly Road, Banbridge, BT32 3UR
Tel (028) 4066 2342
Fax (028) 4066 9400
Web www.banbridgegolf.co.uk
Mem 850
Sec Mrs J Anketell (028) 4066 2211
Holes 18 L 5590 m SSS 69
V'tors U SOC
Fees £10 (£20)
Loc 1 mile W of Banbridge
Arch F Ainsworth

Bangor (1903)

Broadway, Bangor, BT20 4RH
Tel   (028) 9127 0922
Fax   (028) 9145 3394
Mem   1100
Sec   DJ Ryan (Sec/Mgr)
Pro   M Bannon
Holes 18 L 6424 yds SSS 71
V'tors WD–U exc –M 1–2pm
       Wed–U before 4.45pm
       Sat–NA SOC–Mon & Wed
Fees   £25 Sun–£30
Loc   1 mile S of Bangor, off
       Donaghadee road
Arch   James Braid

Blackwood (1995)

*150 Crawfordsburn Road, Bangor,
BT19 1GB*
Tel   (028) 9185 2706
Fax   (028) 9185 3785
Mem   240
Sec   P Edgar, Debbie Hanna
Pro   R Skillen
Holes 18 L 6392 yds SSS 70
V'tors U
Fees   On application
Loc   W of Bangor
Mis   Driving range

Bright Castle (1970)

*14 Coniamstown Road, Bright,
Downpatrick, BT30 8LU*
Tel   (028) 4484 1319
Mem   100
Sec   J McCawl (Hon)
Holes 18 L 6810 yds Par 74 SSS
       74
V'tors U SOC
Fees   £12 (£14)
Loc   5 miles S of Downpatrick, off
       Killough road (B176)

Carnalea (1927)

Station Road, Bangor, BT19 1EZ
Tel   (028) 9146 5004
Fax   (028) 9127 3989
Mem   800
Sec   GY Steele (028) 9127 0368
Pro   T Loughran (028) 9127 0122
Holes 18 L 5647 yds SSS 67
V'tors U SOC–WD
Fees   £16 (£20)
Loc   By Carnalea Station, Bangor

Clandeboye (1933)

Conlig, Newtownards, BT23 3PN
Tel   (028) 9127 1767/9147 3706
Fax   (028) 9147 3711
Web   www.cgc-ni.com
Mem   1291
Sec   R Eddis (Admin Mgr)
       (028) 9127 1767
Pro   P Gregory (028) 9127 1750
Holes Dufferin 18 L 6569 yds
       SSS 71;
       Ava 18 L 5755 yds SSS 68
V'tors WD–U WE–M SOC
Fees   Dufferin–£27.50 (£33)
       Ava–£22 (£27.50)

Loc   Conlig, off A21 Bangor-
       Newtownards road
Arch   Von Limburger/Alliss/Thomas

Crossgar (1993)

*231 Derryboye Road, Crossgar,
BT30 9DL*
Tel   (028) 4483 1523
Mem   105
Sec   D Myles (Sec/Mgr)
Holes 9 L 4170 m Par 64 SSS 63
V'tors U
Fees   £10 (£10)
Loc   6 miles N of Downpatrick
       (A7)

Donaghadee (1899)

*84 Warren Road, Donaghadee,
BT21 0PQ*
Tel   (028) 9188 3624
Fax   (028) 9188 8891
Mem   1135
Sec   K Patton
Pro   G Drew (028) 9188 2392
Holes 18 L 5570 m Par 71
V'tors U exc Sat–NA
       SOC–Mon/Wed/Fri/Sun
Fees   £22 (£25)
Loc   6 miles S of Bangor on coast
       road. 18 miles E of Belfast

Downpatrick (1930)

Saul Road, Downpatrick, BT30 6PA
Tel   (028) 4461 2152/5947
Fax   (028) 4461 7502
Web   www.downpatrickgolfclub
       .com
Mem   960
Sec   L Kennedy (Sec/Mgr)
       (028) 4461 5947
Pro   (028) 4461 5167
Holes 18 L 5702 m SSS 69
V'tors U SOC
Fees   £15 (£20)
Loc   25 miles SE of Belfast (A1).
       Downpatrick 1½ miles
Arch   Hawtree

Helen's Bay (1896)

*Golf Road, Helen's Bay, Bangor,
BT19 1TL*
Tel   (028) 9185 2601
       (Clubhouse)
Fax   (028) 9185 2815
Mem   550
Sec   LWL Mann
       (028) 9185 2815
Holes 9 L 5261 m Par 68 SSS 67
V'tors WD/Sun–U
       Tues/Thurs/Sat–restricted
       SOC–WD
Fees   On application
Loc   9 miles E of Belfast, off A2

Holywood (1904)

*Nuns Walk, Demesne Road, Holywood,
BT18 9LE*
Tel   (028) 9042 2138
Fax   (028) 9042 5040

Web   www.holywoodgolfclub.co.uk
Mem   1000
Sec   GA Fyfe (Gen Mgr)
       (028) 9042 3135
Pro   P Gray (028) 9042 5503
Holes 18 L 5885 yds SSS 68
V'tors WD–U exc 1.30–2.15pm
       Sat–after 5pm
Fees   £16 (£25)
Loc   5 miles E of Belfast on Bangor
       road

Kilkeel (1948)

Mourne Park, Kilkeel, BT34 4LB
Tel   (028) 4176 2296/5095
Fax   (028) 4176 5579
Mem   720
Sec   SC McBride (Hon)
       (028) 4176 5095
Pro   None
Holes 18 L 6579 yds SSS 72
V'tors U SOC–exc Sat
Fees   £18 (£22)
Loc   3 miles W of Kilkeel on Newry
       road
Mis   Driving range
Arch   Badington/Hackett

Kirkistown Castle (1902)

*142 Main Road, Cloughey,
Newtownards, BT22 1JA*
Tel   (028) 4277 1233
Fax   (028) 4277 1699
Web   www.kcgc.org
Mem   948
Sec   R Coulter (028) 4277 1233
Pro   J Peden (028) 4277 1004
Holes 18 L 5616 m Par 69 SSS 70
V'tors WD/Sun–U Sat–NA before
       2.30pm
Fees   £18.75 (£25.75)
Loc   25 miles SE of Belfast
Arch   James Braid

Mahee Island (1930)

Comber, Belfast, BT23 6ET
Tel   (028) 9754 1234
Mem   500
Sec   M Marshall (Hon)
Pro   A McCracken
Holes 9 L 2790 yds SSS 68
V'tors U exc Sat–NA before 5pm
       SOC–WD exc Mon
Fees   £10 (£15)
Loc   Strangford Lough, 14 miles
       SE of Belfast

Mount Ober G&CC (1985)

*Ballymaconaghy Road, Knockbracken,
Belfast, BT8 4SB*
Tel   (028) 9079 2108 (Bookings)
Fax   (028) 9070 5862
Mem   500
Sec   D McNamara (Sec/Mgr)
Pro   G Loughrey (028) 9040 1811
Holes 18 L 5436 yds SSS 68
V'tors WD–U Sat–NA before 3pm
       Sun–NA before 10.30am SOC

Fees £13 (£15)
Loc   2 miles SW of Belfast, nr Four Winds
Mis   Floodlit driving range

Mourne (1946)

Club
36 Golf Links Road, Newcastle, BT33 0AN
Tel   **(028) 4372 3218**
Fax   (028) 4372 2575
Web   www.mournegc.freeserve
      .co.uk
Mem   355
Sec   T Gallagher (Hon)
Holes Play over Royal Co Down

Ringdufferin (1993)

Ringdufferin Road, Toye, Killyleagh, BT30 9PH
Tel   **(028) 4482 8812**
Mem   260
Holes 18 L 4652 m Par 68 SSS 66
V'tors U
Fees £9 (£10)
Loc   2 miles N of Killyleagh, off A22

Rockmount (1995)

28 Drumalig Road, Carryduff, Belfast, BT8 8EQ
Tel   **(028) 9081 2279**
Fax   (028) 9081 5851
Web   www.rockmountgolfclub
      .co.uk
Mem   700
Sec   D Patterson (Mgr)
Holes 18 L 6373 yds Par 72 SSS 71
V'tors U
Fees £20 (£24)
Loc   8 miles S of Belfast (A24)

Royal Belfast (1881)

Holywood, Craigavad, BT18 0BP
Tel   **(028) 9042 8165**
Fax   (028) 9042 1404
Mem   1200
Sec   Mrs SH Morrison
Pro   C Spence (028) 9042 8586
Holes 18 L 6184 yds SSS 70
V'tors I Sat–NA before 4.30pm
Fees £40 (£50)
Loc   E of Belfast on A2

Royal County Down (1889)

Newcastle, BT33 0AN
Tel   **(028) 4372 3314**
Fax   (028) 4372 6281
Mem   450
Sec   PE Rolph
Pro   KJ Whitson (028) 4372 2419
Holes Ch'ship 18 L 7037 yds SSS 74
      Annesley 18 L 4681 yds
      SSS 63
V'tors Contact Sec
Fees Ch'ship–£90 (£100)
      Annesley–£18 (£27)

Loc   30 miles S of Belfast
Arch Tom Morris

Scrabo (1907)

233 Scrabo Road, Newtownards, BT23 4SL
Tel   **(028) 9181 2355**
Fax   (028) 9182 2919
Mem   958
Sec   Christine Hamill (Gen Mgr)
Pro   P McCrystal (028) 9181 7848
Holes 18 L 5699 m SSS 71
V'tors WD–U WE–after 5pm SOC
Fees £15 (£20)
Loc   2 miles W of Newtownards, by Scrabo Tower

The Spa (1907)

Grove Road, Ballynahinch, BT24 8BR
Tel   **(028) 9756 2365**
Fax   (028) 9756 4158
Mem   920
Sec   TG Magee
Holes 18 L 6003 m SSS 72
V'tors U exc Wed–NA after 3pm
      Sat–NA
Fees £15 (£20)
Loc   1 mile S of Ballynahinch. 15 miles S of Belfast

Temple G&CC (1994)

60 Church Road, Boardmills, Lisburn, BT27 6UP
Tel   **(028) 9263 9213**
Fax   (028) 9263 8637
Mem   300
Sec   D Kinnear (Sec/Mgr)
Holes 9 L 5451 yds Par 68 SSS 66
V'tors U
Fees £10 (£14)
Loc   5 miles S of Belfast on Ballynahinch road

Warrenpoint (1893)

Lower Dromore Rd, Warrenpoint, BT34 3LN
Tel   **(028) 4175 2219 (Clubhouse)**
Fax   (028) 4175 2918
Mem   1265
Sec   M Trainor (028) 4175 3695
Pro   N Shaw (028) 4175 2371
Holes 18 L 5628 m SSS 70
V'tors U SOC
Fees £20 (£27)
Loc   5 miles S of Newry
Arch Tom Craddock

Co Dublin

Balbriggan (1945)

Blackhall, Balbriggan
Tel   **(01) 841 2173**
Fax   (01) 841 3927
Web   www.balbriggangolfclub.com
Mem   600
Sec   M O'Halloran (Sec/Mgr)
      (01) 841 2229

Pro   None
Holes 18 L 5881 m SSS 71
V'tors WD–U WE–M SOC
Fees £16 (£18)
Loc   1 mile S of Balbriggan on N1.
      18 miles N of Dublin
Arch Paramour/Stillwell/Ruddy

Balcarrick (1972)

Corballis, Donabate
Tel   **(01) 843 6228**
Fax   (01) 843 6957
Mem   800
Sec   Joan Byrne
Pro   S Rayfus
Holes 18 L 5940 m Par 73 SSS 71
V'tors WD–U Sat–NA before 10am
      Sun–NA SOC
Fees £20 (£25)
Loc   2 miles E of Donabate. 18
      miles N of Dublin

Ballinascorney (1971)

Ballinascorney, Tallaght, Dublin
Tel   **(01) 451 6430**
Mem   500
Holes 18 L 5464 m Par 71 SSS 67
V'tors WD–U
Fees On application
Loc   8 miles SW of Dublin

Beaverstown (1985)

Beaverstown, Donabate
Tel   **(01) 843 6439**
Fax   (01) 843 5059
Web   www.beaverstown.com
Mem   835
Sec   F Ward (Mgr)
Holes 18 L 5855 m Par 71
      SSS 70
V'tors WD–U WE/BH–M SOC
Fees £20 (£25)
Loc   4 miles N of Dublin
      Airport
Arch Eddie Hackett

Beech Park (1983)

Johnstown, Rathcoole
Tel   **(01) 458 0522**
Fax   (01) 458 8365
Mem   550
Sec   E Burke (Hon)
      P Muldowney (Mgr)
Pro   None
Holes 18 L 5730 m SSS 70
V'tors WD–U exc Tues/Wed–M
      WE–M BH–NA
Fees £25
Loc   Rathcoole 2 miles on Kilteel
      road. SW of Dublin
Arch Eddie Hackett

City West (1994)

Saggart
Tel   **(01) 458 8566**
Fax   (01) 831 5779
Mem   270
Sec   B Cooling (Mgr)

Holes	18 L 6441 yds Par 71
	SSS 71
V'tors	U
Fees	£29 (£32)
Loc	10 miles SW of Dublin, off
	N7

Coldwinters (1994)

Newtown House, St Margaret's

Tel	(01) 864 0324
Fax	(01) 834 1400
Mem	375
Sec	Mrs K Yates
Pro	W Noble
Holes	18 L 5973 m SSS 71
	9 L 3133 m SSS 31
V'tors	U
Fees	£11 (£17)
Loc	NW of Dublin. Airport 2
	miles
Mis	Driving range. Golf Academy
Arch	Martin Hawtree

Corrstown (1993)

Corrstown, Killsallaghan

Tel	(01) 864 0533/4
Fax	(01) 864 0537
Mem	1050
Sec	J Kelly
Pro	P Gittens (01) 864 3322
Holes	River 18 L 6077 m Par 72
	SSS 71
	Orchard 9 L 2792 m Par 35
	SSS 69
V'tors	Booking necessary
Fees	£20 (£25)
Loc	Dublin Airport 6 miles
Arch	E Connaughton

Donabate (1925)

Balcarrick, Donabate

Tel	(01) 843 6059/6346/6001
Fax	(01) 843 5012
Mem	913
Sec	B Judd (01) 843 6346
Pro	H Jackson
Holes	18 L 6670 yds SSS 72
	9 L 3200 yds Par 36
V'tors	WE/BH–NA
Fees	£25
Loc	8 miles N of Dublin Airport
	on N1

Dublin Mountain (1993)

Gortlum, Brittas

Tel	(01) 458 2622
Mem	430
Sec	P O'Rourke (Hon)
Holes	18 L 5433 m Par 70 SSS 69
V'tors	U
Fees	£7 (£9)
Loc	SW of Dublin

Dun Laoghaire (1910)

Eglinton Park, Tivoli Road,
Dun Laoghaire

Tel	(01) 280 3916
Fax	(01) 280 4868
Web	www.dunlaoghairegolfclub.ie

Mem	880
Sec	DA Peacock (Gen Mgr)
	(01) 280 3916
Pro	V Carey (01) 280 1694
Holes	18 L 5478 m SSS 69
V'tors	WD–U exc 12–1.30pm SOC
Fees	IR£35
Loc	7 miles S of Dublin. Ferry
	Port 1 mile
Arch	HS Colt

Finnstown

Finnstown House Hotel, Lucan

Tel	(01) 628 0644
Fax	(01) 628 1088
Mem	300
Sec	M Doyle (01) 836 3423
Holes	9 L 5172 yds SSS 64
V'tors	H SOC
Fees	£12 (£16)
Loc	7 miles W of Dublin
Arch	B Browne

Forrest Little (1972)

Forrest Little, Cloghran

Tel	(01) 840 1183/840 1763
Fax	(01) 840 1000
Mem	900
Sec	T Greany (Sec/Mgr)
Pro	T Judd
Holes	18 L 5865 m SSS 70
V'tors	WD–U WE–NA
Fees	IR£20
Loc	Nr Dublin Airport
Arch	F Hawtree

Hermitage (1905)

Lucan

Tel	(01) 626 5396
Mem	1153
Sec	P Maguire (01) 626 8491
Pro	S Byrne (01) 626 8072
Holes	18 L 6032 m SSS 71
V'tors	U SOC–WD
Fees	£50 (£65)
Loc	Lucan 2 miles. 8 miles W of
	Dublin

Hollywood Lakes (1992)

Ballyboughal

Tel	(01) 843 3406/7
Fax	(01) 843 3002
Mem	630
Sec	AC Brogan (Sec/Mgr)
Pro	None
Holes	18 L 6834 yds Par 72 SSS 72
V'tors	WD–U WE/BH–U after noon
Fees	£20 (£25)
Loc	10 miles N of Dublin Airport
Arch	Mel Flanagan

The Island (1890)

Corballis, Donabate

Tel	(01) 843 6104
Fax	(01) 843 6860
Web	www.theislandgolfclub.com
Mem	800
Sec	(01) 843 6462
Pro	K Kelliher (01) 843 5002

Holes	18 L 6195 m SSS 72
V'tors	WD–U WE–NA
Fees	€100
Loc	14 miles N of Dublin
Arch	Hawtree

Killiney (1903)

Ballinclea Road, Killiney

Tel	(01) 285 1983
Fax	(01) 285 2823
Mem	520
Sec	M O'Rourke (01) 285 2823
Pro	P O'Boyle (01) 285 6294
Holes	9 L 6220 yds SSS 70
V'tors	U
Fees	D–£20
Loc	8 miles S of Dublin
Arch	E Connaughton

Kilternan (1987)

Kilternan

Tel	(01) 295 5559
Fax	(01) 295 5670
Mem	906
Sec	J Kinsella
Pro	Shop (01) 295 2986
Holes	18 L 5413 yds SSS 67
V'tors	U SOC
Fees	£18 (£22)
Loc	12 miles S of Dublin
Arch	Eddie Connaughton

Lucan (1897)

Celbridge Road, Lucan

Tel	(01) 628 0246
Fax	(01) 628 2929
Mem	740
Sec	T O'Donnell (Sec/Mgr)
	(01) 628 2106
Holes	18 L 5958 m Par 71 SSS 70
V'tors	WD–U WE/BH–M SOC–WD
	exc Thurs
Fees	£25
Loc	14 miles W of Dublin, nr
	Lucan on N4
Arch	Eddie Hackett

Luttrelstown Castle G&CC (1993)

Castleknock, Dublin 15

Tel	(01) 808 9988
Fax	(01) 808 9989
Web	www.luttrellstown.ie
Mem	400
Pro	E Doyle
Holes	18 L 6384 m Par 72
	SSS 73
V'tors	U SOC
Fees	£50 (£55)
Loc	7 miles W of Dublin
Mis	Driving range
Arch	Bielenberg/Connaughton

Malahide (1892)

Beechwood, The Grange, Malahide

Tel	(01) 846 1611
Fax	(01) 846 1270
Web	www.malahidegolfclub.ie

Mem 850
Sec J McCormack (Sec/Mgr)
Pro J Murray
Holes 27 L 6257-6633 yds SSS 70-72
V'tors WD–U WE–by arrangement SOC
Fees €50 (€85)
Loc 1½ miles S of Malahide. 10 miles N of Dublin, nr Airport
Arch Eddie Hackett

Milltown (1907)

Lower Churchtown Road, Milltown, Dublin 14
Tel (01) 497 6090
Fax (01) 497 6008
Mem 1432
Sec DJ Dalton (Sec/Mgr)
Pro J Harnett (01) 497 7072
Holes 18 L 5638 m Par 71 SSS 69
V'tors WD–U exc Tues & Wed pm Fri/WE–M BH–NA SOC–Mon & Thurs before 3.45pm
Fees IR£35
Loc 4 miles S of Dublin centre
Arch Freddie Davis

Portmarnock (1894)

Portmarnock
Tel (01) 846 2794 (Clubhouse)
Fax (01) 846 2601
Mem 971
Sec JJ Quigley (01) 846 2968
Pro J Purcell (01) 846 2634
Holes 27 holes:
    6361-6497 m SSS 74-75
V'tors I WE–XL
Fees IR£75 (IR£95)
Loc 8 miles NE of Dublin

Portmarnock Hotel Links (1995)

Strand Road, Portmarnock
Tel (01) 846 0611
Fax (01) 846 1077
Web www.portmarnock.com
Sec Moira Cassidy (Golf Dir) (01) 846 1800
Holes 18 L 6260 m Par 71 SSS 73
V'tors U H
Fees £75 Residents–£50
Loc 8 miles NE of Dublin. Airport 15 mins
Arch Bernhard Langer

Rush (1943)

Rush
Tel (01) 843 7548
Fax (01) 843 8177
Mem 360
Sec P Connolly (Hon) (01) 843 8177
Holes 9 L 5598 m SSS 69
V'tors WD–U WE–M
Fees £23
Loc 16 miles N of Dublin, off R127

St Margaret's G&CC (1993)

St Margaret's, Dublin
Tel (01) 864 0400
Fax (01) 864 0289
Web www.st-margarets.net
Mem 260
Sec B Begley (Chief Exec)
Holes 18 L 6900 yds SSS 73
V'tors U SOC
Fees €45 (€80)
Loc 3 miles NW of Dublin Airport, between N1/N2
Mis Driving range
Arch Craddock/Ruddy

Skerries (1905)

Hacketstown, Skerries
Tel (01) 849 1204 (Clubhouse)
Fax (01) 849 1591
Web www.skerriesgolfclub.ie
Mem 1060
Sec A Burns (01) 849 1567
Pro J Kinsella (01) 849 0925
Holes 18 L 6107 m Par 73 SSS 72
V'tors U SOC
Fees IR£25 (IR£30)
Loc 20 miles N of Dublin

Slade Valley (1970)

Lynch Park, Brittas
Tel (01) 458 2739
Fax (01) 458 2784
Mem 800
Sec (01) 458 2183
Pro J Dignam
Holes 18 L 5337 m SSS 68
V'tors WD–U am WE–M
Fees £17
Loc 8 miles W of Dublin, off N4
Arch Sullivan/O'Brien

Swords (1996)

Balheary Avenue, Swords
Tel (01) 840 9819
Fax (01) 840 9819
Mem 400
Sec O McGuinness (Mgr)
Holes 18 L 5677 m Par 71 SSS 70
V'tors U
Fees £9 (£12)
Loc 10 miles N of Dublin, nr Airport
Arch T Halpin

Turvey (1994)

Turvey Avenue, Donabate
Tel (01) 843 5169
Mem 335
Sec R Martin (Mgr)
Holes 18 hole course
V'tors U
Fees £20 (£24)
Loc Donabate
Arch Paddy McGuirk

Westmanstown (1988)

Clonsilla, Dublin 15
Tel (01) 820 5817
Fax (01) 820 5858
Mem 1000
Sec JA Joyce (Hon)
Holes 18 L 5819 m SSS 70
V'tors U SOC
Fees £25 (£30)
Loc 5 miles W of Dublin, nr Lucan
Arch Eddie Hackett

Woodbrook (1921)

Dublin Road, Bray
Tel (01) 282 4799
Fax (01) 282 1950
Web www.woodbrook.ie
Mem 1100
Sec PF Byrne (Gen Mgr)
Pro W Kinsella (01) 282 0205
Holes 18 L 6221 m SSS 72
V'tors WD–U WE–phone Sec SOC
Fees IR£55
Loc 11 miles SE of Dublin on N11
Arch P McEvoy

Dublin City

Carrickmines (1900)

Golf Lane, Carrickmines, Dublin 18
Tel (01) 295 5972
Mem 600
Sec TJB Webb (Hon)
Holes 9 L 6303 yds Par 71 SSS 69
V'tors U exc Wed/Sat–NA
Fees £23 Sun–£26
Loc 6 miles S of Dublin

Castle (1913)

Woodside Drive, Rathfarnham, Dublin 14
Tel (01) 490 4207
Fax (01) 492 0264
Mem 800
Sec LF Blackburne (Sec/Mgr)
Pro D Kinsella (01) 492 0272
Holes 18 L 6270 yds SSS 68
V'tors Mon/Thurs/Fri–U Wed–U before 12.30pm WE/BH–M SOC
Fees £35
Loc 5 miles S of Dublin

Clontarf (1912)

Donnycarney House, Malahide Road, Dublin 3
Tel (01) 833 1892
Fax (01) 833 1933
Mem 1035
Sec A Cahill (Mgr)
Pro M Callan (01) 833 1877
Holes 18 L 5317 m SSS 68
V'tors U SOC
Fees £26 (£35)
Loc 2 miles NE of Dublin city centre
Arch HS Colt

Deer Park (1974)

Deer Park Hotel, Howth Castle, Howth
Tel   **(01) 8222624**
Fax   (01) 8392405
Mem   340
Sec   BM Dunne (Hon)
Pro   None
Holes   18 L 6781 yds Par 72 SSS 71
18 L 6475 yds Par 72 SSS 70
12 hole Par 3 course
V'tors   U SOC
Fees   £9.90 (£12.50)
Loc   8 miles NE of Dublin
Arch   F Hawtree

Edmondstown (1944)

Rathfarnham, Dublin 16
Tel   **(01) 493 2461**
Fax   (01) 493 3152
Web   www.edmondstowngolfclub.ie
Mem   600
Sec   S Davies (01) 493 1082
Pro   A Crofton (01) 494 1049
Holes   18 L 6113 m Par 71 SSS 71
V'tors   WD/BH–U SOC
Fees   £45 Summer. £40 Winter
Loc   5 miles S of Dublin (M50)
Arch   McEvoy/Cooke

Elm Green (1996)

Castleknock, Dublin 15
Tel   **(01) 820 0797**
Fax   (01) 822 6668
Mem   500
Sec   G Carr (Sec/Mgr)
Pro   A O'Connor, P McGahan
Holes   18 L 5300 m Par 71 SSS 66
V'tors   U
Fees   £12 (£18)
Loc   NW Dublin
Mis   Floodlit driving range
Arch   Eddie Hackett

Elm Park (1927)

Nutley House, Donnybrook, Dublin 4
Tel   **(01) 269 3438/269 3014**
Fax   (01) 269 4505
Mem   1750
Sec   A McCormack (01) 269 3438
Pro   S Green (01) 269 2650
Holes   18 L 5374 m SSS 69
V'tors   U–phone Pro
Fees   £45 (£55)
Loc   3 miles S of Dublin

Foxrock (1893)

Torquay Road, Foxrock, Dublin 18
Tel   **(01) 289 5668**
Fax   (01) 289 4943
Mem   660
Sec   WM Daly (01) 289 3992
Pro   D Walker (01) 289 3414
Holes   9 L 5667 m Par 70 SSS 68
V'tors   WD/BH/Sun–M Tues &
Sat–NA
Fees   £30
Loc   5 miles S of Dublin

Grange (1911)

*Whitechurch Road, Rathfarnham,
Dublin 16*
Tel   **(01) 493 2832**
Fax   (01) 493 9490
Mem   1050 235(L) 210(J)
Sec   JA O'Donoghue
(01) 493 2889
Pro   B Hamill (01) 493 2299
Holes   18 L 5517 m SSS 69
V'tors   WD–U exc Tues/Wed
pm–NA WE–M
Fees   £35 (£40)
Loc   Rathfarnham, 5 miles from
centre of Dublin

Hazel Grove (1988)

*Mount Seskin Road, Jobstown,
Tallaght, Dublin 24*
Tel   **(01) 452 0911**
Mem   400 175(L)
Sec   J Matthews
Pro   None
Holes   9 L 5300 m SSS 67
V'tors   Mon/Wed/Fri–U Sun–NA
Tues/Thurs/Sat–restricted
Fees   £9
Loc   3 miles from Tallaght, off
Blessington road
Arch   Eddie Hackett

Howth (1916)

Carrickbrack Road, Sutton, Dublin 13
Tel   **(01) 832 3055**
Fax   (01) 832 1793
Mem   1200
Sec   Ms A MacNeice
Pro   JF McGuirk (01) 839 3895
Holes   18 L 5672 m SSS 69
V'tors   WD–U exc Wed WE–M
Fees   £35
Loc   9 miles NE of Dublin, nr
Sutton Cross
Arch   James Braid

Kilmashogue (1994)

College Road, Whitechurch, Dublin 16
Mem   355
Sec   V O'Kelly (Hon)
Pro   W Sullivan
Holes   9 L 5320 m Par 70 SSS 70
Fees   £10
Loc   Dublin

Newlands (1926)

Clondalkin, Dublin 22
Tel   **(01) 459 2903**
Fax   (01) 459 3498
Mem   1086
Sec   AT O'Neill (01) 459 3157
Pro   K O'Donnell (01) 459 3538
Holes   18 L 6184 yds SSS 70
V'tors   WD–U am WE/BH–NA SOC
Fees   IR£35
Loc   6 miles SW of Dublin at
Newlands Cross (N7)
Arch   James Braid

Rathfarnham (1899)

Newtown, Dublin 16
Tel   **(01) 493 1201/493 1561**
Fax   (01) 493 1561
Mem   561
Sec   DO Tipping (01) 493 1201
Pro   B O'Hara
Holes   9 L 5787 m SSS 70
V'tors   U exc Tues & Sat–NA
Fees   £22.50
Loc   6 miles S of Dublin
Arch   John Jacobs

Royal Dublin (1885)

*North Bull Island Nature Reserve,
Dollymount, Dublin 3*
Tel   **(01) 833 6346/1262**
Fax   (01) 833 6504
Web   www.theroyaldublingolfclub
.com
Mem   1060
Sec   JA Lambe (01) 833 1262
Pro   L Owens (01) 833 6477
(Senior Pro C O'Connor Sr)
Holes   18 L 6925 yds SSS 73
V'tors   U H exc Wed Sat–NA before
4pm Sun–NA exc 10.30–12
noon SOC–WD
Fees   IR£75 (IR£85)
Loc   3 miles NE of Dublin, on
coast road to Howth
Mis   Practice range
Arch   HS Colt

St Anne's (1921)

*North Bull Island, Dollymount,
Dublin 5*
Tel   **(01) 833 6471**
Fax   (01) 833 4618
Web   www.stanneslinksgolf.com
Mem   636
Sec   Shirley Sleator
Pro   P Skerritt
Holes   18 L 5669 m Par 70 SSS 70
V'tors   WE/BH–NA SOC
Fees   £30 (£40)
Loc   Dublin 5 miles. M50, 5 miles
Arch   Eddie Hackett

Stackstown (1975)

*Kellystown Road, Rathfarnham,
Dublin 16*
Tel   **(01) 494 1993**
Fax   (01) 493 3934
Mem   1300
Sec   K Lawlor (Sec/Mgr)
Pro   M Kavanagh (01) 944561
Holes   18 L 6494 m SSS 72
V'tors   WD–U SOC
Fees   £20 (£25)
Loc   7 miles SE of Dublin

Sutton (1890)

Cush Point, Sutton, Dublin 13
Tel   **(01) 832 3013**
Fax   (01) 832 1603
Mem   625
Sec   H O'Neill
Pro   N Lynch

Holes 9 L 5624 m Par 70 SSS 67
V'tors Tues–NA Sat–NA before
5.30pm
Fees £20 (£25)
Loc 7 miles E of Dublin

Co Fermanagh

Castle Hume

Belleek Road, Enniskillen, BT93 7ED
Tel (028) 6632 7077
Fax (028) 6632 7076
Mem 270
Web www.home.btclick.com/
enniskillen.golf
Sec A Frazer
Holes 18 L 5932 m Par 72 SSS 71
V'tors U
Fees £15 (£20)
Loc Enniskillen (A46)
Arch Tony Carroll

Enniskillen (1896)

Castlecoole, Enniskillen, BT74 6HZ
Tel (028) 6632 5250
Fax (028) 6632 5250
Mem 480
Sec W McBrien
Pro None
Holes 18 L 5574 m Par 71 SSS 69
V'tors U SOC
Fees D–£15 (£18)
Loc 1 mile SE of Enniskillen, on
Castlecoole Estate
Arch TJ McAuley

Co Galway

Athenry (1902)

Palmerstown, Oranmore
Tel (091) 794466
Fax (091) 794971
Mem 800
Sec P Flattery (Sec/Mgr)
(091 794466
Pro R Ryan (091) 790599
Holes 18 L 6300 m Par 70 SSS 70
V'tors WD/Sat–U Sun–NA SOC
Fees £20 (£25)
Loc 10 miles E of Galway on
Athenry road (R348)
Arch Eddie Hackett

Ballinasloe (1894)

Rosgloss, Ballinasloe
Tel (0905) 42126
Fax (0905) 42538
Mem 925
Sec M Kelly
Pro None
Holes 18 L 5865 m Par 72 SSS 70
V'tors U SOC
Fees £15 (£18)
Loc Ballinasloe 2 miles
Arch Hackett/Connaughton

Bearna (1996)

Corboley, Bearna
Tel (091) 592677
Fax (091) 592674
Web www.homepage.eircom.net/
bearnagc
Mem 500
Sec M Meade (Sec/Mgr)
(091) 592677
Holes 18 L 5746 m Par 72 SSS 72
V'tors U
Fees £25 (£30)
Arch RJ Browne

Connemara (1973)

Ballyconneely, Clifden
Tel (095) 23502/23602
Fax (095) 23662
Mem 900
Sec R Flaherty (Sec/Mgr)
Pro H O'Neill (095) 23502
Holes 18 L 6560 m SSS 72
V'tors U H SOC
Fees £35
Loc 8 miles SW of Clifden
Arch Eddie Hackett

Connemara Isles

Annaghvane, Lettermore, Connemara
Tel (091) 572498
Fax (091) 572214
Mem 114
Sec P O'Conghaile (Sec/Mgr)
Holes 9 L 5168 yds Par 70 SSS 67
V'tors U SOC
Fees £10–£12
Loc 3 miles W of Costello
Arch Craddock/Ruddy

Curra West (1996)

Curra, Kylebrack, Loughrea
Tel (091) 45121
Mem 60
Sec J Cunningham (Hon)
Holes 9 L 5113 m Par 70 SSS 67
V'tors U
Fees £7 (£7)

Galway (1895)

Blackrock, Salthill, Galway
Tel (091) 522033
Fax (091) 529783
Mem 1020
Sec P Fahy
Pro D Wallace (091) 523038
Holes 18 L 5828 m SSS 70
V'tors Restricted Tues & Sun
Fees £25 (£30)
Loc 3 miles W of Galway City

Galway Bay G&CC
(1993)

Renville, Oranmore
Tel (091) 790500
Fax (091) 792510
Web www.gbaygolf.com
Mem 425
Sec Ann Hanley (Golf Dir)
Pro E O'Connor (091) 790503

Holes 18 L 6350 m SSS 73
V'tors U H SOC
Fees £35–£40
Loc 10 miles E of Galway City
(N18)
Mis Driving range. Golf Academy
Arch C O'Connor Jr

Gort (1924)

Castlequarter, Gort
Tel (091) 632244
Mem 460
Sec S Devlin (Hon)
(091) 631281
Pro None
Holes 18 L 5979 m SSS 71
V'tors U exc Sun am SOC
Fees £12 (£12)
Loc 20 miles S of Galway
Arch C O'Connor Jr

Loughrea (1924)

Graigue, Loughrea
Tel (091) 41049
Mem 400
Sec M Hawkins (Mgr)
Holes 18 L 4987 m Par 69 SSS 66
V'tors U SOC
Fees On application
Loc 1 mile N of Loughrea, off
Dublin–Galway road. 20 miles
E of Galway
Arch Eddie Hackett

Mountbellew (1929)

Mountbellew, Ballinasloe
Tel (0905) 79259
Mem 380
Sec M Meehan (Mgr)
Holes 9 L 5143 m SSS 66
V'tors U SOC
Fees £8
Loc 50km NE of Galway on N63

Oughterard (1973)

Gortreevagh, Oughterard
Tel (091) 552131
Fax (091) 552733
Mem 1000
Sec J Waters
Pro M Ryan (Ext 201)
Holes 18 L 6752 yds SSS 69
V'tors U SOC
Fees £20
Loc 15 miles NW of Galway on
N59
Arch Harris/Merrigan

Portumna (1913)

Ennis Road, Portumna
Tel (0509) 41059
Mem 600
Sec R Clarke (Hon)
Pro R Clarke
Holes 18 L 5474 m Par 68 SSS 67
V'tors U SOC
Fees £15
Loc 40 miles SE of Galway on
Lough Derg
Arch E Connaughton

Tuam (1904)

Barnacurragh, Tuam
Tel	(093) 28993
Fax	(093) 26003
Mem	700
Sec	V Gaffney (Sec/Mgr)
Pro	L Smyth (093) 24091
Holes	18 L 5944 m Par 72 SSS 71
V'tors	Sun–NA SOC–WD
Fees	£15 SOC–£10
Loc	20 miles N of Galway
Arch	Eddie Hackett

Co Kerry

Ardfert (1993)

Sackville, Ardfert, Tralee
Tel	(066) 34744
Fax	(066) 34744
Mem	171
Sec	Sinead Maunsell
Pro	N Cassidy
Holes	9 L 4754 m Par 66
V'tors	U
Fees	9 holes–£9. 18 holes–£14
Loc	60 miles NW of Tralee (R551)
Mis	Driving range
Arch	James Healy

Ballybunion (1893)

Sandhill Road, Ballybunion
Tel	(068) 27146
Fax	(068) 27387
Mem	648
Sec	J McKenna (Sec/Mgr)
Pro	B O'Callaghan
Holes	Old 18 L 6542 yds SSS 72 Cashen 18 L 6477 yds SSS 70
V'tors	U SOC
Fees	Old–£75 New–£40 Old+New D–£95
Loc	2 miles S of Ballybunion. 50 miles W of Limerick, via Tarbert
Mis	Driving range

Ballyheigue Castle (1995)

Ballyheigue, Tralee
Tel	(066) 713 3555
Fax	(066) 713 3147
Mem	250
Sec	JP Broderick (Sec/Mgr)
Holes	9 L 6292 m Par 72 SSS 74
V'tors	U
Fees	£15 (£18)
Loc	11 miles NW of Tralee (R551)
Arch	Roger Jones

Beaufort (1994)

Churchtown, Beaufort, Killarney
Tel	(064) 44440
Fax	(064) 44752

Mem	250
Sec	C Kelly
Pro	H Duggan
Holes	18 L 6605 yds Par 71 SSS 72
V'tors	WD–H SOC
Fees	£30 (£35)
Loc	7 miles W of Killarney, off N72
Arch	Dr Arthur Spring

Castlegregory

Stradbally, Castlegregory
Tel	(066) 39444
Mem	296
Sec	G O'Connor (Sec/Mgr)
Holes	9 L 5340 m SSS 68
V'tors	U SOC
Fees	£18
Loc	18 miles W of Tralee
Arch	Arthur Spring

Ceann Sibeal (1924)

Ballyferriter
Tel	(066) 915 6255/6408
Fax	(066) 915 6409
Mem	460
Sec	S Fahy (Mgr)
Pro	D O'Connor
Holes	18 L 6690 yds SSS 71
V'tors	U SOC
Fees	€20–50 (€32–57)
Loc	Dingle Peninsula, W of Tralee
Arch	Hackett/O'Connor Jr

Dooks (1889)

Glenbeigh
Tel	(066) 976 8205
Fax	(066) 976 8476
Mem	900
Sec	D Mangan
Holes	18 L 5346 m Par 70 SSS 68
V'tors	WD–U H before 5pm WE/BH–phone first SOC
Fees	€40
Loc	3 miles N of Glenbeigh, on Ring of Kerry (N70)

Kenmare (1903)

Kenmare
Tel	(064) 41291
Fax	(064) 42061
Mem	349
Sec	M MacGearailt
Pro	None
Holes	18 L 5441 m SSS 69
V'tors	U SOC
Fees	£20
Loc	20 miles S of Killarney on Cork road
Arch	Eddie Hackett

Kerries (1995)

Tralee
Tel	(066) 22112
Mem	280
Sec	M Barrett (Mgr)

Holes	9 L 2718 m Par 35 SSS 39
V'tors	U
Fees	£14
Loc	Tralee

Killarney (1893)

Mahoney's Point, Killarney
Tel	(064) 31034
Fax	(064) 33065
Web	www.killarney-golf.com
Mem	1500
Sec	T Prendergast
Pro	T Coveney (064) 31615
Holes	Mahoney's Point 18 L 6164 m SSS 72; Killeen 18 L 6475 m SSS 73 Lackabane 18 L 6410 m SSS 73
V'tors	H SOC
Fees	On application
Loc	3 miles W of Killarney (N72)
Arch	Mahoney's Point-Longhurst/ Campbell; Killeen-Hackett/ O'Sullivan; Lackabane-Steel

Killorglin (1992)

Steelroe, Killorglin
Tel	(066) 61979
Fax	(066) 61437
Mem	230
Sec	B Dodd
Pro	None
Holes	18 L 6464 yds SSS 72
V'tors	U SOC
Fees	IR£14 (IR£16)
Loc	1 mile from Killorglin on Tralee road (N70). 12 miles W of Killarney
Arch	Eddie Hackett

Listowel (1993)

Pay and play
Feale View, Listowel
Tel	(068) 21592
Fax	(068) 23387
Sec	Caroline Barrett
Holes	9 L 5728 yds Par 70 SSS 68
V'tors	U SOC
Fees	9 holes–£10. 18 holes–£15
Loc	Nr Listowel on N69
Arch	Eddie Hackett

Parknasilla (1974)

Parknasilla, Sneem
Tel	(064) 45122
Fax	(064) 45323
Mem	180
Sec	M Walsh (Mgr) (064) 45233
Holes	12 L 5284 m Par 69 SSS 67
V'tors	U SOC
Fees	£18
Loc	Great Southern Hotel, 2 miles E of Sneem on Ring of Kerry
Arch	Arthur Spring

For list of abbreviations see page 649

Ring of Kerry G&CC
(1999)

Templenoe, Kenmare

Tel	**(064) 42000**
Fax	(064) 42533
Web	www.ringofkerrygolf.com
Mem	187
Sec	V Devlin (Gen Mgr)
Pro	None
Holes	18 L 6923 yds Par 72 SSS 73
V'tors	U H
Fees	£50 (£50)
Loc	4 miles W of Kenmare on N70
Arch	Hackett/Gaunt/Marnock

Ross (1995)

Ross Road, Killarney

Tel	**(064) 31125**
Fax	(064) 31860
Mem	280
Sec	A O'Meara
Pro	A O'Meara
Holes	9 L 5674 m Par 72 SSS 72
V'tors	U
Fees	18 holes–£18. 9 holes–£12
Loc	In Killarney
Arch	Rodger Jones

Tralee (1896)

West Barrow, Ardfert

Tel	**(066) 713 6379**
Fax	(066) 713 6008
Web	www.tralee-golf.com
Mem	1000
Sec	M O'Brien (Mgr)
Pro	D Power
Holes	18 L 6252 m SSS 71
V'tors	WD–U H before 4.30pm exc Wed–restricted Sat/BH–NA exc 11–1pm–H Sun–NA SOC–WD
Fees	£40 (£60)
Loc	8 miles NW of Tralee on Spa/Fenit road
Arch	Arnold Palmer

Waterville (1889)

Waterville Golf Links, Ring of Kerry, Waterville

Tel	**(066) 947 4102**
Fax	(066) 947 4482
Mem	320
Sec	N Cronin
Pro	L Higgins
Holes	18 L 7225 yds SSS 74
V'tors	U H SOC
Fees	£50–£100
Loc	¹/₄ mile N of Waterville on Ring of Kerry
Mis	Driving range
Arch	Hackett/Mulcahy

Co Kildare

Athy (1906)

Geraldine, Athy

Tel	**(0507) 31729**
Fax	(0507) 34710
Web	www.athygolfclub.com
Mem	700
Sec	EN Wynne (Hon)
Pro	None
Holes	18 L 6308 yds Par 71 SSS 69
V'tors	WD–U (booking necessary) Sat–M SOC
Fees	IR£15 (IR£20)
Loc	1 mile N of Athy on Kildare road

Bodenstown (1983)

Bodenstown, Sallins

Tel	**(045) 97096**
Mem	650
Sec	J Sexton (Hon)
Holes	Old 18 L 6132 m SSS 71 Ladyhill 18 L 5278 m SSS 68
V'tors	U exc WE–NA (Old course)
Fees	Old–£12 Ladyhill–£10
Loc	4 miles N of Naas on Clane road. 18 miles W of Dublin, off N7

Castlewarden G&CC
(1989)

Straffan

Tel	**(01) 458 9254**
Fax	(01) 458 8972
Web	www.castlewardengolfclub .com
Mem	565 225(L)
Sec	P Sheehan (Hon)
Pro	G Egan (01) 458 8219
Holes	18 L 6624 yds Par 72 SSS 71
V'tors	WD–U WE–M SOC
Fees	£17–£23 (£23)
Loc	13 miles W of Dublin, off N7
Arch	Halpin/Browne

Cill Dara (1920)

Little Curragh, Kildare Town

Tel	**(045) 521433/521295**
Mem	400
Sec	P Flanagan (Hon)
Pro	M O'Boyle
Holes	9 L 5842 m SSS 70
V'tors	WD–U before 2pm exc Wed–NA Sat–NA after noon Sun/BH–NA SOC
Fees	£10 (£12)
Loc	1 mile W of Kildare town

Craddockstown (1991)

Blessington Road, Naas

Tel	**(045) 897610**
Fax	(045) 896968
Mem	580
Sec	L Watson
Holes	18 L 6134 m Par 71 SSS 70
V'tors	U
Fees	£14 (£18)
Loc	Naas
Arch	Arthur Spring

The Curragh (1883)

Curragh

Tel	**(045) 441238/441714**

Fax	(045) 442476
Mem	500 176(L)
Sec	Ann Culleton (045) 441714
Pro	G Burke (045) 441896
Holes	18 L 6035 m SSS 71
V'tors	WD–U exc Tues–phone Sec
Fees	€30 (€35)
Loc	3 miles S of Newbridge

Highfield (1992)

Highfield House, Carbury

Tel	**(0405) 31021**
Fax	(0405) 31021
Web	www.highfield-golf.ie
Mem	550
Sec	P Duggan (Sec/Mgr)
Pro	P O'Hagan
Holes	18 L 5707 m SSS 69
V'tors	WD–U WE–U after 12 noon
Fees	£14 (£18)
Loc	32 miles W of Dublin on N4
Arch	Alan Duggan

The K Club (1991)

Kildare Hotel & CC, Straffan

Tel	**(01) 601 7300**
Fax	(01) 601 7399
Mem	527
Sec	P Crowe (Golf Dir)
Pro	E Jones
Holes	18 L 7227 yds SSS 72
V'tors	U H SOC–WD
Fees	€245
Loc	18 miles SW of Dublin (N7)
Mis	Driving range
Arch	Arnold Palmer

Kilkea Castle (1995)

Castledermot

Tel	**(0503) 45555**
Fax	(0503) 45505
Holes	18 L 6200 m Par 71 SSS 71
V'tors	U
Fees	£30 (£35)
Loc	7 miles N of Castledermot (R418)
Arch	David Cassidy

Killeen (1986)

Killeenbeg, Kill

Tel	**(045) 866003**
Fax	(045) 875881
Mem	170
Sec	P Carey
Pro	None
Holes	18 L 5815 m Par 71 SSS 71
V'tors	WD–U WE–NA before 10am
Fees	£17 (£20)
Loc	2 miles off N7 on Sallins road
Arch	Ruddy/Craddock

Knockanally (1985)

Donadea, North Kildare

Tel	**(045) 869322**
Fax	(045) 869322
Mem	500
Sec	N Lyons
Pro	M Darcy

Holes 18 L 6424 yds SSS 71
V'tors U
Fees £20 (£30)
Loc 20 miles W of Dublin on
Galway road (M4)
Arch N Lyons

Leixlip (1994)
Leixlip
Tel (01) 624 4978
Fax (01) 624 6185
Mem 200
Sec J McKone
Holes 9 L 6030 m Par 72 SSS 70
V'tors U
Fees £13 (£15)
Loc 10 miles W of Dublin on N4
Arch Eddie Hackett

Naas (1896)
Kerdiffstown, Naas
Tel (045) 874644
Fax (045) 896109
Mem 1000
Sec M Conway
Holes 18 L 6232 m SSS 69
V'tors U SOC
Fees £18 (£24)
Loc 2 miles N of Naas
Arch Arthur Spring

Newbridge (1997)
Tankardsgarden, Newbridge
Tel (045) 431289
Fax (045) 431289
Mem 110
Sec F Meehan (Hon)
Holes 18 L 5921 m Par 72 SSS 72
V'tors U
Fees £9 (£12)
Loc 30 mins from Dublin on M7
Arch Pat Suttle

Woodlands (1985)
Coolereagh, Coill Dubh
Tel (045) 860777
Fax (045) 860988
Mem 615
Sec J Russell
Holes 18 L 6020 m Par 72 SSS 71
V'tors U
Fees £12 (£15)
Loc Naas
Arch Tommy Halpin

Co Kilkenny

Callan (1929)
Geraldine, Callan
Tel (056) 25136/25949
Fax (056) 55155
Mem 750
Sec M Duggan (Hon)
Pro J O'Dwyer (086) 817 2464
Holes 18 L 6422 yds Par 72 SSS 70
V'tors U SOC

Fees £20
Loc 1 mile SE of Callan. 10 miles
SW of Kilkenny
Arch Bryan Moor

Castlecomer (1935)
Dromgoole, Castlecomer
Tel (056) 41139
Fax (056) 41139
Web www.homepage.eircom.net/
~castlecomergolfclub
Mem 700
Sec M Dooley (Hon)
Holes 9 L 5923 m Par 71 SSS 71
V'tors U SOC–WD
Fees £12
Loc 11 miles N of Kilkenny on N7
Arch Pat Ruddy

Kilkenny (1896)
Glendine, Kilkenny
Tel (056) 65400
Fax (056) 23593
Mem 950
Sec S O'Neill (056) 65400
Pro J Bolger (056) 61730
Holes 18 L 6500 yds SSS 70
V'tors U
Fees £25 (£30)
Loc 1 mile N of Kilkenny, off N77

Mount Juliet (1991)
Thomastown
Tel (056) 73000
Fax (056) 73019
Web www.mountjuliet.com
Sec Kim Thomas
Pro K Morris
Holes 18 L 7299 yds Par 72 SSS 74
V'tors U
Fees £85 (£100)
Loc 10 miles S of Kilkenny, off
Dublin-Waterford road.
Mis Driving range-residents and
green fees. Golf Academy
Arch Jack Nicklaus

Mountain View (1997)
Kiltorcan, Ballyhale
Tel (056) 68122
Fax (056) 24655
Mem 300
Sec M Kelly
Holes 9 L 5025 m Par 70
V'tors U
Fees £11 (£11)
Loc 12 miles S of Kilkenny
Arch John O'Sullivan

Co Laois

Abbeyleix (1895)
Rathmoyle, Abbeyleix
Tel (0502) 31450
Mem 400

Sec GP O'Hara (Hon)
Holes 18 L 6031 yds Par 72 SSS 70
V'tors WD–U WE–NA
SOC–WD/Sat
Fees £12 (£15)
Loc 10 miles S of Portlaoise. 60
miles SW of Dublin on Cork
road
Arch Mel Flanaghan

Heath (Portlaoise) (1930)
The Heath, Portlaoise
Tel (0502) 46533
Fax (0502) 46866
Mem 830
Sec P Carpendale (Hon)
Pro E Doyle (0502) 46622
Holes 18 L 5873 m Par 71 SSS 70
V'tors U
Fees £10 (£17)
Loc 4 miles E of Portlaoise
Mis Floodlit driving range

Mountrath (1929)
Knockanina, Mountrath
Tel (0502) 32558
Mem 500
Sec J Mulhare (0502) 32421
Holes 18 L 6020 yds Par 71 SSS 69
V'tors U
Fees £10
Loc 10 miles W of Portlaoise.
Mountrath 2 miles

Portarlington (1908)
Garryhinch, Portarlington
Tel (0502) 23115
Fax (0502) 23044
Mem 600
Sec D Cunningham (Hon)
Holes 18 L 6004 m Par 71 SSS 71
V'tors WD–U WE–restricted
Fees £14 (£17)
Loc Between Portarlington and
Mountmellick on L116

Rathdowney (1930)
Coulnaboul West, Rathdowney
Tel (0505) 46170
Fax (0505) 46065
Mem 600
Sec S Bolger (Hon)
Holes 18 L 5864 m Par 71 SSS 70
V'tors U exc Sun–NA SOC
Fees £12 (£15)
Loc 1 mile S of Rathdowney.
20 miles SW of Portlaoise
Arch Hackett/Suttle

Co Leitrim

Ballinamore (1941)
Creevy, Ballinamore
Tel (078) 44346
Mem 120
Sec J Cryan

Holes 9 L 5514 m Par 70 SSS 68
V'tors U SOC
Fees £10
Loc 2 miles N of Ballinamore.
20 miles NE of Carrick-on-
Shannon
Arch Arthur Spring

Carrick-on-Shannon
(1910)
Woodbrook, Carrick-on-Shannon
Tel (079) 67015
Mem 210
Sec HP Gralton (Sec/Mgr)
Holes 9 L 5584 yds SSS 68
V'tors U
Fees IR£12
Loc 4 miles W of Carrick-on-
Shannon on N4

Co Limerick

Abbeyfeale (1993)
Dromtrasna Collins, Abbeyfeale
Tel (068) 32033
Mem 85
Sec M O'Riordan (Mgr)
Pro D Power
Holes 9 L 4004 yds Par 62 SSS 61
V'tors U
Fees £6
Loc 12 miles SW of Newcastle
West

Adare Manor (1900)
Adare
Tel (061) 396204
Fax (061) 396800
Mem 400
Sec M Spillane
Pro J Coyle
Holes 18 L 5706 yds SSS 69
V'tors WD–U WE–M
Fees D–£15 (D–£20)
Loc 10 miles SW of Limerick
Arch Sayers/Hackett

Castletroy (1937)
Castletroy, Limerick
Tel (061) 335261
Fax (061) 335373
Mem 940
Sec L Hayes (061) 335753
Pro Shop (061) 330450
Holes 18 L 5802 m SSS 71
V'tors WD–U Sat am–U Sat
pm/Sun–M
SOC–Mon/Wed/Fri
Fees £23 (£30)
Loc 2 miles N of Limerick on
Dublin road

Killeline (1993)
Newcastle West
Tel (069) 61600
Fax (069) 62853

Mem 278
Sec J McCoy
Holes 18 L 6700 yds Par 72
V'tors U
Fees £12
Loc Newcastle West

Limerick (1891)
Ballyclough, Limerick
Tel (061) 414083
Fax (061) 415146
Mem 1325
Sec D McDonogh (061) 415146
Pro L Harrington (061) 412492
Holes 18 L 6479 yds SSS 71
V'tors WD–U before 5pm exc Tues
WE–M SOC–WD
Fees £35
Loc 3 miles S of Limerick

Limerick County G&CC
Ballyneety
Tel (061) 351881
Fax (061) 351384
Web www.limerickcounty.com
Mem 450
Sec J Heaton (Mgr)
Pro P Murphy
Holes 18 L 6137 m Par 72 SSS 74
V'tors U SOC
Fees £20 (£25)
Loc 5 miles S of Limerick (R512)
Mis Driving range
Arch Des Smyth

Newcastle West (1938)
Ardagh
Tel (069) 76500
Fax (069) 76511
Mem 510 120(L)
Sec P Lyons (Sec/Mgr)
Holes 18 L 5905 m SSS 72
V'tors U exc Sun–U after 4pm SOC
Fees £18
Loc 6 miles N of Newcastle West,
off N21
Mis Floodlit driving range
Arch Arthur Spring

Co Londonderry

Benone Par Three
*53 Benone Avenue, Benone, Limavady,
BT49 0LQ*
Tel (028) 7775 0555
Sec MI Clark
Holes 9 L 1427 yds Par 3 course
V'tors U
Fees On application
Loc 12 miles N of Limavady on A2
coast road

Brown Trout (1984)
*209 Agivey Road, Aghadowey,
Coleraine, BT51 4AD*
Tel (028) 7086 8209

Fax (028) 7086 8878
Web www.browntroutinn.com
Mem 150
Sec B O'Hara (Sec/Mgr)
Pro K Revie
Holes 9 L 2800 yds SSS 68
V'tors U SOC
Fees £10 (£15)
Loc 8 miles S of Coleraine at
junction of A54/B66
Arch W O'Hara Sr

Castlerock (1901)
Circular Road, Castlerock, BT51 4TJ
Tel (028) 7084 8314
Fax (028) 7084 9440
Mem 1100
Sec M Steen (Sec/Mgr)
Pro R Kelly
Holes 18 L 6121 m SSS 72
9 L 2457 m SSS 34
V'tors WD–U exc Fri SOC
Fees 18 hole:£30 (£55) 9 hole:£12
(£15)
Loc 5 miles W of Coleraine on A2
Arch Ben Sayers

City of Derry (1912)
*49 Victoria Road, Londonderry,
BT47 2PU*
Tel (01) 504 46369
Mem 775
Pro M Doherty (028) 7131 1496
Holes Prehen 18 L 6487 yds SSS 71
Dunhugh 9 L 4708 yds
SSS 63
V'tors WD–U before 4pm –M after
4pm WE–U H SOC
Fees On application
Loc 3 miles from E end of
Craigavon Bridge towards
Strabane

Foyle (1994)
Alder Road, Londonderry, BT48 8DB
Tel (028) 7135 2222
Fax (028) 7135 3967
Mem 265
Sec M Lapsley
Pro K McLaughlin
Holes 18 L 6678 m SSS 72
9 hole course
V'tors U
Fees £12 (£15)
Loc Londonderry
Mis Driving range
Arch Frank Ainsworth

Kilrea (1920)
Drumagarner Road, Kilrea
Tel (028) 2582 1048
Mem 310
Sec DP Clarke
Holes 9 L 4514 yds SSS 62
V'tors Tues & Wed–NA after 5pm
Sat–NA before 4pm
Fees £10 (£12.50)
Loc Nr Kilrea on Maghera road.
15 miles S of Coleraine

Moyola Park (1976)

15 Curran Road, Castledawson,
Magherafelt, BT45 8DG

Tel	**(028) 7946 8468**
Fax	(028) 7946 8468
Mem	940
Sec	LWP Hastings (Hon)
Pro	V Teague (028) 7946 8830
Holes	18 L 6062 yds Par 71
V'tors	U SOC exc Sat
Fees	£17 (£25)
Loc	40 miles NW of Belfast by M2. 35 miles S of Coleraine
Arch	Don Patterson

Portstewart (1894)

117 Strand Road, Portstewart,
BT55 7PG

Tel	**(028) 7083 2015**
Fax	(028) 7083 4097
Web	www.portstewartgc.co.uk
Mem	1524
Sec	M Moss BA (028) 7083 3839
Pro	A Hunter (028) 7083 2601
Holes	Strand 18 L 6784 yds SSS 73 Riverside 9 L 2662 yds Par 32 Old 18 L 4733 yds SSS 62
V'tors	SOC–by arrangement
Fees	Strand–£55 (£75) Riverside–£12 Old £10 (£14)
Loc	W boundary of Portstewart

Roe Park (1993)

Limavady, BT49 9LB

Tel	**(028) 7172 2212**
Mem	300
Sec	D Brockerton
Pro	S Duffy
Holes	18 L 6318 yds Par 70 SSS 71
V'tors	U
Fees	£20 (£20)
Loc	Limavady
Mis	Driving range

Co Longford

County Longford (1900)

Glack, Dublin Road, Longford

Tel	**(043) 46310**
Fax	(043) 47082
Mem	800
Sec	E Dooley
Pro	D Keenaghan
Holes	18 L 6008 yds SSS 69
V'tors	U SOC
Fees	On application
Loc	Longford ¹/₂ mile on Dublin road
Arch	Eddie Hackett

Co Louth

Ardee (1911)

Ardee

Tel	**(041) 685 3227/6283**
Fax	(041) 685 6137

Mem	650
Sec	MP Conouly (Sec/Mgr) (041) 685 3227
Pro	S Kirkpatrick
Holes	18 L 6348 yds SSS 71
V'tors	U exc Sun–NA SOC
Fees	£20 Sat–£30
Loc	¹/₂ mile N of Ardee
Mis	Driving range
Arch	Eddie Hackett

County Louth (1892)

Baltray, Drogheda

Tel	**(041) 982 2329**
Fax	(041) 982 2969
Mem	1055
Sec	M Delany
Pro	P McGuirk (041) 982 2444
Holes	18 L 6783 yds SSS 72
V'tors	By prior arrangement
Fees	€75 (€95)
Loc	3 miles NE of Drogheda
Arch	Tom Simpson

Dundalk (1904)

Blackrock, Dundalk

Tel	**(042) 932 1731**
Fax	(042) 932 2022
Web	www.eiresoft.com/dundalkgc
Mem	850
Sec	T Sloane (Sec/Mgr)
Pro	L Walker (042) 932 2102
Holes	18 L 6028 m Par 72
V'tors	U SOC
Fees	IR£35
Loc	3 miles S of Dundalk

Greenore (1896)

Greenore

Tel	**(042) 937 3212/3678**
Fax	(042) 937 3678
Mem	700
Sec	R Daly
Holes	18 L 6514 yds Par 71 SSS 71
V'tors	WD–U before 5pm WE/BH–by arrangement SOC
Fees	£20 (£25)
Loc	15 miles E of Dundalk on Carlingford Lough
Arch	Eddie Hackett

Killinbeg (1991)

Killin Park, Bridge a Chrin, Dundalk

Tel	**(042) 39303**
Mem	175
Sec	N Kilco (Sec/Mgr)
Pro	None
Holes	18 L 4717 m Par 69 SSS 64
V'tors	U SOC
Fees	£10 (£14)
Loc	2 miles NW of Dundalk on Castletown road

Seapoint (1993)

Termonfeckin, Drogheda

Tel	**(041) 982 2333**
Fax	(041) 982 2331
Mem	460
Sec	K Carrie

Pro	D Carroll (041) 988 1066
Holes	18 L 6420 m Par 72 SSS 74
V'tors	U SOC
Fees	£25 (£35)
Loc	5 miles NE of Drogheda (R166)
Arch	Des Smyth

Towneley Hall (1994)

Tullyallen, Drogheda

Tel	**(041) 42229**
Fax	(041) 31762
Mem	125
Sec	M Foley (Hon)
Holes	9 L 5221 m Par 71 SSS 69
V'tors	U
Fees	£6 (£7)
Loc	5 miles NW of Drogheda, off R168

Co Mayo

Achill Island (1951)

Keel, Achill

Tel	**(098) 43456**
Mem	100
Sec	E Masterson(Hon)
Holes	9 L 2689 m Par 70 SSS 67
V'tors	U H SOC
Fees	£7
Loc	50 miles NW of Westport, on Achill Island
Arch	P Skerritt

Ashford Castle

Cong

Tel	**(092) 46003**
Holes	9 L 4500 yds SSS 68
V'tors	U SOC
Fees	£15
Loc	25 miles N of Galway on Lough Corrib
Arch	Eddie Hackett

Ballina (1910)

Mossgrove, Shanaghy, Ballina

Tel	**(096) 21050**
Fax	(096) 21050
Mem	460
Sec	V Frawley (096) 21795
Holes	18 L 6103 yds SSS 69
V'tors	WD–U Sun–NA before noon SOC–WD
Fees	£12 (£16)
Loc	1 mile E of Ballina

Ballinrobe (1895)

Clooncastle, Ballinrobe

Tel	**(092) 41118**
Fax	(092) 41889
Mem	590
Sec	Fidelma Butler
Pro	D Kearney
Holes	18 L 6043 m Par 73 SSS 72
V'tors	U exc Sun–NA SOC
Fees	£15–£18

Loc 2 miles NW of Ballinrobe on R331
Misc Driving range
Arch Tony O'Carroll

Ballyhaunis (1929)
Coolnaha, Ballyhaunis
Tel (0907) 30014
Mem 300
Sec T McNicholas (Hon)
Holes 9 L 5413 m Par 70 SSS 68
V'tors U exc Thurs (Ladies Day)–M Sun–NA SOC–WD
Fees £10
Loc 2 miles N of Ballyhaunis

Carne Golf Links (1995)
Carne, Belmullet
Tel (097) 82292
Fax (097) 81477
Web www.carnegolflinks.com
Mem 350
Sec A Valkenburg (097) 82292
Holes 18 L 6119 m SSS 72
V'tors U SOC
Fees £25 W–£100
Loc 2 miles W of Belmullet. 40 miles W of Ballina
Arch Eddie Hackett

Castlebar (1910)
Hawthorn Avenue, Rocklands, Castlebar
Tel (094) 21649
Fax (094) 26088
Web www.castlebar.ie/golf
Mem 950
Sec EJ Lonergan (086) 837 3944
Holes 18 L 6500 yds Par 71 SSS 72
V'tors WD/Sat–U Sun–NA
Fees £20 (£25)
Loc 1 mile S of Castlebar, on Galway road
Arch P McEvoy (1999)

Claremorris (1917)
Castlemagarrett, Claremorris
Tel (094) 71527
Mem 300
Sec W Feeley (Hon)
Holes 18 L 5827 yds Par 73 SSS 70
V'tors WD–U before noon Sat–U before noon SOC
Fees £15 (£18)
Loc 2 miles S of Claremorris (N17)
Arch Tom Craddock

Mulranny (1968)
Mulranny, Westport
Tel (098) 36262
Mem 100
Sec D Nevin (Hon)
Holes 9 L 6255 yds Par 71 SSS 69
V'tors U
Fees £8
Loc 20 miles NW of Castlebar

Swinford (1922)
Brabazon Park, Swinford
Tel (094) 51378
Mem 300
Sec T Regan (094) 51502
Holes 9 L 5901 yds SSS 68
V'tors U SOC–exc Sun
Fees D–£10 (£10)
Loc S of Swinford, off Kiltimagh road

Westport (1908)
Carowholly, Westport
Tel (098) 28262/27070
Fax (098) 27217
Web www.golfing-ireland.com
Mem 750
Sec P Smyth (Mgr)
Pro A Mealia
Holes 18 L 6653 yds SSS 72
V'tors U SOC
Fees £23 (£28)
Loc 2 miles W of Westport
Arch F Hawtree

Co Meath

Ashbourne (1991)
Archerstown, Ashbourne
Tel (01) 835 2005
Fax (01) 835 2561
Mem 645
Sec J Clancy
Pro J Dwyer
Holes 18 L 5778 m Par 71 SSS 70
V'tors WD–U WE–NA before 1pm SOC
Fees £20 (£25)
Loc 12 miles N of Dublin, off N2
Arch Des Smyth

The Black Bush (1987)
Thomastown, Dunshaughlin
Tel (01) 825 0021
Fax (01) 825 0400
Mem 950
Sec M Walsh (Mgr)
Pro S O'Grady
Holes 18 L 6930 yds SSS 73
9 L 2800 yds SSS 35
V'tors WD–U WE–NA before 4pm SOC
Fees On application
Loc 1 mile E of Dunshaughlin, off N3. 20 miles NW of Dublin
Mis Driving range for members and green fees
Arch Robert J Browne

County Meath (1898)
Newtownmoynagh, Trim
Tel (046) 31463
Fax (046) 37554
Web www.trimgolf.net
Mem 800
Sec J McInerney (086) 274 9859
Pro R Machin

Holes 18 L 6720 yds SSS 72
V'tors WD–U exc Thurs WE–restricted SOC–exc Sun
Fees £20 (£25)
Loc 2 miles SW of Trim. 25 miles NW of Dublin
Arch Hackett/Craddock

Gormanston College (1961)
Franciscan College, Gormanston
Tel (01) 841 2203
Fax (01) 841 2874
Mem 160
Sec Br Laurence Brady
Pro B Browne
Holes 9 L 1973 m
V'tors NA
Loc 22 miles N of Dublin

Headfort (1928)
Kells
Tel (046) 40857
Fax (046) 49282
Mem 993
Sec Enda Carroll (046) 40146
Pro B McGovern (046) 40639
Holes 18 L 6007 m SSS 71
18 L 6487 m SSS 75
V'tors U SOC exc Sun
Fees £21 (£26)
Loc 65km NW of Dublin on N3
Arch Christy O'Connor Jr

Kilcock (1985)
Gallow, Kilcock
Tel (01) 628 7592
Fax (01) 628 7283
Mem 575
Sec B Tyrrell (Hon)
Holes 18 L 5794 m SSS 71
V'tors U SOC
Fees £20 (£25)
Loc 20 miles W of Dublin (N4)
Arch E Hackett

Laytown & Bettystown (1909)
Bettystown
Tel (041) 982 7170/7534
Fax (041) 982 8506
Mem 850
Sec Helen Finnegan
Pro RJ Browne (041) 982 8793
Holes 18 L 6454 yds SSS 72
V'tors U SOC–WD
Fees £25 (£30)
Loc 25 miles N of Dublin

Moor Park (1993)
Mooretown, Navan
Tel (046) 27661
Mem 180
Sec M Fagan (Mgr)
Holes 18 L 5600 m Par 72 SSS 69
V'tors U
Fees £8 (£10)
Loc Navan

Royal Tara (1906)

Bellinter, Navan

Tel	(046) 25244/25508/25584
Fax	(046) 25508
Web	www.royaltaragolfclub.com
Mem	1000
Sec	P O'Brien
Pro	A Whiston (046) 26009
Holes	18 L 5757 yds Par 71
	9 L 3184 yds Par 35
V'tors	U
Fees	£20 (£25)
Loc	25 miles N of Dublin, off N3

Co Monaghan

Castleblayney (1985)

Onomy, Castleblayney

Tel	(042) 974 9485
Mem	275
Sec	R Kernan (042) 974 0451
Holes	9 L 2678 yds SSS 66
V'tors	U SOC
Fees	£8 (£10)
Loc	Castleblayney town centre. 18 miles SE of Monaghan
Arch	R Browne

Clones (1913)

Hilton Park, Clones

Tel	(049) 56017
Fax	(042) 974 2333
Mem	305
Sec	P McGrane (042) 42333
Holes	9 L 5790 yds SSS 68
V'tors	WD–U Sun–NA before noon
Fees	£10 (£12)
Loc	Hilton Park, 2½ miles from Clones

Mannan Castle (1993)

Donaghmoyne, Carrickmacross

Tel	(042) 966 3308
Fax	(042) 966 3195
Mem	600
Sec	R Howell (042) 966 2531
Holes	18 L 6020 yds Par 70 SSS 69
V'tors	U
Fees	£15
Loc	4 miles N of Carrickmacross

Nuremore (1964)

Nuremore, Carrickmacross

Tel	(042) 64016
Mem	120
Sec	M McMahon (Hon)
Pro	M Cassidy
Holes	18 L 5870 m Par 71 SSS 69
V'tors	U
Fees	£20 (£25)
Loc	1 mile S of Carrickmacross on Dublin road
Arch	Eddie Hackett

Rossmore (1916)

Rossmore Park, Monaghan

Tel	(047) 81316
Mem	750
Sec	J McKenna (Hon)
Pro	M Nicholson (047) 71222
Holes	18 L 6082 yds Par 70 SSS 69
V'tors	WD–U WE/BH–U SOC
Fees	£20
Loc	2 miles S of Monaghan on Cootehill road
Arch	Des Smyth

Co Offaly

Birr (1893)

The Glenns, Birr

Tel	(0509) 20082
Fax	(0509) 22155
Mem	750
Sec	Mary O'Gorman (Hon)
Pro	S O'Grady (0509) 21606
Holes	18 L 6216 yds SSS 70
V'tors	U SOC–exc Sun–NA 11.30–12
Fees	£12 (£14)
Loc	2 miles W of Birr
Mis	Driving range
Arch	Eddie Connaughton

Castle Barna (1992)

Castlebarnagh, Daingean

Tel	(0506) 53384
Fax	(0506) 53077
Mem	400
Sec	E Mangan
Holes	18 L 5595 m Par 72 SSS 69
V'tors	U
Fees	£10 (£14)
Loc	10 miles E of Tullamore (R402)
Arch	Alan Duggan

Edenderry (1910)

Kishavanna, Edenderry

Tel	(0405) 31072
Web	www.edenderrygolfclub.com
Mem	900
Sec	T Smyth (0405) 31534
Holes	18 L 6121 m Par 72 SSS 72
V'tors	WD–U exc Thurs (Ladies Day) WE–restricted SOC
Fees	£15 (£17)
Loc	1 mile E of Edenderry
Arch	Havers/Hackett

Tullamore (1896)

Brookfield, Tullamore

Tel	(0506) 21439
Fax	(0506) 41806
Web	www.tullamoregolfclub.com
Mem	1000
Sec	P Burns (Hon)
Pro	D McArdle (0506) 51757
Holes	18 L 6428 yds Par 70 SSS 71

V'tors	WD exc Tues–U Sat–restricted Sun–NA SOC
Fees	IR£25 (IR£30)
Loc	2½ miles S of Tullamore, off N52
Arch	Braid/Merrigan

Co Roscommon

Athlone (1892)

Hodson Bay, Athlone

Tel	(0902) 92073/92235
Fax	(0902) 94080
Mem	1000
Sec	L Fagan (Hon)
Pro	M Quinn
Holes	18 L 5854 m SSS 71
V'tors	U SOC
Fees	D–£18 (£20)
Loc	3 miles N of Athlone on Roscommon road
Arch	F Hawtree

Ballaghaderreen (1937)

Aughalustia, Ballaghaderreen

Tel	(0907) 60295
Mem	350
Sec	J Corcoran (Hon)
Holes	9 L 5663 yds Par 70 SSS 66
V'tors	U SOC
Fees	£10
Loc	Ballaghaderreen 3 miles
Arch	P Skerritt

Boyle (1911)

Knockadoobrusna, Roscommon Road, Boyle

Tel	(079) 62192/62594
Mem	145
Sec	D Conlon (Hon)
Holes	9 L 4914 m Par 67 SSS 64
V'tors	U SOC
Fees	£10
Loc	1½ miles S of Boyle
Arch	Eddie Hackett

Castlerea (1905)

Clonallis, Castlerea

Tel	(0907) 20068/20705
Mem	200
Sec	J Mulligan (Hon)
Holes	9 L 5466 yds SSS 66
V'tors	WD/Sat–U Sun–by arrangement
Fees	£8 (£10)
Loc	Knock Road, Castlerea

Roscommon (1904)

Moate Park, Roscommon

Tel	(0903) 26382
Fax	(0903) 26043
Mem	720
Sec	C McConn
Holes	18 L 6059 m Par 72 SSS 71

V'tors WD–U WE/BH–restricted
SOC
Fees £10–15
Loc 1 mile S of Roscommon
Arch Eddie Connaughton

Strokestown (1995)

Bumlin, Strokestown
Mem 200
Sec L Glover (Hon) (078) 33528
Holes 9 L 5230 m Par 68 SSS 67
V'tors U
Fees £10
Loc 15 miles N of Roscommon
(R368)

Co Sligo

Ballymote (1943)

Ballinascarrow, Ballymote
Tel (071) 83158
Mem 250
Sec EJ Stagg (Hon)
Holes 9 L 5302 m SSS 67
V'tors U
Fees D–£7 (£7)
Loc 15 miles S of Sligo

County Sligo (1894)

Rosses Point
Tel (071) 77134/77186
Fax (071) 77460
Web www.countysligogolfclub.ie
Mem 1169
Sec J Ironside (Mgr) (071) 77134
Pro J Robinson (071) 77171
Holes 18 L 6037 m SSS 72
9 L 2795 m SSS 35
V'tors U–booking required
Fees £55 Fri/WE–£70
Loc 5 miles NW of Sligo
Arch Colt/Allison

Enniscrone (1931)

Ballina Road, Enniscrone
Tel (096) 36297
Fax (096) 36657
Web www.homepage.eircom.net/
~enniscronegolf
Mem 740
Sec M Staunton (Sec/Mgr)
Pro C McGoldrick (096) 36666
Holes 18 L 6671 yds SSS 72
9 L 3364 yds Par 72
V'tors WD–U WE/BH–phone first
SOC
Fees €45 (€60)
Loc S of Enniscrone. Ballina 13
km
Mis Driving range
Arch Hackett/Steel

Strandhill (1932)

Strandhill
Tel (071) 68188

Fax (071) 68811
Mem 450
Sec Sandra Corcoran
Pro Golf Shop
Holes 18 L 6032 yds Par 69 SSS 68
V'tors WD–U WE/BH–restricted
SOC
Fees IR£25 (IR£30)
Loc 6 miles W of Sligo

Tubbercurry (1990)

Ballymote Road, Tubbercurry
Tel (071) 85849
Mem 250
Sec B Kilgannon (071) 86124
Holes 9 L 5478 m SSS 69
V'tors U
Fees £10
Loc 20 miles S of Sligo
Arch Eddie Hackett

Co Tipperary

Ballykisteen G&CC
(1994)

Monard
Tel (052) 51439
Mem 260
Sec Josephine Ryan
Pro D Reddan
Holes 18 L 6765 yds Par 72 SSS 73
V'tors U SOC–book in advance
Fees £20
Loc 3 miles W of Tipperary town
Mis Driving range
Arch Des Smyth

Cahir Park (1968)

Kilcommon, Cahir
Tel (052) 41474
Fax (052) 42717
Mem 575
Sec J Costigan (052) 41146
Pro M Joseph (052) 43944
Holes 18 L 6351 yds Par 71 SSS 71
V'tors U SOC–WD/Sat
Fees £18 (£20)
Loc 1 mile S of Cahir
Mis Driving range
Arch Eddie Hackett

Carrick-on-Suir (1939)

Garravoone, Carrick-on-Suir
Tel (051) 640047
Fax (051) 640558
Mem 500
Sec A Murphy (Sec/Mgr)
Holes 18 L 6061 m Par 72 SSS 70
V'tors U exc Sun–NA before 11am
SOC–WD/Sat
Fees £12 (£14)
Loc 2 miles S of Carrick on
Dungarvan road
Arch Eddie Hackett

Clonmel (1911)

Lyreanearla, Mountain Road, Clonmel
Tel (052) 21138/24050
Fax (052) 24050
Mem 931
Sec A Myles-Keating (052) 24050
Pro R Hayes (052) 24050
Holes 18 L 6347 yds SSS 71
V'tors WD–U WE–SOC
Fees £20 (£22)
Loc 2 miles SW of Clonmel
Arch Eddie Hackett

County Tipperary (1993)

Dundrum, Cashel
Tel (062) 71717
Fax (062) 71718
Web www.dundrumhousehotel
.com
Mem 380
Sec W Crowe (Mgr)
Holes 18 L 6955 yds SSS 73
V'tors U SOC
Fees £30 (£35)
Loc 6 miles W of Cashel
Arch Philip Walton

Nenagh (1929)

Beechwood, Nenagh
Tel (067) 31476
Fax (067) 34808
Mem 700
Sec PJ Hayes (Hon)
Pro G Morrison (067) 33242
Holes 18 L 5483 m Par 69 SSS 68
V'tors U SOC
Fees £15
Loc 3 miles NE of Nenagh on old
Birr road
Arch Dr A Mackenzie/Hackett

Roscrea (1892)

Derryvale, Roscrea
Tel (0505) 21130
Fax (0505) 23410
Mem 500
Sec GP Maher (Hon)
Holes 18 L 5782 m SSS 71
V'tors U
Fees £14 (£17)
Loc 2 miles E of Roscrea on
Dublin road (N7)
Arch Arthur Spring

Templemore (1970)

Manna South, Templemore
Tel (0504) 31400/31522
Mem 220
Sec JK Moloughney (Hon)
Holes 9 L 5442 yds SSS 67
V'tors U exc Sun SOC
Fees £5 (£10)
Loc ½ mile S of Templemore

Thurles (1909)

Turtulla, Thurles
Tel (0504) 21983
Fax (0504) 24647

Mem 850
Sec J Irwin
Pro S Hunt
Holes 18 L 5904 m Par 72 SSS 71
V'tors U
Fees £20
Loc 1 mile S of Thurles
Arch Lionel Hewson

Tipperary (1896)
Rathanny, Tipperary
Tel (062) 51119
Mem 550
Sec J Considine (Sec/Mgr)
Holes 18 L 5445 m Par 71 SSS 70
V'tors U SOC
Fees £15 (£17)
Loc Tipperary 1 mile

Co Tyrone

Auchnacloy (1995)
99 Tullyvar Road, Auchnacloy
Tel (028) 8255 7050
Mem 180
Sec S Houston
Holes 9 L 5017 m Par 70 SSS 68
V'tors U
Fees £10 (£12)
Loc 12 miles SW of Dungannon (B35)
Mis Driving range

Dungannon (1890)
34 Springfield Lane, Mullaghmore, Dungannon, BT70 1QX
Tel (028) 8772 7338/2098
Fax (028) 8772 7338
Mem 840
Sec N McGrath
Pro None
Holes 18 L 6046 yds SSS 69
V'tors U
Fees £18 (£22)
Loc ½ mile NW of Dungannon on Donaghmore road

Fintona (1904)
Ecclleville Desmesne, 1 Kiln Street, Fintona, BT78 2BJ
Tel (028) 8284 1480/840777
Fax (028) 8284 1480
Mem 400
Sec V McCarney
Pro P Leonard (01662) 841480
Holes 9 L 5765 m Par 72 SSS 70
V'tors U exc comp days SOC
Fees £15 (£15)
Loc 8 miles S of Omagh

Killymoon (1889)
200 Killymoon Road, Cookstown, BT80 8TW
Tel (028) 8676 3762/62254
Fax (028) 8676 3762

Mem 950
Sec B Rouse (028) 8676 3762
Pro (028) 8676 3460
Holes 18 L 5488 m SSS 69
V'tors U H SOC
Fees £14 (£18)
Loc 1 mile S of Cookstown, off A29

Newtownstewart (1914)
38 Golf Course Road, Newtownstewart, BT78 4HU
Tel (028) 8166 1466
Fax (028) 8166 2506
Web www.globalgolf.com/newtownstewart
Mem 700
Sec JE Mackin (028) 8167 1487
Pro None
Holes 18 L 5341 m Par 70 SSS 69
V'tors WD–U WE–NA after noon SOC
Fees £12 (£17)
Loc 2 miles SW of Newtownstewart on B84
Arch Frank Pennink

Omagh (1910)
83A Dublin Road, Omagh, BT78 1HQ
Tel (028) 8224 3160/1442
Fax (028) 8224 3160
Mem 817
Sec Mrs F Caldwell
Pro None
Holes 18 L 5364 m SSS 68
V'tors U SOC
Fees £12 (£18)
Loc 1 mile from Omagh on Belfast-Dublin road

Strabane (1908)
Ballycolman, Strabane, BT82 9PH
Tel (028) 7138 2271/2007
Fax (028) 7188 6514
Mem 800
Sec G Glover (028) 7138 2007
Pro None
Holes 18 L 5552 m SSS 69
V'tors WD–U WE–by arrangement SOC
Fees £12 (£15)
Loc ½ mile from Strabane, nr Fir Trees Hotel

Co Waterford

Dungarvan (1924)
Knocknagranagh, Dungarvan
Tel (058) 43310/41605
Fax (058) 44113
Mem 680
Sec Irene Howell (Mgr) (058) 43310
Pro (058) 44707
Holes 18 L 6134 m Par 72 SSS 73
V'tors U SOC

Fees £20 (£25)
Loc 2 miles E of Dungarvan on N25. 25 miles W of Waterford
Arch Maurice Fives

Dunmore East (1993)
Dunmore East
Tel (051) 383151
Fax (051) 383151
Web www.dunmore-golf.com
Mem 300
Sec M Skehan
Holes 18 L 6655 yds Par 72 SSS 70
V'tors U
Fees £12 (£18)
Loc 10 miles S of Waterford (R684)
Arch J O'Riordan

Faithlegg (1993)
Faithlegg House, Faithlegg
Tel (051) 382241
Fax (051) 382664
Mem 260
Sec J Santry (Hon)
Pro T Higgins
Holes 18 L 6690 yds SSS 72
V'tors U SOC
Fees €36 (€50)
Loc 6 miles E of Waterford City on Dunmore East road
Arch Patrick Merrigan

Gold Coast (1993)
Ballinacourty, Dungarvan
Tel (058) 42249/44055
Fax (058) 43378
Web www.clonea.com
Mem 400
Sec T Considine (058) 44055
Pro None
Holes 18 L 6171 m Par 72 SSS 72
V'tors U SOC
Fees £25 (£30)
Loc E of Dungarvan, off R675
Arch M Fives

Lismore (1965)
Ballyin, Lismore
Tel (058) 54026
Fax (058) 53338
Mem 450
Sec S Hales
Holes 9 L 5291 m Par 69 SSS 67
V'tors WD–U before 5pm –M after 5pm WE–phone first SOC–exc Sun
Fees £12 (£15)
Loc 1 mile N of Lismore, off N72

Tramore (1894)
Newtown Hill, Tramore
Tel (051) 386170/381247
Fax (051) 390961
Web www.tramoregolfclub.com
Mem 1396
Sec J Cox (Sec/Mgr)
Pro D Kiely
Holes 18 L 6055 m SSS 73

V'tors U
Fees £27 (£33)
Loc 7 miles S of Waterford
Arch Capt Tippett

Waterford (1912)

Newrath, Waterford
Tel (051) 874182
Fax (051) 853405
Mem 961
Sec J Condon
        (Sec/Mgr) (051) 876748
Pro J Condon
Holes 18 L 5722 m Par 71 SSS 70
V'tors U
Fees £22 (£25)
Loc 1 mile N of Waterford (N25)
Arch Willie Park/James Braid

Waterford Castle (1991)

The Island, Waterford
Tel (051) 871633
Fax (051) 871634
Mem 450
Sec D Brennan (051) 841569
Pro None
Holes 18 L 6231 m Par 72 SSS 71
V'tors U H SOC
Fees £27 (£30)
Loc 2 miles E of Waterford, off
        R683. Island in River Suir
Mis Driving range
Arch Des Smyth

West Waterford G&CC

(1993)
Dungarvan
Tel (058) 43216/41475
Fax (058) 44343
Web www.westwaterfordgolf.com
Mem 300
Sec T Whelan
Holes 18 L 6802 yds Par 72
V'tors U SOC
Fees £20 (£25)
Loc 4km W of Dungarvan, off
        N25
Mis Practice range
Arch Eddie Hackett

Co Westmeath

Delvin Castle (1992)

Clonyn, Delvin
Tel (044) 64315
Mem 330
Sec F Dillon
Pro D Keenaghan
Holes 18 L 5818 m Par 70 SSS 68
V'tors U
Fees £10 (£12)
Loc 15 miles NE of Mullingar
        (N52)

Glasson G&CC (1993)

Glasson, Athlone
Tel (0902) 85120
Fax (0902) 85444
Web www.glassongolf.ie
Mem 150
Sec F Reid
Pro None
Holes 18 L 7120 yds Par 72 SSS 72
V'tors U
Fees £35–£40
Loc 6 miles NE of Athlone (N55)
Mis Golf Academy
Arch C O'Connor Jr

Moate (1900)

Aghanargit, Moate
Tel (0902) 81271
Fax (0902) 81267
Mem 600
Sec PJ Higgins
Holes 18 L 6294 yds SSS 70
V'tors U SOC–WD
Fees £12 (£15)
Loc Moate town centre
Arch Bobby Browne

Mount Temple (1991)

Mount Temple, Moate
Tel (0902) 81841/81545
Fax (0902) 81957
Mem 150
Sec M & M Dolan (Props)
Pro None
Holes 18 L 6500 yds SSS 71
V'tors U H SOC
Fees £14 (£16)
Loc 3 miles N of N6, between
        Athlone and Moate
Arch Michael Dolan

Mullingar (1894)

Belvedere, Mullingar
Tel (044) 48366/48629
Fax (044) 41499
Mem 560
Sec B Kiely (Sec/Mgr)
Pro J Burns
Holes 18 L 6370 yds SSS 71
V'tors U SOC
Fees £20 (£25)
Loc 3 miles S of Mullingar (M52)
Arch James Braid

Co Wexford

Courtown (1936)

Kiltennel, Gorey
Tel (055) 25166
Fax (055) 25553
Web www.courtowngolfclub.com
Mem 1200
Sec D Cleere (Mgr)
Pro J Coone (055) 25860
Holes 18 L 6398 yds SSS 71
V'tors U SOC
Fees £25 (£30)
Loc 2 miles SE of Gorey
Arch Harris

Enniscorthy (1908)

Knockmarshall, Enniscorthy
Tel (054) 33191
Fax (054) 36736
Mem 830
Sec B Kenny
Pro M Sludds (054) 37600
Holes 18 L 6115 m Par 72 SSS 72
V'tors U exc Tues & Sun–phone first
        SOC
Fees £16 (£18)
Loc 1½ miles SW of
        Enniscorthy on New Ross
        road
Arch Eddie Hackett

New Ross (1905)

Tinneranny, New Ross
Tel (051) 421433
Fax (051) 420098
Mem 700
Sec Kathleen Daly (Sec/Mgr)
Holes 18 L 5751 m SSS 70
V'tors U exc Sun SOC
Fees £15 (£20)
Loc 1 mile W of New Ross

Rosslare (1905)

Rosslare Strand, Rosslare
Tel (053) 32113 (Clubhouse),
        (053) 32203 (Bookings)
Fax (053) 32263
Web www.iol.ie~rgolfclb
Mem 1000
Sec JF Hall (Mgr)
Pro J Young (053) 32032
Holes 18 L 6719 yds Par 72 SSS 72
        12 L 3887 yds Par 46
V'tors U SOC
Fees 18 hole:€30 (€50)
        12 hole:€17
Loc 10 miles S of Wexford.
        Rosslare Ferry 6 miles
Arch Hawtree/Taylor/
        O'Connor Jr

St Helen's Bay (1993)

St Helen's, Kilrane, Rosslare Harbour
Tel (053) 33234
Fax (053) 33803
Web www.sthelensbay.com
Mem 430
Sec L Byrne
Pro None
Holes 18 L 6091 m SSS 72
V'tors U SOC
Fees £25 (£28)
Loc Nr Rosslare Ferry terminal
Arch Philip Walton

Tara Glen (1993)

Ballymoney, Gorey
Tel (055) 25413
Fax (055) 25612
Sec D Popplewell
Holes 9 L 5826 m Par 72 SSS 70
V'tors U
Fees £14
Loc 4 miles E of Gorey. 12 miles S
        of Arklow

Wexford (1960)

Mulgannon, Wexford

Tel	(053) 42238
Mem	705
Sec	P Daly (Hon)
Pro	D McGrane (053) 46300
Holes	18 L 6338 yds Par 72 SSS 71
V'tors	U SOC
Fees	£18 (£20)
Loc	Wexford ½ mile

Co Wicklow

Arklow (1927)

Abbeylands, Arklow

Tel	(0402) 32492
Fax	(0402) 32971
Mem	500
Sec	B Timmons (Hon)
Pro	None
Holes	18 L 5770 yds SSS 67
V'tors	WD–U Sat–U after 5pm Sun–NA SOC
Fees	£18
Loc	1 mile from Arklow
Arch	Eddie Hackett

Baltinglass (1928)

Baltinglass

Tel	(0508) 81350
Fax	(0508) 81350
Mem	399
Sec	F Doyle (Hon)
Pro	M Murphy
Holes	9 L 6070 yds SSS 69
V'tors	U SOC
Fees	£10 (£12)
Loc	38 miles S of Dublin (N81)

Blainroe (1978)

Blainroe

Tel	(0404) 68168
Fax	(0404) 69369
Mem	960
Sec	W O'Sullivan (Sec/Mgr)
Pro	J McDonald
Holes	18 L 6175 m SSS 72
V'tors	U
Fees	£32 (£43)
Loc	3 miles S of Wicklow on coast
Arch	CW Hawtree

Bray (1897)

Ravenswell Road, Bray

Tel	(01) 286 2484
Fax	(01) 286 2484
Mem	530
Sec	G Montgomery (Sec/Mgr)
Pro	M Walby
Holes	9 L 5642 m Par 70 SSS 69
V'tors	U before 6pm SOC–WD
Fees	£20
Loc	12 miles S of Dublin

Charlesland G&CC (1993)

Greystones

Tel	(01) 287 8200
Fax	(01) 287 4360
Mem	800
Sec	P Bradshaw (Golf Dir)
Pro	P Duignan
Holes	18 L 6739 yds Par 72 SSS 71
V'tors	U SOC
Fees	IR£25 (IR£45)
Loc	18 miles SE of Dublin
Arch	Eddie Hackett

Coollattin (1960)

Coollattin, Shillelagh

Tel	(055) 29125
Fax	(055) 29125
Mem	950
Sec	D Byrne (Hon)
Pro	P Jones
Holes	18 L 6148 yds Par 70 SSS 69
V'tors	U
Fees	€35 (€45)
Loc	50 miles S of Dublin on Wicklow/Carlow border
Arch	Peter McEvoy

Delgany (1908)

Delgany

Tel	(01) 287 4536
Fax	(01) 287 3977
Mem	985
Sec	RJ Kelly (Sec/Mgr)
Pro	G Kavanagh (01) 287 4697
Holes	18 L 6025 yds SSS 69
V'tors	U exc comp days SOC–Mon/Thurs/Fri am
Fees	£30 (£35)
Loc	18 miles S of Dublin, nr Greystones, off N11
Arch	H Vardon

Djouce Mountain (1997)

Roundwood

Tel	(01) 281 8585
Fax	(01) 281 8585
Mem	160
Sec	D McGillycuddy (Mgr)
Pro	None
Holes	9 L 5636 m Par 71 SSS 69
V'tors	U SOC
Fees	£10 (£12)
Loc	15 miles NW of Wicklow (R764), off N11
Arch	Eddie Hackett

Druid's Glen (1995)

Newtownmountkennedy

Tel	(01) 287 3600
Fax	(01) 287 3699
Mem	200
Sec	D Flinn (Gen Mgr)
Pro	E Darcy
Holes	18 L 7026 yds Par 71 SSS 74
V'tors	U SOC
Fees	£85
Loc	20 miles S of Dublin (N11)
Mis	Golf Academy
Arch	Craddock/Ruddy

The European Club (1989)

Brittas Bay, Wicklow

Tel	(0404) 47415
Fax	(0404) 47449
Mem	120
Sec	P Ruddy
Pro	None
Holes	18 L 7089 yds SSS 71
V'tors	H SOC
Fees	£60–£80
Loc	30 miles S of Dublin, off N11
Arch	Pat Ruddy

Glenmalure (1993)

Greenane, Rathdrum

Tel	(0404) 46679
Fax	(0404) 46783
Mem	300
Holes	18 L 5237 m Par 71 SSS 66
V'tors	U SOC
Fees	IR£15 (IR£18)
Loc	2 miles SW of Rathdrum on Glenmalure road

Greystones (1895)

Greystones

Tel	(01) 287 6624/4136
Fax	(01) 287 3749
Web	www.greystonesgc.com
Mem	850
Sec	(01) 287 4136
Pro	K Holmes (01) 287 5308
Holes	18 L 5322 m SSS 69
V'tors	WD–U
Fees	£25 (£30)
Loc	Greystones, 18 miles S of Dublin

Kilcoole (1992)

Kilcoole

Tel	(01) 287 2066
Fax	(01) 287 1803
Mem	250
Sec	G Richardson
Holes	9 L 5506 m Par 70 SSS 69
V'tors	WD–U WE–NA before noon SOC–WD
Fees	£15 (£18)
Loc	S of Kilcoole on Newcastle road, off N11
Arch	Brian Williams

Old Conna (1987)

Ferndale Road, Bray

Tel	(01) 282 6055
Fax	(01) 282 5611
Web	www.oldconna.com
Mem	900
Sec	D Diviney (Sec/Mgr)
Pro	P McDaid (01) 272 0022
Holes	18 L 6551 yds SSS 72
V'tors	WD–U before 4pm WE/BH–NA SOC
Fees	£35 (£45)
Loc	2 miles N of Bray. 12 miles S of Dublin
Arch	Eddie Hackett

Powerscourt (1996)

Powerscourt Estate, Enniskerry

Tel	(01) 204 6033
Fax	(01) 276 1303
Mem	627
Sec	B Gibbons (Mgr)
Pro	P Thompson
Holes	18 L 5858 m Par 72 SSS 72
V'tors	U
Fees	£70 (£75)
Loc	Enniskerry, 5 miles W of Bray
Mis	Driving range
Arch	Peter McEvoy

Rathsallagh (1993)

Dunlavin

Tel	(045) 403316
Fax	(045) 403295
Web	www.rathsallagh.com
Mem	250
Sec	J O'Flynn
Pro	B McDaid (045) 403316
Holes	18 L 5943 m Par 72 SSS 72
V'tors	U
Fees	£45 (£55)
Loc	14 miles S of Naas (R412)
Mis	Driving range
Arch	Peter McEvoy

Roundwood (1995)

Newtownmountkennedy

Tel	(01) 281 8488

Fax	(01) 284 3642
Sec	M McGuirk (Hon)
Holes	18 L 6685 yds Par 72 SSS 72
Loc	15 miles NW of Wicklow (R764)

Tulfarris (1987)

Blessington Lakes

Tel	(045) 867644
Fax	(045) 867000
Mem	200
Sec	A Williams (Mgr)
Pro	AV Williams
Holes	18 L 7172 m SSS 74
V'tors	U SOC
Fees	£60 (£70)
Loc	30 miles S of Dublin, off N81
Mis	Driving range
Arch	Patrick Merrigan

Vartry Lakes

Proprietary

Roundwood

Tel	(01) 281 7006
Fax	(01) 281 7006
Web	www.wicklow.ie
Mem	242
Sec	J & A McDonald
Pro	None
Holes	9 L 5276 m Par 70 SSS 70
V'tors	U SOC–WD/Sat
Fees	£10 (£15)
Loc	Roundwood village. SW of Bray, off N11

Wicklow (1904)

Dunbur Road, Wicklow

Tel	(0404) 67379
Mem	450
Sec	J Kelly (Hon)
Pro	D Daly (0404) 66122
Holes	18 L 5695 m SSS 70
V'tors	SOC–WD/Sat
Fees	£20 (£20)
Loc	32 miles S of Dublin, in Wicklow town
Arch	Craddock/Ruddy

Woodenbridge (1884)

Woodenbridge, Arklow

Tel	(0402) 35202
Fax	(0402) 35754
Web	www.globalgolf.com
Mem	650
Sec	H Crummy
Holes	18 L 6400 yds Par 71 SSS 71
V'tors	U exc Sat & Thurs
Fees	£40 (£50)
Loc	4 miles W of Arklow. 45 miles S of Dublin
Arch	Patrick Merrigan

Scotland

Aberdeenshire

Aboyne (1883)

Formaston Park, Aboyne, AB34 5HP

Tel	(013398) 86328
Fax	(013398) 87078
Mem	725 180(J)
Sec	Mrs M MacLean (013398) 87078
Pro	I Wright (013398) 86328
Holes	18 L 5910 yds SSS 68
V'tors	U
Fees	On application
Loc	E end of Aboyne. 30 miles W of Aberdeen (A93)

Alford

Montgarrie Road, Alford, AB33 8AE

Tel	(019755) 62178
Fax	(019755) 62178
Web	www.golfalford.co.uk
Mem	560
Sec	J Pennet
Pro	None
Holes	18 L 5483 yds Par 69 SSS 66
V'tors	WD–U WE–restricted on comp days SOC

Fees	£13 (£20)
Loc	25 miles W of Aberdeen on A944

Auchenblae (1894)

Public

Auchenblae, Laurencekirk, AB30 1BU

Tel	(01561) 320331 (Bookings)
Mem	85
Sec	J McNicoll (01561) 320678
Holes	9 L 2208 yds SSS 63
V'tors	U exc Wed & Fri 5.30–9pm
Fees	£6 Sat–£7 Sun–£8
Loc	11 miles SW of Stonehaven. 3 miles W of Fordoun

Ballater (1892)

Victoria Road, Ballater, AB35 5QX

Tel	(013397) 55567
Fax	(013397) 55057
Web	www.ballatergolfclub.co.uk
Mem	670
Sec	AE Barclay
Pro	W Yule (013397) 55658
Holes	18 L 6094 yds SSS 69
V'tors	U
Fees	On application

Loc	42 miles W of Aberdeen on A93

Banchory (1904)

Kinneskie, Banchory, AB31 5TA

Tel	(01330) 822365
Fax	(01330) 822491
Mem	800
Sec	Mrs A Smith (Admin)
Pro	D Naylor (01330) 822447
Holes	18 L 5781 yds SSS 68
V'tors	WD–U
Fees	£20 (£23)
Loc	W of Banchory, off A93

Braemar (1902)

Cluniebank Road, Braemar, AB35 5XX

Tel	(013397) 41618
Mem	300
Sec	J Pennet (01224) 704471
Holes	18 L 4916 yds SSS 64
V'tors	U SOC
Fees	£13 D–£17 (£17 D–£23) W–£60
Loc	Braemar ½ mile. 17 miles W of Ballater
Arch	J Anderson

Cruden Bay (1899)

Cruden Bay, Peterhead, AB42 0NN

Tel	(01779) 812285
Fax	(01779) 812945
Mem	1070
Sec	Mrs R Pittendrigh (Sec/Mgr)
Pro	RG Stewart (01779) 812414
Holes	18 L 6395 yds SSS 72
	9 L 5106 yds SSS 65
V'tors	WD–U WE–H exc comp days
Fees	£50 D–£70 (£60)
Loc	22 miles NE of Aberdeen (A90)
Mis	Driving range
Arch	Thomas Simpson

Cullen (1879)

The Links, Cullen, Buckie, AB56 4WB

Tel	(01542) 840685
Fax	(01548) 841977
Mem	625
Sec	LIG Findlay (01542) 840174
Pro	None
Holes	18 L 4610 yds Par 63 SSS 62
V'tors	U SOC
Fees	£12 D–£18 (£16 D–£22)
Loc	5 miles E of Buckie, off A98 between Aberdeen and Inverness
Arch	Tom Morris

Duff House Royal (1910)

The Barnyards, Banff, AB45 3SX

Tel	(01261) 812062
Fax	(01261) 812224
Mem	547 167(L) 132(J)
Sec	Mrs J Corbett
Pro	RS Strachan (01261) 812075
Holes	18 L 6161 yds SSS 69
V'tors	WD–U H WE–H 8.30–11am and 12.30–3pm
Fees	£24 (£30)
Loc	Moray Firth coast, between Buckie and Fraserburgh
Arch	Dr A & Maj CA Mackenzie

Dunecht House (1925)

Dunecht, Skene, AB3 7AX

Mem	400
Sec	K Munn (01330) 860223
Holes	9 L 3135 yds SSS 70
V'tors	M
Fees	£8
Loc	12 miles W of Aberdeen on A944

Fraserburgh (1881)

Philorth, Fraserburgh, AB43 8TL

Tel	(01346) 516616
Fax	(01346) 516616
Mem	642 56(L) 119(J)
Sec	J Mollison
Holes	18 L 6278 yds SSS 70
	9 L 2400 yds Par 64
V'tors	U SOC
Fees	£15 D–£20 (£20 D–£25)
Loc	1 mile SE of Fraserburgh
Arch	James Braid

Huntly (1892)

Cooper Park, Huntly, AB54 4SH

Tel	(01466) 792643
Fax	(01466) 792643
Web	www.huntlygc.com
Mem	800
Sec	EA Stott (01466) 792360
Pro	(01466) 794181 (Shop)
Holes	18 L 5399 yds SSS 66
V'tors	U SOC
Fees	£12 D–£18 (£18 D–£24) W–£65
Loc	N side of Huntly. 38 miles NW of Aberdeen, off A96

Inchmarlo

Glassel Road, Banchory AB31 4BQ

Tel	(01330) 822557
Web	www.inchmarlo.com
Sec	HG Emsie (Gen Mgr) (01330) 822557 Ext 11
Pro	P Lowe (01330) 822557 Ext 20
Holes	18 L 6218 yds Par 71 SSS 70
	9 L 4300 yds Par 64 SSS 62
V'tors	U H SOC-WD
Fees	18 hole: £30 (£35) 9 hole: £10 (£11)
Loc	½ mile W of Banchory on A93
Arch	Graeme Webster

Insch

Golf Terrace, Insch, AB52 6JY

Tel	(01464) 820363
Fax	(01464) 820363
Sec	D Cumming
Holes	18 L 5350 yds SSS 67
V'tors	U
Fees	On application
Loc	28 miles NW of Aberdeen, off A96

Inverallochy

Public

Whitelink, Inverallochy, Fraserburgh, AB43 8XY

Tel	(01346) 582000
Mem	200
Sec	GM Young
Pro	None
Holes	18 L 5300 yds SSS 66
V'tors	U
Fees	D–£12 (£15)
Loc	4 miles E of Fraserburgh, off A92

Inverurie (1923)

Blackhall Road, Inverurie, AB51 5JB

Tel	(01467) 620207
Fax	(01467) 621051
Mem	511 130(L)
Sec	B Rogerson (01467) 624080
Pro	M Lees (01467) 620193
Holes	18 L 5711 yds SSS 68
V'tors	U SOC
Fees	£14 D–£18 (£18 D–£24)
Loc	1 mile W of Inverurie. 16 miles NW of Aberdeen

Keith (1963)

Fife Park, Keith, AB55 5DF

Tel	(01542) 882469
Fax	(01542) 888176
Mem	250
Holes	18 L 5802 yds SSS 68
V'tors	U
Fees	£13 (£15)
Loc	Fife Park, W side of Keith

Kemnay (1908)

Monymusk Road, Kemnay, AB51 5RA

Tel	(01467) 642060 (Clubhouse), (01467) 643746 (Office)
Fax	(01467) 643746
Web	www.kemnaygolfclub.co.uk
Mem	820
Sec	B Robertson
Pro	R McDonald (01647) 642225
Holes	18 L 6342 yds Par 71 SSS 71
V'tors	U
Fees	£18 D–£24 (£22 D–£28)
Loc	15 miles W of Aberdeen (B993, off A96)

Kintore (1911)

Balbithan Road, Kintore, AB51 0UR

Tel	(01467) 632631
Fax	(01467) 632995
Mem	700
Sec	J Black
Holes	18 L 6019 yds SSS 69
V'tors	U
Fees	£13 (£19)
Loc	12 miles NW of Aberdeen on A96

Longside

West End, Longside, Peterhead, AB42 4XJ

Tel	(01779) 821558
Fax	(01779) 821564
Mem	729
Sec	K Allan (01771) 622424
Pro	None
Holes	18 L 5225 yds Par 66 SSS 66
V'tors	U exc Sun–NA before 10.30am SOC
Fees	£12 D–£16 Sat–£16 D–£20 Sun–£18 D–£22
Loc	5 miles W of Peterhead on A590

McDonald (1927)

Hospital Road, Ellon, AB41 9AW

Tel	(01358) 720576
Fax	(01358) 720001
Web	www.freespace.virgin.net/ mcdonald.golf
Mem	750
Sec	IA Shaw
Pro	R Urquhart (01358) 722891
Holes	18 L 5991 yds SSS 70
V'tors	U
Fees	On application
Loc	15 miles N of Aberdeen, off A90

Meldrum House (1998)

Meldrum House Estate, Oldmeldrum,
AB51 0AE

Tel	(01651) 873553
Fax	(01651) 873635
Web	www.meldrumhouse.co.uk
Mem	400
Sec	J Caven (Golf Dir)
Pro	N Marr
Holes	18 L 6379 yds Par 70 SSS 72
V'tors	M
Fees	N/A
Loc	11 miles N of Aberdeen on A947
Arch	Graeme Webster

Newburgh-on-Ythan

(1888)

Newburgh, AB41 6BE

Tel	(01358) 789058
Web	www.newburgh-on-ythan .co.uk
Mem	540 60(L) 80(J)
Sec	V Geoghegan (01358) 789084
Pro	None
Holes	18 L 6162 yds SSS 71
V'tors	U exc Tues after 3pm & Sat before 1pm–NA
Fees	On application
Loc	12 miles N of Aberdeen (A975)
Mis	Driving range

Newmachar (1989)

Swailend, Newmachar, Aberdeen,
AB21 7UU

Tel	(01651) 863002
Fax	(01651) 863055
Web	www.newmachargolfclub. co.uk
Mem	921
Sec	G McIntosh
Pro	G Simpson (01651) 862127
Holes	18 L 6623 yds Par 72 SSS 74 18 L 6388 yds Par 72 SSS 71
V'tors	H SOC
Fees	Hawkshill £30 (£40) Swailend £15 (£20)
Loc	12 miles N of Aberdeen on A947
Mis	Driving range
Arch	Dave Thomas

Oldmeldrum (1885)

Kirk Brae, Oldmeldrum, AB51 0DJ

Tel	(01651) 872648/873555
Fax	(01651) 873555
Mem	800
Sec	J Page (01651) 872315
Pro	H Love (01651) 873555
Holes	18 L 5988 yds Par 70 SSS 69
V'tors	WD–U before 5pm WE–phone first
Fees	£14 (£20)
Loc	17 miles N of Aberdeen on A947

Peterhead (1841)

Craigewan Links, Peterhead,
AB42 1LT

Tel	(01779) 472149/480725
Fax	(01779) 480725

Mem	500 45(L)
Holes	18 L 6173 yds SSS 71 9 L 2237 yds SSS 62
V'tors	U exc Sat–restricted
Fees	On application
Loc	1 mile N of Peterhead
Arch	Willie Park Jr/James Braid

Rosehearty

c/o Mason's Arms Hotel, Rosehearty,
Fraserburgh, AB43 7JJ

Tel	(01346) 571250 (Capt)
Fax	(01346) 571306
Mem	220
Sec	A Watt
Holes	9 L 2197 yds SSS 62
V'tors	U
Fees	D–£10 (D–£12)
Loc	4 miles W of Fraserburgh (B9031)

Rothes (1990)

Blackhall, Rothes, Aberlour, AB38 7AN

Tel	(01340) 831443
Fax	(01340) 831443
Mem	340
Pro	None
Holes	9 L 4972 yds Par 68 SSS 64
V'tors	U
Fees	£12 (£15)
Loc	¹/₂ mile SW of Rothes. 10 miles S of Elgin on A941
Arch	John Souter

Royal Tarlair (1926)

Buchan Street, Macduff, AB44 1TA

Tel	(01261) 832897
Fax	(01261) 833455
Web	www.royaltarlair.co.uk
Mem	520
Sec	Mrs C Davidson
Holes	18 L 5866 yds SSS 68
V'tors	U
Fees	£10 D–£15 (£15 D–£20)
Loc	Macduff, 4 miles E of Banff. 45 miles E of Aberdeen

Stonehaven (1888)

Cowie, Stonehaven, AB39 3RH

Tel	(01569) 762124
Fax	(01569) 765973
Mem	500
Sec	WA Donald
Pro	None
Holes	18 L 5128 yds Par 66 SSS 65
V'tors	Sat–NA before 3.45pm Sun–NA before 10.45am
Fees	£15 (£20)
Loc	1 mile N of Stonehaven
Arch	A Simpson

Strathlene (1877)

Portessie, Buckie, AB56 2DJ

Tel	(01542) 831798
Fax	(01542) 831798
Web	www.scottishholidays.net/ strathlene
Mem	400
Sec	G Jappy
Holes	18 L 5977 yds SSS 69
V'tors	U SOC
Fees	D–£15 (D–£15)

Loc	¹/₂ mile E of Buckie
Arch	G Smith

Tarland (1908)

Aberdeen Road, Tarland, AB34 4TB

Tel	(013398) 81000
Fax	(013398) 81000
Mem	400
Sec	Mrs L Ward (013398) 81967
Holes	9 L 5875 yds SSS 68
V'tors	WD–U WE–enquiry advisable SOC–WD only
Fees	£15 (£20)
Loc	5 miles NW of Aboyne. 30 miles W of Aberdeen
Arch	Tom Morris

Torphins (1896)

Bog Road, Torphins, AB31 4JU

Tel	(013398) 82115
Fax	(013398) 82402
Mem	370
Sec	S MacGregor (013398) 82402
Holes	9 L 4738 yds SSS 64
V'tors	U SOC
Fees	£12 (£14)
Loc	1¹/₂ miles W of Torphins towards Lumphanan

Turriff (1896)

Rosehall, Turriff, AB53 4HD

Tel	(01888) 562982
Fax	(01888) 568050
Mem	814
Sec	R Grieg
Pro	R Smith (01888) 563025
Holes	18 L 6145 yds SSS 69
V'tors	H WE–NA before 10am SOC
Fees	£16 D–£20 (£21 D–£27)
Loc	35 miles N of Aberdeen (A947)
Arch	GM Fraser

Aberdeen Clubs

Bon Accord (1872)

Club
19 Golf Road, Aberdeen, AB2 1QB

Tel	(01224) 633464
Mem	450
Sec	FN Shand
Holes	Play over King's Links

Caledonian (1899)

Club
20 Golf Road, Aberdeen, AB2 1QB

Tel	(01224) 632443
Mem	620
Sec	JA Bridgeford
Holes	Play over King's Links

Northern (1897)

Club
King's Links, Aberdeen, AB24 5BQ

Tel	(01224) 636440
Fax	(01224) 622679

Mem   561
Sec   AW Garner
Holes Play over King's Links

Aberdeen Courses

Auchmill (1975)
Bonnyview Road, West Heatheryfold, Aberdeen, AB2 7FQ
Tel   (01224) 715214
Mem   300
Sec   W Cameron (01464) 821217
Pro   None
Holes 18 L 5883 yds Par 70 SSS 68
V'tors U
Fees   On application
Loc   3 miles NW of Aberdeen city centre
Arch   Coles/Huggett

Balnagask (1955)
Public
St Fitticks Road, Aberdeen
Tel   (01224) 871286
Fax   (01224) 873418
Sec   G Reilly
Pro   None
Holes 18 L 5472 metres SSS 69
V'tors U SOC
Fees   £9 (£11.25)
Loc   1½ miles SE of Aberdeen

Deeside (1903)
Golf Road, Bieldside, Aberdeen, AB15 9DL
Tel   (01224) 869457
Fax   (01224) 869457
Mem   1100
Sec   JW Keefe (Sec/Mgr)
       (01224) 869457
Pro   FJ Coutts (01224) 861041
Holes 18 L 6264 yds SSS 70
       9 L 3316 yds SSS 36
V'tors H
Fees   £40 (£55)
Loc   3 miles SW of Aberdeen on A93

Hazlehead (1927)
Public
Hazlehead Park, Aberdeen, AB15 8BD
Tel   (01224) 321830
Pro   I Smith
Holes 18 L 5673 metres SSS 70
       18 L 5303 metres SSS 68
       9 L 2531 metres SSS 34
V'tors U
Fees   £9 (£11.25)
Loc   4 miles W of Aberdeen

King's Links
Public
Golf Road, King's Links, Aberdeen, AB24 5QB
Tel   (01224) 632269
Pro   B Davidson (01224) 641577
Holes 18 L 5838 metres SSS 71

V'tors U
Fees   £9.50 (£11.50)
Loc   1 mile E of Aberdeen
Mis   Driving range. Bon Accord, Caledonian and Northern Clubs play here

Murcar (1909)
Bridge of Don, Aberdeen, AB23 8BD
Tel   (01224) 704354
Fax   (01224) 704354
Mem   850
Sec   D Corstorphine
       (01224) 704354
Pro   G Forbes (01224) 704370
Holes 18 L 6287 yds SSS 71
       9 L 5369 yds SSS 67
V'tors H Tues–NA before noon
       Wed–NA after 12 noon
       Sat–NA before 4pm Sun–NA
       before 11am
Fees   £45 (£55)
Loc   5 miles N of Aberdeen, off A90
Arch   A Simpson

Peterculter (1989)
Public
Oldtown, Burnside Road, Peterculter, AB14 0LN
Tel   (01224) 735245
Fax   (01224) 735580
Web   www.petercultergolfclub.co.uk
Mem   925
Sec   D Vannet (Mgr)
Pro   D Vannet (01224) 734994
Holes 18 L 5924 yds SSS 69
V'tors WD–U before 4pm WE–U SOC
Fees   £12–£18 (£16–£21)
Loc   8 miles W of Aberdeen on A93

Portlethen (1983)
Badentoy Road, Portlethen, Aberdeen, AB12 4YA
Tel   (01224) 781090
Fax   (01224) 781090
Mem   1100
Pro   Muriel Thomson
       (01224) 782571
Holes 18 L 6670 yds SSS 72
V'tors WD–U exc Wed after 2pm
       Sat–NA before 4pm Sun–NA
       before 1pm
Fees   £15 D–£22 (£22)
Loc   6 miles S of Aberdeen on A90
Arch   Donald Steel

Royal Aberdeen (1780)
Balgownie, Bridge of Don, Aberdeen, AB23 8AT
Tel   (01224) 702571
Fax   (01224) 826591
Mem   350 100(J)
Sec   GF Webster
Pro   R MacAskill (Golf Dir)
       (01224) 702221
Holes 18 L 6415 yds SSS 73
       18 L 4066 yds SSS 60
V'tors I H SOC
Fees   £65 D–£90 (£75)

Loc   2 miles N of Aberdeen on A90
Arch   Simpson/Braid

Westhill (1977)
Westhill Heights, Westhill, AB32 6RY
Tel   (01224) 742567
Fax   (01224) 749124
Mem   900
Sec   Amelia Burt (Admin)
Pro   G Bruce (01224) 740159
Holes 18 L 5849 yds SSS 69
V'tors WD–U before 4.30pm Sat–M
       Sun–U
Fees   £14 D–£20 (£20 D–£25)
Loc   8 miles W of Aberdeen, off A944
Arch   Charles Lawrie

Angus

Arbroath Artisan (1903)
Public
Elliot, Arbroath, DD11 2PE
Tel   (01241) 872069,
       (01241) 875837 (Bookings)
Fax   (01241) 875837
Mem   650
Sec   J Knox
Pro   L Ewart (01241) 875837
Holes 18 L 6185 yds Par 70 SSS 69
V'tors WD–U SOC WE–NA before 10am
Fees   £18 D–£24 (£24 D–£32)
Loc   1 mile SW of Arbroath on A92
Arch   James Braid

Brechin (1893)
Trinity, Brechin, DD9 7PD
Tel   (01356) 622383
Fax   (01356) 626925
Mem   650
Sec   IA Jardine
Pro   S Rennie (01356) 625270
Holes 18 L 6200 yds SSS 70
V'tors U exc Wed SOC
Fees   £17 D–£25 (£22 D–£30)
Loc   1 mile N of Brechin on B90

Caird Park (1926)
Public
Mains Loan, Caird Park, Dundee, DD4 9BX
Tel   (01382) 453606,
       (01382) 438871 (Starter)
Mem   350
Sec   G Martin (01382) 864029
Pro   J Black (01382) 459438
Holes 18 L 6303 yds SSS 70
       Yellow 9 L 1692 yds SSS 29
       Red 9 L 1983 yds SSS 29
V'tors U SOC
Fees   Contact Starter
Loc   Off Kingsway by-pass, N of Dundee

Camperdown (1960)
Public
Camperdown Park, Dundee, DD4 9BX
Tel (01382) 623398
Mem 250
Sec Mrs J Lettice (01382) 660588
Pro R Brown (01382) 623398
Holes 18 L 6561 yds SSS 72
V'tors U
Fees £18 (£18)
Loc 2 miles NW of Dundee (A923)

Downfield (1932)
Turnberry Ave, Dundee, DD2 3QP
Tel (01382) 825595
Fax (01382) 813111
Web www.downfieldgolf.com
Mem 750
Sec Mrs M Stewart
Pro KS Hutton (01382) 889246
Holes 18 L 6822 yds SSS 73
V'tors WD–U 9.30–noon and 2.18–3.42pm WE–limited access after 2pm
Fees £16–£31 D–£26–£46 (£21–£36)
Loc N of Dundee, off A923

Edzell (1895)
High St, Edzell, DD9 7TF
Tel (01356) 647283
Fax (01356) 648094
Mem 700
Sec IG Farquhar (01356) 647283
Pro AJ Webster (01356) 648462
Holes 18 L 6348 yds SSS 71
9 L 2057 yds Par 32
V'tors WD–NA 4.45–6.15pm WE–NA 7.30–10am & 12–2pm SOC
Fees £23 D–£33 (£29 D–£43)
Loc 6 miles N of Brechin on B966
Mis Driving range
Arch Bob Simpson

Forfar (1871)
Cunninghill, Arbroath Road, Forfar, DD8 2RL
Tel (01307) 462120
Fax (01307) 468495
Mem 520 150(L) 100(J)
Sec W Baird (01307) 463773
Pro P McNiven (01307) 465683
Holes 18 L 6052 yds Par 69 SSS 70
V'tors U exc Sat SOC
Fees £20 (£25)
Loc 1½ miles E of Forfar on A932
Arch Tom Morris/James Braid

Kirriemuir (1884)
Northmuir, Kirriemuir, DD8 4PN
Tel (01575) 572144 (Clubhouse), (01575) 573317 (Starter)
Fax (01575) 574608
Mem 850
Sec C Gowrie
Pro Mrs K Dallas (01575) 573317
Holes 18 L 5510 yds SSS 67

V'tors WD–U WE–by arrangement SOC
Fees £20 D–£26 (£25 D–£32)
Loc NE outskirts of Kirriemuir. 17 miles N of Dundee
Arch James Braid

Letham Grange (1987)
Letham Grange, Colliston, Arbroath, DD11 4RL
Tel (01241) 890377
Fax (01241) 890725
Mem 780
Sec D Speed
Pro Shop (01241) 890377
Holes Old 18 L 6968 yds SSS 73
Glens 18 L 5528 yds SSS 68
V'tors WD–U WE–U after 10.30am SOC
Fees Old £35 D–£40 (£35 D–£55) Glens £18 D–£20 (£20 D–£30)
Loc 4 miles NW of Arbroath on A993
Arch Old-Steel/Smith. New-T MacAuley

Monifieth Golf Links
Medal Starter's Box, Princes Street, Monifieth, DD5 4AW
Tel (01382) 532767 (Medal), (01382) 532967 (Ashludie)
Fax (01382) 535553
Web www.monifiethgolf.co.uk
Mem 1850
Sec S Fyffe (01382) 535553
Pro I McLeod (01382) 532945
Holes Medal 18 L 6650 yds SSS 72
Ashludie 18 L 5123 SSS 66
V'tors WD–U Sat–NA before 2pm Sun–NA before 10am SOC
Fees Medal £33 (£36) Ashludie £15 (£16) Medal+Ashludie £50 inc catering
Loc 6 miles E of Dundee
Mis Abertay, Broughty, Grange/Dundee and Monifieth clubs play here

Montrose (1562)
Public
Traill Drive, Montrose, DD10 8SW
Tel (01674) 672932
Fax (01674) 671800
Web www.montroselinks.co.uk
Mem 1300
Sec Mrs M Stewart
Pro J Boyd (01674) 672634
Holes Medal 18 L 6495 yds SSS 72
Broomfield 18 L 4830 yds SSS 63
V'tors Medal–WD–U Sat–NA before 2.30pm Sun–NA before 10am Broomfield–U
Fees Medal £28 (£32) Broomfield £12 (£12)
Loc 1 mile from Montrose centre, off A92
Mis Royal Montrose, Caledonia and Mercantile clubs play here
Arch Willie Park (1903)

Montrose Caledonia (1896)
Club
Dorward Road, Montrose, DD10 8SW
Tel (01674) 672313
Sec M Watson (01674) 672891
Holes Play over Montrose courses

Montrose Mercantile
Club
East Links, Montrose, DD10 8SW
Tel (01674) 672408
Mem 980
Sec R Alexander (01674) 675716
Holes Play over Montrose courses

Panmure (1845)
Barry, Carnoustie, DD7 7RT
Tel (01241) 853120
Fax (01241) 859737
Mem 500
Sec Maj (Retd) GW Paton (01241) 855120
Pro N Mackintosh (01241) 852460
Holes 18 L 6317 yds Par 70 SSS 71
V'tors WD/Sun–U Sat–NA
Fees On application
Loc 2 miles W of Carnoustie, off A930

Royal Montrose (1810)
Club
Dorward Road, Montrose, DD10 8SW
Tel (01674) 672376
Mem 650
Sec JD Sykes (01674) 672785
Holes Play over Montrose courses

Carnoustie Clubs

Carnoustie (1842)
Club
3 Links Parade, Carnoustie, DD7 7JE
Tel (01241) 852480
Fax (01241) 856459
Mem 900
Sec WH Law
Holes Play over Carnoustie courses

Carnoustie Caledonia (1887)
Club
Links Parade, Carnoustie, DD7 7JF
Tel (01241) 852115
Mem 640
Sec JSB Robinson
Holes Play over Carnoustie courses

Carnoustie Ladies (1873)
Club
12 Links Parade, Carnoustie, DD7 7JF
Tel (01241) 855252
Mem 96

Sec Mrs JM Mitchell
(01241) 855035
Holes Play over Carnoustie courses

Carnoustie Mercantile
(1896)
Club
Links Parade, Carnoustie, DD7 7JE
Mem 30
Sec DG Ogilvie
Holes Play over Carnoustie courses

Dalhousie (1868)
Club
c/o Glencoe Hotel, Links Parade,
Carnoustie, DD7 7JF
Tel (01241) 853273
Mem 150
Sec WM Osler
Holes Play over Carnoustie courses

Carnoustie Courses

Buddon Links (1981)
Public
Links Parade, Carnoustie, DD7 7JE
Tel (01241) 853249 (Starter),
(01241) 853789 (Bookings)
Fax (01241) 853720
Sec JM Martin
Holes 18 L 5420 yds SSS 66
V'tors WD–U WE–U after 11am
Fees £20
Loc 12 miles E of Dundee, by A92
or A930

Burnside (1914)
Public
Links Parade, Carnoustie, DD7 7JE
Tel (01241) 855344 (Starter),
(01241) 853789 (Bookings)
Fax (01241) 853720
Sec JM Martin
Holes 18 L 6020 yds SSS 69
V'tors WD–U Sat–U after 2pm
Sun–U after 11.30am
Fees £25 (2001)
Loc 12 miles E of Dundee, by A92
or A930

Carnoustie
Championship (16th)
Public
Links Parade, Carnoustie, DD7 7JE
Tel (01241) 853249 (Starter),
(01241) 853789 (Bookings)
Fax (01241) 853720
Sec JM Martin
Holes 18 L 6941 yds SSS 75
V'tors WD–H Sat–H after 2pm
Sun–H after 11.30am
Fees £70
Loc 12 miles E of Dundee, by A92
or A930

Argyll & Bute

Blairmore & Strone
(1896)
High Road, Strone, Dunoon, PA23 8JJ
Tel (01369) 840676
Mem 120
Sec JC Fleming (01369) 860307
Holes 9 L 2122 yds SSS 62
V'tors Mon–NA after 6pm Sat–NA
12–4pm
Fees D–£8 (D–£10) W–£30
Loc Strone, 8 miles N of Dunoon
Arch James Braid

Bute (1888)
Sithean, Academy Road, Rothesay, Isle
of Bute PA20 0BG
Mem 234
Sec I McDougall (01700) 504369
Holes 9 L 2497 yds SSS 64
V'tors U Sat–U after 11.30am
Fees D–£8
Loc Stravanan Bay, 6 miles S of
Rothesay, off A845

Carradale (1906)
Carradale, Campbeltown, PA28 6SA
Tel (01583) 431321
Mem 324
Sec Dr RJ Abernethy
Pro None
Holes 9 L 2370 yds SSS 64
V'tors U
Fees D–£10
Loc Carradale, 15 miles N of
Campbeltown (B842)

Colonsay
Owned privately
Isle of Colonsay, PA61 7YP
Tel (019512) 316
Mem 100
Sec K Byrne
Holes 18 L 4775 yds Par 72
V'tors U
Fees On application
Loc W coast of Colonsay, at
Machrins

Cowal (1891)
Ardenslate Road, Dunoon, PA23 8LT
Tel (01369) 705673
Fax (01369) 705673
Mem 900
Sec Mrs W Fraser
(01369) 705673
Pro RD Weir (01369) 702395
Holes 18 L 6063 yds SSS 70
V'tors WD–U WE–restricted SOC
Fees £23 (£33)
Loc NE boundary of Dunoon
Arch James Braid (1928)

Craignure (1895)
Scallastle, Craignure, Isle of Mull,
PA64 5AP
Tel (01680) 300402

Mem 85
Sec DS Howitt
Holes 9 L 5351 yds SSS 66
V'tors U
Fees D–£11
Loc 1 mile N of Craignure Ferry
Terminal (Oban 40mins)

Dalmally (1986)
Old Saw Mill, Dalmally, PA33 1AS
Tel (01838) 200370
Web www.loch-awe.com/golfclub
Mem 120
Sec AJ Burke (01838) 200370
Pro None
Holes 9 L 2277 yds Par 64 SSS 63
V'tors U SOC
Fees R/D–£10
Loc 1 mile W of Dalmally on A85

Dunaverty (1889)
Southend, Campbeltown, PA28 6RF
Tel (01586) 830677
Fax (01586) 830677
Web www.redrival.com/dunaverty
Mem 430
Sec D MacBrayne
Holes 18 L 4799 yds SSS 63
V'tors U
Fees £14 (£16)
Loc 10 miles S of Campbeltown

Gigha (1992)
Isle of Gigha, Kintyre, PA41 7AA
Tel (01583) 505242
Mem 30
Sec J Bannatyne
Holes 9 L 5042 yds SSS 65
V'tors U
Fees D–£10
Loc Off W coast of Kintyre

Glencruitten (1908)
Glencruitten Road, Oban, PA34 4PU
Tel (01631) 562868
Mem 400
Sec AG Brown (01631) 564604
Pro Shop (01631) 564115
Holes 18 L 4452 yds SSS 63
V'tors U
Fees £16 (£20)
Loc Oban 1 mile
Arch James Braid

Helensburgh (1893)
25 East Abercromby Street,
Helensburgh, G84 9HZ
Tel (01436) 674173
Fax (01436) 671170
Mem 825
Sec J Stark, K Print
(01436) 674173
Pro D Fotheringham
(01436) 675505
Holes 18 L 6104 yds Par 69 SSS 70
V'tors WD–U WE–NA
Fees £15–£20
Loc N of Helensburgh and A814.
8 miles W of Dumbarton
Arch Tom Morris

Innellan (1891)

Knockamillie Road, Innellan, Dunoon
Tel   (01369) 830242
Mem   200
Sec   A Wilson (01369) 702573
Holes 9 L 4878 yds SSS 64
V'tors U SOC
Fees   18 holes–£12. 9 holes–£8
Loc   4 miles S of Dunoon (A815)

Inveraray (1893)

North Cromalt, Inveraray, Argyll
Tel   (01499) 302508
Mem   175
Sec   R Finnan
Holes 9 L 5600 yds SSS 68
V'tors U SOC
Fees   £10
Loc   1 mile S of Inveraray on A83

Islay (1891)

Western Cottage, Port Ellen, Isle of Islay, PA42 7AT
Tel   (01496) 302409
Web   www.islay.golf.btinternet
.co.uk
Mem   400
Sec   T Dunn
Holes 18 L 6226 yds SSS 70
V'tors U SOC
Fees   £30
Loc   Machrie, 5 miles N of Port Ellen
Mis   Driving range
Arch   Willie Campbell

Isle of Seil (1996)

Pay and play
Balvicar, Isle of Seil, PA34 4TL
Tel   (01852) 300223
Fax   (01852) 300392
Mem   80
Sec   Dr G Hannah
Pro   None
Holes 9 L 2335 yds Par 32
V'tors U
Fees   D–£8
Loc   13 miles S of Oban on island of Seil
Arch   Donald Campbell

Kyles of Bute (1906)

Tighnabruaich, PA21 2EE
Tel   (01700) 811603
Mem   160
Sec   Dr J Thomson
Holes 9 L 2389 yds SSS 32
V'tors U
Fees   D–£8 W–£10
Loc   26 miles W of Dunoon

Lochgilphead (1963)

Blarbuie Road, Lochgilphead, PA31 8LE
Tel   (01546) 602340
Mem   250
Sec   D MacVicar (01546) 602659
Holes 9 L 4484 yds SSS 63
V'tors U SOC

Fees   D–£10 (D–£10)
Loc   ½ mile N of Lochgilphead by Hospital

Lochgoilhead

Drumsynie Estates, Lochgoilhead PA24 8AD
Tel   (01301) 703247
Fax   (01301) 703538
Pro   None
Holes 9 L 1900 yds Par 60
V'tors U
Fees   On application
Loc   N of Lochgoilhead, off Rest & Be Thankful Road

Machrihanish (1876)

Machrihanish, Campbeltown, PA28 6PT
Tel   (01586) 810213
Fax   (01586) 810221
Mem   742 152(L) 178(J)
Sec   Mrs A Anderson
Pro   K Campbell (01586) 810277
Holes 18 L 6225 yds SSS 71
9 hole course
V'tors U
Fees   £30 D–£50 exc Sat £40 D–£60
Loc   5 miles W of Campbeltown

Millport (1888)

Millport, Isle of Cumbrae, KA28 0HB
Tel   (01475) 530311
Fax   (01475) 530306
Mem   288 120(L) 78(J)
Sec   D Donnelly (01475) 530306
Pro   H Lee (01475) 530305
Holes 18 L 5828 yds SSS 69
V'tors U SOC
Fees   £20 D–£25 (£25 D–£31) W–£60
Loc   W of Millport (Largs car ferry)
Arch   James Braid

Port Bannatyne (1912)

Bannatyne Mains Road, Port Bannatyne, Isle of Bute, PA20 0PH
Tel   (01700) 504544
Mem   150
Sec   IL MacLeod (01700) 502009
Holes 13 L 5085 yds Par 68 SSS 65
V'tors U
Fees   £11 (£16)
Loc   2 miles N of Rothesay
Arch   Peter Morrison

Rothesay (1892)

Canada Hill, Rothesay, Isle of Bute, PA20 9HN
Tel   (01700) 503554
Fax   (01700) 503554
Mem   500
Pro   J Dougal (01700) 503554
Holes 18 L 5395 yds SSS 66
V'tors WD–U WE–book with Pro SOC
Fees   On application
Loc   1 mile E of Rothesay
Mis   Practice range
Arch   Braid/Sayers

Tarbert (1910)

Kilberry Road, Tarbert, PA29 6XX
Tel   (01880) 820565
Mem   101
Sec   P Cupples
Holes 9 L 4460 yds SSS 63
V'tors U SOC
Fees   D–£10 W–£30
Loc   1 mile W of Tarbert on B8024, off A83

Taynuilt (1987)

Taynuilt, PA35 1JH
Tel   (01866) 822429
Fax   (01866) 822255 (phone first)
Sec   M Sim (Hon), Laroch, Taynuilt PA35 1JE
Holes 9 L 4510 yds Par 64 SSS 63
V'tors U
Fees   D–£10
Loc   12 miles E of Oban on A85

Tobermory (1896)

Erray Road, Tobermory, Isle of Mull, PA75 6PS
Fax   (01688) 302140
Mem   180
Sec   J Weir (01688) 302338
Holes 9 L 2492 yds SSS 64
V'tors U
Fees   D–£13 W–£50
Loc   Tobermory, Isle of Mull
Mis   Tickets from Western Isles Hotel, Brown's shop and Fairways Lodge.
Arch   David Adams

Vaul (1920)

Scarinish, Isle of Tiree, PA77 6TP
Mem   100
Sec   P Campbell (01879) 220334
Holes 9 L 2837 yds Par 72 SSS 68
V'tors U
Fees   On application
Loc   3 miles N of Scarinish, E end of Tiree. 40 min flight from Glasgow

Ayrshire

Annanhill (1957)

Public
Irvine Road, Kilmarnock, KA3 2RT
Tel   (01563) 521512 (Starter)
Mem   350
Sec   T Denham
(01563) 521644/525557
Holes 18 L 6270 yds SSS 70
V'tors WD/Sun–U Sat–NA SOC–exc Sat
Fees   On application
Loc   1 mile N of Kilmarnock
Arch   J McLean

Ardeer (1880)

Greenhead Avenue, Stevenston, KA20 4JX
Tel   (01294) 464542/465316

Fax (01294) 465316
Mem 700
Sec P Watson (01294) 465316
Pro R Summerfield (Starter)
(01294) 601327
Holes 18 L 6409 yds SSS 72
V'tors U exc Sat–NA SOC–WD
Fees £18 D–£30 Sun–£25 D–£40
Loc 1/2 mile N of Stevenston, off
A78
Arch H Stutt

Auchenharvie (1981)

Public
*Moor Park Road, West Brewery Park,
Saltcoats, KA20 3HU*
Tel **(01294) 603103**
Mem 50
Sec W White (01294) 603775
Pro R Rodgers
Holes 9 L 5300 yds Par 66 SSS 65
V'tors WD–U WE–U after 9.30am
Fees £5.50 (£7.30)
Loc Low road between Saltcoats
and Stevenston
Mis Driving range

Ballochmyle (1937)

Ballochmyle, Mauchline, KA5 6LE
Tel **(01290) 550469**
Fax (01290) 553657
Mem 750
Sec RL Crawford
Pro None
Holes 18 L 5952 yds SSS 69
V'tors WD/WE–U BH–M SOC exc
Sat
Fees On application
Loc 1 mile S of Mauchline on
B705, off A76

Beith (1896)

Threepwood Road, Beith, KA15 2JR
Tel **(01505) 503166 (Clubhouse)**
Fax (01505) 506814
Mem 400
Sec M Murphy (01505) 506814
(am only)
Holes 18 L 5616 yds SSS 68
V'tors WD–U exc Tues–NA after
5pm Sat–NA before 2pm
Sun–NA 1.30–2.30pm
Fees £15 (£20)
Loc Off Beith By-pass on A737

Belleisle (1927)

Public
*Bellisle Park, Doonfoot Road, Ayr,
KA7 4DU*
Tel **(01292) 441258**
Fax (01292) 442632
Web www.golfsouthayrshire.com
Pro D Gemmell (01292) 441314
Holes 18 L 6477 yds SSS 72
V'tors U SOC
Fees £18 (£25)
Loc S of Ayr in Belleisle Park
Arch James Braid

Brodick (1897)

Brodick, Isle of Arran, KA27 8DL
Tel **(01770) 302349**
Fax (01770) 302349
Mem 600
Sec HM Macrae
Pro PS McCalla (01770) 302349
Holes 18 L 4736 yds SSS 64
V'tors U SOC
Fees £18 D–£25 (£22 D–£30)
Loc Brodick Pier 1 mile

Brunston Castle (1992)

*Golf Course Road, Dailly, Girvan,
KA26 9GD*
Tel **(01465) 811471**
Fax (01465) 811545
Web www.brunstoncastle.co.uk
Mem 350
Sec P Muirhead
Pro A Reid
Holes 18 L 6792 yds SSS 72
V'tors U–booking necessary SOC
Fees £26 D–£45
Loc 4 miles E of Girvan
Mis Driving range
Arch Donald Steel

Caprington

Public
*Ayr Road, Caprington, Kilmarnock,
KA1 4UW*
Tel **(01563) 521915 (Starter)**
Mem 400
Sec DR Bray (01292) 474878
Holes 18 L 5810 yds SSS 68
9 hole course
V'tors U
Fees On application
Loc 1 mile S of Kilmarnock
(B7038)

Corrie (1892)

*Corrie, Sannox, Isle of Arran,
KA27 8JD*
Tel **(01770) 810223**
Fax (01770) 810268
Mem 270
Sec GE Welford
(01770) 600403
Holes 9 L 1948 yds SSS 61
V'tors U exc Thurs 12–2.30pm &
Sat–NA
Fees D–£10 W–£45
Loc 6 miles N of Brodick

Dalmilling (1961)

Public
Westwood Avenue, Ayr, KA8 0QY
Tel **(01292) 263893**
Fax (01292) 610543
Pro P Cheyney (Golf Mgr)
Holes 18 L 5724 yds SSS 68
V'tors U
Fees £12 D–£20 (£16 D–£28)
Loc NE boundary of Ayr, nr Ayr
racecourse

Doon Valley (1927)

1 Hillside, Patna, Ayr, KA6 7JT
Tel **(01292) 531607**
Fax (01292) 532489
Mem 90
Sec H Johnstone
Pro None
Holes 9 L 5858 yds SSS 70
V'tors U
Fees £10 (£15)
Loc 8 miles SE of Ayr (A713)

Girvan (1860)

Public
Golf Course Road, Girvan, KA26 9HW
Tel **(01465) 714272/714346
(Starter)**
Fax (01465) 714346
Mem 170
Sec WB Tait
Holes 18 L 5095 yds SSS 64
V'tors U
Fees £13–£25
Loc N side of Girvan (A77). 22
miles S of Ayr
Arch James Braid

Glasgow GC Gailes (1892)

Gailes, Irvine, KA11 5AE
Tel **(01294) 311258**
Fax (01294) 279366
Web www.glasgowgailes-golf.com
Mem 1200
Sec DW Deas (0141) 942 2011
Fax (0141) 942 0770
Pro J Steven (01294) 311561
Holes 18 L 6535 yds Par 71 SSS 72
V'tors WD WE/BH–NA before
2.30pm SOC
Fees £45 D–£60 (£58)
Loc 1 mile S of Irvine, off A78
Arch Willie Park Jr

Irvine (1887)

Bogside, Irvine, KA8 8SN
Tel **(01294) 275979**
Mem 450
Sec W McMahon
Pro K Erskine (01294) 275626
Holes 18 L 6408 yds SSS 71
V'tors U SOC–WD
Fees On application
Loc 1 mile N of Irvine towards
Kilwinning

Irvine Ravenspark (1907)

Public
Kidsneuk Lane, Irvine, KA12 8SR
Tel **(01294) 271293**
Web www.irgc.co.uk
Mem 400
Sec S Howie
Pro P Bond (01294) 276467
Holes 18 L 6429 yds SSS 71
V'tors U
Fees £10.50 D–£21 (£13 D–£21)
Loc N side of Irvine, off A737. 7
miles N of Troon

Kilbirnie Place (1922)

Largs Road, Kilbirnie, KA25 7AT
Tel   (01505) 683398
Mem   450
Sec   JC Walker
Pro   None
Holes   18 L 5411 yds SSS 67
V'tors   WD–U
Fees   On application
Loc   ½ mile W of Kilbirnie, S of
    A760. 15 miles SW of Paisley

Kilmarnock (Barassie)

(1887)
*29 Hillhouse Road, Barassie, Troon,
KA10 6SY*
Tel   (01292) 313920/311077
Fax   (01292) 318300
Web   www.kbgc.co.uk
Mem   600
Sec   D Wilson (01292) 313920
Pro   G Howie (01292) 311322
Holes   18 L 6484 yds SSS 74
    9 L 2888 yds SSS 34
V'tors   WD–U WE–NA before 3pm
    SOC–Mon/Tues & Thurs
Fees   £50 (£60)
Loc   Opp Barassie Railway Station
Arch   Theodore Moone

Lamlash (1889)

Lamlash, Isle of Arran, KA27 8JU
Tel   (01770) 600296 (Clubhouse),
    (01770) 600196 (Starter)
Fax   (01770) 600296
Web   www.arrangolf.co.uk
Mem   450
Sec   J Henderson
Pro   None
Holes   18 L 4640 yds SSS 64
V'tors   U SOC
Fees   On application
Loc   3 miles S of Brodick on A841
Arch   Auchterlonie/Fernie

Largs (1891)

Irvine Road, Largs, KA30 8EU
Tel   (01475) 674681 (Clubhouse)
Fax   (01475) 673594
Web   www.largsgolfclub.co.uk
Mem   800
Sec   DH Macgillivray
    (01475) 673594
Pro   K Docherty (01475) 686192
Holes   18 L 6115 yds Par 70 SSS 71
V'tors   U SOC–WD
Fees   £30 D–£40 (£40)
Loc   1 mile S of Largs on A78

Lochranza (1991)

Pay and play
Lochranza, Isle of Arran, KA27 8HL
Tel   (0177083) 0273
Fax   (0177083) 0600
Web   www.arran.net/lochranza
Sec   IM Robertson
Holes   18 L 5600 yds SSS 70
V'tors   U SOC–May–Oct
Fees   £12
Loc   14 miles N of Brodick
Arch   IM Robertson

Loudoun Gowf (1909)

Galston, KA4 8PA
Tel   (01563) 821993/820551
Fax   (01563) 820011
Mem   650
Sec   WF Dougan (01563) 821993
Holes   18 L 6016 yds SSS 69
V'tors   WD–U WE–M
Fees   £20 D–£30
Loc   5 miles E of Kilmarnock on
    A71

Machrie Bay (1900)

*Machrie Bay, Brodick, Isle of Arran,
KA27 8DZ*
Tel   (01770) 850232
Fax   (01770) 850247
Mem   160
Sec   J Milesi
Pro   None
Holes   9 L 2200 yds Par 66 SSS 62
V'tors   U
Fees   D–£10 W–£35
Loc   10 miles W of Brodick
Arch   William Fernie

Maybole (1970)

Public
Memorial Park, Maybole, KA19
Tel   (01655) 889770
Holes   9 L 2635 yds SSS 65
V'tors   U
Fees   £8 (£9)
Loc   S of Maybole, off A77. 8 miles
    S of Ayr

Muirkirk (1991)

Pay and play
*c/o 65 Main Street, Muirkirk,
KA18 3QR*
Tel   (01290) 660184
Mem   100
Sec   R Bradford
Holes   9 L 5366 yds SSS 67
V'tors   U SOC
Fees   £8
Loc   12 miles W of M74 Junction
    12 on A70

New Cumnock (1902)

*Lochill, Cumnock Road, New Cumnock,
KA18 4BQ*
Tel   (01290) 423659
Mem   250
Sec   D Scott
Holes   9 L 2588 yds SSS 65
V'tors   U exc Sun am–NA
Fees   £5 D–£8
Loc   1 mile W of New Cumnock
Arch   William Fernie

Prestwick (1851)

2 Links Road, Prestwick, KA9 1QG
Tel   (01292) 477404
Fax   (01292) 477255
Web   www.prestwickgc.co.uk
Mem   580
Sec   IT Bunch
Pro   FC Rennie (01292) 479483

Holes   18 L 6668 yds SSS 73
V'tors   WD–I on application only
Fees   £80 D–£120
Loc   Prestwick Airport 1 mile, nr
    Railway Station
Arch   Tom Morris

Prestwick St Cuthbert

(1899)
East Road, Prestwick, KA9 2SX
Tel   (01292) 477101
Fax   (01292) 671730
Web   www.stcuthbert.co.uk
Mem   865
Sec   JC Rutherford
Holes   18 L 6470 yds SSS 71
V'tors   WD–U WE/BH–M SOC–WD
Fees   £24 D–£32
Loc   ½ mile E of Prestwick

Prestwick St Nicholas

(1851)
Grangemuir Road, Prestwick, KA9 1SN
Tel   (01292) 477608
Fax   (01292) 473900
Mem   600 155(L) 68(J)
Sec   GBS Thomson
Pro   Starter (01292) 473904
Holes   18 L 5952 yds SSS 69
V'tors   WD–U WE–NA exc Sun pm
Fees   £30.50 D–£50.30 Sun
    pm–£35.50
Loc   Prestwick
Arch   C Hunter

Routenburn (1914)

Greenock Road, Largs, KA30 9AH
Tel   (01475) 673230
Mem   400
Sec   J Thomson (Mgr)
Pro   G McQueen (01475) 687240
Holes   18 L 5650 yds SSS 68
V'tors   U SOC–WD
Fees   £6.60 (£11)
Loc   N of Largs, off A78
Arch   James Braid

Royal Troon (1878)

Craigend Road, Troon, KA10 6EP
Tel   (01292) 311555
Fax   (01292) 318204
Web   www.royaltroon.com
Mem   800
Sec   JW Chandler
Pro   RB Anderson (01292) 313281
Holes   Old 18 L 7097 yds SSS 74;
    Portland 18 L 6289 yds
    SSS 71
V'tors   Booking required (max 20).
    Mon/Tues/Thurs only–H
    WE–NA
Fees   Old + Portland D–£150
    Portland D–£95 (inc Lunch)
Loc   SE side of Troon (B749).
    Prestwick Airport 3 miles
Mis   Practice range
Arch   W Fernie

Seafield (1930)

Public

Belleisle Park, Doonfoot Road, Ayr,
KA7 4DU

Tel	**(01292) 441258**
Fax	(01292) 442632
Pro	D Gemmell (Golf Mgr)
	(01292) 441314
Holes	18 L 5498 yds SSS 66
V'tors	U
Fees	£13–£25
Loc	S of Ayr in Belleisle Park

Shiskine (1896)

Shiskine, Blackwaterfoot, Isle of Arran,
KA27 8HA

Tel	**(01770) 860226**
Fax	(01770) 860205
Web	www.shiskinegolf.com
Mem	550 154(L) 42(J)
Sec	Mrs F Crawford (Mgr)
	(01770) 860548
Holes	12 L 2990 yds SSS 42
V'tors	U SOC
Fees	£13 (£18)
Loc	11 miles SW of Brodick
Arch	Willie Fernie

Skelmorlie (1891)

Skelmorlie, Largs, PA17 5ES

Tel	**(01475) 520152**
Mem	439
Sec	Mrs A Fahey (Hon)
Holes	18 L 5030 yds SSS 65
V'tors	U exc Sat (Apr–Oct)
Fees	D–£16 Sun–£18
Loc	Wemyss Bay Station 1½ miles
Arch	James Braid

Troon Municipal

Public

Harling Drive, Troon, KA10 6NF

Tel	**(01292) 312464**
Fax	(01292) 312578
Pro	G McKinlay
Holes	Lochgreen 18 L 6785 yds
	SSS 73;
	Darley 18 L 6501 yds SSS 72;
	Fullarton 18 L 4822 yds
	SSS 63
V'tors	U SOC
Fees	Lochgreen £19–£31 Darley
	£15–£29 Fullarton £13–£25
Loc	4 miles N of Prestwick at
	Station Brae

Troon Portland (1894)

Club

1 Crosbie Road, Troon KA10

Tel	**(01292) 313488**
Mem	120
Sec	J Irving
Holes	Play over Portland at Royal
	Troon

Troon St Meddans (1907)

Club

Harling Drive, Troon, KA10 6NF

Mem	200

Sec	R Lamont (01294) 552878
Holes	Play over Troon Municipal
	courses Lochgreen and Darley

Turnberry Hotel (1906)

Turnberry, KA26 9LT

Tel	**(01655) 331000**
Fax	(01655) 331706
Web	www.turnberry.co.uk
Mem	380
Sec	B Gunson (Golf Dir)
	(01655) 334000
Pro	D Fleming (Shop Mgr)
	(01655) 334043
Holes	Ailsa 18 L 6976 yds SSS 72
	Kintyre 18 L 6719 yds SSS 71
V'tors	On application
Fees	On application
Loc	18 miles S of Ayr on A77
Mis	Golf Academy
Arch	Ailsa-Mackenzie Ross.
	Kintyre-Donald Steel

West Kilbride (1893)

Fullerton Drive, Seamill, West Kilbride,
KA23 9HT

Tel	**(01294) 823911**
Fax	(01294) 829573
Mem	900
Sec	H Armour
Pro	G Ross (01294) 823042
Holes	18 L 6452 yds SSS 71
V'tors	WD–U WE–M BH–NA SOC
Fees	On application
Loc	West Kilbride
Arch	Old Tom Morris/James Braid

Western Gailes (1897)

Gailes, Irvine, KA11 5AE

Tel	**(01294) 311649**
Fax	(01294) 312312
Mem	450
Sec	AM McBean
Holes	18 L 6639 yds SSS 73
V'tors	WD–H Mon/Wed/Fri only
	(booking necessary)
Fees	£75 D–£100
Loc	3 miles N of Troon (A78)

Whiting Bay (1895)

Golf Course Road, Whiting Bay, Isle of
Arran, KA27 8PR

Tel	**(01770) 700775**
Mem	290
Sec	Mrs M Auld (01770) 820208
Holes	18 L 4405 yds SSS 63
V'tors	U
Fees	On application
Loc	8 miles S of Brodick

Borders

Duns (1894)

Hardens Road, Duns, TD11 3NR

Tel	**(01361) 882194**
Mem	430
Sec	A Campbell (01361) 882717

Pro	None
Holes	18 L 6209 yds SSS 70
V'tors	U SOC
Fees	£16 (£19)
Loc	1 mile W of Duns, off A6105

Eyemouth (1894)

Gunsgreen House, Eyemouth,
TD14 5DX

Tel	**(018907) 50551 (Clubhouse)**
Mem	400
Sec	M Gibson (018907) 50004
Pro	P Terras (018907) 50004
	C Maltman (Touring)
Holes	18 L 6520 yds SSS 72
V'tors	U SOC
Fees	£20 (£25)
Loc	6 miles N of border, off A1
Arch	JR Bain

Galashiels (1884)

Ladhope Recreation Ground, Galashiels,
TD1 2NJ

Tel	**(01896) 753724**
Mem	366
Sec	R Gass (01896) 755307
Holes	18 L 5309 yds SSS 67
V'tors	U SOC
Fees	£15 D–£20 (£20 D–£25)
Loc	¼ mile NE of Galashiels, off
	A7
Arch	James Braid

Hawick (1877)

Vertish Hill, Hawick, TD9 0NY

Tel	**(01450) 372293**
Mem	600
Sec	J Harley
Holes	18 L 5929 yds SSS 69
V'tors	U
Fees	£21 D–£26
Loc	½ mile S of Hawick

The Hirsel (1948)

Kelso Road, Coldstream, TD12 4NJ

Tel	**(01890) 882678**
Fax	(01890) 882233
Mem	800
Sec	KM Lobban (01890) 883052
Pro	KM Lobban
Holes	18 L 6111 yds SSS 70
V'tors	U SOC
Fees	£20 (£27)
Loc	½ mile W of Coldstream
	(A697)

Innerleithen (1886)

Leithen Water, Leithen Road,
Innerleithen, EH44 6NL

Tel	**(01896) 830951**
Mem	175
Sec	S Wyse (01896) 830071
Holes	9 L 6066 yds SSS 69
V'tors	U
Fees	£11 (£13)
Loc	1 mile N of Innerleithen on
	Heriot road
Arch	Willie Park

For list of abbreviations see page 649

Jedburgh (1892)

Dunion Road, Jedburgh, TD8 6LA
Tel (01835) 863587
Fax (01835) 862360
Web www.tweeddalepress.co.uk/
jedburghgolfclub
Mem 300
Sec G McEwen (01835) 862360
Holes 9 L 5600 yds Par 68 SSS 67
V'tors U
Fees £16 (£16)
Loc Jedburgh 1 mile (signposted
from centre)
Arch Willie Park

Kelso (1887)

Golf Course Road, Kelso, TD5 7SL
Tel (01573) 223009
Fax (01573) 228490
Mem 350
Sec Mrs F Graham
Holes 18 L 6066 yds SSS 69
V'tors U SOC
Fees £16 (£20)
Loc 1 mile N of Kelso, inside
racecourse
Arch James Braid

Langholm (1892)

Langholm, DG13 0JR
Tel (013873) 80673/81247
Web www.langholmgolfclub.co.uk
Mem 150
Sec RA Bell
Holes 9 L 3090 yds SSS 70
V'tors U
Fees £10 (£10)
Loc 21 miles N of Carlisle on A7

Lauder (1896)

Galashiels Road, Lauder, TD2 6QD
Tel (01578) 722526
Mem 250
Sec D Dickson
Holes 9 L 6002 yds SSS 70
V'tors U SOC
Fees £10
Loc ¹/₂ mile W of Lauder
Arch W Park Jr

Melrose (1880)

Dingleton, Melrose
Tel (01896) 822855
Mem 310
Sec W MacRae (01835) 822758
Holes 9 L 5579 yds SSS 68
V'tors U exc during competitions
Fees £16 D–£20
Loc S boundary of Melrose, off
A68

Minto (1928)

Denholm, Hawick, TD9 8SH
Tel (01450) 870220
Fax (01450) 870126
Mem 600
Sec P Brown
Pro None
Holes 18 L 5542 yds SSS 67

V'tors H SOC
Fees £23 (£28)
Loc Denholm, 6 miles E of
Hawick

Newcastleton (1894)

Holm Hill, Newcastleton, TD9 0QD
Tel (013873) 75257
Sec FJ Ewart
Pro None
Holes 9 L 5426 yds Par 70 SSS 68
V'tors U SOC
Fees D–£10
Loc W of Newcastleton, off B6357
(via A7). M6 Junction 44
Arch J Shade

Peebles (1892)

Kirkland Street, Peebles, EH45 8EU
Tel (01721) 720197
Web www.peeblesgolfclub.co.uk
Mem 650
Sec H Gilmore
Pro C Imlah
Holes 18 L 6160 yds SSS 70
V'tors H SOC
Fees £20 D–£27 (£25 D–£34)
Loc 23 miles S of Edinburgh, via
A703
Arch James Braid/HS Colt

The Roxburghe Hotel
(1997)

Heiton, Kelso, TD5 8JZ
Tel (01573) 450331
Fax (01573) 450611
Web www.roxburghe.net
Mem 330
Sec Jeannette Thomson
(Bookings)
Pro C Montgomerie
(01573) 450333
Holes 18 L 6925 yds Par 72 SSS 73
V'tors By arrangement SOC
Fees £40 (£40)
Loc On A698 between Jedburgh
and Kelso
Mis Driving range
Arch Dave Thomas

Selkirk (1883)

The Hill, Selkirk, TD7 4NW
Tel (01750) 20621
Mem 363
Sec A Wilson
Holes 9 L 5560 yds SSS 67
V'tors WD–U exc Mon pm
WE–phone first SOC
Fees D–£16 (£16)
Loc 1 mile S of Selkirk on A7
Arch Willie Park

St Boswells (1899)

St Boswells, Melrose, TD6 0DE
Tel (01835) 823527
Mem 320
Sec JG Phillips
Holes 9 L 5274 yds SSS 66
V'tors U SOC

Fees D–£15 (D–£15)
Loc Off A68 at St Boswells Green,
by River Tweed
Arch Willie Park/Shade

Torwoodlee (1895)

*Edinburgh Road, Galashiels,
Torwoodlee, TD1 2NE*
Tel (01896) 752260
Fax (01896) 752260
Mem 550
Sec G Donnelly
Pro R Elliott
Holes 18 L 6021 yds Par 69 SSS 70
V'tors WD–U from 9.30am–1pm
and after 2pm exc Thurs–NA
from 4–6pm WE–by
arrangement SOC
Fees £20 D–£27 (£25 D–£30)
Loc 1 mile N of Galashiels on A7
Arch Willie Park

Woll

Proprietary
Ashkirk, Selkirkshire TD7 4NY
Tel (01750) 32222
Mem 180
Holes 9 L 6408 yds Par 72 SSS 71
V'tors U
Fees D–£15
Loc Ashkirk, 1 mile off A7

Clackmannanshire

Alloa (1891)

Schawpark, Sauchie, Alloa, FK10 3AX
Tel (01259) 722745
Fax (01259) 218796
Mem 550 80(L) 130(J)
Sec T Crampton (Admin)
Pro W Bennett (01259) 724476
Holes 18 L 6240 yds Par 70 SSS 71
V'tors WD–U WE–parties restricted
Fees £24 D–£30 (£28 D–£35)
Loc Sauchie, N of Alloa on A908
Arch James Braid

Alva

Beauclerc Street, Alva, FK12 5LH
Tel (01259) 760431
Mem 320
Holes 9 L 2423 yds SSS 64
V'tors U
Fees On application
Loc Back Road, Alva, on A91
Stirling-St Andrews road.
Signs to Alva Glen

Braehead (1891)

Cambus, Alloa, FK10 2NT
Tel (01259) 725766
Fax (01259) 214070
Mem 800
Sec P MacMichael
Pro D Boyce (01259) 722078
Holes 18 L 6086 yds SSS 69
V'tors U–booking necessary SOC

Fees £16 D–£24 (£24 D–£32)
Loc   2 miles W of Alloa (A907)
Arch Robert Tait

Dollar (1890)

Brewlands House, Dollar, FK14 7EA
Tel   **(01259) 742400**
Fax   (01259) 743497
Web   www.dollargolfclub.co.uk
Mem   480
Sec   JC Brown
Holes 18 L 5242 yds SSS 66
V'tors U SOC
Fees   £13.50 D–£17.50 (£22)
Loc   Dollar, off A91
Arch   Ben Sayers

Tillicoultry (1899)

Alva Road, Tillicoultry, FK13 6BL
Tel   **(01259) 750124**
Fax   (01259) 750124
Mem   400
Sec   P Brown
Holes 9 L 2528 yds SSS 66
V'tors WD/WE–U SOC
Fees   £12 (£16)
Loc   9 miles E of Stirling

Tulliallan (1902)

Kincardine, Alloa, FK10 4BB
Tel   **(01259) 730396**
Fax   (01259) 733950
Web   www.tulliallan-golf-club.co.uk
Mem   550 71(L) 100(J)
Sec   JS McDowall (01324) 485420
       NC Raleigh (Admin)
Pro   S Kelly (01259) 730798
Holes 18 L 5982 yds SSS 69
V'tors U exc comp days
Fees   £16 (£20)
Loc   5 miles SE of Alloa

Dumfries & Galloway

Brighouse Bay (1999)

Pay and play
Borgue, Kirkcudbright, DG6 4TS
Tel   **(01557) 870409**
Fax   (01557) 870409
Sec   A Prewett-Stansfield
Pro   J Davison (01557) 870409
Holes 18 L 6602 yds Par 74 SSS 73
V'tors WD–U WE–booking advisable
Fees   £18 (£18)
Loc   6 miles SW of Kirkcudbright,
       off B727
Mis   Driving range
Arch   Duncan Gray

Castle Douglas (1905)

*Abercromby Road, Castle Douglas,
DG7 1BA*
Tel   **(01556) 502801**
Mem   510
Sec   AD Millar (01556) 502099

Holes 9 L 5400 yds SSS 66
V'tors U
Fees   £12
Loc   Off A75/A713, NE of Castle
       Douglas

Colvend (1905)

Sandyhills, Dalbeattie, DG5 4PY
Tel   **(01556) 630398**
Fax   (01556) 630495
Mem   500
Sec   JB Henderson
Holes 18 L 5200 yds SSS 67
V'tors U
Fees   D–£20
Loc   6 miles S of Dalbeattie on
       A710
Arch   Fernie/Soutar

Crichton (1884)

Bankend Road, Dumfries, DG1 4TH
Tel   **(01387) 247894/702221**
Fax   (01387) 702223
Mem   500
Holes 9 L 3084 yds SSS 69
V'tors WD–U before 3pm SOC
Fees   £12
Loc   1 mile from Dumfries, nr
       Hospital

Dalbeattie (1894)

Maxwell Park, Dalbeattie, DG5 4LS
Tel   **(01556) 611421 (Clubhouse)**
Fax   (01556) 610311
Mem   400
Sec   A Howatson (01556) 610311
Pro   None
Holes 9 L 5710 yds SSS 68
V'tors U SOC
Fees   £15 (£15)
Loc   14 miles SW of Dumfries on
       A711/B794

Dumfries & County (1912)

*Nunfield, Edinburgh Road, Dumfries,
DG1 1JX*
Tel   **(01387) 253585**
Fax   (01387) 253585
Web   www.dumfriesandcounty-
       gc.fsnet.co.uk
Mem   600 100(J)
Sec   BRM Duguid (01387) 253585
Pro   S Syme (01387) 268918
Holes 18 L 5928 yds SSS 69
V'tors WD–U exc 11.30–2pm–NA
       Sat–NA Sun–NA before 10am
Fees   £26 (£26)
Loc   1 mile NE of Dumfries, on
       A701
Arch   W Fernie

Dumfries & Galloway (1880)

*2 Laurieston Avenue, Maxwelltown,
Dumfries, DG2 7NY*
Tel   **(01387) 253582**
Fax   (01387) 263848
Mem   480

Sec   TM Ross (01387) 263848
Pro   J Fergusson (01387) 256902
Holes 18 L 6325 yds SSS 70
V'tors U
Fees   £26 (£32)
Loc   Dumfries
Arch   Willie Fernie

Gatehouse (1921)

*'Innisfree', Laurieston, Castle Douglas,
DG7 2PW*
Tel   **(01557) 814766 (Clubhouse),
       (01644) 450260 (Bookings)**
Fax   (01644) 450260
Mem   300
Sec   KA Cooper (01644) 450260
Holes 9 L 2521 yds SSS 66
V'tors U
Fees   D–£10 (D–£10)
Loc   ³/₄ mile N of Gatehouse, off
       A75. 9 miles NW of
       Kirkcudbright

Gretna (1991)

Kirtle View, Gretna, DG16 5HD
Tel   **(01461) 338464**
Sec   G & E Birnie (Props)
Holes 9 L 6430 yds SSS 71
V'tors U SOC
Fees   9 holes–£5. 18 holes–£10
Loc   1 mile W of Gretna, off A75
Mis   Driving range
Arch   Nigel Williams

Hoddom Castle (1973)

Pay and play
*Hoddom Bridge, Ecclefechan,
DG11 1AS*
Tel   **(01576) 300251**
Fax   (01576) 300757
Sec   D Laycock
Holes 9 L 2274 yds SSS 33
V'tors U
Fees   £7 (£9)
Loc   2 miles SW of Ecclefechan on
       B725. M74 Junction 6

Kirkcudbright (1893)

*Stirling Crescent, Kirkcudbright,
DG6 4EZ*
Tel   **(01557) 330314**
Mem   500
Sec   DA MacKenzie
Holes 18 L 5739 yds SSS 69
V'tors U H–phone first SOC
Fees   £18 D–£23
Loc   ¹/₂ mile from Kirkcudbright
       town centre

Lochmaben (1926)

*Castlehill Gate, Lochmaben,
DG11 1NT*
Tel   **(01387) 810552**
Mem   650
Sec   JM Dickie
Holes 18 L 5357 yds SSS 66
V'tors WD–U before 5pm WE–U
       exc comp days SOC
Fees   £16 D–£20 (£20 D–£25)

Loc 4 miles W of Lockerbie on
A709. 8 miles NE of Dumfries
Arch James Braid

Lockerbie (1889)

Corrie Road, Lockerbie, DG11 2ND
Tel (01576) 203363
Fax (01576) 203363
Mem 530
Sec J Thomson
Holes 18 L 5418 yds SSS 67
V'tors U exc Sun–NA before
11.30am
Fees £16 (£18)
Loc ¹/₂ mile NE of Lockerbie, on
Corrie road
Arch James Braid

Moffat (1884)

Coatshill, Moffat, DG10 9SB
Tel (01683) 220020
Fax (01683) 220020
Web www.moffatgolfclub.co.uk
Mem 350
Sec JW Mein (01683) 220020
Pro None
Holes 18 L 5259 yds Par 69 SSS 67
V'tors U exc Wed–NA after 3pm
Fees £18.50 D–£22 (£25 D–£31)
Loc Signposted on A701 from
Beattock (A74)
Arch Ben Sayers

New Galloway (1902)

New Galloway, Dumfries, DG7 3RN
Tel (01644) 450685
Mem 280
Sec NE White
Holes 9 L 5006 yds Par 68 SSS 67
V'tors U
Fees D–£12.50
Loc S of New Galloway on A762.
20 miles N of Kirkcudbright
Arch Baillie

Newton Stewart (1981)

*Kirroughtree Avenue, Minnigaff,
Newton Stewart, DG8 6PF*
Tel (01671) 402172
Mem 380
Sec M Large
Holes 18 L 5903 yds Par 69 SSS 70
V'tors U H
Fees £20 D–£23 (£23 D–£27)
Loc N of Newton Stewart, off A75

Portpatrick (1903)

*Golf Course Road, Portpatrick,
DG9 8TB*
Tel (01776) 810273
Fax (01776) 810811
Mem 550
Sec JA Horberry
Holes Dunskey 18 L 5908 yds
SSS 69
Dinvin 9 L 1504 yds Par 27
V'tors U H SOC
Fees £22 D–£33 (£27 D–£38)
W–£110 Dinvin £9 D–£14
Loc 8 miles SW of Stranraer
Arch CW Hunter

Powfoot (1903)

Cummertrees, Annan, DG12 5QE
Tel (01461) 700276 (Bookings)
Fax (01461) 700276
Mem 920
Sec BW Sutherland MBE (Mgr)
Pro G Dick (01461) 700327
Holes 18 L 6266 yds SSS 71
V'tors WD–U Sat–NA Sun–NA
before 1pm
Fees Winter £15 5D–£60 Summer
£25 D–£32 5D–£130
Loc 4 miles W of Annan. 15 miles
SE of Dumfries, off B724
Arch James Braid

St Medan (1904)

Monreith, Newton Stewart, DG8 8NJ
Tel (01988) 700358
Mem 150
Sec DR Graham (01988) 840214
Holes 9 L 2277 yds SSS 63
V'tors U SOC
Fees £15 (£15)
Loc 3 miles S of Port William, off
A747

Sanquhar (1894)

*Blackaddie Road, Sanquhar, Dumfries,
DG4 6JZ*
Tel (01659) 50577
Web www.scottishgolf.com
Mem 180
Sec D Hamilton (01659) 66095
Holes 9 L 5630 yds SSS 68
V'tors U–parties welcome
Fees D–£12 (D–£15)
Loc ¹/₂ mile W of Sanquhar (A76).
30 miles N of Dumfries
Arch W Fernie

Southerness (1947)

Southerness, Dumfries, DG2 8AZ
Tel (01387) 880677
Fax (01387) 880644
Web www.southernessgolfclub.com
Mem 800
Sec IA Robin
Pro None
Holes 18 L 6566 yds SSS 73
V'tors H–phone first SOC
Fees D–£35 (D–£45)
Loc 16 miles S of Dumfries, off
A710
Arch Mackenzie Ross

Stranraer (1905)

*Creachmore, Leswalt, Stranraer,
DG9 0LF*
Tel (01776) 870245
Fax (01776) 870445
Mem 600
Sec BC Kelly
Holes 18 L 6308 yds SSS 72
V'tors WE–NA before 9.30am and
11.45am–1.45pm
Fees D–£20 (£25)
Loc 2 miles NW of Stranraer on
A718
Arch James Braid

Thornhill (1893)

Blacknest, Thornhill, DG3 5DW
Tel (01848) 330546
Mem 625
Sec J Tait
Pro J Davidson (01848) 331779
Holes 18 L 6085 yds SSS 70
V'tors U
Fees On application
Loc 14 miles N of Dumfries (A76)

Wigtown & Bladnoch
(1960)

Lightlands Terrace, Wigtown, DG8 9EF
Tel (01988) 403354
Mem 170
Sec B Kaye
Holes 9 L 2731 yds SSS 67
V'tors U SOC
Fees £15 (£15)
Loc Between Wigtown and
Bladnoch, off A714
Arch J Muir

Wigtownshire
County (1894)

*Mains of Park, Glenluce, Newton
Stewart, DG8 0NN*
Tel (01581) 300420
Web www.glenluce.org.uk/
countygolfclub
Mem 420
Sec R McKnight
Pro None
Holes 18 L 5843 yds SSS 68
V'tors U exc Wed–NA after 6pm
Fees £20 D–£26 (£22 D–£28)
Loc 8 miles E of Stranraer on
A75
Arch W Gordon Cunningham

Dunbartonshire

Balmore (1894)

Balmore, Torrance, G64 4AW
Tel (01360) 620240
Fax (01360) 620284
Mem 750
Sec SB Keir (01360) 620284
Pro D Pirie (01360) 620123
Holes 18 L 5542 yds SSS 67
V'tors WD–U SOC
Fees On application
Loc 4 miles N of Glasgow, off
A807
Arch James Braid

Bearsden (1891)

*Thorn Road, Bearsden, Glasgow,
G61 4BP*
Tel (0141) 942 2351
Mem 600
Sec JL McComish
Holes 9 L 6014 yds SSS 69
V'tors WD only
Loc 6 miles NW of Glasgow

Cardross (1895)

Main Road, Cardross, Dumbarton,
G82 5LB

Tel	**(01389) 841213 (Clubhouse)**
Fax	(01389) 842162
Web	www.cardross.com
Mem	850
Sec	IT Waugh (01389) 841754
Pro	R Farrell (01389) 841350
Holes	18 L 6469 yds SSS 72
V'tors	WD–U WE–M SOC
Fees	£25 D–£35
Loc	4 miles W of Dumbarton on A814
Arch	Fernie (1904)/Braid(1921)

Clober (1951)

Craigton Road, Milngavie, Glasgow,
G62 7HP

Tel	**(0141) 956 1685**
Fax	(0141) 955 1416
Web	www.clober.com
Mem	700
Sec	B Davidson
Pro	(0141) 956 6963 (Golf Shop)
Holes	18 L 4963 yds SSS 65
V'tors	WD–U before 4pm WE–M BH–NA SOC–WD
Fees	£16
Loc	7 miles NW of Glasgow

Clydebank & District (1905)

Hardgate, Clydebank, G81 5QY

Tel	**(01389) 383833**
Fax	(01389) 383831
Mem	780
Sec	(01389) 383831
Pro	PR Jamieson (01389) 383835
Holes	18 L 5823 yds SSS 68
V'tors	WD–H
Fees	On application
Loc	2 miles N of Clydebank

Clydebank Municipal (1927)

Public
Overtoun Road, Dalmuir, Clydebank,
G81 3RE

Tel	**(0141) 952 8698 (Starter)**
Fax	(0141) 952 6372
Pro	R Bowman (0141) 952 6372
Holes	18 L 5349 yds SSS 66
V'tors	U exc Sat–NA 11am–2.30pm
Fees	On application
Loc	8 miles W of Glasgow

Dougalston (1977)

Strathblane Road, Milngavie, Glasgow,
G62 8HJ

Tel	**(0141) 955 2434**
Fax	(0141) 955 2406
Mem	770
Sec	Miss Joanne Young
Pro	C Everett
Holes	18 L 6225 yds SSS 71
V'tors	WD–U SOC
Fees	£20 (£25)
Loc	7 miles N of Glasgow on A81
Arch	J Harris

Douglas Park (1897)

Hillfoot, Bearsden, Glasgow, G61 2TJ

Tel	**(0141) 942 2220 (Clubhouse)**
Fax	(0141) 942 0085
Mem	470 270(L) 120(J)
Sec	JG Fergusson (0141) 942 0085
Pro	D Scott (0141) 942 1482
Holes	18 L 5962 yds SSS 69
V'tors	M SOC
Loc	6 miles NW of Glasgow, nr Hillfoot Station

Dullatur (1896)

1a Glendouglas Drive, Craigmarloch,
Cumbernauld, G68 0DW

Tel	**(01236) 723230**
Fax	(01236) 727271
Mem	580 64(L)
Sec	Carol Millar (01236) 723230
Pro	D Sinclair (01236) 794721
Holes	18 L 6312 yds SSS 70
	18 L 5875 yds SSS 68
V'tors	WD–U WE–M SOC
Fees	£20 (£30)
Loc	3 miles N of Cumbernauld

Dumbarton (1888)

Broadmeadow, Dumbarton, G82 2BQ

Tel	**(01389) 732830**
Fax	(01389) 765995
Mem	500
Sec	DM Mitchell
Holes	18 L 6018 yds SSS 69
V'tors	WD–U WE–NA
Fees	D–£25
Loc	1 mile N of Dumbarton

Hayston (1926)

Campsie Road, Kirkintilloch, Glasgow,
G66 1RN

Tel	**(0141) 776 1244**
Fax	(0141) 776 9030
Mem	440 70(L) 60(J)
Sec	JV Carmichael (0141) 775 0723
Pro	S Barnett (0141) 775 0882
Holes	18 L 6042 yds SSS 70
V'tors	WD–I before 4.30pm –M after 4.30pm WE–M
Fees	£25
Loc	1 mile N of Kirkintilloch
Arch	James Braid

Hilton Park (1927)

Auldmarroch Estate, Stockiemuir Road,
Milngavie, G62 7HB

Tel	**(0141) 956 5124/1215**
Fax	(0141) 956 4657
Mem	1200
Sec	Mrs JA Dawson (0141) 956 4657
Pro	W McCondichie (0141) 956 5125
Holes	Hilton 18 L 6054 yds SSS 70 Allander 18 L 5374 yds SSS 69
V'tors	WD–U before 4pm
Fees	On application

Loc	8 miles NW of Glasgow on A809
Arch	James Braid

Kirkintilloch (1895)

Todhill, Campsie Road, Kirkintilloch,
G66 1RN

Tel	**(0141) 776 1256**
Mem	450 100(L) 100(J)
Sec	IM Gray (0141) 775 2387
Holes	18 L 5860 yds SSS 69
V'tors	M SOC
Fees	SOC–On application
Loc	7 miles N of Glasgow

Lenzie (1889)

19 Crosshill Road, Lenzie, G66 5DA

Tel	**(0141) 776 1535**
Fax	(0141) 777 7748
Web	www.lenziegolfclub.com
Mem	501 125(L) 125(J)
Sec	SM Davidson (0141) 812 3018
Pro	J McCallum (0141) 777 7748
Holes	18 L 5984 yds SSS 69
V'tors	M SOC
Fees	£24 D–£30
Loc	6 miles NE of Glasgow

Loch Lomond

Rossdhu House, Luss, G83 8NT

Tel	**(01436) 655555**
Fax	(01436) 655500
Web	www.lochlomond.com
Sec	K Williams
Pro	C Campbell
Holes	18 L 7060 yds Par 71
V'tors	NA
Loc	20 miles NW of Glasgow on A82
Arch	Weiskopf/Morrish

Milngavie (1895)

Laighpark, Milngavie, Glasgow,
G62 8EP

Tel	**(0141) 956 1619**
Fax	(0141) 956 4252
Mem	390
Sec	S McInnes
Pro	None
Holes	18 L 5818 yds SSS 68
V'tors	M SOC
Fees	On application
Loc	7 miles NW of Glasgow

Palacerigg (1975)

Public
Palacerigg Country Park, Cumbernauld,
G67 3HU

Tel	**(01236) 734969**
Fax	(01236) 721461
Web	www.palaceriggolfclub.co.uk
Mem	360
Sec	DSA Cooper
Holes	18 L 6444 yds SSS 71
V'tors	U SOC
Fees	£8 (£10)
Loc	3 miles SE of Cumbernauld, off A80
Arch	Henry Cotton

Ross Priory

Ross Loan, Gartocharn, Alexandria
G83 8NL

Tel	**(01389) 830398**
Fax	(01389) 830357
Mem	800
Sec	R Cook
Pro	None
Holes	9 L 5758 yds Par 70 SSS 68
V'tors	M
Fees	N/A
Loc	Off A881 at Gartocharn
Arch	George Campbell

Vale of Leven (1907)

Northfield Road, Bonhill, Alexandria,
G83 9ET

Tel	**(01389) 752351**
Mem	600
Sec	A Barclay
Pro	B Campbell (08707) 498914
Holes	18 L 5167 yds Par 67 SSS 66
V'tors	U H SOC (Apr–Sept) SOC (max 36 members)
Fees	£16 D–£24 (£20 D–£30)
Loc	Bonhill, 3 miles N of Dumbarton, off A82

Westerwood Hotel G&CC (1989)

St Andrews Drive, Cumbernauld,
G68 0EW

Tel	**(01236) 725281**
Fax	(01236) 725281
Mem	250
Sec	A Tait
Pro	A Tait
Holes	18 L 6616 yds SSS 72
V'tors	U SOC
Fees	£27.50 (£30)
Loc	13 miles NE of Glasgow, off A80
Arch	Thomas/Ballesteros

Windyhill (1908)

Windyhill, Bearsden, G61 4QQ

Tel	**(0141) 942 2349**
Fax	(0141) 942 5874
Web	www.windyhill.co.uk
Mem	650
Sec	W Proven
Pro	C Duffy (0141) 942 7157
Holes	18 L 6254 yds SSS 70
V'tors	WD–U Sun–M SOC–WD
Fees	£20
Loc	8 miles NW of Glasgow
Arch	James Braid

Fife

Aberdour (1896)

Seaside Place, Aberdour, KY3 0TX

Tel	**(01383) 860688**
Fax	(01383) 860050
Mem	670
Sec	(01383) 860080
Pro	G McCallum (01383) 860256
Holes	18 L 5460 yds Par 67 SSS 66

V'tors	WD–book with Pro Sat–NA SOC
Fees	£17 D–£28
Loc	8 miles SE of Dunfermline, on coast
Arch	Robertson/Anderson

Anstruther (1890)

Marsfield Shore Road, Anstruther,
KY10 3DZ

Tel	**(01333) 310956**
Fax	(01333) 312283
Mem	500
Sec	J Boal
Holes	9 L 4504 yds SSS 63
V'tors	U SOC
Fees	£12 (£15)
Loc	9 miles S of St Andrews

Auchterderran (1904)

Public
Woodend Road, Cardenden, KY5 0NH

Tel	**(01592) 721579**
Mem	100
Sec	G McCrae
Holes	9 L 5400 yds SSS 66
V'tors	U SOC
Fees	£9 (£12)
Loc	1 mile N of Cardenden. 6 miles W of Kirkcaldy, off A910

Balbirnie Park (1983)

Balbirnie Park, Markinch, Glenrothes,
KY7 6NR

Tel	**(01592) 612095**
Fax	(01592) 612383
Mem	800
Sec	S Oliver (Admin)
Pro	C Donnelly (01592) 752006
Holes	18 L 6210 yds SSS 70
V'tors	WE–booking essential
Fees	£25 D–£33 (£30 D–£40)
Loc	2 miles E of Glenrothes
Arch	Fraser Middleton

Ballingry

Pay and play
Lochore Meadows Country Park,
Crosshill, Lochgelly, KY5 8BA

Tel	**(01592) 860086**
Mem	150
Holes	9 L 6482 yds SSS 71
V'tors	U
Fees	On application
Loc	2 miles N of Lochgelly (B920)

Burntisland (1797)

Club
51 Craigkennochie Terrace, Burntisland,
KY3 9EN

Tel	**(01592) 872728**
Web	www.burntislandgolfclub .co.uk
Mem	100
Sec	AD McPherson
Holes	Play over Dodhead Course, Burntisland

Burntisland Golf House Club (1898)

Dodhead, Burntisland, KY3 9LQ

Tel	**(01592) 874093**
Fax	(01592) 874093
Mem	800
Sec	WK Taylor (Mgr) (01592) 874093
Pro	P Wytrazek (01592) 872116
Holes	18 L 5965 yds SSS 70
V'tors	U H SOC
Fees	£17 D–£25 (£25 D–£37)
Loc	1 mile E of Burntisland on B923
Arch	Willie Park jr/James Braid

Canmore (1897)

Venturefair Avenue, Dunfermline,
KY12 0PE

Tel	**(01383) 724969**
Mem	547 70(L) 85(J)
Sec	C Stuart (01383) 513604
Pro	D Gemmell (01383) 728416
Holes	18 L 5437 yds SSS 66
V'tors	WD–U WE–restricted
Fees	£15 D–£20 (£20 D–£30)
Loc	1 mile N of Dunfermline on A823
Arch	Ben Sayers

Charleton (1994)

Pay and play
Charleton, Colinsburgh, KY9 1HG

Tel	**(01333) 340505**
Fax	(01333) 340583
Sec	J Pattison
Pro	A Hutton (01333) 330009
Holes	18 L 6149 yds SSS 70
V'tors	U SOC
Fees	£18 (£22)
Loc	1 mile W of Colinsburgh, off B492
Mis	Driving range. 9 holes pitch & putt course
Arch	John Salvesen

Cowdenbeath (1991)

Public
Seco Place, Cowdenbeath, KY4 8PD

Tel	**(01383) 511918**
Mem	400
Sec	D Ferguson
Holes	18 L 6100 yds SSS 69
V'tors	U
Fees	On application
Loc	In Cowdenbeath, signposted from A909/A92

Crail Golfing Society (1786)

Balcomie Clubhouse, Fifeness, Crail,
KY10 3XN

Tel	**(01333) 450686**
Fax	(01333) 450416
Mem	1700
Sec	JF Horsfield (Mgr) (01333) 451414
Pro	G Lennie (01333) 450960/450967

Holes Balcomie 18 L 5922 yds
SSS 69;
Craighead 18 L 6728 yds Par
71 SSS 73
V'tors U
Fees £30 (£35)
Loc 11 miles SE of St Andrews
Arch Balcomie-Tom Morris.
Craighead-Gil Hanse

Cupar (1855)

Hilltarvit, Cupar, KY15 5JT
Tel (01334) 653549
Mem 475
Sec JM Houston (01334) 654101
Holes 9 L 5074 yds SSS 65
V'tors WD–U Sat–NA
SOC–WD/Sun
Fees D–£15
Loc 10 miles W of St Andrews

Drumoig

Leuchars, St Andrews, KY16 0DW
Tel (01382) 541144
Fax (01382) 541133
Sec N Simpson (Gen Mgr)
Pro JM Farmer (Golf Mgr)
(01382) 541144
Holes 18 hole course
V'tors U
Fees On application
Loc 7 miles NW of St Andrews on
A919
Mis Driving range
Arch Dave Thomas

Dunfermline (1887)

*Pitfirrane, Crossford, Dunfermline,
KY12 8QW*
Tel (01383) 723534
Mem 690
Sec R De Rose
Pro C Nugent (01383) 729061
Holes 18 L 6121 yds SSS 70
V'tors WD–U 10–12 & 2–4pm
WE–M SOC–WD
Fees £21 D–£31
Loc 2 miles W of Dunfermline on
A994
Arch JR Stutt

Dunnikier Park (1963)

Public
Dunnikier Way, Kirkcaldy, KY1 3LP
Tel (01592) 261599
Fax (01592) 642541
Mem 600 35(L) 75(J)
Sec N Crooks
Pro G Whyte (01592) 642121
Holes 18 L 6601 yds SSS 72
V'tors U SOC
Fees £11.50 (£15.50)
Loc N boundary of Kirkcaldy
Arch R Stutt

Earlsferry Thistle (1875)

Club
Melon Park, Elie, KY9 1AS
Mem 60
Sec AJ Stewart (01333) 330639

Holes Play over Golf House Club
Course

Falkland (1976)

Public
The Myre, Falkland, KY15 7AA
Tel (01337) 857404
Mem 350
Sec Mrs H Horsburgh
Holes 9 L 2384 metres SSS 66
V'tors U SOC
Fees On application
Loc 5 miles N of Glenrothes on
A912

Glenrothes (1958)

Public
*Golf Course Road, Glenrothes,
KY6 2LA*
Tel (01592) 754561/758686
Mem 750 35(L) 50(J)
Sec Miss C Dawson
Holes 18 L 6444 yds SSS 71
V'tors U
Fees £11 (£15)
Loc Glenrothes West, off A92.
M90 Junction 29
Arch JR Stutt

Golf House Club (1875)

Elie, Leven, KY9 1AS
Tel (01333) 330327
Fax (01333) 330895
Sec A Sneddon
(01333) 330301
Pro R Wilson (01333) 330955
Holes 18 L 6261 yds SSS 69
9 L 2277 yds SSS 32
V'tors July–Sept ballot. WE–no party
bookings. WE–NA before
3pm (May–Sept)
Fees £32 D–£45 (£40 D–£50)
Loc 12 miles S of St Andrews

Kinghorn Ladies (1894)

Club
*Golf Clubhouse, McDuff Crescent,
Kinghorn, KY3 9RE*
Tel (01592) 890345
Mem 29
Holes Play over Kinghorn Municipal

Kinghorn Municipal (1887)

Public
*McDuff Crescent, Kinghorn,
KY3 9RE*
Tel (01592) 890345
Mem 200
Sec I Gow (01592) 265445
Pro None
Holes 18 L 5629 yds SSS 67
V'tors U SOC
Fees £11 (£16)
Loc 3 miles S of Kirkcaldy (A921)
Mis Kinghorn and Kinghorn
Thistle Clubs play here
Arch Tom Morris

Kingsbarns

Public
*Kingsbarns Golf Links, Kingsbarns, Fife
KY16 8QD*
Tel (01334) 460860
Fax (01334) 460877
Web www.kingsbarns.com
Sec David FG Scott (Dir. of Golf)
(e-mail: info@kingsbarns.com)
Pro David FG Scott
Holes 18
V'tors U 7 days/week
Fees £125 round, £185 day ticket
Loc Coast road A917 St Andrews
to Crail
Mis Full driving range facilities and
caddies available on request
Arch Kyle Phillips in collab. with
Mark Parsinen

Kirkcaldy (1904)

Balwearie Road, Kirkcaldy, KY2 5LT
Tel (01592) 260370
Fax (01592) 205240
Mem 600
Sec AC Thomson (01592) 205240
Pro A Caira (01592) 203258
Holes 18 L 6040 yds SSS 70
V'tors U exc Sat–NA
Fees £22–£28 Sun–£28–£36
Loc S end of Kirkcaldy

Ladybank (1879)

Annsmuir, Ladybank, KY15 7RA
Tel (01337) 830814,
(01337) 830725 **(Starter)**
Fax (01337) 831505
Mem 1000
Sec D Allan
Pro MJ Gray (01337) 830725
Holes 18 L 6601 yds SSS 72
V'tors WD–U 9.30am–4pm M–after
4pm WE–NA
Fees £35 (£45)
Loc 6 miles SW of Cupar, off A92
from Melville Lodges
roundabout

Leslie (1898)

*Balsillie Laws, Leslie, Glenrothes,
KY6 3EZ*
Tel (01592) 620040
Mem 300
Sec G Lewis
Holes 9 L 4940 yds SSS 64
V'tors U
Fees £5 (£8)
Loc 3 miles W of Glenrothes. M90
Junction 5/7, 11 miles

Leven Golfing Society (1820)

Club
Links Road, Leven, KY8 4HS
Tel (01333) 426096/424229
Fax (01333) 424229
Mem 635
Sec RT Wright (01333) 424229
Holes Play over Leven Links

Leven Links (1846)

The Promenade, Leven, KY8 4HS
Tel (01333) 421390 **(Starter)**

Fax (01333) 428859
Mem 1200
Sec (01333) 428859
(Links Joint Committee)
Holes 18 L 6434 yds SSS 71
V'tors WD–U before 5pm Sat–no
parties Sun–NA before
10.30am SOC
Fees £28 (£30)
Loc E of Leven, on promenade.
12 miles SW of St Andrews

Leven Thistle (1867)
Club
Balfour Street, Leven, KY8 4JF
Tel (01333) 426397
Fax (01333) 439910
Mem 500
Sec J Scott (01333) 426333
Holes Play over Leven Links

Lochgelly (1895)
*Cartmore Road, Lochgelly, Kirkcaldy,
KY5 9PB*
Tel (01592) 780174
Mem 450
Sec RF Stuart (01383) 512238
Pro None
Holes 18 L 5454 yds SSS 66
V'tors U
Fees £12 (£17)
Loc NW edge of Lochgelly.
5 miles W of Kirkcaldy

Lundin (1868)
Golf Road, Lundin Links, KY8 6BA
Tel (01333) 320202
Fax (01333) 329743
Web www.lundingolfclub.co.uk
Mem 800
Sec DR Thomson
Pro DK Webster (01333) 320051
Holes 18 L 6394 yds SSS 71
V'tors WD–U H Sat–NA before
2.30pm Sun–M H
Fees £32 D–£40 (£40)
Loc 3 miles E of Leven
Arch James Braid

Lundin Ladies (1891)
*Woodielea Road, Lundin Links,
KY8 6AR*
Tel (01333) 320022 **(Starter)**,
(01333) 320832 **(Sec)**
Mem 350
Sec Marion Mitchell
Holes 9 L 4730 yds SSS 67
V'tors U
Fees On application
Loc 3 miles E of Leven

Methil (1892)
Club
*Links House, Links Road, Leven,
KY8 4HS*
Tel (01333) 425535
Fax (01333) 425187
Mem 50
Sec ATJ Traill
Holes Play over Leven Links

Pitreavie (1922)
*Queensferry Road, Dunfermline,
KY11 8PR*
Tel **(01383) 722591**
Fax (01383) 722591
Mem 800
Sec E Comerford
Pro P Brookes (01383) 723151
Holes 18 L 6031 yds SSS 69
V'tors U–phone Pro SOC
(Parties–max 36–must be
booked in advance)
Fees £19 D–£26 (£38)
Loc 2 miles off M90 Junction 2,
between Rosyth and
Dunfermline
Arch Dr A Mackenzie

St Michaels (1903)
Leuchars, St Andrews, KY16 0DX
Tel **(01334) 839365**
Fax (01334) 838666
Web www.stmichaelsgc.co.uk
Mem 550
Sec J Strain (01334) 838666
Holes 18 L 5802 yds SSS 68
V'tors Sun am–NA (Mar–Oct) SOC
Fees D–£20 (£22)
Loc 5 miles N of St Andrews on
Dundee road (A919)

Saline (1912)
Kinneddar Hill, Saline, KY12 9LT
Tel **(01383) 852591**
Mem 400
Sec R Hutchison
(01383) 852344
Holes 9 L 5302 yds SSS 66
V'tors U exc medal Sat
Fees £9 (£11)
Loc 5 miles NW of Dunfermline

Scoonie (1951)
Public
North Links, Leven, KY8 4SP
Tel **(01333) 307007**
Fax (01333) 307008
Sec S Kuczerepa
Pro None
Holes 18 L 4979 metres SSS 65
V'tors U SOC
Fees On application
Loc Adjoins Leven Links

Scotscraig (1817)
Golf Road, Tayport, DD6 9DZ
Tel **(01382) 552515**
Fax (01382) 553130
Mem 850
Sec BD Liddle
Pro SJ Campbell
Holes 18 L 6550 yds SSS 72
V'tors WD–U WE–by prior
arrangement SOC
Fees On application
Loc 10 miles N of St Andrews

Thornton (1921)
Station Road, Thornton, KY1 4DW
Tel **(01592) 771173 (Starter)**

Fax (01592) 774955
Web www.thorntongolfclubfife
.co.uk
Mem 700
Sec BSL Main (01592) 771111
Holes 18 L 6155 yds Par 70 SSS 69
V'tors U
Fees £15 D–£25 (£22 D–£32)
Loc 5 miles N of Kirkcaldy, off
A92

St Andrews Clubs

New (1902)
Club
*3-5 Gibson Place, St Andrews,
KY16 9JE*
Tel **(01334) 473426**
Fax (01334) 477570
Web www.standrewsnewgolfclub
.com
Mem 1700
Sec H Campbell Graham
(Sec/Mgr)
Holes Play over St Andrews Links
courses

The Royal & Ancient
(1754)
Club
St Andrews, KY16 9JD
Tel **(01334) 460000**
Fax (01334) 460001
Web www.randa.org
www.opengolf.com
Mem 1800
Sec P Dawson
Holes Play over St Andrews Links

St Andrews (1843)
Club
*Links House, 13 The Links, St
Andrews, KY16 9JB*
Tel **(01334) 473017**
Fax (01334) 479577
Web www.thestandrewsgolfclub
.co.uk
Mem 1600
Sec T Gallacher (01334) 473017
Holes Play over St Andrews Links

St Andrews Thistle (1817)
Club
*18 Morton Crescent, St Andrews,
KY16 8RA*
Mem 180
Sec JD Gray (01334) 474668
Holes Play over St Andrews Links

St Regulus Ladies'
Club
*9 Pilmour Links, St Andrews,
KY16 9JG*
Mem 210
Sec Mrs J Lumsden
(01334) 472249
Holes Play over St Andrews Links

The St Rule Club (1898)
Club
12 The Links, St Andrews, KY16 9JB
Tel   **(01334) 472988**
Fax   (01334) 472988
Mem   284
Sec   Mrs J Allan
Holes   Play over St Andrews Links

St Andrews Courses

Balgove Course (1993)
Public
*St Andrews Links Trust, Pilmour House,
St Andrews, KY16 9SF*
Tel   **(01334) 466666**
Fax   (01334) 479555
Web   www.standrews.org.uk
Sec   AJR McGregor (Gen Mgr)
Holes   9 L 1520 yds Par 30
V'tors U
Fees   £7–£10 3D–£12–£18
        W–£25–£36
Loc   St Andrews Links, on A91
Mis   Driving range
Arch   Donald Steel

Duke's Course (1995)
*Craigtoun Park, St Andrews,
KY16 8NS*
Tel   **(01334) 474371**
Fax   (01334) 477668
Web   www.oldcoursehotel.co.uk
Mem   325
Sec   S Toon (01334) 470214
Pro   J Kelly (01334) 470214
Holes   18 L 7271 yds Par 72 SSS 75
V'tors U H SOC
Fees   £55
Loc   3 miles S of St Andrews on
        Pitscottie road
Mis   Golf academy
Arch   Peter Thomson CBE

Eden Course (1914)
Public
*St Andrews Links Trust, Pilmour House,
St Andrews, KY16 9SF*
Tel   **(01334) 466666**
Fax   (01334) 479555
Web   www.standrews.org.uk
Sec   AJR McGregor (Gen Mgr)
Holes   18 L 6112 yds Par 70 SSS 70
V'tors U SOC
Fees   £22–£28
Loc   St Andrews Links, on A91
Mis   3D–£60–£90 W–£120–£190
        (unlimited play over Jubilee,
        New, Eden and Strathtyrum
        courses). Driving range
Arch   HS Colt

Jubilee Course (1897)
Public
*St Andrews Links Trust, Pilmour House,
St Andrews, KY16 9SF*
Tel   **(01334) 466666**
Fax   (01334) 479555

Web   www.standrews.org.uk
Sec   AJR McGregor (Gen Mgr)
Holes   18 L 6805 yds Par 72 SSS 73
V'tors U SOC
Fees   £28–£37
Loc   St Andrews Links, on A91.
        Signs to West Sands
Mis   3D–£60–£95 W–£120–£190
        (unlimited play over Jubilee,
        Strathtyrum, Eden & New
        courses). Driving range
Arch   Angus/Steel

New Course (1895)
Public
*St Andrews Links Trust, Pilmour House,
St Andrews, KY16 9SF*
Tel   **(01334) 466666**
Fax   (01334) 479555
Web   www.standrews.org.uk
Sec   AJR McGregor (Gen Mgr)
Holes   18 L 6604 yds Par 71 SSS 72
V'tors U H SOC
Fees   £31–£42
Loc   St Andrews Links, on A91.
        Signs to West Sands
Mis   3D–£60–£95 W–£120–£190
        (unlimited play over Jubilee,
        New, Eden and Strathtyrum
        courses). Driving range
Arch   Old Tom Morris

Old Course (15th Century)
Public
*St Andrews Links Trust, Pilmour House,
St Andrews, KY16 9SF*
Tel   **(01334) 466666**
Fax   (01334) 479555
Web   www.standrews.org.uk
Sec   AJR McGregor (Gen Mgr)
Holes   18 L 6566 yds Par 72 SSS 72
V'tors H I No Sun play
Fees   £60–£85
Loc   St Andrews Links, on A91.
        Signs to West Sands
Mis   Driving range

Strathtyrum Course (1993)
Public
*St Andrews Links Trust, Pilmour House,
St Andrews, KY16 9SF*
Tel   **(01334) 466666**
Fax   (01334) 479555
Web   www.standrews.org.uk
Sec   AJR McGregor (Gen Mgr)
Holes   18 L 5094 yds Par 69 SSS 64
V'tors U SOC
Fees   £16–£18
Loc   St Andrews Links, on A91
Mis   3D–£60–£95 W–£120–£190
        (unlimited play over Jubilee,
        New, Eden, Strathtyrum and
        Balgove courses). Driving
        range
Arch   Donald Steel

Glasgow

Alexandra Park (1880)
Public
*Alexandra Park, Dennistoun, Glasgow,
G31 8SE*
Tel   **(0141) 556 1294**
Mem   250
Sec   G Campbell
Holes   9 L 4562 yds Par 62
V'tors U
Fees   On application
Loc   ½ mile E of Glasgow, nr M8
Arch   Graham McArthur

Bishopbriggs (1907)
*Brackenbrae Road, Bishopbriggs,
Glasgow, G64 2DX*
Tel   **(0141) 772 1810**
Fax   (0141) 762 2532
Web   www.scottishholidays.net
Mem   400 150(L) 110(J)
Sec   A Smith (0141) 772 8938
Holes   18 L 6041 yds SSS 69
V'tors M or I H SOC
Fees   £20 D–£30
Loc   6 miles N of Glasgow on A803
Arch   James Braid

Cathcart Castle (1895)
Mearns Road, Clarkston, G76 7YL
Tel   **(0141) 638 0082**
Fax   (0141) 638 1201
Mem   950
Sec   IG Sutherland (0141) 638
        9449
Pro   S Duncan (0141) 638 3436
Holes   18 L 5832 yds SSS 68
V'tors M SOC
Fees   £28 D–£40
Loc   1 mile from Clarkston on
        B767

Cawder (1933)
*Cadder Road, Bishopbriggs, Glasgow,
G64 3QD*
Tel   **(0141) 761 1281**
Fax   (0141) 761 1285
Web   www.cawdergolfclub.org.uk
Mem   1400
Sec   HF Tees (0141) 761 1282
Pro   K Stevely (0141) 772 7102
Holes   Cawder 18 L 6279 yds
        SSS 71;
        Keir 18 L 5880 yds SSS 68
V'tors WD–U SOC–WD
Fees   £30
Loc   N of Glasgow, off A803
        Kirkintilloch Road
Arch   Braid/Steel

Cowglen (1906)
*301 Barrhead Road, Glasgow,
G43 1EU*
Tel   **(0141) 632 0556**
Mem   485
Sec   RJG Jamieson
        (01505) 503000
Pro   S Payne (0141) 649 9401

For list of abbreviations see page 649

Holes 18 L 6079 yds SSS 69
V'tors WD–by arrangement with Sec
WE–M
Fees £25.50 D–£35
Loc 3 miles SW of Glasgow
(B762)
Arch James Braid

Glasgow (1787)

Killermont, Bearsden, Glasgow,
G61 2TW
Tel **(0141) 942 1713**
Fax (0141) 942 0770
Mem 800
Sec DW Deas (0141) 942 2011
Pro J Steven (0141) 942 8507
Holes 18 L 5977 yds Par 70 SSS 69
V'tors M
Loc 4 miles NW of Glasgow
Arch Tom Morris Sr

Haggs Castle (1910)

70 Dumbreck Road, Dumbreck,
Glasgow, G41 4SN
Tel **(0141) 427 0480**
Fax (0141) 427 1157
Mem 877
Sec A Williams (0141) 427 1157
Pro J McAlister (0141) 427 3355
Holes 18 L 6419 yds SSS 71
V'tors M SOC–Weds only
Fees SOC–£35
Loc SW Glasgow (B768). M77
Junction 1
Arch Dave Thomas (1998)

King's Park (1934)

Public
150A Croftpark Avenue, Croftfoot,
Glasgow, G54
Tel **(0141) 630 1597**
Sec PJ King
Holes 9 L 4236 yds Par 64 SSS 60
V'tors U
Fees On application
Loc Croftfoot, 3¹/₂ miles S of
Glasgow

Knightswood (1929)

Public
Knightswood Park, Lincoln Avenue,
Glasgow, G13 3DN
Tel **(0141) 959 6358**
Mem 50
Sec J Dean (0141) 954 6495
Pro None
Holes 9 L 2793 yds Par 68 SSS 67
V'tors U exc Wed & Fri before 9am
and 10–11am–NA
Fees £7.40 (£7.40)
Loc 4 miles NW of Glasgow, S of
A82

Lethamhill (1933)

Public
Cumbernauld Road, Glasgow,
G33 1AH
Tel **(0141) 770 6220**
Fax (0141) 770 0520

Holes 18 L 5946 yds SSS 68
V'tors U
Fees £7.20
Loc 3 miles NE of Glasgow (A80)

Linn Park (1924)

Public
Simshill Road, Glasgow, G44 5TA
Tel **(0141) 633 0377**
Holes 18 L 4592 yds SSS 65
V'tors U–phone 1 day in advance
Fees £7.30 (£7.30)
Loc 4 miles S of Glasgow, W of
B766

Littlehill (1926)

Public
Auchinairn Road, Glasgow, G64 1UT
Tel **(0141) 772 1916**
Holes 18 L 6228 yds SSS 70
V'tors U
Fees On application
Loc 3 miles NE of Glasgow, E of
A803

Pollok (1892)

90 Barrhead Road, Glasgow, G43 1BG
Tel **(0141) 632 1080**
Fax (0141) 649 1398
Mem 500
Sec I Cumming (0141) 632 4351
Pro None
Holes 18 L 6358 yds SSS 70
V'tors WD–I XL WE–NA SOC–WD
Fees £32 D–£42 (£40)
Loc 3 miles SW of Glasgow
(B762). M77 Junction 2

Ralston (1903)

Strathmore Avenue, Ralston, Paisley,
PA1 3DT
Tel **(0141) 882 1349**
Fax (0141) 883 9837
Mem 440 165(L) 100(J)
Sec J Pearson
Pro C Munro (0141) 810 4925
Holes 18 L 6100 yds SSS 69
V'tors M SOC
Loc 2 miles E of Paisley (A761)

Rouken Glen (1922)

Public
Stewarton Road, Thornliebank,
Glasgow, G46 7UZ
Tel **(0141) 638 7044**
Holes 18 L 4800 yds SSS 63
V'tors U SOC
Fees On application
Loc 5 miles S of Glasgow, W of
A77
Mis Driving range

Ruchill (1928)

Public
Ruchil Park, Brassey Street, Maryhill,
Glasgow G20
Mem 60
Holes 9 L 2240 yds SSS 31

V'tors U
Fees On application
Loc 2 miles N of Glasgow, W of
A879

Sandyhills (1905)

223 Sandyhills Road, Glasgow,
G32 9NA
Tel **(0141) 778 1179**
Mem 700
Sec CJ Wilson
Holes 18 L 6253 yds SSS 71
V'tors M SOC
Fees £17.50
Loc 4 miles SE of Glasgow, N of
A74

Williamwood (1906)

Clarkston Road, Netherlee, Glasgow,
G44 3YR
Tel **(0141) 637 1783**
Fax (0141) 571 0166
Mem 911
Sec TDM Hepburn
Pro S Marshall (0141) 637 2715
Holes 18 L 5878 yds SSS 69
V'tors WD–H
Fees £27
Loc 5 miles S of Glasgow
Arch James Braid

Highland

Caithness & Sutherland

Bonar Bridge/Ardgay (1904)

Bonar-Bridge, Ardgay, IV24 3EJ
Tel **(01863) 766199**
Web www.bonarbridgegolfclub
.co.uk
Mem 250
Sec J Reid (01863) 766750
Holes 9 L 5284 yds SSS 66
V'tors U
Fees D–£12 (£12)
Loc ¹/₂ mile N of Bonar-Bridge
on A836. 12 miles W of
Dornoch

Brora (1891)

Golf Road, Brora, KW9 6QS
Tel **(01408) 621417/621911**
Fax (01408) 622157
Web www.highlandescape.com
Sec J Fraser
Holes 18 L 6110 yds SSS 69
V'tors U exc comp days –H for open
comps SOC
Fees £25 D–£35 (£30 D–£40)
Loc 18 miles N of Dornoch (A9)
Arch James Braid

The Carnegie Club (1995)
Skibo Castle, Clashmore, Dornoch, IV25 3RQ
Tel	**(01862) 894600**
Fax	(01862) 894601
Sec	A Grant
Pro	D Thomson
Holes	18 L 6671 yds Par 71 SSS 72
V'tors	H–booking required
Fees	£130 inc lunch
Loc	3 miles SW of Dornoch
Arch	Donald Steel

Durness (1988)
Pay and play
Balnakeil, Durness, IV27 4PN
Tel	**(01971) 511364**
Mem	120
Sec	Mrs L Mackay
	(01971) 511364
Holes	9 L 5555 yds SSS 69
V'tors	U
Fees	D–£15 W–£50
Loc	57 miles NW of Lairg on A838

Golspie (1889)
Ferry Road, Golspie, KW10 6ST
Tel	**(01408) 633266**
Fax	(01408) 633393
Web	www.golspie-golf-club.co.uk
Mem	315
Sec	Mrs M MacLeod
Pro	None
Holes	18 L 5890 yds SSS 68
V'tors	U SOC
Fees	£20 D–£25
Loc	11 miles N of Dornoch
Arch	James Braid

Helmsdale (1895)
Golf Road, Helmsdale, KW8 6JA
Mem	50
Sec	R Sutherland
Holes	9 L 3720 yds SSS 61
V'tors	U
Fees	£5 D–£10 W–£25
Loc	30 miles N of Dornoch (A9)

Lybster (1926)
Main Street, Lybster, KW1 6BL
Mem	100
Sec	AD Mackay
Holes	9 L 1896 yds SSS 61
V'tors	U
Fees	D–£8 (£D–£8)
Loc	13 miles S of Wick on A99

Reay (1893)
Reay, Thurso, Caithness, KW14 7RE
Tel	**(01847) 811288**
Fax	(01847) 894189
Web	www.reaygolfclub.co.uk
Mem	345
Sec	W McIntosh (01847) 894189
Pro	None
Holes	18 L 5831 yds Par 69 SSS 69
V'tors	U SOC
Fees	D–£20 W–£60

Loc	11 miles W of Thurso
Arch	James Braid

Royal Dornoch (1877)
Golf Road, Dornoch, IV25 3LW
Tel	**(01862) 810219**
Fax	(01862) 810792
Web	www.royaldornoch.com
Mem	1127 220(L) 72(J)
Sec	JS Duncan (Sec/Mgr)
	(01862) 811220
Pro	A Skinner (01862) 810902
Holes	C'ship 18 L 6514 yds SSS 73
	Struie 18 L 5438 yds SSS 66
V'tors	H
Fees	On application
Loc	45 miles N of Inverness, off A9, N of Dornoch
Mis	Helipad by clubhouse. Airstrip nearby

Thurso (1893)
Newlands of Geise, Thurso, KW14 7XD
Tel	**(01847) 893807**
Mem	300
Sec	Capt D Phillips
	(01847) 895433
Holes	18 L 5828 yds SSS 69
V'tors	U
Fees	£11
Loc	2 miles SW of Thurso

Wick (1870)
Reiss, Wick, KW1 5LJ
Tel	**(01955) 602726**
Web	www.wickgolfclub.fsnet.co.uk
Mem	311
Sec	D Shearer (01955) 602935
Holes	18 L 5976 yds SSS 70
V'tors	U
Fees	On application
Loc	3 miles N of Wick on A99

Inverness

Abernethy (1893)
Nethy Bridge, PH25 3EB
Tel	**(01479) 821305**
Fax	(01479) 821305
Web	www.nethybridge.com
Mem	450
Sec	RH Robbie
Holes	9 L 2520 yds SSS 66
V'tors	U SOC
Fees	£13 (£16)
Loc	5 miles S of Grantown (B970)

Alness (1904)
Ardross Rd, Alness, Ross-shire, IV17 0QA
Tel	**(01349) 883877**
Web	www.alness.com
Mem	300
Sec	Mrs M Rogers
Holes	18 L 4886 yds Par 67 SSS 64

V'tors	U SOC
Fees	£13 (£15)
Loc	¼ mile N of Alness. 23 miles N of Inverness
Arch	I Scott Taylor (New holes)

Boat-of-Garten (1898)
Boat-of-Garten, PH24 3BQ
Tel	**(01479) 831282**
Fax	(01479) 831523
Web	www.boatgolf.com
Mem	650
Sec	P Smyth
Holes	18 L 5866 yds SSS 69
V'tors	U–booking advisable
Fees	£25 D–£30 (£30 D–£35)
Loc	27 miles SE of Inverness (A95)
Arch	James Braid

Carrbridge (1980)
Carrbridge, PH23 3AU
Tel	**(01479) 841623 (Clubhouse)**
Web	www.carrbridgegolf.com
Mem	600
Sec	Mrs AT Baird
Holes	9 L 2623 yds Par 71 SSS 68
V'tors	U exc comp days–NA
Fees	D–£13 (D–£15)
Loc	23 miles SE of Inverness, off A9

Fort Augustus (1926)
Pay and play
Markethill, Fort Augustus, PH32 4AU
Mem	110
Sec	H Fraser (01320) 366309
Holes	9 L 5454 yds SSS 67
V'tors	U
Fees	D–£10
Loc	W end of Fort Augustus on A82

Fort William (1974)
North Road, Fort William, PH33 6SN
Tel	**(01397) 704464**
Mem	430
Sec	R Macintyre
Holes	18 L 5686 metres SSS 71
V'tors	U
Fees	£17
Loc	3 miles N of Fort William (A82)
Arch	JR Stutt

Fortrose & Rosemarkie (1888)
Ness Road East, Fortrose, IV10 8SE
Tel	**(01381) 620529**
Fax	(01381) 621328
Web	www.fortrosegolfclub.co.uk
Mem	750
Sec	Mrs M Collier
Holes	18 L 5885 yds Par 72 SSS 69
V'tors	U SOC
Fees	£21 (£26)
Loc	Black Isle, 12 miles N of Inverness
Arch	James Braid

For list of abbreviations see page 649

Grantown-on-Spey (1890)

Golf Course Road, Grantown-on-Spey,
PH26 3HY

Tel	**(01479) 872079**
Fax	(01479) 873725
Web	www.grantownonspeygolfclub .co.uk
Mem	800
Sec	JS Macpherson
Holes	18 L 5710 yds Par 70 SSS 68
V'tors	WD–U WE–U after 10am SOC
Fees	D–£20 (D–£25)
Loc	E side of Grantown (A95)
Arch	Willie Park

Invergordon (1893)

King George Street, Invergordon,
IV18 0BD

Tel	**(01349) 852715**
Mem	170 30(L) 50(J)
Holes	18 L 6030 yds Par 69 SSS 69
V'tors	U SOC
Fees	£15 (£15)
Loc	15 miles NE of Dingwall (A9/B817)
Arch	A Rae (1994)

Inverness (1883)

Culcabock Road, Inverness, IV2 3XQ

Tel	**(01463) 239882**
Fax	(01463) 239882
Web	www.invernessgolfclub.co.uk
Mem	1100
Sec	JS Thomson
Pro	AP Thomson (01463) 231989
Holes	18 L 6226 yds SSS 70
V'tors	WE/BH–restricted SOC
Fees	£29 D–£39 (£29 D–£39)
Loc	1 mile S of Inverness
Arch	James Braid

Kingussie (1891)

Gynack Road, Kingussie, PH21 1LR

Tel	**(01540) 661374 (Clubhouse)**
Fax	(01540) 662066
Web	www.kingussie-golf.co.uk
Mem	800
Sec	ND MacWilliam (01540) 661600
Pro	None
Holes	18 L 5555 yds SSS 68
V'tors	U
Fees	£18 D–£20 (£20 D–£25)
Loc	Kingussie (A9)
Arch	H Vardon

Loch Ness (1996)

Castle Heather, Inverness, IV2 6AA

Tel	**(01463) 713334/5**
Fax	(01463) 712695
Web	www.golflochness.com
Mem	600
Sec	ND Hampton (01463) 713335
Pro	M Piggot (01463) 713334
Holes	18 L 6772 yds Par 73 SSS 72
V'tors	U SOC
Fees	D–£25 (D–£30)
Loc	Culduthel, SW Inverness (A9)
Mis	Floodlit driving range

Muir of Ord (1875)

Great North Road, Muir of Ord,
IV6 7SX

Tel	**(01463) 870825**
Fax	(01463) 871867
Mem	700
Sec	Mrs J Gibson
Pro	Shop (01463) 871311
Holes	18 L 5557 yds SSS 68
V'tors	U SOC
Fees	D–£16 (£20) W–£50
Loc	15 miles N of Inverness (A862)
Arch	James Braid

Nairn (1887)

Seabank Road, Nairn, IV12 4HB

Tel	**(01667) 452103**
Fax	(01667) 456328
Web	www.nairngolfclub.co.uk
Mem	1100
Sec	J Somerville (01667) 453208
Pro	R Fyfe (01667) 452787
Holes	18 L 6705 yds Par 72 SSS 74 9 hole course
V'tors	U SOC
Fees	On application
Loc	Nairn West Shore (A96). 15 miles E of Inverness
Arch	Old Tom Morris/Braid/ Simpson

Nairn Dunbar (1899)

Lochloy Road, Nairn, IV12 5AE

Tel	**(01667) 452741**
Fax	(01667) 456897
Web	www.nairndunbar.com
Mem	900
Sec	JS Falconer
Pro	DH Torrance (01667) 453964
Holes	18 L 6720 yds SSS 73
V'tors	U
Fees	£33 D–£42 (£40 D–£53)
Loc	In Nairn

Newtonmore (1893)

Golf Course Road, Newtonmore,
PH20 1AT

Tel	**(01540) 673328**
Fax	(01540) 673878
Web	www.newtonmore.com/ golfclub
Mem	450
Sec	G Spinks
Pro	R Henderson (01540) 673611
Holes	18 L 6029 yds SSS 69
V'tors	U SOC
Fees	£15 D–£18 (£17 D–£23)
Loc	4 miles W of Kingussie. 46 miles S of Inverness

Spean Bridge

Spean Bridge, Fort William, PH33

Mem	65
Sec	AJ McLaren (Pres) (01397) 704954
Holes	9 hole course SSS 62
V'tors	U
Fees	On application
Loc	9 miles N of Fort William on A82

Strathpeffer Spa (1888)

Golf Course Road, Strathpeffer,
IV14 9AS

Tel	**(01997) 421011/421219**
Fax	(01997) 421011
Web	www.strathpeffergolf.co.uk
Mem	360 50(L) 85(J)
Sec	N Roxburgh (01997) 421396
Pro	G Lister (01997) 421011
Holes	18 L 4792 yds SSS 64
V'tors	U SOC
Fees	£15 D–£21
Loc	1/4 mile N of Strathpeffer. 5 miles W of Dingwall
Arch	Willie Park/Tom Morris

Tain (1890)

Chapel Road, Tain, IV19 1JE

Tel	**(01862) 892314**
Fax	(01862) 892099
Web	www.tain-golfclub.co.uk
Mem	500
Sec	Mrs KD Ross
Pro	None
Holes	18 L 6404 yds SSS 71
V'tors	U
Fees	£30 D–£36 (£36 D–£46)
Loc	35 miles N of Inverness (A9). 8 miles S of Dornoch
Arch	Tom Morris

Tarbat (1909)

Portmahomack, Tain, IV20 1YB

Tel	**(01862) 871598**
Fax	(01862) 871598
Mem	200
Sec	M Lane
Holes	9 L 2568 yds SSS 65
V'tors	U SOC
Fees	D–£12
Loc	10 miles E of Tain

Torvean (1962)

Public

Glenurquhart Road, Inverness, IV3 6JN

Tel	**(01463) 711434 (Starter)**
Fax	(01463) 225651 (Sec)
Mem	400
Sec	Mrs KM Gray (01463) 225651
Pro	None
Holes	18 L 5784 yds SSS 68
V'tors	U
Fees	£12.90 (£14.80)
Loc	SW of Inverness on A82

Orkney & Shetland

Orkney (1889)

Grainbank, Kirkwall, Orkney,
KW15 1RD

Tel	**(01856) 872457**
Fax	(01856) 872457
Web	www.orkneygc.co.uk
Mem	415
Sec	GR Donaldson (01856) 877533
Holes	18 L 5411 yds SSS 67

V'tors U
Fees D–£15 W–£50
Loc 1 mile W of Kirkwall

Sanday (1977)
Sanday, Orkney, KW17 2BW
Tel (01857) 600341
Fax (01857) 600341
Mem 20
Sec R Thorne
Holes 9 L 2776 yds Par 35
V'tors U
Fees £10
Loc 2 miles N of Lady on B9069

Shetland (1891)
Dale, Gott, Shetland, ZE2 9SB
Tel (01595) 840369
Fax (01595) 840369
Web www.shetlandgolfclub.co.uk
Mem 400
Sec C Lobban (Mgr)
Holes 18 L 5776 yds SSS 68
V'tors U
Fees D–£15
Loc 3 miles N of Lerwick (A907)
Arch Fraser Middleton

Stromness (1890)
Stromness, Orkney, KW16 3DU
Tel (01856) 850772
Web www.stromnessgc.co.uk
Mem 250
Sec GA Bevan (01856) 850885
Holes 18 L 4762 yds SSS 63
V'tors U
Fees D–£15
Loc Stromness, 16 miles W of
Kirkwall on Hoy Sound

Whalsay (1976)
Skaw Taing, Whalsay, Shetland,
ZE2 9AL
Tel (01806) 566373/566450
Mem 100
Sec RP Irvine
Pro None
Holes 18 L 6009 yds Par 70 SSS 68
V'tors U SOC
Fees £10
Loc 5 miles N of Symbister Ferry

West Coast

Askernish (1891)
Lochboisdale, Askernish, South Uist,
HS81 5ST
Tel (01878) 700298
Mem 50
Sec N Elliott
Holes 18 L 5114 yds SSS 67
V'tors U
Fees £10
Loc 5 miles NW of Lochboisdale
Arch Tom Morris Sr

Barra
Cleat, Castlebay, Isle of Barra,
HS9 5XX
Tel (01871) 810591
Fax (01871) 810418
Holes 9 L 2396 yds
V'tors U
Fees D–£5
Loc 6 miles N of Castlebay

Gairloch (1898)
Gairloch, IV21 2BQ
Tel (01445) 712407
Mem 285
Sec A Shinkins
Holes 9 L 2281 yds SSS 64
V'tors U
Fees D–£15 W–£49
Loc 60 miles W of Dingwall in
Wester Ross

Isle of Harris
Scarista, Isle of Harris HS5 3HX
Tel (01859) 502331
Mem 72
Sec A Macsween
Pro None
Holes 9 L 2442 yds Par 68 SSS 64
V'tors U
Fees £10 (£10)
Loc 13 miles S of Tarbert on W
coast

Isle of Skye (1964)
Sconser, Isle of Skye, IV48 8TD
Tel (01478) 650414
Mem 250
Sec I Macmillan
Holes 9 L 4798 yds Par 66 SSS 64
V'tors U
Fees D–£15
Loc Between Broadford and
Sligachan

Lochcarron (1908)
Lochcarron, Strathcarron, IV54 8YU
Mem 132
Sec AG Beattie
(01520) 766211
Holes 9 L 3578 yds Par 62 SSS 60
V'tors U exc Sat 2–5pm–NA
Fees D–£10 W–£40
Loc ½ mile E of Lochcarron in
Wester Ross

Skeabost (1982)
Skeabost Bridge, Isle of Skye, IV5 9NP
Tel (01470) 532202
Fax (01470) 532454
Mem 80
Sec DJ Matheson
(01470) 532319 (Skeabost
House Hotel)
Holes 9 L 3224 yds SSS 59
V'tors U
Fees D–£10
Loc 6 miles NW of Portree on
Dunvegan road

Stornoway (1890)
Lady Lever Park, Stornoway, Isle of
Lewis, HS2 0XP
Tel (01851) 702240
Web www.stornawaygolfclub.co.uk
Mem 400
Sec JDF Watson
Holes 18 L 5252 yds Par 68 SSS 67
V'tors U exc Sun–NA SOC
Fees D–£15 W–£45
Loc Off A857 in Lews Castle, Isle
of Lewis

Traigh
c/o Camusdarach, Arisaig, PH39 4NT
Tel (01687) 450337
Mem 160
Sec H MacDougall
(01687) 450628
Pro None
Holes 9 L 2405 yds Par 68 SSS 65
V'tors U
Fees £12 (£12)
Loc 2 miles N of Arisaig on A830
Fort William-Mallaig road
Arch John Salvesen

Lanarkshire

Airdrie (1877)
Rochsoles, Airdrie, ML6 0PQ
Tel (01236) 762195
Mem 450
Sec DM Hardie
Pro G Monks (01236) 754360
Holes 18 L 6004 yds SSS 69
V'tors M I WE/BH–NA SOC
Fees £15 D–£25
Loc Airdrie 1 mile
Arch James Braid

Bellshill (1905)
Community Road, Orbiston, Bellshill,
ML4 2RZ
Tel (01698) 745124
Mem 680
Sec J Sloan
Holes 18 L 5900 yds Par 69 SSS 69
V'tors WD–U Sun–NA before
1.30pm SOC
Fees D–£20 (£30)
Loc 30 miles W (A725) M74
Junction 5

Biggar (1895)
Public
The Park, Broughton Road, Biggar,
ML12 6AH
Tel (01899) 220618 (Clubhouse),
(01899) 220319 (Bookings)
Mem 180
Sec T Rodger (01698) 382311
Pro None
Holes 18 L 5537 yds SSS 67
V'tors U–booking recommended
Fees £10 (£12)
Loc 12 miles SE of Lanark (A702)
Arch Willie Park

Blairbeth (1910)

Burnside, Rutherglen, Glasgow,
G73 4SF

Tel	**(0141) 634 3355 (Clubhouse),**
	(0141) 634 3325 (Office)
Mem	450
Sec	FT Henderson
	(0141) 569 7266
Holes	18 L 5518 yds SSS 68
V'tors	SOC–WD
Fees	On application
Loc	1 mile S of Rutherglen

Bothwell Castle (1922)

Blantyre Road, Bothwell, Glasgow,
G71 8PJ

Tel	**(01698) 853177**
Fax	(01698) 854052
Mem	1000
Sec	DA McNaught
	(01698) 854052
Pro	A McCloskey (01698) 852052
Holes	18 L 6225 yds SSS 70
V'tors	WD–U 9.30–10.30am &
	2.30–3.30pm
Fees	£24 D–£32
Loc	2 miles N of Hamilton. M74
	Junction 5

Calderbraes (1891)

57 Roundknowe Road, Uddingston,
G71 7TS

Tel	**(01698) 813425**
Mem	300
Sec	S McGuigan (0141) 773 2287
Holes	9 L 5046 yds Par 66 SSS 67
V'tors	WD–U WE–M
Fees	D–£18
Loc	Start of M74

Cambuslang (1892)

30 Westburn Drive, Cambuslang,
G72 7NA

Tel	**(0141) 641 3130**
Mem	200 100(L) 75(J)
Sec	RM Dunlop
Holes	9 L 5942 yds SSS 69
V'tors	M
Fees	On application
Loc	Cambuslang Station ¼ mile

Carluke (1894)

Hallcraig, Mauldslie Road, Carluke,
ML8 5HG

Tel	**(01555) 771070/770574**
Fax	(01555) 770574
Mem	460 100(L)
Sec	T Pheely (01555) 770574
Pro	R Forrest (01555) 751053
Holes	18 L 5805 yds SSS 68
V'tors	WD–U before 4pm
	WE/BH–NA SOC
Fees	£20 D–£25
Loc	20 miles SE of Glasgow

Carnwath (1907)

1 Main Street, Carnwath, ML11 8JX

Tel	**(01555) 840251**
Fax	(01555) 841070

Mem	400
Sec	Mrs L McPate
Pro	None
Holes	18 L 5955 yds SSS 69
V'tors	WD–U before 4pm Sat–NA
	Sun–restricted
Fees	£15 D–£25 Sun–£20 D–£30
Loc	7 miles E of Lanark

Cathkin Braes (1888)

Cathkin Road, Rutherglen, Glasgow,
G73 4SE

Tel	**(0141) 634 6605**
Fax	(0141) 630 9186
Mem	930
Sec	H Millar
Pro	S Bree (0141) 634 0650
Holes	18 L 6208 yds SSS 71
V'tors	WD–I
Fees	£25
Loc	5 miles S of Glasgow (B759)
Arch	James Braid

Coatbridge Municipal (1971)

Public

Townhead Road, Coatbridge,
ML52 2HX

Tel	**(01236) 28975**
Holes	18 L 6020 yds SSS 69
V'tors	U
Fees	On application
Loc	Townhead, E of Glasgow.
	½ mile E of M73
Mis	Driving range

Colville Park (1923)

Jerviston Estate, Motherwell, ML1 4UG

Tel	**(01698) 263017**
Fax	(01698) 230418
Mem	900 64(L) 140(J)
Sec	L Innes (01698) 262808
Pro	J Currie (01698) 265779
Holes	18 L 6301 yds Par 71 SSS 70
V'tors	WD–U 11am–3pm exc
	Fri–NA WE–NA SOC–WD
Fees	£15 D–£25
Loc	1 mile NE of Motherwell on
	A723
Arch	James Braid

Crow Wood (1925)

Cumbernauld Road, Muirhead,
Glasgow, G69 9JF

Tel	**(0141) 799 2011**
Fax	(0141) 779 9148
Mem	700
Sec	I McInnes (0141) 779 4954
Pro	B Moffat (0141) 779 1943
Holes	18 L 6261 yds Par 71 SSS 71
V'tors	WD–H (prior notice required)
	SOC
Fees	£23 D–£34
Loc	5 miles NE of Glasgow, off
	A80
Arch	James Braid

Dalziel Park (1997)

100 Hagen Drive, Motherwell,
ML1 5RZ

Tel	**(01698) 862862**

Fax	(01698) 862863
Mem	400
Sec	I Donnachie
Pro	None
Holes	18 L 6137 yds Par 70
V'tors	WD–U SOC
Fees	£20
Loc	5 miles E of Motherwell via
	A723 and B7029
Mis	Driving range
Arch	Nigel Williams

Douglas Water (1922)

Rigside, Lanark, ML11 9NB

Tel	**(01555) 880361**
Mem	190
Sec	D Hogg
Holes	9 L 2916 yds SSS 69
V'tors	U exc Sat–restricted
Fees	£8 (£10)
Loc	7 miles S of Lanark. M74
	Junctions 11 & 12

Drumpellier (1894)

Drumpellier Ave, Coatbridge,
ML5 1RX

Tel	**(01236) 424139/428723**
Fax	(01236) 428723
Web	www.drumpellier.com
Mem	500
Sec	JM Craig
Pro	D Ross (01236) 432971
Holes	18 L 6227 yds SSS 70
V'tors	I
Fees	£25 D–£35
Loc	8 miles E of Glasgow
Arch	James Braid

East Kilbride (1900)

Chapelside Road, Nerston, East
Kilbride, G74 4PF

Tel	**(01355) 220913 (Clubhouse)**
Mem	834
Sec	WG Gray (01355) 247728
Pro	W Walker (01355) 222192
Holes	18 L 6402 yds SSS 71
V'tors	M SOC
Fees	£25 D–£35
Loc	8 miles S of Glasgow

Easter Moffat (1922)

Mansion House, Plains, Airdrie,
ML6 8NP

Tel	**(01236) 842878**
Fax	(01236) 842904
Mem	450
Sec	JG Timmons (01236) 761440
Pro	G King (01236) 843015
Holes	18 L 6221 yds SSS 70
V'tors	WD only BH–NA
Fees	On application
Loc	3 miles E of Airdrie

Hamilton (1892)

Riccarton, Ferniegair, Hamilton,
ML3 7UE

Tel	**(01698) 282872**
Mem	500
Sec	GM Chapman
	(01698) 459537

Pro   MJ Moir (01698) 282324
Holes 18 L 6255 yds SSS 71
V'tors M or by arrangement with Sec
Fees   On application
Loc   1¹/₂ miles S of Hamilton
Arch   James Braid

Hollandbush (1954)

Public
*Acre Tophead, Lesmahagow, Coalburn,
ML11 0JS*
Tel   (01555) 893484
Mem   420
Sec   R Lynch
Pro   I Rae (01555) 893646
Holes 18 L 6246 yds SSS 70
V'tors U
Fees   £8.20 (9.50)
Loc   10 miles SW of Lanark, off
        A74, between Lesmahagow
        and Coalburn

Kirkhill (1910)

*Greenlees Road, Cambuslang, Glasgow,
G72 8YN*
Tel   (0141) 641 3083
        (Clubhouse)
Fax   (0141) 641 8499
Mem   570
Sec   J Young (0141) 641 8499
Pro   D Williamson (0141) 641
        7972
Holes 18 L 6030 yds SSS 70
V'tors WD–by prior arrangement
        WE/BH–NA SOC
Fees   On application
Loc   Cambuslang, SE Glasgow
Arch   James Braid

Lanark (1851)

The Moor, Lanark, ML11 7RX
Tel   (01555) 663219
Fax   (01555) 663219
Mem   520 130(L) 150(J)
Sec   GH Cuthill
Pro   A White (01555) 661456
Holes 18 L 6426 yds SSS 71
        9 hole course
V'tors WD–U until 4pm WE–M
Fees   18 hole:£26 D–£40
        9 hole:£6
Loc   30 miles S of Glasgow, off
        A74
Arch   Tom Morris

Langlands (1985)

Public
*Langlands Road, East Kilbride,
G75 0QQ*
Tel   (01355) 248173,
        (01355) 224685 (Starter)
Fax   (01355) 248121
Mem   350
Sec   A Craik (01355) 248401
Holes 18 L 6201 yds Par 70 SSS 70
V'tors U
Fees   £8.70 (£10.10)
Loc   2 miles SE of East Kilbride, off
        Strathaven Road
Arch   F Hawtree

Larkhall

Public
Burnhead Road, Larkhall, Glasgow
Tel   (01698) 881113
Mem   150
Sec   M Mallinson
Holes 9 L 6234 yds SSS 70
V'tors U exc Tues 5–8pm & Sat
        7am–5pm
Fees   On application
Loc   SW of Larkhall on B7109.
        10 miles SE of Glasgow

Leadhills (1935)

Leadhills, Biggar, ML12 6XR
Tel   (01659) 74456
Mem   100
Sec   H Shaw
Holes 9 L 2177 yds SSS 64
V'tors U
Fees   D–£5 (£5)
Loc   6 miles S of Abington, off A74

Mount Ellen (1905)

*Lochend Road, Gartcosh, Glasgow,
G69 9EY*
Tel   (01236) 872277
Fax   (01236) 872249
Mem   480
Sec   WJ Dickson
Pro   G Reilly
Holes 18 L 5525 yds SSS 68
V'tors WD–U from 9am–4pm
        WE–NA
Fees   On application
Loc   8 miles NE of Glasgow, W of
        M73

Mouse Valley (1993)

*East End, Cleghorn, Lanark,
ML11 8NR*
Tel   (01555) 870015
Fax   (01555) 870022
Mem   300
Holes 18 L 6300 yds SSS 72
        9 L 2200 yds SSS 65
V'tors U
Fees   18 hole:£12.50 (£15)
        9 hole:£7 (£8)
Loc   2 miles W of Carnwath on
        A721
Arch   Graham Taylor

Shotts (1895)

*Blairhead, Benhar Road, Shotts,
ML7 5BJ*
Tel   (01501) 820431
Mem   700
Sec   GT Stoddart
        (01501) 825868
Pro   J Strachan (01501) 822658
Holes 18 L 6205 yds SSS 70
V'tors WD–U Sat–NA before 4.30pm
Fees   £16 (£22)
Loc   18 miles E of Glasgow on
        B7057. M8 Junction 5,
        1¹/₂ miles
Arch   James Braid

Strathaven (1908)

Glasgow Road, Strathaven, ML10 6NL
Tel   (01357) 520421
Fax   (01357) 520539
Mem   1000
Sec   AW Wallace
Pro   M McCrorie (01357) 521812
Holes 18 L 6226 yds SSS 71
V'tors WD–I before 4pm WE–NA
Fees   On application
Loc   N of Strathaven, off Glasgow
        road (A726)

Strathclyde Park

Public
Mote Hill, Hamilton, ML3 6BY
Tel   (01698) 429350
Mem   200
Sec   K Will
Pro   W Walker (01698) 285511
Holes 9 L 6350 yds SSS 70
V'tors U exc medal days (phone
        booking)
Fees   £3.30 (£3.90)
Loc   Hamilton. M74 Junction 5
Mis   Driving range

Torrance House (1969)

Public
*Strathaven Road, East Kilbride,
Glasgow, G75 0QZ*
Tel   (01355) 248638
Mem   650
Sec   JB Asher (01355) 249720
Pro   J Dunlop (013552) 33451
Holes 18 L 6415 yds SSS 71
V'tors U
Fees   £16
Loc   S of East Kilbride, off
        Strathaven road (A726)

Wishaw (1897)

55 Cleland Road, Wishaw, ML2 7PH
Tel   (01698) 372869 (Clubhouse)
Fax   (01698) 357480
Mem   475 100(L)
Sec   CR Innes (01698) 357480
Pro   S Adair (01698) 358247
Holes 18 L 5999 yds SSS 69
V'tors WD after 4pm–NA Sat–NA
Fees   £15 D–£25 Sun–£20 D–£30
        SOC
Loc   N of Wishaw town centre

Lothians

East Lothian

Aberlady (1912)

Club
Aberlady, EH32 0RR
Mem   43
Sec   I Thompson (01875) 870025
Holes Play over Kilspindie course

Bass Rock (1873)

Club
22 Smileyknowes Court, North Berwick, EH39 4RG
Mem 110
Sec A Thorburn (01620) 893391
Holes Play over North Berwick

Castle Park (1994)

Pay and play
Gifford, Haddington, EH41 4PL
Tel (01620) 810723
Fax (01620) 810723
Web www.castleparkgolfclub.co.uk
Mem 300
Sec S Fortune (01620) 810733
Pro D Small (01368) 862872
Holes 9 L 5810 yds Par 70 SSS 68
V'tors U SOC
Fees £12 D–£18 (£14 D–£22)
Loc 2 miles S of Gifford on Longyester road
Mis Driving range

Dirleton Castle (1854)

Club
15 The Pines, Gullane, EH31 2DT
Tel (01620) 843591
Mem 100
Sec J Taylor
Holes Play over Gullane courses

Dunbar (1856)

East Links, Dunbar, EH42 1LL
Tel (01368) 862317
Fax (01368) 865202
Mem 998
Sec Liz Thom
Pro J Montgomery (01368) 862086
Holes 18 L 6404 yds SSS 71
V'tors U SOC–exc Thurs
Fees £30 D–£40 (£35 D–£45)
Loc ½ mile E of Dunbar. 30 miles E of Edinburgh, off A1
Arch Tom Morris

Gifford (1904)

Edinburgh Road, Gifford, EH41 4JE
Tel (01620) 810591 (Starter)
Mem 570
Sec G MacColl (01620) 810267
Holes 9 L 6256 yds SSS 70
V'tors Booking required
Fees £13–£20
Loc 4 miles S of Haddington. 20 miles SE of Edinburgh (B6355)
Arch Willie Watt

The Glen (1906)

East Links, Tantallon Terrace, North Berwick, EH39 4LE
Tel (01620) 892726
Fax (01620) 895447
Web www.glengolfclub.co.uk
Mem 650
Sec K Fish
Pro Shop (01620) 894596

Holes 18 L 6094 yds SSS 69
V'tors U–booking recommended
Fees £20 D–£30 (£27 D–£38)
Loc 25 miles E of Edinburgh, off A198
Arch Braid/Sayers/Mackenzie Ross

Gullane (1882)

Gullane, EH31 2BB
Tel (01620) 843115 (Starter)
Fax (01620) 842327
Web www.gullanegolfclub.com
Mem 870 300(L) 60(J)
Sec SC Owram (01620) 842255
Pro J Hume (01620) 843111
Holes No 1 18 L 6466 yds SSS 72
No 2 18 L 6244 yds SSS 70
No 3 18 L 5252 yds SSS 66
6 hole children's course
V'tors No 1–H Nos 2/3–U
Fees No 1 £65 D–£90 (£80)
No 2 £29 D–£41 (£35)
No 3 £17 D–£25 (£24)
Children's course free
Loc 18 miles E of Edinburgh on A198
Mis Advance booking advisable

Haddington (1865)

Amisfield Park, Haddington, EH41 4PT
Tel (01620) 823627
Fax (01620) 826580
Mem 650
Sec DM Swarbrick (Mgr)
Pro J Sandilands (01620) 822727
Holes 18 L 6317 yds SSS 70
V'tors WD–U WE–U 10am–12 & 2–4pm
Fees £18 (£26)
Loc 17 miles E of Edinburgh on A1. ¾ mile E of Haddington

The Honourable Company of Edinburgh Golfers (1744)

Muirfield, Gullane, EH31 2EG
Tel (01620) 842123
Fax (01620) 842977
Mem 625
Sec Gp Capt JA Prideaux
Holes 18 L 6601 yds SSS 73 (Championship L 6963 yds)
V'tors WD–Tues & Thurs I H WE/BH–NA SOC
Fees £85 D–£110
Loc NE outskirts of Gullane, opposite sign for Greywalls Hotel on A198

Kilspindie (1867)

Aberlady, EH32 0QD
Tel (01875) 870358
Fax (01875) 870358
Mem 400 150(L) 60(J)
Sec PB Casely
Pro GJ Sked (01875) 870695
Holes 18 L 5012 metres SSS 66
V'tors Phone Sec in advance WD–U after 9.45am WE–U after 11am SOC

Fees £25 D–£40 (£30 D–£50)
Loc Aberlady, 17 miles E of Edinburgh
Arch Ross/Sayers

Longniddry (1921)

Links Road, Longniddry, EH32 0NL
Tel (01875) 852141
Fax (01875) 853371
Web www.longniddrygolfclub.co.uk
Mem 950
Sec N Robertson
Pro WJ Gray (01875) 852228
Holes 18 L 6260 yds SSS 70
V'tors WD–U H SOC–WD after 9.18am
Fees £32 D–£45 (£50)
Loc 13 miles E of Edinburgh, off A1
Arch HS Colt

Luffness New (1894)

Aberlady, EH32 0QA
Tel (01620) 843114
Fax (01620) 842933
Mem 700
Sec DA Leckie (01620) 843336
Pro None
Holes 18 L 6122 yds SSS 70
V'tors H or I XL before 10am WE/BH–NA SOC
Fees £37.50 D–£55
Loc 1 mile W of Gullane (A198)
Arch Morris/Braid

Musselburgh (1938)

Monktonhall, Musselburgh, EH21 6SA
Tel (0131) 665 2005
Mem 1000
Sec G Finlay
Pro F Mann (0131) 665 7055
Holes 18 L 6725 yds SSS 73
V'tors WD–U before 4.30pm WE–NA before 10am
Fees £22 (£30)
Loc 1 mile S of Musselburgh on B6415
Arch James Braid

Musselburgh Old Course

Public
10 Balcarres Road, Musselburgh, EH21 7SD
Tel (0131) 665 6981, (0131) 665 5438 (Starter)
Web www.musselburgholdlinks.co.uk
Mem 200
Sec L Freedman (0131) 665 4861
Pro None
Holes 9 L 5774 yds SSS 69
V'tors WD/BH–U WE–U after 1pm
Fees 9 holes–£8
Loc 7 miles E of Edinburgh on A1

North Berwick (1832)

West Links, Beach Road, North Berwick, EH39 4BB
Tel (01620) 895040

Fax   (01620) 893274
Mem   324
Sec   NA Wilson (01620) 895040
Pro   D Huish (01620) 893233
Holes   18 L 6420 yds SSS 71
V'tors   U H
Fees   £40 D–£60 (£60 D–£80)
        Winter–£22 (£29)
Loc   Centre of North Berwick. 24
        miles E of Edinburgh (A198)

Royal Musselburgh
(1774)
Prestongrange House, Prestonpans,
EH32 9RP
Tel   (01875) 810276
Fax   (01875) 810276
Web   www.royalmusselburgh.co.uk
Mem   800
Sec   TH Hardie (Sec/Mgr)
        J Hanratty (Golf Sec)
        (01875) 819000
Pro   J Henderson (01875) 810139
Holes   18 L 6237 yds SSS 70
V'tors   U SOC
Fees   £22 D–£35 (£35)
Loc   8 miles E of Edinburgh on
        B1361 North Berwick road
Arch   James Braid

Tantallon (1853)
Club
32 Westgate, North Berwick,
EH39 4AH
Tel   (01620) 892114
Fax   (01620) 894399
Mem   300
Sec   T Hill
Holes   Play over North Berwick West
        Links

Thorntree (1856)
Club
Prestongrange House, Prestonpans,
EH32 9RP
Mem   100
Sec   J Hanratty
Holes   Play over Royal
        Musselburgh course

Whitekirk (1995)
Whitekirk, North Berwick, EH39 5PR
Tel   (01620) 870300
Fax   (01620) 870330
Web   www.whitekirk.com
Mem   400
Sec   D Brodie
Pro   P Wardell
Holes   18 L 6526 yds Par 72 SSS 72
V'tors   U SOC
Fees   £20 (£25)
Loc   3 miles SE of North Berwick
        (A198)
Mis   Practice range
Arch   Cameron Sinclair

Winterfield (1935)
Public
St Margarets, North Road, Dunbar,
EH42 1AU
Tel   (01368) 862280

Mem   350
Pro   K Phillips (01368) 863562
Holes   18 L 5053 yds SSS 65
V'tors   U
Fees   On application–phone Pro
Loc   W side of Dunbar. 28 miles E
        of Edinburgh (A1)

Midlothian

Baberton (1893)
50 Baberton Avenue, Juniper Green,
Edinburgh, EH14 5DU
Tel   (0131) 453 3361
Fax   (0131) 453 4678
Web   www.baberton.co.uk
Mem   900
Sec   BM Flockhart
        (0131) 453 4911
Pro   K Kelly (0131) 453 3555
Holes   18 L 6129 yds SSS 70
V'tors   WD–U WE–NA SOC
Fees   £22 D–£32 (£25 D–£35)
Loc   5 miles SW of Edinburgh
        (A70)
Arch   Willie Park Jr

Braid Hills (1893)
Public
Braid Hills Road, Edinburgh,
EH10 6JY
Tel   (0131) 447 6666
        (Starter)
Holes   No 1 18 L 5731 yds SSS 68
        No 2 18 L 4832 yds SSS 63
V'tors   U–phone Starter. No 2 course
        closed Sun
Fees   £11
Loc   3 miles S of Edinburgh
        (A702)
Mis   No 2 course open Apr–Oct

Braids United (1897)
Club
22 Braid Hills Approach, Edinburgh,
EH10 6JY
Tel   (0131) 452 9408
Mem   100
Sec   JS Forson
Holes   Play over Braids 1 and 2

Broomieknowe (1905)
36 Golf Course Road, Bonnyrigg,
EH19 2HZ
Tel   (0131) 663 9317
Fax   (0131) 663 2152
Web   www.broomieknowe.com
Mem   500
Sec   JD Fisher
Pro   M Patchett
        (0131) 660 2035
Holes   18 L 6200 yds Par 70
V'tors   WD–U WE/BH–NA
Fees   £17 D–£25 (£20)
Loc   7 miles SE of Edinburgh
Arch   Braid/Hawtree

Bruntsfield Links Golfing Society (1761)
The Clubhouse, 32 Barnton Avenue,
Edinburgh, EH4 6JH
Tel   (0131) 336 2006
Fax   (0131) 336 5538
Mem   1130
Sec   Cdr DM Sandford
        (0131) 336 1479
Pro   B Mackenzie (0131) 336 4050
Holes   18 L 6407 yds SSS 71
V'tors   WD–U WE–apply to Sec
        SOC–H
Fees   £42 D–£55 (£45 D–£60)
Loc   3 miles NW of Edinburgh, off
        A90 at Davidson Mains
Arch   Willie
        Park/Mackenzie/Hawtree

Carrick Knowe (1930)
Public
Glendevon Park, Edinburgh,
EH12 5VZ
Tel   (0131) 337 1096 (Starter)
Holes   18 L 6184 yds SSS 68
V'tors   U–phone Starter
Fees   £12.50
Loc   3 miles W of Edinburgh centre

Craigentinny (1891)
Public
Fillyside Road, Edinburgh EH7
Tel   (0131) 554 7501 (Starter)
Holes   18 L 5418 yds SSS 66
V'tors   U–phone Starter
Fees   £8.80–£9.65
Loc   2½ miles NE of Edinburgh

Craigmillar Park (1895)
1 Observatory Road, Edinburgh,
EH9 3HG
Tel   (0131) 667 2837
Mem   425 100(L) 70(J)
Sec   T Lawson (0131) 667 0047
Pro   B McGhee (0131) 667 2850
Holes   18 L 5859 yds SSS 69
V'tors   WD–I or H before 3.30pm
        WE/BH–NA
Fees   On application
Loc   Blackford, S of Edinburgh
Arch   James Braid

Duddingston (1895)
Duddingston Road West, Edinburgh,
EH15 3QD
Tel   (0131) 661 7688
Fax   (0131) 652 6057
Web   www.duddingston-golf-
        club.com
Mem   600
Sec   MGG Corsar (0131) 661
        7688
Pro   A McLean (0131) 661 4301
Holes   18 L 6473 yds SSS 72
V'tors   WD–U SOC–Tues & Thurs
Fees   £35 Soc–£25
Loc   SE Edinburgh

Glencorse (1890)

Milton Bridge, Penicuik, EH26 0RD
Tel (01968) 677177
Fax (01968) 674399
Mem 700
Sec W Oliver (01968) 677189
Pro C Jones (01968) 676481
Holes 18 L 5217 yds Par 64 SSS 66
V'tors WD–U SOC–WD/Sun pm
Fees £20 (£26)
Loc 8 miles S of Edinburgh (A701)
Arch Willie Park

Kings Acre (1997)

Pay and play
Lasswade, EH18 1AU
Tel (0131) 663 3456
Fax (0131) 663 7076
Web www.kings-acregolf.com
Sec Lizzie King
Pro A Murdoch (0131) 663 3456
Holes 18 L 5935 yds Par 70
Junior Par 3 course
V'tors U SOC
Fees £17 (£24)
Loc 3 miles S of Edinburgh, off A720
Mis Floodlit driving range
Arch Graeme Webster

Kingsknowe (1907)

326 Lanark Road, Edinburgh, EH14 2JD
Tel (0131) 441 1144
Fax (0131) 441 2079
Mem 819
Sec LI Fairlie (0131) 441 1145
Pro C Morris (0131) 441 4030
Holes 18 L 5981 yds SSS 69
V'tors WD–U before 4pm
WE–phone Pro SOC–WD
before 4pm
Fees £20 (£30)
Loc SW Edinburgh
Arch Herd/Braid

Liberton (1920)

297 Gilmerton Road, Edinburgh, EH16 5UJ
Tel (0131) 664 3009
Fax (0131) 666 0853
Mem 797
Sec TJ Watson
Pro I Seath (0131) 664 1056
Holes 18 L 5299 yds SSS 66
V'tors WD–U before 5pm WE–NA
before 2pm
Fees £20
Loc 3 miles S of Edinburgh

Lothianburn (1893)

106a Biggar Road, Edinburgh, EH10 7DU
Tel (0131) 445 2206
Web www.golfers.net
Mem 600 75(L) 100(J)
Sec WFA Jardine (0131) 445 5067
Pro K Mungall (0131) 445 2288
Holes 18 L 5662 yds SSS 68

V'tors WD–U before 4.30pm –M
after 4.30pm WE–NA
SOC–H
Fees £16.50 D–£22.50 (£22.50 D–£27.50)
Loc S of Edinburgh, on A702. Lothianburn exit from Edinburgh by-pass
Arch James Braid (1928)

Marriott Dalmahoy Hotel & CC

Dalmahoy, Kirknewton, EH27 8EB
Tel (0131) 335 8010
Fax (0131) 335 3577
Sec I Burns (Golf Dir)
Mrs JM Bryans (Sec)
Pro N Graham
Holes East 18 L 6677 yds SSS 72
West 18 L 5185 yds SSS 66
V'tors WD–U H SOC–WD
Fees East–£65 (£80) West–£45 (£55)
Loc 7 miles W of Edinburgh on A71
Mis Floodlit driving range
Arch James Braid

Melville Golf Centre (1995)

Pay and play
Lasswade, Edinburgh, EH18 1AN
Tel (0131) 663 8038,
(0131) 654 0224 (24-hr Bookings)
Fax (0131) 654 0814
Web www.melvillegolf.co.uk
Mem 70
Sec Mr & Mrs MacFarlane (Props)
Pro G Carter (0131) 663 8038
Holes 9 L 4604 yds Par 66 SSS 62
V'tors U SOC
Fees £8–£14 (£10–£18)
Loc 7 miles S of Edinburgh, signposted off city by-pass on A7
Mis Floodlit driving range
Arch G Webster

Merchants of Edinburgh (1907)

10 Craighill Gardens, Morningside, Edinburgh, EH10 5PY
Tel (0131) 447 1219
Mem 730
Sec B Samuel
Pro NEM Colquhoun (0131) 447 8709
Holes 18 L 4889 yds SSS 64
V'tors WD–U before 4pm –M after 4pm WE–M SOC–WD
Fees £15
Loc SW of Edinburgh, off A701

Mortonhall (1892)

231 Braid Road, Edinburgh, EH10 6PB
Tel (0131) 447 2411

Fax (0131) 447 8712
Web www.mortonhallgc.co.uk
Mem 525
Sec Ms BM Giefer (0131) 447 6974
Pro DB Horn (0131) 447 5185
Holes 18 L 6557 yds SSS 72
V'tors H SOC
Fees £30 (£30)
Loc 2 miles S of Edinburgh on A702
Arch James Braid/FW Hawtree

Murrayfield (1896)

43 Murrayfield Road, Edinburgh, EH12 6EU
Tel (0131) 337 1009
Fax (0131) 313 0721
Mem 815
Sec Mrs MK Thomson (0131) 337 3478
Pro J Fisher (0131) 337 3479
Holes 18 L 5764 yds Par 70 SSS 69
V'tors WD–I WE–M
Fees £30 (£35)
Loc 2 miles W of Edinburgh centre

Newbattle (1896)

Abbey Road, Eskbank, Dalkeith, EH22 3AD
Tel (0131) 663 2123
Fax (0131) 654 1810
Mem 600
Sec HG Stanners (0131) 663 1819
Pro S McDonald (0131) 660 1631
Holes 18 L 6012 yds SSS 70
V'tors WD–U before 4pm WE–M
Fees £18 D–£27
Loc 6 miles S of Edinburgh on A7 and A68
Arch HS Colt

Portobello (1853)

Public
Stanley Street, Portobello, Edinburgh, EH15 1JJ
Tel (0131) 669 4361 (Starter)
Holes 9 L 2405 yds SSS 64
V'tors U–phone Starter
Fees £8.80–£9.65
Loc 4 miles E of Edinburgh

Prestonfield (1920)

6 Priestfield Road North, Edinburgh, EH16 5HS
Tel (0131) 667 9665
Fax (0131) 667 9665
Web www.prestonfieldgolfclub.co.uk
Mem 900
Sec AS Robertson
Pro J Macfarlane (0131) 667 8597
Holes 18 L 6214 yds SSS 70
V'tors Sat–NA 8–10.30am and 12–1.30pm Sun–NA before 11.30am SOC
Fees £20 D–£30 (£30 D–£40)
Loc 2 miles SE of Edinburgh, off A7 Dalkeith Road
Arch Peter Robertson

For list of abbreviations see page 649

Ratho Park (1928)

Ratho, Edinburgh, EH28 8NX

Tel	(0131) 335 0069
Fax	(0131) 333 1752
Mem	550 106(L) 72(J)
Sec	JS Yates (0131) 335 0068
Pro	A Pate (0131) 333 1406
Holes	18 L 5932 yds SSS 68
V'tors	U SOC–Tues/Wed/Thurs
Fees	£25 D–£35 (£35)
Loc	8 miles W of Edinburgh centre (A71)
Arch	James Braid

Ravelston (1912)

24 Ravelston Dykes Road, Edinburgh, EH4 5NZ

Tel	(0131) 315 2486
Mem	610
Sec	J Lowrie
Holes	9 L 5218 yds SSS 65
V'tors	WD–H
Fees	WD–£15
Loc	Off Queensferry Road (A90). Turn S at Blackhall
Arch	James Braid

Royal Burgess Golfing Society of Edinburgh (1735)

181 Whitehouse Road, Barnton, Edinburgh, EH4 6BY

Tel	(0131) 339 2075
Fax	(0131) 339 3712
Web	www.royalburgess.co.uk
Mem	620 60(J)
Sec	JP Audis (0131) 339 2075
Pro	G Yuille (0131) 339 6474
Holes	18 L 6494 yds SSS 71
V'tors	I SOC
Fees	On application
Loc	Queensferry Road (A90)
Arch	Tom Morris

Silverknowes (1947)

Public

Silverknowes Parkway, Edinburgh, EH4 5ET

Tel	(0131) 336 3843 (Starter)
Holes	18 L 6214 yds SSS 70
V'tors	U–phone Starter
Fees	£8.80–£9,65
Loc	4 miles N of Edinburgh

Swanston (1927)

111 Swanston Road, Fairmilehead, Edinburgh, EH10 7DS

Tel	(0131) 445 2239
Fax	(0131) 445 2239
Web	www.swanstongolfclub.com
Mem	500
Sec	J Allan
Pro	R Fyfie (0131) 445 4002
Holes	18 L 5004 yds SSS 65
V'tors	U exc comp days–NA WE–NA after 1pm
Fees	£15 D–£20 (£20 D–£25)
Loc	S of Edinburgh, off Biggar road (A702) Edinburgh By-pass

Torphin Hill (1895)

Torphin Road, Edinburgh, EH13 0PG

Tel	(0131) 441 1100
Fax	(0131) 441 7166
Mem	450
Sec	AJ Hepburn
Pro	J Browne
Holes	18 L 5025 yds SSS 66
V'tors	WD–U WE–U exc comp days SOC
Fees	D–£12 (D–£20)
Loc	SW boundary of Edinburgh

Turnhouse (1897)

154 Turnhouse Road, Corstorphine, Edinburgh, EH12 0AD

Tel	(0131) 339 1014
Fax	(0131) 339 1844
Web	www.turnhousegolfclub.co.uk
Mem	640
Sec	AB Hay (0131) 539 5937
Pro	J Murray (0131) 339 7701
Holes	18 L 6153 yds SSS 70
V'tors	M or by arrangement SOC
Fees	On application
Loc	W of Edinburgh (A9080)

Vogrie (1990)

Pay and play

Vogrie Estate Country Park, Gorebridge, EH23 4NU

Tel	(01875) 821716
Holes	9 hole course Par 66
V'tors	U
Fees	£5.70
Loc	SE of Edinburgh, off A68 (B6372)

West Lothian

Bathgate (1892)

Edinburgh Road, Bathgate, EH48 1BA

Tel	(01506) 652232
Fax	(01506) 636775
Mem	580
Sec	WA Osborne (01506) 630505
Pro	S Strachan (01506) 630553
Holes	18 L 6328 yds SSS 70
V'tors	U
Fees	£17 (£33)
Loc	15 miles W of Edinburgh. M8 Junction 4
Arch	Wm Park Sr

Deer Park CC (1978)

Knightsridge, Livingston, EH54 9PG

Tel	(01506) 431037
Fax	(01506) 435608
Mem	500
Pro	B Dunbar
Holes	18 L 6688 yds SSS 72
V'tors	U SOC
Fees	£17 D–£24 (£27 D–£34)
Loc	N of Livingston. M8 Junction 3

Dundas Parks (1957)

South Queensferry, EH30 9SS

Mem	550
Sec	Mrs C Wood (0131) 319 1347

Holes	9 L 6056 yds SSS 70
V'tors	M I SOC
Fees	D–£10
Loc	Dundas Estate (Private). 1 mile S of Queensferry (A8000)

Greenburn (1953)

6 Greenburn Road, Fauldhouse, EH47 9HG

Tel	(01501) 770292
Mem	500
Sec	J Irvine (01506) 635309
Pro	M Leighton (01501) 771187
Holes	18 L 6210 yds SSS 71
V'tors	U
Fees	On application
Loc	4 miles S of M8 Junction 4 (East)/Junction 5 (West)

Harburn (1921)

West Calder, EH55 8RS

Tel	(01506) 871256
Fax	(01506) 870286
Mem	500 80(L) 100(J)
Sec	J McLinden (01506) 871131
Pro	S Mills (01506) 871582
Holes	18 L 5921 yds SSS 69
V'tors	U
Fees	£18 (£25)
Loc	2 miles S of W Calder on B7008, via A70 or A71

Linlithgow (1913)

Braehead, Linlithgow, EH49 6QF

Tel	(01506) 842585
Fax	(01506) 842764
Mem	430
Sec	WS Christie
Pro	S Rosie (01506) 844356
Holes	18 L 5729 yds SSS 68
V'tors	U exc Sat–NA SOC
Fees	£20 D–£25 Sun–£25 D–£30
Loc	SW of Linlithgow, off M9
Arch	Robert Simpson

Niddry Castle (1983)

Castle Road, Winchburgh, EH52 2RQ

Tel	(01506) 891097
Mem	500
Sec	J Thomson
Holes	9 L 5476 yds SSS 67
V'tors	U
Fees	£13 (£19)
Loc	10 miles W of Edinburgh (B9080)

Polkemmet (1981)

Public

Whitburn, Bathgate, EH47 0AD

Tel	(01501) 743905
Holes	9 L 2967 metres SSS 37
V'tors	U
Fees	£4.75 (£5.55)
Loc	Between Whitburn and Harthill on B7066. M8 Junctions 4/5
Mis	Driving range

For list of abbreviations see page 649

Pumpherston (1895)

Drumshoreland Road, Pumpherston, EH53 0LF

Tel	**(01506) 432869**
Mem	443 24(L) 100(J)
Sec	I McArthur (01506) 854584
Holes	18 L 6022 yds Par 70 SSS 69
V'tors	WD–U SOC–WD
Fees	On application
Loc	14 miles W of Edinburgh. M8 Junction 3

Rutherford Castle (1998)

West Linton, EH46 7AS

Tel	**(01968) 661233**
Fax	(01968) 661233
Web	www.ruth-castlegc.co.uk
Mem	315
Sec	Wendy Mitchell (01968) 661233
Pro	None
Holes	18 L 6558 yds Par 72 SSS 71
V'tors	U SOC
Fees	£15 (£25)
Loc	10 miles S of Edinburgh on A702
Arch	Bryan Moor

Uphall (1895)

Houston Mains, Uphall, EH52 6JT

Tel	**(01506) 856404**
Fax	(01506) 855358
Mem	650
Sec	WA Crighton
Pro	G Law (01506) 855553
Holes	18 L 5588 yds Par 69 SSS 67
V'tors	U
Fees	£15 D–£20 (£20 D–£30)
Loc	7 miles W of Edinburgh Airport (A8). M8 Junction 3

West Linton (1890)

West Linton, EH46 7HN

Tel	**(01968) 660970**
Fax	(01968) 660970
Mem	750
Sec	AJ Mitchell (01968) 660970
Pro	I Wright (01968) 660256
Holes	18 L 6132 yds SSS 70
V'tors	WD–U WE–phone Pro
Fees	£20 D–£30 (£30)
Loc	18 miles S of Edinburgh on A702.

West Lothian (1892)

Airngath Hill, Linlithgow, EH49 7RH

Tel	**(01506) 826030**
Fax	(01506) 826030
Mem	850
Sec	MJ Todd
Pro	C Gillies (01506) 825060
Holes	18 L 6406 yds SSS 71
V'tors	WD–NA after 4pm WE–by arrangement
Fees	On application
Loc	1 mile N of Linlithgow, towards Bo'ness
Arch	W Park Jr/Adams/Middleton

Moray

Buckpool (1933)

Barhill Road, Buckie, AB56 1DU

Tel	**(01542) 832236**
Fax	(01542) 832236
Mem	500
Sec	Miss M Coull
Holes	18 L 6257 yds SSS 70
V'tors	U
Fees	£13 D–£16 (£16 D–£22)
Loc	W end of Buckpool, ½ mile off A98

Dufftown (1896)

Tomintoul Road, Dufftown, AB55 4BS

Tel	**(01340) 820325**
Fax	(01340) 820325
Web	www.speyside.moray.org/dufftowngolfclub
Mem	310
Sec	Mrs M Swann (Admin)
Pro	None
Holes	18 L 5308 yds SSS 67
V'tors	U
Fees	£12 D–£15
Loc	1 mile SW of Dufftown on B9009

Elgin (1906)

Hardhillock, Birnie Road, Elgin, IV30 8SX

Tel	**(01343) 542338**
Fax	(01343) 542341
Web	www.elgingolfclub.com
Mem	854 113(L) 150(J)
Sec	DF Black
Pro	K Stables (01343) 542884
Holes	18 L 6411 yds SSS 71
V'tors	WD–U after 9.30am WE–U after 10am SOC–WD SOC–WE by arrangement
Fees	£25 D–£32 (£25 D–£32)
Loc	1 mile S of Elgin on A941
Mis	Driving range
Arch	John MacPherson

Forres (1889)

Muiryshade, Forres, IV36 0RD

Tel	**(01309) 672949**
Mem	716 130(J)
Sec	Margaret Greenaway
Pro	S Aird (01309) 672250
Holes	18 L 6141 yds SSS 70
V'tors	U SOC
Fees	£14 (£20)
Loc	1 mile SE of Forres, off B9010

Garmouth & Kingston (1932)

Garmouth, Fochabers, IV32 7NJ

Tel	**(01343) 870388**
Fax	(01343) 870388
Mem	600
Sec	A Robertson (01343) 870231
Holes	18 L 5935 yds SSS 69
V'tors	U SOC

Fees	£16 D–£18 (£22 D–£25)
Loc	8 miles NE of Elgin

Hopeman (1909)

Hopeman, Moray, IV30 5YA

Tel	**(01343) 830578**
Fax	(01343) 830152
Web	www.hopeman-golf-club.co.uk
Mem	700
Sec	J Fraser
Holes	18 L 5590 yds SSS 67
V'tors	WD–U Sat–NA before 10am and 12.30–2pm Sun–NA before 9am SOC
Fees	£13 (£18)
Loc	7 miles NW of Elgin on B9012
Arch	J McKenzie

Moray (1889)

Stotfield Road, Lossiemouth, IV31 6QS

Tel	**(01343) 812018**
Fax	(01343) 815102
Mem	1500
Sec	B Russell
Pro	A Thomson (01343) 813330
Holes	Old 18 L 6643 yds SSS 73 New 18 L 6005 yds SSS 69
V'tors	U H SOC
Fees	On application
Loc	6 miles N of Elgin
Mis	Practice range
Arch	Old Tom Morris

Spey Bay (1904)

Spey Bay Hotel, Spey Bay, Fochabers, IV32 7PJ

Tel	**(01343) 820424**
Fax	(01343) 829282
Web	www.speybay.com
Mem	200
Sec	Isobell Tesch (Gen Mgr)
Holes	18 L 6092 yds Par 70 SSS 69
V'tors	U
Fees	£20 (£22)
Loc	7 miles W of Buckie, off A96 (B9104)
Mis	Driving range
Arch	Ben Sayers

Perth & Kinross

Aberfeldy (1895)

Taybridge Road, Aberfeldy, PH15 2BH

Tel	**(01887) 820535**
Fax	(01887) 820535
Mem	260
Sec	P Woolley (01887) 829422
Holes	18 L 5600 yds Par 68 SSS 66
V'tors	U
Fees	£16 (£21)
Loc	10 miles W of Ballinluig, off A9
Arch	Souters

Alyth (1894)

Pitcrocknie, Alyth, PH11 8HF
Tel   (01828) 632268
Fax   (01828) 633491
Web   www.alythgolfclub.co.uk
Mem   850
Sec   J Docherty
Pro   T Melville (01828) 632411
Holes 18 L 6205 yds SSS 70
V'tors U SOC
Fees   On application
Loc   16 miles NW of Dundee
       (A91)
Arch   Tom Morris/James Braid

Auchterarder (1892)

Ochil Road, Auchterarder, PH3 1LS
Tel   (01764) 662804
Fax   (01764) 662804
Mem   765
Sec   WM Campbell
       (01764) 664669
Pro   G Baxter (01764) 663711
Holes 18 L 5757 yds SSS 68
V'tors U SOC
Fees   £20 D–£30 Sat–£25 D–£38
       Sun–£38
Loc   1 mile SW of Auchterarder

Bishopshire (1903)

Pay and play
Kinnesswood, Kinross, KY13
Mem   200
Sec   J Proudfoot (01592) 780203
Holes 10 L 4700 metres SSS 64
V'tors U
Fees   £5 (£6)
Loc   3 miles E of Kinross (A911).
       M90 Junction 7
Arch   W Park

Blair Atholl (1896)

Invertilt Road, Blair Atholl, PH18 5TG
Tel   (01796) 481407
Fax   (01796) 481751
Mem   445
Sec   T Boon
Holes 9 L 5816 yds SSS 68
V'tors U
Fees   £14.50 (£16.50)
Loc   35 miles N of Perth, off A9

Blairgowrie (1889)

Rosemount, Blairgowrie, PH10 6LG
Tel   (01250) 872594
Fax   (01250) 875451
Web   www.blairgowrie.golf.co.uk
Mem   1200
Sec   JN Simpson (Managing Sec)
       (01250) 872622
Pro   C Dernie (01250) 873116
Holes Rosemount 18 L 6588 yds
       SSS 72;
       Landsdowne 18 L 6895 yds
       SSS 73;
       Wee 9 L 4614 yds SSS 63
V'tors Mon/Tues/Thurs–U H
       8am–12 & 2–3.30pm
       Wed/Fri/WE–restricted
Fees   On application

Loc   1 mile S of Blairgowrie, off
       A93. 15 miles N of Perth
Arch   Rosemount-Braid;
       Lansdowne-Alliss/Thomas;
       Wee-Old Tom Morris

Callander (1890)

Aveland Road, Callander, FK17 8EN
Tel   (01877) 330090
Fax   (01877) 330062
Web   www.callander.co.uk
Mem   700
Sec   Mrs S Smart
Pro   A Martin (01877) 330975
Holes 18 L 5125 yds SSS 66
V'tors U SOC
Fees   £18 (£26)
Loc   Off A84, E end of Callander
Arch   Tom Morris

Comrie (1891)

Laggan Braes, Comrie, PH6 2LR
Tel   (01764) 670055
Mem   380
Sec   S van der Walt
       (01786) 880727
Holes 9 L 3020 yds Par 70 SSS 70
V'tors U
Fees   £15 (£20)
Loc   7 miles W of Crieff (A85)

Craigie Hill (1911)

Cherrybank, Perth, PH2 0NE
Tel   (01738) 620829
Fax   (01738) 620829
Mem   625
Sec   A Tunnicliffe (01738) 620829
Pro   I Muir (01738) 622644
Holes 18 L 5386 yds SSS 67
V'tors U exc Sat
Fees   £18 (£25)
Loc   W boundary of Perth
Arch   Fernie/Anderson

Crieff (1891)

Perth Road, Crieff, PH7 3LR
Tel   (01764) 652909 (Bookings)
Fax   (01764) 655096
Mem   700
Sec   JS Miller (01764) 652397
Pro   DJW Murchie
Holes Ferntower 18 L 6402 yds
       SSS 72;
       Dornock 9 L 4772 yds SSS 63
V'tors U H NA–12–2pm or after
       5pm SOC
Fees   Ferntower £27 (£36)
       Dornock £12
Loc   1 mile NE of Crieff (A85).
       17 miles W of Perth
Arch   James Braid

Dalmunzie (1948)

Glenshee, Blairgowrie, PH10 7QG
Tel   (01250) 885226
Fax   (01250) 885225
Mem   52
Sec   S Winton (Mgr)
Holes 9 L 2099 yds SSS 60
V'tors U

Fees   D–£11
Loc   22 miles N of Blairgowrie on
       A93. (Dalmunzie Hotel sign)

Dunkeld & Birnam (1892)

Fungarth, Dunkeld, PH8 0HU
Tel   (01350) 727524
Fax   (01350) 728660
Mem   535
Sec   TA Wain
Pro   None
Holes 18 L 5511 yds SSS 67
V'tors WD–U WE–phone first
Fees   On application
Loc   Dunkeld 1 mile, off A923.
       15 miles N of Perth

Dunning (1953)

Rollo Park, Dunning, PH2 0QX
Tel   (01764) 684747
Mem   580
Sec   JR Stockley (01764) 684212
Holes 9 L 4885 yds Par 66 SSS 63
V'tors WD–U Sat–NA before 4pm
Fees   £14 (£16)
Loc   9 miles SW of Perth, off A9

Foulford Inn (1995)

Pay and play
Crieff, Perthshire
Tel   (01764) 652407
Fax   (01764) 652407
Sec   M Beaumont
Holes 9 hole Par 3 course
V'tors U
Fees   £3 D–£5

The Gleneagles Hotel

Auchterarder, PH3 1NF
Tel   (01764) 663543 (Golf),
       (01764) 662231 (Hotel)
Web   www.gleneagles.com
Pro   G Schofield
Holes King's 18 L 6471 yds SSS 71
       Queen's 18 L 5965 yds
       SSS 69
       Monarch 18 L 7081 SSS 74
       9 hole Par 3 course
V'tors U
Fees   May–Sept £100
Loc   16 miles SW of Perth on A9
Mis   Driving range. Golf
       Academy
Arch   James Braid

Glenisla

Proprietary
Pitcrocknie Farm, Alyth PH11 8JJ
Tel   (01828) 632445
Fax   (01828) 633749
Web   www.golf-glenisla.co.uk
Mem   300
Sec   E Wilson (Admin)
Holes 18 L 6402 yds Par 71 SSS 72
V'tors U H
Fees   £22 (£26)
Loc   Nr Alyth (B954)

Green Hotel (1900)

2 The Muirs, Kinross, KY13 8AS

Tel	(01577) 863407
Fax	(01577) 863180
Mem	450
Sec	C Browne
Holes	Red 18 L 6257 yds SSS 70
	Blue 18 L 6456 yds SSS 71
V'tors	U
Fees	£15 D–£25 (£25 D–£35)
Loc	17 miles S of Perth. M90
	Junction 6/7

Kenmore (1992)

Pay and play
Mains of Taymouth, Kenmore,
Aberfeldy, PH15 2HN

Tel	(01887) 830226
Fax	(01887) 830211
Web	www.taymouth.co uk
Mem	120
Sec	R Menzies (Mgr)
Pro	None
Holes	9 L 6052 yds SSS 69
V'tors	U SOC
Fees	9 holes–£9 (£10) 18
	holes–£13 (£14)
Loc	6 miles W of Aberfeldy on
	A827
Arch	D Menzies & Partners

Killin (1913)

Killin, FK21 8TX

Tel	(01567) 820312
Fax	(01567) 820312
Web	www.killingolfclub.co.uk
Mem	298
Sec	TL Taylor (01764) 656291
Holes	9 L 5016 yds Par 66 SSS 65
V'tors	U SOC–Apr–Oct
Fees	£12 (£13.50)
Loc	Killin, W end of Loch Tay
Arch	John Duncan

King James VI (1858)

Moncreiffe Island, Perth, PH2 8NR

Tel	(01738) 625170,
	(01738) 632460 (Starter)
Fax	(01738) 445132
Mem	675
Sec	Mrs H Blair (01738) 445132
Pro	A Crerar (01738) 632460
Holes	18 L 5664 yds SSS 69
V'tors	U exc Sat Sun–by reservation
Fees	£18 D–£25 Sun D–£30
Loc	Island in River Tay, Perth
Arch	Tom Morris

Milnathort (1910)

South Street, Milnathort, Kinross,
KY13 9XA

Tel	(01577) 864069
Mem	575
Holes	9 L 5985 yds SSS 69
V'tors	U SOC
Fees	£12 D–£18 (£14 D–£20)
Loc	1 mile N of Kinross. M90
	Junction 6/7

Muckhart (1908)

Muckhart, Dollar, FK14 7JH

Tel	(01259) 781423
Mem	550 125(L) 100(J)
Sec	AB Robertson
Pro	K Salmoni
Holes	18 L 6034 yds SSS 70
	9 hole course
V'tors	U SOC
Fees	18 hole:£15 D–£22 (£22
	D–£30) 9 hole:£10
Loc	A91, 3 miles E of Dollar,
	towards Rumbling Bridge

Murrayshall (1981)

Murrayshall, New Scone, Perth,
PH2 7PH

Tel	(01738) 551171
Fax	(01738) 552595
Mem	300
Sec	A Bryan (Mgr)
Pro	AT Reid (01738) 552784
Holes	18 L 5877 metres SSS 72
	18 L 4878 metres SSS 67
V'tors	U SOC–WD/WE
Fees	£18–£27 D–£32–£45
	(£20–£30 D–£32–£45)
Loc	3 miles NE of Perth, off A94
Mis	Driving range. Indoor Golf
	Centre
Arch	Hamilton Stutt

Muthill (1935)

Peat Road, Muthill, PH5 2DA

Tel	(01764) 681523
Fax	(01764) 681557
Mem	450
Sec	J Elder
Holes	9 L 2371 yds SSS 63
V'tors	U SOC
Fees	£13 (£16)
Loc	3 miles S of Crieff on A822

North Inch

Public
c/o Perth & Kinross Council, 5 High
Street, Perth, PH1 5JS

Tel	(01738) 636481 (Starter)
Sec	G Harbut (01738) 475215
Holes	18 L 4340 metres SSS 65
V'tors	U SOC
Fees	On application
Loc	Nr Perth and A9, by River
	Tay. Signs to Bell's Sports
	Centre

Pitlochry (1909)

Pitlochry Estate Office, Pitlochry,
PH16 5NE

Tel	(01796) 472792 (Bookings)
Fax	(01796) 473599
Mem	498
Sec	DCM McKenzie JP
	(01796) 472114
Pro	G Hampton (01796) 472792
Holes	18 L 5811 yds SSS 69
V'tors	U SOC
Fees	£17 D–£25 (£20 D–£30)
Loc	N side of Pitlochry (A9).
	28 miles NW of Perth
Arch	Fernie/Hutchison

Royal Perth Golfing Society (1824)

Club
1/2 Atholl Crescent, Perth, PH1 5NG

Tel	(01738) 622265
Fax	(01764) 664049
Mem	250
Sec	DP McDonald (Gen Sec)
	(01738) 622265,
	L Rutherford (Golf Sec)
	(01764) 664049
Holes	Play over Strathmore course

St Fillans (1903)

South Lochearn Rd, St Fillans,
PH26 2NJ

Tel	(01764) 685312
Web	www.st-fillans-golf.com
Mem	400
Sec	J Stanyon (01764) 685300
Holes	9 L 6054 yds SSS 69
V'tors	U SOC
Fees	£14 (£18)
Loc	12 miles W of Crieff, on A85
Arch	W Auchterlonie

Strathmore Golf Centre (1995)

Pay and play
Leroch, Alyth, Blairgowrie, PH11 8NZ

Tel	(01828) 633322
Fax	(01828) 633533
Mem	350
Sec	J Barron
Pro	C Smith
Holes	18 L 6454 yds Par 72 SSS 72
	9 L 1666 yds Par 29 SSS 58
V'tors	U SOC
Fees	18 hole:£19 (£24) 9 hole:£8
	(£10)
Loc	5 miles E of Blairgowrie, off
	A926
Mis	Floodlit driving range
Arch	John Salvesen

Strathtay (1909)

Lyon Cottage, Strathtay, Pitlochry,
PH9 0PG

Tel	(01887) 840211
Mem	237
Sec	IA Ramsay
Holes	9 L 4082 yds SSS 63
V'tors	U exc Thurs–NA after 5pm
	Sat–NA 10–10.30am Sun–NA
	1–4pm SOC
Fees	D–£10
Loc	4 miles W of Ballinluig
	(A827), towards Aberfeldy

Taymouth Castle (1923)

Kenmore, Aberfeldy, PH15 2NT

Tel	(01887) 830228
Fax	(01887) 830228
Mem	200
Sec	AA MacTaggart (Golf Dir)
Pro	G Dott
Holes	18 L 6066 yds SSS 69
V'tors	U WE–booking essential SOC
Fees	£20 D–£30 (£24 D–£38)

Loc   6 miles W of Aberfeldy
(A827)
Arch   James Braid

Whitemoss (1994)

Whitemoss Road, Dunning, Perth,
PH2 0QX
Tel   (01738) 730300
Mem   500
Sec   S Gaden
Pro   None
Holes   18 L 6200 yds Par 69 SSS 69
V'tors   U SOC
Fees   £15 (£15)
Loc   Aberuthven, 10 miles SW of
Perth, off A9

Renfrewshire

Barshaw (1920)

Public
Barshaw Park, Glasgow Road,
Paisley PA2
Tel   (0141) 889 2908
Fax   (0141) 840 2148
Mem   103
Sec   W Collins (0141) 884 2533
Holes   18 L 5703 yds SSS 67
V'tors   U
Fees   £8.50
Loc   1 mile E of Paisley Cross, off
A737

Bonnyton (1957)

Eaglesham, Glasgow, G76 0QA
Tel   (01355) 302781
Fax   (01355) 303151
Mem   950
Sec   A Hughes
Pro   K McWade (01355) 302256
Holes   18 L 6255 yds SSS 71
V'tors   I SOC–WD
Fees   £38
Loc   2 miles W of Eaglesham.
6 miles S of Glasgow

Caldwell (1903)

Caldwell, Uplawmoor, G78 4AU
Tel   (01505) 850329
Fax   (01505) 850604
Mem   450
Sec   HIF Harper (01505) 850366
Pro   S Forbes (01505) 850616
Holes   18 L 6195 yds SSS 70
V'tors   WD–booking before 4pm–M
after 4pm WE–M
Fees   On application
Loc   5 miles SW of Barrhead on
A736 Glasgow-Irvine road

Cochrane Castle (1895)

Scott Avenue, Craigston, Johnstone,
PA5 0HF
Tel   (01505) 320146
Fax   (01505) 325338
Mem   425
Sec   Mrs PIJ Quin

Pro   A Logan (01505) 328465
Holes   18 L 6194 yds Par 71 SSS 71
V'tors   WD–U WE–M
Fees   £22 (£30)
Loc   ½ mile S of Beith Road,
Johnstone
Arch   Charles Hunter

East Renfrewshire (1922)

Pilmuir, Newton Mearns, G77 6RT
Tel   (01355) 500256
Fax   (01355) 500323
Mem   450
Sec   AL Gillespie (0141) 333 9989
DS McKenzie (Mgr)
Pro   S Russell (01355) 500206
Holes   18 L 6097 yds SSS 70
V'tors   On application
Fees   £30 D–£40
Loc   2 miles SW of Newton
Mearns
Arch   James Braid

Eastwood (1893)

Muirshield, Loganswell, Newton
Mearns, Glasgow, G77 6RX
Tel   (01355) 500261
Mem   900
Sec   VE Jones (01355) 500280
Pro   I Darroch (01355) 500285
Holes   18 L 5666 yds SSS 68
V'tors   WD SOC
Fees   £24 D–£30
Loc   9 miles SW of Glasgow
Arch   Theodore Moone

Elderslie (1908)

63 Main Road, Elderslie, PA5 9AZ
Tel   (01505) 323956
Fax   (01505) 340346
Mem   432
Sec   Mrs A Anderson
Pro   R Bowman (01505) 320032
Holes   18 L 6165 yds SSS 70
V'tors   M SOC–WD
Fees   £21 D–£32
Loc   2 miles SW of Paisley

Erskine (1904)

Bishopton, PA7 5PH
Tel   (01505) 862302
Mem   400 140(L)
Sec   TA McKillop
Pro   P Thomson (01505) 862108
Holes   18 L 6287 yds SSS 70
V'tors   WD–I WE–M
Fees   £27
Loc   5 miles NW of Paisley

Fereneze (1904)

Fereneze Avenue, Barrhead, G78 1HJ
Tel   (0141) 881 1519
Mem   700
Sec   A Johnston (0141) 887 4141
Pro   S Kerr (0141) 880 7058
Holes   18 L 5962 yds SSS 70
V'tors   M SOC–WD
Fees   D–£20
Loc   9 miles SW of Glasgow

Gleddoch (1974)

Langbank, PA14 6YE
Tel   (01475) 540304
Fax   (01475) 540459
Mem   600
Sec   DW Tierney
Pro   K Campbell (01475) 540704
Holes   18 L 6375 yds SSS 71
V'tors   WD–U WE–restricted SOC
Fees   £30
Loc   16 miles W of Glasgow
(M8/A8)
Arch   J Hamilton Stutt

Gourock (1896)

Cowal View, Gourock, PA19 1HD
Tel   (01475) 631001
Fax   (01475) 631001
Mem   538 98(L) 86(J)
Sec   AD Taylor
Pro   G Coyle (01475) 636834
Holes   18 L 6512 yds SSS 73
V'tors   WD–I before 4.30pm SOC
Fees   £20 (£25)
Loc   3 miles SW of Greenock, off
A770. 7 miles W of Port
Glasgow

Greenock (1890)

Forsyth Street, Greenock, PA16 8RE
Tel   (01475) 720793
Fax   (01475) 791912
Web   www.greenockgolfclub.co.uk
Mem   500 111(L) 110(J)
Sec   EJ Black (01475) 791912
Pro   P Morrison (01475) 787236
Holes   18 L 5888 yds SSS 68
9 L 2149 yds SSS 32
V'tors   WD–U WE/BH–M
Fees   D–£25 (£30)
Loc   1 mile SW of Greenock on A8
Arch   James Braid

Kilmacolm (1891)

Porterfield Road, Kilmacolm,
PA13 4PD
Tel   (01505) 872139
Fax   (01505) 874007
Mem   888
Sec   DW Tinton
Pro   I Nicholson (01505) 872695
Holes   18 L 5960 yds SSS 69
V'tors   WD–U WE–M
Fees   £20
Loc   10 miles W of Paisley (A761)

Lochwinnoch (1897)

Burnfoot Road, Lochwinnoch,
PA12 4AN
Tel   (01505) 842153
Fax   (01505) 843668
Web   www.lochwinnochgolf.co.uk
Mem   500
Sec   RJG Jamieson
Pro   G Reilly (01505) 843029
Holes   18 L 6243 yds SSS 71
V'tors   WD–U before 4.30pm
SOC–WD
Fees   £20 D–£20
Loc   9 miles SW of Paisley

Old Ranfurly (1905)

Ranfurly Place, Bridge of Weir,
PA11 3DE

Tel	(01505) 613612 (Clubhouse)
Fax	(01505) 613214
Mem	375
Sec	QJ McClymont
	(01505) 613214
Pro	D McIntosh
Holes	18 L 6089 yds SSS 70
V'tors	WD–I WE–M SOC
Fees	On application
Loc	7 miles W of Paisley, off A761

Paisley (1895)

Braehead, Paisley, PA2 8TZ

Tel	(0141) 884 2292 (Clubhouse)
Fax	(0141) 884 3903
Mem	805
Sec	J Hillis (0141) 884 3903
Pro	G Stewart (0141) 884 4114
Holes	18 L 6466 yds Par 71 SSS 72
V'tors	WD–H SOC
Fees	£18 D–£32
Loc	Glenburn, S of Paisley
Arch	Stutt

Port Glasgow (1895)

Devol Farm, Port Glasgow, PA14 5XE

Tel	(01475) 704181
Mem	265
Sec	A Hughes (01475) 791214
Holes	18 L 5712 yds SSS 68
V'tors	WD–U before 5pm –M after 5pm WE–NA SOC
Fees	£15 D–£20 (£20 D–£30)
Loc	1 mile S of Port Glasgow

Ranfurly Castle (1889)

Golf Road, Bridge of Weir, PA11 3HN

Tel	(01505) 612609
Fax	(01505) 610406
Web	www.ranfurlycastle.com
Mem	360 160(L) 100(J)
Sec	J King
Pro	T Eckford (01505) 614795
Holes	18 L 6284 yds SSS 71
V'tors	WD–H WE–M SOC–WD
Fees	£25 D–£35
Loc	7 miles W of Paisley (A761)
Arch	Kirkcaldy/Auchterlonie

Renfrew (1894)

Blythswood Estate, Inchinnan Road,
Renfrew, PA4 9EG

Tel	(0141) 886 6692
Fax	(0141) 886 1808
Web	www.renfrew.scottishgolf.com
Mem	465 110(L) 80(J)
Sec	I Murchison
Pro	D Grant (0141) 885 1754
Holes	18 L 6818 yds SSS 73
V'tors	M SOC
Fees	On application
Loc	3 miles N of Paisley, nr Airport
Arch	Cdr JD Harris

Whinhill (1911)

Beith Road, Greenock, PA16

Tel	(01475) 24694
Mem	250
Sec	R Kirkpatrick (01475) 719260
Pro	None
Holes	18 L 5504 yds SSS 68
V'tors	U
Fees	On application
Loc	Upper Greenock-Largs road
Arch	W Fernie

Whitecraigs (1905)

72 Ayr Road, Giffnock, Glasgow,
G46 6SW

Tel	(0141) 639 4530
Fax	(0141) 639 4530
Web	www.thewhitecraigsgolfclub .co.uk
Mem	1150
Sec	AG Keith CA
Pro	A Forrow (0141) 639 2140
Holes	18 L 6013 yds SSS 70
V'tors	WD–U before 5pm WE–M SOC–WD
Fees	On application
Loc	6 miles S of Glasgow (A77), nr Whitecraigs Station

Stirlingshire

Aberfoyle (1890)

Braeval, Aberfoyle, FK8 3UY

Tel	(01877) 382493
Mem	600
Sec	RD Steele (01877) 382638
Holes	18 L 5218 yds SSS 66
V'tors	WD–U WE–NA before 11.30am
Fees	£15 D–£20 (£20 D–£28)
Loc	Braeval, 18 miles NW of Stirling (A81)

Balfron (1992)

Kepculloch Road, Balfron, G63 0QP

Mem	475
Sec	I Rubython (01360) 440915
Pro	None
Holes	18 L 5903 yds Par 72 SSS 70
V'tors	WD–U before 4pm WE–restricted SOC
Fees	£15 (£15)
Loc	18 miles NW of Glasgow, off A81

Bonnybridge (1925)

Larbert Road, Bonnybridge, Falkirk,
FK4 1NY

Tel	(01324) 812822
Mem	425
Sec	J Mullen
Holes	9 L 6058 yds SSS 70
V'tors	WD–I SOC
Fees	On application to Sec
Loc	3 miles W of Falkirk. M876 Junction 1

Bridge of Allan (1895)

Sunnylaw, Bridge of Allan, Stirling

Tel	(01786) 832332
Mem	471
Sec	Miss M Peattie
Holes	9 L 4932 yds SSS 65
V'tors	U exc Sat
Fees	£10 (£15)
Loc	4 miles N of Stirling, off A9
Arch	Tom Morris Sr

Buchanan Castle (1936)

Proprietary
Drymen, G63 0HY

Tel	(01360) 660307
Fax	(01360) 870382
Mem	830
Sec	R Kinsella
Pro	K Baxter (01360) 660330
Holes	18 L 6015 yds SSS 69
V'tors	By arrangement with Sec SOC
Fees	£30 D–£40 (£30 D–£40)
Loc	18 miles NW of Glasgow. 25 miles W of Stirling, off A811
Arch	James Braid

Campsie (1897)

Crow Road, Lennoxtown, Glasgow,
G66 7HX

Tel	(01360) 310244
Mem	650
Sec	JM Donaldson (01360) 312249
Pro	M Brennan (01360) 310920
Holes	18 L 5517 yds SSS 68
V'tors	WD–U before 4.30pm
Fees	£15 (£20)
Loc	N of Lennoxtown on B822 Fintry road
Arch	Auchterlonie/Stark

Dunblane New (1923)

Perth Road, Dunblane, FK15 0LJ

Tel	(01786) 821521
Fax	(01786) 821522
Mem	700
Sec	JH Dunsmore
Pro	RM Jamieson
Holes	18 L 5957 yds SSS 69
V'tors	WD–U WE–M SOC
Fees	£22
Loc	E side of Dunblane. 6 miles N of Stirling

Falkirk (1922)

Stirling Road, Camelon, Falkirk,
FK2 7YP

Tel	(01324) 611061/612219
Fax	(01324) 639573
Mem	700
Sec	J Elliott
Holes	18 L 6282 yds SSS 70
V'tors	WD–U until 4pm Sat–NA SOC–exc Sat
Fees	£15 D–£25 Sun–£35
Loc	1½ miles W of Falkirk on A9
Arch	James Braid

Falkirk Tryst (1885)
86 Burnhead Road, Larbert, FK5 4BD
Tel   (01324) 562415
Mem   800
Sec   RC Chalmers (01324) 562054
Pro   S Dunsmore (01324) 562091
Holes 18 L 6053 yds SSS 69
V'tors WD–U WE–M SOC–WD
Fees   £18 D–£27
Loc   3 miles NW of Falkirk on A88

Glenbervie (1932)
Stirling Road, Larbert, FK5 4SJ
Tel   (01324) 562605
Fax   (01324) 551054
Mem   600
Sec   Dr Sheila Hartley
Pro   J Chillas (01324) 562725
Holes 18 L 6423 yds Par 71 SSS 71
V'tors WD–U before 4pm WE–M
           SOC–Tues & Thurs
Fees   £30 D–£40
Loc   1 mile N of Larbert on A9.
           M876 Junction 2
Arch   James Braid

Grangemouth (1973)
Public
Polmonthill, Polmont, FK2 0YA
Tel   (01324) 711500
Fax   (01324) 717907

Mem   700
Sec   I Hutton (Hon)
Pro   SJ Campbell (01324) 503840
Holes 18 L 6527 yds SSS 70
V'tors U–book with Pro SOC
Fees   £12.50 D–£18 (£16
           D–£21.50)
Loc   3 miles NE of Falkirk. M9
           Junction 4

Kilsyth Lennox (1900)
Tak-Ma-Doon Road, Kilsyth, G65 0RS
Tel   (01236) 823525 (Bookings)
Mem   250
Sec   AG Stevenson
           (01236) 823213
Holes 18 L 5930 yds Par 70
V'tors WD–U until 5pm –M after
           5pm Sat–NA before 4pm
           Sun–NA before 2pm SOC
Fees   On application
Loc   N of Kilsyth and A803.
           12 miles NE of Glasgow

Polmont (1901)
*Manuel Rigg, Maddiston, Falkirk,
FK2 0LS*
Tel   (01324) 711277
           (Clubhouse)
Fax   (01324) 712504
Mem   300

Sec   P Lees (01324) 713811
Holes 9 L 3044 yds SSS 70
V'tors U exc Sat–NA
Fees   £8 Sun–£15
Loc   4 miles SE of Falkirk on B805

Stirling (1869)
Queen's Road, Stirling, FK8 3AA
Tel   (01786) 473801
Fax   (01786) 450748
Mem   1000
Sec   JG Easson (01786) 464098
Pro   I Collins (01786) 471490
Holes 18 L 6409 yds SSS 71
V'tors WD–U SOC WE–NA
Fees   £25 D–£35
Loc   ½ mile from Stirling centre.
           M9 Junction 10
Arch   Braid/Cotton

Strathendrick (1901)
Glasgow Road, Drymen G63, G63 0AA
Tel   (01360) 660695
Mem   480
Sec   M Quyn (01360) 660733
Holes 9 L 5116 yds SSS 64
V'tors WD–U SOC–WD before 5pm
Fees   £12
Loc   25 miles W of Stirling, off
           A811
Arch   W Fernie

Wales

Cardiganshire

Aberystwyth (1911)
Bryn-y-Mor, Aberystwyth, SY23 2HY
Tel   (01970) 615104
Fax   (01970) 626622
Mem   390
Pro   (01970) 625301
Holes 18 L 6119 yds SSS 71
V'tors U SOC
Fees   £18.50 (£22.50)
Loc   Aberystwyth ½ mile
Arch   H Varden

Borth & Ynyslas (1885)
Borth, Ceredigion, SY24 5JS
Tel   (01970) 871202
Fax   (01970) 871202
Mem   550
Sec   GJ Pritchard
Pro   JG Lewis (01970) 871557
Holes 18 L 6100 yds SSS 70
V'tors WD–U WE/BH–by prior
           arrangement SOC
Fees   £22 (£30)
Loc   8 miles N of Aberystwyth
           (B4353), off A487

Cardigan (1895)
*Gwbert-on-Sea, Cardigan,
SA43 1PR*
Tel   (01239) 612035/621775
Fax   (01239) 621775
Web   www.cardigangolf.sagenet
           .co.uk
Mem   600
Sec   JJ Jones (01239) 621775
Pro   C Parsons (01239) 615359
Holes 18 L 6687 yds SSS 73
V'tors H SOC
Fees   D–£20 (£25) W–£80
Loc   3 miles N of Cardigan
Arch   Grant/Hawtree

Cilgwyn (1977)
Llangybi, Lampeter, SA48 8NN
Tel   (01570) 493286
Mem   290
Sec   JD Morgan
Holes 9 L 5327 yds SSS 67
V'tors U SOC
Fees   £10 (£15) W–£60
Loc   5 miles NE of Lampeter, off
           A485 at Llangybi

Penrhos G&CC (1991)
Llanrhystud, Aberystwyth, SY23 5AY
Tel   (01974) 202999
Fax   (01974) 202100
Web   www.Penrhosgolf.co.uk
Mem   300
Sec   R Rees-Evans
Pro   P Diamond
Holes 18 L 6641 yds SSS 73
           9 hole Par 3 course
V'tors U SOC
Fees   £20 (£25)
Loc   9 miles S of Aberystwyth,
           signposted off A487
Mis   Driving range
Arch   Jim Walters

Carmarthenshire

Ashburnham (1894)
Cliffe Terrace, Burry Port, SA16 0HN
Tel   (01554) 832466
Fax   (01554) 832466
Mem   725
Sec   DK Williams (01554) 832269
Pro   RA Ryder (01554) 833846

For list of abbreviations see page 649

Holes 18 L 6916 yds SSS 72
V'tors H
Fees £27 D–£32 (£32 D–£42)
Loc 5 miles W of Llanelli (A484)

Carmarthen (1907)
Blaenycoed Road, Carmarthen,
SA33 6EH
Tel (01267) 281214
Mem 700
Sec J Coe (01267) 281588
Pro P Gillis (01267) 281493
Holes 18 L 6245 yds SSS 71
V'tors H SOC
Fees £20 (£25)
Loc 4 miles NW of Carmarthen
Arch JH Taylor

Derllys (1993)
Derllys Court, Llysonnen Road,
Carmarthen, SA33 5DT
Tel (01267) 211575/211309
Fax (01267) 211575
Mem 48
Sec R Walters
Holes 9 L 2859 yds Par 70 SSS 66
V'tors U
Fees £10 D–£13 (£11 D–£14)
Loc 4 miles W of Carmarthen, off
A40
Arch P Johnson

Glyn Abbey (1992)
Proprietary
Trimsaran, SA17 4LB
Tel (01554) 810278
Fax (01554) 810889
Web www.glynabbey.co.uk
Mem 240
Sec M Lane (Mgr)
(01554) 810304
Pro N Evans
(01554) 810278
Holes 18 L 6173 yds Par 70 SSS
70
V'tors U SOC
Fees £12 (£15)
Loc 4 miles NW of Llanelli,
between Trimsaran and
Carway
Mis Driving range
Arch Hawtree

Glynhir (1909)
Glynhir Road, Llandybie, Ammanford,
SA18 2TF
Tel (01269) 850472
Fax (01269) 851365
Mem 700
Sec D Kenchington, K Williams
(01269) 851365
Pro D Prior (01269) 851010
Holes 18 L 6006 yds SSS 70
V'tors WD/Sat-H Sun–NA
SOC–WD
Fees Winter £10 (£12) 5D–£45
Summer £16 (£22) 5D–£70
Loc 3½miles N of Ammanford
Arch Hawtree

Saron Golf Course
Pay and play
Penwern, Saron, Llandysul, SA44 4EL
Tel (01559) 370705
Holes 9 L 2300 yds Par 32
V'tors U
Fees 9 holes–£6. 18 holes–£8
Loc On A484 Newcastle Emlyn to
Carmarthen road

Conwy

Abergele (1910)
Tan-y-Gopa Road, Abergele,
LL22 8DS
Tel (01745) 824034
Fax (01745) 824034
Mem 1250
Sec CP Langdon
Pro I Runcie (01745) 823813
Holes 18 L 6520 yds SSS 71
V'tors U SOC
Fees On application
Loc Abergele Castle Grounds
Arch David Williams

Betws-y-Coed (1977)
Clubhouse, Betws-y-Coed, LL24 0AL
Tel (01690) 710556
Mem 400
Sec Mrs P Rowley
Holes 9 L 4996 yds SSS 64
V'tors U SOC
Fees £16 (£21)
Loc ½ mile off A5, in Betws-y-
Coed

Conwy
(Caernarvonshire)
(1890)
Morfa, Conwy, LL32 8ER
Tel (01492) 593400
Fax (01492) 593363
Mem 1000
Sec DL Brown (01492) 592423
Pro JP Lees (01492) 593225
Holes 18 L 6936 yds SSS 74
V'tors H WE–restricted SOC
Fees £25 (£32)
Loc ½ mile W of Conway, off A55

Llandudno (Maesdu)
(1915)
Hospital Road, Llandudno, LL30 1HU
Tel (01492) 876450
Fax (01492) 871570
Mem 1109
Sec G Dean
Pro S Boulden (01492) 875195
Holes 18 L 6513 yds SSS 72
V'tors U H–recognised GC members
SOC
Fees £25 (£30)
Loc 1 mile S of Llandudno
Station, nr Hospital

Llandudno (North
Wales) (1894)
72 Bryniau Road, West Shore,
Llandudno, LL30 2DZ
Tel (01492) 875325
Fax (01492) 873355
Web www.northwales.uk.com/nwgc
Mem 691
Sec WR Williams (01492) 875325
Pro RA Bradbury (01492) 876878
Holes 18 L 6247 yds Par 71 SSS 71
V'tors U SOC–phone Sec
Fees £25 (£35)
Loc ¾ mile from Llandudno on
West Shore

Llanfairfechan (1971)
Llannerch Road, Llanfairfechan,
LL33 0EB
Tel (01248) 680144
Mem 352
Sec MJ Charlesworth
(01248) 680524
Holes 9 L 3119 yds SSS 57
V'tors U
Fees £10 (£10)
Loc 7 miles E of Bangor on A55

Old Colwyn (1907)
Woodland Avenue, Old Colwyn,
LL29 9NL
Tel (01492) 515581
Mem 250
Sec DM Fisher
Holes 9 L 5243 yds SSS 66
V'tors WD–U WE–by arrangement
SOC
Fees £10 (£15)
Loc 2 miles E of Colwyn Bay,
off A55 Chester-Holyhead
road

Penmaenmawr (1910)
Conway Old Road, Penmaenmawr,
LL34 6RD
Tel (01492) 623330
Fax (01492) 622105
Mem 600
Sec Mrs JE Jones
Holes 9 L 5143 yds SSS 66
V'tors U SOC
Fees £12 (£18)
Loc 4 miles W of Conway

Rhos-on-Sea (1899)
Penrhyn Bay, Llandudno,
LL30 3PU
Tel (01492) 549641
Fax (01492) 549100
Mem 600
Sec JM Bray
Pro M Macara
Holes 18 L 6064 yds SSS 69
V'tors U
Fees £20 (£28)
Loc On coast at Rhos-on-Sea.
4 miles E of Llandudno
Arch Simpson

Denbighshire

Bryn Morfydd Hotel
(1982)
Llanrhaeadr, Denbigh, LL16 4NP
Tel   (01745) 890280
Fax   (01745) 890488
Web   www.bryn-morfydd.co.uk
Mem   250
Pro   IP Jones
Holes   18 L 5800 yds Par 70 SSS 67
         9 hole Par 3 course
V'tors   U SOC
Fees   £15 (£20)
Loc   2¹/₂ miles SE of Denbigh on
       A525
Arch   Duchess-Alliss/Thomas
        Dukes-Muirhead/
        Henderson

Denbigh (1922)
Henllan Road, Denbigh, LL16 5AA
Tel   (01745) 814159
Fax   (01745) 814888
Mem   550
Sec   J Raine (01745) 816669
Pro   M Jones (01745) 814159
Holes   18 L 5712 yds SSS 69
V'tors   U SOC
Fees   On application
Loc   1 mile NW of Denbigh
       (B5382)

Kinmel Park (1989)
Pay and play
Bodelwyddan, LL18 5SR
Tel   (01745) 833548
Fax   (01745) 824861
Sec   P Stebbings
Pro   P Stebbings
Holes   9 L 1550 yds Par 29
V'tors   U
Fees   £3.50 (£4)
Loc   Off A55, between Abergele
       and St Asaph
Mis   Driving range
Arch   Peter Stebbings

Prestatyn (1905)
*Marine Road East, Prestatyn,
LL19 7HS*
Tel   (01745) 854320
Fax   (01745) 888327
Web   www.prestatyngc.co.uk
Mem   710
Sec   R Woodruff (Mgr)
       (01745) 888353
Pro   M Staton (01745) 852083
Holes   18 L 6808 yds SSS 73
V'tors   H SOC
Fees   £22 (£27)
Loc   1 mile E of Prestatyn
Arch   S Collins

Rhuddlan (1930)
Meliden Road, Rhuddlan, LL18 6LB
Tel   (01745) 590217
Fax   (01745) 590472
Web   www.rhuddlangolfclub.co.uk

Mem   515 155(L) 80(J)
Sec   BP Jones
Pro   A Carr (01745) 590898
Holes   18 L 6471 yds SSS 71
V'tors   H Sun–M SOC–WD
Fees   £20 (£30)
Loc   2 miles N of St Asaph, off A55
Arch   F Hawtree

Rhyl (1890)
Coast Road, Rhyl, LL18 3RE
Tel   (01745) 353171
Fax   (01745) 353171
Web   www.rhylgolfclub.com
Mem   600
Sec   I StC Doig
Pro   T Leah
Holes   9 L 6220 yds SSS 70
V'tors   U SOC
Fees   £20 (£25)
Loc   On A548 between Rhyl and
       Prestatyn
Arch   James Braid

Ruthin-Pwllglas (1920)
Pwllglas, Ruthin, LL15 2PE
Tel   (01824) 702296
Fax   (01978) 790692
Mem   360
Sec   Mrs BK Tremayne (Hon)
       (01978) 790692
Holes   10 L 5362 yds SSS 66
V'tors   U SOC
Fees   £12.50 (£18)
Loc   2¹/₂ miles S of Ruthin

St Melyd (1922)
*The Paddock, Meliden Road, Prestatyn,
LL18 8NB*
Tel   (01745) 854405
Fax   (01745) 856908
Web   www.stmelydgolf.co.uk
Mem   400
Sec   KJ Woodward
Holes   9 L 5857 yds SSS 68
V'tors   U SOC
Fees   £18 (£22)
Loc   S of Prestatyn on A547

Vale of Llangollen (1908)
Holyhead Road, Llangollen, LL20 7PR
Tel   (01978) 860613
Fax   (01978) 860906
Mem   850
Sec   AD Bluck (01978) 860906
Pro   DI Vaughan (01978) 860040
Holes   18 L 6656 yds Par 72 SSS 73
V'tors   U H SOC
Fees   £20 (£25)
Loc   1¹/₂ miles E of Llangollen on
       A5

Flintshire

Caerwys (1989)
Pay and play
Caerwys, Mold, CH7 5AQ
Tel   (01352) 720692

Mem   200
Sec   E Barlow
Pro   N Lloyd
Holes   9 L 3080 yds SSS 60
V'tors   U SOC
Fees   £4.50 (£5.50)
Loc   SW of Caerwys. 1¹/₂ miles S of
       A55 Express Way, between
       Holywell and St Asaph
Arch   Eleanor Barlow

Devere Northop Country Park (1994)
Northop, Chester, CH7 6WA
Tel   (01352) 840440
Fax   (01352) 840445
Sec   D Llewellyn
Pro   M Pritchard
Holes   18 L 6735 yds Par 72
V'tors   U–phone first
Fees   £30 (£35)
Loc   3 miles S of Flint, off A55
Mis   Driving range
Arch   John Jacobs

Flint (1966)
Cornist Park, Flint, CH6 5HJ
Tel   (01352) 732327,
       (01244) 812974
Fax   (01244) 811885
Mem   390
Sec   TE Owens
Holes   9 L 5953 yds SSS 69
V'tors   WD–U before 5pm SOC–WD
Fees   D–£10 (£10)
Loc   1 mile SW of Flint. End of
       M56, 8 miles

Hawarden (1911)
*Groomsdale Lane, Hawarden, Deeside,
CH5 3EH*
Tel   (01244) 531447
Fax   (01244) 536901
Mem   480
Sec   MB Coppack
Pro   A Rowlands (01244) 520809
Holes   18 L 5842 yds SSS 68
V'tors   H SOC
Fees   £16 (£20)
Loc   6 miles W of Chester, off A55

Holywell (1906)
Brynford, Holywell, CH8 8LQ
Tel   (01352) 710040/713937
Fax   (01352) 713937
Mem   375 60(L)
Sec   SL Roberts (01352) 713937
Pro   M Parsley (01352) 710040
Holes   18 L 6100 yds Par 70 SSS 70
V'tors   WD–U WE–SOC
Fees   £18 (£23)
Loc   2 miles S of Holywell, off
       A5026

Kinsale
Pay and play
Llanerchymor, Holywell, CH8 9DX
Tel   (01745) 561080
Fax   (01745) 561079

Mem 85
Sec A Backhurst (Golf Dir)
Pro A Backhurst
Holes 9 holes Par 71 SSS 70
V'tors U
Fees 9 holes–£6.60. 18
holes–£9.90
Loc 4 miles N of Holywell on
A548
Mis Floodlit driving range
Arch K Smith

Mold (1909)
Cilcain Road, Pantymwyn, Mold,
CH7 5EH
Tel (01352) 740318/741513
Fax (01352) 741517
Mem 450 90(L) 95(J)
Sec P Mather (01352) 741513
Pro M Jordan (01352) 740318
Holes 18 L 5512 yds Par 67 SSS 67
V'tors U SOC
Fees £18 (£25)
Loc 3 miles W of Mold
Arch Hawtree

Old Padeswood (1978)
Station Road, Padeswood, Mold,
CH7 4JL
Tel (01244) 547701 (Clubhouse)
Web www.oldpadeswoodgolfclub
.co.uk
Mem 500
Sec B Slater (Hon)
Pro A Davies (01244) 547401
Holes 18 L 6728 yds SSS 72
9 hole Par 3 course
V'tors U exc comp days SOC–WD
Fees £18 D–£25 (£20)
Loc 2 miles from Mold on A5118

Padeswood & Buckley (1933)
The Caia, Station Lane, Padeswood,
Mold CH7 4JD
Tel (01244) 550537
Fax (01244) 541600
Mem 592
Sec JM Conway
Pro D Ashton (01244) 543636
Holes 18 L 5982 yds Par 70 SSS 69
V'tors WD–U 9am–4pm –M after
4pm Sat–U Sun–NA
SOC–WD Ladies Day–Wed
Fees £20 (£25)
Loc 8 miles W of Chester, off
A5118. 2nd golf club on right
Arch D Williams

Gwynedd

Aberdovey (1892)
Aberdovey, LL35 0RT
Tel (01654) 767210
Fax (01654) 767027
Web www.aberdoveygolf.co.uk
Mem 800
Sec JM Griffiths (01654) 767493

Pro J Davies (01654) 767602
Holes 18 L 6445 yds SSS 71
V'tors NA–8–9.30am & 1–2pm
Fees On application
Loc 1/2 mile W of Aberdovey
(A493)
Arch Braid/Fowler/Swan

Abersoch (1907)
Golf Road, Abersoch, LL53 7EY
Tel (01758) 712636
Fax (01758) 712777
Web www.abersochgolf.co.uk
Mem 700
Sec A Drosinos Jones
(01758) 712622
Pro A Drosinos Jones
Holes 18 L 5819 yds SSS 69
V'tors U H SOC
Fees £18 (£20)
Loc 1/2 mile S of Abersoch (A55).
7 miles S of Pwllheli
Arch Harry Vardon

Bala (1973)
Penlan, Bala, LL23 7BC
Tel (01678) 520359
Fax (01678) 521361
Mem 340
Sec G Rhys Jones (01678) 521361
Pro T Davies
Holes 10 L 4962 yds SSS 64
V'tors WD–U WE–NA pm SOC
Fees £12 (£15) W–£40
Loc 1 mile SW of Bala, off A494
to Dolgellau

Bala Lake Hotel
Bala, LL23 7YF
Tel (01678) 520344/520111
Fax (01678) 521193
Mem 50
Sec D Pickering
Holes 9 L 4280 yds SSS 61
V'tors U
Fees On application
Loc 1 1/2 miles S of Bala on B4403

Criccieth (1905)
Ednyfed Hill, Criccieth, LL52
Tel (01766) 522154
Mem 200
Sec MG Hamilton
(01766) 522697
Holes 18 L 5755 yds SSS 68
V'tors U
Fees £12 Sun–£15
Loc 4 miles W of Portmadoc

Dolgellau (1911)
Hengwrt Estate, Pencefn Road,
Dolgellau, LL4 0SE
Tel (01341) 422603
Mem 300
Sec Ms JM May
Pro H Jones Davies
Holes 9 L 4671 yds Par 66 SSS 63
V'tors U
Fees £15 (£20)

Loc 1/2 miles N of Dolgellau
Arch J Medway

Ffestiniog (1893)
Y Cefn, Ffestiniog
Tel (01766) 762637 (Clubhouse)
Mem 138
Sec A Roberts (01766) 831829
Holes 9 L 5032 metres Par 68
SSS 65
V'tors U
Fees On application
Loc 1 mile E of Ffestiniog on Bala
road (B4391)

Nefyn & District (1907)
Morfa Nefyn, Pwllheli, LL53 6DA
Tel (01758) 720218 (Clubhouse)
Fax (01758) 720476
Mem 750
Sec JB Owens (01758) 720966
Pro J Froom (01758) 720102
Holes 18 L 6548 yds SSS 71
9 L 2618 yds SSS 34
V'tors U SOC
Fees £26 D–£31 (£31 D–£36)
Loc 1 1/2 miles W of Nefyn. 20
miles W of Caernarfon

Porthmadog (1905)
Morfa Bychan, Porthmadog,
LL49 9UU
Tel (01766) 512037 (Clubhouse)
Fax (01766) 514638
Web www.porthmadog-golf-
club.co.uk
Mem 920
Sec Mrs A Richardson (Office
Mgr) (01766) 514124
Pro P Bright (01766) 513828
Holes 18 L 6363 yds Par 71 SSS 71
V'tors U H SOC
Fees D–£25 (D–£30)
Loc 2 miles S of Porthmadog,
towards Black Rock Sands
Arch James Braid

Pwllheli (1900)
Golf Road, Pwllheli, LL53 5PS
Tel (01758) 701644
Fax (01758) 701644
Web www.pwllheligolf.co.uk
Mem 820
Sec E Pritchard
Pro J Pilkington (01758) 612520
Holes 18 L 6091 yds SSS 69
V'tors U
Fees £22 (£27)
Loc 1/2 mile SW of Pwllheli
Arch James Braid

Royal St David's (1894)
Harlech, LL46 2UB
Tel (01766) 780203
Fax (01766) 781110
Web www.royalstdavids.co.uk
Mem 780
Sec DL Morkill (01766) 780361
Pro J Barnett (01766) 780857

For list of abbreviations see page 649

Holes 18 L 6571 yds SSS 73
V'tors U H–booking necessary SOC
Fees £36 (D–£46)
Loc W of Harlech on A496

Royal Town of Caernarfon (1909)

Aberforeshore, LLanfaglan, Caernarfon, LL54 5RP
Tel (01286) 673967
Fax (01286) 672535
Mem 735
Sec G Jones (01286) 673783
Pro A Owen (01286) 678359
Holes 18 L 5891 yds SSS 68
V'tors U SOC
Fees £18 (£22)
Loc 2¹/₂ miles SW of Caernarfon

St Deiniol (1906)

Penybryn, Bangor, LL57 1PX
Tel (01248) 353098
Mem 350
Sec RD Thomas (01248) 370792
Holes 18 L 5654 yds SSS 67
V'tors U SOC
Fees £15 (£19)
Loc Off A5/A55 Junction, 1 mile E of Bangor on A5122
Arch James Braid

Isle of Anglesey

Anglesey (1914)

Station Road, Rhosneigr, LL64 5QX
Tel (01407) 811202
Fax (01407) 811202
Mem 450
Sec K Brown (Sec/Mgr)
Pro P Lovell
Holes 18 L 6330 yds SSS 70
V'tors U H SOC
Fees £15 (£20)
Loc 8 miles SE of Holyhead, off A4080
Arch H Hilton

Baron Hill (1895)

Beaumaris, LL58 8YW
Tel (01248) 810231
Mem 360
Sec A Pleming
Holes 9 L 5062 metres SSS 68
V'tors U exc comp days SOC–WD & Sat (apply Sec)
Fees £15 W–£45
Loc 1 mile SW of Beaumaris

Bull Bay (1913)

Bull Bay Road, Amlwch, LL68 9RY
Tel (01407) 830213
Fax (01407) 832612
Web www.bullbaygc.co.uk
Mem 700
Sec I Furlong (Sec/Mgr) (01407) 830960
Pro J Burns (01407) 831188

Holes 18 L 6276 yds SSS 70
V'tors H SOC
Fees £20 (£25)
Loc ¹/₂ mile W of Amlwch on A5025
Arch WH Fowler

Henllys Hall

Llanfaes, Beaumaris, LL58 8HU
Tel (01248) 811717
Fax (01248) 811511
Pro P Maton
Holes 18 L 6062 yds Par 72
V'tors U SOC
Fees £18 (£22)
Loc 2 miles N of Beaumaris (B5109)
Arch Roger Jones

Holyhead (1912)

Trearddur Bay, Holyhead, LL65 2YL
Tel (01407) 763279/762119
Fax (01407) 763279
Web www.holyheadgolfclub.co.uk
Mem 790 396(L)
Sec JA Williams
Pro S Elliott (01407) 762022
Holes 18 L 5540 metres SSS 70
V'tors H SOC
Fees £19 D–£25 (£25 D–£29)
Loc 2 miles S of Holyhead
Arch James Braid

Llangefni (1983)

Public
Llangefni, LL77 8YQ
Tel (01248) 722193
Pro P Lovell
Holes 9 L 1467 yds Par 28
V'tors U
Fees £3 (£3)
Loc ¹/₂mile S of Llangefni, off A5111
Arch Hawtree

RAF Valley

Anglesey, LL65 3NY
Tel (01407) 762241
Mem 150
Sec MJ Constable (Mgr)
Holes 9 L 5604 yards SSS 68
V'tors U – booking necessary
Fees D–£6 (£6)
Loc RAF Valley base, off A55

Storws Wen (1996)

Brynteg, Benllech, LL78 8JY
Tel (01248) 852673
Fax (01248) 853843
Mem 300
Sec C Purves
Pro J Kelly
Holes 9 L 5002 yds Par 68 SSS 64
V'tors U SOC
Fees £14 (£18)
Loc 2 miles from Benllech on B5108
Arch K Jones

Mid Glamorgan

Aberdare (1921)

Abernant, Aberdare, CF44 0RY
Tel (01685) 871188 (Clubhouse)
Fax (01685) 872797
Mem 500
Sec T Mears (01685) 872797
Pro AW Palmer (01685) 878735
Holes 18 L 5875 yds SSS 69
V'tors H SOC
Fees £16 (£18)
Loc ¹/₂ mile E of Aberdare. 12 miles NW of Pontypridd

Bargoed (1913)

Heolddu, Bargoed, CF81 9GF
Tel (01443) 830143
Mem 548
Sec G Williams (01443) 830608
Pro C Coombs (01443) 836411
Holes 18 L 6233 yds SSS 70
V'tors WD–U WE–M SOC–WD
Fees £18.50
Loc NW boundary of Bargoed. 8 miles N of Caerphilly (A469)

Bryn Meadows Golf Hotel (1973)

The Bryn, Hengoed, CF8 7SM
Tel (01495) 225590/224103
Fax (01495) 228272
Mem 550
Sec B Mayo
Pro B Hunter (01495) 221905
Holes 18 L 6156 yds SSS 69
V'tors U
Fees £17.50 (£22.50)
Loc 6 miles N of Caerphilly (A469)
Arch Mayo/Jefferies

Caerphilly (1905)

Pencapel, Mountain Road, Caerphilly, CF83 1HJ
Tel (029) 2088 3481
Fax (029) 2086 3441
Mem 700
Sec (029) 2086 3441
Pro J Hill (029) 2086 9104
Holes 13 L 6039 yds SSS 70
V'tors WD–U H WE–M
Fees £20 W–£40
Loc 7 miles N of Cardiff, off A469

Castell Heights (1982)

Pay and play
Blaengwynlais, Caerphilly, CF8 1NG
Tel (029) 2088 6666 (Bookings)
Fax (029) 2086 9030
Mem 600
Pro S Bebb
Holes 9 L 2688 yds SSS 66
V'tors U
Fees 9 holes–£4.50 (£5.50)
Loc 4 miles from M4 Junction 32
Mis Driving range
Arch J Page

Coed-y-Mwstwr (1994)
Coychurch, Bridgend, CF35 6TN
Tel (01656) 862121
Fax (01656) 864934
Mem 260
Sec HD James (Sec/Mgr)
Holes 12 L 6144 yds Par 70 SSS 70
V'tors U H Sat–M SOC–WD
Fees £16 (£18)
Loc 2 miles W of M4 Junction 35

Creigiau (1921)
Creigiau, Cardiff, CF15 9NN
Tel (029) 2089 0263
Fax (029) 2089 0706
Mem 700
Sec AJ Greedy
Pro I Luntz (029) 2089 1909
Holes 18 L 6063 yds SSS 70
V'tors WD–U WE/BH–M SOC–WD
Fees £30
Loc 5 miles NW of Cardiff. M4
    Junction 34

Llantrisant & Pontyclun (1927)
Elm Valley Road, Talbot Green,
Llantrisant, CF72 8AL
Tel (01443) 222148
Mem 600
Sec JD Jones (01443) 224601
Pro M Phillips (01443) 228169
Holes 18 L 5328 yds SSS 66
V'tors WD–H WE/BH–M
    SOC–WD
Fees On application
Loc 10 miles NW of Cardiff. 2
    miles N of M4 Junction 34

Maesteg (1912)
Mount Pleasant, Neath Road, Maesteg,
CF34 9PR
Tel (01656) 732037
Fax (01656) 734106
Mem 720
Sec RK Lewis MBE
    (01656) 734106
Pro C Riley (01656) 735742
Holes 18 L 5929 yds SSS 69
V'tors WD–H SOC
Fees £17 (£20)
Loc 1 mile W of Maesteg on
    B4282. M4 Junctions 36 or 40

Merthyr Tydfil (1909)
Cilsanws Mountain, Cefn Coed,
Merthyr Tydfil, CF48 2NU
Tel (01685) 723308
Mem 200
Sec V Price
Pro None
Holes 18 L 5622 yds SSS 68
V'tors U SOC–WD
Fees £10 (£15)
Loc 2 miles N of Merthyr Tydfil,
    off A470 at Cefn Coed
Arch Price/Mathias (new holes)

Morlais Castle (1900)
Pant, Dowlais, Merthyr Tydfil,
CF48 2UY
Tel (01685) 722822
Fax (01685) 722822
Mem 600
Sec M Price
Pro H Jarrett (01685) 388700
Holes 18 L 6320 yds SSS 71
V'tors WD–U Sat–NA 12–4pm
    Sun–NA 8am–12noon SOC
Fees £16 (£20)
Loc 3 miles N of Merthyr Tydfil,
    nr Mountain Railway

Mountain Ash (1907)
Cefnpennar, Mountain Ash, CF45 4DT
Tel (01443) 472265
Fax (01443) 479628
Mem 555
Sec G Matthews (01443) 479459
Pro M Wills (01443) 478770
Holes 18 L 5535 yds SSS 67
V'tors WD–U H WE–M
Fees £15
Loc 9 miles NW of Pontypridd

Mountain Lakes (1988)
Heol Penbryn, Blaengwynlais,
Caerphilly, CF83 1NG
Tel (029) 2086 1128
Fax (029) 2086 3243
Mem 480
Sec DC Rooney (Hon)
Pro S Bebb
Holes 18 L 6300 yds SSS 72
V'tors U SOC
Fees £18 (£18)
Loc 4 miles from M4 Junction 32
Mis Driving range
Arch R Sandow

Pontypridd (1905)
Ty Gwyn Road, Pontypridd, CF37 4DJ
Tel (01443) 402359
Fax (01443) 491622
Mem 850
Sec Vikki Hooley (01443) 409904
Pro W Walters (01443) 491210
Holes 18 L 5725 yds SSS 68
V'tors WD–U H WE/BH–M H
    SOC–WD H
Fees On application
Loc E of Pontypridd, off A470. 12
    miles NW of Cardiff

Pyle & Kenfig (1922)
Waun-y-Mer, Kenfig, Bridgend,
CF33 4PU
Tel (01656) 783093
Fax (01656) 772822
Web www.pyleandkenfiggolfclub
    .co.uk
Mem 860
Sec SD Anthony (Sec/Mgr)
    (01656) 771613
Pro R Evans (01656) 772446
Holes 18 L 6741 yds Par 71 SSS 73
V'tors WD–U H WE–M SOC
Fees D–£30

Loc 2 miles NW of Porthcawl. M4
    Junction 37
Arch HS Colt

Rhondda (1910)
Penrhys, Ferndale, Rhondda,
CF43 3PW
Tel (01443) 433204
Fax (01443) 441384
Mem 500
Sec M Evans JP (01443) 441384
Pro G Bebb (01443) 441385
Holes 18 L 6428 yds SSS 71
V'tors U H SOC
Fees £15 (£20)
Loc 6 miles W of Pontypridd

Royal Porthcawl (1891)
Rest Bay, Porthcawl, CF36 3UW
Tel (01656) 782251
Fax (01656) 771687
Web www.royalporthcawl.com
Mem 800
Sec FW Prescott
Pro P Evans (01656) 773702
Holes 18 L 6685 yds SSS 74
V'tors WD–I or H WE/BH–M
    SOC–H
Fees On application
Loc 22 miles W of Cardiff. M4
    Junction 37
Mis Driving range. Dormy House
Arch Charles Gibson

Southerndown (1905)
Ewenny, Ogmore-by-Sea, Bridgend,
CF32 0QP
Tel (01656) 880326
Fax (01656) 880317
Mem 700
Sec AJ Hughes (01656) 880476
Pro DG McMonagle
Holes 18 L 6449 yds SSS 72
V'tors U H
Fees £30 (£40)
Loc 3 miles S of Bridgend, nr
    Ogmore Castle ruins
Arch W Fernie

Virginia Park (1993)
Pay and play
Virginia Park, Caerphilly, CF83 3SW
Tel (029) 2086 3919
Mem 200
Sec Mrs C Lewis
Pro P Clark (029) 2085 0650
Holes 9 L 4661 yds Par 66 SSS 63
V'tors U SOC
Fees On application
Loc Caerphilly, 7 miles N of
    Cardiff
Mis Driving range

Whitehall (1922)
The Pavilion, Nelson, Treharris,
CF46 6ST
Tel (01443) 740245
Mem 300
Sec PM Wilde

For list of abbreviations see page 649

Holes 9 L 5666 yds SSS 68
V'tors WD–U WE–M SOC
Fees £15
Loc 15 miles NW of Cardiff

Monmouthshire

Alice Springs (1989)
Bettws Newydd, Usk, NP5 1JY
Tel (01873) 880708
Fax (01873) 880838
Mem 350
Sec KR Morgan
Pro M Davies (01873) 880914
Holes Red 18 L 5870 yds SSS 69
Green 18 L 6438 yds SSS 72
V'tors U SOC
Fees £16 (£20)
Loc 3 miles N of Usk on B4598
Mis Driving range
Arch Keith Morgan

Blackwood (1914)
Cwmgelli, Blackwood, NP12 1BR
Tel (01495) 223152
Mem 300
Sec AD Watkins
Pro None
Holes 9 L 5304 yds SSS 66
V'tors WD–I SOC WE/BH–M
Fees £14
Loc 1/4 mile N of Blackwood

Caerleon (1974)
Pay and play
Broadway, Caerleon, NP6 1AY
Tel (01633) 420342
Mem 150
Sec P John
Pro A Campbell
Holes 9 L 3092 yds SSS
V'tors U
Fees 18 holes–£5 9 holes–£3.30
Loc M4 Junction 25, 3 miles
Mis Driving range
Arch Donald Steel

Celtic Manor Hotel G&CC (1995)
Coldra Woods, Newport, NP6 1JQ
Tel (01633) 413000
Fax (01633) 410309
Mem 450
Sec S Wesson (01633) 413000
Pro S Patience
(01633) 413000
Holes 18 L 7001 yds Par 70 SSS 74
18 L 4094 yds Par 61 SSS 60
18 L 7403 yds Par 72 SSS 77
V'tors H SOC
Fees On application
Loc E of Newport on A48. M4
Junction 24
Mis Golf Academy. Driving range
Arch Robert Trent Jones Sr

Dewstow (1988)
Caerwent, NP26 4AH
Tel (01291) 430444
Fax (01291) 425816
Mem 950
Sec E Tose
Pro J Skuse
Holes Valley 18 L 6091 yds Par 72
SSS 70;
Park 18 L 6226 yds Par 69
SSS 69
V'tors WD–U WE–by arrangement
SOC
Fees £14 (£17)
Loc Caerwent, 5 miles W of old
Severn Bridge, off A48
Mis Driving range

Greenmeadow (1980)
Treherbert Road, Croesyceiliog,
Cwmbran, NP44 2BZ
Tel (01633) 869321
Mem 430
Sec PJ Richardson
Pro P Stebbings (01633) 862626
Holes 18 L 5501 yds SSS 69
V'tors U SOC
Fees On application
Loc 4 miles N of Newport on
A4042. M4 Junction 26
Mis Floodlit driving range

Llanwern (1928)
Tennyson Avenue, Llanwern, Newport,
NP18 2DW
Tel (01633) 412380
Fax (01633) 412029
Mem 776
Sec MW Penny (01633) 412029
Pro S Price (01633) 413233
Holes 18 L 6115 yds SSS 69
V'tors WD–U WE–restricted I H
SOC
Fees WD–£20
Loc 1 mile S of M4 Junction 24

Marriott St Pierre Hotel & CC (1962)
St Pierre Park, Chepstow, NP16 6YA
Tel (01291) 625261
Fax (01291) 629975
Mem 840
Sec TJ Cleary
Pro Shop (01291) 635205
Holes Old 18 L 6818 yds SSS 74;
Mathern 18 L 5732 yds
SSS 68
V'tors H SOC–WD
Fees On application
Loc 2 miles W of Chepstow (A48)
Mis Driving range
Arch CK Cotton

Monmouth (1896)
Leasebrook Lane, Monmouth,
NP25 3SN
Tel (01600) 712212/772399
Fax (01600) 772399
Mem 600

Pro None
Holes 18 L 5698 yds SSS 69
V'tors U SOC exc BH
Fees £15 (£20)
Loc Signposted 1 mile along A40
Monmouth-Ross road

Monmouthshire (1892)
Llanfoist, Abergavenny, NP7 9HE
Tel (01873) 852606
Fax (01873) 852606
Mem 555 107(L) 61(J)
Sec R Bradley
Pro (01873) 852532
Holes 18 L 5978 yds SSS 70
V'tors WD–H SOC
Fees £25 (£30)
Loc 2 miles SW of Abergavenny
Arch James Braid

Newport (1903)
Great Oak, Rogerstone, Newport,
NP10 9FX
Tel (01633) 892643/894496
Fax (01633) 896676
Mem 800
Sec JV Dinsdale
(01633) 892643
Pro PM Mayo (01633) 893271
Holes 18 L 6460 yds SSS 71
V'tors WD–H
Fees £30
Loc 3 miles W of Newport on
B4591. M4 Junction 27,
1 mile
Arch Ross/Fernie

Oakdale (1990)
Pay and play
Llwynon Lane, Oakdale, NP2 0NF
Tel (01495) 220044
Sec M Lewis (Dir)
Pro P Glynn (01495) 220440
Holes 9 L 1344 yds Par 28
V'tors U SOC
Fees On application
Loc 15 miles NW of Newport via
A467/B4251. M4 Junction 28
Mis Driving range
Arch Ian Goodenough

Parc (1990)
Pay and play
Church Lane, Coedkernew, Newport,
NP1 9TU
Tel (01633) 680933
Fax (01633) 681011
Mem 450
Sec C Hicks (Mgr),
M Cleary (Sec)
Pro J Skuse (01633) 680955
Holes 18 L 5512 yds SSS 67
V'tors U SOC
Fees £11 (£13)
Loc 2 miles W of Newport on A48.
M4 Junction 28
Mis Floodlit driving range
Arch B Thomas

For list of abbreviations see page 649

Pontnewydd (1875)
Maesgwyn Farm, Upper Cwmbran, NP44 1AB
Tel (01633) 482170
Mem 250
Sec CT Phillips (01633) 484447
Holes 10 L 5353 yds SSS 67
V'tors WD–U WE–M SOC
Fees £15 (£10)
Loc W outskirts of Cwmbran

Pontypool (1903)
Lasgarn Lane, Trevethin, Pontypool, NP4 8TR
Tel (01495) 763655
Mem 544 54(L) 18(J)
Sec L Dodd
Pro J Howard (01495) 755544
Holes 18 L 5712 yds SSS 69
V'tors U H SOC
Fees £20 (£24)
Loc 1 mile N of Pontypool (A4042)

Raglan Parc
Parc Lodge, Raglan, NP5 2ER
Tel (01291) 690077
Mem 380
Sec T Lillistone
Pro C Evans
Holes 18 L 6604 yds Par 73
V'tors U
Fees £15 (£15)
Loc Nr A40/A449 junction

The Rolls of Monmouth (1982)
The Hendre, Monmouth, NP25 5HG
Tel (01600) 715353
Fax (01600) 713115
Mem 200
Sec Mrs SJ Orton
Pro None
Holes 18 L 6733 yds SSS 73
V'tors U SOC
Fees £34 (£38)
Loc 3½ miles W of Monmouth on B4233

Shirenewton (1995)
Shirenewton, Chepstow, NP16 6RL
Tel (01291) 641642
Fax (01291) 641472
Sec L Pagett (Mgr)
Pro L Pagett (01291) 641471
Holes 18 L 6607 yds Par 72 SSS 72
V'tors U SOC
Fees £16 (£18)
Loc 5 miles W of Chepstow, off A48. M4 Junction 22

Tredegar & Rhymney (1921)
Tredegar, Rhymney, NP2 3BQ
Tel (01685) 840743
Mem 180
Sec P Kenealy (07944) 843400
Holes 18 L 5564 yds SSS 68

V'tors U
Fees £10
Loc 1½ miles W of Tredegar (B4256)

Tredegar Park (1923)
Parc-y-Brain Road, Rogerstone, Newport, NP10 9TG
Tel (01633) 895219
Fax (01633) 897152
Mem 800
Sec AJ Trickett (01633) 894433
Pro ML Morgan (01633) 894517
Holes 18 L 6564 yds SSS 72
V'tors H SOC–WD
Fees D–£15 (£20)
Loc W of Newport, off M4 Junction 27
Arch R Sandow

Wernddu Golf Centre
Old Ross Road, Abergavenny, NP7 8NG
Tel (01873) 856223
Fax (01873) 852177
Web www.wernddugolfclub.co.uk
Mem 650
Sec L Turvey
Pro AA Ashmead
Holes 18 L 5500 yds Par 68 SSS 67
V'tors U
Fees 9 holes–£10. 18 holes–£15
Loc 1½ miles NE of Abergavenny on B4521
Mis Floodlit driving range

West Monmouthshire (1906)
Golf Road, Pond Road, Nantyglo, Ebbw Vale, NP23 4QT
Tel (01495) 310233/311361
Fax (01495) 311361
Mem 300
Sec SE Williams (01495) 310233
Holes 18 L 6118 yds SSS 69
V'tors WD/Sat–U Sun–M SOC–WD
Fees £15
Loc Nr Dunlop Semtex, off Brynmawr Bypass, towards Winchestown
Arch Ben Sayers

Woodlake Park (1993)
Glascoed, Usk, NP4 0TE
Tel (01291) 673933
Fax (01291) 673811
Web www.woodlake.co.uk
Mem 500
Sec D Hawker
Pro A Pritchard (01291) 671043
Holes 18 L 6300 yds Par 71 SSS 72
V'tors H SOC
Fees Summer–£20 (£25) Winter–£15 (£20)
Loc 3 miles W of Usk, nr Llandegfedd reservoir

Pembrokeshire

Haverfordwest (1904)
Arnolds Down, Haverfordwest, SA61 2XQ
Tel (01437) 763565
Fax (01437) 764143
Web www.hwestgolf.homestead.com
Mem 800
Sec (01437) 764523
Pro A Pile (01437) 768409
Holes 18 L 5966 yds SSS 69
V'tors U SOC
Fees £19 (£22)
Loc 1 mile E of Haverfordwest on A40

Milford Haven (1913)
Hubberston, Milford Haven, SA72 3RX
Tel (01646) 697762
Fax (01646) 697870
Web www.mhgc.co.uk
Mem 380 65(L) 90(J)
Sec WS Brown
Pro D Williams (01646) 697762
Holes 18 L 6071 yds SSS 71
V'tors U SOC
Fees £15 (£20)
Loc W boundary of Milford Haven

Newport (Pembs) (1925)
Newport, SA42 0NR
Tel (01239) 820244
Fax (01239) 820244
Mem 400
Sec A Payne (Mgr)
Pro J Noott (01239) 615359
Holes 9 L 3089 yds SSS 68
V'tors U SOC
Fees £18 (£22)
Loc 2½ miles NW of Newport, towards Newport Beach
Arch James Braid

Priskilly Forest (1992)
Castle Morris, Haverfordwest, SA62 5EH
Tel (01348) 840276
Fax (01348) 840276
Web www.priskilly-forest.co.uk
Sec P Evans
Holes 9 L 5874 yds Par 70 SSS 69
V'tors U SOC
Fees 9 holes–£8. 18 holes–£12
Loc 2 miles off A40 at Letterston
Arch J Walters

St Davids City (1903)
Whitesands Bay, St Davids, SA62 6PT
Tel (01437) 721751 (Clubhouse)
Mem 200
Sec R Hadfield (01437) 720572
Holes 9 L 6117 yds SSS 70
V'tors U SOC
Fees D–£13
Loc 2 miles W of St Davids. 15 miles NW of Haverfordwest

South Pembrokeshire
(1970)
Military Road, Pembroke Dock,
SA72 6SE
Tel   **(01646) 621453**
Mem 350
Sec   WD Owen
        (01646) 621453/621804
Pro   None
Holes 18 L 5638 yds SSS 69
V'tors U before 4.30pm SOC
Fees   On application
Loc   Pembroke Dock

Tenby (1888)
The Burrows, Tenby, SA70 7NP
Tel   **(01834) 842978**
Fax   (01834) 842978
Web   www.tenbygolf.co.uk
Mem 800
Sec   BSR Warren (01834) 842978
Pro   M Hawkey (01834) 844447
Holes 18 L 6450 yds SSS 71
V'tors H SOC
Fees   £26 (£32)
Loc   Tenby, South Beach
Arch   James Braid

Trefloyne (1996)
Trefloyne Park, Penally, Tenby,
SA70 7RG
Tel   **(01834) 842165**
Web   www.trefloynegolfcourse.co.uk
Mem 250
Pro   S Laidler (01834) 842165
Holes 18 L 6635 yds Par 71
V'tors U SOC
Fees   £21 (£26)
Loc   1¹/₂miles W of Tenby, off
        A4139 Pembroke road
Arch   FH Gilman

Powys

Brecon (1902)
Newton Park, Llanfaes, Brecon,
LD3 8PA
Tel   **(01874) 622004**
Mem 210
Sec   DHE Roderick
        (01874) 625547
Holes 9 L 5256 yds SSS 66
V'tors U SOC
Fees   £10
Loc   ¹/₂ mile W of Brecon on
        A40
Arch   James Braid

Builth Wells (1923)
Golf Club Road, Builth Wells,
LD2 3NF
Tel   **(01982) 553296**
Fax   (01982) 551064
Web   www.builthwellsgolfclub
        .co.uk
Mem 400
Sec   JN Jones

Pro   S Edwards
Holes 18 L 5376 yds SSS 67
V'tors U H SOC
Fees   £15 D–£20 (£20 D–£25)
Loc   W of Builth Wells on
        Llandovery road (A483)

Cradoc (1967)
Penoyre Park, Cradoc, Brecon,
LD3 9LP
Tel   **(01874) 623658**
Fax   (01874) 611711
Web   www.cradoc.co.uk
Mem 750
Sec   Mrs EG Price
        (01874) 623658
Pro   R Davies (01874) 625524
Holes 18 L 6331 yds SSS 72
V'tors U SOC
Fees   £20 (£25)
Loc   2 miles NW of Brecon, off
        B4520
Mis   Driving range
Arch   CK Cotton

Knighton (1905)
Ffrydd Wood, Knighton, LD7 1EF
Tel   **(01547) 528646**
Fax   (01547) 529284
Mem 150
Sec   AW Aspley (Hon)
Holes 9 L 5362 yds Par 68 SSS 66
V'tors U SOC
Fees   £10 (£12)
Loc   SW of Knighton. 20 miles NE
        of Llandrindod Wells
Arch   H Vardon

Llandrindod Wells (1905)
Llandrindod Wells, LD1 5NY
Tel   **(01597) 823873**
Fax   (01597) 823873
Web   www.lwgc.co.uk
Mem 370
Sec   (01597) 823873
Pro   Golf Shop (01597) 822247
Holes 18 L 5759 yds Par 69 SSS 69
V'tors U SOC
Fees   £15 (£20)
Loc   ¹/₂ mile E of Llandrindod
        Wells centre
Arch   Harry Vardon

Machynlleth (1904)
Ffordd Drenewydd, Machynlleth,
SY20 8UH
Tel   **(01654) 702000**
Mem 231
Holes 9 L 5726 yds SSS 67
V'tors U Sun–NA before 11.30am
        SOC
Fees   £12 (£15)
Loc   1 mile E of Machynlleth, off
        A489

Rhosgoch (1991)
Rhosgoch, Builth Wells, LD2 3JY
Tel   **(01497) 851251**
Mem 150
Sec   C Dance

Holes 9 L 5078 yds SSS 65
V'tors U SOC
Fees   £7 (£10)
Loc   5 miles N of Hay-on-Wye

St Giles Newtown (1895)
Pool Road, Newtown, SY16 3AJ
Tel   **(01686) 625844**
Mem 350
Pro   DP Owen
Holes 9 L 6012 yds SSS 70
V'tors U SOC
Fees   £12.50 (£15)
Loc   1 mile E of Newtown (A483).
        14 miles SW of Welshpool

St Idloes (1920)
Owned privately
Penrhallt, Llanidloes, SY18 6LG
Tel   **(01686) 412559**
Fax   (01926) 889536
Mem 292
Sec   JC Green
Pro   P Parkin
Holes 9 L 5510 yds SSS 66
V'tors U H Sun–restricted SOC
Fees   £10 (£12) W–£45
Loc   ¹/₂ mile from Llanidloes on
        Trefeglwys road (B4569)

Welsh Border Golf
Complex (1991)
Bulthy Farm, Bulthy, Middletown,
SY21 8ER
Tel   **(01743) 884247**
Mem 200
Sec   J Watt
Pro   A Griffiths
Holes 9 L 3050 yds SSS 69
        9 hole course
V'tors U SOC
Fees   £14
Loc   Between Shrewsbury and
        Welshpool on A458
Mis   Driving range
Arch   A Griffiths

Welshpool (1929)
Golfa Hill, Welshpool, SY21 9AQ
Tel   **(01938) 850249**
Mem 400
Sec   D Lewis (01938) 810757
Pro   None
Holes 18 L 5708 yds Par 70 SSS 68
V'tors U
Fees   £12.50 D–£20.50
        Winter–£15.50
Loc   4¹/₂ miles W of Welshpool, on
        Dolgellau road (A458)
Arch   James Braid

South Glamorgan

Brynhill (1921)
Port Road, Barry, CF62 8PN
Tel   **(01446) 720277**
Mem 700

Sec P Gershenson
(01446) 720277
Pro P Fountain (01446) 740004
Holes 18 L 6352 yds SSS 71
V'tors WD/Sat–H Sun–NA
SOC–WD
Fees £20 Sat–£25 SOC–£17
Loc A4050, 8 miles SW of
Cardiff

Cardiff (1921)

*Sherborne Avenue, Cyncoed, Cardiff,
CF23 6SJ*
Tel (029) 2075 3067
Fax (029) 2068 0011
Mem 930
Sec K Lloyd (029) 2075 3320
Pro T Hanson (029) 2075 4772
Holes 18 L 6015 yds SSS 70
V'tors WD–H WE–M SOC–Thurs
Fees £35 (£40)
Loc 3 miles N of Cardiff. 2 miles
W of Pentwyn exit of A48(M).
M4 Junction 29

Cottrell Park (1996)

St Nicholas, Cardiff, CF5 6JY
Tel (01446) 781781
Fax (01446) 781187
Mem 1050
Sec DW Marchant
Pro S Birch
Holes 18 L 6606 yds Par 72 SSS 72
9 L 2807 yds Par 70 SSS 67
V'tors U H SOC–WD
Fees 18 hole:£25–£35
9 hole:£10–£15
Loc 4 miles W of Cardiff on A48.
M4 Junction 33
Mis Driving range
Arch Bob Sandow

Dinas Powis (1914)

*Old Highwalls, Dinas Powis,
CF64 4AJ*
Tel (029) 2051 2727
Fax (029) 2051 2727
Mem 490
Sec HL Williams
Pro G Bennett (029) 2051 3682
Holes 18 L 5486 yds SSS 67
V'tors H SOC
Fees D–£25 (£30)
Loc 3 miles SW of Cardiff
(A4055)

Glamorganshire (1890)

*Lavernock Road, Penarth,
CF64 5UP*
Tel (029) 2070 1185
Fax (029) 2070 1185
Mem 1100
Sec BM Williams
(029) 2070 1185
Pro A Kerr-Smith
(029) 2070 7401
Holes 18 L 6181 yds SSS 70
V'tors WD/WE–H SOC
Fees £30 (£35)
Loc 5 miles SW of Cardiff

Llanishen (1905)

Heol Hir, Cardiff, CF14 9UD
Tel (029) 2075 5078
Fax (029) 2075 5078
Mem 850
Sec EW Page (029) 2075 5078
Pro RA Jones (029) 2075 5076
Holes 18 L 5296 yds SSS 67
V'tors WD–U WE–M H SOC–Thurs
& Fri
Fees £30
Loc 5 miles N of Cardiff

Peterstone

Peterstone, Wentloog, Cardiff, CF3 8TN
Tel (01633) 680009
Fax (01633) 680563
Mem 700
Sec R Williams
Pro D Griffiths
Holes 18 L 6555 yds Par 72 SSS 72
V'tors U SOC–WD
Fees £18
Loc 3 miles S of Castleton, off
A48. M4 Junction 28
Arch Robert Sandow

Radyr (1902)

*Drysgol Road, Radyr, Cardiff,
CF15 8BS*
Tel (029) 2084 2408
Fax (029) 2084 3914
Web www.radyrgolf.co.uk
Mem 880
Sec AM Edwards (Mgr)
Pro R Butterworth (029) 2084
2476
Holes 18 L 6031 yds SSS 70
V'tors SOC–Wed/Thurs/Fri
Fees D–£38
Loc 5 miles NW of Cardiff, off
A470. M4 Junction 32

RAF St Athan (1977)

St Athan, Barry, CF62 4WA
Tel (01446) 751043
Fax (01446) 751862
Mem 450
Sec PF Woodhouse
(01446) 797186
Holes 9 L 6452 yds SSS 72
V'tors U exc Sun am–NA
Fees £12 (£17)
Loc 2 miles E of Llantwit Major.
10 miles S of Bridgend

St Andrews Major (1993)

*Coldbrook Road, Cadoxton, Barry,
CF6 3BB*
Tel (01446) 722227
Mem 350
Sec N Edmunds
Holes 9 L 2931 yds
V'tors U SOC
Fees 9 holes–£8. 18 holes–£13
Loc Barry Docks Link road. M4
Junction 33
Arch MRM Leisure

St Mary's Hotel G&CC (1990)

Pay and play
St Mary's Hill, Pencoed, CF35 5EA
Tel (01656) 861100
Fax (01656) 863400
Mem 800
Sec Kay Brazell
Pro J Peters (01656) 861599
Holes 18 L 5291 yds Par 69 SSS 66
9 L 2426 yds Par 35
V'tors H SOC–WD
Fees 18 hole:£15 (£17) 9 hole:£5
(£6)
Loc Off M4 Junction 35
Mis Floodlit driving range

St Mellons (1937)

St Mellons, Cardiff, CF3 2XS
Tel (01633) 680401
Fax (01633) 681219
Mem 500 93(L) 70(J)
Sec Mrs K Newling
(01633) 680408
Pro B Thomas (01633) 680101
Holes 18 L 6225 yds SSS 70
V'tors WD–U WE–M
Fees £32
Loc 4 miles E of Cardiff on A48

Vale of Glamorgan Hotel G&CC

Hensol Park, Hensol, CF7 8JY
Tel (01443) 665899
Fax (01443) 222220
Mem 900
Sec Mrs L Edwards
Pro P Johnson
Holes Lake 18 L 6507 yds Par 72
Hensol 9 L 3115 yds Par 36
V'tors H SOC
Fees £25 (£30)
Loc 1 mile from M 4 Junction 34
Mis Driving range. Golf Academy
Arch Peter Johnson

Wenvoe Castle (1936)

Wenvoe, Cardiff, CF5 6BE
Tel (029) 2059 4371
Fax (029) 2059 4371
Mem 540 100(L) 66(J)
Sec N Sims (029) 2059 4371
Pro J Harris (029) 2059 3649
Holes 18 L 6422 yds SSS 71
V'tors WD–H WE/BH–M SOC–WD
Fees £32
Loc 4 miles W of Cardiff, off
A4050

Whitchurch (1915)

*Pantmawr Road, Whitchurch, Cardiff,
CF4 6XD*
Tel (029) 2062 0125
Fax (029) 2052 9860
Mem 780
Sec JW King (029) 2062 0985
Pro E Clark (029) 2061 4660
Holes 18 L 6212 yds Par 71 SSS 70
V'tors WD–U WE/BH–M H
SOC–Thurs

For list of abbreviations see page 649

Fees £35 (£40)
Loc   3 miles NW of Cardiff on
          A470. M4 Junction 32

West Glamorgan

Allt-y-Graban (1993)
Allt-y-Graban Road, Pontlliw,
Swansea, SA4 1DT
Tel   (01792) 885757
Mem   154
Sec   Mrs M Lewis (Mgr)
Pro   S Rees
Holes 9 L 2210 yds Par 66 SSS 63
V'tors U SOC
Fees   18 holes—£9 (£9)
           9 holes—£6 (£6)
Loc   3 miles of M4 Junction 47, on
           A48
Arch   FG Thomas

Clyne (1920)
120 Owls Lodge Lane, Mayals,
Swansea, SA3 5DP
Tel   (01792) 401989
Fax   (01792) 401078
Mem   900
Sec   RH Thompson FCA (Mgr)
Pro   J Clewett (01792) 402094
Holes 18 L 6334 yds SSS 71
V'tors U H SOC
Fees   £25 (£30)
Loc   3 miles SW of Swansea
Mis   Driving range
Arch   Colt/Harris

Earlswood (1993)
Pay and play
Jersey Marine, Neath, SA10 6JP
Tel   (01792) 321578
Sec   Mrs D Goatcher
           (01792) 812198
Pro   M Day
Holes 18 L 5174 yds SSS 68
V'tors U SOC
Fees   £8
Loc   5 miles E of Swansea, off
           A483 (B4290)

Fairwood Park (1969)
Blackhills Lane, Upper Killay,
Swansea, SA2 7JN
Tel   (01792) 203648
Fax   (01792) 297849
Mem   650
Sec   D Giltrap
           J Pettifer
           (Mgr)
Pro   G Hughes
           (01792) 299194
Holes 18 L 6754 yds SSS 73
V'tors U SOC
Fees   £25 (£30)
Loc   4 miles W of Swansea
           (A4118)
Arch   Hawtree

Glynneath (1931)
Penygraig, Pontneathvaughan,
Glynneath, SA11 5UH
Tel   (01639) 720452
Fax   (01639) 720452
Mem   623
Sec   DA Fellowes
Pro   N Evans
Holes 18 L 5656 yds SSS 68
V'tors U H SOC–WD
Fees   £17 (£22)
Loc   2 miles NW of Glynneath on
           B4242. 15 miles NE of
           Swansea
Arch   Cotton/Pennink/Lawrie

Gower
Cefn Goleu, Three Crosses, Gowerton,
Swansea SA4 3HS
Tel   (01792) 872480
Fax   (01792) 872480
Mem   600
Sec   JD Morgan (01792) 872480
Pro   A Williamson (01792) 879905
Holes 18 L 6450 yds Par 71 SSS 72
V'tors H
Fees   £20
Loc   5 miles W of Swansea, off
           B4295
Arch   Donald Steele

Inco (1965)
Clydach, Swansea, SA6 5QR
Tel   (01792) 841257
Mem   500
Sec   DE Jones (01792) 830949
Holes 18 L 6064 yds SSS 69
V'tors U
Fees   £15 (£20)
Loc   N of Swansea (A4067)

Lakeside (1992)
Pay and play
Water Street, Margam, Port Talbot,
SA13 2PA
Tel   (01639) 899959
Mem   250
Sec   DM Jones
Pro   M Wootton
Holes 18 L 4550 yds Par 63 SSS 63
V'tors U SOC
Fees   £9.50
Loc   Nr M4 Junction 38
Mis   Driving range
Arch   M Wootton

Langland Bay (1904)
Langland Bay Road, Langland,
Swansea, SA3 4QR
Tel   (01792) 366023
Fax   (01792) 361082
Web   www.langlandbaygolfclub.com
Mem   800
Sec   Mrs L Coleman
           (01792) 361721
Pro   M Evans (01792) 366186
Holes 18 L 5857 yds SSS 69
V'tors U H SOC
Fees   £28 (£30)
Loc   6 miles S of Swansea (A4067).
           M4 Junction 45

Morriston (1919)
160 Clasemont Road, Morriston,
Swansea, SA6 6AJ
Tel   (01792) 771079
Fax   (01792) 796528
Mem   585
Sec   WV Thomas (01792) 796528
Pro   DA Rees (01792) 772335
Holes 18 L 5785 yds SSS 68
V'tors U H SOC–WD
Fees   £18 (£30)
Loc   4 miles N of Swansea on A48.
           M4 Junction 46, 1 mile

Neath (1934)
Cadoxton, Neath, SA10 8AH
Tel   (01639) 643615
Fax   (01639) 632759
Mem   750
Sec   DM Hughes (01639) 632759
Pro   EM Bennett (01639) 633693
Holes 18 L 6500 yds SSS 72
V'tors WD–U WE–M SOC
Fees   Summer—£20 (£20) Winter
           £12 (£12)
Loc   2 miles NE of Neath (B4434)
Arch   James Braid

Palleg (1930)
Palleg Road, Lower Cwmtwrch,
Swansea Valley, SA9 2QQ
Tel   (01639) 842193
Mem   250
Sec   B Evans
Pro   Sharon Roberts
           (01639) 845728
Holes 9 L 3209 yds SSS 72
V'tors WD–U Sat–NA
           Sun/BH–phone first SOC
Fees   On application
Loc   15 miles NE of Swansea
           (A4067). M4 Junction 45

Pennard (1896)
2 Southgate Road, Southgate, Swansea,
SA3 2BT
Tel   (01792) 233131
Fax   (01792) 234797
Web   www.golfagent.com/clubsites/
           pennard
Mem   775
Sec   EM Howell (01792) 233131
Pro   MV Bennett (01792) 233451
Holes 18 L 6265 yds SSS 72
V'tors U H SOC–WD only
Fees   £27 (£35) W–£90
Loc   8 miles W of Swansea, by
           A4067 and B4436

Pontardawe (1924)
Cefn Llan, Pontardawe, Swansea,
SA8 4SH
Tel   (01792) 863118
Fax   (01792) 830041
Mem   610
Sec   K Davey (Hon)
           Mrs M Griffiths (Admin)
Pro   G Hopkins (01792) 830977
Holes 18 L 6003 yds SSS 70
V'tors H SOC–WD

For list of abbreviations see page 649

Fees £22
Loc 5 miles N of M4 Junction 45, off A4067

Swansea Bay (1892)
Jersey Marine, Neath, SA10 6JP
Tel (01792) 812198
Mem 400
Sec Mrs D Goatcher
(01792) 814153
Pro M Day (01792) 816159
Holes 18 L 6605 yds SSS 72
V'tors U SOC
Fees £16 (£22)
Loc 5 miles E of Swansea, off A483 (B4290)

Wrexham

Chirk (1990)
Chirk, Wrexham, LL14 5AD
Tel (01691) 774407
Fax (01691) 773878
Web www.chirkgolfclub.com
Mem 700
Sec MCA Moss
Pro M Maddison
Holes 18 L 7045 yds Par 72 SSS 73
9 hole Par 3 course
V'tors U after 10am SOC
Fees £18 D–£25 (£25 D–£30)

Loc 8 miles S of Wrexham on A483
Mis Driving range

Clays Farm (1992)
Bryn Estyn Road, Wrexham, LL13 9UB
Tel (01978) 661406
Mem 410
Pro D Larvin
Holes 18 L 5775 yds Par 67
V'tors U SOC
Fees £14 (£18)
Loc Wrexham, off A534

Moss Valley (1990)
Pay and play
Moss Road, Wrexham, LL11 6HA
Tel (01978) 720518
Fax (01978) 720518
Web www.mossvalleygolf.com
Mem 100
Sec J Parry, J Lloyd (Mgr)
Holes 9 L 2641 yds Par 68 SSS 67
V'tors U
Fees 9 holes–£6 (£8) 18 holes–£9 (£12)
Loc N of Wrexham, off A541

Pen-y-Cae (1993)
Ruabon Road, Pen-y-Cae, Wrexham, LL14 1TW
Tel (01978) 810108
Mem 100

Sec G Williams (Mgr)
Holes 9 L 4280 yds Par 64 SSS 62
V'tors U SOC–WD
Fees 9 holes–£5 (£6)
18 holes–£7.50 (£9.50)
Loc 6 miles S of Wrexham, via A483/A539
Arch John Day

Plassey (1992)
Eyton, Wrexham, LL13 0SP
Tel (01978) 780020
Fax (01978) 781397
Web www.plasseygolf.co.uk
Mem 150
Sec J Taylor (01978) 780020
Holes 9 L 4761 yds Par 64 SSS 62
V'tors U SOC
Fees £10 (£12)
Loc 2 miles SW of Wrexham, off A483
Arch K Williams

Wrexham (1904)
Holt Road, Wrexham, LL13 9SB
Tel (01978) 261033
Fax (01978) 364268
Mem 650
Sec J Johnson (01978) 364268
Pro P Williams (01978) 351476
Holes 18 L 6233 yds Par 70 SSS 70
V'tors H SOC–WD
Fees £20 (£25)
Loc 2 miles NE of Wrexham on A534
Arch James Braid

CONTINENT OF EUROPE – COUNTRY AND REGION INDEX

For list of abbreviations see page 649

Austria

Innsbruck & Tirol

Achensee (1934)
6213 Pertisau/Achensee
Tel   (05243) 5377
Fax   (05243) 6202
Holes 18 L 5501 m SSS 70
V'tors U H
Fees 450s (520s)
Loc   Pertisau, 50km NE of
      Innsbruck

Innsbruck-Igls (1935)
6074 Rinn, Oberdorf 11
Tel   (05223) 78177
Fax   (05223) 78343
Web   www.golfclub-innsbruck-igls
      .at
Holes Rinn 18 L 5945 m Par 71
      Lans 9 L 4657 m Par 66
V'tors H-booking necessary
Fees 560s (690s)
Loc   Rinn, 10km E of Innsbruck.
      Lans, 8km from Innsbruck

Kaiserwinkl GC Kössen
(1988)
6345 Kössen, Mühlau 1
Tel   (05375) 2122
Fax   (05375) 2122-13
Holes 18 L 5927 m SSS 72
V'tors H
Fees 600s (680s)
Loc   30km N of Kitzbühel, nr
      German border
Arch Donald Harradine

Kitzbühel (1955)
Schloss Kaps, 6370 Kitzbühel
Tel   (05356) 63007
Fax   (05356) 63007-7
Holes 9 L 6044 m Par 72
V'tors H
Fees 800s
Loc   Kitzbühel
Arch J Morrison

Kitzbühel-Schwarzsee
(1988)
6370 Kitzbühel, Golfweg Schwarzsee 35
Tel   (05356) 71645
Fax   (05356) 72785
Holes 18 L 6247 m SSS 72
V'tors H-booking necessary
Fees 650-750s
Loc   4km from Kitzbühel
Arch G Hauser

Seefeld-Wildmoos (1968)
6100 Seefeld, Postfach 22
Tel   (05212) 3003-0
Fax   (05212) 3722-22
Web   www.seefeldgolf.com
Holes 18 L 5967 m SSS 72
V'tors H-booking necessary
Fees 450-700s
Loc   7 km W of Seefeld. 24 km W
      of Innsbruck
Arch Donald Harradine

Klagenfurt & South

Austria-Wörther See
9062 Moosburg, Golfstr 2
Tel   (04272) 83486
Fax   (04272) 82055
Holes 18 L 6216 m SSS 72
Fees 550s
Loc   6km N of Wörther See
Arch G Hauser

Bad Kleinkirchheim-Reichenau (1977)
9546 Bad Kleinkirchheim, Postfach 9
Tel   (04275) 594
Fax   (04275) 594-4
Holes 18 L 6074 m Par 72 SSS 72
V'tors H
Fees 600s (600s)
Loc   Kleinkirchheim, 50 km NW of
      Klagenfurt, via Route 95
Arch Donald Harradine

Kärntner (1927)
9082 Maria Wörth, Golfstr 3
Tel   (04273) 2515
Fax   (04273) 2606
Web   www.golf.at
Holes 18 L 5778 m Par 71
V'tors H
Fees 600s (700s)
Loc   Dellach, S side of Wörther
      See. 15km W of Klagenfurt

Klopeiner See-Turnersee (1988)
9122 St Kanzian, Grabelsdorf 94
Tel   (04239) 3800-0
Fax   (04239) 3800-18
Holes 18 L 6114 m Par 72
V'tors U
Fees 600s
Loc   25km E of Klagenfurt
Arch Donald Harradine

Wörther See/Velden
(1988)
9231 Köstenberg, Oberdorf 70
Tel   (04274) 7045/7087
Fax   (04274) 708715
Web   www.golf.at
Holes 18 L 6152 m SSS 72
V'tors H
Fees 600s
Loc   30km W of Klagenfurt. 12km
      from Velden
Arch Erhardt/Rossknecht

Linz & North

Amstetten-Ferschnitz
(1972)
3325 Ferschnitz, Gut Edla 18
Tel   (07473) 8293
Fax   (07473) 82934
Holes 9 L 5948 m SSS 70
V'tors U H
Fees 350s (450s)
Loc   70km E of Linz
Arch McIntosh

Böhmerwald GC Ulrichsberg (1990)
4161 Ulrichsberg, Seitelschlag 50
Tel   (07288) 8200
Fax   (07288) 8422
Holes 18 L 6240 m SSS 73
      9 hole Par 3 course
V'tors U H
Fees 470s (570s)
Loc   65km NW of Linz
Arch Rossknecht/Erhardt

Haugschlag
3874 Haugschlag 160
Tel   (02865) 8441
Fax   (02865) 8441-22
Web   www.golfresort.at
Holes 18 L 6140 m SSS 72
      18 L 6448 m SSS 74
      18 hole Par 3 course
V'tors H
Fees 490s (690s)
Loc   25km N of Gmund. 140km
      NW of Vienna

Herzog Tassilo (1991)
Blankenbergerstr 30, 4540 Bad Hall
Tel   (07258) 5480
Fax   (07258) 5480-11
Web   www.golf.at
Holes 18 L 5710 m SSS 70
V'tors U
Fees 400-500s (600s)
Loc   30km SW of Linz
Arch Peter Mayerhofer

Kremstal (1989)
Schachen 20, 4531 Kematen/Krems
Tel   (07228) 7644-0
Fax   (07228) 7644-7
Web   www.pgckremstal.at
Holes 18 L 5763 m Par 70
V'tors H
Fees €36 (€50)
Loc   20km W of Linz
Arch Peter Mayerhofer

Linz-St Florian (1960)
4490 St Florian, Tillysburg 28
Tel   (07223) 828730
Fax   (07223) 828737
Holes 18 L 5864 m Par 72 SSS 72
V'tors H
Fees 700s (850s)
Loc   St Florian, 15km SE of Linz
Arch Hanz Georg Erhardt

For list of abbreviations see page 649

Linzer Luftenberg (1990)
4222 St Georgen, Am Luftenberg 1a
Tel   (07237) 3893
Fax   (07237) 3893
Holes   18 L 5864 m Par 71 SSS 72
V'tors U H
Fees   €45 (€50)
Loc   15km NE of Linz
Arch   Keith Preston

Maria Theresia (1989)
Letten 5, 4680 Haag am Hausruck
Tel   (07732) 3944
Fax   (07732) 3944-9
Web   www.members.eunet.at/
        gcmariatheresia
Holes   18 L 6055 m Par 72 SSS 72
V'tors H
Fees   500s (600s)
Loc   Between Passau and Wels. A8
        exit Haag
Arch   Angst/Stärk

Ottenstein (1988)
3532 Niedergrünbach 60
Tel   (02826) 7476
Fax   (02826) 7476-4
Web   www.golfclub-ottenstein.at
Holes   18 L 6054 m SSS 72
V'tors U
Fees   490s (590s)
Loc   90km NE of Linz. 100km NW
        of Vienna
Arch   Preston/Zinterl/Erhardt

St Oswald-Freistadt
(1988)
Promenade 22, 4271 St Oswald
Tel   (07945) 7938
Fax   (07945) 79384
Holes   9 L 5888 m Par 72
V'tors WD-UH WE-U H restricted
Fees   350s (450s)
Loc   40km N of Linz
Arch   Mel Flanegan

St Pölten Schloss
Goldegg (1989)
3100 St Pölten Schloss Goldegg
Tel   (02741) 7360/7060
Fax   (02741) 73608
Holes   18 L 6249 m SSS 73
V'tors H or I
Fees   400s (500s)
Loc   8km NW of St Pölten. 60km
        W of Vienna

Schärding-Pramtal
(1994)
Maad 2, 4775 Taufkirchen/Pram
Tel   (07719) 8110
Fax   (07719) 8110 15
Web   www.members.eunet.at/
        gcschaerding
Holes   18 L 6434 m Par 73 SSS 74
V'tors H
Fees   490s (560s)
Loc   10km S of Schärding on B137

Schloss Ernegg (1973)
3261 Steinakirchen, Schloss Ernegg
Tel   (07488) 76770
Fax   (07488) 76771/71171
Web   www.ernegg.at
Holes   18 L 5803 m SSS 71
        9 L 2076 m SSS 62
V'tors U
Fees   450s (550s)
Loc   Steinakirchen, 80km SE of
        Linz. 125km W of Vienna
Arch   Tucker/Day

Traunsee Kircham
4656 Kircham, Kampesberg 38
Tel   (07619) 2576
Fax   (07619) 2576-11
Holes   18 L 5725 m Par 70 SSS 70
V'tors U
Fees   500s (600s)
Loc   10km E of Gmunden. 50km
        SW of Linz

Weitra (1989)
3970 Weitra, Hausschachen
Tel   (02856) 2058
Fax   (02856) 2058-4
Holes   18 L 5916 m Par 72
V'tors WD-U WE-H
Fees   450s (550s)
Loc   75km NE of Linz, nr Czech
        border
Arch   M Gansdorfer

Wels (1981)
4616 Weisskirchen, Weyerbach 37
Tel   (07243) 56038
Fax   (07243) 56685
Holes   18 L 6098 m Par 72
V'tors H
Fees   500s (600s)
Loc   5 km from Salzburg-Vienna
        highway. 8km SE of Wels
Arch   Hauser/Hunt Hastings

Salzburg Region

Bad Gastein (1960)
5640 Bad Gastein, Golfstrasse 6
Tel   (06434) 2775
Fax   (06434) 2775-4
Holes   9 L 5986 m SSS 72
V'tors H
Fees   390s (500s)
Loc   Bad Gastein 2 km. Salzburg
        100km
Arch   B von Limburger

Goldegg
5622 Goldegg, Postfach 6
Tel   (06415) 8585
Fax   (06415) 8585-4
Holes   18 L 4693 m Par 70
V'tors U
Fees   560s (630s)
Loc   60km SW of Salzburg

Gut Altentann (1989)
Hof 54, 5302 Henndorf am Wallersee
Tel   (06214) 6026-0
Fax   (06214) 6105-81
Web   www.gutaltentann.com
Holes   18 L 6223 m SSS 72
V'tors H (max 34) – booking
        necessary
Fees   750–880s
Loc   Henndorf, 16km NE of
        Salzburg
Arch   Jack Nicklaus

Gut Brandlhof G&CC
(1983)
*5760 Saalfelden am Steinernen Meer,
Hohlwegen 4*
Tel   (06582) 7800-555
Fax   (06582) 7800-529
Holes   18 L 6218 m SSS 72
V'tors I H
Fees   550s (650s)
Loc   Saalfelden, 70km SW of
        Salzburg towards Zell am See
Arch   Kofler

Kobernausserwald
5242 St Johann a. Walde, Strass 1
Tel   (07743) 2719
Fax   (07743) 2719
Holes   18 L 5963 m Par 71 SSS 71
V'tors U
Fees   200s (350s)
Loc   30km E of Salzburg
Arch   Heinz Schmidbauer

Lungau/Katschberg (1991)
5582 St Michael, Postfach 44
Tel   (06477) 7448
Fax   (06477) 7448-4
Holes   18 L 6132 m Par 72
        9 L 2502 m Par 56
V'tors U – soft spikes only
Fees   550s (650s)
Loc   St Michael, 120km S of
        Salzburg
Arch   Keith Preston

Am Mondsee (1986)
St Lorenz 400, 5310 Mondsee
Tel   (06232) 3835-0
Fax   (06232) 3835-83
Holes   18 L 6036 m SSS 72
V'tors H
Fees   550s (650s)
Loc   Mondsee, 25km E of Salzburg
Arch   Marc Miller

Radstadt Tauerngolf
(1991)
Römerstrasse 18, 5550 Radstadt
Tel   (06452) 5111
Fax   (06452) 7336
Holes   18 L 6023 m Par 71
        9 hole Par 3 course
V'tors U
Fees   580s (660s)
Loc   70km NW of Salzburg

Salzburg Fuschl (1995)

5322 Hof/Salzburg

Tel	(06229) 2390
Fax	(06229) 2390
Holes	9 L 3650 m Par 62
	9 hole Par 3 course
V'tors	U
Fees	300–400s
Loc	Hof, 12km E of Salzburg

Salzburg Klesheim (1955)

5071 Wals bei Salzburg,
Schloss Klesheim

Tel	(0662) 850851
Fax	(0662) 857925
Holes	9 L 5700 m SSS 70
V'tors	U H–max 28 (men)
	32 (women)
Fees	650s (650s)
Loc	5km N of Salzburg
Arch	Robert Trent Jones Jr

Salzkammergut (1933)

4820 Bad Ischl, Postfach 506

Tel	(06132) 26340
Fax	(06132) 26708
Holes	18 L 5890 m Par 72
V'tors	U
Fees	500 (600s)
Loc	6 km W of Bad Ischl, nr
	Strobl. 50 km E of Salzburg

Urslautal (1991)

Schinking 1, 5760 Saalfelden

Tel	(06584) 2000
Fax	(06584) 7475-10
Web	www.golf-urslautal.at
Holes	18 L 6030 m SSS 71
V'tors	U H
Fees	640s (700s)
Loc	80km SW of Salzburg
Arch	Keith Preston

Zell am See-Kaprun (1983)

5700 Zell am See-Kaprun, Golfstr 25

Tel	(06542) 56161
Fax	(06542) 56161-16
Web	www.europasportregion.at/
	golfclub
Holes	18 L 6218 m Par 72 SSS 72
	18 L 6146 m Par 73 SSS 72
V'tors	H
Fees	€51 (€58)
Loc	Zell am See, 80km SW of
	Salzburg
Arch	Donald Harradine

Steiermark

Bad Gleichenberg (1984)

Am Hoffeld 3, 8344 Bad Gleichenberg

Tel	(03159) 3717
Fax	(03159) 3065
Holes	9 L 5528 m Par 72 SSS 70
V'tors	U
Fees	380s (480s)
Loc	60km SE of Graz
Arch	Hauser

Dachstein Tauern (1990)

8967 Haus/Ennstal, Oberhaus 59

Tel	(03686) 2630
Fax	(03686) 2630-15
Holes	18 L 5910 m SSS 71
V'tors	U
Fees	650s (750s)
Loc	2km from Schladming. 100km
	SE of Salzburg
Arch	Bernhard Langer

Ennstal-Weissenbach G&LC (1978)

8940 Liezen, Postfach 193

Tel	(03612) 24821
Fax	(03612) 24821-4
Holes	18 L 5655 m SSS 70
V'tors	U H I
Fees	450s (500s)
Loc	100km SE of Salzburg. 100km
	NW of Graz
Arch	Gert Aigner

Furstenfeld (1984)

8282 Loipersdorf, Gillersdorf 50

Tel	(03382) 8533
Fax	(03382) 8533-33
Holes	18 L 6192 m SSS 72
V'tors	U
Fees	500s (600s)
Loc	70km E of Graz

Graz (1989)

8051 Graz-Thal, Windhof 137

Tel	(0316) 572867
Fax	(0316) 572867-4
Holes	9 L 5229 m SSS 70
V'tors	U
Fees	400–500s (600s)
Loc	10km W of Graz
Arch	Herwig Zisser

Gut Murstätten (1989)

8403 Lebring, Oedt 14

Tel	(03182) 3555
Fax	(03182) 3688
Web	www.gcmurstaetten.at
Holes	18 L 6398 m SSS 74
	9 L 3034 m SSS 72
V'tors	H
Fees	€46 (€55)
Loc	25km S of Graz
Arch	J Dudok van Heel

Maria Lankowitz (1992)

Puchbacher Str 109, 8591
Maria Lankowitz

Tel	(03144) 6970
Fax	(03144) 6970-4
Holes	18 L 6121 m SSS 72
V'tors	U
Fees	430s (550s)
Loc	40km W of Graz
Arch	Herwig Zisser

Murhof (1963)

8130 Frohnleiten, Adriach 53

Tel	(03126) 3010
Fax	(03126) 3000-29

Holes	18 L 6198 m Par 72
V'tors	U H
Fees	660s (860s)
Loc	Frohnleiten, 25km N of Graz.
	150km S of Vienna
Arch	B von Limburger

Murtal (1995)

Frauenbachstr 51, 8724 Spielberg

Tel	(03512) 75213
Fax	(03512) 75213
Web	www.golf.at
Holes	18 L 5951 m Par 72
V'tors	H I
Fees	550s (600s)
Loc	Knittelfeld, 80km NW of
	Graz, via Route S36
Arch	Jeff Howes

Reiting G&CC (1990)

8772 Traboch, Schulweg 7

Tel	(0663) 833308/(03847) 5008
Fax	(03847) 5682
Holes	9 L 6300 m Par 73 SSS 72
V'tors	U
Fees	350s (390s)
Loc	60km N of Graz

St Lorenzen (1990)

8642 St Lorenzen, Gassing 22

Tel	(03864) 3961
Fax	(03864) 3961-2
Holes	9 L 5374 m Par 70 SSS 70
V'tors	U
Fees	350s (380s)
Loc	60km N of Graz, nr
	Kapfenberg
Arch	Manfred Flasch

Schloss Frauenthal (1988)

8530 Deutschlandsberg, Ulrichsberg 7

Tel	(03462) 5717
Fax	(03462) 5717-5
Web	www.golf.at
Holes	18 L 5447 m SSS 70
V'tors	U H
Fees	500s (600s)
Loc	30km SW of Graz
Arch	Stephan Breisach

Schloss Pichlarn (1972)

8952 Irdning/Ennstal, Gatschen 28

Tel	(03682) 24393
Fax	(03682) 24393
Holes	18 L 6158 m Par 72
V'tors	U
Fees	500s (650s)
Loc	2km E of Irdning, off
	Salzburg-Graz road. 120km
	SE of Salzburg
Arch	Donald Harradine

Vienna & East

Adamstal (1994)

Gaupmannsgraben 21, 3172 Ramsal

Tel	(02764) 3500
Fax	(02764) 3500-15

Holes 9 L 4696-5326 m Par 70
(18 holes from July 1998)
V'tors U
Fees 400s (550s)
Loc 65km SW of Vienna
Arch Jeff Howes

Bad Tatzmannsdorf G&CC (1991)

Am Golfplatz 2, 7431
Bad Tatzmannsdorf
Tel (03353) 8282-0
Fax (03353) 8282-735
Holes 18 L 6304 m SSS 73
9 L 3660 m SSS 60
V'tors U H
Fees 18 hole: 550s (700s)
9 hole: 370s (460s)
Loc 120km SE of Vienna
Arch Rossknecht/Erhardt

Brunn G&CC (1988)

2345 Brunn/Gebirge, Rennweg 50
Tel (02236) 31572/33711
Fax (02236) 33863
Web www.golf.at
Holes 18 L 6138 m Par 70 SSS 70
V'tors H – soft spikes only
Fees 600s (700s)
Loc 10km S of Vienna
Arch G Hauser

Colony Club Gutenhof (1988)

2325 Himberg, Gutenhof
Tel (02235) 87055-0
Fax (02235) 87055-14
Holes East 18 L 6335 m SSS 73
West 18 L 6397 m SSS 73
V'tors H
Fees 500s (750s)
Loc 7km SE of Vienna
Arch Rossknecht/Erhardt

Danube Golf-Wien (1995)

Weingartenallee 22, 1220 Wien
Tel (0222) 25072
Fax (0222) 25072-44
Holes 18 L 6130 m SSS 72
V'tors H
Fees 550s (550s)
Loc 15km NE of Vienna
Arch Rossknecht/Erhardt

Enzesfeld (1970)

2551 Enzesfeld
Tel (02256) 81272
Fax (02256) 81272-4
Holes 18 L 6176 m SSS 72
V'tors H
Fees 500–600s (800s)
Loc 32km S of Vienna. A2
Junction 29 (Leobersdorf)
Arch Cdr John D Harris

Föhrenwald (1968)

2700 Wiener Neustadt, Postfach 105
Tel (02622) 29171
Fax (02622) 29171-4
Holes 18 L 6317 m SSS 72

V'tors H
Fees 450s (600s)
Loc 5 km S of Wiener Neustadt on
Route B54

Fontana (1996)

Fontana Allee 1, 2522 Oberwaltersdorf
Tel (02253) 606401
Fax (02253) 606403
Holes 18 L 6088 m Par 72
V'tors U–booking necessary. Soft
spikes only
Fees 1000s (1300s)
Loc 20km S of Vienna
Arch Carrick/Erhardt

Hainburg/Donau (1977)

2410 Hainburg, Auf der Heide 762
Tel (02165) 62628
Fax (02165) 65331
Holes 18 L 6064 m SSS 72
V'tors H
Fees 400s (600s)
Loc 50km E of Vienna
Arch G Hauser

Lechner 'BN' (1990)

Pichl 1, 2871 Zöbern
Tel (02642) 8451
Fax (02642) 8451
Holes 9 L 4088m Par 64 SSS 63
V'tors H
Fees 300s (400s)
Loc 90km S of Vienna via A2
Arch Anton Reithofer

Lengenfeld (1995)

Am Golfplatz 1, 3552 Lengenfeld
Tel (02719) 8710
Fax (02719) 8738
Holes 18 L 6130 m Par 72
V'tors U
Fees 400s (500s)
Loc 80km W of Vienna. Krems
8km

Neusiedlersee-Donnerskirchen (1988)

7082 Donnerskirchen
Tel (02683) 8171
Fax (02683) 817231
Holes 18 L 5937 m SSS 72
V'tors H
Fees 500s (500s)
Loc 45km SE of Vienna
Arch Rossknecht-Erhardt

Schloss Ebreichsdorf (1988)

2483 Ebreichsdorf, Schlossallee 1
Tel (02254)73888
Fax (02254) 73888-13
Holes 18 L 6246 m Par 72 SSS 73
V'tors WD–H WE–on request
Fees 500s (700s)
Loc 28km S of Vienna
Arch Keith Preston

Schloss Schönborn (1987)

2013 Schönborn 4
Tel (02267) 2863/2879
Fax (02267) 2879-19
Holes 27 L 6265-6474 m Par 72-73
V'tors U H
Fees 600s (800s)
Loc 40km N of Vienna

Schönfeld (1989)

A-2291 Schönfeld, Am Golfplatz 1
Tel (02213) 2063
Fax (02213) 20631
Web www.golf.at
Holes 18 L 6185 m SSS 73
9 hole Par 3 course
V'tors H
Fees 18 hole:500s (700s)
9 hole:300s (400s)
Loc 35km E of Vienna
Arch G Hauser

Semmering (1926)

2680 Semmering
Tel (02664) 8154
Fax (02664) 2114
Holes 9 L 3786 m SSS 60
V'tors H
Fees 350s (450s)
Loc 30km SW of Vienna Neustadt

Thayatal Drosendorf (1994)

Autendorf 18, 2095 Drosendorf
Tel (02915) 2318
Fax (02915) 2318
Holes 18 L 4289 m Par 65
V'tors U
Fees 200s (400s)
Loc 100km NW of Vienna, nr
Czech border (B4)

Wien (1901)

1020 Wien, Freudenau 65a
Tel (0222) 728 9564 (Clubhouse),
(0222) 728 9667
(Caddymaster)
Fax (0222) 728 9564-20
Holes 18 L 5861 m SSS 71
V'tors WE–NA
Fees 800s
Loc 10 mins SE of Vienna

Wienerberg (1989)

1100 Wien, Gutheil Schoder 9
Tel (0222) 66123-7000
Fax (0222) 66123-7789
Holes 9 L 5710 m SSS 70
V'tors H
Fees 500s
Loc Vienna District 10
Arch G Hauser

Wienerwald (1981)

1130 Wien, Altgasse 27
Tel (0222) 877 3111 (Sec)
Holes 9 L 4652 m SSS 65
V'tors H
Fees 300s (500s)

For list of abbreviations see page 649

Loc   Laaben, 35km W of Vienna
Arch   Herbert Illo Holy

Vorarlberg

Bludenz-Braz (1996)
Oberradin 60, 6751 Braz bei Bludenz
Tel   (05552) 33503
Fax   (05552) 33503-3
Holes   12 L 5259 m Par 69 SSS 69
V'tors M H
Fees   D–440s (D–490s)
Loc   5km E of Bludenz
Arch   Maurice O'Fives

Bregenzerwald (1997)
Unterlitten 3a, 6943 Riefensberg
Tel   (05513) 8400
Fax   (05513) 8400-4
Holes   18 L 5702 m Par 71
V'tors U I
Fees   460s (590s)
Loc   32km E of Bregenz. 150km E of Zürich
Arch   Kurt Rossknecht

Montafon-Zelfen (1992)
6774 Tschagguns, Zelfenstrasse 110
Tel   (05556) 77011
Fax   (05556) 77045
Holes   9 L 3708 m Par 62 SSS 60
V'tors U H
Fees   350s
Loc   60km S of Lake Constance
Arch   Stefan Breisach

Belgium

Antwerp Region

Bossenstein (1989)
Moor 16, Bossenstein Kasteel, 2520 Broechem
Tel   (03) 485 64 46
Fax   (03) 485 78 41
Holes   18 L 6203 m SSS 72
          9 hole course
V'tors H
Fees   1000fr (1500fr)
Loc   15km E of Antwerp. 5km N of Lier
Arch   Paul Rolin

Cleydael (1988)
Kasteel Cleydael, 2630 Aartselaar
Tel   (03) 887 00 79/887 18 74
Fax   (03) 887 00 15
Holes   18 L 6059 m SSS 72
V'tors H WE–NA before 2pm
Fees   1800fr (2300fr)
Loc   8km S of Antwerp. 40km N of Brussels
Arch   Paul Rolin

Inter-Mol (1984)
Goorstraat, 2400 Mol
Tel   (011) 39 17 80/60 02 46
Holes   9 L 1557 m Par 29
V'tors H
Fees   500fr (700fr)
Loc   Mol, 60km E of Antwerp

Kempense (1986)
Kiezelweg 78, 2400 Mol
Tel   (014) 81 46 41
(Clubhouse)
Fax   (014) 81 62 78
Holes   18 L 5904 m Par 72
V'tors H
Fees   1200fr (1700fr)
Loc   60km E of Antwerp
Arch   Marc de Keyser

Lilse (1988)
Haarlebeek 3, 2275 Lille
Tel   (014) 55 19 30
Fax   (014) 55 19 31
Holes   9 L 2007 m Par 64
V'tors U
Fees   600fr (800fr)
Loc   Lille, 10km SW of Turnhout, nr E7. 25km E of Antwerp

Rinkven G&CC (1980)
Sint Jobsteenweg 120, 2970 Schilde
Tel   (03) 380 12 85
Fax   (03) 384 29 33
Holes   27 hole course
V'tors H–phone before visit
Fees   1500fr (2500fr)
Loc   17 km NE of Antwerp, off E19

Royal Antwerp (1888)
Georges Capiaulei 2, 2950 Kapellen
Tel   (03) 666 84 56
Fax   (03) 666 44 37
Holes   18 L 6140 m SSS 73
          9 L 2264 m SSS 33
V'tors WD–H (phone first)
Fees   €60–75
Loc   Kapellen, 20km N of Antwerp
Arch   Willie Park/T Simpson

Steenhoven (1985)
Steenhoven 89, 2400 Postel-Mol
Tel   (014) 37 36 61
Fax   (014) 37 36 62
Holes   18 L 5950 m SSS 71
V'tors H–booking necessary
Fees   1500fr (2500fr)
Loc   30 mins W of Antwerp
Arch   Pierre de Broqueville

Ternesse G&CC (1976)
Uilenbaan 15, 2160 Wommelgem
Tel   (03) 355 14 30
Fax   (03) 355 14 35
Holes   18 L 5822 m Par 72
          9 L 1981 m Par 33
V'tors H–30
Fees   2000fr (2500fr)
Loc   5km E of Antwerp on E313
Arch   HJ Baker

Ardennes & South

Andenne (1988)
Ferme du Moulin 52, Stud, 5300 Andenne
Tel   (085) 84 34 04
Fax   (085) 84 34 04
Holes   9 L 2447 m SSS 66
V'tors U
Fees   500fr (700fr)
Loc   Andenne, 20km E of Namur
Arch   C Bertier

Château Royal d'Ardenne
Tour Léopold, Ardenne 6, 5560 Houyet
Tel   (082) 66 62 28
Fax   (082) 66 74 53
Holes   18 L 5363 m SSS 71
V'tors H
Fees   1200fr (1800fr)
Loc   9km SE of Dinant on Rochefort road

Falnuée (1987)
Rue E Pirson 55, 5032 Mazy
Tel   (081) 63 30 90
Fax   (081) 63 37 64
Web   www.falnuee.be
Holes   18 L 5700 m SSS 70
V'tors H
Fees   1000fr (1500fr)
Loc   18km NW of Namur. Mons-Liège highway Junction 13
Arch   J Jottrand

Five Nations C C
Ferme du Grand Scley, 5372 Méan
Tel   (086) 32 32 32
Fax   (086) 32 30 11
Holes   18 L 6066 m Par 72
V'tors U
Fees   1100fr (1500fr)
Loc   30km S of Liège
Arch   Gary Player

Mont Garni (1989)
Rue du Mont Garni 3, 7331 Saint Ghislain
Tel   (065) 62 27 19
Fax   (065) 62 34 10
Web   www.golfmontgarni.be
Holes   18 L 6353 m Par 74
V'tors H
Fees   €30 (€45)
Loc   St Ghislain, 15km W of Mons. 65km SW of Brussels
Arch   T Macauley

Rougemont
Chemin du Beau Vallon 45, 5170 Profondeville
Tel   (081) 41 14 18
Fax   (081) 41 21 42
Web   www.users.skynet.be/ rougemont
Holes   18 L 5645 m Par 72
V'tors U
Fees   1000fr 91500fr)
Loc   Profondeville, 10km S of Namur

For list of abbreviations see page 649

Royal GC du Hainaut
(1933)
Rue de la Vererie 2, 7050 Erbisoeul
Tel   (065) 22 96 10 **(Clubhouse),**
(065) 22 02 00 (Sec)
Fax   (065) 22 02 09
Web   www.viewgolf.net/RGCH
Holes 9 L 3117 m Par 36
           9 L 2925 m Par 36
           9 L 3218 m Par 36
V'tors U H (max 36)
Fees   1500fr (2000fr)
Loc   6km NW of Mons towards
           Ath on N56. Paris-Brussels
           motorway Junction 23
Arch   Martin Hawtree

Brussels &
Brabant

Bercuit (1965)
Les Gottes 3, 1390 Grez-Doiceau
Tel   (010) 84 15 01
Fax   (010) 84 55 95
Holes 18 L 5931 m Par 72 SSS 72
V'tors H
Fees   D–1500–2000fr (3000fr)
Loc   Grez-Doiceau, 27km SE of
           Brussels. Brussels-Namur
           highway exit 8
Arch   Robert Trent Jones Sr

Brabantse (1982)
Steenwagenstraat 11, 1820 Melsbroek
Tel   (02) 751 82 05
Fax   (02) 751 84 25
Holes 18 L 5266 m Par 70
V'tors H
Fees   1200fr (1700fr)
Loc   10km NE of Brussels, nr
           airport
Arch   Paul Rolin

La Bruyère (1988)
*Rue Jumerée 1, 1495 Sart-Dames-
Avelines*
Tel   (071) 87 72 67
Fax   (071) 87 43 38
Holes 18 L 5937 m SSS 71
V'tors U
Fees   €27.5 (€50)
Loc   40km S of Brussels towards
           Charleroi
Arch   Theys

Château de la Bawette
(1988)
*Chaussée du Chateau Bawette 5,
1300 Wavre*
Tel   (010) 22 33 32
Fax   (010) 22 90 04
Holes Parc 18 L 6076 m SSS 72
           Champs 9 L 2146 m SSS 63
V'tors H–booking required
Fees   Parc–1400fr (2200fr)
           Champs–1000fr (1500fr)
Loc   1km N of Wavre. 15km S of
           Brussels. E411 Exit 5
Arch   Tom Macauley

Château de la Tournette
*Chemin de Baudemont 23,
1400 Nivelles*
Tel   (067) 89 42 66/89 42 68
Fax   (067) 21 95 17
Holes 18 L 6031 m Par 72
           18 L 6024 m Par 71
V'tors H
Fees   1200fr (2000fr)
Loc   29km S of Brussels (E19)
Arch   Alliss/Clark

L'Empereur (1989)
*Rue Emile François 9, 1474
Ways (Genappe)*
Tel   (067) 77 15 71
Fax   (067) 77 18 33
Web   www.golfempereur.com
Holes 18 L 6157 m Par 72
           9 L 1660 m Par 31
V'tors U H
Fees   18 hole:1000fr (2000fr)
           9 hole:700fr (1100fr)
Loc   25km S of Brussels
Arch   Marcel Vercruyce

Hulencourt (1989)
*Bruyère d'Hulencourt 15, 1472
Vieux Genappe*
Tel   (067) 79 40 40
Fax   (067) 79 40 48
Holes 18 L 6215 m Par 72
           9 hole Par 3 course
V'tors H–max 36
Fees   1800fr (3000fr)
Loc   30km SE of Brussels
Arch   JM Rossi

Kampenhout (1989)
Wildersedreef 56, 1910 Kampenhout
Tel   (016) 65 12 16
Fax   (016) 65 16 80
Holes 18 L 6142 m SSS 72
V'tors H
Fees   1000fr (1500fr)
Loc   15km NE of Brussels (E19)
Arch   R de Vooght

Keerbergen (1968)
Vlieghavelaan 50, 3140 Keerbergen
Tel   (015) 23 49 61
Fax   (015) 23 57 37
Web   www.golf.be/keerbergen
Holes 18 L 5503 m SSS 70
V'tors H
Fees   1300fr (2000fr)
Loc   30km NE of Brussels
Arch   Frank Pennink

Louvain-la-Neuve
*Rue A Hardy 68, 1348 Louvain-la-
Neuve*
Tel   (010) 45 05 15
Fax   (010) 45 44 17
Holes 18 L 6226 m Par 72
V'tors U
Fees   1200fr (2000fr)
Loc   20km SE of Brussels, off E411
Arch   J Dudok van Heel

Overijse (1986)
Gemslaan 55, 3090 Overijse
Tel   (02) 687 50 30
Fax   (02) 687 37 68
Holes 18 L 5723 m Par 71
V'tors H
Fees   800fr (1500fr)
Loc   10km S of Brussels
Arch   Rossi

Pierpont (1992)
*1 Grand Pierpont, 6210 Frasnes-lez-
Gosselies*
Tel   (071) 85 17 75/85 14 19
Fax   (071) 85 15 43
Web   www.pierpont.be
Holes 18 L 6257 m Par 72
           5 hole Par 3 course
V'tors U
Fees   1200fr (2400fr)
Loc   30km S of Brussels via N5
Arch   J Dudok van Heel

Rigenée (1981)
Rue de Châtelet 62, 1495 Villers-la-Ville
Tel   (071) 87 77 65
Fax   (071) 87 77 83
Holes 18 L 6031 m SSS 73
V'tors H
Fees   1100fr (1800fr)
Loc   35km S of Brussels towards
           Charleroi
Arch   Rolin/Descampe

Royal Amicale
Anderlecht (1987)
Rue Scholle 1, 1070 Bruxelles
Tel   (02) 521 16 87
Fax   (02) 521 51 56
Holes 18 L 5037 m Par 70 CR 68.7
           SR 123
V'tors WD–U H WE–booking
           required
Fees   1200fr (1800fr)
Loc   SW Brussels

Royal Golf Club de
Belgique (1906)
Château de Ravenstein, 3080 Tervuren
Tel   (02) 767 58 01
Fax   (02) 767 28 41
Holes 18 L 6033 m SSS 72
           9 L 1960 m Par 32
V'tors WD–H–max 20 (men)
           24 (ladies)–phone first.
           Course closed Mon
Fees   2500fr
Loc   Tervuren, 10km E of Brussels
Arch   Simpson

Royal Waterloo (1923)
*Vieux Chemin de Wavre 50,
1380 Ohain*
Tel   (02) 633 18 50
Fax   (02) 633 28 66
Holes 18 L 6211 m SSS 72
           18 L 6224 m SSS 73
           9 L 2143 m SSS 33
V'tors WD–H
Fees   D–1750fr (D–2950fr)

Loc 22km SE of Brussels
Arch Hawtree/Rolin

Sept Fontaines (1987)
1021, Chaussée d'Alsemberg, 1420 Braine L'Alleud
Tel (02) 353 02 46/353 03 46
Fax (02) 354 68 75
Web www.golf-7fontaines.be
Holes 18 L 6047 m Par 72 SSS 72
18 L 4870 m Par 69 SSS 67
9 hole short course
V'tors U H
Fees 1500fr (2500fr)
Loc Braine L'Alleud, 15km S of Brussels. Motorway exit 15
Arch Rossi

Winge G&CC (1988)
Leuvensesteenweg 252, 3390 Sint Joris Winge
Tel (016) 63 40 53
Fax (016) 63 21 40
Web www.golfbelgium.be
Holes 18 L 6049 m Par 72 CR 72.4
V'tors H
Fees 1300–1800fr
Loc 35km E of Brussels via Leuven
Arch P Townsend

East

Avernas
Route de Grand Hallet 19A, 4280 Hannut
Tel (019) 51 30 66
Fax (019) 51 53 43
Holes 9 L 2674 m SSS 68
V'tors H
Fees 700fr (900fr)
Loc 40km W of Liège. Brussels 50km
Arch Hawtree/Cappart

Durbuy (1991)
Route d'Oppagne 34, 6940 Barvaux-su-Ourthe
Tel (086) 21 44 54,
Holes 18 L 5963 m SSS 72
9 hole Par 3 course
V'tors U
Fees 1300fr (1800fr)
Loc 45km S of Liège
Arch Martin Hawtree

Flanders Nippon Hasselt (1988)
Vissenbroekstraat 15, 3500 Hasselt
Tel (011) 26 34 82
Fax (011) 26 34 83
Web www.golf.be/flandersnippon
Holes 18 L 5966 m SSS 72
9 L 1750 m SSS 32
V'tors U H
Fees 1200fr (1600fr)
Loc 5km E of Hasselt. 85km E of Brussels
Arch Rolin/Wirtz

Henri-Chapelle (1988)
Rue du Vivier 3, 4841 Henri-Chapelle
Tel (087) 88 19 91
Fax (087) 88 36 55
Holes 18 L 6040 m SSS 72
9 L 2168 m SSS 34
6 hole Par 3 course
V'tors 18 hole:WE–H
Fees 18 hole:1400–1800fr
9 hole:700–1200fr
Loc 15km NE of Liège. 25km N of Maastricht
Arch Steensels/Dudok van Heel

International Gomze (1986)
Sur Counachamps 8, 4140 Gomze Andoumont
Tel (041) 360 92 07
Fax (041) 360 92 06
Holes 18 L 5918 m SSS 72
V'tors U H
Fees On application
Loc 15km S of Liège. Spa 20km
Arch Paul Rolin

Limburg G&CC (1966)
Golfstraat 1, 3530 Houthalen
Tel (089) 38 35 43
Fax (089) 84 12 08
Holes 18 L 6128 m SSS 72
V'tors H
Fees 1600fr (2000fr)
Loc Houthalen, 15km N of Hasselt
Arch Hawtree

Royal GC du Sart Tilman (1939)
Route du Condroz 541, 4031 Liège
Tel (041) 336 20 21
Fax (041) 337 20 26
Holes 18 L 6002 m SSS 72
V'tors H–booking required
Fees D–1550fr (2050fr)
Loc 10km S of Liège on Route 620 (N35), towards Marche
Arch T Simpson

Royal Golf des Fagnes (1930)
1 Ave de l'Hippodrome, 4900 Spa
Tel (087) 79 30 30
Fax (087) 79 30 39
Holes 18 L 6010 m Par 72
V'tors H–booking required
Fees 1500–2000fr (1800–2200fr)
Loc 5km N of Spa. 35km SE of Liège
Arch T Simpson

Spiegelven GC Genk (1988)
Wiemesmeerstraat 109, 3600 Genk
Tel (089) 35 96 16
Fax (089) 36 41 84
Holes 18 L 6198 m SSS 72
9 hole Par 3 course
V'tors H

Fees 1300fr (1800fr)
Loc Genk, 18km E of Hasselt. 20km N of Maastricht
Arch Ron Kirby

West & Oost Vlaanderen

Damme G&CC (1987)
Doornstraat 16, 8340 Damme-Sijsele
Tel (050) 35 35 72
Fax (050) 35 89 25
Web www.golf.be/damme
Holes 18 L 6046 m SSS 72
9 hole short course
V'tors H
Fees €45 (€60)
Loc 7km E of Bruges. Knokke 15km
Arch J Dudok van Heel

Oudenaarde G&CC (1975)
Kasteel Petegem, Kortrykstraat 52, 9790 Wortegem-Petegem
Tel (055) 33 41 61
Fax (055) 31 98 49
Web www.golf.be/oudenaarde
Holes 18 L 6172 m Par 72
9 L 2536 m Par 34
V'tors H
Fees 1300fr (1800fr)
Loc 3 km SW of Oudenaarde
Arch HJ Baker

De Palingbeek (1991)
Eekhofstraat 14, 8902 Hollebeke-Ieper
Tel (057) 20 04 36
Fax (057) 21 89 58
Web www.golfpalingbeek.com
Holes 18 L 6165 m Par 72
V'tors H
Fees 1400fr (1900fr)
Loc 5km SE of Ieper, nr Hollebeke
Arch HJ Baker

Royal Latem (1909)
9830 St Martens-Latem
Tel (092) 82 54 11
Fax (092) 82 90 19
Web www.golf.be/latem
Holes 18 L 5767 m Par 70 SR 123
V'tors H
Fees €50 (€65)
Loc 10 km SW of Ghent on route N43 Ghent-Deinze

Royal Ostend (1903)
Koninklijke Baan 2, 8420 De Haan
Tel (059) 23 32 83
Fax (059) 23 37 49
Web www.golf.be/oostende
Holes 18 L 5618 m Par 70 CR 70.1 SR 123
V'tors H–max 36
Fees 1200–1500fr (1900–2200fr)
Loc 8km N of Ostend towards De Haan
Arch M Hawtree (1993/4)

Royal Zoute (1899)
Caddiespad 14, 8300 Knokke-le-Zoute
Tel   (050) 60 16 17 (Clubhouse)
        (050) 60 37 81 (Starter)
Fax   (050) 62 30 29
Holes No 1 18 L 6172 m Par 72
        No 2 18 L 3607 m Par 64
V'tors H No 1 course–max 20
        WE–restricted
Fees   3500fr
Loc   Knokke-Heist
Arch   HS Colt

Waregem (1988)
Bergstraat 41, 8790 Waregem
Tel   (056) 60 88 08
Fax   (056) 62 18 23
Web   www.golf.be/waregem
Holes 18 L 6038 m SSS 72
V'tors H Sun–NA before 1pm
Fees   1500fr (2000fr)
Loc   30km SW of Ghent (E17)
Arch   Paul Rolin

Czech Republic

Karlovy Vary (1904)
Prazska 125, PO Box 67, 360 01 Karlovy Vary
Tel   (017) 333 1001-2
Fax   (017) 333 1101
Holes 18 L 6226 m SSS 72
V'tors H
Fees   1100czk (1300czk)
Loc   8km from Karlovy Vary
        (Road 6)
Arch   Noskowski

Lísnice (1928)
252 03 Lísnice
Tel   (0305) 92660
Holes 9 L 5002 m SSS 67
V'tors H
Fees   400czk
Loc   30km from Prague towards
        Dobrís

Lokomotiva-Brno (1967)
c/o Chlupova 7, 602 00 Brno
Tel   (05) 744615
Fax   (05) 759309
Holes 9 L 4632 m SSS 68
V'tors H
Fees   100czk (180czk)
Loc   Svratka, 80km NW of Brno.
        100km SE of Prague
Arch   Chocholac

Mariánské Lázne (1905)
PO Box 267, 353 01 Mariánské Lázne
Tel   (0165) 4300
Fax   (0165) 625195
Holes 18 L 6195 m SSS 72

V'tors H
Fees   D–1000czk
Loc   2km NE of Mariánské Lázne,
        opposite Golf Hotel

Park GC Ostrava (1968)
Dolni 412, 747 15 Silherovice
Tel   (069) 505 4144
Fax   (069) 505 4144
Web   www.golf-ostrava.cz
Holes 18 L 5838 m Par 72
V'tors H
Fees   900czk (1100czk)
Loc   15km N of Ostrava
Arch   Jan Cieslar

Podebrady (1964)
Na Zalesi 530, 29080 Podebrady
Tel   (0324) 610928
Fax   (0324) 610981
Web   www.golfpodebrady.cz
Holes 18 L 5790 m CR 70.3 SR 114
V'tors U H
Fees   600czk (800czk)
Loc   E side of Podebrady
Arch   Wagner/Havelka/Kodes

Praha (1926)
Na Morani 4, 128 00 Praha 2
Tel   (02) 292828/644 3828
Fax   (02) 292828
Holes 9 L 5960 m SSS 72
V'tors U
Loc   Prague-Motol, towards Plzen

Semily (1970)
Bavlnarska 521, 513 01 Semily
Tel   (0431) 622443/624428
Fax   (0431) 623000
Web   www.semily.cz
Holes 9 L 4176 m Par 64
V'tors WD–U WE–NA
Fees   400czk (600czk)
Loc   2km from Semily. 100km NE
        of Prague
Arch   Schovánek/Janata

Denmark

Bornholm Island

Bornholm (1972)
Plantagevej 3B, 3700 Rønne
Tel   56 95 68 54
Fax   56 95 68 53
Web   www.hjem.get2net.dk/bgk
Holes 18 L 4819 m Par 68
        9 hole Par 3 course
V'tors H
Fees   180kr
Loc   4km E of Rønne, off Route 38
        towards Aakirkeby
Arch   Frederik Dreyer

Nexø
Dueodde Golfbane, Strandmarksvejen 14, 3730 Nexø
Tel   56 48 89 87
Fax   56 48 89 69
Web   www.dueodde-golf.dk
Holes 18 L 5631 m Par 70 CR 70.4
V'tors H
Fees   200kr (200kr)
Loc   12km S of Nexø, nr Dueodde
        beach
Arch   Frederik Dreyer

Nordbornholm-Rø (1987)
Spellingevej 3, Rø, 3760 Gudhjem
Tel   56 48 40 50
Fax   56 48 40 52
Web   www.roegolfbane.dk
Holes 18 L 5369 m SSS 71
V'tors WD–U WE–H
Fees   D–200kr
Loc   Rø, 8km W of Gudhjem.
        22km NE of Rønne
Arch   Anders Amilon

Funen

Faaborg (1989)
Dalkildegards Allee 1, 5600 Faaborg
Tel   62 61 77 43
Fax   62 61 79 34
Holes 18 L 5715 m Par 72
V'tors U H
Fees   D–200kr
Loc   35km S of Odense
Arch   Frederik Dreyer

Lillebaelt (1990)
O.Hougvej 130, 5500 Middelfart
Tel   64 41 80 11
Fax   64 41 14 11
Web   www.gkl.dk
Holes 18 L 5586 m Par 71 CR 69.1
V'tors H
Fees   D–200kr
Loc   2km from Middelfart. 45km
        W of Odense
Arch   Malling Petersen

Odense (1927)
Hestehaven 200, 5220 Odense SØ
Tel   65 95 90 00
Fax   65 95 90 88
Web   www.odensegolfklub.dk
Holes 18 L 6098 m CR 71
        9 L 4044 m CR 61
V'tors U H
Fees   250kr (300kr)
Loc   SE outskirts of Odense
Arch   Jan Sederholm

Odense Eventyr (1993)
Falen 227, 5250 Odense SV
Tel   66 17 11 44
Fax   66 17 11 37
Web   www.golfin.dk
Holes 18 hole course Par 72
        9 hole course

V'tors H
Fees 230kr (265kr)
Loc 5km SW of Odense
Arch Michael Møller

SCT Knuds (1954)

Slipshavnsvej 16, 5800 Nyborg
Tel 65 31 12 12
Fax 65 30 28 04
Web www.sct-knuds.dk
Holes 18 L 5810 m CR 72
V'tors H
Fees 250kr D–300kr (500kr)
Loc 3km SE of Nyborg
Arch Cotton/Dreyer

Svendborg (1970)

Tordensgaardevej 5, Sørup,
5700 Svendborg
Tel 63 21 12 70
Fax 62 20 29 77
Web www.svendborg-golf.dk
Holes 18 L 5490 m Par 71 CR 70
V'tors H–max 36
Fees 225kr (275kr)
Loc 4km NW of Svendborg
Arch Frederik Dreyer

Vestfyns (1974)

Rønnemosegård, Krengerupvej 27,
5620 Glamsbjerg
Tel 63 72 19 20
Fax 63 72 19 27
Web www.golfonline.dk/klub/
vestfyn
Holes 18 L 5629 m Par 71 CR 71
V'tors H
Fees 200kr (280kr)
Loc Glamsbjerg, 25km SW of
Odense

Greenland

Sondie Arctic Desert
(1990)

Box 58, 3910 Kangerlussuaq, Greenland
Tel 29 91 14 13
Fax 29 91 11 74
Holes 18 L 5521 m SSS 72
V'tors U
Loc 2km E of Kangerlussuaq
Airport, Greenland
Arch Ulf Larson

Jutland

Aalborg (1908)

Jaegersprisvej 35, Restup Enge,
9000 Aalborg
Tel 98 34 14 76
Fax 98 34 15 84
Web www.aalborggk.dk
Holes 18 L 6081 m CR 73.4
V'tors H (max 36)
Fees 300kr
Loc 7 km SW of Aalborg
Arch R Harris

Aarhus (1931)

Ny Moesgaardvej 50, 8270 Hojbjerg
Tel 86 27 63 22
Fax 86 27 63 21
Web www.aarhusgolfclub.dk
Holes 18 L 5725 m Par 72 CR 71
V'tors H
Fees D–200kr (D–250kr)
Loc 6km S of Aarhus, Route 451
Arch Brian Huggett

Blokhus Klit (1993)

Hunetorpvej 115, Box 230,
9490 Pandrup
Tel 98 20 95 00
Fax 98 20 95 01
Holes 18 L 5765 m CR 71
V'tors H
Fees 200kr (280kr)
Loc 35km NW of Aalborg
Arch Frederik Dreyer

Breinholtgård (1992)

Koksspangvej 17-19, 6710 Esbjerg V
Tel 75 11 57 00
Fax 75 11 55 12
Holes 18 L 5855 m Par 71 CR 72
V'tors U
Fees 200kr
Loc 11km N of Esbjerg
Arch Gaunt/Trådsdahl

Brønderslev (1971)

PO Box 94, 9700 Brønderslev
Tel 98 82 32 81
Fax 98 82 45 25
Holes 18 L 5683 m CR 71
9 hole short course
V'tors H WE–booking necessary
Fees 180kr (200kr)
Loc 3km W of Brønderslev
Arch Erik Schnack

Dejbjerg (1966)

Letagervej 1, Dejbjerg, 6900 Skjern
Tel 97 35 00 09
Holes 18 L 5275 m SSS 69
V'tors U H–max 36
Fees D–170kr (D–200kr)
Loc 6km N of Skjern. 25km from
W coast on Skjern-Ringkøbing
road (Route 28)
Arch Schnack/Dreyer

Ebeltoft (1966)

Strandgårdshøj 8a, 8400 Ebeltoft
Tel 86 34 47 87/86 34 01 40
Holes 18 L 5027 m Par 68 CR 67.6
V'tors U
Fees D–200kr
Loc 1km N of Ebeltoft
Arch Frederik Dreyer

Esbjerg (1921)

Sønderhedevej 11, Marbaek,
6710 Esbjerg
Tel 75 26 92 19
Fax 75 26 94 19
Holes 18 L 6434 m CR 71
9 L 5520 m CR 70

V'tors U H
Fees 250kr
Loc 15km N of Esbjerg
Arch Frederik Dreyer

Fanø Golf Links (1901)

Golfvej 1, 6720 Fanø
Tel 76 66 00 77
Fax 76 66 00 44
Web www.fanoe-golf-links.dk
Holes 18 L 4352 m CR 65
V'tors U
Fees D–200kr
Loc W side of Fanø Island. Ferry
from Esbjerg 15 mins

Grenaa (1981)

Vestermarken 1, 8500 Grenaa
Tel (86) 32 79 29
Holes 18 L 5782 m Par 70
V'tors U
Fees 150kr
Loc 1km W of Grenaa. 60km NE
of Aarhus
Arch Dreyer/Sommer

Gyttegård (1974)

Billundvej 43, 7250 Hejnsvig
Tel 75 33 63 82
Fax 75 33 68 20
Holes 18 L 5548 m SSS 70
V'tors H
Fees 150kr (200kr)
Loc 2km NE of Hejnsvig. 5km SW
of Billund
Arch Amilon/Bossen

Haderslev (1971)

Viggo Carstensvej 7, 6100 Haderslev
Tel 74 52 83 01
Fax 74 53 36 01
Holes 18 L 5233 m CR 69
V'tors H
Fees 220kr
Loc 2km NW of Haderslev

Han Herreds

Starkaervej 20, 9690 Fjerritslev
Tel 98 21 26 66
Fax 98 21 24 44
Holes 18 L 5359 m CR 70.5
V'tors H
Fees 150kr
Loc 1km N of Fjerritslev. 40km W
of Aalborg

Henne (1989)

Hennebysvej 30, 6854 Henne
Tel 75 25 56 10
Fax 75 25 56 30
Web www.hennegolf.dk
Holes 18 L 5988 m Par 71
CR 72.5
9 hole Par 3 course
V'tors U H
Fees 200kr
Loc 19km NW of Varde. 35km N
of Esbjerg
Arch Frederik Dreyer

For list of abbreviations see page 649

Herning (1964)
Golfvej 2, 7400 Herning
Tel   97 21 00 33
Fax   97 21 00 34
Holes 18 L 5571 m CR 71.8
V'tors H
Fees   150kr (200kr)
Loc   2km E of Herning on Route 15
Arch   Dreyer/Baekgaard

Himmerland G&CC
(1979)
Centervej 1, Gatten, 9640 Farsö
Tel   96 49 61 00
Fax   98 66 14 56
Holes Old 18 L 5422 m SSS 69
       Par 70;
       New 18 L 6102 m SSS 74
       Par 73;
       18 hole Par 3 course
V'tors H
Fees   180kr D–230kr (270kr
       D–320kr)
Loc   Gatten, 35km NW of Hobro
       towards Løgstør (Route 29)
Arch   Jan Sederström

Hirtshals (1990)
Kjulvej 10, PO Box 51, 9850 Hirtshals
Tel   98 94 94 08
Fax   98 94 19 35
Holes 18 L 5620 m Par 72
V'tors U H max 48 WE–NA 10–12
       noon
Fees   200kr
Loc   12km N of Hjørring
Arch   Erik Nielsen

Hjarbaek Fjord (1992)
Lynderup, 8832 Skals
Tel   86 69 62 88
Fax   86 69 62 68
Holes 27 L 8595 m SSS 72
V'tors H
Fees   230kr (270kr)
Loc   17km NW of Viborg
Arch   Henrik Jacobsen

Hjorring (1985)
*Vinstrupvej, PO Box 215,
9800 Hjorring*
Tel   98 91 18 28
Fax   98 90 31 00
Web   www.hjoerringgolf.dk
Holes 18 L 5945 m SSS 72
V'tors H WE–NA 9–11am &
       1.30–2.30pm
Fees   200kr (220kr)
Loc   N of Hjorring. 50km N of
       Aalborg
Arch   Erik Schnack

Holmsland Klit
*Klevevej 19, Søndervig,
6950 Ringkøbing*
Tel   97 33 88 00
Fax   97 33 86 80
Holes 18 L 5611 m SSS 69
V'tors H
Fees   175kr

Loc   10km W of Ringkøbing
Arch   Leif Baekgaard

Holstebro (1970)
Råsted, 7570 Vemb
Tel   97 48 51 55
Holes 18 L 5853 m CR 70.6
       9 L 2510 m
V'tors H
Fees   200kr (250kr)
Loc   13km W of Holstebro (Route
       16)
Arch   Erik Schnack

Horsens (1972)
Silkeborgvej 44, 8700 Horsens
Tel   75 61 51 21
Holes 18 L 6020 m CR 72.4
       6 hole Par 3 course
Fees   160kr
Loc   1 km W of Horsens towards
       Silkeborg
Arch   Jan Sederholm

Hvide Klit (1972)
Hvideklitvej 28, 9982 Aalbaek
Tel   98 48 90 21/48 84 26
Fax   98 48 91 12
Holes 18 L 5875 m SSS 72
V'tors H
Fees   200kr (230kr)
Loc   3km N of Aalbaek. 24km N of
       Frederikshavn
Arch   Anders Amilon

Juelsminde (1973)
Bobroholtvej 11a, 7130 Juelsminde
Tel   75 69 34 92
Fax   75 69 46 11
Holes 18 L 5680 m SSS 72
V'tors U H
Fees   200kr
Loc   20 km S of Horsens on coast.
       2km N of Juelsminde
Arch   Mehlsen/Jacobsen/Møller

Kaj Lykke
Kirkebrovej 5, 6740 Bramming
Tel   75 10 22 46
Holes 18 L 5975 m Par 72
       Par 3 course
V'tors H
Fees   200kr
Loc   18km E of Esbjerg
Arch   Bent Nielsen

Kalo (1992)
Aarhusvej 32, 8410 Rønde
Tel   86 37 36 00
Fax   86 37 36 46
Holes 18 L 5936 m CR 72.2
V'tors U
Fees   220kr (250kr)
Loc   20km E of Aarhus
Arch   Frederik Dreyer

Kolding (1933)
Egtved Alle 10, 6000 Kolding
Tel   75 52 37 93

Fax   75 52 42 42
Holes 18 L 5376 m SSS 69
       9 L 2065 m
V'tors U
Fees   200kr (250kr)
Loc   3km N of Kolding
Arch   Jan Sederholm

Lemvig (1986)
Søgårdevejen 6, 7620 Lemvig
Tel   97 81 09 20
Fax   97 81 09 20
Web   www.home11.inet.tele.dk/
       lemviggk
Holes 18 L 5890 m CR 72
V'tors H
Fees   200kr (200kr)
Loc   2km N of Lemvig. 35km NE
       of Holsterbro
Arch   Frederik Dreyer

Løkken (1990)
*Vrenstedvej 226, PO Box 43,
9480 Løkken*
Tel   98 99 26 57
Fax   98 99 26 58
Web   www.loekken-golfklub.dk
Holes 18 L 5902 m CR 72.3 SR 127
       9 L 2964 m Par 29
V'tors U H
Fees   200kr (200kr)
Loc   45km NW of Aalborg
Arch   Kaj Andersen

Nordvestjysk (1971)
Nystrupvej 19, 7700 Thisted
Tel   97 97 41 41
Holes 18 L 5675 m CR 72
V'tors H
Fees   150kr (150kr)
Loc   17km NW of Thisted
Arch   Schnack/Jacobsen

Odder (1990)
Akjaervej 200, Postbox 46, 8300 Odder
Tel   86 54 54 51
Holes 18 L 5428 m Par 70 CR 70
V'tors U
Fees   200kr (250kr)
Loc   4km SW of Odder, off Route
       451
Arch   Frederik Dreyer

Randers (1958)
Himmelbovej, Fladbro, 8900 Randers
Tel   86 42 88 69
Fax   86 40 88 69
Web   www.randersgolf.dk
Holes 18 L 5453 m SSS 70
       9 hole Par 3 course
Fees   200kr (250kr)
Loc   5km W of Randers towards
       Langå
Arch   Mogens Harbo

Ribe (1979)
*Rønnehave, Snepsgårdevej 14,
6760 Ribe*
Tel   30 73 65 18
Holes 18 L 5430 m CR 69

V'tors U
Fees 150kr
Loc 8 km SE of Ribe on Haderslev road
Arch Frederik Dreyer

Rold Skov
Golfvej 1, 9520 Skørping
Tel 98 39 26 99
Fax 98 39 26 52
Holes 18 L 5850 m SSS 72
V'tors U H
Fees 220kr (250kr)
Loc 30km S of Aalborg
Arch Henrik Jacobsen

Royal Oak (1992)
Golfvej, Jels, 6630 Rødding
Tel 74 55 32 94
Fax 74 55 32 95
Web www.royal-oak.dk
Holes 18 L 5967 m Par 72
V'tors H–booking necessary. Soft spikes only
Fees 300kr
Loc 25km SW of Kolding

Saeby
Vandløsvej 50, 9300 Saeby
Tel 98 46 76 77
Fax 98 46 11 24
Holes 18 L 5944 m SSS 72
V'tors U
Fees 200kr (200kr)
Loc Saeby, 12km S of Fredrikshavn
Arch Anders Amilon

Silkeborg (1966)
Sensommervej 15C, 8600 Silkeborg
Tel 86 85 33 99
Fax 86 85 35 22
Web www.silkeborggc.dk
Holes 18 L 5975 m SSS 72
V'tors WD–U exc Tues WE–NA pm
Fees 225kr (275kr)
Loc 5km E of Silkeborg
Arch Frederik Dreyer

Sønderjyllands (1968)
Uge Hedegård, 6360 Tinglev
Tel 74 68 75 25
Fax 74 68 75 05
Web www.sdj-golfklub.dk
Holes 18 L 5856 m Par 71
V'tors H
Fees 200kr (240kr)
Loc 9km NE of Tinglev. 9km S of Abenraa
Arch Erik Schnack

Toftlund
Ostergade 63, 6520 Toftlund
Tel 73 83 16 00
Fax 73 83 16 19
Web www.brundtlandbanen.dk
Holes 18 L 5890 m Par 73
9 L 1255 m Par 29
V'tors H
Fees 240kr (280kr)

Loc Toftlund, Central Jutland
Arch Henrik Jacobsen

Varde (1991)
Gellerupvej 111b, 6800 Varde
Tel 75 22 49 44
Fax 75 22 49 44
Holes 18 L 6104 m Par 71
V'tors H
Fees 200kr
Loc 20km N of Esbjerg
Arch Erik Fauerholt

Vejle (1970)
Faellessletgard, Ibaekvej, 7100 Vejle
Tel 75 85 81 85
Fax 75 85 83 01
Holes 27 holes:
5677-6148 m Par 71-73
9 hole Par 3 course
V'tors H
Fees 250kr (300kr)
Loc 5 km SE of Vejle
Arch J Malling Pedersen

Viborg (1973)
Spangsbjerg Alle 50, Overlund, 8800 Viborg
Tel 86 67 30 10
Fax 86 67 34 15
Web www.viborggolfklub.dk
Holes 18 L 5767 m CR 72
V'tors WD–H 48 WE–H 36
Fees 200kr (225kr)
Loc 2 km E of Viborg
Arch Frederik Dreyer

Zealand

Asserbo (1946)
Bødkergaardsvej, 3300 Frederiksvaerk
Tel 47 72 14 90
Fax 47 72 14 26
Holes 18 L 5861 m Par 72
V'tors H
Fees 300kr (350kr)
Loc 3km from Frederiksvaerk towards Liseleje
Arch Ross/Samuelsen

Copenhagen (1898)
Dyrehaven 2, 2800 Kgs. Lyngby
Tel 39 63 04 83
Fax 39 63 46 83
Holes 18 L 5761 m SSS 71
V'tors WD–U WE–NA before noon
Fees 280kr (350kr)
Loc 13 km N of Copenhagen, in deer park

Dragør
Kalvebodvej 100, 2791 Dragør
Tel 32 53 89 75
Fax 32 53 88 09
Web www.dragor-golf.dk
Holes 18 L 5864 m SSS 71
6 hole Par 3 course
V'tors WD–U WE–U H

Fees 250kr (300kr)
Loc 15km SE of Copenhagen centre, nr Airport
Arch Henning Jensen/Kierkegaard

Falster (1994)
Virketvej 44, 4863 Eskilstrup, Falster Island
Tel 54 43 81 43
Fax 54 43 81 23
Holes 18 L 5912 m Par 72
V'tors H
Fees 215kr (275kr)
Loc 20km NE of Nykøbing (Route 271)
Arch Anders Amilon

Frederikssund (1974)
Egelundsgården, Skovnaesvej 9, 3630 Jaegerspris
Tel 47 31 08 77
Fax 47 31 21 88
Holes 18 L 5868 m SSS 71
V'tors WD–U H WE–H 30
Fees 200kr (300kr)
Loc 3km S of Frederikssund towards Skibby (Route 53)
Arch Dreyer/Samuelsen

Furesø (1974)
Hestkøbgård, Hestkøb Vaenge 4, 3460 Birkerød
Tel 45 81 74 44
Fax 45 82 02 24
Web www.furesoegolfklub.dk
Holes 27 holes:
5328-5641 m CR 70-71
V'tors H WD–NA before 9am
WE–NA before noon
Fees 250kr (350kr)
Loc 25 km N of Copenhagen
Arch Jan Sederholm

Gilleleje (1970)
Ferlevej 52, 3250 Gilleleje
Tel 49 71 80 56
Fax 49 71 80 86
Web www.gillelejegolfklub.dk
Holes 18 L 6641 yds Par 72 CR 71
V'tors H–36
Fees 250kr (350kr)
Loc 62km N of Copenhagen
Arch Jan Sederholm

Hedeland (1980)
Staerkendevej 232A, 2640 Hedehusene
Tel 46 13 61 88/46 13 61 69
Fax 46 13 62 78
Holes 18 L 6070 m Par 72
9 hole Par 3 course
V'tors H WE–NA before noon
Fees 200kr (250kr)
Loc 7km SE of Roskilde. 20km SW of Copenhagen
Arch Jan Sederholm

Helsingør
GL Hellebaekvej, 3000 Helsingør
Tel 49 21 29 70
Fax 49 21 09 70

Holes 18 L 5612 m Par 71 CR 71
V'tors U H
Fees 275–400kr (350–500kr)
Loc 2km N of Helsingør

Hillerød (1966)
Nysøgårdsvej 9, Ny Hammersholt,
3400 Hillerød
Tel 48 26 50 46/48 25 40 30 (Pro)
Fax 48 25 29 87
Holes 18 L 5255 m CR 71
V'tors H WE–NA before noon
Fees 250kr (300kr)
Loc 3 km S of Hillerød
Arch Sederholm/Knudsen

Holbaek (1964)
Dragerupvej 50, 4300 Holbaek
Tel 59 43 45 79
Fax 59 44 51 61
Web www.holbaekgolfklub.dk
Holes 18 L 5290 m Par 70
V'tors U H
Fees 220kr (250kr)
Loc Kirsebaerholmen, 2km E of Holbaek
Arch Dreyer/Sederholm

Køge (1970)
Gl.Hastrupvej12, 4600 Køge
Tel 56 65 10 00
Fax 56 65 13 45
Holes 18 L 6042 m Par 72
        9 L 3659 m Par 62
V'tors WE–H max 27
Fees 220kr (260kr)
Loc 3km S of Køge. Copenhagen 38 km

Kokkedal (1971)
Kokkedal Alle 9, 2970 Horsholm
Tel 45 76 99 59
Fax 45 76 99 03
Web www.kokkedalgolf.dk
Holes 18 L 5936 m Par 72
V'tors H–WE pm only
Fees 250kr (300kr)
Loc Hørsholm, 30 km N of Copenhagen
Arch Frank Pennink

Korsør (1964)
Tårnborgparken, Postbox 53,
4220 Korsør
Tel 53 57 18 36
Fax 53 57 18 39
Holes 18 L 5998 m CR 71.1
V'tors H WE–NA before 10am
Fees 160 (200kr)
Loc 1km E of Korsør, on Korsør Bay

Mølleåens (1970)
Stenbaekgård, Rosenlundvej 3,
3540 Lynge
Tel 48 18 86 31/48 18 86 36 (Pro)
Fax 48 18 86 43
Holes 18 L 5494 m SSS 69
V'tors H
Fees 200kr (250kr)

Loc 32 km NW of Copenhagen
Arch Jan Sederholm

Odsherred (1967)
4573 Hojby
Tel 59 30 20 76
Fax 59 30 36 76
Holes 18 L 5536 m Par 71
V'tors H
Fees 200kr (240kr)
Loc 5km SW of Nykøbing
Arch Amilon/Dreyer

Roskilde (1973)
Gedevad, Kongemarken 34,
4000 Roskilde
Tel 46 37 01 81
Fax 46 37 01 81
Holes 18 L 5700 m CR 71
V'tors U H WE–NA before 10am
Fees 200kr (250kr)
Loc 5km W of Roskilde
Arch Jan Sederholm

Rungsted (1937)
Vestre Stationsvej 16, 2960
Rungsted Kyst
Tel 45 86 34 44
Fax 45 86 57 70
Web www.rungstedgolfklub.dk
Holes 18 L 5918 m Par 71 CR 71.2
        SR 129
V'tors H–max 26 (WE–21) WE–NA before noon
Fees 400kr (450kr)
Loc Rungsted, 24km N of Copenhagen
Arch Maj CA Mackenzie

Simon's (1993)
Nybovej 5, 3490 Kvistgaard
Tel 49 19 14 78
Fax 49 19 14 70
Holes 18 L 6200 m SSS 74
V'tors H–max 36
Fees 300kr (450kr)
Loc 10km S of Helsingør. 35km N of Copenhagen
Arch Martin Hawtree

Skjoldenaesholm (1992)
4174 Jystrup
Tel 57 53 87 00
Fax 57 53 87 15
Web www.golfin.dk/sgc
Holes 18 L 5958 m SSS 71
V'tors H–max 36
Fees 260kr (310kr)
Loc 10km N of Ringsted. 60km SW of Copenhagen
Arch Otto Bojesen

Skovlunde Herlev (1980)
Syvendehusvej 111, 2730 Herlev
Tel 44 68 90 09
Fax 44 68 90 04
Holes 18 L 4839 m Par 68 CR 66.7
        9 hole Par 3 course
V'tors H
Fees 200kr (250kr)

Loc Herlev/Ballerup, 15km NW of Copenhagen
Arch Torben Starup

Søllerød
Brillerne 9, 2840 Holte
Tel 45 80 17 84, 45 80 18 77
Fax 45 80 70 08
Web www.sollerodgolf.dk
Holes 18 L 5952 m SSS 72
V'tors U
Fees 260kr (350kr)
Loc 19km N of Copenhagen

Sorø (1979)
Suserupvej 7a, 4180 Sorø
Tel 57 84 93 95
Fax 57 84 85 58
Web www.soroegolf.dk
Holes 18 L 5693 m Par 71 CR 71
V'tors H–max 42
Fees 250kr (300kr)
Loc 6km S of Sorø. 15km W of Ringsted
Arch Jan Sederholm

Sydsjaellands (1974)
Borupgården, Mogenstrup,
4700 Naestved
Tel 55 76 15 55
Fax 55 76 15 88
Holes 18 L 5725 m CR 70.6
V'tors H
Fees 200kr (250kr)
Loc 10km SE of Naestved towards Praestø
Arch Dreyer/Amillon

Vallensbaek (1985)
Golfsvinget 12, 2625 Vallensbaek
Tel 43 62 18 99
Fax 43 62 18 33
Holes 18 L 5965 m Par 71 CR 72
        SR 123
V'tors H
Fees 220kr (260kr)
Loc 15km W of Copenhagen
Arch Frederik Dreyer

Finland

Central

Etelä-Pohjanmaan (1986)
P O Box 136, 60101 Seinäjoki
Tel (06) 423 4545
Fax (06) 423 4547
Web www.ruuhikoskigolf.fi
Holes 18 L 5806 m CR 71.9
V'tors U
Fees 200fmk
Loc 5km E of Seinäjoki. 300km NW of Helsinki
Arch Robert Trent Jones Jr

Karelia Golf (1987)
Vaskiportintie, 80780 Kontioniemi
Tel   (013) 732411
Fax   (013) 732472
Holes   18 L 5619 m CR 71
V'tors   U H
Fees   185fmk
Loc   18km N of Joensuu. 460km
         NE of Helsinki
Arch   Kosti Kuronen

Kokkolan (1957)
P O Box 164, 67101 Kokkola
Tel   (06) 822 1636
Fax   (06) 822 1630
Holes   18 L 5572 m SSS 71
V'tors   U H
Fees   150fmk
Loc   3km S of Kokkola. 500km N
         of Helsinki
Arch   KJ Indola

Laukaan Golf (1989)
41530 Laukaa
Tel   (014) 832801
Fax   (014) 832705
Holes   18 L 5547 m CR 71
V'tors   U
Fees   150fmk (180fmk)
Loc   28km NE of Jyväskylä. 300km
         N of Helsinki

Tarina Golf (1988)
Golftie 135, 71800 Siilinjärvi
Tel   (017) 462 5299
Fax   (017) 462 5269
Holes   Old 18 L 5686 m Par 73
         New 18 holes open 2002
V'tors   U H
Fees   200fmk (250fmk)
Loc   21km N of Kuopio (Route 5)
Arch   Kuronen/Sederholm

Vaasan (1969)
Golfkenttätie 61, 65380 Vaasa
Tel   (06) 356 9989
Fax   (06) 356 9091
Holes   18 L 5602 m Par 72
V'tors   H or Green card
Fees   140fmk
Loc   Kraklund, 6km SE of Vaasa
         on Route 724. 417km NW of
         Helsinki
Arch   Björn Eriksson

Helsinki & South

Aura Golf (1958)
Ruissalon Puistotie 536, 20100 Turku
Tel   (02) 258 9201/9221
Fax   (02) 258 9121
Web   www.auragolf.fi
Holes   18 L 5843 m SSS 71
V'tors   H–max 30 (men) 36 (women)
Fees   250fmk (300fmk)
Loc   Ruissalo Island, 9km W of
         Turku
Arch   Pekka Sivula

Espoo Ringside Golf (1990)
Niipperintie 20, 02920 Espoo
Tel   (09) 849 4940
Fax   (09) 853 7132
Holes   18 L 5855 m SSS 72
V'tors   H
Fees   200fmk (240fmk)
Loc   20km NW of Helsinki
Arch   Kosti Kuronen

Espoon Golfseura (1982)
P O Box 26, 02781 Espoo
Tel   (09) 8190 3444
Fax   (09) 8190 3434
Holes   18 L 5920 m CR 72.3
V'tors   H
Fees   210fmk
Loc   Espoo, 24km W of Helsinki
Arch   Jan Sederholm

Harjattula G&CC (1989)
Harjattulantie 84, 20960 Turku
Tel   (02) 276 2180
Fax   (02) 258 7218
Web   www.harjattula.fi
Holes   18 L 6348 m Par 72 SSS 75
V'tors   H–max 36
Fees   €35 (€43)
Loc   22km S of Turku
Arch   Kosti Kuronen

Helsingin Golfklubi (1932)
Talin Kartano, 00350 Helsinki
Tel   (09) 550235/557899
Fax   (09) 565 3596
Holes   18 L 5428 m CR 68.7
V'tors   H–max 24
Fees   200fmk
Loc   7km W of Helsinki

Hyvinkään (1989)
Golftie 63, 05880 Hyvinkää
Tel   (019) 489390
Fax   (019) 489392
Holes   18 L 5457 m CR 72.1
V'tors   U H
Fees   170fmk
Loc   3km N of Hyvinkää. 50km N
         of Helsinki
Arch   Kosti Kuronen

Keimola Golf (1988)
Kirkantie 32, 01750 Vantaa
Tel   (09) 276 6650
Fax   (09) 896790
Holes   27 L 5870-5924 m SSS 71-74
V'tors   WD–U before 3pm –M after
         3pm WE–M H
Fees   160fmk
Loc   15km N of Helsinki
Arch   Pekka Wesamaa

Kurk Golf (1985)
02550 Evitskog
Tel   (09) 819 0480
Fax   (09) 819 04810
Holes   18 L 5848 m Par 72

V'tors   H
Fees   200fmk
Loc   40km W of Helsinki
Arch   Reijo Hillberg

Master Golf (1988)
Bodomintie 4, 029400 Espoo
Tel   (09) 849 2300
Fax   (09) 849 23011
Holes   18 hole course CR 71.2
         18 hole course CR 70.1
V'tors   WD before 2pm H–max
         30 (M) 36 (L)
Fees   €39 (€46)
Loc   24km NW of Helsinki
Arch   Kuronen/Persson

Meri-Teijo (1990)
*Mathildedalin Kartano,
25660 Mathildedal*
Tel   (02) 736 3955
Fax   (02) 736 3945
Holes   18 L 5842 m CR 70.7
V'tors   U
Fees   110fmk (140fmk)
Loc   20km S of Salo. 70km E of
         Turku

Messilä (1988)
Messiläntie 240, 15980 Messilä
Tel   (03) 753 8171
Fax   (03) 753 8174
Holes   18 L 6013 m Par 73
V'tors   WD–U before 3pm
Fees   D–180fmk
Loc   8km W of Lahti. 100km N of
         Helsinki
Arch   Kosti Kuronen

Nevas Golf (1988)
01190 Box
Tel   (09) 272 6313
Fax   (09) 272 6345
Holes   18 L 5267 m CR 68.5
V'tors   U
Fees   200fmk
Loc   30km E of Helsinki
Arch   Kosti Kuronen

Nordcenter G&CC (1988)
10410 Aminnefors
Tel   (019) 238850
Fax   (019) 238871
Web   www.nordcenter.com
Holes   18 L 6375 m SSS 77
         18 L 6069 m SSS 72
V'tors   H
Fees   350fmk (420fmk)
Loc   80km W of Helsinki
Arch   Fream/Benz

Nurmijärven (1990)
Ratasillantie, 05100 Röykkä
Tel   (09) 276 6230
Fax   (09) 276 62330
Holes   27 L 6002-6214 m SSS 73-75
V'tors   U
Fees   120–180fmk
Loc   23km W of Klaukkala. 50km
         NW of Helsinki

Peuramaa

02400 Kirkkonummi
Tel   **(09) 295 588**
Fax   (09) 2955 8210
Web   www.peuramaagolf.com
Holes 18 L 5878 m CR 72.6
V'tors H
Fees   200fmk (250fmk)
Loc   27km W of Helsinki
Arch   Heikki Kuronen

Pickala Golf (1986)

Golfkuja 5, 02580 Siuntio
Tel   **(09) 221 9080**
Fax   (09) 221 90899
Web   www.pickalagolf.fi
Holes Seaside 18 L 5820 m SSS 72
       Park 18 L 5897 m SSS 72
V'tors H
Fees   200fmk (250fmk)
Loc   42km W of Helsinki, on South
       coast
Arch   Reijo Hillberg

Ruukkigolf (1986)

Brödtorp, 10420 Skuru
Tel   **(019) 245 4485**
Fax   (019) 245 4285
Holes 18 L 6165 m Par 72
V'tors U
Fees   120fmk (170fmk)
Loc   85km W of Helsinki
Arch   Lasse Heikkinen

Sarfvik (1984)

P O Box 27, 02321 Espoo
Tel   **(09) 221 9000**
Fax   (09) 297 7134
Holes 18 L 5690 m CR 70.5
       18 L 5399 m CR 69.8
V'tors WD–U H
Fees   400fmk
Loc   20km W of Helsinki
Arch   Jan Sederholm

Sea Golf Rönnäs (1989)

Rönnäs, 07750 Isnäs
Tel   **(019) 634434**
Fax   (019) 634458
Holes 18 L 5541 m CR 70.5
V'tors U
Fees   30fmk (170fmk)
Loc   27km SE of Porvoo. 80km E
       of Helsinki

St Laurence (1989)

Kaivurinkatu, 08200 Lohja
Tel   **(019) 386603**
Fax   (019) 386666
Holes 18 L 6247 m Par 72
       9 L 3248 m Par 36
V'tors WD–H WE–M H
Fees   250fmk
Loc   50km W of Helsinki
Arch   Kosti Kuronen

Suur-Helsingin (1965)

Rinnekodintie 29, 02980 Espoo
Tel   **(09) 855 8687**
Fax   (09) 855 0648

Holes Lakisto 18 L 5551 m SSS 71
       Luukki 18 L 5085 m SSS 70
V'tors U
Fees   150fmk
Loc   25km N of Helsinki

Golf Talma (1989)

Nygårdintie 115-6, 04240 Talma
Tel   **(09) 274 6540**
Fax   (09) 274 65432
Holes 18 L 5855 m SSS 72
       9 L 2895 m SSS 36
       9 hole Par 3 course
V'tors WD–H WE–M H
Fees   250fmk (300fmk)
Loc   35km N of Helsinki
Arch   Henrik Wartiainen

Tuusula (1983)

Kirkkotie 51, 04310 Tuusula
Tel   **(042) 410241**
Fax   (09) 274 60860
Web   www.golfpiste.com/tgk
Holes 18 L 5626 m CR 71
V'tors H
Fees   220fmk
Loc   30km N of Helsinki, nr airport
Arch   Henrik Wartiainen

Virvik Golf (1981)

Virvik, 06100 Porvoo
Tel   **(915) 579292**
Fax   (915) 579292
Holes 18 L 5855 m SSS 72
V'tors H
Fees   120fmk (140fmk)
Loc   18km SE of Porvoo. 66km E
       of Helsinki
Arch   Reijo Louhimo

North

Green Zone Golf (1987)

Näräntie, 95400 Tornio
Tel   **(016) 431711**
Fax   (016) 431710
Holes 18 L 5870 m SSS 73
V'tors U
Fees   120fmk
Loc   2km N of Tornio. 140km N of
       Oulu, on Finnish/Swedish
       border
Arch   Ake Persson

Katinkulta (1990)

88610 Vuokatti
Tel   **(08) 669 7488**
Fax   (08) 669 7480
Holes 18 L 6000 m Par 72
V'tors H
Fees   160fmk (180fmk)
Loc   36km E of Kajaani. 600km N
       of Helsinki
Arch   Jan Sederholm

Oulu (1964)

Isokatu 99, 90120 Oulu
Tel   **(08) 371666/531 5222**
Fax   (08) 379728/531 5129

Web   www.golfpiste.com/ogk
Holes 18 L 6160 m SSS 73
       9 L 2990 m SSS 73
V'tors H
Fees   200–220fmk
Loc   Sanginsuu, 18km E of Oulu
Arch   Ronald Fream

South East

Imatran Golf (1986)

Golftie 11, 55800 Imatra
Tel   **(05) 473 4954**
Fax   (05) 473 4953
Holes 18 L 5738 m CR 71.4
V'tors U
Fees   170fmk (170fmk)
Loc   6km N of Imatra. 270km E of
       Helsinki
Arch   Kosti Kuronen

Kartano Golf (1988)

P O Box 60, 79601 Joroinen
Tel   **(017) 572257**
Fax   (017) 572263
Holes 18 L 5597 m CR 71
V'tors U
Fees   130fmk (170fmk)
Loc   20km S of Varkaus. 330km
       NE of Helsinki
Arch   Ake Persson

Kerigolf (1990)

Hotellikylä Kerimaa, 58200 Kerimäki
Tel   **(015) 252496**
Fax   (015) 252124
Web   www.kerigolf.fi
Holes 18 L 6218 m Par 72 SSS 75
V'tors H
Fees   200fmk
Loc   15km E of Savonlinna. 350km
       NE of Helsinki
Arch   Ronald Fream

Koski Golf (1987)

Eerolan Golfkeskus, 45700 Kuusankoski
Tel   **(05) 374 7622**
Fax   (05) 374 7820
Web   www.koskigolf.com
Holes 18 L 6375 m Par 73
V'tors H I
Fees   190fmk (220fmk)
Loc   3km E of Kuusankoski. 70km
       E of Lahti
Arch   Kosti Kuronen

Kymen Golf (1964)

Mussalo Golfcourse, 48310 Kotka
Tel   **(05) 260 5333**
Fax   (05) 260 5073
Holes 18 L 5651 m CR 70.6
V'tors H
Fees   160fmk
Loc   5km W of Kotka, Mussalo
       Island. 130km E of Helsinki
Arch   Kosti Kuronen

For list of abbreviations see page 649

Lahden Golf (1959)

P O Box 67, 15141 Lahti
Tel (03) 784 1311
Fax (03) 784 1311
Holes 18 L 5547 m CR 71.7
V'tors U H
Fees 150fmk
Loc 6km NE of Lahti. 110km NE of Helsinki

Porrassalmi (1989)

Annila, 50100 Mikkeli
Tel (015) 335518/335446
Fax (015) 335446
Holes 18 L 4907 m CR 65.8
V'tors H
Fees 140–160fmk
Loc 5km S of Mikkeli

Vierumäen Golfseura (1988)

Suomen Urheiluopisto, 19120 Vierumäki
Tel (03) 842 4501
Fax (03) 842 4630
Holes 18 L 5580 m CR 71.1
V'tors U
Fees 170fmk
Loc 25km NE of Lahti

South West

Porin Golfkerho (1939)

P O Box 25, 28601 Pori
Tel (02) 630 3888
Fax (02) 630 3888
Holes 18 L 6160 m SSS 74
V'tors H
Fees 200fmk
Loc 5km NW of Pori, at Kalafornia
Arch Reijo Louhimo

River Golf (1988)

Taivalkunta, 37120 Nokia
Tel (03) 340 0234
Fax (03) 340 0235
Holes 18 L 5616 m CR 70.8
V'tors U
Fees 150fmk
Loc Nokia, 20km W of Tampere
Arch Kosti Kuronen

Salo Golf (1988)

Liikuntapuisto 8, 24100 Salo
Tel (02) 731 7321
Fax (02) 731 5600
Holes 18 L 5447 m CR 69
V'tors U
Fees 120fmk (150fmk)
Loc 110km W of Helsinki

Tammer Golf (1965)

Toimelankatu 4, 33560 Tampere
Tel (03) 261 3316
Fax (03) 261 3130
Holes 18 L 5717 m CR 70
V'tors U

Fees 150fmk
Loc Ruotula, 5km NE of Tampere

Tawast Golf (1987)

Tawastintie 48, 13270 Hämeenlinna
Tel (03) 619 7502
Fax (03) 619 7503
Web www.htk.fi/tawg
Holes 18 L 6063 m Par 72
V'tors WD–H–max 36 WE–M
Fees 200fmk
Loc 5km E of Hämeenlinna
Arch Reijo Hillberg

Vammala (1991)

38100 Karkku
Tel (03) 513 4070
Fax (03) 513 90711
Holes 18 L 5522 m CR 69.2
V'tors H
Fees 120fmk (160fmk)
Loc 11km N of Vammala. 210km NW of Helsinki
Arch Kosti Kuronen

Wiurila G&CC (1990)

Viurilantie 126, 24910 Halikko
Tel (02) 737 1400
Fax (02) 737 1404
Holes 18 L 5584 m CR 71.7
V'tors U
Fees 130fmk (160fmk)
Loc 5km W of Salo. 115km W of Helsinki

Yyteri Golf (1988)

Karhuluodontie 85, 28840 Pori
Tel (02) 638 0380
Fax (02) 638 0385
Web www.yyterilinks.com
Holes 18 L 5738 m Par 72
V'tors H
Fees 200–250fmk
Loc 20km W of Pori
Arch Reijo Louhimo

France

Bordeaux & South West

Albret (1986)

Le Pusocq, 47230 Barbaste
Tel 05 53 65 53 69
Fax 05 53 65 61 19
Holes 18 L 5911 m SSS 71
V'tors U
Fees 140fr (170fr)
Loc Barbaste, 30km W of Agen
Arch JL Pega

Arcachon (1955)

35 Bd d'Arcachon, 33260 La Teste De Buch
Tel 05 56 54 44 00

Fax 05 56 66 86 32
Holes 18 L 5930 m SSS 71
V'tors U H
Fees 185–270fr (220–270fr)
Loc 60km SW of Bordeaux
Arch CR Blandford

Arcangues (1991)

64200 Arcangues
Tel 05 59 43 10 56
Fax 05 59 43 12 60
Holes 18 L 6142 m Par 72
V'tors U
Fees On application
Loc 3km SE of Biarritz
Arch Ronald Fream

Ardilouse (1980)

Domaine de l'Ardilouse, 33680 Lacanau-Océan
Tel 05 56 03 25 60
Fax 05 56 26 30 57
Holes 18 L 5932 m SSS 72
V'tors H
Loc 45km W of Bordeaux
Arch John Harris

Biarritz (1888)

Ave Edith Cavell, 64200 Biarritz
Tel 05 59 03 71 80
Fax 05 59 03 26 74
Holes 18 L 5402 m SSS 69
V'tors U
Fees €35 (€55)
Loc Biarritz
Arch Willie Dunn

Biscarrosse (1989)

Route d'Ispe, 40600 Biscarrosse
Tel 05 58 09 84 93
Fax 05 58 09 84 50
Holes Lake 9 L 2172 m SSS 32
Forest 9 L 3030 m
SSS 36
V'tors U
Fees 150–270fr
Loc 80km SW of Bordeaux
Arch Brizon/Veyssieres

Blue Green–Artiguelouve (1986)

Domaine St Michel, Pau-Artiguelouve, 64230 Artiguelouve
Tel 05 59 83 09 29
Fax 05 59 83 14 05
Holes 18 L 6063 m Par 71
V'tors U
Fees 190fr (235fr)
Loc 8km NW of Pau, off Bayonne road
Arch J Garaialde

Blue Green–Seignosse (1989)

Avenue du Belvédère, 40510 Seignosse
Tel 05 58 41 68 30
Fax 05 58 41 68 31
Web www.golfseignosse.com

Holes 18 L 6124 m Par 72
V'tors U
Fees 260–390fr
Loc 30km N of Biarritz, nr Airport
Arch Robert von Hagge

Bordeaux-Cameyrac
(1972)
Cameyrac, 33450 St Sulpice
Tel 05 56 72 96 79
Fax 05 56 72 86 56
Holes 18 L 5927 m SSS 72
9 L 1188 m Par 28
Loc 15km E of Bordeaux
Arch Jacques Quenot

Bordeaux-Lac (1977)
Public
Avenue de Pernon, 33300 Bordeaux
Tel 05 56 50 92 72
Fax 05 56 29 01 84
Web www.golfbordeauxlac.com
Holes 18 L 6156 m SSS 72
18 L 6159 m SSS 72
V'tors U
Fees €23 (€33)
Loc 2km N of Bordeaux
Arch Jean Bourret

Bordelais (1900)
Domaine de Kater, Allee F Arago, 33200 Bordeaux-Caudéran
Tel 05 56 28 56 04
Fax 05 56 28 59 71
Holes 18 L 4727 m SSS 67
V'tors H–restricted Tues
Fees 200fr (260fr)
Loc 3km NW of Bordeaux

Casteljaloux (1989)
Avenue du Lac, 47700 Casteljaloux
Tel 05 53 93 51 60
Fax 05 53 93 04 10
Holes 18 L 5916 m SSS 72
V'tors U
Loc 60km NW of Agen
Arch Michel Gayon

Castelnaud (1987)
'La Menuisière', 47290 Castelnaud de Gratecambe
Tel 05 53 01 74 64
Fax 05 53 01 78 99
Holes 18 L 6322 m SSS 73
9 L 2184 m SSS 27
Loc 10km N of Villeneuve on N21. 40km N of Agen

Chantaco (1928)
Route d'Ascain, 64500 St Jean-de-Luz
Tel 05 59 26 14 22/05 59 26 19 22
Fax 05 59 26 48 37
Web www.golfdechantaco.com
Holes 18 L 5722 m SSS 70
V'tors U H
Fees 280fr (350fr)
Loc 2km S of St Jean-de-Luz, on Route d'Ascain
Arch HS Colt

Château des Vigiers
(1990)
24240 Monestier
Tel 05 53 61 50 00
Fax 05 53 61 50 31
Web www.vigiers.com
Holes 18 L 6003 m Par 72
6 hole Academy course
V'tors H
Fees 205–320fr
Loc 15km SW of Bergerac. 75km E of Bordeaux
Arch Donald Steel

Chiberta (1926)
Boulevard des Plages, 64600 Anglet
Tel 05 59 63 83 20
Fax 05 59 63 30 56
Holes 18 L 5650 m SSS 70
V'tors H–booking required
Loc 3km N of Biarritz. Airport 5km
Arch T Simpson

Croix de Mortemart
(1987)
St Felix de Reillac, 24260 Le Bugue
Tel 05 53 03 27 55
Holes 18 L 6222 m Par 72
V'tors U
Loc 30km S of Perigueux, between La Douze and Le Bugue (D710)
Arch Martine Lacroix

Graves et Sauternais
(1989)
St Pardon de Conques, 33210 Langon
Tel 05 56 62 25 43
Holes 18 L 5810 m SSS 71
V'tors U
Loc 5km from Langon. 45km SW of Bordeaux via A62

Gujan (1990)
Route de Souguinet, 33470 Gujan Mestras
Tel 05 57 52 73 73
Fax 05 56 66 10 93
Holes 18 L 6225 m SSS 72
9 L 2635 m SSS 35
V'tors U
Fees 18 hole:180–280fr
9 hole:140–170fr
Loc 12km E of Arcachon on RN 250. 40km W of Bordeaux
Arch Alain Prat

Hossegor (1930)
Ave du Golf, BP 95, 40150 Hossegor
Tel 05 58 43 56 99
Fax 05 58 43 98 52
Holes 18 L 6001 m SSS 71
V'tors H–max 35
Fees 240fr (360fr)
Loc 15km N of Bayonne, on coast
Arch J Morrison

Makila
Route de Cambo, 64200 Bassussarry
Tel 05 59 58 42 42
Fax 05 59 58 42 48
Holes 18 L 6176 m SSS 72
V'tors H
Fees 220–300fr
Loc 5km SE of Biarritz. Airport 2km
Arch R Roquemore

Médoc
Chemin de Courmateau, Louens, 33290 Le Pian Médoc
Tel 05 56 70 11 90
Fax 05 56 70 11 99
Holes Chateaux 18 L 6316 m SSS 73
Vignes 18 L 6220 m SSS 73
V'tors H
Fees 230fr (300fr)
Loc 20km NW of Bordeaux
Arch Coore/Whitman

Moliets (1989)
Public
Rue Mathieu Desbieys, 40660 Moliets
Tel 05 58 48 54 65
Fax 05 58 48 54 88
Web www.golfmoliets.com
Holes 18 L 6172 m SSS 73
9 hole course
V'tors U H–max 30
Fees 220–350fr
Loc Moliets, 40km N of Bayonne. 40km W of Dax
Arch Robert Trent Jones Sr

La Nivelle (1907)
Place William Sharp, 64500 Ciboure
Tel 05 59 47 18 99/
05 59 47 19 72
Holes 18 L 5570 m SSS 69
V'tors U
Loc 2km S of St Jean-de-Luz

Pau (1856)
Rue de Golf, 64140 Pau-Billère
Tel 05 59 13 18 56
Fax 05 59 13 18 57
Holes 18 L 5312 m SSS 69
V'tors H
Fees 200fr (250fr)
Loc 2km S of Pau. Bordeaux 200km
Arch Willie Dunn

Périgueux (1980)
Public
Domaine de Saltgourde, 24430 Marsac
Tel 05 53 53 02 35
Fax 05 53 09 46 29
Holes 18 L 6120 m SSS 72
V'tors U
Loc 3km W of Périgueux, via Angoulême-Riberac road
Arch Robert Berthet

Pessac (1989)
Rue de la Princesse, 33600 Pessac
Tel   05 57 26 03 33
Fax   05 56 36 52 89
Holes 18 L 5567-5935 m SSS 72
       9 L 2911 m SSS 36
       9 hole Par 3 course
V'tors U
Fees   160fr (220fr)
Loc   4km W of Bordeaux
Arch   Olivier Brizon

Scottish Golf Aubertin
(1987)
64290 Aubertin
Tel   05 59 82 70 69
Holes 18 L 4806 m Par 66
V'tors U
Loc   20km S of Pau

Stade Montois (1993)
Pessourdat, 40090 Saint Avit
Tel   05 58 75 63 05
Fax   05 58 06 80 72
Holes 18 L 5944 m Par 71
V'tors U
Fees   180fr (180fr)
Loc   Pau 80km. Biarritz 100km
Arch   J Garaialde

Brittany

Ajoncs d'Or (1976)
Kergrain Lantic, 22410 Saint-Quay Portrieux
Tel   02 96 71 90 74
Fax   02 96 71 40 83
Holes 18 L 6125 m SSS 72
V'tors U
Fees   150-220fr (195-220fr)
Loc   17km N of Saint-Brieuc. 6km
       W of Étables-sur-Mer
Arch   Carlian-Des Heulles

Baden
Kernic, 56870 Baden
Tel   02 97 57 18 96
Fax   02 97 57 22 05
Holes 18 L 6145 m SSS 73
V'tors U
Loc   12km SW of Vannes
Arch   Yves Bureau

Brest Les Abers (1990)
Kerhoaden, 29810 Plouarzel
Tel   02 98 89 68 33
Holes 18 L 5060 m Par 71
V'tors U
Fees   200fr
Loc   15km W 0f Brest (D5)
Arch   Ch Dunoyer

Brest-Iroise (1976)
Parc de Lann-Rohou, Saint-Urbain, 29800 Landerneau
Tel   02 98 85 16 17
Fax   02 98 85 19 39

Holes 18 L 5672 m Par 71
       9 L 3329 m Par 37
V'tors U
Fees   210fr (230fr)
Loc   25km E of Brest
Arch   M Fenn

Cicé-Blossac (1992)
Domaine de Cicé-Blossac, 35170 Bruz
Tel   02 99 52 79 79
Fax   02 99 57 93 60
Holes 18 L 6343 m SSS 72
V'tors U
Loc   Bruz, SW of Rennes (N177)
Arch   Macauley/Quenouille

Coatguelen (1987)
Château de Coatguelen, 22290 Pléhédel
Tel   02 96 55 33 40
Holes 18 hole course
V'tors U
Fees   100fr (150fr)
Loc   10km S of Paimpol on D7.
       35km from Saint-Brieuc

Dinard (1887)
35800 St-Briac-sur-Mer
Tel   02 99 88 32 07
Fax   02 99 88 04 53
Holes 18 L 5137 m Par 68
Loc   8km W of Dinard. 15km W of
       Saint-Malo

La Freslonnière (1989)
Le Bois Briand, 35650 Le Rheu
Tel   02 99 14 84 09
Fax   02 99 14 94 98
Holes 18 L 5756 m SSS 72
V'tors U
Fees   €31 (€40)
Loc   4km SW of Rennes, off N24
Arch   A du Bouexic

L'Odet (1987)
Clohars-Fouesnant, 29950 Benodet
Tel   02 98 54 87 88
Fax   02 98 54 61 40
Holes 18 L 5843 m SSS 72
       9 hole Par 3 course
V'tors U H
Fees   175-290fr
Loc   6km S of Benodet. 15km SE
       of Quimper
Arch   Robert Berthet

Les Ormes (1988)
Château des Ormes, Epiniac, 35120 Dol-de-Bretagne
Tel   02 99 73 54 44
Fax   02 99 73 53 65
Holes 18 L 5801 m SSS 72
V'tors H
Fees   200-270fr
Loc   8km S of Dol, off D795
Arch   A d'Ormesson

Pen Guen (1926)
22380 Saint-Cast-le-Guildo
Tel   02 96 41 91 20

Fax   02 96 41 77 62
Holes 18 L 4967m SSS 68
V'tors U
Fees   195-235fr
Loc   25km W of Dinard. 30km W
       of Saint-Malo

Pléneuf-Val André
Rue de la Plage des Vallées, 22370 Pléneuf-Val André
Tel   02 96 63 01 12
Fax   02 96 63 01 06
Holes 18 L 6052 m Par 72
V'tors U
Fees   160-270fr
Loc   30km E of St Brieuc on coast.
       60km W of St Malo
Arch   Alain Prat

Ploemeur Océan
Kerham Saint-Jude, 56270 Ploemeur
Tel   02 97 32 81 82
Fax   02 97 32 80 90
Web   www.formule-golf.com
Holes 18 L 5957 m SSS 72
V'tors U H
Fees   165-255fr
Loc   10km from Lorient-Brest
       road, exit Ploemeur
Arch   Macauley/Quenouille

Quimper-Cornouaille
(1959)
Manoir du Mesmeur, 29940 La Forêt-Fouesnant
Tel   02 98 56 97 09
Holes 18 L 5657 m SSS 71
Loc   15km SE of Quimper
Arch   F Hawtree

Rennes Saint Jacques
B P 1117, 37136 St-Jacques-de-la-Lande
Tel   02 99 30 18 18
Fax   02 99 31 51 04
Holes 18 L 6135 m Par 72
       9 L 2100 m Par 32
       9 hole short course
V'tors U
Fees   240fr
Loc   5km SW of Rennes
Arch   Robert Berthet

Rhuys-Kerver (1988)
Public
Formule Golf, Domaine de Kerver, 56730 St-Gildas-de-Rhuys
Tel   02 97 45 30 09
Fax   02 97 45 36 58
Holes 18 L 6197 m SSS 73
V'tors U
Fees   230fr
Loc   30km S of Vannes
Arch   Olivier Brizon

Les Rochers (1989)
Route d'Argentré du Plessis 3, 35500 Vitré
Tel   02 99 96 52 52
Fax   02 99 96 79 34

Holes 18 L 5721 m Par 72
V'tors U
Fees 160fr (160fr)
Loc Vitré, 30km E of Rennes
Arch JC Varro

Sables-d'Or-les-Pins
(1925)
22240 Fréhel
Tel 02 96 41 42 57
Fax 02 96 41 51 44
Holes 18 L 5586 m SSS 71
V'tors U
Fees 180–220fr
Loc 6km SW of Fréhel. 30km W of Dinard

St Laurent (1975)
Ploemel, 56400 Auray
Tel 02 97 56 85 18
Fax 02 97 56 89 99
Holes 18 L 6212 m SSS 72
9 L 2705 m SSS 35
V'tors U
Fees 255fr
Loc Ploemel, 16km SW of Auray
Arch Fenn/Bureau

St Malo-Le Tronchet
(1986)
Le Tronchet, 35540 Miniac-Morvan
Tel 02 99 58 96 69
Fax 02 99 58 10 39
Holes 18 L 5936 m SSS 72
9 L 2684 m SSS 36
V'tors U
Fees D–260fr
Loc 23km S of St Malo, off RN 137
Arch Hubert Chesneau

St Samson (1965)
Route de Kérénoc, 22560 Pleumeur-Bodou
Tel 02 96 23 87 34
Fax 02 96 23 84 59
Holes 18 L 5807 m Par 71
V'tors U
Fees 210fr (380fr)
Loc 7km N of Lannion on Tregastel road
Arch Hawtree

Sauzon (1987)
Les Poulins, 56360 Belle-Ile-en-Mer
Tel 02 97 31 64 65
Holes 18 L 5820 m Par 72
V'tors U
Loc Island off S coast of Brittany, near Quiberon
Arch Yves Bureau

Val Queven (1990)
Public
Kerruisseau, 56530 Queven
Tel 02 97 05 17 96
Fax 02 97 05 19 18
Web www.formule-golf.com
Holes 18 L 6127 m SSS 72

V'tors U Sun–restricted
Fees 200–270fr
Loc 10km W of Lorient
Arch Yves Bureau

Burgundy & Auvergne

Beaune-Levernois (1990)
21200 Levernois
Tel 03 80 24 10 29
Fax 03 80 24 03 78
Holes 18 L 6129 m Par 72
9 L 1316 m Par 29
V'tors U
Fees 200fr (260fr)
Loc 5km SE of Beaune (D470/D111)
Arch Christian Piot

Chalon-sur-Saône (1976)
Parc de Saint Nicolas, 71380 Chatenoy-en-Bresse
Tel 03 85 93 49 65
Fax 03 85 93 56 95
Web www.golf_chalon_sur_saone .com
Holes 18 L 5859 m SSS 71
V'tors U
Fees 165fr
Loc 3km SE of Chalon. 125km N of Lyon
Arch Michel Rio

Chambon-sur-Lignon
(1986)
Riondet, La Pierre de la Lune, 43400 Le Chambon-sur-Lignon
Tel 04 71 59 28 10
Fax 04 71 65 87 14
Holes 18 L 6110 m Par 72
V'tors U
Fees On application
Loc 60km NW of Saint Etienne. 120km NW of Lyon
Arch Michel Gayon

Château d'Avoise (1992)
9 Rue de Mâcon, 71210 Montchanin
Tel 03 85 78 19 19
Fax 03 85 78 15 16
Holes 18 L 6350 m Par 72
V'tors WD–U WE–H
Loc 25km W of Chalon
Arch Martin Hawtree

Château de Chailly
Chailly-sur-Armançon, 21320 Pouilly-en-Auxois
Tel 03 80 90 30 40
Fax 03 80 90 30 05
Holes 18 L 6146 m SSS 72
V'tors U
Loc 45km SW of Dijon
Arch Sprecher/Watine

Château de la Salle (1989)
71260 La Salle-Mâcon Nord
Tel 03 85 36 09 71
Fax 03 85 36 06 70
Holes 18 L 6024 m SSS 72
V'tors U
Fees 190fr (235fr)
Loc 12km NW of Mâcon. Lyon 70km
Arch Robert Berthet

Le Coiroux (1977)
Public
19190 Aubazine
Tel 03 55 27 25 66
Fax 03 55 27 29 33
Holes 18 L 5400 m Par 70
V'tors U
Loc 15km E of Brive
Arch Hubert Chesneau

Dijon-Bourgogne (1972)
Bois des Norges, 21490 Norges-la-Ville
Tel 03 80 35 71 10
Fax 03 80 35 79 27
Holes 18 L 6179 m SSS 72
V'tors U
Fees 190fr (250fr)
Loc 7km N of Dijon towards Langres
Arch Fenn/Radcliffe

Domaine de Roncemay (1989)
89110 Chassy
Tel 03 86 73 50 50
Fax 03 86 73 69 46
Holes 18 L 6401 m Par 72 SSS 73
V'tors H WE–restricted
Fees 200fr (280fr)
Loc 15km W of Auxerre
Arch Jeremy Pern

La Fredière (1988)
La Fredière, Céron, 71110 Marcigny
Tel 03 85 25 27 40
Fax 03 85 25 06 12
Holes 18 L 4529 m SSS 68
V'tors U
Fees 150–180fr
Loc 35km NW of Roanne
Arch Gilles Charmat

La Jonchère
Montgrenier, 23230 Gouzon
Tel 05 55 62 23 05
Holes 18 L 5858 m SSS 71
V'tors U
Loc 30km SW of Montluçon. 100km NE of Limoges
Arch J-L Pega

Limoges-St Lazare (1976)
Public
Avenue du Golf, 87000 Limoges
Tel 05 55 28 30 02
Holes 18 L 6238 m SSS 73
V'tors U
Loc 2km S of Limoges on RN20
Arch Hubert Chesneau

Mâcon La Salle (1989)
La Salle-Mâcon Nord, 71260 La Salle
Tel 03 85 36 09 71
Fax 03 85 36 06 70
Web www.golfmacon.com
Holes 18 L 6024 m Par 71
V'tors H or green card
Fees 190fr (235fr)
Loc 5km N of Mâcon (A6)
Arch Robert Berthet

Le Nivernais
Public
Le Bardonnay, 58470 Magny Cours
Tel 03 58 18 30
Fax 03 58 04 04
Holes 18 L 5670 m Par 71
V'tors U
Loc 12km S of Nevers on N7.
50km N of Moulins
Arch Alain Prat

La Porcelaine
Célicroux, 87350 Panazol
Tel 05 55 31 10 69
Fax 05 55 31 10 69
Holes 18 L 6035 m SSS 72
V'tors U
Fees 170–210fr
Loc 6km NE of Limoges
Arch Jean Garaialde

St Junien (1997)
Les Jouberties, 87200 Saint Junien
Tel 05 55 02 96 96
Holes 18 L 5677 m Par 72
9 hole course
V'tors U
Fees 100fr (130fr)
Loc 30km W of Limoges (N141)

Sporting Club de Vichy (1907)
Allée Baugnies, 03700 Bellerive/Allier
Tel 04 70 32 39 11
Fax 04 70 32 00 54
Holes 18 L 5463 m SSS 70
V'tors H
Loc In Vichy
Arch Arnaud Massy

Val de Cher (1975)
03190 Nassigny
Tel 04 70 06 71 15
Holes 18 L 5450 m Par 70
V'tors U
Fees 200fr
Loc 20km N of Montluçon on N144
Arch Bourret/Vigand

Les Volcans (1984)
La Bruyère des Moines, 63870 Orcines
Tel 04 73 62 15 51
Fax 04 73 62 26 52
Web www.golfdesvolcans.com
Holes 18 L 6286 m SSS 73
9 L 1377 m SSS 29
V'tors U H
Fees 240fr (280fr)

Loc 12km W of Clermont-Ferrand on RN41
Arch Lucien Roux

Centre

Les Aisses (1992)
RN20 Sud, 45240 La Ferté St Aubin
Tel 02 38 64 80 87
Fax 02 38 64 80 85
Holes 27 L 6200 m Par 72
V'tors U
Fees 180fr (250fr)
Loc 30km S of Orléans. 140km S of Paris
Arch Olivier Brizon

Ardrée (1988)
37360 St Antoine-du-Rocher
Tel 02 47 56 77 38
Fax 02 47 56 79 96
Holes 18 L 5758 m Par 70
V'tors U
Loc 10km N of Tours
Arch Olivier Brizon

Les Bordes (1987)
41220 Saint Laurent-Nouan
Tel 02 54 87 72 13
Fax 02 54 87 78 61
Web www.lesbordes.com
Holes 18 L 6412 m Par 72
V'tors U
Fees 400fr (600fr)
Loc 30km SW of Orléans
Arch Robert van Hagge

Château de Cheverny
La Rousselière, 41700 Cheverny
Tel 02 54 79 24 70
Fax 02 54 79 25 52
Holes 18 L 6276 m Par 71
V'tors H
Fees 200fr (280fr)
Loc 15km S of Blois. 200km SW of Paris, via A10
Arch O Van der Vynckt

Château de Maintenon (1988)
Route de Gallardon, 28130 Maintenon
Tel 02 37 27 18 09
Fax 02 37 27 10 12
Holes 18 L 6393 m SSS 74
9 L 1541 m SSS 30
V'tors WD–U WE–restricted
Loc 20km W of Rambouillet (D906). 70km SW of Paris
Arch Michel Gayon

Château des Forges (1991)
Domaine des Forges, 79340 Menigoute
Tel 05 49 69 91 77
Holes 18 L 6400 m Par 74
9 L 3200 m Par 37
V'tors U
Fees 200fr (250fr)
Loc 30km W of Poitiers
Arch Bjorn Eriksson

Château des Sept Tours (1989)
Le Vivier des Landes, 37330 Courcelles de Touraine
Tel 02 47 24 69 75
Fax 02 47 24 23 74
Holes 18 L 6194 m Par 72
V'tors U
Fees 200fr (250fr)
Loc 35km NW of Tours
Arch Donald Harradine

Cognac (1987)
Saint-Brice, 16100 Cognac
Tel 05 45 32 18 17
Fax 05 45 35 10 76
Holes 18 L 6142 m SSS 72
V'tors H
Loc 5km E of Cognac
Arch Jean Garaialde

Le Connétable (1987)
Parc Thermal, 86270 La Roche Posay
Tel 05 49 86 25 10
Fax 05 49 19 48 40
Holes 18 L 6014 m SSS 72
V'tors U
Fees 150fr (180fr)
Loc La Roche-Posay, 20km E of Châtellerault. 40km NE of Poitiers
Arch J Garaialde

Domaine de Vaugouard (1987)
Chemin des Bois, Fontenay-sur-Loing, 45210 Ferrières
Tel 02 38 95 81 52
Fax 02 38 95 79 78
Holes 18 L 5914 m SSS 72
V'tors U
Fees 190fr (350fr)
Loc 10km N of Montargis. 100km S of Paris
Arch Fromanger/Adam

Les Dryades (1987)
36160 Pouligny-Notre-Dame
Tel 02 54 30 28 00
Fax 02 54 30 10 24
Holes 18 L 6120 m SSS 72
V'tors U
Fees 200fr (250fr)
Loc 10km S of La Châtre (D940). 60km SW of Bourges
Arch Michel Gayon

Ganay (1991)
Prieuré de Ganay, 41220 St Laurent-Nouan
Tel 02 54 87 26 24
Fax 02 54 87 72 50
Holes 27 hole course
V'tors U
Fees 100fr (140fr)
Loc 130km S of Paris
Arch Jim Shirley

Haut-Poitou (1987)

Public
86130 Saint-Cyr
Tel 05 49 62 53 62
Fax 05 49 88 77 14
Holes 18 L 6590 m SSS 75
9 L 1800 m Par 31
V'tors U
Fees €29 (€33)
Loc 20km N of Poitiers. 70km S of
Tours
Arch HG Baker

Loudun-Roiffe (1985)

Public
Domaine St Hilaire, 86120 Roiffe
Tel 05 49 98 78 06
Fax 05 49 98 72 57
Web www.france-in.com
Holes 18 L 6343 m Par 72
V'tors U
Fees €23 (€29–31)
Loc 18km N of Loudun. 15km S
of Saumur
Arch Hubert Chesneau

Marcilly (1986)

Domaine de la Plaine, 45240 Marcilly-en-Villette
Tel 02 38 76 11 73
Fax 02 38 76 18 73
Holes 18 L 6324 m SSS 73
9 hole course
V'tors U
Fees 130fr (170fr)
Loc 20km SE of Orléans
Arch Olivier Brizon

Mazières (1987)

Le Petit Chêne, 79310 Mazières-en-Gâtine
Tel 05 49 63 20 95
Fax 05 49 63 33 75
Holes 18 L 6060 m SSS 72
V'tors U
Fees 165fr (215fr)
Loc 15km SW of Parthenay. 25km
NE of Niort
Arch Robert Berthet

Mignaloux Beauvoir

*Domaine de Beauvoir, 86550
Mignaloux Beauvoir*
Tel 05 49 46 70 27
Fax 05 49 55 31 95
Holes 18 L 6032 m SSS 71
V'tors WD–U WE–H
Fees 170–200fr
Loc 6km SE of Poitiers (RN147)
Arch Olivier Brizon

Niort

*Chemin du Grand Ormeau, 79000
Niort Romagne*
Tel 05 49 09 01 41
Fax 05 49 73 41 53
Holes 18 L 5865 m Par 71
Fees 180fr (225fr)
Loc 80km W of Poitiers

Orléans Val de Loire

Château de la Touche, 45450 Donnery
Tel 02 38 59 25 15
Fax 02 38 57 01 98
Holes 18 L 5771 m SSS 71
V'tors U
Loc 16km E of Orléans
Arch Trent Jones/Van der Vinckt

Golf du Perche (1987)

*La Vallée des Aulnes, 28400 Souancé
au Perche*
Tel 02 37 29 17 33
Fax 02 37 29 12 88
Holes 18 L 6073 m Par 72
V'tors U
Fees 180fr (250fr)
Loc 60km SW of Chartres (D9).
130km SW of Paris
Arch Laurent Heckly

La Picardière

Chemin de la Picardière, 18100 Vierzon
Tel 02 48 75 21 43
Fax 02 48 71 87 61
Holes 18 L 6077 m Par 72
V'tors U
Fees 190fr (220fr)
Loc 75km S of Orléans, off A71
Arch JL Pega

La Prée-La Rochelle (1990)

Marsilly, 17137 Nieul-sur-Mer
Tel 05 46 01 24 42
Fax 05 46 01 25 84
Web www.golflarochelle.com
Holes 18 L 6012 m SSS 72
V'tors U
Fees 160–250fr
Loc 6km N of La Rochelle
Arch Olivier Brizon

Royan (1977)

Maine-Gaudin, 17420 Saint-Palais
Tel 05 46 23 16 24
Fax 05 46 23 23 38
Holes 18 L 5970 m SSS 71
6 hole short course
V'tors U
Fees 150–270fr
Loc Saint-Palais, 7km W of Royan
Arch Robert Berthet

Saintonge (1953)

Fontcouverte, 17100 Saintes
Tel 05 46 74 27 61
Fax 05 46 92 17 92
Holes 18 L 4971 m Par 68
V'tors U
Fees 150–210fr
Loc 2km NE of Saintes
Arch Hervé Bertrand

Sancerrois (1989)

St Thibault, 18300 Sancerre
Tel 02 48 54 11 22
Fax 02 48 54 28 03
Holes 18 L 5820 m SSS 71
V'tors U

Fees 120–170fr (180–220fr)
Loc 45km NE of Bourges
Arch Didier Fruchet

Sologne (1955)

*Route de Jouy-le-Potier, 45240 La Ferté
St Aubin*
Tel 02 38 76 57 33
Fax 02 38 76 68 79
Holes 18 L 6400 yds SSS 72
V'tors U
Fees 110–120fr (130–170fr)
Loc 25km S of Orléans on
RN20/D18. La Ferté St Aubin
4km

Sully-sur-Loire (1965)

L'Ousseau, 45600 Viglain
Tel 02 38 36 52 08
Holes 18 L 6154 m Par 72
9 L 3155 m Par 36
Loc 3km SW of Sully-sur-Loire

Touraine (1971)

*Château de la Touche, 37510 Ballan-
Miré*
Tel 02 47 53 20 28
Fax 02 47 53 31 54
Holes 18 L 5671 m SSS 71
V'tors WE–H
Fees D–230fr (D–300fr)
Loc Ballan-Miré, 10km SW of
Tours
Arch Michael Fenn

Val de l'Indre (1989)

Villedieu-sur-Indre, 36320 Tregonce
Tel 02 54 26 59 44
Fax 02 54 26 06 37
Holes 18 L 6250 m SSS 72
V'tors U
Fees 180fr (230fr)
Loc 12km NW of Chateauroux.
80km SE of Tours on RN 143
Arch Yves Bureau

Channel Coast & North

Abbeville (1989)

Route du Val, 80132 Grand-Laviers
Tel 03 22 24 98 58
Fax 03 22 24 49 61
Holes 18 L 6080 m Par 73
V'tors U
Fees 150fr (180fr)
Loc 3km NW of Abbeville
Arch Didier Fruchet

L'Ailette

02000 Laon
Tel 23 24 83 99
Fax 23 24 84 66
Holes 18 L 6127 m Par 72
9 hole short course
V'tors WD–H WE–H restricted
Fees 185fr (240fr)

Loc	13km S of Laon. 45km NW of Reims
Arch	Michel Gayon

Amiens (1925)

80115 Querrieu

Tel	03 22 93 04 26
Fax	03 22 93 04 61
Holes	18 L 6114 m SSS 72
V'tors	U
Fees	145–195fr (205–260fr)
Loc	7km NE of Amiens (D929)
Arch	Ross/Pennink

Apremont (1992)

60300 Apremont

Tel	03 44 25 61 11
Fax	03 44 25 11 72
Holes	18 L 6436 m SSS 73
V'tors	H
Fees	250fr (330–480fr)
Loc	45km N of Paris
Arch	John Jacobs

Arras (1989)

Rue Briquet Taillandier, 62223 Anzin-St-Aubin

Tel	03 21 50 24 24
Fax	03 21 50 29 71
Web	www.arras-golfclub.com
Holes	18 L 6150 m SSS 72
	9 L 1550 m SSS 30
V'tors	U
Fees	€30 (€45)
Loc	50km S of Lille. 110km SE of Calais
Arch	JC Cornillot

Belle Dune

Promenade de Marquenterre, 80790 Fort-Mahon-Plage

Tel	03 22 23 45 50
Fax	03 22 23 93 41
Holes	18 L 5909 m Par 72 SSS 71
V'tors	H or Green card
Loc	25km S of Le Touquet on coast
Arch	JM Rossi

Blue Green-Chantilly (1991)

Route d'Apremont, 60500 Vineuil St-Firmin

Tel	03 44 58 47 74
Fax	03 44 58 50 28
Holes	18 L 6209 m SSS 72
V'tors	U
Fees	150–290fr
Loc	40km N of Paris (A1)
Arch	Huau/Nelson

Bois de Ruminghem (1991)

1613 Rue St Antoine, 62370 Ruminghem

Tel	03 21 85 30 33
Fax	03 21 36 38 38
Holes	18 L 6115 m Par 73
V'tors	U
Fees	250fr (250fr)

Loc	20km NE of Calais
Arch	Bill Baker

Bondues (1968)

Château de la Vigne, BP 54, 59587 Bondues Cedex

Tel	03 20 23 20 62
Fax	03 20 23 24 11
Holes	18 L 6163 m SSS 73 SR 130
	18 L 6009 m SSS 72 SR 127
V'tors	H–max 30
Fees	D–200fr (D–300fr)
Loc	10km NE of Lille
Arch	Hawtree/Trent Jones

Brigode (1970)

36 Avenue de Golf, 59650 Villeneuve D'Ascq

Tel	03 20 91 17 86
Fax	03 20 05 96 36
Holes	18 L 6182 m SSS 72
V'tors	WD–H
Loc	8km NE of Lille
Arch	HJ Baker

Champagne (1986)

02130 Villers-Agron

Tel	03 23 71 62 08
Fax	03 23 71 62 08
Holes	18 L 5760 m SSS 72
V'tors	U
Fees	180fr (250fr)
Loc	25km SW of Reims, via E50
Arch	JC Cornillot

Chantilly (1909)

Allée de la Ménagerie, 60500 Chantilly

Tel	03 44 57 04 43
Fax	03 44 57 26 54
Holes	Vineuil 18 L 6597 m SSS 71
	Longeres 18 L 6378 m SSS 72
V'tors	WE–NA
Fees	WD–400fr
Loc	45km N of Paris
Arch	Tom Simpson

Château d'Humières (1990)

Château d'Humières, 60113 Monchy-Humières

Tel	03 44 42 39 51
Fax	03 44 42 48 92
Holes	18 L 6176 m SSS 73
V'tors	U
Fees	180fr (270fr)
Loc	80km N of Paris. A1 Junction 11

Château de Raray

4 Rue Nicolas de Lancy, 60810 Raray

Tel	03 44 54 70 61
Fax	03 44 54 74 97
Holes	18 L 6455 m Par 72
	9 L 2921 m Par 35
V'tors	H
Fees	150–220fr (250–350fr)
Loc	60km N of Paris (A1)
Arch	Patrick Leglise

Chaumont-en-Vexin (1963)

Château de Bertichère, 60240 Chaumont-en-Vexin

Tel	03 44 49 00 81
Fax	03 44 49 32 71
Holes	18 L 6195 m SSS 72
V'tors	H
Fees	150fr (300fr)
Loc	65km NW of Paris
Arch	Donald Harradine

Compiègne (1896)

Ave Royale, 60200 Compiègne

Tel	03 44 38 48 00
Fax	03 44 40 23 59
Holes	18 L 6015 m Par 71
V'tors	U
Fees	150fr (250fr)
Loc	80km NE of Paris
Arch	W Freemantel

Deauville l'Amiraute (1992)

CD 278, Tourgéville, 14800 Deauville

Tel	02 31 14 42 00
Fax	02 31 88 32 00
Web	www.amiraute-resort.com
Holes	18 L 6055 m Par 73
V'tors	U
Fees	280–400fr (350–420fr)
Loc	4km S of Deauville
Arch	Bill Baker

Domaine du Tilleul (1984)

Landouzy-la-Ville, 02140 Vervins

Tel	03 23 98 48 00
Fax	03 23 98 46 46
Holes	18 L 5203 m SSS 71
V'tors	Groups 10+ welcome
Fees	100–150fr (150–180fr)
Loc	7km S of Hirson. 65km N of Reims

Dunkerque (1991)

Public

Fort Vallières, Coudekerque-Village, 59380 Bergues

Tel	03 28 61 07 43
Fax	03 28 60 05 93
Holes	18 L 5710 m Par 71
Fees	140fr (180fr)
Loc	5km E of Dunkerque
Arch	Robert Berthet

Hardelot Dunes Course (1991)

Ave du Golf, 62152 Hardelot

Tel	03 21 83 73 10
Fax	03 21 83 24 33
Holes	18 L 6031 m SSS 73
V'tors	U exc NA 8–9am & 1.15–2.30pm
Fees	240–300fr (360fr D–550fr)
Loc	15km S of Boulogne
Arch	Paul Rolin (1990)

Hardelot Pins Course

Ave du Golf, 62152 Hardelot
Tel   03 21 83 73 10
Fax   03 21 83 24 33
Holes 18 L 5926 m SSS 73
V'tors U
Fees   240–300fr (360fr D–550fr)
Loc   15km S of Boulogne
Arch   Tom Simpson (1931)

International Club du Lys (1929)

Rond-Point du Grand Cerf,
60260 Lamorlaye
Tel   03 44 21 26 00
Fax   03 44 21 35 52
Holes 18 L 6022 m Par 71
       18 L 4770 m Par 66
V'tors WD–H WE–H (booking
       necessary)
Fees   WD–250fr
Loc   5km S of Chantilly. 40km N
       of Paris
Arch   Tom Simpson

Morfontaine (1926)

60128 Mortefontaine
Tel   03 44 54 68 27
Fax   03 44 54 60 57
Holes 18 L 6063 m SSS 72
       9 L 2550 m SSS 35
V'tors Members' guests only
Fees   NA
Loc   10km S of Senlis. N of Paris
Arch   Tom Simpson

Mormal (1991)

Bois St Pierre, 59144 Preux-au-Sart
Tel   03 27 63 07 00
Fax   03 27 39 93 62
Holes 18 L 6022 m Par 72
V'tors H
Fees   180fr (240fr)
Loc   15km E of Valenciennes, off
       RN49
Arch   JC Cornillot

Nampont-St-Martin (1978)

Maison Forte, 80120 Nampont-St-
Martin
Tel   03 22 29 92 90/03 22 29 89 87
Fax   03 22 29 97 54
Holes Cygnes 18 L 6051 m SSS 72
       Belvédère 18 L 5145 m SSS 72
V'tors U
Fees   130–150fr (200–240fr)
Loc   50km S of Boulogne.
       Motorway A16 Junction 25
Arch   Thomas Chatterton

Pelves (1991)

Chemin de l'Enfer, 62118 Pelves
Tel   03 21 58 95 42
Fax   03 21 24 00 04
Holes 18 L 5958 m SSS 72
V'tors U
Loc   40km S of Lille. 180km N of
       Paris
Arch   Ogama

Rebetz (1988)

Route de Noailles, 60240 Chaumont-en-
Vexin
Tel   03 44 49 15 54
Fax   03 44 49 14 26
Web   www.rebetz.com
Holes 18 L 6409 m SSS 73
V'tors H
Fees   150fr (350fr)
Loc   Chaumont-en-Vexin, 65km
       NW of Paris, via D43
Arch   J-P Fourès

Saint-Omer

Chemin des Bois, Acquin-Westbécourt,
62380 Lumbres
Tel   03 21 38 59 90
Fax   03 21 93 02 47
Holes 18 L 6294 m Par 73
       9 L 2038 m Par 31
V'tors U
Fees   170–260fr (220–320fr)
Loc   10km W of Saint-Omer. 40km
       S of Calais
Arch   J Dudok van Heel

Le Sart (1910)

5 Rue Jean-Jaurès, 59650
Villeneuve D'Ascq
Tel   03 20 72 02 51
Fax   03 20 98 73 28
Holes 18 L 5721 m SSS 71
V'tors H
Fees   250fr (300fr 2D–500fr)
Loc   5km E of Lille. Motorway
       Lille-Gand Junction 9
       (Breucq-Le Sart)
Arch   Allan Macbeth

Thumeries (1935)

Bois Lenglart, 59239 Thumeries
Tel   03 20 86 58 98
Fax   03 20 86 52 66
Holes 18 L 5933 m SSS 72
V'tors U
Fees   180fr (250fr)
Loc   10km N of Douai. 15km S of
       Lille
Arch   Boomer/Rossi

Le Touquet 'La Forêt' (1904)

Ave du Golf, BP 41, 62520 Le Touquet
Tel   03 21 06 28 00
Fax   03 21 06 28 01
Holes 18 L 5659 m SSS 70 SR 123
V'tors U H
Fees   €43 (€52)
Loc   2km S of Le Touquet. 30km S
       of Boulogne
Arch   H Hutchinson

Le Touquet 'La Mer' (1930)

Ave du Golf, BP 41, 62520 Le Touquet
Tel   03 21 06 28 00
Fax   03 21 06 28 01
Holes 18 L 6275 m SSS 74 SR 128
V'tors U H
Fees   €49 (€58)

Loc   As 'La Forêt'
Arch   HS Colt

Le Touquet 'Le Manoir' (1994)

Ave du Golf, BP 41, 62520 Le Touquet
Tel   03 21 06 28 00
Fax   03 21 06 28 01
Holes 9 L 2817 m Par 35 SR 118
V'tors U
Fees   €29 (€35)
Loc   As 'La Forêt'
Arch   HJ Baker

Val Secret (1984)

Brasles, 02400 Château Thierry
Tel   03 23 83 07 25
Fax   03 23 83 92 73
Web   www.valsecret.com
Holes 18 L 5540 m Par 70
V'tors U
Fees   160fr (250fr)
Loc   58km W of Reims via A4

Vert Parc (1991)

3 Route d'Ecuelles, 59480 Illies
Tel   03 20 29 37 87
Fax   03 20 49 76 39
Holes 18 L 6328 m SSS 73
V'tors U
Loc   18km SW of Lille
Arch   Patrice Simon

Wimereux (1906)

Route d'Ambleteuse, 62930 Wimereux
Tel   03 21 32 43 20
Fax   03 21 33 62 21
Holes 18 L 6150 m Par 72
V'tors U
Fees   210–260fr (230–290fr)
Loc   6km N of Boulogne on D940.
       30km S of Calais
Arch   Campbell/Hutchinson

Corsica

Spérone (1990)

Domaine de Spérone, 20169 Bonifacio
Tel   04 95 73 17 13
Fax   04 95 73 17 85
Holes 18 L 6106 m SSS 73
V'tors H–max 28
Fees   330–490fr W–1500–2850fr
Loc   S point of Corsica, SE of
       Bonifacio. 25km S of Airport
Arch   Robert Trent Jones Sr

Ile de France

Ableiges (1989)

95450 Ableiges
Tel   01 30 27 97 00
Fax   01 30 27 97 10
Holes 18 L 6261 m Par 72
       9 L 2137 m Par 33
V'tors 18 holes:U H (max 30)

Fees 18 holes:150fr (250fr)
9 holes:120fr (150fr)
Loc 40km NW of Paris, nr Cergy
Pontoise
Arch Pern/Garaialde

Bellefontaine (1987)

95270 Bellefontaine
Tel 01 34 71 05 02
Fax 01 34 71 90 90
Holes 27 holes:
6098-6306 m Par 72
V'tors U
Fees 200fr (350fr)
Loc 27km N of Paris
Arch Michel Gayon

Bondoufle (1990)

Departmentale 31, 91070 Bondoufle
Tel 01 60 86 41 71
Fax 01 60 86 41 56
Holes 18 L 6161 m SSS 73
V'tors U H
Loc 30km S of Paris
Arch Michel Gayon

Bussy-St-Georges (1988)

*Promenade des Golfeurs, 77600 Bussy-
St-Georges*
Tel 01 64 66 00 00
Fax 01 64 66 22 92
Holes 18 L 5924 m SSS 72
V'tors U
Loc 20km E of Paris. Motorway
A4 Junction 12
Arch Rolin/Cornillot

Cély (1990)

*Le Château, Route de Saint-Germain,
77930 Cély-en-Bière*
Tel 01 64 38 03 07
Fax 01 64 38 08 78
Web www.celygolf.com
Holes 18 L 5874 m SSS 72
V'tors U
Fees 220fr (350fr)
Loc Fontainebleau 15km
Arch Adam/Fromanger

Cergy Pontoise (1988)

*2 Allee de l'Obstacle d'Eau,
95490 Vaureal*
Tel 01 34 21 03 48
Fax 01 34 21 03 34
Holes 18 L 6100 m SSS 72
V'tors WD–U WE–U H
Loc 30km NW of Paris. A15
Junction 12
Arch Michel Gayon

Chevannes-Mennecy (1994)

91750 Chevannes
Tel 01 64 99 88 74
Fax 01 64 99 88 67
Holes 18 L 6307 m Par 72
V'tors U
Fees 120fr (200fr)
Loc 45km S of Paris
Arch A d'Ormesson

Clement Ader (1990)

Domaine Château Pereire, 77220 Gretz
Tel 01 64 07 34 10
Fax 01 64 07 82 10
Holes 18 L 6350 m Par 72
V'tors U
Loc 30km SE of Paris
Arch M Saito

Coudray (1960)

*Ave du Coudray, 91830 Le Coudray-
Montceaux*
Tel 01 64 93 81 76
Fax 01 64 93 99 95
Holes 18 L 5761 m Par 71
9 L 1350 m Par 29
V'tors H
Fees 190fr (290fr)
Loc 35km S of Paris on A6
(Junction 11)
Arch CK Cotton

Courson Monteloup (1991)

91680 Bruyères-le-Chatel
Tel 01 64 58 80 80
Fax 01 64 58 83 06
Web www.golf-stadefrancais.com
Holes 36 hole course:
6171-6520 m SSS 72-75
V'tors WD–U WE–M exc Jul/Aug
Fees 250fr (400fr)
Loc 35km SW of Paris, off Route
D3
Arch Robert von Hagge

Crécy-la-Chapelle (1987)

*Ferme de Monpichet, 77580 Crécy-la-
Chapelle*
Tel 01 64 04 70 75
Holes 18 L 6211 m SSS 72
V'tors U
Loc 20km E of Paris by A4

Domaine de Belesbat (1989)

*Courdimanche-sur-Essonne,
91820 Boutigny-sur-Essonne*
Tel 01 69 23 19 10
Fax 01 69 23 19 01
Web www.belesbat.com
Holes 18 L 6033 m SSS 72
SR 132
V'tors H–Booking required
Fees 200fr (400fr)
Loc 50km S of Paris, between
Etampes and Fontainebleau
Arch Fromanger/Adam

Domont-Montmorency

*Route de Montmorency, 95330
Domont*
Tel 01 39 91 07 50
Fax 01 39 91 25 70
Holes 18 L 5775 m SSS 71
V'tors H
Fees 250fr (480fr)
Loc 18km N of Paris
Arch Hawtree

Étiolles (1990)

Vieux Chemin de Paris, 91450 Étiolles
Tel 01 60 75 49 49
Fax 01 60 75 64 20
Holes 18 L 6239 m Par 74
9 L 2665 m SSS 36
V'tors U
Fees 260fr (390fr)
Loc 30km S of Paris
Arch Michel Gayon

Fontainebleau (1909)

Route d'Orleans, 77300 Fontainebleau
Tel 01 64 22 22 95
Fax 01 64 22 63 76
Holes 18 L 6074 m SSS 72
V'tors WD–U WE–Jul/Aug only
Fees WD–350fr
Loc 1km SW of Fontainebleau.
60km SE of Paris
Arch Simpson/M Hawtree

Fontenailles (1991)

*Domaine de Bois Boudran,
77370 Fontenailles*
Tel 01 64 60 51 00
Fax 01 60 67 52 12
Holes 18 L 6256 m SSS 74
9 L 2870 m
V'tors WD–U WE–H
Fees 180–200fr (320–450fr)
Loc 60km SE of Paris
Arch Michel Gayon

Forges-les-Bains (1989)

*Rue du Général Leclerc, 91470 Forges-
les-Bains*
Tel 01 64 91 48 18
Fax 01 64 91 40 52
Web www.golf-forgelesbains.com
Holes 18 L 6167 m SSS 72
V'tors H or Green card
Fees €30 (€50)
Loc 35km S of Paris, off A10
Arch JM Rossi

La Forteresse (1989)

*Domaine de la Forteresse,
77940 Thoury-Ferrottes*
Tel 01 60 96 95 10
Fax 01 60 96 01 41
Web www.golf-forteresse.com
Holes 18 L 5088 m Par 72
V'tors H or Green card
Fees 190fr (350fr)
Loc 25km SE of Fontainebleau
Arch Fromanger/Adam

Greenparc (1993)

*Route de Villepech, 91280 St Pierre-du-
Perray*
Tel 01 60 75 40 60
Fax 01 60 75 40 04
Holes 18 L 5839 m SSS 71
V'tors U
Fees 125fr (250fr)
Loc 30km SW of Paris
Arch Robin Nelson

For list of abbreviations see page 649

L'Isle Adam (1995)

*1 Chemin des Vanneaux, 95290
L'Isle Adam*
Tel   01 34 08 11 11
Fax   01 34 08 11 19
Holes   18 L 6230 m Par 72
V'tors   U
Fees   150–250fr (275–375fr)
Loc   30km N of Paris
Arch   Ronald Fream

Marivaux (1992)

Bois de Marivaux, 91640 Janvry
Tel   01 64 90 85 85
Fax   01 64 90 82 22
Holes   18 L 6116 m Par 72
V'tors   U H–max 36
Fees   150–180fr (250–350fr)
Loc   25km SW of Paris
Arch   Macauley/Quenouille

Meaux-Boutigny (1985)

Rue de Barrois, 77470 Boutigny
Tel   01 60 25 63 98
Fax   01 60 25 60 58
Holes   18 L 5981 m SSS 72
    9 L 1499 m SSS 30
V'tors   U
Fees   180fr (300fr)
Loc   45km E of Paris-Highway 4
Arch   Michel Gayon

Mont Griffon

RD 909, 95270 Luzarches
Tel   01 34 68 10 10
Fax   01 34 68 04 10
Web   www.golfhotelparis.com
Holes   18 L 5905 m SSS 71
V'tors   U
Fees   200fr (340fr)
Loc   27km N of Paris, nr Chantilly
Arch   Nelson/Huau/Dongradi

Ormesson (1969)

*Chemin du Belvedère, 94490 Ormesson-
sur-Marne*
Tel   01 45 76 20 71
Fax   01 45 94 86 85
Holes   18 L 6130 m SSS 72
V'tors   H
Fees   200fr (350fr)
Loc   21km SE of Paris
Arch   Harris/CK Cotton

Ozoir-la-Ferrière (1926)

*Château des Agneaux, 77330 Ozoir-la-
Ferrière*
Tel   01 60 02 60 79
Fax   01 64 40 28 20
Holes   18 L 5859 m Par 71
    9 L 2700 m Par 35
V'tors   U H
Fees   18 hole:210fr (400fr)
    9 hole:140fr (200fr)
Loc   25km SE of Paris via A4
    (Porte de Bercy)
Arch   Sir Henry Cotton

Paris International (1991)

*18 Route du Golf, 95560 Baillet-en-
France*
Tel   01 34 69 90 00

Fax   01 34 69 97 15
Holes   18 L 6319 m SSS 74
V'tors   Members and guests only
Fees   NA
Loc   24km NW of Paris
Arch   Jack Nicklaus

St Aubin (1976)

Public
Route du Golf, 91190 St Aubin
Tel   01 69 41 25 19
Fax   01 69 41 02 25
Holes   18 L 5971 m SSS 71
    9 L 1918 m SSS 31
V'tors   U
Loc   30km SW of Paris
Arch   Berthet/Rio

St Germain-les-Corbeil

*6 Ave du Golf, 91250 St Germain-les-
Corbeil*
Tel   01 60 75 81 54
Fax   01 60 75 52 89
Holes   18 L 5800 m SSS 71
V'tors   U
Loc   30km S of Paris

St Pierre du Perray (1974)

Public
*Melun-Sénart, St Pierre du Perray,
91100 Corbeil*
Tel   01 60 75 17 47
Fax   01 69 89 00 73
Holes   18 L 6169 m SSS 72
V'tors   U
Fees   £15 (£28)
Loc   30km SE of Paris, off N6
Arch   Hubert Chesneau

Seraincourt (1964)

Gaillonnet-Seraincourt, 95450 Vigny
Tel   01 34 75 47 28
Fax   01 34 75 75 47
Holes   18 L 5760 m SSS 70
V'tors   WD–U WE–H
Loc   35km NW of Paris

Villarceaux (1971)

Château du Couvent, 95710 Chaussy
Tel   01 34 67 73 83
Fax   01 34 67 72 66
Holes   18 L 6059 m Par 72
V'tors   H
Fees   220fr (350fr)
Loc   60km NW of Paris
Arch   M Backer

Languedoc-
Roussillon

Cap d'Agde (1989)

Public
4 Ave des Alizés, 34300 Cap d'Agde
Tel   04 67 26 54 40
Fax   04 67 26 97 00
Holes   18 L 6160 m SSS 72
V'tors   U

Loc   25km E of Béziers
Arch   Ronald Fream

Carcassonne (1988)

*Route de Ste-Hilaire,
11000 Carcassonne*
Tel   06 13 20 85 43
Fax   04 68 72 57 30
Holes   18 L 5758 m Par 71
V'tors   U
Fees   180fr (220fr)
Loc   2km SW of Carcassonne
Arch   J-P Basurco

Coulondres (1984)

*72 Rue des Erables, 34980 Saint-Gely-
du-Fesc*
Tel   04 67 84 13 75
Fax   04 67 84 06 33
Web   www.coulondres.com
Holes   18 L 6175 m SSS 73
V'tors   U
Fees   150fr (200fr)
Loc   10km N of Montpellier
    towards Ganges
Arch   Donald Harradine

Domaine de Falgos (1992)

BP 9, 66260 St Laurent-de-Cerdans
Tel   04 68 39 51 42
Fax   04 68 39 52 30
Holes   18 L 5044 m SSS 68
V'tors   U
Fees   200fr (250–300fr)
Loc   60km S of Perpignan, nr
    Spanish border (D115)

Fontcaude (1991)

*Route de Lodève, Domaine de
Fontcaude, 34990 Juvignac*
Tel   04 67 45 90 10
Fax   04 67 45 90 20
Holes   18 L 6992 m SSS 72
    9 hole short course
V'tors   U
Fees   €38–46
Loc   6km W of Montpellier
Arch   C Pitman

La Grande-Motte (1987)

*Clubhouse du Golf, 34280 La Grande-
Motte*
Tel   04 67 56 05 00
Fax   04 67 29 18 84
Holes   18 L 6161 m Par 72
    18 L 3076 m Par 58
    6 hole short course
V'tors   U
Fees   €38 (€46)
Loc   18km E of Montpellier
Arch   Robert Trent Jones Sr

Montpellier Massane (1988)

*Domaine de Massane,
34670 Baillargues*
Tel   04 67 87 87 87
Fax   04 67 87 87 90

Holes 18 L 6231 m Par 72
9 hole Par 3 course
V'tors U
Fees 230fr (290fr)
Loc 9km E of Montpellier. A9
Junction 28
Arch Ronald Fream

Nîmes Campagne (1968)
Route de Saint Gilles, 30900 Nîmes
Tel 04 66 70 17 37
Fax 04 66 70 03 14
Holes 18 L 6135 m SSS 72
V'tors H
Fees 250fr (300fr)
Loc 7km S of Nîmes, by Airport
Arch Morandi/Harradine

Nîmes-Vacquerolles
(1990)
Route de Sauve, 30900 Nîmes
Tel 04 66 23 33 33
Fax 04 66 23 94 94
Holes 18 L 6300 m SSS 72
V'tors U
Fees €28–40 (€37–40)
Loc W of Nîmes centre (D999)
Arch W Baker

St Cyprien (1974)
*Le Mas D'Huston, 66750 St
Cyprien Plage*
Tel 04 68 37 63 63
Fax 04 68 37 64 64
Holes 18 L 6480 m SSS 73
9 L 2724 m SSS 35
V'tors U H
Fees 210fr (270fr)
Loc 15km SE of Perpignan
Arch Wright/Tomlinson

St Thomas (1992)
Route de Bessan, 34500 Béziers
Tel 04 67 39 03 09
Fax 04 67 39 10 65
Holes 18 L 6130 m Par 72
V'tors U
Fees On application
Loc 7km NE of Béziers (RN 113)
Arch Patrice Lambert

Loire Valley

Angers (1963)
*Moulin de Pistrait, 49320 St Jean
des Mauvrets*
Tel 02 41 91 96 56
Holes 18 L 5460 m Par 70
Fees 170fr (220fr)
Loc 14km SE of Angers. Right
bank of Loire.

Anjou G&CC (1990)
Route de Cheffes, 49330 Champigné
Tel 02 41 42 01 01
Fax 02 41 42 04 37
Holes 18 L 6227 m SSS 72
6 hole short course

V'tors U H
Fees 180fr (220fr)
Loc 23km N of Angers
Arch F Hawtree

Avrillé (1988)
Château de la Perrière, 49240 Avrillé
Tel 02 41 69 22 50
Fax 02 41 34 44 60
Holes 18 L 6116 m SSS 71
9 hole Par 3 course
V'tors U
Fees 140fr (200fr)
Loc 5km N of Angers
Arch Robert Berthet

Baugé-Pontigné (1994)
Public
Route de Tours, 49150 Baugé
Tel 02 41 89 01 27
Fax 02 41 89 05 50
Holes 18 L 5558 m Par 72
V'tors U
Fees 135fr (190fr)
Loc 45km E of Angers. 70km SW
of Tours
Arch M Prat

La Bretesche (1967)
*Domaine de la Bretesche,
44780 Missillac*
Tel 02 51 76 86 86
Fax 02 40 88 36 28
Holes 18 L 6080 m SSS 72
V'tors U
Fees 180fr (300fr)
Loc 8km NW of Pontchâteau,
between Nantes and Vannes
Arch Cotton/Baker

Cholet (1989)
Allée du Chêne Landry, 49300 Cholet
Tel 02 41 71 05 01
Fax 02 41 56 06 94
Holes 18 L 5792 m Par 71
V'tors WD–U WE–H
Loc 2km N of Cholet. 52km SE of
Nantes
Arch Olivier Brizon

La Domangère
*La Roche-sur-Yon, Route de la Rochelle,
85310 Nesmy*
Tel 02 51 07 60 15
Fax 02 51 07 64 09
Holes 18 L 6480 m SSS 72
V'tors U
Loc 6km S of La Roche-sur-Yon.
70km S of Nantes
Arch Michel Gayon

Epinay (1991)
*Boulevard de l'Epinay,
44470 Carquefou*
Tel 02 40 52 73 74
Fax 02 40 52 73 20
Holes 18 L 5790 m SSS 71
V'tors U
Fees 170fr (230fr)
Loc NE of Nantes
Arch M Hawtree

Fontenelles
Public
*Saint-Gilles-Croix-de-Vie,
85220 Aiguillon-sur-Vie*
Tel 02 51 54 13 94
Fax 02 51 55 45 77
Holes 18 L 6185 m Par 72
V'tors U
Fees 140–255fr
Loc 6km E of St-Gilles-Croix-de-
Vie. 75km SW of Nantes
Arch Yves Bureau

Ile d'Or (1988)
BP 10, 49270 La Varenne
Tel 02 40 98 58 00
Fax 02 40 98 51 62
Holes 18 L 6292 m Par 72
9 L 1217 m Par 27
V'tors U H
Loc 30km NE of Nantes
Arch Michel Gayon

**International Barriere-
La Baule** (1976)
44117 Saint-André-des Eaux
Tel 02 40 60 46 18
Fax 02 40 60 41 41
Web www.lucienbarriere.com
Holes 18 L 6055 m Par 72 SSS 73
18 L 6301 m Par 72 SSS 74
9 L 2969 m Par 36
V'tors H
Fees €38–56; 9-hole: €21–32
Loc Avrillac, 3km NE of La Baule
Arch Alliss/Thomas/Gayon

Laval-Changé (1972)
Le Jariel, 53000 Changé-les-Laval
Tel 02 43 53 16 03
Fax 02 43 49 35 15
Holes 18 L 6068 m Par 72 SSS 72
9 L 3388 m
V'tors WD–U WE–NA
Fees 180fr (220fr)
Loc 5km N of Laval. 60km E of
Rennes
Arch JP Foures

Le Mans Mulsanne (1961)
Route de Tours, 72230 Mulsanne
Tel 02 43 42 00 36
Fax 02 43 42 21 31
Holes 18 L 5821 m SSS 71
V'tors H
Fees 200–360fr (240–400fr)
Loc Mulsanne, 12km S of Le
Mans

Nantes
44360 Vigneux de Bretagne
Tel 02 40 63 25 82
Fax 02 40 63 64 86
Holes 18 L 5940 m SSS 72
V'tors H
Fees 170fr (250fr)
Loc 12km NW of Nantes
Arch Frank Pennink

For list of abbreviations see page 649

Nantes Erdre (1990)
Chemin du Bout des Landes,
44300 Nantes
Tel   02 40 59 21 21
Fax   02 51 84 94 50
Holes   18 L 6003 m SSS 71
V'tors U
Fees   170fr (220fr)
Loc   Nantes
Arch   Yves Bureau

Les Olonnes
Gazé, 85340 Olonne-sur-Mer
Tel   02 51 33 16 16
Fax   02 51 30 10 45
Holes   18 L 6127 m Par 72
V'tors U
Fees   120–250fr
Loc   3km N of Les Sables d'Olonne
Arch   Bruno Parpoil

Pornic (1912)
49 Boulevard de l'Océan, Sainte-
Marie/Mer, 44210 Pornic
Tel   02 40 82 06 69
Fax   02 40 82 80 65
Holes   18 L 6119 m Par 72
V'tors U
Fees   150–250fr
Loc   1km E of Pornic. 30km S of
        La Baule
Arch   Michel Gayon

Port Bourgenay (1990)
Avenue de la Mine, Port Bourgenay,
85440 Talmont-St-Hilaire
Tel   02 51 23 35 45
Fax   02 51 23 35 48
Holes   18 L 5800 m SSS 72
V'tors U
Fees   110–270fr
Loc   10km SE of Sables d'Olonne.
        100km S of Nantes
Arch   Pierre Thevenin

Sablé-Solesmes
Domaine de l'Outinière, Route de Pincé,
72300 Sablé-sur-Sarthe
Tel   02 43 95 28 78
Fax   02 43 92 39 05
Holes   27 holes SSS 72:
        Forêt 9 L 3197 m
        Rivière 9 L 2992 m
        Cascade 9 L 3069 m
V'tors U
Fees   €40–49
Loc   40km SW of Le Mans
Arch   Michel Gayon

St Jean-de-Monts (1988)
Ave des Pays de la Loire, 85160
Saint Jean-de-Monts
Tel   02 51 58 82 73
Fax   02 51 59 18 32
Holes   18 L 5962 m SSS 72
V'tors U
Loc   60km SW of Nantes on coast

Sargé-Le-Mans (1990)
Rue de Bonnétable, 72190 Sargé-les
Le Mans
Tel   02 43 76 25 07

Fax   02 43 76 45 25
Holes   18 L 6054 m SSS 72
V'tors U
Fees   140fr (200fr)
Loc   6km NE of Le Mans
Arch   Antoine d'Ormesson

Savenay (1990)
44260 Savenay
Tel   02 40 56 88 05
Fax   02 40 56 89 04
Holes   18 L 6335 m Par 73
        9 L 1122 m Par 30
V'tors U
Fees   €24–36
Loc   36km W of Nantes. 30km E of
        La Baule
Arch   Michel Gayon

Normandy

Bellême-St-Martin (1988)
Les Sablons, 61130 Bellême
Tel   02 33 73 00 07
Fax   02 33 73 00 17
Holes   18 L 6011 m SSS 72
V'tors U
Fees   170fr (250fr)
Loc   40km NE of Le Mans
Arch   Eric Vialatel

Beuzeval-Houlgate (1981)
Route de Gonneville, 14510 Houlgate
Tel   02 31 24 80 49
Fax   02 31 28 04 48
Holes   18 L 5558 m SSS 72
V'tors U
Fees   130–240fr
Loc   2km S of Houlgate. 15km SW
        of Deauville
Arch   Alliss/Thomas

Cabourg-Le Home (1907)
38 Av Président Réné Coty, Le Home
Varaville, 14390 Cabourg
Tel   02 31 91 25 56
Fax   02 31 91 18 30
Holes   18 L 5234 m SSS 68
V'tors H
Fees   130–260fr
Loc   4km W of Cabourg
Arch   Jackson/Brizon

Caen (1990)
Le Vallon, 14112 Bieville-Beuville
Tel   02 31 94 72 09
Fax   02 31 47 45 30
Holes   18 holes SSS 72 Par 72
        9 hole course
V'tors U
Loc   5km N of Caen (D60)
Arch   F Hawtree

Champ de Bataille
Château du Champ de Bataille, 27110
Le Neubourg
Tel   02 32 35 03 72
Fax   02 32 35 83 10
Holes   18 L 6575 m SSS 72

V'tors U
Loc   28km NW of Evreux. 45km
        SW of Rouen
Arch   Nelson/Huau

Clécy (1988)
Manoir de Cantelou, 14570 Clécy
Tel   02 31 69 72 72
Fax   02 31 69 70 22
Holes   18 L 5965 m Par 72
V'tors U
Fees   130–250fr
Loc   30km S of Caen, via D562
Arch   W Baker

Coutainville (1925)
Ave du Golf, 50230 Agon-Coutainville
Tel   02 33 47 03 31
Fax   02 33 47 38 42
Holes   18 L 5045 m SSS 68
V'tors H
Fees   200fr
Loc   12km W of Coutances. 75km
        S of Cherbourg

Dieppe-Pourville (1897)
51 Route de Pourville, 76200 Dieppe
Tel   02 35 84 25 05
Fax   02 35 84 97 11
Web   www.golf-dieppe.com
Holes   18 L 5780 m Par 70
V'tors U
Fees   225–275fr (275–300fr)
Loc   2km W of Dieppe towards
        Pourville
Arch   Willie Park Jr

Étretat (1908)
BP No 7, Route du Havre,
76790 Étretat
Tel   02 35 27 04 89
Holes   18 L 5994 m SSS 72
V'tors H
Loc   25km N of Le Havre. Étretat
        1km
Arch   Chantepie/Fruchet

Forêt Verte
Bosc Guerard, 76710 Montville
Tel   02 35 33 62 94
Holes   18 L 7000 yds SSS 72
V'tors U
Loc   10km N of Rouen
Arch   Thierry Huau

Granville (1912)
Bréville, 50290 Bréhal
Tel   02 33 50 23 06
Fax   02 33 61 91 87
Holes   18 L 5854 m Par 71
        9 L 2323 m Par 33
V'tors U
Fees   18 hole:155fr (225fr)
        9 hole:100fr (130fr)
Loc   5km N of Granville
Arch   Colt/Allison/Hawtree

Le Havre (1933)
Hameau Saint-Supplix,
76930 Octeville-sur-Mer
Tel   02 35 46 36 50

Fax 02 35 46 32 66
Holes 18 L 5830 m SSS 70
V'tors H
Loc 10km N of Le Havre

Léry Poses (1989)
BP 7, 27740 Poses
Tel 02 32 59 47 42
Holes 18 L 6242 m SSS 73
9 hole Par 3 course
V'tors U
Loc 25km SE of Rouen
Arch J Baker

New Golf Deauville (1929)
14 Saint Arnoult, 14800 Deauville
Tel 02 31 14 24 24
Fax 02 31 14 24 25
Holes 18 L 5933 m SSS 71
9 L 3033 m SSS 72
V'tors U–booking required
Fees 300–500fr
Loc 3km S of Deauville
Arch Simpson/Cotton

Omaha Beach (1986)
Ferme St Sauveur, 14520 Port-en-Bessin
Tel 02 31 22 12 12
Fax 02 31 22 12 13
Web www.best-channel-golfs.com
Holes 18 L 6216 m SSS 72
9 L 2693 m SSS 35
V'tors U H
Fees 160–280fr
Loc 8km N of Bayeux
Arch Yves Bureau

Parc de Brotonne (1991)
Jumièges, 76480 Duclair
Tel 02 35 05 32 97
Fax 02 35 37 99 97
Holes 18 L 6040 m SSS 72
V'tors U
Fees 120fr (180fr)
Loc 20km W of Rouen
Arch JP Fourès

Rouen-Mont St Aignan (1911)
Rue Francis Poulenc, 76130 Mont St Aignan
Tel 02 35 76 38 65
Fax 02 35 75 13 86
Holes 18 L 5522 m SSS 70
V'tors H WE–H after 4pm
Fees 200fr (300fr)
Loc 4km N of Rouen

St Gatien Deauville (1987)
14130 St Gatien-des-Bois
Tel 02 31 65 19 99
Fax 02 31 65 11 24
Holes 18 L 6272 m Par 72
9 L 3035 m Par 36
V'tors U
Fees 200fr (300fr)
Loc 8km E of Deauville
Arch Olivier Brizon

St Saëns (1987)
Domaine du Vaudichon, 76680 St Saëns
Tel 02 35 34 25 24
Fax 02 35 34 43 33
Web www.golfstsaens.com
Holes 18 L 5791 m SSS 70
V'tors U
Fees 220fr (300fr)
Loc 30km NE of Rouen
Arch D Robinson

St Julien
St Julien-sur-Calonne, 14130 Pont-l'Évêque
Tel 02 31 64 30 30
Fax 02 31 64 12 43
Holes 18 L 6035 m SSS 72
9 L 2275 m SSS 64
V'tors U
Fees 140–190fr (200–250fr)
Loc 3km SE of Pont l'Évêque
Arch Prat/Baker

Le Vaudreuil (1962)
27100 Le Vaudreuil
Tel 02 32 59 02 60
Fax 02 32 59 43 88
Holes 18 L 6320 m SSS 74
V'tors H
Fees 180fr (275fr)
Loc 6km NE of Louviers. 25km SE of Rouen
Arch F Hawtree

North East

Ammerschwihr
BP 19, Route des Trois Épis, 68770 Ammerschwihr
Tel 03 89 47 17 30
Fax 03 89 47 17 77
Holes 18 L 5795 m Par 70
9 hole short course
V'tors U
Fees 200fr (250fr)
Loc 8km W of Colmar. 70km S of Strasbourg
Arch Robert Berthet

Bâle G&CC (1928)
Rue de Wentzwiller, 68220 Hagenthal-le-Bas
Tel 03 89 68 50 91
Fax 03 89 68 55 66
Holes 18 L 6255 m Par 72
SSS 73
V'tors WD–H (max 28) WE–M
Fees 360fr
Loc 15km SW of Basle
Arch B von Limburger

Besançon (1968)
La Chevillotte, 25620 Mamirolle
Tel 03 81 55 73 54
Fax 03 81 55 88 64

Web www.golfbesancon.com
Holes 18 L 6070 m SSS 73
V'tors H
Fees 220fr (260fr)
Loc 12km E of Besançon
Arch Michael Fenn

Bitche (1988)
Rue des Prés, 57230 Bitche
Tel 03 87 96 15 30
Fax 03 87 96 08 04
Holes 18 L 6082 m SSS 72
9 L 2293 m SSS 34
V'tors U
Loc 75km NW of Strasbourg. 55km SE of Saarbrücken
Arch Fromanger

Châlons-en-Champagne (1988)
La Grande Romanie, 51460 Courtisols
Tel 06 07 55 24 30
Fax 03 26 66 66 81
Holes 18 L 6578 m SSS 76
V'tors U
Fees 200–250fr
Loc St Etienne au Temple, 6km from A4 Junction 28
Arch Alain Tribout

Château de Bournel (1990)
25680 Cubry
Tel 03 81 86 00 10
Fax 03 81 86 01 06
Web www.bournel.com
Holes 18 L 5767 m Par 71 CR 71.6 SR 133
V'tors H
Fees €30 (€50)
Loc 50km NE of Besançon
Arch Robert Berthet

Combles-en-Barrois (1948)
14 Rue Basse, 55000 Combles-en-Barrois
Tel 03 29 45 16 03
Fax 03 29 45 16 06
Holes 18 L 6100 m Par 72
V'tors U
Fees 180fr (200fr)
Loc 80km W of Nancy, nr Bar-le-Duc
Arch Michel Gayon

Coteaux de Champagne (1986)
Chemin de Bourdonnerie, BP 41, 51700 Dormans
Tel 03 26 58 25 09
Fax 03 26 59 33 88
Holes 18 L 5969 m Par 72
V'tors U
Loc Dormans, 20km SW of Reims
Arch Olivier Brizon

For list of abbreviations see page 649

Épinal (1985)
Public
Rue du Merle-Blanc, 88001 Épinal
Tel   03 29 34 65 97
Holes 18 L 5700 m SSS 70
V'tors H
Loc   Épinal, 70km S of Nancy
Arch   Michel Gayon

Faulquemont-Pontpierre (1993)
Rue du Golf, 57380 Faulquemont
Tel   03 87 29 21 21
Fax   03 87 90 76 25
Holes 18 L 6000 m SSS 72
       9 hole par 3 course
V'tors U
Loc   30km E of Metz
Arch   Flipo/Fourès

Forêt d'Orient
BP13 Rouilly-Sacey, 10220 Piney
Tel   03 25 46 37 78
Holes 18 L 6120 m Par 72
V'tors U
Loc   20km E of Troyes
Arch   E Rossi

La Grange aux Ormes
La Grange aux Ormes, 57157 Marly
Tel   03 87 63 10 62
Fax   03 87 55 01 77
Holes 18 L 6200 m Par 72
       9 L 2001 m Par 31
V'tors U
Fees   220fr (285fr)
Loc   3km S of Metz
Arch   Philippe Gourdon

Kempferhof (1988)
351 Rue du Moulin, 67115 Plobsheim
Tel   03 88 98 72 72
Fax   03 88 98 74 76
Web   www.kempferhof-golf-
       hotel.com
Holes 18 L 6020 m SSS 72
V'tors H
Fees   400fr (600fr)
Loc   10km S of Strasbourg
Arch   Robert von Hagge

La Largue G&CC (1988)
Rue du Golf, 68580 Mooslargue
Tel   03 89 07 67 67
Fax   03 89 25 62 83
Holes 18 L 6162 m SSS 72
V'tors WD–H WE–NA before noon H
Fees   250fr (350fr)
Loc   25km W of Basle
Arch   Jean Garaialde

Metz Technopole
*Rue Félix Savart, 57070 Metz
Technopole 2000*
Tel   03 87 39 95 95
Holes 18 L 5774 m SSS 71
       6 hole Par 3 course
V'tors H or Green card
Loc   SE of Metz centre
Arch   Robert Berthet

Metz-Cherisey (1963)
Château de Cherisey, 57420 Cherisey
Tel   03 87 52 70 18
Fax   03 87 52 42 44
Holes 18 L 6172 m SSS 72
V'tors H
Fees   200fr (250fr)
Loc   15km SE of Metz
Arch   Donald Harradine

Nancy-Aingeray (1962)
Aingeray, 54460 Liverdun
Tel   03 83 24 53 87
Holes 18 L 5577 m SSS 69
V'tors H
Fees   200fr (250fr)
Loc   17km NW of Nancy
Arch   Michael Fenn

Nancy-Pulnoy (1993)
10 Rue du Golf, 54425 Pulnoy
Tel   03 83 18 10 18
Fax   03 83 18 10 19
Holes 18 L 6000 m SSS 72
       9 hole Par 3 course
V'tors WD–U WE–H
Fees   170fr (250fr)
Loc   10km E of Nancy
Arch   Hawtree/Flipo

Prunevelle (1930)
*Ferme des Petits-Bans,
25420 Dampierre-sur-le-Doubs*
Tel   03 81 98 11 77
Fax   03 81 90 28 65
Holes 18 L 6281 m SSS 73
Loc   10km S of Montbéliard, on
       D126

Reims-Champagne (1928)
*Château des Dames de France,
51390 Gueux*
Tel   03 26 05 46 10
Fax   03 26 05 46 19
Holes 18 L 6026 m SSS 72
V'tors U
Fees   200fr (280fr)
Loc   10km W of Reims
Arch   Michael Fenn

Rhin Mulhouse (1969)
Ile du Rhin, 68490 Chalampe
Tel   03 89 83 28 32
Fax   03 89 83 28 42
Holes 18 L 5991 m SSS 72
V'tors WE–M
Fees   280fr (450fr)
Loc   20km E of Mulhouse
Arch   Donald Harradine

Rochat (1986)
*1305 Route du Noirmont, 39220
Les Rousses*
Tel   03 84 60 06 25
Fax   03 84 60 01 73
Holes 18 L 5388 m Par 71
V'tors U
Fees   180fr (250fr)
Loc   30km N of Geneva (N5)

Rougemont-le-Château (1990)
Route de Masevaux, 90110 Rougemont-le-Château
Tel   03 84 23 74 74
Fax   03 84 23 03 15
Holes 18 L 6002 m SSS 72
V'tors U H
Fees   240fr (320fr)
Loc   18km NE of Belfort. 25km
       NW of Mulhouse
Arch   Robert Berthet

Strasbourg (1934)
Route du Rhin, 67400 Illkirch
Tel   03 88 66 17 22
Fax   03 88 65 05 67
Holes 27 holes:
       6105-6138 m SSS 72-73
V'tors WD–H (max 35)
Fees   WD only–230fr
Loc   10km S of Strasbourg
Arch   Donald Harradine

Troyes-Cordelière (1957)
*Château de la Cordelière,
10210 Chaource*
Tel   03 25 40 18 76
Fax   03 25 40 13 66
Holes 18 L 6154 m SSS 72
V'tors H
Fees   180fr (250fr)
Loc   NE of Chaource on N443.
       30km SE of Troyes
Arch   P Hirigoyen

Val de Sorne
*Domaine de Val de Sorne,
39570 Vernantois*
Tel   03 84 43 04 80
Fax   03 84 47 31 21
Web   www.valdesorne.com
Holes 18 L 6000 m SSS 72
V'tors U
Fees   200–280fr
Loc   5km SE of Lons-le-Saunier,
       between Geneva and Lyon
Arch   Hugues Lambert

Vittel
BP 122, 88804 Vittel-Cedex
Tel   03 29 08 18 80
Holes St Jean 18 L 6326 m SSS 72
       Peulin 18 L 6100 m SSS 72
       9 hole course
Loc   Vittel, 70km S of Nancy
Arch   Allison/Morrison/Begin

La Wantzenau (1991)
C D 302, 67610 La Wantzenau
Tel   03 88 96 37 73
Fax   03 88 96 34 71
Holes 18 L 6400 m SSS 72
V'tors H
Fees   280fr (400fr)
Loc   12km N of Strasbourg
Arch   Pern/Garaialde

Paris Region

Béthemont-Chisan CC
(1989)
12 Rue du Parc de Béthemont,
78300 Poissy
Tel 01 39 75 51 13
Fax 01 39 75 49 90
Holes 18 L 6035 m SSS 72
V'tors U
Fees 250fr (500fr)
Loc 30km W of Paris
Arch Bernhard Langer

La Boulie
La Boulie, 78000 Versailles
Tel 01 39 50 59 41
Holes 18 L 6055 m SSS 71
        18 L 6206 m SSS 72
        9 hole course
V'tors H WE–M
Loc 15km SW of Paris

Disneyland Paris (1992)
1 Allee de la Mare Houleuse,
77400 Magny-le-Hongre
Tel 01 60 45 68 90
Fax 01 60 45 68 33
Holes 18 L 6221 m Par 72
        9 L 2905 m Par 36
V'tors U
Fees On application
Loc 32km E of Paris via A4
Arch Ronald Fream

Feucherolles (1992)
78810 Feucherolles
Tel 01 30 54 94 94
Fax 01 30 54 92 37
Holes 18 L 6358 m Par 72
V'tors U
Fees 300–350fr (380–490fr)
Loc 23km W of Paris
Arch JM Poellot

Fourqueux (1963)
Rue Saint Nom 36, 78112 Fourqueux
Tel 01 34 51 41 47
Fax 01 39 21 00 70
Holes 27 holes:
        5615-6025 m Par 73-74
V'tors WD–U WE–M
Loc 4km SW of St Germain-en-
        Laye, W of Paris

Isabella (1969)
RN12, Sainte-Appoline, 78370 Plaisir
Tel 01 30 54 10 62
Fax 01 30 54 67 58
Holes 18 L 5629 m SSS 71
V'tors WD–H WE–NA
Loc 28km W of Paris (RN12)
Arch Paul Rolin

Joyenval (1992)
Chemin de la Tuilerie,
78240 Chambourcy
Tel 01 39 22 27 50

Fax 01 39 79 12 90
Holes Retz 18 L 6211 m Par 72
        Marly 18 L 6249 m Par 72
V'tors M
Loc 25km N of Paris, nr St
        Germain-en-Laye
Arch Robert Trent Jones Sr

National (1990)
2 Avenue du Golf, 78280
Guyancourt
Tel 01 30 43 36 00
Fax 01 30 43 85 58
Web www.golf-national.com
Holes Albatros 18 L 6495 m Par 72
        Aigle 18 L 5936 m Par 71
        Oiselet 9 L 2010 m Par 32
V'tors H or Green card
Fees 120–310fr (120–490fr)
Loc St Quentin-en-Yvelines,
        SW of Paris (D36)
Arch Chesneau/Von Hagge

Le Prieuré (1965)
78440 Sailly
Tel 01 34 76 70 12
Fax 01 34 76 71 62
Holes Ouest 18 L 6274 m SSS 72
        Est 18 L 6157 m SSS 72
V'tors WD–H
Loc Sailly, 10km NW of
        Meulan (D130). 45km NW
        of Paris
Arch F Hawtree

Rochefort (1964)
78730 Rochefort-en-Yvelines
Tel 01 30 41 31 81
Fax 01 30 41 94 01
Holes 18 L 5735 m SSS 71
V'tors U
Fees 250–450fr
Loc 45km SW of Paris
Arch Hawtree

St Cloud (1911)
60 Rue du 19 Janvier, Garches
92380
Tel 01 47 01 01 85
Fax 01 47 01 19 57
Holes 18 L 5939 m SSS 72
        18 L 4823 m SSS 67
V'tors H
Fees 500fr (600fr)
Loc Porte Dauphine, 9km W of
        Paris
Arch HS Colt

St Germain (1922)
Route de Poissy, 78100 St Germain-en-
Laye
Tel 01 39 10 30 30
Fax 01 39 10 30 31
Web www.golfstgermain.org
Holes 18 L 6117 m SSS 72
        9 L 2030 m SSS 33
V'tors WD–H WE–M
Fees 400fr
Loc 20km W of Paris
Arch HS Colt

St Nom-La-Bretêche
(1959)
Hameau Tuilerie-Bignon, 78860
St Nom-La-Bretêche
Tel 01 30 80 04 40
Fax 01 34 62 60 44
Holes 18 L 6685 yds SSS 72
        18 L 6712 yds SSS 72
V'tors H
Fees WD only–500fr
Loc 24km W of Paris on A-13
Arch F Hawtree

St Quentin-en-Yvelines
Public
RD 912, 78190 Trappes
Tel 01 30 50 86 40
Holes 18 L 5900 m SSS 71
        18 L 5753 m SSS 70
V'tors H
Loc 20km SW of Paris
Arch Hubert Chesneau

La Vaucouleurs (1987)
Rue de l'Eglise, 78910 Civry-la-Forêt
Tel 01 34 87 62 29
Fax 01 34 87 70 09
Holes Rivière 18 L 6138 m Par 73
        Vallons 18 L 5553 m SSS 70
V'tors H or Green card
Fees 220fr (375fr)
Loc 50km W of Paris, between
        Mantes and Houdan
Arch Michel Gayon

Les Yvelines
Château de la Couharde, 78940 La-
Queue-les-Yvelines
Tel 01 34 86 48 89
Fax 01 34 86 50 31
Holes 18 L 6344 m Par 72
        9 L 2065 m Par 31
V'tors U
Fees 170fr (290fr)
Loc Montfort-l'Amaury, 45km W
        of Paris
Arch HJ Baker

Provence & Côte d'Azur

Aix Marseille (1935)
13290 Les Milles
Tel 04 42 24 40 41/04 42 24 23 01
Fax 04 42 39 97 48
Holes 18 L 6291 m SSS 73
V'tors H
Fees D–240fr (D–280fr)
Loc 7km SW of Aix-en-Provence.
        30km N of Marseille
Arch Peter Cannon

Barbaroux (1989)
Route de Cabasse, 83170 Brignoles
Tel 04 94 69 63 63
Fax 04 94 59 00 93
Web www.barbaroux.com
Holes 18 L 6367 m SSS 72

V'tors U
Fees 300fr (300fr)
Loc Brignoles, 50km E of Aix.
40km N of Toulon
Arch Pete Dye/PB Dye

Les Baux de Provence
(1987)
Domaine de Manville, 13520 Les Baux-de-Provence
Tel 04 90 54 40 20
Fax 04 90 54 40 93
Web www.golfsprovence.com
Holes 9 L 2812 m SSS 36
V'tors U H
Fees 145fr (195fr)
Loc 15km NE of Arles. 15km S of Avignon. 80km W of Marseilles
Arch Martin Hawtree

Beauvallon-Grimaud
Boulevard des Collines, 83120 Sainte-Maxime
Tel 04 94 96 16 98
Holes 9 L 2503 m SSS 34
V'tors H
Loc 3km SW of Sainte Maxime

Biot (1930)
La Bastide du Roi, 06410 Biot
Tel 04 93 65 08 48
Fax 04 93 65 05 63
Holes 18 L 5054 m Par 70
V'tors U
Loc Antibes 5km. Nice 15km

Cannes Mandelieu (1891)
Route de Golf, 06210 Mandelieu
Tel 04 92 97 32 00
Fax 04 93 49 92 90
Holes 18 L 5871 m SSS 71
9 L 2852 m SSS 33
V'tors U H
Fees 330fr (330fr)
Loc Mandelieu, 7km W of Cannes

Cannes Mandelieu Riviera (1990)
*Avenue des Amazones,
06210 Mandelieu*
Tel 04 92 97 49 49
Fax 04 92 97 49 42
Holes 18 L 5736 m SSS 71
V'tors U H–max 36
Fees 260fr (290fr)
Loc 10km SW of Cannes, off A8
Arch Robert Trent Jones

Cannes Mougins (1925)
175 Route d'Antibes, 06250 Mougins
Tel 04 93 75 79 13
Fax 04 93 75 27 60
Holes 18 L 6263 m SSS 72
V'tors U
Fees 450fr (500fr)
Loc 8km NE of Cannes (D35)
Arch Colt/Simpson (1925).
Alliss/Thomas (1977)

Château L'Arc (1985)
*Domaine de Château L'Arc,
13710 Fuveau*
Tel 04 42 53 89 09
Fax 04 42 53 89 08
Web www.golfchateaularc.com
Holes 18 L 6300 m SSS 71
V'tors U
Fees 250fr
Loc 15km SE of Aix-en-Provence
Arch Michel Gayon

Châteaublanc
Les Plans, 84310 Morières-les-Avignon
Tel 04 90 33 39 08
Fax 04 90 33 43 24
Web www.golfchateaublanc.com
Holes 18 L 6141 m SSS 72
9 L 1267 m Par 28
V'tors H
Fees 200fr (250fr)
Loc 5km SE of Avignon, nr Airport
Arch Thierry Sprecher

Digne-les-Bains (1990)
Public
St Pierre de Gaubert, 0400 Digne-les-Bains
Tel 04 92 30 58 00
Fax 04 92 30 58 39
Holes 18 L 5861 m SSS 72
V'tors U
Loc 100km NE of Aix-en-Provence
Arch Robert Berthet

Estérel Latitudes (1989)
Ave du Golf, 83700 St Raphaël
Tel 04 94 52 68 30
Fax 04 94 52 68 31
Holes 18 L 5921 m SSS 71
9 L 1392 m Par 29
V'tors U H
Fees 270–300fr
Loc 3km N of St-Raphaël
Arch Robert Trent Jones

Frégate (1992)
*Domaine de Frégate, RD 559, 83270
St Cyr-sur-Mer*
Tel 04 94 29 38 00
Fax 04 94 29 96 94
Holes 18 L 6210 m SSS 72
9 hole short course
V'tors U
Fees 295fr (335fr)
Loc 25km W of Toulon on coast
Arch Ronald Fream

Gap-Bayard (1988)
Centre d'Oxygénation, 05000 Gap
Tel 04 92 50 16 83
Fax 04 92 50 17 05
Holes 18 L 6023 m SSS 72
V'tors U
Fees €30 (€33)
Loc 7km N of Gap. 80km S of Grenoble
Arch Hugues Lambert

Grand Avignon (1989)
*BP 121, Les Chênes Verts,
84270 Vedene*
Tel 04 90 31 49 94
Fax 04 90 31 01 21
Holes 18 L 6046 m Par 72
9 hole short course
V'tors U
Fees 210 fr (250fr)
Loc Vedene, 10km NE of Avignon
Arch Georges Roumeas

La Grande Bastide (1990)
*Chemin des Picholines, 06740
Châteauneuf de Grasse*
Tel 04 93 77 70 08
Fax 04 93 77 72 36
Holes 18 L 6105 m SSS 72
V'tors U H
Fees 290fr (320fr)
Loc Grasse, 17km N of Cannes
Arch Cabell Robinson

Grasse CC (1992)
1 Route des Trois Ponts, 06130 Grasse
Tel 04 93 60 55 44
Fax 04 93 60 55 19
Holes 18 L 6021 m SSS 72
V'tors U
Fees 300fr (320fr)
Loc 18km N of Cannes
Arch JP Fourès

Le Lavandou
*2 Ave du Cap Nègre, Cavalière, 83980
Le Lavandou*
Tel 04 94 05 75 80
Holes 18 L 5649 m Par 72
V'tors U
Loc 50km E of Toulon, between Hyères and St Tropez
Arch Yves Bureau

Luberon (1986)
La Grande Gardette, 04860 Pierrevert
Tel 04 92 72 17 19
Fax 04 92 72 59 12
Web www.golf-pierrevert.com
Holes 18 L 6040 m SSS 72
V'tors U
Fees €38
Loc 5km SW of Manosque. 45km NE of Aix
Arch Artea

Marseille La Salette (1988)
*Impasse des Vaudrans, 13011 La
Valentine Marseille*
Tel 04 91 27 12 16
Fax 04 91 27 21 33
Holes 18 L 5436 m Par 71 SSS 69
V'tors U
Fees 210fr (260fr)
Loc Nr centre of Marseilles
Arch Michel Gayon

Miramas (1993)
Mas de Combe, 13140 Miramas
Tel 04 90 58 56 55

Fax 04 90 17 38 73
Holes 18 L 5670m Par 72
V'tors H or Green card
Fees 110–150fr (150–200fr)
Loc 50km S of Avignon. 50km NW of Marseilles
Arch Serge Giraud

Monte Carlo (1910)
Route du Mont-Agel, 06320 La Turbie
Tel 04 92 41 50 70
Fax 04 93 41 09 55
Holes 18 L 5679 m SSS 71
V'tors H
Fees 400fr (500fr)
Loc Mont Agel, La Turbie, 10km N of Monte Carlo

Opio-Valbonne (1966)
Route de Roquefort-les-Pins, 06650 Opio
Tel 04 93 12 00 08
Fax 04 93 12 26 00
Holes 18 L 5892 m SSS 72
V'tors H
Fees 370fr
Loc 15km N of Cannes
Arch Donald Harradine

Pont Royal (1992)
Pont Royal, 13370 Mallemort
Tel 04 90 57 40 79
Fax 04 90 59 45 83
Holes 18 L 6303 m SSS 72
V'tors H
Fees 200–300fr
Loc 35km SE of Avignon on N7, between Avignon and Aix
Arch Severiano Ballesteros

Provence G&CC (1991)
Route de Fontaine de Vaucluse, L'Isle sur la Sorgue, 84800 Saumane
Tel 04 90 20 20 65
Fax 04 90 20 32 01
Holes 18 L 6045 m SSS 72
9 hole short course
V'tors U
Loc 20km E of Avignon
Arch Jean Garaialde

Roquebrune (1989)
CD 7, 83520 Roquebrune-sur-Argens
Tel 04 94 82 92 91
Fax 04 94 82 94 74
Holes 18 L 6031 m SSS 71
V'tors H
Fees 260fr
Loc 35km N of Saint-Tropez. 40km SW of Cannes
Arch Udo Barth

Royal Mougins (1993)
424 Avenue du Roi, 06250 Mougins
Tel 04 92 92 49 69, 04 92 92 49 79
Fax 04 92 92 49 70
Web www.royalmougins.fr
Holes 18 L 6004 m SSS 72
V'tors H
Fees 1000fr (inc lunch)
Loc 5km N of Cannes
Arch Robert von Hagge

St Endreol (1992)
Route de Bagnols-en-Fôret, 83920 La Motte
Tel 04 94 51 89 89
Fax 04 94 51 89 90
Holes 18 L 6219 m SSS 73
V'tors U H
Fees 300fr
Loc 30km N of St Tropez. 30km W of Cannes
Arch Michel Gayon

La Sainte-Baume (1988)
Golf Hotel, Domaine de Châteauneuf, 83860 Nans-les-Pins
Tel 04 94 78 60 12
Fax 04 94 78 63 52
Holes 18 L 6167 m SSS 72
V'tors U
Fees 220–270fr (270fr)
Loc 30km SE of Aix-en-Provence, via A8 (exit Saint-Maximin)
Arch Robert Berthet

Sainte-Maxime
Route de Débarquement, 83120 Sainte-Maxime
Tel 04 94 55 02 02
Fax 04 94 55 02 03
Holes 18 L 6155 m SSS 71
V'tors H
Loc 15km N of Saint Tropez. 80km W of Nice (RN98)
Arch Donald Harradine

Servanes (1989)
Domaine de Servanes, 13890 Mouriès
Tel 04 90 47 59 95
Fax 04 90 47 52 58
Holes 18 L 6100m SSS 72
V'tors H
Fees 200fr (250fr)
Loc 35km S of Avignon
Arch Sprecher/Watine

Taulane
Domaine du Château de Taulane, RN 85, 83840 La Martre
Tel 04 93 60 31 30
Fax 04 93 60 33 23
Holes 18 L 6250 m Par 72
V'tors H
Fees 200–300fr (350fr)
Loc 55km N of Cannes on N85 (Route Napoleon)
Arch Gary Player

Valcros (1964)
Domaine de Valcros, 83250 La Londe-les-Maures
Tel 04 94 66 81 02
Fax 04 94 66 83 09
Holes 18 L 5274 m SSS 68
V'tors H
Fees 250fr (250fr)
Loc 10km W of Le Lavandou
Arch F Hawtree

Valescure (1895)
BP 451, 83704 St-Raphaël Cedex
Tel 04 94 82 40 46
Fax 04 94 82 41 42
Holes 18 L 5067 m Par 68
V'tors U H
Fees 300fr
Loc 5km E of St-Raphaël
Arch Lord Ashcombe

Rhône-Alps

Aix-les-Bains (1913)
Avenue du Golf, 73100 Aix-les-Bains
Tel 04 79 61 23 35
Fax 04 79 34 06 01
Holes 18 L 5597 m SSS 71
V'tors H
Loc 3km S of Aix

Albon (1989)
Domaine de Senaud, Albon, 26140 St Rambert d'Albon
Tel 04 75 03 03 90
Fax 04 75 03 11 01
Holes 18 L 6108 m Par 72
9 L 1260 m Par 29
V'tors U
Fees 180–240fr
Loc 60km S of Lyon, motorway exit Chanas
Arch Antoine d'Ormesson

Annecy (1953)
Echarvines, 74290 Talloires
Tel 04 50 60 12 89
Fax 04 50 60 08 80
Holes 18 L 5017 m SSS 68
V'tors H
Loc 13km E of Annecy
Arch Cecil Blandford

Annonay-Gourdan (1988)
Domaine de Gourdan, 07430 Saint Clair
Tel 04 75 67 03 84
Fax 04 75 67 79 50
Holes 18 L 5900 m SSS 71
V'tors U
Loc 35km SE of St Etienne. 50km SW of Lyon
Arch Sprecher/Watine

Les Arcs
B P 18, 73706 Les Arcs Cedex
Tel 04 79 07 43 95
Fax 04 79 07 47 65
Holes 18 L 5547 m SSS 70
V'tors H
Loc 90 km E of Chambery on N90

Le Beaujolais (1991)
69480 Lucenay-Anse
Tel 04 74 67 04 44
Fax 04 74 67 09 60
Holes 18 L 6137 m SSS 72

For list of abbreviations see page 649

V'tors U H
Loc 25km N of Lyon

Bossey G&CC (1985)

Château de Crevin, 74160 Bossey
Tel 04 50 43 95 50
Fax 04 50 95 32 57
Holes 18 L 5954 m Par 71
V'tors WD–U WE–NA
Fees 300fr
Loc 6km S of Geneva
Arch Robert Trent Jones Jr

La Bresse

Domaine de Mary, 01400 Condessiat
Tel 04 74 51 42 09
Fax 04 74 51 40 09
Holes 18 L 6217 m Par 72
V'tors WD–U WE–H
Loc 15km SW of Bourg-en-Bresse, via RN73
Arch Jeremy Pern

Chamonix (1934)

35 Route du Golf, 74400 Chamonix
Tel 04 50 53 06 28
Fax 04 50 53 38 69
Web www.golfdechamonix.com
Holes 18 L 6087 m SSS 72
V'tors H
Fees 200–350fr (250–350fr)
Loc 3km N of Chamonix (RN 506). Geneva 80km
Arch Robert Trent Jones Sr

Le Clou (1985)

01330 Villars-les-Dombes
Tel 04 74 98 19 65
Fax 04 74 98 15 15
Holes 18 L 5000 m SSS 67
V'tors WD–U WE–H
Loc 30km NE of Lyon

La Commanderie (1964)

L'Aumusse-Crottet, 01290 Pont-de-Veyle
Tel 04 85 30 44 12
Fax 04 85 30 55 02
Holes 18 L 5560 m SSS 69
V'tors H
Loc 7km E of Mâcon on RN 79

Correçon-en-Vercors (1987)

Les Ritons, 38250 Correçon-en-Vercors
Tel 04 76 95 80 42
Fax 04 76 95 84 63
Holes 18 L 5550 m Par 71
V'tors U
Loc 35km S of Grenoble, off D531
Arch Hugues Lambert

Divonne (1931)

01220 Divonne-les-Bains
Tel 04 50 40 34 11
Fax 04 50 40 34 25
Holes 18 L 5858 m SSS 72
V'tors H–max 35
Fees 300fr (500fr)

Loc Divonne ½ km. 18km N of Geneva
Arch Noskowski

Esery (1990)

Esery, 74930 Reignier
Tel 04 50 36 58 70
Fax 04 50 36 57 62
Holes 18 L 6350 m SSS 73
   9 L 2024 m SSS 31
V'tors WD–H WE–NA
Fees 300fr
Loc 10km S of Geneva
Arch Michel Gayon

Flaine-Les-Carroz (1984)

74300 Flaine
Tel 04 50 90 85 44
Fax 04 50 90 88 21
Holes 18 L 3693 m Par 63
V'tors U
Loc 4km N of Flaine. 60km SE of Geneva Airport
Arch Robert Berthet

Giez (1991)

Lac d'Annecy, 74210 Giez
Tel 04 50 44 48 41
Fax 04 50 32 55 93
Holes 18 L 5820 m Par 72
   9 L 2250 m Par 33
V'tors H or Green card
Fees 220–270fr
Loc 20km SE of Annecy
Arch Didier Fruchet

Le Gouverneur

Château du Breuil, 01390 Monthieux
Tel 04 72 26 40 34
Fax 04 72 26 41 61
Holes 18 L 6477 m Par 72
   18 L 5959 m Par 72
   9 L 2365 m Par 34
V'tors H or green card
Fees 180fr (250fr)
Loc NE of Lyon, off A46
Arch Fruchet/Sprecher

Grenoble-Bresson (1990)

Route de Montavie, 38320 Eybens
Tel 04 76 73 65 00
Fax 04 76 73 65 51
Holes 18 L 6343 m SSS 72
V'tors U
Fees 230fr (270fr)
Loc 10km SE of Grenoble
Arch Robert Trent Jones Jr

Grenoble-Charmeil (1988)

38210 St Quentin-sur-Isère
Tel 04 76 93 67 28
Fax 04 76 93 62 04
Web www.bluegreen.com
Holes 18 L 5733 m Par 73
V'tors U
Fees 200fr (260fr)
Loc 15km NW of Grenoble, off A49
Arch Perl/Garaialde

Grenoble-Uriage (1921)

Les Alberges, 38410 Uriage
Tel 04 76 89 03 47
Fax 04 76 73 15 80
Holes 9 L 2004 m Par 64
V'tors U
Fees 150fr (180fr)
Loc 15km E of Grenoble
Arch Watine/Sprecher

Lyon (1921)

38280 Villette-d'Anthon
Tel 04 78 31 11 33
Fax 04 72 02 48 27
Holes 18 L 6229 m SSS 72
   18 L 6727 m SSS 74
V'tors U H
Fees 220fr (330fr)
Loc 20km E of Lyon
Arch Fenn/Lambert

Lyon-Chassieu

Route de Lyon, 69680 Chassieu
Tel 04 78 90 84 77
Fax 04 78 90 88 85
Holes 18 L 5941 m Par 70
V'tors H
Loc 10km E of Lyon
Arch Chris Pittman

Lyon-Verger (1977)

69360 Saint-Symphorien D'Ozon
Tel 04 78 02 84 20
Fax 04 78 02 08 12
Holes 18 L 5800 m SSS 69
V'tors U
Fees 180fr (250fr)
Loc 14km S of Lyon on A7, or RN7 2km S of Feyzin

Maison Blanche G&CC (1991)

01170 Echenevex
Tel 04 50 42 44 42
Fax 04 50 42 44 43
Holes 18 L 6246 m SSS 72
   9 L 1757 m Par 31
V'tors WD–U H (max 30)
Loc 15km from Geneva
Arch Harradine/Dongradi

Méribel (1973)

BP 54, 73553 Méribel Cedex
Tel 04 79 00 52 67
Fax 04 79 00 38 85
Holes 18 L 5319 m SSS 70
V'tors H
Fees 270fr
Loc 15km S of Moutiers. 35km S of Albertville
Arch Sprecher/Watine

Mionnay La Dombes (1986)

Chemin de Beau-Logis, 01390 Mionnay
Tel 04 78 91 84 84
Fax 04 78 91 02 73
Holes 18 L 6060 m SSS 71

V'tors U
Fees 200fr (260fr)
Loc 20km N of Lyon towards Bourg
Arch Jacques Vouilloux

Mont-d'Arbois (1964)
74120 Megève
Tel 04 50 21 29 79
Fax 04 50 93 02 63
Holes 18 L 6100 m SSS 72
V'tors WE–restricted. Booking required Jul/Aug
Fees 200–300fr
Loc 3km SE of Megève
Arch Henry Cotton

Royal Golf (1904)
Rive Sud du lac de Genève, 74500 Évian
Tel 04 50 75 46 66
Fax 04 50 75 65 54
Holes 18 L 6030 m SSS 72
V'tors H
Fees 210–300fr (D–295–360fr)
Loc 2km W of Évian. 40km NE of Geneva Airport
Arch Cabell Robinson

St Etienne (1989)
62 Rue St Simon, 42000 St Etienne
Tel 04 77 32 14 63
Fax 04 77 33 61 23
Holes 18 L 5700 m Par 72 6 hole Par 3 course
V'tors U
Fees 180fr (230fr)
Loc Nr centre of St Etienne. Lyon 60km
Arch Thierry Sprecher

Salvagny
100 Rue des Granges, 69890 La Tour de Salvagny
Tel 04 78 48 83 60
Fax 04 78 48 00 16
Holes 18 L 6300 m SSS 73 Par 72
V'tors U
Loc Lyon 20km
Arch Drancourt

La Sorelle (1991)
Domaine de Gravagnieux, 01320 Villette-sur-Ain
Tel 04 74 35 47 27
Fax 04 74 35 44 51
Holes 18 L 6100 m SSS 72
V'tors U
Loc 50km NE of Lyon
Arch Patrick Jacquier

Tignes (1968)
Val Claret, 73320 Tignes
Tel 04 79 06 37 42 (Summer)
Fax 04 79 06 35 64
Holes 18 L 4810 m SSS 68
V'tors H–max 35
Fees € 3 2
Loc 50km E of Moutiers, off D902, nr Italian border. 90km S of Chamonix

Valdaine (1989)
Domaine de la Valdaine, Montboucher/Jabron, 26740 Montelimar-Montboucher
Tel 04 75 00 71 33
Fax 04 75 01 24 49
Web www.domainedelavaldaine .com
Holes 18 L 5631 m SSS 71
V'tors U
Fees 200fr (280fr)
Loc 4km E of Montelimar. 50km S of Valence
Arch TJ Macauley

Valence St Didier (1983)
26300 St Didier de Charpey
Tel 04 75 59 67 01
Fax 04 75 59 68 19
Holes 18 L 5807 m SSS 71
V'tors U
Fees 160fr (210fr)
Loc 12km E of Valence
Arch Thierry Sprecher

Toulouse & Pyrenees

Albi Lasbordes (1989)
Château de Lasbordes, 81000 Albi
Tel 05 63 54 98 07
Fax 05 63 47 21 55
Holes 18 L 6200 m SSS 72
V'tors U
Fees 170fr (230fr)
Loc 70km NE of Toulouse
Arch Garaialde/Pern

Ariège (1986)
Unjat, 09240 La Bastide-de-Serou
Tel 05 61 64 56 78
Fax 05 61 64 57 99
Holes 18 L 6000 m SSS 71
V'tors H
Fees 145fr (195fr)
Loc Unjat, 20km NW of Foix
Arch Michel Gayon

La Bigorre (1992)
Pouzac, 65200 Bagnères de Bigorre
Tel 05 62 91 06 20
Holes 18 L 5909 m SSS 72
V'tors U
Loc 18km S of Tarbes. 150km W of Toulouse
Arch Olivier Brizon

Château de Terrides (1986)
Domaine de Terrides, 82100 Labourgade
Tel 05 63 95 61 07
Fax 05 63 95 64 97
Holes 18 L 6420 m SSS 71
V'tors U
Loc 45km NW of Toulouse
Arch J-P Foures

Embats
Route de Montesquiou, 32000 Auch
Tel 05 62 05 20 80/05 62 61 10 11
Fax 05 62 05 92 55
Holes 18 L 4751 m SSS 65
V'tors U
Fees 150fr (170fr)
Loc 4km W of Auch. 80km W of Toulouse
Arch André Migret

Étangs de Fiac (1987)
Brazis, 81500 Fiac
Tel 05 63 70 64 70
Fax 05 63 75 32 91
Holes 18 L 5800 m SSS 71
V'tors U
Fees 170–220fr
Loc 45km NE of Toulouse
Arch M Hawtree

Florentin-Gaillac (1990)
Le Bosc, Florentin, 81150 Marssac-sur-Tarn
Tel 05 63 55 20 50
Fax 05 63 53 26 41
Holes 18 L 6150 m SSS 71
V'tors U
Loc 10km W of Albi. 70km NE of Toulouse
Arch Robert Berthet

Guinlet (1986)
32800 Eauze
Tel 05 62 09 80 84
Fax 05 62 09 84 50
Web www.guinlet.fr
Holes 18 L 5565 m Par 71
V'tors U
Fees € 27 (€ 30)
Loc 60km SW of Agen. 150km SE of Bordeaux
Arch M Larrouy

Lannemezan
La Demi-Lune, 65300 Lannemezan
Tel 05 62 98 01 01
Holes 18 L 5872 m Par 70
V'tors H
Loc 38km SE of Tarbes
Arch Hirigoyen/Laserre

Lourdes (1988)
Chemin du Lac, 65100 Lourdes
Tel 05 62 42 02 06
Fax 05 62 42 02 06
Holes 18 L 5372 m Par 71 CR 70.6
V'tors U
Fees 150fr–180fr (170fr–200fr)
Loc 4km W of Lourdes, off D940
Arch Olivier Brizon

Luchon (1908)
BP 40, 31110 Bagnères de Luchon
Tel 05 61 79 03 27
Holes 9 L 2375 m SSS 66
V'tors H
Loc Luchon, 90km SE of Tarbes. 145km S of Toulouse
Arch Fenn/Hawtree

Mazamet-La Barouge
(1956)
81660 Pont de l'Arn
Tel   05 63 61 08 00/
05 63 67 06 72
Fax   05 63 61 13 03
Holes 18 L 5623 m SSS 70
V'tors U
Fees   175fr (235fr)
Loc   2km N of Mazamet. 80km E
of Toulouse. 80km W of
Béziers
Arch   Mackenzie Ross/Hawtree

Toulouse (1951)
31320 Vieille-Toulouse
Tel   05 61 73 45 48
Fax   05 62 19 04 67
Holes 18 L 5602 m Par 69
V'tors U
Fees   250fr
Loc   8km S of Toulouse
Arch   Hawtree

Toulouse-La Ramée
Ferme Cousturier, 31170 Tournefeuille
Tel   05 61 07 09 09
Fax   05 61 07 15 93
Holes 18 L 5605 m SSS 69
9 hole short course
V'tors H
Loc   SW of Toulouse
Arch   Hawtree

Toulouse-Palmola (1974)
Route d'Albi, 31660 Buzet-sur-Tarn
Tel   05 61 84 20 50
Fax   05 61 84 48 92
Holes 18 L 6156 m SSS 73
V'tors H
Fees   250–350fr
Loc   18km NE of Toulouse. A68
Junction 4
Arch   Michael Fenn

Toulouse-Seilh
Route de Grenade, 31840 Seilh
Tel   05 61 42 59 30
Fax   05 61 42 34 17
Holes Red 18 L 6122 m SSS 72
Yellow 18 L 4202 m SSS 64
V'tors H
Fees   200–250fr
Loc   15km N of Toulouse. Blagnac
Airport 5km
Arch   Jean Garaialde

Toulouse-Teoula
*71 Avenue des Landes, 31830 Plaisance
du Touch*
Tel   05 61 91 98 80
Fax   05 61 91 49 66
Holes 18 L 5500 m Par 69
V'tors H or green card
Fees   200fr
Loc   15km W of Toulouse
Arch   Martin Hawtree

Les Tumulus (1987)
1 Rue du Bois, 65310 Laloubère
Tel   05 62 45 14 50
Fax   05 62 45 11 82
Web   www.perso.fr/tumulus
Holes 18 L 5050 m Par 70 CR 69.2
SR 127
V'tors U
Fees   150fr (180fr)
Loc   2km S of Tarbes, towards
Bagnères
Arch   Charles de Ginestet

Germany

Berlin & East

Balmer See (1995)
Drewinscher Weg 1, 17429 Neppermin
Tel   (038379) 28199
Fax   (038379) 28222
Holes 27 L 5662-6090 m Par 71-73
V'tors U H
Fees   €36 (€46)
Loc   Usedom, 50km E of
Greifswald
Arch   M Skeide

Berlin Motzener See
(1991)
Am Golfplatz 5, 15741 Motzen
Tel   (033769) 50130
Fax   (033769) 50134
Web   www.golfclubmotzen.de
Holes 18 L 6330 m Par 73
9 L 2756 m Par 54
V'tors H–max 45. Booking
necessary
Fees   70–90DM (140DM)
Loc   30km S of Berlin
Arch   Kurt Rossknecht

Berlin Wannsee (1895)
Golfweg 22, 14109 Berlin
Tel   (030) 806 7060
Fax   (030) 806 706-10
Web   www.glcbw.de
Holes 18 L 6088 m SR 127
9 L 4442 m SR 102
V'tors WD–U H WE–M
Fees   110DM
Loc   Berlin (SW)
Arch   Harris Brothers (1925)

Elbflorenz GC Dresden
(1992)
*Ferdinand von Schillstr 4a,
01728 Possendorf*
Tel   (035206) 2430
Fax   (035206) 24317
Web   www.dresdnergolfclub.de
Holes 18 L 5902 m Par 72
V'tors H
Fees   70DM (80DM)
Loc   Dresden 12km
Arch   Dieter Sziedat

Palmerston Golf
Resort (1991)
Parkallee 1, 15526 Bad Sarrow
Tel   (033631) 63300
Fax   (033631) 63310
Web   www.palmerston.de
Holes 18 L 6118 m Par 72
18 L 6084 m Par 72
18 L 5593 m Par 71
9 hole course
V'tors U
Fees   36DM (70DM)
Loc   70km SE of Berlin
Arch   Palmer/Faldo/Eby/McEwan

Potsdamer Tremmen
(1990)
*Tremmener Landstrasse,
14641 Tremmen*
Tel   (033233) 80244
Fax   (033233) 80957
Holes 18 L 5921 m Par 72
V'tors H
Fees   60DM (80DM)
Loc   SW of Berlin

Schloss Meisdorf (1996)
Petersberger Trift 33, 06463 Meisdorf
Tel   (034743) 98450
Fax   (034743) 98499
Holes 18 L 6236 m Par 72
V'tors U H
Fees   40DM (60DM)
Loc   70km S of Magdeburg
Arch   Gerd Osterkamp

Seddiner See (1993)
Zum Weiher 44, 14552 Wildenbruch
Tel   (033205) 7320
Fax   (033205) 73229
Holes North 18 L 6259 m Par 72
South 18 L 6486 m Par 72
V'tors North–U H South–M H
Fees   North–70DM (90DM)
South–100DM (120DM)
Loc   40km SW of Berlin
Arch   North-Preissman
South-Trent Jones jr

Semlin am See (1992)
Ferchesarerstrasse, 14715 Semlin
Tel   (03385) 5540
Fax   (03385) 554400
Web   www.golfhotelsemlin.de
Holes 18 L 6348 m SSS 73
V'tors H
Fees   80DM (100DM)
Loc   75km W of Berlin (B5/B188)
Arch   Christoph Städler

Bremen & North
West

Bremer Schweiz (1991)
Wölpscherstr 4, 28779 Bremen
Tel   (0421) 609 5331
Fax   (0421) 609 5333

Holes 18 L 5858 m Par 72
V'tors H
Loc N of Bremen
Arch Wolfgang Siegmann

Club Zur Vahr (1905)
Bgm-Spitta-Allee 34, 28329 Bremen
Tel Bremen (0421) 204480,
Garlstedt (04795) 417
Fax (0421) 244 9248
Holes Garlstedt 18 L 6408 m CR
73.6 SR 136;
Bremen 9 L 5777 m CR 68.5
SR 111
V'tors WD–H WE–M
Fees Garlstedt–70DM
Bremen–50DM
Loc Garlstedt-30km N of Bremen.
Vahr-Bremen
Arch B von Limburger

Herzogstadt Celle (1985)
Beukenbusch 1, 29229 Celle
Tel (05086) 395
Fax (05086) 8288
Holes 18 L 5915 m SSS 71
V'tors H
Loc 6km NE of Celle, towards
Lüneburg. 40km NE of
Hanover
Arch Wolfgang Siegmann

Küsten GC Hohe Klint
(1978)
Hohe Klint, 27478 Cuxhaven
Tel (04723) 2737
Fax (04723) 5022
Web www.golf-cuxhaven.de
Holes 18 L 6047 m SSS 72
V'tors U H
Fees 50DM (70DM)
Loc 12km SW of Cuxhaven on
Route 6, nr Oxstedt

Münster-Wilkinghege
(1963)
Steinfurterstr 448, 48159 Münster
Tel (0251) 214090
Fax (0251) 261518
Holes 18 L 5990 m SSS 71
V'tors WD–H WE–I
Fees 60DM (80DM)
Loc 2km N of Münster
Arch W Siegmann

Oldenburgischer (1964)
Am Golfplatz 1, 26180 Rastede
Tel (04402) 7240
Fax (04402) 70417
Holes 18 L 6109 m SSS 72
V'tors WD–U WE–U H
Fees 60DM (70DM)
Loc 10km N of Oldenburg, nr
Rastede
Arch Von Limburger/Schnatmeyer

Ostfriesland (1980)
Postbox 1220, 26634 Wiesmoor
Tel (04944) 6440

Fax (04944) 6441
Holes 18 L 6170 m SSS 73
V'tors U
Fees 60DM (70DM)
Loc 25km SW of
Wilhelmshaven
Arch Frank Pennink

Soltau (1982)
Hof Loh, 29614 Soltau
Tel (05191) 967 63 33
Fax (05191) 967 63 34
Holes 18 L 6011 m SSS 73
9 L 2340 m SSS 54
V'tors H
Fees 50DM (60DM)
Loc Tetendorf, S of Soltau

Syke (1989)
Schultenweg 1, 28857 Syke-Okel
Tel (04242) 8230
Fax (04242) 8255
Holes 18 L 6266 m Par 73
V'tors U H
Fees 50DM (60DM)
Loc 20km S of Bremen

Tietlingen (1979)
29683 Fallingbostel
Tel (05162) 3889
Fax (05162) 7564
Holes 18 L 6193 m Par 72
SSS 73
V'tors H
Fees 50DM (60DM)
Loc 65km N of Hanover, between
Walsrode and Fallingbostel
Arch Bruns/Chadwick

Verden (1988)
Holtumer Str 24, 27283 Verden
Tel (04230) 1470
Fax (04230) 1550
Holes 18 hole course Par 72 SSS 72
V'tors U
Fees 50DM (60DM)
Loc 30km E of Bremen, nr Walle

Worpswede (1974)
Giehlermühlen, 27729 Vollersode
Tel (04763) 7313
Fax (04763) 6193
Holes 18 L 6200 m SSS 72
V'tors WD–U H WE–M H
Fees 50DM (60DM)
Loc Giehlermuhlen, 20km N of
Bremen, off B74

Central North

Dillenburg
Auf dem Altscheid, 35687 Dillenburg
Tel (02771) 5001
Fax (02771) 5002
Holes 18 L 6115 m Par 72
V'tors U H
Fees 65DM (80DM)
Loc 30km S of Siegen. 100km N
of Frankfurt

Hofgut Praforst (1992)
Postfach 1137, 36081 Hünfeld
Tel (06652) 9970
Fax (06652) 99755
Web www.praforst.de
Holes 18 hole course
9 hole course
V'tors H–54 max
Fees 70DM (90DM)
Loc Hünfeld, 10km N of Fulda,
off Route 27
Arch Deutsche Golf Consult

Kassel-Wilhelmshöhe
(1958)
Ehlenerstr 21, 34131 Kassel
Tel (0561) 33509
Fax (0561) 37729
Holes 18 L 5586 m SSS 70
V'tors U H
Fees 60DM (80DM)
Loc Wilhelmshöhe, 5km W of
Kassel
Arch Donald Harradine

Kurhessischer GC
Oberaula (1987)
Postfach 31, 36278 Oberaula
Tel (06628) 1573
Fax (06628) 919456
Holes 18 L 6050 m SSS 72
V'tors U H
Fees 50DM (70DM)
Loc 50km S of Kassel, nr
Kircheim
Arch Deutsche Golf Consult

Licher Golf (1992)
35423 Lich
Tel (06404) 91071
Fax (06404) 91072
Holes 18 L 6065m SSS 72
V'tors H–booking necessary Sun–M
Fees 80DM (100DM)
Loc 45km N of Frankfurt
Arch Heinz Fehring

Rhoen (1971)
Am Golfplatz, 36145 Hofbieber
Tel (06657) 1334
Fax (06657) 914809
Web www.golfclub-fulda.de
Holes 18 L 5686 m SSS 70
V'tors H
Fees 50DM (70DM)
Loc Hofbieber, 11km E of Fulda
Arch Kurt Peters

Schloss Braunfels (1970)
Homburger Hof, 35619 Braunfels
Tel (06442) 4530
Fax (06442) 6683
Holes 18 L 6085 m Par 73
V'tors WD–H (max 36) WE–H NA
10am–2pm
Fees D–70DM (90DM)
Loc 70km N of Frankfurt
Arch Bernhard von Limburger

For list of abbreviations see page 649

Schloss Sickendorf (1990)

Schloss Sickendorf, 36341 Lauterbach
Tel   (06641) 96130
Fax   (06641) 961335
Holes 18 L 6045 m Par 72 SSS 72
V'tors H
Fees   50DM (70DM)
Loc   30km W of Fulda. 120km E of
          Frankfurt
Arch   Spangemacher

Winnerod

Parkstr 22, 35447 Reiskirchen
Tel   (06408) 9513-0
Fax   (06408) 9513-13
Holes 18 L 6069 m Par 72
          9 hole Par 3 course
V'tors U H
Fees   50DM (90DM)
Loc   Hessen, 30km N of
          Frankfurt/Main
Arch   Michael Pinner

Zierenberg Gut Escheberg (1995)

Gut Escheberg, 34289 Zierenberg
Tel   (05606) 2608
Fax   (05606) 2609
Web   www.golfclub-escheberg.de
Holes 18 L 6122 m Par 72
V'tors U H WE–booking necessary
Fees   60DM (80DM)
Loc   20km NW of Kassel
Arch   Volker Püschel

Central South

Bad Kissingen (1910)

Euerdorferstr 11, 97688 Bad Kissingen
Tel   (0971) 3608
Fax   (0971) 60140
Holes 18 L 5699 m SSS 70
V'tors U H
Fees   65DM (75DM)
Loc   Bad Kissingen 2km. 65km N
          of Würzburg

Frankfurter (1913)

Golfstrasse 41, 60528 Frankfurt/Main
Tel   (069) 666 2318
Fax   (069) 666 7018
Holes 18 L 6455 yds SSS 71
V'tors H–28 max
Fees   100DM (115DM)
Loc   6km SW of Frankfurt, nr
          Airport
Arch   HS Colt

Hanau-Wilhelmsbad

(1958)
Wilhelmsbader Allee 32, 63454 Hanau
Tel   (06181) 82071
Fax   (06181) 86967
Holes 18 L 6227 m Par 73
V'tors WD–H WE–M H
Fees   80DM (100DM)
Loc   4km NW of Hanau on B8-
          40/AB66. Frankfurt 15km
Arch   Ernst Kothe

Hof Trages

Hofgut Trages, 63579 Freigericht
Tel   (06055) 91380
Fax   (06055) 913838
Web   www.hoftrages.de
Holes 18 L 5940 m CR 71.3 SR 127
V'tors WD–H WE–M
Fees   €50 (€60)
Loc   60 km E of Frankfurt/Main
Arch   Kurt Rossknecht

Homburger (1899)

*Saalburgchaussee 2, 61350
Bad Homburg*
Tel   (06172) 306808
Fax   (06172) 32648
Holes 10 holes Par 70 SSS 69
V'tors H
Fees   50DM (70DM)
Loc   On B456 to Usingen

Idstein (2001)

Am Nassen Berg, 65510 Idstein
Tel   (06126) 9322-13
Fax   (06126) 9322-33
Web   www.golfpark-idstein.de
Holes 18 L 6255 m Par 72
V'tors U
Fees   30DM
Loc   25km N of Wiesbaden
Arch   Siegfried Heinz

Idstein-Wörsdorf (1989)

Gut Henriettenthal, 65510 Idstein
Tel   (06126) 9322-0
Fax   (06126) 9322-22
Web   www.golfpark-idstein.de
Holes 18 L 6140 m Par 72
V'tors WD–H WE–M
Fees   50DM (70DM)
Loc   25km N of Wiesbaden
Arch   Siegfried Heinz

Kitzingen (1980)

Larson Barracks, 97318 Kitzingen
Tel   (09321) 4956
Fax   (09321) 21936
Holes 18 L 5956 m Par 71 SR 118
V'tors H
Fees   50DM (65DM)
Loc   20km E of Würzburg

Kronberg G&LC (1954)

*Schloss Friedrichshof, Hainstr 25,
61476 Kronberg/Taunus*
Tel   (06173) 1426
Fax   (06173) 5953
Holes 18 L 5183 m SSS 68
V'tors WD–U H WE–M H
Fees   90DM (110DM)
Loc   16km NW of Frankfurt
Arch   Harder/Harris

Main-Spessart (1990)

*Postfach 1204, 97821 Marktheidenfeld-
Eichenfürst*
Tel   (09391) 8435
Fax   (09391) 8816
Web   www.main-spessart-golf.de
Holes 18 holes Par 72

V'tors H–max 36

Fees   50DM (70DM)
Loc   80km E of Frankfurt/Main
Arch   Harradine

Main-Taunus (1979)

Lange Seegewann 2, 65205 Wiesbaden
Tel   (06122) 52550/52208(Sec)
Holes 18 L 6045 m SSS 72
V'tors H
Loc   15km NW of Frankfurt
          Airport

Mannheim-Viernheim

(1930)
*Alte Mannheimer Str 3,
68519 Viernheim*
Tel   (06204) 71313 (Clubhouse),
          (06204) 78737 (Sec)
Fax   (06204) 740181
Holes 9 L 6060 m SSS 72
V'tors WD–H WE–M H (Summer)
Loc   10km NE of Mannheim

Maria Bildhausen

Rindhof 1, 97702 Münnerstadt
Tel   (09766) 1601
Fax   (09766) 1602
Holes 18 L 6047 m Par 72
          6 hole short course
V'tors U
Fees   60DM (70DM)
Loc   80km NE of Wurzburg
Arch   Christian Habeck

Neuhof

Hofgut Neuhof, 63303 Dreieich
Tel   (06102) 327927/327010
Fax   (06102) 327012
Holes 18 L 6151 m SSS 72
V'tors WD–H WE–M
Fees   100DM
Loc   Hofgut Neuhof, S of
          Frankfurt, off A3
Arch   Patrick Merrigan

Rhein Main (1977)

Steubenstrasse 9, 65189 Wiesbaden
Tel   (0611) 373014
Holes 18 L 6116 m SSS 71
V'tors M
Loc   Wiesbaden 6km

Rheinblick

*Weisser Weg, 65201 Wiesbaden-
Frauenstein*
Tel   (0611) 420675
Fax   (0611) 941 0434
Holes 18 L 6604 yds SSS 70
V'tors Monday play only
Loc   2km from Wiesbaden at
          Hessen

Rheintal (1971)

*An der Bundesstrr 291,
68723 Oftersheim*
Tel   (06202) 56390
Holes 18 L 5840 m SSS 71
Fees   On application
Loc   Oftersheim, SE of Mannheim

St Leon-Rot (1996)
Opelstrasse 30, 68789 St Leon-Rot
Tel (06227) 86080
Fax (06227) 860888
Holes 18 L 6047 m Par 72
V'tors WD–U before 2pm WE–M
Fees 120DM (150DM)
Loc 20km S of Heidelberg
Arch Hannes Schreiner

Spessart (1972)
Golfplatz Alsberg, 63628 Bad Soden-Salmünster
Tel (06056) 91580
Fax (06056) 915820
Web www.gc-spessart.de
Holes 18 L 5956 m Par 72 SR 135
V'tors H
Fees €32 (€48) W–€135
Loc 70km NE of Frankfurt, via A66 towards Fulda
Arch Elliot Rowan

Taunus Weilrod (1979)
Merzhauser Strasse, 61276 Weilrod-Altweilnau
Tel (06083) 95050
Fax (06083) 950515
Holes 18 L 5981 m SSS 72
V'tors H
Fees 65DM (90DM)
Loc 25km NW of Bad Homburg
Arch Donald Harradine

Wiesbadener (1893)
Chausseehaus 17, 65199 Wiesbaden
Tel (0611) 460238
Fax (0611) 463251
Holes 9 L 5320 m SSS 68
V'tors WD–H (max 36) WE–H (max 25)
Fees 60DM (80DM)
Loc 8km NW of Wiesbaden, towards Schlangenbad
Arch Hirsch

Wiesloch-Hohenhardter Hof G&LC (1983)
Hohenhardter Hof, 69168 Wiesloch-Baiertal
Tel (06222) 78811-0
Fax (06222) 78811-11
Web www.golfclub-wiesloch.de
Holes 18 L 6080 m SSS 72
V'tors WD–H WE–M
Fees 60DM (80DM)
Loc 17km S of Heidelberg
Arch Harradine/Weishaupt

Hamburg & North

Altenhof (1971)
Eckernförde, 24340 Altenhof
Tel (04351) 41227,
(04351) 45800 (Pro)
Fax (04351) 41227
Holes 18 L 6066 m SSS 72
V'tors H

Fees 50DM (70DM)
Loc 3km S of Eckernförde. 25km NW of Kiel
Arch Donald Harradine

Berhinderten (1994)
Gustav-Delle Str 18a, 22926 Ahrensburg
Tel (04102) 41544
Fax (04102) 44516
Holes 18 hole course
V'tors U
Fees On application
Loc 20km NE of Hamburg

Brodauer Mühle (1986)
Baumallee 14, 23730 Gut Beusloe
Tel (04561) 8140
Fax (04561) 407397
Holes 18 L 6113 m Par 72 SSS 72
V'tors U H–36
Fees 50DM (80DM)
Loc 30km N of Lübeck
Arch Siegmann/Osterkamp

Buchholz-Nordheide
An der Rehm 25, 21244 Bucholz
Tel (04181) 36200
Fax (04181) 97294
Holes 18 L 6130 m SSS 72
V'tors WD–U H WE–H I before 10am
Fees 70DM (80DM)
Loc 30km S of Hamburg

Buxtehude (1982)
Zum Lehmfeld 1, 21614 Buxtehude
Tel (04161) 81333
Fax (04161) 87268
Web www.golfclubbuxtehude.de
Holes 18 L 6480 m Par 74 SSS 74
V'tors H
Fees 60DM (70DM)
Loc 30km SW of Hamburg on Route 73 from Harburg
Arch Wolfgang Siegmann

Deinster Mühle (1994)
Im Mühlenfeld 30, 21717 Deinste
Tel (04149) 925112
Fax (04149) 925111
Holes 18 L 6065 m Par 72
V'tors U H
Fees 55DM (75DM)
Loc 50km SW of Hamburg
Arch David Krause

Föhr (1966)
25938 Nieblum
Tel (04681) 580455
Fax (04681) 580456
Holes 18 L 6089 m SSS 72
V'tors H
Fees 65DM (75DM)
Loc 3km SW of Wyk, by Airport

Gut Apeldör (1996)
Gut Apeldör, 25779 Hennstedt
Tel (04836) 8408

Fax (04836) 8409
Web www.apeldoer.de
Holes 18 L 6048 m Par 72
6 hole short course
V'tors U H
Fees 60DM (80DM)
Loc 11km W of Heide. 110km N of Hamburg
Arch DJ Krause

Gut Grambek (1981)
Schlosstr 21, 23883 Grambek
Tel (04542) 841474
Fax (04542) 841476
Web www.gcgrambek.de
Holes 18 L 5877 m SSS 71
V'tors H
Fees 50DM (80DM)
Loc 30km S of Lübeck. 50km E of Hamburg

Gut Kaden (1984)
Kadenerstrasse 9, 25486 Alveslohe
Tel (04193) 9929-0
Fax (04193) 992919
Holes 18 L 6076 m Par 72
9 hole course
V'tors U H
Fees 60DM (90DM)
Loc Alveslohe, 30km N of Hamburg

Gut Uhlenhorst (1989)
24229 Uhlenhorst
Tel (04349) 91700
Fax (04349) 919400
Holes 18 L 6195 m SSS 72
V'tors U
Fees 50DM (60DM)
Loc 8km N of Kiel
Arch Donald Harradine

Gut Waldhof (1969)
Am Waldhof, 24629 Kisdorferwohld
Tel (04194) 99740
Fax (04194) 1251
Web www.gut-waldhof.de
Holes 18 L 5939 m Par 72
V'tors WD–H WE–M
Fees 70DM (90DM)
Loc 34km N of Hamburg via Autobahn A7 to Kaltenkirchen, or via route B432

Gut Waldshagen (1996)
24306 Gut Waldshagen
Tel (04522) 766766
Fax (04522) 766767
Holes 18 L 5688 m Par 72
V'tors U
Fees 60DM (80DM)
Loc 35km S of Kiel. 91km NE of Hamburg

Hamburg (1906)
In de Bargen 59, 22587 Hamburg
Tel (040) 812177
Fax (040) 817315
Holes 18 L 5919 m Par 71 SSS 72

V'tors H WE–M
Fees 75DM (85DM)
Loc Blankenese, 14km W of Hamburg
Arch Colt/Allison/Morrison

Hamburg Ahrensburg (1964)

Am Haidschlag 39-45, 22926 Ahrensburg
Tel (04102) 51309
Fax (04102) 81410
Holes 18 L 5782 m SSS 71
V'tors WD–U WE–M only
Loc 20km NE of Hamburg. Motorway exit Ahrensburg

Hamburg Hittfeld (1957)

Am Golfplatz 24, 21218 Seevetal
Tel (04105) 2331
Fax (04105) 52571
Holes 18 L 5903 m SSS 71
V'tors WD–U WE–M
Fees 60DM (80DM)
Loc 25km S of Hamburg
Arch Morrison/Gärtner

Hamburg Holm (1993)

Haverkamp 1, 25488 Holm
Tel (04103) 91330
Fax (04103) 913313
Web www.gchh.de
Holes 27 hole course
V'tors WD–U WE–M
Fees 65DM (80DM)
Loc 20km W of Hamburg
Arch Harradine/Rossknecht

Hamburg Waldorfer (1960)

Schevenbarg, 22949 Ammersbek
Tel (040) 605 1337
Fax (040) 605 4879
Holes 18 L 6154 m SSS 73
18 hole pitch & putt course
V'tors WD–U H WE–M H
Fees 70DM (85DM)
Loc 20km N of Hamburg
Arch B von Limburger

Hoisdorf (1977)

Hof Bornbek/Hoisdorf, 22952 Lütjensee
Tel (04107) 7831
Fax (04107) 9934
Holes 18 L 5958 m Par 71
V'tors WD–U WE–M only
Fees 70DM (80M)
Loc 25km NE of Hamburg

Jersbek

Oberteicher Weg, 22941 Jersbek
Tel (04532) 20950
Fax (04532) 24779
Holes 18 L 5921 m SSS 71
V'tors WD–H or I WE–M
Fees 60DM (70DM)
Loc 20km N of Hamburg
Arch Von Schinkel

Kieler GC Havighorst (1988)

Havighorster Weg 20, 24211 Havighorst
Tel (04302) 965980
Fax (04302) 965981
Holes 18 L 6242 m Par 73 SSS 73
V'tors WD–U H WE–H
Fees 50DM (60DM)
Loc 10km S of Kiel. 85km N of Hamburg
Arch Udo Barth

Lübeck-Travemünder (1921)

Kowitzberg 41, 23570 Lübeck-Travemünde
Tel (04502) 74018
Fax (04502) 72182
Holes 18 L 6071 m SSS 72
V'tors H
Loc 18km NE of Lübeck. 70km NE of Hamburg

Maritim Timmendorfer Strand (1973)

Am Golfplatz 3, 23669 Timmendorfer Strand
Tel (04503) 5152
Fax (04503) 86344
Holes North 18 L 6065 m SSS 72
South 18 L 3755 m SSS 60
V'tors WE–booking required
Fees North D–60DM (D–90DM)
South D–50DM (D–75DM)
Loc 15km N of Lübeck
Arch B von Limburger

Mittelholsteinischer Aukrug (1969)

Zum Glasberg 9, 24613 Aukrug-Bargfeld
Tel (04873) 595
Fax (04873) 1698
Holes 18 L 6140 m SSS 72
V'tors WD–H WE–H booking necessary
Loc 10km W of Neumunster. Mitte exit on Route 430

An der Pinnau (1982)

Pinnebergerstr 81a, 25451 Quickborn
Tel (04106) 81800
Fax (04106) 82003
Web www.pinnau.de
Holes 18 L 6023 m Par 72 SR 127
18 L 5231 m Par 72 SR 127
V'tors H or I
Fees 60DM (80DM)
Loc 25km NW of Hamburg, nr Quickborn
Arch David Krause

Am Sachsenwald (1985)

Am Riesenbett, 21521 Dassendorf
Tel (04104) 6120
Fax (04104) 6551
Holes 18 L 6118 m SSS 72
V'tors H
Fees 50DM (60DM)

Loc 20km SE of Hamburg
Arch Deutsche Golf Consult

St Dionys (1972)

Widukindweg, 21357 St Dionys
Tel (04133) 6277
Fax (04133) 6281
Holes 18 L 6125 m SSS 72
V'tors By appointment only
Fees 70DM (90DM)
Loc 10km N of Lüneburg

Schloss Breitenberg

25524 Breitenberg
Tel (04828) 8188
Fax (04828) 8100
Web www.golfclubschlossbreiten berg.de
Holes 27 hole course
V'tors H
Fees 60DM (70DM)
Loc 50km N of Hamburg
Arch Osterkamp/Krause

Schloss Lüdersburg (1985)

Lüdersburger Strasse 21, 21379 Lüdersburg
Tel (04139) 6970-0
Fax (04139) 6970 70
Web www.luedersburg.de
Holes 18 L 6091 m SSS 73
18 L 6107 m SSS 72
4 hole Par 3 course
V'tors U H
Fees 60DM (95DM)
Loc 12km E of Lüneburg. 55km SE of Hamburg
Arch Wolfgang Siegmann

Sylt

Am Golfplatz, 25996 Wenningstedt
Tel (04651) 45311
Fax (04651) 45692
Holes 18 L 6200 m Par 72
V'tors H–max 36
Fees 100DM
Loc Sylt Island, 75km W of Flensburg
Arch D Harradine

Treudelberg G&CC (1990)

Lemsahler Landstr 45, 22397 Hamburg
Tel (040) 608 22500
Fax (040) 608 22444
Web www.treudelberg.com
Holes 18 L 6182 m SSS 72
9 hole pitch & putt
V'tors U H
Fees 75DM (90DM)
Loc N of Hamburg centre
Arch Donald Steel

Auf der Wendlohe

Oldesloerstr 251, 22457 Hamburg
Tel (040) 550 5014/5
Fax (040) 550 3668
Holes 27 holes:
5675-6050 m SSS 72

V'tors WD–U WE–M
Loc   15km N of Hamburg
Arch   Ernst-Dietmar Hess

Wentorf-Reinbeker (1901)

Golfstrasse 2, 21465 Wentorf
Tel   (040) 729 78066
Fax   (040) 729 78067
Holes 18 L 5698 m SSS 70
V'tors WD–U H WE–M
Fees   60DM (70DM)
Loc   20km SE of Hamburg
Arch   Ernst Hess

Hanover &
Weserbergland

Bad Lippspringe (1989)

Senne 1, 33173 Bad Lippspringe
Tel   (05252) 53794
Fax   (05252) 53811
Holes 18 L 5826 m Par 73 SSS 72
       9 L 5214 m Par 68 SSS 68
V'tors H
Fees   40–50DM (50–60DM)
Loc   9km E of Paderborn, off
       Route 1

Bad Salzuflen G&LC
(1956)

Schwaghof 4, 32108 Bad Salzuflen
Tel   (05222) 10773
Fax   (05222) 13954
Holes 18 L 6138 m Par 72
V'tors H
Fees   60DM (70DM)
Loc   3km NE of Bad Salzuflen
Arch   B von Limburger

Braunschweig (1926)

*Schwartzkopffstr 10,
38126 Braunschweig*
Tel   (0531) 691369
Holes 18 L 5893 m SSS 71
Loc   Braunschweig 5km

Burgdorf (1970)

*Waldstr 15, 31303 Burgdorf-
Ehlershausen*
Tel   (05085) 7628
Fax   (05085) 6617
Holes 18 L 6426 m SSS 74
V'tors H
Loc   Burgdorf-Ehlershausen, 20km
       NE of Hanover

Gifhorn (1982)

Wilscher Weg 69, 38518 Gifhorn
Tel   (05371) 16737
Fax   (05371) 51092
Holes 18 L 5972 m SSS 72
V'tors H
Fees   50DM (70DM)
Loc   30km N of Braunschweig

Göttingen (1969)

Levershausen, 37154 Northeim
Tel   (05551) 61915

Fax   (05551) 61863
Web   www.gcgoettingen.de
Holes 18 L 6050 m SSS 72
V'tors H
Fees   60DM (80DM)
Loc   20km N of Göttingen,
       towards Northeim
Arch   Dr Siegmann

Gütersloh Garrison

Princess Royal Barracks, BFPO 47
Tel   (05241) 842606
Holes 9 L 5761 yds SSS 68
Fees   £11
Loc   5km W of Gütersloh

Hameln (1985)

Schloss Schwöbber, 31855 Aerzen
Tel   (05154) 9870
Fax   (05154) 9871-11
Holes 18 L 6222 m Par 73
       18 hole short course
Loc   10km SW of Hameln. 60km
       SW of Hanover

Hannover (1923)

Am Blauen See, 30823 Garbsen
Tel   (05137) 73235
Holes 18 L 5855 m SSS 71
Loc   15km NW of Hanover

Isernhagen (1983)

Auf Gut Lohne 22, 30916 Isernhagen
Tel   (05139) 893185
Fax   (05139) 27033
Web   www.golfclub-isernhagen.de
Holes 18 L 6118 m SSS 72
V'tors H–(max 34)
Loc   Gut Lohne, 12km NE of
       Hanover

Langenhagen (1989)

Hainhaus 22, 30688 Langenhagen
Tel   (0511) 736832
Fax   (0511) 726 1990
Holes 27 L 6161 m Par 72
V'tors H
Fees   50DM (70DM)
Loc   25km N of Hanover
Arch   Siegmann

Lipperland zu Lage

Ottenhauserstr 100, 32791 Lage/Lippe
Tel   (05232) 66829
Fax   (05232) 18165
Holes 18 L 6260 m SSS 73
V'tors H
Loc   22km E of Bielefeld
Arch   Heinz Wolters

Lippischer (1980)

Huxoll 14, 32825 Blomberg-Cappel
Tel   (05231) 459
Fax   (05236) 8102
Holes 18 L 5990 m CR 71.5 SR 126
V'tors H
Fees   50DM (70DM)
Loc   12km E of Detmold

Marienfeld (1986)

Remse 27, 33428 Marienfeld
Tel   (05247) 8880
Fax   (05247) 80386
Holes 18 holes Par 71
V'tors U H
Fees   50DM (60DM)
Loc   Bielefeld 20km
Arch   Spangemacher

Paderborner Land
(1983)

Wilseder Weg 25, 33102 Paderborn
Tel   (05251) 4377
Holes 18 L 5670 m SSS 68
V'tors U
Loc   Salzkotten/Thule, between B-
       1 and B-64

Pyrmonter (1961)

Postfach 100 828, 31758 Hameln
Tel   (05281) 8196
Fax   (05281) 8196
Holes 18 L 5775 m SSS 70
V'tors H
Fees   50DM (60DM)
Loc   4km S of Bad Pyrmont. 20km
       SW of Hameln
Arch   Donald Harradine

Ravensberger Land

*Sudstrasse 96, 32130 Enger-
Pödinghausen*
Tel   (09224) 79751
Fax   (09224) 699446
Holes 18 hole course SSS 72
       6 hole pitch & putt
V'tors WD–H WE–M
Fees   40DM (50DM)
Loc   25km NE of Bielefeld towards
       Herford
Arch   Heinz Wolters

Senne GC Gut
Welschof (1992)

*Augustdorferstr 72, 33758 Schloss Holte-
Stukenbrock*
Tel   (05207) 920936
Fax   (05207) 88788
Holes 18 L 6246 m SSS 72
V'tors U H
Fees   60DM (80DM)
Loc   20km S of Bielefeld
Arch   Christoph Städler

Sennelager (British
Army) (1963)

Bad Lippspringe, BFPO 16
Tel   (05252) 53794
Fax   (05252) 53811
Holes Old 18 L 5687 m SSS 72
       New 9 L 5214 m SSS 68
V'tors U
Fees   (Forces) 40DM (50DM)
       (Civilians) 50DM (60DM)
Loc   9km E of Paderborn, off
       Route 1

Sieben-Berge Rheden
(1965)
Postfach 1152, 31021 Gronau
Tel   (05182) 52336
Fax   (05182) 52336
Holes   18 L 5856 m SSS 71
V'tors U H
Fees   50DM (60DM)
Loc   35km S of Hanover
Arch   B von Limburger

Weserbergland (1982)
Weissenfelder Mühle, 37647 Polle
Tel   (05535) 8842
Fax   (05535) 1225
Holes   18 holes SSS 72
V'tors H
Loc   35km S of Hameln

Westfälischer Gütersloh
Gütersloher Str 127, 33397 Rietberg
Tel   (05244) 2340/10528
Fax   (05244) 1388
Holes   18 L 6135 m SSS 72
V'tors U H
Fees   60DM (80DM)
Loc   8km SE of Gütersloh, nr Neuenkirchen
Arch   B von Limburger

Widukind-Land
(1985)
Auf dem Stickdorn 63, 32584 Löhne
Tel   (05228) 7050
Fax   (05228) 1039
Holes   18 hole course
V'tors U H
Fees   60DM (70DM)
Loc   30km NE of Bielefeld
Arch   Dahlmeier/Brinkmeier

Munich & South Bavaria

Allgäuer G&LC (1984)
Hofgut Boschach, 87724 Ottobeuren
Tel   (08332) 1310
Fax   (08332) 5161
Holes   18 L 6215 m SSS 72
         6 hole short course
V'tors H
Fees   60DM (80DM)
Loc   2km S of Ottobeuren. 20km N of Kempten

Altötting-Burghausen
(1986)
Piesing 4, 84533 Haiming
Tel   (08678) 986903
Fax   (08678) 986905
Web   www.gc-altoetting-burghausen.de
Holes   18 L 6281 m SSS 72/73
         9 L 6002 m Par 70
V'tors U
Fees   70DM (90DM)

Loc   Schloss Piesing, 4km N of Burghausen
Arch   G von Mecklenberg

Augsburg (1959)
Engelshofer Str 2, 86399 Bobingen-Burgwalden
Tel   (08234) 5621
Fax   (08234) 7855
Holes   18 L 6077 m Par 72 SSS 72
V'tors U
Fees   60DM (90DM)
Loc   18km SW of Augsburg
Arch   Kurt Rossknecht

Bad Tölz (1973)
83646 Wackersberg
Tel   (08041) 9994
Fax   (08041) 2116
Holes   9 L 2886 m SSS 71
V'tors WD–H WE–M
Fees   50DM (60DM)
Loc   5km W of Bad Tölz. 55km S of Munich

Bad Wörishofen
Schlingenerstr 27, 87668 Rieden
Tel   (08346) 777
Holes   18 L 6318 m SSS 71
Loc   10km S of Bad Wörishofen

Beuerberg (1982)
Gut Sterz, 82547 Beuerberg
Tel   (08179) 671/728
Fax   (08179) 5234
Holes   18 L 6518 m SSS 74
V'tors WD–H WE–M H
Fees   90DM (100DM)
Loc   Beuerberg, 45km SW of Munich
Arch   Donald Harradine

Im Chiemgau (1982)
Kötzing 1, 83339 Chieming
Tel   (08669) 87330
Fax   (08669) 87333
Web   www.Golfchieming.de
Holes   18 L 6221 m SSS 73
         9 hole Par 3 course
V'tors WD–H
Fees   D–80DM (D–110DM)
Loc   40km W of Salzburg
Arch   J Dudok van Heel

Donauwörth (1995)
Lederstatt 1, 86609 Donauwörth
Tel   (0906) 4044
Fax   (0906) 999 8164
Holes   18 L 5939 m Par 72
V'tors U H
Fees   60DM (80DM)
Loc   45km N of Augsburg
Arch   Peter Harradine

Ebersberg (1988)
Postfach 1351, 85554 Ebersberg
Tel   (08094) 8106
Fax   (08094) 8386
Holes   18 L 5907 m Par 72
         6 hole Par 3 course
V'tors U H

Fees   70DM (90DM)
Loc   Zaissing, 35km E of Munich
Arch   Thomas Himmel

Erding-Grünbach (1973)
Am Kellerberg, 85461 Grünbach
Tel   (08122) 49650
Fax   (08122) 49684
Holes   18 L 6109 m SSS 72
V'tors WD–H (max 35) WE–H (max 28)
Fees   70DM (90DM)
Loc   40km NE of Munich

Eschenried (1923)
Kurfürstenweg 10, 85232 Eschenried
Tel   (08131) 567410/567456
Fax   (08131) 567418/567410
Holes   Eschenried 18 L 5935 m Par 72 SR 124;
         Eschenhof 18 L 5550 m Par 70 SR 124;
         Gröbenbach 9 L 1810 m Par 32
V'tors U H
Fees   Eschenried €45 (€55)
         Eschenhof €36 (€46)
         Gröbenbach €23 (€30)
Loc   8km NW of Munich
Arch   G von Mecklenburg

Feldafing (1926)
Tutzinger Str 15, 82340 Feldafing
Tel   (08157) 9334-0
Fax   (08157) 9334-99
Holes   18 L 5724 m SSS 71
V'tors WD–H WE–M
Fees   100DM (120DM)
Loc   32km S of Munich
Arch   B von Limburger

Garmisch-Partenkirchen (1928)
Gut Buchwies, 82496 Oberau
Tel   (08824) 8344
Fax   (08824) 8344
Holes   18 L 6210 m Par 72
V'tors U H
Fees   70DM (90DM)
Loc   10km N of Garmisch-Partenkirchen

Gut Ludwigsberg (1989)
Augsburgerstr 51, 86842 Turkheim
Tel   (08245) 3322
Fax   (08245) 3789
Holes   18 L 6078 m Par 72
         9 hole Par 3 course
V'tors U
Fees   70DM (90DM)
Loc   50km SW of Munich
Arch   Kurt Rossknecht

Gut Rieden
Gut Rieden, 82319 Starnberg
Tel   (08151) 90770
Fax   (08151) 907711
Holes   18 L 6046 yds SSS 72
V'tors H WE–M
Fees   80DM (100DM)
Loc   25km S of Munich

Hohenpähl   (1988)

82396 Pähl
Tel   (08808) 9202-0
Fax   (08808) 9202-22
Holes 18 L 5692 m Par 71 SR 126
V'tors H
Fees   90DM (120DM)
Loc   40km S of Munich on B2
Arch   Kurt Rossknecht

Holledau

Weihern 3, 84104 Rudelzhausen
Tel   (08756) 96010
Fax   (08756) 815
Holes 18 L 6085 m SSS 72
         9 hole course
V'tors U H
Fees   50DM (80DM)
Loc   55km N of Munich

Höslwang im Chiemgau

(1975)
Kronberg 3, 83129 Höslwang
Tel   (08075) 714
Fax   (08075) 8134
Web   www.golfclub-hoeslwang.de
Holes 18 L 6049 m Par 72 SSS 72
V'tors H
Fees   80DM (100DM)
Loc   80km S of Munich
Arch   Thomas Himmel

Iffeldorf

Gut Rettenberg, 82393 Iffeldorf
Tel   (08856) 925555
Fax   (08856) 925559
Holes 18 L 5904 m SSS 71
V'tors U
Fees   80DM (100DM)
Loc   45km S of Munich
Arch   Hery Beer

Landshut   (1989)

Oberlippach 2, 84095 Furth-Landshut
Tel   (08704) 8378
Fax   (08704) 8379
Holes 18 L 6251 m SSS 73
V'tors H
Fees   70DM (90DM)
Loc   65 km E of Munich
Arch   Kurt Rossknecht

Mangfalltal G&LC

Oed 1, 83620 Feldkirchen-Westerham
Tel   (08063) 6300
Fax   (08063) 6958
Web   www.glcm.de
Holes 18 L 5742 m CR 70.4 SR 125
V'tors WD–U WE–M
Loc   40km SE of Munich

Margarethenhof am Tegernsee   (1982)

Gut Steinberg, PF 1101, 83701 Gmund am Tegernsee
Tel   (08022) 7506-0
Fax   (08022) 74818
Web   www.margarethenhof.com
Holes 18 L 6056 m SSS 72

V'tors WD–H WE–before 10am
Fees   100DM (120DM)
Loc   Tegernsee, 45km S of Munich
Arch   Frank Pennink

Memmingen Gut Westerhart   (1994)

Westerhart 1b, 87740 Buxheim
Tel   (08331) 71016
Fax   (08331) 71018
Holes 18 hole course
V'tors U H
Fees   60DM (80DM)
Loc   120km W of Munich.
         Memmingen 5km

München Nord-Eichenried   (1989)

Münchnerstr 57, 85452 Eichenried
Tel   (08123) 93080
Fax   (08123) 930893
Web   www.gc-eichenried.de
Holes 18 L 6318 m Par 73
V'tors WD–U WE–M
Fees   100DM (160DM)
Loc   19km NE of Munich
Arch   Kurt Rossknecht

München West-Odelzhausen   (1988)

Gut Todtenried, 85235 Odelzhausen
Tel   (08134) 1618
Fax   (08134) 7623
Holes 18 L 6169 m Par 72 SSS 72
V'tors I
Fees   60DM (90DM)
Loc   35km NW of Munich

München-Riedhof

82544 Egling-Riedhof
Tel   (08171) 7065
Fax   (08171) 72452
Holes 18 L 6216 m SSS 72
V'tors WD–U H
Loc   25km S of München
Arch   Heinz Fehring

Münchener   (1910)

Tölzerstrasse 95, 82064 Strasslach
Tel   (08170) 450
Fax   (08170) 611
Holes Strasslach 27 L 6177 m
         SSS 72;
         Thalkirchen 9 L 2528 m
         SSS 69
V'tors WD–H WE–M
Fees   WD–120DM
Loc   Strasslach: 10km from
         Munich. Thalkirchen: Munich

Olching   (1979)

Feursstrasse 89, 82140 Olching
Tel   (08142) 48290
Fax   (08142) 482914
Holes 18 L 6028 m Par 72
V'tors H WE–NA
Fees   80DM (100DM)
Loc   15km W of Munich
Arch   J Dudok van Heel

Pfaffing Wasserburger

*München Ost, Köckmühle,
83539 Pfaffing*
Tel   (08076) 1718
Fax   (08076) 8594
Holes 18 L 6212 m SSS 73
         9 hole course
V'tors U H
Loc   50km E of Münich
Arch   Kurt Rossknecht

Reit im Winkl-Kössen

(1986)
Postfach 1101, 83237 Reit im Winkl
Tel   (05375) 628535
Fax   (05375) 628537
Holes 18 L 5221 m Par 70
V'tors U
Fees   60DM (80DM)
Loc   100km SE of Munich
Arch   Georg Böhm

Rottaler G&CC   (1972)

Am Fischgartl 2, 84332 Herbertsfelden
Tel   (08561) 5969
Fax   (08561) 2646
Holes 18 L 6105 m Par 72 SSS 72
V'tors U
Fees   90DM
Loc   5km W of Pfarrkirchen on
         B388. 120km E of Munich
Arch   Donald Harradine

Rottbach   (1995)

Weiherhaus 5, 82216 Rottbach
Tel   (08135) 93290
Fax   (08135) 932911
Holes 18 L 6409 m Par 72
V'tors U
Fees   70DM (90DM)
Loc   20km NW of Munich
Arch   Thomas Himmel

St Eurach G&LC   (1973)

Eurach 8, 82393 Iffeldorf
Tel   (08801) 1332
Fax   (08801) 2523
Holes 18 L 6509 m SSS 74
V'tors H exc Wed & Fri pm–NA
         WE–NA
Fees   100DM
Loc   40km S of Munich
Arch   Donald Harradine

Schloss Maxlrain

Freitung 14, 83104 Maxlrain-Tuntenhausen
Tel   (08061) 1403
Fax   (08061) 30146
Holes 18 L 6357 m Par 72 SSS 73
         9 hole Par 3 course
V'tors U H
Fees   90DM (120DM)
Loc   40km S of Munich
Arch   Paul Krings

Sonnenalp   (1976)

Hotel Sonnenalp, 87527 Ofterschwang
Tel   (08321) 272181 (Sec)

For list of abbreviations see page 649

Fax (08321) 272242
Holes 18 L 5938 m SSS 71
Loc 4km W of Sonthofen
Arch Donald Harradine

Starnberg (1986)

Uneringerstr, 82319 Starnberg
Tel (08151) 12157
Fax (08151) 29115
Web www.gcstarnberg.de
Holes 18 L 6057 m Par 72
V'tors WD–H WE–M
Fees 80DM (100DM)
Loc 30km S of Munich
Arch Kurt Rossknecht

Tegernseer GC Bad Wiessee (1958)

Robognerhof, 83707 Bad Wiessee
Tel (08022) 8769
Fax (08022) 82747
Holes 18 L 5402 m CR 68.3 SR 126
V'tors WD–H WE–H before 10am
Fees 100DM (130DM)
Loc Tegernsee, 50km S of Munich
Arch D Harradine

Tutzing (1983)

82327 Tutzing-Deixlfurt
Tel (08158) 3600
Fax (08158) 7234
Holes 18 L 6159 m SSS 72
V'tors U H
Fees 100DM
Loc Starnberger See, 30km SW of Munich

Waldegg-Wiggensbach (1988)

Hof Waldegg, 87487 Wiggensbach
Tel (08370) 93073
Fax (08370) 93074
Holes 18 L 5462 m SSS 69
V'tors H–max 36
Fees 60DM (80DM)
Loc 10km W of Kempten, nr Swiss/Austrian border

Wittelsbacher GC Rohrenfeld-Neuburg (1988)

Gut Rohrenfeld, 86633 Neuburg/Donau
Tel (08431) 44118
Fax (08431) 41301
Web www.wittelbacher-golf.de
Holes 18 L 6350 m SSS 73
V'tors U H
Fees 70DM (90DM)
Loc 7km E of Neuburg. 70km NW of Munich
Arch J Dudok van Heel

Wörthsee (1982)

Gut Schluifeld, 82237 Wörthsee
Tel (08153) 93477-0
Fax (08153) 4280
Holes 18 L 6300 m SSS 72/73
V'tors WD–H WE–M
Fees 90DM (120DM)

Loc Wörthsee, 20km W of Munich
Arch Kurt Rossknecht

Nuremberg & North Bavaria

Abenberg (1988)

Am Golfplatz 19, 91183 Abenberg
Tel (09178) 98960
Fax (09178) 989696
Holes 18 holes CR 72.3 SR 131
V'tors WD–H
Fees 70DM (90DM)
Loc 10km S of Schwabach. 30km S of Nuremberg

Bad Griesbach

Holzhäuser 8, 94086 Bad Griesbach
Tel (08532) 790-0
Fax (08532) 790-45
Web www.hartl.de
Holes Uttlau 18 L 6115 m SSS 72
Lederbach 18 L 5998 m SSS 71
Brunnwies 18 L 6029 m SSS 71
V'tors I H
Fees 70DM (110DM)
Loc 28km SW of Passau
Arch Kurt Rossknecht

Bad Windsheim (1992)

Am Weinturm 2, 91438 Bad Windsheim
Tel (09841) 5027
Fax (09841) 3448
Holes 18 L 6265 m Par 73 SSS 73
V'tors U
Fees 60DM (80DM)
Loc 40km W of Nuremberg (B470)

Bamberg (1973)

Postfach 1525, 96006 Bamberg
Tel (09547) 7212/7109
Fax (09547) 7817
Holes 18 L 6175 m SSS 72
V'tors H
Fees 60DM (80DM)
Loc Gut Leimershof, 16km N of Bamberg
Arch Dieter Sziedat

Donau GC Passau-Rassbach (1986)

Rassbach 8, 94136 Thyrnau-Passau
Tel (08501) 91313
Fax (08501) 91314
Web www.rassbach.de
Holes 18 L 5864 m Par 72
V'tors U
Fees 70DM (80DM)
Loc 10km E of Passau
Arch Götz Mecklenburg

Fränkische Schweiz (1974)

Kanndorf 8, 91316 Ebermannstadt
Tel (09194) 4827

Fax (09194) 5410
Holes 18 L 6050 m SSS 72
V'tors H
Fees 60DM (80DM)
Loc 5km E of Ebermannstadt. 40km N of Nuremberg

Fürth (1951)

Vacherstrasse 261, 90768 Fürth
Tel (0911) 757522
Fax (0911) 973 2989
Holes 18 L 6478 yds SSS 71
V'tors H
Fees 50DM (80DM)
Loc 20km W of Nuremburg
Arch C Wagner (1992)

Gäuboden (1992)

Gut Fruhstorf, 94330 Aiterhofen
Tel (09421) 72804
Fax (09421) 72804
Holes 18 L 6233 m Par 72
V'tors U H
Fees 60DM (70DM)
Loc 40km SE of Regensburg, nr Straubing
Arch Prof Schmidt

Hof (1985)

Postfach 1324, 95012 Hof
Tel (09281) 43749
Fax (09821) 60318/709999
Holes 18 L 6040 m SSS 72
V'tors H
Fees 50DM (70DM)
Loc 2km NE of Hof (B173)
Arch Dieter Sziedat

Lauterhofen (1987)

Ruppertslohe 18, 92283 Lauterhofen
Tel (09186) 1574
Fax (09186) 1527
Holes 18 L 6054 m SSS 72
V'tors H
Fees 60DM (80DM)
Loc 25km SE of Nuremberg
Arch Dillschnitter

Lichtenau-Weickershof (1980)

Weickershof 1, 91586 Lichtenau
Tel (09827) 92040
Fax (09827) 9204-44
Holes 18 L 6218 m SSS 72
V'tors WD–H (max 35) WE–M
Fees 60DM (80DM)
Loc 10km E of Ansbach
Arch Dieter Sziedat

Oberfranken Thurnau (1965)

Postfach 1349, 95304 Kulmbach
Tel (09228) 319
Fax (09228) 7219
Holes 18 L 6152 m SSS 72
V'tors I H
Loc Thurnau, 18km NW of Bayreuth. 14km SW of Kulmbach
Arch Donald Harradine

Oberpfälzer Wald
G&LC (1977)
Ödengrub, 92431 Kemnath bei Fuhrn
Tel   **(09439) 466**
Fax   (09439) 1247
Holes 18 L 5799 m SSS 71
V'tors I
Fees   50DM (60DM)
Loc   10km E of Schwarzenfeld,
      towards Neunburg
Arch   Max Haseneder

Oberzwieselau (1990)
94227 Lindberg
Tel   **(01049) 9922/2367**
Fax   (01049) 9922/2924
Web   www.golfpark-
      oberzwieselau.de
Holes 18 L 6214 m SSS 72
V'tors U H–(max 36)
Fees   70DM (90DM)
Loc   170km NE of Munich

Regensburg G&LC (1966)
Jagdschloss Thiergarten,
93177 Altenthann
Tel   **(09403) 505**
Fax   (09403) 4391
Holes 18 L 6120 m CR 70.1 SR 127
V'tors U
Fees   60DM (90DM)
Loc   14km E of Regensburg, nr
      Walhalla
Arch   Harradine/Himmel

Regensburg-Sinzing
Minoritenhof 1, 93161 Sinzing
Tel   **(0941) 32504**
Fax   (0941) 36299
Holes 18 L 5984 m SSS 72
      6 hole short course
V'tors U H
Fees   60DM (70DM)
Loc   7km SW of Regensburg

Am Reichswald (1960)
Schiestlstr 100, 90427 Nürnberg
Tel   **(0911) 305730**
Fax   (0911) 301200
Holes 18 L 6345 m CR 71.8 SR 129
V'tors U H
Fees   70DM (100DM)
Loc   10km N of Nuremberg

Sagmühle (1984)
Golfplatz Sagmühle 1, 94086
Bad Griesbach
Tel   **(08532) 2038**
Fax   (08532) 3165
Holes 18 L 6168 m SSS 72
V'tors H
Fees   70DM (80DM)
Loc   25km SW of Passau
Arch   Kurt Rossknecht

Schloss Fahrenbach
(1993)
95709 Tröstau
Tel   **(09232) 882-256**

Fax   (09232) 882-345
Web   www.golfhotel-fahrenbach.de
Holes 18 L 5858 m Par 72 SSS 72
V'tors U
Fees   60DM (70DM)
Loc   15km W of Marktredwitz.
      40km E of Bayreuth
Arch   Deutsche Golf Consult

Schlossberg (1985)
Grünbach 8, 94419 Reisbach
Tel   **(08734) 7035**
Fax   (08734) 7795
Holes 18 L 6070 m SSS 72
V'tors U
Fees   70DM
Loc   Sommershausen, 15km from
      Dingolfing. 100km NE of
      Munich, off Route 11

Schmidmühlen G&CC
(1968)
Am Theilberg, 92287 Schmidmühlen
Tel   **(09474) 701**
Fax   (09474) 8236
Holes 18 L 5946 m Par 72
Loc   35km NW of Regensburg

Schwanhof (1994)
Klaus Conrad Allee 1, 92706 Luhe-
Wildenau
Tel   **(09607) 92020**
Fax   (09607) 920248
Holes 18 hole course SSS 72
V'tors U H
Fees   70DM (90DM)
Loc   80km N of Regensburg
Arch   Pate/Weisshaupt

Die Wutzschleife (1997)
Hillstedt 40, 92444 Rötz
Tel   **(09976) 18460**
Fax   (09976) 18180
Holes 18 L 4728 m Par 65
V'tors U
Fees   50–60DM (60–70DM)
Loc   70km N of Regensburg.
      180km NE of Munich
Arch   Deutsche Golf Consult

Rhineland North

Aachen (1927)
Schürzelter Str 300, 52074 Aachen
Tel   **(0241) 12501**
Fax   (0241) 171075
Holes 18 L 6063 m Par 72
V'tors H
Loc   Seffent, 5km NW of Aachen
Arch   Murray/Morrison/Pennink

Ahaus
Schmäinghook 36, 48683 Ahaus-
Alstätte
Tel   **(02567) 405**
Fax   (02567) 3524
Web   www.glc-ahaus.de
Holes 18 hole course SSS 72
      9 hole course

V'tors U H
Fees   €31 (€45)
Loc   60km W of Münster
Arch   Deutsche Golf Consult

Alten Fliess (1995)
Am Alten Fliess 66, 50129 Bergheim
Tel   **(02238) 94410**
Fax   (02238) 944119
Holes 27 holes:
      6050-6075 m Par 72
V'tors U H–36 max
Fees   45–100DM (60–120DM)
Loc   12km W of Cologne
Arch   Kurt Rossknecht

Artland (1988)
Westerholte 23, 49577 Ankum
Tel   **(05466) 301**
Fax   (05466) 91081
Web   www.artlandgolf.de
Holes 18 holes Par 72
V'tors U H – booking required
Fees   60DM (80DM)
Loc   Ankum, 30km N of
      Osnabrück
Arch   Udo Schmidt

Bergisch-Land
Siebeneickerst 386, 42111 Wuppertal
Tel   **(02053) 7177**
Fax   (02053) 7303
Holes 18 L 6037 m SSS 72
V'tors WD–H WE–M
Fees   80DM
Loc   Elberfeld, 8km W of
      Wuppertal

Bochum (1982)
Im Mailand 127, 44797 Bochum
Tel   **(0234) 799832**
Fax   (0234) 795775
Holes 18 L 5300 m SSS 68
V'tors WD–H
Loc   Bochum-Stiepel, 7km S of
      Bochum

Castrop-Rauxel
Dortmunder Str 383, 44577 Castrop-
Rauxel
Tel   **(02305) 62027**
Fax   (02305) 61410
Holes 18 L 6181 m SSS 72
V'tors U
Loc   10km W of Dortmund

Dortmund (1956)
Reichmarkstr 12, 44265 Dortmund
Tel   **(0231) 774133/774609**
Fax   (0231) 774403
Holes 18 L 6174 m SSS 72
V'tors WE–M
Fees   60DM (80DM)
Loc   8km S of Dortmund
Arch   B von Limburger

Düsseldorf (1961)
Rommerljansweg 12, 40882 Ratingen
Tel   **(02102) 81092**

Fax   (02102) 81782
Holes 18 L 5905 m SSS 71
V'tors WD–U WE–M
Loc   11km N of Düsseldorf

Düsseldorf Hösel

In den Höfen 32, 40883 Ratingen
Tel   (02102) 68629
Holes 18 L 6160 m SSS 72
V'tors U
Loc   Hösel, 15km NE of
       Düsseldorf

Elfrather Mühle (1991)

An der Elfrather Mühle 145,
47802 Krefeld
Tel   (02151) 4969-0
Fax   (02151) 477459
Holes 18 L 6125 m Par 72 SSS 72
V'tors H–max 36
Fees   70DM (90DM)
Loc   Krefeld 7km. Düsseldorf
       25km
Arch   Ron Kirby

Erftaue (1991)

Zur Mühlenerft 1, 41517 Grevenbroich
Tel   (02181) 280637
Fax   (02181) 280639
Holes 18 L 6039 m Par 72
V'tors WD–H WE–H after 1pm
Fees   60DM (80DM)
Loc   25km SW of Düsseldorf
Arch   Karl Grohs

Essen Haus Oefte (1959)

Laupendahler Landstr, 45219 Essen-
Kettwig
Tel   (02054) 83911
Fax   (02054) 83850
Holes 18 L 6011 m CR 71.7 SR 126
V'tors U H
Loc   14km SW of Essen

Essen-Heidhausen (1970)

Preutenborbeckstr 36, 45239 Essen
Tel   (0201) 404111
Holes 18 L 5937 m SSS 71
V'tors U H
Loc   10km S of Essen on B224, nr
       Werden

Euregio Bad Bentheim

(1987)
Postbox 1205, 48443 Bad Bentheim
Tel   (05922) 6700
Fax   (05922) 6701
Holes 18 L 5877 m Par 72
V'tors U exc Wed & Thurs–NA
Fees   50DM (70DM)
Loc   55km N of Münster
Arch   Prof Schmidt

Haus Bey (1992)

41334 Nettetal
Tel   (02153) 9197-0
Fax   (02153) 919750
Web   www.hausbey.de
Holes 18 L 5948 m CR 71.3 SR 117

V'tors U H
Fees   70DM (90DM)
Loc   40km NW of Düsseldorf
Arch   Paul Krings

Haus Kambach (1989)

Kambachstrasse 9-13,
52249 Eschweiler-Kinzweiler
Tel   (02403) 37615
Fax   (02403) 21270
Holes 18 L 6178 m SSS 72
V'tors U
Fees   70DM (90DM)
Loc   20km E of Aachen
Arch   Dieter Sziedat

Hubbelrath (1961)

Bergische Landstr 700,
40629 Düsseldorf
Tel   (02104) 72178/71848
Fax   (02104) 75685
Holes East 18 L 6208 m SSS 72
       West 18 L 4325 m SSS 62
V'tors WD–U WE–M H–max 28
       East, 36 West
Fees   East 100DM (120DM) West
       80DM (100DM)
Loc   Hubbelrath, 13km E of
       Düsseldorf, on Route B7
Arch   B von Limburger

Hummelbachaue Neuss

(1987)
Norfer Kirchstrasse, 41469 Neuss
Tel   (02137) 91910
Fax   (02137) 4016
Holes 18 L 6091 m Par 73
V'tors WD–H WE–M
Fees   40–80DM (80DM)
Loc   5km W of Düsseldorf
Arch   Udo Barth

Issum-Niederrhein (1973)

Pauenweg 68, 47661 Issum 1
Tel   (02835) 92310
Fax   (02835) 9231-20
Holes 18 L 5769 m Par 71 SSS 70
V'tors H
Fees   60DM (80DM)
Loc   10km E of Geldern
Arch   Harradine

Juliana (1979)

Frielinghausen 1, 45549 Sprockhövel
Tel   (0202) 647070/648220
Fax   (0202) 649891
Holes 18 L 6100 m SSS 71
V'tors H
Loc   30km E of Düsseldorf
Arch   De Buer

Köln G&LC

Golfplatz 2, 51429 Bergisch Gladbach
Tel   (02204) 92760
Fax   (02204) 927615
Holes 18 L 6090 m Par 72
V'tors WD–H WE–NA
Fees   WD–100DM
Loc   15km E of Cologne

Krefeld (1930)

Eltweg 2, 47809 Krefeld
Tel   (02151) 570071/72
Holes 18 L 6082 m SSS 72
V'tors WD–U H–max 28
Fees   80DM (100DM)
Loc   7km SE of Krefeld.
       Düsseldorf 16km
Arch   B von Limburger

Mühlenhof (1990)

Mühlenhof, 47546 Kalkar
Tel   (02824) 924040
Fax   (02824) 924093
Web   www.muehlenhof.net
Holes 18 L 6103 m Par 72
V'tors U
Fees   50DM (80DM)
Loc   80km N of Düsseldorf
       (B67)
Arch   Hans Herkberger

Nordkirchen (1974)

Am Golfplatz 6, 59394 Nordkirchen
Tel   (02596) 9191
Fax   (02596) 9195
Web   www.glc-nordkirchen.de
Holes 18 L 5828 m SSS 71
V'tors WD–I WE–H
Fees   60DM (70DM)
Loc   30km S of Münster
Arch   Christoph Städtler

Op de Niep (1995)

Bergschenweg 71, 47506 Neukirchen-
Vluyn
Tel   (02845) 28051
Fax   (02845) 28052
Holes 18 L 6374 m CR 72.8
       SR 130
       9 L 3926 m Par 66 CR 61.8
V'tors WD–U H WE–M
Fees   18 hole: 50DM (80DM)
       9 hole: 35DM (45DM)
Loc   20km W of Duisburg. 30km
       NW of Düsseldorf
Arch   Heinz Wolters

Osnabrück (1955)

Karmannstr 1, 49084 Osnabrück
Tel   (05402) 5636
Fax   (05402) 5257
Web   www.ogc.de
Holes 18 L 5731 m Par 71
V'tors U
Fees   60DM (80DM)
Loc   13km SE of Osnabrück

RAF Germany (1956)

RAF Brüggen, BFPO 25
Tel   (02163) 80049
Fax   (02163) 80934
Holes 18 L 6522 yds SSS 71
V'tors WD–U WE–M
Fees   50DM
Loc   On B230, 1km from
       Dutch/German border. 25km
       W of Mönchengladbach

Ratingen Gut Grashaus
(1988)
Grevemühle, 40882 Ratingen-Homberg

Tel	(02102) 9595-0
Fax	(02102) 959515
Holes	18 L 5864 m Par 72
V'tors	U H
Fees	70DM (90DM)
Loc	10km N of Düsseldorf
Arch	Peter Drecker

Rheine/Mesum (1998)
Wörstr 201, 48419 Rheine

Tel	(05975) 9490
Fax	(05975) 9491
Web	www.golfsportclub.de
Holes	18 L 6036 m Par 72 SSS 72
	9 L 4442 m Par 68 SSS 64
V'tors	U H–max 36
Fees	45–65DM (70–90DM)
Loc	Gut Winterbrock, 40km W of Münster
Arch	Christoph Städler

Rittergut Birkhof
(1996)
Rittergut Birkhof, 41352 Korschenbroich

Tel	(02131) 510660
Fax	(02131) 510616
Holes	18 L 6037 m Par 73
	9 hole Par 3 course
V'tors	I H
Fees	70DM (90DM)
Loc	20km W of Düsseldorf
Arch	Kurt Rossknecht

St Barbara's Royal Dortmund (1969)
Hesslingweg, 44309 Dortmund

Tel	(0231) 202551
Fax	(0231) 259183
Holes	18 L 5967 m SSS 73
V'tors	H–by prior arrangement
Fees	60DM (80DM)
Loc	Dortmund Brackel
Arch	Brig Jones/Maj Coleman

Schloss Georghausen
(1962)
Georghausen 8, 51789 Lindlar-Hommerich

Tel	(02207) 4938
Fax	(02207) 81230
Holes	18 L 6045 m SSS 72
V'tors	H
Fees	70DM (90DM)
Loc	30km E of Cologne

Schloss Haag (1996)
Bartelter Weg 8, 47608 Geldern

Tel	(02831) 94777
Fax	(02831) 94778
Holes	18 L 6193 m Par 73
V'tors	H or I
Fees	50DM (60DM)
Loc	60km NW of Düsseldorf
	(Route 9)
Arch	W Hardes

Schloss Myllendonk
(1965)
Myllendonkerstr 113, 41352 Korschenbroich 1

Tel	(02161) 641049
Fax	(02161) 648806
Holes	18 L 6120 m CR 71.3 SR 128
V'tors	H
Fees	€48 (€55)
Loc	Korschenbroich, 5km E of Mönchengladbach

Schmitzhof (1975)
Arsbeckerstr 160, 41844 Wegberg

Tel	(02436) 39090
Fax	(02436) 390915
Web	www.golfclubschmitzhof.de
Holes	18 L 6115 m CR 71.6 SR 132
V'tors	H
Fees	70DM (90DM)
Loc	Wegberg-Merbeck, 20km SW of Mönchengladbach

Schwarze Heide
Gahlenerstrasse 44, 46244 Bottrop-Kirchellen

Tel	(02045) 82488
Fax	(02045) 83077
Holes	18 L 6051 m SSS 72
V'tors	I H
Fees	50DM (70DM)
Loc	55km N of Düsseldorf
Arch	Peter Drecker

Siegerland (1993)
Berghäuser Weg, 57223 Kreuztal-Mittelhees

Tel	(02732) 59470
Fax	(02732) 594724
Holes	18 L 5865 m Par 72
V'tors	H
Fees	60DM (80DM)
Loc	15km N of Siegen
Arch	Spangemacher

Unna-Fröndenberg
(1985)
Schwarzer Weg 1, 58730 Fröndenberg

Tel	(02373) 70068
Fax	(02373) 70069
Web	www.gcuf.de
Holes	18 L 6177 m SSS 72
	9 hole Par 3 course
V'tors	M H (max 34)
Fees	60DM (80DM)
Loc	25km W of Dortmund
Arch	Karl Grohs

Vechta-Welpe (1989)
Welpe 2, 49377 Vechta

Tel	(04441) 5539/82168
Fax	(04441) 852480
Web	www.golfclub-vechta.de
Holes	18 L 5957 m Par 72
V'tors	H
Fees	50DM (70DM)
Loc	50km SW of Bremen
Arch	Rainer Preissmann

Vestischer GC Recklinghausen (1974)
Bockholterstr 475, 45659 Recklinghausen

Tel	(02361) 93420
Fax	(02361) 934240
Holes	18 L 6111 m SSS 72
V'tors	WD–H exc Mon–NA WE–M
Fees	80DM (100DM)
Loc	Nr Loemühle Airport, N of Recklinghausen
Arch	Donald Harradine

Wasserburg Anholt (1972)
Am Schloss 3, 46419 Isselburg Anholt

Tel	(02874) 3444
Fax	(02874) 29164
Holes	18 L 6115 m SSS 72
V'tors	WD–U WE–H
Loc	Parkhotel, Wasserburg Anholt. 15 km W of Bocholt

Westerwald (1979)
Steinebacherstr, 57629 Dreifelden

Tel	(02666) 8220
Fax	(02666) 8493
Holes	18 holes SSS 72
V'tors	H
Fees	60DM (75DM)
Loc	Hachenburg, 60km E of Bonn

Rhineland South

Bad Neuenahr G&LC
(1979)
Remagener Weg, 53474 Bad Neuenahr-Ahrweiler

Tel	(02641) 950950
Fax	(02641) 950 9595
Holes	18 L 6060 m SSS 72
V'tors	WD–H WE–H before 10am & after 4pm
Fees	80DM (100DM)
Loc	Bad Neuenahr, 40km S of Bonn
Arch	Grohs/Preismann

Bitburger Land (1994)
Zur Weilersheck 1, 54636 Wissmannsdorf

Tel	(06527) 9272-0
Fax	(06527) 9272-30
Web	www.bitgolf.de
Holes	18 L 6168 m Par 72 SR 128
V'tors	H
Fees	€35 (€45)
Loc	25km NE of Trier
Arch	Karl Grohs

Bonn-Godesberg in Wachtberg (1960)
Landgrabenweg, 53343 Wachtberg-Niederbachen

Tel	(0228) 344003
Fax	(0228) 340820
Holes	18 L 5700 m Par 71

V'tors WD–H WE–M
Fees 70DM (90DM)
Loc Niederbachem, 4km from Bad
Godesberg
Arch M Harris

Burg Overbach (1984)
Postfach 1213, 53799 Much
Tel (02245) 5550
Fax (02245) 8247
Web www.golfclub-burg-
overbach.de
Holes 18 L 6056 m SSS 72
V'tors H
Fees 60DM (80DM)
Loc Much, 45km E of Cologne,
off A4
Arch Deutsch Golf Consult

Burg Zievel (1994)
Burg Zievel, 53894 Mechernich
Tel (02256) 1651
Fax (02256) 3479
Holes 18 L 6143 m Par 72
V'tors H
Fees 30–70DM
Loc 30km S of Cologne
Arch G Knappertz

Eifel (1977)
Kölner Str, 54576 Hillesheim
Tel (06593) 1241
Fax (06593) 9421
Holes 18 L 6017 m Par 72
V'tors H–phone before play
Fees 60DM (80DM)
Loc 70km S of Cologne
Arch Grohs/Preismann

Gut Heckenhof (1993)
53783 Eitorf
Tel (02243) 83137
Fax (02243) 83426
Holes 18 L 6214 m SSS 72
V'tors H
Fees On request
Loc 40km SE of Cologne
Arch William Amick

**Internationaler GC
Bonn** (1992)
Gut Grossenbusch, 53757 St Augustin
Tel (02241) 39880
Fax (02241) 398888
Web www.golf-course-bonn.de
Holes 18 L 5927 m Par 72
V'tors U H
Fees 70DM (100DM)
Loc 6km E of Bonn

Jakobsberg (1990)
Im Tal der Loreley, 56154 Boppard
Tel (06742) 808491
Fax (06742) 808493
Web www.jakobsberg.de
Holes 18 L 5950 m Par 72 SSS 72
V'tors U
Fees 70DM (90DM)
Loc 80km N of Mainz
Arch Wolfgang Jersombek

**Mittelrheinischer Bad
Ems** (1938)
Denzerheide, 56130 Bad Ems
Tel (02603) 6541
Fax (02603) 13995
Holes 18 L 6050 m SSS 72
V'tors H
Fees 80DM (110DM)
Loc 13km E of Koblenz, nr Bad
Ems (6km)
Arch Karl Hoffmann

Nahetal (1971)
*Drei Buchen, 55583 Bad Münster
am Stein*
Tel (06708) 2145/3032
Fax (06708) 1731
Web www.golfclub-nahetal.de
Holes 18 L 6065 m Par 72 SSS 72
V'tors H
Fees 70DM (90DM)
Loc 6 km S of Bad Kreuznach.
70km SW of Frankfurt
Arch Armin Keller

Rhein Sieg (1971)
Postfach 1216, 53759 Hennef
Tel (02242) 6501
Holes 18 L 6081 m Par 72
Loc Hennef, 30km SE of Cologne

Stromberg-Schindeldorf
(1987)
*Park Village Golfanlagen, Buchenring 6,
55442 Stromberg*
Tel (06724) 93080
Fax (06724) 930818
Holes 18 L 5161 m Par 68 SSS 68
V'tors U H–booking necessary
Fees 60DM (85DM)
Loc 5km from A61 exit
Stromberg

Trier (1977)
54340 Ensch-Birkenheck
Tel (06507) 993255
Fax (06507) 993257
Holes 18 L 6069 m Par 72
V'tors H–max 36
Fees €20 (€40)
Loc Trier 20km. Koblenz 80km

Waldbrunnen (1983)
Brunnenstr 11, 53578 Windhagen
Tel (02645) 8041
Fax (02645) 8042
Holes 18 L 5787 m Par 71
V'tors U
Fees 60DM (80DM)
Loc 30km S of Bonn
Arch Donald Harradine

Wiesensee (1992)
*Am Wiesensee, 56459 Westerburg-
Stahlhofen*
Tel (02663) 991192
Fax (02663) 991193
Holes 18 L 5917 m Par 72
9 hole Par 3 course

V'tors H
Fees 80DM (90DM)
Loc 100km NW of Frankfurt.
Cologne 80KM
Arch E Bensing

Saar-Pfalz

Pfalz Neustadt (1971)
*Im Lochbusch, 67435 Neustadt-
Geinsheim*
Tel (06327) 97420
Fax (06327) 974218
Holes 18 L 6180 m CR 72.1 SR 130
V'tors U H WE–NA before 3pm
Fees 75DM (100DM)
Loc Geinsheim, 15km SE of
Neustadt towards Speyer
Arch B von Limburger

Saarbrücken (1961)
*Oberlimbergerweg, 66798 Wallerfangen-
Gisingen*
Tel (06837) 91800/1584
Fax (06837) 91801
Web www.golfclub-saarbruecken.de
Holes 18 L 6231 m SSS 73
V'tors H
Fees 80DM (100DM)
Loc B406 towards Wallerfangen.
8km N of Saarlouis
Arch Donald Harradine

Websweiler Hof (1991)
Websweiler Hof, 66424 Homburg/Saar
Tel (06841) 7777-60
Fax (06841) 7777-666
Web www.golf-saar.de
Holes 18 L 6188 m Par 72 SSS 74
V'tors U H
Fees 60DM (80DM)
Loc 35km E of Saarbrücken

**Westpfalz
Schwarzbachtal** (1988)
66509 Rieschweiler
Tel (06336) 6442
Fax (06336) 6408
Holes 18 L 5740 m Par 70
V'tors H
Loc 40km E of Saarbrücken

Woodlawn
6792 Ramstein Flugplatz
Tel (06371) 476240
Fax (06371) 42158
Web www.ramsteingolf.com
Holes 18 L 6225 yds Par 70
V'tors Military GC–visitors
restricted
Fees $16
Loc Ramstein 3km. Kaiserlautern
10km

Stuttgart & South West

Bad Liebenzell
Golfplatz 1-9, 75378 Bad Liebenzell
Tel   (07052) 9325-0
Fax   (07052) 9325-25
Holes 18 L 6113 m Par 72 SSS 72
       18 L 5853 m Par 72 SSS 71
V'tors H–max 33 WE–M
       10.30am–2pm
Fees 80DM (100DM)
Loc   35km W of Stuttgart
Arch Elger/Mühl

Bad Rappenau (1989)
Ehrenbergstrasse 25a, 74906
Bad Rappenau
Tel   (07264) 3666
Fax   (07264) 3838
Holes 18 L 6103 m SSS 72
V'tors U H
Fees 60DM (80DM)
Loc   10km NW of Heilbronn
Arch Karl Gross

Bad Salgau (1995)
Koppelweg 103, 88348 Bad Salgau
Tel   (07581) 527459
Fax   (07581) 527487
Holes 18 L 6190 m CR 71.8 SR 126
V'tors U
Fees €35 (€45)
Loc   5km SW of Bad Salgau

Baden Hills GC Rastatt (1982)
Postfach 2, 76549 Hügelsheim
Tel   (07229) 5346
Fax   (07229) 5347
Holes 18 L 5906 m Par 71
V'tors H–booking necessary WD–U
       before 5pm WE–M before
       3pm
Loc   10km W of Badeb-Baden.
       50km N of Strasbourg

Baden-Baden (1901)
Fremersbergstr 127, 76530 Baden-Baden
Tel   (07221) 23579
Fax   (07221) 23528
Holes 18 L 4282 m Par 64
V'tors U
Fees 65DM (90DM)
Loc   3km S of Baden-Baden
Arch Harry Vardon

Bodensee (1986)
Lampertsweiler 51, 88138 Weissensberg
Tel   (08389) 89190
Fax   (08389) 89191
Holes 18 L 6112 m SSS 72
V'tors H
Fees 75DM (90DM)
Loc   5km NE of Lindau/Bodensee
Arch Robert Trent Jones Sr

Freiburg (1970)
Krüttweg 1, 79199 Kirchzarten
Tel   (07661) 9847-0
Fax   (07661) 984747
Holes 18 L 5945 m CR 71.8 SR 127
V'tors H
Fees €35 (€40)
Loc   Freiburg-Kappel/Kirchzarten
Arch B von Limburger

Fürstlicher Waldsee (1998)
Hopfenweiler, 88339 Bad Waldsee
Tel   (07524) 4017 200
Fax   (07524) 4017 100
Holes 18 L 6474 m Par 72
       9 hole Par 3 course
V'tors U
Fees 18 hole: 60DM (80DM)
       9 hole: 25DM (40DM)
Loc   60km SW of Ulm (Route 30)
Arch Knauss/Himmel

Hechingen Hohenzollern (1955)
Postfach 1124, 72379 Hechingen
Tel   (07471) 6478
Holes 18 holes SSS 72
V'tors WE–M
Fees On application
Loc   Hechingen, 50km S of
       Stuttgart

Heidelberg-Lobenfeld (1968)
Biddersbacherhof, 74931 Lobbach-Lobenfeld
Tel   (06226) 952110
Fax   (06226) 952111
Holes 18 L 5989 m SSS 72
V'tors WD–H WE–M H
Fees 80DM (100DM)
Loc   20km E of Heidelberg
Arch Donald Harradine

Heilbronn-Hohenlohe (1964)
Hofgasse, 74639 Zweiflingen-Friedrichsruhe
Tel   (07941) 920810
Fax   (07941) 920819
Web www.friedrichsruhe.de
Holes 18 L 6039 m Par 72 SSS 72
V'tors H
Fees 60DM (90DM)
Loc   25km W of Heilbronn, nr
       Öhringen

Hetzenhof
Hetzenhof 7, 73547 Larch
Tel   (07172) 9180-0
Fax   (07172) 9180-30
Web www.golfclub-hetzenhof.de
Holes 18 holes Par 72 SR 131
       6 hole short course
V'tors WD-H WE-M
Fees €40
Loc   35km E of Stuttgart Airport,
       via B29 and B297

Hohenstaufen (1959)
Unter den Ramsberg, 73072 Donzdorf-Reichenbach
Tel   (07162) 27171/20050
Holes 18 L 6540 yds SSS 72
Loc   15km E of Goppingen. 45km
       E of Stuttgart

Kaiserhöhe (1995)
Im Laber 4, 74747 Ravenstein
Tel   (06297) 399
Fax   (06297) 599
Web www.gck.geoid.de
Holes 18 L 6049 m CR 71.3 SR 122
       9 hole Par 3 course
V'tors U H
Fees 60DM (80DM)
Loc   60km S of Würzburg
Arch Kurt Rossknecht

Konstanz (1965)
Langenrain, Kargegg, 78476 Allensbach
Tel   (07533) 5124
Fax   (07533) 4897
Holes 18 L 6058 m SSS 72
V'tors WD–I WE–H max 28
Loc   15km NW of Konstanz, nr
       Langenrain

Lindau-Bad Schachen (1954)
Am Schönbühl 5, 88131 Lindau
Tel   (08382) 96170
Fax   (08382) 961750
Holes 18 L 5871 m Par 71 SSS 71
Fees 80DM (100DM)
Loc   Nr Lindau, Bodensee

Markgräflerland Kandern (1984)
Feuerbacher Str 35, 79400 Kandern
Tel   (07626) 1043
Fax   (07626) 1433
Holes 18 L 6044 m Par 72 SSS 72
V'tors WD–U WE–M
Fees 90DM (120DM)
Loc   Kandern, 10km N of Lörrach.
       14km NW of Basle
Arch Grohs/Benz

Neckartal (1974)
Aldingerstr, Gebäude 975, 70806 Kornwestheim
Tel   (07141) 871319
Fax   (07141) 81716/281722
Holes 18 L 6310 m SSS 73
V'tors WD–U WE–M
Fees 60DM (70DM)
Loc   5km NE of Stuttgart, nr
       Kornwestheim
Arch B von Limburger

Nippenburg (1993)
Nippenburg 21, 71701 Schwieberdingen
Tel   (07150) 39530
Fax   (07150) 353518
Holes 18 L 5866 m Par 71
V'tors H
Fees 70DM (100DM)

Loc	16km NW of Stuttgart
Arch	Bernhard Langer

Obere Alp (1989)

Am Golfplatz 1-3, 79780 Stühlingen

Tel	(07703) 9203-0
Fax	(07703) 9203-18
Holes	18 L 6216 m SSS 72
	9 L 3664 m SSS 60
V'tors	H
Fees	18 hole:60DM (90DM)
	9 hole:45DM (60DM)
Loc	40km N of Zürich, nr Swiss border
Arch	Karl Grohs

Oberschwaben-Bad Waldsee (1968)

Hopfenweiler 2d, 88339 Bad Waldsee

Tel	(07524) 5900
Fax	(07524) 6106
Holes	18 L 5986 m CR 72.1 SR 133
V'tors	H–(max 34)
Fees	100DM (120DM)
Loc	Bad Waldsee, 60km SW of Ulm
Arch	Donald Harradine

Oeschberghof L & GC (1976)

Golfplatz 1, 78166 Donaueschingen

Tel	(0771) 84525
Fax	(0771) 84540
Holes	18 L 6580 m SSS 74
	9 L 4120 m SSS 62
V'tors	H
Fees	90DM (120DM)
Loc	Donaueschingen, 60km E of Freiburg
Arch	Deutsche Golf Consult

Owingen-Überlingen

Alte Owinger Str, 88696 Owingen

Tel	(07551) 83040
Fax	(07551) 830422
Holes	18 L 6148 m SSS 72
V'tors	H
Fees	60DM (90DM)
Loc	5km N of Überlingen, nr Lake Konstanz

Pforzheim Karlshäuser Hof

Karlshäuser Weg, 75248 Ölbronn-Dürrn

Tel	(07237) 9100
Fax	(07237) 5161
Holes	18 hole course SSS 72
V'tors	H
Fees	60DM (80DM)
Loc	6km N of Pforzheim. 30km E of Karlsruhe
Arch	Reinhold Weishaupt

Reischenhof (1987)

Industriestrasse 12, 88489 Wain

Tel	(07353) 1732
Fax	(07373) 3824
Holes	18 hole course
V'tors	M H

Fees	65DM (90DM)
Loc	30km S of Ulm
Arch	Wolfgang Jersombeck

Reutlingen-Sonnenbühl (1987)

Im Zerg, 72820 Sonnenbühl

Tel	(07128) 92660
Fax	(07128) 926692
Holes	18 L 6085 m SSS 72
V'tors	H
Fees	60DM (80DM)
Loc	40km S of Stuttgart

Rhein Badenweiler (1971)

79401 Badenweiler

Tel	(07632) 7970
Fax	(07632) 797150
Holes	18 L 6134 m SSS 72
V'tors	WD–H WE–M
Loc	16km W of Badenweiler. 30km SW of Freiburg
Arch	Donald Harradine

Rickenbach (1979)

Hennematt 20, 79736 Rickenbach

Tel	(07765) 777
Fax	(07765) 544
Holes	18 L 5544 m CR 71 SR 134
V'tors	WD/Sat–U H exc Tues/Thurs am Sun–NA before 3pm
Fees	95DM (115DM)
Loc	20km N of Bad Säckingen
Arch	Dudok van Heel/Himmel

Schloss Klingenburg-Günzburg (1978)

Schloss Klingenburg, 89343 Jettingen-Scheppach

Tel	(08225) 3030
Fax	(08225) 30350
Holes	18 L 6237 m SSS 72
V'tors	H
Fees	70DM (100DM)
Loc	40km W of Augsburg. 5km from Stuttgart-Munich motorway, exit Burgau
Arch	Harradine/Sziedat

Schloss Langenstein (1991)

Schloss Langenstein, 78359 Orsingen-Nenzingen

Tel	(07774) 50651
Fax	(07774) 50699
Web	www.schloss-langenstein.com
Holes	18 L 6341 m CR 73.3 SR 124
	9 hole course
V'tors	WD–H WE–H (restricted)
Fees	80DM (120DM)
Loc	120km S of Stuttgart. 75km NE of Zürich
Arch	Rod Whitman

Schloss Liebenstein (1982)

Postfach 27, 74380 Neckarwestheim

Tel	(07133) 9878-0
Fax	(07133) 9878-18

Holes	27 L 5890-6361 m SSS 71-73
V'tors	U
Fees	60DM (80DM)
Loc	35km N of Stuttgart
Arch	Donald Harradine

Schloss Weitenburg (1984)

Sommerhalde 11, 72181 Starzach-Sulzau

Tel	(07472) 8061
Fax	(07472) 8062
Holes	18 L 5978 m CR 71.3 SR 123
	9 hole course
V'tors	I or U
Fees	18 hole:70DM (90DM)
	9 hole:30DM (40DM)
Loc	50km SW of Stuttgart in Neckar Valley
Arch	Heinz Fehring

Steisslingen (1991)

Brunnenstr 4b, 78256 Steisslingen-Wiechs

Tel	(07738) 7196
Fax	(07738) 923297
Web	www.golfclub-steisslingen.de
Holes	18 L 6145 m Par 72
	6 hole course
V'tors	U
Fees	65DM (95DM)
Loc	30km N of Konstanz
Arch	Dave Thomas

Stuttgarter Solitude (1927)

71297 Mönsheim

Tel	(07044) 911 0410
Fax	(07044) 911 0420
Web	www.gc-stuttgart-solitude.de
Holes	18 L 6045 m Par 72
V'tors	WD–H max 28 WE–M (phone first)
Fees	80DM (100DM)
Loc	30km W of Stuttgart
Arch	B von Limburger

Ulm/Neu-Ulm (1963)

Wochenauer Hof 2, 89186 Illerrieden

Tel	(07306) 919420
Fax	(07306) 919422
Holes	18 L 6076 m SSS 72
V'tors	H
Fees	60DM (80DM)
Loc	15km S of Ulm
Arch	Deutsche Golf Consult

Greece

Afandou (1973)

Afandou, Rhodes

Tel	(0241) 51255
Holes	18 L 6060 m Par 72
V'tors	U
Loc	Afandou, 20km S of Rhodes town

For list of abbreviations see page 649

Corfu (1972)

PO Box 71, Ropa Valley, 49100 Corfu
Tel (0661) 94220
Fax (0661) 94220
Web www.corfugolfclub.com
Holes 18 L 6183 m SSS 72
V'tors U
Fees 8000–17.000dra
Loc Ermones Bay, 16km W of Corfu town
Arch Donald Harradine

Glyfada (1962)

PO Box 70116, 166-10 Glyfada, Athens
Tel (01) 894 6459
Fax (01) 894 6834
Holes 18 L 6189 m Par 72
V'tors H
Fees 11.000dra (15.000dra)
Loc 12km S of Athens
Arch Donald Harradine

Porto Carras G&CC (1979)

Porto Carras, Halkidiki
Tel (0375) 71381/71221
Holes 18 L 6086 m SSS 72
V'tors U
Loc Sithonia Peninsula, 100km SE of Thessaloniki

Hungary

Birdland G&CC (1991)

Thermal krt.10, 9740 Bükfürdö
Tel (94) 358060
Fax (94) 359000
Web www.birdland.hu
Holes 18 L 6459 m Par 72 SSS 71-75
9 hole Par 3 course
V'tors U H
Fees £33
Loc 120km SE of Vienna
Arch G Hauser

Budapest G&CC

Becsi u.5, 2024 Kisoroszi
Tel (1) 317 6025
Fax (1) 317 2749
Holes 18 L 6089 m SSS 72
V'tors U
Fees 50DM (60DM)
Loc 35km N of Budapest via Highway 11
Arch D Hajnal

Hencse National

Kossuth u.3, 7232 Hencse
Tel (82) 481245
Fax (82) 481248
Web www.hencsegc.com
Holes 18 L 6231 m Par 72
V'tors U
Fees 55DM (65DM)
Loc 20km from Kaposvar (SW Hungary)
Arch J Dudok van Heel

Old Lake

PO Box 127, 2890 Tata-Remeteségpuszta
Tel (34) 587620
Fax (34) 587623
Web www.oldlakegolf.com
Holes 18 L 5915 m Par 72
V'tors U H
Fees £17 (£27)
Loc 5km from Tata. 60km W of Budapest (M1)
Arch László Soproni

Pannonia G&CC

Alcsútdoboz, 8087 Mariavölgy
Tel (22) 594200
Fax (22) 594205
Holes 18 L 6018 m Par 72
V'tors U
Fees 50DM (100DM)
Loc Budapest 30km
Arch H-G Erhardt

St Lorence G&CC

Pellérdi ut 55, 7634 Pécs
Tel (72) 252844/252142
Fax (72) 252844/252173
Holes 18 holes Par 72
V'tors U
Loc Szentlörinc, 11km W of Pécs

Iceland

Akureyri (1935)

PO Box 317, 602 Akureyri
Tel (462) 2974
Fax (461) 1755
Holes 18 L 5783 m Par 71
V'tors U H
Fees 2000 Ikr
Loc 1km from Akureyri (N coast)
Arch Solnes/Gudmundsson

Borgarness (1973)

Hamar, 310 Borgarnes
Tel (437) 1663
Fax (437) 2063
Holes 9 L 5548 m Par 72
V'tors U
Fees 1200 Ikr
Loc 5km W of Borgarnes. 100km N of Reykjavik (W coast)

Eskifjardar (1976)

735 Eskifjördur
Holes 9 L 4418 m Par 66
Fees 1000 Ikr
Loc 3km W of Eskifjördur (E coast)

Húsavík (1967)

PO Box 23, Kötlum, 640 Húsavík
Tel (464) 1000
Fax (464) 1678
Holes 9 L 2460m Par 70
V'tors U
Fees 1000 Ikr

Loc 2km from Húsavík (N coast)
Arch Nils Skjöld

Isafjardar (1978)

PO Box 367, 400 Isafjördur
Tel (456) 5081
Fax (456) 4547
Holes 9 L 4980 m Par 70
V'tors U
Fees 1000Ikr
Loc 3km W of Isafjördur (NW coast)

Jökull (1973)

Postholf 67, 355 Olafsvík
Tel (436) 1666
Holes 9 L 4598 m Par 68
V'tors U
Fees 1000 Ikr
Loc 5km SE of Olafsvík (W coast)

Keilir (1967)

Box 148, 222 Hafnarfjördur
Tel (565) 3360
Fax (565) 2560
Holes 18 L 5449 m Par 71
9 L 2748 m Par 36
V'tors U
Fees 18 hole: 2000 Ikr 9 hole: 1000 Ikr
Loc Hafnarfjördur, 10km S of Reykjavik
Arch Hannes Thorsteinsson

Kopavogs og Gardabaejar (1994)

Postholf 214, 212 Gardabaer
Tel (565) 7373
Fax (565) 9190
Holes 18 L 5437 m Par 70
V'tors U
Fees 1700 Ikr
Loc Gardabaer, S of Reykjavik

Leynir (1965)

PO Box 9, 300 Akranes
Tel (431) 2711
Fax (431) 3711
Web www.leynir@aknet.is
Holes 18 L 5959 m Par 72
V'tors U
Fees 2000Ikr
Loc 2km from Akranes (SW coast)
Arch H Thorsteinsson

Ness-Nesklúbburinn (1964)

PO Box 66, 172 Seltjarnarnes
Tel (561) 1930
Fax (561) 1966
Holes 9 L 5374 m Par 72
V'tors U
Fees 1500 Ikr
Loc 3km W of Reykjavik

Oddafellowa (1990)

Urridavatnsdölum, 210 Gardabaer
Tel (565) 9094
Fax (565) 9074

Web www.oddur.is
Holes 18 L 5830 m Par 71
V'tors U
Fees 2500 Ikr
Loc Gardabaer, S of Reykjavík

Olafsfjardar (1968)

Skeggjabrekku, 625 Olafsfjördur
Tel (466) 2611
Fax (466) 2611
Holes 9 L 4570 m Par 66
V'tors U
Fees 1000 IkrU
Loc 60 km NW of Akureyri (N coast)

Reykjavíkur (1934)

PO Box 12068, 132 Reykjavík
Tel (587) 2211/2215
Fax (587) 2212
Holes 18 L 5963 m Par 71
      18 L 6214 m Par 72
V'tors U
Fees 1500–2600 Ikr
Loc 8km E of Reykjavík
Arch Skjold/Thorsteinsson

Saudárkróks (1970)

*Hlidarendi, Postholf 56,
550 Saudárkrókur*
Tel (453) 5075
Holes 9 L 5902 m Par 72
V'tors U
Fees 1000 Ikr
Loc 2km W of Saudárkrókur (N coast)

Sudurnesja (1964)

PO Box 112, 232 Keflavik
Tel (421) 4100
Fax (421) 5981
Holes 18 L 5861 m Par 72
V'tors U
Fees 1000–1500 Ikr
Loc N of Keflavik (SW coast). Airport 5 km

Vestmannaeyja (1938)

Postholf 168, 902 Vestmannaeyar
Tel (481) 2363
Fax (481) 2362
Holes 18 L 5322 m Par 70
V'tors U
Fees 1500 Ikr
Loc 2km W of Vestmannaeyar. Island off S coast - 20 min flight from Reykjavík

Italy

Como/Milan/ Bergamo

Ambrosiano (1994)

Cascina Bertacca, 20080 Bubbiano-Milan
Tel (0290) 840820

Fax (0290) 849365
Holes 18 L 6047 m Par 72
V'tors U
Fees 70.000L (110.000L)
Loc 25km SW of Milan
Arch Cornish/Silva

Barlassina CC (1956)

Via Privata Golf 42, 20030 Birago di Cammago (MI)
Tel (0362) 560621/2
Fax (0362) 560934
Holes 18 L 6184 m SSS 72
V'tors WD–U
Fees 110.000L (155.000L)
Loc 22km N of Milan
Arch J Morrison

Bergamo L'Albenza (1961)

Via Longoni 12, 24030 Almenno S. Bartolomeo (BG)
Tel (035) 640028
Fax (035) 643066
Holes 27 L 6129-6253 m SSS 72
V'tors U–book by fax
Fees 80.000L (120.000L)
Loc 13km NW of Bergamo. Milan 45 km
Arch Cotton/Sutton

Bogogno (1996)

Via Sant'Isidoro 1, 28010 Bogogno
Tel (0322) 863339
Fax (0322) 863798
Holes 18 L 6171 m Par 72
V'tors U
Fees 100.000L (130.000L)
Loc Bogogno, 25km N of Novara
Arch Robert von Hagge

Brianza (1996)

Cascina Cazzo, 20040 Usmate Velate
Tel (039) 682 9089
Fax (039) 682 9059
Holes 18 L 5729 m Par 71 SSS 70
V'tors U
Fees 50.000L (80.000L)
Loc 24km NE of Milan. Monza 6km
Arch Marco Croze

Carimate (1962)

Via Airoldi, 22060 Carimate
Tel (031) 790226
Fax (031) 790226
Holes 18 L 5982 m SSS 71
V'tors U H
Fees 80.000L (120.000L)
Loc 15km S of Como. 27km N of Milan
Arch Pier Mancinelli

Castelconturbia (1984)

Via Suno, 28010 Agrate Conturbia
Tel (0322) 832093
Fax (0322) 832428
Holes Red 9 L 3330 m Par 36
      Yellow 9 L 3070 m Par 36
      Blue 9 L 3210 m Par 36

V'tors WD–H WE–M H
Fees 95.000L (150.000L)
Loc 23km N of Novara. Milan 60 km
Arch Robert Trent Jones Sr

Castello di Tolcinasco (1993)

20090 Pieve Emanuele (MI)
Tel (02) 9046 7201
Holes 27 L 6253-6322 m Par 72
      9 hole Par 3 course
V'tors U
Fees 80.000L (100.000L)
Loc 12km S of Milan
Arch Arnold Palmer

Franciacorta (1986)

Via Provinciale 34b, 25040 Nigoline di Corte Franca, (Brescia)
Tel (030) 984167
Fax (030) 984393
Holes 18 L 5924 m Par 72 SSS 72
      9 hole Par 3 course
V'tors WD–U WE–NA before 2pm
Fees 70.000L (100.000L)
Loc Nigoline, 25km E of Bergamo. Autostrada A4 exit Rovato
Arch Dye/Croze

Lanzo Intelvi (1962)

22024 Lanzo Intelvi (CO)
Tel (031) 840169
Holes 9 L 2438 m SSS 66
V'tors U
Loc 32km NW of Como

Menaggio & Cadenabbia (1907)

Via Golf 12, 22010 Grandola E Uniti
Tel (0344) 32103
Fax (0344) 30780
Web www.menaggio.it
Holes 18 L 5455 m Par 70 SSS 69
V'tors WD–U H WE–H restricted
Fees 90.000L (120.000L)
Loc 5km W of Menaggio. 40km N of Como
Arch John Harris

Milano (1928)

20052 Parco di Monza (MI)
Tel (039) 303081/2/3
Fax (039) 304427
Holes 18 L 6414 m SSS 73
      9 L 2976 m SSS 36
V'tors WD–H WE–by appointment
Fees 96.000L (144.000L)
Loc 6km N of Monza. 18km NE of Milan
Arch Gannon/Blandford

Molinetto CC (1982)

SS Padana Superiore 11, 20063 Cernusco S/N (MI)
Tel (02) 9210 5128/9210 5983
Fax (02) 9210 6635
Holes 18 L 6010 m Par 71
V'tors WD–H WE–restricted
Loc Cernusco, 10km E of Milan

Monticello (1975)
Via Volta 4, 22070 Cassina Rizzardi
Tel   (031) 928055
Fax   (031) 880207
Holes 18 L 6413 m SSS 72
       18 L 6056 m SSS 72
V'tors WD–H WE–NA
Fees   80.000L (100.000L)
Loc   10km SE of Como
Arch   Jim Fazio

La Pinetina (1971)
Via al Golf 4, 22070 Carbonate (CO)
Tel   (031) 933202
Fax   (031) 890342
Holes 18 L 5708 m Par 70 SSS 70
V'tors WD–U WE–booking
       necessary
Fees   90.000L (110.000L)
Loc   12km SW of Como. Milan
       25km
Arch   Harris/ Albertini

Le Robinie (1992)
*Via per Busto Arsizio 9, 21058 Solbiate
Olona (VA)*
Tel   (039) 331 329260
Fax   (039) 331 329266
Web   www.lerobinie.com
Holes 18 L 6250 m Par 72 SSS 74
V'tors WD–U WE–H
Fees   90.000L (130.000L)
Loc   25km NW of Milan. Malpensa
       Airport 6km
Arch   Jack Nicklaus

La Rossera (1970)
Via Montebello 4, 24060 Chiuduno
Tel   (035) 838600
Fax   (035) 442 7047
Holes 9 L 2510 m SSS 68
V'tors U
Fees   45.000L (65.000L)
Loc   2km from Chiuduno. 18km
       SE of Bergamo

Le Rovedine (1978)
*Via Carlo Marx, 20090 Noverasco di
Opera (MI)*
Tel   (02) 5760 6420/5760 2730
Fax   (02) 5760 6405
Holes 18 L 6307 m SSS 72
V'tors U
Loc   4km S of Milan

Varese (1934)
*Via Vittorio Veneto 32, 21020
Luvinate (VA)*
Tel   (0332) 227394/229302
Fax   (0332) 222107
Holes 18 L 5936 m SSS 72
V'tors WD–U H
Fees   80.000L (120.000L)
Loc   5km SW of Varese
Arch   Gannon/Blandford

Vigevano (1974)
Via Chitola 49, 27029 Vigevano (PV)
Tel   (0381) 346628/346077
Fax   (0381) 346091
Holes 18 L 5678 m SSS 72

Loc   25km SE of Novara. 35km
       SW of Milan

Villa D'Este (1926)
Via Cantù 13, 22030 Montorfano (CO)
Tel   (031) 200200
Fax   (031) 200786
Holes 18 L 5787 m SSS 71
V'tors I H
Loc   Montorfano, 7km SE of Como
Arch   Peter Gannon

Zoate
20067 Zoate di Tribiano (MI)
Tel   (02) 9063 2183/9063 1861
Fax   (02) 9063 1861
Holes 18 L 6122 m Par 72
V'tors WD–U H
Fees   70.000L (100.000L)
Loc   Zoate, 17km SE of Milan
Arch   Marmori

Elba

Acquabona (1971)
57037 Portoferraio, Isola di Elba (LI)
Tel   (0565) 940066
Fax   (0565) 933410
Holes 9 L 5144 m SSS 67
V'tors U
Fees   45.000L–65.000L
Loc   5km NW of Porto Azzurro.
       6km NW of Porto Ferraio
Arch   Gianni Albertini

Emilia Romagna

Adriatic GC Cervia
(1985)
*Via Jelenia Gora No 6, 48016 Cervia-
Milano Marittima*
Tel   (0544) 992786
Fax   (0544) 993410
Holes 18 L 6246 m SSS 72
V'tors U H
Fees   85.000L (100.000L)
Loc   20km SE of Ravenna
Arch   Marco Croze

Bologna (1959)
*Via Sabattini 69, 40050 Monte San
Pietro (BO)*
Tel   (051) 969100
Fax   (051) 672 0017
Holes 18 L 6171 m SSS 72
V'tors U
Fees   80.000L (100.000L)
Loc   20km W of Bologna
Arch   Harris/Cotton

Croara (1976)
29010 Croara di Gazzola
Tel   (0523) 977105/977148
Fax   (0523) 977100
Holes 18 L 6065 m SSS 72
V'tors H
Fees   60.000L (85.000L)

Loc   16km SW of Piacenza. 84km
       SE of Milan
Arch   Buratti/Croze

Matilde di Canossa (1987)
*Via Casinazzo 1, 42100
San Bartolomeo*
Tel   (0522) 371295
Fax   (0522) 371204
Holes 18 L 6231 m SSS 72
V'tors U
Fees   60.000L (80.000L)
Loc   50km NW of Bologna
Arch   Marco Croze

Modena G&CC (1987)
*Via Castelnuovo Rangone 4, 41050
Colombaro di Formigine (MO)*
Tel   (059) 553482
Fax   (059) 553696
Holes 18 L 6423 m Par 72 SSS 74
       9 hole Par 3 course
V'tors H
Fees   70.000L (100.000L)
Loc   Formigine, 10km SW of
       Modena
Arch   Bernhard Langer

La Rocca (1985)
*Via Campi 8, 43038 Sala
Baganza (PR)*
Tel   (0521) 834037
Fax   (0521) 834575
Web   www.officeitalia.it/golflarocca
Holes 18 L 6076 m SSS 71
V'tors U
Fees   60.000L (80.000L)
Loc   8km S of Parma
Arch   Marco Croze

La Torre (1992)
Via Limisano 10, Riolo Terme (RA)
Tel   (0546) 74035
Fax   (0546) 74076
Holes 18 L 6350 m Par 72
V'tors H
Fees   40.000L (50.000L)
Loc   30km SW of Bologna
Arch   Alberto Croze

Gulf of Genoa

Degli Ulivi (1932)
Via Campo Golf 59, 18038 Sanremo
Tel   (0184) 557093
Fax   (0184) 557388
Web   www.sanremogolf.it
Holes 18 L 5203 m SSS 67
V'tors U
Fees   72.000L (114.000L)
Loc   5km N of Sanremo
Arch   Peter Gannon

Garlenda (1965)
Via Golf 7, 17033 Garlenda
Tel   (0182) 580012
Fax   (0182) 580561
Web   www.garlendagolf.it

Holes 18 L 6085 m Par 72 SSS 72
V'tors H
Fees 80.000L (130.000L)
Loc 15km N of Alassio. Genoa 90km
Arch John Harris

Marigola (1975)

Via Vallata 5, 19032 Lerici (SP)
Tel (0187) 970193
Fax (0187) 970193
Holes 9 L 2116 m Par 49
V'tors U
Loc 6km SE of La Spezia
Arch Franco Marmori

Pineta di Arenzano (1959)

Piazza del Golf 3, 16011 Arenzano (GE)
Tel (010) 911 1817
Fax (010) 911 1270
Holes 9 L 5527 m SSS 70
V'tors H
Fees 60.000L (85.000L)
Loc Arenzano Pineta, 20km W of Genoa
Arch Donald Harradine

Rapallo (1930)

Via Mameli 377, 16035 Rapallo (GE)
Tel (0185) 261777
Fax (0185) 261779
Holes 18 L 5638 m Par 70
V'tors H WE–NA before noon
Fees 80.000L (120.000L)
Loc 25km SE of Genoa. A12 motorway exit Rapallo
Arch Cabell Robinson

Versilia (1990)

Via Sipe 100, 55045 Pietrasanta (LU)
Tel (0584) 88 15 74
Fax (0584) 75 22 72
Holes 18 L 6115 m Par 72
V'tors U H
Fees 80.000L
Loc 30km N of Pisa on coast, nr Forte dei Marmi
Arch Marco Croze

Lake Garda & Dolomites

Asiago (1967)

Via Meltar 2, 36012 Asiago (VI)
Tel (0424) 462721
Fax (0424) 465133
Web www.golfasiago.it
Holes 18 L 6005 m Par 70 SSS 71
V'tors U H
Fees 80.000L (110.000L)
Loc 3km N of Asiago. 50km N of Vicenza
Arch Peter Harradine

Bogliaco (1912)

Via Golf 21, 25088 Toscolano-Maderno
Tel (0365) 643006
Fax (0365) 643006
Web www.bogliaco.com
Holes 9 L 2650 m Par 70 SSS 69
V'tors H
Fees €35 (€40)
Loc Lake Garda, 40km NE of Brescia

Ca' degli Ulivi (1988)

Via Ghiandare 2, 37010 Marciaga di Costermano (VR)
Tel (045) 725 6463/725 6485
Fax (045) 725 6876
Holes 18 L 6000 m SSS 72
9 hole course
Loc Above village of Garda. Verona Airport 35km

Campo Carlo Magno (1922)

Golf Hotel, 38084 Madonna di Campiglio (TN)
Tel (0465) 440622
Fax (0465) 440298
Holes 9 L 5148 m SSS 67
V'tors H
Fees 75.000–100.000L
Loc Madonna di Campiglio 1 km. 74km NW of Trento
Arch Henry Cotton

Folgaria (1987)

Loc Costa di Folgaria, 38064 Folgaria (TN)
Tel (0464) 720480
Fax (0464) 720480
Holes 9 L 2582 m SSS 70
V'tors H
Fees 60.000L (70.000L)
Loc 30km S of Trento, off A22
Arch Marco Croze

Gardagolf CC (1985)

Via Angelo Omodeo 2, 25080 Soiano Del Lago (BS)
Tel (0365) 674707 (Sec)
Fax (0365) 674788
Holes 18 L 6505 m SSS 74
9 L 2635 m Par 35
V'tors H
Fees 95.000L (120.000L)
Loc Lake Garda, 30 km NE of Brescia
Arch Cotton/Pennink/Steel

Karersee-Carezza

Loc Carezza 171, 39056 Welschofen-Nova Levante
Tel (0471) 612200
Fax (0471) 612200
Holes 9 L 5340 m SSS 68
V'tors H
Fees 60.000L (70.000L)
Loc 30km S of Bolzano
Arch Marco Croze

Petersberg (1987)

Unterwinkel 5, 39040 Petersberg (BZ)
Tel (0471) 615122
Fax (0471) 615229
Holes 18 L 5100 m Par 67 SSS 66
V'tors U
Fees 75.000L (95.000L)
Loc 35km SE of Bolzano, nr Nova Ponente
Arch Marco Croze

Ponte di Legno (1980)

Corso Milano 36, 25056 Ponte di Legno (BS)
Tel (0364) 900306
Fax (0364) 900555
Holes 9 L 4803 m SSS 68
V'tors U
Fees 50.000L (70.000L)
Loc 90km W of Trento, nr San Michele
Arch Caremoli

Verona (1963)

Ca' del Sale 15, 37066 Sommacampagna
Tel (045) 510060
Fax (045) 510242
Holes 18 L 6054 m SSS 72
V'tors H
Fees 100.000L (120.000L)
Loc 7km W of Verona
Arch John Harris

Naples & South

Napoli (1983)

Via Campiglione 11, 80072 Arco Felice (NA)
Tel (081) 526 4296
Holes 9 L 4776 m SSS 68
V'tors M
Loc Pozzuoli, 10 km W of Naples

Porto d'Orra (1977)

PB 102, 88063 Catanzaro Lido
Tel (0961) 791045
Fax (0961) 791444
Holes 9 L 5686 m SSS 70
V'tors U
Loc 9km N of Catanzaro Lido on coast

Riva Dei Tessali (1971)

74011 Castellaneta
Tel (099) 843 9251
Fax (099) 843 9255
Holes 18 L 5960 m SSS 71
V'tors U
Fees 60.000L
Loc 34km SW of Taranto
Arch Marco Croze

San Michele

Loc Bosco 8/9, 87022 Cetraro (CS)
Tel (0982) 91012
Fax (0982) 91430
Holes 9 L 2760 m SSS 70

V'tors U H
Fees 30.000L (35.000L)
Loc Cetraro, 50km N of Cosenza.
250km SE of Naples
Arch Piero Mancinelli

Rome & Centre

Castelgandolfo (1987)
Via Santo Spirito 13,
00040 Castelgandolfo
Tel (06) 931 2301/931 3084
Fax (06) 931 2244
Holes 18 L 6025 m SSS 72
V'tors U H Sun–restricted
Fees 60.000L (100.000L)
Loc 22km SE of Rome
Arch Robert Trent Jones

Eucalyptus (1988)
Via Cogna 5, 04011 Aprilia (Roma)
Tel (06) 927 46252
Fax (06) 926 8502
Web www.eucalyptusgolfclub.it
Holes 18 L 6310 m Par 72 SSS 73
V'tors WD–U WE–U H
Fees 50.000L (60.000L)
Loc 20km S of Rome on Aprilia-
Anzio road
Arch D'Onofrio

Fioranello
CP 96, 00134 Roma (RM)
Tel (06) 713 8080
Fax (06) 713 8212
Holes 18 L 5360 m Par 70
V'tors U
Fees 72.000L (84.000L)
Loc Santa Maria, 17km SE of
Rome
Arch David Mezzacane

Fiuggi (1928)
Superstrada Anticolana 1, 03015
Fiuggi (FR)
Tel (0775) 55250
Fax (0775) 506742
Holes 9 L 5697 m SSS 70
V'tors U
Loc 60km SE of Rome

Marco Simone (1989)
Via di Marco Simone, 00012
Guidonia (RM)
Tel (0774) 366469
Fax (0774) 366476
Holes 18 L 6317 m SSS 73
18 hole course Par 64
V'tors U
Loc 17km NE of Rome
Arch Fazio/Mezzacane

Nettuno
Via della Campana 18, 00048
Nettuno (RM)
Tel (06) 981 9419
Fax (06) 981 9419
Holes 18 L 6260 m SSS 72
V'tors U H
Fees 50.000L (70.000L)
Loc 60km S of Rome on coast
Arch Marco Croze

Olgiata (1961)
Largo Olgiata 15, 00123 Roma
Tel (06) 308 89141
Fax (06) 308 89968
Holes 18 L 6347 m SSS 73
9 L 2947 m SSS 71
V'tors U
Fees 90.000L (120.000L)
Loc 19km NW of Rome, nr La
Storta
Arch CK Cotton

Parco de' Medici
(1989)
Viale Parco de' Medici 165,
00148 Roma
Tel (06) 655 3477
Fax (06) 655 3344
Web www.sheraton.com
Holes 18 L 6303 m Par 71 SSS 73
9 L 2620 m Par 34 SSS 68
V'tors U
Fees 100.000L (120.000L)
Loc 15km SW of Rome, nr
Airport
Arch Fabio/Mezzacane/Rebecchini

Pescara (1992)
Contrado Cerreto 58, 66010
Miglianico (CH)
Tel (0871) 959566
Fax (0871) 950363
Holes 18 L 6184 m Par 72 SSS 72
V'tors U
Fees 50.000L (70.000L)
Loc S of Pescara (Adriatic coast)

Le Querce
San Martino, 01015 Sutri (VT)
Tel (0761) 68789
Fax (0761) 68142
Holes 18 L 6433 m SSS 72
V'tors U
Fees 70.000L
Loc 42km N of Rome
Arch Fazio/Mezzacane

Roma (1903)
Via Appia Nuova 716A, 00178 Roma
Tel (06) 780 3407
Fax (06) 783 46219
Holes 18 L 5854 m Par 71 SSS 70
V'tors WD–H WE–M H
Fees 70.000L (100.000L)
Loc 7km SE of Rome towards
Ciampino

Tarquinia
Loc Pian di Spille, Via degli Alina 271,
01016 Marina Velca/Tarquinia (VT)
Tel (0766) 812109
Holes 9 L 5442 m SSS 69
Loc 80km N of Rome on coast

Torvaianica
Via Enna 30, 00040 Marina di Ardea
Tel (06) 913 3250
Fax (06) 913 3592
Holes 9 L 4416 m SSS 64

V'tors H
Loc 30km S of Rome
Arch Leonardo Basili

Sardinia

Is Molas (1975)
CP 49, 09010 Pula
Tel (070) 924 1013/4
Fax (070) 924 1015
Holes 18 L 6383 m SSS 72
Fees 80.000L (100.000L)
Loc Pula, 32km S of Cagliari
Arch Cotton/Pennink/Lurie

Pevero GC Costa Smeralda (1972)
07020 Porto Cervo
Tel (0789) 96072/96210/96211
Fax (0789) 96572
Holes 18 L 6186 m SSS 72
V'tors U H
Fees 80.000–200.000L
Loc Porto Cervo, 30km N of
Olbia, on Costa Smeralda
Arch Robert Trent Jones

Sicily

Il Picciolo (1988)
Via Picciolo, 195012 Castiglione
di Sicilia
Tel (0942) 986252
Fax (0942) 986252
Holes 18 L 5810 m Par 72 SSS 71
V'tors H
Fees 80.000L (100.000L)
Loc 18km E of Taormina
Arch Rota Carcamoli

Turin & Piemonte

Alpino Di Stresa (1924)
Viale Golf Panorama 49, 28839
Vezzo (VB)
Tel (0323) 20642/20101
Fax (0323) 20642
Holes 9 L 5397 m Par 69 SSS 68
V'tors WE–U WE–restricted
Fees 18 holes–50.000L (70.000L)
9 holes–35.000L (50.000L)
Loc 7km W of Stresa. Milan 80km
Arch Peter Gannon

Biella Le Betulle (1958)
Valcarozza, 13887 Magnano (BI)
Tel (015) 679151
Fax (015) 679276
Web www.lebetulle.com
Holes 18 L 6427 m SSS 74
V'tors H
Fees 110.000L (155.000L)
Loc 17km SW of Biella
Arch John Morrison

Cervino (1955)

11021 Cervinia-Breuil (AO)
Tel   (0166) 949131
Fax   (0116) 949131
Holes 9 L 4796 m SSS 66
V'tors U
Fees   50.000L–70.000L
Loc   53km NE of Aosta
Arch   Donald Harradine

Cherasco CC (1982)

Via Fraschetta 8, 12062 Cherasco (CN)
Tel   (0172) 489772/488489
Fax   (0172) 488304
Web   www.golfcherasco.com
Holes 18 L 6041 m Par 72 SSS 72
V'tors H
Fees   65.000L (90.000L)
Loc   Cherasco, 45km S of Turin
Arch   Gianmarco Croze

Claviere (1923)

*Strada Nazionale 45, 10050
Claviere (TO)*
Tel   (0122) 878917
Holes 9 L 4650 m SSS 65
V'tors U
Loc   96km W of Turin
Arch   Luzi

Courmayeur

11013 Courmayeur (AO)
Tel   (0165) 89103
Holes 9 L 2650 m SSS 67
Loc   5km NE of Courmayeur

Cuneo (1990)

*Via degli Angeli 3, 12012 Mellana-
Bóves (CN)*
Tel   (0171) 387041
Fax   (0171) 390763
Holes 18 L 5851 m Par 71 SSS 70
V'tors U H
Fees   70.000L (90.000L)
Loc   80km S of Turin, nr Cúneo
Arch   Graham Cooke

Le Fronde (1973)

*Via Sant-Agostino 68, 10051
Avigliana (TO)*
Tel   (011) 932 8053/0540
Fax   (011) 932 0928
Holes 18 L 5976 m SSS 71
V'tors WD–U WE–H max 34
Fees   60.000L (80.000L)
Loc   Avigliana, 20km W of Turin
Arch   John Harris

I Girasoli (1991)

*Via Pralormo 315, 10022
Carmagnola (TO)*
Tel   (011) 979 5088
Fax   (011) 979 5228
Web   www.girasoligolf.it
Holes 18 L 4585 m Par 65
V'tors H
Fees   40.000L (60.000L)
Loc   25km S of Turin

Iles Borromees

*Loc Motta Rossa, 28833 Brovello
Carpugnino (VB)*
Tel   (0323) 929285/929192
Fax   (0323) 929190
Web   www.golfdesilesborromees.it
Holes 18 L 6445 m SSS 72
V'tors U
Fees   80.000L (120.000L)
Loc   5km S of Stresa. 80km NW of
       Milan
Arch   Marco Croze

Golf dei Laghi (1993)

*Via Trevisani 6, 21028 Travedona
Monate (VA)*
Tel   (0332) 978101
Fax   (0332) 977532
Holes 18 L 6400 m Par 72 SSS 73
V'tors H
Fees   60.000L (100.000L)
Loc   30km SW of Varese. 50km
       NW of Milan
Arch   Piero Mancinelli

Margara (1975)

*Via Tenuta Margara 5, 15043
Fubine (AL)*
Tel   (0131) 778555
Fax   (0131) 778772
Holes 18 L 6045 m SSS 72
V'tors U
Loc   15km NW of Alessandria

La Margherita

Strada Pralormo 29, Carmagnola (TO)
Tel   (011) 979 5113
Fax   (011) 979 5204
Holes 18 L 6339 m SSS 73
V'tors U
Fees   50.000L (80.000L)
Loc   20km S of Turin
Arch   Croze/Ferraris

Piandisole (1964)

Via Pineta 1, 28057 Premeno (NO)
Tel   (0323) 587100
Holes 9 L 2830 m SSS 67
V'tors U
Loc   Premeno, 30km N of Stresa

I Roveri (1971)

Rotta Cerbiatta 24, 10070 Fiano (TO)
Tel   (011) 923 5719/923 5667
Fax   (011) 923 5668
Holes 18 L 6218 m SSS 72
       9 L 3107 m SSS 36
V'tors WE–NA
Loc   16km NW of Turin. Caselle
       Airport 10km
Arch   Robert Trent Jones

La Serra (1970)

*Via Astigliano 42, 15048 Valenza
(AL)*
Tel   (0131) 954778
Fax   (0131) 928294
Holes 9 L 2820 m SSS 70
V'tors H
Fees   40.000L (70.000L)

Loc   4km W of Valenza. 7km N of
       Alessandria
Arch   Migliorini

Sestrieres (1932)

Piazza Agnelli 4, 10058 Sestrieres (TO)
Tel   (0122) 755170/76243
Fax   (0122) 76294
Holes 18 L 4598 m Par 67 SSS 65
V'tors U H
Fees   55.000L (80.000L)
Loc   Sestrieres, 96km W of Turin

Stupinigi (1972)

*Corso Unione Sovietica 506,
10135 Torino*
Tel   (011) 347 2640
Fax   (011) 397 8038
Holes 9 L 2175 m SSS 63
Loc   Mirafiore, Turin

Torino (1924)

Via Agnelli 40, 10070 Fiano Torinese
Tel   (011) 923 5440/923 5670
Fax   (011) 923 5886
Holes 18 L 6216 m SSS 72
       18 L 6214 m SSS 72
V'tors U H
Fees   120.000L (180.000L)
Loc   23km NW of Turin
Arch   Morrison/Croze/Cooke

Vinovo (1986)

Via Stupinigi 182, 10048 Vinovo (TO)
Tel   (011) 965 3880
Fax   (011) 962 3748
Holes 9 L 5732 m Par 72 SSS 71
V'tors U
Fees   50.000L (60.000L)
Loc   Vinovo, 3km SW of Turin
Arch   Croce/Chiaravigcio

Tuscany & Umbria

Casentino (1985)

*Via Fronzola 6, Loc Il Palazzo, 52014
Poppi (Arezzo)*
Tel   (0575) 529810
Fax   (0575) 520167
Web   www.casentino.net/golf
Holes 9 L 5550 m Par 72 SSS 69
V'tors WD–U WE–H
Fees   45.000L (55.000L)
Loc   Poppi, 50km SE of Florence
Arch   Brami/Baracchi

Castelfalfi G&CC

50050 Montaione (FI)
Tel   (0571) 698093/4
Fax   (0571) 698098
Holes 18 L 6095 m SSS 73
V'tors H
Loc   45km SW of Florence
Arch   Pier Mancinelli

Conero GC Sirolo (1987)

Via Betellico 6, 60020 Sirolo (AN)
Tel   (071) 736 0613
Fax   (071) 736 0380
Holes 18 L 6185 m Par 72
        9 hole course Par 29
V'tors U
Loc   Sirolo, 20km SE of Ancona.
        Falconara Airport 25km
Arch   Marco Croze

Cosmopolitan G&CC

(1992)
Viale Pisorno 60, 56018 Tirrenia
Tel   (050) 33633
Fax   (050) 384707
Holes 18 L 6291 m Par 73
V'tors U
Fees   60.000L
Loc   15km SW of Pisa
Arch   David Mezzacane

Firenze Ugolino

Strada Chiantigiana 3, 50015 Grassina
Tel   (055) 205 1009/203 1085
Fax   (055) 230 1141
Holes 18 L 5785 m SSS 70
V'tors U
Loc   Grassina, 9km S of Florence

Lamborghini-Panicale

(1992)
Loc Soderi 1, 06064 Panicale (PG)
Tel   (075) 837582
Fax   (075) 837582
Web   www.lamborghini.com
Holes 9 L 5872 m Par 72 SSS 70
V'tors U H
Fees   50.000L (60.000L)
Loc   30km W of Perugia, nr Lake
        Trasimeno
Arch   Ferruccio Lamborghini

Montecatini (1985)

*Via Dei Brogi 5, Loc Pievaccia, 51015
Monsummano Terme*
Tel   (0572) 62218
Fax   (0572) 617435
Holes 18 L 5932 m SSS 71
V'tors WD–U H
Loc   8km SE of Montecatini Terme.
        50 km SW of Florence (A11)
Arch   Marco Croze

Le Pavoniere (1986)

Via della Fattoria 6, 50047 Prato
Tel   (0574) 620855
Fax   (0574) 624558
Holes 18 L 6464 m Par 72 SSS 73
V'tors U
Fees   50.000L (70.000L)
Loc   Prato 10km. 25km W of
        Florence
Arch   Arnold Palmer

Perugia (1959)

06074 Santa Sabina-Ellera
Tel   (075) 517 2204
Fax   (075) 517 2370

Web   www.golfclubperugia.it
Holes 18 L 5735 m Par 70 SSS 70
V'tors U
Fees   75.000L (90.000L)
Loc   6km NW of Perugia
Arch   David Mezzacane

Poggio dei Medici (1995)

*Via S Gavino 27, 50038
Scarperia Firenze*
Tel   (055) 843 0436
Fax   (055) 843 0439
Web   www.poggiodeimedici.com
Holes 18 L 6368 m Par 73 SSS 73
V'tors U
Fees   €65 (€75)
Loc   27km from Florence
Arch   Fioravanti/Dassù

Punta Ala (1964)

Via del Golf 1, 58040 Punta Ala (GR)
Tel   (0564) 922121/922719
Fax   (0564) 920182
Web   www.puntaAla.net/golf
Holes 18 L 6168 m SSS 72
V'tors U
Fees   60.000L (100.000L)
Loc   40km NW of Grosseto. Siena
        90km. Florence 150km

Tirrenia (1968)

Viale San Guido, 56018 Tirrenia (PI)
Tel   (050) 37518
Fax   (050) 33286
Holes 9 L 3065 m SSS 72
Loc   15km SW of Pisa on coast

Venice & North East

Albarella

Isola di Albarella, 45010 Rosolina (RO)
Tel   (0426) 330124
Fax   (0426) 330628
Holes 18 L 6100 m SSS 72
V'tors H
Fees   80.000L (100.000L)
Loc   80km S of Venice
Arch   Harris/Croze

Ca' della Nave (1986)

Piazza Vittoria 14, 30030 Martellago
Tel   (041) 540 1555
Fax   (041) 540 1926
Holes 18 L 6380 m SSS 73
        9 L 1240 m Par 28
V'tors H
Loc   Martellago, 12km NW of
        Venice
Arch   Arnold Palmer

Cansiglio (1956)

CP 152, 31029 Vittorio Veneto
Tel   (0438) 585398
Fax   (0438) 585398
Holes 18 L 6007 m SSS 71
V'tors WD–U WE–H
Fees   70.000L (90.000L)

Loc   21km NE of Vittorio Veneto.
        80km NE of Venice
Arch   Trent Jones/Croze

Colli Berici (1986)

*Strada Monti Comunali, 36040
Brendola (VI)*
Tel   (0444) 601780
Fax   (0444) 400777
Holes 18 L 5798 m SSS 71
V'tors U
Fees   80.000L (100.000L)
Loc   Vicenza 10km. Venice 70km
Arch   Marco Croze

Frassanelle (1990)

35030 Frassanelle di Rovolon (PD)
Tel   (049) 991 0722
Fax   (049) 991 0722
Holes 18 L 6180 m SSS 72
V'tors H
Fees   80.000L (100.000L)
Loc   20km S of Padova, nr Via dei
        Colli
Arch   Marco Croze

Lignano

*Via Bonifica 3, 33054
Lignano Sabbiadoro*
Tel   (0431) 428025
Fax   (0431) 423230
Holes 18 L 6280 m SSS 72
V'tors H
Fees   60.000L (80.000L)
Loc   90km E of Venice on coast
Arch   Marco Croze

La Montecchia (1989)

*Via Montecchia 12, 35030
Selvazzano (PD)*
Tel   (049) 805 5550
Fax   (049) 805 5737
Holes 18 L 6318 m SSS 73
        9 L 3012 m Par 36
V'tors U H
Fees   100.000L (110.000L)
Loc   8km W of Padova. 40km W of
        Venice
Arch   T Macauley

Padova (1966)

35050 Valsanzibio di Galzigano
Tel   (049) 913 0078
Fax   (049) 913 1193
Holes 18 L 6053 m SSS 72
V'tors U
Loc   Valsanzibio, 20km S of Padua

San Floriano-Gorizia

(1987)
*Castello di San Floriano, 34070 San
Floriano del Collio (GO)*
Tel   (0481) 884252/884234
Fax   (0481) 884252/884052
Holes 9 L 3810 m Par 62
V'tors U
Fees   50.000L
Loc   6km NW of Gorizia. 50km SE
        of Udine, nr Slovenian border
Arch   Pellicciari

Trieste (1954)
Via Padriciano 80, 34012 Trieste
Tel   (040) 226159/227062
Fax   (040) 226159
Holes   9 L 5826 m Par 71
Loc   Padriciano, 7km E of Trieste

Udine (1971)
Via dei Fagi 1, Località Villaverde,
33034 Fagagna (UD)
Tel   (0432) 800418
Fax   (0432) 800418
Holes   9 L 2944 m Par 72
V'tors H
Loc   15km NW of Udine
Arch   Marco Croze

Venezia (1928)
Via del Forte, 30011 Alberoni (Venezia)
Tel   (041) 731015/731333
Fax   (041) 731339
Holes   18 L 6199 m SSS 72
V'tors U H
Fees   100.000L (120.000L)
Loc   Venice Lido
Arch   Cruickshank/Cotton

Villa Condulmer (1960)
Via della Croce 3, 31021 Zerman di
Mogliano Veneto
Tel   (041) 457062
Fax   (041) 457202
Holes   18 L 5995 m SSS 71
        9 hole short course
V'tors H
Fees   80.000L (Sun–100.000L)
Loc   Mogliano Veneto, 17km N of
        Venice
Arch   Harris/Croze

Luxembourg

Christnach (1993)
Am Lahr, 7641 Christnach
Tel   87 83 83
Fax   87 95 64
Web   www.golfclubchristnach.lu
Holes   9 hole course
V'tors Greencard
Fees   300fr (1200fr)
Loc   25km N of Luxembourg city

Clervaux (1992)
Mecherweg, 9748 Eselborn
Tel   92 93 95
Fax   92 94 51
Holes   18 L 6144 m Par 72
V'tors H
Fees   1050fl (1300fl)
Loc   3km from Clervaux, North
        Luxembourg

Gaichel
Rue de Eischen, 8469 Gaichel
Tel   39 71 08
Fax   39 00 75
Holes   9 L 5155 m Par 70
V'tors U H

Fees   700fr (900fr)
Loc   10km W of Mersch on Belgian
        border

**Grand-Ducal de
Luxembourg** (1936)
1 Route de Trèves, 2633 Senningerberg
Tel   34 00 90-1
Fax   34 83 91
Holes   18 L 5765 m SSS 71
V'tors H
Fees   1800fr (2200fr)
Loc   7km N of Luxembourg
Arch   Maj Simpson

**Kikuoka CC Chant
Val** (1991)
Scheierhaff, 5412 Canach
Tel   35 61 35
Fax   35 74 50
Holes   18 L 6404 m SSS 74
V'tors H
Fees   1400fr–2060fr (2575fr)
Loc   Canach, 15km E of
        Luxembourg City
Arch   Iwao Uematsu

Luxembourg Belenhaff
(1993)
Domaine de Belenhaff, 6141 Junglinster
Tel   78 00 68-1
Fax   78 71 28
Holes   18 L 6120 m Par 72
V'tors H or Green card
Fees   1750fl (2100fl)
Loc   17km NE of Luxembourg, nr
        La Rochette

Malta

Royal Malta (1888)
Marsa LQA 06, Malta
Tel   (356) 23 93 02/24 47 14
Fax   (356) 22 70 20
Holes   18 L 5020 m SSS 67
V'tors U exc Thurs–NA before 11am
        Sat–NA before noon
Fees   £M12–£M15
Loc   Marsa, 3 miles from Valetta

Netherlands

Amsterdam &
Noord Holland

**Amsterdam Old
Course** (1990)
Zwarte Laantje 4, 1099 CE Amsterdam
Tel   (020) 694 3650
Fax   (020) 663 4621

Holes   9 L 5264 m SSS 68
V'tors WE–H
Fees   90fl
Loc   5km SE of Amsterdam

Amsterdamse (1934)
Bauduinlaan 35, 1047 HK Amsterdam
Tel   (020) 497 7866
Fax   (020) 497 5966
Holes   18 L 6124 m CR 73.1
V'tors WD–H WE–M
Fees   40–125fl
Loc   10km W of Amsterdam
Arch   Rolin/Jol

Burg Purmerend (1989)
Westerweg 60, 1445 AD Purmerend
Tel   (0299) 689160
Fax   (0299) 647081
Holes   18 L 5994 m SSS 73
        9 hole course
V'tors H
Fees   90–110fl
Loc   16km N of Amsterdam
Arch   Tom McAuley

Haarlemmermeersche
Spieringweg 745, 2141 ED Cruquius
Tel   (023) 558 9000
Fax   (023) 558 9009
Holes   18 L 5747 m Par 73 CR 70
        9 hole short course
V'tors H
Fees   70fl (85fl)
Loc   Haarlemmermeer, W of
        Amsterdam
Arch   O'Connor Jr/Rijks

Heemskerkse (1998)
Communicatieweg 18, 1967
PR Heemskerk
Tel   (0251) 250088
Fax   (0251) 241627
Holes   18 L 6167 m Par 72
V'tors WD–U WE–M
Fees   80fl
Loc   25km NW of Amsterdam

Kennemer G&CC (1910)
Kennemerweg 78, 2042 XT Zandvoort
Tel   (023) 571 2836/8456
Fax   (023) 571 9520
Holes   27 holes CR 71.5-73.2
        Van Hengel 9 L 2951 m
        Pennink 9 L 2916 m
        Colt 9 L 2942 m
V'tors H WE–NA before 3pm
Fees   125fl
Loc   Zandvoort, 6km W of
        Haarlem
Arch   Colt/Pennink

De Noordhollandse
(1982)
Sluispolderweg 6, 1817 BM Alkmaar
Tel   (072) 515 6807
Fax   (072) 520 9918
Holes   18 L 5865 m CR 70.6
V'tors H
Fees   85fl (110fl)

Loc 2km N of Alkmaar
Arch Ryks/Dudok van Heel

Olympus (1973)
Abcouderstraatweg 46, 1105 AA
Amsterdam Zuid-Oost
Tel (0294) 285373
Fax (0294) 286347
Holes 18 L 5926 m SSS 71
V'tors U–phone first
Fees 60fl
Loc SE of Amsterdam, nr A2 and
AMC Hospital
Arch Dudok van Heel/Jol

Spaarnwoude (1977)
Het Hoge Land 2, 1981 LT Velsen-Zuid
Tel (023) 538 2708
Fax (023) 538 7274
Holes 18 L 5668 m Par 71
9 L 2981 m Par 36
V'tors H
Fees 45fl
Loc 14km W of Amsterdam. 10km
NE of Haarlem
Arch Pennink/Jol

Waterlandse (1990)
Buikslotermeerdijk 141, 1027
AC Amsterdam
Tel (020) 632 5650
Fax (0200 634 3506
Holes 18 L 5156 m Par 71
Fees 50fl
Loc 10km N of Amsterdam

Zaanse (1988)
Zuiderweg 68, 1456 NH Wijdewormer
Tel (0299) 479123
Fax (0299) 479123
Web www.zaansegolfclub.com
Holes 9 L 5282 m Par 70
V'tors WD–H WE–M
Fees 85fl (95fl)
Loc 15km NE of Amsterdam
Arch Gerard Jol

Breda &
South West

Brugse Vaart (1993)
Brugse Vaart 10, 4501 NE Oostburg
Tel (0117) 453410
Fax (0117) 455511
Holes 18 L 6305 m SSS 72
V'tors U
Fees 55fl (65fl)
Loc 15km N of Bruges, nr
Knokke
Arch Devos/Bauwens

Domburgsche (1914)
Schelpweg 26, 4357 BP Domburg
Tel (0118) 586106
Fax (0118) 586109
Holes 9 L 5402 m SSS 69

V'tors H
Fees 80fl (90fl)
Loc 15km NW of Middelburg

Efteling (1994)
Veldstraat 6, 5176 NB Kaatsheuvel
Tel (0416) 288399
Fax (0416) 288439
Web www.efteling.com
Holes 18 L 5896 m Par 72
V'tors H
Fees 90fl (110fl)
Loc 20km NE of Breda

Grevelingenhout (1988)
Oudendijk 3, 4311 NA Bruinisse
Tel (0111) 482650
Fax (0111) 481566
Holes 18 L 5951 m CR 70.7
9 hole Par 3 course
V'tors WD–U H WE–NA
Fees 75fl (95fl)
Loc 55km SW of Rotterdam
Arch Donald Harradine

Oosterhoutse (1985)
Dukaatstraat 21, 4903 RN Oosterhout
Tel (0162) 458759
Fax (0162) 433285
Web www.ogcgolf.nl
Holes 18 L 6128 m CR 72 SR 127
V'tors WD–H WE–M
Fees 75fl
Loc 10km NE of Breda
Arch J Dudok van Heel

Princenbosch (1991)
Bavelseweg 153, 5126 NM Gilze
Tel (0161) 431811
Holes 18 L 5542 m Par 70
V'tors H–max 28
Fees 60fl
Loc 10km SW of Breda

Reymerswael (1986)
Grensweg 21, 4411 ST Rilland Bath
Tel (0113) 551265
Fax (0113) 551264
Holes 18 L 5986 m CR 71.4
V'tors H
Fees 45fl (55fl)
Loc 20km W of Bergen op Zoom.
50km W of Breda, off A58
Arch J Dudok van Heel

Toxandria (1928)
Veenstraat 89, 5124 NC Molenschot
Tel (0161) 411200
Fax (0161) 411715
Web www.Toxandria.nl
Holes 18 L 5974 m SSS 71
V'tors WD–I Phone first
Fees 110fl (130fl)
Loc 8km E of Breda
Arch Morrison/Dudok van Heel

De Woeste Kop (1986)
Justaasweg 4, 4571 NB Axel
Tel (0115) 564467/564831 (Pro)
Fax (0115) 564851

Holes 9 L 5424 m SSS 69
V'tors U
Fees 45fl (65fl)
Loc 45km W of Antwerp
Arch Paneels/Bosch

Wouwse Plantage (1981)
Zoomvlietweg 66, 4624 RP Bergen
op Zoom
Tel (0165) 377100
Fax (0165) 377101
Holes 18 L 5909 m Par 72
V'tors H WE–M
Fees 70fl
Loc 10km E of Bergen-op-Zoom,
nr Roosendaal
Arch Pennink/Rolin

East Central

Breuninkhof
Bussloselaan 6, 7383 RP Bussloo
Tel (0571) 261955
Fax (0571) 262089
Holes 9 L 6178 m SSS 72
V'tors H
Fees 55fl (65fl)
Loc 100km E of Amsterdam
Arch Eschauzier

Edese (1978)
Papendallaan 22, 6816 VD Arnhem
Tel (026) 482 1985
Fax (026) 482 1348
Holes 18 L 5740 m SSS 70
V'tors H
Fees 60fl (80fl)
Loc National Sportcentrum
Papendal. NW of Arnhem,
towards Ede
Arch Pennink/Dudok van Heel

De Graafschap (1987)
Sluitdijk 4, 7241 RR Lochem
Tel (0573) 254323
Fax (0573) 258450
Web www.lochemsegolfclub.nl
Holes 18 L 6059 m CR 71.6
V'tors H–booking necessary
Fees 90fl (100fl)
Loc Lochem, 35km NW of
Arnhem

Hattemse G&CC (1930)
Veenwal 11, 8051 AS Hattem
Tel (038) 444 1909
Holes 9 L 5808 yds SSS 68
V'tors WD–H WE–M+H
Fees 40fl (50fl)
Loc Hattem, 5km S of Zwolle
Arch Del Court van Krimpen

Keppelse (1926)
Burg Kehrerstraat 52, 7002
LD Doetinchem
Tel (0314) 343662
Fax (0314) 366523
Holes 9 L 5360 m Par 70

For list of abbreviations see page 649

V'tors H
Fees €35 (€40)
Loc Laag-Keppel, 25km E of
Arnhem
Arch JP Eschauzier

De Koepel (1983)
Postbox 88, 7640 AB Wierden
Tel (0546) 576150/574070
Fax (0546) 578109
Holes 9 L 2863 m SSS 70
V'tors WE–H
Fees 50fl (60fl)
Loc 7km W of Almelo
Arch F Pennink

Nunspeetse G&CC (1987)
Public
Plesmanlaan 30, 8072 PT Nunspeet
Tel (0341) 255255
Fax (0341) 255285
Web www.nunspeetsegolf.nl
Holes 27 L 6100 m Par 72
V'tors U
Fees €45 (€50)
Loc Nunspeet, 80km E of
Amsterdam
Arch Paul Rolin

Rosendaelsche (1895)
Apeldoornseweg 450, 6816 SN Arnhem
Tel (026) 442 1438
Fax (026) 351 1196
Holes 18 L 6057 m CR 72.3 SR 132
V'tors WD–H WE–NA
Fees 100fl
Loc 5km N of Arnhem on Route
N50
Arch Frank Pennink

Sallandsche De Hoek
(1934)
PO Box 24, 7430 AA Diepenveen
Tel (0570) 593269
Fax (0570) 590102
Holes 18 L 5889 m SSS 71
V'tors WD–H WE–M H
Fees 100fl
Loc 6km N of Deventer
Arch Pennink/Steel

Sybrook (1992)
Veendijk 100, 7525 PZ Enschede
Tel (0541) 530331
Fax (0541) 531690
Holes 18 L 5878 m Par 71
V'tors WD–H WE–M
Fees 80fl
Loc 10km N of Enschede
Arch Rolin/Rijks

Twentsche (1926)
*Almelosestraat 17, 7495 TG
Ambt Delden*
Tel (074) 384 1167
Fax (074) 384 1067
Web www.twentschegolfclub.nl
Holes 18 L 6178 m SSS 72
V'tors H
Fees 95fl (100fl)

Loc 4km N of Delden
Arch TJ McAuley

Veluwse (1957)
Nr 57, 7346 AC Hoog Soeren
Tel (055) 519 1275
Fax (055) 519 1275
Holes 9 L 6264 yds SSS 70
V'tors WD–U WD–H
Fees 60fl (70fl)
Loc 5km W of Apeldoorn

Welderen (1994)
Grote Molenstraat 173, 6661 NH Elst
Tel (0481) 376591
Fax (0481) 377055
Holes 18 L 6015 m Par 72
Fees 50fl (60fl)
Loc Elst, S of Arnhem

Eindhoven &
South East

De Berendonck (1985)
Public
*Weg Door de Berendonck 40, 6603
LP Wijchen*
Tel (024) 642 0039
Fax (024) 641 1254
Holes 18 L 5671 m Par 71 SSS 70
V'tors WE–restricted
Fees 55fl (65fl)
Loc 5km SW of Nijmegen
Arch J Dudok van Heel

Best G&CC
Golflaan 1, 5683 RZ Best
Tel (0499) 391443
Fax (0499) 393221
Holes 18 L 6079 m CR 71.7 SR 131
V'tors H
Fees €41 (€50)
Loc Best, 5km NW of Eindhoven
Arch J Dudok van Heel

Crossmoor G&CC (1986)
Laurabosweg 8, 6006 VR Weert
Tel (0495) 518438
Fax (0495) 518709
Holes 18 L 6043 m Par 72
9 hole Par 3 course
V'tors H
Fees 80fl (100fl)
Loc Weert/Altweertheide, 30km
SE of Eindhoven
Arch J Dudok van Heel

De Dommel (1928)
*Zegenwerp 12, 5271 NC
St Michielsgestel*
Tel (07355) 19168
Fax (07355) 19168
Holes 18 L 5607 m SSS 69
V'tors WD–H WE–NA
Fees 75fl (90fl)
Loc 10km S of Hertogenbosch
Arch Colt/Steel

Eindhovensche Golf
(1930)
*Eindhovenseweg 300, 5553
VB Valkenswaard*
Tel (040) 201 4816
Fax (040) 207 6177
Holes 18 L 5918 m SSS 71
V'tors H
Fees 110fl (110fl)
Loc 8km S of Eindhoven
Arch HS Colt

Geijsteren G&CC
(1974)
Het Spekt 2, 5862 AZ Geijsteren
Tel (0478) 531809/532592
Fax (0478) 532963
Holes 18 L 6090 m Par 72
V'tors WD–H WE–M
Fees 80fl (100fl)
Loc Off A73 Junction 9, N270 to
Wanssum. 25km N of Venlo
Arch Pennink/Steel

Gendersteyn (1994)
Locht 140, 5504 RP Veldhoven
Tel (040) 253 4444
Fax (040) 254 9747
Holes 18 L 5770 m Par 72
Fees 65fl (80fl)
Loc 10km SW of Eindhoven

Havelte (1977)
*Postbus 29, Kolonieweg 2, 7970
AA Havelte*
Tel (0521) 342200
Fax (0521) 343134
Holes 18 L 6243 m Par 72
Fees 65fl (75fl)
Loc 30km SW of Assen (N371)

Haviksoord (1976)
*Maarheezerweg Nrd 11, 5595 XG
Leende (NB)*
Tel (040) 206 1818
Fax (040) 206 2761
Holes 9 L 5948 m CR 71.1 SR 136
V'tors H
Fees 55fl (65fl)
Loc 10km S of Eindhoven

Herkenbosch (1991)
Stationsweg 100, 6075 CD Herkenbosch
Tel (0475) 529529
Fax (0475) 533580
Holes 18 L 6307 m Par 72
V'tors U
Fees 100fl (120fl)
Loc 20km S of Venlo, nr German
border

Het Rijk van Nijmegen
(1985)
Postweg 17, 6561 KJ Groesbeek
Tel (024) 397 6644
Fax (024) 397 6942
Web www.golfbaanhetrijkvan
nijmegen.nl

Holes 18 L 6010 m CR 70.7
18 L 5717 m CR 69.1
V'tors H
Fees 70fl (85fl)
Loc 5km E of Nijmegen
Arch Paul Rolin

De Peelse Golf (1991)
Maasduinenweg 1, 5977 NP Eversoord-Sevenum
Tel (077) 467 8030
Fax (077) 467 8031
Holes 18 L 6047 m Par 72
V'tors U H
Fees €35 (€40)
Loc 20km W of Venlo
Arch Alan Rijks

De Schoot (1973)
Schootsedijk 18, 5491 TD Sint Oedenrode
Tel (04134) 73011
Fax (04134) 71358
Holes 9 L 2886 m Par 72
V'tors U
Fees 60fl (70fl)
Loc 20km N of Eindhoven
Arch A Rijks

Tongelreep G&CC (1984)
Charles Roelslaan 15, 5644 ZX Eindhoven
Tel (040) 252 0962
Fax (040) 293 2238
Holes 9 L 5345 m CR 68.4 SR 116
V'tors WD–H WE–H by introduction only
Fees €27.50
Loc Eindhoven
Arch J van Rooy

Welschap (1993)
Welschapsedijk 164, 5657 BB Eindhoven
Tel (040) 251 5797
Fax (040) 252 9297
Holes 18 L 5282 m Par 70
Fees 60fl (70fl)
Loc Eindhoven

Limburg Province

Brunssummerheide (1985)
Rimburgerweg 50, Brunssum
Tel (045) 527 0968
Fax (045) 527 3939
Holes 27 L 5933 m Par 72
9 hole Par 3 course
V'tors U H
Fees 80fl (100fl)
Loc 25km NE of Maastricht

Hoenshuis G&CC (1987)
Hoensweg 17, 6367 GN Voerendaal
Tel (045) 575 3300

Fax (045) 575 0900
Holes 18 L 6074 m CR 71.2
V'tors WE–NA 10am–2pm
Fees 65fl (95fl)
Loc Limburg, 10km NE of Maastricht
Arch Paul Rolin

De Zuid Limburgse G&CC (1956)
Dalbissenweg 22, 6281 NC Mechelen
Tel (043) 455 1397/1254
Fax (043) 455 1576
Holes 18 L 5924 m Par 71
V'tors WD–U WE–H
Fees 75fl (95fl)
Loc Mechelen, 25km SE of Maastricht
Arch Hawtree/Snelder/Rolin

North

Gelpenberg (1970)
Gebbeveenweg 1, 7854 TD Aalden
Tel (0591) 371929
Fax (0591) 372422
Holes 18 L 6031 m Par 71
V'tors H
Fees 65fl (75fl)
Loc 16km W of Emmen
Arch Pennink/Steel

Holthuizen (1985)
Oosteinde 7a, 9301 ZP Roden
Tel (050) 501 5103
Fax (050) 501 3685
Holes 9 L 6079 m SSS 72
V'tors H
Fees 70fl (80fl)
Loc 10km S of Groningen
Arch Rijks/Eschauzier

Lauswolt G&CC (1964)
Van Harinxmaweg 8A, PO Box 36, 9244 ZN Beetsterzwaag
Tel (0512) 383590/382594
Fax (0512) 383739
Holes 18 L 6087 m CR 71.5
V'tors H
Fees 110fl (150fl)
Loc Beetsterzwaag, 5km S of Drachten
Arch Pennink/Steel

Noord Nederlandse G&CC (1950)
Pollselaan 5, 9756 CJ Glimmen
Tel (050) 406 2004
Fax (050) 406 1922
Web www.nngcc.nl
Holes 18 L 5755 m CR 70.2
V'tors H
Fees 80fl (100fl)
Loc 12km S of Groningen, off A28

De Semslanden (1986)
Nieuwe Dijk 1, 9514 BX Gasselternijveen
Tel (0599) 564661/565531

Fax (0599) 565594
Holes 18 L 5973 m CR 127
V'tors H
Fees 60fl (70fl)
Loc 25km E of Assen
Arch Eschauzier/Thate/Jol

Vegilinbosschen
Legemeersterweg 18, 8527 DS Legemeer
Tel (0513) 499466
Fax (0513) 499777
Holes 18 L 5765 m SSS 71
V'tors H
Fees 80fl (90fl)
Loc 120km NE of Amsterdam
Arch Allen Rijks

Rotterdam & The Hague

Broekpolder (1981)
Watersportweg 100, 3138 HD Vlaardingen
Tel (010) 249 5566,
(010) 249 5555/249 5577
Fax (010) 249 5579
Holes 18 L 6048 m SSS 72
V'tors H
Fees 75–100fl (100–125fl)
Loc 15km W of Rotterdam, off A20
Arch Frank Pennink

Capelle a/d IJssel (1977)
Gravenweg 311, 2905 LB Capelle a/d IJssel
Tel (010) 442 2485
Fax (010) 284 0606
Holes 18 L 5214 m SSS 68
V'tors WD–U WE–M
Fees 85fl
Loc 5km S of Rotterdam
Arch Donald Harradine

Cromstrijen (1989)
Veerweg 26, 3281 LX Numansdorp
Tel (0186) 654455
Fax (0186) 654681
Holes 18 L 6099 m Par 72
9 L 3800 m Par 62
V'tors WD–U H WE–M H
Fees 105fl (120fl)
Loc 30km S of Rotterdam (A29)
Arch Tom McAuley

De Hooge Bergsche (1989)
Rottebandreef 40, 2661 JK Bergschenhoek
Tel (010) 522 0052/522 0703
Fax (010) 521 9350
Web www.rottebergen.nl
Holes 18 L 5370 m Par 71 SR 112
V'tors U
Fees 80fl (100fl)
Loc Bergschenhoek, 2km NE of Rotterdam
Arch Gerard Jol

Koninklijke Haagsche G&CC (1893)

Groot Haesebroekeseweg 22, 2243 EC Wassenaar
Tel   (070) 517 9607
Fax   (070) 514 0171
Holes 18 L 5674 m Par 71 SR 129
V'tors WD–H (max 24) WE–M
Fees   180fl
Loc   6km N of The Hague
Arch   Allison/Colt

Kralingen

Kralingseweg 200, 3062 CG Rotterdam
Tel   (010) 452 2283
Holes 9 L 5220 yds CR 66.6
V'tors H
Fees   50fl (65fl)
Loc   5km from centre of Rotterdam
Arch   Copijn/Cotton

Leidschendamse Leeuwenbergh (1988)

Elzenlaan 31, 2267 AT Leidschendam
Tel   (070) 395 4556
Fax   (070) 399 8615
Holes 18 L 5461 m Par 70
Fees   75fl (95fl)
Loc   E side of The Hague

De Merwelanden (1985)

Public
Golfbaan Crayestein, Baanhoekweg 50, 3313 LP Dordrecht
Tel   (078) 621 1221
Fax   (078) 616 1036
Holes 18 L 5722 m Par 71
V'tors U
Fees   50fl (70fl)
Loc   20km SE of Rotterdam
Arch   H & C Kuijsters

Noordwijkse (1915)

Randweg 25, PO Box 70, 2200 AB Noordwijk
Tel   (0252) 373761
Fax   (0252) 370044
Holes 18 L 5879 m CR 71.9
V'tors WD–H before noon and after 3pm
Fees   125fl
Loc   5km N of Noordwijk. 15 km NW of Leiden
Arch   Frank Pennink

Oude Maas (1975)

Veerweg 2a, 3161 EX Rhoon
Tel   (010) 501 5135
Fax   (010) 501 5604
Web   www.golfcluboudemaas.nl
Holes 18 L 5471 m Par 71
V'tors H
Fees   €40 (€45)
Loc   Rhoon, 10km S of Rotterdam via A15
Arch   Pennink/Jol/Rijks

Rijswijkse (1987)

Delftweg 58, 2289 AL Rijswijk
Tel   (070) 395 4864
Fax   (070) 399 5040

Holes 18 L 5863 m Par 71 CR 70.2
V'tors H
Fees   85fl (110fl)
Loc   5km SE of The Hague
Arch   Steel/Rijks

Wassenaarse Rozenstein (1984)

Dr Mansveltkade 1, 2242 TZ Wassenaar
Tel   (070) 511 7846
Fax   (070) 511 9302
Web   www.rozenstein.nl
Holes 18 L 5820 m SSS 70
V'tors H
Fees   €50 (€60)
Loc   14km NE of The Hague
Arch   Dudok van Heel/Jol

Westerpark Zoetermeer (1985)

Heuvelweg 3, 2716 DZ Zoetermeer
Tel   (079) 351 7283
Fax   (079) 352 1335
Holes 18 L 5891 m Par 71
Fees   70fl (80fl)
Loc   10km E of The Hague (A12)

Zeegersloot (1984)

Kromme Aarweg 5, PO Box 190, 2400 AD Alphen a/d Rijn
Tel   (0172) 474567
Fax   (0172) 494660
Holes 18 L 5793 m SSS 70
          9 hole Par 3 course
V'tors U H
Fees   18 hole:70fl (90fl)
          9 hole:30fl (40fl)
Loc   Alphen, 15km N of Gouda. 20km S of Amsterdam
Arch   Gerard Jol

Utrecht & Hilversum

Almeerderhout (1986)

Watersnipweg 19-21, 1341 AA Almere
Tel   (036) 538 4444
Fax   (036) 538 4435
Holes 27 L 6004-6046 m CR 71.9-72.2
          9 hole Par 3 course
V'tors WD–U WE–M (Max h'cap 28)
Fees   55fl (65fl)
Loc   30km N of Hilversum
Arch   Dudok van Heel/Ryks

Anderstein

Woudenbergseweg 13a, 3953 ME Maarsbergen
Tel   (0343) 431330
Fax   (0343) 432062
Holes 18 L 6048 m CR 72
V'tors WD–U WE–M only
Fees   80–110fl
Loc   20km E of Utrecht
Arch   Jol/Dudok van Heel

De Batouwe (1990)

Oost Kanaalweg 1, 4011 LA Zoelen
Tel   (0344) 624370
Fax   (0344) 613096
Holes 18 L 5717 m Par 72 SSS 70
          9 hole Par 3 course
V'tors U H–booking necessary
Fees   95fl (125fl)
Loc   Tiel, 25km SE of Utrecht
Arch   Alan Rijks

Flevoland (1979)

Bosweg 98, 8231 DZ Lelystad
Tel   (0320) 230077
Fax   (0320) 230932
Holes 18 L 5836 m Par 71
V'tors WD–U H WE–M+H
Fees   60fl (75fl)
Loc   Island of Flevoland. 1km NW of Lelystad. 45km N of Hilversum
Arch   JS Eschauzier

De Haar (1974)

PO Box 104, Parkweg 5, 3450 AC Vleuten
Tel   (030) 677 2860
Fax   (030) 677 3903
Holes 9 L 6650 yds SSS 71
V'tors WD–H WE–NA
Fees   120fl (175fl)
Loc   10km NW of Utrecht
Arch   F Pennink

Hilversumsche (1910)

Soestdijkerstraatweg 172, 1213 XJ Hilversum
Tel   (035) 685 7060
Fax   (035) 685 3813
Holes 18 L 6408 m Par 72
V'tors Phone booking necessary
Fees   100fl (125fl)
Loc   3km E of Hilversum, nr Baarn
Arch   Burrows/Colt

De Hoge Kleij (1985)

Appelweg 4, 3832 RK Leusden
Tel   (033) 461 6944
Fax   (033) 465 2921
Holes 18 L 6046 m SSS 72
V'tors WD–H
Fees   135fl
Loc   1km SE of Amersfoort 20km NE of Utrecht via A28
Arch   Donald Steel

Nieuwegeinse (1985)

Postbus 486, 3437 AL Nieuwegein
Tel   (030) 604 2192/0769
Fax   (030) 604 2192
Holes 9 L 4630 m Par 68 SSS 65
V'tors WD–U WE–NA before 4pm
Fees   45fl
Loc   7km S of Utrecht
Arch   Paul Rolin

Utrechtse 'De Pan' (1894)

Amersfoortseweg 1, 3735 LJ Bosch en Duin
Tel   (030) 695 6427
Fax   (030) 696 3769

For list of abbreviations see page 649

Holes 18 L 5707 m Par 72 CR 70.0
V'tors WD–M WE–NA
Fees € 5 0
Loc 10km E of Utrecht, off A28
Arch HS Colt

Zeewolde
Golflaan 1, 3896 LL Zeewolde
Tel (036) 522 2103
Fax (036) 522 4100
Holes 27 L 6259 m Par 72
9 hole course Par 58
V'tors H
Fees 60fl (80fl)
Loc 20km N of Hilversum. 60km
NE of Amsterdam
Arch A Rijks

Norway

Arendal og Omegn (1986)
Nes Verk, 4900 Tvedestrand
Tel 37 19 90 30
Fax 37 16 02 11
Web www.arendalgk.no
Holes 18 L 5528 m Par 72
9 hole course
V'tors U
Fees 250kr (300kr)
Loc Nes Verk, 20km E of Arendal
(E18). 95km NE of
Kristiansand

Baerum (1972)
Hellerudveien 26, 1350 Lommedalen
Tel 67 87 67 00
Fax 67 87 67 20
Holes 18 L 5300 m Par 71
9 hole short course
V'tors WD–U H WE–M H between
11am–4pm. Booking advisable
Fees 350kr
Loc 10km W of Oslo. 10km N of
Sandvika
Arch Jeremy Turner

Bergen (1937)
Erikveien 120, 5080 Eidsvåg
Tel 05 18 20 77
Holes 9 L 4461 m Par 67
V'tors U
Fees 150kr
Loc 8km N of Bergen

Borre (1991)
Semb Hovedgaard, 3186 Horten
Tel 33 07 32 40
Fax 33 07 32 41
Holes 18 L 6120 m Par 73
V'tors H
Fees 200kr (300kr)
Loc Horten, 50km S of Drammen.
100km SW of Oslo
Arch T Nordström

Borregaard (1927)
PO Box 348, 1701 Sarpsborg

Tel 69 12 15 00
Fax 69 15 74 11
Holes 9 L 4500 m SSS 65
V'tors H
Fees 150kr
Loc Opsund, 1km N of Sarpsborg

Drøbak (1988)
Belsjøveien 50, 1440 Drøbak
Tel 64 93 16 80
Fax 64 93 39 80
Holes 18 L 5089 m Par 70
V'tors H
Fees 325kr (375kr)
Loc 40km SE of Oslo
Arch Hauser

Elverum (1980)
PO Box 71, 2401 Elverum
Tel 62 41 35 88
Fax 62 41 55 13
Holes 18 L 5845 m Par 72
V'tors H
Fees 200kr (220kr)
Loc Starmoen Fritidspark, 10km E
of Elverum. 35km E of
Hamar. 150km N of Oslo

Grenland (1976)
Luksefjellvn 578, 3721 Skien
Tel 35 59 07 03
Fax 35 59 06 10
Holes 18 L 5777 m Par 72
V'tors U
Fees 250kr
Loc 6km from Skien
Arch Jan Sederholm

Groruddalen (1988)
Postboks 37, Stovner, 0913 Oslo
Tel 22 79 05 60
Fax 22 79 05 79
Holes 9 L 2798 m Par 54 CR 58.2
SR 102
V'tors U–before 2pm
Fees 150kr
Loc 15km N of Oslo
Arch Leif Nilsson

Hemsedal (1994)
3560 Hemsedal
Tel 32 06 23 77
Fax 32 06 00 84
Holes 9 L 4816 m Par 68
V'tors U H
Fees 160kr (200kr)
Loc 40km N of Gol. 380km NW
of Oslo
Arch Leif Nilsson

Kjekstad (1976)
PO Box 201, 3440 Røyken
Tel 31 29 79 90
Fax 31 29 79 99
Holes 18 L 5100 m SSS 67
V'tors H
Fees 250kr (300kr)
Loc 12km SE of Drammen on
Route 282. 40km SW of Oslo
Arch Jan Sederholm

Kristiansand (1973)
PO Box 6090, Søm, 4602 Kristiansand
Tel 38 04 35 85
Fax 38 04 34 15
Holes 9 L 2485 m SSS 70
V'tors U
Fees D–150kr
Loc 8 km E of Kristiansand (E18)

Larvik (1989)
Fritzøe Gård, 3267 Larvik
Tel 33 14 01 45
Fax 33 14 01 49
Web www.larvikgolf.no
Holes 18 L 6147 m Par 72
V'tors H
Fees 300kr (400kr)
Loc 3km S of Larvik on R301 to
Stavern
Arch Jan Sederholm

Narvik (1992)
8523 Elvegård
Tel 76 95 12 01
Fax 76 95 12 06
Web www.narvikgolf.no
Holes 18 L 5890 m Par 72
V'tors U H
Fees 250kr
Loc 30km S of Narvik
Arch Jan Sederholm

Nes (1988)
Rommen Golfpark, 2160 Vormsund
Tel 63 91 20 30
Fax 63 91 20 31
Holes 18 L 6001 m Par 72
V'tors H or Green card
Fees 250kr (300kr)
Loc 50km NE of Oslo, via E6/RV2
Arch Hauser

Onsøy (1987)
Golfveien, 1626 Manstad
Tel 69 33 91 50
Fax 69 33 35 24
Holes 18 L 5600 m Par 72
V'tors WD–U WE–H
Fees 300kr
Loc 10km W of Fredrikstad. Oslo
80km
Arch Andersen/Mejstedt

Oppdal (1987)
PO Box 19, 7340 Oppdal
Tel 72 42 25 10
Holes 9 L 2621 m Par 72
V'tors U
Fees 150kr
Loc 120km S of Trondheim
Arch Jan Sederholm

Oppegård (1985)
*Kongeveien 198, PO Box 50,
1416 Oppegård*
Tel 66 81 59 90
Fax 66 81 59 91
Web www.oppegardgk.no
Holes 18 L 5280 m Par 71
V'tors U H

Fees   250kr (300kr)
Loc   22km S of Oslo

Oslo (1924)
Bogstad, 0757 Oslo
Tel   22 51 05 60
Fax   22 51 05 61
Holes   18 L 6719 yds SSS 72
V'tors H–Max 20 (men) 28 (ladies)
        WD–restricted before 2pm
        WE–restricted after 2pm
Fees   400kr (400kr)
Loc   8km NW of Oslo. Signs to
         'Bogstad Camping'.

Ostmarka (1989)
Postboks 63, 1914 Ytre Enebakk
Tel   64 92 38 40
Fax   64 92 47 55
Holes   18 L 5640 m
V'tors H
Fees   200kr (300kr)
Loc   35km E of Oslo

Oustoen CC (1965)
PO Box 100, 1330 Fornebu
Tel   67 83 23 80/22 56 33 54
Fax   67 53 95 44/22 59 91 83
Holes   18 L 5590m SSS 72
V'tors M
Fees   500kr
Loc   Small island in Oslofjord,
         10km W of Oslo

Skjeberg (1986)
PO Box 528, 1701 Sarpsborg
Tel   69 16 63 10
Holes   18 L 5500 m Par 72
V'tors U
Fees   150kr (200kr)
Loc   Hevingen, 2km N of
         Sarpsborg
Arch   Jan Sederholm

Sorknes (1990)
Sorknes Gaard, 2450 Rena
Tel   62 44 18 70
Fax   62 44 00 27
Web   www.sorknesgolf.no
Holes   18 L 6150 m SSS 72
V'tors U
Fees   250kr (350kr)
Loc   170km N of Oslo
Arch   Juul Soegaard

Stavanger (1956)
Longebakke 45, 4042 Hafrsfjord
Tel   51 55 54 31
Fax   51 55 73 11
Holes   18 L 5751 m Par 71
V'tors H
Fees   250kr
Loc   6km SW of Stavanger
Arch   F Smith

Trondheim (1950)
PO Box 169, 7401 Trondheim
Tel   73 53 18 85
Fax   73 52 75 05
Web   www.trondheimgolfclubb.no
Holes   9 L 5632 m SSS 72

V'tors H
Fees   200kr
Loc   Trondheim 3 km

Vestfold (1958)
PO Box 64, 3173 Vear
Tel   33 36 25 00
Fax   33 36 25 01
Holes   18 L 5851 m SSS 73
V'tors H
Fees   200kr (300kr)
Loc   Tønsberg 8km
Arch   F Smith

Poland

Amber Baltic (1993)
Baltycka Street 13, 72-514 Kolczewo
Tel   (091) 32 65 110/120
Fax   (091) 32 65 333
Holes   18 L 5802 m Par 72
        9 L 1307 m Par 28
V'tors U
Fees   55DM (80DM)
Loc   80km N of Szczecin
Arch   H-G Erhardt

Portugal

Algarve

Alto Golf (1991)
*Quinta do Alto do Poço, P O Box 1,
8501 906 Alvor*
Tel   (0282) 460870
Fax   (0282) 460879
Holes   18 L 6125 m SSS 73
V'tors H
Fees   12.500esc
Loc   2km W of Portimã
Arch   Cotton/Dobereiner

Floresta Parque (1987)
*Vale do Poço, Budens, 8650 Vila
do Bispo*
Tel   (0282) 695333
Fax   (0282) 695157
Holes   18 L 5787 m SSS 72
V'tors U
Fees   7900esc
Loc   16km W of Lagos, nr Salema
Arch   Pepe Gancedo

Palmares (1975)
*Apartado 74, Meia Praia, 8600
901 Lagos*
Tel   (0282) 762961
Fax   (0282) 762534
Web   www.palmaresgolf.com
Holes   18 L 5961 m Par 71 SSS 72
V'tors U
Fees   11.000esc

Loc   Meia Praia, 5km E of Lagos
Arch   Frank Pennink

Penina (1966)
PO Box 146, Penina, 8502 Portimao
Tel   (0282) 420200
Fax   (0282) 420300
Holes   Ch'ship 18 L 6343 m SSS 73;
        Resort 9 L 3987 m SSS 71;
        Academy 9 L 1851 m Par 30
V'tors H–max 28 (M) or 36 (L) –
        soft spikes only
Fees   Ch'ship–13.000–18.000esc
        Resort–7600esc
        Academy–6600esc
Loc   5km W of Portimao. 12km E
         of Lagos
Arch   Sir Henry Cotton

Pestana (1991)
*Apartado 1011, 8400-908
Carvoeiro Lga*
Tel   (0282) 340900
Fax   (0282) 340901
Web   www.pestana.com
Holes   Gramacho 18 L 5919 m Par
        72 SSS 71
        Pinta 18 L 6727 m Par 71
        SSS 72
V'tors U
Fees   Gramacho 7500–10.000esc
        Pinta 10.000–14.000esc
Loc   10km E of Portimão. 54km W
         of Faro Airport
Arch   Ronald Fream

Pine Cliffs G&CC (1991)
Pinhal do Concelho, 8200 Albufeira
Tel   (0289) 500100/501999
Fax   (0289) 501950
Holes   9 L 2324 m Par 66 SSS 67
V'tors U H
Fees   9 holes–5500esc
Loc   7km W of Vilamoura
Arch   Martin Hawtree

Pinheiros Altos (1992)
Quinta do Lago, 8135 Almancil
Tel   (0289) 359910
Fax   (0289) 394392
Holes   18 L 6236 m Par 72
V'tors H–phone first. Soft spikes only
Fees   20.000esc
Loc   Quinta do Lago, 15km W of
         Faro
Arch   Ronald Fream

Quinta do Lago (1974)
Quinta Do Lago, 8135 Almancil
Tel   (0289) 390700/9
Fax   (0289) 394013
Holes   Quinta do Lago 18 L 6488 m
        SSS 72;
        Ria Formosa 18 L 6205 m
        SSS 72
V'tors H–by prior arrangement
Fees   13.000esc
Loc   15km W of Faro. Airport
         20km
Arch   Mitchell/Lee

Salgados

Apartado 2266, Vale do Rabelho, 8200
917 Albufeira

Tel	(0289) 583030
Fax	(0289) 591112
Holes	18 L 6080 m Par 72
V'tors	U
Fees	On application
Loc	W of Albufeira
Arch	P de Vasconcelos

San Lorenzo (1988)

Quinta do Lago, 8135 Almancil

Tel	(0289) 396522
Fax	(0289) 396908
Holes	18 L 6238 m SSS 73
V'tors	H–restricted
Fees	24.500esc
Loc	16km W of Faro
Arch	Joseph Lee

Vale de Milho (1990)

Apartado 1273, Praia do Carvoeiro,
8401-911 Carvoeiro Lga

Tel	(0282) 358502
Fax	(0282) 358497
Holes	9 hole Par 3 course
V'tors	U
Fees	18 holes–5500esc
	9 holes–3500esc
Loc	2½ km E of Carvoeiro
Arch	Dave Thomas

Vale do Lobo (1968)

Vale Do Lobo, 8135-864 Vale do Lobo-
Almançil

Tel	(0289) 353535
Fax	(0289) 353003
Holes	Ocean 18 L 5424 m Par 71
	Royal 18 L 6050 m Par 72
V'tors	H
Fees	Ocean–18.000esc
	Royal–22.000esc
Loc	19km W of Faro. Airport
	19km
Arch	Cotton/Roquemore

Vila Sol (1991)

Alto do Semino, Vilamoura,
8125 Quarteira

Tel	(0289) 300505
Fax	(0289) 300592
Holes	18 L 6189 m Par SSS 72
V'tors	U H
Fees	15.000 esc
Loc	5km E of Vilamoura. Faro
	Airport 10km
Arch	Donald Steel

Vilamoura Laguna (1990)

Vilamoura, 8125 Quarteira

Tel	(0289) 310180
Fax	(0289) 310183
Web	www.vilamoura.net
Holes	18 L 6133 m Par 72 SSS 73
V'tors	H–max 28(M) 36(L)
Fees	11.500esc
Loc	As Vilamoura Old
Arch	Joseph Lee

Vilamoura Millennium

(2000)

Vilamoura, 8125 Quarteira

Tel	(0289) 310188
Fax	(0289) 310183
Web	www.vilamoura.net
Holes	18 L 6143 m Par 73 SSS 72
V'tors	H–max 24(M) 28(L). Soft
	spikes only
Fees	18.000esc
Loc	As Vilamoura Old
Arch	Martin Hawtree

Vilamoura Old (1969)

Vilamoura, 8125 Quarteira

Tel	(0289) 310340
Fax	(0289) 310321
Web	www.vilamoura.net
Holes	18 L 6254 m Par 73 SSS 72
V'tors	H–max 24(M) 28(L) Soft
	spikes only
Fees	20.000esc
Loc	Quarteira, 25km W of Faro
Arch	Frank Pennink

Vilamoura Pinhal (1976)

Vilamoura, 8125 Quarteira

Tel	(0289) 310390
Fax	(0289) 310393
Web	www.vilamoura.net
Holes	18 L 6206 m Par 72 SSS 71
V'tors	H–max 28(M) 36(L)
Fees	12.500esc
Loc	As Vilamoura Old
Arch	Pennink/Trent Jones

Azores

Batalha (1995)

Rua do Bom Jesus, Aflitos, 9545-234
Fenais da Luz (Açores)

Tel	(0296) 298559/498560
Fax	(0296) 498284
Web	www.virtualazores.com/
	verdegolf
Holes	18 L 6435 m CR 72.8
	SR 131
V'tors	H
Fees	D–7000esc
Loc	Sao Miguel Island. Ponta
	Delgada 10km
Arch	Cameron/Powell

Furnas (1939)

Rua do Bom Jesus, Aflitos, 9545 Fenais
da Luz (Açores)

Tel	(0296) 498559/498560
Fax	(0296) 498284
Web	www.virtualazores.com/
	verdegolf
Holes	18 L 6232 m SSS 72
V'tors	U
Fees	D–7000esc
Loc	São Miguel Island. Furnas
	Villa 5km
Arch	Mackenzie Ross/Cameron/
	Powell

Terceira Island (1954)

Caixa Postal 15, 9760 909 Praia da
Victória (Açores)

Tel	(0295) 902444
Fax	(0295) 902445
Holes	18 L 5790 m Par 72 SSS 70
V'tors	U H
Fees	6000esc
Loc	10km NW of Praia da
	Victoria

Lisbon & Central Portugal

Aroeira (1972)

Herdade da Aroeira, 2815-207
Charneca da Caparica

Tel	(021) 297 9190
Fax	(021) 297 1238
Web	www.sil.pt
Holes	18 L 6170 m CR 71 SR 123
	18 L 6195 m CR 72.3 SR 130
V'tors	U H
Fees	9000esc (12.500esc)
Loc	20km S of Lisbon, off
	Setúbal/Costa da Caparica
	road
Arch	Pennink/Steel

Belas

Alameda do Aqueducto, 2605-199 Belas

Tel	(021) 962 6600
Fax	(021) 962 6601
Holes	18 L 6200 m Par 72
V'tors	U
Loc	W of Lisbon (N117)

Estoril (1945)

Avenida da República, 2765-273 Estoril

Tel	(021) 468 0176
Fax	(021) 468 2796
Holes	18 L 5210 m Par 69 SSS 68
	9 L 2350 m SSS 65
V'tors	WD–U WE–M
Fees	9750esc (12.5000esc)
Loc	N of Estoril on Sintra road.
	30km W of Lisbon
Arch	Mackenzie Ross

Estoril-Sol Golf Academy (1976)

Quinta do Outeira, Linhó, 2710 Sintra

Tel	(01) 923 2461
Fax	(01) 923 2461
Holes	9 L 4118 m Par 66 SSS 66
V'tors	U
Loc	7km N of Estoril. Lisbon
	35km
Arch	Harris/Fream

Lisbon Sports Club (1922)

Casal da Carregueira, 2745 Belas

Tel	(01) 431 0077
Fax	(01) 431 2482
Holes	18 L 5216 m Par 69 SSS 69
V'tors	U
Fees	D–7500esc (9500esc)

Loc Belas, 20km NW of Lisbon
Arch Hawtree

Marvao

*Estrada do Monte Pobre, Sao Salvador
do d'Aramanha, 7330 Marvao*
Tel (045) 93755
Fax (045) 93805
Holes 18 holes Par 72
V'tors U
Loc 25km N of Portalegre, nr
Spanish border (N118/N246)

Montado

Apartado 40, Algeruz, 2950 Palmela
Tel (065) 706648
Fax (065) 706775
Holes 18 L 6060 m SSS 72
V'tors U
Fees 8500P
Loc 5km E of Setúbal. 40km S of
Lisbon
Arch Duarte Sottomayor

Penha Longa (1992)

*Estrada do Lagoa Azul, Linhó, 2714
511 Sintra*
Tel (01) 924 9011
Fax (01) 924 9024
Holes 18 L 6290 m Par 72
9 L 2588 m Par 35
V'tors U H
Fees 18 hole:€76 (€97)
9 hole:€29 (€38)
Loc 8km N of Estoril. 17km W of
Lisbon
Arch Robert Trent Jones Jr

Quinta da Beloura (1994)

Estrada de Albarraque, 2710 444 Sintra
Tel (021) 910 6350
Fax (021) 910 6359
Web www.pestana.com
Holes 18 L 5774 m Par 73 CR 71.2
SR 128
V'tors U
Fees D–7000esc (D–10.500esc)
Loc Between Estoril and Sintra, off
N9. Lisbon 34km
Arch Rocky Roquemore

Quinta da Marinha

(1984)
Quinta da Marinha, 2750 Cascais
Tel (021) 486 0180
Fax (021) 486 9032
Web www.quintadamarinha.com
Holes 18 L 6014 m CR 68.5 SR 114
V'tors U
Fees €61 (€76)
Loc 2km W of Cascais. 32km W of
Lisbon
Arch Robert Trent Jones

Quinta do Perú

Quinta do Perú, 2830 Quinta do Conde
Tel (01) 213 4320/22
Fax (01) 213 4321
Web www.quintadoperu.com
Holes 18 L 6036 m Par 72
V'tors H

Fees 11.000esc (16.500esc)
Loc E of Lisbon on EN10
Arch Rocky Roquemore

Tróia Golf

Torralta, Tróia, 7570 Grandola
Tel (065) 494112
Fax (065) 494315
Holes 18 L 6338 m Par 72 SSS 74
V'tors U
Fees 5500esc
Loc S of Setúbal on Tróia
peninsula. 50km S of Lisbon
Arch Robert Trent Jones

Vimeiro

*Praia do Porto Novo, Vimeiro, 2560
Torres Vedras*
Tel (061) 984157
Fax (061) 984621
Holes 9 L 4781 m Par 68 SSS 67
V'tors U
Fees D–1500esc. Hotel guests free
Loc Vimeiro, 20km N of Torres
Vedras. 65km N of Lisbon
Arch Frank Pennink

Madeira

Madeira (1991)

*Sto Antonio da Serra, 9200
Machico, Madeira*
Tel (091) 552345/552356
Fax (091) 552367
Holes 18 L 6040 m Par 72
V'tors U
Fees 8000esc
Loc 25km E of Funchal. Airport
3km
Arch Robert Trent Jones

Palheiro (1993)

*Sitio do Balancal, Sao Gonçalo, 9050-
296 Funchal, Madeira*
Tel (0291) 792116,
(0291) 790120 (Bookings)
Fax (0291) 792456
Web www.madeira-golf.com
Holes 18 L 6022 m SSS 71
V'tors May–Sept–U Oct–April–H
Fees 13.000esc
Loc 5km from Funchal, off Airport
road to Camacha
Arch Cabell Robinson

North

Amarante (1997)

*Quinta da Deveza, Fregim,
4600 Amarante*
Tel (055) 446060
Fax (055) 446202
Holes 18 L 5085 m Par 68 SSS 68
V'tors U
Fees 5500esc (8000esc)
Loc 50km E of Oporto, off A4
Arch J Santana da Silva

Golden Eagle G&CC

Quinta do Brincal, 2040 Rio Maior
Tel (0243) 908148
Fax (0243) 908149
Holes 18 L 6021 m Par 72
V'tors H
Fees €50 (€60)
Loc 55km N of Lisbon, off N1
towards Leiria
Arch R Roquemore

Miramar (1962)

*Av Sacadura Cabral, Miramar,
4405 Valadares*
Tel (02) 762 2067
Fax (02) 762 7859
Holes 9 L 2477 m Par 68 SSS 67
V'tors H WE–NA after 10am
Fees 7500esc (9000esc)
Loc 8km S of Oporto

Montebelo

Farminhão, 3510 Viseu
Tel (032) 856464
Fax (032) 856401
Holes 18 L 6300 m Par 72 SSS 72
V'tors U
Loc 75km NE of Coimbra

Oporto (1890)

Sisto-Paramos, 4500 Espinho
Tel (022) 734 2008
Fax (022) 734 6895
Holes 18 L 5780 m Par 71 SSS 70
V'tors H WE–restricted
Fees 10.000esc
Loc Espinho, 15km S of Oporto

Ponte de Lima

*Quinta de Pias, Fornelos, 4490 Ponte
de Lima*
Tel (058) 43414
Fax (058) 743424
Holes 18 L 6005 m Par 71 SSS 70
V'tors U
Loc 75km N of Oporto (N201)

Praia d'el Rey G&CC

(1997)
*Vale de Janelas, Apartado 2,
2510 Obidos*
Tel (0262) 905005
Fax (0262) 905009
Web www.praia-del-rey.com
Holes 18 L 6467 m Par 72 SSS 72
V'tors U H
Fees 9500esc (12.500esc)
Loc 65km N of Lisbon,nr Caldas
da Rainha (Motorway A 8)
Arch Cabell Robinson

Quinta da Barca (1997)

*Barca do Lago, Gemezes,
4740 Esposende*
Tel (053) 966723
Fax (053) 969068
Holes 9 L 2015 m Par 62
V'tors U
Fees 6000esc (7500esc)

Loc   25km N of Oporto (IC1)
Arch   J Santana da Silva

Vidago
Pavilhão do Golfe, 5425 Vidago
Tel   (076) 907356
Fax   (076) 996622
Holes 9 L 2256m Par 66 SSS 64
Loc   50km N of Vila Real. 130km
       NE of Oporto
Arch   Mackenzie Ross

Slovenia

G&CC Bled (1937)
Public
Ljublanska 5, 4260 Bled
Tel   (064) 700 777
Fax   (064) 718 225
Holes 18 L 6325 m SSS 73
       9 L 3092 m SSS 72
V'tors H–36 max
Fees   £24 (£27)
Loc   3km W of Bled. 50km NW of
       Ljubljana, nr Austro-Italian
       border
Arch   Donald Harradine

Castle Mokrice (1992)
*Terme Catez, Topliska Cesta 35,
8250 Brezice*
Tel   (0608) 240751
Fax   (0608) 57007
Holes 18 holes SSS 70
V'tors H
Fees   58DM (64DM)
Loc   30km N of Zagreb
Arch   Donald Harradine

Lipica (1989)
Lipica 5, 66210 Sezana
Tel   (067) 31580
Fax   (067) 72818
Holes 9 L 6240 m SSS 71
V'tors U
Fees   £12 (£18)
Loc   11km NE of Trieste. 85km
       SW of Ljubljana
Arch   Donald Harradine

Spain

Alicante & Murcia

Alicante (1997)
*C Vicente Hipolito 37, Playa San Juan,
03540 Alicante*
Tel   (96) 515 37 94/515 20 43
Fax   (96) 516 37 07
Web   www.alicantgolf.com
Holes 18 L 6236 m Par 72
V'tors U H
Fees   9000P

Loc   Playa San Juan, N of Alicante
Arch   Severiano Ballesteros

Altorreal (1994)
*Urb Altorreal, 30500 Molina de
Segura (Murcia)*
Tel   (968) 64 81 44
Fax   (986) 64 82 48
Holes 18 L 6239 m Par 72 SSS 73
V'tors H
Fees   5000P (6000P)
Loc   10km from Murcia on Madrid
       road
Arch   Dave Thomas

Bonalba (1993)
*Partida de Bonalba, 03110
Mutxamiel (Alicante)*
Tel   (96) 595 5955
Web   www.golfbonalba.com
Holes 18 L 6190m Par 72 SSS 73
V'tors U
Fees   8000P
Loc   10km N of Alicante. A7
       Junction 67
Arch   Ramón Espinosa

Don Cayo (1974)
*Apartado 341, 0359 Altea La
Vieja (Alicante)*
Tel   (96) 584 80 46
Fax   (96) 584 11 88
Holes 9 L 6156 m SSS 72
V'tors U H
Loc   4km N of Altea, nr Callosa
Arch   Barber/Sanz

Ifach (1974)
*Crta Moraira-Calpe Km 3, Apdo 28,
03720 Benisa (Alicante)*
Tel   (96) 649 71 14
Fax   (96) 649 71 14
Holes 9 L 3408 m SSS 59
V'tors U
Fees   D–3300P
Loc   9km N of Calpe, towards
       Moraira
Arch   Javier Arana

Jávea (1981)
Apartado 148, 03730 Jávea, (Alicante)
Tel   (96) 579 25 84
Fax   (96) 646 05 54
Holes 9 L 6070 m SSS 71
V'tors H
Fees   D–5500P
Loc   Lluca, Jávea. 90km NE of
       Alicante
Arch   Francisco Moreno

La Manga (1971)
Los Belones, 30385 Cartagena (Murcia)
Tel   (968) 13 72 34
Fax   (968) 15 72 72
Holes North 18 L 5780 m SSS 70
       South 18 L 6259 m SSS 73
       Princesa 18 L 5971 m SSS 72
V'tors U H
Loc   30km NE of Cartagena, nr
       Murcia airport
Arch   RD Putman

La Marquesa (1989)
*Ciudad Quesada II, 03170
Rojales, (Alicante)*
Tel   (96) 671 42 58
Fax   (96) 671 42 67
Holes 18 L 5840 m Par 72 SSS 70
V'tors U
Fees   D–4200P
Loc   Rojales, 40km S of Alicante
Arch   Justo Quesada

Las Ramblas (1991)
*Crta Alicante-Cartagena Km48, 03189
Urb Villamartin, Orihuela (Alicante)*
Tel   (96) 532 20 11
Fax   (96) 532 21 59
Holes 18 L 5770 m SSS 71
V'tors U H
Fees   7000P
Loc   9km S of Torrevieja
Arch   José Gancedo

Real Campoamor (1989)
*Crta Cartagena-Alicante Km48, Apdo
17, 03189 Orihuela-Costa (Alicante)*
Tel   (96) 532 13 66
Fax   (96) 532 24 54
Holes 18 L 6203 m Par 72 SSS 73
V'tors U H
Fees   5000P
Loc   Torrevieja 9km (N332)
Arch   C Gracia Caselles

La Sella (1991)
*Ctra La Jara-Jesús Pobre, 03749
Denia (Alicante)*
Tel   (96) 645 42 52/645 41 10
Fax   (96) 645 42 01
Holes 18 L 6028 m SSS 71
V'tors U H
Fees   6000P
Loc   Denia 5km
Arch   Juan de la Cuadra

Villamartin (1972)
*Crta Alicante-Cartagena Km50, 03189
Urb Villamartin, Orihuela (Alicante)*
Tel   (96) 676 51 27/676 51 60
Fax   (96) 676 51 70
Holes 18 L 6132 m SSS 72
V'tors U H
Fees   8000P
Loc   8km S of Torrevieja
Arch   Paul Putman

Almería

Almerimar (1976)
*Urb Almerimar, 04700 El
Ejido (Almería)*
Tel   (950) 48 02 34
Fax   (950) 49 72 33
Holes 18 L 6111 m SSS 72
V'tors U
Loc   35km W of Almería
Arch   Gary Player

Cortijo Grande (1976)
Apdo 2, Cortijo Grande, 04639
Turre (Almería)
Tel   (951) 47 91 76
Holes   18 L 6024 m Par 72 SSS 71
V'tors U
Loc   20km W of Turre. 85km N of
        Almería, nr Mojácar
Arch   PJ Polansky

La Envia (1993)
Apdo 51, 04720 Aguadulce (Almería)
Tel   (950) 55 96 41
Holes   18 L 5810 m Par 72 SSS 70
V'tors U
Loc   10km from Almería
Arch   F Mendoza

Playa Serena (1979)
Urb Playa Serena, 04740 Roquetas de
Mar (Almería)
Tel   (950) 33 30 55
Fax   (950) 33 30 55
Holes   18 L 6301 m Par 72
V'tors H
Fees   5000–6500P
Loc   20km S of Almería
Arch   Gallardo/Alliss

Badajoz & West

Guadiana (1992)
Crta Madrid-Lisboa Km 393, Apdo
171, 06080 Badajoz
Tel   (924) 44 81 88
Holes   18 L 6381 m Par 72 SSS 73
V'tors U
Loc   Badajoz
Arch   Daniel Calero

Norba (1988)
Apdo 880, 10080 Cáceres
Tel   (927) 23 14 41
Fax   (927) 23 14 80
Holes   18 L 6422 m Par 72 SSS 74
V'tors U
Fees   4000P (6000P)
Loc   4km S of Cáceres
Arch   Carlos Corsini

Salamanca (1988)
Monte de Zarapicos, 37170
Zarapicos (Salamanca)
Tel   (923) 32 91 02
Holes   18 L 6267 m Par 72 SSS 72
V'tors U
Loc   W of Salamanca,nr Parada de
        Arriba (C-517)
Arch   Manuel Piñero

Balearic Islands

Canyamel
Urb Canyamel, Crta de Cuevas, 07580
Capdepera, (Mallorca)
Tel   (971) 56 44 57

Fax   (971) 56 53 80
Holes   18 L 6115 m SSS 72
V'tors H
Loc   70km NE of Palma, nr Cala
        Ratjada
Arch   José Gancedo

Capdepera (1989)
Apdo 6, 07580 Capdepera, Mallorca
Tel   (971) 56 58 75/56 58 57
Fax   (971) 56 58 74
Holes   18 L 6284 m SSS 72
V'tors U H
Loc   71km E of Palma, between
        Artá and Capdepera
Arch   Maples/Pape

Club Son Parc (1977)
Urb Son Parc, Mercadel (Menorca)
Tel   (971) 18 88 75
Fax   (971) 35 95 91
Web   www.clubsonparc.com
Holes   9 L 2791 m SSS 69
V'tors U
Fees   9 holes–4000–5500P
        18 holes–7000–9000P
Loc   Mercadal, 18km N of Mahón
Arch   JF Martinez

Ibiza (1990)
Apdo 1270, 07840 Santa
Eulalia, (Ibiza)
Tel   (971) 19 61 18
Fax   (971) 19 60 51
Holes   18 L 6083 m SSS 72
        9 L 5867 m SSS 70
V'tors U
Fees   6000–12.000P
Loc   7km N of Ibiza town
Arch   Thomas/Rivero

Pollensa (1986)
Ctra Palma-Pollensa Km 49, 07460
Pollensa, (Mallorca)
Tel   (971) 53 32 16
Fax   (971) 53 32 65
Holes   9 L 5304 m Par 70 SSS 70
V'tors U H
Fees   € 5 2
Loc   Pollensa, 45km N of Palma
Arch   José Gancedo

Poniente (1978)
Costa de Calvia, 07181
Calvia (Mallorca)
Tel   (971) 13 01 48
Fax   (971) 13 01 76
Web   www.ponientegolf.com
Holes   18 L 6430 m SSS 72
V'tors U H
Fees   9500P
Loc   12km SW of Palma towards
        Cala Figuera
Arch   John Harris

Pula Golf (1995)
Predio de Pula, 07550 Son
Servera (Mallorca)
Tel   (971) 81 70 34
Fax   (971) 81 70 35
Holes   18 L 5648 m Par 71
V'tors U H

Fees   10.000P
Loc   70km NE of Palma
Arch   F López Segales

Royal Bendinat (1986)
C. Campoamor, 07015
Calviá, (Mallorca)
Tel   (971) 40 52 00
Fax   (971) 70 07 86
Holes   18 L 5768 m SSS 71
V'tors U H
Loc   7km W of Palma
Arch   Martin Hawtree

Santa Ponsa (1976)
Santa Ponsa, 07180 Calvia (Mallorca)
Tel   (971) 69 02 11/69 08 00
Fax   (971) 69 33 64
Holes   18 L 6520 m SSS 74
        18 L 6053 m SSS 73
V'tors No 1–U H No 2–NA
Fees   8700P
Loc   18km W of Palma
Arch   Folco Nardi

Son Antem (1993)
Apartado 102, 07620
Lluchmajor, Mallorca
Tel   (971) 66 11 24
Fax   (971) 66 26 49
Holes   18 L 6325 m Par 72 SSS 72
V'tors U
Fees   8500P
Loc   20km E of Palma
        (Route 717)
Arch   F López Segales

Son Servera (1967)
Costa de Los Pinos, 07759 Son
Servera, (Mallorca)
Tel   (971) 84 00 96
Fax   (971) 84 01 60
Holes   9 L 5956 m SSS 72
V'tors H
Fees   D–7000P
Loc   Son Servera, 64km E of
        Palma
Arch   John Harris

Son Vida (1964)
Urb Son Vida, 07013
Palma (Mallorca)
Tel   (971) 79 12 10
Fax   (971) 79 11 27
Holes   18 L 5740 m SSS 71
V'tors U H
Fees   8100P
Loc   3km NW of Palma
Arch   FW Hawtree

Vall d'Or (1985)
Apdo 23, 07660 Cala D'Or
(Mallorca)
Tel   (971) 83 70 68/83 70 01
Fax   (971) 83 72 99
Holes   18 L 5799 m SSS 71
V'tors H
Fees   10.400P
Loc   60km E of Palma, between
        Cala d'Or and Porto Colóm
Arch   Benz/Bendly

Barcelona & Cataluña

Aro-Mas Nou (1990)
Apdo 429, 17250 Playa de Aro
Tel (972) 82 69 00,
(972) 81 67 27 (Bookings)
Fax (972) 82 69 06
Holes 18 L 6218 m Par 72
9 holes Par 3 course
V'tors U H
Fees 8900P (9500P)
Loc 35km SE of Gerona on coast.
A7 Junction 9 Barcelona
Airport 100km
Arch Ramón Espinosa

Bonmont Terres Noves (1990)
Urb Terres Noves, 43300
Montroig (Tarragona)
Tel (977) 81 81 40
Fax (977) 81 81 46
Web www.bonmont.com
Holes 18 L 6371 m SSS 72
V'tors U H
Fees 5500P (8000P)
Loc S of Tarragona. 130km S of
Barcelona
Arch Robert Trent Jones Jr

Caldes Internacional (1992)
Apdo 200, 08140 Caldes de
Montbui (Barcelona)
Tel (93) 865 38 28
Holes 18 L 6258 m Par 72 SSS 73
V'tors U
Loc 28km from Barcelona
Arch Ramón Espinosa

Can Bosch (1984)
Trav de les Corts 322, 08029 Barcelona
Tel (93) 405 04 22/866 25 71
Fax (93) 419 9659
Holes 9 L 3027 m SSS 71
V'tors U H
Loc 35km NE of Barcelona
Arch Ramon Espinosa

Costa Brava (1962)
La Masia, 17246 Sta Cristina
d'Aro (Gerona)
Tel (972) 83 71 50
Fax (972) 83 72 72
Web www.golfcostabrava.com
Holes 18 L 5573 m SSS 70
V'tors H
Fees 6000–9000P
Loc Playa de Aro 5km. 30km SE
of Gerona
Arch J Hamilton Stutt

Costa Dorada (1983)
Apartado 600, 43080 Tarragona
Tel (977) 65 33 61
Holes 18 L 6223 m SSS 73
Loc Tarragona
Arch José Gancedo

Empordà (1990)
Crta Torroella de Montgri, 17257
Gualta (Gerona)
Tel (972) 76 04 50/76 01 36
Fax (972) 75 71 00
Holes 27 L 5855-6112 m SSS 70-71
V'tors U H
Fees 5500P (8500P)
Loc 35km E of Gerona, nr Pals.
130km N of Barcelona
Arch Robert von Hagge

Fontanals de Cerdanya (1994)
Fontanals de Cerdanya, 17538
Soriguerola (Girona)
Tel (972) 14 43 74
Holes 18 L 6454 m Par 72 SSS 74
V'tors U
Loc 2km from Alp de Puigcerdá

Girona (1992)
Urb Golf Girona, 17481 Sant Juliá de
Ramis, (Girona)
Tel (972) 17 16 41
Fax (972) 17 16 82
Web www.golfgirona.com
Holes 18 L 6100 m Par 72 SSS 72
V'tors H–booking required
Fees 5000P (7000P)
Loc Sant Juliá de Ramis, 4km from
Girona. Barcelona 98km
Arch Hawtree

Llavaneras (1945)
Camino del Golf, 08392 San Andres de
Llavaneras, (Barcelona)
Tel (93) 792 60 50
Fax (93) 795 25 58
Holes 18 L 4644 m SSS 66
V'tors U H
Fees 6000P (12.000P)
Loc 4km N of Mataró. 34km N of
Barcelona (A19)
Arch Hawtree/Espinosa

Masia Bach (1990)
Ctra Martorell-Capellades, 08781 Sant
Esteve Sesrovires
Tel (93) 772 8800
Fax (93) 772 8810
Holes 18 L 6039 m SSS 72
9 L 3578 m SSS 62
V'tors H
Fees 9000P (20.000P)
Loc 30km NW of Barcelona
Arch JM Olazábal

Osona Montanya (1988)
Masia L'Estanyol, 08553 El
Brull (Barcelona)
Tel (93) 884 01 70
Fax (93) 884 04 07
Holes 18 L 6036 m Par 72
V'tors U H
Loc 60km NE of Barcelona
Arch Dave Thomas

Pals (1966)
Playa de Pals, 17526 Gerona
Tel (972) 63 60 06
Fax (972) 63 70 09
Holes 18 L 6222 m Par 73
V'tors U
Loc 40km E of Gerona. 135km
NE of Barcelona
Arch FW Hawtree

Peralada (1993)
La Garriga, 17491 Peralada, Girona
Tel (972) 53 82 87
Fax (972) 53 82 36
Web www.golfperalada.com
Holes 18 L 5990 m SSS 71
V'tors H
Fees €40 (€60)
Loc Costa Brava, on French
border. 40km S of Perpignan
Airport, nr Figueres
Arch Jorge Soler

Real Cerdaña (1929)
Apdo 63, Puigcerdá, (Gerona)
Tel (972) 88 13 38
Holes 18 L 5735 m SSS 70
Loc Cerdaña, 1km from Puigcerdá
Arch Javier Arana

Real Golf El Prat (1956)
Apdo 10, 08820 El Prat de
Llobregat, (Barcelona)
Tel (93) 379 02 78
Fax (93) 370 51 02
Holes 4 x 9 holes:
6070-6266 m SSS 73-74
V'tors H
Fees 12.135P (24.335P)
Loc El Prat, Airport 3km. 15km S
of Barcelona
Arch Arana/Thomas

Reus Aiguesverds (1989)
Crta Cambrils, Mas Guardiá,
43206 Reus
Tel (977) 75 27 25
Fax (977) 75 19 38
Holes 18 L 6905 yds SSS 72
V'tors U
Fees 7000P
Loc 10km W of Tarragona. 100km
S of Barcelona

Sant Cugat (1914)
08190 Sant Cugat del Valles
Tel (93) 674 39 08/674 39 58
Holes 18 L 5209 m SSS 68
Loc 20km NW of Barcelona

Sant Jordi
Urb Sant Jordi d'Alfama, 43860
Ametlla de Mar, (Tarragona)
Tel (977) 49 34 57
Fax (977) 49 32 77
Holes 9 L 5696 m SSS 70
V'tors U H
Loc 50km S of Tarragona
Arch Lauresno Nomen

Terramar (1922)
Apdo 6, 08870 Sitges
Tel (93) 894 05 80/894 20 43
Fax (93) 894 70 51
Holes 18 L 5878 m Par 72
V'tors H
Fees 7000P (11.000P)
Loc Sitges, 37km S of Barcelona
Arch Hawtree/Piñero/Fazio

Torremirona (1994)
Ctra N260 Km46, 17744
Navata (Girona)
Tel (972) 55 37 37
Fax (972) 55 37 16
Holes 18 L 6184 m Par 72
V'tors U
Fees 6500P (8000P)
Loc 30km from Girona. A7
Junction 4
Arch Joan Anglada

Vallromanes (1972)
C/Afveras, 08188
Vallromanes, (Barcelona)
Tel (93) 572 90 64
Fax (93) 572 93 30
Holes 18 L 6038 m Par 72
V'tors H
Loc 23km N of Barcelona between
Alella and Granollers. A7
Junction 13
Arch FW Hawtree

Burgos & North

Barganiza (1982)
Apartado 277, 33080 Oviedo, Asturias
Tel (985) 74 24 68
Holes 18 L 5549 m SSS 70
Loc 12km N of Oviedo on Gijon
old road
Arch Victor García

Castillo de Gorraiz
(1993)
Urb Castillo de Gorraiz, 31620 Valle de
Egues (Navarra)
Tel (948) 33 70 73
Fax (948) 33 73 15
Holes 18 L 6321 m Par 72 SSS 73
V'tors U
Fees 6000P (7000P)
Loc 4km from Pamplona
Arch Cabell B Robinson

La Cuesta
Apdo 40, 33500 Llanes
Tel (98) 541 7084
Fax (98) 540 1973
Holes 9 L 5456 m SSS 69
V'tors U
Loc 3km from Llanes (N-634)

Iski Golf (1992)
01119 Urturi (Alava)
Tel (945) 37 82 62

Fax (945) 37 82 66
Holes 18 L 6576 m Par 73 SSS 74
V'tors U
Fees 3500P (5000P)
Loc Urturi, 39km from Vitoria
Arch Severiano Ballesteros

Larrabea (1989)
Crta de Landa, 01170
Legutiano, (Alava)
Tel (945) 46 58 44/46 58 41
Fax (945) 46 57 25
Holes 18 L 5991 m Par 72
V'tors U
Fees 5000P (6000P)
Loc 14km N of Vitoria, nr Villareal
de Alava
Arch José Gancedo

Laukariz (1976)
Laukariz-Munguía, (Viscaya)
Tel (94) 674 08 58/674 04 62
Holes 18 L 6112 m SSS 72
V'tors U
Loc 15km N of Bilbao towards
Mungía
Arch RD Putman

Lerma (1991)
Ctra Madrid-Burgos Km195, 09340
Lerma (Burgos)
Tel (947) 17 12 14/17 12 16
Fax (947) 17 12 16
Holes 18 L 6235 m SSS 72
V'tors H
Loc 30km S of Burgos, nr Villa
Ducal de Lerma
Arch Pepe Gancedo

La Llorea (1994)
Crta Nacional 632, Km 62, 33394
Lloreda (Gijón)
Tel (985) 33 31 91
Fax (985) 36 47 26
Holes 18 L 5868 m Par 71
V'tors H
Fees 5500P (6500P)
Loc 10km E of Gijón
Arch Roland Fabret

Real Golf Castiello (1958)
Apdo Correos 161, 33200 Gijón
Tel (985) 36 63 13
Fax (985) 13 18 00
Holes 18 L 4817 m Par 70
V'tors WE–restricted
Fees 8000P
Loc 5km S of Gijón

Real Golf Neguri (1911)
Apdo Correos 9, 48990 Algorta
Tel (94) 469 02 00/04/08
Holes 18 L 6319 m SSS 72
6 hole Par 3 course
Loc La Galea, 20km N of Bilbao
Arch Javier Arana

Real Golf Pedreña (1928)
Apartado 233, Santander
Tel (942) 50 00 01/50 02 66

Fax (942) 50 04 21
Holes 18 L 5745 m SSS 70
9 L 2740 m SSS 36
V'tors H
Fees 5600P (9000P)
Loc 20km from Santander, on Bay
of Santander
Arch Colt/Ballesteros

Real San Sebastián (1910)
PO Box 6, Fuenterrabia, (Guipúzcoa)
Tel (943) 61 68 45/61 68 46
Fax (943) 61 14 91
Holes 18 L 6020 m SSS 71
V'tors WD–U H from 9–12 noon
WE–NA
Fees 9000P
Loc Jaizubia Valley, 14km NE of
San Sebastián
Arch P Hirigoyen

Real Zarauz (1916)
Apartado 82, Zarauz, (Guipúzcoa)
Tel (943) 83 01 45
Holes 9 L 5184 m SSS 68
Loc Zarauz, 25km W of San
Sebastián

Ulzama (1965)
31779 Guerendiain (Navarra)
Tel (948) 30 51 62
Fax (948) 30 54 71
Holes 18 L 6246 m Par 72
V'tors U
Fees On application
Loc 20km N of Pamplona
Arch Javier Arana

Canary Islands

Amarilla (1988)
Urb Amarilla Golf, San Miguel de
Abona, 38630 Santa Cruz de Tenerife
Tel (922) 73 03 19
Fax (922) 73 00 85
Holes 18 L 6077 m Par 72
V'tors H
Fees 10.000P
Loc 6km SW of South Airport.
12km from Playa de las
Americas
Arch Donald Steel

Costa Teguise (1978)
Apdo 170, 35080 Arrecife de Lanzarote
Tel (928) 59 05 12
Fax (928) 59 04 90
Holes 18 L 5853 m SSS 72
V'tors U
Fees Summer–5400P
Winter–6000P
Loc 4km N of Arrecife
Arch John Harris

Maspalomas (1968)
Av de Neckerman, Maspalomas, 35100
Gran Canaria
Tel (928) 76 25 81/76 73 43

Fax   (928) 76 82 45
Holes 18 L 6216 m SSS 72
V'tors H
Fees   Summer–6000P
       Winter–10.000P
Loc   Maspalomas, S coast of Gran
       Canaria
Arch   Mackenzie Ross

Real Golf Las Palmas
(1891)
PO Box 93, 35380 Santa Brígida,
Gran Canaria
Tel   (928) 35 10 50/35 01 04
Fax   (928) 35 01 10
Holes 18 L 5690 m SSS 71
V'tors WD–U WE–NA
Fees   12.000P
Loc   Bandama, Las Palmas 14km
Arch   Mackenzie Ross

Real Tenerife (1932)
El Peñón, Tacoronte, Tenerife
Tel   (922) 63 66 07
Fax   (922) 63 64 80
Holes 18 L 5750 m Par 71
V'tors WD–H 8am–1pm
Fees   5720P
Loc   20km N of Santa Cruz. Puerto
       Cruz 15km
Arch   J Laynez

Golf del Sur (1987)
San Miguel de Abona, 38620
Tenerife (Canarias)
Tel   (922) 73 81 70
Fax   (922) 78 82 72
Web   www.golfdelsur.net
Holes North 9 L 2913 m SSS 36
       Links 9 L 2469 m SSS 34
       South 9 L 2957 m SSS 36
V'tors H
Fees   5500–7700P
Loc   Airport 3km. Playa de las
       Américas 12km
Arch   Pepe Gancedo

Córdoba

Córdoba (1976)
Apartado 436, 14080 Córdoba
Tel   (957) 35 02 08
Holes 18 L 5964 m Par 72 SSS 73
V'tors U
Loc   9km N of Córdoba, towards
       Obejo

Pozoblanco (1984)
Apdo 118, 14400
Pozoblanco, (Córdoba)
Tel   (957) 33 91 71
Fax   (957) 33 91 71
Holes 9 L 3020 m Par 72
V'tors U
Loc   Pozoblanco 3km
Arch   Carlos Luca

Galicia

Aero Club de Santiago
(1976)
General Pardiñas 34, Santiago de
Compostela (La Coruña)
Tel   (981) 59 24 00
Holes 9 L 5816 m SSS 70
Loc   Santiago Airport

Aero Club de Vigo (1951)
Reconquista 7, 36201 Vigo
Tel   (986) 48 66 45/48 75 09
Holes 9 L 5622 m SSS 60
Loc   Peinador Airport, 8km from
       Vigo

Domaio (1993)
San Lorenzo-Domaio, 36950
Moaña (Pontevedra)
Tel   (986) 32 70 50
Holes 18 L 6110 m Par 72 SSS 73
V'tors U
Arch   Ramón Espinosa

La Toja (1970)
Isla de La Toja, El Grove, Pontevedra
Tel   (986) 73 01 58/73 08 18
Fax   (986) 73 31 22
Holes 9 L 5178 m SSS 72
V'tors H
Fees   6000–9000P
Loc   La Toja island. 30km W of
       Pontevedra
Arch   Ramón Espinosa

Granada

Granada
Avda de los Corsarios, 18110 Las
Gabias (Granada)
Tel   (958) 58 44 36
Holes 18 L 6037 m Par 71 SSS 73
V'tors U
Loc   Las Gabias, 8km from
       Granada
Arch   Ramón Espinosa

Madrid Region

Barberán (1967)
Apartado 150.239, Cuatro Vientos,
28080 Madrid
Tel   (91) 509 00 59/509 11 40
Fax   (91) 706 2174
Holes 9 L 6042 m SSS 72
V'tors M H
Loc   10km SW of Madrid

La Dehesa (1991)
Calle Real 19, 28691 Villanueva
La Cañada
Tel   (91) 815 70 22/815 70 37
Fax   (91) 815 54 68

Holes 18 L 6456 m SSS 72
Loc   35km NW of Madrid
Arch   Manuel Piñero

Herreria (1966)
PO Box 28200, San Lorenzo del
Escorial, (Madrid)
Tel   (91) 890 51 11
Holes 18 L 6050 m SSS 72
Loc   Escorial, 50km W of Madrid
Arch   Antonio Lucena

Jarama R.A.C.E. (1967)
Urb Ciudalcampo, 28707 San Sebastian
de los Reyes, (Madrid)
Tel   (91) 657 00 01
Fax   (91) 657 04 62
Holes 18 L 6505 m Par 72
       9 hole Par 3 course
Loc   28km N of Madrid on Burgos
       road
Arch   Javier Arana

Lomas-Bosque (1973)
Urb El Bosque, 28670 Villaviciosa de
Odón, (Madrid)
Tel   (91) 616 75 00
Fax   (91) 616 73 93
Holes 18 L 6075 m SSS 72
       9 hole Par 3 course
V'tors WD–U H WE–M H
Fees   4400–13.000P
Loc   20km SW of Madrid
Arch   RD Putman

La Moraleja (1976)
La Moraleja, Alcobendas (Madrid)
Tel   (91) 650 07 00
Holes 18 L 6016 m SSS 72
V'tors M
Loc   9km N of Madrid on Burgos
       road
Arch   Jack Nicklaus

Nuevo De Madrid (1972)
Las Matas (Madrid)
Tel   (91) 630 08 20
Holes 18 L 5647 m SSS 70
V'tors U H
Loc   25km NW of Madrid on La
       Coruña road

Olivar de la Hinojosa
(1995)
Avda de Dublin, Campo de las
Naciones, 28042 Madrid
Tel   (91) 721 18 89
Holes 18 L 6163 m Par 72 SSS 72
V'tors U
Loc   Nr Madrid Airport M40

Puerta de Hierro
(1904)
Avda de Miraflores, 28035 Madrid
Tel   (91) 316 1745
Fax   (91) 373 8111
Holes 18 L 6347 m SSS 73
       18 L 5273 m SSS 68
V'tors M only

Fees 6900P (14.950P)
Loc 4km N of Madrid (Route VI)
Arch Harris/Simpson/Trent Jones

Los Retamares (1991)
Crta Algete-Alalpardo Km 2300, 28130 Valdeolmos (Madrid)
Tel (91) 620 25 40
Holes 18 L 6238 m Par 72 SSS 73
9 hole Par 3 course
V'tors U
Loc 25km N of Madrid via N-1

Somosaguas (1971)
Avda de la Cabaña, 28223 Pozuelo de Alarcón, (Madrid)
Tel (91) 352 16 47
Fax (91) 352 00 30
Holes 9 L 6054 m Par 72
Loc Somosaguas
Arch John Harris

Valdeláguila (1975)
Apdo 9, Alcalá de Henares, (Madrid)
Tel (91) 885 96 59
Fax (91) 885 96 59
Holes 9 L 5724 m Par 72
V'tors WD–U WE–NA
Loc Villalbilla, 10km S of Alcalá

Villa de Madrid CC (1932)
Crta Castilla, 28040 Madrid
Tel (91) 357 21 32
Fax (91) 549 07 97
Holes 27 L 5900-6321 m SSS 73-74
V'tors U H
Fees 6750P (12.775P)
Loc 4km NW of Madrid, in the Casa del Campo
Arch Javier Arana

Málaga Region

Alhaurín (1994)
Crta 426 Km15, Alhaurín el Grande
Tel (952) 59 59 70
Fax (952) 59 45 86
Holes 18 L 6221 m Par 72
18 hole Par 3 course
9 hole Par 3 course
V'tors U
Fees 6000P
Loc 6km from Mijas
Arch Severiano Ballesteros

Añoreta (1989)
Avenida del Golf, 29730 Rincón de la Victoria, (Málaga)
Tel (952) 40 40 00
Fax (952) 40 40 50
Holes 18 L 5976 m SSS 71
V'tors U
Fees 2500P (3000P)
Loc 12km E of Málaga
Arch JM Canizares

La Cala Resort (1991)
La Cala de Mijas, 29647 Mijas-Costa (Málaga)
Tel (952) 66 90 00, (952) 66 90 33

Fax (952) 66 90 34
Web www.lacala.com
Holes North 18 L 6187 m Par 73
South 18 L 5966 m Par 72
6 hole Par 3 course
V'tors U H
Fees 5000–9500P
Loc 6km from Cala de Mijas, between Fuengirola and Marbella
Arch Cabell Robinson

El Candado (1965)
Urb El Candado, El Palo, 29018 Málaga
Tel (952) 29 93 40/1
Holes 9 L 4676 m SSS 66
Loc El Palo, 5km E of Málaga on Route N340
Arch Carlos Fernández

El Chaparral
Urb El Chaparral, Mijas-Costa
Tel (952) 49 38 00
Fax (952) 49 40 51
Holes 18 L 5700 m SSS 71
V'tors U H
Loc 5km W of Fuengirola on N340
Arch Pepe Gancedo

Guadalhorce (1988)
Crtra de Cártama Km7, Apartado 48, 29590 Campanillas (Málaga)
Tel (952) 17 93 78
Fax (952) 17 93 72
Holes 18 L 6194 m SSS 72
9 hole Par 3 course
V'tors WD–H before 1pm (booking necessary) WE–M
Fees 4000–5000P
Loc 8km W of Málaga
Arch Kosti Kuronen

Lauro (1992)
Los Caracolillos, 29130 Alhaurín de la Torre, (Málaga)
Tel (95) 241 27 67
Fax (95) 241 47 57
Web www.laurogolf.com
Holes 18 L 5971 m SSS 71
V'tors U
Fees D–6500P
Loc 15km SW of Málaga airport on Route A-366 towards Coín
Arch Folco Nardi

Málaga Club de Campo (1925)
Parador de Golf, Apdo 324, 29080 Málaga
Tel (952) 38 12 55
Fax (952) 38 21 41
Holes 18 L 6249 m SSS 72
V'tors U
Loc Torremolinos 4km. 12km S of Málaga, nr Airport
Arch Tom Simpson

Mijas (1976)
Apartado 145, Fuengirola, Málaga
Tel (952) 47 68 43
Fax (952) 46 79 43
Holes Lagos 18 L 6548 m Par 71
SSS 74;
Olivos 18 L 6009 m Par 72
SSS 72
V'tors H–booking required Oct–Apr
Fees 6200P
Loc 4km NW of Fuengirola (Mijas Valley)
Arch Robert Trent Jones

Miraflores (1989)
Urb Riviera del Sol, 29647 Mijas-Costa
Tel (952) 93 19 60
Fax (952) 93 19 42
Holes 18 L 5113 m SSS 71
V'tors U H
Fees 8000P
Loc 15km E of Marbella
Arch Folco Nardi

Los Moriscos (1974)
Costa Granada, Motril (Granada)
Tel (958) 82 55 27
Fax (958) 25 52 51
Holes 9 L 5689 m SSS 72 Par 70
V'tors U
Loc 8km W of Motril, nr Salobrena. 80km E of Málaga
Arch Ibergolf

Torrequebrada (1976)
Public
Apdo 120, Crta de Cadiz Km 220, 29630 Benalmadena
Tel (95) 244 27 42
Fax (95) 256 11 29
Holes 18 L 5806 m Par 72 SSS 71
V'tors H
Fees 9500P
Loc Benalmadena, 25km S of Málaga
Arch Pepe Gancedo

Marbella & Estepona

Alcaidesa Links (1992)
CN-340 Km124.6, 11315 La Linea (Cádiz)
Tel (956) 79 10 40
Fax (956) 79 10 41
Holes 18 L 5766 m Par 72 SSS 71
V'tors U–booking advised
Fees 9000P
Loc 15km E of Gibraltar. San Roque 3km
Arch Alliss/Clark

Aloha (1975)
Nueva Andalucía, 29660 Marbella
Tel (952) 81 37 50/90 70 85/86, (952) 81 23 88 (Caddymaster)
Fax (952) 81 23 89

Holes 18 L 6261 m SSS 72
9 hole short course
V'tors H–booking necessary
Fees 18.000P
Loc 8km W of Marbella, nr Puerto
Banus
Arch Javier Arana

Los Arqueros (1991)
Crta de Ronda Km43, 29679
Benahavis (Málaga)
Tel (952) 78 46 00
Fax (952) 78 67 07
Holes 18 L 6130 m SSS 72
V'tors H
Fees 4500P
Loc 5km N of San Pedro de
Alcántara
Arch Severiano Ballesteros

Atalaya G&CC (1968)
Crta Benahavis 7, 29688 Málaga
Tel (952) 88 28 12
Fax (952) 88 78 97
Holes 18 L 5856 m Par 72
18 L 5217 m Par 72
V'tors U H
Fees On application
Loc 12km S of Marbella. 60km
SW of Málaga
Arch Von Limburger/Krings

Las Brisas (1968)
Apdo 147, 29660 Nueva
Andalucía, (Málaga)
Tel (952) 81 08 75/81 30 21
Fax (952) 81 55 18
Holes 18 L 6094 m SSS 72
V'tors H–restricted
Fees 18.000P
Loc 8km S of Marbella, nr Puerto
Banus
Arch Robert Trent Jones

La Cañada (1982)
Ctra Guadiaro Km 1, 11311
Guadiaro (Cádiz)
Tel (956) 79 41 00/79 44 11
Fax (956) 79 42 41
Holes 9 L 2873 m SSS 72
V'tors U
Loc Guadiaro, 2km from
Sotogrande
Arch Robert Trent Jones

La Duquesa G&CC (1987)
Urb El Hacho, 29691
Manilva (Málaga)
Tel (952) 89 04 25/89 04 26
Fax (952) 89 00 57
Holes 18 L 6142 m SSS 72
V'tors U
Loc 10km S of Estepona
Arch Robert Trent Jones

Estepona (1989)
Arroyo Vaquero, Apartado 532, 29680
Estepona (Málaga)
Tel (952) 11 30 81
Fax (952) 11 30 80

Web www.esteponagolf.com
Holes 18 L 5986 m Par 72
V'tors U
Fees 8500P
Loc 5km W of Estepona (CN340)
Arch Luis López

Guadalmina (1959)
Guadalmina Alta, San Pedro de
Alcántara, 29678 Marbella (Málaga)
Tel (952) 88 65 22
Fax (952) 88 34 83
Holes North 18 L 5825 m SSS 70
South 18 L 6075 m SSS 72
9 hole Par 3 course
V'tors H (max 27M/35L)
Fees 7500P
Loc San Pedro, 12km W of
Marbella
Arch Arana/Nardi

Marbella (1994)
CN 340 Km 188, 29600
Marbella (Málaga)
Tel (952) 83 05 00
Holes 18 L 5864 m Par 71 SSS 72
V'tors U
Loc Marbella
Arch Robert Trent Jones

Monte Mayor (1992)
Apdo 962, 29679 Benahavis (Málaga)
Tel (95) 211 30 88
Fax (95) 211 30 87
Holes 18 L 5652 m Par 71 SSS 71
V'tors U
Fees 13.500P (inc buggy)
Loc Between San Pedro and
Estepona, at Cancelada
Arch Pepe Gancedo

Los Naranjos (1977)
Apdo 64, 29660 Nueva
Andalucía, Marbella
Tel (952) 81 52 06/81 24 28
Fax (952) 81 14 28
Holes 18 L 6484 m SSS 72
V'tors U H
Loc 8km S of Marbella, nr Puerto
Banus
Arch Robert Trent Jones Sr

El Paraiso (1974)
Ctra Cádiz-Màlaga Km 167, 29680
Estepona (Málaga)
Tel (95) 288 38 35/288 38 46
Fax (95) 288 58 27
Holes 18 L 6116 m SSS 72
V'tors U
Fees 10.250P
Loc 14km S of Marbella
Arch Player/Kirby

La Quinta G&CC (1989)
Urb La Quinta, 29660
Nueva Andalucía
Tel (952) 76 23 90
Fax (952) 76 23 99
Holes 27 L 5797-5945 m
SSS 71-72

V'tors U H
Fees € 6 6
Loc 3km N of San Pedro de
Alcántara
Arch Piñero/García-Garrido

Rio Real (1965)
Urb Rio Real, PO Box 82, 29600
Marbella (Málaga)
Tel (95) 277 95 09
Fax (95) 277 21 40
Holes 18 L 6130 m SSS 72
V'tors U
Loc 5km E of Marbella. Málaga
Airport 50km
Arch Javier Arana

San Roque (1990)
CN 340 Km 126, San Roque,
11360 Cádiz
Tel (956) 61 30 30/60/90
Fax (956) 61 30 12/61 30 13
Web www.sanroque.com
Holes 18 L 6440 m SSS 74
V'tors U H
Fees 7000P
Loc 3km W of Sotogrande. 15km
E of Gibraltar
Arch Dave Thomas

Santa María G&CC
Coto de los Dolores, Urb Elviria, Crta
N340 Km 192, 29600
Marbella (Málaga)
Tel (952) 83 03 86/83 03 88/
83 10 36
Fax (952) 83 08 70
Holes 9 L 5792 m Par 71
V'tors U
Loc 10km E of Marbella, opp
Hotel Don Carlos
Arch A García Garrido

Sotogrande (1964)
Paseo del Parque, Apartado 14,
Sotogrande (Cádiz)
Tel (956) 79 50 50/79 50 51
Fax (956) 79 50 29
Holes 18 L 6224 m SSS 74
9 L 1299 m Par 29
V'tors U
Loc 30km N of Gibraltar, nr
Guadiaro
Arch Robert Trent Jones

Valderrama (1985)
11310 Sotogrande (Cadiz)
Tel (956) 79 12 00
Fax (956) 79 60 28
Web www.valderrama.com
Holes 18 L 7050 yds SSS 72
9 hole Par 3 course
V'tors H–12–2pm
Fees € 2 2 0
Loc 18km N of Gibraltar
Arch Robert Trent Jones Sr

La Zagaleta (1994)
Crta San Pedro-Ronda Km 9,
29679 Benahavis
Tel (95) 285 54 53

Holes 18 L 6039 m Par 72 SSS 72
V'tors U
Loc S of Marbella on Ronda road
Arch Bradford Benz

Seville & Gulf of Cádiz

Bellavista (1976)
Crta Huelva-Punta Umbría, Apdo 335, Huelva
Tel (955) 31 90 17
Fax (955) 31 90 25
Holes 9 L 6270 m SSS 73
V'tors U
Loc Aljaraque, 6km SW of Huelva, towards Punta Umbria

Costa Ballena (1997)
Crta Sta María-Chipiona, 11520 Rota
Tel (956) 84 70 70
Holes 18 L 6187 m Par 72 SSS 72
V'tors U
Arch J-M Olazábal

Isla Canela (1993)
Crta de la Playa, 21400 Ayamonte (Huelva)
Tel (959) 47 72 63
Fax (959) 47 72 71
Holes 18 L 5937 m Par 72
V'tors U H
Fees 7000P
Loc Ayamonte, 4km from Portuguese border
Arch Juan Caterineu

Islantilla (1993)
Urb Islantilla, Apdo 52, 21410 Isla Cristina (Huelva)
Tel (959) 48 60 39/48 60 49
Fax (959) 48 61 04
Holes 27 L 5926-6142 m SSS 72-73
V'tors U H
Fees 8500P
Loc 30km W of Huelva, nr Portuguese border
Arch Canales/Recasens

Montecastillo (1992)
Carretera de Arcos, 11406 Jérez
Tel (956) 15 12 00
Fax (956) 15 12 09
Holes 18 L 6494 m SSS 72
V'tors H
Fees 15.000P
Loc 10km NE of Jérez. 75km S of Seville
Arch Jack Nicklaus

Montenmedio G&CC (1996)
CN 340 Km42.5, 11150 Vejer-Barbate (Cádiz)
Tel (956) 45 12 16
Fax (956) 45 12 95
Web www.montenmedio.com
Holes 18 L 5897 m Par 72 SSS 72

V'tors H
Fees 12.500P
Loc Cádiz-Algeciras road (CN 340)
Arch A Maldonado

Novo Sancti Petri (1990)
Urb Novo Sancti Petri, Playa de la Barrosa, 11139 Chiclana de la Frontera
Tel (956) 49 40 05
Fax (956) 49 43 50
Web www.golf-novosancti.es
Holes 18 L 6071 m Par 72
       18 L 6476 m Par 72
V'tors U H
Fees 8500P
Loc La Barrosa, 24km SE of Cádiz. Jérez Airport 50km
Arch Severiano Ballesteros

Pineda De Sevilla (1939)
Apartado 1049, 41080 Sevilla
Tel (954) 61 14 00
Holes 18 L 6120 m SSS 72
V'tors U
Loc 3km S of Seville on Cádiz road
Arch R & F Medina

Real Sevilla (1992)
Autovía Sevilla-Utrera, 41089 Montequinto (Sevilla)
Tel (954) 12 43 01
Fax (954) 12 42 29
Web www.sevillagolf.com
Holes 18 L 6321 m SSS 73
V'tors U H WE–booking necessary
Fees 6515P
Loc 3km S of Seville
Arch José María Olazabal

Sevilla Golf (1989)
Hacienda Las Minas, Ctra de Isla Mayor, Aznalcazar (Sevilla)
Tel (955) 75 04 14
Holes 9 L 5910 m Par 71
V'tors U
Loc 15km W of Seville
Arch A García Garrido

Vista Hermosa (1975)
Apartado 77, Urb Vista Hermosa, 11500 Puerto de Santa María, Cádiz
Tel (956) 87 56 05
Holes 9 L 5614 m Par 70
Loc 25km W of Cádiz

Zaudin
Crta Tomares-Mairena, 41940 Tomares (Sevilla)
Tel (954) 15 41 59
Fax (954) 15 33 44
Holes 18 L 6192 m Par 71 SSS 72
V'tors U
Fees €40 (€60)
Loc Cornisa del Aljarafe, 3km from Seville
Arch Gary Player

Valencia & Castellón

El Bosque (1989)
Crta Godelleta, 46370 Chiva-Valencia
Tel (96) 180 41 42
Fax (96) 180 40 09
Holes 18 L 6384 m SSS 74
V'tors U
Loc Nr Chiva, 24km W of Valencia, off Madrid road
Arch Robert Trent Jones Sr

Costa de Azahar (1960)
Crta Grao-Benicasim, Castellón de la Plana
Tel (964) 22 70 64
Holes 9 L 2724 m SSS 70
Loc 5km NE of Castellón, on coast
Arch Angel Pérez

Escorpión (1975)
Apartado Correos 1, Betera (Valencia)
Tel (96) 160 12 11
Fax (96) 169 01 87
Holes 18 L 6345 m SSS 73
V'tors H
Fees 4000P (8000P)
Loc Betera, 20km N of Valencia
Arch Ron Kirby

Manises (1964)
Apartado 22.029, Manises (Valencia)
Tel (96) 152 18 71
Holes 9 L 6094 m Par 73
Loc 8km W of Valencia
Arch Javier Arana

Mediterraneo CC (1978)
Urb La Coma, Borriol, (Castellón)
Tel (964) 32 12 27
Fax (964) 32 13 57
Web www.ccmediterraneo.com
Holes 18 L 6239 m SSS 73
V'tors U
Loc Borriol, 4km NW of Castellón
Arch Ramón Espinosa

Oliva Nova (1995)
46780 Oliva (Valencia)
Tel (096) 285 76 66
Fax (096) 285 76 67
Web www.olivanovagolf.com
Holes 18 L 6270m Par 72
       5 hole Par 3 course
V'tors H
Fees 7000P (8000P)
Loc 15km N of Denia on N332. A7 Junction 61
Arch Severiano Ballesteros

Panorámica (1995)
Urb Panorámica, 12320 San Jorge (Castellón)
Tel (964) 49 30 72
Holes 18 L 6429 m Par 72 SSS 74
V'tors U

Loc   A7 Junction 42 towards
       Vinaroz
Arch   Bernhardt Langer

El Saler (1968)
*Parador Luis Vives, 46012 El
Saler (Valencia)*
Tel   (96) 161 11 86
Fax   (96) 162 70 16
Holes 18 L 6485 m SSS 75
V'tors U
Loc   Oliva, 18km S of Valencia,
       towards Cullera
Arch   Javier Arana

Valladolid

Entrepinos (1990)
*Avda del Golf 2, Urb Entrepinos, 47130
Simancas (Valladolid)*
Tel   (983) 59 05 11/59 05 61
Fax   (983) 59 07 65
Holes 18 L 5215 m Par 69 SSS 69
V'tors U H
Fees   5400P (7500P)
Loc   15km SW of Valladolid
Arch   Manuel Piñero

Zaragoza

Aero Club de Zaragoza
(1966)
Coso 34, 50004 Zaragoza
Tel   (976) 21 43 78
Holes 9 L 5042 m SSS 67
Loc   12km SW of Zaragoza, by
       airbase

La Penaza (1973)
Apartado 3039, Zaragoza
Tel   (976) 34 28 00/34 22 48
Fax   (976) 34 28 00
Holes 18 L 6122 m SSS 72
V'tors H
Loc   15km SW of Zaragoza on
       Madrid road, nr airbase
Arch   FW Hawtree

Sweden

East Central

Ängsö (1979)
Björnövägen 2, 721 30 Västerås
Tel   (0171) 441012
Fax   (0171) 441049
Holes 18 hole course Par 72
V'tors H
Fees   160kr (230kr)
Loc   15km E of Västerås
Arch   Åke Hultström

Arboga
PO Box 263, 732 25 Arboga
Tel   (0589) 70100
Holes 18 L 5890 m Par 71
V'tors U
Fees   160kr
Loc   5km S of Arboga
Arch   Sune Linde

Ärila (1951)
Nicolai, 611 92 Nyköping
Tel   (0155) 216617
Fax   (0155) 267657
Holes 18 L 5826 m Par 72
V'tors H
Fees   200kr (270kr)
Loc   5km SE of Nyköping
Arch   Sköld/Linde

Askersund (1980)
Box 3002, 696 03 Ammeberg
Tel   (0583) 34943
Fax   (0583) 34945
Web   www.golf.se/askersundsgk
Holes 18 L 5835 m SSS 72
V'tors H
Fees   220kr (260kr)
Loc   10km SE of Askersund
       towards Ammeberg. 1km on
       road to Kärra
Arch   Ronald Fream

Burvik
Burvik, 740 12 Knutby
Tel   (0174) 43060
Fax   (0174) 43062
Holes 18 L 5785 m SSS 72
V'tors U
Fees   On application
Loc   45km E of Uppsala. 70km N
       of Stockholm
Arch   Bengt Lorichs

Edenhof (1991)
740 22 Bälinge
Tel   (018) 334185
Fax   (018) 334186
Holes 18 L 5898 m SSS 72
V'tors H
Fees   180kr (240kr)
Loc   17km NW of Uppsala
Arch   Sune Linde

Enköping (1970)
Box 2006, 745 02 Enköping
Tel   (0171) 20830
Fax   (0171) 20823
Holes 18 L 5660 m Par 71
V'tors H
Fees   180kr (220kr)
Loc   1km E of Enköping, off E18

Eskilstuna (1951)
Strängnäsvägen, 633 49 Eskilstuna
Tel   (016) 142629
Fax   (016) 148729
Holes 18 L 5610 m SSS 70
V'tors H
Fees   160kr (200kr)
Loc   2km E of Eskilstuna. 20km E
       of Örebro
Arch   Douglas Brasier

Fagersta (1970)
Box 2051, 737 02 Fagersta
Tel   (0223) 54060
Fax   (0223) 54000
Holes 18 L 5775 m Par 71
V'tors U
Fees   140kr (180kr)
Loc   7km W of Fagersta (Route
       65). 70km N of Västerås

Frösåker (1989)
*Frösåker Gård, Box 17015, 720
17 Västerås*
Tel   (021) 25401
Fax   (021) 25485
Holes 18 L 5820 m Par 72
V'tors U H
Fees   200kr (250kr)
Loc   15km SE of Västerås
Arch   Sune Linde

Fullerö (1988)
Jotsberga, 725 91 Västerås
Tel   (021) 50132
Fax   (021) 50431
Web   www.golf.se/fullerogk
Holes 18 L 5633 m SSS 71
V'tors H
Fees   200kr (280kr)
Loc   6km SW of Västerås
Arch   Hultström/Sjöberg

Gripsholm (1991)
Box 133, 647 32 Mariefred
Tel   (0159) 350050
Fax   (0159) 350059
Web   www.golf.se/gripsholmsgk
Holes 18 holes Par 73 course
V'tors H
Fees   250kr (350kr)
Loc   Mariefred, 70km SW of
       Stockholm
Arch   Bengt Lorichs

Grönlund (1989)
PO Box 38, 740 10 Almunge
Tel   (0174) 20670
Fax   (0174) 20455
Holes 18 L 5865 m SSS 71
V'tors H
Fees   200kr (260kr)
Loc   20km E of Uppsala. 25km NE
       of Arlanda Airport
Arch   Åke Persson

Gustavsvik
Box 22033, 702 02 Örebro
Tel   (019) 244486
Fax   (019) 246490
Holes 18 holes SSS 72
V'tors H
Fees   200kr
Loc   1km S of Örebro
Arch   Turner/Wirhed

Katrineholm (1959)
Jättorp, 641 93 Katrineholm
Tel   (0150) 39270
Fax   (0150) 39011
Holes 18 L 5850 m SSS 72
       9 L 2850 m

V'tors U
Fees 250kr
Loc 7km E of Katrineholm
Arch Skjöld/Lorichs

Köping (1963)
Box 278, 731 26 Köping
Tel (0221) 81090
Fax (0221) 81277
Holes 18 L 5636 m Par 71
V'tors U
Fees 150kr (200kr)
Loc 5km N of Köping (Route 250)
Arch Brasier/Sederholm

Kumla (1987)
Box 46, 692 21 Kumla
Tel (019) 577370
Fax (019) 577373
Holes 18 L 5845 m SSS 72
V'tors U
Fees 200kr
Loc 8km E of Kumla. 20km SE of Örebro
Arch Jan Sederholm

Linde (1984)
Dalkarlshyttan, 711 31 Lindesberg
Tel (0581) 13960
Fax (0581) 12936
Holes 18 L 5539 m Par 71
V'tors H
Fees 180kr (180kr)
Loc 42km N of Örebro on R60. Lindesberg 2km
Arch Jan Sederholm

Mosjö (1989)
Mosjö Gård, 705 94 Örebrö
Tel (019) 225780
Fax (019) 225045
Holes 18 L 6160 m Par 72
V'tors WD–U WE–H
Fees 200kr (200kr)
Loc 10km S of Örebrö
Arch Åke Persson

Nora (1988)
Box 108, 713 23 Nora
Tel (0587) 311660
Fax (0587) 15050
Holes 18 L 5865 m Par 72
V'tors U
Fees 200kr (240kr)
Loc 33km N of Örebro
Arch Jeremy Turner

Örebro (1939)
Lanna, 719 93 Vintrosa
Tel (019) 291065
Fax (019) 291055
Web www.golf.se/golfklubbar/orebrogk
Holes 18 L 5870 m Par 71
V'tors H–max 36
Fees 260kr (320kr)
Loc 18km W of Örebro on Route E18
Arch Sköld/Sundblom/Berglund

Roslagen
Box 110, 761 22 Norrtälje
Tel (0176) 237194
Fax (0176) 237103
Holes 18 L 5614 m SSS 72
9 L 2888 m SSS 36
V'tors H
Fees 18 hole:250kr (300kr)
9 hole:150kr
Loc 7km N of Norrtälje
Arch TG Oxenstierna

Sala (1970)
Fallet, Isätra, 733 92 Sala
Tel (0224) 53077/53055/53064
Fax (0224) 53143
Holes 18 L 5640 m SSS 71
V'tors U
Fees 160kr (200kr)
Loc 8km E of Sala towards Uppsala, Route 67/72
Arch Tedrup/Linde

Sigtunabygden (1961)
Box 89, 193 22 Sigtuna
Tel (08) 592 54012
Fax (08) 592 54167
Holes 18 L 5710 m SSS 72
V'tors H
Fees 220kr (280kr)
Loc Sigtuna, 50km N of Stockholm
Arch Nils Sköld

Skepptuna
Skeptunnam 195 93 Märsta
Tel (08) 512 93069
Fax (08) 512 93163
Web www.skepptunagk.nu
Holes 18 L 5745 m CR 71.4 SR 131
V'tors U H
Fees 250kr (300kr)
Loc 50km N of Stockholm, via Route 273
Arch Jan Sederholm

Södertälje (1952)
Box 91, 151 21 Södertälje
Tel (08) 550 38240
Fax (08) 550 62549
Holes 18 L 5875 m SSS 72
V'tors H WE–NA before 1pm
Fees 225kr (275kr)
Loc 4km W of Södertälje
Arch Nils Sköld

Strängnäs (1968)
Kilenlundavägen, 645 91 Strängnäs
Tel (0152) 14731
Fax (0152) 14716
Holes 18 L 5625 m SSS 72
V'tors H
Fees 200kr (240kr)
Loc 3km S of Strängnäs
Arch Anders Amilon

Torshälla (1960)
Box 128, 64422 Torshälla
Tel (016) 358722
Fax (016) 357491

Holes 18 L 5934 m Par 72
V'tors H
Fees 200kr (250kr)
Loc 5km N of Eskilstuna
Arch Brasier/Linde

Tortuna
Nicktuna, Tortuna, 725 96 Västerås
Tel (021) 65300
Fax (021) 65302
Holes 18 L 5750 m SSS 72
V'tors U
Fees 150kr (180kr)
Loc 10km N of Västerås
Arch Husell/Hultström

Trosa (1972)
Box 80, 619 22 Trosa
Tel (0156) 22458
Fax (0156) 22454
Holes 18 L 5727 m Par 72
V'tors U
Fees 200kr
Loc 5km W of Trosa, towards Uttervik
Arch P Chamberlain

Upsala (1937)
Håmö Gård, Läby, 755 92 Uppsala
Tel (018) 460120
Fax (018) 461205
Holes 18 L 5818 m SSS 72
9 L 2674 m SSS 70
V'tors H
Fees 300kr (350kr)
Loc 10km W of Uppsala
Arch Greger Paulsson

Vassunda (1989)
Smedby Gård, 741 91 Knivsta
Tel (018) 381230/381235
Fax (018) 381416
Holes 18 L 6141 m Par 72
V'tors H
Fees 240kr (340kr)
Loc 45km N of Stockholm
Arch Sune Linde

Västerås (1931)
Bjärby, 724 81 Västerås
Tel (021) 357543
Fax (021) 357573
Holes 18 L 5250 m SSS 69
V'tors U
Fees 200kr (250kr)
Loc 2km N of Västerås
Arch Nils Sköld

Far North

Boden (1946)
Box 107, 961 21 Boden
Tel (0921) 72051
Fax (0921) 72047
Holes 18 L 5495 m SSS 72
V'tors H
Fees 160kr
Loc 7km S of Boden
Arch Björn Eriksson

Funäsdalsfjällen (1972)
Box 66, 840 95 Funäsdalen
Tel (0684) 21100
Fax (0684) 21142
Holes 18 L 5300 m SSS 72
V'tors U
Fees 180kr
Loc Funäsdalen, nr Norwegian border
Arch Sköld/Linde

Gällivare-Malmberget (1973)
Box 35, 983 21 Malmberget
Tel (0970) 20770
Fax (0970) 20776
Web www.gellivare/forening/golf
Holes 18 L 5528 m Par 71
V'tors H
Fees 200kr
Loc 4km NW of Gällivare, towards Malmberget
Arch Jan Sederholm

Haparanda (1989)
Mattiu 140, 953 35 Haparanda
Tel (0922) 10660
Fax (0922) 15040
Holes 18 L 6230 m SSS 73
V'tors H
Fees 160kr
Loc 125km E of Luleå
Arch Peter Chamberlain

Härnösand (1957)
Box 52, 871 22 Härnösand
Tel (0611) 66169
Fax (0611) 66165
Holes 18 L 5819 m SSS 72
V'tors H
Fees D–200kr
Loc Vägnön, 16km N of Härnösand on E4, towards Hemsö Island
Arch Sköld/Turner

Kalix (1990)
Box 32, 952 21 Kalix
Tel (0923) 15945/15935
Fax (0923) 77735
Holes 18 L 5700m SSS 71
V'tors U
Fees 160kr
Loc 80km N of Luleå
Arch Jan Sederholm

Luleå (1955)
Golfbanevåg 80, 975 96 Luleå
Tel (0920) 256300
Fax (0920) 256362
Holes 18 L 5675 m Par 72
V'tors H
Fees 250kr (250kr)
Loc Rutvik, 12km E of Luleå
Arch Skjöld/Tideman

Norrmjöle (1992)
905 82 Umeå
Tel (090) 81581

Fax (090) 81565
Holes 18 L 5619 m Par 72
V'tors U
Fees 200kr (220kr)
Loc 19km S of Umeå
Arch Acke Lundgren

Östersund-Frösö (1947)
Box 40, 832 01 Frösön
Tel (063) 43001
Fax (063) 43765
Holes 18 L 6000 m Par 73
V'tors U
Fees 180kr
Loc Island of Frösö
Arch Nils Sköld

Öviks GC Puttom (1967)
Ovansjö 1970, 891 95 Arnäsvall
Tel (0660) 254001
Fax (0660) 254040
Holes 18 L 5795 m SSS 72
V'tors H
Fees 180kr
Loc 15km N of Örnsköldsvik on E4
Arch Nils Sköld

Piteå (1960)
Nötöv 119, 941 41 Piteå
Tel (0911) 14990
Fax (0911) 14960
Holes 18 L 5325 m Par 69
V'tors H
Fees 160kr
Loc 2km SE of Piteå
Arch Jan Sederholm

Skellefteå (1967)
Rönnbäcken, 931 92 Skellefteå
Tel (0910) 779333
Fax (0910) 779777
Holes 27 L 6135 m SSS 72
Par 3 course
V'tors U H
Fees 200kr
Loc Skellefteå 5km
Arch Sköld/Carlsson/Larsson

Sollefteå (1970)
Box 213, 881 25 Sollefteå
Tel (0620) 21477/12670
Fax (0620) 21477/12670
Holes 18 L 5770 m SSS 72
V'tors H
Fees 180kr
Loc Österforse, 15km SW of Sollefteå (Route 89)
Arch Nils Sköld

Sundsvall (1952)
Golfvägen 5, 862 00 Kvissleby
Tel (060) 561056
Fax (060) 561909
Holes 18 L 5885 m SSS 72
V'tors WD–H before noon WE–H after 10am
Fees 180kr (200r)
Loc Skottsund, 15km S of Sundsvall

Timrå
Golfbanevägen 2, 860 32 Fagervik
Tel (060) 570153
Fax (060) 578136
Holes 18 L 5715 m Par 72
V'tors H
Fees 180kr (200kr)
Loc 1km S of Sundsvall airport
Arch Sune Linde

Umeå (1954)
Lövön, 913 35 Holmsund
Tel (090) 41071/41066
Fax (090) 149120
Holes 18 L 5751 m SSS 72
9 L 2688 m SSS 70
V'tors U
Fees 200kr
Loc 16km SE of Umeå
Arch Bo Engdahl

Gothenburg

Albatross (1973)
Lillhagsvägen, 422 50 Hisings-Backa
Tel (031) 551901/550500
Fax (031) 555900
Holes 18 L 6020 m SSS 72
Fees 220kr (250kr)
Loc 10km N of Gothenburg on Hising Island

Chalmers
PO Box 40, 438 21 Landvetter
Tel (031) 918430
Fax (031) 916338
Holes 18 L 5604 m SSS 71
V'tors WD–U H before 4pm –M H after 4pm WE–M H before 2pm –U H after 2pm
Fees 200kr (200kr)
Loc 20km E of Gothenburg. 2km from Landvetter airport
Arch Gyllenhammar/Henrikson

Delsjö (1962)
Kallebäck, 412 76 Göteborg
Tel (031) 406959
Fax (031) 703 0431
Web www.degk.se
Holes 18 L 5703 m Par 71
V'tors H WE–NA before 1pm
Fees 300kr
Loc 5km E of Gothenburg (Route 40)
Arch Douglas Brasier

Forsgårdens (1982)
Gamla Forsv 1, 434 47 Kungsbacka
Tel (0300) 566350
Fax (0300) 566351
Web www.golf.se/forsgardensgk
Holes 18 L 6110 m SSS 72
9 L 2915 m
V'tors WD–U WE–NA before 2pm
Fees 250kr (300kr)
Loc 1km SE of Kungsbacka. 20km S of Gothenburg
Arch Sune Linde

Göteborg (1902)

Box 2056, 436 02 Hovås
Tel (031) 282444
Fax (031) 685333
Holes 18 L 5935 yds SSS 70
V'tors WD–U H–max 28(M) 32 (L)
WE–M before 2pm
Fees 350kr (400kr)
Loc 11km S of Gothenburg (Route 158)

Gullbringa (1968)

442 95 Kungälv
Tel (0303) 227161
Fax (0303) 227778
Holes 18 L 5775 m Par 70
V'tors U
Fees 220kr
Loc 14km W of Kungälv, towards Marstrand
Arch Douglas Brasier

Kungälv-Kode

Ö Knaverstad 140, 442 97 Kode
Tel (0303) 51300
Fax (0303) 50205
Holes 18 L 5984 m Par 72
V'tors U
Fees 200kr
Loc 30km N of Gothenburg
Arch Lars Andreasson

Kungsbacka (1971)

Hamra Gård 515, 429 44 Särö
Tel (031) 936277
Fax (031) 935085
Holes 18 L 5855 m SSS 72
9 L 2880 m SSS 36
V'tors WD–U WE–NA before 2pm
Fees 250kr (300kr)
Loc 7km N of Kungsbacka on Route 158
Arch Pennink/Davidsson/ Nordström

Lysegården (1966)

Box 532, 442 15 Kungälv
Tel (0303) 223426
Fax (0303) 223075
Holes 18 L 5670 m SSS 71
9 L 5444 m SSS 70
V'tors H
Fees 200kr
Loc 10km N of Kungälv
Arch Röhss/Engström

Mölndals (1979)

Box 77, 437 21 Lindome
Tel (031) 993030
Fax (031) 994901
Holes 18 L 5625 m SSS 73
V'tors H WE–NA before 11am
Fees 220kr (250kr)
Loc Lindome, 20km S of Gothenburg
Arch Ronald Fream

Öijared (1958)

Pl 1082, 448 92 Floda
Tel (0302) 30604

Fax (0302) 35370
Web www.oijaredgk.o.se
Holes 18 L 5875 m Par 72
18 L 5655 m Par 71
V'tors H WE–NA before 1pm
Fees 250kr (250kr)
Loc 35km NE of Gothenburg (E20), nr Nääs
Arch Brasier/Amilon

Partille (1986)

Box 234, 433 24 Partille
Tel (031) 987043
Fax (031) 987757
Web www.golf.se/partillegk
Holes 18 L 5475 m Par 70
V'tors WD–H WE–NA before 1pm
Fees 220kr (220kr)
Loc Öjersjö, 10km E of Gothenburg
Arch Jan Sederholm

Sjögärde

430 30 Frillesås
Tel (0340) 657860
Fax (0340) 657861
Holes 18 L 5723 m SSS 72
6 hole short course
V'tors H
Fees 220kr (250kr)
Loc 20km S of Kungsbacka
Arch Lars Andreasson

Stenungsund (1993)

Lundby Pl 7480, 444 93 Spekeröd
Tel (0303) 778470
Fax (0303) 778350
Web www.golf.se/golfklubbar/ stenungsundgk
Holes 18 L 6245 m Par 72
V'tors WD–H WE–NA 10–12
Fees 220kr (250kr)
Loc 40km N of Gothenburg
Arch Peter Nordwall

Stora Lundby (1983)

Valters Väg 2, 443 71 Grabo
Tel (0302) 44200
Fax (0302) 44125
Web www.storalundbygk.o.se
Holes 18 L 6040 m Par 72
9 hole Par 3 course
V'tors H
Fees 180kr (220kr)
Loc 25km NE of Gothenburg
Arch Frank Pennink

Malmö & South Coast

Abbekas (1989)

Kroppsmarksvagen, 274 56 Abbekas
Tel (0411) 533233
Fax (0411) 533419
Holes 18 L 5817 m Par 72
V'tors U H
Fees 220kr (260kr)
Loc 20km W of Ystad
Arch Tommy Nordström

Barsebäck G&CC (1969)

246 55 Löddeköpinge
Tel (046) 776230
Fax (046) 772630
Holes Old 18 L 5910 m Par 72
New 18 L 6025 m Par 72
V'tors WD–H booking necessary
Fees D–360kr
Loc 35km N of Malmö
Arch Bruce/Steel

Bokskogen (1963)

Torupsvägen 408-140, 230 40 Bara
Tel (040) 406900
Fax (040) 406929
Holes Old 18 L 6006 m Par 72
New 18 L 5542 m Par 71
V'tors H WE–after 1pm Old course
Fees 400kr (400kr)
Loc 15km SE of Malmö, off E65
Arch Amilon/Sederholm/Lorichs

Falsterbo (1909)

Fyrvägen, 239 40 Falsterbo
Tel (040) 470078/475078
Fax (040) 472722
Holes 18 L 6577 yds Par 71
V'tors H WE–M before noon
Fees D–300–400kr
Loc 30km SW of Malmö
Arch Gunnar Bauer

Flommens (1935)

239 40 Falsterbo
Tel (040) 475016
Fax (040) 473157
Web www.flommensgk.com
Holes 18 L 5735 m SSS 72
V'tors U H
Fees 240–280kr (280kr)
Loc 35km SW of Malmö
Arch Bergendorff/Kristersson

Kävlinge (1991)

Box 138, 244 22 Kävlinge
Tel (046) 736270
Fax (046) 728486
Holes 18 L 5800 m SSS 72
V'tors H
Fees 200kr (280kr)
Loc 12km N of Lund
Arch Rolf Collijn

Ljunghusen (1932)

Kinellsvag, Ljunghusen, 236 42 Höllviken
Tel (040) 450384
Fax (040) 454265
Holes 27 holes:
L 5455-5895 m SSS 70-73
V'tors WD–U H WE–M before noon
Fees 300kr (350kr)
Loc Falsterbo Peninsula. 30km SW of Malmö
Arch Douglas Brasier

Lunds Akademiska (1936)

Kungsmarken, 225 92 Lund
Tel (046) 99005
Fax (046) 99146

Holes 18 L 5780 m SSS 72
V'tors H
Fees 160kr (200kr)
Loc 5km E of Lund
Arch Boström/Morrison

Malmö

Segesvängen, 212 27 Malmö
Tel (040) 292535/292536
Fax (040) 292228
Holes 18 L 5720 m SSS 71
V'tors H
Fees 200kr (240kr)
Loc NE of Malmö

Örestad (1986)

Golfvägen, Habo Ljung, 234 22 Lomma
Tel (040) 410580
Fax (040) 416320
Web www.orestadsgk.com
Holes 18 L 6036 m Par 73
9 L 2923 m Par 35
18 hole Par 3 course
V'tors H
Fees 200kr (250kr)
Loc 15km N of Malmö
Arch Åke Persson

Österlen (1945)

Lilla Vik, 272 95 Simrishamn
Tel (0414) 412550
Fax (0414) 412551
Web www.osterlensgk.com
Holes 18 L 5855 m CR 69.8
V'tors H
Fees 220–290kr
Loc Vik, 8km N of Simrishamn
Arch Tommy Nordström

Romeleåsen (1969)

Kvarnbrodda, 240 14 Veberöd
Tel (046) 82012
Fax (046) 82113
Web www.golf.romeleasensgk.com
Holes 18 L 5783 m Par 72
V'tors H
Fees 220kr (280kr)
Loc 6km S of Veberöd. 25km E of Malmö
Arch Douglas Brasier

Söderslätts

Ellaboda Grevier 260, 235 94 Vellinge
Tel (040) 429680
Fax (040) 429684
Holes 18 L 5800 m SSS 72
9 hole Par 3 course
V'tors WD–H WE–M H before noon
Fees 250kr
Loc 15km SE of Malmö
Arch Sune Linde

Tegelberga (1988)

Alstad Pl 140, 231 96 Trelleborg
Tel (040) 485690
Fax (040) 485691
Web www.golf.se/tegelbergagk
Holes 27 L 6011 m CR 73.5
V'tors U H
Fees 250kr (300kr)

Loc 11km N of Trelleborg. 25km E of Malmö
Arch Peter Chamberlain

Tomelilla

Ullstorp, 273 94 Tomelilla
Tel (0417) 13420
Fax (0417) 13657
Web www.tomelillagolfklubb.com
Holes 18 L 6455 m Par 73 SSS 75
V'tors H
Fees 240kr (240kr)
Loc 15km N of Ystad. 60km E of Malmö
Arch Tommy Nordström

Trelleborg (1963)

Maglarp, Pl 431, 231 93 Trelleborg
Tel (0410) 330460
Fax (0410) 330281
Web www.trelleborgsgk.com
Holes 18 L 5278 m Par 70
V'tors U H
Fees 200kr
Loc 5km W of Trelleborg
Arch Brasier/Chamberlain

Vellinge (1991)

Toftadals Gård, 235 41 Vellinge
Tel (040) 443255
Fax (040) 443179
Holes 18 L 5766 m SSS 72
6 hole short course
V'tors WD–U WE–U H
Fees 200kr (250kr)
Loc 10km SE of Malmö
Arch Tommy Nordström

Ystad (1930)

Långrevsvägen, 270 22 Köpingebro
Tel (0411) 550350
Fax (0411) 550392
Holes 18 L 5800 m Par 72
V'tors U
Fees 200–250kr
Loc 7km E of Ystad, towards Simrishamn
Arch Thure Bruce

North

Alvkarleby

Västanåvägen 5, 814 94 Alvkarleby
Tel (026) 72757
Fax (026) 82307
Holes 18 holes Par 70
V'tors U
Fees On application
Loc 25km from Gävle (Route 76)

Avesta (1963)

Åsbo, 774 61 Avesta
Tel (0226) 55913/10866/12766
Fax (0226) 12578
Web www.golf.se/golfklubbar/avestagk
Holes 18 L 5560 m SSS 71
V'tors I

Fees 200kr (260kr)
Loc 3km NE of Avesta
Arch Sune Linde

Bollnäs

Norrfly 4526, 823 91 Kilafors
Tel (0278) 650540
Fax (0278) 651220
Holes 18 L 5870 m Par 72
V'tors H
Fees 180kr (200kr)
Loc 15km S of Bollnäs (Route 83)

Dalsjö (1989)

Dalsjö 3, 781 94 Borlänge
Tel (0243) 220095
Fax (0243) 220140
Holes 18 L 5715 m Par 72
V'tors H
Fees 220kr (270kr)
Loc 5km NE of Borlänge
Arch Jeremy Turner

Falun-Borlänge (1956)

Storgarden 10, 791 93 Falun
Tel (023) 31015
Fax (023) 31072
Holes 18 L 6085 m Par 72
V'tors U
Fees 220kr (270kr)
Loc Aspeboda, 8km N of Borlänge
Arch Nils Sköld

Gävle (1949)

Bönavägen 23, 805 95 Gävle
Tel (026) 120333/120338
Fax (026) 516468
Holes 18 L 5735 m SSS 73
Fees 200kr (250kr)
Loc 3km N of Gävle

Hagge (1963)

Hagge, 771 90 Ludvika
Tel (0240) 28087/28513
Fax (0240) 28515
Holes 18 L 5519 m SSS 71
V'tors H
Fees D–150kr
Loc 7km S of Ludvika
Arch Sune Linde

Hofors (1965)

Box 117, 813 22 Hofors
Tel (0290) 85125
Fax (0290) 85101
Holes 18 L 5400 m Par 70
V'tors U
Fees 180kr (200kr)
Loc 5km SE of Hofors
Arch Sune Linde

Högbo (1962)

Daniel Tilas Väg 4, 811 92 Sandviken
Tel (026) 215015
Fax (026) 215322
Holes 18 L 5760 m Par 72
9 L 2590 m Par 35
V'tors H
Fees 250kr

Loc 6km N of Sandviken (Route 272)
Arch Sköld/Linde

Hudiksvall (1964)
Tjuvskär, 824 01 Hudiksvall
Tel (0650) 15930
Fax (0650) 18630
Holes 18 L 5665 m SSS 72
V'tors U
Fees 160kr
Loc 4km SE of Hudiksvall
Arch Linde/Sköld

Leksand (1977)
Box 25, 793 21 Leksand
Tel (0247) 14640
Fax (0247) 14157
Holes 18 L 5263 m Par 70
V'tors U
Fees 120kr (180kr)
Loc 2km N of Leksand
Arch Nils Sköld

Ljusdal (1973)
Box 151, 827 23 Ljusdal
Tel (0651) 16883
Fax (0651) 16883
Holes 18 L 5920 m Par 72
V'tors U
Fees 200kr
Loc 2km E of Ljusdal
Arch Eriksson/Skjöld

Mora (1980)
Box 264, 792 24 Mora
Tel (0250) 10182
Fax (0250) 10306
Holes 18 L 5600 m Par 72
Fees 150kr
Loc 1km N of Mora. 40km NW of Rättvik
Arch Sune Linde

Rättvik (1954)
Box 29, 795 21 Rättvik
Tel (0248) 51030
Fax (0248) 12081
Holes 18 L 5375 m SSS 70
V'tors U
Fees 160–260kr
Loc 2km N of Rättvik

Sälenfjallens (1991)
Box 20, 780 67 Sälen
Tel (0280) 20670
Fax (0280) 20670
Web www.golf.se/salensfjallensgk
Holes 18 L 5710 m Par 72
V'tors U H
Fees 220kr
Loc 230km NW of Borlänge. 400km NW of Stockholm
Arch Sune Linde

Säter (1984)
Box 89, 783 22 Säter
Tel (0225) 50030
Fax (0225) 51424
Holes 18 L 5781 m Par 72

V'tors U
Fees 160kr
Loc 25km SE of Borlänge. 180km NW of Stockholm
Arch Sune Linde

Snöå (1990)
Snöå Bruk, 780 51 Dala-Järna
Tel (0281) 24072
Fax (0281) 24009
Web www.snoabruk.se/snoagk
Holes 18 L 5738 m SSS 73
V'tors H
Fees 200kr
Loc 80km W of Borlänge, nr Dala-Järna (Route 71)
Arch Åke Persson

Söderhamn (1961)
Box 117, 826 23 Söderhamn
Tel (0270) 281300
Fax (0270) 281003
Web www.soderhamnsgk.com
Holes 18 L 5940 m Par 72
V'tors H
Fees 200–250kr
Loc 8km N of Söderhamn
Arch Nils Sköld

Sollerö (1991)
Levsnäs, 79290 Sollerön
Tel (0250) 22236
Fax (0250) 22854
Holes 18 L 7226 yds Par 72
V'tors H
Fees 160kr
Loc 14km from Mora on Island of Sollerön in Siljan
Arch JR Turner

Skane & South

Allerum (1992)
Pl 7592, 260 35 Ödåkra
Tel (042) 93051
Fax (042) 93045
Holes 18 L 6201 m SSS 73
V'tors U
Fees 130kr (200kr)
Loc 9km NE of Helsingborg
Arch Hans Fock

Ängelholm (1973)
Box 1117, 262 22 Ängelholm
Tel (0431) 430260/431460
Fax (0431) 431568
Web www.golf.se/golfklubbar/angelholmsgk
Holes 18 L 5760 m Par 72
V'tors H (max 36)
Fees 200–250kr
Loc 10km E of Ängelholm on route 114
Arch Jan Sederholm

Araslöv
Starvägen 1, 291 75 Färlöv
Tel (044) 71600

Fax (044) 71575
Holes 18 L 5817 m Par 72
V'tors H or Green card
Fees 160kr (220kr)
Loc 9km NW of Kristianstad (Route 19)
Arch Sune Linde

Båstad (1929)
Box 1037, 269 21 Båstad
Tel (0431) 73136
Fax (0431) 73331
Holes 18 L 5632 m Par 71
          18 L 6163 m Par 72
V'tors H
Fees 330kr
Loc 4km W of Båstad (Route 115)
Arch Hawtree/Taylor/Nordström

Bedinge (1931)
Golfbanevägen, 231 76 Beddingestrand
Tel (0410) 25514
Fax (0410) 25411
Holes 18 L 5444 m Par 70
V'tors H
Fees 120 (160kr)
Loc Beddingestrand, 20km E of Trelleborg
Arch Åke Persson

Bjäre
Salomonhög 3086, 269 93 Båstad
Tel (0431) 361053
Fax (0431) 361764
Holes 18 L 5550 m SSS 71
V'tors H
Fees 290kr
Loc 2km E of Båstad. 60km N of Helsingborg
Arch Svante Dahlgren

Bosjökloster (1974)
243 95 Höör
Tel (0413) 25858
Fax (0413) 25895
Holes 18 L 5890 m Par 72
V'tors H
Fees 180kr (220kr)
Loc 7km S of Höör. 40km NE of Malmö
Arch Douglas Brasier

Carlskrona (1949)
PO Almö, 370 24 Nättraby
Tel (0457) 35123
Fax (0457) 35090
Web www.carlskronagk.com
Holes 18 L 5485 m Par 70
V'tors U
Fees D–220kr
Loc 18km SW of Karlskrona
Arch Jan Sederholm

Degeberga-Widtsköfle
Box 71, 297 21 Degeberga
Tel (044) 355035
Fax (044) 355075
Holes 18 L 6129 m SSS 72
          9 hole Par 3 course
V'tors U

Fees 100–170kr
Loc 20km S of Kristianstad

Eslöv (1966)
Box 150, 241 22 Eslöv
Tel (0413) 18610
Fax (0413) 18613
Web www.golf.se/golfklubbar/
eslovsgk
Holes 18 L 5630 m CR 70
V'tors H
Fees 220kr (270kr)
Loc 4km S of Eslöv (Route 113)
Arch Thure Bruce

Hässleholm (1978)
Skyrup, 282 95 Tyringe
Tel (0451) 53111
Fax (0451) 53138
Holes 18 L 5830 m SSS 72
V'tors U
Fees 200kr (240kr)
Loc 15km NW of Hässleholm
Arch Persson/Bruce/Jensen

Helsingborg (1924)
260 40 Viken
Tel (042) 236147
Holes 9 L 4578 m Par 68
V'tors U
Fees 140kr (160kr)
Loc 15km NW of Helsingborg
Arch W Hester

Karlshamn (1962)
Box 188, 374 23 Karlshamn
Tel (0454) 50085
Fax (0454) 50160
Holes 18 L 5861 m SSS 72
9 holes SSS 36
V'tors H
Fees D–220kr (250kr)
Loc Morrum, 10 km W of
Karlshamn
Arch Douglas Brasier

Kristianstad (1924)
Box 41, 296 21 Åhus
Tel (044) 247656
Fax (044) 247635
Holes 18 L 5810 m SSS 72
9 L 2945 m SSS 36
V'tors H
Fees D–240kr (D–280kr)
Loc 18km SE of Kristianstad.
Airport 20km
Arch Brasier/Nordström

Landskrona (1960)
Erikstorp, 261 61 Landskrona
Tel (0418) 446260
Fax (0418) 446262
Holes Old 18 L 5700 m SSS 71
New 18 L 4300 m SSS 67
V'tors U
Fees 210kr (250kr)
Loc 4km N of Landskrona,
towards Borstahusen

Mölle (1943)
260 42 Mölle
Tel (042) 347520

Fax (042) 347523
Web www.mollegk.m.se
Holes 18 L 5312 m Par 70
V'tors H–max 36
Fees 280kr
Loc Mölle, 35km NW of
Helsingborg
Arch Thure Bruce

Örkelljunga
Rya 472, 286 91 Örkelljunga
Tel (0435) 53690/53640
Fax (0435) 53670
Holes 18 L 5700 m SSS 72
V'tors H
Fees 200kr (240kr)
Loc 8km S of Örkelljunga. 40km
NE of Helsingborg (E4)
Arch Hans Fock

Östra Göinge (1981)
Box 114, 289 21 Knislinge
Tel (044) 60060
Fax (044) 69060
Holes 18 L 5898 m Par 72
V'tors U
Fees 160kr (200kr)
Loc 20km N of Kristianstad
Arch T Nordström

Perstorp (1964)
PO Box 87, 284 22 Perstorp
Tel (0435) 35411
Fax (0435) 35959
Holes 18 L 5675 m Par 71
6 hole short course
V'tors H
Fees 150kr (200kr)
Loc 1km S of Perstorp. 45km E of
Helsingborg
Arch Amilon/Bruce/Persson

Ronneby (1963)
Box 26, 372 21 Ronneby
Tel (0457) 10315
Fax (0457) 10412
Web www.golf.se/ronnebygk
Holes 18 L 5323 m Par 72
V'tors U
Fees 250kr
Loc 3km S of Ronneby

Rya (1934)
PL 5500, 255 92 Helsingborg
Tel (042) 220182
Fax (042) 220394
Holes 18 L 5599 m Par 72
V'tors H
Fees 260kr
Loc 10km S of Helsingborg
Arch Petterson/Sundblom

St Arild (1987)
Golfvagen 48, 260 41 Nyhamnsläge
Tel (042) 346860
Fax (042) 346042
Web www.starild.se
Holes 18 L 5805 m Par 72
V'tors H
Fees 260kr (260kr)
Loc 50km N of Helsingborg
Arch Jan Sederholm

Skepparslov (1984)
Udarpssäteri, 291 92 Kristianstad
Tel (044) 229508
Fax (044) 229503
Web www.golf.se/golfklubbar/
skepparslovsgk
Holes 18 L 5996 m SSS 73
V'tors U
Fees 180kr (250kr)
Loc 7km W of Kristianstad
Arch Rolf Collijn

Söderåsen (1966)
Box 41, 260 50 Billesholm
Tel (042) 73337
Fax (042) 73963
Web www.golf.se/golfklubbar/
soderasensgk
Holes 18 L 5657 m Par 71
V'tors U
Fees 280kr
Loc 20km E of Helsingborg
Arch Thure Bruce

Sölvesborg
Box 63, 294 22 Sölvesborg
Tel (0456) 70650
Fax (0456) 70650
Holes 18 L 5900 m Par 72
V'tors U
Fees 240kr
Loc 30km E of Kristianstad
Arch Sune Linde

Svalöv (1989)
Månstorp Pl 1365, 268 90 Svalöv
Tel (0418) 662462
Fax (0418) 663284
Web www.golf.se/golfklubbar/
svalovsgk
Holes 18 L 5784 m SSS 73
V'tors U
Fees 200kr (250kr)
Loc 20km E of Landskrona
Arch Tommy Nordström

Torekov (1924)
Råledsu 31, 260 93 Torekov
Tel (0431) 449841
Fax (0431) 364916
Holes 18 L 5701 m Par 72
V'tors Jun–Aug–H WE–M before
noon
Fees 220–280kr
Loc 3km N of Torekov
Arch Nils Sköld

Trummenas
373 02 Ramdala
Tel (0455) 60505
Fax (0455) 60571
Holes 18 L 5600 m Par 72
9 hole course
V'tors H
Fees 200kr
Loc 15km SE of Karlskrona, off
Route 22
Arch Ingmar Ericsson

Vasatorp (1973)

Box 13035, 250 13 Helsingborg
Tel   (042) 235058
Fax   (042) 235135
Holes 18 L 5875 m SSS 72
         9 L 2940 m
V'tors H
Fees   280kr
Loc   8km E of Helsingborg
Arch   Thure Bruce

Wittsjö (1962)

Ubbaltsgården, 280 22 Vittsjö
Tel   (0451) 22635
Fax   (0451) 22567
Holes 18 L 5461 m Par 71
V'tors U
Fees   160kr (200kr)
Loc   2km SE of Vittsjö
Arch   Sköld/Amilon

South East

A6 Golfklubb

Centralvägen, 553 05 Jönköping
Tel   (036) 308130
Fax   (036) 308140
Holes 27 hole course:
         9 L 3185 m Par 38
         9 L 3115 m Par 37
         9 L 2935 m Par 36
V'tors U H
Fees   200kr
Loc   2km SE of Jönköping
Arch   Peter Nordwall

Älmhult (1975)

Pl 1215, 343 90 Älmhult
Tel   (0476) 14135
Fax   (0476) 16565
Holes 18 L 5407 m SSS 71
V'tors U H
Fees   D–200kr
Loc   2km E of Älmhult on Route 23
Arch   Persson/Söderberg

Åtvidaberg (1954)

Västantorp, 597 41 Åtvidaberg
Tel   (0120) 35425
Fax   (0120) 13502
Holes 18 L 5565 m Par 71
V'tors H
Fees   250kr (300kr)
Loc   30km SE of Linköping
Arch   Brasier/Nordvall

Ekerum

387 92 Borgholm, Öland
Tel   (0485) 80000
Fax   (0485) 80010
Holes 18 L 6045 m Par 72
         9 L 2875 m Par 36
V'tors U H
Fees   250–340kr
Loc   12km S of Borgholm. 25km N
         of Öland bridge
Arch   Peter Nordwall

Eksjö (1938)

Skedhult, 575 96 Eksjö
Tel   (0381) 13525
Holes 18 L 5930 m SSS 72
V'tors WD–U WE–H
Fees   200kr
Loc   6km W of Eksjö on Nässjö
         road
Arch   Anders Amilon

Emmaboda (1976)

Kyrkogatan, 360 60 Vissefjärda
Tel   (0471) 20505/20540
Fax   (0471) 20440
Web   www.golf.se/golfklubbar/
         emmabodagk
Holes 18 L 6165 m SSS 72
V'tors H
Fees   200kr
Loc   12km S of Emmaboda. 50km
         N of Karlskrona

Finspång (1965)

Viberga Gård, 612 92 Finspång
Tel   (0122) 13940
Fax   (0122) 18888
Holes 27 L 5800 m SSS 72
V'tors U
Fees   220kr (280kr)
Loc   2km E of Finspång, Route 51.
         Norrköping 25km.
Arch   Sköld/Linde/Chamberlain

Gotska (1986)

Box 1119, 621 22 Visby, Gotland
Tel   (0498) 215545
Fax   (0498) 215545
Holes 18 L 5202 m Par 69
         9 L 5414 m Par 72
V'tors U H
Fees   18 hole:220kr 9 hole:120kr
Loc   N outskirts of Visby
Arch   Jack Wenman

Grönhögen (1996)

PL 1270, 380 65 Öland
Tel   (0485) 665990
Fax   (0485) 665999
Web   www.gronhogen.se
Holes 18 L 5100 m Par 70
V'tors H
Fees   160 kr (280kr)
Loc   45km S of Öland Bridge
Arch   Kenneth Nilsson

Gumbalde

Box 35, 620 13 Stånga, Gotland
Tel   (0498) 482880
Fax   (0498) 482884
Holes 18 L 5600 m SSS 71
V'tors U
Fees   200–240kr
Loc   50km SE of Visby, Gotland
         island
Arch   Lars Lagergren

Hook

560 13 Hok
Tel   (0393) 21420
Fax   (0393) 21379

Web www.hooksgk.com

Holes 18 L 5758 m SSS 72
         18 L 5750 m SSS 73
         9 hole Par 3 course
V'tors H
Fees   285kr
Loc   Hok, 30km SE of Jönköping,
         towards Växjö
Arch   Edberg/Bruce/Sederholm

Isaberg (1968)

Nissafors Bruk, 330 27 Hestra
Tel   (0370) 336330
Fax   (0370) 336325
Holes East 18 L 5823 m CR 71.8
         West 18 L 5568 m CR 70.0
V'tors H
Fees   250kr (300kr)
Loc   18km N of Gislaved, nr
         Nissafors. 60km S of
         Jönköping
Arch   Amilon/Bruce/Persson

Jönköping (1936)

Kettilstorp, 556 27 Jönköping
Tel   (036) 76567
Fax   (036) 76511
Web   www.golf.se/jonkopingsgk
Holes 18 L 5313 m Par 70
V'tors Phone in advance H–max 30
Fees   250kr (300kr)
Loc   Kettilstorp, 3km S of
         Jönköping
Arch   Frank Dyer

Kalmar (1947)

Box 278, 391 23 Kalmar
Tel   (0480) 472111
Fax   (0480) 472314
Web   www.golf.se/golfklubbar/
         kalmargk
Holes Blue 18 L 5700 m SSS 72
         Red 18 L 5634 m SSS 72
V'tors H
Fees   300kr (350kr)
Loc   9km N of Kalmar via E22
Arch   Brasier/Sköld/Linde

Lagan (1966)

Box 63, 340 14 Lagan
Tel   (0372) 30450/35460
Fax   (0372) 35307
Holes 18 L 5600 m SSS 71
V'tors U
Fees   160kr
Loc   Lagan, 10km N of Ljungby,
         on Route E4
Arch   Amilon/Persson/
         Magnusson

Landeryd (1987)

Bogestad Gård, 585 93 Linköping
Tel   (013) 362200
Fax   (013) 362208
Holes North 18 L 5675 m SSS 72
         South 18 L 5085 m SSS 68
         9 hole short course
V'tors U
Fees   220kr (240kr)
Loc   7km SE of Linköping
Arch   Nordström/Persson

Lidhems (1988)
360 14 Väckelsång
Tel (0470) 33660
Fax (0470) 33761
Web www.golf.se/lidhemsgk
Holes 18 L 5755 m Par 72
V'tors H
Fees 200kr
Loc 30km S of Växjo (Road 30)
Arch Ingmar Eriksson

Linköping (1945)
Box 10054, 580 10 Linköping
Tel (013) 120646
Fax (013) 140769
Holes 18 L 5664 m SSS 71
V'tors H
Fees 230kr (300kr)
Loc 3km SW of Linköping
Arch Sundblom/Brasier

Mjölby (1986)
Blixberg, Miskarp, 595 92 Mjölby
Tel (0142) 12570
Fax (0142) 16553
Holes 18 L 5485 m SSS 71
V'tors H
Fees 200kr (240kr)
Loc 35km WSW of Linköping (E4)
Arch Åke Persson

Motala (1956)
PO Box 264, 591 23 Motala
Tel (0141) 50840
Fax (0141) 208990
Holes 18 L 5905 m Par 72
V'tors U
Fees 200kr (240kr)
Loc 3km S of Motala via Route 50 or 32
Arch Sköld/Sederholm

Nässjö (1988)
Box 5, 571 21 Nässjö
Tel (0380) 10022
Fax (0380) 12082
Holes 18 L 5783 m Par 72
V'tors U H
Fees 170kr
Loc 40km E of Jönköping
Arch Bjorn Magnusson

Norrköping (1928)
Borg, 605 97 Norrköping
Tel (011) 335235/183654
Fax (011) 335014
Holes 18 L 5860 m SSS 73
V'tors U H
Fees 160kr (200kr)
Loc Klinga, 9km S of Norrköping on E4
Arch Nils Sköld

Oskarshamn (1972)
Box 148, 572 23 Oskarshamn
Tel (0491) 94033
Fax (0491) 94038
Holes 18 L 5545 m SSS 71
V'tors H
Fees 220kr (250kr)

Loc 10km SW of Oskarshamn, nr Forshult
Arch Nils Sköld

Skinnarebo
Skinnarebo, 555 93 Jönköping
Tel (036) 69075
Fax (036) 362975
Holes 18 L 5686 m SSS 71
9 hole Par 3 course
V'tors H
Fees 180kr
Loc 14km SW of Jönköping
Arch Björn Magnusson

Söderköping (1983)
Hylinge, 605 96 Norrköping
Tel (011) 70579
Holes 18 L 5730 m SSS 72
V'tors U
Fees 180kr
Loc Västra Husby, 9km W of Söderköping
Arch Ronald Fream

Tobo (1971)
Fredensborg 133, 598 91 Vimmerby
Tel (0492) 30346
Fax (0492) 30871
Web www.tbgk.h.se
Holes 18 L 5720 m Par 72
V'tors U
Fees 200kr (240kr)
Loc 10km S of Vimmerby, nr Storebro. 60km SW of Västervik
Arch Brasier/Jensen

Tranås (1952)
Box 430, 573 25 Tranås
Tel (0140) 311661
Fax (0140) 16161
Holes 18 L 5830 m SSS 72
V'tors H
Fees 200kr (240kr)
Loc 2km N of Tranås

Vadstena (1957)
Hagalund, Box 122, 592 33 Vadstena
Tel (0143) 12440
Fax (0143) 12709
Holes 18 L 5486 m Par 71
V'tors U
Fees 160kr
Loc 3km S of Vadstena, towards Vaderstad

Värnamo (1962)
Box 146, 331 21 Värnamo
Tel (0370) 23123
Fax (0370) 23216
Holes 18 L 6253 m SSS 72
V'tors U
Fees 200kr
Loc 8km E of Värnamo on Route 127
Arch Nils Sköld

Västervik (1959)
Box 62, Ekhagen, 593 22 Västervik
Tel (0490) 32420

Fax (0490) 32421
Holes 18 L 5760 m Par 72
V'tors U
Fees 200kr (250kr)
Loc 1km E of Västervik
Arch Sune linde

Växjö (1959)
Box 227, 351 05 Växjö
Tel (0470) 21515
Fax (0470) 21557
Web www.vaxjogk.com
Holes 18 L 5860 m Par 71
V'tors H
Fees 250kr
Loc 5km NW of Växjö
Arch Douglas Brasier

Vetlanda (1983)
Box 249, 574 23 Vetlanda
Tel (0383) 18310
Fax (0383) 19278
Holes 18 L 5552 m SSS 71
V'tors U
Fees 160kr
Loc Östanå, 3km W of Vetlanda. 80km SE of Jönköping
Arch Jan Sederholm

Visby
Kronholmen Västergarn, 620 20 Klintehamn, Gotland
Tel (0498) 245058
Fax (0498) 245240
Web www.golf.se/visbygk
Holes 18 L 5765 m Par 72
9 hole course
V'tors Jun–Aug–H
Fees 300kr
Loc Kronholmen, 25km S of Visby, Gotland island
Arch Nordwall/Sköld

Vreta Kloster
Box 144, 590 70 Ljungsbro
Tel (013) 169700
Fax (013) 169707
Holes 18 L 5666 m Par 72
V'tors H
Fees 160kr (200kr)
Loc 15km N of Linköping
Arch Sune Linde

South West

Alingsås (1985)
Hjälmared 4050, 441 95 Alingsås
Tel (0322) 52421
Holes 18 L 5600 m SSS 72
V'tors H
Fees 180kr (200kr)
Loc 5km SE of Alingsås towards Borås

Bäckavattnet (1977)
Marbäck, 305 94 Halmstad
Tel (035) 44270
Fax (035) 44275

Web www.backavattnetsgk.com
Holes 18 L 5740 m Par 71
V'tors H
Fees 220kr (280kr)
Loc 13km E of Halmstad (RD25)

Billingen (1949)
St Kulhult, 540 17 Lerdala
Tel (0511) 80291
Fax (0511) 80244
Holes 18 L 5470 m Par 71
V'tors H
Fees 180kr
Loc 20km NW of Skövde
Arch Douglas Brasier

Borås (1933)
Östra Vik, Kråkered, 504 95 Borås
Tel (033) 250250
Fax (033) 250176
Holes North 18 L 6005 m Par 72
South 18 L 5085 m Par 69
V'tors H–booking necessary
Fees 200kr (200kr)
Loc 6km S of Borås, on Route 41
towards Varberg
Arch Brasier/Persson

Ekarnas (1970)
Balders Väg 12, 467 31 Grästorp
Tel (0514) 12061
Fax (0514) 12062
Holes 18 L 5501 m SSS 71
V'tors H
Fees 200kr (220kr)
Loc 25km E of Trollhättan.
Lidköping 35km
Arch Jan Andersson

Falkenberg (1949)
Golfvägen, 311 72 Falkenberg
Tel (0346) 50287
Fax (0346) 50997
Holes 27 L 5575-5680 m SSS 72
V'tors H
Fees 250–280kr
Loc 5km S of Falkenberg

Falköping (1965)
Box 99, 521 02 Falköping
Tel (0515) 31270
Fax (0515) 31389
Holes 18 L 5835 m Par 72
V'tors H
Fees 120kr (160kr)
Loc 7km E of Falköping on Route
46 towards Skovde
Arch Nils Sköld

Halmstad (1930)
302 73 Halmstad
Tel (035) 30077/30280 (Starter)
Fax (035) 32308
Holes 18 L 6259 m CR 72.4
18 L 5787 m CR 69.9
V'tors H WE–M before 1pm
Fees 400kr
Loc Tylosand, 9km W of
Halmstad
Arch Sundblom/Sköld/Pennink

Haverdals (1988)
Slingervägen 35, 31042 Haverdal
Tel (035) 59530
Fax (035) 53890
Holes 18 L 5840 m Par 72
V'tors H
Fees 220kr
Loc 11km NW of Halmstad
Arch Anders Amilon

Hökensås (1962)
PO Box 116, 544 22 Hjo
Tel (0503) 16059
Fax (0503) 16156
Holes 18 L 5540 m Par 72
9 hole course
V'tors U
Fees 200kr (200kr)
Loc 8km S of Hjo on Route 195
Arch Sune Linde

Hulta (1972)
Box 54, 517 22 Bollebygd
Tel (033) 204340
Fax (033) 204345
Holes 18 L 6000 m SSS 72
V'tors H
Fees 260kr
Loc Bollebygd, 35km E of
Gothenburg
Arch Jan Sederholm

Knistad G&CC
541 92 Skövde
Tel (0500) 463170
Fax (0500) 463075
Holes 18 L 5790 m SSS 72
V'tors H
Fees 200kr
Loc 10km NE of Skövde
Arch Jeremy Turner

Laholm (1964)
Box 101, 312 22 Laholm
Tel (0430) 30601
Fax (0430) 30891
Holes 18 L 5430 m SSS 70
V'tors U H
Fees 170kr (200kr)
Loc 5 miles E of Laholm on Route
24
Arch Jan Sederholm

Lidköping (1967)
Box 2029, 531 02 Lidköping
Tel (0510) 546144
Fax (0510) 546495
Holes 18 L 5382 m CR 68.6
V'tors H
Fees 180kr
Loc 5km E of Lidköping
Arch Douglas Brasier

Mariestad (1975)
*Gummerstadsvägen 45, 542
94 Mariestad*
Tel (0501) 47147
Fax (0501) 78117
Web www.golf.se/mariestadsgk
Holes 18 L 5970 m SSS 73

V'tors H
Fees 200kr
Loc 4km W of Mariestad, at Lake
Vänern

Marks (1962)
Brättingstorpsvägen 28, 511 58 Kinna
Tel (0320) 14220
Fax (0320) 12516
Holes 18 L 5530 m Par 70
V'tors H
Fees 160kr (200kr)
Loc Kinna, 30km S of Borås
Arch Sköld/Sederholm

Onsjö (1974)
Box 6331 A, 462 42 Vänersborg
Tel (0521) 68870
Fax (0521) 17106
Web www.golf.se/golfklubbar/
onsjogk
Holes 18 L 5730 m SSS 72
V'tors U
Fees 200kr (250kr)
Loc 3km S of Vänersborg. 80km N
of Gothenburg
Arch Sköld/Linde

Ringenäs (1987)
Strandlida, 305 91 Halmstad
Tel (035) 161590
Fax (035) 161599
Web www.ringenasgolfbana.com
Holes 27 L 5395-5615 m Par 71-72
V'tors H
Fees 200–320kr (320kr)
Loc 10km NW of Halmstad
Arch Sune Linde

Skogaby (1988)
312 93 Laholm
Tel (0430) 60190
Fax (0430) 60225
Holes 18 L 5555 m Par 71
V'tors U H
Fees 140kr (180kr)
Loc 10km E of Laholm. 30km SE
of Halmstad
Arch J Rosengren

Töreboda (1965)
Box 18, 545 21 Töreboda
Tel (0506) 12305
Fax (0506) 12305
Holes 18 L 5355 m SSS 70
V'tors U
Fees 200kr
Loc 7km E of Töreboda

Trollhättan (1963)
Stora Ekeskogen, 466 91 Sollebrunn
Tel (0520) 441000
Fax (0520) 441049
Holes 18 L 6200 m SSS 73
V'tors U
Fees 200kr
Loc Koberg, 20km SE of
Trollhättan
Arch Nils Sköld

Ulricehamn (1947)

523 33 Ulricehamn
Tel (0321) 10021
Fax (0321) 16004
Holes 18 L 5509 m Par 71
V'tors WD–H
Fees 160kr (200kr)
Loc Lassalyckan, 2km E of
Ulricehamn

Vara-Bjertorp

Bjertorp, 535 91 Kvänum
Tel (0512) 20261
Fax (0512) 20261
Web www.golf.se/golfklubbar/
varabjertorpgk
Holes 18 L 6005 m Par 72
V'tors H
Fees 150kr (220kr)
Loc 10km N of Vara. 110km NE
of Gothenburg (E20)
Arch Jan Sederholm

Varberg (1950)

430 10 Tvååker
Tel (0340) 43446/37496
Fax (0340) 43447
Web www.varbergsgk.com
Holes East 18 L 5440 m Par 71 CR
71
West 18 L 6435 m Par 72 CR
76
V'tors H
Fees 260–320kr
Loc East:15km E of Varberg.
West:8km S of Varberg, nr E6
Arch Sköld/Nordström

Vinberg (1992)

Sannagård, 311 95 Falkenberg
Tel (0346) 19020
Fax (0346) 19042
Holes 18 L 4050 m Par 65
V'tors U
Fees 160kr (180kr)
Loc 5km E of Falkenberg on coast
Arch Nilsson/Haglund

Stockholm

Ågesta (1958)

123 52 Farsta
Tel (08) 604 4538
Fax (08) 604 4397
Holes 18 L 5658 m SSS 72
9 L 3404 m SSS 62
V'tors WD–U
Fees 350kr
Loc Farsta, 15km S of Stockholm
Arch Sköld/Sederholm

Botkyrka

Malmbro Gård, 147 91 Grödinge
Tel (08) 530 29650
Fax (08) 530 29409
Web www.golf.se/botkyrkagk
Holes 18 holes Par 73
9 hole Par 3 course

V'tors WD–U H WE–H after 1pm
Fees 250kr (300kr)
Loc 30km S of Stockholm

Bro-Bålsta (1978)

Ginnlögs Väg, 197 91 Bro
Tel (08) 582 41310
Fax (08) 582 40006
Holes 18 L 6505 m Par 73
9 L 1715 m Par 31
V'tors WD–H (max 30) WE–NA
Fees 330kr (380kr)
Loc 40 km NW of Stockholm
Arch Peter Nordwall

Djursholm (1931)

Hagbardsvägen 1, 182 63 Djursholm
Tel (08) 5449 6451
Fax (08) 5449 6456
Holes 18 L 5595 m SSS 71
9 L 2200 m SSS 34
V'tors WD–U H before 1pm –M
after 3pm WE–M before 1pm
–U H after 3pm
Fees 400kr
Loc 12km N of Stockholm

Drottningholm (1958)

PO Box 183, 178 93 Drottningholm
Tel (08) 759 0085
Fax (08) 759 0851
Holes 18 L 5825 m SSS 72
V'tors WD–U H before 3pm –M
after 3pm WE–M before 3pm
–U H after 3pm
Fees 350kr
Loc 16km W of Stockholm
Arch Sundblom/Sköld

Fågelbro G&CC

Fågelbro Säteri, 139 60 Värmdö
Tel (08) 571 41800
Fax (08) 571 40671
Holes 18 L 5522 m Par 71
V'tors WD–H WE–M
Fees 500kr (600kr)
Loc 35km E of Stockholm
Arch Eriksson/Oredsson

Haninge (1983)

Årsta Slott, 136 91 Haninge
Tel (08) 500 32850
Fax (08) 500 32851
Web www.haningegk.se
Holes 27 L 5930 m Par 73
V'tors WD–U before 1pm –M after
1pm WE–M before 1pm –U
after 1pm
Fees 360kr (420kr)
Loc 30km S of Stockholm towards
Nynäshamn
Arch Jan Sederholm

Ingarö (1962)

Fogelvik, 134 64 Ingarö
Tel (08) 570 28244
Fax (08) 570 28379
Web www.igk.se
Holes Old 18 L 5024 m SSS 71
New 18 L 5203 m SSS 70

V'tors WD–U H WE–NA before
3pm
Fees 270kr (320kr)
Loc 30km E of Stockholm via
Route 222
Arch Sköld/Eriksson

Kungsängen (1992)

Box 133, 196 21 Kungsängen
Tel (08) 584 50730
Fax (08) 581 71002
Holes Kings 18 L 6100 m Par 71
Queens 18 L 5300 m Par 69
V'tors U H
Fees Kings–550kr. Queens–350kr
Loc 25km W of Stockholm via E18
to Brunna
Arch Anders Forsbrand

Lidingö (1933)

Box 1035, 181 21 Lidingö
Tel (08) 765 7911
Fax (08) 765 5479
Holes 18 L 5647 m SSS 72
V'tors WD–U H before 3pm –NA
after 3pm Sat–NA Sun–NA
before 1pm
Fees 400kr
Loc 6km NE of Stockholm
Arch MacDonald/Sundblom

Lindö (1978)

186 92 Vallentuna
Tel (08) 511 72260
Fax (08) 511 74122
Holes 18 L 2850 m Par 71
V'tors U
Fees 300kr (400kr)
Loc Vallentuna, 20 km N of
Stockholm
Arch Åke Persson

Lindo Park

Lindö Park, 186 92 Vallentuna
Tel (08) 511 70055
(Bookings)
Fax (08) 511 70613
Web www.lindopark.se
Holes 18 L 5800 m SSS 72
18 L 5795 m SSS 72
V'tors U H–book day before play
Fees 300kr (400kr)
Loc 30km N of Stockholm
Arch Persson/Bruce/Eriksson

Nya Johannesberg G&CC (1990)

762 95 Rimbo
Tel (08) 514 50000
Fax (08) 512 92390
Web www.golf.se/golfklubbar/
johannesberggcc
Holes 18 L 6328 m SSS 74
9 hole course
V'tors H
Fees 230kr (300kr)
Loc 55km N of Stockholm
Arch Donald Steel

Nynäshamn (1977)
Korunda 40, 148 91 Ösmo
Tel   (08) 524 30590/524 30599
Fax   (08) 524 30598
Web   www.nynashamnsgk.a.se
Holes 27 L 5690 m SSS 72
V'tors H–phone first
Fees   300kr (350kr)
Loc   Ösmo, 40km S of Stockholm
Arch   Sune Linde

Österakers
Hagby 1, 184 92 Åkersberga
Tel   (08) 540 85165
Fax   (08) 540 66832
Holes 18 L 5792 m Par 72
       18 L 5780 m Par 72
V'tors WD–H WE–M before 2pm
       –H after 2pm
Fees   300kr (350kr)
Loc   30km NE of Stockholm
Arch   Sederholm/Tumba

Österhaninge (1992)
Husby, 136 91 Haninge
Tel   (08) 500 32077
Fax   (08) 500 32293
Holes 18 L 5440 m Par 70
V'tors H
Fees   180kr (230kr)
Loc   35km S of Stockholm
Arch   Bengt Lorichs

Saltsjöbaden (1929)
Box 51, 133 21 Saltsjöbaden
Tel   (08) 717 0125
Fax   (08) 5561 6739
Holes 18 L 5436 m SSS 71
       9 L 3640 m SSS 60
V'tors WD–U WE–M H before 2pm
Fees   D–360kr (400kr)
Loc   15km E of Stockholm city, via
       Route 228

Sollentuna (1967)
Skillingegården, 192 77 Sollentuna
Tel   (08) 594 70995
Fax   (08) 594 70999
Holes 18 L 5895 m SSS 72
V'tors WD–H before 3pm WE–H
       after 3pm
Fees   350kr
Loc   19km N of Stockholm. 1km
       W of E4 (Rotebro)
Arch   Nils Sköld

Stockholm (1904)
Kevingestrand 20, 182 57 Danderyd
Tel   (08) 544 90710
Fax   (08) 544 90712
Holes 18 L 5180 m SSS 69
V'tors WD–M after 3pm WE–M
       before 3pm
Fees   340kr (420kr)
Loc   7km NE of Stockholm via
       Route E18

Täby (1968)
Skålhamra Gård, 187 70 Täby
Tel   (08) 510 23261
Fax   (08) 510 23441

Holes 18 L 5776 m SSS 73
V'tors WD–H
Fees   350–450kr
Loc   15km N of Stockholm
Arch   Nils Sköld

Ullna (1981)
Rosenkälla, 184 94 Åkersberga
Tel   (08) 514 41230
Fax   (08) 510 26068
Web   www.ullnagolf.se
Holes 18 L 5825 m Par 72
V'tors H
Fees   600kr
Loc   20km N of Stockholm via
       Route E18
Arch   Sven Tumba

Ulriksdal
Box 8033, 171 08 Solna
Tel   (08) 857931
Holes 18 L 3900 m SSS 61
V'tors H
Fees   130kr (160kr)
Loc   8km N of Stockholm
Arch   Alec Backhurst

Vallentuna
Box 266, 186 24 Vallentuna
Tel   (08) 514 30560/1
Fax   (08) 511 72370
Holes 18 L 5700 m SSS 72
V'tors WD–U WE–U after 1pm
Fees   250kr (300kr)
Loc   35km N of Stockholm
Arch   Sune Linde

Viksjö (1969)
Fjällens Gård, 175 45 Järfälla
Tel   (08) 580 31300/31310
Fax   (08) 580 31340
Web   www.golf.se/viksjogk
Holes 18 L 5930 m SSS 73
       9 L 1830 m Par 30
V'tors U
Fees   9 hole: 150kr (150kr)
       18 hole: 300kr (300kr)
Loc   18km NW of Stockholm

Wäsby
Box 2017, 194 02 Upplands Väsby
Tel   (08) 510 23345/23177
Fax   (08) 510 23364
Holes 18 L 6170 m SSS 72
       9 hole course
V'tors WD–U WE–H
Fees   250kr (350kr)
Loc   20km N of Stockholm. 20km
       S of Airport
Arch   Björn Eriksson

Wermdö G&CC (1966)
Torpa, 139 40 Värmdö
Tel   (08) 574 60700
Fax   (08) 574 60729
Holes 18 L 5555 m Par 72
V'tors H WE–NA before 3pm
Fees   450kr (450kr)
Loc   25km E of Stockholm via
       Route 222
Arch   Nils Sköld

West Central

Arvika (1974)
Box 197, 671 25 Arvika
Tel   (0570) 54133
Fax   (0570) 54233
Web   www.arvikagk.nu
Holes 18 L 5815 m Par 72
V'tors U
Fees   200kr
Loc   11km E of Arvika (Route 61)
Arch   Nils Sköld

Billerud (1961)
Valnäs, 660 40 Segmon
Tel   (0555) 91313
Fax   (0555) 91306
Holes 18 L 5874 m SSS 72
V'tors H
Fees   180kr
Loc   Valnäs, 15km N of Säffle
Arch   Brasier/Sköld

Eda (1992)
Noresund, 670 40 Åmotfors
Tel   (0571) 34101
Fax   (0571) 34191
Web   www.edagk.com
Holes 18 L 5575 m Par 72
V'tors U
Fees   200kr (240kr)
Loc   30km W of Arvika
Arch   Leif Nilsson

Färgelanda
Box 23, 458 21 Färgelanda
Tel   (0528) 20385
Fax   (0528) 20045
Holes 18 L 6000 m SSS 71
V'tors U
Fees   160kr
Loc   23km N of Uddevalla. 100km
       N of Gothenburg
Arch   Åke Persson

Fjällbacka (1965)
450 71 Fjällbacka
Tel   (0525) 31150
Fax   (0525) 32122
Holes 18 L 5850 m SSS 72
V'tors H
Fees   180kr (240kr)
Loc   2km N of Fjällbacka (Route
       163)

Forsbacka (1969)
Box 136, 662 23 Åmål
Tel   (0532) 43073
Fax   (0532) 43116
Web   www.golf.se/golfklubbar/
       forsbackagk
Holes 18 L 5860 m SSS 72
V'tors H
Fees   220kr (300kr)
Loc   6km W of Åmål (Route 164)

Hammarö (1991)
Sätter Tallbacken, 663 91 Hammarö
Tel   (054) 521621

Fax (054) 521863
Holes 18 L 6200 m Par 72
V'tors U
Fees 180kr
Loc 11km S of Karlstad

Karlskoga (1975)
Bricketorp 647, 691 94 Karlskoga
Tel (0586) 728190
Fax (0586) 728417
Holes 18 L 5705 m Par 72
Fees 180kr
Loc Valåsen, 5km E of Karlskoga
via Route E18
Arch Sköld/Sederholm/Engdahl

Karlstad (1957)
Höja 510, 655 92 Karlstad
Tel (054) 866353
Fax (054) 866478
Web www.golf.se/karlstadgk
Holes 18 L 5970 m Par 72
9 L 2875 m Par 36
V'tors H
Fees 250kr (300kr)
Loc 8km N of Karlstad (Route 63)
Arch Sköld/Linde

Kristinehamn (1974)
Box 337, 681 26 Kristinehamn
Tel (0550) 82310
Fax (0550) 19535
Web www.golf.se/golfklubbar/
kristinehamnsgk
Holes 18 L 5800 m SSS 72
V'tors H
Fees 220kr
Loc 3km N of Kristinehamn
Arch Sune Linde

Lyckorna (1967)
Box 66, 459 22 Ljungskile
Tel (0522) 20176
Fax (0522) 22304
Holes 18 L 5820 m SSS 72
V'tors H
Fees 200kr
Loc 20km S of Uddevalla
Arch Anders Amilon

Orust (1981)
Morlanda 9404, 474 93 Ellös
Tel (0304) 53170
Fax (0304) 53174
Holes 18 L 5770 m SSS 72
V'tors H
Fees 160–250kr
Loc Ellös, 10km from Henån.
80km N of Gothenburg
Arch Lars Andreasson

Saxå (1964)
Saxån, 682 92 Filipstad
Tel (0590) 24070
Fax (0590) 24101
Holes 18 L 5680 m Par 72
V'tors U
Fees 160kr
Loc 20km NE of Filipstad (Route
63)
Arch Sköld/Bäckman

Skaftö (1963)
Röd PL 4476, 450 34 Fiskebäckskil
Tel (0523) 23211
Fax (0523) 23215
Holes 18 L 4831 m SSS 69
V'tors WD–H
Fees 150–300kr
Loc 40km W of Uddevalla,
through Fiskebäckskil
Arch Sköld/Sederholm

Strömstad (1967)
Golfbanevägen, 452 90 Strömstad 1
Tel (0526) 61788
Fax (0526) 14766
Web www.golf.se/stromstadgk
Holes 18 L 5615 m SSS 71
V'tors H
Fees 250kr (300kr)
Loc 6km N of Strömstad
Arch Sköld/Sederholm

Sunne (1970)
Box 108, 686 23 Sunne
Tel (0565) 14100/14210
Fax (0565) 14855
Holes 18 hole course SSS 72
V'tors H
Fees 200kr
Loc 2km S of Sunne. 60km N of
Karlstad on Route 45
Arch Jan Sederholm

Torreby (1961)
Torreby Slott, 455 93 Munkedal
Tel (0524) 21365/21109
Fax (0524) 21351
Holes 18 L 5885 m Par 72
V'tors H
Fees 200kr
Loc Munkedal 8km. Uddevalla
30km
Arch Douglas Brasier

Troxhammar
Stenhamra, 179 75 Skå
Tel (08) 564 20610
Fax (08) 560 24870
Web www.golf.se
Holes 27 holes Par 72
V'tors H-max 32
Fees £30 (£35)
Loc 15 km W of Stockholm. nr
Drottningholm Castle
Arch Jan Sederholm

Uddeholm (1965)
Risäter 20, 683 93 Råda
Tel (0563) 60564
Fax (0563) 60017
Holes 18 L 5830 m SSS 72
V'tors U H
Fees D–160kr
Loc Lake Råda, 80km N of
Karlstad, via RD62

Switzerland

Bern

G&CC Blumisberg (1959)
3184 Wünnewil
Tel (026) 496 34 38
Fax (026) 496 35 23
Holes 18 L 6048 m SSS 73
V'tors WD–U H WE–M
Fees 80fr (80fr)
Loc Wünnewil, 16km SW of Bern
Arch B von Limburger

Les Bois (1988)
Case Postale 26, 2336 Les Bois
Tel (032) 961 10 03
Fax (032) 961 10 17
Holes 9 L 3000 m Par 72
V'tors WD–U WE–M
Fees 75fr (90fr)
Loc 12km NE of La Chaux-de-
Fonds, on Basel road
Arch Jeremy Pern

Neuchâtel (1928)
Hameau de Voëns, 2072 Saint-Blaise
Tel (032) 753 55 50
Fax (032) 753 29 40
Holes 18 L 5944 m SSS 71
V'tors H
Fees 70fr (90fr)
Loc Voëns/Saint-Blaise, 5km E of
Neuchâtel. 30km W of Bern

Payerne (1996)
Public
Domaine des Invuardes, 1530 Payerne
Tel (026) 660 2385
Fax (026) 660 4672
Holes 18 L 5450 m Par 70
V'tors U H
Fees 70fr (90fr)
Loc 50km W of Bern. 50km NE of
Lausanne
Arch Yves Bureau

Wallenried (1992)
1784 Wallenried
Tel (026) 684 84 80
Fax (026) 684 84 90
Web www.swissgolfnetwork.ch
Holes 18 L 6000 m Par 72
V'tors WD–U H
Fees 70fr (90fr)
Loc 6km W of Fribourg
Arch Ruzzo Reuss

Wylihof (1994)
4542 Luterbach
Tel (032) 682 28 28
Fax (032) 682 65 17
Web www.golf.ch
Holes 18 L 6580 yds Par 73
V'tors WD–U H–max 36 WE–M H
Fees 90fr (90fr)
Loc 40km N of Bern. 90km W of
Zürich
Arch Ruzzo Reuss von Plauen

Bernese Oberland

Interlaken-Unterseen
(1964)
Postfach 110, 3800 Interlaken
Tel   (033) 823 60 16
Fax   (033) 823 42 03
Web   www.interlakengolf.ch
Holes 18 L 5980 m Par 72
V'tors H
Fees   80fr (90fr)
Loc   Interlaken 3km
Arch   Donald Harradine

Riederalp (1986)
3987 Riederalp
Tel   (027) 927 29 32
Fax   (027) 927 29 32
Holes 9 L 3066 m SSS 55
V'tors U
Fees   45fr
Loc   10km NE of Brig
Arch   Donald Harradine

Lake Geneva & South West

Bonmont (1983)
Château de Bonmont, 1275 Chéserex
Tel   (022) 369 99 00
Fax   (022) 369 99 09
Holes 18 L 6165 m SSS 72
V'tors WD–restricted WE–M
Fees   WD–90fr
Loc   3km from Nyon. 30km NE of Geneva
Arch   Donald Harradine

Les Coullaux (1989)
1846 Chessel
Tel   (024) 481 22 46
Fax   (024) 481 22 46
Holes 9 L 2940 m Par 58
V'tors U
Fees   25–40fr (30–50fr)
Loc   Chessel, between Evian and Montreux
Arch   Donald Harradine

Crans-sur-Sierre (1906)
C P 112, 3963 Crans-sur-Sierre
Tel   (027) 41 21 68
Fax   (027) 41 95 68
Holes 18 L 6170 m SSS 72
        9 L 2729 m SSS 35
        9 hole Par 3 course
V'tors H
Fees   On application
Loc   20km E of Sion. Geneva 2 hrs

Domaine Impérial (1987)
Villa Prangins, 1196 Gland
Tel   (022) 999 06 00
Fax   (022) 999 06 06
Holes 18 L 6297 m SSS 74
V'tors WD–H exc Mon am

Fees   WD–150fr
Loc   Nyon, 20km N of Geneva
Arch   Pete Dye

Geneva (1923)
70 Route de la Capite, 1223 Cologny
Tel   (022) 707 48 00
Fax   (022) 707 48 20
Holes 18 L 6150 m Par 72
V'tors WD–am only Tues–Fri WE–M
Fees   150fr
Loc   4km from centre of Geneva
Arch   Robert Trent Jones Sr

Lausanne (1921)
Route du Golf 3, 1000 Lausanne 25
Tel   (021) 784 84 84
Fax   (021) 784 84 80
Holes 18 L 6295 m SSS 74
V'tors H
Fees   90fr (110fr)
Loc   7km N of Lausanne towards Le Mont
Arch   Narbel/Harradine/Pern

Montreux (1898)
54 Route d'Evian, 1860 Aigle
Tel   (024) 466 46 16
Fax   (024) 466 60 47
Holes 18 L 6143 m Par 72 SSS 73
V'tors H
Fees   80fr (100fr)
Loc   Aigle, 15km S of Montreux
Arch   Donald Harradine

Sion (1995)
CP 639, Rte Vissigen 150, 1951 Sion
Tel   (027) 203 79 00
Fax   (027) 203 79 01
Holes 9 L 2315 m Par 33
V'tors H–booking necessary
Fees   18 holes–61fr (79fr)
        9 holes–37fr (46fr)
Loc   Sion, 80km SE of Montreux
Arch   JL Tronchet

Verbier (1970)
1936 Verbier
Tel   (079) 412 86 48,
(027) 771 53 14 (Season)
Fax   (027) 771 60 93/771 53 34
Holes 18 L 5300 m Par 70
        18 hole Par 3 course
V'tors U
Fees   50fr (65fr)
Loc   Centre of Verbier
Arch   Donald Harradine

Villars (1922)
C P 152, 1884 Villars
Tel   (024) 495 42 14
Fax   (024) 495 42 18
Holes 18 L 5250 m SSS 70
V'tors U
Fees   60fr (80fr)
Loc   7km E of Villars towards Les Diablerets
Arch   Thierry Sprecher

Lugano & Ticino

Lugano (1923)
6983 Magliaso
Tel   (091) 606 15 57
Fax   (091) 606 65 58
Web   www.golflugano.ch
Holes 18 L 5580 m Par 70
V'tors H–max 36
Fees   85fr (110fr)
Loc   8km W of Lugano towards Ponte Tresa
Arch   Harradine/Robinson

Patriziale Ascona (1928)
Via al Lido 81, 6612 Ascona
Tel   (091) 791 21 32
Fax   (091) 791 07 06
Web   www.golf.ascona.ch
Holes 18 L 5933 m Par 71
V'tors H–max 30
Fees   90fr
Loc   5km W of Locarno
Arch   CK Cotton

St Mortiz & Engadine

Arosa (1944)
Postfach 95, 7050 Arosa
Tel   (081) 377 42 42
Fax   (081) 377 46 77
Web   www.arosa.ch/golf
Holes 18 L 4340 m Par 66
V'tors U
Fees   70fr
Loc   30km S of Chur
Arch   D Harradine/P Harradine

Bad Ragaz (1957)
Hans Albrecht Strasse, 7310 Bad Ragaz
Tel   (081) 303 37 17
Fax   (081) 303 37 27
Web   www.resortragaz.ch
Holes 18 L 5750 m Par 70
V'tors H
Fees   D–120fr
Loc   20km N of Chur. 100km SE of Zürich
Arch   Donald Harradine

Davos (1929)
Postfach, 7260 Davos Dorf
Tel   (081) 46 56 34
Fax   (081) 46 25 55
Holes 18 L 5208 yds Par 68
V'tors WD–U
Fees   On application
Loc   1km outside Davos
Arch   Donald Harradine

Engadin (1893)
7503 Samedan
Tel   (081) 851 04 66
Fax   (081) 851 04 67
Holes 18 L 6350 m SSS 73
V'tors H

Fees 90fr
Loc Samedan, 6km NE of St
Moritz
Arch M Verdieri

Lenzerheide Valbella
(1950)
7078 Lenzerheide
Tel (081) 385 13 13
Fax (081) 385 13 19
Holes 18 L 5269 m SSS 69
V'tors H
Fees 60–80fr
Loc 20km S of Chur towards St
Moritz
Arch Donald Harradine

Vulpera (1923)
7552 Vulpera Spa
Tel (081) 864 96 88
Fax (081) 864 96 89
Web www.swissgolfnetwork.
ch-9holes-vulpera
Holes 9 L 1982 m SSS 62
V'tors H
Fees 60fr (70fr) W–290fr
Loc Tarasp, nr Vulpera. 60km NE
of St Moritz
Arch Dell/Spencer

Zürich & North

Breitenloo (1964)
8309 Oberwil b. Bassersdorf
Tel (01) 836 40 80
Fax (01) 837 10 85
Holes 18 L 6125 m Par 72 SSS 72
V'tors WD–H by appointment
WE–M H
Fees 100fr
Loc 10km NE of Zürich Airport
Arch Harradine/Pennink

Bürgenstock (1927)
6363 Bürgenstock
Tel (041) 612 9010
Fax (041) 612 9901
Holes 9 L 2200 m Par 33
V'tors I or H
Fees 60fr (80fr)
Loc 15km S of Lucerne
Arch Fritz Frey

Dolder (1907)
Kurhausstrasse 66, 8032 Zürich
Tel (01) 261 50 45
Fax (01) 261 53 02
Holes 9 L 1735 m SSS 58
V'tors WD–H WE–M
Fees WD–70fr
Loc Zürich

Entfelden (1988)
*Postfach 230, Muhenstrasse 52,
5036 Oberentfelden*
Tel (062) 723 89 84

Fax (062) 723 84 36
Holes 9 L 3960 m SSS 60
V'tors H
Fees 50fr (70fr)
Loc 50km W of Zürich
Arch Donald Harradine

Erlen (1988)
*Schlossgut Eppishausen, Schlossstr 7,
8586 Erlen*
Tel (071) 648 29 30
Fax (071) 648 29 40
Holes 18 L 5913 m SSS 71
V'tors H
Fees 80fr (110fr)
Loc 30km NW of St Gallen. 60km
W of Zürich
Arch Deutsche Golfconsult

Hittnau-Zürich G&CC
(1964)
8335 Hittnau
Tel (01) 950 24 42
Fax (01) 951 01 66
Holes 18 L 5773 m SSS 71
V'tors WD–U WE–M
Fees WD–90fr
Loc Hittnau, 30km E of Zürich

Küssnacht (1994)
*Sekretariat/Grossarni, 6403 Küssnacht
am Rigi*
Tel (041) 850 70 60
Fax (041) 850 70 41
Holes 18 L 5397 m Par 68
V'tors WD–U H WE–M H
Fees 70–80fr (100fr)
Loc 20km NE of Lucerne
Arch Peter Harradine

Lucerne (1903)
Dietschiberg, 6006 Luzern
Tel (041) 420 97 87
Fax (041) 420 82 48
Holes 18 L 6082 m Par 72 SSS 71-73
V'tors H
Fees 80fr (100fr)
Loc Lucerne 2km

Ostschweizerischer
(1948)
9246 Niederbüren
Tel (071) 422 18 56
Fax (071) 422 18 25
Web www.osgc.ch
Holes 18 L 5920 m SSS 71
V'tors WD–H
Fees D–90fr
Loc Niederbüren, 25km NW of St
Gallen
Arch Donald Harradine

Schinznach-Bad (1929)
5116 Schinznach-Bad
Tel (056) 443 12 26
Fax (056) 443 34 83
Holes 9 L 5670 m Par 71
V'tors WD–U

Fees 70fr
Loc 6km S of Brugg. 35km W of
Zürich

Schönenberg (1967)
8824 Schönenberg
Tel (01) 788 90 40
Fax (01) 788 90 45
Web www.swissgolfnetwork.ch
Holes 18 L 6205 m CR 73 SR 137
V'tors WD–H–by appointment
WE–M H
Fees 90fr
Loc 20km S of Zürich
Arch Donald Harradine

Sempachersee (1996)
6024 Hildisrieden, Lucerne
Tel (041) 462 71 71
Fax (041) 462 71 72
Web www.golf-semperachsee.ch
Holes 18 L 6161 m Par 72 SR 127
9 L 3890 m Par 31
V'tors WD–U H WE–M H
Fees 90fr (90fr)
Loc 13km NW of Lucerne
Arch Kurt Rossknecht

Zürich-Zumikon
(1929)
Weid 9, 8126 Zumikon
Tel (01) 918 00 50
Fax (01) 918 00 37
Web www.swissgolfnetwork.ch
Holes 18 L 6350 m Par 72 CR 73
SR 130
V'tors WD–H by appointment
WE–M
Fees WD–150fr
Loc 10km SE of Zürich
Arch Donald Harradine

Turkey

Gloria Golf
*Acisu Mevkii PK27 Belek,
Serik, Antalya*
Tel (242) 715 15 20
Fax (242) 715 15 25
Holes 18 holes Par 72
9 hole Academy course
V'tors U
Loc Antalya
Arch Michel Gayon

Kemer G&CC
*Goturk Koyu Mevkii Kemerburgaz,
Eyup, Istanbul*
Tel (212) 239 70 10
Fax (212) 239 73 76
Holes 18 holes Par 73
V'tors U–phone for booking
Fees $50 ($90)
Loc 30km from Istanbul
Arch J Dudok van Heel

Klassis G&CC

Silivri, Istanbul

Tel	(212) 748 46 00
Fax	(212) 748 46 43
Holes	18 L 6200 m Par 73
	9 hole Par 3 course
V'tors	U
Loc	Istanbul
Arch	Tony Jacklin

National Antalya

*Belek Turizm Merkesi, 07500
Serik, Antalya*

Tel	(242) 725 46 20
Fax	(242) 725 46 23

Web	www.nationalturkey.com
Holes	18 L 6232 m Par 72
	SSS 72
	9 L 1547 m Par 29
V'tors	H
Fees	£50
Loc	Belek, 50km from Antalya
Arch	Feherty/Jones

Nobilis Golf (1998)

*Acisu Mevkii, Belek, 07500
Serik, Antalya*

Tel	(242) 1986/7
Fax	(242) 1985
Holes	18 holes Par 72

V'tors	U
Fees	£35
Loc	35km E of Antalya on
	Mediterranean coast
Arch	Dave Thomas

Tat Golf International

*Belek International Golf, Kum Tepesi
Belek, 07500 Serik, Antalya*

Tel	(242) 725 53 03
Fax	(242) 725 52 99
Holes	27 holes Par 72
V'tors	U
Loc	Antalya
Arch	Hawtree

General Index